ANAGRAM
FINDER

ANAGRAM
FINDER

EDITED BY JOHN DAINTITH

BLOOMSBURY

www.bloomsbury.com/reference

First published 1993
This edition published 2000
Reprinted 2004

Copyright © 1993, 2000 by Bloomsbury Publishing Plc

Bloomsbury Publishing Limited, 38 Soho Square, London W1D 3HB

A CIP record for this title is available from the British Library

ISBN 0 7475 7621 1

10 9 8 7 6 5 4 3 2 1

Compiled and typeset by Market House Books Ltd, Aylesbury
Printed in Great Britain by Clays Ltd, St Ives plc

INTRODUCTION

This dictionary is intended to help crossword-puzzle solvers and other word-game enthusiasts to find anagrams quickly and easily.

It consists of lists of English words and phrases arranged into two-letter words, three-letter words, etc., up to words and phrases that have sixteen letters. Each word or phrase is preceded by an anagram key, composed by taking the letters of the word or phrase and arranging them in alphabetical order. The entries themselves are arranged in alphabetical order of anagram key.

The use of the book can best be illustrated by a simple example. Take the clue 'Ronny can get mixed up and fired'. The answer is an eight-letter word. The words 'mixed-up' in the clue suggest that the answer may be an anagram of 'Ronny can'. Taking the letters of 'Ronny can' and putting them in alphabetical order gives the key ACNNNORY. In the list of eight-letter words, this gives the correct solution – CANNONRY.

We have tried to include as many words and phrases as space permits and short lists of palindromes and backwords are also included. We hope that the book will prove useful to all who enjoy doing crossword puzzles.

JD

May, 2000

AB	AB	CK	KC	EX	EX	IP	PI	OP	OP
AC	AC	CO	CO	EY	YE	IQ	IQ	OR	OR
AD	AD, DA	CP	PC	FI	IF	IT	IT, TI	OS	SO
AF	FA	CQ	QC	FM	FM	JO	JO	OT	TO
AH	AH, HA	CV	CV, VC	FO	OF	JP	JP	OW	OW
AI	AI	CW	WC	GI	GI	KO	KO	OX	OX
AL	AL, LA	CY	CY	GO	GO	KU	UK	PR	PR
AM	AM, MA	DE	ED	GP	GP	LO	LO	PS	PS
AN	AN	DI	ID	GS	GS	LP	LP	PT	PT
AP	PA	DJ	DJ	HI	HI	MO	MO	PU	UP
AS	AS	DO	DO	HM	H'M	MP	MP, PM	PX	PX
AT	AT, TA	DV	VD	HO	HO, OH	MR	MR	QT	QT
BC	CB	EH	EH, HE	HP	PH	MS	MS	SU	US
BE	BE	EM	ME	HQ	HQ	MU	UM	SV	VS
BO	BO	EP	PE	HS	SH	MY	MY	TV	TV
BY	BY	ER	ER, RE	IM	MI	NO	NO, ON		
CD	CD	EW	WE	IN	IN	NU	UN		

Code	Words	Code	Words	Code	Words	Code	Words	Code	Words
AAB	BAA	AEL	ALE, LEA	AJR	JAR, RAJ	ARW	RAW, WAR	BOW	BOW
AAD	ADA	AEM	MAE	AJW	JAW	ARY	RAY	BOX	BOX
AAH	AHA	AEN	ENA	AJY	JAY	ASS	ASS	BOY	BOY, YOB
AAL	A LA	AEP	APE, PEA	AKO	OAK	AST	SAT	BPU	PUB
AAS	ASA	AER	EAR, ERA, RAE	AKR	ARK	ASW	SAW	BRU	BUR, RUB
AAV	AVA	AES	SAE, SEA	AKS	ASK	ASY	SAY	BSU	BUS, SUB
ABB	BAB	AET	ATE, EAT, TEA	AKU	AUK	ATT	TAT	BTU	BUT, TUB
ABC	ABC, CAB	AEV	EVA	AKY	KAY, YAK	ATV	VAT	BUY	BUY
ABD	BAD, DAB	AEW	AWE	AKZ	ZAK	ATW	WAT	CDI	CID
ABE	ABE, BEA	AEX	AXE	ALL	ALL	ATX	TAX	CDL	LCD
ABF	FAB	AEY	AYE, YEA	ALN	LAN	AWX	WAX	CDN	CND
ABG	BAG, GAB	AFG	FAG	ALP	LAP, PAL	AWY	WAY, YAW	CDO	COD, DOC
ABH	BAH	AFL	ALF	ALS	SAL	BBC	BBC	CDS	CDS
ABJ	JAB	AFN	FAN	ALV	VAL	BBE	EBB	CDU	CUD
ABL	LAB	AFO	OAF	ALW	AWL, LAW, WAL	BBI	BIB	CEE	EEC
ABN	BAN, NAB	AFR	FAR, RAF	ALX	LAX	BBO	BOB	CEG	ECG, GCE
ABO	ABO, BOA	AFT	AFT, FAT	ALY	LAY	BBU	BUB	CEI	ICE
ABR	BAR, BRA, RAB	AFX	FAX	AMM	MAM	BCO	COB	CES	CSE, SEC
ABT	BAT, TAB	AFY	FAY	AMN	MAN	BCU	CUB	CET	ECT, ETC
ABY	BAY	AGG	GAG	AMP	AMP, MAP, PAM	BDE	BED, DEB	CEU	CUE
ACD	CAD	AGH	HAG	AMR	ARM, MAR, RAM	BDI	BID	CGO	COG
ACE	ACE	AGJ	JAG	AMS	MAS, SAM	BDO	BOD	CHI	HIC
ACI	CAI, CIA	AGL	GAL, LAG	AMT	MAT, TAM	BDU	BUD, DUB	CIN	INC
ACM	CAM, MAC	AGM	AGM, MAG	AMW	MAW	BEE	BEE	CIS	CIS, SIC
ACN	CAN	AGN	NAG	AMX	MAX	BEG	BEG	CIT	TIC
ACP	CAP, CPA	AGO	AGO	AMY	AMY, MAY, YAM	BEL	BEL	CIV	VIC
ACR	ARC, CAR	AGP	GAP	ANN	ANN, NAN	BEN	BEN	CIY	ICY
ACS	SAC	AGR	RAG	ANO	ONA	BES	SEB	CLM	LCM
ACT	ACT, CAT	AGS	GAS, SAG	ANP	NAP, PAN	BET	BET	CLO	COL
ACV	VAC	AGT	TAG	ANR	RAN, RNA	BEW	WEB	CLP	PLC
ACW	CAW	AGW	WAG	ANT	ANT, NAT, TAN	BEY	BYE	CMS	MSC
ADD	ADD, DAD	AGY	GAY	ANU	UNA	BFI	FBI, FIB	CMU	CUM
ADE	EDA	AHH	HAH	ANV	VAN	BFO	FOB	CMW	CWM
ADF	FAD	AHL	HAL	ANW	WAN	BGI	BIG	CNO	CON, NCO
ADG	GAD	AHM	HAM	ANY	ANY, NAY	BGO	BOG, GOB	COO	COO
ADH	HAD	AHN	HAN	AOP	OAP	BGU	BUG	COP	COP
ADI	AID, DAI, IDA	AHP	HAP	AOR	OAR	BHO	HOB	COR	ROC
ADJ	ADJ	AHS	ASH, HAS	AOV	OVA	BHU	HUB	COS	COS
ADL	LAD	AHT	HAT	APP	PAP	BIJ	JIB	COT	COT
ADM	DAM, MAD	AHW	HAW	APR	PAR, RAP	BIL	LIB	COW	COW
ADN	AND, DAN, DNA	AHY	HAY	APS	ASP, PAS, SAP, SPA	BIN	BIN, NIB	COX	COX
ADO	ADO	AIL	AIL	APT	APT, PAT, PTA, TAP	BIR	RIB	COY	COY
ADP	PAD	AIM	AIM, MIA	APW	PAW	BIT	BIT	CPS	PCS
ADS	ADS, SAD	AIN	IAN, INA	APY	PAY, YAP	BJO	JOB	CPU	CPU, CUP
ADU	AUD	AIP	IPA, PIA	APZ	ZAP	BLO	LOB	CPV	PVC
ADV	ADV	AIR	AIR, IRA, RIA	AQU	QUA	BMO	MOB	CPW	WPC
ADW	WAD	AIS	ISA	ART	ART, RAT, TAR	BMU	BUM	CQS	QCS
ADY	DAY	AIT	ITA			BNO	NOB	CRU	CUR
AEG	AGE	AIV	VIA			BNU	BUN, NUB	CRV	VCR
AEH	HAE	AJM	JAM			BOO	BOO	CRY	CRY
		AJN	JAN			BOP	BOP	CSV	CVS, VCS
						BOR	ORB, ROB	CTU	CUT, TUC
						BOS	SOB	DDI	DID
								DDO	ODD

DDT	DDT	DUV	VDU	EJT	JET	FIS	IFS	HNT	NTH
DDU	DUD	EEF	FEE	EJW	JEW	FIT	FIT	HNU	HUN
DEE	DEE	EEG	GEE	EKL	ELK	FIX	FIX	HOO	HOO, OHO
DEF	FED	EEK	EEK	EKN	KEN	FLU	FLU	HOP	HOP
DEH	HE'D	EEL	EEL, LEE	EKY	KEY	FLY	FLY	HOS	SOH
DEI	DIE	EEN	NEE	ELM	ELM, MEL	FNU	FUN	HOT	HOT
DEJ	JED	EEP	PEE	ELO	LEO	FOO	OOF	HOW	HOW, WHO
DEL	DEL, LED	EER	ERE	ELT	ELT, LET	FOP	FOP	HOY	HOY
DEM	DEM	EES	SEE	ELW	LEW	FOR	FOR, FRO	HPS	PHS
DEN	DEN, END, NED	EET	TEE	EMN	MEN	FOT	OFT	HQS	HQS
DEO	DOE, ODE	EEV	EVE	EMT	MET	FOU	UFO	HSY	SHY
DEP	DEP	EEW	EWE, WEE	EMU	EMU	FOX	FOX	HTU	HUT
DER	RED	EEY	EYE	EMW	MEW	FRU	FUR	HTY	THY
DES	DES	EFF	EFF	ENO	EON, ONE	FRY	FRY	HUW	HUW
DET	TED	EFI	FIE	ENP	PEN	GGI	GIG	HWY	WHY
DEU	DUE	EFL	ELF	ENT	NET, TEN	GHO	HOG	IJM	JIM
DEW	DEW, WED	EFN	FEN	ENW	NEW	GHU	HUG, UGH	IKL	ILK
DEY	DYE	EFO	FOE	ENY	NYE, YEN	GIJ	JIG	IKM	KIM
DEZ	ZED	EFR	REF	ENZ	ZEN	GIL	GIL	IKN	INK, KIN
DGI	DIG	EFW	FEW	EOR	ORE, O'ER, ROE	GIN	GIN	IKP	KIP
DGO	DOG, GOD	EFY	FEY	EOT	TOE	GIP	PIG	IKR	IRK
DGP	GDP	EFZ	FEZ	EOW	OWE, WOE	GIR	RIG	IKS	SKI
DGU	DUG	EGG	EGG	EOZ	ZOE	GIS	GI'S	IKT	KIT
DHI	HID	EGK	EKG, KEG	EPP	PEP	GIW	WIG	ILL	ILL
DHO	DOH, HOD	EGL	GEL, LEG	EPR	PER, REP	GJO	JOG	ILN	NIL
DHP	PHD	EGM	GEM, MEG	EPS	ESP	GJU	JUG	ILO	OIL
DIK	KID	EGN	GEN	EPT	PET	GLO	LOG	ILP	LIP
DIL	LID	EGO	EGO	EPW	PEW	GLU	LUG	ILT	LIT
DIM	DIM, MID	EGP	PEG	EQS	ESQ	GMU	GUM, MUG	ILZ	LIZ
DIN	DIN	EGR	ERG, REG	ERR	ERR	GMY	GYM	IMP	IMP
DIP	DIP	EGT	GET	ERU	RUE	GNP	GNP	IMR	RIM
DIR	RID	EGV	VEG	ERV	REV	GNU	GNU, GUN	IMS	ISM, SIM
DIS	IDS, SDI, SID	EHH	HEH	ERX	REX	GOO	GOO	IMT	TIM
DIU	IUD	EHI	HIE	ERY	RYE	GOP	GOP	IMV	VIM
DIY	DIY, YID	EHL	HEL	EST	SET	GOT	GOT, TOG	IMX	MIX
DJS	DJS	EHM	HEM	ESU	SUE, USE	GOW	WOG	INN	INN
DLO	OLD	EHN	HEN	ESW	SEW	GPS	GPS	INO	ION
DLS	LSD	EHO	HOE	ESX	SEX	GPU	PUG	INP	NIP, PIN
DMO	MOD	EHP	HEP	ESY	YES	GPY	GYP	INS	SIN
DMU	MUD	EHR	HER	ETV	VET	GRU	RUG	INT	NIT, TIN
DNO	DON, NOD	EHS	HE'S, SHE	ETW	WET	GSU	GUS	INV	VIN
DNU	DUN	EHT	HET, THE	ETX	TEX	GTU	GUT, TUG	INW	WIN
DOO	ODO	EHU	HUE	ETY	YET	GUV	GUV	INX	NIX
DOP	POD	EHW	HEW	EVX	VEX	GUY	GUY	INY	YIN
DOR	ROD	EHX	HEX	EWY	YEW	HHU	HUH	IOU	IOU
DOS	DOS, SOD	EHY	HEY	FFO	OFF	HIM	HIM	IOV	IVO
DOT	DOT, TOD	EIK	IKE	FGI	FIG	HIN	HIN	IPP	PIP
DOU	DUO	EIL	ELI, LEI, LIE	FGO	FOG	HIP	HIP	IPR	RIP
DPS	SDP	EIP	PIE	FGU	FUG	HIS	HIS, HSI	IPS	PIS, SIP
DPU	PUD	EIR	IRE	FHU	UHF	HIT	HIT	IPT	PIT, TIP
DRY	DRY	EIT	TIE	FHV	VHF	HMO	HOM, OHM	IPV	VIP
DST	D T'S, STD	EIV	VIE	FIN	FIN	HMU	HUM	IPX	PIX
DSY	SYD	EJM	JEM	FIR	FIR	HNS	NHS	IPZ	ZIP
		EJO	JOE						

3

IQS	IQS	LOP	LOP	MRU	RUM	OPT	OPT, POT, PTO, TOP	OUY	YOU
IRS	SIR	LOS	SOL	MSU	SUM			OVW	VOW
ISS	SIS	LOT	LOT	NNU	NUN	OPW	POW, WOP	OWW	WOW
IST	ITS, SIT	LOU	LOU	NOR	NOR, RON	OPX	POX	PPS	PPS
ISX	SIX	LOW	LOW, OWL	NOS	SON	ORS	ROS	PPU	PUP
ITT	TIT	LOX	LOX	NOT	NOT, TON	ORT	ROT, TOR	PRU	PRU
ITV	ITV	LPS	LPS	NOW	NOW, OWN, WON	ORU	OUR	PRY	PRY
ITW	WIT	LPY	PLY			ORW	ROW	PSU	PUS, SUP
IVV	VIV	LSY	SLY	NPU	PUN	ORY	ROY	PSY	SPY
IVY	IVY	LUV	LUV	NRU	RUN, URN	OSS	SOS	PTU	PUT
IVZ	VIZ	MMO	MOM	NSU	SUN	OST	SOT	PXY	PYX
JNO	JON	MMU	MUM	NTT	TNT	OSU	SOU	RTU	RUT
JOT	JOT	MOO	MOO	NTU	NUT	OSW	SOW	RTY	TRY
JOY	JOY	MOP	MOP	OOT	TOO	OSX	SOX	RWY	WRY
JPS	JPS	MOR	ROM	OOW	WOO	OSY	SOY	STV	TVS
JTU	JUT	MOS	MOS	OOZ	ZOO	OTT	TOT	STY	STY
KOW	WOK	MOT	MOT, TOM	OPP	POP	OTU	OUT	TTU	TUT
KSY	SKY	MOW	MOW	OPR	PRO	OTW	TOW, TWO, WOT		
LNY	LYN	MPS	MPS, PMS	OPS	OPS, SOP				
LOO	LOO	MRS	MRS			OTY	TOY		

AABI	ABIA	ABBU	BABU	ABNO	OBAN
AABJ	BAJA	ABBY	ABBY, BABY	ABNR	BARN, BRAN
AABR	ARAB	ABCH	BACH	ABNS	BANS
AABS	BAAS, SABA	ABCK	BACK	ABNU	BUNA
AACR	CARA	ABCR	CRAB	ABOR	BOAR, BORA
AADH	ADAH	ABCS	ABCS, CABS, SCAB	ABOS	ABOS, BOAS
AADL	ALDA	ABCU	CUBA	ABOT	BOAT
AADM	ADAM	ABDE	ABED, BADE, BEAD	ABOZ	BOAZ
AADN	DANA, NADA	ABDL	BALD	ABRS	BARS, BRAS
AADT	DATA	ABDN	BAND	ABRT	BART, BRAT
AAER	AREA	ABDR	BARD, BRAD, DRAB	ABRY	BRAY
AAFH	HAAF	ABDS	DABS	ABSS	BASS
AAFR	AFAR, AFRA	ABDU	BAUD, DAUB	ABST	BAST, BATS, STAB, TABS
AAGG	GAGA	ABDW	BAWD	ABSW	SWAB
AAGL	GALA	ABEK	BAKE, BEAK	ABSY	BAYS
AAGR	AGRA, RAGA	ABEL	ABEL, ABLE, BALE, ELBA	ABTU	ABUT, TUBA
AAGS	SAGA	ABEM	BEAM	ACCD"	AC/DC
AAGY	GAYA	ABEN	BANE, BEAN	ACCT	ACCT
AAGZ	GAZA	ABER	BARE, BEAR, BRAE	ACCU	UCCA
AAHH	HA-HA	ABES	BASE	ACDH	CHAD
AAHM	HAMA	ABET	ABET, BEAT, BETA	ACDI	ACID
AAHN	NAHA	ABEU	AUBE, BEAU	ACDL	CLAD
AAHR	HAAR	ABEZ	BAEZ	ACDO	CODA
AAHS	HASA	ABFL	FLAB	ACDR	CARD
AAHY	AYAH	ABGI	GABI	ACDS	CADS
AAIL	ALAI	ABGL	BLAG	ACEF	CAFE, FACE
AAIR	ARIA	ABGN	BANG	ACEG	CAGE
AAIS	ASIA	ABGR	BRAG, GARB, GRAB	ACEH	ACHE, EACH
AAJR	AJAR	ABGS	BAGS	ACEK	CAKE
AAKR	KARA	ABGY	GABY	ACEL	ALEC, CELA, LACE
AALM	ALMA, LAMA	ABHL	BLAH	ACEM	ACME, CAME, MACE
AALN	ALAN, ANAL, LANA	ABHS	BASH	ACEN	ACNE, CAEN, CANE
AALS	ALAS	ABHT	BATH	ACEP	CAPE, PACE
AALV	ALVA, LAVA	ABHU	HABU	ACER	ACRE, CARE, RACE
AAMM	MAMA, MA'AM	ABIL	ALBI, BAIL, BALI	ACES	ACES, CASE
AAMR	MARA	ABIM	IAMB	ACEV	CAVE
AAMY	MAYA	ABIN	BINA	ACFL	CALF
AANN	ANNA, NANA	ABIR	BARI	ACFT	FACT
AANR	NARA	ABIS	BIAS	ACGR	CRAG
AANS	NASA, SAN'A	ABIT	BAIT	ACGS	SCAG
AANY	ANYA	ABJM	JAMB	ACHK	HACK
AANZ	ZANA	ABJS	JABS	ACHM	MACH
AAPP	PAPA	ABKL	BALK	ACHP	CHAP
AAQU	AQUA	ABKN	BANK	ACHR	ARCH, CHAR
AARS	SARA	ABKR	BARK	ACHS	CASH, CHAS
AART	TARA	ABKS	BASK	ACHT	CATH, CHAT
AARU	AURA	ABKU	BAKU	ACHY	CHAY
AARZ	ZARA	ABLL	BALL	ACIL	CALI
AATT	TA-TA	ABLM	BALM, LAMB	ACIM	MICA
AAWY	AWAY	ABLS	LABS, SLAB	ACIN	INCA
ABBE	BABE	ABLW	BAWL	ACIP	PICA
ABBL	BLAB	ABLY	ABLY	ACIR	RICA
ABBR	BARB	ABMO	AMBO, BOMA	ACJK	JACK
ABBS	BABS	ABMR	BRAM	ACKL	CALK, LACK

5

Code	Words	Code	Words	Code	Words
ACKP	PACK	ADER	DARE, DEAR, READ	ADRY	DRAY, YARD
ACKR	RACK	ADET	DATE	ADSW	WADS
ACKS	CASK, SACK	ADEU	AUDE	ADSY	DAYS
ACKT	TACK	ADEV	DAVE	ADUV	VAUD
ACKZ	ZACK	ADEW	AWED, WADE	ADVY	DAVY
ACLL	CALL	ADEX	AXED	ADYZ	YAZD
ACLM	CALM, CLAM	ADEZ	ADZE, DAZE	AEES	EASE
ACLN	CLAN	ADFF	DAFF	AEFK	FAKE
ACLO	COAL, COLA	ADFS	FADS	AEFL	FLEA, LEAF
ACLP	CLAP	ADFT	DAFT	AEFM	FAME
ACLR	CARL	ADGL	GLAD	AEFR	FARE, FEAR, RAFE
ACLT	TALC	ADGO	DAGO, GOAD	AEFS	SAFE
ACLU	CAUL	ADGR	DRAG, GARD	AEFT	FATE, FEAT
ACLW	CLAW	ADGY	G'DAY	AEFY	FAYE
ACLX	CALX	ADHJ	HADJ	AEFZ	FAZE
ACLY	CLAY, LACY	ADHK	DHAK	AEGG	GAGE
ACMO	COMA	ADHN	HAND	AEGL	GALE
ACMP	CAMP	ADHO	DOHA, HOAD	AEGM	GAME
ACMR	CRAM, MARC	ADHP	DAPH	AEGP	GAPE, PAGE
ACMS	CAMS, MACS, SCAM	ADHR	HARD	AEGR	AREG, GEAR, GERA, RAGE
ACNS	CANS, SCAN	ADHS	DASH, SHAD	AEGS	AGES, SAGE
ACNT	CANT	ADIL	DIAL, LAID	AEGT	GATE
ACNY	CYAN	ADIM	AMID, MAID	AEGU	AGUE
ACOR	CORA	ADIP	PAID	AEGV	GAVE
ACOT	COAT, TACO	ADIR	ARID, RAID	AEGW	WAGE
ACOX	COAX, COXA	ADIS	AIDS, DAIS, SAID	AEGY	GAYE
ACPR	CARP, CRAP	ADIV	AVID, VIDA	AEGZ	GAZE
ACPS	CAPS	ADIW	WADI	AEHK	HAKE
ACPT	PACT	ADKN	DANK	AEHL	HALE, HEAL, HELA, LEAH
ACRS	ARCS, CARS, SCAR	ADKR	DARK	AEHM	AHEM, HAEM, HAME
ACRT	CART	ADLN	LAND	AEHP	HEAP
ACRY	CARY, RACY	ADLO	ALDO, LOAD	AEHR	HARE, HEAR, HERA, RHEA
ACRZ	CZAR	ADLR	LARD	AEHT	HATE, HEAT, THEA
ACSS	CASS, SACS	ADLS	LADS	AEHV	HAVE
ACST	ACTS, CAST, CATS, SCAT	ADLU	DUAL, LAUD	AEHY	YEAH
ACSV	VACS	ADLY	LADY	AEHZ	HAZE
ACSW	CAWS	ADMN	DAMN	AEIL	ELIA
ACTT	TACT	ADMP	DAMP	AEIN	AINE
ACTY	TACY	ADMR	DRAM	AEIR	AIRE, EIRA
ACVY	CAVY	ADMS	DAMS	AEJK	JAKE
ADDE	DEAD	ADMU	DUMA, MAUD	AEJL	JAEL
ADDO	DADO	ADNR	DARN, RAND	AEJN	JANE, JEAN, JENA
ADDS	DADS	ADNS	SAND	AEJP	JAPE
ADDY	ADDY, DYAD, D-DAY	ADNW	DAWN, WAND	AEKL	KALE, LAKE, LEAK
ADEF	DEAF, FADE	ADNY	ANDY	AEKM	MAKE
ADEG	AGED	ADOR	DORA, ROAD	AEKN	KANE
ADEH	HADE, HEAD	ADOS	SODA	AEKP	PEAK
ADEI	AIDE, IDEA	ADOT	TOAD	AEKR	RAKE
ADEJ	JADE	ADOW	WOAD	AEKS	SAKE
ADEL	ALED, DALE, DEAL, LADE, LEAD	ADPS	PADS	AEKT	KATE, TAKE, TEAK
ADEM	DAME, EDAM, MADE, MEAD	ADQU	QUAD	AEKW	WAKE, WEAK
ADEN	ADEN, DANE, DEAN, EDNA	ADRS	ARDS	AELL	ELLA, LELA
ADEP	APED	ADRT	DART, DRAT, TRAD	AELM	ELMA, LAME, MALE, MEAL
		ADRW	DRAW, WARD		

6

AELN	ELAN, LANE, LEAN, LENA, NEAL
AELO	ALOE
AELP	LEAP, PALE, PEAL, PLEA
AELR	EARL, REAL
AELS	ELSA, LEAS, SALE, SEAL
AELT	ET AL, LATE, LETA, TALE, TEAL
AELU	LAUE
AELV	VALE, VEAL
AELW	WEAL
AELX	ALEX, AXEL, AXLE
AELZ	LAZE, ZEAL
AEMM	EMMA
AEMN	AMEN, MANE, MEAN, NAME
AEMR	MARE, REAM
AEMS	SAME, SEAM
AEMT	MATE, MEAT, META, TAME, TEAM, TEMA
AEMX	AMEX, EXAM
AEMZ	MAZE
AENN	ANNE
AENO	AEON
AENP	NAPE, PANE
AENR	EARN, NEAR, RENA
AENS	SANE, SEAN
AENT	ANTE, NEAT
AENV	EVAN, NAVE, NEVA, VANE
AENW	ANEW, EWAN, WANE, WEAN
AENZ	ZANE, ZENA
AEPR	PARE, PEAR, RAPE, REAP
AEPS	APES, APSE, PEAS
AEPT	PATE, PEAT, PETA, TAPE
AEPV	PAVE
AEPX	APEX
AEPY	PAYE
AERR	RARE, REAR
AERS	ARSE, EARS, ERAS, SEAR, SERA
AERT	RATE, TARE, TEAR
AERV	AVER, RAVE, VERA
AERW	WEAR
AERY	YEAR
AERZ	EZRA, RAZE
AESS	SEAS
AEST	EAST, EATS, SATE, SEAT, SETA, TEAS
AESU	ESAU
AESV	SAVE, VASE
AESX	AXES
AESY	AYES, EASY, YEAS
AETT	ETTA, TEAT
AEUV	UVEA

AEVW	WAVE
AFFF	FAFF
AFFG	GAFF
AFFN	NAFF
AFGL	FLAG
AFGN	FANG
AFGR	GRAF
AFGS	FAGS
AFHL	HALF
AFHT	HAFT
AFIL	FAIL
AFIN	FAIN
AFIR	FAIR
AFIS	SAFI
AFIT	FIAT
AFIW	WAIF
AFKL	FLAK
AFLL	FALL
AFLN	FLAN
AFLO	FOAL, LOAF, OLAF
AFLP	FLAP
AFLT	FLAT
AFLW	FLAW
AFLX	FLAX
AFLY	FLAY
AFMO	FOAM
AFMR	FARM
AFNS	FANS
AFNU	FAUN
AFNW	FAWN
AFOR	AFRO, FORA
AFOS	OAFS, SOFA
AFPR	FRAP
AFRT	FART, RAFT
AFRU	FRAU, URFA
AFRY	FRAY
AFST	FAST, FATS
AFSX	SFAX
AFTW	WAFT
AGGN	GANG
AGGO	AGOG
AGGS	GAGS
AGHI	HAIG
AGHN	HANG
AGHS	GASH, HAGS, SHAG
AGHT	GHAT
AGIL	GAIL
AGIM	MAGI
AGIN	GAIN, GINA, INGA
AGIO	IAGO
AGIR	RIGA
AGIT	GAIT
AGIZ	GIZA
AGJO	JAGO

AGJS	JAGS
AGKW	GAWK
AGLL	GALL
AGLO	GAOL, GOAL, OLGA
AGLS	GALS, LAGS, SLAG
AGLY	ALGY
AGMR	GRAM
AGMS	AGMS, MAGS
AGMU	GUAM
AGMY	GAMY
AGNP	PANG
AGNR	GRAN, RANG
AGNS	NAGS, SANG, SNAG
AGNT	GNAT, TANG
AGNW	GNAW
AGNY	YANG
AGOS	SAGO
AGOT	GOAT, TOGA
AGOY	YOGA
AGPS	GAPS, GASP
AGPW	GAWP
AGRS	RAGS
AGRY	GARY, GRAY
AGRZ	GRAZ
AGSS	SAGS
AGST	STAG, TAGS
AGSW	SWAG, WAGS
AGSY	GAYS
AHHS	HASH, SHAH
AHHT	HATH
AHIK	HAIK
AHIL	HAIL
AHIR	HAIR
AHIV	IVAH
AHJJ	HAJJ
AHKL	LAKH
AHKN	ANKH, HANK, KHAN
AHKO	KOHA
AHKR	HARK
AHKS	HASK
AHKT	KATH
AHKW	HAWK
AHLL	HALL
AHLM	HALM
AHLO	HALO
AHLR	HARL
AHLS	LASH
AHLT	HALT, LATH
AHLU	HAUL, HULA
AHMM	HAMM
AHMO	HAMO, HOMA
AHMR	HARM
AHMS	HAMS, MASH, SHAM
AHMW	WHAM

7

AHNO	NOAH	AINU	AINU	ALLP	PALL
AHNS	HANS	AINV	IVAN, VAIN, VINA	ALLT	TALL
AHNT	TANH, THAN	AINZ	NAZI	ALLW	WALL
AHNW	HWAN	AIOT	IOTA, OITA	ALLY	ALLY
AHOR	HOAR, HORA	AIOW	IOWA	ALMM	MALM
AHOS	SHOA	AIPR	PAIR	ALMO	LOAM
AHOT	OATH	AIPS	PISA	ALMP	LAMP, PALM
AHOU	OAHU	AIQR	IRAQ	ALMR	MARL
AHOW	WHOA	AIRS	AIRS, ASIR, SARI	ALMS	ALMS, SLAM
AHOX	HOAX	AIRT	RITA	ALMT	MALT
AHOY	AHOY, HOYA	AIRY	AIRY	ALMU	ALUM, MAUL
AHPR	HARP	AIST	ASTI	ALNO	LOAN, NOLA
AHPS	HASP	AISV	AVIS, VISA	ALNP	PLAN
AHPT	PATH	AISX	AXIS	ALNU	ALUN, ULNA
AHRS	RASH	AITV	VITA	ALNW	LAWN
AHRT	HART	AITW	WAIT	ALOP	OPAL
AHRZ	HARZ	AITX	TAXI	ALOR	LORA, ORAL
AHSS	SASH	AITZ	ZITA	ALOS	ALSO, LAOS
AHST	HAST, HATS, SHAT	AIVV	VIVA	ALOT	ALTO
AHSW	SHAW, WASH	AJMS	JAMS	ALOV	OLAV, OVAL
AHSY	ASHY	AJNO	JOAN	ALOW	AWOL
AHTT	THAT	AJNU	JUAN	ALOZ	ZOLA
AHTU	UTAH	AJRS	JARS	ALPP	LAPP, PALP
AHTW	THAW, WHAT	AJRU	JURA	ALPS	ALPS, LAPS, PALS, SLAP
AHYZ	HAZY	AJSW	JAWS	ALPU	PAUL, PULA
AIIN	IAIN	AJSY	JAYS	ALPW	PAWL
AIJL	JAIL	AJZZ	JAZZ	ALPY	PLAY
AIKN	AKIN	AKLN	LANK	ALRS	LARS
AIKP	PAKI	AKLR	KARL, LARK	ALRY	LYRA
AIKR	RIKA	AKLS	SALK	ALSS	LASS
AILL	LILA	AKLT	TALK	ALST	LAST, SALT, SLAT
AILM	ILMA, LIAM, LIMA, MAIL, MALI	AKLW	WALK	ALSU	SAUL
AILN	LAIN, LINA, NAIL	AKMO	AMOK	ALSV	SLAV
AILO	IOLA	AKMR	MARK	ALSW	AWLS, LAWS
AILP	PAIL	AKMS	MASK	ALSY	ALYS, LAYS, SLAY
AILR	LAIR, LIAR, LIRA, RAIL, RIAL	AKNO	KANO	ALTU	TULA
AILS	ISLA, LIAS, LISA, SAIL	AKNP	KNAP	ALTW	WALT
AILT	ALIT, LITA, TAIL	AKNR	NARK, RANK	ALUW	WAUL
AILV	VIAL	AKNS	SANK	ALWY	YAWL
AILW	WAIL	AKNT	TANK	ALYZ	LAZY
AILX	ALIX	AKNW	WANK	AMMS	MAMS
AILZ	LIZA	AKNY	YANK	AMNO	MOAN, MONA, OMAN
AIMM	IMAM, MAIM, MIMA	AKOR	OKRA	AMNX	MANX
AIMN	MAIN, MINA	AKOS	OAKS, SOAK	AMNY	MANY, MYNA
AIMR	AMIR, IRMA, MAIR, MIRA	AKOT	KOTA	AMOR	OMAR, ROAM, ROMA
AIMS	AIMS, AMIS	AKOY	OKAY	AMOS	AMOS, SOMA
AIMU	MAUI	AKPR	PARK	AMOT	ATOM, MOAT
AINN	NINA	AKRS	ARKS, SARK	AMOY	AMOY, MOYA
AINO	IONA	AKST	TASK	AMPR	PRAM, RAMP
AINP	PAIN	AKSU	AUKS, SKUA	AMPS	AMPS, MAPS, SPAM
AINR	IRAN, RAIN, RANI, RINA	AKSY	YAKS	AMPT	TAMP
AINS	ANIS, SIAN	AKTY	KATY	AMPU	PUMA
AINT	AIN'T, NITA, TINA	ALLM	MALL	AMPV	VAMP
		ALLO	LOLA	AMRS	ARMS, MARS, RAMS

8

AMRT	TRAM	ARSW	WARS	BDLO	BOLD
AMRW	WARM	ARSY	RAYS	BDMU	DUMB
AMRY	ARMY, MARY, MYRA	ARTT	TART	BDNO	BOND
AMSS	MASS	ARTW	WART	BDOS	BODS
AMST	MAST, MATS	ARTY	ARTY, TRAY, TYRA	BDOY	BODY, BOYD
AMSW	MAWS, SWAM	ARTZ	TZAR	BDRU	DRUB
AMSX	XMAS	ARVY	VARY	BDSU	BUDS
AMSY	MAYS, YAMS	ARWY	AWRY, WARY	BEEF	BEEF
AMTT	MATT	ARXY	X-RAY	BEEH	HEBE
AMYZ	MAZY	ASSS	SASS	BEEL	ELBE
ANNO	ANON, NONA	ASSW	SAWS	BEEN	EBEN
ANOO	OONA	ASSY	SAYS	BEER	BEER
ANOR	NORA, ORAN, ROAN,	ASTT	TATS	BEES	BEES
RONA		ASTV	VAST, VATS	BEET	BEET
ANOT	NATO	ASTW	SWAT	BEGI	GIBE
ANOV	AVON, NOVA	ASTY	STAY	BEGY	GYBE
ANPS	NAPS, PANS, SNAP, SPAN	ASUV	SUVA	BEHR	HERB
ANPT	PANT	ASWY	SWAY, WAYS, YAWS	BEHT	BETH
ANPW	PAWN	ATTU	TAUT	BEIJ	JIBE
ANRT	RANT, TARN	ATTW	TWAT, WATT	BEIK	BIKE
ANRW	WARN	AVWY	WAVY	BEIL	BIEL, BILE
ANRY	RYAN, YARN	AWXY	WAXY	BEIN	BE IN
ANST	ANTS, STAN, TANS	BBES	EBBS	BEIR	BIER
ANSU	ANUS	BBIS	BIBS	BEIT	BITE
ANSV	VANS	BBIY	IBBY	BEIX	IBEX
ANSW	SAWN, SWAN	BBLO	BLOB	BEKO	KOBE
ANSY	NAYS	BBLU	BULB	BEKR	BERK, KERB
ANTU	AUNT, TUNA	BBMO	BOMB	BELL	BELL
ANTW	WANT	BBOO	BOOB	BELO	BOLE, LOBE
ANUY	YUAN	BBOS	BOBS	BELP	PLEB
ANVY	NAVY	BBOU	BUBO	BELT	BELT
ANWY	YAWN	BBSU	BUBS	BELU	BLUE
ANYZ	ZANY	BCEH	CHEB	BELW	BLEW
AOPS	OAPS, SOAP	BCEK	BECK	BENO	BONE
AOPT	ATOP	BCEU	CUBE	BENR	BERN
AORR	ROAR	BCIM	ICBM	BENS	BENS
AORS	OARS, ROSA, SOAR	BCIR	CRIB	BENT	BENT
AORT	ROTA, TARO	BCKU	BUCK	BEOO	OBOE
AORZ	ZORA	BCLO	BLOC	BEOR	BOER, BORE, ROBE
AOST	OATS	BCLU	CLUB	BEOY	OBEY
AOTU	AUTO	BCMO	COMB	BERT	BERT, BRET
AOVW	AVOW	BCOS	COBS	BERV	VERB
APPS	PAPS	BCRU	CURB	BERW	BREW
APPU	PUPA	BCSU	CUBS	BERY	BYRE
APRS	PARS, RAPS, RASP, SPAR	BDEI	BIDE	BESS	BESS
APRT	PART, PRAT, RAPT, TRAP	BDEL	BLED	BEST	BEST, BETS
APRW	WARP, WRAP	BDEN	BEND	BESW	WEBS
APRY	PRAY	BDEO	BODE	BESY	BYES
APSS	ASPS, PASS, SAPS, SPAS	BDES	BEDS, DEBS	BETU	BUTE, TUBE
APST	PAST, PATS, SPAT, TAPS	BDET	DEBT	BETY	BYTE
APSW	PAWS, SWAP, WASP	BDII	IBID	BEUZ	ZEBU
APSY	SPAY, YAPS	BDIN	BIND	BEVY	BEVY
AQUY	QUAY	BDIR	BIRD	BFFI	BIFF
ARST	ARTS, RATS, STAR, TARS,	BDIS	BIDS	BFFU	BUFF
TSAR					

9

BFIS	FIBS	BNOR	BORN, BRNO	CEGS	ECGS, GCES, GCSE
BFMU	BUMF	BNOS	NOBS, SNOB	CEHK	HECK
BFOS	FOBS	BNOY	BONY	CEHO	ECHO
BGIL	GLIB	BNRU	BURN	CEHR	CHER
BGIN	BING	BNRY	BRYN	CEHT	ETCH
BGIO	GOBI, IGBO	BNSU	BUNS, NUBS, SNUB	CEHW	CHEW
BGNU	BUNG	BOOR	BOOR	CEIL	LICE
BGOO	GOBO	BOOS	BOOS	CEIM	MICE
BGOS	BOGS, GOBS	BOOT	BOOT	CEIN	NICE
BGRU	GRUB	BOOZ	BOZO	CEIP	EPIC
BGSU	BUGS	BOPS	BOPS	CEIR	CERI, ERIC, RICE
BHOO	HOBO	BORS	ORBS	CEIS	ICES
BHOS	BOSH, HOBS	BORT	BORT	CEIT	CITE
BHOT	BOTH	BORW	BROW	CEIV	VICE
BHSU	BUSH, HUBS	BORZ	BROZ	CEKN	NECK
BIIS	IBIS	BOSS	BOSS, SOBS	CEKO	COKE
BIJS	JIBS	BOSW	BOWS	CEKP	PECK
BIKL	BILK	BOSY	BOYS, YOBS	CEKR	RECK
BIKS	IKBS	BOTU	BOUT	CELL	CELL
BILL	BILL	BOTY	TOBY	CELM	CLEM
BILM	LIMB	BOUY	BUOY	CELO	CLEO
BILO	BOIL	BPRU	BURP	CELU	CLUE, LUCE
BILP	BLIP	BPSU	PUBS	CELW	CLEW
BILR	BIRL	BRRU	BURR	CEMO	COME
BIMR	BRIM	BRSU	BURS, RUBS	CEMY	CYME
BINS	BINS, NIBS	BRTU	BURT	CENO	CONE, ONCE
BIOR	BIRO	BRUY	BURY, RUBY	CENT	CENT
BIOZ	ZIBO	BSSU	BUSS, SUBS	CEOP	COPE, OPEC
BIRS	RIBS	BSTU	BUST, BUTS, STUB, TUBS	CEOR	CORE
BIRT	BRIT	BSUY	BUSY, BUYS	CEOV	COVE
BIST	BITS	BTTU	BUTT	CEPS	SPEC
BJOS	JOBS	BUZZ	BUZZ	CEPU	PUCE
BKLU	BULK	CCHI	CHIC	CERT	CERT
BKNO	KNOB	CCIN	C-IN-C	CERU	CURE, ECRU
BKNU	BUNK	CCKO	COCK	CERW	CREW
BKOO	BOOK	CCOR	CROC	CESS	CSES, SECS
BKRU	BURK	CDEE	CEDE	CEST	SECT
BKSU	BUSK	CDEI	DICE, ICED	CESU	CUES
BLLO	BOLL	CDEK	DECK	CETU	CUTE
BLLU	BULL	CDEO	CODE, COED	CFFU	CUFF
BLOS	LOBS, SLOB	CDEU	CUED	CFIO	COIF, FOCI
BLOT	BLOT, BOLT	CDHI	CHID	CFKU	FUCK
BLOW	BLOW, BOWL	CDIK	DICK	CGHU	CHUG
BLRU	BLUR	CDIS	DISC	CGLO	CLOG
BLSU	SLUB	CDKO	DOCK	CGOS	COGS
BMNU	NUMB	CDKU	DUCK	CHIK	HICK
BMOO	BOOM	CDLO	CLOD, COLD	CHIN	CHIN, INCH
BMOS	MOBS	CDOR	CORD	CHIP	CHIP
BMOT	TOMB	CDOS	CODS, DOCS	CHIR	RICH
BMOW	WOMB	CDRU	CURD	CHIT	CHIT, ITCH
BMPU	BUMP	CDSU	SCUD	CHKO	HOCK
BMSU	BUMS	CDTU	DUCT	CHLO	LOCH
BNNO	BONN	CEFH	CHEF	CHMU	CHUM, MUCH
BNOO	BOON	CEFL	CLEF	CHOP	CHOP

10

CHOS	COSH	CMSU	SCUM	DEFR	FRED
CHOU	CHOU, OUCH	CNNO	CONN	DEFT	DEFT
CHOW	CHOW	CNOO	COON	DEFU	FEUD
CHRU	CHUR	CNOR	CORN	DEFY	DEFY
CHSU	SUCH	CNOS	CONS, NCOS	DEGL	GELD
CIKK	KICK	CNOY	CONY	DEGO	DOGE
CIKL	LICK	CNSY	SYNC	DEGY	EDGY
CIKM	MICK	CNTU	CUNT	DEHI	HIDE, HIED
CIKN	NICK	COOP	COOP	DEHL	HELD
CIKP	PICK	COOS	COOS	DEHO	HOED
CIKR	RICK	COOT	COOT	DEHR	HERD
CIKS	SICK	COPR	CROP	DEHS	SHED
CIKT	TICK	COPS	COPS	DEHU	HUED
CIKV	VICK	COPU	COUP	DEHY	HEDY, HYDE
CIKW	WICK	COPY	COPY	DEIK	DIKE
CILO	COIL, LOCI	CORS	ROCS	DEIL	IDLE, LIED
CILP	CLIP	CORW	CROW	DEIM	DIME, IDEM
CINO	COIN, ICON	COST	COST, COTS, SCOT	DEIN	DINE, ENID
CINZ	ZINC	COSW	COWS	DEIP	PIED
CIOR	COIR	COSY	COSY	DEIR	DIRE, RIDE
CIPS	SPIC	COYZ	COZY	DEIS	IDES, SIDE
CIRU	URIC	CPSU	CUPS, CUSP	DEIT	DIET, EDIT, TIDE, TIED
CISS	CISS	CPSW	WPCS	DEIV	DIVE, VIED
CIST	TICS	CRSU	CRUS, CURS	DEIW	DEWI, WIDE
CITY	CITY	CRTU	CURT	DEJN	NEJD
CJKO	JOCK	CRUX	CRUX	DEJU	JUDE
CJLU	CLUJ	CSSU	CUSS	DEKS	DESK
CKLO	LOCK	CSTU	CUTS	DEKU	DUKE
CKLU	LUCK	CSTY	CYST	DEKY	DYKE
CKMO	MOCK	DDEE	DEED	DELL	DELL
CKMU	MUCK	DDEI	DIED	DELN	LEND
CKNO	CONK	DDEO	EDDO	DELO	DOLE, LODE
CKOO	COOK	DDEU	DUDE	DELP	PLED
CKOR	CORK, ROCK	DDEY	DYED, EDDY	DELS	SLED
CKOS	SOCK	DDJU	JUDD	DELU	DUEL
CKPU	PUCK	DDOO	DODO	DELV	VELD
CKRU	RUCK	DDOS	ODDS	DELW	LEWD, WELD
CKSU	SUCK	DDOT	TODD	DEMN	MEND
CKTU	TUCK	DDSU	DUDS	DEMO	DEMO, DOME, EDOM,
CKUY	YUCK	DEEF	FEED		MODE
CLLU	CULL	DEEG	EDGE	DENO	DONE, NODE
CLMO	COLM	DEEH	HEED	DENR	NERD, REND
CLMU	CULM	DEEI	EDIE	DENS	DENS, ENDS, SEND
CLOO	COOL, LOCO	DEEL	DELE	DENT	DENT, TEND
CLOP	CLOP	DEEM	DEEM	DENU	DUNE, NUDE
CLOS	COLS	DEEN	EDEN, NEED	DENV	VEND
CLOT	CLOT, COLT	DEEP	DEEP, PEED	DENW	WEND
CLOW	COWL	DEER	DEER, REED	DENY	DENY, DYNE
CLOY	CLOY	DEES	SEED	DEOP	DOPE
CLRU	CURL	DEET	TEED	DEOR	DOER, REDO, RODE
CLTU	CULT	DEEW	WEED	DEOS	DOES, DOSE, ODES
CLUY	LUCY	DEEY	EYED	DEOT	DOTE, TOED
CMOO	COMO	DEFL	FLED	DEOV	DOVE
CMOR	CORM	DEFN	FEND	DEOW	OWED

DEOZ	DOZE	DINR	RIND	DORW	WORD
DEPS	SPED	DINS	DINS, SIND	DORY	DORY
DEPU	DUPE	DINT	DINT	DOSS	DOSS, SODS
DERS	REDS	DINW	WIND	DOST	DOTS, TODS
DERU	RUDE, RUED	DIOV	VOID	DOSU	DUOS
DERV	DERV	DIPR	DRIP	DOYZ	DOZY
DERW	DREW	DIPS	DIPS	DPSU	PUDS, SPUD
DERY	DYER	DIQU	QUID	DRSU	SURD
DESU	DUES, SUED, USED	DIRT	DIRT	DRTU	TURD
DESY	DYES	DIRU	RUDI	DRUU	URDU
DESZ	ZEDS	DISS	DISS	DRUY	RUDY
DETU	DUET	DISU	IUDS	DSSU	SUDS
DEWY	DEWY	DISY	YIDS	DSTU	DUST, STUD
DFFO	DOFF	DITY	TIDY	DSUV	VDUS
DFFU	DUFF	DJOU	JUDO	DTUY	DUTY
DFIN	FIND	DJOY	JODY	EEEP	EPEE
DFLO	FOLD	DJUY	JUDY	EEFL	FEEL, FLEE
DFNO	FOND	DKNU	DUNK	EEFR	FREE, REEF
DFNU	FUND	DKSU	DUSK	EEFS	FEES
DFOO	FOOD	DKUU	KUDU	EEFT	FEET, FETE
DFOR	FORD	DLLO	DOLL	EEGH	GHEE
DGIL	GILD	DLLU	DULL	EEGK	GEEK
DGIR	GIRD, GRID	DLMO	MOLD	EEGL	GLEE
DGIS	DIGS	DLNU	LUND	EEGN	GENE
DGLO	GOLD	DLOP	PLOD	EEGR	EGER
DGNU	DUNG	DLOR	LORD	EEHL	HEEL
DGOO	GOOD	DLOS	SOLD	EEHR	HERE
DGOS	DOGS, GODS	DLOT	DOLT, TOLD	EEHT	THEE
DGOU	DOUG	DLOU	LOUD, LUDO	EEIR	EIRE, ERIE
DGRU	DRUG	DLOW	WOLD	EEIV	EVIE
DGSU	DUGS	DLOZ	LODZ	EEJP	JEEP
DHIN	HIND	DLUY	DULY	EEJR	JEER
DHIS	DISH	DMOO	DOOM, MOOD	EEKL	KEEL, LEEK
DHLO	HOLD	DMOS	MODS	EEKM	MEEK
DHOO	HOOD	DMPU	DUMP	EEKN	KEEN, KNEE
DHOS	DOSH, HODS, SHOD	DMRU	DRUM	EEKP	KEEP, PEEK
DHOU	OUDH	DNOO	ONDO	EEKR	REEK
DHOW	DHOW	DNOP	POND	EEKS	SEEK
DHRU	HURD	DNOR	NORD	EEKW	WEEK
DHTU	THUD	DNOS	DONS, NODS	EELP	PEEL
DIIM	MIDI	DNOT	DON'T	EELR	ERLE, LEER, REEL
DIJO	JODI	DNOU	UNDO	EELS	EELS, ELSE, LEES
DIJU	JUDI	DNOW	DOWN	EELU	UELE
DIKN	KIND	DNOZ	ZOND	EEMR	MERE
DIKR	DIRK	DNSU	DUNS	EEMS	ESME, SEEM, SEME
DIKS	DISK, KIDS, SKID	DOOR	DOOR, ROOD	EEMT	MEET, METE, TEEM
DILL	DILL	DOOT	TO-DO	EENR	ERNE, NE'ER, RENE
DILM	MILD	DOOW	WOOD	EENS	SEEN
DILO	IDOL, LIDO, LODI	DOPR	DROP, PROD	EENV	EVEN
DILS	LIDS, SLID	DOPS	PODS	EENW	EWEN
DILW	WILD	DOQU	QUOD	EEPP	PEEP
DILY	IDLY	DORS	RODS	EEPR	PEER
DIMN	MIND	DORT	TROD	EEPS	SEEP
DINO	DION	DORU	DOUR	EEPT	PETE

12

EEPW	WEEP	EGNU	GENU	EIKL	KIEL, LIKE
EERS	ERSE, SEER, SERE	EGNW	GWEN	EIKM	MIKE
EERT	TREE	EGOR	ERGO, GOER, GORE,	EIKN	KINE
EERU	EURE		OGRE, ROEG	EIKP	PIKE
EERV	EVER, VEER, VERE	EGOS	EGOS, GOES	EIKR	ERIK, KEIR, KERI
EERW	EWER	EGPS	PEGS	EIKT	KITE
EERY	EYRE	EGPU	PEGU	EIKV	KIEV
EESS	SEES	EGRS	ERGS	EILM	EMIL, LIME, MILE
EEST	TEES	EGRT	GERT	EILN	LIEN, LINE, NEIL
EESV	EVES	EGRU	URGE	EILP	PILE
EESW	EWES	EGRW	GREW	EILR	LIRE, RILE
EESX	EXES	EGRY	GREY	EILS	ILSE, ISLE, LEIS, LIES, LISE,
EESY	EYES	EHHT	HETH	SILE	
EETW	TWEE	EHIK	HIKE	EILT	LITE, TILE
EFFI	FIFE	EHIR	HEIR, HIRE	EILU	LIEU
EFFJ	JEFF	EHIV	HIVE	EILV	EVIL, LEVI, LIVE, VEIL, VILE
EFHT	HEFT	EHKO	HOKE	EILX	ILEX
EFIK	EFIK	EHLL	HELL	EILY	EILY
EFIL	FILE, LIEF, LIFE	EHLM	HELM	EIMM	MIME
EFIN	FINE	EHLO	HOLE	EIMN	MIEN, MINE
EFIR	FIRE, RIFE	EHLP	HELP	EIMR	EMIR, MIRE, RIME
EFIV	FIVE	EHLR	HERL	EIMS	SEMI
EFIW	WIFE	EHMO	HOME	EIMT	EMIT, ITEM, MITE, TIME
EFLL	FELL	EHMP	HEMP	EINN	NINE
EFLO	FLOE	EHMR	HERM	EINP	PINE
EFLS	SELF	EHMS	HEMS, MESH, SHEM	EINR	ERIN, REIN
EFLT	FELT, LEFT	EHMT	THEM	EINS	SINE
EFLU	FLUE, FUEL	EHMU	HUME	EINT	TINE
EFLW	FLEW	EHNO	HONE	EINU	NIUE
EFLX	FLEX	EHNR	HERN	EINV	VEIN, VINE
EFMU	FUME	EHNS	HENS	EINW	WINE
EFNR	FERN	EHNT	HENT, THEN	EINZ	INEZ, ZEIN, ZINE
EFNS	FENS	EHNW	HEWN, WHEN	EIOS	OISE
EFOR	FORE, FROE	EHOP	HOPE	EIPP	PIPE
EFOS	FOES	EHOR	HERO, HOER	EIPR	PIER, RIPE
EFRS	REFS, SERF	EHOS	HOES, HOSE, SHOE	EIPS	PIES
EFRT	FRET	EHOT	THEO	EIPW	WIPE
EFSU	FUSE	EHOV	HOVE	EIRS	RISE, SIRE
EFTW	WEFT	EHOW	HOWE	EIRT	RITE, TIER, TIRE
EGGR	GREG	EHPW	PHEW	EIRV	RIVE
EGGS	EGGS	EHPY	HYPE	EIRW	WEIR, WIRE
EGHU	HUGE	EHRR	HERR	EIST	SITE, TIES
EGIN	INGE	EHRS	HERS	EISV	IVES, VIES, VISE
EGIV	GIVE	EHSS	HESS	EISW	WISE
EGKN	GENK	EHST	HEST, SETH	EISZ	SIZE
EGKS	KEGS	EHSU	HUES	EITX	EXIT
EGLN	GLEN	EHSW	SHEW	EITY	YETI
EGLO	OGLE	EHTW	WHET	EIVW	VIEW
EGLS	GELS, LEGS	EHTY	THEY	EJKO	JOKE
EGLU	GLUE	EHUY	HUEY	EJKR	JERK
EGMR	GERM	EHWW	WHEW	EJLL	JELL
EGMS	GEMS	EHWY	WHEY	EJLO	JOEL
EGNO	GONE	EIJV	JIVE	EJNU	JUNE
EGNT	GENT	EIKK	KIKE	EJOS	JOSE

13

EJOV	JOVE	ELTU	LUTE	EORU	EURO, ROUE
EJOY	JOEY	ELTW	WELT	EORV	OVER, ROVE
EJSS	JESS	ELUY	YULE	EORW	WORE
EJST	JEST, JETS	ELVY	LEVY	EORY	YORE
EJSW	JEWS	EMMO	MEMO	EORZ	ZERO
EJTU	JUTE	EMNO	OMEN	EOST	TOES
EKLM	MELK	EMNU	MENU	EOSW	WOES
EKLP	KELP	EMOP	MOPE, POEM	EOTT	TOTE
EKLS	ELKS	EMOR	MORE, ROME	EOTV	VETO, VOTE
EKLU	LUKE	EMOS	SOME	EOTY	EYOT
EKLY	KYLE	EMOT	MOTE, TOME	EOVW	WOVE
EKMO	MOKE	EMOV	MOVE	EOYZ	OYEZ
EKNR	KERN	EMOW	MEOW	EPPR	PREP
EKNS	KENS	EMPR	PERM	EPRS	REPS
EKNT	KENT	EMPT	TEMP	EPRT	PERT
EKNU	NUKE	EMRT	TERM	EPRU	PERU, PRUE, PURE
EKNW	KNEW	EMRV	MERV	EPRY	PREY, PYRE
EKOP	POKE	EMSS	MESS	EPST	PEST, PETS, STEP
EKOS	KEOS	EMST	STEM	EPSW	PEWS, SPEW
EKOW	WOKE	EMSU	EMUS, MUSE	EPSY	ESPY
EKOY	YOKE	EMSW	MEWS	EPTW	WEPT
EKPR	PERK	EMTU	MUTE	EPTY	TYPE
EKPT	KEPT	EMTZ	METZ	ERST	REST
EKPU	PUKE	ENNO	NEON, NONE	ERSU	REUS, RUSE, SUER, SURE,
EKRT	TREK	ENNP	PENN		USER
EKRU	KURE	ENOP	NOPE, OPEN	ERSV	REVS
EKSW	SKEW	ENOR	ORNE, RENO	ERSY	RYES
EKSY	KEYS, SKYE	ENOS	ENOS, EONS, NOES, NOSE,	ERTU	TRUE
ELLN	NELL		ONES	ERTV	TVER
ELLS	SELL	ENOT	ETON, NOTE, TONE	ERTY	TYRE
ELLT	TELL	ENOV	OVEN	ERVY	VERY
ELLW	WELL	ENOW	OWEN	ESST	SETS, TESS
ELLY	LYLE, YELL	ENOX	OXEN	ESSU	USES
ELMO	MOLE	ENOZ	ZONE	ESTT	STET, TEST
ELMS	ELMS	ENPS	PENS	ESTU	SUET
ELMT	MELT	ENRT	RENT, TERN	ESTV	VEST, VETS
ELMU	MULE	ENRU	RUNE	ESTW	STEW, WEST, WETS
ELMY	YLEM	ENRW	WREN	ESTY	STYE
ELNO	LEON, LONE, NOEL	ENST	NEST, NETS, SENT, TENS	ESTZ	ZEST
ELNS	LENS	ENSW	NEWS, SEWN	ESUZ	SUEZ
ELNT	LENT	ENSY	YENS	ESVY	YVES
ELOP	LOPE, POLE	ENTT	NETT, TENT	ESWY	YEWS
ELOR	LORE, OREL, ROLE	ENTU	TUNE	ESXY	SEXY
ELOS	LEOS, LOSE, SLOE, SOLE	ENTV	VENT	ETTX	TEXT
ELOV	LOVE, VOLE	ENTW	NEWT, WENT	ETTY	ETTY
ELPR	PERL	ENTX	NEXT	FFGU	GUFF
ELPT	PELT	ENVY	ENVY	FFHU	HUFF
ELPY	YELP	EOOZ	OOZE	FFII	FIFI
ELRU	LURE, RULE	EOPP	POPE	FFIN	NIFF
ELRY	LYRE, RELY	EOPR	PORE, ROPE, REPO	FFIR	RIFF
ELSS	LESS	EOPS	PESO, POSE	FFIT	TIFF
ELST	LEST, LETS	EOPT	POET	FFIY	IFFY
ELSU	SLUE	EORS	ORES, ROES, ROSE, SORE	FFLU	LUFF
ELSW	SLEW	EORT	ROTE, TORE	FFMU	MUFF

FFOT	TOFF	FOOW	WOOF	GJOS	JOGS
FFPU	PUFF	FOPR	PROF	GJSU	JUGS
FFRU	RUFF	FOPS	FOPS	GLLU	GULL
FGIS	FIGS	FOPU	POUF	GLMU	GLUM
FGIT	GIFT	FORT	FORT	GLNO	LONG
FGIU	GIFU	FORU	FOUR	GLNU	LUNG
FGLO	FLOG, GOLF	FOST	SOFT	GLNY	GLYN
FGLU	GULF	FOSU	UFOS	GLOO	LOGO
FGOO	GOOF	FOXY	FOXY	GLOS	LOGS, SLOG
FGOR	FROG	FRSU	FURS, SURF	GLOU	LUGO
FGOS	FOGS	FRTU	TURF	GLOW	GLOW
FGOY	FOGY	FRUY	FURY	GLOY	LOGY
FHII	HI-FI	FSSU	FUSS	GLPU	GULP, PLUG
FHIS	FISH	FTTU	TUFT	GLSU	LUGS, SLUG
FHNO	FOHN	FUZZ	FUZZ	GLTU	GLUT
FHOO	HOOF	GGHO	HOGG	GLUY	UGLY
FHOW	HOWF	GGIS	GIGS	GMOS	SMOG
FIIJ	FIJI	GGNO	GONG	GMSU	GUMS, MUGS, SMUG
FIJU	FUJI	GGOO	GO-GO	GMSY	GYMS
FILL	FILL	GGOR	GROG	GNNU	GUNN
FILM	FILM	GHHI	HIGH	GNOO	GOON, NO GO
FILO	FOIL	GHHU	HUGH	GNOP	PONG
FILP	FLIP	GHIN	NIGH	GNOS	SNOG, SONG
FILT	FLIT, LIFT	GHIS	GISH, SIGH	GNOU	OGUN
FILW	WILF	GHIW	WHIG	GNOW	GOWN
FIMR	FIRM	GHNO	HONG	GNRU	RUNG
FINN	FINN	GHNU	HUNG	GNSU	GNUS, GUNS, SNUG,
FINO	INFO	GHOS	GOSH, HOGS		SUNG
FINS	FINS	GHOU	HUGO	GNWY	GWYN
FIOR	IFOR	GHSU	GUSH, HUGS	GOOP	GOOP
FIRS	FIRS	GHTU	THUG	GOOT	TOGO
FIRT	RIFT	GIJS	JIGS	GORW	GROW
FIST	FIST, FITS, SIFT	GIKN	KING	GORY	GORY, ORGY
FIZZ	FIZZ	GIKO	KOGI	GOST	TOGS
FKLO	FOLK	GILL	GILL	GOSW	WOGS
FKNU	FUNK	GILN	LING	GOTU	GOUT
FKOR	FORK	GILR	GIRL	GPSU	PUGS
FKOU	KOFU	GILT	GILT	GRSU	RUGS
FLLU	FULL	GIMP	GIMP	GRTU	TRUG
FLOO	FOOL	GIMR	GRIM	GRUU	GURU
FLOP	FLOP	GINP	PING	GSTU	GUST, GUTS, TUGS
FLOR	ROLF	GINR	GRIN, RING	GSUV	GUVS
FLOT	LOFT	GINS	GINS, SIGN, SING	GSUY	GUYS
FLOU	FOUL	GINT	TING	HHSU	HUSH
FLOW	FLOW, FOWL, WOLF	GINW	WING	HIKS	SIKH
FLOY	FLOY	GIOR	GIRO, IGOR	HILL	HILL
FLRU	FURL	GIOY	YOGI	HILP	PHIL
FLUX	FLUX	GIPR	GRIP, PRIG	HILT	HILT
FMOR	FORM, FROM	GIPS	PIGS	HIMS	SHIM
FMUY	FUMY	GIRS	RIGS	HIMW	WHIM
FNOT	FONT	GIRT	GIRT, GRIT	HINS	SHIN, SINH
FOOP	POOF	GIST	GIST	HINT	HINT, THIN
FOOR	ROOF	GISW	SWIG, WIGS	HIOO	OHIO
FOOT	FOOT	GITW	TWIG	HIOP	HOPI, IPOH

15

HIPS	HIPS, PISH, SHIP	HPSU	PUSH	ILMN	LIMN
HIPT	PITH	HPTU	PHUT	ILMO	MILO
HIPW	WHIP	HRRU	RUHR	ILMP	LIMP
HIRW	WHIR	HRSU	RUSH	ILMS	SLIM
HISS	HISS	HRSY	RHYS	ILMT	MILT
HIST	HIST, HITS, SHIT, THIS	HRTU	HURT, RUTH, THRU	ILMY	LIMY
HISW	WISH	HSSU	HUSS	ILNO	LION, LOIN
HITW	WHIT, WITH	HSTU	HUTS, SHUT, THUS, TUSH	ILNT	LINT
HIWZ	WHIZ	HSWY	WHYS	ILNZ	LINZ
HJNO	JOHN	HTUU	HUTU	ILOO	IOLO
HJOS	JOSH	HUUW	WUHU	ILOR	LORI
HKLO	KOHL	IIKW	KIWI	ILOS	LOIS, OILS, SILO, SOIL
HKLU	HULK	IILL	LILI	ILOT	TOIL
HKNO	HONK	IIMM	MIMI	ILOV	VIOL
HKNU	HUNK	IIMN	MINI	ILOY	OILY
HKOO	HOOK	IIMP	IMPI	ILPS	LIPS, LISP, SLIP
HKSU	HUSK	IINS	NISI	ILST	LIST, SILT, SLIT
HLLU	HULL	IINT	INTI	ILTT	TILT
HLMO	HOLM	IIRS	IRIS	ILTW	WILT
HLOP	HOLP	IJLL	JILL	ILVV	LVIV
HLOS	HOLS	IJLT	JILT	ILWY	WILY
HLOT	HOLT, LOTH	IJNN	JINN	IMMY	IMMY
HLOW	HOWL	IJNO	JOIN	IMNT	MINT
HLOY	HOLY	IJNX	JINX	IMNX	MINX
HLRU	HURL	IKKN	KINK	IMOT	OMIT
HLSU	LUSH	IKKR	KIRK	IMPP	PIMP
HLWY	HWYL	IKLL	KILL	IMPR	PRIM
HMNY	HYMN	IKLM	MILK	IMPS	IMPS
HMOO	HOMO	IKLN	KILN, LINK	IMPW	WIMP
HMOS	HOMS, OHMS	IKLO	KILO	IMRS	RIMS
HMOT	MOTH, THOM	IKLS	SILK	IMRT	TRIM
HMOW	WHOM	IKLT	KILT	IMRU	MUIR
HMOY	HOMY	IKMN	MINK	IMRY	MIRY, RIMY
HMPU	HUMP	IKMS	SKIM	IMSS	ISMS, MISS
HMSU	HUMS, MUSH	IKNO	IKON, OINK	IMST	MIST
HMTY	MYTH	IKNP	PINK	IMSW	SWIM
HNOP	PHON	IKNR	RINK	IMTT	MITT
HNOR	HORN	IKNS	INKS, SINK, SKIN	IMTU	MUTI
HNOS	NOSH	IKNT	KNIT	INNS	INNS
HNOU	HUON	IKNW	WINK	INOP	PION
HNSU	SHUN	IKNY	INKY	INOR	IRON
HNTU	HUNT, THUN	IKPS	KIPS, SKIP, SPIK	INOS	IONS, SION
HOOP	HOOP, POOH	IKRS	KRIS, RISK	INOT	INTO, TONI
HOOS	SHOO	IKSS	KISS, SKIS	INOV	VINO
HOOT	HOOT, OTHO	IKST	KITS, SKIT	INOZ	ZION
HOPS	HOPS, POSH, SHOP	IKUV	KIVU	INPS	NIPS, PINS, SNIP, SPIN
HOPT	PHOT	ILLM	MILL	INPT	PINT
HOPW	WHOP	ILLO	LILO	INPY	PINY
HOPY	HYPO	ILLP	PILL	INQU	QUIN
HORT	ROTH	ILLR	RILL	INRU	RUIN
HORU	HOUR	ILLS	ILLS, SILL	INSS	SINS
HOST	HOST, HOTS, SHOT	ILLT	LILT, TILL	INST	NITS, TINS
HOSW	SHOW	ILLW	WILL	INSW	WINS
HOTU	THOU	ILLY	LILY	INTT	TINT

INTU	UNIT	
INTW	TWIN	
INTY	TINY	
INWY	WINY	
IOPR	PORI	
IORT	RIOT, TIRO, TRIO	
IORV	IVOR	
IOST	OTIS	
IOSU	IOUS	
IPPS	PIPS	
IPQU	QUIP	
IPRS	RIPS	
IPRT	TRIP	
IPRU	PURI	
IPSS	PISS, SIPS	
IPST	PITS, SPIT, TIPS	
IPSV	SPIV, VIPS	
IPSW	WISP	
IPSZ	ZIPS	
IPTY	PITY	
IQTU	QUIT	
IQUZ	QUIZ	
IRSS	SIRS	
IRST	STIR	
IRTW	WRIT	
IRTX	TRIX	
IRWY	WIRY	
ISSY	ISSY	
ISTT	TITS	
ISTU	SUIT	
ISTW	WITS	
ISTZ	ZITS	
ITTW	TWIT	
IYZZ	IZZY	
IZZZ	ZIZZ	
JJUU	JUJU	
JKNU	JUNK	
JLOT	JOLT	
JLOW	JOWL	
JLUY	JULY	
JM00	MOJO	
JMPU	JUMP	
JNOU	JUNO	
JOSS	JOSS	
JOSY	JOYS	
JRUY	JURY	
JSTU	JUST	
KK00	KOOK	
KL00	LOOK	
KLOY	YOLK	
KLRU	LURK	
KLSU	SULK	
KMNO	MONK	
KMOS	OMSK	
KMRU	MURK	
KMSU	MUSK	
KN00	NOOK	
KNOT	KNOT	
KNOW	KNOW	
KNPU	PUNK	
KNSU	SUNK	
KNUU	NUUK	
KOOR	ROOK	
KOOT	TOOK	
KOPR	PORK	
KOPY	POKY	
KORS	ORSK	
KORW	WORK	
KORY	YORK	
KOSW	WOKS	
KRSU	RUSK	
KRTU	KURT	
KSTU	TUSK	
LLLO	LOLL	
LLLU	LULL	
LLMO	MOLL	
LLMU	MULL	
LLNU	NULL	
LLOP	POLL	
LLOR	ROLL	
LLOT	TOLL	
LLPU	PULL	
LLUU	LULU	
LM00	LOOM	
LMOT	MOLT	
LMPU	LUMP, PLUM	
LMSU	SLUM	
LNNY	LYNN	
LN00	LOON	
LNOR	LORN	
LNOY	LYON, ONLY	
LNUY	LUNY	
LNXY	LYNX	
LOOP	LOOP, POLO, POOL	
LOOS	LOOS, OSLO, SOLO	
LOOT	LOOT, TOOL	
LOOW	WOOL	
LOPP	PLOP	
LOPS	SLOP	
LOPT	PLOT	
LOPW	PLOW	
LOPY	PLOY, POLY	
LORU	LOUR	
LORY	ORLY, ROLY	
LOSS	LOSS	
LOST	LOST, LOTS, SLOT, STOL	
LOSU	SOUL	
LOSW	LOWS, OWLS, SLOW	
LOTU	LOUT, TOUL	
LOTV	VOLT, VTOL	
LOUU	OULU	
LOWY	YOWL	
LPPU	PULP	
LPRU	PURL	
LPSU	PLUS	
LRSU	SLUR	
LSTU	LUST, SLUT	
LSUV	LUVS	
LUUZ	ZULU	
MMOS	MOMS	
MMSU	MUMS	
MN00	MONO, MOON	
MNOR	MORN, NORM	
MNOS	MONS	
MNOU	MUON	
MNOW	MOWN	
MOOR	MOOR, ROOM	
MOOS	MOOS	
MOOT	MOOT	
MOOZ	ZOOM	
MOPP	POMP	
MOPR	PROM, ROMP	
MOPS	MOPS	
MORS	ROMS	
MORT	MORT	
MORW	WORM	
MOSS	MOSS	
MOST	MOST, MOTS	
MOUV	OVUM	
MPPU	PUMP	
MPRU	RUMP	
MPSU	SUMP	
MRSU	RUMS	
MSSU	MUSS, SUMS	
MSTU	MUST, SMUT, STUM	
MSUW	SWUM	
MSUY	SUMY	
MTTU	MUTT	
NNNU	NUNN	
NN00	NOON	
NNOU	NON-U, NOUN	
NNSU	NUNS	
NNWY	WYNN	
NOOS	SOON	
NOOT	ONTO	
NOPR	PORN	
NOPU	UPON	
NOPY	PONY	
NORT	TORN	
NORW	WORN	
NOSS	SONS	
NOST	SNOT, TONS	

NOSU	NOUS, ONUS, OSUN	OPPS	POPS	OSST	SOTS, TOSS
NOSW	SNOW, SOWN	OPRS	PROS	OSSW	SOWS
NOSY	NOSY	OPRT	PORT	OSSY	OSSY
NOTU	UNTO	OPRU	POUR	OSTT	TOTS
NOTW	TOWN, WONT	OPRW	PROW	OSTU	OUST
NOTY	TONY	OPRY	ROPY	OSTW	STOW, SWOT, TOWS, TWOS
NOXY	ONYX	OPSS	SOPS		
NPSU	PUNS, SPUN	OPST	POST, POTS, SPOT, STOP, TOPS	OSTY	TOYS
NPTU	PUNT			OSVW	VOWS
NPUY	PUNY	OPSU	OPUS, SOUP	OTTU	TOUT
NRSU	RUNS, URNS	OPSW	POWS, SWOP, WOPS	OYZZ	OZZY
NRTU	RUNT, TURN	OPSY	POSY	PPSU	PUPS
NSSU	SUNS	OPTU	POUT	PRRU	PURR
NSTU	NUTS, STUN	ORRT	RORT	PRSU	SPUR
OOPP	POOP	ORRY	RORY	PRSY	SPRY
OOPR	POOR	ORSS	ROSS	PRTU	PRUT
OOPS	OOPS	ORST	ROTS, SORT, TORS	PSST	PSST
OORT	ROOT	ORSU	OURS, SOUR	PSSU	PUSS, SUPS
OOSS	SO-SO	ORSW	ROWS	PTTU	PUTT
OOST	SOOT	ORSY	ROSY	PTUZ	PUTZ
OOSZ	ZOOS	ORTT	TORT, TROT	RSSU	RUSS
OOTT	OTTO, TOOT, TOTO	ORTU	ROUT, TOUR	RSTT	TRST
OOUZ	OUZO	ORTY	TORY, TROY, TYRO	RSTU	RUST, RUTS
OOYY	YOYO	ORUX	ROUX	SSSU	SUSS
OOYZ	OOZY	ORUY	YOUR	SUYZ	SUZY
OPPR	PROP	ORXY	ORYX, ROXY	TTUU	TUTU

AAABC	ABACA	AADEH	AHEAD	AAFIM	MAFIA
AAABQ	AQABA	AADEL	ADELA	AAFIN	NAAFI
AAADN	ADANA	AADFR	DARAF, FARAD	AAFIT	TAFIA
AAAGM	AGAMA	AADGG	DAGGA	AAFLT	FATAL
AAALN	ALANA	AADGM	MAGDA	AAFNU	FAUNA
AAAMT	AMATA	AADGN	GANDA	AAGHL	GALAH
AAARU	AARAU	AADGR	GARDA	AAGHN	GHANA
AAASV	VAASA	AADHI	HAIDA	AAGHR	HAGAR
AABCK	ABACK	AADHK	DHAKA	AAGIN	AGAIN
AABCL	CABAL	AADHL	HADAL	AAGIS	SAIGA
AABDE	BAAED	AADIL	ADLAI	AAGIT	TAIGA
AABDN	BANDA	AADIN	AIDAN, DIANA, NADIA,	AAGJN	GANJA
AABEM	ABEAM, AMEBA	NAIAD		AAGKN	KANGA
AABES	ABASE	AADIR	ADAIR	AAGLL	ALGAL, GALLA
AABET	ABATE, BEATA	AADIS	SAIDA	AAGLN	LAGAN
AABFT	ABAFT	AADJW	WAJDA	AAGLO	LAOAG
AABGR	BRAGA	AADKR	DAKAR	AAGLR	ALGAR
AABHI	BAHAI, BAHIA	AADLN	ALDAN	AAGLS	GALAS
AABHS	ABASH, SABAH, SHABA	AADLS	SALAD	AAGLV	VAGAL
AABJU	ABUJA	AADLU	DUALA	AAGMM	GAMMA, MAGMA
AABLN	ALBAN, BANAL, LABAN	AADLV	VALDA	AAGMR	GRAMA
AABLS	BALAS, BALSA, BASAL	AADMM	MADAM	AAGNP	PAGAN
AABMM	MAMBA	AADMN	ADMAN, DAMAN	AAGNT	TANGA
AABMR	ABRAM	AADMR	DRAMA	AAGOR	AGORA
AABMS	SAMBA	AADMS	ADAMS	AAGRS	RAGAS
AABNW	BWANA	AADNP	PANDA	AAGRZ	ZARGA
AABRR	BARRA	AADNV	VANDA	AAGSS	SAGAS
AABRS	ARABS, BASRA, SABRA	AADNW	WANDA	AAGUV	GUAVA
AABRT	RABAT	AADPT	ADAPT	AAHHS	HA-HAS
AABRU	ARUBA	AADPU	PADUA	AAHJR	RAJAH
AACCD	DACCA	AADRR	RADAR	AAHLL	ALLAH, HALAL
AACCO	CACAO	AADRU	AUDRA	AAHLM	HALMA, HAMAL
AACCR	ACCRA	AADRW	AWARD	AAHLP	ALPHA
AACEN	CANEA	AADUW	ADUWA	AAHLS	LHASA
AACEP	APACE	AAEGL	ALGAE, GALEA	AAHLV	ALVAH
AACER	ARECA, CEARA	AAEGP	AGAPE	AAHMO	OMAHA
AACFI	FACIA	AAEGT	AGATE	AAHMR	MARAH
AACHS	SACHA	AAEGV	AGAVE	AAHMZ	HAMZA
AACIR	ARICA	AAEHK	HAKEA	AAHNS	HANSA
AACIS	ISAAC	AAEKP	APEAK	AAHNU	HANAU
AACKL	ALACK	AAEKW	AWAKE	AAHPR	APHRA
AACLL	CALLA	AAELP	PALEA	AAHPS	PASHA
AACLN	CANAL	AAELR	AREAL	AAHRR	HARAR
AACLR	CARLA, CLARA	AAELT	ALATE	AAHRS	SARAH
AACLT	TALCA	AAELX	ALEXA	AAHSU	HAUSA
AACMO	MACAO	AAEMR	MARAE	AAHSW	AWASH
AACMW	MACAW	AAEMZ	AMAZE	AAHSY	AYAHS
AACNN	CANNA	AAENP	PAEAN	AAHWZ	AHWAZ
AACNV	CAVAN	AAENR	ARENA	AAIIL	AALII
AACNZ	ANZAC	AAERS	AREAS	AAIKS	KASAI, SAKAI
AACPU	CAPUA	AAERU	AUREA	AAIKU	KAUAI
AACRT	CARAT	AAERW	AWARE	AAIKZ	IZAAK
AADDX	ADDAX	AAFFJ	JAFFA	AAILN	ALAIN, ALINA, LANAI,
AADEG	ADAGE	AAFHI	HAIFA	LIANA	

AAILS	AILSA, ALIAS
AAILT	ALTAI
AAILV	AVAIL
AAILX	AXIAL
AAIMN	ANIMA, MANIA
AAIMR	MARIA
AAIMS	AMIAS, MASAI
AAIMZ	ZAMIA
AAINP	APIAN
AAINR	ARIAN, RAINA
AAINS	ASIAN
AAINT	ANITA, TANIA
AAINV	AVIAN
AAIPV	PAVIA
AAIRS	ARIAS, SARAI
AAIRT	ATRIA, TIARA
AAIRV	VARIA
AAIRZ	ZARIA
AAISS	ASSAI
AAITW	AWAIT
AAJLP	JALAP
AAJNP	JAPAN
AAKKY	KAYAK
AAKLO	KOALA
AAKLR	KRAAL
AAKLT	KALAT
AAKMR	KARMA
AAKNZ	KAZAN
AAKOS	OSAKA
AAKPR	PARKA
AAKRT	KARAT
AAKRW	KWARA
AALLM	LLAMA
AALLN	ALLAN
AALLO	ALLOA
AALLV	LAVAL
AALLY	ALLAY
AALMO	ALAMO
AALMP	PALMA
AALMR	ALARM, MALAR, MARLA
AALMS	LAMAS
AALMT	MALTA
AALMY	MALAY
AALNN	ANNAL
AALNS	NASAL
AALNT	NATAL
AALNU	NUALA
AALNV	NAVAL
AALNY	NYALA
AALPP	APPAL, PAPAL
AALPS	SALPA
AALPU	PAULA
AALPZ	LA PAZ, PLAZA
AALRT	ALTAR, RATAL

AALRU	AURAL, LAURA
AALRV	ALVAR, LARVA
AALRY	ALARY
AALST	ATLAS, SALTA
AALTY	YALTA
AALUY	AULAY
AAMMM	MAMMA
AAMMN	AMMAN
AAMMS	MAMAS
AAMNN	ANNAM, MANNA
AAMNS	MASAN
AAMNT	MANTA
AAMNY	MAYAN
AAMOR	AROMA
AAMOS	SAMOA
AAMPR	PARMA
AAMPT	TAMPA
AAMRS	SAMAR
AAMRT	MARTA, TAMAR
AAMRU	MAURA
AAMSS	AMASS, ASSAM, MASSA
AAMSY	AMYAS
AANNN	ANNAN
AANNO	ANONA
AANNY	YANAN
AANOR	AARON
AANPP	NAPPA
AANPT	PATNA
AANRR	ARRAN
AANRS	SARAN
AANRV	NARVA, NAVAR, VARNA
AANRY	ARYAN
AANST	SATAN
AANSU	SAUNA
AANSW	ASWAN
AANTT	TANTA
AANTY	TANYA
AAORT	AORTA
AAOST	AOSTA
AAPPS	PAPAS
AAPPU	PAPUA
AAPPW	PAPAW
AAPRS	PARAS
AAPRT	APART
AAPST	PASTA
AAPSY	PASAY
AAQRT	QATAR
AAQRZ	ZARQA
AARRS	ARRAS, SARRA
AARRY	ARRAY
AARST	ASTRA
AARSU	AURAS
AARTT	ATTAR, TATAR, TATRA
AARTY	TAYRA

AASSY	ASSAY
AATZZ	TAZZA
ABBCY	CABBY
ABBEI	ABBIE
ABBEK	KEBAB
ABBEL	BABEL
ABBEM	BEMBA
ABBES	BABES
ABBEY	ABBEY
ABBGY	GABBY
ABBIR	RABBI
ABBLU	BABUL, BUBAL
ABBMO	A-BOMB
ABBNO	NABOB
ABBOT	ABBOT
ABBRS	BABRS
ABBSU	BABUS
ABBTY	TABBY
ABCCY	BACCY
ABCEH	BEACH
ABCEI	CEIBA
ABCEL	CABLE, CALEB
ABCER	BRACE, CABER
ABCHI	CHIBA
ABCHT	BATCH
ABCIN	CABIN
ABCIO	COBIA
ABCIR	BARIC, RABIC
ABCIS	BASIC
ABCJO	JACOB
ABCKL	BLACK
ABCKS	BACKS
ABCLN	BLANC
ABCNO	BACON
ABCNU	CUBAN
ABCOR	CAROB, COBRA
ABCOV	VOCAB
ABCRS	CRABS
ABCRT	BRACT
ABCSS	SCABS
ABCSU	SCUBA
ABDEG	BADGE
ABDEI	ABIDE
ABDEK	BAKED
ABDEL	BALED, BLADE
ABDEO	ABODE, ADOBE
ABDER	BARED, BEARD, BREAD, BREDA, DEBAR, DEBRA
ABDES	BASED, BEADS
ABDET	BATED
ABDEY	BAYED, BEADY
ABDIL	AD-LIB
ABDIR	BRAID, RABID
ABDIU	DUBAI

ABDLN	BLAND
ABDLY	BADLY, BALDY
ABDNR	BRAND, R AND B
ABDNS	BANDS
ABDNY	BANDY
ABDOR	BOARD, BROAD
ABDRS	BARDS, DRABS
ABDRY	DARBY
ABDSU	DAUBS
ABDSW	BAWDS
ABDUY	DAUBY
ABDWY	BAWDY
ABDYY	BY DAY
ABEEL	ABELE, ALBEE
ABEFL	FABLE
ABEGL	BAGEL, GABLE
ABEGN	BEGAN
ABEGR	BARGE
ABEGS	GABES
ABEGT	BEGAT
ABEHO	BOHEA, OBEAH
ABEHR	HABER
ABEHS	SHEBA
ABEHT	BATHE
ABEIM	I-BEAM
ABEIR	BEIRA
ABEIS	BASIE
ABEIZ	BAIZE
ABEJZ	JABEZ
ABEKL	BLAKE, BLEAK
ABEKR	BAKER, BRAKE, BREAK
ABEKS	BEAKS
ABEKY	BEAKY
ABELL	BELLA, LABEL
ABELM	AMBLE, BLAME, MABEL, MABLE, MELBA
ABELN	BLANE
ABELR	BALER, BLARE, BLEAR
ABELS	BALES, BASEL, BLASE, SABLE
ABELT	BLEAT, TABLE
ABELY	BELAY
ABELZ	BLAZE
ABEMP	PEMBA
ABEMR	AMBER, BREAM
ABEMS	BEAMS
ABEMY	EMBAY, MAYBE
ABENO	BEANO
ABENR	ABNER
ABENS	BANES, BEANS
ABEOV	ABOVE
ABERR	ARBER, BARER, BARRE
ABERS	BASER, BEARS, BRAES, SABER, SABRE
ABERT	BERTA

ABERV	BRAVE
ABERY	BARYE, BY EAR, YERBA
ABERZ	BRAZE, ZEBRA
ABESS	BASES
ABEST	BASTE, BEAST, BEATS, BETAS, TABES
ABESU	ABUSE, BEAUS
ABETU	BEAUT
ABEUX	BEAUX
ABFFN	BANFF
ABFRY	BY FAR
ABGGR	BRAGG
ABGGY	BAGGY
ABGHN	BHANG
ABGNO	GABON
ABGNS	BANGS
ABGRS	GRABS
ABHIJ	BHAJI
ABHIR	BIHAR
ABHIS	SAHIB
ABHIT	HABIT
ABHKL	BALKH
ABHMO	ABOHM
ABHOR	ABHOR
ABHRS	BRASH
ABHRT	BARTH
ABHST	BATHS
ABIIL	ALIBI
ABIIT	TIBIA
ABIIZ	IBIZA
ABIJM	JAMBI
ABIKT	BATIK
ABILN	ALBIN, BINAL, BLAIN
ABILR	BLAIR, BRAIL, LIBRA
ABILS	BAILS, BASIL
ABILT	BALTI
ABILY	LIBYA
ABIMS	IAMBS
ABIMT	AMBIT
ABINR	BAIRN, BRAIN, BRIAN, RABIN
ABINS	BASIN, SABIN
ABIOT	BIOTA
ABIRR	BRIAR
ABIRT	BRITA
ABIRY	BY AIR
ABISS	BASIS
ABJMS	JAMBS
ABJNO	BANJO
ABJOT	JABOT
ABKLN	BLANK
ABKLS	BALKS
ABKLU	BAULK, KABUL
ABKNS	BANKS
ABKRS	BARKS

ABLLS	BALLS
ABLLU	BULLA
ABLLY	BALLY
ABLMS	BALMS, LAMBS
ABLMU	ALBUM
ABLMY	BALMY
ABLOP	PABLO
ABLOR	LOBAR
ABLOT	BLOAT
ABLRW	BRAWL
ABLSS	SLABS
ABLST	BLAST
ABLTU	TUBAL
ABLWY	BYLAW
ABLYY	LAY-BY
ABMMO	MAMBO
ABMOZ	ZOMBA
ABMRU	BURMA, RUMBA, UMBRA
ABMRY	AMBRY, BARMY
ABMSU	SUMBA
ABMTU	BATUM
ABNNS	BANNS
ABNOR	BARON, BONAR
ABNOT	BATON
ABNRS	BARNS
ABNRU	UNBAR, URBAN
ABNRW	BRAWN
ABNRY	BRYAN
ABNTU	BANTU
ABOOT	TABOO
ABORR	ARBOR
ABORS	BOARS
ABORT	ABORT, TABOR
ABORV	BRAVO
ABORX	BORAX
ABOSS	BASSO
ABOST	BOAST, BOATS, SABOT
ABOTU	ABOUT, U-BOAT
ABOUY	BAYOU
ABQSU	SQUAB
ABRRY	BARRY
ABRSS	BRASS
ABRST	BRATS
ABRSU	BURSA
ABRSY	BRAYS
ABRXY	BRAXY
ABSST	STABS
ABSSW	SWABS
ABSSY	ABYSS
ABSTU	TUBAS
ABTTY	BATTY, BYATT
ABWYY	BYWAY
ACCDY	CYCAD

21

ACCEH	CACHE	ACEHK	HACEK	ACETY	TACEY
ACCEM	MECCA	ACEHL	CHELA, LEACH	ACETZ	AZTEC
ACCHO	COACH	ACEHN	HANCE	ACFFH	CHAFF
ACCHT	CATCH	ACEHP	CHEAP, PEACH	ACFHU	CHUFA
ACCIR	CIRCA	ACEHR	REACH	ACFIR	FARCI
ACCIT	CACTI	ACEHS	ACHES, CHASE	ACFKL	FLACK
ACCKL	CLACK	ACEHT	CHEAT, TEACH, THECA	ACFLO	FOCAL
ACCKR	CRACK	ACEIL	ALICE, CELIA, ILEAC	ACFNR	FRANC
ACCLU	LUCCA	ACEIM	AMICE	ACFNY	FANCY
ACCOO	COCOA	ACEIN	CAINE	ACFRS	SCARF
ACCUY	YUCCA	ACEIR	ERICA	ACFRT	CRAFT
ACDDY	CADDY	ACEIV	AVICE	ACFRY	FARCY
ACDEF	FACED	ACEKL	ALECK	ACFST	FACTS
ACDEG	CADGE, CAGED	ACEKR	CRAKE, CREAK	ACGIM	GAMIC, MAGIC
ACDEH	ACHED	ACEKS	CAKES	ACGIR	CIGAR, CRAIG
ACDEK	CAKED	ACELL	CELLA	ACGLN	CLANG
ACDEL	CADEL, CLADE, DECAL,	ACELM	CAMEL, MACLE	ACGNO	CONGA
	LACED	ACELN	ANCEL, CLEAN, LANCE	ACGOR	CARGO
ACDEN	CANED, DANCE	ACELP	PLACE	ACGOU	GUACO
ACDEP	PACED	ACELR	CLARE, CLEAR, LACER	ACGRS	CRAGS, SCRAG
ACDER	CADRE, CARED, CEDAR,	ACELS	LACES, SCALE	ACHHT	HATCH
	RACED	ACELT	CLEAT, ECLAT	ACHIL	HALIC
ACDES	CASED	ACELV	CALVE, CLAVE	ACHIM	MICAH
ACDET	ACTED, CADET	ACEMO	CAMEO	ACHIN	CHAIN, CHINA
ACDEV	CAVED	ACEMR	CREAM	ACHIR	CHAIR
ACDEW	CAWED	ACEMS	MACES	ACHIT	AITCH, CHITA
ACDEY	DECAY	ACENN	NANCE	ACHKL	CHALK
ACDHO	AD HOC	ACENO	CANOE, OCEAN	ACHKS	HACKS, SHACK
ACDHR	CHARD	ACENP	PECAN	ACHKW	WHACK
ACDIR	ACRID	ACENR	CANER, CARNE, CRANE,	ACHLO	LOACH
ACDIS	ACIDS, ASDIC		NACRE, RANCE	ACHLR	LARCH
ACDIT	DICTA	ACENS	CANES	ACHLS	CLASH
ACDIZ	CADIZ	ACENT	ENACT	ACHLT	LATCH
ACDLS	SCALD	ACEOR	OCREA	ACHMO	MACHO, MOCHA
ACDLU	CLAUD, DUCAL	ACEPR	CAPER, CRAPE, PACER,	ACHMP	CHAMP
ACDMO	MADOC		RECAP	ACHMR	CHARM, MARCH
ACDNY	CANDY	ACEPS	CAPES, PACES, SCAPE,	ACHMS	CHASM
ACDOS	CODAS		SPACE	ACHMT	MATCH
ACDOT	OCTAD	ACEPT	EPACT	ACHNR	RANCH
ACDRS	CARDS	ACERR	RACER	ACHNT	CHANT
ACDRY	DARCY	ACERS	ACRES, CARES, RACES,	ACHNU	NUCHA
ACDSS	SCADS		SCARE, SERAC	ACHOP	POACH
ACDTU	DUCAT	ACERT	CARET, CATER, CRATE,	ACHOR	ORACH, ROACH
ACEEK	ACKEE		REACT, TRACE	ACHOS	CHAOS
ACEEP	PEACE	ACERV	CARVE, CRAVE	ACHOV	HAVOC
ACEES	CEASE	ACERY	CAREY	ACHPR	PARCH
ACEFH	CHAFE	ACERZ	CRAZE	ACHPS	CHAPS
ACEFL	FECAL	ACESS	CASES	ACHPT	PATCH
ACEFR	FACER, FARCE	ACEST	CASTE	ACHRS	CHARS, CRASH
ACEFS	CAFES, FACES	ACESU	CAUSE, SAUCE	ACHRT	CHART
ACEFT	FACET	ACESV	CAVES	ACHRY	ARCHY, CHARY
ACEGL	GLACE	ACESY	CASEY	ACHST	CHATS
ACEGR	GRACE	ACETT	TACET	ACHSW	SCHWA
ACEGS	CAGES	ACETU	ACUTE, CEUTA	ACHTW	WATCH
ACEGY	CAGEY	ACETX	EXACT		

ACHTY	CATHY, YACHT	ACLOP	COPAL	ACRSZ	CZARS
ACIIL	ILIAC	ACLOR	CALOR, CARLO, CAROL,	ACRTT	TRACT
ACIIS	ASCII		CLARO, CORAL	ACRTY	TRACY
ACIKL	ALICK	ACLOS	COALS	ACRYZ	CRAZY
ACILL	CILLA, LILAC	ACLOT	OCTAL	ACSST	CASTS
ACILM	CLAIM	ACLOV	VOCAL	ACSSU	ASCUS
ACILP	PLICA	ACLOX	COXAL	ACSTY	STACY
ACILS	SALIC	ACLOY	COALY	ACSUY	SAUCY
ACILT	TICAL	ACLOZ	COLZA	ACTTY	CATTY
ACILU	LUCIA	ACLPS	CLAPS, CLASP, SCALP	ADDDE	ADDED
ACILV	CAVIL	ACLPU	CULPA	ADDDY	DADDY
ACILX	CALIX	ACLRW	CRAWL	ADDEF	FADED
ACIMN	MANIC	ACLRY	CARLY, CARYL, CLARY	ADDEH	HEDDA
ACINP	PANIC	ACLSS	CLASS	ADDEI	ADDIE, AIDED
ACINR	CAIRN	ACLSU	LUCAS	ADDEJ	JADED
ACINT	ACTIN, ANTIC, CAN IT!	ACLSW	CLAWS	ADDEL	ADDLE
ACIOR	CAIRO	ACLSY	SCALY	ADDER	ADDER, DARED, DREAD,
ACIOZ	AZOIC	ACLXY	CALYX		DREDA
ACIPR	CAPRI	ACMMO	COMMA	ADDET	DATED
ACIPS	ASPIC, SPICA	ACMNO	MACON	ADDEV	VEDDA
ACIRU	AURIC, CURIA	ACMOP	CAMPO	ADDEW	WADED
ACIRV	VICAR	ACMOR	ARMCO, MACRO,	ADDEZ	DAZED
ACISU	CAIUS		MARCO	ADDFY	FADDY
ACITT	ATTIC, TACIT	ACMOS	COMAS	ADDGI	GADID
ACJKS	JACKS	ACMPR	CRAMP	ADDIJ	JIDDA
ACJKY	JACKY	ACMPS	CAMPS, SCAMP	ADDIV	DAVID
ACJNU	CAJUN	ACMRS	SCRAM	ADDMY	MADDY
ACKKN	KNACK	ACMRY	CYMAR, MARCY	ADDNO	ADD-ON
ACKLN	CLANK	ACMSS	SCAMS	ADDNR	R AND D
ACKLO	CLOAK	ACNNO	ANCON, CANON,	ADDNY	DANDY
ACKLR	CLARK		CONAN	ADDPY	PADDY
ACKLS	SLACK	ACNNY	CANNY, NANCY	ADDRY	DRYAD
ACKLU	CAULK	ACNOP	CAPON	ADDWY	WADDY
ACKMS	SMACK	ACNOR	ACORN	ADEEL	ADELE
ACKMU	AMUCK	ACNOT	CANTO	ADEEM	EDEMA
ACKNR	CRANK	ACNPU	UNCAP	ADEER	EARED
ACKNS	SNACK	ACNSS	SCANS	ADEES	AEDES, EASED
ACKOR	CROAK	ACNST	CANTS, SCANT	ADEEV	EVADE
ACKPS	PACKS	ACOPR	COPRA	ADEFK	FAKED
ACKQU	QUACK	ACORS	OSCAR	ADEFM	FAMED
ACKRS	RACKS	ACORT	ACTOR, CROAT	ADEFR	FADER, FARED, FREDA
ACKRT	TRACK	ACOST	ASCOT, COAST, COATS,	ADEFT	FATED
ACKRW	WRACK		COSTA, TACOS	ADEFX	FAXED
ACKSS	CASKS, SACKS	ACOTT	COTTA	ADEFZ	FAZED
ACKST	STACK, TACKS	ACPPU	CUPPA	ADEGG	GAGED
ACKTY	TACKY	ACPRS	CARPS, CRAPS, SCARP,	ADEGL	GLADE
ACKWY	WACKY		SCRAP	ADEGM	GAMED, MADGE
ACLLO	LOCAL	ACPST	PACTS	ADEGP	GAPED, PAGED
ACLLS	CALLS, SCALL	ACPSU	SCAUP	ADEGR	EDGAR, GERDA, GRADE,
ACLMO	COMAL	ACPTU	CAPUT		RAGED
ACLMP	CLAMP	ACRRU	CRURA	ADEGS	DEGAS
ACLMS	CLAMS	ACRRY	CARRY	ADEGT	GATED
ACLMU	CALUM	ACRSS	CRASS, SCARS	ADEGW	WADGE, WAGED
ACLNS	CLANS	ACRST	CARTS	ADEGZ	GAZED
		ACRSY	CARYS, SCARY	ADEHK	KEDAH

ADEHR	HARED, HEARD	ADEPV	PAVED	ADIKN	DINKA
ADEHS	HADES, HEADS, SHADE	ADEPW	PAWED	ADILN	LINDA, NIDAL
ADEHT	DEATH, HATED	ADERR	DARER, DREAR	ADILP	PLAID
ADEHX	HEXAD	ADERS	DARES, DEARS	ADILR	DRAIL, LAIRD
ADEHY	HEADY	ADERT	DATER, RATED, TRADE,	ADILS	ALDIS, DIALS
ADEHZ	HAZED	TREAD		ADILT	TIDAL, TILDA
ADEIL	AILED, DELIA, IDEAL	ADERV	RAVED	ADILU	DULIA
ADEIM	AIMED, AMIDE, MEDIA	ADERW	DEWAR, WADER	ADILV	VALID, VIDAL
ADEIN	DIANE	ADERY	DEARY, READY	ADILY	DAILY, LYDIA
ADEIP	A PIED	ADERZ	RAZED	ADIMS	MAIDS
ADEIR	AIRED, REDIA	ADEST	DATES, SATED, STEAD	ADIMT	ADMIT
ADEIS	AIDES, ASIDE, IDEAS,	ADESV	SAVED	ADIMX	ADMIX
SADIE		ADESW	SAWED	ADINO	DANIO
ADEIU	ADIEU	ADESZ	ADZES, DAZES	ADINR	DINAR, DRAIN, NADIR
ADEIZ	AZIDE	ADETX	TAXED	ADINV	DIVAN, VIAND
ADEJR	JARED	ADEUX	A DEUX	ADIOP	PODIA
ADEJS	JADES	ADEVW	WAVED	ADIOR	AROID, DORIA, RADIO
ADEJW	JAWED	ADEWX	WAXED	ADIOS	ADIOS
ADEKL	KELDA	ADEWY	YAWED	ADIOU	AUDIO, DOUAI
ADEKN	KNEAD, NAKED	ADFFR	DRAFF	ADIOV	AVOID
ADEKR	DRAKE, RAKED	ADFLO	ADOLF, FALDO	ADIOZ	DIAZO
ADEKS	ASKED	ADFRT	DRAFT	ADIPR	RAPID
ADEKW	WAKED	ADFRU	FRAUD	ADIPS	SAPID
ADELL	DELLA, LADLE	ADFRW	DWARF	ADIPV	VAPID
ADELM	LAMED, MEDAL	ADGIL	ALGID, GILDA	ADIRS	RAIDS
ADELN	ALDEN, ELAND, LADEN	ADGLN	GLAND	ADIRT	TRIAD
ADELP	PALED, PEDAL, PLEAD	ADGMO	DOGMA	ADIRX	RADIX
ADELR	ALDER, LADER	ADGNO	GONAD	ADIRY	DAIRY, DIARY
ADELS	DALES, DEALS, LEADS	ADGNR	GRAND	ADIST	STAID
ADELT	DEALT, DELTA	ADGOS	DAGOS, GOADS	ADISW	WADIS
ADELV	VELDA	ADGOU	GOUDA	ADISY	DAISY
ADELW	WEALD	ADGRS	DRAGS	ADITU	AUDIT
ADELY	DELAY, LEADY	ADGRU	GUARD	ADITV	DAVIT
ADELZ	LAZED, ZELDA	ADGUY	GAUDY	ADJOU	OUJDA
ADEMN	ADMEN, AMEND,	ADHIJ	HADJI, JIHAD	ADJSU	JUDAS
MANDE, MANED, MEDAN,		ADHIL	HALID, HILDA	ADKLY	ALKYD
NAMED		ADHIN	DINAH	ADKNR	DRANK
ADEMR	AD REM, ARMED,	ADHIO	IDAHO	ADKNY	KANDY
DERMA, DREAM		ADHIP	APHID	ADKOV	VODKA
ADEMS	DAMES, MEADS	ADHJU	JUDAH	ADKRS	DARKS
ADEMT	MATED, TAMED	ADHLU	HULDA	ADKRY	DARKY
ADEMU	MAUDE	ADHLY	HYLDA	ADLLO	ALDOL
ADENO	ANODE	ADHNS	HANDS	ADLLY	DALLY
ADENR	ANDRE, ARDEN, DENAR,	ADHNT	HADN'T	ADLMO	MODAL
REDAN		ADHNY	HANDY, HAYDN	ADLMY	MADLY
ADENS	ANDES, DEANS, SEDAN	ADHOR	HOARD, RHODA	ADLNO	DONAL, NDOLA, NODAL
ADENT	ANTED, DANTE	ADHRS	HARDS, SHARD	ADLNS	LANDS
ADENU	DUANE	ADHRY	HARDY, HYDRA	ADLNY	DYLAN, LYNDA
ADENV	VENDA	ADHST	HADST	ADLOR	ROALD
ADENW	WANED, WENDA	ADHSU	SADHU	ADLOS	LOADS
ADEOR	ADORE, OARED	ADHSY	HYADS, SHADY	ADLOU	ALOUD
ADEPR	DRAPE, PADRE, PARED,	ADIIL	ILIAD	ADLOW	WALDO
RAPED		ADIIN	INDIA	ADLRW	DRAWL
ADEPS	SPADE	ADIIR	RADII	ADLRY	DARYL
ADEPT	ADEPT, TAPED				

ADLSU	ALDUS	AEESV	EAVES	AEGNS	AGNES, SENGA
ADLSY	SADLY	AEEVW	WEAVE	AEGNT	AGENT, TEGAN
ADLTU	ADULT	AEFFG	GAFFE	AEGNV	VEGAN
ADLUY	DYULA	AEFHS	SHEAF	AEGNW	AGNEW
ADMNO	DAMON, MONAD, NOMAD	AEFIL	ALFIE	AEGPR	GAPER, GRAPE, PAGER
		AEFIR	AFIRE, FERIA	AEGPS	GAPES, PAGES
ADMNY	MANDY	AEFKL	FLAKE	AEGRS	GEARS, RAGES, SARGE
ADMOR	RADOM	AEFKR	FAKER, FREAK	AEGRT	GRATE, GREAT, GRETA
ADMRS	DRAMS	AEFKS	FAKES	AEGRU	ARGUE, AUGER
ADMTU	DATUM	AEFLM	FLAME, FLEAM	AEGRV	GRAVE
ADNNO	DONNA	AEFLR	FARLE, FERAL, FLARE	AEGRW	WAGER
ADNNY	DANNY	AEFLS	FALSE, FLEAS	AEGRY	GAYER
ADNOR	ADORN, DORAN, RADON	AEFLT	FETAL	AEGRZ	GAZER, GRAZE
		AEFLY	LEAFY	AEGSS	GASES, SAGES
ADNRS	DARNS	AEFMR	FRAME	AEGST	GATES, STAGE
ADNRW	DRAWN	AEFOV	FOVEA	AEGSU	AGUES, USAGE
ADNRY	RANDY	AEFRR	FARER	AEGSW	SWAGE, WAGES
ADNSS	SANDS	AEFRS	FARES, FEARS, SAFER	AEGTU	TAEGU
ADNST	STAND	AEFRT	AFTER	AEGUV	VAGUE
ADNSU	SUDAN	AEFRW	WAFER	AEGUZ	GAUZE
ADNSW	DAWNS, WANDS	AEFRY	FAERY, FREYA	AEHHT	HEATH
ADNSY	SANDY	AEFSS	SAFES	AEHJZ	HEJAZ
ADNTU	DAUNT	AEFST	FATES, FEAST, FEATS	AEHKL	HEKLA
ADOPT	ADOPT	AEGGI	AGGIE	AEHKS	HAKES, SHAKE
ADORS	ROADS	AEGGR	AGGER	AEHLL	HALLE
ADOSS	SODAS	AEGGS	GAGES	AEHLR	HALER
ADOST	TOADS	AEGGU	GAUGE	AEHLS	LEASH, SHALE
ADOSV	DAVOS	AEGHL	HELGA	AEHLT	LATHE
ADOTY	TOADY, TODAY	AEGHM	EGHAM	AEHLV	HALVE
ADQSU	QUADS, SQUAD	AEGHN	HAGEN	AEHLW	WHALE, WHEAL
ADRRU	DURRA	AEGHU	HAGUE	AEHLY	HEALY
ADRST	DARTS	AEGIL	AGILE, ALGIE	AEHLZ	HAZEL
ADRSU	DURAS	AEGIM	IMAGE	AEHMN	HE-MAN
ADRSW	DRAWS, SWARD, WARDS	AEGIN	ANGIE	AEHMR	HAREM
		AEGIS	AEGIS	AEHMS	SHAME
ADRSY	DRAYS, YARDS	AEGLL	GALLE, LEGAL	AEHMT	MEATH
ADRTY	TARDY	AEGLM	GLEAM	AEHNN	HENAN, HENNA
ADUVZ	VADUZ	AEGLN	ANGEL, ANGLE, GLEAN	AEHNR	AHERN
AEEFZ	FEAZE	AEGLP	PLAGE	AEHNS	ASHEN, HANSE, SHANE, SHENA
AEEGL	EAGLE	AEGLR	ALGER, GLARE, LAGER, LARGE, REGAL		
AEEGR	AGREE, EAGER, EAGRE			AEHNT	ETHAN, THANE, 'NEATH
AEEHV	HEAVE	AEGLS	GALES	AEHNV	HAVEN
AEEIM	AIMEE	AEGLT	AGLET	AEHNY	HYENA
AEELN	ELENA	AEGLV	GAVEL, GAVLE	AEHOR	HORAE
AEELS	EASEL, LEASE	AEGLY	GAYLE	AEHOS	HOSEA
AEELT	ELATE	AEGLZ	GLAZE	AEHPR	RAPHE
AEELV	LEAVE	AEGMM	GEMMA	AEHPS	HEAPS, PHASE, SHAPE
AEEMN	ENEMA, NEMEA	AEGMN	MANGE, MEGAN	AEHRS	ASHER, HARES, RHEAS, SHARE, SHEAR
AEEMV	MAEVE, MEAVE	AEGMO	OMEGA		
AEENR	RANEE	AEGMR	MARGE	AEHRT	EARTH, HEART, HERAT, THERA
AEENT	EATEN, ENATE	AEGMS	GAMES		
AEEPY	PAYEE	AEGMY	GAMEY	AEHRV	HAVER, HAVRE
AEERS	EASER, ERASE	AEGNO	GENOA, ONEGA	AEHRZ	HAZER
AEERT	ARETE, EATER	AEGNR	ANGER, RANGE	AEHSS	ASHES
AEEST	TEASE			AEHST	HASTE, HATES

25

AEHSV	HAVES, SHAVE
AEHSW	HAWES, HAWSE
AEHSZ	HAZES
AEHTT	THETA
AEHTW	WHEAT
AEHVY	HEAVY
AEIIL	AILIE
AEIJK	IKEJA
AEIJM	JAMIE
AEIJN	JANIE
AEIKL	ALIKE
AEIKR	ERIKA
AEIKT	KATIE
AEIKZ	KEZIA
AEILL	ALLIE, LEILA, LELIA
AEILN	ALIEN, ALINE, ANILE, ELAIN
AEILR	ARIEL
AEILS	AISLE, ELIAS
AEILT	EILAT
AEILV	ALIVE, ALVIE
AEILX	AXILE
AEILZ	ELIZA
AEIMM	MAMIE
AEIMN	AMINE, MAINE, MENAI
AEIMR	MAIRE, MARIE, RAMIE
AEIMZ	MAIZE
AEINN	ANNIE, INANE
AEINR	ARIEN, RAINE
AEINS	AISNE, ANISE, SIENA
AEINT	TINEA
AEINV	NAIVE
AEINX	XENIA
AEINZ	AZINE
AEIPS	SEPIA
AEIPT	PIETA
AEIRS	AESIR, ARIES, ARISE, RAISE
AEIRT	ARTIE, IRATE
AEIRZ	ZAIRE
AEITV	EVITA
AEIVW	WAIVE
AEJMM	JEMMA
AEJMR	AJMER
AEJMS	JAMES
AEJNN	JENNA
AEJNS	JEANS
AEJNT	JANET
AEJNY	JANEY, JAYNE
AEJPR	JAPER
AEJPS	JAPES
AEKLN	ANKLE
AEKLR	KAREL, LAKER
AEKLS	LAKES, LEAKS, SLAKE
AEKLW	KWELA

AEKLY	LEAKY
AEKMN	EKMAN
AEKMR	MAKER
AEKMS	MAKES
AEKNO	OAKEN
AEKNR	KAREN
AEKNS	SNAKE, SNEAK
AEKNT	TAKEN
AEKNV	KNAVE
AEKNW	WAKEN
AEKNY	KENYA
AEKOR	KOREA
AEKOW	AWOKE
AEKPR	PERAK
AEKPS	PEAKS, SPEAK
AEKPY	PEAKY
AEKQU	QUAKE
AEKRR	RAKER
AEKRS	ASKER, RAKES, SAKER
AEKRT	TAKER
AEKRU	AKURE
AEKRW	WAKER, WREAK
AEKSS	SAKES
AEKST	SKATE, STAKE, STEAK, TAKES, TEAKS
AEKSW	ASKEW, WAKES
AEKTW	TWEAK
AELLM	MALLE
AELLN	ALLEN
AELLP	LAPEL
AELLY	ALLEY
AELMM	LEMMA
AELMP	AMPLE, MAPLE
AELMR	LAMER, REALM
AELMS	MALES, MEALS, SALEM, SELMA
AELMT	METAL
AELMV	MELVA, VELMA
AELMY	MEALY
AELMZ	ZELMA
AELNO	ALONE, ANOLE, LEONA
AELNP	NEPAL, PANEL, PENAL, PLANE
AELNR	LARNE, LEARN, RENAL
AELNS	ANSEL, LANES
AELNT	LEANT
AELNV	NAVEL, VENAL
AELOV	OLAVE
AELOZ	AZOLE
AELPP	APPEL, APPLE
AELPR	PALER, PEARL
AELPS	LAPSE, LEAPS, PALES, PEALS, PLEAS, SALEP, SEPAL
AELPT	LEAPT, PETAL, PLATE, PLEAT

AELQU	EQUAL, QUALE
AELRS	ARLES, EARLS, LASER
AELRT	ALERT, ALTER, ARTEL, LATER, RATEL
AELRU	UREAL
AELRV	LAVER, RAVEL, VELAR
AELRX	RELAX
AELRY	EARLY, LAYER, RELAY
AELSS	SALES, SEALS
AELST	LEAST, SETAL, SLATE, STALE, STEAL, TALES, TESLA
AELSV	SALVE, SELVA, SLAVE, VALES, VALSE
AELSW	WALES, WEALS
AELSX	AXLES
AELTV	VALET
AELTX	EXALT, LATEX
AELUV	UVEAL, VALUE
AELVV	VALVE
AEMMT	MAMET
AEMMY	MAMEY
AEMNN	NEMAN
AEMNO	EAMON
AEMNR	MARNE
AEMNS	MANES, MANSE, MEANS, NAMES
AEMNT	AMENT, MEANT
AEMRR	REARM
AEMRS	MARES, MASER, REAMS, SMEAR
AEMRT	MATER, TAMER
AEMSS	SEAMS
AEMST	MATES, SATEM, STEAM, TEAMS
AEMSU	AMUSE
AEMSX	EXAMS
AEMSY	SAMEY, SEAMY
AEMSZ	MAZES
AEMTT	MATTE
AEMTY	MATEY, MEATY
AEMUV	MAUVE
AENNP	PANNE, PENNA
AENNS	SENNA
AENNW	ANWEN
AENNX	ANNEX
AENOP	PAEON
AENOS	AEONS
AENOT	ATONE, OATEN
AENOV	NOVAE
AENOW	OWENA
AENPP	NAPPE
AENPS	ASPEN, NAPES, PANES
AENPT	PATEN
AENPZ	PENZA
AENRR	RERAN

AENRS	NARES, SANER, SNARE
AENRV	RAVEN, VERNA
AENRY	YEARN
AENSS	ASSEN, NESSA
AENST	ANTES, NATES, NESTA
AENSV	AVENS, NAVES, VANES
AENSW	WANES
AENSZ	SENZA
AENTT	NETTA
AENTZ	ZANTE
AENWX	WAXEN
AENWY	WANEY, WAYNE
AEOPR	OPERA
AEORS	AROSE
AEORT	ORATE
AEOSS	OASES
AEOTV	OVATE
AEOTZ	AZOTE
AEPPR	PAPER
AEPPU	PUPAE
AEPRR	PARER
AEPRS	ASPER, PARSE, PEARS, PRASE, PRESA, RAPES, SPARE, SPEAR
AEPRT	PATER, PETRA, PRATE, TAPER
AEPRY	APERY, REPAY
AEPSS	APSES, PASSE
AEPST	PASTE, PATES, PEATS, SPATE, TAPES
AEPSU	PAUSE
AEPTU	TAUPE
AEPTY	PEATY
AERRR	RARER
AERRS	REARS
AERRT	TERRA
AERRV	RAVER
AERRW	RAWER
AERRZ	RAZER
AERSS	ARSES
AERST	ASTER, RATES, RESAT, STARE, TARES, TEARS
AERSV	SAVER
AERSW	SAWER, SWEAR, WARES
AERSY	SAYER, YEARS
AERTT	TETRA, TREAT
AERTU	URATE
AERTV	AVERT, TRAVE
AERTW	TAWER, WATER
AERTX	EXTRA, TAXER
AERUZ	AZURE
AERVV	VARVE
AERVW	WAVER
AERVY	AVERY
AERWX	WAXER

AERWY	WEARY
AESSS	ASSES
AESST	ASSET, EASTS, SEATS, TESSA
AESSV	SAVES, VASES
AESSY	ESSAY
AESTT	STATE, TASTE, TEATS, TESTA
AESTU	SAUTE
AESTV	STAVE, VESTA
AESTW	SWEAT, WASTE
AESTX	TAXES, TEXAS
AESTY	AS YET, YEAST
AESUV	SUAVE
AESVW	WAVES
AFFGS	GAFFS
AFFIX	AFFIX
AFFLO	OFFAL
AFFLU	LUFFA
AFFQU	QUAFF
AFFST	STAFF
AFFTY	TAFFY
AFGHU	FAUGH
AFGLS	FLAGS
AFGLU	FUGAL
AFGNO	FANGO
AFGNS	FANGS
AFGRT	GRAFT
AFHIT	FAITH
AFHIZ	HAFIZ
AFHLS	FLASH
AFHRW	WHARF
AFHST	HAFTS, SHAFT
AFIKR	FAKIR
AFILL	FLAIL
AFILN	FINAL
AFILP	PILAF
AFILR	FILAR, FLAIR, FRAIL
AFILS	FAILS
AFINO	FIONA
AFINT	FAINT, FANTI
AFIOS	SOFIA
AFIRR	FRIAR
AFIRS	FAIRS
AFIRY	FAIRY
AFIST	FIATS
AFISW	WAIFS
AFKLN	FLANK
AFKLS	FLASK
AFKLY	FLAKY
AFKNR	FRANK
AFKRT	KRAFT
AFLLO	ALL OF
AFLLS	FALLS
AFLMY	FLAMY

AFLNS	FLANS
AFLNU	FALUN
AFLOO	ALOOF
AFLOR	FLORA
AFLOS	FOALS, SOL-FA
AFLOT	ALOFT, FLOAT
AFLOU	AFOUL
AFLPS	FLAPS
AFLST	FLATS
AFLSW	FLAWS
AFLTU	FAULT
AFLUW	AWFUL
AFLWY	FLAWY
AFMOX	OXFAM
AFMOY	FOAMY
AFMRS	FARMS
AFNNO	FANON
AFNNY	FANNY
AFNOR	FARON
AFNRU	FURAN
AFNSU	FAUNS, SNAFU
AFNSW	FAWNS
AFOOT	AFOOT
AFORS	AFROS, SOFAR
AFORY	FORAY
AFOSS	FOSSA, SOFAS
AFOST	SOFTA
AFRST	FARTS, RAFTS
AFRSW	SWARF
AFSST	FASTS
AFSUV	FAVUS
AFTTY	FATTY
AGGGO	GOGGA
AGGIN	AGING
AGGLU	GULAG
AGGNS	GANGS
AGGOR	AGGRO
AGGSY	SAGGY
AGHHU	HAUGH
AGHLU	LAUGH
AGHMO	OMAGH
AGHNO	HOGAN
AGHNS	GNASH
AGHNW	WHANG
AGHOT	GOTHA
AGHPR	GRAPH
AGHRT	GARTH
AGHSS	SHAGS
AGHST	GHATS
AGHTU	AUGHT
AGIIV	VIGIA
AGIKN	KIANG
AGILN	ALGIN, ALIGN
AGILR	ARGIL, GLAIR, GRAIL

27

AGILS	SIGLA
AGILY	GAILY
AGIMN	GAMIN
AGIMO	IMAGO
AGIMS	AGISM, SIGMA
AGINP	APING
AGINR	GRAIN
AGINS	GAINS
AGINT	GIANT
AGINV	GAVIN
AGINW	WIGAN
AGINX	AXING
AGIOS	GOIAS
AGIRV	VIRGA
AGIST	AGIST, GAITS
AGISU	GAIUS
AGJLU	JUGAL
AGKWY	GAWKY
AGLLO	ALGOL
AGLLS	GALLS
AGLMU	MULGA
AGLNO	ALONG
AGLNR	GNARL
AGLNS	GLANS, SLANG
AGLOR	ALGOR, ARGOL, GORAL, LARGO
AGLOS	GAOLS, GOALS, LAGOS
AGLOT	GLOAT
AGLOW	AGLOW
AGLRU	GULAR
AGLRY	GLARY, GYRAL
AGLSS	GLASS, SLAGS
AGMMU	GUMMA
AGMMY	GAMMY
AGMNO	AMONG, MANGO
AGMNY	MANGY
AGMOR	MARGO, MORAG
AGMRS	GRAMS
AGMSU	MAGUS
AGMTU	GAMUT
AGNOR	ARGON, GROAN, ORGAN
AGNOT	TANGO, TONGA
AGNOU	GUANO
AGNOW	WAGON
AGNOY	AGONY
AGNPS	PANGS
AGNRS	GRANS
AGNRT	GRANT
AGNRY	ANGRY, RANGY
AGNSS	SNAGS
AGNST	ANGST, GNATS
AGNSU	ANGUS, GANSU
AGNTU	GAUNT
AGNTW	TWANG

AGNTY	TANGY
AGOOT	OTAGO
AGORS	ARGOS
AGORT	ARGOT, GROAT
AGOST	GOATS, TOGAS
AGPRS	GRASP, SPRAG
AGPSS	GASPS
AGRRY	GARRY
AGRSS	GRASS
AGRSU	SUGAR
AGRSY	GRAYS
AGRUU	AUGUR
AGRVY	GRAVY
AGSST	STAGS
AGSSU	GAUSS
AGSSY	GASSY
AGSTU	GUSTA
AGSTY	STAGY
AGSUV	VAGUS
AGTTU	GUTTA
AGUYZ	GAUZY
AHHIS	SHIAH
AHHOO	HOO-HA
AHHRS	HARSH
AHHSS	SHAHS
AHIIT	HAITI
AHIJJ	HAJJI
AHIJZ	HIJAZ
AHIKK	KHAKI
AHIKM	HAKIM
AHIKS	KASHI
AHIKU	HAIKU
AHILL	HILLA
AHILP	PHIAL
AHILR	HILAR
AHILS	HAILS
AHILT	LAHTI
AHIMR	HIRAM
AHINO	HANOI
AHINS	HSIAN, SHANI
AHINT	HAIN'T
AHINU	ANHUI
AHIPS	APHIS, APISH
AHIRS	HAIRS, SHARI
AHIRU	URIAH
AHIRY	HAIRY
AHIST	TISHA
AHJNO	JONAH
AHJTU	THUJA
AHKNS	HANKS, KHANS, SHANK
AHKNT	THANK
AHKNY	HANKY
AHKOS	SHAKO
AHKRS	SHARK

AHKSW	HAWKS
AHKSY	SHAKY
AHKTY	KATHY
AHLLO	HALLO, HOLLA
AHLLS	HALLS, SHALL
AHLMU	HAULM
AHLOR	HORAL
AHLOS	HALOS, SHOAL
AHLOT	ATHOL, LOATH
AHLPR	RALPH
AHLPS	PLASH
AHLPY	HAPLY, PHYLA
AHLSS	SLASH
AHLST	HALTS, LATHS, SHALT
AHLSU	HAULS
AHLSW	SHAWL
AHLSY	SHALY
AHMMY	HAMMY
AHMNO	HAMON
AHMNU	HUMAN, NAHUM
AHMNY	HYMAN, MYNAH
AHMRS	MARSH
AHMSS	SHAMS, SMASH
AHMSW	WHAMS
AHMTY	MY HAT
AHNNO	HONAN
AHNNU	HUNAN
AHNOR	NORAH, RHONA
AHNOS	SHONA
AHNOT	HOTAN
AHNST	HANTS, HASN'T, SHAN'T, SNATH
AHNSU	SHAUN
AHNSW	SHAWN
AHNTU	HAUNT
AHNUW	WUHAN
AHOOW	WAHOO
AHOOY	YAHOO
AHORS	HORSA
AHORT	THORA, TORAH
AHORY	HOARY
AHORZ	ZORAH
AHOST	ATHOS, HOSTA, OATHS, SHOAT
AHOSX	XHOSA
AHPPY	HAPPY
AHPRS	HARPS, SHARP
AHPRY	HARPY
AHPSS	HASPS
AHPST	PATHS
AHQSU	QUASH
AHRRY	HARRY
AHRST	HARTS, RASHT, TRASH
AHRSU	SURAH
AHRTW	WRATH

AHRTY	THYRA	AILRU	LAURI	AIORY	ORIYA
AHSST	STASH	AILRV	AVRIL, RIVAL, VIRAL	AIOSS	OASIS
AHSSW	SWASH	AILRY	RIYAL	AIOST	IOTAS
AHSTW	SWATH, THAWS	AILSS	SAILS, SILAS, SISAL	AIPPP	PIPPA
AHSTY	HASTY	AILST	A LIST, TAILS	AIPRS	PAIRS, PARIS
AHSWY	WASHY	AILSV	ALVIS, VIALS	AIPRT	ATRIP, TAPIR
AHTTY	HATTY	AILSY	ISLAY	AIPRU	PIURA
AIILS	AILIS	AILTV	VITAL	AIPSS	APSIS
AIIMM	MIAMI	AILTY	ITALY, LAITY	AIPST	TAPIS
AIINS	SINAI	AIMMS	IMAMS	AIPTT	PATTI
AIIPU	PIAUI	AIMMX	MAXIM	AIPZZ	PIZZA
AIIQR	IRAQI	AIMNN	MINNA	AIRRS	ARRIS
AIIVV	VIVIA	AIMNO	AMINO, NAOMI	AIRSS	ARSIS, SARIS
AIJJN	JINJA	AIMNR	ARMIN, MARNI	AIRST	ASTIR, SITAR, STAIR,
AIJKT	TAJIK	AIMNS	MAINS		STRIA, TARSI
AIJLS	JAILS	AIMNT	MATIN	AIRSY	SYRIA
AIJLU	JULIA	AIMNZ	MAINZ	AIRSZ	SIZAR
AIJNN	JINAN	AIMOR	MAORI, MARIO, MOIRA	AIRTT	TRAIT
AIJNS	JANIS	AIMOW	MIAOW	AIRVX	VARIX
AIJOU	OUIJA	AIMOX	AXIOM	AISSV	SIVAS, VISAS
AIKMU	UMIAK	AIMRS	AMIRS	AISTV	VISTA
AIKNR	KARIN	AIMRT	MARTI	AISTW	WAIST
AIKNS	NASIK	AIMRZ	MIZAR	AISTX	TAXIS
AIKNT	TAKIN	AIMSS	AMISS	AISWZ	SWAZI
AIKOP	OKAPI	AIMSV	MAVIS	AISXX	X-AXIS
AIKRT	KRAIT	AIMSW	SWAMI	AISXY	Y-AXIS
AIKRU	KAURI	AIMSY	ISMAY	AISXZ	Z-AXIS
AIKST	SITKA	AIMTY	AMITY	AITTV	VITTA
AILLL	LILLA	AINNO	ANION	AITZZ	TA'IZZ
AILLN	NIALL	AINNP	PINNA	AJLRU	JURAL
AILLV	VILLA	AINNS	ANNIS	AJMMU	JAMMU
AILLW	WILLA	AINOP	PIANO	AJMMY	JAMMY
AILMN	MILAN	AINOR	ON-AIR	AJMOR	MAJOR
AILMS	ISLAM, SIMLA	AINOS	SONIA	AJNOS	JASON, JONAS, SONJA
AILMV	VILMA	AINOT	TONIA	AJNOU	ANJOU
AILMW	WILMA	AINOW	OWAIN	AJNTU	JAUNT, JUNTA
AILNO	ALOIN, ILONA	AINOZ	ANZIO	AJRTU	JURAT
AILNP	PLAIN	AINPR	PIRAN	AJRUU	JURUA
AILNS	NAILS, SLAIN, SNAIL	AINPS	PAINS, SPAIN	AJYZZ	JAZZY
AILNT	LATIN	AINPT	INAPT, PAINT, PINTA	AKKLU	KULAK
AILNV	ALVIN, ANVIL, NIVAL	AINRS	RAINS	AKKOP	KAPOK
AILNW	IN-LAW	AINRT	TRAIN, TRINA	AKKPU	PUKKA
AILNY	INLAY	AINRV	INVAR	AKLLY	ALKYL
AILOS	LAOIS	AINRY	RAINY	AKLNP	PLANK
AILOV	OLIVA, VIOLA	AINST	SAINT, SATIN, STAIN	AKLNY	LANKY
AILOZ	LAZIO	AINSV	SAVIN	AKLOP	POLKA
AILPP	PIPAL	AINSW	SWAIN	AKLOR	KAROL
AILPR	APRIL	AINSZ	NAZIS	AKLRS	LARKS
AILPS	PAILS	AINTT	TAINT, TITAN	AKLST	STALK, TALKS
AILPT	PLAIT	AINTU	UNIAT	AKLSW	WALKS
AILQU	QUAIL	AINTW	TWAIN	AKMOU	OAKUM
AILRS	LAIRS, LIARS, LIRAS,	AINUX	AUXIN	AKMRS	MARKS
	RAILS, RIALS	AIOPT	PATIO	AKMSS	MASKS
AILRT	TRAIL, TRIAL	AIORT	RATIO	AKMUZ	MUZAK

AKNOR	KORAN, KRONA	ALMQU	QUALM	ALTTY	LYTTA
AKNOY	KONYA	ALMRU	MURAL	ALTUV	VAULT
AKNPR	PRANK	ALMST	SMALT	ALTWZ	WALTZ
AKNPS	SPANK	ALMTY	MALTY	ALUUV	UVULA
AKNPU	PUNKA	ALNNO	NOLAN	ALUVV	VULVA
AKNRS	NARKS, RANKS	ALNNU	ANNUL	AMMMO	MOMMA
AKNRY	NARKY	ALNOP	NOPAL	AMMMY	MAMMY
AKNST	STANK, TANKS	ALNOR	ARLON, LORAN, LORNA	AMMOY	MYOMA
AKNSU	KANSU	ALNOS	LOANS, SALON	AMMRS	SMARM
AKNSW	SWANK	ALNOT	TALON, TOLAN, TONAL	AMMSY	SAMMY
AKNSY	SNAKY, YANKS	ALNOZ	ZONAL	AMMTY	TAMMY
AKOOR	KAROO	ALNPS	PLANS	AMNNU	UNMAN
AKOOZ	KAZOO	ALNPT	PLANT	AMNNY	MANNY
AKOPY	YAPOK	ALNRS	SNARL	AMNOR	MANOR, MORNA,
AKOSS	SOAKS	ALNRU	LUNAR, ULNAR		NORMA, RAMON, ROMAN
AKOSY	OKAYS	ALNST	SLANT	AMNOS	MASON, MOANS
AKOTY	TOKAY	ALNSU	ULNAS	AMNOW	WOMAN
AKPRS	PARKS, SPARK	ALNSW	LAWNS	AMNOY	MOYNA
AKPRY	PARKY	ALNTY	LANTY	AMNOZ	MONZA
AKPTU	KAPUT	ALNUY	UNLAY, YULAN	AMNRU	NAMUR
AKPWY	PAWKY	ALNWY	ALWYN, LAWNY,	AMNRY	MYRNA
AKQRU	QUARK		WANLY	AMNSU	MANUS
AKQUY	QUAKY	ALNXY	XYLAN	AMNTY	MAYN'T
AKRST	KARST, STARK	ALOOP	PAOLO	AMNUY	YUMAN
AKRSY	SARKY	ALOPR	PAROL, POLAR	AMOPR	PRO-AM
AKSST	TASKS	ALOPS	OPALS, SALOP	AMORU	AMOUR
AKSSU	SKUAS	ALORS	LAROS, SOLAR	AMORY	MAYOR, MORAY,
AKTUY	YAKUT	ALORU	RAOUL		MOYRA
ALLLY	ALLYL	ALORV	ORVAL, VOLAR	AMOSS	SAMOS
ALLMO	MOLAL	ALORY	ROYAL	AMOST	ATOMS, MOATS,
ALLMS	MALLS, SMALL	ALOSS	LASSO		STOMA
ALLMY	MYALL	ALOST	ALTOS	AMOTU	OMUTA
ALLNO	LLANO	ALOSV	OVALS, SALVO	AMPRS	PRAMS, RAMPS
ALLOS	SALOL	ALOTT	TOTAL	AMPRT	TRAMP
ALLOT	ALLOT, ATOLL	ALOTV	LOVAT, VOLTA	AMPSS	SPASM
ALLOW	ALLOW	ALOVV	VOLVA	AMPST	STAMP
ALLOY	ALLOY, LOYAL	ALPPU	PUPAL	AMPSU	PUMAS
ALLPS	PALLS, SPALL	ALPPY	APPLY	AMPSV	VAMPS
ALLPY	PALLY	ALPSS	SLAPS	AMPSW	SWAMP
ALLRY	RALLY	ALPST	SPLAT	AMRRY	MARRY
ALLST	STALL	ALPSY	PALSY, PLAYS, SPLAY	AMRST	SMART, TRAMS
ALLSW	WALLS	ALPTY	APTLY, PLATY	AMRSU	RAMUS
ALLSY	SALLY	ALRRU	RURAL	AMRSW	SWARM
ALLTY	TALLY	ALRRY	LARRY	AMRTY	MARTY, TRYMA
ALLWY	WALLY	ALRSU	SURAL, URALS	AMSST	MASTS
ALLXY	LAXLY	ALRTW	TRAWL	AMSTU	MATSU
ALMMO	MALMO	ALRWY	RAWLY	AMSTY	MAYST
ALMNO	MONAL	ALSST	LASTS, SALTS, SLATS	AMTTY	MATTY
ALMNY	MANLY	ALSSV	SLAVS	ANNNY	NANNY
ALMOR	MOLAR, MORAL	ALSTU	TALUS, TULSA	ANNOR	RONNA
ALMOY	LOAMY	ALSTY	SALTY, SLATY	ANNOT	ANTON
ALMPS	LAMPS, PALMS, PLASM,	ALSUU	USUAL	ANNOY	ANNOY
	PSALM	ALSVY	SYLVA	ANOOP	POONA
ALMPY	AMPLY, PALMY	ALSWY	YAWLS	ANOPR	APRON, NO-PAR
				ANOPW	POWAN

ANORS	ARSON, ROANS, SONAR	AOSSY	SAY-SO	BBEWY	WEBBY
ANORT	TRONA	AOSTT	STOAT, TOAST	BBHMO	H-BOMB
ANORW	ROWAN	AOSTU	AUTOS	BBHOS	HOBBS
ANORY	RAYON	AOSVY	SAVOY	BBHOY	HOBBY
ANOSV	NOVAS	APPPY	PAPPY	BBHUY	HUBBY
ANOSX	NAXOS, SAXON	APPSU	PUPAS	BBILY	LIBBY
ANOSY	SONYA	APPSY	SAPPY	BBISY	SIBBY
ANOTT	TANTO	APPYZ	ZAPPY	BBITY	TIBBY
ANOTX	TAXON	APRRY	PARRY	BBLOS	BLOBS
ANOTY	ATONY, TONYA	APRSS	RASPS, SPARS	BBLOY	LOBBY
ANOWY	NO WAY	APRST	PARTS, PRATS, SPRAT,	BBLRU	BLURB
ANPPY	NAPPY		STRAP, TRAPS	BBLSU	BULBS
ANPRW	PRAWN	APRSU	SUPRA	BBMOS	BOMBS
ANPRY	PYRAN	APRSW	WARPS, WRAPS	BBOOS	BOOBS
ANPSS	SNAPS	APRSY	SPRAY	BBOOY	BOOBY
ANPST	PANTS	APRTY	PARTY	BBSUY	BUSBY
ANPSU	PUSAN	APSST	PASTS, SPATS	BBTUY	TUBBY
ANPSW	PAWNS, SPAWN	APSSW	SWAPS, WASPS	BCCIU	CUBIC
ANPSY	PANSY	APSTY	PATSY, PASTY, PATSY	BCDEU	CUBED
ANPTU	UNAPT	APTTY	PATTY	BCEEH	BEECH
ANPTY	PANTY	AQRTU	QUART	BCEHL	BELCH
ANQRU	QUR'AN	AQSTU	SQUAT	BCEHN	BENCH
ANQTU	QUANT	AQSUW	SQUAW	BCEHO	BOCHE
ANRST	TARNS	AQSUY	QUAYS	BCEIR	BRICE
ANRSY	YARNS	ARRTY	TARRY	BCEKS	BECKS
ANRUU	NAURU	ARSST	STARS, TRASS, TSARS	BCEKY	BECKY
ANRUY	UNARY	ARSTT	START, TARTS	BCEOY	BOYCE
ANSST	STANS	ARSTU	SURAT	BCERU	BRUCE
ANSSU	SUSAN	ARSTW	STRAW, WARTS	BCERY	CYBER
ANSSW	SWANS	ARSTY	SATYR, STRAY, TRAYS	BCESU	CUBES
ANSTU	AUNTS, TUNAS	ARSTZ	TZARS	BCHIR	BIRCH
ANSTW	WANTS	ARSUV	VARUS	BCHIT	BITCH
ANSTY	NASTY, TANSY	ARSUY	SAURY	BCHLO	BLOCH
ANSUY	UNSAY	ARSXY	X-RAYS	BCHNU	BUNCH
ANSWY	YAWNS	ARTTU	TARTU	BCHOT	BOTCH
ANTTU	TAUNT	ARTTY	RATTY	BCHTU	BUTCH
ANTTY	NATTY	ARTWY	WARTY	BCHUU	BUCHU
ANTUV	VAUNT	ASSSY	SASSY	BCIKR	BRICK
ANTWY	TAWNY	ASSTW	SWATS	BCILM	CLIMB
ANVVY	NAVVY	ASSTY	STAYS	BCIOR	BORIC
AOPPP	POPPA	ASTTW	TWATS, WATTS	BCIPU	PUBIC
AOPRT	APORT, OP ART, PRATO	ASTTY	TASTY	BCIRS	CRIBS
AOPSS	PSOAS, SOAPS	ASVVY	SAVVY	BCITU	CUBIT
AOPST	PASTO	ATTTY	TATTY	BCKLO	BLOCK
AOPSY	SOAPY	ATTWY	WYATT	BCKOR	BROCK
AOPTZ	TOPAZ	BBBOY	BOBBY	BCKSU	BUCKS
AOQTU	QUOTA	BBCEU	CUBEB	BCLOS	BLOCS
AORRS	ROARS	BBDEE	EBBED	BCLSU	CLUBS
AORRW	ARROW	BBDOY	DOBBY	BCMOO	COMBO
AORRZ	RAZOR	BBEII	IBBIE	BCMOS	COMBS
AORSS	SAROS	BBEIL	BIBLE	BCMRU	CRUMB
AORST	ROAST, ROTAS, TAROS	BBEIR	BRIBE	BCRSU	CURBS, SCRUB
AORTT	TAROT	BBEMO	BOMBE	BDDEI	BIDED
AORVY	OVARY	BBEOP	BEBOP	BDDEO	BODED

BDDIY	BIDDY	BEEIL	BELIE	BEISV	BEVIS, VIBES
BDDUY	BUDDY	BEELL	BELLE	BEITT	TIBET
BDEEL	BLEED	BEELM	BELEM	BEITZ	ZIBET
BDEEM	EMBED	BEELP	BLEEP	BEJNY	BENJY
BDEER	BREED	BEELR	REBEL	BEKLO	BLOKE
BDEGO	BODGE	BEELT	BETEL	BEKOR	BROKE
BDEGU	BUDGE, DEBUG	BEELV	BEVEL	BEKRS	BERKS, KERBS
BDEIJ	JIBED	BEELZ	BEZEL	BEKRU	BURKE
BDEIK	BIKED	BEEMR	EMBER	BEKUZ	UZBEK
BDEIM	IMBED	BEENT	BENET	BELLS	BELLS
BDEIP	BIPED	BEENU	BENUE	BELLY	BELLY
BDEIR	BRIDE	BEEOS	OBESE	BELMU	UMBEL
BDEIS	B-SIDE	BEERS	BEERS	BELNO	NOBLE
BDEIT	BIDET, DEBIT	BEERT	BERET	BELOR	ROBLE
BDELN	BLEND	BEERV	BREVE	BELOS	BOLES, LOBEŠ
BDELO	LOBED	BEERW	WEBER	BELOU	BOULE
BDEMO	DEMOB	BEERY	BEERY	BELOW	BELOW, BOWEL, ELBOW
BDENO	BONED	BEEST	BEETS, BESET	BELPS	PLEBS
BDENS	BENDS	BEETT	BETTE	BELRU	BLUER, RUBLE
BDEOO	BOOED	BEFGO	BEFOG	BELRY	BERYL
BDEOR	BORED, ROBED	BEFIR	BRIEF, FIBRE	BELSS	BLESS
BDEOW	BOWED	BEFIT	BEFIT	BELST	BELTS, BLEST
BDEOX	BOXED	BEGIL	BILGE	BELSU	BLUES
BDERY	DERBY	BEGIN	BEGIN, BEING, BINGE	BELSY	SELBY
BDEST	DEBTS	BEGIO	BOGIE	BEMOR	BROME
BDESU	BUSED	BEGIR	GIBER	BEMOS	BESOM
BDETU	DEBUT	BEGIS	GIBES	BEMOW	EMBOW
BDFII	BIFID	BEGLO	GLOBE	BEMRU	BRUME, UMBER
BDGIY	DIGBY	BEGLU	BUGLE, BULGE	BEMSU	SEBUM
BDIIR	IRBID	BEGMU	BEGUM	BENNY	BENNY
BDILN	BLIND	BEGNU	BEGUN	BENOR	BORNE
BDILU	BUILD	BEGOT	BEGOT	BENOS	BONES
BDINO	BONDI	BEGOY	BOGEY	BENOT	T-BONE
BDINU	IN BUD	BEHIU	HUBEI	BENOY	EBONY
BDIOP	BIPOD	BEHOR	HOREB	BENOZ	BONZE
BDIOV	BOVID	BEHRS	HERBS	BENRT	BRENT
BDIRS	BIRDS, DRIBS	BEHRT	BERTH	BENRY	BERNY
BDLNO	BLOND	BEHRY	HERBY	BENST	BENTS
BDLOO	BLOOD	BEIJS	JIBES	BEOOS	OBOES
BDLOY	DOLBY	BEIKM	MBEKI	BEOOZ	BOOZE
BDNOS	BONDS	BEIKS	BIKES	BEOPR	PROBE
BDNOU	BOUND	BEILL	LIBEL	BEORR	BORER
BDNUU	BUNDU	BEILR	ERBIL	BEORS	BOERS, BORES, ROBES, SOBER
BDOOR	BROOD, DOBRO	BEIMO	BIOME		
BDOSU	DOUBS	BEIMU	IMBUE	BEORW	BOWER
BDOTU	DOUBT	BEINN	BENIN	BEORX	BOXER
BEEFY	BEEFY	BEINR	BRINE	BEOSU	BOUSE
BEEGI	BEIGE	BEINX	BENXI	BEOSX	BOXES
BEEGL	GLEBE	BEIOS	BOISE	BEPSU	PUBES
BEEGR	GREBE	BEIOW	BOWIE	BERRY	BERRY
BEEGT	BEGET	BEIRR	BRIER	BERST	BREST
BEEHI	HEBEI	BEIRS	BIERS	BERSU	BURSE, REBUS
BEEHP	PHEBE	BEIRT	TRIBE	BERSV	VERBS
BEEHR	HEBER	BEIST	BITES	BERSY	BYRES

32

BERTT	BRETT	BILLS	BILLS	BMOOR	BROOM
BERTU	BRUTE, REBUT, TUBER	BILLY	BILLY	BMOOS	BOOMS, BOSOM
BERUY	BUYER	BILMO	LIMBO	BMOST	TOMBS
BESSU	BUSES	BILMP	BLIMP	BMOSW	WOMBS
BESSY	BESSY	BILMS	LIMBS	BMOTY	BYTOM
BESTU	TUBES	BILOR	BROIL	BMOUX	BUXOM
BESTY	BETSY, BYTES	BILOS	BLOIS, BOILS	BMPSU	BUMPS
BETTU	BUTTE	BILPS	BLIPS	BMPUY	BUMPY
BETTY	BETTY	BILSS	BLISS	BNNOY	BONNY
BFFIS	BIFFS	BILST	B LIST	BNNUY	BUNNY
BFFLU	BLUFF	BILSY	SIBYL, SYBIL	BNOOR	BORNO, BORON
BFFSU	BUFFS	BILTU	BUILT	BNOOS	BOONS, BOSON
BFLYY	FLYBY	BILTZ	BLITZ	BNORU	BORNU, BOURN, BRUNO
BGGOY	BOGGY	BINOR	ROBIN	BNORW	BROWN
BGGUY	BUGGY	BINOS	BISON	BNORX	BRONX
BGHIT	BIGHT	BINRU	BRUIN, BURIN	BNORY	BYRON, ROBYN
BGHOU	BOUGH	BINRY	BRINY	BNOSS	SNOBS
BGHRU	BURGH	BIORS	BIROS, BORIS	BNOSU	BONUS, BOSUN
BGINO	BINGO	BIORT	ORBIT	BNRSU	BURNS
BGINR	BRING	BIPSU	PUBIS	BNRTU	BRUNT, BURNT
BGIOT	BIGOT	BIQSU	SQUIB	BNSSU	SNUBS
BGIPU	BIG UP	BIRST	BRITS	BOOPX	PO BOX
BGLUY	BULGY	BIRTT	BRITT	BOORS	BOORS
BGMOU	GUMBO	BIRTU	BRUIT	BOORT	ROBOT
BGNOO	BONGO	BISVY	VISBY	BOOST	BOOST, BOOTS
BGNSU	BUNGS	BITTY	BITTY	BOOSZ	BOZOS
BGOOR	BOGOR	BIYZZ	BIZZY	BOOTY	BOOTY
BGOSU	BOGUS	BJMOU	JUMBO	BOOWX	OXBOW
BGRSU	GRUBS	BJNOR	BJORN	BOOYZ	BOOZY
BGRUY	RUGBY	BKLSU	BULKS	BOPUW	UP-BOW
BHILU	HUBLI	BKLUY	BULKY	BORRU	BURRO
BHIRT	BIRTH	BKNOS	KNOBS	BORSW	BROWS
BHLOO	BOHOL	BKNSU	BUNKS	BOSSY	BOSSY
BHLSU	BLUSH	BKOOR	BROOK	BOSTU	BOUTS
BHMPU	BUMPH	BKOOS	BOOKS	BOSUY	BUOYS
BHMRU	RHUMB	BKOSY	BOSKY	BPRSU	BURPS
BHMTU	THUMB	BKRSU	BURKS	BRRSU	BURRS
BHOOS	HOBOS	BLLOS	BOLLS	BRRUY	BURRY
BHOOT	BOOTH	BLLSU	BULLS	BRSTU	BURST
BHORT	BROTH, THROB	BLLUY	BULLY	BSSTU	BUSTS, STUBS
BHRSU	BRUSH, SHRUB	BLMOO	BLOOM	BSTTU	BUTTS
BHSUY	BUSHY	BLMPU	PLUMB	BSTUY	BUSTY
BIILN	BLINI	BLNOW	BLOWN	BTTUY	BUTTY
BIIMN	NIMBI	BLNOY	NOBLY	CCEEL	LECCE
BIINY	YIBIN	BLNTU	BLUNT	CCEHK	CHECK
BIIOR	ORIBI	BLOSS	SLOBS	CCEHZ	CZECH
BIISU	SIBIU	BLOST	BLOTS, BOLTS	CCEIL	CECIL
BIJOU	BIJOU	BLOSU	BOLUS	CCEIR	CERIC
BIKLN	BLINK	BLOSW	BLOWS, BOWLS	CCELY	CYCLE
BIKNR	BRINK	BLOTY	BY LOT	CCEOS	SECCO
BIKRS	BRISK	BLOWY	BLOWY	CCESU	CUSEC
BIKRY	KIRBY	BLRTU	BLURT	CCHIK	CHICK
BIKSY	BIYSK	BLRUY	BURLY	CCHIN	CINCH
BILLR	BRILL	BLTUY	BUTYL	CCHKO	CHOCK

CCHKU	CHUCK	CDHIT	DITCH	CEFHS	CHEFS
CCHLU	CULCH	CDHOR	CHORD	CEFHT	FETCH
CCHNO	CONCH	CDHTU	DUTCH	CEFIT	FECIT
CCHOU	COUCH	CDHUY	DUCHY	CEFKL	FLECK
CCHRU	CURCH	CDIIN	INDIC	CEFLS	CLEFS
CCIIT	ICTIC	CDIIO	IODIC	CEFLT	CLEFT
CCIIV	CIVIC	CDIKS	DICKS	CEFOR	FORCE
CCIKL	CLICK	CDIKY	DICKY	CEGIN	GENIC
CCIKR	CRICK	CDILU	LUCID	CEGKO	GECKO
CCILO	COLIC	CDINY	CINDY	CEGNO	CONGE
CCIMO	COMIC	CDIOR	DORIC	CEGSS	GCSES
CCINO	CONIC	CDIOS	DISCO	CEHIL	CHILE
CCINY	CYNIC	CDIPU	CUPID	CEHIM	CHIME
CCIOS	CISCO	CDISS	DISCS	CEHIN	CHINE, NICHE
CCKLO	CLOCK	CDJOU	JUDOC	CEHIR	REICH
CCKLU	CLUCK	CDKOS	DOCKS	CEHIT	ETHIC
CCKOR	CROCK	CDKSU	DUCKS	CEHJU	CHEJU
CCKOS	COCKS	CDKUY	DUCKY	CEHKO	CHOKE
CCKOY	COCKY	CDLOS	CLODS, COLDS, SCOLD	CEHKR	KERCH
CCORU	OCCUR	CDLOU	CLOUD, COULD	CEHKT	KETCH
CCOUZ	CUZCO	CDLWY	CLWYD	CEHLO	CHLOE
CDDEE	CEDED	CDMOR	CD-ROM	CEHLW	WELCH
CDDEI	DICED	CDNOO	CODON	CEHLY	CHYLE
CDDEO	CODED	CDNOS	CORDS	CEHMY	CHYME
CDDUY	CUDDY	CDORU	DUROC	CEHNO	ENOCH
CDEEI	DE-ICE	CDORW	CROWD	CEHNT	TENCH
CDEER	CEDER, CREED	CDRUY	CURDY	CEHNW	WENCH
CDEEU	DEUCE, EDUCE	CDSTU	DUCTS	CEHOP	EPOCH
CDEHI	CHIDE	CEEEM	EMCEE	CEHOR	CHORE, OCHRE
CDEIM	MEDIC	CEEFN	FENCE	CEHOS	CHOSE, SOCHE
CDEIR	CIDER, CRIED, DICER	CEEFS	FECES	CEHPR	PERCH
CDEIT	CITED, EDICT	CEEHK	CHEEK	CEHRT	CHERT, RETCH
CDEIV	VEDIC	CEEHL	ELCHE, LEECH	CEHRU	RUCHE
CDEIY	DICEY	CEEHN	HENCE	CEHSS	CHESS
CDEKS	DECKS	CEEHP	CHEEP	CEHST	CHEST
CDELO	DOLCE	CEEHR	CHEER	CEHSW	CHEWS
CDELU	DULCE	CEEIN	NIECE	CEHTU	CHUTE
CDELY	CLYDE	CEEIP	PIECE	CEHTV	VETCH
CDEMO	MEDOC	CEEJT	EJECT	CEHTY	TECHY
CDENS	SCEND	CEEKL	CLEEK	CEHWY	CHEWY
CDENU	DUNCE	CEEKR	CREEK	CEIIR	ICIER
CDEOO	COOED	CEELL	CELLE	CEIJU	JUICE
CDEOP	COPED	CEELR	CREEL	CEILM	CLIME
CDEOR	CODER, CORED, CREDO, DECOR	CEELT	ELECT	CEILN	CLINE
CDEOS	CODES, COEDS	CEELX	EXCEL	CEILR	RELIC
CDEOU	COUDE	CEELY	LYCEE	CEILS	SLICE
CDEOW	COWED	CEEMR	CREME	CEILT	TELIC
CDEOX	CODEX, COXED	CEENP	PENCE	CEILU	LUCIE
CDEOY	DECOY	CEENS	CENSE, SCENE	CEILV	CLIVE
CDERU	CRUDE, CURED	CEEPR	CREEP, CREPE, PERCE	CEIMN	MINCE
CDERY	CYDER, DECRY	CEERS	CERES, SCREE	CEIMR	CRIME
CDETU	EDUCT	CEERT	CRETE, ERECT	CEIMS	MESIC
CDHIL	CHILD	CEERW	CREWE	CEIMX	CIMEX
		CEFHI	CHIEF	CEINO	ON ICE

CEINR	NICER	CEORS	CORES, CORSE, SCORE	CGIOR	CORGI
CEINS	SINCE	CEORT	RECTO	CGIOY	YOGIC
CEINV	VINCE	CEORV	COVER	CGIRU	UGRIC
CEINW	WINCE	CEORW	COWER	CGLNU	CLUNG
CEINZ	ZENIC	CEORZ	CROZE	CGLOS	CLOGS
CEIOV	VOICE	CEOSV	COVES	CGNOO	COGON, CONGO
CEIPR	PRICE	CEOSW	COWES	CHHIT	HITCH
CEIPS	EPICS, SPICE	CEOSX	COXES	CHHIW	WHICH
CEIPT	TEPIC	CEOTT	OCTET	CHHNU	HUNCH
CEIRR	CRIER	CEOTV	COVET	CHHOO	HOOCH
CEIRS	CRIES	CEOVY	COVEY	CHHTU	HUTCH
CEIRT	TRICE	CEPRT	CREPT	CHIKN	CHINK
CEIRU	CURIE	CEPRY	PERCY	CHIKO	HOICK, KOCHI
CEIRX	XERIC	CEPSS	SPECS	CHIKS	HICKS
CEISV	VICES	CERRU	RECUR	CHIKT	THICK
CEITV	CIVET, EVICT	CERSS	CRESS	CHILL	CHILL
CEITW	TWICE	CERST	CERTS, CREST	CHILM	MILCH
CEJOY	JOYCE	CERSU	CRUSE, CURES, CURSE, SUCRE	CHILZ	ZILCH
CEKLR	CLERK			CHIMR	CHIRM
CEKNS	NECKS, SNECK	CERSW	CREWS, SCREW	CHIMT	MITCH
CEKNV	V-NECK	CERSY	CERYS	CHIMU	HUMIC
CEKOS	COKES	CERTU	CRUET, CURET, CUTER, ERUCT, TRUCE	CHINP	PINCH
CEKPS	PECKS, SPECK			CHINS	CHINS
CEKRW	WRECK	CERUV	CURVE	CHINW	WINCH
CELLO	CELLO	CESST	SECTS	CHIOR	CHOIR
CELLS	CELLS	CESTU	CETUS, SCUTE	CHIOS	CHIOS, SOCHI
CELMO	OLMEC	CFFHU	CHUFF	CHIPR	CHIRP
CELNO	CLONE	CFFIL	CLIFF	CHIPS	CHIPS
CELNU	UNCLE	CFFOS	SCOFF	CHIPT	PITCH
CELOS	CLOSE, SOCLE	CFFSU	CUFFS, SCUFF	CHIPV	V-CHIP
CELOV	CLOVE	CFHIL	FILCH	CHIRR	CHIRR
CELOY	COLEY	CFHIN	FINCH	CHIRS	CHRIS
CELPU	CUPEL	CFHIT	FITCH	CHIST	CHITS, STICH
CELRU	CRUEL, LUCRE, ULCER	CFHIU	FICHU	CHITW	WITCH
CELSU	CLUES	CFIKL	FLICK	CHITY	ITCHY
CELSW	CLEWS	CFIKU	KUFIC	CHIVY	CHIVY, VICHY
CELTU	CULET	CFILO	FOLIC	CHKNU	CHUNK
CELUX	CULEX	CFIOS	COIFS	CHKOO	CHOKO
CEMOR	COMER	CFKLO	FLOCK	CHKOS	HOCKS, SHOCK
CEMOT	COMET	CFKOR	FROCK	CHKOY	CHOKY
CEMRY	MERCY	CFKSU	FUCKS	CHKSU	SHUCK
CENNO	NONCE	CFMOY	COMFY	CHKTU	KUTCH
CENOP	PONCE	CFORT	CROFT	CHLMU	MULCH
CENOR	CRONE	CFORU	CORFU	CHLNU	LUNCH
CENOS	CONES, SCONE	CFOSU	FOCUS	CHLNY	LYNCH
CENOT	CENTO, CONTE	CFRSU	SCURF	CHLOS	LOCHS
CENOU	OUNCE	CFSUU	FUCUS	CHLOT	CLOTH
CENOV	COVEN	CGHIN	CHING	CHLRU	CHURL, LURCH
CENOY	CONEY	CGHLU	GULCH	CHMNU	MUNCH
CENOZ	COZEN	CGHOU	COUGH	CHMOO	MOOCH
CENST	CENTS, SCENT	CGIIN	ICING	CHMOP	CHOMP
CEOPS	COPES, COPSE, SCOPE	CGILN	CLING	CHMPU	CHUMP
CEOPU	COUPE	CGILO	LOGIC	CHMSU	CHUMS
CEORR	CORER, CRORE	CGINO	COIGN	CHNOT	NOTCH
		CGINU	CUING		

CHNPU	PUNCH	CIMPR	CRIMP	CLOSW	COWLS, SCOWL
CHNRU	CHURN	CIMRS	SCRIM	CLOTU	CLOUT
CHOOP	POOCH	CIMSU	MUSIC	CLOYY	COYLY
CHOPR	PORCH	CINOS	COINS, ICONS, SCION,	CLRSU	CURLS
CHOPS	CHOPS		SONIC	CLRUY	CURLY
CHOPU	POUCH	CINOT	TONIC	CLSTU	CULTS
CHORT	TORCH	CINOV	COVIN	CMOOP	COMPO
CHOSU	HOCUS	CINRU	INCUR, RUNIC	CMOOS	COSMO
CHOSW	CHOWS	CINSU	INCUS	CMORS	CORMS
CHOTU	TOUCH	CINTU	CUTIN, TUNIC	CMORU	MUCRO
CHOUV	VOUCH	CIOPT	OPTIC, PICOT, TOPIC	CMPRU	CRUMP
CHOUX	CHOUX	CIORT	TORIC	CMRSU	SCRUM
CHPSY	PSYCH	CIORU	CURIO	CMRYY	CYMRY
CHRSU	CRUSH	CIOST	STOIC	CMSUU	MUCUS
CHSUY	CUSHY	CIOTX	TOXIC	CNOOR	CONOR, CROON
CIIKR	RICKI	CIPRS	CRISP, SCRIP	CNOOS	COONS
CIIKV	VICKI	CIPRY	PRICY	CNOPY	PONCY
CIILT	LICIT	CIPSS	SPICS	CNORS	CORNS, SCORN
CIILV	CIVIL	CIPSY	SPICY	CNORU	CORNU
CIILY	ICILY	CISSY	CISSY	CNORW	CROWN
CIIMM	MIMIC	CISTU	CUTIS, ICTUS	CNORY	CORNY, CRONY
CIINO	IONIC	CJKOS	JOCKS	CNOTU	COUNT
CIINR	RICIN	CJNOU	JUNCO	CNOTY	CYTON
CIINV	VINIC	CKKNO	KNOCK	CNOWY	CONWY
CIJUY	JUICY	CKLNU	CLUNK	CNSTU	CUNTS
CIIKS	KICKS	CKLOS	LOCKS	CNSUU	UNCUS
CIKLN	CLINK	CKLPU	PLUCK	CNTUU	UNCUT
CIKLS	LICKS, SLICK	CKLUY	LUCKY	COOPS	COOPS, SCOOP
CIKMS	MICKS	CKMNO	MONCK	COOPT	CO-OPT
CIKMY	MICKY	CKMOS	MOCKS, SMOCK	COOST	COOTS, SCOOT
CIKNS	NICKS, SNICK	CKMUY	MUCKY	COPRS	CORPS, CROPS
CIKNY	NICKY	CKNOS	CONKS	COPRU	CROUP
CIKPR	PRICK	CKOOR	CROOK	COPSU	COUPS
CIKPS	PICKS	CKOOS	COOKS	COPUY	COYPU
CIKPY	PICKY	CKOPS	SPOCK	CORSS	CROSS
CIKQU	QUICK	CKORS	CORKS, ROCKS	CORSU	SCOUR
CIKRS	RICKS	CKORY	ROCKY	CORSW	CROWS
CIKRT	TRICK	CKOSS	SOCKS	CORTU	COURT
CIKRY	RICKY	CKOST	STOCK	CORWY	COWRY
CIKST	STICK, TICKS	CKPSU	PUCKS	COSST	COSTS, SCOTS
CIKSW	WICKS	CKRSU	RUCKS	COSTT	SCOTT
CIKVY	VICKY	CKRTU	TRUCK	COSTU	SCOUT
CILNO	COLIN, NICOL	CKSTU	STUCK, TUCKS	CPRTY	CRYPT
CILNT	CLINT	CKUYY	YUCKY	CPSSU	CUSPS
CILOS	COILS	CLLSU	CULLS, SCULL	CPTUU	CUT UP
CILOT	LOTIC	CLMOU	COLUM, LOCUM	CRRUY	CURRY
CILOW	WILCO	CLMPU	CLUMP	CRSTU	CRUST
CILPS	CLIPS	CLMTU	MULCT	CRSUY	CYRUS
CILRU	ULRIC	CLNOO	COLON	CSSTY	CYSTS
CILRY	CYRIL, LYRIC	CLNOW	CLOWN	DDEEG	EDGED
CILTY	LYTIC	CLNUY	CLUNY	DDEEI	EDDIE
CIMNU	CUMIN, MUCIN	CLOOS	COOLS	DDEEN	ENDED
CIMOR	MICRO	CLOST	CLOTS, COLTS	DDEES	DEEDS
CIMOS	OSMIC	CLOSU	LOCUS	DDEFY	DYFED

DDEGO	DODGE	DEELS	LEEDS	DEGLY	LEDGY
DDEIL	IDLED	DEELU	ELUDE	DEGNO	OGDEN
DDEIN	DINED	DEELV	DELVE	DEGNU	NUDGE
DDEIO	DIODE, DODIE	DEEMN	EMDEN, EMEND	DEGOR	GORED, RODGE
DDEIR	DRIED, REDID	DEEMT	METED	DEGOS	DOGES
DDEIS	SIDED	DEEMW	MEWED	DEGRS	DREGS
DDEIT	TIDED	DEENO	DONEE	DEGRU	URGED
DDEIV	DIVED	DEENR	ENDER	DEGSY	SEDGY
DDELO	DOLED	DEENS	DENSE, NEEDS	DEGUY	GUYED
DDEMO	DOMED	DEENU	ENDUE	DEGWY	WEDGY
DDENY	NEDDY	DEENY	NEEDY	DEHII	HEIDI
DDEOP	DOPED	DEEOP	EPODE	DEHIK	HIKED
DDEOR	ODDER	DEEOR	ERODE	DEHIL	DELHI
DDEOS	DOSED	DEEPS	SPEED	DEHIR	HIDER, HIRED
DDEOT	DOTED	DEERR	ERRED	DEHIS	HIDES, SHIED
DDEOZ	DOZED	DEERS	REEDS	DEHIT	EDITH
DDEPU	DUPED	DEERT	DETER	DEHIV	HIVED
DDERU	UDDER	DEERY	REEDY	DEHLO	DHOLE
DDESU	DUDES	DEESS	SEEDS	DEHNO	HONED
DDETY	TEDDY	DEEST	STEED	DEHOP	HOPED
DDGIY	GIDDY	DEESU	SUEDE	DEHOR	HEROD, HORDE
DDGOY	DODGY	DEESW	SEWED, SWEDE, WEEDS	DEHOS	HOSED, SHOED
DDILO	DILDO	DEESX	SEXED	DEHPT	DEPTH
DDILY	LIDDY	DEESY	SEEDY	DEHPY	HYPED
DDIMY	MIDDY	DEETU	ETUDE	DEHRS	HERDS, SHERD, SHRED
DDINU	UNDID	DEETW	TWEED	DEHSS	SHEDS
DDIRU	DRUID	DEEUX	EXUDE	DEHSY	SHYED
DDLOY	ODDLY	DEEVX	VEXED	DEIIM	IMIDE
DDMUY	MUDDY	DEEWY	WEEDY	DEIIV	IVIED
DDNOY	NODDY	DEFGU	FUDGE	DEIIX	DIXIE
DDOOS	DODOS	DEFIL	FIDEL, FIELD, FILED	DEIJO	JODIE
DDORY	RODDY	DEFIN	FIEND, FINED	DEIJV	JIVED
DDOTY	TODDY	DEFIR	FIRED, FRIED	DEIKL	LIKED
DDOWY	DOWDY	DEFIT	FETID	DEIKN	INKED
DDRUY	RUDDY	DEFIX	FIXED	DEIKR	IRKED
DEEFF	EFFED	DEFIY	DEIFY, EDIFY	DEIKS	DIKES, SKIED
DEEFR	DEFER, FREED	DEFJL	FJELD	DEILM	LIMED
DEEFS	FEEDS	DEFLT	DELFT	DEILN	LINED
DEEFT	FETED	DEFLU	FLUED	DEILO	ODILE, OILED
DEEGH	HEDGE	DEFLY	FYLDE	DEILP	PILED, PLIED
DEEGK	KEDGE	DEFMU	FUMED	DEILR	IDLER, RILED
DEEGL	LEDGE	DEFOX	FOXED	DEILS	SIDLE, SLIDE
DEEGO	GEODE	DEFPU	FED UP	DEILT	TILDE, TILED
DEEGR	EDGER, GREED	DEFSU	FEUDS, FUSED	DEILV	DEVIL, LIVED
DEEGS	EDGES, SEDGE	DEGHY	HEDGY	DEILW	WIELD
DEEGW	WEDGE	DEGIL	GELID, GLIDE	DEILY	YIELD
DEEHW	HEWED	DEGIM	MIDGE	DEIMM	MIMED
DEEHX	HEXED	DEGIN	DEIGN	DEIMN	DENIM, MINED
DEEIL	ELIDE	DEGIO	DOGIE, GEOID	DEIMR	DIMER, MIRED
DEEIR	EIDER	DEGIR	DIRGE, RIDGE	DEIMS	DEISM, DIMES
DEEKN	KNEED	DEGIU	GUIDE	DEIMT	TIMED
DEEKR	DEREK	DEGJU	JUDGE	DEIMX	MIXED
DEEKY	KEYED	DEGLO	LODGE, OGLED	DEINO	DIONE
DEELR	ELDER	DEGLU	GLUED	DEINP	PINED

DEINR	DINER, INDRE	DEMNS	MENDS	DEOTY	TOYED
DEINS	DENIS, SNIDE	DEMOO	MOOED	DEOVW	VOWED
DEINU	UDINE	DEMOP	MOPED	DEOWW	WOWED
DEINW	EDWIN, WIDEN, WINED	DEMOR	DROME	DEPRU	DRUPE, DUPER, PRUDE
DEINX	INDEX, NIXED	DEMOS	DEMOS, DOMES,	DEPSU	DUPES, PSEUD
DEIOV	VIDEO		MODES	DEPTY	TYPED
DEIOX	OXIDE	DEMOU	ODEUM	DERRU	RUDER
DEIPP	PIPED	DEMOV	MOVED	DERRY	DERRY, DRYER
DEIPR	PRIDE, PRIED	DEMOW	MOWED	DERSS	DRESS
DEIPS	SPIED	DEMRU	DEMUR	DERSU	DRUSE
DEIPT	TEPID	DEMSU	MUSED, SEDUM	DERSY	DYERS
DEIPW	WIPED	DEMTU	MUTED	DERUX	DUREX
DEIRR	DIRER, DRIER, RIDER	DENNY	DENNY	DESTU	DUETS
DEIRS	RIDES, SIRED	DENOR	DRONE	DETUV	DUVET
DEIRT	TIRED, TRIED	DENOS	NODES, NOSED, SONDE	DFFSU	DUFFS
DEIRV	DIVER, DRIVE	DENOT	NOTED, TONED	DFILU	FLUID
DEIRW	WEIRD, WIDER, WIRED,	DENOV	DEVON	DFINS	FINDS
	WRIED	DENOW	ENDOW, OWNED	DFIOR	FIORD
DEISS	SIDES	DENOY	DOYEN	DFIRT	DRIFT
DEIST	DEIST, DIETS, SITED,	DENOZ	DOZEN, ZONED	DFJOR	FJORD
	TIDES	DENPS	SPEND	DFLOO	FLOOD, OF OLD
DEISV	DIVES	DENPU	UPEND	DFLOS	FOLDS
DEISW	WIDES	DENRS	NERDS	DFLOY	FLOYD
DEISZ	SIZED	DENRT	TREND	DFNOR	FROND
DEITY	DEITY	DENRU	UNDER	DFNOU	FOUND
DEJKO	JOKED	DENRY	DERYN	DFNSU	FUNDS
DEJOY	JOYED	DENST	DENTS	DFOOS	FOODS
DEKKO	DEKKO	DENSU	DUNES, NUDES	DFORS	FORDS
DEKNU	NUKED	DENSY	DENYS	DGGOO	DOGGO
DEKOP	POKED	DENTU	TUNED	DGGOY	DOGGY
DEKOY	YOKED	DENUU	UNDUE	DGHOU	DOUGH
DEKPU	PUKED	DENWY	EDWYN, WENDY	DGIIR	RIGID
DEKRY	DERYK	DEOOR	RODEO	DGIIT	DIGIT
DEKSS	DESKS	DEOOW	WOOED	DGILU	GUILD
DEKSU	DUKES	DEOOZ	OOZED	DGINO	DINGO, DOING, GONDI
DEKSY	DYKES	DEOPR	PEDRO, PORED, ROPED	DGINR	GRIND
DELLN	LENDL	DEOPS	DOPES, POSED, SPODE	DGINY	DINGY, DYING
DELLS	DELLS	DEOPT	DEPOT, OPTED	DGIOU	GUIDO
DELLW	DWELL	DEOPY	DOPEY	DGIRS	GRIDS
DELMO	MODEL	DEORR	ORDER	DGIRY	RIDGY
DELNO	ELDON, LODEN, OLDEN	DEORS	DOERS, DOSER	DGLOS	GOLDS
DELOP	LOPED, POLED	DEORT	DOTER	DGLOY	GODLY
DELOR	OLDER	DEORU	UREDO	DGNUY	DUNGY
DELOS	DELOS, LODES, SOLED	DEORV	DOVER, DROVE, ROVED	DGOOR	DROGO
DELOV	LOVED	DEORW	DOWER, ROWED	DGOOS	GOODS
DELOW	DOWEL, LOWED	DEORZ	DOZER	DGOOY	GOODY
DELOY	YODEL	DEOSS	DOSES	DGOPY	PODGY
DELPU	DUPLE	DEOSU	DOUSE	DGORU	GOURD
DELRU	LURED, RULED	DEOSV	DOVES	DGPUY	PUDGY
DELSS	SLEDS	DEOSW	DOWSE, SOWED	DGRSU	DRUGS
DELSU	DUELS, DULSE, SLUED	DEOTT	TOTED	DHIIN	HINDI
DELSW	WELDS	DEOTV	VOTED	DHILP	D PHIL
DELTW	DWELT	DEOTW	TOWED	DHIMU	HUMID
DEMMO	MODEM	DEOTX	DETOX	DHINS	HINDS
DEMNO	DEMON				

38

DHINU	HINDU	DIOTT	DITTO	DOOSW	WOODS
DHIOT	DHOTI	DIOTV	DIVOT	DOOTU	OUTDO
DHIRT	THIRD	DIOWW	WIDOW	DOOWY	WOODY
DHISY	DISHY	DIPRS	DRIPS	DOPRS	DROPS, PRODS
DHITW	WIDTH	DIQSU	SQUID	DOPRU	PROUD
DHLOS	HOLDS	DIRTU	TRUDI	DORSS	DROSS
DHNOO	HONDO	DIRTY	DIRTY	DORSU	SUDOR
DHNOU	HOUND	DITTY	DITTY	DORSW	SWORD, WORDS
DHOOS	HOODS	DITYZ	DITZY	DORTU	TUDOR
DHORY	HYDRO	DIYZZ	DIZZY	DORWY	DOWRY, ROWDY,
DHOSW	DHOWS	DKNRU	DRUNK		WORDY
DHOWY	HOWDY	DKNSU	DUNKS	DOTTY	DOTTY
DHRSU	HURDS	DKOSU	KUDOS	DPSSU	SPUDS
DHSTU	THUDS	DKSUY	DUSKY	DRSSU	SURDS
DIILP	LIPID	DKUUZ	KUDZU	DRSTU	TURDS
DIILV	LIVID	DLLOR	DROLL	DRTUY	TRUDY
DIIMO	IDIOM	DLLOS	DOLLS	DSSTU	STUDS
DIIMT	TIMID	DLLOY	DOLLY, LLOYD	DSSUY	SUDSY
DIIOT	IDIOT	DLLUY	DULLY	DSTUY	DUSTY, STUDY
DIIRS	IDRIS	DLMOS	MOLDS	EEEGS	GEESE
DIIVV	VIVID	DLMOU	MOULD	EEEIR	EERIE
DIJNN	DJINN	DLMOY	MOLDY	EEELM	MELEE
DIJNO	DIJON	DLOOR	DROOL	EEELV	LEVEE
DIKNR	DRINK	DLORS	LORDS	EEEMS	ESMEE
DIKNS	KINDS	DLORW	WORLD	EEENR	RENEE
DIKNY	DINKY	DLOST	DOLTS	EEEPS	EPEES
DIKRS	DIRKS	DLOSW	WOLDS	EEEPT	TEPEE
DIKSS	DISKS, SKIDS	DLOUW	WOULD	EEEPV	PEEVE
DILLR	DRILL	DLRYY	DRYLY	EEEPW	PEWEE
DILLY	IDYLL	DMMUY	DUMMY	EEERV	REEVE
DILMY	DIMLY	DMNOU	MOUND	EEFFI	EFFIE
DILNY	LINDY	DMOOS	DOOMS, MOODS	EEFHI	HEFEI
DILOS	IDOLS, LIDOS, SOLID	DMOOY	MOODY	EEFIL	EIFEL
DILOY	DOILY	DMPSU	DUMPS	EEFLR	FLEER
DILRU	LURID	DMPUY	DUMPY	EEFLT	FLEET
DILRY	DRILY	DMRSU	DRUMS	EEFRR	FREER, REFER
DILSW	WILDS	DMRUU	DURUM	EEFRS	REEFS
DILSY	DILYS	DNNOY	DONNY	EEFRV	FEVER
DIMNO	MID-ON	DNOOR	DONOR, RONDO	EEFSS	FESSE
DIMNS	MINDS	DNOOS	SNOOD	EEFST	FETES
DIMOU	ODIUM	DNOOT	TONDO	EEFSU	FUSEE
DIMST	MIDST	DNOPS	PONDS	EEFSZ	FEZES
DIMTU	TUMID	DNOPU	POUND	EEGGR	EGGER
DINRS	RINDS	DNORU	ROUND	EEGHL	HEGEL
DINSU	INDUS, NIDUS	DNORW	DROWN	EEGHN	HENGE
DINSW	WINDS	DNOSU	NODUS, SOUND	EEGIL	LIEGE
DINWY	WINDY	DNOSW	DOWNS	EEGIN	GENIE
DIOOT	OOTID	DNOSY	SYNOD	EEGIR	EIGER
DIOOV	OVOID	DNOUW	WOUND	EEGIS	SIEGE
DIOOZ	ZOOID	DNOWY	DOWNY	EEGKR	GREEK
DIOPY	PYOID	DOOPR	DROOP	EEGLR	LEGER
DIORS	DORIS	DOORS	DOORS, ROODS	EEGLS	GLEES
DIORT	DROIT	DOORU	DOURO, ODOUR	EEGLT	GLEET
DIOSV	VOIDS	DOOST	STOOD, TO-DOS	EEGLY	ELEGY

EEGMR	MERGE	EEJRZ	JEREZ	EENST	TEENS, TENSE
EEGNR	GENRE, GREEN	EEJSS	JESSE	EENSU	ENSUE
EEGNS	GENES	EEKLN	KNEEL	EENSV	EVENS, SEVEN
EEGNT	GENET	EEKLS	KEELS, LEEKS, SLEEK	EENTT	TENET
EEGNV	NEGEV	EEKLV	KEVEL	EENTV	EVENT
EEGRR	GREER	EEKNR	KEREN	EENTW	'TWEEN
EEGRS	SERGE	EEKNS	KEENS, KNEES	EENTY	TEENY
EEGRT	EGRET, GREET	EEKOP	PEKOE	EENUV	VENUE
EEGRV	VERGE	EEKOV	EVOKE	EENWY	WEENY
EEGST	EGEST, GEEST	EEKPS	KEEPS	EEOPT	TOPEE
EEHIN	HENIE	EEKRS	ESKER	EEORS	EROSE
EEHLL	HELLE	EEKRY	REEKY	EEOXY	OXEYE
EEHLN	HELEN	EEKST	SKEET	EEPPS	PEEPS
EEHLS	HEELS	EEKSW	WEEKS	EEPRS	PERES, PEERS, PER SE,
EEHLT	ETHEL	EELLN	ELLEN		SPREE
EEHLV	HELVE	EELLV	LEVEL	EEPRT	PETER
EEHLW	WHEEL	EELMR	ELMER, MERLE	EEPRU	PUREE, RUPEE
EEHMN	HE-MEN	EELNO	NOELE	EEPST	STEEP
EEHMT	THEME	EELNW	NEWEL	EEPSW	SWEEP
EEHNR	HERNE	EELOP	ELOPE	EEPWY	WEEPY
EEHNS	SHEEN	EELPR	LEPER, REPEL	EEQRU	QUEER
EEHNT	ETHNE	EELPS	SLEEP	EEQUU	QUEUE
EEHNZ	HENZE	EELPX	EXPEL	EERSS	SEERS
EEHPS	SHEEP	EELRS	LEERS, REELS	EERST	ESTER, RESET, STEER,
EEHRS	ESHER, HERES, SHEER	EELRV	ELVER, LEVER, REVEL		STERE, TERSE, TREES
EEHRT	ETHER, THERE, THREE	EELRY	LEERY	EERSU	REUSE
EEHRV	HERVE	EELSS	SELES	EERSV	SERVE, SEVER, VERSE
EEHRW	HEWER, WHERE	EELST	SLEET, STEEL, STELE	EERSW	EWERS, SEWER, WESER
EEHRX	HEXER	EELSV	ELVES	EERSX	REXES
EEHSS	HESSE	EELSW	LEWES	EERTV	EVERT, REVET
EEHST	SHEET, THESE	EELTU	ELUTE	EERTX	EXERT
EEHSX	HEXES	EELTX	TELEX	EERUV	REVUE
EEHTT	TEETH	EELTY	LEYTE	EERVV	VERVE
EEILL	ELLIE	EEMMN	EMMEN	EERVX	VEXER
EEILM	ELEMI, EMILE	EEMMR	EMMER	EERVY	EVERY, VEERY
EEILS	ELISE, ELSIE	EEMNS	MESNE, SEMEN	EESSX	ESSEX, SEXES
EEILT	ELITE	EEMNY	ENEMY, YEMEN	EESTV	STEVE
EEILV	ELVIE	EEMOT	EMOTE	EESTW	SWEET
EEILX	EXILE	EEMRS	MERES, MERSE	EETTU	TUTEE
EEIMM	EMMIE	EEMRT	METER, METRE	EETTW	TWEET
EEINR	ERNIE, IRENE, REINE,	EEMRX	REMEX	EFFGO	GEOFF
	RENIE	EEMRY	EMERY	EFFIR	FIFER
EEINS	SEINE	EEMST	MEETS	EFFIS	FIFES
EEIPP	EPPIE	EEMSU	MEUSE	EFFOR	OFFER
EEIRS	ISERE	EENPR	NEPER, PREEN	EFFRU	RUFFE
EEIRT	TIREE	EENQU	QUEEN	EFGIN	FEIGN
EEIRY	EYRIE	EENRS	SNEER	EFGIR	GRIEF
EEISS	ESSIE, SEISE	EENRT	ENTER, RENTE, TERNE,	EFGOR	FORGE, GOFER
EEISV	SIEVE		TREEN	EFGOY	FOGEY
EEISZ	SEIZE	EENRU	ENURE	EFGUU	FUGUE
EEITT	ETTIE	EENRV	NERVE, NEVER	EFHIO	HOFEI
EEJLW	JEWEL	EENRW	NEWER, RENEW	EFHIT	THIEF
EEJPS	JEEPS	EENRY	NYREE	EFHLS	FLESH, SHELF
EEJRS	JEERS	EENSS	ESSEN, SENSE	EFHRS	FRESH
				EFHTT	THEFT

EFHTY	HEFTY	EGGMY	MEGGY	EGOOS	GOOSE
EFIKN	KNIFE	EGGNU	GUNGE	EGOOY	GOOEY
EFILN	ELFIN	EGGOP	POGGE	EGOPR	GROPE
EFILR	FILER, FLIER, LIFER, RIFLE	EGGOR	GORGE	EGORR	ROGER
EFILS	FILES, FLIES	EGGOU	GOUGE	EGORS	GOERS, GORES, GORSE,
EFILT	FILET	EGGPY	PEGGY		OGRES
EFILX	FELIX	EGHIL	LEIGH	EGORT	ERGOT
EFIMR	FERMI	EGHIN	HINGE, NEIGH	EGORU	ROGUE, ROUGE
EFINR	FINER, INFER	EGHIT	EIGHT	EGORV	GROVE
EFINS	FINES	EGHIW	WEIGH	EGORW	GOWER
EFINT	FEINT	EGHNT	GHENT, THEGN	EGOSS	GESSO
EFIRR	FIRER, FRIER	EGHRU	HUGER	EGOUV	VOGUE
EFIRS	FIRES, FRIES, FRISE, SERIF	EGIIN	GENII	EGPRU	PURGE
EFIRT	REFIT	EGIJR	REJIG	EGPTU	GETUP
EFIRV	FIVER	EGILN	ELGIN, NIGEL	EGPTY	EGYPT
EFIRX	FIXER	EGILR	LIGER	EGRRU	URGER
EFIRY	FIERY, REIFY	EGILS	GILES	EGRRY	GERRY
EFISV	FIVES	EGILT	GILET, LEGIT	EGRSU	SURGE, URGES
EFISX	FIXES	EGILU	GUILE	EGRSY	GREYS
EFKLU	FLUKE	EGIMR	GRIME	EGRUW	GWERU
EFLLS	FELLS	EGINR	NIGER, REIGN	EGSSU	GUESS
EFLMU	FLUME	EGINS	SINGE	EGSTU	GUEST
EFLNO	FELON	EGINT	TINGE	EHHOP	HOPEH
EFLOS	FLOES	EGINV	GIVEN	EHHPU	HUPEH
EFLRU	FLEUR	EGINW	WINGE	EHIKR	HIKER
EFLRY	FLYER	EGINY	EYING	EHIKS	HIKES, SHEIK
EFLSU	FLUES, FUELS, FUSEL	EGIOV	OGIVE	EHIKT	KEITH
EFLSW	FLEWS	EGIPR	GRIPE	EHILT	ITHEL, LITHE
EFLTU	FLUTE	EGIRT	TIGER, TIGRE	EHILU	ELIHU
EFLTY	LEFTY	EGIRV	GIVER	EHILW	WHILE
EFMOR	FORME	EGISU	GUISE	EHILX	HELIX
EFMRU	FEMUR, FUMER	EGLMO	GOLEM, GOMEL	EHIMY	HYMIE
EFMSU	FUMES	EGLMU	GLUME	EHINR	HENRI, RHINE
EFNNU	FUNEN	EGLNN	GLENN	EHINS	HINES, SHINE
EFNNY	FENNY	EGLNS	GLENS	EHINT	THINE
EFNOR	FREON	EGLNU	LUNGE	EHINW	WHINE
EFNOT	OFTEN	EGLOO	GOOLE	EHIRR	HIRER
EFNRS	FERNS	EGLOR	OGLER	EHIRS	HEIRS, SHIER, SHIRE
EFNRY	FERNY	EGLOT	LET GO	EHIRT	THEIR
EFORT	FETOR, FORTE	EGLOV	GLOVE	EHISS	SHIES
EFORY	FOYER	EGLRU	GLUER, GRUEL, LUGER	EHIST	HEIST
EFORZ	FROZE	EGLSU	GULES	EHISV	HIVES, SHIVE
EFOSS	FOSSE	EGLSY	GYLES	EHITT	TITHE
EFOSX	FOXES	EGLUY	GLUEY	EHITW	WHITE, WITHE
EFOWY	FOWEY	EGMNO	GNOME	EHJLO	JEHOL
EFRRY	FERRY, FRYER	EGMRS	GERMS	EHKLW	WHELK
EFRSS	SERFS	EGNOR	GONER, NEGRO	EHKMR	KHMER
EFRST	FRETS	EGNOS	SEGNO	EHKOO	HOOKE
EFRUZ	FURZE	EGNOT	GET ON	EHLLO	HELLO
EFSSU	FUSES	EGNPU	UNPEG	EHLLS	HELLS, SHELL
EFSTU	FETUS	EGNST	GENTS	EHLMS	HELMS
EGGGR	GREGG	EGNSU	GENUS, NEGUS	EHLMU	HULME
EGGIU	GIGUE	EGNTW	GWENT	EHLOS	HOLES
EGGLY	LEGGY	EGNUU	ENUGU	EHLOT	HELOT, HOTEL, THOLE

EHLOV	HOVEL	EIINT	TIE-IN	EILTT	TITLE
EHLOW	HOWEL, WHOLE	EIIPX	PIXIE	EIMMR	MIMER
EHLOY	HOLEY, HOYLE	EIISV	IVIES	EIMMS	MIMES
EHLPS	HELPS	EIJLU	JULIE	EIMNR	MINER
EHLPW	WHELP	EIJOS	JOSIE	EIMNS	MIENS, MINES, NIMES
EHLPY	PHYLE	EIKKS	KIKES	EIMNV	VIMEN
EHLSW	WELSH	EIKLN	INKLE, LIKEN	EIMOR	MOIRE
EHLTY	ETHYL	EIKLS	LIKES	EIMOV	MOVIE
EHLWY	HYWEL	EIKLY	KYLIE	EIMOX	OXIME
EHLXY	HEXYL	EIKMS	MIKES	EIMPR	PRIME
EHMNY	HYMEN	EIKNO	EIKON, KOINE	EIMPT	TEMPI
EHMOR	HOMER, HORME	EIKNS	SKEIN, SKIEN	EIMRS	EMIRS, MIRES, MISER,
EHMOS	HOMES, MOSHE	EIKNV	KEVIN		REIMS
EHMOY	HOMEY	EIKPR	PIKER	EIMRT	MERIT, MITRE, REMIT,
EHMRT	THERM	EIKPS	PIKES, SPIKE		TIMER
EHMRU	RHEUM	EIKRR	KERRI	EIMRX	MIXER
EHMRY	RHYME	EIKRS	SKIER	EIMSS	SEISM, SEMIS
EHMST	METHS	EIKRT	TRIKE	EIMST	ITEMS, MITES, SMITE,
EHMTY	THYME	EIKSS	SKIES		TIMES
EHNNY	HENNY	EIKST	KITES	EIMSX	MIXES
EHNOP	PHONE	EIKSV	SKIVE	EIMSY	MYSIE
EHNOR	HERON, RHONE	EIKTW	KITWE	EINNR	INNER, RENIN
EHNOS	SHONE	EILLL	LILLE	EINNS	ENNIS, NINES
EHNOY	HONEY	EILLN	NEILL	EINNU	ENNUI
EHNRY	HENRY	EILLO	OLLIE	EINNV	VENIN
EHNSW	SHEWN	EILLS	ELLIS, LIESL, LISLE	EINOP	OPINE
EHNTT	TENTH	EILMN	LIMEN	EINOS	EOSIN, NOISE
EHOOY	HOOEY	EILMP	IMPEL	EINOT	TIE-ON, TOE-IN
EHOPR	HOPER	EILMR	MILER	EINOV	OVINE
EHOPS	HOPES	EILMS	LIMES, MILES, SLIME,	EINPP	PEPIN
EHORS	HORSE, SHOER, SHORE		SMILE	EINPR	RIPEN
EHORT	OTHER	EILMU	ILEUM	EINPS	PENIS, PINES, SNIPE,
EHORV	HOVER	EILMY	EMILY, LIMEY		SPINE
EHORW	WHORE	EILNN	LINEN	EINPT	INEPT
EHOSS	HOSES, SHOES	EILNR	LINER	EINPY	PINEY
EHOST	ETHOS, THOSE	EILNS	LENIS, LIENS, LINES	EINQU	QUINE
EHOSU	HOUSE	EILNT	INLET	EINRS	REINS, RESIN, RINSE,
EHOSV	SHOVE	EILNV	ELVIN, LIVEN, NEVIL		RISEN, SERIN, SIREN
EHOSW	WHOSE	EILOR	LOIRE, OILER, ORIEL	EINRT	INERT, INTER, NITRE,
EHPRT	PERTH	EILOT	ELIOT, TOILE		TERNI, TRINE
EHPRY	HYPER	EILOU	LOUIE	EINRU	INURE, URINE
EHPSY	HEPSY	EILOV	OLIVE, VOILE	EINRV	RIVEN
EHPTU	HET UP	EILPR	PERIL, PLIER	EINRW	ERWIN
EHRSU	USHER	EILPS	PILES, SPIEL, SPILE	EINSS	SINES
EHRSW	SHREW	EILPX	PIXEL	EINST	INSET, STEIN, TINES
EHRSY	SHYER	EILRT	LITER, LITRE, TILER	EINSV	NEVIS, VEINS, VINES
EHRTW	THREW	EILRV	LIVER, VILER	EINSW	SINEW, SWINE, WINES
EHRTZ	HERTZ	EILRY	RILEY	EINTU	UNITE, UNTIE
EHSTW	THEWS	EILSS	ISLES	EINTW	TWINE
EHTTY	HETTY	EILST	ISLET, ISTLE, STILE, TILES	EINVX	VIXEN
EIIKR	REIKI	EILSU	ILEUS, LIEUS	EINVY	VEINY
EIILN	LIE-IN	EILSV	ELVIS, EVILS, LEVIS,	EINWZ	WINZE, WIZEN
EIIMN	IMINE		LIVES, VEILS	EIOPS	POISE
EIINS	NISEI	EILSW	LEWIS, WILES	EIORS	OSIER, ROSIE
		EILSX	LEXIS, SILEX	EIORV	VIREO

EIOSS	OSSIE	EJLRU	JUREL	ELMOY	MOYLE
EIOZZ	OZZIE	EJLSU	JULES	ELMPU	PLUME
EIPPR	PIPER	EJMMY	JEMMY	ELMRU	LEMUR
EIPPS	PIPES	EJNNY	JENNY	ELMRY	MERYL
EIPQU	EQUIP, PIQUE	EJNOY	ENJOY	ELMST	SMELT
EIPRR	PRIER, RIPER	EJNSU	JUNES	ELMSU	MULES
EIPRS	PIERS, PRISE, SPIRE	EJOSV	JOVES	ELMSY	MYLES
EIPRT	TRIPE	EJRRY	JERRY	ELMUV	VELUM
EIPRV	VIPER	EJRWY	JEWRY	ELMUY	MULEY
EIPRW	WIPER	EJSST	JESTS	ELMXY	XYLEM
EIPRZ	PRIZE	EJSSU	JESUS	ELNNY	LENNY, LYNNE
EIPSS	SPIES	EJTTY	JETTY	ELNOR	ENROL, LONER, LOREN,
EIPST	PISTE, SPITE, STIPE	EKLLN	KNELL	LORNE	
EIPSW	SWIPE, WIPES	EKLLS	KELLS	ELNOT	ELTON, LENTO
EIPTT	PETIT	EKLLY	KELLY	ELNOV	NOVEL
EIPTU	TIE-UP	EKLNT	KNELT	ELNOW	OLWEN
EIPTW	PEWIT	EKLOY	YOKEL	ELNPZ	PLZEN
EIPTY	PIETY	EKLPS	SKELP	ELNWY	ELWYN, NEWLY
EIPXY	PYXIE	EKMOS	MOKES, SMOKE	ELOOP	POOLE
EIQRU	QUIRE	EKMRS	KREMS	ELOOS	LOOSE
EIQTU	QUIET, QUITE	EKNNY	KENNY	ELOPR	LOPER, PROLE
EIRRS	RISER	EKNOR	KRONE	ELOPS	POLES, SLOPE
EIRRT	TERRI, TRIER	EKNOS	SNOEK	ELOPU	LOUPE
EIRRV	RIVER	EKNOT	TOKEN	ELORR	ERROL
EIRRW	WIRER, WRIER	EKNOW	WOKEN	ELORS	LOSER, ROLES
EIRSS	RISES, SIRES	EKOPR	POKER	ELORV	LOVER
EIRST	RESIT, RITES, TIERS,	EKOPS	POKES, SPOKE	ELORW	LOWER, ROWEL
TIRES, TRIES		EKOST	STOKE	ELORY	ELROY, LEROY
EIRSW	WEIRS, WIRES, WISER	EKOSY	YOKES	ELOSS	LOESS, SLOES, SOLES
EIRTT	TITRE, TRITE	EKPRS	PERKS	ELOST	STOLE, TESOL
EIRTU	UTERI	EKPRY	PERKY	ELOSU	LOUSE, SEOUL
EIRTV	RIVET	EKPSY	PESKY	ELOSV	LOVES, SOLVE, VOLES
EIRTW	WRITE	EKRRY	KERRY	ELOTW	OWLET, TOWEL
EISST	SITES, STIES	EKRST	TREKS	ELOTX	EXTOL
EISSU	ISSUE, SUSIE	EKSSW	SKEWS	ELOUV	OVULE
EISSV	VISES	EKSUY	SUKEY	ELOUZ	OUZEL
EISSX	SIXES	ELLMS	SMELL	ELOVW	VOWEL
EISSZ	SIZES	ELLNY	NELLY	ELOVY	LOVEY
EISTU	SUITE	ELLPS	SPELL	ELPRU	PULER
EISTX	EXIST, EXITS, SIXTE	ELLQU	QUELL	ELPRY	REPLY
EISTY	YETIS	ELLSW	SWELL, WELLS	ELPST	PELTS, SLEPT, SPELT
EISTZ	ZEIST	ELLSY	YELLS	ELPSU	PULSE
EISUV	VISEU	ELLTU	TULLE	ELPSY	SLYPE, YELPS
EISVW	VIEWS, WIVES	ELLTY	TELLY	ELPTU	LETUP
EITTW	TWITE	ELLWY	WELLY	ELRRU	LURER, RULER
EJKOR	JOKER	ELMMU	LUMME	ELRSU	LURES, RULES
EJKOS	JOKES	ELMMY	LEMMY	ELRSY	LYRES, SLYER
EJKRS	JERKS	ELMNO	LEMON, MELON	ELRUX	LUREX
EJKRY	JERKY	ELMNU	LUMEN	ELSSW	SLEWS
EJLLO	JELLO	ELMNY	EMLYN	ELSTU	LUTES
EJLLY	JELLY	ELMOR	MOREL	ELSTW	WELTS
EJLOP	POLJE	ELMOS	MELOS, MOLES	ELSTY	STYLE
EJLOU	JOULE	ELMOT	METOL, MOTEL	ELTTY	LETTY
EJLPU	JULEP	ELMOU	OLEUM	ELTUX	EXULT

ELTWY	WETLY
EMMOS	MEMOS, SOMME
EMNOS	MESON, OMENS
EMNOT	MONTE
EMNOV	VENOM
EMNOW	WOMEN
EMNOY	MONEY
EMNRU	RUMEN
EMNSU	MENUS
EMOOR	ROMEO
EMOOS	MOOSE
EMOOT	ME-TOO
EMOPR	MOPER, PROEM
EMOPS	EPSOM, POEMS
EMOPT	TEMPO
EMOPY	MYOPE
EMORR	ORMER
EMORS	MOERS, MORES
EMORT	METRO
EMORV	MOVER, VOMER
EMORW	MOWER
EMOSS	MOSES
EMOST	MOTES, SMOTE, TOMES
EMOSU	MOUSE
EMOSV	MOVES
EMOSW	MEOWS
EMOSY	MOSEY
EMOTT	MOTET, TOTEM
EMOZZ	MEZZO
EMPRS	SPERM
EMPST	TEMPS
EMPSU	SPUME
EMPTT	TEMPT
EMPTY	EMPTY
EMRRY	MERRY
EMRST	TERMS
EMRSU	MUSER, SERUM
EMRSY	EMRYS
EMRUW	MWERU
EMRUX	MUREX
EMSST	STEMS
EMSSU	MUSES
EMSSY	MESSY
EMSTU	MUTES
ENNOO	NO ONE
ENNOT	TENON, TONNE
ENNOX	XENON
ENNOY	YONNE
ENNPY	PENNY
ENNWY	WYNNE
ENOOS	NOOSE
ENOOZ	OZONE
ENOPR	PRONE
ENOPY	PEONY

ENORS	NORSE, SENOR, SNORE
ENORT	TENOR, TONER
ENORU	ROUEN
ENORW	OWNER
ENOSS	NOSES
ENOST	NOTES, ONSET, STONE, TONES
ENOSV	OVENS
ENOSZ	ZONES
ENOVW	WOVEN
ENOVY	ENVOY
ENPRU	PRUNE
ENPST	SPENT
ENQRU	QUERN
ENRRU	RERUN
ENRST	RENTS, STERN, TERNS
ENRSU	NURSE, RUNES
ENRSW	WRENS
ENRSY	NERYS
ENRTU	TUNER
ENRTY	ENTRY
ENRVY	NERVY
ENRWY	NEWRY
ENSST	NESTS
ENSSU	NEUSS
ENSTT	TENTS
ENSTU	TUNES, UNSET
ENSTV	VENTS
ENSTW	NEWTS
ENSUV	VENUS
ENSUX	NEXUS, UNSEX
ENSWY	NEWSY
EOOPS	ESPOO
EOORW	WOOER
EOPPS	POPES
EOPRS	PORES, POSER, PROSE, ROPES, SPORE
EOPRT	TOPER, TROPE
EOPRV	PROVE
EOPRW	POWER
EOPRY	ROPEY
EOPSS	PESOS, POSES, POSSE
EOPST	ESTOP, POETS, STOEP, STOPE
EOPSX	POXES
EOPSY	POESY, SEPOY
EOPXY	EPOXY
EOQTU	QUOTE, TOQUE
EORRR	ERROR
EORRV	ROVER
EORRW	ROWER
EORSS	ROSES, SORES
EORST	STORE
EORSU	ROUES, ROUSE
EORSV	OVERS, SERVO, VERSO

EORSW	SEROW, SOWER, SWORE, WORSE
EORSZ	ZEROS
EORTT	OTTER, TOTER
EORTU	OUTER, OUTRE, ROUTE
EORTV	OVERT, TROVE, VOTER
EORTW	TOWER, WROTE
EORTY	TOYER
EORVW	VOWER
EORXX	XEROX
EOSSU	SOUSE
EOSTT	SET-TO, TOTES
EOSTV	STOVE, VOTES
EOSTY	EYOTS
EPPRS	PREPS
EPPRU	UPPER
EPRRU	PURER
EPRRY	PERRY
EPRSS	PRESS
EPRSU	PURSE, SPRUE, SUPER
EPRSY	PYRES, YPRES
EPRTU	ERUPT
EPRTW	TWERP
EPRXY	PYREX
EPSST	PESTS, STEPS
EPSTU	SET UP, STUPE, UPSET
EPSTW	SWEPT
EPSTY	TYPES
EPSXY	PYXES
EPTTY	PETTY
EQRUY	QUERY
EQSTU	QUEST
EQTUU	TUQUE
ERRSU	SURER
ERRTU	TRUER
ERRTY	RETRY, TERRY
ERRWY	WRYER
ERSST	RESTS, TRESS
ERSSU	RUSES, USERS
ERSTU	TRUES
ERSTW	STREW, TREWS, WREST
ERSTY	STEYR, TYRES
ERTTU	UTTER
ESSTT	TESTS
ESSTV	VESTS
ESSTW	STEWS
ESTTX	TEXTS
ESTTY	TESTY
ESTUY	SUETY
ESTYZ	ZESTY
ETTTY	TETTY
FFFLU	FLUFF
FFGRU	GRUFF
FFHIT	FIFTH

FFHIW	WHIFF	FILPS	FLIPS	FOOPR	PROOF
FFHOU	HOFUF	FILRT	FLIRT	FOOPS	POOFS, SPOOF
FFHUU	HUFUF	FILST	LIFTS	FOOPY	POOFY
FFHUY	HUFFY	FILSU	FUSIL	FOORS	ROOFS
FFIJY	JIFFY	FILTY	FITLY	FOOST	FOOTS
FFIKS	SKIFF	FIMOS	FOISM	FOOSW	WOOFS
FFILO	OLIFF	FIMOT	MOTIF	FOPRS	PROFS
FFIMY	MIFFY	FIMRS	FIRMS	FOPSU	POUFS
FFINS	SNIFF	FIMTU	MUFTI	FORST	FORTS, FROST
FFINY	NIFFY	FINNY	FINNY	FORSU	FOURS
FFIQU	QUIFF	FINTU	UNFIT	FORTY	FORTY
FFIRS	RIFFS	FINTY	NIFTY	FOSTY	SOFTY
FFIST	STIFF, TIFFS	FINUX	UNFIX	FPRUY	FRY-UP
FFITY	FIFTY	FINUY	UNIFY	FRRUY	FURRY
FFMSU	MUFFS	FIOST	FOIST	FRSTU	TURFS
FFNSU	SNUFF	FIRRY	FIRRY	FRSUU	RUFUS
FFOST	TOFFS	FIRST	FIRST, RIFTS	FRSUY	SURFY
FFPSU	PUFFS	FIRTT	FRITT	FRTUY	TURFY
FFPUY	PUFFY	FIRTU	FRUIT	FRUYZ	FURZY
FFRSU	RUFFS	FIRZZ	FRIZZ	FSSUY	FUSSY
FFSTU	STUFF	FISST	FISTS	FSTTU	TUFTS
FGGOY	FOGGY	FISTW	SWIFT	FSTUY	FUSTY
FGGUY	FUGGY	FIYZZ	FIZZY	FTTUY	TUFTY
FGHIT	FIGHT	FKLNU	FLUNK	FUYZZ	FUZZY
FGILN	FLING	FKLOS	FOLKS	GGGLO	GLOGG
FGINO	FINGO	FKLUY	FLUKY	GGINO	GOING
FGINU	FUNGI	FKNSU	FUNKS	GGIOT	GIGOT
FGIST	GIFTS	FKNUY	FUNKY	GGIPY	PIGGY
FGLNO	FLONG	FKORS	FORKS	GGMOY	MOGGY
FGLNU	FLUNG	FLLOY	FOLLY	GGMUY	MUGGY
FGLSU	GULFS	FLLUY	FULLY, LYULF	GGNOS	GONGS
FGOOR	FORGO	FLNOW	FLOWN	GGOSY	SOGGY
FGOOS	GOOFS	FLOOR	FLOOR	GHHIS	HIGHS
FGOOY	GOOFY	FLOOS	FOOLS	GHHIT	HIGHT, THIGH
FGORS	FROGS	FLOOW	WOLOF	GHHOU	HOUGH
FHIIS	HI-FIS	FLOPS	FLOPS	GHILT	LIGHT
FHILT	FILTH	FLORU	FLOUR, FLUOR	GHIMT	MIGHT
FHIRT	FIRTH	FLORY	FLORY	GHINT	NIGHT, THING
FHIST	SHIFT	FLOSS	FLOSS	GHINY	HYING
FHISY	FISHY	FLOST	LOFTS	GHIRT	GIRTH, RIGHT
FHLSU	FLUSH	FLOSU	FOULS	GHISS	SIGHS
FHORT	FORTH, FROTH	FLOSW	FOWLS	GHIST	SIGHT
FIINS	FINIS	FLOTU	FLOUT	GHISW	WHIGS
FIINX	INFIX	FLOTY	LOFTY	GHITT	TIGHT
FIKRS	FRISK	FLTUY	FLUTY	GHITW	WIGHT
FILLR	FRILL	FMORS	FORMS	GHLLY	GHYLL
FILLY	FILLY	FMORU	FORUM	GHLOU	GHOUL, LOUGH
FILMS	FILMS	FMPRU	FRUMP	GHLPY	GLYPH
FILMU	FILUM	FNNUY	FUNNY	GHNOT	THONG
FILMY	FILMY	FNORS	FRONS	GHORU	ROUGH
FILNT	FLINT	FNORT	FRONT	GHOST	GHOST
FILOO	FOLIO	FNORW	FROWN	GHOSU	SOUGH
FILOR	FORLI	FNOST	FONTS	GHOTU	OUGHT, TOUGH
FILOS	FOILS	FNOTU	FOUNT, FUTON	GHRSU	SHRUG

45

GHSTU	THUGS	GLMOU	MOGUL	HIKSW	WHISK
GIILV	VIGIL	GLNSU	LUNGS, SLUNG	HILLS	HILLS
GIINO	INIGO	GLOOS	LOGOS	HILLY	HILLY
GIINP	PIING	GLORW	GROWL	HILMU	HILUM
GIJNO	GIJON, JINGO	GLORY	GLORY	HILOT	THIOL
GIKNS	KINGS	GLOSS	GLOSS, SLOGS	HILRS	SHIRL
GIKOR	GORKI	GLOUV	VOGUL	HILRW	WHIRL
GILLR	GRILL	GLPSU	GULPS, PLUGS	HILST	HILTS
GILLS	GILLS	GLRUY	LURGY	HILSU	HILUS
GILNO	LOG IN, LINGO	GLSSU	SLUGS	HILSY	SHILY
GILNS	SLING	GLSTU	GLUTS	HILTT	TILTH
GILNT	GLINT	GMMUY	GUMMY	HIMRT	MIRTH
GILNY	LYING	GMNOU	MUNGO	HIMST	SMITH
GILOO	IGLOO	GMOOR	GROOM	HIMSW	WHIMS
GILOS	SLIGO	GMPYY	PYGMY	HINNT	NINTH
GILRS	GIRLS	GNOOS	GOONS	HINNY	HINNY
GILST	GILTS	GNOPR	PRONG	HINOR	RHINO
GILTU	GUILT	GNOPS	PONGS	HINOT	HIT ON
GILTZ	GLITZ	GNOPY	PONGY	HINSS	SHINS
GIMNY	MINGY	GNORW	GROWN, WRONG	HINST	HINTS
GIMOZ	GIZMO	GNOSS	SNOGS, SONGS	HINSY	SHINY
GIMPY	PIGMY	GNOST	TONGS	HINWY	WHINY
GIMRY	GRIMY	GNOSW	GOWNS	HIOPP	HIPPO
GINNY	GINNY	GNOUY	YOUNG	HIORU	HOURI
GINOP	PINGO	GNRSU	RUNGS	HIOST	HOIST
GINOR	GIRON, GROIN	GNRTU	GRUNT	HIPPY	HIPPY
GINOT	INGOT, TIGON	GNRUW	WRUNG	HIPSS	SHIPS
GINOW	OWING	GNSSU	SNUGS	HIPSW	WHIPS
GINRS	GRINS, RINGS	GNSTU	STUNG	HIPTY	PITHY
GINRU	RUING, UNRIG	GNSUW	SWUNG	HIRRS	SHIRR
GINRW	WRING	GOORS	SORGO	HIRRW	WHIRR
GINSS	SIGNS	GOOSY	GOOSY	HIRST	HIRST, SHIRT
GINST	STING, TINGS	GOOTU	OUTGO	HIRSW	WHIRS
GINSU	SUING, USING	GOPRU	GROUP	HISST	SHITS
GINSV	V-SIGN	GOPRY	PORGY	HISSU	SUSHI
GINSW	SWING, WINGS	GORSS	GROSS	HISSW	SWISH
GINTY	TYING	GORTU	GROUT, TRUGO	HISTW	WHIST, WHITS
GINVY	VYING	GOSTU	GUSTO	HISTX	SIXTH
GINYZ	ZINGY	GOTUY	GOUTY, GUYOT	HISUW	WUSIH
GIORR	RIGOR	GPPUY	GUPPY	HITWY	WITHY
GIORV	VIRGO	GPSYY	GYPSY	HIWZZ	WHIZZ
GIOSY	YOGIS	GRSTU	TRUGS	HKKOU	HOKKU
GIPRS	GRIPS, PRIGS, SPRIG	GRSUU	GURUS	HKLSU	HULKS
GIPSY	GIPSY	GSSTU	GUSTS	HKMOU	HOKUM
GIRST	GRIST, GRITS	GSTUY	GUSTY, GUTSY	HKNOS	HONKS
GIRUU	UIGUR	HHLSU	SHLUH	HKNOY	HONKY
GISSW	SWIGS	HHMOU	HO-HUM	HKNSU	HUNKS
GISTW	TWIGS	HHMPU	HUMPH	HKOOS	HOOKS, SHOOK
GJMUU	JUGUM	HHSSU	SHUSH	HKOOY	HOOKY
GKNOO	KONGO	HIILN	NIHIL	HKSSU	HUSKS
GLLOY	GOLLY	HIIRS	IRISH	HKSUY	HUSKY
GLLSU	GULLS	HIKNT	THINK	HLLOO	HOLLO
GLLUY	GULLY	HIKRS	SHIRK	HLLOU	HULLO
GLMOO	GLOOM	HIKSS	SIKHS	HLLOY	HOLLY

HLLSU	HULLS	HOSST	HOSTS, SHOTS	IKLRS	SKIRL
HLMPY	LYMPH	HOSSW	SHOWS	IKLRU	KURIL
HLOPR	ROLPH	HOSTT	SHOTT	IKLSS	SILKS
HLOPX	PHLOX	HOSTU	SHOUT, SOUTH	IKLST	KILTS
HLORW	WHORL	HOSWY	SHOWY	IKLSY	SILKY
HLOSS	SLOSH	HOTUY	YOUTH	IKMNS	MINSK
HLOST	HOLST, SLOTH	HPSTU	PHUTS	IKMPS	SKIMP
HLOSW	HOWLS	HPSUY	PUSHY	IKMRS	SMIRK
HLOTU	LOUTH	HRRUY	HURRY	IKNOP	PINKO
HLOTY	HOTLY	HRSTU	HURST, HURTS	IKNOS	IKONS, OINKS
HLPSU	PLUSH	HRSUY	RUSHY	IKNPR	PRINK
HLPSY	SYLPH	HRTTU	TRUTH	IKNPS	PINKS, PINSK
HLSSU	SLUSH	HRUUU	UHURU	IKNRS	RINKS
HLSYY	SHYLY	HSSUY	HUSSY	IKNSS	SINKS, SKINS
HMNOT	MONTH	IIJLN	JILIN	IKNST	SKINT, STINK
HMNPY	NYMPH	IIJNN	JINNI	IKNSW	WINKS
HMNSY	HYMNS	IIKKN	NIKKI	IKORV	KIROV
HMOOP	OOMPH	IIKKR	RIKKI	IKPSS	SKIPS, SPIKS
HMOPR	MORPH	IIKKV	VIKKI	IKPSY	SPIKY
HMOST	MOTHS	IIKNN	INK IN, KININ	IKQRU	QUIRK
HMOTU	MOUTH	IIKNR	KIRIN	IKRSS	RISKS
HMOTY	MOTHY	IIKSW	KIWIS	IKRST	SKIRT, STIRK
HMPSU	HUMPS	IILMT	LIMIT	IKRSY	RISKY
HMPTU	THUMP	IILMU	ILIUM	IKRTU	TURKI
HMPUY	HUMPY	IILNN	LININ	IKSST	SKITS
HMRRY	MYRRH	IIMMN	MINIM	IKTTY	KITTY
HMRTU	THRUM	IIMNS	MINIS	ILLMS	MILLS
HMSTU	MUSTH	IIMRZ	IZMIR	ILLMY	MILLY
HMSTY	MYTHS	IIMST	MITIS	ILLOS	LILOS
HMSUU	HUMUS	IIMTZ	IZMIT, MITZI	ILLPR	PRILL
HMSUY	MUSHY	IINNO	INION	ILLPS	PILLS, SPILL
HNOOR	HONOR	IINRV	IRVIN	ILLQU	QUILL
HNOOW	NOHOW	IINRW	IRWIN	ILLRS	RILLS
HNORS	HORNS, SHORN	IINST	SIT-IN	ILLRT	TRILL
HNORT	NORTH, THORN	IINTU	INUIT	ILLSS	SILLS
HNORU	HURON	IIPPT	PIPIT	ILLST	LILTS, STILL, TILLS
HNORY	HORNY	IISTV	VISIT	ILLSW	SWILL, WILLS
HNOSW	SHOWN	IJKNS	JINKS	ILLSY	SILLY, SLILY
HNSTU	HUNTS, SHUNT	IJMMY	JIMMY	ILLTW	TWILL
HOOPS	HOOPS	IJNNY	JINNY	ILLTY	TILLY
HOOPT	PHOTO	IJNOS	JOINS	ILLWY	WILLY
HOOPW	WHOOP	IJNOT	JOINT	ILMPY	IMPLY
HOOST	HOOTS, SHOOT, SOTHO	IJOST	JOIST	ILMSY	SLIMY
HOOTT	TOOTH	IKKNO	NIKKO	ILNOR	LORIN
HOPSS	SHOPS	IKKNS	KINKS, SKINK	ILNOS	LIONS, LOINS
HOPSY	HYPOS, SOPHY	IKKNY	KINKY	ILNPU	LUPIN
HOQTU	QUOTH	IKKOS	KIOSK	ILNSY	LYSIN
HORRY	HORRY	IKKRS	KIRKS	ILNTU	UNTIL
HORST	HORST, SHORT	IKKRU	KUKRI	ILNTY	LINTY
HORSU	HORUS, HOURS	IKLLR	KRILL	ILNVY	VINYL
HORSY	HORSY	IKLLS	KILLS, SKILL	ILOOP	POLIO
HORTT	TROTH	IKLMY	MILKY	ILOPS	SPOIL
HORTW	THROW, WORTH,	IKLNS	KILNS, LINKS, SLINK	ILOPT	PILOT
	WROTH	IKLOS	KILOS	ILOPU	POILU

ILOPX	OXLIP	INNVY	VINNY	IPSTZ	SPITZ
ILORS	LORIS	INOOR	ORION	IPSWY	WISPY
ILORT	TRIOL	INOPR	RIPON	IPSXY	PYXIS
ILOSS	SILOS, SOILS	INOPT	PINTO, PITON, POINT	IQRTU	QUIRT
ILOST	SOLTI, TOILS	INOQU	QUOIN	IQSTU	QUITS
ILOSU	LOUIS	INORS	IRONS, ROSIN	IRSST	STIRS
ILOSV	VIOLS	INORT	INTRO	IRSTW	WRIST, WRITS
ILPPU	PUPIL	INORY	IRONY	IRSUV	VIRUS
ILPSS	SLIPS	INOSW	OSWIN	IRTUV	VIRTU
ILPST	SPILT, SPLIT	INOSY	NOISY	IRTYZ	RITZY
ILPTU	TULIP	INOTW	IN TOW, IN TWO	ISSSW	SWISS
ILQTU	QUILT	INOTX	TOXIN	ISSSY	SISSY
ILRSW	SWIRL	INPPU	PINUP	ISSTU	SITUS, SUITS
ILRTW	TWIRL	INPPY	NIPPY	ISTTU	TITUS
ILSST	LISTS, SLITS	INPRT	PRINT	ISTTW	TWIST, TWITS
ILSSY	LYSIS	INPRU	UNRIP	ISTUV	VITUS
ILSTT	STILT, TILTS	INPSS	SNIPS, SPINS	ISTXY	SIXTY
ILSTY	SILTY	INPST	PINTS	ITTTU	TUTTI
ILYZZ	LIZZY	INPSY	SPINY	ITTTY	TITTY
IMMTY	TIMMY	INPTU	INPUT	ITTWX	TWIXT
IMNOR	MINOR	INPUZ	UNZIP	ITTWY	WITTY
IMNOS	SIMON	INQSU	QUINS	ITYZZ	TIZZY
IMNST	MINTS	INQTU	QUINT	JJSUU	JUJUS
IMNSU	IN SUM, MINUS	INRSU	RUINS	JKNSU	JUNKS
IMNTY	MINTY	INRTU	TURIN	JLLOY	JOLLY
IMOPR	PRIMO	INSSU	NISUS, SINUS	JLOST	JOLTS
IMOPU	OPIUM	INSTT	STINT, TINTS	JLOSW	JOWLS
IMOSS	MOSSI	INSTU	SUINT, TUNIS, UNITS	JMORU	JORUM
IMOST	MOIST	INSTW	TWINS	JMPSU	JUMPS
IMOSX	SIXMO	INTTY	NITTY	JMPUY	JUMPY
IMOTV	VOMIT	INTUX	X-UNIT	JNOTU	JUNTO
IMPPR	PRIMP	INTUY	UNITY	JORRU	JUROR
IMPPS	PIMPS	IOPRR	PRIOR	JOSTU	JOUST
IMPRS	PRISM	IOPST	POSIT	KKLSU	SKULK
IMPSW	WIMPS	IOPSU	PIOUS	KKNSU	SKUNK
IMPUX	MIX-UP	IOPTV	PIVOT	KKOOS	KOOKS
IMPWY	WIMPY	IOQTU	QUITO, QUOIT	KKOOY	KOOKY
IMRST	TRIMS	IORRS	ORRIS	KKRSU	KURSK
IMSST	MISTS	IORST	RIOTS, TIROS, TRIOS	KLLNO	KNOLL
IMSSW	SWIMS	IORSV	VISOR	KLLSU	SKULL
IMSSY	MISSY	IORVY	IVORY	KLNOP	PLONK
IMSTT	MITTS	IOSUX	SIOUX	KLNPU	PLUNK
IMSTY	MISTY	IOTTW	TO WIT	KLNRU	KNURL
INNNO	NINON	IPPYZ	ZIPPY	KLNSU	SLUNK
INNNY	NINNY	IPQSU	QUIPS	KLOOS	LOOKS
INNOO	ONION	IPRST	SPRIT, STRIP, TRIPS	KLOSY	YOLKS
INNOU	UNION	IPRSY	SPIRY	KLOYY	YOLKY
INNOW	NO-WIN	IPRTW	TWIRP	KLSSU	SULKS
INNPU	UNPIN	IPRVY	PRIVY	KLSUY	SULKY
INNPY	PINNY	IPSST	SPITS	KMNOS	MONKS
INNQU	QUINN	IPSSV	SPIVS	KMOOP	MOKPO
INNRU	INURN, RUN-IN	IPSSW	WISPS	KMOST	TOMSK
INNSU	SUNNI	IPSTU	SIT UP	KMOSY	SMOKY
INNTY	TINNY	IPSTY	TIPSY	KMRUY	MURKY

KMSUY	MUSKY	LNOOR	ORLON	MNOOY	MOONY
KNNOW	KNOWN	LNOOS	LOONS	MNORS	MORNS, NORMS
KNOOR	KROON	LNOOY	LOONY	MNORU	MOURN
KNOOS	NOOKS, SNOOK	LNOPY	PYLON	MNORY	MYRON
KNORT	TRONK	LNOTU	LUTON	MNOTU	MOUNT, NOTUM
KNOST	KNOTS	LNOUZ	LUZON	MNOTY	MONTY
KNOSW	KNOWS	LNOWY	OLWYN	MOOPR	PROMO
KNOSY	YONKS	LOOOV	OVOLO	MOORS	MOORS, ROOMS
KNOUY	YUKON	LOOPR	ORLOP	MOORT	MOTOR
KNOWY	WONKY	LOOPS	LOOPS, POOLS, SLOOP,	MOORY	ROOMY
KNPSU	PUNKS, SPUNK		SPOOL	MOOSS	MOSSO
KNRTU	TRUNK	LOOPY	LOOPY	MOOTT	MOTTO
KNSTU	STUNK	LOOSS	SOLOS	MOPPU	MOP-UP
KNSUU	NUKUS	LOOST	STOOL, TOOLS	MOPRS	PROMS, ROMPS
KOOPS	SPOOK	LOPPY	POLYP	MOPST	STOMP
KOORS	ROOKS	LOPRW	PROWL	MORST	STORM
KOOST	STOOK	LOPSS	SLOPS	MORSW	WORMS
KOOTY	KYOTO, TOKYO	LOPST	PLOTS	MORTY	MORTY
KOPRY	PORKY	LOPSW	PLOWS	MORWY	WORMY
KOPSV	PSKOV	LOPSY	PLOYS, POLYS	MOSSY	MOSSY
KORST	STORK, TORSK	LOPTU	PLUTO, POULT	MOSUY	MOUSY
KORSW	WORKS	LOPUU	UPOLU	MPPSU	PUMPS
KRSSU	RUSKS	LORRY	LORRY	MPRSU	RUMPS
KRTUU	TURKU	LORTY	TYROL	MPRTU	TRUMP
KSSTU	TUSKS	LORUX	LUXOR	MPSSU	SUMPS
LLLOY	LOLLY	LOSST	SLOTS	MPSTU	STUMP
LLMOS	MOLLS	LOSSU	SOULS	MRSTU	STRUM
LLMOY	MOLLY	LOSSY	LOSSY	MSSTU	SMUTS
LLMSU	MULLS	LOSTU	LOTUS, LOUTS	MSTTU	MUTTS
LLOOR	ROLLO	LOSTV	VOLTS	MSTUY	MUSTY
LLOPS	POLLS	LOSUY	LOUSY	MUYZZ	MUZZY
LLOPY	POLLY	LOSWY	YOWLS	NNOOY	NOYON
LLORS	ROLLS	LOTTY	LOTTY	NNOSU	NOUNS
LLORT	TROLL	LOTYZ	ZLOTY	NNOSY	SONNY
LLORY	ROLLY	LPPSU	PULPS	NNRUY	RUNNY
LLOST	TOLLS	LPPUY	PULPY	NNSUY	SUNNY
LLOSY	LYSOL, SOLLY	LPRSU	SLURP	NNTUY	TUNNY
LLOTY	TOLLY, TOLYL	LPSUU	LUPUS	NOOPR	PORNO
LLOWY	LOWLY	LRSSU	SLURS	NOOPS	SNOOP, SPOON
LLOXY	XYLOL	LRSUY	SURLY	NOORS	ORSON
LLPSU	PULLS	LRTUY	TRULY	NOOSW	SWOON
LLSTU	STULL	LRUUU	ULURU	NOOTW	ON TOW
LLSUY	SULLY	LRWYY	WRYLY	NOPTU	PUT-ON, TON-UP,
LLXYY	XYLYL	LSSTU	LUSTS, SLUTS		UPTON
LMOOS	LOOMS	LSTUY	LUSTY	NORST	SNORT
LMOOT	MOLTO	MMMOY	MOMMY	NORSW	SWORN
LMOST	MOLTS, SMOLT	MMMUY	MUMMY	NORTU	TORUN
LMOSU	MOSUL, SOLUM	MMOPY	POMMY	NORTY	TRY-ON
LMOTU	MOULT	MMOTY	TOMMY	NOSSW	SNOWS
LMPPU	PLUMP	MMPSU	MUMPS	NOSTU	SNOUT, TONUS
LMPSU	LUMPS, PLUMS, SLUMP	MMRUY	RUMMY	NOSTW	TOWNS
LMPUY	LUMPY, PLUMY	MMTUY	TUMMY	NOSTY	STONY, TYSON
LMSSU	SLUMS	MNOOR	MORON	NOSWY	SNOWY
LNNOY	NYLON	MNOOS	MOONS	NPRSU	SPURN

49

NPRUU	RUN-UP	OPRST	PORTS, PROST, SPORT, STROP	ORSUY	YOURS
NPSTU	PUNTS	OPRSW	PROWS	ORTTU	TROUT, TUTOR
NPSUU	SUN-UP	OPRSY	PROSY	OSSST	STOSS
NPTUY	PUNTY	OPRUY	ROUPY	OSSTW	SWOTS
NRSTU	RUNTS, TURNS	OPRXY	PROXY	OSTTU	STOUT, TOUTS
NRTUU	U-TURN	OPSST	POSTS, SPOTS, STOPS	OSUYZ	SOYUZ
NRTUY	RUNTY	OPSSU	SOUPS	OTTTY	TOTTY
NSTTU	STUNT	OPSSW	SWOPS	PPPUY	PUPPY
NTTUY	NUTTY	OPSTU	POUTS, SPOUT, STOUP	PRRSU	PURRS
OOPPS	POOPS	OPSTY	TOPSY	PRSSU	SPURS
OOPRS	SOPOR, SPOOR	OPSUY	SOUPY	PRSTU	SPURT, TURPS
OOPRT	TROOP	OPSWY	POWYS	PRSUU	USURP
OOPST	STOOP, TOPOS	OPTTU	PUTTO	PRSUY	SYRUP
OOPSW	SWOOP	OPTTY	POTTY	PSSUY	PUSSY
OOPTT	POTTO	OPTUZ	TZU-PO	PSTTU	PUTTS
OORRT	ROTOR	ORRSY	SORRY	PTTUY	PUTTY
OORRU	ORURO	ORRTU	TRURO	RSSTU	TRUSS
OORST	ROOST, ROOTS, TORSO	ORRWY	WORRY	RSTTU	STRUT, TRUST
OOSTT	TOOTS	ORSST	SORTS	RSTTY	TRYST
OOSTY	SOOTY	ORSSU	SORUS	RSTUW	WURST
OOSYY	YOYOS	ORSTT	TORTS, TROTS	RSTUY	RUSTY
OOWYZ	WOOZY	ORSTU	ROUST, ROUTS, STOUR, TORUS, TOURS	RSUUY	USURY
OPPPU	POP-UP	ORSTW	WORST	RTTUY	RUTTY
OPPPY	POPPY	ORSTY	STORY, TYROS	STTUU	TUTUS
OPPRS	PROPS			TTTUY	TUTTY
OPPSY	POPSY, SOPPY				

AAABBN	BANABA	AAAMRY	AYMARA	AABINS	SABINA
AAABCN	CABANA	AAANPR	PARANA	AABIST	ABATIS, BASTIA
AAABCS	CASABA	AAANST	ASTANA	AABISW	SWABIA
AAABDN	ABADAN	AAAPPY	PAPAYA	AABKLN	BALKAN
AAABHN	HABANA	AAARRT	ARARAT	AABKMO	BAMAKO
AAABIR	ARABIA	AAARTV	AVATAR	AABKNN	KANBAN
AAABKN	ABAKAN	AAARTW	TARAWA	AABLMO	MALABO
AAABLM	AMBALA	AABBBO	BAOBAB	AABLMS	BALSAM
AAABLT	BALATA	AABBCY	ABBACY	AABLNY	ALBANY
AAABNN	ANNABA, BANANA	AABBLL	LABLAB	AABLOR	ABORAL
AAABNS	ANABAS	AABBLO	BALBOA	AABLOV	LAVABO
AAABRT	ATBARA	AABBRR	BARBRA	AABLRU	RABAUL
AAABRZ	BAZAAR	AABBST	SABBAT	AABLSS	BALSAS
AAACCI	ACACIA	AABCIN	BIANCA	AABLST	BASALT
AAACDI	ACADIA	AABCIR	ARABIC	AABLTU	ABLAUT
AAACDN	CANADA	AABCIU	CUIABA	AABMMS	MAMBAS
AAACEH	ACHAEA	AABCJO	JACOBA	AABMNR	BARMAN
AAACGI	AGACIA	AABCLS	CABALS	AABMNT	BANTAM, BATMAN
AAACJN	JACANA	AABCMN	CABMAN	AABMRS	SAMBAR
AAACLP	ALPACA	AABCRS	SCARAB	AABMRY	AMBARY
AAACMR	MARACA	AABCSU	ABACUS	AABMSS	SAMBAS
AAACNR	ARCANA	AABDER	ABRADE	AABNNY	BANYAN
AAACOX	OAXACA	AABDES	ABASED	AABORR	ARROBA
AAADLM	ALMADA	AABDET	ABATED	AABORT	ABATOR, RABATO
AAADMN	AMANDA	AABDEU	AUBADE	AABRSS	SABRAS
AAADMR	ARMADA, DAMARA	AABDIN	IBADAN	AABTTW	ABWATT
AAADNP	PANADA	AABDLL	BALLAD	AACCDI	CICADA
AAAELZ	AZALEA	AABDLM	LAMBDA	AACCHH	CHA-CHA
AAAGHT	AGATHA	AABDOR	ABOARD, ABROAD,	AACCHM	CHACMA
AAAGLM	MALAGA		BARODA	AACCLO	CLOACA
AAAGLT	GALATA	AABDRT	TABARD	AACCLP	CALPAC
AAAGNN	NAGANA	AABEGT	TEABAG	AACCLR	CALCAR
AAAGRU	AARGAU	AABELM	AMABEL	AACCMO	MACACO
AAAHLM	MAHALA	AABELR	ARABLE	AACCNN	CANCAN
AAAHLS	AL HASA	AABELZ	ABLAZE	AACDDU	CAUDAD
AAAHMR	AMHARA	AABEMO	AMOEBA	AACDEF	FACADE
AAAHNV	HAVANA	AABEMS	AMEBAS	AACDER	ARCADE
AAAHRS	SAHARA	AABERZ	ZAREBA	AACDHU	DACHAU
AAAILM	AMALIA	AABFIN	FABIAN	AACDIR	ACARID
AAAITX	ATAXIA	AABFIR	BIAFRA	AACDLU	CAUDAL
AAAJLP	JALAPA	AABGGR	RAGBAG	AACDMP	MADCAP
AAAJMP	PAJAMA	AABGGS	GASBAG	AACDNR	CANARD
AAAJRW	JAWARA	AABGIM	GAMBIA	AACEFL	FAECAL
AAAKLM	KAMALA	AABGIN	BAAING	AACEFR	CARAFE
AAAKLS	ALASKA	AABGRT	RATBAG	AACEHN	AACHEN
AAAKNR	ANKARA, KANARA	AABHKS	KASBAH	AACEHP	APACHE
AAALMS	SALAAM	AABHKZ	ABKHAZ	AACEHT	CHAETA
AAALMY	MALAYA	AABHRS	BASRAH	AACELP	PALACE
AAALNN	ALANNA	AABIKL	KABILA	AACELS	ALSACE
AAAMMN	MANAMA	AABIKR	KARIBA	AACELT	ACETAL
AAAMNN	MANANA	AABILL	LABIAL	AACELY	CELAYA
AAAMNP	PANAMA	AABILN	ALBINA	AACEMO	CAEOMA
AAAMRS	ASMARA, SAMARA	AABILU	ABULIA	AACEMR	CAMERA
AAAMRT	TAMARA	AABIMZ	ZAMBIA	AACENP	CANAPE

AACENR	ARCANE	AACLSU	CASUAL, CAUSAL	AADIMN	DAMIAN
AACENT	CATENA	AACLTU	ACTUAL	AADIMT	MATADI
AACERS	CAESAR	AACMNR	CARMAN	AADINR	ADRIAN, RADIAN
AACETV	CAVEAT, VACATE	AACMNU	CUMANA	AADINS	NAIADS
AACFIL	FACIAL	AACMNY	CAYMAN	AADINT	DANITA
AACFIR	AFRICA	AACMOT	TACOMA	AADINV	DAVINA
AACFIS	FASCIA	AACMRT	TARMAC	AADIST	STADIA
AACFLU	FACULA, FAUCAL	AACMSS	CAMASS	AADKMS	DAMASK
AACFNR	FRANCA	AACMSW	MACAWS	AADKNU	KADUNA
AACFNT	CAFTAN	AACNNO	ANCONA	AADKOT	DAKOTA
AACFRS	FRACAS	AACNPT	CATNAP	AADKPU	PADAUK
AACFTT	FAT CAT	AACNRY	CANARY	AADLLS	DALLAS
AACGIM	AGAMIC	AACNSV	CANVAS	AADLMY	MALADY
AACGIR	AGARIC	AACNTV	VACANT	AADLNR	RANALD, RANDAL
AACHIN	CHANIA	AACPPY	PAPACY	AADLNS	SANDAL
AACHIT	ITHACA	AACPRS	CASPAR	AADLNU	LANDAU, LUANDA
AACHKW	KWACHA	AACRST	CARATS	AADLNV	VANDAL
AACHLS	CALASH	AACRSU	ACARUS	AADLOP	APODAL
AACHNO	CHAOAN	AACRTV	CRAVAT	AADLOU	DOUALA
AACHTT	ATTACH	AADDIL	LA-DI-DA	AADLRU	RADULA
AACIIL	ALICIA	AADDIV	DAVIDA	AADLSS	SALADS
AACIIM	AMICIA	AADDOU	AOUDAD	AADMMN	MADMAN
AACILL	LAICAL	AADEGL	GELADA	AADMMR	DAMMAR
AACILP	APICAL	AADEGM	DAMAGE	AADMMS	MADAMS
AACILR	ALARIC, RACIAL	AADEGN	AGENDA	AADMNR	ARMAND
AACILS	CALAIS	AADEGS	ADAGES	AADMOU	AMADOU
AACILT	ALTAIC	AADEHN	HADEAN	AADMRS	DRAMAS, MADRAS
AACIMN	MANIAC	AADEJU	JUDAEA	AADMRU	MARAUD
AACIMR	MARCIA	AADEKW	AWAKED	AADMYY	MAY DAY
AACINR	ARNICA, CARINA,	AADEMM	MADAME	AADNNR	RANDAN
CRANIA		AADEMN	MAENAD	AADNPS	PANDAS
AACIPS	CAPIAS	AADEMZ	AMAZED	AADNRS	SANDRA
AACIRT	CARITA	AADENN	ANDEAN, DEANNA	AADNRU	ARNAUD
AACIRV	CAVIAR	AADENR	ANDREA	AADNRW	RWANDA
AACISS	CASSIA	AADENT	ADNATE	AADNRY	ANADYR
AACITT	ATTICA	AADENV	NEVADA	AADNRZ	ZANDRA
AACITX	ATAXIC	AADEOR	ORADEA	AADNTU	DANUTA
AACJKL	JACKAL	AADEPR	PARADE	AADNTW	WANT AD
AACJOU	ACAJOU	AADFIR	AFRAID	AADPYY	PAYDAY
AACKMY	MACKAY	AADGIO	ADAGIO	AADRRV	VARDAR
AACKRR	ARRACK	AADGIR	AGADIR	AADRSW	AWARDS
AACKTT	ATTACK	AADGLO	LADOGA	AADRTU	DATURA
AACLLO	CALLAO	AADGMR	DAGMAR	AADRTY	DATARY
AACLMT	LACTAM	AADGNN	DA NANG	AAEEGN	AEGEAN
AACLMU	MACULA	AADGNP	PADANG	AAEENS	AENEAS
AACLNR	CARNAL	AADGNU	UGANDA	AAEERT	AERATE
AACLNS	CANALS	AADGOP	PAGODA	AAEEST	AT EASE
AACLNT	CANTAL	AADHIL	DAHLIA	AAEFLM	AFLAME
AACLNU	LACUNA	AADHIN	HAIDAN	AAEFLR	RAFAEL
AACLOR	CAROLA	AADHLR	HARALD	AAEFNZ	FAENZA
AACLPR	CARPAL	AADHRZ	ADZHAR, HAZARD	AAEGGR	GARAGE
AACLPS	PASCAL	AADILN	DALIAN	AAEGGV	GAVAGE
AACLPU	PAUCAL	AADILR	RADIAL	AAEGLL	LALAGE
AACLRS	LASCAR, RASCAL,	AADILS	DALASI		
SACRAL, SCALAR					

AAEGLN	ANGELA, ANLAGE, GALENA, LAGENA	AAFFJN	JAFFNA	AAGNOR	ANGORA, ARAGON
AAEGLR	ALEGAR, LAAGER	AAFFRY	AFFRAY	AAGNOY	NAGOYA
AAEGLV	LAVAGE	AAFGHN	AFGHAN	AAGNPR	PARANG
AAEGMN	MANAGE	AAFIKS	SIFAKA	AAGNPS	PAGANS
AAEGMR	MEGARA	AAFILV	FLAVIA	AAGNRY	ANGARY
AAEGNT	AGNATE, AGNETA	AAFINR	FARINA	AAGNUY	GUYANA
AAEGRV	RAVAGE	AAFINS	NAAFIS	AAGPRS	GASPAR
AAEGST	AGATES	AAFIRS	SAFARI	AAGRSU	RAGUSA
AAEGSV	SAVAGE	AAFITU	AU FAIT	AAGRVY	VAGARY
AAEGTU	GATEAU	AAFKNT	KAFTAN	AAGSUV	GUAVAS
AAEHLM	HAEMAL, MEHALA	AAFLLL	FALLAL	AAHHLL	HALLAH
AAEHLT	ALTHEA	AAFLNU	FAUNAL	AAHHLV	HALVAH
AAEHMT	HAMATE	AAFLOT	AFLOAT	AAHHNN	HANNAH
AAEHNT	ANTHEA	AAFNNT	FAN-TAN	AAHHPT	APHTHA
AAEHNY	HYAENA	AAFNRR	FARRAN	AAHHWW	HAWHAW
AAEHRR	HARARE	AAFNSU	FAUNAS	AAHIIS	ISAIAH
AAEHRT	EARTHA	AAGGHI	HAGGAI	AAHIIW	HAWAII
AAEILM	AMALIE, AMELIA	AAGGQU	QUAGGA	AAHILT	HIATAL
AAEILR	AERIAL	AAGGRS	SAGGAR	AAHINN	HAINAN
AAEILX	ALEXIA	AAGGRT	RAGTAG	AAHIOT	TAIHOA
AAEIMN	ANEMIA	AAGHMR	ARMAGH, GRAHAM	AAHIPR	PARIAH
AAEINR	ANEIRA, ARIANE	AAGHNP	PAHANG	AAHIRS	SHARIA
AAEITV	AVIATE	AAGHNR	HANGAR	AAHJRR	JARRAH
AAEKLN	ALKANE	AAGHST	AGHAST	AAHJRS	RAJAHS
AAEKLR	KERALA	AAGIJW	JIGAWA	AAHKKZ	KAZAKH
AAEKNW	AWAKEN	AAGILR	ARGALI	AAHKMO	OAKHAM
AAEKRT	KARATE	AAGILT	GALATI	AAHKNO	HAAKON
AAELLP	PAELLA	AAGILV	GAVIAL	AAHLLW	WALLAH
AAELMP	PAMELA	AAGIMN	MAGIAN	AAHLMT	MALTHA
AAELMT	MALATE	AAGINN	ANGINA	AAHLNT	ANHALT
AAELNN	ANNEAL	AAGINR	GRANIA	AAHLPS	ALPHAS
AAELNS	SALENA	AAGINU	GUIANA, IGUANA	AAHLRS	ASHLAR
AAELNT	LANATE	AAGINV	VAGINA	AAHLRT	HARTAL
AAELNV	LAVENA	AAGINW	GAWAIN	AAHMNS	SHAMAN
AAELOR	AREOLA	AAGIRV	VIAGRA	AAHMRS	MARSHA
AAELPP	APPEAL	AAGJRU	JAGUAR	AAHMRT	MARTHA
AAELPT	PALATE	AAGKLU	KALUGA	AAHMST	ASTHMA
AAELRV	LARVAE	AAGKLY	GALYAK	AAHNNS	ANSHAN
AAELTV	VALETA	AAGKNS	KANGAS	AAHNNT	NATHAN
AAEMNP	APEMAN	AAGLLN	LALANG	AAHNOV	NAVAHO
AAEMNS	SEAMAN	AAGLLP	PLAGAL	AAHNPT	PATHAN
AAENOP	APNOEA	AAGLMN	MALANG	AAHNSS	HASSAN
AAENPS	PAEANS	AAGLNO	ANALOG, ANGOLA	AAHNSU	SHAUNA
AAENPV	PAVANE	AAGLNR	RAGLAN	AAHNTU	UTAHAN
AAENRS	ARENAS	AAGLRT	TRAGAL	AAHNTV	HAVANT
AAENRT	RENATA	AAGLST	STALAG	AAHOSW	OSHAWA
AAENST	ANSATE	AAGLWY	GALWAY	AAHPPR	PARAPH
AAENSU	NAUSEA	AAGLXY	GALAXY	AAHPTY	APATHY
AAEPPR	APPEAR	AAGMMS	GAMMAS	AAHRRR	HARRAR
AAERRT	ERRATA	AAGMNR	RAGMAN	AAHRSS	HARASS
AAERWX	EARWAX	AAGMNS	GASMAN	AAHRSU	AARHUS
AAESWY	SEAWAY	AAGMRY	MAGYAR, MARGAY	AAHSSY	SASHAY
AAFFIR	AFFAIR, RAFFIA	AAGNNO	NAGANO	AAIIMM	MAI MAI
		AAGNNY	ANYANG	AAIISV	SAVAÏ

AAIKLL	ALKALI	AAIRST	ARISTA, SARITA,	AAMNOR	RAMONA
AAIKLM	KALMIA	TIARAS		AAMNOS	SAMOAN
AAIKNN	ANNIKA	AAIRVY	AVIARY	AAMNOZ	AMAZON
AAIKNR	KARINA	AAIRWY	AIRWAY	AAMNPS	SAMPAN
AAILLX	AXILLA	AAITUY	YAUTIA	AAMNST	TASMAN
AAILMN	ANIMAL, LAMINA,	AAJLMR	AL MARJ	AAMNSU	MANAUS
MANILA		AAJNNO	JOANNA	AAMNTU	MANTUA
AAILMP	IMPALA	AAJPRU	JAPURA	AAMNTX	TAXMAN
AAILMR	LARIAM	AAKKMR	MARKKA	AAMOPR	PARAMO
AAILMS	SALAMI	AAKKOP	KAKAPO	AAMORS	AROMAS
AAILMW	MALAWI	AAKKSY	KAYAKS	AAMOSS	SAMOSA
AAILNR	NARIAL	AAKLMO	AKMOLA	AAMOTY	TOYAMA
AAILNS	NASIAL, SALINA	AAKLMR	KALMAR	AAMPPS	PAMPAS
AAILNT	LATINA	AAKLMU	MAKALU	AAMQSU	SQUAMA
AAILNV	ALVINA, LAVINA	AAKLOS	KOALAS	AAMRSU	ASARUM
AAILPS	PALAIS	AAKLRS	KRAALS	AAMRSW	ASWARM
AAILPU	APULIA	AAKLSU	LUSAKA	AAMRSY	RAMSAY
AAILQU	AQUILA	AAKNOR	ANORAK	AAMRTU	TRAUMA
AAILRS	LARISA	AAKNSS	KANSAS	AAMTTU	UMTATA
AAILRT	ALTAIR, LARIAT,	AAKNSU	KAUNAS	AANNOR	ANNORA
LATRIA		AAKPRS	PARKAS	AANNRU	ANURAN
AAILSS	ASSAIL	AAKRST	KARATS	AANNTT	NATANT
AAILSV	SALIVA, SALVIA,	AALLMS	LLAMAS	AANORV	NOVARA
VALAIS		AALLPS	PALLAS	AANORX	ROXANA
AAILTU	AU LAIT	AALLRV	LARVAL	AANOST	SONATA
AAILTV	LATVIA	AALMMM	MAMMAL	AANOSV	SAVONA
AAIMMR	MARIAM	AALMMS	LAMMAS	AANPPU	PAPUAN
AAIMMS	MIASMA	AALMNP	NAPALM	AANPRT	TARPAN
AAIMMX	MAXIMA	AALMNU	ALUMNA, MANUAL	AANQTU	QUANTA
AAIMNR	AIRMAN, ARMINA,	AALMNY	LAYMAN	AANRRT	ARRANT
MARIAN, MARINA		AALMOR	AMORAL	AANRTT	RATTAN, TARTAN
AAIMNS	MANIAS, MANISA	AALMOT	AMATOL	AANRYZ	RYAZAN
AAIMNT	AMINTA	AALMPR	PALMAR	AANSSU	ASSUAN, NASSAU,
AAIMRS	MARISA	AALMPS	LAMPAS, PLASMA	SAUNAS	
AAIMRT	AMRITA, MARITA	AALMRS	ALARMS	AANSTV	SAVANT
AAINNT	TAINAN	AALMRT	RATLAM	AANSTW	TSWANA
AAINOR	ORIANA	AALMTY	ALMATY, AMYTAL	AANSTZ	STANZA
AAINOX	ANOXIA	AALNNO	AL-ANON	AANWYY	ANYWAY
AAINPP	PAPAIN	AALNNS	ANNALS	AAOPST	SAPOTA
AAINPR	PARIAN	AALNNU	ANNUAL	AAORRU	AURORA
AAINPS	SAIPAN	AALNOT	ALTONA, ATONAL	AAORST	AORTAS
AAINPT	PATINA, TAIPAN	AALNPR	PLANAR	AAOTTV	OTTAVA
AAINRS	SARINA, SARNIA	AALNPT	PLATAN	AAOTTW	OTTAWA
AAINRT	TIRANA	AALNRX	LARNAX	AAPPWW	PAWPAW
AAINRU	ANURIA	AALNSS	NASALS	AAPRST	PATRAS
AAINSS	ASIANS	AALNST	ASLANT	AAPWXX	PAXWAX
AAINTT	ATTAIN	AALOPY	PAYOLA	AAQRSU	QUASAR
AAINTW	TAIWAN	AALOVW	AVOWAL	AARRSY	ARRAYS
AAINTY	YANTAI	AALPSZ	PLAZAS	AARRTT	TARTAR
AAIOTU	AOUITA	AALRST	ALTARS, ASTRAL,	AARSTT	STRATA
AAIPRU	AU PAIR	TARSAL		AARSTY	ASTRAY
AAIPRY	APIARY	AALRSY	SALARY	AARSWW	WARSAW
AAIPZZ	PIAZZA	AALSSV	VASSAL	AARTTT	RAT-TAT
AAIQRT	QATARI	AALSWY	ALWAYS	AARTTY	TATARY
		AALWYY	WAYLAY		

AASSSY	ASSAYS	ABCEJT	ABJECT	ABDEHS	BASHED
ABBBEL	BABBLE	ABCEKR	BACKER	ABDEHT	BATHED
ABBCEI	CABBIE	ABCELS	CABLES	ABDEIL	BAILED, BALDIE
ABBCOT	BOBCAT	ABCELT	CABLET	ABDEIR	ABIDER, AIRBED
ABBCRY	CRABBY	ABCEMR	CAMBER	ABDEIS	BIASED
ABBCSY	SCABBY	ABCENO	BEACON	ABDEIT	BAITED
ABBDDE	DABBED	ABCENU	CUBANE	ABDEKL	BALKED
ABBDEG	GABBED	ABCERR	BRACER	ABDEKN	BANKED
ABBDEI	BABIED	ABCERS	BRACES, CABERS	ABDEKR	BARKED, BRAKED, DEBARK
ABBDEJ	JABBED	ABCEST	BE CAST	ABDEKS	BASKED
ABBDEL	DABBLE	ABCFIR	FABRIC	ABDELM	AMBLED, BEDLAM, BLAMED, LAMBED
ABBDEN	NABBED	ABCGIT	BIG CAT	ABDELO	ALBEDO, DOABLE
ABBDER	BARBED, DABBER	ABCHIU	BAUCHI	ABDELR	BLARED
ABBDET	TABBED	ABCHLN	BLANCH	ABDELS	BLADES
ABBDEU	BEDAUB	ABCHNR	BRANCH	ABDELT	TABLED
ABBEGI	GABBIE	ABCHOR	BROACH	ABDELW	BAWLED
ABBEGL	GABBLE	ABCHPU	HUBCAP	ABDELY	DYABLE
ABBEGR	GABBER	ABCIIM	IAMBIC	ABDELZ	BLAZED
ABBEIR	BARBIE, RABBIE	ABCILT	BALTIC	ABDENN	BANNED
ABBEIS	BABIES	ABCILU	ABULIC	ABDENP	BEDPAN
ABBEIU	BAUBIE	ABCINS	CABINS	ABDENR	BRENDA
ABBEJR	JABBER	ABCISS	BASICS	ABDENU	DANUBE
ABBEKS	KEBABS	ABCISY	BISCAY	ABDEOS	ABODES
ABBELR	BARBEL, RABBLE	ABCKLS	BLACKS	ABDEOT	BOATED
ABBELU	BAUBLE	ABCKPU	BACK UP	ABDEPY	PAYBED
ABBERR	BARBER	ABCLMY	CYMBAL	ABDERR	BARRED
ABBERT	BARBET	ABCLOT	COBALT	ABDERS	BEARDS
ABBESS	ABBESS	ABCMOR	CRAMBO	ABDERU	DAUBER
ABBESY	ABBEYS	ABCMOT	COMBAT, TOMBAC	ABDERV	ADVERB, BRAVED
ABBFLY	FLABBY	ABCNOR	CARBON, CORBAN	ABDERY	BRAYED
ABBGOR	GABBRO	ABCORS	CAROBS, COBRAS	ABDEST	BASTED
ABBHSY	SHABBY	ABCORX	BOXCAR	ABDESU	ABUSED
ABBILO	BILBAO	ABCORY	CARBOY	ABDETT	BATTED
ABBIRS	RABBIS	ABCOSU	VOCABS	ABDFOR	FORBAD
ABBIRT	RABBIT	ABCSSU	SCUBAS	ABDHRY	HARD BY
ABBLRU	BULBAR	ABDDEE	BEADED	ABDIJM	DJAMBI
ABBMOO	BAMBOO	ABDDEI	ABIDED	ABDILR	BRIDAL, RIBALD
ABBMOY	BOMBAY	ABDDEN	BANDED	ABDINT	BANDIT
ABBNOO	BABOON	ABDDER	BADDER	ABDIRS	BRAIDS, DISBAR
ABBNOS	NABOBS	ABDDEU	DAUBED	ABDLLY	BALDLY
ABBORS	ABSORB	ABDDHU	BUDDHA	ABDLNO	BOLAND
ABBOST	ABBOTS	ABDEEH	BEHEAD	ABDLRY	DRABLY
ABBRSU	BUSBAR	ABDEEL	BEADLE	ABDNOR	BRANDO, ROBAND
ABCCLU	BUCCAL	ABDEEM	BEAMED	ABDNOU	ABOUND
ABCDEK	BACKED	ABDEES	DEBASE, SEABED	ABDNRS	BRANDS
ABCDEL	CABLED	ABDEET	DEBATE	ABDNRT	BRANDT
ABCDER	BRACED	ABDEFL	FABLED	ABDNRU	DUNBAR, DURBAN
ABCDIR	BARDIC	ABDEGG	BAGGED	ABDNRY	BRANDY
ABCDTU	ABDUCT	ABDEGL	GABLED	ABDORS	ADSORB, BOARDS, BROADS
ABCEEM	BECAME	ABDEGN	BANGED	ABDORY	BYROAD
ABCEHL	BLEACH	ABDEGO	BODEGA	ABDOYY	DAYBOY
ABCEHR	BREACH	ABDEGR	BADGER, BARGED, GARBED	ABDRRU	DURBAR
ABCEHU	HECUBA	ABDEGS	BADGES		
ABCEIM	AMEBIC				

ABDRSU	ABSURD	
ABEEGL	BEAGLE	
ABEEGR	BARGEE	
ABEEHV	BEHAVE	
ABEEIL	BAILEE	
ABEEKR	BEAKER	
ABEEKT	BETAKE	
ABEELN	BALEEN, ENABLE	
ABEENT	BEATEN	
ABEENU	BEAUNE	
ABEEOR	AEROBE	
ABEEOU	EUBOEA	
ABEERR	BEARER	
ABEERT	BEATER, BERATE, REBATE	
ABEERV	BEAVER	
ABEERW	BEWARE	
ABEFFL	BAFFLE	
ABEFHL	BEHALF	
ABEFLL	BEFALL	
ABEFLM	FLAMBE	
ABEFLR	FABLER	
ABEFLS	FABLES	
ABEFMR	FERBAM	
ABEFPR	PREFAB	
ABEGGR	BEGGAR	
ABEGIT	GIBE AT	
ABEGIU	IBAGUE	
ABEGLM	GAMBLE	
ABEGLN	BANGLE, BENGAL	
ABEGLR	GARBLE	
ABEGLS	BAGELS, GABLES	
ABEGLU	BELUGA	
ABEGMR	BREGMA	
ABEGMU	MUGABE	
ABEGNR	BANGER, GRABEN	
ABEGOR	BORAGE	
ABEGOZ	GAZEBO	
ABEGRS	BARGES	
ABEGRZ	ZAGREB	
ABEHIL	HABILE	
ABEHIT	BETHIA	
ABEHLR	HERBAL	
ABEHLU	BEULAH	
ABEHNT	BETHAN	
ABEHRT	BATHER, BERTHA	
ABEHSS	BASHES	
ABEIIR	IBERIA	
ABEIIT	TIBIAE	
ABEILL	LABILE, LIABLE	
ABEILN	BLAINE	
ABEILR	BAILER	
ABEILS	ABSEIL, BLAISE, ISABEL	
ABEILT	ALBEIT, ALBITE	

ABEILV	VIABLE	
ABEILW	BEWAIL	
ABEILY	BAILEY	
ABEINT	BENITA, BINATE	
ABEIRR	BARRIE, RIBERA	
ABEIRS	BRAISE, RABIES, SERBIA	
ABEISS	BIASES	
ABEJOR	JERBOA	
ABEJRU	ABJURE	
ABEKLR	BALKER	
ABEKLY	KABYLE	
ABEKMN	EMBANK	
ABEKMR	EMBARK	
ABEKNR	BANKER	
ABEKOU	BOUAKE	
ABEKRR	BARKER	
ABEKRS	BAKERS, BRAKES, BREAKS	
ABEKRY	BAKERY	
ABEKST	BASKET	
ABELLS	LABELS	
ABELLT	BALLET	
ABELMM	EMBALM	
ABELMR	AMBLER, MARBLE, RAMBLE	
ABELNU	NEBULA, UNABLE	
ABELOR	BOREAL	
ABELOT	LOBATE, OBLATE	
ABELPU	PUEBLA	
ABELRR	BARREL	
ABELRT	ALBERT, BARTLE, LABRET	
ABELRV	VERBAL	
ABELRW	BAWLER, WARBLE	
ABELRY	BARELY, BARLEY, BLEARY	
ABELRZ	BLAZER	
ABELSS	SABLES	
ABELST	BLEATS, STABLE, TABLES	
ABELSU	SUABLE, USABLE	
ABELSY	BASELY	
ABELSZ	BLAZES	
ABELTT	BATTLE, TABLET	
ABELTY	BATLEY	
ABEMNO	BEMOAN	
ABEMNR	BARMEN	
ABEMNT	BATMEN	
ABENNR	BANNER	
ABENOR	BORANE	
ABENRR	BARREN	
ABENRT	BANTER, BARNET	
ABENRU	URBANE	
ABENRY	BARNEY, NEARBY	

ABENRZ	BRAZEN	
ABENST	ABSENT	
ABENTT	BATTEN	
ABENTU	BUTANE	
ABEORT	BOATER, BORATE	
ABEORZ	BEZOAR	
ABEOSS	SASEBO	
ABEPTU	UPBEAT	
ABEQRU	BARQUE	
ABEQSU	BASQUE	
ABERRT	BARTER	
ABERRV	BRAVER	
ABERRY	BRAYER	
ABERRZ	BRAZER	
ABERSS	SABERS, SABRES	
ABERST	BAREST, BREAST, TARBES	
ABERSU	ABUSER	
ABERSV	BRAVES	
ABERSZ	ZEBRAS	
ABERTT	BATTER	
ABERTU	AUBERT	
ABERTY	BETRAY	
ABERUU	BUREAU	
ABERUY	AUBREY	
ABERZZ	ZABRZE	
ABESSS	BASSES	
ABESST	BASEST, BASSET, BEASTS	
ABESSU	ABUSES	
ABESTU	BEAUTS	
ABETTU	BATTUE	
ABETTY	BEATTY	
ABETUY	BEAUTY	
ABEUXY	BAYEUX	
ABFILU	FIBULA	
ABFISY	BASIFY	
ABGHTU	HAGBUT	
ABGIIL	GALIBI	
ABGIKN	BAKING	
ABGIKT	KIT BAG	
ABGILN	BALING	
ABGIMT	GAMBIT	
ABGIMY	BIGAMY	
ABGINO	GABION, GOBIAN	
ABGINR	BARING	
ABGINS	BASING	
ABGINU	BANGUI, URBANGI	
ABGINY	BAYING	
ABGIOU	BAGUIO	
ABGLLO	GLOBAL	
ABGLMO	GAMBOL	
ABGNOR	BANGOR	
ABGOOT	BOGOTA, TOBAGO	
ABGRSU	BURGAS	

ABHIIR	BIHARI	ABKUUV	BUKAVU	ABOSTU	U-BOATS
ABHINR	HARBIN	ABLLNO	NO-BALL	ABOSUY	BAYOUS
ABHINS	BANISH	ABLLOO	LOBOLA	ABOSWW	BOWSAW
ABHIOP	PHOBIA	ABLLOT	BALLOT	ABPRTU	ABRUPT
ABHISS	SAHIBS	ABLLTU	ALL BUT	ABPSSY	BYPASS
ABHIST	HABITS	ABLMOP	APLOMB	ABQSSU	SQUABS
ABHLOP	BHOPAL	ABLMOR	BROMAL	ABRRSU	BURSAR
ABHMOU	HUAMBO	ABLMRU	BRUMAL, LABRUM,	ABRSSY	BRASSY
ABHMSU	AMBUSH		LUMBAR, UMBRAL	ABRTUY	BURYAT
ABHNTU	BHUTAN	ABLMRY	MARBLY	ABSUWY	SUBWAY
ABHORT	HOBART	ABLMSU	ALBUMS	ABSWYY	BYWAYS
ABHOST	BATHOS	ABLNOZ	BLAZON	ACCCIL	CALCIC
ABHOTX	HATBOX	ABLNSU	NABLUS	ACCDEE	ACCEDE
ABHOXY	HAYBOX	ABLOOR	ROBALO	ACCDEN	DECCAN
ABHRSY	BRASHY	ABLORU	LABOUR	ACCDII	ACIDIC
ABIILS	ALIBIS	ABLOST	OBLAST	ACCDOR	ACCORD
ABIIST	TIBIAS	ABLOTT	TALBOT	ACCEHN	CHANCE
ABIJRU	JABIRU	ABLOTV	ABVOLT	ACCEHS	CACHES
ABIKMO	AKIMBO	ABLPRU	BURLAP	ACCEHT	CACHET
ABIKRS	BISKRA	ABLPYY	BYPLAY	ACCEIN	CANICE
ABILMT	TIMBAL	ABLRSU	BURSAL	ACCEIP	ICE CAP, IPECAC
ABILMU	LABIUM	ABLRSW	BRAWLS	ACCEIT	ACETIC
ABILNO	ALBINO, ALBION	ABLRTU	BRUTAL	ACCEKL	CACKLE
ABILNR	LIBRAN	ABLSST	BLASTS	ACCELN	CANCEL
ABILNY	LIBYAN	ABLSTY	STABLY	ACCELR	CERCAL
ABILOR	BAILOR	ABLSWY	BYLAWS	ACCELS	CALCES
ABILPU	BAIL UP	ABLSYY	LAY-BYS	ACCEMS	MECCAS
ABILRT	TRIBAL	ABLTTY	TYBALT	ACCEMU	CAECUM
ABILRU	BURIAL	ABMNOW	BOWMAN	ACCENR	CANCER
ABILRZ	BRAZIL	ABMNOY	BONAMY	ACCENT	ACCENT
ABILVY	VIABLY	ABMNTU	NUMBAT	ACCEPT	ACCEPT
ABIMNN	BINMAN	ABMOTV	TAMBOV	ACCERS	SCARCE
ABIMRU	BARIUM, UMBRIA	ABMOTW	WOMBAT	ACCERU	ACCRUE
ABIMST	AMBITS	ABMRSU	RUMBAS	ACCESS	ACCESS
ABIMSU	IAMBUS	ABMRUY	AUMBRY	ACCESU	ACCUSE
ABINOR	ROBINA	ABNORR	BARRON	ACCGNO	COGNAC
ABINOS	BASION, BONSAI,	ABNORS	BARONS	ACCHIR	CHIRAC
BOSNIA		ABNORT	BARTON	ACCHNO	CONCHA
ABINOT	BONITA, OBTAIN	ABNORY	BARONY, BARYON	ACCHNY	CHANCY
ABINRS	BAIRNS, BRAINS	ABNOST	BATONS	ACCHOU	CACHOU
ABINRU	RUBINA	ABNOTY	BOTANY	ACCHTY	CATCHY
ABINRY	BINARY, BRAINY	ABNRTU	TURBAN	ACCIIN	ACINIC
ABINSS	BASINS	ABNRUU	AUBURN	ACCILO	CALICO
ABIORS	ISOBAR	ABNRWY	BRAWNY	ACCILT	LACTIC
ABIOST	TOBIAS	ABOOST	TABOOS	ACCIMM	MICMAC
ABIRSU	AIRBUS	ABOOTU	BAOTOU	ACCINT	CANTIC
ABIRTZ	TABRIZ	ABORRU	ARBOUR	ACCINY	CYANIC
ABISSU	BISSAU	ABORRW	BARROW	ACCIOS	CAICOS
ABJLNU	BANJUL	ABORSV	BRASOV, BRAVOS	ACCIRT	ARCTIC
ABJNOS	BANJOS	ABORTU	RUBATO	ACCITT	TACTIC
ABJNPU	PUNJAB	ABORTW	TOWBAR	ACCKRS	CRACKS
ABKLNS	BLANKS	ABORTY	TORBAY	ACCLOU	COUCAL
ABKLSU	BAULKS	ABORUY	YORUBA	ACCMOR	CORMAC
ABKLSY	SKYLAB	ABOSST	BOASTS	ACCORW	CRACOW

ACCOST	ACCOST	ACDENR	CRANED, DANCER, NACRED	ACEENR	CAREEN
ACCRUY	CURACY			ACEENS	ENCASE, SEANCE, SENECA
ACCSTU	CACTUS	ACDENS	ASCEND, DANCES		
ACCSUU	CAUCUS	ACDENT	CADENT, CANTED, DECANT	ACEENT	CETANE, TENACE
ACCSUY	YUCCAS			ACEEPS	ESCAPE, PEACES
ACCTUU	CUCUTA	ACDEOT	COATED	ACEERR	CAREER
ACDDEE	DECADE	ACDEOX	COAXED	ACEERS	CREASE
ACDDEG	CADGED	ACDEPP	CAPPED	ACEERT	CERATE, CREATE, ECARTE
ACDDEI	CADDIE	ACDEPR	CARPED, REDCAP		
ACDDEN	DANCED	ACDEPS	SPACED	ACEFFT	AFFECT
ACDDER	CARDED	ACDERS	CADRES, CEDARS, SACRED, SCARED	ACEFHR	CHAFER
ACDDEU	ADDUCE			ACEFIL	FACILE
ACDDII	DIACID	ACDERT	CARTED, CRATED, REDACT, TRACED	ACEFIN	FIANCE
ACDDIN	CANDID			ACEFIR	FIACRE
ACDDIR	DARDIC, ID CARD	ACDERV	CARVED, CRAVED	ACEFIS	FACIES
ACDDIS	CADDIS	ACDERZ	CRAZED	ACEFLU	FECULA
ACDDIT	ADDICT	ACDEST	CADETS	ACEFNR	FRANCE
ACDDIY	DYADIC	ACDESU	CAUSED, SAUCED	ACEFRS	FARCES
ACDDTU	ADDUCT	ACDEUX	CAUDEX	ACEFST	FACETS
ACDEEF	DEFACE	ACDHIR	DIARCH	ACEFSU	FAUCES
ACDEEN	DECANE	ACDHMR	DRACHM	ACEFSY	CASEFY
ACDEER	DECARE	ACDHRS	CHARDS	ACEFTU	FAUCET
ACDEES	CEASED	ACDIIM	AMIDIC	ACEGHN	CHANGE
ACDEFH	CHAFED	ACDIJU	JUDAIC	ACEGHR	CHARGE
ACDEGR	CADGER, GRACED	ACDILP	PLACID	ACEGHU	GAUCHE
ACDEGT	GEDACT	ACDINO	ANODIC	ACEGIL	GAELIC
ACDEHK	HACKED	ACDINR	RANCID	ACEGIR	CAGIER, GRACIE
ACDEHR	ARCHED, ECHARD	ACDIOT	DACOIT	ACEGLN	GLANCE
ACDEHS	CASHED, CHASED	ACDIOZ	ZODIAC	ACEGLY	LEGACY
ACDEHT	DETACH	ACDIPS	CAPSID	ACEGNY	AGENCY
ACDEIM	DECIMA	ACDLNU	UNCLAD	ACEGOS	SOCAGE
ACDEIV	ADVICE	ACDLSS	SCALDS	ACEGOW	COWAGE
ACDEJK	JACKED	ACDLTY	DACTYL	ACEGRS	GRACES
ACDEKL	CALKED, LACKED	ACDMTU	MUDCAT	ACEHIM	HAEMIC
ACDEKP	PACKED	ACDNNU	DUNCAN	ACEHIR	ARCHIE, CAHIER
ACDEKR	RACKED	ACDNOR	CONRAD, DACRON	ACEHIS	CHAISE
ACDEKS	SACKED	ACDORS	DORCAS	ACEHKL	HACKLE
ACDEKT	TACKED	ACDORW	COWARD	ACEHKR	HACKER
ACDELL	CADELL, CALLED	ACDSTU	DUCATS	ACEHLP	CHAPEL, PLEACH
ACDELM	CALMED	ACEEFF	EFFACE	ACEHLR	RACHEL
ACDELN	CANDLE, DECLAN, LANCED	ACEEFN	ENFACE	ACEHLS	LACHES
		ACEEFR	REFACE	ACEHLT	CHALET, THECAL, THECLA
ACDELO	COALED	ACEEFS	FAECES		
ACDELP	PLACED	ACEEGI	ICE AGE	ACEHMN	MANCHE
ACDELR	CRADLE	ACEEGN	ENCAGE	ACEHMR	MARCHE
ACDELS	DECALS, SCALED	ACEEHN	ACHENE	ACEHMS	SCHEMA
ACDELU	CAUDLE, CLAUDE	ACEEHT	HECATE	ACEHNS	ENCASH
ACDELV	CALVED	ACEEIP	APIECE	ACEHOR	CHOREA, HORACE
ACDELW	CLAWED	ACEEJT	EJECTA	ACEHPR	EPARCH, PREACH
ACDEMN	CAMDEN	ACEELN	ENLACE	ACEHPT	HEPCAT
ACDEMP	CAMPED, DECAMP	ACEELR	CEREAL	ACEHPY	PEACHY
ACDENN	CANNED	ACEELV	CLEAVE	ACEHRR	ARCHER
ACDENO	ACNODE, CANOED, DEACON	ACEEMN	MENACE	ACEHRS	ARCHES, CHASER, ESCHAR, SEARCH
		ACEEMR	RACEME		
		ACEEMZ	ECZEMA	ACEHRX	EXARCH

ACEHSS	CHASES, CHASSE
ACEHST	CHASTE, CHEATS, SACHET
ACEHSU	HUESCA
ACEHSW	CASHEW
ACEIJK	JACKIE
ACEIJN	JANICE
ACEILM	MALEIC, MALICE
ACEILN	CELINA
ACEILP	PLAICE
ACEILR	CLAIRE, ECLAIR, LACIER
ACEIMN	ANEMIC, CINEMA, ICEMAN
ACEIMO	MACEIO
ACEIMR	CRIMEA, MARCIE, MERCIA
ACEIMS	CAMISE
ACEIMU	AECIUM
ACEINN	ANNICE, CANINE
ACEINS	CASEIN
ACEINT	ENATIC
ACEINV	CAVE-IN
ACEINX	AXENIC
ACEIPS	APICES
ACEIQU	CAIQUE
ACEIRR	CARRIE, RACIER
ACEIRS	CARIES
ACEIRU	CURIAE
ACEISS	CASSIE
ACEISV	VESICA
ACEITV	ACTIVE
ACEIVV	VIVACE
ACEJKT	JACKET
ACEJLO	CAJOLE
ACEKLM	MACKLE
ACEKLR	CLARKE
ACEKLS	ALECKS
ACEKLT	TACKLE
ACEKLY	LACKEY
ACEKNR	CANKER, NECKAR
ACEKPR	PACKER
ACEKPT	PACKET
ACEKRR	RACKER
ACEKRS	CREAKS, SACKER
ACEKRT	RACKET, TACKER
ACEKRY	CREAKY
ACEKST	CASKET
ACELLO	LOCALE
ACELLR	CALLER, CELLAR, RECALL
ACELMR	CALMER, CARMEL, MARCEL
ACELMS	CAMELS, MASCLE, MESCAL

ACELMT	CAMLET
ACELMU	ALMUCE, CAELUM
ACELNN	CANNEL
ACELNR	LANCER
ACELNS	LANCES
ACELNT	CANTLE, CENTAL, LANCET
ACELNU	CUNEAL, LAUNCE, UNLACE
ACELOR	CAROLE, COALER, ORACLE
ACELOS	SOLACE
ACELOT	LOCATE
ACELOV	ALCOVE, COEVAL
ACELPR	CARPEL, PARCEL, PLACER
ACELPS	PLACES
ACELPT	PLACET
ACELQU	CALQUE, CLAQUE
ACELRR	CARREL
ACELRS	SCALER, SCLERA
ACELRT	CARTEL, CLARET, RECTAL
ACELRW	CLAWER
ACELSS	SCALES
ACELST	CASTLE, CLEATS
ACELSU	CLAUSE
ACELSV	CALVES
ACELTT	CATTLE
ACELTY	ACETYL
ACELYY	CLAYEY
ACEMNP	ENCAMP
ACEMNR	CARMEN
ACEMNU	ACUMEN
ACEMNW	MCEWAN
ACEMOP	POMACE
ACEMOS	CAMEOS
ACEMOT	COMATE
ACEMPR	CAMPER
ACEMRS	CREAMS, SCREAM
ACEMRY	CREAMY
ACEMTU	ACETUM
ACENNS	CANNES
ACENNU	NUANCE
ACENNY	ANNECY
ACENOR	CORNEA
ACENOS	CANOES, OCEANS
ACENOT	OCTANE
ACENPR	PRANCE
ACENPS	PECANS
ACENRS	CARNES, CASERN, CRANES
ACENRT	CANTER, CARNET, CRETAN, NECTAR, RECANT, TRANCE

ACENRV	CAVERN, CRAVEN
ACENST	ASCENT, SECANT, STANCE
ACENSU	USANCE
ACEOPS	PASCOE
ACEOPT	CAPOTE, TOE CAP
ACEOPW	COWPEA
ACEORS	COARSE
ACEORX	COAXER
ACEOTV	AVOCET, OCTAVE
ACEPPR	CAPPER
ACEPRS	CAPERS, ESCARP, PARSEC, RECAPS, SCRAPE, SPACER
ACEPRT	CARPET
ACEPRU	APERCU
ACEPSS	SPACES
ACEPST	ASPECT
ACEPTU	TEACUP
ACEQSU	CASQUE
ACERRS	RACERS, SCARER
ACERRT	CARTER, CRATER, TRACER
ACERRU	CURARE
ACERRV	CARVER
ACERSS	CARESS, SCARES
ACERST	CARETS, CASTER, CRATES, RECAST, TRACES
ACERSU	SAUCER
ACERSY	SCAREY
ACERSZ	CRAZES
ACERTU	CURATE
ACERTY	TRACEY
ACESST	CASTES
ACESSU	CAUSES, SAUCES
ACESTU	CUESTA
ACESTY	STACEY
ACFFHY	CHAFFY
ACFFLS	SCLAFF
ACFGIN	FACING
ACFILO	AFL-CIO
ACFILS	FISCAL
ACFINT	IN FACT
ACFIOS	FIASCO
ACFIPY	PACIFY
ACFLNO	FALCON, FLACON
ACFLRU	FULCRA
ACFMOR	CORFAM
ACFNOR	FRANCO
ACFNRS	FRANCS
ACFORT	FACTOR
ACFRSS	SCARFS
ACFRST	CRAFTS
ACFRTY	CRAFTY
ACGGIN	CAGING

ACGGIO	AGOGIC
ACGGRY	CRAGGY
ACGHIN	ACHING, ICHANG
ACGHOU	GAUCHO
ACGHTU	CAUGHT
ACGIKN	CAKING
ACGILL	GALLIC
ACGILN	LACING
ACGILR	GARLIC
ACGILS	GLACIS
ACGILY	CAGILY
ACGINN	CANING
ACGINO	AGONIC
ACGINP	PACING
ACGINR	CARING, RACING
ACGINS	CASING
ACGINT	ACTING
ACGINV	CAVING
ACGINW	CAWING
ACGIOR	GORICA
ACGIRS	CIGARS
ACGIRT	TRAGIC
ACGIUU	IGUACU
ACGNOR	GARCON
ACGNOS	CONGAS, GASCON
ACGORS	CARGOS
ACGORU	COUGAR
ACGTTU	CATGUT
ACHHNU	HAUNCH
ACHHTT	THATCH
ACHIIS	ISCHIA
ACHIJK	HIJACK
ACHIKW	HAWICK
ACHILO	LOCHIA
ACHILP	CALIPH
ACHINR	INARCH, RANCHI
ACHINS	CHAINS
ACHIPS	PHASIC
ACHIPT	HAPTIC
ACHIRS	CHAIRS, CHARIS, RACHIS
ACHKKU	CHUKKA
ACHKLS	CHALKS
ACHKLY	CHALKY
ACHKRU	CHUKAR
ACHKSS	SHACKS
ACHKSW	WHACKS
ACHKTW	THWACK
ACHLLO	CHOLLA
ACHLNU	LAUNCH, NUCHAL
ACHLOR	CHORAL
ACHLRY	ARCHLY
ACHMNU	MANCHU
ACHMOR	CHROMA

ACHMPS	CHAMPS
ACHMRS	CHARMS
ACHMSS	CHASMS
ACHMSU	SUMACH
ACHNOR	ANCHOR
ACHNOS	NACHOS
ACHNPU	PAUNCH
ACHNST	CHANTS, SNATCH, STANCH
ACHNTU	NAUTCH
ACHNTY	CHANTY
ACHOPR	CARHOP
ACHORS	SORCHA
ACHPTU	CHAT UP
ACHPTY	PATCHY
ACHRST	CHARTS, STARCH
ACHSSW	SCHWAS
ACHSTW	SWATCH
ACHSTY	YACHTS
ACHTTY	CHATTY
ACIILS	SIALIC, SILICA
ACIILT	ITALIC
ACIIRT	TRICIA
ACIJQU	JACQUI
ACIKLN	CALKIN
ACIKMR	KARMIC
ACIKNP	INK-CAP
ACIKNS	INK SAC
ACIKNT	CATKIN
ACILLN	CALL-IN, CLINAL
ACILLP	PLICAL
ACILLS	LILACS, SCILLA
ACILLY	LACILY
ACILMO	COLIMA
ACILMS	CLAIMS
ACILMX	CLIMAX
ACILNO	ALNICO, COLINA, NICOLA, OILCAN
ACILNT	TINCAL
ACILNU	LUCIAN, LUCINA, UNCIAL
ACILNV	CALVIN
ACILOR	LORICA
ACILOS	SOCIAL
ACILOT	COITAL
ACILRT	CITRAL, RICTAL
ACILRU	ULRICA, URACIL, URALIC
ACILRY	RACILY
ACILSV	SLAVIC
ACIMNO	ANOMIC, CAMION, MONICA
ACIMNT	MANTIC
ACIMOR	ROMAIC
ACIMOS	MOSAIC

ACIMOT	ATOMIC
ACIMPS	SCAMPI
ACIMPT	IMPACT
ACIMRS	RACISM
ACIMRU	MURCIA
ACIMRY	MYRICA
ACIMST	MASTIC
ACINNT	TANNIC
ACINOP	PACINO
ACINOS	CASINO
ACINOT	ACTION, ATONIC, CATION
ACINOX	ANOXIC
ACINPS	PANICS
ACINPT	CATNIP
ACINRS	CAIRNS
ACINRT	CATRIN
ACINRU	URANIC
ACINST	ANTICS
ACINSU	ACINUS
ACINTT	INTACT
ACINTU	TUNICA
ACINUV	VICUNA
ACIORS	SCORIA
ACIORT	AORTIC
ACIOST	SCOTIA
ACIOSV	OVISAC
ACIOTZ	AZOTIC
ACIPRS	PRISCA
ACIPRY	PIRACY
ACIQTU	ACQUIT
ACIRSS	CRASIS
ACIRST	CRISTA, RACIST
ACIRSV	VICARS
ACIRTU	URATIC
ACISSS	CASSIS
ACISTT	ATTICS, STATIC
ACITUY	ACUITY
ACITVY	CAVITY
ACKLOS	CLOAKS
ACKLSS	SLACKS
ACKMSS	SMACKS
ACKNPU	UNPACK
ACKNRS	CRANKS
ACKNRY	CRANKY
ACKNSS	SNACKS
ACKORS	CROAKS
ACKPSY	SKYCAP
ACKQSU	QUACKS
ACKRST	TRACKS
ACKSST	STACKS
ACLLMU	CALLUM
ACLLMY	CALMLY
ACLLNO	CLONAL

ACLLOR	COLLAR	ACNOTU	TOUCAN	ADDENW	DAWNED
ACLLOS	LOCALS	ACNOTX	CAXTON	ADDEOR	ADORED, DEODAR
ACLLOW	CALLOW	ACNSTU	CANTUS, TUSCAN	ADDEOS	DADOES
ACLLPU	CALL-UP	ACNSTY	SCANTY	ADDEPP	DAPPED
ACLLSU	CALLUS	ACOOTV	OCTAVO	ADDEPR	DRAPED
ACLLSY	SCYLLA	ACOPRT	CAPTOR	ADDERS	ADDERS, DREADS,
ACLMMY	CLAMMY	ACOPTW	COWPAT		SADDER
ACLMOP	COPALM	ACORRT	CARROT, TROCAR	ADDERT	DARTED, TRADED
ACLMOR	COLMAR	ACORSS	ACROSS, OSCARS	ADDERW	EDWARD, WARDED
ACLMPS	CLAMPS	ACORST	ACTORS, CASTOR,	ADDGIN	ADDING
ACLMTU	TALCUM		CASTRO, CO-STAR, SCROTA	ADDGIO	GADOID
ACLNOS	CASLON	ACORTV	CAVORT	ADDGIY	GIDDAY
ACLNUY	LUNACY	ACORTX	OXCART	ADDGLU	DUGALD
ACLOPU	COPULA, CUPOLA	ACORYZ	CORYZA	ADDGOO	OGDOAD
ACLORR	CORRAL	ACOSST	ASCOTS, COASTS	ADDGOR	GODARD
ACLORS	CARLOS, CAROLS,	ACPPRY	CRAPPY	ADDHOS	ASHDOD
	CORALS	ACPPSU	CUPPAS	ADDIMR	MADRID
ACLORU	OCULAR	ACPRSS	SCARPS, SCRAPS	ADDIMY	MIDDAY
ACLORW	CARLOW	ACPRSU	CARPUS	ADDLNO	DONALD
ACLOST	COSTAL	ACPSTU	CATSUP, UPCAST	ADDMOO	DODOMA
ACLOSV	VOCALS	ACRRWY	WAR CRY	ADDNOS	ADD-ONS
ACLOTU	TOLUCA	ACRSTT	TRACTS	ADDNRU	DURAND
ACLPSS	CLASPS, SCALPS	ACSTTY	SCATTY	ADDORS	DORSAD
ACLRRU	CRURAL	ADDDEG	GADDED	ADDORT	DOTARD
ACLRSW	CRAWLS, SCRAWL	ADDDEL	ADDLED	ADDOST	AT ODDS
ACLSSY	CLASSY	ADDDEN	ADDEND	ADDRSY	DRYADS
ACMMOS	COMMAS	ADDDEP	PADDED	ADEEFM	DEFAME
ACMNNO	CONMAN	ADDDFY	DAFYDD	ADEEFN	DEAFEN
ACMNOO	MONACO	ADDEEH	HEADED	ADEEFR	FEARED
ACMNOR	MACRON	ADDEEN	DEADEN	ADEEFT	DEFEAT
ACMNOS	MASCON, SOCMAN	ADDEEV	EVADED	ADEEGG	DEGAGE
ACMNOW	COWMAN	ADDEGO	GOADED	ADEEGR	AGREED, DRAGEE,
ACMOPS	CAMPOS	ADDEGR	GADDER, GRADED		GEARED
ACMOST	MASCOT	ADDEHN	HANDED	ADEEHI	HAIDEE
ACMOTT	TOMCAT	ADDEHS	DASHED, SHADED	ADEEHL	HEALED
ACMPRS	CRAMPS	ADDEIL	DIALED, LADDIE	ADEEHP	HEAPED
ACMPSS	SCAMPS	ADDEIM	DIADEM, MADDIE	ADEEHR	ADHERE, HEADER
ACMPSU	CAMPUS	ADDEIR	RAIDED	ADEEHT	HEATED
ACMRSU	MARCUS, SACRUM	ADDELL	LADLED	ADEEHV	HEAVED
ACMSTU	MUSCAT	ADDELN	DANDLE, LANDED	ADEEIL	AEDILE
ACMUUV	VACUUM	ADDELO	LOADED	ADEEIT	IDEATE
ACNNNO	CANNON	ADDELP	PADDLE	ADEEKL	LEAKED
ACNNOS	CANONS	ADDELR	ALDRED, LADDER,	ADEEKP	PEAKED
ACNNOT	CANNOT, CANTON		LARDED, RADDLE	ADEELN	LEADEN, LEANED
ACNNOY	CANYON	ADDELS	SADDLE	ADEELP	LEAPED, PEALED
ACNNRY	CRANNY	ADDELU	LAUDED	ADEELR	DEALER, LEADER
ACNOOR	CORONA, RACOON	ADDELW	DAWDLE, WADDLE	ADEELS	LEASED, SEALED
ACNOPS	CAPONS	ADDELY	DEADLY	ADEELT	ELATED
ACNOPY	CANOPY	ADDEMM	DAMMED	ADEELV	LEAVED
ACNORS	ACORNS, CARSON	ADDEMN	DAMNED, DEMAND,	ADEEMN	DEMEAN
ACNORT	CANTOR, CARTON		MADDEN	ADEEMO	OEDEMA
ACNORY	CRAYON	ADDEMP	DAMPED	ADEEMR	REAMED, REMADE
ACNOST	CANTOS	ADDEMR	MADDER	ADEEMT	TEAMED
ACNOTT	OCTANT	ADDENR	DANDER, DARNED	ADEENN	DEANNE, ENNEAD
		ADDENS	SADDEN, SANDED		

61

ADEENR	ANDREE, EARNED, ENDEAR, NEARED
ADEENT	ANTEED
ADEENV	EVADNE
ADEENW	WEANED
ADEEPR	REAPED
ADEEPS	PESADE
ADEEPT	PEDATE
ADEERR	DEARER, READER, REARED, REREAD
ADEERS	ERASED, RESEDA, SEARED
ADEERV	EVADER
ADEERW	DRAWEE
ADEERX	EXEDRA
ADEEST	SEATED, SEDATE, TEASED
ADEFGG	FAGGED
ADEFGN	FAG END, FANGED
ADEFIL	AFIELD, FAILED
ADEFIN	FADE-IN
ADEFIR	FRIEDA
ADEFKL	FLAKED
ADEFLM	FLAMED
ADEFLO	FOALED, LOAFED
ADEFLR	ALFRED, FLARED
ADEFLU	FEUDAL
ADEFLW	FLAWED
ADEFLY	FLAYED
ADEFMO	FOAMED
ADEFMR	FARMED, FRAMED
ADEFNN	FANNED
ADEFNW	FAWNED
ADEFOR	FEDORA
ADEFRT	DAFTER, FARTED, RAFTED
ADEFRY	DEFRAY, FRAYED
ADEFST	FASTED
ADEFTW	WAFTED
ADEGGG	GAGGED
ADEGGJ	JAGGED
ADEGGL	LAGGED
ADEGGN	GANGED, NAGGED
ADEGGR	DAGGER, RAGGED
ADEGGS	SAGGED
ADEGGT	GADGET, TAGGED
ADEGGU	GAUGED
ADEGGW	WAGGED
ADEGHS	GASHED
ADEGII	EGIDIA
ADEGIN	GAINED
ADEGIY	ADYGEI
ADEGKW	GAWKED
ADEGLL	GALLED

ADEGLN	ANGLED, DANGLE, GLENDA
ADEGLO	GAOLED, OLD AGE
ADEGLR	GERALD, GLARED
ADEGLS	GLADES
ADEGLZ	GLAZED
ADEGMM	GAMMED
ADEGNO	OGADEN
ADEGNR	DANGER, GANDER, GARDEN, RANGED
ADEGNU	AUGEND
ADEGNW	GNAWED, GWENDA
ADEGOR	DOG-EAR
ADEGOS	DAGOES, DOSAGE, SEA DOG
ADEGOT	DOTAGE
ADEGPP	GAPPED
ADEGPS	GASPED
ADEGPW	GAWPED
ADEGRR	GERARD, GRADER, REGARD
ADEGRS	GRADES
ADEGRT	GRATED
ADEGRU	ARGUED
ADEGRY	GRAYED
ADEGRZ	GRAZED
ADEGSS	GASSED
ADEGST	STAGED
ADEGSW	WADGES
ADEHHS	HASHED
ADEHIL	HAILED, HALIDE
ADEHIR	HARDIE
ADEHJS	HADJES
ADEHJZ	HEDJAZ
ADEHKR	HARKED
ADEHKW	HAWKED
ADEHLN	HANDEL, HANDLE
ADEHLR	HERALD
ADEHLS	LASHED
ADEHLT	HALTED
ADEHLU	HAULED
ADEHLV	HALVED
ADEHMM	HAMMED
ADEHMR	HARMED
ADEHMS	MASHED, SHAMED
ADEHNO	HEAD-ON
ADEHNP	DAPHNE
ADEHNR	HARDEN
ADEHNY	HAYDEN
ADEHOX	HOAXED
ADEHPR	HARPED
ADEHPS	PHASED, SHAPED
ADEHPT	HEPTAD
ADEHRR	HARDER
ADEHRS	DASHER, SHARED

ADEHRT	DEARTH, HATRED, THREAD
ADEHSS	DASHES, SHADES
ADEHST	DEATHS
ADEHSV	SHAVED
ADEHSW	WASHED
ADEHSY	HYADES
ADEHTW	THAWED
ADEHYY	HEYDAY
ADEIIM	MAIDIE
ADEIJL	JAILED
ADEILL	ALLIED
ADEILM	MAILED, MEDIAL
ADEILN	DANIEL, DELIAN, DENIAL, LEAD-IN, NAILED
ADEILP	ALIPED, ELAPID, PLEIAD
ADEILR	DERAIL, RAILED, RELAID
ADEILS	IDEALS, LADIES, SAILED
ADEILT	DETAIL, DILATE, TAILED
ADEILU	AUDILE
ADEILW	WAILED
ADEIMM	MAIMED
ADEIMN	DAMIEN, MAIDEN, MEDIAN, MEDINA
ADEIMR	ADMIRE
ADEIMU	MAUDIE
ADEINN	DIANNE, NADINE
ADEINO	IDONEA
ADEINP	PAINED
ADEINR	RAINED
ADEINS	SANDIE, SENDAI, SINEAD
ADEINT	DETAIN
ADEINV	INVADE
ADEINW	EDWINA
ADEIOT	IODATE
ADEIPR	DIAPER, PAIRED, REPAID
ADEIRR	RAIDER
ADEIRS	RAISED
ADEIRT	TIRADE
ADEIRV	VARIED
ADEISS	ASIDES, DAISES
ADEISU	ADIEUS
ADEISV	ADVISE, DAVIES, VISAED
ADEITV	DATIVE
ADEITW	WAITED
ADEITX	TAXIED
ADEIUX	ADIEUX
ADEIVW	WAIVED

ADEJMM	JAMMED
ADEJRR	JARRED
ADEJRU	ADJURE
ADEJUV	DEJA VU
ADEJZZ	JAZZED
ADEKKY	YAKKED
ADEKLN	KENDAL
ADEKLR	LARKED
ADEKLS	SLAKED
ADEKLT	TALKED
ADEKLW	WALKED
ADEKMR	MARKED
ADEKMS	MASKED
ADEKNR	DANKER, DARKEN, KENDRA, NARKED, RANKED
ADEKNS	SNAKED
ADEKNW	WANKED
ADEKNY	YANKED
ADEKOS	SOAKED
ADEKOY	OKAYED
ADEKPR	PARKED
ADEKQU	QUAKED
ADEKRR	DARKER
ADEKRS	DRAKES
ADEKST	SKATED, STAKED
ADELLP	PALLED
ADELLR	LADLER
ADELLS	DALLES, LADLES
ADELLU	ALLUDE, ALUDEL
ADELLW	WALLED
ADELMP	PALMED
ADELMR	DERMAL, MEDLAR
ADELMS	DAMSEL, MEDALS
ADELMT	MALTED
ADELMU	MAULED
ADELNO	LOANED
ADELNP	PLANED
ADELNR	DARNEL
ADELNS	ELANDS, LANDES
ADELNT	DENTAL
ADELNU	UNLEAD
ADELOR	LAREDO, LOADER, ORDEAL, RELOAD
ADELOS	ALDOSE
ADELPP	DAPPLE, LAPPED
ADELPR	PEDLAR
ADELPS	LAPSED, PEDALS
ADELPT	PLATED
ADELPW	DEWLAP
ADELPY	PLAYED
ADELRR	DARREL, LARDER
ADELRU	ALURED, LAUDER
ADELRY	DEARLY
ADELST	DELTAS, LASTED, SALTED, SLATED, STALED

ADELSV	SALVED, SLAVED
ADELSY	DELAYS
ADELUV	VALUED
ADELZZ	DAZZLE
ADEMMN	MADMEN
ADEMMR	RAMMED
ADEMNN	MANNED
ADEMNO	DAEMON, MENADO, MOANED, MODENA
ADEMNP	DAMPEN
ADEMNR	REMAND
ADEMNS	AMENDS, DESMAN
ADEMNT	TANDEM
ADEMNU	UNMADE
ADEMOP	POMADE
ADEMOR	RADOME, ROAMED
ADEMOT	MOATED
ADEMOW	MEADOW
ADEMPP	MAPPED
ADEMPR	DAMPER
ADEMPT	TAMPED
ADEMPU	MADE-UP
ADEMRR	MARRED
ADEMRS	DREAMS
ADEMRT	DREAMT
ADEMRW	WARMED
ADEMRY	DREAMY
ADEMSS	MASSED
ADEMSU	AMUSED
ADEMTT	MATTED
ADENNP	PANNED
ADENNT	TANNED
ADENNU	DUENNA
ADENNW	WANNED
ADENOS	ANODES
ADENOT	ATONED, DONATE
ADENPP	APPEND, NAPPED
ADENPR	PANDER, REPAND
ADENPT	PANTED, PEDANT, PENTAD
ADENPW	PAWNED
ADENPX	EXPAND
ADENRR	DARNER, DARREN, ERRAND
ADENRS	SANDER, SNARED
ADENRT	ARDENT, RANTED
ADENRU	UNREAD
ADENRW	ANDREW, WANDER, WARDEN, WARNED
ADENRY	DENARY, YARNED
ADENSS	SEDANS
ADENSU	SUNDAE
ADENTT	ATTEND
ADENTV	ADVENT
ADENTW	WANTED

ADENWY	DWAYNE, YAWNED
ADEOPS	SOAPED
ADEORR	ROARED
ADEORS	SOARED
ADEORW	REDOWA
ADEOSS	ODESSA
ADEOSV	VADOSE
ADEOTT	TO DATE
ADEOVW	AVOWED
ADEPPR	DAPPER, RAPPED
ADEPPS	SAPPED
ADEPPT	TAPPED
ADEPPY	YAPPED
ADEPPZ	ZAPPED
ADEPRR	DRAPER
ADEPRS	DRAPES, PADRES, PARSED, RASPED, SPADER, SPARED, SPREAD
ADEPRT	DEPART, PARTED, PETARD, PRATED
ADEPRW	WARPED
ADEPRY	PRAYED
ADEPSS	PASSED, SPADES
ADEPST	ADEPTS, PASTED
ADEPSU	PAUSED
ADEPSY	SPAYED
ADEPTT	PATTED
ADEPTU	UPDATE
ADERRT	DARTER, RETARD, TARRED, TRADER
ADERRW	DRAWER, REWARD, WARDER, WARRED
ADERRY	DREARY
ADERST	STARED, TRADES, TREADS
ADERSW	SEWARD, WADERS
ADERTT	RATTED, TETRAD
ADERTV	ADVERT
ADERTW	WARTED
ADERUY	AUDREY
ADERXY	X-RAYED
ADESSS	SASSED
ADESST	STEADS
ADESSU	DESSAU
ADESTT	STATED, TASTED
ADESTV	STAVED
ADESTW	WASTED
ADESTY	STAYED, STEADY
ADESWY	SWAYED
ADETTT	TATTED
ADFFOR	AFFORD
ADFFRY	DRAFFY
ADFGIN	FADING
ADFGLY	GADFLY
ADFGRU	FUGARD

ADFIRT	ADRIFT
ADFIRY	FRIDAY
ADFLTY	DAFTLY
ADFNOU	AU FOND
ADFRRU	DARFUR
ADFRST	DRAFTS
ADFRSU	FRAUDS
ADFRSW	DWARFS
ADFRTY	DRAFTY
ADGGOT	DOG TAG
ADGGRY	DRAGGY
ADGIIN	AIDING
ADGILN	LADING, LIGAND
ADGILO	ALGOID
ADGIMY	DIGAMY
ADGINO	GANOID
ADGINR	DARING, GRADIN, IN DRAG
ADGINT	DATING
ADGINW	WADING
ADGINY	GDYNIA
ADGINZ	DANZIG, DAZING
ADGIRV	GRAVID
ADGKNS	GDANSK
ADGLLO	OLD LAG
ADGLLY	GLADLY
ADGLNS	GLANDS
ADGLOP	LAPDOG
ADGLOU	DOUGAL
ADGLOY	DAYGLO
ADGLSY	GLADYS
ADGMOS	DOGMAS
ADGNNO	ANDONG
ADGNOR	DRAGON, GONDAR
ADGNOS	GONADS
ADGNRS	GRANDS
ADGRSU	GRADUS, GUARDS
ADHHIT	HADITH
ADHHLU	HULDAH
ADHHOW	HOWDAH
ADHHWY	WHYDAH
ADHIJS	HADJIS, JIHADS
ADHIKU	HAIDUK
ADHILO	HALOID
ADHILT	ALDITH
ADHIMR	DIRHAM
ADHINS	DANISH, SANDHI
ADHIOR	HAIRDO
ADHIPS	APHIDS
ADHIRS	RADISH
ADHIRY	HYDRIA, RIYADH
ADHLMO	OLDHAM
ADHLOP	ADOLPH
ADHLOR	HAROLD

ADHLOT	OLD HAT
ADHLRY	HARDLY
ADHMNO	HODMAN
ADHMRU	DURHAM
ADHNNU	UNHAND
ADHNOR	HADRON, HARD-ON, RHONDA
ADHNOU	HOUDAN
ADHNOY	HAYDON
ADHNSY	SHANDY
ADHORS	HOARDS
ADHORW	HOWARD
ADHOSW	SHADOW
ADHPRU	HARD UP, PURDAH
ADHRSS	SHARDS
ADHRSY	HYDRAS
ADHSSU	SADHUS
ADIIKO	AIKIDO
ADIILN	INLAID
ADIILO	ODILIA
ADIILW	DIWALI
ADIIMR	MIDAIR
ADIINN	INDIAN
ADIINV	AVIDIN
ADIIPR	DIAPIR
ADIJMS	MASJID
ADIJNO	ADJOIN
ADIKKO	KODIAK
ADIKKS	SKIKDA
ADIKMO	MIKADO
ADIKNP	INKPAD, KIDNAP
ADIKTT	DIKTAT
ADILLP	PALLID
ADILMO	AMIDOL
ADILMS	DISMAL
ADILMY	MILADY
ADILNN	INLAND
ADILNO	LADINO
ADILNR	ALDRIN
ADILNS	ISLAND
ADILNU	UNLAID
ADILNW	ALDWIN
ADILOS	ISOLDA
ADILOZ	OZALID
ADILPS	PLAIDS
ADILRS	LAIRDS
ADILRZ	LIZARD
ADILSS	ALDISS
ADILST	DISTAL
ADILVY	AVIDLY
ADIMNO	DOMAIN
ADIMOT	DIATOM
ADIMRS	DISARM
ADIMRU	RADIUM

ADIMRY	MYRIAD
ADIMSS	SADISM
ADIMST	AMIDST
ADIMSY	DISMAY
ADIMWY	MIDWAY
ADINOR	DORIAN, INROAD, ORDAIN
ADINOX	DIOXAN
ADINPT	PANDIT
ADINPU	UNPAID
ADINRS	DINARS, DRAINS, NADIRS
ADINRU	DURIAN
ADINRW	DARWIN, INWARD
ADINSU	UNSAID
ADINSV	DIVANS, VIANDS
ADINTY	DAINTY
ADIORS	RADIOS
ADIORT	ADROIT, DORITA
ADIPPU	PAID-UP
ADIPRS	RAPIDS, SPARID
ADIPSX	SPADIX
ADIRRY	AIR-DRY
ADIRST	ASTRID, TRIADS
ADIRSU	RADIUS
ADIRWZ	WIZARD
ADISST	SADIST
ADISTU	AUDITS
ADISTV	DAVITS
ADJKOU	JUDOKA
ADJNOR	JORDAN
ADJORR	JARROD
ADJSTU	ADJUST
ADKKNO	KOKAND
ADKLRY	DARKLY
ADLLOR	DOLLAR
ADLMNO	ALMOND, DOLMAN, MALDON, OLD MAN
ADLMOS	DOLMAS
ADLMPY	DAMPLY
ADLMTU	TALMUD
ADLNOP	POLAND
ADLNOR	ARNOLD, LARDON, ROLAND, RONALD
ADLNOT	DALTON
ADLNOU	UNLOAD
ADLNPU	UPLAND
ADLNWY	ALDWYN
ADLORS	DORSAL
ADLOSS	DOSSAL
ADLOSU	ALDOUS
ADLOSW	OSWALD
ADLRRY	DARRYL
ADLRSW	DRAWLS
ADLRWY	DRAWLY

ADLSTU	ADULTS	AEEHHW	HEE-HAW	AEELRT	ELATER, RELATE,
ADMNOR	RANDOM	AEEHJN	JEHANE		TRALEE
ADMNOS	DAMSON, NOMADS	AEEHKT	HEKATE	AEELRV	LEAVER, REVEAL
ADMNOY	DYNAMO, MONDAY	AEEHLN	HELENA	AEELSS	EASELS, LEASES
ADMNPY	DYMPNA	AEEHLR	HEALER	AEELST	TEASEL
ADMNUY	MAUNDY	AEEHLX	EXHALE	AEELSV	LEAVES, SLEAVE
ADMORR	RAMROD	AEEHLY	HEALEY	AEELSW	WEASEL
ADMORU	MADURO	AEEHMR	HAREEM	AEELSZ	SLEAZE
ADNNOU	ADNOUN	AEEHMU	HEAUME	AEELTV	VELATE, VELETA
ADNOPR	PARDON	AEEHNN	HEENAN	AEELWY	LEEWAY
ADNOPT	DOPANT	AEEHNP	PEAHEN	AEEMNR	MEANER, RENAME
ADNORS	ANDROS	AEEHNS	SHEENA	AEEMNS	ENEMAS, SEAMEN
ADNORU	AROUND	AEEHNT	ATHENE, ETHANE	AEEMNX	EXAMEN
ADNORW	ONWARD	AEEHNV	HEAVEN	AEEMPR	AMPERE
ADNOTY	DAYTON	AEEHNX	HEXANE	AEEMRR	REAMER
ADNRST	STRAND	AEEHNY	HEANEY	AEEMRS	SEAMER
ADNRTU	TUNDRA	AEEHPR	HEAPER	AEEMSS	SESAME
ADNSST	STANDS	AEEHRR	HEARER, REHEAR	AEEMTX	TAXEME
ADNSTY	DYNAST	AEEHRS	HAERES, HEARSE	AEENNT	NEATEN
ADNSUY	SUNDAY	AEEHRT	AETHER, HEATER,	AEENNX	ANNEXE
ADOOTW	ATWOOD		HEREAT, REHEAT	AEENQU	QUEENA
ADOPRY	PARODY	AEEHRV	HEAVER	AEENRR	EARNER, NEARER
ADORRU	ARDOUR	AEEHSV	HEAVES, SHEAVE	AEENRS	RANEES, SERENA
ADPRUW	UPWARD	AEEHTX	THE AXE	AEENRT	NEATER
ADQSSU	SQUADS	AEEIJN	JEANIE	AEENRV	VERENA
ADRSSW	SWARDS	AEEILM	MEALIE	AEENST	SATEEN, SENATE
ADRTWY	TAWDRY	AEEILN	AILEEN, ELAINE	AEENSU	UNEASE
AEEFIR	FAERIE	AEEIRS	EASIER	AEENUV	AVENUE
AEEFLM	FEMALE	AEEJNN	JEANNE	AEEPRR	REAPER
AEEFRR	FEARER	AEEKLN	ALKENE	AEEPRS	PARSEE
AEEGGN	ENGAGE	AEEKLR	LEAKER	AEEPRT	REPEAT
AEEGGR	REGGAE	AEEKMR	REMAKE	AEEPST	PESETA
AEEGIR	ARIEGE	AEEKNW	WEAKEN	AEEPSX	APEXES
AEEGKN	KEEGAN	AEEKNY	YANKEE	AEEPSY	PAYEES
AEEGLL	ALLEGE	AEEKRT	RETAKE	AEEQTU	EQUATE
AEEGLP	PELAGE	AEEKRU	EUREKA	AEERRR	REARER
AEEGLR	GALERE, REGALE	AEEKRW	WEAKER	AEERRS	ERASER
AEEGLS	EAGLES	AEELLL	ALLELE	AEERRT	TEARER
AEEGLT	EAGLET, LEGATE	AEELLM	MALLEE	AEERRW	WEARER
AEEGLU	LEAGUE	AEELLS	SALLEE	AEERST	ARETES, EASTER,
AEEGMN	MANEGE, MENAGE	AEELLV	A LEVEL		EATERS, RESEAT, SEATER,
AEEGMR	GRAEME, MEAGRE	AEELMN	ENAMEL		TEASER, TERESA
AEEGMT	GAMETE, METAGE	AEELMP	EMPALE	AEERSU	RESEAU, UREASE
AEEGNN	ENNAGE	AEELNN	LEANNE	AEERSV	AVERSE, VARESE
AEEGNR	ENRAGE, GENERA	AEELNR	ARLEEN, ARLENE,	AEERVW	WEAVER
AEEGNS	SENEGA		LEANER	AEESST	TEASES
AEEGNT	NEGATE	AEELNS	SELENA	AEESSW	SEESAW
AEEGNV	AVENGE, GENEVA	AEELNT	LATEEN	AEESTT	ESTATE
AEEGNW	NEW AGE	AEELNV	LEAVEN	AEESVW	WEAVES
AEEGOP	APOGEE	AEELOT	OLEATE	AEFFGR	GAFFER
AEEGOT	GOATEE	AEELPR	LEAPER, REPEAL	AEFFGS	GAFFES
AEEGRS	GREASE	AEELPS	ASLEEP, ELAPSE,	AEFFIN	AFFINE
AEEGST	EGESTA		PLEASE, SAPELE	AEFFIP	PIAFFE
AEEGSW	SEWAGE	AEELRS	LEASER, RESALE,	AEFFLR	RAFFLE
			SEALER	AEFFLW	WAFFLE

AEFFRZ	ZAFFER	AEFRST	AFTERS, FASTER, STRAFE	AEGJTU	JUGATE
AEFGLN	FLANGE	AEFRSW	WAFERS	AEGKRW	GAWKER
AEFGOR	FORAGE	AEFRTT	FATTER	AEGKST	GASKET
AEFHRS	AFRESH	AEFRTW	WAFTER	AEGLLU	ULLAGE
AEFHRT	FATHER, HAFTER	AEFSST	FEASTS, SAFEST	AEGLLY	GALLEY
AEFIJO	FEIJOA	AEFSTY	SAFETY	AEGLMN	MANGLE
AEFILL	FAILLE	AEGGGL	GAGGLE	AEGLMS	GLEAMS
AEFILN	FINALE	AEGGGR	GAGGER	AEGLMY	GAMELY
AEFILR	FERIAL	AEGGHL	HAGGLE	AEGLNN	GLENNA
AEFILT	FETIAL	AEGGIM	MAGGIE	AEGLNO	ANGELO
AEFIMN	FAMINE	AEGGIN	AGEING	AEGLNR	ANGLER, ERLANG, LANGER
AEFINN	FENIAN	AEGGLR	GARGLE		
AEFIRR	FAIRER	AEGGLW	WAGGLE	AEGLNS	ANGELS, ANGLES
AEFIRY	AERIFY	AEGGNR	GANGER, GRANGE, NAGGER	AEGLNT	TANGLE
AEFIST	FIESTA			AEGLNU	LANGUE
AEFITX	FIXATE	AEGGNS	GANGES	AEGLNW	WANGLE
AEFJNT	FANJET	AEGGNU	GANGUE	AEGLOR	GALORE, GAOLER
AEFKLR	FLAKER	AEGGRT	GARGET	AEGLOT	LEGATO
AEFKLS	FLAKES	AEGGRU	GAUGER	AEGLOV	LOVAGE
AEFKRS	FAKERS, FREAKS	AEGGSU	GAUGES	AEGLPU	PLAGUE
AEFKRY	FREAKY	AEGHIR	HEGIRA	AEGLRR	LARGER
AEFLLN	FALLEN	AEGHIS	GEISHA	AEGLRS	GLARES, LAGERS
AEFLLR	FALLER	AEGHIW	AWEIGH	AEGLRT	TERGAL
AEFLMR	FLAMER	AEGHMN	MEGHAN	AEGLRV	GRAVEL
AEFLMS	FLAMES	AEGHMO	HOMAGE, OHMAGE	AEGLRY	ARGYLE
AEFLNX	FLAXEN	AEGHNO	EOGHAN	AEGLRZ	GLAZER
AEFLOR	LOAFER	AEGHNR	HANGER	AEGLSV	GAVELS
AEFLOT	FOETAL	AEGHRT	GARETH, GATHER	AEGLSY	SAGELY
AEFLOV	FOVEAL	AEGHSS	GASHES	AEGLSZ	GLAZES
AEFLRS	FALSER, FLARES	AEGILN	EALING, GENIAL, LINAGE	AEGMMR	GRAMME
AEFLRT	FALTER			AEGMMS	SMEGMA
AEFLRU	EARFUL, FERULA	AEGILS	GISELA, SILAGE	AEGMNR	ENGRAM, GERMAN, MANGER
AEFLRY	FLAYER	AEGILT	LIGATE		
AEFLST	FESTAL	AEGILZ	EL GIZA	AEGMNS	GASMEN
AEFLSY	SAFELY	AEGIMN	ENIGMA, GAMINE	AEGMNT	MAGNET
AEFLTY	FEALTY	AEGIMP	MAGPIE	AEGMOS	OMEGAS
AEFMOR	FEMORA	AEGIMR	GAMIER, MARGIE, MIRAGE	AEGMUY	MAGUEY
AEFMRR	FARMER, FRAMER			AEGMUZ	ZEUGMA
AEFMRS	FRAMES	AEGIMS	AGEISM, IMAGES	AEGNNO	NONAGE
AEFMRT	FERMAT	AEGINR	EARING, GAINER, REGAIN, REGINA	AEGNNP	PENANG
AEFNNR	FANNER			AEGNNT	GANNET
AEFNRR	FARREN	AEGINS	EASING	AEGNOR	GAENOR, ONAGER, ORANGE
AEFNRU	FRAUEN	AEGINT	EATING		
AEFNRW	FAWNER	AEGINU	GUINEA	AEGNRR	GARNER, RANGER
AEFNST	FASTEN	AEGIPP	PIPAGE	AEGNRS	ANGERS, RANGES
AEFNSU	UNSAFE	AEGIRT	GAITER, TRIAGE	AEGNRT	ARGENT, GARNET
AEFNTT	FATTEN	AEGIRW	EARWIG	AEGNRV	GRAVEN
AEFNZZ	FEZZAN	AEGIRZ	GEZIRA	AEGNRW	GNAWER
AEFPPR	FRAPPE	AEGIST	AGEIST	AEGNRY	ANERGY
AEFRRS	FRASER	AEGISV	VISAGE	AEGNST	AGENTS
AEFRRT	FRATER, RAFTER	AEGITU	AUGITE	AEGNSV	VEGANS
AEFRRY	RAREFY	AEGITY	GAIETY	AEGOPT	POTAGE
AEFRRZ	FRAZER	AEGJLN	JANGLE	AEGORT	ORGEAT
		AEGJLT	JET LAG	AEGORU	AERUGO
				AEGOTU	OUTAGE

AEGOTW	TOWAGE	AEHIST	HESTIA, SAITHE	AEHNST	ATHENS, HASTEN, THANES
AEGOVY	VOYAGE	AEHITT	HATTIE		
AEGPRS	GASPER, GRAPES	AEHJJS	HAJJES	AEHNSV	HAVENS, SHAVEN
AEGPRT	PARGET	AEHKLT	THEKLA	AEHNSY	HYENAS
AEGPRU	PRAGUE	AEHKNR	HANKER, HARKEN	AEHNTV	HAVEN'T
AEGRRT	GARRET, GARTER, GRATER	AEHKNS	SHAKEN	AEHNTX	XANTHE
		AEHKRS	SHAKER	AEHORS	ASHORE, HOARSE
AEGRRU	ARGUER	AEHKRW	HAWKER	AEHORX	HOAXER
AEGRRV	GRAVER	AEHKSS	SHAKES	AEHOSX	HOAXES
AEGRRY	GRAYER	AEHLLL	HALLEL	AEHPRR	HARPER
AEGRRZ	GRAZER	AEHLLS	HELLAS	AEHPRS	PHRASE, SERAPH, SHERPA
AEGRSS	GASSER, SARGES	AEHLLT	LETHAL		
AEGRST	GRATES, GREATS, STAGER	AEHLLY	HALLEY	AEHPSS	PHASES, SHAPES
		AEHLMN	HAMELN	AEHPST	SPATHE
AEGRSU	AUGERS, SAUGER	AEHLMP	PELHAM	AEHRRS	RASHER, SHARER
AEGRSV	GRAVES	AEHLMR	HARLEM	AEHRRT	RATHER
AEGRSW	SWAGER, WAGERS	AEHLMT	HAMLET, THELMA	AEHRSS	RASHES, SHARES, SHEARS
AEGRSY	GREASY	AEHLNS	HANSEL		
AEGRSZ	GRAZES	AEHLOR	LAHORE	AEHRST	EARTHS, HEARST, HEARTS, SARTHE
AEGRTT	TARGET	AEHLOS	HALOES		
AEGRTU	TUAREG	AEHLOT	LOATHE	AEHRSV	SHAVER
AEGRTY	GYRATE	AEHLRS	LASHER	AEHRSW	HAWSER, WASHER
AEGSSS	GASSES	AEHLRT	HALTER, LATHER	AEHRTT	HATTER, THREAT
AEGSST	STAGES	AEHLRU	HAULER	AEHRTW	THAWER, WREATH
AEGSSU	USAGES	AEHLRW	WHALER	AEHRTY	EARTHY, HEARTY
AEGSTY	GAYEST, STAGEY	AEHLRY	HARLEY	AEHRVW	WHARVE
AEHHLT	HEALTH	AEHLSS	HASSLE, LASHES	AEHRVY	HARVEY
AEHHRS	REHASH	AEHLST	HALEST, HASLET, LATHES	AEHSSS	SASHES
AEHHRT	HEARTH			AEHSSV	SHAVES
AEHHSS	HASHES	AEHLSV	HALVES	AEHSSW	WASHES
AEHHST	HEATHS, SHEATH	AEHLSW	WHALES	AEHSTW	SWATHE
AEHHTY	HEATHY	AEHLSY	ASHLEY	AEIILM	EMILIA
AEHIIW	WEIHAI	AEHLSZ	HAZELS	AEIILS	LIAISE
AEHIJL	ELIJAH	AEHLTW	WEALTH	AEIIMS	MAISIE
AEHIJR	HEJIRA	AEHLUV	HUELVA	AEIINR	EIRIAN
AEHIKN	HANKIE	AEHLYY	HAYLEY	AEIIPT	TAIPEI
AEHIKZ	KEZIAH	AEHMMR	HAMMER	AEIIRR	AIRIER
AEHILL	LEILAH	AEHMMY	MAYHEM	AEIJKR	RIJEKA
AEHILM	HIEMAL	AEHMNR	ARNHEM, HERMAN	AEIJLR	JAILER
AEHILN	INHALE	AEHMNT	ANTHEM, HAMNET, HETMAN	AEIJMM	JEMIMA
AEHILP	PHILAE			AEIJNN	JANINE
AEHILR	HAILER	AEHMNU	HUMANE	AEIKLS	ALSIKE
AEHILS	ELISHA, ILESHA, SHEILA	AEHMNW	NEWHAM	AEIKLT	TALKIE
		AEHMOT	AT-HOME	AEIKNR	KIERAN
AEHILT	HALITE	AEHMPR	HAMPER	AEIKNS	KINASE
AEHILW	AWHILE	AEHMRR	HARMER	AEIKNT	INTAKE
AEHIMN	HAEMIN	AEHMRS	HAREMS, MASHER	AEIKNZ	KAIZEN
AEHIMR	HERMIA	AEHMSS	MASHES	AEIKRS	KAISER
AEHIMS	MASHIE	AEHMST	THAMES	AEILLN	LIENAL, LINEAL
AEHIMT	HAMITE	AEHNNS	HANSEN	AEILLR	ALLIER
AEHINR	HERNIA	AEHNPP	HAPPEN	AEILLS	ALLIES
AEHINT	AITHNE, IANTHE	AEHNPT	HAPTEN	AEILLT	TELIAL
AEHINW	ANHWEI	AEHNRT	ANTHER, TEHRAN, THENAR	AEILMN	MENIAL
AEHIRS	ASHIER, SHERIA			AEILMP	IMPALE
AEHIRZ	HAZIER	AEHNRY	HARNEY	AEILMR	MAILER, MARIEL

AEILMS	MALISE	AEINST	TISANE	AEKMPU	MAKE-UP
AEILNN	LIANNE	AEINSV	NAVIES	AEKMRR	MARKER, REMARK
AEILNP	ALPINE, NEPALI, PINEAL	AEINTV	NATIVE	AEKMRS	MAKERS, MASKER
AEILNR	ARLINE, LARINE, LINEAR, NAILER	AEINTY	YENTAI	AEKMRT	MARKET
		AEIOPR	PEORIA	AEKNNY	KENYAN
AEILNS	ALIENS, SALINE, SELINA	AEIOPT	OPIATE	AEKNOR	KOREAN
		AEIORV	AVEIRO	AEKNOW	AWOKEN
AEILNT	ENTAIL, TINEAL	AEIOSV	SAVOIE	AEKNRR	RANKER
AEILNV	ALVINE, ELVINA, VALINE, VEINAL, VENIAL	AEIPPT	PEPITA	AEKNRT	TANKER
		AEIPRR	RAPIER, REPAIR	AEKNRW	NEWARK, WANKER
AEILNX	XENIAL	AEIPRS	ASPIRE, PARIES, PERSIA, PRAISE	AEKNSS	SNAKES, SNEAKS
AEILOS	ELOISA			AEKNSV	KNAVES
AEILPS	ESPIAL, LIPASE	AEIPRT	PIRATE	AEKNSY	SNEAKY
AEILPT	APLITE	AEIPTT	PATTIE	AEKOPT	TOPEKA
AEILRR	RAILER	AEIRRS	RAISER, SIERRA	AEKORS	ARKOSE, SOAKER
AEILRS	ISRAEL, SAILER, SERIAL	AEIRRT	ARTIER	AEKPRR	PARKER
AEILRT	RETAIL, RETIAL	AEIRRV	ARRIVE	AEKPTU	TAKEUP, UPTAKE
AEILRU	AURIEL, LAURIE	AEIRRW	WARIER	AEKQRU	QUAKER
AEILRV	AVERIL, ELVIRA	AEIRSS	RAISES, SISERA	AEKQSU	QUAKES, SQUEAK
AEILRW	LAWRIE, WAILER	AEIRST	SATIRE	AEKRST	SKATER, STRAKE, STREAK, TAKERS, TASKER
AEILRX	RAILEX	AEIRTT	ATTIRE, RATITE		
AEILRZ	LAZIER	AEIRTW	WAITER	AEKSST	SKATES, STAKES, STEAKS
AEILSS	AISLES, ELISSA	AEIRVW	WAIVER, WAVIER		
AEILSV	VALISE	AEIRVX	XAVIER	AEKSTW	TWEAKS
AEILSX	ALEXIS	AEIRWX	WAXIER	AEKWYY	KEYWAY
AEILSY	EASILY	AEISST	SIESTA	AELLLU	LUELLA
AEIMMN	AMMINE	AEISSU	AUSSIE	AELLMT	MALLET
AEIMMR	MAIMER	AEISSZ	ASSIZE	AELLMY	LAMELY
AEIMNN	IN NAME	AEJMMR	JAMMER	AELLNS	ANSELL
AEIMNO	ANOMIE	AEJMRT	RAMJET	AELLPS	LAPELS
AEIMNR	AIRMEN, ARMINE, MARINE, MARNIE, REMAIN	AEJMST	JETSAM	AELLPT	L-PLATE, PALLET, TELPAL
		AEJNNO	JOANNE		
AEIMNS	AMIENS	AEJNOT	TAEJON	AELLPY	PALELY
AEIMNT	INMATE	AEJNST	SEJANT	AELLRT	TALLER
AEIMNX	MAXINE, XIAMEN	AEJNUU	JUNEAU	AELLRU	ALLURE, LAUREL
AEIMNY	NIAMEY	AEJPRS	JASPER	AELLRY	REALLY
AEIMRS	ARMIES	AEJPRY	JAPERY	AELLST	STELLA
AEIMRT	MARTIE	AEKLNR	LANKER, RANKLE	AELLSY	ALLEYS
AEIMRW	WEIMAR	AEKLNS	ANKLES	AELLTU	LUTEAL
AEIMST	SAMITE	AEKLNT	ANKLET	AELLTW	WALLET
AEIMTT	MATTIE	AEKLNW	KNAWEL	AELLTY	LATELY
AEINNR	NERINA	AEKLNY	ALKYNE	AELLVY	VALLEY
AEINNS	INSANE, SIENNA	AEKLPS	SPLAKE	AELMNS	ANSELM, LE MANS, MANSEL
AEINNT	INNATE	AEKLRR	LARKER		
AEINNV	VIENNA	AEKLRS	SLAKER	AELMNT	LAMENT, MANTEL, MANTLE, MENTAL
AEINPR	NAPIER, RAPINE	AEKLRT	TALKER		
AEINRR	RAINER	AEKLRV	KEVLAR	AELMNU	MANUEL
AEINRS	ARISEN, ARSINE, SARNIE	AEKLRW	WALKER	AELMNY	LAYMEN, MANLEY, MEANLY, NAMELY
		AEKLSS	KASSEL		
AEINRT	RATINE, RETAIN, RETINA	AEKLST	LASKET	AELMOR	MORALE
		AEKLTU	AUKLET	AELMOS	SALOME
AEINRV	RAVINE, VAINER	AEKLWY	WEAKLY	AELMPR	PALMER
AEINRZ	ZANIER	AEKMNR	KERMAN	AELMPS	MAPLES, SAMPLE
AEINSS	SANIES	AEKMNU	UNMAKE	AELMPU	AMPULE
				AELMRS	REALMS

AELMRT	ARMLET
AELMRU	MAULER
AELMRV	MARVEL
AELMRY	AYLMER
AELMST	LAMEST, METALS
AELMSU	SAMUEL
AELMSY	MEASLY
AELMTU	AMULET
AELMTY	TAMELY
AELNNR	LANNER
AELNOR	LOANER
AELNOT	ETALON, LEAN-TO
AELNPP	PEN PAL
AELNPR	PARNEL, PLANER, REPLAN
AELNPS	NAPLES, PANELS, PLANES
AELNPT	PLANET, PLATEN
AELNPU	PLAUEN
AELNRT	ANTLER, LEARNT, RENTAL
AELNRU	LAUREN, NEURAL, UNREAL
AELNRV	VERNAL
AELNRY	NEARLY
AELNSU	UNSEAL
AELNSV	NAVELS
AELNSY	SANELY
AELNTT	LATENT, LATTEN, TALENT
AELNTU	LUNATE
AELNTV	LEVANT
AELNTY	NEATLY
AELOPP	ALEPPO
AELOPR	PAROLE
AELOPS	EL PASO
AELOPT	PELOTA
AELOST	OSTEAL
AELOSV	LOAVES
AELOTZ	ZEALOT
AELPPR	LAPPER, RAPPEL
AELPPS	APPLES
AELPPT	APPLET, LAPPET
AELPPU	PAPULE
AELPQU	PLAQUE
AELPRR	PARREL
AELPRS	LAPSER, PEARLS
AELPRT	PALTER, PLATER
AELPRU	PLEURA
AELPRY	PARLEY, PEARLY, PLAYER, REPLAY
AELPSS	LAPSES, SEPALS
AELPST	PALEST, PASTEL, PETALS, PLATES, PLEATS, SEPTAL, STAPLE

AELPTU	PETULA
AELQSU	EQUALS, SQUEAL
AELQUY	QUAYLE
AELRRY	RARELY
AELRSS	LASERS
AELRST	ALERTS, LASTER, SALTER, SLATER, STALER, STELAR
AELRSV	SALVER, SERVAL, SLAVER, VELARS
AELRSY	LAYERS, RELAYS, SLAYER
AELRTT	LATTER, RATTLE
AELRTV	TRAVEL, VARLET
AELRTW	WALTER
AELRTY	LYRATE
AELRUV	VALUER
AELRWY	LAWYER, WARLEY
AELRYY	YEARLY
AELRZZ	RAZZLE
AELSSS	LASSES
AELSST	SLATES, TASSEL
AELSSV	SALVES, SLAVES
AELSTT	LATEST
AELSTU	SALUTE
AELSTV	VALETS, VESTAL
AELSUV	VALUES
AELSUX	SEXUAL
AELSVV	VALVES
AELSYZ	SLEAZY
AELTTT	TATTLE
AELTTW	WATTLE
AELTUX	LUXATE
AELUUV	UVULAE
AELUVV	VULVAE
AEMMNR	MERMAN
AEMMRR	RAMMER
AEMMRY	YAMMER
AEMNNO	EAMONN
AEMNNP	PENMAN
AEMNNR	MANNER
AEMNNW	NEWMAN
AEMNOR	MERANO, MOANER
AEMNOY	YEOMAN
AEMNPU	PNEUMA
AEMNQU	MANQUE
AEMNRT	MARTEN
AEMNRU	MANURE
AEMNST	STAMEN
AEMNSU	UNSEAM
AEMNSY	YES-MAN
AEMNTX	TAXMEN
AEMORR	REMORA, ROAMER
AEMORS	RAMOSE
AEMORX	XEROMA
AEMPPR	PAMPER

AEMPRT	TAMPER
AEMPRV	REVAMP
AEMQRU	MARQUE
AEMQSU	MASQUE
AEMRRR	MARRER
AEMRRU	ARMURE
AEMRRW	WARMER
AEMRSS	MASERS, SMEARS
AEMRST	MASTER, STREAM, TAMERS
AEMRSU	MASERU, MAUSER
AEMRSY	RAMSEY, SMEARY
AEMRTT	MATTER
AEMRTU	MATURE, MUTARE
AEMSSS	MASSES
AEMSSU	ASSUME, SEAMUS, SEUMAS
AEMSSX	XMASES
AEMSTT	TAMEST
AEMSTU	MEATUS
AEMSTY	STEAMY
AEMSYZ	ZYMASE
AEMTTU	MUTATE
AENNOV	NOVENA
AENNOY	ANYONE
AENNRS	SENNAR
AENNRT	TANNER
AENNRW	WANNER
AENNST	NANTES
AENNTT	TENANT
AENOPW	WEAPON
AENOPY	PAEONY
AENORS	REASON, SENORA
AENORT	ATONER, ORNATE
AENORV	VERONA
AENORW	ROWENA
AENORX	ROXANE
AENOSS	SEASON
AENOTZ	ZONATE
AENOWY	ONE-WAY
AENPPR	NAPPER
AENPRT	ENTRAP, PARENT, TREPAN
AENPRW	ENWRAP
AENPRZ	PANZER
AENPTT	PATENT, PATTEN
AENPTU	PEANUT
AENRRS	SNARER
AENRRT	ERRANT, RANTER
AENRRW	WARNER, WARREN
AENRRY	RAYNER
AENRSS	SNARES
AENRST	ASTERN, SANTER, STERNA
AENRSV	RAVENS

AENRSW	ANSWER	AEQRSU	SQUARE	AFGINZ	FAZING
AENRSY	SENARY	AEQRUV	QUAVER	AFGISY	GASIFY
AENRTT	NATTER	AEQSUY	QUEASY	AFGLNO	FLAGON
AENRTU	NATURE	AERRST	ARREST, RAREST,	AFGLNU	FUNGAL
AENRTV	TAVERN		RASTER, STARER	AFGLRU	FRUGAL
AENRTW	WANTER	AERRSV	RAVERS	AFGOTU	FUGATO
AENRWY	YAWNER	AERRTT	RATTER	AFGRST	GRAFTS
AENSST	ASSENT, SANEST	AERRTY	ARTERY	AFGSTU	GUSTAF
AENSSU	ANUSES	AERSST	ASSERT, STARES	AFHIIR	HAIRIF
AENSTU	AUSTEN, UNSEAT	AERSSU	ASSURE	AFHIKL	KHALIF
AENSTY	ANSTEY	AERSSV	SAVERS	AFHIMS	FAMISH
AENSUV	NAEVUS	AERSSW	WRASSE	AFHIOS	OAFISH
AENSUY	UNEASY	AERSTT	AT REST, STATER,	AFHIST	FAITHS
AENTTU	ATTUNE, TAUTEN,		TASTER, TREATS	AFHLOO	LOOFAH
TETUAN		AERSTV	STARVE	AFHLSY	FLASHY
AENTTX	EXTANT	AERSTW	RAWEST, WASTER,	AFHMOT	FATHOM
AEOPPS	APPOSE		WATERS	AFHNOS	FOSHAN
AEOPQU	OPAQUE	AERSTX	EXTRAS	AFHRSW	WHARFS
AEOPRS	OPERAS, PESARO	AERSTY	ESTRAY, STAYER	AFHSST	SHAFTS
AEOPRT	PROTEA	AERSTZ	ERSATZ	AFIIJN	FIJIAN
AEOPTT	TEAPOT	AERSUU	AUREUS	AFIILL	FILIAL
AEOPTY	TEAPOY	AERSWY	SAWYER, SWAYER	AFIILN	FINIAL
AEORRR	ROARER	AERTTT	TATTER	AFIJNU	FUJIAN
AEORRS	SOARER	AERTTU	TAUTER	AFIKRS	FAKIRS
AEORRU	AURORE	AERTTY	TREATY	AFILLS	FLAILS
AEORSS	SEROSA, SOARES	AERTUU	AUTEUR	AFILMY	FAMILY
AEORSU	AROUSE	AERTWY	WATERY	AFILNO	FINOLA
AEORSZ	AZORES	AESSSS	ASSESS, SASSES	AFILNS	FINALS
AEORTT	ROTATE	AESSST	ASSETS	AFILNU	FULANI
AEORVW	AVOWER	AESSSY	ESSAYS	AFILNV	FLAVIN
AEORZZ	AREZZO	AESSTT	STATES, TASTES	AFILNY	FINLAY
AEPPRR	RAPPER	AESSTV	STAVES	AFILOR	FOLIAR
AEPPRS	PAPERS, SAPPER	AESSTW	SWEATS, WASTES	AFILPS	PILAFS
AEPPRT	TAPPER	AESTTT	ATTEST	AFILRY	FAIRLY
AEPPRU	PAUPER	AESTTU	ASTUTE, STATUE	AFILRZ	FRAZIL
AEPPRY	PAPERY, PREPAY,	AESTWY	SWEATY	AFILSY	SALIFY
YAPPER		AESTYY	YEASTY	AFIMNY	INFAMY
AEPPTT	TAPPET	AFFFOR	FAR-OFF	AFIMRY	RAMIFY
AEPPTU	PUPATE	AFFGUW	GUFFAW	AFIMSS	MASSIF
AEPRRS	PARSER, RASPER,	AFFIKR	KAFFIR	AFINNO	FANION
SPARER		AFFIMR	AFFIRM	AFINNT	INFANT
AEPRRT	PRATER	AFFIRT	TARIFF	AFINRU	UNFAIR
AEPRRU	PARURE, UPREAR	AFFLOY	LAY-OFF, OFFALY	AFINST	FAINTS
AEPRRW	PREWAR, WARPER	AFFLUX	AFFLUX	AFINSU	FUSAIN
AEPRRY	PRAYER	AFFOPY	PAYOFF	AFIRRS	FRIARS
AEPRSS	SPARES, SPARSE,	AFFORR	FORFAR	AFIRRY	FRIARY
SPEARS		AFFSST	STAFFS	AFIRTY	RATIFY
AEPRST	PATERS, REPAST,	AFGGIO	FOGGIA	AFKLNS	FLANKS
TAPERS		AFGGLY	FLAGGY	AFKLSS	FLASKS
AEPRSU	PAUSER	AFGGOT	FAGGOT	AFLLOR	FLORAL
AEPRTT	PATTER	AFGIKN	FAKING	AFLLOW	FALLOW
AEPRUV	RAVE-UP	AFGILN	FINGAL	AFLLTY	FLATLY
AEPSSS	PASSES	AFGINO	FANGIO	AFLLUW	LAWFUL
AEPSST	PASTES, STAPES	AFGINR	FARING	AFLMNU	MANFUL
AEPSSU	PAUSES	AFGINX	FAXING		

AFLMOR	FORMAL	AGHOQU	QUAHOG	AGINSY	SAYING
AFLMRU	ARMFUL, FULMAR	AGHPRS	GRAPHS	AGINTX	TAXING
AFLMYY	MAYFLY	AGHTTU	TAUGHT	AGINVW	WAVING
AFLNOT	FONTAL	AGIIKL	KIGALI	AGINWX	WAXING
AFLNTU	FLAUNT	AGIILN	AILING, ILIGAN, NILGAI	AGINWY	YAWING
AFLOST	FLOATS			AGIORU	GIAOUR
AFLOTY	FLOATY	AGIIMN	AIMING	AGIORV	VIRAGO
AFLRTU	ARTFUL	AGIINR	AIRING	AGIOTU	AGOUTI
AFLSTU	FAULTS, FLATUS	AGIJNW	JAWING	AGIRST	GRATIS
AFLSWY	SAWFLY	AGIJSW	JIGSAW	AGIRTU	GUITAR
AFLTUY	FAULTY	AGIKMN	MAKING	AGJLMO	LOGJAM
AFMNOR	FORMAN	AGIKNN	ANKING	AGJNOR	JARGON
AFMORT	FORMAT	AGIKNR	RAKING	AGKLNO	KALONG
AFMOSU	FAMOUS	AGIKNS	ASKING, GASKIN	AGKNOR	ANGKOR
AFNNRY	FRANNY	AGIKNT	TAKING	AGKNRU	KURGAN
AFNSSU	SNAFUS	AGIKNW	WAKING	AGKORT	GO-KART
AFORRW	FARROW	AGILLU	LIGULA	AGLLNO	GALLON
AFORSY	FORAYS	AGILMM	GIMMAL	AGLLOP	GALLOP
AFORTU	FAR-OUT	AGILMN	LAMING, MALIGN	AGLLRY	ARGYLL
AFORUV	FAVOUR	AGILMO	GLIOMA	AGLNNO	LONGAN
AGGGIN	GAGING	AGILNP	PALING	AGLNOO	LAGOON
AGGHIS	HAGGIS	AGILNS	SIGNAL	AGLNOS	SLOGAN
AGGHSY	SHAGGY	AGILNU	LINGUA	AGLNOU	LANUGO, LUGANO
AGGILO	LOGGIA	AGILNY	GAINLY, LAYING	AGLNOY	LOYANG
AGGIMN	GAMING	AGILNZ	LAZING	AGLNRU	LANGUR
AGGINP	GAPING, PAGING	AGILOR	GLORIA	AGLNSY	SLANGY
AGGINR	RAGING	AGILOT	GALIOT	AGLNTY	TANGLY
AGGINW	WAGING	AGILOV	OGIVAL	AGLNUU	UNGUAL, UNGULA
AGGINZ	GAZING	AGILRY	GLAIRY	AGLORS	LARGOS
AGGIWW	WIGWAG	AGIMNN	NAMING	AGLOSS	GLOSSA
AGGIZZ	ZIGZAG	AGIMNR	ARMING, INGRAM,	AGLOST	GLOATS
AGGLSY	SLAGGY		MARGIN	AGLPUY	PLAGUY
AGGLWY	WAGGLY	AGIMNT	MATING, TAMING	AGLRSU	GLARUS
AGGMOT	MAGGOT	AGIMST	STIGMA	AGLRUV	VULGAR
AGGNSY	SNAGGY	AGIMWW	WIGWAM	AGLSSY	GLASSY
AGGQUY	QUAGGY	AGINNQ	ANQING	AGLSUV	VALGUS
AGHILT	ALIGHT	AGINNW	AWNING, WANING	AGMMNO	GAMMON
AGHINN	HANG IN	AGINOR	ORIGAN	AGMMNU	MAGNUM
AGHINR	HARING	AGINOS	SAIGON	AGMNNU	GUNMAN
AGHINS	HSIANG	AGINPR	PARING, RAPING	AGMNOR	MORGAN
AGHINT	HATING	AGINPT	TAPING	AGMNOS	MANGOS
AGHINV	HAVING	AGINPV	PAVING	AGMNSU	MAGNUS
AGHINZ	HAZING	AGINPW	PAWING	AGMOOY	OOGAMY
AGHIRS	GARISH	AGINPY	PAYING	AGMORS	ORGASM
AGHIRT	ARIGHT	AGINRR	RARING	AGMORT	MARGOT
AGHKRU	GURKHA	AGINRS	GRAINS	AGMOYZ	ZYGOMA
AGHLLU	GULLAH	AGINRT	RATING	AGMPUZ	GAZUMP
AGHLOS	GALOSH	AGINRU	AIRGUN, UGRIAN	AGNNOT	TONGAN
AGHLSU	LAUGHS	AGINRV	INGVAR, RAVING	AGNNOY	YANGON
AGHNOO	OONAGH	AGINRY	GRAINY	AGNNRY	GRANNY
AGHNPU	HANG-UP	AGINRZ	RAZING	AGNNTU	ANTUNG
AGHNTU	NAUGHT	AGINSS	ASSIGN	AGNOQU	QUANGO
AGHNUV	VAUGHN	AGINST	GIANTS, SATING	AGNORS	GROANS, ORGANS,
AGHNUY	GUNYAH	AGINSV	SAVING		SARONG
		AGINSW	SAWING		

AGNORY	GAYNOR	AHIMOR	MOHAIR	AHMNPY	NYMPHA
AGNOST	SONTAG, TANGOS,	AHIMPS	MISHAP	AHMNSU	HUMANS
	TSONGA	AHINPT	HATPIN	AHMNSY	MYNAHS
AGNOSW	WAGONS	AHINRU	UNHAIR	AHMORY	MORYAH
AGNOTU	NOUGAT	AHINSS	SHANSI	AHMOST	THOMAS
AGNPRS	SPRANG	AHINSU	HUSAIN	AHMOTU	MAHOUT
AGNPRU	NAGPUR	AHINSV	VANISH	AHMOWY	HAYMOW
AGNRST	GRANTS	AHINSW	WASHIN	AHMRSY	MARSHY
AGNRTY	GANTRY	AHINSX	SHANXI	AHMRTW	WARMTH
AGNSTW	TWANGS	AHINTT	TANITH, TIN HAT	AHMSSU	SHAMUS
AGNTWY	TWANGY	AHIOPS	SOPHIA	AHNNSY	SHANNY
AGORST	ARGOTS, GROATS	AHIORT	HOT AIR	AHNOOR	HONORA
AGORSY	ARGOSY	AHIPRS	PARISH	AHNOPR	ORPHAN
AGORTU	RAGOUT	AHIPRU	RUPIAH	AHNORS	SHARON, SHORAN
AGOSTU	OUTGAS	AHIRRS	HARRIS, SIRRAH	AHNOSX	XHOSAN
AGOTTU	TAUTOG	AHIRST	THIRSA, TRISHA	AHNOWY	ANYHOW
AGRSSU	SUGARS	AHIRSV	RAVISH	AHNSTU	HAUNTS
AGRSSY	GRASSY	AHIRSZ	SHIRAZ	AHNSTY	SHANTY
AGRSTU	TRAGUS	AHIRTW	WRAITH	AHOORY	HOORAY
AGRSUY	SUGARY	AHIRTZ	THIRZA, TIRZAH	AHOPPS	PAPHOS
AGRUUY	AUGURY	AHISTU	HIATUS	AHOPST	PASHTO, PATHOS,
AGSSTU	AUGUST	AHISTV	VASHTI		POTASH
AGSTUV	GUSTAV	AHJMOT	JOTHAM	AHOPTT	TOP HAT
AHHIMS	HAMISH	AHJOSU	JOSHUA	AHORRW	HARROW
AHHKOO	HOOKAH	AHKLNU	KHULNA	AHORRY	HORARY
AHHOOR	HOORAH	AHKMOW	MOHAWK	AHORTT	THROAT
AHHORT	HATHOR	AHKNOW	HANKOW	AHORTU	AUTHOR
AHHORW	HOWRAH	AHKNPU	PUNKAH	AHORTX	THORAX
AHHPPU	HUPPAH	AHKNRS	SHRANK	AHPRSS	SHARPS
AHHRRU	HURRAH	AHKNSS	SHANKS	AHQSSU	SQUASH
AHHRST	THRASH	AHKNST	THANKS	AHRRTU	ARTHUR
AHHUZZ	HUZZAH	AHKRSS	SHARKS	AHRRUY	HURRAY
AHIILT	AILITH, LITHIA	AHLLMU	MULLAH	AHRSSU	HUSSAR
AHIITT	TAHITI	AHLLOO	HALLOO	AHRSTY	TRASHY
AHIJJS	HAJJIS	AHLLOS	HALLOS	AHRTTW	THWART
AHIJNS	JHANSI	AHLLOW	HALLOW	AHSSTU	TUSSAH
AHIJOS	JOSIAH	AHLLRT	THRALL	AHSSTW	SWATHS
AHIKMO	KOHIMA	AHLLUX	HALLUX	AIIKLS	LIKASI
AHIKMS	HAKIMS	AHLMNY	HAMLYN, HYMNAL	AIILLN	LILIAN
AHIKRS	RAKISH	AHLMOS	SHALOM	AIILLS	LILIAS
AHILLL	LILLAH	AHLNOT	HALTON	AIILNS	IN SAIL
AHILLZ	ZILLAH	AHLNSU	UNLASH	AIILOV	OLIVIA
AHILMP	IMPHAL	AHLOOP	HOOP-LA	AIILRY	AIRILY
AHILNR	RHINAL	AHLORT	HARLOT	AIILSV	SILVIA
AHILNU	INHAUL	AHLORW	HARLOW	AIIMMN	MINIMA
AHILNY	HYALIN	AHLOSS	SHOALS	AIIMMR	MIRIAM
AHILOS	LASHIO	AHLOSY	SHOALY	AIIMNR	MAIRIN
AHILPS	PALISH, PHIALS	AHLPSS	SPLASH	AIIMNS	SIMIAN
AHILRY	HILARY	AHLPSU	LASH-UP	AIIMNT	INTIMA
AHILST	LATISH	AHLPSY	PLASHY	AIIMPR	IMPAIR
AHILSV	LAVISH	AHLRSY	RASHLY	AIIMRY	MARY II
AHILTW	WITHAL	AHLSSW	SHAWLS	AIINNN	NINIAN
AHILYZ	HAZILY	AHMMSY	SHAMMY	AIINNO	IONIAN
AHIMNT	HIT MAN	AHMNOS	HANSOM	AIINNZ	ZINNIA

AIINRS	RAISIN
AIINST	ISATIN
AIINVV	VIVIAN
AIIPTW	WAPITI
AIIRST	ISTRIA
AIIRTV	TRIVIA
AIISSS	ASSISI
AIJJNU	UJJAIN
AIJLNU	JULIAN
AIJLOV	JOVIAL
AIJMNP	PANJIM
AIJOSS	JOSIAS
AIJPRU	JAIPUR
AIJRSV	JARVIS
AIKLNO	KAOLIN
AIKLNW	WALK-IN
AIKLSU	SALUKI
AIKLSZ	KALISZ
AIKMNR	KIRMAN
AIKMOP	MAIKOP
AIKMSU	KUMASI
AIKNNP	NAPKIN
AIKNPR	PARKIN
AIKNRU	KIRUNA
AIKNRV	NARVIK
AIKNSU	SUAKIN
AIKORT	TROIKA
AIKTUW	KUWAIT
AILLMU	ALLIUM
AILLOT	LOLITA
AILLPR	PILLAR
AILLSV	VILLAS
AILLSW	WALLIS
AILLTW	AT WILL
AILLYZ	LAZILY
AILMNO	OILMAN
AILMNR	MARLIN
AILMNU	ALUMNI
AILMNV	MALVIN
AILMNY	MAINLY
AILMOP	LIPOMA
AILMOS	SOMALI
AILMPR	PRIMAL
AILMRT	MITRAL, RAMTIL
AILMSS	MISSAL
AILMSX	SMILAX
AILMSY	MISLAY
AILMTU	LATIUM, ULTIMA
AILMUV	VALIUM
AILMYZ	MAZILY
AILNOS	ALISON
AILNOT	TALION
AILNPS	PLAINS, SPINAL
AILNPT	PLAINT, PLIANT

AILNRT	TRINAL
AILNRU	URINAL
AILNSS	SNAILS
AILNST	LATINS
AILNSU	INSULA
AILNSV	ANVILS, SILVAN
AILNSW	IN-LAWS
AILNSY	INLAYS
AILNTY	LITANY
AILNVY	VAINLY
AILNWY	AYLWIN
AILNYZ	ZANILY
AILORS	SAILOR
AILORT	RIALTO, TAILOR
AILORU	AURIOL
AILOSU	LOUISA
AILOSV	VIOLAS
AILOSX	OXALIS
AILOTX	OXTAIL
AILPPS	PIPALS
AILPRS	APRILS, SPIRAL
AILPST	PLAITS, SPITAL
AILQSU	QUAILS
AILRRW	WIRRAL
AILRST	TRAILS, TRIALS
AILRSV	RIVALS
AILRSY	RIYALS
AILRTU	RITUAL
AILRWY	WARILY
AILSTV	VITALS
AILSUV	VISUAL
AILSVY	SYLVIA
AILTXY	LAXITY
AILVWY	WAVILY
AILWXY	WAXILY
AIMMOS	MAOISM, MIMOSA
AIMMSX	MAXIMS
AIMNNO	AMNION, MINOAN
AIMNOP	MOPANI
AIMNOR	MARION
AIMNOS	SIMONA
AIMNPT	PITMAN
AIMNRT	ANTRIM, MARTIN
AIMNRV	MARVIN
AIMNST	MANTIS, MATINS, TAMSIN
AIMNSU	ANIMUS
AIMNSY	YASMIN
AIMNSZ	NAZISM
AIMOPY	MYOPIA
AIMOST	MAOIST, TAOISM
AIMOSW	MIAOWS
AIMOSX	AXIOMS
AIMPRS	PAMIRS

AIMPRT	ARMPIT, IMPART
AIMPSS	PASSIM
AIMQSU	MAQUIS
AIMRSU	MARIUS
AIMRSW	WISMAR
AIMRTU	ATRIUM, TIMARU
AIMRTX	MATRIX
AIMSSW	SWAMIS
AIMSTU	AUTISM
AINNNT	TANNIN
AINNOS	NASION
AINNOT	ANOINT, NATION
AINNPW	IN PAWN
AINNST	TSINAN
AINOPS	PIANOS
AINORS	ROSINA
AINORT	RATION
AINOSU	SIOUAN
AINPRS	SPRAIN
AINPST	PAINTS, PINTAS, PTISAN
AINPSV	SPAVIN
AINQRT	QINTAR
AINQTU	QUAINT
AINRST	INSTAR, STRAIN, TRAINS
AINRSY	SYRIAN
AINRTU	IN A RUT, NUTRIA
AINRYZ	ZYRIAN
AINSST	SAINTS, STAINS
AINSSW	SWAINS
AINSTT	TITANS
AINSTU	AUSTIN
AINSTY	SANITY, SATINY
AINTVY	VANITY
AIOORS	ARIOSO
AIOPRT	PORTIA
AIOPST	PATIOS, PATOIS
AIOPTU	UTOPIA
AIORSS	ORISSA
AIORST	AORIST, ARTOIS, RATIOS, ROSITA
AIOSTT	TAOIST
AIOSYZ	ZOYSIA
AIPPRY	PAPYRI
AIPPST	PAPIST
AIPRST	RAPIST, TAPIRS
AIPRSW	RIPSAW
AIPRSX	PRAXIS
AIPRTY	PARITY
AIPRUY	PYURIA
AIPSTW	PITSAW
AIPSZZ	PIZZAS
AIRRTY	RARITY
AIRSST	SITARS, STAIRS

73

AIRSSU	RUSSIA	
AIRSTT	ARTIST, STRAIT, TRAITS	
AIRSTV	TRAVIS	
AIRSTY	STYRIA	
AIRTTY	YTTRIA	
AISSST	ASSIST, STASIS	
AISSTV	VISTAS	
AISSTW	WAISTS	
AISTUW	WATUSI	
AJKORT	RAJKOT	
AJLOPY	JALOPY	
AJMORS	MAJORS	
AJNORT	TROJAN	
AJNSTU	JAUNTS, JUNTAS	
AJNTUY	JAUNTY	
AJORRW	JARROW	
AJPRTU	RAJPUT	
AKLLNY	LANKLY	
AKLMOY	KOLYMA	
AKLNOW	WALK-ON	
AKLNOX	KLAXON	
AKLNPS	PLANKS	
AKLNRY	RANKLY	
AKLOPS	POLKAS	
AKLOSV	SLOVAK	
AKLPUW	WALK-UP	
AKLSST	STALKS	
AKLSTY	STALKY	
AKMNSU	UNMASK	
AKMPRU	MARKUP	
AKNORU	KORUNA	
AKNPRS	PRANKS	
AKNPRU	KANPUR	
AKNPSS	SPANKS	
AKNRUU	NAKURU	
AKNSSW	SWANKS	
AKNSWY	SWANKY	
AKOPRV	KARPOV	
AKOTVY	VOTYAK	
AKPRSS	SPARKS	
AKQRSU	QUARKS	
AKQSUW	SQUAWK	
ALLMOS	SLALOM	
ALLMOW	MALLOW	
ALLMSS	SMALLS	
ALLNOP	POLLAN	
ALLNUU	LUNULA	
ALLOOP	APOLLO	
ALLOPR	PALLOR	
ALLOPW	WALLOP	
ALLORY	ORALLY	
ALLOST	ATOLLS	
ALLOSW	SALLOW	
ALLOSY	ALLOYS	

ALLOTW	TALLOW	
ALLOWW	WALLOW	
ALLPRU	PLURAL	
ALLQSU	SQUALL	
ALLSST	STALLS	
ALLSTY	LASTLY	
ALLUVV	VULVAL	
ALMMOW	MOWLAM	
ALMMUY	AMYLUM	
ALMNOR	NORMAL	
ALMNOS	SALMON	
ALMNRY	MARLYN	
ALMNTU	MULTAN	
ALMORS	MOLARS, MORALS	
ALMORT	MORTAL	
ALMORU	MORULA	
ALMORY	MALORY	
ALMOST	ALMOST, SMALTO	
ALMPSS	PSALMS	
ALMQSU	QUALMS	
ALMRSU	MURALS	
ALMRWY	WARMLY	
ALMSUY	ASYLUM	
ALMTUU	MUTUAL, UMLAUT	
ALNNOU	NOUNAL	
ALNOOS	ALONSO, SALOON	
ALNOOZ	ALONZO	
ALNOSS	SALONS	
ALNOST	TALONS	
ALNOTV	VOLANT	
ALNOTW	WALTON	
ALNOTY	LAYTON	
ALNPST	PLANTS	
ALNRSS	SNARLS	
ALNRSY	SNARLY	
ALNRUY	URANYL	
ALNRXY	LARYNX	
ALNSST	SLANTS	
ALNSTU	SULTAN	
ALNSVY	SYLVAN	
ALNTUW	WALNUT	
ALOOPS	SALOOP	
ALOPPR	POPLAR	
ALOPPT	LAPTOP	
ALOPRT	PATROL, PORTAL	
ALOPST	POSTAL	
ALOQTU	LOQUAT	
ALORSV	SALVOR	
ALORSY	ROYALS	
ALORTY	TAYLOR	
ALORUV	LOUVAR, OVULAR, VALOUR	
ALOSSS	LASSOS	
ALOSSV	SALVOS	

ALOSTT	TOTALS	
ALOTUW	OUTLAW	
ALOTUY	LAY OUT, OUTLAY	
ALPPSU	SLAP-UP	
ALPRSU	PULSAR	
ALPRSW	SPRAWL	
ALPRTY	PALTRY, PARTLY	
ALPSSU	LAPSUS	
ALRSTW	TRAWLS	
ALRSTY	STYLAR	
ALRSUU	URSULA	
ALRSUW	WALRUS	
ALRTTY	RATTLY, TARTLY	
ALRUUV	UVULAR	
ALSSTU	SALTUS	
ALSTUV	VAULTS	
ALSTUY	SALYUT	
ALSTVY	VASTLY	
ALSUUV	UVULAS	
ALSUVV	VULVAS	
ALTTUY	TAUTLY	
ALTUUV	TUVALU	
AMMMNO	MAMMON	
AMMMOS	MOMMAS	
AMMORT	MARMOT	
AMMOSU	OMASUM	
AMMOXY	MYXOMA	
AMMPUW	WAMPUM	
AMMRSY	SMARMY	
AMMSTU	SUMMAT	
AMNNOR	NORMAN	
AMNOOR	MAROON, ROMANO	
AMNOPT	TAMPON	
AMNORR	MARRON	
AMNORS	MANORS, RANSOM, ROMANS	
AMNORT	MATRON	
AMNORY	MORNAY, ROMANY	
AMNOSS	MASONS, SAMSON	
AMNOTU	AMOUNT, OUTMAN	
AMNPTY	TYMPAN	
AMNRTU	ANTRUM, TRUMAN	
AMNRTY	MARTYN	
AMNRVY	MARVYN	
AMNSSU	SAMSUN	
AMNTTU	MUTANT	
AMNTUU	AUTUMN	
AMOOTT	TOMATO	
AMOPRS	PRO-AMS	
AMOPST	PATMOS	
AMOPTU	MAPUTO	
AMORRT	MORTAR	
AMORRU	ARMOUR	
AMORRW	MARROW	

AMORSS	MORASS
AMORST	STROMA
AMORSU	AMOURS
AMORSY	MAYORS
AMPRRU	RAMPUR
AMPRST	TRAMPS
AMPRUW	WARM-UP
AMPSSS	SPASMS
AMPSST	STAMPS
AMPSSW	SWAMPS
AMPSWY	SWAMPY
AMRRTY	MARTYR
AMRRUY	MURRAY
AMRSSW	SWARMS
AMRSTU	STRUMA
ANNNUY	YUNNAN
ANNOPZ	POZNAN
ANNORT	NATRON
ANNOST	SONANT
ANNOSW	WONSAN
ANNOTW	WANTON
ANNOTY	ANTONY, TANNOY
ANNPSU	UNSNAP
ANNRTY	TRANNY
ANNSTU	SUNTAN
ANNTTU	NUTANT
ANOOPS	NO SOAP
ANOOPX	A POX ON
ANOORS	SONORA
ANOORT	RATOON
ANOPRS	APRONS, PARSON
ANOPRT	PARTON, PATRON, TARPON
ANOPUY	YAUPON
ANORRW	NARROW
ANORRY	RAYNOR
ANORSW	ROWANS
ANORTT	ATTORN
ANORTU	OUTRAN
ANORTY	NOTARY
ANORWY	NORWAY
ANOSST	SANTOS
ANOSSX	SAXONS
ANOSXY	SAXONY
ANPPSY	SNAPPY
ANPRSW	PRAWNS
ANPRTY	PANTRY
ANPRUW	UNWRAP
ANRSTU	SATURN
ANRSUU	URANUS
ANRSUY	SUNRAY
ANRSYZ	SYZRAN
ANRTTU	TRUANT
ANRTTY	TYRANT

ANRUWY	RUNWAY, UNWARY
ANSTTU	TAUNTS, TUTSAN
ANSTUV	VAUNTS
ANSTWY	WYSTAN
ANSTXY	SYNTAX
ANSYZZ	SNAZZY
ANVVYY	VYVYAN
AOOPTT	POTATO
AOOPTW	PAOTOW
AOORRT	ORATOR
AOOTTT	TATTOO
AOPPPS	POPPAS
AOPPRT	POP ART
AOPRRT	PARROT, RAPTOR
AOPRRU	UPROAR
AOPRST	PASTOR
AOPRUV	VAPOUR
AOPTUY	PAYOUT
AOQRTU	QUARTO
AOQSTU	QUOTAS
AORRST	ROSTRA
AORRSW	ARROWS
AORRSY	ROSARY
AORRSZ	RAZORS
AORRTY	ROTARY
AORRWY	YARROW
AORSST	ASSORT, ROASTS
AORSTT	STATOR, TAROTS
AORSTX	STORAX
AORSUU	AUROUS
AORSUV	SAVOUR
AORSVY	SAVORY
AORTVY	VOTARY
AOSSTT	STOATS, TOASTS
AOSSVY	SAVOYS
AOSTWW	SWATOW
AOTUWY	WAY-OUT
AOTWWY	TWO-WAY
APPPSU	PAPPUS
APRRSY	SPARRY
APRSST	SPRATS, STRAPS
APRSSY	SPRAYS
APRSTY	PASTRY
AQRRUY	QUARRY
AQRSTU	QUARTS
AQRTUZ	QUARTZ
AQSSTU	SQUATS
AQSSUW	SQUAWS
ARRSTY	STARRY
ARSSTT	STARTS
ARSSTU	TARSUS
ARSSTW	STRAWS
ARSSTY	SATYRS, STRAYS
ARSTTU	STUART

ARSTUU	TAURUS
ARSTUX	SURTAX
ARSTWY	STRAWY
ARSTXY	STYRAX
ASSTTU	STATUS
BBBDEO	BOBBED
BBBEIO	BOBBIE
BBBELO	BOBBLE
BBBELU	BUBBLE
BBBHUU	HUBBUB
BBBINO	BOBBIN
BBBLUY	BUBBLY
BBCDEU	CUBBED
BBCELO	COBBLE
BBCEOR	COBBER
BBCEOW	COBWEB
BBCHUY	CHUBBY
BBCLUY	CLUBBY
BBDDEI	DIBBED
BBDDEU	DUBBED
BBDEEI	DEBBIE
BBDEEW	WEBBED
BBDEFI	FIBBED
BBDEFO	FOBBED
BBDEGI	GIBBED
BBDEGU	BEDBUG
BBDEIJ	JIBBED
BBDEIL	DIBBLE
BBDEIR	DIBBER, RIBBED
BBDEIY	BIDE BY
BBDEJO	JOBBED
BBDELO	LOBBED
BBDEMO	BOMBED, MOBBED
BBDEOO	BOOBED
BBDEOR	ROBBED
BBDEOS	SOBBED
BBDERU	RUBBED
BBDESU	SUBBED
BBDETU	TUBBED
BBDINO	DOBBIN
BBDINU	DUBBIN
BBEELP	PEBBLE
BBEFIR	FIBBER
BBEGIN	EBBING
BBEGIR	GIBBER
BBEGIT	GIBBET
BBEGLO	GOBBLE
BBEGNU	BENGBU
BBEGOT	GOBBET
BBEHLO	HOBBLE
BBEHLU	HUBBLE
BBEHOS	HOBBES
BBEIIM	IMBIBE
BBEIIS	SIBBIE

BBEIJR	JIBBER	BCEIPS	BICEPS	BDDELU	BUDDLE
BBEILN	NIBBLE	BCEIRS	SCRIBE	BDDENO	BONDED
BBEILR	LIBBER	BCEIRT	TERBIC	BDDERU	REDBUD
BBEILS	BIBLES	BCEIST	BISECT	BDDIOR	DO BIRD
BBEIOR	ROBBIE	BCEJOT	OBJECT	BDDISU	DISBUD
BBEIRR	BRIBER	BCEKLU	BUCKLE, LUBECK	BDEEEF	BEEFED
BBEJOR	JOBBER	BCEKNO	BECKON	BDEEGG	BEGGED
BBELMU	BUMBLE	BCEKTU	BUCKET	BDEEHL	BEHELD
BBELNO	NOBBLE	BCELNO	EN BLOC	BDEEIL	BELIED, EDIBLE
BBELNU	NUBBLE	BCELOR	CORBEL	BDEEIS	BESIDE
BBELOW	WOBBLE	BCELOU	BOUCLE	BDEEIT	BETIDE
BBELPY	PEBBLY, PLEBBY	BCEMOR	COMBER	BDEELN	BLENDE
BBELRU	BURBLE, LUBBER, RUBBLE	BCEMRU	CUMBER	BDEELT	BELTED
		BCENOR	BRECON	BDEEOY	OBEYED
BBEMNU	BENUMB	BCENOU	BOUNCE	BDEEST	BESTED
BBEMOR	BOMBER, MOBBER	BCEOTT	OBTECT	BDEETT	BETTED
BBEORR	ROBBER	BCGINU	CUBING	BDEFFI	BIFFED
BBEORS	SOBBER	BCGORU	COBURG	BDEFFU	BUFFED
BBERRU	RUBBER	BCHIOP	PHOBIC	BDEFIR	FIBRED
BBGINO	GIBBON	BCHITY	BITCHY	BDEGGO	BOGGED
BBGRUY	GRUBBY	BCHLOT	BLOTCH	BDEGGU	BUGGED
BBHMOS	H-BOMBS	BCHMOU	BOCHUM	BDEGIN	BIG END
BBHNOO	HOBNOB	BCHNRU	BRUNCH	BDEGIR	BRIDGE
BBIIIO	IBIBIO	BCHNUY	BUNCHY	BDEGLU	BULGED
BBIKOS	SKIBOB	BCHOOR	BROOCH	BDEGNU	BUNGED
BBILLU	BULBIL	BCHOTY	BOTCHY	BDEGTU	BUDGET
BBINOR	RIBBON, ROBBIN	BCIILM	LIMBIC	BDEHIN	BEHIND
BBLLUU	BULBUL	BCIINO	BIONIC, NIOBIC	BDEHLO	BEHOLD
BBLNUY	NUBBLY	BCIINU	INCUBI	BDEHOT	HOTBED
BBLOWY	BY-BLOW, WOBBLY	BCIIOP	BIOPIC	BDEHSU	BUSHED
BBLRSU	BLURBS	BCIIOT	BIOTIC	BDEIIR	BIRDIE, BRIDIE
BBLRUY	RUBBLY	BCILMS	CLIMBS	BDEIKL	BILKED
BBMRUY	BRUMBY	BCILPU	PUBLIC	BDEILL	BILLED
BBNNOO	BONBON	BCIMOR	BROMIC	BDEILO	BOILED, BOLIDE
BBNSUY	SNUBBY	BCIMSU	CUBISM	BDEILR	BRIDLE
BBORTU	BURBOT	BCINOR	BICORN	BDEIMU	IMBUED
BBOSUY	BUS BOY	BCIORS	SORBIC	BDEINN	BINNED
BBRSUU	SUBURB	BCIRRU	RUBRIC	BDEINR	BINDER, INBRED, REBIND
BBSTUY	STUBBY	BCISTU	CUBIST, CUBITS		
BCDEEK	BEDECK	BCKLOS	BLOCKS	BDEINT	IN DEBT
BCDEIO	BODICE	BCMOOS	COMBOS	BDEIOR	BORIDE
BCDEKU	BUCKED	BCMORY	CORYMB	BDEIOS	BODIES
BCDEMO	COMBED	BCMRSU	CRUMBS	BDEIPS	BIPEDS
BCDERU	CURBED	BCMRUY	CRUMBY	BDEIRS	DEBRIS
BCDIOU	CUBOID	BCNOOR	BRONCO	BDEIRU	BURIED
BCEEHR	BREECH	BCNOTU	COBNUT	BDEIRV	VERBID
BCEEKT	BECKET	BCNOUY	BOUNCY	BDEIST	BEDSIT, BIDETS, DEBITS
BCEEMO	BECOME	BCOOWY	COWBOY		
BCEEQU	QUEBEC	BCRSSU	SCRUBS	BDEISU	BUSIED
BCEHLN	BLENCH	BDDDEE	BEDDED	BDEKLU	BULKED
BCEHOR	BROCHE	BDDDEU	BUDDED	BDEKNU	BUNKED, DEBUNK
BCEHRU	CHERUB	BDDEER	BEDDER	BDEKOO	BOOKED
BCEIKR	BICKER	BDDEGU	BUDGED	BDEKSU	BUSKED
BCEIOX	ICEBOX	BDDEIN	BIDDEN	BDELNO	BLONDE
				BDELNS	BLENDS

BDELNU	BUNDLE	BDLOUY	DOUBLY	BEENOR	ENROBE
BDELOR	BOLDER	BDNOOY	NOBODY	BEENRU	REUBEN
BDELOT	BOLTED	BDNOSU	BOUNDS	BEENTU	BUTENE
BDELOU	DOUBLE	BDOORS	BROODS	BEEOOT	BOOTEE
BDELOW	BOWLED	BDOORY	BROODY	BEEOPP	PEEPBO
BDEMMU	BUMMED	BDORWY	BYWORD	BEEORY	OBEYER
BDEMNU	NUMBED	BDOSTU	DOUBTS	BEERRW	BREWER
BDEMOO	BOOMED	BEEEFL	FEEBLE	BEERST	BERETS
BDEMOY	EMBODY	BEEELT	BEETLE	BEERTT	BETTER
BDEMPU	BUMPED	BEEEMS	BESEEM	BEERTV	BREVET
BDEMRU	DUMBER	BEEERZ	BREEZE	BEERYZ	BREEZY
BDENNU	UNBEND	BEEFIL	BELIEF	BEFFRU	BUFFER, REBUFF
BDENOY	BEYOND	BEEFLL	BEFELL	BEFFTU	BUFFET
BDENRU	BURDEN, BURNED	BEEFLY	FEEBLY	BEFILM	FIMBLE
BDENSU	SUNBED	BEEFOR	BEFORE	BEFILO	FOIBLE
BDEOOT	BOOTED	BEEFRT	BEREFT	BEFIRS	FIBRES
BDEOOZ	BOOZED	BEEGLS	GLEBES	BEFLMU	FUMBLE
BDEOPP	BOPPED	BEEGNO	BEGONE	BEFLOO	BEFOOL
BDEOPR	PROBED	BEEGNR	BERGEN	BEFLOU	BEFOUL
BDEORR	BORDER	BEEGRS	GREBES	BEFLRY	BELFRY
BDEORS	DESORB	BEEGRT	EGBERT	BEGGII	BIGGIE
BDEORT	DEBTOR	BEEGRU	BURGEE	BEGGIR	BIGGER
BDEOSS	BOSSED	BEEHIR	HERBIE	BEGGLO	BOGGLE
BDEOUY	BUOYED	BEEHLT	BETHEL	BEGGRU	BUGGER
BDEPRU	BURPED	BEEHOP	PHOEBE	BEGILO	OBLIGE
BDERRU	BURRED	BEEHOV	BEHOVE	BEGILR	GERBIL
BDESSU	BUSSED	BEEHRW	HEBREW	BEGILS	BILGES
BDESTU	BUSTED, DEBUTS	BEEHRY	HEREBY	BEGINN	BENIGN, BINGEN
BDESUU	SUBDUE	BEEHST	BEHEST	BEGINO	BIOGEN, GIBEON
BDETTU	BUTTED	BEEILR	BELIER	BEGINR	BERING
BDEUZZ	BUZZED	BEEILZ	BELIZE	BEGINS	BEINGS, BINGES
BDFIOR	FORBID	BEEINR	BERNIE	BEGIOO	BOOGIE
BDGIIN	BIDING	BEEIRT	BERTIE	BEGIOS	BOGIES
BDGIIR	BRIGID	BEEIRZ	BEZIER	BEGIOU	BOUGIE
BDGINO	BODING	BEEISS	BESSIE	BEGLNO	BELONG
BDHIRY	HYBRID	BEEISV	BEVIES	BEGLNU	BLUNGE, BUNGLE
BDIILO	LIBIDO	BEEISW	BE WISE	BEGLOS	GLOBES
BDIIMR	MIDRIB	BEEISX	IBEXES	BEGLOT	GOBLET
BDIITT	TIDBIT	BEEKRU	REBUKE	BEGLRU	BUGLER, BURGLE
BDIKNO	BODKIN	BEELLS	BELLES	BEGLSU	BUGLES, BULGES
BDILNS	BLINDS	BEELMM	EMBLEM	BEGMSU	BEGUMS
BDILNU	DUBLIN	BEELNO	LEOBEN	BEGNOY	BYGONE
BDILOY	BODILY	BEELNS	BELSEN	BEGOPX	PEG BOX
BDILSU	BUILDS	BEELPS	BLEEPS	BEGORU	BROGUE
BDIMNO	BODMIN	BEELRS	REBELS	BEGOSY	BOGEYS
BDIMOR	MORBID	BEELRT	BELTER, TREBLE	BEGRRU	BURGER
BDINNU	UNBIND	BEELRY	BERLEY	BEGRSU	BRUGES
BDIOTU	OUTBID	BEELSV	BEVELS	BEHILS	ISHBEL
BDIRTU	TURBID	BEELXY	BEXLEY	BEHILT	BLITHE
BDLLOY	BOLDLY	BEEMMR	MEMBER	BEHINT	HENBIT
BDLMUY	DUMBLY	BEEMNR	BREMEN	BEHKOR	RHEBOK
BDLNOY	BLODYN	BEEMRS	EMBERS	BEHKRY	KHYBER
BDLOOS	BLOODS	BEEMSU	BEMUSE	BEHLMU	HUMBLE
BDLOOY	BLOODY, OLD BOY	BEENNT	BENNET	BEHLSU	BUSHEL

BEHLTY	BLYTHE	BELLOU	BOULLE, LOBULE	BEOPRS	PROBES
BEHMOR	HOMBRE	BELLOW	BELLOW	BEORRS	BORERS, RESORB
BEHMRU	HUMBER	BELLTU	BULLET	BEORRT	ROBERT
BEHNOR	HEBRON	BELMMU	MUMBLE	BEORST	OSBERT, SORBET,
BEHOOS	HOBOES	BELMNY	EMBLYN		STROBE
BEHORT	BOTHER	BELMOY	EMBOLY	BEORSU	BOURSE
BEHRST	BERTHS	BELMRU	LUMBER, RUMBLE	BEORSW	BOWERS, BOWSER,
BEHRTU	HUBERT	BELMTU	TUMBLE		BROWSE
BEHSSU	BUSHES	BELNNY	BLENNY	BEORSX	BOXERS
BEIILL	BILLIE	BELNOR	NOBLER	BEORTV	OBVERT
BEIISS	IBISES	BELNOS	NOBLES	BEORTY	BY ROTE
BEIKLR	BILKER	BELNOZ	BENZOL	BEORVV	BOVVER
BEIKOO	BOOKIE	BELNTU	UNBELT	BEORWY	BOWERY, BOWYER
BEILLS	LIBELS	BELNYZ	BENZYL	BEOSSS	BOSSES, OBSESS
BEILLT	BILLET	BELOOR	BOLERO	BEOSTU	OBTUSE
BEILMN	NIMBLE	BELOOT	BOOTLE	BEOSTW	BESTOW
BEILMO	MOBILE	BELOPU	PUEBLO	BEPRSU	SUPERB
BEILMR	LIMBER	BELORT	BOLTER	BERSTU	BRUTES, BUSTER,
BEILMW	WIMBLE	BELORU	ROUBLE		TUBERS
BEILMY	BLIMEY	BELORW	BLOWER, BOWLER	BERSUX	EXURBS
BEILNR	BERLIN	BELOSS	LESBOS	BERSUY	BUYERS
BEILNU	NUBILE	BELOSU	BLOUSE, BOULES,	BERTTU	BUTTER
BEILNY	BY-LINE		OBELUS	BERTWY	WYBERT
BEILOR	BOILER	BELOSW	BOWELS, ELBOWS	BERUZZ	BUZZER
BEILOS	ISOBEL	BELOTT	BOTTLE	BESSTU	SUBSET
BEIMOV	B-MOVIE	BELRRU	BURLER	BESTTU	BUTTES
BEIMOZ	ZOMBIE	BELRSU	RUBLES	BESUZZ	BUZZES
BEIMRT	TIMBER, TIMBRE	BELRSY	BERYLS	BFFIIN	BIFFIN
BEIMRU	ERBIUM, IMBRUE	BELRTU	BUTLER	BFFINO	BOFFIN
BEINNO	BENONI, BONNIE	BELRTY	TREBLY	BFFLSU	BLUFFS
BEINOR	BONIER	BELRUY	BURLEY	BFGOOW	FOGBOW
BEINOT	BENITO	BELSTU	BLUEST, BUSTLE,	BFIILR	FIBRIL
BEINOV	BOVINE		SUBLET, SUBTLE	BFIINR	FIBRIN
BEINRU	BRUNEI	BELTUU	TUBULE	BFINOW	BOWFIN
BEINTT	BITTEN	BEMNOT	ENTOMB	BFLOOT	BOTOLF
BEIORS	RIBOSE	BEMNOW	BOWMEN, ENWOMB	BFLOTU	BOTULF
BEIOTW	BOW TIE	BEMNRU	NUMBER	BFLOTY	BOTFLY
BEIQSU	BISQUE	BEMORS	SOMBRE	BFLSYY	FLYBYS
BEIRRU	BURIER	BEMORY	EMBRYO	BGGIIW	BIGWIG
BEIRRY	BRIERY	BEMOSS	BESOMS, EMBOSS	BGHIIL	GHIBLI
BEIRST	BESTIR, BISTRE, TRIBES	BEMPRU	BUMPER	BGHILT	BLIGHT
BEIRSU	BRUISE, BUSIER,	BENNOT	BONNET	BGHIRT	BRIGHT
	RUBIES	BENNTU	UNBENT	BGHIST	BIGHTS
BEIRTT	BITTER	BENOOR	BORNEO, OBERON	BGHMUU	HUMBUG
BEIRTU	BEIRUT	BENORR	REBORN	BGHOSU	BOUGHS
BEJJUU	JUJUBE	BENORT	BRETON	BGHOTU	BOUGHT
BEJLMU	JUMBLE	BENORZ	BONZER, BRONZE	BGHRSU	BURGHS
BEKLOS	BLOKES	BENOST	T-BONES	BGIIJN	JIBING
BEKNOR	BROKEN	BENOTY	BETONY	BGIIKN	BIKING
BEKNRU	BUNKER	BENRRU	BURNER	BGIINT	BITING
BEKOOT	BETOOK	BENRTU	BURNET	BGIIRT	BIRGIT, BRIGIT
BEKORR	BROKER	BEOORR	OREBRO	BGILLY	GLIBLY
BEKOST	BOSKET	BEOORT	REBOOT	BGILNO	GLOBIN, GOBLIN
BEKRSU	BUSKER	BEOORZ	BOOZER	BGINNO	BONING, NINGBO
		BEOPRR	PROBER	BGINOO	BOOING

BGINOR	BORING, ROBING	BILOOT	LOBITO
BGINOS	BINGOS, GIBSON	BILOTW	BLOW IT!
BGINOW	BOWING	BILRTY	TRILBY
BGINOX	BOXING	BILRUW	WILBUR
BGINSU	BUSING	BILSSY	SIBYLS
BGINTU	TUBING	BILSUY	BUSILY
BGINUY	BUYING	BIMNSU	NIMBUS
BGIOPT	BIG TOP	BIMSTU	SUBMIT
BGIORV	VIBORG	BINNOR	INBORN
BGIOST	BIGOTS	BINNOU	BUNION
BGLNOO	OBLONG	BINOOT	BONITO
BGMOSU	GUMBOS	BINORS	ROBINS
BGNOOS	BONGOS	BINORT	BRITON
BGORSU	BURGOS	BINORY	BRIONY
BGORVY	VYBORG	BINOSS	BISONS
BHIKOS	KIBOSH	BIOORZ	BORZOI
BHILSU	BLUISH	BIOOST	OBOIST
BHIMTU	THIMBU	BIOPSY	BIOPSY
BHIOPS	BISHOP	BIORST	BISTRO, ORBITS
BHIOSY	BOYISH	BIOSTU	SUBITO
BHIRST	BIRTHS	BIOTTW	TWO-BIT
BHIRSU	HUBRIS	BIQSSU	SQUIBS
BHIRSY	HYBRIS	BIRTTU	TURBIT
BHITWY	WHITBY	BJLOOT	JOB LOT
BHLMUY	HUMBLY	BKLMOO	LOMBOK
BHLOSY	BOLSHY	BKMNUU	BUNKUM
BHMSTU	THUMBS	BKNPUU	BUNK-UP
BHOOOO	BOOHOO	BKOORS	BROOKS
BHOOPS	PHOBOS	BKORTU	TOBRUK
BHOOST	BOOTHS	BLLORY	BROLLY
BHORST	THROBS	BLMNUY	NUMBLY
BHOTTU	BHUTTO	BLMOOS	BLOOMS
BHRSSU	SHRUBS	BLMOSY	SYMBOL
BIIIKN	BIKINI	BLMRUY	RUMBLY
BIINOT	BIOTIN	BLNOOS	BOLSON
BIIORV	VIBRIO	BLNOOT	BOLTON
BIISTV	VIBIST	BLNOTU	UNBOLT
BIITTT	TITBIT	BLOOTT	BLOTTO
BIJLOT	BITOLJ	BLOPUW	BLOW-UP
BIKKRY	KIRKBY	BLOSWY	BLOWSY
BIKLNS	BLINKS	BLOWYZ	BLOWZY
BIKLNU	IN BULK	BLRRUY	BLURRY
BIKNSU	BUSKIN	BLSTUY	SUBTLY
BILLNO	BILLON	BMNOOT	BON MOT
BILLNU	LUBLIN	BMOORS	BROOMS
BILLOW	BILLOW	BMOOSS	BOSOMS
BILLOY	BILLY-O	BMOOSY	BOSOMY
BILMNY	NIMBLY	BMOOTT	BOTTOM
BILMOS	LIMBOS	BMOOTY	TOMBOY
BILMPS	BLIMPS	BNNORU	UNBORN
BILMSU	LIMBUS	BNOORS	OSBORN, ROBSON
BILNOS	LISBON	BNOOST	BOSTON
BILNOY	BONILY	BNORSU	BOURNS, SUBORN
BILNTZ	BLINTZ	BNORSW	BROWNS

BNORTU	BRUTON, BURTON
BNORYY	BRYONY
BNORYZ	BRONZY
BNOSSU	BOSUNS
BNOSUW	SUNBOW
BNOTTU	BUTTON
BNOTUX	BUXTON
BNOTUY	BOUNTY
BOOOTT	TO BOOT
BOOPTY	POTBOY
BOORRW	BORROW
BOORST	ROBOTS
BOOSST	BOOSTS
BOOWWW	BOWWOW
BORRSU	BURROS
BORRUW	BURROW
BORSTU	ROBUST
BORTTU	TURBOT
BOTUUY	BUYOUT
BPSTUU	BUST-UP
BRSSTU	BURSTS
BSSSUY	BYSSUS
CCCDIO	COCCID
CCCILY	CYCLIC
CCCOSU	COCCUS
CCCOXY	COCCYX
CCDEIR	CEDRIC, CERDIC
CCDEKO	COCKED
CCDELY	CYCLED
CCDEOT	DECOCT
CCEEHR	CRECHE
CCEEIL	CECILE
CCEEOR	COERCE
CCEHIL	CHICLE, CLICHE
CCEHIO	CHOICE, ECHOIC
CCEHIT	HECTIC
CCEHKS	CHECKS
CCEHKY	CHECKY
CCEHLN	CLENCH
CCEHLO	CLOCHE
CCEHOS	COSECH
CCEIIL	CILICE, ICICLE
CCEILR	CIRCLE, CLERIC
CCEILT	CELTIC
CCEILY	CECILY, CICELY
CCEINS	SCENIC
CCEIOR	CICERO
CCEIPT	PECTIC
CCEIRS	CERCIS
CCEIRT	CRETIC
CCEKLO	COCKLE
CCELSY	CYCLES
CCENOS	SCONCE
CCEORS	SOCCER

CCERSU	CERCUS	CDDEEI	DECIDE, DE-ICED	CDEHIU	HEIDUC
CCHHII	CHICHI	CDDEEK	DECKED	CDEHKO	CHOKED, HOCKED
CCHHRU	CHURCH	CDDEEO	DECODE	CDEHNR	DRENCH
CCHIKS	CHICKS	CDDEEU	DEDUCE, DEUCED	CDEHOS	COSHED
CCHILN	CLINCH	CDDEHI	CHIDED	CDEHOU	DOUCHE
CCHILY	CHICLY	CDDEIU	CUDDIE	CDEIIK	DICKIE
CCHINO	COCHIN	CDDEKO	DOCKED	CDEIIR	DICIER
CCHIOR	CHORIC	CDDEKU	DUCKED	CDEIJU	JUICED
CCHIPU	HICCUP	CDDELO	CODDLE	CDEIKK	KICKED
CCHKOS	CHOCKS	CDDELU	CUDDLE	CDEIKL	LICKED
CCHKSU	CHUCKS	CDDEOR	CORDED	CDEIKM	MEDICK
CCHLTU	CLUTCH	CDDETU	DEDUCT	CDEIKN	NICKED
CCHNOY	CONCHY	CDDLOY	CLODDY	CDEIKP	PICKED
CCHNRU	CRUNCH	CDDLUY	CUDDLY	CDEIKR	DICKER, RICKED
CCHORS	SCORCH	CDEEER	DECREE, RECEDE	CDEIKS	SICKED
CCHORT	CROTCH	CDEEES	SECEDE	CDEIKT	TICKED
CCHORU	CROUCH	CDEEEX	EXCEED	CDEIKW	WICKED
CCHOST	SCOTCH	CDEEFN	FENCED	CDEILO	COILED, DOCILE
CCHRTU	CRUTCH	CDEEFT	DEFECT	CDEILS	SLICED
CCHSTU	SCUTCH	CDEEHO	ECHOED	CDEILT	DELICT
CCIILN	CLINIC	CDEEHT	ETCHED	CDEILU	DULCIE
CCIILT	CLITIC	CDEEHW	CHEWED	CDEIMN	MINCED
CCIINO	ICONIC	CDEEIL	DECILE	CDEIMO	MEDICO
CCIINP	PICNIC	CDEEIP	PIECED	CDEIMR	DERMIC
CCIINZ	ZINCIC	CDEEIR	DE-ICER	CDEIMS	MEDICS
CCIIRT	CITRIC, CRITIC	CDEEIT	DECEIT	CDEINO	COINED
CCIISV	CIVICS	CDEEIV	DEVICE	CDEINR	CINDER
CCIKLS	CLICKS	CDEEJT	DEJECT	CDEINU	INDUCE
CCIKRS	CRICKS	CDEEKL	DECKLE	CDEINW	WINCED
CCILNO	CLONIC	CDEEKN	NECKED	CDEIOP	COPIED
CCILTU	CULTIC	CDEEKO	DECOKE	CDEIOR	DORICE
CCIMOS	COMICS, COSMIC	CDEEKP	PECKED	CDEIOV	VOICED
CCIMRY	CYMRIC	CDEEKR	RECKED	CDEIPR	PRICED
CCINOS	CONICS	CDEENO	ENCODE	CDEIPS	SPICED
CCINSY	CYNICS	CDEENT	DECENT	CDEIPT	DEPICT
CCIOPT	COPTIC	CDEERS	CREEDS, SCREED	CDEIRS	CIDERS
CCIPRU	CUPRIC	CDEERU	REDUCE	CDEIRT	CREDIT, DIRECT
CCIRSU	CIRCUS	CDEERW	CREWED	CDEIRV	CERVID
CCISTY	CYSTIC	CDEESU	SEDUCE	CDEIRY	DRY ICE
CCKLOO	O'CLOCK	CDEETT	DETECT	CDEIST	EDICTS
CCKLOS	CLOCKS	CDEFFU	CUFFED	CDEKLO	LOCKED
CCKLSU	CLUCKS	CDEFII	DEIFIC	CDEKMO	MOCKED
CCKLUY	CLUCKY	CDEFKU	FUCKED	CDEKMU	MUCKED
CCKOOU	CUCKOO	CDEFNU	FECUND	CDEKNO	CONKED
CCKOPU	COCK-UP	CDEFOR	FORCED	CDEKOO	COOKED
CCKORS	CROCKS	CDEGGO	COGGED	CDEKOP	POCKED
CCLOTU	OCCULT	CDEGIN	CEDING	CDEKOR	CORKED, DOCKER,
CCNOOO	COCOON	CDEGIO	GEODIC		ROCKED
CCNORU	CONCUR	CDEGLU	CUDGEL	CDEKOS	SOCKED
CCOOOR	ROCOCO	CDEGOR	CODGER	CDEKOT	DOCKET
CCOPUY	OCCUPY	CDEHIM	CHIMED	CDEKRU	DUCKER, RUCKED
CCORSU	CROCUS	CDEHIN	INCHED	CDEKRY	DERYCK
CCOSTU	STUCCO	CDEHIR	CHIDER, HERDIC	CDEKSU	SUCKED
CCSSUU	CUSCUS	CDEHIT	ITCHED	CDEKTU	TUCKED

CDELLU	CULLED
CDELOO	COOLED
CDELOR	COLDER
CDELOS	CLOSED
CDELOY	CLOYED
CDELRU	CURDLE, CURLED
CDELTU	DULCET
CDEMOO	COMEDO
CDEMOY	COMEDY
CDENNO	CONNED
CDENOS	SECOND
CDENOT	DOCENT
CDENSU	DUNCES, SECUND
CDEOOP	COOPED
CDEOPP	COPPED
CDEORR	RECORD
CDEORS	CREDOS, DECORS, SCORED
CDEORW	CROWED
CDEOSU	ESCUDO
CDEOSY	DECOYS
CDEPPU	CUPPED
CDERRU	CRUDER
CDERSU	CURSED
CDERSY	CYDERS, DESCRY
CDERUV	CURVED
CDESSU	CUSSED
CDFINU	FUNDIC
CDFIOU	FUCOID
CDFIOY	CODIFY
CDGIIN	DICING
CDGINO	CODING
CDHIOR	ORCHID, RHODIC
CDHIRY	HYDRIC
CDHORS	CHORDS
CDIIIM	IMIDIC
CDIIIR	IRIDIC
CDIINT	INDICT
CDIIOY	IDIOCY
CDIISV	VISCID
CDIKNO	DICKON
CDIMOU	MUCOID
CDIMOY	CYMOID
CDIMSU	MUSCID
CDIMTU	DICTUM
CDINOO	CONOID
CDINOR	NORDIC
CDINSY	SYNDIC
CDINTU	INDUCT
CDIOSS	DISCOS
CDIPSU	CUPIDS, CUSPID
CDISSU	DISCUS
CDJNOU	JOCUND
CDLLOY	COLDLY

CDLOSS	SCOLDS
CDLOSU	CLOUDS
CDLOUY	CLOUDY
CDMNOO	CONDOM, MOD CON
CDMORS	CD-ROMS
CDNOOR	CONDOR, CORDON
CDOORT	DOCTOR
CDORSW	CROWDS
CEEEFL	FLEECE
CEEEGR	GREECE
CEEEHS	CHEESE
CEEELS	CLEESE
CEEENO	EOCENE
CEEFFO	COFFEE
CEEFFT	EFFECT
CEEFHL	FLECHE
CEEFIL	FELICE
CEEFIR	FIERCE, RECIFE
CEEFLY	FLEECY
CEEFNN	FENNEC
CEEFNR	FENCER
CEEFNS	FENCES
CEEFSU	FESCUE
CEEHIR	CHERIE
CEEHIS	SEICHE
CEEHKL	HECKLE
CEEHKS	CHEEKS
CEEHKY	CHEEKY
CEEHLR	LECHER
CEEHLY	LYCHEE
CEEHMS	SCHEME
CEEHNT	THENCE
CEEHNW	WHENCE
CEEHOR	COHERE, REECHO
CEEHOS	ECHOES
CEEHPS	CHEEPS, SPEECH
CEEHQU	CHEQUE
CEEHRS	CHEERS
CEEHRT	ETCHER
CEEHRU	EUCHRE
CEEHRW	CHEWER
CEEHRY	CHEERY
CEEHSW	ESCHEW
CEEHSY	CHEESY
CEEIKL	KIELCE
CEEILN	CELINE
CEEILS	SIECLE
CEEIMN	ICEMEN
CEEIMT	EMETIC
CEEINS	NIECES
CEEINT	ENTICE
CEEINU	EUNICE
CEEINV	EVINCE, VENICE
CEEIPR	PIECER, PIERCE, RECIPE

CEEIPS	PIECES, SPECIE
CEEIRS	CERISE
CEEIRT	RECITE, TIERCE
CEEIRU	ECURIE
CEEISS	ECESIS
CEEISX	EXCISE
CEEITX	EXCITE
CEEJRT	REJECT
CEEKNR	NECKER
CEEKPR	PECKER
CEEKRS	CREEKS
CEEKRT	ECKERT
CEELMO	CLEOME
CEELNR	CRENEL
CEELOR	CREOLE
CEELOU	COULEE
CEELOV	VELOCE
CEELRS	CREELS
CEELRT	TERCEL
CEELRV	CLEVER
CEELRW	CREWEL
CEELRY	CELERY
CEELST	SELECT
CEELSY	LYCEES
CEEMNT	CEMENT
CEEMNY	CYMENE
CEEMRR	MERCER
CEEMRT	CERMET
CEENOR	ENCORE
CEENPT	PECTEN
CEENRS	CENSER, SCREEN
CEENRT	CENTER, CENTRE, RECENT, TENREC
CEENSS	SCENES
CEEPRS	CREEPS
CEEPRT	RECEPT
CEEPRY	CREEPY
CEEPTX	EXCEPT, EXPECT
CEEPTY	ECTYPE
CEERSS	RECESS
CEERST	RESECT, SECRET
CEERSU	CEREUS, CERUSE, CREUSE, RESCUE, SECURE
CEERTT	TERCET
CEESSX	EXCESS
CEESUX	EXCUSE
CEFFIO	OFFICE
CEFFOR	COFFER
CEFHIS	CHIEFS
CEFHLT	FLETCH
CEFHNR	FRENCH
CEFIKL	FICKLE
CEFINT	INFECT
CEFINU	UNICEF
CEFIRR	FERRIC

CEFKLS	FLECKS
CEFKRU	FUCKER
CEFLOS	FO'C'SLE
CEFLST	CLEFTS
CEFNOR	CONFER
CEFORR	FORCER
CEFORS	FORCES, FRESCO
CEFRUW	CURFEW
CEGGPU	EGGCUP
CEGHIO	CHIGOE
CEGINR	CRINGE
CEGKOS	GECKOS
CEGLRY	CLERGY
CEGNOR	CONGER
CEGNOS	CONGES
CEGNOT	COGENT
CEGNTY	CYGNET
CEGORR	GROCER
CEHHIT	HI-TECH
CEHIIR	RICHIE
CEHIKY	HICKEY
CEHILN	LICHEN
CEHILS	CHILES, CHISEL
CEHIMS	CHIMES
CEHINP	PENCHI
CEHINR	ENRICH
CEHINS	CHINES, INCHES, NICHES
CEHINT	ETHNIC
CEHIOR	COHEIR, HEROIC
CEHIPR	CIPHER
CEHIQU	QUICHE
CEHIRR	RICHER
CEHIRS	RICHES
CEHIRT	THRICE
CEHIST	ETHICS, ITCHES
CEHISV	CHIVES
CEHITT	THETIC
CEHKLU	HUCKLE
CEHKOR	CHOKER, HOCKER
CEHKOS	CHOKES
CEHKOY	HOCKEY
CEHKST	SKETCH
CEHLOR	CHOLER
CEHLOT	CLOTHE
CEHLPS	SCHLEP
CEHLRY	CHERYL
CEHMOR	CHROME
CEHNOS	CHOSEN
CEHNOU	COHUNE
CEHNQU	QUENCH
CEHNRT	TRENCH
CEHNRW	WRENCH
CEHNST	STENCH

CEHNUU	EUNUCH
CEHOOS	CHOOSE
CEHORS	CHORES
CEHORT	HECTOR, ROCHET, TROCHE
CEHOSS	COSHES
CEHOTU	TOUCHE
CEHPRY	CYPHER
CEHPSY	PSYCHE
CEHRRY	CHERRY
CEHRTW	WRETCH
CEHRTY	CHERTY
CEHSST	CHESTS
CEHSTU	CHUTES, TUSCHE
CEHSTY	CHESTY, SCYTHE
CEHTTY	TETCHY
CEIIKS	CISKEI, SICKIE
CEIIKV	VICKIE
CEIILT	ELICIT
CEIILX	EXILIC
CEIINR	IRENIC
CEIINS	INCISE
CEIINT	INCITE
CEIISS	CISSIE
CEIIST	CITIES, ICIEST
CEIISV	CIVIES
CEIJNT	INJECT
CEIJSU	JUICES
CEIKKR	KICKER
CEIKLN	NICKEL
CEIKLP	PICKLE
CEIKLR	LICKER
CEIKLS	SICKLE
CEIKLT	KELTIC, TICKLE
CEIKMY	MICKEY
CEIKNR	NICKER
CEIKNS	SICKEN
CEIKOO	COOKIE
CEIKOS	KOSICE
CEIKPR	PICKER
CEIKPT	PICKET
CEIKRS	SICKER
CEIKRT	TICKER
CEIKRW	WICKER
CEIKRY	CRIKEY
CEIKTT	TICKET
CEIKTW	WICKET
CEILLO	COLLIE
CEILMS	CLIMES
CEILNO	CINEOL, NICOLE
CEILNP	PENCIL
CEILNS	CLINES
CEILNT	CLIENT, LENTIC
CEILNU	LUCIEN, NUCLEI

CEILNY	NICELY
CEILOO	COOLIE
CEILOP	POLICE
CEILOR	COILER, RECOIL
CEILPS	SPLICE
CEILPV	PELVIC
CEILQU	CLIQUE
CEILRS	RELICS, SLICER
CEILRT	RELICT
CEILSS	SLICES
CEILSU	SLUICE
CEILSV	CLEVIS
CEIMNO	INCOME
CEIMNR	MINCER
CEIMOX	MEXICO
CEIMPU	PUMICE
CEIMRS	CRIMES
CEIMRT	METRIC
CEIMRU	CERIUM
CEIMSU	MISCUE
CEINNO	CONNIE
CEINOR	COINER, ORCEIN
CEINOS	CONIES, COSINE, OSCINE
CEINOT	NOETIC, NOTICE
CEINOV	NOVICE
CEINPR	PINCER, PRINCE
CEINPT	INCEPT, PECTIN
CEINQU	CINQUE, QUINCE
CEINRT	CRETIN
CEINRW	WINCER
CEINST	INCEST, INSECT, NICEST
CEINSU	INCUSE
CEINSW	WINCES
CEINTY	NICETY
CEINWY	WINCEY
CEIOOZ	EOZOIC
CEIOPR	COPIER
CEIOPS	COPIES
CEIOPT	POETIC
CEIORS	COSIER
CEIORT	EROTIC
CEIORV	VOICER
CEIORW	COWRIE
CEIORZ	COZIER
CEIOSS	COSIES
CEIOSV	VOICES
CEIOTX	EXOTIC
CEIPPT	PEPTIC
CEIPRS	CRIPES, PRECIS, PRICES, SPICER
CEIPRY	PRICEY
CEIPSS	PISCES, SPICES
CEIPST	SEPTIC

CEIPTU	CUP TIE	CELORU	COLURE	CEORRW	CROWER
CEIQRU	CIRQUE	CELORV	CLOVER, VELCRO	CEORSS	CORSES, CROSSE, SCORES
CEIRRS	CRIERS	CELOSS	CLOSES	CEORST	CORSET, ESCORT, RECTOS, SCOTER, SECTOR
CEIRSS	CRISES	CELOST	CLOSET		
CEIRST	STERIC, TRICES	CELOSU	COLEUS	CEORSU	CEROUS, COURSE, SOURCE
CEIRSU	CRUISE	CELOSV	CLOVES		
CEIRTU	URETIC	CELOSX	SCOLEX	CEORSV	COVERS
CEIRVX	CERVIX	CELOSY	COLEYS	CEORSW	ESCROW
CEISTV	CIVETS	CELPUU	CUPULE	CEORTT	COTTER
CEJKOY	JOCKEY	CELRRU	CURLER	CEORTV	COVERT, VECTOR
CEJNOU	JOUNCE	CELRSU	ULCERS	CEORTX	CORTEX
CEJOOS	JOCOSE	CELRTU	CUTLER	CEOSST	COSSET
CEKKOP	KOPECK	CELRUW	CURLEW	CEOSSU	SCOUSE
CEKLOR	LOCKER	CELTTU	CUTLET	CEOSTT	OCTETS
CEKLOT	LOCKET	CELTUY	CUTELY	CEOSVY	COVEYS
CEKLRS	CLERKS	CEMNNO	CONMEN, NEM CON	CEPRSU	SPRUCE
CEKLSU	SUCKLE	CEMNOO	COME ON	CERSST	CRESTS
CEKMOR	MOCKER	CEMNOW	COWMEN	CERSSU	CRUSES, CURSES
CEKMRU	MUCKER	CEMNTU	CENTUM	CERSSW	SCREWS
CEKNOR	CONKER, RECKON	CEMOOS	COMOSE	CERSTU	CRUETS, RECTUS, TRUCES
CEKNSV	V-NECKS	CEMOPR	COMPER		
CEKOOR	COOKER	CEMORS	COMERS	CERSUV	CURVES
CEKOPT	POCKET	CEMOST	COMETS	CERSUX	CRUXES
CEKORR	CORKER, ROCKER	CEMOSY	CYMOSE	CERSWY	SCREWY
CEKORT	ROCKET	CEMOTU	TEMUCO	CERTTU	CUTTER
CEKOST	SOCKET	CEMRTU	RECTUM	CERTUV	CURVET
CEKPRU	PUCKER	CENNOS	NONCES	CESSSU	CUSSES
CEKPSS	SPECKS	CENOPS	PONCES	CESTTU	CUTEST
CEKRSU	SUCKER	CENOPU	POUNCE	CFFILS	CLIFFS
CEKRSW	WRECKS	CENOPY	PONCEY	CFFINO	COFFIN
CEKRTU	TUCKER	CENORR	CORNER	CFFOSS	SCOFFS
CELLOS	CELLOS	CENORS	CENSOR, CRONES	CFFOTU	CUTOFF
CELLOT	COLLET	CENORT	CORNET	CFFRSU	SCRUFF
CELLOU	LOCULE	CENORY	CORNEY	CFFSSU	SCUFFS
CELLOY	COLLEY	CENOSS	SCONES	CFGINU	FUNGIC
CELLRU	CULLER	CENOSU	OUNCES, UNESCO	CFHILN	FLINCH
CELLTU	CULLET	CENOSV	COVENS	CFHILT	FLITCH
CELMOO	COELOM	CENOSY	CONEYS	CFHLSY	FLYSCH
CELMOP	COMPEL	CENOVX	CONVEX	CFHOUU	FU-CHOU
CELMOR	CORMEL	CENOVY	CONVEY	CFIILM	FILMIC
CELMOY	COMELY	CENSST	SCENTS	CFIINN	FINNIC
CELMSU	MUSCLE	CENSSU	CENSUS	CFIIST	FISTIC
CELMUY	LYCEUM	CENSTY	ENCYST	CFIITY	CITIFY
CELNOR	CORNEL	CEOOPR	COOPER	CFIKLS	FLICKS
CELNOS	CLONES	CEOOTY	COYOTE, OOCYTE	CFILOR	FROLIC
CELNOV	CLOVEN	CEOPPR	COPPER	CFIMOR	FORMIC
CELNOY	CEYLON	CEOPRS	CORPSE	CFIMOT	COMFIT
CELNSU	UNCLES	CEOPRU	RECOUP	CFISTU	FUSTIC
CELNTU	LUCENT	CEOPSS	COPSES	CFKLOS	FLOCKS
CELOOR	COOLER	CEOPSU	COUPES	CFKLOY	FLOCKY
CELOOT	OCELOT	CEOQTU	COQUET	CFKORS	FROCKS
CELOPU	COUPLE	CEORRS	CORERS, CRORES, SCORER	CFKPUU	FUCK-UP
CELORS	CLOSER, CRESOL			CFORST	CROFTS
CELORT	LECTOR	CEORRT	RECTOR	CFRSUY	SCURFY

CGGLOY CLOGGY	CHIPRY CHIRPY	CIKNPY PYKNIC
CGHHOU CHOUGH	CHIPSY PHYSIC	CIKNSS SNICKS
CGHILT GLITCH	CHIPTY PITCHY	CIKNTU TUCK-IN
CGHIOT GOTHIC	CHIRST CHRIST	CIKNYZ ZINCKY
CGHORU GROUCH	CHIRUZ ZURICH	CIKPPU PICK-UP
CGHOSU COUGHS	CHISST SCHIST	CIKPRS PRICKS
CGIINT CITING	CHISTT STITCH	CIKRST STRICK, TRICKS
CGILNY CLINGY	CHISTW SWITCH	CIKRTU TURKIC
CGIMNO COMING, GNOMIC	CHITTW TWITCH	CIKRTY TRICKY
CGINOO COOING	CHITTY TITCHY	CIKSST STICKS
CGINOP COPING	CHJNOU CHONJU	CIKSTY STICKY
CGINOR CORING	CHKNSU CHUNKS	CILLSU CULLIS
CGINOW COWING	CHKNUY CHUNKY	CILNOP CLIP-ON
CGINOX COXING	CHKOSS SHOCKS	CILNOU UNCOIL
CGINRU CURING	CHKSSU SHUCKS	CILOPU OILCUP
CGINRY CRYING	CHLMOO MOLOCH	CILOPY POLICY
CGIORS CORGIS	CHLOOS SCHOOL	CILOSY COSILY
CGLLOY GLYCOL	CHLORS SCHORL	CILOYZ COZILY
CGLNOU UNCLOG	CHLOST CLOTHS	CILRSY LYRICS
CGNOOU CONGOU	CHLOSU SLOUCH	CILSUU LUCIUS
CGNSUY CYGNUS, SCUNGY	CHLRSU CHURLS	CIMMOS COMMIS
CHHOOS COHOSH	CHMMUY CHUMMY	CIMMOT COMMIT
CHIILL CHILLI	CHMOOS SMOOCH	CIMNOR MICRON
CHIILT LITCHI, LITHIC	CHMPSU CHUMPS	CIMNOU CONIUM
CHIINT CHITIN	CHMSTU SMUTCH	CIMNRU CRINUM
CHIKKO HICKOK	CHNOOP PONCHO	CIMOOS COSIMO
CHIKNO IN HOCK	CHNPUY PUNCHY	CIMOPY MYOPIC
CHIKNS CHINKS	CHNRSU CHURNS	CIMORS MICROS
CHIKOS HOICKS	CHOORT COHORT	CIMORU CORIUM
CHIKOT THICKO	CHOOSY CHOOSY	CIMOST SITCOM
CHIKRS KIRSCH	CHOPPY CHOPPY	CIMOTY COMITY
CHIKST KITSCH	CHOPUY POUCHY	CIMPRS SCRIMP
CHILLS CHILLS	CHORSU CHORUS	CIMRUU CURIUM
CHILLY CHILLY	CHOSUU SUCHOU	CIMSTY MYSTIC
CHILMO HOLMIC	CHOTUY TOUCHY	CINNOU NUNCIO
CHILOR ORCHIL	CHPSTU PUTSCH	CINOOP COIN-OP
CHILRY RICHLY	CHSSSU SCHUSS	CINOPT PONTIC
CHIMNU MUNICH	CHSWYZ SCHWYZ	CINORT CITRON
CHIMOR HORMIC	CIIIRT IRITIC	CINORZ ZIRCON
CHIMRS CHRISM, SMIRCH	CIIKKN KICK IN	CINOSS SCIONS
CHIMSS SCHISM	CIILMU CILIUM	CINOST TOCSIN, TONICS
CHIMTY THYMIC	CIILSY SICILY	CINOSU COUSIN
CHINNO INCHON	CIIMMS MIMICS	CINQUY QUINCY
CHINOP PHONIC	CIIMOT MIOTIC	CINSTU TUNICS
CHINOT CHITON	CIIMTV VICTIM	CIOOPT OCTOPI
CHINRU URCHIN	CIINOR IRONIC	CIOORT OCTROI
CHINST SNITCH	CIINOT TICINO	CIOPRT TROPIC
CHINTZ CHINTZ	CIINRT CITRIN, NITRIC	CIOPST OPTICS, TOPICS
CHIOPT PHOTIC	CIIRSS CRISIS	CIORSU CURIOS
CHIORS CHOIRS, ORCHIS	CIIRTV VITRIC	CIORTT TRICOT
CHIORT THORIC	CIKLSS SLICKS	CIORTV VICTOR
CHIOST SOTHIC	CIKLSY SICKLY	CIOSST STOICS
CHIPPY CHIPPY	CIKNOT ON TICK	CIOSTU COITUS
CHIPRS CHIRPS	CIKNPU UNPICK	CIPRSS CRISPS

CIPRST	SCRIPT	CMSTUU	SCUTUM	DDEEGW	WEDGED
CIPRSY	CRISPY	CNNOOR	CONNOR	DDEEHL	HEDDLE
CIRRSU	CIRRUS	CNOOPU	COUPON	DDEEHR	HERDED
CIRSTT	STRICT	CNOORT	CROTON	DDEEIL	ELIDED
CIRSTU	CITRUS, CURTIS,	CNOOST	NOSTOC, ONCOST	DDEEIN	DENIED, INDEED,
RICTUS, RUSTIC		CNOOTT	COTTON		NEDDIE
CIRTTY	YTTRIC	CNOOTY	TYCOON	DDEEIR	DERIDE
CKKNOS	KNOCKS	CNOOVY	CONVOY	DDEEIS	EDDIES
CKLNOU	UNLOCK	CNORSS	SCORNS	DDEEIT	DIETED, EDITED,
CKLNUY	CLUNKY	CNORSW	CROWNS		TEDDIE
CKLOPU	LOCKUP	CNOSTU	COUNTS, TUCSON	DDEELM	MEDDLE
CKLPSU	PLUCKS	CNOTUY	COUNTY	DDEELP	PEDDLE
CKLPUY	PLUCKY	COOPRS	SCROOP	DDEELR	ELDRED
CKMOPU	MOCK-UP	COOPSS	SCOOPS	DDEELU	DELUDE, DUELED,
CKMOSS	SMOCKS	COOPTU	COP-OUT		ELUDED
CKNORU	UNCORK	COOPWX	COWPOX	DDEELV	DELVED
CKNTUU	UNTUCK	COPRSU	CORPUS, CROUPS	DDEELW	WELDED
CKOORS	CROOKS	COPSUY	COYPUS	DDEEMN	MENDED
CKOSST	STOCKS	CORRSU	CURSOR	DDEEMO	DEMODE
CKOSTY	STOCKY	CORSTU	COURTS	DDEENN	DENNED
CKRSTU	STRUCK, TRUCKS	CORTUY	OUTCRY	DDEENP	DEPEND
CKRSUU	RUCKUS	COSSTU	SCOUTS	DDEENR	REDDEN
CLLOOY	COOLLY	COTTUU	CUTOUT	DDEENT	DENTED, TENDED
CLLORS	SCROLL	CPRSTY	CRYPTS	DDEENU	DENUDE, DUDEEN,
CLMNOU	COLUMN	CPRSUY	CYPRUS		DUNDEE, ENDUED
CLMOPY	COMPLY	CPSTUU	CUTUPS	DDEENV	VENDED
CLMOSU	LOCUMS	CRRSUY	SCURRY	DDEENW	WENDED
CLMPSU	CLUMPS	CRSSTU	CRUSTS	DDEEOR	ERODED
CLMPUY	CLUMPY	CRSTUY	CRUSTY, CURTSY	DDEERR	REDDER
CLMSUY	CLUMSY, MUSCLY	CRSUVY	SCURVY	DDEERT	TEDDER
CLNOOS	COLONS	CSUYZZ	SCUZZY	DDEEUX	EXUDED
CLNOOY	COLONY	DDDEEI	EDDIED	DDEFFO	DOFFED
CLNOSU	CLONUS, CONSUL	DDDEEW	WEDDED	DDEFGU	FUDGED
CLNOSW	CLOWNS	DDDEGO	DODGED	DDEFIL	FIDDLE
CLNRUU	UNCURL	DDDEIK	KIDDED	DDEFLO	FOLDED
CLOORU	COLOUR	DDDEIL	DIDDLE, LIDDED	DDEFLU	FUDDLE
CLOSSW	SCOWLS	DDDEIR	RIDDED	DDEFNU	FUNDED
CLOSTU	CLOUTS, LOCUST	DDDELO	DODDLE	DDEFOR	FODDER, FORDED
CLOSTY	COSTLY	DDDEMU	MUDDED	DDEFRY	FREDDY
CLPRUU	CURL UP	DDDENO	NODDED	DDEGGO	DOGGED
CLPSTU	SCULPT	DDDEOP	PODDED	DDEGIL	GILDED, GLIDED
CLRTUY	CURTLY	DDDEOR	DODDER	DDEGIR	GIRDED, RIDGED
CLSSUU	SULCUS	DDDEOS	SODDED	DDEGIU	GUIDED
CMMNOO	COMMON	DDEEEH	HEEDED	DDEGJU	JUDGED
CMMRUY	CRUMMY	DDEEEM	DEEMED	DDEGLO	LODGED
CMMSUY	SCUMMY	DDEEEN	NEEDED	DDEGMO	DODGEM
CMNOSY	SYNCOM	DDEEES	SEEDED	DDEGNU	NUDGED
CMOOOR	COMORO	DDEEEW	WEEDED	DDEGOR	DODGER
CMOOSS	COSMOS	DDEEFI	DEFIED	DDEGOS	DODGES
CMOOSW	MOSCOW	DDEEFN	DEFEND, FENDED	DDEGRU	DRUDGE
CMOSTU	CUSTOM	DDEEFU	FEUDED	DDEHIN	HIDDEN
CMOSUU	MUCOUS	DDEEGH	HEDGED	DDEHIS	DISHED
CMPRSU	SCRUMP	DDEEGL	GELDED	DDEHLU	HUDDLE
CMRSSU	SCRUMS	DDEEGR	DREDGE	DDEHNO	HODDEN
				DDEHOO	HOODED

DDEIIK	KIDDIE	DDFILY	FIDDLY	DEEGGP	PEGGED
DDEIIO	IODIDE	DDHINO	HODDIN	DEEGHR	HEDGER
DDEIIV	DIVIDE	DDHOSY	SHODDY	DEEGHS	HEDGES
DDEIKR	KIDDER	DDIIKK	DIK-DIK	DEEGIR	EDGIER
DDEILM	MIDDLE	DDILNR	DIRNDL	DEEGLL	GELLED
DDEILP	PIDDLE	DDILOS	DILDOS	DEEGLN	LEGEND
DDEILR	RIDDLE	DDILTY	TIDDLY	DEEGLP	PLEDGE
DDEILS	SIDLED	DDIOOS	DO-SI-DO	DEEGLR	LEDGER
DDEIMM	DIMMED	DDIOPY	DIPODY	DEEGLS	LEDGES, SLEDGE
DDEIMN	MIDDEN, MINDED	DDIORS	SORDID	DEEGLU	DELUGE
DDEIMS	DESMID	DDIOTU	OUTDID	DEEGMM	GEMMED
DDEINN	DINNED	DDIOTY	ODDITY	DEEGMR	MERGED
DDEINR	RIDDEN	DDIRSU	DRUIDS	DEEGNO	ON EDGE
DDEINW	WINDED	DDLPUY	PUDDLY	DEEGNR	GENDER
DDEIOV	DEVOID, VOIDED	DDMMUU	DUMDUM	DEEGNU	DENGUE
DDEIPP	DIPPED	DDNOOS	ODDS-ON	DEEGRV	VERGED
DDEIPR	PRIDED	DDOOOO	DOO-DOO	DEEGRY	GREEDY, GREYED
DDEIRR	RIDDER	DEEEFR	FEEDER, REEFED	DEEGSW	WEDGES
DDEITY	TIDYED	DEEEGR	DEGREE	DEEGSZ	SZEGED
DDEJRU	JUDDER	DEEEHL	HEELED	DEEHLP	HELPED
DDEKNU	DUNKED	DEEEHR	HEEDER	DEEHLY	HEDLEY
DDELLO	DOLLED	DEEEJR	JEERED	DEEHMM	HEMMED
DDELLU	DULLED	DEEEKL	KEELED	DEEHMS	MESHED
DDELMO	MOLDED	DEEEKN	KEENED	DEEHRR	HERDER
DDELMU	MUDDLE	DEEEKP	PEEKED	DEEHRT	THREE-D
DDELNO	NODDLE	DEEEKR	REEKED	DEEHSW	SHEWED
DDELOO	DOODLE	DEEELN	NEEDLE	DEEILN	ELINED, LEIDEN
DDELOR	LORDED	DEEELP	PEELED	DEEILR	RELIED
DDELOT	TODDLE	DEEELR	LEERED, REELED	DEEILS	DIESEL, SEDILE
DDELPU	PUDDLE	DEEELT	DELETE	DEEILV	LEVIED, VEILED
DDELRU	RUDDLE	DEEEMR	REDEEM	DEEILX	EXILED
DDELUY	DUDLEY	DEEEMS	SEEMED	DEEILY	EYELID
DDEMNO	EDMOND	DEEEMT	TEEMED	DEEIMP	IMPEDE
DDEMNU	EDMUND	DEEENP	DEEPEN	DEEIMS	DEMISE
DDEMOO	DOOMED	DEEENV	VENDEE	DEEINN	DENNIE, INDENE
DDEMPU	DUMPED	DEEEPP	PEEPED	DEEINR	DENIER, EDIRNE,
DDENNO	DONNED	DEEEPR	DEEPER, PEERED		NEREID, REINED
DDENNU	DUNNED	DEEEPS	SEEPED	DEEINS	DENISE
DDENOR	DONDER, DRONED	DEEEPV	PEEVED	DEEINV	ENDIVE, ENVIED,
DDENOS	SODDEN	DEEERS	SEEDER		VEINED
DDENOW	DOWNED	DEEERV	VEERED	DEEIPP	DIEPPE
DDENOY	DYNODE	DEEERW	WEEDER	DEEIPS	ESPIED
DDENSU	SUDDEN	DEEFGL	FLEDGE	DEEIRS	DESIRE, RESIDE
DDEOOS	DODOES	DEEFIL	DEFILE	DEEIRT	DIETER
DDEOOW	WOODED	DEEFIN	DEFINE	DEEIRU	UREIDE
DDEORW	WORDED	DEEFIR	DEFIER	DEEIRV	DERIVE
DDEOSS	DOSSED	DEEFLL	FELLED	DEEIRW	DEWIER
DDEOST	ODDEST	DEEFLU	FUELED	DEEISS	SEISED
DDEOSU	DOUSED	DEEFLX	FLEXED	DEEISV	DEVISE, SIEVED
DDEOSW	DOWSED	DEEFNR	FENDER	DEEISZ	SEIZED
DDEOTT	DOTTED	DEEFRT	RED EFT	DEEITX	EXITED
DDERRU	RUDDER	DEEFSU	DEFUSE	DEEITY	TIE-DYE
DDERSU	UDDERS	DEEFZZ	FEZZED	DEEIVW	VIEWED
DDESTU	DUSTED	DEEGGL	LEGGED	DEEJKR	JERKED
		DEEGGL	LEGGED	DEEJLL	JELLED

DEEJRU	DE JURE	DEEORT	TEREDO	DEFINS	FIENDS
DEEJST	JESTED	DEEORZ	ZEROED	DEFIOO	FOODIE
DEEJTT	JETTED	DEEOTT	ODETTE	DEFIOT	FOETID
DEEKNN	KENNED	DEEOTV	DEVOTE, VETOED	DEFIRV	FERVID
DEEKOV	EVOKED	DEEPPP	PEPPED	DEFIST	SIFTED
DEEKPR	PERKED	DEEPRU	PUREED	DEFITT	FITTED
DEEKSW	SKEWED	DEEPRY	PREYED	DEFIZZ	FIZZED
DEELLW	WELLED	DEEPSS	SPEEDS	DEFKNU	FUNKED
DEELLY	YELLED	DEEPSW	SPEWED	DEFKOR	FORKED
DEELMT	MELTED	DEEPSY	SPEEDY	DEFLNO	ENFOLD, FONDLE
DEELMY	MEDLEY	DEEPTT	PETTED	DEFLOO	FOOLED
DEELNR	LENDER	DEEPTU	DEPUTE	DEFLOR	FOLDER
DEELNU	ELUNED	DEEQUU	QUEUED	DEFLOT	LOFTED
DEELNW	DELWEN, WEDELN	DEERST	DESERT, RESTED	DEFLOU	FOULED
DEELOP	ELOPED	DEERSU	REUSED	DEFLOW	FLOWED, WOLFED
DEELPT	PELTED	DEERSV	SERVED, VERSED	DEFLRU	FURLED
DEELPY	DEEPLY, YELPED	DEERTX	DEXTER	DEFLTU	FLUTED
DEELRS	ELDERS	DEERVV	REVVED	DEFLTY	DEFTLY
DEELRU	ELUDER	DEESST	STEEDS	DEFMOR	DEFORM, FORMED
DEELRV	DELVER	DEESSW	SWEDES	DEFNOR	FONDER
DEELRW	WELDER	DEESTT	DETEST, TESTED	DEFNOU	FONDUE
DEELST	ELDEST	DEESTV	VESTED	DEFNRU	REFUND
DEELSW	SLEWED	DEESTW	STEWED, TWEEDS	DEFOOR	ROOFED
DEELTU	TELEDU	DEETTV	VETTED	DEFRRU	FURRED
DEELUX	DE LUXE	DEETTW	WETTED	DEFRSU	SURFED
DEEMNR	MENDER	DEETWY	TWEEDY	DEFRTU	TURFED
DEEMOT	DEMOTE	DEFFHU	HUFFED	DEFSSU	FUSSED
DEEMOW	MEOWED	DEFFIM	MIFFED	DEFTTU	TUFTED
DEEMPR	PERMED	DEFFIR	DIFFER	DEFUZZ	FUZZED
DEEMPT	TEMPED	DEFFLU	DUFFEL, LUFFED	DEGGHO	HOGGED
DEEMRT	TERMED	DEFFMU	MUFFED	DEGGHU	HUGGED
DEEMRU	DEMURE	DEFFNO	OFFEND	DEGGIJ	JIGGED
DEEMRY	REMEDY	DEFFOR	DOFFER	DEGGIN	EDGING
DEEMSS	MESSED	DEFFPU	PUFFED	DEGGIP	PIGGED
DEENNP	PENNED	DEFFRU	DUFFER	DEGGIR	DIGGER, RIGGED
DEENNT	NEEDN'T	DEFGGO	FOGGED	DEGGIU	DUGGIE
DEENOP	OPENED	DEFGIR	FRIDGE	DEGGIW	WIGGED
DEENOR	DOREEN, REDONE	DEFGIT	FIDGET, GIFTED	DEGGJO	JOGGED
DEENOS	ODENSE	DEFGLO	GELDOF	DEGGJU	JUGGED
DEENOT	DENOTE	DEFGOO	GOOFED	DEGGLO	DOGLEG, LOGGED
DEENPX	EXPEND	DEFGOR	FORGED	DEGGLU	LUGGED
DEENRR	RENDER	DEFHIS	FISHED	DEGGMU	MUGGED
DEENRS	DENSER, SENDER	DEFHOO	HOOFED	DEGGOR	DOGGER, GORGED
DEENRT	RENTED, TENDER	DEFIKN	KNIFED	DEGGOT	TOGGED
DEENRU	ENDURE	DEFILL	FILLED	DEGGOU	GOUGED
DEENRV	DENVER, NERVED	DEFILM	FILMED	DEGGPU	PUGGED
DEENSS	SENSED	DEFILO	FOILED	DEGGRU	GRUDGE, RUGGED
DEENST	NESTED, TENSED	DEFILR	RIFLED	DEGGRY	DREGGY
DEENSU	ENSUED	DEFILS	FIELDS	DEGGTU	TUGGED
DEENSW	SWEDEN	DEFILT	LIFTED	DEGHIN	HINGED
DEENTT	DETENT, NETTED	DEFIMR	FIRMED	DEGHIS	SIGHED
DEENTV	VENTED	DEFINN	FINNED	DEGHIW	HEDWIG
DEENTX	DENTEX, EXTEND	DEFINR	FINDER, FRIEND,	DEGHSU	GUSHED
DEEOPS	DEPOSE		REDFIN	DEGILL	GILLED

DEGILN	DINGLE	
DEGILO	GOLDIE	
DEGILR	GILDER, GIRDLE, GLIDER	
DEGILS	GLIDES	
DEGILY	EDGILY	
DEGIMS	MIDGES	
DEGIMT	MIDGET	
DEGINN	ENDING	
DEGINO	GIDEON	
DEGINP	PINGED	
DEGINR	RINGED	
DEGINS	DESIGN, SIGNED, SINGED	
DEGINT	TINGED	
DEGINW	WINGED	
DEGINY	DYEING	
DEGIOS	DOGIES	
DEGIOU	DOUGIE	
DEGIPR	GRIPED	
DEGIRR	GIRDER	
DEGIRS	DIRGES, RIDGES	
DEGIRU	GUIDER	
DEGIST	DIGEST	
DEGISU	GUIDES	
DEGITW	WIDGET	
DEGJRU	JUDGER	
DEGJSU	JUDGES	
DEGLLU	GULLED	
DEGLNO	GOLDEN, LONGED	
DEGLNU	GULDEN, LUNGED	
DEGLOR	LODGER	
DEGLOS	LODGES	
DEGLOV	GLOVED	
DEGLOW	GLOWED	
DEGLPU	GULPED	
DEGLSU	SLUDGE	
DEGMMU	GUMMED	
DEGMSU	SMUDGE	
DEGNNU	GUNNED	
DEGNOP	PONGED	
DEGNRU	GERUND, NUDGER	
DEGNSU	NUDGES	
DEGOPR	GROPED	
DEGORR	RODGER	
DEGORU	DROGUE, ROUGED	
DEGOST	STODGE	
DEGPPY	GYPPED	
DEGPRU	PURGED	
DEGRSU	SURGED	
DEGRTU	TRUDGE	
DEGSTU	GUSTED	
DEGTTU	GUTTED	
DEHHSU	HUSHED	
DEHILP	DELPHI	
DEHILS	SHIELD	
DEHILW	WHILED	
DEHINO	HOIDEN, HONIED	
DEHINR	HINDER	
DEHINT	HINTED	
DEHINW	WHINED	
DEHIOS	HESIOD	
DEHIPP	HIPPED	
DEHIRT	DITHER	
DEHISS	DISHES, HISSED	
DEHISW	WISHED	
DEHIUY	YEHUDI	
DEHJOS	JOSHED	
DEHKNO	HONKED	
DEHKOO	HOOKED	
DEHLLU	HULLED	
DEHLNO	HOLDEN	
DEHLOR	HOLDER	
DEHLOW	HOWLED	
DEHLPU	UPHELD	
DEHLRU	HURDLE, HURLED	
DEHLTY	DELYTH	
DEHMMU	HUMMED	
DEHMNY	HYMNED	
DEHMOT	METHOD	
DEHMPU	HUMPED	
DEHMRY	RHYMED	
DEHNOP	PHONED	
DEHNOR	DEHORN, HORNED	
DEHNOS	NOSHED	
DEHNOY	HOYDEN	
DEHNRY	HENDRY	
DEHNTU	HUNTED	
DEHOOP	HOOPED	
DEHOOS	SHOOED	
DEHOOT	HOOTED	
DEHOPP	HOPPED	
DEHORS	HORDES, RHODES, SHORED	
DEHORT	RED-HOT	
DEHOST	HOSTED	
DEHOSU	HOUSED	
DEHOSV	SHOVED	
DEHOSW	SHOWED	
DEHPST	DEPTHS	
DEHPSU	PUSHED	
DEHRSS	SHERDS, SHREDS	
DEHRSU	RUSHED	
DEHRSW	SHREWD	
DEHRTY	RHEYDT	
DEIIKR	KEDIRI	
DEIINO	IODINE	
DEIINS	INSIDE	
DEIINT	INDITE, TINEID	
DEIINV	DIVINE	
DEIIOS	IODISE	
DEIIOZ	IODIZE	
DEIIPT	PITIED	
DEIIRT	TIDIER	
DEIISS	DIESIS	
DEIISX	DEIXIS	
DEIJLT	JILTED	
DEIJNO	JOINED	
DEIJNX	JINXED	
DEIKLL	KILLED	
DEIKLM	MILKED	
DEIKLN	KINDLE, LINKED	
DEIKLO	KELOID	
DEIKLT	KILTED	
DEIKNO	OINKED	
DEIKNP	PINKED	
DEIKNR	KINDER	
DEIKNW	WINKED	
DEIKNY	KIDNEY	
DEIKPP	KIPPED	
DEIKPS	SPIKED	
DEIKPU	UPDIKE	
DEIKRS	RISKED	
DEIKRU	DUIKER	
DEIKSS	KISSED	
DEIKSV	SKIVED	
DEIKTT	KITTED	
DEILLM	MILLED	
DEILLT	TILLED	
DEILLW	WILLED	
DEILMN	LIMNED, MINDEL	
DEILMO	MELOID	
DEILMP	DIMPLE, LIMPED	
DEILMR	MILDER	
DEILMS	MISLED, SMILED	
DEILMW	MILDEW	
DEILNN	LINDEN	
DEILNO	DOLINE, INDOLE, LEONID	
DEILNT	DENTIL	
DEILNZ	DENZIL	
DEILOP	DIPLOE, DIPOLE, POLDIE	
DEILOS	ISOLDE, SOILED	
DEILOT	TOILED	
DEILPS	DISPEL, LISPED	
DEILPX	DIPLEX	
DEILRS	SIDLER	
DEILRV	DRIVEL	
DEILRW	WILDER	
DEILSS	SLIDES	
DEILST	IDLEST, LISTED, SILTED, TILDES	
DEILSV	DEVILS	

DEILSY	YIELDS
DEILTT	TILTED, TITLED
DEILTU	DILUTE
DEILTW	WILTED
DEILWY	DEWILY, WIDELY, WIELDY
DEIMMR	DIMMER, RIMMED
DEIMMU	MEDIUM
DEIMNP	IMPEND
DEIMNR	MINDER, REMIND
DEIMNS	DENIMS
DEIMNT	MINTED
DEIMOR	DORMIE
DEIMOT	DO TIME
DEIMPP	PIMPED
DEIMPR	PRIMED
DEIMPU	MUD PIE
DEIMRS	DERMIS
DEIMSS	MISSED
DEIMST	DEMIST, MISTED
DEIMTU	TEDIUM
DEINNO	DIONNE
DEINNP	PINNED
DEINNR	DINNER
DEINNS	DENNIS, SINNED
DEINNT	DENTIN, INDENT, INTEND, TINNED
DEINNW	ENWIND
DEINOP	OPINED
DEINOR	DE NIRO, INDORE, IRONED
DEINOS	NO-SIDE, ONSIDE, SIDE-ON
DEINPP	NIPPED
DEINPS	SNIPED
DEINRS	DINERS, RINSED, SNIDER
DEINRT	TINDER
DEINRU	INURED, RUINED
DEINRV	DRIVEN, VERDIN
DEINRW	REWIND, WINDER
DEINSU	UNDIES
DEINSW	WIDNES
DEINSY	SIDNEY
DEINTT	TINTED
DEINTU	DUNITE, UNITED, UNTIED
DEINTW	TWINED
DEIOOR	OROIDE
DEIOOV	OVIEDO
DEIOPR	DOPIER, PERIOD
DEIOPS	POISED
DEIORR	DORRIE
DEIORS	DORIES

DEIORT	EDITOR, RIOTED, TRIODE
DEIORV	VOIDER
DEIORW	WEIRDO
DEIORZ	DOZIER
DEIOSV	VIDEOS
DEIOSX	OXIDES
DEIOTT	DOTTIE
DEIPPP	PIPPED
DEIPPR	DIPPER, RIPPED
DEIPPS	SIPPED
DEIPPT	TIPPED
DEIPPZ	ZIPPED
DEIPQU	PIQUED
DEIPRS	PRIDES, PRISED, SPIDER
DEIPRZ	PRIZED
DEIPSS	PISSED
DEIPST	SPITED
DEIPSU	UPSIDE
DEIPSV	VESPID
DEIPSW	SWIPED
DEIPTT	PITTED
DEIRRS	DERRIS, DRIERS, RIDERS
DEIRRV	DRIVER
DEIRST	DIREST, DRIEST, STRIDE
DEIRSU	DISEUR
DEIRSV	DIVERS, DRIVES
DEIRTU	TRUDIE
DEIRTV	DIVERT
DEISST	DEISTS, DESIST
DEISSU	DISUSE, ISSUED
DEISTU	DUTIES, SUITED
DEISTV	DIVEST
DEISTW	WIDEST
DEJKNU	JUNKED
DEJLOT	JOLTED
DEJMPU	JUMPED
DEJOTT	JOTTED
DEJTTU	JUTTED
DEKLOO	LOOKED
DEKLRU	LURKED
DEKLSU	SULKED
DEKMOS	SMOKED
DEKNOY	DONKEY
DEKNOZ	ZONKED
DEKNRU	DUNKER
DEKOOR	ROOKED
DEKORW	WORKED
DEKOST	STOKED
DELLLO	LOLLED
DELLLU	LULLED
DELLMU	MULLED
DELLOP	POLLED
DELLOR	ROLLED

DELLOT	TOLLED
DELLOU	DUELLO
DELLPU	PULLED
DELLRU	DULLER
DELLWY	LEWDLY
DELMNO	DOLMEN
DELMOO	LOOMED
DELMOR	MOLDER
DELMOS	MODELS, SELDOM
DELMOT	MOLTED
DELMOU	MODULE
DELMOY	MELODY
DELMPU	LUMPED, PLUMED
DELNOO	NOODLE
DELNOR	RONDEL
DELNOU	LOUDEN, NODULE
DELNOW	WELDON
DELNRU	RUNDLE
DELNWY	DELWYN
DELOOP	LOOPED, POODLE, POOLED
DELOOS	LOOSED, OODLES
DELOOT	LOOTED, TOLEDO, TOOLED
DELOPP	LOPPED
DELOPR	POLDER
DELOPS	SLOPED
DELOPW	PLOWED
DELOPY	DEPLOY
DELORS	SOLDER
DELORT	RETOLD
DELORU	LOUDER, LOURED
DELOST	OLDEST
DELOSU	LOUSED
DELOSV	SOLVED
DELOSW	SLOWED
DELOSY	YODELS
DELOTT	DOTTLE, LOTTED
DELOWY	YOWLED
DELOYY	DOYLEY
DELPPU	PULPED
DELPRU	PURLED
DELPSU	PULSED
DELPTU	DUPLET
DELPUX	DUPLEX
DELRUY	RUDELY
DELSTU	LUSTED
DELSTY	STYLED
DEMMOS	MODEMS
DEMMSU	SUMMED
DEMNOO	MOONED
DEMNOR	MODERN
DEMNOS	DEMONS, ESMOND
DEMOOR	MOORED, ROOMED
DEMOOT	MOOTED

DEMOOZ	ZOOMED
DEMOPP	MOPPED
DEMOPR	ROMPED
DEMOPS	MOPEDS
DEMORR	DORMER
DEMORT	DERMOT
DEMORW	WORMED
DEMOST	MODEST
DEMPPU	PUMPED
DEMPRU	DUMPER
DEMRRU	MURDER
DEMRSU	DEMURS
DEMSSU	MUSSED
DENNOT	TENDON
DENNOU	UNDONE
DENNPU	PUNNED
DENNRU	DUNNER
DENNSU	SUNNED
DENOOS	DO ONE'S, NODOSE
DENOOW	WOODEN
DENOPR	PERNOD, PONDER
DENORS	DRONES, SNORED
DENORT	RODENT
DENORU	UNDOER
DENORV	VENDOR
DENORW	DOWNER, WONDER
DENORY	RODNEY, YONDER
DENOST	OSTEND, STONED
DENOSW	SNOWED
DENOSY	DOYENS
DENOSZ	DOZENS
DENOTW	WONTED
DENPRU	PRUNED
DENPSU	SEND-UP
DENPTU	PUNTED
DENRST	TRENDS
DENRSU	NURSED, SUNDER
DENRTU	TURNED
DENRTY	TRENDY
DENRUV	VERDUN
DENSUU	UNUSED
DENSUW	SUNDEW
DENSYY	SYDNEY
DENTTU	NUTTED
DEOOPP	POOPED
DEOORS	RODEOS
DEOORT	ROOTED
DEOORV	OVERDO
DEOOTT	TOOTED
DEOPPP	POPPED
DEOPPS	SOPPED
DEOPPT	TOPPED
DEOPRT	DEPORT, DE TROP, PORTED

DEOPRU	POURED
DEOPRV	PROVED
DEOPRW	POWDER
DEOPST	DEPOTS, DESPOT, POSTED
DEOPTT	POTTED
DEOPTU	POUTED
DEOQTU	QUOTED
DEORRS	ORDERS
DEORRU	ORDURE
DEORRV	DROVER
DEORRW	REWORD
DEORSS	DOSSER
DEORST	DORSET, SORTED, STORED, STRODE
DEORSU	DOUSER, ROUSED, SOURED
DEORSV	DROVES
DEORSW	DOWSER, DROWSE
DEORTT	DOTTER, ROTTED
DEORTU	DETOUR, ROUTED, TOURED
DEORUV	DEVOUR
DEOSST	TOSSED
DEOSSU	SOUSED
DEOSTU	USED TO, OUSTED
DEOSTW	STOWED
DEOSUX	EXODUS
DEOTTT	TOTTED
DEOTTU	TOUTED
DEOTUV	DEVOUT
DEOTUX	TUXEDO
DEPPPU	PUPPED
DEPPSU	SUPPED
DEPPTU	TUPPED
DEPRRU	PURRED
DEPRSU	PRUDES, PURSED
DEPRUY	DUPERY
DEPSSU	PSEUDS
DEPSUY	PUDSEY, PSEUDY
DEPTTU	PUTTED
DEPTUY	DEPUTY
DERRSY	DRYERS
DERSSU	DURESS
DERSSY	DRESSY
DERSTU	DUSTER, RUDEST, RUSTED
DERTTU	RUTTED
DESSSU	SUSSED
DESTUV	DUVETS
DFFIMO	MID-OFF
DFGGOO	FOGDOG
DFGIIR	FRIGID
DFIINY	NIDIFY
DFIIRT	TRIFID

DFIKNO	KIND OF
DFILOR	FLORID
DFILSU	FLUIDS
DFIMOY	MODIFY
DFIORS	FIORDS
DFIRST	DRIFTS
DFIRTY	DRIFTY
DFJORS	FJORDS
DFLNOU	UNFOLD
DFLNOY	FONDLY
DFLOOS	FLOODS
DFLORU	RUDOLF
DFNORS	FRONDS
DFNSUU	FUNDUS
DFOORX	OXFORD
DGGNOU	DUGONG, GUNDOG
DGHIIN	HIDING
DGHINY	DINGHY
DGHITW	DWIGHT
DGHOOT	HOT DOG
DGHOUY	DOUGHY
DGIILN	IDLING
DGIINN	DINING
DGIINO	INDIGO
DGIINP	PIDGIN
DGIINR	INGRID, RIDING
DGIINS	SIDING
DGIINT	TIDING
DGIINV	DIVING
DGIIST	DIGITS
DGIJOU	JUDOGI
DGILNO	DOLING
DGILOT	DIGLOT
DGILSU	GUILDS
DGIMTU	MIDGUT
DGINOP	DOPING, PONGID
DGINOS	DOINGS, DOSING
DGINOT	DOTING, TIN GOD
DGINOU	GUIDON
DGINOW	GODWIN
DGINOZ	DOZING
DGINPU	DUPING
DGINRS	GRINDS
DGINRU	DURING
DGINRY	DRYING
DGIOTW	GODWIT
DGIRTU	TURGID
DGLOOY	GOODLY
DGLSUY	SLUDGY
DGMSUY	SMUDGY
DGNOOR	DRONGO, GORDON, GRODNO
DGNOOS	GODSON
DGNORU	GROUND

DGNOSU	SUN GOD	DILNTU	INDULT	DMNOOS	OSMOND
DGOOPT	TOP DOG	DILOSS	SOLIDS	DMNOSU	MOUNDS, OSMUND
DGORSU	GOURDS	DILOST	STOLID	DMOOSY	SODOMY
DGOSTY	STODGY	DILOXY	XYLOID	DMORSU	DORSUM
DGOTUU	DUGOUT	DILOYZ	DOZILY	DMRTUU	UDMURT
DHIINS	SINDHI	DIMMSU	DIM SUM	DNOORS	DONORS, RONDOS
DHIIPS	HISPID	DIMNOO	DOMINO	DNOPSU	POUNDS
DHIISW	WIDISH	DIMNSU	NUDISM	DNORSU	ROUNDS
DHIJTU	JUDITH	DIMOPU	PODIUM	DNORTU	ROTUND
DHILOS	OLDISH	DIMOSU	SODIUM	DNOSSU	SOUNDS
DHIMOS	MODISH	DIMOSW	WISDOM	DNOSSY	SYNODS
DHINOO	HINDOO	DIMSST	MIDSTS	DNOSUW	WOUNDS
DHINSU	HINDUS	DINNUW	UNWIND	DNRSUY	SUNDRY
DHIORR	HORRID	DINOOR	INDOOR	DOOOOV	VOODOO
DHIOST	DHOTIS	DINOPU	UNIPOD	DOOPRU	UROPOD
DHIOSV	DOVISH	DINOSW	DISOWN	DOOPRY	DROOPY
DHIRST	THIRDS	DINOSY	SIDONY	DOORSU	ODOURS
DHISTW	WIDTHS	DINOWW	WINDOW	DOPRSY	DROPSY
DHLOPU	HOLDUP, UPHOLD	DINPTU	PUNDIT	DORRTY	DRY ROT
DHLOSU	SHOULD	DINPUW	UPWIND	DORSSW	SWORDS
DHLTUU	DULUTH	DINSTU	DUSTIN, NUDIST	DORSSY	DROSSY
DHNOSU	HOUNDS, HUDSON	DINTUY	NUDITY, UNTIDY	DORSTU	STROUD
DHOOOO	HOODOO	DIOOPS	ISOPOD	DORSWY	DROWSY
DHOORT	HOT ROD	DIOORT	TOROID	DPSTUU	DUSTUP
DHORSU	SHROUD	DIOOSU	IODOUS, ODIOUS	DRSTUY	STURDY
DIILMP	LIMPID	DIOOSV	OVOIDS	EEEEGG	GEE-GEE
DIILOP	LIPOID	DIOOTX	TOXOID	EEEEPT	TEEPEE
DIILOS	SOLIDI	DIOPRT	TORPID, TRIPOD	EEEEWW	WEE-WEE
DIILPS	LIPIDS	DIORRT	TORRID	EEEFFT	EFFETE
DIILQU	LIQUID	DIOSTT	DITTOS	EEEFLR	FEELER
DIILST	DISTIL	DIOSTU	STUDIO	EEEFRR	REEFER
DIILTY	TIDILY	DIOSWW	WIDOWS	EEEFRZ	FREEZE
DIIMNU	INDIUM	DIPPRY	DRIPPY	EEEGMR	EMERGE
DIIMOS	IDIOMS, IODISM	DIPRTU	PUTRID	EEEGNO	EOGENE
DIIMOU	OIDIUM	DIPSTU	STUPID	EEEGNR	RENEGE
DIIMTW	DIMWIT	DIQSSU	SQUIDS	EEEGNU	EUGENE
DIIMTY	DIMITY	DJNNOO	DONJON	EEEGRZ	GEEZER
DIINOX	DIOXIN	DKNOOP	PONDOK	EEEHLN	HELENE
DIINRS	INDRIS	DKNRSU	DRUNKS	EEEHLR	HEELER
DIIOST	IDIOTS	DLLOOP	DOLLOP	EEEHNT	ETHENE
DIJNNS	DJINNS	DLLORY	DROLLY, LORDLY	EEEHST	SEETHE
DIKLNY	KINDLY	DLLOUW	LUDLOW	EEEHTT	TEETHE
DIKMNU	DINKUM	DLLOUY	LOUDLY	EEEHWZ	WHEEZE
DIKNNU	UNKIND	DLMOSU	MOULDS	EEEILN	EILEEN
DIKNRS	DRINKS	DLMOUY	MOULDY	EEEJRR	JEERER
DIKOOS	SKIDOO	DLNNOO	LONDON	EEEKLY	KEELEY
DILLMY	MILDLY	DLNNOY	LYNDON	EEEKMR	MEEKER
DILLNO	DILLON	DLNOOS	SOLD ON	EEEKNR	KEENER
DILLRS	DRILLS	DLNOTU	UNTOLD	EEEKNT	KETENE
DILLSY	IDYLLS	DLNUUY	UNDULY	EEEKPR	KEEPER
DILLWY	WILDLY	DLOOPZ	PODZOL	EEEKRS	SEEKER
DILMOR	MILORD	DLOORU	DOLOUR	EEELMS	MELEES
DILMPY	DIMPLY	DLORSW	WORLDS	EEELNV	ELEVEN
DILNNU	DUNLIN	DLORUY	DOURLY	EEELPR	PEELER

EEELRR	REELER	EEFSZZ	FEZZES	EEHLSV	HELVES, SHELVE
EEELSS	LESSEE	EEGGIM	MEGGIE	EEHLSW	WHEELS
EEELSV	LEVEES, SLEEVE	EEGGIR	REGGIE	EEHMMR	HEMMER
EEELSY	ELYSEE	EEGGLP	PEG LEG	EEHMNP	HEMPEN
EEELTY	EYELET	EEGGOR	GEORGE	EEHMNS	ENMESH
EEEMMS	SEMEME	EEGILS	LIEGES	EEHMRS	HERMES
EEEMRS	SEEMER	EEGILT	ELEGIT	EEHMSS	MESHES
EEEMRT	MEETER	EEGIMR	EMIGRE, REGIME	EEHMST	THEMES
EEEMST	ESTEEM	EEGINN	ENGINE	EEHMUX	EXHUME
EEENRS	SERENE	EEGINP	PEEING	EEHNOR	HEREON
EEENRT	ENTREE, RETENE	EEGINS	GENIES, SEEING	EEHNOX	HEXONE
EEENRV	VENEER	EEGINT	TEEING	EEHNPS	SPHENE
EEENSZ	SNEEZE	EEGINW	WEEING	EEHNPW	NEPHEW
EEEOPP	EPOPEE	EEGINY	EYEING	EEHNRR	HERREN
EEEPPR	PEEPER	EEGIRS	SERGEI	EEHNRT	NETHER
EEEPRW	WEEPER	EEGIRT	GERTIE	EEHNTY	ETHYNE
EEEPST	TEPEES	EEGIRV	GRIEVE	EEHORR	HERERO
EEERRV	REVERE	EEGISS	SIEGES	EEHORS	HEROES
EEERSV	REEVES, SEVERE	EEGLMU	LEGUME	EEHORT	HERETO
EEERTT	TEETER, TERETE	EEGLNT	GENTLE	EEHORW	HOWE'ER
EEERTX	EXETER	EEGLRS	LEGERS	EEHOSX	HEXOSE
EEERVW	WEEVER	EEGLRT	GRETEL, REGLET	EEHOTW	TOWHEE
EEESTT	SETTEE	EEGLTY	GLEETY	EEHPRS	HERPES, SPHERE
EEESTV	STEEVE	EEGMNO	GENOME	EEHPSY	HEPSEY
EEFFOT	TOFFEE	EEGMNR	GERMEN	EEHRST	ESTHER, HESTER,
EEFFSU	EFFUSE	EEGMNT	TEGMEN	THREES	
EEFGIR	FERGIE	EEGMRR	MERGER	EEHRSW	HEWERS
EEFGRU	REFUGE	EEGNOP	PONGEE	EEHRSY	HERESY
EEFHIR	HEIFER	EEGNRS	GENRES, GREENS	EEHRTT	TETHER
EEFHOR	HEREOF	EEGNRT	REGENT	EEHRTW	WETHER
EEFHRT	HEFTER	EEGNRY	ENERGY	EEHRVY	HERVEY
EEFILN	FELINE	EEGNTW	TEGWEN	EEHSST	SHEETS, THESES
EEFILR	RELIEF	EEGRRT	REGRET	EEHWYY	WHEYEY
EEFINR	REFINE	EEGRRV	VERGER	EEHWYZ	WHEEZY
EEFIRZ	FRIEZE	EEGRRY	GREYER	EEIJNN	JENNIE
EEFLLO	FELLOE	EEGRSS	EGRESS	EEIJSS	JESSIE
EEFLLR	FELLER	EEGRST	EGRETS	EEIKLL	KELLIE
EEFLNN	FENNEL	EEGRSV	VERGES	EEIKLP	KELPIE
EEFLNS	FLENSE	EEGRSY	GEYSER	EEIKRR	KERRIE
EEFLRT	REFLET	EEGRTT	GETTER	EEILLL	LILLEE
EEFLRU	FERULE, REFUEL	EEHIMP	PHEMIE	EEILLN	NELLIE
EEFLRX	REFLEX	EEHINN	HENNIE	EEILLS	LESLIE, LIESEL
EEFLRY	FREELY	EEHINR	HEREIN, INHERE	EEILMR	MERIEL
EEFLST	FLEETS	EEHINT	EITHNE, THEINE	EEILNN	LENNIE
EEFLSX	FLEXES	EEHIPS	HEPSIE	EEILNO	LEONIE
EEFLTT	FETTLE	EEHIRT	EITHER	EEILNR	LIERNE, RELINE
EEFLUY	EYEFUL	EEHITV	THIEVE	EEILNS	ENSILE, SENILE
EEFPRR	PREFER	EEHKLS	SHEKEL	EEILNW	EILWEN
EEFPTY	TEPEFY	EEHLLN	HELLEN	EEILOS	ELOISE
EEFRRT	FERRET	EEHLLR	HELLER	EEILPS	ELSPIE
EEFRST	FESTER, FREEST	EEHLLS	HELLES	EEILPT	PELITE
EEFRSU	REFUSE	EEHLMT	HELMET	EEILRS	RESILE
EEFRTT	FETTER	EEHLNY	HENLEY	EEILRV	EVILER, LEVIER, RELIVE,
EEFRTU	REFUTE	EEHLPR	HELPER	REVILE, VEILER	
				EEILRY	EERILY

EEILSV	LEVIES	EEKLLR	KELLER	EELPRT	PELTER, PETREL
EEILSX	EXILES, ILEXES	EEKLMN	KENELM	EELPRY	YELPER
EEILTT	LETTIE	EEKLMY	MEEKLY	EELPST	PESTLE
EEILVW	WEEVIL	EEKLNN	KENNEL	EELPSV	PELVES
EEIMNR	ERMINE	EEKLNR	KERNEL	EELPSY	SLEEPY
EEIMNY	YEMENI	EEKLNY	KEENLY	EELQSU	SEQUEL
EEIMPR	EMPIRE	EEKLTT	KETTLE	EELRSS	LESSER
EEIMRS	MIERES, MISERE,	EEKLWY	WEEKLY	EELRST	LESTER
	REMISE	EEKMNS	MEKNES	EELRSV	LEVERS
EEIMRT	METIER	EEKMRS	KERMES	EELRTT	LETTER
EEIMSS	EMESIS	EEKNOT	KETONE	EELRTU	TERUEL
EEIMST	SEMITE	EEKORV	EVOKER, REVOKE	EELRTW	WELTER
EEINNP	PINENE	EEKOST	KETOSE	EELRUV	VELURE
EEINNV	VIENNE	EEKPPU	UPKEEP	EELSST	STEELS
EEINPR	REPINE	EEKPRU	PERUKE	EELSSV	SELVES, VESSEL
EEINQU	EQUINE	EEKRST	KESTER	EELSTT	SETTLE
EEINRS	NEREIS, SEREIN, SERINE	EEKRSW	SKEWER, WESKER	EELSTV	SVELTE
EEINRT	ENTIRE	EEKRSY	KERSEY	EELSTY	SLEETY, STEELY
EEINRV	ENVIER, NIEVRE,	EELLMU	LEMUEL	EELSWY	WESLEY
	VENIRE	EELLNO	NOELLE	EELTVV	VELVET
EEINSS	NESSIE, SEINES	EELLOV	O LEVEL	EELTVW	TWELVE
EEINSV	ENVIES	EELLPT	PELLET	EEMNOR	MOREEN
EEINTT	NETTIE	EELLRS	SELLER	EEMNOY	YEOMEN
EEINTX	EXTINE	EELLRT	RETELL, TELLER	EEMNSS	MENSES
EEIORS	SOIREE	EELLRY	ELLERY, YELLER	EEMNSY	YES-MEN
EEIPPY	YIPPEE	EELLSV	LEVELS	EEMNYZ	ENZYME
EEIPRR	PIERRE	EELLSY	LESLEY	EEMOPT	METOPE
EEIPRS	ESPIER	EELMNY	EMELYN	EEMORT	EMOTER, METEOR,
EEIPRX	EXPIRE	EELMPT	PELMET, TEMPLE		REMOTE
EEIPTT	PETITE	EELMRT	MELTER	EEMORV	REMOVE
EEIPTW	PEEWIT	EELMRW	MEWLER	EEMPRS	SEMPRE
EEIRRT	RETIRE	EELMRY	MERELY	EEMPRT	TEMPER
EEIRRW	REWIRE	EELMSY	SEEMLY	EEMPTX	EXEMPT
EEIRSS	SEISER, SERIES	EELMTT	METTLE	EEMRST	METERS, METRES
EEIRSV	REVISE	EELNNT	LENTEN	EEMRSU	RESUME
EEIRSX	SEXIER	EELNOR	LENORE, LOREEN	EEMRTU	MEERUT
EEIRSY	EYRIES	EELNOV	ELEVON	EEMSSS	MESSES
EEIRSZ	SEIZER	EELNPS	SPLEEN	EEMSTU	MUSTEE
EEIRVV	REVIVE	EELNPV	PLEVEN	EEMSTX	SEMTEX
EEIRVW	REVIEW, VIEWER	EELNRT	RELENT	EENNOR	NOREEN
EEISST	TESSIE	EELNSS	LENSES, LESSEN	EENNOV	EVONNE
EEISSV	SIEVES	EELNST	NESTLE	EENNPY	PENNEY
EEISTV	STEVIE	EELNSV	VELSEN	EENNRS	RENNES
EEJJNU	JEJUNE	EELNTT	NETTLE	EENNRT	RENNET, TENNER
EEJKRR	JERKER	EELNUV	VENULE	EENNSU	UNSEEN
EEJLNO	JOLEEN, JOLENE	EELNVY	EVELYN, EVENLY	EENNUV	UNEVEN
EEJLSW	JEWELS	EELNXY	XYLENE	EENOPR	OPENER, REOPEN,
EEJMOR	JEROME	EELOPP	PEOPLE		REPONE
EEJMRY	JEREMY	EELOPR	ELOPER	EENOPT	POTEEN
EEJNNT	JENNET	EELORS	OR ELSE	EENORS	ORENSE
EEJRST	JESTER	EELORZ	LOZERE	EENOSV	VENOSE
EEJRSY	JERSEY	EELOVV	EVOLVE	EENOTV	VENETO
EEJSSW	JEWESS	EELPPU	PEEPUL	EENOTW	TOWNEE
EEJSTT	JET SET	EELPRS	LEPERS	EENOVZ	EVZONE
EEKKLR	LEKKER			EENPRT	REPENT

EENPRY	PYRENE	EEPTTU	PUTTEE	EFGOOR	FOREGO
EENQSU	QUEENS	EEQRSU	QUEERS	EFGORR	FORGER
EENQUY	QUEENY	EEQSUU	QUEUES	EFGORS	FORGES, GOFERS
EENRRT	RENTER	EERRST	RESTER	EFGORT	FORGET
EENRSS	SNEERS	EERRSV	REVERS, SERVER	EFGRSU	FERGUS
EENRST	ERNEST, NESTER,	EERRTT	TERRET	EFGSUU	FUGUES
	RESENT, TENSER	EERRTU	URETER	EFHILS	ELFISH
EENRSU	ENSURE	EERRTV	REVERT	EFHIRS	FISHER
EENRSV	NERVES, NEVERS	EERSST	STEERS	EFHISS	FISHES
EENRTT	TENTER	EERSSV	SERVES, SEVRES,	EFHIST	FETISH
EENRTU	NEUTER, RETUNE,		VERSES	EFHLSY	FLESHY
	TENURE, TUREEN	EERSSW	SEWERS	EFHRRU	FUHRER
EENRTV	VENTER	EERSTT	SETTER, STREET,	EFHSTT	THEFTS
EENRTX	EXTERN		TESTER	EFIINT	FINITE
EENRVY	VENERY	EERSTU	RETUSE	EFIKNR	KNIFER
EENSSS	SENSES	EERSTV	REVEST	EFIKNU	FUKIEN
EENSST	TENSES	EERSTW	WESTER	EFILLR	FILLER, REFILL
EENSSV	SEVENS	EERSTX	EXSERT	EFILLT	FILLET
EENSTT	TENETS	EERSUV	REVUES	EFILNY	FINELY
EENSTV	EVENTS, STEVEN	EERSVW	SWERVE	EFILOS	FILOSE
EENSTW	NEWEST	EERTTT	TETTER	EFILPP	FIPPLE
EENSUV	VENUES	EERTTW	WETTER	EFILPR	PILFER
EENSWY	SWEENY	EERTUY	TUYERE	EFILRR	RIFLER
EENSYZ	SNEEZY	EERTVV	VERVET	EFILRS	FLIERS, LIFERS, RIFLES
EENTTX	EXTENT	EERTVX	VERTEX	EFILRT	FILTER, LIFTER, TRIFLE
EENTUX	EXEUNT	EESSTT	SESTET, TESTES	EFILRU	IREFUL
EEOPRS	REPOSE	EESSTW	SWEETS	EFILST	FILETS, ITSELF, STIFLE
EEOPRU	EUROPE	EESTTU	SUTTEE	EFILSU	FUSILE
EEOPST	TOPEES	EESTTW	TWEETS	EFILTU	FUTILE
EEOPSX	EXPOSE	EESTTX	SEXTET	EFILWY	WIFELY
EEOPTU	TOUPEE	EETTVY	YVETTE	EFILZZ	FIZZLE
EEORST	STEREO	EFFFFO	EFF OFF	EFIMRR	FIRMER
EEORSV	SOEVER	EFFGIN	EFFING	EFINRY	FINERY
EEORSZ	ZEROES	EFFGIR	GRIFFE	EFINST	FEINTS, FINEST, INFEST
EEORTV	VETOER	EFFGIY	EFFIGY	EFINSU	INFUSE
EEORUV	OEUVRE	EFFGOR	GOFFER	EFIORX	FOXIER
EEOSST	SETOSE	EFFILP	PIFFLE	EFIOST	SOFTIE
EEOSTV	VETOES	EFFILR	RIFFLE	EFIPRX	PREFIX
EEPPPR	PEPPER	EFFILY	LIFFEY	EFIRRS	FRIERS
EEPPST	STEPPE	EFFLMU	MUFFLE	EFIRSS	SERIFS
EEPRRY	PREYER	EFFLRU	RUFFLE	EFIRST	REFITS, SIFTER, STRIFE
EEPRSS	SPREES	EFFLUX	EFFLUX	EFIRSU	FURIES
EEPRST	PESTER, PETERS,	EFFNOO	ONE-OFF	EFIRSV	FIVERS
	PRESET, STREEP	EFFORS	OFFERS	EFIRSX	FIXERS
EEPRSU	PERUSE, PUREES,	EFFORT	EFFORT	EFIRTT	FITTER, TITFER
	RUPEES	EFFOST	OFFSET, SET-OFF	EFIRVY	VERIFY
EEPRSV	VESPER	EFFPRU	PUFFER	EFIRZZ	FIZZER
EEPRSW	SPEWER	EFFRSU	SUFFER	EFISTY	FEISTY
EEPRSY	SPEYER	EFFTTU	TUFFET	EFKLSU	FLUKES
EEPRTT	PETTER	EFGINR	FINGER, FRINGE	EFKLUY	FLUKEY
EEPRTU	REPUTE	EFGINT	FETING	EFKNRU	FUNKER
EEPRTW	PEWTER	EFGIOS	FOGIES	EFLLOW	FELLOW
EEPRTX	EXPERT	EFGIRU	FIGURE	EFLLRU	FULLER
EEPSSW	SWEEPS	EFGLNU	ENGULF	EFLMSY	MYSELF
EEPSTT	SEPTET	EFGLOR	GOLFER		

EFLNNU	FUNNEL	EGGIJR	JIGGER	EGIKNP	PEKING
EFLNOS	FELONS	EGGILN	NIGGLE	EGIKNY	KEYING
EFLNOT	TEFLON	EGGILW	WIGGLE	EGILLR	GRILLE
EFLNOY	FELONY	EGGINR	GINGER, NIGGER	EGILLU	LIGULE
EFLNTU	FLUENT	EGGIRR	RIGGER	EGILMN	MINGLE
EFLOOT	FOOTLE	EGGJLO	JOGGLE	EGILMP	MEGILP
EFLOOZ	FOOZLE	EGGJLU	JUGGLE	EGILMT	GIMLET
EFLORT	FLORET, LOFTER	EGGJOR	JOGGER	EGILNO	LEGION
EFLORU	FOULER	EGGLOR	LOGGER	EGILNP	LI PENG
EFLORW	FLOWER, FOWLER	EGGLOT	TOGGLE	EGILNR	LINGER
EFLORX	FLEXOR	EGGLRU	GURGLE, LUGGER	EGILNS	GLENIS, SINGLE
EFLOSW	FOWLES	EGGMRU	MUGGER	EGILNT	TINGLE
EFLOUW	WOEFUL	EGGNTU	NUGGET	EGILOR	LOGIER
EFLPRU	PURFLE	EGGORR	GORGER, GREGOR	EGILPT	PIGLET
EFLRRU	FURLER	EGGORS	GORGES	EGILRS	GRILSE
EFLRSY	FLYERS	EGGORU	GOUGER	EGILRU	UGLIER
EFLRTU	FLUTER	EGGOSU	GOUGES	EGILRZ	GRIZEL
EFLRUU	RUEFUL	EGGRTU	TUGGER	EGILST	LEGIST
EFLRUX	REFLUX	EGHHIR	HIGHER	EGIMNO	IMOGEN
EFLSTU	FLUTES	EGHHIT	EIGHTH, HEIGHT	EGIMNT	METING
EFLSUU	USEFUL	EGHHIU	HUGHIE	EGIMNW	MEWING
EFMNOT	FOMENT	EGHHSU	HUGHES	EGIMOS	EGOISM
EFMORR	FORMER, REFORM	EGHIIN	HIEING	EGIMPU	GUIMPE
EFMRSU	FEMURS	EGHILS	SLEIGH	EGINNS	ENSIGN
EFMTUY	TUMEFY	EGHINO	HOEING	EGINOP	PIGEON
EFNNOT	FENTON	EGHINR	HINGER	EGINOR	IGNORE, REGION
EFNORS	FRESNO	EGHINS	HINGES, NEIGHS	EGINOS	SOIGNE
EFNORZ	FROZEN	EGHINT	GETHIN	EGINOT	TOEING
EFNOST	SEFTON, SOFTEN	EGHINW	HEWING, WHINGE	EGINOW	WIGEON
EFNRUZ	FRUNZE	EGHINX	HEXING	EGINPP	EPPING
EFNRYZ	FRENZY	EGHIOT	HOGTIE	EGINRR	ERRING, RINGER
EFOORT	FOETOR, FOOTER	EGHIRS	SIGHER	EGINRS	REIGNS, RESIGN,
EFOORW	WOOFER	EGHIST	EIGHTS		SIGNER, SINGER
EFORRT	TREFOR	EGHITW	WEIGHT	EGINRW	WINGER
EFORRU	FURORE	EGHITY	EIGHTY	EGINSS	GNEISS, SINGES
EFORST	FOREST, FORTES,	EGHLMP	PHLEGM	EGINST	INGEST, SIGNET
	FOSTER, SOFTER	EGHLNT	LENGTH	EGINSU	GENIUS
EFORSY	FOYERS	EGHLPU	GUELPH	EGINSW	SEWING, SWINGE,
EFOSTU	FOETUS	EGHLUY	HUGELY		WINGES
EFRRSU	SURFER	EGHMMO	MEGOHM	EGINSX	SEXING
EFRRSY	FRYERS	EGHNOU	ENOUGH	EGINTW	TWINGE
EFRRTU	ERFURT	EGHNRU	HUNGER	EGINVX	VEXING
EFRSSU	FUSSER	EGHNST	THEGNS	EGIOOR	GOOIER
EFRTTU	TUFTER	EGHOPR	GOPHER	EGIORR	GORIER
EFRTUU	FUTURE	EGHORZ	HERZOG	EGIORS	ORGIES, SERGIO
EFSSSU	FUSSES	EGHOTT	GHETTO	EGIORT	GOITRE
EGGGIL	GIGGLE	EGHRSU	GUSHER	EGIOST	EGOIST
EGGGLO	GOGGLE	EGHSTU	HUGEST	EGIPRR	GRIPER
EGGGNO	EGGNOG	EGIILL	GILLIE	EGIPRS	GRIPES
EGGHIL	HIGGLE	EGIILR	GIRLIE	EGIRRT	TRIGER
EGGHOR	HOGGER	EGIIMN	GEMINI	EGIRST	TIGERS
EGGHOT	HOGGET	EGIINT	IGNITE	EGIRTV	GRIVET
EGGHRU	HUGGER	EGIJLN	JINGLE	EGISSU	GUISES, GUSSIE
EGGIJL	JIGGLE	EGIJRS	REJIGS	EGJLNU	JUNGLE
				EGKMNO	MEKONG

EGKRRU	KRUGER	EGOSYZ	ZYGOSE	EHIRSW	WISHER
EGLLTU	GULLET	EGOTYZ	ZYGOTE	EHIRTT	HITTER, TITHER
EGLNNU	GUNNEL	EGPRRU	PURGER	EHIRTU	RUTHIE
EGLNOR	LONGER	EGPRSU	PURGES, SUPER-G,	EHIRTV	THRIVE
EGLNOU	LOUNGE		SPURGE	EHIRTW	WHITER, WITHER,
EGLNPU	PLUNGE	EGPSTU	GETUPS		WRITHE
EGLNRU	LUNGER	EGRRSU	SURGER	EHIRTZ	ZITHER
EGLNSU	LUNGES	EGRSSU	SURGES	EHISSS	HISSES
EGLNSY	GLENYS	EGRTTU	GUTTER	EHISST	SHIEST, THESIS
EGLNTU	GLUTEN	EGSSTU	GUESTS, GUSSET	EHISSW	WISHES
EGLNTY	GENTLY	EHHIKS	SHEIKH	EHISTT	THEIST, TITHES
EGLOPR	PROLEG	EHHIRT	HITHER	EHISTW	WHITES
EGLOPS	GOSPEL	EHHNPY	HYPHEN	EHJOOR	JOHORE
EGLORU	REGULO	EHHRST	THRESH	EHJOPS	JOSEPH
EGLORV	GLOVER, GROVEL	EHIIJM	HIMEJI	EHJORT	JETHRO
EGLORW	GLOWER	EHIIPP	HIPPIE	EHJOSS	JOSHES
EGLOSV	GLOVES	EHIIST	SHIITE	EHKLSW	WHELKS
EGLOUY	EULOGY	EHIJSW	JEWISH	EHKNOR	HONKER
EGLPRU	GULPER	EHIKRS	HIKERS, SHRIEK,	EHKOOR	HOOKER
EGLUZZ	GUZZLE		SHRIKE	EHKORS	KOSHER
EGMNNU	GUNMEN	EHILLL	HILLEL	EHKOTY	HOT KEY
EGMNOR	MONGER	EHILLR	HILLER	EHKPTU	PHUKET
EGMNOS	GNOMES	EHILMU	HELIUM	EHKRSU	HUSKER
EGMNTU	NUTMEG	EHILOR	HOLIER	EHLLOR	HOLLER
EGMORU	MORGUE	EHILOS	HELIOS, ISOHEL	EHLLOS	HELLOS
EGMRTU	TERGUM	EHILOT	EOLITH	EHLLOW	HOWELL
EGNNOO	NONEGO	EHILRS	RELISH	EHLLRU	HULLER
EGNNOU	GUENON	EHILRT	HITLER, LITHER	EHLLSS	SHELLS
EGNNRU	GUNNER	EHIMNR	MENHIR	EHLLSY	SHELLY
EGNOOR	OREGON	EHIMNT	HIT MEN	EHLMMU	HUMMEL
EGNOPS	SPONGE	EHIMNU	INHUME	EHLMOO	MOHOLE
EGNORS	GONERS, NEGROS	EHIMOR	HOMIER	EHLMOP	PHLOEM
EGNORV	GOVERN	EHIMRT	HERMIT	EHLMOS	HOLMES
EGNORY	ERYNGO, GROYNE	EHIMST	THEISM, THEMIS	EHLMOY	HOMELY
EGNOTU	TONGUE	EHINOR	HEROIN, ON HIRE	EHLMTY	METHYL
EGNOXY	OXYGEN	EHINOT	HOTIEN	EHLNOP	HOLPEN, PHENOL
EGNPPU	PENGPU	EHINRS	SHINER, SHRINE	EHLNPY	PHENYL
EGNRTU	GUNTER, URGENT	EHINRT	HINTER	EHLOPP	HOPPLE
EGNRTY	GENTRY	EHINRW	WHINER	EHLORW	HOWLER
EGNRWY	GERWYN	EHINSS	SHENSI	EHLOST	HOSTEL, HOTELS
EGOORV	GROOVE	EHINSW	NEWISH, WHINES	EHLOSU	HOUSEL
EGOOST	STOOGE	EHINTW	WHITEN	EHLOSV	HOVELS, SHOVEL
EGOPRR	GROPER	EHINTZ	ZENITH	EHLOTW	HOWLET
EGOPRS	GROPES	EHIOPS	SOPHIE	EHLPSW	WHELPS
EGORRS	ROGERS	EHIOPT	OPHITE	EHLRRU	HURLER
EGORRV	GROVER	EHIORS	HOSIER	EHLRSY	SHERYL
EGORRW	GROWER	EHIORT	HERIOT	EHLRTU	HURTLE, LUTHER
EGORSS	OGRESS	EHIOST	HOSTIE	EHLRUY	HURLEY
EGORSU	GROUSE, ROGUES,	EHIOTT	HOTTIE	EHLSSU	LUSHES
	RUGOSE	EHIPPR	HIPPER	EHLSTU	HUSTLE, SLEUTH
EGORSV	GROVES	EHIPRS	PERISH, RESHIP	EHLUXY	HUXLEY
EGORSY	GYROSE	EHIRRS	SHERRI	EHMMRU	HUMMER
EGOSSV	VOSGES	EHIRSS	HISSER, SHIRES	EHMNOR	HERMON
EGOSUV	VOGUES	EHIRST	THEIRS	EHMNSY	HYMENS
		EHIRSV	SHIVER, SHRIVE		

EHMORT	MOTHER	EIILMR	LIMIER	EIKLNW	WELKIN, WINKLE
EHMRST	THERMS	EIILMS	SIMILE	EIKLRT	KILTER
EHMRSY	RHYMES	EIILMU	MILIEU	EIKMOS	ESKIMO
EHMRUY	RHEUMY	EIILNN	IN LINE	EIKMST	KISMET
EHMSSU	MUSHES	EIILNR	INLIER	EIKMSU	MUSKIE
EHNOPS	PHONES	EIILNS	LIE-INS	EIKNOV	INVOKE
EHNOPY	PHONEY	EIILNU	IN LIEU	EIKNPR	PERNIK, PINKER
EHNORS	HERONS	EIILNV	LIVE-IN	EIKNRS	SINKER
EHNORT	HORNET, THRONE	EIILOR	OILIER	EIKNRT	TINKER
EHNOST	HONEST	EIILRV	VIRILE	EIKNRW	WINKER
EHNRTU	HUNTER	EIILRW	WILIER	EIKNSS	SKEINS
EHNSTT	TENTHS	EIILRX	ELIXIR	EIKNSV	KNIVES
EHOOOP	HOOPOE	EIILZZ	LIZZIE	EIKNTT	KITTEN
EHOOPR	HOOPER	EIIMNN	MINNIE	EIKOOR	ROOKIE
EHOOPY	PHOOEY	EIINNT	INTINE	EIKOPP	KOPPIE
EHOORT	HOOTER	EIINNV	VINNIE	EIKOPR	POKIER
EHOORV	HOOVER	EIINNW	WINNIE	EIKPPR	KIPPER
EHOOST	SOOTHE	EIINOS	IONISE	EIKPSS	SPIKES
EHOOSV	HOOVES	EIINOZ	IONIZE	EIKRRS	RISKER
EHOPPR	HOPPER	EIINPR	PINIER	EIKRSS	KISSER, KRISES, SKIERS
EHOPRS	POSHER	EIINPT	PINITE, TIEPIN	EIKRST	STRIKE, TRIKES
EHOPRT	POTHER	EIINRT	TINIER	EIKRSV	SKIVER
EHOPRU	UPHROE	EIINRV	IRVINE	EIKSSS	KISSES
EHORSS	SHORES	EIINSS	SEISIN	EILLMR	MILLER
EHORST	OTHERS, THROES	EIINST	TIE-INS	EILLMT	MILLET
EHORSV	SHOVER	EIINTV	INVITE	EILLNO	LIONEL, NIELLO
EHORSW	SHOWER, WHORES	EIINVV	VIVIEN	EILLNT	LENTIL, LINTEL
EHORSY	HORSEY	EIIPST	PITIES	EILLOT	ELLIOT
EHORTT	HOTTER	EIIPSX	PIXIES	EILLPU	PILULE
EHORTV	THROVE	EIIRRW	WIRIER	EILLRT	RILLET, TILLER
EHORTX	EXHORT	EIIRSS	IRISES	EILLRW	WILLER
EHORTY	THEORY	EIIRTX	TRIXIE	EILLSU	ILL-USE
EHOSSU	HOUSES	EIIRVZ	VIZIER	EILLTT	LITTLE
EHOSSV	SHOVES	EIISSS	SISSIE	EILLTW	WILLET
EHPRSU	PUSHER	EIJKNR	JERKIN	EILLVY	EVILLY, LIVELY, VILELY
EHPRSY	SYPHER	EIJKNU	JUNKIE	EILMNO	OILMEN
EHPRYZ	ZEPHYR	EIJKOS	OSIJEK	EILMNR	LIMNER, MERLIN
EHPSSU	PUSHES	EIJLRT	JILTER	EILMNS	SIMNEL
EHRRSU	RUSHER	EIJLSU	JULIES	EILMNV	MELVIN
EHRRSY	SHERRY	EIJLTU	JULIET	EILMNY	MYELIN
EHRRTU	HURTER	EIJNNO	ENJOIN	EILMOS	MOLISE
EHRRWY	WHERRY	EIJNOR	JOINER, REJOIN	EILMOT	MOTILE
EHRSSU	RHESUS, RUSHES, USHERS	EIJNRU	INJURE	EILMPP	PIMPLE
		EIJNSX	JINXES	EILMPR	LIMPER
EHRSSW	SHREWS	EIJRSU	JURIES	EILMPS	SIMPLE
EHRSTY	THYRSE	EIJRTT	JITTER	EILMPT	LIMPET
EHSSTU	TUSHES	EIJSTU	JESUIT	EILMPU	PILEUM
EHSSTY	SHYEST	EIKLLR	KILLER	EILMPW	WIMPLE
EIIKNP	PINKIE	EIKLLY	ILKLEY, LIKELY	EILMRS	MILERS, SMILER
EIIKNR	INKIER	EIKLMR	MILKER	EILMRT	MILTER
EIILLL	LILLIE	EIKLNS	SILKEN	EILMRU	MURIEL
EIILLM	MILLIE	EIKLNT	TINKLE	EILMRW	WILMER
EIILLS	LILIES	EIKLNU	UNLIKE	EILMSS	SMILES
EIILLW	WILLIE	EIKLNV	KELVIN	EILMSU	MUESLI

97

EILMSY	LIMEYS, SMILEY
EILMTU	TELIUM
EILMTY	TIMELY
EILNNO	LONNIE, ONLINE
EILNNT	LINNET
EILNOR	ELINOR
EILNOS	INSOLE, LESION
EILNPP	NIPPLE
EILNPS	SPINEL, SPLINE
EILNPT	PINTLE
EILNPU	LINEUP, LUPINE
EILNRS	LINERS
EILNRT	LINTER
EILNST	ENLIST, INLETS, LISTEN, SILENT, TINSEL
EILNSV	SNIVEL
EILNSY	LYSINE
EILNTY	LENITY
EILNUV	UNLIVE, UNVEIL
EILOOR	ORIOLE
EILOOT	OOLITE
EILOPS	PILOSE
EILOPT	POLITE
EILORT	LOIRET, LOITER, TOILER
EILORU	LOURIE
EILORV	OLIVER
EILOSU	LOUISE
EILOSV	OLIVES
EILOSX	ISOLEX
EILOTT	LOTTIE, TOILET
EILOTV	OLIVET, VIOLET
EILPPR	RIPPLE
EILPPT	TIPPLE
EILPPU	PILEUP
EILPRS	LISPER, PERILS, PERLIS, PLIERS
EILPRT	TRIPLE
EILPSS	PLISSE, SPIELS
EILPST	STIPEL
EILPSU	PILEUS
EILPSV	PELVIS
EILPSX	PIXELS
EILRST	LITERS, LITRES, TILERS
EILRSV	LIVERS, SILVER, SLIVER
EILRSY	RILEYS
EILRTT	LITTER, TILTER
EILRTU	RUTILE
EILRVY	LIVERY, VERILY
EILSST	ISLETS, STILES
EILSSY	SISLEY
EILSTT	TITLES
EILSTU	ISEULT
EILSTV	VILEST
EILSVW	SWIVEL
EILSVY	SYLVIE

EILSWY	WISELY
EILSXY	SEXILY
EILSZZ	SIZZLE
EILTTT	TITTLE
EILTVY	LEVITY
EIMMNU	IMMUNE
EIMMOR	MEMOIR
EIMMRS	SIMMER
EIMMRU	IMMURE
EIMNOR	MERINO
EIMNOS	EONISM, MONIES, SIMEON, SIMONE
EIMNPT	PITMEN
EIMNRS	MERSIN, MINERS
EIMNRT	MINTER
EIMNRU	MURINE
EIMNRV	MERVIN, VERMIN
EIMNSX	MINXES
EIMNTT	MITTEN
EIMNTU	MINUET, MINUTE
EIMNTY	ENMITY
EIMNZZ	MIZZEN
EIMOPS	IMPOSE
EIMORS	ISOMER, RIMOSE
EIMOSS	MOSSIE
EIMOST	SOMITE
EIMOSV	MOVIES
EIMOTV	MOTIVE
EIMOTY	MOIETY
EIMPRR	PRIMER
EIMPRS	PRIMES, SIMPER
EIMPRT	PERMIT
EIMPRU	IMPURE, UMPIRE
EIMPTU	IMPUTE
EIMRRT	TRIMER
EIMRSS	MISERS, REMISS
EIMRST	MERITS, MISTER, MITRES, SMITER, TIMERS
EIMRSV	VERISM, VERMIS
EIMRSX	MIXERS
EIMRSY	MISERY
EIMSSS	MISSES
EIMSST	TMESIS
EIMSSU	MISUSE
EIMSSX	SEXISM
EIMSTY	STYMIE
EINNNR	RENNIN
EINNOO	IONONE
EINNOR	RONNIE
EINNOT	INTONE
EINNPR	PINNER
EINNPT	TENPIN
EINNRS	SINNER
EINNRT	INTERN
EINNRW	WINNER

EINNST	SENNIT, TENNIS
EINNTT	INTENT
EINNTU	IN TUNE
EINNTV	INVENT
EINNTY	NINETY
EINOPR	ORPINE
EINOPS	PONIES
EINOPT	POINTE
EINORR	IRONER
EINORS	NOSIER, SENIOR
EINORT	NORITE, ORIENT
EINORV	RENVOI
EINOSS	ENOSIS, NOESIS, NOISES, OSSEIN
EINOSW	NOWISE
EINOTW	TOWNIE
EINPPR	NIPPER
EINPPS	PEPSIN
EINPRS	SNIPER
EINPRT	PINTER
EINPRU	PUNIER, PURINE, UNRIPE
EINPRY	PINERY
EINPSS	SNIPES, SPINES
EINPST	INSTEP, SPINET
EINPSU	SUPINE
EINQSU	SEQUIN
EINQUU	UNIQUE
EINRRS	RINSER
EINRRU	RUINER
EINRSS	RESINS, RINSES, SIRENS
EINRST	INSERT, SINTER
EINRSU	INSURE, URSINE
EINRTU	TRIUNE, UNITER
EINRTV	INVERT
EINRTW	TWINER, WINTER
EINRVY	VINERY
EINSST	INSETS, STEINS
EINSSW	SINEWS, SWINES
EINSTV	INVEST
EINSTZ	ZENIST
EINSUW	UNWISE
EINSUX	UNISEX
EINSVX	VIXENS
EINSWY	SINEWY
EINTTY	ENTITY
EIOORZ	OOZIER
EIOOST	OTIOSE
EIOPRR	ROPIER
EIOPSS	POSIES
EIOPST	POSTIE
EIOPTT	TIPTOE
EIORRS	ROSIER
EIORRT	RIOTER
EIORRW	OWERRI

EIORSS	OSIERS
EIORST	SORTIE, TORIES, TRIOSE
EIOSTV	SOVIET
EIOTVV	VOTIVE
EIPPRR	RIPPER
EIPPRS	PIPERS, SIPPER
EIPPRT	PRIPET, TIPPER
EIPPRZ	ZIPPER
EIPPST	SIPPET
EIPPTT	TIPPET
EIPPUY	YUPPIE
EIPQSU	PIQUES
EIPQTU	PIQUET
EIPRRS	SPRIER
EIPRSS	PRISES, SPIRES
EIPRST	ESPRIT, PRIEST, RIPEST, SPRITE, STRIPE
EIPRSU	EPIRUS, UPRISE
EIPRSV	VIPERS
EIPRSZ	PRIZES
EIPRTV	PRIVET
EIPRTY	PYRITE
EIPRXY	EXPIRY
EIPSSS	PISSES, SEPSIS, SPEISS
EIPSST	STIPES
EIPSSW	SWIPES
EIPSTU	TIE-UPS
EIPSTW	PEWITS
EIQRSU	QUIRES, RISQUE, SQUIRE
EIQRUV	QUIVER
EIQTUY	EQUITY
EIRRSS	RISERS
EIRRST	TRIERS
EIRRSV	RIVERS
EIRRTW	WRITER
EIRSST	RESIST, RESITS, SISTER
EIRSSU	ISSUER
EIRSTT	SITTER
EIRSTV	RIVETS, STRIVE, VERIST
EIRSTW	WRIEST
EIRTTT	TITTER
EIRTTV	TRIVET
EIRTUV	VIRTUE
EIRTVY	VERITY
EISSSU	ISSUES
EISSTT	TESTIS
EISSTU	SUITES, TISSUE
EISSTW	WISEST
EISSTX	SEXIST
EJKNTU	JUNKET
EJKOPS	SKOPJE
EJKORS	JOKERS
EJLOST	JOSTLE

EJLOSU	JOULES
EJLPSU	JULEPS
EJMPRU	JUMPER
EJNOTT	JETTON
EJOPRT	PROJET
EJORTT	JOTTER
EJRTTU	JUTTER
EKLLNS	KNELLS
EKLLSY	SKELLY
EKLMMU	KUMMEL
EKLMOW	WELKOM
EKLOOR	LOOKER
EKLOSY	YOKELS
EKLOWY	LOW-KEY
EKLRRU	LURKER
EKLRSU	SULKER
EKMNOY	MONKEY
EKMOOP	MOPOKE
EKMORS	SMOKER
EKMOSS	SMOKES
EKMSTU	MUSKET
EKNNOT	KENTON, NEKTON
EKNNSU	SUNKEN
EKNOPS	SPOKEN
EKNORR	KRONER
EKNORW	KNOWER
EKNOST	TOKENS
EKNOUY	UNYOKE
EKOORT	RETOOK
EKOPRR	PORKER
EKOPRS	POKERS
EKOPSS	SPOKES
EKORRW	REWORK, WORKER
EKORRY	YORKER
EKORST	STOKER, STROKE
EKOSST	STOKES
EKRSTU	TUSKER
EKRTUY	TURKEY
ELLLOR	LOLLER
ELLLOV	LOVELL
ELLLOW	LOWELL
ELLMOW	MELLOW
ELLMRU	MULLER
ELLMSS	SMELLS
ELLMSY	SMELLY
ELLMTU	MULLET
ELLMUV	VELLUM
ELLNOP	POLLEN
ELLNOW	NOWELL
ELLNOY	LONELY
ELLNSU	SULLEN
ELLNUW	UNWELL
ELLOPW	POWELL
ELLOPX	POLLEX

ELLORR	ORRELL, ROLLER
ELLOSY	SOLELY
ELLOVY	LOVELY, VOLLEY
ELLOWY	YELLOW
ELLOWZ	ZWOLLE
ELLPSS	SPELLS
ELLPTU	PULLET
ELLPUY	PULLEY
ELLSSW	SWELLS
ELMMOP	POMMEL
ELMMOS	MOSLEM
ELMMPU	PUMMEL
ELMNOR	MERLON
ELMNOS	LEMNOS, LEMONS, MELONS, SOLEMN
ELMNOT	LOMENT, MELTON, MOLTEN
ELMNOY	LEMONY
ELMNPU	LUMPEN, PLENUM
ELMNVY	MELVYN
ELMOPY	EMPLOY
ELMORS	MORSEL
ELMORY	MORLEY
ELMOST	MOLEST, MOTELS
ELMOTT	MOTTLE
ELMOTY	MOTLEY
ELMOUV	VOLUME
ELMPPU	PEPLUM
ELMPRU	RUMPLE
ELMPSU	PLUMES
ELMRSU	LEMURS
ELMRTY	MYRTLE, TERMLY
ELMSST	SMELTS
ELMSSU	MUSSEL
ELMTUU	MUTULE
ELMTUY	MUTELY
ELMUZZ	MUZZLE
ELNNOS	NELSON
ELNNOX	LENNOX
ELNNRU	RUNNEL
ELNNTU	TUNNEL
ELNOOS	LOOSEN
ELNOOY	LOONEY
ELNOPT	LEPTON
ELNOPY	OPENLY, POLEYN
ELNORS	LONERS
ELNOSS	LESSON
ELNOST	SOLENT, STOLEN, TELSON
ELNOSU	ENSOUL
ELNOSV	NOVELS, SLOVEN
ELNOUZ	ZONULE
ELNOZZ	NOZZLE
ELNPTU	PENULT
ELNPTY	PENTYL, PLENTY

ELNSSU	UNLESS	ELRRSU	RULERS	ENNORU	NEURON
ELNSWY	SELWYN	ELRSSU	RUSSEL	ENNORV	VERNON
ELNSXY	LYNXES	ELRSTU	LUSTRE, RESULT,	ENNORW	RENOWN
ELNSYY	LYNSEY		RUSTLE, ULSTER	ENNOST	SONNET, TENONS,
ELNTTU	NUTLET	ELRSTY	STYLER		TONNES
ELNTTY	NETTLY	ELRSUY	SURELY	ENNOTW	NEWTON
ELNUZZ	NUZZLE	ELRTTU	TURTLE	ENNOVY	YVONNE
ELOOOT	O'TOOLE	ELRTTY	TETRYL	ENNPTU	PUNNET
ELOOPR	LOOPER	ELSSTU	TUSSLE	ENNRRU	RUNNER
ELOORS	LOOSER	ELSSTY	SLYEST, STYLES	ENOOPR	OPERON
ELOORT	LOOTER, RETOOL,	ELSTTY	STYLET	ENOORS	SOONER
	TOOLER	EMMMRU	MUMMER	ENOORT	ENROOT
ELOOSS	LOOSES	EMMNOT	MOMENT	ENOOSS	NOOSES
ELOOTT	TOOTLE	EMMORY	MEMORY	ENOOSZ	SNOOZE
ELOPPP	POPPLE	EMMRRU	RUMMER	ENOPRR	PERRON
ELOPPR	LOPPER, PROPEL	EMMRSU	SUMMER	ENOPRS	PERSON
ELOPPT	TOPPLE	EMMSUU	MUSEUM	ENOPRV	PROVEN
ELOPRS	PROLES, SLOPER	EMNNOT	MENTON	ENOPRY	PYRONE
ELOPRT	PETROL	EMNOPY	EPONYM	ENOPTT	POTENT
ELOPRV	PLOVER	EMNORS	SERMON	ENORRS	SNORER
ELOPRX	PLEXOR	EMNORT	MENTOR, MERTON	ENORRY	ORNERY
ELOPSS	SLOPES	EMNOSY	MONEYS	ENORSS	SENORS, SENSOR,
ELOPTU	TUPELO	EMNOTY	ETYMON		SNORES
ELORRS	SORREL	EMNOXY	EXONYM	ENORST	STONER, TENORS,
ELORSS	LESSOR, LOSERS	EMNRVY	MERVYN		TENSOR
ELORST	OSTLER, STEROL	EMNTUY	TYUMEN	ENORSW	OWNERS, WORSEN
ELORSV	LOVERS, SOLVER	EMOORR	ROOMER	ENORTT	ROTTEN
ELORSW	SLOWER	EMOORS	MOROSE, ROMEOS	ENORTY	TYRONE
ELORSY	SORELY	EMOORT	MOOTER	ENOSST	STONES
ELORTV	REVOLT	EMOOSS	OSMOSE	ENOSTX	SEXTON
ELORTW	TROWEL	EMOPPT	MOPPET	ENOSUV	VENOUS
ELORUV	LOUVRE, VELOUR	EMOPRT	PRO TEM, TROMPE	ENOSVY	ENVOYS
ELORVW	WOLVER	EMOPRU	EURO MP	ENOTTU	TENUTO, TEUTON
ELORVY	OVERLY	EMOPST	TEMPOS	ENPPTU	PENT UP
ELORWY	YOWLER	EMOQSU	MOSQUE	ENPRRU	PRUNER
ELOSSS	LOSSES	EMOQUY	QUEMOY	ENPRSU	PRUNES
ELOSST	STOLES	EMORRT	TERMOR, TREMOR	ENPRTU	PUNTER
ELOSTU	SOLUTE, TOUSLE	EMORRW	WORMER	ENPRUY	PENURY
ELOSTW	LOWEST, OWLETS,	EMORST	METROS	ENPSTU	UNSTEP
	TOWELS	EMORSU	MOUSER	ENPTUU	TUNE-UP
ELOSVW	VOWELS, WOLVES	EMORSV	MOVERS	ENPTUW	UNWEPT
ELOSVY	LOVEYS	EMORSW	MOWERS	ENRRSU	RERUNS
ELOSXY	XYLOSE	EMORSY	MYSORE	ENRRTU	RETURN, TURNER
ELOTTU	OUTLET	EMOSSU	MOUSSE	ENRSST	STERNS
ELOTUV	VOLUTE	EMOSTT	MOTETS, TOTEMS	ENRSSU	NURSES
ELOTWY	OWELTY	EMOSZZ	MEZZOS	ENRSTU	TUNERS, UNREST
ELPPRU	PURPLE	EMPRSS	SPERMS	ENRSTW	STREWN
ELPPSU	SUPPLE	EMPSSU	MESS-UP	ENRSTY	SENTRY
ELPPRU	PURLER	EMPSTU	SEPTUM	ENRSUU	UNSURE
ELPRTY	PELTRY, PERTLY	EMRSSU	SERUMS	ENRTTU	NUTTER
ELPRUY	PURELY	EMRSTU	MUSTER, STUMER	ENRTUU	UNTRUE
ELPSSU	PLUSES, PULSES	EMRTTU	MUTTER	ENRVWY	WYVERN
ELPSTU	LETUPS	EMSSTY	SYSTEM	ENSSTU	SUNSET
ELPSUX	PLEXUS	ENNNOP	PENNON	ENTTWY	TWENTY
ELPUZZ	PUZZLE			EOOPPR	POOPER

EOOPPS	OPPOSE	EORTTT	TOTTER	FFIOPR	RIP-OFF
EOOPRR	POORER	EORTTX	EXTORT	FFIOPT	TIP-OFF
EOORRT	ROOTER, TORERO	EORTVX	VORTEX	FFIOST	SOFFIT
EOORST	TOROSE	EORUVY	VOYEUR	FFIQSU	QUIFFS
EOORSW	WOOERS	EOSSST	TOSSES	FFISST	STIFFS
EOORTT	TOOTER	EOSSSU	SOUSSE	FFISUX	SUFFIX
EOOSTW	SOWETO	EOSSTV	STOVES	FFLRUY	RUFFLY
EOPPPR	POPPER	EOSTTU	OUTSET	FFNORU	RUN OFF
EOPPPT	POPPET	EPPPRY	PREPPY	FFNSUY	SNUFFY
EOPPRR	PER PRO, PROPER	EPPPTU	PUPPET	FFOPTU	PUT-OFF
EOPPRT	TOPPER	EPPRSU	SUPPER, UPPERS	FFRRUU	FURFUR
EOPPRY	POPERY, PYROPE	EPRRSU	PURSER	FFSTUY	STUFFY
EOPPRT	PORTER, REPORT	EPRRTU	RUPERT	FGGIIZ	FIZGIG
EOPRRU	POURER	EPRSSU	PURSES	FGGINU	FUGING
EOPRSS	POSERS, PROSES,	EPRSTU	PUREST	FGGORY	FROGGY
	SPORES	EPRSTW	TWERPS	FGHILT	FLIGHT
EOPRST	POSTER, PRESTO,	EPRSUU	PURSUE	FGHIRT	FRIGHT
	TROPES	EPRTTU	PUTTER	FGHIST	FIGHTS
EOPRSU	POSEUR	EPRTTY	PRETTY	FGHOTU	FOUGHT
EOPRSW	POWERS	EPRUVY	PURVEY	FGIILN	FILING
EOPRSY	OSPREY	EPSSSU	PUSSES	FGIINN	FINING
EOPRTT	POTTER	EPSSTU	SET-UPS, UPSETS	FGIINR	FIRING
EOPRTU	POUTER, TROUPE	EQRTWY	QWERTY	FGIINX	FIXING
EOPRTX	EXPORT	EQSSTU	QUESTS	FGILNY	FLYING
EOPRTY	POETRY	ERRSUU	USURER	FGILUY	UGLIFY
EOPSSS	POSSES	ERRSUY	SURREY	FGIMNU	FUMING
EOPSST	POSSET	ERRTTU	TURRET	FGINOX	FOXING
EOPSSU	OPUSES, SPOUSE	ERSSST	STRESS	FGINRY	FRINGY, FRYING
EOPSTX	SEXPOT	ERSSTU	RUSSET, SUREST	FGINSU	FUSING
EOQRTU	ROQUET, TORQUE	ERSSTY	TRESSY	FGKNUU	KUNG FU
EOQSTU	QUOTES	ERSSUV	VERSUS	FGNSUU	FUNGUS
EORRRS	ERRORS	ERSTTU	TRUEST	FGOORT	FORGOT
EORRRT	TERROR	ERSTUU	SUTURE, UTERUS	FHIINS	FINISH
EORRRY	ORRERY	ERSTUV	TURVES	FHILTY	FILTHY
EORRST	RESORT, ROSTER,	ERSTUY	SURETY	FHIRST	FIRTHS, SHRIFT
	SORTER	ERSTVY	VESTRY	FHIRTT	THRIFT
EORRSU	ROUSER, SOURER	ERSTWY	WRYEST	FHISST	SHIFTS
EORRSV	ROVERS	ERSTXY	XYSTER	FHISTU	SHUFTI
EORRSW	ROWERS	ERSUVY	SURVEY	FHISTY	SHIFTY
EORRTT	RETORT, ROTTER	ERTTUX	URTEXT	FHNSUU	FUSHUN
EORRTU	ROUTER, TOURER	ESSTUX	SEXTUS	FHORST	FROTHS
EORRTV	TREVOR, TROVER	FFFLUY	FLUFFY	FHORTU	FOURTH
EORRZZ	ROZZER	FFGINO	OFFING	FHORTY	FROTHY
EORSST	STORES, TOSSER	FFHIST	FIFTHS	FHOUUZ	FUZHOU
EORSSU	SEROUS	FFHISW	WHIFFS	FHSTUY	SHUFTY
EORSSV	SERVOS, VERSOS	FFHIWY	WHIFFY	FIIKNR	FIRKIN
EORSSW	SOWERS	FFIINT	TIFFIN	FIILLN	FILL-IN
EORSTT	OTTERS	FFIKSS	SKIFFS	FIILLP	FILLIP
EORSTU	OUSTER, ROUTES	FFILLU	FULFIL	FIILRU	FRIULI
EORSTV	STOVER, STROVE,	FFILTU	FITFUL	FIILST	TIFLIS
	TROVES, VOTERS	FFIMNU	MUFFIN	FIILVY	VILIFY
EORSTW	TOWERS	FFINPU	PUFFIN	FIIMNR	INFIRM
EORSTY	OYSTER, STOREY,	FFINSS	SNIFFS	FIIMNY	MINIFY
	TROYES	FFINSY	SNIFFY	FIIMST	MISFIT
EORSTZ	ZOSTER				

FIINOR	FIORIN	FLOPTU	POTFUL	GHIKNT	KNIGHT
FIITXY	FIXITY	FLOPUU	FOUL-UP	GHILPT	PLIGHT
FIIVVY	VIVIFY	FLORUY	FLOURY	GHILST	LIGHTS, SLIGHT
FIJLOR	FRIJOL	FLOSSY	FLOSSY	GHIMNO	HOMING
FIKRSS	FRISKS	FLOSTY	SOFTLY	GHIMTY	MIGHTY
FIKRSY	FRISKY	FLRRUY	FLURRY	GHINNO	HONING
FILLRS	FRILLS	FMORSU	FORUMS	GHINOP	HOPING
FILLRY	FRILLY	FMPRSU	FRUMPS	GHINOS	HOSING
FILLUW	WILFUL	FMPRUY	FRUMPY	GHINPY	HYPING
FILMOU	FOLIUM	FNNRUU	FUN RUN	GHINST	NIGHTS, THINGS
FILMRY	FIRMLY	FNORST	FRONTS	GHINSY	SHYING
FILMSY	FLIMSY	FNORSW	FROWNS	GHIOPZ	PHIZOG
FILNOR	FLORIN	FNOSTU	FOUNTS, FUTONS	GHIRST	GIRTHS, RIGHTS
FILNOW	INFLOW	FOOPRS	PROOFS	GHIRTW	WRIGHT
FILNST	FLINTS	FOOPSS	SPOOFS	GHISST	SIGHTS
FILNSU	SINFUL	FOORST	SORT OF	GHISTT	TIGHTS
FILNTY	FLINTY	FOOTUX	OUTFOX	GHISTW	WIGHTS
FILNUX	INFLUX	FORRUW	FURROW	GHLLSY	GHYLLS
FILOOS	FOLIOS	FORSST	FROSTS	GHLOPU	PLOUGH
FILORV	FRIVOL	FORSTY	FROSTY	GHLOSU	GHOULS, LOUGHS,
FILOSS	FOSSIL	FORSUU	RUFOUS		SLOUGH
FILOXY	FOXILY	FORWYZ	FROWZY	GHNORT	THRONG
FILPTU	UPLIFT	FPRSUY	FRY-UPS	GHNOST	THONGS
FILRST	FLIRTS	GGGILY	GIGGLY	GHNOSU	SHOGUN
FIMNOR	INFORM	GGGORY	GROGGY	GHNOTU	HOGNUT, NOUGHT
FIMOST	MOTIFS	GGHNOU	GUNG-HO	GHNRUY	HUNGRY
FIMSTU	MUFTIS	GGIINP	PIGGIN	GHNSUY	GUNSHY
FINORX	FORNIX	GGIINV	GIVING	GHORTU	TROUGH
FINOSU	FUSION	GGIIRR	GRIGRI	GHORTW	GROWTH
FINOTY	NOTIFY	GGIJLY	JIGGLY	GHOSST	GHOSTS
FIOOTT	FOOT IT	GGIKNO	GINKGO	GHOSSU	SOUGHS
FIOPRT	PROFIT	GGILNO	OGLING	GHOSTU	SOUGHT
FIORST	FORTIS	GGILNU	GLUING	GHRSSU	SHRUGS
FIOSSY	OSSIFY	GGILOO	GIGOLO	GIIJNV	JIVING
FIOTTU	OUTFIT	GGILWY	WIGGLY	GIIKLN	LIKING
FIPRUY	PURIFY	GGINNO	NOGGIN	GIIKNN	INKING
FIPTYY	TYPIFY	GGINOR	GORING, GRINGO	GIIKNR	IRKING
FIRSST	FIRSTS	GGINOZ	ZIGONG	GIIKNS	SKIING
FIRSTU	FRUITS	GGINRU	URGING	GIIKNV	VIKING
FIRTUY	FRUITY	GGINUY	GUYING	GIILMN	LIMING
FIRYZZ	FRIZZY	GGITWY	TWIGGY	GIILNN	LIGNIN, LINING
FISSTW	SWIFTS	GGLLOO	LOGLOG	GIILNO	OILING
FJLOUY	JOYFUL	GGLOOO	GOOGOL	GIILNP	PILING
FKLNUY	FLUNKY	GGLOOY	GOOGLY	GIILNR	RILING
FKLOSY	FOLKSY	GGMOSY	SMOGGY	GIILNT	TILING
FLLNOU	FULL-ON	GGNOOR	GORGON	GIILNU	GUILIN
FLLOOW	FOLLOW	GGNRUY	GRUNGY	GIILNV	LIVING
FLLOUY	FOULLY	GGRRUU	GRUGRU	GIILOR	OILRIG
FLMOOS	FOLSOM	GHHILY	HIGHLY	GIILRV	VIRGIL
FLMORY	FORMYL	GHHIST	THIGHS	GIILSV	VIGILS
FLNRUU	UNFURL	GHHOTU	THOUGH	GIIMMN	MIMING
FLOORS	FLOORS	GHIIKN	HIKING	GIIMNN	MINING
FLOOYZ	FLOOZY	GHIINR	HIRING	GIIMNR	MIRING
FLOPPY	FLOPPY	GHIINV	HIVING	GIIMNT	TIMING

GIIMNX	MIXING	GIMNTU	MUTING	GIRTTY	GRITTY
GIINNN	INNING	GIMOSY	YOGISM	GJLNUY	JUNGLY
GIINNP	PINING	GIMOTU	GOMUTI	GJNRUU	GURJUN
GIINNR	RING IN	GINNOO	GONION	GKRYYZ	KYRGYZ
GIINNS	SINING	GINNOP	NINGPO	GLLMUY	GLUMLY
GIINNW	WINING	GINNOS	NOSING, SIGN ON	GLLOOP	GOLLOP
GIINNX	NIXING	GINNOT	NOTING, TONING	GLMNOO	MONGOL
GIINOR	ORIGIN	GINNOW	OWNING	GLMOOY	GLOOMY
GIINPP	PIPING	GINNOZ	ZONING	GLMOSU	MOGULS
GIINPW	WIPING	GINNTU	TUNING	GLMSUY	SMUGLY
GIINRS	RISING, SIRING	GINOOS	ISOGON	GLNOOO	OOLONG
GIINRT	TIRING	GINOOW	WOOING	GLNPUU	UNPLUG
GIINRV	IRVING, VIRGIN	GINOOZ	OOZING	GLNSUY	SNUGLY
GIINRW	WIRING	GINOPR	PORING, ROPING	GLOOOY	OOLOGY
GIINST	SITING	GINOPS	POSING	GLOOPR	PROLOG
GIINSZ	SIZING	GINOPT	OPTING	GLOOSW	GO-SLOW
GIIRST	TIGRIS	GINORS	GRISON, GROINS,	GLOOTU	LOG OUT
GIJKNO	JOKING		SIGNOR	GLOPTU	PUTLOG
GIJLNY	JINGLY	GINORV	ROVING	GLORSW	GROWLS
GIJNOY	JOYING	GINORW	ROWING	GLOSSY	GLOSSY
GIKLNY	KINGLY	GINOSS	GNOSIS	GMNNOO	GNOMON
GIKNNU	NUKING	GINOST	INGOTS	GMOOPR	POGROM
GIKNOP	POKING	GINOSW	SOWING	GMOORS	GROOMS
GIKNOW	WOKING	GINOTT	TOTING	GMPRUY	GRUMPY
GIKNOY	YOKING	GINOTU	OUTING	GMPSUY	GYPSUM
GIKNPU	PUKING	GINOTV	VOTING	GNNOOS	ON SONG
GILLRS	GRILLS	GINOTW	TOWING	GNNSUU	UNSUNG
GILMRY	GRIMLY	GINOTY	TOYING	GNOORT	TROGON
GILMWY	GWILYM, GWYLIM	GINOVW	VOWING	GNOPPU	OPPUGN, POPGUN
GILNOO	LOGION	GINOWW	WOWING	GNOPRS	PRONGS
GILNOP	LOPING, POLING	GINPRS	SPRING	GNOPSY	SPONGY
GILNOS	LOSING, SOLING	GINPRY	PRYING	GNORST	STRONG
GILNOV	LOVING	GINPSU	PIGNUS	GNORSW	WRONGS
GILNOW	LOWING	GINPSY	SPYING	GNORUV	GUVNOR
GILNPY	PLYING	GINPTU	PIGNUT	GNORYZ	GROZNY
GILNRU	LURING, RULING	GINPTY	TYPING	GNPRSU	SPRUNG
GILNSS	SLINGS	GINRST	STRING	GNRSTU	GRUNTS, STRUNG
GILNST	GLINTS	GINRTY	TRYING	GNRTUU	GUNTUR
GILNSU	SLUING	GINRWY	WRYING	GNSTUU	TUNGUS
GILNSY	GLINYS, GLYNIS,	GINSST	STINGS	GOOPST	STOP-GO
	SINGLY	GINSSV	V-SIGNS	GOORTT	GROTTO
GILNTY	TINGLY	GINSSW	SWINGS	GOORVY	GROOVY
GILOOS	IGLOOS	GINSTY	STINGY	GOPRSU	GROUPS
GILORY	GILROY, GORILY	GINSUU	UNGUIS	GORRTU	TURGOR
GILRSY	GRISLY	GIOPSS	GOSSIP	GORSTU	GROUTS
GILTUY	GUILTY	GIOPST	SPIGOT	GORTTU	ROTGUT
GILTYZ	GLITZY	GIORRU	RIGOUR	GORTTY	GROTTY
GIMNNO	MIGNON	GIORSV	VIRGOS	GORTUY	YOGURT
GIMNOO	MOOING	GIORTU	RIG-OUT	GSYYYZ	SYZYGY
GIMNOP	MOPING	GIORUV	VIGOUR	HHHOOT	HOHHOT
GIMNOV	MOVING	GIOSTU	GIUSTO	HHMRTY	RHYTHM
GIMNOW	MOWING	GIPRSS	SPRIGS	HHNOSU	HONSHU
GIMNPU	IMPUGN	GIPSTY	PIGSTY	HHOOSW	WHOOSH
GIMNSU	MUSING	GIRSST	GRISTS	HHPSUU	HUSH-UP

HHRSTU	THRUSH	HJNNOY	JOHNNY	HOPSTU	TOPHUS, UPSHOT
HIILLT	LILITH	HJNOST	ST JOHN	HORSST	SHORTS
HIILPP	PHILIP	HKNOOU	UNHOOK	HORSTT	TROTHS
HIIMPS	IMPISH	HKNRSU	SHRUNK	HORSTW	THROWS
HIIMST	MISHIT	HKOOPU	HOOKUP	HORSTY	SHORTY
HIINTW	WITHIN	HKSUUY	KYUSHU	HORTWY	WORTHY
HIKNRS	SHRINK	HLLOOW	HOLLOW	HOSSTU	SHOUTS
HIKSSW	WHISKS	HLLOSU	HULLOS	HOSTUY	YOUTHS
HIKSWY	WHISKY	HLLOWY	WHOLLY	HOSUUZ	SUZHOU
HILLOY	HOLILY	HLLPUY	LYULPH	HOUUXZ	XUZHOU
HILLPU	UPHILL	HLMOTY	THYMOL	HPPSUU	PUSH-UP
HILLRS	SHRILL	HLMPUY	PHYLUM	HPSTUY	TYPHUS
HILLRT	THRILL	HLNOUY	UNHOLY	HRSTTU	THRUST, TRUTHS
HILMOS	HOLISM	HLNSUU	LU-SHUN	IIIMNR	RIMINI
HILMOY	HOMILY	HLOOST	SHOLTO, THOLOS	IIIRST	IRITIS
HILMSU	MULISH	HLOPSS	SPLOSH	IIKKMS	SIKKIM
HILNPT	PLINTH	HLORSW	WHORLS	IIKNPP	PIPKIN
HILNTY	THINLY	HLORUY	HOURLY	IIKNSS	SISKIN
HILOPS	POLISH	HLOSST	SLOTHS	IIKPST	SKIP IT!
HILOSW	OWLISH	HLOSSY	SLOSHY	IILLOO	ILOILO
HILRSW	WHIRLS	HLSSUY	SLUSHY	IILLOY	OILILY
HILSTW	WHILST	HMMSUU	HUMMUS	IILLSW	WILLIS
HIMMSU	HUMISM	HMNOST	MONTHS	IILMMU	MILIUM
HIMNOY	HOMINY	HMNPSY	NYMPHS	IILMST	LIMITS
HIMPRS	SHRIMP	HMOOST	SMOOTH	IILNNU	INULIN
HIMSST	SMITHS	HMORUU	HUMOUR	IILNOR	ILORIN
HIMSTY	SMITHY	HMORUZ	HORMUZ	IILNOV	VIOLIN
HIMSWY	WHIMSY	HMOSTU	MOUTHS	IILNST	INSTIL
HINNST	NINTHS	HMOSTY	MYTHOS	IILOTV	TIVOLI
HINNSY	SHINNY	HMPSTU	THUMPS	IILPST	PISTIL
HINNWY	WHINNY	HMPTUY	HUMPTY	IILRWY	WIRILY
HINOOS	SHOO-IN	HMSTUY	THYMUS	IILTTW	TWILIT
HINOPS	SIPHON	HNNOOP	PHONON	IIMMNS	MINIMS
HINOST	SHINTO	HNOOPT	PHOTON	IIMMNU	MINIUM
HINPSU	PUNISH, UNSHIP	HNOORT	THORON	IIMNNO	MINION
HINPSX	SPHINX	HNOORU	HONOUR	IIMOSS	MIOSIS
HINRSU	INRUSH	HNOPSU	NOSH-UP	IIMSSS	MISSIS
HINSTY	SHINTY	HNOPSY	SYPHON	IINNOP	PINION
HIOPPS	POPISH	HNOPTY	PHYTON, PYTHON	IINNTU	INNUIT
HIOPST	PITHOS	HNORST	NORTHS, THORNS	IINORS	ROISIN
HIOPSY	PHYSIO	HNORSU	ONRUSH	IINOSV	VISION
HIORSU	HOURIS	HNORTW	THROWN	IINPPP	PIPPIN
HIOSST	HOISTS	HNORTY	RHYTON, THORNY	IINPTX	PINXIT
HIPPSU	UPPISH	HNOSTU	HUSTON	IINSST	INSIST, SIT-INS
HIPPWY	WHIPPY	HNSSTU	SHUNTS	IINSTU	IN SITU, INUITS
HIPRST	THRIPS	HOOPST	PHOTOS	IINTTU	INTUIT
HIQSSU	SQUISH	HOOPSW	WHOOPS	IINTTW	NITWIT
HIRSST	SHIRTS	HOOPTT	HOTPOT	IIOSTT	OTITIS
HIRSTT	THIRST, T-SHIRT	HOORRR	HORROR	IIPPST	PIPITS
HIRSTY	IRTYSH, SHIRTY	HOOSST	SHOOTS	IIPRST	SPIRIT
HIRTTY	THIRTY	HOOSSW	SWOOSH	IIRSSU	SIRIUS
HISSTX	SIXTHS	HOOTTY	TOOTHY	IISSTV	VISITS
HISTTY	SHITTY	HOPPSU	HOPPUS	IJLSUU	JULIUS
HIWYZZ	WHIZZY	HOPRTY	TROPHY	IJNORU	JUNIOR

IJNOST	JOINTS	ILMPSY	SIMPLY	IMOPST	IMPOST
IJNRUY	INJURY	ILMRTY	TRIMLY	IMORRR	MIRROR
IJNSTU	JUSTIN	ILMSTU	LITMUS	IMORRS	MORRIS
IJOSST	JOISTS	ILMTUU	TUMULI	IMOSTU	OSTIUM
IJRSTU	JURIST	ILNOOT	LOTION	IMPRSS	PRISMS
IKKKRU	KIRKUK	ILNOPP	POPLIN	IMPRSU	PRIMUS, PURISM
IKKOSS	KIOSKS	ILNOPS	SLIP-ON	IMPSUX	MIX-UPS
IKKRSU	KUKRIS	ILNOPT	PONTIL	IMQRSU	SQUIRM
IKKUUY	KIKUYU	ILNOQU	QUINOL	IMRSTU	TRUISM
IKLLSS	SKILLS	ILNOST	TONSIL	IMSSSU	MISSUS
IKLNOO	LOOK-IN	ILNOSW	WILSON	INNOOS	ONIONS
IKLNPU	LINKUP	ILNOSY	NOSILY	INNOOT	NOTION
IKLNSY	SLINKY	ILNPRU	PURLIN	INNOPP	NIPPON
IKLNTY	TINKLY	ILNPST	SPLINT	INNOSU	UNIONS, UNISON
IKLOPY	POKILY	ILNPSU	LUPINS	INNOWW	WINNOW
IKLSSU	SUSLIK	ILNSTU	INSULT, SUNLIT	INNRTU	TURN IN
IKMNOO	KIMONO	ILNSVY	VINYLS	INNSSU	SUNNIS
IKMPSY	SKIMPY	ILOOYZ	OOZILY	INOOPS	POISON
IKMRSS	SMIRKS	ILOPRX	PROLIX	INOOPT	OPTION, POTION
IKMSSU	KUMISS	ILOPRY	ROPILY	INOORS	ORISON
IKMSUU	KISUMU	ILOPSS	SPOILS	INOOTT	IN TOTO
IKNNOT	TONKIN	ILOPST	PILOTS, PISTOL,	INOPRS	PRISON
IKNNSY	SKINNY	POSTIL, SPOILT		INOPST	PISTON, POINTS
IKNNTU	UNKNIT	ILOPTY	POLITY	INOPTT	TIN-POT
IKNOPS	PINKOS	ILOQRU	LIQUOR	INORRS	NORRIS
IKNSST	STINKS	ILORSY	ROSILY	INORST	INTROS
IKOOPU	KUOPIO	ILPPRY	RIPPLY	INORSY	ROSINY
IKQRSU	QUIRKS	ILPPSU	PUPILS, SLIP-UP	INORTT	TRITON
IKQRUY	QUIRKY	ILPPSY	SLIPPY	INORTU	TURION
IKRSST	SKIRTS	ILPPTU	PULPIT	INOSTX	TOXINS
IKRSTY	KIRSTY	ILPSST	SPLITS	INOSUV	VINOUS
IKSUUY	SUU KYI	ILPSTU	TULIPS	INPPSU	PINUPS
IKSVVY	SKIVVY	ILPTTU	UPTILT	INPPSY	SNIPPY
ILLMPY	LIMPLY	ILQSTU	QUILTS	INPRST	PRINTS, SPRINT
ILLMSY	SLIMLY	ILRSSW	SWIRLS	INPRTU	TURNIP
ILLNOS	LLINOS	ILRSTW	TWIRLS	INQSTU	SQUINT
ILLNPU	PULL-IN	ILRSTY	LYRIST	INQSUY	QUINSY
ILLOPW	PILLOW	ILRSWY	SWIRLY	INRSXY	SYRINX
ILLOWW	WILLOW	ILRTWY	TWIRLY	INRTWY	WINTRY
ILLPSS	SPILLS	ILSSTT	STILTS	INSSTT	STINTS
ILLQSU	QUILLS, SQUILL	IMMMOS	MOMISM	IOPPTT	TIP-TOP
ILLRST	TRILLS	IMMNOS	MONISM, NOMISM	IOPRRS	PRIORS
ILLSST	STILLS	IMMOOS	SIMOOM	IOPRRY	PRIORY
ILLSSW	SWILLS	IMMOSU	OSMIUM	IOPRST	TRIPOS
ILLSTY	STILLY	IMMSTU	MUTISM, SUMMIT	IOPSST	PTOSIS
ILLSUV	VILLUS	IMNNOW	MINNOW	IOPSSY	PYOSIS
ILMMSU	MUSLIM	IMNOOR	MORION, MORONI	IOPSTV	PIVOTS
ILMNOT	MILTON	IMNOOT	MOTION	IOQSTU	QUOITS
ILMNOU	MOULIN	IMNORS	MINORS	IORSSV	VISORS
ILMNSU	MUSLIN	IMNOST	INMOST, MONIST	IORSTU	SUITOR
ILMOSS	LISSOM	IMNOSY	MYOSIN, SIMONY	IOSSTT	TSOTSI
ILMOTW	WILMOT	IMNTUY	MUTINY	IOTTUW	OUTWIT
ILMPPY	PIMPLY	IMOPRS	PORISM	IPPPSU	PUPPIS
ILMPRY	PRIMLY	IMOPRT	IMPORT	IPPRTY	TRIPPY

IPPSSU	PISS-UP	LMOOOP	MOLOPO
IPPTUY	UPPITY	LMOORU	ORMOLU
IPRRTU	IRRUPT	LMOSTU	MOULTS
IPRSST	STIRPS, STRIPS	LMOSTY	MOSTLY
IPRSSY	PRISSY	LMPRUY	RUMPLY
IPRSTU	PURIST, SPRUIT	LMPSSU	SLUMPS
IPRSTW	TWIRPS	LMTTUU	TUMULT
IPRSTY	STRIPY	LNNOSY	NYLONS
IPRTUY	PURITY	LNOOPY	POLONY
IPSSTU	SIT-UPS	LNOOST	STOLON
IPSTTY	TYPIST	LNOOTU	TOULON
IPTTTU	TITTUP	LNOPSY	PYLONS
IQRSTU	SQUIRT	LNOPTU	PLUTON
IRSSTW	WRISTS	LNRUUY	UNRULY
IRSTWY	WRISTY	LOOPPT	POL POT
ISSSTU	SUSS IT, TUSSIS	LOOPRY	POORLY
ISSTTW	TWISTS	LOOPSS	SLOOPS, SPOOLS
ISTTWY	TWISTY	LOOSST	STOOLS
JLNOOY	JOLYON	LOOVVX	VOLVOX
JLSTUY	JUSTLY	LOPPRY	PROPYL
JNOORU	JOURNO	LOPPSY	POLYPS, SLOPPY
JNSTUU	UNJUST	LOPRSW	PROWLS
JOOSUY	JOYOUS	LOPRTY	PORTLY
JORRSU	JURORS	LOPTWY	TWO-PLY
JOSSTU	JUST SO	LORSUY	SOURLY
KKLMUU	MUKLUK	LPPSUY	SUPPLY
KKNSSU	SKUNKS	LRRSUY	SLURRY
KLLNOS	KNOLLS	LRSTUY	SULTRY
KLLSSU	SKULLS	LRUUXY	LUXURY
KLNNUU	KUNLUN	LSSTUY	STYLUS
KNOORR	KRONOR	MMNNOR	MORMON
KNOTTY	KNOTTY	MMNOSU	SUMMON
KNPSUY	SPUNKY	MMOOPP	POMPOM
KNRSTU	TRUNKS	MMOOTT	MOTMOT, TOM-TOM
KOOOST	SOKOTO	MMRRUU	MURMUR
KOOPSS	SPOOKS	MNOOPP	POMPON
KOOPSY	SPOOKY	MNOORS	MORONS
KOORVV	KOVROV	MNOORU	UNMOOR
KOOSTV	VOSTOK	MNOOTW	MOTOWN
KOOTWW	KOWTOW	MNOSTU	MOUNTS
KORSST	STORKS	MNOTTU	MUTTON
KORSSY	SKYROS	MNSTTU	MUSTN'T
LLLOOP	LOLLOP	MOOPRS	PROMOS
LLNOOR	ROLL-ON	MOORRW	MORROW
LLNOPU	PULL-ON	MOORST	MOTORS
LLNORU	UNROLL	MOOSTT	MOTTOS
LLOOWY	WOOLLY	MOPPRT	PROMPT
LLOPUX	POLLUX	MOPSSU	POSSUM
LLORST	STROLL, TROLLS	MOQRUU	QUORUM
LLOSWY	SLOWLY	MORRUU	RUMOUR
LLOTUY	TOLUYL	MORSST	STORMS
LMMOUX	LUMMOX	MORSTY	STORMY
LMMPUY	PLUMMY	MORTUU	TUMOUR
LMMSUY	SLUMMY	MOSTTU	UTMOST

MPRSTU	TRUMPS
MPRSUU	RUMPUS
MPSSTU	STUMPS
MPSTUU	SPUTUM
MPSTUY	STUMPY
MSTTUY	SMUTTY
NNOOWW	NOW NOW!
NNORTU	TURN-ON
NOOPRT	PRONTO, PROTON
NOOPSS	SNOOPS, SPOONS
NOOPST	SPOT-ON
NOOPSY	SNOOPY
NOOSSW	SWOONS
NOOSTY	SNOOTY
NOOSYZ	SNOOZY
NOPSTU	PUT-ONS, UNSTOP
NOPTUW	UPTOWN
NORSST	SNORTS
NORTUU	OUTRUN
NOSSTU	SNOUTS
NOSTTY	SNOTTY
NPRSUU	RUN-UPS
NPRTUU	TURN-UP, UPTURN
NRSTUU	U-TURNS
NSSTTU	STUNTS
OOOPRT	OPORTO
OOPPVX	VOX POP
OOPRRT	TORPOR
OOPRSS	SPOORS
OOPRST	TROOPS
OOPRSU	POROUS
OOPRTU	UPROOT
OOPSSW	SWOOPS
OOPWWW	POWWOW
OORRST	ROTORS
OORRSW	SORROW
OORSST	ROOSTS, TORSOS
OORSTV	ROSTOV
OPRSST	SPORTS, STROPS
OPRSTU	SPROUT, STUPOR
OPRSTY	SPORTY
OPSSTU	SPOUTS, STOUPS, TOSS-UP
OPSTTY	SPOTTY
OPTTUU	OUTPUT
ORSTTU	TROUTS, TUTORS
ORTTUY	TRY-OUT
PRSSTU	SPURTS
PRSUYY	SYRUPY
RSSTTU	STRUTS, TRUSTS
RSSTTY	TRYSTS
RSTTUY	TRUSTY
TTTTUU	TUT-TUT

AAAABLM	ALABAMA	AAACNST	CANASTA	AAAIKLT	LATAKIA
AAAADMW	ADAMAWA	AAACNTT	CANTATA	AAAILMR	MALARIA
AAAALMT	ALMA-ATA	AAACRRR	CARRARA	AAAILNT	NATALIA
AAABBCL	CABBALA	AAACRWY	CARAWAY	AAAILPS	APLASIA
AAABBMR	BAMBARA	AAACSST	CASSATA	AAAILPT	PATIALA
AAABBRR	BARBARA	AAACSSV	CASSAVA	AAAIMNT	AMANITA
AAABCLR	CALABAR	AAADDMO	AMADODA	AAAINNR	ARIANNA
AAABCMR	CARAMBA	AAADFRY	FARADAY	AAAINTT	TATIANA
AAABCOR	CARABAO	AAADGNR	GRANADA	AAAIPRX	APRAXIA
AAABDFR	ABFARAD	AAADHMN	HAMADAN	AAAIPSS	ASPASIA
AAABDGN	BAGANDA	AAADHWY	HADAWAY	AAAIQRU	AQUARIA
AAABFIN	FABIANA	AAADILX	ADAXIAL	AAAJKRT	JAKARTA
AAABFLL	FALBALA	AAADIMN	ADAMINA	AAAJMPS	PAJAMAS
AAABHMR	ABRAHAM	AAADINR	ADRIANA	AAAKLMP	KAMPALA
AAABHMS	BAHAMAS	AAADKNN	KANNADA	AAAKLMR	ALKMAAR
AAABILN	ALBANIA	AAADMNN	ADAMNAN	AAAKLNS	ALASKAN
AAABILX	ABAXIAL	AAADMNR	RAMADAN	AAAKLSS	KASSALA
AAABINR	ARABIAN	AAADMNT	ADAMANT	AAAKMOY	OKAYAMA
AAABIPR	PARAIBA	AAADMRS	ARMADAS	AAAKMRS	MAKASAR
AAABIRV	BAVARIA	AAAEFLR	RAFAELA	AAAKRSW	SARAWAK
AAABKLR	KARBALA	AAAEGLT	GALATEA	AAALLMP	LA PALMA
AAABLLU	LUALABA	AAAEGNP	PANGAEA	AAALLPT	LA PLATA, PALATAL
AAABLMR	MALABAR	AAAEHLT	ALTHAEA	AAALMNY	MALAYAN
AAABMNR	ANAMBRA	AAAEIMN	ANAEMIA	AAALMRS	MARSALA
AAABNNS	BANANAS	AAAELRS	ARAL SEA	AAALMSS	SALAAMS
AAABNPR	PAN-ARAB	AAAENST	ANATASE	AAALMTY	MALATYA
AAABORR	ARAROBA	AAAERWY	AREAWAY	AAALNNT	LANTANA
AAABRSZ	BAZAARS	AAAFFLL	ALFALFA	AAALNTT	ATLANTA
AAACCIS	ACACIAS	AAAFIRT	RATAFIA	AAALRRY	ARRAYAL
AAACCLM	MALACCA	AAAFRSS	AS FAR AS	AAAMNPS	PANAMAS
AAACCLR	CARACAL	AAAFRWY	FARAWAY	AAAMRTU	TAMARAU
AAACCRS	CARACAS,	AAAGHIP	APHAGIA	AAAMSSW	MASSAWA
	CASCARA	AAAGHPR	AGRAPHA	AAANNRS	SARANNA
AAACDIN	ACADIAN	AAAGINR	NIAGARA	AAANNSV	SAVANNA
AAACDIR	ARCADIA	AAAGKNN	KANANGA	AAAPPSY	PAPAYAS
AAACDLU	ACAUDAL	AAAGKNT	KATANGA	AAARRST	TARRASA
AAACDMM	MACADAM	AAAGLMM	AMALGAM	AAARSTV	AVATARS
AAACEHN	ACHAEAN	AAAGLNS	LASAGNA	AAARTTT	RAT-A-TAT
AAACENP	PANACEA	AAAGLOS	ALAGOAS	AAARTTU	TUATARA
AAACHLZ	CHALAZA	AAAGMNR	ANAGRAM	AABBCEG	CABBAGE
AAACIJM	JAMAICA	AAAGMNU	MANAGUA	AABBDRU	BARBUDA
AAACIMR	ARAMAIC	AAAHHKL	HALAKAH	AABBEKL	BAALBEK
AAACINT	CATANIA	AAAHHLM	MAHALAH	AABBEMN	MBABANE
AAACJMR	JACAMAR	AAAHHLV	HALAVAH	AABBERT	BARBATE
AAACJRU	ARACAJU	AAAHILM	MAHALIA	AABBGGR	GRAB BAG
AAACLLV	CAVALLA	AAAHIPS	APHASIA	AABBHMR	BRABHAM
AAACLMN	ALMANAC	AAAHIRZ	AZARIAH	AABBHST	SABBATH
AAACLNT	CANTALA, CATALAN	AAAHMMT	MAHATMA	AABBMRU	RUM BABA
AAACLPS	ALPACAS	AAAHMRT	MARATHA	AABBNRT	BRABANT
AAACLPT	CATALPA	AAAHNRS	SAHARAN	AABBNRY	BARNABY
AAACLRZ	ALCAZAR	AAAHNRY	HARYANA	AABBRRY	BARBARY
AAACMRS	MARACAS,	AAAHNST	NATASHA	AABBSSU	BABASSU
	MARASCA, MASCARA	AAAHOPR	ARAPAHO	AABBSTY	BABY-SAT
AAACMRY	MARACAY	AAAHPPR	HARAPPA	AABCCET	BACCATE
AAACNRV	CARAVAN				

AABCDIN	CABINDA	AABDLRW	BRADAWL	AABGINS	ABASING
AABCDIR	CARABID	AABDMNR	ARMBAND	AABGINT	ABATING
AABCEFR	FACEBAR	AABDNNO	ABANDON	AABGLOR	AALBORG
AABCELN	BALANCE	AABDNNR	BRANDAN	AABGRST	RATBAGS
AABCELP	CAPABLE	AABDNRR	BARNARD	AABHIMS	BAHAISM
AABCELT	ACTABLE	AABDNRS	SANDBAR	AABHINR	BAHRAIN
AABCEMR	MACABRE	AABDORV	BRAVADO	AABHIST	BAHAIST
AABCERT	ABREACT, CABARET	AABDRRW	DRAWBAR	AABHITT	HABITAT, TABITHA
AABCFKT	FATBACK	AABDRST	BASTARD	AABHKRU	BUKHARA
AABCHNR	BARCHAN	AABDSTU	DATA BUS	AABHLTY	BATHYAL
AABCILM	CAMBIAL	AABEELT	EATABLE	AABHMNR	BRAHMAN
AABCIMR	CAMBRAI	AABEEMO	AMOEBAE	AABHMTT	BATH MAT
AABCIMS	CABIMAS	AABEFFL	AFFABLE	AABHSUU	BAUHAUS
AABCIOP	COPAIBA	AABEFGL	FLEABAG	AABIILN	ALBINIA
AABCIRT	BACTRIA	AABEFNR	ABERFAN	AABIILS	BASILIA
AABCITX	TAXICAB	AABEGGG	BAGGAGE	AABIILX	BIAXIAL
AABCKNR	CAB RANK	AABEGGR	GARBAGE	AABIIMN	NAMIBIA
AABCKRR	BARRACK	AABEGLR	ALGEBRA	AABIKNS	BANKSIA
AABCKSW	BACKSAW	AABEGRR	BARRAGE	AABILLR	BARILLA
AABCLPY	CAPABLY	AABEGSS	BAGASSE	AABILLS	BASILLA, LABIALS
AABCLRY	BARCLAY	AABEGST	TEABAGS	AABILMY	AMIABLY
AABCORT	ACROBAT	AABEIKN	IKEBANA	AABILNS	BASILAN
AABCOST	TABASCO	AABEILM	AMIABLE	AABILNT	TALIBAN
AABCOTT	CATBOAT	AABEILT	LABIATE	AABILRS	BASILAR
AABCRSS	SCARABS	AABEIRS	AIRBASE	AABIMMR	MARIMBA
AABDDER	ABRADED	AABEJLL	JELLABA	AABIMNZ	ZAMBIAN
AABDDGH	BAGHDAD	AABEKLT	TAKABLE	AABINOU	OUABAIN
AABDDHN	DAB HAND	AABELLM	MABELLA	AABINRS	SABRINA
AABDDIK	KABADDI	AABELLN	BALNEAL	AABINST	ABSTAIN, BASTIAN
AABDEFL	FADABLE	AABELLS	SALABLE	AABINSW	SWABIAN
AABDEGN	BANDAGE	AABELMN	NAMABLE	AABIORZ	ORIZABA
AABDEHS	ABASHED	AABELMT	TAMABLE	AABIRST	ARABIST
AABDEIS	DIABASE	AABELNN	ANNABEL	AABIRSV	BRAVAIS
AABDELL	BALLADE	AABELNO	ABALONE	AABKMRU	MUBARAK
AABDELR	ABELARD, ALBREDA	AABELPR	PARABLE	AABKNPR	BRAKPAN
AABDELT	DATABLE	AABELPY	PAYABLE	AABKNRT	TANBARK
AABDELW	WADABLE	AABELRT	ALBERTA, RATABLE	AABKOOZ	BAZOOKA
AABDENU	BANDEAU	AABELSV	SAVABLE	AABLLST	BALLAST
AABDERR	ABRADER	AABELTU	TABLEAU	AABLLWY	WALLABY
AABDFYZ	FYZABAD	AABELTX	TAXABLE	AABLMOS	ABSALOM
AABDGHN	HANDBAG	AABEMOS	AMOEBAS	AABLMSS	BALSAMS
AABDGLY	BAG LADY	AABEMRR	BRAEMAR	AABLMST	LAMBAST
AABDGMO	GAMBADO	AABEMST	MASBATE	AABLMSY	ABYSMAL
AABDGNS	SANDBAG	AABENTY	ABEYANT	AABLNOT	BALATON
AABDGNU	BUGANDA	AABERST	ABREAST	AABLNRU	BARNAUL
AABDHIO	OBADIAH	AABFFLY	AFFABLY	AABLNTT	BLATANT
AABDHNT	HATBAND	AABFINS	FABIANS	AABLORT	ABLATOR
AABDIJN	ABIDJAN	AABGGRS	RAGBAGS	AABLOTW	AT A BLOW
AABDIMR	BARMAID	AABGGSS	GASBAGS	AABLRTU	TABULAR
AABDINT	TABANID	AABGHNR	BRANAGH	AABLRTY	RATABLY
AABDIOT	BIODATA	AABGIIL	ABIGAIL	AABLSSY	ABYSSAL
AABDJOZ	BADAJOZ	AABGILM	MAILBAG	AABLTTU	ABUTTAL
AABDLLR	BALLARD	AABGIMN	GAMBIAN	AABMMOS	MOMBASA
AABDLLS	BALLADS	AABGINR	BARGAIN	AABMNOT	BOATMAN

AABMNOY	AMBOYNA, BAYAMON
AABMNST	BANTAMS, BATSMAN
AABMORU	MARABOU
AABMSUW	SUMBAWA
AABNNOZ	BONANZA
AABNNSY	BANYANS
AABORRS	RASBORA
AABQSUU	SUB-AQUA
AABRRUV	BRAVURA
AABSSSY	SASSABY
AABSTUX	SAXTUBA
AACCDEN	CANDACE
AACCDES	CASCADE
AACCDIR	CARDIAC
AACCDIS	CICADAS
AACCDOR	CARADOC
AACCEST	SACCATE
AACCHHS	CHA-CHAS
AACCHIR	ARCHAIC
AACCHMP	CHAMPAC
AACCHPU	PACHUCA
AACCIJO	AJACCIO
AACCILM	ACCLAIM
AACCILU	ACICULA
AACCIOR	CARIOCA
AACCITT	ATACTIC
AACCLLO	CLOACAL
AACCLLT	CATCALL
AACCLRU	ACCRUAL, CARACUL
AACCNNS	CANCANS
AACCNVY	VACANCY
AACCORU	CURACAO
AACCOTT	TOCCATA
AACCRSS	CARCASS
AACDDEL	DECADAL
AACDDIN	CANDIDA
AACDEEM	ACADEME
AACDEFS	FACADES
AACDEHL	CHALDEA
AACDEHR	CHARADE
AACDEHT	CATHEAD
AACDELN	CANDELA, DECANAL
AACDELR	CALDERA
AACDEMY	ACADEMY
AACDENV	ADVANCE
AACDENZ	CADENZA
AACDERS	ARCADES
AACDERV	CADAVER
AACDERY	DAY-CARE
AACDETU	CAUDATE
AACDETV	VACATED
AACDFIR	FARADIC

AACDGOR	CARADOG
AACDHMR	DRACHMA
AACDIJU	JUDAICA
AACDILR	RADICAL
AACDILU	CLAUDIA
AACDINT	ANTACID
AACDINV	VANADIC
AACDIOR	ACAROID
AACDIRR	RICARDA
AACDIRS	ASCARID
AACDJKW	JACKDAW
AACDLNO	ACNODAL
AACDLNS	SCANDAL
AACDLPR	PLACARD
AACDNRS	CANARDS
AACDOOV	AVOCADO
AACDRSZ	CZARDAS
AACEEGR	ACREAGE
AACEEHR	EARACHE
AACEEKT	TEACAKE
AACEEPT	AT PEACE
AACEERT	ACERATE
AACEESS	CASEASE
AACEEST	CASEATE
AACEETT	ACETATE
AACEFLT	FALCATE
AACEFRR	CARFARE
AACEFRS	CARAFES
AACEGKP	PACKAGE
AACEGNR	CARNAGE
AACEGRT	CARTAGE
AACEHLR	RACHAEL
AACEHNP	PANACHE
AACEHPU	CHAPEAU
AACEHRT	TRACHEA
AACEHTT	ATTACHE
AACEHTU	CHATEAU
AACEHWY	EACH WAY
AACEIMN	ANAEMIC
AACEIMR	AMERICA
AACEINO	OCEANIA
AACEIPP	CAP-A-PIE
AACEIRV	AVARICE
AACEKNP	PANCAKE
AACEKNS	ASKANCE
AACEKOT	OATCAKE
AACELLN	CANELLA
AACELLP	CAPELLA, LAPLACE
AACELLT	LACTEAL
AACELLW	WALLACE
AACELMN	MACLEAN, MANACLE
AACELMR	CAMERAL, CARAMEL, CARMELA
AACELNU	LACUNAE

AACELNV	VALANCE
AACELPR	CARPALE
AACELPS	PALACES, PASCALE
AACELPT	PLACATE
AACELRV	CARAVEL
AACELST	LACTASE
AACELTT	LACTATE
AACELTV	CLAVATE
AACEMMR	MACRAME
AACEMNV	CAVEMAN
AACEMQU	MACAQUE
AACEMRS	CAMERAS
AACENPS	CANAPES
AACENRS	SARACEN
AACENTY	CYANATE
AACEPRS	PESCARA
AACEPRT	RATE-CAP
AACERRT	RAT RACE
AACERST	CASERTA, CAT'S-EAR
AACERSU	CAESURA
AACERTU	ARCUATE
AACESTV	CAVEATS
AACETTU	ACTUATE
AACFILS	FACIALS, FASCIAL
AACFINR	AFRICAN
AACFINT	FANATIC
AACFISS	FASCIAS
AACFLLY	FALLACY
AACFLRU	FACULAR
AACFLTU	FACTUAL
AACFNST	CAFTANS
AACFSTT	FAT CATS
AACGIIL	GALICIA
AACGILL	GLACIAL
AACGILM	MAGICAL
AACGLOS	COAL GAS
AACGLRY	CALGARY
AACGNOU	GUANACO
AACHHKR	CHARKHA
AACHHLL	CHALLAH
AACHHMT	CHATHAM
AACHIKL	HALAKIC
AACHIKR	KARACHI
AACHILM	MALACHI
AACHILR	RACHIAL
AACHIMN	MAHICAN
AACHIMR	AMHARIC
AACHIMS	CHIASMA
AACHINS	SANCHIA
AACHINT	ITHACAN
AACHIPS	CHIAPAS
AACHIPT	CHAPATI
AACHIRT	CITHARA

AACHKRY	HAYRACK	
AACHKSW	HACKSAW	
AACHLLN	LACHLAN	
AACHLMS	CHASMAL	
AACHLMY	MALACHY	
AACHLPP	CHAPPAL	
AACHLPS	PASCHAL	
AACHMNR	CAM RANH	
AACHNOP	PANOCHA	
AACHNPX	PANCHAX	
AACHNRY	ANARCHY	
AACHNSU	ANCHUSA	
AACHRRT	CATARRH	
AACHRWY	ARCHWAY	
AACHRYZ	ZACHARY	
AACIINT	ACTINIA	
AACIIST	ASIATIC	
AACIJLP	JALAPIC	
AACIJNT	JACINTA	
AACIKLL	ALKALIC	
AACIKLR	CLARKIA	
AACILLM	CAMILLA	
AACILLS	CALLAIS	
AACILNR	ACRILAN, CRANIAL	
AACILNT	ACTINAL	
AACILNU	LUCIANA	
AACILOS	ASOCIAL	
AACILOX	COAXIAL	
AACILPT	CAPITAL	
AACIMNS	MANIACS	
AACINOR	OCARINA	
AACINPS	CASPIAN	
AACINPT	CAPTAIN	
AACINRZ	CZARINA	
AACINST	SATANIC	
AACINTV	VATICAN	
AACIOPT	TAPIOCA	
AACIORT	CROATIA	
AACIORV	CRAIOVA	
AACIOTV	OCTAVIA	
AACIPRX	APRAXIC	
AACIQTU	AQUATIC	
AACISTT	ASTATIC	
AACJKLS	JACKALS	
AACJKMN	MAN JACK	
AACJKRT	JACK TAR	
AACJKSS	JACKASS	
AACJMOR	MAJORCA	
AACJOST	JOCASTA	
AACKKLO	KAOLACK	
AACKLTW	CATWALK	
AACKNRS	RANSACK	
AACKPRR	CAR PARK	
AACKSTT	ATTACKS	

AACLLNT	CALLANT	
AACLLSU	CLAUSAL	
AACLMNT	CLAMANT	
AACLMRU	MACULAR	
AACLMSU	CALAMUS	
AACLNNO	ANCONAL	
AACLNNU	CANNULA	
AACLNPY	CLAYPAN	
AACLNRU	LACUNAR	
AACLNSU	LACUNAS	
AACLOPR	CAPORAL	
AACLORT	COAL TAR	
AACLOST	COASTAL	
AACLOTT	CATTALO	
AACLPSU	SCAPULA	
AACLPTY	PLAY-ACT	
AACLRSS	RASCALS, SCALARS	
AACLRVY	CALVARY, CAVALRY	
AACLSTU	LUCASTA	
AACLSUX	LASCAUX	
AACLTTU	TACTUAL	
AACMNNO	MONACAN	
AACMNRU	ARCANUM	
AACMNTX	MANX CAT	
AACMORS	SARCOMA	
AACMRRT	TRAMCAR	
AACMRSS	SARCASM	
AACMRST	TARMACS	
AACNNOZ	CANZONA	
AACNOST	SACATON	
AACNPST	CAPSTAN, CATNAPS	
AACNSSV	CANVASS	
AACNTUY	YUCATAN	
AACOPPR	APOCARP	
AACPSTW	CAT'S PAW	
AACRSTV	CRAVATS	
AACRTTT	ATTRACT	
AACRTUY	ACTUARY	
AACTUWY	CUTAWAY	
AADDDEN	ADDENDA	
AADDEFI	DEAF-AID	
AADDEGM	DAMAGED	
AADDEIL	ALIDADE	
AADDELR	ALDREDA	
AADDENP	DEADPAN	
AADDEPR	PARADED	
AADDEPT	ADAPTED	
AADDERW	AWARDED	
AADDGNR	GRANDAD	
AADDHKR	KHADDAR	
AADDIMS	DADAISM	
AADDIST	DADAIST	
AADDLNO	DONALDA	
AADDNVV	DVANDVA	

AADEELT	DEALATE	
AADEERT	AERATED	
AADEERW	AWARDEE	
AADEFHO	AHEAD OF	
AADEFHT	FATHEAD	
AADEFLR	ALFREDA	
AADEGGR	AGGRADE, GARAGED	
AADEGHO	GO-AHEAD	
AADEGMN	MANAGED	
AADEGMR	DAMAGER	
AADEGMS	DAMAGES	
AADEGNR	GRENADA	
AADEGNS	AGENDAS	
AADEGRT	GRADATE	
AADEGRV	RAVAGED	
AADEGRY	YARDAGE	
AADEGSV	SAVAGED	
AADEHLN	HALDANE	
AADEHMN	HEADMAN	
AADEHMS	ASHAMED	
AADEHRW	WARHEAD	
AADEHWY	HEADWAY	
AADEILN	ADELINA	
AADEILV	AVAILED, VEDALIA	
AADEIMR	MADEIRA	
AADEINR	ARANEID, ARIADNE	
AADEINS	NAIADES	
AADEINZ	IN A DAZE	
AADEIRT	RADIATE	
AADEITW	AWAITED	
AADEJNU	JUDAEAN	
AADELLY	ALLAYED	
AADELMN	MANDELA	
AADELMO	A LA MODE	
AADELMR	ALARMED	
AADELNR	ADRENAL	
AADELNZ	ZEALAND	
AADELRW	RAW DEAL	
AADELRY	ALREADY	
AADELTU	ADULATE	
AADEMMN	MAN-MADE	
AADEMNO	ADENOMA	
AADEMNS	MAENADS	
AADEMNT	MANDATE	
AADEMNY	NAME DAY	
AADEMSS	AMASSED	
AADENNT	ANDANTE	
AADENRS	ANDREAS	
AADENRV	VERANDA	
AADEPRR	PARADER	
AADEPRS	PARADES	
AADEPRT	ADAPTER	
AADEPSS	PASSADE	

AADERRW	AWARDER	AADINRT	RADIANT	AAEERTU	AUREATE
AADERRY	ARRAYED	AADIORS	ISADORA	AAEERTX	EXARATE
AADERSY	DARESAY	AADKLNO	OAKLAND	AAEFFGR	AGRAFFE
AADESSY	ASSAYED	AADKNOT	DAKOTAN	AAEFFIR	AFFAIRE
AADFGLY	FLAG DAY	AADKNRT	TANKARD	AAEFFLL	FALAFEL
AADGGHR	HAGGARD	AADKRWW	AWKWARD	AAEFFNR	FANFARE
AADGGLR	LAGGARD	AADLLMR	MALLARD	AAEFFTT	TAFFETA
AADGHNZ	GANDZHA	AADLLMS	SMALL AD	AAEFGLN	FALANGE
AADGIMM	DIGAMMA	AADLLNP	LAPLAND	AAEFGNR	FERGANA
AADGIMR	DIAGRAM	AADLLNR	RANDALL	AAEFGTW	WAFTAGE
AADGIOS	ADAGIOS	AADLNOR	RONALDA	AAEFLPR	EARFLAP
AADGIPR	PADRAIG	AADLNOY	YOLANDA	AAEFMRT	FERMATA
AADGLLW	GADWALL	AADLNRY	LANYARD	AAEFNST	SANTA FE
AADGLNO	GONADAL	AADLNSS	SANDALS	AAEFRRR	FERRARA
AADGLNR	GARLAND	AADLNSU	LANDAUS	AAEFRRW	WARFARE
AADGLNT	LANDTAG	AADLNSV	VANDALS	AAEFRST	FAR EAST
AADGLNU	LUGANDA	AADLOPY	PAYLOAD	AAEGGNO	ANAGOGE
AADGLRU	GRADUAL	AADLPPU	APPLAUD	AAEGGOP	APAGOGE
AADGMNR	GRANDMA	AADLRRU	RADULAR	AAEGGRS	GARAGES
AADGNNU	UGANDAN	AADMNNO	MADONNA	AAEGHLU	HAULAGE
AADGNPR	GRANDPA	AADMNOR	MADRONA,	AAEGHMR	GRAHAME
AADGOPR	PODAGRA		MONARDA, ROADMAN	AAEGHOV	HAVE-A-GO
AADGOPS	PAGODAS	AADMNRS	MANSARD	AAEGILR	ALGERIA, REGALIA
AADHHMS	MASHHAD	AADMNRY	MAYNARD	AAEGISS	ASSEGAI
AADHHNR	DHAHRAN	AADMORT	MATADOR	AAEGITT	AGITATE
AADHILS	DAHLIAS	AADMRRY	YARDARM	AAEGKNT	TANKAGE
AADHINP	DAPHNIA	AADMRZZ	MAZZARD	AAEGKOS	SOAKAGE
AADHINR	HADRIAN	AADMSYY	MAY DAYS	AAEGLLR	ALLEGRA
AADHLRY	HALYARD	AADNOPR	PANDORA	AAEGLLT	TALLAGE
AADHMNO	DAHOMAN	AADNORR	ANDORRA	AAEGLMN	GAMELAN
AADHNPR	HARDPAN	AADNRVW	VANWARD	AAEGLMT	GAMETAL
AADHNRS	HANSARD	AADNSTW	WANT ADS	AAEGLNS	LASAGNE
AADHNSW	HANDSAW	AADOPRT	ADAPTOR	AAEGLRR	REALGAR
AADHOSS	SODA ASH	AADOPRX	PARADOX	AAEGLRV	ALGARVE
AADHRRV	HARVARD	AADORTX	ROAD TAX	AAEGLSV	SALVAGE
AADHRSZ	HAZARDS	AADORWY	ROADWAY	AAEGMNR	MANAGER
AADHRWY	HAYWARD	AADQRTU	QUADRAT	AAEGMNT	MAGENTA,
AADHSWY	WASHDAY	AADRWWY	WAYWARD		MAGNATE
AADIINN	INDIANA	AAEEFGL	LEAFAGE	AAEGMPR	RAMPAGE
AADIINO	DIANOIA	AAEEFLT	TEALEAF	AAEGMRT	MARGATE
AADIINV	DAVINIA	AAEEGKL	LEAKAGE	AAEGMRW	WAR GAME
AADIIRR	AIR RAID	AAEEGLT	GALEATE	AAEGMSS	MASSAGE
AADIISV	ADIVASI	AAEEGMT	AGAMETE	AAEGNNT	TANNAGE
AADILMR	ADMIRAL	AAEEGNO	NEOGAEA	AAEGNPT	PAGEANT
AADILMT	MATILDA	AAEEGRV	AVERAGE	AAEGNPW	PAWNAGE
AADILNP	PALADIN	AAEEHLT	ALETHEA	AAEGNRR	ARRANGE
AADILPS	APSIDAL	AAEEHRT	HETAERA	AAEGNRT	TANAGER
AADILRS	RADIALS	AAEELLP	PALE ALE	AAEGNSU	GUANASE
AADILTV	DATIVAL	AAEELMT	MALEATE	AAEGNTV	VANTAGE
AADILWY	WAYLAID	AAEELNS	SEA-LANE	AAEGPRW	WARPAGE
AADIMNR	MIRANDA	AAEELRZ	ELEAZAR	AAEGPRY	GAP YEAR
AADIMOR	DIORAMA	AAEEMNT	EMANATE,	AAEGPSS	PASSAGE
AADIMRS	DAMARIS		MANATEE	AAEGQUY	QUAYAGE
AADIMRU	MADURAI	AAEEPPS	APPEASE	AAEGRRV	RAVAGER
		AAEERSW	SEAWARE		

AAEGRST	TEAR GAS	AAEIPTT	APATITE	AAENNRV	RAVENNA
AAEGRSV	RAVAGES	AAEIRSU	EURASIA	AAENNST	ANNATES
AAEGRTT	REGATTA	AAEIRTT	ARIETTA	AAENNTT	TANNATE
AAEGSSU	ASSUAGE, SAUSAGE	AAEIRTV	VARIATE	AAENPST	ANAPEST, PEASANT
AAEGSSV	SAVAGES	AAEISTT	SATIATE	AAENPSV	PAVANES
AAEGSTW	WASTAGE	AAEJNTT	JANETTA	AAENRRT	NARRATE
AAEGTTW	WATTAGE	AAEKKRY	KAYAKER	AAENRRV	NAVARRE
AAEGTUX	GATEAUX	AAEKLNT	ALKANET	AAENRTU	TAUREAN
AAEGTWY	GATEWAY, GETAWAY	AAEKMRR	EARMARK	AAENRUW	UNAWARE
		AAEKMRS	SEAMARK	AAENSSV	VANESSA
AAEHHIL	HIALEAH	AAEKMWY	MAKE WAY	AAENSSW	SWANSEA
AAEHHLM	MEHALAH	AAEKPRT	PARTAKE	AAENSTV	AVESTAN
AAEHILM	MEHALIA	AAEKSTT	AT STAKE	AAEORRT	AERATOR
AAEHIMN	ANAHEIM	AAELLLM	LAMELLA	AAEORRU	AURORAE
AAEHIRT	HETAIRA	AAELLLS	LA SALLE	AAEPPRT	PARAPET
AAEHKLN	ELKANAH	AAELLPT	PATELLA	AAERRRS	ARREARS
AAEHKMY	MAKE HAY	AAELLRS	ALL EARS	AAERSSY	ASSAYER
AAEHKNT	KHANATE	AAELLRT	LATERAL	AAESSWY	SEAWAYS
AAEHLLL	ALLHEAL	AAELLSV	SAVE-ALL	AAETTUW	WATTEAU
AAEHLMR	HAARLEM	AAELLSW	SEAWALL	AAFFINS	SAFFIAN
AAEHLPR	RAPHAEL	AAELMNS	ANSELMA	AAFFIRS	AFFAIRS
AAEHLPX	HEXAPLA	AAELMNU	ALUMNAE, MANUELA	AAFFRSY	AFFRAYS
AAEHLRT	TREHALA			AAFGHNS	AFGHANS
AAEHNPR	HANAPER	AAELMOT	OATMEAL	AAFGLMN	FLAGMAN
AAEHNPS	SAPHENA	AAELMPT	PALMATE	AAFGORR	FARRAGO
AAEHNSY	HYAENAS	AAELMST	MALTASE	AAFHILX	HALIFAX
AAEHRSY	HEARSAY	AAELMSY	AMYLASE	AAFHINS	ISFAHAN
AAEHSTT	HASTATE	AAELNNP	ANNAPLE	AAFHLMO	HALF A MO
AAEIKLR	KARELIA	AAELNRS	ARSENAL	AAFHLWY	HALFWAY
AAEIKLS	AS ALIKE	AAELNST	SEALANT	AAFHNST	FATSHAN
AAEIKMT	TAKE AIM	AAELNSY	ANALYSE	AAFIILR	FILARIA
AAEILLU	EULALIA	AAELORR	AREOLAR	AAFIJST	FAJITAS
AAEILMN	MELANIA	AAELORU	AUREOLA	AAFILNT	FANTAIL
AAEILMP	PAMELIA	AAELOTX	OXALATE	AAFIMRY	MAYFAIR
AAEILMR	ALMERIA	AAELPPR	APPAREL	AAFINNT	INFANTA
AAEILMS	MALAISE	AAELPPS	APPEALS	AAFIPRT	PARFAIT
AAEILNN	ALANINE	AAELPPT	PALPATE	AAFIRSS	SAFARIS
AAEILNR	AIRLANE, LARAINE	AAELPRT	APTERAL	AAFIRWY	FAIRWAY
AAEILNT	NATALIE	AAELPRV	PALAVER	AAFKNST	KAFTANS
AAEILOT	AETOLIA	AAELPST	PALATES	AAFLLTY	FATALLY
AAEILRS	AERIALS	AAELPTT	TAPETAL	AAFLWYY	FLYAWAY
AAEILRU	AURELIA	AAELPTU	PLATEAU	AAFNSTT	FANTAST
AAEILRV	VALERIA	AAELPTY	APETALY	AAFNSTY	FANTASY
AAEILSS	ALIASES	AAELRTT	ARLETTA	AAFPSUX	FAUX PAS
AAEIMMT	IMAMATE	AAELSST	ATLASES	AAGGIUZ	GAGAUZI
AAEIMNR	ARMENIA	AAELSUX	ASEXUAL	AAGGIZZ	ZAGAZIG
AAEIMNS	AMNESIA	AAELTVV	VALVATE	AAGGNWY	GANGWAY
AAEIMNT	AMENTIA, ANIMATE	AAEMMMR	MAREMMA	AAGHILR	ALIGARH
AAEIMPY	PYAEMIA	AAEMNPP	PAMPEAN	AAGHILZ	GHAZALI
AAEIMRU	URAEMIA	AAEMNRS	MANRESA	AAGHITU	GAUHATI
AAEINNO	AEONIAN	AAEMRSS	AMASSER	AAGHKRS	KASHGAR
AAEINST	ENTASIA	AAEMRST	ARTEMAS	AAGHMNN	HANGMAN
AAEIPRR	PAREIRA	AAEMRTU	AMATEUR	AAGHNNY	HANYANG
AAEIPRS	SPIRAEA	AAENNNT	ANTENNA	AAGHNRS	HANGARS

112

AAGHNUV	VAUGHAN	
AAGIINO	GOIANIA	
AAGIINT	NIIGATA	
AAGIKNW	AWAKING	
AAGILMY	MYALGIA	
AAGILNN	ANGINAL, ANGLIAN	
AAGILNP	PAGINAL	
AAGILNV	VAGINAL	
AAGILTW	WAGTAIL	
AAGIMNO	ANGIOMA	
AAGIMNS	SIAMANG	
AAGIMNZ	AMAZING	
AAGINRR	ARRAIGN	
AAGINRS	SANGRIA	
AAGINRU	GUARANI	
AAGINST	AGAINST	
AAGINSU	IGUANAS	
AAGINSV	VAGINAS·	
AAGINSY	GAINSAY	
AAGINTU	ANTIGUA	
AAGIOTT	AGITATO	
AAGJRSU	JAGUARS	
AAGJRTU	GUJARAT	
AAGKMSS	GAS MASK	
AAGKNRS	ANGARSK	
AAGLLNT	GALLANT	
AAGLNNO	ANGOLAN	
AAGLNOR	GRANOLA	
AAGLNOY	ANALOGY	
AAGLNRU	ANGULAR	
AAGLRUU	AUGURAL	
AAGMMRR	GRAMMAR	
AAGMNOR	ROMAGNA	
AAGMNRT	TANGRAM	
AAGMOPY	APOGAMY	
AAGMRUX	MARGAUX	
AAGNOPR	PARAGON	
AAGNORS	ANGORAS	
AAGNORZ	ORGANZA	
AAGNRRY	GRANARY	
AAGNRTV	VAGRANT	
AAGOPSS	SAPSAGO	
AAGORSU	SAGUARO	
AAGSTUU	AUGUSTA	
AAHHKKL	KHALKHA	
AAHHNPT	NAPHTHA	
AAHHOPR	PHARAOH	
AAHIINT	HAITIAN	
AAHIJNR	HARIJAN	
AAHIKNT	INKATHA	
AAHIKRU	HAURAKI	
AAHILTT	TALITHA	
AAHIMNO	MAHONIA	
AAHIMRT	MARATHI	

AAHINNU	HUAINAN
AAHINOP	APHONIA
AAHINOR	HONIARA
AAHINPR	PIRANHA
AAHINST	ASHANTI
AAHINSX	SHAANXI
AAHINTU	HAINAUT
AAHIORT	HORATIA
AAHIPRS	PARIAHS
AAHIPTY	HYPATIA
AAHJNNO	JOHANNA
AAHKKSS	KHAKASS
AAHKMSY	YASHMAK
AAHLLSW	WALLAHS
AAHLLWY	HALLWAY, WHYALLA
AAHLMRS	MARSHAL
AAHLMRU	HAMULAR
AAHLNPX	PHALANX
AAHLNRW	NARWHAL
AAHLNTU	NAHUATL
AAHLPRS	PHRASAL
AAHLPST	ASPHALT
AAHMNNU	HANUMAN
AAHMNSS	SHAMANS
AAHMOPR	AMPHORA
AAHMRTU	MATHURA
AAHNNOS	HOSANNA
AAHNPST	PATHANS
AAHNRTX	ANTHRAX
AAHNRTY	RHATANY
AAHPRTW	WARPATH
AAHPTWY	PATHWAY
AAHRSTY	ASHTRAY
AAHRTTW	ATHWART
AAIILMR	AIRMAIL
AAIILNT	ITALIAN
AAIILNV	LAVINIA
AAIILOS	ALOISIA
AAIILPT	TILAPIA
AAIINNR	IRANIAN
AAIINTT	TITANIA
AAIINVV	VIVIANA
AAIJLNU	JULIANA
AAIJNTU	JUANITA, TIJUANA
AAIKLLS	ALKALIS
AAIKMNN	MANAKIN
AAIKNNT	KANTIAN
AAIKNOW	OKINAWA
AAIKNRT	KATRINA
AAIKNST	KATSINA
AAIKPPR	PAPRIKA
AAIKPTZ	KAPITZA
AAILLMM	MAMILLA

AAILLMX	MAXILLA
AAILLNV	VANILLA
AAILLPP	PAPILLA
AAILLUV	ALLUVIA
AAILMMN	MAILMAN
AAILMMS	LAMAISM, MIASMAL
AAILMMX	MAXIMAL
AAILMNR	LAMINAR
AAILMNS	ANIMALS
AAILMNV	MALVINA
AAILMOS	SOMALIA
AAILMPR	PALMIRA
AAILMPS	IMPALAS
AAILMRT	MARITAL, MARTIAL
AAILMSS	SALAMIS
AAILMST	LAMAIST
AAILNOP	PIANOLA
AAILNOS	SINALOA
AAILNOT	LAOTIAN
AAILNOV	VALONIA
AAILNPT	PLATINA
AAILNPU	NAIPAUL
AAILNRU	LAURINA
AAILNRY	LANIARY
AAILNSV	SILVANA
AAILNTV	LATVIAN, VALIANT
AAILNWY	WAYLAIN
AAILORS	ROSALIA, SOLARIA
AAILORV	VARIOLA
AAILOSY	ALOYSIA
AAILPRT	PARTIAL, PATRIAL
AAILPRY	AIRPLAY
AAILPST	SPATIAL
AAILRRV	ARRIVAL
AAILRSS	LARISSA
AAILRST	LARIATS
AAILRTV	TRAVAIL
AAILRWY	RAILWAY
AAILSSW	WASSAIL
AAILSTU	LUSATIA
AAIMMNO	AMMONIA
AAIMMSS	MIASMAS
AAIMNOR	ROMANIA
AAIMNOS	ANOSMIA
AAIMNOT	ANIMATO
AAIMNRS	MARINAS
AAIMNRT	MARTIAN, MARTINA, TAMARIN
AAIMNRU	RUMANIA
AAIMNRX	MARXIAN
AAIMNST	STAMINA
AAIMORR	RORAIMA
AAIMORV	MORAVIA
AAIMRSS	MARISSA

AAIMRSU	MASURIA, SAMURAI	AALMNOS	SALAMON	AANNSUZ	SUZANNA
AAIMSTV	ATAVISM	AALMNOY	ANOMALY	AANORTT	TARANTO
AAINNOT	ANTONIA	AALMNSU	MANUALS	AANOSST	SONATAS
AAINNRU	URANIAN	AALMORY	MAYORAL	AANPRST	SPARTAN
AAINNRV	NIRVANA	AALMPRY	PALMYRA	AANPRUU	URUAPAN
AAINORV	OVARIAN	AALMPRY	PALMYRA	AANPSST	PASSANT
AAINORZ	ARIZONA	AALNNRU	ANNULAR	AANQRTU	QUARTAN
AAINPRT	TRAPANI	AALNNSU	ANNUALS	AANRRTW	WARRANT
AAINRST	ARTISAN, TSARINA	AALNORS	ALSO-RAN	AANRSTT	TARTANS
AAINRSU	SAURIAN	AALNOUV	ULANOVA	AANRUWY	RUNAWAY
AAINRTV	VARIANT	AALNPRT	PLANTAR	AANSSTV	SAVANTS
AAINRTY	NAYARIT	AALNPST	SALTPAN	AANSSTZ	STANZAS
AAINRTZ	TZARINA	AALNQTU	QUANTAL	AANSTTT	STATANT
AAINSVY	VISAYAN	AALNRTU	NATURAL	AANTUUV	VANUATU
AAINTTT	ATTAINT	AALNSTT	SALTANT	AAOPRRT	PRO RATA
AAINTUY	TAIYUAN	AALNSTU	SULTANA	AAOQSSU	OQUASSA
AAIOPRR	PAIR-OAR	AALNSTY	ANALYST	AAORRSU	AURORAS
AAIORTV	AVIATOR	AALOPRS	PARASOL	AAORSTV	OSTRAVA, SARATOV
AAIPPTT	PIT-A-PAT	AALOPTV	POLTAVA	AAOTTUY	TATOUAY
AAIPRSU	AU PAIRS	AALORRU	AURORAL	AAPPSWW	PAWPAWS
AAIPRTT	PARTITA	AALORSU	AROUSAL	AAPRRTT	RAT TRAP
AAIPSZZ	PIAZZAS	AALOSVW	AVOWALS	AAQRSSU	QUASARS
AAIQSSU	QUASSIA	AALPPSU	UPPSALA	AARRSTT	TARTARS
AAIQTUV	AQUAVIT	AALPSTU	SPATULA	AARSSTT	STRATAS
AAIRSSS	SASSARI	AALRSTT	STRATAL	ABBBDEL	BABBLED, BLABBED
AAIRSSY	ASSYRIA	AALRSTU	AUSTRAL	ABBBELR	BABBLER, BLABBER
AAIRSTU	AUSTRIA	AALRSTY	ASTYLAR	ABBBITT	BABBITT
AAIRSWY	AIRWAYS	AALRSUZ	LAZARUS	ABBCDER	CRABBED
AAISTTV	ATAVIST	AALSSSV	VASSALS	ABBCEIS	CABBIES
AAITWXY	TAXIWAY	AALSSTU	ASSAULT	ABBCELS	SCABBLE
AAJKLWY	JAYWALK	AAMMMRY	MAMMARY	ABBCRYY	CRYBABY
AAJMPSY	PYJAMAS	AAMMNNX	MANXMAN	ABBDDEL	DABBLED
AAJNNSU	SAN JUAN	AAMMNRY	MYANMAR	ABBDDET	BAD DEBT
AAJNRUY	JANUARY	AAMMNOT	MONTANA	ABBDEGL	GABBLED
AAKKLRU	KARAKUL	AAMMNOT	MONTANA	ABBDEGR	GRABBED
AAKLMNW	WALKMAN	AAMNORS	OARSMAN	ABBDELR	DABBLER, DRABBLE
AAKMNUU	MANUKAU	AAMNOSZ	AMAZONS	ABBDERR	DRABBER
AAKMRUZ	MAZURKA	AAMNOTY	ANATOMY	ABBDEST	STABBED
AAKNNTU	NUNATAK	AAMNPRT	RAMPANT	ABBDESW	SWABBED
AAKNORS	ANORAKS	AAMNPSS	SAMPANS	ABBDGIN	DABBING
AAKNOSU	ANOUSKA	AAMNPTY	TYMPANA	ABBDINR	RIBBAND
AAKNRSS	SARANSK	AAMORSV	SAMOVAR	ABBDMOR	BOMBARD
AAKPRWY	PARKWAY	AAMORTY	AMATORY	ABBDNOX	BANDBOX
AAKRTUY	AUTARKY	AAMOSSS	SAMOSAS	ABBEERR	BERBERA
AALLLNS	LALLANS	AAMOTTU	AUTOMAT	ABBEETT	BABETTE
AALLLSW	WALSALL	AAMPRRT	RAMPART	ABBEGLR	GABBLER, GRABBLE
AALLMPU	AMPULLA	AAMPRSS	SAMPRAS	ABBEGMR	BAMBERG
AALLNPU	PLANULA	AAMRSTU	SUMATRA,	ABBEGNU	BUGBANE
AALLNSY	NASALLY		TRAUMAS	ABBEGRR	GRABBER
AALLOWY	ALLOWAY	AAMRTWY	TRAMWAY	ABBEGRU	BUGBEAR
AALLRST	ALL-STAR	AAMSSTU	SATSUMA	ABBEHMO	HOBBEMA
AALLRUY	AURALLY	AANNORS	ROSANNA	ABBEIST	TABBIES
AALMMMS	MAMMALS	AANNORX	ROXANNA	ABBELLR	BARBELL
AALMMNO	AMMONAL	AANNOTT	ANNATTO	ABBELMR	BRAMBLE
		AANNRUU	NAURUAN		
		AANNSSU	SUSANNA		

ABBELRR	RABBLER	ABCEEHS	BEACHES	ABCGKLO	BACKLOG
ABBELRS	RABBLES	ABCEEMR	EMBRACE	ABCHHII	HIBACHI
ABBELRU	BARBULE	ABCEENR	CARBENE	ABCHILS	CHABLIS
ABBELSU	BAUBLES	ABCEENS	ABSENCE	ABCHILU	BALUCHI
ABBERRS	BARBERS	ABCEERR	CEREBRA	ABCHIOT	COHABIT
ABBERST	STABBER	ABCEESU	BECAUSE	ABCHKTU	HACKBUT
ABBERSW	SWABBER	ABCEGIR	RIB CAGE	ABCHLOR	CHABROL
ABBESSU	SUBBASE	ABCEGOS	BOSCAGE	ABCHPSU	HUBCAPS
ABBGGIN	GABBING	ABCEHIR	HEBRAIC	ABCIILL	BACILLI
ABBGIJN	JABBING	ABCEHLN	BLANCHE	ABCIILN	ALBINIC
ABBGINN	NABBING	ABCEHMR	CHAMBER	ABCIILS	BASILIC
ABBGINT	TABBING	ABCEHST	BATCHES	ABCIILT	ALBITIC
ABBGINY	BABYING	ABCEILL	ICEBALL	ABCIIMN	MINICAB
ABBGOOU	BUGABOO	ABCEILM	ALEMBIC	ABCIIMS	IAMBICS
ABBHISY	BABYISH	ABCEILR	ALBERIC, CALIBRE	ABCIJNO	JACOBIN
ABBHRRU	RHUBARB	ABCEILT	CITABLE	ABCIKSY	SICKBAY
ABBHTTU	BATHTUB	ABCEIMO	AMOEBIC	ABCILRS	SCRIBAL
ABBILOT	BOBTAIL	ABCEINR	CARBINE	ABCILST	BALTICS
ABBIMNO	BAMBINO	ABCEINT	CABINET	ABCILTU	CUBITAL
ABBIRST	RABBITS	ABCEIOR	AEROBIC	ABCIMMU	CAMBIUM
ABBISTY	BABY-SIT	ABCEIRS	ASCRIBE, BRESCIA	ABCIMOR	COIMBRA
ABBKLOU	BLAUBOK	ABCEISS	ABSCISE, SCABIES	ABCIMRU	CUMBRIA
ABBMOOS	BAMBOOS	ABCEKLN	BLACKEN	ABCIMST	CAMBIST
ABBMOST	BOMBAST	ABCEKLR	BLACKER	ABCINOR	NICOBAR
ABBMOTU	BUMBOAT	ABCEKNR	BRACKEN	ABCIORU	CARIBOU
ABBNOOS	BABOONS	ABCEKRS	BACKERS	ABCIOUV	BIVOUAC
ABBNRUY	BANBURY	ABCEKRT	BRACKET	ABCKLLY	BLACKLY
ABBOSTY	BOBSTAY	ABCEKST	SETBACK	ABCKMRU	BUCKRAM
ABBQSUY	SQUABBY	ABCELLU	BULLACE	ABCKNNO	BANNOCK
ABBSSSU	SUBBASS	ABCELMO	CEMBALO	ABCKOTU	OUTBACK
ABCCEER	REBECCA	ABCELMR	CLAMBER	ABCKPSU	BACKUPS
ABCCEIR	ACERBIC, BRECCIA	ABCELOP	PLACEBO	ABCKSUW	BUCKSAW
ABCCILU	CUBICAL	ABCELOV	VOCABLE	ABCLLOX	CALL BOX
ABCCIMR	CAMBRIC	ABCELRU	CURABLE	ABCLLOY	CALLBOY
ABCCIOR	BORACIC	ABCELRY	CYBALER	ABCLMNU	CLUBMAN
ABCCKTU	CUTBACK	ABCELSU	BASCULE	ABCLMOU	COLUMBA
ABCCOOT	TOBACCO	ABCEMRS	CAMBERS	ABCLMSY	CYMBALS
ABCDEEH	BEACHED	ABCENOS	BEACONS	ABCLMUU	BACULUM
ABCDEEL	DEBACLE	ABCENOW	COWBANE	ABCLNOY	BALCONY
ABCDEHU	DEBAUCH	ABCENOZ	CABEZON	ABCLRUY	CURABLY
ABCDEIK	DIEBACK	ABCENRU	UNBRACE	ABCMNRW	CWMBRAN
ABCDEIR	CARBIDE	ABCEOOS	CABOOSE	ABCMOST	COMBATS
ABCDEKL	BLACKED	ABCESSS	ABSCESS	ABCNORS	CARBONS
ABCDEMP	CAMP BED	ABCFFKO	BACK OFF	ABCORRW	CROWBAR
ABCDEOR	BAR CODE,	ABCFIKN	FINBACK	ABCORSX	BOXCARS
	BROCADE	ABCFILO	BIFOCAL	ABCORSY	CARBOYS
ABCDERU	CUDBEAR	ABCFIRS	FABRICS	ABDDEER	BEARDED
ABCDHIO	ICHABOD	ABCFKLY	FLYBACK	ABDDEES	DEBASED
ABCDIIS	DIBASIC	ABCFLNU	FAN CLUB	ABDDEET	DEBATED
ABCDIRT	CATBIRD	ABCGHKO	HOGBACK	ABDDEIN	BANDIED
ABCDISU	SUBACID	ABCGIKN	BACKING	ABDDEIR	BRAIDED
ABCDLOO	BACOLOD	ABCGILN	CABLING	ABDDELR	BLADDER
ABCDNOS	ABSCOND	ABCGINR	BRACING	ABDDENR	BRANDED
ABCDOOR	CORDOBA	ABCGIST	BIG CATS		

ABDDEOR	BOARDED, ROADBED
ABDDEST	BADDEST
ABDDINS	DISBAND
ABDDLLO	ODDBALL
ABDEEFG	FEEDBAG
ABDEEFL	FEEL BAD
ABDEEHV	BEHAVED
ABDEEIL	BEDELIA
ABDEEIR	BEADIER
ABDEELL	LABELED
ABDEELN	ENABLED
ABDEELS	BEADLES
ABDEELT	BELATED, BLEATED
ABDEELY	BELAYED
ABDEERS	DEBASER
ABDEERT	BERATED, DEBATER
ABDEEST	DEBATES
ABDEETT	ABETTED
ABDEFFL	BAFFLED
ABDEFLT	FLAT-BED
ABDEFOR	FORBADE
ABDEGGR	BRAGGED
ABDEGHI	BIGHEAD
ABDEGIL	BIG DEAL
ABDEGIN	BEADING
ABDEGIR	ABRIDGE, BRIGADE
ABDEGLM	GAMBLED
ABDEGLR	GARBLED
ABDEGNO	BONDAGE, DOGBANE
ABDEGOR	BEOGRAD, BOGARDE
ABDEGRS	BADGERS
ABDEHIL	HIDABLE
ABDEHIT	HABITED
ABDEHLR	HALBERD
ABDEHOR	DEBORAH
ABDEHOW	BOWHEAD
ABDEHRT	BREADTH
ABDEILN	BELINDA
ABDEILP	PIEBALD
ABDEILR	BEDRAIL
ABDEILS	DISABLE
ABDEILU	AUDIBLE
ABDEILY	BEADILY
ABDEINR	BANDIER, BRAINED
ABDEIRR	BRAIDER
ABDEIRS	AIRBEDS, BRAISED, SEABIRD
ABDEIRT	TRIBADE
ABDEIRW	BAWDIER
ABDEISS	BIASSED
ABDEJRU	ABJURED
ABDEKLU	BAULKED

ABDELMR	MARBLED, RAMBLED
ABDELMS	BEDLAMS
ABDELNR	BLANDER
ABDELOT	BLOATED
ABDELOW	DOWABLE
ABDELPU	DUPABLE
ABDELRU	DURABLE
ABDELRW	BRAWLED, WARBLED
ABDELRY	BRADLEY, DRYABLE
ABDELST	BLASTED, STABLED
ABDELTT	BATTLED
ABDEMNO	ABDOMEN
ABDEMRU	BERMUDA
ABDENNR	BRENDAN
ABDENOR	BROADEN
ABDENPS	BEDPANS
ABDENRR	BERNARD, REBRAND
ABDENSS	BADNESS
ABDEORR	BOARDER, BROADER
ABDEORT	ABORTED
ABDEOST	BOASTED
ABDEPSY	PAYBEDS
ABDERSV	ADVERBS
ABDERUY	DAUBERY
ABDETTU	ABUTTED
ABDFIIR	BID FAIR
ABDFMOR	BAD FORM
ABDGIIN	ABIDING
ABDGILN	BALDING
ABDGINN	BANDING
ABDGINO	BAODING
ABDGINR	BRIGAND
ABDGINU	DAUBING
ABDGINW	WINDBAG
ABDGNNU	BANDUNG
ABDHMTU	MUD BATH
ABDHNSU	HUSBAND
ABDHOSW	BAD SHOW
ABDIKOR	KOBARID
ABDILNW	BALDWIN
ABDILOO	DIABOLO
ABDILOR	LABROID
ABDILOT	TABLOID
ABDILUY	AUDIBLY
ABDILWY	BAWDILY
ABDINOR	INBOARD
ABDINOT	BANTOID
ABDINST	BANDITS
ABDIPRU	UPBRAID
ABDIRSU	SUBARID
ABDJORU	DOBRUJA
ABDKNOU	DO A BUNK
ABDKOOY	DAYBOOK

ABDLLNY	BLANDLY
ABDLLOR	BOLLARD
ABDLMOR	LOMBARD
ABDLNOY	BLAYDON
ABDLORY	BROADLY
ABDLRUY	DURABLY
ABDLSUU	SUBDUAL
ABDNNOR	BRANDON
ABDNOSS	DONBASS
ABDNOSX	SANDBOX
ABDNOYY	ANYBODY
ABDNSTY	STANDBY
ABDOOWY	BAYWOOD
ABDOSYY	DAYBOYS
ABDRSTU	BUSTARD
ABDRUZZ	BUZZARD
ABEEEFT	BEEF TEA
ABEEERV	BEREAVE
ABEEGHR	HERBAGE
ABEEGLS	BEAGLES
ABEEGLT	GETABLE
ABEEGRS	BARGEES
ABEEGRU	AUBERGE
ABEEGRW	BREWAGE
ABEEHKR	REBEKAH
ABEEHNN	HENBANE
ABEEHNS	BANSHEE, HAS-BEEN
ABEEHNT	BENEATH
ABEEHRT	BREATHE
ABEEHTY	EYEBATH
ABEEINT	BETAINE
ABEEITT	BEATTIE
ABEEKLR	BLEAKER
ABEEKNT	BETAKEN
ABEEKPS	BESPEAK
ABEEKRR	BREAKER
ABEEKRS	BEAKERS
ABEELLM	MABELLE
ABEELLY	EYEBALL
ABEELNR	ENABLER
ABEELNT	TENABLE
ABEELNU	NEBULAE
ABEELOR	EARLOBE
ABEELQU	EQUABLE
ABEELRT	BLEATER, RETABLE
ABEEMRS	BESMEAR
ABEENOU	EUBOEAN
ABEENRS	BENARES
ABEENRV	VERBENA
ABEERRS	BEARERS
ABEERRT	REBATER
ABEERST	BEATERS, REBATES
ABEERSV	BEAVERS
ABEESWX	BEESWAX

ABEFFLR	BAFFLER	ABEHITU	HABITUE	ABEIRSS	BRASSIE
ABEFFLS	BAFFLES	ABEHKRU	HAUBERK	ABEIRTT	BATTIER, BIRETTA
ABEFFOT	OFFBEAT	ABEHLMS	SHAMBLE	ABEIRTV	VIBRATE
ABEFGST	GABFEST	ABEHLMT	LAMBETH	ABEIRTX	BEATRIX
ABEFILN	FINABLE	ABEHLRS	HERBALS	ABEIRUX	EXURBIA
ABEFILR	FRIABLE	ABEHLRT	BLATHER	ABEISTT	BATISTE
ABEFILU	FIBULAE	ABEHNRY	ABHENRY	ABEISUV	ABUSIVE
ABEFILX	FIXABLE	ABEHNTY	BETHANY	ABEITUX	BAUXITE
ABEFITY	BEATIFY	ABEHRRS	BRASHER	ABEJLUY	BLUE JAY
ABEFLLU	BALEFUL	ABEHRST	BATHERS	ABEJNOW	JAWBONE
ABEFLLY	FLYABLE	ABEHRTY	BREATHY	ABEJRRU	ABJURER
ABEFLNT	FAN BELT	ABEIILR	LIBERIA	ABEKLLY	BLEAKLY
ABEFLNU	BANEFUL	ABEIILS	BASILIE	ABEKLNT	BLANKET
ABEFLST	BELFAST	ABEIINR	IBERIAN	ABEKNRS	BANKERS
ABEFORR	FORBEAR	ABEIINT	BAINITE	ABEKRRS	BARKERS
ABEFPRS	PREFABS	ABEIIRS	SIBERIA	ABEKSST	BASKETS
ABEGGIM	BIG GAME	ABEIJNS	BASENJI	ABELLNT	NETBALL
ABEGGIR	BAGGIER	ABEIKLL	LIKABLE	ABELLOS	LOSABLE
ABEGGMO	GAMBOGE	ABEIKLS	SKIABLE	ABELLOV	LOVABLE
ABEGGRR	BRAGGER	ABEIKNR	BIKANER, BREAK-IN	ABELLRU	RUBELLA, RULABLE
ABEGGRS	BEGGARS	ABEIKNT	BEATNIK	ABELLST	BALLETS
ABEGGRY	BEGGARY	ABEILLN	LINABLE	ABELLSY	SYBELLA
ABEGHMR	MAGHREB	ABEILLO	LOBELIA	ABELLTU	BULLATE
ABEGHNS	SHEBANG	ABEILLP	PLIABLE	ABELLUW	BLUE LAW
ABEGHRU	BEAR HUG	ABEILLR	BRAILLE, LIBERAL	ABELMNT	BELT MAN, LAMBENT
ABEGILN	BELGIAN, BENGALI	ABEILLS	SIBELLA		
ABEGILR	GABRIEL	ABEILLV	LIVABLE	ABELMNU	ALBUMEN
ABEGILV	GIVABLE	ABEILMN	MINABLE	ABELMOV	MOVABLE
ABEGIMN	BEAMING, BIG NAME	ABEILMR	BALMIER, MIRABEL	ABELMRR	MARBLER, RAMBLER
		ABEILMT	LIMBATE, TIMBALE	ABELMRS	MARBLES, RAMBLES
ABEGIMR	GAMBIER	ABEILMX	MIXABLE	ABELMRT	LAMBERT
ABEGINO	BEGONIA	ABEILNP	BIPLANE	ABELMRY	BRAMLEY
ABEGINR	BEARING	ABEILNS	LESBIAN	ABELMTU	MUTABLE
ABEGINT	BEATING	ABEILRT	LIBRATE, TRIABLE	ABELNNO	LEBANON
ABEGIPP	BAGPIPE	ABEILST	BESTIAL, STABILE	ABELNOT	NOTABLE
ABEGLMR	GAMBLER, GAMBREL	ABEILSY	BAILEYS	ABELNOY	BALONEY
		ABEILSZ	SIZABLE	ABELNRU	NEBULAR
ABEGLMU	BELGAUM	ABEILVV	BIVALVE	ABELNRY	BLARNEY
ABEGLNS	BANGLES	ABEIMNT	AMBIENT	ABELNSU	NEBULAS
ABEGLOT	GLOBATE	ABEIMRR	BARMIER	ABELNTU	TUNABLE
ABEGLRR	GARBLER	ABEIMZZ	ZAMBEZI	ABELOPT	POTABLE
ABEGMOR	BERGAMO, EMBARGO	ABEINOR	BONAIRE	ABELORS	ROSABEL
		ABEINOZ	ZENOBIA	ABELORT	BLOATER
ABEGMRU	UMBRAGE	ABEINRS	SERBIAN	ABELORU	RUBEOLA
ABEGNOS	NOSEBAG	ABEINRW	WINE BAR	ABELOSV	ABSOLVE
ABEGNRS	BANGERS	ABEINSS	BASSEIN	ABELOTV	VOTABLE
ABEGOPY	PAGEBOY	ABEINST	ANTIBES	ABELQUY	EQUABLY
ABEGORX	GEARBOX	ABEINTT	BETTINA, TIBETAN	ABELRRS	BARRELS
ABEGOSZ	GAZEBOS	ABEIOTV	OBVIATE	ABELRRW	BRAWLER, WARBLER
ABEGOTT	TOTE BAG	ABEIPST	BAPTISE	ABELRSU	BELARUS
ABEGOUY	BUOYAGE	ABEIPTZ	BAPTIZE	ABELRSZ	BLAZERS
ABEHILR	HIRABLE	ABEIRRR	BARRIER	ABELRTT	BARTLET
ABEHIMO	BOHEMIA	ABEIRRT	ARBITER, RAREBIT	ABELRVY	BRAVELY
ABEHINO	BIEN HOA	ABEIRRZ	BIZARRE, BRAZIER	ABELSST	STABLES
ABEHIRS	BEARISH				

ABELSTT	BATTLES	ABFLOTY	FLYBOAT	ABHINOS	SIOBHAN
ABELSTY	BEASTLY	ABGGGIN	BAGGING	ABHINRS	BAS-RHIN
ABELTWY	BELTWAY	ABGGILY	BAGGILY	ABHINST	ABSINTH
ABEMNOT	BOATMEN	ABGGINN	BANGING	ABHIOPS	PHOBIAS
ABEMNST	BATSMEN, BEST MAN	ABGGINR	BARGING, GARBING	ABHIORS	BOARISH
ABEMNSU	SUNBEAM	ABGHINS	BASHING	ABHIOST	ISOBATH
ABEMORS	AMBROSE	ABGHINT	BATHING	ABHIRTY	YATHRIB
ABEMORT	BROMATE	ABGHLRU	BURGHAL	ABHISTU	HABITUS
ABEMRRT	BERTRAM	ABGHMRU	HAMBURG	ABHLRSY	BRASHLY
ABEMSSY	EMBASSY	ABGIILN	BAILING	ABHMNSU	BUSHMAN
ABENNOY	BAYONNE	ABGIINS	BIASING	ABHOOST	BASOTHO
ABENNRS	BANNERS	ABGIINT	BAITING	ABHORRU	HARBOUR
ABENNRW	BRANWEN	ABGIKLN	BALKING	ABHOTUY	HAUTBOY
ABENORT	BARONET	ABGIKLT	TALK BIG	ABHSTUW	WASHTUB
ABENORU	AUBERON	ABGIKNN	BANKING	ABIILLS	SIBILLA
ABENOTY	BAYONET	ABGIKNR	BARKING, BRAKING	ABIILMU	BULIMIA
ABENOWX	BONE WAX	ABGIKNS	BASKING	ABIILOV	BOLIVIA
ABENQTU	BANQUET	ABGIKST	KIT BAGS	ABIILRY	BILIARY
ABENRST	BARENTS	ABGILMN	AMBLING, BLAMING, LAMBING	ABIILTY	ABILITY
ABENRSY	BARNEYS	ABGILMS	GIMBALS	ABIINOR	NAIROBI
ABENSTT	BATTENS, TEST BAN	ABGILNR	BLARING	ABIIOSS	ABIOSIS
ABENTUZ	BAUTZEN	ABGILNT	TABLING	ABIJNPU	PUNJABI
ABEOOTV	OBOVATE	ABGILNW	BAWLING	ABIJPRU	BIJAPUR
ABEOPRS	SAPROBE	ABGILNZ	BLAZING	ABIKLLM	KIMBALL
ABEOPRT	PROBATE	ABGIMST	GAMBITS	ABILLMY	BALMILY
ABEOQRU	BAROQUE	ABGINNN	BANNING	ABILLNP	PINBALL
ABEORRT	ROBERTA	ABGINOT	BOATING	ABILLSW	SAWBILL
ABEORST	BAROTSE, BOASTER, BOATERS	ABGINRR	BARRING	ABILLSY	SIBYLLA, SYBILLA, SYLLABI
ABEORTT	ABETTOR, TABORET	ABGINRV	BRAVING	ABILLWX	WAXBILL
ABEOSTX	BOX SEAT	ABGINRY	BRAYING	ABILLWY	WAYBILL
ABEPRTY	TYPEBAR	ABGINST	BASTING	ABILMNU	ALBUMIN
ABEQRSU	BARQUES	ABGINSU	ABUSING	ABILMOX	MAILBOX
ABERRTT	BARRETT	ABGINTT	BATTING	ABILNOS	ALBINOS
ABERRVY	BRAVERY	ABGINTW	BATWING	ABILOPR	BIPOLAR, PARBOIL
ABERSSS	BRASSES	ABGKKNO	BANGKOK	ABILORT	ORBITAL
ABERSSU	SURBASE	ABGKORW	WORKBAG	ABILORV	BOLIVAR
ABERSTT	BATTERS	ABGLMOS	GAMBOLS	ABILOTU	BAIL OUT
ABERSTV	BRAVEST	ABGLMOU	LUMBAGO	ABILRRY	LIBRARY
ABERSTY	BARYTES	ABGLNOO	BOLOGNA	ABILRSU	BURIALS
ABERTTU	ABUTTER	ABGLRRU	BURGLAR	ABIMNRU	UMBRIAN
ABERTTY	BATTERY	ABGMORW	BAGWORM	ABIMORR	MARIBOR
ABERUUX	BUREAUX	ABGMRRU	MARBURG	ABIMOSS	BIOMASS
ABESSST	BASSETS	ABGNOPR	PROBANG	ABIMPST	BAPTISM
ABESSSY	ABYSSES	ABGNOTU	GUNBOAT	ABINNOS	BOSNIAN
ABFFIIL	BAILIFF	ABGOPST	POSTBAG	ABINORT	TABORIN
ABFFLOU	BUFFALO	ABHHIPT	HIPBATH	ABINORW	RAINBOW
ABFHIST	BATFISH	ABHHOOP	POOH-BAH	ABINOST	BASTION
ABFHLSU	BASHFUL	ABHHSUY	HUSHABY	ABINRTV	VIBRANT
ABFIILR	BIFILAR	ABHIINT	INHABIT	ABIORSS	ISOBARS
ABFIIMR	FIMBRIA	ABHIKRS	BASHKIR	ABIORTV	VIBRATO
ABFILRU	FIBULAR	ABHILNO	HOBNAIL	ABIORUX	ROUBAIX
ABFILSU	FIBULAS	ABHILOS	ABOLISH	ABIPRTT	BIT PART
ABFIMOR	FIBROMA	ABHILTU	HALIBUT	ABIPSTT	BAPTIST

ABIRUZZ	ABRUZZI	ACCDEHN	CHANCED	ACCENST	ACCENTS
ABISSST	BASSIST	ACCDEHO	COACHED	ACCEPRY	PECCARY
ABKLLNY	BLANKLY	ACCDEIN	CANDICE	ACCERRS	SCARCER
ABKLRUW	BULWARK	ACCDEKL	CACKLED, CLACKED	ACCERSU	ACCUSER
ABKNRSY	BRYANSK	ACCDEKO	COCKADE	ACCFIIP	PACIFIC
ABLLLUY	LULLABY	ACCDEKR	CRACKED	ACCFILY	CALCIFY
ABLLNOO	BALLOON	ACCDENY	CADENCY	ACCGHIO	CHICAGO
ABLLNOS	NO BALLS	ACCDERU	ACCRUED	ACCGNOS	COGNACS
ABLLORR	ROLL BAR	ACCDESU	ACCUSED	ACCHILS	CHALCIS
ABLLORU	LOBULAR	ACCDFIL	FLACCID	ACCHINO	CHICANO
ABLLOST	BALLOTS	ACCDHIL	CHALCID	ACCHIOT	CHAOTIC
ABLLOTY	TALLBOY	ACCDINS	SCANDIC	ACCHIOU	ACOUCHI
ABLLPSU	BALLS-UP	ACCDIOT	OCTADIC	ACCHKNO	HANCOCK
ABLMMUU	LUMUMBA	ACCDORS	ACCORDS	ACCHKOY	HAYCOCK
ABLMOOT	TOMBOLA	ACCEELN	CENACLE	ACCHLNO	CONCHAL
ABLMOVY	MOVABLY	ACCEERT	ACCRETE	ACCHNUY	CHAUNCY
ABLMPUU	PABULUM	ACCEFLU	FELUCCA	ACCHOTW	CHOCTAW
ABLMSTU	STAMBUL	ACCEHIL	CALICHE, CHALICE	ACCHRST	SCRATCH
ABLMTUY	MUTABLY	ACCEHIN	CHICANE	ACCIINT	ACTINIC
ABLNOOZ	BOLZANO	ACCEHLN	CHANCEL	ACCIIST	ASCITIC, SCIATIC
ABLNOSZ	BLAZONS	ACCEHLO	COCHLEA	ACCIKRR	CARRICK
ABLNOTU	BUTANOL	ACCEHNR	CHANCRE	ACCIKRS	CARSICK
ABLNOTY	NOTABLY	ACCEHNS	CHANCES	ACCIKRT	CRACK IT
ABLOPYY	PLAYBOY	ACCEHOS	COACHES	ACCILLU	CALCULI
ABLORST	BORSTAL	ACCEHRT	CATCHER	ACCILMO	COMICAL
ABLORSU	LABOURS	ACCEHST	CACHETS, CATCHES	ACCILMU	CALCIUM
ABLOSTX	SALTBOX	ACCEHTU	CATECHU	ACCILNO	CONICAL, LACONIC
ABLRTUU	TUBULAR	ACCEIIL	CECILIA	ACCILNU	CLUNIAC
ABMORTU	TAMBOUR	ACCEIKP	ICE PACK, PACK ICE	ACCILNY	CYNICAL
ABMOSTW	WOMBATS	ACCEILN	CALCINE	ACCILOR	CALORIC
ABNNORS	BRANSON	ACCEILO	COELIAC	ACCILOS	CALICOS
ABNOORZ	BORAZON	ACCEILR	CLARICE	ACCILOV	VOCALIC
ABNOOSS	BASSOON	ACCEILT	CALCITE	ACCILRU	CRUCIAL
ABNORTZ	TRABZON	ACCEIMR	CERAMIC, RACEMIC	ACCILRY	ACRYLIC
ABNORUY	YORUBAN	ACCEINO	COCAINE, OCEANIC	ACCILSS	CLASSIC
ABNOTUY	BOUYANT,	ACCEINV	VACCINE	ACCILST	CLASTIC
BUOYANT		ACCEIPR	CAPRICE	ACCIORS	CORSICA
ABNRSTU	TURBANS	ACCEIPS	ICE CAPS	ACCISTT	TACTICS
ABOOPSX	SOAPBOX	ACCEIPV	PECCAVI	ACCISTU	CAUSTIC
ABOOTTU	ABOUT TO	ACCEIST	ASCETIC	ACCKNNO	CANNOCK
ABOOTTW	TOWBOAT	ACCEKLR	CACKLER, CRACKLE	ACCKOSS	CASSOCK
ABORRSU	ARBOURS	ACCEKLS	CACKLES	ACCKPRU	CRACK UP
ABORRSW	BARROWS	ACCEKOP	PEACOCK	ACCKTTU	CUTTACK
ABORSSU	SUB ROSA	ACCEKOS	SEACOCK	ACCMOOY	COCOYAM
ABORSTU	ROBUSTA	ACCEKPU	CUP CAKE	ACCMOPT	COMPACT
ABRRSSU	BURSARS	ACCEKRR	CRACKER	ACCMRUU	CURCUMA
ABRRSUY	BURSARY	ACCELLY	CALYCLE	ACCNOOR	RACCOON
ABRRTUY	TURBARY	ACCELNO	CONCEAL	ACCNOTT	CONTACT
ABRSTUU	ARBUTUS	ACCELOR	CORACLE	ACCNOTU	ACCOUNT
ABSSUWY	SUBWAYS	ACCELSU	SACCULE	ACCOPTY	COPYCAT
ACCCILY	ACYCLIC	ACCELSY	CALYCES	ACCOQSU	SQUACCO
ACCDDEE	ACCEDED	ACCENOV	CONCAVE	ACDDDEI	CADDIED
ACCDEEN	CADENCE	ACCENPT	PECCANT	ACDDDEU	ADDUCED
ACCDEER	ACCEDER	ACCENRS	CANCERS	ACDDEEF	DEFACED

ACDDEES	DECADES
ACDDEEY	DECAYED
ACDDEHR	CHEDDAR
ACDDEIN	CANDIED
ACDDEIS	CADDIES
ACDDEIU	DECIDUA
ACDDELO	CLADODE
ACDDELR	CRADLED
ACDDELS	SCALDED
ACDDEOP	DECAPOD
ACDDERR	RED CARD
ACDDHIS	CADDISH
ACDDHKO	HADDOCK
ACDDIRS	DISCARD, ID CARDS
ACDDIRY	DRYADIC
ACDDIST	ADDICTS
ACDDKOP	PADDOCK
ACDEEES	DECEASE
ACDEEFF	EFFACED
ACDEEFR	DEFACER, REFACED
ACDEEHL	LEACHED
ACDEEHR	ARDECHE, REACHED
ACDEEHT	CHEATED
ACDEEIR	DECIARE
ACDEEJT	DEJECTA
ACDEEKR	CREAKED
ACDEELL	CADELLE
ACDEELN	CLEANED
ACDEELR	CLEARED, CREEDAL, DECLARE
ACDEELS	DESCALE
ACDEELV	CLEAVED
ACDEEMN	MENACED
ACDEEMR	CREAMED
ACDEENS	ENCASED
ACDEENT	ENACTED
ACDEENV	VENDACE
ACDEEPR	CAPERED, RECAPED
ACDEEPS	ESCAPED
ACDEERS	CREASED
ACDEERT	CATERED, CERATED, CREATED, REACTED
ACDEETU	EDUCATE
ACDEETX	EXACTED
ACDEFFH	CHAFFED
ACDEFIN	FANCIED
ACDEFOP	PO-FACED
ACDEFOT	DE FACTO
ACDEFRT	CRAFTED
ACDEGHN	CHANGED
ACDEGHR	CHARGED
ACDEGKO	DOCKAGE
ACDEGLN	CLANGED, GLANCED
ACDEGNO	DECAGON

ACDEGNU	UNCAGED
ACDEGOR	CORDAGE
ACDEGRS	CADGERS
ACDEHHT	HATCHED
ACDEHIN	CHAINED, ECHIDNA
ACDEHIP	EDAPHIC
ACDEHIR	CHAIRED
ACDEHIX	HEXADIC
ACDEHKL	CHALKED
ACDEHKS	SHACKED
ACDEHKW	WHACKED
ACDEHLS	CLASHED
ACDEHLT	LATCHED
ACDEHMP	CHAMPED
ACDEHMR	CHARMED, MARCHED
ACDEHMT	MATCHED
ACDEHNR	ENDARCH
ACDEHNT	CHANTED
ACDEHOP	POACHED
ACDEHOT	CATHODE
ACDEHPP	CHAPPED
ACDEHPR	PARCHED
ACDEHPT	PATCHED
ACDEHRR	CHARRED
ACDEHRS	CRASHED
ACDEHRT	CHARTED
ACDEHTT	CHATTED
ACDEHTW	WATCHED
ACDEILL	CEDILLA
ACDEILM	CLAIMED, DECIMAL, DECLAIM, MEDICAL
ACDEILN	ICELAND
ACDEILR	DECRIAL, RADICEL, RADICLE
ACDEILT	CITADEL, DELTAIC, DIALECT, EDICTAL
ACDEILV	CAVILED
ACDEIMY	MEDIACY
ACDEINS	CANDIES
ACDEINY	CYANIDE
ACDEIPR	PERACID
ACDEIRR	CARRIED
ACDEIRS	RADICES, SIDECAR
ACDEIST	DIE-CAST
ACDEISV	ADVICES
ACDEITT	DICTATE
ACDEITY	EDACITY
ACDEJLO	CAJOLED
ACDEKLN	CLANKED
ACDEKLO	CLOAKED
ACDEKLS	SLACKED
ACDEKLT	TACKLED
ACDEKLU	CAULKED
ACDEKMS	SMACKED

ACDEKNR	CRANKED
ACDEKNS	SNACKED
ACDEKOR	CROAKED
ACDEKQU	QUACKED
ACDEKRT	TRACKED
ACDEKST	STACKED
ACDELMM	CLAMMED
ACDELMP	CLAMPED
ACDELNO	CELADON
ACDELNR	CANDLER
ACDELNS	CALENDS, CANDLES
ACDELOP	PEDOCAL
ACDELOR	CAROLED
ACDELOS	SOLACED
ACDELOT	LOCATED
ACDELPP	CLAPPED
ACDELPS	CLASPED, SCALPED
ACDELRS	CRADLES
ACDELRW	CRAWLED
ACDELSS	CLASSED, DECLASS
ACDELST	CASTLED
ACDELWW	DEWCLAW
ACDEMMR	CRAMMED
ACDEMNO	MACEDON
ACDEMOR	COMRADE
ACDEMPR	CRAMPED
ACDENNS	SCANNED
ACDENOS	DEACONS
ACDENOT	TACNODE
ACDENPR	PRANCED
ACDENPT	PANDECT
ACDENRS	DANCERS
ACDENRT	TANCRED
ACDENRY	ARDENCY
ACDENST	DESCANT
ACDEORR	CORRADE
ACDEORT	ART DECO, CORDATE, REDCOAT
ACDEORU	ECUADOR
ACDEOST	COASTED
ACDEOUV	COUVADE
ACDEPPR	CRAPPED
ACDEPRS	SCRAPED
ACDEQSU	CASQUED
ACDERRS	SCARRED
ACDERSU	CRUSADE
ACDERTT	DETRACT
ACDERTU	TRADUCE
ACDESTT	SCATTED
ACDFFIR	CARDIFF
ACDFIIY	ACIDIFY
ACDGGIN	CADGING
ACDGHLO	CLODAGH
ACDGINN	DANCING

ACDGINR	CARDING	ACEEEPS	ESCAPEE	ACEEPST	PECTASE
ACDGKLO	DAGLOCK	ACEEEUV	EVACUEE	ACEEPTT	PECTATE
ACDGORT	DOGCART	ACEEFFR	EFFACER	ACEERRS	CAREERS
ACDHIIL	CHILIAD	ACEEFIN	FAIENCE	ACEERRT	CATERER, RETRACE,
ACDHIIS	HASIDIC	ACEEFPR	PREFACE	TERRACE	
ACDHIRR	RICHARD	ACEEGIL	ELEGIAC	ACEERSS	CREASES
ACDHIRY	DIARCHY	ACEEGIS	ICE AGES	ACEERSV	VERSACE
ACDHLOR	CHORDAL	ACEEHHT	CHEETAH	ACEERTX	EXCRETA
ACDHMRS	DRACHMS	ACEEHIV	ACHIEVE	ACEESTU	EUSTACE
ACDHNOW	COWHAND	ACEEHLR	LEACHER	ACEESTY	CAT'S EYE
ACDHOPR	POCHARD	ACEEHLT	CHELATE	ACEFFFO	FACE-OFF
ACDHORR	ORCHARD	ACEEHMT	MACHETE	ACEFFHR	CHAFFER
ACDHRYY	DYARCHY	ACEEHNN	ENHANCE	ACEFHMR	CHAMFER
ACDIIIN	INDICIA	ACEEHNP	CHEAPEN	ACEFIIL	FELICIA
ACDIINN	INDICAN	ACEEHPR	CHEAPER	ACEFILL	ICEFALL
ACDIIRT	TRIACID, TRIADIC	ACEEHPS	PEACHES	ACEFILM	MALEFIC
ACDIITY	ACIDITY	ACEEHRR	REACHER	ACEFINN	FINANCE
ACDILMO	DOMICAL	ACEEHRS	REACHES	ACEFINR	FANCIER, FRANCIE
ACDILNO	NODICAL	ACEEHRT	CHEATER, HECTARE,	ACEFINS	FANCIES, FASCINE,
ACDILNU	LUCINDA	TEACHER		FIANCES	
ACDILOP	PLACOID	ACEEILP	CALIPEE	ACEFITY	ACETIFY
ACDILOR	CORDIAL	ACEEILT	ELEATIC	ACEFLRU	CAREFUL
ACDILOT	COTIDAL	ACEEINU	EUCAINE	ACEFNRS	FRANCES
ACDILTW	WILDCAT	ACEEKNP	KNEECAP	ACEFNRU	FURNACE
ACDIMMU	CADMIUM	ACEELLN	NACELLE	ACEFOTU	OUTFACE
ACDIMNO	MONADIC,	ACEELMP	EMPLACE	ACEFRRT	REFRACT
NOMADIC		ACEELNR	CARLEEN, CARLENE,	ACEFRRU	FARCEUR
ACDIMNY	DYNAMIC	CLEANER		ACEFRSU	SURFACE
ACDINSU	SUDANIC	ACEELNS	CLEANSE, SCALENE	ACEFRTU	FURCATE
ACDIOPR	PARODIC, PICADOR	ACEELNV	ENCLAVE, VALENCE	ACEFSTU	FAUCETS
ACDIORR	CORRIDA, RICARDO	ACEELPR	PERCALE, REPLACE	ACEGHNR	CHANGER
ACDIORS	SARCOID	ACEELRR	CLEARER	ACEGHNS	CHANGES
ACDIORT	CAROTID	ACEELRS	CEREALS	ACEGHOU	GOUACHE
ACDIOSZ	ZODIACS	ACEELRT	TREACLE	ACEGHRR	CHARGER
ACDIOXY	OXYACID	ACEELRV	CLEAVER	ACEGHRS	CHARGES
ACDIPRY	PICARDY	ACEELST	CELESTA	ACEGILN	ANGELIC, GALENIC,
ACDIQRU	QUADRIC	ACEELVX	EXCLAVE	LEGNICA	
ACDIRST	DRASTIC	ACEEMNR	MENACER	ACEGILP	PELAGIC
ACDITUV	VIADUCT	ACEEMNS	MENACES	ACEGILR	GLACIER, GRACILE
ACDJNTU	ADJUNCT	ACEEMNV	CAVEMEN	ACEGIMR	GRIMACE
ACDKLOP	PADLOCK	ACEEMNY	MYCENAE	ACEGINO	COINAGE
ACDKMPU	MUDPACK	ACEEMRR	CREAMER	ACEGINR	ANERGIC, GRECIAN
ACDLLOR	COLLARD	ACEEMRT	CREMATE	ACEGINS	CEASING
ACDLNOR	CALDRON	ACEENNP	PENANCE	ACEGIST	CAGIEST
ACDLORW	COLD WAR	ACEENNT	CANTEEN	ACEGKLO	LOCKAGE
ACDLSTY	DACTYLS	ACEENNY	CAYENNE	ACEGKLR	GRACKLE
ACDMMNO	COMMAND	ACEENOT	ACETONE	ACEGKOR	CORKAGE
ACDMOOW	CAMWOOD	ACEENRT	CRENATE	ACEGLLO	COLLAGE
ACDNOOR	CARDOON	ACEENSS	SEANCES	ACEGLNO	CONGEAL
ACDNORU	CANDOUR	ACEENTU	CUNEATE	ACEGLNR	CLANGER
ACDORST	COSTARD	ACEEORS	ACEROSE	ACEGLNS	GLANCES
ACDORSW	COWARDS	ACEEORT	OCREATE	ACEGLOU	CAGOULE
ACDORUZ	CRUZADO	ACEEOSS	CASEOSE	ACEGNOR	ACROGEN
ACDRSTU	CUSTARD	ACEEPRS	ESCAPER	ACEGNOT	COGNATE
		ACEEPSS	ESCAPES		

ACEGORS	CARGOES, CORSAGE, SOCAGER
ACEGORU	COURAGE
ACEGOTT	COTTAGE
ACEHHLR	HARLECH
ACEHHLT	HATCHEL
ACEHHRT	HATCHER
ACEHHRU	HACHURE
ACEHHST	HATCHES
ACEHHTT	HATCHET
ACEHILL	HELICAL
ACEHILM	MICHAEL
ACEHILN	CHILEAN
ACEHILR	CHARLIE
ACEHILT	ETHICAL
ACEHIMN	MACHINE
ACEHIMP	IMPEACH
ACEHIMR	CHIMERA
ACEHINN	ENCHAIN, CHENNAI
ACEHINR	ARCHINE
ACEHINT	TEACH-IN
ACEHINY	HYAENIC
ACEHIPT	HEPATIC
ACEHIRR	CHARIER
ACEHIRS	CASHIER
ACEHIRT	RHAETIC
ACEHIRV	ARCHIVE
ACEHISS	CHAISES
ACEHIST	AITCHES
ACEHITT	CHATTIE
ACEHKLR	HACKLER
ACEHKLS	HACKLES, SHACKLE
ACEHKNY	HACKNEY
ACEHKRS	HACKERS
ACEHKRW	WHACKER
ACEHLLS	SHELLAC
ACEHLLT	HELLCAT
ACEHLMY	ALCHEMY
ACEHLNN	CHANNEL
ACEHLNO	CHALONE
ACEHLNR	CHARNEL
ACEHLOP	EPOCHAL
ACEHLOR	CHOLERA, CHORALE, CHOREAL
ACEHLPS	CHAPELS
ACEHLPT	CHAPLET
ACEHLPY	CHEAPLY
ACEHLRS	CHARLES, CLASHER, LARCHES
ACEHLRY	CHARLEY
ACEHLSS	CLASHES
ACEHLST	CHALETS, LATCHES, SATCHEL
ACEHLTT	CHATTEL, LATCHET

ACEHMRR	CHARMER, MARCHER
ACEHMRS	MARCHES, MESARCH
ACEHMRT	REMATCH
ACEHMST	MATCHES
ACEHMTY	ECTHYMA
ACEHNNT	ENCHANT
ACEHNRR	RANCHER
ACEHNRS	RANCHES
ACEHNRT	CHANTER, TRANCHE
ACEHNST	CHASTEN
ACEHOOT	OOTHECA
ACEHOPR	POACHER
ACEHORS	ROACHES
ACEHOTY	CHAYOTE
ACEHPRT	CHAPTER, PATCHER
ACEHPRY	EPARCHY
ACEHPST	PATCHES
ACEHQUU	QUECHUA
ACEHRRS	ARCHERS
ACEHRRT	CHARTER
ACEHRRX	XERARCH
ACEHRRY	ARCHERY
ACEHRSS	CHASERS, CRASHES
ACEHRST	CHASTER
ACEHRTT	CHATTER, RATCHET
ACEHRTW	WATCHER
ACEHRTY	CYTHERA
ACEHSST	SACHETS
ACEHSSW	CASHEWS
ACEHSTW	WATCHES
ACEIILS	LAICISE
ACEIILT	CILIATE
ACEIILZ	LAICIZE
ACEIJSS	JESSICA
ACEIKPX	PICKAXE
ACEIKRT	TACKIER
ACEIKSS	SEASICK
ACEIKST	TACKIES
ACEILLL	ALLELIC
ACEILLM	CAMILLE
ACEILLX	LEXICAL
ACEILMN	MELANIC
ACEILMR	CLAIMER, MIRACLE, RECLAIM
ACEILMT	CLIMATE
ACEILMX	EXCLAIM
ACEILNP	CAPELIN, IN PLACE, PANICLE, PELICAN
ACEILNR	CARLINE
ACEILNS	SANICLE
ACEILNU	CAULINE
ACEILOR	CALORIE, CARIOLE, CORALIE

ACEILOT	ALOETIC
ACEILPR	REPLICA
ACEILPS	SPECIAL
ACEILPT	PLICATE
ACEILRR	CLARRIE
ACEILRS	ECLAIRS, SCALIER
ACEILRT	ARTICLE, RECITAL
ACEILRU	AURICLE
ACEILRV	CLAVIER, VALERIC
ACEILST	CASTILE, ELASTIC, LACIEST
ACEILSV	VESICAL
ACEILTT	LATTICE, TACTILE
ACEIMNO	ENCOMIA
ACEIMNR	CARMINE, CRIMEAN
ACEIMNS	CINEMAS
ACEIMNT	NEMATIC
ACEIMNX	MEXICAN
ACEIMPY	PYAEMIC
ACEIMRU	MAURICE, URAEMIC
ACEIMST	SEMATIC
ACEIMSU	CAESIUM
ACEINNP	PINNACE
ACEINNR	CANNIER
ACEINNS	CANINES
ACEINNT	ANCIENT
ACEINNY	CYANINE
ACEINOT	ACONITE
ACEINRS	ARSENIC
ACEINRT	CERTAIN
ACEINST	ANSTICE
ACEINSV	CAVE-INS
ACEINTT	TETANIC
ACEINTV	VENATIC
ACEINTX	INEXACT
ACEINTY	CYANITE
ACEINTZ	ZINCATE
ACEINVZ	VICENZA
ACEIOPT	ECTOPIA
ACEIORT	EROTICA
ACEIOTX	EXOTICA
ACEIPPR	CRAPPIE, EPICARP
ACEIPRT	PARETIC, PICRATE
ACEIPSS	CAPSISE
ACEIPST	ASEPTIC, SPICATE
ACEIPSU	AUSPICE
ACEIPSZ	CAPSIZE
ACEIPTV	CAPTIVE
ACEIQRU	ACQUIRE
ACEIQSU	CAIQUES
ACEIRRR	CARRIER
ACEIRRS	CARRIES, SCARIER
ACEIRRT	CIRRATE, ERRATIC
ACEIRRW	AIRCREW

ACEIRRZ	CRAZIER
ACEIRST	RACIEST, STEARIC
ACEIRSU	SAUCIER
ACEIRSV	VISCERA
ACEIRTT	CATTIER, CITRATE
ACEISST	ASCITES
ACEJKST	JACKETS
ACEJNOT	JACONET
ACEJQSU	JACQUES
ACEJRTT	TRAJECT
ACEKLNS	SLACKEN
ACEKLPT	PLACKET
ACEKLRS	SLACKER
ACEKLRT	TACKLER
ACEKLRU	CAULKER
ACEKLST	TACKLES
ACEKLSY	LACKEYS
ACEKMRS	SMACKER
ACEKNRS	CANKERS
ACEKORR	CROAKER
ACEKPPR	PREPACK
ACEKPRS	PACKERS
ACEKPST	PACKETS
ACEKRRT	TRACKER
ACEKRST	RACKETS, STACKER
ACEKRTY	RACKETY
ACEKSST	CASKETS
ACELLMO	CALOMEL
ACELLNY	CLEANLY
ACELLOR	OCELLAR
ACELLOS	LOCALES
ACELLOT	COLLATE
ACELLPS	SCALPEL
ACELLPY	CLYPEAL
ACELLRS	CALLERS, CELLARS, RECALLS
ACELLRU	CURE-ALL
ACELLRY	CLEARLY
ACELMOT	CAMELOT
ACELMOU	LEUCOMA
ACELMPR	CLAMPER
ACELMST	CALMEST
ACELNNU	UNCLEAN
ACELNNY	LYNCEAN
ACELNOP	NO-PLACE
ACELNOR	CORNEAL
ACELNOT	LACTONE
ACELNPS	SPANCEL
ACELNPU	CLEANUP
ACELNRS	LANCERS
ACELNRT	CENTRAL
ACELNRU	NUCLEAR, UNCLEAR
ACELNRY	LARCENY
ACELNST	LANCETS

ACELNSU	CENSUAL
ACELNTY	LATENCY
ACELNVY	VALENCY
ACELOPT	POLECAT
ACELOQU	COEQUAL
ACELORS	ESCOLAR, ORACLES, SOLACER
ACELORT	LOCATER
ACELOSS	SOLACES
ACELOST	LACTOSE, TALCOSE
ACELOSV	ALCOVES, COEVALS
ACELOTT	CALOTTE
ACELOTY	ACOLYTE
ACELOUV	VACUOLE
ACELPPR	CLAPPER
ACELPRS	CLASPER, PARCELS, SCALPER
ACELPRY	PRELACY
ACELPSU	CAPSULE
ACELPSY	CYPSELA
ACELPTY	ECTYPAL
ACELQRU	LACQUER
ACELQSU	CLAQUES
ACELRRW	CRAWLER
ACELRST	CARTELS, SCARLET
ACELRSU	SECULAR
ACELRTT	CLATTER
ACELRTY	TREACLY
ACELRWY	CRAWLEY
ACELSSS	CLASSES
ACELSST	CASTLES
ACELSSU	CLAUSES
ACELSTU	SULCATE
ACELSUU	ACULEUS
ACELSUX	EXCUSAL
ACELSXY	CALYXES
ACELTTU	LUCETTA
ACELTUY	ACUTELY
ACELTXY	EXACTLY
ACEMMRR	CRAMMER
ACEMNOR	CAMERON, CREMONA, ROMANCE
ACEMOPR	COMPARE
ACEMORU	MORCEAU
ACEMPRS	CAMPERS, SCAMPER
ACEMRSS	SCREAMS
ACENNOS	SONANCE
ACENNOT	CONNATE
ACENNOZ	CANZONE
ACENNRS	SCANNER
ACENNRY	CANNERY
ACENNST	NASCENT
ACENNSU	NUANCES
ACENNTY	TENANCY
ACENOOR	CORONAE

ACENORS	COARSEN
ACENORT	ENACTOR, NOT CARE
ACENOST	OCTANES
ACENOSZ	COSENZA
ACENOTV	CENTAVO
ACENPRR	PRANCER
ACENPTY	PATENCY
ACENRRY	ERRANCY
ACENRST	CANTERS, TRANCES
ACENRSV	CAVERNS
ACENRTU	CENTAUR
ACENRTY	NECTARY
ACENSST	ASCENTS, STANCES
ACENSTU	NUTCASE
ACEOOPP	APOCOPE
ACEOPSS	SCAPOSE
ACEOPST	TOE CAPS
ACEOPTU	OUTPACE
ACEOPTZ	ZAPOTEC
ACEORRS	COARSER
ACEORRT	ACROTER, CREATOR, REACTOR
ACEORST	COASTER
ACEORSU	CAROUSE
ACEORTV	OVERACT
ACEORTW	EAT CROW
ACEORTX	EXACTOR
ACEOSSU	CASEOUS
ACEOSTT	COSTATE
ACEOSTU	ACETOUS
ACEOSTV	OCTAVES
ACEOSTY	TEA COSY
ACEOTTV	CAVETTO
ACEOTUU	AUTOCUE
ACEPRRS	SCARPER, SCRAPER
ACEPRSS	SCRAPES
ACEPRST	CARPETS, PRECAST, SPECTRA
ACEPRTU	CAPTURE
ACEPSST	ASPECTS
ACEPSTU	CUSPATE, TEACUPS
ACEQRTU	RACQUET
ACEQSSU	CASQUES
ACERRST	CARTERS, CRATERS, TRACERS
ACERRSV	CARVERS
ACERRTT	RETRACT
ACERRTY	TRACERY
ACERRUV	VERRUCA
ACERSST	ACTRESS, CASTERS
ACERSSU	SAUCERS, SUCRASE
ACERSSV	SCARVES
ACERSTT	SCATTER
ACERSTU	CURATES

123

ACERSTY	SECTARY	ACGIKLN	CALKING, LACKING	ACHILLO	LOCHIAL
ACERTTX	EXTRACT	ACGIKNP	PACKING	ACHILLP	PHALLIC
ACERTTY	CATTERY	ACGIKNR	RACKING	ACHILLS	CHALLIS
ACERTUY	CAUTERY	ACGIKNS	SACKING	ACHILLT	THALLIC
ACESSTY	ECSTASY	ACGIKNT	TACKING	ACHILLV	VILLACH
ACESTTU	SCUTATE	ACGIKRR	GARRICK	ACHILMR	RICHMAL
ACESTTY	TESTACY	ACGILLN	CALLING	ACHILNO	NICHOLA
ACFFILT	AFFLICT	ACGILLO	LOGICAL	ACHILPS	CALIPHS
ACFFIRT	TRAFFIC	ACGILMN	CALMING	ACHILRY	CHARILY
ACFFLTU	FACTFUL	ACGILMY	MYALGIC	ACHIMNO	MOHICAN
ACFFOST	CAST-OFF	ACGILNN	LANCING	ACHIMOS	CHAMOIS
ACFGHIN	CHAFING	ACGILNO	COALING	ACHINNU	UNCHAIN
ACFGINS	FACINGS	ACGILNP	PLACING	ACHINOP	APHONIC
ACFHIST	CATFISH	ACGILNR	CARLING	ACHINOT	ANTIOCH
ACFHISU	FUCHSIA	ACGILNS	SCALING	ACHINPS	SPINACH
ACFHLNU	FLAUNCH, FUNCHAL	ACGILNT	CATLING	ACHINSU	SICHUAN
ACFHLTU	HALF-CUT	ACGILNV	CALVING	ACHINTX	XANTHIC
ACFILNO	FOLACIN	ACGILNW	CLAWING	ACHINTY	CYNTHIA
ACFILNY	FANCILY	ACGIMNO	COAMING	ACHIOPT	APHOTIC
ACFILRY	CLARIFY	ACGIMNP	CAMPING	ACHIORT	CHARIOT, HARICOT
ACFILSS	FISCALS	ACGIMNN	CANNING	ACHIPST	SPATHIC
ACFIMOR	FORMICA	ACGINNR	CRANING	ACHIQRU	CHARQUI
ACFIMRU	FUMARIC	ACGINNT	CANTING	ACHIRTU	HAIRCUT
ACFIMSS	FASCISM	ACGINOR	ORGANIC	ACHIRTY	CHARITY
ACFINNY	INFANCY	ACGINOT	COATING, COTINGA	ACHISSS	CHASSIS
ACFINOT	FACTION	ACGINOX	COAXING	ACHISTT	CATTISH
ACFINRS	FRANCIS	ACGINPP	CAPPING	ACHITTW	WATCH IT!
ACFINRT	FRANTIC, INFARCT, INFRACT	ACGINPR	CARPING	ACHKMMO	HAMMOCK
		ACGINPS	SPACING	ACHKOPS	HOPSACK
ACFINRY	CARNIFY	ACGINRS	SCARING	ACHKOSS	HASSOCK
ACFIOSS	FIASCOS	ACGINRT	CARTING, CRATING, TRACING	ACHKSTW	THWACKS
ACFIRSY	SCARIFY			ACHLLOO	ALCOHOL
ACFISST	FASCIST	ACGINRV	CARVING, CRAVING	ACHLLOR	CHLORAL
ACFKLLU	FUCK ALL	ACGINSS	CASINGS	ACHLLOU	CHOLULA
ACFLNOS	FALCONS	ACGINST	CASTING	ACHLNOW	LANCHOW
ACFLRUU	FURCULA	ACGINSU	CAUSING, SAUCING	ACHLNOY	HALCYON
ACFLTTU	TACTFUL	ACGIORT	ARGOTIC	ACHLNTU	UNLATCH
ACFLTUY	FACULTY	ACGIRST	GASTRIC	ACHLORS	SCHOLAR
ACFOQRT	Q-FACTOR	ACGLNOR	CLANGOR	ACHLORT	TROCHAL
ACFORST	FACTORS	ACGNOOT	OCTAGON	ACHMNOR	MONARCH
ACFORTY	FACTORY	ACGNORS	GARCONS	ACHMOPR	CAMPHOR
ACFRSTU	FRACTUS	ACGNOSY	GASCONY	ACHMOST	STOMACH
ACGGINR	GRACING	ACGORSU	COUGARS	ACHNNOS	CHANSON
ACGGRSY	SCRAGGY	ACHHIIT	HITACHI	ACHNORS	ANCHORS
ACGHIKN	HACKING	ACHHIRW	HARWICH	ACHNOTY	TACHYON
ACGHINR	ARCHING, CHAGRIN	ACHHSUV	CHUVASH	ACHNOVY	ANCHOVY
ACGHINS	CASHING, CHASING	ACHIILS	ISCHIAL	ACHNPUY	PAUNCHY
ACGHINT	GNATHIC	ACHIIMT	HAMITIC	ACHNRTY	CHANTRY
ACGHINW	CHINWAG	ACHIINT	CHIANTI	ACHNRUY	RAUNCHY
ACGHINY	YICHANG	ACHIITW	WICHITA	ACHNSTU	CANTHUS, STAUNCH
ACGHIPR	GRAPHIC	ACHIJKS	HIJACKS		
ACGHOSU	GAUCHOS	ACHIJMO	JOACHIM	ACHNSTY	SNATCHY
ACGIITU	AUGITIC	ACHIJNT	JACINTH	ACHOOST	CAHOOTS
ACGIJKN	JACKING	ACHIKLN	NALCHIK	ACHOPRS	CARHOPS

ACHOPRT	TOPARCH	ACILRTY	CLARITY	ACJKLOW	LOCKJAW
ACHOPRY	CHARPOY	ACILRYZ	CRAZILY	ACJKNOS	JACKSON
ACHRSTY	STARCHY	ACILSSS	CLASSIS	ACJKOPT	JACKPOT
ACIIKRS	AIRSICK	ACILSUV	CLAVIUS	ACJLORU	JOCULAR
ACIILMS	ISLAMIC, LAICISM	ACILSUY	SAUCILY	ACJMNTU	MUNTJAC
ACIILNS	SALICIN	ACILTTY	CATTILY, TACITLY	ACJPTUU	CAJUPUT
ACIILNT	CAITLIN	ACILTUV	VICTUAL	ACKKLMU	KALMUCK
ACIILNV	VICINAL	ACIMMNO	AMMONIC	ACKLLOP	POLLACK
ACIILPT	APLITIC	ACIMNOP	CAMPION	ACKLLSY	SLACKLY
ACIILRY	CILIARY	ACIMNOR	MINORCA	ACKLMOT	MATLOCK
ACIILSS	LIASSIC	ACIMNOS	MASONIC	ACKLNOU	UNCLOAK
ACIILST	ITALICS	ACIMNRU	CRANIUM	ACKLOOR	OARLOCK
ACIIMRS	CASIMIR	ACIMNTT	CATMINT	ACKLORW	WARLOCK
ACIINNO	ANIONIC	ACIMOPT	APOMICT, TAMPICO	ACKMOTT	MATTOCK
ACIINOS	NICOSIA	ACIMOSS	MOSAICS	ACKNORY	CONAKRY
ACIINOV	AVIONIC	ACIMOST	SOMATIC	ACKNPRU	CRANK UP
ACIINPS	PISCINA	ACIMPRY	PRIMACY	ACKPSSY	SKYCAPS
ACIINTT	TITANIC	ACIMPST	IMPACTS	ACLLLOY	LOCALLY
ACIIPRT	PIRATIC	ACIMSST	MISCAST	ACLLMMO	MALCOLM
ACIJLOS	JALISCO	ACINNOR	CORINNA	ACLLOOR	COROLLA
ACIJUZZ	JACUZZI	ACINNOT	ACTINON, CONTAIN	ACLLOPS	SCALLOP
ACIKLOR	AIRLOCK	ACINNST	STANNIC	ACLLORS	COLLARS
ACIKLTY	TACKILY	ACINOPT	CAPTION	ACLLORU	LOCULAR
ACIKNPY	PANICKY	ACINOQU	COQUINA	ACLLOSU	CALLOUS
ACIKNST	CATKINS	ACINORR	CARRION	ACLLOVY	VOCALLY
ACIKNTT	TINTACK	ACINORS	SARONIC	ACLLRYY	ACRYLYL
ACIKPRT	PATRICK	ACINOSS	CAISSON, CASINOS,	ACLMNUY	CALUMNY
ACIKPSX	SIX-PACK		CASSINO	ACLMORU	CLAMOUR
ACIKPSY	SICK PAY	ACINOST	ACTIONS	ACLNOOR	CORONAL,
ACIKRST	KARSTIC	ACINOTU	AUCTION, CAUTION		LOCARNO
ACIKRWW	WARWICK	ACINOUV	IN VACUO	ACLNOOT	COOLANT
ACIKUWZ	ZWICKAU	ACINPRY	CYPRIAN	ACLNOOV	VOLCANO
ACILLLU	LUCILLA	ACINQTU	QUANTIC	ACLNORT	CARLTON
ACILLMS	MISCALL	ACINRTU	CURTAIN	ACLNORU	CORNUAL
ACILLNS	CALL-INS	ACINSUV	VICUNAS	ACLNORY	CAROLYN
ACILLRY	LYRICAL	ACIOPRS	PROSAIC	ACLNOTY	CLAYTON
ACILMNO	LIMACON	ACIOPRT	APRICOT, PAROTIC	ACLNPSU	UNCLASP
ACILMPS	PSALMIC	ACIOPTY	OPACITY	ACLOOPR	CAR POOL
ACILMSU	MUSICAL	ACIORRS	CORSAIR	ACLOPRT	CALTROP
ACILNNY	CANNILY	ACIORSU	CARIOUS, CURIOSA	ACLOPRU	COPULAR
ACILNOR	CLARINO, CLARION	ACIORTT	RIOT ACT	ACLOPSU	CUPOLAS, SCOPULA
ACILNOS	NICOLAS, OILCANS	ACIPRSY	PISCARY	ACLOPSY	CALYPSO
ACILNPY	PLIANCY	ACIPRVY	PRIVACY	ACLORRS	CORRALS
ACILNTU	LUNATIC	ACIPSST	SPASTIC	ACLORSU	CAROLUS, OSCULAR
ACILOOR	AIR-COOL	ACIPTUY	PAUCITY	ACLORWW	WROCLAW
ACILOPT	CAPITOL, OPTICAL,	ACIQRTU	QUARTIC	ACLOTTW	WALCOTT
	TOPICAL	ACIRSST	RACISTS	ACLPRTY	CRYPTAL
ACILOSS	SOCIALS	ACIRSSU	CUIRASS	ACLRSSW	SCRAWLS
ACILOST	STOICAL	ACIRSTY	SATYRIC	ACLRSSY	CRASSLY
ACILOTV	VOLTAIC	ACISSTT	STATICS	ACLRSTU	CRUSTAL
ACILPST	PLASTIC	ACISSTU	CASUIST	ACLRSTY	CRYSTAL
ACILPTY	TYPICAL	ACISTTU	CATSUIT	ACLRSWY	SCRAWLY
ACILRSS	CRISSAL	ACITUVY	VACUITY	ACLSSTU	CUTLASS
ACILRTU	CURTAIL	ACJKKSY	SKYJACK	ACMNOPR	CRAMPON

125

ACMNOPY	COMPANY	ADDDEIS	DADDIES
ACMNORY	ACRONYM	ADDDELN	DANDLED
ACMNSTU	SANCTUM	ADDDELP	PADDLED
ACMNTUU	TUCUMAN	ADDDELS	SADDLED
ACMOOPT	POTOMAC	ADDDELW	DAWDLED, WADDLED
ACMOOST	SCOTOMA	ADDEEEY	DEADEYE
ACMOPSS	COMPASS	ADDEEFM	DEFAMED
ACMOSST	MASCOTS	ADDEEGR	DEGRADE
ACMOSTT	TOMCATS	ADDEEHR	ADHERED, REDHEAD
ACMQTUU	CUMQUAT	ADDEEIR	READIED
ACMSUUV	VACUUMS	ADDEEKN	KNEADED
ACNNNOS	CANNONS	ADDEELP	PEDALED, PLEADED
ACNNNUY	UNCANNY	ADDEELR	ELDREDA, RED DEAL
ACNNORY	CANONRY	ADDEELY	DELAYED
ACNNOST	CANTONS	ADDEEMN	AMENDED
ACNNOSY	CANYONS	ADDEEMR	DREAMED
ACNOORS	CORONAS, RACOONS	ADDEEST	SEDATED
ACNOORT	CARTOON, CORTONA	ADDEFRT	DRAFTED
ACNOPSU	CANOPUS	ADDEFRU	DEFRAUD
ACNOPSW	SNOWCAP	ADDEFRW	DWARFED
ACNORRU	RANCOUR	ADDEGGR	DRAGGED
ACNORRY	CARRY-ON	ADDEGHO	GODHEAD
ACNORST	CANTORS, CARTONS	ADDEGJU	ADJUDGE
ACNORSY	CRAYONS	ADDEGLN	DANGLED, GLADDEN
ACNOSTU	CONATUS, TOUCANS	ADDEGLR	GLADDER
ACNPRSY	SYNCARP	ADDEGRU	GUARDED
ACNRRTU	CURRANT	ADDEHIO	HODEIDA
ACNRSWY	SCRAWNY	ADDEHIR	DIEHARD
ACNRTUY	TRUANCY	ADDEHLN	HANDLED
ACNSSTU	SANCTUS	ADDEHOR	HOARDED
ACNSTUY	TUSCANY	ADDEILL	DALLIED, DIALLED
ACOOPRR	CORPORA	ADDEILS	LADDIES
ACOOPTT	TOPCOAT	ADDEILT	DILATED
ACOORTU	TOURACO	ADDEIMR	ADMIRED
ACOPPRR	PROCARP	ADDEIMS	DIADEMS
ACOPRRT	CARPORT	ADDEINO	ADENOID
ACOPRST	CAPTORS	ADDEINR	DANDIER, DRAINED
ACOPSTW	COWPATS	ADDEINS	DANDIES
ACORRST	CARROTS	ADDEINU	UNAIDED
ACORRTT	TRACTOR	ADDEINV	INVADED
ACORRTU	CURATOR	ADDEIOR	RADIOED
ACORRTY	CARROTY	ADDEIOT	TOADIED
ACORSST	CASTORS, CO-STARS	ADDEIOV	AVOIDED
ACORSSU	SARCOUS	ADDEIPS	PADDIES
ACORSTU	SURCOAT	ADDEISV	ADVISED
ACORSTX	OXCARTS	ADDEITU	AUDITED
ACORSUU	RAUCOUS	ADDEJRU	ADJURED
ACOSTTU	OUTCAST	ADDELLU	ALLUDED
ACOSUUV	VACUOUS	ADDELNR	DANDLER
ACPPRSY	SCRAPPY	ADDELPP	DAPPLED
ADDDEEN	DEAD END	ADDELPR	PADDLER
ADDDEER	DREADED	ADDELPS	PADDLES
		ADDELRS	LADDERS, SADDLER

ADDELRW	DAWDLER, DRAWLED, WADDLER
ADDELSS	SADDLES
ADDELST	STADDLE
ADDELSW	SWADDLE, WADDLES
ADDELTW	TWADDLE
ADDELYZ	DAZEDLY
ADDELZZ	DAZZLED
ADDEMNS	DEMANDS
ADDEMST	MADDEST
ADDENOR	ADORNED
ADDENOT	DONATED
ADDENOU	DUODENA
ADDENPU	PUDENDA
ADDENRS	DANDERS
ADDENTU	DAUNTED
ADDEOPT	ADOPTED
ADDEPTU	UPDATED
ADDERSS	ADDRESS
ADDERTT	DRATTED
ADDESST	SADDEST
ADDFHIS	FADDISH
ADDFIMS	FADDISM
ADDFINY	DANDIFY
ADDFIST	FADDIST
ADDGGIN	GADDING
ADDGINP	PADDING
ADDGINW	WADDING
ADDGMNO	GODDAMN
ADDGOOY	GOOD DAY
ADDGOSY	DOG DAYS
ADDHITY	HYDATID
ADDHLNO	OLD HAND
ADDHNOR	RHONDDA
ADDIINS	DISDAIN
ADDIKTY	KATYDID
ADDILMN	MIDLAND
ADDILMO	OLD MAID
ADDIMNO	DIAMOND
ADDINOR	ANDROID, DORINDA
ADDKLNU	DUNDALK
ADDLLOY	OLD LADY
ADDLLRU	DULLARD
ADDLNRY	DRY LAND
ADDLOSY	LAY ODDS
ADEEESW	SEAWEED
ADEEFKR	FREAKED
ADEEFLR	ELFREDA, FEDERAL
ADEEFLT	DEFLATE
ADEEFMR	DEFAMER
ADEEFRT	DRAFTEE
ADEEFST	DEFEATS, FEASTED
ADEEGGH	EGGHEAD
ADEEGGN	ENGAGED

ADEEGLL	ALLEGED	ADEELQU	EQUALED	ADEFINR	FRIEDAN
ADEEGLM	GLEAMED	ADEELRS	DEALERS, LEADERS	ADEFINT	DEFIANT, FAINTED
ADEEGLN	GLEANED	ADEELRT	ALERTED, ALTERED,	ADEFITX	FIXATED
ADEEGLU	LEAGUED		RELATED, TREADLE	ADEFKLN	FLANKED
ADEEGLY	GLAD EYE	ADEELRV	RAVELED	ADEFKNR	FRANKED
ADEEGMN	END GAME	ADEELRW	LEEWARD	ADEFLOT	FLOATED
ADEEGNR	ANGERED,	ADEELRX	RELAXED	ADEFLPP	FLAPPED
DERANGE, EN GARDE,		ADEELRY	DELAYER, LAYERED,	ADEFLTU	DEFAULT, FAULTED
ENRAGED, GRANDEE, GRENADE		RELAYED		ADEFMNR	MANFRED
ADEEGNT	NEGATED	ADEELTX	EXALTED	ADEFOOR	FEODORA
ADEEGNV	AVENGED	ADEELUV	DEVALUE	ADEFOOS	SEAFOOD
ADEEGOT	GOATEED	ADEEMNR	AMENDER,	ADEFORS	FEDORAS
ADEEGRS	GREASED	MEANDER, RENAMED		ADEFORY	FORAYED
ADEEGRW	RAGWEED,	ADEEMRR	DREAMER,	ADEFOTU	FADEOUT
WAGERED		REARMED		ADEFRRT	DRAFTER, REDRAFT
ADEEHIR	HEADIER	ADEEMRS	SMEARED	ADEFRST	STRAFED
ADEEHLX	EXHALED	ADEEMRT	RED MEAT	ADEFSTT	DAFTEST
ADEEHMN	HEADMEN	ADEEMST	STEAMED	ADEGGHL	HAGGLED
ADEEHNS	DASHEEN	ADEEMWY	MAYWEED	ADEGGHS	SHAGGED
ADEEHRS	HEADERS, SHEARED	ADEENNX	ANNEXED	ADEGGLR	DRAGGLE, GARGLED
ADEEHRT	EARTHED	ADEENRY	DEANERY, YEARNED	ADEGGLS	SLAGGED
ADEEHST	HEADSET	ADEENST	EAST END	ADEGGLW	WAGGLED
ADEEHSY	HAYSEED	ADEENTT	DANETTE, DENTATE	ADEGGNS	SNAGGED
ADEEIJT	JADEITE	ADEEPPR	PAPERED	ADEGGRS	DAGGERS
ADEEILM	LIMEADE	ADEEPRS	SPEARED	ADEGGST	GADGETS
ADEEILN	ADELINE, DELAINE	ADEEPRT	PREDATE, RED TAPE,	ADEGGTY	GADGETY
ADEEIMT	MEDIATE	TAPERED		ADEGHIN	HEADING
ADEEINN	ADENINE	ADEEPRV	DEPRAVE, PERVADE	ADEGHLU	LAUGHED
ADEEINS	ANISEED	ADEEQTU	EQUATED	ADEGHNS	GNASHED
ADEEIRR	READIER	ADEERRS	READERS	ADEGILN	ALIGNED, DEALING,
ADEEIRS	DEARIES, READIES	ADEERRT	RETREAD, TREADER	LEADING	
ADEEIRW	WEARIED	ADEERRV	AVERRED, EVERARD	ADEGINR	READING
ADEEISS	DISEASE, SEASIDE	ADEERST	DEAREST	ADEGINV	EVADING
ADEEITV	DEVIATE	ADEERSV	ADVERSE	ADEGINW	WINDAGE
ADEEKNP	KNEEPAD	ADEERTT	TREATED	ADEGIRU	GAUDIER
ADEEKNR	KNEADER	ADEERTV	AVERTED	ADEGJLN	JANGLED
ADEEKNS	SNEAKED	ADEERTW	WATERED	ADEGLLU	ULLAGED
ADEEKNW	WAKENED	ADEERVW	WAVERED	ADEGLMN	MANGLED
ADEEKRW	WREAKED	ADEESSY	ESSAYED	ADEGLNN	ENGLAND
ADEEKTW	TWEAKED	ADEESTU	SAUTEED	ADEGLNO	DONEGAL
ADEEKWY	WEEKDAY	ADEESTW	SWEATED	ADEGLNR	DANGLER, GNARLED
ADEELLS	ALLSEED	ADEFFIX	AFFIXED	ADEGLNS	SLANGED
ADEELMR	EMERALD	ADEFFLR	RAFFLED	ADEGLNT	TANGLED
ADEELMT	METALED	ADEFFLW	WAFFLED	ADEGLNW	WANGLED
ADEELMZ	DEMELZA	ADEFFST	STAFFED	ADEGLOT	GLOATED
ADEELNP	PANELED	ADEFGGL	FLAGGED	ADEGLPU	PLAGUED
ADEELNR	DARLENE, LEANDER,	ADEFGLR	RED FLAG	ADEGLSS	GLASSED
LEARNED		ADEFGNS	FAG ENDS	ADEGMNU	AGENDUM
ADEELNT	AL DENTE	ADEFGOR	FORAGED	ADEGNNU	DUNNAGE
ADEELNW	ALEDWEN, NEW	ADEFGRT	GRAFTED	ADEGNOR	GROANED
DEAL		ADEFHLS	FLASHED	ADEGNOS	SONDAGE
ADEELNZ	ZEELAND	ADEFHST	SHAFTED	ADEGNOT	TANGOED
ADEELPR	PLEADER	ADEFIIL	FIDELIA	ADEGNOV	DOGVANE
ADEELPS	ELAPSED, PLEASED	ADEFILL	FLAILED	ADEGNPU	UNPAGED
ADEELPT	PLEATED	ADEFILR	ELFRIDA		

ADEGNRR	GRANDER	ADEHORR	HOARDER	ADEIMRY	MIDYEAR
ADEGNRS	DANGERS,	ADEHOTW	TOWHEAD	ADEIMTU	IDEATUM
	GANDERS, GARDENS	ADEHPRS	PHRASED	ADEIMTY	DAYTIME
ADEGNRT	DRAGNET, GRANTED	ADEHQSU	QUASHED	ADEINOR	ANEROID
ADEGNTW	TWANGED	ADEHRST	HARDEST, THREADS,	ADEINOS	ANODISE
ADEGNUW	UNWAGED		TRASHED	ADEINOV	NAEVOID
ADEGORW	DOWAGER,	ADEHRTY	HYDRATE, THREADY	ADEINOZ	ANODIZE
	WORDAGE	ADEHSST	STASHED	ADEINPT	PAINTED
ADEGOSS	DOSAGES, SEA	ADEHSTW	SWATHED	ADEINRR	DRAINER, RANDIER
	DOGS	ADEIILS	DAILIES, LIAISED,	ADEINRS	SANDIER, SARDINE
ADEGOST	DOTAGES		SEDILIA	ADEINRT	DETRAIN, TRADE-IN,
ADEGOVY	VOYAGED	ADEIIMN	DIAMINE		TRAINED
ADEGPRS	GRASPED	ADEIINZ	DIAZINE	ADEINRU	URANIDE
ADEGPRU	UPGRADE	ADEIIRR	AIRDRIE	ADEINRV	INVADER
ADEGRRR	GERRARD	ADEIIRS	DAIRIES, DIARIES	ADEINST	INSTEAD, SAINTED,
ADEGRRS	REGARDS	ADEIISS	DAISIES		STAINED
ADEGRRU	GUARDER	ADEIJSU	JUDAISE	ADEINTT	TAINTED
ADEGRSS	GRASSED	ADEIJUZ	JUDAIZE	ADEINTV	DEVIANT
ADEGRSU	SUGARED	ADEIKLM	LIKE MAD	ADEIOPS	ADIPOSE
ADEGRTY	GYRATED, TRAGEDY	ADEIKLR	KILDARE	ADEIORV	AVOIDER
ADEGRUU	AUGURED	ADEIKRS	DARKIES	ADEIOST	TOADIES
ADEGRUY	GAUDERY	ADEILLR	DIALLER, RALLIED	ADEIOSX	OXIDASE
ADEGSSU	DEGAUSS	ADEILLS	SALLIED	ADEIOTX	OXIDATE
ADEHHOP	HOPHEAD	ADEILLT	TALLIED	ADEIPPR	PREPAID
ADEHHOT	HOTHEAD	ADEILLY	IDEALLY	ADEIPRR	PARRIED
ADEHILL	DELILAH	ADEILMM	DILEMMA	ADEIPRS	ASPIRED, DESPAIR,
ADEHILN	HIELAND, INHALED	ADEILMN	MELINDA		DIAPERS, PRAISED
ADEHILY	HEADILY	ADEILMP	IMPALED, IMPLEAD	ADEIPRT	PARTIED, PERDITA,
ADEHIMO	HAEMOID	ADEILMS	MISDEAL, MISLEAD		PIRATED
ADEHINP	HEADPIN, PINHEAD	ADEILNN	ANNELID, LINDANE	ADEIRRS	RAIDERS
ADEHINR	HANDIER	ADEILNR	IRELAND	ADEIRRT	TARDIER, TARRIED
ADEHIPR	RAPHIDE	ADEILNS	DENIALS, LEAD-INS	ADEIRRV	ARRIVED
ADEHIPS	DIPHASE	ADEILNT	TAIL END	ADEIRST	ASTRIDE, DIASTER,
ADEHIPT	PITHEAD	ADEILNU	ALIUNDE		DISRATE, TIRADES
ADEHIRR	HARDIER, HARRIED	ADEILOP	OEDIPAL	ADEIRSV	ADVISER
ADEHIRS	SHADIER	ADEILOR	DARIOLE	ADEIRTT	ATTIRED
ADEHIRW	RAWHIDE	ADEILOZ	DIAZOLE	ADEIRTY	DIETARY
ADEHKNT	THANKED	ADEILPP	APPLIED	ADEISTV	DATIVES, VISTAED
ADEHLLM	ALDHELM	ADEILPR	LIP-READ	ADEISTW	WAISTED
ADEHLMN	HELMAND	ADEILPS	PALSIED	ADEISWY	WAYSIDE
ADEHLNR	HANDLER	ADEILPT	PLAITED, TALIPED	ADEITUZ	DEUTZIA
ADEHLNS	HANDLES, HANDSEL	ADEILQU	QUAILED	ADEITWY	TIDEWAY
ADEHLOP	ADOLPHE	ADEILRT	TRAILED	ADEJMOR	MAJORED
ADEHLOT	LOATHED	ADEILRU	UREDIAL	ADEJNTU	JAUNTED
ADEHLRS	HERALDS	ADEILRV	RIVALED	ADEJRRU	ADJURER
ADEHLSS	HASSLED, SLASHED	ADEILRY	READILY	ADEJSSU	JUDASES
ADEHLTY	DEATHLY	ADEILST	DETAILS	ADEKLLN	KENDALL
ADEHMMS	SHAMMED	ADEILSV	DEVISAL	ADEKLNR	RANKLED
ADEHMNP	HAMPDEN	ADEILSY	DIALYSE	ADEKLNS	KALENDS
ADEHMOY	DAHOMEY	ADEIMMR	MERMAID	ADEKLNY	NAKEDLY
ADEHMSS	SMASHED	ADEIMNS	MAIDENS, MEDIANS	ADEKLST	STALKED
ADEHNRU	UNHEARD	ADEIMNT	MEDIANT	ADEKMNR	DENMARK
ADEHNST	HANDSET	ADEIMOW	MIAOWED	ADEKNPS	SPANKED
ADEHNTU	HAUNTED	ADEIMRR	ADMIRER, MARRIED	ADEKNRU	KUNDERA
ADEHOPX	HEXAPOD	ADEIMRS	MISREAD, SIDEARM	ADEKNST	DANKEST

ADEKNSW	SWANKED	ADEMNRS	REMANDS	ADEORTU	READOUT
ADEKPRS	SPARKED	ADEMNRU	MANURED,	ADEORTY	YEAR DOT
ADEKRST	DARKEST		MAUNDER, UNARMED	ADEORYZ	ZEDOARY
ADELLMU	MEDULLA	ADEMNSS	MADNESS	ADEOSTT	TOASTED
ADELLOW	ALLOWED	ADEMNST	TANDEMS	ADEOTTU	OUTDATE
ADELLOY	ALLOYED	ADEMORS	MODERAS	ADEPPRT	TRAPPED
ADELLRR	DARRELL	ADEMOSW	MEADOWS	ADEPPRW	WRAPPED
ADELLRU	ALLURED	ADEMOSY	SAMOYED,	ADEPPSW	SWAPPED
ADELLST	STALLED		SOMEDAY	ADEPRRS	DRAPERS, SPARRED
ADELMMS	SLAMMED	ADEMPRS	DAMPERS	ADEPRRY	DRAPERY
ADELMNR	MANDREL	ADEMPRT	TRAMPED	ADEPRSS	SPREADS
ADELMNT	MANTLED	ADEMPST	DAMPEST, STAMPED	ADEPRST	PETARDS
ADELMOR	EARLDOM	ADEMPSW	SWAMPED	ADEPRSY	SPRAYED
ADELMPS	SAMPLED	ADEMRRU	EARDRUM	ADEPRTU	UPDATER
ADELMRS	MEDLARS	ADEMRST	SMARTED	ADEPSTU	UPDATES
ADELMSS	DAMSELS	ADEMRSW	SWARMED	ADEQRSU	SQUARED
ADELNNP	PLANNED	ADEMRTU	MATURED	ADERRST	STARRED, TRADERS
ADELNOR	LEONARD	ADEMSSU	ASSUMED	ADERRSW	DRAWERS,
ADELNOY	YOLANDE	ADENNOY	ANNOYED,		REWARDS, WARDERS
ADELNPT	PLANTED		ANODYNE	ADERSSU	ASSURED
ADELNRS	SLANDER, SNARLED	ADENNPS	SPANNED	ADERSTT	STARTED
ADELNRU	ARUNDEL, LAUNDER	ADENNPT	PENDANT	ADERSTV	STARVED
ADELNST	SLANTED	ADENNSU	DUENNAS	ADERSTW	STEWARD
ADELNUU	ULAN-UDE	ADENNSW	SWANNED	ADERSTY	STRAYED
ADELOPR	LEOPARD, PAROLED	ADENOPR	OPERAND,	ADERSUY	DASYURE
ADELOPS	DEPOSAL		PADRONE, PANDORE	ADERSVW	DWARVES
ADELOPT	TADPOLE	ADENOPT	NOTEPAD	ADESTTU	STATUED
ADELORS	ORDEALS	ADENORR	RED ROAN	ADESTTW	SWATTED
ADELORT	LEOTARD	ADENORU	RONDEAU	ADESTUY	TUESDAY
ADELOSS	LASSOED	ADENOUY	YAOUNDE	ADFFHNO	OFFHAND
ADELOTT	TOTALED	ADENPPS	SNAPPED	ADFFIST	DISTAFF
ADELOVY	LOVEDAY	ADENPST	PEDANTS	ADFFLOO	OFF-LOAD
ADELPPS	SLAPPED	ADENPSW	SPAWNED	ADFHLNU	HANDFUL
ADELPRS	PEDLARS	ADENRRS	ERRANDS, RANDERS	ADFHOOS	SHADOOF
ADELPST	STAPLED	ADENRRY	REYNARD	ADFHORS	ASHFORD
ADELPSW	DEWLAPS	ADENRSS	SANDERS	ADFIINO	IN AID OF
ADELPSY	SPLAYED	ADENRST	STANDER	ADFILLU	FLUIDAL
ADELPTY	ADEPTLY	ADENRSU	ASUNDER, DANSEUR	ADFILNN	FINLAND
ADELRRS	LARDERS			ADFILOR	FLORIDA
ADELRRU	RUDERAL	ADENRSW	WARDENS	ADFILOT	DO A FLIT
ADELRRW	DRAWLER	ADENRTU	DAUNTER	ADFIMNY	DAMNIFY
ADELRTT	RATTLED	ADENRTV	VERDANT	ADFIRSY	FRIDAYS
ADELRTW	TRAWLED	ADENRTX	DEXTRAN	ADFLMPU	MUDFLAP
ADELRTX	DEXTRAL	ADENRUY	UNREADY	ADFLMTU	MUDFLAT
ADELSTT	SLATTED	ADENSSU	SADNESS	ADFLNOP	PLAFOND
ADELSTU	SALUTED	ADENSSU	SUNDAES	ADFLNSY	SAND FLY
ADELTTT	TATTLED	ADENSTV	ADVENTS	ADFLORS	SALFORD
ADELTUV	VAULTED	ADENSWY	ENDWAYS	ADFLORT	ALTDORF
ADELTWZ	WALTZED	ADENTTU	ATTUNED, TAUNTED	ADFLORU	FOULARD
ADEMNNU	MUNDANE,	ADENTUV	VAUNTED	ADFNNOT	FONDANT
	UNNAMED	ADEOPST	PODESTA	ADFOOPT	FOOTPAD
ADEMNOR	ROADMEN	ADEORRW	ARROWED	ADFORRW	FORWARD,
ADEMNOS	DAEMONS	ADEORST	ROASTED, TORSADE		FROWARD
ADEMNOZ	MENDOZA	ADEORSU	AROUSED	ADFORTW	WATFORD
		ADEORTT	ROTATED	ADFPRTU	UPDRAFT

ADGGHNO	HANGDOG
ADGGINO	GOADING
ADGGINR	GRADING, NIGGARD
ADGGOST	DOG TAGS
ADGHILO	HIDALGO
ADGHINN	HANDING
ADGHINR	HARDING
ADGHINS	DASHING, SHADING
ADGHIPR	DIGRAPH
ADGHNNU	HANDGUN
ADGHOOR	ROAD HOG
ADGHRTU	DRAUGHT
ADGIILN	DIALING, GLIADIN
ADGIILT	DIGITAL
ADGIINR	RAIDING
ADGILLN	LADLING
ADGILNN	LANDING
ADGILNO	LOADING
ADGILNR	DARLING, LARDING
ADGILNS	LADINGS
ADGILNU	LANGUID, LAUDING
ADGILUY	GAUDILY
ADGIMMN	DAMMING
ADGIMNN	DAMNING
ADGIMNP	DAMPING
ADGINNR	DARNING
ADGINNS	SANDING
ADGINNW	DAWNING
ADGINOQ	QINGDAO
ADGINOR	ADORING
ADGINPP	DAPPING
ADGINPR	DRAPING
ADGINRT	DARTING, TRADING
ADGINRW	DRAWING, WARDING
ADGINWY	GWYNIAD
ADGIRZZ	GIZZARD
ADGKNOZ	DZONGKA
ADGLLOS	OLD LAGS
ADGLNOO	GONDOLA
ADGLNOT	GOTLAND
ADGLNOY	DAYLONG
ADGLNRY	GRANDLY
ADGLOOV	VOLOGDA
ADGLOPS	LAPDOGS
ADGLORY	GAYLORD
ADGLOSU	DOUGLAS
ADGLSWY	GWLADYS
ADGMOOR	MOGADOR
ADGNOOR	DRAGOON, GADROON
ADGNORS	DRAGONS
ADGNORU	AGROUND, DURANGO
ADGNRRU	GURNARD

ADHHMOS	SHAHDOM
ADHHOSW	HOWDAHS
ADHIIKS	DASHIKI
ADHIIMS	HASIDIM
ADHIKTZ	TADZHIK
ADHILMO	HALIDOM
ADHILNY	HANDILY
ADHILOP	HAPLOID
ADHILOY	HOLIDAY, HYALOID
ADHILRY	HARDILY
ADHILSY	SHADILY
ADHIMPS	DAMPISH, PHASMID
ADHINPU	DAUPHIN
ADHIORS	HAIRDOS
ADHLLLO	HOLDALL
ADHLLNO	HOLLAND
ADHLNOW	HOWLAND
ADHMMNO	HAMMOND
ADHMNOO	MANHOOD
ADHMNPY	DYMPHNA
ADHMNWY	WYNDHAM
ADHNNOS	HANDS-ON
ADHNORS	HARD-ONS
ADHNOSW	ASHDOWN
ADHNOTU	HANDOUT
ADHNOVZ	ZHDANOV
ADHNPSU	HANDS UP
ADHNRTU	HARD NUT
ADHNRTY	HYDRANT
ADHOPRT	HARDTOP
ADHOSSW	SHADOWS
ADHOSWY	SHADOWY
ADIIJNU	JUNDIAI
ADIILMS	MISLAID
ADIILNO	LIANOID
ADIILNV	INVALID
ADIILOS	SIALOID
ADIINNS	INDIANS
ADIINOS	SIDONIA
ADIIORS	ISIDORA
ADIIRST	DIARIST
ADIIRTY	ARIDITY
ADIITVY	AVIDITY
ADIJMSU	JUDAISM
ADIJNOT	ADJOINT
ADIJSTU	JUDAIST
ADIKMNN	MANKIND
ADIKMOS	MIKADOS
ADIKMRU	MAKURDI
ADIKNPS	INKPADS, SKIDPAN
ADIKNSW	DAWKINS
ADILLMM	MILLDAM
ADILLRW	WILLARD
ADILLVY	VALIDLY

ADILMNU	MAUDLIN
ADILMOP	DIPLOMA
ADILMOY	AMYLOID
ADILMSU	DUALISM
ADILNOR	LORINDA, ORDINAL
ADILNRU	DIURNAL
ADILNSS	ISLANDS
ADILNSU	SUNDIAL
ADILNSY	LINDSAY
ADILOPR	DIPOLAR
ADILORT	DILATOR
ADILOUV	OLDUVAI
ADILPRY	PYRALID, RAPIDLY
ADILPST	PLASTID
ADILPSY	DISPLAY
ADILPTU	PLAUDIT
ADILPVY	VAPIDLY
ADILQSU	SQUALID
ADILRSZ	LIZARDS, SZILARD
ADILRTY	TARDILY
ADILSTU	DUALIST
ADILSTY	STAIDLY
ADILTUY	DUALITY
ADIMNOS	DOMAINS, MADISON
ADIMORR	MIRADOR
ADIMOST	MASTOID
ADIMPRY	PYRAMID
ADIMRSY	MYRIADS
ADIMSST	DISMAST
ADIMSTU	STADIUM
ADINNOP	DIPNOAN
ADINNOR	ANDIRON
ADINNRS	INNARDS
ADINNRW	INDRAWN
ADINNST	STAND-IN
ADINOPR	PONIARD
ADINORS	INROADS, SADIRON
ADINOSV	NOVI SAD
ADINOTX	OXIDANT
ADINPST	PANDITS, SANDPIT
ADINRSW	INWARDS
ADINSTT	DISTANT
ADINTTY	DITTANY
ADIOOSW	WOODSIA
ADIOPRR	AIRDROP
ADIOPRT	PAROTID
ADIORST	ASTROID
ADIORTU	AUDITOR
ADIOSUV	VAUDOIS
ADIOSVW	DISAVOW
ADIPRTY	PAY DIRT
ADIPRUU	UDAIPUR
ADIRSSU	SARDIUS

ADIRSTY	SATYRID	ADMRSTU	DURMAST, MUSTARD	AEEGGLT	GATE-LEG
ADIRSUY	DYSURIA			AEEGGNR	ENGAGER
ADIRSWZ	WIZARDS	ADNNOOV	DONOVAN	AEEGHNW	WHANGEE
ADISSST	SADISTS	ADNNOOY	NOONDAY	AEEGILL	GALILEE
ADJLNTU	JUTLAND	ADNNSTU	DUNSTAN	AEEGILM	MILEAGE
ADJNNOU	DON JUAN	ADNOORT	DONATOR, TORNADO	AEEGILN	LINEAGE
ADJNORU	ADJOURN			AEEGILP	EPIGEAL
ADKORWY	WORKDAY	ADNOOSS	SO-AND-SO	AEEGILW	WEIGELA
ADLLLNO	LOLLAND	ADNOPRS	PARDONS	AEEGINU	EUGENIA
ADLLLOR	LOLLARD	ADNORSW	ONWARDS	AEEGIRT	REIGATE
ADLLMOY	MODALLY	ADNORTU	ROTUNDA	AEEGISS	AEGISES
ADLLNOW	LOWLAND	ADNOSTU	ASTOUND	AEEGLLZ	GAZELLE
ADLLOPR	POLLARD	ADNPPUU	UP-AND-UP	AEEGLMN	MELANGE
ADLLORS	DOLLARS	ADNPSTU	DUSTPAN, STAND-UP	AEEGLMT	MELTAGE
ADLMNOS	ALMONDS			AEEGLNR	ENLARGE, GENERAL, GLEANER
ADLMNUU	ALUNDUM	ADNRSST	STRANDS		
ADLMOOV	MOLDOVA	ADNSSUY	SUNDAYS	AEEGLNS	SENEGAL
ADLMORU	MODULAR	ADNSTYY	DYNASTY	AEEGLNT	ELEGANT
ADLNOOR	ORLANDO	ADOOPSW	SAPWOOD	AEEGLNU	EUGLENA
ADLNOPU	POUNDAL	ADOORWY	DOORWAY	AEEGLNV	EVANGEL
ADLNORU	NODULAR	ADORSTW	TOWARDS	AEEGLOR	AEROGEL
ADLNORW	ROWLAND	ADORSUU	ARDUOUS	AEEGLRY	EAGERLY
ADLNOSY	SYNODAL	ADORTUW	OUTWARD	AEEGLSS	AGELESS, SEA LEGS
ADLNPSU	UPLANDS	ADPRSUW	UPWARDS	AEEGLST	EAGLETS, LEGATES
ADLNRTU	RUTLAND	ADSSTUW	SAWDUST	AEEGLSU	LEAGUES
ADLNRUY	LAUNDRY	AEEEGLT	LEGATEE	AEEGLSV	SELVAGE
ADLNTWY	TYNWALD	AEEEGNT	TEENAGE	AEEGLTV	VEGETAL
ADLOORW	LARWOOD	AEEEGPR	PEERAGE	AEEGMMT	GEMMATE, TAGMEME
ADLOPRU	POULARD	AEEEGPS	SEEPAGE		
ADLORRW	WARLORD	AEEEGRT	ETAGERE	AEEGMNR	GERMANE
ADLORUY	OUR LADY	AEEEILN	ALIENEE	AEEGMNS	MENAGES
ADLOSSW	SOD'S LAW	AEEELNR	RAELENE	AEEGMSS	MESSAGE
ADLRSTY	DRY-SALT	AEEELRS	RELEASE	AEEGNNV	GENEVAN
ADMMNSU	SUMMAND	AEEELTV	ELEVATE	AEEGNPP	GENAPPE
ADMNOOR	DOORMAN	AEEEPPT	PAPEETE	AEEGNRT	GRANTEE, REAGENT
ADMNOOW	WOODMAN	AEEERTT	TEA TREE	AEEGNRV	AVENGER, ENGRAVE, GENEVRA
ADMNOQU	QUONDAM	AEEFFLL	FELAFEL		
ADMNORS	RANDOMS	AEEFHRT	FEATHER	AEEGNTT	TENTAGE
ADMNORT	DORMANT, MORDANT	AEEFILR	LEAFIER	AEEGNTV	VENTAGE
		AEEFIRS	FREESIA	AEEGOPS	APOGEES
ADMNORY	RAYMOND	AEEFLLN	FENELLA	AEEGORV	OVERAGE
ADMNOSS	DAMSONS	AEEFLLT	LEAFLET	AEEGOST	GOATEES
ADMNOSU	OSMUNDA	AEEFLMS	FEMALES	AEEGPRS	PRESAGE
ADMNOSY	DYNAMOS, MONDAYS	AEEFLRT	REFLATE	AEEGRRS	GREASER
		AEEFLRW	WELFARE	AEEGRRT	GREATER, REGRATE
ADMNRUY	RAYMUND	AEEFLSU	EASEFUL	AEEGRRW	WAGERER
ADMNSTU	DUSTMAN	AEEFMNR	FREEMAN	AEEGRSV	GERVASE, GREAVES
ADMOORT	DOORMAT	AEEFORS	FAEROES	AEEGSTT	GESTATE
ADMOORY	DAYROOM	AEEFOTV	FOVEATE	AEEGTTZ	GAZETTE
ADMOPPU	POPADUM	AEEFRRT	FERRATE	AEEHHNT	HEATHEN
ADMOPST	POTSDAM	AEEFRST	FEASTER	AEEHHRT	HEATHER
ADMORRS	RAMRODS	AEEFRTU	FEATURE	AEEHHST	SHEATHE
ADMORST	STARDOM, TSARDOM	AEEFRTX	TAX-FREE	AEEHIRV	HEAVIER
		AEEFRWY	FREEWAY	AEEHISV	HEAVIES
ADMORTW	MADWORT	AEEGGLM	GAME LEG	AEEHKNR	HEARKEN

AEEHLPT	HEELTAP	AEEINRT	ARENITE, RETINAE,	AEELORU	AUREOLE
AEEHLRS	HEALERS		TRAINEE	AEELPRR	PEARLER
AEEHLRT	HALTERE, LEATHER	AEEINST	ETESIAN	AEELPRS	PLEASER, RELAPSE
AEEHLRV	LE HAVRE	AEEINTV	NAIVETE, VENETIA	AEELPRT	PLEATER, PRELATE
AEEHLSS	LEASHES	AEEINVW	INWEAVE	AEELPTT	PALETTE, PELTATE
AEEHLSY	EYELASH	AEEIPRR	PEREIRA	AEELPTU	EPAULET
AEEHLTT	ATHLETE	AEEIPTX	EXPIATE	AEELQSU	SEQUELA
AEEHMNT	METHANE	AEEIRRT	ERITREA	AEELRRT	RELATER
AEEHMSV	EVESHAM	AEEIRRW	WEARIER	AEELRRX	RELAXER
AEEHNPS	PEAHENS	AEEIRST	SERIATE	AEELRSS	SEALERS
AEEHNPT	HAPTENE, HEPTANE	AEEIRSZ	ZAIRESE	AEELRST	STEALER
AEEHNRT	EARTHEN, HEARTEN,	AEEIRTT	ITERATE	AEELRSV	SEVERAL
TEHERAN		AEEISST	EASIEST	AEELRSY	SEALERY
AEEHNSV	HEAVENS	AEEISVV	EVASIVE	AEELRTT	ARLETTE
AEEHNSW	SHAWNEE	AEEIUVX	EXUVIAE	AEELRTX	EXALTER
AEEHNTW	WHEATEN	AEEJNTT	JANETTE	AEELRUV	REVALUE
AEEHPRS	RESHAPE	AEEJRSW	JEW'S-EAR	AEELSST	TEASELS
AEEHPRT	PREHEAT	AEEKKNO	KOKANEE	AEELSSW	WEASELS
AEEHPTT	PET HATE	AEEKMRS	REMAKES	AEELSTT	SEATTLE
AEEHPUV	UPHEAVE	AEEKMRT	MEERKAT	AEELTTY	LAYETTE
AEEHRRS	SHEARER	AEEKNNN	NANKEEN	AEELTVW	WAVELET
AEEHRSS	HEARSES	AEEKNRS	SNEAKER	AEEMMPY	EMPYEMA
AEEHRST	HEATERS, THERESA	AEEKNRT	RETAKEN	AEEMMRT	AMMETER,
AEEHRSW	WHEREAS	AEEKNRW	WAKENER	METAMER	
AEEHRTT	THEATRE, THEREAT	AEEKNSY	YANKEES	AEEMNNO	ANEMONE
AEEHRTW	WEATHER,	AEEKPRS	SPEAKER	AEEMNNP	PEN NAME
WHEREAT, WREATHE		AEEKRRT	RETAKER	AEEMNNY	MAYENNE
AEEHSSV	SHEAVES	AEEKRRW	WREAKER	AEEMNPT	PET NAME
AEEHSTT	THE EAST	AEEKRST	RETAKES	AEEMNRU	MAUREEN
AEEHSWY	EYEWASH	AEEKSTW	WEAKEST	AEEMNSS	EN MASSE
AEEIJNN	JEANNIE	AEELLST	ESTELLA	AEEMNST	MEANEST
AEEIKLP	APELIKE	AEELLSV	A LEVELS	AEEMORT	EROTEMA
AEEIKLR	LEAKIER	AEELLWY	WALLEYE	AEEMOSW	AWESOME
AEEIKPR	PEAKIER	AEELMNP	EMPANEL	AEEMPRT	TAMPERE, TEMPERA
AEEILLU	EULALIE	AEELMNR	MARLENE, REELMAN	AEEMPTU	AMPUTEE
AEEILMN	MELANIE	AEELMNU	EMANUEL	AEEMQRU	MARQUEE
AEEILMR	MEALIER	AEELMNV	VELAMEN	AEEMRRS	REAMERS, SMEARER
AEEILMS	SEA MILE	AEELMNY	AMYLENE	AEEMRST	STEAMER
AEEILMT	ELAMITE	AEELMPR	EMPALER	AEEMRSU	MEASURE
AEEILNT	LINEATE	AEELMPX	EXAMPLE	AEENNOT	NEONATE
AEEILNV	AVELINE, EVELINA	AEELMSS	MEASLES	AEENNPT	PENNATE, PENTANE
AEEILPR	PEARLIE	AEELMST	MALTESE	AEENNRS	ENSNARE
AEEILPT	PILEATE	AEELMTU	EMULATE	AEENNSX	ANNEXES
AEEILRR	EARLIER	AEELNNP	ENPLANE	AEENNTT	ANNETTE, NANETTE
AEEILRS	REALISE	AEELNOR	ELEANOR	AEENOPU	EUPNOEA
AEEILRT	ATELIER	AEELNRR	LEARNER	AEENPSX	EXPANSE
AEEILRV	VALERIE	AEELNRT	ETERNAL, TELERAN	AEENRRS	EARNERS
AEEILRZ	REALIZE	AEELNRU	LAUREEN	AEENRRT	TERRANE
AEEILTV	ELATIVE	AEELNRV	LAVERNE	AEENRRV	RAVENER
AEEIMNT	ETAMINE, MATINEE	AEELNRW	RENEWAL	AEENRRY	YEARNER
AEEIMNX	EXAMINE	AEELNST	LEANEST	AEENRST	EARNEST, EASTERN,
AEEIMRS	SEAMIER, SERIEMA	AEELNSV	ENSLAVE, LEAVENS	NEAREST	
AEEIMRT	EMIRATE, MEATIER	AEELNSW	SALWEEN	AEENRTT	ENTREAT, TERNATE
AEEIMSS	SIAMESE	AEELOPX	POLEAXE	AEENRTV	NERVATE, TAVENER,
				VETERAN	

AEENRVY	YEREVAN
AEENRWY	NEW YEAR
AEENSST	SENATES, SENSATE
AEENSTT	NEATEST
AEENSUV	AVENUES
AEENVWW	NEW WAVE
AEEOPRT	OPERATE
AEEORST	ROSEATE
AEEORVW	OVERAWE
AEEPPRR	PAPERER, PREPARE
AEEPPRS	REAPERS, SPEARER
AEEPRRT	TAPERER
AEEPRSS	ASPERSE, PARSEES
AEEPRST	REPEATS
AEEPRTX	EX PARTE
AEEPRTZ	TRAPEZE
AEEPSST	PESETAS
AEEPSTT	SEPTATE
AEERRSS	ERASERS
AEERRST	SERRATE
AEERRSU	ERASURE
AEERRSW	SWEARER
AEERRTT	RETREAT, TREATER
AEERRTW	WATERER
AEERRUX	AUXERRE
AEERRVW	WAVERER
AEERSST	EASTERS, TEASERS, TESSERA
AEERSTT	ESTREAT, RESTATE
AEERSTU	AUSTERE
AEERSTW	SWEATER
AEERSVW	WEAVERS
AEESSSW	SEESAWS
AEESSTT	ESTATES
AEESTTT	TESTATE
AEFFGIL	FIG LEAF
AEFFGIR	GIRAFFE
AEFFGRS	GAFFERS
AEFFIST	TAFFIES
AEFFISX	AFFIXES
AEFFKOP	OFF-PEAK
AEFFKOR	RAKE-OFF
AEFFKOT	TAKEOFF
AEFFLLY	FLYLEAF
AEFFLNS	SNAFFLE
AEFFLRR	RAFFLER
AEFFLRS	RAFFLES
AEFFLRU	FEARFUL
AEFFLSW	WAFFLES
AEFFLTU	FATEFUL
AEFFMRU	EARMUFF
AEFFOVW	WAVEOFF
AEFFQRU	QUAFFER
AEFFRST	STAFFER

AEFGGLR	FLAGGER
AEFGIKN	KAIFENG
AEFGILN	FINAGLE
AEFGILO	FOLIAGE
AEFGILR	FRAGILE
AEFGINR	FEARING
AEFGINU	FUEGIAN
AEFGIRT	FRIGATE
AEFGITU	FATIGUE
AEFGLNR	FLANGER
AEFGLNS	FLANGES
AEFGLOT	FLOTAGE
AEFGLOW	FLOWAGE
AEFGNOR	FAR GONE
AEFGNRT	ENGRAFT
AEFGOOT	FOOTAGE
AEFGORR	FORAGER
AEFGORS	FORAGES
AEFGORV	FORGAVE
AEFGRRT	GRAFTER
AEFGRSU	FEARGUS
AEFHLRS	FLASHER
AEFHLSS	FLASHES
AEFHLTU	HATEFUL
AEFHRRT	FARTHER
AEFHRST	FATHERS
AEFIILT	FILIATE
AEFIIRS	FAIRIES
AEFIKLR	FLAKIER
AEFIKNR	FRANKIE
AEFILLM	FAMILLE
AEFILMN	INFLAME
AEFILNS	FINALES
AEFILNT	INFLATE
AEFILOT	FOLIATE
AEFILPT	FLEAPIT
AEFILRR	FRAILER
AEFILRU	FAILURE
AEFILRV	FAVRILE
AEFILSS	FALSIES
AEFIMNR	FIREMAN
AEFIMNS	FAMINES
AEFIMOR	FOAMIER
AEFIMRR	FIREARM
AEFINNR	FRANNIE
AEFINNS	FANNIES
AEFINNT	INFANTE
AEFINNZ	FANZINE
AEFINPR	FIREPAN
AEFINRR	REFRAIN
AEFINRT	FAINTER, FINE ART
AEFINTX	ANTEFIX
AEFIQRU	AQUIFER
AEFIRRR	FARRIER

AEFIRRZ	FRAZIER
AEFIRST	FAIREST
AEFIRSX	FAIR SEX
AEFIRTT	FATTIER
AEFISST	FIESTAS
AEFISTT	FATTIES
AEFKLNR	FLANKER
AEFKLRT	FARTLEK
AEFKLST	FLASKET
AEFKLUW	WAKEFUL
AEFKNRR	FRANKER
AEFKORS	FORSAKE
AEFLLNN	FLANNEL
AEFLLSY	FALSELY
AEFLLTT	FLATLET
AEFLMOR	FEMORAL
AEFLNOV	FLAVONE
AEFLNRU	FLANEUR, FUNERAL
AEFLNTT	FLATTEN
AEFLOOV	FOVEOLA
AEFLOPW	PEAFOWL
AEFLORS	LOAFERS, SAFROLE
AEFLORT	FLOATER
AEFLPPR	FLAPPER
AEFLPRS	FELSPAR
AEFLPRU	FLARE-UP
AEFLPRY	PALFREY
AEFLRST	FALSTER
AEFLRSU	REFUSAL
AEFLRTT	FLATTER
AEFLRTU	TEARFUL
AEFLRZZ	FRAZZLE
AEFLSST	FALSEST
AEFMNOR	FORAMEN, FOREMAN
AEFMNRU	FRAENUM
AEFMORR	FOREARM
AEFMORT	FORMATE
AEFMPRU	FRAME-UP
AEFMRRS	FARMERS
AEFNOPR	PROFANE
AEFNORT	TORFAEN
AEFNRSS	FARNESS
AEFNSST	FATNESS
AEFOPRW	FOREPAW
AEFORRY	FORAYER
AEFORSW	FORESAW
AEFPPRS	FRAPPES
AEFRRST	RAFTERS, STRAFER
AEFRSTW	FRETSAW
AEFSSTT	FASTEST
AEFSTTT	FATTEST
AEGGGLU	LUGGAGE
AEGGHLR	HAGGLER

AEGGINR	GEARING	AEGILNV	LEAVING	AEGJLNR	JANGLER
AEGGIOR	GEORGIA	AEGILOS	SOILAGE	AEGKRSW	GAWKERS
AEGGIOS	ISAGOGE	AEGILOU	EULOGIA	AEGKSST	GASKETS
AEGGIRS	SAGGIER	AEGILPS	LEGASPI	AEGLLLY	LEGALLY
AEGGJRY	JAGGERY (	AEGILRS	ALGIERS	AEGLLNO	GALLEON
AEGGLRR	GARGLER	AEGILRZ	GLAZIER	AEGLLOR	ALLEGRO
AEGGLRS	GARGLES	AEGIMNN	MEANING	AEGLLRY	ALLERGY, GALLERY,
AEGGLRY	GREYLAG	AEGIMNR	GERMAIN,		LARGELY, REGALLY
AEGGLSW	WAGGLES		MANGIER, REAMING	AEGLLSU	SEA GULL, SULLAGE
AEGGNRS	GANGERS,	AEGIMNS	ENIGMAS	AEGLLSY	GALLEYS
	GRANGES, NAGGERS	AEGIMNT	MINTAGE, TEAMING	AEGLLTU	GLUTEAL
AEGGNTU	GAUTENG	AEGIMPR	EPIGRAM	AEGLMNR	MANGLER
AEGGRSS	AGGRESS	AEGIMPS	MAGPIES	AEGLMNS	MANGLES
AEGGRST	STAGGER, TAGGERS	AEGIMRR	ARMIGER	AEGLMPU	PLUMAGE
AEGGRSW	SWAGGER	AEGIMRS	GISARME, MIRAGES	AEGLNOT	TANGELO
AEGGRTY	GARGETY	AEGIMRT	MIGRATE, RAGTIME	AEGLNOU	ANGELOU
AEGHHIT	HIGH TEA	AEGIMRY	IMAGERY	AEGLNPR	GRAPNEL
AEGHHLS	SHELAGH	AEGIMST	GAMIEST, SIGMATE	AEGLNPS	SPANGLE
AEGHIKL	HAGLIKE	AEGINNR	EARNING, ENGRAIN,	AEGLNRS	LANGRES
AEGHILN	HEALING		GRAINNE, NEARING	AEGLNRT	TANGLER
AEGHILR	RALEIGH	AEGINNT	ANTEING, ANTIGEN,	AEGLNRU	GRANULE
AEGHINP	HEAPING		GENTIAN	AEGLNRW	WANGLER,
AEGHINR	HEARING	AEGINNU	ANGUINE, GUANINE,		WRANGLE
AEGHINT	GAHNITE, HEATING		GUINEAN	AEGLNST	TANGLES
AEGHINV	HEAVING	AEGINNV	ANGEVIN	AEGLNSU	ANGELUS
AEGHISS	GEISHAS	AEGINNW	WEANING	AEGLNSW	WANGLES
AEGHLNO	HALOGEN	AEGINOR	IRON AGE	AEGLNTT	GANTLET
AEGHLRU	LAUGHER	AEGINOS	AGONIES, AGONISE	AEGLNUW	GUNWALE
AEGHMNN	HANGMEN	AEGINOZ	AGONIZE	AEGLOPR	PERGOLA
AEGHNOX	HEXAGON	AEGINPP	GENIPAP	AEGLORS	GAOLERS
AEGHNRS	HANGERS	AEGINPR	REAPING	AEGLORT	GLOATER, LEGATOR
AEGHNSS	GNASHES	AEGINRR	ANGRIER, EARRING,	AEGLORV	VORLAGE
AEGHOST	HOSTAGE		GRAINER, REARING	AEGLOTV	VOLTAGE
AEGHRST	GATHERS	AEGINRS	ERASING, GAINERS,	AEGLPPR	GRAPPLE
AEGIIMN	IMAGINE		REGINAS, SEARING, SERINGA	AEGLPRU	EARPLUG, GRAUPEL,
AEGIINR	NIGERIA	AEGINRT	GERAINT, GRANITE,		PLAGUER
AEGIKLN	LEAKING, LINKAGE		INGRATE, TANGIER, TEARING	AEGLPSU	PLAGUES
AEGIKNP	PEAKING	AEGINRV	GINEVRA, VINEGAR	AEGLRRU	REGULAR
AEGIKNT	KEATING	AEGINRW	WEARING	AEGLRSS	LARGESS
AEGIKPR	GARPIKE	AEGINST	EASTING, INGESTA,	AEGLRST	LARGEST
AEGIKRW	GAWKIER		SEATING, TEASING	AEGLRSV	VERGLAS
AEGILLL	ILLEGAL	AEGINSU	GUINEAS	AEGLRTU	TEGULAR
AEGILLN	GILLEAN	AEGINTV	VINTAGE	AEGLRTY	GREATLY
AEGILLP	PILLAGE	AEGINVW	WEAVING	AEGLRVY	GRAVELY
AEGILLT	TILLAGE	AEGIOSV	SEGOVIA	AEGLSSS	GLASSES
AEGILLV	VILLAGE	AEGIPRU	PERUGIA	AEGLSTT	GESTALT
AEGILLY	AGILELY	AEGIRRZ	GRAZIER	AEGLTUV	VULGATE
AEGILMR	GREMIAL	AEGIRSS	GASSIER	AEGLUUY	GUAYULE
AEGILMT	TIME LAG	AEGIRST	GAITERS, SEAGIRT	AEGLUVY	VAGUELY
AEGILNN	LEANING	AEGIRSV	GERVAIS	AEGMMRS	GRAMMES
AEGILNP	LEAPING, PEALING	AEGIRSW	EARWIGS	AEGMMRU	RUMMAGE
AEGILNR	ENGRAIL, REALIGN	AEGIRTV	VIRGATE	AEGMNNO	AGNOMEN
AEGILNS	LEASING, SEALING	AEGIRUZ	GAUZIER	AEGMNOS	MANGOES
AEGILNT	GELATIN, GENITAL,	AEGISST	AGEISTS	AEGMNOT	MAGNETO,
	TAG LINE	AEGISSV	VISAGES		MEGATON, MONTAGE

AEGMNRS	GERMANS, MANGERS	AEHHJPT	JAPHETH	AEHLMNO	MANHOLE
AEGMNRT	GARMENT	AEHHLST	HEALTHS	AEHLMOR	ARMHOLE
AEGMNRY	GERMANY	AEHHLTY	HEALTHY	AEHLMRT	THERMAL
AEGMNST	MAGNETS	AEHHMSY	HEYSHAM	AEHLMRU	HUMERAL
AEGMNTU	AUGMENT, MUTAGEN	AEHHRRS	HARSHER	AEHLMST	HAMLETS
AEGMOOR	MOORAGE	AEHHRST	HEARTHS	AEHLNOT	ETHANOL
AEGMOXY	EXOGAMY	AEHHSST	SHEATHS	AEHLNRT	ENTHRAL
AEGMRRY	MARGERY	AEHIIRR	HAIRIER	AEHLNSU	UNLEASH
AEGNNOR	ARGONNE, GARONNE	AEHIKLT	HATLIKE	AEHLOPT	TAPHOLE
AEGNNOT	TONNAGE	AEHIKNS	HANKIES	AEHLORT	LOATHER
AEGNNRT	REGNANT	AEHIKRS	SHAKIER	AEHLOSS	ASSHOLE
AEGNNST	GANNETS	AEHILMN	HAMELIN	AEHLPRS	SPHERAL
AEGNNTT	TANGENT	AEHILMO	HEMIOLA	AEHLPSS	HAPLESS
AEGNOOR	OREGANO	AEHILNR	HERNIAL, INHALER	AEHLPSY	SHAPELY
AEGNORR	GROANER	AEHILNY	HYALINE	AEHLRSS	SLASHER
AEGNORS	ORANGES	AEHILOP	OPHELIA	AEHLRST	HALTERS, HARSLET
AEGNORT	NEGATOR	AEHILPR	HARELIP	AEHLRSW	WHALERS
AEGNORW	WAGONER	AEHILPT	HAPLITE	AEHLRTY	EARTHLY, HARTLEY, LATHERY
AEGNOSY	NOSEGAY	AEHILRU	HAULIER	AEHLSSS	HASSLES, SLASHES
AEGNPRT	TREPANG	AEHILSS	SHEILAS	AEHLSST	HASSLET, HATLESS
AEGNRRS	RANGERS	AEHILTY	HYALITE	AEHLSTT	STEALTH
AEGNRRT	GRANTER	AEHILVY	HEAVILY	AEHLTWY	WEALTHY
AEGNRST	GARNETS, STRANGE	AEHIMNS	HSIA-MEN	AEHMMRS	HAMMERS, SHAMMER
AEGNSSY	GAYNESS	AEHIMPR	EPHRAIM	AEHMNNR	HERMANN
AEGNTYZ	YANGTZE	AEHIMRS	MISHEAR	AEHMNST	ANTHEMS
AEGOORT	ROOTAGE	AEHIMSS	MESSIAH	AEHMOPT	APOTHEM
AEGOPRS	GO SPARE	AEHIMST	ATHEISM	AEHMPRS	HAMPERS
AEGOPRT	PORTAGE	AEHINOT	HIONATE	AEHMPTY	EMPATHY
AEGOPST	GESTAPO, POSTAGE	AEHINPR	HEPARIN	AEHMRSS	MARSHES, SMASHER
AEGOPTT	POTTAGE	AEHINPS	IN PHASE, PHINEAS	AEHMRST	HAMSTER
AEGORST	STORAGE	AEHINRS	HERNIAS	AEHMRWX	WREXHAM
AEGORTU	OUTRAGE	AEHINRT	HAIRNET	AEHMSSS	SMASHES
AEGORVY	VOYAGER	AEHINSS	HESSIAN	AEHMTTW	MATTHEW
AEGOSSU	GASEOUS	AEHIORR	HOARIER	AEHNNPY	HA'PENNY
AEGOSTW	STOWAGE	AEHIPPR	HAPPIER	AEHNOPT	PHAETON, PHONATE
AEGOSVY	VOYAGES	AEHIPPT	EPITAPH	AEHNORS	HOARSEN
AEGOTTV	GAVOTTE	AEHIPRS	HARPIES	AEHNORT	ANOTHER
AEGOTTW	GET A TOW	AEHIPSS	APHESIS	AEHNORV	HANOVER
AEGPRRS	GRASPER	AEHIRRR	HARRIER	AEHNOSX	HEXOSAN
AEGPSTU	UPSTAGE	AEHIRRT	HARRIET	AEHNPRS	SHARPEN
AEGRRST	GARRETS, GARTERS, GRATERS	AEHIRSU	HERISAU	AEHNPRT	PANTHER
AEGRRTT	GARRETT	AEHIRWY	HAYWIRE	AEHNRSS	HARNESS
AEGRRUV	GRAVURE	AEHISST	ASHIEST	AEHNRST	ANTHERS
AEGRSSS	GRASSES	AEHISTT	ATHEIST	AEHNRTU	HAUNTER, UNEARTH
AEGRSTT	TARGETS	AEHISTZ	HAZIEST	AEHNRTX	NARTHEX
AEGRSTV	GRAVEST	AEHISVY	YESHIVA	AEHOORT	TOHEROA
AEGRSTY	GRAYEST	AEHJOPS	JOSEPHA	AEHOPST	TEASHOP
AEGSTUV	GUSTAVE	AEHKLOY	HOYLAKE	AEHORRS	HOARSER
AEGTTTU	GUTTATE	AEHKPSU	SHAKE-UP	AEHORST	EARSHOT
AEHHILS	SHEILAH	AEHKRSS	SHAKERS	AEHORSX	HOAXERS
AEHHJOV	JEHOVAH	AEHKRSW	HAWKERS	AEHORTX	OXHEART
		AEHKRTU	KETURAH	AEHOSTT	HOT SEAT
		AEHLLUV	HELLUVA	AEHPPRS	PERHAPS

AEHPRRS	SHARPER	
AEHPRSS	PHRASES, SERAPHS, SHERPAS	
AEHPRTY	THERAPY	
AEHPSTT	THE PAST	
AEHRRSS	RASHERS, SHARERS	
AEHRRTU	URETHRA	
AEHRSST	RASHEST	
AEHRSSV	SHAVERS	
AEHRSSW	HAWSERS, WASHERS	
AEHRSTT	HATTERS, SHATTER, THREATS	
AEHRSTV	HARVEST	
AEHRSTW	WREATHS	
AEHRSVW	WHARVES	
AEHRSWY	WASHERY	
AEHRTUU	HAUTEUR	
AEHSSST	STASHES	
AEHSTUX	EXHAUST	
AEIIJMS	JAMES II	
AEIIKNT	KAINITE	
AEIILNN	ANILINE	
AEIILNR	AIRLINE	
AEIILNS	AINSLIE	
AEIILRS	ISRAELI	
AEIILSS	SILESIA	
AEIILTT	LETITIA	
AEIIMTT	IMITATE	
AEIINNR	ANEIRIN	
AEIINNS	ASININE	
AEIINNR	RAINIER	
AEIINRT	INERTIA	
AEIIPRR	PRAIRIE	
AEIIRRV	RIVIERA	
AEIIRST	AIRIEST	
AEIITTV	VITIATE	
AEIJLNV	JAVELIN	
AEIJLRS	JAILERS	
AEIJMMR	JAMMIER	
AEIJMNS	JASMINE	
AEIJRZZ	JAZZIER	
AEIKLMN	MALINKE, MANLIKE	
AEIKLNR	LANKIER	
AEIKLOT	KEITLOA	
AEIKLRW	WARLIKE	
AEIKLST	TALKIES	
AEIKLSW	WALKIES	
AEIKLUZ	ZULEIKA	
AEIKLWX	WAXLIKE	
AEIKMNP	PIKEMAN	
AEIKMNR	RAMEKIN	
AEIKMST	MISTAKE	
AEIKNRR	NARKIER	
AEIKNRT	KATRINE, KERATIN	

AEIKNRU	UKRAINE	
AEIKNST	INTAKES	
AEIKNSY	KYANISE	
AEIKNYZ	KYANIZE	
AEIKPRR	PARKIER	
AEIKPRW	PAWKIER	
AEIKRRS	SARKIER	
AEIKRSS	KAISERS	
AEIKRSY	KAYSERI	
AEILLLM	MELILLA	
AEILLMT	ALL-TIME	
AEILLNR	RALLINE	
AEILLPR	PALLIER	
AEILLRR	RALLIER	
AEILLRS	RALLIES, SALLIER	
AEILLRT	LITERAL, TALLIER	
AEILLSS	SALLIES	
AEILLST	LIESTAL, TALLIES	
AEILLSW	WALLIES	
AEILLUV	ELUVIAL	
AEILLVY	VIYELLA	
AEILMMN	MAILMEN	
AEILMMS	MELISMA	
AEILMNN	LINEMAN, MELANIN	
AEILMNP	IMPANEL	
AEILMNR	MANLIER, MARLINE, MINERAL	
AEILMNS	MALINES, MENIALS, SEMINAL	
AEILMNT	AILMENT, ALIMENT	
AEILMNV	MELVINA	
AEILMNY	EL MINYA	
AEILMOR	MELIORA, MORELIA	
AEILMPR	IMPALER, PALMIER	
AEILMRS	REALISM	
AEILMRT	LATIMER, MARLITE	
AEILMSS	AIMLESS, MELISSA	
AEILMTY	MEATILY	
AEILNNY	INANELY	
AEILNNZ	LIZANNE	
AEILNOP	OPALINE	
AEILNOR	AILERON, ALIENOR, LORAINE	
AEILNOS	ANISOLE, SEA LION	
AEILNOT	ELATION, TOENAIL	
AEILNPR	PLAINER, PRALINE	
AEILNPS	SPANIEL	
AEILNPT	PANTILE	
AEILNPU	PAULINE	
AEILNPX	EXPLAIN	
AEILNRS	LINARES	
AEILNRT	LATRINE, RATLINE, RELIANT, RETINAL	
AEILNRV	RAVELIN	
AEILNRX	RELAXIN	

AEILNRY	INLAYER	
AEILNST	ELASTIN, SALIENT	
AEILNSY	AINSLEY, ELYSIAN	
AEILNTU	ALUNITE	
AEILNVY	NAIVELY	
AEILOPR	PELORIA	
AEILORS	ROSALIE	
AEILORV	VARIOLE	
AEILOST	ISOLATE	
AEILOTV	VIOLATE	
AEILPPR	APPLIER	
AEILPRV	PREVAIL	
AEILPST	TALIPES	
AEILPSY	PAISLEY	
AEILQTU	LIQUATE, TEQUILA	
AEILRRT	RETRIAL, TRAILER	
AEILRSS	AIRLESS, SERIALS	
AEILRST	REALIST, SALTIER, SALTIRE	
AEILRSV	REVISAL	
AEILRTT	TERTIAL	
AEILRTU	URALITE	
AEILRTY	IRATELY, REALITY	
AEILRVV	REVIVAL	
AEILRVY	VIRELAY	
AEILRWY	WEARILY	
AEILSST	SET SAIL	
AEILSSV	VALISES	
AEILSTZ	LAZIEST	
AEILTVV	TEL AVIV	
AEILUVX	EXUVIAL	
AEIMMMS	MAMMIES	
AEIMMNS	MISNAME	
AEIMMRT	MARMITE	
AEIMNNT	MANNITE	
AEIMNOR	MORAINE, ROMAINE	
AEIMNPR	PERMIAN	
AEIMNRR	MARINER	
AEIMNRS	MARINES, REMAINS, SEMINAR	
AEIMNRT	MARTINE, MINARET, RAIMENT	
AEIMNRV	MINERVA	
AEIMNSS	MESSINA, SAMISEN	
AEIMNST	INMATES	
AEIMNTV	VIETNAM	
AEIMNTY	AMENITY	
AEIMOOP	IPOMOEA	
AEIMOPR	EMPORIA	
AEIMORR	ARMOIRE	
AEIMOST	ATOMISE	
AEIMOTZ	ATOMIZE	
AEIMPRS	IMPRESA	
AEIMPRT	PRIMATE	
AEIMPRV	VAMPIRE	

AEIMPSS	IMPASSE	AEIOPST	OPIATES	AEKLPRS	SPARKLE
AEIMPST	IMPASTE, PASTIME, SEPTIMA	AEIOQSU	SEQUOIA	AEKLRST	STALKER, TALKERS
AEIMRRR	MARRIER	AEIORSV	OVARIES	AEKLRSW	WALKERS
AEIMRST	MAESTRI	AEIORSV	OVARIES	AEKMNRU	UNMAKER
AEIMRTW	WARTIME	AEIOSST	OSSETIA	AEKMRRS	MARKERS, REMARKS
AEIMSST	SEA MIST	AEIPPPS	PAPPIES	AEKMRST	MARKETS
AEIMSSV	MASSIVE	AEIPPRS	APPRISE, SAPPIER	AEKNOPS	SPOKANE
AEIMSTZ	MESTIZA	AEIPPRZ	ZAPPIER	AEKNPPR	KNAPPER
AEINNNS	NANNIES	AEIPRRS	ASPIRER, PARRIES, PRAISER, RAPIERS, REPAIRS	AEKNPRS	SPANKER
AEINNOT	ANTOINE			AEKNRRS	RANKERS
AEINNPR	PANNIER	AEIPRSS	PARESIS, PRAISES	AEKNRST	TANKERS
AEINNPT	PINNATE	AEIPRST	PARTIES, PASTIER, PIASTRE, PIRATES, TRAIPSE	AEKNRSW	WANKERS
AEINNRT	ENTRAIN			AEKNRVY	KNAVERY
AEINNRU	ANEURIN	AEIPRSU	PIRAEUS, UPRAISE	AEKOTTU	OUT-TAKE, TAKEOUT
AEINOPR	OPEN-AIR	AEIPRTT	PARTITE		
AEINOPZ	APIEZON	AEIPRTV	PRIVATE	AEKPSSY	PASSKEY
AEINORS	ERASION	AEIPRTW	WIRETAP	AEKPSTU	TAKEUPS, UPTAKES
AEINOST	ESTONIA	AEIPRXY	PYREXIA	AEKQRSU	QUAKERS
AEINOSV	EVASION	AEIPSSS	ASEPSIS	AEKQSSU	SQUEAKS
AEINOXZ	OXAZINE	AEIPSST	PASTIES	AEKQSUY	SQUEAKY
AEINPPS	NAPPIES	AEIPSSV	PASSIVE	AEKRRST	STARKER
AEINPRS	PERSIAN	AEIPSTT	PATTIES	AEKRSST	STREAKS
AEINPRT	PAINTER, PERTAIN, PETRINA	AEIPSTU	IAPETUS	AEKRSTY	STREAKY
		AEIPTXY	EPITAXY	AELLLOU	LOUELLA
AEINPSS	PANSIES	AEIRRRV	ARRIVER	AELLMNS	MANSELL
AEINPST	PANTIES, SAPIENT	AEIRRSS	RAISERS, SIERRAS	AELLMNU	LUMENAL
AEINPTT	PATIENT	AEIRRST	TARSIER	AELLMRS	SMALLER
AEINPTU	PETUNIA	AEIRRTT	RATTIER	AELLMST	MALLETS
AEINQTU	ANTIQUE, QUINATE	AEIRRTU	ETRURIA	AELLMSU	MALLEUS
AEINRRS	SIERRAN	AEIRSSS	SASSIER	AELLMWX	MAXWELL
AEINRRT	TERRAIN, TRAINER	AEIRSST	SATIRES	AELLNOV	NOVELLA
AEINRSS	NERISSA, SARNIES	AEIRSTT	ARTIEST, ARTISTE, STRIATE, TASTIER	AELLNPR	PARNELL
AEINRST	NASTIER, RETINAS, RETSINA, STAINER, STEARIN			AELLNPY	PENALLY
		AEIRSTW	WAITERS, WARIEST	AELLNVY	VENALLY
AEINRSV	RAVINES	AEIRSVW	WAIVERS	AELLORS	ROSELLA
AEINRTT	ITERANT, NATTIER, NITRATE, TERTIAN	AEIRTTT	TATTIER, TITRATE	AELLORV	ALL OVER, OVERALL
		AEIRTUZ	AZURITE	AELLPRU	PLEURAL
AEINRTU	TAURINE, URANITE, URINATE	AEIRTVY	VARIETY	AELLPST	L-PLATES, PALLETS
		AEISSSS	ASSISES	AELLPTY	PLAYLET
AEINRTW	TINWARE	AEISSST	SIESTAS	AELLQUY	EQUALLY
AEINRVV	VERVAIN	AEISSSU	AUSSIES	AELLRRU	ALLURER
AEINSST	ENTASIS, SESTINA, STAINES	AEISSSZ	ASSIZES	AELLRST	STELLAR
		AEISSUX	AUXESIS	AELLRSU	LAURELS
AEINSSV	VINASSE	AEISTTU	SITUATE	AELLRTY	ALERTLY
AEINSTT	INSTATE, SATINET	AEISTTV	STATIVE	AELLRVY	RAVELLY
AEINSTU	SINUATE	AEISTTY	SATIETY	AELLSSW	LAWLESS
AEINSTV	NATIVES, VAINEST	AEISTVW	WAVIEST	AELLSTT	TALLEST
AEINSTW	IN A STEW	AEISSTW	WAXIEST	AELLSTW	WALLETS
AEINSTZ	ZANIEST	AEITTTV	VITTATE	AELLSVY	VALLEYS
AEINSVV	NAVVIES	AEJJLNU	JEJUNAL	AELLTUU	ULULATE
AEINSWY	ANYWISE	AEJLOSU	JEALOUS	AELLUVV	VALVULE
AEINTVY	NAIVETY	AEJMSTY	MAJESTY	AELMMOY	MYELOMA
AEINTXY	ANXIETY	AEJNOSS	SAN JOSE	AELMMRT	TRAMMEL
AEIOPRS	SOAPIER	AEKLNST	ANKLETS, LANKEST	AELMMST	STAMMEL
		AEKLOST	SKATOLE		
		AEKLPPT	PEP TALK		

AELMMSY	MALMSEY	AELOPRV	OVERLAP	AELSTTY	STATELY
AELMNOR	ALMONER	AELOPST	APOSTLE, PELOTAS	AELSTWZ	WALTZES
AELMNOT	TELAMON	AELOPSX	EXPOSAL	AELSUVY	SUAVELY
AELMNPR	LAMPERN	AELORRT	REALTOR, RELATOR	AELTTUX	TEXTUAL
AELMNRU	NUMERAL	AELORSS	LASSOER	AEMMNOT	MOMENTA
AELMNRV	MALVERN	AELORTT	LORETTA	AEMMRST	STAMMER
AELMNST	LAMENTS, MANTLES	AELORTV	LEVATOR	AEMNNOS	MANNOSE
AELMOPR	PALERMO	AELORUU	ROULEAU	AEMNNOT	MONTANE
AELMOPU	AMPOULE	AELORVY	OVERLAY	AEMNNRS	MANNERS
AELMOPY	MAYPOLE	AELOSSV	SALVOES	AEMNNRT	REMNANT
AELMORV	REMOVAL	AELOSTV	SOLVATE	AEMNNTU	UNMEANT
AELMOST	MALTOSE	AELOSTZ	ZEALOTS	AEMNOPR	MANROPE
AELMOSY	AMYLOSE	AELOSUZ	ZEALOUS	AEMNORS	MOANERS,
AELMPRS	SAMPLER	AELOTTU	TOLUATE		OARSMEN, SAN REMO
AELMPRT	TRAMPLE	AELOTUV	OVULATE	AEMNORU	ENAMOUR,
AELMPRY	LAMPREY	AELOTVV	VOLVATE		NEUROMA
AELMPSS	SAMPLES	AELPPRS	SLAPPER	AEMNORV	OVERMAN
AELMPTU	PLUMATE	AELPPSU	APPULSE	AEMNPTU	PUTAMEN
AELMRSS	ARMLESS	AELPQSU	PLAQUES	AEMNPTY	PAYMENT
AELMRSU	SERUMAL	AELPRST	PLASTER, PSALTER,	AEMNRRU	MANURER
AELMRSV	MARVELS		STAPLER	AEMNRST	MARTENS, SMARTEN
AELMRTU	RELATUM	AELPRSU	PERUSAL	AEMNRSU	SURNAME
AELMSTU	AMULETS	AELPRSY	PARLEYS, PARSLEY,	AEMNSST	STAMENS
AELNNPR	PLANNER		PLAYERS, REPLAYS	AEMNSTY	AMNESTY
AELNNRT	LANTERN	AELPRTT	PLATTER, PRATTLE	AEMOORT	TEAROOM
AELNNRU	UNLEARN	AELPRTY	PTERYLA	AEMOORW	WOOMERA
AELNNTU	ANNULET	AELPSSS	SAPLESS	AEMOOST	OSTEOMA
AELNOOR	LEONORA	AELPSST	PASTELS, STAPLES	AEMOOSV	VAMOOSE
AELNOPT	LEPANTO	AELPSSU	PAS SEUL	AEMOPRS	PASMORE
AELNOPU	APOLUNE	AELPSTU	PULSATE	AEMOPST	PETSAMO
AELNORS	ORLEANS, SALERNO	AELQRRU	QUARREL	AEMORRS	ROAMERS
AELNORV	VERONAL	AELQSSU	SQUEALS	AEMORRV	OVERARM
AELNOST	LEAN-TOS	AELQTUZ	QUETZAL	AEMORST	MAESTRO
AELNPPS	PEN PALS	AELRRSU	SURREAL	AEMORTU	EURATOM
AELNPPY	PLAYPEN	AELRRTW	TRAWLER	AEMOSWY	SOMEWAY
AELNPRT	PLANTER	AELRSST	ARTLESS	AEMOTTY	MAYOTTE
AELNPRY	PLENARY	AELRSSV	SALVERS, SLAVERS	AEMPRRT	TRAMPER
AELNPST	PLANETS	AELRSSY	SLAYERS	AEMPRST	STAMPER
AELNPTX	EXPLANT	AELRSTT	RATTLES, STARLET,	AEMPTTT	ATTEMPT
AELNPTY	APLENTY, PENALTY		STARTLE, TELSTAR	AEMPTTU	TAPETUM
AELNQUU	UNEQUAL	AELRSTU	SALUTER	AEMQSSU	MASQUES
AELNRRS	SNARLER	AELRSTV	TRAVELS, VARLETS,	AEMRRRY	REMARRY
AELNRST	ANTLERS, RENTALS,		VESTRAL	AEMRRST	ARMREST, SMARTER
	SALTERN, STERNAL	AELRSTW	WASTREL	AEMRRTU	ERRATUM
AELNRTU	NEUTRAL	AELRSUV	VALUERS	AEMRSST	MASTERS, STREAMS
AELNRTV	VENTRAL	AELRSVY	SLAVERY	AEMRSSU	ASSUMER,
AELNRUV	UNRAVEL, VENULAR	AELRSWY	LAWYERS		ERASMUS, MASSEUR
AELNSSU	SENSUAL	AELRSZZ	RAZZLES	AEMRSTT	MATTERS, SMATTER
AELNSSX	LAXNESS	AELRTTT	TATTLER	AEMRSTU	ARTEMUS
AELNSTT	TALENTS	AELRTUV	VAULTER	AEMRSTW	WARMEST
AELNSTY	STANLEY	AELRTWZ	WALTZER	AEMRSTY	MASTERY
AELOORS	AEROSOL, ROSEOLA	AELSSST	TASSELS	AEMRTTZ	ZERMATT
AELOPRS	PAROLES, REPOSAL	AELSSTT	STALEST	AENNNPT	PENNANT
AELOPRT	PROLATE	AELSSTU	SALUTES	AENNORS	ROSANNE, ROSEANN
		AELSTTW	WATTLES	AENNORX	ROXANNE

AENNOTU	TONNEAU
AENNPRS	SPANNER
AENNRST	TANNERS
AENNRTT	ENTRANT
AENNRTY	TANNERY
AENNSSU	SUSANNE
AENNSSW	WANNESS
AENNSTT	TENANTS
AENNSTW	WANNEST
AENNSUZ	SUZANNE
AENOPPR	PROPANE
AENOPRS	PERSONA
AENOPRT	OPERANT, PRONATE, PROTEAN
AENOPSW	WEAPONS
AENORRV	OVERRAN
AENORSS	REASONS, SENORAS
AENORST	ONE-STAR, SENATOR, TREASON
AENORSY	REYNOSA
AENORVY	AVEYRON
AENOSSS	SEASONS
AENOSTU	SOUTANE
AENOUUV	NOUVEAU
AENPPRS	SNAPPER
AENPRRT	PARTNER
AENPRRW	PRAWNER
AENPRST	PARENTS, PASTERN
AENPRSW	SPAWNER
AENPRSZ	PANZERS
AENPRTT	PATTERN, REPTANT
AENPRTW	ANTWERP
AENPRUV	PARVENU
AENPSST	APTNESS
AENPSSY	SYNAPSE
AENPSTT	PATENTS, PATTENS
AENPSTU	PEANUTS
AENRRST	RANTERS
AENRRSW	WARRENS
AENRRTY	TERNARY
AENRSSW	ANSWERS, RAWNESS
AENRSTU	NATURES, SAUNTER
AENRSTV	SERVANT, TAVERNS, VERSANT
AENRSUW	UNSWEAR
AENRTTU	TAUNTER
AENRTUV	VAUNTER
AENSTTU	TETANUS
AENSTTX	SEXTANT
AEOOPPS	PAPOOSE
AEOPPPS	PAPPOSE
AEOPPRV	APPROVE
AEOPRST	ESPARTO, SEAPORT
AEOPRVY	OVERPAY

AEOPSTT	TEAPOTS
AEOPSTZ	TOPAZES
AEOQRTU	EQUATOR, QUORATE
AEOQSUU	AQUEOUS
AEORRST	ROASTER
AEORRSU	AROUSER
AEORSTT	ROSETTA, TOASTER
AEORSVW	OVERSAW
AEORTUW	OUTWEAR
AEORTVX	OVERTAX
AEPPRRT	TRAPPER
AEPPRRW	WRAPPER
AEPPRSS	SAPPERS
AEPPRSU	PAUPERS
AEPPRSW	SWAPPER
AEPPSTT	TAPPETS
AEPPSTU	PASTE-UP
AEPQRTU	PARQUET
AEPRRSS	PARSERS, SPARSER
AEPRRSY	PRAYERS, SPRAYER
AEPRRTU	RAPTURE, RUPERTA
AEPRSST	REPASTS
AEPRSSY	PESSARY
AEPRSTT	PATTERS, SPATTER
AEPRSTU	PASTURE
AEPRSUV	RAVE-UPS
AEQRRSU	SQUARER
AEQRRTU	QUARTER
AEQRSSU	SQUARES
AEQRSTU	T-SQUARE
AEQRSUV	QUAVERS
AEQRTTU	QUARTET
AEQRUVY	QUAVERY
AERRSST	ARRESTS
AERRSSU	ASSURER
AERRSTT	STARTER
AERRSTV	STARVER, TRAVERS
AERRSTY	STRAYER
AERSSTT	TASTERS
AERSSTW	WASTERS .
AERSSTY	STAYERS
AERSTTT	STRETTA, TATTERS
AERSTTU	STATURE
AERSTTW	STEWART, SWATTER
AERSTUY	ESTUARY
AESSTTU	STATUES
AESSTUY	EUSTASY
AESTTTU	STATUTE, TAUTEST
AFFGSUW	GUFFAWS
AFFHINU	IN A HUFF
AFFHIRS	RAFFISH
AFFHLLY	FLY HALF
AFFHLUU	AL HUFUF

AFFHMNO	HOFFMAN
AFFIKRS	KAFFIRS
AFFILSY	FALSIFY
AFFIMST	MASTIFF
AFFINRU	FUNFAIR, RUFFIAN
AFFINTY	TIFFANY
AFFIRST	TARIFFS
AFFKLOW	WALK OFF
AFFLOPY	PLAY-OFF
AFFLOSY	LAY-OFFS
AFFNORS	SAFFRON
AFFNORT	AFFRONT
AFFNOSW	SAWN-OFF
AFGGGIN	FAGGING
AFGGOST	FAGGOTS
AFGHHIS	HAGFISH
AFGHIRS	GARFISH
AFGHRTU	FRAUGHT
AFGIILN	FAILING
AFGIINR	FAIRING
AFGIKLN	FLAKING
AFGILLN	FALLING
AFGILMN	FLAMING
AFGILNO	FOALING, LOAFING
AFGILNR	FLARING
AFGILNT	FATLING
AFGILNU	GAINFUL
AFGILNW	FLAWING
AFGILNY	ANGLIFY, FLAYING
AFGILRU	FIGURAL
AFGIMNO	FOAMING
AFGIMNR	FARMING, FRAMING
AFGIMNY	MAGNIFY
AFGINNN	FANNING
AFGINNW	FAWNING
AFGINRT	FARTING, RAFTING
AFGINRY	FRAYING
AFGINST	FASTING
AFGINTW	WAFTING
AFGIRTY	GRATIFY
AFGKORT	KOFTGAR
AFGLLLY	GALLFLY
AFGLLUY	FALL GUY
AFGLMOP	FOG LAMP
AFGLNOS	FLAGONS
AFGMNOR	FROGMAN
AFHIIRS	FAIRISH
AFHIKLS	KHALIFS
AFHILTW	HALF-WIT
AFHIMNU	HAFNIUM
AFHINOS	FASHION
AFHIORS	OARFISH
AFHISSW	SAWFISH
AFHISTT	FATTISH

AFHKORY	HAYFORK	AFMNORT	FORMANT	AGHHHMNU	HAMHUNG
AFHLMRU	HARMFUL	AFMNWYY	MYFANWY	AGHHNOW	HWANG HO
AFHLOOS	LOOFAHS	AFMOORS	FORMOSA	AGHHORT	HOGARTH
AFHMOST	FATHOMS	AFMORST	FORMATS	AGHHOSW	HOGWASH
AFHMOUZ	MAHFOUZ	AFMOSTU	SFUMATO	AGHHTUY	HAUGHTY
AFHORTW	WHAT FOR	AFOORST	OF A SORT	AGHIILN	HAILING
AFIILRT	AIRLIFT	AFOOTWY	FOOTWAY	AGHIKNN	KHINGAN
AFIINRS	FRISIAN	AFORSUV	FAVOURS	AGHIKNR	HARKING
AFIKKLR	FALKIRK	AFORUWY	FOUR-WAY	AGHIKNS	SHAKING
AFIKNNU	IN A FUNK	AFOSTUU	FATUOUS	AGHIKNW	HAWKING
AFILLNY	FINALLY	AGGGGIN	GAGGING	AGHILNS	LASHING
AFILLPT	PITFALL	AGGGIJN	JAGGING	AGHILNT	ALTHING, HALTING
AFILLUV	FLUVIAL	AGGGILN	LAGGING	AGHILNU	HAULING
AFILLUW	WAILFUL	AGGGINN	GANGING,	AGHILNV	HALVING
AFILMOR	ALIFORM		NAGGING	AGHILNW	WHALING
AFILMPY	AMPLIFY	AGGGINR	RAGGING	AGHILOT	GOLIATH
AFILNOR	FLORIAN	AGGGINS	SAGGING	AGHILRS	LARGISH
AFILNPU	PAINFUL	AGGGINT	TAGGING	AGHILRT	ALRIGHT
AFILNTY	FAINTLY	AGGGINU	GAUGING	AGHIMMN	HAMMING
AFILORW	AIRFLOW	AGGGINW	WAGGING	AGHIMNR	HARMING
AFILOTX	FOXTAIL	AGGHHIS	HAGGISH	AGHIMNS	MASHING,
AFILQUY	QUALIFY	AGGHIMN	GINGHAM		SHAMING
AFILRTY	FRAILTY	AGGHINN	HANGING	AGHINOX	HOAXING
AFILSSY	SALSIFY	AGGHINS	GASHING	AGHINPR	HARPING
AFILSTU	FISTULA	AGGHISW	WAGGISH	AGHINPS	PHASING, SHAPING
AFILSTY	FALSITY	AGGIINN	GAINING	AGHINRS	GARNISH, SHARING
AFILTTY	FATTILY	AGGIINV	GINGIVA	AGHINSU	ANGUISH
AFIMOOS	MAFIOSO	AGGIKNW	GAWKING	AGHINSV	SHAVING
AFIMSSS	MASSIFS	AGGILLN	GALLING	AGHINSW	WASHING
AFIMSUV	FAUVISM	AGGILNN	ANGLING	AGHINTT	AT NIGHT
AFINNST	INFANTS	AGGILNO	GAOLING	AGHINTW	THAWING
AFINORS	INSOFAR	AGGILNR	GLARING	AGHJMNO	MAH JONG
AFINRTU	UT INFRA	AGGILNZ	GLAZING	AGHKOSW	GOSHAWK
AFINSTU	FUSTIAN	AGGILOS	LOGGIAS	AGHLMPU	GALUMPH
AFISSTY	SATISFY	AGGINNR	RANGING	AGHLOSU	GOULASH
AFISTUV	FAUVIST	AGGINNW	GNAWING	AGHLSTY	GHASTLY
AFITTUY	FATUITY	AGGINPP	GAPPING	AGHMNNU	HUNGNAM
AFKKOUU	FUKUOKA	AGGINPS	GASPING	AGHMRTU	MURTAGH
AFKLNRY	FRANKLY	AGGINPW	GAWPING	AGHNOTU	HANGOUT
AFKRRTU	FRAKTUR	AGGINRT	GRATING	AGHNPSU	HANG-UPS
AFLLOOY	ALOOFLY	AGGINRU	ARGUING	AGHNRUY	HUNGARY
AFLLOTU	FALLOUT, OUTFALL	AGGINRY	GRAYING	AGHNTUY	NAUGHTY
AFLLPUY	PLAYFUL	AGGINRZ	GRAZING	AGHORTW	WARTHOG
AFLLUWY	AWFULLY	AGGINSS	GASSING	AGHRTUU	THURGAU
AFLMORU	FORMULA	AGGINST	STAGING	AGIIJLN	JAILING
AFLMORW	WOLFRAM	AGGINUY	GUIYANG	AGIIJNX	JIANGXI
AFLMOST	FLOTSAM	AGGISZZ	ZIGZAGS	AGIIKNS	KIANGSI
AFLMRSU	ARMFULS, FULMARS	AGGKNOT	GANGTOK	AGIILLN	GILLIAN
AFLNOOS	ALFONSO	AGGLOSW	GLASGOW	AGIILMN	MAILING
AFLNORT	FRONTAL	AGGMORR	GROGRAM	AGIILNN	NAILING
AFLORUV	FLAVOUR	AGGMOST	MAGGOTS	AGIILNR	RAILING
AFLPRTY	FLYTRAP	AGGMOTY	MAGGOTY	AGIILNS	AISLING, SAILING
AFLPSTY	FLYPAST	AGHHINS	HASHING	AGIILNT	TAILING
AFMNOOT	FOOTMAN	AGHHIWY	HIGHWAY	AGIILNW	WAILING

140

AGIILPT	PIGTAIL	AGILMNY	MANGILY	AGINOPS	SOAPING
AGIILRU	LIGURIA	AGILNNO	LOANING	AGINOPT	PAOTING
AGIILTY	AGILITY	AGILNNP	PLANING	AGINORR	ROARING
AGIIMMN	MAIMING	AGILNNS	LANSING, LINSANG	AGINORS	SIGNORA, SOARING
AGIIMMS	IMAGISM	AGILNPP	LAPPING	AGINORV	VIRGOAN
AGIIMOR	ORIGAMI	AGILNPS	LAPSING, PALINGS,	AGINOST	AGONIST
AGIIMST	IMAGIST		SAPLING	AGINOVW	AVOWING
AGIINNP	PAINING	AGILNPT	PLATING	AGINPPR	RAPPING
AGIINNR	INGRAIN, RAINING	AGILNPW	LAPWING	AGINPPS	SAPPING
AGIINPR	PAIRING	AGILNPY	PLAYING	AGINPPT	TAPPING
AGIINRS	AIRINGS, ARISING,	AGILNRY	ANGRILY, RANGILY	AGINPPY	YAPPING
	RAISING	AGILNSS	SIGNALS	AGINPPZ	ZAPPING
AGIINSV	VISAING	AGILNST	LASTING, SALTING,	AGINPRS	PARINGS, PARSING,
AGIINTW	WAITING		SLATING, STALING		RASPING, SPARING
AGIINTX	TAXIING	AGILNSV	SALVING, SLAVING	AGINPRT	GIN TRAP, PARTING,
AGIINVW	WAIVING	AGILNSY	SLAYING		PRATING
AGIIORZ	GORIZIA	AGILNUV	VALUING	AGINPRW	WARPING
AGIJMMN	JAMMING	AGILOPT	GALIPOT	AGINPRY	PRAYING
AGIJNNN	NANJING	AGILORS	ARGOLIS, GIRASOL	AGINPSS	PASSING
AGIJNNU	JUNGIAN	AGILORW	AIRGLOW, GWALIOR	AGINPST	PASTING
AGIJNRR	JARRING	AGILSTY	STAGILY	AGINPSU	PAUSING
AGIJNSU	JIANGSU	AGIMMNR	RAMMING	AGINPSV	PAVINGS
AGIJNZZ	JAZZING	AGIMMNN	MANNING	AGINPSY	SPAYING
AGIJSSW	JIGSAWS	AGIMMNO	MOANING	AGINPTT	PATTING
AGIKKNY	YAKKING	AGIMNOR	ROAMING	AGINRRT	TARRING
AGIKLNR	LARKING	AGIMNPP	MAPPING	AGINRRW	WARRING
AGIKLNS	SLAKING	AGIMNPT	TAMPING	AGINRST	GASTRIN, RATINGS,
AGIKLNT	TALKING	AGIMNRR	MARRING		STARING
AGIKLNW	WALKING	AGIMNRS	MARGINS	AGINRSU	AIRGUNS
AGIKMNR	MARKING	AGIMNRT	MIGRANT	AGINRSV	RAVINGS
AGIKMNS	MAKINGS, MASKING	AGIMNRW	WARMING	AGINRSY	SYRINGA
AGIKNNN	NANKING	AGIMNSS	MASSING	AGINRTT	RATTING
AGIKNNR	NARKING, RANKING	AGIMNSU	AMUSING	AGINRVY	VARYING
AGIKNNS	SNAKING	AGIMNTT	MATTING	AGINRXY	X-RAYING
AGIKNNW	WANKING	AGIMORU	GOURAMI	AGINSSS	SASSING
AGIKNNY	YANKING	AGIMOSY	ISOGAMY	AGINSSV	SAVINGS
AGIKNOS	SOAKING	AGIMSST	STIGMAS	AGINSSY	SAYINGS
AGIKNOY	OKAYING	AGIMSWW	WIGWAMS	AGINSTT	STATING, TASTING
AGIKNPR	PARKING	AGINNNN	NANNING	AGINSTV	STAVING
AGIKNQU	QUAKING	AGINNNP	PANNING	AGINSTW	WASTING
AGIKNRT	KARTING	AGINNNT	TANNING	AGINSTY	STAYING, STYGIAN
AGIKNST	SKATING, STAKING,	AGINNNW	WANNING	AGINSWY	SWAYING
	TAKINGS	AGINNOT	ATONING	AGINTTT	TATTING
AGIKNSU	KIANGSU	AGINNOV	AVIGNON	AGINWWX	WAXWING
AGILLMU	GALLIUM	AGINNPP	NAPPING	AGIORSV	VIRAGOS
AGILLNP	PALLING	AGINNPT	PANTING	AGIRSTU	GUITARS
AGILLNU	LINGUAL	AGINNPW	PAWNING	AGIRTVY	GRAVITY
AGILLNW	WALLING	AGINNRS	SNARING	AGJKNUW	KWANGJU
AGILLNY	ALLYING	AGINNRT	RANTING	AGJLMOS	LOGJAMS
AGILLOR	GORILLA	AGINNRW	WARNING	AGJLRUU	JUGULAR
AGILLRU	LIGULAR	AGINNRY	YARNING	AGJNORS	JARGONS
AGILLSU	LUGSAIL	AGINNSW	AWNINGS	AGKLNSU	LUGANSK
AGILMNP	PALMING	AGINNTW	WANTING	AGKORST	GO-KARTS
AGILMNT	MALTING	AGINNWY	YAWNING	AGLLNOO	GALLOON
AGILMNU	MAULING	AGINOOP	POGONIA	AGLLNOS	GALLONS

AGLLNTU	GALLNUT, NUTGALL	AHIILSW	SWAHILI	AHKMORR	MARKHOR
AGLLOPS	GALLOPS	AHIINPR	HAIRPIN	AHKNPSU	PUNKAHS
AGLLOSS	GLOSSAL	AHIINRT	THIN AIR	AHKNRTY	KATHRYN
AGLLOSU	GALLOUS	AHIIPRS	AIRSHIP	AHLLMSU	MULLAHS
AGLLOSW	GALLOWS	AHIKLSY	SHAKILY	AHLLOPS	SHALLOP
AGLLOTT	GLOTTAL	AHIKMNS	KHAMSIN	AHLLOST	SHALLOT
AGLMORU	GLAMOUR	AHIKMRS	KASHMIR	AHLLOSW	SHALLOW
AGLNOOS	LAGOONS	AHIKMSW	MAWKISH	AHLLOTY	LOATHLY, TALLYHO
AGLNOOW	OWN GOAL	AHIKNOS	KHOISAN	AHLLPSU	PHALLUS
AGLNOPS	GOSPLAN	AHIKNRS	KRISHNA	AHLLPYY	APHYLLY
AGLNORU	LANGUOR	AHIKNSV	KNAVISH	AHLLRST	THRALLS
AGLNOSS	SLOGANS	AHIKNSW	HAWKINS	AHLLSTU	THALLUS
AGLNOUY	LUOYANG	AHIKOSU	HOKUSAI	AHLMNPY	NYMPHAL
AGLNPSY	SPANGLY	AHILLNT	ANT HILL	AHLMNSY	HYMNALS
AGLNRUU	UNGULAR	AHILLRY	HILLARY	AHLMNUY	HUMANLY
AGLOOPY	APOLOGY	AHILLST	TALLISH	AHLMORU	HUMORAL
AGMMNSU	MAGNUMS	AHILNPS	PLANISH	AHLMOSW	OHM'S LAW
AGMNORU	ORGANUM	AHILORY	HOARILY	AHLMSUU	HAMULUS
AGMNOTU	MONTAGU	AHILPPY	HAPPILY	AHLNOPR	ALPHORN
AGMNSTU	MUSTANG	AHILSSV	SLAVISH	AHLNORT	ALTHORN
AGMNSTY	GYMNAST	AHILSTY	HASTILY	AHLORST	HARLOTS
AGMNSYY	SYNGAMY	AHILTTZ	HAZLITT	AHLOTUU	OUTHAUL
AGMOPRR	PROGRAM	AHIMMRS	RAMMISH	AHLPRSY	SHARPLY
AGMORRW	RAGWORM	AHIMNNS	MANNISH	AHLPSSU	LASH-UPS
AGMORSS	ORGASMS	AHIMNNU	INHUMAN	AHLPSSY	SPLASHY
AGMPRSU	GRAMPUS	AHIMPSS	MISHAPS	AHMMMOT	MAMMOTH
AGNNNOO	NONAGON	AHIMRST	MITHRAS	AHMNNTU	MANHUNT
AGNNNOT	NANTONG	AHIMSSU	HASSIUM	AHMNOPT	HAMPTON,
AGNNNTU	NANTUNG	AHIMTUZ	AZIMUTH	PHANTOM	
AGNNOOP	GO NAP ON	AHIMTVZ	MITZVAH	AHMNORU	MANHOUR
AGNNOOR	ORGANON,	AHINNTX	XANTHIN	AHMNORY	HARMONY
RANGOON		AHINOOR	HONORIA	AHMNOSS	HANSOMS
AGNNTTU	TAN-TUNG	AHINOST	ONITSHA	AHMNOSU	HOUSMAN
AGNOQSU	QUANGOS	AHINOTZ	HOATZIN	AHMNOSW	SHOWMAN
AGNORRT	GRANTOR	AHINPRS	HARPINS	AHMOOPS	SHAMPOO
AGNORSS	SARONGS	AHINPSS	SPANISH	AHMOSTU	MAHOUTS
AGNOSTU	NOUGATS	AHINPST	HATPINS	AHMPSSU	SMASH-UP
AGOPPST	STOPGAP	AHINRST	TARNISH	AHNNNOS	SHANNON
AGORRTW	RAGWORT	AHINRSV	VARNISH	AHNNOTY	ANTHONY
AGORRTY	GYRATOR	AHINSTT	TIN HATS	AHNOOPR	HARPOON
AGORSTU	RAGOUTS	AHIOORT	HORATIO	AHNOPRS	ORPHANS
AGORTTU	TORTUGA	AHIORRT	HARRIOT	AHNORRS	SHARRON
AGOSUYZ	AZYGOUS	AHIPRST	HARPIST	AHNORSX	SAXHORN
AGPRSSU	GRASS UP	AHIPRSW	WARSHIP	AHNOSTU	SHANTOU
AGRUUUY	URUGUAY	AHIPSSW	WASPISH	AHNOTTW	WHATNOT
AHHHISS	HASHISH	AHIPSWW	WHIPSAW	AHNPPUY	UNHAPPY
AHHIKSW	HAWKISH	AHIPSWY	SHIPWAY	AHNPRXY	PHARYNX
AHHIMNU	HAHNIUM	AHIRRSS	SIRRAHS	AHOORSY	HOORAYS
AHHKOOS	HOOKAHS	AHIRSTT	RATTISH	AHOPRTY	ATROPHY
AHHKSTY	SHAKHTY	AHIRSTW	WRAITHS	AHOPSTT	TOP HATS
AHHLRSY	HARSHLY	AHISTTW	WHATSIT	AHOPTTW	TOWPATH
AHHOPRT	HAP'ORTH	AHKKORV	KHARKOV	AHORRSW	HARROWS
AHHORTW	HAWORTH	AHKLNSY	SHANKLY	AHORSTT	THROATS
AHIIKNT	HAITINK	AHKLTUY	HAKLUYT	AHORSTU	AUTHORS

AHORTTY	THROATY	AIINSTU	TUNISIA	AILMPST	PALMIST
AHOSTUW	OUTWASH, WASHOUT	AIIOOTV	VOIOTIA	AILMPSY	MISPLAY
		AIIOPRR	A PRIORI	AILMRST	MISTRAL
AHPRRTY	PHRATRY	AIIOPST	PISTOIA	AILMRSU	SIMULAR
AHQSSUY	SQUASHY	AIIORTV	VITORIA	AILMSSS	MISSALS
AHRRSUY	HURRAYS	AIIPSTW	WAPITIS	AILNNOT	ANTLION
AHRSSSU	HUSSARS	AIISSVV	VIS-A-VIS	AILNORT	ON TRIAL
AHRSTWY	SWARTHY	AIJJMMS	JIMJAMS	AILNOSV	NOVALIS
AHRTUWY	THRUWAY	AIJLTTU	JULITTA	AILNOUV	LOUVAIN
AIIILMT	MILITIA	AIJLYZZ	JAZZILY	AILNPST	PLAINTS
AIIILNT	INITIAL	AIJNORT	JANITOR	AILNPSX	SALPINX
AIIJLLN	JILLIAN	AIJNSTU	JUSTINA	AILNPTU	NUPTIAL
AIIJNNT	TIANJIN	AIKLLNY	LANKILY	AILNPTY	INAPTLY, PTYALIN
AIIKLNN	KALININ	AIKLMMN	MILKMAN	AILNQTU	QUINTAL
AIIKMMS	SKIMMIA	AIKLMNN	LINKMAN	AILNRSU	INSULAR, URINALS
AIIKMNN	MANIKIN	AIKLMOO	MOLOKAI	AILNSTY	NASTILY, SAINTLY
AIIKSTU	KUTAISI	AIKLNSY	SNAKILY	AILNTTY	NATTILY
AIIKTUW	KUWAITI	AIKLOST	SIALKOT	AILOPRS	POLARIS
AIILLLN	LILLIAN	AIKLPWY	PAWKILY	AILOPST	APOSTIL, TOPSAIL
AIILLLS	LILLIAS	AIKLQUY	QUAKILY	AILOPSY	SOAPILY
AIILLMN	LIMINAL	AIKLSSY	SKYSAIL	AILOPTT	TALIPOT
AIILLMW	WILLIAM	AIKMNNS	KINSMAN	AILOPTV	PIVOTAL
AIILLNV	VILLAIN	AIKMRUY	KUMAYRI	AILOQTU	ALIQUOT
AIILMMN	MINIMAL	AIKNNPS	NAPKINS	AILORSS	SAILORS
AIILMNT	INTIMAL	AIKORST	TROIKAS	AILORST	TAILORS
AIILMRS	SIMILAR	AILLMOP	PALM OIL	AILORUX	UXORIAL
AIILMRY	MILIARY	AILLMPU	PALLIUM	AILORVY	OLIVARY
AIILNNS	AISLINN	AILLMSW	SAWMILL	AILOSSU	SAO LUIS
AIILNOS	LIAISON	AILLNNO	LANOLIN	AILPPSY	PAYSLIP, SAPPILY
AIILNOV	LIVONIA	AILLNNT	TALLINN	AILPRSS	SPIRALS
AIILNPT	PINTAIL	AILLNOS	ALLISON	AILPRSU	SPIRULA
AIILNRY	RAINILY	AILLNPY	PLAINLY	AILPSTU	PAULIST
AIILNTY	ANILITY	AILLNST	INSTALL	AILPSTY	PASTILY
AIILORV	RAVIOLI	AILLORZ	ZORILLA	AILPSWY	SLIPWAY, WASPILY
AIILOTT	OTTILIA	AILLPRS	PILLARS	AILQTUY	QUALITY
AIILQSU	SILIQUA	AILLPRU	PILULAR	AILRRVY	RIVALRY
AIILRTV	TRIVIAL	AILLPUV	PLUVIAL	AILRSTT	STARLIT
AIIMMNS	ANIMISM	AILLQSU	SQUILLA	AILRSTU	RITUALS
AIIMMNX	MAXIMUM, MINIMAX	AILLSTY	SALTILY	AILRSTY	TRYSAIL
AIIMNPS	PIANISM	AILLTVY	VITALLY	AILRTTU	TITULAR
AIIMNPT	TIMPANI	AILMMOR	IMMORAL	AILRTTY	RATTILY
AIIMNRT	MARTINI	AILMMSY	MYALISM	AILRTUV	VIRTUAL
AIIMNSS	SIMIANS	AILMNNO	NOMINAL	AILSTTW	SALT WIT
AIIMNST	ANIMIST	AILMNOY	ALIMONY	AILSTTY	TASTILY
AIIMNTV	VITAMIN	AILMNPS	PLASMIN	AILSTUV	VISTULA
AIIMSSY	MYIASIS	AILMNPT	IMPLANT	AILSTUW	LAWSUIT
AIINNTY	INANITY	AILMNRS	MARLINS	AILTTTY	TATTILY
AIINORV	IVORIAN	AILMNRY	MARILYN	AILTTUU	TUTUILA
AIINPRS	ASPIRIN	AILMOOV	MOVIOLA	AIMMMUX	MAXIMUM
AIINPST	PIANIST	AILMOPT	OPTIMAL	AIMMNSU	SAMNIUM
AIINRSS	RAISINS	AILMOPY	OLYMPIA	AIMMORZ	MIZORAM
AIINRST	ISTRIAN	AILMOST	SOMITAL	AIMMOST	ATOMISM
AIINRSY	RAISINY	AILMOZZ	MILAZZO	AIMMRSX	MARXISM
AIINRTV	VITRAIN	AILMPRU	PRIMULA	AIMMSUX	MAXIMUS

AIMNNOS	MANSION	AINRTTT	TITRANT	AKQSSUW	SQUAWKS
AIMNOPR	RAMPION	AINRTUY	UNITARY	ALLLOYY	LOYALLY
AIMNOPT	MAINTOP	AINSSTU	SUSTAIN	ALLMNOY	ALLONYM
AIMNOTU	TINAMOU	AIOORRS	ROSARIO	ALLMNPU	PULLMAN
AIMNPRU	MANIPUR	AIOPRRT	AIRPORT	ALLMORY	MALLORY,
AIMNRRU	MURRAIN	AIOPRRU	PORIRUA	MORALLY	
AIMNRST	MARTINS	AIOPRTT	PATRIOT	ALLMOSS	SLALOMS
AIMNRSU	SURINAM	AIOPRTY	TOPIARY	ALLMOSW	MALLOWS
AIMNRTV	VARMINT	AIOPRUV	PAVIOUR	ALLNOOW	WALLOON
AIMNRUU	URANIUM	AIOPSTU	UTOPIAS	ALLNOYZ	ZONALLY
AIMNSTT	MATTINS	AIORRRW	WARRIOR	ALLNTUU	ULULANT
AIMNSTU	TSUNAMI	AIORRTT	TRAITOR	ALLOOTX	AXOLOTL
AIMOPRX	PROXIMA	AIORSTV	TRAVOIS	ALLOPRY	PAYROLL
AIMOPST	IMPASTO	AIORSUV	SAVIOUR, VARIOUS	ALLOPSW	WALLOPS
AIMORST	AMORIST	AIOSSTT	TAOISTS	ALLOPTX	POLL TAX
AIMOSST	MAOISTS	AIPPSST	PAPISTS	ALLORWY	ROLLWAY
AIMOSTT	ATOMIST	AIPRRTU	TRIPURA	ALLORYY	ROYALLY
AIMPRRY	PRIMARY	AIPRSST	RAPISTS	ALLOSSW	SALLOWS
AIMPRST	ARMPITS	AIPRSSU	PRUSSIA	ALLOSWW	SWALLOW,
AIMQRSU	MARQUIS	AIPRSSW	RIPSAWS	WALLOWS	
AIMRSTX	MARXIST	AIPZZZZ	PIZZAZZ	ALLOTTY	TOTALLY
AIMSSTT	STATISM	AIRSSTT	ARTISTS, STRAITS,	ALLOTYY	LOYALTY
AINNOOT	ANTONIO	TSARIST		ALLPRSU	PLURALS
AINNOOX	OXONIAN	AIRSTVY	VARSITY	ALLQSSU	SQUALLS
AINNOPS	SAPONIN	AISSTTT	STATIST	ALLQSUY	SQUALLY
AINNOST	NATIONS	AISTTVY	VASTITY	ALLRSTU	LUSTRAL
AINNQTU	QUINTAN	AISTUVY	SUAVITY	ALLSUUY	USUALLY
AINNRTU	URINANT	AJLLMOR	JAM ROLL	ALMNNUY	UNMANLY
AINNSTT	INSTANT	AJLMORY	MAJORLY	ALMNOOP	LAMPOON
AINNTUY	ANNUITY	AJLNORU	JOURNAL	ALMNOPS	PLASMON
AINOORT	ONTARIO, ORATION	AJMNRUY	JURYMAN	ALMNORU	UNMORAL
AINOOTV	OVATION	AJNORST	TROJANS	ALMNOSS	SALMONS
AINOOVV	IVANOVO	AKKLRSY	SKYLARK	ALMNOSU	SOLANUM
AINOPPT	APPOINT	AKKSTUY	YAKUTSK	ALMNOWY	WOMANLY
AINOPSS	PASSION	AKLLNOW	KNOW-ALL	ALMNPSU	SUNLAMP
AINOPTU	OPUNTIA, UTOPIAN	AKLMNOO	KOLOMNA	ALMNSSU	ALUMNUS
AINORST	RATIONS	AKLNOSW	WALK-ONS	ALMORRU	MORULAR
AINORTU	RAINOUT, TOURNAI	AKLNOSX	KLAXONS	ALMORST	MORTALS
AINOSTT	STATION	AKLOPUV	VOLAPUK	ALMOTTU	MULATTO
AINOSUX	ANXIOUS	AKLOTTU	OUTTALK	ALMRSTY	SMARTLY
AINOSVY	SYNOVIA	AKLOTUW	WALKOUT	ALMRTUU	TUMULAR
AINPPRS	PARSNIP	AKLPSUW	WALK-UPS	ALMSSUY	ALYSSUM, ASYLUMS
AINPQTU	PIQUANT	AKLRSTY	STARKLY	ALMSTUU	UMLAUTS
AINPRSS	SPRAINS	AKLUUWZ	KWAZULU	ALNNRSU	UNSNARL
AINPRST	SPIRANT	AKMNORU	RUN AMOK	ALNNSUU	ANNULUS
AINPRTU	PURITAN	AKMNORW	WORKMAN	ALNOOPT	PLATOON
AINQRTU	TARQUIN	AKMORST	OSTMARK	ALNOORT	ORTOLAN
AINQRUY	QUINARY	AKMPRSU	MARKUPS	ALNOOSS	SALOONS
AINRRTY	TRINARY	AKMQTUU	KUMQUAT	ALNOPPY	PANOPLY
AINRRUY	URINARY	AKMRSTU	MUSKRAT	ALNOPYY	POLYNYA
AINRSST	STRAINS	AKNORTU	OUTRANK	ALNORSY	ROSALYN
AINRSSU	RUSSIAN	AKOOPRT	PARTOOK	ALNORUZ	ZONULAR
AINRSTT	TRANSIT, TRISTAN	AKORRTW	ARTWORK	ALNPRSU	SNARL-UP
AINRSTU	NUTRIAS	AKORWWX	WAXWORK	ALNSSTU	SULTANS
				ALNSTUW	WALNUTS

ALNSUUU	UNUSUAL	AMOORSU	AMOROUS	ARSSTTU	STRATUS
ALOOPRW	POOR LAW	AMOPSTT	TOPMAST	BBBDELU	BUBBLED
ALOORTT	TORTOLA	AMORRST	MORTARS	BBBEIOS	BOBBIES
ALOPPRS	POPLARS	AMORRSW	MARROWS	BBBELOS	BOBBLES
ALOPPRU	POPULAR	AMORRUY	ARMOURY	BBBELRU	BLUBBER, BUBBLER
ALOPRRU	PARLOUR	AMPRSUW	WARM-UPS	BBBELSU	BUBBLES
ALOPRST	PATROLS, PORTALS	AMRRSTY	MARTYRS	BBBEORY	BOBBERY
ALOPRSU	PARLOUS	AMRRTYY	MARTYRY	BBBGINO	BOBBING
ALOPSSU	SPOUSAL	AMRSTTU	STRATUM	BBBINOS	BOBBINS
ALOPSTT	SALTPOT	ANNOTTU	TAUNTON	BBCCIKO	BIBCOCK
ALOPTUY	OUTPLAY	ANNRTYY	TYRANNY	BBCDEIR	CRIBBED
ALOQRRU	RORQUAL	ANNSSTU	SUNTANS	BBCDELO	COBBLED
ALOQRSU	SQUALOR	ANNTUUV	NUNAVUT	BBCDELU	CLUBBED
ALOQSTU	LOQUATS	ANOOPRS	SOPRANO	BBCELOR	CLOBBER, COBBLER
ALORRST	ROSTRAL	ANOORTT	OTRANTO	BBCEORS	COBBERS
ALORTWW	AWLWORT	ANOPRRS	SPORRAN	BBCEOSW	COBWEBS
ALORTYY	ROYALTY	ANOPRSS	PARSONS	BBCGINU	CUBBING
ALOSTTU	OUTLAST	ANOPRST	PATRONS	BBCINOU	BUBONIC
ALOSTUW	OUTLAWS	ANORRSW	NARROWS	BBCJLOU	JOBCLUB
ALOSTUY	LAYOUTS, OUTLAYS	ANORSUU	ANUROUS,	BBCKLOU	LUBBOCK
ALOSTXY	OXYSALT		URANOUS	BBCRSUY	SCRUBBY
ALOTTUU	TUTUOLA	ANPRSTU	SUNTRAP, UNSTRAP	BBDDEIL	DIBBLED
ALPRSSU	PULSARS	ANRSSTU	SUNSTAR	BBDEEIT	EBB TIDE
ALPRSSW	SPRAWLS	ANRSTTU	TRUANTS	BBDEGLO	GOBBLED
ALPRSWY	SPRAWLY	ANRSTTY	TYRANTS	BBDEGRU	GRUBBED
ALRSTUU	SUTURAL	ANRSUWY	RUNWAYS	BBDEGSU	BEDBUGS
ALRSUUV	UVULARS	AOOPPRS	APROPOS, SAPPORO	BBDEHLO	HOBBLED
AMMNRUY	NUMMARY	AOOPRTT	TAPROOT	BBDEIIM	IMBIBED
AMMORST	MARMOTS	AOORRST	ORATORS	BBDEILN	NIBBLED
AMMRSUY	SUMMARY	AOORRTT	ROTATOR	BBDEILO	LOBBIED
AMNNORS	NORMANS	AOORRTU	ROTORUA	BBDEILR	DIBBLER, DRIBBLE
AMNNOSW	SNOWMAN	AOORRTY	ORATORY	BBDEILS	DIBBLES
AMNNOTY	ANTONYM	AOOSTTT	TATTOOS	BBDELMU	BUMBLED
AMNOOPP	POMPANO	AOPPRRT	RAPPORT	BBDELNO	NOBBLED
AMNOORS	MAROONS	AOPPRTU	UP TO PAR	BBDELOS	BOBSLED
AMNOOTT	OTTOMAN	AOPRRST	PARROTS	BBDELOW	WOBBLED
AMNOOTY	TOO MANY	AOPRRSW	SPARROW	BBDELRU	BURBLED
AMNOPRY	PARONYM	AOPRRTY	PORTRAY	BBDENSU	SNUBBED
AMNOPSS	SAMPSON	AOPRSST	PASTORS	BBDERRU	DRUBBER
AMNOPST	POSTMAN,	AOPRSTW	POSTWAR	BBDESTU	STUBBED
	TAMPONS	AOPRSUV	VAPOURS	BBDGIIN	DIBBING
AMNOPTU	PANTOUM	AOPSTUY	AUTOPSY, PAYOUTS	BBDGINU	DUBBING
AMNORSS	RAMSONS,	AOQRSTU	QUARTOS	BBEEENT	ENTEBBE
	RANSOMS	AOQRTUY	TORQUAY	BBEELPS	PEBBLES
AMNORST	MATRONS,	AORSSUY	OSSUARY	BBEESTT	BEST BET
	TRANSOM	AORSTTW	AT WORST,	BBEESUY	BUSY BEE
AMNORSY	MASONRY		TWO-STAR	BBEESYY	BYE-BYES
AMNOSTU	AMOUNTS	AORSUVY	SAVOURY	BBEFILR	FRIBBLE
AMNPTTU	PUTTNAM	AORTTUY	OUT-TRAY	BBEFIRS	FIBBERS
AMNQTUU	QUANTUM	AOSTTUY	OUTSTAY	BBEGILR	GLIBBER, GRIBBLE
AMNRTTU	TANTRUM	APPRRUU	PURPURA	BBEGINW	WEBBING
AMNSTTU	MUTANTS	APPRSUY	PAPYRUS	BBEGIST	GIBBETS
AMNSTUU	AUTUMNS	APRSSSU	SURPASS	BBEGLOR	GOBBLER
AMOOORS	AMOROSO	APRSTTU	UPSTART	BBEGLOS	GOBBLES
AMOOPRT	TAPROOM	APRSTUU	UT SUPRA		

BBEGOST	GOBBETS	BBIKOSS	SKIBOBS	BCEHIOT	BIOTECH
BBEGRRU	GRUBBER	BBIKTUZ	KIBBUTZ	BCEHIRS	BIRCHES
BBEHIOS	HOBBIES	BBINORS	RIBBONS	BCEHIST	BITCHES
BBEHISU	HUBBIES	BBKLNOY	KNOBBLY	BCEHISW	WISBECH
BBEHLOR	HOBBLER	BBLOSUU	BULBOUS	BCEHITW	BEWITCH
BBEIIMR	IMBIBER	BBLSTUY	STUBBLY	BCEHNSU	BUNCHES
BBEILNR	NIBBLER	BBNNOOS	BONBONS	BCEHORT	BOTCHER
BBEILNS	NIBBLES	BBNOORU	BOURBON	BCEHORW	COWHERB
BBEILOS	BILBOES, LOBBIES	BBOSSUY	BUS BOYS	BCEHRSU	CHERUBS
BBEILOT	BIBELOT	BBRSSUU	SUBURBS	BCEHRTU	BUTCHER
BBEILQU	QUIBBLE	BCCEILO	ECBOLIC	BCEILMO	EMBOLIC
BBEILRS	LIBBERS	BCCEILU	CUBICLE	BCEILMR	CLIMBER
BBEIOOS	BOOBIES	BCCEILY	BICYCLE	BCEILOR	BRICOLE, CORBEIL
BBEIRRY	BRIBERY	BCCIIMR	CIMBRIC	BCEIMNO	COMBINE
BBEIRTU	TUBBIER	BCCILOU	BUCOLIC	BCEIMOR	MICROBE
BBEISSU	BUSBIES	BCCINOO	OBCONIC	BCEINOZ	BENZOIC
BBEJORS	JOBBERS	BCCISUU	SUCCUBI	BCEINRU	BRUCINE
BBEJORY	JOBBERY	BCCMOOX	COXCOMB	BCEIRRS	SCRIBER
BBEKLOS	BLESBOK	BCCMSUU	SUCCUMB	BCEIRSS	SCRIBES
BBELLOY	BELLBOY	BCCNOOR	CORNCOB	BCEJOST	OBJECTS
BBELMRU	BUMBLER	BCDEEHL	BELCHED	BCEJSTU	SUBJECT
BBELNOR	NOBBLER	BCDEEIL	DECIBEL	BCEKLRU	BUCKLER
BBELORS	SLOBBER	BCDEHIR	BIRCHED	BCEKLSU	BUCKLES
BBELORW	WOBBLER	BCDEHIT	BITCHED	BCEKORT	BROCKET
BBELORY	LOBBYER	BCDEHNU	BUNCHED	BCEKORU	ROEBUCK
BBELOSW	WOBBLES	BCDEHOT	BOTCHED	BCEKSTU	BUCKETS
BBELRRU	BURBLER	BCDEHOU	DEBOUCH	BCELLOW	COWBELL
BBELSTU	STUBBLE	BCDEIIO	BIOCIDE	BCELMRU	CRUMBLE
BBEMORS	BOMBERS	BCDEIKS	SICKBED	BCELMSU	SCUMBLE
BBENRSU	SNUBBER	BCDEILM	CLIMBED	BCELORS	CORBELS
BBEORRS	ROBBERS	BCDEIOS	BODICES	BCELORT	COLBERT
BBEORRY	ROBBERY	BCDEKLO	BLOCKED	BCEMORS	COMBERS
BBERRSU	RUBBERS	BCDEKLU	BUCKLED	BCENORU	BOUNCER
BBERRUY	RUBBERY	BCDEKOR	BEDROCK	BCENOSU	BOUNCES
BBFGIIN	FIBBING	BCDENOU	BOUNCED	BCEOORT	OCTOBER
BBFGINO	FOBBING	BCDIIRU	RUBIDIC	BCEORSU	OBSCURE
BBGGIIN	GIBBING	BCDINOW	COWBIND	BCFSSUU	SUBFUSC
BBGIIJN	JIBBING	BCDIORW	COWBIRD	BCGIKNU	BUCKING
BBGIINR	RIBBING	BCDKORU	BURDOCK	BCGIMNO	COMBING
BBGIJNO	JOBBING	BCDSTUU	SUBDUCT	BCGINRU	CURBING
BBGILNO	LOBBING	BCEEEHS	BEECHES, BESEECH	BCHIINT	BITCHIN'
BBGIMNO	BOMBING,	BCEEELS	CELEBES	BCHIKOU	CHIBOUK
	MOBBING	BCEEGIR	ICEBERG	BCHIMOR	RHOMBIC
BBGINOO	BOOBING	BCEEHIT	HEBETIC	BCHINOR	BRONCHI
BBGINOR	ROBBING	BCEEHLS	BELCHES	BCHIOPR	PIBROCH
BBGINOS	GIBBONS, SOBBING	BCEEHNR	BENCHER	BCHIOPS	PHOBICS
BBGINRU	RUBBING	BCEEHNS	BENCHES	BCHKOOY	BOK CHOY
BBGINSU	SUBBING	BCEEHOU	BOUCHEE	BCHLOTY	BLOTCHY
BBGINTU	TUBBING	BCEEILR	LIBEREC	BCHOPTU	BOTCH-UP
BBGIOSU	GIBBOUS	BCEEINR	BERNICE	BCHORST	BORSCHT
BBHIMOS	HOBBISM	BCEEKTT	BECKETT	BCIINOS	BIONICS
BBHIOST	HOBBIST	BCEEKUY	BUCKEYE	BCIIOPS	BIOPICS
BBHIRSU	RUBBISH	BCEENOS	OBSCENE	BCIIOPT	BIOPTIC
BBHRSUY	SHRUBBY	BCEHIOR	BRIOCHE	BCIISTU	BISCUIT

BCIKKRU	KUBRICK	BDEEKRU	REBUKED	BDEITUY	DUBIETY
BCILMPU	PLUMBIC	BDEELNR	BLENDER	BDEJLMU	JUMBLED
BCINORU	RUBICON	BDEELOV	BELOVED	BDEKNOO	BOOKEND
BCINORY	BYRONIC	BDEELOW	ELBOWED	BDEKOOR	BROOKED, RED
BCINSUU	INCUBUS	BDEELRT	TREBLED	BOOK	
BCIORST	STROBIC	BDEELSS	BLESSED	BDELMMU	MUMBLED
BCIRRSU	RUBRICS	BDEEMSU	BEMUSED	BDELMOO	BLOOMED
BCIRTUY	BUTYRIC	BDEENPR	PREBEND	BDELMPU	PLUMBED
BCKLLOU	BULLOCK	BDEEORS	BEDSORE, SOBERED	BDELMRU	RUMBLED
BCKOTTU	BUTTOCK	BDEEOTW	WEB-TOED	BDELMTU	TUMBLED
BCLMOOO	COLOMBO	BDEERUW	BURWEED	BDELNOR	BLONDER
BCLMOOU	COULOMB	BDEFFLU	BLUFFED	BDELNOS	BLONDES
BCLMRUY	CRUMBLY	BDEFLMU	FUMBLED	BDELNOW	BLODWEN
BCLOOSU	COLOBUS	BDEGGLO	BOGGLED	BDELNRU	BLUNDER, BUNDLER
BCMOOTU	COMB-OUT	BDEGILO	OBLIGED	BDELNSU	BUNDLES
BCMOSTU	COMBUST	BDEGINN	BENDING	BDELNTU	BLUNTED
BCNOORS	BRONCOS	BDEGINO	BENDIGO	BDELORU	BOULDER, DOUBLER
BCOOSWY	COWBOYS	BDEGINS	BIG ENDS	BDELOST	BOLDEST
BCOOTTY	BOYCOTT	BDEGIOT	BIGOTED	BDELOSU	DOUBLES
BDDEEES	SEEDBED	BDEGIRT	BRIDGET	BDELOTT	BLOTTED, BOTTLED
BDDEEEW	BEDEWED	BDEGLNU	BUNGLED	BDELOTU	DOUBLET
BDDEEIS	BEDSIDE	BDEGLRU	BURGLED	BDELOUW	WOULD-BE
BDDEEIT	BETIDED, DEBITED	BDEGOOY	GOODBYE	BDELRRU	BLURRED
BDDEELN	BLENDED	BDEGSTU	BUDGETS	BDELRTU	BLURTED
BDDEFOR	BEDFORD	BDEHINS	BEHINDS	BDELSTU	BUSTLED
BDDEGIN	BEDDING	BDEHLMU	HUMBLED	BDEMOOR	BEDROOM,
BDDEILN	BLINDED	BDEHLSU	BLUSHED	BOREDOM	
BDDEISU	BUDDIES	BDEHMTU	THUMBED	BDEMSTU	DUMBEST
BDDELNU	BUNDLED	BDEHOST	HOTBEDS	BDENNOU	BOUNDEN,
BDDELOO	BLOODED	BDEHRSU	BRUSHED	UNBONED	
BDDELOU	DOUBLED	BDEIIRS	BIRDIES	BDENORU	BOUNDER,
BDDENOU	BOUNDED	BDEIKLN	BLINKED	REBOUND	
BDDEOOR	BROODED	BDEILLR	ILL-BRED	BDENORW	BROWNED
BDDEOTU	DOUBTED	BDEILLU	BULLIED	BDENORY	BONE-DRY
BDDESUU	SUBDUED	BDEILNR	BRINDLE	BDENORZ	BRONZED
BDDGIIN	BIDDING	BDEILOR	BROILED	BDENOUW	UNBOWED
BDDGINU	BUDDING	BDEILRT	DRIBLET	BDENRSU	BURDENS
BDDGIOR	BIRD DOG	BDEILRU	BUILDER, REBUILD	BDENSSU	SUNBEDS
BDEEELP	BLEEPED	BDEILTZ	BLITZED	BDENSTU	SUBTEND
BDEEELR	BLEEDER	BDEIMOR	BROMIDE	BDEOORR	BROODER
BDEEELT	BEETLED	BDEINOU	BEDOUIN	BDEOOST	BOOSTED
BDEEELV	BEVELED	BDEINRS	BINDERS	BDEOPST	BEDPOST
BDEEERR	BREEDER	BDEINRY	BINDERY	BDEORRS	BORDERS
BDEEERT	RED BEET	BDEINTW	TWIN BED	BDEORRU	BORDURE
BDEEFIR	DEBRIEF	BDEIORS	DISROBE	BDEORST	DEBTORS
BDEEGUY	BUG-EYED	BDEIORT	ORBITED	BDEORSU	ROSEBUD
BDEEHRT	BERTHED	BDEIORV	OVERBID	BDEORSW	BROWSED
BDEEILL	LIBELED	BDEIOSY	DISOBEY	BDEORTU	DOUBTER, OBTRUDE,
BDEEILO	EL OBEID	BDEIOWY	WIDE BOY	REDOUBT	
BDEEILV	BEDEVIL	BDEIRST	BESTRID	BDFIIOR	FIBROID
BDEEIMT	BEDTIME	BDEIRSU	BRUISED	BDGGINU	BUDGING
BDEEINR	INBREED	BDEIRTU	BRUITED	BDGHIIR	BRIGHID
BDEEIRS	DERBIES	BDEISSU	SUBSIDE	BDGIINN	BINDING
BDEEISS	BESIDES	BDEISTU	SUBEDIT	BDGIIOO	GOBIOID
				BDGILOO	GLOBOID

BDGINNO	BONDING	BEEFIRS	FRISBEE	BEENOST	BONESET
BDGLLOU	BULLDOG	BEEFLOR	FROEBEL	BEEOOST	BOOTEES
BDHIRSY	HYBRIDS	BEEFLTY	BEETFLY	BEEORSV	OBSERVE, OBVERSE,
BDHOOOY	BOYHOOD	BEEGILL	LEGIBLE		VERBOSE
BDIILOR	OILBIRD	BEEGILO	OBLIGEE	BEEORWY	EYEBROW
BDIILOS	LIBIDOS	BEEGILU	BEGUILE	BEEQSTU	BEQUEST
BDIISTT	TIDBITS	BEEGINR	BIGENER	BEERRWY	BREWERY
BDIKNOS	BODKINS	BEEGJRS	ESBJERG	BEERSSU	REBUSES
BDILLNY	BLINDLY	BEEGLMR	LEMBERG	BEERSTT	BETTERS
BDILPUU	BUILDUP, UPBUILD	BEEHLLT	BETHELL	BEERSTW	BESTREW
BDIMNUU	DUBNIUM	BEEHLRT	BLETHER	BEERTTU	BURETTE
BDINNOU	INBOUND	BEEHLST	BETHELS	BEFFLRU	BLUFFER
BDINOOR	BRIDOON	BEEHRRT	HERBERT	BEFFOST	BEST-OFF
BDINOTU	IN DOUBT	BEEHRST	SHERBET	BEFFRSU	BUFFERS, REBUFFS
BDINRSU	SUNBIRD	BEEHRSW	HEBREWS	BEFFSTU	BUFFETS
BDINRUU	BURUNDI	BEEHRTY	THEREBY	BEFGIIL	FILIBEG
BDINSTU	DUSTBIN	BEEHRWY	WHEREBY	BEFGIRU	FIREBUG
BDIOOOV	OBOVOID	BEEIJLU	JUBILEE	BEFILOS	FOIBLES
BDIOORU	BOUDOIR	BEEILLS	BELLIES	BEFILOU	BIOFUEL
BDIOSUU	DUBIOUS	BEEILOS	OBELISE	BEFILRT	FILBERT
BDIRSTU	DISTURB	BEEILOZ	OBELIZE	BEFILSU	FUSIBLE
BDISSUY	SUBSIDY	BEEIMST	BETIMES	BEFINOR	BONFIRE
BDLOOOT	OLD BOOT	BEEINNZ	BENZINE	BEFIORX	FIREBOX
BDLOOOX	OXBLOOD	BEEINOS	EBONISE	BEFIRVY	VERBIFY
BDLOOSY	OLD BOYS	BEEINOT	EBONITE	BEFITUX	TUBIFEX
BDLORWY	BLOW-DRY	BEEINOZ	EBONIZE	BEFLMRU	FUMBLER
BDNNOUU	UNBOUND	BEEINRZ	ZEBRINE	BEFLMSU	FUMBLES
BDNOORU	BOURDON	BEEIQUZ	BEZIQUE	BEFLORT	BELFORT
BDNOOWW	DOWN-BOW	BEEIRRS	BERRIES	BEFLRTU	FULBERT
BDNORUW	RUBDOWN	BEEIRRV	BREVIER	BEFOORR	FORBORE
BDOOOWX	BOXWOOD	BEEIRST	BISERTE	BEFOOTW	WEBFOOT
BDORSWY	BYWORDS	BEEIRTZ	BIZERTE	BEGGGIN	BEGGING
BDRSUUY	SUDBURY	BEEKNOT	BETOKEN	BEGGIIS	BIGGIES
BEEEFIR	BEEFIER, FREEBIE	BEEKOPS	BESPOKE	BEGGIOR	BOGGIER
BEEEFLR	FEEBLER	BEEKRRS	BERSERK	BEGGIST	BIGGEST
BEEEGIS	BESIEGE	BEEKRRU	REBUKER	BEGGISU	BUGGIES
BEEEHIV	BEEHIVE	BEEKRSU	REBUKES	BEGGRSU	BUGGERS
BEEEHNS	SHEBEEN	BEELMMS	EMBLEMS	BEGGRUY	BUGGERY
BEEEILN	BEELINE	BEELMRT	TREMBLE	BEGHRRU	BURGHER
BEEEILV	BELIEVE	BEELMSS	BLESS ME!	BEGIIJN	BEIJING
BEEEJLW	BEJEWEL	BEELMWY	WEMBLEY	BEGIIMT	BIG TIME
BEEEJLZ	JEZEBEL	BEELNNO	ENNOBLE	BEGIKNR	KERBING
BEEEKLL	BELLEEK	BEELNOR	BORNEEL	BEGILLY	LEGIBLY
BEEELPR	BLEEPER	BEELNTY	BENTLEY	BEGILMU	BELGIUM
BEEELPS	PEEBLES	BEELNUX	BENELUX	BEGILNO	GOBELIN, IGNOBLE
BEEELST	BEETLES	BEELOTY	EYEBOLT	BEGILNT	BELTING
BEEEMRS	BERSEEM	BEELRST	TREBLES	BEGILNU	BLUEING
BEEENNZ	BENZENE	BEELRVY	BEVERLY	BEGILNY	BELYING
BEEENRS	BERNESE	BEEMMRS	MEMBERS	BEGILOR	BROGLIE, OBLIGER
BEEENTW	BETWEEN	BEEMNRU	E NUMBER	BEGILRS	GERBILS
BEEFGIN	BEEFING	BEEMRSU	BURMESE	BEGILRT	GILBERT
BEEFILR	FEBRILE	BEENNRR	BRENNER	BEGILRU	BULGIER
BEEFILS	BELIEFS	BEENNTT	BENNETT	BEGILST	GIBLETS
BEEFINT	BENEFIT	BEENORR	ENROBER	BEGINOY	OBEYING

BEGINRW	BREWING	BEHRSSU	BRUSHES
BEGINSS	BIGNESS	BEIILLS	BILLIES
BEGINST	BESTING	BEIILRS	RISIBLE
BEGINTT	BETTING	BEIILSV	VISIBLE
BEGKMOS	GEMSBOK	BEIINOT	NIOBITE
BEGLLOU	GLOBULE	BEIINST	STIBINE
BEGLMRU	GRUMBLE	BEIIOTT	BIOTITE
BEGLMUU	BLUE GUM	BEIIRTT	BITTIER
BEGLNRU	BLUNGER, BUNGLER	BEIKKLU	KUBELIK
BEGLNSU	BUNGLES	BEIKLNR	BLINKER
BEGLOOS	GLOBOSE	BEIKLOS	OBELISK
BEGLOOT	BOOTLEG	BEIKLRU	BULKIER
BEGLOST	GOBLETS	BEIKRRS	BRISKER
BEGLOUY	BEYOGLU	BEIKRST	BRISKET
BEGLRSU	BUGLERS	BEIKSTV	VITEBSK
BEGNOOS	BONGOES	BEILLST	BILLETS
BEGNORU	BURGEON	BEILLSU	BULLIES
BEGNOSY	BYGONES	BEILMNR	NIMBLER
BEGORSU	BOURGES, BROGUES	BEILMOR	EMBROIL
BEGRRSU	BURGERS	BEILMOS	MOBILES
BEGRSSU	BURGESS	BEILMRT	TIMBREL, TRIMBLE
BEHIITX	EXHIBIT	BEILMRU	UMBRIEL
BEHIKKS	BISHKEK	BEILMSU	SUBLIME
BEHIKLO	HOBLIKE	BEILNOW	BOWLINE
BEHIKNT	BETHINK	BEILNSY	BY-LINES
BEHILLX	BEXHILL	BEILOPY	EPIBOLY
BEHILMS	BLEMISH	BEILOQU	OBLIQUE
BEHILMT	THIMBLE	BEILORR	BROILER
BEHILOS	BOLSHIE	BEILORS	BOILERS
BEHILRT	HILBERT	BEILORW	BLOWIER
BEHILST	LISBETH	BEILRRU	BURLIER
BEHILTZ	LIZBETH	BEILRST	BLISTER, BRISTLE
BEHIMOR	BIOHERM	BEILRTT	BRITTLE
BEHINOP	HIPBONE	BEILRTU	REBUILT
BEHIOTW	HOWBEIT	BEILRTW	WILBERT
BEHIRRT	REBIRTH	BEILRTY	LIBERTY
BEHIRSU	BUSHIER, BUSHIRE	BEILSTW	BLEWITS
BEHKKOO	KOKOBEH	BEILSTZ	BLITZES
BEHKNOO	HOBOKEN	BEILTTU	BLUETIT
BEHLLOX	HELLBOX	BEIMMRR	BRIMMER
BEHLMRU	HUMBLER	BEIMNOR	BROMINE
BEHLORT	BROTHEL	BEIMNTU	BITUMEN
BEHLRSU	BLUSHER	BEIMOSV	B-MOVIES
BEHLSSU	BLUSHES, BUSHELS	BEIMOSZ	ZOMBIES
BEHMOTT	THE TOMB	BEIMPRU	BUMPIER
BEHMRTU	HUMBERT	BEIMRST	TIMBERS, TIMBRES
BEHNOST	BENTHOS	BEIMRTU	IMBRUTE, TERBIUM
BEHNPRU	HEPBURN	BEINNOR	BONNIER
BEHNRTU	BURTHEN	BEINNOZ	BENZOIN
BEHOPRT	POTHERB	BEINNSU	BUNNIES
BEHORRT	BROTHER	BEINOOT	EOBIONT
BEHORTT	BETROTH	BEINORT	BORNITE
BEHOSTY	THE BOYS	BEINORW	BROWNIE
BEHRRSU	BRUSHER	BEINOST	BONIEST

BEINRSU	SUBERIN
BEINRTT	BITTERN
BEINRTU	TRIBUNE, TURBINE
BEIOOPT	BIOTOPE
BEIOORZ	BOOZIER
BEIOPTY	BIOTYPE
BEIORSS	BOSSIER
BEIOSTW	BOW TIES
BEIOSTY	OBESITY
BEIRRSU	BRUISER
BEIRSSU	BRUISES
BEIRSTT	BITTERS
BEIRSTU	BUSTIER
BEIRTTU	TRIBUTE
BEIRTVY	BREVITY
BEISSTU	BUSIEST
BEISTTU	BUTTIES
BEITTWX	BETWIXT
BEJJSUU	JUJUBES
BEJKOUX	JUKEBOX
BEJLMRU	JUMBLER
BEJLMSU	JUMBLES
BEJLOSS	JOBLESS
BEKLNOZ	KOBLENZ
BEKLOOT	BOOKLET
BEKLSUY	BLUE-SKY, SKY-BLUE
BEKNORS	BONKERS
BEKNRSU	BUNKERS
BEKORRS	BROKERS
BEKRSSU	BUSKERS
BELLOSU	SOLUBLE
BELLOSW	BELLOWS
BELLOUV	VOLUBLE
BELLSTU	BULLETS
BELMMRU	MUMBLER
BELMNOU	NELUMBO
BELMOOR	BLOOMER
BELMOPR	PROBLEM
BELMORY	BROMLEY
BELMOSU	EMBOLUS
BELMPRU	PLUMBER
BELMRRU	RUMBLER
BELMRSU	RUMBLES, SLUMBER
BELMRTU	TUMBLER, TUMBREL
BELMRTY	TREMBLY
BELMSTU	STUMBLE, TUMBLES
BELNOOY	BOLONEY
BELNOST	NOBLEST
BELNOYZ	BENZOYL
BELNRUY	BURNLEY
BELNSTU	SUNBELT
BELOOPR	BLOOPER
BELOORS	BOLEROS
BELOOVY	BYELOVO

BELORST	BOLSTER, LOBSTER	BFFNOOU	BUFFOON	BGINOPP	BOPPING
BELORSU	ROUBLES	BFGIORT	FROG-BIT	BGINOPR	PROBING
BELORSW	BLOWERS, BOWLERS	BFHIRSU	FURBISH	BGINOSS	BOSSING
BELORSY	SOBERLY	BFIINOR	FIBROIN	BGINOUY	BUOYING
BELORTT	BLOTTER	BFILMRU	BRIMFUL	BGINPRU	BURPING
BELORTU	TROUBLE	BFIORSU	FIBROUS	BGINRRU	BURRING
BELOSSU	BLOUSES	BFKLOOY	FLYBOOK	BGINRUY	BURYING
BELOSTT	BOTTLES	BFLLOWY	BLOWFLY, FLYBLOW	BGINSSU	BUSSING
BELOSTU	BOLETUS	BFOOOTY	FOOTBOY	BGINSTU	BUSTING
BELRSTU	BLUSTER, BUSTLER,	BGGGINO	BOGGING	BGINSUY	BUSYING
BUTLERS, SUBTLER		BGGGINU	BUGGING	BGINTTU	BUTTING
BELRTUY	BUTLERY	BGGIISW	BIGWIGS	BGINUZZ	BUZZING
BELSSTU	BUSTLES	BGGILNU	BULGING	BGIOPST	BIG TOPS
BEMNRSU	NUMBERS	BGGINNU	BUNGING	BGIORTY	BIGOTRY
BEMORST	MOBSTER	BGHHIOY	HIGHBOY	BGJOTUY	TOBY JUG
BEMORSY	EMBRYOS	BGHILST	BLIGHTS	BGKLOOO	LOGBOOK
BEMPRSU	BUMPERS	BGHINOR	BIGHORN	BGLNOOS	OBLONGS
BEMSSUU	SUBSUME	BGHINSU	BUSHING	BGLNOOW	LONGBOW
BENNORT	BRENTON	BGHINTY	BY NIGHT	BGLOSSU	BUGLOSS
BENNORW	BRONWEN,	BGHIOST	BIG SHOT	BGMOOTU	GUMBOOT
NEWBORN		BGHIPSU	BUSHPIG	BHIIINT	INHIBIT
BENNOST	BONNETS	BGHMORU	HOMBURG	BHIIRST	BRITISH
BENOORS	OSBORNE	BGHMSUU	HUMBUGS	BHIKOOS	BOOKISH
BENORRT	NORBERT	BGHOOOS	OSHOGBO	BHILLSU	BULLISH
BENORRW	BROWNER	BGHOORU	BOROUGH	BHILOTU	HOLIBUT
BENORSZ	BRONZES	BGIIKLN	BILKING	BHILPSU	PUBLISH
BENORTY	RENT BOY	BGIILLN	BILLING	BHIMOOS	HOBOISM
BENOSSU	BONUSES	BGIILNO	BOILING	BHIMOPR	BIMORPH
BENRRSU	BURNERS	BGIILNS	SIBLING	BHIMORU	BOHRIUM
BENRUWY	NEWBURY	BGIIMNU	IMBUING	BHIMSTU	BISMUTH
BEOOPSX	PO BOXES	BGIINNN	BINNING	BHINRSU	BURNISH
BEOOPUZ	BOOZE-UP	BGIJNOY	BY JINGO	BHIOORS	BOORISH
BEOORSS	SORBOSE	BGIKLNU	BULKING	BHIOPSS	BISHOPS
BEOORST	BOOSTER	BGIKNNU	BUNKING	BHIRSTU	BRUTISH
BEOORSZ	BOOZERS	BGIKNOO	BOOKING	BHISTTU	BUSHTIT
BEOPRRV	PROVERB	BGIKNSU	BUSKING	BHLOOPT	BOTOLPH
BEOQTUU	BOUQUET	BGILMOU	GUMBOIL	BHLRSUU	BULRUSH
BEORRSW	BROWSER	BGILMRU	LIMBURG	BHMORSU	RHOMBUS
BEORSST	SORBETS	BGILNOS	GOBLINS	BHOOSTW	BOWSHOT
BEPRRTU	PERTURB	BGILNOT	BILTONG, BOLTING	BHPRSUU	BRUSH-UP
BEPRTUY	PUBERTY	BGILNOW	BLOWING, BOWLING	BIIIKNS	BIKINIS
BEPSTUY	SUBTYPE	BGILNOY	IGNOBLY	BIIILST	TBILISI
BEQRSUU	BRUSQUE	BGILOOR	OBLIGOR	BIIILTZ	TBILIZI
BERRSTU	BURSTER	BGILOOY	BIOLOGY	BIILLNO	BILLION
BERSSTU	BUSTERS	BGILRTU	TILBURG	BIILNTU	BUILT-IN
BERSTTY	BETTRYS	BGIMMNU	BUMMING	BIILOSU	BILIOUS
BERSTUV	SUBVERT	BGIMNNU	NUMBING	BIILRSY	RISIBLY
BERSUZZ	BUZZERS	BGIMNOO	BOOMING	BIILSVY	VISIBLY
BERTTUY	BUTTERY	BGIMNPU	BUMPING	BIIMNOU	NIOBIUM
BESSSTU	SUBSETS	BGIMRSY	GRIMSBY	BIIMNSU	MINIBUS
BESTTUX	SUBTEXT	BGINNRU	BURNING	BIISTTT	TITBITS
BFFGIIN	BIFFING	BGINNTU	BUNTING	BIJNOSU	SUBJOIN
BFFGINU	BUFFING	BGINOOT	BOOTING	BIKLLUY	BULKILY
BFFINOS	BOFFINS	BGINOOZ	BOOZING	BIKLRSY	BRISKLY
BFFLLUY	BLUFFLY				

BIKMNPU	BUMPKIN	BMNOOSU	UNBOSOM	CCEEHOR	ECORCHE
BIKNRSY	RYBINSK	BMOOORX	BOXROOM	CCEEHRS	CRECHES, SCREECH
BILLNOU	BULLION	BMOOSTT	BOTTOMS	CCEEIIL	CECILIE
BILLOPX	PILLBOX	BMOOSTY	TOMBOYS	CCEEILN	LICENCE
BILLOSW	BILLOWS	BMORSUU	BRUMOUS	CCEEINR	ECCRINE
BILLOWY	BILLOWY	BNNORWY	BRONWYN	CCEEINS	SCIENCE
BILLRWY	WRYBILL	BNNOUUY	NUN BUOY	CCEEIRV	CREVICE
BILMNOO	IN BLOOM	BNNRSUU	SUNBURN	CCEELRU	LUCRECE
BILMNOR	NOMBRIL	BNORSTU	BURTONS	CCEELRY	RECYCLE
BILMNRU	MILBURN	BNORSUU	BURNOUS	CCEERSY	SECRECY
BILMPUY	BUMPILY	BNORTUU	BURNOUT	CCEFNOT	CONFECT
BILNOTU	BOTULIN	BNOSTTU	BUTTONS	CCEGNOY	COGENCY
BILNRSU	LISBURN	BOOPRTT	BOTTROP	CCEHIKN	CHECK-IN, CHICKEN
BILOOYZ	BOOZILY	BOOPSTX	POSTBOX	CCEHILS	CLICHES
BILORST	BRISTOL	BOPSSTU	BUS STOP	CCEHINT	TECHNIC
BILOSSU	SUBSOIL	BORRSUW	BURROWS	CCEHIOR	CHOICER
BILOSSY	BOSSILY	BORSTTU	TURBOTS	CCEHIOS	CHOICES
BILPTUU	BUILT-UP	BOSTUUY	BUYOUTS	CCEHKLU	CHUCKLE
BILRSTY	BRISTLY	BPSSTUU	BUST-UPS	CCEHKPU	CHECKUP
BIMMORS	BROMISM	CCCDIOO	COCCOID	CCEHLOS	CLOCHES
BIMNOSU	OMNIBUS	CCCEHIO	CHOC-ICE	CCEHNOS	CONCHES
BINNOSU	BUNIONS	CCCNOOT	CONCOCT	CCEHORT	CROCHET
BINOOSU	NIOBOUS	CCCOOSU	COCCOUS	CCEHORU	COUCHER
BINORST	BRITONS	CCDEEHK	CHECKED	CCEHOSU	COUCHES
BINOTUY	BUY INTO	CCDEENO	CONCEDE	CCEIIKP	ICE PICK
BINRTUY	BUTYRIN	CCDEENY	DECENCY	CCEIILS	ICICLES
BIOORSZ	BORZOIS	CCDEEOR	COERCED	CCEIIRT	ICTERIC
BIOOSST	OBOISTS	CCDEESU	SUCCEED	CCEIKLR	CLICKER
BIOOSUV	OBVIOUS	CCDEHIL	CLICHED	CCEIKOR	COCKIER
BIOPRTY	PROBITY	CCDEHKO	CHOCKED	CCEIKRT	CRICKET
BIORRTU	BURRITO	CCDEHKU	CHUCKED	CCEILRR	CIRCLER
BIORRTW	RIBWORT	CCDEHOU	COUCHED	CCEILRS	CIRCLES, CLERICS
BIORSST	BISTROS	CCDEHRY	CEDRYCH	CCEILRT	CIRCLET
BIORSTT	BISTORT	CCDEIIL	ICICLED	CCEILTU	CUTICLE
BIORSUU	RUBIOUS	CCDEIIT	DEICTIC	CCEIMST	SMECTIC
BISSSTU	SUBSIST	CCDEIKL	CLICKED	CCEINOR	CORNICE, CROCEIN
BJLOOST	JOB LOTS	CCDEIKR	CRICKED	CCEINOS	CONCISE
BJNOORU	BONJOUR	CCDEILO	ICE-COLD	CCEINOT	CONCEIT
BJORUXY	JURY BOX	CCDEILR	CIRCLED	CCEINRT	CENTRIC
BKLOOST	TOBOLSK	CCDEIMO	COMEDIC	CCEIOPP	COPPICE
BKNOOTW	BOWKNOT	CCDEIOS	CODICES	CCEIOPT	ECTOPIC
BKNPSUU	BUNK-UPS	CCDEKLO	CLOCKED	CCEIORT	ORECTIC
BKOORWX	WORKBOX	CCDEKLU	CLUCKED	CCEIPST	SCEPTIC
BLLNTUY	BLUNTLY	CCDELOU	OCCLUDE	CCEKLOS	COCKLES
BLLOUVY	VOLUBLY	CCDENOU	CONDUCE	CCEKNOY	COCKNEY
BLMOOOT	TOMBOLO	CCDHIIL	CICHLID	CCEKOPT	PETCOCK
BLMOOSS	BLOSSOM	CCDIILO	CODICIL	CCEKORT	CROCKET
BLMOSSY	SYMBOLS	CCDIILU	CULICID	CCELLOT	COLLECT
BLNOORW	LOWBORN	CCDIIOR	CRICOID	CCELNOY	CYCLONE
BLOOQUY	OBLOQUY	CCDILOY	CYCLOID	CCEMNOO	COMECON
BLOORWW	LOWBROW	CCDKLOU	CUCKOLD	CCENNOR	CONCERN
BLOOTUW	BLOWOUT	CCDNOOR	CONCORD	CCENNOT	CONNECT
BLOPSTU	SUBPLOT	CCDNOTU	CONDUCT	CCENOPT	CONCEPT
BLOPSUW	BLOW-UPS	CCEEHHN	CHECHEN	CCENORT	CONCERT

CCENOSS	SCONCES	CDDDELU	CUDDLED	CDEEILN	DECLINE
CCEOOTT	COCOTTE	CDDDESU	SCUDDED	CDEEILP	PEDICEL, PEDICLE
CCEORRT	CORRECT	CDDEEER	DECREED, RECEDED	CDEEIMN	ENDEMIC
CCERTUW	CREW CUT	CDDEEES	SECEDED	CDEEINO	CODEINE
CCESSSU	SUCCESS	CDDEEII	DEICIDE	CDEEINT	ENTICED
CCFIRUY	CRUCIFY	CDDEEIR	DECIDER, DECRIED	CDEEINV	EVINCED
CCFLOSU	FLOCCUS	CDDEENO	ENCODED	CDEEIOS	DIOCESE
CCGHINO	GNOCCHI	CDDEENS	DESCEND	CDEEIOV	DEVOICE
CCGIKNO	COCKING	CDDEEOY	DECOYED	CDEEIPR	PIERCED
CCGILNY	CYCLING	CDDEERU	REDUCED	CDEEIRR	DECRIER
CCHHIKU	CHUKCHI	CDDEESU	SEDUCED	CDEEIRT	RECITED
CCHIIST	STICHIC	CDDEEUW	CUDWEED	CDEEISV	DEVICES
CCHIKNU	CHUCK IN	CDDEHIN	CHIDDEN	CDEEISX	EXCISED
CCHILOR	CHLORIC	CDDEHIT	DITCHED	CDEEITV	EVICTED
CCHIMOR	CHROMIC	CDDEILM	MIDDLE C	CDEEITX	EXCITED
CCHINOR	CHRONIC	CDDEINU	INDUCED	CDEEKLR	CLERKED
CCHIORY	CHICORY	CDDELOS	SCOLDED	CDEEKNR	REDNECK
CCHIPSU	HICCUPS	CDDELOU	CLOUDED	CDEEKNV	V-NECKED
CCHIPSY	PSYCHIC	CDDELRU	CURDLED	CDEEKRW	WRECKED
CCHKMSU	SCHMUCK	CDDEORW	CROWDED	CDEELPU	DECUPLE
CCHNRSU	SCRUNCH	CDDIIOS	DISCOID	CDEELSU	SECLUDE
CCHNRUY	CRUNCHY	CDDIIOY	DIDICOY	CDEELUX	EXCLUDE
CCIIILS	SILICIC	CDDIIRU	DRUIDIC	CDEENOR	ENCODER
CCIILNS	CLINICS	CDDIKOP	PIDDOCK	CDEENOZ	COZENED
CCIILOT	COLITIC	CDDIORS	DISCORD	CDEENRT	CENTRED, CREDENT,
CCIINPS	PICNICS	CDDKORY	DRY DOCK		RED CENT
CCIIRST	CRITICS	CDEEEFL	FLEECED	CDEENST	DESCENT, SCENTED
CCIIRTU	CIRCUIT	CDEEEFN	DEFENCE	CDEEOPR	PROCEED
CCIKLOW	COWLICK	CDEEEHK	CHEEKED	CDEEORV	COVERED
CCIKLOY	COLICKY	CDEEEHP	CHEEPED	CDEEORW	COWERED
CCIKOPT	COCKPIT	CDEEEHR	CHEERED	CDEEORY	DECOYER
CCILNOO	COLONIC	CDEEEIV	DECEIVE	CDEEOST	CESTODE
CCILNOU	COUNCIL	CDEEEJT	EJECTED	CDEEOTV	COVETED
CCILOOP	PICCOLO	CDEEELT	ELECTED	CDEERRU	REDUCER
CCILSTY	CYCLIST	CDEEEPR	PRECEDE	CDEERSS	SCREEDS
CCIMOTY	MYCOTIC	CDEEERR	DECREER	CDEERST	CRESTED
CCINOTV	CONVICT	CDEEERS	DECREES, SECEDER	CDEERSU	RESCUED, SECURED,
CCIOORS	SIROCCO	CDEEERT	ERECTED		SEDUCER
CCIOPTU	OCCIPUT	CDEEFHT	FETCHED	CDEESUX	EXCUSED
CCIPRTY	CRYPTIC	CDEEFII	EDIFICE	CDEFFHU	CHUFFED
CCKOOSU	CUCKOOS	CDEEFKL	FLECKED	CDEFFOS	SCOFFED
CCKOPSU	COCK-UPS	CDEEFLT	DEFLECT	CDEFFSU	SCUFFED
CCLOPSY	CYCLOPS	CDEEFOR	DEFORCE	CDEFHIL	FILCHED
CCMOOOR	MOROCCO	CDEEFST	DEFECTS	CDEFIIT	DEFICIT
CCNOOOS	COCOONS	CDEEHIS	DEHISCE	CDEFIKL	FLICKED
CCNOOPU	PUCCOON	CDEEHKL	HECKLED	CDEFINO	CONFIDE
CCNOOTU	COCONUT	CDEEHLW	WELCHED	CDEFIRR	FREDRIC
CCNOSSU	CONCUSS	CDEEHMS	SCHEMED	CDEFKLO	FLOCKED
CCORSUU	SUCCOUR	CDEEHNW	WENCHED	CDEFKOR	DEFROCK
CCSSSUU	SUCCUSS	CDEEHOR	COHERED	CDEFNTU	DEFUNCT
CDDDEEI	DECIDED	CDEEHPR	PERCHED	CDEFOSU	FOCUSED
CDDDEEO	DECODED	CDEEHRT	RETCHED	CDEGGHU	CHUGGED
CDDDEEU	DEDUCED	CDEEHST	CHESTED	CDEGGLO	CLOGGED
CDDDELO	CODDLED	CDEEIIT	EIDETIC	CDEGHOU	COUGHED

CDEGIIN	DE-ICING	CDEIISU	SUICIDE	CDELLSU	SCULLED
CDEGIKN	DECKING	CDEIJST	DISJECT	CDELMPU	CLUMPED
CDEGINR	CRINGED	CDEIKLN	CLINKED	CDELMSU	MUSCLED
CDEGLSU	CUDGELS	CDEIKLP	PICKLED	CDELMTU	MULCTED
CDEGORS	CODGERS	CDEIKLS	SLICKED	CDELNOO	CONDOLE
CDEHHIT	HITCHED	CDEIKLT	TICKLED	CDELNOW	CLOWNED
CDEHHNU	HUNCHED	CDEIKNS	DICKENS, SNICKED	CDELNOY	CONDYLE
CDEHIIV	CHIVIED	CDEIKPR	PRICKED	CDELNWY	CLEDWYN
CDEHIKN	CHINKED	CDEIKRR	DERRICK	CDELOPP	CLOPPED
CDEHILL	CHILLED	CDEIKRT	TRICKED	CDELOPU	COUPLED
CDEHILP	DELPHIC	CDEIKSU	DUCKIES	CDELORS	SCOLDER
CDEHINO	HEDONIC	CDEILLO	COLLIDE	CDELOST	COLDEST
CDEHINP	PINCHED	CDEILMO	MELODIC	CDELOSW	SCOWLED
CDEHINW	WINCHED	CDEILNU	INCLUDE, NUCLIDE	CDELOTT	CLOTTED
CDEHIOW	COWHIDE	CDEILOP	POLICED	CDELOTU	CLOUTED
CDEHIPP	CHIPPED	CDEILPP	CLIPPED	CDELRUY	CRUDELY
CDEHIPR	CHIRPED	CDEILPS	SPLICED	CDEMMNO	COMMEND
CDEHIPT	PITCHED	CDEILPU	CLUPEID	CDEMMOO	COMMODE
CDEHIRT	DITCHER	CDEILSU	SLUICED	CDEMNNO	CONDEMN
CDEHIST	DITCHES	CDEILTU	DUCTILE	CDEMORU	DECORUM
CDEHISU	DUCHIES	CDEIMNO	DEMONIC	CDENNOO	CONDONE
CDEHKOS	SHOCKED	CDEIMOR	DORMICE	CDENNOT	CONTEND
CDEHKSU	SHUCKED	CDEIMOS	MEDICOS	CDENOOR	CROONED
CDEHKUY	HEYDUCK	CDEIMOT	DEMOTIC	CDENOOS	SECONDO
CDEHLMU	MULCHED	CDEIMPR	CRIMPED	CDENOPU	POUNCED
CDEHLNU	LUNCHED	CDEIMSU	DECIMUS	CDENORS	SCORNED
CDEHLNY	LYNCHED	CDEINOT	CTENOID, DEONTIC,	CDENORU	CRUNODE
CDEHLOT	CLOTHED		D-NOTICE, NOTICED	CDENORW	CROWNED
CDEHLRU	LURCHED	CDEINRS	CINDERS, DISCERN,	CDENOSS	SECONDS
CDEHMMU	CHUMMED		RESCIND	CDENOTU	COUNTED
CDEHMNU	MUNCHED	CDEINRU	INDUCER	CDEOOPP	COPEPOD
CDEHMOO	MOOCHED	CDEINRY	CINDERY	CDEOOPS	SCOOPED
CDEHMOP	CHOMPED	CDEINSX	EXSCIND	CDEOOPT	CO-OPTED
CDEHNOT	NOTCHED	CDEIOPR	PERCOID	CDEOORR	CORRODE
CDEHNPU	PUNCHED	CDEIOPZ	ZIP CODE	CDEOORT	COTE-D'OR
CDEHNRU	CHURNED	CDEIORT	CORDITE	CDEOOST	SCOOTED
CDEHOPP	CHOPPED	CDEIORV	DIVORCE	CDEOPPR	CROPPED
CDEHOPU	POUCHED	CDEIOST	CESTOID	CDEOPRU	PRODUCE
CDEHORW	CHOWDER,	CDEIPRS	CRISPED	CDEORRS	RECORDS
	COWHERD	CDEIPRT	PREDICT	CDEORSS	CROSSED
CDEHOSU	DOUCHES	CDEIRRU	CURRIED	CDEORSU	COURSED, SCOURED
CDEHOSW	COWSHED	CDEIRST	CREDITS	CDEORTU	COURTED
CDEHOTU	TOUCHED	CDEIRSU	CRUISED	CDEORWY	COWDREY
CDEHOUV	VOUCHED	CDEIRTV	VERDICT	CDEOSTU	SCOUTED
CDEHPSY	PSYCHED	CDEISST	DISSECT	CDEPRSU	SPRUCED
CDEHRSU	CRUSHED	CDEISSY	ECDYSIS	CDERSTU	CRUDEST
CDEHSSU	DUCHESS	CDEKKNO	KNOCKED	CDFHIOS	CODFISH
CDEHSTY	SCYTHED	CDEKLOW	WEDLOCK	CDFIILU	FLUIDIC
CDEIIKR	DICKIER	CDEKLPU	PLUCKED	CDGHIIN	CHIDING
CDEIIKS	DICKIES	CDEKLSU	SUCKLED	CDGIKNO	DOCKING
CDEIINR	DINERIC	CDEKOOR	CROOKED	CDGIKNU	DUCKING
CDEIINS	INCISED	CDEKORS	DOCKERS	CDGILNO	CODLING, LINGCOD
CDEIINT	IDENTIC, INCITED	CDEKOST	DOCKETS, STOCKED	CDGINNO	CONDIGN
CDEIIST	DEISTIC, DICIEST	CDEKRTU	TRUCKED	CDGINOR	CORDING
		CDELLOU	COLLUDE		

CDHIIST	DISTICH	CEEELST	CELESTE	CEEHPSU	CEPHEUS
CDHILOS	COLDISH	CEEENNO	NEOCENE	CEEHQRU	CHEQUER
CDHIOOR	CHOROID, OCHROID	CEEENRT	TERENCE	CEEHQSU	CHEQUES
CDHIORS	ORCHIDS	CEEENSS	ESSENCE	CEEHRST	CHESTER, ETCHERS
CDHIPTY	DIPTYCH	CEEEOTZ	COETZEE	CEEHSTV	VETCHES
CDHMORU	MURDOCH	CEEEPRR	CREEPER	CEEIIPR	EPEIRIC
CDIIIOT	IDIOTIC	CEEERRT	ERECTER	CEEIJNT	CETINJE
CDIILLY	IDYLLIC	CEEERST	SECRETE	CEEIJOR	REJOICE
CDIILNY	DICLINY	CEEERTX	EXCRETE	CEEIKNT	NECKTIE
CDIIMNO	DOMINIC	CEEETUX	EXECUTE	CEEILLM	MICELLE
CDIINOR	CRINOID	CEEFFNO	OFFENCE	CEEILNR	RECLINE
CDIINOT	DICTION	CEEFFST	EFFECTS	CEEILNS	LICENSE, SELENIC,
CDIINOV	VIDICON	CEEFHRT	FETCHER		SILENCE
CDIIORS	CIRSOID	CEEFIRR	FIERCER	CEEILNU	LEUCINE
CDIIOSS	CISSOID	CEEFKLR	FRECKLE	CEEILPS	ECLIPSE
CDIIOSV	VISCOID	CEEFLRT	REFLECT	CEEILRT	RETICLE
CDIKLNO	OLD NICK	CEEFNOR	ENFORCE	CEEILST	SECTILE
CDIKNOR	DORNICK	CEEFNRS	FENCERS	CEEILSV	VESICLE
CDILLOO	COLLOID	CEEFPRT	PERFECT, PREFECT	CEEILTT	LETTICE
CDILLUY	LUCIDLY	CEEGINR	GENERIC	CEEILTU	LEUCITE
CDILOTZ	COLDITZ	CEEGINT	GENETIC	CEEIMNO	MIOCENE
CDILOUV	LUDOVIC	CEEGINU	EUGENIC	CEEIMNT	CENTIME
CDILPPU	CUDLIPP	CEEGKOS	GECKOES	CEEIMRS	MERCIES
CDIMMOU	MODICUM	CEEGLLO	COLLEGE	CEEIMST	EMETICS
CDIMOOS	COSMOID	CEEGLNO	GLENCOE	CEEINNS	INCENSE
CDIMSTU	DICTUMS	CEEGLNT	NEGLECT	CEEINNW	CEINWEN
CDINOSY	SYNODIC	CEEGLOU	ECLOGUE	CEEINRS	SINCERE
CDINOTU	CONDUIT, NOCTUID	CEEGNRY	REGENCY	CEEINRT	ENTERIC, ENTICER
CDIOPRR	RIPCORD	CEEGORT	CORTEGE	CEEINRV	CERVINE
CDIOSTY	CYSTOID	CEEHILM	MICHELE	CEEIOPT	PICOTEE
CDIOTUV	OVIDUCT	CEEHILS	HELICES	CEEIORT	COTERIE
CDIRSUY	DYSURIC	CEEHILV	VEHICLE	CEEIORV	REVOICE
CDIRTUY	CRUDITY	CEEHIMR	CHIMERE	CEEIPRR	PIERCER
CDISSSU	DISCUSS	CEEHIMS	CHEMISE	CEEIPRS	PRECISE, RECIPES
CDLNOTU	COULDN'T	CEEHINS	CHINESE	CEEIPRT	RECEIPT
CDLOOPY	LYCOPOD	CEEHIOR	CHEERIO	CEEIPRU	EPICURE
CDLOSTU	COULDST	CEEHIRT	ETHERIC, HERETIC	CEEIPSS	SPECIES
CDMNOOS	CONDOMS, MOD	CEEHIRW	CHEWIER	CEEIPST	PECTISE
CONS		CEEHKLR	HECKLER	CEEIPTZ	PECTIZE
CDNOORS	CONDORS,	CEEHKNP	HENPECK	CEEIRRT	RECITER
CORDONS		CEEHKST	KETCHES	CEEIRSV	SERVICE
CDNOORY	CROYDON	CEEHLNO	ECHELON	CEEIRTX	EXCITER
CDOOOPT	OCTOPOD	CEEHLRS	LECHERS	CEEJORT	EJECTOR
CDOORST	DOCTORS	CEEHLRY	LECHERY	CEEJRST	REJECTS
CDOOTUW	WOODCUT	CEEHLSY	LYCHEES	CEEKLNT	NECKLET
CDOPRTU	PRODUCT	CEEHMRS	SCHEMER	CEEKLPS	SPECKLE
CDOSTUY	CUSTODY	CEEHMSS	SCHEMES	CEEKNSY	EYSENCK
CEEEFLS	FLEECES	CEEHNRW	WENCHER	CEEKOSY	SOCKEYE
CEEEHLS	LEECHES	CEEHNST	TENCHES	CEEKPRS	PECKERS
CEEEHPR	CHEEPER	CEEHNSW	WENCHES	CEEKRRW	WRECKER
CEEEHSS	CHEESES	CEEHOPS	EPOCHES	CEELLLU	CELLULE
CEEEINP	EPICENE	CEEHORT	TROCHEE	CEELLNO	COLLEEN
CEEEIRV	RECEIVE	CEEHPRR	PERCHER	CEELMNT	CLEMENT
CEEEKNW	EWE-NECK	CEEHPRS	PERCHES	CEELMOW	WELCOME
CEEELRT	RE-ELECT				

CEELNOS	ENCLOSE	CEFIILT	FICTILE	CEGOORS	SCROOGE
CEELNRT	LECTERN	CEFIIOR	ORIFICE	CEGOOTY	CETOOGY
CEELNRU	LUCERNE	CEFIKLR	FLICKER	CEGORRS	GROCERS
CEELORS	CREOLES	CEFILNT	INFLECT	CEGORRY	GROCERY
CEELORT	ELECTOR	CEFILNU	FUNICLE	CEGORSU	SCOURGE
CEELOTT	COLETTE	CEFILOR	LEOFRIC	CEHHIRS	CHERISH
CEELRSU	RECLUSE	CEFILRU	LUCIFER	CEHHIRT	HITCHER
CEELRTU	LECTURE	CEFIMOR	COMFIER	CEHHIST	HITCHES
CEELRTY	ERECTLY	CEFINNO	CONFINE	CEHHITU	HUTCHIE
CEELTTU	LETTUCE, LUCETTE	CEFINOR	CONIFER	CEHHNSU	HUNCHES
CEEMNOR	MCENROE	CEFINTU	FINE-CUT	CEHHSTU	HUTCHES
CEEMNRU	CERUMEN	CEFIPSY	SPECIFY	CEHIIKT	THICKIE
CEEMOPR	COMPEER, COMPERE	CEFIRTY	CERTIFY, RECTIFY	CEHIILS	CHILIES
CEEMOPT	COMPETE	CEFKLOT	FETLOCK	CEHIINR	HIRCINE
CEENNOU	ENOUNCE	CEFKRSU	FUCKERS	CEHIINT	ICHNITE
CEENNOV	CONVENE	CEFLNOU	FLOUNCE	CEHIIRT	ITCHIER
CEENNRT	CENTNER	CEFLNUY	FLUENCY	CEHIJOR	JERICHO
CEENOOT	ECOTONE	CEFLOSS	FO'C'SLES	CEHIKNT	KITCHEN, THICKEN
CEENORS	ENCORES, NECROSE	CEFMORY	COMFREY	CEHIKPS	PECKISH
CEENORZ	COZENER	CEFNOSS	CONFESS	CEHIKRR	HERRICK
CEENPRS	SPENCER	CEFNOSU	CONFUSE	CEHIKRT	THICKER
CEENPRT	PER CENT	CEFNOTU	CONFUTE	CEHIKRW	WHICKER
CEENRSS	SCREENS	CEFOPRS	FORCEPS	CEHIKTT	THICKET
CEENRST	CENTERS, CENTRES	CEFORRT	CROFTER	CEHILNO	CHOLINE, HELICON
CEENRSU	CENSURE	CEFORSS	FRESCOS	CEHILRR	RICHLER
CEENRSY	SCENERY	CEFORSU	FOCUSER	CEHILRV	CHERVIL
CEEOPTY	ECOTYPE	CEFOSSU	FOCUSES	CEHILSS	CHISELS
CEEORRT	ERECTOR	CEFRSUW	CURFEWS	CEHILTY	ETHYLIC, TECHILY
CEEORRV	COVERER, RECOVER	CEGGHIR	CHIGGER	CEHIMNY	CHIMNEY
CEEORRZ	CORREZE	CEGGIOR	GEORGIC	CEHIMOR	HOMERIC
CEEORTV	COVETER	CEGGPSU	EGGCUPS	CEHIMOS	ECHOISM
CEEPPRT	PERCEPT, PRECEPT	CEGHINO	ECHOING	CEHIMRT	THERMIC
CEEPPRU	PREPUCE	CEGHINT	ETCHING	CEHIMRU	RHEUMIC
CEEPRSS	PRECESS	CEGHINW	CHEWING	CEHIMST	CHEMIST
CEEPRST	RESPECT, SCEPTRE, SPECTRE	CEGHLSU	GULCHES	CEHINOP	PHOCINE
CEEPRTX	EXCERPT	CEGHNTU	CHENGTU	CEHINPR	PHRENIC
CEERRSU	RESCUER, SECURER	CEGIILN	CEILING	CEHINPS	PINCHES, SPHENIC
CEERRSW	SCREWER	CEGIILW	GLIWICE	CEHINRW	WINCHER
CEERRUV	RECURVE	CEGIINP	PIECING	CEHINST	STHENIC
CEERSST	CRESSET, SECRETS	CEGIKNN	NECKING	CEHINSU	ECHINUS
CEERSSU	RESCUES	CEGIKNP	PECKING	CEHINSW	WINCHES
CEERTTU	CURETTE	CEGIKNR	RECKING	CEHIOPS	HOSPICE
CEESSUX	EXCUSES	CEGILNR	CLINGER, CRINGLE	CEHIOPT	POTICHE
CEFFIOR	OFFICER	CEGILNY	GLYCINE	CEHIORS	HEROICS
CEFFIOS	OFFICES	CEGINOS	COGNISE	CEHIOTV	CHEVIOT
CEFFISU	SUFFICE	CEGINOZ	COGNIZE	CEHIPPR	CHIPPER
CEFFLSU	SCUFFLE	CEGINRW	CREWING	CEHIPRR	CHIRPER
CEFFORS	COFFERS, SCOFFER	CEGLNOO	COLOGNE	CEHIPRS	CIPHERS
CEFGINN	FENCING	CEGLOOY	ECOLOGY	CEHIPRT	PITCHER
CEFHILR	FILCHER	CEGLOSU	GLUCOSE	CEHIPST	PITCHES
CEFHILY	CHIEFLY	CEGNORY	CRYOGEN	CEHIQSU	QUICHES
CEFHINS	FINCHES	CEGNOST	CONGEST	CEHIRRT	RICHTER
CEFHIRS	FISCHER	CEGNRUY	URGENCY	CEHIRST	RICHEST
		CEGNSTY	CYGNETS	CEHIRSU	CUSHIER

CEHISTW	WITCHES	CEIILPP	CLIPPIE	CEIKRST	RICKETS, STICKER,
CEHKKRU	CHUKKER	CEIILPT	PELITIC		TICKERS
CEHKLMO	HEMLOCK	CEIIMMT	MIMETIC	CEIKRTY	RICKETY
CEHKNOY	HOCKNEY	CEIIMOT	MEIOTIC	CEIKRUY	YUCKIER
CEHKORS	CHOKERS, SHOCKER	CEIIMPR	EMPIRIC	CEIKSST	SICKEST
CEHKPTU	KETCHUP	CEIIMSS	SEISMIC	CEIKSTT	TICKETS
CEHKRSU	SHUCKER	CEIIMST	SEMITIC	CEIKSTW	WICKETS
CEHKSTY	SKETCHY	CEIIMTT	TITMICE	CEILLLU	LUCILLE
CEHLMWY	WYCH-ELM	CEIINNO	CONIINE	CEILLOR	COLLIER
CEHLNRU	LUNCHER	CEIINNR	CINERIN	CEILLOS	COLLIES
CEHLNRY	LYNCHER	CEIINOS	EOSINIC	CEILLST	CELLIST
CEHLNSU	LUNCHES	CEIINOV	INVOICE	CEILMOP	COMPILE, POLEMIC
CEHLORT	CHORTLE	CEIINPS	PISCINE	CEILMPR	CRIMPLE
CEHLORY	CHORLEY	CEIINRS	IRENICS, SERICIN	CEILNNU	NUCLEIN
CEHLOST	CLOTHES	CEIINRT	CITRINE, CRINITE,	CEILNOS	INCLOSE
CEHLQSU	SQUELCH		INCITER, NERITIC	CEILNOT	LECTION
CEHLRRU	LURCHER	CEIINSS	ICINESS	CEILNOX	LEXICON
CEHLRSU	LURCHES	CEIINSU	CUISINE	CEILNPS	SPLENIC
CEHMNRU	MUNCHER	CEIINTZ	CITIZEN, ZINCITE	CEILNST	CLIENTS, STENCIL
CEHMNUW	NEW CHUM	CEIIOPZ	EPIZOIC	CEILNTU	TUNICLE
CEHMOOR	MOOCHER	CEIIPRR	PRICIER	CEILOOS	COOLIES
CEHMOOW	HOW COME?	CEIIPRS	SPICIER	CEILOSS	OSSICLE
CEHNOOP	HENCOOP	CEIIPRT	PICRITE	CEILPPR	CLIPPER, CRIPPLE
CEHNORV	CHEVRON	CEIIRST	ERISTIC	CEILPRS	SPLICER
CEHNOST	NOTCHES	CEIISSS	CISSIES	CEILPSS	SPLICES
CEHNPRU	PUNCHER	CEIISVV	CIVVIES	CEILPSU	SPICULE
CEHNPSU	PUNCHES	CEIITUV	UVEITIC	CEILQSU	CLIQUES
CEHNSUU	EUNUCHS	CEIJSTU	JUSTICE	CEILQUY	CLIQUEY
CEHNTUY	CHUTNEY	CEIKKNR	KENRICK	CEILRRU	CURLIER
CEHOOPS	POOCHES	CEIKKSW	KESWICK	CEILRTU	UTRICLE
CEHOORS	CHOOSER	CEIKLNR	CLINKER, CRINKLE	CEILSSU	CELSIUS, SLUICES
CEHOORT	CHEROOT	CEIKLNS	NICKELS	CEIMNOS	COSMINE, INCOMES
CEHOPPR	CHOPPER	CEIKLPR	PICKLER, PRICKLE	CEIMNOT	CENTIMO
CEHOPRS	PORCHES	CEIKLPS	PICKLES	CEIMNRS	MINCERS
CEHOPSU	POUCHES	CEIKLRS	SLICKER	CEIMOPT	METOPIC
CEHORST	TORCHES	CEIKLRT	TICKLER, TRICKLE	CEIMOTT	TOTEMIC
CEHORSZ	SCHERZO	CEIKLRU	LUCKIER	CEIMOTV	VICOMTE
CEHORTU	RETOUCH, TOUCHER	CEIKLRW	LERWICK	CEIMPRR	CRIMPER
CEHORTW	WOTCHER	CEIKLSS	SICKLES	CEIMRST	METRICS
CEHORUV	VOUCHER	CEIKLST	STICKLE, TICKLES	CEINNOR	CORINNE
CEHOSTU	TOUCHES	CEIKMRU	MUCKIER	CEINNOV	CONNIVE
CEHPRSY	CYPHERS	CEIKMSY	MICKEYS	CEINNTV	VINCENT
CEHPSSY	PSYCHES	CEIKNOT	KENOTIC, KETONIC	CEINOOT	COONTIE
CEHRSSU	CRUSHES	CEIKNQU	QUICKEN	CEINOOZ	NEOZOIC
CEHRSTT	STRETCH	CEIKNRS	SNICKER	CEINOPR	PORCINE
CEHRTTU	UTRECHT	CEIKOOS	COOKIES	CEINOPT	ENTOPIC, NEPOTIC
CEHSSTY	SCYTHES	CEIKORR	ROCKIER	CEINORR	CORNIER
CEIIJRU	JUICIER	CEIKORS	ROCKIES	CEINORS	COINERS, CRONIES
CEIIKNR	ICE RINK	CEIKPRR	PRICKER	CEINORV	CORVINE
CEIIKNT	KINETIC	CEIKPRS	PICKERS	CEINOSS	CESSION, COSINES
CEIIKPR	PICKIER	CEIKPRT	PRICKET	CEINOST	NOTICES, SECTION
CEIIKQU	QUICKIE	CEIKPST	PICKETS, SKEPTIC	CEINOSV	NOVICES
CEIILLS	SILICLE	CEIKQRU	QUICKER	CEINOTT	TONETIC
CEIILNN	INCLINE	CEIKRRT	TRICKER	CEINOTX	EXCITON

CEINOUV	UNVOICE	CEKMORS	MOCKERS	CEMMNOU	COMMUNE
CEINPRS	PINCERS, PRINCES	CEKMORY	MOCKERY	CEMMOTU	COMMUTE
CEINPST	INSPECT	CEKNOOV	CONVOKE	CEMMRSU	SCUMMER
CEINQSU	QUINCES	CEKNORS	CONKERS	CEMNNOT	CONTEMN
CEINRST	CISTERN, CRETINS	CEKNRWY	WRYNECK	CEMNOOY	ECONOMY
CEINRUV	INCURVE	CEKOOPR	PRECOOK	CEMNOSU	CONSUME
CEINSST	INSECTS	CEKOORS	COOKERS	CEMNRTU	CENTRUM
CEINSTY	CYSTINE	CEKOORY	COOKERY	CEMOOPS	COMPOSE
CEINTTX	EXTINCT	CEKOPST	POCKETS	CEMOOPT	COMPOTE
CEIOPRS	COPIERS	CEKORRS	CORKERS, ROCKERS	CEMOOTU	OUTCOME
CEIOPST	POETICS	CEKORRY	ROCKERY	CEMOPTU	COMPUTE
CEIOPSU	PICEOUS	CEKORST	RESTOCK, ROCKETS, STOCKER	CEMOSTU	COSTUME
CEIORRS	CROSIER	CEKOSST	SOCKETS	CEMPRTU	CRUMPET
CEIORRU	COURIER	CEKPRSU	PUCKERS	CEMRRUY	MERCURY
CEIORRZ	CROZIER	CEKRRTU	TRUCKER	CEMRSTU	RECTUMS
CEIORSW	COWRIES	CEKRSSU	SUCKERS	CENNOOT	CONNOTE
CEIORTV	EVICTOR	CELLMNO	CLONMEL	CENNORY	CONNERY
CEIORTX	EXCITOR, XEROTIC	CELLNOO	COLONEL	CENNOST	CONSENT
CEIORVY	VICEROY	CELLOSU	OCELLUS	CENNOTT	CONTENT
CEIOSST	COSIEST, OSSETIC	CELLOSY	CLOSELY	CENNOTV	CONVENT
CEIOSSV	VISCOSE	CELLPRU	PURCELL	CENOORR	CORONER, CROONER
CEIOSTV	COSTIVE	CELLRSU	SCULLER	CENOORT	CORONET
CEIOSTX	COEXIST	CELLRUY	CRUELLY	CENOPSU	POUNCES
CEIOSTY	SOCIETY	CELMNOO	MONOCLE	CENOPSY	SYNCOPE
CEIOSTZ	COZIEST	CELMOPX	COMPLEX	CENOPTY	POTENCY
CEIPRST	TRICEPS	CELMPRU	CRUMPLE	CENOQRU	CONQUER
CEIPRSY	SPICERY	CELMSSU	MUSCLES	CENORRS	CORNERS, SCORNER
CEIPRTU	CUPRITE, PICTURE	CELMTUU	CUMULET	CENORSS	CENSORS
CEIPRTY	PYRETIC	CELNNOU	NUCLEON	CENORST	CORNETS, COSTNER
CEIPSST	CESSPIT	CELNOOS	CONSOLE	CENORTU	CORNUTE, COUNTER, RECOUNT, TROUNCE
CEIPSTU	CUP TIES	CELNOSU	COUNSEL, UNCLOSE	CENORTV	CONVERT
CEIQRSU	CIRQUES	CELNOTU	NOCTULE	CENORUV	UNCOVER
CEIRRRU	CURRIER	CELNSUU	NUCLEUS	CENOSSY	COYNESS
CEIRRSU	CRUISER, CURRIES	CELOORS	COOLERS, CREOSOL	CENOSTT	CONTEST
CEIRRTT	CRITTER	CELOOST	COOLEST, OCELOTS	CENOSTU	CONTUSE
CEIRRTU	RECRUIT	CELOPRU	COUPLER	CENOTTX	CONTEXT
CEIRRTX	RECTRIX	CELOPSU	CLOSE-UP, COUPLES	CENRRTU	CURRENT
CEIRSSU	CRUISES	CELOPTU	COUPLET, OCTUPLE	CENRSTU	ENCRUST
CEIRSTT	TRISECT	CELORSU	CLOSURE	CENRSUW	UNSCREW
CEIRSTU	ICTERUS	CELORSW	SCOWLER	CENRTUY	CENTURY
CEIRSUV	CURSIVE	CELORTU	CLOTURE, COULTER	CEOOPRS	COOPERS, SCOOPER
CEIRTTX	TECTRIX	CELOSST	CLOSEST, CLOSETS	CEOORST	SCOOTER
CEJKOSY	JOCKEYS	CELPRSU	SCRUPLE	CEOOSTY	COYOTES
CEJLNOY	JOCELYN	CELPSUY	CLYPEUS	CEOPPRR	CROPPER
CEJNORU	CONJURE	CELRRSU	CURLERS	CEOPPRS	COPPERS
CEJOPRT	PROJECT	CELRSTU	CLUSTER, CUTLERS	CEOPPRY	COPPERY
CEKKLNU	KNUCKLE	CELRSUW	CURLEWS	CEOPRRS	SCORPER
CEKKNOR	KNOCKER	CELRTTU	CLUTTER	CEOPRRU	PROCURE
CEKKOPS	KOPECKS	CELRTUU	CULTURE	CEOPRSS	CORPSES, PROCESS
CEKLORS	LOCKERS	CELRTUV	CULVERT	CEOPRTT	PROTECT
CEKLOST	LOCKETS	CELRTUY	CRUELTY, CUTLERY	CEOPRUV	COVER-UP
CEKLPRU	PLUCKER	CELSTTU	CUTLETS, SCUTTLE	CEOQRTU	CROQUET
CEKLRSU	SUCKLER	CEMMNOT	COMMENT	CEORRSS	CROSSER, SCORERS
CEKLRTU	TRUCKLE				

CEORRST	RECTORS	CGHIKNU	KUCHING	CGINOST	COSTING, GNOSTIC
CEORRSU	COURSER, SCOURER	CGHILNU	CHILUNG	CGINOSU	CONGIUS
CEORRSY	SORCERY	CGHILPY	GLYPHIC	CGINPPU	CUPPING
CEORRTY	RECTORY	CGHINNO	CHIGNON	CGINRSU	CURSING
CEORSSS	CROSSES	CGHINOS	COSHING	CGINRUV	CURVING
CEORSST	CORSETS, ESCORTS, SECTORS	CGHINRU	RUCHING	CGINSSU	CUSSING
		CGHORUY	GROUCHY	CGINTTU	CUTTING
CEORSSU	COURSES, SOURCES, SUCROSE	CGIIJNU	JUICING	CGIOTYZ	ZYGOTIC
		CGIIKKN	KICKING	CGKLNOU	GUNLOCK
CEORSTU	SCOUTER	CGIIKLN	LICKING	CHHOSUU	HSU-CHOU
CEORSTV	COVERTS, VECTORS	CGIIKMM	GIMMICK	CHIILST	LITCHIS
CEORTUU	COUTURE	CGIIKNN	NICKING	CHIIMSU	ISCHIUM
CEOSSSU	SCOUSES	CGIIKNP	PICKING	CHIINOT	THIONIC
CEPPRRU	CRUPPER	CGIIKNR	RICKING	CHIIOPT	OPHITIC
CEPPRSU	SCUPPER	CGIIKNS	SICKING	CHIIPST	PICTISH
CEPRSSU	PERCUSS, SPRUCES	CGIIKNT	TICKING	CHIIPSW	IPSWICH
CEPRSSY	CYPRESS	CGIIKNW	WICKING	CHIKLLO	HILLOCK
CEPRSUW	SCREW UP	CGIILNO	COILING	CHIKLTY	THICKLY
CEPSSTU	SUSPECT	CGIILNS	SLICING	CHIKNOO	CHINOOK
CERSTTU	CUTTERS	CGIIMNN	MINCING	CHIKORY	HICKORY
CERSTUY	CURTESY	CGIINNO	COINING	CHIKPSU	PUCKISH
CFFGINU	CUFFING	CGIINNW	WINCING	CHIKSTY	KITSCHY
CFFHINO	CHIFFON	CGIINOV	VOICING	CHILLMU	CHILLUM
CFFIKKO	KICKOFF	CGIINPR	PRICING	CHILNSY	LYCHNIS
CFFINOS	COFFINS	CGIINPS	SPICING	CHILOOS	COOLISH
CFFOSTU	CUTOFFS	CGIKLNO	LOCKING	CHILOST	COLTISH
CFFRSSU	SCRUFFS	CGIKMNO	MOCKING	CHILPSY	SYLPHIC
CFFRSUY	SCRUFFY	CGIKMNU	MUCKING	CHILSTU	CULTISH
CFGIKNU	FUCKING	CGIKNNO	CONKING	CHIMMTU	MITCHUM
CFGINOR	FORCING	CGIKNOO	COOKING	CHIMRUU	URUMCHI
CFHINSU	FUCHSIN	CGIKNOR	CORKING, ROCKING	CHIMSSS	SCHISMS
CFHIOSW	COWFISH	CGIKNOS	SOCKING	CHIMSTY	TYCHISM
CFHOOOW	FOOCHOW	CGIKNPU	KINGCUP	CHINOOR	CHORION
CFIIKNY	FINICKY	CGIKNRU	RUCKING	CHINOPS	PHONICS
CFIILNT	INFLICT	CGIKNSU	SUCKING	CHINORS	CORNISH
CFIINOT	FICTION	CGIKNTU	TUCKING	CHINORT	CORINTH
CFILNOT	CLIFTON	CGILLNU	CULLING	CHINORW	NORWICH
CFILORS	FROLICS	CGILNOO	COOLING	CHINOSU	CUSHION
CFILORU	FLUORIC	CGILNOS	CLOSING	CHINOTU	IN TOUCH
CFIMNOR	CONFIRM	CGILNOW	COWLING	CHINQSU	SQUINCH
CFIMOST	COMFITS	CGILNOY	CLOYING	CHINRSU	URCHINS
CFIORSY	SCORIFY	CGILNRU	CURLING	CHINTYZ	CHINTZY
CFKNORU	UNFROCK	CGILORW	COWGIRL	CHIOORS	ISOCHOR
CFKOTTU	FUTTOCK	CGILOTT	GLOTTIC	CHIOPRT	TROPHIC
CFKPSUU	FUCK-UPS	CGILPTY	GLYPTIC	CHIPRRU	CHIRRUP
CFLMRUU	FULCRUM	CGIMNOS	COMINGS	CHIPRRY	PYRRHIC
CFLORWY	CRY WOLF	CGINNNO	CONNING	CHIPSSY	PHYSICS
CFMNOOR	CONFORM	CGINNNU	CUNNING	CHIRRSU	CURRISH
CFMOORT	COMFORT	CGINNOS	CONSIGN	CHIRSSY	CHRISSY
CFOSSUU	FUSCOUS	CGINOPP	COPPING	CHIRSTY	CHRISTY
CGGGINO	COGGING	CGINOPS	COPINGS	CHKLOSY	SHYLOCK
CGHIIMN	CHIMING	CGINOPY	COPYING	CHKMMOU	HUMMOCK
CGHIINN	INCHING	CGINORS	SCORING	CHLMORY	CHROMYL
CGHIINT	ITCHING	CGINORW	CROWING		
CGHIKNO	CHOKING, HOCKING				

CHLOOSS	SCHOOLS	CIKPSTU	STICK-UP	CIORSUU	CURIOUS
CHLOSUY	SLOUCHY	CIKRSTY	TRICKSY	CIORTVY	VICTORY
CHMOSUY	CHYMOUS	CILLNNO	LINCOLN	CIOSSSY	SYCOSIS
CHMSTUY	SMUTCHY	CILLOOR	CRIOLLO	CIOSSUV	VISCOUS
CHNNOOR	CHRONON	CILMNOP	COMPLIN	CIPRSST	SCRIPTS
CHNNOPY	PYNCHON	CILMOOS	LOCOISM	CIPRTTY	TRYPTIC
CHNOOPS	PONCHOS	CILMOPY	OLYMPIC	CIPSTTY	STYPTIC
CHNORSY	SYNCHRO	CILMSTU	CULTISM	CIRSSTU	RUSTICS
CHNOTUU	UNCOUTH	CILNNOT	CLINTON	CKKLNUY	KNUCKLY
CHNPPUU	PUNCH-UP	CILNOOR	ORCINOL	CKKNNOO	KNOCK-ON
CHOOOSW	SOOCHOW	CILNOTU	LINOCUT	CKKNOPU	KNOCK-UP
CHOORST	COHORTS	CILNPSU	SCULPIN	CKLNOTU	LOCKNUT
CHOORWZ	CHORZOW	CILNSTU	LINCTUS	CKLNOUW	LUCKNOW
CIIILLT	ILLICIT	CILOOPT	COPILOT	CKLNUUY	UNLUCKY
CIIINPT	INCIPIT	CILOORU	COULOIR	CKLOORW	ROWLOCK
CIIINST	SINITIC	CILOOSS	COLOSSI	CKLOOTU	LOCKOUT
CIIJLUY	JUICILY	CILOPSW	COWSLIP	CKLOPSU	LOCKUPS
CIIKKLL	KILLICK	CILOSTU	OCULIST	CKLOPTU	POT LUCK
CIILLVY	CIVILLY	CILPRSY	CRISPLY	CKMOPSU	MOCK-UPS
CIILNOP	CIPOLIN	CILPRTU	CULPRIT	CKNOOOR	ROCKOON
CIILNOS	SILICON	CILSTTU	CULTIST	CKNOOOS	COOKSON
CIILNOT	NILOTIC	CIMNOOR	MORONIC,	CKNSTUU	UNSTUCK
CIILNUV	UNCIVIL		OMICRON	CKOOOTU	COOKOUT
CIILOOT	OOLITIC	CIMNORS	CRIMSON, MICRONS	CKOORST	ROSTOCK
CIILOPT	POLITIC	CIMOOST	OSMOTIC	CKORTUW	CUTWORK
CIILOST	COLITIS, SOLICIT	CIMOSST	SITCOMS	CKOSSTU	TUSSOCK
CIILPSY	SPICILY	CIMOSSY	MYCOSIS	CKPSTUU	STUCK-UP
CIIMMRY	MIMICRY	CIMOTYZ	ZYMOTIC	CLLMOSU	MOLLUSC
CIIMOTT	MITOTIC	CIMPRSY	SCRIMPY	CLLOOPS	SCOLLOP
CIIMRST	TRISMIC	CIMRSSU	CRISSUM	CLLORSS	SCROLLS
CIIMSTV	VICTIMS	CIMSSTY	MYSTICS	CLMNOSU	COLUMNS
CIINORS	INCISOR	CINNORU	UNICORN	CLMOOOU	OLOMOUC
CIINPRS	CRISPIN	CINNOSU	NUNCIOS	CLMOSUU	OSCULUM
CIINQTU	QUINTIC	CINNOTU	UNCTION	CLMPRUY	CRUMPLY
CIIOSUV	VICIOUS	CINNSUU	UNCINUS	CLMSUUU	CUMULUS
CIIPRTY	PYRITIC	CINOOOR	ORINOCO	CLNOORT	CONTROL
CIJMORW	JIM CROW	CINOOPS	OPSONIC	CLNOOSS	CONSOLS
CIJNNOO	CONJOIN	CINORRT	TRICORN	CLNOSSU	CONSULS
CIKKNNO	KINNOCK	CINORSS	INCROSS	CLNOSTU	CONSULT
CIKLLOP	PILLOCK	CINORST	CISTRON, CITRONS	CLOORSU	COLOURS
CIKLLOR	ROLLICK	CINORTU	RUCTION	CLORSSY	CROSSLY
CIKLLSY	SLICKLY	CINORTY	TYRONIC	CLORTUY	COURTLY
CIKLLUY	LUCKILY	CINOSST	CONSIST, TOCSINS	CLOSSTU	LOCUSTS
CIKLMOS	MISKOLC	CINOSSU	COUSINS	CMMNOOS	COMMONS
CIKLMUY	MUCKILY	CINOSTU	SUCTION	CMNNOOT	MONCTON
CIKLNRY	CRINKLY	CIOOPRS	SCORPIO	CMNOOPT	COMPTON
CIKLOWW	WICKLOW	CIOOPRT	PORTICO	CMNOOPY	COMPONY
CIKLPRY	PRICKLY	CIOOPSU	COPIOUS	CMOOORS	COMOROS
CIKLQUY	QUICKLY	CIOOQTU	COQUITO	CMOOPRT	COMPORT
CIKLRTY	TRICKLY	CIOPRST	TROPICS	CMOOPST	COMPOST
CIKMORR	RIMROCK	CIOPRTY	CYPRIOT	CMOORSU	CORMOUS
CIKNOST	STICK-ON	CIOPSTY	COPYIST	CMORSTU	SCROTUM
CIKNSTU	UNSTICK	CIORSSS	SCISSOR	CMORTUW	CUTWORM
CIKPPSU	PICK-UPS	CIORSTV	VICTORS	CMOSSTU	CUSTOMS

159

CMPRSUY	SCRUMPY	DDEEELT	DELETED	DDEFLNO	FONDLED
CNNORRU	RUNCORN	DDEEEMN	EMENDED	DDEFLOO	FLOODED
CNNORTU	NOCTURN	DDEEEPS	SPEEDED	DDEFLSU	FUDDLES
CNOOOTU	COTONOU	DDEEERR	RED DEER	DDEFNOR	FRONDED
CNOOPPR	POPCORN	DDEEFII	DEIFIED, EDIFIED	DDEFNOU	FOUNDED
CNOOPSU	COUPONS,	DDEEFIL	DEFILED, FIELDED	DDEFORR	REDFORD
SOUPCON		DDEEFIN	DEFINED	DDEGGRU	DRUGGED,
CNOORST	CONSORT	DDEEFIR	FREDDIE	GRUDGED	
CNOORTT	CONTORT	DDEEFSU	DEFUSED	DDEGIIR	GIDDIER
CNOORTU	CONTOUR,	DDEEGIN	DEIGNED	DDEGILR	GIRDLED, GRIDDLE
CROUTON		DDEEGLP	PLEDGED	DDEGIMO	DEMIGOD
CNOOSTY	TYCOONS	DDEEGLS	SLEDGED	DDEGINW	WEDDING
CNOOSVY	CONVOYS	DDEEGLU	DELUGED	DDEGINY	EDDYING
CNOOTTY	COTTONY	DDEEGRR	DREDGER	DDEGIOR	DODGIER
CNORSSU	UNCROSS	DDEEHRS	SHEDDER	DDEGMOS	DODGEMS
CNORTUY	COUNTRY	DDEEIIT	TIE-DIED	DDEGMSU	SMUDGED
COOPRRT	PROCTOR	DDEEILV	DEVILED	DDEGNOS	GODSEND
COOPRTU	OUTCROP	DDEEILW	WIELDED	DDEGNOU	DUDGEON
COOPSTU	COP-OUTS,	DDEEILY	YIELDED	DDEGNWY	GWYNEDD
OCTOPUS		DDEEIMP	IMPEDED	DDEGORS	DODGERS
COOSTTY	OTOCYST	DDEEIMS	MISDEED	DDEGOSS	GODDESS
COPRRTU	CORRUPT	DDEEINW	WIDENED	DDEGRRU	DRUDGER
COPRSUU	CUPROUS	DDEEINX	INDEXED	DDEGRSU	DRUDGES
CORRSSU	CURSORS	DDEEIOV	VIDEOED	DDEGRTU	TRUDGED
CORRSUY	CURSORY	DDEEIPS	DEPSIDE	DDEHIRS	REDDISH
COSTTUU	CUTOUTS	DDEEIRR	DEIRDRE, DERIDER	DDEHIRY	HYDRIDE
DDDDEIL	DIDDLED	DDEEIRS	DESIRED, RESIDED	DDEHLRU	HUDDLER, HURDLED
DDDEEGR	DREDGED	DDEEIRV	DERIVED	DDEHLSU	HUDDLES
DDDEEIR	DERIDED	DDEEISV	DEVISED	DDEHNOU	HOUNDED
DDDEELM	MEDDLED	DDEELLU	DUELLED	DDEHNRU	HUNDRED
DDDEELP	PEDDLED	DDEELLW	DWELLED	DDEHRSU	SHUDDER
DDDEELS	SLEDDED	DDEELMO	MODELED	DDEIIKS	KIDDIES
DDDEELU	DELUDED	DDEELMR	MEDDLER	DDEIINV	DIVINED
DDDEENU	DENUDED	DDEELOY	YODELED	DDEIIOX	DIOXIDE
DDDEFIL	FIDDLED	DDEELPR	PEDDLER	DDEIIRT	DIRTIED
DDDEFLU	FUDDLED	DDEELRS	SLEDDER	DDEIIRV	DIVIDER
DDDEGRU	DRUDGED	DDEELRU	DELUDER	DDEIISV	DIVIDES
DDDEHLU	HUDDLED	DDEEMOT	DEMOTED	DDEIKLN	KINDLED
DDDEHTU	THUDDED	DDEENOT	DENOTED	DDEIKNR	KINDRED
DDDEIIV	DIVIDED	DDEENOW	ENDOWED	DDEIKRS	KIDDERS
DDDEIKS	SKIDDED	DDEENPU	UPENDED	DDEILLR	DRILLED
DDDEILP	PIDDLED	DDEENRS	DRESDEN	DDEILMR	MILDRED
DDDEILR	RIDDLED	DDEENRU	DENUDER, ENDURED	DDEILNW	DWINDLE
DDDEIMU	MUDDIED	DDEEOPS	DEPOSED	DDEILOS	DILDOES
DDDEIOV	VEDDOID	DDEEORR	ORDERED	DDEILOT	DELTOID
DDDELMU	MUDDLED	DDEEOTV	DEVOTED	DDEILRR	RIDDLER
DDDELOO	DOODLED	DDEEPTU	DEPUTED	DDEILRS	RIDDLES
DDDELOP	PLODDED	DDEERSS	DRESSED	DDEILRT	TIDDLER
DDDELOS	DODDLES	DDEERST	REDDEST	DDEILTU	DILUTED, LUDDITE
DDDELOT	TODDLED	DDEERTU	DETRUDE	DDEILTW	TWIDDLE
DDDELPU	PUDDLED	DDEERYY	DRY-EYED	DDEILTY	LYDDITE
DDDEOPR	PRODDED	DDEFILR	FIDDLER	DDEIMNS	MIDDENS
DDDEORY	DODDERY	DDEFILS	FIDDLES	DDEIMOR	DERMOID
DDDESTU	STUDDED	DDEFIRT	DRIFTED	DDEIMOS	DESMOID
DDDEEELN	NEEDLED				

DDEIMRU	MUDDIER	DDGOOOW	DOGWOOD	DEEERRV	REVERED
DDEINNU	DUNEDIN	DDHIISY	YIDDISH	DEEERST	STEERED
DDEINOT	DENTOID	DDHIORY	HYDROID	DEEERSV	DESERVE, SEVERED
DDEINST	DISTEND	DDHORSY	DRY-SHOD	DEEERTX	EXERTED
DDEIOOR	DO-OR-DIE	DDIILOP	DIPLOID	DEEETTV	VEDETTE
DDEIORV	OVERDID	DDILMUY	MUDDILY	DEEETTW	TWEETED
DDEIORW	DOWDIER	DDILNRS	DIRNDLS	DEEFFOR	OFFERED
DDEIOST	TODDIES	DDILOWY	DOWDILY	DEEFGIN	FEEDING, FEIGNED
DDEIOWW	WIDOWED	DDILRUY	RUDDILY	DEEFHLS	FLESHED
DDEIPPR	DRIPPED	DDILTWY	TWIDDLY	DEEFHLU	HEEDFUL
DDEIRRU	RUDDIER	DDIMOOS	DODOISM	DEEFIIR	DEIFIER, EDIFIER
DDEISSU	DISUSED	DDIPRRY	DRIP-DRY	DEEFILN	ENFIELD
DDEISTU	STUDIED	DEEEFRS	FEEDERS	DEEFILR	DEFILER, FIELDER
DDEKMOU	DUKEDOM	DEEEFRV	FEVERED	DEEFILS	DEFILES
DDELMOU	MOULDED	DEEEGMR	EMERGED	DEEFILT	FILETED
DDELMRU	MUDDLER	DEEEGNR	GREENED, RENEGED	DEEFINR	DEFINER, REFINED
DDELMSU	MUDDLES	DEEEGRS	DEGREES	DEEFINT	FEINTED
DDELNOS	NODDLES	DEEEGRT	DETERGE, GREETED	DEEFIRR	FERRIED
DDELOOR	DOODLER, DROOLED	DEEEHLW	WHEEDLE, WHEELED	DEEFKLR	KREFELD
DDELOOS	DOODLES	DEEEHRS	HEREDES, SHEERED	DEEFLLU	FUELLED
DDELOPR	PLODDER	DEEEHST	SEETHED	DEEFLLW	WELL-FED
DDELORT	TODDLER	DEEEHWZ	WHEEZED	DEEFLNU	NEEDFUL
DDELPRU	PUDDLER	DEEEILT	LEE TIDE	DEEFLOT	FEEDLOT
DDELPSU	PUDDLES	DEEEINR	NEEDIER	DEEFMOR	FREEDOM
DDEMMRU	DRUMMED	DEEEIPY	PIE-EYED	DEEFNRS	FENDERS
DDEMNOS	DESMOND	DEEEIRR	REEDIER	DEEFPRY	DEEP FRY
DDEMNOT	ODDMENT	DEEEIRS	DESIREE, SEEDIER	DEEFRSU	REFUSED
DDENOPS	DESPOND	DEEEIRW	WEEDIER	DEEFRTT	FRETTED
DDENOPU	POUNDED	DEEEISV	DEVISEE	DEEFRTU	REFUTED
DDENORT	TRODDEN	DEEEKLN	KNEELED	DEEGHIN	HEEDING, NEIGHED
DDENORU	REDOUND,	DEEEKLS	SLEEKED	DEEGHIW	WEIGHED
ROUNDED, UNDERDO		DEEEKNW	WEEKEND	DEEGHOW	HOGWEED
DDENORW	DROWNED	DEEELLV	LEVELED	DEEGILS	LEG SIDE
DDENOSS	ODDNESS	DEEELNS	NEEDLES	DEEGIMN	DEEMING
DDENOSU	SOUNDED	DEEELPT	DEPLETE	DEEGIMV	DEMIVEG
DDENOUW	WOUNDED	DEEELRV	LEVERED, REVELED	DEEGINN	NEEDING
DDEOOPR	DROOPED	DEEELST	SLEETED, STEELED	DEEGINR	ENERGID, REEDING,
DDEOORW	REDWOOD	DEEELTX	TELEXED	REIGNED	
DDEOOWY	DYEWOOD	DEEEMNS	DEMESNE	DEEGINS	SEEDING
DDEOPPR	DROPPED	DEEEMRS	EMERSED	DEEGINW	WEEDING
DDEOPRR	PRODDER	DEEEMRT	METERED	DEEGIOR	GEORDIE
DDEOPRW	DEWDROP	DEEENPR	PREENED	DEEGIPW	PIGWEED
DDEORSW	DROWSED	DEEENQU	QUEENED	DEEGIRV	DIVERGE, GRIEVED
DDGGINO	DODGING	DEEENRS	SNEERED	DEEGIST	EDGIEST
DDGHOOO	GODHOOD	DEEENRT	ENTERED	DEEGLNS	LEGENDS
DDGIIKN	KIDDING	DEEENRW	RENEWED	DEEGLOY	GOLDEYE
DDGIILY	GIDDILY	DEEENSZ	SNEEZED	DEEGLPR	PLEDGER
DDGIINR	RIDDING	DEEENTT	DETENTE	DEEGLPS	PLEDGES
DDGIMNU	MUDDING	DEEENUV	DENEUVE	DEEGLPT	PLEDGET
DDGINNO	NODDING	DEEEORR	ROE DEER	DEEGLRS	LEDGERS
DDGINOP	PODDING	DEEEOTV	DEVOTEE	DEEGLSS	SLEDGES
DDGINOS	SODDING	DEEEPRS	SPEEDER	DEEGLSU	DELUGES
DDGINPU	PUDDING	DEEEPST	DEEPEST, STEEPED	DEEGNRS	GENDERS
		DEEEQRU	QUEERED	DEEGOSY	GEODESY

DEEGSSU	GUESSED
DEEGSTU	GUESTED
DEEHITV	THIEVED
DEEHLLS	SHELLED
DEEHLSV	SHELVED
DEEHLSW	WELSHED
DEEHMUX	EXHUMED
DEEHNOY	HONEYED
DEEHNRT	DRENTHE
DEEHORV	HOVERED
DEEHRSU	USHERED
DEEHTTW	WHETTED
DEEIINS	SINE DIE
DEEIIRW	WEIRDIE
DEEIIST	DEITIES
DEEIJLL	JELLIED
DEEIJMM	JEMMIED
DEEIKLN	LIKENED
DEEIKMW	MIDWEEK
DEEILMO	MELODIE
DEEILNR	RELINED
DEEILNS	LINSEED
DEEILNU	EILUNED
DEEILNV	LIVENED
DEEILNY	DYELINE
DEEILPR	REPLIED
DEEILRV	DELIVER, EVERILD,
RELIVED, REVILED	
DEEILRW	WIELDER
DEEILRY	YIELDER
DEEILSS	DIESELS
DEEILSY	EYELIDS, SEEDILY
DEEILTU	DILUTEE
DEEILWY	WEEDILY
DEEIMNO	DOMINEE
DEEIMPR	IMPEDER, PER DIEM
DEEIMPT	EMPTIED
DEEIMRT	DEMERIT, DIMETER,
MERITED	
DEEIMTT	EMITTED
DEEINNS	DENISEN
DEEINNT	DENTINE
DEEINNZ	DENIZEN
DEEINPR	DNIEPER, REPINED,
RIPENED	
DEEINRS	DENIERS, NEREIDS
DEEINRW	WIDENER
DEEINRX	INDEXER
DEEINST	DESTINE
DEEINSV	ENDIVES
DEEINSW	WISENED
DEEINSX	INDEXES
DEEINTT	DINETTE
DEEINTU	DETINUE
DEEINTV	EVIDENT

DEEINWZ	WIZENED
DEEIOPS	EPISODE
DEEIOPT	EPIDOTE
DEEIPPT	PEPTIDE
DEEIPRS	DEPISER, PERSEID,
PRESIDE	
DEEIPRV	DEPRIVE
DEEIPRX	EXPIRED
DEEIPSS	DESPISE
DEEIPST	DESPITE
DEEIQRU	QUERIED
DEEIRRS	DESIRER, RESIDER,
SERRIED	
DEEIRRT	RETIRED
DEEIRRV	DERIVER
DEEIRRW	REWIRED, WEIRDER
DEEIRSS	DESIRES
DEEIRSU	RESIDUE
DEEIRSV	DEVISER, DIVERSE,
REVISED	
DEEIRTU	ERUDITE
DEEIRTV	RIVETED
DEEIRVV	REVIVED
DEEISSU	DISEUSE
DEEISTW	DEWIEST
DEEISTX	EXISTED
DEEISVZ	DEVIZES
DEEJNOY	ENJOYED
DEEKKLR	DE KLERK
DEEKKRT	TREKKED
DEEKNNY	KENNEDY
DEEKNRW	KENDREW
DEEKORV	REVOKED
DEEKPUY	KEYED UP
DEELLMS	SMELLED
DEELLNR	RENDELL
DEELLNW	WENDELL
DEELLPS	SPELLED
DEELLQU	QUELLED
DEELLRU	DUELLER
DEELLRW	DWELLER
DEELLRY	ELDERLY
DEELLSW	SWELLED
DEELMOR	REMODEL
DEELMPU	DEPLUME
DEELMST	SMELTED
DEELMSY	MEDLEYS
DEELNRS	LENDERS, SLENDER
DEELNSS	ENDLESS
DEELNST	NESTLED
DEELNSY	DENSELY
DEELNTT	NETTLED
DEELOPP	PEOPLED
DEELOPR	DEPLORE
DEELOPV	DEVELOP

DEELOPX	EXPLODE
DEELORU	URODELE
DEELORW	LOWERED
DEELOSU	DELOUSE
DEELOTW	TOWELED
DEELOVV	DEVOLVE, EVOLVED
DEELPRU	PRELUDE
DEELRSW	WELDERS
DEELSTT	SETTLED
DEELTUX	EXULTED
DEELVXY	VEXEDLY
DEEMMST	STEMMED
DEEMNOY	MONEYED
DEEMNRS	MENDERS
DEEMORV	REMOVED
DEEMORX	EXODERM
DEEMOSY	MOSEYED
DEEMPTT	TEMPTED
DEEMRRU	DEMURER
DEEMRSU	RESUMED
DEENNPT	PENDENT
DEENOPS	SPONDEE
DEENOPT	PENTODE
DEENORS	ENDORSE
DEENORT	ERODENT
DEENORW	ENDOWER
DEENPPR	PERPEND
DEENPRS	SPENDER
DEENPRT	PRETEND
DEENRSS	REDNESS, SENDERS
DEENRST	TENDERS
DEENRSU	END USER, ENSURED
DEENRTU	DENTURE
DEENSST	DENSEST
DEENSTW	WEST END
DEEOPPY	POP-EYED
DEEOPRS	DEPOSER, REPOSED
DEEOPRW	POWERED
DEEOPSX	EXPOSED
DEEORRR	ORDERER, REORDER
DEEORRS	REREDOS
DEEORST	OERSTED
DEEORTT	DORETTE, TETRODE
DEEORTW	TOWERED
DEEORUV	OVERDUE
DEEORXX	XEROXED
DEEPPST	STEPPED
DEEPRSS	DEPRESS, PRESSED
DEEPRSU	PERUSED
DEEPRTU	ERUPTED, REPUTED
DEEQSTU	QUESTED
DEERRSS	DRESSER, REDRESS
DEERRSV	REDVERS
DEERRUV	VERDURE

DEERSSS	DRESSES	DEFIRRT	DRIFTER	DEGHOST	GHOSTED
DEERSST	DESERTS, DESSERT	DEFIRTU	FRUITED	DEGHOSU	SOUGHED
DEERSTW	STREWED, WRESTED	DEFIRZZ	FRIZZED	DEGIILN	ELIDING
DEERSVW	SWERVED	DEFKLNU	FLUNKED	DEGIINR	DINGIER
DEERTTU	UTTERED	DEFLLOU	DOLEFUL	DEGIINT	DIETING, EDITING,
DEERTUX	EXTRUDE	DEFLNOR	FONDLER		IGNITED
DEESSTU	SUDETES	DEFLNOT	TENFOLD	DEGIISU	EGIDIUS
DEFFFLU	FLUFFED	DEFLOOR	FLOODER, FLOORED	DEGIJLN	JINGLED
DEFFILR	RIFFLED	DEFLOPP	FLOPPED	DEGIKLO	GODLIKE
DEFFINS	SNIFFED	DEFLORS	FOLDERS	DEGILLR	GRILLED
DEFFIOS	OFFSIDE	DEFLORT	TELFORD	DEGILMN	MINGLED
DEFFISU	DIFFUSE	DEFLORU	FLOURED	DEGILNN	LENDING
DEFFLMU	MUFFLED	DEFLOSS	FLOSSED	DEGILNO	GLENOID, ON-GLIDE
DEFFLRU	RUFFLED	DEFLOTU	FLOUTED	DEGILNS	DINGLES, SINGLED
DEFFNOS	SEND-OFF	DEFMORS	SERFDOM	DEGILNT	GLINTED, TINGLED
DEFFNSU	SNUFFED	DEFNORT	FRONTED	DEGILNU	DUELING, ELUDING,
DEFFRSU	DUFFERS	DEFNORU	FOUNDER		INDULGE
DEFFSTU	STUFFED	DEFNORW	FROWNED	DEGILNV	DELVING
DEFGGLO	FLOGGED	DEFNOST	FONDEST	DEGILNW	WELDING
DEFGINN	FENDING	DEFNOSU	FONDUES	DEGILOR	GLORIED, GODLIER
DEFGINR	FRINGED	DEFNRSU	REFUNDS	DEGILRR	GIRDLER
DEFGINU	FEUDING	DEFOOPR	PROOFED	DEGILRS	GIRDLES, GLIDERS
DEFGINY	DEFYING	DEFORST	DEFROST, FROSTED	DEGILRU	GUILDER
DEFGIOR	FIREDOG	DEFORWX	WEXFORD	DEGILUV	DIVULGE
DEFGIRS	FRIDGES	DEGGGIL	GIGGLED	DEGIMNN	MENDING
DEFGIRU	FIGURED	DEGGGLO	GOGGLED	DEGIMST	MIDGETS
DEFGIST	FIDGETS	DEGGHIN	HEDGING	DEGINNN	DENNING
DEFGITY	FIDGETY	DEGGIJL	JIGGLED	DEGINNP	PENDING
DEFGORY	GODFREY	DEGGILN	GELDING, NIGGLED	DEGINNR	GRINNED, RENDING
DEFHIRS	REDFISH	DEGGILW	WIGGLED	DEGINNS	ENDINGS, SENDING
DEFHIST	SHIFTED	DEGGINS	EDGINGS	DEGINNT	DENTING, TENDING
DEFHLSU	FLUSHED	DEGGINW	WEDGING	DEGINNU	ENDUING
DEFHORT	FROTHED	DEGGIOS	DOGGIES	DEGINNV	VENDING
DEFIILN	INFIDEL, INFIELD	DEGGIRS	DIGGERS	DEGINNW	WENDING
DEFIIMS	FIDEISM	DEGGISW	SWIGGED	DEGINNY	DENYING
DEFIIMW	MIDWIFE	DEGGITW	TWIGGED	DEGINOR	ERODING, GIRONDE,
DEFIINU	UNIFIED	DEGGJLO	JOGGLED		IGNORED, NEGROID, REDOING
DEFIIST	FIDEIST	DEGGJLU	JUGGLED	DEGINOS	DINGOES
DEFIKRS	FRISKED	DEGGLOS	DOGLEGS, SLOGGED	DEGINOW	WIDGEON
DEFILLR	FRILLED	DEGGLPU	PLUGGED	DEGINRR	GRINDER
DEFILPP	FLIPPED	DEGGLRU	GURGLED	DEGINRW	REDWING
DEFILRT	FLIRTED, TRIFLED	DEGGLSU	SLUGGED	DEGINSS	DESIGNS
DEFILRU	DIREFUL	DEGGNOO	DOGGONE	DEGINUX	EXUDING
DEFILRW	WILFRED	DEGGNOS	SNOGGED	DEGIOOS	GOODIES
DEFILST	STIFLED	DEGGNOU	GUDGEON	DEGIOPR	PODGIER
DEFILTT	FLITTED	DEGGORY	DOGGERY	DEGIPPR	GRIPPED
DEFILXY	FIXEDLY	DEGGRRU	GRUDGER	DEGIPRU	PUDGIER
DEFIMOR	DEIFORM	DEGGRSU	GRUDGES	DEGIRRS	GIRDERS
DEFINRS	FRIENDS	DEGGRTU	DRUGGET	DEGIRSS	DIGRESS
DEFINRW	WINFRED	DEGHILT	DELIGHT, LIGHTED	DEGIRTT	GRITTED
DEFINSU	INFUSED	DEGHINR	HERDING	DEGISST	DIGESTS
DEFIOOS	FOODIES	DEGHINW	WHINGED	DEGLNOU	LOUNGED
DEFIOST	FOISTED	DEGHIRT	RIGHTED	DEGLNPU	PLUNGED
DEFIPRY	PERFIDY	DEGHIST	SIGHTED	DEGLNSU	GULDENS
				DEGLOPR	PLEDGOR

DEGLOPS	SPLODGE	
DEGLORS	LODGERS	
DEGLORW	GROWLED	
DEGLOSS	GLOSSED, GODLESS	
DEGLTTU	GLUTTED	
DEGLUZZ	GUZZLED	
DEGMOOR	GROOMED	
DEGMSSU	SMUDGES	
DEGNNOU	DUNGEON	
DEGNOPS	SPONGED	
DEGNORU	UNDERGO	
DEGNORW	WRONGED	
DEGNRSU	GERUNDS	
DEGNRTU	GRUNTED, TRUDGEN	
DEGOORV	GROOVED	
DEGOPRU	GROUPED	
DEGORSS	GROSSED	
DEGORSU	GROUSED	
DEGRRTU	TRUDGER	
DEGRSTU	TRUDGES	
DEHHSSU	SHUSHED	
DEHIIRS	DISHIER	
DEHIKRS	SHIRKED	
DEHIKSW	WHISKED	
DEHILRW	WHIRLED	
DEHILSS	SHIELDS	
DEHIMOP	HEMIPOD	
DEHIMOR	HEIRDOM	
DEHIMOT	ETHMOID	
DEHINNS	SHINNED	
DEHINNT	THINNED	
DEHINOR	HORDEIN	
DEHINPT	IN-DEPTH	
DEHINRX	HENDRIX	
DEHINSW	WENDISH	
DEHIORT	THEROID	
DEHIOST	HOISTED	
DEHIOSU	HIDEOUS	
DEHIPPS	SHIPPED	
DEHIPPW	WHIPPED	
DEHIRRU	HURRIED	
DEHIRRW	WHIRRED	
DEHIRSU	RUSHDIE	
DEHIRSV	DERVISH	
DEHIRTV	THRIVED	
DEHIRTW	WRITHED	
DEHISSW	SWEDISH, SWISHED	
DEHISTT	SHITTED	
DEHIWZZ	WHIZZED	
DEHJNOO	JOHN DOE	
DEHLMNO	DENHOLM	
DEHLNOS	SHELDON	
DEHLOOT	TOEHOLD	
DEHLORS	HOLDERS	
DEHLORW	WHORLED	
DEHLOSS	SLOSHED	
DEHLRRU	HURDLER	
DEHLRSU	HURDLES	
DEHLRTU	HURTLED	
DEHLSTU	HUSTLED	
DEHMOST	METHODS	
DEHMOTU	MOUTHED	
DEHMPTU	THUMPED	
DEHNNSU	SHUNNED	
DEHNOOW	HOEDOWN	
DEHNORR	HORDERN	
DEHNORU	HOUNDER	
DEHNOSY	HOYDENS	
DEHNOTZ	DOZENTH	
DEHNRTU	THUNDER	
DEHNSTU	SHUNTED	
DEHOOPW	WHOOPED	
DEHOOST	SOOTHED	
DEHOOWY	HEYWOOD	
DEHOPPS	SHOPPED	
DEHOPPW	WHOPPED	
DEHOQTU	QUOTHED	
DEHORST	SHORTED	
DEHOSTU	SHOUTED	
DEHPPUY	HYPED UP	
DEIIKLS	DISLIKE	
DEIIKNR	DINKIER	
DEIILMP	IMPLIED	
DEIILMT	DELIMIT, LIMITED	
DEIILOS	DOILIES, IDOLISE	
DEIILOZ	IDOLIZE	
DEIINOS	IONISED, SIDONIE	
DEIINOT	EDITION	
DEIINOZ	IONIZED	
DEIINRS	INSIDER	
DEIINRT	NITRIDE	
DEIINRU	URIDINE	
DEIINRV	DIVINER, DRIVE-IN	
DEIINRW	WINDIER	
DEIINSS	INSIDES	
DEIINTV	INVITED	
DEIIORS	IODISER, ISIDORE	
DEIIORT	DIORITE	
DEIIORZ	IODIZER	
DEIIOSX	OXIDISE	
DEIIOXZ	OXIDIZE	
DEIIPRT	RIPTIDE	
DEIIRRT	DIRTIER	
DEIIRZZ	DIZZIER	
DEIISTT	DITTIES, TIDIEST	
DEIISTV	VISITED	
DEIJLLO	JOLLIED	
DEIJNOR	JOINDER	
DEIJNOT	JOINTED	
DEIJNRU	INJURED	
DEIJORY	JOYRIDE	
DEIKLLS	SKILLED	
DEIKLNR	KINDLER	
DEIKLNT	TINKLED	
DEIKLNW	WINKLED	
DEIKLOR	RODLIKE	
DEIKMMS	SKIMMED	
DEIKMPS	SKIMPED	
DEIKMRS	SMIRKED	
DEIKNNS	SKINNED	
DEIKNOS	DOESKIN, SEKONDI	
DEIKNOV	INVOKED	
DEIKNRR	DRINKER	
DEIKNRS	REDSKIN	
DEIKNST	KINDEST	
DEIKNSY	KIDNEYS	
DEIKNTT	KNITTED	
DEIKPPS	SKIPPED	
DEIKRST	SKIRTED	
DEIKRSU	DUSKIER	
DEIKSVY	SKYDIVE	
DEILLOS	DOLLIES	
DEILLPS	SPILLED	
DEILLRR	DRILLER	
DEILLRT	TRILLED	
DEILLST	STILLED	
DEILLSU	SULLIED	
DEILLSW	SWILLED	
DEILMMS	SLIMMED	
DEILMOP	IMPLODE	
DEILMOR	MOLDIER	
DEILMOT	OLDTIME	
DEILMOY	MYELOID	
DEILMPP	PIMPLED	
DEILMPS	DIMPLES	
DEILMST	MILDEST	
DEILMWY	MILDEWY	
DEILNNS	LINDENS	
DEILNOO	EIDOLON	
DEILNOW	LIE-DOWN	
DEILNPS	SPINDLE	
DEILNRT	TENDRIL	
DEILNSW	SWINDLE	
DEILNSY	LINDSEY, SNIDELY	
DEILNTU	DILUENT	
DEILOPR	LEPORID	
DEILOPS	DESPOIL, SPOILED	
DEILOPT	PILOTED	
DEILOPU	EUPLOID	
DEILORS	SOLDIER	
DEILOTW	LOW TIDE	
DEILPPR	RIPPLED	

164

DEILPPS	SLIPPED	DEINSST	DISSENT, SNIDEST	DELLOPR	REDPOLL
DEILPRT	TRIPLED	DEINSTT	DENTIST, STINTED	DELLORR	DROLLER
DEILPTY	TEPIDLY	DEINSTY	DENSITY, DESTINY	DELLORT	TROLLED
DEILQTU	QUILTED	DEIOORW	WOODIER	DELLSTU	DULLEST
DEILRRV	L-DRIVER	DEIOOST	OSTEOID	DELMMSU	SLUMMED
DEILRSW	SWIRLED	DEIOPRS	PERIODS	DELMNOS	DOLMENS
DEILRTU	DILUTER	DEIOPRT	DIOPTRE, PERIDOT	DELMORS	SMOLDER
DEILRTW	TWIRLED	DEIOPRV	PROVIDE	DELMORU	MOULDER,
DEILRTY	TIREDLY	DEIOPSS	DISPOSE	REMOULD	
DEILRVY	DEVILRY	DEIOPST	DEPOSIT, DOPIEST,	DELMOSU	MODULES
DEILRWY	WEIRDLY	POSITED, TOPSIDE		DELMOTT	MOTTLED
DEILRZZ	DRIZZLE	DEIOPTT	TIPTOED	DELMOTU	MOULTED
DEILSTT	SLITTED, STILTED	DEIOPTV	PIVOTED	DELMOUV	VOLUMED
DEILSTW	WILDEST	DEIORRW	ROWDIER, WORDIER,	DELMPPU	PLUMPED
DEILSZZ	SIZZLED	WORRIED		DELMPRU	RUMPLED
DEIMMRS	DIMMERS	DEIORSS	DOSSIER	DELMPSU	SLUMPED
DEIMMRT	MIDTERM, TRIMMED	DEIORST	EDITORS, STEROID,	DELMUZZ	MUZZLED
DEIMMRU	IMMURED	STORIED		DELNOOS	NOODLES
DEIMMST	DIMMEST	DEIORSV	DEVISOR, DEVOIRS	DELNORU	ROUNDEL
DEIMMSU	DUMMIES,	DEIORSW	DOWRIES, WEIRDOS	DELNORY	REYNOLD
MEDIUMS		DEIORTT	DETROIT, DOTTIER	DELNOSU	NODULES
DEIMNPS	MENDIPS	DEIORTU	OUTRIDE	DELNOTW	LETDOWN
DEIMNRS	MINDERS	DEIORWW	WIDOWER	DELNPRU	PLUNDER
DEIMNSS	DIMNESS	DEIOSTU	OUTSIDE, TEDIOUS	DELNRTU	TRUNDLE
DEIMNTU	MINUTED	DEIOSTZ	DOZIEST	DELNUZZ	NUZZLED
DEIMOOR	MOIDORE, MOODIER	DEIOSUV	DEVIOUS	DELOOPS	POODLES
DEIMOPS	IMPOSED	DEIPPQU	QUIPPED	DELOORS	DOLORES
DEIMOST	MODISTE	DEIPPRS	DIPPERS	DELOOTT	TOOTLED
DEIMOTT	OMITTED	DEIPPRT	TRIPPED	DELOPPP	PLOPPED
DEIMOTV	VOMITED	DEIPRSS	SPIDERS	DELOPPS	SLOPPED
DEIMPRU	DUMPIER, UMPIRED	DEIPRST	STRIPED	DELOPPT	TOPPLED
DEIMPSU	MUD PIES	DEIPRSY	SPIDERY	DELOPRT	DROPLET
DEIMPTU	IMPUTED	DEIPSTU	DISPUTE	DELOPRW	PROWLED
DEIMPUX	MIXED UP	DEIQTTU	QUITTED	DELOPTT	PLOTTED
DEIMRUU	UREDIUM	DEIQUZZ	QUIZZED	DELORRY	ORDERLY
DEIMSSU	MISUSED	DEIRRST	STIRRED	DELORST	OLDSTER
DEIMSTW	MIDWEST	DEIRRSV	DRIVERS	DELORSU	LOURDES
DEIMSTY	STYMIED	DEIRSST	STRIDES	DELOSTT	SLOTTED
DEINNOT	INTONED	DEIRSTU	DUSTIER	DELOSTU	LOUDEST, TOUSLED
DEINNRS	DINNERS	DEISSTU	STUDIES	DELOSYY	DOYLEYS
DEINNST	INDENTS	DEISTTW	TWISTED	DELOSZZ	SOZZLED
DEINNTU	DUNNITE	DEITTTW	TWITTED	DELPRSU	SLURPED
DEINNTW	TWINNED	DEJLOST	JOSTLED	DELPUZZ	PUZZLED
DEINOPT	POINTED	DEJOSTU	JOUSTED	DELRRSU	SLURRED
DEINORS	INDORSE, ROSINED	DEKKLSU	SKULKED	DELRSTU	RUSTLED, STRUDEL
DEINORU	DOURINE	DEKLNOP	PLONKED	DELSSTU	TUSSLED
DEINORW	DOWNIER	DEKNNRU	DRUNKEN	DEMMRRU	DRUMMER
DEINPPS	SNIPPED	DEKNOST	DONETSK	DEMNOOR	DOORMEN
DEINPRT	PRINTED	DEKNOSY	DONKEYS	DEMNORS	MODERNS
DEINPST	STIPEND	DEKNOTT	KNOTTED	DEMNORT	MORDENT
DEINRSU	INSURED	DEKNRRU	DRUNKER	DEMNORU	MOURNED
DEINRTT	TRIDENT	DEKOOPS	SPOOKED	DEMNOST	ENDMOST
DEINRTU	INTRUDE, TURDINE,	DEKOPST	DESKTOP	DEMNOTU	DEMOUNT,
UNTRIED		DEKORST	STROKED	MOUNTED	
DEINRTX	DEXTRIN	DELLOOP	LEOPOLD	DEMNOUV	UNMOVED

DEMNSTU	DUSTMEN	DEOPSST	DESPOTS	DGGNOSU	GUNDOGS
DEMOOPP	POPEDOM	DEOPSTT	SPOTTED	DGHIINS	DISHING, HIDINGS, SHINDIG
DEMOORT	MOTORED	DEOPSTU	SPOUTED		
DEMOPST	STOMPED	DEORRSV	DROVERS	DGHIKNO	HODGKIN
DEMORRS	DORMERS	DEORSSS	DOSSERS	DGHILNO	HOLDING
DEMORST	STORMED	DEORSSW	DOWSERS	DGHINTU	HINDGUT
DEMOSTY	MODESTY	DEORSTU	DETOURS	DGHIOOS	GOODISH
DEMPRSU	DUMPERS	DEORSTW	WORSTED	DGHOOST	HOT DOGS
DEMPRTU	TRUMPED	DEORSTY	DESTROY	DGHORTU	DROUGHT
DEMPSTU	STUMPED	DEORTTT	TROTTED	DGHOTUY	DOUGHTY
DEMRRSU	MURDERS	DEORTTU	TUTORED	DGIIILNS	SIDLING, SLIDING
DENNOST	TENDONS	DEOSSYY	ODYSSEY	DGIILNW	WILDING
DENNOUW	UNOWNED	DEOSTTW	SWOTTED	DGIILNY	DINGILY
DENNSTU	DUNNEST, STUNNED	DEOSTUX	TUXEDOS	DGIILRY	RIGIDLY
DENOOPS	SNOOPED, SPOONED	DEPRRSU	SPURRED	DGIIMMN	DIMMING
DENOOSW	SWOONED	DEPRRUY	PRUDERY	DGIIMNN	MINDING
DENOOSZ	SNOOZED	DEPRSTU	SPURTED	DGIIMNS	SMIDGIN
DENOOTU	DUOTONE, OUTDONE	DEPRSUU	PURSUED, USURPED	DGIIMOS	SIGMOID
DENOPPR	PROPEND	DERSSTU	DUSTERS, TRUSSED	DGIINNN	DINNING
DENOPRS	RESPOND	DERSTTU	TRUSTED	DGIINNW	WINDING
DENOPRT	PORTEND	DERSTUU	SUTURED	DGIINOV	VOIDING
DENOPRU	POUNDER	DFFGINO	DOFFING	DGIINPP	DIPPING
DENOPUX	EXPOUND	DFFIIMR	MIDRIFF	DGIINPR	PRIDING
DENORRU	RONDURE, ROUNDER	DFGGINU	FUDGING	DGIINPS	PIDGINS
DENORRW	DROWNER	DFGHIOS	DOGFISH	DGIINPU	PINGUID
DENORST	RODENTS, SNORTED	DFGIINN	FINDING	DGIINRV	DRIVING
DENORSU	RESOUND, SOUNDER	DFGIINY	DIGNIFY	DGIINSS	SIDINGS
DENORSV	VENDORS	DFGILNO	FOLDING	DGIINST	TIDINGS
DENORSW	DOWNERS, WONDERS	DFGINNU	FUNDING	DGIINTY	DIGNITY, TIDYING
DENORUW	WOUNDER	DFGINOR	FORDING	DGIKLNO	KOLDING
DENPRSU	SPURNED	DFGINOU	FUNGOID	DGIKMNO	KINGDOM
DENPRTU	PRUDENT	DFGLOOY	OLD FOGY	DGIKNNU	DUNKING
DENPSSU	SEND-UPS, SUSPEND	DFHILSU	DISHFUL	DGILLNO	DOLLING
DENRSSU	UNDRESS	DFHIMSU	MUDFISH	DGILLNU	DULLING
DENRSSY	DRYNESS	DFIILRW	WILFRID	DGILMNO	MOLDING
DENSTTU	STUDENT, STUNTED	DFIINRW	WINFRID	DGILNOR	LORDING
DENTUVY	DUVETYN	DFILMNU	MINDFUL	DGILNOW	GOLDWIN
DEOOPPS	OPPOSED	DFILNOO	IN FLOOD	DGILOPY	PODGILY
DEOOPRT	TORPEDO, TROOPED	DFILNOP	PINFOLD	DGILPUY	PUDGILY
DEOOPST	STOOPED	DFILOSX	SIXFOLD	DGIMNOO	DOOMING
DEOOPSW	SWOOPED	DFILTUU	DUTIFUL	DGIMNPU	DUMPING
DEOORRT	REDROOT	DFLOOTU	FOLDOUT	DGIMNSU	SIGMUND
DEOORST	ROOSTED	DFLOOTW	TWOFOLD	DGINNNO	DONNING
DEOORTU	OUTRODE	DFNORUY	FOUNDRY	DGINNNU	DUNNING
DEOPPPR	PROPPED	DFNORWY	WYNFORD	DGINNOR	DRONING
DEOPPRR	DROPPER	DGGGIIN	DIGGING	DGINNOU	UNDOING
DEOPPST	STOPPED	DGGGINO	DOGGING	DGINNOW	DOWNING
DEOPPSW	SWOPPED	DGGIILN	GILDING, GLIDING	DGINNUY	UNDYING
DEOPRRU	PROUDER	DGGIINR	GIRDING, RIDGING	DGINORW	WORDING
DEOPRST	RED SPOT, SPORTED	DGGIINU	GUIDING	DGINOSS	DOSSING
DEOPRSW	POWDERS	DGGIJNU	JUDGING	DGINOST	TIN GODS
DEOPRWY	POWDERY	DGGILNO	LODGING	DGINOSU	DOUSING
		DGGINNU	NUDGING	DGINOSW	DOWSING
		DGGIORY	DIGGORY	DGINOTT	DOTTING

DGINSTU	DUSTING	DIILLVY	LIVIDLY	DLMOSUU	MODULUS
DGIOORR	RODRIGO	DIILMTY	TIMIDLY	DLNOOWW	LOW-DOWN
DGIOPRY	PRODIGY	DIILNWY	WINDILY	DLNORUY	ROUNDLY
DGIQSUY	SQUIDGY	DIILQSU	LIQUIDS	DLNOSUY	SOUNDLY
DGISSTU	DISGUST	DIILRSU	SILURID	DLNOTUW	WOULDN'T
DGLNOUY	UNGODLY	DIILRTY	DIRTILY	DLOOPPY	POLYPOD
DGLNOWY	GOLDWYN	DIILVVY	VIVIDLY	DLOOPWY	PLYWOOD
DGLOOOW	LOGWOOD	DIILYZZ	DIZZILY	DLOORRU	OUR LORD
DGLOPSY	SPLODGY	DIIMNOR	MIDIRON	DLOOSTU	OUTSOLD
DGMOPRU	GUMDROP	DIIMSSS	DISMISS	DLOPRUY	PROUDLY
DGNORSU	GROUNDS	DIIMSTW	DIMWITS	DNNORUW	RUN-DOWN
DGNOSSU	SUN GODS	DIIOPRS	SPIROID	DNNOSUW	UNSOUND
DGOOPST	TOP DOGS	DIIORSV	DIVISOR	DNNOSUW	SUNDOWN
DGOORTT	DOGTROT	DIJOSTU	JUDOIST	DNNOUUW	UNWOUND
DGOSTUU	DUGOUTS	DIKKNRU	DUNKIRK	DNOORTU	OROTUND
DHIILOT	LITHOID	DIKORSW	SKID ROW	DNOOTUW	NUTWOOD
DHIIMNO	HOMINID	DILLOSY	SOLIDLY	DNOPRUU	ROUNDUP
DHIINOU	HOUDINI	DILLPSY	PSYLLID	DNOPTUW	PUT-DOWN
DHIINRU	HIRUDIN	DILLRUY	LURIDLY	DNOPUUW	WOUND-UP
DHIIOPX	XIPHOID	DILMNRU	DRUMLIN	DOOORSU	ODOROUS
DHIIORZ	RHIZOID	DILMOOY	MOODILY	DOOORTU	OUTDOOR
DHIIOST	HISTOID	DILNOPT	DIPLONT	DOOORWW	WOODROW
DHIKRSU	KURDISH	DILNOXY	INDOXYL	DOOPRSY	PROSODY
DHILLOS	DOLLISH	DILNPSY	SPINDLY	DOOPRTU	DROPOUT
DHILMUY	HUMIDLY	DILOPVV	PLOVDIV	DPSSTUU	DUSTUPS
DHILNOP	DOLPHIN	DILORWY	ROWDILY, WORDILY	EEEEFRR	REFEREE
DHILOST	DOLTISH	DILOSSU	DULOSIS, SOLIDUS	EEEEGGS	GEE-GEES
DHILPSY	SYLPHID	DILOSTY	STYLOID	EEEEGTX	EXEGETE
DHIMOPR	DIMORPH	DILRYZZ	DRIZZLY	EEEELNV	EVELEEN
DHIMORU	HUMIDOR,	DIMMOST	MIDMOST	EEEEPST	TEEPEES
	RHODIUM	DIMNOOR	MINDORO	EEEFGRU	REFUGEE
DHINNOS	DONNISH	DIMNOPU	IMPOUND	EEEEFLRS	FEELERS
DHINORS	DRONISH	DIMNORV	MORDVIN	EEEFLRT	FLEETER
DHIOPTY	TYPHOID	DIMOPSU	PODIUMS	EEEFMNR	FREEMEN
DHIORTY	THYROID	DIMRTUU	TRIDUUM	EEEFORS	FORESEE
DHIPRSU	PRUDISH	DINNOSW	SWINDON	EEEFRRS	REEFERS
DHIPRSY	SYRPHID	DINOORS	INDOORS, SORDINO	EEEFRRZ	FREEZER
DHJOPRU	JODHPUR	DINORSW	WINDSOR	EEEGILS	ELEGIES, ELEGISE
DHKORSY	DROSHKY	DINORWW	WINDROW	EEEGILZ	ELEGIZE
DHLMOOU	HOODLUM	DINOSTW	SIT-DOWN	EEEGINP	EPIGENE
DHLOOPR	RODOLPH	DINOSWW	WINDOWS	EEEGINU	EUGENIE
DHLOPRU	RUDOLPH	DINPRSY	SPIN-DRY	EEEGIPR	PERIGEE
DHLOPSU	HOLDUPS	DINPSTU	PUNDITS	EEEGLNT	GENTEEL
DHMMRUU	HUMDRUM	DINSSTU	NUDISTS	EEEGNNO	NEOGENE
DHOOOOS	HOODOOS	DIOORTT	RIDOTTO	EEEGNOS	GENOESE
DHOORST	HOT RODS	DIOPRST	DISPORT, TRIPODS	EEEGNPR	EPERGNE
DHOORTY	DOROTHY	DIOPRTY	TRIPODY	EEEGNRR	GREENER, RENEGER
DHOPRSU	PUSHROD	DIORRST	STRIDOR	EEEGNRV	REVENGE
DHORSSU	SHROUDS	DIORSTT	DISTORT	EEEGRRT	GREETER
DIIIMRU	IRIDIUM	DIOSSTU	STUDIOS	EEEGRSZ	GEEZERS
DIIINPS	INSIPID	DIPRSTU	DISRUPT	EEEGRUX	EXERGUE
DIIIJNOS	DISJOIN	DKLOOPS	PODOLSK	EEEHILW	WHEELIE
DIIKKNS	KIDSKIN	DLLOOPS	DOLLOPS	EEEHLLN	HELLENE
DIIKNRU	KIRUNDI	DLLORWY	WORLDLY	EEEHLNR	HEERLEN

167

EEEHLRW	WHEELER
EEEHRRS	SHEERER
EEEHRST	THERESE
EEEHRWZ	WHEEZER
EEEHSTT	ESTHETE
EEEHSWZ	WHEEZES
EEEIKLL	EEL-LIKE
EEEIKLZ	EZEKIEL
EEEILMN	EMELINE
EEEILNV	EVELINE
EEEILRR	LEERIER
EEEILRV	RELIEVE
EEEILVY	EVIL EYE
EEEIMNS	ENEMIES
EEEIMNT	EMETINE
EEEIMPR	EPIMERE
EEEIMRT	EREMITE
EEEINQU	QUEENIE
EEEINRS	ESERINE
EEEINRW	WEENIER
EEEINST	STEENIE
EEEIPST	EPEEIST
EEEIRRV	REVERIE
EEEISTW	SWEETIE
EEEKLNX	KLEENEX
EEEKLRS	SLEEKER
EEEKMST	MEEKEST
EEEKNPT	KEEPNET
EEEKNST	KEENEST
EEEKPRS	KEEPERS
EEEKRSS	SEEKERS
EEELLST	ESTELLE
EEELMNT	ELEMENT
EEELNNO	NOELEEN
EEELNSV	ELEVENS
EEELPRS	SLEEPER
EEELPRT	REPLETE
EEELPST	STEEPLE
EEELRTV	LEVERET
EEELSSS	LESSEES
EEELSSV	SLEEVES
EEELSSY	EYELESS
EEELSTX	TELEXES
EEELSTY	EYELETS
EEEMNSS	NEMESES
EEEMRTX	EXTREME
EEENNPT	PENTENE
EEENNTT	ENTENTE
EEENPRR	PREENER
EEENPRT	PRETEEN, TERPENE
EEENPST	STEEPEN
EEENPSX	EXPENSE
EEENRRS	SNEERER

EEENRRT	ENTERER, RE-ENTER, TERRENE
EEENRRW	RENEWER
EEENRST	ENTREES
EEENRSV	VENEERS
EEENRSZ	SNEEZER
EEENRUV	REVENUE, UNREEVE
EEENSSZ	SNEEZES
EEENSTW	SWEETEN
EEEORSV	OVERSEE
EEEORSY	EYESORE
EEEPPRS	PEEPERS
EEEPRSS	PEERESS
EEEPRST	STEEPER
EEEPRSW	SWEEPER
EEEQRRU	QUEERER
EEEQSUZ	SQUEEZE
EEERRRV	REVERER
EEERRST	STEERER
EEERRSV	RESERVE, REVERSE
EEERSTV	EVEREST
EEERSTW	SWEETER
EEERTTW	TWEETER
EEESSTT	SETTEES
EEFFFNO	ENFEOFF
EEFFINT	FIFTEEN
EEFFJRY	JEFFERY, JEFFREY
EEFFORR	OFFERER
EEFFOST	TOFFEES
EEFGILN	FEELING, FLEEING
EEFGINR	FEIGNER, FREEING, REEFING
EEFGLLU	GLEEFUL
EEFGLOR	FORELEG
EEFGRSU	REFUGES
EEFHIRS	HEIFERS
EEFHIRT	HEFTIER
EEFHISY	FISH-EYE
EEFHITZ	HEIFETZ
EEFHLRS	FLESHER, HERSELF
EEFHLSS	FLESHES
EEFHNRS	FRESHEN
EEFHORT	THEREOF
EEFHORW	WHEREOF
EEFHRRS	FRESHER, REFRESH
EEFHRST	FRESHET
EEFIIRR	FIERIER, REIFIER
EEFIJNR	JENIFER
EEFILLX	FLEXILE
EEFILNO	OLEFINE
EEFILNS	FELINES
EEFILOS	FIESOLE
EEFILRS	RELIEFS
EEFILRT	FERTILE
EEFILST	FELSITE, LEFTIES

EEFIMNR	FIREMEN
EEFINRR	REFINER
EEFINSS	FINESSE
EEFIRRS	FERRIES
EEFIRRT	FERRITE, FIRTREE
EEFIRSZ	FRIEZES
EEFISTV	FESTIVE
EEFLLRS	FELLERS
EEFLLRU	FUELLER
EEFLNOS	ONESELF
EEFLNRS	FLENSER, FRESNEL
EEFLRRU	FERRULE
EEFLRUX	FLEXURE
EEFMNOR	FOREMEN
EEFMNRT	FERMENT
EEFMOTT	MOFETTE
EEFMPRU	PERFUME
EEFNRRW	RENFREW
EEFNRRY	FERNERY
EEFNRTV	FERVENT
EEFNSSW	FEWNESS
EEFNSSY	FEYNESS
EEFNSTU	FUENTES
EEFORRV	FOREVER
EEFOTTU	FOUETTE
EEFPRSU	PERFUSE
EEFRRST	FERRETS
EEFRRSU	REFUSER
EEFRRTU	REFUTER
EEFRRTY	FERRETY
EEFRSTT	FETTERS
EEFSSTU	FETUSES
EEGGILR	LEGGIER
EEGGIOR	GEORGIE
EEGGLNO	GEELONG
EEGGLPS	PEG LEGS
EEGGNOR	ENGORGE
EEGGNST	NEST EGG
EEGHILN	HEELING
EEGHINY	HYGIENE
EEGHIRW	WEIGHER
EEGHLNO	HENGELO
EEGHMNU	HEGUMEN
EEGHNRY	GREYHEN
EEGIJNR	JEERING
EEGIKLN	KEELING
EEGIKNN	KEENING, KNEEING
EEGIKNP	KEEPING, PEEKING
EEGIKNR	REEKING
EEGIKNS	SEEKING
EEGILLS	GISELLE
EEGILNP	PEELING
EEGILNR	LEERING, REELING
EEGILNT	GENTILE

EEGILRV	VELIGER	EEHINRR	ERRHINE	EEHSTTW	THE WEST
EEGILST	ELEGIST	EEHINRT	NEITHER, THEREIN	EEHSTUY	SHUT-EYE
EEGIMNR	REGIMEN	EEHINRW	WHEREIN	EEIIMST	ITEMISE
EEGIMNS	SEEMING	EEHIPRT	PRITHEE	EEIIMTZ	ITEMIZE
EEGIMNT	MEETING, TEEMING	EEHIPSV	PEEVISH	EEIINSY	YENISEI
EEGIMRS	EMIGRES, REGIMES	EEHIPTT	EPITHET	EEIIPST	PIETIES
EEGINNS	ENGINES	EEHIRSS	HEIRESS	EEIIRRV	RIVIERE
EEGINNU	GENUINE, INGENUE	EEHIRST	HEISTER	EEIJKRR	JERKIER
EEGINNV	EVENING	EEHISST	HESSITE	EEIJLLS	JELLIES
EEGINOP	EPIGONE	EEHISTV	THIEVES	EEIJMMS	JEMMIES
EEGINPP	PEEPING	EEHKLOY	KEYHOLE	EEIJNNS	JENNIES
EEGINPR	PEERING	EEHKLSS	SHEKELS	EEIJSTT	JETTIES
EEGINPS	SEEPING	EEHKNNT	KENNETH	EEIKMNP	PIKEMEN
EEGINPV	PEEVING	EEHLLMP	PHELLEM	EEIKNPY	PINKEYE
EEGINPW	WEEPING	EEHLLRY	HELLERY	EEIKNRT	KERNITE
EEGINRS	GREISEN	EEHLLSY	SHELLEY	EEIKPRR	PERKIER
EEGINRT	INTEGER	EEHLMST	HELMETS	EEIKPRS	PESKIER
EEGINRV	VEERING	EEHLNUW	HEULWEN	EEIKTTT	TEKTITE
EEGINSS	GENESIS, GIESSEN	EEHLOSY	HOLY SEE	EEILLNO	LEOLINE
EEGINTT	GINETTE	EEHLPRT	TELPHER	EEILLNS	NELLIES
EEGINTX	EXIGENT	EEHLPST	ELSPETH	EEILLNV	NEVILLE
EEGIPRS	SERGIPE	EEHLRST	SHELTER	EEILLOR	LORELEI
EEGIRRV	GRIEVER	EEHLRSV	SHELVER	EEILLPS	ELLIPSE
EEGISTV	VESTIGE	EEHLRSW	WELSHER	EEILLRV	EVILLER
EEGISTW	GET WISE	EEHLSSV	SHELVES	EEILLST	TELLIES
EEGKNRU	GERENUK	EEHMNOP	PHONEME	EEILLSV	SEVILLE
EEGLLSS	LEGLESS	EEHMNRY	MYNHEER	EEILLSW	WELLIES
EEGLMMU	GEMMULE	EEHMORT	THEOREM	EEILMNN	LINEMEN
EEGLMSU	LEGUMES	EEHMRUX	EXHUMER	EEILMRV	VERMEIL
EEGLNOU	EUGENOL	EEHNNRY	HENNERY	EEILNNO	LEONINE, NOELINE
EEGLNOZ	LOZENGE	EEHNOPT	POTHEEN	EEILNNT	LENIENT
EEGMNST	SEGMENT	EEHNORT	THEREON	EEILNNV	ENLIVEN
EEGMRRS	MERGERS	EEHNORW	NOWHERE, WHEREON	EEILNPS	PENSILE
EEGMRTU	GUM TREE	EEHNPST	STEPHEN	EEILNRV	LIVENER
EEGNORS	NEGROES	EEHNPSW	NEPHEWS	EEILNST	SETLINE, TENSILE
EEGNPUX	EXPUNGE	EEHNSTU	ENTHUSE	EEILNTT	ENTITLE, LINETTE
EEGNRSS	NEGRESS	EEHNSTV	SEVENTH	EEILNTV	VEINLET
EEGNRST	REGENTS	EEHOOPW	WHOOPEE	EEILOPT	PETIOLE
EEGOPRT	PROTEGE	EEHOPRT	THE ROPE	EEILORV	OVERLIE
EEGRRSS	REGRESS	EEHOPRU	EUPHROE	EEILOTZ	ZEOLITE
EEGRRST	REGRETS	EEHOPST	HEPTOSE	EEILPRR	REPLIER
EEGRRSV	VERGERS	EEHORRV	HOVERER	EEILPRS	REPLIES, SPIELER
EEGRRUY	GRUYERE	EEHORST	HERE'S TO	EEILPRT	PERLITE, REPTILE
EEGRSSU	GUESSER	EEHORSU	REHOUSE	EEILPRU	PUERILE
EEGRSSY	GEYSERS	EEHORTT	THERETO	EEILPST	EPISTLE
EEGRSTU	GESTURE	EEHORTW	WHERETO	EEILRRV	REVILER
EEGRSTY	GREYEST	EEHORVW	HOWEVER, WHOEVER	EEILRST	LEISTER, STERILE
EEGSSSU	GUESSES	EEHOSTY	EYESHOT	EEILRSU	LEISURE
EEHHRTW	WHETHER	EEHPPSY	SHEPPEY	EEILRSV	SERVILE
EEHIKLO	HOELIKE	EEHPRSS	SPHERES	EEILSSS	SESSILE
EEHILMN	HEMLINE	EEHRRST	THREE R'S	EEILSST	TELESIS
EEHILOS	HELOISE	EEHRSTT	TETHERS	EEILSSU	ELEUSIS
EEHINOR	HEROINE	EEHRTTW	WHETTER	EEILSTT	LISETTE
EEHINOS	HESIONE			EEILSTV	EVILEST

EEILSTX	SEXTILE	EEIPQRU	PERIQUE	EELMPST	PELMETS, TEMPLES
EEILSUV	ELUSIVE	EEIPRRS	REPRISE, RESPIRE	EELMRST	SMELTER
EEILSVW	WEEVILS	EEIPRRX	EXPIRER	EELNOPR	PERONEL
EEILTTX	TEXTILE	EEIPRST	RESPITE	EELNOPV	ENVELOP
EEILVWY	WEEVILY	EEIPRTT	PETTIER	EELNOSV	SLOVENE
EEIMMNS	IMMENSE	EEIPRVW	PREVIEW	EELNOTT	NOTELET
EEIMMRS	IMMERSE	EEIPRZZ	PREZZIE	EELNOTU	TOLUENE
EEIMNNO	NOMINEE	EEIPSTW	PEEWITS	EELNPSS	SPLEENS
EEIMNNT	EMINENT	EEIQRRU	REQUIRE	EELNQUY	QUEENLY
EEIMNOT	ONETIME	EEIQRSU	ESQUIRE, QUERIES	EELNRST	NESTLER
EEIMNRS	ERMINES	EEIQRTU	QUIETER, REQUITE	EELNSTT	NETTLES
EEIMNSS	MEISSEN, NEMESIS,	EEIRRRT	RETIRER, TERRIER	EELNSTY	TENSELY
	SIEMENS	EEIRRSV	REVISER	EELNTTU	LUNETTE
EEIMOPS	EPISOME	EEIRRTV	RIVETER	EELNTTY	LYNETTE
EEIMOPT	EPITOME	EEIRRTW	REWRITE	EELOPPS	PEOPLES
EEIMOTV	EMOTIVE	EEIRRVV	REVIVER	EELOPRS	LEPROSE
EEIMPRR	PREMIER	EEIRSSU	REISSUE	EELOPRX	EXPLORE
EEIMPRS	EMPIRES, EPIMERS,	EEIRSTT	TESTIER, TRIESTE	EELOPTU	EELPOUT
	PREMISE, SPIREME	EEIRSTV	RESTIVE	EELORSV	RESOLVE
EEIMPRT	EMPTIER	EEIRSUZ	SEIZURE	EELORTT	LORETTE
EEIMPST	EMPTIES, SEPTIME	EEIRSVW	REVIEWS, VIEWERS	EELORVV	EVOLVER, REVOLVE
EEIMQRU	REQUIEM	EEIRTVV	VETIVER	EELOSTT	TELEOST
EEIMRRR	MERRIER	EEISSTX	SEXIEST	EELOTUV	EVOLUTE
EEIMRRT	TRIREME	EEJNORY	ENJOYER	EELPPRX	PERPLEX
EEIMRSS	MESSIER	EEJNOSS	JONESES	EELPRST	PETRELS, SPELTER
EEIMRST	METIERS	EEJOSTT	JOSETTE	EELPRSU	REPULSE
EEIMRTT	EMITTER, TERMITE	EEJPRRU	PERJURE	EELPRTZ	PRETZEL
EEINNPS	PENNIES	EEJRSST	JESTERS	EELPRVY	REPLEVY
EEINNRV	INNERVE, NERVINE	EEJRSSY	JERSEYS	EELPSST	PESTLES
EEINNST	INTENSE	EEKKRRT	TREKKER	EELPSTY	STEEPLY
EEINNTT	NINETTE	EEKLLSY	SLEEKLY	EELQRUY	QUEERLY
EEINNTW	ENTWINE	EEKLLUU	UKULELE	EELQSSU	SEQUELS
EEINOPR	PIONEER	EEKLNNS	KENNELS	EELRRVY	REVELRY
EEINOPS	PEONIES	EEKLNOS	KEELSON	EELRSTT	LETTERS, SETTLER,
EEINORT	ORIENTE	EEKLNRS	KERNELS		STERLET, TRESTLE
EEINPRR	RIPENER	EEKLRST	KESTREL	EELRSTW	SWELTER, WRESTLE
EEINPRS	EREPSIN	EEKLSTT	KETTLES	EELRSTY	RESTYLE, TERSELY
EEINPSS	PENISES	EEKNOTY	KEYNOTE	EELRSTZ	SELTZER
EEINPSV	PENSIVE, VESPINE	EEKNSTU	NETSUKE	EELSSSU	USELESS
EEINQRU	ENQUIRE	EEKORRV	REVOKER	EELSSSV	VESSELS
EEINQTU	QUIETEN	EEKOSTV	VOETSEK	EELSSSX	SEXLESS
EEINRRT	RENTIER, TERRINE	EEKRSSW	SKEWERS	EELSSTT	SETTLES
EEINRRV	NERVIER, VERNIER	EELLMOS	MOSELLE	EELSTVW	TWELVES
EEINRST	ENTRIES	EELLNOV	NOVELLE	EELSTWY	SWEETLY
EEINRSV	INVERSE	EELLORV	VELLORE	EELTVVY	VELVETY
EEINRTU	RETINUE, REUNITE,	EELLOSV	O LEVELS	EEMMNOT	MEMENTO
	UTERINE	EELLPRS	SPELLER	EEMMRST	STEMMER
EEINSTV	TENSIVE	EELLPST	PELLETS	EEMNNOV	ENVENOM
EEINSTX	SIXTEEN	EELLQRU	QUELLER	EEMNOOS	SOMEONE
EEINSTY	SYENITE	EELLRSS	SELLERS	EEMNOOY	MOONEYE
EEIORSS	SOIREES	EELLRST	TELLERS	EEMNPTU	UMPTEEN
EEIORSV	EROSIVE	EELLSTW	WELL-SET	EEMNSYZ	ENZYMES
EEIPPST	PEPTISE	EELMORW	EELWORM	EEMOPRR	EMPEROR
EEIPPTT	PIPETTE	EELMOSY	MOSELEY	EEMOPRW	EMPOWER
EEIPPTZ	PEPTIZE				

EEMORRS	REMORSE	EEORSST	STEREOS	EFFIORX	FOXFIRE
EEMORRT	REMOTER	EEORSTT	ROSETTE	EFFIPRU	PUFFIER
EEMORRV	REMOVER	EEORSTV	OVERSET	EFFIRST	STIFFER
EEMORST	METEORS	EEORSUV	OVERUSE	EFFJKOR	JERK OFF
EEMORSV	REMOVES	EEORSVW	OVERSEW	EFFLLOW	WELL-OFF
EEMPPRT	PREEMPT	EEORSXX	XEROXES	EFFLMRU	MUFFLER
EEMPRSS	EMPRESS	EEPPPRS	PEPPERS	EFFLNSU	SNUFFLE
EEMPRST	TEMPERS	EEPPPRY	PEPPERY	EFFLOSU	SOUFFLE
EEMPRSU	PRESUME, SUPREME	EEPPPRST	STEPPER	EFFLRRU	RUFFLER
EEMPRTT	TEMPTER	EEPPRSX	PERSPEX	EFFLRSU	RUFFLES
EEMPRTU	PERMUTE	EEPPSST	STEPPES	EFFLRTU	FRETFUL, TRUFFLE
EEMPSTT	TEMPEST	EEPPSUW	UPSWEEP	EFFNOOS	ONE-OFFS
EEMRSSU	RESUMES	EEPRSS	REPRESS	EFFNRSU	SNUFFER
EENNORT	ENTERON, TENONER	EEPRRSU	PERUSER	EFFOPRR	PROFFER
EENNORU	NEURONE	EEPRRTV	PERVERT	EFFORST	EFFORTS
EENNOSS	ESSONNE, ONENESS	EEPRSSS	PRESSES	EFFRSTU	STUFFER
EENNOTY	NEOTENY	EEPRSSV	VESPERS	EFFSSUU	SUFFUSE
EENNPTU	NEPTUNE	EEPRSSX	EXPRESS	EFGGIOR	FOGGIER
EENNRST	TENNERS	EEPRSTT	PRETEST	EFGGIRU	FUGGIER
EENNRUV	UNNERVE	EEPRSTX	EXPERTS	EFGGLOR	FLOGGER
EENNSSW	NEWNESS	EEPRTTX	PRETEXT	EFGHIRT	FIGHTER, FREIGHT
EENOPPR	PROPENE	EEPSSTT	SEPTETS	EFGILLN	FELLING
EENOPPT	PEPTONE	EEPSTTY	TYPESET	EFGILMN	FLEMING
EENOPRS	OPENERS, PENROSE	EEQRRUY	EQUERRY	EFGILNR	FLINGER
EENOPST	ONE-STEP, PENTOSE	EEQRSTU	QUESTER, REQUEST	EFGILNT	FELTING
EENOPTY	NEOTYPE	EERRSSV	SERVERS	EFGILNU	FUELING
EENORTU	EN ROUTE	EERRSTW	STREWER, WRESTER	EFGILNX	FLEXING
EENPRST	PRESENT, SERPENT	EERRSVW	SWERVER	EFGIMNT	FIGMENT
EENPRTV	PREVENT	EERRSVY	SERVERY	EFGINNP	PFENNIG
EENQSTU	SEQUENT	EERRTTU	UTTERER	EFGINOR	FOREIGN
EENRRST	RENTERS, STERNER	EERSSST	TRESSES	EFGINRS	FINGERS, FRINGES
EENRRSU	ENSURER	EERSSTT	SETTERS, STREETS,	EFGINRU	GUNFIRE
EENRRTY	RE-ENTRY		TESTERS	EFGIOOR	GOOFIER
EENRRUV	NERVURE	EERSSVW	SWERVES	EFGIORV	FORGIVE
EENRSTU	TUREENS	EERSTTU	TRUSTEE	EFGIRRU	FIGURER
EENRSTW	WESTERN	EERSTUV	VESTURE	EFGIRSU	FIGURES
EENRSTY	STYRENE	EERTTUX	TEXTURE	EFGLNTU	FULGENT
EENRTUV	VENTURE	EESSTTX	SEXTETS	EFGLORS	GOLFERS
EENSSTT	TENSEST	EESTTTW	WETTEST	EFGMNOR	FROGMEN
EENSSTW	WETNESS	EESTTUZ	SUZETTE	EFGNOOR	FORGONE
EENSSUX	NEXUSES	EFFGRRU	GRUFFER	EFGOORR	FORGOER
EENSTTX	EXTENTS	EFFHILW	WHIFFLE	EFGORRS	FORGERS
EENSTVY	SEVENTY	EFFHIRS	SHERIFF	EFGORRY	FORGERY
EEOPRRS	REPOSER	EFFHIRU	HUFFIER	EFGORTU	FOREGUT
EEOPRRV	REPROVE	EFFHIRW	WHIFFER	EFHIIRS	FISHIER
EEOPRSX	EXPOSER	EFFHLSU	SHUFFLE	EFHIJSW	JEWFISH
EEOPSST	POETESS	EFFIIST	FIFTIES	EFHILMS	FLEMISH, HIMSELF
EEOPSSU	ESPOUSE	EFFIKLS	SKIFFLE	EFHILSS	SELFISH
EEOPSSX	EXPOSES	EFFILNS	SNIFFLE	EFHILTY	HEFTILY
EEOPSTU	TOUPEES	EFFILRR	RIFFLER	EFHINST	FISHNET
EEOPSTY	EYESPOT	EFFILRY	FIREFLY	EFHIORR	FOR HIRE
EEORRST	RESTORE	EFFINRS	SNIFFER	EFHIRST	SHIFTER
EEORRTV	EVERTOR	EFFINST	STIFFEN	EFHIRSY	FISHERY
EEORRTW	REWROTE	EFFIORT	FORFEIT	EFHLLPU	HELPFUL

EFHLLSY	FLESHLY	EFINRST	SNIFTER	EFMOPRR	PERFORM
EFHLOOX	FOXHOLE	EFINRSU	INFUSER	EFMORRS	REFORMS
EFHLOPU	HOPEFUL	EFINRUY	REUNIFY	EFNOOST	FESTOON
EFHLRSU	FLUSHER	EFINSST	FITNESS	EFNORRU	FORERUN
EFHLRSY	FRESHLY	EFIOOPR	POOFIER	EFNORRW	FROWNER
EFHLSSU	FLUSHES	EFIOOST	FOOTSIE	EFNORTU	FORTUNE
EFHLSTY	THYSELF	EFIORRT	ROTIFER	EFNORTW	FORWENT
EFHLTTW	TWELFTH	EFIORRU	FOURIER	EFNRSSU	FURNESS
EFHRRTU	FURTHER	EFIORST	FORTIES	EFOOPRR	REPROOF
EFHRTTU	THE TURF	EFIOSST	SOFTIES	EFOOPRS	SPOOFER
EFIILLS	FILLIES	EFIOSTX	FOXIEST	EFOOPRT	FORETOP
EFIILMR	FILMIER	EFIPRTY	PETRIFY	EFOORSW	WOOFERS
EFIILMS	MISFILE	EFIRRRU	FURRIER	EFOPPRY	FOPPERY
EFIILSS	FISSILE	EFIRRSU	FRISEUR	EFOPRSS	PROFESS
EFIIMRR	RIM-FIRE	EFIRRTT	FRITTER	EFOPRSU	PROFUSE
EFIIMRS	MISFIRE	EFIRRTU	FRUITER	EFORRSU	FERROUS
EFIINRT	NIFTIER	EFIRRTY	TERRIFY	EFORRTY	TORREFY
EFIINRU	UNIFIER	EFIRRZZ	FRIZZER	EFORRUV	FERVOUR
EFIIRZZ	FIZZIER	EFIRSST	SIFTERS	EFORSST	FORESTS
EFIJLLY	JELLIFY	EFIRSSU	FISSURE, FUSSIER	EFOSSTT	SOFTEST
EFIJLOT	JETFOIL	EFIRSTT	FITTERS, TITFERS	EFPRTUY	PUTREFY
EFIKLNU	LIKE FUN	EFIRSTU	FUSTIER, SURFEIT	EFPSTUY	STUPEFY
EFIKLOX	FOXLIKE	EFIRSTW	SWIFTER	EFRRSSU	SURFERS
EFIKNRU	FUNKIER	EFIRSVY	VERSIFY	EFRSTUU	FUTURES
EFIKRRS	FRISKER	EFIRTUV	FURTIVE	EGGGILN	LEGGING
EFIKRST	FRISKET	EFIRTUX	FIXTURE	EGGGILR	GIGGLER
EFILLOS	FOLLIES	EFIRUZZ	FUZZIER	EGGGILS	GIGGLES
EFILLOW	LOW LIFE	EFISTTT	FITTEST	EGGGINP	PEGGING
EFILLRS	REFILLS	EFISTTY	TESTIFY	EGGGLOS	GOGGLES
EFILLST	FILLETS	EFKLMNO	MENFOLK	EGGIIPR	PIGGIER
EFILMST	FILMSET, LEFTISM	EFKLNUY	FLUNKEY	EGGIIPS	PIGGIES
EFILNOX	FLEXION	EFLLOSW	FELLOWS	EGGIJLS	JIGGLES
EFILOOS	FOLIOSE	EFLLSTU	FULLEST	EGGIJRS	JIGGERS
EFILOPR	PROFILE, PRO-LIFE	EFLMOSU	FULSOME	EGGILLN	GELLING
EFILORR	FLORRIE	EFLMSUU	MUSEFUL	EGGILNR	NIGGLER
EFILORT	LOFTIER, TREFOIL	EFLNNSU	FUNNELS	EGGILNS	SNIGGLE
EFILOSS	FLOSSIE	EFLNORU	FLEURON	EGGILNU	GLUEING
EFILPPR	FLIPPER	EFLNORY	FELONRY	EGGILRW	WIGGLER, WRIGGLE
EFILQUY	LIQUEFY	EFLNSSU	FULNESS	EGGILSW	WIGGLES
EFILRRT	FLIRTER, TRIFLER	EFLNTUU	TUNEFUL	EGGIMMN	GEMMING
EFILRRY	RIFLERY	EFLOORY	FOOLERY	EGGIMNR	MERGING
EFILRST	FILTERS, STIFLER, TRIFLES	EFLOORZ	FOOZLER	EGGIMOS	MOGGIES
EFILRTT	FLITTER	EFLORSU	OURSELF	EGGIMRU	MUGGIER
EFILRVV	FLIVVER	EFLORSW	FLOWERS	EGGINNS	GINSENG
EFILRZZ	FRIZZLE	EFLORTU	FLOUTER	EGGINRS	NIGGERS, SNIGGER
EFILSTT	LEFTIST	EFLORTW	FELWORT	EGGINRV	VERGING
EFIMMRU	FERMIUM	EFLORVY	FLYOVER, OVERFLY	EGGINRY	GINGERY, GREYING
EFIMNOR	FERMION	EFLORWY	FLOWERY	EGGINTT	GETTING
EFIMNTT	FITMENT	EFLOSTU	FOULEST	EGGIORS	SOGGIER
EFIMRST	FIRMEST	EFLRSTU	FLUSTER, RESTFUL	EGGIPRY	PIGGERY
EFIMRTY	METRIFY	EFLRTTU	FLUTTER	EGGIRRT	TRIGGER
EFINNOR	INFERNO	EFLSTUZ	ZESTFUL	EGGIRSW	SWIGGER
EFINNRU	FUNNIER	EFMNOOT	FOOTMEN	EGGJLOR	JOGGLER
		EFMNORT	FREMONT	EGGJLOS	JOGGLES

EGGJLRU	JUGGLER	EGHNTWY	GWYNETH	EGILNOS	LEGIONS, LINGOES
EGGLLOR	EGG ROLL	EGHOPRS	GOPHERS	EGILNOT	LENTIGO
EGGLMSU	SMUGGLE	EGHORRU	ROUGHER	EGILNPS	SPIGNEL
EGGLNSU	SNUGGLE	EGHORTU	TOUGHER	EGILNPT	PELTING
EGGLOOY	GEOLOGY	EGHORTZ	HERTZOG	EGILNPY	YELPING
EGGLORS	LOGGERS, SLOGGER	EGHOSTT	GHETTOS	EGILNRS	SLINGER
EGGLOST	TOGGLES	EGHRSSU	GUSHERS	EGILNRT	RINGLET, TINGLER
EGGLRSU	LUGGERS	EGHRTUY	THEURGY	EGILNRY	RELYING
EGGMRSU	MUGGERS,	EGIILLS	GILLIES	EGILNSS	SINGLES
SMUGGER		EGIILNT	LIGNITE	EGILNST	GLISTEN, SINGLET
EGGNSTU	NUGGETS	EGIILNV	VEILING	EGILNSW	SLEWING, SWINGLE
EGGNTUY	NUGGETY	EGIILNX	EXILING	EGILNTT	LETTING
EGGORRY	GREGORY	EGIILPZ	LEIPZIG	EGILNTW	WINGLET
EGGSSTU	SUGGEST	EGIIMNP	IMPINGE	EGILNVY	LEVYING
EGHHHIO	HEIGH-HO	EGIIMNR	MINGIER	EGILORR	GROLIER
EGHHIST	EIGHTHS, HEIGHTS,	EGIIMPS	PIGMIES	EGILORS	GLORIES
HIGHEST		EGIIMRR	GRIMIER	EGILOST	LOGIEST
EGHIILL	GHILLIE	EGIINNR	REINING	EGILPST	PIGLETS
EGHIINT	NIGHTIE	EGIINNV	VEINING	EGILRST	GRISTLE
EGHIINV	INVEIGH	EGIINRT	IGNITER	EGILRSU	LURGIES
EGHIKLO	HOGLIKE	EGIINSV	SIEVING	EGILRTT	GLITTER
EGHIKNR	GHERKIN	EGIINSZ	SEIZING	EGILRUV	VIRGULE
EGHILNP	HELPING	EGIINTX	EXITING	EGILRZZ	GRIZZEL, GRIZZLE
EGHILNS	ENGLISH, SHINGLE	EGIINVW	VIEWING	EGILSTU	UGLIEST
EGHILNT	LIGHTEN	EGIIPRW	PERIWIG	EGIMMRR	GRIMMER
EGHILRT	LIGHTER	EGIIPSS	GIPSIES	EGIMMRU	GUMMIER
EGHILSS	SLEIGHS	EGIJKNR	JERKING	EGIMMTU	GUMMITE
EGHILST	SLEIGHT	EGIJLLN	JELLING	EGIMNOW	MEOWING
EGHIMMN	HEMMING	EGIJLNR	JINGLER	EGIMNPR	PERMING
EGHIMNS	MESHING	EGIJLNS	JINGLES	EGIMNPT	PIGMENT, TEMPING
EGHINNU	UNHINGE	EGIJNST	JESTING	EGIMNRT	TERMING
EGHINOS	SHOEING	EGIJNTT	JETTING	EGIMNSS	MESSING
EGHINRR	HERRING	EGIKNNN	KENNING	EGIMOST	EGOTISM
EGHINST	HENGIST	EGIKNOV	EVOKING	EGIMPSY	PYGMIES
EGHINSW	SHEWING	EGIKNPR	PERKING	EGINNNP	PENNING
EGHINTT	TIGHTEN	EGIKNRY	KEY RING	EGINNOP	OPENING
EGHIORS	OGREISH	EGIKNSW	SKEWING	EGINNPU	PENGUIN
EGHIOTV	EIGHTVO	EGILLNS	SELLING	EGINNRR	GRINNER
EGHIRRT	RIGHTER	EGILLNT	TELLING	EGINNRT	RENTING, RINGENT
EGHIRST	SIGHTER	EGILLNW	WELLING	EGINNRV	NERVING
EGHIRSY	GREYISH	EGILLNY	YELLING	EGINNSS	ENSIGNS, SENSING
EGHIRTT	TIGHTER	EGILLRR	GRILLER	EGINNST	NESTING, TENSING
EGHISTW	WEIGHTS	EGILLRS	GRILLES	EGINNSU	ENSUING
EGHITWY	WEIGHTY	EGILLSU	GULLIES	EGINNTT	NETTING
EGHLLOU	LUGHOLE	EGILMMN	LEMMING	EGINNTV	VENTING
EGHLNOR	LEGHORN	EGILMMR	GLIMMER	EGINNVY	ENVYING
EGHLNST	LENGTHS	EGILMNR	GREMLIN	EGINOPR	PERIGON, PONGIER
EGHLNTY	LENGTHY	EGILMNT	MELTING	EGINOPS	PIGEONS
EGHMORS	GERSHOM	EGILMNU	LEGUMIN	EGINORR	IGNORER
EGHMOSU	GUMSHOE	EGILMOS	LIMOGES	EGINORS	REGIONS, SIGNORE
EGHNOOS	HOGNOSE	EGILMOV	MOGILEV	EGINORT	GENITOR, NEGRITO
EGHNORU	ROUGHEN	EGILMPS	GLIMPSE	EGINORZ	ZEROING
EGHNOTU	TOUGHEN	EGILMST	GIMLETS	EGINOSU	IGNEOUS
EGHNRTU	GUNTHER	EGILNOP	ELOPING	EGINOSY	ISOGENY
EGHNSUY	HUYGENS				

EGINOTV	VETOING	EGLNOST	LONGEST	EHHILLS	HELLISH
EGINOUV	IN VOGUE	EGLNOSU	LOUNGES	EHHIRTT	THITHER
EGINPPP	PEPPING	EGLNPRU	PLUNGER	EHHIRTW	WHITHER
EGINPRS	SPRINGE	EGLOORS	REGOSOL	EHHMPTU	THE HUMP
EGINPRY	PREYING	EGLOPSS	GOSPELS	EHHNPSY	HYPHENS
EGINPSW	SPEWING	EGLORRW	GROWLER	EHIIIKT	HEITIKI
EGINPSY	ESPYING	EGLORSS	GLOSSER	EHIIKLP	HIPLIKE
EGINPTT	PETTING	EGLORSU	REGULOS	EHIILLR	HILLIER
EGINPYY	EPIGYNY	EGLPRSU	SPLURGE	EHIINRS	SHINIER
EGINQUU	QUEUING	EGLRSUU	REGULUS	EHIINRT	INHERIT
EGINRRS	RINGERS	EGLRUZZ	GUZZLER	EHIIPPS	HIPPIES
EGINRRW	WRINGER	EGLSSTU	GUTLESS	EHIIPRT	PITHIER
EGINRSS	INGRESS	EGLSTUU	GLUTEUS	EHIISST	SHIITES
EGINRST	RESTING, STINGER	EGMMORT	GROMMET	EHIITTT	HITTITE
EGINRSU	REUSING	EGMNOYZ	ZYMOGEN	EHIJNNO	JOHNNIE
EGINRSV	SERVING	EGMNSTU	NUTMEGS	EHIKLNU	HUNLIKE
EGINRSW	SWINGER, WINGERS	EGMOORR	GROOMER	EHIKLTU	HUTLIKE
EGINRSY	SYRINGE	EGMORSU	MORGUES	EHIKNOS	HONKIES
EGINRTT	GITTERN	EGMORTU	GOURMET	EHIKNRT	RETHINK
EGINRVV	REVVING	EGNNORT	RONTGEN	EHIKNST	KENTISH
EGINSST	SIGNETS	EGNNPTU	PUNGENT	EHIKOOS	HOOKIES
EGINSTT	SETTING, TESTING	EGNNRSU	GUNNERS	EHIKPPS	PISHPEK
EGINSTV	VESTING	EGNNRUY	GUNNERY	EHIKRRS	SHIRKER
EGINSTW	STEWING, TWINGES,	EGNNSTU	STEN GUN	EHIKRSS	SHRIEKS, SHRIKES
	WESTING	EGNNTUU	UNGUENT	EHIKRSU	HUSKIER
EGINTTV	VETTING	EGNOORY	OROGENY	EHIKRSW	WHISKER
EGINTTW	WETTING	EGNOPRS	SPONGER	EHIKSSU	HUSKIES
EGIOOST	GOOIEST	EGNOPRY	PROGENY, PYROGEN	EHIKSVZ	IZHEVSK
EGIOPRS	SERPIGO	EGNOPSS	SPONGES	EHIKSWY	WHISKEY
EGIOPRT	EGO TRIP	EGNORRW	WRONGER	EHILLNO	HELLION
EGIOPRU	GROUPIE	EGNORSS	ENGROSS	EHILLRY	HILLERY
EGIORST	GORIEST	EGNORSU	SURGEON	EHILLTY	LITHELY
EGIORTV	VERTIGO	EGNORSY	GROYNES	EHILNOP	PINHOLE
EGIOSST	EGOISTS	EGNORUY	YOUNGER	EHILNOT	HOTLINE, NEOLITH
EGIOSTT	EGOTIST	EGNOSTU	TONGUES	EHILOPT	HOPLITE
EGIPPRR	GRIPPER	EGNRRTU	GRUNTER	EHILOST	HOLIEST, HOSTILE,
EGIPRRS	GRIPERS	EGNRSYY	SYNERGY		THE SOIL
EGIPRUU	GUIPURE	EGOORSV	GROOVES	EHILPRT	PHILTRE
EGIPSSY	GYPSIES	EGOOSST	STOOGES	EHILPSS	HIPLESS
EGIRSST	TIGRESS	EGOPRRU	GROUPER, REGROUP	EHILRRW	WHIRLER
EGIRSSU	SERGIUS	EGORRSS	GROSSER	EHILRST	SLITHER
EGIRSTU	GUSTIER, GUTSIER	EGORRSU	GROUSER	EHILRSV	SHRIVEL
EGIRTTU	TURGITE	EGORRSW	GROWERS	EHILRSY	SHIRLEY
EGISUWY	WISE GUY	EGORRTU	GROUTER	EHILSTT	LITHEST, THISTLE
EGJLNSU	JUNGLES	EGORRUY	ROGUERY	EHILSTW	WHISTLE
EGKLORW	LEGWORK	EGORSSS	GROSSES	EHILTTW	WHITTLE
EGLLLPU	LEG-PULL	EGORSSU	GROUSES	EHIMMPS	MEMPHIS
EGLLOUY	YULE LOG	EGORTUW	OUTGREW	EHIMMRS	SHIMMER
EGLLSTU	GULLETS	EGPRSUU	UPSURGE	EHIMNRU	INHUMER, RHENIUM
EGLMMRU	GLUMMER	EGRRSUY	SURGERY	EHIMNTY	THYMINE
EGLMNOR	MONGREL	EGRSTTU	GUTTERS	EHIMORS	HEROISM, MOREISH
EGLMOOR	LEGROOM	EGSSSTU	GUSSETS	EHIMORZ	RHIZOME
EGLNNSU	GUNNELS	EHHHOTU	HUHEHOT	EHIMOST	HOMIEST
EGLNORU	LOUNGER	EHHIKSS	SHEIKHS	EHIMPRW	WHIMPER

EHIMRST	HERMITS	EHLOPPR	HOPPLER	EHORSSW	SHOWERS
EHIMRSU	MUSHIER	EHLOPSX	PHLOXES	EHORSTU	SHOUTER, SOUTHER
EHIMRTT	THERMIT	EHLORST	HOLSTER, HOSTLER	EHORSWY	SHOWERY
EHINNOP	PHONE-IN	EHLORSW	HOWLERS	EHORTUX	THEROUX
EHINNRT	THINNER	EHLORTY	HELOTRY, THORLEY	EHOSSST	HOSTESS
EHINOPR	PHONIER	EHLOSST	HOSTELS	EHOSTTT	HOTTEST
EHINOPX	PHOENIX	EHLOSSV	SHOVELS	EHPRSSU	PUSHERS
EHINORR	HORNIER	EHLPRSU	PLUSHER	EHPRSYZ	ZEPHYRS
EHINORS	INSHORE	EHLRSTU	HUSTLER	EHPRTTU	TURPETH
EHINOST	HISTONE	EHLSSTU	SLEUTHS	EHRSSTY	SHYSTER
EHINOSU	HEINOUS, IN-HOUSE	EHLSTTU	SHUTTLE	EHRSTTU	SHUTTER
EHINPRT	PENRITH	EHMNOOR	HORMONE, MOORHEN	EHRSTTW	STREWTH
EHINRSS	SHRINES	EHMNORU	HOME RUN	EIIILST	ILEITIS
EHINRSW	WHINERS	EHMNOSW	SHOWMEN	EIIJMMS	JIMMIES
EHINSSU	HUSSEIN	EHMNPTY	NYMPHET	EIIKKNR	KINKIER
EHINSTZ	ZENITHS	EHMNTTU	HUTMENT	EIIKLMR	MILKIER
EHIOPRS	ROSE HIP	EHMOOSW	SOMEHOW	EIIKLNW	KWEILIN
EHIORRS	HORSIER	EHMORST	MOTHERS, SMOTHER, THERMOS	EIIKLRS	SILKIER
EHIORRT	HERITOR			EIIKNPS	PINKIES
EHIORSS	HOSIERS	EHMORTU	MOUTHER	EIIKNST	INKIEST
EHIORST	HOISTER, SHORTIE	EHMOTUX	EXMOUTH	EIIKPRS	SPIKIER
EHIORSW	SHOWIER	EHMPRTU	THUMPER	EIIKRRS	RISKIER
EHIORSY	HOSIERY	EHMRSUU	HUMERUS	EIIKSTT	KITTIES
EHIORTT	THORITE	EHNNOPR	NEPHRON	EIILLMN	MILLINE
EHIOSTY	ISOHYET	EHNNORW	RHONWEN	EIILLNV	VILLEIN
EHIPPRS	SHIPPER	EHNNRSU	SHUNNER	EIILLRS	SILLIER
EHIPPRW	WHIPPER	EHNOORS	ONSHORE	EIILLSS	SILLIES
EHIPPST	HIPPEST	EHNOPSY	PHONEYS	EIILLSW	WILLIES
EHIPPTW	WHIPPET	EHNOPUY	EUPHONY	EIILMPR	IMPERIL
EHIPRST	HIPSTER	EHNORRY	HERONRY	EIILMRS	SLIMIER
EHIPRSU	PUSHIER	EHNORSS	HORSENS	EIILMRT	LEITRIM, LIMITER
EHIPRSW	WHISPER	EHNORST	HORNETS, SHORTEN, THRONES	EIILMSS	MISSILE, SIMILES
EHIPSTT	PETTISH			EIILMST	ELITISM, LIMIEST
EHIRRSV	SHRIVER	EHNORSU	UNHORSE	EIILMSU	MILIEUS
EHIRRTW	WHERRIT, WRITHER	EHNOSST	HOTNESS	EIILMUX	MILIEUX
EHIRSSV	SHIVERS	EHNOSTT	SHOTTEN	EIILNOS	ELISION, ISOLINE, LIONISE
EHIRSSW	SWISHER	EHNOSTY	HONESTY		
EHIRSTU	HIRSUTE	EHNRSTU	HUNTERS, SHUNTER	EIILNOV	OLIVINE
EHIRSTW	WITHERS	EHNSSSY	SHYNESS	EIILNOZ	LIONIZE
EHIRSTZ	ZITHERS	EHOOPRW	WHOOPER	EIILNRT	NITRILE
EHIRSVY	SHIVERY	EHOOPTY	OOPHYTE	EIILNTU	INUTILE
EHISSSU	HUSSIES	EHOORST	HOOTERS, SHOOTER, SOOTHER	EIILORV	OLIVIER
EHISSSW	SWISHES			EIILOST	OILIEST
EHISSTT	THEISTS	EHOORSV	HOOVERS	EIILOTT	OTTILIE
EHISSTU	HUSSITE	EHOOSST	SESOTHO	EIILRSX	ELIXIRS
EHISTTW	WETTISH, WHITEST	EHOPPRS	HOPPERS, SHOPPER	EIILSTT	ELITIST
EHISWZZ	WHIZZES	EHOPPRT	PROPHET	EIILSTU	UTILISE
EHKNORS	KHERSON	EHOPPRW	WHOPPER	EIILSTW	WILIEST
EHKNRSU	HUNKERS	EHOPRRY	ORPHREY	EIILSUX	LISIEUX
EHKOORS	HOOKERS	EHOPRST	STROPHE	EIILTUZ	UTILIZE
EHLLORS	HOLLERS	EHOPSST	POSHEST	EIIMMSS	MIMESIS
EHLMNOT	MENTHOL	EHOPSTT	THE TOPS	EIIMMST	MISTIME
EHLOOPT	POTHOLE	EHORRST	SHORTER	EIIMNOR	MEIRION
EHLOOST	LESOTHO	EHORRTW	THROWER	EIIMNPR	PRIMINE

EIIMNRT	INTERIM, TERMINI	EIJNORT	JOINTER	EIKOORS	ROOKIES
EIIMNRV	MINIVER	EIJNORY	JOINERY	EIKOPPR	PORK PIE
EIIMNTV	MINIVET	EIJNPRU	JUNIPER	EIKOPRR	PORKIER
EIIMOPP	POMPEII	EIJNRRU	INJURER	EIKOPST	POKIEST
EIIMOSS	MEIOSIS	EIJNSTU	JUSTINE	EIKOSST	KETOSIS
EIIMPSW	WIMPIES	EIJPRTU	JUPITER	EIKPPRS	KIPPERS, SKIPPER
EIIMPTY	IMPIETY	EIJRSTT	JITTERS	EIKPPST	SKIPPET
EIIMSSS	MISSIES	EIJRTTY	JITTERY	EIKRRST	SKIRRET, STRIKER
EIIMSSV	MISSIVE	EIJSSTU	JESUITS	EIKRSSS	KISSERS
EIINNNP	NINEPIN	EIJSSUV	JUSSIVE	EIKRSST	STRIKES
EIINNNS	NINNIES	EIKKOOR	KOOKIER	EIKRSSV	SKIVERS
EIINNPS	PINNIES	EIKKOPS	KOPEISK	EIKRSTT	SKITTER
EIINNQU	QUININE	EIKLLNW	INKWELL	EILLLOS	LOLLIES
EIINNRT	TINNIER	EIKLLRS	KILLERS	EILLLOW	OIL WELL
EIINORS	IONISER, IRONIES, NOISIER	EIKLLST	SKILLET	EILLMNU	MULLEIN
EIINORT	NITEROI	EIKLMMN	MILKMEN	EILLMOT	MELILOT
EIINORZ	IONIZER	EIKLMNR	KREMLIN	EILLMOU	MOUILLE
EIINPPR	NIPPIER	EIKLMRS	MILKERS	EILLMRS	MILLERS
EIINPRS	INSPIRE	EIKLNRU	URNLIKE	EILLMTU	MULLITE
EIINPST	PINIEST, TIEPINS	EIKLNRW	WRINKLE	EILLNSS	ILLNESS
EIINQRU	INQUIRE	EIKLNST	TINKLES	EILLNST	LENTILS, LINTELS
EIINQTU	INQUIET	EIKLNSV	KELVINS	EILLORV	ORVILLE
EIINRTT	NITRITE	EIKLNSW	WINKLES	EILLORW	LOWLIER
EIINRTV	INVITER, VITRINE	EIKLNSY	SKYLINE	EILLOTT	ELLIOTT
EIINRTW	WRITE-IN	EIKLNTW	TWINKLE	EILLPPP	PEP PILL
EIINSTT	TINIEST	EIKLOPS	SKI POLE	EILLPRS	SPILLER
EIINSTU	UNITIES	EIKLPRY	PERKILY	EILLRST	STILLER, TILLERS, TRELLIS
EIINTUV	UNITIVE	EIKLPST	LIPETSK	EILLRSW	SWILLER
EIIORSV	IVORIES	EIKLRST	KILTERS	EILMMRS	SLIMMER
EIIOSTZ	ZOISITE	EIKLRSU	SULKIER	EILMNRY	MERILYN
EIIPPRZ	ZIPPIER	EIKLSTT	SKITTLE	EILMOPR	IMPLORE
EIIPRRV	PRIVIER	EIKMMRS	SKIMMER	EILMPPS	PIMPLES
EIIPRST	TIPSIER	EIKMNNS	KINSMEN	EILMPRS	PRELIMS, SIMPLER
EIIPRSV	PRIVIES	EIKMORS	IRKSOME, SMOKIER	EILMPRU	LUMPIER
EIIPRSW	WISPIER	EIKMOSS	ESKIMOS	EILMPST	LIMPEST, LIMPETS
EIIQQUU	IQUIQUE	EIKMRRS	SMIRKER	EILMPSU	IMPULSE
EIIQUVV	QUI VIVE	EIKMRRU	MURKIER	EILMPSW	WIMPLES
EIIRSSS	SISSIER	EIKMRSU	MUSKIER	EILMPSX	SIMPLEX
EIIRSST	TRISSIE	EIKNNOR	EINKORN	EILMPTY	EMPTILY
EIIRSTW	WIRIEST	EIKNNRS	SKINNER	EILMQSU	QUILMES
EIIRSVZ	VIZIERS	EIKNOOR	ROOINEK	EILMRRY	MERRILY
EIIRTTW	WITTIER	EIKNOPS	PINKOES	EILMRSS	RIMLESS
EIISSSS	SISSIES	EIKNORV	INVOKER	EILMRSU	MISRULE
EIISSTX	SIXTIES	EIKNORW	WONKIER	EILMRSY	MISERLY
EIISTTT	TITTIES	EIKNOSS	KENOSIS	EILMSSY	MESSILY
EIISTUV	UVEITIS	EIKNPRR	PRINKER	EILMSUY	ELYSIUM
EIISTZZ	TIZZIES	EIKNPST	PINKEST	EILMUUV	ELUVIUM
EIJKLRY	JERKILY	EIKNRSS	SINKERS	EILNNPU	PINNULE
EIJKNRS	JERKINS	EIKNRST	KIRSTEN, KRISTEN, STINKER, TINKERS	EILNNST	LINNETS
EIJKNSU	JUNKIES	EIKNRSW	WINKERS	EILNOOR	LOONIER
EIJLLOR	JOLLIER	EIKNRTT	KNITTER, TRINKET	EILNOOS	LOONIES
EIJMPRU	JUMPIER	EIKNSTT	KITTENS	EILNOPR	PROLINE
EIJNORS	JOINERS	EIKNTUZ	KUNZITE	EILNOPS	EPSILON

EILNORT	LORIENT, RETINOL	EILRSVY	SILVERY	EIMPRSU	UMPIRES
EILNOSS	INSOLES, LESIONS,	EILRSZZ	SIZZLER	EIMPRTU	IMPUTER
	LIONESS	EILRTTY	TRITELY	EIMPSTU	IMPETUS
EILNOSU	ELUSION	EILRTUV	RIVULET	EIMRSST	MISTERS
EILNOTU	LINE-OUT, OUTLINE	EILSSTW	WITLESS	EIMRSSU	MISUSER, SURMISE
EILNOTV	VIOLENT	EILSSTY	STYLISE	EIMRSTT	METRIST
EILNOTW	TOWLINE	EILSSVW	SWIVELS	EIMRSTU	MUSTIER
EILNOVV	INVOLVE	EILSTTY	TESTILY	EIMRTUX	MIXTURE
EILNPPS	NIPPLES	EILSTVY	SYLVITE	EIMRUZZ	MUZZIER
EILNPRS	PILSNER	EILSTYZ	STYLIZE	EIMSSSU	MISUSES
EILNPSU	LINEUPS, SPINULE	EILSWZZ	SWIZZLE	EINNOPS	PENSION
EILNPTY	INEPTLY	EIMMMOS	MOMMIES	EINNOPT	PONTINE
EILNPUV	VULPINE	EIMMMSU	MUMMIES	EINNOQU	QUINONE
EILNRTY	INERTLY	EIMMOPS	POMMIES	EINNORT	INTONER
EILNRVY	NERVILY	EIMMORS	MEMOIRS	EINNORU	REUNION
EILNSSS	SINLESS	EIMMPRR	PRIMMER	EINNORV	ENVIRON
EILNSST	SILENTS	EIMMPRU	PREMIUM	EINNOST	TENSION
EILNSTU	UTENSIL	EIMMRRT	TRIMMER	EINNOSV	VENISON
EILOOST	OSTIOLE	EIMMRSW	SWIMMER	EINNOTT	TONTINE
EILOPRS	SPOILER	EIMMSTU	TUMMIES	EINNPRS	SPINNER
EILOPST	PLOESTI	EIMNNOT	MENTION	EINNPST	TENPINS
EILOPSU	PILEOUS	EIMNOOS	NOISOME	EINNPSY	SPINNEY
EILOPSV	PLOSIVE	EIMNOOT	EMOTION	EINNPTU	PINE NUT
EILOPTX	EXPLOIT	EIMNOPT	PIMENTO	EINNQTU	QUENTIN
EILORRS	LORRIES	EIMNOQU	MONIQUE	EINNRRU	RUNNIER
EILORSS	RISSOLE	EIMNORR	MERRION	EINNRSS	SINNERS
EILORST	ESTORIL	EIMNOST	MOISTEN	EINNRST	INTERNS
EILORSU	LOUSIER	EIMNOSW	WINSOME	EINNRSU	SUNNIER
EILORSW	LOW-RISE	EIMNOTU	MOUNTIE	EINNRSW	WINNERS
EILORTT	TRIOLET	EIMNPTU	PINETUM	EINNRTV	VINTNER
EILORTU	OUTLIER	EIMNRST	MINSTER	EINNSTU	TUNNIES
EILOSTT	LITOTES, TOILETS	EIMNSSU	MINUSES	EINOOPZ	EPIZOON
EILOSTV	VIOLETS	EIMNSTT	MITTENS, SMITTEN	EINOORS	EROSION
EILOTUV	OUTLIVE	EIMNSTU	MINUETS, MINUTES	EINOOST	ISOTONE
EILPPRR	RIPPLER	EIMNUZZ	MUEZZIN	EINOOSZ	OZONISE
EILPPRS	RIPPLES, SLIPPER	EIMOORR	ROOMIER	EINOOZZ	OZONIZE
EILPPRT	RIPPLET, TIPPLER	EIMOPRS	IMPOSER, PROMISE	EINOPRT	POINTER, PROTEIN
EILPPRU	PULPIER	EIMOPRV	IMPROVE	EINOPSS	IN POSSE, SPINOSE
EILPPST	STIPPLE, TIPPLES	EIMORRW	WORMIER	EINOQUX	EQUINOX
EILPPSU	PILEUPS	EIMORSS	MOSSIER	EINORSS	SENIORS
EILPPSW	SWIPPLE	EIMORST	MORTISE, TRISOME	EINORST	IN STORE, STONIER
EILPRTT	TRIPLET	EIMORSU	MOUSIER	EINORSV	VERSION
EILPRTX	TRIPLEX	EIMORSV	VERISMO	EINORSW	SNOWIER
EILPRUU	PURLIEU	EIMORTT	OMITTER	EINORTT	TRITONE
EILPSTT	SPITTLE	EIMORTV	VOMITER	EINORTU	ROUTINE
EILPSTU	STIPULE	EIMOSTV	MOTIVES	EINOSSS	SESSION
EILPTTY	PETTILY	EIMOSTZ	MESTIZO	EINOSST	NOSIEST
EILQRTU	QUILTER	EIMOTTU	TIME-OUT	EINOSUV	ENVIOUS, NIVEOUS
EILQRUU	LIQUEUR	EIMOTTW	TWO-TIME	EINPPRS	NIPPERS
EILQTUY	QUIETLY	EIMPQRU	QUIMPER	EINPPST	SNIPPET
EILRRSU	SURLIER	EIMPRRS	PRIMERS	EINPRRT	PRINTER, REPRINT
EILRRTW	TWIRLER	EIMPRSS	IMPRESS, PREMISS,	EINPRSS	SNIPERS
EILRSSV	SILVERS, SLIVERS		SIMPERS	EINPSST	INSTEPS, SPINETS
EILRSTT	LITTERS, SLITTER	EIMPRST	IMPREST, PERMITS	EINPSTU	PUNIEST

EINPTTY	TINTYPE	EIPRRST	STRIPER	EKMNPTU	UNKEMPT
EINQRUY	ENQUIRY	EIPRRSU	UPRISER	EKMNRTU	TURKMEN
EINQSSU	SEQUINS	EIPRRUV	UPRIVER	EKMORSS	SMOKERS
EINQSTU	INQUEST	EIPRSST	PERSIST, PRIESTS,	EKMSSTU	MUSKETS
EINQTTU	QUINTET		SPRIEST, SPRITES, STRIPES	EKNOORS	SNOOKER
EINQTUU	UNQUIET	EIPRSTT	SPITTER, TIPSTER	EKNORSY	ORKNEYS, YONKERS
EINRRSU	INSURER	EIPRSTY	PYRITES, STRIPEY	EKNORTT	KNOTTER
EINRRSU	INSURER	EIPRSUU	EURIPUS	EKNORTW	NETWORK
EINRSSU	INSERTS	EIPRTUW	WRITE-UP	EKNORUY	YUKONER
EINRSSU	SUNRISE	EIPRUVW	PURVIEW	EKNORWY	NEW YORK
EINRSTT	STINTER	EIPSSSU	PUSSIES	EKNRTUY	TURNKEY
EINRSTV	STRIVEN	EIQRSSU	SQUIRES	EKOOPRV	PROVOKE
EINRSTW	WINTERS	EIQRSTU	QUERIST	EKOORRY	ROOKERY
EINRTTU	NUTTIER	EIQRSUV	QUIVERS	EKOORST	STOOKER
EINRTTW	WRITTEN	EIQRTTU	QUITTER	EKOPRRS	PORKERS
EINSSSU	SINUSES	EIQRUVY	QUIVERY	EKORRSW	WORKERS
EINSSSY	SYNESIS	EIQRUZZ	QUIZZER	EKORSST	STOKERS, STROKES
EINSSTW	WITNESS	EIQSTUU	QUIETUS	EKORSWX	EX-WORKS
EINSSUW	SUNWISE	EIQSUZZ	QUIZZES	EKRSSTU	TUSKERS
EINSTTW	TWIN SET	EIRRRST	STIRRER	EKRSTUY	TURKEYS
EINTTUY	TENUITY	EIRRSTU	RUSTIER	ELLMOOR	MORELLO
EIOOPST	ISOTOPE	EIRRSTV	STRIVER	ELLMPUU	PLUMULE
EIOORST	SOOTIER	EIRRSTW	WRITERS	ELLMSTU	MULLETS
EIOORTV	ORVIETO	EIRSSST	SISTERS	ELLNOOW	WOOLLEN
EIOORWZ	WOOZIER	EIRSSTT	SITTERS	ELLNOSW	SWOLLEN
EIOOSTT	TOOTSIE	EIRSSUV	VIRUSES	ELLNSTU	NULL SET
EIOOSTZ	OOZIEST	EIRSTTT	TITTERS	ELLOOSY	LOOSELY
EIOPPPS	POPPIES	EIRSTTU	TERTIUS	ELLOPTU	POLLUTE
EIOPPRS	SOPPIER	EIRSTTV	TRIVETS	ELLORRS	ROLLERS
EIOPRRS	PROSIER	EIRSTTW	TWISTER	ELLORTY	TROLLEY
EIOPRST	REPOSIT, RIPOSTE,	EIRSTUV	VIRTUES	ELLOSTU	OUTSELL, SELL-OUT
	ROPIEST	EIRSUVV	SURVIVE	ELLOSVY	VOLLEYS
EIOPRSX	PROXIES	EIRTTTW	TWITTER	ELLOSWY	YELLOWS
EIOPRTT	POTTIER	EISSSTU	TISSUES	ELLPSTU	PULLETS
EIOPSST	POSTIES	EISSSTX	SEXISTS	ELLPSUY	PULLEYS
EIOPSTT	POTTIES, TIPTOES	EISSTUV	TUSSIVE	ELLRSSU	RUSSELL
EIOPSTU	PITEOUS	EISTTUW	WET SUIT	ELMMOPS	POMMELS
EIORRRS	SORRIER	EJJMNUU	JEJUNUM	ELMMORT	TROMMEL
EIORRRW	WORRIER	EJKNSTU	JUNKETS	ELMMOSS	MOSLEMS
EIORRST	RIOTERS, ROISTER	EJLORST	JOSTLER	ELMMPTU	PLUMMET
EIORRSW	WORRIES	EJLOSSY	JOYLESS	ELMMRSU	SLUMMER
EIORSST	ROSIEST, SORITES,	EJMPRSU	JUMPERS	ELMOORS	MORELOS
	SORTIES, STORIES	EJNORUY	JOURNEY	ELMOORT	TREMOLO
EIORSSU	SERIOUS	EJOORVY	OVERJOY	ELMOPRY	POLYMER
EIORSSX	XEROSIS	EJOPRTT	JETPORT	ELMORSS	MORSELS
EIORSTV	TREVISO	EJORSTT	JOTTERS	ELMORTU	MOULTER
EIOSSTU	OUTSISE	EJORSTU	JOUSTER	ELMOSUU	EMULOUS
EIOSSTV	SOVIETS	EJPRRUY	PERJURY	ELMOSUV	VOLUMES
EIOSTUZ	OUTSIZE	EKKLRSU	SKULKER	ELMPPRU	PLUMPER
EIPPPSU	PUPPIES	EKLNORS	SNORKEL	ELMRSTY	MYRTLES
EIPPRRT	TRIPPER	EKLOORS	LOOKERS	ELMRUZZ	MUZZLER
EIPPRST	TIPPERS	EKLOOTW	WET-LOOK	ELMSSSU	MUSSELS
EIPPRSZ	ZIPPERS	EKMNORW	WORKMEN	ELMSUZZ	MUZZLES
EIPPRTT	TRIPPET	EKMNOSY	MONKEYS	ELNNRSU	RUNNELS
EIPPSUY	YUPPIES				
EIPPTTT	TIPPETT				

ELNNSTU	TUNNELS	ELSSSTU	TUSSLES	ENNOTWW	NEWTOWN
ELNOORZ	LORENZO	ELSSSUY	ULYSSES	ENNPSTU	PUNNETS
ELNOOSU	UNLOOSE	EMMMRSU	MUMMERS	ENNRRSU	RUNNERS
ELNOPRU	PLEURON	EMMMRUY	MUMMERY	ENNRRSTU	STUNNER
ELNOPTU	OPULENT	EMMNOOR	MONOMER	ENOOPRS	SNOOPER
ELNORSY	ROSELYN	EMMNOST	MOMENTS	ENOORRT	TORREON
ELNORTY	ELYTRON	EMMNOTU	OMENTUM	ENOORSU	ONEROUS
ELNOSSS	LESSONS	EMMNOTY	METONYM	ENOORSZ	SNOOZER
ELNOSSW	LOWNESS	EMMOOTY	MYOTOME	ENOOSSZ	SNOOZES
ELNOSTV	SOLVENT	EMMRSSU	SUMMERS	ENOOTTW	TWO-TONE
ELNOSZZ	NOZZLES	EMMRSTU	RUMMEST	ENOOTXY	OXYTONE
ELNOTVY	NOVELTY	EMMRSUY	SUMMERY	ENOPRSS	PERSONS
ELNRSTY	STERNLY	EMMSSUU	MUSEUMS	ENOPRST	POSTERN, PRESTON
ELNSSSU	SUNLESS	EMNNOOW	NEW MOON	ENOPRTT	PORTENT
ELNSSSY	SLYNESS	EMNNOSW	SNOWMEN	ENOPRTW	NEWPORT
ELOORST	LOOTERS	EMNOOST	MOONSET	ENOPRTY	ENTROPY
ELOORTT	ROOTLET, TOOTLER	EMNOPST	POSTMEN	ENOPSST	STEPSON
ELOOSST	LOOSEST	EMNOPSU	SPUMONE	ENOQTUU	UNQUOTE
ELOOSTT	TOOTLES	EMNOPYY	EPONYMY	ENORRSS	SNORERS
ELOOSTU	OUTSOLE	EMNORRU	MOURNER	ENORRST	SNORTER
ELOPRRW	PROWLER	EMNORSS	SERMONS	ENORRTT	TORRENT
ELOPRRY	PYRROLE	EMNORST	MENTORS,	ENORRUV	OVERRUN
ELOPRSU	LEPROUS, PELORUS,		MONSTER	ENORSSS	SENSORS
	SPORULE	EMNORTT	TORMENT	ENORSSY	SENSORY
ELOPRSV	PLOVERS	EMNORTU	MOUNTER,	ENORSTT	STENTOR
ELOPRSY	LEPROSY		REMOUNT	ENORSTU	TONSURE
ELOPRTT	PLOTTER	EMNORTV	VERMONT	ENORSUV	NERVOUS
ELOPRTY	PROTYLE	EMNOSST	STEMSON	ENORTUY	TOURNEY
ELOPSST	TOPLESS	EMNRSTU	MUNSTER, STERNUM	ENOSSTT	STETSON
ELORRSU	ROULERS	EMOOPRS	OOSPERM	ENOSSTX	SEXTONS
ELORSSS	LESSORS	EMOOPRT	PROMOTE	ENOSTUU	TENUOUS
ELORSST	OSTLERS	EMOOORRS	ROOMERS	ENPRRSU	SPURNER
ELORSSV	SOLVERS	EMOOSTT	MOTTOES	ENPRSTU	PUNSTER, PUNTERS
ELORSTT	SLOTTER	EMOOSTW	TWOSOME	ENRRSTU	RETURNS, TURNERS
ELORSTV	REVOLTS	EMOPPST	MOPPETS	ENRRSUY	NURSERY
ELORSTW	TROWELS	EMOPRRS	ROMPERS	ENRRTUU	NURTURE
ELORSUV	LOUVRES, VELOURS	EMOPRST	STOMPER	ENRRTUY	TURNERY
ELORTTY	LOTTERY	EMOPRSU	SUPREMO	ENRSSWY	WRYNESS
ELORTVY	OVERTLY	EMOQSSU	MOSQUES	ENRSTTU	ENTRUST
ELOSSTU	LOTUSES	EMORRST	TREMORS	ENRSVWY	WYVERNS
ELOSSTW	SLOWEST	EMORSSU	MOUSERS	ENSSSTU	SUNSETS
ELOSSTY	SYSTOLE	EMORSUY	SEYMOUR	EOOOPRS	OOSPORE
ELOSTTU	OUTLETS	EMOSSSU	MOUSSES	EOOPPRS	OPPOSER, POOPERS,
ELOSTUU	LUTEOUS	EMPRSTU	STUMPER		PROPOSE
ELPPRSU	PURPLES, SUPPLER	EMPRTTU	TRUMPET	EOOPPRV	POPOVER
ELPRUZZ	PUZZLER	EMPSSSU	MESS-UPS	EOOPRRS	SPOORER
ELPSTUU	PUSTULE	EMRRUUZ	ERZURUM	EOOPRRT	TROOPER
ELPSUZZ	PUZZLES	EMRSSTU	MUSTERS	EOOPRST	POOREST, STOOPER
ELRRSTU	RUSTLER	EMRSTYY	MYSTERY	EOOPRTV	OVERTOP
ELRRTTU	TURTLER	EMSSSTY	SYSTEMS	EOOPRTW	TOWROPE
ELRSSTU	LUSTRES, RESULTS	ENNNOPS	PENNONS	EOORRST	ROOSTER
ELRSTTU	TURTLES	ENNNRUY	NUNNERY	EOOSSSU	OSSEOUS
ELRTTUY	UTTERLY	ENNORTT	TRENTON	EOOTTUV	OUTVOTE
ELRTUUV	VULTURE	ENNORTU	NEUTRON	EOPPPRS	POPPERS
		ENNOSST	SONNETS		

EOPPPST	POPPETS	ERSSTUU	SUTURES	FGIILNR	RIFLING
EOPPRRS	PROSPER	ERSSUVY	SURVEYS	FGIILNS	FILINGS
EOPPRSS	OPPRESS	ERSTTTU	STUTTER	FGIILNT	LIFTING
EOPPRST	STOPPER, TOPPERS	FFFILOT	LIFTOFF	FGIILNY	LIGNIFY
EOPPRSU	PURPOSE	FFGHINU	HUFFING	FGIIMNR	FIRMING
EOPPSSU	SUPPOSE	FFGIINR	GRIFFIN	FGIINNN	FINNING
EOPRRSS	PRESSOR	FFGILNU	LUFFING	FGIINNS	FININGS
EOPRRST	PORTERS, REPORTS, SPORTER	FFGIMNU	MUFFING	FGIINST	SIFTING
		FFGINOR	GRIFFON	FGIINSY	SIGNIFY
EOPRRTU	TROUPER	FFGINOS	OFFINGS, SIGN OFF	FGIINTT	FITTING
EOPRSST	POSTERS, PRESTOS	FFGINPU	PUFFING	FGIINZZ	FIZZING
EOPRSSU	POSEURS	FFGLRUY	GRUFFLY	FGIKNNU	FUNKING
EOPRSSW	PROWESS	FFHHISU	HUFFISH	FGIKNOR	FORKING
EOPRSSY	OSPREYS	FFHILSY	FLY-FISH	FGILNOO	FOOLING
EOPRSTT	POTTERS, PROTEST, SPOTTER	FFHILUY	HUFFILY	FGILNOT	LOFTING
		FFHOOSW	SHOW-OFF	FGILNOU	FOULING
EOPRSTU	PETROUS, POSTURE, SPOUTER, TROUPES	FFHOSTU	SHUT-OFF	FGILNOW	FLOWING, FOWLING, WOLFING
		FFILPUY	PUFFILY		
EOPRSTX	EXPORTS	FFILSTY	STIFFLY	FGILNRU	FURLING
EOPRTTY	POTTERY	FFIMNSU	MUFFINS	FGILNTU	FLUTING
EOPRTVY	POVERTY	FFINOOT	FINFOOT	FGILOOY	GOOFILY
EOPSSSS	POSSESS	FFINOPS	SPIN-OFF	FGILORY	GLORIFY
EOPSSST	POSSETS	FFINOPT	PONTIFF	FGIMNOR	FORMING
EOPSSSU	SPOUSES	FFINPSU	PUFFINS	FGINOOR	ROOFING
EOPSSTX	SEXPOTS	FFINSTU	SNUFF IT	FGINOOT	FOOTING
EOPSTTW	TWO-STEP	FFIOPRS	RIP-OFFS	FGINRRU	FURRING
EOQRSTU	TORQUES	FFIOPST	TIP-OFFS	FGINRSU	SURFING
EORRRST	TERRORS	FFIORTY	FORTIFY	FGINRTU	TURFING
EORRSST	RESORTS, ROSTERS	FFIQSUY	SQUIFFY	FGINSSU	FUSSING
EORRSTT	RETORTS, ROTTERS, STERTOR	FFJMOPU	JUMP-OFF	FGINUZZ	FUZZING
		FFKLORU	FORKFUL	FGIOORT	GO FOR IT
EORRSTU	TROUSER	FFKLOSU	SUFFOLK	FGIORTW	FIGWORT
EORRSZZ	ROZZERS	FFLNSUY	SNUFFLY	FGLNOOR	FOR LONG
EORRTTT	TROTTER	FFNORSU	RUN-OFFS	FGLNORU	FURLONG
EORRTTU	TORTURE	FFNORTU	TURN-OFF	FGLNOSU	SONGFUL
EORSSTU	OESTRUS, OUSTERS, SOUREST	FFOPSTU	PUT-OFFS	FGNORWY	GWYNFOR
		FGGGINO	FOGGING	FGNOSUU	FUNGOUS
EORSSTY	OYSTERS, STOREYS	FGGHIIS	FISHGIG	FHIINNS	FINNISH
EORSTTT	STRETTO	FGGILNO	GOLFING	FHIINPS	PINFISH
EORSTTU	STOUTER	FGGILOY	FOGGILY	FHIKLOS	FOLKISH
EORSUVY	VOYEURS	FGGINOO	GOOFING	FHILOOS	FOOLISH
EORTTTY	TOTTERY	FGGINOR	FORGING	FHILOSW	WOLFISH
EPPPSTU	PUPPETS	FGHHIOS	HOGFISH	FHILSUW	WISHFUL
EPPRRUU	PURPURE	FGHIINS	FISHING	FHINRSU	FURNISH
EPPRSSU	PRESS-UP, SUPPERS	FGHIIPS	PIGFISH	FHINSSU	SUNFISH
EPPRSSU	PURSERS	FGHILST	FLIGHTS	FHIOPPS	FOPPISH
EPPRSUU	PURSUER, USURPER	FGHILTY	FLIGHTY	FHIORRY	HORRIFY
EPRRTUU	RUPTURE	FGHIOSY	FOGYISH	FHIRSST	SHRIFTS
EPRSTTU	PUTTERS, SPUTTER	FGHIRST	FRIGHTS	FHIRSTT	THRIFTS
ERRSSTU	TRUSSER	FGHNOOR	FOGHORN	FHIRTTY	THRIFTY
ERRSSUU	USURERS	FGIIKNN	KNIFING	FHLRTUU	HURTFUL
ERRSSUY	SURREYS	FGIILLN	FILLING	FHNOTUX	FOXHUNT
ERRSTTU	TRUSTER, TURRETS	FGIILMN	FILMING	FHOOOTT	HOTFOOT
ERRSTTY	TRYSTER	FGIILNO	FOILING	FHORSTU	FOURTHS
ERSSSTU	TRUSSES				

FHORSTY	FORSYTH	FLMOOOT	TOMFOOL	GGILNNO	LONGING
FIIKLST	SKI LIFT	FLMOORU	ROOMFUL	GGILNNU	LUNGING
FIILLMY	FILMILY	FLNOORR	FORLORN	GGILNOS	GOSLING
FIILLNS	FILL-INS	FLOOTUW	OUTFLOW	GGILNOW	GLOWING
FIILLPS	FILLIPS	FLOPSTU	POTFULS	GGILNPU	GULPING
FIILNOT	TINFOIL	FLOPSUU	FOUL-UPS	GGILOOS	GIGOLOS
FIILNTY	NIFTILY	FLOSUUV	FULVOUS	GGILOSY	SOGGILY
FIILPTU	PITIFUL	FMOOPRR	PRO-FORM	GGILRWY	WRIGGLY
FIIMSST	MISFITS	FMRSTUU	FRUSTUM	GGIMMNU	GUMMING
FIINOSS	FISSION	FNNRSUU	FUN RUNS	GGIMNSU	MUGGINS
FIINRTY	NITRIFY	FNOOOTT	FOOT-TON	GGINNNU	GUNNING
FIIOPST	POSITIF	FNOORSU	SUNROOF	GGINNOO	ONGOING
FIIRTVY	VITRIFY	FNOPRTU	UPFRONT	GGINNOP	PONGING
FIJLLOY	JOLLIFY	FNORSTY	Y-FRONTS	GGINNOS	NOGGINS
FIJSTUY	JUSTIFY	FOOOPRT	ROOFTOP	GGINOPR	GROPING
FIKKLNO	KINFOLK	FOORSST	OF SORTS	GGINORS	GRINGOS
FIKLLSU	SKILFUL	FOORTTX	FOXTROT	GGINORU	ROUGING
FIKLNSU	SKINFUL	FOPSSTU	FUSSPOT	GGINORW	GROWING
FILLMOY	MOLLIFY	FORRSUW	FURROWS	GGINPPY	GYPPING
FILLNUY	NULLIFY	FORRUWY	FURROWY	GGINPRU	PURGING
FILLOTY	LOFTILY	FORSTWY	FROWSTY	GGINRST	G-STRING
FILNNUY	FUNNILY	GGGHINO	HOGGING	GGINRSU	SURGING
FILNORS	FLORINS	GGGHINU	HUGGING	GGINSTU	GUSTING
FILNOSW	INFLOWS	GGGIIJN	JIGGING	GGINTTU	GUTTING
FILNOUX	FLUXION	GGGIINP	PIGGING	GGIPRSY	SPRIGGY
FILORST	FLORIST	GGGIINR	RIGGING	GGNOORS	GORGONS
FILORTU	FLORUIT	GGGIINW	WIGGING	GHHIKSY	SKY-HIGH
FILOSSS	FOSSILS	GGGIJNO	JOGGING	GHHINSU	HUSHING
FILRSTY	FIRSTLY	GGGIJNU	JUGGING	GHHLOOY	HOOGHLY
FILSSUY	FUSSILY	GGGILNO	LOGGING	GHHORTU	THROUGH
FILSTTU	FLUTIST	GGGILNU	LUGGING	GHHOTTU	THOUGHT
FILSTUW	WISTFUL	GGGIMNU	MUGGING	GHIIKRZ	KIRGHIZ
FILSTWY	SWIFTLY	GGGINNO	NOGGING	GHIILNW	WHILING
FILUYZZ	FUZZILY	GGGINOR	GORGING	GHIILRS	GIRLISH
FIMMMUY	MUMMIFY	GGGINOT	TOGGING	GHIINNS	HSINING, SHINING
FIMNORU	UNIFORM	GGGINOU	GOUGING	GHIINNT	HINTING
FIMOORV	OVIFORM	GGGINPU	PUGGING	GHIINNW	WHINING
FIMORTY	MORTIFY	GGGINTU	TUGGING	GHIINSS	HISSING
FIMSTYY	MYSTIFY	GGHHIOS	HOGGISH	GHIINST	INSIGHT
FINOPSU	SOUPFIN	GGHIINN	HINGING	GHIINSW	WISHING
FINORSS	FRISSON	GGHIINS	SIGHING	GHIINTT	HITTING, TITHING
FIOORSU	FURIOSO	GGHIIPS	PIGGISH	GHIINTW	WHITING
FIOPRST	PROFITS	GGHINSU	GUSHING	GHIJNOS	JOSHING
FIOPSTX	POSTFIX	GGIIILN	GINGILI	GHIKLNU	HULKING
FIORSUU	FURIOUS	GGIINNO	INGOING	GHIKNNO	HONKING
FIORTYZ	FITZROY	GGIINNP	PINGING	GHIKNOO	HOOKING
FIOSTTU	OUTFITS	GGIINNR	RINGING	GHIKNST	KNIGHTS
FIRRSTY	STIR-FRY	GGIINNS	SIGNING, SINGING	GHILLNU	HULLING
FKLNOOR	NORFOLK	GGIINNT	TINGING	GHILLTY	LIGHTLY
FKOOORS	FORSOOK	GGIINNW	WINGING	GHILNOS	LONGISH
FLLOSUU	SOULFUL	GGIINPR	GRIPING	GHILNOW	HOWLING
FLLSTUU	LUSTFUL	GGIINSU	GUISING	GHILNRU	HURLING
FLMMOUX	FLUMMOX	GGILLNU	GULLING	GHILNSY	SHINGLY
FLMNOOU	MOUFLON	GGILMUY	MUGGILY	GHILNTY	NIGHTLY

GHILPST	PLIGHTS	GIIJNNO	JOINING	GIINNTW	TWINING
GHILRTY	RIGHTLY	GIIJNNX	JINXING	GIINOPR	PIG IRON
GHILSST	SLIGHTS	GIIKLLN	KILLING	GIINOPS	POISING
GHILSTY	SIGHTLY	GIIKLMN	MILKING	GIINORS	ORIGINS
GHILTTY	TIGHTLY	GIIKLNN	INKLING, LINKING	GIINORT	RIOTING
GHIMMNU	HUMMING	GIIKLNS	LIKINGS	GIINPPP	PIPPING
GHIMMNY	HYMNING	GIIKNNO	OINKING	GIINPPR	RIPPING
GHIMNOS	GNOMISH	GIIKNNP	KINGPIN, PINK GIN,	GIINPPS	SIPPING
GHIMNPU	HUMPING		PINKING	GIINPPT	TIPPING
GHIMNRY	RHYMING	GIIKNNS	SINKING	GIINPPZ	ZIPPING
GHIMNTT	MIGHTN'T	GIIKNNW	WINKING	GIINPQU	PIQUING
GHINNOP	PHONING	GIIKNPP	KIPPING	GIINPRS	PRISING
GHINNOS	NOSHING	GIIKNPS	PIGSKIN, SPIKING	GIINPRZ	PRIZING
GHINNOT	NOTHING	GIIKNRS	RISKING	GIINPSS	PISSING
GHINNTU	HUNTING	GIIKNSS	KISSING	GIINPST	SPITING
GHINOOS	SHOOING	GIIKNSV	SKIVING, VIKINGS	GIINPSW	SWIPING
GHINOOT	HOOTING	GIIKNTT	KITTING	GIINPTT	PITTING
GHINOPP	HOPPING	GIILLMN	MILLING	GIINPTY	PITYING
GHINORS	SHORING	GIILLNT	LILTING, TILLING	GIINRSS	RISINGS
GHINORT	RIGHT-ON	GIILLNW	WILLING	GIINRSV	VIRGINS
GHINOST	HOSTING	GIILMNN	LIMNING	GIINRTW	WRITING
GHINOSU	HOUSING	GIILMNP	LIMPING	GIINSSU	ISSUING
GHINOSV	SHOVING	GIILMNS	SMILING	GIINSTT	SITTING
GHINOSW	SHOWING	GIILMPR	PILGRIM	GIINSTU	SUITING
GHINOTT	TONIGHT	GIILNNS	LININGS	GIJKNNU	JUNKING
GHINOTU	HOUTING	GIILNNY	LYING-IN	GIJLNOT	JOLTING
GHINPSU	PUSHING	GIILNOR	LIGROIN	GIJMNPU	JUMPING
GHINRSU	RUSHING	GIILNOS	SOILING	GIJNOTT	JOTTING
GHINRTU	HURTING	GIILNOT	TOILING	GIJNTTU	JUTTING
GHIOPSZ	PHIZOGS	GIILNPS	LISPING	GIKLNOO	LOOKING
GHIORSU	ROGUISH	GIILNST	LISTING, SILTING	GIKLNRU	LURKING
GHIOUUZ	GUIZHOU	GIILNSV	LIVINGS	GIKLNSU	SULKING
GHIPRTU	UPRIGHT	GIILNTT	TILTING	GIKMNNU	KUNMING
GHIPTTU	UPTIGHT	GIILNTW	WILTING	GIKMNOS	SMOKING
GHLMOOO	HOMOLOG	GIILORS	OILRIGS	GIKNNOO	KONGONI,
GHLOPSU	PLOUGHS	GIIMMNR	RIMMING		KOONING
GHLORUY	ROUGHLY	GIIMNNT	MINTING	GIKNNOW	KNOWING
GHLOSSU	SLOUGHS	GIIMNPP	PIMPING	GIKNOOR	ROOKING
GHLOSTY	GHOSTLY	GIIMNPR	PRIMING	GIKNORW	WORKING
GHLOSUY	SLOUGHY	GIIMNSS	MISSING	GIKNOST	STOKING
GHLOTUY	TOUGHLY	GIIMNST	MISTING, SMITING	GIKNOUY	YINGKOU
GHMORSU	SORGHUM	GIINNNP	PINNING	GIKNOWY	YINGKOW
GHMOSTU	MUGSHOT	GIINNNS	INNINGS, SINNING	GILLLNO	LOLLING
GHNOPRY	GRYPHON	GIINNNT	TINNING	GILLLNU	LULLING
GHNORST	THRONGS	GIINNNW	WINNING	GILLMNU	MULLING
GHNOSSU	SHOGUNS	GIINNOP	OPINING	GILLNOP	POLLING
GHNOSTU	GUNSHOT,	GIINNOR	IRONING	GILLNOR	ROLLING
	NOUGHTS, SHOTGUN	GIINNPP	NIPPING	GILLNOT	TOLLING
GHNOTTU	OUGHTN'T	GIINNPS	SNIPING	GILLNPU	PULLING
GHORSTU	TROUGHS	GIINNRS	RINSING	GILMNOO	LOOMING
GHORSTW	GROWTHS	GIINNRU	INURING, RUINING	GILMNOT	MOLTING
GHORTUW	WROUGHT	GIINNSW	INSWING	GILMNPU	LUMPING, PLUMING
GHORTUY	YOGHURT	GIINNTT	TINTING	GILMPSY	GYMSLIP
GIIJLNT	JILTING	GIINNTU	UNITING	GILNNSU	UNSLING

GILNOOP	LOOPING, POOLING	GINNTUW	WING NUT	GLNORWY	WRONGLY
GILNOOS	LOOSING	GINNTUY	UNTYING	GLNOSUW	SUNGLOW
GILNOOT	LOOTING, TOOLING	GINOORT	ROOTING	GLNOTTU	GLUTTON
GILNOPP	LOPPING	GINOOTT	TOOTING	GLOOORY	OROLOGY
GILNOPS	SLOPING	GINOOTW	OWING TO	GLOOOTY	OTOLOGY
GILNOPW	PLOWING	GINOPPP	POPPING	GLOOOYZ	ZOOLOGY
GILNORU	LOURING	GINOPPS	SOPPING	GLOORUY	UROLOGY
GILNOSS	LOSINGS	GINOPPT	TOPPING	GLOOSSW	GO-SLOWS
GILNOSU	LOUSING	GINOPRT	PORTING	GLORSSY	GROSSLY
GILNOSV	SOLVING	GINOPRU	IN-GROUP, POURING	GMMPUUW	MUGWUMP
GILNOSW	SLOWING	GINOPRV	PROVING	GMOOPRS	POGROMS
GILNOTT	LOTTING	GINOPST	POSTING, STOPING	GMORSUU	GRUMOUS
GILNOWY	YOWLING	GINOPTT	POTTING	GMORTUW	MUGWORT
GILNPPU	PULPING	GINOPTU	POUTING	GMRUYYZ	ZYMURGY
GILNPRU	PURLING	GINOQTU	QUOTING	GNOPPSU	POPGUNS
GILNPSU	PULSING	GINORSS	SIGNORS	GNOPRUW	GROWN-UP
GILNRSU	RULINGS	GINORST	SORTING, STORING	GNORSUV	GUVNORS
GILNSTU	LUSTING	GINORSU	ROUSING, SOURING	GOOPRST	GOSPORT
GILNSTY	STYLING	GINORTT	ROTTING	GOORSTT	GROTTOS
GILORTY	TRILOGY	GINORTU	ROUTING, TOURING	GOORTUW	OUTGROW
GILOSTT	GLOTTIS	GINOSST	TOSSING	HHINNSU	HUNNISH
GILRSTY	GRISTLY	GINOSSU	SOUSING	HHIORSW	WHORISH
GILRTUY	LITURGY	GINOSTU	OUSTING, OUTINGS	HHMRSTY	RHYTHMS
GILRYZZ	GRIZZLY	GINOSTW	STOWING	HIIKNPS	KINSHIP, PINKISH
GILSTUY	GUSTILY	GINOTTT	TOTTING	HIILLPP	PHILLIP
GIMMMNU	MUMMING	GINOTTU	TOUTING	HIILLPS	PHILLIS
GIMMNSU	SUMMING	GINPPPU	PUPPING	HIILMTU	LITHIUM
GIMNNOO	MOONING	GINPPSU	SUPPING	HIILPTY	PITHILY
GIMNNOR	MORNING	GINPPTU	TUPPING	HIILSTT	HIT LIST
GIMNOOR	MOORING, ROOMING	GINPRRU	PURRING	HIIMNSX	MINXISH
GIMNOOT	MOOTING	GINPRSS	SPRINGS	HIIMPSW	WIMPISH
GIMNOOZ	ZOOMING	GINPRSU	PURSING	HIINSSW	SWINISH
GIMNOPP	MOPPING	GINPRSY	SPRINGY	HIINSTW	SWITHIN
GIMNOPR	ROMPING	GINPSUW	UPSWING	HIJNOUZ	JINZHOU
GIMNORW	WORMING	GINPTTU	PUTTING	HIKKOSU	SHIKOKU
GIMNOSU	MOUSING	GINRSST	STRINGS	HIKLNOT	HOT LINK
GIMNOWY	WYOMING	GINRSTU	RUSTING	HIKLSUY	HUSKILY
GIMNPPU	PUMPING	GINRSTY	STRINGY	HIKMNOS	MONKISH
GIMNSSU	MUSSING	GINRTTU	RUTTING	HIKMSUU	SUKHUMI
GINNNPU	PUNNING	GINSSSU	SUSSING	HIKNNTU	UNTHINK
GINNNRU	RUNNING	GIOPRRU	PRURIGO	HIKNOOU	HOKONUI
GINNNSU	SUNNING	GIOPSSS	GOSSIPS	HIKNOPS	HOPKINS
GINNOPS	SPONGIN	GIOPSST	SPIGOTS	HIKNPSU	PUSHKIN
GINNORS	SNORING	GIOPSSY	GOSSIPY	HIKNRSS	SHRINKS
GINNORW	INGROWN	GIORSTU	RIG-OUTS	HIKRSTU	TURKISH
GINNORY	GIRONNY	GIOSSYZ	ZYGOSIS	HILLPSY	PHYLLIS
GINNOST	STONING	GJOORTT	JOG TROT	HILLRST	THRILLS
GINNOSW	SNOWING	GLMNOOS	MONGOLS	HILLRSY	SHRILLY
GINNPRU	PRUNING	GLMOOYY	MYOLOGY	HILMMOU	HOLMIUM
GINNPTU	PUNTING	GLMORUW	LUGWORM	HILMPSU	LUMPISH
GINNRSU	NURSING	GLNNOOR	LORGNON	HILMSUY	MUSHILY
GINNRTU	TURNING	GLNNOOT	LONG TON	HILMTUU	THULIUM
GINNTTU	NUTTING	GLNOOPR	PROLONG	HILNORY	HORNILY
		GLNOOPY	POLYGON	HILNOTY	THIONYL

HILNPST	PLINTHS	HNOORSU	HONOURS	IIMOPSU	IMPIOUS
HILOOTT	OTOLITH	HNOOSTU	HOUSTON	IIMOSST	MITOSIS
HILORSY	HORSILY	HNOPSSY	SYPHONS	IIMOSSU	SIMIOUS
HILORTU	UROLITH	HNOPSTY	PYTHONS	IIMOSTT	TITOISM
HILOSTU	LOUTISH	HNRTTUU	UNTRUTH	IIMRTTU	TRITIUM
HILOSWY	SHOWILY	HOOPSTT	HOTPOTS, HOT	IINNOOP	OPINION
HILOTWW	WHITLOW		SPOT, POTSHOT	IINNOPS	PINIONS
HILPSUY	PUSHILY	HOORRRS	HORRORS	IINNORS	IN IRONS
HILSSTY	STYLISH	HOPRSTU	HOTSPUR	IINNQTU	QUINTIN
HILSTTY	THISTLY	HOPRTUW	UPTHROW	IINORST	IRONIST
HIMOORS	MOORISH	HOPSTTU	SHOT PUT	IINORTT	INTROIT
HIMOPSS	SOPHISM	HOPSTUY	TYPHOUS	IINORTV	IN VITRO
HIMORTU	THORIUM	HOSTTUU	SHUTOUT	IINOSSV	VISIONS
HIMOTTY	TIMOTHY	HPPSSUU	PUSH-UPS	IINOSTZ	ZIONIST
HIMPRSS	SHRIMPS	HRSSTTU	THRUSTS	IINOTTU	TUITION
HIMPRTU	TRIUMPH	HRSSTUY	THYRSUS	IINPPPS	PIPPINS
HIMSSSU	HUSSISM	IIJNSUU	SINUIJU	IINQRUY	INQUIRY
HIMSSTU	ISTHMUS	IIKKLNY	KINKILY	IINRTTY	TRINITY
HINNOOT	HONITON	IIKLLMY	MILKILY	IINSTTW	NITWITS
HINOORZ	HORIZON	IIKLLSY	SILKILY	IIOQSTU	IQUITOS
HINOOST	IN SOOTH	IIKLMNP	LIMPKIN	IIORSTV	VISITOR
HINOPSS	SIPHONS	IIKLNOS	OILSKIN	IIOSTTT	TITOIST
HINORSU	NOURISH	IIKLPSY	SPIKILY	IIPRSST	SPIRITS
HINORTT	IN TROTH	IIKLRSY	RISKILY	IIPRTVY	PRIVITY
HINORTW	THROW-IN	IIKNRST	KRISTIN	IJJSTUU	JUJITSU
HINRSTU	RUNTISH	IILLLLW	ILL WILL	IJKLLOY	KILLJOY
HINSTUW	WHITSUN	IILLMNO	MILLION	IJKMPSU	SKI JUMP
HIOPRSW	WORSHIP	IILLMSY	SLIMILY	IJLLLOY	JOLLILY
HIOPSST	SOPHIST	IILLNOP	PILLION	IJLLOTY	JOLLITY
HIOPSSY	PHYSIOS	IILLNOZ	ZILLION	IJLMPUY	JUMPILY
HIORSTY	HISTORY	IILMSTU	STIMULI	IJLNOQU	JONQUIL
HIOSSTT	SOTTISH	IILMSTY	MISTILY	IJLNOTY	JOINTLY
HIOTTUW	WITHOUT	IILNNSU	INSULIN	IJNORSU	JUNIORS
HIQSSUY	SQUISHY	IILNNTY	TINNILY	IJRSSTU	JURISTS
HIRSSTT	THIRSTS, T-SHIRTS	IILNORS	SIRLOIN	IKKRSTU	IRKUTSK
HIRSTTU	RUTTISH	IILNOSV	VIOLINS	IKLLPSU	UPSKILL
HIRSTTY	THIRSTY	IILNOSY	NOISILY	IKLLSUY	SULKILY
HJNNOOS	JOHNSON	IILNPPY	NIPPILY	IKLMNRU	MILK RUN
HKKLOOZ	KOLKHOZ	IILNSUV	VILNIUS	IKLMOPS	MILKSOP
HKNOOOS	SHOOK ON	IILOPRT	TRIPOLI	IKLMOSY	SMOKILY
HKNOOWW	KNOW-HOW	IILORTV	VITRIOL	IKLMRUY	MURKILY
HKOOOPT	POTHOOK	IILOSTV	VIOLIST	IKLNOOT	KILOTON
HKOOPSU	HOOKUPS	IILPRVY	PRIVILY	IKLNPSU	LINKUPS
HKOOSVZ	SOVKHOZ	IILPSST	PISTILS	IKLNRWY	WRINKLY
HKORSWY	WORKSHY	IILPSTY	TIPSILY	IKMNOOS	KIMONOS
HLLOOSW	HOLLOWS	IILPSWY	WISPILY	IKMNPPU	PUMPKIN
HLMNOTY	MONTHLY	IILTTUY	UTILITY	IKMOOST	MISTOOK
HLORSTY	SHORTLY	IILTTWY	WITTILY	IKNOPRW	PINWORK
HLPRSUU	SULPHUR	IIMMMNU	MINIMUM	IKNOPST	SKIPTON
HMMNOOY	HOMONYM	IIMMNSU	MINIMUS	IKNORTW	TINWORK
HMOOOST	MOSOTHO	IIMMNNOS	MINIONS	IKNPSTU	SPUTNIK
HMOOSUU	HOUMOUS	IIMMNOSS	MISSION	IKORSTY	YORKIST
HMORSUU	HUMOURS	IIMNOSZ	ZIONISM	ILLMNOU	MULLION
HNOOPTY	TYPHOON	IIMNPRT	IMPRINT	ILLMNRU	MILLRUN

184

ILLMPUY	LUMPILY	ILSSTTY	STYLIST	IOORSTT	RISOTTO
ILLMSUU	LIMULUS	IMMOPTU	OPTIMUM	IOORSTU	RIOTOUS
ILLNPSU	PULL-INS	IMMSSTU	SUMMITS	IOOSSST	OSTOSIS
ILLNPUU	LUPULIN	IMNNOSW	MINNOWS	IOPPPRT	PIT PROP
ILLNTUY	NULLITY	IMNOORT	MONITOR	IOPRSSY	PYROSIS
ILLOPRY	PILLORY	IMNOOST	MOTIONS	IOPRSTT	PROTIST
ILLOPSW	PILLOWS	IMNOOSU	OMINOUS	IOQRTTU	QUITTOR
ILLOSUV	VILLOUS	IMNOOSY	ISONOMY	IORSSTU	SUITORS
ILLOSUY	LOUSILY	IMNOPRW	PINWORM	IORSTTU	TOURIST
ILLOSWW	WILLOWS	IMOOSSS	OSMOSIS	IPPSSSU	PISS-UPS
ILLOTUW	WILL OUT	IMOOSSU	OSMIOUS	IPRRSTU	STIRRUP
ILLOWWY	WILLOWY	IMOPRST	IMPORTS, TROPISM	IPRSSTU	PURISTS
ILLRSUY	SURLILY	IMOPRTU	PROTIUM	IPRSTUU	PURSUIT
ILLSTUY	LUSTILY	IMORRRS	MIRRORS	IPSSSTY	STYPSIS
ILMMSSU	MUSLIMS	IMORSTU	TOURISM	IPSSTTY	TYPISTS
ILMNOOT	MOONLIT	IMORSTY	TORYISM	IQRSSTU	SQUIRTS
ILMNOOY	MOONILY	IMOSSYZ	ZYMOSIS	JNOORSU	JOURNOS, SOJOURN
ILMOOPP	LIMPOPO	IMOSTUV	VOMITUS	KLNOOOW	KOWLOON
ILMOORY	ROOMILY	IMQRSSU	SQUIRMS	KLOOOTU	LOOKOUT,
ILMORTU	TURMOIL	IMQRSUY	SQUIRMY		OUTLOOK
ILMOSTY	MOISTLY	IMRSSTU	TRISMUS, TRUISMS	KMNOOSY	MYKONOS
ILMSTUY	MUSTILY	IMRTTUY	YTTRIUM	KNNNOUW	UNKNOWN
ILMUYZZ	MUZZILY	INNNOOR	NON-IRON	KNNOOTW	NOT KNOW
ILNNSUY	SUNNILY	INNOOPS	OPSONIN	KNOOPTT	TOPKNOT
ILNOOPS	PLOSION	INNOOST	NOTIONS	KNOOSSS	KNOSSOS
ILNOORV	LIVORNO	INNOSTU	NONSUIT	KNOPRTY	KRYPTON
ILNOOST	LOTIONS	INNOSTW	WINSTON	KOOPRSW	WORKSOP
ILNOPRU	PURLOIN	INOOPRT	PORTION	KOOPRTW	WORKTOP
ILNOPSS	SLIP-ONS	INOOPSS	POISONS	KOORTUW	OUTWORK,
ILNOPSU	UPSILON	INOOPST	OPTIONS, POTIONS		WORKOUT
ILNORST	NOSTRIL	INOORSS	ORISONS	KOOSSUU	SOUKOUS
ILNOSST	TONSILS	INOORST	ISOTRON, NITROSO,	LLMOOPR	ROLLMOP
ILNOSTT	STILTON		TORSION	LLNOORS	ROLL-ONS
ILNOSTY	STONILY	INOORTT	TORTONI	LLOOPRT	ROLL-TOP, TROLLOP
ILNOSWY	SNOWILY	INOOSUX	NOXIOUS	LLOPTUU	PULLOUT
ILNPSST	SPLINTS	INOPPST	TOPSPIN	LLORSST	STROLLS
ILNSSTU	INSULTS	INOPPTY	PIT PONY	LMMPSUU	LUMP SUM
ILNTTUY	NUTTILY	INOPRSS	PRISONS	LMNOOOS	SOLOMON
ILOOPST	TOPSOIL	INOPSST	PISTONS	LMOPSUY	OLYMPUS
ILOOSST	SOLOIST	INOPSSU	SPINOUS	LMSTTUU	TUMULTS
ILOOSTY	SOOTILY	INORSTU	NITROUS	LMSTUUU	TUMULUS
ILOOWYZ	WOOZILY	INORSUU	RUINOUS, URINOUS	LNNOPSU	NONPLUS
ILOPPSY	SOPPILY	INORTTY	TRY IT ON	LNORSSY	ROSSLYN
ILOPRSY	PROSILY	INOSSUU	SINUOUS	LNOSTYZ	OLSZTYN
ILOPSST	PISTOLS	INPRSST	SPRINTS	LOPPSUY	POLYPUS
ILOPSTT	SPOTLIT	INPRSTU	TURNIPS	LOPRSUY	PYLORUS
ILOPSUY	PIOUSLY	INPRSTY	TRYPSIN	LOPRTUY	POULTRY
ILOQRTU	TORQUIL	INQSSTU	SQUINTS	LOPSSTY	STYLOPS
ILORRSY	SORRILY	INQSTUY	SQUINTY	LOSTTUY	STOUTLY
ILOSSTY	TYLOSIS	INRSTTU	INTRUST	LPRSSUU	SURPLUS
ILPPSSU	SLIP-UPS	IOOPRRT	PRIOR TO	MMNOORS	MORMONS
ILPPSTU	PULPITS	IOOPRSV	PROVISO	MMNOSSU	SUMMONS
ILRSTUY	RUSTILY	IOOPSTY	ISOTOPY	MMOOPPS	POMPOMS
ILRTTUY	RUTTILY	IOORSSS	SOROSIS	MMOOSTT	TOM-TOMS
				MMOPSTY	SYMPTOM

MMRRSUU	MURMURS	MORRSTU	ROSTRUM	NPRSTUU	TURN-UPS, UPTURNS
MNNOOOS	MONSOON	MORRSUU	RUMOURS	NRSSTUU	UNTRUSS
MNNOSYY	SYNONYM	MORSTUU	TUMOURS	OOPPSVX	VOX POPS
MNOOPTY	TOPONYM	NNOOOPT	PONTOON	OOPRSSU	SOURSOP
MNOPRTU	NO-TRUMP	NNOOPRS	NON-PROS	OOPRSTV	PROVOST
MNORSTU	NOSTRUM,	NNOOPRU	PRONOUN	OOPRTTU	OUTPORT
URMSTON		NNOOPSS	SPONSON	OOPRTUU	OUTPOUR
MNOTTUY	MUTTONY	NNOOPST	NONSTOP	OOPSTTU	OUTPOST
MOOOTYZ	ZOOTOMY	NNORSTU	TURN-ONS	OOPSWWW	POWWOWS
MOOPPSU	POMPOUS	NOOORTT	TORONTO	OORRSSW	SORROWS
MOOPSSU	OPOSSUM	NOOPRSS	SPONSOR	OORSTTU	SORT-OUT
MOOPSTT	TOPMOST	NOOPRST	PROTONS	OPPRRTU	PURPORT
MOORRSW	MORROWS	NOORSTY	ROYSTON	OPPRSTU	SUPPORT
MOOSTTU	OUTMOST	NOORTUW	OUTWORN,	OPPRSTY	STROPPY
MOPPRST	PROMPTS	WORN-OUT		OPRSSTU	SPROUTS, STUPORS
MOPSSSU	POSSUMS	NOPPTUU	PUT-UPON	OPSSSTU	TOSS-UPS
MOPSSUU	SPUMOUS	NOPSSTU	SUNSPOT	OPSTTUU	OUTPUTS
MOQRSUU	QUORUMS	NORTTUU	TURNOUT		

AAAABENN	ANABAENA	AAACDNRS	SANDARAC	AAAEIMRV	AVE MARIA
AAAACCRR	CARACARA	AAACDOTV	ADVOCAAT	AAAEKTWY	TAKEAWAY
AAAACNRS	ANASARCA	AAACEHNR	ARCHAEAN	AAAELMMN	ANALEMMA
AAAADTVV	AVADAVAT	AAACELRT	A LA CARTE	AAAELNPT	PANATELA
AAAAGLRT	AGARTALA	AAACELST	CATALASE	AAAENPRV	PARAVANE
AAAAHJMR	MAHARAJA	AAACENNP	PANACEAN	AAAENPST	ANAPAEST
AAAAIMPR	ARAPAIMA	AAACENPS	PANACEAS	AAAERTWY	TEARAWAY
AAAAIRTX	ATARAXIA	AAACGLSW	SCALAWAG	AAAFGLNO	FANAGALO
AAAAKKNT	KATAKANA	AAACGMNP	CAMPAGNA	AAAFHHRT	HAFTARAH
AAAAKMWY	WAKAYAMA	AAACGMNR	ARMAGNAC	AAAFHILN	HALAFIAN
AAAAKNRW	ARAWAKAN	AAACGNRU	RANCAGUA	AAAFINST	FANTASIA
AAAAKNWZ	KANAZAWA	AAACHLLZ	CHALAZAL	AAAFINUV	AVIFAUNA
AAAANNST	SANTA ANA	AAACIJMN	JAMAICAN	AAAGGLLN	GALANGAL
AAABBILT	ABBATIAL	AAACILMN	MANIACAL	AAAGHINN	GHANAIAN
AAABBNRS	BARNABAS	AAACILRV	CALVARIA	AAAGHINR	HIRAGANA
AAABCCRT	BACCARAT	AAACILSY	CALISAYA	AAAGHIPR	AGRAPHIA
AAABCHLS	CALABASH	AAACIMNP	CAMPANIA	AAAGIKNS	NAGASAKI
AAABCILR	CALABRIA	AAACINTV	CAVATINA	AAAGILRU	LA GUAIRA
AAABCINT	ANABATIC	AAACKMRT	TAMARACK	AAAGINRR	AGRARIAN
AAABCITT	CIABATTA	AAACLLTX	TLAXCALA	AAAGJMNR	JAMNAGAR
AAABCNRU	CARNAUBA	AAACLMNS	ALMANACS	AAAGLMMS	AMALGAMS
AAABCPRY	CAPYBARA	AAACLRTZ	ALCATRAZ	AAAGLMSY	MALAGASY
AAABDEST	DATABASE	AAACNOSV	CASANOVA	AAAGLNRW	WARANGAL
AAABDFIZ	FAIZABAD	AAACNRSV	CARAVANS	AAAGLRST	ASTRAGAL
AAABDLNO	BADALONA	AAACNSTT	CANTATAS	AAAGMMRY	GAMMA RAY
AAABDNNN	BANDANNA	AAACRSWY	CARAWAYS	AAAGMNNN	NAMANGAN
AAABDNRS	SARABAND	AAACSTWY	CASTAWAY	AAAGMNRS	ANAGRAMS
AAABDNRT	ABRADANT	AAADDORV	VADODARA	AAAGMNRT	RAMAT GAN
AAABEHNR	HABANERA	AAADELMS	SALAAMED	AAAGNRTU	TAURANGA
AAABEHRT	BARATHEA	AAADELRW	A RAW DEAL	AAAGORZZ	ZARAGOZA
AAABELLR	ARABELLA	AAADENPS	PASADENA	AAAGPRUY	PARAGUAY
AAABGNST	BATANGAS	AAADENTV	VANADATE	AAAHHITW	HIAWATHA
AAABGRTU	RUTABAGA	AAADGGHH	HAGGADAH	AAAHHTWY	HATHAWAY
AAABHIKZ	ABKHAZIA	AAADGHNR	ANGHARAD	AAAHIINW	HAWAIIAN
AAABHIMN	BAHAMIAN	AAADGLMY	AMYGDALA	AAAHIKLR	KALAHARI
AAABHLMR	ALHAMBRA	AAADGLNN	NAGALAND	AAAHIMNR	MAHARANI
AAABHPRT	BHATPARA	AAADHHSS	HADASSAH	AAAHINNY	HINAYANA
AAABILNN	ALBANIAN	AAADHKNR	KANDAHAR	AAAHJLMT	TAJ MAHAL
AAABINRV	BAVARIAN	AAADHRTZ	AT HAZARD	AAAHKNSW	WAKASHAN
AAABINSS	ANABASIS	AAADILMT	DALMATIA	AAAHMMST	MAHATMAS
AAABLLRT	BALLARAT	AAADILRS	ALASDAIR	AAAHMNOR	MARANHAO
AAABLOPR	PARABOLA	AAADILRU	ADULARIA	AAAHMNRT	AMARANTH
AAABMNRT	MARTABAN	AAADIMNY	ADYNAMIA	AAAHMNST	SAMANTHA
AAABRSUY	SURABAYA	AAADJKRT	DJAKARTA	AAAHNNSV	SAVANNAH
AAACCEPR	CARAPACE	AAADKNNS	SANDAKAN	AAAHNOPR	ANAPHORA
AAACCISU	CAUCASIA	AAADKRRV	AARDVARK	AAAHNPPR	HARAPPAN
AAACCRTT	CATARACT	AAADLMNY	MANDALAY	AAAIINPR	APIARIAN
AAACDEIM	ACADEMIA	AAADLNRS	SAARLAND	AAAIKKSW	KAWASAKI
AAACDENR	DRACAENA	AAADMNTU	TAMANDUA	AAAIKMNO	KAI MOANA
AAACDIMM	MACADMIA	AAADNSTZ	ZAANSTAD	AAAILLMR	MALARIAL
AAACDINN	CANADIAN	AAAEGNPP	APPANAGE	AAAILLPT	PALATIAL
AAACDINR	ARCADIAN	AAAEHLPR	RAPHAELA	AAAILMSV	MALVASIA
AAACDNNO	ANACONDA	AAAEHMNT	ANATHEMA	AAAILMSY	MALAYSIA
AAACDNPR	PANDA CAR	AAAEHNPS	ANAPHASE	AAAILNNS	ANNALISA

AAAILNOT	ANATOLIA	
AAAILNST	ALSATIAN	
AAAILRST	ALASTAIR	
AAAIMNOR	MARIANAO	
AAAIMNRT	ARAMINTA	
AAAIMNST	TASMANIA	
AAAIMRST	SARMATIA	
AAAIMRTV	AMRAVATI	
AAAINNTZ	TANZANIA	
AAAINOPR	PARANOIA	
AAAINRSV	VARANASI	
AAAINRTT	TATARIAN	
AAAIPSSV	PIASSAVA	
AAAIRRSV	RARA AVIS	
AAAJPRUY	JAYAPURA	
AAAKKMRU	KAMAKURA	
AAAKKORT	KRAKATOA	
AAAKLWWY	WALKAWAY	
AAAKMTUU	KAUMATUA	
AAAKNRSS	ARKANSAS	
AAALLPRX	PARALLAX	
AAALLPST	PALATALS	
AAALMNTZ	MAZATLAN	
AAALNRTT	TARLATAN	
AAAMNOPR	PANORAMA	
AAAMNOSZ	AMAZONAS	
AAAMNSSS	MANASSAS	
AAAMNSTZ	MATANZAS	
AAAMOTTU	AUTOMATA	
AAANNSSV	SAVANNAS	
AAANOPRZ	PARAZOAN	
AAANQTUU	AQUANAUT	
AAAPQRTU	PARAQUAT	
AABBCDRS	SCABBARD	
AABBCEGS	CABBAGES	
AABBCEKR	BAREBACK	
AABBCINR	BARBICAN	
AABBCIRR	BARBARIC	
AABBCIST	SABBATIC	
AABBDHIU	ABU DHABI	
AABBDORS	BARBADOS	
AABBEELR	BEARABLE	
AABBEELT	BEATABLE	
AABBEILL	BAILABLE	
AABBEKLN	BANKABLE	
AABBELLM	BLAMABLE	
AABBELLS	BASEBALL	
AABBELRY	BEARABLY	
AABBGGRS	GRAB BAGS	
AABBIILL	BILABIAL	
AABBIRSU	BABIRUSA	
AABBKLTY	BABY TALK	
AABBOORR	BORA BORA	
AABCCEHK	BACKACHE	

AABCCELR	CABLE CAR	
AABCCHKT	BACKCHAT	
AABCCINN	CANNABIC	
AABCCKKP	BACKPACK	
AABCCKLP	BLACKCAP	
AABCCMOT	CATACOMB	
AABCDEIN	ABIDANCE	
AABCDEIT	ABDICATE	
AABCDEKT	BACKDATE	
AABCDELN	BALANCED	
AABCDHKN	BACKHAND	
AABCDHKR	HARDBACK	
AABCDIIS	DIABASIC	
AABCDIKL	LAID-BACK	
AABCDIMO	CAMBODIA	
AABCDKRW	BACKWARD,	
	DRAWBACK	
AABCDKRY	BACKYARD	
AABCEEFL	FACEABLE	
AABCEENY	ABEYANCE	
AABCEERT	ACERBATE	
AABCEGOT	CABOTAGE	
AABCEHLS	CASHABLE	
AABCEILM	AMICABLE	
AABCEILR	BALEARIC	
AABCEIRT	BACTERIA	
AABCEJNO	JACOBEAN	
AABCEKLM	CLAMBAKE	
AABCEKLP	PACKABLE	
AABCEKST	BACK SEAT	
AABCELLL	CALLABLE	
AABCELLP	PLACABLE	
AABCELLS	SCALABLE	
AABCELNR	BALANCER,	
	BARNACLE	
AABCELNS	BALANCES	
AABCELOR	ALBACORE	
AABCELRT	BRACTEAL	
AABCELSU	CAUSABLE	
AABCELWY	CABLEWAY	
AABCEMRV	VAMBRACE	
AABCENRR	CANBERRA	
AABCEPRS	SPACE-BAR	
AABCERST	CABARETS	
AABCESSU	ABACUSES	
AABCFHKL	HALFBACK	
AABCFIIL	BIFACIAL	
AABCFKST	FASTBACK	
AABCGIMO	CAMBOGIA	
AABCHILR	BRACHIAL	
AABCHINR	BRANCHIA	
AABCHKLS	BACKLASH	
AABCHKSW	BACKWASH	
AABCHMRY	CHAMBRAY	
AABCHRRT	BAR CHART	

AABCIILR	BIRACIAL	
AABCIILS	BASILICA	
AABCIJNO	JACOBIAN,	
	JACOBINA	
AABCIKLT	TAILBACK	
AABCILLR	CABRILLA	
AABCILMS	BALSAMIC	
AABCILMY	AMICABLY	
AABCILNN	CANNIBAL	
AABCILNO	ANABOLIC	
AABCIMNR	CAMBRIAN	
AABCINNN	CANNABIN	
AABCINNR	CINNABAR	
AABCINNS	CANNABIS	
AABCINRT	BACTRIAN	
AABCIRSS	BRASSICA	
AABCISSS	ABSCISSA	
AABCKKLT	BACK TALK	
AABCKLPY	PLAYBACK	
AABCKLRT	BLACK ART	
AABCKNPS	SNAPBACK	
AABCKNRS	CAB RANKS,	
	SNACK BAR	
AABCKRRS	BARRACKS	
AABCKSTY	BACKSTAY	
AABCKSWY	SWAY-BACK	
AABCLLSY	SCALABLY	
AABCLNTY	BLATANCY	
AABCLOOR	COOLABAR	
AABCOORS	SOROCABA	
AABCORST	ACROBATS	
AABCRSTT	ABSTRACT	
AABDDEET	DEADBEAT	
AABDDEGN	BANDAGED	
AABDDEHN	HEADBAND	
AABDDHNS	DAB HANDS	
AABDDLNS	BADLANDS	
AABDEELR	READABLE	
AABDEELT	DATEABLE	
AABDEELV	EVADABLE	
AABDEERR	ABERDARE	
AABDEGIN	BADINAGE	
AABDEGLR	GRADABLE	
AABDEGNS	BANDAGES	
AABDEHKR	HARDBAKE	
AABDEKRY	DAYBREAK	
AABDELLS	BALLADES,	
	SABADELL	
AABDELLU	LAUDABLE	
AABDELMN	DAMNABLE	
AABDELOR	ADORABLE	
AABDELPR	DRAPABLE	
AABDELRT	TRADABLE	
AABDELRW	DRAWABLE	
AABDELRY	READABLY	

AABDENOS	A BAD NOSE
AABDENST	BANSTEAD
AABDENTU	UNABATED
AABDENVW	WAVE BAND
AABDEORS	SEABOARD
AABDFHIT	BAD FAITH
AABDFHLN	FAHLBAND
AABDGHNS	HANDBAGS
AABDGHOT	GODTHAAB
AABDGINR	ABRADING
AABDGNOV	VAGABOND
AABDGNSS	SANDBAGS
AABDGORR	GARBOARD
AABDGOTU	GADABOUT
AABDHLLN	HANDBALL
AABDHLLR	HARDBALL
AABDHNST	HATBANDS
AABDHRUY	BURAYDAH
AABDHRYZ	BY HAZARD
AABDIILR	BIRADIAL
AABDIILS	BASIDIAL
AABDIMRS	BARMAIDS
AABDINNR	RAINBAND
AABDINNU	DANUBIAN
AABDIOST	BIODATAS
AABDKNNS	SANDBANK
AABDLLRY	BALLADRY
AABDLLUY	LAUDABLY
AABDLMNU	LABDANUM
AABDLMNY	DAMNABLY
AABDLMRU	ADUMBRAL
AABDLOOT	BOATLOAD
AABDLOPR	LAPBOARD
AABDLORR	LABRADOR, LARBOARD
AABDLRSV	SVALBARD
AABDLRSW	BRADAWLS
AABDMNNS	BANDSMAN
AABDMNRS	ARMBANDS
AABDNNTU	ABUNDANT
AABDNRRY	BARNYARD
AABDNRSS	SANDBARS
AABDORWY	BROADWAY
AABDRRSS	BRASSARD
AABDRSST	BASTARDS
AABDRSTY	BASTARDY
AABEEFLN	FLEABANE
AABEEGKR	BREAKAGE
AABEEGNT	ABNEGATE
AABEEHLL	HEALABLE
AABEEHLR	HEARABLE
AABEEHLT	HATEABLE
AABEEHMR	HARAMBEE
AABEEKRT	TEA BREAK

AABEELLS	LEASABLE, SALEABLE, SEALABLE
AABEELMN	AMENABLE
AABEELMT	MATABELE, TAMEABLE
AABEELPR	REAPABLE
AABEELRS	ERASABLE
AABEELRT	TEARABLE
AABEELRW	WEARABLE
AABEEMPR	ABAMPERE
AABEENOR	ANAEROBE
AABEERST	BASE RATE
AABEFGLS	FLEABAGS
AABEFHKL	HALFBEAK
AABEFLMR	FARMABLE, FRAMABLE
AABEFLMU	FLAMBEAU
AABEGGGS	BAGGAGES
AABEGILN	GAINABLE
AABEGLLL	GLABELLA
AABEGLLM	BALL GAME
AABEGLNW	GNAWABLE
AABEGLRU	ARGUABLE
AABEGMNY	MANGABEY
AABEGNOR	BARONAGE
AABEGORT	ABROGATE
AABEGOST	SABOTAGE
AABEGRRS	BARRAGES
AABEGRTW	WATER BAG
AABEHIMS	MAEBASHI
AABEHKLS	SHAKABLE
AABEHLMS	SHAMABLE
AABEHLPS	SHAPABLE
AABEHLPT	ALPHABET
AABEHLRS	SHARABLE
AABEHLSV	SHAVABLE
AABEHLSW	WASHABLE
AABEIKRR	AIRBRAKE
AABEILLM	MAILABLE
AABEILLS	ISABELLA, SAILABLE
AABEILMN	LIMA BEAN
AABEILRS	RAISABLE
AABEILRV	VARIABLE
AABEILST	SATIABLE
AABEILTV	ABLATIVE
AABEIRSS	AIRBASES
AABEIRSV	ABRASIVE
AABEISUV	BEAUVAIS
AABEKLLS	SLAKABLE
AABEKLLT	TALKABLE
AABEKLLW	WALKABLE
AABEKNRS	NEBRASKA
AABEKNRT	BANK RATE
AABEKOTU	ABEOKUTA

AABELLMT	MEATBALL
AABELLNO	LOANABLE
AABELLOV	ABOVE ALL
AABELLPP	PALPABLE
AABELLPS	LAPSABLE
AABELLPY	PLAYABLE
AABELLSV	SALVABLE
AABELLSY	SALEABLY
AABELLUV	VALUABLE
AABELMPP	MAPPABLE
AABELMST	BLASTEMA, LAMBASTE
AABELMTT	TABLEMAT
AABELMTU	AMBULATE
AABELNOT	ATONABLE
AABELNPS	ANABLEPS
AABELORR	ARBOREAL
AABELOVW	AVOWABLE
AABELPPT	TAPPABLE
AABELPRS	PARABLES, PARSABLE, SPARABLE
AABELPSS	PASSABLE
AABELRTT	BARLETTA
AABELRTY	BETRAYAL
AABELSTT	STATABLE, TASTABLE
AABELSTU	TABLEAUS
AABELSTW	WASTABLE
AABELSWY	SWAYABLE
AABELTTU	TABULATE
AABELTUX	TABLEAUX
AABENOSY	SOYA BEAN
AABENRRT	ABERRANT
AABENRST	RATSBANE, STRABANE
AABENSTU	ANTABUSE
AABFLOTT	FALTBOAT, FLATBOAT
AABGGGNN	GANG-BANG
AABGGRRT	BRAGGART
AABGHKRS	SHAGBARK
AABGHPRR	BAR GRAPH
AABGILMS	MAILBAGS
AABGILRU	BULGARIA
AABGINRS	BARGAINS
AABGLMNU	GALBANUM
AABGLNPS	SLAP-BANG
AABGLRUW	WALBURGA
AABGLRUY	ARGUABLY
AABGMORR	BAROGRAM
AABHHORU	BROUHAHA
AABHIINR	BAHRAINI
AABHIINU	BAUHINIA
AABHILLR	HAIRBALL
AABHILNN	HANNIBAL

AABHILTU	HABITUAL	AABNOSTW	BOTSWANA	AACDEEPS	ESCAPADE
AABHIMNR	BRAHMANI	AABORRRT	BARRATOR	AACDEGKP	PACKAGED
AABHINTT	HABITANT	AABORSTT	BAROSTAT	AACDEHHY	HEADACHY
AABHISTT	HABITATS	AABRRRTY	BARRATRY	AACDEHIN	HACIENDA
AABHKKKU	HABAKKUK	AACCCHHU	CACHUCHA	AACDEHLP	CEPHALAD
AABHMNRS	BRAHMANS	AACCCLOO	COCA-COLA	AACDEHMR	DRACHMAE
AABHMSTT	BATH MATS	AACCCRUY	ACCURACY	AACDEHRS	CHARADES
AABHNOTU	AUTOBAHN	AACCDDES	CASCADED	AACDEHRT	CATHEDRA
AABHORRT	ARBROATH	AACCDEFR	FACE CARD	AACDEHTT	ATTACHED
AABHRSST	BRASS HAT	AACCDEIM	ACADEMIC	AACDEIMN	MAENADIC
AABIILRS	BRASILIA	AACCDELO	ACCOLADE	AACDEINR	RADIANCE
AABIIMNN	NAMIBIAN	AACCDESS	CASCADES	AACDEJNT	ADJACENT
AABIKLNU	KINABALU	AACCDHRS	CASH CARD	AACDEKTT	ATTACKED
AABILMNS	BAILSMAN	AACCDOVY	ADVOCACY	AACDELMN	MANACLED
AABILNNU	BIANNUAL	AACCEENT	CETACEAN	AACDELNR	CALENDAR,
AABILNOR	BARONIAL	AACCEFKP	FACE PACK		CARDENAL, LANDRACE
AABILNOT	ABLATION	AACCEFLO	COALFACE	AACDELNV	VALANCED
AABILNRU	BINAURAL	AACCEHIX	CACHEXIA	AACDELPT	PLACATED
AABILNTY	BANALITY	AACCEIRR	CERCARIA	AACDENPT	TAP DANCE
AABILRRT	ARBITRAL	AACCEKRS	SACK RACE	AACDENRV	ADVANCER
AABILRSY	BASILARY	AACCELOR	CARACOLE	AACDENRW	WAR DANCE
AABILRVY	VARIABLY	AACCELTY	CALYCATE	AACDENSV	ADVANCES
AABILSTY	SATIABLY	AACCENTU	ACUTANCE	AACDENSZ	CADENZAS
AABIMMRS	MARIMBAS	AACCERTU	ACCURATE	AACDEOTV	ADVOCATE
AABIMNOT	MANITOBA	AACCFILR	FARCICAL	AACDEQUY	ADEQUACY
AABIMORS	AMBROSIA	AACCGILT	GALACTIC	AACDERST	CADASTER
AABINNPR	BRAINPAN	AACCHHRT	CARTHACH	AACDERSV	CADAVERS
AABINORS	ABRASION	AACCHINR	ANARCHIC,	AACDETTU	ACTUATED
AABINRTZ	BARTIZAN		CHARACIN	AACDFIST	ACID-FAST
AABINRZZ	ZANZIBAR	AACCHISV	VISCACHA	AACDGGHI	HAGGADIC
AABIORTT	ABATTOIR	AACCHLLT	CATCH-ALL	AACDGINR	CARANGID,
AABIOSSY	BIO-ASSAY	AACCHLOR	CHARCOAL		CARDIGAN
AABIOSTV	BOA VISTA	AACCHLOT	CACHALOT	AACDHHKR	HARDHACK
AABISTUZ	ZAIBATSU	AACCHMNO	COACHMAN	AACDHHRS	HARD CASH
AABJLPRU	JABALPUR	AACCIINV	VACCINIA	AACDHINP	HANDICAP
AABKLLPR	BALL PARK	AACCIIST	SCIATICA	AACDHINR	ARACHNID
AABKOOSZ	BAZOOKAS	AACCILNU	CULIACAN	AACDHKRT	HARD TACK
AABKOPRS	SOAPBARK	AACCILNV	VACCINAL	AACDHLNP	HANDCLAP
AABLLMOR	BALMORAL	AACCILRU	ACICULAR	AACDHLRY	CHARLADY
AABLLPPY	PALPABLY	AACCILTT	TACTICAL	AACDHMRS	DRACHMAS
AABLLSTU	BLASTULA	AACCIPTY	CAPACITY	AACDHNRT	HANDCART
AABLLSVY	SALVABLY	AACCLLST	CATCALLS	AACDIINR	ACID RAIN
AABLMNOR	ABNORMAL	AACCLOPU	ACAPULCO	AACDIINS	ASCIDIAN
AABLMNTU	AMBULANT	AACCLTTU	CALCUTTA	AACDIIRT	ADRIATIC
AABLOTUY	LAYABOUT	AACCOPRS	ASCOCARP	AACDILLP	PALLADIC
AABLOUWY	BULAWAYO	AACCOSTT	STACCATO,	AACDILMT	DALMATIC
AABLPSSY	PASSABLY		TOCCATAS	AACDILMU	CALADIUM
AABLSTTU	ABUTTALS	AACCSSUU	CAUCASUS	AACDILNO	DIACONAL
AABMMOSU	ABOMASUM	AACDDENV	ADVANCED	AACDILNR	CARDINAL,
AABMMOSY	MAMA'S BOY	AACDDETY	TEA CADDY		CLARINDA
AABMNRTU	RAMBUTAN	AACDDINR	RADICAND	AACDILNU	DULCIANA
AABMORSU	MARABOUS	AACDEEHH	HEADACHE	AACDILOZ	ZODIACAL
AABNNORR	ANN ARBOR	AACDEEHR	HEADRACE	AACDILRS	RADICALS
AABNNOSZ	BONANZAS	AACDEELS	ESCALADE	AACDIMNY	ADYNAMIC
		AACDEEOR	AREA CODE	AACDIMRT	DRAMATIC

AACDIOTU	AUTACOID	AACEHIRS	ARCHAISE	AACELNPT	PLACENTA
AACDIRTY	CARYATID	AACEHIRZ	ARCHAIZE	AACELNPY	ANYPLACE
AACDITUY	AUDACITY	AACEHLRT	TRACHEAL	AACELNRT	LACERANT
AACDJKSW	JACKDAWS	AACEHLRX	EXARCHAL	AACELNST	ANALECTS
AACDJQRU	JACQUARD	AACEHMRS	MARCHESA	AACELNSV	VALANCES
AACDKLNU	AUCKLAND	AACEHMST	SCHEMATA	AACELRWY	CLEARWAY
AACDLLUY	CAUDALLY	AACEHRST	TRACHEAS	AACELSTY	CATALYSE
AACDLNSS	SCANDALS	AACEHRTT	ATTACHER	AACELTTY	CATTLEYA
AACDLOSV	CALVADOS	AACEHSTT	ATTACHES	AACEMNPS	SPACEMAN
AACDLPRS	PLACARDS	AACEIKMT	KAMACITE	AACEMRRS	ARMS RACE
AACDMMOR	CARDAMOM	AACEILLM	CAMELLIA	AACEMRSS	MASSACRE
AACDMSSU	DAMASCUS	AACEILLN	ALLIANCE,	AACENPRS	PANCREAS
AACDNSST	SAND-CAST		CANAILLE	AACENPSU	SAUCEPAN
AACDOOSV	AVOCADOS	AACEILMN	CALAMINE	AACENRSS	SARACENS
AACDQRSU	SQUAD CAR	AACEILMT	CALAMITE	AACENRTT	REACTANT
AACEEFIT	FACETIAE	AACEILNP	PALENCIA	AACENRTY	CATENARY
AACEEFLP	PALEFACE	AACEILNS	CANALISE	AACENSSV	CANVASES
AACEEGLV	CLEAVAGE	AACEILNT	ALICANTE,	AACENTUV	EVACUANT
AACEEGPS	SPACE-AGE		ANALCITE	AACEORTV	CAVEATOR
AACEEHLR	HERACLEA	AACEILNV	VALENCIA,	AACEOSST	SEACOAST
AACEEIMT	EMACIATE		VALIANCE	AACERRRS	CARRERAS
AACEEINN	ENCAENIA	AACEILNZ	CANALIZE	AACERRTU	ARCATURE
AACEEIRT	ACIERATE	AACEILOP	ALOPECIA	AACERSSU	CAESURAS
AACEEKST	TEACAKES	AACEILRT	TAILRACE	AACERSTT	CASTRATE
AACEELRT	LACERATE	AACEILRV	CAVALIER	AACERTTT	TRACTATE
AACEELST	ESCALATE	AACEIMNR	AMERICAN,	AACESUWY	CAUSEWAY
AACEELTU	ACULEATE		CINERAMA, IN CAMERA	AACFHMST	CAMSHAFT
AACEEMRT	MACERATE	AACEIMNS	AMNESIAC	AACFILLY	FACIALLY
AACEEMST	CASEMATE	AACEIMTT	CATAMITE	AACFINRS	AFRICANS
AACEENNT	CATENANE	AACEINNO	OCEANIAN	AACFINST	FANATICS
AACEENRS	CESAREAN	AACEINPZ	PIACENZA	AACFIOPR	A FAIR COP
AACEENTT	CATENATE	AACEINRS	CANARIES	AACFIRRT	AIRCRAFT
AACEEPSS	SEASCAPE	AACEINRT	CARINATE,	AACFIRTT	ARTIFACT
AACEERTV	ACERVATE		CRANIATE	AACFJKLP	FLAPJACK
AACEETUV	EVACUATE	AACEINRV	VARIANCE	AACFMNNY	FANCY MAN
AACEETVX	EXCAVATE	AACEINST	ESTANCIA	AACGGINO	ANAGOGIC
AACEFFIN	AFFIANCE	AACEIPPS	PAPACIES	AACGGIOP	APAGOGIC
AACEFIST	FASCIATE	AACEIPRS	AIRSPACE	AACGHHNS	CHANGSHA
AACEFRTT	ARTEFACT	AACEIPTT	APATETIC,	AACGHNNN	NANCHANG
AACEGHRT	CARTHAGE		CAPITATE	AACGHOPZ	GAZPACHO
AACEGILN	ANGELICA	AACEISTU	EUSTACIA	AACGIILN	GALICIAN
AACEGILT	GLACIATE	AACEITTV	ACTIVATE	AACGIILR	CAGLIARI
AACEGINR	CANAIGRE	AACEKKLW	CAKEWALK	AACGIIMN	MAGICIAN
AACEGIRR	CARRIAGE	AACEKLST	SALT CAKE	AACGILNN	ANGLICAN
AACEGIRV	VICARAGE	AACEKNPS	PANCAKES	AACGILNV	GALVANIC
AACEGKPR	PACKAGER	AACEKOST	OATCAKES	AACGILOU	GUAIACOL
AACEGKPS	PACKAGES	AACEKRTT	ATTACKER	AACGILOX	COXALGIA
AACEGMUY	CAMAGUEY	AACELLLR	ALL CLEAR	AACGIMNN	MANGANIC
AACEHILL	HELIACAL	AACELLMR	MARCELLA	AACGIMNP	CAMPAIGN
AACEHILM	MICHAELA	AACELLOT	ALLOCATE	AACGIMOP	APOGAMIC
AACEHILN	ACHENIAL	AACELMNS	MANACLES	AACGIMRR	MARGARIC
AACEHIMR	CHIMAERA	AACELMPT	PLACE MAT	AACGIMUU	GUAIACUM
AACEHIMT	HAEMATIC	AACELMPU	MEA CULPA	AACGINTV	VACATING
AACEHIPT	HEPATICA	AACELMRS	CARAMELS	AACGISTY	SAGACITY
		AACELNPR	PARLANCE		

AACGLMOU	GLAUCOMA
AACGLORS	CALOR GAS
AACGNRVY	VAGRANCY
AACHHKNU	CHANUKAH
AACHHTWY	HATCHWAY
AACHILMS	CHIASMAL
AACHILMT	THALAMIC
AACHILNP	CHAPLAIN
AACHILOU	COAHUILA
AACHILPS	CALIPASH
AACHILRV	ARCHIVAL
AACHIMNN	CHINAMAN, CHAINMAN,
AACHIMNR	CHAIRMAN, CHARMIAN
AACHIMRR	ARMCHAIR
AACHIMRS	ARCHAISM, CHARISMA
AACHINSW	CHAIN SAW
AACHIPTT	CHAPATTI
AACHIRSS	CHARISSA
AACHIRST	ARCHAIST
AACHKSSW	HACKSAWS
AACHKSTY	HAYSTACK
AACHLMNO	MONACHAL
AACHLPRT	LAP-CHART
AACHLSTU	CALATHUS
AACHMNTW	WATCHMAN
AACHMORT	ACHROMAT, TRACHOMA
AACHMPRY	PHARMACY
AACHNORT	AT ANCHOR
AACHNRST	TRASHCAN
AACHNSTU	ACANTHUS
AACHOPPR	APPROACH
AACHRSWY	ARCHWAYS
AACHRTUY	AUTARCHY
AACIILRV	VICARIAL
AACIILTV	VIATICAL
AACIIPRT	PATRICIA
AACIJLMO	MAJOLICA
AACIJNOP	JAPONICA
AACIKRTU	AUTARKIC
AACILLMR	LACRIMAL
AACILLRY	RACIALLY
AACILMNT	CALAMINT, CLAIMANT
AACILMTY	CALAMITY
AACILNOR	CAROLINA
AACILNRV	CARNIVAL
AACILNTT	ATLANTIC, TANTALIC
AACILNTU	NAUTICAL
AACILNTY	ANALYTIC

AACILOTT	COAT-TAIL, TAILCOAT
AACILPRU	PIACULAR
AACILPST	APLASTIC, CAPITALS
AACILPTY	ATYPICAL
AACILRSS	CLARISSA
AACILRTY	ALACRITY
AACILRUU	AURICULA
AACILSTT	STATICAL
AACILSTY	SALACITY
AACIMMNO	AMMONIAC
AACIMMRS	MARASMIC
AACIMNOR	MACARONI
AACIMNPS	CAMPINAS
AACIMORT	AROMATIC
AACINORS	OCARINAS
AACINORT	CATRIONA, CROATIAN, RAINCOAT
AACINOTV	OCTAVIAN, VACATION
AACINPST	CAPTAINS
AACINQTU	ACQUAINT
AACINRSZ	CZARINAS
AACINSTZ	STANZAIC
AACIPRTY	RAPACITY
AACIQSTU	AQUATICS
AACIRRTT	TARTARIC
AACJKRST	JACK TARS
AACJKSTY	JACKSTAY
AACKKNPS	KNAPSACK
AACKLSTW	CATWALKS
AACKPRRS	CAR PARKS
AACLLRRY	CARRYALL
AACLLRSY	RASCALLY
AACLLSUY	CASUALLY, CAUSALLY
AACLLTUY	ACTUALLY
AACLMNNS	CLANSMAN
AACLMRRU	MACRURAL
AACLNNOT	CANTONAL
AACLNNOW	CANON LAW
AACLNOPR	COPLANAR
AACLNORU	LA CORUNA
AACLNTVY	VACANTLY
AACLORRU	ORACULAR
AACLORSU	CAROUSAL
AACLORTT	CARLOTTA
AACLORUV	VACUOLAR
AACLPPRT	CLAPTRAP
AACLPRSU	CAPSULAR, SCAPULAR
AACLPRTY	CALYPTRA
AACLPSSU	SCAPULAS
AACLPTTU	CATAPULT

AACLRSUV	VASCULAR
AACLSTTY	CATALYST
AACLSTUY	CASUALTY
AACMNOOR	MACAROON
AACMNPRY	RAMPANCY
AACMNRRU	MACRURAN
AACMNSTX	MANX CATS
AACNPSST	CAPSTANS
AACNRSTT	TRANSACT
AACOPRSU	ACARPOUS
AACOPSTV	POSTCAVA
AACORRTV	VARACTOR
AACORSTT	CASTRATO
AACORTTU	ACTUATOR, AUTOCRAT
AACPSSTW	CAT'S PAWS
AACSTUWY	CUTAWAYS
AADDDEEH	DEADHEAD
AADDEEHT	DEAD HEAT
AADDEEIL	ADELAIDE
AADDEFIS	DEAF-AIDS
AADDEFLL	DEADFALL
AADDEHLN	HEADLAND
AADDEHMN	HANDMADE
AADDEHRW	HEADWARD
AADDEHRZ	HAZARDED
AADDEIRT	RADIATED
AADDEMNT	MANDATED
AADDEMRY	DAYDREAM
AADDGHLN	GLAD HAND
AADDGNRS	GRANDADS
AADDHHIL	LAH-DI-DAH
AADDLLNY	LANDLADY
AADDLNRW	LANDWARD
AADDNRST	STANDARD
AADDOTYY	DAY-TO-DAY
AADEEGHR	HEADGEAR
AADEEGHT	GET AHEAD
AADEEGMN	ENDAMAGE
AADEEGRV	AVERAGED
AADEEILR	AIREDALE
AADEEIRT	ERADIATE
AADEEKNW	AWAKENED
AADEELNN	ANNEALED
AADEELPP	APPEALED
AADEELRW	DELAWARE
AADEEMNT	EMANATED
AADEEMRR	DEMERARA
AADEENPT	TAPENADE
AADEENTT	ANTEDATE
AADEEPPR	APPEARED
AADEEPPS	APPEASED
AADEEQTU	ADEQUATE
AADEFHLT	FLATHEAD

AADEFHST	FATHEADS, HEADFAST
AADEFILR	FAIRLEAD
AADEFIRS	FARADISE
AADEFIRZ	FARADIZE
AADEFLLR	FALDERAL, LEAF-LARD
AADEFLRY	DEFRAYAL
AADEGILL	DIALLAGE, LEGAL AID
AADEGILT	GLADIATE
AADEGINR	DRAINAGE, GARDENIA
AADEGITT	AGITATED
AADEGKRS	DARK AGES
AADEGLMN	MAGDALEN
AADEGLMY	AMYGDALE
AADEGLSV	SALVAGED
AADEGMPR	RAMPAGED
AADEGMSS	MASSAGED
AADEGNRR	ARRANGED
AADEGNST	DAGESTAN
AADEGORR	ROAD RAGE
AADEGPRT	TRADE GAP
AADEGRRT	RAG TRADE
AADEGRTU	GRADUATE
AADEGSSU	ASSUAGED
AADEHILN	NAILHEAD
AADEHILR	HEADRAIL, RAILHEAD
AADEHILS	HEADSAIL
AADEHIWY	HIDEAWAY
AADEHKOT	HAKODATE
AADEHLNR	ANHEDRAL
AADEHMNS	HEADSMAN
AADEHMST	MASTHEAD
AADEHRRW	HARDWARE
AADEHRSS	HARASSED
AADEHRSW	WARHEADS
AADEHSSY	SASHAYED
AADEHSWY	HEADWAYS
AADEIIMV	VIA MEDIA
AADEIKLP	KLAIPEDA
AADEILLN	DANIELLA
AADEILMN	MADELINA
AADEILMR	ARMIDALE
AADEILMS	MALADIES
AADEILPR	PRAEDIAL
AADEILPS	PALISADE
AADEILRS	SALARIED
AADEILSS	ASSAILED
AADEILTV	VALIDATE
AADEIMNR	MARINADE
AADEIMNT	ANIMATED, DIAMANTE

AADEIMPZ	DIAZEPAM
AADEIMST	ADAMSITE, DIASTEMA
AADEINNR	ADRIANNE
AADEINTT	ATTAINED
AADEIPRS	PARADISE
AADEIPSU	DIAPAUSE
AADEIPTV	ADAPTIVE
AADEISST	DIASTASE
AADEISTT	SATIATED
AADEJMNN	NDJAMENA
AADEJNNP	JAPANNED
AADEJNOT	ONDAATJE
AADEKMNR	MANDRAKE
AADELLPP	APPALLED
AADELMNR	ALDERMAN
AADELMNS	DALESMAN, LEADSMAN
AADELNSY	ANALYSED
AADELPPT	PALPATED
AADELRSW	RAW DEALS
AADEMNST	MANDATES
AADEMNSY	NAME DAYS
AADEMRRU	MARAUDER
AADENNST	ANDANTES
AADENRRT	NARRATED
AADENRSV	VERANDAS
AADEPRST	ADAPTERS
AADEQRTU	QUADRATE
AADERRRW	REARWARD
AADERRST	RAT-ARSED
AADERSSW	SEAWARDS
AADERSTW	EASTWARD
AADFFLLN	LLANDAFF
AADFGLSY	FLAG DAYS
AADFGNNO	FANDANGO
AADFHMNR	FARMHAND
AADFHNST	HANDFAST
AADFIMRS	FARADISM
AADFKLLN	FALKLAND
AADFLLLN	LANDFALL
AADFLMNR	FARMLAND
AADFLORW	AARDWOLF
AADFLOTX	TOADFLAX
AADFLOWY	FOLDAWAY
AADFMRRY	FARMYARD
AADGGIMN	DAMAGING
AADGGLNN	GANGLAND
AADGGLRS	GLAD RAGS, LAGGARDS
AADGGRST	STAGGARD
AADGHINN	GANDHIAN
AADGHIPR	DIAGRAPH
AADGHJNU	JUNAGADH
AADGHORS	SARGODHA

AADGIINS	GAINSAID
AADGILLR	GALLIARD
AADGILMR	MADRIGAL
AADGILNO	DIAGONAL
AADGIMPR	PARADIGM
AADGIMRS	DIAGRAMS
AADGINPR	PARADING
AADGINPT	ADAPTING
AADGINRU	GUARDIAN
AADGINRW	AWARDING
AADGLMNR	GRAND MAL
AADGLNRS	GARLANDS
AADGLOPR	PODAGRAL
AADGMNOR	DRAGOMAN, GARAMOND
AADGMNRS	GRANDMAS
AADGNPRS	GRANDPAS
AADGNRTU	GUARDANT
AADGNRUV	VANGUARD
AADHILLR	HALLIARD
AADHILNR	HANDRAIL
AADHILNT	THAILAND
AADHILNU	LUDHIANA
AADHILRV	HAVILDAR
AADHINNZ	ANDIZHAN
AADHINRR	HARRIDAN
AADHLMST	HALMSTAD
AADHLPSS	SLAPDASH
AADHLRSY	HALYARDS
AADHMNNY	HANDYMAN
AADHMNRU	DAMANHUR
AADHSSWY	WASHDAYS
AADIILVV	VALDIVIA
AADIIMRT	DIARMAIT
AADIINRS	SARDINIA
AADIIRRS	AIR RAIDS
AADIKLLO	ALKALOID
AADIKORT	TAKORADI
AADILLLO	ALLODIAL
AADILLRY	RADIALLY
AADILMNN	MAINLAND
AADILMOV	MOLDAVIA
AADILMRS	ADMIRALS
AADILMVY	LIMAVADY
AADILNPR	PRANDIAL
AADILNPS	PALADINS
AADILNRU	LAURINDA
AADILNTT	DILATANT
AADILORR	RAILROAD
AADILPRY	LAPIDARY
AADILRST	DIASTRAL
AADIMNNO	MINDANAO
AADIMNNR	MANDARIN
AADIMNOT	MANATOID

193

AADIMNRT	TAMARIND	AAEEGNRS	SANGAREE	AAEGGIOT	AGIOTAGE
AADIMNRY	DAIRYMAN	AAEEGRRY	GREY AREA	AAEGGLNU	LANGUAGE
AADIMNUV	VANADIUM	AAEEGRSV	AVERAGES	AAEGGLNY	LAY AN EGG
AADIMSTZ	SAMIZDAT	AAEEGRTW	WATERAGE	AAEGGNRY	GARGANEY
AADINOPR	PARANOID	AAEEHHRR	HEAR! HEAR!	AAEGGOPR	PARAGOGE
AADINOPS	DIAPASON	AAEEHIMR	HAEREMAI	AAEGHIRS	HARGEISA
AADINPRS	SPANIARD	AAEEHRTW	AWEATHER,	AAEGHLNP	PHALANGE
AADIOPRS	DIASPORA	WHEATEAR		AAEGHLPS	SLAGHEAP
AADIORRT	RADIATOR	AAEEHTVW	HEAT WAVE	AAEGHMRX	HEXAGRAM
AADIRRSY	DISARRAY	AAEEILNT	ALIENATE	AAEGHNRU	HARANGUE
AADJNTTU	ADJUTANT	AAEEJNPS	JAPANESE	AAEGILLM	GAMALIEL
AADJNTUV	ADJUVANT	AAEEJNSV	JAVANESE	AAEGILLN	GALILEAN
AADJRTZZ	TRAD JAZZ	AAEEKMNS	NAMESAKE	AAEGILNN	ANGELINA
AADKLMNR	LANDMARK	AAEEKMRT	TEA-MAKER	AAEGILNR	ALGERIAN,
AADKLNPR	PARKLAND	AAEEKNRS	KANARESE	GERANIAL	
AADKMNTU	KATMANDU	AAEEKNRW	REAWAKEN	AAEGILNT	AGENTIAL,
AADKNRST	TANKARDS	AAEEKPRT	PARAKEET	ALGINATE	
AADKORWY	WORKADAY	AAEEKPTW	TAKE A PEW	AAEGILSX	GALAXIES
AADLLMRS	MALLARDS	AAEEKQSU	SEAQUAKE	AAEGILTT	TAILGATE
AADLLMSS	SMALL ADS	AAEELLMR	AMARELLE	AAEGIMNO	EGOMANIA
AADLMNOR	MANDORLA	AAEELLMT	METAMALE	AAEGIMNS	MAGNESIA
AADLMNRY	MARYLAND	AAEELMNU	EMANUELA	AAEGIMNT	AGMINATE
AADLMNSS	LANDMASS	AAEELNNR	ANNEALER	AAEGIMNZ	MAGAZINE
AADLMNUU	LAUDANUM	AAEELNOR	ELEANORA	AAEGIMRR	MARRIAGE
AADLNOPR	PARLANDO	AAEELNPS	SEAPLANE,	AAEGINPS	PAGANISE
AADLNRSY	LANYARDS	SPELAEAN		AAEGINPT	PAGINATE
AADLOPRV	PAVLODAR	AAEELPPR	APPEALER	AAEGINPZ	PAGANIZE
AADLOPSY	PAYLOADS	AAEELPRY	LEAP YEAR	AAEGINRT	AERATING
AADLORST	LOADSTAR	AAEELRTU	LAUREATE	AAEGINTV	NAVIGATE,
AADLORSV	SALVADOR	AAEELTUV	EVALUATE	VAGINATE	
AADLORTU	ADULATOR	AAEEMMTT	TEAM-MATE	AAEGIRSV	VAGARIES
AADMMNSU	MANDAMUS	AAEEMNPT	NAMETAPE	AAEGIRTX	EX GRATIA
AADMNNOS	MADONNAS	AAEEMNRT	MAN-EATER	AAEGISSS	ASSEGAIS
AADMNRSS	MANSARDS	AAEEMSSS	ASSAMESE	AAEGIVWY	GIVEAWAY
AADMORST	MATADORS	AAEENNRZ	NAZARENE	AAEGKTTT	KATTEGAT
AADMRRSY	YARDARMS	AAEENRST	ARSENATE, NEAR	AAEGLLMN	MAGELLAN
AADNNORR	ANDORRAN	EAST, SERENATA		AAEGLLPR	PELLAGRA
AADNNPSU	PANDANUS	AAEENRTT	ANTEATER	AAEGLLSS	GALLEASS
AADNOPSS	SANDSOAP	AAEENSTU	NAUSEATE	AAEGLNOU	ANALOGUE
AADNOSUV	VANADOUS	AAEEPPRR	REAPPEAR	AAEGLNTU	ANGULATE
AADNOSWY	NOWADAYS	AAEEPRST	SEPARATE	AAEGLRST	AGRESTAL
AADNPRST	SAND TRAP	AAEERSTT	STEARATE	AAEGLRSV	SALVAGER
AADNPSTT	STAND PAT	AAEFFILS	FAIL-SAFE	AAEGLSSV	LAS VEGAS
AADNQRTU	QUADRANT	AAEFFNRS	FANFARES	AAEGLSVY	SAVAGELY
AADNQRUY	QUANDARY	AAEFGHRW	WHARFAGE	AAEGMNRS	MANAGERS,
AADOPPRR	PARADROP	AAEFGIMR	FAIR GAME	SEMARANG	
AADORSVY	SAVOYARD	AAEFGLOT	FLOATAGE	AAEGMNRV	GRAVAMEN
AADRSTUY	SATURDAY	AAEFHLRY	HALF-YEAR	AAEGMNST	MAGNATES
AAEEFLNW	A NEW LEAF	AAEFILTY	FAYALITE	AAEGMORR	AEROGRAM
AAEEFRRS	SEAFARER	AAEFIMRR	AIRFRAME	AAEGMPRR	RAMPAGER
AAEEGILN	ALIENAGE	AAEFINNT	FAINEANT	AAEGMRRT	MARGARET
AAEEGKLS	LEAKAGES	AAEFLMTT	FLATMATE	AAEGMRSS	MASSAGER
AAEEGMPR	AMPERAGE	AAEFLPSY	PLAY SAFE	AAEGMRST	RAMSGATE
AAEEGNNO	NEOGAEAN	AAEFLRTW	FLATWARE	AAEGMRSW	WAR GAMES
		AAEFRRWY	WAYFARER	AAEGMRTU	AGERATUM

AAEGMSSS	MASSAGES	AAEILLRT	ARILLATE	AAEKKRSY	KAYAKERS
AAEGMTTW	MEGAWATT	AAEILLRY	AERIALLY	AAEKLMRY	MALARKEY
AAEGNOOR	NO-GO AREA	AAEILMNT	LAMINATE	AAEKLNNT	KELANTAN
AAEGNOOT	NOTOGAEA	AAEILMRT	ARMALITE,	AAEKNPRT	PARTAKEN
AAEGNPST	PAGEANTS		MATERIAL	AAEKPRRT	PARTAKER
AAEGNRRR	ARRANGER	AAEILMSS	MALAISES	AAELLLMR	LAMELLAR
AAEGNSTT	STAGNATE	AAEILNPR	AIRPLANE	AAELLLPR	PARALLEL
AAEGORRT	ARROGATE	AAEILNPT	PALATINE	AAELLORV	ALVEOLAR
AAEGORTT	AEGROTAT	AAEILNRR	LARRAINE	AAELLPRT	PATELLAR
AAEGPSSS	PASSAGES	AAEILNRS	AIRLANES	AAELLPST	PATELLAS
AAEGRSSU	ASSUAGER	AAEILNRU	AURELIAN,	AAELLRST	LATERALS
AAEGRSTT	REGATTAS		LAURAINE	AAELLSSW	SEAWALLS
AAEGRSTZ	STARGAZE	AAEILNRV	VALERIAN	AAELLSWY	WALLASEY
AAEGRSVY	SAVAGERY	AAEILNSS	NASALISE	AAELLTTV	VALLETTA
AAEGSSSU	SAUSAGES	AAEILNSZ	NASALIZE	AAELLWYY	ALLEYWAY
AAEGSTWY	GATEWAYS	AAEILNTT	LATINATE	AAELMMNO	MELANOMA
AAEHHRST	HEAT RASH	AAEILPRT	PARIETAL	AAELMNRT	MATERNAL
AAEHILNP	APHELIAN	AAEILPRX	PREAXIAL	AAELMNSS	SALESMAN
AAEHIMNT	HAEMATIN	AAEILPST	STAPELIA	AAELMNST	TALESMAN
AAEHINNT	ATHENIAN	AAEILPSZ	LA SPEZIA	AAELMPTY	PLAYMATE
AAEHINPT	APHANITE	AAEILRRT	ARTERIAL	AAELMRSY	LAMASERY
AAEHINRT	RHAETIAN	AAEILRSS	ASSAILER,	AAELMRTT	MALTREAT
AAEHINST	ASTHENIA		SALARIES	AAELNNOT	NEONATAL
AAEHKLST	ALKAHEST	AAEILRTV	VARIETAL	AAELNNSU	LAUSANNE
AAEHKMRY	HAYMAKER	AAEILSTV	SALIVATE	AAELNNTU	ANNULATE
AAEHLMSY	SEALYHAM	AAEILTVX	LAXATIVE	AAELNOSS	SEASONAL
AAEHLNTX	EXHALANT	AAEIMMNR	MARIAMNE	AAELNPRT	PARENTAL,
AAEHLPRX	HEXAPLAR	AAEIMNNR	ARMENIAN,		PATERNAL, PRENATAL
AAEHLPUV	UPHEAVAL		MARIANNE	AAELNPRW	WARPLANE
AAEHMNSS	MANASSEH	AAEIMNPR	PEARMAIN	AAELNPST	PLEASANT
AAEHMOPR	AMPHORAE	AAEIMNRT	MARINATE	AAELNRSS	ARSENALS
AAEHMORT	ATHEROMA	AAEIMNST	TAMASINE	AAELNRST	ASTERNAL
AAEHNPST	PHEASANT	AAEIMOTX	TOXAEMIA	AAELNRSY	ANALYSER
AAEHNRTZ	NAZARETH	AAEIMOTZ	AZOTEMIA	AAELNRTX	RELAXANT
AAEHNTTX	XANTHATE	AAEIMPRT	PIA MATER	AAELNSSY	ANALYSES
AAEHNTVX	TAX HAVEN	AAEIMRTT	MARIETTA	AAELOPRS	PSORALEA
AAEHPRSW	PESHAWAR	AAEINORT	AERATION	AAELORTY	ALEATORY
AAEHRRSS	HARASSER	AAEINORX	ANOREXIA	AAELPPSU	APPLAUSE
AAEHRSTT	HATTERAS	AAEINRST	ARTESIAN	AAELPRSV	PALAVERS
AAEHRSTU	ARETHUSA	AAEINRSU	EURASIAN	AAELPRSY	PARALYSE
AAEIILTT	LAETITIA	AAEINRSY	ARYANISE	AAELPRUV	PAR VALUE
AAEIIPRS	APIARIES	AAEINRYZ	ARYANIZE	AAELRTTU	LAURETTA
AAEIIRSV	AVIARIES	AAEINSTT	ASTATINE, IN A	AAELRWYY	WAYLAYER
AAEIJMNS	JAMESINA		STATE	AAELSSTX	SALES TAX
AAEIKKMZ	KAMIKAZE	AAEINSTW	IN A SWEAT	AAEMMNRT	ARMAMENT
AAEIKLLN	ALKALINE	AAEINTTT	TITANATE	AAEMNORT	EMANATOR
AAEIKLLS	ALKALIES,	AAEIPPRS	APPRAISE	AAEMNOTZ	METAZOAN
	ALKALISE	AAEIPQRU	AREQUIPA	AAEMNPRS	PARMESAN
AAEIKLLZ	ALKALIZE	AAEIPRST	ASPIRATE,	AAEMNPRT	PARAMENT
AAEIKLMS	MAKE SAIL		PARASITE	AAEMNRST	SANTAREM
AAEIKLNR	KARELIAN	AAEIPRTZ	TRAPEZIA	AAEMNRTW	WATERMAN
AAEILLLU	ALLELUIA	AAEIRSTT	ARISTATE	AAEMNSSS	MANASSES
AAEILLNT	ALLANITE	AAEIRSVW	AIRWAVES	AAEMORTT	TERATOMA
AAEILLPT	PALLIATE	AAEIRTTZ	ZARATITE	AAEMOTTU	AUTOMATE
		AAEJORSV	SARAJEVO		

AAEMPTTU	AMPUTATE	AAFMNORW	MAN-OF-WAR	AAGINSSY	ASSAYING
AAEMQSTU	SQUAMATE	AAGGGINR	GARAGING	AAGIORTT	AGITATOR
AAEMRRTU	ARMATURE	AAGGILLN	GANGLIAL	AAGIRSTV	GRAVITAS
AAEMRSTU	AMATEURS	AAGGIMNN	MANAGING	AAGKMSSS	GAS MASKS
AAEMRTTU	MATURATE	AAGGINRV	RAVAGING	AAGKNOOR	KANGAROO
AAENNNST	ANTENNAS	AAGGINSV	SAVAGING	AAGKNOOV	OKAVANGO
AAENNORS	ROSEANNA	AAGGNORT	TAGANROG	AAGLLMOY	ALLOGAMY
AAENNOTT	ANNOTATE	AAGGNSWY	GANGWAYS	AAGLLNST	GALLANTS
AAENORTU	AERONAUT	AAGGOOPP	PAGO PAGO	AAGLLOPY	POLYGALA
AAENPPRT	APPARENT	AAGHHINS	SHANGHAI	AAGLLOWY	GALLOWAY
AAENPSST	PEASANTS	AAGHHINW	HWANG HAI	AAGLMNSS	GLASSMAN
AAENRSUW	UNAWARES	AAGHHNUU	HUANG HUA	AAGLNQUU	AQUALUNG
AAEOPSTT	APOSTATE	AAGHILNN	HANGNAIL	AAGLNRRU	GRANULAR
AAEORSTT	AEROSTAT	AAGHKMNY	GYMKHANA	AAGLRSTU	GASTRULA
AAEPPRST	PARAPETS	AAGHLNPY	ANAGLYPH	AAGMNORT	MARTAGON
AAEPPSTT	APPESTAT	AAGHMNNO	MONAGHAN	AAGMOTUY	AUTOGAMY
AAEPRTTY	TEA PARTY	AAGHMNOY	HOGMANAY,	AAGNNSTT	STAGNANT
AAEPRTXY	TAXPAYER	MAHOGANY		AAGNOPRS	PARAGONS
AAERRSTU	SARRAUTE	AAGHMNRT	GRANTHAM	AAGNOPRT	TRAGOPAN
AAERRTTT	TARTRATE	AAGHMRSS	MARSH GAS	AAGNORRT	ARROGANT,
AAERRTTW	WATER RAT	AAGHNNRT	NHA TRANG	TARRAGON	
AAERSSTV	VASTERAS	AAGHNNST	TANGSHAN	AAGNRSTV	VAGRANTS
AAERSTTU	SATURATE	AAGIILMN	IMAGINAL	AAGNRTUY	GUARANTY
AAERTWWY	WATERWAY	AAGIILNV	AVAILING	AAGORSSS	SARGASSO
AAFFGILS	GAFFSAIL	AAGIINNU	IGUANIAN	AAGRSSTU	SASTRUGA
AAFFGLLL	FLAG FALL	AAGIINTW	AWAITING	AAHHKKNU	HANUKKAH
AAFFILRT	TAFFRAIL	AAGIJRTU	GUJARATI	AAHHNSSU	SHUSHANA
AAFFINPR	PARAFFIN	AAGIKLNO	KAOLIANG	AAHHOPRS	PHARAOHS
AAFFLSTU	AFFLATUS	AAGIKNNW	KINGWANA	AAHIIKRR	HARA-KIRI,
AAFFMNST	STAFFMAN	AAGILLNU	ANGUILLA	HARIKARI	
AAFFMORR	FROM AFAR	AAGILLNY	ALLAYING	AAHIILRT	HAIRTAIL
AAFGLLNU	LANGLAUF	AAGILMNO	MAGNOLIA	AAHIINPS	HISPANIA
AAFGLNRT	FLAGRANT	AAGILMNR	ALARMING,	AAHIINTT	TAHITIAN
AAFGNRRT	FRAGRANT	MARGINAL		AAHILNOT	HALATION
AAFHLMST	HALF-MAST	AAGILNOY	LIAOYANG	AAHIMNRR	HARRIMAN
AAFHLSTY	LAYSHAFT	AAGILNRR	LARRIGAN	AAHIMSTT	MATTHIAS
AAFHQRRU	FARQUHAR	AAGILOOP	APOLOGIA	AAHINNST	TIAN SHAN
AAFHRSUU	HAUSFRAU	AAGILRRW	WARRIGAL	AAHINORT	HORATIAN
AAFIILLM	FAMILIAL	AAGILSTT	SAGITTAL	AAHINPRS	PIRANHAS
AAFIILLR	FILARIAL	AAGILSTW	WAGTAILS	AAHINPRT	PARTHIAN
AAFIILMR	FAMILIAR	AAGIMNNN	MANGANIN	AAHIPPRS	SAPPHIRA
AAFIKLLY	ALKALIFY	AAGIMNPR	GRAMPIAN	AAHIPSXY	ASPHYXIA
AAFILLNR	RAINFALL	AAGIMNPS	PAGANISM	AAHITWWY	AWAY WITH
AAFILMST	FATALISM	AAGIMNSS	AMASSING	AAHJNNOT	JONATHAN
AAFILPRS	PARSIFAL	AAGIMPTU	PATAGIUM	AAHKLLMR	HALLMARK
AAFILSTT	FATALIST	AAGIMSTT	STIGMATA	AAHKLMOO	OKLAHOMA
AAFILTTY	FATALITY	AAGINNST	SIANGTAN	AAHKMOOY	YOKOHAMA
AAFINNOV	FAVONIAN	AAGINNTX	XIANGTAN	AAHKMOTW	TOMAHAWK
AAFINNST	INFANTS	AAGINNUW	WANGANUI	AAHKMSSY	YASHMAKS
AAFINRRW	WARFARIN	AAGINOST	SANTIAGO	AAHKRSTV	HRVATSKA
AAFINSTU	FAUSTIAN,	AAGINPRU	PAGURIAN	AAHLLLTU	TALLULAH
FAUSTINA		AAGINPST	PAGANIST	AAHLLMRS	MARSHALL
AAFIRSWY	FAIRWAYS	AAGINRRS	SRINAGAR		
AAFLSTWY	FLATWAYS	AAGINRRY	ARRAYING		
		AAGINSST	ASSIGNAT		

AAHLLOPT	ALLOPATH	AAILMRST	ALARMIST	AAINPRST	ASPIRANT,
AAHLLSWY	HALLWAYS	AAILMTTU	ULTIMATA		PARTISAN
AAHLMRSS	MARSHALS	AAILNNOT	NATIONAL	AAINPRTW	WAR PAINT
AAHLMSTU	THALAMUS	AAILNNPT	PLANTAIN	AAINQRTU	QUATRAIN
AAHMNORT	MARATHON	AAILNNST	ANNALIST	AAINQTTU	AQUATINT
AAHMNOTX	XANTHOMA	AAILNOPP	APPOLINA	AAINRSST	ARTISANS,
AAHMNPST	PHANTASM	AAILNOPS	PIANOLAS		TSARINAS
AAHMOPRS	AMPHORAS	AAILNOPT	TALAPOIN	AAINRSSY	ASSYRIAN
AAHNNOSS	HOSANNAS	AAILNORS	ORINASAL	AAINRSTU	AUSTRIAN
AAHNNSSU	SUSANNAH	AAILNORT	NOTARIAL,	AAINRSTV	VARIANTS
AAHNPSTY	PHANTASY		RATIONAL	AAINRSTY	SANITARY
AAHNRTTY	HANRATTY	AAILNOSV	SLAVONIA	AAINRSTZ	TZARINAS
AAHPRSTW	WARPATHS	AAILNOTV	LAVATION	AAINSSSS	ASSASSIN
AAHPSTWY	PATHWAYS	AAILNOTX	LAXATION	AAINSSTT	SATANIST
AAHRSSTY	ASHTRAYS	AAILNQTU	ALIQUANT	AAIORSTV	AVIATORS
AAIIILMR	MILIARIA	AAILNSSY	ANALYSIS	AAIQRSTU	AQUARIST
AAIIILMS	ISMAILIA	AAILNSTT	ATLANTIS	AAIQRSUU	AQUARIUS
AAIIJJPP	JIPIJAPA	AAILNSTU	LUSATIAN	AAIRSSTU	ASTURIAS
AAIILMNS	MAINSAIL	AAILNSTY	NASALITY	AAIRSTWY	STAIRWAY
AAIILNRZ	ALIZARIN	AAILORRS	RASORIAL	AAJMMORR	MARJORAM
AAIILNST	ITALIANS	AAILORRV	VARIOLAR	AAKLMNSW	WALKMANS
AAIILNUX	UNIAXIAL	AAILPPRU	PUPARIAL	AAKMMNRS	MARKSMAN
AAIILRST	ALISTAIR	AAILPRST	PATRIALS	AAKMOSSU	MOUSSAKA
AAIILRTX	TRIAXIAL	AAILPRVZ	PARZIVAL	AAKMRSUZ	MAZURKAS
AAIIMNNT	MAINTAIN	AAILRRSV	ARRIVALS	AAKORSUW	KUROSAWA
AAIIMNPX	PANMIXIA	AAILRSVY	SALIVARY	AAKPRSWY	PARKWAYS
AAIIMNRS	ARIANISM	AAILRSWY	RAILWAYS	AALLLLMP	PALL MALL
AAIINNTZ	ANTI-NAZI	AAILSSTY	STAYSAIL	AALLMNTY	TALLYMAN
AAIINOTV	AVIATION	AAIMMNST	MAINMAST	AALLMNUY	MANUALLY
AAIINPRR	RIPARIAN	AAIMMRSU	SAMARIUM	AALLMPRU	AMPULLAR
AAIINPRS	PARISIAN	AAIMNNRU	RUMANIAN	AALLNNUY	ANNUALLY
AAIINRST	INTARSIA	AAIMNORT	ANIMATOR	AALLNOTY	ATONALLY
AAIIORRT	AIR-TO-AIR	AAIMNORV	MORAVIAN	AALLNPRU	PLANULAR
AAIIPRST	APIARIST	AAIMNORW	AIRWOMAN	AALLOOPT	PALO ALTO
AAIIRTVX	AVIATRIX	AAIMNPRZ	MARZIPAN	AALLOORW	WALLAROO
AAIKLNRS	SRI LANKA	AAIMNRRT	TRIMARAN	AALLORWY	ROLLAWAY
AAIKLOSV	SLOVAKIA	AAIMNRST	MARTIANS	AALLPRST	PLASTRAL
AAIKMRST	TAMARISK	AAIMNRSU	MASURIAN	AALLRUVV	VALVULAR
AAIKNNTT	ANTITANK	AAIMNSST	MANTISSA,	AALMNOPP	PAMPLONA
AAIKNORU	KAIROUAN		SATANISM	AALMNORT	MATRONAL
AAIKNPST	PAKISTAN	AAIMNSTY	MAINSTAY	AALMNORU	MONAURAL
AAIKNRTX	TAXI RANK	AAIMOPRS	MARIPOSA	AALMNORW	ROMAN LAW
AAIKSSTW	SWASTIKA	AAIMPRST	PASTRAMI	AALMNOWY	LAYWOMAN
AAILLLUV	ALLUVIAL	AAIMQRUU	AQUARIUM	AALMNTTU	TANTALUM
AAILLMNT	MANTILLA	AAIMRRST	AMRITSAR	AALMNTUU	AUTUMNAL
AAILLMOR	AMARILLO	AAIMRSSU	SAMURAIS	AALMOSTT	STOMATAL
AAILLMRX	MAXILLAR	AAINNNOT	ANTONINA	AALNNOST	SONANTAL
AAILLRXY	AXILLARY	AAINNOST	SONATINA	AALNOPRT	PATRONAL
AAILMMRS	ALARMISM	AAINNOTT	NATATION	AALNORSS	ALSO-RANS
AAILMNOR	MANORIAL,	AAINNRSV	NIRVANAS	AALNPSST	SALTPANS
	MORAINAL	AAINNSST	NAISSANT	AALNPTWX	WAXPLANT
AAILMNOS	SOMALIAN	AAINOPRV	PAR AVION	AALNRSTU	NATURALS
AAILMNST	STAMINAL,	AAINORRS	ROSARIAN	AALNSSTU	SULTANAS
	TALISMAN	AAINORRT	ROTARIAN	AALNSSTY	ANALYSTS
AAILMORR	ARMORIAL	AAINOTTX	TAXATION	AALNSTTU	TANTALUS

AALOOPSU	SAO PAULO	ABBCINOY	CABIN BOY	ABBHRRSU	RHUBARBS
AALOPPRV	APPROVAL	ABBCKLOX	BLACK BOX	ABBHSTTU	BATHTUBS
AALOPRSS	PARASOLS	ABBDDEEU	BEDAUBED	ABBILLSU	SILLABUB
AALOPRST	PASTORAL	ABBDDEIL	AD-LIBBED,	ABBILOST	BOBTAILS
AALORTUV	VALUATOR		BIDDABLE	ABBIRRTY	RABBITRY
AALORTVY	LAVATORY	ABBDDEST	BAD DEBTS	ABBIRSUU	SUBURBIA
AALPRSTU	SPATULAR	ABBDDLOO	BAD BLOOD	ABBKKNOO	BANKBOOK
AALPSSTU	SPATULAS	ABBDEEER	BEEBREAD	ABBLLRSU	BULL BARS
AALRSTTW	STALWART	ABBDEEJR	JABBERED	ABBCIKKK	KICKBACK
AALRSTUY	SALUTARY	ABBDEILR	AD-LIBBER	ABBLLSUY	SYLLABUB
AALSSSTU	ASSAULTS	ABBDEINR	BREAD BIN	ABBLOPRY	PROBABLY
AAMMNNOT	MAN-TO-MAN	ABBDEIRT	RABBITED	ABBMMOOT	ATOM BOMB
AAMMRSSU	MARASMUS	ABBDELRS	DABBLERS	ABBNRSUU	SUBURBAN
AAMNRSTU	SUMATRAN	ABBDEORS	ABSORBED	ABCCDHIK	DABCHICK
AAMNRSTW	STRAW MAN	ABBDERST	DRABBEST	ABCCEELP	PECCABLE
AAMOPRRU	PARAMOUR	ABBDGILN	DABBLING	ABCCEIKL	BLACK ICE
AAMORSSV	SAMOVARS	ABBDHIRT	BIRDBATH	ABCCEILY	CELIBACY
AAMOSTTU	AUTOMATS	ABBDHOOY	BABYHOOD	ABCCEKMO	COMEBACK
AAMPRRST	RAMPARTS	ABBDOORX	BOXBOARD	ABCCHISU	BACCHIUS
AAMSSSTU	SATSUMAS	ABBDRRUY	BRADBURY	ABCCHNOO	CABOCHON
AANNOSST	ASSONANT	ABBEEJRR	JABBERER	ABCCILOR	CARBOLIC
AANNRSTY	STANNARY	ABBEELLN	BEN BELLA	ABCCILOT	COBALTIC
AANOOSSS	AS SOON AS	ABBEELVW	EBBW VALE	ABCCINOR	CARBONIC
AANORRRT	NARRATOR	ABBEESSS	ABBESSES	ABCCIORS	ASCORBIC
AANRRSTW	WARRANTS	ABBEFILR	FLABBIER	ABCCKLLO	BALLCOCK
AANRRTWY	WARRANTY	ABBEGLRR	GRABBLER	ABCCKSTU	CUTBACKS
AANRSTTU	SATURANT	ABBEGRSU	BUGBEARS	ABCCOOST	TOBACCOS
AANRSUWY	RUNAWAYS	ABBEHIRS	SHABBIER	ABCDDEOR	BROCADED
AAOPSSTY	APOSTASY	ABBEHORT	BATHROBE	ABCDDETU	ABDUCTED
AAOSTWWY	STOWAWAY	ABBEILLO	BOILABLE	ABCDEEFK	FEEDBACK
AAPRRSTT	RAT TRAPS	ABBEILNU	BUBALINE	ABCDEEHL	BLEACHED
AARRSSTW	STAR WARS	ABBEILOT	BILOBATE	ABCDEEHR	BREACHED
AARSTTUY	STATUARY	ABBEIMWZ	ZIMBABWE	ABCDEELM	BECALMED
ABBBEILR	BRIBABLE	ABBEINRS	BRISBANE	ABCDEELS	DEBACLES
ABBBELRS	BABBLERS	ABBEIRRT	RABBITER	ABCDEELU	EDUCABLE
ABBBELUY	BLUE BABY	ABBEKLOO	BOOKABLE	ABCDEEMR	EMBRACED
ABBBGILN	BABBLING,	ABBELMRS	BRAMBLES	ABCDEFLO	BOLDFACE
	BLABBING	ABBELOPR	PROBABLE	ABCDEGIR	BIRDCAGE
ABBBHSUY	BUSHBABY	ABBELORU	BELABOUR	ABCDEGKL	GLADBECK
ABBCCKMO	BACKCOMB	ABBELQSU	SQUABBLE	ABCDEHLN	BLANCHED
ABBCEERU	BARBECUE	ABBENORY	NABOBERY	ABCDEHNR	BRANCHED
ABBCEGIR	CRIBBAGE	ABBEORRS	ABSORBER	ABCDEHOR	BROACHED
ABBCEIKT	BACKBITE	ABBEORTW	BROWBEAT	ABCDEIIT	DIABETIC
ABBCEILR	BARBICEL	ABBERRRY	BARBERRY	ABCDEIKS	BACKSIDE
ABBCEIRR	CRABBIER	ABBERRYY	BAYBERRY	ABCDEILR	CALIBRED
ABBCEIRS	SCABBIER	ABBERSST	STABBERS	ABCDEIRS	ASCRIBED
ABBCEKNO	BACKBONE	ABBFILLY	FLABBILY	ABCDEKLO	BLOCKADE
ABBCEKNU	BUCKBEAN	ABBGGILN	GABBLING	ABCDEKNN	NECKBAND
ABBCELRS	SCRABBLE	ABBGGINR	GRABBING	ABCDEKNU	UNBACKED
ABBCGINR	CRABBING	ABBGHRSU	HABSBURG	ABCDELOO	CABOODLE
ABBCGIOR	GABBROIC	ABBGINST	STABBING	ABCDEMNU	DUMB-CANE
ABBCIILL	BIBLICAL	ABBGINSW	SWABBING	ABCDEMOT	COMBATED
ABBCIKRT	BRICKBAT	ABBGOOSU	BUGABOOS	ABCDEMPS	CAMP BEDS
ABBCILSY	SCABBILY	ABBHILSY	SHABBILY	ABCDENTU	ABDUCENT

ABCDEORS	BAR CODES	
ABCDIILO	BIOCIDAL,	
	DIABOLIC	
ABCDIIRT	TRIBADIC	
ABCDIKLS	BACKSLID	
ABCDKOOR	BACK DOOR	
ABCDKOPR	BACKDROP	
ABCDOPRU	CUPBOARD	
ABCDORUY	OBDURACY	
ABCEEEFK	BEEFCAKE	
ABCEEHLM	BECHAMEL	
ABCEEHLR	BLEACHER	
ABCEEHLW	CHEWABLE	
ABCEEHRS	BREACHES	
ABCEEILT	CELIBATE	
ABCEEIMN	AMBIENCE	
ABCEEIRT	BEATRICE	
ABCEEKLY	BLACK EYE	
ABCEELOV	EVOCABLE	
ABCEELRR	CEREBRAL	
ABCEELRT	BRACELET	
ABCEEMRR	EMBRACER	
ABCEEMRS	EMBRACES	
ABCEENSS	ABSENCES	
ABCEFIIT	BEATIFIC	
ABCEFIKR	BACKFIRE,	
	FIREBACK	
ABCEFINO	BONIFACE	
ABCEFLSS	BASS CLEF	
ABCEGHIN	BEACHING	
ABCEGIRS	RIB CAGES	
ABCEGKLL	BLACKLEG	
ABCEGKLO	BLOCKAGE	
ABCEGKRY	GREYBACK	
ABCEHITT	BATHETIC	
ABCEHLOR	BACHELOR	
ABCEHLSU	CHASUBLE	
ABCEHMOT	HECATOMB	
ABCEHMRS	CHAMBERS	
ABCEHNRS	BRANCHES	
ABCEHOOT	COHOBATE	
ABCEHORR	BROACHER	
ABCEHORU	BAROUCHE	
ABCEIJOT	JACOBITE	
ABCEIKKL	KICKABLE	
ABCEIKLP	PICKABLE	
ABCEIKLT	BLACK-TIE	
ABCEIKWZ	ZWIEBACK	
ABCEILLR	CLARIBEL	
ABCEILNN	BINNACLE	
ABCEILOR	CABRIOLE	
ABCEILOS	SOCIABLE	
ABCEILRS	CALIBRES	
ABCEINRS	BRISANCE,	
	CARBINES	

ABCEINRT	BACTERIN	
ABCEINST	CABINETS	
ABCEINTU	INCUBATE	
ABCEIORS	AEROBICS	
ABCEIORT	BORACITE	
ABCEIRSW	CRABWISE	
ABCEIRTT	BRATTICE	
ABCEIRTY	ACERBITY	
ABCEJKLT	JET-BLACK	
ABCEJLTY	ABJECTLY	
ABCEKKSW	SKEWBACK	
ABCEKLLO	LOCKABLE	
ABCEKLMO	MOCKABLE	
ABCEKLOO	COOKABLE	
ABCEKLSS	BACKLESS	
ABCEKLST	BLACKEST	
ABCEKOOS	BOOKCASE	
ABCEKRST	BRACKETS	
ABCEKSST	SETBACKS	
ABCELLMP	CAMPBELL	
ABCELLPU	CULPABLE	
ABCELMNY	LAMBENCY	
ABCELMRS	SCRAMBLE	
ABCELNUU	NUBECULA	
ABCELOOT	BOOTLACE	
ABCELOPS	PLACEBOS	
ABCELOST	OBSTACLE	
ABCEMORT	COMBATER	
ABCENNOS	BESANCON	
ABCEOOSS	CABOOSES	
ABCERRTU	CARBURET	
ABCERTUU	CUBATURE	
ABCESTUU	SUBACUTE	
ABCFHOTW	FOB WATCH	
ABCFIKLL	BACKFILL	
ABCFILOS	BIFOCALS	
ABCFKLLU	FULLBACK	
ABCFKLLY	BLACKFLY	
ABCGHNPU	PUNCHBAG	
ABCGIKLN	BLACKING	
ABCGIKNS	BACKINGS	
ABCGILNO	LOG CABIN	
ABCGKLOS	BACKLOGS	
ABCHIKLS	BLACKISH	
ABCHIKRS	BRACKISH	
ABCHILOO	COOLIBAH	
ABCHIMOR	CHORIAMB	
ABCHIMRU	BRACHIUM	
ABCHINOR	BRONCHIA	
ABCHIRRT	TRIBRACH	
ABCHKMPU	HUMPBACK	
ABCHKOOP	CHAPBOOK	
ABCHKOOS	CASH-BOOK	
ABCHLLUU	CLUBHAUL	

ABCHMOTX	MATCHBOX	
ABCIIKRR	AIRBRICK	
ABCIIMNR	CIMBRIAN	
ABCIIMNS	MINICABS	
ABCIIORS	ISOBARIC	
ABCIIRST	TRIBASIC	
ABCIIRTU	CURITIBA	
ABCIISTY	BASICITY	
ABCIKLST	BACKLIST	
ABCIKMRS	BISMARCK	
ABCIKNPS	BACKSPIN	
ABCIKSSY	SICKBAYS	
ABCILLSU	BACILLUS	
ABCILLSY	SYLLABIC	
ABCILMOO	COLOMBIA	
ABCILMOU	COLUMBIA	
ABCILNPU	PUBLICAN	
ABCILOSY	SOCIABLY	
ABCILRRU	RUBRICAL	
ABCIMNRU	CUMBRIAN	
ABCINRVY	VIBRANCY	
ABCIOPRS	SAPROBIC	
ABCIORSU	CARIBOUS	
ABCIOSSU	SCABIOUS	
ABCIOSTU	SUBOTICA	
ABCIOSUV	BIVOUACS	
ABCJKOOT	JACKBOOT	
ABCKKOOR	BOOKRACK	
ABCKLOPT	BLACKTOP	
ABCKLOTU	BLACKOUT	
ABCKNNOS	BANNOCKS	
ABCKOORU	BUCKAROO	
ABCKOPST	BACKSTOP	
ABCLLPUY	CULPABLY	
ABCLNORY	CARBONYL	
ABCLPRUW	PUB-CRAWL	
ABCLSSSU	SUBCLASS	
ABCMOOPT	BOOT CAMP	
ABCMOORT	MOBOCRAT	
ABCNOUYY	BUOYANCY	
ABCORRSS	CROSSBAR	
ABCORRSW	CROWBARS	
ABCORRTU	TURBOCAR	
ABCORSSU	SCABROUS	
ABCRSTTU	SUBTRACT	
ABDDEEEH	BEHEADED	
ABDDEEGR	BADGERED	
ABDDEEHT	DEATHBED	
ABDDEEKR	DEBARKED	
ABDDEERR	DEBARRED	
ABDDEEST	BEDSTEAD	
ABDDEGIR	ABRIDGED	
ABDDEHMO	HEBDOMAD	
ABDDEILS	DISABLED	

ABDDEILU	BUDDLEIA	
ABDDEINS	SIDEBAND	
ABDDELRS	BLADDERS	
ABDDENOU	ABOUNDED	
ABDDFORR	BRADFORD	
ABDDILMO	LAMBDOID	
ABDDILRY	LADYBIRD	
ABDDLLOS	ODDBALLS	
ABDEEEFL	FEEDABLE	
ABDEEEIW	BIDE A WEE	
ABDEEEKR	BAEDEKER	
ABDEEENR	ABERDEEN	
ABDEEERV	BEAVERED,	
BEREAVED		
ABDEEFGS	FEEDBAGS	
ABDEEGGR	BEGGARED	
ABDEEGLR	BELGRADE	
ABDEEHLS	SHEDABLE	
ABDEEHNO	BONEHEAD	
ABDEEILN	DENIABLE	
ABDEEILS	ABSEILED	
ABDEEILW	BEWAILED	
ABDEEIST	BEADIEST,	
DIABETES		
ABDEEKMR	EMBARKED	
ABDEELLL	LABELLED	
ABDEELLW	WELDABLE	
ABDEELMM	EMBALMED	
ABDEELMN	MENDABLE	
ABDEELNS	SENDABLE	
ABDEELOR	LEEBOARD	
ABDEELPT	BEDPLATE	
ABDEELZZ	BEDAZZLE	
ABDEEMNO	BEMOANED	
ABDEEMNS	BEAM-ENDS	
ABDEENRT	BANTERED	
ABDEENRZ	BRAZENED	
ABDEENST	ABSENTED	
ABDEENTT	BATTENED	
ABDEERRT	BARTERED	
ABDEERST	DEBATERS	
ABDEERTT	BATTERED	
ABDEERTW	WATERBED	
ABDEERTY	BETRAYED	
ABDEESTT	BEAD TEST	
ABDEFILN	FINDABLE	
ABDEFINO	BONA FIDE	
ABDEFLLO	FOLDABLE	
ABDEFLOR	FORDABLE	
ABDEGHIS	BIGHEADS	
ABDEGILN	BLINDAGE	
ABDEGILU	GUIDABLE	
ABDEGIMX	MIXED BAG	
ABDEGINR	BEARDING	

ABDEGINS	BEADINGS,
DEBASING	
ABDEGINT	DEBATING
ABDEGIRR	ABRIDGER
ABDEGLMO	GAMBOLED
ABDEGOPR	PEGBOARD
ABDEHINS	BANISHED
ABDEHITU	HABITUDE
ABDEHKLU	BULKHEAD
ABDEHLLN	HANDBELL
ABDEHLLO	HOLDABLE
ABDEHLLU	BULLHEAD
ABDEHLMS	SHAMBLED
ABDEHLOT	THEOBALD
ABDEHLRS	HALBERDS
ABDEHMSU	AMBUSHED
ABDEHNRR	BERNHARD
ABDEHNSU	DUSHANBE
ABDEHORR	ABHORRED
ABDEHRST	BREADTHS
ABDEIIRT	DIATRIBE
ABDEIKQU	QUAD BIKE
ABDEILLS	SLIDABLE
ABDEILMN	MANDIBLE
ABDEILNO	BODLEIAN
ABDEILNW	WINDABLE
ABDEILOV	VOIDABLE
ABDEILPS	PIEBALDS
ABDEILRV	DRIVABLE
ABDEILTU	DUTIABLE
ABDEIMOO	AMOEBOID
ABDEIMOR	AMBEROID
ABDEINNR	ENDBRAIN
ABDEINOR	DEBONAIR
ABDEINOT	OBTAINED
ABDEINRS	BRANDIES
ABDEINST	BANDIEST
ABDEINSU	UNBIASED
ABDEIOTV	OBVIATED
ABDEIPST	BAPTISED
ABDEIPTZ	BAPTIZED
ABDEIRSS	SEABIRDS
ABDEIRTV	VIBRATED
ABDEISSU	DISABUSE
ABDEISTW	BAWDIEST
ABDEKLSW	SKEWBALD
ABDEKNSU	SUNBAKED
ABDEKORY	KEYBOARD
ABDELLOT	BALLOTED
ABDELNOR	OBERLAND
ABDELNOZ	BLAZONED
ABDELNRY	BENADRYL
ABDELNSS	BALDNESS
ABDELNST	BLANDEST

ABDELORU	LABOURED
ABDELOSV	ABSOLVED
ABDELOSW	DOWSABEL
ABDEMNNS	BANDSMEN
ABDEMNOS	ABDOMENS
ABDEMRTU	DRUMBEAT
ABDENNOS	NOSEBAND
ABDENNPY	BAD PENNY
ABDENNRW	BRAND-NEW
ABDENORW	RAW-BONED
ABDENOTW	DOWNBEAT
ABDENRRT	BERTRAND
ABDENRRU	UNBARRED
ABDENRSS	DRABNESS
ABDENRTU	BREADNUT,
TURBANED	
ABDEOPRT	PROBATED
ABDEORRS	BOARDERS
ABDEORRW	DRAWBORE,
WARDROBE	
ABDEORST	BROADEST
ABDEORSW	SOWBREAD
ABDEORTU	OBDURATE
ABDEORUX	BORDEAUX
ABDEPSSY	BYPASSED
ABDEPSTU	BUDAPEST
ABDERSTW	BEDSTRAW
ABDERTUW	DRAWTUBE
ABDESTTU	TASTE BUD
ABDFFLOY	BADLY-OFF
ABDFLOOT	FOLDBOAT
ABDGGGOY	DOGGY BAG
ABDGHINR	HANGBIRD
ABDGIINR	BRAIDING
ABDGILOR	GAOLBIRD
ABDGINNO	ABINGDON
ABDGINNR	BRANDING
ABDGINNY	BANDYING
ABDGINOR	BOARDING
ABDGINSW	WINDBAGS
ABDHILLN	HANDBILL
ABDHILNS	BLANDISH
ABDHINRS	BRANDISH
ABDHIRTY	BIRTHDAY
ABDHKNOO	HANDBOOK
ABDHLOPR	BARDOLPH
ABDHLORW	BLOWHARD
ABDHMOTU	BAD-MOUTH
ABDHMSTU	MUD BATHS
ABDHNSSU	HUSBANDS
ABDIIJLR	JAILBIRD
ABDIILLR	BILLIARD
ABDIIMNR	MIDBRAIN
ABDIIMSU	BASIDIUM
ABDIINOS	OBSIDIAN

ABDIIRTY	RABIDITY
ABDILNOS	BASILDON
ABDILORW	WILD BOAR
ABDILOST	TABLOIDS
ABDILRRY	RIBALDRY
ABDILRZZ	BLIZZARD
ABDINOTY	ANTIBODY
ABDINRTY	BANDITRY
ABDJMOOR	DOORJAMB
ABDLLORS	BOLLARDS
ABDLMORY	LOMBARDY
ABDLRSUY	ABSURDLY
ABDNORUY	BOUNDARY
ABDNSSTY	STANDBYS
ABDOORTU	OUTBOARD
ABDOOSSW	BASSWOOD
ABDRSUZZ	BUZZARDS
ABEEEERT	BEE-EATER
ABEEEFRS	FREE-BASE
ABEEEGRV	BEVERAGE
ABEEEHTT	HEBETATE
ABEEELLR	REELABLE
ABEEENST	ABSENTEE
ABEEFILN	FINEABLE
ABEEFILR	AFEBRILE, FIREABLE
ABEEFILS	FEASIBLE
ABEEFILT	FLEABITE
ABEEFLLL	FELLABLE
ABEEFLLN	BEFALLEN
ABEEFORR	FOREBEAR
ABEEGIRV	VERBIAGE
ABEEGLNU	BENGUELA
ABEEGMRT	BERGAMET
ABEEGMUU	MAUBEUGE
ABEEGNOS	GABONESE
ABEEGTTU	BAGUETTE
ABEEHINT	THEBAINE
ABEEHIRS	HEBRAISE
ABEEHIRZ	HEBRAIZE
ABEEHLLL	HEELBALL
ABEEHLLP	HELPABLE
ABEEHLLR	HAREBELL
ABEEHNNS	HENBANES
ABEEHNSS	BANSHEES, HAS-BEENS
ABEEHORS	RHEOBASE
ABEEHQTU	BEQUEATH
ABEEHRRT	BREATHER
ABEEIKLT	BAKELITE
ABEEIKRS	BAKERIES
ABEEIKRT	TIE-BREAK
ABEEILLR	RELIABLE
ABEEILLS	ISABELLE
ABEEILLV	LEVIABLE
ABEEILNP	PLEBEIAN
ABEEILNS	BALINESE, BASELINE
ABEEILNV	ENVIABLE
ABEEILPX	EXPIABLE
ABEEILRR	BLEARIER
ABEEILRT	LIBERATE
ABEEILRW	BEWAILER
ABEEILSS	SEISABLE, SISEABLE
ABEEILSZ	SEIZABLE, SIZEABLE
ABEEILUU	BEAULIEU
ABEEINRZ	BEREZINA
ABEEISTU	BEAUTIES
ABEEJMOR	JAMBOREE
ABEEKLST	BLEAKEST
ABEEKOOP	PEEKABOO
ABEEKRRS	BREAKERS
ABEELLLR	LABELLER
ABEELLLT	TELLABLE
ABEELLMT	MELTABLE
ABEELLRY	REELABLY
ABEELLSY	EYEBALLS
ABEELMMR	EMBALMER
ABEELMNO	BONE MEAL
ABEELMPR	PREAMBLE
ABEELMSS	ASSEMBLE
ABEELMTT	EMBATTLE
ABEELNOP	BEANPOLE
ABEELNRT	RENTABLE
ABEELOPR	OPERABLE
ABEELORS	EARLOBES
ABEELORX	EXORABLE
ABEELRSU	REUSABLE
ABEELRSV	SERVABLE
ABEELSSS	BASELESS
ABEELSSU	SUBLEASE
ABEELSTT	SEAT BELT, TESTABLE
ABEELTTW	WETTABLE
ABEEMMNR	MEMBRANE
ABEEMNRS	SEREMBAN
ABEEMNST	BASEMENT
ABEENNOT	NOTA BENE
ABEENNTU	UNBEATEN
ABEENORS	SEABORNE
ABEENOTZ	BENZOATE
ABEENRRT	BANTERER
ABEENRSS	BARENESS
ABEENRST	ABSENTER
ABEENSSS	BASENESS
ABEEORRV	OVERBEAR
ABEERRRT	BARTERER
ABEERRTT	BARRETTE, BATTERER
ABEERRTV	VERTEBRA
ABEERRTY	BETRAYER, TEABERRY
ABEFFKOR	OFF BREAK
ABEFGLLU	BLUE FLAG
ABEFHILS	FISHABLE
ABEFILLL	FALLIBLE
ABEFILLO	FOILABLE
ABEFILLR	FIREBALL
ABEFILLT	LIFTABLE
ABEFILOT	LIFEBOAT
ABEFILSY	FEASIBLY
ABEFILTT	FITTABLE
ABEFIORT	FIREBOAT
ABEFIRRT	FIREBRAT
ABEFITUY	BEAUTIFY
ABEFLLMU	BLAMEFUL
ABEFLLRU	FURLABLE
ABEFLMOR	FORMABLE
ABEFLNST	FAN BELTS
ABEFLRSU	SURFABLE
ABEFOORT	BAREFOOT
ABEFORRS	FORBEARS
ABEFRRUY	FEBRUARY
ABEGGHLU	HUGGABLE
ABEGGILN	BEAGLING
ABEGGIST	BAGGIEST
ABEGGLRY	BEGGARLY
ABEGHIMR	MAGHREBI
ABEGHINS	SIEGBAHN
ABEGHINV	BEHAVING
ABEGHINZ	BENGHAZI
ABEGHRSU	BEAR HUGS
ABEGIJTU	BIJUGATE
ABEGIKNR	BREAKING
ABEGIKNT	BETAKING
ABEGILLN	LABELING
ABEGILNN	ENABLING
ABEGILNS	SINGABLE
ABEGILNT	BLEATING, TANGIBLE
ABEGILNY	BELAYING
ABEGILOT	OBLIGATE
ABEGILRT	GILBERTA
ABEGIMNS	BIG NAMES
ABEGINRS	BEARINGS
ABEGINRT	BERATING
ABEGINRW	BEWARING
ABEGINST	BEATINGS
ABEGINTT	ABETTING
ABEGIPPS	BAGPIPES
ABEGKORS	GROSBEAK
ABEGLMRS	GAMBLERS
ABEGLORW	GROWABLE
ABEGLRSS	GARBLESS
ABEGMNOY	BOGEYMAN

ABEGMRSU	UMBRAGES
ABEGNOOR	GABORONE
ABEGNOSS	NOSEBAGS
ABEGNOST	BASTOGNE
ABEGNSTU	SUBAGENT
ABEGOSTT	TOTE BAGS
ABEGSSTU	SUBSTAGE
ABEHHIPZ	HEPZIBAH
ABEHIINR	HIBERNIA
ABEHILNR	HIBERNAL
ABEHILPS	SHIPABLE
ABEHILTT	TITHABLE
ABEHIMMS	MEMSAHIB
ABEHIMNO	BOHEMIAN
ABEHIMRS	HEBRAISM
ABEHINST	ABSINTHE
ABEHIRST	HEBRAIST
ABEHISTU	HABITUES
ABEHLMSS	SHAMBLES
ABEHMNOR	HORNBEAM
ABEHMOOR	REHOBOAM
ABEHMSSU	AMBUSHES
ABEHNSTU	SUNBATHE
ABEHORRR	ABHORRER
ABEHRSST	BRASHEST
ABEHRTUY	BAYREUTH
ABEIILMT	IMITABLE
ABEIILNN	BIENNIAL
ABEIILNR	BILINEAR, LIBERIAN
ABEIILNV	INVIABLE
ABEIILPT	PITIABLE
ABEIILST	SIBILATE
ABEIILTV	VITIABLE
ABEIINRR	BRAINIER
ABEIINRS	SIBERIAN
ABEIIRST	TIBERIAS
ABEIJLTU	JUBILATE
ABEIJMNN	BENJAMIN
ABEIKLLN	LINKABLE
ABEIKLNS	SINKABLE
ABEIKLSS	KISSABLE
ABEIKNRS	BEARSKIN, BREAK-INS
ABEIKNST	BEATNIKS
ABEILLLM	MILLABLE
ABEILLLT	TILLABLE
ABEILLLW	WILLABLE
ABEILLOS	ISOLABLE
ABEILLOV	VIOLABLE
ABEILLRS	LIBERALS
ABEILLRY	BAREILLY, BLEARILY, RELIABLY
ABEILLST	BASTILLE, LISTABLE
ABEILMNT	BAILMENT
ABEILMST	BALMIEST

ABEILNNW	WINNABLE
ABEILNPS	BIPLANES
ABEILNPT	PINTABLE
ABEILNRS	RINSABLE
ABEILNRU	RUINABLE
ABEILNSS	LESBIANS
ABEILNTV	BIVALENT
ABEILNVY	ENVIABLY
ABEILPPR	RIPPABLE
ABEILPPT	TIPPABLE
ABEILPRT	PARTIBLE
ABEILPSS	PASSIBLE
ABEILPST	EPIBLAST
ABEILRYY	BIYEARLY
ABEILSSU	ISSUABLE
ABEILSTU	SUITABLE
ABEILSUX	BISEXUAL
ABEILSVV	BIVALVES
ABEIMRST	BARMIEST
ABEIMRTV	AMBIVERT, VERBATIM
ABEIMSSU	IAMBUSES
ABEINORR	AIRBORNE
ABEINORS	BARONIES
ABEINORT	BARITONE, OBTAINER
ABEINOST	BOTANISE, OBEISANT
ABEINOTZ	BOTANIZE
ABEINRRW	BRAWNIER
ABEINRST	BANISTER
ABEINRSU	URBANISE
ABEINRSW	WINE BARS
ABEINRTU	BRAUNITE
ABEINRUZ	URBANIZE
ABEINSST	BASSINET
ABEINTTU	INTUBATE
ABEIORTV	ABORTIVE
ABEIPRRS	SPARERIB
ABEIRRRS	BARRIERS
ABEIRRSS	BRASSIER
ABEIRRST	ARBITERS
ABEIRRSZ	BRAZIERS
ABEIRRVY	BREVIARY
ABEIRSSU	AIRBUSES
ABEIRSTT	BIRETTAS
ABEIRSTY	BESTIARY, SYBARITE
ABEIRTTY	YTTERBIA
ABEISTTT	BATTIEST
ABEJLMPU	JUMPABLE
ABEJLSUY	BLUE JAYS
ABEJMOOR	JEROBOAM
ABEJNOSW	JAWBONES

ABEKLMOS	ABELMOSK, SMOKABLE
ABEKLNOW	KNOWABLE
ABEKLNST	BLANKETS
ABEKLORW	WORKABLE
ABEKNNOT	BANK NOTE
ABEKNSTW	WEST BANK
ABEKOORY	YEARBOOK
ABEKORTU	OUTBREAK
ABEKRSTY	BASKETRY
ABELLLMU	LABELLUM
ABELLLSY	SYLLABLE
ABELLMRU	UMBRELLA
ABELLNOT	BALLONET
ABELLOSV	SOLVABLE
ABELLRVY	VERBALLY
ABELLSUW	BLUE LAWS
ABELMNNO	NOBLEMAN
ABELMNOP	BELMOPAN
ABELMNOZ	EMBLAZON
ABELMNTU	NEMBUTAL
ABELMOSV	MOVABLES
ABELMRRS	RAMBLERS
ABELMSSY	ASSEMBLY
ABELNORU	BLUE ROAN
ABELNOST	NOTABLES, STONABLE
ABELNPRU	PRUNABLE
ABELNRSY	BARNSLEY
ABELNRTU	TURNABLE
ABELNRUY	URBANELY
ABELNRYZ	BRAZENLY
ABELNSTU	UNSTABLE
ABELNSTY	ABSENTLY
ABELNSUU	UNUSABLE
ABELNUVY	NAVY BLUE
ABELOPRT	PORTABLE
ABELOPRV	PROVABLE
ABELOPRY	OPERABLY
ABELOQTU	QUOTABLE
ABELORRU	LABOURER, RUBEOLAR
ABELORST	BLOATERS, SORTABLE, STORABLE
ABELORSV	ABSOLVER
ABELOSTU	ABSOLUTE
ABELOSTW	BESTOWAL
ABELOVVW	BLOW-WAVE
ABELRRSW	BRAWLERS, WARBLERS
ABELRSTU	BALUSTER
ABELRTTT	BARTLETT
ABELRTTU	REBUTTAL
ABELSTUU	SUBULATE
ABELSTWY	BELTWAYS

ABELTTUU	TUBULATE
ABEMMNOO	MOONBEAM
ABEMNOTU	BEAUMONT,
UMBONATE	
ABEMNPRU	PENUMBRA
ABEMNSSU	SUNBEAMS
ABEMNTTU	ABUTMENT
ABENNNOR	NARBONNE
ABENNOTU	BUTANONE
ABENOPSU	SUBPOENA
ABENORSS	BARONESS
ABENORST	BARONETS
ABENORTT	BETATRON
ABENORTV	BEVATRON
ABENOSSW	SAWBONES
ABENOSTY	BAYONETS
ABENQSTU	BANQUETS
ABENRTTU	BRUNETTA
ABENSSTT	TEST BANS
ABEOPPRY	PAPERBOY
ABEOPRST	PROBATES
ABEORSST	BOASTERS
ABEORSTT	ABETTORS
ABEORSTU	SABOTEUR
ABEORTUV	OUTBRAVE
ABEOSSST	ASBESTOS
ABEOSTWX	SWEATBOX
ABEPRSSY	PASSERBY
ABEPSSSY	BYPASSES
ABERRWXY	WAXBERRY
ABERSSTU	ABSTRUSE
ABERTTUY	BUTYRATE
ABERTUXY	X-RAY TUBE
ABFFGILN	BAFFLING
ABFFIILS	BAILIFFS
ABFFLLPU	PUFFBALL
ABFFLOST	BLAST-OFF
ABFFLOSU	BUFFALOS
ABFFNOTU	BOUFFANT
ABFGLLLO	GOLF BALL
ABFGORNU	FAUBOURG
ABFHIORS	BOARFISH
ABFIILMR	FIMBRIAL
ABFIILRR	FIBRILAR
ABFILSTU	FABULIST
ABFIRTTU	FRUIT BAT
ABFLLOOT	FOOTBALL
ABFLLORU	FOUR-BALL
ABFLLOST	SOFTBALL
ABFLOSTU	BOASTFUL
ABFLOSUU	FABULOUS
ABFNORTU	TURBOFAN
ABFORSTU	SURFBOAT
ABGGGINR	BRAGGING

ABGGILMN	GAMBLING
ABGGILNR	GARBLING
ABGGNOOT	TOBOGGAN
ABGGRSUU	AUGSBURG
ABGHHILL	HIGHBALL
ABGHINWZ	WHIZ-BANG
ABGHMORU	BROUGHAM
ABGHMOTU	TOMBAUGH
ABGHPRSU	HAPSBURG
ABGIIMST	BIGAMIST
ABGIINNO	BIGNONIA
ABGIINNR	BRAINING
ABGIINRS	BRAISING
ABGIINSS	BIASSING
ABGIIRTT	BIRGITTA,
BRIGITTA	
ABGIJNRU	ABJURING
ABGIKLNU	BAULKING
ABGILMNR	MARBLING,
RAMBLING	
ABGILNRW	BRAWLING,
WARBLING	
ABGILNST	BLASTING,
STABLING	
ABGILNTT	BATTLING
ABGILNTY	TANGIBLY
ABGIMOSU	BIGAMOUS
ABGINORT	ABORTING
ABGINOST	BOASTING
ABGINTTU	ABUTTING
ABGKORSW	WORKBAGS
ABGLLLOY	GLOBALLY
ABGLLORU	GLOBULAR
ABGLMOPU	PLUMBAGO
ABGLNOOT	LONGBOAT
ABGLNOUW	BUNGALOW
ABGLORSU	GLABROUS
ABGLRRSU	BURGLARS
ABGLRRUY	BURGLARY
ABGLRSUZ	SALZBURG
ABGNORSU	OSNABURG
ABGNOSTU	GUNBOATS
ABGOPSST	POSTBAGS
ABGRRTUW	WARTBURG
ABHHIPST	HIPBATHS
ABHIKLLW	HAWKBILL
ABHIKLOR	KOHLRABI
ABHILNOS	HOBNAILS
ABHILNOT	BIATHLON
ABHILOPS	BASOPHIL
ABHILSTU	HALIBUTS
ABHIMNOR	MORBIHAN
ABHIOSTU	HAUTBOIS
ABHIRRSU	AIRBRUSH
ABHKOOOT	BOAT HOOK

ABHLLMOT	MOTHBALL
ABHLLOOY	BALLYHOO
ABHLOSWW	WASHBOWL
ABHLSSTU	SALTBUSH
ABHMNSUU	SUBHUMAN
ABHMOORT	BATHROOM
ABHOORST	TARBOOSH
ABHOOSTW	SHOWBOAT
ABHORRSU	HARBOURS
ABHOSTUY	HAUTBOYS
ABHRSTTU	BATHURST
ABIIIKRT	KIRIBATI
ABIIINOT	AB INITIO
ABIIKLSS	BASILISK
ABIILLMR	MILLIBAR
ABIILLTY	LABILITY
ABIILMNO	BINOMIAL
ABIILMNS	ALBINISM
ABIILNOT	LIBATION
ABIILNOV	BOLIVIAN
ABIILNRZ	BRAZILIN
ABIILNST	SIBILANT
ABIILPTY	PITIABLY
ABIIMNOT	AMBITION
ABIIRRTZ	BIARRITZ
ABIIRSSV	VIBRISSA
ABIJLNTU	JUBILANT
ABIKLMNS	LAMBSKIN
ABIKNORR	IRONBARK
ABILLLPY	PLAYBILL
ABILLSWY	WAYBILLS
ABILMNOU	OLIBANUM
ABILMOPS	BIOPLASM
ABILNOOT	BOLTONIA,
OBLATION	
ABILNOTU	ABLUTION,
ABUTILON	
ABILNRTU	TRIBUNAL
ABILNRWY	BRAWNILY
ABILNSTU	ISTANBUL
ABILORST	STROBILA
ABILRSSY	BRASSILY
ABILSTUY	SUITABLY
ABIMNOSU	BIMANOUS
ABIMORSU	BIRAMOUS
ABIMPSST	BAPTISMS
ABINOORT	ABORTION
ABINORSW	RAINBOWS
ABINOSST	BASTIONS
ABINOSTT	BOTANIST
ABINRTTY	BRITTANY
ABINRTUY	URBANITY
ABIOPRSU	BIPAROUS
ABIORRTV	VIBRATOR
ABIORSTV	VIBRATOS

ABIORTUY	OBITUARY	ACCDELSU	CUL-DE-SAC	ACCEILLU	CAULICLE
ABIPRSTT	BIT PARTS	ACCDELSY	CYCLADES	ACCEILLV	CLAVICLE
ABIPRSUU	UBI SUPRA	ACCDEORR	ACCORDER	ACCEILNT	CANTICLE
ABIPSSTT	BAPTISTS	ACCDEOST	ACCOSTED	ACCEILNY	CALYCINE
ABIRRSTU	AIRBURST	ACCDERSU	ACCURSED	ACCEILRV	CERVICAL
ABISSSST	BASSISTS	ACCDESUU	CADUCEUS	ACCEIMRS	CERAMICS
ABKKMOOR	BOOKMARK	ACCDHIIR	DIARCHIC	ACCEINRT	ACENTRIC,
ABKLLNOR	BANKROLL	ACCDHIOT	CATHODIC		NEARCTIC
ABKLRSUW	BULWARKS	ACCDHIRY	DYARCHIC	ACCEINSV	VACCINES
ABKNPRTU	BANKRUPT	ACCDHPTU	DUTCH CAP	ACCEIOTV	COACTIVE
ABKOOPSS	PASSBOOK	ACCDIIOT	ACIDOTIC	ACCEIPRS	CAPRICES
ABLLMOOR	BALLROOM	ACCDILTY	DACTYLIC	ACCEIPRT	PRACTICE
ABLLMOPW	BLOWLAMP	ACCDINOR	CANCROID,	ACCEIRTU	CRUCIATE
ABLLNOOS	BALLOONS		DRACONIC	ACCEISST	ASCETICS
ABLLNOSW	SNOWBALL	ACCDIOOR	CORACOID	ACCEISTT	ECSTATIC
ABLLORRS	ROLL BARS	ACCDITUY	CADUCITY	ACCEKKOR	ROCK CAKE
ABLLOSTY	TALLBOYS	ACCDOSUU	CADUCOUS	ACCEKLNR	CRACKNEL
ABLLPSSU	BALLS-UPS	ACCEEHLO	COCHLEAE	ACCEKLRS	CACKLERS
ABLLRTUY	BRUTALLY	ACCEEHMP	CAMPECHE	ACCEKOPS	PEACOCKS
ABLLSSUY	SYLLABUS	ACCEEILR	CELERIAC	ACCEKPSU	CUP CAKES
ABLMNRUU	LABURNUM	ACCEEILS	ECCLESIA	ACCEKRRS	CRACKERS
ABLNORYZ	BLAZONRY	ACCEEIMR	ICE CREAM	ACCELMNY	CYCLAMEN
ABLOORTY	OBLATORY	ACCEEKLN	NECKLACE	ACCELNOV	CONCLAVE
ABLOPRVY	PROVABLY	ACCEELNR	CLARENCE	ACCELNRU	CARUNCLE
ABLOPSYY	PLAYBOYS	ACCEELOS	COALESCE	ACCELNTU	CLEAN-CUT
ABLORSST	BORSTALS	ACCEENNS	NASCENCE	ACCELORS	CORACLES
ABLORSSU	SUBSOLAR	ACCEENST	ACESCENT	ACCELRSY	SCARCELY
ABLOSSUU	SABULOUS	ACCEESSS	ACCESSES	ACCELRTU	CLEAR-CUT
ABLOSTTU	SUBTOTAL	ACCEFFIY	EFFICACY	ACCENOPT	CONCEPTA
ABLPRTUY	ABRUPTLY	ACCEFILS	FASCICLE	ACCENORT	ACCENTOR
ABMORSTU	TAMBOURS	ACCEGKMO	GAMECOCK	ACCENOST	COSECANT
ABNOORYZ	BRYOZOAN	ACCEHIKP	CHICKPEA	ACCENOTT	CONCETTA
ABNOOSSS	BASSOONS	ACCEHILM	ALCHEMIC,	ACCEOPRT	ACCEPTOR
ABNORTSU	RUN-ABOUT		CHEMICAL	ACCEORST	ECTOSARC
ABNOSSUU	AUBUSSON	ACCEHILP	CEPHALIC	ACCERSST	SCARCEST
ABOPRSST	TOP BRASS	ACCEHILS	CHALICES	ACCERSSU	ACCUSERS
ACCCENPY	PECCANCY	ACCEHIMN	MECHANIC	ACCESSTU	CACTUSES
ACCCFIIL	CALCIFIC	ACCEHINO	ANECHOIC	ACCESSUU	CAUCUSES
ACCCIILT	CALCITIC	ACCEHINR	ACRE-INCH,	ACCFHKLO	HALF COCK
ACCDDEOR	ACCORDED		CHANCIER, CHICANER	ACCFHLTY	CATCHFLY
ACCDDIII	DIACIDIC	ACCEHINT	CATECHIN	ACCFLNOO	CONFOCAL
ACCDDIIT	DIDACTIC	ACCEHIRT	CATCHIER	ACCGHINN	CHANCING
ACCDEELN	CANCELED	ACCEHKPY	PAYCHECK	ACCGHINO	COACHING
ACCDEENS	CADENCES	ACCEHLNS	CHANCELS	ACCGHINT	CATCHING
ACCDEENT	ACCENTED	ACCEHLOR	COCHLEAR	ACCGIKLN	CACKLING,
ACCDEEPT	ACCEPTED	ACCEHLOT	CATECHOL		CLACKING
ACCDEESS	ACCESSED	ACCEHMNO	COACHMEN,	ACCGIKMR	GIMCRACK
ACCDEGIN	ACCEDING		COMANCHE	ACCGIKNR	CRACKING
ACCDEILY	DELICACY	ACCEHNNO	CHACONNE	ACCGILOX	COXALGIC
ACCDEINO	DECANOIC	ACCEHNOR	ENCROACH	ACCGINRU	ACCRUING
ACCDEINT	ACCIDENT	ACCEHNRY	CHANCERY	ACCGINSU	ACCUSING
ACCDEIRT	ACCREDIT	ACCEHNUY	CHAUNCEY	ACCHHITT	CHITCHAT
ACCDEKLR	CRACKLED	ACCEHOPT	CACHEPOT	ACCHHOOW	CHAOCHOW
ACCDEKOS	COCKADES	ACCEIKPS	ICE PACKS	ACCHIIMS	CHIASMIC
		ACCEILLR	CLERICAL	ACCHIIST	CHIASTIC

ACCHILNY	CHANCILY	ACCKOOOT	COCKATOO	ACDEEENR	CAREENED
ACCHILOT	CATHOLIC	ACCKOPRT	CRACKPOT	ACDEEENT	ANTECEDE
ACCHILOY	CHICLAYO	ACCKORST	STOCKCAR	ACDEEERR	CAREERED
ACCHILTY	CATCHILY	ACCKOSSS	CASSOCKS	ACDEEERS	DECREASE
ACCHIMOR	ACHROMIC	ACCKPRSU	CRACKUPS	ACDEEESS	SEEDCASE
ACCHINNO	CINCHONA	ACCLLOSU	OCCLUSAL	ACDEEFFT	AFFECTED
ACCHINOS	CHICANOS	ACCLLSUU	CALCULUS	ACDEEFIN	DEFIANCE
ACCHINPU	CAPUCHIN	ACCLMOSU	MOLUCCAS	ACDEEFPR	PREFACED
ACCHIORT	THORACIC,	ACCMNOOR	MOROCCAN	ACDEEGLY	DELEGACY
	TROCHAIC	ACCMOPST	COMPACTS	ACDEEHIV	ACHIEVED
ACCHKLOR	CHARLOCK	ACCMOSTU	ACCUSTOM	ACDEEHMR	DEMARCHE
ACCHKOSY	HAYCOCKS	ACCNOORS	RACCOONS	ACDEEHNN	ENHANCED
ACCHNNOT	CONNACHT	ACCNOPTU	OCCUPANT	ACDEEHPR	PREACHED
ACCHNOTU	COUCHANT	ACCNORTT	CONTRACT	ACDEEHRS	SEARCHED
ACCHOPRS	CASH CROP	ACCNORTU	ACCUTRON	ACDEEHRT	DETACHER
ACCHORTY	OCTARCHY	ACCNOSTT	CONTACTS	ACDEEILT	DELICATE
ACCHORVY	CRY HAVOC	ACCNOSTU	ACCOUNTS	ACDEEIMR	MEDICARE
ACCHRSTY	SCRATCHY	ACCOPSTY	COPYCATS	ACDEEIMT	DECIMATE,
ACCIILLN	CLINICAL	ACCORRTY	CARRYCOT		MEDICATE
ACCIILMT	CLIMATIC	ACDDDEIT	ADDICTED	ACDEEINN	ENNEADIC
ACCIILRT	CRITICAL	ACDDDEKU	DEAD DUCK	ACDEEINU	AUDIENCE
ACCIINNP	PICCANIN	ACDDEEES	DECEASED	ACDEEINV	DEVIANCE
ACCIINOT	ACONITIC,	ACDDEEFR	RED-FACED	ACDEEKPT	TAPE DECK
	CATIONIC	ACDDEEHT	DETACHED	ACDEELLR	RECALLED
ACCIINTY	CYANITIC	ACDDEEIT	DEDICATE	ACDEELNR	CALENDER
ACCIIRTX	CICATRIX	ACDDEELR	DECLARED	ACDEELNS	CLEANSED
ACCIKKNN	NICKNACK	ACDDEELS	DESCALED	ACDEELPR	PARCELED,
ACCIKKRR	RICKRACK	ACDDEEMP	DECAMPED		REPLACED
ACCIKKTT	TICKTACK	ACDDEENS	ASCENDED	ACDEELRR	DECLARER
ACCIKLLS	SICK CALL	ACDDEENT	DECADENT,	ACDEELRT	DECRETAL
ACCIKLOT	COCKTAIL		DECANTED	ACDEELSS	DECLASSE
ACCILMUU	ACICULUM	ACDDEETU	EDUCATED	ACDEEMNP	ENCAMPED
ACCILNOT	LACTONIC	ACDDEHKN	DECKHAND	ACDEEMRS	SCREAMED
ACCILNOV	VOLCANIC	ACDDEIIL	DEICIDAL	ACDEEMRT	CREMATED
ACCILORT	CORTICAL	ACDDEIIM	MEDICAID	ACDEENOT	ANECDOTE
ACCILRRU	CIRCULAR	ACDDEILU	DECIDUAL	ACDEENRS	ASCENDER
ACCILRSY	ACRYLICS	ACDDEINR	RIDDANCE	ACDEENRT	CANTERED,
ACCILSSS	CLASSICS	ACDDEITT	DICTATED		DECANTER, RECANTED
ACCILTUU	CUTICULA	ACDDEKLO	DEADLOCK	ACDEENRZ	CREDENZA
ACCIMNOS	MOCCASIN	ACDDENTU	ADDUCENT	ACDEEORT	DECORATE
ACCIMORU	COUMARIC	ACDDERSU	CRUSADED	ACDEEPPR	RECAPPED
ACCIMPSU	CAPSICUM	ACDDERTU	TRADUCED	ACDEEPRT	CARPETED
ACCINOOS	OCCASION	ACDDGINU	ADDUCING	ACDEERRT	RETRACED
ACCINOOT	COACTION	ACDDGINY	CADDYING	ACDEERSS	CARESSED
ACCINORT	NARCOTIC	ACDDHIRY	HYDRACID	ACDEFGIN	DEFACING
ACCINORV	CAVICORN	ACDDHKOS	SHADDOCK	ACDEFIIP	PACIFIED
ACCINOTY	CYANOTIC	ACDDIIOR	CARDIOID	ACDEFILN	CANFIELD
ACCIOPST	SPICCATO	ACDDILNY	CANDIDLY	ACDEFILR	FILECARD
ACCIORST	ACROSTIC,	ACDDIRSS	DISCARDS	ACDEFINN	FINANCED
	SOCRATIC	ACDDKLNO	DOCKLAND	ACDEFIRR	FREDRICA
ACCIORSY	ISOCRACY	ACDDKOPS	PADDOCKS	ACDEFOTU	OUTFACED
ACCIOSTU	ACOUSTIC	ACDDKORY	DOCKYARD	ACDEFOTW	TWOFACED
ACCIRRTT	TRICTRAC	ACDDORTU	ADDUCTOR	ACDEFRSU	SURFACED
ACCIRSTY	SCARCITY	ACDEEEFT	DEFECATE	ACDEFRTU	FURCATED
ACCKKRSU	RUCKSACK			ACDEGGRS	SCRAGGED

ACDEGIMR	GRIMACED
ACDEGINU	GUIDANCE
ACDEGINY	DECAYING
ACDEGIRS	DISGRACE
ACDEHHNU	HAUNCHED
ACDEHHTT	THATCHED
ACDEHIJK	HIJACKED
ACDEHILL	HELLADIC
ACDEHILR	HERALDIC
ACDEHIMN	MACHINED
ACDEHIMS	SCHIEDAM
ACDEHINR	RICHENDA
ACDEHIRT	TRACHEID
ACDEHKLO	HEADLOCK
ACDEHKLS	SHACKLED
ACDEHKRU	ARCHDUKE
ACDEHKSS	CASH DESK
ACDEHKTW	THWACKED
ACDEHLNR	CHANDLER
ACDEHLNU	LAUNCHED
ACDEHLOR	ROCHDALE
ACDEHNOR	ANCHORED
ACDEHNST	SNATCHED, STANCHED
ACDEHORR	HARDCORE
ACDEHORT	CHORDATE
ACDEHOST	CATHODES
ACDEHOTT	COT DEATH
ACDEHPST	DESPATCH
ACDEHRRS	CHRESARD
ACDEHRST	STARCHED
ACDEIILN	ALCIDINE
ACDEIINR	ACRIDINE
ACDEIINS	SCIAENID
ACDEIINT	ACTINIDE, INDICATE
ACDEIJNU	JAUNDICE
ACDEIKNP	PANICKED
ACDEILLM	MEDALLIC
ACDEILLS	CEDILLAS
ACDEILLV	CAVILLED
ACDEILMS	DECIMALS, MEDICALS
ACDEILMX	CLIMAXED
ACDEILNP	PANICLED
ACDEILNU	CLAUDINE
ACDEILOR	CORDELIA
ACDEILPS	DISPLACE
ACDEILRT	ARTICLED
ACDEILST	CITADELS, DIALECTS
ACDEILSY	ECDYSIAL
ACDEIMNO	COMEDIAN, DAEMONIC, DEMONIAC
ACDEIMNP	PANDEMIC

ACDEIMOR	MORDECAI
ACDEIMPT	IMPACTED
ACDEIMRT	TIMECARD
ACDEINNR	CRANNIED
ACDEINOS	DIOCESAN
ACDEINOT	CATENOID
ACDEINOV	VOIDANCE
ACDEINPT	PEDANTIC
ACDEINRT	DICENTRA
ACDEINSS	ACIDNESS
ACDEINST	DISTANCE
ACDEINTU	INCUDATE
ACDEIOPS	DIASCOPE
ACDEIORT	CERATOID
ACDEIOSU	EDACIOUS
ACDEIPSS	CAPSISED
ACDEIPSZ	CAPSIZED
ACDEIQRU	ACQUIRED
ACDEIRSS	CRESSIDA, SIDECARS
ACDEIRTT	TETRACID
ACDEISTT	ACID TEST, DICTATES
ACDEKLMU	LAME DUCK
ACDEKNPU	UNPACKED
ACDEKOST	STOCKADE
ACDELLOR	CAROLLED, COLLARED
ACDELLOS	SO-CALLED
ACDELLOT	COLLATED
ACDELMOS	DAMOCLES
ACDELNOO	CANOODLE
ACDELNOR	COLANDER
ACDELNPU	UNPLACED
ACDELNRY	DRY-CLEAN
ACDELRSW	SCRAWLED
ACDELRSY	SACREDLY
ACDEMMRS	SCRAMMED
ACDEMNOR	ROMANCED
ACDEMOPR	COMPARED
ACDEMORS	COMRADES
ACDEMORT	DEMOCRAT
ACDEMUUV	VACUUMED
ACDENNNO	CANNONED
ACDENNOR	ORDNANCE
ACDENOPR	ENDOCARP
ACDENORY	CRAYONED, DEACONRY
ACDENRTU	UNDERACT
ACDENRVY	VERDANCY
ACDENSST	DESCANTS
ACDEORRT	REDACTOR
ACDEORST	REDCOATS, SACRED TO
ACDEORSU	CAROUSED

ACDEORTU	EDUCATOR
ACDEORTV	CAVORTED
ACDEPPRS	SCRAPPED
ACDEPRTU	CAPTURED
ACDEQTUU	AQUEDUCT
ACDERRSU	CRUSADER
ACDERRTU	TRADUCER
ACDERSSU	CRUSADES
ACDERSTT	TEST CARD
ACDFFHNU	HANDCUFF
ACDFFILR	RADCLIFF
ACDFFIRT	DIFFRACT
ACDFFLOS	SCAFFOLD
ACDFGOOT	ACT OF GOD
ACDFIILU	FIDUCIAL
ACDFILOU	FUCOIDAL
ACDGHOTW	DOGWATCH, WATCHDOG
ACDGILNR	CRADLING
ACDGILNS	SCALDING
ACDGIMOT	DOGMATIC
ACDGORST	DOGCARTS
ACDHILPR	PILCHARD
ACDHINOR	HADRONIC
ACDHINSW	SANDWICH
ACDHIPST	DISPATCH
ACDHIQRU	CHARQUID
ACDHKLRU	HARD LUCK
ACDHKORS	ROCK DASH
ACDHLNOR	CHALDRON
ACDHMNTU	DUTCHMAN
ACDHNOSW	CASH DOWN, COWHANDS
ACDHOOTW	WOODCHAT
ACDHOPRY	HARD COPY
ACDHORRS	ORCHARDS
ACDIIILN	INDICIAL
ACDIIJLU	JUDICIAL
ACDIILMS	DISCLAIM
ACDIILNO	CONIDIAL
ACDIILSU	SUICIDAL
ACDIILTY	DIALYTIC
ACDIIMNO	DOMINICA
ACDIIMOR	DIORAMIC
ACDIIMOT	DIATOMIC
ACDIIMSU	ASCIDIUM
ACDIINNT	INDICANT
ACDIINOT	ACTINOID, DIATONIC
ACDIIOSS	ACIDOSIS
ACDIIOSX	OXIDASIC
ACDIIRST	CARDITIS
ACDIIRTY	ACRIDITY
ACDIISST	SADISTIC
ACDILLOT	CLOTILDA

ACDILLPY	PLACIDLY	ACEEEPSS	ESCAPEES	ACEEIMRR	CREAMIER
ACDILMTU	TALMUDIC	ACEEERRT	RECREATE	ACEEINNR	NARCEINE
ACDILNOO	CONOIDAL	ACEEERTX	EXECRATE	ACEEINPS	SAPIENCE
ACDILNOR	IRONCLAD	ACEEESUV	EVACUEES	ACEEINPT	PATIENCE
ACDILNOT	DALTONIC	ACEEFFIN	CAFFEINE	ACEEINRS	INCREASE
ACDILNSY	SYNDICAL	ACEEFHWY	WHEYFACE	ACEEINRT	CENTIARE,
ACDILNUU	NUDICAUL	ACEEFLPU	PEACEFUL		CREATINE
ACDILORS	CORDIALS	ACEEFLSS	FACELESS	ACEEINST	CINEASTE
ACDILOUV	OVIDUCAL	ACEEFPRR	PREFACER	ACEEINTV	ENACTIVE
ACDILSTW	WILDCATS	ACEEFPRS	PREFACES	ACEEINTX	EXITANCE
ACDILSUU	CLAUDIUS	ACEEFPTY	TYPEFACE	ACEEIRRT	TERCEIRA
ACDIMNOO	CODOMAIN,	ACEEFRSU	FARCEUSE	ACEEIRSU	CAUSERIE
	MONOACID	ACEEGHNX	EXCHANGE	ACEEIRSW	WISEACRE
ACDIMNSU	SCANDIUM	ACEEGHRR	RECHARGE	ACEEIRTV	CREATIVE,
ACDIMNSY	DYNAMICS	ACEEGILS	LEGACIES		REACTIVE
ACDINOPS	SPONDAIC	ACEEGIMY	MAGIC EYE	ACEEIRTW	ICE WATER,
ACDINORS	SARDONIC	ACEEGINS	AGENCIES		WATER ICE
ACDINORT	TORNADIC	ACEEGINT	AGENETIC	ACEEISTV	VESICATE
ACDINSTY	DYNASTIC	ACEEGKRW	WRECKAGE	ACEEKLMR	MACKEREL
ACDIOPRS	PICADORS,	ACEEGNOZ	COZENAGE	ACEEKNPS	KNEECAPS
	SPORADIC	ACEEGNSV	SCAVENGE	ACEELLMR	MARCELLE
ACDIORTT	DICTATOR	ACEEGORV	COVERAGE	ACEELLNS	NACELLES
ACDIOSTX	DOXASTIC	ACEEHHST	CHEETAHS	ACEELLNT	LANCELET
ACDIRSTT	DISTRACT	ACEEHINS	EISENACH	ACEELLRR	CELLARER
ACDISTUV	VIADUCTS	ACEEHINT	ECHINATE	ACEELLRT	CELLARET
ACDJNSTU	ADJUNCTS	ACEEHIPT	PETECHIA	ACEELNOR	CAERLEON
ACDKLOPS	PADLOCKS	ACEEHIRT	HETAERIC	ACEELNPT	PENTACLE
ACDKMPSU	MUDPACKS	ACEEHIRV	ACHIEVER	ACEELNRS	CLEANERS,
ACDLNOPS	COLD SNAP	ACEEHLNR	CHARLENE		CLEANSER
ACDLNORS	CALDRONS	ACEEHLNT	CATHLEEN	ACEELNRU	CERULEAN,
ACDLNORU	CAULDRON,	ACEEHLOS	SHOELACE		LAURENCE
	COURLAND	ACEEHLRS	HERACLES	ACEELNRW	LAWRENCE
ACDLNORY	CONDYLAR	ACEEHLSW	ESCHEWAL	ACEELNST	CLEANEST
ACDLNOST	SCOTLAND	ACEEHMNP	CAMPHENE	ACEELNSU	NUCLEASE
ACDLOOOR	COLORADO	ACEEHMNR	MENARCHE	ACEELNSV	ENCLAVES
ACDLOORT	DOCTORAL	ACEEHMRS	CASHMERE,	ACEELNTT	TENTACLE
ACDLORWY	COWARDLY		MARCHESE	ACEELNTU	NUCLEATE
ACDMMNOO	COMMANDO	ACEEHMST	MACHETES	ACEELOPS	ESCALOPE,
ACDMMNOS	COMMANDS	ACEEHNNR	ENHANCER		OPALESCE
ACDMNORY	DORMANCY,	ACEEHNRT	CHARENTE	ACEELORT	RELOCATE
	MORDANCY	ACEEHPRR	PREACHER	ACEELPRR	REPLACER
ACDNOORT	ACRODONT	ACEEHPST	CHEAPEST	ACEELPRV	PERCEVAL
ACDNOORV	CORDOVAN	ACEEHRRS	RESEARCH,	ACEELPTU	PECULATE
ACDNOSTW	DOWNCAST		SEARCHER	ACEELRSS	CARELESS
ACDOOPSU	DOCU-SOAP	ACEEHRSS	SEARCHES	ACEELRST	CLEAREST
ACDOORST	OSTRACOD	ACEEHRST	HECTARES,	ACEELRSV	CLEAVERS
ACDOPRST	POSTCARD		TEACHERS	ACEELRTU	ULCERATE
ACDRSSTU	CUSTARDS	ACEEHRTT	CATHETER	ACEELRTV	CERVELAT
ACDRSTTU	DUSTCART	ACEEHRTY	CYTHEREA	ACEELRTX	EXCRETAL
ACEEEFRR	CAREFREE	ACEEHSTT	TEA CHEST	ACEELSSY	LES CAYES
ACEEEGLN	ELEGANCE	ACEEIKRR	CREAKIER	ACEELSTT	TELECAST
ACEEEIPR	EARPIECE	ACEEIKST	ICE SKATE	ACEEMNPS	SPACEMEN
ACEEEKPV	KEEP CAVE	ACEEILNR	RELIANCE	ACEEMNST	CASEMENT
ACEEELMR	CAMELEER	ACEEILNS	SALIENCE	ACEEMORS	RACEMOSE
ACEEENSV	EVANESCE	ACEEILPS	ESPECIAL	ACEEMORV	OVERCAME

ACEEMRRS	CREAMERS, SCREAMER
ACEEMRRY	CREAMERY
ACEENNPS	PENANCES
ACEENNPZ	PENZANCE
ACEENNRT	ENTRANCE
ACEENNST	CANTEENS
ACEENORT	CAROTENE
ACEENOST	NOTECASE
ACEENPRR	PARCENER
ACEENRRT	RECANTER, RECREANT
ACEENRTT	ENTR'ACTE
ACEEPSTT	SPECTATE
ACEERRSS	CARESSER
ACEERRST	TERRACES
ACEERRSU	ECRASEUR
ACEERRTU	CREATURE
ACEERRUV	VERRUCAE
ACEERSSS	CARESSES
ACEERSST	CERASTES
ACEERSSV	CREVASSE
ACEESSTT	CASSETTE, TEST CASE
ACEESSTY	CAT'S EYES
ACEFFGIN	EFFACING
ACEFFHRU	CHAUFFER
ACEFFILT	FACE-LIFT
ACEFFLRS	SCLAFFER
ACEFGINR	REFACING
ACEFGLNO	LONG FACE
ACEFGLRU	GRACEFUL
ACEFHIKS	FISHCAKE
ACEFHISV	CAVEFISH
ACEFHORU	FAROUCHE
ACEFIIPR	PACIFIER
ACEFIIRT	ARTIFICE
ACEFILLY	FACILELY
ACEFILOP	EPIFOCAL
ACEFILOS	FOCALISE
ACEFILOZ	FOCALIZE
ACEFIMPR	CAMPFIRE
ACEFINNR	FRANCINE
ACEFINNS	FINANCES
ACEFINRS	FANCIERS
ACEFINST	FANCIEST
ACEFIORR	AIRFORCE
ACEFIOSS	FIASCOES
ACEFIRRT	CRAFTIER
ACEFLLOV	CALF LOVE
ACEFLMNO	FLAMENCO
ACEFLNOR	FALCONER
ACEFLNOT	CONFLATE, FALCONET
ACEFLNRY	CRANE FLY

ACEFLORS	ALFRESCO
ACEFMNNY	FANCY MEN
ACEFNORV	CONFERVA
ACEFNRSU	FURNACES
ACEFOOPT	FOOTPACE
ACEFOORT	ACRE-FOOT, FOOTRACE
ACEFORST	FORECAST
ACEFRRSU	SURFACER
ACEFRRTU	FRACTURE
ACEFRSSU	SURFACES
ACEGGILN	CAGELING
ACEGGIRR	CRAGGIER
ACEGHHNT	CHANGTEH
ACEGHIIT	CHIGETAI
ACEGHIKN	CHEKIANG
ACEGHILN	LEACHING
ACEGHILT	LICH GATE
ACEGHINR	REACHING
ACEGHINT	CHEATING, TEACHING
ACEGHLTY	LYCH GATE
ACEGHOSU	GOUACHES
ACEGHRRS	CHARGERS
ACEGIKNR	CREAKING
ACEGILLR	ALLERGIC
ACEGILMU	MUCILAGE
ACEGILNN	CLEANING
ACEGILNR	CLEARING
ACEGILNV	CLEAVING
ACEGILNW	LACEWING
ACEGILRS	GLACIERS
ACEGIMMT	TAGMEMIC
ACEGIMNN	MENACING
ACEGIMNR	CREAMING, GERMANIC
ACEGIMNT	MAGNETIC
ACEGIMRR	GRIMACER
ACEGIMRS	GRAECISM, GRIMACES
ACEGINNO	CANOEING
ACEGINNS	ENCASING
ACEGINNT	ENACTING
ACEGINOS	COINAGES
ACEGINPR	CAPERING
ACEGINPS	ESCAPING
ACEGINRS	CREASING
ACEGINRT	ARGENTIC, CATERING, CREATING, REACTING
ACEGINSS	CAGINESS
ACEGINTX	EXACTING
ACEGIOTT	COGITATE
ACEGIPRT	PRICE TAG
ACEGLLNO	COLLAGEN

ACEGLLOS	COLLAGES
ACEGLNRS	CLANGERS
ACEGLOSU	CAGOULES
ACEGMNOY	GEOMANCY
ACEGNNOY	CYANOGEN
ACEGNNTY	TANGENCY
ACEGNOST	COGNATES
ACEGORSS	CORSAGES
ACEGORTT	COTTAGER
ACEGORTY	CATEGORY
ACEGOSTT	COTTAGES
ACEHHIRR	HIERARCH
ACEHHIRT	THE CHAIR
ACEHHMNN	HENCHMAN
ACEHHNRT	ETHNARCH
ACEHHNSU	HAUNCHES
ACEHHPRT	HEPTARCH
ACEHHRRT	THATCHER
ACEHHRTY	HATCHERY, THEARCHY
ACEHHSTT	HATCHETS, THATCHES
ACEHIIRT	HIERATIC
ACEHIJKR	HIJACKER
ACEHIKLR	CHALKIER
ACEHILLS	ACHILLES
ACEHILNP	CEPHALIN
ACEHILPR	PARHELIC
ACEHILRS	CHARLIES
ACEHILTT	ATHLETIC
ACEHIMNR	CHAIRMEN
ACEHIMNS	MACHINES
ACEHIMPT	EMPATHIC, EMPHATIC
ACEHIMRS	CHIMERAS
ACEHIMTT	THEMATIC
ACEHINOT	INCHOATE
ACEHINOX	HEXANOIC
ACEHINST	ASTHENIC, CHANTIES, TEAK-INS
ACEHIPRS	SERAPHIC
ACEHIPRT	PATCHIER, PHREATIC, PIE CHART
ACEHIPST	PASTICHE
ACEHIPTT	PATHETIC
ACEHIPTW	WHITECAP
ACEHIRSS	CASHIERS
ACEHIRST	CHARIEST
ACEHIRSU	EUCHARIS
ACEHIRSV	ARCHIVES
ACEHIRTT	CHATTIER
ACEHISST	CHASTISE
ACEHISTX	CATHEXIS
ACEHKLOV	HAVELOCK
ACEHKLRS	SHACKLER

ACEHKLSS	SHACKLES	ACEHPRSU	PURCHASE	ACEILMST	CLEMATIS,
ACEHKLSV	ALCHEVSK	ACEHRRST	CHARTERS,		CLIMATES
ACEHKLTY	LATCHKEY	CHARTRES, STARCHER		ACEILMSU	MUSICALE
ACEHKMPU	MUCKHEAP	ACEHRRTT	TETRARCH	ACEILMSX	CLIMAXES
ACEHKNSY	HACKNEYS	ACEHRSST	STARCHES	ACEILNNP	PINNACLE
ACEHKORV	HAVOCKER	ACEHRSSU	CHASSEUR	ACEILNOR	ACROLEIN,
ACEHKRTW	THWACKER	ACEHRSTT	RATCHETS	CAROLINE, CORNELIA
ACEHLLOO	COALHOLE	ACEHRTTY	TRACHYTE	ACEILNPS	PELICANS
ACEHLLST	HELLCATS	ACEHSSTT	CHASTEST	ACEILNRT	CLARINET
ACEHLNNS	CHANNELS	ACEHSSTW	SWATCHES	ACEILNSS	LACINESS
ACEHLNOU	EULACHON	ACEIILMN	LIMACINE	ACEILOPR	CAPRIOLE
ACEHLNOY	HALCYONE	ACEIILMX	MEXICALI	ACEILOPT	POETICAL
ACEHLNPT	PLANCHET	ACEIILST	SILICATE	ACEILORS	CALORIES
ACEHLNRU	LAUNCHER	ACEIIMTU	MAIEUTIC	ACEILORT	LORICATE
ACEHLNSU	LAUNCHES	ACEIINRT	ANTI-ICER,	ACEILOST	SOCIETAL
ACEHLOOT	OOTHECAL	ARENITIC, IN A TRICE		ACEILOSV	VOCALISE
ACEHLORS	CHORALES	ACEIINTV	INACTIVE	ACEILOTV	LOCATIVE
ACEHLORT	CHLORATE,	ACEIIPRS	PIRACIES	ACEILOVZ	VOCALIZE
TROCHLEA		ACEIIRRT	CRITERIA	ACEILPPY	PIPECLAY
ACEHLOTT	TEA CLOTH	ACEIISTV	CAVITIES	ACEILPRS	CALIPERS,
ACEHLPST	CHAPLETS	ACEIJMST	MAJESTIC	REPLICAS, SPIRACLE
ACEHLSSS	CASHLESS	ACEIKKLS	SACKLIKE	ACEILPRT	PARTICLE,
ACEHLSST	SATCHELS	ACEIKLLY	CLAYLIKE	PRELATIC
ACEHLSTT	CHATTELS	ACEIKLRY	CREAKILY	ACEILPRU	PECULIAR
ACEHLSTY	CHASTELY	ACEIKMNN	NICKNAME	ACEILPRV	PERCIVAL
ACEHMNRT	MERCHANT	ACEIKMRV	MAVERICK	ACEILPSS	SLIPCASE,
ACEHMNSS	CHESSMAN	ACEIKNPS	CAPESKIN	SPECIALS
ACEHMNTW	WATCHMEN	ACEIKNRR	CRANKIER	ACEILPXY	EPICALYX
ACEHMORT	CHROMATE	ACEIKOTW	KATOWICE	ACEILRSS	CLASSIER
ACEHMRRS	CHARMERS,	ACEIKPPR	PIPE RACK	ACEILRST	ARTICLES,
MARCHERS		ACEIKPSX	PICKAXES	RECITALS
ACEHMSTU	MUSTACHE	ACEIKSTT	TACKIEST	ACEILRSU	AURICLES
ACEHNNPT	PENCHANT	ACEILLMR	MICELLAR,	ACEILRSV	VISCERAL
ACEHNOPR	CHAPERON	MILLRACE		ACEILRTT	TRACTILE
ACEHNOPT	CENOTAPH	ACEILLMT	METALLIC	ACEILRTU	LUCRETIA
ACEHNPSU	PAUNCHES	ACEILLMY	MYCELIAL	ACEILRTV	VERTICAL
ACEHNQUU	QUECHUAN	ACEILLNT	CLIENTAL	ACEILRTY	LITERACY
ACEHNRRS	RANCHERS	ACEILLOP	CALLIOPE	ACEILRUZ	LUCREZIA
ACEHNRSS	ARCHNESS	ACEILLOR	ROCAILLE	ACEILSST	SCALIEST
ACEHNRST	SNATCHER,	ACEILLOS	LOCALISE	ACEILSTT	LATTICES
STANCHER		ACEILLOT	TEOCALLI	ACEILTVY	ACTIVELY
ACEHNSST	SNATCHES	ACEILLOZ	LOCALIZE	ACEIMMNP	PEMMICAN
ACEHNSTU	UNCHASTE	ACEILLPR	CALLIPER	ACEIMMRS	RACEMISM
ACEHNSWZ	SZECHWAN	ACEILLPS	ALLSPICE	ACEIMNRU	MANICURE
ACEHNUVX	CUXHAVEN	ACEILLRS	CARLISLE	ACEIMNST	SEMANTIC
ACEHOPRR	REPROACH	ACEILLRV	CAVILLER	ACEIMNSY	SYCAMINE
ACEHOPRS	POACHERS	ACEILMMO	CAMOMILE	ACEIMOTX	TOXAEMIC
ACEHORRV	OVERARCH	ACEILMMR	CLAMMIER	ACEIMOTZ	AZOTEMIC,
ACEHORST	THORACES	ACEILMNO	COALMINE	METAZOIC
ACEHORTT	THEOCRAT	ACEILMNP	MANCIPLE	ACEIMPSS	ESCAPISM
ACEHORTU	OUTREACH	ACEILMNS	MESCALIN	ACEIMPST	CAMPSITE
ACEHOSSW	SHOWCASE	ACEILMOS	CAMISOLE	ACEIMRRW	WAR CRIME
ACEHOSTU	SOUTACHE	ACEILMPS	MISPLACE	ACEIMRST	CERAMIST,
ACEHPRRT	PETRARCH	ACEILMRS	MIRACLES	MATRICES
ACEHPRST	CHAPTERS	ACEILMRT	METRICAL	ACEIMRTU	MURICATE

ACEINNOS	CANONISE
ACEINNOZ	CANONIZE
ACEINNPS	PINNACES
ACEINNRS	CRANNIES
ACEINNST	ANCIENTS,
CANNIEST, INSTANCE	
ACEINNSU	NUISANCE
ACEINNTU	UNCINATE
ACEINOPR	APOCRINE,
PROCAINE	
ACEINOPS	CANOPIES,
CAPONISE	
ACEINOPZ	CAPONIZE
ACEINORS	SCENARIO
ACEINORT	CREATION,
REACTION	
ACEINORV	VERONICA
ACEINOST	CANOEIST
ACEINOTT	TACONITE
ACEINOTV	CONATIVE
ACEINOTX	EXACTION
ACEINPTT	PITTANCE
ACEINRRY	CINERARY
ACEINRSS	RACINESS
ACEINRST	CANISTER,
CISTERNA, SCANTIER	
ACEINRTT	INTERACT
ACEINRTV	NAVICERT
ACEINRVY	VICENARY
ACEINSSU	ISSUANCE
ACEINSTV	VESICANT
ACEINTTU	TUNICATE
ACEINTTX	EXCITANT
ACEINTTY	TENACITY
ACEIOPRT	OPERATIC
ACEIORSV	VARICOSE
ACEIOTVV	VOCATIVE
ACEIOVVV	VIVA VOCE
ACEIPPRR	CRAPPIER,
PERICARP	
ACEIPRRS	PERISARC
ACEIPRST	CRISPATE,
PRACTISE	
ACEIPRTY	APYRETIC
ACEIPSST	ESCAPIST
ACEIPSSU	AUSPICES
ACEIPSTV	CAPTIVES
ACEIQRRU	ACQUIRER
ACEIRRRS	CARRIERS
ACEIRRSU	CURARISE
ACEIRRSW	AIRCREWS,
AIRSCREW, WAR CRIES	
ACEIRRUZ	CURARIZE
ACEIRSST	CASTRIES,
SCARIEST	

ACEIRSTT	CRISTATE,
SCATTIER	
ACEIRSTU	SURICATE
ACEIRSTZ	CRAZIEST
ACEIRTTU	URTICATE
ACEIRTTV	TRACTIVE
ACEIRTUV	CURATIVE
ACEIRTVY	VERACITY
ACEISSTU	SAUCIEST,
SUITCASE	
ACEISTTT	CATTIEST
ACEISTTU	EUSTATIC
ACEJLORY	CAJOLERY
ACEKKMRU	MUCKRAKE
ACEKLSST	SLACKEST
ACEKMRSS	SMACKERS
ACEKNORT	ONE-TRACK
ACEKNPRU	UNPACKER
ACEKNRRT	RACK-RENT
ACEKORSW	CASEWORK
ACEKQRUY	QUACKERY
ACELLLRU	CELLULAR
ACELLNOT	LANCELOT
ACELLNRU	NUCELLAR
ACELLOPS	COLLAPSE
ACELLORV	OVERCALL
ACELLOSW	COLESLAW
ACELLPSS	SCALPELS
ACELLRSU	CURE-ALLS
ACELLRTY	RECTALLY
ACELLSSU	CALLUSES
ACELMNNS	CLANSMEN
ACELMNSS	CALMNESS
ACELMNSU	UNCLE SAM
ACELMORS	SCLEROMA
ACELMORY	CLAYMORE
ACELMSTU	MUSCATEL
ACELNOOT	ECOTONAL
ACELNORT	CARLETON
ACELNOSU	LACUNOSE
ACELNOTV	COVALENT
ACELNRVY	CRAVENLY
ACELNSSU	SCALENUS
ACELOPPU	POPULACE
ACELOPRT	PECTORAL
ACELOPST	POLECATS
ACELOPTU	COPULATE
ACELOQSU	COEQUALS
ACELORSS	LACROSSE
ACELORST	SECTORAL
ACELORSU	CAROUSEL
ACELORSY	COARSELY
ACELORTU	CLEAROUT
ACELOSTU	OSCULATE
ACELOSTY	ACOLYTES

ACELPPRS	CLAPPERS
ACELPRSS	SCALPERS
ACELPRST	SPECTRAL
ACELPRSU	SPECULAR
ACELPSSU	CAPSULES
ACELPTUU	CUPULATE
ACELRRSW	CRAWLERS,
SCRAWLER	
ACELRSTT	CLATTERS,
SCARLETT	
ACELRTTU	CULTRATE
ACELRTTY	CLATTERY
ACELSSTT	TACTLESS
ACELSUUV	VAUCLUSE
ACEMMOTY	MYCETOMA
ACEMMRRS	CRAMMERS
ACEMNOOR	CAMEROON
ACEMNORS	ROMANCES
ACEMNRUY	NUMERACY
ACEMOOST	COMATOSE
ACEMOPRR	COMPARER
ACEMOPRS	COMPARES,
MESOCARP	
ACEMORRT	CREMATOR
ACEMORSY	SYCAMORE
ACEMPSSU	CAMPUSES
ACENNNOU	ANNOUNCE
ACENNOSS	CANONESS
ACENNOTT	COTENANT
ACENNOTV	COVENANT
ACENNOTZ	CANZONET
ACENNRSS	SCANNERS
ACENOPST	CAPSTONE,
OPENCAST	
ACENOPTW	CAPE TOWN
ACENORRT	TORRANCE
ACENORRW	CAREWORN
ACENORST	ANCESTOR
ACENORSU	NACREOUS
ACENORTU	COURANTE
ACENORTY	ENACTORY
ACENOSTV	CENTAVOS
ACENPTTU	PUNCTATE
ACENRSTT	TRANSECT
ACENRSTU	CENTAURS,
ETRUSCAN, RECUSANT	
ACENRSTY	ANCESTRY
ACENRTTU	TRUNCATE
ACENRTUY	CENTAURY
ACENSSTU	NUTCASES
ACENSSTW	NEWSCAST
ACEOOPSU	POACEOUS
ACEOORTV	EVOCATOR,
OVERCOAT	
ACEOPPRS	COPPERAS

ACEORRST	CREATORS, REACTORS
ACEORRTT	RETROACT
ACEORRTU	EUROCRAT
ACEORSST	COARSEST, COASTERS
ACEORSTV	OVERCAST
ACEOSSUY	SOY SAUCE
ACEOSTTU	OUTCASTE
ACEOSTUU	AUTOCUES, COUSTEAU
ACEPRRSS	SCRAPERS
ACEPRSTU	CAPTURES
ACEPSTTY	TYPECAST
ACEQRSTU	RACQUETS
ACERRSUV	VERRUCAS
ACERRUVZ	VERACRUZ
ACERSSUY	SYRACUSE
ACERSTTX	EXTRACTS
ACERSTTY	CYTASTER
ACERTTUW	CUTWATER
ACFFGHIN	CHAFFING
ACFFIILO	OFFICIAL
ACFFILNU	FANCIFUL
ACFGIIPR	CAPRIFIG
ACFGINNY	FANCYING
ACFGINRT	CRAFTING
ACFGITUY	FUGACITY
ACFHHINW	HAWFINCH
ACFHIJKS	JACKFISH
ACFHILNO	FALCHION
ACFHILOS	COALFISH
ACFHIRSW	CRAWFISH
ACFHIRSY	CRAYFISH
ACFHISSU	FUCHSIAS
ACFHLOSW	CASH FLOW
ACFHLTUW	WATCHFUL
ACFHORRT	RH FACTOR
ACFIILTY	FACILITY
ACFIIMPS	PACIFISM
ACFIIPST	PACIFIST
ACFIKLNS	CALFSKIN
ACFILLSY	FISCALLY
ACFILNOR	FORNICAL
ACFILNPU	CUP FINAL
ACFILORT	TRIFOCAL
ACFILRTY	CRAFTILY
ACFILSSY	CLASSIFY
ACFIMNRU	FRANCIUM
ACFINORT	FRACTION
ACFINOST	FACTIONS
ACFINSTY	SANCTIFY
ACFIOPRY	FAIR COPY
ACFIOSTU	FACTIOUS
ACFISSST	FASCISTS
ACFKLLOR	ROCKFALL
ACFKOORR	ROOF RACK
ACFLLMRU	CRAM-FULL
ACFLMNOO	MOONCALF
ACFLNORY	FALCONRY
ACFLOOPS	FOOLSCAP
ACFLORSU	SCROFULA
ACFMOTTU	FACTOTUM
ACFOOSTT	CAT'S-FOOT
ACGGHINN	CHANGING
ACGGHINR	CHARGING
ACGGIINT	GIGANTIC
ACGGIIOS	ISAGOGIC
ACGGILNN	CLANGING, GLANCING
ACGGLNOU	GLUCAGON
ACGGLRSY	SCRAGGLY
ACGHHIJK	HIGHJACK
ACGHHINT	HATCHING
ACGHHNOW	HANGCHOW
ACGHIIMN	MICHIGAN
ACGHIINN	CHAINING
ACGHIINR	CHAIRING
ACGHIKLN	CHALKING
ACGHIKNS	SHACKING
ACGHIKNW	WHACKING
ACGHILNS	CLASHING
ACGHILNT	LATCHING
ACGHILOR	OLIGARCH
ACGHIMNP	CHAMPING
ACGHIMNR	CHARMING, MARCHING
ACGHIMNT	MATCHING
ACGHINNT	CHANTING
ACGHINOP	POACHING
ACGHINPP	CHAPPING
ACGHINPR	PARCHING
ACGHINPT	NIGHTCAP, PATCHING
ACGHINRR	CHARRING
ACGHINRS	CRASHING
ACGHINRT	CHARTING
ACGHINRU	CHURINGA
ACGHINST	SCATHING
ACGHINTT	CHATTING
ACGHINTU	TAICHUNG
ACGHINTW	WATCHING
ACGHINTY	YACHTING
ACGHIPRS	GRAPHICS
ACGHNRYY	GYNARCHY
ACGIILMN	CLAIMING
ACGIILNO	LOGICIAN
ACGIILNV	CAVILING
ACGIINRT	GRANITIC
ACGIJLNO	CAJOLING
ACGIKLNN	CLANKING
ACGIKLNO	CLOAKING
ACGIKLNS	SLACKING
ACGIKLNT	TACKLING
ACGIKLNU	CAULKING
ACGIKLRY	GARLICKY
ACGIKMNS	SMACKING
ACGIKNNR	CRANKING
ACGIKNNS	SNACKING
ACGIKNOR	CROAKING
ACGIKNQU	QUACKING
ACGIKNRT	TRACKING
ACGIKNST	STACKING
ACGILLLR	CALL GIRL
ACGILLNS	CALLINGS
ACGILLRS	SCARGILL
ACGILMMN	CLAMMING
ACGILMNP	CLAMPING
ACGILNOR	CAROLING
ACGILNOS	SOLACING
ACGILNOT	LOCATING
ACGILNPP	CLAPPING
ACGILNPS	CLASPING, SCALPING
ACGILNRW	CRAWLING
ACGILNSS	CLASSING
ACGILRSU	SURGICAL
ACGIMMNR	CRAMMING
ACGIMNPR	CRAMPING
ACGIMNSY	SYNGAMIC
ACGIMORS	ORGASMIC
ACGINNNS	SCANNING
ACGINNPR	PRANCING
ACGINOST	AGNOSTIC, COASTING, COATINGS
ACGINPPR	CRAPPING
ACGINPRS	SCRAPING
ACGINRRS	SCARRING
ACGINRRY	CARRYING
ACGINRST	TRACINGS
ACGINRSV	CARVINGS, CRAVINGS
ACGINSST	CASTINGS
ACGINSTT	SCATTING
ACGIORSU	GRACIOUS
ACGJKLPU	JACK PLUG
ACGJLNOU	CONJUGAL
ACGLMOUU	COAGULUM
ACGLOSUU	GLAUCOUS
ACGLSSTU	CUT GLASS
ACGNNOOT	CONTANGO
ACGNOOST	OCTAGONS
ACGNORST	CONGRATS
ACHHILPT	PHTHALIC
ACHHINTW	WHINCHAT

ACHHINTY	HYACINTH	ACHLNORT	CHARLTON	ACIIORTV	VICTORIA
ACHHIORT	HATHORIC	ACHLORSS	SCHOLARS	ACIIRSST	TRIASSIC
ACHHIPPR	HIPPARCH	ACHLRSTY	CHRYSTAL	ACIIRSTT	ARTISTIC
ACHHLNOR	RHONCHAL	ACHMNORS	MONARCHS,	ACIISTTU	AUTISTIC
ACHHNTTU	NUTHATCH		ROMANSCH	ACIISTTV	ACTIVIST
ACHHOSTW	CHAT SHOW	ACHMNORY	MONARCHY	ACIITTVY	ACTIVITY
ACHHPTUZ	CHUTZPAH	ACHMOSST	STOMACHS	ACIITVVY	VIVACITY
ACHHSTTU	SUCH THAT	ACHMOSTY	STOMACHY	ACIJKKPS	SKIPJACK
ACHIILMS	CHILIASM	ACHNOPRU	UP-ANCHOR	ACIJRSSU	JURASSIC
ACHIILPT	HAPLITIC	ACHNPPSS	SCHNAPPS	ACIJSUZZ	JACUZZIS
ACHIILST	CHILIAST	ACHNRSYY	SYNARCHY	ACIKLLST	SALTLICK
ACHIINPS	HISPANIC	ACHOORTU	COAUTHOR	ACIKLORS	AIRLOCKS
ACHIINRT	TRICHINA	ACHOPRTY	TOPARCHY	ACIKLORY	CROAKILY
ACHIKKSW	KICKSHAW	ACHPRSTU	PUSHCART	ACIKNNPR	CRANKPIN
ACHIKOOW	KIAOCHOW	ACIIILMN	INIMICAL	ACIKNSTT	TINTACKS
ACHIKRSW	RICKSHAW	ACIIILNS	SICILIAN	ACIKPSSX	SIX-PACKS
ACHIKRTT	HAT TRICK	ACIIILNV	CIVILIAN	ACILLLOP	POLLICAL
ACHILLTY	CITY HALL	ACIIINST	ISATINIC, SINAITIC	ACILLMMY	CLAMMILY
ACHILMRS	CHRISMAL	ACIIKLNO	KAOLINIC	ACILLMOS	LOCALISM
ACHILMTY	MYTHICAL	ACIIKNNN	CANNIKIN	ACILLMSU	CAMILLUS
ACHILNNS	CLANNISH	ACIIKNPT	PACK IT IN	ACILLNOO	COLONIAL
ACHILNOS	NICHOLAS	ACIILLNV	VANILLIC	ACILLNOR	CARILLON
ACHILORT	ACROLITH	ACIILLTV	VILLATIC	ACILLNOS	SCALLION
ACHILPSY	PHYSICAL	ACIILLVW	CIVIL LAW	ACILLORT	CLITORAL
ACHILPTY	PATCHILY	ACIILMNR	CRIMINAL	ACILLOST	CALLISTO,
ACHILRVY	CHIVALRY	ACIILNPT	PLATINIC		LOCALIST
ACHILTTY	CHATTILY	ACIILNRS	SINCLAIR	ACILLOSY	SOCIALLY
ACHIMMOS	MACHISMO	ACIILRTU	URALITIC	ACILLOTY	LOCALITY
ACHIMMST	MISMATCH	ACIILRVW	CIVIL WAR	ACILMNOP	COMPLAIN
ACHIMNOP	CHAMPION	ACIILSST	SILASTIC	ACILMOPR	PROCLAIM
ACHIMNOR	HARMONIC	ACIIMNNT	MANNITIC	ACILMOSV	VOCALISM
ACHIMNOX	CHAMONIX	ACIIMNOS	SIMONIAC	ACILMSSS	CLASSISM
ACHIMNSU	INASMUCH	ACIIMNOT	AMNIOTIC	ACILMSSU	MUSICALS
ACHIMPSS	SCAMPISH	ACIIMNST	ACTINISM	ACILMSTY	MYSTICAL
ACHIMRST	CHARTISM	ACIIMNSU	MUSICIAN	ACILNOOT	LOCATION
ACHIMSSU	CHIASMUS	ACIIMNTU	ACTINIUM	ACILNOPS	SALPICON
ACHINORS	NIARCHOS	ACIIMNTY	INTIMACY	ACILNOPT	PLATONIC
ACHINOTZ	HOACTZIN	ACIIMOST	IOTACISM	ACILNORS	CLARIONS
ACHIOPRT	ATROPHIC	ACIIMOTT	AMITOTIC	ACILNORT	CONTRAIL
ACHIORST	CHARIOTS,	ACIIMPRV	VAMPIRIC	ACILNOSU	UNSOCIAL
	HARICOTS	ACIIMRST	SCIMITAR	ACILNOSV	SLAVONIC
ACHIPRRT	PHRATRIC	ACIIMSTV	ACTIVISM	ACILNOUV	UNIVOCAL
ACHIRRTY	TRIARCHY	ACIIMTUV	VIATICUM	ACILNRSU	CISLUNAR
ACHIRSTT	CHARTIST	ACIINNOT	INACTION	ACILNRUY	CULINARY,
ACHIRSTU	HAIRCUTS	ACIINNQU	CINQUAIN		URANYLIC
ACHISTTY	CHASTITY	ACIINNRV	NIRVANIC	ACILNSTU	LUNATICS,
ACHKKORW	HACKWORK	ACIINOPT	OPTICIAN		SULTANIC
ACHKMMOS	HAMMOCKS	ACIINORZ	ZIRCONIA	ACILNSTY	SCANTILY
ACHKMORS	SHAMROCK	ACIINOSV	AVIONICS	ACILOPRT	TROPICAL
ACHKNOOT	CANT HOOK	ACIINOTT	CITATION	ACILORTV	VORTICAL
ACHKOSSS	HASSOCKS	ACIINPRS	CRISPIAN	ACILOSTV	VOCALIST
ACHLLNWY	LYNCH LAW	ACIINRSS	NARCISSI	ACILOTVY	VOCALITY
ACHLLOOS	ALCOHOLS	ACIINRTU	URANITIC	ACILPSST	PLASTICS
ACHLMSTZ	SCHMALTZ	ACIIORST	AORISTIC	ACILRSTU	RUSTICAL
				ACILRTUV	CULTIVAR

ACILSSST	CLASSIST	ACIPSSST	SPASTICS	ACNOORRY	CORONARY
ACILSTTY	SCATTILY	ACIRSSTY	SACRISTY	ACNOORST	CARTOONS
ACILSTUV	VICTUALS	ACISSSTU	CASUISTS	ACNORRTY	CONTRARY
ACILSTVY	SYLVATIC	ACISSTTU	CATSUITS	ACNORSTT	CONTRAST
ACIMMTUY	CYMATIUM	ACJKOPST	JACKPOTS	ACNORTTU	TURNCOAT
ACIMNNNO	CINNAMON	ACKKMOPR	POCKMARK	ACNPRSYY	SYNCARPY
ACIMNNOR	MINORCAN	ACKLLPSU	SKULLCAP	ACNRRSTU	CURRANTS
ACIMNOOR	ACROMION	ACKLOOPW	WOOLPACK	ACOOPSTT	TOPCOATS
ACIMNORT	ROMANTIC	ACKLOORS	OARLOCKS	ACOPRRST	CARPORTS
ACIMNORU	COUMARIN	ACKLOOSW	WOOLSACK	ACOPRRTT	PROTRACT
ACIMNORY	ACRIMONY	ACKLORST	ROCK SALT	ACOPRTUY	PAY COURT
ACIMNOST	MONASTIC	ACKLORSW	WARLOCKS	ACORRSTT	TRACTORS
ACIMNPTY	TYMPANIC	ACKMNOST	STOCKMAN	ACORRSTU	CURATORS
ACIMNRSU	CRANIUMS	ACLLLLOR	ROLL CALL	ACORRTUY	CARRYOUT
ACIMOSST	MASSICOT	ACLLNORW	CORNWALL	ACORRTUZ	RAZOR-CUT
ACIMOSTT	STOMATIC	ACLLOORT	COLLATOR	ACORSSTU	SURCOATS
ACIMRRSY	MISCARRY	ACLLOOSS	COLOSSAL	ACORSSUW	CURASSOW
ACINNOOT	CONATION	ACLLOPSS	SCALLOPS	ACORSTTY	CRYOSTAT
ACINNOSS	SCANSION	ACLLRTUU	CULTURAL	ACOSSTTU	OUTCASTS
ACINNOST	CANONIST,	ACLMMNOU	COMMUNAL	ACPSSTUY	PUSSYCAT
	SANCTION	ACLMNORU	COLUMNAR	ACRRSTUU	ARCTURUS
ACINNOSU	ASUNCION	ACLMORSU	CLAMOURS	ADDDEEEN	DEADENED
ACINNOTU	CONTINUA	ACLMRSUU	MUSCULAR	ADDDEEGR	DEGRADED
ACINOOTV	VOCATION	ACLMSTUU	CUSTUMAL	ADDDEELR	LADDERED
ACINOPPT	PANOPTIC	ACLMSUUV	VASCULUM	ADDDEEMN	DEMANDED,
ACINOPST	CAPTIONS	ACLNOORT	COLORANT		MADDENED
ACINORSS	NARCOSIS	ACLNOOST	COOLANTS	ADDDEENS	DEAD ENDS,
ACINORST	CAST-IRON	ACLNOOSV	VOLCANOS		SADDENED
ACINORTT	TRACTION	ACLNORSU	CONSULAR	ADDDEGJU	ADJUDGED
ACINOSSS	CAISSONS	ACLNORTU	CALUTRON	ADDDELSW	SWADDLED
ACINOSSY	CYANOSIS	ACLNOSTU	OSCULANT	ADDDEMNU	ADDENDUM
ACINOSTT	OSCITANT	ACLNPTUU	PUNCTUAL	ADDDEOOW	DEAD WOOD
ACINOSTU	AUCTIONS,	ACLOOPRR	CORPORAL	ADDDEOPR	DROP-DEAD
	CAUTIONS	ACLOOPRS	CAR POOLS	ADDEEEFN	DEAFENED
ACINOSTW	WAINSCOT	ACLOOPRT	COALPORT	ADDEEEFT	DEFEATED
ACINOSWX	COXSWAIN	ACLOPRRW	PROWL CAR	ADDEEEMN	DEMEANED
ACINOTTX	TOXICANT	ACLOPRXY	XYLOCARP	ADDEEENR	DEADENER,
ACINPQUY	PIQUANCY	ACLOPSSY	CALYPSOS		ENDEARED
ACINPSTY	SYNAPTIC	ACLOSSTU	OUTCLASS	ADDEEFHN	HANDFEED
ACINRSTU	CURTAINS	ACLRSSTY	CRYSTALS	ADDEEFLT	DEFLATED
ACINRTTU	TACITURN	ACMMNOSY	SCAMMONY	ADDEEFRY	DEFRAYED
ACINSTTY	SANCTITY	ACMNOOPR	MONOCARP	ADDEEGNR	DERANGED,
ACIOOPST	SCOTOPIA	ACMNOORT	MONOCRAT		GARDENED
ACIOOPTX	COTOPAXI	ACMNOPRS	CRAMPONS	ADDEEGOR	DOG-EARED
ACIOPRST	APRICOTS	ACMNORSY	ACRONYMS	ADDEEGRR	DEGRADER,
ACIOPRST	POTASSIC	ACMNOSST	SCOTSMAN		REGARDED
ACIOPSSU	SPACIOUS	ACMNSSTU	SANCTUMS	ADDEEHIL	ADELHEID
ACIOPSTU	CAPTIOUS	ACMOORRT	MOTORCAR	ADDEEHLR	HERALDED
ACIORRSS	CORSAIRS	ACMORSTW	WORM CAST	ADDEEHLY	ALDEHYDE
ACIORSSU	SCARIOUS	ACMORSTY	COSTMARY	ADDEEHNR	HARDENED
ACIORSTT	RIOT ACTS	ACMQSTUU	CUMQUATS	ADDEEHRS	REDHEADS
ACIORTTY	ATROCITY	ACNNNORY	CANNONRY	ADDEEHRT	THREADED
ACIORTVY	VORACITY	ACNNORST	SCRANTON	ADDEEILN	DEADLINE
ACIOSTUU	CAUTIOUS	ACNNOSTT	CONSTANT	ADDEEILP	DEEP-LAID
ACIOSTUV	OCTAVIUS				

ADDEEILR	DEADLIER, DERAILED
ADDEEILT	DETAILED
ADDEEIMT	MEDIATED
ADDEEINT	DETAINED
ADDEEISS	DISEASED
ADDEEIST	STEADIED
ADDEEITV	DEVIATED
ADDEEKNR	DARKENED
ADDEELLP	PEDALLED
ADDEELOR	RELOADED
ADDEELUV	DEVALUED
ADDEEMNP	DAMPENED
ADDEEMNR	DEMANDER, REDEMAND, REMANDED
ADDEENPP	APPENDED
ADDEENPR	PANDERED
ADDEENPX	EXPANDED
ADDEENRW	WANDERED
ADDEENSS	DEADNESS
ADDEENTT	ATTENDED
ADDEENTU	DENUDATE
ADDEEPRT	DEPARTED, PREDATED
ADDEEPRV	DEPRAVED, PERVADED
ADDEERRT	RETARDED
ADDEERRW	REWARDED
ADDEERTV	ADVERTED
ADDEFFOR	AFFORDED
ADDEFILY	FIELD DAY
ADDEFLRU	DREADFUL
ADDEFORW	WORD-DEAF
ADDEGGLR	DRAGGLED
ADDEGHOR	DROGHEDA
ADDEGINR	DREADING
ADDEGLST	GLADDEST
ADDEGPRU	UPGRADED
ADDEHIIJ	JEDIDIAH
ADDEHILR	DIHEDRAL
ADDEHINW	HEADWIND
ADDEHIRS	DIEHARDS
ADDEHMRU	DRUMHEAD
ADDEHNNU	UNHANDED
ADDEHORW	HEADWORD
ADDEHOSW	SHADOWED
ADDEHRTY	HYDRATED
ADDEHSTU	THADDEUS
ADDEIITV	ADDITIVE
ADDEIJNO	ADJOINED
ADDEIKNP	KIDNAPED
ADDEIMOS	SODAMIDE
ADDEIMRS	DISARMED
ADDEIMSY	DISMAYED
ADDEIMTT	ADMITTED

ADDEINOR	ORDAINED
ADDEINOS	ADENOIDS
ADDEINST	DANDIEST
ADDEIOPR	PARODIED
ADDEIORS	ROADSIDE
ADDEISSU	DISSUADE
ADDEJSTU	ADJUSTED
ADDELNOU	DUODENAL, UNLOADED
ADDELNSU	UNSADDLE
ADDELOOR	EL DORADO
ADDELRSS	SADDLERS
ADDELRST	STRADDLE
ADDELRSW	DAWDLERS
ADDELRSY	SADDLERY
ADDELRTW	TWADDLER
ADDEMNPU	UNDAMPED
ADDENNSU	SAND DUNE
ADDENOPR	PARDONED
ADDENRST	STRANDED
ADDENRYY	YARN-DYED
ADDEOTTU	OUTDATED
ADDFFILO	DAFFODIL
ADDFFNRU	DANDRUFF
ADDFORRT	DARTFORD
ADDGILNN	DANDLING
ADDGILNP	PADDLING
ADDGILNS	SADDLING
ADDGILNW	DAWDLING, WADDLING
ADDGLORU	OLD GUARD
ADDGMRUU	MUDGUARD
ADDHHLNO	HANDHOLD
ADDHIKRS	HARD DISK
ADDHINSY	DANDYISH
ADDHLNOS	OLD HANDS
ADDHOORW	HARDWOOD
ADDIIMRU	DIARMUID
ADDIINOT	ADDITION
ADDIINRT	TRINIDAD
ADDILMNS	MIDLANDS
ADDILMOS	OLD MAIDS
ADDIMNOS	DIAMONDS
ADDIMNSY	DANDYISM
ADDINNOR	ORDINAND
ADDINORS	ANDROIDS
ADDINRWW	WINDWARD
ADDIORRT	DIRT ROAD
ADDKNRRU	DRUNKARD
ADDLLNOR	LANDLORD
ADDLLRSU	DULLARDS
ADDLNOOW	DOWNLOAD, WOODLAND
ADDMOOSY	DOOMSDAY
ADDNORWW	DOWNWARD

ADEEEFRT	DEFEATER, FEDERATE
ADEEEGLT	DELEGATE
ADEEEGNR	RENEGADE
ADEEEGUW	AGUEWEED
ADEEEHSY	EYESHADE
ADEEEINT	DETAINEE
ADEEEKNW	WEAKENED
ADEEELMN	ENAMELED
ADEEELNV	LEAVENED
ADEEELPR	REPEALED
ADEEELRS	RELEASED
ADEEELRV	REVEALED
ADEEELSW	WEASELED
ADEEELTV	ELEVATED
ADEEENRS	SERENADE
ADEEENTT	ATTENDEE, EDENTATE
ADEEEPRS	RAPESEED
ADEEEPRT	REPEATED
ADEEESSW	SEESAWED
ADEEFHNR	FREEHAND
ADEEFHOR	FOREHEAD
ADEEFHRT	FATHERED
ADEEFILN	ENFILADE
ADEEFIRR	RAREFIED
ADEEFLMS	SELF-MADE
ADEEFLOR	FREELOAD
ADEEFLPR	PEDALFER
ADEEFLRT	FALTERED, REFLATED
ADEEFLSS	FADELESS
ADEEFLSX	FLAXSEED
ADEEFMNR	FREEDMAN
ADEEFMTU	DEAF-MUTE
ADEEFNOT	TONE-DEAF
ADEEFNSS	DEAFNESS
ADEEFNST	FASTENED
ADEEFNTT	FATTENED
ADEEFRRY	DEFRAYER
ADEEFRST	DRAFTEES
ADEEFRTU	FEATURED
ADEEGGHS	EGGHEADS
ADEEGHRT	GATHERED
ADEEGINN	ENGADINE
ADEEGINR	REGAINED
ADEEGIRS	DISAGREE
ADEEGLLN	GLENDALE
ADEEGLNR	ENLARGED
ADEEGLRV	GRAVELED
ADEEGMNR	GENDARME
ADEEGMNS	END GAMES
ADEEGMNY	GANYMEDE
ADEEGNNR	ENDANGER

ADEEGNRR	GARDENER,
	GARNERED
ADEEGNRS	GRANDEES,
	GRENADES
ADEEGNRU	DUNGAREE,
	UNDERAGE
ADEEGNRV	ENGRAVED
ADEEGORT	DEROGATE
ADEEGPRS	PRESAGED
ADEEGRRV	REDGRAVE
ADEEGRSS	DEGASSER,
	DRESSAGE
ADEEGRTT	TARGETED
ADEEGSWY	EDGEWAYS
ADEEHHRS	REHASHED
ADEEHHST	SHEATHED
ADEEHIKL	HEADLIKE
ADEEHIKZ	ZEDEKIAH
ADEEHILN	HEADLINE
ADEEHIST	HEADIEST
ADEEHISV	ADHESIVE
ADEEHKNR	HANKERED,
	HARKENED
ADEEHKWW	HAWKWEED
ADEEHKWY	HAWK-EYED
ADEEHLLW	WELLHEAD
ADEEHLRT	LATHERED
ADEEHLSS	HEADLESS
ADEEHLTY	HEATEDLY
ADEEHMMO	HOMEMADE
ADEEHMMR	HAMMERED
ADEEHMNN	MENHADEN
ADEEHMPR	HAMPERED
ADEEHMST	STEMHEAD
ADEEHNPP	HAPPENED
ADEEHNRR	HARDENER
ADEEHNRT	ADHERENT
ADEEHNST	HASTENED
ADEEHORV	OVERHEAD
ADEEHRRT	THREADER
ADEEHRRW	HEREWARD
ADEEHRST	HEADREST
ADEEHRTW	WREATHED
ADEEHSST	HEADSETS
ADEEIILS	IDEALISE
ADEEIILZ	IDEALIZE
ADEEIITV	IDEATIVE
ADEEIJMR	JEREMIAD
ADEEILLN	DANIELLE
ADEEILMN	ENDEMIAL,
	MADELINE
ADEEILMR	REMEDIAL
ADEEILMT	LEAD TIME
ADEEILMV	MEDIEVAL

ADEEILNT	DATELINE,
	ENTAILED
ADEEILPS	PLEIADES
ADEEILPT	DEPILATE
ADEEILRS	REALISED,
	SIDEREAL
ADEEILRT	ELATERID,
	RETAILED
ADEEILRZ	REALIZED
ADEEIMNR	REMAINED
ADEEIMNT	DEMENTIA
ADEEIMNX	EXAMINED
ADEEIMRT	DIAMETER
ADEEIMST	TAMESIDE
ADEEIMTT	MEDITATE
ADEEINNR	ADRIENNE
ADEEINNS	ANDESINE
ADEEINPT	NEAP TIDE
ADEEINRS	ARSENIDE,
	NEARSIDE
ADEEINRT	DETAINER,
	RETAINED
ADEEINST	ANDESITE
ADEEIPRR	REPAIRED
ADEEIPRS	AIRSPEED
ADEEIPTX	EXPIATED
ADEEIRRR	DREARIER
ADEEIRST	READIEST,
	STEADIER
ADEEISSS	DISEASES
ADEEISST	EAST SIDE
ADEEISTV	SEDATIVE
ADEEKKRR	KERKRADE
ADEEKMRR	REMARKED
ADEEKMRT	MARKETED
ADEEKNPW	KNAPWEED
ADEEKNRR	DARKENER
ADEEKQSU	SQUEAKED
ADEEKRST	STREAKED
ADEEKSWY	WEEKDAYS
ADEELLLP	LAPELLED
ADEELLMT	METALLED
ADEELLNP	PANELLED
ADEELLPR	PREDELLA
ADEELLPS	SEPALLED
ADEELLQU	EQUALLED
ADEELLRV	RAVELLED
ADEELLRW	WELL-READ
ADEELLWY	WALLEYED
ADEELMMR	MAL DE MER
ADEELMNO	LEMONADE
ADEELMNR	ALDERMEN
ADEELMNT	LAMENTED
ADEELMRS	DEMERSAL,
	EMERALDS

ADEELMRV	MARVELED
ADEELMTU	EMULATED
ADEELNOR	OLEANDER
ADEELNPT	ENDPLATE
ADEELNRV	LAVENDER
ADEELNRY	ALDERNEY
ADEELNSV	ENSLAVED
ADEELNSW	NEW DEALS
ADEELNTT	TALENTED
ADEELOPR	LOP-EARED
ADEELOPX	POLEAXED
ADEELOST	DESOLATE
ADEELPPT	LAPPETED
ADEELPRS	RELAPSED
ADEELPRY	PARLEYED,
	REPLAYED
ADEELPST	PEDESTAL
ADEELQSU	SQUEALED
ADEELRRT	RED ALERT,
	TREADLER
ADEELRRS	TREADLES
ADEELRSV	SLAVERED
ADEELRTV	TRAVELED
ADEELRUV	REVALUED
ADEELSST	TASSELED
ADEELSTY	SEDATELY
ADEEMMRY	YAMMERED
ADEEMMSS	MESDAMES
ADEEMNNR	MANNERED
ADEEMNOT	NEMATODE
ADEEMNPR	DAMPENER
ADEEMNSS	SEEDSMAN
ADEEMORT	MODERATE
ADEEMPPR	PAMPERED
ADEEMPRT	TAMPERED
ADEEMPRV	REVAMPED
ADEEMPST	STAMPEDE
ADEEMRRS	DREAMERS
ADEEMRST	MASTERED,
	STREAMED
ADEEMRSU	MADURESE,
	MEASURED
ADEEMRTT	MATTERED
ADEEMRTW	WET DREAM
ADEENNRS	ARDENNES,
	ENSNARED
ADEENNRU	UNEARNED
ADEENOPW	WEAPONED
ADEENORS	REASONED
ADEENORY	AERODYNE
ADEENOSS	SEASONED
ADEENOTT	DETONATE
ADEENPPR	ENDPAPER
ADEENPRR	PANDERER
ADEENPRX	EXPANDER

ADEENPTT	PATENTED	ADEFIIMR	RAMIFIED	ADEGILNS	DEALINGS,
ADEENRRW	WANDERER	ADEFIIRT	RATIFIED	SIGNALED	
ADEENRSS	DEARNESS	ADEFIKRR	FREDRIKA	ADEGILNY	DELAYING
ADEENRSU	UNDERSEA	ADEFILLT	ILL-FATED	ADEGILOU	DIALOGUE
ADEENRSW	ANSWERED	ADEFILMN	INFLAMED	ADEGILRS	GRISELDA
ADEENRTT	NATTERED	ADEFILNT	INFLATED	ADEGILSS	GLISSADE
ADEENRTU	DENATURE	ADEFILOT	FOLIATED	ADEGIMNN	AMENDING
ADEENSST	ASSENTED	ADEFILRW	WILFREDA	ADEGIMNR	DREAMING
ADEENSSU	SUDANESE	ADEFIMPR	FIREDAMP	ADEGIMOR	IDEOGRAM
ADEENSTU	UNSEATED	ADEFINRR	INFRARED	ADEGIMRT	MIGRATED
ADEENTTU	TAUTENED	ADEFINRU	FREUDIAN	ADEGINOR	ORGANDIE
ADEENTTV	VENDETTA	ADEFINRW	FINE-DRAW	ADEGINOS	AGONISED,
ADEEOPRT	OPERATED	ADEFIRRT	DRAFTIER	DIAGNOSE, SAN DIEGO	
ADEEORVW	OVERAWED	ADEFLLMO	OLD FLAME	ADEGINOZ	AGONIZED
ADEEPPRR	PREPARED	ADEFLNOR	FORELAND	ADEGINRS	READINGS
ADEEPPRS	SPREADER	ADEFLNRS	FLANDERS	ADEGINRT	GRADIENT, RED
ADEEPPRV	DEPRAVER,	ADEFLNTU	FLAUNTED	GIANT, TREADING	
PERVADER		ADEFLORT	DEFLATOR	ADEGINRY	READYING
ADEEPRST	PEDERAST	ADEFLORU	FOUR-DEAL	ADEGINSS	ASSIGNED
ADEEPRSU	PERSUADE	ADEFLPRS	FELDSPAR	ADEGINST	SEDATING
ADEEPRTT	PATTERED	ADEFLRTW	LEFTWARD	ADEGISTU	GAUDIEST
ADEEPRTU	DEPURATE	ADEFLRZZ	FRAZZLED	ADEGLLNU	GLANDULE
ADEEPSWY	SPEEDWAY	ADEFLSTU	DEFAULTS	ADEGLLOP	GALLOPED
ADEEQRUV	QUAVERED	ADEFNNOR	FERNANDO	ADEGLNPS	SPANGLED
ADEERRRT	RETARDER	ADEFNOPR	PROFANED	ADEGLNRS	GLANDERS
ADEERRRW	REWARDER	ADEFNSST	DAFTNESS	ADEGLNRW	WRANGLED
ADEERRST	ARRESTED,	ADEFORRW	FARROWED	ADEGLNSS	GLADNESS
RETREADS, SERRATED		ADEFORRY	FOREYARD	ADEGLPPR	GRAPPLED
ADEERSST	ASSERTED,	ADEFORUV	FAVOURED	ADEGMMRU	RUMMAGED
DEARESTS		ADEFOSTU	FADEOUTS	ADEGMNOY	ENDOGAMY
ADEERSTT	RESTATED	ADEGGIRR	DRAGGIER	ADEGMPUZ	GAZUMPED
ADEERTTT	TATTERED	ADEGGJLY	JAGGEDLY	ADEGNNOR	ANDROGEN
ADEERVYY	EVERYDAY	ADEGGLRY	RAGGEDLY	ADEGNOPU	POUNDAGE
ADEESSSS	ASSESSED	ADEGGMOY	DEMAGOGY	ADEGNORT	DRAGONET
ADEESTTT	ATTESTED	ADEGGOPY	PEDAGOGY	ADEGNRRU	GRANDEUR
ADEFFGUW	GUFFAWED	ADEGGRTY	GADGETRY	ADEGNRST	DRAGNETS,
ADEFFIMR	AFFIRMED	ADEGHHOS	HOGSHEAD	GRANDEST	
ADEFFLNS	SNAFFLED	ADEGHILT	ALIGHTED,	ADEGOPRR	DRAGROPE
ADEFFORT	TRADE-OFF	GILTHEAD		ADEGORSW	DOWAGERS
ADEFGILR	GARFIELD	ADEGHINR	ADHERING	ADEGORTU	OUTRAGED
ADEFGILS	GADFLIES	ADEGHINS	HEADINGS,	ADEGPRRU	UPGRADER
ADEFGIMN	DEFAMING	SHEADING		ADEGPSTU	UPSTAGED
ADEFGIRT	DRIFTAGE	ADEGHLNO	HEADLONG	ADEHHIPS	HEADSHIP
ADEFGITU	FATIGUED	ADEGHORT	GOATHERD	ADEHHLOY	HOLYHEAD
ADEFGLLO	GOLD LEAF	ADEGHRTU	DAUGHTER	ADEHHNTU	HEADHUNT
ADEFGLOT	GATEFOLD	ADEGIILP	DIPLEGIA	ADEHHOST	HOTHEADS
ADEFGLRS	RED FLAGS	ADEGIIMN	IMAGINED	ADEHHRST	THRASHED
ADEFHILS	DEALFISH	ADEGIITT	DIGITATE	ADEHIKLN	HANDLIKE
ADEFHILT	HATFIELD	ADEGIKNN	KNEADING	ADEHIKNS	SKINHEAD
ADEFHIMS	FAMISHED	ADEGILLP	PILLAGED	ADEHILLM	HEIMDALL
ADEFHLNT	LEFT-HAND	ADEGILMN	MALIGNED	ADEHILNP	DELPHIAN
ADEFHMOT	FATHOMED	ADEGILNP	PEDALING,	ADEHILNR	HARD LINE
ADEFHNOR	FOREHAND	PLEADING		ADEHILRY	HYDER ALI
ADEFIILN	FINIALED	ADEGILNR	DRAGLINE,	ADEHILSV	LAVISHED
ADEFIILR	AIRFIELD	REGINALD		ADEHIMRS	MISHEARD

ADEHINOP	DIAPHONE	ADEHRSTY	HYDRATES	ADEILPRS	SPIRALED
ADEHINOS	ADHESION	ADEHRTTW	THWARTED	ADEILPRT	DIPTERAL
ADEHINPS	DEANSHIP,	ADEIILMS	IDEALISM	ADEILPRU	EPIDURAL
PINHEADS		ADEIILST	IDEALIST	ADEILRRY	DREARILY
ADEHINPU	DAUPHINE	ADEIILTV	DILATIVE	ADEILRSU	RESIDUAL
ADEHINRS	SHERIDAN	ADEIILTY	IDEALITY	ADEILRSY	DIALYSER
ADEHINSS	SHANDIES	ADEIIMNN	INDAMINE	ADEILRTT	DETRITAL
ADEHINST	HANDIEST	ADEIIMNR	MERIDIAN	ADEILSTY	DIASTYLE,
ADEHINSV	VANISHED	ADEIIMPR	IMPAIRED	STEADILY	
ADEHIORS	HERODIAS,	ADEIIMRS	SEMIARID	ADEILSXY	DYSLEXIA
RHODESIA		ADEIIMTT	IMITATED	ADEILTTU	ALTITUDE,
ADEHIPRS	SEPHARDI	ADEIINOT	IDEATION	LATITUDE	
ADEHIPST	PITHEADS	ADEIINRT	DAINTIER	ADEIMMRS	MERMAIDS
ADEHIRSS	RADISHES	ADEIINST	ADENITIS,	ADEIMNNT	IN TANDEM
ADEHIRST	HARDIEST	DAINTIES		ADEIMNOT	DOMINATE
ADEHIRSV	RAVISHED	ADEIIPRS	PRESIDIA	ADEIMNRY	DAIRYMEN
ADEHIRSW	RAWHIDES	ADEIITTV	VITIATED	ADEIMNSS	MAN-SISED,
ADEHISST	SHADIEST	ADEIJRSU	JUDAISER	SIDESMAN	
ADEHKNRS	REDSHANK	ADEIJRUZ	JUDAIZER	ADEIMNSZ	MAN-SIZED
ADEHKORW	HEADWORK	ADEIKLLO	KELOIDAL	ADEIMNTY	DYNAMITE
ADEHLLOW	HALLOWED	ADEIKLLY	LADYLIKE	ADEIMORT	MEDIATOR
ADEHLLRS	HARD SELL	ADEIKLSW	SIDEWALK	ADEIMOSS	SESAMOID
ADEHLMNO	HOMELAND	ADEIKMRT	TIDEMARK	ADEIMPRT	IMPARTED
ADEHLNRS	HANDLERS	ADEIKORT	KERATOID	ADEIMRRS	ADMIRERS,
ADEHLNSS	HANDLESS	ADEILLMY	MEDIALLY	DISARMER, MARRIEDS	
ADEHLNST	SHETLAND	ADEILLOR	ARILLODE	ADEIMRSS	SIDEARMS
ADEHLOPS	ASPHODEL	ADEILLRV	RIVALLED	ADEIMRXY	READY-MIX
ADEHLPSS	SPLASHED	ADEILLSW	SIDEWALL	ADEIMSTY	DAYTIMES
ADEHLRRY	HERALDRY	ADEILMMS	DILEMMAS	ADEINNOT	ANOINTED,
ADEHMMMO	MOHAMMED	ADEILMNN	LANDMINE	ANTINODE	
ADEHMNNY	HANDYMEN	ADEILMNO	MELANOID	ADEINNOV	DEVONIAN
ADEHMNOS	HANDSOME	ADEILMNY	MAIDENLY	ADEINNRZ	RENDZINA
ADEHMNRS	HERDSMAN	ADEILMOX	ALDOXIME	ADEINNTU	INUNDATE
ADEHMOOR	HEADROOM	ADEILMPS	MISPLEAD	ADEINORR	ORDAINER
ADEHMORW	HOMEWARD	ADEILMRY	DREAMILY	ADEINORT	ORDINATE,
ADEHMOST	HEADMOST	ADEILMSV	MALDIVES	RATIONED	
ADEHMOSU	MADHOUSE	ADEILNNR	INLANDER	ADEINOST	SEDATION
ADEHNOPR	ORPHANED	ADEILNNT	DENTINAL	ADEINOTT	ANTIDOTE
ADEHNORV	HANDOVER,	ADEILNOP	PALINODE	ADEINOTV	DONATIVE
OVERHAND		ADEILNRS	ISLANDER	ADEINPPX	APPENDIX
ADEHNOSS	SANDSHOE	ADEILNST	TAIL ENDS	ADEINPRS	SPRAINED
ADEHNPRS	SHARP END	ADEILNTV	DIVALENT	ADEINPRT	DIPTERAN
ADEHNRSS	HARDNESS	ADEILOPS	SEPALOID	ADEINPSS	IN SPADES
ADEHNRTU	UNTHREAD	ADEILOPT	PETALOID	ADEINRRS	SERRANID
ADEHNSSU	SUNSHADE	ADEILORT	IDOLATER,	ADEINRSS	SARDINES
ADEHNSUW	UNWASHED	TAILORED		ADEINRST	RANDIEST,
ADEHOORT	DOROTHEA,	ADEILORV	OVERLAID	STRAINED	
THEODORA		ADEILORX	EXORDIAL	ADEINRSV	INVADERS
ADEHOPXY	HEXAPODY	ADEILOST	DIASTOLE,	ADEINRTU	URINATED
ADEHORRW	HARROWED	ISOLATED, SODALITE		ADEINRVY	VINEYARD
ADEHORSW	SHADOWER	ADEILOSV	VAL-D'OISE	ADEINSST	SANDIEST
ADEHORTU	AUTHORED	ADEILOTT	DATOLITE	ADEINSSV	AVIDNESS
ADEHORTW	DEATH ROW	ADEILOTV	DOVETAIL,	ADEINSTV	DEVIANTS
ADEHPSUW	WASHED-UP	VIOLATED		ADEIOPRS	DIASPORE,
ADEHQSSU	SQUASHED	ADEILPPP	PEDIPALP	PARODIES	

ADEIOPRV	OVERPAID	ADELNRTY	ARDENTLY	ADEOPPRV	APPROVED
ADEIOPST	DIOPTASE	ADELNRUY	UNDERLAY	ADEOPRRS	EARDROPS
ADEIOPTV	ADOPTIVE	ADELNTUU	UNDULATE	ADEOPRRT	PARROTED,
ADEIORST	ASTEROID	ADELNUUV	UNVALUED	PREDATOR, TEARDROP	
ADEIORTT	TERATOID	ADELOORV	OVERLOAD	ADEOPRTT	TETRAPOD
ADEIORTV	DEVIATOR	ADELOPRS	LEOPARDS	ADEOPSTT	POSTDATE
ADEIPPRS	APPRISED	ADELOPST	TADPOLES	ADEOPTTU	UP-TO-DATE
ADEIPRST	TRAIPSED	ADELOPTY	PETALODY	ADEORRST	ROADSTER
ADEIPRSY	PRISE DAY	ADELORST	LEOTARDS,	ADEORRVW	OVERDRAW
ADEIPRYZ	PRIZE DAY	LODESTAR		ADEORSST	ASSORTED
ADEIPTTU	APTITUDE	ADELORTW	LEADWORT	ADEORSTT	ROAD TEST
ADEIQRRU	QUARRIED	ADELOTUV	OVULATED	ADEORSTU	READOUTS
ADEIRRWW	WIREDRAW	ADELOTUW	OUTLAWED	ADEORSTX	EXTRADOS
ADEIRSST	DISASTER	ADELPRSW	SPRAWLED	ADEORSUV	SAVOURED
ADEIRSSV	ADVISERS	ADELPRTT	PRATTLED	ADEPPRST	STRAPPED
ADEIRSTT	STRIATED,	ADELPSTT	SPLATTED	ADEPRSTU	PASTURED
TARDIEST		ADELPSTU	PULSATED	ADEQSTTU	SQUATTED
ADEIRTUV	DURATIVE	ADELRSTT	STARTLED	ADERRSSW	WARDRESS
ADEIRVWY	DRIVEWAY	ADELRTUY	ADULTERY	ADERRSTT	REDSTART
ADEISSST	ASSISTED	ADEMNNNU	UNMANNED	ADERSSTW	STEWARDS
ADEISSTT	DISTASTE	ADEMNOOR	MAROONED	ADERSTWW	WESTWARD
ADEISSWY	SIDEWAYS	ADEMNOPR	NAMEDROP,	ADESSTUY	TUESDAYS
ADEISTTU	SITUATED	POMANDER		ADFFHNOS	HANDS-OFF
ADEISTWY	TIDEWAYS	ADEMNORS	RANSOMED	ADFFISST	DISTAFFS
ADEITTTU	ATTITUDE	ADEMNORY	RAYMONDE	ADFFNOST	STANDOFF
ADEJOPRY	JEOPARDY	ADEMNOTU	AMOUNTED	ADFFOOST	FAST FOOD
ADEJRSTU	READJUST	ADEMNPSS	DAMPNESS	ADFFORRT	TRAFFORD
ADEKLMRY	MARKEDLY	ADEMNRRU	UNDERARM	ADFFORST	STAFFORD
ADEKLPRS	SPARKLED	ADEMOORT	MODERATO	ADFGIINR	INFRA DIG
ADEKMNRU	UNMARKED	ADEMOOSV	VAMOOSED	ADFGINRT	DRAFTING
ADEKMNSU	UNMASKED	ADEMOPRY	PYODERMA	ADFGINRW	DWARFING
ADEKNNSS	DANKNESS	ADEMORRU	ARMOURED	ADFGLOUW	GOD-AWFUL
ADEKNPTU	TANKED UP	ADEMRRSU	EARDRUMS	ADFHIOST	TOADFISH
ADEKNRSS	DARKNESS	ADEMRRTY	MARTYRED	ADFHIRSW	DWARFISH
ADEKQSUW	SQUAWKED	ADENNORS	ANDERSON	ADFHLNSU	HANDFULS
ADELLNNU	ANNULLED	ADENNOSY	ANODYNES	ADFHLOST	HOLDFAST
ADELLNSW	SANDWELL,	ADENNPST	PENDANTS	ADFHORRT	HARTFORD
WALLSEND		ADENOORW	WANDEROO	ADFIILRW	WILFRIDA
ADELLOPW	WALLOPED	ADENOPRR	PARDONER	ADFIIRST	FIRST AID
ADELLOTT	ALLOTTED,	ADENOPST	NOTEPADS	ADFILNSW	WINDFALL
TOTALLED		ADENOPSY	DYSPNOEA	ADFILMNO	MANIFOLD
ADELLOWW	WALLOWED	ADENORRW	NARROWED	ADFILNOR	FLORINDA
ADELLQSU	SQUALLED	ADENORTW	DANEWORT	ADFIMRSW	DWARFISM
ADELMOPS	MALPOSED	ADENORUY	DOUNREAY	ADFIRSTY	FIRST-DAY
ADELMORS	EARLDOMS	ADENPPTU	UNTAPPED	ADFKNOOR	KORDOFAN
ADELMOTU	MODULATE	ADENPRTY	PEDANTRY	ADFLLNOU	ALL FOUND
ADELMPRT	TRAMPLED	ADENPRUY	UNDERPAY	ADFLLNOW	DOWNFALL
ADELMRRU	DEMURRAL	ADENQRSU	SQUANDER	ADFLMNOR	LANDFORM
ADELMSSY	MASSEDLY	ADENRRWY	WARDENRY	ADFLMSTU	MUDFLATS
ADELNORS	SOLANDER	ADENRSTU	TRANSUDE	ADFMORST	STAMFORD
ADELNORU	UNLOADER	ADENRTVY	DAVENTRY	ADFNNOST	FONDANTS
ADELNORV	OVERLAND	ADENSTUY	UNSTEADY	ADFNOORT	TO-AND-FRO
ADELNOVY	DONLEAVY	ADEOORRT	TOREADOR	ADFNOORZ	FORZANDO
ADELNPRS	SPANDREL	ADEOOSTW	EASTWOOD	ADFNORST	STANFORD
ADELNRSS	SLANDERS	ADEOOTTT	TATTOOED		

218

ADFOOPST	FOOTPADS	ADGINOPT	ADOPTING	ADHNOSWW	DOWNWASH
ADFORRSW	FORWARDS	ADGINORR	RING ROAD	ADHNRSTU	HARD NUTS
ADGGGINR	DRAGGING	ADGINOTY	TOADYING	ADHNRSTY	HYDRANTS
ADGGILNN	DANGLING	ADGINPTU	UPDATING	ADHOOPRS	HOSPODAR
ADGGINRS	NIGGARDS	ADGINRSW	DRAWINGS	ADHOORSW	ROADSHOW
ADGGINRU	GUARDING	ADGINRTT	DRATTING	ADHOPRST	HARDTOPS
ADGGLRSU	SLUGGARD	ADGIORTT	TITOGRAD	ADHOPRSY	RHAPSODY
ADGHHILN	HIGHLAND	ADGIRSZZ	GIZZARDS	ADHORRTY	HYDRATOR
ADGHHIOR	HIGH ROAD	ADGLNOOS	GONDOLAS	ADHORSTY	SHORT-DAY
ADGHILNN	HANDLING	ADGMNOOR	ONDOGRAM	ADHRSTUY	THURSDAY
ADGHILTY	DAYLIGHT	ADGMNNOU	GOURMAND	ADIIINRV	VIRIDIAN
ADGHINOR	HOARDING	ADGNNOQU	QUANDONG	ADIIIQRU	DAIQUIRI
ADGHINPR	HANDGRIP	ADGNNORS	GRANDSON	ADIIKLMM	MILKMAID
ADGHINSS	SHADINGS	ADGNNRYY	GYNANDRY	ADIIKLST	TAILSKID
ADGHIPRS	DIGRAPHS	ADGNOORS	DRAGOONS	ADIILLMR	MILLIARD
ADGHLNNO	LONGHAND	ADHHINPW	WHIP HAND	ADIILLOP	LIPOIDAL
ADGHNNOS	SHANDONG	ADHHIPRS	HARDSHIP	ADIILLUV	DILUVIAL
ADGHNNSU	HANDGUNS	ADHHNRTY	HYDRANTH	ADIILMRV	VLADIMIR
ADGHOORS	ROAD HOGS	ADHIILLP	PHILLIDA	ADIILNOT	DILATION
ADGHRSTU	DRAUGHTS	ADHIILLR	HILLIARD	ADIILNSU	INDUSIAL
ADGHRTUY	DRAUGHTY	ADHIIMSS	HASIDISM	ADIILNSV	INVALIDS
ADGIILLN	DIALLING	ADHIINOP	OPHIDIAN	ADIILNSW	WINDSAIL
ADGIILLO	GLADIOLI	ADHIKKOO	HOKKAIDO	ADIILNTW	TAILWIND
ADGIILNO	GONIDIAL	ADHILLOT	THALLOID	ADIILNTY	DAINTILY
ADGIILNT	DILATING	ADHILLOY	HOLLIDAY	ADIILOPP	DIPLOPIA
ADGIILPY	PYGIDIAL	ADHILLPY	PHYLLIDA	ADIILSSY	DIALYSIS
ADGIIMNR	ADMIRING	ADHILNOR	RHODINAL	ADIILTVY	VALIDITY
ADGIIMST	DIGAMIST	ADHILOOW	HAILWOOD	ADIIMRST	TRIADISM
ADGIINNR	DRAINING	ADHILOPS	SHIPLOAD	ADIINOOT	IODATION
ADGIINNV	INVADING	ADHILOSY	HOLIDAYS	ADIINOSY	DIONYSIA
ADGIINOR	RADIOING	ADHILPSY	LADYSHIP	ADIINOTU	AUDITION
ADGIINOV	AVOIDING	ADHIMNOS	ADMONISH	ADIINRST	DISTRAIN
ADGIINSV	ADVISING	ADHIMNOU	HUMANOID	ADIIPRTY	RAPIDITY
ADGIINTU	AUDITING	ADHIMOPP	AMPHIPOD	ADIIPSTY	SAPIDITY
ADGIJNRU	ADJURING	ADHINOPY	DIAPHONY	ADIIPTVY	VAPIDITY
ADGILLNU	ALLUDING	ADHINPSU	DAUPHINS	ADIIRSST	DIARISTS
ADGILLNW	WINDGALL	ADHINSST	STANDISH	ADIIRSTT	DISTRAIT
ADGILLNY	DALLYING	ADHINSTU	DIANTHUS	ADIKNNST	INKSTAND
ADGILMOR	MARIGOLD	ADHIPRSW	WARDSHIP	ADIKNOPY	PYINKADO
ADGILNNS	LANDINGS	ADHIPRSY	SHIPYARD	ADIKNPSS	SKIDPANS
ADGILNOS	LOADINGS	ADHIRTWW	WITHDRAW	ADILLLNW	LINDWALL
ADGILNRS	DARLINGS	ADHLLLOS	HOLDALLS	ADILLLPY	PALLIDLY
ADGILNRW	DRAWLING	ADHLLNOS	HOLLANDS	ADILLMNR	MANDRILL
ADGILNRY	DARINGLY	ADHLMNOO	HANDLOOM	ADILLMOU	ALLODIUM
ADGILNZZ	DAZZLING	ADHLMORT	THRALDOM	ADILLMSY	DISMALLY
ADGILOOS	SOLIDAGO	ADHLNOPR	RANDOLPH	ADILLNPS	LANDSLIP
ADGILOPR	PRODIGAL	ADHLNOUW	DOWNHAUL	ADILLOSW	DISALLOW
ADGILOST	DOG'S-TAIL	ADHLNSTU	LANDSHUT	ADILLOSY	DISLOYAL
ADGIMOSU	DIGAMOUS	ADHLOPSU	ADOLPHUS	ADILLRSU	DRUSILLA
ADGINNOR	ADORNING	ADHNNORU	HONDURAN	ADILMNNO	MANDOLIN
ADGINNOT	DONATING	ADHNOPRU	HARD UPON	ADILMOPS	DIPLOMAS
ADGINNST	STANDING	ADHNORSU	HONDURAS	ADILMOPT	DIPLOMAT
ADGINNTU	DAUNTING	ADHNOSTU	HANDOUTS,	ADILMOPY	OLYMPIAD
ADGINOOR	RIGADOON		THOUSAND	ADILMOTY	MODALITY

ADILNNOR	LONDRINA	ADIORTUY	AUDITORY	ADNRSSUW	SUNWARDS
ADILNNSU	DISANNUL	ADIRRWYZ	WIZARDRY	ADOOPRRT	TRAPDOOR
ADILNOOR	DOORNAIL	ADJKNRUY	JUNKYARD	ADOOPRSU	SAUROPOD
ADILNORS	ORDINALS,	ADJNNOSU	DON JUANS	ADOORSWY	DOORWAYS
ROSALIND		ADKLOOPT	POLKA DOT	ADOPPRST	STOPPARD
ADILNOTY	NODALITY	ADKLOORW	WOODLARK,	ADOPRSSW	PASSWORD
ADILNRWY	INWARDLY	WORKLOAD		ADOPSSSU	SOAPSUDS
ADILNSSU	SUNDIALS	ADKMNORW	MARKDOWN	ADORSTUW	OUTWARDS
ADILNSSW	WINDLASS	ADKMOORR	DARKROOM	ADORSTUY	SUDATORY
ADILOOPR	POLAROID	ADKOORRW	ROADWORK	ADRSSTTU	STARDUST
ADILOORT	TOROIDAL	ADKORSWY	WORKDAYS	AEEEFORS	FAEROESE
ADILOPRS	SLIP ROAD	ADKRSSWY	SKYWARDS	AEEEFRRW	FREEWARE
ADILOPRT	DIOPTRAL,	ADLLLORY	LOLLARDY	AEEEGGLU	LEE GAUGE
TRIPODAL		ADLLNORU	ALL-ROUND	AEEEGLLS	LEGALESE
ADILOPSS	DISPOSAL	ADLLNOSW	LOWLANDS	AEEEGLRT	REGELATE,
ADILORSY	SOLIDARY	ADLLNUUZ	ZULULAND	RELEGATE	
ADILORTY	ADROITLY,	ADLLOPRS	POLLARDS	AEEEGLRV	LEVERAGE
DILATORILY, IDOLATRY		ADLMNOOR	MOORLAND	AEEEGLST	LEGATEES
ADILOSTW	WILD OATS	ADLMNOOW	OLD WOMAN	AEEEGNPR	PEA GREEN
ADILPSSY	DISPLAYS	ADLMNORY	RANDOMLY	AEEEGNRT	GENERATE, GREEN
ADILPSTU	PLAUDITS	ADLMOPSY	PSALMODY	TEA, TEENAGER	
ADILRTWY	TAWDRILY	ADLNNTUU	UNDULANT	AEEEGPRS	PEERAGES
ADIMMNOS	MONADISM,	ADLNOORW	LOANWORD	AEEEGRST	STEERAGE
NOMADISM		ADLNOPRT	PORTLAND	AEEEGRSW	SEWERAGE
ADIMMNSY	DYNAMISM	ADLNOPWY	DOWNPLAY	AEEEGTTV	VEGETATE
ADIMNNOT	DOMINANT	ADLOOPRU	UROPODAL	AEEEHLRT	ETHEREAL
ADIMNSTY	DYNAMIST	ADLOPRWY	WORDPLAY	AEEEHMPR	EPHEMERA
ADIMOPRY	MYRIAPOD	ADLORRSW	WARLORDS	AEEEHRRS	REHEARSE
ADIMOSST	MASTOIDS	ADLORSTW	LAST WORD	AEEEHRRT	REHEATER
ADIMOSTY	TOADYISM	ADMMNORU	OMDURMAN	AEEEHSTT	AESTHETE
ADIMPRSY	PYRAMIDS	ADMMNORY	MONANDRY,	AEEEIMNX	EXAMINEE
ADIMSSTU	STADIUMS	NORMANDY		AEEEJNTT	JEANETTE
ADINNNTU	INUNDANT	ADMNOORS	ROSAMOND	AEEEKKPS	KEEPSAKE
ADINNOOT	DONATION	ADMNOOST	MASTODON	AEEEKNRW	WEAKENER
ADINNORS	ANDIRONS	ADMNOOSW	WOODSMAN	AEEELLPP	APPELLEE
ADINNSST	STAND-INS	ADMNORRU	ROUND-ARM	AEEELLSV	SEA LEVEL
ADINOOPS	ISOPODAN	ADMNORSU	ROSAMUND	AEEELNPS	NEPALESE
ADINOOPT	ADOPTION	ADMNORSW	SANDWORM	AEEELNRV	VENEREAL
ADINOORT	TANDOORI	ADMOOPPP	POPPADOM	AEEELNST	SELENATE
ADINOOTT	DOTATION	ADMOORRW	WARDROOM	AEEELPRR	REPEALER
ADINOPRR	RAINDROP	ADMOORST	DOORMATS	AEEELRRS	RELEASER
ADINOPRS	PONIARDS	ADMOORSY	DAYROOMS	AEEELRRV	REVEALER
ADINORRY	ORDINARY	ADMOPPSU	POPADUMS	AEEELRSS	RELEASES
ADINORST	INTRADOS	ADNNORTY	DYNATRON	AEEELRTX	AXLETREE
ADINORSU	DINOSAUR	ADNOOQRU	QUADROON	AEEEMMRT	METAMERE
ADINORTU	DURATION	ADNOORST	TORNADOS	AEEEMNST	EASEMENT
ADINPSST	SANDPITS	ADNOOSSS	SO-AND-SOS	AEEEMPRT	PERMEATE
ADIOOPRT	PAROTOID	ADNOQRSU	SQUADRON	AEEENPTT	PATENTEE
ADIOOPSS	APODOSIS	ADNORSTU	ROTUNDAS	AEEENRTV	ENERVATE,
ADIOPPST	POSTPAID	ADNORSTW	SANDWORT	VENERATE	
ADIOPRST	PARODIST, PORT	ADNORSXY	SARDONYX	AEEEPPRS	PRAESEPE
SAID		ADNORTUW	UNTOWARD	AEEEPRRT	REPARTEE,
ADIOPRTY	PODIATRY	ADNOSTTU	OUTSTAND	REPEATER	
ADIORSTU	AUDITORS	ADNPPSUU	UP-AND-UPS	AEEEPSTW	SWEET PEA
ADIORSVY	ADVISORY	ADNPSSTU	DUSTPANS	AEEERSST	ESTERASE

AEEFFLLR	FREE-FALL
AEEFFLTT	FLAT FEET
AEEFFNRT	AFFERENT
AEEFGILN	FINE GAEL
AEEFGILR	FILAGREE
AEEFGIRR	FERRIAGE
AEEFGLSU	FUSELAGE
AEEFHLLS	SELFHEAL
AEEFHRST	FEATHERS
AEEFHRTY	FEATHERY
AEEFHRVY	HAY FEVER
AEEFILMN	FILENAME
AEEFILNR	FLANERIE
AEEFILST	FETIALES, LEAFIEST
AEEFINST	STEFANIE
AEEFIRRR	RAREFIER
AEEFIRSS	FREESIAS
AEEFISST	SAFETIES
AEEFKOPR	FOREPEAK
AEEFLLRW	FAREWELL
AEEFLLST	LEAFLETS
AEEFLMSS	SELFSAME
AEEFLNRU	FUNEREAL
AEEFLORV	OVERLEAF
AEEFLRRR	REFERRAL
AEEFLRRT	FALTERER
AEEFLRSS	FEARLESS
AEEFLTTT	FLATETTE
AEEFMNOR	FORENAME
AEEFMORS	FEARSOME
AEEFNRST	FASTENER, FENESTRA
AEEFNRTT	FATTENER
AEEFNSSS	SAFENESS
AEEFPRSS	FREE PASS
AEEFRSTU	FEATURES
AEEFRSWY	FREEWAYS
AEEGGIRV	AGGRIEVE
AEEGGKOR	OAK EGGER
AEEGGNNR	GANGRENE
AEEGHHLS	SHEELAGH
AEEGHILN	HEGELIAN
AEEGHIRT	HERITAGE
AEEGHMOP	HOME PAGE
AEEGHMPR	GRAPHEME
AEEGHNRS	SHAGREEN
AEEGHRRT	GATHERER
AEEGILLS	LEGALISE
AEEGILLZ	LEGALIZE
AEEGILMS	MILEAGES
AEEGILNN	ANGELINE
AEEGILNR	ALGERINE
AEEGILNS	ENSILAGE, LINEAGES

AEEGILNT	GELATINE, LEGATINE
AEEGILTV	LEVIGATE
AEEGIMNR	GERMAINE
AEEGIMNT	GEMINATE
AEEGIMRT	EMIGRATE
AEEGINPR	PERIGEAN
AEEGINRR	REGAINER
AEEGINSS	AGENESIS, ASSIGNEE
AEEGINSU	GUIANESE
AEEGINSV	ENVISAGE
AEEGINTV	AGENTIVE, NEGATIVE
AEEGIPQU	EQUIPAGE
AEEGIRRS	GREASIER
AEEGIRTT	AIGRETTE
AEEGLLNR	ALLERGEN
AEEGLLSZ	GAZELLES
AEEGLMNS	MELANGES
AEEGLMOS	MESOGLEA
AEEGLMRT	TELEGRAM
AEEGLMRY	MEAGRELY
AEEGLNNO	ANGELENO
AEEGLNNR	ERLANGEN
AEEGLNNT	ENTANGLE
AEEGLNOT	ELONGATE
AEEGLNRR	ENLARGER
AEEGLNRS	GENERALS
AEEGLNRT	REGENTAL
AEEGLNSY	ANGLESEY
AEEGLORT	ALTER EGO
AEEGLRSS	EELGRASS, LARGESSE
AEEGLRTU	REGULATE
AEEGLRUX	EXERGUAL
AEEGLSSV	SELVAGES
AEEGLSSY	EYEGLASS
AEEGLTTU	TUTELAGE
AEEGMNSS	GAMENESS
AEEGMRST	GAMESTER
AEEGMSSS	MESSAGES
AEEGMSSU	MESSUAGE
AEEGNNNO	ENNEAGON
AEEGNOST	STONE AGE
AEEGNRRV	ENGRAVER
AEEGNRST	ESTRANGE, REAGENTS, SERGEANT
AEEGNRSV	AVENGERS
AEEGNRUV	AUVERGNE
AEEGNSUY	GUYANESE
AEEGPRRS	PRESAGER
AEEGPRSS	PRESAGES
AEEGRRRT	REGRATER
AEEGRRSS	GREASERS

AEEGRSTT	GREATEST
AEEGSTTZ	GAZETTES
AEEHHIKZ	HEZEKIAH
AEEHHIMN	NEHEMIAH
AEEHHLNZ	HAZELHEN
AEEHHNST	HEATHENS
AEEHHRSS	REHASHES
AEEHHRTY	HEATHERY
AEEHIJMR	JEREMIAH
AEEHIKLR	HARELIKE
AEEHILTV	HELVETIA
AEEHIMPU	EUPHEMIA
AEEHIPRS	HESPERIA, PHARISEE
AEEHIRRT	EARTHIER, HEARTIER
AEEHIRST	THERESIA
AEEHISTT	HESITATE
AEEHISTV	HEAVIEST
AEEHKLNT	KATHLEEN
AEEHKNRR	HANKERER, HARKENER
AEEHLLRT	HEAR TELL
AEEHLLSS	SEASHELL
AEEHLMNY	HYMENEAL
AEEHLMPT	HELPMATE
AEEHLNOT	ANETHOLE
AEEHLNPT	ELEPHANT
AEEHLNSS	HALENESS
AEEHLNVY	HEAVENLY
AEEHLOSU	ALEHOUSE
AEEHLRTY	LEATHERY
AEEHLSST	HEATLESS
AEEHLSTT	ATHLETES
AEEHLTTY	ETHYLATE
AEEHMMRR	HAMMERER
AEEHMPRR	HAMPERER
AEEHMPSS	EMPHASES
AEEHMRTY	ERYTHEMA
AEEHNNTX	XANTHENE
AEEHNNVW	NEWHAVEN
AEEHNOPR	EARPHONE
AEEHNRST	HASTENER
AEEHNRTT	THREATEN
AEEHNRTU	URETHANE
AEEHNRTW	ENWREATH
AEEHNRWY	ANYWHERE
AEEHNSTW	ENSWATHE
AEEHORRV	OVERHEAR
AEEHORSS	SEAHORSE, SEASHORE
AEEHORTV	OVERHEAT
AEEHOSTU	TEAHOUSE
AEEHPRRS	REPHRASE
AEEHRSTT	THEATRES

AEEHRTVW	WHATEVER
AEEHSTVY	HEAVY-SET
AEEIJMNR	JERMAINE
AEEIJMRS	JEREMIAS
AEEIJNNN	JEANNINE
AEEIKLMU	LEUKEMIA
AEEIKLST	LEAKIEST
AEEIKLVW	WAVELIKE
AEEIKNRS	SNEAKIER
AEEIKNRT	ANKERITE
AEEIKNTW	KEEWATIN
AEEIKPST	PEAKIEST
AEEILMMN	MELAMINE
AEEILMNS	MILANESE
AEEILMNT	MELANITE
AEEILMRT	MATERIEL, REAL-TIME
AEEILMSS	SEA MILES
AEEILMST	MEALIEST
AEEILNPS	PENALISE
AEEILNPT	PETALINE
AEEILNPZ	PENALIZE
AEEILNRT	ELATERIN, ENTAILER, TREENAIL
AEEILNSV	VASELINE
AEEILORT	AEROLITE
AEEILOTT	ETIOLATE
AEEILPPP	APPLE PIE
AEEILPRR	PEARLIER
AEEILPRS	ESPALIER
AEEILPRT	PEARLITE
AEEILQSU	EQUALISE
AEEILQUZ	EQUALIZE
AEEILRRS	REALISER
AEEILRRT	RETAILER
AEEILRRZ	REALIZER
AEEILRST	EARLIEST
AEEILRSV	VELARISE
AEEILRSZ	SLEAZIER
AEEILRTT	LATERITE, LITERATE
AEEILRTV	RELATIVE
AEEILRVW	LIVEWARE, REVIEWAL
AEEILRVZ	VELARIZE
AEEILTTV	LEVITATE
AEEIMMNT	MEANTIME
AEEIMNRT	ANTIMERE
AEEIMNRX	EXAMINER
AEEIMNSS	MESSENIA
AEEIMNST	MATINEES
AEEIMORV	AVIEMORE
AEEIMRST	EMIRATES, STEAMIER
AEEIMRTT	MARIETTE
AEEIMSST	SEAMIEST

AEEIMSTT	ESTIMATE, MEATIEST
AEEINNRS	ANSERINE
AEEINNTV	VENETIAN
AEEINOPS	PAEONIES
AEEINPRT	APERIENT
AEEINRRT	RETAINER
AEEINRSS	ASNIERES
AEEINRST	ARSENITE, RESINATE, TERESINA, TRAINEES
AEEINRSU	UNEASIER
AEEINSSS	EASINESS
AEEINSTT	ANISETTE, TETANISE
AEEINTTZ	TETANIZE
AEEIPPSU	EUPEPSIA
AEEIPPTT	APPETITE
AEEIPRRR	REPAIRER
AEEIQRSU	QUEASIER
AEEIRRST	ARTERIES
AEEIRSTT	TREATIES, TREATISE
AEEIRSTW	AS IT WERE, SWEATIER, WEARIEST
AEEIRSVV	AVERSIVE
AEEIRTTZ	TREATIZE
AEEISTTT	STEATITE
AEEITUVX	EXUVIATE
AEEJMPPS	JEMAPPES
AEEJORSV	SERAJEVO
AEEKLLST	SKELETAL
AEEKLMRT	TELEMARK
AEEKLSSW	WAKELESS
AEEKLSTY	EYESTALK
AEEKMRRR	REMARKER
AEEKMRRT	MARKETER
AEEKNPSW	NEWSPEAK
AEEKNRSS	SNEAKERS
AEEKNSSW	WEAKNESS
AEEKORST	KERATOSE
AEEKORTV	OVERTAKE, TAKEOVER
AEEKPRSS	SPEAKERS
AEEKQRSU	SQUEAKER
AEEKRRST	STREAKER
AEELLLTT	TELLTALE
AEELLMNW	MEAN WELL
AEELLNOT	LET ALONE
AEELLOTT	ALLOTTEE
AEELLPPY	ALLEPPEY
AEELLPTT	PLATELET
AEELLPTY	TELEPLAY
AEELLRRV	RAVELLER
AEELLSTT	STELLATE
AEELLSWY	WEASELLY

AEELMMNU	EMMANUEL
AEELMNRT	LAMENTER
AEELMNSS	LAMENESS, MALENESS, NAMELESS, SALESMEN
AEELMPRX	EXEMPLAR
AEELMPRY	EMPYREAL
AEELMPSX	EXAMPLES
AEELMPTT	PALMETTE, TEMPLATE
AEELMSSS	SEAMLESS
AEELNNRT	LANNERET
AEELNNSS	LEANNESS
AEELNOOR	ELEONORA
AEELNOPR	PERONEAL
AEELNOPT	ANTELOPE
AEELNORS	ROSALEEN
AEELNPSS	PALENESS
AEELNQSU	SQUALENE
AEELNRRS	LEARNERS
AEELNRSS	REALNESS
AEELNRSV	ENSLAVER
AEELNRSW	RENEWALS
AEELNRTV	LEVANTER, RELEVANT
AEELNRTX	EXTERNAL
AEELNSST	LATENESS
AEELNSWY	WESLEYAN
AEELNTUV	EVENTUAL
AEELORST	OLEASTER
AEELORSU	AUREOLES
AEELORTT	TOLERATE
AEELORTV	ELEVATOR
AEELOTTT	TEETOTAL
AEELOTTW	TEA TOWEL
AEELPRRS	RELAPSER
AEELPRRT	PALTERER
AEELPRRY	PARLEYER
AEELPRSS	RELAPSES
AEELPRST	PRELATES
AEELPRSU	PLEASURE
AEELPRSV	VESPERAL
AEELPSTT	PALETTES
AEELPSTU	EPAULETS
AEELPTTU	PAULETTE
AEELQRSU	SQUEALER
AEELRRSV	REVERSAL, SLAVERER
AEELRRTU	URETERAL
AEELRSST	TESSERAL
AEELRSTT	LETRASET
AEELRSTY	EASTERLY
AEELRTTU	LAURETTE
AEELSTTY	LAYETTES
AEEMMRRY	YAMMERER

AEEMMRST	AMMETERS	AEEORSSV	OVERSEAS	AEFHILMS	FISHMEAL
AEEMMSST	MESSMATE	AEEOSTTU	TEASE OUT	AEFHILMT	HALF TIME
AEEMNNOS	ANEMONES	AEEPPRTU	PERPETUA	AEFHILRS	FLASHIER
AEEMNNPS	PEN NAMES	AEEPPRRT	PARTERRE	AEFHLMRT	HALF TERM
AEEMNNSS	MEANNESS	AEEPRRSS	ASPERSER	AEFHLMSU	SHAMEFUL
AEEMNPRT	PERMEANT	AEEPRRTU	APERTURE	AEFHLNOT	HALF NOTE,
AEEMNPRY	EMPYREAN	AEEPRSTZ	TRAPEZES		HALFTONE
AEEMNPST	PET NAMES	AEEQRRUV	QUAVERER	AEFHLRRU	HARFLEUR
AEEMNPTV	PAVEMENT	AEERRRST	ARRESTER	AEFHLRSS	FLASHERS
AEEMNRSW	MENSWEAR	AEERRSST	ASSERTER	AEFHLRTY	FATHERLY
AEEMNRTU	NUMERATE	AEERRSSU	ERASURES,	AEFHLSST	FLASHEST
AEEMNRTV	AVERMENT		REASSURE	AEFHLSTU	HASTEFUL
AEEMNRUV	MANEUVER	AEERRSTT	RETREATS	AEFHMNRS	FRESHMAN
AEEMNRVY	EVERYMAN	AEERRSTU	TREASURE	AEFHMORT	FATHOMER
AEEMNSSS	SAMENESS	AEERRSTV	TRAVERSE	AEFHRSTT	FARTHEST
AEEMNSST	TAMENESS	AEERRSVW	WAVERERS	AEFIILLN	NAIL FILE
AEEMPPRR	PAMPERER	AEERSSTW	SWEATERS	AEFIILMS	FAMILIES
AEEMPRRT	TAMPERER	AEFFGIIL	EFFIGIAL	AEFIILNS	FINALISE
AEEMPRRV	REVAMPER	AEFFGILS	FIG LEAFS	AEFIILNZ	FINALIZE
AEEMPSTU	AMPUTEES	AEFFGIRS	GIRAFFES	AEFIIMNS	INFAMIES
AEEMPSTW	SWAP MEET	AEFFGOST	OFFSTAGE	AEFIINRS	FRIESIAN
AEEMQRRU	REMARQUE	AEFFGRSU	SUFFRAGE	AEFIIPRT	APERITIF
AEEMQRSU	MARQUEES	AEFFHILL	HALF-LIFE	AEFIIRRS	FRIARIES
AEEMQTTU	MAQUETTE	AEFFIMRR	AFFIRMER,	AEFIIRRT	RATIFIER
AEEMRRST	STREAMER		REAFFIRM	AEFIITVX	FIXATIVE
AEEMRRSU	MEASURER	AEFFKORS	RAKE-OFFS	AEFIKLMO	FOAMLIKE
AEEMRSTU	MASSETER,	AEFFKOST	TAKEOFFS	AEFIKLST	FLAKIEST
	STEAMERS	AEFFLNSS	SNAFFLES	AEFIKLTY	FLY A KITE
AEEMRSSU	MEASURES	AEFFLNTU	AFFLUENT	AEFILLOT	FELLATIO
AEEMRSTT	TEAMSTER	AEFFLORU	FOUR-LEAF	AEFILLRW	FIREWALL
AEENNORS	ROSEANNE	AEFFMRSU	EARMUFFS	AEFILMNR	INFLAMER,
AEENNPRY	PYRENEAN	AEFFORST	AFFOREST		RIFLEMAN
AEENNRRS	ENSNARER	AEFGIIRS	GASIFIER	AEFILMNT	FILAMENT
AEENNRRT	NANTERRE	AEFGIKMN	MAFIKENG	AEFILMUY	EL FAIYUM
AEENNRSS	NEARNESS	AEFGIKNR	FREAKING	AEFILNNR	INFERNAL
AEENNRTV	REVENANT	AEFGILNR	FINAGLER	AEFILNPS	LIFESPAN
AEENNSSS	SANENESS	AEFGIMTU	FUMIGATE	AEFILNRT	INFLATER
AEENNSST	NEATNESS	AEFGINST	FEASTING	AEFILNRU	FRAULEIN
AEENOPRU	EUROPEAN	AEFGIORS	FOIE GRAS	AEFILOOR	AEROFOIL
AEENORRS	REASONER	AEFGIRST	FRIGATES	AEFILORS	FORESAIL
AEENORSS	SEASONER	AEFGIRTU	FIGURATE,	AEFILPRX	PREFIXAL
AEENORST	RESONATE		FRUITAGE	AEFILPST	FLEAPITS
AEENORTV	RENOVATE	AEFGISTU	FATIGUES	AEFILRST	FRAILEST
AEENORVW	OVENWARE	AEFGLLOP	FLAGPOLE	AEFILRSU	FAILURES
AEENRRSS	RARENESS	AEFGLLPU	FULL-PAGE	AEFILRTT	FILTRATE
AEENRRTV	TAVERNER	AEFGLMNU	FUGLEMAN	AEFILRTU	FAULTIER,
AEENRSTV	VETERANS	AEFGLOOR	FLOORAGE		FILATURE
AEENRTTV	ANTEVERT	AEFGLOPR	LEAPFROG	AEFILSTV	FESTIVAL
AEENRTTY	ENTREATY	AEFGLRTU	GRATEFUL	AEFILTUU	FAUTEUIL
AEENSVWW	NEW WAVES	AEFGMNRT	FRAGMENT	AEFIMNST	MANIFEST
AEEOPRRT	PERORATE	AEFGNORT	FRONTAGE	AEFIMOST	FOAMIEST
AEEOPRSW	SEA POWER	AEFGOORT	FOOTGEAR	AEFIMRRS	FIREARMS
AEEOPRTT	OPERETTA	AEFGRRST	GRAFTERS	AEFIMRRW	FIRMWARE
AEEORRTV	OVERRATE	AEFHIKRS	FREAKISH	AEFINNNS	ANFINSEN
		AEFHIKSW	WEAKFISH	AEFINNSZ	FANZINES

AEFINOPR	PINAFORE	AEFNRRST	TRANSFER	AEGHLOSS	GALOSHES
AEFINORS	FARINOSE	AEFNRRUY	FUNERARY	AEGHLRTU	LAUGHTER
AEFINOTT	FETATION	AEFNSSST	FASTNESS	AEGHLRTY	LETHARGY
AEFINRRS	REFRAINS	AEFOORTW	FOOTWEAR	AEGHNNOR	HANGER-ON
AEFINRRU	UNFAIRER	AEFOPRRT	FOREPART	AEGHNNSY	SHENYANG
AEFINRSS	FAIRNESS	AEFORRSW	FORSWEAR	AEGHNOPT	HEPTAGON,
AEFINRST	FINE ARTS	AEFORRUV	FAVOURER	PATHOGEN	
AEFINSTT	FAINTEST	AEFORSTW	SOFTWARE	AEGHNORV	HANGOVER,
AEFIPRRT	FIRETRAP	AEFORSTY	FORESTAY	OVERHANG	
AEFIRRRS	FARRIERS	AEFRSSTW	FRETSAWS	AEGHNOSX	HEXAGONS
AEFIRRRY	FARRIERY	AEGGGINN	ENGAGING	AEGHOPPR	PROPHAGE
AEFIRSTV	FIVE-STAR	AEGGHIRS	SHAGGIER	AEGHOPPY	APOPHYGE
AEFISTTT	FATTIEST	AEGGHNNY	HENGYANG	AEGHORST	SHORTAGE
AEFKLLOT	FOLKTALE	AEGGHOPY	GEOPHAGY	AEGHOSST	HOSTAGES
AEFKNORS	FORSAKEN	AEGGHORU	ROUGHAGE	AEGIILLU	AIGUILLE
AEFKNRST	FRANKEST	AEGGILLN	ALLEGING	AEGIILMR	REMIGIAL
AEFKORRS	FORSAKER	AEGGILLR	GRILLAGE	AEGIILTT	LITIGATE
AEFLLNNS	FLANNELS	AEGGILMN	GLEAMING	AEGIILTV	LIGATIVE
AEFLLRUX	FLEXURAL	AEGGILNN	GLEANING	AEGIIMNR	IMAGINER,
AEFLLSSW	FLAWLESS	AEGGILNU	LEAGUING	MIGRAINE	
AEFLLSTT	FLATLETS	AEGGINNR	ANGERING,	AEGIIMTT	MITIGATE
AEFLMORU	FORMULAE,	ENRAGING		AEGIINNR	ARGININE,
FUMAROLE		AEGGINNT	NEGATING	NIGERIAN	
AEFLMOTU	FLAMEOUT	AEGGINNV	AVENGING	AEGIIRRT	IRRIGATE
AEFLNORS	FARNESOL	AEGGINOR	GEORGIAN,	AEGIKLNS	LINKAGES
AEFLNRSU	FUNERALS	GEORGINA		AEGIKLNW	WEAKLING
AEFLNRTU	FLAUNTER	AEGGINOS	SEAGOING	AEGIKMNR	REMAKING
AEFLNSST	FLATNESS	AEGGINRS	GREASING	AEGIKNNS	SNEAKING
AEFLOORV	FOVEOLAR	AEGGINRW	WAGERING	AEGIKNNW	WAKENING
AEFLOPRY	FOREPLAY	AEGGIOPR	ARPEGGIO	AEGIKNPS	SPEAKING
AEFLOPSW	PEAFOWLS	AEGGISST	SAGGIEST	AEGIKNRT	RETAKING
AEFLORST	FLOATERS,	AEGGLNPT	EGGPLANT	AEGIKNRW	WREAKING
FORESTAL		AEGGLORY	GARGOYLE	AEGIKNTW	TWEAKING
AEFLORTT	FLORETTA	AEGGLRST	STRAGGLE	AEGIKNWY	KWEIYANG
AEFLORTW	FLEAWORT	AEGGMMSU	MUG'S GAME	AEGIKSTW	GAWKIEST
AEFLOSTT	FALSETTO	AEGGMORT	MORTGAGE	AEGILLMS	LEGALISM
AEFLPPRY	FLYPAPER	AEGGNRST	GANGSTER	AEGILLMU	GULIELMA
AEFLPRSU	FLARE-UPS	AEGGOPRU	AGE GROUP	AEGILLNO	GOAL LINE
AEFLPRSY	PALFREYS	AEGGRSST	STAGGERS	AEGILLNY	GENIALLY
AEFLRSSU	REFUSALS	AEGHHISS	HIGH SEAS	AEGILLPR	PILLAGER
AEFLRTTU	AFLUTTER	AEGHIJNZ	ZHEJIANG	AEGILLPS	SPILLAGE
AEFLRTTY	FLATTERY	AEGHILLT	LIGHT ALE	AEGILLRV	VILLAGER
AEFLSTTT	FLATTEST	AEGHILMT	MEGALITH	AEGILLST	LEGALIST
AEFLSTTU	TASTEFUL	AEGHILNX	EXHALING	AEGILLSV	VILLAGES
AEFLSTUW	WASTEFUL	AEGHILRT	LITHARGE	AEGILLTU	LIGULATE
AEFMNORW	MEN-OF-WAR	AEGHINRS	HEARINGS,	AEGILLTY	LEGALITY
AEFMNRRY	FERRYMAN	SHEARING		AEGILMNR	GERMINAL,
AEFMORRS	FOREARMS	AEGHINRT	EARTHING,	MALINGER, MALINGER	
AEFMORST	FOREMAST	INGATHER		AEGILMNS	GALENISM
AEFMORVW	WAVEFORM	AEGHINRV	HAVERING	AEGILMNT	LIGAMENT,
AEFMPRSU	FRAME-UPS	AEGHINRY	HARINGEY	METALING, TEGMINAL	
AEFNNSTU	UNFASTEN	AEGHINTT	GNATHITE	AEGILMST	TIME LAGS
AEFNOPRR	PROFANER	AEGHIPPR	EPIGRAPH	AEGILN	EALING
AEFNORRW	FOREWARN	AEGHIPRT	GRAPHITE	AEGILNNP	PANELING
AEFNORST	SEAFRONT			AEGILNNR	LEARNING

AEGILNNS	LEANINGS
AEGILNNT	GANTLINE
AEGILNNW	WEANLING
AEGILNNY	YEANLING
AEGILNOR	GERANIOL, REGIONAL
AEGILNOS	GASOLINE
AEGILNOT	GELATION, LEGATION
AEGILNPS	ELAPSING, PLEASING
AEGILNPT	PLEATING
AEGILNQU	EQUALING
AEGILNRS	SALINGER
AEGILNRT	ALERTING, ALTERING, INTEGRAL, RELATING, TRIANGLE
AEGILNRV	RAVELING
AEGILNRX	RELAXING
AEGILNRY	LAYERING, RELAYING, YEARLING
AEGILNSS	GLASSINE
AEGILNST	GALENIST, GENITALS, STEALING
AEGILNSV	LEAVINGS
AEGILNTX	EXALTING
AEGILOPS	SPOILAGE
AEGILOPT	PILOTAGE
AEGILORS	GASOLIER, SERAGLIO
AEGILPPS	SLIPPAGE
AEGILRSS	GLASSIER
AEGILRSY	GREASILY
AEGILRSZ	GLAZIERS
AEGILRTU	LIGATURE
AEGILRTY	REGALITY
AEGILRVW	LAWGIVER
AEGILRYZ	GLAZIERY
AEGIMNNR	RENAMING
AEGIMNNS	MEANINGS
AEGIMNRR	REARMING
AEGIMNRS	SMEARING
AEGIMNRT	EMIGRANT
AEGIMNRU	GERANIUM
AEGIMNSS	GAMINESS
AEGIMNST	MANGIEST, STEAMING
AEGIMPRS	EPIGRAMS
AEGIMQRU	QUAGMIRE
AEGIMRST	STERIGMA
AEGIMSSU	MISUSAGE
AEGINNNX	ANNEXING
AEGINNOS	ANGINOSE
AEGINNOT	NEGATION

AEGINNRS	EARNINGS, GRANNIES
AEGINNRV	RAVENING
AEGINNRY	YEARNING
AEGINNST	ANTIGENS, GENTIANS
AEGINNSU	SANGUINE
AEGINORS	ORGANISE
AEGINORZ	ORGANIZE
AEGINOTV	GO NATIVE
AEGINPPR	PAPERING
AEGINPRS	SPEARING
AEGINPRT	TAPERING
AEGINPRY	REPAYING
AEGINPTY	EGYPTIAN
AEGINQTU	EQUATING
AEGINRRS	EARRINGS
AEGINRRV	AVERRING
AEGINRSS	ASSIGNER
AEGINRST	ANGRIEST, GANISTER, GANTRIES, INGRATES
AEGINRSW	SWEARING
AEGINRTT	TREATING
AEGINRTV	AVERTING, VINTAGER
AEGINRTW	WATERING
AEGINRVW	WAVERING
AEGINRVY	VINEGARY
AEGINRWY	WEARYING
AEGINSST	GIANTESS
AEGINSSY	ESSAYING
AEGINSTT	TANGIEST
AEGINSTU	SAUTEING
AEGINSTV	VINTAGES
AEGINSTW	SWEATING
AEGIORSV	VIRAGOES
AEGIOSTX	GEOTAXIS
AEGIRRSS	GRASSIER
AEGIRSST	SEAGIRTS
AEGIRSUU	AUGURIES
AEGISSST	GASSIEST
AEGISTUZ	GAUZIEST
AEGLLNOS	GALLEONS
AEGLLOPR	GALLOPER
AEGLLORY	ALLEGORY
AEGLLOTT	TOLLGATE
AEGLLRVY	GRAVELLY
AEGLLSSU	SEAGULLS
AEGLMNNO	MANGONEL
AEGLMNTU	GUNMETAL
AEGLMOTV	MEGAVOLT
AEGLNNOR	ALGERNON
AEGLNNPT	PLANGENT
AEGLNNTU	UNTANGLE
AEGLNORS	SELANGOR

AEGLNORY	YEARLONG
AEGLNOVW	LONG WAVE
AEGLNPRS	GRAPNELS
AEGLNPSS	SPANGLES
AEGLNRRW	WRANGLER
AEGLNRST	STRANGLE
AEGLNRSU	GRANULES
AEGLNRSW	WRANGLES
AEGLNRSY	LARYNGES
AEGLNSUW	GUNWALES
AEGLNTTU	GAUNTLET
AEGLNTUU	UNGULATE
AEGLOOOZ	ZOOGLOEA
AEGLOOPU	APOLOGUE
AEGLOORY	AEROLOGY
AEGLOPRS	PERGOLAS
AEGLOPRY	PLAYGOER
AEGLOSTV	VOLTAGES
AEGLPPRR	GRAPPLER
AEGLPRSU	EARPLUGS
AEGLRRSU	REGULARS
AEGLRSTU	GESTURAL
AEGLSSTT	GESTALTS
AEGMMNOR	GAMMONER
AEGMMRRU	RUMMAGER
AEGMMRSU	RUMMAGES
AEGMNNOT	MAGNETON
AEGMNORV	MANGROVE
AEGMNOST	MAGNETOS, MEGATONS, MONTAGES
AEGMNOTU	MONTAGUE
AEGMNOXY	XENOGAMY
AEGMNRST	GARMENTS
AEGMNRTU	ARGUMENT
AEGMOPRW	GAPEWORM
AEGMORRW	WORM GEAR
AEGMORSS	GOSSAMER
AEGMPRUZ	GAZUMPER
AEGNNOPT	PENTAGON
AEGNNOST	TONNAGES
AEGNNPRT	PREGNANT
AEGNNSTT	TANGENTS
AEGNORRY	ORANGERY
AEGNORST	ESTRAGON
AEGNORSX	SEX ORGAN
AEGNOSSY	NOSEGAYS
AEGNPPRU	GUNPAPER
AEGNRRST	STRANGER
AEGOPPST	STOPPAGE
AEGOPSST	GESTAPOS
AEGOPSTT	GATEPOST
AEGORRTT	GARROTTE
AEGORSTU	GOAT'S-RUE, OUTRAGES
AEGORSVY	VOYAGERS

AEGORTTU	TUTORAGE	AEHINRTZ	HERTZIAN	AEHLPSST	PATHLESS
AEGOSTTV	GAVOTTES	AEHINSSS	HESSIANS	AEHLPSTU	SULPHATE
AEGRRSSY	RYEGRASS	AEHINSST	ANTHESIS,	AEHLRRTU	URETHRAL
AEGRSTTY	STRATEGY		SHANTIES	AEHLSSTY	THESSALY
AEHHHJPT	JEPHTHAH	AEHINSSZ	HAZINESS	AEHLSTTY	STEALTHY
AEHHINPR	HA-ERH-PIN	AEHINSTT	HESITANT	AEHMNORS	HORSEMAN
AEHHINPS	PHINEHAS	AEHINTTW	WHITE ANT	AEHMNOSU	HOUSEMAN
AEHHRRST	THRASHER	AEHINTWY	IN THE WAY	AEHMOPRT	METAPHOR
AEHHRSST	HARSHEST	AEHIOPRS	APHORISE	AEHMOSTW	SOMEWHAT
AEHIIKLR	HAIRLIKE	AEHIOPRU	EUPHORIA	AEHMPPTU	HEAT PUMP
AEHIILNR	HAIRLINE	AEHIOPRZ	APHORIZE	AEHMRSSS	SMASHERS
AEHIIMNT	THIAMINE	AEHIORST	HOARIEST	AEHMRSST	HAMSTERS
AEHIINTZ	THIAZINE	AEHIORTU	THIOUREA	AEHMSTTY	AMETHYST
AEHIIOPT	ETHIOPIA	AEHIPPRS	SAPPHIRE	AEHNNOPT	PANTHEON
AEHIIRST	HAIRIEST	AEHIPPST	EPITAPHS,	AEHNNORV	HANNOVER
AEHIJNOV	JEHOVIAN		HAPPIEST	AEHNNPSU	UNSHAPEN
AEHIKKLW	HAWKLIKE	AEHIPRSS	PARISHES	AEHNNSUV	UNSHAVEN
AEHIKLLO	HALO-LIKE	AEHIRRRS	HARRIERS	AEHNOPPY	PAY PHONE
AEHIKMNR	KHMERIAN	AEHIRRST	TRASHIER	AEHNOPRT	HAPTERON
AEHIKSST	SHAKIEST	AEHIRRSV	RAVISHER	AEHNOPST	PHAETONS
AEHILMSW	LEWISHAM,	AEHIRRSY	AYRSHIRE	AEHNORST	SHERATON
	LIMEWASH	AEHIRSTY	HYSTERIA	AEHNOSTV	HAVE-NOTS
AEHILNOP	APHELION	AEHISSTT	ATHEISTS,	AEHNPRST	PANTHERS
AEHILNOT	IOLANTHE		HASTIEST	AEHNPRTY	HEN PARTY,
AEHILNRS	INHALERS	AEHISSTU	HIATUSES		TRYPHENA
AEHILNTX	ANTHELIX	AEHJNNOS	JOHANNES	AEHNRSSS	RASHNESS
AEHILNTZ	ZENITHAL	AEHJPRSW	JEW'S HARP	AEHNRTTU	EARTHNUT
AEHILOTZ	THIAZOLE	AEHKLOOY	HOLYOAKE	AEHNSTUW	UNSWATHE
AEHILRSS	HAIRLESS	AEHKNSTT	TASHKENT	AEHOPPRS	PROPHASE
AEHILRSU	HAULIERS	AEHKOSTU	SHAKEOUT	AEHOPPST	PHASE-OUT
AEHILRSV	LAVISHER,	AEHKPSSU	SHAKE-UPS	AEHOPSTW	TWO-PHASE
	SHRIEVAL	AEHLLLTY	LETHALLY	AEHOPTVY	TOP-HEAVY
AEHILRTY	EARTHILY,	AEHLLMTY	METHYLAL	AEHORRRW	HARROWER
	HEARTILY	AEHLLNRT	HARTNELL	AEHORRSW	WARHORSE
AEHIMMNN	MANNHEIM	AEHLLORW	HALLOWER	AEHORSST	EARSHOTS,
AEHIMMSS	SHAMMIES	AEHLMMNS	HELMSMAN		HOARSEST
AEHIMNNU	INHUMANE	AEHLMNNP	HELPMANN	AEHORSSW	SAWHORSE
AEHIMNOR	HOMERIAN	AEHLMNOS	MANHOLES	AEHORSTT	RHEOSTAT
AEHIMNSU	HUMANISE	AEHLMNOT	METHANOL	AEHORSTU	ART HOUSE,
AEHIMNUZ	HUMANIZE	AEHLMNUY	HUMANELY		SHARE-OUT
AEHIMOTT	TIMOTHEA	AEHLMORS	ARMHOLES	AEHORSTX	THORAXES
AEHIMPRS	SAMPHIRE,	AEHLMPPT	PAMPHLET	AEHORSTY	ROTHESAY
	SERAPHIM	AEHLMRSS	HARMLESS	AEHORTTW	HOT WATER
AEHIMPSS	EMPHASIS,	AEHLMRST	THERMALS	AEHPRSST	SHARPEST,
	MISSHAPE	AEHLNOPS	ALPHONSE		SHARP-SET
AEHIMPST	SHIPMATE	AEHLNPRS	SHRAPNEL	AEHPRSUX	HARUSPEX
AEHIMSSS	MESSIAHS	AEHLNPTY	ENTHALPY	AEHPRSUY	EUPHRASY
AEHINNTX	XANTHEIN,	AEHLNRTU	LUTHERAN	AEHQRSSU	SQUASHER
	XANTHINE	AEHLNTUZ	HAZELNUT	AEHQSSSU	SQUASHES
AEHINORT	ANTIHERO	AEHLOPRT	PLETHORA	AEHRRSTU	URETHRAS
AEHINPPY	EPIPHANY	AEHLOPTT	HOTPLATE	AEHRRTTW	THWARTER
AEHINPRT	PERIANTH	AEHLORSY	HOARSELY	AEHRSSTV	HARVESTS
AEHINPST	THESPIAN	AEHLORUV	OVERHAUL	AEHSSTUX	EXHAUSTS
AEHINRST	HAIRNETS	AEHLOSSS	ASSHOLES	AEIIINTT	INITIATE
AEHINRSV	VANISHER	AEHLPRSS	SPLASHER	AEIILLTV	ILLATIVE

AEIILMNN	MAIN LINE	AEIKLLOV	OAKVILLE	AEILMPRV	PRIMEVAL
AEIILMNS	ALIENISM	AEIKLNPS	SKI PLANE	AEILMPST	PALMIEST
AEIILMPR	IMPERIAL	AEIKLNSS	SEALSKIN	AEILMPTT	PETIT MAL
AEIILMRS	AIR MILES	AEIKLNST	LANKIEST	AEILMPTY	PLAYTIME
AEIILMTT	MILITATE	AEIKLNSY	SNEAKILY	AEILMRSY	MISLAYER
AEIILNPR	PLEIN-AIR	AEIKLOSV	LEVKOSIA	AEILMSTT	SMALTITE
AEIILNQU	AQUILINE	AEIKLRST	STARLIKE	AEILMSTU	SIMULATE
AEIILNRR	AIRLINER	AEIKMNOS	ESKIMOAN	AEILMSTY	STEAMILY
AEIILNRS	AIRLINES	AEIKMNRS	RAMEKINS	AEILMTTU	MUTILATE,
AEIILNRT	INERTIAL	AEIKMNST	MISTAKEN	ULTIMATE	
AEIILNST	ALIENIST, LATINISE,	AEIKMSST	MISTAKES	AEILNNRT	INTERNAL
LITANIES, TALIESIN		AEIKNRST	NARKIEST,	AEILNNSY	INSANELY
AEIILNTZ	LATINIZE	TRANSKEI		AEILNNTY	INNATELY
AEIILPPT	TAIL PIPE	AEIKNRSW	SWANKIER	AEILNOPP	APPOLINE
AEIILRSS	ISRAELIS	AEIKNRTW	KNITWEAR	AEILNORR	LORRAINE
AEIILRTT	LITERATI	AEIKPRSS	APRES-SKI	AEILNORS	AILERONS,
AEIILSTV	VITALISE	AEIKPRST	PARKIEST	ROSALINE	
AEIILTVZ	VITALIZE	AEIKPSST	PISS-TAKE	AEILNORT	ORIENTAL,
AEIIMMRT	MARITIME	AEIKPSTW	PAWKIEST	RELATION	
AEIIMMSX	MAXIMISE	AEIKRSST	ASTERISK,	AEILNORV	OVERLAIN
AEIIMMXZ	MAXIMIZE	SARKIEST		AEILNOSS	SEA LIONS
AEIIMNTT	INTIMATE	AEIKRSTW	WATER-SKI	AEILNOST	INSOLATE,
AEIIMNTU	MINUTIAE	AEILLLLN	LLANELLI	TOENAILS	
AEIIMPRR	IMPAIRER	AEILLLMS	ALLELISM	AEILNOSV	SLOVENIA
AEIIMRST	SERIATIM	AEILLLNY	LINEALLY	AEILNOSX	SILOXANE
AEIINNRS	SIRENIAN	AEILLMNY	MENIALLY	AEILNPRS	PRALINES
AEIINRSS	AIRINESS	AEILLNPS	SPLENIAL	AEILNPRT	TRIPLANE
AEIINRST	RAINIEST	AEILLNST	ANTILLES	AEILNPSS	PAINLESS,
AEIINRTZ	TRIAZINE	AEILLNUV	LAEVULIN	SPANIELS	
AEIINSST	SANITISE	AEILLOSS	LOESSIAL	AEILNPST	PANTILES,
AEIINSTZ	SANITIZE	AEILLOTV	VOLATILE	PLAINEST	
AEIINSVV	INVASIVE	AEILLPRS	PIS ALLER	AEILNPTT	TINPLATE
AEIINTTT	TITANITE	AEILLPST	PALLIEST, PASTILLE	AEILNRSS	RAINLESS
AEIIPRRS	PRAIRIES	AEILLRRY	RAILLERY	AEILNRST	ENTRAILS,
AEIIPRZZ	PIZZERIA	AEILLRST	LITERALS	LATRINES	
AEIIPSST	EPITASIS	AEILLRSY	SERIALLY	AEILNRTU	TENURIAL
AEIIRRST	RARITIES	AEILLRTT	ILL-TREAT	AEILNRTV	INTERVAL
AEIIRRSV	RIVIERAS	AEILLSST	TAILLESS	AEILNRTY	INTERLAY
AEIIRRTT	IRRITATE	AEILLSUV	ALLUSIVE	AEILNSST	SALIENTS
AEIIRSST	SATIRISE, TIRESIAS	AEILLSYZ	SLEAZILY	AEILNSSZ	LAZINESS
AEIIRSTW	WISTERIA	AEILLTUZ	LAZULITE	AEILNSTU	INSULATE
AEIIRSTZ	SATIRIZE	AEILMMNS	MELANISM	AEILNSUY	UNEASILY
AEIITTTV	TITIVATE	AEILMMOR	MEMORIAL	AEILNTVY	VENALITY
AEIJLNNU	JULIANNE	AEILMMOT	IMMOLATE	AEILNUVV	UNIVALVE
AEIJLNSV	JAVELINS	AEILMMRT	TRILEMMA	AEILOPPT	OPPILATE
AEIJLOPS	JALOPIES	AEILMNNS	LINESMAN	AEILOPRS	POLARISE
AEIJLOSU	JALOUSIE	AEILMNOS	SEMOLINA	AEILOPRZ	POLARIZE
AEIJMMST	JAMMIEST	AEILMNRS	MINERALS	AEILOPST	SPOLIATE
AEIJMNSS	JASMINES	AEILMNRT	TERMINAL,	AEILORSS	SOLARISE
AEIJMORR	MARJORIE	TRAMLINE		AEILORSV	VALORISE
AEIJNRTU	JAUNTIER	AEILMNST	AILMENTS,	AEILORSZ	SOLARIZE
AEIJORST	JAROSITE	MANLIEST, MELANIST		AEILORTZ	TRIAZOLE
AEIJSTZZ	JAZZIEST	AEILMOPR	PROEMIAL	AEILORVZ	VALORIZE
AEIKLLLW	WALL-LIKE	AEILMORS	MORALISE	AEILOSTT	TOTALISE
		AEILMORZ	MORALIZE	AEILOTTV	VIOLETTA

AEILOTTZ	TOTALIZE
AEILPPQU	APPLIQUE
AEILPPST	SPLIT PEA
AEILPRRS	REPRISAL
AEILPRRT	PALTRIER
AEILPRST	PILASTER
AEILPRTV	LIVETRAP
AEILPRXY	PYREXIAL
AEILPSUV	PLAUSIVE
AEILQRTU	QUARTILE, REQUITAL
AEILQSUY	QUEASILY
AEILQTUY	EQUALITY
AEILRRST	RETRIALS, TRAILERS
AEILRRSU	RURALISE
AEILRRTY	LITERARY
AEILRRUZ	RURALIZE
AEILRSST	REALISTS
AEILRSVV	REVIVALS
AEILRTUZ	LAZURITE
AEILSSTT	SALTIEST
AEILSSUW	SULAWESI
AEILSTWY	SWEATILY
AEILSTYY	YEASTILY
AEIMMNNT	IMMANENT
AEIMMNOT	AMMONITE
AEIMMRRS	SMARMIER
AEIMMRTU	IMMATURE
AEIMNNNR	INNER MAN
AEIMNNOT	NOMINATE
AEIMNOPT	PTOMAINE
AEIMNORS	MORAINES, ROMANIES
AEIMNORW	AIRWOMEN
AEIMNOSW	WOMANISE
AEIMNOTZ	MONAZITE
AEIMNOWZ	WOMANIZE
AEIMNRRS	MARINERS
AEIMNRSS	NEAR MISS, SEMINARS
AEIMNRST	MINARETS
AEIMNRSY	SEMINARY
AEIMNRTT	MARTINET
AEIMNRTU	RUMINATE
AEIMNRTY	TYRAMINE
AEIMNSST	MANTISES
AEIMORST	AMORTISE, ATOMISER
AEIMORTZ	AMORTIZE, ATOMIZER
AEIMOTTV	MOTIVATE
AEIMPRRT	IMPARTER
AEIMPRST	PRIMATES
AEIMPRSV	VAMPIRES

AEIMPRTT	PART-TIME
AEIMPSSS	IMPASSES
AEIMPSST	PASTIMES
AEIMQRSU	MARQUISE
AEIMRSST	ASTERISM
AEIMRSSY	EMISSARY
AEIMRSTT	MISTREAT, TERATISM
AEIMRSTX	MATRIXES
AEIMSSST	SEA MISTS
AEIMSSTT	MISSTATE
AEINNOPV	PAVONINE
AEINNORT	ANOINTER
AEINNOST	ESTONIAN
AEINNOTT	INTONATE
AEINNOTV	INNOVATE, VENATION
AEINNPRS	PANNIERS
AEINNRST	TRANNIES
AEINNSSV	VAINNESS
AEINNSSZ	ZANINESS
AEINNSTT	STANNITE
AEINNSUV	VENUSIAN
AEINOPRT	ATROPINE
AEINOPST	SAPONITE
AEINOQTU	EQUATION
AEINORRT	ANTERIOR
AEINORRW	IRONWARE
AEINORST	NOTARIES, NOTARISE, SENORITA
AEINORSV	AVERSION
AEINORTU	TOURAINE
AEINORTZ	NOTARIZE
AEINOSSV	EVASIONS
AEINOTVX	VEXATION
AEINPPPS	PANPIPES
AEINPPRS	SNAPPIER
AEINPRRT	TERRAPIN
AEINPRST	PAINTERS, PANTRIES, PINASTER
AEINPRTT	TRIPTANE
AEINPRUV	PERUVIAN
AEINPSST	STEAPSIN
AEINPSTT	PATIENTS
AEINPSTU	PETUNIAS, SUPINATE
AEINPSTY	EPINASTY
AEINQSTU	ANTIQUES, QUANTISE
AEINQTTU	EQUITANT
AEINQTUZ	QUANTIZE
AEINRRST	RESTRAIN, STRAINER, TERRAINS, TRAINERS
AEINRRTW	INTERWAR
AEINRSST	ARTINESS

AEINRSSU	ANURESIS
AEINRSSW	WARINESS
AEINRSTT	NITRATES, STRAITEN, TRAIN SET
AEINRSUZ	SUZERAIN
AEINRSZZ	SNAZZIER
AEINSSTT	NASTIEST
AEINSSVW	WAVINESS
AEINSSWX	WAXINESS
AEINSTTT	NATTIEST
AEINSUVV	VESUVIAN
AEINTTUU	AUTUNITE
AEIOPPST	APPOSITE
AEIOPRRT	PRETORIA, PRIORATE
AEIOPRSV	VAPORISE
AEIOPRTX	EXPIATOR
AEIOPRVZ	VAPORIZE
AEIOPSST	SOAPIEST
AEIOPTTV	OPTATIVE
AEIOQSSU	SEQUOIAS
AEIORRSS	ROSARIES
AEIORRUV	AU REVOIR
AEIORSSV	SAVORIES
AEIORSTV	VOTARIES
AEIORTTV	ROTATIVE
AEIPPSST	SAPPIEST
AEIPPSTZ	ZAPPIEST
AEIPQRTU	PRATIQUE
AEIPRRSU	UPRAISER
AEIPRSST	PASTRIES, PIASTRES
AEIPRSTV	PRIVATES
AEIPRSTW	WIRETAPS
AEIPRSTY	ASPERITY
AEIPRSVY	VESPIARY
AEIPRTVY	VARITYPE
AEIPSSTT	PASTIEST
AEIPTTUV	PUTATIVE
AEIQRRRU	QUARRIER
AEIQRRSU	QUARRIES
AEIRRRST	STARRIER
AEIRRTTY	TERTIARY
AEIRSSST	ASSISTER
AEIRSSTT	ARTISTES
AEIRSSTW	WAITRESS
AEIRSTTT	RATTIEST
AEISSSST	SASSIEST
AEISSSTY	ESSAYIST
AEISSTTT	TASTIEST
AEISTTTT	TATTIEST
AEJLOSUY	JEALOUSY
AEJMNSSY	JESSAMYN
AEJMOOSW	MOOSE JAW
AEKKMNOO	KAKEMONO

AEKLMORS	LARKSOME	AELMOORS	SALEROOM
AEKLMRUW	LUKEWARM	AELMOPRR	PREMOLAR
AEKLNNSS	LANKNESS	AELMOPRT	TEMPORAL
AEKLNOSY	ANKYLOSE	AELMOPSU	AMPOULES
AEKLOPRW	ROPEWALK	AELMOPSY	MAYPOLES
AEKLORVW	WALKOVER	AELMOPTT	PALMETTO
AEKLPPST	PEP TALKS	AELMORSU	RAMULOSE
AEKLPRRS	SPARKLER	AELMORSV	REMOVALS
AEKLPRSS	SPARKLES	AELMORTU	EMULATOR
AEKLRSST	STALKERS	AELMOSSS	MOLASSES
AEKMMNRS	MARKSMEN	AELMPRRT	TRAMPLER
AEKMNRSU	UNMASKER	AELMPRSS	SAMPLERS
AEKMORTW	TEAMWORK	AELMPRSY	LAMPREYS
AEKMPRTU	UP-MARKET	AELMRSTT	MALTSTER
AEKNNRSS	RANKNESS	AELMRSTY	MASTERLY
AEKNOOTY	KOOTENAY	AELMRTUY	MATURELY
AEKNPPSS	SPANSPEK	AELNNOOP	NAPOLEON
AEKOSTTU	OUT-TAKES,	AELNNOPP	OPEN-PLAN
TAKEOUTS		AELNNOSU	ANNULOSE
AEKOSTVW	TAKE VOWS	AELNNPRS	PLANNERS
AEKPSSSY	PASSKEYS	AELNNRST	LANTERNS
AEKQRSUW	SQUAWKER	AELNOPRS	PERSONAL
AEKRRSST	STARKERS	AELNOPST	TONLE SAP
AEKRSSTT	STARKEST	AELNORTT	TOLERANT
AELLMNTY	MENTALLY	AELNORTY	ORNATELY
AELLMORT	MARTELLO	AELNOSSV	OVALNESS
AELLMSST	SMALLEST	AELNPPSY	PLAYPENS
AELLNOPV	VOLPLANE	AELNPRST	PLANTERS
AELLNOSV	NOVELLAS	AELNPRSU	PURSLANE,
AELLNPRU	PRUNELLA	SUPERNAL	
AELLNSST	TALLNESS	AELNPTTU	PETULANT
AELLNTUU	LUNULATE	AELNPTTY	PATENTLY
AELLOPRW	WALLOPER	AELNRSTT	SLATTERN
AELLOPRY	ROLE PLAY	AELNRSTU	NEUTRALS
AELLORSV	OVERALLS	AELNRSXY	LARYNXES
AELLORWW	WALLOWER	AELNSSST	SALTNESS
AELLOSUV	ALVEOLUS	AELNTTUX	EXULTANT
AELLPPSU	SELL A PUP	AELOORRS	ROSEOLAR
AELLQRSU	SQUALLER	AELOORSS	AEROSOLS
AELLRTTY	LATTERLY	AELOORTW	WATERLOO
AELLSSTY	TASSELLY	AELOORTZ	ZOOLATER
AELLSUXY	SEXUALLY	AELOPPRS	PROLAPSE,
AELMMORW	MEALWORM	SAPROPEL	
AELMMRST	TRAMMELS	AELOPPTU	POPULATE
AELMNNOT	NONMETAL	AELOPPXY	APOPLEXY
AELMNNRY	MANNERLY	AELOPQUY	OPAQUELY
AELMNOPS	NEOPLASM,	AELOPRRV	REPROVAL
PLEONASM		AELOPRST	PETROSAL, POLE
AELMNORS	ALMONERS	STAR	
AELMNORT	MONTREAL	AELOPRSV	OVERLAPS
AELMNOSU	MELANOUS	AELOPRVY	OVERPLAY
AELMNOWY	LAYWOMEN	AELOPRYZ	PYRAZOLE
AELMNOYY	YEOMANLY	AELOPSSS	SOAPLESS
AELMNRSU	MENSURAL,	AELOPSST	APOSTLES
NUMERALS		AELOPSSU	ESPOUSAL

AELORRST	REALTORS		
AELORSVY	OVERLAYS		
AELORTWW	LOW WATER		
AELORTYZ	ZEALOTRY		
AELOSTUY	AUTOLYSE		
AELPRRSW	SPRAWLER		
AELPRRTT	PRATTLER		
AELPRRST	PLASTERS,		
PSALTERS, STAPLERS			
AELPRSSU	PERUSALS		
AELPRSSY	SPARSELY		
AELPRSTT	PLATTERS,		
SPLATTER			
AELPRSTY	PSALTERY		
AELQRRSU	QUARRELS		
AELQRSUV	SERVQUAL		
AELQRSUY	SQUARELY		
AELRRSTT	STARTLER		
AELRRSTW	TRAWLERS		
AELRSSST	STARLESS		
AELRSSTT	STARLETS		
AELRSSTW	WASTRELS		
AELRSSUW	WALRUSES		
AELRSTTT	TATTLERS		
AELRSTTU	LUSTRATE		
AELRSTUV	VAULTERS,		
VESTURAL			
AELRTTUX	TEXTURAL		
AELRTTUY	TUTELARY		
AELSTTUY	ASTUTELY		
AEMMNRTU	RAMENTUM		
AEMMOORT	ROOMMATE		
AEMMOORT	MARMOSET		
AEMMRSST	STAMMERS		
AEMMNORS	NORSEMAN		
AEMMNORT	ORNAMENT		
AEMMNORW	MORWENNA		
AEMMNPRU	PER ANNUM		
AEMMNRST	REMNANTS		
AEMNOORT	ANTEROOM		
AEMNOPRW	MANPOWER		
AEMNORRS	RANSOMER		
AEMNORST	ONSTREAM		
AEMNORTY	MONETARY		
AEMNORYY	YEOMANRY		
AEMNOSTU	SEAMOUNT		
AEMNPRSS	PRESSMAN		
AEMNPRSU	SUPERMAN		
AEMNPSTY	PAYMENTS		
AEMNRRUY	NUMERARY		
AEMNRSSU	SURNAMES		
AEMNRSSW	WARMNESS		
AEMNRSTW	STRAW MEN		
AEMNRSUY	ANEURYSM		
AEMOORST	TEAROOMS		

AEMOORTT	AMORETTO	
AEMOOSST	MAESTOSO	
AEMOOSTT	TOMATOES	
AEMOOSTU	AUTOSOME	
AEMOPRTW	TAPEWORM	
AEMORRRU	ARMOURER	
AEMORRST	REARMOST	
AEMORRSY	ROSEMARY	
AEMORSSS	MORASSES	
AEMORSST	MAESTROS	
AEMORSSY	MAYORESS	
AEMORTTU	TAUTOMER	
AEMORUWZ	MUZOREWA	
AEMOTTZZ	MOZZETTA	
AEMPRRSY	SPERMARY	
AEMPRSTU	UPSTREAM	
AEMPSTTT	ATTEMPTS	
AEMQRSSU	MARQUESS	
AEMRSSSU	MASSEURS	
AEMRSSTT	MATTRESS,	
SMARTEST		
AENNNOTU	NUNEATON	
AENNNPST	PENNANTS	
AENNOPST	PENTOSAN	
AENNORST	RESONANT	
AENNORSU	UNREASON	
AENNOSTV	EVANSTON	
AENNPRSS	SPANNERS	
AENNRSTT	ENTRANTS	
AENNRSWY	SWANNERY	
AENNRTTY	TENANTRY	
AENOOPST	TEASPOON	
AENOPRSS	PERSONAS	
AENOPRST	PATERSON	
AENOPRTT	PATENTOR	
AENOPRWY	WEAPONRY	
AENOPSTT	ANTE-POST	
AENORRST	ANTRORSE	
AENORSST	ASSENTOR,	
SENATORS		
AENORSUV	RAVENOUS	
AENORTTY	ATTORNEY	
AENOSSUU	NAUSEOUS	
AENPPRSS	SNAPPERS	
AENPRRST	PARTNERS	
AENPRSST	PASTERNS,	
RAPTNESS		
AENPRSTT	PATTERNS,	
TRANSEPT		
AENPRSUV	PARVENUS	
AENQRRTU	QUARTERN	
AENRRRTY	ERRANTRY	
AENRSSTT	TARTNESS	
AENRSSTU	SAUNTERS	
AENRSSTV	SERVANTS	

AENRSTWY	STERNWAY	
AENRTWYY	ENTRYWAY	
AENSSSTV	VASTNESS	
AENSSTTU	TAUTNESS	
AENSSTTX	SEXTANTS	
AEOOPPSS	PAPOOSES	
AEOOPRRT	OPERATOR	
AEOOPSTT	POTATOES	
AEOORRST	SORORATE	
AEOORTTT	TATTOOER	
AEOPRRUV	VAPOURER	
AEOPRRVW	WRAPOVER	
AEOPRSST	SEAPORTS	
AEOPRSSV	OVERPASS,	
PASSOVER		
AEOPRSTT	PROSTATE	
AEOPRSTU	APTEROUS	
AEOPTTUY	AUTOTYPE	
AEOQRTTU	TORQUATE	
AEORRSST	ASSORTER,	
ROASTERS		
AEORRTZZ	TERRAZZO	
AEORSSSS	ASSESSOR	
AEORSSTT	TOASTERS	
AEORSSTV	VOTARESS	
AEORSTTT	TESTATOR	
AEORSTTU	OUTSTARE	
AEORSTVY	OVERSTAY	
AEPPRRST	TRAPPERS	
AEPPRRSW	WRAPPERS	
AEPPSSTU	PASTE-UPS	
AEPRRSSY	SPRAYERS	
AEPRRSTU	RAPTURES	
AEPRSSST	SPARSEST,	
TRESPASS		
AEPRSSTT	SPATTERS	
AEPRSSTU	PASTURES	
AEPRSTTY	TAPESTRY	
AEPRSTUX	SUPERTAX	
AEQRRSTU	QUARTERS	
AEQRSSTU	SQUAREST,	
T-SQUARES		
AEQRSTTU	QUARTETS,	
SQUATTER		
AERRSSTT	STARTERS	
AERRSTUY	TREASURY	
AERSSTTU	STATURES	
AERSSTTW	SWATTERS	
AERSTTVY	TRAVESTY	
AERTTUXY	TEXTUARY	
AESSSTTU	STATUSES	
AESSTTTU	STATUTES	
AFFFFIRR	RIFFRAFF	
AFFGIINX	AFFIXING	
AFFGIIRT	GRAFFITI	

AFFGILNR	RAFFLING	
AFFGILNW	WAFFLING	
AFFGINST	STAFFING	
AFFGIORT	GRAFFITO	
AFFGLNRU	FAR-FLUNG	
AFFHILLS	FALLFISH	
AFFHILST	FLATFISH	
AFFHILTU	FAITHFUL	
AFFHIMRS	FISH FARM	
AFFIINTY	AFFINITY	
AFFILLMM	FLIMFLAM	
AFFILSUX	SUFFIXAL	
AFFIMSST	MASTIFFS	
AFFINOSU	AFFUSION	
AFFINRSU	FUNFAIRS,	
RUFFIANS		
AFFIPSTT	TIPSTAFF	
AFFLLOOT	FOOTFALL	
AFFLOOTT	FLATFOOT	
AFFLOPSY	PLAY-OFFS	
AFFNORST	AFFRONTS	
AFFNRRUU	FURFURAN	
AFGGGILN	FLAGGING	
AFGGINOR	FORAGING	
AFGGINRT	GRAFTING	
AFGHILNS	FLASHING	
AFGHILNT	FANLIGHT	
AFGHILPS	FLAGSHIP	
AFGHINRT	FARTHING	
AFGHINST	SHAFTING	
AFGHLNSU	FLASHGUN	
AFGIILLN	FLAILING	
AFGIILNS	FAILINGS	
AFGIINNT	FAINTING	
AFGIINRS	FAIRINGS	
AFGIKLNN	FLANKING	
AFGIKNNR	FRANKING	
AFGIKORT	KOFTGARI	
AFGILMNO	FLAMINGO	
AFGILNOT	FLOATING	
AFGILNOW	FOWLIANG	
AFGILNPP	FLAPPING	
AFGILNTT	FLATTING	
AFGILNTU	FAULTING	
AFGIMNTU	FUMIGANT	
AFGIMORS	GASIFORM	
AFGINORY	FORAYING	
AFGINRST	STRAFING	
AFGINRTU	FIGURANT	
AFGIPRTW	GIFT-WRAP	
AFGJNRUU	JUNGFRAU	
AFGLLRUY	FRUGALLY	
AFGLLSUY	FALL GUYS	
AFGLMOPS	FOG LAMPS	

AFGNOORS	FOR A SONG	AFKLOSWY	FOLKWAYS	AGGILNSS	GLASSING
AFGORTUW	TUG-OF-WAR	AFKMOORT	FOOTMARK	AGGINNOR	GROANING
AFHIILSS	SAILFISH	AFLLLORY	FLORALLY	AGGINNOT	TANGOING
AFHIILST	FISHTAIL	AFLLLUWY	LAWFULLY	AGGINNRT	GRANTING
AFHIINST	FAINTISH	AFLLMNUY	MANFULLY	AGGINNTW	TWANGING
AFHIKLPS	HIP FLASK	AFLLMORY	FORMALLY	AGGINOOX	GAOXIONG
AFHIKNRS	FRANKISH	AFLLMRSY	SMALL FRY	AGGINOVY	VOYAGING
AFHILLSY	FLASHILY	AFLLNOSW	SNOWFALL	AGGINPRS	GRASPING
AFHILOSY	OAFISHLY	AFLLNUUW	UNLAWFUL	AGGINRSS	GRASSING
AFHILSTT	FLATTISH	AFLLOOTW	FOOTWALL	AGGINRST	GRATINGS
AFHILSTW	HALF-WITS	AFLLOPUY	FOUL PLAY	AGGINRSU	SUGARING
AFHINOSS	FASHIONS	AFLLOSTU	FALLOUTS,	AGGINRTY	GYRATING
AFHIRSST	STARFISH		OUTFALLS	AGGINRUU	AUGURING
AFHKLNTU	THANKFUL	AFLLRTUY	ARTFULLY	AGGINSST	STAGINGS
AFHKORSY	HAYFORKS	AFLMNOPR	PLANFORM	AGGLLOOY	ALGOLOGY
AFHLMNOO	HALF MOON	AFLMOPRT	PLATFORM	AGGLMOOR	LOGOGRAM
AFHLMOTU	FALMOUTH	AFLMORSU	FORMULAS	AGGLOORY	AGROLOGY
AFHLRTUW	WRATHFUL	AFLMORTW	FLATWORM	AGGLRSTY	STRAGGLY
AFHOOPTT	FOOTPATH	AFLMOSUY	FAMOUSLY	AGGNUWZZ	ZUGZWANG
AFIILLNU	UNFILIAL	AFLORSUV	FLAVOURS	AGHHIILT	HIGHTAIL
AFIILMNS	FINALISM	AFLPSSTY	FLYPASTS	AGHHIMSS	HIGH MASS
AFIILLNU	FRIULIAN	AFMNNORT	FRONT MAN	AGHHINOP	HAIPHONG
AFIILNST	FINALIST	AFMOOPRR	PRO FORMA	AGHHISWY	HIGHWAYS
AFIILNTY	FINALITY	AFMOORTZ	FROM A TO Z	AGHHLOTU	ALTHOUGH
AFIILRST	AIRLIFTS	AFMORTUY	FUMATORY	AGHHNOUZ	HANGZHOU
AFIINNOS	SAINFOIN,	AFOOPSST	SOFT SOAP	AGHIILNN	INHALING
SINFONIA		AFORRSTU	FOUR-STAR	AGHIINST	TSINGHAI
AFIINOTX	FIXATION	AFPPPTUY	PUPPY FAT	AGHIIPRR	HAIRGRIP
AFIKLNNR	FRANKLIN	AGGGHILN	HAGGLING	AGHIIRTT	AIRTIGHT
AFIKMNNR	FINNMARK	AGGGHINS	SHAGGING	AGHIJNRT	NIGHTJAR
AFILLLOT	FLOTILLA	AGGGILNN	GANGLING	AGHIKLRU	GURKHALI
AFILLPST	PITFALLS	AGGGILNR	GARGLING	AGHIKNNT	THANKING
AFILLTUY	FAULTILY	AGGGILNS	SLAGGING	AGHILLRT	ALL RIGHT
AFILMNOR	FORMALIN,	AGGGILNW	WAGGLING	AGHILMTY	ALMIGHTY
INFORMAL		AGGGINNS	SNAGGING	AGHILNOO	HOOLIGAN
AFILMNOS	FOILSMAN	AGGHILNU	LAUGHING	AGHILNOT	LOATHING
AFILMRST	FILM STAR	AGGHILST	GASLIGHT	AGHILNRS	RINGHALS
AFILMRUU	MUFULIRA	AGGHILSY	SHAGGILY	AGHILNSS	HASSLING,
AFILNPPT	FLIPPANT	AGGHINNS	GNASHING,	LASHINGS, SLASHING	
AFILNPST	FLAT SPIN	HANGINGS		AGHILNSU	LANGUISH
AFILNRUY	UNFAIRLY	AGGHISTT	GASTIGHT	AGHILOST	GOLIATHS
AFILSTTU	FLAUTIST	AGGIILNN	ALIGNING	AGHILRSY	GARISHLY
AFIMMNOY	AMMONIFY	AGGIILNV	GINGIVAL	AGHIMMNS	SHAMMING
AFIMNOPR	NAPIFORM	AGGIINNR	GRAINING	AGHIMNSS	SMASHING
AFIMNOSU	INFAMOUS	AGGIJLNN	JANGLING	AGHINNOT	GNATHION
AFIMORRV	VARIFORM	AGGILMNN	MANGLING	AGHINNTU	HAUNTING
AFINNOOP	ON PAIN OF	AGGILMNO	GLOAMING	AGHINNTY	ANYTHING
AFINNOTU	FOUNTAIN	AGGILNNO	GANGLION	AGHINPRS	HARPINGS,
AFINNRTY	INFANTRY	AGGILNNS	SLANGING	PHRASING	
AFINOPSY	SAPONIFY	AGGILNNT	TANGLING	AGHINQSU	QUASHING
AFINORUV	IN FAVOUR	AGGILNNW	WANGLING	AGHINRRY	HARRYING
AFINQTUY	QUANTIFY	AGGILNOT	GLOATING	AGHINRST	TRASHING
AFINRSTX	TRANSFIX	AGGILNPU	PLAGUING	AGHINSST	HASTINGS,
AFIRSTTY	STRATIFY	AGGILNPY	GAPINGLY	STASHING	
AFKLNOTU	OUTFLANK	AGGILNRY	GRAYLING	AGHINSSV	SHAVINGS

231

AGHINSTW	SWATHING
AGHIPRRT	TRIGRAPH
AGHIRSTT	STRAIGHT
AGHLLNOU	LONG-HAUL
AGHLMOOR	HOLOGRAM
AGHMMOOY	HOMOGAMY
AGHMNPSU	SPHAGNUM
AGHMOPRY	MYOGRAPH
AGHNNSTU	SHANTUNG
AGHNOSTU	HANGOUTS
AGHNTTUU	UNTAUGHT
AGHORSTW	WARTHOGS
AGIIIKMR	KIRIGAMI
AGIIILNS	LIAISING
AGIIINNS	INSIGNIA
AGIIINRV	VIRGINIA
AGIIJJNN	JINJIANG
AGIILLMN	MILLIGAN
AGIILMNP	IMPALING
AGIILNNO	LIAONING
AGIILNNU	INGUINAL
AGIILNOR	ORIGINAL
AGIILNOT	INTAGLIO, LIGATION
AGIILNOX	GLOXINIA
AGIILNPT	PLAITING
AGIILNQU	QUAILING
AGIILNRS	RAILINGS
AGIILNRT	TRAILING
AGIILNRU	LIGURIAN
AGIILNRV	RIVALING, VIRGINAL
AGIILNSS	SAILINGS
AGIILNST	TAILINGS
AGIILNTT	LITIGANT
AGIILNTV	VIGILANT
AGIILORU	OLIGURIA
AGIILPST	PIGTAILS
AGIIMNOW	MIAOWING
AGIINNPT	PAINTING
AGIINNRT	TRAINING
AGIINNST	STAINING
AGIINNTT	TAINTING
AGIINORT	RIGATONI
AGIINPRS	ASPIRING, PRAISING
AGIINPRT	PIRATING
AGIINRRV	ARRIVING
AGIINRTT	ATTIRING
AGIINRUU	UIGURIAN
AGIINSTU	IGNATIUS
AGIJLNPY	JAPINGLY
AGIJMNOR	MAJORING
AGIJNNTU	JAUNTING
AGIKLMOR	KILOGRAM
AGIKLNNP	PLANKING
AGIKLNNR	RANKLING
AGIKLNST	STALKING
AGIKMNRS	MARKINGS
AGIKNNPS	SPANKING
AGIKNNSW	SWANKING
AGIKNOST	GOATSKIN
AGIKNPRS	SPARKING
AGILLMNY	MALIGNLY
AGILLMSU	GAULLISM
AGILLNOW	ALLOWING
AGILLNOY	ALLOYING
AGILLNRU	ALLURING
AGILLNRY	RALLYING
AGILLNST	STALLING
AGILLNSY	SALLYING, SIGNALLY, SLANGILY
AGILLNTY	TALLYING
AGILLOPT	GALLIPOT
AGILLORS	GORILLAS
AGILLPUY	PLAGUILY
AGILLSSU	LUGSAILS
AGILLSTU	GAULLIST
AGILMMNS	SLAMMING
AGILMNNT	MANTLING
AGILMNOO	MONGOLIA
AGILMNPS	SAMPLING
AGILMOPR	LIPOGRAM
AGILMORS	ALGORISM
AGILNNNP	PLANNING
AGILNNOP	PANGOLIN
AGILNNPT	PLANTING
AGILNNRS	SNARLING
AGILNNST	SLANTING
AGILNNUY	UNGAINLY
AGILNOOO	OOGONIAL
AGILNOPR	PAROLING
AGILNORT	TRIGONAL
AGILNOSS	LASSOING
AGILNOTT	TOTALING
AGILNOTU	LIAOTUNG
AGILNOTW	WAGON-LIT
AGILNPPS	SLAPPING
AGILNPPY	APPLYING
AGILNPRS	SPARLING
AGILNPSS	SAPLINGS
AGILNPST	STAPLING
AGILNPSW	LAPWINGS
AGILNPSY	SPLAYING
AGILNRST	STARLING
AGILNRSU	SINGULAR
AGILNRTT	RATTLING
AGILNRTW	TRAWLING
AGILNSTU	SALUTING
AGILNTTT	TATTLING
AGILNTUV	VAULTING
AGILNTWZ	WALTZING
AGILNTXY	TAXINGLY
AGILOOPY	APIOLOGY
AGILOOXY	AXIOLOGY
AGILSYYZ	SYZYGIAL
AGIMMOSY	MISOGAMY
AGIMNNRU	MANURING
AGIMNORS	ORGANISM
AGIMNORY	AGRIMONY
AGIMNPPS	MAPPINGS
AGIMNPRT	TRAMPING
AGIMNPST	STAMPING
AGIMNPSW	SWAMPING
AGIMNRRY	MARRYING
AGIMNRST	MIGRANTS, SMARTING
AGIMNRSW	SWARMING
AGIMNRTU	MATURING
AGIMNSSU	ASSUMING
AGIMORRT	MIGRATOR
AGINNNOY	ANNOYING
AGINNNPS	SPANNING
AGINNNSW	SWANNING
AGINNOPT	POIGNANT
AGINNORT	IGNORANT
AGINNPPS	SNAPPING
AGINNPSW	SPAWNING, WINGSPAN
AGINNRSW	WARNINGS
AGINNTTU	ATTUNING, TAUNTING
AGINNTUV	VAUNTING
AGINOORT	ROGATION
AGINORRS	GARRISON
AGINORRW	ARROWING
AGINORSS	ASSIGNOR, SIGNORAS
AGINORST	ORGANIST, ROASTING
AGINORSU	AROUSING
AGINORTT	ROTATING
AGINORTV	GRAVITON
AGINORTY	GYRATION
AGINOSTT	TANGOIST, TOASTING, TSINGTAO
AGINPPRT	TRAPPING
AGINPPRW	WRAPPING
AGINPPSW	SWAPPING
AGINPRRS	SPARRING
AGINPRRY	PARRYING
AGINPRSS	RASPINGS
AGINPRST	GIN TRAPS, PARTINGS

AGINPRSY	SPRAYING	AHHIPRSS	SHARPISH	AHIQRSSU	SQUARISH
AGINPRTY	PARTYING	AHHLNOPT	NAPHTHOL	AHISSTTW	WHATSITS
AGINPSST	PASTINGS	AHHLNPTY	NAPHTHYL	AHKLLOOY	HOLLY OAK
AGINQRSU	SQUARING	AHHLOOPU	HULA HOOP	AHKLOPRU	KOLHAPUR
AGINRRST	STARRING	AHHMPRRU	HARRUMPH	AHKLOPST	SHOPTALK, TALK
AGINRRTY	TARRYING	AHHNORTW	HAWTHORN	SHOP	
AGINRSST	STAR SIGN	AHIIKMRS	KASHMIRI	AHKLOSTW	TALK SHOW
AGINRSSU	ASSURING	AHIILLPP	PHILLIPA	AHKMORTU	KHARTOUM
AGINRSTT	STARTING	AHIILPPP	PHILIPPA	AHKNOTUY	THANKYOU
AGINRSTV	STARVING	AHIILRTY	HILARITY	AHLLNOOS	SHALLOON
AGINRSTY	STINGRAY,	AHIIMNOT	HIMATION	AHLLNOTW	TOWN HALL
STRAYING		AHIIMNRS	IRISHMAN	AHLLOSST	SHALLOTS
AGINSTTW	SWATTING	AHIIMNST	ISTHMIAN	AHLLOSSW	SHALLOWS
AGINSTUU	AUGUSTIN	AHIINPRS	HAIRPINS	AHLLOSTU	THALLOUS
AGIOORTU	AUTOGIRO	AHIIPRSS	AIRSHIPS	AHLMMOPY	LYMPHOMA
AGIOPPRT	AGITPROP	AHIKLNRS	RINKHALS	AHLMNOOR	HORMONAL
AGIRTTUY	GRATUITY	AHIKLRSY	RAKISHLY	AHLMNOST	MANSHOLT
AGJLRSUU	JUGULARS	AHIKNPRS	PRANKISH	AHLMOOPS	OMPHALOS
AGKLOORV	GORLOVKA	AHIKOSUZ	SHIZUOKA	AHLMOPTY	POLYMATH
AGKORSSW	GASWORKS	AHILLMSS	SMALLISH	AHLNOOPS	ALPHONSO
AGLLRUVY	VULGARLY	AHILLMTU	THALLIUM	AHLOPRSU	SHOLAPUR
AGLMOPYY	POLYGAMY	AHILLNST	ANTHILLS	AHLORRTY	HARLOTRY
AGLNOOSW	OWN GOALS	AHILLSVY	LAVISHLY	AHMMMOST	MAMMOTHS
AGLNOSWY	LONGWAYS	AHILMNOT	HAMILTON	AHMNNSTU	HUNTSMAN,
AGLNSSSU	SUNGLASS	AHILMOST	MAILSHOT	MANHUNTS	
AGLOOPST	GOALPOST	AHILMQSU	QUALMISH	AHMNOPST	PHANTOMS
AGLOPRTU	PORTUGAL	AHILNOPS	SIPHONAL	AHMNORSU	MANHOURS
AGLORSSY	GLOSSARY	AHILNORT	HORNTAIL	AHMOOPPT	PHOTOMAP
AGLOSUVY	YUGOSLAV	AHILNOST	LOTHIANS	AHMOOPSS	SHAMPOOS
AGLPSSSY	SPYGLASS	AHILOORT	LOTHARIO	AHMOORSW	WASHROOM
AGLRTTUU	GUTTURAL	AHILOPSS	ALPHOSIS,	AHMORTTW	TAMWORTH
AGLSTUUY	AUGUSTLY	HAPLOSIS		AHMPSSSU	SMASH-UPS
AGMMNOOR	MONOGRAM	AHILOPST	HOSPITAL	AHMPSTYY	SYMPATHY
AGMMNOOY	MONOGAMY	AHILRSTY	TRASHILY	AHMQSSUU	MUSQUASH
AGMMORSY	MYOGRAMS	AHIMMNSU	HUMANISM	AHNOOPRS	HARPOONS
AGMNOORY	AGRONOMY	AHIMNOST	THOMASIN	AHNOORRY	HONORARY
AGMNORST	ANGSTROM	AHIMNOSW	WOMANISH	AHNOPPSW	PAWNSHOP
AGMNSSTU	MUSTANGS	AHIMNSTU	HUMANIST	AHNOPPSY	PANSOPHY
AGMNSSTY	GYMNASTS	AHIMNTUY	HUMANITY	AHNOPSST	SNAP SHOT
AGMOOOSU	OOGAMOUS	AHIMOOSY	YAHOOISM	AHNOSTTW	WHATNOTS
AGMOOTVY	VAGOTOMY	AHIMOPRS	APHORISM	AHNOSTUX	XANTHOUS
AGMOPRRS	PROGRAMS	AHIMORRW	HAIRWORM	AHNRSTTU	THURSTAN
AGNNOSSW	SWANSONG	AHIMSSTU	TSUSHIMA	AHOOSSTY	SOOTHSAY
AGNOPRST	PART-SONG	AHIMSTUZ	AZIMUTHS	AHOOSTTW	SAWTOOTH
AGNORTUY	NUGATORY	AHINNNOR	RHIANNON	AHOPSTTW	TOWPATHS
AGNPRSUY	SPRAY GUN	AHINNOPT	ANTIPHON	AHOPSTUW	SOUTHPAW
AGOORRTY	ROGATORY	AHINORRS	HARRISON	AHORTTUW	WATT-HOUR
AGOPPSST	STOPGAPS	AHINOSST	ASTONISH	AHOSSTUW	WASHOUTS
AGORRTYY	GYRATORY	AHINPPSS	SNAPPISH	AHRSTUWY	THRUWAYS
AGSSTUUU	AUGUSTUS	AHINQSUV	VANQUISH	AIIILMST	MILITIAS
AGSSTUUV	GUSTAVUS	AHIOOPPT	PHOTOPIA	AIIILNST	INITIALS
AHHILPSW	WHIPLASH	AHIOPRST	APHORIST	AIIKLNOR	IRAKLION
AHHIMMSS	MISHMASH	AHIPRSST	HARPISTS	AIIKLNRR	LARRIKIN
AHHINRTU	HAUT-RHIN	AHIPRSSW	WARSHIPS	AIIKMNNS	MANIKINS
				AIIKNNNP	PANNIKIN

AIIKNRST	KRISTINA
AIIKTTZZ	TZATZIKI
AIILLMRY	MILLIARY
AIILLNNV	VANILLIN
AIILLNSV	VILLAINS
AIILLNVY	VILLAINY
AIILLWWW	WILLIWAW
AIILMNPS	ALPINISM
AIILMNPT	PALMITIN
AIILMNST	LATINISM
AIILMNTT	MILITANT
AIILMRST	MISTRIAL
AIILMRTY	LIMITARY, MILITARY
AIILMSST	ISLAMIST
AIILMSTV	VITALISM
AIILNNOV	LIVONIAN
AIILNOPT	OIL PAINT
AIILNOPV	PAVILION
AIILNOSS	LIAISONS
AIILNOSV	VISIONAL
AIILNPST	ALPINIST, TAILSPIN
AIILNRSU	SILURIAN
AIILNSTT	LATINIST
AIILNSTY	SALINITY
AIILNTTY	LATINITY
AIILSTTV	VITALIST
AIILTTVY	VITALITY
AIIMNNOS	INSOMNIA
AIIMNPSS	SINAPISM
AIIMNRST	MARTINIS
AIIMNSST	ANIMISTS
AIIMNSTT	TITANISM
AIIMNSTV	NATIVISM, VITAMINS
AIIMNTTU	TITANIUM
AIIMOPSX	APOMIXIS
AIIMORTT	IMITATOR
AIIMOSST	AMITOSIS
AIIMPPRS	PRIAPISM
AIIMPRTY	IMPARITY
AIIMRUVV	VIVARIUM
AIIMSSTT	MASTITIS
AIINNOSV	INVASION
AIINNOTV	NIVATION
AIINNSTU	TUNISIAN
AIINNSTV	VINNITSA
AIINNSTY	INSANITY
AIINORTT	ANTI-RIOT
AIINPRSS	ASPIRINS
AIINPSST	PIANISTS
AIINRRTT	IRRITANT
AIINSTTV	NATIVIST, VISITANT
AIINTTVY	NATIVITY
AIIORSTV	OVARITIS
AIIORTTV	VITIATOR
AIIPRRST	AIRSTRIP
AIIRSSTT	SATIRIST, SITARIST
AIJKKNOU	KINKAJOU
AIJKLMNU	JUNK MAIL
AIJLLOVY	JOVIALLY
AIJLNTUY	JAUNTILY
AIJMORTY	MAJORITY
AIJNOPPY	POPINJAY
AIJNORST	JANITORS
AIKKLLRW	KIRKWALL
AIKLLSTY	STALKILY
AIKLMWYY	MILKY WAY
AIKLNOPS	POLANSKI
AIKLNSWY	SWANKILY
AIKLOTTW	KILOWATT
AIKMRSTZ	SITZMARK
AIKNNOOS	NAINSOOK
AIKNNSSW	SWANSKIN
AIKNRSST	SANSKRIT
AILLLNOO	LINALOOL
AILLLOST	SALTILLO
AILLLPSU	LAPILLUS
AILLMOSS	LIMASSOL
AILLMOSY	LOYALISM
AILLMOTY	MOLALITY
AILLMRTY	MYRTILLA
AILLMRUY	ARUM LILY
AILLMSSW	SAWMILLS
AILLMUUV	ALLUVIUM
AILLNOPP	PAPILLON
AILLNOST	STALLION
AILLNOSU	ALLUSION
AILLNPTY	PLIANTLY
AILLORSY	SAILORLY
AILLORTT	LITTORAL, TORTILLA
AILLOSTY	LOYALIST
AILLPRTY	PALTRILY
AILLPSTY	PLAYLIST
AILLPSWY	SPILLWAY
AILLRTUY	RITUALLY
AILLSUVY	VISUALLY
AILMMNOO	MONOMIAL
AILMMORS	MORALISM
AILMMORT	IMMORTAL
AILMMSTU	SUMMITAL
AILMNNOT	MANNITOL
AILMNOOP	PALOMINO
AILMNOOR	MONORAIL
AILMNOPY	OLYMPIAN
AILMNPST	IMPLANTS
AILMNPTU	PLATINUM
AILMNRUY	LUMINARY
AILMNSTU	SIMULANT
AILMOPRX	PROXIMAL
AILMORST	MORALIST
AILMORSU	SOLARIUM
AILMORSY	ROYALISM
AILMORTY	MORALITY
AILMOSTU	SOLATIUM
AILMOSTV	VOLTAISM
AILMPPSY	MISAPPLY
AILMPRSU	PRIMULAS
AILMPSST	PALMISTS, PSALMIST
AILMPSTY	PTYALISM
AILMRRSU	RURALISM
AILMRSTU	ALTRUISM, MURALIST, ULTRAISM
AILNNOOT	NOTIONAL
AILNNOSW	SON-IN-LAW
AILNNOSY	LYONNAIS
AILNNOTU	LUNATION
AILNNSTU	INSULANT
AILNOOPT	OPTIONAL
AILNOPRU	UNIPOLAR
AILNOPTY	PONYTAIL
AILNOSUV	AVULSION
AILNOSVY	SYNOVIAL
AILNOTTY	TONALITY
AILNOTUX	LUXATION
AILNPPSY	SNAPPILY
AILNPSTU	NUPTIALS
AILNPSUU	NAUPLIUS
AILNQRTU	TRANQUIL
AILNQTUY	QUAINTLY
AILNRRTU	TRIAL RUN
AILNSSUV	SILVANUS
AILNSTTU	LUTANIST
AILNSTUU	NAUTILUS
AILNSYZZ	SNAZZILY
AILOORST	ISOLATOR, OSTIOLAR
AILOORTV	VIOLATOR
AILOPRTU	TROUPIAL
AILOPRTY	POLARITY
AILOPRUY	POLYURIA
AILORSTY	ROYALIST, SOLITARY
AILORTTU	TUTORIAL
AILORTUV	OUTRIVAL
AILOSSUY	ALOYSIUS
AILOTTTY	TOTALITY
AILPPSSY	PAYSLIPS
AILPRSTU	STIPULAR
AILPSSWY	SLIPWAYS
AILPSTUY	PLAYSUIT

AILRRSTU	RURALIST	AINPSSTU	PUISSANT	ALNNOTWY	WANTONLY
AILRRSTY	STARRILY	AINQTTUY	QUANTITY	ALNOOPST	PLATOONS
AILRRTUY	RURALITY	AINRSSTT	TRANSITS	ALNOOPYZ	POLYZOAN
AILRSTTU	ALTRUIST,	AINRSTTU	NATURIST	ALNOPPTT	POT PLANT
	ULTRAIST	AIOOORRT	ORATORIO	ALNOPRST	PLASTRON
AILRSUVV	SURVIVAL	AIOPRRST	AIRPORTS	ALNORRWY	NARROWLY
AILSSTUW	LAWSUITS	AIOPRRTT	PORTRAIT	ALNPPSTU	SUPPLANT
AIMMMNOU	AMMONIUM	AIOPRSST	PROTASIS	ALNPRSSU	SNARL-UPS
AIMMMSUX	MAXIMUMS	AIOPRSTT	PATRIOTS	ALNSSUVY	SYLVANUS
AIMMNORT	MORTMAIN	AIORRRSW	WARRIORS	ALOOPPRS	PROPOSAL
AIMNNOSS	MANSIONS	AIORRRST	TRAITORS	ALOOPRSW	POOR LAWS
AIMNNOTU	MOUNTAIN	AIORRSTV	VARISTOR	ALOORSUV	VALOROUS
AIMNNOTY	ANTIMONY,	AIORSSUV	SAVIOURS	ALOORTYZ	ZOOLATRY
	ANTINOMY	AIORSTTV	VOTARIST	ALOPPRYY	POLYPARY
AIMNNRTU	RUMINANT	AIOSSSTY	ISOSTASY	ALOPPTUY	PLAY UP TO
AIMNOORV	MONROVIA	AIPPRSTT	TRAPPIST	ALOPRRSU	PARLOURS
AIMNOOTY	MYOTONIA	AIPPRSTY	PAPISTRY	ALOPRSTU	POSTURAL,
AIMNOQRU	MAROQUIN	AIPRSSTU	UPSTAIRS		PULSATOR
AIMNORTU	MINOTAUR	AIRRSTTY	ARTISTRY	ALOPSSTT	LAST POST
AIMNORTY	MINATORY	AJLNORSU	JOURNALS	ALOPSTUU	PATULOUS
AIMNOTTU	MUTATION	AJORRTUY	JURATORY	ALORSTTW	SALTWORT
AIMNRRSU	MURRAINS	AKKLRSSY	SKYLARKS	ALORTUWY	OUTLAWRY
AIMNRSTT	TRANSMIT	AKKOOSUY	YOKOSUKA	ALOSTTUZ	ZLATOUST
AIMNRSTU	NATURISM	AKKORSTW	TASKWORK	ALPPSTUY	PLATYPUS
AIMNRSTV	VARMINTS	AKLLNOSW	KNOW-ALLS	ALPRSTUU	PUSTULAR
AIMOPRSS	PROSAISM	AKLNNOPT	PLANKTON	AMMNOORT	MOTORMAN
AIMOPSSY	SYMPOSIA	AKLOSTUW	WALKOUTS	AMMNPTUY	TYMPANUM
AIMORRUV	VARIORUM	AKLPRRSU	LARKSPUR	AMNNOSTW	TOWNSMAN
AIMORSTY	RAMOSITY	AKMMNRSU	MURMANSK	AMNNOSTY	ANTONYMS
AIMPPRUU	PUPARIUM	AKMMOOTU	KUMAMOTO	AMNNSTTU	STUNT MAN
AIMRRSTT	TRISTRAM	AKMNORTU	TURKOMAN	AMNOOSTT	OTTOMANS
AIMRSSTX	MARXISTS	AKMOORST	KOSTROMA	AMNOOTUY	AUTONOMY
AIMRTTUY	MATURITY	AKMOPRST	POSTMARK	AMNOOTXY	TAXONOMY
AINNNOST	SANTONIN	AKMQSTUU	KUMQUATS	AMNORSST	TRANSOMS
AINNOOTT	NOTATION	AKOPRRTW	PART WORK	AMNOTTUY	TAUTONYM
AINNOOTV	NOVATION	AKORSWWX	WAXWORKS	AMNRSTTU	TANTRUMS
AINNOOTZ	ZONATION	ALLLPRUY	LYALLPUR	AMOORRTY	MORATORY
AINNOTTU	NUTATION	ALLMNORY	NORMALLY	AMOORTWY	MOTORWAY
AINNRSTU	NURISTAN	ALLMNPSU	PULLMANS	AMOOTTUY	AUTOTOMY
AINNSSTT	INSTANTS	ALLMOPSX	SMALLPOX	AMOPRSXY	PAROXYSM
AINNSTTY	NYSTATIN	ALLMORTY	MORTALLY	AMOQSSUU	SQUAMOUS
AINOOPTT	POTATION	ALLMTUUY	MUTUALLY	AMORRTUY	MORTUARY
AINOORST	ORATIONS	ALLNOOPS	PLANOSOL	AMORSTTU	OUTSMART
AINOORTT	ROTATION	ALLOPRSY	PAYROLLS	ANNOORST	SONORANT
AINOOSTT	OSTINATO	ALLOSSWW	SWALLOWS	ANNOSSTU	STANNOUS
AINOOSTV	OVATIONS	ALMMNRUU	NUMMULAR	ANOOPRRT	PRONATOR
AINOPPTU	PUPATION	ALMNOOPS	LAMPOONS	ANOOPRSS	SOPRANOS
AINOPSSS	PASSIONS	ALMNORTY	MATRONLY	ANOPRRSS	SPORRANS
AINORSST	ARSONIST	ALMNPSSU	SUNLAMPS	ANOPRTTU	TRAPUNTO
AINOSSTT	STATIONS	ALMOOPRY	PLAYROOM	ANPRSSTU	SUNTRAPS
AINOSTTU	TITANOUS	ALMOORTU	ALUMROOT	ANPRSTUU	PURSUANT
AINPPRSS	PARSNIPS	ALMOPPST	LAMPPOST	AOOOPRTZ	PROTOZOA
AINPRSSU	PRUSSIAN	ALMOSTTU	MULATTOS, SUM	AOOPPRSY	APOSPORY
AINPRSTU	PURITANS		TOTAL	AOOPRSTT	TAPROOTS
AINPSSSY	SYNAPSIS				

AOOPRSTW	SOAPWORT	BBEHIOTW	BOBWHITE	BCCILMOU	COLUMBIC
AOOPRSUV	VAPOROUS	BBEILORW	WOBBLIER	BCCILOOR	BROCCOLI
AOORRTTY	ROTATORY	BBEILQRU	QUIBBLER	BCCIRTUU	CUCURBIT
AOORSSUV	SAVOROUS	BBEILQSU	QUIBBLES	BCCMOOSX	COXCOMBS
AOPPRSST	PASSPORT	BBEILRRY	BILBERRY	BCCNOORS	CORNCOBS
AOPRRSSW	SPARROWS	BBEIMMOT	TIME BOMB	BCCSSUUU	SUCCUBUS
AOPRSTTY	PYROSTAT	BBEIMOPP	PIPE BOMB	BCDDEEEK	BEDECKED
AOPTTUYY	AUTOTYPY	BBEIMOST	BOMBSITE	BCDEEEMR	DECEMBER
AORRSTTW	STARWORT	BBEIRSTU	STUBBIER	BCDEEENR	DEBRECEN
APRSSTTU	UPSTARTS	BBEISTTU	TUBBIEST	BCDEEEHLN	BLENCHED
BBBCEOWY	COBWEBBY	BBEKLOOU	BLUE BOOK	BCDEEIKN	BENEDICK
BBBEILRU	BUBBLIER	BBEKNOOT	BONTEBOK	BCDEEIKR	BICKERED
BBBEINOT	BOBBINET	BBELLOSY	BELLBOYS	BCDEEILR	CREDIBLE
BBBGILNU	BUBBLING	BBELORSY	SLOBBERY	BCDEEILS	DECIBELS
BBBINOPY	BOBBY PIN	BBENORSY	SNOBBERY	BCDEEILU	EDUCIBLE
BBCDERSU	SCRUBBED	BBEORRXY	BOXBERRY	BCDEEINT	BENEDICT
BBCDIMOY	BOMBYCID	BBERRRUY	BURBERRY	BCDEEIRS	DESCRIBE
BBCEHIRU	CHUBBIER	BBGGILNO	GOBBLING	BCDEEIST	BISECTED
BBCEILRS	SCRIBBLE	BBGGINRU	GRUBBING	BCDEEJOT	OBJECTED
BBCELORS	COBBLERS	BBGHILNO	HOBBLING	BCDEEKNO	BECKONED
BBCERRSU	SCRUBBER	BBGIIIMN	IMBIBING	BCDEEKRU	REEDBUCK
BBCGIINR	CRIBBING	BBGIILNN	NIBBLING	BCDEEKTU	BUCKETED
BBCGILNO	COBBLING	BBGILMNU	BUMBLING	BCDEEMRU	CUMBERED
BBCGILNU	CLUBBING	BBGILNNO	NOBBLING	BCDEIIRR	RICEBIRD
BBCHKSUU	BUSHBUCK	BBGILNOW	WOBBLING	BCDEIKRR	REDBRICK
BBCKLOOU	BOOK CLUB	BBGILNOY	LOBBYING	BCDEIKSS	SICKBEDS
BBDDEEMO	DEMOBBED	BBGILNRU	BURBLING	BCDEILRY	CREDIBLY
BBDDEILR	DRIBBLED	BBGILRUY	GRUBBILY	BCDEIMNO	COMBINED
BBDDEIRY	BY-BIDDER	BBGINNSU	SNUBBING	BCDEINOU	ICEBOUND
BBDEEGIR	GIBBERED	BBGINRSU	RUBBINGS	BCDELMRU	CRUMBLED
BBDEEIST	EBB TIDES	BBGINSTU	STUBBING	BCDEORSU	OBSCURED
BBDEEMNU	BENUMBED	BBHINOSS	SNOBBISH	BCDIIPSU	BICUSPID
BBDEHORT	THROBBED	BBHIOSTY	HOBBYIST	BCDILMOY	MOLYBDIC
BBDEILLR	BELLBIRD	BBHIRSUY	RUBBISHY	BCDILORU	COLUBRID
BBDEILQU	QUIBBLED	BBHRSSUU	SUBSHRUB	BCDINRUU	RUBICUND
BBDEILRR	DRIBBLER	BBIKLNOO	BOBOLINK	BCEEEFIN	BENEFICE
BBDEILRS	DRIBBLES	BBIKORSU	BOBRUISK	BCEEEHRS	BREECHES
BBDEILRU	BLUEBIRD	BBILMOSY	LOBBYISM	BCEEEINR	BERENICE
BBDEIMOV	DIVE-BOMB	BBILOSTY	LOBBYIST	BCEEERSU	BERCEUSE
BBDELLMU	DUMBBELL	BBILOSUU	BIBULOUS	BCEEFLTU	CLUBFEET
BBDELSTU	STUBBLED	BBILSTUY	STUBBILY	BCEEGIRS	ICEBERGS
BBDGIILN	DIBBLING	BBLLOUYY	BULLYBOY	BCEEHHNT	THE BENCH
BBDGINRU	DRUBBING	BBNORSTU	STUBBORN	BCEEHHSU	BUCHSHEE
BBDLOOWY	BODY BLOW	BCCCIILY	BICYCLIC	BCEEHKSU	BUCKSHEE
BBDOSUYY	BUSYBODY	BCCDEILY	BICYCLED	BCEEHLNR	BLENCHER
BBEEHTYY	BY THE BYE	BCCEEIRR	CEREBRIC	BCEEHNTU	BEECHNUT
BBEEIIRR	BERIBERI	BCCEHIRU	CHERUBIC	BCEEIILM	IMBECILE
BBEEILPR	PLEBBIER	BCCEIILO	LIBECCIO	BCEEIKRR	BICKERER
BBEELLLU	BLUEBELL	BCCEILOY	BIOCYCLE	BCEEIOSX	ICEBOXES
BBEFILRR	FRIBBLER	BCCEILRU	CRUCIBLE	BCEEKNOR	BECKONER
BBEGIIST	GIBBSITE	BCCEILSU	CUBICLES	BCEELRTU	TUBERCLE
BBEGILNP	PEBBLING	BCCEILSY	BICYCLES	BCEEMNRU	ENCUMBER
BBEGILST	GLIBBEST	BCCEMRUU	CUCUMBER	BCEEMRRU	CEREBRUM
BBEGIRRU	GRUBBIER	BCCIISTU	CUBISTIC	BCEEPRTY	CYBERPET

BCEERTVY	BREVETCY	BCFIMORU	CUBIFORM
BCEFFIIR	FEBRIFIC	BCFLOOTU	CLUBFOOT
BCEFILOR	FORCIBLE	BCGHIINR	BIRCHING
BCEGHILN	BELCHING	BCGHIINT	BITCHING
BCEGIMNO	BECOMING	BCGHINNU	BUNCHING
BCEHHIRT	THE BIRCH	BCGHINOT	BOTCHING
BCEHIIRT	BITCHIER	BCGIIKST	BIG STICK
BCEHILPU	BLUE CHIP	BCGIILMN	CLIMBING
BCEHIMOT	CHIMBOTE	BCGIKLNO	BLOCKING
BCEHIMRS	BESMIRCH	BCGIKLNU	BUCKLING
BCEHIORS	BRIOCHES	BCGINNOU	BOUNCING
BCEHIORT	BOTCHIER	BCHIILTY	BITCHILY
BCEHIRST	BRITCHES	BCHIISSU	HIBISCUS
BCEHLOST	BLOTCHES	BCHILOTY	BOTCHILY
BCEHNRSU	BRUNCHES	BCHIOORY	CHOIRBOY
BCEHOORS	BROOCHES	BCHKNORU	BUCKHORN
BCEHORRU	BROCHURE	BCHKOSTU	BUCKSHOT
BCEHORST	BOTCHERS	BCHNOORS	BRONCHOS
BCEHRSTU	BUTCHERS	BCHNORSU	BRONCHUS
BCEHRTTU	CUTHBERT	BCHOPSTU	BOTCH-UPS
BCEHRTUY	BUTCHERY	BCIIIOTT	BIOTITIC
BCEIIKLN	ICEBLINK	BCIILOTY	BIOLYTIC
BCEIILMS	MISCIBLE	BCIIMNOO	BIONOMIC
BCEIILOP	EPIBOLIC	BCIIMORU	CIBORIUM
BCEIINRS	INSCRIBE	BCIINORV	VIBRONIC
BCEIKNNT	BENTINCK	BCIIOPTY	BIOTYPIC
BCEILMRS	CLIMBERS	BCIISSTU	BISCUITS, CUBIST
BCEILPRU	REPUBLIC	BCIKKNSU	BUCKSKIN
BCEIMNOR	COMBINER	BCIKOSTT	BITSTOCK
BCEIMNOS	COMBINES	BCILLPUY	PUBLICLY
BCEIMORS	MICROBES	BCILMOSY	SYMBOLIC
BCEINORU	BOUNCIER	BCILNOUY	BOUNCILY
BCEINOVX	BICONVEX	BCILOORU	BICOLOUR
BCEIOOPS	BIOSCOPE	BCINORSU	RUBICONS
BCEIOOVX	VOICE BOX	BCINOSSU	SUBSONIC
BCEIORST	BISECTOR	BCINOSTU	SUBTONIC
BCEJNOOT	NO OBJECT	BCIOOPSY	BIOSCOPY
BCEJOORT	OBJECTOR	BCIOORST	ROBOTICS
BCEJSSTU	SUBJECTS	BCKKOOOO	COOKBOOK
BCEKLLNU	BULLNECK	BCKLLOOS	BOLLOCKS
BCEKLNUU	UNBUCKLE	BCKLLOSU	BULLOCKS
BCEKLRSU	BUCKLERS	BCKOOOPY	COPYBOOK
BCEKORSU	ROEBUCKS	BCKOSTTU	BUTTOCKS
BCELLOSW	COWBELLS	BCLMOSUU	COLUMBUS
BCELMOOS	COLOMBES	BCOOORTW	CROWBOOT
BCELMRSU	CRUMBLES	BCOORSSW	CROSSBOW
BCENORSU	BOUNCERS	BCOOSTTY	BOYCOTTS
BCEOORST	OCTOBERS	BCOOSTUY	BOY SCOUT
BCEOORTU	CUBE ROOT	BCORSTTU	OBSTRUCT
BCEORRWY	COWBERRY	BDDDEEEM	EMBEDDED
BCFGLLOU	GOLF CLUB	BDDDEEIM	IMBEDDED
BCFIIMOR	MORBIFIC	BDDEEESS	SEEDBEDS
BCFIIORT	FIBROTIC	BDDEEGGU	DEBUGGED
BCFILORY	FORCIBLY	BDDEEGTU	BUDGETED

BDDEEIMM	BEDIMMED
BDDEEIMO	EMBODIED
BDDEEINT	INDEBTED
BDDEEINW	BINDWEED
BDDEEIRS	BIRDSEED
BDDEEISS	BEDSIDES
BDDEEKNU	DEBUNKED
BDDEENRU	BURDENED
BDDEEORR	BORDERED
BDDEGINR	BRIDGEND
BDDEINNU	UNBIDDEN
BDDEINOU	UNBODIED
BDDEINRU	UNDERBID
BDDEIORS	DISROBED
BDDEISSU	SUBSIDED
BDDELOOR	BLOOD RED
BDDEORTU	OBTRUDED
BDDEOTYY	TEDDY BOY
BDDGIORS	BIRD DOGS
BDDGOOSY	DOGSBODY
BDDHIIRY	DIHYBRID
BDDHIMSU	BUDDHISM
BDDHISTU	BUDDHIST
BDDMNOUW	DUMB DOWN
BDEEEGIS	BESIEGED
BDEEEHTU	HEBETUDE
BDEEEILV	BELIEVED
BDEEELLR	REBELLED
BDEEELLV	BEVELLED
BDEEELRS	BLEEDERS
BDEEERTT	BETTERED
BDEEFFRU	BUFFERED, REBUFFED
BDEEFFTU	BUFFETED
BDEEFINR	BEFRIEND
BDEEFITT	BEFITTED
BDEEFOOR	FOREBODE
BDEEFOOW	BEEFWOOD
BDEEGGIW	BEWIGGED
BDEEGGRU	BEGRUDGE, BUGGERED
BDEEGILN	BLEEDING
BDEEGILU	BEGUILED
BDEEGINR	BREEDING
BDEEGLNO	BELONGED
BDEEHIRS	HEBRIDES
BDEEHLNO	BEHOLDEN
BDEEHLOR	BEHOLDER
BDEEHMOR	HOMEBRED
BDEEHORT	BOTHERED
BDEEIILL	ELIDIBLE
BDEEIILN	INEDIBLE
BDEEILLL	LIBELLED
BDEEILLT	BILLETED
BDEEILNN	BED LINEN

BDEEILNO	BONE-IDLE	BDEILLMU	BDELLIUM	BDEORRUW	BURROWED
BDEEILNR	RENDIBLE	BDEILLOW	BILLOWED	BDEORSTU	DOUBTERS,
BDEEILNV	VENDIBLE	BDEILNRS	BLINDERS		REDOUBTS
BDEEILRW	BEWILDER	BDEILNRU	UNBRIDLE	BDFFIPRU	PUFFBIRD
BDEEIMST	BEDTIMES	BDEILORV	LOVEBIRD	BDFGNOOU	FOGBOUND
BDEEINOT	OBEDIENT	BDEILOSS	BODILESS	BDFIIITY	BIFIDITY
BDEEIRRV	RIVERBED	BDEILRRY	LYREBIRD	BDFILLLO	BILLFOLD
BDEEIRST	BESTRIDE	BDEILRST	BRISTLED,	BDFILNOO	BLOODFIN
BDEEIRSY	BIRD'S-EYE		DRIBLETS	BDFIRRSU	SURFBIRD
BDEEKNRU	DEBUNKER	BDEILRSU	BUILDERS	BDFLOTUU	DOUBTFUL
BDEELLOW	BELLOWED	BDEIMORS	BROMIDES	BDGGIINR	BRIDGING
BDEELLRW	WELL-BRED	BDEIMORY	EMBRYOID	BDGIIKNR	KINGBIRD
BDEELMNO	EMBOLDEN	BDEINOOS	NOBODIES	BDGIILNN	BLINDING
BDEELMRT	TREMBLED	BDEINOOW	WOODBINE	BDGIILNU	BUILDING
BDEELMRU	LUMBERED	BDEINORV	OVENBIRD	BDGIINNS	BINDINGS
BDEELNNO	ENNOBLED	BDEINOSU	BEDOUINS	BDGILNNU	BUNDLING
BDEELNRS	BLENDERS	BDEINSTW	TWIN BEDS	BDGILNOO	BLOODING
BDEELORU	REDOUBLE	BDEIOORR	BROODIER	BDGILNOU	DOUBLING
BDEELOSV	BELOVEDS	BDEIORRS	DISROBER	BDGINNOU	BOUNDING
BDEEMNOT	ENTOMBED	BDEIORSV	OVERBIDS	BDGINOOR	BROODING
BDEEMNRU	NUMBERED	BDEIOSUX	SUBOXIDE	BDGINORS	SONGBIRD
BDEEMOSS	EMBOSSED	BDEIOSWY	WIDE BOYS	BDGINOTU	DOUBTING
BDEENPRS	PREBENDS	BDEIRSSU	DISBURSE,	BDGINSUU	SUBDUING
BDEEORRR	BORDERER		SUBSIDER	BDGIRSUU	DUISBURG
BDEEORSS	BEDSORES	BDEKNOOS	BOOKENDS	BDGKOOOO	GOOD BOOK
BDEEORST	BESTRODE	BDELLOOR	BORDELLO,	BDGLLOSU	BULLDOGS
BDEEORSV	OBSERVED		DOORBELL	BDGNRUUY	BURGUNDY
BDEEORTU	OUTBREED	BDELLOUZ	BULLDOZE	BDHIMOOR	RHOMBOID
BDEEOSSS	OBSESSED	BDELMSTU	STUMBLED	BDHLMOTU	HUMBOLDT
BDEEOSSY	BOSS-EYED	BDELNNOW	END-BLOWN	BDHMOSUW	DUMB SHOW
BDEEOSTT	BESOTTED	BDELNOOW	NEW BLOOD	BDIIINRS	BRINDISI
BDEEOSTW	BESTOWED	BDELNOSS	BOLDNESS	BDIIIORV	VIBRIOID
BDEEPRRU	PUREBRED	BDELNOST	BLONDEST	BDIIJOTU	DJIBOUTI
BDEERRWY	DEWBERRY	BDELNOTU	UNBOLTED	BDIIMRRU	RUBIDIUM
BDEERTTU	BUTTERED,	BDELNRSU	BLUNDERS	BDILLOOY	BLOODILY
	REBUTTED	BDELORSU	BOULDERS	BDILMORY	MORBIDLY
BDEGHILT	BLIGHTED	BDELORTU	TROUBLED	BDILNPRU	PURBLIND
BDEGIINT	BETIDING,	BDELORUU	DOUBLURE	BDILOORY	BROODILY
	DEBITING	BDELOSTU	DOUBLETS	BDILPSUU	BUILDUPS
BDEGILNN	BLENDING	BDEMNSSU	DUMBNESS	BDIMNORU	MORIBUND
BDEGIORX	OXBRIDGE	BDEMOORS	BEDROOMS	BDINNRUW	WINDBURN
BDEGLMRU	GRUMBLED	BDEMOOSY	SOMEBODY	BDINORSW	SNOWBIRD
BDEGLNOU	BLUDGEON	BDEMSSUU	SUBSUMED	BDINSSTU	DUSTBINS
BDEGOOSY	GOODBYES	BDENNOTU	DUBONNET	BDIOORSU	BOUDOIRS
BDEGORRY	DOGBERRY	BDENNRUU	UNBURDEN	BDKNOOOR	DOORKNOB
BDEHLORT	BERTHOLD	BDENOOTW	BENTWOOD	BDKOOORW	WORDBOOK
BDEHLSUV	BUSHVELD	BDENORSU	BOUNDERS,	BDKOORWY	BODYWORK
BDEHMOOY	HOMEBODY		REBOUNDS, SUBORNED	BDKOOSTU	STUDBOOK
BDEHOOOO	BOOHOOED	BDENOTTU	BUTTONED	BDLNOOOU	DOUBLOON
BDEHORTW	BEDWORTH	BDENRUUY	UNDERBUY	BDLOSTUW	DUSTBOWL
BDEIIKLR	BIRDLIKE	BDEOORRS	BROODERS	BDNOOPTU	POTBOUND
BDEIIKRT	DIRT BIKE	BDEOORRW	BORROWED	BDNOOSUX	SOUNDBOX
BDEIILMR	BIRDLIME	BDEOPSST	BEDPOSTS	BDNOOTUU	OUTBOUND
BDEIILNY	INEDIBLY	BDEORRSU	SUBORDER	BDNORSUW	RUBDOWNS
BDEIILTY	DEBILITY	BDEORRTU	OBTRUDER		

BDORUWZZ	BUZZWORD	BEEHNRRT	BRETHREN	BEESTTTU	TEST TUBE
BEEEEFLN	ENFEEBLE	BEEHRSST	SHERBETS	BEFGIINR	BRIEFING
BEEEEENRT	TEREBENE	BEEIILNZ	ZIBELINE	BEFGILNU	FUNGIBLE
BEEEEENRZ	EBENEZER	BEEIJLSU	JUBILEES	BEFGIRRU	FREIBURG
BEEEFIRS	FREEBIES	BEEIKLWY	BIWEEKLY	BEFGIRSU	FIREBUGS
BEEEFIST	BEEFIEST	BEEILLLR	LIBELLER	BEFHILSU	BLUEFISH
BEEEFLNT	BENFLEET	BEEILLNO	LOBELINE	BEFHINOS	BONEFISH
BEEEFLST	FEEBLEST	BEEILLTT	BELITTLE	BEFILLMU	BLUE FILM
BEEEGIRS	BESIEGER	BEEILMPR	PERIBLEM	BEFILLXY	FLEXIBLY
BEEEGNRR	BERENGER	BEEILNNO	BENNE OIL	BEFILMOR	FORELIMB
BEEEGRTT	BEGETTER	BEEILNRY	BERYLINE	BEFILOUY	LIFE BUOY
BEEEHISV	BEEHIVES	BEEILNSS	SENSIBLE	BEFINORS	BONFIRES
BEEEHNOY	HONEYBEE	BEEILNST	STILBENE, TENSIBLE	BEFLLLUY	BELLYFUL
BEEEHNSS	SHEBEENS	BEEILNSU	NEBULISE	BEFLORUW	FURBELOW
BEEEILLL	LIBELLEE	BEEILNUZ	NEBULIZE	BEFNOORR	FORBORNE
BEEEILNS	BEELINES	BEEILRRT	TERRIBLE	BEGGIINN	BEGINING
BEEEILRV	BELIEVER	BEEILRTU	RUBELITE	BEGGINOR	INGEBORG
BEEEJLSZ	JEZEBELS	BEEILRYZ	BREEZILY	BEGGINRS	GINSBERG
BEEEKLRY	BERKELEY	BEEIMRTT	EMBITTER	BEGGIOST	BOGGIEST
BEEELMNS	ENSEMBLE	BEEIRSSU	SUBERISE	BEGGOORT	GOTEBORG
BEEELMRS	RESEMBLE	BEEIRSUZ	SUBERIZE	BEGHILRT	BLIGHTER
BEEELMZZ	EMBEZZLE	BEEIRTVY	EVERY BIT	BEGHINRT	BERTHING, BRIGHTEN
BEEELPRS	BLEEPERS	BEEKMOPR	PEMBROKE	BEGHIOST	GOBSHITE
BEEELRVY	BEVERLEY	BEEKNOPS	BESPOKEN	BEGHLNOU	BUNGHOLE
BEEEMMRR	REMEMBER	BEELLORW	BELLOWER	BEGHOSTU	BESOUGHT
BEEFFRTU	BUFFETER	BEELLSUY	BULL'S-EYE	BEGHRRSU	BURGHERS
BEEFILLT	LIFE BELT	BEELMNNO	NOBLEMEN	BEGIILLN	LIBELING
BEEFILLX	FLEXIBLE	BEELMRRT	TREMBLER	BEGIIMRT	BIG-TIMER
BEEFILNU	UNBELIEF	BEELMRRU	LUMBERER	BEGIIRTT	BRIGITTE
BEEFILRS	BELFRIES	BEELMRST	TREMBLES	BEGIKNRU	REBUKING
BEEFINST	BENEFITS	BEELNNOR	ENNOBLER	BEGILLLU	BLUEGILL, GULLIBLE
BEEFIRSS	FRISBEES	BEELNOSS	BONELESS	BEGILNNY	BENIGNLY
BEEFLORU	BEFOULER	BEELNSSU	BLUENESS	BEGILNOW	ELBOWING
BEEFNORR	FREEBORN	BEELOOST	OBSOLETE	BEGILNRT	TREBLING
BEEFOORT	FREEBOOT	BEELRTUU	TRUE-BLUE	BEGILNSS	BLESSING, GLIBNESS
BEEGHILW	BIG WHEEL	BEELSSTU	TUBELESS	BEGILSTU	BULGIEST
BEEGHLTU	THE BULGE	BEEMNORV	NOVEMBER	BEGINNOR	RINGBONE
BEEGIILL	ELIGIBLE	BEEMNRSU	E NUMBERS	BEGINORS	GISBORNE, SOBERING
BEEGIILX	EXIGIBLE	BEEMOORY	RYE-BROME	BEGLLOSU	GLOBULES
BEEGILNP	BLEEPING	BEEMORSS	EMBOSSER	BEGLMRRU	GRUMBLER
BEEGILNT	BEETLING	BEENORTV	VERBOTEN	BEGLMRSU	GRUMBLES
BEEGILNV	BEVELING	BEENRSTW	BESTREWN	BEGLMSUU	BLUE GUMS
BEEGILRU	BEGUILER	BEENRTTU	BRUNETTE	BEGLNOOU	BOULOGNE
BEEGINNR	BEGINNER	BEEOORRT	ROOT BEER	BEGLNRSU	BUNGLERS
BEEGINSW	BEESWING	BEEOORRV	OVERBORE	BEGLNRUU	LUNEBURG
BEEGLNOR	GRENOBLE	BEEOORTT	BEETROOT	BEGNORRU	ORENBURG
BEEGMRSU	SUBMERGE	BEEORRSV	OBSERVER	BEGNSSUU	SUBGENUS
BEEGNOTT	BEGOTTEN	BEEORRSU	SUBEROSE	BEHIISTX	EXHIBITS
BEEHIKLR	HERBLIKE	BEEORSTU	TUBEROSE	BEHIKLOS	BLOKEISH
BEEHILMN	BLENHEIM	BEEORSTW	BESTOWER	BEHIKOSS	KIBOSHES
BEEHIMOT	BOEHMITE	BEEORSWY	EYEBROWS	BEHIKPSU	PUSHBIKE
BEEHLLNT	HELL-BENT	BEEQSSTU	BEQUESTS		
BEEHLOOR	BOREHOLE	BEERRTTU	REBUTTER		
BEEHMORW	HOME BREW	BEERSSUV	SUBSERVE		

BEHILLOS	SHOEBILL	BEILMRST	TIMBRELS	BELMOPRS	PROBLEMS
BEHILLTY	BLITHELY	BEILNNTU	BUNTLINE	BELMORSY	SOMBRELY
BEHILMRW	WHIMBREL	BEILNSSY	SENSIBLY	BELMPRSU	PLUMBERS
BEHILMST	THIMBLES	BEILOPPW	BLOWPIPE	BELMPRUY	PLUMBERY
BEHILNPY	BIPHENYL	BEILOPSS	POSSIBLE	BELMRRUY	MULBERRY
BEHILORR	HORRIBLE	BEILOQSU	OBLIQUES	BELMRSTU	STUMBLER,
BEHILORS	BOLSHIER	BEILORRS	BROILERS		TUMBLERS, TUMBRELS
BEHILRTU	THURIBLE	BEILORTT	LIBRETTO	BELMSSTU	STUMBLES
BEHIMNOO	BONHOMIE	BEILORWZ	BLOWZIER	BELNOSUU	NEBULOUS
BEHINNOS	SHINBONE	BEILOSTW	BLOWIEST	BELNSSTU	SUNBELTS
BEHINOSW	WISHBONE	BEILRRTY	TERRIBLY	BELOOOSX	LOOSEBOX
BEHISSTU	BUSHIEST	BEILRSST	BLISTERS, BRISTLES	BELOOPRS	BLOOPERS
BEHLLOOT	BOLTHOLE	BEILRSTU	BURLIEST	BELOOPRT	BOLTROPE
BEHLLOOW	BLOWHOLE	BEILRTTY	BITTERLY	BELOOSST	BOOTLESS
BEHLMSTU	HUMBLEST	BEILSTTU	SUBTITLE	BELOOTUV	OBVOLUTE
BEHLORST	BROTHELS	BEIMNORY	IN EMBRYO	BELORRTU	TROUBLER
BEHLRSSU	BLUSHERS	BEIMNSSU	NIMBUSES	BELORSST	BOLSTERS,
BEHMNOTU	ON THE BUM	BEIMOORS	RIBOSOME		LOBSTERS
BEHNOOPX	PHONE BOX	BEIMORTY	BIOMETRY	BELORSTT	BLOTTERS
BEHNRSTU	BURTHENS	BEIMPSTU	BUMPIEST	BELORSTU	TROUBLES
BEHOORSX	HORSEBOX	BEINNOSS	BONINESS	BELOSSUY	BLESS YOU!
BEHOOSUY	HOUSEBOY	BEINNOST	BONNIEST	BELOSTUY	OBTUSELY
BEHORRST	BROTHERS	BEINOQRU	QUIBERON	BELPRSUY	SUPERBLY
BEHORSSU	ROSEBUSH	BEINORSW	BROWNIES	BELRSSSU	BRUSSELS
BEIILMMO	IMMOBILE	BEINOSTU	BOUNTIES	BELRSTTU	RUST BELT
BEIILMOS	MOBILISE	BEINRSTT	BITTERNS	BELRSTUY	BLUSTERY
BEIILMOZ	MOBILIZE	BEINRSTU	TRIBUNES,	BELSSTTU	SUBTLEST
BEIILNNR	BIN-LINER		TURBINES	BELSTTUY	SUBTLETY
BEIILRST	TRILBIES	BEINSSSU	BUSINESS	BEMNNSSU	NUMBNESS
BEIILRSX	EX LIBRIS	BEIOOSTZ	BOOZIEST	BEMNOORT	TROMBONE
BEIILRTT	LIBRETTI	BEIOQTUU	BOUTIQUE	BEMNOORW	NEW BROOM
BEIILSTT	STILBITE	BEIORSTY	SOBRIETY	BEMNOOXY	MONEYBOX
BEIINSTT	STIBNITE	BEIOSSST	BOSSIEST	BEMOORRS	SOMBRERO
BEIIOPSS	BIOPSIES	BEIRRSSU	BRUISERS	BEMORSST	MOBSTERS
BEIISTTT	BITTIEST	BEIRSTTU	TRIBUTES	BENNOORS	SORBONNE
BEIJNORT	TJIREBON	BEISSTTU	BUSTIEST	BENOORSU	BURNOOSE
BEIKLMOT	TOMBLIKE	BEJJMOTU	JUMBO JET	BENORRSU	SUBORNER
BEIKLMOW	WOMBLIKE	BEJORTTU	TURBOJET	BENORRTU	TRUEBORN
BEIKLMRY	KIMBERLY	BEKLNORY	BROKENLY	BENORSTW	BROWNEST
BEIKLNRS	BLINKERS	BEKLNTTU	BLUNKETT	BENORSTY	RENT BOYS
BEIKLOSS	OBELISKS	BEKLOORU	RULEBOOK	BENSSSUY	BUSYNESS
BEIKLOTY	KILOBYTE	BEKLOOST	BOOKLETS	BEOOPSUZ	BOOZE-UPS
BEIKLSTU	BULKIEST	BEKNNORU	UNBROKEN	BEOORRRW	BORROWER
BEIKNOST	STEINBOK	BEKNOOOT	NOTEBOOK	BEOORSST	BOOSTERS
BEIKNRRY	INKBERRY	BEKNOORR	BROOKNER	BEOPRRSV	PROVERBS
BEIKOORT	BROOKITE	BEKOOORV	OVERBOOK	BEOPRSSX	PRESS BOX
BEIKRSST	BRISKEST	BEKOOTTX	TEXTBOOK	BEOQSTUU	BOUQUETS
BEILLMSS	LIMBLESS	BELLLLPU	BELLPULL	BEORRRUW	BURROWER
BEILLNTU	BULLETIN	BELLOPTY	POTBELLY	BEORSTUU	TUBEROUS
BEILLORS	BROLLIES	BELLORTW	BELLWORT	BERSSTTU	BUTTRESS
BEILLMMOS	EMBOLISM	BELLOSWX	SWELL BOX	BFFGILNU	BLUFFING
BEILMNOU	NOBELIUM	BELMNOOU	BLUE MOON	BFFHORSU	BRUSH-OFF
BEILMNRU	UNLIMBER	BELMOORS	BLOOMERS	BFFLLOUY	BULLY-OFF
BEILMNST	NIMBLEST	BELMOORY	BLOOMERY	BFFLMOPU	OFF PLUMB
				BFFLOTUU	OUTBLUFF

BFFNOOSU	BUFFOONS	BGILMNTU	TUMBLING	BIIQTUUY	UBIQUITY
BFFNOSUX	SNUFFBOX	BGILMOSU	GUMBOILS	BIIRSSTU	BURSITIS
BFGILMNU	FUMBLING	BGILMOTU	GUMBOTIL	BIKMNPSU	BUMPKINS
BFGIORRU	FRIBOURG	BGILNNTU	BLUNTING	BIKMTTUU	TIMBUKTU
BFGLLORU	BULLFROG	BGILNORT	RINGBOLT	BIKOOUUZ	BOUZOUKI
BFHIILLS	BILLFISH	BGILNORY	BORINGLY	BILLNOOU	BOUILLON,
BFHILOST	FISHBOLT	BGILNOTT	BLOTTING,		BOULLION
BFHILOSW	BLOWFISH,	BGILNOTT	BOTTLING	BILLOWYZ	BLOWZILY
FISHBOWL		BGILNRRU	BLURRING	BILMMPSU	PLUMBISM
BFHIMNSU	NUMBFISH	BGILNRTU	BLURTING	BILMOSTU	BOTULISM
BFIIORSS	FIBROSIS	BGILNSTU	BUSTLING	BILNNOOY	LOONY BIN
BFILLSSU	BLISSFUL	BGINNORW	BROWNING	BILOORST	SORBITOL
BFIMORTU	TUBIFORM	BGINNORZ	BRONZING	BILOPSSY	POSSIBLY
BFLLNOWY	FLYBLOWN	BGINOOST	BOOSTING	BIMNORSY	BYRONISM
BFLOORSU	SUBFLOOR	BGINORSW	BROWSING	BIMNOSTY	SYMBIONT
BGGGILNO	BOGGLING	BGINRSTU	BURSTING	BIMNRUUV	VIBURNUM
BGGIILNO	OBLIGING	BGJOSTUY	TOBY JUGS	BIMOORST	ROBOTISM
BGGIILNY	GIBINGLY	BGKLOOOS	LOGBOOKS	BINNOORS	ROBINSON
BGGILNNU	BUNGLING	BGKNOOOS	SONGBOOK	BIOOPSTT	POST-OBIT
BGGILNRU	BURGLING	BGLNOOSW	LONGBOWS	BIOPRSTW	BOWSPRIT
BGHHINOR	HIGHBORN	BGLOORYY	BRYOLOGY	BIORRSTU	BURRITOS
BGHHIORW	HIGHBROW	BGMNOOOR	GOMBROON	BIORSTUY	BISTOURY
BGHHIOSY	HIGHBOYS	BGMOOSTU	GUMBOOTS	BJOPPTUU	PUT-UP JOB
BGHIIKNT	THINK BIG	BGOPRSSU	SUBGROUP	BKKOOORW	WORKBOOK
BGHILMNU	HUMBLING	BGRRUUWZ	WURZBURG	BKLNOORY	BROOKLYN
BGHILNSU	BLUSHING	BHIILMPS	BLIMPISH	BKMOOORW	BOOKWORM
BGHILOTX	LIGHT BOX	BHIIOPRT	PROHIBIT	BLLLLOOY	LOBLOLLY
BGHIMNTU	THUMBING	BHIKLLOO	BILLHOOK	BLLMOORW	BOLLWORM
BGHINORT	BRIGHTON	BHILLNOR	HORNBILL	BLMOOOTY	LOBOTOMY
BGHINRSU	BRUSHING	BHILLSTU	BULLSHIT	BLMOOSSS	BLOSSOMS
BGHIOSST	BIG SHOTS	BHILORRY	HORRIBLY	BLMOPSUU	PLUMBOUS
BGHMORSU	HOMBURGS	BHILOSYY	BOYISHLY	BLOORSWW	LOWBROWS
BGHOORSU	BOROUGHS	BHIMNORT	THROMBIN	BLOOSTUW	BLOWOUTS
BGIIKLNN	BLINKING	BHINORSW	BROWNISH	BLOPSSTU	SUBPLOTS
BGIILNOR	BROILING	BHINORTU	THONBURI	BLORSTUY	ROBUSTLY
BGIILNRS	BRISLING	BHJLLNOU	JOHN BULL	BLOSTUUU	TUBULOUS
BGIILNSS	SIBLINGS	BHKNOOOR	HORNBOOK	BMNOOSST	BONS MOTS
BGIILNTY	BITINGLY	BHKOOOPS	BOOKSHOP	BMOOORSX	BOXROOMS
BGIILNTZ	BLITZING	BHLLNORU	BULLHORN	BMOORSSU	SOMBROUS
BGIINORT	ORBITING	BHLMNOOR	BORNHOLM	BMOORSTU	MOTORBUS
BGIINRSU	BRUISING	BHMNTTUU	THUMBNUT	BMOORTTY	BOTTOMRY
BGIINRTU	BRUITING	BHMORSTU	THROMBUS	BNNORTUW	NUT-BROWN
BGIJLMNU	JUMBLING	BHMPSTUU	THUMBS UP	BNNOTTUU	UNBUTTON
BGIKLNOT	KINGBOLT	BHOOSSTW	BOWSHOTS	BNNRSTUU	SUNBURNT
BGIKNOOR	BROOKING	BHPRSSUU	BRUSH-UPS	BNOOOSUY	SONOBUOY
BGIKNOOS	BOOKINGS	BIIKMRSS	SIMBIRSK	BNORSTUU	BURNOUTS
BGILLLUY	GULLIBLY	BIIKNOUV	BUKOVINI	BNRSSTUU	SUNBURST
BGILLNOU	GLOBULIN	BIILLNOS	BILLIONS	BOOPRSSU	BOSPORUS
BGILLNRU	BULLRING	BIILMOTY	MOBILITY	BOORSSTY	SOB STORY
BGILLNUY	BULLYING	BIILNOOV	OBLIVION	BOPSSSTU	BUS STOPS
BGILMMNU	MUMBLING	BIILNOTY	NOBILITY	BORSTTUU	OUTBURST
BGILMNOO	BLOOMING	BIILNTUY	NUBILITY	CCCEIILT	ECLECTIC
BGILMNPU	PLUMBING	BIILOSSY	BIOLYSIS	CCCEGOSY	COCCYGES
BGILMNRU	RUMBLING	BIIMMOSZ	ZOMBIISM	CCCEHIOS	CHOC-ICES

241

CCCEILNY	ENCYCLIC	CCEEITTU	EUTECTIC
CCCIINSU	SUCCINIC	CCEEKLOR	COCKEREL
CCCILNOY	CYCLONIC	CCEEKNRW	CREW NECK
CCCINSTU	SUCCINCT	CCEELMNY	CLEMENCY
CCCKOORW	COCKCROW	CCEEMMNO	COMMENCE
CCDDEENO	CONCEDED	CCEEMMOR	COMMERCE
CCDDENOU	CONDUCED	CCEENNOS	ENSCONCE
CCDEEENR	CREDENCE	CCEENORT	CONCRETE
CCDEEHLN	CLENCHED	CCEENRST	CRESCENT
CCDEEIOP	CODPIECE	CCEFIIPS	SPECIFIC
CCDEEKOY	COCKEYED	CCEFIRRU	CRUCIFER
CCDEELRY	RECYCLED	CCEFLLOU	FLOCCULE
CCDEHILN	CLINCHED	CCEFLOOS	FLOCCOSE
CCDEHIPU	HICCUPED	CCEGHIKN	CHECKING
CCDEHKLU	CHUCKLED	CCEGILRY	GLYCERIC
CCDEHLTU	CLUTCHED	CCEGINOR	COERCING
CCDEHNRU	CRUNCHED	CCEHHRSU	CHURCHES
CCDEHORS	SCORCHED	CCEHIIMS	ISCHEMIC
CCDEHORU	CROUCHED	CCEHIKNS	CHECK-INS,
CCDEHOST	SCOTCHED		CHICKENS
CCDEIINO	COINCIDE	CCEHILNR	CLINCHER
CCDEINOT	OCCIDENT	CCEHILNS	CLINCHES
CCDEIOPU	OCCUPIED	CCEHILOR	CHOLERIC
CCDELNOU	CONCLUDE	CCEHILOY	CHOICELY
CCDENOOO	COCOONED	CCEHINOR	CORNICHE
CCDENORU	CONDUCER	CCEHINOZ	ZECCHINO
CCDEORRU	OCCURRED	CCEHINST	TECHNICS
CCDEOSTU	STUCCOED	CCEHIORT	RICOCHET
CCDHIILO	CICHLOID	CCEHIOST	CHOICEST
CCDHIIOR	DICHROIC	CCEHKLRU	CHUCKLER
CCDHINOO	CONCHOID	CCEHKLSU	CHUCKLES
CCDIILOS	CODICILS	CCEHKOTU	CHECKOUT
CCDIINOS	SCINCOID	CCEHKPSU	CHECKUPS
CCDIIORT	DICROTIC	CCEHLMOR	CROMLECH
CCDKLOOR	OLD CROCK	CCEHLNNU	UNCLENCH
CCDKLOSU	CUCKOLDS	CCEHLSTU	CLUTCHES
CCDKOOOW	WOODCOCK	CCEHORRS	SCORCHER
CCDLOSTU	COLD CUTS	CCEHORSS	SCORCHES
CCEEELMN	CLEMENCE	CCEHORST	CROTCHES
CCEEHKRS	CHECKERS	CCEHORTT	CROTCHET
CCEEHLNS	CLENCHES	CCEHRSTU	CRUTCHES
CCEEHRSY	SCREECHY	CCEIIKLN	NICKELIC
CCEEILNR	ENCIRCLE	CCEIIKPS	ICE PICKS
CCEEILNS	LICENCES	CCEIILNT	ENCLITIC
CCEEILNT	ELENCTIC	CCEIILOR	LICORICE
CCEEILPY	EPICYCLE	CCEIILPT	ECLIPTIC
CCEEILRT	ELECTRIC	CCEIILST	SCILICET
CCEEIMNU	ECUMENIC	CCEIILTU	LEUCITIC
CCEEINOR	CICERONE	CCEIKOST	COCKIEST
CCEEINOV	CONCEIVE	CCEIKRST	CRICKETS
CCEEINSS	SCIENCES	CCEILNUY	UNICYCLE
CCEEIORV	COERCIVE	CCEILRRU	CURRICLE
CCEEIRSV	CERVICES,	CCEILRST	CIRCLETS
	CREVICES	CCEILRSY	CRESYLIC

CCEILRTY	TRICYCLE
CCEILRUU	CURLICUE
CCEILSTU	CUTICLES
CCEIMNOO	ECONOMIC
CCEIMOST	COSMETIC
CCEIMRRU	MERCURIC
CCEINNOV	CONVINCE
CCEINOOR	COERCION
CCEINOOZ	CENOZOIC
CCEINORS	CORNICES
CCEINORT	NECROTIC
CCEINOST	CONCEITS
CCEINOTT	TECTONIC
CCEINPRT	PRECINCT
CCEINRTU	CINCTURE
CCEINSZZ	SZCZECIN
CCEIOORT	CROCOITE
CCEIOPRU	OCCUPIER
CCEIOPTY	ECOTYPIC
CCEIORST	CORTICES
CCEIPRTU	CUT-PRICE
CCEIPSST	SCEPTICS
CCEIRSSU	CIRCUSES
CCEKNOSY	COCKNEYS
CCEKORRY	CROCKERY
CCEKORSU	COCKSURE
CCELLOST	COLLECTS
CCELNOSY	CYCLONES
CCENNORS	CONCERNS
CCENOORT	CONCERTO
CCENOPST	CONCEPTS
CCENORST	CONCERTS
CCENRRUY	CURRENCY
CCEORSSU	CROCUSES
CCERSTUW	CREW CUTS
CCFFHKOU	CHUCK OFF
CCFIIRUX	CRUCIFIX
CCFILNOT	CONFLICT
CCGHIKNO	CHOCKING
CCGHIKNU	CHUCKING
CCGHINOU	COUCHING
CCGIIKLN	CLICKING
CCGIIKNR	CRICKING
CCGIILNR	CIRCLING
CCGIKLNO	CLOCKING
CCGIKLNU	CLUCKING
CCGILLOY	GLYCOLIC
CCGILOSU	GLUCOSIC
CCGINOTW	TWOCCING
CCHHIITY	ICHTHYIC
CCHHINOU	CHIN-CHOU
CCHHNRUU	UNCHURCH
CCHHOOPP	CHOP-CHOP
CCHHOOWW	CHOW-CHOW

CCHIINUZ	ZUCCHINI	CDDEELUY	DEUCEDLY	CDEEERTT	DETECTER
CCHIIORT	ORCHITIC	CDDEENOS	SECONDED	CDEEERTX	EXCRETED
CCHILMOW	MILCH COW	CDDEEORR	RECORDED	CDEEETUX	EXECUTED
CCHIPSSY	PSYCHICS	CDDEERUV	DECURVED	CDEEFFOR	FORCE-FED
CCHKMSSU	SCHMUCKS	CDDEFIIO	CODIFIED	CDEEFIIS	EDIFICES
CCIILLRY	CYRILLIC	CDDEFINO	CONFIDED	CDEEFIIT	FETICIDE
CCIIMNSY	CYNICISM	CDDEGIIN	DECIDING	CDEEFINT	INFECTED
CCIINORZ	ZIRCONIC	CDDEGINO	DECODING	CDEEFIRR	FREDERIC
CCIIRSTU	CIRCUITS	CDDEGINU	DEDUCING	CDEEFKLR	FRECKLED
CCIIRTUY	CIRCUITRY	CDDEHIRT	REDDITCH	CDEEFKOR	FOREDECK
CCIKKLOP	PICKLOCK	CDDEIINT	INDICTED	CDEEFLOT	COLD FEET
CCIKKOTT	TICKTOCK	CDDEIKOS	DOCKSIDE	CDEEFNOR	ENFORCED
CCIKLOSW	COWLICKS	CDDEILLO	COLLIDED	CDEEFORT	DEFECTOR
CCIKOPST	COCKPITS	CDDEILMS	MIDDLE CS	CDEEGIIR	REGICIDE
CCILNOSU	COUNCILS	CDDEILNU	INCLUDED	CDEEGINO	GENOCIDE
CCILOOPS	PICCOLOS	CDDEILRU	CUDDLIER	CDEEGINR	RECEDING
CCILORUU	CURCULIO	CDDEINTU	INDUCTED	CDEEGINS	SECEDING
CCILOSSY	CYCLOSIS	CDDEIORV	DIVORCED	CDEEGIOS	GEODESIC
CCILSSTY	CYCLISTS	CDDELLOU	COLLUDED	CDEEGIOT	GEODETIC
CCINOPSY	SYNCOPIC	CDDELLOW	COLD-WELD	CDEEHILS	CHISELED
CCINORSY	CRYONICS	CDDELNOO	CONDOLED	CDEEHINR	ENRICHED
CCINOSTV	CONVICTS	CDDENNOO	CONDONED	CDEEHIPR	CIPHERED,
CCIOOPST	SCOTOPIC	CDDENOOR	CORDONED		DECIPHER
CCIOORSS	SIROCCOS	CDDEOORR	CORRODED	CDEEHKST	SKETCHED
CCIOOTXY	OXYTOCIC	CDDEOORT	DOCTORED	CDEEHLSU	SCHEDULE
CCJNNOTU	CONJUNCT	CDDEOPRU	PRODUCED	CDEEHNQU	QUENCHED
CCKMOORU	MOORCOCK	CDDGHILO	GODCHILD	CDEEHNRR	DRENCHER
CCKNORTU	TURNCOCK	CDDGILNO	CODDLING	CDEEHNRW	WRENCHED
CCKOOPST	STOPCOCK	CDDGILNU	CUDDLING	CDEEHORT	HECTORED
CCKOPRSU	COCKSPUR	CDDGINSU	SCUDDING	CDEEHPRY	CYPHERED
CCNOOSTU	COCONUTS	CDDHILOS	CLODDISH	CDEEHRTW	WRETCHED
CCOOSSUU	COUSCOUS	CDDIISTY	DYTISCID	CDEEIILT	ELICITED
CCOOTTUU	TUCOTUCO	CDDIORSS	DISCORDS	CDEEIIMN	MEDICINE
CCORSSTU	CROSSCUT	CDDKORSY	DRY DOCKS	CDEEIIMP	EPIDEMIC
CDDDEETU	DEDUCTED	CDDOOORW	CORDWOOD	CDEEIINT	INDICTEE
CDDEEEEX	EXCEEDED	CDEEEERX	EXCEEDER	CDEEIIRT	DIERETIC
CDDEEEFT	DEFECTED	CDEEEFFT	EFFECTED	CDEEIISV	DECISIVE
CDDEEEIV	DECEIVED	CDEEEFNS	DEFENCES	CDEEIITT	DIETETIC
CDDEEEJT	DEJECTED	CDEEEHNS	ENSCHEDE	CDEEIJNT	INJECTED
CDDEEEPR	PRECEDED	CDEEEHOR	REECHOED	CDEEIJOR	REJOICED
CDDEEETT	DETECTED	CDEEEHSW	ESCHEWED	CDEEIKLN	NICKELED
CDDEEGLU	CUDGELED	CDEEEINV	EVIDENCE	CDEEIKNS	SICKENED
CDDEEHIT	CHEDDITE	CDEEEIRV	DECEIVER,	CDEEIKPT	PICKETED
CDDEEHNR	DRENCHED		RECEIVED	CDEEIKTT	TICKETED
CDDEEIKR	DICKERED	CDEEEJRT	REJECTED	CDEEILNP	PENCILED
CDDEEILN	DECLINED	CDEEELLX	EXCELLED	CDEEILNR	DECLINER,
CDDEEIPT	DEPICTED	CDEEELST	SELECTED		RECLINED
CDDEEIRS	DESCRIED	CDEEEMNT	CEMENTED	CDEEILNS	DECLINES,
CDDEEIRT	CREDITED,	CDEEEMRS	MERCEDES		LICENSED, SILENCED
	DIRECTED	CDEEENRS	SCREENED	CDEEILNT	DENTICLE
CDDEEKOT	DOCKETED	CDEEENRT	CENTERED	CDEEILOR	RECOILED
CDDEEKUW	DUCKWEED	CDEEEPTX	EXCEPTED,	CDEEILPS	ECLIPSED
CDDEELSU	SECLUDED		EXPECTED	CDEEILRT	DERELICT
CDDEELUX	EXCLUDED	CDEEERSS	RECESSED	CDEEIMNR	ENDERMIC
		CDEEERST	SECRETED	CDEEIMOR	MEDIOCRE

CDEEIMOS	COMEDIES	CDEEORTT	DETECTOR	CDEIIIOS	IDIOCIES
CDEEINNS	INCENSED	CDEERRRU	RECURRED	CDEIIKKS	SIDEKICK
CDEEINNT	INDECENT	CDEERSSU	SEDUCERS	CDEIIKMM	MIMICKED
CDEEINRW	CERIDWEN	CDEFFISU	SUFFICED	CDEIIKST	DICKIEST
CDEEIORV	DIVORCEE	CDEFFLSU	SCUFFLED	CDEIILMO	DOMICILE
CDEEIOSS	DIOCESES	CDEFHILN	FLINCHED	CDEIILNN	INCLINED
CDEEIPRT	DECREPIT,	CDEFIIIL	FILICIDE	CDEIILNO	INDOCILE
DEPICTER		CDEFIIIT	CITIFIED	CDEIILOT	IDIOLECT
CDEEIPRU	PEDICURE	CDEFIIOR	CODIFIER	CDEIILPS	DISCIPLE
CDEEIRRS	DESCRIER	CDEFIIST	DEFICITS	CDEIILRU	RIDICULE
CDEEIRRT	REDIRECT	CDEFIKRR	FREDRICK	CDEIIMRT	DIMETRIC
CDEEIRST	DISCREET,	CDEFINNO	CONFINED	CDEIINNT	INCIDENT
DISCRETE		CDEFINOR	CONFIDER	CDEIINOS	DECISION
CDEEIRSV	SERVICED	CDEFLNOU	FLOUNCED	CDEIINOV	INVOICED
CDEEITUV	EDUCTIVE	CDEFNORU	UNFORCED	CDEIINRT	INDIRECT
CDEEJKOY	JOCKEYED	CDEFNOSU	CONFUSED	CDEIINTY	CYTIDINE
CDEEKLPS	SPECKLED	CDEFNOTU	CONFUTED	CDEIIOPR	PERIODIC
CDEEKNOR	RECKONED	CDEFOSSU	FOCUSSED	CDEIIOPS	EPISODIC
CDEEKNRS	REDNECKS	CDEGHORU	GROUCHED	CDEIIOPT	EPIDOTIC
CDEEKOPT	POCKETED	CDEGIILO	GOIDELIC	CDEIIRTU	DIURETIC
CDEEKORT	ROCKETED	CDEGINNO	ENCODING	CDEIISSU	SUICIDES
CDEEKORW	ROCKWEED	CDEGINOY	DECOYING	CDEIKLNR	CRINKLED
CDEEKPRU	PUCKERED	CDEGINRU	REDUCING	CDEIKLPR	PRICKLED
CDEEKRTU	TUCKERED	CDEGINRY	DECRYING	CDEIKLRT	TRICKLED
CDEELMOW	WELCOMED	CDEGINSU	SEDUCING	CDEIKLWY	WICKEDLY
CDEELNOS	ENCLOSED	CDEGINSY	DYSGENIC	CDEIKNOS	SOCKED IN
CDEELNPU	PEDUNCLE	CDEGORSU	SCOURGED	CDEIKNPU	UNPICKED
CDEELNTY	DECENTLY	CDEHIILO	HELICOID	CDEIKORR	RODERICK
CDEELOOW	LOCOWEED	CDEHIIMO	HOMICIDE	CDEIKOST	DIESTOCK
CDEELOST	CLOSETED	CDEHIINO	ECHINOID	CDEIKRRS	DERRICKS
CDEELPRU	PRECLUDE	CDEHIIOS	HESIODIC	CDEILLOU	CELULOID,
CDEELRTU	LECTURED	CDEHIKOT	HOCKTIDE	LODICULE	
CDEELRUX	EXCLUDER	CDEHIKRW	HERDWICK	CDEILLPU	PELLUCID
CDEEMOPR	COMPERED	CDEHILNR	CHILDREN	CDEILMOP	COMPILED,
CDEEMOPT	COMPETED	CDEHILOR	CHLORIDE	COMPLIED	
CDEEMORT	ECTODERM	CDEHILRT	ELDRITCH	CDEILMOY	MYCELOID
CDEENNOS	CONDENSE	CDEHIMRS	SMIRCHED	CDEILMRU	DULCIMER
CDEENNOU	DENOUNCE	CDEHINOS	HEDONICS	CDEILNOS	INCLOSED
CDEENNOV	CONVENED	CDEHINST	SNITCHED	CDEILNRY	CYLINDER
CDEENNTY	TENDENCY	CDEHIOSW	COWHIDES	CDEILOOW	WOODLICE
CDEENORR	CORNERED	CDEHISTT	STITCHED	CDEILOPU	CLUPEOID
CDEENORS	CENSORED,	CDEHISTW	SWITCHED	CDEILORS	SCLEROID
SECONDER, SEEDCORN		CDEHITTW	TWITCHED	CDEILORU	CLOUDIER
CDEENOSY	ECDYSONE	CDEHKLSU	SHELDUCK	CDEILOSS	DISCLOSE
CDEENOTX	COEXTEND	CDEHLOOS	SCHOOLED	CDEILPPR	CRIPPLED
CDEENOVY	CONVEYED	CDEHLORT	CHORTLED	CDEILRTY	DIRECTLY
CDEENPRU	PRUDENCE	CDEHLOSU	SLOUCHED	CDEILSTU	DUCTILES
CDEENRSU	CENSURED	CDEHMOOS	SMOOCHED	CDEILSXY	DYSLEXIC
CDEENSST	DESCENTS	CDEHNOOP	CHENOPOD	CDEIMOST	DOMESTIC
CDEEOOTV	DOVECOTE	CDEHORSU	CHORUSED	CDEIMPRS	SCRIMPED
CDEEOPRS	PROCEEDS	CDEHORSW	COWHERDS	CDEINNOU	UNCOINED
CDEEOPRU	RECOUPED	CDEHOSSW	COWSHEDS	CDEINNOV	CONNIVED
CDEEORRR	RECORDER	CDEIIILS	SILICIDE	CDEINORS	CONSIDER
CDEEORST	CORSETED,	CDEIIIMT	MITICIDE	CDEINORT	CENTROID,
ESCORTED				DOCTRINE	

CDEINOST	D-NOTICES	CDENNOOT	CONNOTED	CDIKNOSW	WINDSOCK
CDEINOTU	EDUCTION	CDENOORT	CREODONT	CDILLOUY	CLOUDILY
CDEINOUV	UNVOICED	CDENOOVY	CONVOYED	CDILOOPZ	PODZOLIC
CDEINPRU	UNPRICED	CDENORTU	TROUNCED	CDILOORT	LORDOTIC
CDEINRRU	INCURRED	CDENOSTU	CONTUSED	CDILOOTY	COTYLOID
CDEINSTY	SYNDETIC	CDENRTUU	UNDERCUT	CDIMOORT	MICRODOT
CDEIOPST	DESPOTIC	CDEOOPST	POSTCODE	CDINNQUU	QUIDNUNC
CDEIOPSZ	ZIP CODES	CDEOORRR	CORRODER	CDINORTU	INDUCTOR
CDEIOPTY	COPY-EDIT	CDEOORSU	DECOROUS	CDINOSTU	CONDUITS,
CDEIORRT	CREDITOR,	CDEOPRRU	PROCURED,		DISCOUNT
	DIRECTOR		PRODUCER	CDIOOPRS	PROSODIC
CDEIORRV	DIVORCER	CDEOORSS	RED CROSS	CDIOORRR	CORRIDOR
CDEIORSV	DISCOVER,	CDEPRRUY	RYDER CUP	CDIOPRRS	RIPCORDS
	DIVORCES	CDERSTTU	DESTRUCT	CDIOPRSU	CUSPIDOR
CDEIPRST	SCRIPTED	CDFFILOR	CLIFFORD	CDKOOORW	CORKWOOD
CDEIPRTU	PICTURED	CDFHILOS	COLD FISH	CDLOOSTW	COTSWOLD
CDEIRRSU	SCURRIED	CDFIILMS	DISC FILM	CDMNOOPU	COMPOUND
CDEIRSTU	CRUDITES,	CDFIILSU	FLUIDICS	CDMNORUU	CORUNDUM
	CURTSIED	CDFKOORR	ROCKFORD	CDNNOOOT	CONODONT
CDEIRSTV	VERDICTS	CDGHIINT	DITCHING	CDOORRUY	CORDUROY
CDEISSSU	DISCUSSES	CDGHINOR	CHORDING	CDOOSTUW	WOODCUTS
CDEJNORU	CONJURED	CDGIINNU	INDUCING	CDOPRSTU	PRODUCTS
CDEKKLNU	KNUCKLED	CDGIKLNU	DUCKLING	CEEEEIPY	EYEPIECE
CDEKLMOR	CLERKDOM	CDGIKLOR	GRIDLOCK	CEEEFFRT	EFFECTER
CDEKLNOU	UNLOCKED	CDGILNOS	SCOLDING	CEEEFNOR	CONFEREE
CDEKLRTU	TRUCKLED	CDGILNOU	CLOUDING	CEEEGITX	EXEGETIC
CDEKNOOV	CONVOKED	CDGILNRU	CURDLING	CEEEGMNR	MERGENCE
CDEKNORU	UNCORKED	CDGINORW	CROWDING	CEEEHIKR	CHEEKIER
CDELLORS	SCROLLED	CDHHIILS	CHILDISH	CEEEHIRR	CHEERIER
CDELLOTU	CLOUDLET	CDHIINNW	CHINDWIN	CEEEHIST	ICE SHEET
CDELMNOU	COLUMNED	CDHIIORT	HIDROTIC,	CEEEHKOR	CHEROKEE
CDELMPRU	CRUMPLED		TRICHOID	CEEEHLMN	MECHELEN
CDELNOOR	CONDOLER	CDHIIOSZ	SCHIZOID	CEEEHNNY	CHEYENNE
CDELNOOS	CONSOLED	CDHILOOP	CHILOPOD	CEEEHPSS	SPEECHES
CDELNOSS	COLDNESS	CDHIMNOR	RICHMOND	CEEEHRSW	ESCHEWER
CDELNOSY	SECONDLY	CDHIOORT	TROCHOID	CEEEIJTV	EJECTIVE
CDELOORS	COLD SORE	CDHIOPRW	WHIPCORD	CEEEILNS	LICENSEE
CDELOORU	COLOURED,	CDHLOOPY	COPYHOLD	CEEEILRT	ERECTILE
	DECOLOUR	CDHOORRU	UROCHORD	CEEEILTV	CLEVEITE,
CDELORSS	CORDLESS	CDIIIORT	DIORITIC		ELECTIVE
CDELPRSU	SCRUPLED	CDIIKMNO	DOMINICK	CEEEIMNN	EMINENCE
CDELRSUY	CURSEDLY	CDIIKPST	DIPSTICK	CEEEINOP	ONE-PIECE
CDELRTUU	CULTURED	CDIILOPP	DIPLOPIC	CEEEIPRR	CREEPIER
CDELSSUY	CUSSEDLY	CDIILOTY	DOCILITY	CEEEIPRV	PERCEIVE
CDELSTTU	SCUTTLED	CDIILTUY	LUCIDITY	CEEEIPST	SET PIECE
CDEMMNOU	COMMUNED	CDIIMNOU	CONIDIUM	CEEEIRRV	RECEIVER
CDEMMOOS	COMMODES	CDIINPRY	CYPRINID	CEEEIRSX	EXERCISE
CDEMMOTU	COMMUTED	CDIINSTT	DISTINCT	CEEEJRRT	REJECTER
CDEMNOOW	COMEDOWN	CDIIOPRT	DIOPTRIC	CEEELRTT	ELECTRET
CDEMNOSU	CONSUMED	CDIIORSU	SCIUROID	CEEEMNRT	CEMENTER,
CDEMNOTU	DOCUMENT	CDIIPTUY	CUPIDITY		CEREMENT
CDEMOOPS	COMPOSED	CDIIRSTT	DISTRICT	CEEEMORT	ECTOMERE
CDEMOPTU	COMPUTED	CDIJNSTU	DISJUNCT	CEEEMRTY	CEMETERY
CDEMPRSU	SCRUMPED	CDIKLPUY	LUCKY DIP	CEEEMSUX	EXCUSE ME!
CDENNOOR	CONDONER			CEEENNST	SENTENCE

CEEENNSV	CEVENNES	
CEEENPRS	PRESENCE	
CEEENPRT	PRETENCE	
CEEENQSU	SEQUENCE	
CEEENRRS	SCREENER	
CEEENRRT·	TERRENCE	
CEEENSSS	ESSENCES	
CEEEPRRS	CREEPERS	
CEEERRTX	EXCRETER	
CEEERSSS	RECESSES	
CEEERTUX	EXECUTER	
CEEESSSX	EXCESSES	
CEEFFINT	IN EFFECT	
CEEFFNOS	OFFENCES	
CEEFFORT	EFFECTOR	
CEEFGILN	FLEECING	
CEEFHIKR	KERCHIEF	
CEEFHLRT	FLETCHER	
CEEFHLRU	CHEERFUL	
CEEFIKKR	FREE KICK	
CEEFILRY	FIERCELY	
CEEFINRT	FRENETIC	
CEEFIRRU	FIRE-CURE	
CEEFIRST	FIERCEST	
CEEFKLRS	FRECKLES	
CEEFKLSS	FECKLESS	
CEEFLNOR	FLORENCE	
CEEFLNTU	FECULENT	
CEEFLRUU	FLUE-CURE	
CEEFNORR	CONFRERE, ENFORCER	
CEEFNRVY	FERVENCY	
CEEFOPRR	PERFORCE	
CEEFORSS	FRESCOES	
CEEFORST	SCOT-FREE	
CEEFPRST	PREFECTS	
CEEGHIKN	CHEEKING	
CEEGHINP	CHEEPING	
CEEGHINR	CHEERING	
CEEGHLOW	COGWHEEL	
CEEGHNRT	GRETCHEN	
CEEGIJNT	EJECTING	
CEEGILNT	ELECTING	
CEEGILOT	ECLOGITE	
CEEGINPR	CREEPING	
CEEGINRT	ERECTING	
CEEGINST	GENETICS	
CEEGINSU	EUGENICS	
CEEGINXY	EXIGENCY	
CEEGIORX	EXOERGIC	
CEEGKNOR	GREENOCK	
CEEGLLMR	GERM CELL	
CEEGLLOS	COLLEGES	
CEEGMNOY	CYMOGENE	

CEEGNNOR	CONGENER	
CEEGNORV	CONVERGE	
CEEGORST	CORTEGES	
CEEHHIRS	CHESHIRE	
CEEHHLRS	HERSCHEL	
CEEHHMNN	HENCHMEN	
CEEHIIST	ETHICISE	
CEEHIITZ	ETHICIZE	
CEEHIKLY	CHEEKILY	
CEEHILLM	MICHELLE	
CEEHILLN	CHENILLE, HELLENIC	
CEEHILRW	CLERIHEW	
CEEHILRY	CHEERILY	
CEEHILSV	VEHICLES	
CEEHILTV	HELVETIC	
CEEHIMRT	HERMETIC	
CEEHIMSS	CHEMISES	
CEEHINPR	ENCIPHER	
CEEHINPT	PHENETIC	
CEEHINRR	ENRICHER	
CEEHINTT	ENTHETIC	
CEEHIOSV	COHESIVE	
CEEHIPRT	HERPETIC	
CEEHIRRS	CHERRIES	
CEEHIRST	CHESTIER, HERETICS	
CEEHIRTT	TETCHIER	
CEEHISTW	CHEWIEST	
CEEHKLRS	HECKLERS	
CEEHKRST	SKETCHER	
CEEHKSST	SKETCHES	
CEEHLLOR	ROCHELLE	
CEEHLNOO	HOLOCENE	
CEEHLNOS	ECHELONS	
CEEHLNSU	ELENCHUS	
CEEHLRSU	HERCULES	
CEEHMRSS	SCHEMERS	
CEEHNNRT	ENTRENCH	
CEEHNORT	COHERENT	
CEEHNQRU	QUENCHER	
CEEHNRRT	RETRENCH, TRENCHER	
CEEHNRST	TRENCHES	
CEEHNRSW	WRENCHES	
CEEHNSST	STENCHES	
CEEHOPRY	CORYPHEE	
CEEHORRT	TORCHERE	
CEEHORST	THE SCORE, TROCHEES	
CEEHQRSU	CHEQUERS	
CEEHRSTW	WRETCHES	
CEEHRSTY	CHERTSEY	
CEEIIKLV	VICELIKE	
CEEIIMNP	MINCE PIE	

CEEIIMRT	EREMITIC	
CEEIINST	NICETIES	
CEEIINVV	EVINCIVE	
CEEIJNOT	EJECTION	
CEEIJORR	REJOICER	
CEEIJRUV	VERJUICE	
CEEIKLNN	NECKLINE	
CEEIKLPR	PICKEREL	
CEEIKNRS	SICKENER	
CEEIKNST	NECKTIES	
CEEIKPRT	PICKETER	
CEEILLLP	PELLICLE	
CEEILLNT	LENTICEL	
CEEILLRV	VERCELLI	
CEEILMNT	MELICENT	
CEEILMOR	COMELIER	
CEEILMPS	SEMPLICE	
CEEILNNU	LUCIENNE	
CEEILNNY	LENIENCY	
CEEILNOP	PLIOCENE	
CEEILNOT	ELECTION	
CEEILNOV	VIOLENCE	
CEEILNRR	RECLINER	
CEEILNRS	LICENSER, SILENCER	
CEEILNSS	SILENCES	
CEEILORR	RECOILER	
CEEILPRS	ECLIPSER	
CEEILPRY	CREEPILY	
CEEILPSS	ECLIPSES	
CEEILQSU	LIQUESCE	
CEEILRST	SCLERITE	
CEEILRSV	VERSICLE	
CEEILRTU	RETICULE	
CEEILRTY	CELERITY	
CEEILSSV	VESICLES	
CEEILSTT	TESTICLE	
CEEIMMPY	EMPYEMIC	
CEEIMMRS	MESMERIC	
CEEIMNPS	SPECIMEN	
CEEIMNST	CENTIMES, TENESMIC	
CEEIMORT	CORE TIME, METEORIC	
CEEINNPZ	PINCE-NEZ	
CEEINNSS	NICENESS	
CEEINNST	NESCIENT	
CEEINOPU	EUPNOEIC	
CEEINORT	ERECTION, NEOTERIC	
CEEINORX	EXOCRINE	
CEEINOTV	EVECTION	
CEEINPRT	TERPENIC	
CEEINPSX	SIXPENCE	
CEEINQRU	QUERCINE	

CEEINRST	SECRETIN	CEEMNOYZ	COENZYME	CEFIIRRT	TERRIFIC
CEEINRSU	INSECURE,	CEEMOORV	OVERCOME	CEFIKLRY	FLICKERY
SINECURE		CEEMOPRS	COMPEERS,	CEFILLLO	FOLLICLE
CEEINRTT	RETICENT	COMPERES		CEFILMRU	MERCIFUL
CEEINRTU	ENURETIC	CEENNOOS	NOSECONE	CEFILNOT	FLECTION
CEEINSSX	IN EXCESS	CEENNORS	ON-SCREEN	CEFILOUV	VOICEFUL
CEEINSTY	CYSTEINE	CEENNORT	CRETONNE	CEFIMOST	COMFIEST
CEEIOPPS	EPISCOPE	CEENNORU	RENOUNCE	CEFINNOS	CONFINES
CEEIOPTW	TWO-PIECE	CEENNORV	CONVENER	CEFINORS	CONIFERS,
CEEIORST	COTERIES,	CEENOOOV	ONCE-OVER	FORENSIC	
ESOTERIC		CEENOPRV	PROVENCE	CEFINORT	INFECTOR
CEEIORSX	EXORCISE	CEENOPTW	TWOPENCE	CEFINOTT	CONFETTI
CEEIORTX	EXOTERIC	CEENORSV	CONSERVE,	CEFIORTY	FEROCITY
CEEIORXZ	EXORCIZE	CONVERSE		CEFKLOOR	FORELOCK
CEEIPPTU	EUPEPTIC	CEENORTT	CORNETTE	CEFKLOST	FETLOCKS
CEEIPRST	RECEIPTS	CEENORVY	CONVEYER	CEFKLPSY	FLYSPECK
CEEIPRSU	EPICURES	CEENPPTU	TUPPENCE	CEFLNOSU	FLOUNCES
CEEIRRST	RECITERS	CEENRSSU	CENSURES	CEFLNRUU	FURUNCLE
CEEIRRSW	SCREWIER	CEENSSSU	CENSUSES	CEFNORTU	CONFUTER
CEEIRSSV	SERVICES	CEENSSTU	CUTENESS	CEFORRST	CROFTERS
CEEIRSTV	VERTICES	CEEOORST	CREOSOTE	CEFORSTU	FRUCTOSE
CEEIRSVX	CERVIXES	CEEOPRRT	RECEPTOR	CEGGHIRS	CHIGGERS
CEEKLNST	NECKLETS	CEEOPRTY	CEROTYPE	CEGGLNOY	GLYCOGEN
CEEKLPSS	SPECKLES	CEEOQTTU	COQUETTE	CEGHHHIT	HIGH TECH
CEEKLRSS	RECKLESS	CEEORRRS	SORCERER	CEGHIINY	HYGIENIC
CEEKNORR	RECKONER	CEEORRSU	RECOURSE,	CEGHIKLN	HECKLING
CEEKOPRX	OXPECKER	RESOURCE		CEGHILLW	CHIGWELL
CEEKRRSW	WRECKERS	CEEORRVY	RECOVERY	CEGHILNW	WELCHING
CEELLMOU	MOLECULE	CEEORSSS	SCORSESE	CEGHILST	GLITCHES
CEELLNOS	COLLEENS	CEEORSSY	CROSS-EYE	CEGHIMNS	SCHEMING
CEELLRVY	CLEVERLY	CEEORTTV	CORVETTE	CEGHINNW	WENCHING
CEELLSSU	CLUELESS	CEEORTUX	EXECUTOR	CEGHINOR	COHERING
CEELMOPT	COMPLETE	CEEOSSTX	TO EXCESS	CEGHINPR	PERCHING
CEELMORW	WELCOMER	CEEPPRST	PRECEPTS	CEGHINRT	RETCHING
CEELMOSW	WELCOMES	CEEPRSST	RESPECTS,	CEGHINST	ETCHINGS
CEELMRTU	ELECTRUM	SCEPTRES, SPECTRES		CEGHIRTU	THEURGIC
CEELNOPU	OPULENCE	CEEPRSTX	EXCERPTS	CEGHMRUY	CHEMURGY
CEELNORS	ENCLOSER	CEERRSSU	RESCUERS	CEGHNORS	GROSCHEN
CEELNORT	ELECTRON	CEERRSTU	REST CURE	CEGHORSU	GROUCHES
CEELNRST	LECTERNS	CEERSSTU	SECUREST	CEGIILNS	CEILINGS
CEELNRTY	RECENTLY	CEERSSTW	SETSCREW	CEGIINNT	ENTICING
CEELNSTU	ESCULENT	CEFFIORS	OFFICERS	CEGIINNV	EVINCING
CEELORST	CORSELET,	CEFFIORU	COIFFEUR,	CEGIINPR	PIERCING
ELECTORS, SELECTOR		COIFFURE		CEGIINRT	NEGRITIC,
CEELORTV	COVERLET	CEFFIRSU	SUFFICER	RECITING	
CEELOSST	CLOSE-SET	CEFFLORU	FORCEFUL	CEGIINSS	GNEISSIC
CEELRRTU	LECTURER	CEFFLSSU	SCUFFLES	CEGIINSX	EXCISING
CEELRSSU	RECLUSES	CEFGHINT	FETCHING	CEGIINTV	EVICTING
CEELRSTU	LECTURES	CEFGIKLN	FLECKING	CEGIINTX	EXCITING
CEELRSTY	SECRETLY	CEFHIIMS	MISCHIEF	CEGIIOST	EGOISTIC
CEELRSUY	SECURELY	CEFHILNR	FLINCHER	CEGIKLNR	CLERKING
CEELSTTU	LETTUCES	CEFIILNO	OLEFINIC	CEGIKNRW	WRECKING
CEEMMNTU	CEMENTUM	CEFIILST	FELSITIC	CEGILNRY	GLYCERIN
CEEMNORW	NEWCOMER	CEFIILTY	FELICITY	CEGILNTU	CULTIGEN
CEEMNORY	CEREMONY	CEFIIORS	ORIFICES	CEGIMNOY	MYOGENIC

CEGINNOZ	COZENING	CEHIKSTT	THICKEST,	CEHISTTW	TWITCHES
CEGINNRT	CENTRING		THICKETS, THICKSET	CEHKKRSU	CHUKKERS
CEGINNST	SCENTING	CEHILLMT	MITCHELL	CEHKLMOS	HEMLOCKS
CEGINOOP	GEOPONIC	CEHILLRS	SCHILLER	CEHKNPUY	KEYPUNCH
CEGINOOR	OROGENIC	CEHILMTY	METHYLIC	CEHKORSS	SHOCKERS
CEGINOPY	PYOGENIC	CEHILNOP	PHENOLIC,	CEHKRSTU	HUCKSTER
CEGINORV	COVERING		PINOCHLE	CEHLNNOU	LUNCHEON
CEGINORW	COWERING	CEHILNOR	CHLORINE	CEHLNOTU	UNCLOTHE
CEGINOTV	COVETING,	CEHILNSS	CHINLESS	CEHLORST	CHORTLES
	VIETCONG	CEHILOOS	SCHOOLIE	CEHLORSU	SLOUCHER
CEGINOXY	OXYGENIC	CEHILORT	CHLORITE,	CEHLOSUY	SQUELCHY
CEGINRST	CRESTING		CLOTHIER	CEHMNSSU	MUCHNESS
CEGINRSU	RESCUING,	CEHILOSU	CHOISEUL	CEHMORUV	OVERMUCH
	SECURING	CEHILPTY	PHYLETIC	CEHNNOPU	PUNCHEON
CEGINRSW	SCREWING	CEHILSTY	CHESTILY	CEHNNOSU	NONESUCH
CEGINRSY	SYNERGIC	CEHILTTY	TETCHILY	CEHNOORS	SCHOONER
CEGINSUX	EXCUSING	CEHIMMRU	CHUMMIER	CEHNORSV	CHEVRONS
CEGLLOOU	COLLOGUE	CEHIMNOP	PHONEMIC	CEHNSTTU	CHESTNUT
CEGLLORY	GLYCEROL	CEHIMNOR	NICHROME	CEHOOORZ	ZOOCHORE
CEGLLRYY	GLYCERYL	CEHIMNOW	CHOW MEIN	CEHOORST	CHEROOTS
CEGLNOTY	COGENTLY	CEHIMNSY	CHIMNEYS	CEHOORSU	OCHREOUS
CEGMNNOO	COGNOMEN	CEHIMNTZ	CHEMNITZ	CEHOPPRS	CHOPPERS
CEGNNPUY	PUNGENCY	CEHIMORT	CHROMITE,	CEHOPPRY	PROPHECY
CEGNOOTY	GONOCYTE		TRICHOME	CEHOPSTW	CHEPSTOW
CEGNORSS	CONGRESS	CEHIMRRS	SMIRCHER	CEHOPSUY	CHOP SUEY
CEGNORSU	SCROUNGE	CEHIMSST	CHEMISTS	CEHORSSU	CHORUSES
CEGOORSS	SCROOGES	CEHINNRT	INTRENCH	CEHORSSZ	SCHERZOS
CEGORRSU	SCOURGER	CEHINOOS	COHESION	CEHORSUV	VOUCHERS
CEGORSSU	SCOURGES	CEHINOPT	PHONETIC	CEHPSSTU	PUTSCHES
CEHIILLR	CHILLIER	CEHINOPU	EUPHONIC	CEHRSTTY	STRETCHY
CEHIILLS	CHILLIES	CEHINPRU	PUNCHIER	CEIIILSV	CIVILISE
CEHIILMO	HEMIOLIC	CEHINRSS	RICHNESS	CEIIILVZ	CIVILIZE
CEHIILNN	LICHENIN	CEHINRST	CHRISTEN	CEIIINSV	INCISIVE
CEHIILNT	LECITHIN	CEHINRSW	SCHWERIN	CEIIJSTU	JESUITIC, JUICIEST
CEHIILOT	EOLITHIC	CEHINRTU	RUTHENIC	CEIIKLMR	LIMERICK
CEHIIMOS	ISOCHEIM	CEHINSST	SNITCHES	CEIIKLRS	SICKLIER
CEHIIMPT	MEPHITIC	CEHIOORS	CHOOSIER	CEIIKMMR	MIMICKER
CEHIIMRT	HERMITIC	CEHIOPPR	CHOPPIER	CEIIKNRS	ICE RINKS
CEHIIOPT	ETHIOPIC	CEHIOPRU	EUPHORIC	CEIIKNST	KINETICS
CEHIIPPS	CHIPPIES	CEHIOPSS	HOSPICES	CEIIKPST	PICKIEST
CEHIIPRR	CHIRPIER	CEHIOPST	POSTICHE	CEIIKQSU	QUICKIES
CEHIIRSS	CHRISSIE	CEHIOPTU	EUPHOTIC	CEIIKRRT	TRICKIER
CEHIIRST	CHRISTIE	CEHIORRT	RHETORIC,	CEIIKRST	STICKIER
CEHIIRTT	TITCHIER, TRICHITE		TORCHIER	CEIIKSST	EKISTICS
CEHIISTT	ETHICIST, ITCHIEST,	CEHIORTU	TOUCHIER	CEIILMNT	LIMNETIC
	THEISTIC	CEHIPRSS	SPHERICS	CEIILMNY	MYELINIC
CEHIKLNY	HINCKLEY	CEHIPRST	PITCHERS	CEIILNNR	INCLINER
CEHIKLSU	SUCHLIKE	CEHIRSTT	STITCHER	CEIILNNS	INCLINES
CEHIKMNT	CHIMKENT	CEHIRSTW	SWITCHER	CEIILNOP	PICOLINE
CEHIKMOS	HOMESICK	CEHIRSTY	HYSTERIC	CEIILNOS	ISOCLINE,
CEHIKNRU	CHUNKIER	CEHIRTTW	TWITCHER		SILICONE
CEHIKNST	KITCHENS	CEHIRTWY	WITCHERY	CEIILOPS	POLICIES
CEHIKOWW	KWEICHOW	CEHISSTT	STITCHES	CEIILORT	ELICITOR
CEHIKRSW	WHICKERS	CEHISSTU	CUSHIEST	CEIILOTZ	ZEOLITIC
		CEHISSTW	SWITCHES		

CEIILPPS	CLIPPIES	CEIKNRSS	SNICKERS	CEIMMRRU	CRUMMIER
CEIILPRT	PERLITIC	CEIKNRST	STRICKEN	CEIMNNOY	NEOMYCIN
CEIILPSS	ECLIPSIS	CEIKNSSS	SICKNESS	CEIMNOPT	PENTOMIC
CEIILPTX	EXPLICIT	CEIKORST	ROCKIEST,	CEIMNOPY	EPONYMIC
CEIILPTY	PYELITIC		STOCKIER	CEIMNORS	SERMONIC
CEIILRTV	VERTICIL	CEIKPSST	SKEPTICS	CEIMNORT	INTERCOM
CEIILSSS	SCISSILE	CEIKQSTU	QUICKEST,	CEIMNSSU	MENISCUS
CEIIMOPT	EPITOMIC		QUICKSET	CEIMOOSZ	MESOZOIC
CEIIMORS	ISOMERIC	CEIKRRTY	TRICKERY	CEIMOPRS	COMPRISE
CEIIMOST	COMITIES,	CEIKRRST	STICKERS	CEIMORSX	EXORCISM
	SEMIOTIC	CEIKSTUY	YUCKIEST	CEIMRRTU	TURMERIC
CEIIMRST	MERISTIC	CEILLLOY	ICE LOLLY	CEIMSSTY	SYSTEMIC
CEIIMRTT	TERMITIC	CEILLOQU	COQUILLE	CEINNNOT	INNOCENT
CEIIMSST	SEMITICS	CEILLORS	COLLIERS	CEINNORU	NEURONIC
CEIINNOT	NICOTINE	CEILLORY	COLLIERY	CEINNORV	CONNIVER
CEIINORS	RECISION,	CEILLRTU	TELLURIC	CEINNOTU	CONTINUE
	SORICINE	CEILLSST	CELLISTS	CEINOOTZ	ENTOZOIC,
CEIINOSV	INVOICES	CEILMMUY	MYCELIUM		ENZOOTIC
CEIINOSX	EXCISION	CEILMNOP	COMPLINE	CEINOPRS	CONSPIRE
CEIINOTV	EVICTION	CEILMOPR	COMPILER,	CEINOPRT	INCEPTOR
CEIINPPR	PRINCIPE		COMPLIER	CEINOPRV	PROVINCE
CEIINRSU	INCISURE,	CEILMOPS	POLEMICS	CEINORSS	NECROSIS
	SCIURINE	CEILMOSS	SOLECISM	CEINORST	CORNIEST
CEIINRTU	NEURITIC	CEILMOSU	COLISEUM	CEINORSU	COINSURE
CEIINSST	CITISENS	CEILMRSU	CLUMSIER	CEINORSW	IN ESCROW
CEIINSTU	CUTINISE	CEILNNOT	NON LICET	CEINORTT	CONTRITE
CEIINSTY	SYENITIC	CEILNNSY	SYNCLINE	CEINORTU	NEUROTIC
CEIINSTZ	CITIZENS	CEILNOOS	COLONIES,	CEINORTV	CONTRIVE
CEIINTUZ	CUTINIZE		COLONISE, ECLOSION	CEINOSSS	CESSIONS,
CEIIOPRT	PERIOTIC	CEILNOOZ	COLONIZE		COSINESS
CEIIOSTT	OSTEITIC	CEILNORV	IN CLOVER	CEINOSST	SECTIONS
CEIIPRRS	CRISPIER	CEILNOST	TELSONIC	CEINOSSZ	COZINESS
CEIIPRST	PRICIEST	CEILNOSX	LEXICONS	CEINOSTT	STENOTIC
CEIIPSST	SPICIEST	CEILNPRY	PRINCELY	CEINOSTU	COUNTIES
CEIIQRTU	CRITIQUE	CEILNRUV	CULVERIN	CEINOSTY	CYTOSINE
CEIIRSTV	VERISTIC	CEILNSST	STENCILS	CEINOTTU	TEUTONIC
CEIISTVV	VIVISECT	CEILOPPS	POPSICLE	CEINPRSS	PRINCESS
CEIJLNOS	JOSCELIN	CEILOPRT	PETROLIC	CEINRSST	CISTERNS
CEIJNORT	INJECTOR	CEILOPTU	POULTICE	CEINRSTT	CENTRIST
CEIJSSTU	JUSTICES	CEILOPTY	EPICOTYL	CEINRTTU	TINCTURE
CEIKKNRS	KNICKERS	CEILORST	CLOISTER,	CEIOOTXX	EXOTOXIC
CEIKKRRS	SKERRICK		COSTLIER	CEIOPRRU	CROUPIER
CEIKLNRS	CLINKERS,	CEILORTY	CRYOLITE	CEIOPRSU	PRECIOUS
	CRINKLES	CEILOSST	SOLECIST,	CEIOPSSU	SPECIOUS
CEIKLOSV	LOVESICK		SOLSTICE	CEIORRSS	CROSIERS
CEIKLPRS	PRICKLES	CEILOSSU	COULISSE	CEIORRSZ	CROZIERS
CEIKLPRU	PLUCKIER	CEILOTVY	VELOCITY	CEIORRTU	COURTIER
CEIKLRSS	SLICKERS	CEILPPRS	CLIPPERS, CRIPPLES	CEIORRUZ	CRUZEIRO
CEIKLRST	STICKLER,	CEILPRSS	SPLICERS	CEIORSTU	CITREOUS,
	STRICKLE	CEILPRSU	SURPLICE		OUTCRIES
CEIKLSST	SLICKEST	CEILRSTU	CURLIEST	CEIORSTV	VORTICES
CEIKLSTU	LUCKIEST	CEIMMNNO	MNEMONIC	CEIORSTX	EXORCIST
CEIKMPPU	PICK-ME-UP	CEIMMNOU	ENCOMIUM,	CEIORSVY	VICEROYS
CEIKMSTU	MUCKIEST		MECONIUM	CEIORTTU	TOREUTIC
CEIKNNOT	NEKTONIC	CEIMMORT	RECOMMIT	CEIPRRST	RESCRIPT

CEIPRSTU	PICTURES, PIECRUST
CEIPSSST	CESSPITS
CEIRRRUY	CURRIERY
CEIRRSSU	CRUISERS
CEIRRSTT	CRITTERS, RESTRICT, STRICTER
CEIRRSTU	CRUSTIER, RECRUITS
CEIRSSTU	CITRUSES, CURTSIES
CEIRSTUY	SECURITY
CEJLOOSY	JOCOSELY
CEJNORRU	CONJURER
CEJNRTUU	JUNCTURE
CEJOPRST	PROJECTS
CEKKLNSU	KNUCKLES
CEKKNORS	KNOCKERS
CEKKNTUY	KENTUCKY
CEKLLSSU	LUCKLESS
CEKLNOOP	POLO NECK
CEKMNOST	STOCKMEN
CEKNOORV	CONVOKER
CEKNOPST	PENSTOCK
CEKOOORV	OVERCOOK
CEKOORRS	ROCKROSE
CEKOORRW	CO-WORKER
CEKOPRST	SPROCKET
CEKORRTY	ROCKETRY
CEKRRSTU	TRUCKERS
CEKRSSUU	RUCKUSES
CELLNOOS	COLONELS
CELLNSUU	NUCELLUS
CELLRSSU	SCULLERS
CELLRSUY	SCULLERY
CELMNOOS	MONOCLES
CELMNOTU	UNCLE TOM
CELMPRTU	PLECTRUM
CELMPSUU	SPECULUM
CELNOORS	CONSOLER
CELNOOSS	CONSOLES, COOLNESS
CELNOPUU	UNCOUPLE
CELNORWY	CLOWNERY
CELNOSUV	CONVULSE
CELNOSVY	SOLVENCY
CELNOVXY	CONVEXLY
CELOOPSS	CESSPOOL
CELOPSSU	CLOSE-UPS
CELOPSTU	COUPLETS
CELORSST	CROSSLET
CELORSSU	CLOSURES, SCLEROUS
CELORSUU	ULCEROUS
CELORTVY	COVERTLY
CELOSTTU	CULOTTES
CELPRSSU	SCRUPLES
CELPRSUY	SPRUCELY
CELRSSTU	CLUSTERS
CELRSTUU	CULTURES
CELRSTUV	CULVERTS
CELRSTUY	CLUSTERY
CELSSTTU	SCUTTLES
CEMMNOOR	COMMONER
CEMMNOOS	CONSOMME
CEMMNOST	COMMENTS
CEMMNOSU	COMMUNES
CEMMORTU	COMMUTER
CEMNOOTY	MONOCYTE
CEMNOPTT	CONTEMPT
CEMNORSU	CONSUMER
CEMOOPRS	COMPOSER
CEMOOPST	COMPOTES
CEMOOSTU	OUTCOMES
CEMOPRSS	COMPRESS
CEMOPRTU	COMPUTER
CEMORSTU	CUSTOMER
CEMOSSTU	COSTUMES
CEMPRSTU	CRUMPETS, SPECTRUM
CEMRSSTU	SET SCRUM
CENNOOPR	CORN PONE
CENNORTU	NOCTURNE
CENNOSTT	CONTENTS
CENNOSTV	CONVENTS
CENOORRS	CORONERS, CROONERS
CENOORST	CORONETS
CENOORSU	CORNEOUS
CENOORVY	CONVEYOR
CENOQSTU	CONQUEST
CENORSTU	CONSTRUE, COUNTERS, RECOUNTS
CENORSTV	CONVERTS
CENORSUU	CERNUOUS, COENERUS
CENORSUY	CYNOSURE
CENORTUY	COURTNEY
CENORTVY	COVENTRY
CENOSSTT	CONTESTS
CENOSSTU	COUNTESS
CENOSTTX	CONTEXTS
CENPRTUU	PUNCTURE
CENRRSTU	CURRENTS
CENRSSTU	CURTNESS
CEOOOPST	OTOSCOPE
CEOOPRRV	OVERCROP
CEOORSST	SCOOTERS
CEOOSTUV	COVETOUS
CEOPPRRS	CROPPERS
CEOPPRST	PROSPECT
CEOPRRRU	PROCURER
CEOPRSTT	PRESCOTT
CEOPRSTW	SCREW TOP
CEOPRSUU	CUPREOUS
CEOPRSUV	COVER-UPS
CEOQRTUY	COQUETRY
CEORRSSU	SCOURERS
CEORRSTY	CORSETRY
CEORSSST	CROSSEST
CEORSTUY	COURTESY
CEPPRSSU	SCUPPERS
CEPPRTUU	UPPERCUT
CEPRSTUU	CUTPURSE
CEPSSSTU	SUSPECTS
CERSSUUX	EXCURSUS
CFFGINOS	SCOFFING
CFFGINSU	SCUFFING
CFFIKKOS	KICKOFFS
CFFIKLNU	CUFF LINK
CFFIRTUY	FRUCTIFY
CFGHIILN	FILCHING
CFGIIKLN	FLICKING
CFGIKLNO	FLOCKING
CFGIKNOR	FROCKING
CFGINOSU	FOCUSING
CFHIINOO	FINOCHIO
CFHIIORR	HORRIFIC
CFHIKORS	ROCKFISH
CFIIILSY	SILICIFY
CFIILMNU	FULMINIC
CFIILOPR	PROLIFIC
CFIINORT	FRICTION
CFIINOST	FICTIONS
CFIKLSTU	STICKFUL
CFIMNORU	UNCIFORM
CFINNOTU	FUNCTION
CFKKLOOR	FOLK-ROCK
CFLMRSUU	FULCRUMS
CFLNORSU	SCORNFUL
CFMOORST	COMFORTS
CFNNOORT	CONFRONT
CFOOORTW	CROWFOOT
CFOOPSTY	SOFT COPY
CFRSTUUU	USUFRUCT
CGGGHINU	CHUGGING
CGGGILNO	CLOGGING
CGGHINOU	COUGHING
CGGIILNN	CLINGING
CGGIINNR	CRINGING
CGHHIINT	HITCHING
CGHHINNU	HUNCHING
CGHIIKNN	CHINKING
CGHIILLN	CHILLING

CGHIINNP	PINCHING
CGHIINNW	WINCHING
CGHIINPP	CHIPPING
CGHIINPR	CHIRPING
CGHIINPT	PITCHING
CGHIINTW	WITCHING
CGHIINVY	CHIVYING
CGHIJNNO	CHONGJIN
CGHIKNOS	SHOCKING
CGHIKNSU	SHUCKING
CGHILMNU	MULCHING
CGHILNNU	LUNCHING
CGHILNNY	LYNCHING
CGHILNOT	CLOTHING
CGHILNRU	LURCHING
CGHIMMNU	CHUMMING
CGHIMNNU	MUNCHING
CGHIMNOO	MOOCHING
CGHIMNOP	CHOMPING
CGHIMPSY	SPHYGMIC
CGHINNOS	CHIGNONS
CGHINNOT	NOTCHING
CGHINNPU	PUNCHING
CGHINNRU	CHURNING
CGHINOPP	CHOPPING
CGHINOTU	TOUCHING
CGHINOUV	VOUCHING
CGHINPSY	PSYCHING
CGHINRSU	CRUSHING
CGHINSTY	SCYTHING
CGHNOOSU	SOUCHONG
CGIIILNT	LIGNITIC
CGIIINNS	INCISING
CGIIINNT	INCITING
CGIIKLNN	CLINKING
CGIIKLNP	PICKLING
CGIIKLNS	LICKINGS, SLICKING
CGIIKLNT	TICKLING
CGIIKMMS	GIMMICKS
CGIIKMMY	GIMMICKY
CGIIKNNS	SNICKING
CGIIKNPR	PRICKING
CGIIKNPS	PICKINGS
CGIIKNRT	TRICKING
CGIIKNST	STICKING
CGIIKPST	PIGSTICK
CGIILMOS	LOGICISM
CGIILNOP	POLICING
CGIILNPP	CLIPPING
CGIILNPS	SPLICING
CGIILNSU	SLUICING
CGIILOST	LOGISTIC
CGIIMNNO	INCOMING

CGIIMNPR	CRIMPING
CGIINNOT	NOTICING
CGIINOOS	ISOGONIC
CGIINPRS	CRISPING
CGIINRSU	CRUISING
CGIKKNNO	KNOCKING
CGIKLNOR	ROCKLING
CGIKLNPU	PLUCKING
CGIKLNSU	SUCKLING
CGIKMNOS	SMOCKING
CGIKNOOR	CROOKING
CGIKNOST	STOCKING
CGIKNRTU	TRUCKING
CGILLNSU	SCULLING
CGILMNOO	MONGOLIC
CGILMNPU	CLUMPING
CGILMNSU	MUSCLING
CGILMNTU	MULCTING
CGILMNUU	CINGULUM, GLUCINUM
CGILMOOY	MYOLOGIC
CGILNNOW	CLOWNING
CGILNOPP	CLOPPING
CGILNOPU	COUPLING
CGILNOSW	COWLINGS, SCOWLING
CGILNOTT	CLOTTING
CGILNOTU	CLOUTING
CGILOORU	UROLOGIC
CGILPSTY	GLYPTICS
CGIMNNOO	GNOMONIC, ONCOMING
CGIMNOPU	UPCOMING
CGINNOOR	CROONING
CGINNOPU	POUNCING
CGINNORS	SCORNING
CGINNORW	CROWNING
CGINNOTU	COUNTING
CGINOOPS	SCOOPING
CGINOOPT	COOPTING
CGINOOST	SCOOTING
CGINOPPR	CROPPING
CGINORSS	CROSSING
CGINORSU	COURSING, SCOURING
CGINORTU	COURTING
CGINOSTU	SCOUTING
CGINPRSU	SPRUCING
CGINRRUY	CURRYING
CGINSTTU	CUTTINGS, TUNGSTIC
CGINSTUU	TUNGUSIC
CGKNOSTU	GUNSTOCK
CGLMOOYY	MYCOLOGY
CGLNOOOY	ONCOLOGY

CGLOOOTY	TOCOLOGY
CGLOOTYY	CYTOLOGY
CHHHHOTU	HOCHHUTH
CHHIIPST	PHTHISIC
CHHILRSU	CHURLISH
CHHIMRTY	RHYTHMIC
CHHNORSU	RHONCHUS
CHHOOPTT	HOTCHPOT
CHIIKLST	TICKLISH
CHIILNNP	LINCHPIN
CHIILOPT	HOPLITIC
CHIILOST	HOLISTIC
CHIILPRY	CHIRPILY
CHIILQSU	CLIQUISH
CHIINORT	ORNITHIC
CHIIORST	HISTORIC, ORCHITIS
CHIIRSTT	TRISTICH
CHIKLLOS	HILLOCKS
CHIKMNPU	CHIPMUNK
CHIKOPTY	KYPHOTIC
CHILLOOT	OILCLOTH
CHILMMUY	CHUMMILY
CHILMOSU	SCHOLIUM
CHILMPSU	CLUMPISH
CHILNNPY	LYNCHPIN
CHILNOSW	CLOWNISH
CHILOOOZ	HOLOZOIC
CHILOPPY	CHOPPILY
CHILOTUY	TOUCHILY
CHIMMORU	CHROMIUM
CHIMNOSU	INSOMUCH
CHIMNOSY	CHYMOSIN
CHINOPTY	HYPNOTIC, PYTHONIC, TYPHONIC
CHINOSSU	CUSHIONS
CHINOSTZ	SCHIZONT
CHINOSUY	CUSHIONY
CHIOOPPT	PHOTOPIC
CHIOOPTY	OOPHYTIC
CHIOPRST	STROPHIC
CHIOSSTT	SCOTTISH
CHIPRRUY	CHIRRUPY
CHIPRTTY	TRIPTYCH
CHIPSTTU	STITCH UP
CHIRRSSU	SCIRRHUS
CHKMMOSU	HUMMOCKS
CHKMMOUY	HUMMOCKY
CHKORRTU	THURROCK
CHLNOOOP	COLOPHON
CHLOORSU	CHLOROUS
CHMNORRU	CRUMHORN
CHMOORSU	CHROMOUS
CHNOOPTT	TOP-NOTCH
CHNPPSUU	PUNCH-UPS

CHORSTTU	SHORT CUT	CILLMSUY	CLUMSILY	CIPSSTTY	STYPTICS
CIIILMPT	IMPLICIT	CILLNOSU	SCULLION	CJNOORRU	CONJUROR
CIIILTVY	CIVILITY	CILLOOOT	OCOTILLO	CKKNOOTU	KNOCKOUT
CIIINNOS	INCISION	CILMNOPU	PULMONIC	CKKNOPSU	KNOCK-UPS
CIIINNOT	COIN IT IN	CILMNOUU	INOCULUM	CKLOORSW	ROWLOCKS
CIIINTVY	VICINITY	CILMNUUV	VINCULUM	CKLOOSTU	LOCKOUTS
CIIJRSTU	JURISTIC	CILMPSUU	SPICULUM	CKLOPSTU	POTLUCKS
CIIKLLOS	OIL SLICK	CILNOOST	COLONIST	CKMMORUW	MUCKWORM
CIIKLPST	LIPSTICK	CILNOOTU	LOCUTION	CKNOOSTT	STOCKTON
CIIKLRTY	TRICKILY	CILNOPTU	PLUTONIC	CKOOOSTU	COOKOUTS
CIIKLSTY	STICKILY	CILNOSTU	LINOCUTS	CKOOPSTT	STOCKPOT
CIIKNPPR	PINPRICK	CILOOPST	COPILOTS	CKOSSSTU	TUSSOCKS
CIIKNPST	STICKPIN	CILOOPYZ	POLYZOIC	CKOSSTUY	TUSSOCKY
CIILLMTU	TILLICUM	CILOPRRY	PYRROLIC	CLLMOSSU	MOLLUSCS
CIILLNOP	POLLINIC	CILOPRUY	POLYURIC	CLLOOPSS	SCOLLOPS
CIILMNOT	MILTONIC	CILOPSSW	COWSLIPS	CLLOOQUY	COLLOQUY
CIILMOPY	IMPOLICY	CILOSSTU	OCULISTS	CLLOSUUY	CULOUSLY
CIILMRSY	LYRICISM	CILOSSTY	SYSTOLIC	CLMMNOOY	COMMONLY
CIILOOPT	POLITICO	CILOSSUU	LUSCIOUS	CLMOOOTY	COLOTOMY
CIILOPST	COLPITIS, POLITICS	CILPRSTU	CULPRITS	CLMOSUUU	CUMULOUS
CIILORST	CLITORIS	CILPSSTU	SCULPSIT	CLNOORST	CONTROLS
CIILRSTY	LYRICIST	CILRSTTY	STRICTLY	CLOOOPRT	PROTOCOL
CIIMNOST	MONISTIC,	CILRSTUY	CRUSTILY	CLOOSSSU	COLOSSUS
	NOMISTIC	CILRSUVY	SCURVILY	CLOPRSSY	CROSSPLY
CIIMORST	TRISOMIC	CIMNOOTY	MYOTONIC	CLOPRSTU	SCULPTOR
CIIMOSST	STOICISM	CIMNORSS	CRIMSONS	CLOPSSTU	COST-PLUS
CIIMRTTU	TRITICUM	CIMNOSTU	MISCOUNT	CMMNNOOU	UNCOMMON
CIINNSTT	INSTINCT	CIMNOSUU	MUCINOUS	CMORSSTU	SCROTUMS
CIINOOST	ISOTONIC	CIMNOSUY	SYCONIUM	CNOOOORT	OCTOROON
CIINOPSU	OPINICUS	CIMOOOTZ	ZOOTOMIC	CNOORRTY	CRYOTRON
CIINORSS	INCISORS	CIMOSTUU	MUTICOUS	CNOORSST	CONSORTS
CIINOSSS	SCISSION	CIMOSTUY	MUCOSITY	CNOORSTU	CONTOURS,
CIINOTTY	TONICITY	CINNOOTU	CONTINUO		CROUTONS
CIINPSTU	SINCIPUT	CINNOOTX	NONTOXIC	CNOSTUUU	UNCTUOUS
CIIOOPST	ISOTOPIC	CINNOOVY	IN CONVOY	COOOPRRT	ROOT CROP
CIIOQTUX	QUIXOTIC	CINNORSU	UNICORNS	COOPRRST	PROCTORS
CIIOTTXY	TOXICITY	CINNOSTY	SYNTONIC	COOPRSTU	OUTCROPS
CIIPRRTU	PRURITIC	CINNQUUX	QUINCUNX	COOPRSUU	CROUPOUS
CIIPRSTU	PURISTIC	CINOOOPT	COOPTION	COOPRSUY	UROSCOPY
CIIRSTTU	TRUISTIC	CINOOPRS	SCORPION	COORSSTU	OUTCROSS
CIISSTTY	CYSTITIS	CINOOTXY	OXYTOCIN	DDDDEEOR	DODDERED
CIJKOSTY	JOYSTICK	CINOPSTY	SYNOPTIC	DDDEEEFN	DEFENDED
CIJNNOOT	CONJOINT	CINOSTUV	VISCOUNT	DDDEEENP	DEPENDED
CIJNNOTU	JUNCTION	CINRSTTU	INSTRUCT	DDDEEENR	REDDENED
CIJOOSTY	JOCOSITY	CINRSTUY	SCRUTINY	DDDEEHRS	SHREDDED
CIKLLOPS	PILLOCKS	CIOOOPRS	OOSPORIC	DDDEEJRU	JUDDERED
CIKLLPUY	PLUCKILY	CIOOOTXZ	ZOOTOXIC	DDDEEORR	DODDERER
CIKLNOST	LINSTOCK	CIOOPRSS	SCORPIOS	DDDEIINV	DIVIDEND
CIKLOSTY	STOCKILY	CIOOPRST	PORTICOS	DDDEILNW	DWINDLED
CIKMOORS	SICKROOM	CIOPRSSU	SCORPIUS	DDDEILTW	TWIDDLED
CIKNNOOS	COONSKIN	CIOPSSTY	COPYISTS	DDDEINOR	DENDROID
CIKNNOST	NONSTICK	CIORSSSS	SCISSORS	DDDGIILN	DIDDLING
CIKOSSTT	STOCKIST	CIOTTTUU	CUT IT OUT	DDEEEEMR	REDEEMED
CIKPSSTU	STICK-UPS	CIPRRUVY	PYRRUVIC	DDEEEENP	DEEPENED

DDEEEFLX	DEFLEXED
DDEEEFNR	DEFENDER,
FENDERED	
DDEEEFRR	DEFERRED
DDEEEHLW	WHEEDLED
DDEEEIMR	REMEDIED
DDEEEIWY	WIDE-EYED
DDEEELPT	DEPLETED
DDEEEMNT	DEMENTED
DDEEENPX	EXPENDED
DDEEENRR	RENDERED
DDEEENRT	TENDERED
DDEEENSU	UNSEEDED
DDEEENTX	EXTENDED
DDEEERRT	DETERRED
DDEEERST	DESERTED
DDEEERSV	DESERVED
DDEEESTT	DETESTED
DDEEEWYY	DEWY-EYED
DDEEFFIR	DIFFERED
DDEEFFNO	OFFENDED
DDEEFGIT	FIDGETED
DDEEFLNO	ENFOLDED
DDEEFMOR	DEFORMED
DDEEFNRU	REFUNDED
DDEEGINS	DESIGNED
DDEEGIRV	DIVERGED
DDEEGIST	DIGESTED
DDEEGOPS	GODSPEED
DDEEGOTW	TWO-EDGED
DDEEGRRS	DREDGERS
DDEEHILS	SHIELDED
DDEEHINR	HINDERED
DDEEHIRT	DITHERED
DDEEHRRS	SHREDDER
DDEEIINT	INEDITED
DDEEILLV	DEVILLED
DDEEILMW	MILDEWED
DDEEILRV	DRIVELED
DDEEILWY	WILD-EYED
DDEEIMNR	REMINDED
DDEEIMSS	MISDEEDS
DDEEIMST	DEMISTED
DDEEINNT	INDENTED,
INTENDED	
DDEEINOS	ONE-SIDED
DDEEINRT	DENDRITE
DDEEINST	DESTINED
DDEEIPRS	PRESIDED
DDEEIPRV	DEPRIVED
DDEEIPSS	DESPISED
DDEEIRTV	DIVERTED
DDEEISST	DESISTED
DDEEISTV	DIVESTED
DDEELLMO	MODELLED

DDEELLOP	DEED POLL
DDEELLOY	YODELLED
DDEELMOR	MOLDERED
DDEELMRS	MEDDLERS
DDEELOPR	DEPLORED
DDEELOPX	EXPLODED
DDEELOPY	DEPLOYED
DDEELORS	SOLDERED
DDEELOSU	DELOUSED
DDEELOVV	DEVOLVED
DDEELPRS	PEDDLERS
DDEEMNOR	ENDODERM
DDEEMRRU	DEMURRED,
MURDERED	
DDEENOPR	PONDERED
DDEENOPW	PONDWEED
DDEENORS	ENDORSED
DDEENORW	WONDERED
DDEENRSU	SUNDERED
DDEEOPRT	DEPORTED
DDEEOPRW	POWDERED
DDEEORRW	REWORDED
DDEEORUV	DEVOURED
DDEERTUX	EXTRUDED
DDEFFISU	DIFFUSED
DDEFIILM	MIDFIELD
DDEFIIMO	MODIFIED
DDEFLNOU	UNFOLDED
DDEGGINR	DREDGING
DDEGGLOY	DOGGEDLY
DDEGGNOO	DOGGONED
DDEGHINS	SHEDDING
DDEGIINR	DERIDING
DDEGIIST	GIDDIEST
DDEGILMN	MEDDLING
DDEGILNP	PEDDLING
DDEGILNS	SLEDDING
DDEGILNU	DELUDING,
INDULGED	
DDEGILOS	DISLODGE
DDEGILRS	GRIDDLES
DDEGILUV	DIVULGED
DDEGIMOS	DEMIGODS
DDEGINNU	DENUDING
DDEGINSW	WEDDINGS
DDEGIORT	DOG-TIRED
DDEGIOST	DODGIEST
DDEGIOSV	GIVE ODDS
DDEGNOOR	DORDOGNE
DDEGNORU	GROUNDED,
UNDERDOG	
DDEGNOSS	GODSENDS
DDEGOOOR	DO-GOODER
DDEGOOWW	WEDGWOOD
DDEGRRUY	DRUDGERY

DDEHIISS	SIDE DISH
DDEHILNY	HIDDENLY
DDEHINOR	DIHEDRON
DDEHIORS	SHODDIER
DDEHNRSU	HUNDREDS
DDEHOOSW	WOODSHED
DDEHORSU	SHROUDED
DDEHRSSU	SHUDDERS
DDEHRSUY	SHUDDERY
DDEIIKLS	DISLIKED
DDEIILNR	DIELDRIN
DDEIILOS	IDOLISED
DDEIILOZ	IDOLIZED
DDEIIOPS	DIOPSIDE
DDEIIOST	ODDITIES
DDEIIOSX	DIOXIDES,
OXIDISED	
DDEIIOXZ	OXIDIZED
DDEIIRSV	DIVIDERS
DDEIIRUV	REDUVIID
DDEIKNRS	KINDREDS
DDEILMOP	IMPLODED
DDEILNPS	SPLENDID
DDEILNRU	UNRIDDLE
DDEILNSW	SWINDLED
DDEILOPS	LOP-SIDED
DDEILRST	TIDDLERS
DDEILRTW	TWIDDLER
DDEILRZZ	DRIZZLED
DDEILSTU	LUDDITES
DDEILSTW	TWIDDLES
DDEIMOSU	MEDUSOID
DDEIMSTU	MUDDIEST
DDEINORS	INDORSED
DDEINOSW	DISENDOW,
DISOWNED	
DDEINRST	STRIDDEN
DDEINRTU	INTRUDED
DDEIOPRS	DROPSIED
DDEIOPRV	PROVIDED
DDEIOPSS	DISPOSED
DDEIORRS	DISORDER
DDEIOSTW	DOWDIEST,
TWO-SIDED	
DDEIPSTU	DISPUTED
DDEIRSTU	RUDDIEST
DDEKMOSU	DUKEDOMS
DDELNRTU	TRUNDLED
DDELNSUY	SUDDENLY
DDELOPRS	PLODDERS
DDELORST	TODDLERS
DDEMNOST	ODDMENTS
DDEMNOUU	DUODENUM
DDEMNPUU	PUDENDUM
DDEMOOTU	OUTMODED

DDEOORSW	REDWOODS	
DDEOPRSW	DEWDROPS	
DDFGIILN	FIDDLING	
DDFGILNU	FUDDLING	
DDGGINNO	DINGDONG	
DDGGINRU	DRUDGING	
DDGHILNU	HUDDLING	
DDGHINTU	THUDDING	
DDGIIINO	INDIGOID	
DDGIIINV	DIVIDING	
DDGIIKNS	SKIDDING	
DDGIILMN	MIDDLING	
DDGIILNP	PIDDLING	
DDGIILNR	RIDDLING	
DDGILMNU	MUDDLING	
DDGILNOO	DOODLING	
DDGILNOP	PLODDING	
DDGILNOT	TODDLING	
DDGILNPU	PUDDLING	
DDGIMNUY	MUDDYING	
DDGINOPR	PRODDING	
DDGINPSU	PUDDINGS	
DDGINSTU	STUDDING	
DDGLOSTU	GOLD DUST	
DDGOOOOW	GOODWOOD	
DDGOOORW	GOOD WORD	
DDGOOOSW	DOGWOODS	
DDGOORSY	DRY GOODS	
DDHILOSY	SHODDILY	
DDIIIVVV	DIVI-DIVI	
DDIIMMUY	DIDYMIUM	
DDIIMRSU	DRUIDISM	
DDIIQTUY	QUIDDITY	
DDILOOPP	DIPLOPOD	
DDILORSY	SORDIDLY	
DDIMOSUY	DIDYMOUS	
DDINNOWW	DOWNWIND	
DDINOOOT	ODONTOID	
DDINOOWW	WOODWIND	
DDLLOORW	OLD WORLD	
DDLMORSU	DOLDRUMS	
DDMNORTU	DORTMUND	
DEEEEFRR	REFEREED	
DEEEEGKR	KEDGEREE	
DEEEEKNP	KNEE-DEEP	
DEEEEMRR	REDEEMER	
DEEEEMST	ESTEEMED	
DEEEENPR	DEEPENER	
DEEEENRV	VENEERED	
DEEEERTT	TEETERED	
DEEEFIIX	IDEE FIXE	
DEEEFIRW	FIREWEED	
DEEEFLRU	REFUELED	
DEEEFNRT	DEFERENT	

DEEEFRRR	DEFERRER, REFERRED
DEEEFRRT	FERRETED	
DEEEFRST	FESTERED	
DEEEFRTT	FETTERED	
DEEEGIPR	PEDIGREE	
DEEEGIRR	GREEDIER	
DEEEGNNR	ENGENDER	
DEEEGNRV	REVENGED	
DEEEHLMT	HELMETED	
DEEEHLRT	ETHELRED	
DEEEHLRW	WHEEDLER	
DEEEHLSS	HEEDLESS	
DEEEHMNS	ENMESHED	
DEEEHRTT	TETHERED	
DEEEILRV	RELIEVED	
DEEEILST	LEE TIDES	
DEEEIMRS	REMEDIES	
DEEEINRR	REINDEER	
DEEEINST	NEEDIEST	
DEEEINTV	EVENTIDE	
DEEEIPRS	SPEEDIER	
DEEEIPTX	EXPEDITE	
DEEEIRSS	DIERESES	
DEEEIRST	REEDIEST	
DEEEIRVW	REVIEWED	
DEEEISST	SEEDIEST, TEESSIDE
DEEEISTW	WEEDIEST	
DEEEJLLW	JEWELLED	
DEEEKLNN	KENNELED	
DEEEKNSW	WEEKENDS	
DEEEKOPW	POKEWEED	
DEEEKRSW	SKEWERED	
DEEELLLV	LEVELLED	
DEEELLPR	REPELLED	
DEEELLPX	EXPELLED	
DEEELLRV	REVELLED	
DEEELNRT	RELENTED	
DEEELNSS	LESSENED, NEEDLESS
DEEELOSY	SLOE-EYED	
DEEELRTT	LETTERED	
DEEELSSS	SEEDLESS	
DEEEMNSS	DEMESNES, SEEDSMEN
DEEEMPRT	TEMPERED	
DEEEMPTX	EXEMPTED	
DEEEMRST	DEEMSTER	
DEEENNRT	ENTENDRE	
DEEENOPR	REOPENED	
DEEENOPY	OPEN-EYED	
DEEENORS	ENDORSEE	
DEEENPRT	REPENTED, REPETEND
DEEENPRX	EXPENDER	

DEEENPSS	DEEPNESS	
DEEENRRR	RENDERER	
DEEENRRT	TENDERER	
DEEENRRV	REVEREND	
DEEENRST	RESENTED	
DEEENRTU	NEUTERED	
DEEENRTX	EXTENDER	
DEEENRUV	REVENUED	
DEEENSTT	DETENTES	
DEEEOPRT	DEPORTEE	
DEEEOSTV	DEVOTEES	
DEEEPPPR	PEPPERED	
DEEEPRST	PESTERED	
DEEEQSUZ	SQUEEZED	
DEEERRST	DESERTER	
DEEERRSV	DESERVER, RESERVED, REVERSED
DEEERRTV	REVERTED	
DEEERSTT	DETESTER	
DEEFFNOR	OFFENDER	
DEEFFRSU	SUFFERED	
DEEFGINR	FINGERED	
DEEFGLNU	ENGULFED	
DEEFGLUW	GULFWEED	
DEEFHLOR	FREEHOLD	
DEEFHORR	HEREFORD	
DEEFIINT	DEFINITE	
DEEFIIRS	FIRESIDE	
DEEFIIRV	VERIFIED	
DEEFILLR	REFILLED	
DEEFILLT	FILLETED	
DEEFILNX	INFLEXED	
DEEFILPR	PILFERED	
DEEFILRS	DEFILERS, FIELDERS
DEEFILRT	FILTERED	
DEEFINRR	INFERRED	
DEEFINRW	WINEFRED	
DEEFINRZ	FRENZIED	
DEEFINST	INFESTED	
DEEFIORS	FORESIDE	
DEEFIPRX	PREFIXED	
DEEFIRTT	REFITTED	
DEEFLNNU	FUNNELED	
DEEFLNOR	ENFOLDER	
DEEFLORW	DEFLOWER, FLOWERED
DEEFMNOT	FOMENTED	
DEEFMORR	DEFORMER, REFORMED
DEEFMPRU	PERFUMED	
DEEFNOST	SOFTENED	
DEEFNRRU	REFUNDER	
DEEFNSST	DEFTNESS	
DEEFORST	DEFOREST, FORESTED, FOSTERED

DEEFORUY	FOUR-EYED
DEEFRTUY	DUTY-FREE
DEEGGHHO	HEDGEHOG
DEEGGIJR	JIGGERED, REJIGGED
DEEGGINR	GINGERED
DEEGGLOR	DOGGEREL
DEEGHHOP	HEDGEHOP
DEEGHITW	WEIGHTED
DEEGHNRU	HUNGERED
DEEGHOPS	SHEEPDOG
DEEGHORW	HEDGEROW
DEEGIINN	INDIGENE
DEEGILNN	NEEDLING
DEEGILNP	IN PLEDGE
DEEGILNR	LINGERED, REEDLING
DEEGILNS	SEEDLING
DEEGILNT	DELETING
DEEGILRY	GREEDILY
DEEGILSS	LEG SIDES
DEEGIMNN	EMENDING
DEEGINPS	SPEEDING
DEEGINRS	DESIGNER, REDESIGN, RESIGNED
DEEGINSS	EDGINESS
DEEGINST	INGESTED
DEEGIORS	GEORDIES
DEEGIRST	DIGESTER
DEEGJPRU	PREJUDGE
DEEGLNRY	LEGENDRY
DEEGLORV	GROVELED
DEEGLORW	GLOWERED
DEEGNNOY	ENDOGENY
DEEGNORV	GOVERNED
DEEGNPUX	EXPUNGED
DEEGOTUW	GOUTWEED
DEEGRRTU	GERTRUDE
DEEGRSTU	GESTURED
DEEGRTTU	GUTTERED
DEEHHPRS	SHEPHERD
DEEHHRST	THRESHED
DEEHIKRS	SHRIEKED
DEEHILNP	DELPHINE
DEEHILRS	RELISHED, SHIELDER
DEEHILSS	HIDELESS
DEEHILSV	DISHEVEL
DEEHIMOP	HEMIPODE
DEEHIMRT	MEREDITH
DEEHINRR	HINDERER
DEEHINTW	WHITENED
DEEHIOTX	ETHOXIDE
DEEHIPPS	SHEEPDIP
DEEHIPRS	PERISHED

DEEHIRRT	DITHERER
DEEHIRSV	SHIVERED
DEEHIRTW	WITHERED
DEEHIRTY	HEREDITY
DEEHKNOS	KEESHOND
DEEHLLOR	HOLLERED
DEEHLOSV	SHOVELED
DEEHMNRS	HERDSMEN
DEEHMORT	MOTHERED
DEEHNORT	DETHRONE
DEEHNOWY	HONEYDEW
DEEHNSTU	ENTHUSED
DEEHOORT	THEODORE
DEEHOORV	HOOVERED
DEEHORSU	REHOUSED
DEEHORSW	SHOWERED
DEEHORTX	EXHORTED
DEEHRRSW	SHREWDER
DEEIILNS	SIDELINE
DEEIILRV	LIVERIED
DEEIIMST	ITEMISED
DEEIIMTZ	ITEMIZED
DEEIIPRU	PRIE-DIEU
DEEIIRSS	DIERESIS
DEEIIRST	SIDERITE
DEEIIRSV	DERISIVE
DEEIISSS	DISSEISE
DEEIJNNO	ENJOINED
DEEIJNOR	REJOINED
DEEIKLLR	KILLDEER
DEEIKLMO	DOMELIKE
DEEIKLMW	MILKWEED
DEEIKLNN	ENKINDLE
DEEIKLNR	REKINDLE
DEEIKNPS	SKIN-DEEP
DEEIKNRS	DEERSKIN
DEEIKNRT	TINKERED
DEEIKSTT	DISKETTE
DEEILLMN	MEDELLIN
DEEILLMP	IMPELLED
DEEILLST	LET SLIDE
DEEILLVY	VEILEDLY
DEEILMNU	DEMILUNE
DEEILMOS	MELODIES, MELODISE
DEEILMOZ	MELODIZE
DEEILNOT	DELETION
DEEILNRU	UNDERLIE
DEEILNSS	IDLENESS
DEEILNST	ENLISTED, LISTENED
DEEILNSV	SNIVELED
DEEILNTT	ENTITLED
DEEILNUV	UNVEILED
DEEILOPT	LEPIDOTE

DEEILORT	DOLERITE, LOITERED
DEEILORV	EVILDOER
DEEILPRX	DIPLEXER
DEEILPSY	SPEEDILY
DEEILRSU	LEISURED
DEEILRSV	SILVERED
DEEILRSW	WIELDERS
DEEILRTT	LITTERED
DEEILRVY	DELIVERY
DEEILSUV	DELUSIVE
DEEILSVW	SWIVELED
DEEILTUY	YULETIDE
DEEIMMNS	ENDEMISM
DEEIMMOS	SEMIDOME
DEEIMMRS	IMMERSED, SIMMERED
DEEIMNOR	DOMINEER
DEEIMNOS	DEMONISE
DEEIMNOZ	DEMONIZE
DEEIMNPT	PEDIMENT
DEEIMNRR	REMINDER
DEEIMNST	SEDIMENT
DEEIMNSY	MIND'S EYE
DEEIMPRR	PERIDERM
DEEIMPRS	SIMPERED
DEEIMRST	DEMERITS, DEMISTER
DEEIMRTT	REMITTED
DEEINNRT	INDENTER, INTENDER, INTERNED
DEEINNSS	DENISENS
DEEINNST	DESINENT
DEEINNSZ	DENIZENS
DEEINNTV	INVENTED
DEEINNTW	ENTWINED
DEEINOPW	WIDE-OPEN
DEEINOSV	NOSEDIVE
DEEINPSS	DISPENSE
DEEINQRU	ENQUIRED
DEEINQSU	SEQUINED
DEEINRRT	INTERRED, TRENDIER
DEEINRRW	REWINDER
DEEINRST	DNIESTER, INSERTED, RESIDENT, TRENDIES
DEEINRSX	INDEXERS
DEEINRTU	RETINUED, REUNITED
DEEINRTV	INVERTED
DEEINRTW	WINTERED
DEEINSSW	DEWINESS, WIDENESS
DEEINSTT	INSETTED
DEEINSTV	INVESTED

DEEINSTY	TYNESIDE	DEELOPRX	EXPLODER,
DEEIOPRX	PEROXIDE		EXPLORED
DEEIOPSS	EPISODES	DEELOPRY	REDEPLOY
DEEIORRV	OVERRIDE	DEELORRS	SOLDERER
DEEIORSV	OVERSIDE	DEELORSV	RESOLVED
DEEIPPQU	EQUIPPED	DEELORTT	DOTTEREL
DEEIPRRS	PRESIDER,	DEELORTV	REVOLTED
RESPIRED		DEELORVV	REVOLVED
DEEIPRRV	DEPRIVER	DEELPRRU	PRELUDER
DEEIPRSS	DISPERSE	DEELPRSU	PRELUDES,
DEEIPSST	SIDESTEP		REPULSED
DEEIPSTU	DEPUTIES,	DEELPRTU	DRUPELET
DEPUTISE		DEELPSUX	DUPLEXES
DEEIPTUZ	DEPUTIZE	DEELRSTU	RESULTED
DEEIQRRU	REQUIRED	DEELRSTW	WRESTLED
DEEIQRTU	REQUITED	DEEMMORS	MESODERM
DEEIQRUV	QUIVERED	DEEMMRSU	SUMMERED
DEEIQTUU	QUIETUDE	DEEMNOOS	ENDOSOME,
DEEIRRSS	DRESSIER		MOONSEED
DEEIRRTV	DIVERTER	DEEMNOQU	QUEENDOM
DEEIRSST	RESISTED	DEEMNOORT	ENTODERM
DEEIRSSU	REISSUED,	DEEMOORT	ODOMETER
RESIDUES		DEEMORSW	WORMSEED
DEEIRSSV	DISSEVER	DEEMPRST	DEMPSTER
DEEIRSTW	WEIRDEST	DEEMPRSU	PRESUMED
DEEIRTTT	TITTERED	DEEMPRTU	PERMUTED
DEEJPRRU	PERJURED	DEEMRRRU	DEMURRER,
DEEKMNOY	MONKEYED		MURDERER
DEEKNOTW	KNOTWEED	DEEMRSTU	DEMUREST,
DEEKORRW	REWORKED		MUSTERED
DEELLMOR	MODELLER	DEEMRTTU	MUTTERED
DEELLMOW	MELLOWED	DEENNOPT	DEPONENT
DEELLNOR	ENROLLED	DEENNOPU	UNOPENED
DEELLNOW	WELL-DONE	DEENNORW	RENOWNED
DEELLORY	YODELLER	DEENNRUV	UNNERVED
DEELLOTW	TOWELLED	DEENNSSU	NUDENESS
DEELLOTX	EXTOLLED	DEENOORV	OVERDONE
DEELLOVY	VOLLEYED	DEENOPRR	PONDERER
DEELLOWY	YELLOWED	DEENOPSS	SPONDEES
DEELMMPU	PUMMELED	DEENORRS	ENDORSER
DEELMNOO	MELODEON	DEENORRW	WONDERER
DEELMOPY	EMPLOYED	DEENORSW	WORSENED
DEELMOST	MOLESTED	DEENORTU	DEUTERON
DEELMRUY	DEMURELY	DEENPRSS	SPENDERS
DEELNNTU	TUNNELED	DEENPSTU	TENSED UP
DEELNOOS	LOOSE END,	DEENRRTU	RETURNED
LOOSENED		DEENRSSU	END USERS,
DEELNORT	REDOLENT,		RUDENESS
RONDELET		DEENRSTU	DENTURES,
DEELNRTU	UNDERLET		UNDERSET
DEELNRTY	TENDERLY	DEENRSUV	UNVERSED
DEELNSSW	LEWDNESS	DEENRTUV	VENTURED
DEELNWWY	NEWLYWED	DEEOORRV	OVERRODE
DEELOPRR	DEPLORER	DEEOORSV	OVERDOSE
		DEEOPRRT	REPORTED
DEEOPRRV	REPROVED
DEEOPRRW	POWDERER
DEEOPRTT	POTTERED
DEEOPRTX	EXPORTED
DEEOPSSU	ESPOUSED
DEEORRST	RESORTED,
RESTORED
DEEORRTT	RETORTED
DEEORRUV	DEVOURER
DEEORRVW	OVERDREW
DEEORSTX	DEXTROSE
DEEORSTY	STOREYED
DEEORTTT	TOTTERED
DEEORTTX	EXTORTED
DEEORTUV	DEVOUTER
DEEPRTTU	PUTTERED
DEEPRUVY	PURVEYED
DEERRSSS	DRESSERS
DEERRTTU	TURRETED
DEERSSST	DESSERTS,
STRESSED
DEERSUVY	SURVEYED
DEFFGILO	OFF-GLIDE
DEFFHLSU	SHUFFLED
DEFFILNS	SNIFFLED
DEFFILOV	FIVEFOLD
DEFFIRSU	DIFFUSER
DEFFLNSU	SNUFFLED
DEFFNOSS	SEND-OFFS
DEFFSSUU	SUFFUSED
DEFFSTUY	DYESTUFF
DEFGIILN	DEFILING, FIELDING
DEFGIINN	DEFINING
DEFGIINY	DEIFYING,
EDIFYING
DEFGIIST	DIGESTIF
DEFGINSU	DEFUSING
DEFGIORS	FIREDOGS
DEFGJORU	FORJUDGE
DEFGLOOS	GOOD SELF
DEFHIINS	FIENDISH, FINISHED
DEFHIRST	RED SHIFT
DEFHLOOS	SELFHOOD
DEFHORRT	HERTFORD
DEFIIILV	VILIFIED
DEFIIILO	OILFIELD
DEFIIILLW	WILDLIFE
DEFIILNS	INFIDELS
DEFIILOR	OIL-FIRED
DEFIILPS	FLIP SIDE
DEFIILRW	WILDFIRE
DEFIILSU	FLUIDISE
DEFIILTY	FIDELITY
DEFIILUZ	FLUIDIZE
DEFIIMOR	MODIFIER

DEFIIMRS	MISFIRED	DEGGLNSU	SNUGGLED	DEGILRUV	DIVULGER
DEFIINOT	NOTIFIED	DEGGLORY	GORGEDLY	DEGILRZZ	GRIZZLED
DEFIINRW	WINIFRED	DEGGLRUY	RUGGEDLY	DEGIMNOT	DEMOTING
DEFIINTY	IDENTIFY	DEGGRSTU	DRUGGETS	DEGIMNPU	IMPUGNED
DEFIIOSS	OSSIFIED	DEGHHIIT	HIGH TIDE	DEGIMORR	GORDIMER
DEFIIPRU	PURIFIED	DEGHHILV	HIGHVELD	DEGINNNU	UNENDING
DEFIIPSS	FISSIPED	DEGHIINS	DINGHIES	DEGINNOT	DENOTING
DEFIIPTY	TYPIFIED	DEGHIKNT	KNIGHTED	DEGINNOW	ENDOWING
DEFILNNO	NINEFOLD	DEGHILPT	PLIGHTED	DEGINNPS	SPENDING
DEFILNRU	UNRIFLED,	DEGHILRT	RED LIGHT	DEGINNPU	UPENDING
URNFIELD		DEGHILST	DELIGHTS,	DEGINNRU	ENDURING
DEFILNRY	FRIENDLY	SLIGHTED		DEGINOPS	DEPOSING
DEFILOPR	PROFILED	DEGHINNU	UNHINGED	DEGINORR	ORDERING
DEFILORU	FLUORIDE	DEGHLOPU	PLOUGHED	DEGINORV	RINGDOVE
DEFILOTU	OUTFIELD	DEGHLOSU	SLOUGHED	DEGINOSW	WIDGEONS
DEFILPRU	PRIDEFUL	DEGHNORT	THRONGED	DEGINOTV	DEVOTING
DEFILPTU	UPLIFTED	DEGHNORY	HYDROGEN	DEGINPTU	DEPUTING
DEFILRRU	FLURRIED	DEGHOOSU	DOGHOUSE	DEGINRRS	GRINDERS
DEFILRVY	FERVIDLY	DEGIIIST	DIGITISE	DEGINRRY	GRINDERY
DEFILRZZ	FRIZZLED	DEGIIITZ	DIGITIZE	DEGINRSS	DRESSING
DEFIMNOR	INFORMED	DEGIILNT	DILIGENT	DEGINRSY	SYRINGED
DEFIMOPR	PEDIFORM	DEGIILNV	DEVILING	DEGIOPRR	PORRIDGE
DEFIMRRU	DRUMFIRE	DEGIILNW	WIELDING	DEGIOPSS	GOSSIPED
DEFIMRSU	DUMFRIES	DEGIILNY	YIELDING	DEGIOPST	PODGIEST
DEFINORW	FOREWIND	DEGIILTY	GELIDITY	DEGIORST	STODGIER
DEFIOORW	FIREWOOD	DEGIIMNP	IMPEDING,	DEGIPSTU	PUDGIEST
DEFIOOST	SIDE-FOOT	IMPINGED		DEGJMNTU	JUDGMENT
DEFIOPRT	PROFITED	DEGIIMSU	MISGUIDE	DEGLMNOT	LODGMENT
DEFIRRST	DRIFTERS	DEGIINNT	INDIGENT	DEGLOOPY	PEDOLOGY
DEFLLOOW	FOLLOWED	DEGIINNW	WIDENING	DEGLOOUU	DUOLOGUE
DEFLNORU	FLOUNDER,	DEGIINNX	INDEXING	DEGLOPSS	SPLODGES
UNFOLDER		DEGIINOV	VIDEOING	DEGLPRSU	SPLURGED
DEFLNRUU	UNFURLED	DEGIINRS	DESIRING,	DEGNNOSU	DUNGEONS
DEFLOORT	FORETOLD	RESIDING, RINGSIDE		DEGNOOSS	GOODNESS
DEFMNORU	UNFORMED	DEGIINRV	DERIVING	DEHHILTW	WITHHELD
DEFMOOOR	FOREDOOM	DEGIINST	DINGIEST	DEHIILLS	HILLSIDE
DEFNNOSS	FONDNESS	DEGIINSV	DEVISING	DEHIILSV	DEVILISH
DEFNNOUW	NEW-FOUND	DEGIINTY	TIE-DYING	DEHIIMST	DITHEISM
DEFNOOPS	SPOON-FED	DEGIISSU	DISGUISE	DEHIINNS	SHINNIED
DEFNORRU	FRONDEUR	DEGIJMSU	MISJUDGE	DEHIINNW	WHINNIED
DEFNORSU	FOUNDERS	DEGIKLOV	KID-GLOVE	DEHIISST	DISHIEST
DEFNRRUU	UNDERFUR	DEGIKNRY	RING-DYKE	DEHIISTT	DITHEIST
DEFOORRW	FOREWORD	DEGILLNU	DUELLING	DEHIJMNO	DEMIJOHN
DEFOOTUX	OUTFOXED	DEGILLNW	DWELLING	DEHIKLOO	HOODLIKE
DEFORRUW	FURROWED	DEGILMNO	GOLDMINE,	DEHIKMOS	SHEIKDOM
DEGGHRSU	SHRUGGED	MODELING		DEHIKNOW	WINDHOEK
DEGGIINN	DEIGNING	DEGILMPS	GLIMPSED	DEHILLRT	THRILLED
DEGGILNP	PLEDGING	DEGILNOS	SIDELONG	DEHILMOS	DEMOLISH
DEGGILNS	GELDINGS,	DEGILNOY	YODELING	DEHILNOY	HONIEDLY
SLEDGING		DEGILNRU	INDULGER	DEHILNPY	DIPHENYL
DEGGIINN	DELUGING	DEGILOOR	GOODLIER	DEHILOPS	POLISHED
DEGGILOO	LIE DOGGO	DEGILOOY	IDEOLOGY	DEHILOTY	HOLYTIDE
DEGGILRW	WRIGGLED	DEGILOST	GODLIEST	DEHILPSU	SULPHIDE
DEGGIORS	DISGORGE	DEGILRSU	GUILDERS,	DEHILSTW	WHISTLED
DEGGLMSU	SMUGGLED	SLUDGIER			

DEHILTTW	WHITTLED	DEIILNVY	DIVINELY	DEIKSSTU	DUSKIEST
DEHIMNOS	HEDONISM	DEIILNXY	XYLIDINE	DEILLOPW	PILLOWED
DEHINOPS	SIPHONED,	DEIILORS	IDOLISER	DEILLORR	LORDLIER
SPHENOID		DEIILORZ	IDOLIZER	DEILLSTU	DUELLIST
DEHINOST	HEDONIST	DEIILPSS	SIDESLIP	DEILMNSS	MILDNESS,
DEHINPSU	PUNISHED	DEIILSTU	UTILISED	MINDLESS	
DEHINSUW	UNWISHED	DEIILTUZ	UTILIZED	DEILMOOT	DOLOMITE
DEHIOPRS	SPHEROID	DEIIMMRS	DIMERISM	DEILMOPR	IMPLORED
DEHIOSSW	SIDESHOW	DEIIMMST	MISTIMED	DEILMORT	OLD-TIMER
DEHIOSSU	SQUISHED	DEIIMNRT	DIRIMENT	DEILMORU	LEMUROID,
DEHIRTWW	WITHDREW	DEIIMNTU	MUTINIED	MOULDIER	
DEHKLNOU	ELKHOUND	DEIIMPRU	PERIDIUM	DEILMOST	MELODIST,
DEHLLOOW	HOLLOWED	DEIIMSVW	MIDWIVES	MOLDIEST	
DEHLLOPY	PHYLLODE	DEIINNOP	PINIONED	DEILMOSU	EMULSOID
DEHLMORY	HYDROMEL	DEIINNPP	PINNIPED	DEILMOTV	DEMIVOLT
DEHLNTUY	HUNTEDLY	DEIINORS	DERISION,	DEILMPTU	MULTIPED
DEHLOORV	HOLDOVER	RESINOID		DEILNNOT	INDOLENT
DEHLOOSS	HOODLESS	DEIINOST	EDITIONS,	DEILNOOS	SOLENOID
DEHLOOST	TOEHOLDS	SEDITION		DEILNOSU	DELUSION
DEHLOPRU	UPHOLDER	DEIINPPW	WINDPIPE	DEILNOSW	LIE-DOWNS
DEHLOPSS	SPLOSHED	DEIINPRS	INSPIRED	DEILNOTU	OUTLINED
DEHLORSU	SHOULDER	DEIINPRT	INTREPID	DEILNOVV	INVOLVED
DEHLRRSU	HURDLERS	DEIINPRY	PYRIDINE	DEILNPSS	SPINDLES
DEHLRSWY	SHREWDLY	DEIINQRU	INQUIRED	DEILNPST	SPLIT END
DEHLSTTU	SHUTTLED	DEIINRSS	INSIDERS	DEILNRST	TENDRILS
DEHMMRTU	THRUMMED	DEIINRST	DISINTER	DEILNRSW	SWINDLER
DEHMOORW	WHOREDOM	DEIINRSV	DIVINERS,	DEILNRTY	TRENDILY
DEHMOOST	SMOOTHED	DRIVE-INS		DEILNSSW	SWINDLES,
DEHMORUU	HUMOURED	DEIINSST	INSISTED, TIDINESS	WILDNESS	
DEHNOORU	HONOURED	DEIINSTU	DISUNITE	DEILNSTU	INSULTED,
DEHNOPSY	SYPHONED	DEIINSTW	WINDIEST	UNLISTED	
DEHNORSU	ENSHROUD,	DEIINTTU	INTUITED	DEILNTTU	UNTITLED
UNHORSED		DEIINTTY	IDENTITY	DEILNTUY	UNITEDLY
DEHNORTY	THRENODY	DEIIOPRS	PRESIDIO	DEILNUWY	UNWIELDY
DEHNOSSW	SNOWSHED	DEIIORSX	OXIDISER	DEILOOPW	WOODPILE
DEHNRSTU	THUNDERS	DEIIORTX	TRIOXIDE	DEILORSS	SOLDIERS
DEHNRTUY	THUNDERY	DEIIORXZ	OXIDIZER	DEILORSY	SOLDIERY
DEHOOPRT	THEROPOD	DEIIPRST	RIPTIDES, SPIRITED	DEILORTY	ELYTROID
DEHOORTU	OUT-HEROD	DEIIPTTY	TEPIDITY	DEILOSSV	DISSOLVE
DEHOPRST	POTSHERD	DEIIQSTU	DISQUIET	DEILOSTU	SOLITUDE
DEIIINSV	DIVINISE	DEIIRSSU	DIURESIS	DEILOSTW	LOW TIDES
DEIIINVZ	DIVINIZE	DEIIRSTT	DIRTIEST	DEILOTUV	OUTLIVED
DEIIISVV	DIVISIVE	DEIISTZZ	DIZZIEST	DEILPPST	STIPPLED
DEIIKLNR	KINDLIER	DEIJORRY	JOYRIDER	DEILPPSU	SUPPLIED
DEIIKLSS	DISLIKES	DEIJORSY	JOYRIDES	DEILPRSU	SERPULID
DEIIKMOS	ESKIMOID	DEIKKLNO	KLONDIKE	DEILRRSV	L-DRIVERS
DEIIKNST	DINKIEST	DEIKLNRW	WRINKLED	DEILRSSY	DRESSILY
DEIIKNSV	SKIN-DIVE	DEIKLNTW	TWINKLED	DEILSSTY	STYLISED
DEIIKSVV	SKIVVIED	DEIKLORS	ROSKILDE	DEILSTUY	SEDULITY
DEIILLMT	ILL-TIMED	DEIKMNOO	KIMONOED	DEILSTWW	WILD WEST
DEIILMRU	DELIRIUM	DEIKNNRU	UNKINDER	DEILSTYZ	STYLIZED
DEIILNNU	INDULINE	DEIKNNSS	KINDNESS	DEIMMNOS	DEMONISM
DEIILNOS	LIONISED	DEIKNRRS	DRINKERS	DEIMMOST	IMMODEST
DEIILNOT	TOLIDINE	DEIKNRSS	REDSKINS	DEIMNOOS	DOMINOES
DEIILNOZ	LIONIZED	DEIKRSVY	SKYDIVER		

258

DEIMNOOT	DEMOTION,
	MOTIONED
DEIMNOOX	MONOXIDE
DEIMNOPT	PIEDMONT
DEIMNOST	DEMONIST
DEIMNOTW	DOWNTIME
DEIMNPSS	MISSPEND
DEIMNPTU	IMPUDENT
DEIMNRTU	RUDIMENT
DEIMOOST	MOODIEST,
	SODOMITE
DEIMOOSZ	SODOMIZE
DEIMOPRS	PROMISED
DEIMOPRT	IMPORTED
DEIMOPRV	IMPROVED
DEIMORRR	MIRRORED
DEIMORSU	DIMEROUS,
	SOREDIUM
DEIMORUX	EXORDIUM
DEIMOSTT	DEMOTIST
DEIMOTTW	TWO-TIMED
DEIMPSTU	DUMPIEST
DEIMQRSU	SQUIRMED
DEIMRSSU	SURMISED
DEIMRSUU	RESIDUUM
DEINNNOU	INNUENDO
DEINNOWW	WINNOWED
DEINNPRU	UNDERPIN
DEINNRSU	IN SUNDER
DEINNRTV	TV DINNER
DEINNRUW	UNWINDER
DEINOOPS	POISONED
DEINOOPW	PINEWOOD
DEINOOTV	DEVOTION
DEINOPPW	DOWNPIPE
DEINOPRY	PYRENOID
DEINOPSS	DOPINESS
DEINORSU	SOURDINE
DEINORSW	DISOWNER
DEINORVW	OVERWIND
DEINOSSZ	DOZINESS
DEINOSTW	DOWNIEST
DEINOSWZ	DOWNSIZE
DEINPPUZ	UNZIPPED
DEINPRST	SPRINTED
DEINPSST	STIPENDS
DEINPTTU	INPUTTED
DEINQSTU	SQUINTED
DEINRRTU	INTRUDER
DEINRSSU	SUNDRIES
DEINRSTT	STRIDENT,
	TRIDENTS
DEINSSST	DISSENTS
DEINSSSY	SYNDESIS
DEINSTUU	UNSUITED

DEIOORTV	OVERDO IT
DEIOOSTW	WOODIEST
DEIOPRRV	PROVIDER
DEIOPRSS	DISPOSER
DEIOPRST	RIPOSTED
DEIOPRSV	DISPROVE
DEIOPSST	DEPOSITS
DEIOPTUW	WIPED OUT
DEIORRSY	DERISORY
DEIORRTU	OUTRIDER
DEIORSSS	DOSSIERS
DEIORSST	STEROIDS
DEIORSSU	DESIROUS
DEIORSTU	OUTSIDER
DEIORSTW	ROWDIEST,
	WORDIEST
DEIORSWW	WIDOWERS
DEIOSSTU	OUTSIDES
DEIOSTTT	DOTTIEST
DEIPPRST	STRIPPED
DEIPRSTU	DISPUTER,
	STUPIDER
DEIPSSTU	DISPUTES
DEIQRSTU	SQUIRTED
DEIRRSTU	STURDIER
DEIRSSST	DISTRESS
DEIRSTTU	DETRITUS
DEIRSUVV	SURVIVED
DEISSTTU	DUSTIEST
DEISTTTU	DUETTIST
DEJMPPUU	JUMPED-UP
DEKKORSW	DESKWORK
DEKNRSTU	DRUNKEST
DEKOOPRV	PROVOKED
DEKOOTWW	KOWTOWED
DEKOPRUW	WORKED UP
DELLLOOP	LOLLOPED
DELLNOPU	UNPOLLED
DELLNORU	UNROLLED
DELLNSSU	DULLNESS
DELLOOTW	WELL-TO-DO
DELLOPTU	POLLUTED
DELLORRY	DROLLERY
DELLORST	DROLLEST,
	STROLLED
DELMNOOW	OLD WOMEN
DELMNOTW	MELTDOWN
DELMNPUU	PENDULUM
DELMORSU	REMOULDS,
	SMOULDER
DELMOSTY	MODESTLY
DELNNOOR	LONDONER
DELNOOSU	UNLOOSED
DELNOOWY	WOODENLY
DELNORSU	ROUNDELS

DELNORSY	REYNOLDS
DELNORWW	NEW WORLD
DELNOSSU	LOUDNESS
DELNOSTW	LETDOWNS
DELOORRV	OVERLORD
DELOORSV	OVERSOLD
DELOPRST	DROPLETS
DELOPSTU	POSTLUDE
DELOPSTW	SPOT-WELD
DELORSST	OLDSTERS
DELORSSW	WORDLESS
DELORSUY	DELUSORY
DELOSSUU	SEDULOUS
DELOTUVY	DEVOUTLY
DELRSSTU	STRUDELS
DEMMNOSU	SUMMONED
DEMMRRSU	DRUMMERS
DEMMRRUU	MURMURED
DEMMRSTU	STRUMMED
DEMNNOOT	EDMONTON
DEMNOOSW	WOODSMEN
DEMNORSY	SYNDROME
DEMNOSTU	MUDSTONE
DEMOOPRR	PRODROME
DEMOOPRT	PROMOTED
DEMOORSU	DORMOUSE
DEMOPPRT	PROMPTED
DEMORRUU	RUMOURED
DENNOORW	NO WONDER
DENNOSTY	SYNDETON
DENNOTUW	UNWONTED
DENOOOTW	WOODNOTE
DENOORRS	ENDORSOR
DENOORTX	NEXT-DOOR
DENORRSU	ROUNDERS
DENORSSU	DOURNESS
DENORSTU	ROUNDEST
DENORSTY	DRY-STONE
DENORTUW	UNDERTOW
DENPRTUU	UPTURNED
DENRRTUU	NURTURED
DENSSTTU	STUDENTS
DEOOORSW	ROSEWOOD
DEOOPPRS	PROPOSED
DEOOPPRT	PTEROPOD
DEOOPRST	DOORSTEP
DEOOPRTU	UPROOTED
DEOORRSW	SORROWED
DEOOSTWW	WESTWOOD
DEOOTTUV	OUTVOTED
DEOPPRRS	DROPPERS
DEOPPRSU	PURPOSED
DEOPPSSU	SUPPOSED
DEOPRRTU	PROTRUDE

DEOPRSST	TOP-DRESS	DGHOOOSW	GOOD SHOW	DHIJOPRU	JODHPURI
DEOPRSTU	POSTURED,	DGHOOOTT	DOGTOOTH	DHIKNOOW	HOODWINK
PROUDEST, SPROUTED		DGHORRUY	ROUGH-DRY	DHILLNOW	DOWNHILL
DEORRTTU	TORTURED	DGHORSTU	DROUGHTS	DHILLOPY	PHYLLOID
DEOSSSYY	ODYSSEYS	DGHORTUY	DROUGHTY	DHILMOPY	LYMPHOID
DEPRRTUU	RUPTURED	DGIIINNV	DIVINING	DHILMOSY	MODISHLY
DERSTTTU	STRUTTED	DGIIIRTY	RIGIDITY	DHILNOPS	DOLPHINS
DFFIIMRS	MIDRIFFS	DGIIKLNN	KINDLING	DHILOPRS	LORDSHIP
DFFLOORU	FOURFOLD	DGIIKNNR	DRINKING	DHILOPSS	SLIPSHOD
DFFOORUW	WOODRUFF	DGIILLNR	DRILLING	DHILORRY	HORRIDLY
DFGGHIOT	DOGFIGHT	DGIILLOU	LIGULOID	DHIMNOST	HINDMOST
DFGHILOS	GOLDFISH	DGIILNTU	DILUTING	DHINORSU	ROUNDISH
DFGIILRY	FRIGIDLY	DGIIMNOU	GONIDIUM	DHINOTUW	WHODUNIT
DFGIINNS	FINDINGS	DGIIMPUY	PYGIDIUM	DHIOOPRZ	RHIZOPOD
DFGIINRT	DRIFTING	DGIINORR	GRIDIRON	DHIORSTY	THYROIDS,
DFGILNNO	FONDLING	DGIINORT	DIGITRON	THYRSOID	
DFGILNOO	FLOODING	DGIINPPR	DRIPPING	DHJOPRSU	JODHPURS
DFGINNOU	FOUNDING	DGIINRTY	DIRTYING	DHKMNOOO	MONKHOOD
DFGLNOOR	LONGFORD	DGIKMNOS	KINGDOMS	DHLMOOSU	HOODLUMS
DFHIIMUY	HUMIDIFY	DGIKNOOW	KINGWOOD	DHLNOSTU	SHOULDN'T
DFHILSSU	DISHFULS	DGILLOOW	GOODWILL	DHMNOOOT	HOMODONT
DFHIMRSU	DRUMFISH	DGILMNOS	MOLDINGS	DHNOOSWW	SHOWDOWN
DFHLOOOT	FOOTHOLD	DGILMNOU	MOULDING	DHNOSTUW	SHUTDOWN
DFHNOOUX	FOXHOUND	DGILMNPU	DUMPLING	DHOOORTX	ORTHODOX
DFIILMTU	MULTIFID	DGILMSUY	SMUDGILY	DHOOPRST	DROP SHOT
DFIILOSY	SOLIDIFY	DGILNOOR	DROOLING	DHOORSUW	WOODRUSH
DFIILTUY	FLUIDITY	DGILNOOY	INDOLOGY	DIIILLQU	ILLIQUID
DFILLOOT	FLOODLIT	DGILNOTY	DOTINGLY	DIIIMTTY	TIMIDITY
DFILLORY	FLORIDLY	DGILOSTY	STODGILY	DIIINOSV	DIVISION
DFILLOWW	WILDFOWL	DGILRTUY	TURGIDLY	DIIINTVY	DIVINITY
DFIMOOOR	IODOFORM	DGIMMNNRU	DRUMMING	DIIIPRST	DISPIRIT
DFIOOPRS	DISPROOF	DGINNOPU	POUNDING	DIIIRTVY	VIRIDITY
DFJKNOOU	JUNK FOOD	DGINNORU	ROUNDING	DIIJNOST	DISJOINT
DFLOOOSU	SOUL FOOD	DGINNORW	DROWNING	DIILLMNW	WINDMILL
DFNOOPRU	PROFOUND	DGINNOSU	SOUNDING	DIILLMPY	LIMPIDLY
DFOOOSTW	SOFTWOOD	DGINNOUW	WOUNDING	DIILLSTY	IDYLLIST
DGGGIINS	DIGGINGS	DGINOOPR	DROOPING	DIILNOTU	DILUTION
DGGGINRU	DRUGGING,	DGINOOPS	GOSPODIN	DIILNTUY	UNTIDILY
GRUDGING		DGINOOTU	OUTDOING	DIILOPRT	TRIPLOID
DGGIILNR	GIRDLING	DGINOPPR	DROPPING	DIILOPSS	DIPLOSIS
DGGIINNR	GRINDING	DGINORSW	DROWSING	DIILOSTY	SOLIDITY
DGGILNOS	LODGINGS	DGINSTUY	STUDYING	DIIMMNOU	DOMINIUM
DGGIMNSU	SMUDGING	DGLOOOXY	DOXOLOGY	DIIMNNOO	DOMINION
DGGINRTU	TRUDGING	DGMOPRSU	GUMDROPS	DIIMNOPT	MIDPOINT
DGGIRSTU	DRUGGIST	DGNOOORV	NOVGOROD	DIIMNSUU	INDUSIUM
DGHIIINN	IN HIDING	DGOORSTT	DOGTROTS	DIIMOPRS	PRISMOID
DGHIIMNT	MIDNIGHT	DHHILOTW	WITHHOLD	DIIMPUXY	PYXIDIUM
DGHIINSS	SHINDIGS	DHIIIMNS	DIMINISH	DIIMTTUY	TUMIDITY
DGHILLNU	DUNGHILL	DHIIKWZZ	WHIZZ KID	DIINNOSU	DISUNION
DGHILNOS	HOLDINGS	DHIIMNOO	HOMINOID	DIINOOPS	IODOPSIN
DGHILNRU	HURDLING	DHIIMNSU	HINDUISM	DIINOSSU	SINUSOID
DGHILOOR	GIRLHOOD	DHIIMOST	ISTHMOID	DIINSTUY	DISUNITY
DGHINNOU	HOUNDING	DHIIMTUY	HUMIDITY	DIIORSST	SISTROID
DGHLORSU	GOLD RUSH	DHIIORSS	HIDROSIS	DIIORSSV	DIVISORS
DGHNOTUU	DOUGHNUT				

DIKLNNUY	UNKINDLY
DILLMNOP	MILLPOND
DILLOORS	DOORSILL
DILLOSTY	STOLIDLY
DILMNOSW	SLIM DOWN
DILMOOSU	MODIOLUS
DILOOPPY	POLYPOID
DILOOPRY	DROOPILY
DILOORSS	LORDOSIS
DILOOSUY	ODIOUSLY
DILOPRTY	TORPIDLY
DILORRTY	TORRIDLY
DILORSWY	DROWSILY
DILPSTUY	STUPIDLY
DILRSTUY	STURDILY
DIMNOSTU	DISMOUNT
DIMORSWY	ROWDYISM
DINOOORW	IRONWOOD
DINOOSTY	NODOSITY
DINOSSTW	SIT-DOWNS
DINRSTUY	INDUSTRY
DIOSSTUU	STUDIOUS
DIRSSTTU	DISTRUST
DKOOORWW	WOODWORK
DKORSTUW	STUDWORK
DLNOOSWW	SLOWDOWN
DLOOOORS	DOLOROSO
DLOOORSU	DOLOROUS
DLOOPPUW	PULPWOOD, WOOD PULP
DLOOPPYY	POLYPODY
DMMNRUUY	DUMMY RUN
DMOOORWW	WOODWORM, WORMWOOD
DNNOOTWW	DOWNTOWN
DNNORSUW	RUNDOWNS
DNNORTUW	DOWNTURN
DNOOPPRU	PROPOUND
DNOOPRSW	SNOWDROP
DNOOPRUW	DOWNPOUR
DNOORSUW	WONDROUS
DNOPRSUU	ROUNDUPS
DNOPSTUW	PUT-DOWNS
DNORRSUU	SURROUND
DOOOPRST	DOORPOST, DOORSTOP
DOOORSTU	OUTDOORS
DOOPRRTW	DROPWORT
DOOPRSTU	DROPOUTS
EEEEFRRS	REFEREES
EEEEGQSU	SQUEEGEE
EEEEGSSX	EXEGESES
EEEEHTTY	EYETEETH
EEEELLPX	EXPELLEE
EEEENRRV	VENEERER

EEEFFINT	TENEFIFE
EEEFFNOR	FREEFONE
EEEFFNRT	EFFERENT
EEEFFORT	FOREFEET
EEEFFRVW	FEVERFEW
EEEFGRSU	REFUGEES
EEEFILPR	LIFE PEER
EEEFINRR	FREE REIN
EEEFINRT	TENERIFE
EEEFLRSX	REFLEXES
EEEFLSTT	FLEETEST
EEEFNORS	FORESEEN
EEEFNRRT	REFERENT, RENT-FREE, TREE FERN
EEEFNRUZ	UNFREEZE
EEEFORRS	FORESEER
EEEFPRUZ	FREEZE-UP
EEEFRRRR	REFERRER
EEEFRRRT	FERRETER
EEEFRRSZ	FREEZERS
EEEFRRTT	FETTERER
EEEGGILN	NEGLIGEE
EEEGHINT	EIGHTEEN
EEEGINNR	ENGINEER
EEEGINRS	ENERGISE
EEEGINRZ	ENERGIZE
EEEGIPRS	PERIGEES
EEEGISSX	EXEGESIS
EEEGISTV	EGESTIVE
EEEGLNRT	GREENLET
EEEGMNRT	EMERGENT
EEEGMORT	GEOMETER
EEEGNRRV	REVENGER
EEEGNRRY	GREENERY
EEEGNRST	GREENEST
EEEGOPRT	PROTEGEE
EEEHILSW	HELEWISE, WHEELIES
EEEHIRSS	HERESIES
EEEHIRST	ETHERISE
EEEHIRTZ	ETHERIZE
EEEHITWY	WHITE-EYE
EEEHLLNS	HELLENES
EEEHLLSS	HEELLESS
EEEHLMPT	HELPMEET
EEEHLNTV	ELEVENTH
EEEHLNTY	ETHYLENE
EEEHLOPP	PEEPHOLE
EEEHLORS	LEE SHORE
EEEHMNTV	VEHEMENT
EEEHNNPT	NEPENTHE
EEEHNNQU	HENEQUEN
EEEHNPRS	ENSPHERE
EEEHNRVW	WHENEVER
EEEHORST	SHOETREE

EEEHRRVW	WHEREVER
EEEHRSST	SHEEREST
EEEHSSTT	ESTHETES
EEEIKLSW	WEEKLIES
EEEIKNPS	PEKINESE
EEEILLRV	REVEILLE
EEEILMMN	EMMELINE
EEEILNRT	TREELINE
EEEILNRY	EYELINER
EEEILNST	SELENITE
EEEILPRS	SLEEPIER
EEEILRRV	RELIEVER
EEEILRST	LEERIEST, STEELIER
EEEILSTV	TELEVISE
EEEIMNRU	MEUNIERE
EEEIMPRR	PREMIERE
EEEIMRRS	MISERERE
EEEIMRSZ	MEZIERES
EEEINNNT	NINETEEN
EEEINNRT	INTERNEE, RETINENE
EEEINNSV	VIENNESE
EEEINPRT	PINETREE
EEEINRSS	EERINESS
EEEINRST	ETERNISE
EEEINRTZ	ETERNIZE
EEEINSTW	WEENIEST
EEEINTUX	EUXENITE
EEEIPRRV	REPRIEVE
EEEIQSUX	EXEQUIES
EEEIRRSV	REVERIES
EEEIRRTV	RETRIEVE
EEEIRRVW	REVIEWER
EEEIRTVX	EXERTIVE
EEEISSTW	SWEETIES
EEEJKKNR	KNEE-JERK
EEEJLLRW	JEWELLER
EEEKLSST	SLEEKEST
EEEKMNNS	MEEKNESS
EEEKNNSS	KEENNESS
EEEKNORS	KEROSENE
EEEKNSTV	KESTEVEN
EEELLLRV	LEVELLER
EEELLNOR	ENROLLEE
EEELLPRR	REPELLER
EEELLPRX	EXPELLER
EEELLRRV	REVELLER
EEELMNST	ELEMENTS
EEELMOPY	EMPLOYEE
EEELMOTT	OMELETTE
EEELMRTU	MULETEER
EEELNOPP	PENELOPE
EEELNOPV	ENVELOPE
EEELNRSW	NEWSREEL

EEELNRSY	SERENELY	EEFFISUV	EFFUSIVE	EEFKNORT	REEF KNOT
EEELNRTY	TERYLENE	EEFFLNTU	EFFLUENT	EEFLLLNU	FLUELLEN
EEELOPPR	REPEOPLE	EEFFRRSU	SUFFERER	EEFLLORR	EL FERROL
EEELPRSS	PEERLESS,	EEFGIILR	FILIGREE	EEFLLORT	FORETELL,
	SLEEPERS	EEFGILNS	FEELINGS		TOLL-FREE
EEELPSST	STEEPLES	EEFGILNT	FLEETING	EEFLLRSU	SELF-RULE
EEELPTTY	TELETYPE	EEFGINRR	FINGERER	EEFLLSSS	SELFLESS
EEELRRTT	LETTERER	EEFGINRZ	FREEZING	EEFLMSSU	FUMELESS
EEELRSST	TREELESS	EEFGLNRY	GREENFLY	EEFLNORU	FLUORENE
EEELRSTT	RESETTLE	EEFGLNUV	VENGEFUL	EEFLNTUV	EVENTFUL
EEELRSTV	LEVERETS	EEFGLORS	FORELEGS	EEFLORRW	FLOWERER
EEELRSVY	SEVERELY	EEFGNOOR	FOREGONE	EEFLORTT	FLORETTE
EEELTTTX	TELETEXT	EEFGOORR	FOREGOER	EEFLORTV	LEFTOVER
EEEMMRUZ	MEZEREUM	EEFHILLR	HELLFIRE	EEFLORVW	OVERFLEW
EEEMNNTT	TENEMENT	EEFHILRS	FLESHIER	EEFLORWW	WEREWOLF
EEEMNORZ	MEZEREON	EEFHIRSV	FEVERISH	EEFLRRSU	FERRULES
EEEMORRV	EVERMORE	EEFHIRTY	ETHERIFY	EEFLRSST	FRETLESS
EEEMPRRT	TEMPERER	EEFHISST	FETISHES	EEFMNORT	FOMENTER
EEEMRSST	SEMESTER	EEFHISTT	HEFTIEST	EEFMNRRY	FERRYMEN
EEEMRSTX	EXTREMES	EEFHLLPS	SELF-HELP	EEFMORRR	REFORMER
EEENNOPR	NEOPRENE	EEFHLLWY	FLYWHEEL	EEFMPRRU	PERFUMER
EEENNSSV	EVENNESS	EEFHLSTY	FLYSHEET	EEFMPRSU	PERFUMES
EEENNSTT	ENTENTES	EEFHMNRS	FRESHMEN	EEFNORST	SOFTENER
EEENORSV	OVERSEEN,	EEFHRSST	FRESHEST	EEFNORTU	FOURTEEN
	VERONESE	EEFIIKLL	LIFELIKE	EEFNORTW	FOREWENT,
EEENORVY	EVERYONE	EEFIILLN	LIFELINE		FREETOWN
EEENPPRS	PREPENSE	EEFIILMT	LIFETIME	EEFNQRTU	FREQUENT
EEENPRRT	REPENTER	EEFIILSS	LIFE-SISE	EEFNRTTU	UNFETTER
EEENPRSY	PYRENEES	EEFIILSZ	LIFE-SIZE	EEFOORRT	ROOFTREE
EEENPSSX	EXPENSES	EEFIIMNN	FEMININE	EEFOPRRT	FREE PORT
EEENRRTV	REVERENT	EEFIIMNS	FEMINISE	EEFOPRST	FREEPOST,
EEEORRSV	OVERSEER	EEFIIMNZ	FEMINIZE		POST-FREE
EEEORRSX	XEROSERE	EEFIIRRV	VERIFIER	EEFORRST	FORESTER,
EEEORSSY	EYESORES	EEFIIRST	FIERIEST		FOSTERER, REFOREST
EEEPRRST	PESTERER	EEFIJNNR	JENNIFER	EEFORRSU	FERREOUS
EEEPRRSV	PERVERSE,	EEFIKNNP	PENKNIFE	EEFORRTY	FERETORY
	PRESERVE	EEFILLRW	FREE WILL	EEFORSUY	FOUREYES
EEEPRRTW	PEWTERER	EEFILLSS	LIFELESS	EEFOSSTT	FOSSETTE
EEEPRSSW	SWEEPERS	EEFILMST	FISTMELE	EEFOSSTU	FOETUSES
EEEPSSTT	STEEPEST	EEFILNOS	FELONIES	EEGGHLLS	EGGSHELL
EEEQRSTU	QUEEREST	EEFILPRR	PILFERER	EEGGHNOR	HONEGGER
EEEQRSUZ	SQUEEZER	EEFILRTU	TRUE-LIFE	EEGGILST	LEGGIEST
EEEQSSUZ	SQUEEZES	EEFIMORT	FORETIME	EEGGIMNR	EMERGING
EEERRRSV	RESERVER,	EEFINNSS	FINENESS	EEGGIMRT	EGG TIMER
	REVERSER	EEFINNTU	FINE-TUNE	EEGGINNR	GREENING,
EEERRRTV	REVERTER	EEFINRRR	INFERRER		RENEGING
EEERRSSV	RESERVES,	EEFINRRY	REFINERY	EEGGINRT	GREETING
	REVERSES	EEFINRSS	RIFENESS	EEGGNSST	NEST EGGS
EEERRSTT	RESETTER	EEFINRST	INFESTER	EEGGORTT	GO-GETTER
EEERSTTW	TWEETERS	EEFIPRSX	PREFIXES	EEGHHIKN	KNEE-HIGH
EEERSTVX	VERTEXES	EEFIRRST	FIRTREES	EEGHHINT	HEIGHTEN
EEERSTWZ	TWEEZERS	EEFIRRSU	SUREFIRE	EEGHIIST	EIGHTIES
EEESSTTW	SWEETEST	EEFIRSTT	FRISETTE	EEGHIKLY	KEIGHLEY
EEFFGIIS	EFFIGIES	EEFIRSTY	ESTERIFY	EEGHILNW	WHEELING
EEFFGORY	GEOFFREY			EEGHILRS	SLEIGHER

EEGHINRS	GREENISH, SHEERING	
EEGHINST	SEETHING, SHEETING	
EEGHINTT	TEETHING	
EEGHINWZ	WHEEZING	
EEGHIOTT	GOETHITE	
EEGHIRST	THESIGER	
EEGHIRTW	WEIGHTER	
EEGHISST	SIGHTSEE	
EEGHISTY	EYESIGHT	
EEGHLNNT	LENGTHEN	
EEGHMNOY	HEGEMONY	
EEGHNOPS	PHOSGENE	
EEGHNSSU	HUGENESS	
EEGHOPTY	GEOPHYTE	
EEGHORTT	TOGETHER	
EEGHOSTT	GHETTOES	
EEGIILNR	LINGERIE	
EEGIILNV	INVEIGLE	
EEGIINTV	GENITIVE	
EEGIJMNN	NIJMEGEN	
EEGIKLNN	KNEELING	
EEGIKLNS	SLEEKING	
EEGILLNV	LEVELING	
EEGILNPS	PEELINGS, SLEEPING	
EEGILNRR	LINGERER	
EEGILNRU	REGULINE	
EEGILNRV	LEVERING, REVELING	
EEGILNST	GENTILES, SLEETING, STEELING	
EEGILNSV	SLEEVING	
EEGILNTX	TELEXING	
EEGILOPU	EPILOGUE	
EEGILOSU	EULOGISE, EULOGIES	
EEGILRTV	VERLIGTE	
EEGILOUZ	EULOGIZE	
EEGIMNNS	MENINGES	
EEGIMNRS	REGIMENS	
EEGIMNRT	METERING, REGIMENT	
EEGIMNRU	MERINGUE	
EEGIMNST	MEETINGS	
EEGINNPR	PREENING	
EEGINNQU	QUEENING	
EEGINNRS	SNEERING	
EEGINNRT	ENTERING	
EEGINNRW	RENEWING	
EEGINNRY	ENGINERY	
EEGINNSU	INGENUES, UNSEEING	
EEGINNSV	EVENINGS	

EEGINNSZ	SNEEZING	
EEGINORR	ERIGERON	
EEGINOST	EGESTION	
EEGINPRU	PUREEING	
EEGINPST	STEEPING	
EEGINPSW	SWEEPING	
EEGINQRU	QUEERING	
EEGINRRS	RESIGNER	
EEGINRRV	REVERING	
EEGINRST	INTEGERS, STEERING	
EEGINRSU	SEIGNEUR	
EEGINRSV	SEVERING	
EEGINRTX	EXERTING	
EEGINSSU	GENIUSES	
EEGINTTV	VIGNETTE	
EEGINTTW	TWEETING	
EEGIPRST	PRESTIGE	
EEGIRRST	REGISTER	
EEGIRSTT	GRISETTE	
EEGISSTV	VESTIGES	
EEGLNOPY	POLYGENE	
EEGLNOSZ	LOZENGES	
EEGLNOTY	TELEGONY	
EEGLOOST	TOGOLESE	
EEGMNOST	GEMSTONE	
EEGMNSST	SEGMENTS	
EEGMORSU	GRUESOME	
EEGMORTY	GEOMETRY	
EEGMRSTU	GUM TREES	
EEGNNORT	ROENTGEN	
EEGNNOSV	EVENSONG	
EEGNOPTY	GENOTYPE	
EEGNORSU	GENEROUS	
EEGNOTYZ	ZYGOTENE	
EEGNPRUX	EXPUNGER	
EEGNRSSY	GREYNESS	
EEGNRSUY	GUERNSEY	
EEGOPRST	PROTEGES	
EEGOPRSU	SUPEREGO	
EEGORRRU	GUERRERO	
EEGRRSTU	GESTURER	
EEGRSSTU	GESTURES	
EEHHIPSS	SHEEPISH	
EEHHIRST	THIS HERE	
EEHHIRTW	HEREWITH	
EEHHLLLO	HELLHOLE	
EEHHLMOP	HOME HELP	
EEHHLSTW	THE WELSH	
EEHHNOSU	HEN HOUSE	
EEHHRRST	THRESHER	
EEHHRSST	THRESHES	
EEHIIKLV	HIVELIKE	
EEHIILTV	HELVETII	

EEHIILTW	WHITE LIE	
EEHIITTW	WHITE-TIE	
EEHIKLMO	HOMELIKE	
EEHIKRRS	SHRIEKER	
EEHILMNS	HEMLINES	
EEHILMOR	HOMELIER	
EEHILNPW	PINWHEEL	
EEHILORT	HOTELIER	
EEHILRSS	HEIRLESS, RELISHES	
EEHILWYZ	WHEEZILY	
EEHIMNOR	HERMIONE	
EEHIMNRT	THEREMIN	
EEHIMRST	ERETHISM	
EEHIMRTT	THERMITE	
EEHINNRS	ENSHRINE	
EEHINNRT	INHERENT	
EEHINORT	HEREINTO	
EEHINPRT	NEPHRITE, TREPHINE	
EEHINRTT	THIRTEEN	
EEHINRTW	WHITENER	
EEHIORRT	EITHER-OR	
EEHIORST	ISOTHERE, THEORIES, THEORISE	
EEHIORTZ	THEORIZE	
EEHIPPST	PSEPHITE	
EEHIPPTY	EPIPHYTE	
EEHIPRRS	PERISHER	
EEHIPRTT	TEPHRITE	
EEHIPSTT	EPITHETS	
EEHIRRSV	SHIVERER	
EEHIRRTW	WITHERER	
EEHIRSTT	TEE SHIRT	
EEHIRTVY	THIEVERY	
EEHKLOSY	KEYHOLES	
EEHKLOWY	HOLY WEEK	
EEHLLMSS	HELMLESS	
EEHLLPSS	HELPLESS	
EEHLMMNS	HELMSMEN	
EEHLMORU	HOME RULE	
EEHLMOSS	HOMELESS	
EEHLNOSW	HENSLOWE	
EEHLOPSS	HOPELESS	
EEHLOPST	HEELPOST, PESTHOLE	
EEHLORSV	SHOVELER	
EEHLPRSU	SPHERULE	
EEHLPRTY	THREE-PLY	
EEHLRSST	SHELTERS	
EEHLRSSW	WELSHERS	
EEHMMOPR	MORPHEME	
EEHMMORT	OHMMETER	
EEHMNOPS	PHONEMES	
EEHMNORS	HORSEMEN	
EEHMNOSU	HOUSEMEN	

EEHMORST	REST HOME, THEOREMS
EEHMORVW	WHOMEVER
EEHNNOOT	ETHONONE
EEHNNORT	ENTHRONE
EEHNOORS	ONE-HORSE
EEHNOPRU	HEREUPON
EEHNOPTY	NEOPHYTE
EEHNORST	HORTENSE, THE NORSE
EEHNORTU	HEREUNTO
EEHNSSTV	SEVENTHS
EEHOOPRS	OOSPHERE
EEHOOPSW	WHOOPEES
EEHOORSV	OVERSHOE
EEHOOTTY	EYETOOTH
EEHOPPSW	PEEPSHOW
EEHORRSV	HOVERERS
EEHORRTX	EXHORTER
EEHPRSSU	HESPERUS
EEIIKLLR	LIKELIER
EEIIKLSW	LIKEWISE
EEIILLRV	LIVELIER
EEIILMNT	ILMENITE, MELINITE
EEIILMRT	TIMELIER
EEIILNPP	PIPELINE
EEIILNTV	LENITIVE
EEIILRSV	LIVERIES
EEIILRVW	LIVE WIRE
EEIILSTW	LEWISITE
EEIIMMTT	MIMETITE
EEIIMOST	MOIETIES
EEIIMRSS	MISERIES
EEIIMSSV	EMISSIVE
EEIINNST	NINETIES
EEIINNVV	VIVIENNE
EEIINPPR	PIPERINE
EEIINPRV	VIPERINE
EEIINRRV	RIVERINE
EEIINRSS	IN SERIES
EEIINRTT	RETINITE
EEIINSSV	INESSIVE
EEIINSTT	ENTITIES
EEIIOPTZ	EPIZOITE
EEIIQSTU	EQUITIES
EEIIRSTV	VERITIES
EEIJKRST	JERKIEST
EEIJLNNU	JULIENNE
EEIJLNRT	JETLINER
EEIJLNUV	JUVENILE
EEIJLTTU	JULIETTE
EEIJNNOR	ENJOINER
EEIKKLRS	KIRKLEES
EEIKLNSS	LIKENESS

EEIKLORT	LORIKEET
EEIKLPST	SPIKELET
EEIKMOTX	KETOXIME
EEIKNOTW	ENIWETOK
EEIKNRRT	TINKERER
EEIKPRST	PERKIEST
EEIKPSST	PESKIEST
EEILLLMV	MELVILLE
EEILLMPR	IMPELLER
EEILLMRS	SMELLIER
EEILLNOR	LONELIER
EEILLORV	LOVELIER
EEILLOSV	LOVELIES
EEILLPSS	ELLIPSES
EEILLPSY	SLEEPILY
EEILLSTT	STELLITE
EEILLSTV	EVILLEST
EEILMNNO	LIMONENE
EEILMNNS	LINESMEN
EEILMNST	MELISENT
EEILMNSU	SELENIUM
EEILMNTY	MYTILENE
EEILMSST	TIMELESS
EEILMSUV	EMULSIVE
EEILNNST	SENTINEL
EEILNOPR	LEPORINE
EEILNORS	ROSELINE
EEILNPPZ	ZEPPELIN
EEILNPRU	PERILUNE
EEILNPRV	REPLEVIN
EEILNRST	ENLISTER, LEINSTER, LISTENER
EEILNRTY	ENTIRELY, LIENTERY
EEILNSSV	EVILNESS, VILENESS
EEILNSVY	YVELINES
EEILORRT	LOITERER
EEILOSVW	VOWELISE
EEILOTTT	TOILETTE
EEILOTTV	VIOLETTE
EEILOVWZ	VOWELIZE
EEILPPSY	EPILEPSY
EEILPRST	EPISTLER, REPTILES
EEILPSST	EPISTLES
EEILPSSV	PELVISES
EEILPSTY	EPISTYLE
EEILRRSV	REVILERS, SILVERER, SLIVERER
EEILRSST	TIRELESS
EEILRSSW	WIRELESS
EEILSSVW	VIEWLESS
EEILSTTX	TEXTILES
EEIMMORS	MEMORIES, MEMORISE

EEIMMORZ	MEMORIZE
EEIMMOST	SOMETIME
EEIMMRST	MERISTEM
EEIMNNOS	NOMINEES
EEIMNORS	EMERSION
EEIMNORV	VOMERINE
EEIMNOST	MONETISE, SEMITONE
EEIMNOTZ	MONETIZE, TIME ZONE, ZONETIME
EEIMNPRS	SPERMINE
EEIMNPRU	PERINEUM
EEIMNRTU	MUTINEER
EEIMOPRS	REIMPOSE
EEIMORST	TIRESOME
EEIMORTV	OVERTIME
EEIMPRRS	PREMIERS, SIMPERER
EEIMPRSS	PREMISES
EEIMPSTT	EMPTIEST
EEIMQRSU	REQUIEMS
EEIMQSTU	MESQUITE
EEIMRRST	MERRIEST, TRIREMES
EEIMRRTT	REMITTER, TRIMETER
EEIMRSTT	TERMITES
EEIMRSTU	EMERITUS
EEIMRTTY	TEMERITY
EEIMSSST	MESSIEST
EEINNNPS	PENNINES
EEINNPTT	PENITENT
EEINNRRT	INTERNET
EEINNSTT	SENTIENT
EEINOPRS	ISOPRENE, PIONEERS
EEINORST	SEROTINE
EEINORSV	EVERSION
EEINORTT	TENORITE
EEINORTX	EXERTION
EEINOSTT	TEOSINTE
EEINPRSS	RIPENESS
EEINPRTX	INEXPERT
EEINQRRU	ENQUIRER
EEINRRST	INSERTER, RENTIERS
EEINRRSU	REINSURE
EEINRRTU	REUNITER
EEINRRTV	INVERTER
EEINRRTW	WINTERER
EEINRRTX	INTERREX
EEINRSST	SENTRIES
EEINRSSU	ENURESIS
EEINRSTT	INSETTER, INTEREST

EEINRSTU	ESURIENT,	EEJLPSTU	PULSEJET	EELORTUV	REVOLUTE,
	RETINUES	EEJPRRRU	PERJURER		TRUELOVE
EEINRSTV	NERVIEST,	EEKLLSUU	UKULELES	EELPPSTU	SEPTUPLE
	REINVEST	EEKLNNNU	UNKENNEL	EELPRRSU	REPULSER
EEINRSTX	INTERSEX	EEKLNOST	SKELETON	EELPRSSU	REPULSES
EEINRSTY	SERENITY	EEKLRSST	KESTRELS	EELPRSTZ	PRETZELS
EEINRSUV	UNIVERSE	EEKMNOYY	KEY MONEY	EELPRTXY	EXPERTLY
EEINRTTY	ENTIRETY,	EEKMOORV	KEMEROVO	EELPSTUX	SEXTUPLE
	ETERNITY	EEKNOSTY	KEYNOTES,	EELRRSTW	WRESTLER
EEINSSSW	WISENESS		KEYSTONE	EELRSSST	RESTLESS
EEINSSSX	SEXINESS	EELLLLMP	PELL-MELL	EELRSSTT	SETTLERS,
EEINSSTX	SIXTEENS	EELLLNWY	LLEWELYN		TRESTLES
EEINSTTW	TWENTIES	EELLMNOY	MELLONEY	EELRSSTU	STREUSEL
EEINSTTX	EXISTENT	EELLMORW	MELLOWER	EELRSTWY	WESTERLY
EEIOPRRT	PORTIERE	EELLNORR	ENROLLER	EEMMNOST	MEMENTOS
EEIOPRRV	OVERRIPE	EELLNPRU	PRUNELLE	EEMMNOTV	MOVEMENT
EEIORRRS	ORRERIES	EELLNRSU	SULLENER	EEMMNNORS	NORSEMEN
EEIORRTV	OVERTIRE	EELLNSTU	ENTELLUS	EEMNOOPT	TONE POEM
EEIORRTX	EXTERIOR	EELLOPTV	TOP-LEVEL	EEMNORTY	MONTEREY
EEIORSSV	OVERSISE	EELLORSV	OVERSELL	EEMNPRSS	PRESSMEN
EEIORSVZ	OVERSIZE	EELLORTX	EXTOLLER	EEMNPRSU	SUPERMEN
EEIORVVW	OVERVIEW	EELLORVY	VOLLEYER	EEMNPRTU	ERUMPENT
EEIORVWW	WIRE-WOVE	EELLOSSV	LOVELESS	EEMNRSTU	MUENSTER
EEIPPQRU	EQUIPPER	EELMMPUX	EXEMPLUM	EEMNSSTU	MUTENESS,
EEIPPRRS	PERSPIRE	EELMNOOS	LONESOME		TENESMUS
EEIPPRST	PEPTISER	EELMNSUY	UNSEEMLY	EEMNSTTV	VESTMENT
EEIPPRTZ	PEPTIZER	EELMOPRY	EMPLOYER,	EEMOORRT	OROMETER
EEIPPSTT	PIPETTES		RE-EMPLOY	EEMOORRV	MOREOVER
EEIPRRSS	REPRISES	EELMORST	MOLESTER	EEMOPRRS	EMPERORS,
EEIPRRTT	PRETTIER	EELMORTY	REMOTELY		PREMORSE
EEIPRSST	RESPITES	EELMOTVW	TWELVEMO	EEMOORSU	MORESQUE
EEIPRSTX	PRE-EXIST	EELMRRTU	MURRELET	EEMOQTTU	MOQUETTE
EEIPRSVW	PREVIEWS	EELMRSST	TERMLESS	EEMORRSV	REMOVERS
EEIPRSZZ	PREZZIES	EELMRSTY	SMELTERY	EEMORSST	SOMERSET
EEIPRTUV	ERUPTIVE	EELNNRTU	TUNNELER	EEMORSTT	REMOTEST
EEIPSSTW	STEPWISE	EELNNTTY	LYNNETTE	EEMPRRSU	PRESUMER
EEIPSTTT	PETTIEST	EELNNUVY	UNEVENLY	EEMPRSTT	TEMPTERS
EEIQRRRU	REQUIRER	EELNOORS	LOOSENER	EEMPSSTT	TEMPESTS
EEIQRRTU	REQUITER	EELNOPPU	UNPEOPLE	EEMRRRTU	MUTTERER
EEIQRRUV	QUIVERER	EELNOQTU	ELOQUENT	EENNNOOO	ONE-ON-ONE
EEIQSTTU	QUIETEST	EELNORST	ENTRESOL	EENNNOSS	NONSENSE
EEIRRRST	TERRIERS	EELNOSST	TONELESS	EENNNOTV	NON-EVENT
EEIRRSST	RESISTER	EELNOSTT	NOTELETS	EENNOOOT	ONE-TO-ONE
EEIRRSSU	REISSUER	EELNSSTU	TUNELESS	EENNOORT	ROTENONE
EEIRRSSV	REVISERS	EELNSTTU	UNSETTLE	EENNOPSS	OPENNESS
EEIRRSTV	RIVETERS	EELOPPST	ESTOPPEL	EENNOPTX	EXPONENT
EEIRRSTW	REWRITES	EELOPRRX	EXPLORER	EENNORTT	RONNETTE
EEIRRTTT	TITTERER	EELORRSV	RESOLVER	EENOORST	OESTRONE
EEIRSSSU	REISSUES	EELORRTV	REVOLTER	EENOORTU	EURONOTE
EEIRSSTU	SURETIES	EELORRUV	OVERRULE	EENOORTV	OVERTONE
EEIRSSTV	VESTRIES	EELORRVV	REVOLVER	EENOPRSS	RESPONSE
EEIRSSUZ	SEIZURES	EELORSSV	RESOLVES	EENOPRTT	ENTREPOT
EEIRSTVY	SEVERITY	EELORSTU	RESOLUTE	EENOPRTU	PURE TONE
EEISSTTT	TESTIEST	EELORSTY	TYROLESE	EENOPRXY	PYROXENE
EEJKNRTU	JUNKETER	EELORTTU	ROULETTE	EENORSSS	SORENESS

EENORSSU	NEUROSES	EFFHIIRW	WHIFFIER	EFGINRTT	FRETTING
EENORSTX	EXTENSOR	EFFHIISW	FISHWIFE	EFGINRTU	REFUTING
EENPRSST	PERTNESS,	EFFHIITT	FIFTIETH	EFGINRTY	GENTRIFY
PRESENTS, SERPENTS		EFFHIOTW	OFF-WHITE	EFGIOOST	GOOFIEST
EENPRSSU	PURENESS	EFFHIRSS	SHERIFFS	EFGIOPTT	PETTIFOG
EENPSSSU	SUSPENSE	EFFHISTU	HUFFIEST	EFGIORRV	FORGIVER
EENPSTTU	PETUNTSE	EFFHLRSU	SHUFFLER	EFGIORTT	FORGET IT!
EENRRRTU	RETURNER	EFFHLSSU	SHUFFLES	EFGLOOVX	FOXGLOVE
EENRRTUV	VENTURER	EFFHOORS	OFFSHORE	EFGNSSUU	FUNGUSES
EENRRSSU	SURENESS	EFFILNRS	SNIFFLER	EFHIILRT	FILTHIER
EENRSSTT	STERNEST	EFFILNSS	SNIFFLES	EFHIILST	TILEFISH
EENRSSTU	TRUENESS	EFFINOSU	EFFUSION	EFHIINRS	FINISHER, REFINISH
EENRSSTW	WESTERNS	EFFIORST	FORFEITS	EFHIINSS	FINISHES
EENRSTUV	VENTURES	EFFIORTW	WRITE-OFF	EFHIIPPS	PIPEFISH
EENRSTUW	WET NURSE	EFFIPSTU	PUFFIEST	EFHIIRST	SHIFTIER
EEOOPRST	PROTEOSE	EFFIRSTU	STUFFIER	EFHIISST	FISHIEST
EEOOPRSX	EXOSPORE	EFFISSTT	STIFFEST	EFHIKLOO	HOOFLIKE
EEOORRVV	ROVE-OVER	EFFISSUX	SUFFIXES	EFHIKSTY	SHIFT KEY
EEOPRRRT	REPORTER	EFFLMRSU	MUFFLERS	EFHILTWY	WHITEFLY
EEOPRRRV	REPROVER	EFFLNRSU	SNUFFLER	EFHINSST	FISHNETS
EEOPRRTT	POTTERER	EFFLNSSU	SNUFFLES	EFHIORRT	FROTHIER
EEOPRRTX	EXPORTER,	EFFLOSSU	SOUFFLES	EFHIORSS	ROSEFISH
RE-EXPORT		EFFLRSTU	TRUFFLES	EFHIORTT	FORTIETH
EEOPRSSS	ESPRESSO	EFFNRSSU	SNUFFERS	EFHIRRTU	THURIFER
EEOPRSSU	ESPOUSER,	EFFOOORT	FOREFOOT	EFHLNORS	HORNFELS
REPOUSSE		EFFOORSW	WORSE-OFF	EFHLOOSS	HOOFLESS
EEOPRSTV	OVERSTEP	EFGGIINN	FEIGNING	EFHLOOSX	FOXHOLES
EEOPRSUX	EXPOSURE	EFGGIOST	FOGGIEST	EFHLOPST	FLESHPOT
EEOPSSTW	SWEETSOP	EFGGISTU	FUGGIEST	EFHLOPSU	HOPEFULS
EEORRRST	RESORTER,	EFGHHIIL	HIGH LIFE	EFHLORSY	HORSEFLY
RESTORER, RETRORSE		EFGHILNS	FLESHING	EFHLOSUU	HOUSEFUL
EEORRRTT	RETORTER	EFGHINRT	FRIGHTEN	EFHLOSUY	HOUSEFLY
EEORRSTX	EXTRORSE	EFGHIRST	FIGHTERS	EFHLSTTW	TWELFTHS
EEORRTTT	TOTTERER	EFGIILNT	FILETING	EFHRSTTU	FURTHEST
EEORRTTX	EXTORTER	EFGIILRU	UGLIFIER	EFIIILRV	VILIFIER
EEORRTUV	OVERTURE	EFGIINNR	INFRINGE,	EFIIINNT	INFINITE
EEORSSTT	ROSETTES	REFINING		EFIIIRVV	VIVIFIER
EEORSSTV	ESTOVERS	EFGIINNT	FEINTING	EFIIKRRS	FRISKIER
EEORSTVX	VORTEXES	EFGIINRU	FIGURINE	EFIILLRR	FRILLIER
EEORTTTZ	TERZETTO	EFGIITUV	FUGITIVE	EFIILMRS	FLIMSIER
EEPRRSSU	PRESSURE	EFGILLNO	LIFELONG,	EFIILMST	FILMIEST
EEPRRSTV	PERVERTS	LONG-LIFE		EFIILNOU	IN LIEU OF
EEPRSSUX	SUPERSEX	EFGILLNU	FUELLING	EFIILNRT	FLINTIER
EEPRSTTU	UPSETTER	EFGILLUU	GUILEFUL	EFIILNTY	FELINITY, FINITELY
EEPRSTTX	PRETEXTS	EFGILNOR	FLORIGEN	EFIILRSU	FUSILIER
EEQRSSTU	REQUESTS	EFGILNTT	FETTLING	EFIIMMNS	FEMINISM
EERRSSTU	TRESSURE	EFGILNTW	LEFT WING	EFIIMNST	FEMINIST
EERSSSST	STRESSES	EFGILPRU	FIRE-PLUG	EFIIMRSS	MISFIRES
EERSSTTU	TRUSTEES	EFGIMNST	FIGMENTS	EFIINNNS	SINN FEIN
EERSSTUU	UTERUSES	EFGIMRUU	REFUGIUM	EFIINORR	INFERIOR
EERSTTUX	TEXTURES	EFGINNPS	PFENNIGS	EFIINORT	NOTIFIER
EFFFILRU	FLUFFIER	EFGINORV	FORGIVEN	EFIINPSV	FIVEPINS
EFFGINOR	OFFERING	EFGINORW	FOREWING	EFIINPSX	SPINIFEX
EFFGRSTU	GRUFFEST	EFGINRRY	FERRYING	EFIINRRT	FERRITIN
EFFHIILS	FILEFISH	EFGINRSU	REFUSING		

EFIINSTT	NIFTIEST	EFIOOPST	POOFIEST	EFNNOOOR	FORENOON
EFIINSUV	INFUSIVE	EFIOOSST	FOOTSIES	EFNOOOTT	FOOTNOTE
EFIIORSS	OSSIFIER	EFIOPRRT	PROFITER	EFNOOSST	FESTOONS
EFIIPRRU	PURIFIER	EFIORRST	FROSTIER	EFNORSTU	FORTUNES
EFIIPRST	SPITFIRE	EFIORRTT	RETROFIT	EFNOSSST	SOFTNESS
EFIIPRTY	TYPIFIER	EFIORRWZ	FROWZIER	EFOOOPRT	FOOTROPE
EFIIRRTU	FRUITIER	EFIPPRRY	FRIPPERY	EFOOORST	FOOTSORE
EFIIRRZZ	FRIZZIER	EFIPRSUX	SUPERFIX	EFOOPRRS	REPROOFS
EFIIRVVY	REVIVIFY	EFIPRTTY	PRETTIFY	EFOOPSTT	FOOTSTEP
EFIISTVW	FIVE WITS	EFIRRRSU	FURRIERS	EFOORRSW	FORSWORE
EFIISTZZ	FIZZIEST	EFIRRRUY	FURRIERY	EFOORSTT	FOOTREST
EFIJLOST	JETFOILS	EFIRRSTT	FRITTERS	EFORRRUW	FURROWER
EFIKLLOW	WOLFLIKE	EFIRRSTU	FURRIEST	EFORRSST	FORTRESS
EFIKLORW	LIFE WORK	EFIRSSSU	FISSURES	EFORRSTY	FORESTRY
EFIKLRSU	SURFLIKE	EFIRSTUX	FIXTURES	EGGGILNS	LEGGINGS
EFIKLRUY	LIKE FURY	EFISSSTU	FUSSIEST	EGGGIORR	GROGGIER
EFIKNORS	FORESKIN	EFISSTTU	FUSTIEST	EGGHIINN	NEIGHING
EFIKNSTU	FUNKIEST	EFISSTTW	SWIFTEST	EGGHIINW	WEIGHING
EFIKORRW	FIREWORK	EFISTUZZ	FUZZIEST	EGGHIRWY	WHIGGERY
EFILLLSW	SELF-WILL	EFKLLOOR	FOLKLORE	EGGHRTUY	THUGGERY
EFILLMTU	FULL-TIME	EFKLNSUY	FLUNKEYS	EGGIINNR	REIGNING
EFILLSTY	STELLIFY	EFKNOORW	FOREKNOW	EGGIINNS	SINGEING
EFILMSUY	EMULSIFY	EFKORRTW	FRETWORK	EGGIINRV	GRIEVING
EFILNNTU	INFLUENT	EFLLLLUW	FULL WELL	EGGIIPST	PIGGIEST
EFILNORU	FLUORINE	EFLLNOOW	LONE WOLF	EGGILNRS	NIGGLERS,
EFILNSUX	INFLUXES	EFLLNSSU	FULLNESS		SNIGGLER
EFILOOSZ	FLOOZIES	EFLLNTUY	FLUENTLY	EGGILNRY	GINGERLY
EFILOPPR	FLOPPIER	EFLLOORW	FOLLOWER	EGGILOOS	GOOGLIES
EFILOPRS	PROFILES	EFLLOSST	SOFT SELL	EGGILQSU	SQUIGGLE
EFILORST	TREFOILS	EFLLOUWY	WOEFULLY	EGGILRRW	WRIGGLER
EFILOSTT	LOFTIEST	EFLLRUUY	RUEFULLY	EGGILRSW	WRIGGLES
EFILPPRS	FLIPPERS	EFLLSUUY	USEFULLY	EGGIMSTU	MUGGIEST
EFILPPST	FLIPPEST	EFLMMRUY	FLUMMERY	EGGINORR	GORGERIN
EFILPRTU	UPLIFTER	EFLMNRUU	FRENULUM	EGGINRSS	SNIGGERS
EFILPSTU	SPITEFUL	EFLMORRY	FORMERLY	EGGINSSU	GUESSING
EFILPSTY	SELF-PITY	EFLMORSS	FORMLESS	EGGINSTU	GUESTING
EFILRRSU	FLURRIES	EFLNORTT	FRONTLET	EGGIOSST	SOGGIEST
EFILRRZZ	FRIZZLER	EFLNOSSU	FOULNESS	EGGIPRRS	SPRIGGER
EFILSSTT	LEFTISTS	EFLNOSTY	STONEFLY	EGGIPRRY	PRIGGERY
EFIMNORR	INFORMER,	EFLOORSS	ROOFLESS	EGGIRRST	TRIGGERS
RENIFORM		EFLOORVW	OVERFLOW	EGGJLRSU	JUGGLERS
EFIMNORS	ENSIFORM	EFLOPRUW	POWERFUL	EGGJLRUY	JUGGLERY
EFIMNRSS	FIRMNESS	EFLOPSTW	FOWL PEST	EGGLLORS	EGG ROLLS
EFIMNSTT	FITMENTS	EFLORSUY	YOURSELF	EGGLMOOY	GEMOLOGY
EFIMORST	SETIFORM	EFLORSVY	FLYOVERS	EGGLMRSU	SMUGGLER
EFIMPRRU	FRUMPIER	EFLOSUUX	FLEXUOUS	EGGLORSS	SLOGGERS
EFIMRSTU	FREMITUS	EFLRSTTU	FLUTTERS	EGGLRSTU	STRUGGLE
EFINNORS	INFERNOS	EFLRSTUU	FRUSTULE	EGGMSSTU	SMUGGEST
EFINNPSU	FINESPUN	EFLRTTUY	FLUTTERY	EGGNOOSY	GEOGNOSY
EFINNSTU	FUNNIEST	EFMNNORT	FRONT MEN	EGGNRSUY	SNUGGERY
EFINOPTX	PONTIFEX	EFMNORTY	FROMENTY	EGGOORSU	GORGEOUS
EFINORRT	FRONTIER	EFMNRTUY	FRUMENTY	EGHHIIMT	HIGH TIME
EFINOSSX	FOXINESS	EFMOORST	FOREMOST	EGHHIIRS	HIGH-RISE
EFINRSST	SNIFTERS	EFMOORSU	FOURSOME	EGHHINSS	HIGHNESS

EGHHIPRU	HIGHER-UP
EGHHIPTY	TYPE-HIGH
EGHHORUW	ROUGH-HEW
EGHIILNR	HIRELING
EGHIILNS	SHIELING
EGHIIMRT	MIGHTIER
EGHIINTV	THIEVING
EGHIKNRS	GHERKINS
EGHILLNS	SHELLING
EGHILLNW	WELL-NIGH
EGHILNOT	LEIGHTON
EGHILNPS	HELPINGS
EGHILNRS	SHINGLER
EGHILNSS	SHINGLES
EGHILNSV	SHELVING
EGHILNSW	WELSHING
EGHILPRT	PLIGHTER
EGHILRST	LIGHTERS, SLIGHTER
EGHILSTT	LIGHTEST
EGHIMNUX	EXHUMING
EGHINORV	HOVERING
EGHINOST	HISTOGEN
EGHINRRS	HERRINGS
EGHINRRU	HUNGRIER
EGHINRSU	USHERING
EGHINTTW	WHETTING
EGHIOTUW	OUTWEIGH
EGHISTTT	TIGHTEST
EGHLLNUW	WELL-HUNG
EGHLLOPU	PLUGHOLE
EGHLLOSU	LUGHOLES
EGHLOOOR	HOROLOGE
EGHLOORY	RHEOLOGY
EGHLOOTY	ETHOLOGY, THEOLOGY
EGHLOPRU	PLOUGHER
EGHMNOOY	HOMOGENY
EGHMOSSU	GUMSHOES
EGHNNTWY	GWYNNETH
EGHNORUV	HUNG OVER, OVERHUNG
EGHNOTUU	HUGUENOT
EGHNRSTT	STRENGTH
EGHOOOSW	HOOSEGOW
EGHORRTW	REGROWTH
EGHORSTU	ROUGHEST
EGHOSTTU	TOUGHEST
EGIIKLNN	LIKENING
EGIIKLNR	KINGLIER
EGIIKLNW	WINGLIKE
EGIIKNSS	KING-SISE
EGIIKNSZ	KING-SIZE
EGIILNNR	RELINING
EGIILNNV	LIVENING

EGIILNOR	RELIGION
EGIILNRS	RIESLING
EGIILNRV	RELIVING, REVILING
EGIILRRS	GRISLIER
EGIILRTU	GUILTIER
EGIILRTZ	GLITZIER
EGIIMNPR	IMPINGER
EGIIMNRT	MERITING
EGIIMNST	MINGIEST
EGIIMNTT	EMITTING
EGIIMOPT	IMPETIGO
EGIIMRST	GRIMIEST
EGIINNPR	REPINING, RIPENING
EGIINNPW	WINNIPEG
EGIINOPR	PEIGNOIR
EGIINPRX	EXPIRING
EGIINRRT	RETIRING
EGIINRRW	REWIRING
EGIINRST	STINGIER
EGIINRSV	REVISING
EGIINRTU	INTRIGUE
EGIINRTV	RIVETING
EGIINRVV	REVIVING
EGIINSTX	EXISTING
EGIIPRSW	PERIWIGS
EGIIPSST	PIGSTIES
EGIIRRTT	GRITTIER
EGIITUXY	EXIGUITY
EGIJMMNY	JEMMYING
EGIJNNOY	ENJOYING
EGIKKNRT	TREKKING
EGIKLNSY	KINGSLEY
EGIKNORV	REVOKING
EGIKNRSY	KEY RINGS
EGILLMNS	SMELLING
EGILLNOR	NEGRILLO
EGILLNOV	LIVELONG
EGILLNOW	LILONGWE
EGILLNPS	SPELLING
EGILLNQU	QUELLING
EGILLNSW	SWELLING
EGILLNTU	GLUTELIN
EGILMMNS	LEMMINGS
EGILMMRS	GLIMMERS
EGILMNRS	GREMLINS
EGILMNST	SMELTING
EGILMOOR	GLOOMIER
EGILMPRS	GLIMPSER
EGILMPSS	GLIMPSES
EGILNNOS	SOLINGEN
EGILNNST	NESTLING
EGILNNTT	NETTLING
EGILNOPP	PEOPLING

EGILNORW	LOWERING
EGILNOSU	LIGNEOUS
EGILNOTW	TOWELING
EGILNOVV	EVOLVING
EGILNPRY	REPLYING
EGILNRST	RINGLETS, STERLING
EGILNSST	SINGLETS
EGILNSSU	UGLINESS
EGILNSSW	WINGLESS
EGILNSTT	LETTINGS, SETTLING
EGILNTUX	EXULTING
EGILNVXY	VEXINGLY
EGILOOSU	ISOLOGUE
EGILOOTY	ETIOLOGY
EGILORSS	GLOSSIER
EGILOSTU	EULOGIST
EGILRRZZ	GRIZZLER
EGILRSTT	GLITTERS
EGILRTTY	GLITTERY
EGIMMNST	STEMMING
EGIMMRST	GRIMMEST
EGIMMSTU	GUMMIEST
EGIMNORS	NEGROISM
EGIMNORV	REMOVING
EGIMNOSY	MOSEYING
EGIMNPRU	IMPUGNER
EGIMNPST	PIGMENTS
EGIMNPTT	TEMPTING
EGIMNPTY	EMPTYING
EGIMNRSS	GRIMNESS
EGIMNRSU	RESUMING
EGIMORST	ERGOTISM
EGIMPRRU	GRUMPIER
EGINNOPS	OPENINGS
EGINNORT	NITROGEN
EGINNPSU	PENGUINS
EGINNRRU	UNERRING
EGINNRSU	ENSURING
EGINOPRS	REPOSING, SPONGIER
EGINOPRW	POWERING
EGINOPST	PONGIEST
EGINOPSX	EXPOSING
EGINORRY	IRON-GREY
EGINORSS	GORINESS
EGINORTW	TOWERING
EGINORVW	WINGOVER
EGINORXX	XEROXING
EGINPPST	STEPPING
EGINPRRS	SPRINGER
EGINPRSS	PRESSING
EGINPRSU	PERUSING
EGINPRTU	ERUPTING

EGINPRYY	PERIGYNY	EGMNOOOS	MONGOOSE	EHIIMSSW	WHIMSIES
EGINQRUY	QUERYING	EGMNSSSU	SMUGNESS	EHIINNOT	THIONINE
EGINQSTU	QUESTING	EGMORSTU	GOURMETS	EHIINNSW	WHINNIES
EGINRRST	STRINGER	EGNNOOTY	ONTOGENY	EHIINSST	SHINIEST
EGINRRSW	WRINGERS	EGNNORST	RONTGENS	EHIINSVX	VIXENISH
EGINRRST	STINGERS	EGNNOTUV	VONNEGUT	EHIIPSTT	PITHIEST
EGINRSSV	SERVINGS	EGNNSSSU	SNUGNESS	EHIIRRST	SHIRTIER
EGINRSSW	SWINGERS	EGNNSSTU	STEN GUNS	EHIIRSTT	SHITTIER, THIRTIES
EGINRSSY	SYRINGES	EGNNSTTU	TUNGSTEN	EHIISTTX	SIXTIETH
EGINRSTW	STREWING,	EGNNSTUU	UNGUENTS	EHIJNNOS	JOHNNIES
	WRESTING	EGNOOOPR	GONOPORE	EHIKKLOO	HOOKLIKE
EGINRSVW	SWERVING	EGNOORRV	GOVERNOR	EHIKKLSU	HUSKLIKE
EGINRTTU	UTTERING	EGNOOTUX	OXTONGUE	EHIKLMPU	HUMPLIKE
EGINSSTT	SETTINGS	EGNOPPRU	OPPUGNER	EHIKLNOR	HORNLIKE
EGINSTTW	WETTINGS	EGNOPRSS	SPONGERS	EHIKLNOS	SINKHOLE
EGIOORRV	GROOVIER	EGNORRST	STRONGER	EHIKLOOP	HOOPLIKE
EGIOPRSS	GOSSIPER	EGNORSST	SONGSTER	EHIKLOSY	YOKELISH
EGIOPRST	EGO TRIPS	EGNORSSU	SURGEONS	EHIKNRRS	SHRINKER
EGIOPRSU	GROUPIES	EGNORSTU	STURGEON	EHIKRRSS	SHIRKERS
EGIORRTT	GROTTIER	EGNOSTUY	YOUNGEST	EHIKRSSW	WHISKERS
EGIORSST	STRIGOSE	EGNRSTUU	TEN GURUS	EHIKRSWY	WHISKERY
EGIORSSU	GRISEOUS	EGOOPRRU	PROROGUE	EHIKSSTU	HUSKIEST
EGIORSUV	GRIEVOUS	EGOORRVW	OVERGROW	EHILLLMO	MOLEHILL
EGIOSSTT	EGOTISTS	EGOORSTT	GROTTOES	EHILLPTY	PHYLLITE
EGIOSUUX	EXIGUOUS	EGOPRRSS	PROGRESS	EHILLRRS	SHRILLER
EGIRRSTY	REGISTRY	EGOPSSUY	GYPSEOUS	EHILLRRT	THRILLER
EGISSTTU	GUSTIEST,	EGORSSST	GROSSEST	EHILMNOP	PHILEMON
	GUTSIEST	EGPRSSUU	UPSURGES	EHILMOOR	HEIRLOOM
EGISSUWY	WISE GUYS	EHHIIPRS	HEIRSHIP	EHILMOST	HELOTISM
EGLLLPSU	LEG-PULLS	EHHIIRST	THE IRISH	EHILMPSY	SYMPHILE
EGLLMORW	GROMWELL	EHHIISTV	THIEVISH	EHILNOSS	HOLINESS
EGLLOOPR	GOLLOPER	EHHILMNT	HELMINTH	EHILNOST	HOLSTEIN, HOT
EGLLOSUY	YULE LOGS	EHHIORTT	HITHERTO		LINES
EGLMMSTU	GLUMMEST	EHHIOTTW	WHITE-HOT	EHILNOTX	XENOLITH
EGLMNOOY	MENOLOGY	EHHIRSSW	SHREWISH	EHILOOPZ	ZOOPHILE
EGLMNORS	MONGRELS	EHHMPRUY	HUMPHREY	EHILOPRS	POLISHER
EGLMNORT	LONG-TERM	EHHNOORS	SHOEHORN	EHILOPRT	HELIPORT
EGLMNSSU	GLUMNESS	EHHNORTT	THE NORTH	EHILOPSS	POLISHES
EGLMORSS	GORMLESS	EHHOOSSW	WHOOSHES	EHILOPST	ISOPLETH
EGLNNOOR	LONGERON	EHHOOSTU	HOTHOUSE	EHILORTY	RHYOLITE
EGLNOOOY	OENOLOGY	EHHOPRTW	HEPWORTH	EHILPRST	PHILTRES
EGLNOOPY	PENOLOGY	EHHOSTTU	THE SOUTH	EHILPSTU	SULPHITE
EGLNOORV	OVERLONG	EHHRSSTU	THRUSHES	EHILRSSU	SLUSHIER
EGLNORSU	LOUNGERS	EHIIKLNS	HELSINKI	EHILRSTW	WHISTLER
EGLNORUU	LONGUEUR	EHIIKLPW	WHIPLIKE	EHILRSTY	SLITHERY
EGLNPRSU	PLUNGERS	EHIIKNSV	KISHINEV	EHILRTTW	WHITTLER
EGLNRTUY	URGENTLY	EHIIKSSW	WHISKIES	EHILSSTT	THISTLES
EGLOOPRU	PROLOGUE	EHIILLST	HILLIEST	EHILSSTW	WHISTLES
EGLOOPTY	LOGOTYPE	EHIILMOS	HOMILIES	EHIMMRSY	SHIMMERY
EGLOORSY	SEROLOGY	EHIILRSV	LIVERISH	EHIMNOPR	MORPHINE
EGLOOSXY	SEXOLOGY	EHIIMNRS	IRISHMEN	EHIMNORT	THERMION
EGLORRSW	GROWLERS	EHIIMNTV	VIETMINH	EHIMNOSS	HOMINESS
EGLPRSSU	SPLURGES	EHIIMPST	MEPHITIS	EHIMNOTT	MONTEITH
EGLRSUZZ	GUZZLERS	EHIIMSST	SMITHIES	EHIMNPST	SHIPMENT
EGMNNOOY	MONOGENY				

EHIMNRRU	MURRHINE	EHLMOORW	WORMHOLE	EHOORSST	SHOOTERS
EHIMOOST	SMOOTHIE	EHLMORTY	MOTHERLY	EHOORSTV	OVERSHOT
EHIMORST	ISOTHERM	EHLMOSUU	MULHOUSE	EHOORSUW	ROW HOUSE
EHIMORSZ	RHIZOMES	EHLNOPSU	SULPHONE	EHOOSTUU	OUTHOUSE
EHIMPRRS	SHRIMPER	EHLNORSS	HORNLESS	EHOPPRSS	SHOPPERS
EHIMPRSW	WHIMPERS	EHLNOSTY	HONESTLY, ON	EHOPPRST	PROPHETS
EHIMPSUU	EUPHUISM		THE SLY	EHOPPRSW	WHOPPERS
EHIMRSTY	SMITHERY	EHLNSSSU	LUSHNESS	EHOPPRSY	PROPHESY
EHIMSSTU	MUSHIEST	EHLOOPRT	PORTHOLE,	EHOPRSST	STROPHES
EHINNOPS	PHONE-INS		POTHOLER	EHOPRSUV	PUSHOVER
EHINNOTW	NONWHITE	EHLOOPST	POTHOLES	EHORSSTT	SHORTEST
EHINNSST	THINNESS	EHLOOPTY	HOLOTYPE	EHRRSTTU	THRUSTER
EHINNSSU	SUNSHINE	EHLOPSSS	SPLOSHES	EHRSSSTY	SHYSTERS
EHINNSTT	THINNEST	EHLORSST	HOLSTERS,	EHRSSTTU	SHUTTERS
EHINOOPS	ISOPHONE		HOSTLERS	EIIIMMNS	MINIMISE
EHINOPPR	HORNPIPE	EHLORSTY	HOSTELRY	EIIIMMNZ	MINIMIZE
EHINOPST	PHONIEST	EHLORTTT	THROTTLE	EIIJNRSU	INJURIES
EHINORRT	THORNIER	EHLPSSTU	PLUSHEST	EIIKKNST	KINKIEST
EHINORST	HORNIEST	EHLRSSTU	HUSTLERS,	EIIKLLMN	LIMEKILN
EHINORTY	IN THEORY		RUTHLESS	EIIKLMST	MILKIEST
EHINOSTU	OUTSHINE	EHLSSTTU	SHUTTLES	EIIKLNRS	SLINKIER
EHINPRSU	PUNISHER	EHMMOOPR	ROMP HOME	EIIKLSST	SILKIEST
EHINPSSX	SPHINXES	EHMMRRTU	THRUMMER	EIIKMPRS	SKIMPIER
EHIOORTT	TOOTHIER	EHMNNSTU	HUNTSMEN	EIIKNNRS	SKINNIER
EHIOPRSS	ROSE HIPS	EHMNOORS	HORMONES,	EIIKNNSS	INKINESS
EHIOPRST	TROPHIES		MOORHENS	EIIKNNSW	WINESKIN
EHIORRTW	IORWERTH,	EHMNOOST	SMOOTHEN	EIIKNRST	KRISTINE
	WORTHIER	EHMNOOTW	HOMETOWN	EIIKPSST	SPIKIEST
EHIORSST	HORSIEST,	EHMNOPSU	HOMESPUN	EIIKQRRU	QUIRKIER
	SHORTIES	EHMNORSU	HOME RUNS	EIIKRSST	RISKIEST
EHIORSTT	THEORIST	EHMNPSTY	NYMPHETS	EIIKSSVV	SKIVVIES
EHIORSTW	WORTHIES	EHMOORST	SMOOTHER	EIILLMNR	MILLINER
EHIORTWZ	HOWITZER	EHMOPRSU	MORPHEUS	EIILLNST	NIELLIST
EHIOSSTW	SHOWIEST	EHMORSTY	SMOTHERY	EIILLNSV	VILLEINS
EHIOTTUW	WHITEOUT	EHMORTUV	VERMOUTH	EIILLNTV	VITELLIN
EHIPPRSS	SHIPPERS	EHMOTUWY	WEYMOUTH	EIILLPSS	ELLIPSIS
EHIPPSTW	WHIPPETS	EHNNOPRT	PENN'ORTH	EIILLSST	SILLIEST
EHIPQSUY	PHYSIQUE	EHNNORRT	NORTHERN	EIILMMOT	IMMOTILE
EHIPRSST	HIPSTERS	EHNNORSY	HENRYSON	EIILMNNS	LENINISM
EHIPRSSW	WHISPERS	EHNOOPPS	OPEN SHOP	EIILMNNT	LINIMENT
EHIPSSTU	PUSHIEST	EHNOORRU	HONOURER	EIILMNOT	LIMONITE
EHIPSTUU	EUPHUIST	EHNOORTW	HONEWORT	EIILMNSS	LIMINESS
EHISSSTW	SWISHEST	EHNOORVZ	VORONEZH	EIILMOPT	IMPOLITE
EHKLNOOT	KNOTHOLE	EHNOOSSW	SNOWSHOE	EIILMSSS	MISSILES
EHKLOOSS	HOOKLESS	EHNOOSTU	OUTSHONE	EIILMSST	SLIMIEST
EHKMMNOR	MON-KHMER	EHNORSSU	ONRUSHES	EIILMSTY	MYELITIS
EHKMOORW	HOMEWORK	EHNORSTU	SOUTHERN	EIILNNST	LENINIST
EHKNNRSU	SHRUNKEN	EHNOSTUU	NUTHOUSE	EIILNORS	LIONISER
EHKNOOOS	HOOKNOSE	EHNRSSTU	HUNTRESS,	EIILNORZ	LIONIZER
EHLLLSSU	HULL-LESS		SHUNTERS	EIILNOSS	ELISIONS, OILINESS
EHLLMOPY	PHYLLOME	EHOOPRTY	ORTHOEPY	EIILNQTU	QUINTILE
EHLLNSTU	NUTSHELL	EHOOPSST	PHOTOSET	EIILNSSW	WILINESS
EHLLOOOP	LOOPHOLE	EHOOPSTU	HOUSETOP	EIILNSTY	SENILITY
EHLLOORW	HOLLOWER	EHOOPTYZ	ZOOPHYTE	EIILNTUV	VITULINE
EHLLOPST	TOP-SHELL	EHOORRUZ	ZERO HOUR		

EIILOPST	PISOLITE, POLITIES	EIIOPRRS	PRIORIES	EIKNRSTT	KNITTERS, TRINKETS
EIILOTVV	VOLITIVE	EIIOPRST	POITIERS	EIKOOPRS	SPOOKIER
EIILPPRS	SLIPPIER	EIIOPSTV	POSITIVE	EIKOPPRS	PORK PIES
EIILPSST	PITILESS	EIIOSSTT	OSTEITIS	EIKOPRST	PORKIEST
EIILPSTY	PYELITIS	EIIPPSTZ	ZIPPIEST	EIKORRWW	WIREWORK
EIILRSTU	UTILISER	EIIPRRSS	PRISSIER	EIKPPRSS	SKIPPERS
EIILRTUZ	UTILIZER	EIIPRRST	STRIPIER	EIKRRSST	STRIKERS
EIILSSTT	ELITISTS	EIIPRRTW	TRIPWIRE	EILLLOSW	OIL WELLS
EIILTUVV	VITI LEVU	EIIPRSTV	PRIVIEST	EILLMNOU	LINOLEUM
EIIMMNNT	IMMINENT	EIIPSSTT	TIPSIEST	EILLMPSS	MISSPELL
EIIMMNSU	IMMUNISE	EIIPSSTW	WISPIEST	EILLMPTU	MULTIPLE
EIIMMNUZ	IMMUNIZE	EIIQSTTU	QUIETIST	EILLMUVX	VEXILLUM
EIIMMPRU	IMPERIUM	EIIRSTTW	TWISTIER	EILLNOTU	LUTEOLIN
EIIMMSSS	SEISMISM	EIISSSST	SISSIEST	EILLNSTY	SILENTLY, TINSELLY
EIIMNOPT	PIMIENTO	EIISTTTW	WITTIEST	EILLNSVY	SNIVELLY
EIIMNOSS	EMISSION	EIJKORRS	SKIJORER	EILLOORW	WOOLLIER
EIIMNRST	INTERIMS, MINISTER	EIJLLOST	JOLLIEST	EILLOOSW	WOOLLIES
EIIMNRTT	INTERMIT	EIJMPSTU	JUMPIEST	EILLOPTY	POLITELY
EIIMNRTX	INTERMIX	EIJNORTU	JOINTURE	EILLOSTW	LOWLIEST
EIIMNSTU	MUTINIES	EIJNOSTT	JETTISON	EILLPPPS	PEP PILLS
EIIMOPRX	MIREPOIX	EIJNPRSU	JUNIPERS	EILLSSST	LISTLESS
EIIMOPST	OPTIMISE	EIKKLNNY	KILKENNY	EILLSSTT	STILLEST
EIIMOPSZ	EPIZOISM	EIKKLSTU	TUSKLIKE	EILMMNOU	MOULMEIN
EIIMOPTZ	OPTIMIZE	EIKKOOST	KOOKIEST	EILMMPRU	PLUMMIER
EIIMOTVV	VOMITIVE	EIKLLNSW	INKWELLS	EILMMRSS	SLIMMERS
EIIMQSTU	QUIETISM	EIKLLNTW	WELL-KNIT	EILMMSST	SLIMMEST
EIIMRSTT	METRITIS	EIKLLNUY	UNLIKELY	EILMNOSU	EMULSION
EIIMSSSV	MISSIVES	EIKLLORV	OVERKILL	EILMNOTY	MYLONITE
EIIMSSTT	SEMITIST	EIKLLSST	SKILLETS	EILMNPSS	LIMPNESS
EIINNNPS	NINEPINS	EIKLMNOS	MOLESKIN	EILMNRRY	MERRILYN
EIINNOSU	UNIONISE	EIKLMORW	WORMLIKE	EILMNRST	MINSTREL
EIINNOSV	ENVISION	EIKLNOST	ILKESTON	EILMNSSS	SLIMNESS
EIINNOUZ	UNIONIZE	EIKLNPRS	SPRINKLE	EILMNTUY	MINUTELY, UNTIMELY
EIINNSTT	TIENTSIN, TINNIEST	EIKLNRSW	WRINKLES	EILMOOST	TOILSOME
EIINOPTT	PETITION	EIKLNRTW	TWINKLER	EILMOPRR	IMPLORER
EIINORRT	INTERIOR	EIKLNSSS	SKINLESS	EILMOPST	MILEPOST
EIINORSS	IONISERS	EIKLNSSY	SKYLINES	EILMPSST	MISSPELT, SIMPLEST
EIINORSV	REVISION	EIKLOORT	ROOTLIKE	EILMPSSU	IMPULSES
EIINORSZ	IONIZERS	EIKLOPSS	SKI POLES	EILMPSTU	LUMPIEST
EIINOSST	NOISIEST	EIKLSSTT	SKITTLES	EILMTTUU	LUTETIUM
EIINPPST	NIPPIEST	EIKLSSTU	SULKIEST	EILNNOST	INSOLENT
EIINPRRS	INSPIRER	EIKMMRSS	SKIMMERS	EILNNOSW	SNOWLINE
EIINPRST	PRISTINE	EIKMNOST	TOKENISM	EILNNPTY	IN PLENTY
EIINPSST	PINT-SISE	EIKMORTW	TIMEWORK	EILNNTTY	INTENTLY
EIINPSTZ	PINT-SIZE	EIKMOSST	SMOKIEST	EILNOOST	LOONIEST, OILSTONE
EIINPTUV	PUNITIVE	EIKMPSST	SKEPTISM	EILNOPRT	INTERPOL
EIINQRRU	INQUIRER	EIKMRSTU	MURKIEST	EILNOPTY	LINOTYPE
EIINQTUY	EQUINITY, INEQUITY	EIKMSSTU	MUSKIEST	EILNORTT	TROTLINE
EIINRRTW	WINTRIER	EIKNOPSS	POKINESS	EILNORTV	IN REVOLT
EIINRSST	INSISTER, SINISTER	EIKNORTT	KNOTTIER	EILNORVV	INVOLVER
EIINRSSW	WIRINESS	EIKNOSTW	WONKIEST	EILNOSTU	OUTLINES
EIINRSTU	NEURITIS	EIKNPRSU	SPUNKIER		
EIINRSTW	WRITE-INS	EIKNPRTU	TURNPIKE		
		EIKNRSST	STINKERS		

EILNOSTV	NOVELIST	EIMMPRSU	PREMIUMS	EIMQRRSU	SQUIRMER
EILNOTUV	INVOLUTE	EIMMRRST	TRIMMERS	EIMQSTUY	MYSTIQUE
EILNPRST	SPLINTER	EIMMRSSW	SWIMMERS	EIMRRSSU	SURMISER
EILNPSSU	SPLENIUS	EIMMRSTT	TRIMMEST	EIMRSSST	MISTRESS
EILNPSUY	SUPINELY	EIMNNOOT	NOONTIME	EIMRSSSU	SURMISES
EILNQUUY	UNIQUELY	EIMNNOPY	PIN MONEY	EIMRSTTU	SMUTTIER
EILNRSTU	INSULTER	EIMNNOST	MENTIONS	EIMRSTUX	MIXTURES
EILNRSUU	URSULINE	EIMNNOTT	OINTMENT	EIMSSTTU	MUSTIEST
EILNRTUV	VIRULENT	EIMNOORS	MOONRISE	EIMSTUZZ	MUZZIEST
EILNSSTU	UTENSILS	EIMNOORT	MOTIONER	EINNOPSS	PENSIONS
EILNSTTU	LUTENIST	EIMNOORV	OMNIVORE	EINNORSU	REUNIONS
EILOOPRR	POORLIER	EIMNOOST	EMOTIONS	EINNORSV	ENVIRONS
EILOORST	OESTRIOL	EIMNOPRT	ORPIMENT	EINNORTU	NEUTRINO
EILOORWW	WIRE WOOL	EIMNOPST	NEPOTISM,	EINNORTV	INVENTOR
EILOPPRS	SLOPPIER		PIMENTOS	EINNORWW	WINNOWER
EILOPRRT	PORTLIER	EIMNOPTT	IMPOTENT	EINNOSSS	NOSINESS
EILOPRSS	SPOILERS	EIMNORSU	MONSIEUR	EINNOSST	TENSIONS
EILOPRSU	PERILOUS	EIMNORTW	TIMEWORN	EINNPRSS	SPINNERS
EILOPRTW	PILEWORT	EIMNORTY	ENORMITY	EINNPSSU	PUNINESS
EILOPSSV	PLOSIVES	EIMNOSTU	MOUNTIES	EINNPSSY	SPINNEYS
EILOPSTX	EXPLOITS	EIMNPRSS	PRIMNESS	EINNPSXY	SIXPENNY
EILORRTU	ULTERIOR	EIMNPSST	MISSPENT	EINNRSTU	RUNNIEST
EILORSSS	RISSOLES	EIMNRSST	MINSTERS,	EINNRSTV	VINTNERS
EILORTTY	TOILETRY		TRIMNESS	EINNRTTU	NUTRIENT
EILOSSTU	LOUSIEST	EIMNRSTU	TERMINUS	EINNSSTU	SUNNIEST
EILOSTTT	STILETTO	EIMNRSTY	ENTRYISM	EINOOPRS	POISONER
EILPPRSS	SLIPPERS	EIMNSUZZ	MUEZZINS	EINOOPSS	OPSONISE
EILPPRST	STIPPLER, TIPPLERS	EIMOORST	MOTORISE,	EINOOPSZ	OPSONIZE
EILPPRSU	SUPPLIER		ROOMIEST	EINOOPTT	ON TIPTOE
EILPPRSY	SLIPPERY	EIMOORTZ	MOTORIZE	EINOORST	SNOOTIER
EILPPSSU	SUPPLIES	EIMOPPRR	IMPROPER	EINOORSZ	OZONISER
EILPPSTU	PULPIEST	EIMOPRRS	PRIMROSE,	EINOORZZ	OZONIZER
EILPRSTT	SPLITTER, TRIPLETS		PROMISER	EINOOSSZ	OOZINESS
EILPRSTY	PRIESTLY	EIMOPRRT	IMPORTER,	EINOOTXX	EXOTOXIN
EILPRSUU	PURLIEUS		REIMPORT	EINOPRRS	PRISONER
EILPRSUY	PLEURISY	EIMOPRRV	IMPROVER	EINOPRSS	ROPINESS
EILPRTTY	PRETTILY	EIMOPRSS	PROMISES	EINOPRST	POINTERS,
EILQRRSU	SQUIRREL	EIMOPRUU	EUROPIUM		PROTEINS
EILQRSUU	LIQUEURS	EIMOQSTU	MISQUOTE	EINOPRSU	PRUINOSE
EILRRSTU	SULTRIER	EIMORRST	MORTISER,	EINOPRTU	ERUPTION
EILRRSTW	TWIRLERS		STORMIER	EINOPSTT	NEPOTIST, STEP ON
EILRSSTU	SURLIEST	EIMORRWW	WIREWORM		IT
EILRSSTY	SISTERLY, STYLISER	EIMORSST	MORTISES	EINOPSWX	SWINEPOX
EILRSSZZ	SIZZLERS	EIMORSTU	MOISTURE	EINOQSTU	QUESTION
EILRSTTW	WRISTLET	EIMORSTW	WORMIEST	EINOQTTU	QUOTIENT
EILRSTUV	RIVULETS	EIMORSTY	ISOMETRY	EINORRST	INTRORSE
EILRSTYZ	STYLIZER	EIMORTTW	TWO-TIMER	EINORSSS	ROSINESS
EILRSUUX	LUXURIES	EIMOSSST	MOSSIEST	EINORSSU	NEUROSIS,
EIMMNNTU	MUNIMENT	EIMOSSTU	MOUSIEST		RESINOUS
EIMMNORS	MISNOMER	EIMOSSTZ	MESTIZOS	EINORSSV	VERSIONS
EIMMOPRU	EMPORIUM	EIMOSTTT	TOTEMIST	EINORSTT	SNOTTIER
EIMMORRT	MORTIMER	EIMOSTTU	TITMOUSE	EINORSTU	ROUTINES
EIMMOSTT	TOTEMISM	EIPRSSTU	PRIMUSES	EINORSTV	INVESTOR
EIMMPRST	PRIMMEST	EIMPRSTU	STUMPIER	EINORSUV	SOUVENIR
		EIMPSSTU	SEPTIMUS	EINORTTU	RITENUTO

EINOSSSS	SESSIONS	EIRSTTTW	TWITTERS	ELNOOSTZ	SOLONETZ
EINOSSST	STENOSIS	EIRTTTWY	TWITTERY	ELNOPRVY	PROVENLY
EINOSSTT	STONIEST	EISSTTUW	WET SUITS	ELNOPSTU	PLEUSTON
EINOSSTW	SNOWIEST	EISSUUVV	VESUVIUS	ELNOPTTY	POTENTLY
EINOSTVY	VENOSITY	EJMOSTTU	MOT JUSTE	ELNORSTU	TURNSOLE
EINPPSST	SNIPPETS	EJNORSUY	JOURNEYS	ELNORTTY	ROTTENLY
EINPRRST	PRINTERS,	EJNSSSTU	JUSTNESS	ELNOSSSW	SLOWNESS
REPRINTS, SPRINTER		EKKNSTUZ	KUZNETSK	ELNOSSTV	SOLVENTS
EINPRRTU	PRURIENT	EKLMNOSS	SMOLENSK	ELNPRTUU	PURULENT
EINPRSST	SPINSTER	EKLNOOOR	LOOKER-ON,	ELOORSST	ROOTLESS
EINQRSTU	SQUINTER	ONLOOKER		ELOOSTUU	TOULOUSE
EINQSSTU	INQUESTS	EKLNORSS	SNORKELS	ELOPPRRY	PROPERLY
EINQSTTU	QUINTETS	EKLNOSWY	KNOWSLEY	ELOPRRSW	PROWLERS
EINRRSSU	INSURERS	EKLOOORV	OVERLOOK	ELOPRSTY	PROSTYLE
EINRSSSU	SUNRISES	EKMRSTUY	MUSKETRY	ELOPSSST	SPOTLESS
EINSSTTW	TWIN SETS	EKNNOPSU	UNSPOKEN	ELORSTUY	UROSTYLE
EINSTTTU	NUTTIEST	EKNOOPRW	OPENWORK	ELPPSSTU	SUPPLEST
EIOOPPRS	PORPOISE	EKNORSTW	NETWORKS	ELPRSTTU	SPLUTTER
EIOOPPST	OPPOSITE	EKNRSTUY	TURNKEYS	ELPRSUZZ	PUZZLERS
EIOOPSST	ISOTOPES	EKOOORTV	OVERTOOK	ELPSSTUU	PUSTULES
EIOORSTT	TORTOISE	EKOORRVW	OVERWORK	ELRRSSTU	RUSTLERS
EIOOSSTT	SOOTIEST,	EKOORTWW	KOWTOWER	ELRSTUUV	VULTURES
TOOTSIES		EKOPRSTU	UPSTROKE	ELSSSTUY	STYLUSES
EIOOSTWZ	WOOZIEST	ELLLMOWY	MELLOWLY	EMMMNOTU	MOMENTUM
EIOPPRTW	PIPEWORT	ELLLNSUY	SULLENLY	EMMNNOTU	MONUMENT
EIOPPSST	SOPPIEST	ELLMNOSY	SOLEMNLY	EMMNOOSS	MONOSOME
EIOPRRSS	PRIORESS	ELLNOORV	LOVELORN	EMMNOORS	MEN'S ROOM
EIOPRRST	SPORTIER	ELLNOOSW	WOOLLENS	EMMNOORT	MOTORMEN
EIOPRRSU	SUPERIOR	ELLNORRT	RENT-ROLL	EMMNOOSY	MONOSEMY
EIOPRSST	PROSIEST,	ELLNORWW	WELL-WORN	EMMNOTTU	TOMENTUM
RIPOSTES, TRIPOSES		ELLNOSVY	SLOVENLY	EMMNOTYY	METONYMY
EIOPRSTT	SPOTTIER	ELLNOUVY	UNLOVELY	EMMRRRUU	MURMURER
EIOPRSTV	SPORTIVE	ELLNSSTU	NULL SETS	EMMRRSTU	STRUMMER
EIOPRSUV	PERVIOUS,	ELLOORRV	ROLL OVER	EMMRSTYY	SYMMETRY
PREVIOUS, VIPEROUS		ELLOPRST	POLLSTER	EMNNOOOT	MONOTONE
EIOPSTTT	POTTIEST	ELLOPRTU	POLLUTER	EMNNOOSW	NEW MOONS
EIORRRSW	WORRIERS	ELLOPRUV	PULLOVER	EMNNOSTW	TOWNSMEN
EIORRSST	RESISTOR,	ELLORRST	STROLLER	EMNNSTTU	STUNT MEN
SORRIEST		ELLORSTY	TROLLEYS	EMNOOPTY	MONOTYPE
EIORRSTV	SERVITOR	ELLOSSSU	SOULLESS	EMNOORSU	ENORMOUS
EIORRSVY	REVISORY	ELLOSSTU	SELL-OUTS	EMNOORSW	NEWSROOM
EIORSSTY	SEROSITY	ELMNOOSS	MOONLESS	EMNOOSUV	VENOMOUS
EIORSTUV	VITREOUS	ELMNOOSZ	ZOOM LENS	EMNOOTTY	TENOTOMY
EIPPRRST	STRIPPER, TRIPPERS	ELMNUUZZ	UNMUZZLE	EMNORRSU	MOURNERS
EIPQRSTU	QUIPSTER	ELMOORST	TREMOLOS	EMNORSST	MONSTERS
EIPRRSSU	SURPRISE	ELMOORSY	MOROSELY	EMNORSTT	TORMENTS
EIPRSSTT	TIPSTERS	ELMOOSSY	LYSOSOME	EMNORSTU	REMOUNTS
EIPRSTUW	WRITE-UPS	ELMOPRSY	POLYMERS	EMNORSUU	NUMEROUS
EIQRRSTU	SQUIRTER	ELMOPSYY	POLYSEMY	EMNORTUX	MONTREUX
EIQRSTTU	QUITTERS	ELMOSTUU	TUMULOSE	EMNOSUUY	EUONYMUS
EIRRRSST	STIRRERS	ELMOSYYZ	LYSOZYME	EMNOSUVY	EVONYMUS
EIRRSTTU	TRUSTIER	ELMPPSTU	PLUMPEST	EMNRSSTU	STERNUMS
EIRSSTTU	RUSTIEST,	ELNNOOSU	UNLOOSEN	EMOOPRRT	PROMOTER
TRUSTIES		ELNOOPRT	TERNOPOL	EMOOPRSZ	ZOOSPERM
EIRSSTTW	TWISTERS				

EMOORRST	REST ROOM	EOPRRSTU	POSTURER,	FGGGILNO	FLOGGING
EMOORTYZ	ZOOMETRY		TROUPERS	FGGHIINT	FIGHTING
EMOOSSTW	TWOSOMES	EOPRRUVY	PURVEYOR	FGGIILNN	FLINGING
EMOPPRRT	PROMPTER	EOPRSSTT	PROTESTS,	FGGIINNR	FRINGING
EMOPRSSU	SPERMOUS,		SPOTTERS	FGGIINRU	FIGURING
SUPREMOS		EOPRSSTU	POSTURES,	FGGINOOR	FORGOING
EMPRRTUY	TRUMPERY		SPOUTERS	FGGINORS	FORGINGS
EMPRSTTU	STRUMPET,	EOPSSTTW	TWO-STEPS	FGHIIKNS	KINGFISH
TRUMPETS		EORRRTTU	TORTURER	FGHIILNT	IN-FLIGHT
ENNOOOTZ	ENTOZOON	EORRSSTU	TROUSERS	FGHIINST	SHIFTING
ENNOOPPT	OPPONENT	EORRSTTT	TROTTERS	FGHILNSU	FLUSHING,
ENNOORTV	NONVOTER	EORRSTTU	TORTURES	LUNGFISH	
ENNOPRUV	UNPROVEN	EORRSUVY	SURVEYOR	FGHILRTU	RIGHTFUL
ENNOPTWY	TWOPENNY	EOSSTTTU	STOUTEST	FGHINORT	FROTHING
ENNORSST	STERNSON	EPPPRTUY	PUPPETRY	FGHIOTTU	OUTFIGHT
ENNORSTU	NEUTRONS	EPPRSSSU	PRESS-UPS,	FGHLORUU	FURLOUGH
ENNOSTWW	NEW TOWNS	SUPPRESS		FGHNOORS	FOGHORNS
ENNPPTUY	TUPPENNY	EPRRSSUU	PURSUERS,	FGIIKNRS	FRISKING
ENNPRRUU	RUNNER-UP	USURPERS		FGIILLNS	FILLINGS
ENNRSSTU	STUNNERS	EPRRSTUU	RUPTURES	FGIILNPP	FLIPPING
ENOOPPST	POSTPONE	EPRSSTTU	SPUTTERS	FGIILNRT	FLIRTING, TRIFLING
ENOOPRSS	POORNESS,	ERRSTTTU	STRUTTER	FGIILNST	STIFLING
SNOOPERS		ERRSTTTU	STUTTERS	FGIILNTT	FLITTING
ENOOPSTT	POTSTONE	FFFGILNU	FLUFFING	FGIINNSU	INFUSING
ENOORRST	SORRENTO	FFFILOST	LIFT-OFFS	FGIINNUY	UNIFYING
ENOPRSTT	PORTENTS	FFGHIIRT	GRIFFITH	FGIINOST	FOISTING
ENOPSSSY	SYNOPSES	FFGHIORS	FROGFISH	FGIINRTU	FRUITING
ENORRSST	SNORTERS	FFGHIRSU	GRUFFISH	FGIINRZZ	FRIZZING
ENORRSTT	TORRENTS	FFGIILNP	PIFFLING	FGIINSST	SIFTINGS
ENORRTUV	OVERTURN,	FFGIILNR	RIFFLING	FGIINSTT	FITTINGS
TURNOVER		FFGIINNS	SNIFFING	FGIKLNNU	FLUNKING
ENORSSSU	SOURNESS	FFGIINRS	GRIFFINS	FGILMNUY	FUMINGLY
ENORSSTU	TONSURES	FFGILMNU	MUFFLING	FGILNNTU	GUNFLINT
ENORSTUY	TOURNEYS	FFGILNRU	RUFFLING	FGILNOOR	FLOORING
ENOSSSTT	STETSONS	FFGINNSU	SNUFFING	FGILNOOT	FOOTLING
ENOSSSUU	SENSUOUS	FFGINSTU	STUFFING	FGILNOPP	FLOPPING
ENPRSSSY	SPRYNESS	FFHILOSW	WOLFFISH	FGILNORU	FLOURING
ENPRSSTU	PUNSTERS	FFHOOOST	OFFSHOOT	FGILNOSS	FLOSSING
ENRRRTUU	NURTURER	FFHOOSSW	SHOW-OFFS	FGILNOTU	FLOUTING
EOOORSPZ	ZOOSPORE	FFHOSTTU	HOT STUFF	FGILNPRU	PURFLING
EOOORRST	ROSE-ROOT	FFIILMOR	FILIFORM	FGINNORT	FRONTING
EOOPPRRS	PROPOSER	FFIKLORT	FORK-LIFT	FGINNORW	FROWNING
EOOPPRSV	POPOVERS	FFILLOPP	FLIP-FLOP	FGINOOPR	PROOFING
EOOPPTTY	TOPOTYPE	FFILLTUY	FITFULLY	FGINORST	FROSTING
EOOPRRST	TROOPERS	FFILRTUU	FRUITFUL	FGLLMOOU	GLOOMFUL
EOOPRRTU	UPROOTER	FFILRTUY	FRUIT FLY	FGLNORSU	FURLONGS
EOOPRSTV	STOPOVER	FFILSTUY	STUFFILY	FGLNORUW	WRONGFUL
EOOPRSTW	TOWROPES	FFIMORSU	FUSIFORM	FGLOOOST	FOOTSLOG
EOORRRSW	SORROWER	FFINOPRT	OFFPRINT	FHHIKOOS	FISH-HOOK
EOORRSST	ROOSTERS	FFINOPSS	SPIN-OFFS	FHHLOSTU	HOT FLUSH
EOORSSTU	OESTROUS	FFINOPST	PONTIFFS	FHIIKLMS	MILKFISH
EOPPRRTY	PROPERTY	FFNORSTU	TURN-OFFS	FHIIKNSS	FISHSKIN
EOPPRSST	STOPPERS	FFOORRUU	FROUFROU	FHIILLTY	FILTHILY
EOPPRSSU	PURPOSES,	FFOORSTW	WORST-OFF	FHIILMNT	THIN-FILM
SUPPOSER		FGGGIINR	FRIGGING		

FHIILNOS	LIONFISH	
FHIILSTY	SHIFTILY	
FHIKLSWY	FLYWHISK	
FHIKMNOS	MONKFISH	
FHILLOOT	FOOTHILL	
FHILLORT	HILLFORT	
FHILMPSU	LUMPFISH	
FHILMRTU	MIRTHFUL	
FHILOPST	SHOPLIFT	
FHILORSU	FLOURISH	
FHILORTY	FROTHILY	
FHIMNOOS	MOONFISH	
FHIMPRSU	FRUMPISH	
FHIOOPTT	PHOTOFIT	
FHLLOSTU	SLOTHFUL	
FHLMOTUU	MOUTHFUL	
FHLOTUUY	YOUTHFUL	
FHLRTTUU	TRUTHFUL	
FHNOSTUX	FOXHUNTS	
FHOOORST	FORSOOTH	
FIIILNOP	FILIPINO	
FIIINNOX	INFIXION	
FIIINNTY	INFINITY	
FIIKLRSY	FRISKILY	
FIIKLSST	SKI LIFTS	
FIILLMSY	FLIMSILY	
FIILMOPR	PILIFORM	
FIILMPSY	SIMPLIFY	
FIILTTUY	FUTILITY	
FIIMOPRS	PISIFORM	
FIINNOSU	INFUSION	
FIINORTU	FRUITION	
FIKKLNOS	KINSFOLK	
FILLLUWY	WILFULLY	
FILLNSUY	SINFULLY	
FILLOPPY	FLOPPILY	
FILORSST	FLORISTS	
FILORSTY	FROSTILY	
FILSSTTU	FLUTISTS	
FILSTTUY	STULTIFY	
FIMNORSU	UNIFORMS	
FIMOPRRY	PYRIFORM	
FIMORTUY	FUMITORY	
FIMRSTUU	FUTURISM	
FINORSSS	FRISSONS	
FIORTTUY	FORTUITY	
FIRSTTUU	FUTURIST	
FIRTTUUY	FUTURITY	
FJLLOUYY	JOYFULLY	
FKMOORRW	FORMWORK	
FKNOORTX	FORT KNOX	
FKOOORTW	FOOTWORK	
FLLMNOOU	FULL MOON	
FLLNOOOW	FOLLOW-ON	

FLLOOPUW	FOLLOW-UP
FLLOPSTU	FULL STOP
FLLOSSTU	FULL TOSS
FLMNORUU	MOURNFUL
FLNOOPSU	SPOONFUL
FLOOSTUW	OUTFLOWS
FLOPRSTU	SPORTFUL
FLRSTTUU	TRUSTFUL
FNOOORTW	FOOTWORN
FNOORRSW	FORSWORN
FNOORSSU	SUNROOFS
FOOOPRST	ROOFTOPS
FOOPSSTT	SOFT SPOT
FOORSTTX	FOXTROTS
FOPSSSTU	FUSSPOTS
GGGGIILN	GIGGLING
GGGGILNO	GOGGLING
GGGIIJLN	JIGGLING
GGGIILNN	NIGGLING
GGGIILNW	WIGGLING
GGGIINSW	SWIGGING, WIGGINGS
GGGIINTW	TWIGGING
GGGIJLNO	JOGGLING
GGGIJLNU	JUGGLING
GGGILNOS	SLOGGING
GGGILNPU	PLUGGING
GGGILNRU	GURGLING
GGGILNSU	SLUGGING
GGGILORY	GROGGILY
GGGIMNSU	MUGGINGS
GGGINNOS	SNOGGING
GGHHIISW	WHIGGISH
GGHIILNT	LIGHTING
GGHIINNW	WHINGING
GGHIINRT	RIGHTING
GGHIINST	SIGHTING
GGHIIPRS	PRIGGISH
GGHILSSU	SLUGGISH
GGHINORU	ROUGHING
GGHINOST	GHOSTING
GGHINOSU	SOUGHING
GGHKNNOO	HONG KONG
GGIIINNT	IGNITING
GGIIJLNN	JINGLING
GGIILLNR	GRILLING
GGIILMNN	MINGLING
GGIILNNS	GIN SLING, SINGLING, SLINGING
GGIILNNT	GLINTING, TINGLING
GGIIMPRS	PRIGGISM
GGIINNNR	GRINNING
GGIINNOR	IGNORING
GGIINNRW	WRINGING

GGIINNSS	SIGNINGS
GGIINNST	STINGING
GGIINNSW	SWINGING
GGIINPPR	GRIPPING
GGIINRTT	GRITTING
GGILLOOW	GOLLIWOG
GGILNNOS	LONGINGS
GGILNNOU	LOUNGING
GGILNNPU	PLUNGING
GGILNORW	GROWLING
GGILNORY	GLORYING
GGILNOSS	GLOSSING, GOSLINGS
GGILNRUY	URGINGLY
GGILNTTU	GLUTTING
GGILNUZZ	GUZZLING
GGILOSUY	SQUIGGLY
GGIMNOOR	GROOMING
GGINNOOS	GOINGS-ON
GGINNOPP	PING-PONG
GGINNOPS	SPONGING
GGINNORW	WRONGING
GGINNOSS	SINGSONG
GGINNRTU	GRUNTING
GGINOOTU	OUTGOING
GGINOPRU	GROUPING
GGINORSS	GROSSING
GGINORSU	GROUSING
GGINRSST	G-STRINGS
GHHIJMPU	HIGH JUMP
GHHILOSU	GHOULISH
GHHINSSU	SHUSHING
GHHIOPST	HIGH SPOT
GHHOORTU	THOROUGH
GHHOSTTU	THOUGHTS
GHIIKNNS	HSINKING
GHIIKNNT	THINKING
GHIIKNPS	KINGSHIP
GHIIKNRS	SHIRKING
GHIIKNSW	WHISKING
GHIILLNS	SHILLING
GHIILMTY	MIGHTILY
GHIILNRW	WHIRLING
GHIILTTW	TWILIGHT
GHIIMRST	RIGHTISM
GHIINNNS	SHINNING
GHIINNNT	THINNING
GHIINOST	HOISTING
GHIINPPS	SHIPPING
GHIINPPW	WHIPPING
GHIINRRS	SHIRRING
GHIINRRW	WHIRRING
GHIINRST	SHIRTING
GHIINRTV	THRIVING

GHIINRTW	WRITHING	GHNOSSTU	GUNSHOTS,	GIILPSTU	PUGILIST
GHIINSST	INSIGHTS		SHOTGUNS	GIILRTTY	GRITTILY
GHIINSSW	SWISHING	GHOPRTUW	UPGROWTH	GIIMMNRT	TRIMMING
GHIINSTT	SHITTING	GIIILMNT	LIMITING	GIIMMNRU	IMMURING
GHIINSTW	WHITINGS	GIIILOTV	VITILIGO	GIIMMNSW	SWIMMING
GHIINWZZ	WHIZZING	GIIINNOT	IGNITION	GIIMNNOY	IGNOMINY
GHIIRSTT	RIGHTIST	GIIINNOZ	IONIZING	GIIMMNTU	MINUTING
GHIKLNTY	KNIGHTLY	GIIINNTV	INVITING	GIIMNOPS	IMPOSING
GHIKLSTY	SKYLIGHT	GIIINSTV	VISITING	GIIMNOTT	OMITTING
GHILLNOS	SHILLONG	GIIJMNOS	JINGOISM	GIIMNOTV	VOMITING
GHILLSTY	SLIGHTLY	GIIJNNOT	JOINTING	GIIMNPRU	UMPIRING
GHILNOPS	LONGSHIP	GIIJNNRU	INJURING	GIIMNPTU	IMPUTING
GHILNOSS	SLOSHING	GIIJNOST	JINGOIST	GIIMNSSU	MISUSING
GHILNOTW	NIGHT OWL	GIIKLLNS	KILLINGS	GIIMORRS	RIGORISM
GHILNRTU	HURTLING	GIIKLNNS	SLINKING	GIINNNOT	INTONING
GHILNRUY	HUNGRILY	GIIKLNNT	TINKLING	GIINNNPS	SPINNING
GHILNSTU	HUSTLING,	GIIKLNNW	WINKLING	GIINNNSW	WINNINGS
	SUNLIGHT	GIIKMMNS	SKIMMING	GIINNNTW	TWINNING
GHILOPRS	SHOPGIRL	GIIKMNPS	SKIMPING	GIINNOPT	POINTING
GHILORSW	SHOWGIRL	GIIKMNRS	SMIRKING	GIINNORS	ROSINING
GHILPRTY	TRIGLYPH	GIIKNNNS	SKINNING	GIINNORT	IGNITRON
GHIMNOTU	MOUTHING	GIIKNNOV	INVOKING	GIINNPPS	SNIPPING
GHIMNPTU	THUMPING	GIIKNNPS	KINGPINS, PINK	GIINNPRT	PRINTING
GHIMNSTU	GUNSMITH		GINS	GIINNRSU	INSURING
GHINNNSU	SHUNNING	GIIKNNST	STINKING	GIINNRTU	UNTIRING
GHINNOQU	QUI NHONG	GIIKNNTT	KNITTING	GIINNSTT	STINTING
GHINNORT	NORTHING	GIIKNPPS	SKIPPING	GIINOPST	POSITING
GHINNSTU	SHUNTING	GIIKNPSS	PIGSKINS	GIINOPTV	PIVOTING
GHINOOPW	WHOOPING	GIIKNRST	SKIRTING,	GIINORUV	IN VIGOUR
GHINOOST	SHOOTING,		STRIKING	GIINPPQU	QUIPPING
	SOOTHING	GIILLNPS	SPILLING	GIINPPRT	TRIPPING
GHINOPPS	SHOPPING	GIILLNRT	TRILLING	GIINPRSU	UPRISING
GHINOPPW	WHOPPING	GIILLNST	STILLING	GIINPSTT	SPITTING
GHINOQTU	QUOTHING	GIILLNSW	SWILLING	GIINQTTU	QUITTING
GHINORST	SHORTING	GIILLPSW	PIGSWILL	GIINQUZZ	QUIZZING
GHINORTW	INGROWTH,	GIILLTUY	GUILTILY	GIINRRST	STIRRING
	THROWING, WORTHING	GIILMMNS	SLIMMING	GIINRSTW	WRITINGS
GHINOSSU	HOUSINGS	GIILMNPY	IMPLYING	GIINSSTT	SITTINGS
GHINOSSW	SHOWINGS	GIILMPRS	PILGRIMS	GIINSTTW	TWISTING
GHINOSTU	SHOUTING,	GIILMPSU	PUGILISM	GIINTTTW	TWITTING
	SOUTHING	GIILNNSY	LYINGS-IN	GIIORRST	RIGORIST
GHINOSUY	YOUNGISH	GIILNOPS	SPOILING	GIJKLNOY	JOKINGLY
GHINRRUY	HURRYING	GIILNOPT	PILOTING	GIJLLNOY	JOLLYING
GHINSSTU	HUSTINGS	GIILNPPR	RIPPLING	GIJLNOST	JOSTLING
GHINSTTU	SHUTTING	GIILNPPS	SLIPPING	GIJNOSTT	JOTTINGS
GHIORTTU	OUTRIGHT	GIILNPRT	TRIPLING	GIJNOSTU	JOUSTING
GHLMOOOY	HOMOLOGY	GIILNQSU	QUISLING	GIKKLNSU	SKULKING
GHLNNOOR	LONGHORN	GIILNQTU	QUILTING	GIKLNNOP	PLONKING
GHLNOOST	LONG SHOT	GIILNRST	STIRLING	GIKNNOST	KINGSTON
GHLOOORY	HOROLOGY	GIILNRSW	SWIRLING	GIKNNOTT	KNOTTING
GHLORTUU	TURLOUGH	GIILNRTW	TWIRLING	GIKNOOPS	SPOOKING
GHMNOOOY	HOMOGONY	GIILNSTT	SLITTING	GIKNORST	STROKING
GHMOSSTU	MUGSHOTS	GIILNSTU	LINGUIST	GIKNORSW	WORKINGS
GHNNOPUU	HUNG UP ON	GIILNSTY	STINGILY	GILLMOOY	GLOOMILY
GHNOPRSY	GRYPHONS	GIILNSZZ	SIZZLING		

GILLNORT	TROLLING
GILLNOVY	LOVINGLY
GILLNOWY	LOW-LYING
GILLNRUY	LURINGLY
GILLNSUY	SULLYING
GILLOSSY	GLOSSILY
GILMMNSU	SLUMMING
GILMNOPY	MOPINGLY
GILMNOTU	MOULTING
GILMNOVY	MOVINGLY
GILMNPPU	PLUMPING
GILMNPRU	RUMPLING
GILMNPSU	SLUMPING
GILMNSUY	MUSINGLY
GILMNUZZ	MUZZLING
GILMOOSY	MISOLOGY
GILMPRUY	GRUMPILY
GILMPSSY	GYMSLIPS
GILNNRSU	NURSLING
GILNNUZZ	NUZZLING
GILNOOSY	SINOLOGY
GILNOOTT	TOOTLING
GILNOPPP	PLOPPING
GILNOPPS	SLOPPING
GILNOPPT	TOPPLING
GILNOPRW	PROWLING
GILNOPSY	SPONGILY
GILNOPTT	PLOTTING
GILNOSTT	SLOTTING
GILNOSTU	LONG SUIT, TOUSLING
GILNOTUY	OUTLYING
GILNPRSU	SLURPING
GILNPUZZ	PUZZLING
GILNRRSU	SLURRING
GILNRSTU	RUSTLING
GILNSSTU	TUSSLING
GILOOOST	OOLOGIST
GILOORSU	GLORIOUS
GILOORVY	VIROLOGY
GILOOSSS	ISOGLOSS
GILOOSTY	SITOLOGY
GIMMNRUY	GIN RUMMY
GIMMOSSU	GUMMOSIS
GIMNNORS	MORNINGS
GIMNNORU	MOURNING
GIMNNOTU	MOUNTING
GIMNOOOU	OOGONIUM
GIMNOORS	MOORINGS
GIMNOORT	MOTORING
GIMNOPST	STOMPING
GIMNOPTU	GUMPTION
GIMNORRW	RINGWORM
GIMNORST	STORMING
GIMNOSYY	MISOGYNY
GIMNPRTU	TRUMPING
GIMNPSTU	STUMPING
GIMNSTYY	STYMYING
GINNNSTU	STUNNING
GINNOOPS	SNOOPING, SPOONING
GINNOOSW	SWOONING
GINNOOSZ	SNOOZING
GINNOPTU	GUNPOINT
GINNORST	SNORTING
GINNPRSU	SPURNING
GINNRSTU	TURNINGS, UNSTRING
GINNSTTU	STUNTING
GINNSTUW	WING NUTS
GINOOPPS	OPPOSING
GINOOPRT	TROOPING
GINOOPST	STOOPING
GINOOPSW	SWOOPING
GINOORST	ROOSTING
GINOOPPR	PROPPING
GINOOPPT	STOPPING, TOPPINGS
GINOPPSW	SWOPPING
GINOPRST	SPORTING
GINOPRSU	IN-GROUPS
GINOPSST	POSTINGS, SIGNPOST
GINOPSTT	SPOTTING
GINOPSTU	SPOUTING
GINORRWY	WORRYING
GINORSTW	WORSTING
GINORTTT	TROTTING
GINORTTU	TUTORING
GINOSTTW	SWOTTING
GINOSTUW	OUTSWING
GINPRRSU	SPURRING
GINPRSTU	SPURTING
GINPRSUU	PURSUING, USURPING
GINPSSUW	UPSWINGS
GINRSSTU	TRUSSING
GINRSTTU	TRUSTING
GINRSTUU	SUTURING
GIOOORSV	VIGOROSO
GIOORRSU	RIGOROUS
GIOORSTU	GOITROUS
GIOORSUV	VIGOROUS
GIORSTUY	RUGOSITY
GJLMNOPU	LONG JUMP
GLLOOPTY	POLYGLOT
GLMNOOOY	MONOLOGY, NOMOLOGY
GLMNORUW	LUNGWORM
GLMOOOPY	POMOLOGY
GLMOORWW	GLOW-WORM
GLMOOYYZ	ZYMOLOGY
GLMORSUW	LUGWORMS
GLNOOOST	LONG TONS
GLNOOOSY	NOSOLOGY
GLNOOOTY	ONTOLOGY
GLNOOPSY	POLYGONS
GLNOPYYY	POLYGYNY
GLNORSTY	STRONGLY
GLNORTUW	LUNGWORT
GLNOSTTU	GLUTTONS
GLNOTTUY	GLUTTONY
GLOOOPSY	POSOLOGY
GLOOOPTY	TOPOLOGY
GLOOPSSY	GOSSYPOL
GLOOPTYY	LOGOTYPY, TYPOLOGY
GMMNOTUY	TOMMY GUN
GMMPSUUW	MUGWUMPS
GMNNOOYY	MONOGYNY
GNOOOTTW	GO TO TOWN
GNOORTUW	OUTGROWN
GNOPPUUY	YOUNG PUP
GNOPRSUW	GROWN-UPS
GNPRSTUU	STRUNG-UP
GOOPRTUU	OUT-GROUP
HHHHSSUU	HUSH-HUSH
HHIIKKOO	KHOIKHOI
HHIIOORT	HIROHITO
HHIIPSST	PHTHISIS
HHKKSSUU	KHUSKHUS
HHOOOOPP	POOH-POOH
HHOOPPRS	PHOSPHOR
HHORRSUU	RUSH HOUR
HIIILMNS	NIHILISM
HIIILNST	NIHILIST
HIIILNTY	NIHILITY
HIIINRST	RHINITIS
HIIKMRSS	SKIRMISH
HIIKSSTT	SKITTISH
HIILLPPS	PHILLIPS
HIILMOST	HOMILIST
HIILMPSY	IMPISHLY
HIILMTUY	HUMILITY
HIILOPST	PISOLITH
HIILPSSY	SYPHILIS
HIILSSTT	HIT LISTS
HIIMNSTT	TINSMITH
HIIMOPSS	PHIMOSIS
HIIMORTU	HIRI MOTU
HIIMORTZ	ZHITOMIR

HIISSSSY	SISSYISH	HNNOORTT	THORNTON	IIMNNOSU	UNIONISM
HIKNOOOR	KOHINOOR	HNOOOSTT	NOT SO HOT	IIMNNOTU	MUNITION
HIKOOPSS	SPOOKISH	HNOOPRST	POST HORN	IIMNOOSS	OMISSION
HIKOPSSY	KYPHOSIS	HNOOPSTY	TYPHOONS	IIMNOPRS	IMPRISON
HILLLOSU	SOLIHULL	HNOORRTW	HORNWORT	IIMNORTY	MINORITY
HILLMSUY	MULISHLY	HNORSTTU	THURSTON	IIMNOSSS	MISSIONS
HILLOSWY	OWLISHLY	HNORTUWY	UNWORTHY	IIMNOSST	SIMONIST
HILMNOOT	MONOLITH	HNRSTTUU	UNTRUTHS	IIMNPRST	IMPRINTS,
HILNORTY	THORNILY	HOOOSTTU	OUTSHOOT,		MISPRINT
HILOOTTY	TOOTHILY		SHOOT-OUT	IIMNPTUY	IMPUNITY
HILORSUU	URUSHIOL	HOOPSSTT	HOT SPOTS,	IIMNRSTY	MINISTRY
HILORTWY	HOLY WRIT,		POTSHOTS	IIMOPSTT	OPTIMIST
	WORTHILY	HOPPRRYY	PORPHYRY	IIMORSSU	MISSOURI
HILOSTWW	WHITLOWS	HPRSTTUU	UPTHRUST	IIMORSTY	RIMOSITY
HILPPRSU	PURPLISH	IIILLNOS	ILLINOIS	IIMOTTVY	MOTIVITY
HILSSTTU	SLUTTISH	IIILMRSV	VIRILISM	IIMPRTUY	IMPURITY
HIMOOPRS	ISOMORPH	IIILMUVX	LIXIVIUM	IIMSSTUW	SWIMSUIT
HIMOPRRT	TRIMORPH	IIILRTVY	VIRILITY	IINNNOSU	IN UNISON
HIMOPRSW	SHIPWORM	IIINPRST	INSPIRIT	IINNOOPS	OPINIONS
HIMOPRWW	WHIPWORM	IIINQTUY	INIQUITY	IINNOPPT	PINPOINT
HIMOPSSS	SOPHISMS	IIJJKRSW	RIJSWIJK	IINNOSTU	UNIONIST
HIMORSTU	HUMORIST	IIJJSTUU	JIUJITSU	IINNSTTU	TINNITUS
HIMPRSTU	TRIUMPHS	IIKLLNSY	SLINKILY	IINOOPST	POSITION
HINNSSUY	SUNSHINY	IIKLMPSY	SKIMPILY	IINOSSTZ	ZIONISTS
HINOORSZ	HORIZONS	IIKLNOSS	OILSKINS	IINOSTVY	VINOSITY
HINOPRTW	WINTHROP	IIKLQRUY	QUIRKILY	IINRTTUY	TRIUNITY
HINOPSSY	HYPNOSIS	IILLMNOS	MILLIONS	IIOOPSTV	OVIPOSIT
HINOPSTW	TOWNSHIP	IILLMRTU	TRILLIUM	IIOOQRSU	IROQUOIS
HINORSTW	THROW-INS	IILLMUUV	ILLUVIUM	IIOOSTTY	OTIOSITY
HIOORTWZ	HOROWITZ	IILLNOPS	PILLIONS	IIOPRRTY	PRIORITY
HIOPRSSW	WORSHIPS	IILLNORT	TRILLION	IIORSSTV	VISITORS
HIOPRSUZ	RHIZOPUS	IILLNOSU	ILLUSION	IIORSTUV	VIRTUOSI
HIOPSSST	SOPHISTS	IILLNOSZ	ZILLIONS	IJKLLOSY	KILLJOYS
HIPPPSUY	PUPPYISH	IILMMPSS	SIMPLISM	IJKMPSSU	SKI JUMPS
HKMOOORW	HOOKWORM	IILMNOSU	LIMOUSIN	IJLLORTU	TRUJILLO
HKOOPRSW	WORKSHOP	IILMOTTY	MOTILITY	IJMPSTUU	JUMPSUIT
HLLLOOWY	HOLLOWLY	IILNOOST	INOSITOL	IKKLNORW	LINKWORK
HLLMNOOU	MONOHULL	IILNOOTV	VOLITION	IKKLNOSY	KOLINSKY
HLLNOOUU	HONOLULU	IILNORSS	SIRLOINS	IKKLSSUY	ISSYK-KUL
HLLPPSUU	PUSH-PULL	IILNPPSY	SNIPPILY	IKLLOOTV	KILOVOLT
HLMOOSTY	SMOOTHLY	IILNRTWY	WINTRILY	IKLMNRSU	MILK RUNS
HLMOPTUY	PLYMOUTH	IILPRSSY	PRISSILY	IKLMOPSS	MILKSOPS
HLNOOSUW	HOUNSLOW	IILSTUUV	UVULITIS	IKLMORSW	SILKWORM
HMMNOOSY	HOMONYMS	IILSTUVV	VULVITIS	IKLMORTW	MILKWORT
HMMNOOTU	MONMOUTH	IIMMMNSU	MINIMUMS	IKLNOPST	SLIPKNOT
HMMOORSU	MUSHROOM	IIMMNTUY	IMMUNITY	IKLNOTTY	KNOTTILY
HMNOOOST	MOON SHOT	IIMMOPST	OPTIMISM	IKLNPSUY	SPUNKILY
HMNOPSYY	SYMPHONY	IIMMOPSU	OPIUMISM	IKLOOPSY	SPOOKILY
HMOOORSW	SHOWROOM	IIMMSTTU	MITTIMUS	IKMNPPSU	PUMPKINS
HMOORSUU	HUMOROUS	IIMNNOOT	MONITION	IKNOOPRT	PINKROOT

IKNOORRW	IRONWORK	INNNNOOU	NONUNION	KOOORSTV	VOORSKOT
IKORSSTU	KURTOSIS	INNNORTU	TRUNNION	KOOPRSTW	WORKTOPS
ILLLMOPS	PLIMSOLL	INNOOPSS	SPONSION	KOORSTUW	OUTWORKS,
ILLLOOPP	LOLLIPOP	INNOORST	NOTORNIS		WORKOUTS
ILLLOOWY	WOOLLILY	INOOOSSZ	ZOONOSIS	LLMOOPRS	ROLLMOPS
ILLMNOSU	MULLIONS	INOOOTXZ	ZOOTOXIN	LLOOPRST	TROLLOPS
ILLMOSSY	LISSOMLY	INOOPRST	PORTIONS,	LLOOPRYY	ROLY-POLY
ILLMPTUY	MULTIPLY		POSITRON, SORPTION	LLOPSTUU	PULLOUTS
ILLOPPSY	SLOPPILY	INOOPSTT	SPITTOON	LLOSUUVV	VOLVULUS
ILLORSUY	ILLUSORY	INOOPTTU	OUTPOINT	LMMPSSUU	LUMP SUMS
ILLRSTUY	SULTRILY	INOORSTY	SONORITY	LMNOOOPY	MONOPOLY
ILMNOOPU	POLONIUM	INOOSSSS	SOISSONS	LMOOPRTU	PULMOTOR
ILMNOSUU	LUMINOUS	INOPRTTU	PRINTOUT	LMOORSWW	SLOWWORM
ILMOPPSU	POPULISM	INOPSSXY	SYNOPSIS	LMOOTXYY	XYLOTOMY
ILMORSTY	STORMILY	INORSSUV	SUN VISOR	LMOPPRTY	PROMPTLY
ILMSSTUU	STIMULUS	INPPRRUU	PURPURIN	LNOOOPRT	POLTROON
ILMSTTUY	SMUTTILY	INPRRSTU	SURPRINT	LOOPPSUU	POPULOUS
ILNOOSTU	SOLUTION	IOOPRSSV	PROVISOS	LOOPPSUY	POLYPOUS
ILNOOSTY	SNOOTILY	IOOPRSTY	ISOTROPY,	LORSSTUU	LUSTROUS
ILNOOTUV	VOLUTION		POROSITY	MMOOPPRU	PUMP ROOM
ILNORSST	NOSTRILS	IOORRSTY	SORORITY	MMOORTTY	TOMMYROT
ILNORSTY	NITROSYL	IOORSSTT	RISOTTOS	MMOPSSTY	SYMPTOMS
ILNOSTTY	SNOTTILY	IOORSSUV	VOUSSOIR	MNNOOOSS	MONSOONS
ILNPSUUV	PULVINUS	IOORSTTU	TORTIOUS	MNNOOOTY	MONOTONY
ILOOPPRS	PROPOLIS	IOORSTUV	VIRTUOSO	MNNOOSSYY	SYNONYMS
ILOOPUZZ	POZZUOLI	IOORSUUX	UXORIOUS	MNNOSYYY	SYNONYMY
ILOOSSST	SOLOISTS	IOPPPRST	PIT PROPS	MNOOORTW	MOONWORT
ILOPPSTU	POPULIST	IOPRRSSU	SPURIOUS	MNOOORXY	OXYMORON
ILOPRSTY	SPORTILY	IOPRSTTU	OUTSTRIP	MNOOPTYY	TOPONYMY
ILOPSTTY	SPOTTILY	IORRSUVV	SURVIVOR	MNOORSTT	STORMONT
ILOPSUUV	PLUVIOUS	IORSSTTU	TOURISTS	MNORSSTU	NOSTRUMS
ILOQRTUU	LOQUITUR	IORSSUUU	USURIOUS	MNORSTUU	SURMOUNT
ILRSTTUY	TRUSTILY	IORSTTUY	TOURISTY	MOOORRTW	MOORWORT,
ILSSSTTY	STYLISTS	IORSTUUV	VIRTUOUS		TOMORROW
IMMNOORS	MORONISM	IPRRSSTU	STIRRUPS	MOOPSSSU	OPOSSUMS
IMNNOSUU	NUMINOUS	IPRRSTUU	PRURITUS	MOORSTUU	TUMOROUS
IMNOORRS	MORRISON	IPRSSTUU	PURSUITS	MORRSSTU	ROSTRUMS
IMNOORST	MONITORS	JLOOSUYY	JOYOUSLY	NNOOOPST	PONTOONS
IMNOORTY	MONITORY	JNNOORRU	NONJUROR	NNOOPRSU	PRONOUNS
IMNOSTUU	MUTINOUS	JNOORSSU	SOJOURNS	NNOORTUU	RUN OUT ON
IMOOPRRS	PROMISOR	KLLMNSUU	NUMSKULL	NOOORSSU	SONOROUS
IMOOPRST	IMPOSTOR	KLMMOOOS	KOMSOMOL	NOOPRSSS	SPONSORS
IMOOQSTU	MOSQUITO	KLNORSTY	KLYSTRON	NOPSSSTU	SUNSPOTS
IMOORSTT	MOTORIST	KLOOOSTU	LOOKOUTS,	NORSTTUU	TURNOUTS
IMOORSTU	TIMOROUS		OUTLOOKS	OOPRSSTV	PROVOSTS
IMOORTVY	VOMITORY	KLOOPRSW	SLOPWORK	OOPSSTTU	OUTPOSTS
IMOOSSTY	MYOSOTIS	KMOOORRW	WORKROOM	OORSTTUU	TORTUOUS
IMRSSTTU	MISTRUST	KNNNOSUW	UNKNOWNS	OPPRSSTU	SUPPORTS
		KNOOPSTT	TOPKNOTS	OPRSSSUU	SOURPUSS

AAAABCLLV	BALACLAVA	AAAABEHLLV	HAVE A BALL	AAACILLNN	ANACLINAL
AAAABDHLL	ALLAHABAD	AAAABEILLV	AVAILABLE	AAACILNOT	CATALONIA
AAAABGNRU	GUANABARA	AAABEKRWY	BREAKAWAY	AAACILNPT	APLANATIC
AAAABIKLL	BALALAIKA	AAABELLNN	ANNABELLA	AAACILRTU	ACTUARIAL
AAAABILMN	ALABAMIAN	AAABELLPT	PALATABLE	AAACINOPR	PARANOIAC
AAAABKLLV	BALAKLAVA	AAABELRST	ALABASTER	AAACINOTT	CATATONIA
AAAACCHMT	TACAMAHAC	AAABELSSY	ASSAYABLE	AAACINRSU	CASUARINA
AAAACDJNR	JACARANDA	AAABGHNRV	BHAVNAGAR	AAACLMNPU	CAMPANULA
AAAACHSUY	AYAHUASCA	AAABGLORR	ALGARROBA	AAACLMPST	CATAPLASM
AAAACINRU	ARAUCANIA	AAABGMNOZ	ZAMBOANGA	AAACMRTUX	TARAXACUM
AAAACIRRU	ARAUCARIA	AAABGRSTU	RUTABAGAS	AAACNOSSV	CASANOVAS
AAAACLMNS	SALAMANCA	AAABHIRTY	BHARATIYA	AAACSSTWY	CASTAWAYS
AAAACMNRT	CATAMARAN	AAABHKNRT	BAKHTARAN	AAADDHMRY	HAMADRYAD
AAAADGKNR	KARAGANDA	AAABHLRST	BALTHASAR	AAADDLSSY	SALAD DAYS
AAAADILLM	DALAI LAMA	AAABHLRTZ	BALTHAZAR	AAADEGLMN	MAGDALENA
AAAAEHKLL	HALEAKALA	AAABILLVY	AVAILABLY	AAADEGNTV	ADVANTAGE
AAAAGHJMN	MAHAJANGA	AAABJKLNU	BANJA LUKA	AAADELMMR	MARMALADE
AAAAGIKMS	AMAGASAKI	AAABLLPTY	PALATABLY	AAADELNRX	ALEXANDRA
AAAAHHJMR	MAHARAJAH	AAABLOPRS	PARABOLAS	AAADEMNSU	AD NAUSEAM
AAAAHJMRS	MAHARAJAS	AAABLPRST	PARABLAST	AAADHHPRZ	HAPHAZARD
AAAAILNPS	ANAPLASIA	AAACCCHHH	CHA-CHA-CHA	AAADHIILR	HAIDAR ALI
AAAAINSST	ANASTASIA	AAACCDELV	CAVALCADE	AAADHJLNR	JALANDHAR
AAAAKKNRT	KARNATAKA	AAACCELLN	CALCANEAL	AAADHMRSY	HAMADRYAS
AAAALLMMY	MALAYALAM	AAACCEPRS	CARAPACES	AAADILLNP	PALLADIAN
AAAAMPRTT	PARAMATTA	AAACCESTZ	ZACATECAS	AAADILMNT	DALMATIAN
AAABBDINR	BARBADIAN	AAACCGIMU	GUM ACACIA	AAADILNSU	ANDALUSIA
AAABBINRR	BARBARIAN	AAACCIRTT	ATARACTIC	AAADILPRS	PARADISAL
AAABCCHLN	BACCHANAL	AAACCLMNO	CALAMANCO	AAADJJPRU	DJAJAPURA
AAABCCHNR	CHARABANC	AAACCRSTT	CATARACTS	AAADKMNRS	SAMARKAND
AAABCCITT	CATABATIC	AAACDEHRS	A HARD CASE	AAADLMNTY	ADAMANTLY
AAABCDIIT	ADIABATIC	AAACDEHRZ	AZEDARACH	AAADLNNSY	ANALYSAND,
AAABCDRRU	BARRACUDA	AAACDNNOS	ANACONDAS		NYASALAND
AAABCELTV	VACATABLE	AAACDNPRS	PANDA CARS	AAADMNRTY	MANDATARY
AAABCEMRT	CARBAMATE	AAACDNRSS	CASSANDRA	AAAEELQRU	EQUAL-AREA
AAABCIKTT	KATABATIC	AAACEENRS	CAESAREAN	AAAEGGRTV	AGGRAVATE
AAABCILNT	ABACTINAL	AAACEGNRT	CARTAGENA	AAAEGHLMY	MEGHALAYA
AAABCIMOR	MARACAIBO	AAACEGORT	ARCTOGAEA	AAAEGILNS	ANALGESIA
AAABCISST	CATABASIS	AAACEHLNV	AVALANCHE	AAAEGLMNU	MALAGUENA
AAABCLNOT	CANAL BOAT	AAACEIMNR	AMERICANA	AAAEGLMTU	GUATEMALA
AAABDDEHM	AHMEDABAD	AAACEIMNT	CATAMENIA	AAAEGLSSV	VASSALAGE
AAABDDMOR	MORADABAD	AAACEINNT	CANAANITE	AAAEGMNNT	MANGANATE
AAABDELNR	ALDEBARAN	AAACELNRV	CANAVERAL	AAAEGMRRT	MARGARETA
AAABDELPT	ADAPTABLE	AAACEMMNR	CAMERAMAN	AAAEHHLMR	HALMAHERA
AAABDELRW	AWARDABLE	AAACENRTT	AT A CANTER	AAAEHLNNT	NATHANAEL
AAABDENRS	SARABANDE	AAACFILNT	FANATICAL	AAAEHMMOT	HAEMATOMA
AAABDESST	DATABASES	AAACGILSU	CAUSALGIA	AAAEHMNST	ANATHEMAS
AAABDHHKS	ASHKHABAD	AAACGINRU	NICARAGUA	AAAEIMNOX	ANOXAEMIA
AAABDILLS	SABADILLA	AAACGLSSW	SCALAWAGS	AAAEIMPRS	SAPRAEMIA
AAABDILMS	ISLAMABAD	AAACHHIRZ	ZACHARIAH	AAAEKSTWY	TAKEAWAYS
AAABDINNT	ANABANTID	AAACHIRSZ	ZACHARIAS	AAAELMMRT	ALMA MATER
AAABDLLOR	ALL ABOARD!	AAACHKKMT	KAMCHATKA	AAAELNNTT	ANTENATAL,
AAABDNNNS	BANDANNAS	AAACHLNRT	CHARLATAN		ATLANTEAN
AAABDNRSS	SARABANDS	AAACHLRRT	CATARRHAL	AAAELNPQU	AQUAPLANE
AAABEEMNO	AMOEBAEAN	AAACIIRSS	ACARIASIS	AAAELNPST	PANATELAS
				AAAELNTTT	TANTALATE

AAAENPSST	ANAPAESTS	AAAINNNTZ	TANZANIAN	AABCCEKPS	BACKSPACE
AAAERSTWY	TEARAWAYS	AAAINORST	SANATORIA	AABCCELRS	CABLE CARS
AAAFGLRRT	TRAFALGAR	AAAINPSTV	VANASPATI	AABCCHHKT	HATCHBACK
AAAFGMSTU	FAMAGUSTA	AAAIPPRZZ	PAPARAZZI	AABCCHKKU	HUCKABACK
AAAFIILLR	ALFILARIA	AAAIPRSTX	PARATAXIS	AABCCILOT	CATABOLIC
AAAFIKNRS	AFRIKAANS	AAAKKMORR	KARAKORAM	AABCCIORT	ACROBATIC
AAAFILNUV	AVIFAUNAL	AAAKLMOOZ	KALAMAZOO	AABCCJKKL	BLACKJACK
AAAFINORS	AFRO-ASIAN	AAAKLSWWY	WALKAWAYS	AABCCKKPS	BACKPACKS
AAAFLLPRT	FALL APART	AAAKMSTTU	TAKAMATSU	AABCCKKRT	BACKTRACK
AAAFLORST	SOLFATARA	AAAKRRSTU	SURAKARTA	AABCCMOST	CATACOMBS
AAAFRSSSS	SASSAFRAS	AAALLMPSS	LAS PALMAS	AABCDDEIT	ABDICATED
AAAGGLOPS	GALAPAGOS	AAALMPPRS	PARAPLASM	AABCDDEKT	BACKDATED
AAAGHPPRR	PARAGRAPH	AAALNPSTY	ANAPLASTY	AABCDDORR	CARDBOARD
AAAGILMNS	SALAAMING	AAALNRSTV	TRANSVAAL	AABCDEEFR	BAREFACED
AAAGIMRRT	MARGARITA	AAALNRTTU	TARANTULA	AABCDEEHH	BEACHHEAD
AAAGINNRV	VARANGIAN	AAALOOPPS	APPALOOSA	AABCDEHKL	BLACKHEAD
AAAGINOPT	PATAGONIA	AAAMMNRST	MAN-AT-ARMS	AABCDEILL	CABLE-LAID
AAAGINSST	AS AGAINST	AAAMMSTUY	MATSUYAMA	AABCDEIRR	BARRICADE
AAAGMMRSY	GAMMA RAYS	AAAMNOPRS	PANORAMAS	AABCDEKLL	BLACK LEAD
AAAGNORRT	TARRAGONA	AAANNNPRU	ANNAPURNA	AABCDEKLP	BACKPEDAL
AAAGPRSSU	ASPARAGUS	AAAOPPRZZ	PAPARAZZO	AABCDEKRR	BARRACKED
AAAHHHPRT	HAPHTARAH	AAAPPRSTU	APPARATUS	AABCDENNR	BARN DANCE
AAAHIKRTW	KATHIAWAR	AABBBEJNO	BOBBEJAAN	AABCDENNU	ABUNDANCE
AAAHILMSY	HIMALAYAS	AABBCCIRR	BRIC-A-BRAC	AABCDENPS	SPACEBAND
AAAHIMNRS	MAHARANIS	AABBCDEIL	ABDICABLE	AABCDHILR	ARCHIBALD
AAAHINRRT	ANARTHRIA	AABBCDKOR	BACKBOARD	AABCDHKNS	BACKHANDS
AAAHJNRST	RAJASTHAN	AABBCDRSS	SCABBARDS	AABCDHKRS	HARDBACKS
AAAHKNRST	ASTRAKHAN	AABBCEHLL	BEACH BALL	AABCDIORS	SCARABOID
AAAHLLOTY	AYATOLLAH	AABBCEINR	CARIBBEAN	AABCDIORT	ABDICATOR
AAAHLNNTU	NAHUATLAN	AABBCHKOR	BAR KOCHBA	AABCDKLMP	BLACKDAMP
AAAHLNOPR	ANAPHORAL	AABBCINRS	BARBICANS	AABCDKRSW	BACKWARDS,
AAAHMMSTU	HAMAMATSU	AABBCKLLL	BLACKBALL	DRAWBACKS	
AAAHMNNTT	MANHATTAN	AABBDEELT	DEBATABLE	AABCDKRSY	BACKYARDS
AAAHMNRTT	HARMATTAN	AABBDENOR	BROAD BEAN	AABCDLOPR	CLAPBOARD
AAAHTTUYY	AYUTTHAYA	AABBDEORS	BASEBOARD	AABCDNOOR	CARBONADO
AAAIIJNRY	IRIAN JAYA	AABBDNRSS	BRASS BAND	AABCDORST	BROADCAST
AAAIILMNR	LAMINARIA	AABBEEKLR	BREAKABLE	AABCEEELP	PEACEABLE
AAAIINRST	SANITARIA	AABBEELRT	REBATABLE	AABCEEHLR	REACHABLE
AAAIJMNRU	MARIJUANA	AABBEHHST	BATHSHEBA	AABCEEHLT	TEACHABLE
AAAIKLLNT	ANTALKALI	AABBEHILT	HABITABLE	AABCEEHRW	BEACHWEAR
AAAILLRRW	ILLAWARRA	AABBEIILT	BILABIATE	AABCEEKLS	LEASEBACK
AAAILMMMN	MAMMALIAN	AABBEINRT	RABBINATE	AABCEELLN	CLEANABLE
AAAILMNSY	MALAYSIAN	AABBEIRRS	BARBARISE	AABCEELLR	LACERABLE
AAAILNNOT	ANATOLIAN	AABBEIRRZ	BARBARIZE	AABCEELPS	ESCAPABLE
AAAILNNPR	PLANARIAN	AABBEKMMO	MAKE A BOMB	AABCEELPY	PEACEABLY
AAAILNSST	ALSATIANS,	AABBELLSS	BASEBALLS	AABCEELRT	TRACEABLE
ASSAILANT		AABBELLTU	TABULABLE	AABCEELTX	EXACTABLE
AAAILPPRS	APPRAISAL	AABBHILTY	HABITABLY	AABCEENRR	ABERRANCE
AAAILRSTU	AUSTRALIA	AABBIILLS	BILABIALS	AABCEERTT	BRACTEATE
AAAIMNNOZ	AMAZONIAN	AABBIMRRS	BARBARISM	AABCEFIRT	FABRICATE
AAAIMNNST	TASMANIAN	AABBIRRTY	BARBARITY	AABCEFOSU	FABACEOUS
AAAIMNORT	INAMORATA	AABBORRSU	BARBAROUS	AABCEGILR	ALGEBRAIC
AAAIMNOST	TOAMASINA	AABCCEFKL	BLACKFACE	AABCEGKST	BACKSTAGE
AAAIMNRST	SAMARITAN	AABCCEHKS	BACKACHES	AABCEGLMR	CABLEGRAM

AABCEGPRT	CARPETBAG	AABCKLMSS	BLACK MASS	AABDEMRTU	ADUMBRATE
AABCEHHLT	HATCHABLE	AABCKLPSY	PLAYBACKS	AABDENNPY	A BAD PENNY
AABCEHIRT	BRACHIATE	AABCKNRSS	SNACK BARS	AABDENSTW	SWEATBAND
AABCEHITZ	CHABAZITE	AABCKORRZ	RAZORBACK	AABDENSVW	WAVE BANDS
AABCEHLMP	PALM BEACH	AABCMNOTT	COMBATANT	AABDEORSS	SEABOARDS
AABCEHLPT	PATCHABLE	AABCNORTX	CARBON TAX	AABDEORST	ADSORBATE
AABCEHLRT	CHARTABLE	AABCOSTTU	CAST ABOUT	AABDESSTU	DATA BUSES
AABCEILLM	CLAIMABLE	AABCRSSTT	ABSTRACTS	AABDFHLOR	HALF BOARD
AABCEILMN	IMBALANCE	AABDDEEST	DEADBEATS	AABDFILOT	BIT OF A LAD
AABCEILNP	INCAPABLE	AABDDEGLS	SADDLEBAG	AABDFKNRT	BANK DRAFT
AABCEILNT	CANTABILE	AABDDEHNS	HEADBANDS	AABDGGINN	BANDAGING
AABCEILRT	BACTERIAL,	AABDDEHOR	HEADBOARD	AABDGIILR	GARIBALDI
	CALIBRATE	AABDDEHRY	HYDERABAD	AABDGNNOW	BANDWAGON
AABCEINOR	ANAEROBIC	AABDDENNO	ABANDONED	AABDGNOSV	VAGABONDS
AABCEIORT	AEROBATIC	AABDDGHUY	BUDDH GAYA	AABDGOSTU	GADABOUTS
AABCEJKMR	AMBERJACK	AABDDHORR	HARDBOARD	AABDHLRSU	HASDRUBAL
AABCEKLMS	CLAMBAKES	AABDDHORS	DASHBOARD	AABDHORSW	WASHBOARD
AABCEKLRT	TRACKABLE	AABDDNNST	BANDSTAND	AABDIJNOR	JABORANDI
AABCEKPPR	PAPERBACK	AABDDORRT	DARTBOARD	AABDIKORV	KIROVABAD
AABCEKRTW	BACKWATER	AABDEELLP	PLEADABLE	AABDILMNO	ABDOMINAL
AABCEKSST	BACK SEATS	AABDEELMN	AMENDABLE	AABDILMRY	ADMIRABLY
AABCELLOR	CABALLERO	AABDEEMNO	ENDAMOEBA	AABDILORS	SAILBOARD
AABCELLOT	LOCATABLE	AABDEERTT	TRABEATED	AABDILORT	BROADTAIL,
AABCELMNU	AMBULANCE	AABDEFHKL	HALF-BAKED		TAILBOARD
AABCELNNU	UNBALANCE	AABDEFLOR	BROADLEAF	AABDILSSU	DISABUSAL
AABCELNOR	BARCELONA	AABDEGILS	BAG LADIES	AABDINOST	BASTINADO
AABCELNRS	BARNACLES	AABDEGINO	GABIONADE	AABDINSTW	WAISTBAND
AABCELOOS	CALABOOSE	AABDEGINR	BARGAINED,	AABDKLORW	BOARDWALK
AABCELORR	BARCAROLE		GABARDINE	AABDKNNSS	SANDBANKS
AABCELORZ	CARBAZOLE	AABDEGLRU	GUARDABLE	AABDLLORW	WALLBOARD
AABCELPPR	CRAB APPLE	AABDEGORT	ABROGATED	AABDLNSST	SANDBLAST
AABCELPRS	SCRAPABLE	AABDEGOST	SABOTAGED	AABDLNTWY	WANT BADLY
AABCELRTT	TRACTABLE	AABDEHKNR	HANDBRAKE	AABDLORRS	LABRADORS
AABCELRTU	TRABECULA	AABDEHLNR	HANDLEBAR	AABDLORUY	LABOUR DAY
AABCENORT	CARBONATE	AABDEHLSY	ABASHEDLY	AABDMORRU	BURMA ROAD
AABCFHKLS	FLASHBACK,	AABDEHNSU	UNABASHED	AABDNRRSY	BARNYARDS
	HALFBACKS	AABDEILLT	DILATABLE	AABDORRST	STARBOARD
AABCGILNN	BALANCING	AABDEILMR	ADMIRABLE	AABEEEGLR	AGREEABLE
AABCHHIRT	BATH CHAIR	AABDEILMN	LENINABAD	AABEEGGLU	GAUGEABLE
AABCHINR	BRANCHIAL	AABDEILNR	DRAINABLE	AABEEGKRS	BREAKAGES
AABCHRRST	BAR CHARTS	AABDEILNV	INVADABLE	AABEEGLLN	GLEANABLE
AABCIILNS	BASILICAN	AABDEILOV	AVOIDABLE	AABEEGLLT	BAGATELLE
AABCIILSS	BASILICAS	AABDEILRV	ADVERBIAL	AABEEGLRY	AGREEABLY
AABCIKLLM	BLACKMAIL	AABDEILSV	ADVISABLE	AABEEGRRT	GREAT BEAR
AABCIKLLT	BLACKTAIL	AABDEIMNR	MARIENBAD	AABEEHLLX	EXHALABLE
AABCIKLST	TAILBACKS	AABDEINNR	BERNADINA	AABEEHRTT	HEARTBEAT
AABCILLRY	BACILLARY	AABDEINST	ABSTAINED	AABEEILLN	ALIENABLE
AABCILLSY	ASYLLABIC,	AABDELLNT	TABLELAND	AABEEINRS	BEARNAISE
	BASICALLY	AABDELLST	BALLASTED	AABEEKLPS	SPEAKABLE
AABCILNNS	CANNIBALS	AABDELMST	LAMBASTED	AABEEKRST	TEA BREAKS
AABCILNOT	BOTANICAL	AABDELTTU	TABULATED	AABEELLLM	MALLEABLE
AABCILNPY	INCAPABLY	AABDELTWY	TWAYBLADE	AABEELLNN	ANNABELLE
AABCILOPR	PARABOLIC	AABDEMNNR	BRAND NAME	AABEELLNR	LEARNABLE
AABCINNOR	CARBANION	AABDEMORT	DREAMBOAT	AABEELLPS	PLEASABLE
AABCKLLMP	LAMP-BLACK				

AABEELLRS	RESALABLE	AABEIKLNZ	BALKANIZE	AABGGIMNO	GAMBOGIAN
AABEELLRT	ALTERABLE,	AABEIKNRR	KARABINER	AABGGRRST	BRAGGARTS
RELATABLE		AABEIKRRS	AIRBRAKES	AABGHLLUY	LAUGHABLY
AABEELLRV	ALLA BREVE	AABEILLMN	LAMINABLE	AABGHLPRU	BHAGALPUR
AABEELLRX	RELAXABLE	AABEILLMR	MIRABELLA	AABGHOPRR	BAROGRAPH
AABEELMST	BASE METAL	AABEILLNR	BALLERINA	AABGHPRRS	BAR GRAPHS
AABEELNTU	UNEATABLE	AABEILLRT	BILATERAL	AABGIINNY	IN A BIG WAY
AABEELORT	ELABORATE	AABEILLSW	WALLABIES	AABGILNRU	BULGARIAN
AABEELPRR	REPARABLE	AABEILMNS	LIMA BEANS	AABGILNVY	NAVIGABLY
AABEELPRS	SEPARABLE	AABEILNOT	ANABOLITE	AABGILRRT	GIBRALTAR
AABEELPRY	REPAYABLE	AABEILNRT	ALBERTINA,	AABGINNOR	BORN-AGAIN
AABEELQTU	EQUATABLE	TRAINABLE		AABGOORRT	ABROGATOR
AABEELRTT	TREATABLE	AABEILNST	STAINABLE	AABGORTVY	GRAVY BOAT
AABEELRTW	TABLEWARE	AABEILPST	BASIPETAL	AABHIILRZ	BILHARZIA
AABEELRTY	BETA LYRAE	AABEILRSV	VARIABLES	AABHIIMNP	AMPHIBIAN
AABEELTTX	BATTLEAXE	AABEIMNOT	ABOMINATE	AABHIMMRU	HAMMURABI
AABEEMNOT	ENTAMOEBA	AABEIMNZZ	ZAMBEZIAN	AABHINRSW	BRAINWASH
AABEEMNST	ABASEMENT	AABEIMRSU	BEAUMARIS	AABHINSSW	WASHBASIN
AABEEMNTT	ABATEMENT	AABEINORS	ARABINOSE	AABHKORTU	KOTA BHARU
AABEEQRSU	ARABESQUE	AABEINRST	ABSTAINER	AABHRSSST	BRASS HATS
AABEERSST	BASE RATES	AABEINRVW	BRAINWAVE	AABIILLMS	LABIALISM
AABEFGILT	FATIGABLE	AABEINSST	SEBASTIAN	AABIILLTY	LABIALITY
AABEFKLNR	FRANKABLE	AABEIRRTT	ARBITRATE	AABIILNRR	LIBRARIAN
AABEFKRST	BREAKFAST	AABEIRSSV	ABRASIVES	AABIILNRZ	BRAZILIAN
AABEFLLMM	FLAMMABLE	AABEKMNRS	BRAKESMAN	AABIINNRT	BRITANNIA
AABEFLLOT	FLOATABLE	AABELLLOW	ALLOWABLE	AABIINOSS	ANABIOSIS
AABEGGLUY	GAUGEABLY	AABELLMNY	BALLYMENA	AABIINRZZ	ZANZIBARI
AABEGHLLU	LAUGHABLE	AABELLMST	MEATBALLS	AABIINSSY	ABYSSINIA
AABEGILLR	GABRIELLA	AABELLNPT	PLANTABLE	AABILLORS	ISALLOBAR
AABEGILNV	NAVIGABLE	AABELLOPR	PAROLABLE	AABILMNOS	ANABOLISM
AABEGILRV	BELGRAVIA	AABELLORS	ROSABELLA	AABILMNRU	MANUBRIAL
AABEGINRR	BARGAINER	AABELLPPR	PALPEBRAL	AABILMOPY	AMBLYOPIA
AABEGIRRT	ARBITRAGE	AABELLSUV	VALUABLES	AABILMORS	AMBROSIAL
AABEGIRRU	BIGARREAU	AABELMSSU	ASSUMABLE	AABILMPST	BAPTISMAL
AABEGLLLR	GLABELLAR	AABELMSTT	TABLEMATS	AABILNOTT	BATTALION
AABEGLLMS	BALL GAMES	AABELNPPS	SNAPPABLE	AABILRRSU	BURSARIAL
AABEGLMNP	PALEMBANG	AABELOPRR	POLAR BEAR	AABILSVWY	WALVIS BAY
AABEGLNOR	BANGALORE	AABELORST	ASTROLABE	AABIMNORS	AMBROSINA
AABEGLNRT	GRANTABLE	AABELORTT	ROTATABLE	AABIMORSU	SIMAROUBA
AABEGLPRS	GRASPABLE	AABELPRRY	REPARABLY	AABINORSS	ABRASIONS
AABEGNORT	ABNEGATOR	AABELPRSY	SEPARABLY	AABINORTT	BOAT TRAIN
AABEHILRR	HERBARIAL	AABELRSSU	ASSURABLE	AABINOSTW	BOATSWAIN
AABEHIMNN	INHAMBANE	AABELRSTU	SATURABLE	AABIORSTT	ABATTOIRS
AABEHITTU	HABITUATE	AABELRSTY	BETRAYALS	AABIRRRTY	ARBITRARY
AABEHLMSS	SMASHABLE	AABELRTTU	TABLATURE	AABJJLLNU	LJUBLJANA
AABEHLOTW	WHALEBOAT	AABEMOSTT	STEAMBOAT	AABKLOTUW	WALKABOUT
AABEHLPST	ALPHABETS	AABEMRRSS	EMBARRASS	AABKRSSSY	SASSY BARK
AABEHLSTW	SWATHABLE	AABENOSSY	SOYA BEANS	AABLLLOWY	ALLOWABLY
AABEIILLS	LABIALISE	AABEOPPRT	APPROBATE	AABLLNTTY	BLATANTLY
AABEIILLZ	LABIALIZE	AABERSTUX	BEAUX-ARTS	AABLLRSTU	BLASTULAR
AABEIIMNR	BAIN-MARIE	AABFIIMNS	FABIANISM	AABLLRSYY	SYLLABARY
AABEIIRTU	AUBRIETIA	AABFIKNRS	FAIRBANKS	AABLMNORY	MYROBALAN
AABEIJKLR	JAILBREAK	AABFORTTU	FART ABOUT	AABLNOORS	SALOON BAR
AABEIKLNS	BALKANISE	AABGGGNNS	GANG-BANGS	AABLNORTU	ULAN BATOR

AABLORSST	ALBATROSS
AABLORTTU	TABULATOR
AABLOSTUY	LAYABOUTS
AABMMOSSY	MAMA'S BOYS
AABMNNOTU	MONTAUBAN
AABNNSTTU	BANTUSTAN
AABRSSTTU	SUBSTRATA
AACCCLOOS	COCA-COLAS
AACCDDINY	CANDIDACY
AACCDEFRS	FACE CARDS
AACCDEILM	ACCLAIMED
AACCDEIMS	ACADEMICS
AACCDEJNY	ADJACENCY
AACCDELLT	CATCALLED
AACCDELOS	ACCOLADES
AACCDELPR	PLACE CARD
AACCDGINS	CASCADING
AACCDHLRU	ARCHDUCAL
AACCDHRSS	CASH CARDS
AACCDIILM	MALIC ACID
AACCDIINR	CIRCADIAN
AACCDIOSU	CAUCASOID
AACCDNORT	ACCORDANT
AACCEELNR	CLEARANCE
AACCEENRT	REACTANCE
AACCEENST	CETACEANS
AACCEFKPS	FACE PACKS
AACCEFLOS	COALFACES
AACCEFNRS	FRANCESCA
AACCEHJKP	CHEAP-JACK
AACCEHRRT	CHARACTER
AACCEHSUZ	ZACCHAEUS
AACCEIILN	CAECILIAN
AACCEILNT	ANALECTIC
AACCEILRR	CERCARIAL
AACCEILTU	ACICULATE
AACCEINRS	SARACENIC
AACCEINRY	CYRENAICA
AACCEINSV	VACANCIES
AACCEINTV	VACCINATE
AACCEKNRS	CRANKCASE
AACCEKRRT	RACETRACK
AACCEKRSS	SACK RACES
AACCELLTU	CALCULATE
AACCELMTY	CYCLAMATE
AACCELNSU	CALCANEUS
AACCELNTU	ACCENTUAL
AACCELSTU	SACCULATE
AACCENPTT	ACCEPTANT
AACCEORTT	COARCTATE
AACCEPRTU	CUT A CAPER
AACCERSSS	CARCASSES
AACCFINRS	FRANCISCA
AACCHILMO	MAILCOACH

AACCHIMNO	MICHOACAN
AACCHINRS	SACCHARIN
AACCHIPRR	ARCHICARP
AACCHIRTT	CATHARTIC
AACCHIRTU	AUTARCHIC
AACCHLORS	CHARCOALS
AACCIILNT	ANACLITIC
AACCIILNV	VACCINIAL
AACCIINPS	CAPSAICIN
AACCIINTT	TACTICIAN
AACCIIRSS	CIRCASSIA
AACCILLSS	CLASSICAL
AACCILMNU	CACUMINAL
AACCILNNO	CANONICAL
AACCILNRU	CANICULAR
AACCILPRT	PRACTICAL
AACCILTTY	CATALYTIC
AACCIMNOR	CARCINOMA, MACARONIC
AACCINOTT	CATATONIC
AACCINPTY	CAPTAINCY
AACCINRTT	ANTARCTIC
AACCIOPRT	CAPACITOR
AACCIOPSU	CAPACIOUS
AACCIORST	COSTA RICA
AACCIRSST	SARCASTIC
AACCKMNRS	CRACKSMAN
AACCKRRTT	CART TRACK
AACCLMORY	CYCLORAMA
AACCLMSTY	CATACLYSM
AACCMNOPY	ACCOMPANY
AACCOPRRS	SARCOCARP
AACCORTUY	AUTOCRACY
AACDDEERT	A DEAD CERT
AACDDEHMR	DEAD MARCH
AACDDEINT	CANDIDATE
AACDDELOP	DECAPODAL
AACDDELPR	PLACARDED
AACDDEOTV	ADVOCATED
AACDDGNOT	CAT-AND-DOG
AACDDIIST	DADAISTIC
AACDEEFLT	DEFALCATE
AACDEEHHR	HEADREACH
AACDEEHHS	HEADACHES
AACDEEIMT	ACETAMIDE, EMACIATED
AACDEEIRT	ERADICATE
AACDEELRS	ESCALADER
AACDEELRT	LACERATED
AACDEELST	ESCALATED
AACDEEMNS	DAMASCENE
AACDEEMRT	DEMARCATE, MACERATED
AACDEEORS	AREA CODES
AACDEEPSS	ESCAPADES

AACDEETUV	EVACUATED
AACDEETUX	EXCAUDATE
AACDEETVX	EXCAVATED
AACDEFFIN	AFFIANCED
AACDEFHRS	HEADSCARF
AACDEGLNO	DECAGONAL
AACDEHILN	ENCHILADA
AACDEHINS	HACIENDAS
AACDEHLRT	CATHEDRAL
AACDEILLN	DALLIANCE
AACDEILLT	DIALECTAL
AACDEILNO	LAODICEAN
AACDEILNS	CANALISED
AACDEILNZ	CANALIZED
AACDEILTU	ACIDULATE
AACDEIMNO	MACEDONIA
AACDEIMNY	CYANAMIDE
AACDEIMPR	PARAMEDIC
AACDEINOT	DIACONATE
AACDEINOV	AVOIDANCE
AACDEINPT	CAPTAINED
AACDEINRS	RADIANCES
AACDEINRT	ERADICANT
AACDEITTV	ACTIVATED
AACDEJKMP	JAM-PACKED
AACDEKMRT	TARMACKED
AACDEKNRS	RANSACKED
AACDELLNU	CALENDULA
AACDELLOT	ALLOCATED
AACDELMNS	CANDLEMAS
AACDELNOT	ANECDOTAL
AACDELNPS	LANDSCAPE
AACDELNRS	CALENDARS
AACDELNRT	DECLARANT
AACDELPTY	PLAY-ACTED
AACDEMRSS	MASSACRED
AACDENNNO	CANNONADE
AACDENNST	ASCENDANT
AACDENOTU	COADUNATE
AACDENPRT	TAP DANCER
AACDENPST	TAP DANCES
AACDENRSW	WAR DANCES
AACDENRSW	CANVASSED
AACDEOSTV	ADVOCATES
AACDERSTT	CASTRATED
AACDERTTT	ATTRACTED
AACDFHNRT	HANDCRAFT
AACDGIMNW	MAGIC WAND
AACDGINNV	ADVANCING
AACDGINRS	CARDIGANS
AACDHIILL	CHILIADAL
AACDHIILS	DICHASIAL
AACDHINOR	ARACHNOID
AACDHINOT	ACANTHOID

284

AACDHINPS	HANDICAPS	AACEFGNRR	FRAGRANCE
AACDHLNPS	HANDCLAPS,	AACEFGORT	FACTORAGE
HANDCLASP		AACEFGOSU	FAGACEOUS
AACDHLNPU	LAUNCH PAD	AACEFHLST	HALF-CASTE
AACDHLNRS	CRASH-LAND	AACEFILLS	FALLACIES
AACDHNRST	HANDCARTS	AACEFINST	FASCINATE
AACDHPRRS	CARDSHARP	AACEFRSTT	ARTEFACTS
AACDIINNO	AMINO ACID	AACEGHLNR	ARCHANGEL
AACDIINNR	CNIDARIAN	AACEGHMNP	CHAMPAGNE
AACDIISST	DIASTASIC	AACEGHNOR	ANCHORAGE
AACDIISTT	DIASTATIC	AACEGHRST	GATECRASH
AACDILLRY	RADICALLY	AACEGILLN	ANGELICAL,
AACDILNRS	CARDINALS	ENGLACIAL, GALENICAL	
AACDILNTY	DILATANCY	AACEGILNS	ANALGESIC
AACDILORT	CAROTIDAL	AACEGILRS	ALGECIRAS
AACDIMRST	DRAMATICS	AACEGILRT	CARTILAGE
AACDINNOR	DRACONIAN	AACEGIMNO	EGOMANIAC
AACDINOTU	CAUDATION	AACEGIRRS	CARRIAGES
AACDIOSUU	AUDACIOUS	AACEGIRSV	VICARAGES
AACDIQRTU	QUADRATIC	AACEGISTT	CASTIGATE
AACDIRSTY	CARYATIDS	AACEGKPRS	PACKAGERS
AACDJNTUY	ADJUTANCY	AACEGLOST	GALACTOSE
AACDQRSSU	SQUAD CARS	AACEGLOSU	COAGULASE
AACEEFINN	FAINEANCE	AACEGLOTU	CATALOGUE,
AACEEFIRT	CAFETERIA	COAGULATE	
AACEEFLPS	PALEFACES	AACEGNORR	ARROGANCE
AACEEFLPT	FACEPLATE	AACEGNRSU	SUGAR CANE
AACEEFLUV	FACE VALUE	AACEGOPST	SCAPEGOAT
AACEEFRRT	AFTERCARE	AACEGORTT	GREATCOAT
AACEEFRSV	FACE-SAVER	AACEHHIRZ	ZECHARIAH
AACEEGHNS	SEA CHANGE	AACEHIIMS	ISCHAEMIA
AACEEGLLR	CELLARAGE	AACEHILLO	ECHOLALIA
AACEEGLSV	CLEAVAGES	AACEHILMR	CAMELHAIR
AACEEGNRR	CARRAGEEN	AACEHILMT	MALACHITE
AACEEHHRT	HEARTACHE	AACEHILNS	SELACHIAN
AACEEHLNR	HERACLEAN	AACEHILNT	CHATELAIN
AACEEJLTU	EJACULATE	AACEHILNU	ACHEULIAN
AACEEKMPR	PACEMAKER	AACEHILPR	EPARCHIAL
AACEEKRRT	CARETAKER	AACEHILPT	CALIPHATE
AACEELNPS	PLEASANCE	AACEHIMNO	HEOMANIAC
AACEELNPT	PLACENTAE	AACEHIMNR	CHARMAINE
AACEELNST	ELASTANCE	AACEHIMNT	MACHINATE
AACEELRTT	ALTERCATE	AACEHINNT	ACANTHINE
AACEELTTY	ACETYLATE	AACEHINRT	CATHARINE
AACEEMMNR	CAMERAMEN	AACEHINRW	CHINAWARE
AACEEMNNY	MYCENAEAN	AACEHINST	HANSEATIC
AACEEMRRT	MACERATER	AACEHIPTT	APATHETIC
AACEENRSS	CESAREANS	AACEHIRRS	ARCHAISER
AACEEOPRS	AEROSPACE	AACEHIRRZ	ARCHAIZER
AACEEPRSS	CASSAREEP	AACEHIRSY	EASY CHAIR
AACEEPSSS	SEASCAPES	AACEHKMOR	HACKAMORE
AACEERSTT	ESTATE CAR	AACEHKMPU	KAMPUCHEA
AACEFFIRT	AFFRICATE	AACEHKMRR	MARRAKECH
AACEFGLNR	FLAGRANCE	AACEHKRSV	HAVERSACK
AACEFGLNR	FLAGRANCE	AACEHLRSU	ARCHELAUS

AACEHLRTT	CLATHRATE
AACEHMNRU	HUMAN RACE
AACEHNSSS	SASSENACH
AACEHPPRS	SCRAP HEAP
AACEHPRTU	PARACHUTE
AACEHRSST	CATHARSES
AACEIILNT	LACINIATE
AACEIINRR	CINERARIA
AACEIIRTV	VICARIATE
AACEILLMS	CAMELLIAS
AACEILLNS	ALLIANCES
AACEILLRV	VARICELLA
AACEILLTV	VACILLATE
AACEILMNN	ALEMANNIC
AACEILMNP	CAMPANILE
AACEILMPS	ECLAMPSIA
AACEILMRT	CARMELITA
AACEILMTV	CALMATIVE
AACEILNNR	CARNELIAN
AACEILNNT	LANCINATE
AACEILNPP	APPLIANCE
AACEILNPT	ANALEPTIC
AACEILNRS	ARSENICAL
AACEILNRT	LACERTIAN,
NECTARIAL	
AACEILNRU	LAURENCIA
AACEILPTU	APICULATE
AACEILRSV	CALVARIES,
CAVALIERS	
AACEILSTU	ACTUALISE
AACEILTUZ	ACTUALIZE
AACEIMNOX	ANOXAEMIC
AACEIMNRS	AMERICANS
AACEIMNSS	AMNESIACS
AACEIMNTU	ACUMINATE
AACEIMPRS	SAPRAEMIC
AACEIMRST	MARCASITE
AACEIMSTT	MASTICATE
AACEINNRT	INCARNATE
AACEINOST	CASEATION
AACEINPST	ANAPESTIC
AACEINRST	ASCERTAIN,
CARTESIAN, SECTARIAN	
AACEINRSV	VARIANCES
AACEIOSST	ASSOCIATE
AACEIPPRT	PER CAPITA
AACEIPTTV	CAPTIVATE
AACEIRSST	STAIRCASE
AACEIRSTU	ACTUARIES
AACEISTUV	CAUSATIVE
AACEJKLPP	APPLEJACK
AACEJKSSS	JACKASSES
AACEJQTTU	JACQUETTA
AACEKLPRT	PLATE RACK
AACEKLPSW	SPACEWALK

AACEKNRRS	RANSACKER	AACFINSTT	FANTASTIC	AACHINRST	ANARCHIST
AACEKPPTY	PAY PACKET	AACFIRSTT	ARTIFACTS	AACHINSSW	CHAIN SAWS
AACEKRSTT	ATTACKERS	AACFJKLPS	FLAPJACKS	AACHIPRRT	PATRIARCH
AACELLLRU	ACELLULAR	AACFLLTUY	FACTUALLY	AACHIRSST	CATHARSIS
AACELLLUV	VALLECULA	AACFLOPSW	SCAPA FLOW	AACHKMMRT	MATCHMARK
AACELLNOR	OLECRANAL	AACFLRRTU	FRACTURAL	AACHKSSTY	HAYSTACKS
AACELLNOW	ALLOWANCE	AACFMNRST	CRAFTSMAN	AACHLLMRY	LACHRYMAL
AACELLNPT	PLACENTAL	AACGGHINN	CHAIN GANG	AACHLLPTY	CATAPHYLL
AACELMNTT	CATTLEMAN	AACGGIKNP	PACKAGING	AACHLLRTW	WALLCHART
AACELMPST	PLACE MATS	AACGGIOPR	PARAGOGIC	AACHLMNOR	MONARCHAL
AACELMSST	CLASSMATE	AACGHHIRY	HAGIARCHY	AACHLMPTY	MATCH PLAY
AACELNNTU	CANNULATE	AACGHIKUW	KAWAGUCHI	AACHLMRSY	MARSHALCY
AACELNPST	PLACENTAS	AACGHIMNP	CHAMPAIGN	AACHLOPVY	PLAY HAVOC
AACELNRST	ANCESTRAL,	AACGHINTT	ATTACHING	AACHMNORW	CHARWOMAN
	LANCASTER	AACGHMORT	TACHOGRAM	AACHMNSTY	YACHTSMAN
AACELOPRT	ACROPETAL,	AACGHOPRR	ARCOGRAPH	AACHMPRST	MARCH-PAST
	CLEOPATRA	AACGIIMNS	MAGICIANS	AACHNOSTU	ACANTHOUS
AACELORST	ESCALATOR	AACGIKNTT	ATTACKING	AACHNOTTY	CHATOYANT
AACELOTUV	AUTOCLAVE,	AACGILLMY	MAGICALLY	AACHNRSST	TRASHCANS
	VACUOLATE	AACGILLOS	SCAGLIOLA	AACHOPPRY	APOCRYPHA
AACELPPRT	APPLE CART	AACGILMNN	MANACLING	AACIILLRT	ALTRICIAL
AACELPSTU	CAPSULATE	AACGILMNS	ANGLICANS	AACIILMRS	RACIALISM
AACELPSTY	CATALEPSY	AACGILNPT	PLACATING	AACIILMST	LAMAISTIC
AACELPTXY	CATAPLEXY	AACGIMNPS	CAMPAIGNS	AACIILNPT	ANCIPITAL
AACELRRTU	CREATURAL	AACGIMPRT	PRAGMATIC	AACIILNSS	ANACLISIS
AACELRSTY	CATALYSER	AACGINORV	CRAIGAVON	AACIILNST	CASTILIAN
AACELRSWY	CLEARWAYS	AACGINTTU	ACTUATING	AACIILPRT	PIRATICAL
AACELRTUW	CATERWAUL	AACGIOSSU	SAGACIOUS	AACIILRST	RACIALIST,
AACEMNNOR	CONNEMARA	AACGLLSWY	SCALLYWAG		SATIRICAL
AACEMNPRT	MERCAPTAN	AACGLNOOT	OCTAGONAL	AACIIMOTX	AXIOMATIC
AACEMNRST	SACRAMENT	AACGLNOTU	COAGULANT	AACIINNOP	POINCIANA
AACEMRRSS	ARMS RACES,	AACGLOORY	ACAROLOGY	AACIINNOT	NICOTIANA
	MASSACRER	AACGMORRT	CARTOGRAM	AACIINPRT	PATRICIAN
AACEMRSSS	MASSACRES	AACGNNSTY	STAGNANCY	AACIIPRST	PARASITIC
AACENNNOY	ANNOYANCE	AACHHHIUU	CHIHUAHUA	AACIIRRTU	URTICARIA
AACENNOSS	ASSONANCE	AACHHINTY	HYACINTHA	AACIISTTV	ATAVISTIC
AACENOPTZ	ZAPOTECAN	AACHHSTWY	HATCHWAYS	AACIJNOPS	JAPONICAS
AACENPRRY	PARCENARY	AACHIILMN	CHAIN MAIL	AACIKMNNY	KANAMYCIN
AACENPSSU	SAUCEPANS	AACHIILPT	ALIPHATIC	AACILLNOT	ALLANTOIC
AACENRSSU	ASSURANCE	AACHIINRT	CARINTHIA	AACILLNRY	ANCILLARY
AACENRSSV	CANVASSER	AACHIIPRS	PHARISAIC	AACILLNTU	LUNATICAL
AACENRTTU	CAUTERANT	AACHIIRRV	CHARIVARI	AACILLNTV	VACILLANT
AACENSSSV	CANVASSES	AACHILNPS	CHAPLAINS	AACILLPRY	CAPILLARY
AACENSSTT	CASTANETS	AACHILOPR	PAROCHIAL	AACILMMNO	AMMONICAL
AACEOOPPT	APOCOPATE	AACHILOPT	CHIPOLATA	AACILMNST	CLAIMANTS
AACEORTUV	EVACUATOR	AACHILPST	ASPHALTIC	AACILMRSU	SIMULACRA
AACEORTVX	EXCAVATOR	AACHILSST	THALASSIC	AACILNNOR	NONRACIAL
AACEOSTUX	TAXACEOUS	AACHIMNOR	HARMONICA	AACILNNUV	VULCANIAN
AACESSUWY	CAUSEWAYS	AACHIMNRS	ANARCHISM	AACILNOPT	PLACATION
AACFGLNRY	FLAGRANCY	AACHIMNRU	MANCHURIA	AACILNOTT	LACTATION
AACFHJKST	JACKSHAFT	AACHIMRRS	ARMCHAIRS	AACILNOTY	CLAYTONIA
AACFHMSST	CAMSHAFTS	AACHIMRRT	MATRIARCH	AACILNPPT	APPLICANT
AACFIILLN	FINANCIAL	AACHIMRSS	ARCHAISMS	AACILNRST	CARNALIST
AACFILNOT	FACTIONAL	AACHIMSTT	ASTHMATIC	AACILNRSV	CARNIVALS
AACFILORT	FACTORIAL				

AACILNRTY	CARNALITY	AACNNOSTT	CONSTANTA	AADEEGNRT	GREAT DANE,
AACILNRUV	NAVICULAR	AACNORTUU	AU COURANT		TEAGARDEN
AACILNSTY	ANALYTICS	AACNRSTUY	SANCTUARY	AADEEHPRS	SPEARHEAD
AACILORTU	AUCTORIAL	AACNRSTUZ	SANTA CRUZ	AADEEHRTT	DEATH RATE
AACILOSSU	SALACIOUS	AACORRSTT	CASTRATOR	AADEEIKWW	WIDE-AWAKE
AACILOSTT	COAT TAILS,	AACORRSTU	TUSCARORA	AADEEILMV	MEDIAEVAL
	TAILCOATS	AACORRTTT	ATTRACTOR	AADEEILNT	ALIENATED
AACILPRTU	CAPITULAR	AACORSSWY	CASSOWARY	AADEEIMNT	DEAMINATE
AACILPRTY	PARALYTIC	AACORSTTU	AUTOCRATS	AADEEKMRR	EARMARKED
AACILQTTU	ACQUITTAL	AADDDGNRY	GRANDADDY	AADEELMRS	ESMERALDA
AACILRRTU	ARTICULAR	AADDEEFHT	FATHEADED	AADEELNNR	LEND AN EAR
AACILRRUU	AURICULAR	AADDEEHRT	DEAD HEART	AADEELNPS	ESPLANADE
AACILRSTY	RASCALITY	AADDEEHST	DEAD HEATS	AADEELNRX	ALEXANDER
AACILSSTY	CATALYSIS	AADDEEMRY	READY-MADE	AADEELRRY	LAY READER
AACILSTUY	CAUSALITY	AADDEENRV	VERANDAED	AADEELTUV	DEVALUATE,
AACILTTUY	ACTUALITY	AADDEENTT	ANTEDATED		EVALUATED
AACIMNNNU	MANCUNIAN	AADDEGLNR	GARLANDED	AADEEMNRT	TRADE NAME
AACIMNOPR	PANORAMIC	AADDEGRTU	GRADUATED	AADEEMRSU	ADMEASURE
AACIMNOST	ANOSMATIC	AADDEHHRS	HARDHEADS	AADEENSTU	NAUSEATED
AACIMORTU	AMAUROTIC	AADDEHLNS	HEADLANDS	AADEEPRST	PAEDERAST,
AACIMOTTU	AUTOMATIC	AADDEHNST	HEADSTAND		SEPARATED
AACIMRRSU	SACRARIUM	AADDEHOST	A DEAD SHOT	AADEERRTT	RETARDATE
AACIMRTTU	TRAUMATIC	AADDEHRSW	HEADWARDS	AADEESTTV	DEVASTATE
AACINNORT	CARNATION	AADDEILNO	ADENOIDAL	AADEFFILR	FAR AFIELD
AACINNOST	SANTONICA	AADDEILTV	VALIDATED	AADEFGLNN	FANDANGLE
AACINOOTV	AVOCATION	AADDEIMNW	WAD MEDANI	AADEFGRSU	SAFEGUARD
AACINOPRS	CAPARISON	AADDEINRT	ANDRADITE	AADEFILNT	FAN-TAILED
AACINORST	RAINCOATS	AADDEINRW	EDWARDIAN	AADEFIORS	AFORESAID
AACINORTU	ARCUATION	AADDEKRST	STARK DEAD	AADEFIRRS	FARADISER
AACINOSST	CASSATION	AADDELLNS	SANDALLED	AADEFIRRZ	FARADIZER
AACINOSTU	CAUSATION	AADDELMNR	DREAMLAND	AADEFLNOR	FARANDOLE
AACINOSTV	VACATIONS	AADDELPPU	APPLAUDED	AADEFMPRT	AFTERDAMP
AACINOTTU	ACTUATION	AADDELRST	ASTRADDLE	AADEFMRST	FARMSTEAD
AACINRRTU	ARCTURIAN	AADDEMNNT	DEMANDANT	AADEFSSTT	STEADFAST
AACINRSST	SACRISTAN	AADDEMNOR	ANDROMEDA	AADEGHNRU	HARANGUED
AACINRSSU	ANACRUSIS	AADDEMRSY	DAYDREAMS	AADEGHNRY	HYDRANGEA
AACIOPRSU	RAPACIOUS	AADDEMRYY	DAYDREAMY	AADEGHNST	STAGEHAND
AACIORTTV	ACTIVATOR	AADDEORST	ROADSTEAD	AADEGILRT	TALIGRADE
AACIOSTTW	WAISTCOAT	AADDHLNNO	AN OLD HAND	AADEGILTT	TAILGATED
AACKKNPSS	KNAPSACKS	AADDHNNST	HANDSTAND	AADEGIMNT	DIAMAGNET
AACLLOPRS	COLLAPSAR	AADDIIMRY	DAIRYMAID	AADEGINRR	ARRAIGNED
AACLLRRSY	CARRYALLS	AADDIINRV	DRAVIDIAN	AADEGINRS	GARDENIAS
AACLNOPTU	CANTALOUP	AADDILNNO	DONALDINA	AADEGINRT	TRAGEDIAN
AACLNRUUV	AVUNCULAR	AADDIRRWY	IRRAWADDY	AADEGINTV	NAVIGATED
AACLOPRRR	PARLOR CAR	AADDLNRSW	LANDWARDS	AADEGIPRS	DISPARAGE
AACLOPRRT	PATROL CAR	AADDLRSTY	DASTARDLY	AADEGLNNT	LAND AGENT
AACLOPRTU	PORTULACA	AADDMRSTT	DARMSTADT	AADEGNNRR	REGARDANT
AACLOPRTY	PLACATORY	AADDNRSST	STANDARDS	AADEGNSTT	STAGNATED
AACLORSSU	CAROUSALS	AADEEGHMT	MEGADEATH	AADEGORRT	ARROGATED
AACLPSTTU	CATAPULTS	AADEEGHST	GATESHEAD	AADEGPRST	TRADE GAPS
AACLRRTUY	CARTULARY	AADEEGLMN	MAGDALENE	AADEGRRRU	REARGUARD
AACLSSTTY	CATALYSTS	AADEEGNOR	ORANGEADE	AADEGRRVY	GRAVEYARD
AACMNOORS	MACAROONS	AADEEGNPP	APPENDAGE	AADEGRSTU	GRADUATES
AACMNOTTU	CATAMOUNT			AADEHHKNS	HANDSHAKE
				AADEHILRS	RAILHEADS

AADEHIMOT	HAEMATOID	AADEIPRST	ASPIRATED,
AADEHIORR	DIARRHOEA		DISPARATE
AADEHIPRT	APARTHEID, HIT	AADEJKLWY	JAYWALKED
	PARADE	AADEKMMRU	MARMADUKE
AADEHIRST	STAIRHEAD	AADEKMNRS	MANDRAKES
AADEHISWY	HIDEAWAYS	AADEKMRRT	TRADEMARK
AADEHKMST	DEATH MASK	AADELLNOT	LANOLATED
AADEHLLST	HEADSTALL	AADELLNPR	LAPLANDER
AADEHLMNN	MANHANDLE	AADELLNTU	LANDAULET
AADEHLMPS	LAMPSHADE	AADELMMOR	MELODRAMA
AADEHLMRS	MARSHALED	AADELMNRS	MALANDERS
AADEHLMSY	ASHAMEDLY	AADELMORV	AD VALOREM
AADEHLNNP	PANHANDLE	AADELNSTW	WASTELAND
AADEHLNRT	HEARTLAND	AADELPPRU	APPLAUDER
AADEHLPST	ASPHALTED	AADELPRSY	PARALYSED
AADEHMNSU	UNASHAMED	AADELPRTW	DRAWPLATE
AADEHMPST	HAMPSTEAD	AADELRTTY	LATTER-DAY
AADEHMSST	MASTHEADS	AADELSSTU	ASSAULTED
AADEHORRW	ARROWHEAD	AADEMMNOR	MEMORANDA
AADEHPRTT	DEATH TRAP	AADEMMRST	AMSTERDAM
AADEHRRTW	EARTHWARD	AADEMNPRS	AMPERSAND
AADEHRSTT	HEAD START	AADEMNRST	TRADESMAN
AADEIIPRS	PRAESIDIA	AADEMOTTU	AUTOMATED
AADEIIRRT	IRRADIATE	AADEMPTTU	AMPUTATED
AADEIIRTV	RADIATIVE	AADEMRRSU	MARAUDERS
AADEIKKVY	KADIYEVKA	AADEMRRTU	DURA MATER
AADEILLPT	PALLIATED	AADEMSTTU	STATE DUMA
AADEILMNN	ALMANDINE	AADENNOTT	ANNOTATED
AADEILMNS	LADIES' MAN	AADENNPPT	APPENDANT
AADEILMNT	LAMINATED	AADENNRST	SANTANDER
AADEILMRT	DIAMETRAL	AADENNTTT	ATTENDANT
AADEILNNN	ANNELIDAN	AADENPPRS	SANDPAPER
AADEILNNR	ADRENALIN	AADENPRTU	PANDURATE
AADEILNOT	DEALATION	AADENRRTT	RETARDANT
AADEILNSV	VANDALISE	AADENRRTW	WARRANTED
AADEILNVZ	VANDALIZE	AADEOPRSX	PARADOXES
AADEILPSS	PALISADES	AADEORSTW	SODA WATER
AADEILPST	STAPEDIAL	AADEORSTX	ROAD TAXES
AADEILRTV	TRAVAILED	AADERRRSW	REARWARDS
AADEILSTV	SALIVATED	AADERRSVY	ADVERSARY
AADEILTVW	TIDAL WAVE	AADERSSTW	EASTWARDS
AADEIMMNR	DRAMAMINE	AADERSTTU	SATURATED
AADEIMMSS	MASS MEDIA	AADFFIITV	AFFIDAVIT
AADEIMNRS	MARINADES	AADFGHRRT	HARD GRAFT
AADEIMNRT	MARINATED	AADFGNNOS	FANDANGOS
AADEIMNSW	ADAM'S WINE	AADFGNORR	FRAGONARD
AADEIMRST	DRAMATISE	AADFHMNRS	FARMHANDS
AADEIMRTZ	DRAMATIZE	AADFILNRY	FAIRYLAND
AADEINPRT	PINTADERA	AADFIMNRY	MAN FRIDAY
AADEINRST	STERADIAN	AADFIMRYY	DAIRY FARM
AADEINRTT	ATTAINDER	AADFLLLNS	LANDFALLS
AADEIPPRS	APPRAISED,	AADFMNRST	DRAFTSMAN
	DISAPPEAR	AADFMRRSY	FARMYARDS
AADEIPRSS	PARADISES	AADFRRSTW	DWARF STAR

AADGGHIST	HAGGADIST		
AADGGHLRY	HAGGARDLY		
AADGHIMPR	DIAPHRAGM		
AADGHINRZ	HAZARDING		
AADGHIPSY	DYSPHAGIA		
AADGIINRT	RADIATING		
AADGILMNY	AMYGDALIN		
AADGILMRS	MADRIGALS		
AADGILNOS	DIAGONALS		
AADGILORT	GLADIATOR		
AADGILRRU	GUARDRAIL		
AADGIMMNO	GAMMADION		
AADGIMNNT	MANDATING		
AADGIMNRU	MARAUDING		
AADGIMORR	RADIOGRAM		
AADGIMPRS	PARADIGMS		
AADGIMRRS	MARDI GRAS		
AADGINORT	GRADATION		
AADGINRSU	GUARDIANS		
AADGINRUZ	DZUNGARIA		
AADGLLNRU	GLANDULAR		
AADGLLRUY	GRADUALLY		
AADGLMNRS	GRAND SLAM		
AADGLNOOW	WAGONLOAD		
AADGLNRSS	GRASSLAND		
AADGMNORS	DRAGOMANS		
AADGMNRSU	GUARDSMAN		
AADGNRSUV	GUARD'S VAN,		
	VANGUARDS		
AADGORRTU	GRADUATOR		
AADHILLNO	HOLLANDIA		
AADHILLRS	HALLIARDS		
AADHILLSS	ALLIS SHAD		
AADHILNRS	HANDRAILS		
AADHINRRS	HARRIDANS		
AADHIPSSY	DYSPHASIA		
AADHNSSTW	WASHSTAND		
AADHORRSU	HADROSAUR		
AADHORSUZ	HAZARDOUS		
AADIILLNP	PLAIN-LAID		
AADIILMNV	MALDIVIAN		
AADIILSUV	VISUAL AID		
AADIINNRS	SARDINIAN		
AADIINORT	RADIATION		
AADIINRRT	IRRADIANT		
AADIISSST	DIASTASIS		
AADIJNNOR	JORDANIAN		
AADILLMOR	ARMADILLO		
AADILLMPU	PALLADIUM		
AADILLNOT	ALLANTOID		
AADILLOPS	SAPODILLA		
AADILLPRY	RADIAL-PLY		
AADILMNNO	ADNOMINAL		
AADILMNOV	MOLDAVIAN		

AADILMNSV	VANDALISM	AAEEGNPRT	PARENTAGE	AAEENRSSW	AWARENESS
AADILMNTU	TAMIL NADU	AAEEGNRRR	REARRANGE	AAEENRSTT	ANTEATERS
AADILMORT	MALADROIT	AAEEGNRTU	GUARANTEE	AAEENTTTU	ATTENUATE
AADILMPRY	PYRAMIDAL	AAEEGNRWY	GREENAWAY	AAEEOPRSU	AEROPAUSE
AADILMRTY	ADMIRALTY	AAEEGPRUV	AVERAGE UP	AAEEOPRTV	EVAPORATE
AADILNNOT	ANTINODAL	AAEEGRRSY	GREY AREAS	AAEEPPPRT	PAPER TAPE
AADILNOPT	ANTIPODAL	AAEEHIMNT	HAEMATEIN	AAEEPPRTY	RATEPAYER
AADILNORS	ROSALINDA	AAEEHIMTT	HAEMATITE	AAEEPRSST	SEPARATES
AADILNOTU	ADULATION,	AAEEHISST	AESTHESIA	AAEERRTTW	WATER RATE
LAUDATION		AAEEHKMST	MAKE HASTE	AAEFFIILT	AFFILIATE
AADILNRTY	RADIANTLY	AAEEHLRRS	REHEARSAL	AAEFFILRS	RAFFLESIA
AADILNSWZ	SWAZILAND	AAEEHMNTU	ATHENAEUM	AAEFGHMNR	FERMANAGH
AADILORRS	RAILROADS	AAEEHMNTX	EXANTHEMA	AAEFGINRS	SEAFARING
AADILOSVW	DISAVOWAL	AAEEHMPST	METAPHASE	AAEFGIRSX	SAXIFRAGE
AADILPSSY	DYSPLASIA	AAEEHRRRT	RARE EARTH	AAEFGLLLR	FLAGELLAR
AADIMNNOT	DAMNATION	AAEEHSTVW	HEAT WAVES	AAEFGLRVW	FLAG-WAVER
AADIMNNRS	MANDARINS	AAEEIKLMP	MAKE A PILE	AAEFGORRS	FARRAGOES
AADIMNRST	TAMARINDS	AAEEIKLMU	LEUKAEMIA	AAEFHLLPT	HALF-PLATE
AADIMRSTT	DRAMATIST	AAEEILLMN	EL ALAMEIN	AAEFHLPRT	FLARE PATH
AADINNNOT	ANDANTINO	AAEEILLST	ILL AT EASE	AAEFHMRTT	AFTERMATH
AADINOORT	ADORATION	AAEEILLTV	ALLEVIATE	AAEFIKNRR	AFRIKANER
AADINPRSS	SPANIARDS	AAEEILMNS	MELANESIA	AAEFILMRR	FIRE ALARM
AADINSSTY	SAINT'S DAY	AAEEILRTT	RETALIATE	AAEFILNTX	ANTEFIXAL
AADIORRST	RADIATORS	AAEEIMNRT	REANIMATE	AAEFILRTY	FAIRY-TALE
AADJNSTTU	ADJUTANTS	AAEEIMNTV	EMANATIVE	AAEFIMMNR	MAINFRAME
AADKLMNRS	LANDMARKS	AAEEIMNTX	EXANIMATE	AAEFINNRS	SAFRANINE
AADKLRWWY	AWKWARDLY	AAEEINSTW	TAIWANESE	AAEFINSST	FANTASIES,
AADKNORRS	KRASNODAR	AAEEIPTTX	EXPATIATE	FANTASISE	
AADLLNORU	ALL-AROUND	AAEEISTTV	AESTIVATE	AAEFINSTZ	FANTASIZE
AADLLOPSU	PALLADOUS	AAEEKKMVY	MAKEYEVEKA	AAEFINTTU	INFATUATE
AADLMNPSW	SWAMPLAND	AAEEKMNSS	NAMESAKES	AAEFKLLST	LEAFSTALK
AADLORSST	LOADSTARS	AAEEKPRST	PARAKEETS	AAEFLLLRY	FALLALERY
AADLORTUY	ADULATORY,	AAEEKPSSY	SPEAKEASY	AAEFLLRTW	WATERFALL
LAUDATORY		AAEELLOTV	ALVEOLATE	AAEFLMSTT	FLATMATES
AADMMNOOR	MONODRAMA	AAEELLPPT	APPELLATE	AAEFLNRRT	FRATERNAL
AADMNORTY	DAMNATORY,	AAEELLPTT	PATELLATE	AAEFLORTZ	FORTALEZA
MANDATORY		AAEELLQRU	AQUARELLE	AAEFRRSWY	WAYFARERS
AADNNORSU	ANANDROUS	AAEELLRWW	WELL-AWARE	AAEGGILLN	GALINGALE
AADNPRSST	SAND TRAPS	AAEELMMNU	EMMANUELA	AAEGGILNW	GALWEGIAN
AADNQRSTU	QUADRANTS	AAEELMMRT	METAMERAL	AAEGGINOR	GEORGIANA
AADRSSTUY	SATURDAYS	AAEELMNPT	NAMEPLATE	AAEGGINRU	RAIN GAUGE
AAEEEHLRT	AETHEREAL	AAEELMSST	MATELASSE	AAEGGINRV	AVERAGING
AAEEELSTV	TEALEAVES	AAEELMSTT	STALEMATE	AAEGGLLNO	GALLONAGE
AAEEFHRTT	AFTERHEAT	AAEELNOPR	AEROPLANE	AAEGGLNSU	LANGUAGES
AAEEFKPRT	AFTERPEAK	AAEELNPSS	SEAPLANES	AAEGHIILM	HEMIALGIA
AAEEFLOTV	FAVEOLATE	AAEELNRTT	ALTERNATE	AAEGHINRW	WHANGAREI
AAEEGGGRT	AGGREGATE	AAEELPPSX	SEX APPEAL	AAEGHLNOX	HEXAGONAL
AAEEGINTV	EVAGINATE	AAEELPRSY	LEAP YEARS	AAEGHLNPR	PHALANGER
AAEEGIRTV	VARIEGATE	AAEELRRTT	RETREATAL	AAEGHLNPS	PHALANGES
AAEEGKNST	KATANGESE	AAEELRSTU	LAUREATES	AAEGHLPSS	SLAGHEAPS
AAEEGLMNT	MENTAL AGE	AAEEMMNTZ	AMAZEMENT	AAEGHMRSX	HEXAGRAMS
AAEEGLSVW	WAGE SLAVE	AAEEMNRST	MAN-EATERS	AAEGHNOPR	ORPHANAGE
AAEEGMNNS	MANGANESE	AAEEMPRRT	PARAMETER	AAEGHNRRU	HARANGUER
AAEEGMNST	STAGE NAME	AAEENRRTW	WARRANTEE	AAEGHNRSU	HARANGUES
AAEEGNORS	ARAGONESE				

AAEGHORRT	HARROGATE	AAEGNRTTU	GREAT-AUNT	AAEILMNOS	ANOMALIES
AAEGIILQU	AQUILEGIA	AAEGOPPRT	PROPAGATE	AAEILMNST	LAMINATES
AAEGIKNNW	AWAKENING	AAEGPRSTU	PASTURAGE	AAEILMNSZ	MANIZALES
AAEGILMRT	METRALGIA	AAEGRRSTZ	STARGAZER	AAEILMNTU	ALUMINATE
AAEGILNNN	ANNEALING	AAEHHINPZ	ZEPHANIAH	AAEILMPRV	PRIMAEVAL
AAEGILNNT	GALANTINE	AAEHHLNOT	HALOTHANE	AAEILMPTT	PALMITATE
AAEGILNOS	ANALOGIES,	AAEHIKNRT	KATHARINE	AAEILMRST	MATERIALS
	ANALOGISE	AAEHIKNSZ	ASHKENAZI	AAEILNNTV	VALENTINA
AAEGILNOZ	ANALOGIZE	AAEHILNNT	NATHANIEL	AAEILNORT	ALIENATOR,
AAEGILNPP	APPEALING	AAEHILNTV	LEVIATHAN		RATIONALE
AAEGILNRU	NEURALGIA	AAEHIMMNR	MARIEHAMN	AAEILNPRS	AIRPLANES
AAEGILNSV	GALVANISE	AAEHIMNOT	THEOMANIA	AAEILNPRT	PERINATAL
AAEGILNVZ	GALVANIZE	AAEHINPRS	SERAPHINA	AAEILNRTU	LAURENTIA
AAEGILSTT	TAILGATES	AAEHINPRT	PARTHENIA	AAEILNSTT	TANTALISE
AAEGIMMNS	MISMANAGE	AAEHINRSV	HAVERSIAN	AAEILNTTT	TANTALITE
AAEGIMNNS	MAGNESIAN	AAEHJLLLU	HALLELUJA	AAEILNTTZ	TANTALIZE
AAEGIMNNT	EMANATING,	AAEHLLNOP	ALLOPHANE	AAEILORTV	VARIOLATE
	MANGANITE, MAN-EATING	AAEHLMSSY	SEALYHAMS	AAEILPPTT	PALPITATE
AAEGIMNRR	MARGARINE	AAEHLNPSX	PHALANXES	AAEILPRTZ	TRAPEZIAL
AAEGIMNRT	MARGINATE	AAEHLNPSY	SYNALEPHA	AAEILRSSW	WASSAILER
AAEGIMNSZ	MAGAZINES	AAEHLNSTT	ATHELSTAN	AAEILRSTU	ESTUARIAL
AAEGIMRRS	MARRIAGES	AAEHLOPPR	PHALAROPE	AAEILSSSV	VASSALISE
AAEGIMRRT	MARGARITE	AAEHLPSUV	UPHEAVALS	AAEILSSVZ	VASSALIZE
AAEGIMNRT	ARGENTINA	AAEHMOSTT	HAEMOSTAT	AAEILSTVX	LAXATIVES
AAEGINORT	ARAGONITE	AAEHMRSTU	SHAMATEUR	AAEIMMNOT	AMMONIATE
AAEGINPPR	APPEARING	AAEHNNTUY	NETANYAHU	AAEIMNNOT	EMANATION
AAEGINPPS	APPEASING	AAEHNPSST	PHEASANTS	AAEIMNNSS	ANAMNESIS
AAEGINPRS	PAGANISER	AAEHNSSTT	SHAN STATE	AAEIMNOPR	POMERANIA
AAEGINPRZ	PAGANIZER	AAEHNSSTY	SEA SHANTY	AAEIMNOST	ANATOMIES,
AAEGINPTZ	GAZIANTEP	AAEHNSTVX	TAX HAVENS		ANATOMISE
AAEGINRRR	ARRAIGNER	AAEHRRSTT	EARTHSTAR	AAEIMNOTZ	AMAZONITE,
AAEGINRRS	GRANARIES	AAEIIKNRT	AIR-INTAKE		ANATOMIZE
AAEGINRSY	GAINSAYER	AAEIILMNS	ANIMALISE	AAEIMNPRR	REPAIRMAN
AAEGIRTTV	GRAVITATE	AAEIILMNZ	ANIMALIZE	AAEIMNPRS	PEARMAINS
AAEGISTTT	SAGITTATE	AAEIILMRT	LATIMERIA	AAEIMNRTW	WATER MAIN
AAEGISVWY	GIVEAWAYS	AAEIILNRT	INTER ALIA	AAEIMNSTT	STAMINATE
AAEGKKRRS	SKAGERRAK	AAEIILPTX	EPITAXIAL	AAEIMOPRT	AMETROPIA
AAEGLLMPS	PLASMAGEL	AAEIIMNNT	INANIMATE	AAEIMORST	AROMATISE
AAEGLLNRY	LARYNGEAL	AAEIIMRST	ARTEMISIA	AAEIMORTZ	AROMATIZE
AAEGLMNOR	MANGALORE	AAEIINQTU	AQUITAINE	AAEIMRRST	AIRSTREAM
AAEGLNOSU	ANALOGUES	AAEIINSST	TAENIASIS	AAEINNRSW	RAW SIENNA
AAEGLNRTU	GRANULATE	AAEIJNRSU	JANUARIES	AAEINPPRT	APPERTAIN
AAEGLRSSW	GLASSWARE	AAEIKLNNN	LENINAKAN	AAEINPRST	SEPTARIAN
AAEGMNNOR	ORANGEMAN	AAEIKLTTV	TALKATIVE	AAEINQTTU	ANTIQUATE
AAEGMNORT	MATRONAGE	AAEIKMNRR	RAINMAKER	AAEINRRRS	IN ARREARS
AAEGMNPRT	PENTAGRAM	AAEIKNPST	TAKE PAINS	AAEINRRTV	NARRATIVE
AAEGMNRTT	TERMAGANT	AAEIKRSTU	AUTARKIES	AAEINRRTW	RAINWATER
AAEGMRRTT	TETRAGRAM	AAEILLLSU	ALLELUIAS	AAEINRRVY	INVERARAY
AAEGMRSTT	STRATAGEM	AAEILLMMT	MAMILLATE	AAEIORSSU	ESSAOUIRA
AAEGNNOOT	NOTOGAEAN	AAEILLNPS	SAILPLANE	AAEIPPRRS	APPRAISER
AAEGNOORS	NO-GO AREAS	AAEILLNPT	TAILPLANE	AAEIPRSST	ASPIRATES,
AAEGNOPRS	PARSONAGE	AAEILLNTV	ELAN VITAL		PARASITES
AAEGNOPRT	PATRONAGE	AAEILLPSS	PAILLASSE,	AAEIRRSTT	TARTARISE
AAEGNPRTY	PAGEANTRY		PALLIASSE	AAEIRRTTZ	TARTARIZE
AAEGNRSTV	STAVANGER			AAEISSSUV	ASSUASIVE

AAEJKLRWY	JAYWALKER	AAERRSTTU	SATURATER	AAGIJNNNP	JAPANNING
AAEKLLSST	SALES TALK	AAERRSTTW	WATER RATS	AAGIKNPRT	PARTAKING
AAEKMRRTW	WATERMARK	AAERSTWWY	WATERWAYS	AAGILLNST	SAINT GALL
AAELLLMOR	MALLEOLAR	AAFFFGLST	FLAGSTAFF	AAGILLNTV	GALLIVANT
AAELLLPRS	PARALLELS	AAFFGNRSU	SUFFRAGAN	AAGILLORT	ALLIGATOR
AAELLLRTY	LATERALLY	AAFGILMNS	FALANGISM	AAGILLPSW	GALLIWASP
AAELLNPPT	APPELLANT	AAFGILNRS	FRANGLAIS	AAGILMNNO	AGNOMINAL
AAELLORSV	ALVEOLARS	AAFGILNST	FALANGIST	AAGILMNNS	SIGNALMAN
AAELLPPRW	WALLPAPER	AAFGINRWY	WAYFARING	AAGILMNNT	MALIGNANT
AAELLSUXY	ASEXUALLY	AAFGORTTU	AUTOGRAFT	AAGILMNOS	MAGNOLIAS
AAELLSWYY	ALLEYWAYS	AAFIILMRS	FAMILIARS	AAGILMNSV	GALVANISM
AAELMMORR	MARMOREAL	AAFILLNOP	FALLOPIAN	AAGILMNYZ	AMAZINGLY
AAELMMPST	METAPLASM	AAFILLNRS	RAINFALLS	AAGILMRST	MAGISTRAL
AAELMNOSU	MAUSOLEAN	AAFILMMNY	FAMILY MAN	AAGILNNSY	ANALYSING
AAELMNRSU	EL MANSURA	AAFILMNOR	FORAMINAL	AAGILNOST	ANALOGIST,
AAELMPSTY	PLAYMATES	AAFILNNOU	FIONNUALA		NOSTALGIA
AAELNPRTY	PLANETARY	AAFILNOOV	OF NO AVAIL	AAGILNPPT	PALPATING
AAELNRSTT	TRANSLATE	AAFILNOTX	AFLATOXIN	AAGILNRUU	INAUGURAL
AAELNRTUU	AU NATUREL	AAFILORUW	RAUWOLFIA	AAGILNRUV	VULGARIAN
AAELNSTTU	SULTANATE	AAFILSSTT	FATALISTS	AAGILNWYY	WAYLAYING
AAELOPRST	PASTORALE	AAFINORSS	IN SO FAR AS	AAGILOOPS	APOLOGIAS
AAELOPSSU	ASEPALOUS	AAFIOTTTU	TOUT A FAIT	AAGILQUUY	GUAYAQUIL
AAELOPSTU	APETALOUS	AAFKLNOUU	NUKU'ALOFA	AAGIMMMST	MAGMATISM
AAELORRSY	SOLAR YEAR	AAFKLOOST	ASK A LOT OF	AAGIMNOSY	ANISOGAMY
AAELORSTV	SALVATORE	AAFLORSWY	FOR ALWAYS	AAGIMNPRT	PTARMIGAN
AAELORTTZ	LAZARETTO	AAFMOPRRT	APART FROM	AAGINNNRT	NARRATING
AAELORTUV	EVALUATOR	AAFMORRTW	MARROWFAT	AAGINOOTV	VAGOTONIA
AAELPPRST	STAR-APPLE	AAGGIINTT	AGITATING	AAGINORTV	NAVIGATOR
AAELPRRSY	PARALYSER	AAGGILNSV	SALVAGING	AAGINRSTT	GIANT STAR
AAELPRSSY	PARALYSES	AAGGIMNPR	RAMPAGING	AAGINSTTU	AUGUSTINA
AAELPSTTU	SPATULATE	AAGGIMNSS	MASSAGING	AAGIORSTT	AGITATORS
AAELRRSTV	TRAVERSAL	AAGGINNRR	ARRANGING	AAGIPRSTZ	GAZA STRIP
AAELRSSTU	ASSAULTER,	AAGGINSSU	ASSUAGING	AAGKMORYY	KARYOGAMY
	SALERATUS	AAGGKLNNP	GANGPLANK	AAGKNOORS	KANGAROOS
AAELRSTTW	SALTWATER	AAGGLMNOR	GLAMORGAN	AAGLLLNTY	GALLANTLY
AAELSSTWY	LEASTWAYS	AAGHIKMNY	HAYMAKING	AAGLLNRTY	GALLANTRY
AAEMMNRST	ARMAMENTS,	AAGHIKMOS	KAGOSHIMA	AAGLMMMOY	MAMMALOGY
	MEN-AT-ARMS	AAGHILNNS	HANGNAILS	AAGLMNORU	GRANULOMA
AAEMNORTY	EMANATORY	AAGHILNRS	SHANGRI-LA	AAGLNNNOO	NONAGONAL
AAEMNPRTT	APARTMENT	AAGHIMOOP	OMOPHAGIA	AAGLNOOSU	ANALOGOUS
AAEMNSSTT	STATESMAN	AAGHINNRU	HUNGARIAN	AAGLNQSUU	AQUALUNGS
AAEMPRSTY	PAYMASTER	AAGHINRSS	HARASSING	AAGLRRSTU	GASTRULAR
AAEMRRSTU	ARMATURES	AAGHINSSY	SASHAYING	AAGMNNOSU	MANGANOUS
AAENNPSST	EN PASSANT	AAGHKMNSY	GYMKHANAS	AAGMOOPSU	APOGAMOUS
AAENNTTTU	ATTENUANT	AAGHLLOPR	ALLOGRAPH	AAGMRSSSU	SARGASSUM
AAENPRSTY	PEASANTRY	AAGHOPRTU	AUTOGRAPH	AAGNNNOTY	NANNY GOAT
AAENRRRST	STRANRAER	AAGIIKNNS	KISANGANI	AAGNNORTU	ORANG-UTAN
AAENRRRTW	WARRANTER	AAGIILNSS	ASSAILING	AAGNORRTU	GUARANTOR
AAENSTTTT	ATTESTANT	AAGIIMNNT	ANIMATING	AAGNORSTU	ANGOSTURA
AAEOOPPRS	SOAP OPERA	AAGIIMNRY	IMAGINARY	AAGNRUUUY	URUGUAYAN
AAEOPRRST	SEPARATOR	AAGIILNTT	ATTAINING	AAGOORRRT	ARROGATOR
AAEOPRSTT	PASTORATE	AAGIINOTT	AGITATION	AAGPRSTTY	STAG PARTY
AAEOPSSTT	APOSTATES	AAGIINSTT	SATIATING	AAHHNNSSU	SHUSHANNA
AAEPPRRST	SPARE PART	AAGIIRRTU	AIR GUITAR	AAHIILNSW	SWAHILIAN
AAEPRSTXY	TAXPAYERS				

AAHIILNTU	LITHUANIA	AAIINOPRT	TOPIARIAN
AAHILMNOT	MALATHION	AAIINORTV	VARIATION
AAHILMTUZ	AZIMUTHAL	AAIINOSTT	SATIATION
AAHILNNST	INHALANTS	AAIINPRSS	PARISIANS
AAHILNORT	INHALATOR	AAIJNRSSY	JANISSARY
AAHILNSTU	AILANTHUS	AAIKLLOSS	ALKALOSIS
AAHILORTU	AUTHORIAL	AAIKLNOSV	SLOVAKIAN
AAHILPSXY	ASPHYXIAL	AAIKNNOPT	PONTIANAK
AAHIMMNSS	SHAMANISM	AAIKNRSTX	TAXI RANKS
AAHIMNOST	THOMASINA	AAIKSSSTW	SWASTIKAS
AAHIMNSST	SHAMANIST	AAILLLNOT	LALLATION
AAHIMNSTU	AMIANTHUS	AAILLMMRY	MAMILLARY
AAHINOORR	HONORARIA	AAILLMMXY	MAXIMALLY
AAHINOPRT	PARATHION	AAILLMNST	MANTILLAS
AAHINORRV	HARROVIAN	AAILLMOPP	PAPILLOMA
AAHINPTTY	ANTIPATHY	AAILLMRSY	AMARYLLIS
AAHINRRTU	ARTHURINA	AAILLMRTY	MARITALLY
AAHIOPPSS	APOPHASIS	AAILLMRXY	MAXILLARY
AAHJNRTUV	THANJAVUR	AAILLNOOP	APOLLONIA
AAHKLLMRS	HALLMARKS	AAILLNOPT	ALTIPLANO
AAHKLMNOO	OKLAHOMAN	AAILLNOST	ALLANTOIS
AAHKMOSTW	TOMAHAWKS	AAILLNOTV	VALLATION
AAHLLMOSW	HALLOWMAS	AAILLNPRU	NULLIPARA
AAHLLOPTY	ALLOPATHY	AAILLNTVY	VALIANTLY
AAHLLSTTT	HALLSTATT	AAILLOPRT	PALLIATOR
AAHLMNNTU	LANTHANUM	AAILLPPRY	PAPILLARY
AAHLMPSTU	ASPHALTUM	AAILLPRTY	PARTIALLY
AAHLPPPSY	SLAPHAPPY	AAILLPSTY	SPATIALLY
AAHMNORST	MARATHONS	AAILMNNPS	PLAINSMAN
AAHMNPSST	PHANTASMS	AAILMNOPT	PALMATION
AAHMOPPRR	PARAMORPH	AAILMNORT	LAMINATOR
AAHNNOOTZ	ANTHOZOAN	AAILMNOST	ATONALISM
AAHNNOSTU	ANANTHOUS	AAILMNSST	TALISMANS
AAHNOTTXY	ANTHOTAXY	AAILMNTTU	MATUTINAL
AAHORTWWY	THROWAWAY	AAILMORTY	AMORALITY
AAIIKNNRU	UKRAINIAN	AAILMPRSU	MARSUPIAL
AAIIKNPST	PAKISTANI	AAILMPRTU	MULTIPARA
AAIILLMNS	SNAIL MAIL	AAILMRSST	ALARMISTS
AAIILMNNS	ANIMALISM	AAILNNOPS	ANNAPOLIS
AAIILMNSS	MAINSAILS	AAILNNOPT	PLANATION
AAIILMNST	ANIMALIST	AAILNNOST	NATIONALS
AAIILMNTY	ANIMALITY	AAILNNOSV	SLAVONIAN
AAIILMPRT	IMPARTIAL, PRIMATIAL	AAILNNPQU	PALANQUIN
AAIILNOSU	LOUISIANA	AAILNNPRU	UNIPLANAR
AAIILNRTV	ANTIVIRAL	AAILNNPST	PLANTAINS
AAIILRUXY	AUXILIARY	AAILNNSST	ANNALISTS
AAIIMMNST	ANIMATISM	AAILNOOTV	OVATIONAL
AAIIMNNOT	ANIMATION	AAILNOPPT	PALPATION
AAIIMNRTU	MAURITIAN	AAILNOPSS	PASSIONAL
AAIIMORST	TIMISOARA	AAILNOPUW	PAULOWNIA
AAIIMPPRR	PRIMIPARA	AAILNOSTT	SALTATION
AAIINNRTU	UNITARIAN	AAILNOSTV	SALVATION
AAIINNRTV	INVARIANT	AAILNOTTY	ATONALITY
		AAILNOTUV	VALUATION
AAILNPRTU	TARPAULIN		
AAILNPSTU	SAINT PAUL		
AAILNSSST	STANISLAS		
AAILOPRRT	RAPTORIAL		
AAILOPSTX	POSTAXIAL		
AAILORRST	SARTORIAL		
AAILPRSSY	PARALYSIS		
AAIMMNNOO	MONOMANIA		
AAIMMNNRT	MARTINMAS		
AAIMMNNST	MAINMASTS		
AAIMNNORS	SAN MARINO		
AAIMNOPRY	PYROMANIA		
AAIMNOSTT	ANATOMIST		
AAIMNPRSZ	MARZIPANS		
AAIMNNRRT	TRIMARANS		
AAIMNRSTT	TARANTISM		
AAIMNSSTY	MAINSTAYS		
AAIMOORRT	MORATORIA		
AAIMORSSU	AMAUROSIS		
AAIMQRSUU	AQUARIUMS		
AAINNNTTU	ANNUITANT		
AAINNORRT	NARRATION		
AAINNPRSY	SPIN A YARN		
AAINNRSTU	SATURNIAN		
AAINORRST	ROTARIANS		
AAINPRSST	ASPIRANTS, PARTISANS		
AAINPSTXY	ANAPTYXIS		
AAINQRSTU	QUATRAINS		
AAINQRTUY	ANTIQUARY		
AAINQSTTU	AQUATINTS		
AAINSSSSS	ASSASSINS		
AAINSSSTT	ASSISTANT, SATANISTS		
AAIOPPRRT	APPARITOR, PRO PATRIA		
AAIOPRRST	ASPIRATOR		
AAIORRTTT	TRATTORIA		
AAIPPRSSU	PARI PASSU		
AAJMORRSU	URSA MAJOR		
AAKKMORRU	KARAKORUM		
AAKLLLMST	SMALL TALK		
AAKNOOSST	SASKATOON		
AALLLMMSS	SMALL SLAM		
AALLLMOPS	ALLOPLASM		
AALLMMRSS	SMALL ARMS		
AALLMOOSS	LOS ALAMOS		
AALLMOPSS	PLASMASOL		
AALLNNOPY	POLLYANNA		
AALLNRTUY	NATURALLY		
AALLORSVY	YAROSLAVL		
AALLPRTWY	PARTY WALL		
AALMNOOSU	ANOMALOUS		
AALMNOPRT	PATROLMAN		
AALMNPRTY	RAMPANTLY		

AALMOOSTU	AUTOSOMAL	ABBDEGNRU	BUNDABERG	ABCCCEFIO	BECCAFICO
AALMOQSSU	SQUAMOSAL	ABBDEILOT	BOBTAILED	ABCCCKKLO	BLACKCOCK
AALMORTYY	MAYORALTY	ABBDEILTU	DUBITABLE	ABCCEEFRY	CYBERCAFE
AALNNRTUU	UNNATURAL	ABBDEINRS	BREAD BINS	ABCCEEHKL	CHECKABLE
AALNOPSTT	POSTNATAL	ABBDEIRTT	RABBITTED	ABCCEENRU	BUCCANEER
AALNOSTTU	TANTALOUS	ABBDELOTU	DOUBTABLE	ABCCEIIST	SCABIETIC
AALNPRTWY	LAWN PARTY	ABBDELOSU	SQUABBLED	ABCCEINOV	BICONCAVE
AALOPRRTY	PORTRAYAL	ABBDELSUU	SUBDUABLE	ABCCEKMOS	COMEBACKS
AALOPRSST	PASTORALS	ABBDGIILN	AD-LIBBING	ABCCELNRU	CARBUNCLE
AALRSSTTW	LAST STRAW,	ABBDHLOOT	BLOODBATH	ABCCEMNRU	CUMBRANCE
	STALWARTS	ABBDILLOR	BILLBOARD,	ABCCEMNTU	ACCUMBENT
AAMMOORST	MATAMOROS		BROADBILL	ABCCFIINO	FIBONACCI
AAMNNOTUY	ANY AMOUNT	ABBDKLNOO	BLOOD BANK	ABCCFIMOR	BACCIFORM
AAMNOOTTU	AUTOMATON	ABBDMNOOR	BOMBARDON	ABCCGHLTU	CLUTCH BAG
AAMNOPRTU	PARAMOUNT	ABBEEEHRS	BEERSHEBA	ABCCHHKNU	HUNCHBACK
AAMOPRRSU	PARAMOURS	ABBEEHTTY	BABY TEETH	ABCCHKLOT	BACKCLOTH
AANNOORTT	ANNOTATOR	ABBEEJRRS	JABBERERS	ABCCIKKKS	KICKBACKS
AANORRRST	NARRATORS	ABBEEKLRU	REBUKABLE	ABCCIKRST	CRABSTICK
AANORRRTW	WARRANTOR	ABBEELMOT	BE TO BLAME	ABCCILORU	CORBICULA
AANORSTTU	ASTRONAUT	ABBEELOPR	PROBEABLE	ABCCIRSTU	SUBARCTIC
AANPRSSSU	PARNASSUS	ABBEENORS	BARE BONES	ABCCKLLOS	BALLCOCKS
AAOORRTTV	ROTAVATOR	ABBEENRRY	BANEBERRY	ABCCKORSS	BACKCROSS
AAORRSTTU	TARTAROUS	ABBEERRRY	BEARBERRY	ABCCMOORY	MOBOCRACY
AAOSSTWWY	STOWAWAYS	ABBEFILST	FLABBIEST	ABCDEEHHU	DEBAUCHED
ABBBCELLU	CLUBBABLE	ABBEGIJNR	JABBERING	ABCDEEIL	DECIDABLE
ABBBDEELR	BLABBERED	ABBEGILLO	OBLIGABLE	ABCDDEFLO	BOLDFACED
ABBCCEHKN	BACKBENCH	ABBEHINOS	HOBBESIAN	ABCDDEKLO	BLOCKADED
ABBCCKKLU	BLACKBUCK	ABBEHISST	SHABBIEST	ABCDDENOS	ABSCONDED
ABBCDEERU	BARBECUED	ABBEHORST	BATHROBES	ABCDDKORU	DUCKBOARD
ABBCDELRS	SCRABBLED	ABBEILMSU	ABU SIMBEL	ABCDEEEHU	DEBAUCHEE
ABBCDELRY	CRABBEDLY	ABBEIMNOZ	BOMBAZINE	ABCDEEHRU	DEBAUCHER
ABBCDIKLR	BLACKBIRD	ABBEINORT	BARBITONE	ABCDEEHSU	DEBAUCHES
ABBCDKORU	BUCKBOARD	ABBEKLOOR	BROOKABLE	ABCDEEILM	MEDICABLE
ABBCEEIRS	CARIBBEES	ABBELLMPU	PLUMBABLE	ABCDEEINT	BENEDICTA
ABBCEERSU	BARBECUES	ABBELMOOZ	BAMBOOZLE	ABCDEEKLN	BLACKENED
ABBCEIKRT	BACKBITER	ABBELOPRS	PROBABLES	ABCDEEKRT	BRACKETED
ABBCEIRST	CRABBIEST	ABBELOSTY	STABLE BOY	ABCDEELMR	CLAMBERED
ABBCEIRSY	CRYBABIES	ABBELQRSU	SQUABBLER	ABCDEFIKR	BACKFIRED
ABBCEISST	SCABBIEST	ABBELQSSU	SQUABBLES	ABCDEGIMR	CAMBRIDGE
ABBCEKLLT	BLACK BELT	ABBENORST	ABSORBENT	ABCDEHIOT	COHABITED
ABBCEKLLU	BLUE-BLACK	ABBFHLLSU	FLASHBULB	ABCDEHKLO	BLOCKHEAD
ABBCEKLNO	BONEBLACK	ABBGIINRT	RABBITING	ABCDEIIST	DIABETICS
ABBCEKNOS	BACKBONES	ABBGILMNR	BRAMBLING	ABCDEIJLU	JUDICABLE
ABBCELRRS	SCRABBLER	ABBGILOOT	OBBLIGATO	ABCDEIKLS	BACKSLIDE
ABBCILPRU	PUBLIC BAR	ABBGINORS	ABSORBING	ABCDEIKRU	RUDBECKIA
ABBCIMOST	BOMBASTIC	ABBHHOOTY	BABY TOOTH	ABCDEIKSS	BACKSIDES
ABBCINOSY	CABIN BOYS	ABBILLSSU	SILLABUBS	ABCDEILMY	MEDICABLY
ABBCKLNRU	BLACKBURN	ABBJMRUUU	BUJUMBURA	ABCDEINTU	INCUBATED
ABBCKLOOT	BOOTBLACK	ABBKKNOOS	BANKBOOKS	ABCDEIORT	BACTEROID
ABBCLMOOU	ABCOULOMB	ABBLLSSUY	SYLLABUBS	ABCDEIPRU	PARDUBICE
ABBDDEMOR	BOMBARDED	ABBMMOOST	ATOM BOMBS	ABCDEKLNY	CLYDEBANK
ABBDEELRU	BLUEBEARD	ABBOOPRTY	BOOBY TRAP	ABCDEKLOR	BLOCKADER
ABBDEGINR	BANBRIDGE	ABBOORRWY	BARROW BOY	ABCDEKLOS	BLOCKADES
ABBDEGINU	BEDAUBING	ABCCCCIOO	BOCCACCIO	ABCDEKNNS	NECKBANDS

ABCDELLOS	SCOLDABLE	ABCEELOPS	PLACEBOES
ABCDELMRS	SCRAMBLED	ABCEELORT	BRACTEOLE
ABCDELOOS	CABOODLES	ABCEELORV	REVOCABLE
ABCDEMOTT	COMBATTED	ABCEELRST	BRACELETS
ABCDENORR	CORN BREAD	ABCEELRSU	RESCUABLE,
ABCDENORS	ABSCONDER		SECURABLE
ABCDENOSU	CASEBOUND,	ABCEELRXY	EXECRABLY
	SUBDEACON	ABCEELSUX	EXCUSABLE
ABCDEOORT	OBCORDATE	ABCEEMMOR	MORECAMBE
ABCDGINOR	BROCADING	ABCEEMMRT	CAMEMBERT
ABCDGINTU	ABDUCTING	ABCEEMORR	EMBRACEOR
ABCDHINRS	DISBRANCH	ABCEEMORT	EMBROCATE
ABCDHIOPR	CHIPBOARD	ABCEEMRRY	EMBRACERY
ABCDHNRTU	DUTCH BARN	ABCEENRTY	CYBERNATE
ABCDIKRRY	BRICKYARD	ABCEENSTT	TABESCENT
ABCDILMOR	LOMBARDIC	ABCEEOSSU	SEBACEOUS
ABCDILOPR	CLIPBOARD	ABCEEPRRU	CUPBEARER
ABCDINOOT	BANDICOOT	ABCEESSSS	ABSCESSES
ABCDINOTU	ABDUCTION	ABCEFFHNO	OFFENBACH
ABCDIOOSU	BODACIOUS	ABCEFHLSU	FLASHCUBE
ABCDKLNOU	CLOUDBANK	ABCEFIRTU	BIFURCATE
ABCDKLOOR	ROADBLOCK	ABCEFLOSU	FOCUSABLE
ABCDKOORR	CORKBOARD	ABCEFLSSS	BASS CLEFS
ABCDKOORS	BACK DOORS	ABCEFOSTU	OBFUSCATE
ABCDKOOSW	BACKWOODS	ABCEGHILN	BLEACHING
ABCDKOPRS	BACKDROPS	ABCEGHINR	BREACHING
ABCDLNRSU	SCRUBLAND	ABCEGHLNO	LONG BEACH
ABCDNOOXX	BOX AND COX	ABCEGILOR	BRICOLAGE
ABCDOPRSU	CUPBOARDS	ABCEGIMNR	EMBRACING
ABCEEELRT	CELEBRATE,	ABCEGKLLS	BLACKLEGS
	ERECTABLE	ABCEGKLOS	BLOCKAGES
ABCEEELRX	EXECRABLE	ABCEGKRTU	TUCKER-BAG
ABCEEFFOR	COFFEE BAR	ABCEHINNO	BONE CHINA
ABCEEFIRS	BRIEFCASE	ABCEHINOT	AITCHBONE
ABCEEFLOR	FORCEABLE	ABCEHKLLO	BLACK HOLE
ABCEEFOSU	BECAUSE OF	ABCEHKLOS	SHOCKABLE
ABCEEGKNR	GREENBACK	ABCEHKMNR	BENCHMARK
ABCEEHKLO	CHOKEABLE	ABCEHKORS	HORSEBACK
ABCEEHLLY	BELLYACHE	ABCEHKRRY	HACKBERRY
ABCEEHLRS	BLEACHERS	ABCEHKTUW	BUCKWHEAT
ABCEEILLS	SLICEABLE	ABCEHLORS	BACHELORS
ABCEEILPR	PIERCABLE	ABCEHLOTU	TOUCHABLE
ABCEEILRT	RECITABLE	ABCEHLSSU	CHASUBLES
ABCEEILST	CELIBATES	ABCEHOQRU	QUEBRACHO
ABCEEILSX	EXCISABLE	ABCEHRSTU	BUCHAREST
ABCEEILTX	EXCITABLE	ABCEIILNS	SIBILANCE
ABCEEIMNS	AMBIENCES	ABCEIILRS	IRASCIBLE
ABCEEINOS	OBEISANCE	ABCEIIMRT	IMBRICATE
ABCEEINRR	CARBINEER	ABCEIJLNU	JUBILANCE
ABCEEKKNR	BREAKNECK	ABCEIJNOT	ABJECTION
ABCEEKLSY	BLACK EYES	ABCEIJOST	JACOBITES
ABCEEKPSW	SWEEPBACK	ABCEIKLLS	BLACK ISLE
ABCEELMNS	SEMBLANCE	ABCEILLOS	OBELISCAL
ABCEELNRT	CELEBRANT	ABCEILMOT	METABOLIC
ABCEELNST	ALBESCENT		

ABCEILMST	BLASTEMIC
ABCEILNOS	BALCONIES
ABCEILNOV	INVOCABLE
ABCEILNRU	BINUCLEAR,
	INCURABLE
ABCEILORS	CARBOLISE
ABCEILORT	CABRIOLET
ABCEILORZ	CARBOLIZE
ABCEILOTT	COBALTITE
ABCEILRTU	LUBRICATE
ABCEILRUX	EXCALIBUR
ABCEILSTU	BISULCATE
ABCEIMOTV	COMBATIVE
ABCEIMRTU	BACTERIUM
ABCEINORS	CARBONISE
ABCEINORZ	CARBONIZE
ABCEIRRSU	CARBURISE
ABCEIRRTU	RUBRICATE
ABCEIRRUZ	CARBURIZE
ABCEJNSTU	SUBJACENT
ABCEKLLNR	BRACKNELL
ABCEKLNSS	BLACKNESS
ABCEKLPRU	PARBUCKLE
ABCEKOOSS	BOOKCASES
ABCEKPSTW	BACKSWEPT,
	SWEPT-BACK
ABCEKRTUW	WATERBUCK
ABCELLOSX	CALL BOXES
ABCELLRSW	SCREWBALL
ABCELMRRS	SCRAMBLER
ABCELMRSS	SCRAMBLES
ABCELNOST	CONSTABLE
ABCELNOTU	COUNTABLE
ABCELOOST	BOOTLACES
ABCELORVY	REVOCABLY
ABCELOSST	OBSTACLES
ABCELOSTT	ECTOBLAST
ABCELRTTY	BATTLE CRY
ABCELRTUU	LUCUBRATE
ABCELSUXY	EXCUSABLY
ABCEMORSS	CROSSBEAM
ABCENORTY	BARONETCY
ABCENRRRY	CRANBERRY
ABCENSSTU	SUBSTANCE
ABCEOOPRS	BAROSCOPE
ABCEOPRRY	REPROBACY
ABCFHIKLS	BLACKFISH
ABCFHIKST	BACK SHIFT
ABCFKLLSU	FULLBACKS
ABCGGIKPY	PIGGYBACK
ABCGHIKST	BACKSIGHT
ABCGHILNN	BLANCHING
ABCGHINNR	BRANCHING
ABCGHINOR	BROACHING

ABCGIINRS	ASCRIBING	ABCKLOSTU	BLACKOUTS	ABDEEHLRT	BLATHERED
ABCGILNOS	LOG CABINS	ABCKNORSU	OSNABRUCK	ABDEEHNOS	BONEHEADS
ABCGILNRY	BRACINGLY	ABCKOOPRS	SCRAPBOOK	ABDEEIILR	DIABLERIE
ABCGIMNOT	COMBATING	ABCLMNNOT	MONT BLANC	ABDEEIILW	WIELDABLE
ABCHHKSUW	BUSHWHACK	ABCLNOWYY	COLWYN BAY	ABDEEIILY	YIELDABLE
ABCHIILLN	CHILBLAIN	ABCLOORRU	COLOUR BAR	ABDEEILMS	AMBLESIDE,
ABCHIIOST	ISOBATHIC	ABCLOOSTU	COBALTOUS		DEMISABLE
ABCHILMOS	SHAMBOLIC	ABCLPRSUW	PUB-CRAWLS	ABDEEILNR	BREADLINE
ABCHILNOR	BRONCHIAL	ABCMOSSUU	SUBMUCOSA	ABDEEILNS	DISENABLE
ABCHKMPSU	HUMPBACKS	ABCNOORSU	CARBONOUS	ABDEEILRS	DESIRABLE
ABCHKMTTU	THUMBTACK	ABCNORSTU	OBSCURANT	ABDEEILRT	LIBERATED
ABCHKNORT	THORNBACK	ABCORRSSS	CROSSBARS	ABDEEILRV	DERIVABLE
ABCHKORTW	THROWBACK	ABDDDEINS	DISBANDED	ABDEEILSV	DEVISABLE
ABCHLLNPU	PUNCHBALL	ABDDEEHIJ	JIB-HEADED	ABDEEINNR	BERNADINE
ABCHLRWYZ	WALBRZYCH	ABDDEEHST	DEATHBEDS	ABDEEINSS	BEADINESS
ABCIIIKLW	BAILIWICK	ABDDEELNY	NEED BADLY	ABDEEINSW	WIESBADEN
ABCIIILPT	BICIPITAL	ABDDEENOR	BROADENED	ABDEEINTT	BIDENTATE
ABCIIKNRS	BRAINSICK	ABDDEEPRS	BEDSPREAD	ABDEEINTU	BUTADIENE
ABCIILLMU	UMBILICAL	ABDDEERTY	TEDDY BEAR	ABDEEITTU	BEATITUDE
ABCIILLST	BALLISTIC	ABDDEESST	BEDSTEADS	ABDEEKLNT	BLANKETED
ABCIILMOR	MICROBIAL	ABDDEFILN	DEAFBLIND	ABDEELLTY	BELATEDLY
ABCIILRSY	IRASCIBLY	ABDDEHNSU	HUSBANDED	ABDEELMSS	ASSEMBLED
ABCIINNRT	BRITANNIC	ABDDEIILV	DIVIDABLE	ABDEELMTT	EMBATTLED
ABCIINRRU	RUBRICIAN	ABDDEILNT	BLIND DATE	ABDEELNOR	BANDEROLE,
ABCIIOSTT	BIOSTATIC	ABDDEIORS	BROADSIDE,		BANDOLEER
ABCIIRSTY	SYBARITIC		SIDEBOARD	ABDEELNOT	DENOTABLE
ABCIKLLST	BLACKLIST	ABDDEIPRU	UPBRAIDED	ABDEELNPR	PREBENDAL
ABCILLMRU	LUMBRICAL	ABDDEIRRS	DISBARRED	ABDEELNPS	SPENDABLE
ABCILLORU	BILOCULAR	ABDDEISSU	DISABUSED	ABDEELNRU	ENDURABLE
ABCILMNOO	COLOMBIAN	ABDDELOSW	SADDLEBOW	ABDEELNST	STEEL BAND
ABCILMNOU	COLUMBIAN,	ABDDGORUY	BODYGUARD	ABDEELOPS	DEPOSABLE
	COLUMBINA	ABDDHINTW	BANDWIDTH	ABDEELRSS	BEARDLESS
ABCILMOPY	AMBLYOPIC	ABDDHNORU	HARDBOUND	ABDEELSSU	SUBLEASED
ABCILMSTY	CYMBALIST	ABDDILNNS	SAND-BLIND	ABDEEMNOU	BEAU MONDE
ABCILMSUX	SUBCLIMAX	ABDDILRSY	LADYBIRDS	ABDEEMNRT	DEBARMENT
ABCILNNOU	CONNUBIAL	ABDDJMNOO	ODD-JOB MAN	ABDEENOTY	BAYONETED
ABCILNORU	BINOCULAR	ABDEEEFRS	FREE-BASED	ABDEENOTU	BANQUETED
ABCILNPSU	PUBLICANS	ABDEEEGLL	DELEGABLE	ABDEENRRT	BARTENDER
ABCILNRTU	LUBRICANT	ABDEEELLY	EYEBALLED	ABDEENTTU	DEBUTANTE
ABCILNRUY	INCURABLY	ABDEEELMN	EMENDABLE	ABDEEOPST	SPEEDBOAT
ABCILOPSY	POLYBASIC	ABDEEEMRS	BESMEARED	ABDEERRST	REDBREAST
ABCILORRU	ORBICULAR	ABDEEFHLR	HALF-BREED	ABDEFFGLU	DUFFEL BAG
ABCILOSSU	SUBSOCIAL	ABDEEFIIT	BEATIFIED	ABDEFIISX	BASIFIXED
ABCIMNOOS	MONOBASIC	ABDEEFILN	DEFINABLE	ABDEFINOS	BONA FIDES
ABCIMOSTU	SUBATOMIC	ABDEEFORR	FREEBOARD	ABDEFINRR	FIREBRAND
ABCIMRSTY	CAMBISTRY	ABDEEGGLR	BEDRAGGLE	ABDEFLLOO	FLOODABLE
ABCINOORR	RIO BRANCO	ABDEEGHIN	BEHEADING	ABDEFORTY	AFTERBODY
ABCINORTU	INCUBATOR	ABDEEGINR	GABERDINE	ABDEGGINR	BADGERING
ABCINOSTY	OBSTINACY	ABDEEGJLU	JUDGEABLE	ABDEGGMRU	MAGDEBURG
ABCIOPRRT	PORTACRIB	ABDEEGLLO	LODGEABLE	ABDEGHLRU	ALDEBURGH
ABCJKOOST	JACKBOOTS	ABDEEGMOR	EMBARGOED	ABDEGIINU	BIGUANIDE
ABCKLLLOP	BLACKPOLL	ABDEEGRRY	GREYBEARD	ABDEGIIRR	BRIGADIER
ABCKLLOOP	BLACKPOOL	ABDEEGRSY	SAGE DERBY	ABDEGIKNR	DEBARKING
ABCKLOPST	BLACK SPOT	ABDEEHINR	HEBRIDEAN	ABDEGILOT	OBLIGATED
				ABDEGINRR	DEBARRING

ABDEGNOTU	ON A BUDGET	ABDENORST	ADSORBENT	ABDINRSTW	WRISTBAND
ABDEGNSTU	BUNDESTAG	ABDENOSSX	SANDBOXES	ABDIRSTUY	ABSURDITY
ABDEGRTUY	BUDGETARY	ABDENOSTU	EASTBOUND	ABDJMOPRU	BROAD JUMP
ABDEHIINT	INHABITED	ABDENRRST	ST BERNARD	ABDKLNORW	WORLD BANK
ABDEHILNO	HOBNAILED	ABDENRRSTU	BUNDESRAT	ABDKNOOST	BOOKSTAND
ABDEHILOS	ABOLISHED	ABDENRSTY	BYSTANDER	ABDLMOOOR	BROADLOOM
ABDEHKLSU	BULKHEADS	ABDEOORRT	BREADROOT	ABDMMNOSU	OMBUDSMAN
ABDEHLOOT	BLOOD HEAT	ABDEOORRV	OVERBOARD	ABDMNORTU	DUMBARTON
ABDEHLOTW	DEATHBLOW	ABDEOORWZ	ZEBRAWOOD	ABDMOOORR	BOARDROOM
ABDEHNRSU	HUSBANDER	ABDEOORRSW	WARDROBES	ABDNNOSTY	ON STAND-BY
ABDEHORRU	HARBOURED	ABDEORTUV	OUTBRAVED	ABEEEEFRT	BEEFEATER
ABDEIILNU	INAUDIBLE	ABDESSTTU	TASTE BUDS	ABEEEERSZ	SEA BREEZE
ABDEIILNV	DIVINABLE	ABDFHORSU	SHUFBOARD	ABEEEFKST	BEEFSTEAK
ABDEIILOS	DIABOLISE	ABDFIIKOR	FABRIKOID	ABEEEFLRR	REFERABLE
ABDEIILOZ	DIABOLIZE	ABDFIIRRR	FRIARBIRD	ABEEEFLRZ	FREEZABLE
ABDEIILRST	DIATRIBES	ABDFLLORU	FULL BOARD	ABEEEGLNR	GENERABLE
ABDEIKLNR	DRINKABLE	ABDFNORRT	BRANTFORD	ABEEEGLNS	BENGALESE
ABDEIKMRS	DISEMBARK	ABDFOOORT	FOOTBOARD	ABEEEGLRU	BELEAGUER
ABDEIKNRW	WINDBREAK	ABDFORRSU	SURFBOARD	ABEEEGLTV	VEGETABLE
ABDEILLLO	LABELLOID	ABDGGGOSY	DOGGY BAGS	ABEEEGNNR	GREEN BEAN
ABDEILLLR	DRILLABLE	ABDGGIINR	ABRIDGING	ABEEEGRSV	BEVERAGES
ABDEILMNS	MANDIBLES	ABDGIILNS	DISABLING	ABEEEHLMT	MEHETABEL
ABDEILMOR	BROMELIAD	ABDGIILNY	ABIDINGLY	ABEEEHLSW	WHEELBASE
ABDEILNOR	BANDOLIER	ABDGILNNR	BRANDLING	ABEEEKNRV	BREAKEVEN
ABDEILOPR	PARBOILED	ABDGILORS	GAOLBIRDS	ABEEELMPR	PERMEABLE
ABDEILORV	OLIVE DRAB	ABDGINNOU	ABOUNDING	ABEEELNRT	ENTERABLE
ABDEILRRY	EARLY BIRD	ABDGINORS	SIGNBOARD	ABEEELNRV	VENERABLE
ABDEILRSY	DESIRABLY	ABDGINOXY	BOXING DAY	ABEEELNRW	RENEWABLE
ABDEINOST	BOTANISED	ABDGLOPRU	PLUGBOARD	ABEEELRRV	REVERABLE
ABDEINOTZ	BOTANIZED	ABDHIINNR	HINDBRAIN	ABEEELRST	STEERABLE
ABDEINSSW	BAWDINESS	ABDHILLNS	HANDBILLS	ABEEELRSV	SEVERABLE
ABDEIPRRU	UPBRAIDER	ABDHIMRTY	DITHYRAMB	ABEEENSST	ABSENTEES
ABDEIRRTW	WATER BIRD	ABDHIOPRS	SHIPBOARD	ABEEERRTV	VERTEBRAE
ABDEJORTT	OBJET D'ART	ABDHIRSTY	BIRTHDAYS	ABEEERTUX	EXUBERATE
ABDEKLSSW	SKEWBALDS	ABDHKNOOS	HANDBOOKS	ABEEFFILN	INEFFABLE
ABDEKNORW	BREAKDOWN	ABDHLORSW	BLOWHARDS	ABEEFGLOR	FORGEABLE
ABDEKORRW	WORDBREAK	ABDHNOORU	BOARHOUND	ABEEFIKRR	FIREBREAK
ABDEKORSY	KEYBOARDS	ABDHNRSUY	HUSBANDRY	ABEEFILNR	INFERABLE,
ABDELLMOU	MOULDABLE	ABDHOOSWX	SHADOW-BOX		REFINABLE
ABDELLNOO	BALLOONED	ABDIIILLN	LIBIDINAL	ABEEFILRS	BAS-RELIEF
ABDELMOTY	MOLYBDATE	ABDIIJLRS	JAILBIRDS	ABEEFILST	FLEABITES
ABDELNNSS	BLANDNESS	ABDIILLRS	BILLIARDS	ABEEFLRSU	REFUSABLE
ABDELNOST	ENDOBLAST	ABDIILMOS	DIABOLISM	ABEEFLRTU	REFUTABLE
ABDELNOSU	SOUNDABLE	ABDIILNUY	INAUDIBLY	ABEEFLSSU	SELF-ABUSE
ABDELNOUW	WOUNDABLE	ABDIILOST	DIABOLIST,	ABEEFORRR	FORBEARER
ABDELNSTU	DUNSTABLE		IDIOBLAST	ABEEFORRS	FOREBEARS
ABDELOOPS	PASO DOBLE	ABDIIMRST	TRIBADISM	ABEEGGLOR	GORGEABLE
ABDELORTX	EXTRABOLD	ABDIKOOOU	AUDIO BOOK	ABEEGHILW	WEIGHABLE
ABDELORUV	BOULEVARD	ABDILLMOR	MILLBOARD	ABEEGHNOR	HABERGEON
ABDEMRSTU	DRUMBEATS	ABDILORSW	WILD BOARS	ABEEGHRTU	HAGBUTEER
ABDENNTTU	BUTENANDT	ABDILRSZZ	BLIZZARDS	ABEEGILLR	GABRIELLE
ABDENOPRR	PADERBORN	ABDIMNNOT	BADMINTON	ABEEGILLV	GIVE A BELL
ABDENORSS	BROADNESS	ABDIMPQSU	DAMP SQUIB	ABEEGILNN	BENGALINE
		ABDINOWWY	BAY WINDOW	ABEEGINRU	AUBERGINE

ABEEGINRV BEAVERING, BEREAVING	ABEEIRRSS BRASSERIE, BRASSIERE	ABEFGILLN BEFALLING
ABEEGKORR BROKERAGE	ABEEIRRST BISERRATE	ABEFGILNR FRANGIBLE
ABEEGLLRU REGULABLE	ABEEIRSTT BATTERIES	ABEFGLOOR GABLE ROOF
ABEEGLNPR PREGNABLE	ABEEJLLNY JELLY BEAN	ABEFIILNU UNIFIABLE
ABEEGLOPR BARGE POLE, PORBEAGLE	ABEEJLNOY ENJOYABLE	ABEFIILOT BIFOLIATE
ABEEGLRTT GREAT BELT	ABEEJLNSU BLUE JEANS	ABEFIIMRT FIMBRIATE
ABEEGLSSU GUESSABLE	ABEEJMORS JAMBOREES	ABEFILLRS FIREBALLS
ABEEGMORS EMBARGOES	ABEEKLNNO ANKLEBONE	ABEFILOST LIFEBOATS
ABEEGNORZ BRONZE AGE	ABEEKLNSS BLEAKNESS	ABEFILTUU BEAUTIFUL
ABEEGORSX GEARBOXES	ABEEKLORV REVOKABLE	ABEFIMORS FRAMBOISE
ABEEGRSTU SUGAR BEET	ABEELLLPS SPELLABLE	ABEFINORR FOREBRAIN
ABEEHILMT MEHITABEL	ABEELLMRS SMALL BEER	ABEFLLLMU FLABELLUM
ABEEHILRT HERITABLE	ABEELLMSS BLAMELESS	ABEFLLLUY BALEFULLY
ABEEHILST ELISABETH	ABEELLMTU UMBELLATE	ABEFLLNUY BANEFULLY
ABEEHILTZ ELIZABETH	ABEELLORS ROSABELLE	ABEFLNOSW WOLFSBANE
ABEEHIMSV MISBEHAVE	ABEELLORT TOLERABLE	ABEFOORST BEAR'S-FOOT
ABEEHINRT HIBERNATE	ABEELLORW LOWERABLE	ABEFRTTTU BUTTERFAT
ABEEHIRRS HEBRAISER	ABEELLOVV EVOLVABLE	ABEGGGINR BEGGARING
ABEEHIRRZ HEBRAIZER	ABEELMMOR MEMORABLE	ABEGGINSS BAGGINESS
ABEEHKORS BRAKE SHOE	ABEELMMRS EMBALMERS	ABEGGLLRU BUGGER ALL
ABEEHLLRS HAREBELLS	ABEELMNRU NUMERABLE	ABEGGNOPS SPONGE BAG
ABEEHLMPS BLASPHEME	ABEELMORV REMOVABLE	ABEGHHILT HIGH TABLE
ABEEHLNOW WHALEBONE	ABEELMOSV MOVEABLES	ABEGHILST SIGHTABLE
ABEEHNSTU BHUTANESE	ABEELMPRS PREAMBLES	ABEGHINRR HARBINGER
ABEEHRSTT HARTBEEST	ABEELMPTT TEMPTABLE	ABEGHINRT BREATHING
ABEEIINRT INEBRIATE	ABEELMRSS ASSEMBLER	ABEGHMRRU HAMBURGER
ABEEIKLRZ ZEBRA-LIKE	ABEELMRSU RESUMABLE	ABEGHRSSU SAGEBRUSH
ABEEIKNST SNAKEBITE	ABEELNNTU UNTENABLE	ABEGIILLT LITIGABLE
ABEEILLMR MIRABELLE	ABEELOPSX EXPOSABLE	ABEGIILMT MITIGABLE
ABEEILLRV RELIVABLE	ABEELPRSU SUPERABLE	ABEGIILNS ABSEILING
ABEEILMPT EMPTIABLE	ABEELPRTU REPUTABLE	ABEGIILNT IGNITABLE
ABEEILMRS MISERABLE	ABEELRRTV VERTEBRAL	ABEGIILNW BEWAILING
ABEEILMST ESTIMABLE	ABEELRSVW SWERVABLE	ABEGIILRR IRRIGABLE
ABEEILMTT TIMETABLE	ABEELRTTU UTTERABLE	ABEGIINOR ABORIGINE
ABEEILNPS PLEBEIANS	ABEELSSSU SUBLEASES	ABEGIKMNR EMBARKING
ABEEILNRT ALBERTINE	ABEELSSTT SEAT BELTS	ABEGILLLN LABELLING
ABEEILNSS BASELINES	ABEEMMNRS MEMBRANES	ABEGILMMN EMBALMING
ABEEILNTW TABLE WINE	ABEEMMNTY EMBAYMENT	ABEGIMNNO BEMOANING
ABEEILQTU EQUITABLE	ABEEMNSST BASEMENTS	ABEGIMRRS AMBERGRIS
ABEEILRRW REWIRABLE	ABEEMORRT BAROMETER	ABEGINNNT BENIGNANT
ABEEILRST BEASTLIER, BLEARIEST	ABEEMRRSU EMBRASURE	ABEGINNOW WINNEBAGO
ABEEILRSV REVISABLE, VERBALISE	ABEEMRSTU A BUM STEER	ABEGINNRT BANTERING
ABEEILRTT ALBERTITE, BEAR TITLE	ABEENQTTU BANQUETTE	ABEGINNRZ BRAZENING
ABEEILRTV AVERTIBLE, VERITABLE	ABEENRSSV BRAVENESS	ABEGINNST ABSENTING
	ABEENRTUX EXUBERANT	ABEGINNTT BATTENING
	ABEEOPRRT PERBORATE, REPROBATE	ABEGINRRT BARTERING
ABEEILRVV REVIVABLE	ABEEOPRSW POWER BASE	ABEGINRTT BATTERING
ABEEILRVZ VERBALIZE	ABEEOSTUU BEAUTEOUS	ABEGINRTY BETRAYING
ABEEIMSSS EMBASSIES	ABEEPRSTT BESPATTER	ABEGJORTU OBJURGATE
ABEEIPSTT A BIT STEEP	ABEERRSST BARRETTES	ABEGJSTUU SUBJUGATE
	ABEERRSTY BETRAYERS	ABEGKRSTU GRUBSTAKE
	ABEFFILNY INEFFABLY	ABEGLNORU LOUNGE BAR
	ABEFFLOSU BUFFALOES	ABEGLRSSU BLUEGRASS
		ABEGMNOOR BOOMERANG

ABEGMNOSY	MONEYBAGS	ABEILLRTX	BELLATRIX	ABEIRSSST	BRASSIEST
ABEGORSTU	SUBROGATE	ABEILLSTY	BESTIALLY	ABEIRSSTY	SYBARITES
ABEHHHIPZ	HEPHZIBAH	ABEILMMOV	IMMOVABLE	ABEIRTTTU	ATTRIBUTE
ABEHIINNR	HIBERNIAN	ABEILMMSW	SWIMMABLE	ABEJLNOYY	ENJOYABLY
ABEHIIITTW	WHITEBAIT	ABEILMMTU	IMMUTABLE	ABEJMOORS	JEROBOAMS
ABEHIKLNT	THINKABLE	ABEILMNSS	BALMINESS	ABEKKMOOR	BOOKMAKER
ABEHILMOP	AMPHIBOLE	ABEILMOPS	IMPOSABLE	ABEKLNNSS	BLANKNESS
ABEHILORS	ABOLISHER	ABEILMORT	BALTIMORE	ABEKLOOPT	BOOKPLATE
ABEHILRST	HERBALIST	ABEILMOSX	MAILBOXES	ABEKLORTW	WORKTABLE
ABEHILRSY	BEARISHLY	ABEILMPTU	IMPUTABLE	ABEKLORVY	REVOKABLY
ABEHILRTY	BREATHILY,	ABEILMRSV	VERBALISM	ABEKNNOST	BANK NOTES
HERITABLY		ABEILMRSY	MISERABLY	ABEKOORSY	YEARBOOKS
ABEHILSST	ESTABLISH	ABEILMSTU	SUBLIMATE	ABEKORSTU	OUTBREAKS
ABEHIMMSS	MEMSAHIBS	ABEILNPRT	PRINTABLE	ABELLLSSY	SYLLABLES
ABEHIMNOS	BOHEMIANS	ABEILNPST	PINTABLES	ABELLMRSU	UMBRELLAS
ABEHIMRRU	HERBARIUM	ABEILNPSU	SUBALPINE	ABELLORTY	TOLERABLY
ABEHIOPRU	EUPHORBIA	ABEILNRSS	BRAINLESS	ABELLORUY	ROYAL BLUE
ABEHIORUV	BEHAVIOUR	ABEILNRSU	INSURABLE	ABELLOSWY	BOYLE'S LAW
ABEHIRRTT	BIRTHRATE	ABEILORRT	LIBERATOR	ABELMMNRU	LUMBERMAN
ABEHLMPSY	BLASPHEMY	ABEILORTT	TRILOBATE	ABELMMORY	MEMORABLY
ABEHLNNSU	SHUNNABLE	ABEILORTU	LABOURITE	ABELMNOTU	MOUNTABLE
ABEHLOPRY	HYPERBOLA	ABEILQTUY	EQUITABLY	ABELMNPRU	PENUMBRAL
ABEHLORTT	BETROTHAL	ABEILRRST	STIRRABLE	ABELMNRUY	NUMERABLY
ABEHNORRT	ABHORRENT	ABEILRRYZ	BIZARRELY	ABELMNSTU	SUBMENTAL
ABEHNRRTU	HEARTBURN	ABEILRSTU	BRUTALISE	ABELMORVY	REMOVABLY
ABEHNRSSS	BRASHNESS	ABEILRSTV	VERBALIST	ABELNNORV	NONVERBAL
ABEHNRSTU	SUNBATHER	ABEILRTUZ	BRUTALIZE	ABELNOOTW	AT ONE BLOW
ABEHOOSTU	BOATHOUSE,	ABEILRTVY	VERITABLY	ABELNOSTT	ENTOBLAST
HOUSEBOAT		ABEILRVVY	REVIVABLY	ABELNOSYZ	LAZYBONES
ABEHORRRU	HARBOURER	ABEILSSUX	BISEXUALS	ABELNRSTU	SUBALTERN
ABEHQRSUU	HARQUEBUS	ABEILSTTW	TWISTABLE	ABELNRTTU	TURNTABLE
ABEIIILST	ABILITIES	ABEILSUVY	ABUSIVELY	ABELOOPPS	OPPOSABLE
ABEIILLLR	ILLIBERAL	ABEIMNORS	AMBROSINE	ABELOPPST	STOPPABLE
ABEIILLMT	LIMITABLE	ABEIMNORT	BROMINATE	ABELOPSTT	SPOTTABLE
ABEIILNRZ	BRAZILEIN	ABEIMNRST	TRIBESMAN	ABELORRSU	LABOURERS
ABEIILRRS	LIBRARIES	ABEIMNRSU	SUBMARINE	ABELORTTX	RATTLEBOX
ABEIILRRT	IRRITABLE	ABEIMNSTU	SEMI-BANTU	ABELOSTTY	STYLOBATE
ABEIILRTV	VIBRATILE	ABEINNRST	BANNISTER	ABELPRTUY	REPUTABLY
ABEIILSST	STABILISE	ABEINNSTT	ABSTINENT	ABELRSTTU	REBUTTALS,
ABEIILSTV	VISITABLE	ABEINNTYZ	BYZANTINE	TRUSTABLE	
ABEIILSTZ	STABILIZE	ABEINORST	BARITONES	ABEMMNOOS	MOONBEAMS
ABEIINNPT	BIPINNATE	ABEINOSTT	OBSTINATE	ABEMNPRSU	PENUMBRAS
ABEIINNRT	INEBRIANT	ABEINRSST	BANISTERS	ABEMNSTTU	ABUTMENTS
ABEIINRST	BRAINIEST	ABEINRSTW	BRAWNIEST	ABEMOOPRR	BROOMRAPE
ABEIIPRTT	BIPARTITE	ABEINRTTU	TRIBUNATE,	ABEMOPRTY	AMBROTYPE
ABEIIRTVV	VIBRATIVE	TURBINATE		ABEMORRTU	ARBORETUM
ABEIJLNRU	INJURABLE	ABEINSSST	BASSINETS	ABENNSTTU	SUBTENANT
ABEIKLNTT	KNITTABLE	ABEINSSTT	BATTINESS	ABENOPSSU	SUBPOENAS
ABEIKNORW	WAKE-ROBIN	ABEIOORSV	BERIOSOVA	ABENORSTV	OBSERVANT
ABEIKNRSS	BEARSKINS	ABEIOPRTV	PROBATIVE	ABEOOPRTW	POWERBOAT
ABEILLLNT	LIBELLANT	ABEIPRRSS	SPARERIBS	ABEOOPSSX	SOAPBOXES
ABEILLLRY	LIBERALLY	ABEIRRRST	BARRISTER	ABEOORRSU	ARBOREOUS
ABEILLLSU	LULLABIES,	ABEIRRSST	ARBITRESS	ABEOPPRSY	PAPERBOYS
SULLIABLE		ABEIRRSSU	BURSARIES	ABEOPRRSY	SOAPBERRY
ABEILLPSU	PLAUSIBLE				

ABEORSSTU	SABOTEURS	ABHILMSTU	BISMUTHAL	ABILOPRRT	PORT BLAIR
ABEPRRRSY	RASPBERRY	ABHILNOOT	HALOBIONT	ABILORRTY	LIBRATORY
ABEPRSSSY	PASSERSBY	ABHILNRSU	NAILBRUSH	ABILORSTU	LABOURIST
ABERSSTTU	SUBSTRATE	ABHILNRTY	LABYRINTH	ABILRSSUY	SALISBURY
ABERTTTUW	WATER BUTT	ABHIOOOPZ	ZOOPHOBIA	ABILRTTUY	BRUTALITY
ABFGLLLOS	GOLF BALLS	ABHKOOOST	BOAT HOOKS	ABIMMNRUU	MANUBRIUM
ABFHLLSUY	BASHFULLY	ABHLLMOST	MOTHBALLS	ABIMNTUYZ	BYZANTIUM
ABFIILOTT	BIT OF TAIL	ABHLLMSTU	ALL THUMBS	ABIMORSSU	AMBROSIUS
ABFIIORSU	BIFARIOUS	ABHLPRSUY	SUBPHYLAR	ABINNOTVV	BON VIVANT
ABFILLSYY	SYLLABIFY	ABHMNRTUY	URBAN MYTH	ABINOOPRT	PROBATION
ABFILMSUY	SUBFAMILY	ABHMOORST	BATHROOMS	ABINOORST	ABORTIONS
ABFIRSTTU	FRUIT BATS	ABIIILLTY	LIABILITY	ABINOSSTT	BOTANISTS
ABFLLOOST	FOOTBALLS	ABIIILNTY	INABILITY	ABINRRTUY	TRIBUNARY
ABGGIKNPY	PIGGYBANK	ABIIILTVY	VIABILITY	ABIOORRRT	BRIARROOT
ABGGILMNO	GAMBOLING	ABIIJMMUY	MBUJIMAYI	ABIORRSTV	VIBRATORS
ABGGLOORY	GARBOLOGY	ABIIKLSSS	BASILISKS	ABIRRTTUY	TRIBUTARY
ABGGNOOST	TOBOGGANS	ABIILLMRS	MILLIBARS	ABKKMOORS	BOOKMARKS
ABGHHILLS	HIGHBALLS	ABIILLNOT	BALLOTINI	ABKLLNORS	BANKROLLS
ABGHIINNS	BANISHING	ABIILLNRT	BRILLIANT	ABKLLOOST	BOOKSTALL
ABGHILMNS	SHAMBLING	ABIILMNOS	BINOMIALS	ABKNPRSTU	BANKRUPTS
ABGHIMNSU	AMBUSHING	ABIILMRST	TRIBALISM	ABKOOPSSS	PASSBOOKS
ABGHINORR	ABHORRING	ABIILNOOT	ABOLITION	ABLLMOORS	BALLROOMS
ABGHINWZZ	WHIZZ-BANG	ABIILNORT	LIBRATION	ABLLMOPSW	BLOWLAMPS
ABGHIOPRY	BIOGRAPHY	ABIILNORY	NOBILIARY	ABLLNOSSW	SNOWBALLS
ABGHMORSU	BROUGHAMS	ABIILNOST	LIBATIONS	ABLMNORSU	SUBNORMAL
ABGIILLNU	BILINGUAL	ABIILNSST	SIBILANTS	ABLMNRSUU	LABURNUMS
ABGIIMSST	BIGAMISTS	ABIILRRTY	IRRITABLY	ABLNOTUYY	BUOYANTLY
ABGIIMTUY	AMBIGUITY	ABIILRSSV	VIBRISSAL	ABLNRSUUY	SUBLUNARY
ABGIINNOT	OBTAINING	ABIILRSTT	TRIBALIST	ABLOOPPSY	OPPOSABLY
ABGIINOTV	OBVIATING	ABIILSTTY	STABILITY	ABLORTTUU	TUBULATOR
ABGIINPTZ	BAPTIZING	ABIILSTUY	SUABILITY,	ABLOSSTTU	SUBTOTALS
ABGIINRTV	VIBRATING	USABILITY		ABMNORRST	BARNSTORM
ABGILLMOS	GLOBALISM	ABIIMNOST	AMBITIONS	ABMOOOOTW	TOOWOOMBA
ABGILLNOT	BALLOTING	ABIIMORSS	ISOBARISM	ABMOOORTT	MOTORBOAT
ABGILLOST	GLOBALIST	ABIIMOSTU	AMBITIOUS	ABNNSTUUY	BUNYA NUTS
ABGILLOTY	BILLY GOAT	ABIINOOTV	OBVIATION	ABNORSTUU	RUN-ABOUTS
ABGILNNOZ	BLAZONING	ABIINORTV	VIBRATION	ABNORTTUU	ABOUT-TURN,
ABGILNORU	LABOURING	ABIKLMNSS	LAMBSKINS	TURNABOUT	
ABGILNOSV	ABSOLVING	ABIKLOSTY	BIALYSTOK	ABOOPRSTT	BOOTSTRAP
ABGILNOSX	SIGNAL BOX	ABILLMSSY	SYLLABISM	ABRRSSTTU	STARBURST
ABGILOORT	OBLIGATOR	ABILLNOPT	BALLPOINT	ACCCCEHIT	CACHECTIC
ABGIMOSUU	AMBIGUOUS	ABILLOPRX	PILLAR BOX	ACCCDEEEN	ACCEDENCE
ABGINNNRU	UNBARRING	ABILLORRZ	RAZORBILL	ACCCDEEIN	ACCIDENCE
ABGINOPRT	PROBATING	ABILLPSUY	PLAUSIBLY	ACCCDIIMU	MUCIC ACID
ABGINPSSY	BYPASSING	ABILMMOVY	IMMOVABLY	ACCCEEENS	ACESCENCE
ABGLMNOOS	BOOMSLANG	ABILMMTUY	IMMUTABLY	ACCCEGLOY	COCCYGEAL
ABGLNOOST	LONGBOATS	ABILMOORS	RIBOSOMAL	ACCCEHIOT	CACOETHIC
ABGLNOSUW	BUNGALOWS	ABILMORSU	LABOURISM	ACCCEIIRT	CICATRICE
ABHHIRUVI	BAHUVRIHI	ABILMSTTU	SUBMITTAL	ACCCEILLO	CALCICOLE
ABHHILOTT	BATHOLITH	ABILNOOST	OBLATIONS	ACCCHKOOR	COCKROACH
ABHHIRRSU	HAIRBRUSH	ABILNOSTU	ABLUTIONS	ACCCHOPRT	CATCH CROP
ABHIKLLSW	HAWKSBILL	ABILNRSTU	TRIBUNALS	ACCCIILLY	ALICYCLIC
ABHIKMRRT	BIRTHMARK	ABILNRTVY	VIBRANTLY	ACCCIILMT	CLIMACTIC
ABHILMNTU	THUMBNAIL	ABILOORSU	LABORIOUS	ACCCIIOPR	CAPRICCIO

ACCCNOPUY	OCCUPANCY
ACCDDEEEN	DECADENCE
ACCDDEILS	DISCALCED
ACCDDIIST	DIDACTICS
ACCDDIORS	DISACCORD
ACCDEEHIK	CHICKADEE
ACCDEEIST	DESICCATE
ACCDEELLN	CANCELLED
ACCDEELNO	CONCEALED
ACCDEELOS	COALESCED
ACCDEFIIL	CALCIFIED
ACCDEFILS	FASCICLED
ACCDEFILY	DECALCIFY
ACCDEHIKR	DECKCHAIR
ACCDEHKOT	COCKED HAT
ACCDEHRST	SCRATCHED
ACCDEIILN	ICELANDIC
ACCDEIILT	DIALECTIC
ACCDEINOT	ANECDOTIC
ACCDEINST	ACCIDENTS,
	DESICCANT
ACCDEIORW	COWARDICE
ACCDEKOSS	CASSOCKED
ACCDELMOR	COLD CREAM
ACCDELSSU	CUL-DE-SACS
ACCDEMNOO	CACODEMON
ACCDEMOPT	COMPACTED
ACCDEMORY	DEMOCRACY
ACCDENOTT	CONTACTED
ACCDENOTU	ACCOUNTED
ACCDENPSU	DUNCE'S CAP
ACCDEORRS	SCORECARD
ACCDEORSW	SACRED COW
ACCDFILLY	FLACCIDLY
ACCDGINOR	ACCORDING
ACCDHHRUY	ARCHDUCHY
ACCDHINOR	CHANCROID
ACCDHNPRU	CARD PUNCH
ACCDHORTW	CATCHWORD
ACCDHPSTU	DUTCH CAPS
ACCDIIINT	DIACTINIC
ACCDIIIRT	DIACRITIC
ACCDIIOPT	APODICTIC
ACCDILLOY	CYCLOIDAL
ACCDILSTY	DACTYLICS
ACCDINOOR	ACCORDION
ACCDKNORW	CRACKDOWN
ACCDNOORT	CONCORDAT
ACCDORRTU	COURT CARD
ACCEEGLMY	MEGACYCLE
ACCEEHHIN	CHECHENIA
ACCEEHILR	CHELICERA
ACCEEHIST	CATECHISE
ACCEEHITY	HAECCEITY

ACCEEHITZ	CATECHIZE
ACCEEHKMN	NAMECHECK
ACCEEHKMT	CHECKMATE
ACCEEHLOT	COCHLEATE
ACCEEHNPR	PERCHANCE
ACCEEHOST	CACOETHES
ACCEEIMRS	ICE CREAMS
ACCEEIPRS	PECCARIES
ACCEEIQSU	ACQUIESCE
ACCEEIRTV	ACCRETIVE
ACCEEISTX	EXSICCATE
ACCEEKLNS	NECKLACES
ACCEELLNR	CANCELLER
ACCEELNPR	PRECANCEL
ACCEELPST	SPECTACLE
ACCEENNST	CANESCENT
ACCEEORSU	CERACEOUS
ACCEFGILU	CALCIFUGE
ACCEFHLOT	FACECLOTH
ACCEFIIRS	SACRIFICE
ACCEFILSU	FASCICULE
ACCEFNORS	FRANCESCO
ACCEGHLNO	CHALCOGEN
ACCEGILNN	CANCELING
ACCEGINNT	ACCENTING
ACCEGINOR	ACROGENIC
ACCEGINPT	ACCEPTING
ACCEGINSS	ACCESSING
ACCEGIOTT	GEOTACTIC
ACCEGKMOS	GAMECOCKS
ACCEHHIRT	THEARCHIC
ACCEHIKNR	RAIN CHECK
ACCEHIKPS	CHICKPEAS
ACCEHILLO	ECHOLALIC
ACCEHILMS	CHEMICALS
ACCEHILNO	COCHINEAL
ACCEHILNT	TECHNICAL
ACCEHILOT	CHICALOTE
ACCEHIMNS	MECHANICS,
	MISCHANCE
ACCEHIMST	CATECHISM,
	SCHEMATIC
ACCEHINRY	CHICANERY
ACCEHINST	CHANCIEST
ACCEHIRTT	ARCHITECT
ACCEHISTT	CATCHIEST,
	CATECHIST
ACCEHKPSY	PAYCHECKS
ACCEHLOOT	CHOCOLATE
ACCEHMNTT	CATCHMENT
ACCEHORTU	CARTOUCHE
ACCEHORTY	THEOCRACY
ACCEHRRST	SCRATCHER
ACCEHRSST	SCRATCHES
ACCEIILMN	CALCIMINE

ACCEIIMNT	CINEMATIC
ACCEIINOS	COCAINISE
ACCEIINOZ	COCAINIZE
ACCEIINRT	CIRCINATE
ACCEIIPRT	ACCIPITER
ACCEIIRST	CICATRISE
ACCEIIRTZ	CICATRIZE
ACCEIISTV	SICCATIVE
ACCEIKLOT	COCKATIEL
ACCEIKRSW	WISECRACK
ACCEILLSV	CLAVICLES
ACCEILMPT	ECLAMPTIC
ACCEILNST	CANTICLES
ACCEILNTU	INCULCATE
ACCEILOPR	PRECOCIAL
ACCEILPST	SCEPTICAL
ACCEILRTU	CIRCULATE
ACCEIMOSU	MICACEOUS
ACCEINORT	ACCRETION
ACCEINOSS	ACCESSION
ACCEINSTU	ENCAUSTIC,
	SUCCINATE
ACCEIORTT	CORTICATE
ACCEIPRST	PRACTICES
ACCEISSTT	ECSTATICS
ACCEKKORS	ROCK CAKES
ACCEKMNRS	CRACKSMEN
ACCEKNORR	CORNCRAKE
ACCELLLOS	CLOSE CALL
ACCELLOOT	COLLOCATE
ACCELLTUU	CUCULLATE
ACCELNOSV	CONCLAVES
ACCELNOVY	COVALENCY
ACCEMNRTU	ACCRUMENT
ACCEMNRTY	MCCARTNEY
ACCEMOPRT	COMPACTER
ACCEMORTY	MACROCYTE
ACCEMPRSU	CREAMCUPS
ACCENNOST	CONSTANCE
ACCENNOTY	COTENANCY
ACCENOORS	COENOSARC
ACCENORSU	CANCEROUS
ACCENRSUY	RECUSANCY
ACCEORRSW	SCARECROW
ACCEORSSY	ACCESSORY
ACCEORSTU	CORUSCATE
ACCFFHHIN	CHAFFINCH
ACCFIILOR	CALORIFIC
ACCFIISST	FASCISTIC
ACCFINNOU	CONFUCIAN
ACCFINORS	FRANCISCO
ACCFKOORT	FROCK COAT
ACCGHHNNU	CHANGCHUN
ACCGHHNOW	CHANGCHOW

ACCGHINRY	GYNARCHIC	ACCINOPRR	CAPRICORN	ACDDEKOST	STOCKADED
ACCGIKLNR	CRACKLING	ACCINORST	NARCOTICS	ACDDELNOO	CANOODLED
ACCGINOST	ACCOSTING	ACCINOSTY	OSCITANCY	ACDDEMMNO	COMMANDED
ACCHHMNRU	CHURCHMAN	ACCINOTVY	CONCAVITY	ACDDHHNSU	DACHSHUND
ACCHIILRV	CHIVALRIC	ACCINSTTY	SYNTACTIC	ACDDIILOS	DISCOIDAL
ACCHILLOO	ALCOHOLIC	ACCIOPRTT	CATOPTRIC	ACDDIINOT	ADDICTION
ACCHILLOT	LACCOLITH	ACCIORSST	ACROSTICS	ACDDINOTU	ADDUCTION
ACCHILORT	HOLARCTIC	ACCIOSSTU	ACOUSTICS	ACDDKORSY	DOCKYARDS
ACCHILOST	CATHOLICS	ACCKKRSSU	RUCKSACKS	ACDDLNORW	COLD-DRAWN
ACCHILPSY	PSYCHICAL	ACCKOOOST	COCKATOOS	ACDEEEHIP	HEADPIECE
ACCHIMOPR	CAMPHORIC	ACCKOPRST	CRACKPOTS	ACDEEEHNP	CHEAPENED
ACCHIMORT	CHROMATIC	ACCKORSST	STOCKCARS	ACDEEEHNR	ADHERENCE
ACCHIMOST	STOMACHIC	ACCLLOSUU	CALCULOUS	ACDEEELRY	CLEAR-EYED
ACCHIRTTY	TRACHYTIC	ACCLMOPTY	COMPACTLY	ACDEEEPRT	DEPRECATE
ACCHKLOST	SACKCLOTH	ACCMMOORS	MACROCOSM	ACDEEEPRV	CAPE VERDE
ACCHKOOOP	COCK-A-HOOP	ACCMNOORY	MONOCRACY,	ACDEEERRT	RECREATED
ACCHKOORW	COACHWORK		NOMOCRACY	ACDEEERSS	DECREASES
ACCHLOORT	COLCOTHAR,	ACCMNOTUY	CONTUMACY	ACDEEERST	DESECRATE
	OCHLOCRAT	ACCMORSTY	MACROCYST	ACDEEERTU	RE-EDUCATE
ACCHLOOSW	SLOWCOACH	ACCNNOOTU	NO-ACCOUNT	ACDEEERTX	EXECRATED
ACCHLOOTY	CHOCOLATY	ACCNNOSTY	CONSTANCY	ACDEEFIRR	FREDERICA
ACCHNOOPY	CACOPHONY	ACCNOORTT	CONTACTOR	ACDEEFKRT	AFTERDECK
ACCHNORSU	CHANCROUS	ACCNOPSTU	OCCUPANTS	ACDEEFNOP	OPEN-FACED
ACCHOPRSS	CASH CROPS	ACCNORSTT	CONTRACTS	ACDEEFNTU	FECUNDATE
ACCIIILNN	CLINICIAN	ACCOPRSTY	CYSTOCARP	ACDEEFORT	DEFECATOR
ACCIILLVY	CIVICALLY	ACCORRSTY	CARRYCOTS	ACDEEFRRT	REFRACTED
ACCIILNOR	CONCILIAR	ACDDDEEIT	DEDICATED	ACDEEGHNX	EXCHANGED
ACCIILOPT	OCCIPITAL	ACDDDEIRS	DISCARDED	ACDEEGHRR	RECHARGED
ACCIILRTU	CIRCUITAL	ACDDDEKSU	DEAD DUCKS	ACDEEGLNO	CONGEALED
ACCIILTVY	ACCLIVITY	ACDDEEEFT	DEFECATED	ACDEEGLOU	DECALOGUE
ACCIIMNOS	COCAINISM	ACDDEEEIT	DEDICATEE	ACDEEGNSV	SCAVENGED
ACCIINRTY	INTRICACY	ACDDEEERS	DECREASED	ACDEEGOPU	DECOUPAGE
ACCIIORST	ISOCRATIC	ACDDEEILM	DECLAIMED	ACDEEHIMP	IMPEACHED
ACCIIOSTT	ISOTACTIC	ACDDEEIMT	DECIMATED,	ACDEEHINN	ENCHAINED
ACCIISSTU	CASUISTIC		MEDICATED	ACDEEHIRS	CASHIERED
ACCIKKNNS	NICKNACKS	ACDDEEORT	DECORATED	ACDEEHKNY	HACKNEYED
ACCIKLOST	COCKTAILS	ACDDEERTT	DETRACTED	ACDEEHLLN	CHANDELLE
ACCILLMOY	COMICALLY	ACDDEFIII	ACIDIFIED	ACDEEHLNN	CHANNELED
ACCILLNOY	CONICALLY	ACDDEGIRS	DISGRACED	ACDEEHLPT	CHAPLETED
ACCILLNYY	CYNICALLY	ACDDEGNOO	DODECAGON	ACDEEHNNT	ENCHANTED
ACCILLRUY	CRUCIALLY	ACDDEHIRR	HARD CIDER	ACDEEHNST	CHASTENED
ACCILNORV	CLAVICORN	ACDDEHKNS	DECKHANDS	ACDEEHPSY	SPEECH DAY
ACCILNOTU	NOCTILUCA	ACDDEHNRU	DUDE RANCH	ACDEEHRRT	CHARTERED
ACCILRRSU	CIRCULARS	ACDDEIINT	INDICATED	ACDEEHRTT	CHATTERED
ACCILRRUU	CURRICULA	ACDDEIITV	ADDICTIVE	ACDEEIJTV	ADJECTIVE
ACCILRTUU	CUTICULAR	ACDDEIJNU	JAUNDICED	ACDEEIKST	ICE-SKATED
ACCIMNORY	ACRONYMIC	ACDDEILPS	DISPLACED	ACDEEILMR	DECLAIMER,
ACCIMNOSS	MOCCASINS	ACDDEINRS	RIDDANCES		RECLAIMED
ACCIMNOSY	SCIOMANCY	ACDDEINRX	CARD INDEX	ACDEEILMX	EXCLAIMED
ACCIMORSY	COSMIC RAY	ACDDEINST	DISTANCED	ACDEEILNN	CELANDINE,
ACCIMORTY	TIMOCRACY	ACDDEIORT	DEDICATOR		DECENNIAL
ACCIMPSSU	CAPSICUMS	ACDDEIPRY	RICE PADDY	ACDEEILNR	ICELANDER
ACCINNOTT	IN CONTACT	ACDDEIRRS	DISCARDER	ACDEEILNT	DECLINATE
ACCINOOSS	OCCASIONS	ACDDEKLOP	PADLOCKED	ACDEEILNU	EUCLIDEAN
		ACDDEKLOS	DEADLOCKS	ACDEEILTU	ELUCIDATE

ACDEEILTY	ACETYLIDE	ACDEFILLO	COALFIELD	ACDEHNSTU	STAUNCHED,
ACDEEIMNO	MACEDOINE	ACDEFINRT	INFARCTED		UNSCATHED
ACDEEIMNP	IMPEDANCE	ACDEFKLNO	FOLK DANCE	ACDEHNTUW	UNWATCHED
ACDEEINRS	INCREASED	ACDEFLMOR	COLD FRAME	ACDEHOOPT	CHAETOPOD
ACDEEINSU	AUDIENCES	ACDEFLNOT	CONFLATED	ACDEHORRS	HARD CORES
ACDEEIOPR	ADIPOCERE	ACDEFMNOO	MOON-FACED	ACDEHORRV	HARDCOVER
ACDEEIPRT	PREDICATE	ACDEFRRTU	FRACTURED	ACDEHORSS	CROSSHEAD
ACDEEITUV	EDUCATIVE	ACDEGGIMO	DEMAGOGIC	ACDEHOSTT	COT DEATHS
ACDEEKKNR	KNACKERED	ACDEGGIOP	PEDAGOGIC	ACDEHPRSU	PURCHASED
ACDEEKLNS	SLACKENED	ACDEGHINR	CHAGRINED	ACDEIIINT	DIETICIAN
ACDEEKPPR	PREPACKED	ACDEGHINT	DETACHING	ACDEIILMN	ADMINICLE,
ACDEEKPST	TAPE DECKS	ACDEGHIRS	DISCHARGE		MEDICINAL
ACDEELLNV	CLEVELAND	ACDEGHNRU	UNCHARGED	ACDEIILNT	IDENTICAL
ACDEELLOT	DECOLLATE,	ACDEGIILR	REGICIDAL	ACDEIILNX	INDEXICAL
	OCELLATED	ACDEGILNO	GENOCIDAL	ACDEIILRV	LARVICIDE,
ACDEELLPR	PARCELLED	ACDEGILNR	DECLARING		VERIDICAL
ACDEELLTW	WELL-ACTED	ACDEGILNS	DESCALING	ACDEIIMMY	IMMEDIACY
ACDEELNRS	CALENDERS	ACDEGILOO	LOGAOEDIC	ACDEIIMNR	AMERINDIC
ACDEELORT	RELOCATED	ACDEGIMNP	DECAMPING	ACDEIIMRT	DIAMETRIC,
ACDEELPTU	PECULATED	ACDEGINNS	ASCENDING		MATRICIDE
ACDEELQRU	LACQUERED	ACDEGINNT	DECANTING	ACDEIINOT	DIANOETIC
ACDEELRTT	CLATTERED	ACDEGINOY	GYNAECOID	ACDEIINTV	VINDICATE
ACDEELRTU	ULCERATED	ACDEGINTU	EDUCATING	ACDEIIOPR	APERIODIC
ACDEELSTY	DECASTYLE	ACDEGIOTT	COGITATED	ACDEIIPRR	PARRICIDE
ACDEELTTU	CLAUDETTE	ACDEGIRRS	DISGRACER	ACDEIIPRT	PATRICIDE
ACDEEMPRS	SCAMPERED	ACDEGIRRT	CARTRIDGE	ACDEIKMNN	NICKNAMED
ACDEENNRT	ENTRANCED	ACDEGLNOU	LANGUEDOC	ACDEIKRST	SIDETRACK
ACDEENNRU	ENDURANCE	ACDEGNNOU	UNDECAGON	ACDEILLMS	MISCALLED
ACDEENORS	COARSENED	ACDEHHIKT	THICKHEAD	ACDEILLMY	DECIMALLY,
ACDEENOSS	DEACONESS	ACDEHHORX	HEXACHORD		MEDICALLY
ACDEENOST	ANECDOTES	ACDEHIITT	DIATHETIC	ACDEILLOS	LOCALISED
ACDEENRST	DECANTERS,	ACDEHINNR	HINDRANCE	ACDEILLOZ	LOCALIZED
	DESCANTER	ACDEHINSV	CAVENDISH	ACDEILMPS	MISPLACED
ACDEENRTU	UNCREATED	ACDEHIOPX	HEXAPODIC	ACDEILNVY	DIVALENCY
ACDEEOPRR	CROP-EARED	ACDEHIPRS	SEPHARDIC	ACDEILOPT	PETALODIC
ACDEEORTV	OVERACTED	ACDEHIPRT	DIRT CHEAP	ACDEILOST	DISLOCATE
ACDEEPRRS	SCARPERED	ACDEHIRSV	CRASH-DIVE	ACDEILPRS	DISPLACER
ACDEEPRRT	RED CARPET	ACDEHISST	CHASTISED	ACDEILPRU	PEDICULAR
ACDEEPSTT	SPECTATED	ACDEHKMPU	CHEMPADUK	ACDEILPTU	DUPLICATE
ACDEERRTT	RETRACTED	ACDEHKOST	HEADSTOCK	ACDEILRTU	CURTAILED
ACDEERSTT	SCATTERED	ACDEHKPST	SKETCHPAD	ACDEILTUV	VICTUALED
ACDEERSTU	REDUCTASE	ACDEHKRSU	ARCHDUKES	ACDEIMNNO	DOMINANCE
ACDEERTTX	EXTRACTED	ACDEHKSSS	CASH DESKS	ACDEIMNNT	MENDICANT
ACDEESSTU	DECUSSATE	ACDEHLNOR	CHLORDANE	ACDEIMNOP	COMPENDIA
ACDEFFILR	RADCLIFFE	ACDEHLNOT	DECATHLON	ACDEIMNOS	COMEDIANS
ACDEFFILT	AFFLICTED	ACDEHLNRS	CHANDLERS	ACDEIMNPS	PANDEMICS
ACDEFFIST	DISAFFECT	ACDEHLNRY	CHANDLERY	ACDEIMNRU	MANICURED
ACDEFFLLU	FULL-FACED	ACDEHLRSU	SCHEDULAR	ACDEIMNSU	MUSCADINE
ACDEFFMOR	COFFERDAM	ACDEHMNTU	UNMATCHED	ACDEIMNTY	MENDACITY
ACDEFHINR	ARCHFIEND	ACDEHMOST	STOMACHED	ACDEIMORT	DECIMATOR
ACDEFIIIL	EDIFICIAL	ACDEHMPRY	PACHYDERM	ACDEINNOR	ORDINANCE
ACDEFIILR	ACIDIFIER	ACDEHNRTU	UNCHARTED	ACDEINNOS	CANONISED
ACDEFIILR	CLARIFIED	ACDEHNRUY	HUE AND CRY	ACDEINNOT	CONTAINED
ACDEFIILT	FETICIDAL			ACDEINNOZ	CANONIZED
ACDEFIIRS	SCARIFIED				

ACDEINNST	INSTANCED
ACDEINORR	CORIANDER
ACDEINORS	DINOCERAS
ACDEINORT	REDACTION
ACDEINOTU	AUCTIONED,
CAUTIONED, EDUCATION	
ACDEINOTV	ADVECTION
ACDEINPRT	PREDICANT
ACDEINRTU	CURTAINED
ACDEINSST	DISTANCES
ACDEINSTY	ASYNDETIC,
SYNDICATE	
ACDEIPRST	PRACTISED
ACDEIPSTU	CUSPIDATE
ACDEIQTTU	ACQUITTED
ACDEIRTTX	DIRECT TAX
ACDEISSTT	ACID TESTS
ACDEJKKSY	SKYJACKED
ACDEKLMSU	LAME DUCKS
ACDEKOPTU	PACKED-OUT
ACDEKOSST	STOCKADES
ACDELLOPS	COLLAPSED,
SCALLOPED	
ACDELLORR	CORRALLED
ACDELMOPR	PLACODERM
ACDELMORU	CLAMOURED
ACDELMORY	COMRADELY
ACDELNNOO	COLONNADE
ACDELNNOR	CLARENDON
ACDELNNTU	CANDLENUT
ACDELNNUU	UNDULANCE
ACDELNOOW	LANCEWOOD
ACDELNORS	COLANDERS
ACDELNRUY	UNDERCLAY
ACDELOPTU	COPULATED,
CUPOLATED	
ACDELOSTW	COLD SWEAT
ACDEMMMNO	COMMENDAM
ACDEMMNOR	COMMANDER
ACDEMNOPR	COMPANDER
ACDEMOORR	ACRODROME
ACDEMOORT	MOTORCADE
ACDEMORST	DEMOCRATS
ACDENNNOU	ANNOUNCED
ACDENNRST	TRANSCEND
ACDENOOTT	COTTONADE
ACDENORST	DONCASTER
ACDENORSY	SECONDARY
ACDENORTU	UNDERCOAT
ACDENRTTU	TRUNCATED
ACDEOORRT	DECORATOR
ACDEOORTT	DOCTORATE
ACDEOPSTU	SPACED OUT
ACDEOPTTU	COUP D'ETAT
ACDEOORRST	CO-STARRED

ACDEORRTT	DETRACTOR
ACDEORSTU	CERATODUS,
EDUCATORS	
ACDEORSUU	RUDACEOUS
ACDEORTUY	EDUCATORY
ACDEORTUZ	COTE D'AZUR
ACDEQSTUU	AQUEDUCTS
ACDERRSSU	CRUSADERS
ACDERRSTU	TRADUCERS
ACDERSSTT	TEST CARDS
ACDESSTUY	CASE STUDY
ACDFFHNSU	HANDCUFFS
ACDFFLOSS	SCAFFOLDS
ACDFGOOST	ACTS OF GOD
ACDFHILSS	SCALDFISH
ACDFIIILL	FILICIDAL
ACDFIIRUY	FIDUCIARY
ACDFINNOT	CONFIDANT
ACDFNTTUY	CANDYTUFT
ACDFOORTW	WOODCRAFT
ACDGHIIPR	DIGRAPHIC
ACDGHIMOY	DICHOGAMY
ACDGHIPSY	DYSPHAGIC
ACDGHOSTW	WATCHDOGS
ACDGIILNO	GADOLINIC
ACDGIINNR	DINING CAR
ACDGIINTT	DICTATING
ACDGIIRST	DIGASTRIC
ACDGIMOST	DOGMATICS
ACDGINRSU	CRUSADING
ACDGINRTU	TRADUCING
ACDGLLOOR	DOG COLLAR
ACDHIILMO	HOMICIDAL
ACDHIILOP	ACIDOPHIL
ACDHIILST	DISTICHAL
ACDHIIMSU	DICHASIUM
ACDHIINNO	INDOCHINA
ACDHIINOP	DIAPHONIC
ACDHIKPRT	PITCH-DARK
ACDHILNOO	CONHOIDAL
ACDHILPRS	PILCHARDS
ACDHILRUY	HYDRAULIC
ACDHILSTT	LAST-DITCH
ACDHIMORT	CHROMATID
ACDHIOPRS	RHAPSODIC
ACDHIORYZ	HYDRAZOIC
ACDHIPSSY	DYSPHASIC
ACDHLOOSY	DAY SCHOOL
ACDHMNOOR	CHONDROMA
ACDHMOOTW	MATCHWOOD
ACDHOOPPS	SCAPHOPOD
ACDHORTWW	WATCHWORD
ACDIIIILMT	MITICIDAL
ACDIIIMOT	IDIOMATIC

ACDIIJLRU	JURIDICAL
ACDIIJRUY	JUDICIARY
ACDIILMNO	DOMINICAL
ACDIILMSX	DISCLIMAX
ACDIILOST	DIASTOLIC
ACDIILPTY	PLACIDITY
ACDIILSTU	DUALISTIC
ACDIIMNNO	DOMINICAN
ACDIIMNTY	DYNAMITIC
ACDIIMRTY	MYDRIATIC
ACDIINORT	INDICATOR
ACDIINOTT	DICTATION
ACDIINRTY	RANCIDITY
ACDIIOPRT	DIATROPIC
ACDIJORTU	JUDICATOR
ACDIKKLRY	KIRKCALDY
ACDIKNQSU	QUICKSAND
ACDIKRRTT	DIRT TRACK
ACDIKRSTY	YARDSTICK
ACDILLLOO	COLLOIDAL
ACDILLOOR	CORALLOID
ACDILLORY	CORDIALLY
ACDILMOPS	PSALMODIC
ACDILMOPY	DIPLOMACY
ACDILMOTU	COMATULID
ACDILNOOR	COORDINAL
ACDILNORT	DOCTRINAL
ACDILOPRS	DROPSICAL
ACDILORSY	CORYDALIS
ACDILOSTU	CUSTODIAL
ACDILOSUU	ACIDULOUS
ACDILRTTY	TRIDACTYL
ACDIMOPSS	SPASMODIC
ACDIMORRU	MACRUROID
ACDIMORTY	MORDACITY
ACDINOOPT	ACTINOPOD
ACDINOSTU	CUSTODIAN
ACDIORSTT	DICTATORS
ACDJOORTU	COADJUTOR
ACDKLORTU	TRUCKLOAD
ACDKMNNOO	MONADNOCK
ACDKORSTY	STOCKYARD
ACDLMNOOY	CONDYLOMA
ACDLMNOPW	CLAMPDOWN
ACDLNOPSS	COLD SNAPS
ACDLNORSU	CAULDRONS
ACDLNSTYY	SYNDACTYL
ACDLORSUW	WAR CLOUDS
ACDMMNOOS	COMMANDOS
ACDMOOSUV	MUSCOVADO
ACDMPRRTU	TRUMP CARD
ACDNOORRT	CORRODANT
ACDOPRSST	POSTCARDS
ACDORRTUY	COURTYARD

ACDRSSTTU	DUSTCARTS	ACEEGNORU	ENCOURAGE	ACEEILLST	CELESTIAL
ACEEEFIRS	CEASEFIRE	ACEEGNRSV	SCAVENGER	ACEEILMNS	MESCALINE
ACEEEFLNR	FREELANCE	ACEEGNRSY	SERGEANCY	ACEEILMNT	CLEMENTIA
ACEEEGHPR	REPECHAGE	ACEEGOOPR	COOPERAGE	ACEEILMRT	CARMELITE
ACEEEGNNV	VENGEANCE	ACEEGRTTU	CURETTAGE	ACEEILMRX	EXCLAIMER
ACEEEILMP	PIECEMEAL	ACEEHHORT	EACH OTHER	ACEEILNOR	COLERAINE
ACEEEIMPT	PEACETIME	ACEEHHTUX	HEXATEUCH	ACEEILNPR	PERCALINE
ACEEEIPPP	PEACE PIPE	ACEEHIIPR	HAIRPIECE	ACEEILNRS	LARCENIES
ACEEEIPRS	EARPIECES	ACEEHILMS	ALCHEMISE	ACEEILNRT	INTERLACE,
ACEEEKRRT	RACKETEER	ACEEHILMZ	ALCHEMIZE	RECLINATE	
ACEEELNRV	RELEVANCE	ACEEHILPT	PETECHIAL	ACEEILNST	CELESTINA
ACEEELNTU	ENUCLEATE	ACEEHILRT	HERETICAL	ACEEILNSV	VALENCIES
ACEEELNTY	ACETYLENE	ACEEHILRV	CHEVALIER	ACEEILPRS	PERICLASE
ACEEELSSS	CEASELESS	ACEEHIMNS	MECHANISE	ACEEILPRT	REPLICATE
ACEEEMNNR	REMANENCE	ACEEHIMNZ	MECHANIZE	ACEEILPTX	EXPLICATE
ACEEEMNPR	PERMEANCE	ACEEHIMPR	IMPEACHER	ACEEIMMNN	IMMANENCE
ACEEENPPT	APPETENCE	ACEEHINNV	ENHANCIVE	ACEEIMMNT	MINCEMEAT
ACEEENRSV	SEVERANCE	ACEEHINPT	PHENACITE	ACEEIMMRT	METAMERIC
ACEEERSTT	ETCETERAS	ACEEHINRT	CATHERINE	ACEEIMNPR	MEPACRINE
ACEEFFHRU	RECHAUFFE	ACEEHISTT	AESTHETIC	ACEEIMNSX	EXCISEMAN
ACEEFFITV	AFFECTIVE	ACEEHLMNO	CHAMELEON	ACEEIMPRT	IMPRECATE
ACEEFFLNU	AFFLUENCE	ACEEHLMOO	HAEMOCOEL	ACEEIMPST	SPACE-TIME
ACEEFFLTU	EFFECTUAL	ACEEHLMPV	CHAMPLEVE	ACEEIMRRS	CAREERISM
ACEEFFNRY	FANCY-FREE	ACEEHLNRU	HERCULEAN	ACEEIMRSS	CASSIMERE
ACEEFHLNP	HALFPENCE	ACEEHLNRW	WALCHEREN	ACEEIMRST	CREAMIEST,
ACEEFHMRR	CHAMFERER	ACEEHLNSS	SENESCHAL	MISCREATE	
ACEEFHORR	FOREREACH	ACEEHLNTU	NEUCHATEL	ACEEINNRS	CANNERIES
ACEEFIIRT	ACETIFIER	ACEEHLOSS	SHOELACES	ACEEINNRT	NECTARINE
ACEEFILPR	FIREPLACE	ACEEHLRTW	CARTWHEEL	ACEEINNST	INSECTEAN,
ACEEFINNR	REFINANCE	ACEEHMMRT	MACHMETER	TENANCIES	
ACEEFINRT	INTERFACE	ACEEHMNRY	ARCHENEMY	ACEEINNTU	ENUNCIATE
ACEEFIRSS	FRICASSEE	ACEEHMOTY	HAEMOCYTE	ACEEINPRU	EPICUREAN
ACEEFKOPR	POKER FACE	ACEEHMRSU	CHARMEUSE	ACEEINPTT	PECTINATE
ACEEFLOTV	VOLTE-FACE	ACEEHNNRT	ENCHANTER	ACEEINRRS	INCREASER
ACEEFMORT	FORCEMEAT	ACEEHNPSS	CHEAPNESS	ACEEINRSS	INCREASES
ACEEFPSTY	TYPEFACES	ACEEHNPTY	PACHYTENE	ACEEIORTX	EXCORIATE
ACEEFRRSU	RESURFACE	ACEEHNRST	CHASTENER	ACEEIOSST	TEA COSIES
ACEEGHIRU	GAUCHERIE	ACEEHNRTT	ENTRECHAT	ACEEIOTVV	EVOCATIVE
ACEEGHLLN	CHALLENGE	ACEEHNSTU	CHANTEUSE	ACEEIPPRR	RICE PAPER
ACEEGHNRX	EXCHANGER	ACEEHORRS	RACEHORSE	ACEEIPRTT	CREPITATE
ACEEGHNSX	EXCHANGES	ACEEHORRV	OVERREACH	ACEEIRRST	CAREERIST
ACEEGILRS	SACRILEGE	ACEEHOSTU	THEACEOUS	ACEEIRSTT	CATTERIES
ACEEGILRV	VICEGERAL,	ACEEHPRRS	PREACHERS	ACEEIRSTU	CAUTERISE
VICEREGAL		ACEEHPRTY	ARCHETYPE	ACEEIRSTW	WATER ICES
ACEEGIMSY	MAGIC EYES	ACEEHRRTT	CHATTERER	ACEEIRSVV	VICE VERSA
ACEEGINNR	CAREENING	ACEEHRRTY	TREACHERY	ACEEIRTTX	EXTRICATE
ACEEGINRR	CAREERING	ACEEHRSTT	CATHETERS	ACEEIRTUZ	CAUTERIZE
ACEEGINRV	GRIEVANCE	ACEEHSSTT	TEA CHESTS	ACEEISSST	ECSTASIES
ACEEGIRTT	CIGARETTE	ACEEIILPT	TAILPIECE	ACEEKLMRS	MACKERELS
ACEEGKRWY	GREYWACKE	ACEEIKLSV	SICK LEAVE	ACEELLLSU	CELLULASE
ACEEGLLOU	COLLEAGUE	ACEEIKMNZ	MACKENZIE	ACEELLORT	ELECTORAL
ACEEGLNRT	RECTANGLE	ACEEIKRST	CREAKIEST,	ACEELMNPT	PLACEMENT
ACEEGLRSS	GRACELESS	ICE-SKATER		ACEELMOPS	SOMEPLACE
ACEEGMNOR	GEOMANCER	ACEEIKSST	ICE SKATES	ACEELMORT	LATECOMER
				ACEELNNRU	CANNELURE

ACEELNNSS	CLEANNESS	ACEERRSTY	SECRETARY	ACEFORRRT	REFRACTOR
ACEELNORT	TOLERANCE	ACEERSSST	ACTRESSES	ACEFORRRU	CARREFOUR
ACEELNPTU	PETULANCE	ACEERSSSV	CREVASSES	ACEFORSST	FORECASTS
ACEELNRSS	CLEANSERS,	ACEERSSTT	TESSERACT	ACEFRRSTU	FRACTURES
CLEARNESS		ACEERSSTU	SECATEURS	ACEGGIRRS	SCRAGGIER
ACEELNRTU	CALENTURE,	ACEESSSTT	CASSETTES, TEST	ACEGGIRST	CRAGGIEST
CRENULATE		CASES		ACEGHHPTU	HUGH CAPET
ACEELNRVY	RELEVANCY	ACEFFGINT	AFFECTING	ACEGHIINV	ACHIEVING
ACEELNSTT	TENTACLES	ACEFFHRUU	CHAUFFEUR	ACEGHILRT	LETHARGIC
ACEELNSTW	NEWCASTLE	ACEFFIIOT	OFFICIATE	ACEGHINNN	ENHANCING
ACEELOOSU	OLEACEOUS	ACEFFILST	FACE-LIFTS	ACEGHINPR	PREACHING
ACEELOPRT	PERCOLATE	ACEFFINOT	AFFECTION	ACEGHINRS	SEARCHING
ACEELOPSS	ESCALOPES	ACEFFIORT	FORFICATE	ACEGHLSTY	LYCHGATES
ACEELORRT	CORRELATE	ACEFFOSTU	SUFFOCATE	ACEGHMNOS	CHEONGSAM
ACEELORSS	CASSEROLE	ACEFGINPR	PREFACING	ACEGHMORT	HECTOGRAM
ACEELORSW	LOWER CASE	ACEFGLNOS	LONG FACES	ACEGHOPRY	CREOPHAGY
ACEELORTT	LECTORATE	ACEFHIINT	CHIEFTAIN	ACEGHOPTY	PHAGOCYTE
ACEELORTU	URCEOLATE	ACEFHIKLT	THICKLEAF	ACEGHRRSU	SURCHARGE
ACEELPSSS	SPACELESS	ACEFHIKSS	FISHCAKES	ACEGIILLS	GALLICISE
ACEELPSTU	SPECULATE	ACEFHINRS	FRANCHISE	ACEGIILLZ	GALLICIZE
ACEELPTUX	EXCULPATE	ACEFHIPRY	PREACHIFY	ACEGIILNS	ANGLICISE
ACEELQRRU	LACQUERER	ACEFHMNNR	FRENCHMAN	ACEGIILNT	GENITALIC
ACEELRTUY	ELECTUARY	ACEFHOSUV	VOUCHSAFE	ACEGIILNV	VIGILANCE
ACEELSSTT	TELECASTS	ACEFIILMS	FACSIMILE	ACEGIILNZ	ANGLICIZE
ACEEMMOOT	AMMOCOETE	ACEFIILRR	CLARIFIER	ACEGIIMNT	ENIGMATIC
ACEEMNNTT	ENACTMENT	ACEFIINNR	FINANCIER	ACEGIINNT	ANTIGENIC
ACEEMNRRY	MERCENARY	ACEFIIPRS	PACIFIERS	ACEGIIRRT	GERIATRIC
ACEEMORTT	OCTAMETER	ACEFIIRRS	SCARIFIER	ACEGILLLO	COLLEGIAL
ACEEMPRRS	SCAMPERER	ACEFIIRRT	ARTIFICER	ACEGILLNO	COLLEGIAN
ACEEMRRTU	MERCURATE	ACEFIIRST	ARTIFICES	ACEGILLNR	RECALLING
ACEENNOPR	CAN OPENER	ACEFIIRTV	FRICATIVE	ACEGILLOT	COLLIGATE
ACEENNORS	RESONANCE	ACEFIITTV	FACTITIVE	ACEGILNNO	CONGENIAL
ACEENNOST	CANTONESE	ACEFIJKKN	JACK KNIFE	ACEGILNNS	CLEANSING
ACEENNRST	ENTRANCES,	ACEFIKRTU	FRUITCAKE	ACEGILNPR	PARCELING,
RENASCENT		ACEFILNNO	FALCONINE	REPLACING	
ACEENNRTY	CENTENARY	ACEFILORT	FORTALICE	ACEGILNRS	CLEARINGS
ACEENPRRT	CARPENTER	ACEFILSTU	FACULTIES	ACEGILNRU	NEURALGIC
ACEENPTTX	EXPECTANT	ACEFIMPRS	CAMPFIRES	ACEGILNRW	CLEARWING
ACEENRRST	RECREANTS	ACEFINNSS	FANCINESS	ACEGILNTU	CINGULATE
ACEENRSSY	NECESSARY	ACEFINORT	FORNICATE	ACEGILOOR	AEROLOGIC
ACEENRTTU	UTTERANCE	ACEFINSTU	INFUSCATE	ACEGILRTU	CURTILAGE,
ACEENSSTU	ACUTENESS	ACEFIORRS	AIRFORCES	GRATICULE	
ACEENSSTX	EXACTNESS	ACEFIORST	FACTORIES,	ACEGIMMNR	ENGRAMMIC
ACEENTTUX	EXECUTANT	FACTORISE		ACEGIMMRS	SCRIMMAGE
ACEEOOPRT	COOPERATE	ACEFIORTZ	FACTORIZE	ACEGIMMST	TAGMEMICS
ACEEOPRRT	PROCREATE	ACEFIOSTU	FACETIOUS	ACEGIMNNP	ENCAMPING
ACEEORRRT	RE-CREATOR	ACEFIRSTT	CRAFTIEST	ACEGIMNOT	GEOMANTIC
ACEEORRTT	RECTORATE	ACEFKORST	TASK FORCE	ACEGIMNRS	SCREAMING
ACEEORRTV	OVERREACT	ACEFLLLSU	FULL-SCALE	ACEGIMNRT	CENTIGRAM,
ACEEOSSTU	SETACEOUS	ACEFLLRUY	CAREFULLY	CREMATING	
ACEEPPRSU	UPPER CASE	ACEFLNORS	FALCONERS	ACEGIMNST	MAGNETICS
ACEEPRRTU	RECAPTURE	ACEFLNORV	CONFERVAL	ACEGIMNTU	MUTAGENIC
ACEERRSTT	SCATTERER,	ACEFLTTUU	FLUCTUATE	ACEGIMTUZ	ZEUGMATIC
STREETCAR		ACEFMNRST	CRAFTSMEN	ACEGINNOR	IGNORANCE
ACEERRSTU	CREATURES	ACEFOORST	FOOTRACES		

ACEGINNRT	CANTERING, RECANTING	ACEHIMMNS	MECHANISM	ACEHMSTTT	TEST MATCH
ACEGINNSU	UNCEASING	ACEHIMNRY	MACHINERY	ACEHNNPST	PENCHANTS
ACEGINNPPR	RECAPPING	ACEHIMNST	MECHANIST	ACEHNNRTT	TRENCHANT
ACEGINPRT	CARPETING	ACEHIMRTU	RHEUMATIC	ACEHNOOTT	ON THE COAT
ACEGINPRY	PANEGYRIC	ACEHINNRY	HERCYNIAN	ACEHNOPRS	CHAPERONS
ACEGINRRT	RETRACING	ACEHINORT	ANCHORITE, ANTECHOIR	ACEHNOPST	CENOTAPHS
ACEGINRSS	CARESSING	ACEHINORX	CHRONAXIE	ACEHNORSS	ANCHORESS
ACEGINRST	RECASTING	ACEHINOSV	ANCHOVIES	ACEHNOSTT	STONECHAT
ACEGIOPRR	PAREGORIC	ACEHINPST	CATHEPSIN	ACEHNPRTY	PENTARCHY
ACEGIOSTT	GEOSTATIC	ACEHINRRU	HURRICANE, RAUNCHIER	ACEHNRSTU	STAUNCHER
ACEGIPRST	PRICE TAGS	ACEHINRSS	CHARINESS	ACEHNRSUZ	SCHNAUZER
ACEGIRSTT	STRATEGIC	ACEHINRSU	SEA URCHIN	ACEHOOSTU	HOUSECOAT
ACEGJNOTU	CONJUGATE	ACEHINRTT	IN THE CART	ACEHOPRRS	SHARECROP
ACEGLMNRY	CLERGYMAN	ACEHINSST	CAITHNESS	ACEHORRST	CARTHORSE, ORCHESTRA
ACEGLNNPY	PLANGENCY	ACEHINSTY	HESITANCY	ACEHORSTY	THEOCRASY
ACEGMMNOO	COMMONAGE	ACEHINTTU	AUTHENTIC	ACEHOSSSW	SHOWCASES
ACEGMMRSU	SCRUMMAGE	ACEHIPPSS	SPACESHIP	ACEHPRRSU	PURCHASER
ACEGNNOTT	COTANGENT	ACEHIPRST	PIE CHARTS	ACEHPRSSU	PURCHASES
ACEGNNPRY	PREGNANCY	ACEHIPSST	PASTICHES	ACEHPSTTY	PETTY CASH
ACEGORRTU	CORRUGATE	ACEHIPSTT	PATCHIEST	ACEHRRTTY	TETRARCHY
ACEGORSTT	COTTAGERS	ACEHIPSTW	WHITECAPS	ACEIIILST	ITALICISE
ACEHHILPS	CHELASHIP	ACEHIRRST	STARCHIER	ACEIIILTZ	ITALICIZE
ACEHHIRRY	HIERARCHY	ACEHIRSTT	THEATRICS	ACEIIKLST	EKISTICAL
ACEHHISTX	HEXASTICH	ACEHIRSTU	EUCHARIST	ACEIILLOT	CILIOLATE
ACEHHLWYZ	WYCH-HAZEL	ACEHISTTT	CHATTIEST	ACEIILMOV	VOICE MAIL
ACEHHMNTT	HATCHMENT	ACEHKLNSU	UNSHACKLE	ACEIILMPR	EMPIRICAL
ACEHHNRTY	ETHNARCHY	ACEHKLSTY	LATCHKEYS	ACEIILMPT	IMPLICATE
ACEHHOOTT	TOOTHACHE	ACEHKMPSU	MUCKHEAPS	ACEIILNNT	ANTICLINE
ACEHHPRTY	HEPTARCHY	ACEHKNORT	ON THE RACK	ACEIILNNV	VICENNIAL
ACEHHRSTT	THATCHERS	ACEHKOPRS	PACKHORSE	ACEIILNPR	CIRALPINE
ACEHHSSTY	HESYCHAST	ACEHKORST	SHORTCAKE	ACEIILNST	INELASTIC, SCIENTIAL
ACEHIINOP	PHOENICIA	ACEHLLLOR	CHLORELLA	ACEIILOSS	SOCIALISE
ACEHIINPP	EPIPHANIC	ACEHLLOOS	COALHOLES	ACEIILOST	SOCIALITE
ACEHIIPPT	EPITAPHIC	ACEHLMOST	MOSCHATEL	ACEIILOSZ	SOCIALIZE
ACEHIIRST	CHARITIES	ACEHLMSST	MATCHLESS	ACEIILPRT	PEARLITIC
ACEHIISTT	ATHEISTIC	ACEHLNPTY	PHLYCTENA	ACEIILRST	ERISTICAL, REALISTIC
ACEHIJKRS	HIJACKERS	ACEHLOOSU	COALHOUSE	ACEIILRTT	LATERITIC
ACEHIKLST	CHALKIEST	ACEHLOPSW	SHOWPLACE	ACEIILSST	SILICATES
ACEHIKORT	ARTICHOKE	ACEHLORRT	TROCHLEAR	ACEIILSTV	CALVITIES
ACEHIKRST	HEARTSICK	ACEHLORSU	HOUSECARL	ACEIIMMNR	CIMMERIAN
ACEHILLLY	HELICALLY	ACEHLORTT	CHARLOTTE	ACEIIMMRU	AMERICIUM
ACEHILLTY	ETHICALLY	ACEHLOSTT	TEA CLOTHS	ACEIIMNRT	ANTIMERIC
ACEHILMMO	CHAMOMILE	ACEHLTTYY	TACHYLYTE	ACEIIMNSS	MESSIANIC
ACEHILMST	ALCHEMIST	ACEHMNOPY	CYMOPHANE	ACEIIMRST	ARMISTICE
ACEHILNNO	CHELONIAN	ACEHMNORW	CHARWOMEN	ACEIINNTV	VINCENTIA
ACEHILNOO	HOLOCAINE	ACEHMNPRT	PARCHMENT	ACEIINPRS	PRECISIAN
ACEHILNOR	ENCHORIAL	ACEHMNRST	MERCHANTS	ACEIINPST	EPINASTIC
ACEHILNOT	CHELATION	ACEHMNSTY	YACHTSMEN	ACEIINRTT	INTRICATE
ACEHILNTU	UNETHICAL	ACEHMNTTU	HUMECTANT	ACEIINTTT	NICTITATE
ACEHILNTY	THYLACINE	ACEHMOSTT	CHEMOSTAT	ACEIIPSTT	EPISTATIC
ACEHILPRS	SPHERICAL	ACEHMOSTU	MOUSTACHE	ACEIIRSTV	VARISCITE
ACEHILRUV	VEHICULAR	ACEHMPRTY	CHAMPERTY		
ACEHILSTT	ATHLETICS	ACEHMSSTU	MUSTACHES		

ACEIISTTT	STEATITIC	
ACEIJKNPS	JACKSNIPE	
ACEIJMSST	MAJESTICS	
ACEIKLPST	SKEPTICAL	
ACEIKMNNS	NICKNAMES	
ACEIKMRSV	MAVERICKS	
ACEIKNRST	CRANKIEST	
ACEIKNSST	TACKINESS	
ACEIKNSSW	WACKINESS	
ACEIKOPRT	AIRPOCKET	
ACEIKOPSS	SKIASCOPE	
ACEIKPPRS	PIPE RACKS	
ACEIKPRRT	PERITRACK	
ACEIKRSTW	WATER-SICK	
ACEILLLXY	LEXICALLY	
ACEILLMOP	POLEMICAL	
ACEILLMOT	COLLIMATE, LOCAL TIME	
ACEILLMSY	MESICALLY	
ACEILLNOR	COLLINEAR, CORALLINE	
ACEILLORS	LOCALISER	
ACEILLORZ	LOCALIZER	
ACEILLOST	OSCILLATE	
ACEILLOTV	COLLATIVE	
ACEILLPSY	SPECIALLY	
ACEILLRSV	CAVILLERS	
ACEILLRXY	XERICALLY	
ACEILMMST	CLAMMIEST	
ACEILMNNU	LUMINANCE	
ACEILMNOP	POLICEMAN	
ACEILMNOS	COALMINES	
ACEILMNRU	NUMERICAL	
ACEILMNSU	CALUMNIES, MASCULINE	
ACEILMNTU	CULMINATE	
ACEILMOPT	PTOLEMAIC	
ACEILMOSS	CAMISOLES, COSEISMAL	
ACEILMOSV	SEMIVOCAL	
ACEILMRRU	MERCURIAL	
ACEILNNOR	CORNELIAN	
ACEILNNOT	OCTENNIAL	
ACEILNNPS	PINNACLES	
ACEILNOPR	PORCELAIN	
ACEILNORS	CENSORIAL	
ACEILNOST	COASTLINE, SECTIONAL	
ACEILNOSV	VOLCANISE	
ACEILNOTU	INOCULATE	
ACEILNOVZ	VOLCANIZE	
ACEILNPTU	INCULPATE	
ACEILNRST	CLARINETS, LARCENIST	
ACEILNRTU	CENTURIAL	
ACEILNRTY	CERTAINLY	
ACEILNSSS	SCALINESS	
ACEILNSUV	VULCANISE	
ACEILNTUV	VULCANITE	
ACEILNUVZ	VULCANIZE	
ACEILOPPS	EPISCOPAL	
ACEILOPST	SCAPOLITE	
ACEILOQUV	EQUIVOCAL	
ACEILORRT	RECTORIAL	
ACEILORST	SECTORIAL	
ACEILORSV	VOCALISER	
ACEILORTV	VECTORIAL	
ACEILORVZ	VOCALIZER	
ACEILOTVY	COEVALITY	
ACEILPPPR	PAPER CLIP	
ACEILPRST	PARTICLES	
ACEILPSSS	SLIPCASES	
ACEILPSTU	EUPLASTIC, SPICULATE	
ACEILPSTY	SPECIALTY	
ACEILRSUV	VESICULAR	
ACEILRTUV	LUCRATIVE	
ACEILSSST	CLASSIEST	
ACEILTTUV	CULTIVATE	
ACEIMMNNY	IMMANENCY	
ACEIMNOPS	COMPANIES	
ACEIMNORT	CREMATION	
ACEIMNOST	ENCOMIAST	
ACEIMNOTX	INCOME TAX	
ACEIMNPTU	PNEUMATIC	
ACEIMNRST	MISCREANT	
ACEIMNRSU	MANICURES, MUSCARINE	
ACEIMNSST	SEMANTICS	
ACEIMNTYZ	ENZYMATIC	
ACEIMORVW	MICROWAVE	
ACEIMOSTU	AUTOECISM	
ACEIMPRST	SPERMATIC	
ACEIMPSST	CAMPSITES	
ACEIMRRSW	WAR CRIMES	
ACEINNNRU	UNCANNIER	
ACEINNNSS	CANNINESS	
ACEINNOOV	NOVOCAINE	
ACEINNORT	CONTAINER, CRENATION	
ACEINNOSS	ASCENSION	
ACEINNRSU	INSURANCE	
ACEINNRTU	RUNCINATE, UNCERTAIN	
ACEINNSST	INCESSANT, INSTANCES	
ACEINNSSU	NUISANCES	
ACEINOOST	ISOOCTANE	
ACEINOOTV	EVOCATION	
ACEINOPRT	RECAPTION	
ACEINOPSU	PINACEOUS	
ACEINORRV	CARNIVORE	
ACEINORSS	SCENARIOS	
ACEINORST	CREATIONS, NARCOTISE, REACTIONS	
ACEINORTT	CARNOTITE	
ACEINORTU	COINTREAU	
ACEINORTZ	NARCOTIZE	
ACEINOSST	CANOEISTS, CESSATION	
ACEINOSTU	TENACIOUS	
ACEINOSUV	VINACEOUS	
ACEINOTTY	TO A NICETY	
ACEINPRTT	CREPITANT	
ACEINPRUY	PECUNIARY	
ACEINPSSU	PUISSANCE	
ACEINPSTT	PITTANCES	
ACEINQTTU	QUITTANCE	
ACEINRRSW	SCRAWNIER	
ACEINRSST	CANISTERS, SCENARIST	
ACEINRSSZ	CRAZINESS	
ACEINRTTY	CERTAINTY	
ACEINRTUV	INCURVATE	
ACEINSSSU	SAUCINESS	
ACEINSSTT	CATTINESS, SCANTIEST, TACITNESS	
ACEINSTTY	INTESTACY	
ACEIOPRRS	ACROSPIRE	
ACEIOPRTV	PROACTIVE	
ACEIOPTTT	PETTICOAT	
ACEIORRSV	CORRASIVE	
ACEIORSST	OSTRACISE	
ACEIORSTZ	OSTRACIZE	
ACEIORSUV	VERACIOUS	
ACEIOSTUV	VITACEOUS	
ACEIOSTVV	VOCATIVES	
ACEIOSVVV	VIVA VOCES	
ACEIPPRRS	SCRAPPIER	
ACEIPPRST	CRAPPIEST	
ACEIPSSST	ESCAPISTS	
ACEIPSSTU	SPACESUIT	
ACEIQRTTU	ACQUITTER	
ACEIQSTUY	SEQUACITY	
ACEIRSSSU	CUIRASSES	
ACEIRSTTU	RUSTICATE	
ACEIRSTUV	CURATIVES	
ACEISSSTU	SUITCASES	
ACEISSTTT	SCATTIEST	
ACEISTTTY	CITY-STATE	
ACEJKKRSY	SKYJACKER	
ACEJKLMST	JACKSMELT	
ACEJLMSUU	MAJUSCULE	
ACEJLNQUY	JACQUELYN	
ACEKKMRRU	MUCKRAKER	

ACEKLLMMU	MALLEMUCK	ACEMOOPSU	POMACEOUS
ACEKLNSSS	SLACKNESS	ACEMOORSU	MORACEOUS
ACEKLOPRW	WORKPLACE	ACEMOPSSS	COMPASSES
ACEKLRSST	TRACKLESS	ACEMORRSU	SOUR CREAM
ACEKNNTTU	NANTUCKET	ACEMORRTY	CREMATORY
ACEKNORSU	CANKEROUS	ACEMORSSY	SYCAMORES
ACEKOPRRT	RETROPACK	ACEMOSSUU	MUSACEOUS
ACEKPRSSU	SAPSUCKER	ACEMOSTVY	VASECTOMY
ACEKRSTUW	AWESTRUCK	ACEMPRSUY	SUPREMACY
ACELLLMOU	COLUMELLA	ACENNNORU	ANNOUNCER
ACELLLORS	SOLAR CELL	ACENNOSTV	COVENANTS
ACELLMORU	MOLECULAR	ACENNSSST	SCANTNESS
ACELLMRSU	MARCELLUS	ACENOPRRT	COPARTNER,
ACELLNORU	NUCLEOLAR	PROCREANT	
ACELLNOTU	LAUNCELOT	ACENOPSTW	TOWNSCAPE
ACELLNRTY	CENTRALLY	ACENOPSTY	SYNCOPATE
ACELLOPRS	SCALLOPER	ACENOPTYY	CYANOTYPE
ACELLOPSS	COLLAPSES	ACENORRTU	RACONTEUR
ACELLOQUY	COEQUALLY	ACENORSST	ANCESTORS
ACELLORSS	SCLEROSAL	ACENORSTU	COURTESAN
ACELLORSV	COVERALLS	ACENORSUV	CAVERNOUS
ACELLRSTU	SCUTELLAR	ACENORTUY	COURTENAY
ACELLSSSS	CLASSLESS	ACENORUVV	VANCOUVER
ACELMMNOS	COMMENSAL	ACENOSTUU	CUTANEOUS
ACELMMNSU	MUSCLEMAN	ACENPRRTY	CARPENTRY
ACELMNTUU	TENACULUM	ACENPRSUU	PURSUANCE
ACELMOPST	ECTOPLASM	ACENPTTUU	PUNCTUATE
ACELMORSY	CLAYMORES	ACENRSSSS	CRASSNESS
ACELMOSUU	ULMACEOUS	ACENRSSTU	RECUSANTS
ACELMSSTU	MUSCATELS	ACENRSTUU	CENTAURUS
ACELNNOOR	OLECRANON	ACEOOPRRT	CORPORATE
ACELNOOSV	VOLCANOES	ACEOOPRSS	ASCOSPORE
ACELNOPRV	PROVENCAL	ACEOORSSU	ROSACEOUS
ACELNORSU	LARCENOUS	ACEOORSTV	OVERCOATS
ACELNORTU	NUCLEATOR,	ACEOPPRST	SPACEPORT
RECOUNTAL		ACEOPRSTT	SPECTATOR
ACELNOSTU	CONSULATE	ACEORRRTT	RETRACTOR
ACELNOSTY	CLAYSTONE	ACEORRRVY	CARRY-OVER
ACELNRTTU	RELUCTANT	ACEORRSTU	CRATEROUS,
ACELOOPRR	CORPORALE,	EUROCRATS	
CORPOREAL		ACEORRTTX	EXTRACTOR
ACELOORTW	WATER-COOL	ACEORSTTY	ASTROCYTE
ACELOOSTT	COELOSTAT	ACEORSTUU	RUTACEOUS
ACELOPRRU	OPERCULAR	ACEOSSTTU	OUTCASTES
ACELOPRTU	PECULATOR	ACERRTUUV	CURVATURE
ACELOPSTU	SCOPULATE	ACFFIILOS	OFFICIALS
ACELORSSU	CAROUSELS	ACFFIINOT	OFFICIANT
ACELOSSTU	CASSOULET,	ACFFIIORY	OFFICIARY
LOST CAUSE		ACFGHMORR	FROGMARCH
ACELPPRRU	CURLPAPER	ACFGIIMNO	MAGNIFICO
ACELSSSTU	CUTLASSES	ACFGIINNN	FINANCING
ACEMMOTTU	COMMUTATE	ACFGIINPY	PACIFYING
ACEMNOOPS	MOONSCAPE	ACFGINORT	FACTORING
ACEMNOPSS	ENCOMPASS	ACFGINOTU	OUTFACING
ACEMNORTU	MUCRONATE	ACFGINRSU	SURFACING
ACFGIOSUU	FUGACIOUS		
ACFGLNORY	GYRFALCON		
ACFHIILRT	CHAIRLIFT		
ACFHKORST	ROCKSHAFT		
ACFHLMRSU	SCRUMHALF		
ACFHLNORW	HALF CROWN		
ACFHLORTW	FLOWCHART		
ACFHORRST	RH FACTORS		
ACFIILNOT	FICTIONAL		
ACFIIMNOR	ACINIFORM		
ACFIIOPRV	VAPORIFIC		
ACFIIPSST	PACIFISTS		
ACFIJKRTU	JACKFRUIT		
ACFIKNRSS	SCARFSKIN		
ACFILMORU	FORMULAIC,		
FUMAROLIC			
ACFILNNOR	FRANCOLIN		
ACFILNOOT	OLFACTION		
ACFILNPPY	FLIPPANCY		
ACFILNPSU	CUP FINALS		
ACFILNRUU	FUNICULAR		
ACFIMORRY	FORMICARY		
ACFINORRT	INFRACTOR		
ACFINORST	FRACTIONS		
ACFINORTU	FURCATION		
ACFIOOPST	IPSO FACTO		
ACFIORSTU	FRACTIOUS		
ACFJKORST	JACK FROST		
ACFKLLORS	ROCKFALLS		
ACFKMRRTU	TRUCK FARM		
ACFKNORWY	FANCYWORK		
ACFKOORRS	ROOF RACKS		
ACFLLTTUY	TACTFULLY		
ACFLMNOOR	CONFORMAL		
ACFLNTTUU	FLUCTUANT		
ACFLOORTY	OLFACTORY		
ACFOOSTUU	AUTOFOCUS		
ACGGGINRS	SCRAGGING		
ACGGIIMNR	GRIMACING		
ACGGIIOSS	ISAGOGICS		
ACGGILRSY	SCRAGGILY		
ACGHHHIIR	HIGH CHAIR		
ACGHHILNT	HATCHLING		
ACGHHILSS	HIGH-CLASS		
ACGHHINOT	HOATCHING		
ACGHHINTT	THATCHING		
ACGHIIJKN	HIJACKING		
ACGHIIKNN	CHINKIANG		
ACGHIIMNN	MACHINING		
ACGHIIPRT	GRAPHITIC		
ACGHIKLNS	SHACKLING		
ACGHIKNSW	WHACKINGS		
ACGHIKNTW	THWACKING		
ACGHILNNU	LAUNCHING		

ACGHILORY	OLIGARCHY	ACGINNOOT	COGNATION,
ACGHIMOOP	OMOPHAGIC		CONTAGION
ACGHINNOR	ANCHORING	ACGINNOPY	POIGNANCY
ACGHINNST	SNATCHING,	ACGINNORY	CRAYONING
STANCHING		ACGINNOTZ	COGNIZANT
ACGHINPST	NIGHTCAPS	ACGINORSU	CAROUSING
ACGHINRST	STARCHING	ACGINORTV	CAVORTING
ACGHINSTY	YACHTINGS	ACGINOSST	AGNOSTICS
ACGHLMOOY	LOGOMACHY	ACGINPPRS	SCRAPPING
ACGHMOPRY	CYMOGRAPH	ACGINPRSS	SCRAPINGS
ACGHORSTU	ROUGHCAST	ACGINPRTU	CAPTURING
ACGIIIMST	IMAGISTIC	ACGINPTUY	PUGNACITY
ACGIIKNNP	PANICKING	ACGIOORTT	COGITATOR
ACGIILLLO	ILLOGICAL	ACGJNNOTU	CONJUGANT
ACGIILLMS	GALLICISM	ACGLOOPRY	CARPOLOGY
ACGIILLNV	CAVILLING	ACGLOOSTY	SCATOLOGY
ACGIILLOR	CIGARILLO	ACGMOPRTY	CRYPTOGAM
ACGIILMNS	ANGLICISM	ACGORRSUY	SURROGACY
ACGIILMNX	CLIMAXING	ACHHILORT	HAIRCLOTH
ACGIILNOS	GASOLINIC,	ACHHINNOT	CHTHONIAN
LOGICIANS		ACHHINSTY	HYACINTHS
ACGIILNRT	ARTICLING	ACHHIPRSU	PUSHCHAIR
ACGIIMNPT	IMPACTING	ACHHLOSTU	SLOUCH HAT
ACGIIMSTT	STIGMATIC	ACHHLOSTW	WASHCLOTH
ACGIINNOR	INORGANIC	ACHHOSSTW	CHAT SHOWS
ACGIINOST	AGONISTIC	ACHIIIMOS	CHISIMAIO
ACGIINPSZ	CAPSIZING	ACHIILMSW	WHIMSICAL
ACGIINQRU	ACQUIRING	ACHIIMNST	MACHINIST
ACGIIORST	ORGIASTIC	ACHIINPSY	PHYSICIAN
ACGIIRSTT	GASTRITIC	ACHIINRST	CHRISTIAN,
ACGIKNNPU	UNPACKING	CHRISTINA	
ACGILLLOY	LOGICALLY	ACHIIOPST	PISTACHIO
ACGILLLRS	CALL GIRLS	ACHIIPRSV	VICARSHIP
ACGILLNOR	CAROLLING,	ACHIIRRTT	ARTHRITIC
COLLARING		ACHIIRSTV	ARCHIVIST
ACGILLNOT	COLLATING	ACHIKLPTU	CHALK IT UP
ACGILLOOO	OOLOGICAL	ACHIKRSSW	RICKSHAWS
ACGILLOST	COLLAGIST	ACHIKRSTT	HAT TRICKS
ACGILNNST	SCANTLING	ACHILLMSU	MUSIC HALL
ACGILNOST	NOSTALGIC	ACHILLNTY	CHANTILLY
ACGILNOXY	COAXINGLY	ACHILLOST	SAILCLOTH
ACGILNRSW	SCRAWLING	ACHILLSTY	CITY HALLS
ACGILNRSY	SCARINGLY	ACHILMPTY	ITCHY PALM,
ACGIMMNRS	SCRAMMING	LYMPHATIC	
ACGIMNNOR	ROMANCING	ACHILNORT	ANTICHLOR
ACGIMNNOR	AGRONOMIC	ACHILNRUY	RAUNCHILY
ACGIMNOPR	COMPARING	ACHILNSTY	SNATCHILY
ACGIMNORR	CAIRNGORM	ACHILOPTU	PATCHOULI
ACGIMNOTU	CONTAGIUM	ACHILORTV	ARCHIVOLT
ACGIMNSTY	GYMNASTIC,	ACHILOSST	SCHOLIAST
NYSTAGMIC		ACHILPSSY	PHYSICALS
ACGIMNUUV	VACUUMING	ACHILRSSY	CHRYSALIS
ACGIMOTYZ	ZYGOMATIC	ACHILRSTY	STARCHILY
ACGINNNNO	CANNONING	ACHIMMNOS	MONACHISM
		ACHIMMOSS	MASOCHISM

ACHIMNOPS	CHAMPIONS
ACHIMNORS	HARMONICS
ACHIMNORT	CHROMATIN
ACHIMOOTX	HOMOTAXIC
ACHIMORST	RHOTACISM
ACHIMOSST	MASOCHIST
ACHIMOSTU	MUSTACHIO
ACHIMRSST	CHRISTMAS
ACHIMRSSW	SCRIMSHAW
ACHINNOST	STANCHION
ACHINNOTW	CHINATOWN
ACHINOPPS	PANSOPHIC
ACHINPRST	CHINSTRAP
ACHIOOPST	SOCIOPATH
ACHIOPPRS	HIPPOCRAS
ACHIORSTT	RHOTACIST
ACHIPRSUY	HARUSPICY
ACHISTUWZ	AUSCHWITZ
ACHKLNOOS	SOLONCHAK
ACHKMORTU	TOUCHMARK
ACHKOPRTW	PATCHWORK
ACHKORRXY	ROCK HYRAX
ACHLLORSY	SCHOLARLY
ACHLMSTYZ	SCHMALTZY
ACHLNSTUY	STAUNCHLY
ACHLOOSTU	HOLOCAUST
ACHNOPSTY	SYCOPHANT
ACHOPSTTW	STOPWATCH
ACHORSSST	TROSSACHS
ACHORTTTU	CUT-THROAT
ACHPRSSTU	PUSHCARTS
ACIIILNOT	CILIATION
ACIIILNSV	CIVILIANS
ACIIIMNST	ANIMISTIC
ACIIIMNTV	VITAMINIC
ACIIINPST	PIANISTIC
ACIIJRSTU	JUSTICIAR
ACIIKMNRT	MINITRACK
ACIILLNOS	COLLINSIA,
ISOCLINAL	
ACIILLNST	SCINTILLA
ACIILLOPT	POLITICAL
ACIILLPRS	PRISCILLA
ACIILMNPU	MUNICIPAL
ACIILMNRS	CRIMINALS
ACIILMNSV	CALVINISM
ACIILMNTY	MILITANCY
ACIILMOSS	SOCIALISM
ACIILMOSU	MALICIOUS
ACIILMQTU	QUITCLAIM
ACIILNNOT	CLINTONIA
ACIILNOOT	COALITION
ACIILNOPT	PLICATION
ACIILNOVV	CONVIVIAL

ACIILNOVY	INVIOLACY	ACILLLOUV	COLLUVIAL	ACIMNORST	NARCOTISM,
ACIILNPPR	PRINCIPAL	ACILLLRYY	LYRICALLY		ROMANTICS
ACIILNRSU	INCISURAL	ACILLMSUY	MUSICALLY	ACIMNOSUU	ACUMINOUS
ACIILNSTV	CALVINIST	ACILLNNSY	SYNCLINAL	ACIMOOTTU	AUTOTOMIC
ACIILOPRT	PICTORIAL	ACILLNOOS	COLONIALS	ACIMOPSSY	SYMPOSIAC
ACIILORST	SORITICAL	ACILLNOOT	COLLATION	ACIMORSST	OSTRACISM
ACIILORTZ	TRIAZOLIC	ACILLNORS	CARILLONS	ACIMORSTT	STROMATIC
ACIILOSST	SOCIALIST	ACILLNOSS	SCALLIONS	ACIMPRSTY	SYMPATRIC
ACIILOSTY	SOCIALITY	ACILLOPTY,	OPTICALLY,	ACIMRSTTU	STRUMATIC
ACIILQUZZ	QUIZZICAL	TOPICALLY		ACINNORST	CONSTRAIN,
ACIILRSVW	CIVIL WARS	ACILLORST	CLOISTRAL		TRANSONIC
ACIILTTTY	TACTILITY	ACILLORYZ	ZIRCALLOY	ACINNOSST	SANCTIONS
ACIIMMNOT	AMMONITIC	ACILLOSTY	CALLOSITY,	ACINNOSTT	TOCANTINS
ACIIMNNOS	INSOMNIAC	STOICALLY		ACINOORRS	CORRASION
ACIIMNNOT	ANTIMONIC,	ACILLOTXY	TOXICALLY	ACINOORST	CONSORTIA
ANTINOMIC		ACILLPTYY	TYPICALLY	ACINOOSTV	VOCATIONS
ACIIMNOPT	IMPACTION	ACILMMOTT	COMMITTAL	ACINORSST	CROISSANT
ACIIMNORT	MORTICIAN	ACILMNNTU	CULMINANT	ACINORSTY	CRAYONIST
ACIIMNSSU	MUSICIANS	ACILMNOPT	COMPLAINT,	ACINOSSTW	WAINSCOTS
ACIIMOPST	SIMPATICO	COMPLIANT		ACINOSTTU	SCUTATION
ACIIMORTT	TRIATOMIC	ACILMNOSV	VOLCANISM	ACINRSSSU	NARCISSUS
ACIIMOSST	MOSAICIST	ACILMNSSU	UNMUSICAL	ACIOOPRSU	PAROICOUS
ACIIMOSTT	ATOMISTIC	ACILMOPRS	COMPRISAL	ACIOOPRSZ	SAPROZOIC
ACIIMOTTY	ATOMICITY	ACILMPTUU	CAPITULUM	ACIOORSTU	ATROCIOUS
ACIIMPRST	PRISMATIC	ACILNNNUY	UNCANNILY	ACIOORSUV	VORACIOUS
ACIIMPSSS	SIC PASSIM	ACILNNOTU	CONTINUAL	ACIOOSTUU	AUTOICOUS
ACIIMRSST	SCIMITARS	ACILNNQTU	CLINQUANT	ACIOOTTUX	AUTOTOXIC
ACIINNOTU	INCAUTION	ACILNOOST	LOCATIONS	ACIOPRSSY	CARYOPSIS
ACIINOPST	OPTICIANS	ACILNOPRT	PROLACTIN	ACIOPRSTT	PROSTATIC
ACIINORTV	VICTORIAN	ACILNORST	CONTRAILS	ACIOPTTUY	AUTOTYPIC
ACIINOSTT	CITATIONS	ACILNOSTT	CLINOSTAT	ACIRSSTUY	CASUISTRY
ACIINOTTX	ANTITOXIC	ACILNOSTU,	SUCTIONAL,	ACJKOPRST	JOCKSTRAP
ACIINOTTY	ATONICITY	SULCATION		ACJLLORUY	JOCULARLY
ACIIOPRST	PSORIATIC	ACILNPTUY	UNTYPICAL	ACKKMOPRS	POCKMARKS
ACIIOPRTT	PATRIOTIC	ACILNRSWY	SCRAWNILY	ACKLLNRTU	TRUNK CALL
ACIIOPTZZ	PIZZICATO	ACILOOPRS	ACROPOLIS	ACKLLPSSU	SKULLCAPS
ACIIORSSV	VARICOSIS	ACILOOPST	APOSTOLIC	ACKLMOOOR	CLOAKROOM
ACIIORSTY	CARIOSITY	ACILOORST	CASTOR OIL	ACKLNOPRT	ROCK PLANT
ACIIORSUV	VICARIOUS	ACILOQTUY	LOQUACITY	ACKLNORST	CORNSTALK
ACIIOSSTT	ISOSTATIC	ACILORRSU	CURSORIAL	ACKLORSST	CROSS TALK
ACIIOSUVV	VIVACIOUS	ACILORSSU	OSSICULAR	ACKLORSSW	CROSSWALK
ACIIPRSTT	PATRISTIC	ACILORSTU	SUCTORIAL	ACLLLLORS	ROLL CALLS
ACIIPTTVY	CAPTIVITY	ACILOSSTV	VOCALISTS	ACLLLOSUY	CALLOUSLY
ACIISSTTT	STATISTIC	ACILOTTUY	AUTOLYTIC	ACLLMNOSU	MOLLUSCAN
ACIISSTTV	ACTIVISTS	ACILPPRSY	SCRAPPILY	ACLLOORRY	COROLLARY
ACIJKNNOU	UNION JACK	ACILPSTTY	STYPTICAL	ACLLOORST	COLOSTRAL
ACIKKNNOT	ANTIKNOCK	ACILRRTUU	UTRICULAR	ACLMMNOOW	COMMON-LAW
ACIKKRSTT	KICK-START	ACILSSTTY	SYSTALTIC	ACLMNOORU	MONOCULAR
ACIKLLSST	SALTLICKS	ACIMMNOOT	MONATOMIC	ACLMOORSS	CLASSROOM
ACIKLMSTU	MAULSTICK	ACIMMORSS	COMMISSAR	ACLMOORSU	CLAMOROUS
ACIKLOSTT	TAILSTOCK	ACIMNNOOP	COMPANION	ACLMOPSTY	CYTOPLASM
ACIKLPSST	SLAPSTICK	ACIMNOOST	ONOMASTIC	ACLNNORTU	NOCTURNAL
ACIKOPSSY	SKIASCOPY	ACIMNOOTU	AUTONOMIC	ACLNOORTT	CONTRALTO
ACIKRSTTU	TRACKSUIT	ACIMNOOTX	TAXONOMIC	ACLOOORRT	CORALROOT
		ACIMNOPRY	PARONYMIC	ACLOOPRRS	CORPORALS

ACLOPPRYY	POLYCARPY	ADDEEGLNR	GLADDENER,	ADDEGLLMO	GOLD MEDAL
ACLOPRRSW	PROWL CARS		GLANDERED	ADDEGLRUY	GUARDEDLY
ACLOPRSUU	CRAPULOUS	ADDEEGNSW	SAND WEDGE	ADDEGNOOR	DRAGOONED,
ACLOPRTTU	PLUTOCRAT	ADDEEGORT	DEROGATED		GADROONED
ACLOPSTTY	CYTOPLAST	ADDEEHHOT	HOTHEADED	ADDEGNORW	DOWNGRADE
ACLORSUUY	RAUCOUSLY	ADDEEHILN	HEADLINED	ADDEGNRUU	UNGUARDED
ACLOSUUVY	VACUOUSLY	ADDEEHRSS	HEADDRESS	ADDEHHOTY	HYDATHODE
ACMNOORRT	CORMORANT	ADDEEHRTY	DEHYDRATE	ADDEHILOY	HOLIDAYED
ACMNOOSTU	COSMONAUT	ADDEEIILS	IDEALISED	ADDEHINRY	ANHYDRIDE
ACMNOPRYY	PYROMANCY	ADDEEIILZ	IDEALIZED	ADDEHINSW	HEADWINDS
ACMOORRST	MOTORCARS	ADDEEILNS	DEADLINES	ADDEHINSY	HENDIADYS
ACMORRSUU	MACRUROUS	ADDEEILRV	DAREDEVIL	ADDEHNNRU	UNDERHAND
ACMORSSTW	WORM CASTS	ADDEEILST	DEADLIEST	ADDEHNORS	HARD-NOSED
ACMORSTUY	CUSTOMARY	ADDEEIMTT	MEDITATED	ADDEHNORU	ROUNDHEAD
ACNNNOOST	CONSONANT	ADDEEINRT	DETRAINED	ADDEHNOTW	TWO-HANDED
ACNNOSSTT	CONSTANTS	ADDEEIPRR	DRAPERIED	ADDEHORSW	HEADWORDS
ACNOOPRST	CORPOSANT	ADDEEIPRS	DESPAIRED	ADDEHTTUY	DEATH DUTY
ACNOORRSU	RANCOROUS	ADDEEIPRU	DEPARDIEU	ADDEIIIMT	DIMIDIATE
ACNORRSST	CONTRASTS	ADDEELNRS	SLANDERED	ADDEIILNV	INVALIDED
ACNORSTTU	TURNCOATS	ADDEELNRU	LAUNDERED	ADDEIILNX	DIXIELAND
ACNORSTTY	CONTRASTY	ADDEELOST	DESOLATED	ADDEIIMNS	DESMIDIAN
ACOOPPRRS	SPOROCARP	ADDEEMMNO	DESDEMONA	ADDEIINNR	RED INDIAN
ACOORSSTU	AUTOCROSS	ADDEEMNRU	MAUNDERED	ADDEIISTV	ADDITIVES
ACOPRRSST	SPORTS CAR	ADDEEMNST	DAMNEDEST	ADDEIKNPP	KIDNAPPED
ACOSSTTTY	STATOCYST	ADDEEMORT	MODERATED	ADDEILLNS	LANDSLIDE
ADDDEEEHR	RED-HEADED	ADDEEMPST	STAMPEDED	ADDEILMMN	MIDDLEMAN
ADDDEEFRU	DEFRAUDED	ADDEENNPT	DEPENDANT	ADDEILNNO	DANDELION
ADDDEEGLN	GLADDENED	ADDEENOST	STONE-DEAD	ADDEILNSY	DEADLY SIN
ADDDEEHNR	RED-HANDED	ADDEENOTT	DETONATED	ADDEILPSY	DISPLAYED
ADDDEEKLS	SKEDADDLE	ADDEENSST	DATEDNESS	ADDEILSVY	ADVISEDLY
ADDDEERSS	ADDRESSED	ADDEENSWY	WEDNESDAY	ADDEIMNOT	DEMANTOID,
ADDDEFIIN	DANDIFIED	ADDEEOPRS	DESPERADO		DOMINATED
ADDDEGLOP	DOG PADDLE	ADDEEPRSU	PERSUADED	ADDEIMNSY	MANY-SIDED
ADDDEIINS	DISDAINED	ADDEEPSUX	PAS DE DEUX	ADDEIMNTY	DYNAMITED
ADDDEISSU	DISSUADED	ADDEERRSS	ADDRESSER,	ADDEIMORT	DERMATOID
ADDDELNSU	UNSADDLED		READDRESS	ADDEIMSST	DISMASTED
ADDDELRST	STRADDLED	ADDEERSSS	ADDRESSES	ADDEINNTU	INUNDATED
ADDEEEFRT	FEDERATED	ADDEFFHNO	OFFHANDED	ADDEINPRU	UNDERPAID
ADDEEEGLT	DELEGATED	ADDEFFLOO	OFF-LOADED	ADDEINRTT	DITTANDER
ADDEEEGRY	DEGREE-DAY	ADDEFIIPT	PEDATIFID	ADDEINRTW	TRADE WIND
ADDEEEMNR	MEANDERED	ADDEFILSY	FIELD DAYS	ADDEINSUV	UNADVISED
ADDEEENRS	SERENADED	ADDEFINNR	FERDINAND	ADDEIOSVW	DISAVOWED
ADDEEERRT	RETREADED	ADDEFINSS	FADDINESS	ADDEIRSSU	DISSUADER
ADDEEERSS	ADDRESSEE	ADDEFORRW	FORWARDED	ADDEIRSSW	SIDEWARDS
ADDEEFHIX	FIXED-HEAD	ADDEGGINR	DEGRADING	ADDEJNORU	ADJOURNED
ADDEEFILN	ENFILADED	ADDEGGOOT	DOG-EAT-DOG	ADDELLOPR	POLLARDED
ADDEEFLTU	DEFAULTED	ADDEGHILR	HILDEGARD	ADDELMOTU	MODULATED
ADDEEFNNT	DEFENDANT	ADDEGHILT	DEADLIGHT	ADDELNTUU	UNDULATED
ADDEEFNSS	FADEDNESS	ADDEGHINR	HAG-RIDDEN	ADDELRRST	STRADDLER
ADDEEFRRU	DEFRAUDER	ADDEGILNR	LADDERING	ADDEMORRY	DROMEDARY
ADDEEGHIP	PIGHEADED	ADDEGIMNN	DEMANDING,	ADDENNRTU	REDUNDANT
ADDEEGILM	MIDDLE AGE		MADDENING	ADDENNSSU	SAND DUNES
ADDEEGINN	DEADENING	ADDEGINNS	SADDENING	ADDENNTUU	UNDAUNTED
ADDEEGIRS	DISAGREED	ADDEGINOS	DIAGNOSED	ADDENOORT	DEODORANT
		ADDEGIRRS	DISREGARD	ADDENOPTU	UNADOPTED

ADDENORUY	DUODENARY	ADEEEELMNP	EMPANELED	ADEEGINRR	GRENADIER
ADDENOSTU	ASTOUNDED	ADEEEELNRZ	ZEELANDER	ADEEGINRT	DENIGRATE
ADDEOPSTT	POSTDATED	ADEEEELPRR	REPLEADER	ADEEGINST	DESIGNATE
ADDEPPRSU	SUPPERADD	ADEEEMMNRR	MEANDERER	ADEEGINSV	ENVISAGED
ADDEPQRUU	QUADRUPED	ADEEEMPRT	PERMEATED	ADEEGINTV	NEGATIVED
ADDFFILOS	DAFFODILS	ADEEENRRS	SERENADER	ADEEGIRST	TRAGEDIES
ADDFHILSY	FADDISHLY	ADEEENRSS	SERENADES	ADEEGIUVW	WAVEGUIDE
ADDFIIQRU	QUADRIFID	ADEEENRST	EAST ENDER	ADEEGLLLY	ALLEGEDLY
ADDGGIJNU	ADJUDGING	ADEEENRTT	ENTREATED	ADEEGLLRV	GRAVELLED
ADDGHNORU	DRAGHOUND	ADEEENRTV	ENERVATED,	ADEEGLNNR	GREENLAND
ADDGILNSW	SWADDLING		VENERATED	ADEEGLNNT	ENTANGLED
ADDGMRSUU	MUDGUARDS	ADEEEPRST	DESPERATE	ADEEGLNOT	ELONGATED
ADDHHIOOR	HARDIHOOD	ADEEERRTT	RETREATED	ADEEGLNRY	ENRAGEDLY,
ADDHIKNRR	HARD DRINK	ADEEERTWW	WATERWEED		LEGENDARY
ADDHIKRSS	HARD DISKS	ADEEFFILR	FIELDFARE	ADEEGLOOW	EAGLEWOOD
ADDHNNOSW	HANDS DOWN	ADEEFFLOT	FLOAT-FEED	ADEEGLRTU	REGULATED
ADDHOORSW	HARDWOODS	ADEEFGINN	DEAFENING	ADEEGMNRR	GERMANDER
ADDIINOST	ADDITIONS	ADEEFGINT	DEFEATING	ADEEGMNRS	GENDARMES
ADDINORSU	DIANDROUS	ADEEFHORS	FOREHEADS	ADEEGMNTU	AUGMENTED
ADDIOPRTY	ODD PARITY	ADEEFIKLW	WAKEFIELD	ADEEGMRRU	DEMURRAGE
ADDIORRST	DIRT ROADS	ADEEFIKRR	FREDERIKA	ADEEGNNRS	GREENSAND
ADDKNRRSU	DRUNKARDS	ADEEFILNS	ENFILADES	ADEEGNRRS	GARDENERS
ADDLLNNOU	LLANDUDNO	ADEEFILOT	DEFOLIATE	ADEEGNRST	ESTRANGED
ADDLLNORS	LANDLORDS	ADEEFILSU	FEUDALISE	ADEEGNRSU	DUNGAREES
ADDLNNOOP	PONDOLAND	ADEEFILUZ	FEUDALIZE	ADEEGNRSV	GRAVESEND
ADDMNOOTU	ODD MAN OUT	ADEEFIMST	DEFEATISM	ADEEGORRZ	RAZOR EDGE
ADDNNOPUW	UP-AND-DOWN	ADEEFINRR	REFRAINED	ADEEGRRSS	DEERGRASS
ADDNORSWW	DOWNWARDS	ADEEFISTT	DEFEATIST	ADEEHHLRY	HEYERDAHL
ADEEEEGLY	EAGLE-EYED	ADEEFLLNN	FLANNELED	ADEEHIISV	HEAVISIDE
ADEEEEFHRT	FEATHERED	ADEEFLLST	STALL-FEED	ADEEHIKLT	DEATHLIKE
ADEEEFLLT	LEAFLETED	ADEEFLNTT	FLATTENED	ADEEHILNR	HEADLINER
ADEEEFNRR	REFERENDA	ADEEFLRTT	FLATTERED	ADEEHILNS	HEADLINES
ADEEEFRRT	FREE TRADE	ADEEFLRTU	DEFAULTER	ADEEHILNT	ETHELINDA
ADEEEGHNR	GREENHEAD	ADEEFMNOR	FORENAMED	ADEEHILTW	WHITE DEAL,
ADEEEGLRT	RELEGATED	ADEEFMORR	FOREARMED		WHITE LEAD
ADEEEGLST	DELEGATES	ADEEFMSTU	DEAF-MUTES	ADEEHIMNV	MIDHEAVEN
ADEEEGNRS	RENEGADES	ADEEFNOST	STONE-DEAF	ADEEHINRT	HERNIATED
ADEEEGNRT	GENERATED	ADEEGGINS	DISENGAGE	ADEEHINSS	HEADINESS
ADEEEGTTV	VEGETATED	ADEEGGIRV	AGGRIEVED	ADEEHIRRV	RIVERHEAD
ADEEEHHRT	HEATHERED	ADEEGGLNO	GOLDEN AGE	ADEEHISSV	ADHESIVES
ADEEEHKNR	HEARKENED	ADEEGGMOU	DEMAGOGUE	ADEEHISTT	HESITATED
ADEEEHLST	STEELHEAD	ADEEGGOPU	PEDAGOGUE	ADEEHLLOS	LEASEHOLD
ADEEEHNRT	HEARTENED	ADEEGGRST	STAGGERED	ADEEHLNSU	UNLEASHED
ADEEEHPRT	PREHEATED	ADEEGGRSW	SWAGGERED	ADEEHLOSU	HEAD LOUSE
ADEEEHRRS	REHEARSED	ADEEGILLR	GALLERIED	ADEEHLSST	DEATHLESS
ADEEEHRTW	WEATHERED	ADEEGILLS	LEGALISED	ADEEHMNOT	METHADONE
ADEEEILMN	MADELEINE	ADEEGILLZ	LEGALIZED	ADEEHMOST	HOMESTEAD
ADEEEILNT	DELINEATE	ADEEGILNR	GERALDINE,	ADEEHNOST	HEADSTONE
ADEEEINRS	DEANERIES		REALIGNED	ADEEHNPPR	APPREHEND
ADEEEINST	DETAINEES	ADEEGILNW	WIDE-ANGLE	ADEEHNPRS	SHARPENED
ADEEEIRSS	DIAERESES	ADEEGIMNN	DEMEANING	ADEEHNRSS	HARNESSED
ADEEEKKNW	WEAK-KNEED	ADEEGIMOV	VIDEO GAME	ADEEHNRST	ADHERENTS
ADEEELLMN	ENAMELLED	ADEEGIMRT	EMIGRATED	ADEEHNRTU	UNEARTHED
ADEEELLNS	LEND-LEASE	ADEEGINNR	ENDEARING,	ADEEHORRV	OVERHEARD
			GRENADINE	ADEEHORSV	OVERHEADS

ADEEHOSWY	EYE SHADOW	ADEEINRTT	DENITRATE	ADEEMNRST	SMARTENED,
ADEEHPRRS	REPHRASED	ADEEINRUW	UNWEARIED		TRADESMEN
ADEEHPRSY	SHARP-EYED	ADEEINTVV	ADVENTIVE	ADEEMNRTY	DYNAMETER
ADEEHRSST	HEADRESTS	ADEEIOPRT	PERIODATE	ADEEMOORR	AERODROME
ADEEHRSTT	SHATTERED	ADEEIOPTV	VIDEOTAPE	ADEEMOPRR	MADREPORE
ADEEHRSTV	HARVESTED	ADEEIPPST	PEPTIDASE	ADEEMORRX	XERODERMA
ADEEHRSTW	WATERSHED	ADEEIPRRS	DRAPERIES	ADEEMORST	MODERATES
ADEEHSTUX	EXHAUSTED	ADEEIPRTU	REPUDIATE	ADEEMORTT	TREMATODE
ADEEIILRS	IDEALISER	ADEEIRRST	DREARIEST	ADEEMOSTU	EDEMATOUS
ADEEIILRZ	IDEALIZER	ADEEIRSTV	ADVERTISE	ADEEMPRST	STAMPEDER
ADEEIIMMT	IMMEDIATE	ADEEIRSTW	WATERSIDE	ADEEMPSST	STAMPEDES
ADEEIIMST	MEDIATISE	ADEEIRTTW	TIDEWATER	ADEEMPSTU	DESPUMATE,
ADEEIIMTV	MEDIATIVE	ADEEIRTTX	EXTRADITE		STEAMED-UP
ADEEIIMTZ	MEDIATIZE	ADEEISSTT	STATESIDE,	ADEEMPTTT	ATTEMPTED
ADEEIIRSS	DIAERESIS		STEADIEST	ADEEMRSTW	WET DREAMS
ADEEIJMRS	JEREMIADS	ADEEISSTV	SEDATIVES	ADEENNPRT	TREPANNED
ADEEIKLMR	DREAMLIKE	ADEEITUVX	EXUDATIVE	ADEENORST	RESONATED
ADEEILLUV	DEAUVILLE	ADEEKNNSS	NAKEDNESS	ADEENORTV	RENOVATED
ADEEILMNN	MENDELIAN	ADEEKNRTU	UNDERTAKE	ADEENORUV	ENDEAVOUR
ADEEILMNS	LADIES' MEN,	ADEELLMRV	MARVELLED	ADEENORVY	OVEN-READY
MELISANDE		ADEELLNRY	LEARNEDLY	ADEENPPRT	ENTRAPPED
ADEEILMPR	EPIDERMAL,	ADEELLPSY	PLEASEDLY	ADEENPRRT	PARTNERED
IMPLEADER		ADEELLRTV	TRAVELLED	ADEENPRTT	PATTERNED
ADEEILMRS	MISDEALER,	ADEELLRXY	RELAXEDLY	ADEENRRSW	WANDERERS
MISLEADER		ADEELLTXY	EXALTEDLY	ADEENRRTU	UNDERRATE
ADEEILMST	LEAD TIMES	ADEELMRSS	DREAMLESS	ADEENRRUW	UNDERWEAR
ADEEILNPS	PENALISED	ADEELNNRU	UNLEARNED	ADEENRSTU	SAUNTERED
ADEEILNPX	EXPLAINED	ADEELNORS	OLEANDERS	ADEENRSTY	SEDENTARY
ADEEILNPZ	PENALIZED	ADEELNORV	OVERLADEN	ADEENRTTU	UNTREATED
ADEEILNST	DATELINES	ADEELNOST	ENDOSTEAL	ADEENRTUV	ADVENTURE
ADEEILOTT	ETIOLATED	ADEELNRRS	SLANDERER	ADEENSTTV	VENDETTAS
ADEEILPPR	LIP-READER	ADEELNRRU	LAUNDERER	ADEEOPRSV	EAVESDROP
ADEEILPRS	PEARLISED	ADEELNRSU	UNDERSEAL	ADEEORRTV	OVERRATED,
ADEEILPRV	PREVAILED	ADEELNRTU	UNRELATED	OVERTRADE	
ADEEILPRZ	PEARLIZED	ADEELNRUV	UNRAVELED	ADEEORTVX	OVERTAXED
ADEEILPSS	DISPLEASE	ADEELORST	DESOLATER	ADEEPPRSS	APPRESSED
ADEEILQSU	EQUALISED	ADEELORTT	TOLERATED	ADEEPPRST	SPEED TRAP
ADEEILQUZ	EQUALIZED	ADEELPRST	PLASTERED	ADEEPRRSU	PERSUADER
ADEEILTTV	LEVITATED	ADEELPSST	PEDESTALS	ADEEPRRTU	DEPARTURE
ADEEIMMRT	DREAMTIME	ADEELQRRU	QUARRELED	ADEEPRRST	PEDERASTS
ADEEIMNNO	MENADIONE	ADEELRRST	RED ALERTS	ADEEPRSTT	SPATTERED
ADEEIMNOU	EUDEMONIA	ADEELRRTT	RED RATTLE	ADEEPRSTU	DEPASTURE
ADEEIMNRR	REMAINDER	ADEELRRTU	ADULTERER	ADEEPRSTY	PEDERASTY
ADEEIMNRT	MINARETED	ADEELRSTY	STEELYARD	ADEEPSSWY	SPEEDWAYS
ADEEIMPPR	PIPE DREAM	ADEELRSVY	ADVERSELY	ADEEQRRTU	QUARTERED
ADEEIMRRR	REMARRIED	ADEEMMNNT	AMENDMENT	ADEERRSSU	REASSURED
ADEEIMRST	DIAMETERS	ADEEMMORT	DERMATOME	ADEERRSTU	TREASURED
ADEEIMSST	DEMITASSE	ADEEMMOXY	MYXOEDEMA	ADEERRSTV	TRAVERSED
ADEEIMSTT	ESTIMATED	ADEEMMRST	STAMMERED	ADEERSTYY	YESTERDAY
ADEEINNOS	ADENOSINE	ADEEMNOPR	PROMENADE	ADEFFIILS	FALSIFIED
ADEEINNRT	ENTRAINED	ADEEMNORT	EMENDATOR	ADEFFNORT	AFFRONTED
ADEEINPRT	PERTAINED	ADEEMNORU	DEMEANOUR,	ADEFFOORR	OFF-ROADER
ADEEINPST	NEAP TIDES	ENAMOURED		ADEFFORST	TRADE-OFFS
ADEEINRSS	READINESS	ADEEMNRRU	MAUNDERER	ADEFGHORT	GODFATHER
ADEEINRST	RESINATED			ADEFGIIMN	MAGNIFIED

313

ADEFGIIRT	GRATIFIED	ADEFOOPRR	PROOFREAD	ADEGILNPS	PLEADINGS
ADEFGILLO	FIELD GOAL	ADEFOOTTU	OUT-OF-DATE	ADEGILNRU	GERUNDIAL
ADEFGILNT	DEFLATING	ADEFORRRW	FORWARDER	ADEGILNUV	DEVALUING
ADEFGILRU	LIFEGUARD	ADEFORRTV	OVERDRAFT	ADEGILNVY	EVADINGLY
ADEFGIMTU	FUMIGATED	ADEFORRTW	AFTERWORD,	ADEGILORU	DIALOGUER
ADEFGINRY	DEFRAYING	WATERFORD		ADEGILOSU	DIALOGUES
ADEFGIRRU	FIREGUARD	ADEFORTUY	FEUDATORY	ADEGILRSS	GLISSADER
ADEFGLOOT	FLOODGATE	ADEGGGIZZ	ZIGZAGGED	ADEGIMNNP	DAMPENING
ADEFGLRRU	REGARDFUL	ADEGGHHIR	HIGH-GRADE	ADEGIMNNR	REMANDING
ADEFHIMST	HAM-FISTED	ADEGGINNR	GARDENING	ADEGIMNTU	MAGNITUDE
ADEFHINOS	FASHIONED	ADEGGINRR	REGARDING	ADEGIMORS	IDEOGRAMS
ADEFHINRT	THREADFIN	ADEGGINUW	WIND GAUGE	ADEGIMOST	DOGMATISE
ADEFHIPSS	SPADEFISH	ADEGGIRST	DRAGGIEST	ADEGIMOTZ	DOGMATIZE
ADEFHIRST	HEADFIRST	ADEGGLORY	GARGOYLED	ADEGIMNNP	DAMPENING
ADEFHLNOZ	HALF-DOZEN	ADEGGLRST	STRAGGLED	ADEGINNPP	APPENDING
ADEFHLOOS	FALSEHOOD	ADEGGMORT	MORTGAGED	ADEGINNPR	PANDERING
ADEFHNORS	FOREHANDS	ADEGGNORU	GROUNDAGE	ADEGINNPX	EXPANDING
ADEFHNORU	UNHEARD-OF	ADEGHHILT	HEADLIGHT	ADEGINNRT	INTEGRAND
ADEFIILMP	AMPLIFIED	ADEGHHOSS	HOGSHEADS	ADEGINNRW	WANDERING
ADEFIILNS	FINALISED	ADEGHILNR	HERALDING	ADEGINNTT	ATTENDING
ADEFIILNZ	FINALIZED	ADEGHINNR	HARDENING	ADEGINORR	RIO GRANDE
ADEFIILQU	QUALIFIED	ADEGHINRS	GARNISHED	ADEGINORS	GRANDIOSE,
ADEFIILRS	AIRFIELDS	ADEGHINRT	THREADING	ORGANISED	
ADEFIILRT	AIRLIFTED	ADEGHINSU	ANGUISHED	ADEGINORZ	ORGANIZED
ADEFIIPRR	RAPID-FIRE	ADEGHIRST	SIGHT-READ	ADEGINOSS	DIAGNOSES
ADEFIISST	SATISFIED	ADEGHLLNO	HELGOLAND	ADEGINPRS	SPREADING
ADEFIKNRW	DRAWKNIFE	ADEGHLMPU	GALUMPHED	ADEGINPRT	DEPARTING,
ADEFILLSU	FUSILLADE	ADEGHLORS	GASHOLDER	PREDATING	
ADEFILMNS	FIELDSMAN,	ADEGHMORU	HOME GUARD	ADEGINPRV	DEPRAVING,
MANSFIELD		ADEGHNOPR	HOP GARDEN	PERVADING	
ADEFILMSU	FEUDALISM	ADEGHNOUZ	GAZEHOUND	ADEGINRRT	RETARDING
ADEFILNOT	DEFLATION,	ADEGHORST	GOATHERDS	ADEGINRRW	REWARDING
DEFOLIANT		ADEGHRRTU	DRAUGHTER	ADEGINRST	GRADIENTS, RED
ADEFILNRS	FRIESLAND	ADEGHRSTU	DAUGHTERS	GIANTS	
ADEFILNSS	SAND FLIES	ADEGIILNR	DERAILING,	ADEGINRTV	ADVERTING
ADEFILNTY	DEFIANTLY	GRINDELIA		ADEGINSSU	GAUDINESS
ADEFILORT	FLORIATED	ADEGIILNT	DETAILING	ADEGINSTT	DIGESTANT
ADEFILSTU	FEUDALIST	ADEGIILOS	DIALOGISE	ADEGINSTY	STEADYING
ADEFILTUY	FEUDALITY	ADEGIILOZ	DIALOGIZE	ADEGIPRRT	PARTRIDGE
ADEFIMORS	ASIDE FROM	ADEGIILPT	PIGTAILED	ADEGIRTTU	GRATITUDE
ADEFINOST	INSTEAD OF	ADEGIILTT	LITIGATED	ADEGLLLOU	DOLGELLAU
ADEFIRSTT	DRAFTIEST	ADEGIIMNT	MEDIATING	ADEGLLOPT	GOLD PLATE
ADEFIRSTX	FIXED STAR	ADEGIIMTT	MITIGATED	ADEGLNNTU	UNTANGLED
ADEFLLMOS	OLD FLAMES	ADEGIINNR	INGRAINED	ADEGLNRST	STRANGLED
ADEFLLMOU	LEAF MOULD	ADEGIINNT	DETAINING	ADEGLOOPY	PAEDOLOGY
ADEFLLMSY	DAMSELFLY	ADEGIINNU	GUANIDINE	ADEGLORST	OLD STAGER
ADEFLMMOR	MALFORMED	ADEGIINTV	DEVIATING	ADEGMNRSU	GUARDSMEN
ADEFLOPST	SOFT-PEDAL	ADEGIIRRT	IRRIGATED	ADEGMOPRR	PROGRAMED
ADEFLORUV	FLAVOURED	ADEGIKNNR	DARKENING	ADEGNNOPR	PENDRAGON
ADEFLORWY	DAYFLOWER	ADEGILLNP	PEDALLING	ADEGNNORW	DOWNRANGE
ADEFLRSTW	LEFTWARDS	ADEGILLNS	SIGNALLED	ADEGNNRSS	GRANDNESS
ADEFMNNTU	FUNDAMENT	ADEGILNNR	LENINGRAD	ADEGNOOOS	A GOOD NOSE
ADEFMNRST	DRAFTSMEN	ADEGILNOR	GIRANDOLE,	ADEGNOORS	GOOSANDER
ADEFMOORR	DOORFRAME	RELOADING		ADEGNOPRT	GODPARENT
ADEFMORTT	FORMATTED	ADEGILNOS	ALONGSIDE	ADEGNORSS	DRAGONESS
				ADEGNORSU	DANGEROUS

ADEGNOSTW	DOWNSTAGE	ADEHNOSSS	SANDSHOES	ADEILLPRS	SPIRALLED
ADEGOORST	STAGE DOOR	ADEHNPPRU	UPPER HAND	ADEILLPRU	PRELUDIAL
ADEGORRTT	GARROTTED	ADEHNSSSU	SUNSHADES	ADEILLQRU	QUADRILLE
ADEHHIPSS	HEADSHIPS	ADEHOORSU	ROADHOUSE	ADEILMMOT	IMMOLATED
ADEHHISTW	DEATH WISH	ADEHOORTW	HEARTWOOD	ADEILMNNS	LANDMINES
ADEHIILRS	HAIR SLIDE	ADEHOOSTT	STATEHOOD	ADEILMNPT	IMPLANTED
ADEHIISST	DIATHESIS	ADEHOPPPY	POPPYHEAD	ADEILMNST	DISMANTLE
ADEHIKNPS	HANDSPIKE	ADEHOSTUW	WASHED-OUT	ADEILMNTU	DENTALIUM
ADEHIKNRT	IN THE DARK	ADEHTUVYY	HEAVY-DUTY	ADEILMOPT	DIPLOMATE
ADEHIKNSS	SKINHEADS	ADEIIILNT	INITIALED	ADEILMOPY	POLYAMIDE
ADEHILLMR	HEIMDALLR	ADEIIINTT	DIETITIAN,	ADEILMORR	MAIL ORDER
ADEHILMNS	MISHANDLE		INITIATED	ADEILMORS	MORALISED
ADEHILMOT	ETHMOIDAL	ADEIILMNN	MAINLINED	ADEILMORZ	MORALIZED
ADEHILNNR	RHINELAND	ADEIILMOZ	IMIDAZOLE	ADEILMOTV	MOLDAVITE
ADEHILNPR	PHILANDER	ADEIILMTT	MILITATED	ADEILMPTU	AMPLITUDE
ADEHILNRR	HARD-LINER	ADEIILNRT	DELIRIANT	ADEILMSTU	SIMULATED
ADEHILNRS	HARD LINES	ADEIILNST	DISENTAIL	ADEILMTTU	MUTILATED
ADEHILRRT	TRIHEDRAL	ADEIILORT	EDITORIAL	ADEILNNRU	UNDERLAIN
ADEHILRST	HERALDIST	ADEIILQTU	LIQUIDATE	ADEILNOPP	PANOPLIED
ADEHIMNOR	RHODAMINE	ADEIILSST	IDEALISTS	ADEILNOPT	PLANETOID
ADEHIMNSU	HUMANISED	ADEIIMMSX	MAXIMISED	ADEILNOPU	ANEUPLOID
ADEHIMNUZ	HUMANIZED	ADEIIMMXZ	MAXIMIZED	ADEILNRRT	INTERLARD
ADEHIMOSU	HOUSEMAID	ADEIIMNOT	MEDIATION	ADEILNRSS	ISLANDERS
ADEHIMPTW	WHITEDAMP	ADEIIMNRS	MERIDIANS	ADEILNRSU	LAUNDRIES
ADEHIMRTY	DIATHERMY	ADEIIMNRT	AD INTERIM	ADEILNRTU	UITLANDER
ADEHINNSS	HANDINESS	ADEIIMNTT	INTIMATED	ADEILNSSV	VALIDNESS
ADEHINOPU	AUDIPHONE	ADEIIMOTT	DIATOMITE	ADEILNSTU	INSULATED
ADEHINORS	RHODESIAN	ADEIIMSSV	ADMISSIVE,	ADEILOPRS	POLARISED
ADEHINOSS	ADHESIONS		MISADVISE	ADEILOPRT	DEPILATOR
ADEHINRSS	HARDINESS	ADEIINNOS	INDONESIA	ADEILOPRZ	POLARIZED
ADEHINRST	TARNISHED	ADEIINOTV	DEVIATION	ADEILOQSU	ODALISQUE
ADEHINRSV	VARNISHED	ADEIINPPR	DRAINPIPE	ADEILORST	IDOLATERS
ADEHINRTY	ANHYDRITE	ADEIINSST	SANITISED	ADEILOSTV	DOVETAILS
ADEHINRYZ	HYDRAZINE	ADEIINSTT	DAINTIEST	ADEILPPRY	REPLY-PAID
ADEHINSSS	SHADINESS	ADEIINSTZ	SANITIZED	ADEILPRSS	DISPERSAL
ADEHIOOST	THEODOSIA	ADEIIOSTZ	DIAZOTISE	ADEILPRSU	EPIDURALS
ADEHIOPRT	ATROPHIED	ADEIIOTVX	OXIDATIVE	ADEILPRSY	DISPLAYER
ADEHIORSW	SHADOWIER	ADEIIOTZZ	DIAZOTIZE	ADEILPTTU	PLATITUDE
ADEHIPRST	THERAPSID	ADEIIPRRS	DISREPAIR	ADEILRTTU	RUTILATED
ADEHIRRTT	THIRD-RATE	ADEIIPRSS	DISPRAISE	ADEILSSTU	LASSITUDE
ADEHIRSTW	DISHWATER	ADEIIPSST	DISSIPATE	ADEILSTTU	ALTITUDES,
ADEHKNOSW	SHAKEDOWN	ADEIIRRTT	IRRITATED		LATITUDES
ADEHKORRS	DARK HORSE	ADEIIRSST	SATIRISED	ADEIMNNOT	NOMINATED
ADEHLLNOR	HOLLANDER	ADEIIRSTZ	SATIRIZED	ADEIMNOPT	ADEMPTION
ADEHLLOSW	SHALLOWED	ADEIITTTV	TITIVATED	ADEIMNORS	RANDOMISE
ADEHLLOTT	DEATH TOLL	ADEIKKSST	KIDSTAKES	ADEIMNORZ	RANDOMIZE
ADEHLMNOS	HOMELANDS	ADEIKMORS	KAISERDOM	ADEIMNOST	MAIDSTONE
ADEHLORST	ALDERSHOT	ADEIKMRST	TIDEMARKS	ADEIMNOSW	WOMANISED
ADEHMOOPS	SHAMPOOED	ADEIKNPPR	KIDNAPPER	ADEIMNOWZ	WOMANIZED
ADEHMORSW	HOMEWARDS	ADEIKNPRS	SPIKENARD	ADEIMNPRR	REPRIMAND
ADEHMOSSU	MADHOUSES	ADEILLMNO	MEDALLION	ADEIMNPRS	SPIDERMAN
ADEHNOOPR	HARPOONED	ADEILLMOT	METALLOID	ADEIMNRRU	UNMARRIED
ADEHNOPRS	HORNED ASP	ADEILLMRT	TREADMILL	ADEIMNRSU	NURSEMAID
ADEHNORSV	HANDOVERS	ADEILLMST	MEDALLIST	ADEIMNRTU	RUMINATED
		ADEILLNST	INSTALLED		

ADEIMNRTY	DYNAMITER	ADEKLOTTU	OUTTALKED	ADENORRVW	OVERDRAWN
ADEIMORST	AMORTISED,	ADEKNORTU	OUTRANKED	ADENOTTWY	WYANDOTTE
MEDIATORS		ADEKOPRSW	SPADEWORK	ADENPRSSU	UNDERPASS
ADEIMORTT	MEDITATOR	ADELLLOWY	ALLOWEDLY	ADEOORRST	TOREADORS
ADEIMORTZ	AMORTIZED	ADELLMRUY	MEDULLARY	ADEOPRRST	PREDATORS,
ADEIMOTTV	MOTIVATED	ADELLNORW	LOWLANDER	TEARDROPS	
ADEIMPRST	SPERMATID	ADELLNOUY	UNALLOYED	ADEOPRRTU	DEPURATOR
ADEIMRTUX	ADMIXTURE	ADELLOPRT	PATROLLED	ADEOPRRTW	TOP DRAWER
ADEIMRTXY	TAXIDERMY	ADELLORRT	TALL ORDER	ADEOPRRTY	PORTRAYED,
ADEIMSSTT	MISSTATED	ADELLOSWW	SWALLOWED	PREDATORY	
ADEINNNSU	DUNSINANE	ADELMNNUY	MUNDANELY	ADEOPRSTU	OUTSPREAD
ADEINNNTT	INTENDANT	ADELMNOOP	LAMPOONED	ADEOPRTTY	TETRAPODY
ADEINNOTT	DENTATION	ADELMNOPS	ENDOPLASM	ADEORRSST	ROADSTERS
ADEINNOTV	INNOVATED	ADELMORST	OLD MASTER	ADEORRSWW	SWEARWORD
ADEINNRSS	RANDINESS	ADELNNORW	LANDOWNER	ADEORSSTT	ROAD TESTS
ADEINNSSS	SANDINESS	ADELNOOPR	APELDOORN	ADEORSTTU	OUTSTARED
ADEINOOTX	EXODONTIA	ADELNOOST	LOADSTONE	ADEOSTTUY	OUTSTAYED
ADEINOPPT	APPOINTED	ADELNOPSY	DYSPNOEAL	ADEPPPRUW	WRAPPED UP
ADEINOPRR	PREORDAIN	ADELNORRV	LAND ROVER	ADEPRSSSU	SURPASSED
ADEINOPRT	PREDATION	ADELNORSU	UNLOADERS	ADERSSTWW	WESTWARDS
ADEINOPST	ANTIPODES	ADELNORUY	ROUNDELAY	ADFFGINOR	AFFORDING
ADEINORST	NOTARISED	ADELNPRUY	UNDERPLAY	ADFFIIMRS	DISAFFIRM
ADEINORTY	ARYTENOID	ADELNRSSU	LAUNDRESS	ADFGHIOOT	GOOD FAITH
ADEINORTZ	NOTARIZED	ADELNRSUY	UNDERLAYS	ADFGHIRSU	FISHGUARD
ADEINOSTT	ANTIDOTES,	ADELNSSTU	DAUNTLESS	ADFGINORS	SANGFROID
STATIONED		ADELOOPRT	DOORPLATE	ADFGLNORY	DRAGONFLY
ADEINOTUX	EXUDATION	ADELOORSV	OVERLOADS	ADFHINRST	FIRSTHAND
ADEINPPRS	SANDPIPER	ADELOPPRS	PROLAPSED	ADFHLOORY	FOOLHARDY
ADEINPPST	STANDPIPE	ADELOPPTU	POPULATED	ADFILLNSW	WINDFALLS
ADEINPRSS	RAPIDNESS	ADELOPTUY	OUTPLAYED,	ADFILMNOS	MANIFOLDS
ADEINPSSV	VAPIDNESS	PLAYED-OUT		ADFILRSTY	FIRST LADY
ADEINRSST	STREISAND,	ADELORSST	LODESTARS	ADFIORSUV	DISAVOUR
TARDINESS		ADELOSTTU	OUTLASTED	ADFLLNOSW	DOWNFALLS
ADEINRSVY	VINEYARDS	ADELPQRUU	QUADRUPLE	ADFLLOOST	FALDSTOOL
ADEINSSST	STAIDNESS	ADELRSSUY	ASSUREDLY	ADFLORRWY	FORWARDLY
ADEINSSTU	SUSTAINED	ADEMMORST	MASTERDOM	ADFMOOPST	FOOD STAMP
ADEINSSTY	DYNASTIES	ADEMNNORT	ADORNMENT	ADFNOORSZ	SFORZANDO
ADEIOPRSV	VAPORISED	ADEMNOPRS	POMANDERS	ADGGGNNOU	GUANGDONG
ADEIOPRTZ	TRAPEZOID	ADEMNORSU	MEANDROUS	ADGGILNRY	NIGGARDLY
ADEIOPRVZ	VAPORIZED	ADEMNRRSU	SNARE DRUM	ADGGINPRU	UPGRADING
ADEIORSST	ASTEROIDS	ADEMNSSUU	UNASSUMED	ADGGLOORV	VOLGOGRAD
ADEIORSVW	DISAVOWER	ADEMOORRT	MODERATOR	ADGGLRSSU	SLUGGARDS
ADEIORTVY	DEVIATORY	ADEMOORST	ASTRODOME,	ADGHHILNS	HIGHLANDS
ADEIPPSSY	DYSPEPSIA	MODERATOS		ADGHHINRT	RIGHT-HAND
ADEIPRSSY	PRISE DAYS	ADEMORRTT	ROTTERDAM	ADGHHIORS	HIGH ROADS
ADEIPRSYZ	PRIZE DAYS	ADENNNSTU	SUNTANNED	ADGHIIMNS	GANDHIISM
ADEIPRTVY	DEPRAVITY	ADENNOPSS	SENNA PODS	ADGHILLLU	GUILDHALL
ADEIPSTTU	APTITUDES	ADENNOSST	SANDSTONE	ADGHILNSY	DASHINGLY
ADEIRRSUY	RESIDUARY	ADENNOSTY	ASYNDETON	ADGHILSTY	DAYLIGHTS
ADEIRSSST	DISASTERS	ADENNSSTW	NEWSSTAND	ADGHIMOSU	MOGADISHU
ADEIRSTVY	ADVERSITY	ADENOORST	TORNADOES	ADGHINNNU	UNHANDING
ADEIRSVWY	DRIVEWAYS	ADENOORTT	DETONATOR	ADGHINORS	DRAGONISH,
ADEISTTTU	ATTITUDES	ADENOOSTT	TOADSTONE	HOARDINGS	
ADEJLNRTU	JUTLANDER	ADENOPRRS	PARDONERS	ADGHINOSW	SHADOWING
ADEKKLRSY	SKYLARKED	ADENOPRTV	DAVENPORT	ADGHINRTU	INDRAUGHT

ADGHIRRTW	RIGHTWARD	ADHILMNPY	NYMPHALID	ADIKNNSST	INKSTANDS
ADGHLOPUY	PLAY DOUGH	ADHILOPTY	TYPHOIDAL	ADIKNRSTU	KURDISTAN
ADGHNOOPR	ONDOGRAPH	ADHILPSSY	LADYSHIPS	ADILLMNRS	MANDRILLS
ADGHNOSTU	STAGHOUND	ADHIMNOSU	HUMANOIDS	ADILLNPSS	LANDSLIPS
ADGIIILNT	DIGITALIN	ADHIMNOTU	ANTHODIUM	ADILLNRUY	DIURNALLY
ADGIIILST	DIGITALIS	ADHIMSTYY	DYSTHYMIA	ADILLQSUY	SQUALIDLY
ADGIIJNNO	ADJOINING	ADHINNOTY	HYDANTOIN	ADILMMSTU	TALMUDISM
ADGIIKNNP	KIDNAPING	ADHINNRTU	HIT-AND-RUN	ADILMNNOS	MANDOLINS
ADGIILMOS	DIALOGISM	ADHINNSTU	HINDUSTAN	ADILMNOOS	SALMONOID
ADGIILOST	DIALOGIST	ADHINOOST	SAINTHOOD	ADILMNOST	DALTONISM
ADGIIMNRS	DISARMING	ADHINOPSY	DYSPHONIA	ADILMNRUU	DURALUMIN
ADGIIMNSY	DISMAYING	ADHINORTY	HYDRATION	ADILMOPST	DIPLOMATS
ADGIIMNTT	ADMITTING	ADHINRTWW	WITHDRAWN	ADILMOPSY	OLYMPIADS,
ADGIIMRUU	MAIDUGURI	ADHINSTTW	WITHSTAND	SYMPODIAL	
ADGIINNNT	INDIGNANT	ADHIOPRSY	DYSPHORIA	ADILMSTTU	TALMUDIST
ADGIINNOR	ORDAINING	ADHIPRSSY	SHIPYARDS	ADILNOORS	DOORNAILS
ADGIINOSS	DIAGNOSIS	ADHIRSSTY	HYDRASTIS	ADILNORTW	ANTIWORLD
ADGIINRTY	DIGNITARY	ADHLLMORT	THRALLDOM	ADILNSTTY	DISTANTLY
ADGIIRTVY	GRAVIDITY	ADHLMNOOS	HANDLOOMS	ADILOOPRS	POLAROIDS
ADGIJNSTU	ADJUSTING	ADHMNOOOW	WOMANHOOD	ADILOPRSS	SLIP ROADS
ADGILLNUY	LANGUIDLY	ADHMORTTU	DARTMOUTH	ADILOPRSV	DISPROVAL
ADGILLOSU	GLADIOLUS	ADHNORRTW	NORTHWARD	ADILOPRXY	PYRIDOXAL
ADGILMNSU	GUILDSMAN	ADHNORSUY	ANHYDROUS	ADILORSTW	SWORDTAIL
ADGILMORS	MARIGOLDS	ADHNOSSTU	THOUSANDS	ADIMNOORT	DOMINATOR
ADGILNNOU	UNLOADING	ADHNRSSTU	SANDHURST	ADIMNOSTY	STAMINODY
ADGILNOSS	GLISSANDO	ADHOOPRRT	ARTHROPOD	ADINNOOST	DONATIONS
ADGILOORY	RADIOLOGY	ADHOORSSW	ROADSHOWS	ADINNOOSW	SNOWDONIA
ADGILOOUY	AUDIOLOGY	ADHORSTUW	SOUTHWARD	ADINNORTU	INUNDATOR
ADGILOPRS	PRODIGALS	ADHRSSTUY	THURSDAYS	ADINNOSST	DISSONANT
ADGIMMOST	DOGMATISM	ADIIIKNNN	INDIAN INK	ADINOOPST	ADOPTIONS
ADGIMOSTT	DOGMATIST	ADIIINOSZ	ISONIAZID	ADINOORST	TANDOORIS
ADGINNOOU	IGUANODON	ADIIIQRSU	DAIQUIRIS	ADINOOSTW	SATINWOOD
ADGINNOPR	PARDONING	ADIIKLMMS	MILKMAIDS	ADINOPRRS	RAINDROPS
ADGINOORS	GRANDIOSO	ADIILLNTU	LUNITIDAL	ADINORSSU	DINOSAURS
ADGINOPRY	PARODYING	ADIILLNVY	INVALIDLY	ADINPSTTU	DISPUTANT
ADGINORRS	RING ROADS	ADIILMSSS	DISMISSAL	ADIOPRSST	PARODISTS
ADGINPRRX	GRAND PRIX	ADIILNOPT	PLATINOID	ADIOSSSUU	ASSIDUOUS
ADGJNRRUY	GRAND JURY	ADIILNOTU	NAUTILOID	ADJMMOOOR	MAJORDOMO
ADGLNOORY	ANDROLOGY	ADIILNSTW	TAILWINDS	ADJMMORRU	DRUM MAJOR
ADGMNORSU	GOURMANDS	ADIILOORV	VARIOLOID	ADKLOOPST	POLKA DOTS
ADGMOORRU	GUARDROOM	ADIIMNOSS	ADMISSION	ADKLOORSW	WORKLOADS
ADGNNNNOU	DUNGANNON	ADIIMNOUZ	DIAZONIUM	ADKMNORSW	MARKDOWNS
ADGNNORSS	GRANDSONS	ADIIMRSSY	MYDRIASIS	ADKMOORRS	DARKROOMS
ADGOOPRST	GASTROPOD	ADIINOOTX	OXIDATION	ADKNORRTU	TRUNK ROAD
ADHHIPRSS	HARDSHIPS	ADIINOQTU	QUOTIDIAN	ADKNORSTT	KRONSTADT
ADHHNOORU	HOARHOUND	ADIINORTT	TRADITION	ADKOOORRSW	ROADWORKS
ADHHNORST	SHORTHAND	ADIINOSST	SOI-DISANT	ADLLNSSUV	SUNDSVALL
ADHIILORZ	RHIZOIDAL	ADIINOSTU	AUDITIONS	ADLLOOPRT	TOP DOLLAR
ADHIIMPSS	AMIDSHIPS	ADIINRSTT	DISTRAINT	ADLMNORTY	MORDANTLY
ADHIIOPSS	APHIDIOUS	ADIINRSSTU	SATURNIID	ADLMOOPRR	PRODROMAL
ADHIIOPTY	IDIOPATHY	ADIIPRSTY	DISPARITY	ADLMOORTU	MODULATOR
ADHIIPSSY	DIAPHYSIS	ADIISSTUY	ASSIDUITY	ADLNOORSW	LOANWORDS
ADHIKMNNU	HUMANKIND	ADIJNOOVV	VOJVODINA	ADLNOPRYY	POLYANDRY
ADHIKNORW	HANDIWORK	ADIKMNNOW	WOMANKIND	ADLNORTUU	UNDULATOR

ADLNRSSTU	STRALSUND	AEEEILNNS	ANNELIESE	AEEFLLOOS	LOOSE-LEAF
ADLOOOSTT	TOADSTOOL	AEEEILRTT	ELATERITE	AEEFLLRSW	FAREWELLS
ADLOPRSWY	SWORDPLAY	AEEEIMNRX	RE-EXAMINE	AEEFLLSVY	FLYLEAVES
ADLORSUUY	ARDUOUSLY	AEEEIPPRT	PAPETERIE	AEEFLMNRT	FREMANTLE
ADLORTUWY	OUTWARDLY	AEEEIRRTT	REITERATE	AEEFLNORW	ON WELFARE
ADLPQRUUY	QUADRUPLY	AEEEJNNTT	JEANNETTE	AEEFLNRST	FENESTRAL
ADMMNOOPW	MOP AND MOW	AEEEKKPSS	KEEPSAKES	AEEFLNRTT	FLATTENER
ADMMORRTY	MARTYRDOM	AEEEKLTTT	TEAKETTLE	AEEFLNSSS	FALSENESS
ADMNNORSU	ROUNDSMAN	AEEEKMRRT	MARKETEER	AEEFLOOTV	FOVEOLATE
ADMNOORTY	DYNAMOTOR	AEEEKRSWX	WEAKER SEX	AEEFLRRRS	REFERRALS
ADMNOOSST	MASTODONS	AEEELLMNR	ENAMELLER	AEEFLRRTT	FLATTERER
ADMNORSST	SANDSTORM	AEEELLMNT	ELEMENTAL	AEEFMNORS	FORENAMES,
ADMNORSSW	SWORDSMAN	AEEELNPRT	PLANE TREE		FREEMASON
ADMOOPPRU	POMPADOUR	AEEELNUVZ	VENEZUELA	AEEFMPTTT	TEMPT FATE
ADMOORRSW	WARDROOMS	AEEELPSSY	YES PLEASE	AEEFNRSST	FASTENERS
ADNNORRUU	RUN-AROUND	AEEEMNNRT	NEMERTEAN	AEEFNSTTY	SAFETY NET
ADNNOSSWW	SWAN'S-DOWN	AEEEMNRTU	ENUMERATE	AEEFOPRRT	PERFORATE
ADNOOPRTW	PORTADOWN	AEEEMORRT	AEROMETER	AEEFORSTT	FORETASTE
ADNOOTTUU	OUT-AND-OUT	AEEEMPRTT	TEMPERATE	AEEGGILLR	GELLIGAER
ADNOPRRTY	PROTANDRY	AEEEMRRTT	ETRAMETER	AEEGGILNR	GINGER ALE
ADNOPRSTU	PORT SUDAN	AEEEMRTVW	WAVEMETER	AEEGGINRR	GREGARINE
ADNOPSTTU	STAND UP TO	AEEEMSTTW	SWEETMEAT	AEEGGIRUW	WIRE-GAUGE
ADNOQRSSU	SQUADRONS	AEEENNPRT	PERENNATE	AEEGGLNOY	GENEALOGY
ADOOORRWW	ARROWWOOD	AEEENOPRW	WEAPONEER	AEEGGMORT	MORTGAGEE
ADOOPRRST	TRAPDOORS	AEEENORTX	EXONERATE	AEEGGNRSU	GREASE GUN
ADOPRSSSW	PASSWORDS	AEEENPRTT	PENETRATE	AEEGGRRST	STAGGERER
ADOPSSSUY	SOAPSUDSY	AEEENPSTT	PATENTEES	AEEGGRRSW	SWAGGERER
AEEEETTTT	TETE-A-TETE	AEEENRRST	EASTERNER	AEEGHILST	EASTLEIGH
AEEEFGNRR	FREE-RANGE	AEEENRRTW	TREENWARE	AEEGHIMRT	HERMITAGE
AEEEFGNRT	FREE AGENT	AEEENTTUV	EVENTUATE	AEEGHLPRT	TELEGRAPH
AEEEFHRRT	HEREAFTER	AEEENTTUX	EXTENUATE	AEEGHMNOP	MEGAPHONE
AEEEFIRRT	FIRE-EATER	AEEEPRRST	REPARTEES,	AEEGHMNOT	ON THE GAME
AEEEFRSTT	FREE STATE		REPEATERS	AEEGHMRTW	WHEAT GERM
AEEEGGGNR	GREENGAGE	AEEEPSSTW	SWEET PEAS	AEEGHMRTZ	MEGAHERTZ
AEEEGGRST	EASTER EGG,	AEEFFILRT	AFTERLIFE	AEEGHOSTU	GATEHOUSE
	SEGREGATE	AEEFFILPR	PILFERAGE	AEEGIKNNW	WEAKENING
AEEEGHLRW	GEARWHEEL	AEEFGINPY	FEE-PAYING	AEEGILLRS	ALLERGIES,
AEEEGHTTX	GET THE AXE	AEEFGINRS	FAR-SEEING		GALLERIES
AEEEGIMNR	MENAGERIE	AEEFGLLOT	FLAGEOLET	AEEGILLRT	TREILLAGE
AEEEGLRRV	GEAR LEVER	AEEFGLORW	FLOWERAGE	AEEGILLST	LEGISLATE
AEEEGMNNP	EMPENNAGE	AEEFGLSSU	FUSELAGES	AEEGILMNN	ENAMELING
AEEEGMNRT	AGREEMENT	AEEFGORST	FOSTERAGE	AEEGILNNT	EGLANTINE,
AEEEGNRSS	EAGERNESS	AEEFHIKPT	KEEP FAITH		INELEGANT
AEEEGNRST	TEENAGERS	AEEFHLRTT	HEARTFELT	AEEGILNNV	LEAVENING
AEEEGNSTV	STEVENAGE	AEEFHOSSU	SAFE HOUSE	AEEGILNPR	REPEALING
AEEEGRTTZ	GAZETTEER	AEEFIKLLM	FLAMELIKE	AEEGILNQU	ANGELIQUE
AEEEHHSTV	THE HEAVES	AEEFILLMN	EN FAMILLE	AEEGILNRS	RELEASING
AEEEHKNRR	HEARKENER	AEEFILMPR	RELIEF MAP	AEEGILNRV	REVEALING
AEEEHLMPR	EPHEMERAL	AEEFILNRT	INTERLEAF	AEEGILNST	ANGLESITE
AEEEHLSSY	EYELASHES	AEEFILNSS	LEAFINESS	AEEGILNSW	WEASELING
AEEEHMRTX	HEXAMETER	AEEFILOTX	EXFOLIATE	AEEGILNTV	ELEVATING
AEEEHRRRS	REHEARSER	AEEFILRSV	LIFE-SAVER	AEEGILPTT	TITLE PAGE
AEEEHRRTW	WEATHERER	AEEFINRRR	REFRAINER	AEEGILRTU	GAULEITER
AEEEHSSTT	AESTHETES	AEEFIRRTW	FIREWATER	AEEGILUVY	IVY LEAGUE
				AEEGIMNNV	GIVEN NAME

AEEGIMNRS	GERMANISE	
AEEGIMNRT	GERMANITE,	
GERMINATE		
AEEGIMNRZ	GERMANIZE	
AEEGIMNST	MAGNESITE,	
MAGNETISE		
AEEGIMNTT	MAGNETITE	
AEEGIMNTZ	MAGNETIZE	
AEEGIMOST	ISOGAMETE	
AEEGIMPTT	PEGMATITE	
AEEGINNRT	ARGENTINE,	
TANGERINE		
AEEGINOPS	ESPIONAGE	
AEEGINOTT	NEGOTIATE	
AEEGINPRT	REPEATING	
AEEGINPRV	GRAPEVINE	
AEEGINRTT	ARGENTITE,	
INTEGRATE		
AEEGINSSW	SEESAWING	
AEEGINSTV	NEGATIVES	
AEEGIORTV	GIVE EAR TO	
AEEGIRSST	GREASIEST	
AEEGLLNOR	ORGANELLE	
AEEGLLNRY	GENERALLY	
AEEGLLNTY	ELEGANTLY	
AEEGLMNNT	GENTLEMAN	
AEEGLMNST	SEGMENTAL	
AEEGLMORT	ALGOMETER,	
GLOMERATE		
AEEGLMRRW	LEG-WARMER	
AEEGLMRST	TELEGRAMS	
AEEGLNNRT	ENTANGLER	
AEEGLNRSS	LARGENESS	
AEEGLORST	ALTER EGOS	
AEEGLORVZ	OVERGLAZE	
AEEGMNNRS	MERGANSER	
AEEGMOPRS	MEGASPORE	
AEEGMORST	GASOMETER	
AEEGNNSTW	NEWSAGENT	
AEEGNOPRS	PERSONAGE	
AEEGNORRT	GENERATOR	
AEEGNORTU	ENTOURAGE	
AEEGNOTTW	WAGONETTE	
AEEGNOTXY	OXYGENATE	
AEEGNPRSS	PASSENGER	
AEEGNRRST	ESTRANGER	
AEEGNRRSV	ENGRAVERS	
AEEGNRRST	GREATNESS,	
SERGEANTS		
AEEGNRSSV	GRAVENESS	
AEEGNSSUV	VAGUENESS	
AEEGOPPST	ESTOPPAGE	
AEEGOPRRT	PORTERAGE,	
REPORTAGE		
AEEGPRTUX	EXPURGATE	

AEEGRRTWY	GREY WATER	
AEEGRSTTY	GREY-STATE	
AEEHHIKLT	HEATHLIKE	
AEEHHILRT	HEALTHIER	
AEEHHIMST	HASHEMITE	
AEEHHITTW	WHITE HEAT	
AEEHHLMTT	AT THE HELM	
AEEHHLOSW	HAWSEHOLE	
AEEHHNNPT	NAPHTHENE	
AEEHHNPTY	HYPHENATE	
AEEHHNSTU	UNSHEATHE	
AEEHIKNRT	KATHERINE	
AEEHILLNN	HELLENIAN	
AEEHILMNW	MEANWHILE	
AEEHILNSS	SINHALESE	
AEEHILNTV	HELVETIAN	
AEEHILPRS	SHAPELIER	
AEEHILRRT	EARTHLIER	
AEEHILRTW	WEALTHIER	
AEEHIMNST	MAINSHEET	
AEEHIMPSS	EMPHASISE	
AEEHIMPST	EMPATHISE	
AEEHIMPSZ	EMPHASIZE	
AEEHIMPTZ	EMPATHIZE	
AEEHIMRST	HETAERISM	
AEEHIMTTW	WHITE MEAT	
AEEHINNPZ	PHENAZINE	
AEEHINPRS	HESPERIAN	
AEEHINPST	STEPHANIE	
AEEHINRSV	HAVERSINE	
AEEHINRTT	HENRIETTA	
AEEHINRTU	EUTHERIAN	
AEEHINSSV	HEAVINESS	
AEEHIPPSW	HAWSEPIPE	
AEEHIPRSS	APHERESIS,	
PHARISEES		
AEEHIPRST	THERAPIES	
AEEHIRRST	EARTHRISE	
AEEHIRRTT	HARRIETTE	
AEEHIRSTT	EARTHIEST,	
HEARTIEST, HESITATER,		
HETAERIST		
AEEHKLPSW	SHEEPWALK	
AEEHKMMOR	HOMEMAKER	
AEEHKMORS	SHOEMAKER	
AEEHKMPRT	THEME PARK	
AEEHKMRTT	THE MARKET	
AEEHLLMOW	WHOLEMEAL	
AEEHLLNOW	HALLOWEEN	
AEEHLLOSW	WHOLESALE	
AEEHLLSSS	SEASHELLS	
AEEHLMNNT	EMMENTHAL	
AEEHLMPST	HELPMATES	
AEEHLMRSY	HAMERSLEY	
AEEHLMSSS	SHAMELESS	

AEEHLMTTY	METHYLATE	
AEEHLNOPS	ANOPHELES	
AEEHLNOPT	PHENOLATE	
AEEHLNOSW	HALESOWEN	
AEEHLNPST	ELEPHANTS	
AEEHLNSSV	HAVENLESS	
AEEHLOPST	TELOPHASE	
AEEHLORST	TREHALOSE	
AEEHLORTW	WATERHOLE	
AEEHLOSSU	ALEHOUSES	
AEEHLPSSS	SHAPELESS	
AEEHLPTTY	TELEPATHY	
AEEHLRSST	HEARTLESS	
AEEHLSTXY	HEXASTYLE	
AEEHMMORT	HAMMERTOE	
AEEHMMPSY	EMPHYSEMA	
AEEHMNNOP	PHENOMENA	
AEEHMNOTT	MOTH-EATEN	
AEEHMOPRS	SEMAPHORE	
AEEHMORST	HEARTSOME	
AEEHMPRST	PETERSHAM	
AEEHMSTTW	WESTMEATH	
AEEHNNOTW	ON THE WANE	
AEEHNOOPR	AEROPHONE	
AEEHNOPRS	EARPHONES	
AEEHNOPTX	TOXAPHENE	
AEEHNPRRS	SHARPENER	
AEEHNRRSS	HARNESSER	
AEEHNRSSS	HARNESSES	
AEEHORSSS	SEAHORSES	
AEEHORSUW	WAREHOUSE	
AEEHOSSTU	TEAHOUSES	
AEEHPRSTU	EUPHRATES,	
SUPERHEAT		
AEEHRRSTT	SHATTERER,	
THREE-STAR		
AEEHRRSTV	HARVESTER	
AEEHRSTUX	EXHAUSTER	
AEEIILLOP	AEOLIPILE	
AEEIILMNT	ELIMINATE	
AEEIILRSS	SERIALISE	
AEEIILRST	ISRAELITE,	
REALITIES		
AEEIILRSZ	SERIALIZE	
AEEIIMNST	AMENITIES	
AEEIINNTV	VIENTIANE	
AEEIINRTT	ITINERATE	
AEEIINSTV	NAIVETIES	
AEEIINSTX	ANXIETIES	
AEEIIRSTV	VARIETIES	
AEEIIRTTV	ITERATIVE	
AEEIJMNSS	JESSAMINE	
AEEIJMSST	MAJESTIES	
AEEIKLLPT	PETAL-LIKE	
AEEIKLMUW	MILWAUKEE	

AEEIKLNNP	LENIN PEAK
AEEIKLNSS	LEAKINESS
AEEIKMNSY	YANKEEISM
AEEIKNRSV	KNAVERIES
AEEIKNSST	SNEAKIEST
AEEIKQRSU	SQUEAKIER
AEEIKRRST	STREAKIER
AEEILLMNT	METALLINE
AEEILLMRS	MARSEILLE
AEEILLMST	METALLISE
AEEILLMTZ	METALLIZE
AEEILLNOT	LINEOLATE, LINOLEATE
AEEILLPTT	PAILLETTE
AEEILLSTT	SATELLITE
AEEILLTVW	WAVELLITE
AEEILLTVX	VEXILLATE
AEEILMNNT	LINEAMENT
AEEILMNRY	MINELAYER
AEEILMNSS	MESSALINE
AEEILMORT	MELIORATE
AEEILMPST	TIME-LAPSE
AEEILMRST	SALIMETER
AEEILMRTT	ALTIMETER
AEEILMRTU	ELATERIUM
AEEILMRTW	LIMEWATER
AEEILMTUV	EMULATIVE
AEEILNNPP	PENEPLAIN
AEEILNNPR	PERENNIAL
AEEILNNSX	SEXENNIAL
AEEILNNTV	LEVANTINE, VALENTINE
AEEILNOTV	ELEVATION
AEEILNPPP	PINEAPPLE
AEEILNPRX	EXPLAINER
AEEILNPST	PALESTINE, PENALTIES
AEEILNPSX	EXPANSILE
AEEILNRSS	EARLINESS
AEEILNRSV	VERNALISE
AEEILNRTW	WATERLINE
AEEILNRVZ	VERNALIZE
AEEILNSST	ESSENTIAL
AEEILNTTV	VENTILATE
AEEILOPTT	PETIOLATE
AEEILORRT	ARTERIOLE
AEEILPPPS	APPLE PIES
AEEILPRRV	PREVAILER
AEEILPRST	PEARLIEST
AEEILQRSU	EQUALISER
AEEILQRUZ	EQUALIZER
AEEILRRST	RETAILERS
AEEILRRTT	AIRLETTER
AEEILRRTV	RETRIEVAL

AEEILRSTV	RELATIVES, VERSATILE
AEEILRTTU	ELUTRIATE
AEEILSSTZ	SLEAZIEST
AEEILSVVY	EVASIVELY
AEEIMMNST	MEANTIMES
AEEIMNNZZ	MEZZANINE
AEEIMNRSX	EXAMINERS
AEEIMNRTT	TERMINATE
AEEIMNSSS	SEAMINESS
AEEIMNSST	AMNESTIES, MEATINESS
AEEIMNSTT	ESTAMINET
AEEIMORRS	ROSEMARIE
AEEIMORSW	WEARISOME
AEEIMPRRT	PRIME RATE
AEEIMPRTT	IMPETRATE
AEEIMRSTT	TASIMETER
AEEIMRSTV	TIMESAVER
AEEIMRTTX	TAXIMETER
AEEIMSSTT	ESTIMATES, STEAMIEST
AEEINNNPS	APENNINES
AEEINNRST	IN EARNEST, TANNERIES
AEEINNRTT	ENTERTAIN
AEEINNRTV	INNERVATE
AEEINNSST	INSENSATE
AEEINNSSV	NAIVENESS
AEEINOPPT	APPOINTEE
AEEINOPRT	PERITONEA
AEEINORTT	ORIENTATE
AEEINPPST	PEPSINATE
AEEINPRSS	PASSERINE
AEEINPRST	SPARTEINE
AEEINPSVX	EXPANSIVE
AEEINRRST	RETAINERS
AEEINRRTT	REITERANT
AEEINRRTV	VERATRINE
AEEINRSSW	WEARINESS
AEEINRSTT	REINSTATE
AEEINRSTU	ESTUARINE
AEEINRSTV	INVERTASE
AEEINRSTY	EYESTRAIN
AEEINSSTU	UNEASIEST
AEEINSTTT	ENSTATITE, INTESTATE
AEEINSTTU	AUSTENITE
AEEINTTTV	ATTENTIVE, TENTATIVE
AEEIOPRTV	EVAPORITE, OPERATIVE
AEEIPPRST	APPETISER
AEEIPPRSU	PAUPERISE
AEEIPPRTW	WATER PIPE

AEEIPPRTZ	APPETIZER
AEEIPPRUZ	PAUPERIZE
AEEIPPSTT	APPETITES
AEEIPRRTV	PRIVATEER
AEEIPRSSS	PESSARIES
AEEIPRSSV	ASPERSIVE
AEEIPRSVV	PERVASIVE
AEEIPRTTX	EXTIRPATE
AEEIQSSTU	QUEASIEST
AEEIRSSTT	TREATISES
AEEIRSSTU	ESTUARIES
AEEIRSSTV	ASSERTIVE
AEEISSTTW	SWEATIEST
AEEJLMRSU	JERUSALEM
AEEJMORTT	MAJORETTE
AEEJMRSTT	JET STREAM
AEEKKOPRT	KAPOK TREE
AEEKLLPSW	SLEEPWALK
AEEKLSTTW	SWEET TALK
AEEKMMRRY	MAKE MERRY
AEEKMNRTW	NEWMARKET
AEEKMRRST	MARKETERS
AEEKMRSTY	MASTER KEY
AEEKNORTV	OVERTAKEN
AEEKORSTV	TAKEOVERS
AEEKORTUY	EUKARYOTE
AEEKQRSSU	SQUEAKERS
AEEKRRSST	STREAKERS
AEELLLSTT	TELLTALES
AEELLMNTW	WELL-MEANT
AEELLNPPZ	APPENZELL
AEELLNPTX	EXPELLANT
AEELLNRTY	ENTERALLY, ETERNALLY
AEELLOPST	SELLOTAPE
AEELLOSUV	LAEVULOSE
AEELLPSTT	PLATELETS
AEELLRRTV	TRAVELLER
AEELLRSVY	SEVERALLY
AEELLRTTU	TELLURATE
AEELLSSUV	VALUELESS
AEELLSSVV	VALVELESS
AEELMMRRT	TRAMMELER
AEELMMTXY	METAXYLEM
AEELMORST	ELASTOMER
AEELMPRXY	EXEMPLARY
AEELMPSTT	TEMPLATES
AEELMRSST	SEMESTRAL
AEELMRTTW	MELTWATER
AEELNNNTU	ANTENNULE
AEELNOPST	ANTELOPES
AEELNPRTV	PREVALENT
AEELNRSST	ALERTNESS
AEELNRSTX	EXTERNALS

AEELNRSTY	EARNESTLY
AEELNRTTV	TERVALENT
AEELNSSST	STALENESS
AEELNSSWY	WESLEYANS
AEELORRTV	REVELATOR
AEELORSTV	ELEVATORS
AEELORTVW	WATER VOLE
AEELOSTTW	TEA TOWELS
AEELPPRRU	PUERPERAL
AEELPPRTU	PERPETUAL
AEELPRRST	PLASTERER
AEELPRRTU	PRELATURE
AEELPRSSU	PLEASURES
AEELPRSTT	SALTPETRE
AEELQRSSU	SQUEALERS
AEELRRSSV	REVERSALS
AEELRRSTU	SERRULATE
AEELRSSTW	WATERLESS
AEELRSTUY	AUSTERELY
AEELRSTVY	SEVERALTY
AEELSSSTT	STATELESS, TASTELESS
AEEMMNORT	MANOMETER
AEEMMNSTU	AMUSEMENT
AEEMMORTT	ATMOMETER
AEEMMPRUY	EMPYREUMA
AEEMMRRST	STAMMERER
AEEMNNORT	NANOMETER
AEEMNNOTT	ATONEMENT
AEEMNNPRT	PERMANENT
AEEMNOPRT	TREPONEMA
AEEMNOPSU	MENOPAUSE
AEEMNOPYZ	APOENZYME
AEEMNORTW	WORM-EATEN
AEEMNORUV	MANOEUVRE
AEEMNPRTY	REPAYMENT
AEEMNPSTV	PAVEMENTS
AEEMNRSST	MARE'S NEST, STEERSMAN
AEEMNRSUV	MANEUVERS
AEEMNRTTT	TREATMENT
AEEMNSSTT	MEANS TEST, STATESMEN
AEEMNSSTY	MATEYNESS
AEEMNSTTT	STATEMENT, TESTAMENT
AEEMOPRRT	PERMEATOR
AEEMOPSSU	MESOPAUSE
AEEMORRTT	ROTAMETER
AEEMORRTY	AEROMETRY
AEEMPRRTU	PREMATURE
AEEMPRTTT	ATTEMPTER
AEEMPSSTW	SWAP MEETS
AEEMRRSST	STREAMERS
AEEMRRSTT	SMATTERER

AEEMRSSTT	SMEAR TEST, TEAMSTERS
AEEMRSSTY	EASY TERMS
AEEMRTTTW	WATTMETER
AEENNPRTT	PENETRANT, REPENTANT
AEENNRRTT	RE-ENTRANT
AEENOPPRT	NOTEPAPER
AEENOPRST	ESPERANTO, PERSONATE
AEENOPTTT	POTENTATE
AEENOQRSU	SQUARE ONE
AEENORRTV	ENERVATOR, VENERATOR
AEENORSTW	STONEWARE
AEENPPRRT	ENTRAPPER
AEENPPRSW	NEWSPAPER
AEENPRRTU	ENRAPTURE
AEENPRSSS	SPARENESS
AEENPRSTT	AT PRESENT
AEENPRSTY	SEPTENARY
AEENRRSTU	SAUNTERER
AEENRSSTU	SAUTERNES
AEENSSSUV	SUAVENESS
AEEOOPRTZ	AZEOTROPE
AEEOPPRSU	PEA SOUPER
AEEOPRSSW	SEA POWERS
AEEOPRSTT	OPERETTAS, POETASTER
AEEOQRRTU	QUERETARO
AEEORRSTW	ROSEWATER
AEEORSTTV	OVERSTATE
AEEORSTTW	TWO-SEATER
AEEPRRRST	PARTERRES
AEEPRRSTU	APERTURES
AEEPRRSTY	SPARE TYRE
AEEQRSSTU	SETSQUARE
AEEQRTUUX	EXEQUATUR
AEERRRSSU	REASSURER
AEERRRSTU	TREASURER
AEERRRSTV	TRAVERSER
AEERRSSTU	TREASURES
AEERRSSTV	TRAVERSES
AEERRTTVX	EXTRAVERT
AEESTTTTU	STATUETTE
AEFFFLTUW	LUFTWAFFE
AEFFGRSSU	SUFFRAGES
AEFFHMOPT	OFF THE MAP
AEFFIILRS	FALSIFIER
AEFFIKPST	PIKESTAFF
AEFFILLUV	EFFLUVIAL
AEFFINORS	RAFFINOSE
AEFFIRTUX	AFFIXTURE
AEFFKMNOU	MAKE FUN OF
AEFFLLRUY	FEARFULLY

AEFFLLTUY	FATEFULLY
AEFFLORSW	SAFFLOWER
AEFFMORST	OFF STREAM
AEFGHILNS	ANGELFISH
AEFGHILST	SAFELIGHT
AEFGHILTW	WHITE FLAG
AEFGHINRT	FATHERING
AEFGHORRT	FORGATHER
AEFGIIMNR	MAGNIFIER
AEFGIINNR	FINE-GRAIN
AEFGIIRRT	GRATIFIER
AEFGILMOR	GALEIFORM
AEFGILNRT	FALTERING, REFLATING
AEFGILRUY	LAY FIGURE
AEFGINNST	FASTENING
AEFGINNTT	FATTENING
AEFGINRTU	FEATURING
AEFGIORSS	OSSIFRAGE
AEFGIRSTT	GAS FITTER
AEFGLLLMU	FLAGELLUM
AEFGLLOPS	FLAGPOLES
AEFGLNOST	FLAGSTONE
AEFGLORTW	AFTERGLOW
AEFGMNRST	FRAGMENTS
AEFGNOPRT	FRONT-PAGE
AEFGNORST	FRONTAGES
AEFHHISST	SHEATFISH
AEFHHLLTU	HEALTHFUL
AEFHHLOTW	HEATHFOWL
AEFHIKMST	MAKESHIFT
AEFHILLSV	HALF-LIVES
AEFHILPST	FISHPLATE
AEFHILSST	FAITHLESS, FLASHIEST
AEFHIMNRS	FISHERMAN
AEFHINORS	FASHIONER
AEFHINRTW	WAFER-THIN
AEFHKNORS	FORESHANK
AEFHLLSVY	FLY HALVES
AEFHLLTUY	HATEFULLY
AEFHLNNPY	HALFPENNY
AEFHLNOST	HALF NOTES, HALFTONES
AEFHLORSV	FLASHOVER
AEFHMORSU	FARMHOUSE
AEFHORRTU	OUR FATHER
AEFIIKLRY	FAIRY-LIKE
AEFIILLNS	NAIL FILES
AEFIILMNS	SEMIFINAL
AEFIILMPR	AMPLIFIER
AEFIILNNT	INFANTILE
AEFIILQRU	QUALIFIER
AEFIILRST	FRAILTIES
AEFIILSST	FALSITIES

AEFIINRSS	FRIESIANS	AEFLNOPRY	PROFANELY	AEGHHRRTU	HEARTHRUG
AEFIINRTU	INFURIATE	AEFLNSSUW	AWFULNESS	AEGHIILNS	GHISLAINE
AEFIIPRST	APERITIFS	AEFLOOPTT	FOOTPLATE	AEGHIKNNR	HANKERING,
AEFIIRSST	SATISFIER	AEFLORRUV	FLAVOURER		HARKENING
AEFIISTVX	FIXATIVES	AEFLORTWW	WATERFOWL	AEGHIKNRS	SHRINKAGE
AEFIKLNSS	FLAKINESS	AEFLPRRUY	PRAYERFUL	AEGHILLNY	HEALINGLY
AEFILLNOX	FLEXIONAL	AEFMNOORW	FOREWOMAN	AEGHILMST	MEGALITHS
AEFILLOOT	FOLIOLATE	AEFNNOORT	AFTERNOON	AEGHILNRS	SHEARLING
AEFILMMNY	FAMILY MEN	AEFNORSST	SEAFRONTS	AEGHILNRT	EARTHLING,
AEFILMNST	FILAMENTS	AEFNORTTU	FORTUNATE		LATHERING
AEFILMNTU	FULMINATE	AEFNRRSST	TRANSFERS	AEGHILRRT	REAR LIGHT
AEFILMORS	FORMALISE	AEFNRRSTU	TRANSFUER	AEGHILRST	GHASTLIER
AEFILMORZ	FORMALIZE	AEFNRSSTU	TRANSFUSE	AEGHILRSV	GRAVELISH
AEFILNNUZ	INFLUENZA	AEFOOPRRW	WEARPROOF	AEGHILRTY	LIGHT YEAR
AEFILNORT	REFLATION	AEFOPRRTY	PREFATORY	AEGHIMMNR	HAMMERING
AEFILNPSS	LIFESPANS	AEFRRSTTU	FRUSTRATE	AEGHIMNPR	HAMPERING
AEFILORRT	ROTIFERAL	AEGGGIRWW	WIGWAGGER	AEGHIMNRT	NIGHTMARE
AEFILSSTV	FESTIVALS	AEGGGIRZZ	ZIGZAGGER	AEGHIMNWY	HEMINGWAY
AEFILSTTU	FAULTIEST	AEGGHINRT	GATHERING	AEGHIMORR	HIEROGRAM
AEFIMMNRT	FIRMAMENT	AEGGHIRTZ	GIGAHERTZ	AEGHIMPPR	EPIPHRAGM
AEFIMNOSS	FOAMINESS	AEGGHISST	SHAGGIEST	AEGHINNPP	HAPPENING
AEFIMNOST	MANIFESTO	AEGGHOPRR	ERGOGRAPH	AEGHINNRT	NEAR THING
AEFIMNRST	FIRST NAME	AEGGHOPRY	GEOGRAPHY	AEGHINNST	HASTENING
AEFIMNSST	MANIFESTS	AEGGIINNR	REGAINING	AEGHINOPS	SIPHONAGE
AEFIMORTV	FORMATIVE	AEGGIINPU	GUINEA PIG	AEGHINRRS	GARNISHER
AEFINNSST	FAINTNESS	AEGGIIORV	VIAREGGIO	AEGHINRSS	GARNISHES
AEFINOOTT	FOETATION	AEGGILNNR	ENLARGING	AEGHINRTU	NAUGHTIER
AEFINOPRR	PORIFERAN	AEGGILNNS	GLEANINGS	AEGHINRTW	NIGHTWEAR,
AEFINOPRS	PINAFORES	AEGGILNRV	GRAVELING		WREATHING
AEFINORSS	SANFORISE	AEGGINNRR	GARNERING	AEGHIORWY	GO HAYWIRE
AEFINORSU	NEFARIOUS	AEGGINNRV	ENGRAVING	AEGHIPPRY	EPIGRAPHY
AEFINORSZ	SANFORIZE	AEGGINORR	GREGORIAN	AEGHIPRRS	SERIGRAPH
AEFINOSTY	SAINTE FOY	AEGGINORT	AGRIGENTO	AEGHIPSTT	SPAGHETTI
AEFINPSTY	SAFETY PIN	AEGGINOSY	EASYGOING	AEGHLOOPR	OLEOGRAPH
AEFINRSSS	SANS SERIF	AEGGINPRS	PRESAGING	AEGHLORTT	LARGHETTO
AEFINRSTU	UNFAIREST	AEGGINPRT	PARGETING	AEGHLRSTU	SLAUGHTER
AEFINSSTT	FATTINESS	AEGGINRTT	TARGETING	AEGHMNOPR	NEPHOGRAM
AEFIORTUV	FAVOURITE	AEGGIOPRS	ARPEGGIOS	AEGHNNORS	HANGERS-ON
AEFIPRRST	FIRETRAPS	AEGGLNNOR	LONG-RANGE	AEGHNOORR	GONORRHEA
AEFIRRSTT	FIRST-RATE	AEGGLNPST	EGGPLANTS	AEGHNOPST	HEPTAGONS
AEFKLLOST	FOLKTALES	AEGGLNRRY	GLENGARRY	AEGHNORSV	HANGOVERS,
AEFKLLUWY	WAKEFULLY	AEGGLORSY	GARGOYLES		OVERHANGS
AEFKLNOSW	SNOWFLAKE	AEGGLRRST	STRAGGLER	AEGHOPRST	GRAPESHOT
AEFKMORRW	FRAMEWORK	AEGGMORST	MORTGAGES	AEGHOPSSU	ESOPHAGUS
AEFKNNRSS	FRANKNESS	AEGGNNRTU	TRENGGANU	AEGHORSST	SHORTAGES
AEFKNOPTU	POKE FUN AT	AEGGNOSUY	SYNAGOGUE	AEGIILLRS	GRISAILLE
AEFLLNTTU	FLATULENT	AEGGNPRSS	PRESSGANG	AEGIILLRT	ARGILLITE
AEFLLORST	FORESTALL	AEGGNRSST	GANGSTERS	AEGIILMSV	VIGESIMAL
AEFLLRTUY	TEARFULLY	AEGGOPRSU	AGE GROUPS	AEGIILNNT	ENTAILING
AEFLLSSTU	FAULTLESS	AEGGORRSS	AGGRESSOR	AEGIILNRT	RETAILING
AEFLMORTU	FORMULATE	AEGHHINRS	REHASHING	AEGIILNRZ	REALIZING
AEFLMORWY	MAYFLOWER	AEGHHINST	SHEATHING	AEGIILNSS	SIGNALISE
AEFLMRSTU	MASTERFUL	AEGHHIRTU	HAUGHTIER	AEGIILNSZ	SIGNALIZE
AEFLNOOSS	ALOOFNESS	AEGHHIRTW	HIGH WATER	AEGIILNTV	GENITIVAL,
					VIGILANTE

AEGIILNTY	GENIALITY	AEGILNNSV	ENSLAVING	AEGIMQRSU	QUAGMIRES
AEGIILSTV	VESTIGIAL	AEGILNOPX	POLEAXING	AEGIMRSTY	MAGISTERY
AEGIIMMRT	IMMIGRATE	AEGILNORU	NEUROGLIA	AEGINNNRS	ENSNARING
AEGIIMNNR	REMAINING	AEGILNORY	LEGIONARY	AEGINNORS	REASONING
AEGIIMNNX	EXAMINING	AEGILNOST	LEGATIONS	AEGINNORW	NORWEGIAN
AEGIIMNRS	MIGRAINES	AEGILNPRS	RELAPSING	AEGINNORZ	ORGANZINE
AEGIINNRT	RETAINING	AEGILNPRY	PARLEYING,	AEGINNOSS	SEASONING
AEGIINORT	ORIGINATE		REPLAYING	AEGINNOST	NEGATIONS
AEGIINOTT	GONIATITE	AEGILNQSU	SQUEALING	AEGINNOSU	GUANOSINE
AEGIINPRR	REPAIRING	AEGILNRST	TRIANGLES	AEGINNOTT	NEGOTIANT
AEGIINPTX	EXPIATING	AEGILNRSV	SLAVERING	AEGINNPPR	PERPIGNAN
AEGIINRTT	GRANITITE	AEGILNRSY	SYRINGEAL,	AEGINNPRT	PARENTING
AEGIINSTT	INSTIGATE		YEARLINGS	AEGINNPTT	PATENTING
AEGIJNORS	JARGONISE	AEGILNRTU	GRANULITE	AEGINNRSS	RANGINESS
AEGIJNORZ	JARGONIZE	AEGILNRTV	TRAVELING	AEGINNRSW	ANSWERING
AEGIJNTUU	UNIJUGATE	AEGILNRTY	TEARINGLY	AEGINNRSY	YEARNINGS
AEGIKKMNR	KINGMAKER	AEGILNRUV	REVALUING	AEGINNRRT	INTEGRANT,
AEGIKLNSW	WEAKLINGS	AEGILNRWY	WEARINGLY		NATTERING
AEGIKMNNP	PEKING MAN	AEGILNSSW	WINEGLASS	AEGINNSST	ASSENTING
AEGIKMNRR	REMARKING	AEGILNSTY	TEASINGLY	AEGINNSTU	UNSEATING
AEGIKMNRT	MARKETING	AEGILOOPS	APOLOGIES,	AEGINNTTU	TAUTENING
AEGIKNQSU	SQUEAKING		APOLOGISE	AEGINOPRS	SINGAPORE
AEGIKNRST	STREAKING	AEGILOOPZ	APOLOGIZE	AEGINOPRT	OPERATING
AEGIKNSSW	GAWKINESS	AEGILOOTY	AETIOLOGY	AEGINORRS	ORGANISER
AEGILLLLY	ILLEGALLY	AEGILORSS	SERAGLIOS	AEGINORRV	GRANIVORE
AEGILLLNU	GALLINULE	AEGILORSU	GLAIREOUS	AEGINORRZ	ORGANIZER
AEGILLMNT	METALLING	AEGILORTV	LEVIGATOR	AEGINORVW	OVERAWING
AEGILLMRU	MALGRE LUI	AEGILPPSS	SLIPPAGES	AEGINOSTT	GESTATION
AEGILLNNP	PANELLING	AEGILRRRU	IRREGULAR	AEGINPPRR	PREPARING
AEGILLNNW	GWENLLIAN	AEGILRRTW	WRIT LARGE	AEGINPPRY	PREPAYING
AEGILLNOS	GOAL LINES	AEGILRSTU	LIGATURES	AEGINPRTT	PATTERING
AEGILLNOT	NO-TILLAGE	AEGILRSUV	VULGARISE	AEGINPSTY	EGYPTIANS
AEGILLNQU	EQUALLING	AEGILRTUV	VIRGULATE	AEGINQRUV	QUAVERING
AEGILLNRS	SIGNALLER	AEGILRUVZ	VULGARIZE	AEGINRRST	ARRESTING
AEGILLNRV	GRANVILLE,	AEGILSSST	GLASSIEST	AEGINRRTU	GARNITURE
	RAVELLING	AEGIMMNNOT	GEMMATION	AEGINRSST	ASSERTING
AEGILLNTU	LINGULATE	AEGIMMNRS	GERMANISM	AEGINRSTT	RESTATING
AEGILLNTY	GENITALLY	AEGIMMNRU	GERMANIUM	AEGINRSTU	SIGNATURE
AEGILLPPR	GRAPPELLI	AEGIMMNRY	YAMMERING	AEGINSSSS	ASSESSING,
AEGILLPPU	PUPILLAGE	AEGIMMNST	MAGNETISM		GASSINESS
AEGILLPRS	PILLAGERS	AEGIMMNSU	MAGNESIUM	AEGINSSST	STAGINESS
AEGILLRRU	GUERRILLA	AEGIMMNNU	UNMEANING	AEGINSSUZ	GAUZINESS
AEGILLRSS	SALESGIRL	AEGIMMNOR	OMNIRANGE	AEGINSTTT	ATTESTING
AEGILLRST	ALLERGIST	AEGIMMNRT	GERMINANT	AEGINSTUU	AUGUSTINE
AEGILLRSV	VILLAGERS	AEGIMMNSS	MANGINESS	AEGIPRTUV	PURGATIVE
AEGILMNNS	SIGNALMEN	AEGIMNORS	ORANGEISM	AEGIRRRST	REGISTRAR
AEGILMNNT	ALIGNMENT,	AEGIMNORT	MORGANITE	AEGIRSSST	GRASSIEST
	LAMENTING	AEGIMNPPR	PAMPERING	AEGKORSTT	AGTERSKOT
AEGILMNRV	MARVELING	AEGIMNPRT	TAMPERING	AEGLLNOPW	ALPENGLOW
AEGILMNST	LIGAMENTS	AEGIMNPRV	REVAMPING	AEGLLNOST	GALLSTONE
AEGILMNTU	EMULATING,	AEGIMNRST	EMIGRANTS,	AEGLLOOOZ	ZOOGLOEAL
	GLUTAMINE		MASTERING, STREAMING	AEGLLOSTT	TOLLGATES
AEGILMORR	RIGMAROLE	AEGIMNRSU	GERANIUMS,	AEGLLRRUY	REGULARLY
AEGILMORS	GLAMORISE		MEASURING	AEGLMNOOY	ANEMOLOGY
AEGILMORZ	GLAMORIZE	AEGIMNRTT	MATTERING	AEGLMNORW	ANGLEWORM

AEGLMORTY	ALGOMETRY	AEHHMORRT	ROTHERHAM
AEGLNNOOT	LONG EATON	AEHHNORTW	HAWTHORNE
AEGLNOSTU	LANGOUSTE	AEHHNRSSS	HARSHNESS
AEGLNRRST	STRANGLER	AEHHOPPST	PHOSPHATE
AEGLNRRSW	WRANGLERS	AEHHOPRSS	SHARE SHOP
AEGLNRSST	STRANGLES	AEHIILMTU	HUMILIATE
AEGLNRSTY	STRANGELY	AEHIILNRS	HAIRLINES
AEGLNSTTU	GAUNTLETS	AEHIIMNRT	HERMITIAN
AEGLOPPRU	PROPAGULE	AEHIIMNST	HISTAMINE
AEGLOPRSY	PLAYGOERS	AEHIIMRST	HETAIRISM
AEGLORRTU	REGULATOR	AEHIIMRTY	HIMYARITE
AEGLORTTY	TETRALOGY	AEHIINOPT	ETHIOPIAN
AEGMMOPRR	PROGRAMME	AEHIINRSS	HAIRINESS
AEGMNNORT	MAGNETRON	AEHIIPSTT	HEPATITIS
AEGMNORRW	WARMONGER	AEHIKKLMS	MILK SHAKE
AEGMNORSU	GERMANOUS	AEHIKLMNU	HUMAN-LIKE
AEGMNORSV	MANGROVES	AEHIKMOTT	MAKE IT HOT
AEGMNORTU	AUGMENTOR	AEHIKNOST	SHAKE ON IT
AEGMNOTTU	MANGETOUT	AEHIKNSSS	SHAKINESS
AEGMNRSTU	ARGUMENTS	AEHILLNRT	ALLETHRIN
AEGMOOSUX	EXOGAMOUS	AEHILLNSV	NASHVILLE
AEGMOPRRR	PROGRAMER	AEHILLPTY	PHILATELY
AEGMORRSW	WORM GEARS	AEHILLTTY	LETHALITY
AEGMORSTY	GASOMETRY	AEHILLTWW	WHITEWALL
AEGMPRSSU	GRAMPUSES	AEHILLTWY	WEALTHILY
AEGNNOPST	PENTAGONS	AEHILMNOP	PHILOMENA
AEGNNPRTU	REPUGNANT	AEHILNNOT	ANTHELION
AEGNNSSTU	GAUNTNESS	AEHILNOOZ	HELIOZOAN
AEGNORSSX	SEX ORGANS	AEHILNOPR	PARHELION
AEGNORSTU	ARGENTOUS	AEHILNOST	HAILSTONE
AEGNRRSST	STRANGERS	AEHILNPRS	PLANISHER
AEGNRSSTT	STRANGEST	AEHILNQRU	HARLEQUIN
AEGNRSSTU	ASSURGENT	AEHILORST	HORSETAIL,
AEGOPPSST	STOPPAGES		ISOTHERAL
AEGOPRRUW	GROUPWARE	AEHILOSTT	HELIOSTAT
AEGOPSSTT	GATEPOSTS	AEHILPRSS	SPLASHIER
AEGORRRTT	GARROTTER	AEHILRSTY	HAIRSTYLE
AEGORRSTT	GARROTTES	AEHIMNNOT	ANTHEMION
AEGORRSTU	SURROGATE	AEHIMNORS	HARMONIES,
AEGORSTTY	GESTATORY		HARMONISE
AEGPRRRUY	PRAYER RUG	AEHIMNORZ	HARMONIZE
AEHHHITTY	HIT THE HAY	AEHIMNOST	THOMASINE
AEHHHOOTU	HU-HO-HAO-T'E	AEHIMNPSS	MISSHAPEN
AEHHILLTW	WHITEHALL	AEHIMNPST	PANTHEISM
AEHHILLTY	HEALTHILY	AEHIMNRSU	HUMANISER
AEHHILNPT	PHTHALEIN	AEHIMNRUZ	HUMANIZER
AEHHILOPT	THEOPHILA	AEHIMPSST	SHIPMATES,
AEHHIMPRS	HAMPSHIRE		STEAMSHIP
AEHHIORRS	HORSEHAIR	AEHIMQSSU	SQUEAMISH
AEHHIPPSS	SHIPSHAPE	AEHINNRSS	IN HARNESS
AEHHISTWW	WHITEWASH	AEHINNRTU	RUTHENIAN
AEHHLNTUY	UNHEALTHY	AEHINORSS	HOARINESS
AEHHLOPTY	HALOPHYTE	AEHINORST	HORTENSIA
AEHHMOOPT	HOMEOPATH	AEHINORTT	ANORTHITE
		AEHINPPSS	HAPPINESS
AEHINPSSS	APISHNESS		
AEHINPSST	THESPIANS		
AEHINPSSY	SISYPHEAN		
AEHINPSTT	PANTHEIST		
AEHINRRST	TARNISHER		
AEHINRRSV	VARNISHER		
AEHINRRTU	ARTHURINE		
AEHINRSSV	VARNISHES		
AEHINSSST	HASTINESS		
AEHINSSSW	WASHINESS		
AEHINSTTW	WHITE ANTS		
AEHIORRTT	THROATIER		
AEHIORSTU	AUTHORISE		
AEHIORSTX	RHEOTAXIS		
AEHIORTTV	HORTATIVE		
AEHIORTUZ	AUTHORIZE		
AEHIPPRSS	SAPPHIRES		
AEHIPRSTT	THERAPIST		
AEHIQRSSU	SQUASHIER		
AEHIRRSTW	SWARTHIER		
AEHIRSSTT	TRASHIEST		
AEHJLLNOS	HALL-JONES		
AEHJPRSSW	JEW'S HARPS		
AEHKLNSST	THANKLESS		
AEHKLRRSU	KARLSRUHE		
AEHKORRTW	EARTHWORK		
AEHKOSSTU	SHAKEOUTS		
AEHLLLNPU	ALEPH-NULL		
AEHLLNOOP	ALLOPHONE		
AEHLLORSW	SHALLOWER		
AEHLLPSSU	PHALLUSES		
AEHLLPSSY	HAPLESSLY		
AEHLMOOST	LOATHSOME		
AEHLMOSSU	ALMSHOUSE		
AEHLMPPST	PAMPHLETS		
AEHLNRTUY	UNEARTHLY		
AEHLOPPSY	POLYPHASE		
AEHLOPRSY	HORSEPLAY		
AEHLOPSTT	HOTPLATES		
AEHLOPSUY	PLAYHOUSE		
AEHLORSUV	OVERHAULS		
AEHLPRRSU	SPHERULAR		
AEHLPSSTU	SULPHATES		
AEHMMOORT	HARMOTOME		
AEHMNNRTU	MANHUNTER		
AEHMNNSSU	HUMANNESS		
AEHMNRRWY	WHERRYMAN		
AEHMOOPRS	SHAMPOOER		
AEHMOPRST	METAPHORS		
AEHMORRTW	EARTHWORM,		
	HEARTWORM		
AEHMORTWW	WHEATWORM		
AEHMPPSTU	HEAT PUMPS		
AEHMSSTTY	AMETHYSTS		

AEHNNOPRT	PARTHENON	AEIILNPTZ	PLATINIZE
AEHNNOPST	PANTHEONS	AEIILNRRS	AIRLINERS
AEHNNRSSU	UNHARNESS	AEIILNRRT	TRILINEAR
AEHNOOPRR	HARPOONER	AEIILNRST	LATINISER
AEHNOOPSX	SAXOPHONE	AEIILNRTY	LINEARITY
AEHNOPPSY	PAY PHONES	AEIILNRTZ	LATINIZER
AEHNOPRTU	NEUROPATH	AEIILNSTW	WAISTLINE
AEHNOPRTY	HONEYTRAP	AEIILNTVY	VENIALITY
AEHNOPRWY	PHONEY WAR	AEIILORST	SOLITAIRE
AEHNOPSSU	SAPHENOUS	AEIILORTV	VARIOLITE
AEHNOPSTY	PANTY HOSE	AEIILOSTV	ISOLATIVE
AEHNORSTT	NORTHEAST	AEIILOTVV	VIOLATIVE
AEHNPRSSS	SHARPNESS	AEIILPPST	TAIL PIPES
AEHNPRSXY	PHARYNXES	AEIILQSTU	QUALITIES
AEHOOPRRY	PYORRHOEA	AEIILRRST	TRISERIAL
AEHOOPSTT	OSTEOPATH	AEIILRRSV	RIVALRIES
AEHOOSSTU	OAST HOUSE	AEIILRSTU	RITUALISE
AEHOPSSTT	POSTHASTE	AEIILRSTV	VITALISER
AEHOPSSTU	PHASE-OUTS	AEIILRTUZ	RITUALIZE
AEHOPSSTW	SWEATSHOP	AEIILRTVZ	VITALIZER
AEHOPTTUY	AUTOPHYTE	AEIILSSUV	VISUALISE
AEHORRSSW	WARHORSES	AEIILSUVZ	VISUALIZE
AEHORSSTT	RHEOSTATS	AEIIMMRSX	MAXIMISER
AEHORSSTU	AUTHORESS	AEIIMMRXZ	MAXIMIZER
AEHORSTTW	HOT WATERS	AEIIMNNRT	NITRAMINE
AEHORSTVW	SHORT WAVE	AEIIMNPST	IMPATIENS
AEHORSTWY	SEAWORTHY	AEIIMNPTT	IMPATIENT
AEHOSSTTU	SOUTHEAST	AEIIMNRTU	MINIATURE
AEHRSSTUU	THESAURUS	AEIIMNSTT	INTIMATES
AEIIILNRT	INITIALER	AEIIMPRRS	PRIMARIES
AEIIILNTW	LIE IN WAIT	AEIIMPSSV	IMPASSIVE
AEIIIMTTV	IMITATIVE	AEIINNNTV	ANTIVENIN
AEIIINNST	INANITIES	AEIINNPTT	IN-PATIENT
AEIIINSTT	INITIATES	AEIINNRSS	RAININESS
AEIIJLNUV	JUVENILIA	AEIINNRSV	NIVERNAIS
AEIIKKTTW	KITTIWAKE	AEIINNRTT	ITINERANT
AEIIKLLNS	SILKALINE	AEIINNRTU	URANINITE
AEIIKLNOT	KAOLINITE	AEIINNSTU	ANNUITIES,
AEIIKRSTT	KERATITIS		INSINUATE
AEIILLMNN	MILLENNIA	AEIINOPTX	EXPIATION
AEIILLTTT	TITILLATE	AEIINORTT	ITERATION
AEIILLMNNS	MAIN LINES	AEIINOTTV	NOVITIATE
AEIILMNNT	ELIMINANT	AEIINRRTY	ITINERARY
AEIILMNSU	ALUMINISE	AEIINRTUV	URINATIVE
AEIILMNUZ	ALUMINIZE	AEIIPRSTV	PRIVATISE
AEIILMOSV	MALVOISIE	AEIIPRTTV	PARTITIVE
AEIILMRSS	SERIALISM	AEIIPRTVV	PRIVATIVE
AEIILMRTT	LITERATIM	AEIIPRTVZ	PRIVATIZE
AEIILNNOT	LINEATION	AEIIPSSST	EPISTASIS
AEIILNNRT	TRIENNIAL	AEIIPSSTX	EPISTAXIS
AEIILNOTV	INVIOLATE	AEIIPSTTT	STIPITATE
AEIILNPRT	REPTILIAN	AEIIRRSST	SATIRISER
AEIILNPST	PLATINISE	AEIIRRSTT	ARTERITIS
AEIILNPTV	PLAINTIVE	AEIIRRSTV	ARRIVISTE

AEIIRRSTZ	SATIRIZER
AEIIRSSTV	VARSITIES
AEIIRTTTV	ATTRITIVE
AEIJKKRVY	REYKJAVIK
AEIJMNNSS	JANSENISM
AEIJNNSST	JANSENIST
AEIJNSTTU	JAUNTIEST
AEIKKLLOO	LOOK-ALIKE
AEIKKNNSS	SNAKESKIN
AEIKLLNRY	KILLARNEY
AEIKLMNOW	WOMAN-LIKE
AEIKLNNSS	LANKINESS
AEIKLNORT	OIL TANKER
AEIKLNOVY	NIKOLAYEV
AEIKLNPSS	SKI PLANES
AEIKLRSTY	STREAKILY
AEIKMQRSU	QUAKERISM
AEIKNNPRS	SPINNAKER
AEIKNNSSS	SNAKINESS
AEIKNORTU	KETONURIA
AEIKNPSSW	PAWKINESS
AEIKNQSSU	QUAKINESS
AEIKNSSTW	SWANKIEST
AEIKORSST	KERATOSIS
AEIKPPQSU	PIPSQUEAK
AEIKPRSTY	STRIKE PAY
AEIKPSSST	PISS-TAKES
AEIKRSSST	ASTERISKS
AEILLLRTY	LITERALLY
AEILLMMST	SMALL-TIME
AEILLMNRY	MILLENARY
AEILLMRTW	WATERMILL
AEILLMSSY	AIMLESSLY
AEILLMSTT	METALLIST
AEILLNOPT	POLLINATE
AEILLNPRY	PLENARILY
AEILLNPST	PANELLIST
AEILLNRST	INSTALLER,
REINSTALL	
AEILLNRTU	TELLURIAN
AEILLOPPT	PAPILLOTE,
POPLITEAL	
AEILLOSTY	LOYALTIES
AEILLPRSU	PLURALISE
AEILLPRUZ	PLURALIZE
AEILLPSSS	SALES SLIP
AEILLPSST	PASTILLES
AEILLPSTU	PULSATILE
AEILLQRSU	SQUALLIER
AEILLRRTY	ARTILLERY
AEILLRSTW	STAIRWELL
AEILLRTWY	WATER LILY
AEILLRVXY	VEXILLARY
AEILMMNPS	PELMANISM
AEILMMNST	MENTALISM

AEILMMORS	MEMORIALS
AEILMMNOT	MELATONIN
AEILMNNSS	MANLINESS
AEILMNOOT	EMOTIONAL
AEILMNOPR	PROLAMINE
AEILMNORS	NORMALISE
AEILMNORT	MENTORIAL
AEILMNORZ	NORMALIZE
AEILMNOSS	LOAMINESS,
MELANOSIS	
AEILMNOTU	EMULATION
AEILMNPRT	IMPLANTER
AEILMNRST	TERMINALS,
TRAMLINES	
AEILMNRSU	SEMILUNAR
AEILMNRVY	LIVERYMAN
AEILMNSST	MALTINESS
AEILMNTTY	MENTALITY
AEILMORRS	MORALISER
AEILMORRZ	MORALIZER
AEILMOSTU	MOUSETAIL
AEILMPRST	PRELATISM
AEILMRSTY	SALIMETRY
AEILMRTTY	ALTIMETRY
AEILMSSVY	MASSIVELY
AEILMSTTU	STIMULATE
AEILMSTUU	MUTUALISE
AEILMTUUZ	MUTUALIZE
AEILNNNOR	NONLINEAR
AEILNNOPR	NONPAREIL
AEILNNOST	TENSIONAL
AEILNNOSV	SLOVENIAN
AEILNNOSY	LYONNAISE
AEILNNPSS	PLAINNESS
AEILNNPSU	PENINSULA
AEILNNTUV	UNIVALENT
AEILNOOPS	POLONAISE
AEILNOORS	EROSIONAL
AEILNOPPR	PIPERONAL
AEILNOPST	SEAL-POINT
AEILNOPSY	POLYNESIA
AEILNOPTT	PELTATION,
POTENTIAL	
AEILNORST	ORIENTALS,
RELATIONS, SEROTINAL,	
TENSORIAL	
AEILNORSV	VERSIONAL
AEILNORTT	NATROLITE
AEILNOSSS	SESSIONAL
AEILNPRTY	INTERPLAY,
PAINTERLY, PARTY LINE	
AEILNPSTY	SAPIENTLY
AEILNPTTY	PATIENTLY
AEILNPTUV	PULVINATE
AEILNRSTT	STERILANT

AEILNRSTV	INTERVALS
AEILNRSUV	UNIVERSAL
AEILNRTTV	TRIVALENT
AEILNRTUV	AVIRULENT
AEILNRTUY	UNREALITY
AEILNSSST	SALTINESS,
SLATINESS, STAINLESS	
AEILNSSTW	SLANTWISE
AEILNSTVY	SYLVANITE
AEILNSUUX	UNISEXUAL
AEILOPRRS	POLARISER
AEILOPRRZ	POLARIZER
AEILOPRST	SAPROLITE
AEILORSTT	TOTALISER
AEILORSTY	ROYALTIES
AEILORTTV	LEVITATOR
AEILORTTZ	TOTALIZER
AEILPPRTU	PREPUTIAL
AEILPPSST	SPLIT PEAS
AEILPPSUV	APPULSIVE
AEILPRRSS	REPRISALS
AEILPRSST	PILASTERS
AEILPRSTT	PALTRIEST,
PRELATIST	
AEILPRTVY	PRIVATELY
AEILPSSVY	PASSIVELY
AEILPSTTU	STIPULATE
AEILPSTUV	PULSATIVE
AEILQRRUY	RELIQUARY
AEILRSSTY	LAY SISTER
AEILRTUUX	LUXURIATE
AEILSTUXY	SEXUALITY
AEIMMNNRS	MANNERISM
AEIMMNOPT	PANTOMIME
AEIMMRSST	SMARMIEST
AEIMMRSSU	SUMMARIES,
SUMMARISE	
AEIMMRSUZ	SUMMARIZE
AEIMNNNQU	MANNEQUIN
AEIMNNOPU	PNEUMONIA
AEIMNNOST	MINNESOTA
AEIMNNRST	MANNERIST
AEIMNOPRT	PROTAMINE
AEIMNORST	STEAM IRON
AEIMNORSW	WOMANISER
AEIMNORTV	NORMATIVE
AEIMNORWZ	WOMANIZER
AEIMNPRST	SPEARMINT
AEIMNRSTT	MARTINETS
AEIMNRSTU	ANTISERUM
AEIMNRTTY	MATERNITY
AEIMOPRTX	PROXIMATE
AEIMORRSU	ARMOURIES
AEIMORSST	ATOMISERS
AEIMORSTT	ESTIMATOR

AEIMORSTV	MOVIE STAR
AEIMORSTZ	ATOMIZERS
AEIMORTTU	AUTOTIMER
AEIMPPRSU	PAUPERISM
AEIMPRSTU	SEPTARIUM
AEIMPRTUZ	TRAPEZIUM
AEIMQRSSU	MARQUISES
AEIMRRRTU	TERRARIUM
AEIMRSTTY	TASIMETRY
AEINNNOTW	NEWTONIAN
AEINNNPTU	NEPTUNIAN
AEINNOPSX	EXPANSION
AEINNORTV	VERNATION
AEINNOSST	SENSATION
AEINNOSTU	SAINT-OUEN
AEINNOTTT	ATTENTION,
TENTATION	
AEINNPPSS	NAPPINESS
AEINNPSST	INAPTNESS
AEINNRSTT	INSTANTER,
TRANSIENT	
AEINNRSTU	SATURNINE
AEINNRSTY	TYRANNIES,
TYRANNISE	
AEINNRTYZ	TYRANNIZE
AEINNSSST	NASTINESS
AEINNSSTT	NATTINESS
AEINOOPRT	OPERATION
AEINOOPSU	IONOPAUSE
AEINOPPRT	APPOINTER,
REAPPOINT	
AEINOPRSS	ASPERSION
AEINOPRST	PATRONISE
AEINOPRSY	AEPYORNIS
AEINOPRTZ	PATRONIZE
AEINOPSSS	SOAPINESS
AEINOQRTU	INQUORATE,
ORTANIQUE	
AEINOQSTU	EQUATIONS
AEINOQTTU	TOTAQUINE
AEINORRST	SERRATION
AEINORSST	ASSERTION,
SENORITAS	
AEINORSSU	ARSENIOUS
AEINORSSV	AVERSIONS
AEINORSTT	STATIONER
AEINOSTVX	VEXATIONS
AEINPPSSS	SAPPINESS
AEINPPSST	SNAPPIEST
AEINPRRST	TERRAPINS,
TRANSPIRE	
AEINPRTTY	PATERNITY
AEINPSSST	PASTINESS
AEINPSSSW	WASPINESS
AEINRRSST	STRAINERS

AEINRRSTT	RESTRAINT
AEINRSSTT	RATTINESS,
RESISTANT, TRAIN SETS	
AEINRSSTU	SUSTAINER
AEINRSSUZ	SUZERAINS
AEINRSTTT	IN TATTERS
AEINSSSTT	TASTINESS
AEINSSTTT	TATTINESS
AEINSSTZZ	SNAZZIEST
AEIOORRST	ORATORIES
AEIOPRRSV	VAPORISER
AEIOPRRVZ	VAPORIZER
AEIOPRTTV	PORTATIVE
AEIOPRTXY	EXPIATORY
AEIOPSSTU	AUTOPSIES
AEIORTUVV	UVAROVITE
AEIOSTUVX	VEXATIOUS
AEIPPRRTY	TIPPERARY
AEIPRRTVY	VARITYPER
AEIPRSSTU	PRUSSIATE
AEIPRSTUZ	TRAPEZIUS
AEIQRRTTUZ	QUARTZITE
AEIRRSSTT	STARRIEST
AEIRRTTTU	TRITURATE
AEIRSSTTU	TESSITURA
AEIRSTTTX	TESTATRIX
AEIRSTTUY	AUSTERITY
AEISSSSTY	ESSAYISTS
AEJLLOSUY	JEALOUSLY
AEJMPRTUW	WATER JUMP
AEJOPSTUX	JUXTAPOSE
AEKKLRRSY	SKYLARKER
AEKLMOORT	TOOL-MAKER
AEKLMORTW	METALWORK
AEKLORSVW	WALKOVERS
AEKLPRRSS	SPARKLERS
AEKMNOORR	MOONRAKER
AEKMNOPSS	SPOKESMAN
AEKMNOPTW	KEPT WOMAN
AEKMOORSY	KARYOSOME
AEKMPRRSS	PRESSMARK
AEKNOORST	SNAKEROOT
AEKNOOTTU	TAKE OUT ON
AEKNPRRST	PRANKSTER
AEKNRSSST	STARKNESS
AEKNRSTTU	TURKESTAN
AEKOPPRRW	PAPERWORK
AEKOPRTYY	KARYOTYPE
AEKORRWWX	WAXWORKER
AEKQRSSUW	SQUAWKERS
AELLLMOSU	MALLEOLUS
AELLLPTUU	PULLULATE
AELLLRSTU	STELLULAR
AELLLSSWY	LAWLESSLY

AELLMNOTT	ALLOTMENT
AELLMNSSS	SMALLNESS
AELLMOPRY	PERMALLOY
AELLMORTU	TULLAMORE
AELLMORTY	ALLOMETRY
AELLNNOTW	ALLENTOWN
AELLNOSTW	STONEWALL
AELLNQUUY	UNEQUALLY
AELLNRTUY	NEUTRALLY
AELLOOPRT	ALLOTROPE
AELLOPRRT	PATROLLER
AELLOPRSY	ROLE PLAYS
AELLOPSTX	POLL TAXES
AELLOPTUV	POLE VAULT
AELLORSWW	SWALLOWER
AELLOSUYZ	ZEALOUSLY
AELLRSSTY	ARTLESSLY
AELMMORST	MAELSTROM
AELMMOSUU	MAUSOLEUM
AELMNNNTU	ANNULMENT
AELMNNOOP	MONOPLANE
AELMNOOPR	LAMPOONER
AELMNOORT	MONOLATER
AELMNOORY	MONOLAYER
AELMNOPRT	PATROLMEN
AELMNOPSS	PLEONASMS
AELMNOPTU	PULMONATE
AELMNORST	MESTRANOL
AELMNORWW	LAWNMOWER
AELMNRSTU	MENSTRUAL
AELMNRTTU	TREMULANT
AELMOORSS	SALEROOMS,
SALESROOM	
AELMOOSTT	LOOM-STATE
AELMOPSTT	PALMETTOS
AELMOSTTU	MULATTOES
AELMRSSTT	MALTSTERS
AELNOOSSW	LOW SEASON
AELNOPRSS	PERSONALS
AELNOPRSY	LAYPERSON
AELNOPSTY	NEOPLASTY
AELNORSTU	SOLUTREAN
AELNOTUVV	VOL-AU-VENT
AELNRRUVY	VULNERARY
AELNRSSTT	SLATTERNS
AELNRSTTU	RESULTANT
AELNSSSUU	USUALNESS
AELOOPRTW	WATER POLO
AELOORRTT	TOLERATOR
AELOPPRSS	PROLAPSES
AELOPRSTU	SPORULATE
AELOPSSSU	ESPOUSALS
AELOPSTTU	POSTULATE
AELPPRTUW	WUPPERTAL

AELPRRSTT	PRATTLERS
AELPRSSST	STRAPLESS
AELPSTTUU	PUSTULATE
AELQRRTUY	QUARTERLY
AEMMNORTY	MANOMETRY,
MOMENTARY	
AEMMOORST	ROOMMATES
AEMMORRST	MARMOSETS
AEMMORTTY	ATMOMETRY
AEMMRSTYY	ASYMMETRY
AEMNNOORS	ROMAN NOSE
AEMNNORST	ORNAMENTS
AEMNNORTT	REMONTANT
AEMNOOPRT	PROTONEMA
AEMNOORST	ANTEROOMS
AEMNORRSS	RANSOMERS
AEMNORRTU	NUMERATOR
AEMNORSTY	MONASTERY
AEMNPRTUY	PRYTANEUM
AEMNRSSST	SMARTNESS
AEMNRSTTU	TRANSMUTE
AEMNRSTVY	VESTRYMAN
AEMOORRST	STATEROOM
AEMOPRRTY	TEMPORARY
AEMOPRSTU	MOUSETRAP
AEMOPRSTW	TAPEWORMS
AEMOPSTTY	ASYMPTOTE
AEMORRRSU	ARMOURERS
AEMORRTUY	MARQUETRY
AENNORRST	RESNATRON
AENNPSSTU	UNAPTNESS
AENNRSTTU	TRANSEUNT
AENOOPSST	SOAPSTONE,
TEASPOONS	
AENOORRST	RESONATOR
AENOORRTV	RENOVATOR
AENOPPRRT	EN RAPPORT
AENOPRSST	PATRONESS,
TRANSPOSE	
AENOPRSUV	SUPERNOVA
AENORRTWW	WATERWORN
AENORSSTU	ANOESTRUS
AENORSTTY	ATTORNEYS
AENPRSSTT	TRANSEPTS
AENQSSSTU	SQUATNESS
AENRSTWYY	ENTRYWAYS
AEOOPRRST	OPERATORS
AEOOPRTTV	VAPORETTO
AEOPRRRTY	PORTRAYER
AEOPRRSTT	PROSTRATE
AEOPRRSTW	SPEARWORT
AEOPRSSSV	PASSOVERS
AEOPRSSTT	PROSTATES
AEOQRRSSU	SQUARROSE
AEORSSSSS	ASSESSORS

AEORSSTTT	TESTATORS	AFGNNOOSU	SON-OF-A-GUN	AFLOSTUUY	FATUOUSLY
AEORSSTUU	TROUSSEAU	AFGNOPRSW	FROGSPAWN	AFMNORRST	TRANSFORM
AEPPRSSUY	PAPYRUSES	AFGORSTUW	TUGS-OF-WAR	AFMNORRTW	WARM FRONT
AEPPRSTUU	SUPPURATE	AFHHLRTTU	HALF-TRUTH	AFMOORSTY	STYROFOAM
AEPQRRTUY	PARQUETRY	AFHIILNTU	HIFALUTIN	AGGHHILSY	HAGGISHLY
AEPRRSSTU	SUPERSTAR	AFHIKLOTT	OF THAT ILK	AGGHIILNT	ALIGHTING
AEQRRSSTU	TRY SQUARE	AFHIKLPSS	HIP FLASKS	AGGHILOOY	HAGIOLOGY
AEQRSSTTU	SQUATTERS	AFHIKMSUU	FUKUSHIMA	AGGHILSST	GASLIGHTS
AEQSSTTTU	SQUATTEST	AFHIORSTY	FORSYTHIA	AGGHILSWY	WAGGISHLY
AERRSSTUU	SUSURRATE	AFHLLMRUY	HARMFULLY	AGGIIIMNN	IMAGINING
AFFGGINUW	GUFFAWING	AFHLLORST	SHORTFALL	AGGIILLNP	PILLAGING
AFFGIIMNR	AFFIRMING	AFHLMNOOS	HALF MOONS	AGGIILMNN	MALIGNING
AFFGILNNS	SNAFFLING	AFHOOPSTT	FOOTPATHS	AGGIILNNS	SIGNALING
AFFGIORST	SGRAFFITO	AFHOORRST	HOARFROST	AGGIILNNT	TINGALING
AFFHILRSY	RAFFISHLY	AFIIILNOT	FILIATION	AGGIILNVW	LAWGIVING
AFFHILSTU	FAITHFULS	AFIILLNOT	INFLATION	AGGIIMNRT	MIGRATING
AFFHIMRSS	FISH FARMS	AFIILNOOT	FOLIATION	AGGIIMNST	GIGANTISM
AFFIILNPT	PLAINTIFF	AFIILNSST	FINALISTS	AGGIINNOZ	AGONIZING
AFFILNRUY	RUFFIANLY	AFIILORRT	TRIFORIAL	AGGIINNSS	ASSIGNING
AFFKNORRT	FRANKFORT	AFIIMNRRY	INFIRMARY	AGGILLNOP	GALLOPING
AFFLLOOST	FOOTFALLS	AFIINOSTX	FIXATIONS	AGGILLNRY	GLARINGLY
AFFLOOTTU	FOOT FAULT	AFIIOORRT	A FORTIORI	AGGILNNOS	GANGLIONS
AFFMNNRUY	FUNNY FARM	AFIKLLMOT	MILK FLOAT	AGGILNNPS	SPANGLING
AFGGGINOT	FAGGOTING	AFILLLOST	FLOTILLAS	AGGILNNRW	WRANGLING
AFGGIINTU	FATIGUING	AFILLNOUX	FLUXIONAL	AGGILNOOY	ANGIOLOGY
AFGHHILLT	HALF-LIGHT	AFILLNPUY	PAINFULLY	AGGILNPPR	GRAPPLING
AFGHILLNT	NIGHTFALL	AFILLOOPR	APRIL FOOL	AGGILNPSY	GASPINGLY
AFGHILNST	FANLIGHTS	AFILMMORS	FORMALISM	AGGILNRTY	GRATINGLY
AFGHILPSS	FLAGSHIPS	AFILMNNTU	FULMINANT	AGGIMMNRU	RUMMAGING
AFGHILSTT	LIGHT-FAST	AFILMOPRS	SALPIFORM	AGGIMNPUZ	GAZUMPING
AFGHIMNOT	FATHOMING	AFILMORST	FORMALIST	AGGINNOOR	GORGONIAN
AFGHINRST	FARTHINGS	AFILMORTY	FORMALITY	AGGINORRS	GROSGRAIN
AFGHLNSSU	FLASHGUNS	AFILMRSST	FILM STARS	AGGINORTU	OUTRAGING
AFGHMOORT	HOMOGRAFT	AFILNOOTT	FLOTATION	AGGINPSTU	UPSTAGING
AFGIILMNN	INFLAMING	AFILNPSST	FLAT SPINS	AGGKNNTUW	KWANGTUNG
AFGIILNNT	INFLATING	AFILOORSS	FOSSORIAL	AGGMOORRT	MORTGAGOR
AFGIILNNU	UNFAILING	AFILSSTTU	FLAUTISTS	AGGMOSTYY	MYSTAGOGY
AFGIILRTY	FRAGILITY	AFIMNNORT	INFORMANT	AGGNNOPYY	PYONGYANG
AFGIIMNRY	RAMIFYING	AFIMNOORT	FORMATION	AGHHIKNTW	NIGHTHAWK
AFGIINRTY	RATIFYING	AFINNOSTU	FOUNTAINS	AGHHILTUY	HAUGHTILY
AFGIKNORS	FORSAKING	AFINOOPRR	RAINPROOF	AGHHINRST	THRASHING
AFGIKNRST	SKIN GRAFT	AFINOPRTY	PROFANITY	AGHHLOOPR	HOLOGRAPH
AFGILLNUY	GAINFULLY	AFIORTTTT	TIT FOR TAT	AGHHMOOPR	HOMOGRAPH
AFGILMNOS	FLAMINGOS	AFIOSTTUU	FATUITOUS	AGHHNOUZZ	ZHANGZHOU
AFGILNNOU	UNION FLAG	AFKLOOSTT	FOOTSTALK	AGHIIIKRZ	KIRGHIZIA
AFGILNNTU	FLAUNTING	AFLLLPUYY	PLAYFULLY	AGHIILLRT	LIGHT RAIL
AFGILNNWY	FAWNINGLY	AFLLNORTY	FRONTALLY	AGHIILLTT	TAIL-LIGHT
AFGILRTUY	FRUGALITY	AFLLNOSSW	SNOWFALLS	AGHIILNSV	LAVISHING
AFGIMORTU	FUMIGATOR	AFLLOOSTT	FOOTSTALL	AGHIIMMMN	IMMINGHAM
AFGINNOPR	PROFANING	AFLMOPRST	PLATFORMS	AGHIINNSV	VANISHING
AFGINNPRY	FRYING PAN	AFLMORRUY	FORMULARY	AGHIINRSV	RAVISHING
AFGINORRW	FARROWING	AFLOOPSTY	SPLAYFOOT	AGHIINRTU	THURINGIA
AFGINORUV	FAVOURING	AFLOORSUV	FLAVOROUS	AGHIIPRRS	HAIRGRIPS
AFGINSTTU	FUNGISTAT	AFLOPRRSU	FLUORSPAR	AGHIKMNOW	WOKINGHAM

AGHIKNOSU	KAOHSIUNG	AGIILLMMR	MILLIGRAM	AGILLNSTY	LASTINGLY
AGHILLNOW	HALLOWING	AGIILLNOR	GORILLIAN	AGILMNNOO	MONGOLIAN
AGHILLNSY	LASHINGLY	AGIILLNRV	RIVALLING	AGILMNNOY	MOANINGLY
AGHILLNTY	HALTINGLY	AGIILLNWY	WAILINGLY	AGILMNPRT	TRAMPLING
AGHILLORY	HOLY GRAIL	AGIILMNSY	MISLAYING	AGILMNSUY	AMUSINGLY
AGHILMORT	ALGORITHM,	AGIILMNTY	MALIGNITY	AGILMRSUV	VULGARISM
	LOGARITHM	AGIILNORS	ORIGINALS	AGILNNOPS	PLAINSONG
AGHILNOOS	HOOLIGANS	AGIILNORT	TAILORING	AGILNNOQU	ALGONQUIN
AGHILNORT	GRANOLITH	AGIILNOST	INTAGLIOS,	AGILNNRSY	SNARINGLY
AGHILNOTW	ALONG WITH		ISOLATING	AGILNNRTY	RANTINGLY
AGHILNPSS	SPLASHING	AGIILNOTV	VIOLATING	AGILNNWYY	YAWNINGLY
AGHILNPTY	PLAYTHING	AGIILNPRS	SPIRALING	AGILNORSY	SOARINGLY
AGHILNTUY	NAUGHTILY	AGIILNRSV	VIRGINALS	AGILNORVY	VAINGLORY
AGHILRSTT	STARLIGHT	AGIILNSSS	ISINGLASS	AGILNOTUV	OVULATING
AGHIMNRST	HAMSTRING	AGIILNSTT	LITIGANTS	AGILNOTUW	OUTLAWING
AGHIMOPRY	AMPHIGORY	AGIILORTT	LITIGATOR	AGILNOTUY	OUTLAYING
AGHIMORST	HISTOGRAM	AGIILOTTT	TOGLIATTI	AGILNPRSW	SPRAWLING
AGHINNOPR	ORPHANING	AGIIMMNRT	IMMIGRANT	AGILNPRSY	RASPINGLY,
AGHINORRW	HARROWING	AGIIMNNRT	INMIGRANT		SPARINGLY
AGHINPSUW	WASHING-UP	AGIIMNORT	MIGRATION	AGILNPRTT	PRATTLING
AGHINQSSU	SQUASHING	AGIIMNOST	SIGMATION	AGILNPRTY	PRATINGLY
AGHINRTTW	THWARTING	AGIIMNPRT	IMPARTING	AGILNPSTT	SPLATTING
AGHIRSSTT	STRAIGHTS	AGIIMORTT	MITIGATOR	AGILNPSTU	PULSATING
AGHKMOPRY	KYMOGRAPH	AGIINNNOT	ANOINTING	AGILNPSUY	PAUSINGLY
AGHKOPRRU	GORAKHPUR	AGIINNORS	SIGNORINA	AGILNRSST	STARLINGS
AGHLLOOPY	HAPLOLOGY	AGIINNORT	RATIONING	AGILNRSSU	SINGULARS
AGHLMNOPU	PLOUGHMAN	AGIINNPRS	SPRAINING	AGILNRSTT	STARTLING
AGHLMOOPR	LAGOMORPH	AGIINNPSS	IN PASSING	AGILNRVYY	VARYINGLY
AGHLMOORS	HOLOGRAMS	AGIINNPST	PAINTINGS	AGILNSWYY	SWAYINGLY
AGHLMOOTU	GOALMOUTH	AGIINNRST	STRAINING,	AGILOOPST	APOLOGIST
AGHLNOOTY	ANTHOLOGY		TRAININGS	AGILOPRUY	UROPYGIAL
AGHLNOSTU	ONSLAUGHT	AGIINNRTU	URINATING	AGILRRTUY	GARRULITY
AGHLOOPTY	PATHOLOGY	AGIINOORT	IGNORATIO	AGILRTUVY	VULGARITY
AGHLOOPRY	POLYGRAPH	AGIINPPRS	APPRISING	AGIMMNSUY	GYMNASIUM
AGHLOPRXY	XYLOGRAPH	AGIINPRST	TRAIPSING	AGIMNNOOR	MAROONING
AGHLORSSU	HOURGLASS	AGIINSSST	ASSISTING	AGIMNNORS	RANSOMING
AGHMNOOPR	MONOGRAPH,	AGIINSTTU	SITUATING	AGIMNNOTU	AMOUNTING
	NOMOGRAPH, PHONOGRAM	AGIIORRRT	IRRIGATOR	AGIMNNOVV	MOVING VAN
AGHMNOOPY	MONOPHAGY	AGIIRSSTT	GASTRITIS	AGIMNOOSV	VAMOOSING
AGHMNPSSU	SPHAGNUMS	AGIIRSTTU	GUITARIST	AGIMNORSS	ORGANISMS
AGHMNRSTU	HAMSTRUNG	AGIKLMORS	KILOGRAMS	AGIMNORSU	IGNORAMUS
AGHMOOPRT	PHOTOGRAM	AGIKLNOSY	SOAKINGLY	AGIMNRRTY	MARTYRING
AGHMOPRYY	MYOGRAPHY	AGIKLNOTT	TALKING-TO	AGIMOOSSU	ISOGAMOUS
AGHNNSTUU	HSUAN T'UNG	AGIKLNPRS	SPARKLING	AGIMORRTY	MIGRATORY
AGHNOPSSU	SPHAGNOUS	AGIKMNNSU	UNMASKING	AGINNORRW	NARROWING
AGHOOPRRY	OROGRAPHY	AGIKNNPSS	SPANKINGS	AGINNPRSU	UNSPARING
AGHOOPRYZ	ZOOGRAPHY	AGIKNOSST	GOATSKINS	AGINNPSSW	WINGSPANS
AGIIIMNPR	IMPAIRING	AGIKNQSUW	SQUAWKING	AGINNSTUU	TUNGUSIAN
AGIIIMNTT	IMITATING	AGILLMNRU	MULLINGAR	AGINOOPSS	POISON GAS
AGIIINNRV	VIRGINIAN	AGILLNNNU	ANNULLING	AGINOOTTT	TATTOOING
AGIIINSTV	VAGINITIS	AGILLNOPW	WALLOPING	AGINOPPRV	APPROVING
AGIIINTTV	VITIATING	AGILLNOTT	ALLOTTING,	AGINOPRRT	PARROTING
AGIIKLMNR	GRIMALKIN		TOTALLING	AGINOPRTU	PURGATION
AGIIKMNST	MISTAKING	AGILLNOWW	WALLOWING	AGINORRSS	GARRISONS
AGIILLLOP	GALLIPOLI	AGILLNQSU	SQUALLING		

AGINORSST	ASSORTING, ORGANISTS, ROASTINGS	
AGINORSTY	GYRATIONS, SIGNATORY	
AGINORSUV	SAVOURING	
AGINPPRST	STRAPPING, TRAPPINGS	
AGINPPRSW	WRAPPINGS	
AGINPRSTU	PASTURING	
AGINQRRUY	QUARRYING	
AGINQSTTU	SQUATTING	
AGINRSSST	STAR SIGNS	
AGINRSSTY	STINGRAYS	
AGIOPRRSY	SPIROGYRA	
AGIQRSSTU	GRASSQUIT	
AGJKNORRU	KURRAJONG	
AGKLLNOOO	A LONG LOOK	
AGKLORSSW	GLASSWORK	
AGKLPPRSU	SPARK PLUG	
AGKNORSST	KNOTGRASS	
AGLLNOOPY	POLYGONAL	
AGLMOORSU	GLAMOROUS	
AGLOOPSST	GOALPOSTS	
AGLOORSTY	ASTROLOGY	
AGLOOTTUY	TAUTOLOGY	
AGLOPPRUY	PLAYGROUP	
AGLORRSUU	GARRULOUS	
AGLORSSTW	GLASSWORT	
AGMMNOORS	GROOMSMAN, MONOGRAMS	
AGMMOSTUU	GUMMATOUS	
AGMNORRST	STRONGARM	
AGMNSSTUY	NYSTAGMUS	
AGNNOSSSW	SWANSONGS	
AGNOPRSST	PART-SONGS	
AGNPRSSUY	SPRAY GUNS	
AGNRRSSUY	STRANGURY	
AGOPRRTUY	PURGATORY	
AGORSSTTU	GUSTATORY	
AGRSTTTTU	STUTTGART	
AHHIIMORS	HIROSHIMA	
AHHIIRRST	HAIR SHIRT	
AHHLORSTU	SHORT-HAUL	
AHHMOSTUW	MOUTHWASH	
AHHNORRST	HARTSHORN	
AHHNORSTW	HAWTHORNS	
AHHOPPRUY	HAPPY HOUR	
AHIIILSST	LITHIASIS	
AHIILLPPP	PHILLIPPA	
AHIILLTWW	WITH A WILL	
AHIILOOPZ	ZOOPHILIA	
AHIILORSU	HILARIOUS	
AHIILOSST	HALITOSIS	
AHIILRSTT	SHIRTTAIL	
AHIINORST	HISTORIAN	

AHIIPRSSZ	SIZARSHIP
AHIIRRSTT	ARTHRITIS
AHIIRSSTT	TSITSIHAR
AHIJNNOST	SAINT JOHN
AHIKKNNTT	THINK TANK
AHIKKNRSS	SHARKSKIN
AHIKLMSWY	MAWKISHLY
AHIKLNSVY	KNAVISHLY
AHILLPSSY	SPLASHILY
AHILLPSTW	WHIPSTALL
AHILLSSVY	SLAVISHLY
AHILMNNSY	MANNISHLY
AHILMOPSY	SYPHILOMA
AHILMORST	HAILSTORM
AHILMOSST	MAILSHOTS
AHILMPRTU	TRIUMPHAL
AHILNORTT	TRIATHLON
AHILNPPUY	UNHAPPILY
AHILOPPTY	HIPPOLYTA
AHILOPSST	HOSPITALS
AHILORSTW	SHOW TRIAL
AHILORTTY	THROATILY
AHILOSTTT	STATOLITH
AHILPSSWY	WASPISHLY
AHILQSSUY	SQUASHILY
AHILRSTWY	SWARTHILY
AHIMMNORU	HARMONIUM
AHIMMOPRS	AMORPHISM
AHIMNNORY	INHARMONY
AHIMNORST	HARMONIST
AHIMNPSTY	SYMPATHIN
AHIMNRTUU	ANTHURIUM
AHIMNSSTU	HUMANISTS
AHIMOOSTX	HOMOTAXIS
AHIMOPRSS	APHORISMS
AHIMOPRSY	MAYORSHIP
AHIMOPSUX	AMPHIOXUS
AHINNOOPT	PHONATION
AHINNOPTY	ANTIPHONY
AHINOOPRS	SOPHRONIA
AHINOOSTU	HOUSTONIA
AHINPRSST	TRANSSHIP
AHIOPPSSY	APOPHYSIS
AHIOPRSUV	VAPOURISH
AHIORRTWY	AIRWORTHY
AHIORTTUY	AUTHORITY
AHKLOOPYY	PLAY HOOKY
AHKLOSSTW	TALK SHOWS
AHKNOSTUY	THANKYOUS
AHKORSTUW	SOUTHWARK
AHLLLOSWY	SHALLOWLY
AHLLMOOPR	ALLOMORPH
AHLLNOSTW	TOWN HALLS
AHLLOPSUY	APHYLLOUS

AHLMOOOPR	HOMOPOLAR
AHLMOOPSY	HOMOPLASY
AHLMOPSTY	POLYMATHS
AHLNOPSSU	ALPHONSUS
AHMOOPRSU	AMORPHOUS
AHMOORSSW	WASHROOMS
AHMOPRTTU	MOUTHPART
AHNNNOOTY	HOOTNANNY
AHNOOPRTY	PHONATORY
AHNOPPSSW	PAWNSHOPS
AHNOPSSST	SNAPSHOTS
AHNORRTTY	THYRATRON
AHOOOPTTT	HOT POTATO
AHOOPRRTX	PROTHORAX
AHOOPSTTT	PHOTOSTAT
AHOORRTTY	HORTATORY
AHOPSSTUW	SOUTHPAWS
AIIILLNTY	INITIALLY
AIIILMNST	LAMINITIS
AIIIMNOTT	IMITATION
AIIINNNOT	INANITION
AIIINNSTY	ASININITY
AIIINORTT	INITIATOR
AIIINOTTV	VITIATION
AIIJLOTVY	JOVIALITY
AIIKNNNPS	PANNIKINS
AIILLMMNY	MINIMALLY
AIILLMRSY	SIMILARLY
AIILLNSTY	SAINTLILY
AIILLPRRS	SPIRILLAR
AIILLRSTT	TRIALLIST
AIILLRTVY	TRIVIALLY
AIILMMNUU	ALUMINIUM
AIILMNORT	TRINOMIAL
AIILMNSST	STALINISM
AIILMNSTT	MILITANTS
AIILMOSST	ALTISSIMO
AIILMPRRY	PRIMARILY
AIILMRSST	MISTRIALS
AIILMRSTU	RITUALISM
AIILNOOST	ISOLATION
AIILNOOTV	VIOLATION
AIILNOPST	OIL PAINTS
AIILNOPSV	PAVILIONS
AIILNOQTU	LIQUATION
AIILNORTT	INTROITAL
AIILNOSTT	SILTATION
AIILNOTTU	TUITIONAL
AIILNPSST	TAILSPINS
AIILNRSST	SINISTRAL
AIILNSSTT	STALINIST
AIILPRSST	SPRITSAIL
AIILPRSTU	SPIRITUAL
AIILRSTTU	RITUALIST

AIIMMPRSV	VAMPIRISM
AIIMNNTUY	UNANIMITY
AIIMNOPRS	PROSIMIAN
AIIMNOPSS	IMPASSION
AIIMNOSTY	ANIMOSITY
AIIMNPSTT	TIMPANIST
AIIMORSTT	IMITATORS
AIIMPSSSV	PASSIVISM
AIIMRSTUU	MAURITIUS
AIIMRSUVV	VIVARIUMS
AIINNNOOT	ANTONIONI
AIINNNOPT	PINNATION
AIINNORTT	NITRATION
AIINNORTU	RUINATION, URINATION
AIINNOSSV	INVASIONS
AIINNOTTX	ANTITOXIN
AIINNRSTT	IN TRANSIT
AIINOOQRU	IROQUOIAN
AIINOPRTT	PARTITION
AIINOPRTV	PRIVATION
AIINORSTT	STRIATION
AIINORSVY	VISIONARY
AIINORTTT	ATTRITION, TITRATION
AIINOSTTU	SITUATION
AIINQTTUY	ANTIQUITY
AIINRRSTT	IRRITANTS
AIIOPRRTY	APRIORITY
AIIOPRSSS	PSORIASIS
AIIOPRSTT	PAROTITIS, TOPIARIST
AIIORRRTT	IRRITATOR
AIIORTTTV	TITIVATOR
AIIPPRRST	PARTI PRIS
AIIPRRSST	AIRSTRIPS
AIIPRTTUY	PITUITARY
AIIPSSSTV	PASSIVIST
AIIPSSTVY	PASSIVITY
AIJMORSTU	MAJOR SUIT
AIJNOPPSY	POPINJAYS
AIKLNOSSY	ANKYLOSIS
AIKLOSTTW	KILOWATTS
AIKMNNOSW	KINSWOMAN
AIKNOPRTW	PAINTWORK
AILLMMORY	IMMORALLY
AILLMNNOY	NOMINALLY
AILLMPRSU	PLURALISM
AILLMSUUV	ALLUVIUMS
AILLNORST	TONSILLAR
AILLNORSU	LUNISOLAR
AILLNOSST	STALLIONS
AILLNOSSU	ALLUSIONS
AILLNOTUU	ULULATION

AILLORSTT	LITTORALS, TORTILLAS
AILLOSSTY	LOYALISTS
AILLPPRUY	PUPILLARY
AILLPRSTU	PLURALIST
AILLPRTUY	PLURALITY
AILLPSSWY	SPILLWAYS
AILLRTUVY	VIRTUALLY
AILMMOORT	IMMOLATOR
AILMMORST	IMMORTALS
AILMMRSUY	SUMMARILY
AILMMTTUU	ULTIMATUM
AILMNNOTY	ANTIMONYL
AILMNOOPS	PALOMINOS
AILMNOORS	MONORAILS
AILMNOPSY	AMYLOPSIN, OLYMPIANS
AILMNORST	MORTAL SIN
AILMNORTY	NORMALITY
AILMNOSUU	ALUMINOUS
AILMNSTTU	STIMULANT
AILMORSST	MORALISTS
AILMORSSU	SOLARIUMS
AILMORSTU	SIMULATOR
AILMORTTU	MUTILATOR
AILMORTTY	MORTALITY
AILMOSSTY	ATMOLYSIS
AILMPRSTY	PALMISTRY
AILMPSSST	PSALMISTS
AILMTTUUY	MUTUALITY
AILNNOSSW	SONS-IN-LAW
AILNNSTTY	INSTANTLY
AILNOORST	TONSORIAL, TORSIONAL
AILNOOSTV	SOLVATION
AILNOOTUV	OVULATION
AILNOPSTU	PLATINOUS, PULSATION
AILNOPSTY	PONYTAILS
AILNORSTU	INSULATOR
AILNOSTUY	AUTOLYSIN
AILNOSUXY	ANXIOUSLY
AILNPPSTU	SUPPLIANT
AILNPQTUY	PIQUANTLY
AILNRRSTU	TRIAL RUNS
AILNRTUUX	LUXURIANT
AILNSSTTU	LUTANISTS
AILOORSTV	VIOLATORS
AILOORSUV	VARIOLOUS
AILORRSUV	RIVALROUS
AILORSSTY	ROYALISTS
AILORSTTU	TUTORIALS
AILORSUVY	VARIOUSLY
AILOSSTUY	AUTOLYSIS
AILRSSTTU	ALTRUISTS

AILRSSUVV	SURVIVALS
AIMMMMNOS	MAMMONISM
AIMMMNOST	MAMMONIST
AIMMNORTY	MATRIMONY
AIMMNOSTU	SUMMATION
AIMMPRSUU	MARSUPIUM
AIMNNOORT	NOMINATOR
AIMNNOPST	POINTSMAN
AIMNNOSTU	MOUNTAINS
AIMNNOSUU	UNANIMOUS
AIMNNOTYY	ANONYMITY
AIMNNRSTU	RUMINANTS
AIMNOPRSY	PARSIMONY
AIMNOPRTT	IMPORTANT
AIMNOPRTY	PATRIMONY
AIMNORRST	RAINSTORM
AIMNORRTU	RUMINATOR
AIMNORSUU	UNIRAMOUS
AIMNOSTTU	MUTATIONS
AIMNPSTTY	TYMPANIST
AIMNRSSTU	SATURNISM
AIMOPSSTU	POTASSIUM
AINNOOPRS	SOPRANINO
AINNOOPRT	PRONATION
AINNOORTV	INNOVATOR
AINNOOSTT	NOTATIONS
AINNORSTT	STRONTIAN
AINOOPPRT	APPOINTOR, APPORTION
AINOOPSTT	POTATIONS
AINOOQTTU	QUOTATION
AINOORSTT	ROTATIONS
AINOOTTUX	AUTOTOXIN
AINOOPRSTU	PUT ON AIRS, SUPINATOR
AINOPRSUU	UNIPAROUS
AINORSSST	ARSONISTS
AINRSSTTU	NATURISTS
AIOOORRST	ORATORIOS
AIOOPRSUV	APIVOROUS, OVIPAROUS
AIOOSTTTT	TATTOOIST
AIOPRRSTT	PORTRAITS
AIORRSSTT	SARTORIUS
AIPPRSSTT	TRAPPISTS
AJMMNNOPU	PANMUNJOM
AJMPRSTTU	JUMP-START
AKKRSTVYY	SYKTYVKAR
AKLNOOTUW	WALK OUT ON
AKLNOSUVY	ULYANOVSK
AKLOPRRRY	LORRY PARK
AKLORSSTW	SALTWORKS
AKLPRRSSU	LARKSPURS
AKMOPRSST	POSTMARKS
AKNNORSYY	SYNKARYON

AKOPRRSTW PART WORKS	BBBEGLMUU BUBBLE GUM	BBEKLOOSU BLUE BOOKS
ALLMOOSSY LYSOSOMAL	BBBEILSTU BUBBLIEST	BBEMNORUX BOX NUMBER
ALLNOOPTY POLYTONAL	BBBINOPSY BOBBY PINS	BBERRTTUU BUTTERBUR
ALLNOPPTU POLLUTANT	BBCDEELOR CLOBBERED	BBFMOOOPR BOMBPROOF
ALLNOPTTU POLLUTANT	BBCDEILRS SCRIBBLED	BBGGINOPU GO PUBBING
ALLNSUUUY UNUSUALLY	BBCEHISTU CHUBBIEST	BBGHILLTU LIGHT BULB
ALLOOPRTY ALLOTROPY	BBCEHLOUY CUBBYHOLE	BBGHILNOO HOBGOBLIN
ALLOPPRUY POPULARLY	BBCEILRRS SCRIBBLER	BBGHIMOST BOMBSIGHT
ALLOPRSTW STRAW POLL	BBCEILRSS SCRIBBLES	BBGHINORT THROBBING
ALLORSTTY TALL STORY	BBCEIRRSU SCRUBBIER	BBGIILNQU QUIBBLING
ALMNOORTY MONOLATRY	BBCEIRSSU SUBSCRIBE	BBGILNOSY SOBBINGLY
ALMNOPRUY PULMONARY	BBCEKTUUY BUCKYTUBE	BBIIILNRU BILIRUBIN
ALMOOPRSY PLAYROOMS	BBCERRSSU SCRUBBERS	BBIIKMTUZ KIBBUTZIM
ALMOORSUY AMOROUSLY	BBCGINRSU SCRUBBING	BBIKMNOST STINK-BOMB
ALMOPPSST LAMPPOSTS	BBCIIILOT BIBLIOTIC	BBLLOSUYY BULLYBOYS
ALNOPPRUU UNPOPULAR	BBCKLOOSU BOOK CLUBS	BCCCKMOOS COCKSCOMB
ALNOPPSTT POT PLANTS	BBDDEELOU DOUBLE BED	BCCDEHKOY BODYCHECK
ALNOPSTTU POSTULANT	BBDEELORS SLOBBERED	BCCDEMSUU SUCCUMBED
ALNORTUVY VOLUNTARY	BBDEGIMNO DEMOBBING	BCCEEILOR COERCIBLE
ALNPSTTUU PUSTULANT	BBDEHIRSU RUBBISHED	BCCEHIKNP PINCHBECK
ALOOPPRSS PROPOSALS	BBDEILRSU BLUEBIRDS	BCCEILRSU CRUCIBLES
ALOOPRSTV STAVROPOL	BBDEIORRW BOWERBIRD	BCCEINNOU CONCUBINE
ALOOPSTYZ ZOOPLASTY	BBDELLMSU DUMBBELLS	BCCEKLORU COCKLEBUR
ALOPRSTUY PULSATORY	BBDELLOOU BLUE BLOOD	BCCEKOSTU STOCK CUBE
AMMNPSTUY TYMPANUMS	BBDGIILNR DRIBBLING	BCCEMRSUU CUCUMBERS,
AMMOOSTTU MATSUMOTO	BBDGINRSU DRUBBINGS	SUCCUMBER
AMNNOOSUY ANONYMOUS	BBDLOOSWY BODY BLOWS	BCCGIILNY BICYCLING
AMNOORSTY ASTRONOMY	BBEEEEINR BEBEERINE	BCCIILSTY BICYCLIST
AMNOPRSST SPORTSMAN	BBEEEHLMU HUMBLEBEE	BCCIOOPRS BROSCOPIC
AMNOTTUYY TAUTONYMY	BBEEEINRR BERBERINE	BCCIORSTU SCORBUTIC
AMOOORSTV VASOMOTOR	BBEEFLLUY BULLY BEEF	BCCMOORXY COXCOMBRY
AMOORRRWW ARROWWORM	BBEEILPST PLEBBIEST	BCCMORRUY CURRYCOMB
AMOORSTWY MOTORWAYS	BBEEIORRS ROBBERIES	BCCOSSTUU CUB SCOUTS
AMOPRSSXY PAROXYSMS	BBEEIRRSU RUBBERISE	BCDDEEHOU DEBOUCHED
AMPRSTUUY SUMPTUARY	BBEEIRRUZ RUBBERIZE	BCDDEEILU DEDUCIBLE
ANNOOPRSU NONPAROUS	BBEELLLSU BLUEBELLS	BCDDEEIRS DESCRIBED
ANNORSTUY TYRANNOUS	BBEELORRS SLOBBERER	BCDDIIKRY DICKYBIRD
ANOOOPRSZ SPOROZOAN	BBEELRRUY BLUEBERRY	BCDEEEEHS BESEECHED
ANOOOPRTZ PROTOZOAN	BBEGGIINR GIBBERING	BCDEEEINO OBEDIENCE
ANOORSTWY STORNOWAY	BBEGHIIRS GIBBERISH	BCDEEEMRS DECEMBERS
ANOPRRSTT TRANSPORT	BBEGHILOS BOBSLEIGH	BCDEEGIKN BEDECKING
ANORSUUVY UNSAVOURY	BBEGINNOT BEBINGTON	BCDEEHIIR HERBICIDE
ANRRSSTUU SUSURRANT	BBEGIRSTU GRUBBIEST	BCDEEHITW BEWITCHED
AOOOORRTW ARROWROOT	BBEHKOOTY BY THE BOOK	BCDEEHRTU BUTCHERED
AOOORRTTV ROTOVATOR	BBEHLLMOS BOMBSHELL	BCDEEILRU REDUCIBLE
AOOPRRSTT PROTOSTAR	BBEHRRSUY SHRUBBERY	BCDEEILSU SEDUCIBLE
AOPPRSSST PASSPORTS	BBEIKLNOR KNOBBLIER	BCDEEIORR CEREBROID
AOPRRSTUU RAPTUROUS	BBEIKSTUZ KIBBUTZES	BCDEEIRRS DESCRIBER
AOQSSTTUU STATUS QUO	BBEILLOSTW WOBBLIEST	BCDEEJSTU SUBJECTED
AORRRTTWWY WORRYWART	BBEILQRSU QUIBBLERS	BCDEEMNTU DECUMBENT
AORSTTTUY STATUTORY	BBEIMMOST TIME BOMBS	BCDEIILNU INDUCIBLE
BBBDEELRU BLUBBERED	BBEIMOSST BOMBSITES	BCDEIINRS INSCRIBED
BBBDEHNOO HOBNOBBED	BBEINSSTU TUBBINESS	BCDEIJSUU SUB JUDICE
BBBEEELMU BUMBLEBEE	BBEISSTTU STUBBIEST	BCDEIKORR BRODERICK
BBBEEELUZ BEELZEBUB		

BCDEIKRRS	REDBRICKS	BCEHILPSU	BLUE CHIPS	BCHILLOTY	BLOTCHILY
BCDEKLNUU	UNBUCKLED	BCEHIMORS	CHEMISORB	BCHILOOPY	LYOPHOBIC
BCDEOOTTY	BOYCOTTED	BCEHIOSTT	BOTCHIEST	BCHINORTY	BRYTHONIC
BCDEORRSS	CROSSBRED	BCEHKNORW	WORKBENCH	BCHIOORSY	CHOIRBOYS
BCDGOSYZZ	BYDGOSZCZ	BCEHLOSUU	CLUBHOUSE	BCHKNORTU	BUCKTHORN
BCDHKNOUU	BUCKHOUND	BCEHMNOOY	HONEYCOMB	BCHKOOTTU	BUCKTOOTH
BCDILMNOW	CLIMB-DOWN	BCEHORRSU	BROCHURES	BCHLNOPUW	PUNCH BOWL
BCDIMOORS	SCOMBROID	BCEIIJNOT	BIJECTION	BCHLOOOSY	SCHOOLBOY
BCDKLOOOW	WOODBLOCK	BCEIILPSU	PUBLICISE	BCHLOORTW	BLOWTORCH
BCDKNOOOS	BOONDOCKS	BCEIILPUZ	PUBLICIZE	BCHMOOOTT	TOOTHCOMB
BCDKNOORU	ROCKBOUND	BCEIIMORT	BIOMETRIC	BCIIIMRST	BRITICISM
BCDOPRTUY	BY-PRODUCT	BCEIINNTY	BENIN CITY	BCIILMSUU	UMBILICUS
BCEEEFINS	BENEFICES	BCEIINOST	BISECTION	BCIILPSTU	PUBLICIST
BCEEEGHIS	BIG CHEESE	BCEIINRRS	INSCRIBER	BCIILPTUY	PUBLICITY
BCEEEHKNO	CHEEKBONE	BCEIIRSTX	BISECTRIX	BCIILRTUY	LUBRICITY
BCEEEELQRU	BECQUEREL	BCEIJLOPU	JOE PUBLIC	BCIIMNOOS	BIONOMICS
BCEEGHINR	BREECHING	BCEIJNOOT	OBJECTION	BCIIMOSTY	SYMBIOTIC
BCEEHKTTU	BUCKTEETH	BCEILLMRU	CRIBELLUM	BCIISSSTU	CUBISISTS
BCEEHORTT	BROCHETTE	BCEILMNOU	COLUMBINE	BCIKKORRW	BRICKWORK
BCEEIIJTV	BIJECTIVE	BCEILMORY	COR BLIMEY	BCIKNNRSU	INNSBRUCK
BCEEIILMS	IMBECILES	BCEILMOTU	COLUMBITE	BCIKNRSUW	BRUNSWICK
BCEEIILNV	EVINCIBLE	BCEILMRRU	CRUMBLIER	BCILLORSS	CROSSBILL
BCEEIJOTV	OBJECTIVE	BCEILNOOT	BOLECTION	BCILMMOUU	COLUMBIUM
BCEEIKLOR	LOCKERBIE	BCEILNORU	COLUBRINE	BCILMNOPU	PLUMBICON
BCEEIILLOS	BELLICOSE	BCEILPRSU	REPUBLICS	BCILORSUU	LUBRICOUS
BCEEILRTY	CELEBRITY	BCEIMNNTU	INCUMBENT	BCILPRSTU	STRIP CLUB
BCEEINOOT	COENOBITE	BCEIMNORY	EMBRYONIC	BCIMNOOOS	SONIC BOOM
BCEEIOQSU	QUEBECOIS	BCEINORRW	BROWN RICE	BCIOOPRSS	PROBOSCIS
BCEEIPRRS	PRESCRIBE	BCEINOSTU	BOUNCIEST	BCIORSTUY	OBSCURITY
BCEEJNORT	JOBCENTRE	BCEINOSTY	OBSCENITY	BCIPRSSTU	SUBSCRIPT
BCEEJOSTX	SEX OBJECT	BCEINSSUU	INCUBUSES	BCKOOOPSY	COPYBOOKS
BCEELNOSY	OBSCENELY	BCEIOPRRS	PROSCRIBE	BCMNOOORR	BROOMCORN
BCEELOOSS	OBSOLESCE	BCEIORSTT	OBSTETRIC	BCMOORSTU	COMBUSTOR
BCEEMNRTU	RECUMBENT	BCEJOORST	OBJECTORS	BCOORSSSW	CROSSBOWS
BCEEMRRSU	CEREBRUMS	BCEKLOOTV	BLOCK VOTE	BCOOSSTUY	BOY SCOUTS
BCEENPSTU	PUBESCENT	BCELMOOTY	LOBECTOMY	BDDDEEINR	BEDRIDDEN
BCEENRSTU	RUBESCENT	BCELORSUY	OBSCURELY	BDDEEEFIR	DEBRIEFED
BCEFFIOOX	BOX OFFICE	BCEMOORSY	CORYMBOSE	BDDEEEILV	BEDEVILED
BCEFFIOOY	OFFICE BOY	BCENOORTY	CON BY ROTE	BDDEEFOOR	FOREBODED
BCEFIIKRR	FIREBRICK	BCEOORSTU	CUBE ROOTS	BDDEEGGRU	BEGRUDGED
BCEFIIRTY	FEBRICITY	BCEORRRWY	CROWBERRY	BDDEEGIMN	EMBEDDING
BCEFIJOTY	OBJECTIFY	BCEORSTUX	SUBCORTEX	BDDEEGIRR	REDBRIDGE
BCEGHILNN	BLENCHING	BCEPRTTUU	BUTTERCUP	BDDEEIOSY	DISOBEYED
BCEGHORRU	CHERBOURG	BCFGLLOSU	GOLF CLUBS	BDDEEISTU	SUBEDITED
BCEGIIKNR	BICKERING	BCFHILLNU	BULLFINCH	BDDEELNRU	BLUNDERED
BCEGIINST	BISECTING	BCGHILNTU	NIGHTCLUB	BDDEELORU	REDOUBLED
BCEGIJNOT	OBJECTING	BCGIIMNNO	COMBINING	BDDEENORU	REBOUNDED
BCEGIKNNO	BECKONING	BCGIKRSUV	VICKSBURG	BDDEENRRU	UNDERBRED
BCEGIKNTU	BUCKETING	BCGILMNRU	CRUMBLING	BDDEENSTU	SUBTENDED
BCEGIMNRU	CUMBERING	BCGINORSU	OBSCURING	BDDEFINOR	FORBIDDEN
BCEHIILPT	PHLEBITIC	BCHIIMSTU	BISMUTHIC	BDDEFIORR	FORBIDDER
BCEHIISTT	BITCHIEST	BCHIIOPRS	BISHOPRIC	BDDEFLOOU	BLOOD FEUD
BCEHILORT	BLOTCHIER	BCHIIRSTU	HUBRISTIC	BDDEGIIMN	IMBEDDING
		BCHIIRSTY	HYBRISTIC	BDDEGLOOU	DOODLEBUG

BDDEHINOU	HIDEBOUND	BDEEIINNZ	BENZIDINE	BDEHIIRYZ	HYBRIDIZE
BDDEHLOOS	BLOODSHED	BDEEIKLNR	BLINKERED	BDEHILPSU	PUBLISHED
BDDEIIMOR	DIBROMIDE	BDEEILLTT	BELITTLED	BDEHINRSU	BURNISHED
BDDEIISUV	SUBDIVIDE	BDEEILMOR	EMBROILED	BDEHIORSU	BIRDHOUSE
BDDEILNRU	UNBRIDLED	BDEEILMSS	DISSEMBLE	BDEHNOSTU	SOUTH BEND
BDDEILORW	BLOW-DRIED	BDEEILNNO	NONEDIBLE	BDEIIILSV	DIVISIBLE
BDDEIMOSY	DISEMBODY	BDEEILRST	BLISTERED	BDEIIILTY	EDIBILITY
BDDEINRSU	DISBURDEN	BDEEIMMRS	DISMEMBER	BDEIIJNOS	INSIDE JOB
BDDEIRSSU	DISBURSED	BDEEIMORR	EMBROIDER	BDEIIKRST	DIRT BIKES
BDDEIRSTU	DISTURBED	BDEEINRRT	INTERBRED	BDEIILLNY	INDELIBLY
BDDELLOUZ	BULLDOZED	BDEEIORSY	DISOBEYER	BDEIILMOS	MOBILISED
BDDELSUUY	SUBDUEDLY	BDEEIPRSW	SPIDERWEB	BDEIILMOZ	MOBILIZED
BDDENNOUU	UNBOUNDED	BDEEIRRST	BESTIRRED	BDEIILNNO	BLENNIOID
BDDENORUY	UNDERBODY	BDEEIRRSV	RIVERBEDS	BDEIISSSU	SUBSIDIES,
BDDENOTUU	UNDOUBTED	BDEEIRSTT	BED-SITTER		SUBSIDISE
BDDEOSTYY	TEDDY BOYS	BDEEKNRSU	DEBUNKERS	BDEIISSUZ	SUBSIDIZE
BDDFILLNO	BLINDFOLD	BDEEKOORW	BROOKWEED	BDEIJNOSU	SUBJOINED
BDDFMNOUU	DUMBFOUND	BDEELLSSY	BLESSEDLY	BDEILLNPS	SPELLBIND
BDDHISSTU	BUDDHISTS	BDEELMRSU	SLUMBERED	BDEILMOOR	DORMOBILE
BDDILLORY	DOLLY BIRD	BDEELNRRU	BLUNDERER	BDEILNNSS	BLINDNESS
BDDINNOUW	WINDBOUND	BDEELNSSU	UNBLESSED	BDEILOQTU	QUODLIBET
BDEEEEFLN	ENFEEBLED	BDEELORST	BOLSTERED	BDEILORSV	LOVEBIRDS
BDEEEELRV	BELVEDERE	BDEELRSTU	BLUSTERED	BDEILORSW	BLOW-DRIES
BDEEEFILL	BIELEFELD	BDEEMMOOS	EMBOSOMED	BDEILORUV	OVERBUILD
BDEEEFINT	BENEFITED	BDEEORSTY	OYSTER BED	BDEILPRUU	UPBUILDER
BDEEEGLUW	BUGLEWEED	BDEEORVYY	EVERYBODY	BDEILRRSY	LYREBIRDS
BDEEEHLRT	BLETHERED	BDEEPRRSU	PUREBREDS	BDEILSTTU	SUBTITLED
BDEEEIOTW	WOE BETIDE	BDEEPRRTU	PERTURBED	BDEIMSTTU	SUBMITTED
BDEEEKNOT	BETOKENED	BDEERSTUV	SUBVERTED	BDEINNORW	WIND-BORNE
BDEEELMRS	RESEMBLED	BDEFFLORU	OLD BUFFER	BDEINORTX	TINDERBOX
BDEEELMZZ	EMBEZZLED	BDEFHIRSU	FURBISHED	BDEINRSSU	SIDEBURNS
BDEEELNOS	NOSEBLEED	BDEFIILRR	RIFLEBIRD	BDEIOORST	BROODIEST
BDEEELOSU	SEE DOUBLE	BDEFILLOO	LIFEBLOOD	BDEIORSTU	SUBEDITOR
BDEEEMMNT	EMBEDMENT	BDEFINORY	BOYFRIEND	BDEIPRSTU	BUPRESTID
BDEEENRTU	DEBENTURE	BDEFLOSTU	SELF-DOUBT	BDEIRRSSU	DISBURSER
BDEEERSTW	BESTREWED	BDEGGGINU	DEBUGGING	BDEIRRSTU	DISTURBER
BDEEFIILS	DISBELIEF	BDEGGINTU	BUDGETING	BDEISSSTU	SUBSISTED
BDEEFLLOW	BEDFELLOW	BDEGGNUUY	DUNE BUGGY	BDELLOORS	BORDELLOS,
BDEEFLORW	FLOWERBED	BDEGHILNO	BEHOLDING		DOORBELLS
BDEEFLOTT	BOTTLE-FED	BDEGHINRU	EDINBURGH	BDELLOOSS	BLOODLESS
BDEEFOORR	FOREBODER	BDEGIIILR	DIRIGIBLE	BDELLORUZ	BULLDOZER
BDEEFOOTW	WEB-FOOTED	BDEGIILOS	DISOBLIGE	BDELLRRUY	BLURREDLY
BDEEGGLOW	BOW-LEGGED	BDEGIINNR	REBINDING	BDELMNPUU	UNPLUMBED
BDEEGGORS	GODESBERG	BDEGIIPPR	BIG DIPPER	BDELMOOSS	BLOSSOMED
BDEEGHINT	BENIGHTED	BDEGIKNNU	DEBUNKING	BDELMRTUY	TUMBLE-DRY
BDEEGMRSU	SUBMERGED	BDEGIMNOY	EMBODYING	BDELNNOSS	BLONDNESS
BDEEGNORU	BURGEONED	BDEGINNNU	UNBENDING	BDELNOOTU	DOUBLETON
BDEEHIITX	EXHIBITED	BDEGINNRU	BURDENING	BDELNOSSU	BOUNDLESS
BDEEHILMS	BLEMISHED	BDEGINORR	BORDERING	BDELOOPTY	BLOOD TYPE
BDEEHLORS	BEHOLDERS	BDEGINORT	TONBRIDGE	BDELOOSUY	BODY LOUSE
BDEEHNRTU	BURTHENED	BDEGLNORU	OLDENBURG	BDELOSSTU	DOUBTLESS
BDEEHORTT	BETROTHED	BDEGLNOSU	BLUDGEONS	BDEMMNOSU	OMBUDSMEN
BDEEIIILLN	INDELIBLE	BDEHIIINT	INHIBITED	BDEMNOOSU	UNBOSOMED
BDEEIILRS	DERISIBLE	BDEHIIRSY	HYBRIDISE	BDENNOSSU	SNUB-NOSED
				BDENNRSUU	SUNBURNED

BDENOORTW	BRENTWOOD	BEEEILMNT	BELEMNITE	BEEHNORRS	SHERBORNE
BDENOSTUW	WESTBOUND	BEEEILRSV	BELIEVERS,	BEEIIKNRZ	BEREZNIKI
BDEOOORRW	WOODBORER		EVERSIBLE	BEEIIILNRT	LIBERTINE
BDFHIILNS	BLINDFISH	BEEEIMRSV	SEMIBREVE	BEEIILRST	LIBERTIES
BDFHNOOOU	HOOFBOUND	BEEEINORT	BETE-NOIRE	BEEIINRTY	INEBRIETY
BDFILLLOS	BILLFOLDS	BEEEINRSS	BEERINESS	BEEIKLMRU	BERKELIUM
BDFIOORST	BIRD'S-FOOT	BEEELMNSS	ENSEMBLES	BEEIKLMRY	KIMBERLEY
BDGIILNSU	BUILDINGS	BEEELMRRS	RESEMBLER	BEEILLNOR	REBELLION
BDGIINNNU	UNBINDING	BEEELMRZZ	EMBEZZLER	BEEILLNTU	EBULLIENT
BDGIINORS	DISROBING	BEEELPRTU	BLUE PETER	BEEILLRTT	BELITTLER
BDGIINSSU	SUBSIDING	BEEELSSSU	SUBLESSEE	BEEILMORR	EMBROILER
BDGINORSS	SONGBIRDS	BEEEMPRST	SEPTEMBER	BEEILNOPX	EXPONIBLE
BDGINORTU	OBTRUDING	BEEENNOTV	BENEVENTO	BEEILNRSU	NEBULISER
BDHIIMRSY	HYBRIDISM	BEEFFGIRU	FEBRIFUGE	BEEILNRUZ	NEBULIZER
BDHIIRTYY	HYBRIDITY	BEEFFORTT	BETTER OFF	BEEILORTT	BRIOLETTE
BDHIMOORS	RHOMBOIDS	BEEFFOSTW	WEB OFFSET	BEEILOTTU	OUBLIETTE
BDHLOOOST	BLOODSHOT	BEEFIILMS	MISBELIEF	BEEILPRTU	ERUPTIBLE
BDHMOSSUW	DUMB SHOWS	BEEFILLST	LIFE BELTS	BEEILRRSV	VERS LIBRE
BDHOOORTY	BOOTHROYD	BEEFIORSX	FIREBOXES	BEEILSTUV	VESTIBULE
BDHOORSUW	BRUSHWOOD	BEEGGIINS	BESIEGING	BEEIMNRST	TENEBRISM,
BDIIMORTY	MORBIDITY	BEEGGINTT	BEGETTING		TRIBESMEN
BDIIRTTUY	TURBIDITY	BEEGHILSW	BIG WHEELS	BEEIMRRSU	REIMBURSE
BDIKNORUV	DUBROVNIK	BEEGHIRTY	EYEBRIGHT	BEEINNOTT	BENTONITE
BDILLORSW	SWORDBILL	BEEGIILLL	ILLEGIBLE	BEEINNRTU	INNER TUBE
BDILNNOSW	SNOW-BLIND	BEEGIILNV	BELIEVING	BEEINRSTT	TENEBRIST
BDILNNOWW	WINDBLOWN	BEEGILLNR	REBELLING	BEEINRTTU	BUTTERINE
BDILNOPST	BLIND SPOT	BEEGILLNV	BEVELLING	BEEIOQSUU	OBSEQUIES
BDILOSUUY	DUBIOUSLY	BEEGILLNW	WELLBEING	BEEIOSSSV	OBSESSIVE
BDINNOORU	IRONBOUND	BEEGILNRS	INSELBERG	BEEIQRTTU	BRIQUETTE
BDINNRTUW	WINDBURNT	BEEGILPRS	SPIELBERG	BEEIRTTTY	YTTERBITE
BDINOOWWW	BOW WINDOW	BEEGINNRS	BEGINNERS	BEEJKOSUX	JUKEBOXES
BDINOOWWX	WINDOW BOX	BEEGINRTT	BETTERING	BEEKNORST	KERBSTONE
BDKNOOORS	DOORKNOBS	BEEGINSST	BEESTINGS	BEEKOPRRY	POKEBERRY
BDKOOSSTU	STUDBOOKS	BEEGINSTT	BESETTING	BEELLLMUU	UMBELLULE
BDLLOOSTU	BLOOD LUST	BEEGKORRS	GO BERSERK	BEELLORSU	RESOLUBLE
BDLMOOORW	BLOODWORM	BEEGMNRRU	NUREMBERG	BEELLSSUY	BULL'S-EYES
BDLMOOSUY	MOLYBDOUS	BEEGMRRSU	MERSEBURG	BEELMMNRU	LUMBERMEN
BDLNOOOSU	DOUBLOONS	BEEGMSTUY	BE MY GUEST	BEELMNORU	MELBOURNE
BDLOOORRT	BLOODROOT	BEEGNRSUV	VENUSBERG	BEELMOORT	BOLOMETER
BDLOSSTUW	DUSTBOWLS	BEEGRSSSU	BURGESSES	BEELMRRSU	SLUMBERER
BDNNOOSUW	SNOWBOUND	BEEHIKRRS	BERKSHIRE	BEELNNOSS	NOBLENESS
BDORSUWZZ	BUZZWORDS	BEEHILLMS	EMBELLISH	BEELNOSTU	BLUESTONE
BEEEEEKPR	BEEKEEPER	BEEHILMRS	BLEMISHER	BEELORRST	BOLSTERER
BEEEEFLNR	ENFEEBLER	BEEHILMSS	BLEMISHES	BEELORSVY	VERBOSELY
BEEEFINSS	BEEFINESS	BEEHILTUZ	BUTHELEZI	BEELORTTX	LETTERBOX
BEEEGGRUZ	ZEEBRUGGE	BEEHINRTT	TEREBINTH	BEELQRSUU	BURLESQUE
BEEEGLNOS	BOLEGNESE	BEEHIOPRS	BIOSPHERE	BEELRRSTU	BLUSTERER
BEEEGLNRT	GREEN BELT	BEEHIORRV	HERBIVORE	BEEMMNOTW	EMBOWMENT
BEEEGNOOW	WOEBEGONE	BEEHIRSTU	BUTESHIRE	BEEMNNORU	NUMBER ONE
BEEEGNOTW	GO-BETWEEN	BEEHLLRSU	BUSHELLER	BEEMNNTRU	NUMBER TEN
BEEEHHLMT	BETHLEHEM	BEEHLOORS	BOREHOLES	BEEMNORSV	NOVEMBERS
BEEEHLLOR	HELLEBORE	BEEHLOPRY	HYPERBOLE	BEENOORRV	OVERBORNE
BEEEHLRTT	ETHELBERT	BEEHLOTTT	THE BOTTLE	BEENOQSTU	OBSEQUENT
BEEEHNOSY	HONEYBEES	BEEHNOOPX	XENOPHOBE	BEENORRST	RESORBENT

BEENORSSS	SOBERNESS	BEGILNSSS	BLESSINGS	BEIKLNSSU	BULKINESS
BEENORSTU	TENEBROUS	BEGILNSSU	BULGINESS	BEIKLOORT	ROBOT-LIKE
BEENRSTTU	BRUNETTES	BEGIMNNOT	ENTOMBING	BEIKLOSTY	KILOBYTES
BEEOORSTT	BEETROOTS	BEGIMNNRU	NUMBERING	BEIKMOORT	MOTORBIKE
BEEORRSSV	OBSERVERS	BEGIMNOSS	EMBOSSING	BEIKNRSSS	BRISKNESS
BEEORSTTU	SOUBRETTE	BEGINORSU	SUBREGION	BEILLLOSU	LIBELLOUS
BEEPRRSTY	PRESBYTER	BEGINORSV	OBSERVING	BEILLMNPU	PLUMB LINE
BEEQRSTUY	BY REQUEST	BEGINOSSS	OBSESSING	BEILLMRUY	BERYLLIUM
BEERRSTUV	SUBVERTER	BEGINOSTW	BESTOWING	BEILLMSUY	SUBLIMELY
BEESSTTTU	TEST TUBES	BEGINRTTU	BUTTERING,	BEILLNOSU	INSOLUBLE
BEFFGINRU	BUFFERING,		REBUTTING	BEILLNRSU	BULLETINS
	REBUFFING	BEGIOORSU	BOURGEOIS	BEILNORTU	IN TROUBLE
BEFFGINTU	BUFFETING	BEGLMRRSU	GRUMBLERS	BEILNPRTU	BLUEPRINT
BEFFHINTU	IN THE BUFF	BEGLMRUUX	LUXEMBURG	BEILNRSSU	BURLINESS
BEFFIILLR	FIBREFILL	BEHIIINRT	INHIBITER	BEILOOPRT	POTBOILER
BEFFLNSSU	BLUFFNESS	BEHIILPRT	PHILIBERT	BEILOPPSW	BLOWPIPES
BEFGIINTT	BEFITTING	BEHIILPST	PHLEBITIS	BEILOPSSS	POSSIBLES
BEFGLNRSU	FLENSBURG	BEHIIMNOY	YOHIMBINE	BEILORSSU	SUBSOILER
BEFHIRRSU	FURBISHER,	BEHIIORTX	EXHIBITOR	BEILORSTT	LIBRETTOS
	REFURBISH	BEHIIRRST	BRITISHER	BEILOSTWZ	BLOWZIEST
BEFHKLOOS	BOOKSHELF	BEHIKLOSV	BOLSHEVIK	BEILSSTTU	SUBTITLES
BEFIILNSU	INFUSIBLE	BEHIKPSSU	PUSHBIKES	BEIMMNORR	MERBROMIN
BEFIILRTY	FEBRILITY	BEHIKSUVY	KUIBYSHEV	BEIMNOORS	BROMEOSIN
BEFILLMSU	BLUE FILMS	BEHILNNOR	HEILBRONN	BEIMNORST	BRIMSTONE
BEFILLOSW	BLOWFLIES	BEHILNOOT	ON THE BOIL	BEIMNOSSU	OMNIBUSES
BEFILOSUY	LIFE BUOYS	BEHILOSST	BOLSHIEST	BEIMNPSSU	BUMPINESS
BEFIORSTT	FROSTBITE	BEHILPRSU	PUBLISHER,	BEIMOORST	BIOSTROME
BEFLLLOPY	BELLY FLOP		REPUBLISH	BEIMRSTTU	SUBMITTER
BEFLRTTUY	BUTTERFLY	BEHINNOSS	SHINBONES	BEIMRTTUY	YTTERBIUM
BEFNNNOUY	FUNNY BONE	BEHINOSSW	WISHBONES	BEINOOPRT	OBREPTION
BEGGGINRU	BUGGERING	BEHINRRSU	BURNISHER	BEINOORSV	OBVERSION
BEGGGLOOX	GOGGLE BOX	BEHINSSSU	BUSHINESS	BEINOOSSS	OBSESSION
BEGGHMRUU	HUMBUGGER	BEHKNOOOP	PHONE BOOK	BEINOOSSZ	BOOZINESS
BEGGIILNU	BEGUILING	BEHKNOSUU	BUNKHOUSE	BEINOSSSS	BOSSINESS
BEGGIINNN	BEGINNING	BEHLLOOST	BOLTHOLES	BEINRTTTU	BITTERNUT
BEGGIILNNO	BELONGING	BEHLLOOSW	BLOWHOLES	BEIOOPRRU	POURBOIRE
BEGGINOSS	BOGGINESS	BEHLORRTY	BROTHERLY	BEIOPTTTU	PITOT TUBE
BEGHHINOT	THIGHBONE	BEHLRSSUU	BULRUSHES	BEIOQRSTU	SOBRIQUET
BEGHHOTTU	BETHOUGHT	BEHMORSSU	RHOMBUSES	BEIOQSTUU	BOUTIQUES
BEGHIINTW	BEGIN WITH	BEHNORSTU	BUHRSTONE	BEIORSTUV	OBTRUSIVE
BEGHILRST	BLIGHTERS	BEHOOPTTU	PHOTOTUBE	BEIORSTVY	VERBOSITY
BEGHINORT	BOTHERING	BEHOOSSUY	HOUSEBOYS	BEIRSSSTU	SUBSISTER
BEGHINORU	NEIGHBOUR	BEHOPRTYY	BRYOPHYTE	BEJJMOSTU	JUMBO JETS
BEGHIORSU	BRIGHOUSE	BEIIILNSV	INVISIBLE	BEJORSTTU	TURBOJETS
BEGHLNOSU	BUNGHOLES	BEIILLNSY	SIBYLLINE	BEJORSUXY	JURY BOXES
BEGIILLLN	LIBELLING	BEIILMOSS	OMISSIBLE	BEKKNOOOT	BOOK TOKEN
BEGIILLLY	ILLEGIBLY	BEIILLNNRS	BIN-LINERS	BEKLOORSU	RULEBOOKS
BEGIILLNT	BILLETING	BEIILNRTT	LITTERBIN	BEKLOOSTY	STYLEBOOK
BEGIIMRST	BIG-TIMERS	BEIILORTT	TRILOBITE	BEKNNNOUW	UNBEKNOWN
BEGIINNTY	BENIGNITY	BEIILSSTU	SUBTILISE		
BEGIJRTTU	JITTERBUG	BEIILSTUZ	SUBTILIZE		
BEGILLNOW	BELLOWING	BEIIMNSSU	MINIBUSES		
BEGILMNRT	TREMBLING	BEIINNRSS	BRININESS		
BEGILMNRU	LUMBERING	BEIINSSTT	BITTINESS		
BEGILNNNO	ENNOBLING	BEIKLMOOR	BROOKLIME		

BEKNOOOST	NOTEBOOKS	BGILMNSTU	STUMBLING	BILOOPRTU	POLITBURO
BEKOOSTTX	TEXTBOOKS	BGILNNRUY	BURNINGLY	BILOOSUVY	OBVIOUSLY
BELMOOORW	ELBOWROOM	BGILNOPRY	PROBINGLY	BILORSSTU	STROBILUS
BELMOPSUU	PLUMBEOUS	BGILNORTU	TROUBLING	BIMOPSTUU	BUMPTIOUS
BELNNSSTU	BLUNTNESS	BGILOORTY	TRIBOLOGY	BINOOOSUX	OBNOXIOUS
BELNOORVW	OVERBLOWN	BGILOOSTY	GLOBOSITY	BINOORSTU	OBTRUSION
BELNRTTUU	TURBULENT	BGILORSUU	LOUISBURG	BIOPRSSTW	BOWSPRITS
BELORSSSU	SUBLESSOR	BGIMNSSUU	SUBSUMING	BJOPPSTUU	PUT-UP JOBS
BELQRSUUY	BRUSQUELY	BGINNNOOT	BONINGTON	BKKOOORSW	WORKBOOKS
BEMNOORST	TROMBONES	BGINNORSU	SUBORNING	BKLLMNSUU	NUMBSKULL
BEMNOORSW	NEW BROOMS	BGINNORTU	BINTURONG	BKMOOORSW	BOOKWORMS
BEMNOOSTT	TOMBSTONE	BGINNOTTU	BUTTONING	BKOOORSTY	STORYBOOK
BEMNORTUU	OUTNUMBER	BGINOORRW	BORROWING	BLOORSTUU	TROUBLOUS
BEMNOSSUX	BUXOMNESS	BGINORRUW	BURROWING	BOOPPRRTU	TURBOPROP
BEMOORRSS	SOMBREROS	BGINORSTW	BOWSTRING	BORSSTTUU	OUTBURSTS
BENOOSTTU	BOUNTEOUS	BGKNOOOSS	SONGBOOKS	CCCDENOOT	CONCOCTED
BENORRSWY	SNOWBERRY	BGLMOOSYY	SYMBOLOGY	CCCEEINRT	ECCENTRIC
BENORSSUU	BURNOUSES	BGNOORSTX	STRONGBOX	CCCEIILPY	EPICYCLIC
BENORSTTU	OBSTRUENT	BHIIINORT	INHIBITOR	CCCENOORT	CONCOCTER
BENORSTXY	SENTRY BOX	BHIILLLLY	HILLBILLY	CCCHHIKOT	HITCHCOCK
BENRTTTUU	BUTTERNUT	BHIILLNOT	BILLIONTH	CCCHIKNOP	PINCHCOCK
BEOOPSTTX	SET-TOP BOX	BHIIMORUZ	RHIZOBIUM	CCCHILMOU	COLCHICUM
BEOORRRSW	BORROWERS	BHIKLLOOS	BILLHOOKS	CCCHILOOT	COCCOLITH
BFFHORSSU	BRUSH-OFFS	BHILLLSUY	BULLISHLY	CCCIILRTY	TRICYCLIC
BFFIIMORR	FIBRIFORM	BHILLNORS	HORNBILLS	CCDDEEESU	SUCCEEDED
BFFLLOSUY	BULLY-OFFS	BHILLNORT	THORNBILL	CCDDEIINO	COINCIDED
BFGHILLTU	BULLFIGHT	BHILMNOTY	BIMONTHLY	CCDDEKLOU	CUCKOLDED
BFGLLORSU	BULLFROGS	BHILOORSY	BOORISHLY	CCDDELNOU	CONCLUDED
BFGLORSUW	WOLFSBURG	BHILRSTUY	BRUTISHLY	CCDDENOTU	CONDUCTED
BFIILMORR	LIBRIFORM	BHIMOOSTY	TOMBOYISH	CCDEEEHKR	CHECKERED
BFIINORSU	FIBRINOUS	BHIOORRTT	BIRTHROOT	CCDEEEHRS	SCREECHED
BFILNOTUU	BOUNTIFUL	BHIORRTTW	BIRTHWORT	CCDEEEINS	DECENCIES
BFIMORRSU	BURSIFORM	BHKOOOPSS	BOOKSHOPS	CCDEEERSU	SUCCEEDER
BFINORRST	FIRSTBORN	BHKORRSUW	BRUSHWORK	CCDEEHIKW	CHICKWEED
BFLLLNOUW	FULL-BLOWN	BHLLNORSU	BULLHORNS	CCDEEHKNU	UNCHECKED
BFMMOOORR	BROMOFORM	BHLLOOOTT	TOLLBOOTH	CCDEEHORT	CROCHETED
BFOORTUWY	TWO-BY-FOUR	BHLMPSUUY	SUBPHYLUM	CCDEEIINN	INCIDENCE
BGGHIILNT	BLIGHTING	BIIILNSVY	INVISIBLY	CCDEEILNR	ENCIRCLED
BGGILLNUY	BULGINGLY	BIILMSTUY	SUBLIMITY	CCDEEILOW	COLICWEED
BGGILMNRU	GRUMBLING	BIILOOSUV	OBLIVIOUS	CCDEEINNY	INDECENCY
BGHHIORSW	HIGHBROWS	BIILOQTUY	OBLIQUITY	CCDEEINOT	CONCEITED
BGHINOOOO	BOOHOOING	BIIMNOOST	BIONOMIST	CCDEEINOV	CONCEIVED
BGHLOOPUY	PLOUGHBOY	BIIMOPRTY	IMPROBITY	CCDEEIOPS	CODPIECES
BGHMOOOOS	OGBOMOSHO	BIIMOSSSY	SYMBIOSIS	CCDEELLOT	COLLECTED
BGHORRSUU	BURROUGHS	BIISSTTYY	ITSY-BITSY	CCDEEMMNO	COMMENCED
BGIILLNOW	BILLOWING	BIKLNNOSW	SNOWBLINK	CCDEENNOR	CONCERNED
BGIILLNOY	BOILINGLY	BILLNOOPS	SPOONBILL	CCDEENNOS	ENSCONCED
BGIILMOOR	IMBROGLIO	BILLNOOSU	BOUILLONS	CCDEENNOT	CONNECTED
BGIILNRST	BRISTLING	BILLNORST	STILLBORN	CCDEENORS	CRESCENDO
BGIILOOST	BIOLOGIST	BILMMOSSY	SYMBOLISM	CCDEENORT	CONCERTED,
BGIKNOPRS	SPRINGBOK	BILMNOOSS	IN BLOSSOM		CONCRETED
BGILLNRSU	BULLRINGS	BILMOSSTY	SYMBOLIST	CCDEEORRT	CORRECTED
BGILMNOOY	MYOGLOBIN	BILNNOOSY	LOONY BINS	CCDEFIIRU	CRUCIFIED
BGILMNRSU	RUMBLINGS	BILNOSTUU	BOTULINUS	CCDEGINNO	CONCEDING

CCDEHNRSU	SCRUNCHED	CCEFFIIIL	FELICIFIC	CCEINSSTY	SYNECTICS
CCDEIIKNP	PICNICKED	CCEFIIPSS	SPECIFICS	CCEIOORST	CREOSOTIC
CCDEILOOR	CROCODILE	CCEFIIRRU	CRUCIFIER	CCEIOPRST	COST PRICE
CCDEILSTY	DYSLECTIC	CCEFKNOYY	COCKNEYFY	CCEIOPRSU	OCCUPIERS
CCDEINNOV	CONVINCED	CCEGGHOST	SCOTCH EGG	CCEIOPRTY	PRECOCITY
CCDEINOOT	DECOCTION	CCEGHHNOW	CHENGCHOW	CCEKORRSW	CORKSCREW
CCDEINOTV	CONVICTED	CCEGHILNN	CLENCHING	CCELLNOOY	COLONELCY
CCDEINOUV	CONDUCIVE	CCEGHIMRU	CHEMURGIC	CCELLOORT	COLLECTOR
CCDEKLOOR	OLD COCKER	CCEGILNRY	RECYCLING	CCELMOOTY	COLECTOMY
CCDELNOTU	OCCLUDENT	CCEHHNRTU	THE CRUNCH	CCELNSTUU	SUCCULENT
CCDENORRU	CONCURRED	CCEHIILRS	SCHLIERIC	CCELOPRSU	CORPUSCLE
CCDENOSSU	CONCUSSED	CCEHIKLST	CHECKLIST	CCELOPSSY	CYCLOPSES
CCDEORSUU	SUCCOURED	CCEHILNOR	CHRONICLE	CCELORRTY	CORRECTLY
CCDGINNOU	CONDUCING	CCEHILNRS	CLINCHERS	CCENNNORU	UNCONCERN
CCDHIILOR	CHLORIDIC	CCEHINNRU	CRUNCHIER	CCENNOORT	CONNECTOR
CCDHIIMOR	DICHROMIC	CCEHIORST	RICOCHETS	CCENOORST	CONCERTOS
CCDHKOOUW	WOODCHUCK	CCEHIKLNOT	NECKCLOTH	CCENOORSU	CONCOURSE
CCDKOOOSW	WOODCOCKS	CCEHKMOOR	CHECKROOM	CCENOORTV	CONVECTOR
CCDNOORTU	CONDUCTOR	CCEHKOORS	COCKHORSE	CCENORRTU	OCCURRENT
CCEEEFLNU	FECULENCE	CCEHKOPST	SPOT CHECK	CCENORSTU	SUCCENTOR
CCEEEHHRR	RECHERCHE	CCEHKOSTU	CHECKOUTS	CCEOOPRSY	CRYOSCOPE
CCEEEHNOR	COHERENCE	CCEHLMORS	CROMLECHS	CCEOOPRTT	ECTOPROCT
CCEEEHRRS	SCREECHER	CCEHNOSTU	SCUTCHEON	CCEOORRRT	CORRECTOR
CCEEEHRSS	SCREECHES	CCEHORRSS	SCORCHERS	CCEOPPRUY	PREOCCUPY
CCEEEIKNP	NECKPIECE	CCEHORSTT	CROTCHETS	CCEORRSUU	SUCCOURER
CCEEEINNS	NESCIENCE	CCEHORTTY	CROTCHETY	CCEORSSSU	SUCCESSOR
CCEEEINRT	RETICENCE	CCEIIIPRT	EPICRITIC	CCFGHIKOT	COCKFIGHT
CCEEELORT	RECTOCELE	CCEIIIRST	CRITICISE	CCFHKLLOU	CHOCK-FULL
CCEEFILLY	LIFE CYCLE	CCEIIIRTZ	CRITICIZE	CCFIILOOR	COLORIFIC
CCEEGINOR	CONCIERGE	CCEIIKNPR	PICNICKER	CCFILNOST	CONFLICTS
CCEEHIKOY	ICE HOCKEY	CCEIILNOT	NICCOLITE	CCFIMORRU	CRUCIFORM
CCEEHILMY	HEMICYCLE	CCEIILRST	SCLERITIC	CCFKOOOST	COCKSFOOT
CCEEHKORV	OVERCHECK	CCEIILSTT	CELTICIST	CCFLLOSUU	FLOCCULUS
CCEEHLORT	CERECLOTH	CCEIINSTY	CYSTEINIC	CCGHIILNN	CLINCHING
CCEEHORRT	CROCHETER	CCEIKLLOY	KILOCYCLE	CCGHIINPU	HICCUPING
CCEEHOTTU	COUCHETTE	CCEIKLOSW	CLOCKWISE	CCGHIKLNU	CHUCKLING
CCEEIIPPR	PRECIPICE	CCEIKNOSS	COCKINESS	CCGHILNTU	CLUTCHING
CCEEIKRRT	CRICKETER	CCEILNNOU	NUCLEONIC	CCGHILOOP	CHOPLOGIC
CCEEILNOR	RECONCILE	CCEILNOSY	CONCISELY	CCGHINNRU	CRUNCHING
CCEEILOST	SCOLECITE	CCEILNOTY	CYCLONITE	CCGHINORS	SCORCHING
CCEEILPRY	PERICYCLE	CCEILORST	SCLEROTIC	CCGHINORU	CROUCHING
CCEEILRST	ELECTRICS	CCEILOSUV	OCCLUSIVE	CCGHINOST	SCOTCHING
CCEEIMORT	ECTOMERIC	CCEILRSTY	TRICYCLES	CCGINNOOO	COCOONING
CCEEINNNO	INNOCENCE	CCEILRSUU	CURLICUES	CCGINOPUY	OCCUPYING
CCEEINORS	CICERONES	CCEIMNOOS	ECONOMICS	CCGINORRU	OCCURRING
CCEEKLORS	COCKERELS	CCEIMORTY	MICROCYTE	CCHHOOPST	HOPSCOTCH
CCEEKNRSW	CREW NECKS	CCEIMOSST	COSMETICS	CCHIIIRTT	TRICHITIC
CCEELLORT	RECOLLECT	CCEINNORV	CONVINCER	CCHIILORT	CHLORITIC
CCEELOSTY	CYSTOCELE	CCEINOOSS	CONSOCIES	CCHIIMOPR	MICROCHIP
CCEELOTUY	LEUCOCYTE	CCEINORRT	INCORRECT	CCHIIMORT	TRICHOMIC
CCEENNORT	CONCENTRE	CCEINOSTT	TECTONICS	CCHIINOOR	CHORIONIC
CCEENOOTY	COENOCYTE	CCEINPRST	PRECINCTS	CCHIINSUZ	ZUCCHINIS
CCEENRSST	CRESCENTS	CCEINRSTU	CINCTURES	CCHIIOORS	ISOCHORIC
CCEESSSSU	SUCCESSES	CCEINRSTY	SYNCRETIC		

CCHIIORRT	CIRRHOTIC,	CDDEELPRU	PRECLUDED	CDEEENPRT	PRECEDENT
	TRICHROIC	CDDEEMMNO	COMMENDED	CDEEEOPRR	PROCEEDER
CCHIKOPST	CHOPSTICK	CDDEEMNNO	CONDEMNED	CDEEEOORRT	RETROCEDE
CCHILMOSW	MILCH COWS	CDDEEMNRU	CREDENDUM	CDEEEOORRV	RE-COVERED
CCHILNRUY	CRUNCHILY	CDDEENNOS	CONDENSED	CDEEEPRST	RESPECTED
CCHILOORT	CHLOROTIC	CDDEENNOT	CONTENDED	CDEEFGINT	DEFECTING
CCHINRSTY	STRYCHNIC	CDDEENNOU	DENOUNCED	CDEEFIINT	DEFICIENT
CCHIOPSTY	PSYCHOTIC	CDDEEORSS	DRESS CODE	CDEEFIIOT	FOETICIDE
CCHLNOOTY	COLOCYNTH	CDDEGINTU	DEDUCTING	CDEEFIIPS	SPECIFIED
CCIIILNOP	PICOLINIC	CDDEGIOTY	DODGE CITY	CDEEFIIRT	CERTIFIED,
CCIIILNRT	TRICLINIC	CDDEHORRT	DORDRECHT		RECTIFIED
CCIIIMRST	CRITICISM	CDDEIILMO	DOMICILED	CDEEFIKLR	FLICKERED
CCIIINNOT	NICOTINIC	CDDEIILRU	RIDICULED	CDEEFIKRR	FREDERICK
CCIILNOTY	CLONICITY	CDDEIINRT	DENDRITIC	CDEEFILNT	INFLECTED
CCIILOOST	SCOLIOTIC	CDDEIIOSV	VIDEODISC	CDEEFILTU	DECEITFUL
CCIILOPRT	PROCLITIC	CDDEIIRST	DISCREDIT	CDEEFINOT	DEFECTION
CCIINNOOS	CONCISION	CDDEILOSS	DISCLOSED	CDEEFLORT	DEFLECTOR
CCIIORRTT	TRICROTIC	CDDEILSTU	CUDDLIEST	CDEEFNORR	CONFERRED
CCIIRRTUY	CIRCUITRY	CDDEIMOOU	DUODECIMO	CDEEFNOSS	CONFESSED
CCILMOSTU	OCCULTISM	CDDEINOTU	DEDUCTION	CDEEFORST	DEFECTORS
CCILNOOSU	OCCLUSION	CDDEIOSUU	DECIDUOUS	CDEEGIILN	DILIGENCE
CCILOOORT	COLICROOT	CDDEISSSU	DISCUSSED	CDEEGIIMR	GERMICIDE
CCILOSTTU	OCCULTIST	CDDHHILOO	CHILDHOOD	CDEEGIINN	INDIGENCE
CCIMMOORS	MICROCOSM	CDDHIIORY	HYDRIODIC	CDEEGIINT	DIGENETIC
CCIMNOOTY	MONOCYTIC	CDDIIILOP	DIPLOIDIC	CDEEGIINV	DECEIVING
CCIMOOPRY	MICROCOPY	CDDILNOOY	CONDYLOID	CDEEGIIRS	REGICIDES
CCINOOSSU	CONSCIOUS	CDEEEEFNR	DEFERENCE	CDEEGILRY	GLYCERIDE
CCINOPRST	CONSCRIPT	CDEEEELRT	RE-ELECTED	CDEEGINOR	ENDOERGIC
CCINORSTT	CONSTRICT	CDEEEFFOR	FORCE-FEED	CDEEGINPR	PRECEDING
CCIOOOPST	OTOSCOPIC	CDEEEFITV	DEFECTIVE	CDEEGINTT	DETECTING
CCIOOPRSU	UROSCOPIC	CDEEEFLRT	REFLECTED	CDEEGLLRU	CUDGELLER
CCIOOSTTY	OTOCYSTIC	CDEEEFPRT	PERFECTED	CDEEGNORV	CONVERGED
CCKKLOORW	CLOCKWORK	CDEEEGINR	DECREEING	CDEEGNOST	CONGESTED
CCKNORSTU	TURNCOCKS	CDEEEGINX	EXCEEDING	CDEEHHIRS	CHERISHED
CCKOOPPPY	POPPYCOCK	CDEEEGLNT	NEGLECTED	CDEEHIKNT	THICKENED
CCKOOPSST	STOPCOCKS	CDEEEHKNP	HENPECKED	CDEEHIKRW	WHICKERED
CCLNOORTY	CYCLOTRON	CDEEEHQRU	CHEQUERED	CDEEHILLS	CHISELLED
CCNORSTTU	CONSTRUCT	CDEEEIMRT	DECIMETRE	CDEEHIMRS	REMSCHEID
CCOOPRSYY	CRYOSCOPY	CDEEEINNS	DESINENCE	CDEEHINST	DEHISCENT
CDDDEEENS	DESCENDED	CDEEEINPT	CENTIPEDE	CDEEHKOSU	DECKHOUSE
CDDDEEILY	DECIDEDLY	CDEEEINRS	RESIDENCE	CDEEHLORY	HYDROCELE
CDDDEEINU	UNDECIDED	CDEEEINRT	INTERCEDE	CDEEHLPPS	SCHLEPPED
CDDEEEFLT	DEFLECTED	CDEEEINUV	UNDECEIVE	CDEEHLQSU	SQUELCHED
CDDEEEIPY	PIECE-DYED	CDEEEIPRV	PERCEIVED	CDEEHLSSU	SCHEDULES
CDDEEENRS	DESCENDER	CDEEEIPTV	DECEPTIVE	CDEEHORTU	RETOUCHED
CDDEEEOPR	PROCEEDED	CDEEEIRSV	DECEIVERS	CDEEHRSTT	STRETCHED
CDDEEFKOR	DEFROCKED	CDEEEIRSX	EXERCISED	CDEEHSSSU	DUCHESSES
CDDEEGLLU	CUDGELLED	CDEEEIRTV	DECRETIVE	CDEEIILTV	VIDELICET
CDDEEHLSU	SCHEDULED	CDEEEITTV	DETECTIVE	CDEEIIMNS	MEDICINES
CDDEEINRS	DISCERNED,	CDEEELLOT	DECOLLETE	CDEEIIMPS	EPIDEMICS
	RESCINDED	CDEEELNOR	REDOLENCE	CDEEIIMRV	VERMICIDE
CDDEEIPRT	PREDICTED	CDEEELORT	ELECTRODE	CDEEIIPRR	CIRRIPEDE
CDDEEISST	DISSECTED	CDEEEMNRT	DECREMENT	CDEEIIPST	PESTICIDE
CDDEEITUV	DEDUCTIVE	CDEEENNST	SENTENCED	CDEEIIPTV	DEPICTIVE
CDDEELNPU	PEDUNCLED				

CDEEIIRTV	DIRECTIVE	CDEEMMNOT	COMMENTED	CDEGIINPT	DEPICTING
CDEEIISTT	DIETETICS	CDEEMNNOR	CONDEMNER	CDEGIINRT	CREDITING, DIRECTING
CDEEIJNOT	DEJECTION	CDEEMOOPS	DECOMPOSE		
CDEEIJPRU	PREJUDICE	CDEEMOORS	MORSE CODE	CDEGIKNOT	DOCKETING
CDEEIKLLN	NICKELLED	CDEENNORS	CONDENSER	CDEGILNSU	SECLUDING
CDEEIKNQU	QUICKENED	CDEENNORT	CONTENDER	CDEGILNUX	EXCLUDING
CDEEIKNRS	SNICKERED	CDEENNORU	DENOUNCER, RENOUNCED	CDEGILOSU	GLUCOSIDE
CDEEIKSST	STICKSEED			CDEGILOSY	GLYCOSIDE
CDEEIKSTW	STICKWEED	CDEENNOST	CONSENTED	CDEGINNOS	CONSIGNED, SECONDING
CDEEILLNP	PENCILLED	CDEENNOTT	CONTENTED		
CDEEILNNO	INDOLENCE	CDEENOOPS	ENDOSCOPE	CDEGINORR	RECORDING
CDEEILNPR	RED-PENCIL	CDEENOQRU	CONQUERED	CDEGINRSY	DESCRYING
CDEEILNST	STENCILED	CDEENORSS	SECONDERS	CDEGINSSY	DYSGENICS
CDEEILORS	CREOLISED	CDEENORSV	CONSERVED, CONVERSED	CDEGLORST	GOLDCREST
CDEEILORZ	CREOLIZED			CDEGNORSU	SCROUNGED
CDEEILRST	DERELICTS	CDEENORTU	COUNTERED, RECOUNTED	CDEHIIKLL	CHILDLIKE
CDEEILTXY	EXCITEDLY			CDEHIILNO	LICHENOID
CDEEIMNOU	EUDEMONIC	CDEENORTV	CONVERTED	CDEHIIMOS	HOMICIDES
CDEEIMNPU	IMPUDENCE	CDEENORUV	UNCOVERED	CDEHIIORT	DICHROITE
CDEEINNOR	ENDOCRINE	CDEENOSTT	CONTESTED	CDEHIKLLO	HILLOCKED
CDEEINNSU	SECUNDINE	CDEENRRTU	DECURRENT	CDEHIKOOY	DOOHICKEY
CDEEINOPT	DECEPTION	CDEENRSTU	ENCRUSTED	CDEHILLOV	LOVECHILD
CDEEINORT	RECONDITE	CDEENRSUU	UNSECURED	CDEHILLSS	CHILDLESS
CDEEINOST	SECTIONED	CDEENRSUW	UNSCREWED	CDEHILOOR	CHOLEROID
CDEEINOTT	DETECTION	CDEEOORST	CREOSOTED	CDEHILORS	CHLORIDES
CDEEINPST	INSPECTED	CDEEOOSTV	DOVECOTES	CDEHILPST	STEPCHILD
CDEEINRRS	DISCERNER, RESCINDER	CDEEOPRRR	PRERECORD	CDEHINORT	CHONDRITE
		CDEEOPRRU	PROCEDURE, REPRODUCE	CDEHINOSU	CUSHIONED
CDEEINRST	STRIDENCE			CDEHIOORT	THEODORIC
CDEEINRSY	RESIDENCY	CDEEOPRSS	PROCESSED	CDEHIORRS	CIRRHOSED
CDEEIORSV	DIVORCEES	CDEEOPRTT	PROTECTED	CDEHIORTW	DOWITCHER
CDEEIORSX	EXORCISED	CDEEORRRS	RECORDERS	CDEHKLSSU	SHELDUCKS
CDEEIORXZ	EXORCIZED	CDEEORRTY	DECRETORY	CDEHLNORU	CHONDRULE
CDEEIOSTX	COEXISTED	CDEEORSSY	CROSS-EYED	CDEHNOOTT	THECODONT
CDEEIPRSU	PEDICURES	CDEEORSTT	DETECTORS	CDEHNOTUU	UNTOUCHED
CDEEIPRTU	DEPICTURE	CDEEOSSTT	COSSETTED	CDEHNOTUV	DUTCH OVEN
CDEEIRRTU	RECRUITED	CDEEPPRSU	SCUPPERED	CDEHOOOPS	HODOOSCOPE
CDEEIRSTT	TRISECTED	CDEEPSSTU	SUSPECTED	CDEIIILSV	CIVILISED
CDEEIRTTU	CERTITUDE, RECTITUDE	CDEFFIORU	COIFFURED	CDEIIILVZ	CIVILIZED
		CDEFGIINU	FUNGICIDE	CDEIIIRST	SIDERITIC
CDEEISTUV	SEDUCTIVE	CDEFIIIST	FIDEISTIC	CDEIIKKSS	SIDEKICKS
CDEEJOPRT	PROJECTED	CDEFIILNT	INFLICTED	CDEIIKMTW	MID-WICKET
CDEEKLNOW	LOW-NECKED	CDEFIINST	DISINFECT	CDEIILLNO	CELLOIDIN, DECILLION
CDEEKOOPR	PRECOOKED	CDEFIKLOR	FROLICKED		
CDEEKORST	RESTOCKED	CDEFILNOR	CORNFIELD	CDEIILMOS	DOMICILES
CDEELLMOP	COMPELLED	CDEFIMNOR	CONFIRMED	CDEIILMTU	MULTICIDE
CDEELLNRU	CULLENDER	CDEFINNOT	CONFIDENT	CDEIILNTU	INDUCTILE
CDEELLOST	COLD STEEL	CDEFINTUY	FECUNDITY	CDEIILORT	DOLERITIC
CDEELMNTU	DEMULCENT	CDEFKNORU	UNFROCKED	CDEIILOST	IDIOLECTS, SOLICITED
CDEELMOPT	COMPLETED	CDEFMNOOR	CONFORMED		
CDEELNOSU	COUNSELED	CDEFMOORT	COMFORTED	CDEIILOSU	DELICIOUS
CDEELORSS	SCLEROSED	CDEGGILNU	CUDGELING	CDEIILPSS	DISCIPLES
CDEELRSTU	CLUSTERED	CDEGHINNR	DRENCHING	CDEIILRRU	RIDICULER
CDEELRTTU	CLUTTERED	CDEGIIKNR	DICKERING	CDEIILTVY	DECLIVITY
CDEEMMNOR	RECOMMEND	CDEGIILNN	DECLINING	CDEIIMNOS	MENISCOID

CDEIIMNTU	CTENIDIUM	
CDEIIMRST	MISDIRECT	
CDEIINNST	INCIDENTS	
CDEIINOPT	DEPICTION	
CDEIINORT	CRETINOID,	
	DIRECTION	
CDEIINOSS	DECISIONS	
CDEIINRTT	INTERDICT	
CDEIINTUV	INDUCTIVE	
CDEIIOOSU	DIOECIOUS	
CDEIIORST	SIDEROTIC	
CDEIIORUX	UXORICIDE	
CDEIIORVV	DIVORCIVE	
CDEIIRRTX	DIRECTRIX	
CDEIIRSTU	CRUDITIES,	
	DIURETICS	
CDEIJNNOO	CONJOINED	
CDEIKNSTY	STICKY END	
CDEIILLLOU	CELLULOID	
CDEILMRSU	DULCIMERS	
CDEILNNOU	CLOUD NINE	
CDEILNOOS	COLONISED	
CDEILNOOZ	COLONIZED	
CDEILNRSY	CYLINDERS	
CDEILORSS	DISCLOSER	
CDEILOSTU	CLOUDIEST	
CDEILOTTW	TWICE-TOLD	
CDEILRTUY	CREDULITY	
CDEIMMNOO	INCOMMODE	
CDEIMMOTT	COMMITTED	
CDEIMNNOT	CONDIMENT	
CDEIMNOPR	PRINCEDOM	
CDEIMNORS	CRIMSONED	
CDEIMNORU	INDECORUM	
CDEIMNOSU	NICODEMUS	
CDEIMOPRS	COMPRISED	
CDEIMOSST	DOMESTICS	
CDEINNOTU	CONTINUED,	
	UNNOTICED	
CDEINOOTX	ENDOTOXIC	
CDEINOPRS	CONSPIRED	
CDEINORST	DOCTRINES	
CDEINORTU	INTRODUCE,	
	REDUCTION	
CDEINORTV	CONTRIVED	
CDEINOSST	CONSISTED	
CDEINOSTU	SEDUCTION	
CDEINRSSU	CURDINESS	
CDEINRSTY	STRIDENCY	
CDEIOPRRT	PREDICTOR	
CDEIORRST	CREDITORS,	
	DIRECTORS	
CDEIORRTY	DIRECTORY	
CDEIORSST	DISSECTOR	
CDEIORSSU	DISCOURSE	

CDEIORSTV	DISCOVERT	
CDEIORSVY	DISCOVERY	
CDEIPPSTY	DYSPEPTIC	
CDEKLOORY	CROOKEDLY	
CDELLOOPS	SCOLLOPED	
CDELLOSSU	CLOUDLESS	
CDELMNORU	LEMON CURD	
CDELMOOWY	LOW COMEDY	
CDELNOORT	DECONTROL	
CDELNOOST	STONE-COLD	
CDELNOOSW	CLOSEDOWN	
CDELNOOTY	COTYLEDON	
CDELNOPUU	UNCOUPLED	
CDELNORSU	SCOUNDREL	
CDELNOSTU	CONSULTED	
CDELNOSUV	CONVULSED	
CDELOORSS	COLD SORES	
CDELOORSU	COLOUREDS	
CDELOORUV	OVERCLOUD	
CDELORSUU	CREDULOUS	
CDEMMOOOR	COMMODORE	
CDEMNOORW	DOWNCOMER	
CDEMNOOSW	COMEDOWNS	
CDEMNOSTU	DOCUMENTS	
CDEMOOPRT	COMPORTED	
CDEMOOPST	COMPOSTED	
CDENNORUW	UNCROWNED	
CDENNOTUU	UNCOUNTED	
CDENOOPSY	ENDOSCOPY	
CDENOORST	CONSORTED	
CDENOORTT	CONTORTED	
CDENOORTU	CONTOURED	
CDENORSTU	CONSTRUED	
CDENPRTUU	PUNCTURED	
CDEOOPRRT	PROCTORED	
CDEOOPSST	POSTCODES	
CDEOORRVW	OVERCROWD	
CDEOORSWW	WOODSCREW	
CDEOPRRSU	PRODUCERS	
CDEOPRRTU	CORRUPTED	
CDFFIILTU	DIFFICULT	
CDFGHILNO	GOLDFINCH	
CDFGIINNO	CONFIDING	
CDFGIINOY	CODIFYING	
CDFHINORY	CHONDRIFY	
CDFIIMOST	DISCOMFIT	
CDFIIORSU	SUDORIFIC	
CDFIMOORR	CORDIFORM	
CDFLNOORT	COLD FRONT	
CDGIIINNT	INDICTING	
CDGIIINOT	INDIGOTIC	
CDGIILLNO	COLLIDING	
CDGIILNNU	INCLUDING	
CDGIILOTT	DIGLOTTIC	

CDGIINNTU	INDUCTING	
CDGIINORV	DIVORCING	
CDGIKLNSU	DUCKLINGS	
CDGILLNOU	COLLUDING	
CDGILNNOO	CONDOLING	
CDGILNNOY	CONDIGNLY	
CDGILNOSS	SCOLDINGS	
CDGINNNOO	CONDONING	
CDGINNOOR	CORDONING	
CDGINOORR	CORRODING	
CDGINOORT	DOCTORING	
CDGINOPRU	PRODUCING	
CDHHIILTW	WITH CHILD	
CDHHIIOTY	ICHTHYOID	
CDHHILOST	DISHCLOTH	
CDHIIINOT	CHITINOID	
CDHIIMORS	DICHROISM	
CDHIIORRS	SCIRRHOID	
CDHIIPSTW	DIPSWITCH	
CDHIIRRTY	TRIHYDRIC	
CDHIMOOTY	DICHOTOMY	
CDHIMSTYY	DYSTHYMIC	
CDHINOPSY	DYSPHONIC	
CDHIOOPRY	CHIROPODY	
CDHIOOPSZ	SCHIZOPOD	
CDHIOPRSY	DYSPHORIC	
CDHLLOOOS	OLD SCHOOL	
CDHMNOOOR	MONOCHORD	
CDHNOOORT	NOTOCHORD	
CDHNOOTUW	TOUCHDOWN	
CDHOOORTW	TORCHWOOD	
CDHOOOTUW	TOUCHWOOD	
CDIIILMNS	DICLINISM	
CDIIISTVY	VISCIDITY	
CDIIJOSUU	JUDICIOUS	
CDIIKPSST	DIPSTICKS	
CDIILMOOT	DOLOMITIC	
CDIILNOSU	DICLINOUS	
CDIILPTUY	DUPLICITY	
CDIILTTUY	DUCTILITY	
CDIIMNPUY	PYCNIDIUM	
CDIIMORST	DICROTISM	
CDIINNOOT	CONDITION	
CDIINNOTU	INDUCTION	
CDIINOPRY	CYPRINOID	
CDIIOOPRS	SCORPIOID	
CDIIORRTT	TORTRICID	
CDIIPRSTU	TRICUSPID	
CDIIRSSTT	DISTRICTS	
CDIJNOTUY	JOCUNDITY	
CDIKLPSUY	LUCKY DIPS	
CDIKMRSTU	DRUMSTICK	
CDIKNOSSW	WINDSOCKS	
CDILLNOOO	COLLODION	

CDILOORSU	DISCOLOUR	CEEEILNSS	LICENSEES	CEEFHIPSY	SPEECHIFY
CDILORSUU	LUDICROUS	CEEEILNST	CELESTINE	CEEFHITTY	ITCHY FEET
CDIMMNOOS	DISCOMMON	CEEEILRST	LEICESTER	CEEFHMNNR	FRENCHMEN
CDIMMOOTY	COMMODITY	CEEEILSTT	CELESTITE	CEEFIINTV	INFECTIVE
CDIMNOORT	MICRODONT	CEEEILSTV	SELECTIVE	CEEFIIPRS	SPECIFIER
CDIMNOORU	DORONICUM	CEEEIMNNS	EMINENCES	CEEFIIRRT	RECTIFIER
CDIMNORSY	SYNDROMIC	CEEEIMNTT	CEMENTITE	CEEFIKKRS	FREE KICKS
CDINORSSW	CROSSWIND	CEEEIMRRS	MERCERISE	CEEFILNNU	INFLUENCE
CDINOSSTU	DISCOUNTS	CEEEIMRRZ	MERCERIZE	CEEFILRTY	ELECTRIFY
CDINOSTUY	IN CUSTODY	CEEEINNPT	PENITENCE	CEEFIMPRT	IMPERFECT
CDIOORRRS	CORRIDORS	CEEEINNSS	IN ESSENCE	CEEFINORR	REINFORCE
CDIOPRSSU	CUSPIDORS	CEEEINNST	SENTIENCE	CEEFINORT	REFECTION
CDKKNNOOW	KNOCKDOWN	CEEEINPRT	EPICENTRE	CEEFINTTU	FETTUCINE
CDKOOOSTW	WOODSTOCK	CEEEINRSU	ESURIENCE	CEEFIRRST	FIRECREST
CDMNNORUU	CONUNDRUM	CEEEINSTX	EXISTENCE	CEEFLOORS	FORECLOSE
CDMNOOPSU	COMPOUNDS	CEEEIPRRV	PERCEIVER	CEEFLORRT	REFLECTOR
CDNNOOTUW	COUNTDOWN	CEEEIPRST	CREEPIEST	CEEFLORSU	FLUORESCE
CDOORRSSW	CROSSWORD	CEEEIPRTV	RECEPTIVE	CEEFLPRTY	PERFECTLY
CEEEEFFNR	EFFERENCE	CEEEIPSST	SET PIECES	CEEFNORRR	CONFERRER
CEEEEFNRR	REFERENCE	CEEEIPTVX	EXCEPTIVE	CEEFNORRS	CONFRERES
CEEEEGMNR	EMERGENCE	CEEEIRRSV	RECEIVERS	CEEFNORUY	FREQUENCY
CEEEEHILP	HEELPIECE	CEEEIRRSX	EXERCISER	CEEFNRSTU	RUFESCENT
CEEEEHMNV	VEHEMENCE	CEEEIRSSV	RECESSIVE	CEEFORRTY	REFECTORY
CEEEEIPSY	EYEPIECES	CEEEIRSSX	EXERCISES	CEEFORSTW	CROW'S FEET
CEEEENRRV	REVERENCE	CEEEIRSTV	SECRETIVE	CEEGHIMNO	HEGEMONIC
CEEEFFITV	EFFECTIVE	CEEEIRTVX	EXCRETIVE	CEEGHINOR	RE-ECHOING
CEEEFFLNU	EFFLUENCE	CEEEISSVX	EXCESSIVE	CEEGHINRW	GREENWICH
CEEEFINNR	INFERENCE	CEEEITUVX	EXECUTIVE	CEEGHINSW	ESCHEWING
CEEEFNORR	FERROCENE,	CEEEKORRT	ROCKETEER	CEEGHLOSW	COGWHEELS
	RE-ENFORCE	CEEELLNRV	NERVE CELL	CEEGIINRV	RECEIVING
CEEEFNORU	FREQUENCE	CEEELLNTX	EXCELLENT	CEEGIJNRT	REJECTING
CEEEFPRRT	PERFECTER	CEEELNOQU	ELOQUENCE	CEEGILLNX	EXCELLING
CEEEGILNT	TELEGENIC	CEEELOPST	TELESCOPE	CEEGILNOO	OLIGOCENE
CEEEGINRS	REGENCIES	CEEEMNRRT	RECREMENT	CEEGILNOT	TELEGONIC
CEEEGINRT	ENERGETIC	CEEEMNRTX	EXCREMENT	CEEGILNRY	GLYCERINE
CEEEGISTX	EXEGETICS	CEEENNSST	SENESCENT,	CEEGILNST	SELECTING
CEEEGLNNO	GENE CLONE		SENTENCES	CEEGIMNNT	CEMENTING
CEEEGLNOR	CONGER EEL	CEEENORTT	ENTRECOTE	CEEGIMORT	GEOMETRIC
CEEEGLNRT	NEGLECTER	CEEENPRSS	PRESENCES	CEEGINNOS	CONSIGNEE
CEEEGMNRY	EMERGENCY	CEEENPRST	PRETENCES	CEEGINNRS	SCREENING
CEEEHIKST	CHEEKIEST	CEEENQRSU	SEQUENCER	CEEGINNRT	CENTERING
CEEEHILST	SCHEELITE	CEEENQSSU	SEQUENCES	CEEGINNST	IGNESCENT
CEEEHINNR	INHERENCE	CEEENRSST	ERECTNESS	CEEGINOOT	OOGENETIC
CEEEHIRST	CHEERIEST	CEEEORRRV	RECOVERER	CEEGINORS	CONGERIES,
CEEEHISST	ICE SHEETS	CEEEPRRST	RESPECTER		RECOGNISE
CEEEHLNTY	ENTELECHY	CEEEPRRTX	EXCERPTER	CEEGINORZ	RECOGNIZE
CEEEHLRSS	CHEERLESS	CEEEPRSTU	PERSECUTE	CEEGINPTX	EXCEPTING,
CEEEHOPRS	ECOSPHERE	CEEFFFORT	FOR EFFECT		EXPECTING
CEEEHQRUX	EXCHEQUER	CEEFFGINT	EFFECTING	CEEGINRSS	RECESSING
CEEEHRRTV	CHEVRETTE	CEEFFIINT	EFFICIENT	CEEGINRST	SECRETING
CEEEIIMPT	TIMEPIECE	CEEFFOOPT	COFFEEPOT	CEEGINRTX	EXCRETING
CEEEIINRV	VICEREINE	CEEFGLNTU	GENUFLECT	CEEGINTUX	EXECUTING
CEEEIJRTV	REJECTIVE	CEEFHHNRT	THE FRENCH	CEEGIORRS	GROCERIES
CEEEILLNT	CLIENTELE	CEEFHIKRS	KERCHIEFS	CEEGKNOOS	GOOSENECK
				CEEGLLMRS	GERM CELLS

CEEGLMNRY	CLERGYMEN
CEEGLNOOS	CONGOLESE
CEEGORTTU	COURGETTE
CEEHHIRRS	CHERISHER
CEEHHIRVW	WHICHEVER
CEEHHOPST	HOPE CHEST
CEEHIILLN	HELICLINE
CEEHIIPTT	EPITHETIC
CEEHIKNNT	IN THE NECK
CEEHIKNRT	KITCHENER,
THICKENER	
CEEHIKPPR	PIKEPERCH
CEEHIKRST	SKETCHIER
CEEHILLRS	CHISELLER
CEEHILNRS	SCHLIEREN
CEEHILNTY	ETHYLENIC
CEEHILPRT	TELPHERIC
CEEHILRSW	CLERIHEWS
CEEHILSTT	TELESTICH
CEEHINQTU	TECHNIQUE
CEEHINRVY	EVERY INCH
CEEHINSST	TECHINESS
CEEHINSTU	EUTHENICS
CEEHIOPSW	SHOWPIECE
CEEHISSTT	CHESTIEST,
ESTHETICS	
CEEHISTTT	TETCHIEST
CEEHKRSST	SKETCHERS
CEEHLORSU	LECHEROUS
CEEHLPRSU	SEPULCHRE
CEEHLQRSU	SQUELCHER
CEEHMNORZ	CHERNOZEM
CEEHNOPRR	PERCHERON
CEEHNRRST	TRENCHERS
CEEHOPTTY	ECTOPHYTE
CEEHORRST	ROCHESTER
CEEHORRTU	RETOUCHER
CEEHRRSTT	STRETCHER
CEEHRSSTT	STRETCHES
CEEIIJNTV	INJECTIVE
CEEIILNPR	PERICLINE
CEEIILNRT	LIENTERIC
CEEIILPPT	EPILEPTIC
CEEIIMMNN	IMMINENCE
CEEIIMNPS	EPICENISM,
MINCE PIES	
CEEIIMNRS	REMINISCE
CEEIIMPRS	IMPRECISE
CEEIIMPST	EPISTEMIC
CEEIIMRST	METRICISE
CEEIIMRTZ	METRICIZE
CEEIINNOR	EIRENICON
CEEIINNRS	INSINCERE
CEEIINNRT	ENCRINITE
CEEIINNTV	INCENTIVE

CEEIINPRT	RECIPIENT
CEEIINPTV	INCEPTIVE
CEEIINPTX	EXCIPIENT
CEEIINRSV	IN SERVICE
CEEIINTVV	INVECTIVE
CEEIIOPST	POETICISE
CEEIIOPTZ	POETICIZE
CEEIIOSST	SOCIETIES
CEEIJNORT	REJECTION
CEEIJNRTT	INTERJECT
CEEIKLNNS	NECKLINES
CEEIKMORS	MOCKERIES
CEEIKOPRW	PIECEWORK,
WORKPIECE	
CEEIKORRS	ROCKERIES
CEEILLNPR	PENCILLER
CEEILLNTT	INTELLECT
CEEILMNNT	INCLEMENT
CEEILMNOP	POLICEMEN
CEEILMNPR	CRIMPLENE
CEEILMNSU	LUMINESCE
CEEILMOST	COMELIEST
CEEILMRSS	MERCILESS
CEEILNNOS	INSOLENCE
CEEILNORT	CENTRIOLE
CEEILNOST	ELECTIONS,
SELECTION	
CEEILNOTT	NICOLETTE
CEEILNPST	SPLENETIC
CEEILNRSS	SILENCERS
CEEILNRSY	SINCERELY
CEEILNRTV	VENTRICLE
CEEILNRUV	VIRULENCE
CEEILORSX	EXCELSIOR
CEEILOSSS	ISOSCELES
CEEILOSSV	VOICELESS
CEEILPRSS	PRICELESS
CEEILPRSY	PRECISELY
CEEILRSTU	CRUELTIES,
RETICULES	
CEEILRSTW	CREWELIST
CEEILRSUV	RECLUSIVE
CEEILSSTT	TESTICLES
CEEILSSUV	SECLUSIVE
CEEILSUVX	EXCLUSIVE
CEEIMMNSU	ECUMENISM
CEEIMMOTT	COMMITTEE
CEEIMNNRT	INCREMENT
CEEIMNOOS	ECONOMIES,
ECONOMISE	
CEEIMNOOZ	ECONOMIZE
CEEIMNOPT	IMPOTENCE
CEEIMNORR	MEROCRINE
CEEIMNOST	CENTESIMO
CEEIMNOWX	NEW MEXICO

CEEIMNPSS	SPECIMENS
CEEIMNSTU	INTUMESCE
CEEINNNSV	VINCENNES
CEEINNORS	RECENSION
CEEINOPRS	PRECONISE
CEEINOPRT	RECEPTION
CEEINOPRZ	PRECONIZE
CEEINOPTX	EXCEPTION
CEEINORSS	RECESSION
CEEINORST	ERECTIONS,
RESECTION, SECRETION	
CEEINORSU	CINEREOUS
CEEINORTX	EXCRETION
CEEINOSSS	SECESSION
CEEINOSTX	EXSECTION
CEEINOTUX	EXECUTION
CEEINPRRU	PRURIENCE
CEEINPRST	PRESCIENT
CEEINPRTT	INTERCEPT
CEEINPSSX	SIXPENCES
CEEINQRTU	QUERCETIN
CEEINQSTU	QUIESCENT
CEEINRSSU	SINECURES
CEEINRSTT	INTERSECT
CEEINRSTU	CENTURIES
CEEINRSTV	VIRESCENT
CEEINSSTY	NECESSITY
CEEIOORTZ	OZOCERITE
CEEIOORVV	VOICE-OVER
CEEIOPPRS	PERISCOPE
CEEIOPRRV	OVERPRICE
CEEIORRST	RECTORIES
CEEIORRSX	EXORCISER
CEEIORSSU	SERICEOUS
CEEIPRSST	TRICEPSES
CEEIRRRTU	RECRUITER
CEEIRSSTU	CERUSSITE
CEEIRSSTW	SCREWIEST
CEEIRSUVX	EXCURSIVE
CEEIRTUXX	EXECUTRIX
CEELLLOSU	CELLULOSE
CEELLMNTY	CLEMENTLY
CEELLMOPR	COMPELLER
CEELLMOSU	MOLECULES
CEELLORTU	COURTELLE
CEELMMNSU	MUSCLEMEN
CEELMNOUW	UNWELCOME
CEELMOPRT	COMPLETER
CEELMOPSX	COMPLEXES
CEELNORST	ELECTRONS
CEELNORSU	ENCLOSURE
CEELNOSSS	CLOSENESS
CEELNPRUU	PURULENCE
CEELNSSST	SCENTLESS

CEELOPSTY	TELESCOPY
CEELORSSS	SCLEROSES
CEELORSST	CORSELETS, SELECTORS
CEELORSSV	COVERLESS
CEELORSTV	COVERLETS
CEELRRSTU	LECTURERS
CEEMMNORT	COMMENTER
CEEMNNORT	CONTEMNER
CEEMNOPTT	COMPETENT
CEEMNORSW	NEWCOMERS
CEEMNSTTU	TUMESCENT
CEEMOOPRS	RECOMPOSE
CEEMORRTY	CRYOMETER
CEEMOSSTY	ECOSYSTEM
CEENNOOSS	NOSECONES
CEENNORRU	RENOUNCER
CEENNORST	CONSENTER
CEENNORSV	CONVENERS
CEENNORTU	ENCOUNTER
CEENOOPST	COPESTONE
CEENOORSV	ONCE-OVERS
CEENOORTV	COVER NOTE
CEENOPRRT	PRECENTOR
CEENOPSTT	PENTECOST
CEENOPSTW	TWOPENCES
CEENORRSV	CONSERVER, CONVERSER
CEENORRTV	CONVERTER, RECONVERT
CEENORSSV	CONSERVES
CEENORSTT	CONTESTER
CEENORSTW	SWEET CORN
CEENORSVY	CONVEYERS
CEENPPSTU	TUPPENCES
CEENRRRTU	RECURRENT
CEENRRTUX	EXCURRENT
CEEOORRSV	OVERSCORE
CEEOPPRRT	PRECEPTOR
CEEOPPRSS	REPROCESS
CEEOPRSSS	PROCESSES
CEEOPRSTT	TOP-SECRET
CEEOPRSTU	PROSECUTE
CEEOQRTTU	CROQUETTE
CEEOQSTTU	COQUETTES
CEEORRRSS	SORCERERS
CEEORRSSS	SORCERESS
CEEORRSST	CROSSTREE
CEEORRSSU	RESOURCES
CEEORRSTW	WORCESTER
CEEORRSTY	SECRETORY
CEEORRSUV	VERRUCOSE
CEEORRTUV	COVERTURE
CEEORRTXY	EXCRETORY
CEEORSTTV	CORVETTES
CEEORSTUX	EXECUTORS
CEEORTUXY	EXECUTORY
CEEPRSSSY	CYPRESSES
CEEPRSSTU	SUSPECTER
CEERRRSTU	RESURRECT
CEERRSSTU	REST CURES
CEFFHINRY	FRENCHIFY
CEFFIIOOX	EX OFFICIO
CEFFIORSU	COIFFEURS, COIFFURES
CEFFIRRSU	SCRUFFIER
CEFGIINNT	INFECTING
CEFGINNOR	ENFORCING
CEFHIILSS	FISH SLICE
CEFHIIMSS	MISCHIEFS
CEFHIKRSW	WRECKFISH
CEFHILMOR	CHELIFORM
CEFHKOORS	FORESHOCK
CEFHPRRSU	SURFPERCH
CEFIILNRT	INFLICTER
CEFIILNRU	LUCIFERIN
CEFIINNOT	INFECTION
CEFIIORRS	SCORIFIER
CEFIKLORR	FROLICKER
CEFILLLOS	FOLLICLES
CEFILNORT	INFLECTOR
CEFIMNORU	CUNEIFORM
CEFINORSS	FORENSICS
CEFINORTU	CONFITURE
CEFIOORSU	FEROCIOUS
CEFIORRSS	CROSSFIRE
CEFKLOORS	FORELOCKS
CEFKLOPTU	POCKETFUL
CEFKOORRW	WORKFORCE
CEFLNNOTU	CONFLUENT
CEFMNOORR	CONFORMER
CEFMOORRT	COMFORTER
CEFNOORSS	CONFESSOR
CEFOORRTU	FORECOURT
CEGHIILNS	CHISELING
CEGHIINNR	ENRICHING
CEGHIINPR	CIPHERING
CEGHIKNST	SKETCHING
CEGHILLOU	GUILLOCHE
CEGHILMTU	GEMUTLICH
CEGHILNTV	VETCHLING
CEGHILOOT	ETHOLOGIC
CEGHINNQU	QUENCHING
CEGHINNRW	WRENCHING
CEGHINORT	HECTORING
CEGHINPRY	CYPHERING
CEGHIOPTY	GEOPHYTIC
CEGHIORRU	GROUCHIER
CEGHKNORU	ROUGHNECK
CEGHMNOOR	CHROMOGEN
CEGIIILNT	ELICITING
CEGIIJNNT	INJECTING
CEGIIJNOR	REJOICING
CEGIIKLNN	NICKELING
CEGIIKNNS	SICKENING
CEGIIKNPT	PICKETING
CEGIIKNTT	TICKETING
CEGIILNNP	PENCILING
CEGIILNNR	RECLINING
CEGIILNNS	LICENSING, SILENCING
CEGIILNOR	RECOILING
CEGIILNPS	ECLIPSING
CEGIINNNS	INCENSING
CEGIINOTV	COGNITIVE
CEGIINRSV	SERVICING
CEGIIOSTT	EGOTISTIC
CEGIJKNOY	JOCKEYING
CEGIKNNOR	RECKONING
CEGIKNOPT	POCKETING
CEGIKNORT	ROCKETING
CEGIKNPRU	PUCKERING
CEGIKNRTU	TUCKERING
CEGILLMOU	COLLEGIUM
CEGILMMNO	COMMINGLE
CEGILMNOW	WELCOMING
CEGILNNOS	ENCLOSING
CEGILNOST	CLOSETING
CEGILNRSU	SURCINGLE
CEGILNRTU	LECTURING
CEGILOORS	SEROLOGIC
CEGILOOST	ECOLOGIST
CEGIMNNOO	MONOGENIC
CEGIMNOOR	ERGONOMIC
CEGIMNOPR	COMPERING
CEGIMNOPT	COMPETING
CEGIMNOUY	GYNOECIUM
CEGIMNOYZ	ZYMOGENIC
CEGINNNOV	CONVENING
CEGINNOOT	ONTOGENIC
CEGINNORR	CORNERING
CEGINNORS	CENSORING
CEGINNOVY	CONVEYING
CEGINNRSU	CENSURING
CEGINOOPS	GEOPONICS
CEGINOPRU	RECOUPING
CEGINOPRY	PYROGENIC
CEGINOPTY	GENOTYPIC
CEGINORST	ESCORTING
CEGINORSV	COVERINGS
CEGINRRRU	RECURRING
CEGIOOPRT	GEOTROPIC
CEGLNOORY	NECROLOGY

CEGMNNOOS	COGNOMENS	CEHIOOPRT	ORTHOEPIC	CEIILNPPR	PRINCIPLE
CEGNNORTU	CONGRUENT	CEHIOOSST	CHOOSIEST	CEIILNSUV	INCLUSIVE
CEGNORRSU	SCROUNGER	CEHIOPPRT	PROPHETIC	CEIILOQRU	LIQUORICE
CEGNORSUY	SURGEONCY	CEHIOPPST	CHOPPIEST	CEIILOSSU	SILICEOUS
CEGOOPRSY	GYROSCOPE	CEHIOPRRT	CHIROPTER	CEIILPRST	LIST PRICE
CEHHHIIKT	HITCHHIKE	CEHIOPRTT	PROTHETIC	CEIILPRTU	PLEURITIC
CEHHIIMST	HEMISTICH	CEHIOPRTU	EUTROPHIC	CEIILRSST	SCLERITIS
CEHHIMSTT	HEMSTITCH	CEHIOPRTY	HYPOCRITE	CEIILSTTY	SECTILITY
CEHHOOPSU	CHOPHOUSE	CEHIORRST	CHORISTER	CEIIMNOST	SEMITONIC
CEHIIKLTW	WITCHLIKE	CEHIORSST	OSTRICHES	CEIIMNRST	CRETINISM
CEHIIKORS	HICKORIES	CEHIOSSST	SCHISTOSE	CEIIMNSST	SCIENTISM
CEHIIKTTW	HIT WICKET	CEHIOSTTU	TOUCHIEST	CEIIMORST	EROTICISM,
CEHIILLST	CHILLIEST	CEHIPRRRU	CHIRRUPER		ISOMETRIC
CEHIILMOT	HOMILETIC	CEHIPRSTW	PRESTWICH	CEIIMOSST	SEMIOTICS
CEHIILNOT	NEOLITHIC	CEHIPRTTT	PRITCHETT	CEIIMOSTX	EXOTICISM
CEHIIMSTY	MYTHICISE	CEHIRSSTY	HYSTERICS	CEIIMPRSU	EPICURISM
CEHIIMTYZ	MYTHICIZE	CEHKLNORS	SCHNORKEL	CEIIMRRTT	TRIMETRIC
CEHIINNOT	ON THIN ICE	CEHKOOOSU	COOKHOUSE	CEIINNOPT	INCEPTION
CEHIINPRT	NEPHRITIC,	CEHKRSSTU	HUCKSTERS	CEIINNORT	INCRETION
	PHRENITIC	CEHLLOOPT	PHOTOCELL	CEIINNRTY	INNER CITY
CEHIINRST	CHRISTINE	CEHLOOPRS	PRESCHOOL	CEIINOPRS	PRECISION
CEHIINRTZ	CHINTZIER	CEHMOOPRT	ECTOMORPH	CEIINORRT	CRITERION
CEHIINSST	ITCHINESS	CEHMOORRU	UROCHROME	CEIINORTT	TRICOTINE
CEHIINTWZ	ZINC WHITE	CEHNNORTU	TRUNCHEON	CEIINORTV	VICTORINE
CEHIIPPTY	EPIPHYTIC	CEHNOOPPY	PHENOCOPY	CEIINOSSX	EXCISIONS
CEHIIPRST	CHIRPIEST	CEHNOORSS	SCHOONERS	CEIINOSTV	EVICTIONS
CEHIIPRTT	TEPHRITIC	CEHNSSTTU	CHESTNUTS	CEIINPRSS	PRICINESS
CEHIIRSTU	HEURISTIC	CEHOOOPRS	HOROSCOPE	CEIINPSSS	SPICINESS
CEHIISTTT	TITCHIEST	CEHOPRTYY	CRYOPHYTE	CEIINRSTX	EXTRINSIC
CEHIKLPRS	CLERKSHIP	CEHOPSSSY	PSYCHOSES	CEIINRSTY	CITISENRY,
CEHIKLSTY	SKETCHILY	CEHOPTTUY	TOUCH-TYPE		SINCERITY
CEHIKNSST	THICKNESS	CEIIILRSV	CIVILISER	CEIINRSUV	INCURSIVE
CEHIKNSTU	CHUNKIEST	CEIIILRVZ	CIVILIZER	CEIINRTTY	INTERCITY
CEHIKOPPT	HIP POCKET	CEIIIMSTV	VICTIMISE	CEIINRTYZ	CITIZENRY
CEHIKPRSW	SHIPWRECK	CEIIIMTVZ	VICTIMIZE	CEIINSSTT	SCIENTIST
CEHILNNPU	PUNCH LINE	CEIIINNPT	INCIPIENT	CEIIOOPTZ	EPIZOOTIC
CEHILNOOR	HOLOCRINE	CEIIIPRSS	EPICRISIS	CEIIORSST	ISOSTERIC
CEHILNOSU	LICHENOUS	CEIIJNNOT	INJECTION	CEIIORSTV	VICTORIES
CEHILNOTU	TOUCHLINE	CEIIJNSSU	JUICINESS	CEIIPRSST	CRISPIEST
CEHILNSTZ	SCHNITZEL	CEIIJNSTU	INJUSTICE	CEIIPSTTY	SEPTICITY
CEHILORST	CLOTHIERS	CEIIKLMQU	QUICKLIME	CEIIQRSTU	CRITIQUES
CEHIMMOPR	MORPHEMIC	CEIIKLMRS	LIMERICKS	CEIJNNOOR	CONJOINER
CEHIMMORS	MICROMESH	CEIIKLMST	KELTICISM	CEIJNORTT	INTROJECT
CEHIMMSTU	CHUMMIEST	CEIIKLNRR	CRINKLIER	CEIKLNORT	INTERLOCK
CEHIMNNOU	ICHNEUMON	CEIIKLPRR	PRICKLIER	CEIKLNOST	CLOSE-KNIT
CEHIMNOPS	PHONEMICS	CEIIKLSST	SICKLIEST	CEIKLNOSU	NICKELOUS
CEHIMRSTY	CHEMISTRY	CEIIKLSTT	KELTICIST	CEIKLNSSS	SLICKNESS
CEHINOPRT	NEPHROTIC	CEIIKNPRT	NITPICKER	CEIKLNSSU	LUCKINESS
CEHINOPST	PHONETICS	CEIIKNPSS	PICKINESS	CEIKLOPST	STOCKPILE
CEHINOPTY	NEOPHYTIC	CEIIKRSTT	TRICKIEST	CEIKLOSTV	LIVESTOCK
CEHINPRST	SPHINCTER	CEIIKSSTT	STICKIEST	CEIKLPSTU	PLUCKIEST
CEHINPSTU	PUNCHIEST	CEIILLMNT	MILLICENT	CEIKLRSST	STICKLERS
CEHINSSSU	CUSHINESS	CEIILMNSU	MINISCULE	CEIKMNSSU	MUCKINESS
CEHINSTTY	SYNTHETIC	CEIILNNOR	CRINOLINE	CEIKMPPSU	PICK-ME-UPS
				CEIKNORSS	ROCKINESS

CEIKNOSTT	STOCKINET	CEIMMOORT	MICROTOME	CEIRRSTTU	STRICTURE
CEIKNQSSU	QUICKNESS	CEIMMORTT	COMMITTER	CEIRSSTTT	STRICTEST
CEIKORRTV	OVERTRICK	CEIMMRSTU	CRUMMIEST	CEIRSSTTU	CRUSTIEST
CEIKOSSTT	STOCKIEST	CEIMNNOPU	PNEUMONIC	CEJNORRSU	CONJURERS
CEIKPQSTU	QUICKSTEP	CEIMNOORT	MICROTONE	CEJNRSTUU	JUNCTURES
CEIKPRSTW	PRESTWICK	CEIMNOOST	ECONOMIST	CEJOOPRRT	PROJECTOR
CEIKRRSTT	TRICKSTER	CEIMNORST	INTERCOMS	CEKKORSTY	SKYROCKET
CEILLLMTU	CLITELLUM	CEIMNORTT	METRIC TON	CEKLNOOPS	POLO NECKS
CEILLNOOR	COLOR LINE	CEIMOOPRR	POROMERIC	CEKLNORTW	TOWN CLERK
CEILLNOUV	INVOLUCEL	CEIMOOPST	COMPOSITE	CEKOORRSW	CO-WORKERS
CEILLOPTU	POLLUCITE	CEIMOORTZ	ZOOMETRIC	CEKOORSTV	OVERSTOCK
CEILLOSUV	COLLUSIVE	CEIMOOSTX	EXOSMOTIC	CEKOPRSST	SPROCKETS
CEILLPSTY	SYLLEPTIC	CEIMOPRST	PRIME COST	CELLMSTUU	SCUTELLUM
CEILMNNOO	MONOCLINE	CEIMOPSUU	PUMICEOUS	CELLNOSUU	NUCLEOLUS
CEILMNOOS	SEMICOLON	CEIMORSSX	EXORCISMS	CELLOOPTY	COLLOTYPE
CEILMNOTU	MONTICULE	CEIMORSTU	COSTUMIER	CELMNOTUY	CONTUMELY
CEILMNSSU	LEMNISCUS	CEIMOSSTU	CUSTOMISE	CELMOOPRY	COPOLYMER
CEILMNSUU	MINUSCULE	CEIMOSTUV	MUSCOVITE	CELMOOTUY	LEUCOTOMY
CEILMOPRS	COMPILERS	CEIMOSTUZ	CUSTOMIZE	CELMOPRUU	OPERCULUM
CEILMOPRY	MICROPYLE,	CEINNNOTT	CONTINENT	CELMPRSTU	PLECTRUMS
POLYMERIC		CEINNNOTV	CONNIVENT	CELNOOSTU	CONSOLUTE
CEILMOSSS	SOLECISMS	CEINNOPRT	PRINCETON	CELNOOTUV	CONVOLUTE
CEILMRTUU	RETICULUM	CEINNORTU	CENTURION,	CELNOPRTU	CORPULENT
CEILMSSTU	CLUMSIEST	CONTINUER		CELNORSTU	CONSULTER
CEILNNOOS	CLOISONNE	CEINNRRTU	INCURRENT	CELNOSSTU	COUNTLESS
CEILNOOPS	SCOPOLINE	CEINOORST	CORTISONE	CELNRRTUY	CURRENTLY
CEILNOORS	COLONISER	CEINOOSSW	SOSNOWIEC	CELNRTTUU	TRUCULENT
CEILNOORZ	COLONIZER	CEINOPPRU	PORCUPINE	CELOOPRSU	SUPERCOOL
CEILNOOTU	ELOCUTION	CEINOPRRT	INTERCROP	CELORSSUU	SURCULOSE
CEILNOPRV	PIN CLOVER	CEINOPRST	INSPECTOR	CELPRSTUU	SCULPTURE
CEILNORSU	CORNELIUS,	CEINOPRSV	PROVINCES	CEMMNOORS	COMMONERS
INCLOSURE, RECLUSION		CEINOPRXY	PYROXENIC	CEMMORSTU	COMMUTERS
CEILNORUV	INVOLUCRE	CEINORRTW	TOWN CRIER	CEMMNOOPT	COMPONENT
CEILNOSSU	SECLUSION	CEINORSTT	CORNETIST	CEMNOOOQU	MONOCOQUE
CEILNOSUX	EXCLUSION	CEINORSTU	COUNTRIES,	CEMNOORTY	NECROTOMY
CEILNRSSU	CURLINESS	CRETINOUS, NEUROTICS		CEMNORSSU	CONSUMERS
CEILNRUVY	VIRULENCY	CEINORSUX	EXCURSION	CEMNORTUY	EMUNCTORY
CEILOOPRT	COPROLITE	CEINOSTUV	CONTUSIVE	CEMOOPRSS	COMPOSERS
CEILOPPRT	PROLEPTIC	CEINOTVXY	CONVEXITY	CEMOOPRSU	COMPOSURE
CEILOPPSS	POPSICLES	CEINPRSSS	CRISPNESS	CEMOPRSTU	COMPUTERS
CEILOPSTU	POULTICES	CEINRSSTT	CENTRISTS	CEMORRSUU	MERCUROUS
CEILORRTU	COURTLIER	CEINRSTTU	TINCTURES	CEMORRSWW	SCREWWORM
CEILORSSS	SCLEROSIS	CEIOOPRST	COREOPSIS	CEMORRTYY	CRYOMETRY
CEILORSST	CLOISTERS	CEIOOPRST	PORTICOES	CEMORSSTU	CUSTOMERS
CEILOSSST	SOLSTICES	CEIOORRSV	CORROSIVE	CENNOOPPY	OPPONENCY
CEILOSSTT	COSTLIEST	CEIOPRRSU	CROUPIERS	CENNOOPRU	PRONOUNCE
CEILPRSSU	SURPLICES	CEIORRSTT	TRISECTOR	CENNORSTU	NOCTURNES
CEILRSUVY	CURSIVELY	CEIORRSTU	COURTIERS	CENNOSSSU	CONSENSUS
CEIMMNNOS	MNEMONICS	CEIORRTUU	COUTURIER	CENOOPRST	STONECROP
CEIMMNOOR	MONOMERIC	CEIORSSSW	CROSSWISE	CENOOQRRU	CONQUEROR
CEIMMNOSU	COMMUNISE,	CEIORSSTX	EXORCISTS	CENOORRST	CONSORTER
ENCOMIUMS		CEIORSTTU	TOREUTICS	CENOQSSTU	CONQUESTS
CEIMMNOTU	COMMINUTE	CEIPPRRST	PRESCRIPT	CENORRSTU	CONSTRUER
CEIMMNOUZ	COMMUNIZE	CEIPRRSTU	SCRIPTURE	CENORSSSS	CROSSNESS
CEIMMOORS	MICROSOME	CEIPRSSTU	PIECRUSTS		

CENORSSTW	CROW'S NEST	CFINNOSTU	FUNCTIONS
CENORSSUY	CYNOSURES	CFLLOORUU	COLOURFUL
CENORSTXY	XENOCRYST	CFLNOORRU	CORNFLOUR
CENPRRTUU	PUNCTURER	CFLOOOSTT	COLTSFOOT
CENPRSTUU	PUNCTURES	CFOOORSTW	CROW'S FOOT
CEOOOSTTV	SOTTO VOCE	CFORSTUUU	FRUCTUOUS
CEOOPRRSS	PROCESSOR	CGGHIKNNU	CHUNGKING
CEOOPRRST	PROSECTOR	CGGHINNOQ	CHONGQING
CEOOPRRTT	PROTECTOR	CGGHINORU	GROUCHING
CEOOPRSTY	SPOROCYTE	CGGINORSU	SCOURGING
CEOOPSSTU	OCTOPUSES	CGHHIORTU	HIGH COURT
CEOORRSSU	SORCEROUS	CGHIILLNS	SCHILLING
CEOORRSSV	CROSSOVER	CGHIIMNRS	SMIRCHING
CEOORSTUU	COURTEOUS	CGHIIMOST	GOTHICISM
CEOPPRSST	PROSPECTS	CGHIINNST	SNITCHING
CEOPRRRSU	PRECURSOR,	CGHIINPPS	CHIPPINGS
PROCURERS		CGHIINSTT	STITCHING
CEOPRRRTU	CORRUPTER	CGHIINSTW	SWITCHING
CEOPRRSSU	PERCUSSOR	CGHIINTTW	TWITCHING
CEOPRSSTW	SCREW TOPS	CGHILNOOS	SCHOOLING
CEPPRSTUU	UPPERCUTS	CGHILNOOY	ICHNOLOGY
CEPRSSTUU	CUTPURSES	CGHILNORT	CHORTLING
CERRSTTUU	STRUCTURE	CGHILNOSU	SLOUCHING
CFFGIINSU	SUFFICING	CGHILOOOR	HOROLOGIC
CFFGILNSU	SCUFFLING	CGHILORUY	GROUCHILY
CFFIIOOSU	OFFICIOUS	CGHIMNOOS	SMOOCHING
CFFIKLNSU	CUFF LINKS	CGHINORSU	CHORUSING
CFFLOOORU	OFF COLOUR	CGHIOPRTY	COPYRIGHT
CFGHIILNN	FLINCHING	CGHKLOTUU	TOUGH LUCK
CFGHIILNS	CLINGFISH	CGHLLNOOT	LONGCLOTH
CFGIILLMN	CLINGFILM	CGHLOOORY	CHOROLOGY
CFGILNNOU	FLOUNCING	CGHLOOPYY	PHYCOLOGY
CFGILNORY	FORCINGLY	CGIIIKMMN	MIMICKING
CFGINNOSU	CONFUSING	CGIIILNNN	INCLINING
CFGINNOTU	CONFUTING	CGIIINNOV	INVOICING
CFGINOSSU	FOCUSSING	CGIIKLNNR	CRINKLING
CFHIIKSST	FISH STICK	CGIIKLNPR	PRICKLING
CFHIINOOR	HONORIFIC	CGIIKLNRT	TRICKLING
CFHIKOPRT	PITCHFORK	CGIIKMMRY	GIMMICKRY
CFHIKOSST	STOCKFISH	CGIIKNNPU	UNPICKING
CFHMNOOTU	NOT MUCH OF	CGIILMNNY	MINCINGLY
CFHOOSTTU	SOFT TOUCH	CGIILMNOP	COMPILING
CFIIKKLNS	SKIN FLICK	CGIILNNOS	INCLOSING
CFIILMMOR	MICROFILM	CGIILNNWY	WINCINGLY
CFIILORST	FLORISTIC	CGIILNPPR	CRIPPLING
CFIIOOPRS	SOPORIFIC	CGIILNPPS	CLIPPINGS
CFIIOPRRT	TRPORIFIC	CGIILOSST	GLOSSITIC,
CFIKLLNOT	FLINTLOCK	LOGISTICS	
CFIKLLOOR	FOLKLORIC	CGIILRSTU	LITURGICS
CFIKLMOST	FILM STOCK	CGIIMNPRS	SCRIMPING
CFILNSUUU	FUNICULUS	CGIINNNOV	CONNIVING
CFIMORSTU	SCUTIFORM	CGIINNOOT	COGNITION,
CFINNOOSU	CONFUSION	INCOGNITO	
		CGIINNRRU	INCURRING
		CGIINPRTU	PICTURING

CGIJNNORU	CONJURING
CGIKKLNNU	KNUCKLING
CGIKLMNOY	MOCKINGLY
CGIKLNNOU	UNLOCKING
CGIKLNRTU	TRUCKLING
CGIKLNSSU	SUCKLINGS
CGIKNNOOV	CONVOKING
CGIKNNOOR	UNCORKING
CGIKNOSST	STOCKINGS
CGIKOOPST	POGO STICK
CGILLNORS	SCROLLING
CGILLNOYY	CLOYINGLY
CGILMNOOO	MONOLOGIC
CGILMNOPY	COMPLYING
CGILMNPRU	CRUMPLING
CGILMOOYZ	ZYMOLOGIC
CGILNNNUY	CUNNINGLY
CGILNNOOR	LONGICORN
CGILNNOOS	CONSOLING
CGILNOOOY	ICONOLOGY
CGILNOORU	COLOURING
CGILNOPSU	COUPLINGS
CGILNOPUV	LOVING CUP
CGILNPRSU	SCRUPLING
CGILNSTTU	SCUTTLING
CGILNTTUY	CUTTINGLY
CGILOOOPT	TOPOLOGIC
CGILOOOSY	SOCIOLOGY
CGIMMNNOU	COMMUNING
CGIMMNOTU	COMMUTING
CGIMMNOSU	CONSUMING
CGIMNOOPS	COMPOSING
CGIMNOPTU	COMPUTING
CGIMNPRSU	SCRUMPING
CGINNNOOT	CONNOTING
CGINNOORS	CONSIGNOR
CGINNOOTT	COTTON GIN
CGINNOOVY	CONVOYING
CGINNORTU	TROUNCING
CGINNOSTU	CONTUSING
CGINOORTU	TOURCOING
CGINOPRRU	PROCURING
CGINORSSS	CROSSINGS
CGINORSSU	SCOURINGS
CGINORTUY	CONGRUITY
CGINRRSUY	SCURRYING
CGINRSTUY	CURTSYING
CGLMOOOSY	COSMOLOGY
CGMNOOOSY	COSMOGONY
CGNNOOTTU	GUN COTTON
CGNOORSUU	CONGRUOUS
CHHHIIMNO	HO CHI MINH
CHHIMRSTY	RHYTHMICS
CHHINORTW	NORTHWICH

CHHINTTUW	WITCH-HUNT	CIIIMSTTW	WITTICISM	CIKLORSTW	WRISTLOCK
CHHKLLOOY	HOLLYHOCK	CIIINNOSS	INCISIONS	CIKMOORSS	SICKROOMS
CHIIILPPP	PHILIPPIC	CIIINNRST	INTRINSIC	CIKOSSSTT	STOCKISTS
CHIILLOPY	LYOPHILIC	CIIINOSTZ	ZIONISTIC	CILLMORUY	COLLYRIUM
CHIILLPTY	PHYLLITIC	CIIJLNOPT	CLIP JOINT	CILLMOUUV	COLLUVIUM
CHIILNNPS	LINCHPINS	CIIKLLOSS	OIL SLICKS	CILLNOOSU	COLLUSION
CHIILOOPZ	ZOOPHILIC	CIIKLPSST	LIPSTICKS	CILLNOSSU	SCULLIONS
CHIILOOTT	OTOLITHIC	CIIKNPPRS	PINPRICKS	CILLOOOTY	COYOTILLO
CHIILORTU	UROLITHIC	CIIKNPSST	STICKPINS	CILMNOSTU	COLUMNIST
CHIILORTY	RHYOLITIC	CIILLNOOS	COLLISION	CILMOOPSY	POLYSOMIC
CHIILPSTU	SULPHITIC	CIILLNOOT	COTILLION,	CILMOSSUU	SOUL MUSIC
CHIILPTTY	TYPHLITIC		OCTILLION	CILMOTYYZ	ZYMOLYTIC
CHIINOSTU	CHITINOUS	CIILLOPTY	LIPOLYTIC	CILNOORUU	UNICOLOUR
CHIIOPSST	SOPHISTIC	CIILMPRSY	SCRIMPILY	CILNOOSST	COLONISTS
CHIIORRSS	CIRRHOSIS	CIILMRSSY	LYRICISMS	CILNOOSTU	LOCUTIONS
CHIIORSST	TRICHOSIS	CIILNNOSU	INCLUSION	CILNOSTYY	CYTOLYSIN
CHIIPSSTY	PHYSICIST	CIILNOPTU	PUNCTILIO,	CILOOPSUY	COPIOUSLY
CHIKLMOST	LOCKSMITH		UNPOLITIC	CILOORRTU	TRICOLOUR
CHIKLPSUY	PUCKISHLY	CIILOOPST	POLITICOS	CILOORSTU	COLOURIST
CHIKMNPSU	CHIPMUNKS	CIILOORST	SOLICITOR	CILOPPTYY	POLYTYPIC
CHIKOOPTT	TOOTHPICK	CIILOOSSS	SCOLIOSIS	CILORRSUY	CURSORILY
CHIKOPSTW	WHIPSTOCK	CIILOPRTY	PYROLITIC	CILORSUUY	CURIOUSLY
CHILLMOPY	PHYLLOMIC	CIILOSUVY	VICIOUSLY	CILOSSTYY	CYTOLYSIS
CHILLNOOT	LOINCLOTH	CIILRSSTY	LYRICISTS	CILRSTTUU	CULTURIST
CHILLOSTY	COLTISHLY	CIILSSTTY	STYLISTIC	CIMMMNOSU	COMMUNISM
CHILLOSUY	SLOUCHILY	CIIMMSSTY	MYSTICISM	CIMMNNOOU	COMMUNION
CHILMOOTY	HOMOLYTIC	CIIMNORUZ	ZIRCONIUM	CIMMNOOOS	MONOSOMIC
CHILNNOOS	NICHOLSON	CIIMOOSST	ISOSMOTIC	CIMMNOOOT	COMMOTION
CHILOOPTY	HOLOTYPIC	CIIMORSTV	VORTICISM	CIMMNOSTU	COMMUNIST
CHILOORSS	CHLOROSIS	CIINNNOTU	INUNCTION	CIMMNOTUY	COMMUNITY
CHILORTUY	ULOTRICHY	CIINNORSU	INCURSION	CIMMOORTY	MICROTOMY
CHILOSTTY	CYSTOLITH	CIINNOSSW	WISCONSIN	CIMNNOOOT	MONOTONIC
CHIMMNNOY	HOMONYMIC	CIINNSSTT	INSTINCTS	CIMNNOSYY	SYNONYMIC
CHIMNOOST	MONOSTICH	CIINOOPRT	INOTROPIC	CIMNNOTUU	CONTINUUM
CHIMNOPSY	SYMPHONIC	CIINOPSSU	SUSPICION	CIMNOOPTY	MONOTYPIC,
CHIOOPRTT	ORTHOPTIC	CIINORSUU	INCURIOUS		TOPONYMIC
CHIOOPTYZ	ZOOPHYTIC	CIINOSTVY	SYNOVITIC	CIMNOSSTU	MISCOUNTS
CHIOPRSTU	COURTSHIP	CIIOOPRST	ISOTROPIC	CIMNSTUYY	SYNCYTIUM
CHIOPRSYY	HYPOCRISY	CIIOOSSTX	TOXICOSIS	CINNOOSTU	CONTINUOS,
CHIOPSSSY	PSYCHOSIS	CIIOPRSTT	TROPISTIC		CONTUSION
CHIORRSSU	SCIRRHOUS	CIIORSTTU	TOURISTIC	CINNOOSUU	INNOCUOUS
CHIPRSTTY	TRIPTYCHS	CIIORSTTV	VORTICIST	CINOOORRS	CORROSION
CHKLMOOST	STOCKHOLM	CIIORSTUV	VIRTUOSIC	CINOOPRSS	SCORPIONS
CHLNOTUUY	UNCOUTHLY	CIIORSTUY	CURIOSITY	CINOPRRTU	INCORRUPT
CHLOPPTYY	POLYPTYCH	CIIOSSTVY	VISCOSITY	CINOSSTUV	VISCOUNTS
CHNNORSYY	SYNCHRONY	CIIRSTTUY	RUSTICITY	CIOOOPRSZ	ZOOSPORIC
CHOOOPPTY	PHOTOCOPY	CIJKOSSST	JOSS STICK	CIOOPSSTU	POSTICOUS
CHOOOPRSY	HOROSCOPY	CIJKOSSTY	JOYSTICKS	CKKNOOSTU	KNOCKOUTS
CHORSSTTU	SHORT CUTS	CIJNNOSTU	JUNCTIONS	CKLLNOORR	ROCK 'N' ROLL
CIIIILLTY	ILLICITLY	CIJNNOTTU	T-JUNCTION	CKMOOORST	STOCKROOM
CIIILLSTV	CIVIL LIST	CIKKOOSSU	KOSCIUSKO	CKNOOOSTW	COOKSTOWN
CIIILMOPT	IMPOLITIC	CIKLLNUUY	UNLUCKILY	CKNOORRWW	CROWNWORK
CIIILORTV	VITRIOLIC	CIKLNORSS	CROSS-LINK	CKOOORSTT	ROOTSTOCK
CIIILOSSS	SILICOSIS	CIKLOOPST	POLO STICK	CKOOPRSTT	STOCKPORT
		CIKLOORSU	COKULORIS	CKOOPSSTT	STOCKPOTS

CKOPRSTTU	TRUCK STOP	DDEEGHILT	DELIGHTED	DDEEOORSV	OVERDOSED
CLMOOOORT	LOCOMOTOR	DDEEGINNP	DEPENDING	DDEEORSTY	DESTROYED
CLMOOOSTY	COLOSTOMY	DDEEGINNR	REDDENING	DDEFFIINT	DIFFIDENT
CLMOORSTU	COLOSTRUM	DDEEGIRSS	DIGRESSED	DDEFGIIIN	DIGNIFIED
CLNOOPRSU	PROCONSUL	DDEEGJPRU	PREJUDGED	DDEFGILLO	GOLDFIELD
CLOOOPRST	PROTOCOLS	DDEEHIINT	HIDDENITE	DDEFILOOT	FLOOD TIDE
CLOPRRTUY	CORRUPTLY	DDEEHNORT	DETHRONED	DDEFNNOUU	UNFOUNDED
CLOPRSSTU	SCULPTORS	DDEEHNORU	DEERHOUND	DDEGGIORS	DISGORGED
CMMNOOOORS	ROSCOMMON	DDEEHNRTU	THUNDERED	DDEGHINRS	SHREDDING
CMNOOORST	COSMOTRON	DDEEHRRSS	SHREDDERS	DDEGIIIST	DIGITISED
CMOOORRTU	COURTROOM	DDEEIILMT	DELIMITED	DDEGIIITZ	DIGITIZED
CMOOORSST	MOTOCROSS	DDEEIILNS	SIDELINED	DDEGIIMSU	MISGUIDED
CMOOOSTTY	COSTOTOMY	DDEEIIOSX	DEOXIDISE	DDEGIINSS	GIDDINESS
CMOOSTTYY	CYSTOTOMY	DDEEIIOXZ	DEOXIDIZE	DDEGIISSU	DISGUISED
CNNNOOTUU	COUNT NOUN	DDEEIKLNR	REKINDLED	DDEGIJMSU	MISJUDGED
CNOPRTUUY	UP-COUNTRY	DDEEILLPS	DISPELLED	DDEGIJNRU	JUDDERING
COOOPRRST	ROOT CROPS	DDEEILLRV	DRIVELLED	DDEGINORR	DERRING-DO
COOPRSSTY	SPOROCYST	DDEEILMMN	MIDDLEMEN	DDEGINRRU	UNDERGIRD
COORRSSTW	CROSSWORT	DDEEILMSX	MIDDLESEX	DDEGIOOSS	GOOD-SISED
DDDEEHRSU	SHUDDERED	DDEEILOPS	DESPOILED	DDEGIOOSZ	GOOD-SIZED
DDDEEINST	DISTENDED	DDEEILORS	SOLDIERED	DDEGISSTU	DISGUSTED
DDDEENORU	REDOUNDED	DDEEIMMNO	DEMIMONDE	DDEGLNOOR	GOLDENROD
DDDEEORRS	DODDERERS	DDEEINNST	INTENDEDS	DDEGNORSU	UNDERDOGS
DDDEGILOS	DISLODGED	DDEEINORW	EIDERDOWN	DDEGOOORS	DO-GOODERS
DDDEGINOR	DODDERING	DDEEINOSV	NOSEDIVED	DDEHHNRTU	HUNDREDTH
DDDEIINSV	DIVIDENDS	DDEEINPSS	DISPENSED	DDEHIOSST	SHODDIEST
DDDEIINUV	UNDIVIDED	DDEEINRST	DISTENDER	DDEHOOSSW	WOODSHEDS
DDDEIIPRR	DRIP-DRIED	DDEEINRSU	UNDERSIDE,	DDEIIKNSV	SKIN-DIVED
DDDEEEKNW	WEEKENDED		UNDESIRED	DDEIIKRSV	DISK DRIVE
DDDEEEFIPR	DEEP FRIED	DDEEINSST	DISSENTED	DDEIILLST	DISTILLED
DDDEEFNRS	DEFENDERS	DDEEIOORS	DEODORISE	DDEIIMSSS	DISMISSED
DDEEEFNRU	UNDERFEED	DDEEIOORZ	DEODORIZE	DDEIIMTTW	DIM-WITTED
DDEEEGIPR	PEDIGREED	DDEEIOPST	DEPOSITED	DDEIINPRS	SPIN-DRIED
DDEEEILRV	DELIVERED	DDEEIORRS	SIDE ORDER	DDEIINSST	DISSIDENT
DDEEEILTT	TITLE DEED	DDEEIPRSS	DISPERSED	DDEIINSTU	DISUNITED
DDEEEINRX	DEXEDRINE	DDEEIPSTU	DEPUTISED	DDEILMNOT	MIDDLETON
DDEEEIPTX	EXPEDITED	DDEEIPTUZ	DEPUTIZED	DDEILMNOW	LOW-MINDED
DDEEEIRTU	DEUTERIDE	DDEEIRSSS	SIDE-DRESS	DDEILNRRU	UNRIDDLER
DDEEELMOR	REMODELED	DDEELLOPS	DEED POLLS,	DDEILORWW	WORLDWIDE
DDEEELOPV	DEVELOPED		DEEDS POLL	DDEILOSSV	DISSOLVED
DDEEENNOP	OPEN-ENDED	DDEELMORS	SMOLDERED	DDEIMNOPU	IMPOUNDED
DDEEENNPT	DEPENDENT	DDEELMORU	MOULDERED,	DDEIMNSSU	MUDDINESS
DDEEENPRT	PRETENDED		REMOULDED	DDEINORTU	OUTRIDDEN
DDEEEPRSS	DEPRESSED	DDEELNPRU	PLUNDERED	DDEINOSSW	DOWDINESS
DDEEERRSS	REDRESSED	DDEELOTVY	DEVOTEDLY	DDEINRSSU	RUDDINESS
DDEEERSWY	DYER'S-WEED	DDEEMOPUY	PUY DE DOME	DDEINSTUU	UNSTUDIED
DDEEESTUU	DESUETUDE	DDEENNORU	UNDERDONE	DDEIOPRST	DISPORTED
DDEEFGHNU	HEDGE FUND	DDEENOPRS	RESPONDED	DDEIOPRSV	DISPROVED
DDEEFGINN	DEFENDING	DDEENOPRT	PORTENDED	DDEIORRSS	DISORDERS
DDEEFGLNU	UNFLEDGED	DDEENOPUX	EXPOUNDED	DDEIORSTT	DISTORTED
DDEEFNORU	FOUNDERED	DDEENORSU	RESOUNDED	DDEIPRSTU	DISRUPTED
DDEEFORST	DEFROSTED	DDEENOSTY	EDDYSTONE	DDELNORSU	UNDERSOLD
DDEEGGGLO	DOGLEGGED	DDEENPSSU	SUSPENDED	DDEMNOOTU	ODD MEN OUT
DDEEGGILT	GILT-EDGED	DDEENRSSU	UNDRESSED	DDEMNOSUU	DUODENUMS
		DDEEOOPRT	TORPEDOED		

DDENNORUU	UNROUNDED	DEEEINQTU	QUIETENED
DDENOOPRS	DROPSONDE	DEEEINRSS	REEDINESS
DDENOORSW	DO WONDERS	DEEEINRST	TENDERISE
DDENORSSW	DRESS DOWN	DEEEINRTZ	TENDERIZE
DDEOPRRTU	PROTRUDED	DEEEINSSS	SEEDINESS
DDFGILORU	GUILDFORD	DEEEINSSW	WEEDINESS
DDFIOORTW	DRIFTWOOD	DEEEIPRRV	REPRIEVED
DDGGINNOS	DINGDONGS	DEEEIPRTX	EXPEDITER
DDGIILNNW	DWINDLING	DEEEIPRVW	PREVIEWED
DDGIILNTW	TWIDDLING	DEEEIPSST	SPEEDIEST
DDGOOORSW	GOOD WORDS	DEEEIRRTV	RETRIEVED
DDHIOOOWW	WIDOWHOOD	DEEEIRSTV	DETERSIVE
DEEEEKNRW	WEEKENDER	DEEEIRUZZ	ZUIDER ZEE
DEEEEMRRS	REDEEMERS	DEEEKLLNN	KENNELLED
DEEEENPST	STEEPENED	DEEELLPSW	SPEEDWELL
DEEEFGIKN	KNIFE-EDGE	DEEELNOPV	ENVELOPED
DEEEFHNRS	FRESHENED	DEEELNRWY	RENEWEDLY
DEEEFHRRS	REFRESHED	DEEELOPRV	DEVELOPER,
DEEEFINSV	DEFENSIVE		REDEVELOP
DEEEFLLRU	REFUELLED	DEEELPPRX	PERPLEXED
DEEEFMNRT	DEFERMENT,	DEEELRSTT	RESETTLED
	FERMENTED	DEEELRSTW	SWELTERED
DEEEFPRRR	PREFERRED	DEEEMNRTT	DETERMENT
DEEEFRRYZ	FREEZE-DRY	DEEEMOPRW	EMPOWERED
DEEEGIMNR	REDEEMING	DEEEMPPRT	PRE-EMPTED
DEEEGINNP	DEEPENING	DEEENNRST	ENTENDRES
DEEEGINRS	ENERGISED	DEEENNSSS	DENSENESS
DEEEGINRZ	ENERGIZED	DEEENPRRT	PRETENDER
DEEEGIPRS	PEDIGREES	DEEENPRST	PRESENTED
DEEEGIRST	GREEDIEST	DEEENPRTV	PREVENTED
DEEEGKLNT	KENTLEDGE	DEEENRRSV	REVERENDS
DEEEGLNOY	GOLDENEYE	DEEENRRTT	DETERRENT
DEEEGMNST	SEGMENTED	DEEENRSTT	TENDEREST
DEEEGNRTT	DETERGENT	DEEENSSVX	VEXEDNESS
DEEEGRRSS	REGRESSED	DEEEOPRST	DEPORTEES
DEEEGRRTT	REGRETTED	DEEEORRSS	REREDOSES
DEEEHIMPR	EPHEMERID	DEEEORSTV	STEVEDORE
DEEEHINPR	EPHEDRINE	DEEEOSRVX	OVERSEXED
DEEEHLRST	SHELTERED	DEEEPPPRR	RED PEPPER
DEEEHNPRR	REPREHEND	DEEEPPRSS	REPRESSED
DEEEHNRRU	HEREUNDER	DEEEPPRSV	PRESERVED
DEEEHORSW	HORSEWEED	DEEEPPRTV	PERVERTED
DEEEIILLMP	MILLEPEDE	DEEEPRSST	SPEEDSTER
DEEEILNNV	ENLIVENED	DEEEPRSSU	SUPERSEDE
DEEEILPTV	DEPLETIVE	DEEEPRSSX	EXPRESSED
DEEEILRRV	DELIVERER,	DEEEQRSTU	REQUESTED
	REDELIVER	DEEERRRSS	REDRESSER
DEEEILSSW	EDELWEISS	DEEERRSST	DESERTERS
DEEEILSTV	TELEVISED	DEEFFHILS	SHEFFIELD
DEEEIMNRT	DETERMINE	DEEFFINRT	DIFFERENT
DEEEIMPRR	PREMIERED	DEEFFINST	STIFFENED
DEEEIMSST	DISESTEEM	DEEFFIORT	FORFEITED
DEEEINNSS	NEEDINESS	DEEFFNORS	OFFENDERS
DEEEINOPR	PIONEERED	DEEFFOPRR	PROFFERED
DEEEINPTX	EXPEDIENT		

DEEFGHIRT	FREIGHTED
DEEFGIIRS	SIEGFRIED
DEEFGINNU	UNFEIGNED
DEEFGINRR	DEFERRING
DEEFGINRR	DEFERRING
DEEFGJORU	FOREJUDGE
DEEFGLNNO	DOG FENNEL
DEEFHLLUY	HEEDFULLY
DEEFHLOPS	SHEEPFOLD
DEEFHLORS	FREEHOLDS
DEEFHLORT	THREEFOLD
DEEFHRRTU	FURTHERED
DEEFIILMN	MINEFIELD
DEEFIILNR	INFIELDER
DEEFIILQU	LIQUEFIED
DEEFIINNS	DEFINIENS
DEEFIIPRS	PERFIDIES
DEEFIIPRT	PETRIFIED
DEEFIIRRT	TERRIFIED
DEEFIIRSS	FIRESIDES
DEEFIISTT	TESTIFIED
DEEFILMNS	FIELDSMEN
DEEFILMPS	FILM SPEED
DEEFILRSV	SELF-DRIVE
DEEFILSTT	FIELD-TEST
DEEFINNPR	PEN FRIEND
DEEFINNRU	UNREFINED
DEEFINNTU	FINE-TUNED
DEEFIPRTU	PUTREFIED
DEEFIPSTU	STUPEFIED
DEEFIRRTT	FRITTERED
DEEFIRSTU	SURFEITED
DEEFLLNNU	FUNNELLED
DEEFLLNUY	NEEDFULLY
DEEFLNOSV	SEVENFOLD
DEEFLNRTU	UNDERFELT
DEEFLOOTW	FLEETWOOD
DEEFLORRW	FREE WORLD
DEEFLRSTU	FLUSTERED
DEEFLRTTU	FLUTTERED
DEEFMOPRR	PERFORMED
DEEFNOOPS	SPOON-FEED
DEEFNOOST	FESTOONED
DEEFOPRSS	PROFESSED
DEEFORRST	DEFROSTER
DEEFRSTUY	DUTY-FREES
DEEGGGILN	LEGGINGED
DEEGGHHOS	HEDGEHOGS
DEEGGINRS	SNIGGERED
DEEGGIRRT	TRIGGERED
DEEGGSSTU	SUGGESTED
DEEGHHIPS	HIGH-SPEED
DEEGHIINV	INVEIGHED
DEEGHILNT	LIGHTENED
DEEGHILNW	WHEEDLING

DEEGHILRT	DELIGHTER	DEEHHINST	IN THE SHED	DEEIIRTVV	DIVERTIVE
DEEGHINTT	TIGHTENED	DEEHHIORS	HORSEHIDE	DEEIISSSU	SIDE ISSUE
DEEGHINUW	UNWEIGHED	DEEHHPRSS	SHEPHERDS	DEEIJNORR	REJOINDER
DEEGHNORU	ROUGHENED	DEEHIINRT	INHERITED	DEEIKLNNR	ENKINDLER
DEEGHNOTU	TOUGHENED	DEEHIKRSW	WHISKERED	DEEIKNSTW	STINKWEED
DEEGHOPSS	SHEEPDOGS	DEEHILLRV	HELLDIVER	DEEIKPPRS	SKIPPERED
DEEGHORSW	HEDGEROWS	DEEHILORU	HIERODULE	DEEIKRSTT	SKITTERED
DEEGIILNU	GUIDELINE	DEEHILPRS	ELDERSHIP	DEEIKSSTT	DISKETTES
DEEGIILNV	INVEIGLED	DEEHILRST	SLITHERED	DEEILLLNW	WELL-LINED
DEEGIINSS	DIGENESIS	DEEHILRSV	SHRIVELED	DEEILLLOW	WELL-OILED
DEEGIINTY	TIE-DYEING	DEEHIMMRS	SHIMMERED	DEEILLMNO	ILL-OMENED
DEEGIISTV	DIGESTIVE	DEEHIMOST	METHODISE	DEEILLMTW	WELL-TIMED
DEEGILLOR	LIEGE LORD	DEEHIMOTX	METHOXIDE	DEEILLNSV	SNIVELLED
DEEGILMMR	GLIMMERED	DEEHIMOTZ	METHODIZE	DEEILLPRS	DISPELLER
DEEGILNPT	DEPLETING	DEEHIMPRW	WHIMPERED	DEEILLRRV	DRIVELLER
DEEGILNSS	SEEDLINGS	DEEHINNOV	EINDHOVEN	DEEILLRSU	SLIDE RULE
DEEGILNST	GLISTENED	DEEHINNRS	ENSHRINED	DEEILLRTU	TELLURIDE
DEEGILOOU	IDEOLOGUE	DEEHINNTU	IN THE NUDE	DEEILLRTW	WELL-TRIED
DEEGILOPR	RIDGEPOLE	DEEHINOPX	PHENOXIDE	DEEILLSVW	SWIVELLED
DEEGILOSU	EULOGISED	DEEHINORT	DINOTHERE	DEEILMMNS	MENDELISM
DEEGILOUZ	EULOGIZED	DEEHINPRT	TREPHINED	DEEILMNTV	DEVILMENT
DEEGILRTT	GLITTERED	DEEHINRSW	SWINEHERD	DEEILMORS	MELODISER
DEEGIMNRY	REMEDYING	DEEHIORST	THEORISED	DEEILMORZ	MELODIZER
DEEGIMORT	GEOMETRID	DEEHIORTZ	THEORIZED	DEEILMRTY	MERITEDLY
DEEGINNPX	EXPENDING	DEEHIOSTU	TIED HOUSE	DEEILNNRU	UNDERLINE
DEEGINNRR	RENDERING	DEEHIPPSS	SHEEPDIPS	DEEILNOPT	DEPLETION,
DEEGINNRT	TENDERING	DEEHIPRSW	WHISPERED		DIPLOTENE
DEEGINNTX	EXTENDING	DEEHIRSSV	DERVISHES	DEEILNOST	DELETIONS
DEEGINRRR	DERRINGER	DEEHLLOSV	SHOVELLED	DEEILNPTU	PLENITUDE
DEEGINRRT	DETERRING	DEEHLNOYY	HONEYEDLY	DEEILNRRU	UNDERLIER
DEEGINRSS	DESIGNERS	DEEHLORST	HOLSTERED	DEEILNRTU	INTERLUDE
DEEGINRST	DESERTING	DEEHMNNOT	ON THE MEND	DEEILNTVY	EVIDENTLY
DEEGINRSV	DESERVING	DEEHMOORT	HODOMETER	DEEILOPRS	DESPOILER
DEEGINRTU	NEGRITUDE	DEEHMORST	SMOTHERED	DEEILOPTX	EXPLOITED
DEEGINRTV	DIVERGENT	DEEHNNORT	ENTHRONED	DEEILORRS	ORDERLIES
DEEGINRUV	GERUNDIVE	DEEHNOPTY	ENDOPHYTE	DEEILORSV	EVILDOERS
DEEGINSTT	DETESTING	DEEHNORRT	DETHRONER	DEEILRRSS	RIDERLESS
DEEGIOSST	GEODESIST	DEEHNORST	SHORTENED	DEEILRSVY	DIVERSELY
DEEGIPRST	PREDIGEST	DEEHNRRTU	THUNDERER	DEEILRTUY	ERUDITELY
DEEGIRRSS	DIGRESSER	DEEHOORTX	HETERODOX	DEEIMMORS	MEMORISED
DEEGIRRUU	DE RIGUEUR	DEEHOPSTU	DEEP SOUTH	DEEIMMORZ	MEMORIZED
DEEGJMNTU	JUDGEMENT	DEEHRSSTW	SHREWDEST	DEEIMNNOT	MENTIONED
DEEGJPRRU	PREJUDGER	DEEHRSTTU	SHUTTERED	DEEIMNNRU	UNDERMINE
DEEGKLNOW	KNOWLEDGE	DEEHSSTTU	DUSTSHEET	DEEIMNORS	MODERNISE
DEEGKOPRW	POWDER KEG	DEEIIINPR	PIERIDINE	DEEIMNORZ	MODERNIZE
DEEGLLORV	GROVELLED	DEEIILLMP	MILLIPEDE	DEEIMNOSS	DES MOINES
DEEGLNNOU	GUENDOLEN	DEEIILMPR	IMPERILED	DEEIMNOST	MOISTENED
DEEGLNNOW	GWENDOLEN	DEEIILNSS	SIDELINES	DEEIMNPST	PEDIMENTS
DEEGNNORU	UNDERGONE	DEEIIMPRS	EPIDERMIS	DEEIMNNRS	REMINDERS
DEEGNNSSU	DUNGENESS	DEEIIMRTV	DRIVE-TIME	DEEIMNRTT	DETRIMENT
DEEGNOORW	GREENWOOD	DEEIINSST	DENSITIES,	DEEIMNSST	SEDIMENTS
DEEGNORRU	UNDERGOER		DESTINIES	DEEIMOORT	METEOROID
DEEGNORSS	ENGROSSED	DEEIIPSSW	SIDESWIPE	DEEIMORST	DOSIMETER
DEEGOPRRU	REGROUPED	DEEIIRRSV	RIVERSIDE	DEEIMPRSS	IMPRESSED

DEEIMPRST	DISTEMPER	DEELNSWWY	NEWLYWEDS	DEFGIIINS	SIGNIFIED
DEEIMPRTT	PERMITTED	DEELOPRSY	REPOSEDLY	DEFGIILOR	GLORIFIED
DEEIMRTUU	DEUTERIUM	DEELORRUV	OVERRULED	DEFGIINNR	INFRINGED
DEEINNOPS	PENSIONED	DEELPRTUY	REPUTEDLY	DEFGIIRSU	DISFIGURE
DEEINNORT	INTERNODE	DEEMNNOTW	ENDOWMENT	DEFGILNNO	ENFOLDING
DEEINNOTT	DETENTION	DEEMNNRUY	RUNNYMEDE	DEFGIMNOR	DEFORMING
DEEINNRTU	INDENTURE	DEEMNOORT	ONDOMETER	DEFGINNRU	REFUNDING
DEEINNSSS	SNIDENESS	DEEMNOPRS	ENDOSPERM	DEFHIILSV	DEVILFISH
DEEINOPTX	PENTOXIDE	DEEMNOPSU	SPODUMENE	DEFHIIORR	HORRIFIED
DEEINORST	DESERTION	DEEMNORTT	TORMENTED	DEFHINRSU	FURNISHED
DEEINORSW	ROSINWEED	DEEMNORTU	REMOUNTED	DEFHLOOOW	WHOLEFOOD
DEEINOSSV	NOSEDIVES	DEEMNOSTU	ENDOSTEUM	DEFHOOOTT	HOTFOOTED
DEEINPRRT	REPRINTED	DEEMOORST	ODOMETERS	DEFIIIRTV	VITRIFIED
DEEINPRSS	DISPENSER	DEEMPRTTU	TRUMPETED	DEFIIJSTU	JUSTIFIED
DEEINPRST	PRESIDENT	DEEMRRRSU	MURDERERS	DEFIILLMO	MOLLIFIED
DEEINRRSU	REINSURED	DEEMRRSSU	MURDERESS	DEFIILLNU	NULLIFIED
DEEINRSST	DISSENTER,	DEENNORTU	UNDERTONE	DEFIILLOS	OILFIELDS
RESIDENTS, TIREDNESS		DEENNRTUW	UNDERWENT	DEFIILLRR	FIRE DRILL
DEEINRSSW	WEIRDNESS	DEENOOPRS	ENDOSPORE	DEFIILMSU	SEMIFLUID
DEEINRSTT	TRENDIEST	DEENOPRRS	RESPONDER	DEFIILPRT	FIELD TRIP
DEEINSSTW	WITNESSED	DEENOPRRV	PROVENDER	DEFIILRSU	FLUIDISER
DEEIOPRVW	POWER DIVE	DEENOPRSV	OVERSPEND	DEFIILRSW	WILDFIRES
DEEIORRRV	OVERRIDER	DEENOPRUX	EXPOUNDER	DEFIILRUZ	FLUIDIZER
DEEIORRVV	OVERDRIVE	DEENPRSSU	SUSPENDER	DEFIIMMMU	MUMMIFIED
DEEIORSSV	OVERSISED	DEENRRRSU	SURRENDER	DEFIIMNNY	INDEMNIFY
DEEIORSVZ	OVERSIZED	DEENRSTTU	ENTRUSTED	DEFIIMORS	MODIFIERS
DEEIORTTX	TETROXIDE	DEENRSTUW	WET-NURSED	DEFIIMORT	MORTIFIED
DEEIPPRRS	PERSPIRED	DEENRSTYY	DYSENTERY	DEFIIMRWY	MIDWIFERY
DEEIPRRSS	DISPERSER	DEEOOPRST	TORPEDOES	DEFIIMSTY	MYSTIFIED
DEEIPRSST	PERSISTED	DEEOOORSV	OVERDOSES	DEFIINNRW	WINNIFRED
DEEIPRSTU	DISREPUTE	DEEOPPRRS	PROSPERED	DEFIINRTY	DENITRIFY
DEEIPSSST	SIDESTEPS	DEEOPPRSS	OPPRESSED	DEFIINSST	DISINFEST
DEEIRSSST	DRESSIEST	DEEOPPRST	STOPPERED	DEFIIRRST	STIR-FRIED
DEEIRSTUV	SERVITUDE	DEEOPRRSS	DEPRESSOR	DEFIIRSVY	DIVERSIFY
DEEIRTTTW	TWITTERED	DEEOPSSSS	POSSESSED	DEFIIRTVY	DEVITRIFY
DEEIRTTXY	DEXTERITY	DEEORRSSV	OVERDRESS	DEFIKLORW	FIELDWORK
DEEISTTTU	DESTITUTE	DEEORRSTX	DEXTRORSE	DEFILLRUY	DIREFULLY
DEEJNORUY	JOURNEYED	DEEORRSTY	DESTROYER	DEFILMNRU	REMINDFUL
DEEJOORVY	OVERJOYED	DEEORSTUX	DEXTEROUS	DEFILMSUY	DEMULSIFY
DEEKNOORS	SNOOKERED	DEEOSTTUV	DEVOUTEST	DEFILNOSW	SNOWFIELD
DEEKNORTW	NETWORKED	DEEPRRSSU	PRESSURED	DEFIMNORT	DENTIFORM
DEEKNQRUU	DUNKERQUE	DEEPRSTTU	SPUTTERED	DEFIMNORU	UNIFORMED
DEELLMMPU	PUMMELLED	DEERSTTTU	STUTTERED	DEFIMORTY	DEFORMITY
DEELLMOOR	ROLE MODEL	DEFFGIINR	DIFFERING	DEFIMSTYY	DEMYSTIFY
DEELLNNTU	TUNNELLED	DEFFGINNO	OFFENDING	DEFINORSU	FOUNDRIES
DEELLNRSU	UNDERSELL	DEFFIIORT	FORTIFIED	DEFIORSST	DISFOREST
DEELLNSSY	ENDLESSLY	DEFFIISUV	DIFFUSIVE	DEFIORTTU	FORTITUDE
DEELLOPPR	PROPELLED	DEFFILLLU	FULFILLED	DEFIOTTTU	OUTFITTED
DEELMMPTU	PLUMMETED	DEFFILSUY	DIFFUSELY	DEFLLLOUY	DOLEFULLY
DEELMOORV	VELODROME	DEFFLNRUU	UNRUFFLED	DEFLLNOUW	WELL-FOUND
DEELNOOSS	LOOSE ENDS	DEFGGIINT	FIDGETING	DEFLLRSSU	FULL DRESS
DEELNOOST	LODESTONE	DEFGGILLN	FLEDGLING	DEFLMMOUX	FLUMMOXED
DEELNPRRU	PLUNDERER	DEFGHILOT	EIGHTFOLD	DEFLNORSU	FLOUNDERS
DEELNSTTU	UNSETTLED	DEFGHIOSS	DOGFISHES	DEFLNORUW	WONDERFUL

DEFNOORTU	UNDERFOOT
DEFOORRSW	FOREWORDS
DEFORRSTT	STRETFORD
DEGGIILNR	RIDGELING
DEGGIILRU	GIRL GUIDE
DEGGIINNS	DESIGNING
DEGGIINRV	DIVERGING
DEGGIINST	DIGESTING
DEGGIORRS	DISGORGER
DEGGLNPUU	UNPLUGGED
DEGGLRSTU	STRUGGLED
DEGHHIIST	HIGH TIDES
DEGHHINOT	HIGH-TONED
DEGHIILNS	SHIELDING
DEGHIILST	SIDELIGHT
DEGHIINNR	HINDERING
DEGHIINRT	DITHERING
DEGHIJPSU	JUDGESHIP
DEGHILMSU	GUMSHIELD
DEGHILRST	RED LIGHTS
DEGHIMNRU	HUMDINGER
DEGHINSTU	UNSIGHTED
DEGHIORTU	DOUGHTIER
DEGHMOORT	GODMOTHER
DEGHNNRUU	UNDERHUNG
DEGHNORUY	GREYHOUND
DEGHOOSSU	DOGHOUSES
DEGIIIMRS	SEMIRIGID
DEGIIINST	DIGNITIES
DEGIIIRST	DIGITISER
DEGIIIRTZ	DIGITIZER
DEGIILLNV	DEVILLING
DEGIILNOV	EVILDOING
DEGIILNRV	DRIVELING
DEGIIMNNP	IMPENDING
DEGIIMNNR	REMINDING
DEGIIMNST	DEMISTING
DEGIIMRSU	MISGUIDER
DEGIINNNT	INDENTING,
INTENDING	
DEGIINNSS	DINGINESS
DEGIINOST	DIGESTION
DEGIINPRS	PRESIDING
DEGIINPRV	DEPRIVING
DEGIINPSS	DESPISING
DEGIINRTU	INTRIGUED
DEGIINRTV	DIVERTING
DEGIINSST	DESISTING
DEGIINSTU	DISTINGUE
DEGIINSTV	DIVESTING
DEGIIOPRS	PRODIGIES
DEGIIQRSU	SQUIDGIER
DEGIIRRSV	VERDIGRIS
DEGIIRSSU	DISGUISER

DEGIISSSU	DISGUISES
DEGIJMRSU	MISJUDGER
DEGIKLOSV	KID GLOVES
DEGILLMNO	MODELLING
DEGILLNOV	LONG-LIVED
DEGILLNOY	YODELLING
DEGILLNSW	DWELLINGS
DEGILMNOR	GOLD-MINER,
MOLDERING	
DEGILMNOS	GOLDMINES
DEGILNNRU	UNDERLING
DEGILNNTU	INDULGENT
DEGILNOOR	GONDOLIER
DEGILNOPR	DEPLORING
DEGILNOPX	EXPLODING
DEGILNOPY	DEPLOYING
DEGILNORS	SOLDERING
DEGILNOSS	GODLINESS
DEGILNOSU	DELOUSING
DEGILNOTU	LONGITUDE
DEGILNOVV	DEVOLVING
DEGILOOST	GOODLIEST
DEGILOSTT	GLOTTIDES
DEGILSSTU	SLUDGIEST
DEGIMNRRU	DEMURRING,
MURDERING	
DEGINNOPR	PONDERING
DEGINNORS	ENDORSING
DEGINNORW	WONDERING
DEGINNRSU	SUNDERING
DEGINNRUW	UNDERWING
DEGINOORV	OVERDOING
DEGINOPRT	DEPORTING
DEGINOPRW	POWDERING
DEGINOPSS	PODGINESS
DEGINORRW	REWORDING
DEGINORUV	DEVOURING
DEGINPSSU	PUDGINESS
DEGINRSSS	DRESSINGS
DEGINRTUX	EXTRUDING
DEGIOPRTY	PTERYGOID
DEGIOPSTU	GUIDEPOST
DEGIOSSTT	STODGIEST
DEGJMNSTU	JUDGMENTS
DEGLLOSSY	GODLESSLY
DEGLNNOWY	GWENDOLYN
DEGLNOOPR	PROLONGED
DEGLNORSU	GROUNDSEL
DEGLOOSUU	DUOLOGUES
DEGNOORRW	WRONGDOER
DEGNOPRUW	GUNPOWDER
DEGOOPRRU	PROROGUED
DEGORRSTU	DRUGSTORE
DEHHIINOS	HOIDENISH
DEHHIKMOS	SHEIKHDOM

DEHHILNOS	HOLINSHED
DEHHINOSY	HOYDENISH
DEHHIOPPS	PHOSPHIDE
DEHHLLNOU	HELLHOUND
DEHHLOOSU	HOUSEHOLD
DEHHLORST	THRESHOLD
DEHHNOORU	HOREHOUND
DEHIIINST	HISTIDINE
DEHIILLSS	HILLSIDES
DEHIILRSS	DISRELISH
DEHIIMNTY	THYMIDINE
DEHIINNRU	HIRUNDINE
DEHIINOOP	IDIOPHONE
DEHIIPRST	PETRI DISH
DEHIISTWW	WIDTHWISE
DEHIJMNOS	DEMIJOHNS
DEHIKKOOZ	KOZHIKODE
DEHILOORT	RHODOLITE
DEHILORSW	WILD HORSE
DEHILOSTW	DISH TOWEL
DEHILOSUY	HIDEOUSLY
DEHILPSSU	SULPHIDES
DEHILRRUY	HURRIEDLY
DEHIMMOST	METHODISM
DEHIMNOOT	IN THE MOOD
DEHIMNORT	TRONDHEIM
DEHIMNSSU	HUMIDNESS
DEHIMOSTT	METHODIST
DEHIMPRTU	TRIUMPHED
DEHINOORT	RHODONITE
DEHINORRT	TRIHEDRON
DEHINORSU	NOURISHED
DEHINOSST	DISHONEST,
HEDONISTS	
DEHINRRUU	UNHURRIED
DEHIOOTWW	HOWTOWDIE,
WHITEWOOD	
DEHIOPRSS	SPHEROIDS
DEHIOPRSW	WORSHIPED
DEHIOSSSW	SIDESHOWS
DEHKLOOST	STOKEHOLD
DEHKNOOOS	HOOK-NOSED
DEHLMNOPY	ENDOLYMPH
DEHLOORSV	HOLDOVERS
DEHLOPRSU	UPHOLDERS
DEHLORSSU	SHOULDERS
DEHLORSYY	HYDROLYSE
DEHLORTTT	THROTTLED
DEHLORTYY	HYDROLYTE
DEHMNOOPR	ENDOMORPH
DEHMOORTY	HODOMETRY
DEHNNOOPS	SPHENODON
DEHNNOSUW	NEWSHOUND
DEHNORSTU	UNDERSHOT
DEHOORSTU	HERODOTUS

DEHOOSSSU	DOSSHOUSE	
DEHOPRSST	POTSHERDS	
DEHORSSTU	STUDHORSE	
DEIIIKNTT	IDENTIKIT	
DEIIILQSU	LIQUIDISE	
DEIIILQUZ	LIQUIDIZE	
DEIIIMMNS	MINIMISED	
DEIIIMMNZ	MINIMIZED	
DEIIINNQU	QUINIDINE	
DEIIINSSS	DISSEISIN	
DEIIKLNST	KINDLIEST	
DEIIKNRSV	SKIN DIVER	
DEIILLNST	INSTILLED	
DEIILLOPR	PILLORIED	
DEIILLOPS	ELLIPSOID	
DEIILLRST	DISTILLER	
DEIILMNTU	UNLIMITED	
DEIILMOSS	SEMISOLID	
DEIILMRSU	DELIRIUMS	
DEIILNPRS	SPINDLIER	
DEIILNSSV	LIVIDNESS	
DEIILOPRT	REPTILOID	
DEIILORSU	DELIRIOUS	
DEIILPSSS	SIDESLIPS	
DEIILSUVV	DIVULSIVE	
DEIIMMNSU	IMMUNISED	
DEIIMMNUZ	IMMUNIZED	
DEIIMNNOS	DIMENSION	
DEIIMNNTY	INDEMNITY	
DEIIMNOQU	DOMINIQUE	
DEIIMNPRT	IMPRINTED	
DEIIMNRSS	MINIDRESS	
DEIIMNRTW	MIDWINTER	
DEIIMOPST	OPTIMISED	
DEIIMOPTZ	OPTIMIZED	
DEIIMPRSU	PRESIDIUM	
DEIINNNOT	INDENTION	
DEIINNORT	RENDITION	
DEIINNOSU	UNIONISED	
DEIINNOTT	DENTITION	
DEIINNOTV	VENDITION	
DEIINNOUZ	UNIONIZED	
DEIINNSSW	WINDINESS	
DEIINOPRT	PERDITION	
DEIINOPSS	INDISPOSE	
DEIINORSS	IRONSIDES	
DEIINORSV	DIVERSION	
DEIINORTT	DETRITION	
DEIINORTU	ERUDITION	
DEIINPPSW	WINDPIPES	
DEIINRSST	DIRTINESS	
DEIINSSVV	VIVIDNESS	
DEIINSSZZ	DIZZINESS	

DEIIORSSS	DISSEISOR,
	SIDEROSIS
DEIIOSSTU	SEDITIOUS
DEIIRSTVY	DIVERSITY
DEIJORRSY	JOYRIDERS
DEIKLLNSU	UNSKILLED
DEIKLNPRS	SPRINKLED
DEIKNNSTU	UNKINDEST
DEIKNSSSU	DUSKINESS
DEIKRSSVY	SKYDIVERS
DEILLMNOU	MULLIONED
DEILLORRW	WORLDLIER
DEILLORST	LORDLIEST
DEILLORSY	SOLDIERLY
DEILLSSTU	DUELLISTS
DEILLSTTY	STILTEDLY
DEILMNOSS	MOLDINESS
DEILMOOST	DOLOMITES
DEILMOOSU	MELODIOUS
DEILMORST	OLD-TIMERS
DEILMOSTU	MOULDIEST
DEILMTTUU	MULTITUDE
DEILNOPRU	PURLOINED
DEILNOPTY	POINTEDLY
DEILNORSU	UNDERSOIL
DEILNOSSS	SOLIDNESS
DEILNOSSU	DELUSIONS
DEILNPSST	SPLIT ENDS
DEILNRSSU	LURIDNESS
DEILNRSSW	SWINDLERS
DEILORRWY	WORRIEDLY
DEILORSSV	DISSOLVER
DEILOSSTU	DISSOLUTE
DEILOSTUY	TEDIOUSLY
DEILOSUVY	DEVIOUSLY
DEILPTUXY	DUPLEXITY
DEILSTTWY	TWISTEDLY
DEIMMMRSU	MIDSUMMER
DEIMMNORS	MODERNISM
DEIMMNOUY	NEODYMIUM
DEIMMOSTY	IMMODESTY
DEIMNOORT	MONITORED
DEIMNOOSS	MOODINESS
DEIMNOOST	DEMOTIONS
DEIMNOOSX	MONOXIDES
DEIMNOPRU	IMPOUNDER
DEIMNORST	MODERNIST
DEIMNORTY	MODERNITY
DEIMNPRTU	IMPRUDENT
DEIMNPSTU	DUMPINESS
DEIMNRSTU	RUDIMENTS
DEIMOOORT	IDEOMOTOR
DEIMOORST	MOTORISED
DEIMOORTY	IODOMETRY

DEIMOORTZ	MOTORIZED
DEIMOOSST	SODOMITES
DEIMOPSST	DESPOTISM
DEIMOQSTU	MISQUOTED
DEIMORSTY	DOSIMETRY
DEINNNOSU	INNUENDOS
DEINNOOTX	ENDOTOXIN
DEINNOSTU	TENDINOUS
DEINNRSTV	TV DINNERS
DEINNRSUU	UNINSURED
DEINNRTTU	UNDERTINT
DEINOOPRT	PORTIONED
DEINOOPSW	PINEWOODS
DEINOOSSW	WOODINESS
DEINOOSTV	DEVOTIONS
DEINOPRST	DRIPSTONE
DEINOPRTV	PROVIDENT
DEINORRWW	WINDROWER
DEINORSSW	ROWDINESS,
	WORDINESS
DEINORSTU	DETRUSION
DEINOSSTT	DOTTINESS
DEINPRRSY	SPIN-DRYER
DEINPRSTU	UNSTRIPED
DEINPSTWW	WINDSWEPT
DEINRRSTU	INTRUDERS
DEINRSTTU	INTRUSTED
DEINRSTTY	DENTISTRY
DEIOOPRST	DEPOSITOR
DEIOOPRTX	PROTOXIDE
DEIOPRRSV	PROVIDERS
DEIOPRSTU	DIPTEROUS
DEIORRSTT	DISTORTER
DEIORRSTU	OUTRIDERS
DEIORSSTU	DIOESTRUS,
	OUTSIDERS
DEIOTTTUW	OUTWITTED
DEIPRRSSU	SURPRISED
DEIPRRSTU	DISRUPTER
DEIPRTTUU	TURPITUDE
DEIPSSTTU	STUPIDEST
DEIRSSTTU	STURDIEST
DEJNOORSU	SOJOURNED
DEKLNNRUY	DRUNKENLY
DEKNOORTU	UNDERTOOK
DELLNORSS	DROLLNESS
DELMNOSTW	MELTDOWNS
DELMNPSUU	PENDULUMS
DELNNOOOS	SOLENODON
DELNOPRSU	SPLENDOUR
DELNOPRTU	UNDERPLOT
DELNOPSUU	PENDULOUS
DELNOSSSU	SOUNDLESS
DELNPRTUY	PRUDENTLY
DELOOOSUW	WOODLOUSE

DELOORRSV	OVERLORDS	DGGHINOOT	GOODNIGHT	DGINOPPRS	DROPPINGS
DELOORSSU	ODOURLESS	DGGIILLNY	GLIDINGLY	DGKLOOOOS	GOOD LOOKS
DELORSTUY	DESULTORY	DGGIILNNU	INDULGING	DGNNORTUU	GROUNDNUT
DEMMNOSSU	SUMMONSED	DGGIILNUV	DIVULGING	DHHIKNSUU	HINDU KUSH
DEMNNORSU	ROUNDSMEN	DGGIILNUY	GUIDINGLY	DHIIIPSTY	HISPIDITY
DEMNOPSUY	PSEUDONYM	DGGIJLNUY	JUDGINGLY	DHIIKSWZZ	WHIZZ KIDS
DEMNORSSW	SWORDSMEN	DGGINNORU	GROUNDING	DHIILNRWW	WHIRLWIND
DEMNORSSY	SYNDROMES	DGGIRSSTU	DRUGGISTS	DHIILOPSY	SYPHILOID
DEMNORSTU	UNDERMOST	DGHHIINST	HINDSIGHT	DHIIMNOOS	HINDOOISM
DEMORRSUU	MURDEROUS	DGHHINOPT	DIPHTHONG	DHIINOPTY	TYPHOIDIN
DENNOOSTU	DO ONE'S NUT	DGHHOORSU	ROUGHHOOD	DHILLOSTY	DOLTISHLY
DENNORSSU	ROUNDNESS	DGHIIMNST	MIDNIGHTS	DHILNNOSY	DONNISHLY
DENNORSUW	SUNDOWNER	DGHILMOST	GOLDSMITH	DHILOPRSS	LORDSHIPS
DENNOSSSU	SOUNDNESS	DGHILNOPU	UPHOLDING	DHILPRSUY	PRUDISHLY
DENOOPPST	POSTPONED	DGHILOPRT	DROPLIGHT	DHIMOOOOS	HOODOOISM
DENOOPPSU	UNOPPOSED	DGHIMOPSY	SPHYGMOID	DHINNOTUU	WHODUNNIT
DENOOPRSS	SPONSORED	DGHINORSU	SHROUDING	DHINOOPRS	DONORSHIP,
DENOOPRSU	PONDEROUS	DGHINORTW	DOWNRIGHT	DHINOORSU	RHODOPSIN
DENOPPRRU	UNDERPROP	DGHLOORYY	HYDROLOGY	DHINOORSU	DISHONOUR
DENOPPSTU	UNSTOPPED	DGHNOSTUU	DOUGHNUTS	DHINOPRUW	WHIP-ROUND
DENOPRSSU	PROUDNESS	DGIIIKLNS	DISLIKING	DHINOSTUW	WHODUNITS
DENOPSTTU	UNSPOTTED	DGIIILNOZ	IDOLIZING	DHIOOSTTW	WITHSTOOD
DENORTTUU	UNTUTORED	DGIIINNRT	NITRIDING	DHKMNOOOS	MONKSHOOD
DEOOPRSST	DOORSTEPS	DGIIINNTY	INDIGNITY	DHKNORUYY	HUNKY-DORY
DEOPPRRTU	PURPORTED	DGIIINOTX	DIGITOXIN	DHLLOOOWY	HOLLYWOOD
DEOPPRSTU	SUPPORTED	DGIIINOXZ	OXIDIZING	DHLMOOTUU	LOUDMOUTH
DEORRSUUV	VERDUROUS	DGIIJNORY	JOYRIDING	DHLNOOOTU	HOLD OUT ON
DEPRSSSTU	PRESS-STUD	DGIIKNSVY	SKYDIVING	DHNNOORTW	NORTH DOWN
DETTTTTUU	TUT-TUTTED	DGIILLOOR	GORILLOID	DHNOORTWW	DOWNTHROW
DFFFOOSTU	FOODSTUFF	DGIILLMNOP	IMPLODING	DHNOOSSWW	SHOWDOWNS
DFFGIINSU	DIFFUSING	DGIILNNSW	SWINDLING	DHNOOSTUW	SOUTHDOWN
DFFIINOSU	DIFFUSION	DGIILNNWY	WINDINGLY	DHNOSSTUW	SHUTDOWNS
DFGGHIOST	DOGFIGHTS	DGIILNRZZ	DRIZZLING	DHOOORTXY	ORTHODOXY
DFGIIIRTY	FRIGIDITY	DGIIMNORS	GIRONDISM	DHOOPPSUY	PUPPYHOOD
DFGIIMNOY	MODIFYING	DGIIMNSSU	SIGISMUND	DHOPRSTYY	DYSTROPHY
DFGILNNOU	FOUNDLING,	DGIINNNUW	UNWINDING	DIIILMPTY	LIMPIDITY
	UNFOLDING	DGIINNORS	INDORSING	DIIILNPSY	INSIPIDLY
DFHILOORY	HYDROFOIL	DGIINNOSW	DISOWNING	DIIILQTUY	LIQUIDITY
DFHIORSSW	SWORDFISH	DGIINNRTU	INTRUDING	DIIINOSSU	INSIDIOUS
DFHLNOOUW	WOLFHOUND	DGIINOPRV	PROVIDING	DIIINOSSV	DIVISIONS
DFHLNSSUU	SLUSH FUND	DGIINOPSS	DISPOSING	DIIINOSUV	INVIDIOUS
DFHLOOOST	FOOTHOLDS	DGIINORRS	GRIDIRONS	DIILLMNOO	MODILLION
DFHNOOSUX	FOXHOUNDS	DGIINORST	GIRONDIST	DIILLMNSW	WINDMILLS
DFIILORTY	FLORIDITY	DGIINORTU	OUTRIDING	DIILNOSTU	DILUTIONS
DFIINPRST	SPINDRIFT	DGIINPSTU	DISPUTING	DIILNOSUV	DIVULSION
DFIKOOPRS	SKIDPROOF	DGIIRTTUY	TURGIDITY	DIILOSTTY	STOLIDITY
DFILLMOTU	MULTIFOLD	DGILLNORW	WORLDLING	DIIMNNOOS	DOMINIONS
DFILLTUUY	DUTIFULLY	DGILMNOOO	MONGOLOID	DIIMNOPST	MIDPOINTS
DFILMNNUU	UNMINDFUL	DGILMNOSU	MOULDINGS	DIIMOORTY	IRIDOTOMY
DFINORSTW	SNOWDRIFT	DGILMNPSU	DUMPLINGS	DIIMORSSY	DIMISSORY
DFNOOOPTU	FOOT-POUND	DGILNNRTU	TRUNDLING	DIINNOOQU	QUINONOID
DFNOOORRT	FRONT DOOR	DGINNOPSU	POUNDINGS	DIINOSSUY	DIONYSIUS
DFNRSTTUU	TRUST FUND	DGINNOSSU	SOUNDINGS	DIIOPRTTY	TORPIDITY
DFOOOSSTW	SOFTWOODS	DGINNOSWW	DOWNSWING	DIIORRTTY	TORRIDITY

DIIPRTTUY	PUTRIDITY	EEEFHNOPR	FREEPHONE
DIIPSTTUY	STUPIDITY	EEEFHNRRS	FRESHENER
DIKNOOSTW	STINKWOOD	EEEFHORRT	THEREFORE
DIKORRTWY	DIRTY WORK	EEEFHORRW	WHEREFORE
DILLMNOPS	MILLPONDS	EEEFHORST	FORESHEET
DILLOOPPY	POLYPLOID	EEEFHORSU	FREE HOUSE
DILOOPTUW	TULIPWOOD	EEEFHRRRS	REFRESHER
DIMMOPSUY	SYMPODIUM	EEEFILPRS	LIFE PEERS
DIMNORSTW	WINDSTORM	EEEFILRRV	FREE-LIVER
DIMOOOOSV	VOODOOISM	EEEFILRVX	REFLEXIVE
DIMOORRTY	DORMITORY	EEEFINRRT	INTERFERE
DINOOPRTW	WOODPRINT	EEEFLNSST	FLEETNESS
DINOPRRTU	ROUND-TRIP	EEEFLRSTY	FREESTYLE
DINOPTTUY	POINT DUTY	EEEFLRTTU	FLEURETTE
DINORTTUY	ROTUNDITY	EEEFMNRRT	FERMENTER
DIOOOOSTV	VOODOOIST	EEEFNORST	FREESTONE
DIOOPRSST	PROSODIST	EEEFNRRST	TREE FERNS
DJLLNRUUU	JULLUNDUR	EEEGGILNS	NEGLIGEES
DKORSTUWY	WORK-STUDY	EEEGGORTT	GEORGETTE
DLLNORUWY	UNWORLDLY	EEEGHILNT	GEHLENITE
DLNOOSSWW	SLOWDOWNS	EEEGHLRSS	SHEERLEGS
DMMNRSUUY	DUMMY RUNS	EEEGIISSS	EISEGESIS
DMNOORRUW	ROUNDWORM	EEEGIJNNT	JET ENGINE
DMORSSTTU	DUST STORM	EEEGIKNPS	PEKINGESE
DNNORRTUU	TURNROUND	EEEGIMNST	ESTEEMING
DNNORSTUW	DOWNTURNS	EEEGINNRS	ENGINEERS
DNOOPRSSW	SNOWDROPS	EEEGINNRV	VENEERING
DNOOPRSUW	DOWNPOURS	EEEGINPRR	PEREGRINE
DNOOPSSTU	SOUNDPOST	EEEGINRRS	ENERGISER
DNOOPSTUW	DOWNSPOUT	EEEGINRRZ	ENERGIZER
DNOORTUWW	WOUNDWORT	EEEGINRTT	TEETERING
DNORRSSUU	SURROUNDS	EEEGINRUV	GUINEVERE
EEEEELRTY	EYELETEER	EEEGIRSTY	GEYSERITE
EEEEFHLRW	FREEWHEEL	EEEGLLNTY	GENTEELLY
EEEEFHRST	FREESHEET	EEEGLMNNT	GENTLEMEN
EEEEFRRSV	FREE VERSE	EEEGLNSTX	GENTLE SEX
EEEEGINVV	GENEVIEVE	EEEGMNNRU	ENERGUMEN
EEEEGNRRV	EVERGREEN	EEEGMNRSS	MESSENGER
EEEEGQSSU	SQUEEGEES	EEEGMORRT	ERGOMETER
EEEEHLRSW	ELSEWHERE	EEEGNNRSS	GREENNESS
EEEEKLNSX	KLEENEXES	EEEGRRRTT	REGRETTER
EEEELLMRS	ELLESMERE	EEEHILLNS	HELLENISE
EEEELMRTT	TELEMETER	EEEHILLNZ	HELLENIZE
EEEELNOPT	ELEOPTENE	EEEHILNNP	NEPHELINE
EEEELNSSV	ELEVENSES	EEEHILNST	HESELTINE
EEEELNTVV	VELVETEEN	EEEHIMPRS	EPHEMERIS
EEEENNSST	TENNESSEE	EEEHIMPSU	EUPHEMISE
EEEENNSTV	SEVENTEEN	EEEHIMPUZ	EUPHEMIZE
EEEENOPRY	EYE-OPENER	EEEHIMSTT	TIME SHEET
EEEENPRST	PRESENTEE	EEEHINNRT	HENRIETTE
EEEENRSTW	SWEETENER	EEEHIRRST	ETHERISER
EEEEPRRSV	PERSEVERE	EEEHIRRTZ	ETHERIZER
EEEEPRSSS	PEERESSES	EEEHIRSSS	HEIRESSES
EEEFGKNRU	FENUGREEK	EEEHKLOSU	HOUSELEEK

EEEHLMNTY	METHYLENE
EEEHLNOPT	PHENETOLE, TELEPHONE
EEEHLNSTV	ELEVENTHS
EEEHLOPPS	PEEPHOLES
EEEHLOPPT	THE PEOPLE
EEEHLORSS	LEE SHORES
EEEHLRRST	SHELTERER
EEEHMMNTY	ENTHYMEME
EEEHMNOPR	EPHEMERON
EEEHMORRT	RHEOMETER
EEEHMORRT	THREESOME
EEEHMORSW	SOMEWHERE
EEEHNRSSS	SHEERNESS
EEEHNSSTW	NEWSSHEET
EEEHOPRSX	EXOSPHERE
EEEHORSST	SHOETREES
EEEHRRSTW	TREE SHREW
EEEHRSTTU	USHERETTE
EEEIIKRST	KIESERITE
EEEIKNNPR	INNKEEPER
EEEIKNPSS	PEKINESES
EEEILNNRV	ENLIVENER
EEEILPRTV	REPLETIVE
EEEILPSST	SLEEPIEST
EEEILPTVX	EXPLETIVE
EEEILRSTX	EXSERTILE
EEEILSSTT	STEELIEST
EEEIMMRSS	MESMERISE
EEEIMMRSZ	MESMERIZE
EEEIMORTT	METEORITE
EEEIMPRRS	PREMIERES
EEEIMPRRT	PERIMETER
EEEIMSSTW	SEMISWEET
EEEINNNST	NINETEENS
EEEINNRST	ERNESTINE, INTERNEES
EEEINNRTV	INTERVENE
EEEINPRRS	RESERPINE
EEEINPRST	PINETREES
EEEINPSSW	WEEPINESS
EEEINPSVX	EXPENSIVE
EEEINQSUZ	QUEEN-SIZE
EEEINRRST	RE-ENTRIES
EEEINRRTW	WERNERITE
EEEINRTTV	RETENTIVE
EEEINSSTV	SEVENTIES
EEEINSTVX	EXTENSIVE
EEEIPRRRV	REPRIEVER
EEEIPRRSV	REPRIEVES
EEEIPRRTT	PRETERITE
EEEIPRSTX	EXPERTISE
EEEIQRRSU	EQUERRIES
EEEIQTTTU	ETIQUETTE
EEEIRRRTV	RETRIEVER

EEEIRRSSV	SERVERIES
EEEIRRSVW	REVIEWERS
EEEIRRTVV	REVERTIVE
EEEIRSTTV	SERVIETTE
EEEJLLRSW	JEWELLERS
EEEJLLRWY	JEWELLERY
EEEJNRSWY	NEW JERSEY
EEEJRSTTT	JET-SETTER
EEEKLNSSS	SLEEKNESS
EEEKMRSTU	MUSKETEER
EEEKNOSTY	SYNOEKETE
EEELLLRSV	LEVELLERS
EEELLNPRT	REPELLENT
EEELLPSSS	SLEEPLESS
EEELMNOPT	ELOPEMENT
EEELMNRTV	REVELMENT
EEELMOPSY	EMPLOYEES
EEELMOSTT	OMELETTES
EEELMRSTU	MULETEERS
EEELMRTTY	TELEMETRY
EEELMRTXY	EXTREMELY
EEELNOPSV	ENVELOPES
EEELNOPTT	LEPTOTENE
EEELNOTTV	NOVELETTE
EEELNRSSV	NERVELESS
EEELNRSSW	NEWSREELS
EEELNSSSS	SENSELESS
EEELOPRSV	OVERSLEEP
EEEMMNNPRS	PER MENSEM
EEEMNNSTT	TENEMENTS
EEEMNORRV	NEVERMORE
EEEMNOXYZ	EXOENZYME
EEEMNRSST	STEERSMEN
EEEMNRSTT	ENTREMETS
EEEMNRSTY	MESENTERY
EEEMNRTTV	REVETMENT
EEEMOPRTX	EXTEMPORE
EEEMPRSSS	EMPRESSES
EEEMRSSST	SEMESTERS
EEENNORST	SONNETEER
EEENNSSST	TENSENESS
EEENPRRST	PRESENTER,
REPRESENT	
EEENPRRTV	PREVENTER
EEENPRSUV	SUPERVENE
EEENPSSST	STEEPNESS
EEENQRSSU	QUEERNESS
EEENRRSTW	WESTERNER
EEENRRSUV	UNRESERVE
EEENRSSST	TERSENESS
EEENSSSTW	SWEETNESS
EEEOPSSST	POETESSES
EEEORRSSV	OVERSEERS
EEEPPPRTU	PUPPETEER
EEEPRRRSS	REPRESSER
EEEPRRRSV	PRESERVER
EEEPRRRTV	PERVERTER
EEEPRRSSV	PRESERVES
EEEPRRSSX	EXPRESSER
EEEPRRSTT	PRESETTER
EEEPRSSSX	EXPRESSES
EEEQRRSTU	REQUESTER
EEEQRSSTU	SEQUESTER
EEEQRSSUZ	SQUEEZERS
EEFFFKLRU	KERFUFFLE
EEFFGLNTU	EFFULGENT
EEFFHILLS	SHELF LIFE
EEFFHINTT	FIFTEENTH
EEFFHLRSU	RESHUFFLE
EEFFIILRS	FIREFLIES
EEFFINOSV	OFFENSIVE
EEFFINRST	STIFFENER
EEFFIORRT	FORFEITER
EEFFJNORS	JEFFERSON
EEFFLNSTU	EFFLUENTS
EEFFOPRRR	PROFFERER
EEFFORSTT	OFF-STREET
EEFFRRSSU	SUFFERERS
EEFGHIRRT	FREIGHTER
EEFGILLNY	FEELINGLY
EEFGILNNU	UNFEELING
EEFGILNRU	REFUELING
EEFGIMRUV	VERMIFUGE
EEFGINORR	FOREIGNER
EEFGINRRR	REFERRING
EEFGINRRT	FERRETING
EEFGINRST	FESTERING
EEFGINRTT	FETTERING
EEFGIORRS	FORGERIES
EEFGIPRRU	PREFIGURE
EEFGLLLUY	GLEEFULLY
EEFGLNRTU	REFULGENT
EEFGLRRTU	REGRETFUL
EEFGORRTT	FORGETTER
EEFHIIRSS	FISHERIES
EEFHIJLSW	JEWELFISH
EEFHILLRS	SHELLFIRE
EEFHILSST	FLESHIEST
EEFHIMNRS	FISHERMEN
EEFHINSST	HEFTINESS
EEFHIOSUW	HOUSEWIFE
EEFHLLSWY	FLYWHEELS
EEFHLORUW	FOUR-WHEEL
EEFHLSSTY	FLYSHEETS
EEFHMORRT	THE FORMER
EEFHNRSSS	FRESHNESS
EEFHOORRS	FORESHORE
EEFHOORTT	TO THE FORE
EEFHRRRTU	FURTHERER
EEFIILLNS	LIFELINES
EEFIILMST	LIFETIMES
EEFIILMTX	FLEXITIME
EEFIILNRT	INFERTILE,
INTERFILE	
EEFIILQRU	LIQUEFIER
EEFIILRST	FERTILISE
EEFIILRTZ	FERTILIZE
EEFIIMRRT	METRIFIER
EEFIINRST	FINISTERE
EEFIIPRRT	PETRIFIER
EEFIIRRRT	TERRIFIER
EEFIIRRSV	VERSIFIER
EEFIIRSTT	TESTIFIER
EEFILLLOS	FILOSELLE
EEFILLSTY	LIFESTYLE
EEFILMPXY	EXEMPLIFY
EEFILNTUW	WULFENITE
EEFILOORS	FOOLERIES
EEFILPRRS	PILFERERS
EEFINORST	FIRESTONE
EEFINPRSU	SUPERFINE
EEFINRSTU	INTERFUSE
EEFIOPRRT	PROFITEER
EEFIOPRRW	FIREPOWER
EEFIORRRT	RETROFIRE
EEFIPRRTU	PUTREFIER
EEFIPRSTU	STUPEFIER
EEFIPRSUV	PERFUSIVE
EEFIRRRTT	FRITTERER
EEFIRRRTU	FRUITERER
EEFIRRSTU	SURFEITER
EEFKNOORT	FORETOKEN
EEFKNORST	REEF KNOTS
EEFLLNPSU	SPLEENFUL
EEFLMRTUX	FLUXMETER
EEFLNRSTU	RESENTFUL
EEFLNRTVY	FERVENTLY
EEFLOPRSU	REPOSEFUL
EEFLORRTX	RETROFLEX
EEFLORSTV	LEFTOVERS
EEFLRRTTU	FLUTTERER
EEFLSSTTY	TSETSE FLY
EEFLTTYYZ	TZETZE FLY
EEFMNOORW	FOREWOMEN
EEFMOPRRR	PERFORMER
EEFMORRRS	REFORMERS
EEFMPRRUY	PERFUMERY
EEFOPRRST	FREE PORTS
EEFOPRRTY	FERROTYPE
EEFORRSST	FORESTERS
EEFORRTVW	FEVERWORT
EEGGHLLSS	EGGSHELLS

EEGGIILNT	GELIGNITE
EEGGIIPRS	PIGGERIES
EEGGILNNR	GREENLING
EEGGILNNT	NEGLIGENT
EEGGILNSS	LEGGINESS
EEGGILOOS	GEOLOGISE
EEGGILOOZ	GEOLOGIZE
EEGGIMRST	EGG TIMERS
EEGGINNRV	REVENGING
EEGGINRST	GREETINGS
EEGGIORSU	EGREGIOUS
EEGGORSTT	GO-GETTERS
EEGGRSSTU	SUGGESTER
EEGHHIITT	EIGHTIETH
EEGHHILLV	HIGH-LEVEL
EEGHIIKLN	HINGELIKE
EEGHIINRV	INVEIGHER
EEGHIKNTW	WEEKNIGHT
EEGHILNNT	ENLIGHTEN
EEGHILNOR	RHIGOLENE
EEGHILNRT	LENGTHIER
EEGHILNSS	HINGELESS
EEGHIMNNS	ENMESHING
EEGHINRTT	TETHERING, TIGHTENER
EEGHIORVW	OVERWEIGH
EEGHIRSST	SIGHTSEER
EEGHLLNOP	PHELLOGEN
EEGHMNOST	THEME SONG
EEGHMNOSU	HEGUMENOS
EEGHNNORR	GREENHORN
EEGHNNOTY	ETHNOGENY
EEGHNORTU	TOUGHENER
EEGHRTTTU	THE GUTTER
EEGIILNRV	INVEIGLER, RELIEVING
EEGIILORS	RELIGIOSE
EEGIILPRV	PRIVILEGE
EEGIINRVW	REVIEWING
EEGIINSTV	GENITIVES, INGESTIVE
EEGIISTTZ	ZEITGEIST
EEGIJLLNW	JEWELLING
EEGIJLNRY	JEERINGLY
EEGIKLNNN	KENNELING
EEGIKLNRY	REEKINGLY
EEGIKNNRT	KENTIGERN
EEGIKNRSW	SKEWERING
EEGIKNRTT	KETTERING
EEGILLLNV	LEVELLING
EEGILLNPR	REPELLING
EEGILLNPX	EXPELLING
EEGILLNRT	RETELLING
EEGILLNRV	GRENVILLE, REVELLING

EEGILLNRY	LEERINGLY
EEGILLSSU	GUILELESS
EEGILMMSU	GELSEMIUM
EEGILMNSY	SEEMINGLY
EEGILMRSY	LYME REGIS
EEGILNNRT	RELENTING
EEGILNNSS	ESSLINGEN, LESSENING
EEGILNNUY	GENUINELY
EEGILNOOS	NEOLOGISE
EEGILNOOZ	NEOLOGIZE
EEGILNPWY	WEEPINGLY
EEGILNRRS	LINGERERS
EEGILNRTT	LETTERING
EEGILNRVY	VEERINGLY
EEGILOPSU	EPILOGUES
EEGILORST	SORTILEGE
EEGIMNPRT	TEMPERING
EEGIMNPTX	EXEMPTING
EEGIMNRST	REGIMENTS
EEGIMNRSU	MERINGUES
EEGINNOPR	REOPENING
EEGINNPRT	REPENTING
EEGINNRST	RESENTING
EEGINNRTU	NEUTERING
EEGINOOSS	OOGENESIS
EEGINOPRY	EPIROGENY
EEGINOPSU	EPIGENOUS
EEGINORSV	SOVEREIGN
EEGINORVY	ROVING EYE
EEGINOSXY	OXYGENISE
EEGINOXYZ	OXYGENIZE
EEGINPPPR	PEPPERING
EEGINPRST	PESTERING
EEGINPSSW	SWEEPINGS
EEGINQSUZ	SQUEEZING
EEGINRRSV	RESERVING, REVERSING
EEGINRRTV	REVERTING
EEGINRSSU	SEIGNEURS
EEGINRSTT	RESETTING
EEGINRSTW	WESTERING
EEGINSTTV	VIGNETTES
EEGIORRSU	ROGUERIES
EEGIPRSST	PRESTIGES
EEGIRRSST	REGISTERS
EEGIRRSSU	SURGERIES
EEGIRSSST	TIGRESSES
EEGLLMORU	GLOMERULE
EEGLLOOTY	TELEOLOGY
EEGLLOPRS	GOSPELLER
EEGLLORRV	GROVELLER
EEGLMNNOU	MELUNGEON
EEGLNORTT	LORGNETTE
EEGMNOORR	GREENROOM

EEGNNORST	ROENTGENS
EEGNOORST	OESTROGEN
EEGNOORSU	EROGENOUS
EEGNOOSUX	EXOGENOUS
EEGNORRSS	ENGROSSER
EEGNORSSV	GOVERNESS
EEGNRRSTU	RESURGENT
EEGOOPSST	GOOSESTEP
EEGOPRSSU	SUPEREGOS
EEGOQRSTU	GROTESQUE
EEGORRRSS	REGRESSOR
EEHHHLNOO	HOHENLOHE
EEHHINOPT	THIOPHENE
EEHHINOSS	SHOESHINE
EEHHIOPTW	WHITE HOPE
EEHHIORTT	THIO-ETHER
EEHHIRSST	THE SHIRES
EEHHIRTTW	THEREWITH
EEHHIRTWW	WHEREWITH
EEHHLMOPS	HOME HELPS
EEHHNOPPS	PHOSPHENE
EEHHNOSSU	HEN HOUSES
EEHHOORSS	HORSESHOE
EEHHRRSST	THRESHERS
EEHIIKRSS	ESKISEHIR
EEHIILSTW	WHITE LIES
EEHIINNTT	NINETIETH
EEHIIRTTW	WITHERITE
EEHIJNOPS	JOSEPHINE
EEHIKLNOY	HONEY-LIKE
EEHIKLORS	HORSELIKE
EEHIKNPSS	SHEEPSKIN
EEHILLLMW	MILLWHEEL
EEHILLMNS	HELLENISM
EEHILLNST	HELLENIST
EEHILMOST	HOMELIEST
EEHILNNOO	HOLE IN ONE
EEHILNOPX	XENOPHILE
EEHILNORS	SHORELINE
EEHILNOSU	HOUSELINE
EEHILNPRS	REPLENISH
EEHILNPSS	SPLEENISH
EEHILNPSW	PINWHEELS
EEHILNSST	LITHENESS
EEHILOPRU	EUROPHILE
EEHILOPTY	HELIOTYPE
EEHILORST	HOTELIERS
EEHILPSST	SLIPSHEET
EEHILPSVY	PEEVISHLY
EEHILRSTW	ERSTWHILE
EEHILSTUV	HELVETIUS
EEHIMMOOV	HOME MOVIE
EEHIMMPSU	EUPHEMISM
EEHIMOPRT	HEMITROPE

EEHIMPRRW	WHIMPERER	EEHNOPRUW	WHEREUPON	EEIINSSTV	SENSITIVE
EEHIMPSTU	EUPHEMIST	EEHNOPSTU	PENTHOUSE	EEIINSSTZ	SENSITIZE
EEHINNORT	THREONINE	EEHNOPSTY	NEOPHYTES	EEIIOPQSU	EQUIPOISE
EEHINOPSU	EUPHONISE	EEHNOPTTY	ENTOPHYTE	EEIIOSSTV	SOVIETISE
EEHINOPSX	PHOENIXES	EEHNORRST	SHORTENER	EEIIOSTVZ	SOVIETIZE
EEHINOPUZ	EUPHONIZE	EEHNORSST	OTHERNESS	EEIIQRSTU	REQUISITE
EEHINORTT	THEREINTO	EEHNOSTTW	WHETSTONE	EEIIQSTUX	EXQUISITE
EEHINOSST	HESSONITE	EEHNPPRSU	PEN PUSHER	EEIJKNRSS	JERKINESS
EEHINPRST	TREPHINES	EEHNSSSTY	SYNTHESES	EEIJLNSUV	JUVENILES
EEHINSSTW	WHITENESS	EEHOORSSV	OVERSHOES	EEIJPRRSU	PERJURIES
EEHINSTTU	EUTHENIST	EEHOORSVW	HOWSOEVER,	EEIKLMORT	KILOMETRE
EEHINSTTX	SIXTEENTH	WHOSOEVER		EEIKLMORT	KILOMETRE
EEHINTTTW	TWENTIETH	EEHOPRSTY	HEY PRESTO	EEIKLRTWY	TRIWEEKLY
EEHIORRST	THEORISER	EEHOPRTXY	XEROPHYTE	EEIKNNPSV	PENKNIVES
EEHIORRTZ	THEORIZER	EEHORRTVW	OVERTHREW	EEIKNPRSS	PERKINESS
EEHIORSST	HETEROSIS	EEHORSTTY	SET THEORY	EEIKOORRS	ROOKERIES
EEHIORSTW	OTHERWISE	EEHOSSSST	HOSTESSES	EEILLMNOT	EMOLLIENT
EEHIPPRRY	PERIPHERY	EEIIIMPST	IMPIETIES	EEILLMNPT	IMPELLENT
EEHIPRRSS	PERISHERS	EEIIKKMSS	SIKKIMESE	EEILLMOPR	MILLEPORE
EEHIPRRSW	WHISPERER	EEIIKLLST	LIKELIEST	EEILLMSST	SMELLIEST
EEHIRRSST	HERITRESS	EEIIKNNTZ	ZINKENITE	EEILLNNTY	LENIENTLY
EEHIRRTTY	ERYTHRITE	EEIILLMRT	MILLERITE	EEILLNOST	LONELIEST
EEHIRSSTT	TEE SHIRTS	EEIILLMTW	WILLEMITE	EEILLNRSV	SNIVELLER
EEHKLOOST	STOKEHOLE	EEIILLNTV	VITELLINE	EEILLNSSS	ILLNESSES
EEHKLORWW	WHEELWORK	EEIILLSTV	LIVELIEST	EEILLOPTU	PETIOLULE
EEHKORSTW	WORKSHEET	EEIILMSTT	TIMELIEST	EEILLORTT	TITLE ROLE
EEHLLLNVY	HELVELLYN	EEIILNNRT	INTERLINE	EEILLOSTV	LOVELIEST
EEHLLORST	HOSTELLER	EEIILNORT	TRIOLEIN	EEILLRSST	TRELLISES
EEHLMOOSW	WHOLESOME	EEIILNOTV	OLIVENITE	EEILLRSTU	TELLURISE
EEHLMORVW	OVERWHELM	EEIILNPPS	PIPELINES	EEILLRSUY	LEISURELY
EEHLMORWW	WORM WHEEL	EEIILNRST	RESILIENT	EEILLRSVY	SERVILELY
EEHLNOOTW	WHOLE NOTE	EEIILOPST	SEPIOLITE	EEILLRTTU	TELLURITE
EEHLNOPTY	POLYTHENE,	EEIILRSST	STERILISE	EEILLRTUZ	TELLURIZE
TELEPHONY		EEIILRSTU	REUTILISE,	EEILLSUVY	ELUSIVELY
EEHLNOSSW	WHOLENESS	TUILERIES		EEILMMNPT	IMPLEMENT
EEHLOPPTU	UP THE POLE	EEIILRSTZ	STERILIZE	EEILMMNSY	IMMENSELY
EEHLORSSS	HORSELESS,	EEIILRSVW	LIVE WIRES	EEILMMORS	SOMMELIER
SHORELESS		EEIILRTUZ	REUTILIZE	EEILMMORT	MILOMETER
EEHLOSSSU	HOUSELESS	EEIIMMPRT	PRIME TIME	EEILMNNTY	EMINENTLY
EEHMMOPRS	MORPHEMES	EEIIMMRST	EREMITISM	EEILMNOSS	SOLEMNISE
EEHMNOOPR	PHEROMONE	EEIIMOPST	EPITOMISE	EEILMNOST	LIMESTONE,
EEHMNOORW	HOMEOWNER	EEIIMOPTZ	EPITOMIZE	MILESTONE	
EEHMNORTY	HETERONYM	EEIIMORSS	ISOMERISE	EEILMNOSZ	SOLEMNIZE
EEHMNOSSY	HOMEYNESS	EEIIMORSZ	ISOMERIZE	EEILMNPPR	PIMPERNEL
EEHMNPTTU	UMPTEENTH	EEIIMRSSV	REMISSIVE	EEILMNRVY	LIVERYMEN
EEHMOPSTY	MESOPHYTE	EEIINNNPT	PENNINITE	EEILMNSTU	MUSTELINE
EEHMORRTY	RHEOMETRY	EEIINNSTT	INTESTINE	EEILMORTT	TREMOLITE
EEHMORSST	REST HOMES,	EEIINNSTV	INTENSIVE	EEILMOSTT	MISTLETOE
THERMOSES		EEIINNTVV	INVENTIVE	EEILMOSVW	SEMIVOWEL
EEHMRRSTY	RHYMESTER	EEIINQRSU	ENQUIRIES	EEILMOTVY	EMOTIVELY
EEHMRSSUU	HUMERUSES	EEIINRRVV	VIVERRINE	EEILMRSST	MERITLESS
EEHMSSTTY	THE SYSTEM	EEIINRSTT	ENTERITIS	EEILMRSTY	LYSIMETER
EEHNOOPSU	OPEN HOUSE	EEIINRSVV	INVERSIVE	EEILNNOPT	LEPONTINE
EEHNOPPTY	PHENOTYPE	EEIINRTVW	INTERVIEW	EEILNNPSS	PENNILESS
EEHNOPRTU	THEREUPON	EEIINSSST	SENSITISE	EEILNNSST	SENTINELS

EEILNNNSTY	INTENSELY	EEIMOPRST	PERISTOME,	EEINSSSTT	TESTINESS
EEILNOORS	OLEORESIN		TEMPORISE	EEINSSSTW	WITNESSES
EEILNOPRT	INTERLOPE,	EEIMOPRTZ	TEMPORIZE	EEINSTTXY	EXTENSITY
REPLETION, TERPINEOL		EEIMPPRRS	PERISPERM	EEIOPPSTV	STOVEPIPE
EEILNORVW	WOLVERINE	EEIMPRRSS	IMPRESSER	EEIOPRSTT	POTTERIES
EEILNOSSS	NOISELESS	EEIMPRRTT	PERMITTER	EEIOPRSTV	POVERTIES
EEILNOSSU	SELENIOUS	EEIMPRRTY	PERIMETRY	EEIOPRTTU	PIROUETTE
EEILNOSTV	NOVELTIES	EEIMPRSSS	IMPRESSES	EEIOQQUUV	EQUIVOQUE
EEILNPPSZ	ZEPPELINS	EEIMPSSTU	IMPETUSES	EEIORRRST	ROISTERER,
EEILNPSSS	SPINELESS	EEIMQSTUU	EQUISETUM	TERRORISE	
EEILNPSTT	PESTILENT	EEIMRRSTT	TRIMESTER	EEIORRRSV	RESERVOIR
EEILNPSVY	PENSIVELY	EEIMRSSSU	MESSIEURS	EEIORRRTZ	TERRORIZE
EEILNRSST	LISTENERS	EEIMRSSTY	MYSTERIES	EEIORRSTX	EXTERIORS
EEILNRSVY	INVERSELY	EEIMRSTTX	EXTREMIST	EEIORRTVW	OVERWRITE
EEILOPRTX	EXPLOITER	EEIMRTTXY	EXTREMITY	EEIORSSUV	OVERISSUE
EEILOPSST	POLITESSE	EEINNNRSU	NUNNERIES	EEIORSVVW	OVERVIEWS
EEILOPSVX	EXPLOSIVE	EEINNOPPS	NIPPONESE	EEIORTTVX	EXTORTIVE
EEILORRST	LOITERERS	EEINNOPRS	PENSIONER	EEIPRRSST	PERSISTER
EEILORSTT	LOTTERIES	EEINNOPRT	TIN OPENER	EEIPRSSST	PRIESTESS
EEILPRSTX	TRIPLEXES	EEINNORTT	RETENTION	EEIPRSSUV	SUPERVISE
EEILPRSTY	PERISTYLE	EEINNOSTV	VEINSTONE	EEIPRSTTT	PRETTIEST
EEILPRSUV	PRELUSIVE,	EEINNOSTX	EXTENSION	EEIPRTTWY	TYPEWRITE
PULVERISE, REPULSIVE		EEINNPRST	SPINNERET	EEIQSSTUU	QUIETUSES
EEILPRUVZ	PULVERIZE	EEINNPRTT	PERTINENT	EEIRRSSST	RESISTERS
EEILPSUVX	EXPULSIVE	EEINNPSST	INEPTNESS	EEIRRSSTV	RESERVIST
EEILRSSTV	SILVESTER	EEINNPSTT	PENITENTS	EEIRRTTTW	TWITTERER
EEILRSTVY	RESTIVELY	EEINNPSWY	PENNY-WISE	EEIRSTUVX	EXTRUSIVE
EEILRSUVV	REVULSIVE	EEINNRSST	INERTNESS	EEJMNNOTY	ENJOYMENT
EEIMMMRSS	MESMERISM	EEINNRSSV	INVERNESS,	EEJMPQUUU	QUEUE-JUMP
EEIMMNRRT	MERRIMENT	NERVINESS		EEJNOQSUU	JUNOESQUE
EEIMMORRS	MEMORISER	EEINNSSSW	NEWSINESS	EEJNORRUY	JOURNEYER
EEIMMORRZ	MEMORIZER	EEINOPPST	PEPTONISE,	EEJPRRRSU	PERJURERS
EEIMMOSST	SOMETIMES	PIPESTONE		EEKKORSTY	KEYSTROKE
EEIMMRSST	MESMERIST	EEINOPPTZ	PEPTONIZE	EEKLMOSSS	SMOKELESS
EEIMMRSTW	SWIMMERET	EEINOPRST	INTERPOSE	EEKLNOSST	SKELETONS
EEIMMRSTX	EXTREMISM	EEINOQRUV	VERONIQUE	EEKLNPRSU	SPELUNKER
EEIMNNORT	MENTIONER	EEINOQSUX	EQUINOXES	EEKLORSTW	STEELWORK
EEIMNNRTT	INTERMENT	EEINORRSV	REVERSION	EEKMNOPTW	KEPT WOMEN
EEIMNNSTT	SENTIMENT	EEINORSTX	EXERTIONS,	EEKNOSSTY	KEYSTONES
EEIMNOOTV	MOVIETONE	EXSERTION		EELLLLNWY	LLEWELLYN
EEIMNOPTX	EXEMPTION	EEINORTVW	INTERWOVE	EELLMNOOS	LEMON SOLE
EEIMNORSS	SERMONISE	EEINOSSTV	OSTENSIVE	EELLMOSTW	MELLOWEST
EEIMNORST	MOISTENER	EEINPRRRT	REPRINTER	EELLNNRTU	TUNNELLER
EEIMNORSZ	SERMONIZE	EEINPRRTT	INTERPRET	EELLNSSTU	SULLENEST
EEIMNOSST	SEMITONES	EEINPRSSW	WINEPRESS	EELLOOSTW	STEEL WOOL
EEIMNOSTX	SIXTEENMO	EEINPSSTT	PETTINESS	EELLOPPRR	PROPELLER
EEIMNOSTZ	TIME ZONES	EEINQRSTU	IN REQUEST	EELLORRTW	TROWELLER
EEIMNPQTU	EQUIPMENT	EEINQSSTU	QUIETNESS	EELLSSSTY	STYLELESS
EEIMNPRSS	PRIMENESS	EEINRRRSU	REINSURER	EELLSSSUY	USELESSLY
EEIMNPSST	EMPTINESS	EEINRRSSU	NURSERIES	EELMMNOTU	EMOLUMENT
EEIMNRRSS	MERRINESS	EEINRSSSY	SYNERESIS	EELMNNORT	ENROLMENT
EEIMNRSTU	MUTINEERS	EEINRSSTT	INTERESTS,	EELMNOSSY	MONEYLESS
EEIMNSSSS	MESSINESS	TRITENESS		EELMNOTTX	EXTOLMENT
EEIMOOPRS	MEIOSPORE	EEINRSSTW	WITNESSER	EELMOOPST	LEPTOSOME
EEIMOORTZ	MEROZOITE	EEINRSSUV	UNIVERSES		

EELMOOPTT	TOTEM POLE	EENNOPSTX	EXPONENTS	EFFINOOSS	NOISES OFF
EELMOPRSY	EMPLOYERS	EENNORSTU	ENTRE NOUS	EFFINOSSU	EFFUSIONS
EELMOPRTU	PETROLEUM	EENNRSSST	STERNNESS	EFFINPSSU	PUFFINESS
EELMORSST	MOLESTERS	EENOOPPSS	POPE'S NOSE	EFFINSSST	STIFFNESS
EELMORTTV	VOLTMETER	EENOORRSU	ERRONEOUS	EFFIOOPRR	FIREPROOF
EELMORTUV	VOLUMETER	EENOORSTV	OVERTONES	EFFIORSTW	WRITE-OFFS
EELMPRSUY	SUPREMELY	EENOPPRTT	PREPOTENT	EFFIORTVY	FORTY-FIVE
EELNNOOUV	NUEVO LEON	EENOPRRSS	RESPONSER	EFFISSTTU	STUFFIEST
EELNNOPRS	PERSONNEL	EENOPRSSS	RESPONSES	EFFISSUUV	SUFFUSIVE
EELNNRSTU	TUNNELERS	EENOPSTTY	STENOTYPE	EFFLLRTUY	FRETFULLY
EELNOOSSS	LOOSENESS	EENOORSTU	ON REQUEST	EFFNOORRT	FOREFRONT
EELNOPSTU	PLENTEOUS	EENORTTTU	NEUTRETTO	EFFOORRTY	OFFERTORY
EELNORSTV	RESOLVENT	EENRRSTUV	VENTURERS	EFGGIINNR	FINGERING
EELNORTUV	VOLUNTEER	EENRSSTUW	WET NURSES	EFGGILNNU	ENGULFING
EELNOSSST	STONELESS	EEOOPRRVW	OVERPOWER	EFGGILOOS	SOLFEGGIO
EELNPRSTY	PRESENTLY	EEOOPPPRT	PEPPER POT	EFGGINOOR	FOREGOING
EELNRSTTU	NET RESULT	EEOOPPRSU	SUPERPOSE	EFGGINOSS	FOGGINESS
EELOPRRSX	EXPLORERS	EEOOPRRRST	REPORTERS	EFGHHIILR	HIGH-FLIER
EELOPRRTU	POULTERER	EEOOPRRRTY	REPERTORY	EFGHHILRY	HIGH-FLYER
EELOPRSSW	POWERLESS	EEOOPRRSTT	PROTESTER	EFGHIILNT	NIGHTLIFE
EELOPRSTV	OVERSLEPT	EEOOPRRSTX	EXPORTERS	EFGHIILRT	FIRELIGHT,
EELOPRSTY	POLYESTER,	EEOOPRSSSS	ESPRESSOS,		FLIGHTIER
PROSELYTE		REPOSSESS		EFGHIINRT	INFIGHTER
EELORRSUV	REVELROUS	EEOOPRSSSW	PROWESSES	EFGHILNSS	FLESHINGS
EELORRSVV	REVOLVERS	EEOOPRSSUX	EXPOSURES	EFGHILPRT	PREFLIGHT
EELORRSUV	OURSELVES	EEORRRSST	RESTORERS	EFGHILTWY	FLYWEIGHT
EELORSTUV	TRUELOVES	EEORRRSSTU	RETROUSSE	EFGHIORST	FORESIGHT, GIFT
EELPPSTTU	SEPTUPLET	EEORRSTUV	OVERTURES		HORSE
EELPRSSXY	EXPRESSLY	EEORRTTVX	EXTROVERT	EFGHOOSTT	GET SHOT OF
EELPRSTUU	SEPULTURE	EEORSSTUW	SOU'WESTER	EFGHOSTTU	GET SHUT OF
EELPSTTUX	SEXTUPLET	EEPRRSSST	PRESTRESS	EFGIIINRS	SIGNIFIER
EELRRSSTW	WRESTLERS	EEPRRSSSU	PRESSURES	EFGIILLNR	REFILLING
EELRSSTTU	UTTERLESS	EEPRRSTTU	SPUTTERER	EFGIILLNT	FILLETING
EELRSSTVY	SYLVESTER	EERRSTTTU	STUTTERER	EFGIILNPR	PILFERING
EEMMNOORT	METRONOME,	EFFFILSTU	FLUFFIEST	EFGIILNRT	FILTERING
MONOMETER, MONOTREME		EFFFLORTU	EFFORTFUL	EFGIILORR	GLORIFIER
EEMMNOSTV	MOVEMENTS	EFFGINORS	OFFERINGS	EFGIINNRR	INFERRING,
EEMMOORST	OSMOMETER	EFFGINRSU	SUFFERING	INFRINGER	
EEMMORTYZ	ZYMOMETER	EFFGLORTU	FORGETFUL	EFGIINNST	INFESTING
EEMNNORWY	NEW ROMNEY	EFFGNRSSU	GRUFFNESS	EFGIINPRT	FINGERTIP
EEMNOOPST	TONE POEMS	EFFHIIKNS	FISH KNIFE	EFGIINPRX	PREFIXING
EEMNOORTT	TONOMETER	EFFHIISTT	FIFTIETHS	EFGIINRSU	FIGURINES
EEMNORRTV	VERMONTER	EFFHIISTW	WHIFFIEST	EFGIINRTT	REFITTING
EEMNORRTY	MONTERREY	EFFHIKSWW	SKEW-WHIFF	EFGIINRVY	VERIFYING
EEMNSSTTV	VESTMENTS	EFFHILRSY	FLY-FISHER	EFGIISTUV	FUGITIVES
EEMOOOSTT	OSTEOTOME	EFFHINSSU	HUFFINESS	EFGILNNNU	FUNNELING
EEMOOPRTT	OPTOMETER	EFFHLRSSU	SHUFFLERS	EFGILNORW	FLOWERING
EEMOPPRRT	PRE-EMPTOR	EFFIIMNSS	MIFFINESS	EFGILPRSU	FIRE-PLUGS
EEMOPRRTY	PYROMETER	EFFIIORRT	FORTIFIER	EFGILRTUU	FULGURITE
EEMPRRTTU	TRUMPETER	EFFIIQRSU	SQUIFFIER	EFGIMNNOT	FOMENTING
EEMPRSSTT	TEMPTRESS	EFFILLLRU	FULFILLER	EFGIMNORR	REFORMING
EEMRRSTTU	MUTTERERS	EFFILMUUV	EFFLUVIUM	EFGIMNPRU	PERFUMING
EENNNOSTV	NON-EVENTS	EFFILNRSS	SNIFFLERS	EFGINNOST	SOFTENING
EENNOOSTU	NEOTENOUS	EFFILORRS	FLOS FERRI	EFGINOOSS	GOOFINESS
EENNOPRSS	PRONENESS			EFGINORST	FOSTERING

EFGLOOSVX	FOXGLOVES
EFGLOOTUV	TUG-OF-LOVE
EFGNOORTT	FORGOTTEN
EFGOOOOST	GOOSEFOOT
EFHHIISTW	WHITEFISH
EFHHILLSS	SHELLFISH
EFHHNOOOT	ON THE HOOF
EFHIILSTT	FILTHIEST
EFHIIMSST	FETISHISM
EFHIINPSS	SNIPEFISH
EFHIINSSS	FISHINESS
EFHIIRRTT	THRIFTIER
EFHIISSTT	FETISHIST,
	SHIFTIEST
EFHIJLLSY	JELLYFISH
EFHIKSSTY	SHIFT KEYS
EFHILLSSW	SWELLFISH
EFHILLSSY	SELFISHLY
EFHILNSSU	UNSELFISH
EFHILSSST	SHIFTLESS
EFHIMOPRZ	PFORZHEIM
EFHINOOTT	FINE-TOOTH
EFHINORRT	FIRETHORN
EFHINOSST	STONEFISH
EFHINRRSU	FURNISHER
EFHIORSTT	FORTIETHS,
	FROTHIEST
EFHLLLPUY	HELPFULLY
EFHLLOPUY	HOPEFULLY
EFHLLOSUU	FULL HOUSE
EFHLOOPSU	FLOPHOUSE
EFHLOPSST	FLESHPOTS
EFHMNOORT	HOME FRONT
EFHNORTUX	FOXHUNTER
EFHOOORTT	FORETOOTH
EFIIJRSTU	JUSTIFIER
EFIIKRSST	FRISKIEST
EFIILLLST	STILL LIFE
EFIILLMOR	MOLLIFIER
EFIILLNRU	NULLIFIER
EFIILLRST	FILLISTER,
	FRILLIEST
EFIILMNSS	FILMINESS
EFIILMOTT	LEITMOTIF
EFIILMSST	FLIMSIEST
EFIILNSTT	FLINTIEST
EFIILOSSS	FOSSILISE
EFIILOSSZ	FOSSILIZE
EFIILPRTT	FILTER TIP
EFIILRTTY	FERTILITY
EFIIMNSST	FEMINISTS
EFIIMORRT	MORTIFIER
EFIIMRSTY	MYSTIFIER
EFIINNNOT	NON-FINITE
EFIINNPRT	FINE PRINT

EFIINNSST	NIFTINESS
EFIINNSTY	INTENSIFY
EFIINOPST	IN SPITE OF
EFIIINORRS	FIRE IRONS,
	INFERIORS
EFIINSSZZ	FIZZINESS
EFIIPRRSU	PURIFIERS
EFIIPRSST	SPITFIRES
EFIIRSTTU	FRUITIEST
EFIIRSTZZ	FRIZZIEST
EFIISTTVY	FESTIVITY
EFIKLNSSU	FLUKINESS
EFIKNORSS	FORESKINS
EFIKORRSW	FIREWORKS
EFILLMOPU	FILOPLUME
EFILLNPTU	PLENTIFUL
EFILLORRV	FRIVOLLER
EFILMNOSY	SOLEMNIFY
EFILMOPRX	PLEXIFORM
EFILNNOOS	NO FLIES ON
EFILNNORT	FRONT LINE
EFILNOORS	SOLFERINO
EFILNOOSU	FELONIOUS
EFILNOOTU	OUT OF LINE
EFILNOSST	LOFTINESS
EFILOPPST	FLOPPIEST
EFILORSTY	LIFE STORY
EFILQRUUV	QUIVERFUL
EFILRSSTU	FRUITLESS
EFILRTUVY	FURTIVELY
EFIMMORRS	REFORMISM
EFIMMORRV	VERMIFORM
EFIMNORRS	INFORMERS
EFIMNORST	IN TERMS OF
EFIMORRST	SERRIFORM
EFIMORRST	FIRESTORM,
	REFORMIST, RESTIFORM
EFIMPRSTU	FRUMPIEST
EFINNNSSU	FUNNINESS
EFINNSSTU	UNFITNESS
EFINOPRSU	PERFUSION
EFINOPRSY	PERSONIFY
EFINORRST	FRONTIERS
EFINRRSSU	FURRINESS
EFINRRTUU	FURNITURE
EFINRSSTU	TURFINESS
EFINSSSSU	FUSSINESS
EFINSSSTU	FUSTINESS
EFINSSSTW	SWIFTNESS
EFINSSUZZ	FUZZINESS
EFIOORSTX	SIX-FOOTER
EFIOORSUV	OVIFEROUS
EFIOPRTTU	PETIT FOUR
EFIORRSTW	FROWSTIER
EFIORSSTT	FROSTIEST

EFIORSTWZ	FROWZIEST
EFIORTTTU	OUTFITTER
EFKLMNOOW	WOMENFOLK
EFKNOOPRS	SPOKEN FOR
EFKORRSTW	FRETWORKS
EFLLMOSUY	FULSOMELY
EFLLNOOSW	LONE WOLFS
EFLLNTUUY	TUNEFULLY
EFLLOORSW	FOLLOWERS
EFLLRSTUY	RESTFULLY
EFLLSTUYZ	ZESTFULLY
EFLNOORVW	OVERFLOWN
EFLNOPRTU	PROFLUENT
EFLNORSUW	SUNFLOWER
EFLOOOOST	FOOTLOOSE
EFLOOPRTW	FLOWERPOT
EFLOORSVW	OVERFLOWS
EFLOOSTTW	LOWESTOFT
EFLOPRSUY	PROFUSELY
EFLORRRTU	TERRORFUL
EFLRSSSTU	STRESSFUL
EFMOORSSU	FOURSOMES
EFNOOOSTT	FOOTNOTES
EFNOOTTUU	OUT OF TUNE
EFOOOPRRV	OVERPROOF
EFOOPRRSS	PROFESSOR
EFOOPSSTT	FOOTSTEPS
EFOOQRRTU	ROQUEFORT
EGGGIIJNR	REJIGGING
EGGGIINNR	GINGERING
EGGGIORST	GROGGIEST
EGGHIINTW	WEIGHTING
EGGHINNRU	HUNGERING
EGGIILNNR	LINGERING
EGGIINNRS	RESIGNING
EGGIINNST	INGESTING
EGGIINNSW	SWINGEING
EGGILLNRU	GRUELLING
EGGILNORV	GROVELING
EGGILNORW	GLOWERING
EGGILOOST	GEOLOGIST
EGGILQRSU	SQUIGGLER
EGGILQSSU	SQUIGGLES
EGGIMNNOR	MONGERING
EGGIMNNSU	MUGGINESS,
	MUGGINESS
EGGINNNOR	GRONINGEN
EGGINNORV	GOVERNING
EGGINNOTT	GOTTINGEN
EGGINNPTU	TUNING PEG
EGGINNPUX	EXPUNGING
EGGINNRTU	GINGER NUT
EGGINOORV	GOING-OVER
EGGINOSSS	SOGGINESS

EGGINRSTU	GESTURING
EGGINRTTU	GUTTERING
EGGIORRTU	OUTRIGGER
EGGJLMNUY	JUNGLE GYM
EGGLMRSSU	SMUGGLERS
EGGLRRSTU	STRUGGLER
EGGLRSSTU	STRUGGLES
EGHHHIORS	HIGH HORSE
EGHHIIORS	HIROSHIGE
EGHHIIRSS	HIGH-RISES
EGHHINRST	THRESHING
EGHHIPRSU	HIGHER-UPS
EGHHNORUW	ROUGH-HEWN
EGHHNOUZZ	ZHENGZHOU
EGHHORTTU	RETHOUGHT
EGHIIKNRS	SHRIEKING
EGHIILLMT	LIMELIGHT
EGHIILNRS	HIRELINGS, RELISHING
EGHIILTWY	WEIGHTILY
EGHIIMNTT	NIGHTTIME
EGHIIMSTT	MIGHTIEST
EGHIINNTW	WHITENING
EGHIINPRS	PERISHING
EGHIINRSV	SHIVERING
EGHIINRTW	WITHERING
EGHIINSTY	HYGIENIST
EGHIIRSTZ	RIGHTSIZE
EGHILLNOR	HOLLERING
EGHILLNTY	LENGTHILY
EGHILNNOT	NEON LIGHT
EGHILNOSV	SHOVELING
EGHILNSST	LIGHTNESS
EGHILOORY	HIEROLOGY
EGHILORST	GHOSTLIER
EGHILRTVY	VERY LIGHT
EGHILSSTT	SIGHTLESS
EGHILSSTT	SLIGHTEST
EGHIMNORT	MOTHERING
EGHIMNOST	SOMETHING
EGHIMPPSU	PEMPHIGUS
EGHINNSTU	ENTHUSING
EGHINOORV	HOOVERING
EGHINORSU	REHOUSING
EGHINORSW	SHOWERING
EGHINORTV	OVERNIGHT
EGHINORTX	EXHORTING
EGHINOSTY	HISTOGENY
EGHINPRSY	SYPHERING
EGHINRSST	RIGHTNESS
EGHINRSTU	HUNGRIEST, SURE THING
EGHINSSTT	TIGHTNESS
EGHIOPRTT	TIGHTROPE
EGHIORSTU	RIGHTEOUS

EGHIORSTV	OVERSIGHT
EGHIRSTTU	THEURGIST
EGHLLOORY	GLORY HOLE
EGHLLOPSU	PLUGHOLES
EGHLMNOPU	PLOUGHMEN
EGHLNOOPY	NEPHOLOGY, PHENOLOGY
EGHLNOORS	LONGSHORE
EGHLNOOTY	ETHNOLOGY
EGHLNOPYY	PHYLOGENY
EGHMNOORW	HOMEGROWN
EGHNOOOPR	GONOPHORE
EGHNOOPRY	GYNOPHORE
EGHNORSSU	ROUGHNESS
EGHNOSSTU	TOUGHNESS
EGHNRSSTT	STRENGTHS
EGHOPTYYZ	ZYGOPHYTE
EGIIIMNTZ	ITEMIZING
EGIIIJNNNO	ENJOINING
EGIIJNNOR	REJOINING
EGIIKLNST	KINGLIEST
EGIIKLNSV	KING'S EVIL
EGIIKNNRT	TINKERING
EGIIKNRSS	KISSINGER
EGIIKRSTZ	SITZKRIEG
EGIILLMNP	IMPELLING
EGIILLNNST	ENLISTING, LISTENING
EGIILNNSV	SNIVELING
EGIILNNTT	ENTITLING
EGIILNNUV	UNVEILING
EGIILNORS	RELIGIONS
EGIILNORT	LOITERING
EGIILNOST	GILSONITE
EGIILNRSV	SILVERING
EGIILNRTT	LITTERING
EGIILNSVW	SWIVELING
EGIILNTTY	GENTILITY
EGIILOPST	EPILOGIST
EGIILORST	TRILOGIES
EGIILORSU	RELIGIOUS
EGIILRRST	GRISTLIER
EGIILRSST	GRISLIEST
EGIILRSTU	LITURGIES
EGIILSTTU	GUILTIEST
EGIILSTTZ	GLITZIEST
EGIIMMNRS	IMMERSING, SIMMERING
EGIIMNPRS	SIMPERING
EGIIMNRSS	GRIMINESS
EGIIMNRTT	REMITTING
EGIINNNRT	INTERNING
EGIINNNTV	INVENTING
EGIINNNTW	ENTWINING
EGIINNORS	NIGROSINE

EGIINNOST	INGESTION
EGIINNOSU	INGENIOUS
EGIINNQRU	ENQUIRING
EGIINNRRT	INTERRING
EGIINNRST	INSERTING
EGIINNRSW	INSWINGER
EGIINNRTU	REUNITING
EGIINNRTV	INVERTING
EGIINNRTW	WINTERING
EGIINNSTT	INSETTING
EGIINNSTV	INVESTING
EGIINNTUY	INGENUITY
EGIINPPQU	EQUIPPING
EGIINPRRS	RESPIRING, SPRINGIER
EGIINQRRU	REQUIRING
EGIINQRTU	REQUITING
EGIINQRUV	QUIVERING
EGIINRRST	STRINGIER
EGIINRRTU	INTRIGUER
EGIINRRTW	REWRITING
EGIINRSST	RESISTING
EGIINRSSU	REISSUING
EGIINRSTT	RESITTING
EGIINRSTU	INTRIGUES
EGIINRTTT	TITTERING
EGIINRTTY	INTEGRITY
EGIINSSTT	STINGIEST
EGIIRSTTT	GRITTIEST
EGIJKLNRY	JERKINGLY
EGIJKNNTU	JUNKETING
EGIJLNSTY	JESTINGLY
EGIJNPRRU	PERJURING
EGIKLNNOO	INGLENOOK
EGIKMNNOY	MONKEYING
EGIKNORRW	REWORKING
EGILLLNTY	TELLINGLY
EGILLMNOW	MELLOWING
EGILLMNTY	MELTINGLY
EGILLMOTU	GUILLEMOT
EGILLNNOR	ENROLLING
EGILLNOTT	ILL-GOTTEN
EGILLNOTW	TOWELLING
EGILLNOTX	EXTOLLING
EGILLNOUU	LONGUEUIL
EGILLNOVY	VOLLEYING
EGILLNOWY	YELLOWING
EGILLNPSS	SPELLINGS
EGILLNSSW	SWELLINGS
EGILLOSSY	SYLLOGISE
EGILLOSYZ	SYLLOGIZE
EGILLSSTU	GUILTLESS
EGILMMNPU	PUMMELING
EGILMNOOS	NEOLOGISM

EGILMNOPY	EMPLOYING
EGILMNOST	MOLESTING
EGILMOOST	GLOOMIEST
EGILNNNTU	TUNNELING
EGILNNOOS	LOOSENING
EGILNNOST	SINGLETON
EGILNNOTX	LEXINGTON
EGILNNRSU	NURSELING
EGILNNSST	NESTLINGS
EGILNNSUY	ENSUINGLY
EGILNNVYY	ENVYINGLY
EGILNOOST	NEOLOGIST
EGILNOOSU	SINOLOGUE
EGILNOPRX	EXPLORING
EGILNORSV	RESOLVING
EGILNORTV	REVOLTING
EGILNORVV	REVOLVING
EGILNORVY	OVERLYING
EGILNOTVY	LONGEVITY
EGILNPRSU	REPULSING
EGILNRSTU	RESULTING
EGILNRSTW	WRESTLING
EGILNSSTT	SETTLINGS
EGILNSTTY	TESTINGLY
EGILOSSST	GLOSSIEST
EGILOSSTT	GLOTTISES
EGILOSSTU	EULOGISTS
EGIMMNRSU	SUMMERING
EGIMMNSSU	GUMMINESS
EGIMNORST	GERMISTON
EGIMNORSV	MISGOVERN
EGIMNPRSU	PRESUMING
EGIMNPRTU	PERMUTING
EGIMNRSSY	SYNERGISM
EGIMNRSTU	MUSTERING
EGIMNRTTU	MUTTERING
EGIMPRSTU	GRUMPIEST
EGINNNRSU	RERUNNING
EGINNNRUV	UNNERVING
EGINNORSW	WORSENING
EGINNOSUU	INGENUOUS
EGINNRRTU	RETURNING
EGINNRSTT	STRINGENT
EGINNRSTU	INSURGENT
EGINNRTUV	VENTURING
EGINOOSSS	GOOSINESS
EGINOOSSU	ISOGENOUS
EGINOPRRR	PORRINGER
EGINOPRRT	REPORTING
EGINOPRRV	REPROVING
EGINOPRST	PROGESTIN
EGINOPRTT	POTTERING
EGINOPRTX	EXPORTING
EGINOPSST	SPONGIEST

EGINOPSSU	ESPOUSING
EGINOPSUY	EPIGYNOUS
EGINORRST	RESORTING, RESTORING
EGINORRTT	RETORTING
EGINORSTU	GERONTIUS
EGINORTTT	TOTTERING
EGINORTTX	EXTORTING
EGINOSSTU	GOUTINESS
EGINPRSSS	PRESSINGS
EGINPRTTU	PUTTERING
EGINPRUVY	PURVEYING
EGINPSTTU	UPSETTING
EGINPSTWW	SWEPTWING
EGINRSSST	STRESSING
EGINRSSTY	SYNERGIST
EGINRSUVY	SURVEYING
EGINSSSTU	GUSTINESS
EGINSTTTU	TUNGSTITE
EGIOORSTV	GROOVIEST
EGIORSTTT	GROTTIEST
EGIPSTUZZ	ZUGSPITZE
EGKORSSUW	GUESSWORK
EGLMNOOOU	MONOLOGUE
EGLMOORTY	METROLOGY
EGLMOOTYY	ETYMOLOGY
EGLNNOSUU	SUN LOUNGE
EGLNNPTUY	PUNGENTLY
EGLNOOPRR	PROLONGER
EGLNOORUY	NEUROLOGY
EGLNOOSUV	LONGEVOUS
EGLNORSTY	STRONGYLE
EGLNORSUU	LONGUEURS
EGLNOSTUU	GLUTENOUS
EGLOOOSTY	OSTEOLOGY
EGLOOPRSU	PROLOGUES
EGLOOPRTY	PETROLOGY
EGMNOOOSS	MONGOOSES
EGMOORSTU	GUESTROOM
EGNNNRRUU	GUNRUNNER
EGNNORSSW	WRONGNESS
EGNOOPRSS	PROGNOSES
EGNOORRSV	GOVERNORS
EGNOORRVW	OVERGROWN
EGNOORSUU	UROGENOUS
EGNOPRSUW	NEWSGROUP
EGNORSSSS	GROSSNESS
EGNORSSST	SONGSTERS
EGNORSSTT	STRONGEST
EGNORSSTU	STURGEONS
EGNORSTUY	YOUNGSTER
EGOOPRSYZ	ZYGOSPORE
EHHIINSTT	IN THE SHIT
EHHIIRTTT	THIRTIETH

EHHILLLSY	HELLISHLY
EHHILMOOP	HOMOPHILE
EHHINOPPS	PHOSPHINE
EHHIOPPST	PHOSPHITE
EHHIOPRSW	HORSEWHIP
EHHIORSST	HORSESHIT
EHHIORTTT	THITHERTO
EHHLOOPTY	HOLOPHYTE
EHHMNNOPP	PHNOM PENH
EHHMNOOOP	HOMOPHONE
EHHMNOSUY	HUSH MONEY
EHHMORTTU	HOME TRUTH
EHHMRTUYY	EURHYTHMY
EHHNOORSS	SHOEHORNS
EHHOOPSTY	THEOSOPHY
EHHOOSSTU	HOTHOUSES
EHIIKNSTT	KITTENISH
EHIILLTWY	LILY-WHITE
EHIILMRST	HITLERISM
EHIILRSTW	WILTSHIRE
EHIINNORT	ORNITHINE
EHIINNSSS	SHININESS
EHIINORRT	INHERITOR
EHIINPPRW	WHIPPER-IN
EHIINPRST	NEPHRITIS, PHRENITIS
EHIINPSST	PITHINESS
EHIIORSST	HISTORIES
EHIIPPSSY	EPIPHYSIS
EHIIQRSSU	SQUISHIER
EHIIRRSTT	THIRSTIER
EHIIRSSTT	SHIRTIEST
EHIIRSSTW	IRISH STEW
EHIIRSTTZ	ZITHERIST
EHIISSTTT	SHITTIEST
EHIISSTTX	SIXTIETHS
EHIKLLPSY	SYLPHLIKE
EHIKLORTZ	KILOHERTZ
EHIKNSSSU	HUSKINESS
EHIKORRSY	YORKSHIRE
EHIKPRSSU	SPIKE-RUSH
EHILLLMOS	MOLEHILLS
EHILLOSTY	HOSTILELY
EHILLOSWY	YELLOWISH
EHILLRRST	THRILLERS
EHILLRSST	SHRILLEST
EHILMNOST	MONTHLIES
EHILMOORS	HEIRLOOMS
EHILMPPRY	PERILYMPH
EHILMRSST	MIRTHLESS
EHILMRSTU	LUTHERISM
EHILMRSUV	HILVERSUM
EHILNOOPT	LITHOPONE, PHONOLITE
EHILNOSST	HOLSTEINS

EHILNOSUY	HEINOUSLY
EHILOPPTY	HIPPOLYTE
EHILOPRST	HELIPORTS
EHILOPRXY	XEROPHILY
EHILPSTTY	PETTISHLY
EHILRSTTW	WHITTLERS
EHILSSSTU	SLUSHIEST
EHIMNNOOS	MOONSHINE
EHIMNOPUU	EUPHONIUM
EHIMNORST	HORSEMINT
EHIMNPSST	SHIPMENTS
EHIMNPSSU	HUMPINESS
EHIMNRTUU	RUTHENIUM
EHIMNSSSU	MUSHINESS
EHIMOOSST	SMOOTHIES
EHIMOPPRR	PERIMORPH
EHIMORSST	ISOTHERMS
EHIMORSTT	SHORT TIME
EHIMPRRTU	TRIUMPHER
EHIMRRSTY	ERYTHRISM
EHIMSSSTU	ISTHMUSES
EHINNOPSS	PHONINESS
EHINNORSS	HORNINESS
EHINNOSST	THONINESS
EHINNOSTW	NONWHITES,
	WHINSTONE
EHINNSSTU	NISSEN HUT
EHINOPPRS	HORNPIPES
EHINOPRSS	NEPHROSIS
EHINOPRSW	OWNERSHIP,
	SHIPOWNER
EHINOPSTU	IN THE SOUP
EHINOPSTY	HYPNOTISE
EHINOPTYZ	HYPNOTIZE
EHINORRSU	NOURISHER
EHINORSSS	HORSINESS
EHINORSTT	THORNIEST
EHINORTXY	THYROXINE
EHINOSSSW	SHOWINESS
EHINOSTWW	SNOW-WHITE
EHINPRRTY	PYRETHRIN
EHINPSSSU	PUSHINESS
EHINRSSSU	RUSHINESS
EHINSSSTY	SYNTHESIS
EHIOOPRTW	POOR WHITE
EHIOOSTTT	TOOTHIEST
EHIOPRSST	PROTHESIS,
	SOPHISTER
EHIORSSTT	THEORISTS
EHIORSTTW	WORTHIEST
EHIORSTWZ	HOWITZERS
EHIPQSSUY	PHYSIQUES
EHIRSSSTU	RUSSETISH
EHKNPRRSU	PRESHRUNK
EHKOORRSW	WORKHORSE

EHKOORSUW	HOUSEWORK,
	WORKHOUSE
EHLLMOPSY	MESOPHYLL
EHLLNSSTU	NUTSHELLS
EHLLOOOPS	LOOPHOLES
EHLLOOSTU	TOLLHOUSE
EHLLOOSTW	HOLLOWEST
EHLMOORSW	WORMHOLES
EHLNOOPPY	POLYPHONE
EHLNOOPRT	NORTH POLE
EHLNOOPXY	XYLOPHONE
EHLNOOSTY	HOLYSTONE
EHLNORRTY	NORTHERLY
EHLNPSSSU	PLUSHNESS
EHLOOPRST	PORTHOLES,
	POTHOLERS
EHLOOPSTU	SOUTH POLE
EHLOOSSTT	TOOTHLESS
EHLOPRSTU	UPHOLSTER
EHLORRTTT	THROTTLER
EHLORSSTW	WORTHLESS
EHLORSTTT	THROTTLES
EHLORSTUY	SOUTHERLY
EHLPRSTUU	SULPHURET
EHMMOOPRS	MESOMORPH
EHMNNOOOY	HONEYMOON
EHMNOOSTW	HOMETOWNS
EHMNOTTUY	TYNEMOUTH
EHMOOOPRS	SOPHOMORE
EHMOOORSU	HOUSEROOM
EHMOOOSTT	TOOTHSOME
EHMOOPSTU	SHOOT-'EM-UP
EHMOOSSTT	SMOOTHEST
EHMORRSTT	SHORT-TERM
EHMPRRTUY	PYRETHRUM
EHNNOORST	HORNSTONE
EHNNOOTTW	ON THE TOWN
EHNNOPRST	PENN'ORTHS
EHNOOPPSS	OPEN SHOPS
EHNOOPPTY	PHONOTYPE
EHNOORSSW	SNOWSHOER
EHNOOSSSW	SNOWSHOES
EHNOOSTUW	TOWN HOUSE
EHNOOTTTT	HOTTENTOT
EHNOPRTTU	POTHUNTER
EHNORRTTU	TRUE NORTH
EHNORSSST	SHORTNESS
EHNORSTTW	NORTHWEST
EHNOSSTUU	NUTHOUSES
EHOOOPRSU	POORHOUSE
EHOOORSTV	OVERSHOOT
EHOOPPTTY	PHOTOTYPE
EHOOPRRTT	ORTHOPTER
EHOOPRRTV	HOVERPORT
EHOOPSSTU	HOUSETOPS

EHOORRTVW	OVERTHROW
EHOORSSUW	ROW HOUSES
EHOORSTTW	SHOT TOWER
EHOOSSTUU	OUTHOUSES
EHOPRSTXY	EXSTROPHY
EHORRSTTW	THROWSTER
EHOSSTTUW	SOUTHWEST
EHRRSSTTU	THRUSTERS
EIIILMMTT	TIME LIMIT
EIIILNNQU	INQUILINE
EIIILSTTU	UTILITIES
EIIIMMNRS	MINIMISER
EIIIMMNRZ	MINIMIZER
EIIIMPRTV	PRIMITIVE
EIIINQRSU	INQUIRIES
EIIINRSTT	RETINITIS,
	TRINITIES
EIIINTTUV	INTUITIVE
EIIJMSSTU	JESUITISM
EIIKKNNSS	KINKINESS
EIIKLLORT	KILOLITRE
EIIKLMNSS	MILKINESS
EIIKLNNRT	INTERLINK
EIIKLNSSS	SILKINESS
EIIKLNSST	SLINKIEST
EIIKMPSST	SKIMPIEST
EIIKNNSST	SKINNIEST
EIIKNPSSS	SPIKINESS
EIIKNRSSS	RISKINESS
EIIKQRSTU	QUIRKIEST
EIILLMNRS	MILLINERS
EIILLMNRY	MILLINERY
EIILLMSST	LIMITLESS
EIILLNRST	INSTILLER
EIILLNSSS	SILLINESS
EIILLNSTU	NULLITIES
EIILLOPRS	PILLORIES
EIILMMORS	MELIORISM
EIILMNORV	VERMILION
EIILMNOSU	LIMOUSINE
EIILMNSSS	SLIMINESS
EIILMOPSV	IMPLOSIVE
EIILMOTTV	LEITMOTIV
EIILMPRSU	PUERILISM
EIILMPSUV	IMPULSIVE
EIILMRSST	LISTERISM
EIILMRSSY	MISSILERY
EIILNNOQU	QUINOLINE
EIILNPSST	SPLENITIS
EIILNPSTY	PENSILITY
EIILNSTTY	TENSILITY
EIILOQSSU	SILIQUOSE
EIILPPSST	SLIPPIEST
EIILPRTUY	PUERILITY

EIILRSTTY	STERILITY	EIINSTTTU	INSTITUTE	EILMNOPSU	ON IMPULSE
EIILRSTVY	SERVILITY	EIIOPSSTV	POSITIVES	EILMNORTT	TORMENTIL
EIILSSSTY	SESSILITY	EIIOSSTTV	SOVIETIST	EILMNORTU	MONTREUIL
EIIMMNORS	IMMERSION	EIIPRRSTW	TRIPWIRES	EILMNOSSU	EMULSIONS
EIIMMNOSS	MISONEISM	EIIPRRTUV	IRRUPTIVE	EILMNOSTY	SOLEMNITY
EIIMMNRSU	IMMUNISER	EIIPRSSST	PRISSIEST	EILMNOSWY	WINSOMELY
EIIMMNRUZ	IMMUNIZER	EIIPRSSTT	STRIPIEST	EILMNPSSU	LUMPINESS
EIIMMNSTY	IMMENSITY	EIIQSSTTU	QUIETISTS	EILMNRSST	MINSTRELS
EIIMMORSS	ISOMERISM	EIISSTTTW	TWISTIEST	EILMOOSTY	ILEOSTOMY
EIIMMOSTV	EMOTIVISM	EIJLLNOSS	JOLLINESS	EILNNOOSS	LOONINESS
EIIMMPSSS	PESSIMISM	EIJLMNPTU	MINT JULEP	EILNNOSTV	INSOLVENT
EIIMMPSUY	EPIMYSIUM	EIJMNPSSU	JUMPINESS	EILNOOPSS	SLIPNOOSE
EIIMNNRTU	TRIENNIUM	EIJNORSST	JOINTRESS	EILNOOPSX	EXPLOSION
EIIMNORSS	MISSIONER,	EIKKNOOSS	KOOKINESS	EILNOOTUV	EVOLUTION
REMISSION		EIKLLNOVX	KNOXVILLE	EILNOPRRU	PURLOINER
EIIMNOSSS	EMISSIONS	EIKLMNOSS	MOLESKINS	EILNOPRSU	PRELUSION,
EIIMNOSST	MISONEIST	EIKLNPRRS	SPRINKLER	REPULSION	
EIIMNOSUV	VIMINEOUS	EIKLNPRSS	SPRINKLES	EILNOPRTY	LINOTYPER
EIIMNPRRT	IMPRINTER	EIKLNSSSU	SULKINESS	EILNOPSST	POINTLESS
EIIMNRSST	MINISTERS	EIKMNOSSS	SMOKINESS	EILNOPSSU	SPINULOSE
EIIMNSSST	MISTINESS	EIKMNRSSU	MURKINESS	EILNOPSUX	EXPULSION
EIIMOPRSU	IMPERIOUS	EIKMNSSSU	MUSKINESS	EILNORSTY	STORY LINE
EIIMOPRSV	IMPROVISE	EIKNOPRSS	PORKINESS	EILNORSUV	REVULSION
EIIMOPSTT	EPITOMIST	EIKNOSTTT	KNOTTIEST	EILNORTUY	ROUTINELY
EIIMOSSTV	SOVIETISM	EIKNPRSTU	TURNPIKES	EILNOSSSU	LOUSINESS
EIIMPSSST	PESSIMIST	EIKNPSSTU	SPUNKIEST	EILNOSSTV	NOVELISTS
EIINNNOST	INTENSION	EIKOOPSST	SPOOKIEST	EILNOSUVY	ENVIOUSLY
EIINNNOTT	INTENTION	EIKORRSTV	OVERSKIRT	EILNPPSSU	PULPINESS
EIINNNOTV	INVENTION	EIKORRSWW	WIREWORKS	EILNPQTUU	QUINTUPLE
EIINNNSST	TINNINESS	EIKRRSTWY	SKYWRITER	EILNPRSST	SPLINTERS
EIINNORST	INSERTION	EILLMNOST	MILLSTONE	EILNPRSTY	SPLINTERY
EIINNORSV	INVERSION	EILLMNSSU	SENSILLUM	EILNRSSSU	SURLINESS
EIINNOSSS	NOISINESS	EILLMOOPT	MELITOPOL	EILNRSTTU	TURNSTILE
EIINNPPSS	NIPPINESS	EILLMPSTU	MULTIPLES	EILNRTUUV	VULTURINE
EIINNPSSS	SPININESS	EILLMPTTU	MULTIPLET	EILNSSSTU	LUSTINESS
EIINNRSTT	INTERNIST	EILLMPTUX	MULTIPLEX	EILOOPRST	POORLIEST
EIINNSSTT	INSISTENT	EILLMRTUU	TELLURIUM	EILOPPRSS	PROLEPSIS
EIINNSTTY	INTENSITY	EILLNOPRU	NULLIPORE	EILOPPRTY	PROPYLITE
EIINOPPST	PIT PONIES	EILLNORTU	TELLURION	EILOPPSST	SLOPPIEST
EIINOPRSV	PREVISION	EILLNOSSW	LOWLINESS	EILOPRSTT	PORTLIEST
EIINOPSTT	PETITIONS	EILLNOSTY	STONE-LILY	EILOPRSTU	POULTRIES
EIINOPTVW	VIEWPOINT	EILLNOTVY	VIOLENTLY	EILOPSSTY	STYLOPISE
EIINORRST	INTERIORS	EILLNSSST	STILLNESS	EILOPSTTT	TEST PILOT
EIINORRSV	REVISIONS	EILLOOPRV	LIVERPOOL	EILOPSTUY	PITEOUSLY
EIINORSTY	SENIORITY	EILLOOSTW	WOOLLIEST	EILOPSTYZ	STYLOPIZE
EIINPPRST	PINSTRIPE	EILLOPPRS	OVERSPILL	EILORRTVW	LIVERWORT
EIINPSSST	TIPSINESS	EILLOPRTY	PELLITORY	EILORSSUY	SERIOUSLY
EIINPSSSW	WISPINESS	EILLOPRWW	WILLPOWER	EILOSSTTT	STILETTOS
EIINRSTTW	WINTRIEST	EILLOSTTY	STYLOLITE	EILPPRSSU	SUPPLIERS
EIINRSTUV	INTRUSIVE	EILLPSSSY	SYLLEPSIS	EILQRRSSU	SQUIRRELS
EIINRTTUV	NUTRITIVE	EILLSSTWY	WITLESSLY	EILRSSTTU	SULTRIEST,
EIINSSSSY	SYNISESIS	EILMMNTUU	NUMMULITE	SURTITLES	
EIINSSSYZ	SYNIZESIS	EILMMPSTU	PLUMMIEST	EILRSSTTW	WRISTLETS
EIINSSTTW	WITTINESS	EILMNOPST	SIMPLETON	EIMMNNSTU	MUNIMENTS
				EIMMNOPRS	PERSIMMON

EIMMNORRS	MORRIS MEN	EINNRTTUW	UNWRITTEN	EIPRRRSSU	SURPRISER
EIMMNORSS	MISNOMERS	EINNSSTTU	NUTTINESS	EIPRRSSSU	SURPRISES
EIMMOPRSU	EMPORIUMS	EINOOPRSS	POISONERS	EIPRSSSTU	PERTUSSIS
EIMNNOOSS	MOONINESS	EINOOORRST	RETORSION	EIQRRSSTU	SQUIRTERS
EIMNNOOTZ	MONZONITE	EINOOORRTT	RETORTION	EIRSSTTTU	TRUSTIEST
EIMNNOPRT	PROMINENT	EINOOORSST	ROOTINESS	EJLLLLORY	JELLY ROLL
EIMNNORST	INNERMOST	EINOOORTTX	EXTORTION	EJLLOSSYY	JOYLESSLY
EIMNNOSTT	OINTMENTS	EINOOORTTY	NOTORIETY	EJNOORRSU	SOJOURNER
EIMNNPTUU	NEPTUNIUM	EINOOOSSST	SOOTINESS	EKKOOPRRW	POKERWORK
EIMNNRTTU	NUTRIMENT	EINOOOSSTT	SNOOTIEST	EKLLNNOWW	WELL-KNOWN
EIMNOORRT	REMONTOIR	EINOOOSSWZ	WOOZINESS	EKLMMNOSU	MUSKMELON
EIMNOORSS	ROOMINESS	EINOOPPSSS	SOPPINESS	EKLNOOORS	ONLOOKERS
EIMNOPRTU	IMPORTUNE	EINOOPRSS	PRISONERS	EKMNNOORS	NONSMOKER
EIMNORSST	MONITRESS	EINOOPRRTV	OVERPRINT	EKMNNOTUY	MONKEY NUT
EIMNORSSU	SENSORIUM	EINOOPRSS	PROSINESS	EKNOOPSTU	OUTSPOKEN
EIMNORSUV	VERMINOUS	EINOOPRSTU	ERUPTIONS	EKNOORSTW	STONEWORK
EIMNOSSSS	MOSSINESS	EINOOPSSSU	PIOUSNESS	EKNORSSTU	SUNSTROKE
EIMNOSSST	MOISTNESS	EINOOPSST	POTTINESS	EKOORRTUW	OUTWORKER
EIMNOSSSU	MOUSINESS	EINOOQSSTU	QUESTIONS	EKOORSTTW	TWO-STROKE
EIMNOSTTY	TESTIMONY	EINOOQSTTU	QUOTIENTS	EKOPRRSSW	PRESSWORK
EIMNOTTZZ	MEZZOTINT	EINOORRSSS	SORRINESS	ELLMORSTU	ROSTELLUM
EIMNSSSTU	MUSTINESS	EINOORRTTV	INTROVERT	ELLNOPTUY	OPULENTLY
EIMNSSUZZ	MUZZINESS	EINOORRUWZ	RUWENZORI	ELLOPRSST	POLLSTERS
EIMOOPRTV	PROMOTIVE	EINOORSSUV	SOUVENIRS	ELLOPRSUV	PULLOVERS
EIMOORRSW	WORRISOME	EINOORSTUX	EXTRUSION	ELLORRSST	STROLLERS
EIMOORSSU	ISOMEROUS	EINOSSTTT	SNOTTIEST	ELLORSTUU	TELLUROUS
EIMOOSSSX	EXOSMOSIS	EINPRRSST	SPRINTERS	ELMNNOOST	SOMNOLENT
EIMOPRRSS	PRIMROSES	EINPRRTTU	INTERRUPT	ELMNPPSSU	PLUMPNESS
EIMOPRRST	IMPORTERS,	EINPRSSST	SPINSTERS	ELMOOOPRW	POWER LOOM
MISREPORT		EINRSSSTU	RUSTINESS	ELMOORSTW	LOWERMOST
EIMOPRSTU	IMPOSTURE	EINRSSTTU	RUTTINESS	ELMORSTUU	TREMULOUS
EIMOPSTUU	IMPETUOUS	EIOOPPRSS	PORPOISES	ELMORTUVY	VOLUMETRY
EIMORRRST	TERRORISM	EIOOPPSST	OPPOSITES	ELMSSTUUU	TUMULUSES
EIMORRSTU	TRIMEROUS	EIOOPRRST	POSTERIOR	ELNOOOPRV	PROVOLONE
EIMORRSWW	WIREWORMS	EIOOPRSTX	EXPOSITOR	ELNOORSUY	ONEROUSLY
EIMORRTTW	MITREWORT	EIOORSSTT	TORTOISES	ELNORSUVY	NERVOUSLY
EIMORSSTT	STORMIEST	EIOORSTTT	TROOSTITE	ELNOSTUUY	TENUOUSLY
EIMORSTTW	TWO-TIMERS	EIOOSSSTX	EXOSTOSIS	ELOOORSTZ	ZOOSTEROL
EIMORSUVY	VOYEURISM	EIOOSSTTV	OVOTESTIS	ELOORSTUW	LOUSEWORT
EIMPRSTUY	SUPREMITY	EIOPPRRST	STROPPIER	ELOPPPUVY	PUPPY LOVE
EIMPSSTTU	STUMPIEST	EIOPPRRTY	PROPRIETY	ELOPPRSUY	PURPOSELY
EIMQSSTUY	MYSTIQUES	EIOPPRSUV	PURPOSIVE	ELOQRSUUU	QUERULOUS
EIMSSTTTU	SMUTTIEST	EIOPRRSSU	SUPERIORS	ELPRSSSUU	SURPLUSES
EINNNOTTY	NONENTITY	EIOPRSSTT	SPORTIEST	ELPRSSTTU	SPLUTTERS
EINNNSSSU	SUNNINESS	EIOPRSTTU	PROUSTITE	EMMMNOSTU	MOMENTUMS
EINNOOPST	ON POINTES	EIOPRSTTY	POSTERITY	EMMNNOSTU	MONUMENTS
EINNOORST	IRONSTONE,	EIOPSSTTT	SPOTTIEST	EMMNOOOST	MONOSTOME
SEROTONIN		EIOQRSTUU	TURQUOISE	EMMNOORSS	MEN'S ROOMS
EINNORSTV	INVENTORS	EIORRRSST	TERRORIST	EMMNOOSTU	MOMENTOUS
EINNORTVY	INVENTORY	EIORRRTTY	TERRITORY	EMMNOSSSU	SUMMONSES
EINNOSSST	STONINESS	EIORRSSST	RESISTORS	EMMNRSTUU	MENSTRUUM
EINNOSSSW	SNOWINESS	EIORRSSTV	SERVITORS	EMMOORSTY	OSMOMETRY
EINNPRSTW	NEWSPRINT	EIPPRRSST	STRIPPERS	EMNNOOOST	MOONSTONE
EINNRSSTU	RUNTINESS			EMNOOPRTY	MONOTYPER
EINNRSTTU	NUTRIENTS				

EMNOOPSUY	EPONYMOUS	FFGILNOXY	FLYING FOX	FHLMORUUU	HUMOURFUL
EMNOORRTT	TORMENTOR	FFGIMNORU	FUNGIFORM	FHLMOSTUU	MOUTHFULS
EMNOORSSW	NEWSROOMS	FFGINOPRS	OFFSPRING	FHLOOOPRS	SHOP FLOOR
EMNOORTTY	TONOMETRY	FFGINSSUU	SUFFUSING	FHLOOORSW	FLOOR SHOW
EMNOORTUY	NEUROTOMY	FFHOOOSST	OFFSHOOTS	FHMOOOPRT	MOTHPROOF
EMNOORTWY	MONEYWORT	FFIINOSUX	SUFFIXION	FHOORRTTW	FORT WORTH
EMNOPRSST	SPORTSMEN	FFILLOPPS	FLIP-FLOPS	FIIILSSTY	FISSILITY
EMNORSSTT	STERNMOST	FFINOSSUU	SUFFUSION	FIIIMNRTY	INFIRMITY
EMOOORRST	STOREROOM	FFIORSTTU	SOFT FRUIT	FIIKLNNST	SKINFLINT
EMOOOSTTY	OSTEOTOMY	FFLOOOOPR	FOOLPROOF	FIILLMORV	VILLIFORM
EMOOPRRSS	PRESSROOM	FFLOOOPRY	POORLY OFF	FIILLMOTU	MULTIFOIL
EMOOPRRST	PROMOTERS	FFNOPSTUU	UP TO SNUFF	FIILLMORTU	TRIFOLIUM
EMOOPRTTY	OPTOMETRY	FGGGILNOS	FLOGGINGS	FIILMPRST	FILMSTRIP
EMOORRSST	REST ROOMS	FGGIINORV	FORGIVING	FIILORTVY	FRIVOLITY
EMOORRSTU	TREMOROUS	FGHHILNOW	HIGH-FLOWN	FIIMMNORS	MISINFORM
EMOORSTTU	OUTERMOST	FGHHIOSTW	SHOW FIGHT	FIIMNOSSU	FUSIONISM
EMOPPRSTU	UPPERMOST	FGHIIINNS	FINISHING	FIIMOPRST	STIPIFORM
EMOPRRTUV	OVERTRUMP	FGHIIILLTY	FLIGHTILY	FIIMORRTU	TRIFORIUM
EMOPRRTYY	PYROMETRY	FGHILOPTT	TOP-FLIGHT	FIIMORRTV	VITRIFORM
EMPRSSTTU	STRUMPETS	FGHINORTT	FORTNIGHT	FIINNOSSU	INFUSIONS
ENNOOPPRT	PROPONENT	FGHLORSUU	FURLOUGHS	FIINOSSTU	FUSIONIST
ENNOOPPST	OPPONENTS	FGHMOORTU	FROGMOUTH	FIKLLLSUY	SKILFULLY
ENNOPRTWY	PENNYWORT	FGHOOTTUU	OUTFOUGHT	FIKLLNSUU	UNSKILFUL
ENNORRTUU	OUTRUNNER	FGIIILNVY	VILIFYING	FILLLMORU	FLOURMILL
ENNORSTTU	TURNSTONE	FGIIIMNRS	MISFIRING	FILLSTUWY	WISTFULLY
ENNPRRSUU	RUNNERS-UP,	FGIILMNOR	LIGNIFORM	FILMMORSU	FORMULISM
RUNNER-UPS		FGIILNOPR	PROFILING	FILMMORTU	MULTIFORM
ENOOPPRST	POSTPONER	FGIILNPTU	UPLIFTING	FILMNORUY	UNIFORMLY
ENOOPPRSU	ON PURPOSE	FGIILNRST	FIRSTLING	FILMORSTU	FORMULIST
ENOOPPRTU	OPPORTUNE	FGIILNRZZ	FRIZZLING	FILMORUVV	VULVIFORM
ENOORSTTW	STONEWORT	FGIIMNNOR	INFORMING	FILOOOPRT	PORTFOLIO
ENOOSSTTU	SOSTENUTO	FGIINNOTY	NOTIFYING	FILOORSSU	FLUOROSIS
ENOPRSSSU	SUSPENSOR	FGIINOPRT	PROFITING	FILOORSUV	FRIVOLOUS
ENOPRSSTT	STERNPOST	FGIINOSSY	OSSIFYING	FILORSUUY	FURIOUSLY
ENOPSTTYY	STENOTYPY	FGIINPRUY	PURIFYING	FILOSSTUU	FISTULOUS
ENORRSTUV	TURNOVERS	FGIINPTYY	TYPIFYING	FINOOPRSU	PROFUSION
ENORRSTUU	STRENUOUS	FGIKLLNOS	GOLF LINKS	FINOOPRTT	FOOTPRINT
ENOSSSTTU	STOUTNESS	FGILLNOOW	FOLLOWING	FIOPRSSTT	FIRST POST
EOOOPRRTU	EUROPOORT	FGILLNOWY	FLOWINGLY	FIRSSTTUU	FUTURISTS
EOOPPRRSS	OPPRESSOR,	FGILNNRUU	UNFURLING	FKOORRSTW	FROSTWORK
PROPOSERS		FGILNRRUY	FLURRYING	FLLLOSUUY	SOULFULLY
EOOPPRTTY	PROTOTYPE	FGINOOTUX	OUTFOXING	FLLLSTUUY	LUSTFULLY
EOOPRSSSS	POSSESSOR	FGINORRUW	FURROWING	FLLMNOOSU	FULL MOONS
EOOPRSSTV	STOPOVERS	FGLLNORUW	FULL-GROWN	FLLMNOTUY	FULL MONTY
EOPPRRSTU	SUPPORTER	FGLORSUUU	FULGUROUS	FLLNOORRY	FORLORNLY
EOPPRSSST	STOP PRESS	FHHIORTTW	FORTHWITH	FLLOOPSUW	FOLLOW-UPS
EOPRRSUVY	PURVEYORS	FHIIIKLLS	KILLIFISH	FLLOPSSTU	FULL STOPS
EORRRSTTU	TORTURERS	FHIILRTTY	THRIFTILY	FLNOOPSSU	SPOONFULS,
EORRSSUVY	SURVEYORS	FHIKLSSWY	FLYWHISKS	SPOONSFUL	
FFFOOPTUU	OUT OF PUFF	FHIKNRSTU	TRUNKFISH	FLOOOOSTT	FOOTSTOOL
FFGHILNSU	SHUFFLING	FHILLOOST	FOOTHILLS	FLOORRSUW	SORROWFUL
FFGHILRTU	FRIGHTFUL	FHILLOOSY	FOOLISHLY	FLOPRSSUU	PLUS FOURS
FFGIILLNU	IN FULL FIG	FHIMORSTX	SIXTH FORM	FMNOOORRT	FRONT ROOM
FFGIILNNS	SNIFFLING	FHLLRTUUY	HURTFULLY		
FFGILNNSU	SNUFFLING				

FOOPRRSTU	RUSTPROOF	GHHLOOSTY	HOLY GHOST	GHINOTUWY	WITH YOUNG
FOOPSSSTT	SOFT SPOTS	GHIIKNNRS	SHRINKING	GHINRSTTU	THRUSTING
FOOPSSTUY	PUSSYFOOT	GHIIKNSTT	SKIN-TIGHT	GHJLNNOOS	LONG JOHNS
GGGHINRSU	SHRUGGING	GHIIKNTTT	TIGHTKNIT	GHLLOOOPY	HOPLOLOGY
GGGIILNRW	WRIGGLING	GHIILLNRT	THRILLING	GHLMOOTYY	MYTHOLOGY
GGGILMNSU	SMUGGLING	GHIILLNSS	SHILLINGS	GHLNOOOPY	PHONOLOGY
GGGILNNSU	SNUGGLING	GHIILLRSY	GIRLISHLY	GHLNOOSST	LONG SHOTS
GGHHHIILT	HIGHLIGHT	GHIILNNWY	WHININGLY	GHNNOOPRR	PRONGHORN
GGHHILOSY	HOGGISHLY	GHIILNOPS	POLISHING	GHNOOSTTW	GHOST TOWN
GGHIIILRW	WHIRLIGIG	GHIILNOST	NIGHT SOIL	GHOORTTUW	OUTGROWTH
GGHIIKNNT	KNIGHTING	GHIILNSTW	WHISTLING	GHOPRTUUW	WROUGHT-UP
GGHIIILNNT	LIGHTNING	GHIILNTTW	WHITTLING	GIIILLNNOZ	LIONIZING
GGHIILNPT	PLIGHTING	GHIINNNSY	SHINNYING	GIIILNTUZ	UTILIZING
GGHIILNST	SLIGHTING	GHIINNNWY	WHINNYING	GIIILOSTU	LITIGIOUS
GGHIILPSY	PIGGISHLY	GHIINNOPS	SIPHONING	GIIIMMNST	MISTIMING
GGHIINNNU	UNHINGING	GHIINNPSU	PUNISHING	GIIINNNOP	PINIONING
GGHIINRTW	RIGHT WING	GHIINOPPT	PIPING HOT	GIIINNPRS	INSPIRING
GGHIINSST	SIGHTINGS	GHIINPPSW	WHIPPINGS	GIIINNQRU	INQUIRING
GGHILNNOT	NIGHTLONG	GHIINQSSU	SQUISHING	GIIINNSST	INSISTING
GGHILNOPU	PLOUGHING	GHIIRSSTT	RIGHTISTS	GIIINNTTU	INTUITING
GGHILNOSU	SLOUGHING	GHIKLSSTY	SKYLIGHTS	GIIINPRST	SPIRITING
GGHILNSUY	GUSHINGLY	GHILLNOOW	HOLLOWING	GIIINRTVY	VIRGINITY
GGHILOOPR	LOGOGRIPH	GHILLNOWY	HOWLINGLY	GIIJKNORS	SKIJORING
GGHINNORT	THRONGING	GHILLOOPY	PHILOLOGY	GIIKLLLNY	KILLINGLY
GGHINNOTW	NIGHTGOWN	GHILLOOTY	LITHOLOGY	GIIKLNNOP	LINKOPING
GGIIIMNNP	IMPINGING	GHILMNOOT	MOONLIGHT	GIIKLNNRW	WRINKLING
GGIIIMNSV	MISGIVING	GHILNOOPT	POTHOLING	GIIKLNNTW	TWINKLING
GGIILMNPS	GLIMPSING	GHILNOORY	RHINOLOGY	GIIKMMNSS	SKIMMINGS
GGIILNNSS	GIN SLINGS	GHILNOPSS	LONGSHIPS,	GIIKNSVVY	SKIVVYING
GGIILNNSY	SINGINGLY		SPLOSHING	GIILLLNWY	WILLINGLY
GGIILNPRY	GRIPINGLY	GHILNOSST	SLINGSHOT	GIILLMNPY	LIMPINGLY
GGIILNRZZ	GRIZZLING	GHILNOSTW	NIGHT OWLS	GIILLMNSY	SMILINGLY
GGIIMNNPU	IMPUGNING	GHILNPSUY	PUSHINGLY	GIILLMRST	GRISTMILL
GGIINNORW	INGROWING	GHILNRSUY	RUSHINGLY	GIILLNNUW	UNWILLING
GGIINNPRS	SPRINGING	GHILNSTTU	SHUTTLING	GIILLNOPW	PILLOWING
GGIINNRST	STRINGING	GHILNSTUY	UNSIGHTLY	GIILLNPSY	LISPINGLY
GGIINNRSY	SYRINGING	GHILOOOPY	OPHIOLOGY	GIILMNOPR	IMPLORING
GGIINNSWW	SWING-WING	GHILOOSTY	HISTOLOGY	GIILMRSTU	LITURGISM
GGIINOPSS	GOSSIPING	GHILOPSTT	SPOTLIGHT,	GIILNNOST	ISLINGTON
GGILLNNOY	LONGINGLY		STOPLIGHT	GIILNNOTU	OUTLINING
GGILLNOWY	GLOWINGLY	GHILORSSW	SHOWGIRLS	GIILNNOVV	INVOLVING
GGILLNPUY	GULPINGLY	GHILORSUY	ROGUISHLY	GIILNNSTU	INSULTING
GGILLOOSW	GOLLIWOGS	GHILOSTTU	LIGHTS-OUT	GIILNOTUV	OUTLIVING
GGILNOPRY	GROPINGLY	GHILPRSTY	SPRIGHTLY	GIILNPPST	STIPPLING
GGILNPRSU	SPLURGING	GHILPRTUY	UPRIGHTLY	GIILNPRST	SPLIT RING,
GGINNOSSS	SINGSONGS	GHIMMNRTU	THRUMMING		STRIPLING
GGINOOSTU	OUTGOINGS	GHIMNOOST	SMOOTHING	GIILNPRSY	SPRINGILY
GGINOPRSU	GROUPINGS	GHIMNORUU	HUMOURING	GIILNPSTT	SPLITTING
GGHIIJKNS	HIGH JINKS	GHIMNSSTU	GUNSMITHS	GIILNPTYY	PITYINGLY
GGHIILPST	LIGHTSHIP	GHIMOOPSS	GOMPHOSIS	GIILNQSSU	QUISLINGS
GGHIINOPT	HIGH POINT	GHINNOORU	HONOURING	GIILNRSTY	STRINGILY
GGHIJMPSU	HIGH JUMPS	GHINNOPSY	SYPHONING	GIILNSSTU	LINGUISTS
GGHILRSTU	RUSHLIGHT	GHINNORSU	ONRUSHING,	GIILNSTYZ	STYLIZING
GGHIOPSST	HIGH SPOTS		UNHORSING	GIILOSSST	GLOSSITIS
		GHINOOSST	SHOOTINGS		

GIILPSSTU PUGILISTS	GILNOPTUY POUTINGLY	HIILOSTTY HOSTILITY
GIILRSTTU LITURGIST	GILNOSTUU GLUTINOUS	HIILPSTTY TYPHLITIS
GIIMMNNRST TRIMMINGS	GILNPPSUY SUPPLYING	HIILRSTTY THIRSTILY
GIIMMNNOOT MOTIONING	GILNSSTUU SINGULTUS	HIIMOPSTU HOSPITIUM
GIIMMNNTUY MUTINYING	GILOOOORST OROLOGIST	HIIMORSST HIT-OR-MISS
GIIMMNOPRS PROMISING	GILOOOSSU ISOLOGOUS	HIKLMOOTT MILK TOOTH
GIIMMNOPRT IMPORTING	GILOOOSTT OTOLOGIST	HIKNNORST STINKHORN
GIIMMNOPRV IMPROVING	GILOOOSTZ ZOOLOGIST	HILLLMTUU MULTIHULL
GIIMMNORRR MIRRORING	GILOORSTU UROLOGIST	HILLOOPRW WHIRLPOOL
GIIMNNOTTW TWO-TIMING	GIMMNNOSU SUMMONING	HILLSSTYY STYLISHLY
GIIMMNQRSU SQUIRMING	GIMMNNPSUU SUMMING-UP	HILMNOOST MONOLITHS
GIIMMNRSSU SURMISING	GIMMNRRUU MURMURING	HILMOOSSY HOMOLYSIS
GIINNNOWW WINNOWING	GIMMNRSTU STRUMMING	HILMOOTTY LITHOTOMY
GIINNOOPS POISONING	GIMNNOORS MONSIGNOR	HILOOPTXY TOXOPHILY
GIINNPPUZ UNZIPPING	GIMNOOPRT PROMOTING	HILORSSTT SHORT LIST
GIINNPRST PRINTINGS,	GIMNOPPRT PROMPTING	HIMNOPSTY HYPNOTISM
SPRINTING	GIMOPRUUY UROPYGIUM	HIMOOPRSS MORPHOSIS
GIINNPTTU INPUTTING	GINNOSUUU UNGUINOUS	HIMOORTYZ RHIZOTOMY
GIINNQSTU SQUINTING	GINNRRTUU NURTURING	HIMORSSTU HUMORISTS
GIINNTTUW UNWITTING	GINOOPPRS PROPOSING	HIMPSSSYY SYMPHYSIS
GIINOPRST RIPOSTING	GINOOPRSS PROGNOSIS	HINNOOPSU UNION SHOP
GIINPPRST STRIPPING	GINOOPRTU UPROOTING	HINOPPRRY PORPHYRIN
GIINPRSSU UPRISINGS	GINOORRSW SORROWING	HINOPRSUU ONUPHRIUS
GIINQRSTU SQUIRTING	GINOORSTU TRIGONOUS	HINOPSSTW TOWNSHIPS
GIINRSUVV SURVIVING	GINOOTTUV OUTVOTING	HINOPSTTY HYPNOTIST
GIJKNNOOP JONKOPING	GINOPPRSU PURPOSING	HIOOPPRST TROOPSHIP
GIKLLNRUY LURKINGLY	GINOPPSSU SUPPOSING	HIOPRSSTY SOPHISTRY
GIKLNNNSY KING'S LYNN	GINOPRSTU POSTURING,	HIORRSTTY THYRISTOR
GIKLNNOOO ONLOOKING	SPROUTING	HKKNNOOTY HONKY-TONK
GIKLNNOWY KNOWINGLY	GINOPSSST SIGNPOSTS	HKMOOORSW HOOKWORMS
GIKLNOOOY KONIOLOGY	GINORRTTU TORTURING	HKOOPRSSW WORKSHOPS
GIKNNNOUW UNKNOWING	GINPRRTUU RUPTURING	HLLNOOORR HONOR ROLL
GIKNNOSTW KINGSTOWN	GINRSTTTU STRUTTING	HLLPRSUUY SULPHURYL
GIKNOOPRV PROVOKING	GIOPRSTWY GIPSYWORT	HLMOOPPRY POLYMORPH
GIKNOOTWW KOWTOWING	GLLNOOOOS SONGOLOLO	HLNOOPPYY POLYPHONY
GIKOORRVY KRIVOY ROG	GLLOOPSTY POLYGLOTS	HLNOORSTU SOLOTHURN
GILLLLNOY LOLLINGLY	GLMNOOPUY POLYGONUM	HMMOORSSU MUSHROOMS
GILLLLNUY LULLINGLY	GLMOORSWW GLOW-WORMS	HMNNOOOPY MONOPHONY
GILLLNOOP LOLLOPING	GLNOOOSTY NOSTOLOGY	HMNOOOSST MOON SHOTS
GILLLNORY ROLLINGLY	GLOOOPRTY TROPOLOGY	HMOOOPRSY HOMOSPORY
GILLMNOOY LIMNOLOGY	GMMNOSTUY TOMMY GUNS	HMOOORSSW SHOWROOMS
GILLMOORR GRILLROOM	GMNOORSSW MOSS-GROWN	HNOOPPTYY PHONOTYPY
GILLMOSSY SYLLOGISM	GNOOOPRSY SPOROGONY	HNOOPRSST POST HORNS
GILLNNORU UNROLLING	GNOOPRTYY PROTOGYNY	HNOOPRTTY PHYTOTRON
GILLNOPSY SLOPINGLY	GNORSTTUU STRUNG-OUT	HOOORTTTW TOOTHWORT
GILLNOPTU POLLUTING	HHIILNNSY HUNNISHLY	HOOOSSTTU SHOOT-OUTS
GILLNORST STROLLING	HHLMOOPYY HOMOPHYLY	HOOPRSTTU SOUTHPORT
GILLOOOPY OLIGOPOLY	HHMNOOOPY HOMOPHONY	IIIKLLNPS SPILLIKIN
GILMMNOOS MONGOLISM	HHNOORRST SHORTHORN	IIIKMNRST MINISKIRT
GILMNNOTY LYMINGTON	HHORRSSUU RUSH HOURS	IIILNOSTV VIOLINIST
GILMNOPRY ROMPINGLY	HIIILNSST NIHILISTS	IIILNTTUY INUTILITY
GILMOOSTY MYOLOGIST	HIILLMNOT MILLIONTH	IIINNOTTU INTUITION
GILNNOOSU UNLOOSING	HIILLOOOP HOI POLLOI	IIINPRSSU NISI PRIUS
GILNNRSSU NURSLINGS	HIILNSSWY SWINISHLY	IIINSSSTU SINUSITIS

IIJNORSUU	INJURIOUS	IINOSSTVY	SYNOVITIS	IMNORSTTU	STRONTIUM
IIKLLMPST	SPILT MILK	IIOOPRSST	SPIRITOSO	IMOOOSTTZ	ZOOTOMIST
IIKNNNOOS	ONIONSKIN	IIOPSTTTU	SPIT IT OUT	IMOOPPSTY	POMPOSITY
IILLMNOPU	POLLINIUM	IIORSTTTU	TUTIORIST	IMOOPRSST	IMPOSTORS
IILLMPRSU	SPIRILLUM	IJMNOORTW	JOINTWORM	IMOOQSSTU	MOSQUITOS
IILLNNNOO	NONILLION	IJMPSSTUU	JUMPSUITS	IMOORSSTT	MOTORISTS
IILLNORST	TRILLIONS	IKLMORSSW	SILKWORMS	IMORSUVXY	MYXOVIRUS
IILLNOSSU	ILLUSIONS	IKLNOPSST	SLIPKNOTS	INNOOSSUU	UNISONOUS
IILLOPSSY	LIPOLYSIS	IKNOORRSW	IRONWORKS	INOOOPSSU	POISONOUS
IILLOSTVY	VILLOSITY	IKORSSTTU	OUTSKIRTS	INOOORSTU	NOTORIOUS
IILMMMSSU	MUSLIMISM	ILLLMOPSS	PLIMSOLLS	INOOPPTTU	PUT OPTION
IILMNOOPS	IMPLOSION	ILLLOOPPS	LOLLIPOPS	INOOPRSST	POSITRONS
IILMNOPSU	IMPULSION	ILLLPSUUV	PULVILLUS	INOOPSSTT	SPITTOONS
IILMOPSSS	SOLIPSISM	ILLNOOPTU	POLLUTION	INOPRSTTU	PRINTOUTS
IILMOPSSY	IMPIOUSLY	ILLNOPVYY	POLYVINYL	INORSSSUV	SUN VISORS
IILNOOPST	POSTILION	ILLOOQSUY	SOLILOQUY	INRSTTTUU	UNIT TRUST
IILOPRTXY	PROLIXITY	ILLOORSSW	SLOW LORIS	IOOPPRRTU	POTPOURRI
IILOPSSST	SOLIPSIST	ILLOQRTUW	QUILLWORT	IOOPPRSST	PROPTOSIS
IILOSTVVZ	SLIVOVITZ	ILLORSSSW	SWISS ROLL	IOOPPRSVY	PROVISORY
IIMNNOSTU	MUNITIONS	ILMNOOSUY	OMINOUSLY	IOORSSTUV	VIRTUOSOS
IIMNOOSSS	OMISSIONS	ILMNOPTUU	PLUTONIUM	IORRSSUVV	SURVIVORS
IIMNORSTU	MINOR SUIT,	ILMNOPXYY	POLYMYXIN	KLLMNSSUU	NUMSKULLS
ROUTINISM		ILMOSSYYZ	ZYMOLYSIS	KMOOORRSW	WORKROOMS
IIMNPRSST	MISPRINTS	ILNOOPRSU	PROLUSION	LMOOPPSUY	POMPOUSLY
IIMOPRTXY	PROXIMITY	ILNOOSSTU	SOLUTIONS	LMOORSSWW	SLOWWORMS
IIMOPSSTT	OPTIMISTS	ILNOOSUXY	NOXIOUSLY	LNOOOPPTY	PONTYPOOL
IIMOQSTUX	QUIXOTISM	ILNOPRXYY	PYROXYLIN	LNOOOPRST	POLTROONS
IIMORSTTU	TUTIORISM	ILNORSUUY	RUINOUSLY	LOOPRRSUY	PROLUSORY
IINNOORST	INTORSION	ILNOSSUUY	SINUOUSLY	LORSTUUUV	VULTUROUS
IINNOPPST	PINPOINTS	ILOOPPRSY	ISOPROPYL	MMOOPPRSU	PUMP ROOMS
IINNORSTU	INTRUSION	ILOOPRSTU	PORT LOUIS	MNNOOOPSY	MONOPSONY
IINNORTTU	NUTRITION	ILOORSTUY	RIOTOUSLY	MNOORSSTU	MONSTROUS
IINNOSSTU	UNIONISTS	ILOPPSSTU	POPULISTS	MNOORSSTW	SNOWSTORM
IINOOPRSV	PROVISION	ILOPRSSYY	PYROLYSIS	MOOORRSTW	TOMORROWS
IINOOPSST	POSITIONS	ILORSUUUX	LUXURIOUS	MOPSSTUUU	SUMPTUOUS
IINOOPSVY	POISON IVY	IMMMNOORS	MORMONISM	NOOOOPRTV	PORTO NOVO
IINOORSTT	SORTITION	IMMOPPRTU	IMPROMPTU	NOOOPPSSU	SOUP SPOON
IINOPRRTU	IRRUPTION	IMMOPSSUY	SYMPOSIUM	OOPRSSTUU	STUPOROUS
IINOPSSTY	SPINOSITY	IMNNOOPTW	TOPMINNOW	OOPRTTTUY	PUTTYROOT
IINORSTTU	ROUTINIST	IMNOOOPRT	PROMOTION		
IINOSSTUY	SINUOSITY	IMNOOOPTT	MOOT POINT		

AAAAABCCRS	ASARABACCA	AAABCINNRT	CANTABRIAN
AAAAABBDDIS	ADDIS ABABA	AAABCLLMRU	AMBULACRAL
AAAABCCLNS	CASABLANCA	AAABCLNOST	CANAL BOATS
AAAABCLLSV	BALACLAVAS	AAABDDHIRY	BAD HAIR DAY
AAAABCNNTU	CABANATUAN	AAABDEEGLM	DAMAGEABLE
AAAABDFILS	FAISALABAD	AAABDEHLRZ	HAZARDABLE
AAAABGKORY	KABARAGOYA	AAABDEORVW	ABOVE
AAAABHJRSY	RAJYA SABHA		AWARD
AAAABIKLLS	BALALAIKAS	AAABDMNNRU	BARRAMUNDA
AAAACDGMNS		AAABDMORSS	AMBASSADOR
	MADAGASCAN	AAABEEGLMN	MANAGEABLE
AAAACDGMRS	MADAGASCAR	AAABEELLPP	APPEALABLE
AAAACGMNRT	MAGNA	AAABEELMNS	ABLE SEAMAN
	CARTA	AAABEELPPS	APPEASABLE
AAAACHILPP	APPALACHIA	AAABEGLMNY	MANAGEABLY
AAAACILPST	CATAPLASIA	AAABEIJNRZ	AZERBAIJAN
AAAACINNRU	ARAUCANIAN	AAABEILLMR	MARIABELLA
AAAACLNRST	SANTA CLARA	AAABEILLSS	ASSAILABLE
AAAACMNRST	CATAMARANS	AAABEILNTT	ATTAINABLE
AAAADFNRWY	FAR AND	AAABEKRSWY	BREAKAWAYS
	AWAY	AAABELLNSY	ANALYSABLE
AAAADIJVWY	VIJAYAWADA	AAABELNRRT	NARRATABLE
AAAADILLMS	DALAI LAMAS	AAABELRSTW	BASALTWARE
AAAAEGLMMT	AMALGAMATE	AAABHIOPQU	AQUAPHOBIA
AAAAGGGGWW	WAGGA	AAABHLPRUW	BAHAWALPUR
	WAGGA	AAABHNRSSU	SUB-SAHARAN
AAAAGMSSSU	MASSASAUGA	AAABIKLNPP	BALIKPAPAN
AAAAGNPRUY	PARAGUAYAN	AAABIKNNNS	BANANA SKIN
AAAAIMNNNP	PANAMANIAN	AAABILLNOS	LABIONASAL
AAAAIMNNRST	SANTA MARIA	AAABILRSTV	BRATISLAVA
AAAAKKKLPR	KARA-KALPAK	AAABIMNPRS	PAN-ARABISM
AAAAKMNNORY	ARAKAN	AAABIMOPRR	PARAMARIBO
	YOMA	AAACCDELSV	CAVALCADES
AAAALMNRSZ	SALMANAZAR	AAACCEHRSS	SACCHARASE
AAAAMNRSTT	SANTA MARTA	AAACCEHRST	SACCHARATE
AAAARTTTTT	RAT-A-TAT-TAT	AAACCEIPTT	CAPACITATE
AAABBCCHMO	COCHABAMBA	AAACCENRUV	CUERNAVACA
AAABBCILST	SABBATICAL	AAACCILLNT	CATACLINAL
AAABBEIRSS	BESSARABIA	AAACCILLRS	CASCARILLA
AAABBINRRS	BARBARIANS	AAACCINRTT	ANTARCTICA
AAABCCHLNS	BACCHANALS	AAACCIPRTT	PARATACTIC
AAABCCHNRS	CHARABANCS	AAACDEIMMS	MACADAMISE
AAABCCKNSV	CANVASBACK	AAACDEIMMZ	MACADAMIZE
AAABCDEIRS	SCARABAEID	AAACDEKNPY	PANCAKE DAY
AAABCDELNR	CANDELABRA	AAACDELMNR	CALAMANDER
AAABCDRRSU	BARRACUDAS	AAACDELMRS	SALAD CREAM
AAABCEGGGR	BAGGAGE CAR	AAACDGIILR	CARDIALGIA
AAABCEGGNR	GARBAGE CAN	AAACDHINNR	ARACHNIDAN
AAABCEHLSS	CALABASHES	AAACDILNOP	PINA COLADA
AAABCEHLTT	ATTACHABLE	AAACDILRTY	CARYATIDAL
AAABCELLRS	CLARABELLA	AAACEENPPR	APPEARANCE
AAABCERSSU	SCARABAEUS	AAACEENRSS	CAESAREANS
AAABCIILST	BASILICATA	AAACEFLQTU	CATAFALQUE
AAABCIKLMR	BLACK MARIA	AAACEGNORT	ARCTOGAEAN
AAABCIKRSS	CASSIA BARK		

AAACEHLNSV	AVALANCHES		
AAACEILMNT	CATAMENIAL		
AAACEINNRT	CATENARIAN		
AAACEINPST	ANAPAESTIC,		
	SEA CAPTAIN		
AAACEINRRS	SARRACENIA		
AAACEJKNPS	JACKANAPES		
AAACELLNPT	APLACENTAL		
AAACELMPRT	METACARPAL		
AAACGGIORV	CARAVAGGIO		
AAACGHNRTT	TRAGACANTH		
AAACGILLMY	AGAMICALLY		
AAACGILLNO	ANALOGICAL		
AAACGINNRU	NICARAGUAN		
AAACHINPRT	CARPATHIAN		
AAACHLNOTU	TALCAHUANO		
AAACHLNRST	CHARLATANS		
AAACHNPRTY	PYRACANTHA		
AAACIINNPR	INCAPARINA		
AAACIIRSSS	ASCARIASIS		
AAACIKLMNP	PACK ANIMAL		
AAACIKLMNR	LAMARCKIAN		
AAACILLMNY	MANIACALLY		
AAACILLRTU	URAL-ALTAIC		
AAACILMMNO	AMMONIACAL		
AAACILMNOT	ANATOMICAL		
AAACILNPST	ANAPLASTIC		
AAACILNRSS	CARNASSIAL		
AAACILNRST	SCARLATINA		
AAACIMNPTY	PANAMA CITY		
AAACINOPRS	PARANOIACS		
AAACISSSTT	CATASTASIS		
AAACLMNRVY	CAVALRYMAN		
AAACLNSSTU	SANTA CLAUS		
AAACNORSSU	ANASARCOUS		
AAADEELLNV	AVELLANEDA		
AAADEELNRW	DELAWAREAN		
AAADEFIOST	ASAFOETIDA		
AAADEGGRTV	AGGRAVATED		
AAADEGHMNR	AHMEDNAGAR		
AAADEGLMTY	AMYGDALATE		
AAADEGNRTV	AVANT-GARDE		
AAADEGNSTV	ADVANTAGES		
AAADEHLPRT	HARD PALATE		
AAADEILNRX	ALEXANDRIA		
AAADEIMNNT	ADAMANTINE		
AAADELMNRS	SALAMANDER		
AAADELMPPS	ADAM'S APPLE		
AAADELNPQU	AQUAPLANED		
AAADGHNQRY	QARAGHANDY		
AAADGIILLR	GAILLARDIA		
AAADGILLNR	GRANADILLA		
AAADGINNPT	GIANT PANDA		
AAADGLLNOR	ALLARGANDO		

AAADGNOPPR	PROPAGANDA
AAADHHMRTU	HADHRAMAUT
AAADHMMMNU	MUHAMMADAN
AAADIILNPR	LAPIDARIAN
AAADILMNST	DALMATIANS
AAADILMORR	RADIO ALARM
AAADILNOPS	DIAPASONAL
AAADINOPTT	ADAPTATION
AAADLNQRTU	QUADRANTAL
AAADORSTTU	AUTOSTRADA
AAAEEGGLRS	GARAGE SALE
AAAEFLLMRS	FALSE ALARM
AAAEFLMNST	MALFEASANT
AAAEGHIOPR	AEROPHAGIA
AAAEGHLLNP	PHALANGEAL
AAAEGILMNR	MANAGERIAL
AAAEGILNST	EAST ANGLIA
AAAEGILPPR	PARAPLEGIA
AAAEGINPRS	ASPARAGINE
AAAEGLMTXY	METAGALAXY
AAAEGMRRTT	MARGARETTA
AAAEGNNTTT	AT A TANGENT
AAAEGPSSWY	PASSAGEWAY
AAAEHHLSSV	HAVE A SLASH
AAAEHIMRTU	HAEMATURIA
AAAEHINSTU	EUTHANASIA
AAAEHKNOTT	TAKE AN OATH
AAAEHPPRRS	PARAPHRASE
AAAEIILNTT	ITALIANATE
AAAEILLPST	PALATALISE
AAAEILLPTZ	PALATALIZE
AAAEILMPST	METAPLASIA
AAAEILMRTU	TULARAEMIA
AAAEILNPRT	PLANETARIA
AAAEILNPTT	PALATINATE
AAAEIMNPRS	PARAMNESIA
AAAEIMNQRU	AQUAMARINE
AAAEINNRTV	TANANARIVE
AAAELLNRTT	TARANTELLA
AAAELMMRST	ALMA MATERS
AAAELNPQSU	AQUAPLANES
AAAFFIILNN	FIANNA FAIL
AAAFIJNNRS	RAFSANJANI
AAAFIKPRRS	SAFARI PARK
AAAGGILLNO	ALGOLAGNIA
AAAGGILRST	GASTRALGIA
AAAGGNNRTU	GARGANTUAN
AAAGHILRRT	ARTHRALGIA
AAAGHIMNOP	PHAGOMANIA
AAAGHNPSTU	AGAPANTHUS
AAAGHPPRRS	PARAGRAPHS
AAAGIILMNR	MARGINALIA
AAAGIKNNTY	TANGANYIKA

AAAGIMMNRR	GRAMMARIAN
AAAGIMNSTT	ANASTIGMAT
AAAGIMRRST	MARGARITAS
AAAGJJKORT	JOGJAKARTA
AAAGJLNRUW	GUJRANWALA
AAAGJNOTUU	GUANAJUATO
AAAGKORTYY	YOGYAKARTA
AAAGLMMNPU	MPUMALANGA
AAAGLNRSTU	NATURAL GAS
AAAGLRSSTU	ASTRAGALUS
AAAGMNNOTU	GUANTANAMO
AAAHKKNSTZ	KAZAKHSTAN
AAAHLLOSTY	AYATOLLAHS
AAAHLMNPST	PHANTASMAL
AAAHNPRRSU	SAHARANPUR
AAAIIMNRTU	MAURITANIA
AAAIINNRST	SANITARIAN
AAAIKLMNRS	KARAMANLIS
AAAILLLPTY	PALATIALLY
AAAILLMNNZ	MANZANILLA
AAAILLMRTW	MARTIAL LAW
AAAILLNOTV	LAVATIONAL
AAAILLORTV	LAVATORIAL
AAAILMPSTU	TAMAULIPAS
AAAILMRRTT	MARTIAL ART
AAAILNNOTT	NATATIONAL
AAAILNOTTX	TAXATIONAL
AAAILNRSTU	AUSTRALIAN, SATURNALIA
AAAILNSSST	ASSAILANTS
AAAILOPRSV	VALPARAISO
AAAILPPRSS	APPRAISALS
AAAIMNORST	INAMORATAS
AAAIMNRSST	SAMARITANS
AAAIPPRRSX	PARAPRAXIS
AAALMNOPRR	PARANORMAL
AAALNNOSST	ASSONANTAL
AAALNRSTTU	TARANTULAS
AAAMRTZZZZ	RAZZMATAZZ
AABBBELORS	ABSORBABLE
AABBCDKLOR	BLACKBOARD
AABBCEEHLL	BLEACHABLE
AABBCEHLLS	BEACH BALLS
AABBCEILRS	ASCRIBABLE
AABBCELMOT	COMBATABLE
AABBCENORS	ABSORBANCE
AABBCIILNR	RABBINICAL
AABBCIJKRT	JACKRABBIT
AABBDDEENN	BADEN-BADEN
AABBDDEORR	BREADBOARD
AABBDEGILR	ABRIDGABLE
AABBDEIRRS	BARBARISED
AABBDEIRRZ	BARBARIZED

AABBDELORS	ADSORBABLE
AABBDENORS	BROAD BEANS
AABBDEOORV	ABOVEBOARD
AABBDNRSSS	BRASS BANDS
AABBEEHLRT	BREATHABLE
AABBEEIRTV	ABBREVIATE
AABBEELLRT	BARBELLATE
AABBEELNRU	UNBEARABLE
AABBEELNTU	UNBEATABLE
AABBEILMNO	ABOMINABLE
AABBEILNOT	OBTAINABLE
AABBEILRRT	ARBITRABLE
AABBEKLLST	BASKETBALL
AABBELLOSV	ABSOLVABLE
AABBELNRUY	UNBEARABLY
AABBILMNOY	ABOMINABLY
AABBIMRSSS	BARBARISMS
AABBMMNPYY	NAMBY-PAMBY
AABBNNUUYY	BUNYA-BUNYA
AABCCDELOR	ACCORDABLE
AABCCEELPT	ACCEPTABLE
AABCCEHHIR	BEACHCHAIR
AABCCEKKPR	BACKPACKER
AABCCEKPSS	BACKSPACES
AABCCELLLU	CALCULABLE
AABCCELOST	ACCOSTABLE
AABCCELPTY	ACCEPTABLY
AABCCGIKLM	BLACK MAGIC
AABCCHHKST	HATCHBACKS
AABCCIINRT	BACITRACIN
AABCCIKNRR	CRACKBRAIN
AABCCILNSS	CABIN CLASS
AABCCIORST	ACROBATICS
AABCCJKKLS	BLACKJACKS
AABCDDEELU	ADDUCEABLE
AABCDDEHKN	BACKHANDED
AABCDDEIRR	BARRICADED
AABCDDEKLS	SADDLEBACK
AABCDEEEFL	DEFACEABLE
AABCDEEHHS	BEACHHEADS
AABCDEEHLT	DETACHABLE
AABCDEEILR	ERADICABLE
AABCDEELLR	DECLARABLE
AABCDEFIRT	FABRICATED
AABCDEHKLS	BLACKHEADS
AABCDEHKLT	BLACK DEATH
AABCDEHKNR	BACKHANDER
AABCDEIITV	ABDICATIVE
AABCDEILRT	CALIBRATED
AABCDEIRRR	BARRICADER
AABCDEIRRS	BARRICADES
AABCDELNNU	UNBALANCED
AABCDELORS	SCALEBOARD

AABCDELORT	CARBOLATED	AABCEINORT	ABREACTION	AABDDEELMN	DEMANDABLE
AABCDENNRS	BARN DANCES	AABCEIORST	AEROBATICS	AABDDEGGNS	SANDBAGGED
AABCDENORT	CARBONATED	AABCEIRSTT	TETRABASIC	AABDDEGLSS	SADDLEBAGS
AABCDERSTT	ABSTRACTED	AABCEKKLNS	BLACKSNAKE	AABDDEHLMO	HEBDOMADAL
AABCDGIINT	ABDICATING	AABCEKMRTT	BACK MATTER	AABDDEHLRS	BALDERDASH
AABCDGIKNT	BACKDATING	AABCEKPPRS	PAPERBACKS	AABDDEHORS	HEADBOARDS
AABCDGKLRU	BLACKGUARD	AABCEKRSTW	BACKWATERS	AABDDEILRY	DAILY BREAD
AABCDHKLOR	CHALKBOARD	AABCELMNSU	AMBULANCES	AABDDEMRTU	ADUMBRATED
AABCDHMORT	MATCHBOARD	AABCELMOPR	COMPARABLE	AABDDHORSS	DASHBOARDS
AABCDIILLO	DIABOLICAL	AABCELMTUU	ACETABULUM	AABDDNNSST	BANDSTANDS
AABCDIINOT	ABDICATION	AABCELNOTU	OUTBALANCE	AABDDORRST	DARTBOARDS
AABCDILMMS	LAMBDACISM	AABCELOOSS	CALABOOSES	AABDEEELMS	SEALED-BEAM
AABCDKLRWY	BACKWARDLY	AABCELPPRS	CRAB APPLES	AABDEEFLRY	DEFRAYABLE
AABCDNNORT	CONTRABAND	AABCELRRTU	TRABECULAR	AABDEEGLRR	REGARDABLE
AABCDORSST	BROADCASTS	AABCERRTUU	BUREAUCRAT	AABDEEHLLN	HANDLEABLE
AABCEEEFFL	EFFACEABLE	AABCFHKLSS	FLASHBACKS	AABDEEHRRT	THREADBARE
AABCEEEMRR	MACEBEARER	AABCFIORRT	FABRICATOR	AABDEEILNT	DETAINABLE
AABCEEERTT	EBRACTEATE	AABCGIKNRR	BARRACKING	AABDEELNPX	EXPANDABLE
AABCEEERTX	EXACERBATE	AABCGILLSU	SUBGLACIAL	AABDEELNRU	UNREADABLE
AABCEEGHLN	CHANGEABLE	AABCGKMMNO		AABDEELORT	ELABORATED
AABCEEGHLR	CHARGEABLE	BACKGAMMON		AABDEELPRS	SPREADABLE
AABCEEHILV	ACHIEVABLE	AABCGLRRTU	CAT BURGLAR	AABDEELRRW	REWARDABLE
AABCEEHLMP	PEACH MELBA	AABCHHIMPR	AMPHIBRACH	AABDEFFLOR	AFFORDABLE
AABCEEHLNS	ENCASHABLE	AABCHHIRST	BATH CHAIRS	AABDEGGGNN	
AABCEEHLRS	SEARCHABLE	AABCHHPSTY	BATHYSCAPH	GANG-BANGED	
AABCEEHLTY	CHALYBEATE	AABCHILRTY	CHARITABLY	AABDEGGNRS	SANDBAGGER
AABCEEIRTU	EUBACTERIA	AABCHINOTT	COHABITANT	AABDEGGORU	BROAD GAUGE
AABCEEKLSS	LEASEBACKS	AABCHIOOPR	ACROPHOBIA	AABDEGHLNS	BANGLADESH
AABCEELLLR	RECALLABLE	AABCHKLPSS	SPLASHBACK	AABDEGINRS	GABARDINES
AABCEELLNS	CLEANSABLE	AABCHNRRUY	BRACHYURAN	AABDEGORST	GOATSBEARD
AABCEELNRT	TABERNACLE	AABCIILLMY	IAMBICALLY	AABDEHITTU	HABITUATED
AABCEESTTU	SUBACETATE	AABCIILNOT	ANABOLITIC	AABDEHKNRS	HANDBRAKES
AABCEFLORT	FACTORABLE	AABCIILPTY	CAPABILITY	AABDEHLLNR	HANDBALLER
AABCEGHLNY	CHANGEABLY	AABCIILTTY	ACTABILITY	AABDEHLNRS	HANDLEBARS
AABCEGIRRR	CARRIER BAG	AABCIIOPRT	PARABIOTIC	AABDEIKNUZ	ADZUKI BEAN
AABCEGLLOU	COAGULABLE	AABCIKRSST	BACKSTAIRS	AABDEILLNR	BANDERILLA
AABCEGLMNN	BLANCMANGE	AABCILMOPR	PROCAMBIAL	AABDEILLSY	DIALYSABLE
AABCEHIIMM	MIAMI BEACH	AABCILMOST	CATABOLISM	AABDEILRSV	ADVERBIALS
AABCEHILMN	MACHINABLE	AABCILNNUU	INCUNABULA	AABDEIMNOT	ABOMINATED
AABCEHILRT	CHARITABLE	AABCILNSUV	SUBCLAVIAN	AABDEINNRR	BERNARDINA
AABCEHINRT	BRANCHIATE	AABCILORRT	CALIBRATOR	AABDEIORTU	BIQUADRATE
AABCEHKLRT	BLACKHEART	AABCILRRUV	VIBRACULAR	AABDEIRRTT	ARBITRATED
AABCEHKLSS	BACKLASHES	AABCIQSTUU	SUBAQUATIC	AABDEIRSST	BASTARDISE
AABCEHLNST	STANCHABLE	AABCKLMOOR	BLACKAMOOR	AABDEIRSTZ	BASTARDIZE
AABCEHRRTT	TETRABRACH	AABCKRSSST	BRASS TACKS	AABDEJLSTU	ADJUSTABLE
AABCEIINTU	BEAUTICIAN	AABCLLNNNO	CANNONBALL	AABDEKLNRU	DARK NEBULA
AABCEILLMP	IMPLACABLE	AABCLMMRUU	AMBULACRUM	AABDEKORST	SKATEBOARD
AABCEILLPP	APPLICABLE	AABCLMOPRY	COMPARABLY	AABDELLNNO	BELLADONNA
AABCEILMNS	IMBALANCES	AABCLORUVY	VOCABULARY	AABDELLNST	TABLELANDS
AABCEILMST	MASTICABLE	AABCMNOSTT	COMBATANTS	AABDELNOPR	PARDONABLE
AABCEILNOT	ACTIONABLE	AABCNORSST	CONTRABASS	AABDELNRUY	UNREADABLY
AABCEILOSS	ASSOCIABLE	AABDDDEEHL	BALDHEADED	AABDELRSTU	BALUSTRADE
AABCEILOTT	CATABOLITE	AABDDEEEHR	BAREHEADED	AABDEMNNNO	ONE-MAN
AABCEILQRU	ACQUIRABLE	AABDDEEGLR	DEGRADABLE	BAND	
				AABDEMNNRS	BRAND NAMES

AABDEMNRST	BANDMASTER	AABEEKLRRW	LAW-BREAKER
AABDEMORST	DREAMBOATS	AABEEKRRTW	BREAKWATER
AABDENSSTW	SWEATBANDS	AABEELLMNT	LAMENTABLE
AABDEOPPRR	PAPERBOARD	AABEELLNSU	UNSEALABLE
AABDEOPRST	PASTEBOARD	AABEELLPRR	PALLBEARER
AABDFHIINT	IN BAD FAITH	AABEELMRSU	MEASURABLE
AABDFHLORS	FLASHBOARD	AABEELMSST	BASE METALS
AABDFKNRST	BANK DRAFTS	AABEELMSTT	METASTABLE
AABDGIILNW	LAW-ABIDING	AABEELNORS	REASONABLE
AABDGIKNOS	BAKING SODA	AABEELNOSS	SEASONABLE
AABDGINNNO	ABANDONING	AABEELNPTT	PATENTABLE
AABDGNNOSW		AABEELNRSW	ANSWERABLE
	BANDWAGONS	AABEELOPRV	EVAPORABLE
AABDHLORRU	HARD LABOUR	AABEELPPRT	PALPEBRATE
AABDHMNNSU	HUSBANDMAN	AABEELPPRY	PREPAYABLE
AABDHNORRW	HANDBARROW	AABEELRTTW	WATER TABLE
AABDIIKRRY	DIYARBAKIR	AABEELSSSS	ASSESSABLE
AABDIINNRR	BRAIN DRAIN	AABEELSTTT	ATTESTABLE
AABDIJOORU	OUIJA BOARD	AABEELSTTX	BATTLEAXES
AABDILOOPR	PARABOLOID	AABEEQRSSU	ARABESQUES
AABDILORSS	SAILBOARDS	AABEERRSTT	STREET ARAB
AABDILORST	TAILBOARDS	AABEFGIILS	GASIFIABLE
AABDIMNRRU	BARRAMUNDI	AABEFGKLNR	KLANGFARBE
AABDINSSTW	WAISTBANDS	AABEFHIKRT	BREAK FAITH
AABDKLORSW	BOARDWALKS	AABEFHLMOT	FATHOMABLE
AABDLNNTUY	ABUNDANTLY	AABEFIILLS	SALIFIABLE
AABDLNOPRY	PARDONABLY	AABEFIILRT	RATIFIABLE
AABDLNOSTU	BASUTOLAND	AABEFILLNT	INFLATABLE
AABDLORSUY	LABOUR DAYS	AABEFINRRT	AFTERBRAIN
AABDORRSTW	STRAWBOARD	AABEFKRSST	BREAKFASTS
AABEEELLPR	REPEALABLE	AABEFLORUV	FAVOURABLE
AABEEELLRV	REVEALABLE	AABEGGGNNR	
AABEEEELMNS	ABLE SEAMEN		GANG-BANGER
AABEEELPRT	REPEATABLE	AABEGHORRU	HARBOURAGE
AABEEELRRT	TALEBEARER	AABEGIILMN	IMAGINABLE
AABEEFHORT	FEATHER BOA	AABEGILNSS	ASSIGNABLE
AABEEFILRR	RAREFIABLE	AABEGILRST	ALGEBRAIST
AABEEFLLLT	FLABELLATE	AABEGINNOT	ABNEGATION
AABEEFLNTT	FATTENABLE	AABEGLOPPR	PROPAGABLE
AABEEGHLRT	GATHERABLE	AABEHIILTT	HABILITATE
AABEEGILNR	REGAINABLE	AABEHIOOPR	AEROPHOBIA
AABEEGIMNS	SENEGAMBIA	AABEHKLNSU	UNSHAKABLE
AABEEGINRR	BERENGARIA	AABEIILNRV	INVARIABLE
AABEEGLMSS	ASSEMBLAGE	AABEIILNST	BANALITIES,
AABEEGNORT	BARONETAGE		INSATIABLE
AABEEHKRRT	HEARTBREAK	AABEIILPRT	BIPARIETAL
AABEEHRSTT	HEARTBEATS	AABEIILSST	ASSIBILATE
AABEEILLRZ	REALIZABLE	AABEIIMOSS	AMOEBIASIS
AABEEILMNX	EXAMINABLE	AABEIINNST	IN ABSENTIA
AABEEILMNR	RETAINABLE	AABEIIRRTT	ABIRRITATE
AABEEILPRR	REPAIRABLE	AABEIJKLRS	JAILBREAKS
AABEEJKRRW	JAWBREAKER	AABEIJLOSU	BEAUJOLAIS
AABEEKLMRR	REMARKABLE	AABEIKLMST	MISTAKABLE
AABEEKLMRT	MARKETABLE	AABEILLMPP	IMPALPABLE
		AABEILLNRS	BALLERINAS

AABEILLNUV	INVALUABLE
AABEILLORV	LABIOVELAR
AABEILLRYZ	REALIZABLY
AABEILMMRU	BARIUM MEAL
AABEILMNTU	ALBUMINATE
AABEILMNTV	AMBIVALENT
AABEILMPSS	IMPASSABLE
AABEILNNTU	BIANNULATE
AABEILOPRS	PARABOLISE
AABEILOPRZ	PARABOLIZE
AABEILRSTU	TABULARISE
AABEILRSVY	ABRASIVELY
AABEILRTTT	TITRATABLE
AABEILRTUZ	TABULARIZE
AABEIMPRTV	VAMPIRE BAT
AABEINORRT	ABERRATION
AABEINORTT	TRABEATION
AABEINRSST	ABSTAINERS
AABEINRSVW	BRAINWAVES
AABEIRRTTT	BITARTRATE
AABEKLMRRY	REMARKABLY
AABEKLMRTY	MARKETABLY
AABEKNNRRU	RUN A BANKER
AABEKRSSTT	BASKET-STAR
AABELLLNNU	ANNULLABLE
AABELLMNTY	LAMENTABLY
AABELLNPUY	UNPLAYABLE
AABELMPRRU	PREAMBULAR
AABELMRSUY	MEASURABLY
AABELNORSY	REASONABLY
AABELNOSSY	SEASONABLY
AABELNPRST	BARNSTAPLE
AABELNRSWY	ANSWERABLY
AABELOORRT	ELABORATOR
AABELOPRRS	POLAR BEARS
AABELOPRUV	VAPOURABLE
AABELSTTTU	STATUTABLE
AABEMOSSTT	STEAMBOATS
AABEMRSTTU	MASTURBATE
AABFFIILTY	AFFABILITY
AABFLMNOTY	FLAMBOYANT
AABFLORUVY	FAVOURABLY
AABGGIINNR	BARGAINING
AABGGILNRZ	GLAZING-BAR
AABGGINORT	ABROGATING
AABGGINOST	SABOTAGING
AABGHILOOP	ALGOPHOBIA
AABGIILNOR	ABORIGINAL
AABGIINNST	ABSTAINING
AABGILLNST	BALLASTING
AABGILMNST	LAMBASTING
AABGILNTTU	TABULATING
AABGINNOTW	ANGWANTIBO
AABGINOORT	ABROGATION

AABGIRSSTU	BASS GUITAR	AACCCEENPT	ACCEPTANCE	AACCEKOPPT	COP A PACKET
AABGORSTVY	GRAVY BOATS	AACCCEILTT	CATALECTIC	AACCEKRRST	RACETRACKS
AABHIIMNPS	AMPHIBIANS	AACCCEIORT	CACCIATORE	AACCELMSTY	CYCLAMATES
AABHIINNTT	INHABITANT	AACCCEOSTU	CACTACEOUS	AACCELMTUU	ACCUMULATE
AABHIINOTT	HABITATION	AACCCILRSS	CLASSIC CAR	AACCELORSU	CALCAREOUS
AABHIKLLRU	RUB' AL KHALI	AACCCINRUY	INACCURACY	AACCELRTUY	ACCURATELY
AABHILLTUY	HABITUALLY	AACCDDEHKN		AACCENRSTU	CRUSTACEAN
AABHIMMNRS	BRAHMANISM		CACK-HANDED	AACCFGILLU	CALCIFUGAL
AABHIMRTVZ	BAR MITZVAH	AACCDEGHRR	CHARGE CARD	AACCFHIRSY	SACCHARIFY
AABHINSSSW	WASHBASINS	AACCDEHIRS	SACCHARIDE	AACCFILLRY	FARCICALLY
AABHKKORSV	KHABAROVSK	AACCDEHNOR	ARCHDEACON	AACCFILRSU	FASCICULAR
AABHLLLOOU	HULLABALOO	AACCDEIIPR	EPICARDIAC	AACCFINNRS	FRANCISCAN
AABIIILMTY	AMIABILITY	AACCDEILNT	ACCIDENTAL	AACCGHIORY	HAGIOCRACY
AABIIILNOT	LIBATIONAL	AACCDEINTV	VACCINATED	AACCGHOPRY	CACOGRAPHY
AABIIILLRWY	AIR WAYBILL	AACCDELLTU	CALCULATED	AACCGIILMN	ACCLAIMING
AABIIILLSTY	SALABILITY	AACCDELNOR	CLADOCERAN	AACCGILLNT	CATCALLING
AABIIILMTTY	TAMABILITY	AACCDELPRS	PLACE CARDS	AACCHIIRST	ARCHAISTIC
AABIIILNRRS	LIBRARIANS	AACCDELRST	CAT'S CRADLE	AACCHILNPY	CHAPLAINCY
AABIIILNRVY	INVARIABLY	AACCDENNSY	ASCENDANCY	AACCHIMORT	ACHROMATIC
AABIIILNSTY	INSATIABLY	AACCDERSTY	SCAREDY CAT	AACCHKLLUW	CHUCKWALLA
AABIIILRTTY	RATABILITY	AACCDGIILR	CARDIALGIC	AACCHLNORY	ACRONYCHAL
AABIIILTTXY	TAXABILITY	AACCDHIORS	SACCHAROID	AACCHNORST	CAST ANCHOR
AABIINNSSY	ABYSSINIAN	AACCDHPRST	SCRATCH PAD	AACCHNOTYY	CHATOYANCY
AABIINPRST	BIPARTISAN	AACCDIISTU	DIACAUSTIC	AACCIILORS	SACROILIAC
AABIINRRTT	ABIRRITANT	AACCEEELRT	ACCELERATE	AACCIILPRT	ACCIPITRAL
AABIIOPRSS	PARABIOSIS	AACCEEFFOT	FACE-TO-FACE	AACCIINPTY	INCAPACITY
AABIJNORTU	ABJURATION	AACCEEGPRS	SCAPEGRACE	AACCIINSTT	TACTICIANS
AABIKLMSTY	MISTAKABLY	AACCEEKMRS	MAKE SCARCE	AACCILLRUV	CLAVICULAR
AABILLRUVV	BIVALVULAR	AACCEELLNT	CANCELLATE	AACCILLTTY	TACTICALLY
AABILMNOTU	AMBULATION	AACCEELNRS	CLEARANCES	AACCILMMUY	IMMACULACY
AABILMRSST	STRABISMAL	AACCEELNRT	ACCELERANT	AACCILNNOT	CLACTONIAN
AABILNOORT	ABORTIONAL	AACCEENTTU	ACCENTUATE	AACCILNOOS	OCCASIONAL
AABILNOSTT	BATTALIONS	AACCEEORTV	COACERVATE	AACCILPRST	PRACTICALS
AABILNOTTU	TABULATION	AACCEFPRST	SPACECRAFT	AACCINORST	COSTA RICAN
AABILOPRST	PARABOLIST	AACCEGHOST	STAGECOACH	AACCINOSTU	ACCUSATION,
AABIMNOORT	ABOMINATOR	AACCEHILMN	MECHANICAL		ANACOUSTIC
AABINNORTY	ANTIBARYON	AACCEHIMNN	MAIN CHANCE	AACCINPTTY	ANAPTYCTIC
AABINORSTT	BOAT TRAINS	AACCEHINNT	CACHINNATE	AACCINRSTU	ANACRUSTIC
AABINOSSTW	BOATSWAINS	AACCEHINRS	SACCHARINE	AACCIOPRST	CAPACITORS
AABINRRXYY	X-RAY BINARY	AACCEHINRT	CHAIN-REACT	AACCIORTTU	AUTOCRATIC
AABIORRRTT	ARBITRATOR	AACCEHLNOT	COELACANTH	AACCKLLMOR	ALARM CLOCK
AABKKOORRU	KOOKABURRA	AACCEHMNNO		AACCKRRSTT	CART TRACKS
AABKLOSTUW	WALKABOUTS		COMANCHEAN	AACCLLORTU	CALCULATOR
AABLLMNORY	ABNORMALLY	AACCEHORSS	SACCHAROSE	AACCLMSSTY	CATACLYSMS
AABLMORTUY	AMBULATORY	AACCEHRRST	CHARACTERS	AACCLNOTTU	CONTACTUAL
AABLNOORSS	SALOON BARS	AACCEIIPST	CAPACITIES	AACCLNRRUU	CARUNCULAR
AABLOORRTY	LABORATORY	AACCEIIPTV	CAPACITIVE	AACCMNORTY	CARTOMANCY
AABLOSSTTT	STATOBLAST	AACCEILPTT	CATALEPTIC	AACCNNOTTU	ACCOUNTANT
AABNOORRTW	NARROW	AACCEINNOT	CANONICATE	AACCNORSST	SACROSANCT
	BOAT	AACCEINORV	COVARIANCE	AACDDEEHLR	DECAHEDRAL
AABORRRSTU	BARRATROUS	AACCEINPRT	PANCREATIC	AACDDEEIMP	AIDE-DE-CAMP
AACCCDEIIT	ACETIC ACID	AACCEINRTT	CANTATRICE	AACDDEEIRT	ERADICATED
AACCCDENOR	ACCORDANCE	AACCEINRTU	INACCURATE	AACDDEEIST	TEA CADDIES
AACCCDIILT	LACTIC ACID	AACCEIRRTU	CARICATURE	AACDDEELLR	CALDERDALE
		AACCEISTUV	ACCUSATIVE		

AACDDEEMRT	DEMARCATED	AACDEILMNR	ALDERMANIC	AACDIILMRT	MATRICIDAL
AACDDEERRR	CARD READER	AACDEILNNO	CALEDONIAN	AACDIILPRR	PARRICIDAL
AACDDEIJTU	ADJUDICATE	AACDEILNOR	ANDROECIAL	AACDIILPRT	PATRICIDAL
AACDDEINST	CANDIDATES	AACDEILNSS	SCANDALISE	AACDIILSTT	DIASTALTIC
AACDDEKLPS	PACKSADDLE	AACDEILNSZ	SCANDALIZE	AACDIIMNOS	AMINO ACIDS
AACDDIKNOR	ADIRONDACK	AACDEIMNNO	MACEDONIAN	AACDILMNNO	CALAMONDIN
AACDEEEFNS	DEFEASANCE	AACDEIMNTT	ADMITTANCE	AACDILMORY	MYOCARDIAL
AACDEEEHNX	HEXADECANE	AACDEIMPRS	PARAMEDICS	AACDINOOTV	ADVOCATION
AACDEEELST	DE-ESCALATE	AACDEIMSTT	MASTICATED	AACDIQRSTU	QUADRATICS
AACDEEFHMS	SHAMEFACED	AACDEINNRT	INCARNATED	AACDJNOTTU	COADJUTANT
AACDEEFHNR	FACE-HARDEN	AACDEINORU	ECUADORIAN	AACDLNOSSU	SCANDALOUS
AACDEEGNOT	ANECDOTAGE	AACDEINOTV	VACATIONED	AACDLOSTUY	ADACTYLOUS
AACDEEHNRS	CASE-HARDEN	AACDEINQTU	ACQUAINTED	AACDMMNNOT	
AACDEEHRTX	EX CATHEDRA	AACDEINQUY	INADEQUACY	COMMANDANT	
AACDEEIINT	TAENIACIDE	AACDEINRTX	TAXI DANCER	AACDNOORST	OSTRACODAN
AACDEEINRT	DERACINATE	AACDEIORRT	ERADICATOR	AACDOORTVY	ADVOCATORY
AACDEEINRV	CADAVERINE	AACDEIOSST	ASSOCIATED	AACEEEHKPS	CHESAPEAKE
AACDEEIPTT	DECAPITATE	AACDEIPTTV	CAPTIVATED	AACEEEKMPR	PEACEMAKER
AACDEEITTV	DEACTIVATE	AACDELMRSU	CLEAR AS	AACEEELMNP	ELECAMPANE
AACDEEJLTU	EJACULATED	MUD		AACEEELNOP	PALAEOCENE
AACDEENNTT	ATTENDANCE	AACDELNOPR	ENDOCARPAL	AACEEFIRST	CAFETERIAS
AACDEEPPRT	RATE-CAPPED	AACDELNPSS	LANDSCAPES	AACEEFLSUV	FACE VALUES
AACDEFINRU	FRICANDEAU	AACDELNSST	SANDCASTLE	AACEEFRSSV	FACE-SAVERS
AACDEFINST	FASCINATED	AACDELORST	SACERDOTAL	AACEEGHNSS	SEA CHANGES
AACDEFLORT	DEFALCATOR	AACDELPTTU	CATAPULTED	AACEEGILLN	ALLEGIANCE
AACDEFPSTY	PASTY-FACED	AACDEMORRT	DEMARCATOR	AACEEGKPPR	PREPACKAGE
AACDEGHHNR	CHARGE HAND	AACDEMRRST	MASTER CARD	AACEEGKPTT	GET A PACKET
AACDEGIMNP	CAMPAIGNED	AACDENNNOS	CANNONADES	AACEEGLLRS	LARGE-SCALE
AACDEGISTT	CASTIGATED	AACDENNSST	ASCENDANTS	AACEEGNOST	ACT ONE'S
AACDEGLOTU	CATALOGUED,	AACDENPRST	TAP DANCERS	AGE	
COAGULATED		AACDENRSTT	TRANSACTED	AACEEHIKLN	HAECKELIAN
AACDEHHTTW	DEATHWATCH	AACDEOPRRS	RADARSCOPE	AACEEHILNT	CHATELAINE
AACDEHILNR	HERACLIDAN	AACDEORSUV	CADAVEROUS	AACEEHINNP	PHENACAINE
AACDEHILNS	ENCHILADAS	AACDFHINRT	HANDICRAFT	AACEEHKPST	CHEAPSKATE
AACDEHILRS	CHARLADIES	AACDFIINOO	AFICIONADO	AACEEHLMNR	MENARCHEAL
AACDEHILRT	TRACHEIDAL	AACDGHHINR	CHANDIGARH	AACEEHMNRY	AERENCHYMA
AACDEHINRS	SEDAN CHAIR	AACDGHNORR	DRAG	AACEEHNNRT	ANTHRACENE
AACDEHJKLT	JACK THE LAD	ANCHOR		AACEEHPPRS	PAPER CHASE
AACDEHKPRT	PACKTHREAD	AACDGILNNP	LAP DANCING	AACEEILMRS	CARAMELISE
AACDEHLMTY	CHLAMYDATE	AACDGILNPR	PLACARDING	AACEEILMRZ	CARAMELIZE
AACDEHLNNS	CLEAN HANDS	AACDGIMNSW	MAGIC	AACEEILPRT	ALTARPIECE
AACDEHLORT	OCTAHEDRAL	WANDS		AACEEILRTV	CALAVERITE,
AACDEHLRST	CATHEDRALS	AACDGIMORR	CARDIOGRAM	LACERATIVE	
AACDEHNTTU	UNATTACHED	AACDGINNPT	TAP DANCING	AACEEIMNPT	EMANCIPATE
AACDEHOPPR	APPROACHED	AACDGINOTV	ADVOCATING	AACEEIMRTV	MACERATIVE
AACDEHPRTU	PARACHUTED	AACDGNNOPW	CAP AND	AACEEIMSST	SIAMESE CAT
AACDEIINRR	IRRADIANCE	GOWN		AACEEIPPRT	APPRECIATE
AACDEIIPRT	PAEDIATRIC	AACDGORSTU	COASTGUARD	AACEEIRTTV	REACTIVATE
AACDEIIRTV	DIVARICATE	AACDHINORT	ANTHRACOID	AACEEITUVV	EVACUATIVE
AACDEIJLTV	ADJECTIVAL	AACDHLNPSU	LAUNCH PADS	AACEEKMPRS	PACEMAKERS
AACDEIKPRS	SICK PARADE	AACDHNNORY	CHARDONNAY	AACEEKRRST	CARETAKERS
AACDEILLTV	VACILLATED	AACDHPRRSS	CARDSHARPS	AACEELLNOT	LANCEOLATE
AACDEILMNO	DEMONIACAL	AACDIIILMR	MIRACIDIAL	AACEELLNST	CLEAN SLATE
		AACDIIILRV	LARVICIDAL	AACEELLORT	REALLOCATE
		AACDIILMRS	RADICALISM	AACEELLPRT	CARPELLATE

AACEELMSTU	EMASCULATE	AACEHIKLMR	LIKE A CHARM	AACEILLSTY	SALICYLATE
AACEELNTTU	CATENULATE	AACEHILMMS	MICHAELMAS	AACEILMMTU	IMMACULATE
AACEELOPRT	CAPREOLATE	AACEHILNOP	CEPHALONIA	AACEILMNPS	CAMPANILES
AACEELOPSU	PALEACEOUS	AACEHILNPT	CHAINPLATE	AACEILMNRT	RECLAIMANT
AACEENORSU	ARENACEOUS	AACEHILNRS	LANCASHIRE	AACEILMNRU	UNICAMERAL
AACEENPRSS	PANCREASES	AACEHILOPT	APOTHECIAL	AACEILMNSU	MAIN CLAUSE
AACEEPRSTW	WATERSCAPE	AACEHILPST	CALIPHATES	AACEILMNTU	CALUMNIATE
AACEERSSTT	ESTATE CARS	AACEHILRTT	THEATRICAL	AACEILMRTU	TULARAEMIC
AACEERSSTV	STAVESACRE	AACEHIMMPR	AMPHIMACER	AACEILNNRS	CARNELIANS
AACEFFIRST	AFFRICATES	AACEHIMPRS	PHARMACIES	AACEILNORT	CREATIONAL,
AACEFGHNOR	FOR A	AACEHIMPRT	AMPHEATRIC		LACERATION, REACTIONAL
CHANGE		AACEHIMRTU	HAEMATURIC	AACEILNOST	ESCALATION
AACEFGINSV	FACE-SAVING	AACEHINNOU	OUANANICHE	AACEILNPPS	APPLIANCES
AACEFGLMOU	CAMOUFLAGE	AACEHINRRT	CATARRHINE	AACEILNPSS	SNAIL'S PACE
AACEFGNRRS	FRAGRANCES	AACEHINRTT	ANTHRACITE	AACEILNPTU	PANICULATE
AACEFGRSTT	STAGECRAFT	AACEHINSTU	EUSTACHIAN	AACEILOOPZ	PALAEOZOIC
AACEFHLLNP	CHAPFALLEN	AACEHIOPRX	ECHOPRAXIA	AACEILPRRS	PERISARCAL
AACEFHLSST	HALF-CASTES	AACEHIRRTV	ARCHITRAVE	AACEILPTTU	CAPITULATE
AACEFIILLT	FACILITATE	AACEHIRSSY	EASY CHAIRS	AACEILRTTU	ARTICULATE
AACEFIIMPR	PRIMA FACIE	AACEHIRSTU	AUTARCHIES	AACEILRTUU	AURICULATE
AACEFIINST	FANATICISE	AACEHJKMMR	JACKHAMMER	AACEILSSTU	CASUALTIES
AACEFIINTZ	FANATICIZE	AACEHKLMRS	RAMSHACKLE	AACEILSTTT	STALACTITE
AACEFLMORT	MALEFACTOR	AACEHKMMRT	MATCHMAKER	AACEIMMPRU	PARAMECIUM
AACEFRRTTW	WATERCRAFT	AACEHKMRTW	WATCHMAKER	AACEIMNNRU	UN-AMERICAN
AACEFRSTTT	STATECRAFT	AACEHKRSSV	HAVERSACKS	AACEIMNNST	ANAMNESTIC
AACEGHILNR	ALCHERINGA	AACEHLOPSU	ACEPHALOUS	AACEIMNORT	MACERATION
AACEGHLNRS	ARCHANGELS	AACEHLPRTY	ARCHETYPAL	AACEIMNORU	OCEANARIUM
AACEGHMOPR	MACROPHAGE	AACEHMNPRY	PARENCHYMA	AACEIMOPST	APOSEMATIC
AACEGHNORS	ANCHORAGES	AACEHMNRRT	CARMARTHEN	AACEIMORRT	CREMATORIA
AACEGHNORT	COAT HANGER	AACEHMNRTY	ATHERMANCY	AACEIMPRRT	PARAMETRIC
AACEGILLPR	PREGLACIAL	AACEHMNTTT	ATTACHMENT	AACEIMSTTT	METASTATIC
AACEGILNRT	LACERATING	AACEHMOPRT	CAMPHORATE	AACEINNNTU	ANNUNCIATE
AACEGILNSS	ANALGESICS	AACEHMORST	SAMOTHRACE	AACEINNOTT	CATENATION
AACEGILNST	ESCALATING	AACEHOPPRS	APPROACHES	AACEINNPRT	PANCREATIN
AACEGILPPR	PARAPLEGIC	AACEHOPRTY	APOTHECARY	AACEINORTU	AERONAUTIC
AACEGILRST	CARTILAGES	AACEHPPRSS	SCRAP HEAPS	AACEINORTV	VACATIONER
AACEGIMNPR	CAMPAIGNER	AACEHPRSTU	PARACHUTES	AACEINOTUV	EVACUATION
AACEGIMNRT	MACERATING	AACEIILMST	CALAMITIES	AACEINOTVX	EXCAVATION
AACEGINTUV	EVACUATING	AACEIILPST	CAPITALISE	AACEINPRST	PERSIAN CAT
AACEGINTVX	EXCAVATING	AACEIILPTZ	CAPITALIZE	AACEINPRTY	AT ANY PRICE
AACEGJKRUV	KRAGUJEVAC	AACEIIMNOT	EMACIATION	AACEINRSST	INCRASSATE
AACEGLMORY	ACROMEGALY	AACEIINNRV	INVARIANCE	AACEINSSST	ASSISTANCE
AACEGLORTU	CATALOGUER	AACEIINORT	ACIERATION	AACEIORSTT	AEROSTATIC
AACEGLOSTU	CATALOGUES	AACEIINPTT	ANTICIPATE	AACEIOSSST	ASSOCIATES
AACEGMNRTY	TERMAGANCY	AACEIINTTV	INACTIVATE	AACEIRSSST	STAIRCASES
AACEGOPRRS	APGAR SCORE	AACEIIOPSS	CASSIOPEIA	AACEIRTTTV	ATTRACTIVE
AACEGOPSST	SCAPEGOATS	AACEIIPRTT	PATRICIATE	AACEJKNRTT	NATTERJACK
AACEGORSTT	GREATCOATS	AACEIIPTTV	CAPITATIVE	AACEJLORTU	EJACULATOR
AACEHHILRR	HIERARCHAL	AACEILLMNU	ANIMALCULE	AACEKKMRST	MAKE TRACKS
AACEHHKLMS	HAMSHACKLE	AACEILLMNY	ANEMICALLY	AACEKLMRST	SMART ALECK
AACEHHMNTT	HATCHET MAN	AACEILLNRT	CARNALLITE	AACEKLPRST	PLATE RACKS
AACEHIIMNT	HAEMATINIC	AACEILLNTT	CANTILLATE	AACEKLRRTY	TRACKLAYER
AACEHIIMTT	HAEMATITIC	AACEILLOSU	ALLIACEOUS	AACEKPPSTY	PAY PACKETS
AACEHIINPT	CAP-HAITIEN	AACEILLRRV	VARICELLAR	AACELLLMSS	SMALL-SCALE

AACELLLORT	COLLATERAL
AACELLLRST	SALTCELLAR
AACELLLRUV	VALLECULAR
AACELLNOSW	ALLOWANCES
AACELLPRRY	CARPELLARY
AACELLPSST	CAST A SPELL
AACELMNRVY	CAVALRYMEN
AACELMOPSU	PALMACEOUS
AACELMOSUV	MALVACEOUS
AACELMOSUY	AMYLACEOUS
AACELMPRST	CAMPESTRAL
AACELMSSST	CLASSMATES
AACELNNOTV	COVENANTAL
AACELNOPTU	CANTALOUPE
AACELNOTTV	OCTAVALENT
AACELNRRUV	VERNACULAR
AACELNRTTU	TENTACULAR
AACELNSSSU	CASUALNESS
AACELNTUUV	AVUNCULATE
AACELOPPSY	APOCALYPSE
AACELORSST	ESCALATORS
AACELORSUU	LAURACEOUS
AACELPPRST	APPLE CARTS
AACELPRTTY	CALYPTRATE
AACELSTTUU	AUSCULTATE
AACEMNOPSW	SPACEWOMAN
AACEMNORST	SACRAMENTO
AACEMNRSST	SACRAMENTS
AACEMPRSTU	METACARPUS
AACENNNOSY	ANNOYANCES
AACENNSSTV	VACANTNESS
AACENOTTUZ	UTO-AZTECAN
AACENRRSTU	EARN A CRUST
AACENRSSSU	ASSURANCES
AACENRSSSV	CANVASSERS
AACEORRTTT	TERRACOTTA
AACEORSTVX	EXCAVATORS
AACEPPPRRS	SCRAP PAPER
AACFFIJMRT	TRAFFIC JAM
AACFGILNRT	FLAT RACING
AACFHKNRST	CRANKSHAFT
AACFHLNORW	HALF A CROWN
AACFIIILRT	ARTIFICIAL
AACFIILNOR	CALIFORNIA
AACFIILSTT	FATALISTIC
AACFIIMNST	FANATICISM
AACFIINOST	FASCIATION
AACFILLOSU	FALLACIOUS
AACFILMSTU	FACTUALISM
AACFILNORT	FRACTIONAL
AACFILORST	SOLFATARIC
AACFILSTTU	FACTUALIST
AACFINNNOR	FRANCONIAN

AACFLNNOTU	NONFACTUAL
AACFMNNOWY	FANCY WOMAN
AACFMOORST	COAT OF ARMS
AACFNRSTTU	SURFACTANT
AACFRRTTYY	ARTY-CRAFTY
AACGGHINNS	CHAIN GANGS
AACGGIILOS	SIALAGOGIC
AACGGILLNO	ALGOLAGNIC
AACGGILRST	GASTRALGIC
AACGHHOPRT	TACHOGRAPH
AACGHILNPY	ANAGLYPHIC
AACGHILRRT	ARTHRALGIC
AACGHIOPRS	SARCOPHAGI
AACGHMOPRR	MACROGRAPH
AACGHNRTTT	GANTT CHART
AACGIILLST	GLACIALIST
AACGIILNNZ	CANALIZING
AACGIILNOT	GLACIATION
AACGIIMSTT	ASTIGMATIC
AACGIINNPT	CAPTAINING
AACGIINPST	PAGANISTIC
AACGIINTTV	ACTIVATING
AACGIKMNRT	TARMACKING
AACGIKMORY	KARYOGAMIC
AACGIKNNRS	RANSACKING
AACGILLNOT	ALLOCATING
AACGILLRTY	TRAGICALLY
AACGILMNNY	MALIGNANCY
AACGILNORS	COR ANGLAIS
AACGILNPTY	PLAY-ACTING
AACGIMNORT	MORGANATIC
AACGIMNRSS	MASSACRING
AACGIMPRST	PRAGMATICS
AACGIMRSTY	MAGISTRACY
AACGINNSSV	CANVASSING
AACGINRSTT	CASTRATING
AACGINRTTT	ATTRACTING
AACGIORSTT	CASTIGATOR
AACGLLMOOY	MALACOLOGY
AACGLLSSWY	SCALLYWAGS
AACGLNORTU	OCTANGULAR
AACHHHISUU	CHIHUAHUAS
AACHIINRST	CHRISTIANA
AACHILLOPT	ALLOPATHIC
AACHILMNRT	ALTRINCHAM
AACHILNNPT	PLAINCHANT
AACHILOPST	CHIPOLATAS
AACHILPRSU	HARUSPICAL
AACHIMMNRS	RACHMANISM
AACHIMMNRU	MANCHURIAN
AACHIMNOPR	ANAMORPHIC
AACHIMNORS	ANACHORISM, HARMONICAS, MARASCHINO

AACHIMNORT	ACHROMATIN, MACHINATOR
AACHIMNORW	CHAIRWOMAN
AACHIMPRST	PHARMACIST
AACHIMRRST	MATRIARCHS
AACHIMRRTY	MATRIARCHY
AACHIMRSTT	MAASTRICHT
AACHIMSSTT	ASTHMATICS
AACHINRSST	ANARCHISTS
AACHINRSTU	CARTHUSIAN
AACHIPRRST	PATRIARCHS
AACHIPRRTY	PATRIARCHY
AACHIPRSTY	PARASTICHY
AACHLLRSTW	WALLCHARTS
AACHLMOPRS	ARCHOPLASM
AACHLNNNOT	NONCHALANT
AACHLOPPRY	APOCRYPHAL
AACHMOOPRT	APOCHROMAT
AACHMORTUY	TAUROMACHY
AACHMPRSST	MARCH-PASTS
AACHPRSTTW	WATCHSTRAP
AACIILLNNT	ANTICLINAL
AACIILLOPT	APOLITICAL
AACIILMNOS	SIMONIACAL
AACIILMNST	TALISMANIC
AACIILMNTX	ANTICLIMAX
AACIILMPST	CAPITALISM
AACIILNNOR	CAROLINIAN
AACIILNNST	ANNALISTIC
AACIILNORS	SALICORNIA
AACIILNOST	ANTISOCIAL
AACIILNSTU	SAINT LUCIA
AACIILPPST	PAPISTICAL
AACIILPSTT	CAPITALIST
AACIILRRTU	URTICARIAL
AACIILRSST	RACIALISTS
AACIIMNNRT	MARTINICAN
AACIIMSSTT	ASTATICISM
AACIINNPTT	ANTICIPANT
AACIINOPTT	CAPITATION
AACIINORTV	VICTORIANA
AACIINOTTV	ACTIVATION, CAVITATION
AACIINPRST	PATRICIANS
AACIINSTTT	ANTISTATIC
AACIIORSUV	AVARICIOUS
AACIKLMMRS	LAMARCKISM
AACIKNSSTY	KANSAS CITY
AACILLMNTY	MANTICALLY
AACILLMORT	MATRILOCAL
AACILLMOTY	ATOMICALLY, LAY CLAIM TO
AACILLNOOT	ALLOCATION
AACILLNTUY	NAUTICALLY
AACILLOOPR	COPROLALIA

AACILLOPRT	ALLOPATRIC,	AACNNNOSTT	CONSTANTAN	AADEEHHLRX	HEXAHEDRAL
PATRILOCAL		AACNORRSTT	TRANSACTOR	AADEEHHMMR	HAMMERHEAD
AACILLORTV	VACILLATOR	AACOOPPRSU	APOCARPOUS	AADEEHLNVY	HEAVY-LADEN
AACILLPTYY	ATYPICALLY	AACORRSTTT	STRATOCRAT	AADEEHLTWY	LEAD THE WAY
AACILLRWXY	WAX LYRICAL	AADDDEEHHR	HARDHEADED	AADEEHMRST	HEADMASTER,
AACILLTVWY	CAVITY WALL	AADDDEEMRY	DAYDREAMED	HEADSTREAM	
AACILMNOTU	MACULATION	AADDDEILPR	PARADIDDLE	AADEEHNRVW	HEAVENWARD
AACILMORRT	LACRIMATOR	AADDDGRSUY	SUGAR DADDY	AADEEHPPRS	PEAR-SHAPED
AACILMORSU	MARLACIOUS	AADDEEHHST	DEATH'S-HEAD	AADEEHPRSS	SPEARHEADS
AACILMOSTU	CALAMITOUS	AADDEEHIMN	MAIDENHEAD	AADEEHQRSU	HEADSQUARE
AACILNNRTY	TYRANNICAL	AADDEEIRST	DESIDERATA	AADEEHRSTT	DEATH RATES
AACILNOOTV	VOCATIONAL	AADDEEMRRY	DAYDREAMER	AADEEHRSTW	HEADWATERS
AACILNOPTY	NYCTALOPIA	AADDEESTTV	DEVASTATED	AADEEILLTV	ALLEVIATED
AACILNORSS	SCANSORIAL	AADDEFINRW	FAR AND WIDE	AADEEILMNT	DELAMINATE
AACILNORTT	TRACTIONAL	AADDEGHNOR	DRAGONHEAD	AADEEILNNR	ADRENALINE
AACILNPPST	APPLICANTS	AADDEGIPRS	DISPARAGED	AADEEILNST	DESALINATE
AACILOORRT	ORATORICAL	AADDEGIRRT	TARDIGRADE	AADEEILRTT	RETALIATED
AACILOPPRT	APPLICATOR	AADDEGMNOR	ARMAGEDDON	AADEEIMMNN	MAIDEN NAME
AACILOPRTT	OPTICAL ART	AADDEHIMNN	HANDMAIDEN	AADEEIMNRT	REANIMATED
AACILORRTU	CURATORIAL	AADDEHLMNN	MANHANDLED	AADEEIMPRT	PREADAMITE
AACILORSTU	ALACRITOUS	AADDEHLMOT	THE OLD	AADEEINQTU	INADEQUATE
AACILPRRSU	SPIRACULAR	ADAM		AADEEIPTTX	EXPATIATED
AACILPRRTU	PARTICULAR	AADDEHLNNP	PANHANDLED	AADEEIRSTT	ASTERIATED
AACILPRSTT	PLASTIC ART	AADDEHQSTU	DEATH SQUAD	AADEEKKKOT	TAKE A DEKKO
AACILPRSTY	PARALYTICS	AADDEIILPT	DILAPIDATE	AADEELLLMT	LAMELLATED
AACILQSTTU	ACQUITTALS	AADDEIIRRT	IRRADIATED	AADEELLLPR	PARALLELED
AACIMMNNOO		AADDEILLNS	LANDLADIES	AADEELLPPR	APPARELLED
MONOMANIAC		AADDEILMRR	RED ADMIRAL	AADEELLMNRV	
AACIMNNNSU	MANCUNIANS	AADDEILNSV	VANDALISED	VAL-DE-MARNE	
AACIMNOPRY	PYROMANIAC	AADDEILNVZ	VANDALIZED	AADEELMRTT	MALTREATED
AACIMORSTT	MASTICATOR	AADDEILORR	RAILROADED	AADEELMSTT	STALEMATED
AACIMOSTTU	AUTOMATICS	AADDEIMRST	DRAMATISED	AADEELNNWZ	NEW ZEALAND
AACINNOOTZ	ACTINOZOAN	AADDEIMRTZ	DRAMATIZED	AADEELNPSS	ESPLANADES
AACINNORST	CARNATIONS	AADDEINRSW	EDWARDIANS	AADEELNRTT	ALTERNATED
AACINNOSTT	CONSTANTIA	AADDELMNRS	DREAMLANDS	AADEELQTUY	ADEQUATELY
AACINOOSTV	AVOCATIONS,	AADDELMRSS	MALADDRESS	AADEELRRSY	LAY READERS
NOVA SCOTIA		AADDGILMOY	AMYGDALOID	AADEELRSTV	SLAVE TRADE
AACINOPRSS	CAPARISONS	AADDGNNRST	GRANDSTAND	AADEELRTTU	ADULTERATE
AACINORSTT	CASTRATION	AADDHNNSST	HANDSTANDS	AADEEMNRST	TRADE NAMES
AACINORTTT	ATTRACTION	AADDIILNOT	ADDITIONAL	AADEEMQRSU	MASQUERADE
AACINORTUY	CAUTIONARY	AADDIIMRSY	DAIRYMAIDS	AADEEMQSTU	DESQUAMATE
AACINRSSST	SACRISTANS	AADDILLLOV	VALLADOLID	AADEENTTTU	ATTENUATED
AACIOOPPRT	APOTROPAIC	AADDINORRT	RITARDANDO	AADEEOPRTV	EVAPORATED
AACIOPRTTV	CAPTIVATOR	AADDLNOOSW	SANDALWOOD	AADEEPPRWX	WAXED PAPER
AACIORRSTT	ARISTOCRAT	AADEEEPPRR	REAPPEARED	AADEEPRSST	PAEDERASTS
AACIOSSTTW	WAISTCOATS	AADEEFGHOR	FORGE AHEAD	AADEEPRSTY	PAEDERASTY
AACJLMRSUU	MAJUSCULAR	AADEEFGLRT	DEFLAGRATE	AADEERRTTW	TREAD WATER
AACLMNNOSW		AADEEFHRRZ	HAZARD-FREE	AADEFFIILT	AFFILIATED
CLANSWOMAN		AADEEGGGRT	AGGREGATED	AADEFFNORT	FORE AND AFT
AACLNOPSTU	CANTALOUPS	AADEEGIRTV	VARIEGATED	AADEFGRSSU	SAFEGUARDS
AACLOORRTU	COLORATURA	AADEEGNPPS	APPENDAGES	AADEFHHIOR	HEAD OF HAIR
AACLOPRRRS	PARLOR CARS	AADEEGNRRR	REARRANGED	AADEFHLNRT	FATHERLAND
AACLOPRRST	PATROL CARS	AADEEGNRST	GREAT DANES,	AADEFIKNRR	AFRIKANDER
AACMOOPRRT	COMPARATOR	TEAGARDENS		AADEFIMNOT	DEFAMATION
		AADEEGNRTU	GUARANTEED	AADEFINSST	FANTASISED

AADEFINSTZ	FANTASIZED	
AADEFINTTU	INFATUATED	
AADEFLLMNO	AN OLD FLAME	
AADEFMORTY	DEFAMATORY	
AADEFMRSST	FARMSTEADS	
AADEFRRSTW	AFTERWARDS	
AADEGGINRS	AGGRANDISE	
AADEGGINRZ	AGGRANDIZE	
AADEGGNOOR	DRAGOONAGE	
AADEGGOSSU	SAUSAGE DOG	
AADEGHHINS	SHANGHAIED	
AADEGHIINR	HEARING AID	
AADEGHNRSY	HYDRANGEAS	
AADEGHNSST	STAGEHANDS	
AADEGILMNY	AMYGDALINE	
AADEGILNSV	GALVANISED	
AADEGILNVZ	GALVANIZED	
AADEGILRST	SALTIGRADE	
AADEGIMMNS	MISMANAGED	
AADEGIMRST	SMARAGDITE	
AADEGINNTT	ANTEDATING	
AADEGINRRS	DISARRANGE	
AADEGINRST	TRAGEDIANS	
AADEGIPRRS	DISPARAGER	
AADEGIRTTV	GRAVITATED	
AADEGLNNST	LAND AGENTS	
AADEGLNQRU	QUADRANGLE	
AADEGLNRTU	GRANULATED	
AADEGLNSTW	SWEAT GLAND	
AADEGMRRTU	DRAMATURGE	
AADEGNOPRR	GRAND OPERA	
AADEGOPPRT	PROPAGATED	
AADEGRRRSU	REARGUARDS	
AADEGRRSVY	GRAVEYARDS	
AADEHHKNSS	HANDSHAKES,
SHAKE HANDS		
AADEHIIMNR	MAIDENHAIR	
AADEHILNNT	LANTHANIDE	
AADEHILORR	DIARRHOEAL	
AADEHIPRST	HIT PARADES	
AADEHKLLMR	HALLMARKED	
AADEHKMSST	DEATH MASKS	
AADEHLLMRS	MARSHALLED	
AADEHLMNNR	ARNHEM LAND	
AADEHLMPSS	LAMPSHADES	
AADEHLNNPR	PANHANDLER	
AADEHLNNPS	PANHANDLES	
AADEHMMMNO	
MOHAMMEDAN		
AADEHORRSW	ARROWHEADS	
AADEHPRSTT	DEATH TRAPS	
AADEHRRSTW	EARTHWARDS	
AADEIILNNR	DAIL EIRANN	
AADEIILNOT	IDEATIONAL	
AADEIILNTV	INVALIDATE	

AADEIILPRS	LAPIDARIES	
AADEIIMNNR	AMERINDIAN	
AADEIIMNNT	MAINTAINED	
AADEIINNST	EAST INDIAN	
AADEIINNTV	VANADINITE	
AADEIINORT	ERADIATION	
AADEIINTTV	ADVENTITIA	
AADEIIRRRT	TRIRADIATE	
AADEILMNRV	VINA DEL MAR	
AADEILMNTY	ANIMATEDLY	
AADEILMORT	TAILOR-MADE	
AADEILMRTX	TAXIDERMAL	
AADEILNSTT	TANTALISED	
AADEILNSTU	ANDALUSITE	
AADEILNTTZ	TANTALIZED	
AADEILORST	ASTEROIDAL	
AADEILPPTT	PALPITATED	
AADEILSTVW	TIDAL WAVES	
AADEIMNRTV	ANIMADVERT	
AADEIMRRST	DRAMATISER	
AADEIMRRTZ	DRAMATIZER	
AADEINNOPT	ANTIPODEAN	
AADEINPQSU	PASQUINADE	
AADEINQRSU	QUANDARIES	
AADEINQTTU	ANTIQUATED	
AADEINRSTT	ANTITRADES	
AADEIOPQRU	RADIOPAQUE	
AADEKLMORW	MEADOWLARK	
AADEKMRRST	TRADEMARKS	
AADELLNPTT	PLATTELAND	
AADELLORSV	EL SALVADOR	
AADELMMORS	MELODRAMAS	
AADELMNSSS	LANDMASSES	
AADELMOOST	STOMODAEAL	
AADELMOPRR	MADREPORAL	
AADELNRSTT	TRANSLATED	
AADELNRTTU	ADULTERANT	
AADELNRTUY	DAY-NEUTRAL	
AADELNSSTW	WASTELANDS	
AADELRSTWY	EASTWARDLY	
AADEMNPRSS	AMPERSANDS	
AADENNRTTU	DENATURANT	
AADENNSTTT	ATTENDANTS	
AADENOPPRU	PAPANDREOU	
AADENRSTTU	TRANSUDATE	
AADEORSTTV	DEVASTATOR	
AADEQRRTUU	QUADRATURE	
AADEQRRTUY	QUARTER DAY	
AADFFIISTV	AFFIDAVITS	
AADFILNRSY	FAIRYLANDS	
AADFILRSTU	FRUIT SALAD	
AADFIMNRSY	MAN FRIDAYS	
AADFIMRRSY	DAIRY FARMS	
AADFNORRTU	FART AROUND	

AADGGILNNR	GARLANDING	
AADGGINRTU	GRADUATING	
AADGHIMPRS	DIAPHRAGMS	
AADGHINSWY	WASHING DAY	
AADGHIOPRR	RADIOGRAPH	
AADGIILNTV	VALIDATING	
AADGIINNRT	GRANT-IN-AID	
AADGIJNORU	JAGUARONDI	
AADGILLNOY	DIAGONALLY	
AADGILMRSU	GRADUALISM	
AADGILNOOT	ODONTALGIA	
AADGILNPPU	APPLAUDING	
AADGILORST	GLADIATORS	
AADGILPSUV	DAUGAVPILS	
AADGILRRSU	GUARDRAILS	
AADGILRSTU	GRADUALIST	
AADGIMORRS	RADIOGRAMS	
AADGINNOPR	GRAND PIANO	
AADGINORST	GRADATIONS	
AADGINORTU	GRADUATION	
AADGLMNRSS	GRAND SLAMS	
AADGMRRTUY	DRAMATURGY	
AADGMRSSTU	MUSTARD GAS	
AADGNNOPRS	SNAPDRAGON	
AADGNRSSUV	GUARD'S
VANS		
AADHIILPSY	DIAPHYSIAL	
AADHIIOPRS	APHRODISIA	
AADHILRTWW	WITHDRAWAL	
AADHINOPSU	DIAPHANOUS	
AADHNSSSTW	WASHSTANDS	
AADIIKLNST	SAINT KILDA	
AADIILLNST	TILLANDSIA	
AADIILMMOT	OMMATIDIAL	
AADIILNOTT	DILATATION	
AADIILNOTV	VALIDATION	
AADIILNPRW	RAWALPINDI	
AADIILQRUV	QUADRIVIAL	
AADIILSSTT	DIASTALSIS	
AADIILSSUV	VISUAL AIDS	
AADIIMNOPS	DIPSOMANIA	
AADIIMNORT	ADMIRATION	
AADIINORST	RADIATIONS	
AADIINORTX	X-RADIATION	
AADIIORRRT	IRRADIATOR	
AADIIPRSST	ASPIDISTRA	
AADIJNORTU	ADJURATION	
AADILLMNOS	SOMALILAND	
AADILLMORS	ARMADILLOS	
AADILNORTU	DURATIONAL	
AADILORSTU	AUSTRALOID	
AADILORTVY	VALIDATORY	
AADILOSSVW	DISAVOWALS	
AADIMNNOPR	PRIMA DONNA	

AADIMNOPRY	MYRIAPODAN
AADIMOPPRU	PARAPODIUM
AADIMRSSTT	DRAMATISTS
AADINSSSTY	SAINT'S DAYS
AADIOOPSSY	OOPS-A-DAISY
AADJMNNPRU	PANJANDRUM
AADJORRTUY	ADJURATORY
AADLMNNNOS	NO-MAN'S-LAND
AADLMNNRUY	LAUNDRYMAN
AADLMNPSUY	PALM SUNDAY
AADMNOORSU	ANADROMOUS
AADNOOPPSW	SAPPANWOOD
AAEEEFLMMT	METAFEMALE
AAEEEGGMMT	MEGAGAMETE
AAEEEGGRTX	EXAGGERATE
AAEEEGLNOP	PALAEOGENE
AAEEEHRSST	HEARTSEASE
AAEEELMNRW	ENAMELWARE
AAEEELNPRS	PARASELENE
AAEEELRSTT	REAL ESTATE
AAEEEMNNOS	SEA ANEMONE
AAEEEPRSTX	EXASPERATE
AAEEERSSTV	ASSEVERATE
AAEEFGIMRT	AFTERIMAGE
AAEEFGINTU	TAENIAFUGE
AAEEFGLLLT	FLAGELLATE
AAEEFHRSTV	AFTERSHAVE
AAEEFKLMRT	FLEA MARKET
AAEEFNRRST	FAR EASTERN
AAEEFRSTTT	AFTERTASTE
AAEEGGGRST	AGGREGATES
AAEEGGHMOU	HAEMAGOGUE
AAEEGHLLRT	ALL THE RAGE
AAEEGHLNOT	HALOGENATE
AAEEGHRRSV	HARGREAVES
AAEEGILLTT	TAGLIATELE
AAEEGILNNV	EVANGELINA
AAEEGIMNRT	EMARGINATE
AAEEGIMSSX	SEXAGESIMA
AAEEGINRTV	VEGETARIAN
AAEEGIRSSV	SAVAGERIES
AAEEGLMNPS	PLASMAGENE
AAEEGLMNST	MENTAL AGES
AAEEGLSSVW	WAGE SLAVES
AAEEGMMNNT	MANAGEMENT
AAEEGMMORR	AEROGRAMME
AAEEGMNRSS	MANAGERESS
AAEEGMNRST	EAST GERMAN
AAEEGMNRTV	RAVAGEMENT
AAEEGMNSST	STAGE NAMES
AAEEGNPRRR	PREARRANGE
AAEEGNRRRR	REARRANGER
AAEEGNRSTU	GUARANTEES
AAEEGNRSXY	SEXAGENARY
AAEEGNSSSV	SAVAGENESS
AAEEGQRRTU	QUARTERAGE
AAEEHHRSST	HEAT RASHES
AAEEHILRTX	EXHILARATE
AAEEHINSST	ANESTHESIA
AAEEHKMOSU	MAKE A HOUSE
AAEEHKQRTU	EARTHQUAKE
AAEEHLMTVY	HEAVY METAL
AAEEHLNTTT	LATENT HEAT
AAEEHLNTVX	HEXAVALENT
AAEEHLRRSS	REHEARSALS
AAEEHMNRTU	HAUTE-MARNE
AAEEHMNRTW	WEATHERMAN
AAEEHMPRST	METAPHRASE
AAEEHPTVWY	PAVE THE WAY
AAEEHRRRST	RARE EARTHS
AAEEHRRSTW	SHEARWATER
AAEEHRTVWY	HEAVY WATER
AAEEIKLMNS	SEAMANLIKE
AAEEILLNST	LATEEN SAIL
AAEEILLRTT	ALLITERATE
AAEEILMNNS	MELANESIAN
AAEEILMORT	AMELIORATE
AAEEILMRSS	LAMASERIES
AAEEILNPRT	PENETRALIA
AAEEILRTTV	ALTERNATIVE
AAEEILTUVV	EVALUATIVE
AAEEINPPRV	PAPAVERINE
AAEEIPPRRS	REAPPRAISE
AAEEIPRRTT	REPATRIATE
AAEEIPRRTV	REPARATIVE
AAEEIPRSTT	TEA PARTIES
AAEEIPRSTV	SEPARATIVE
AAEEIPRTTX	EXPATRIATE
AAEEKKWWYY	WAKEY WAKEY
AAEEKNQRSU	NEAR SQUEAK
AAEELLPRTY	PLATELAYER
AAEELLTTTT	TATTLETALE
AAEELMNPST	NAMEPLATES
AAEELMQRSU	SQUARE MEAL
AAEELMRRTT	MALTREATER
AAEELMSSTT	STALEMATES
AAEELNOPRS	AEROPLANES
AAEELNPRRT	PARENTERAL
AAEELNPRST	PLEASANTER
AAEELPRSTY	SEPARATELY
AAEELSSSTX	SALES TAXES
AAEELSSTUV	ASSET VALUE
AAEEMMNNRT	REARMAMENT
AAEEMNNSSU	AMANUENSES
AAEEMPRRST	PARAMETERS
AAEEPPRSTW	WASTE PAPER
AAEERRSTTW	WATER RATES
AAEFFHRSTT	AFTERSHAFT
AAEFFIILST	AFFILIATES
AAEFFILORV	LOVE AFFAIR
AAEFGIISTT	FASTIGIATE
AAEFGLLLNT	FLAGELLANT
AAEFGLLNRU	LANGLAUFER
AAEFGLMNRT	FRAGMENTAL
AAEFHLPRST	FLARE PATHS
AAEFHMRSTT	AFTERMATHS
AAEFIILSTT	FATALITIES
AAEFIKNRRS	AFRIKANERS
AAEFILLNRX	FRAXINELLA
AAEFILMMNY	FAMILY NAME
AAEFILMRRS	FIRE ALARMS
AAEFILRSTY	FAIRY TALES
AAEFIMMNRS	MAINFRAMES
AAEFIMRRRT	TERRA FIRMA
AAEFINPRST	AFTERPAINS
AAEFKLMOOT	MAKE A LOT OF
AAEFLLNSTU	FUSTANELLA
AAEFLLRSTW	WATERFALLS
AAEFLMPSTY	SAFETY LAMP
AAEFLOPSTT	SOFT PALATE
AAEFLORTZZ	TO A FRAZZLE
AAEFLRSSTT	FALSE START
AAEGGGLNUV	LUGGAGE VAN
AAEGGILNSW	GLASWEGIAN
AAEGGILOSU	SIALAGOGUE
AAEGGINRSU	RAIN GAUGES
AAEGHILLSS	GALASHIELS
AAEGHILNPR	NEPHRALGIA
AAEGHILORT	HAGIOLATER
AAEGHILRTU	GAULTHERIA
AAEGHINNNS	SHENANIGAN
AAEGHLNOPT	HEPTAGONAL
AAEGHLNPRY	PHARYNGEAL
AAEGHLNRUX	HEXANGULAR
AAEGHMNOPR	ANEMOGRAPH, PHANEROGAM
AAEGHNOPRS	ORPHANAGES
AAEGHOPRRY	AEROGRAPHY, AREOGRAPHY
AAEGHPPPRR	GRAPH PAPER
AAEGIILNNT	ALIENATING
AAEGIILPRS	PLAGIARISE
AAEGIILPRZ	PLAGIARIZE
AAEGIINNTV	INVAGINATE
AAEGIINRTT	INGRATIATE
AAEGIKMNRR	EARMARKING
AAEGIKNNSW	AWAKENINGS
AAEGILLNOT	ALLEGATION
AAEGILLORT	LEGATORIAL
AAEGILMNRT	MARTINGALE

AAEGILMSTT	STALAGMITE	AAEHIPSTXY	ASPHYXIATE	AAEILNOTTX	EXALTATION
AAEGILNNTT	TANGENTIAL	AAEHKLRSST	SALT SHAKER	AAEILNOTUV	EVALUATION
AAEGILNRSV	GALVANISER	AAEHLLMRRS	MARSHALLER	AAEILNRSTT	TANTALISER
AAEGILNRVZ	GALVANIZER	AAEHMNRSST	HARASSMENT	AAEILNRSTU	NATURALISE
AAEGILNSWX	SEALING WAX	AAEHMNRSTV	HARVESTMAN	AAEILNRTTZ	TANTALIZER
AAEGILNTUV	EVALUATING	AAEHMORTTX	METATHORAX	AAEILNRTUZ	NATURALIZE
AAEGILPRTY	APTERYGIAL	AAEHMOSTTY		AAEILOQRTU	EQUATORIAL
AAEGIMMNRS	MISMANAGER		STAY-AT-HOME	AAEILORRTT	RETALIATOR
AAEGIMRRTU	MARGUERITA	AAEHMPRSTT	METAPHRAST	AAEILORSTV	LAVATORIES
AAEGIMRSTT	MAGISTRATE	AAEHMRSSTU	SHAMATEURS	AAEILSTUXY	ASEXUALITY
AAEGINNOST	ANTAGONISE	AAEHOPPSTY	APOPHYSATE	AAEIMMNRST	MAINSTREAM
AAEGINNOTZ	ANTAGONIZE	AAEHRRTTTU	ARTHURETTA	AAEIMMPRTU	AT A PREMIUM
AAEGINNSTU	NAUSEATING	AAEIILLPTV	PALLIATIVE	AAEIMMRSTU	AMATEURISM
AAEGINPRST	SEPARATING	AAEIILMMRT	IMMATERIAL	AAEIMNNOPR	POMERANIAN
AAEGINRSTU	GUARANTIES	AAEIILMNRS	SEMINARIAL	AAEIMNNOST	EMANATIONS
AAEGINRTTV	GRAVETTIAN	AAEIILMSST	ASSIMILATE	AAEIMNNOSY	MAYONNAISE
AAEGINRTUU	INAUGURATE	AAEIILNNOT	ALIENATION	AAEIMNNSSU	AMANUENSIS
AAEGIORRTV	ARROGATIVE	AAEIILNPST	SAPIENTIAL	AAEIMNNTTT	ATTAINMENT
AAEGIRRTTV	GRAVITATER	AAEIILNSTV	INSALIVATE	AAEIMNOORT	EROTOMANIA
AAEGKLMRSS	GLASS-MAKER	AAEIIMNNRR	RIEMANNIAN	AAEIMNORST	ANATOMISER
AAEGLLPSST	PLATE GLASS	AAEIIMNNRS	SEMINARIAN	AAEIMNORTZ	ANATOMIZER
AAEGLNNOPT	PENTAGONAL	AAEIIMNNRT	MAINTAINER	AAEIMNRSTW	WATER MAINS
AAEGLNORTT	TETRAGONAL	AAEIIPPRSV	APPRAISIVE	AAEIMNRTTT	ANTIMATTER
AAEGMMNOST	MOSTAGANEM	AAEIIPRSST	PARASITISE	AAEIMPRSST	SEPARATISM
AAEGMNPRST	PENTAGRAMS	AAEIIPRSTZ	PARASITIZE	AAEIMQRSTU	MARQUISATE
AAEGMNRSTT	TERMAGANTS	AAEIKMRSST	SAMARSKITE	AAEIMRSTTU	TRAUMATISE
AAEGMOPRSU	RAMPAGEOUS	AAEIKNNRST	TRANSKEIAN	AAEIMRTTUV	MATURATIVE
AAEGMRSSTT	STRATAGEMS	AAEILLLLNV	VILLANELLA	AAEIMRTTUZ	TRAUMATIZE
AAEGNNNOTT	ON A	AAEILLLNPR	IN PARALLEL	AAEIMSSSTT	METASTASIS
	TANGENT	AAEILLMPRX	PREMAXILLA	AAEINNNOTX	ANNEXATION
AAEGNOPRSS	PARSONAGES	AAEILLMRTY	MATERIALLY	AAEINNOSTU	NAUSEATION
AAEGRRSSTZ	STARGAZERS	AAEILLNORT	RELATIONAL	AAEINNOTTV	ANNOTATIVE
AAEHHINOPT	THEOPHANIA	AAEILLNPSS	SAILPLANES	AAEINNQRTU	QUARANTINE
AAEHHJLLLU	HALLELUJAH	AAEILLNRTU	UNILATERAL	AAEINOPRRT	REPARATION
AAEHHKMNRS	KERMANSHAH	AAEILLORTV	ALLEVIATOR	AAEINOPRST	SEPARATION
AAEHIILMNS	LEISHMANIA	AAEILLPSSS	PAILLASSES,	AAEINOPSST	PASSIONATE
AAEHIILNNT	ANNIHILATE		PALLIASSES	AAEINRRSTV	NARRATIVES
AAEHIIMNNT	AMIANTHINE	AAEILLRRTT	TRILATERAL	AAEINRRSTW	WARRANTIES
AAEHIKRRST	HAIRSTREAK	AAEILMNNSU	SEMIANNUAL	AAEIOPRTTX	EXPATIATOR
AAEHILLOPT	PALAEOLITH	AAEILMNORT	AMELIORANT	AAEIOPSSST	APOSTASIES
AAEHILNOTX	EXHALATION	AAEILMNPRT	PARLIAMENT	AAEIOPSSTT	APOSTATISE
AAEHILNRTX	EXHILARANT	AAEILMNPTU	MANIPULATE	AAEIOPSTTZ	APOSTATIZE
AAEHILNSST	THESSALIAN	AAEILMNRTY	ALIMENTARY	AAEIORSTTV	AESTIVATOR
AAEHILNSTV	LEVIATHANS	AAEILMNSST	ASSAILMENT	AAEIPRRSTX	SEPARATRIX
AAEHILPSTT	ASPHALTITE	AAEILMPRRT	PREMARITAL	AAEIPRSSTT	SEPARATIST
AAEHILPSTW	WESTPHALIA	AAEILNNOPT	NEAPOLITAN	AAEJKLRSWY	JAYWALKERS
AAEHIMNPSS	SEAMANSHIP	AAEILNNOTV	VENATIONAL	AAEKKOSTTT	TAKE TO TASK
AAEHIMNSTY	MYASTHENIA	AAEILNNRTU	LAURENTIAN	AAEKMRRSTW	WATERMARKS
AAEHIMOSST	HAEMATOSIS	AAEILNOORT	AREOLATION	AAEKMRSSTT	TASKMASTER
AAEHIMPRST	AMPHIASTER	AAEILNOQTU	EQUATIONAL	AAEKRRSTUU	SAUERKRAUT
AAEHIMRSTU	AMATEURISH	AAEILNORST	RATIONALES,	AAELLLMNOS	SALMONELLA
AAEHINNORV	HANOVERIAN		SENATORIAL	AAELLLORST	SALTARELLO
AAEHINOPST	ASTHENOPIA	AAEILNORTT	ALTERATION	AAELLMNRTY	MATERNALLY
AAEHINPSST	PHANTASIES	AAEILNORTU	LAUREATION	AAELLMORTT	MARTELLATO
		AAEILNORTX	RELAXATION		

AAELLMORZZ	MOZZARELLA	AAFMNORSTW	MAN OF
AAELLNOPRS	SOLAR PANEL	STRAW	
AAELLNPRTY	PATERNALLY,	AAGGHINNRU	HARANGUING
PRENATALLY		AAGGIILNTT	TAILGATING
AAELLNPSTY	PLEASANTLY	AAGGIINNRR	ARRAIGNING
AAELLPPRSW	WALLPAPERS	AAGGIINNSY	GAINSAYING
AAELLRSTTT	TATTERSALL	AAGGIINNTV	NAVIGATING
AAELMNNORT	ORNAMENTAL	AAGGINNSTT	STAGNATING
AAELMNOPSU	MENOPAUSAL	AAGGINORRT	ARROGATING
AAELMNORVV	REMOVAL VAN	AAGGINRSTZ	STARGAZING
AAELMNOSSW	SALESWOMAN	AAGGKLNNPS	GANGPLANKS
AAELMNRSUY	ANEURYSMAL	AAGGLLLOSS	GALLOGLASS
AAELMRRTUX	EXTRAMURAL	AAGGLLNNYY	YLANG-YLANG
AAELNNPSTU	UNPLEASANT	AAGGNNORTU	ORANGUTANG
AAELNORRTT	ALTERNATOR	AAGHHIMNWY	HIGHWAYMAN
AAELNPPRTY	APPARENTLY	AAGHHINORT	HOGARTHIAN
AAELNPRRSU	SUPRARENAL	AAGHIILMNP	MALPIGHIAN
AAELNPRSTT	TRANSEPTAL	AAGHIILMNRS	MARSHALING
AAELNPRSTY	PLEASANTRY	AAGHIILNPST	ASPHALTING
AAELNRSTUV	TRANSVALUE	AAGHILOPPY	POLYPHAGIA
AAELNSSTTU	SULTANATES,	AAGHILORTY	HAGIOLATRY
TANTALUSES		AAGHINPRSS	SPRINGHAAS
AAELOOPSST	APOSTOLATE	AAGHNOPPRT	PANTOGRAPH
AAELORRSSY	SOLAR YEARS	AAGHOPRSTU	AUTOGRAPHS
AAELPRRTTT	RATTLETRAP	AAGHOPRSTY	PYTHAGORAS
AAELSTTTUW	STATUTE LAW	AAGHOPRTUY	AUTOGRAPHY
AAEMNNORTT	TRAMONTANE	AAGIIKMNNR	RAINMAKING
AAEMNNRSTV	MANSERVANT	AAGIILLNPT	PALLIATING
AAEMNOOSST	ANASTOMOSE	AAGIILMNNT	LAMINATING
AAEMNPRSTT	APARTMENTS	AAGIILMPRS	PLAGIARISM
AAEMPRSSTT	PAST MASTER	AAGIILNNPS	SALPINGIAN
AAEMPRSSTY	PAYMASTERS	AAGIILNNUV	UNAVAILING
AAEMRSSTTU	METATARSUS	AAGIILNRTV	TRAVAILING
AAENORTTTU	ATTENUATOR	AAGIILNSTV	SALIVATING
AAENORTUUV	ART NOUVEAU	AAGIILPRST	PLAGIARIST
AAENQRRTUY	QUATERNARY	AAGIIMNNRT	MARINATING
AAENRRSTTU	RESTAURANT	AAGIINNOPT	PAGINATION
AAEOOPPRSS	SOAP OPERAS	AAGIINNOTV	NAVIGATION
AAEOOPRRTV	EVAPORATOR	AAGIINOSTT	AGITATIONS
AAEOPRRSST	SEPARATORS	AAGIINPPRS	APPRAISING
AAEPPRRSST	SPARE PARTS	AAGIINPRST	ASPIRATING
AAEQRRSTUW	QUARTERSAW	AAGIJKLNWY	JAYWALKING
AAFFFGLSST	FLAGSTAFFS	AAGILLMNRY	ALARMINGLY,
AAFFGIMNRU	RAGAMUFFIN	MARGINALLY	
AAFGGILNVW	FLAG-WAVING	AAGILLORSS	GLOSSARIAL
AAFGIINNPR	FRANGIPANI	AAGILLORST	ALLIGATORS
AAFGILNNTU	ANTIFUNGAL	AAGILMNORS	ORGANISMAL
AAFGLLNRTY	FLAGRANTLY	AAGILMOPRS	PARALOGISM
AAFGLNRRTY	FRAGRANTLY	AAGILNNOQU	ALGONQUIAN
AAFHIINNOS	IN A FASHION	AAGILNNOTU	ANGULATION
AAFIIILRSS	FILARIASIS	AAGILNOORT	GORNO-ALTAI
AAFIILLMRY	FAMILIARLY	AAGILNOPRS	SPORANGIAL
AAFIILMNRU	UNFAMILIAR	AAGILNPRSY	PARALYSING
AAFILNOOTT	FLOATATION	AAGILNRRTU	TRIANGULAR
		AAGILNRTUY	ANGULARITY

AAGILNSSTU	ASSAULTING
AAGILOPRST	PARALOGIST
AAGILOSUVY	YUGOSLAVIA
AAGIMMPRST	PRAGMATISM
AAGIMNNOST	ANTAGONISM
AAGIMNNPRW	WARMING
PAN	
AAGIMNNOTTU	AUTOMATING
AAGIMNPTTU	AMPUTATING
AAGIMNSSTY	GYMNASIAST
AAGIMPRSTT	PRAGMATIST
AAGINNNOTT	ANNOTATING
AAGINNOSTT	ANTAGONIST,
STAGNATION	
AAGINNRRTW	WARRANTING
AAGINNRSUY	SANGUINARY
AAGINOORRT	ARROGATION
AAGINORSTV	NAVIGATORS
AAGINOSSTT	GAS STATION
AAGINRRTVY	GRAVY TRAIN
AAGINRSTTU	ANTITRAGUS,
SATURATING	
AAGLLMOOSU	ALLOGAMOUS
AAGLLNOPTT	TOPGALLANT
AAGLMOOPRR	POLAROGRAM
AAGLNNOOSX	ANGLO-SAXON
AAGLNNSTTY	STAGNANTLY
AAGLNORRTU	GRANULATOR
AAGLNORRTY	ARROGANTLY
AAGMOOSTUU	AUTOGAMOUS
AAGNNNOSTY	NANNY GOATS
AAGNORRSTU	GUARANTORS
AAGOOPPRRT	PROPAGATOR
AAHHILMOPT	OPHTHALMIA
AAHHIMRRTY	ARRHYTHMIA
AAHHLORSTT	THROATLASH
AAHIIKMNRS	KASHMIRIAN
AAHIILLNNOT	INHALATION
AAHIILNNTU	LITHUANIAN
AAHIILNOPS	HISPANIOLA
AAHIIMPRSS	PHARISAISM
AAHIINNSTY	HINAYANIST
AAHILMNSTU	MALTHUSIAN
AAHILMTTUZ	ALTAZIMUTH
AAHILNNOPT	ANTIPHONAL
AAHILOPPSY	APOPHYSIAL
AAHILORSTU	HAUSTORIAL
AAHIMMNOTY	MYTHOMANIA
AAHIMMNSSS	SHAMANISMS
AAHIMNSSST	SHAMANISTS
AAHINNOTTX	XANTHATION
AAHINOPRTW	ON A PAR
WITH	
AAHINPSTXY	ASPHYXIANT
AAHIPPRSSY	PARAPHYSIS

AAHKKNNPYY	HANKY-PANKY	AAILNNPQSU	PALANQUINS
AAHKLOORSY	YOSHKAR-OLA	AAILNOORTT	ROTATIONAL
AAHLLMOPSY	HYALOPLASM	AAILNOPPST	PALPATIONS
AAHNOPRTTU	NATUROPATH	AAILNOSTTU	SALUTATION
AAHNORRSTU	ANARTHROUS	AAILNOSTUV	VALUATIONS
AAIIILLMNW	WILLIAMINA	AAILNPPPTU	AN APT PUPIL
AAIIILMMNT	MILITIAMAN	AAILNPRSTU	TARPAULINS
AAIIILMMNX	MAXIMILIAN	AAILNRSTTU	NATURALIST
AAIIILMNRT	LIMITARIAN	AAILNSSSTU	STANISLAUS
AAIIJKNSTT	TAJIKISTAN	AAIMMOSTTU	AUTOMATISM
AAIIJLNORT	JANITORIAL	AAIMMRSTTU	TRAUMATISM
AAIIKLLNTY	ALKALINITY	AAIMNOOTTU	AUTOMATION
AAIIKMNNST	KANTIANISM	AAIMNOPTTU	AMPUTATION
AAIIKNPSST	PAKISTANIS	AAIMNOQSTU	SQUAMATION
AAIIILLNOPT	PALLIATION	AAIMNORSTU	SANATORIUM
AAIILMMRST	MARTIALISM	AAIMNORTTU	MATURATION
AAIILMMSTX	MAXIMALIST	AAIMNOSSTT	ANATOMISTS
AAIILMNNOT	ANTIMONIAL,	AAIMNPRSST	SPARTANISM
LAMINATION		AAIMOSTTTU	AUTOMATIST
AAIILMRSTT	MARTIALIST	AAINNNOOST	SAN ANTONIO
AAIILNORRT	IRRATIONAL	AAINNNOOTT	ANNOTATION
AAIILNOSTV	SALIVATION	AAINNORRST	NARRATIONS
AAIILNRSTY	SANITARILY	AAINNRSTUY	UNSANITARY
AAIILPRTTY	PARTIALITY	AAINOOPPRT	PROTANOPIA
AAIILPSTTY	SPATIALITY	AAINOPSTTY	PAY STATION
AAIIMMNNRSX	MARXIANISM	AAINORSTTU	SATURATION
AAIIMNNOPT	IMPANATION	AAINORSTTV	STARVATION
AAIIMNNORT	MARINATION	AAINORSTTY	STATIONARY
AAIIMNRSTU	SANITARIUM	AAINSSSSTT	ASSISTANTS
AAIIMPRSST	PARASITISM	AAIOPRRSTY	ASPIRATORY
AAIINNOSTT	SANITATION	AAKKLNORRS	KARLSKRONA
AAIINNRRTU	RURITANIAN	AAKKMORRST	KRAMATORSK
AAIINNRSTU	UNITARIANS	AAKLMOPRSY	KARYOPLASM
AAIINNRSTY	INSANITARY	AAKLNORSUY	ANKYLOSAUR
AAIINOPPRT	APPARITION	AAKMMNORSW	
AAIINOPRST	ASPIRATION	MARKSWOMAN	
AAIINOPRTT	TRITANOPIA	AALLLLOTWW	
AAIINORSTV	VARIATIONS	WALL-TO-WALL	
AAIIRSSSTY	SATYRIASIS	AALLMNTUUY	AUTUMNALLY
AAIKLLNOTY	ALKYLATION	AALLPRSTWY	PARTY WALLS
AAILLNNOTY	NATIONALLY	AALLPSSWYY	PALSY-WALSY
AAILLNNOVV	VILLANOVAN	AALLRSTTWY	STALWARTLY
AAILLNOPST	SPALLATION	AALMOOPPRS	MALAPROPOS
AAILLNORTY	RATIONALLY	AALMOOPRTY	LAPAROTOMY
AAILLRSTUY	SALUTARILY	AALMOPRSXY	PAROXYSMAL
AAILMNOTTU	MUTATIONAL	AALNNOOPST	PANTALOONS
AAILMNRRTU	INTRAMURAL	AALNNPRSTT	TRANSPLANT
AAILMNRSTU	NATURALISM	AALNNRRSTU	TRANSLUNAR
AAILMOPPRX	APPROXIMAL	AALNOOPPRV	ON APPROVAL
AAILMPRSSU	MARSUPIALS	AALNOOPUZZ	POZZUOLANA
AAILNNNOTU	ANNULATION	AALNOPRRST	TRANSPOLAR
AAILNNOOTT	NOTATIONAL	AALNORRSTT	TRANSLATOR
AAILNNOPTT	PLANTATION	AALOPRRSTU	AUSTRALORP
AAILNNOTTU	NUTATIONAL	AALOPRRSTY	PORTRAYALS

AALOPSTTUY	AUTOPLASTY		
AALORSTTUY	SALUTATORY		
AAMNNOTTTU	TANTAMOUNT		
AAMNOOSTTU	AUTOMATONS		
AAMOOSSTTU	ASTOMATOUS		
AAMOOSTTUU	AUTOMATOUS		
AANOOPRSTU	ANATROPOUS		
AANORSSTTU	ASTRONAUTS		
AAOOPPRRST	PARATROOPS		
ABBBDENRRU	RUBBER BAND		
ABBBEEILSU	BLUE BABIES		
ABBBEGILNR	BLABBERING		
ABBBEHISSU	BUSHBABIES		
ABBBELOPSU	SOAP BUBBLE		
ABBBELPRUW	BUBBLE WRAP		
ABBCCDEKMO	BACKCOMBED		
ABBCDEKLOU	DOUBLE BACK		
ABBCDEMRRU	BREADCRUMB		
ABBCDIKLRS	BLACKBIRDS		
ABBCDKORSU	BUCKBOARDS		
ABBCEGGHUY	BEACH BUGGY		
ABBCEGINRU	BARBECUING		
ABBCEIKRST	BACKBITERS		
ABBCEILMNO	COMBINABLE		
ABBCEILRSU	SUBCALIBRE		
ABBCEINSSS	SCABBINESS		
ABBCEKLLST	BLACK BELTS		
ABBCEKLOSX	BLACK BOXES		
ABBCEKLRRY	BLACKBERRY		
ABBCEKMNRU	BACK NUMBER		
ABBCENORSY	ABSORBENCY		
ABBCGIIKNT	BACKBITING		
ABBCGILNRS	SCRABBLING		
ABBCILPRSU	PUBLIC BARS		
ABBCIMMOOT	ATOMIC BOMB		
ABBCKLOOST	BOOTBLACKS		
ABBDDEEILO	ABLE-BODIED		
ABBDEEGILR	BRIDGEABLE		
ABBDEEHLPS	PEBBLEDASH		
ABBDEEIRRW	BARBED WIRE		
ABBDEEKNOR	DONER KEBAB		
ABBDEELNNU	UNBENDABLE		
ABBDEELORU	BELABOURED		
ABBDEELRSU	BLUEBEARDS		
ABBDEFIORR	FIBREBOARD		
ABBDEGIINR	BAINBRIDGE		
ABBDEIMNRY	BABY-MINDER		
ABBDEIMORR	BOMBARDIER		
ABBDELLNRU	LANDLUBBER		
ABBDELMOOZ	BAMBOOZLED		
ABBDELORSY	ABSORBEDLY		
ABBDELOSSU	DOUBLE BASS		
ABBDGIMNOR	BOMBARDING		
ABBDHLOOST	BLOODBATHS		
ABBDILLORS	BILLBOARDS		

Code	Word	Code	Word	Code	Word
ABBDKLNOOS	BLOOD BANKS	ABCCHKLOST	BACKCLOTHS	ABCDERSTTU	SUBTRACTED
ABBDNORSSU	BRASSBOUND	ABCCIMOORT	MOBOCRATIC	ABCDGIKLNO	BLOCKADING
ABBEEEILLV	BELIEVABLE	ABCCINORTU	BUCCINATOR	ABCDGINNOS	ABSCONDING
ABBEEILLVY	BELIEVABLY	ABCCMOPSTU	SUBCOMPACT	ABCDGKNORU	BACKGROUND
ABBEELORSV	OBSERVABLE	ABCCNOOPRY	CARBON COPY	ABCDHIILNR	BRAINCHILD
ABBEELRTTU	REBUTTABLE	ABCDDKORSU	DUCKBOARDS	ABCDHINNRU	NUDIBRANCH
ABBEENORST	BREASTBONE	ABCDEEEELR	DECREEABLE	ABCDHIOOPR	BRACHIOPOD
ABBEENORTW	BROWBEATEN	ABCDEEEELX	EXCEEDABLE	ABCDHLOORT	BROADCLOTH
ABBEENRTTU	BUTTER BEAN	ABCDEEEHSU	DEBAUCHEES	ABCDHNOPRU	PUNCHBOARD
ABBEFILNSS	FLABBINESS	ABCDEEEILV	DECEIVABLE	ABCDHNRSTU	DUTCH BARNS
ABBEFMORRU	FOAM RUBBER	ABCDEEELLT	DELECTABLE	ABCDIIISTY	DIBASICITY
ABBEGJLSUU	SUBJUGABLE	ABCDEEELRT	CELEBRATED	ABCDIILLSY	DISYLLABIC
ABBEHHIKSS	SHISH KEBAB	ABCDEEELTT	DETECTABLE	ABCDIIMNOY	BIODYNAMIC
ABBEHINSSS	SHABBINESS	ABCDEEHLLY	BELLYACHED	ABCDIISTUY	SUBACIDITY
ABBEILLMSU	SUBLIMABLE	ABCDEEHRUY	DEBAUCHERY	ABCDIKLOWW	BLACK WIDOW
ABBEILMOPR	IMPROBABLE	ABCDEEILLN	DECLINABLE	ABCDIKOPRR	DROP A BRICK
ABBEIRSTTY	BABY-SITTER	ABCDEEILNU	INEDUCABLE	ABCDILLNOO	BILL AND COO
ABBEKLNOTT	BOTTLE BANK	ABCDEEILPR	PREDICABLE	ABCDILNOST	CNIDOBLAST
ABBELMOORZ	BAMBOOZLER	ABCDEEILPS	DESPICABLE	ABCDILOPRS	CLIPBOARDS
ABBELMSSUU	SUBSUMABLE	ABCDEEILRT	CREDITABLE	ABCDKLNOSU	CLOUDBANKS
ABBELORSVY	OBSERVABLY	ABCDEELLNY	BELLY DANCE	ABCDKLOORS	ROADBLOCKS
ABBELOSSTY	STABLE BOYS	ABCDEELLTY	DELECTABLY	ABCEEEHKRS	SCHAERBEEK
ABBENORSST	ABSORBENTS	ABCDEELLUX	EXCLUDABLE	ABCEEEIKRR	ICEBREAKER
ABBFHIIRST	RABBITFISH	ABCDEELORR	RECORDABLE	ABCEEEILRV	RECEIVABLE
ABBFHLLSSU	FLASHBULBS	ABCDEFIRTU	BIFURCATED	ABCEEEJLRT	REJECTABLE
ABBFILORST	FIBROBLAST	ABCDEFOSTU	OBFUSCATED	ABCEEELLRR	CEREBELLAR
ABBGIINRTT	RABBITTING	ABCDEGHINU	DEBAUCHING	ABCEEELNRS	SCREENABLE
ABBGILNQSU	SQUABBLING	ABCDEHIILR	HERBICIDAL	ABCEEELPTX	EXCEPTABLE,
ABBHILMSUU	LUBUMBASHI	ABCDEHKLOS	BLOCKHEADS	EXPECTABLE	
ABBILMOPRY	IMPROBABLY	ABCDEHKMPU	HUMPBACKED	ABCEEELTUX	EXECUTABLE
ABBILORSTU	SUBORBITAL	ABCDEHLNUW	BUCHENWALD	ABCEEENRUX	EXUBERANCE
ABBOOPRSTY	BOOBY TRAPS	ABCDEHORSS	CHESSBOARD	ABCEEFFORS	COFFEE BARS
ABBOORRSWY	BARROW BOYS	ABCDEHORSY	BODY SEARCH	ABCEEFHNNR	FRENCH BEAN
ABCCCEMNUY	ACCUMBENCY	ABCDEIILNT	INDICTABLE	ABCEEFIILN	BENEFICIAL
ABCCDEEIRT	BRECCIATED	ABCDEIILNV	VINDICABLE	ABCEEFNORT	BENEFACTOR
ABCCEEELNS	ALBESCENCE	ABCDEIIMRT	IMBRICATED	ABCEEGKNRS	GREENBACKS
ABCCEEENST	TABESCENCE	ABCDEIIORT	ABORTICIDE	ABCEEHILNR	HIBERNACLE
ABCCEEILMP	IMPECCABLE	ABCDEIIRSS	SACRED IBIS	ABCEEHKLPS	BLACK SHEEP
ABCCEEILSS	ACCESSIBLE	ABCDEIKLRS	BACKSLIDER	ABCEEHKKST	SKETCHABLE
ABCCEENRSU	BUCCANEERS	ABCDEIKOUV	BIVOUACKED	ABCEEHKRTU	HACKBUTEER
ABCCEHHOOR	COOCH BEHAR	ABCDEIKRSS	DISC BRAKES	ABCEEHLLSY	BELLYACHES
ABCCEHILRU	CHERUBICAL	ABCDEILLLU	DULCIBELLA	ABCEEHLNQU	QUENCHABLE
ABCCEILMPY	IMPECCABLY	ABCDEILLNU	INCLUDABLE	ABCEEHNORR	ABHORRENCE
ABCCEINOSU	SUBOCEANIC	ABCDEILLPU	DUPLICABLE	ABCEEHORSU	HERBACEOUS
ABCCEJNSUY	SUBJACENCY	ABCDEILNUY	INEDUCABLY	ABCEEIILLT	ELICITABLE
ABCCELNRSU	CARBUNCLES	ABCDEILPSY	DESPICABLY	ABCEEIJLNT	INJECTABLE
ABCCGHLSTU	CLUTCH BAGS	ABCDEILRTU	LUBRICATED,	ABCEEILLNR	RECLINABLE
ABCCHHKNSU	HUNCHBACKS	TRADUCIBLE		ABCEEILLNS	LICENSABLE
ABCCHIIMOR	CHORIAMBIC	ABCDEILRTY	CREDITABLY	ABCEEILLOT	BIOCELLATE
ABCCHIIRRT	TRIBRACHIC	ABCDEINORS	CARBONISED	ABCEEILLPX	EXPLICABLE
ABCCHIKLPT	PITCH-BLACK	ABCDEINORZ	CARBONIZED	ABCEEILMMT	EMBLEMATIC
ABCCHIKSTT	BACKSTITCH	ABCDELLORY	LOCAL DERBY	ABCEEILNNU	ENUNCIABLE
ABCCHIKSTW	SWITCHBACK	ABCDELPRUW	PUB-CRAWLED	ABCEEILNOT	NOTICEABLE
ABCCHIOOPR	ACROPHOBIC	ABCDEOORRS	SCOREBOARD	ABCEEILNTU	BINUCLEATE

ABCEEILPTZ	PECTIZABLE	ABCEIILMTU	UMBILICATE	ABCGHLORYY	BRACHYLOGY
ABCEEILRTX	EXTRICABLE	ABCEIILPST	EPIBLASTIC	ABCGIILLOO	BIOLOGICAL
ABCEEINNOZ	BENZOCAINE	ABCEIINTUV	INCUBATIVE	ABCGIINNTU	INCUBATING
ABCEEINNST	ABSTINENCE	ABCEIIOORT	AEROBIOTIC	ABCGILMNRS	SCRAMBLING
ABCEEINOSS	OBEISANCES	ABCEIKLRRY	BRICKLAYER	ABCGIMNOTT	COMBATTING
ABCEEKLOPT	POCKETABLE	ABCEILLNOU	INOCULABLE	ABCHHIOPRS	ARCHBISHOP
ABCEEKRSTT	BACK STREET	ABCEILLNPU	INCULPABLE	ABCHIILLNS	CHILBLAINS
ABCEEKSTTU	BUCKET SEAT	ABCEILLNRS	CRANESBILL	ABCHIILMOP	AMPHIBOLIC
ABCEELLNOS	ENCLOSABLE	ABCEILLPXY	EXPLICABLY	ABCHIKLMST	BLACKSMITH
ABCEELLORT	BROCATELLE	ABCEILLSSU	CASUS BELLI	ABCHIKLRST	BLACKSHIRT
ABCEELLPUX	EXCULPABLE	ABCEILLTUV	CULTIVABLE	ABCHKKOOTU	CHUKKA BOOT
ABCEELLRRY	CEREBRALLY	ABCEILMOPT	COMPATIBLE	ABCHKLNORT	BLACKTHORN
ABCEELNNOV	CONVENABLE	ABCEILNOSU	UNSOCIABLE	ABCHKMSTTU	THUMBTACKS
ABCEELNORS	CENSORABLE	ABCEILNOTY	NOTICEABLY	ABCHKORSTW	THROWBACKS
ABCEELNOVY	CONVEYABLE	ABCEILNPRU	REPUBLICAN	ABCHLLNPSU	PUNCH BALLS
ABCEELNRSU	CENSURABLE	ABCEILNRRU	INCURRABLE	ABCIIINOTT	ANTIBIOTIC
ABCEELOPRU	RECOUPABLE	ABCEILPRSU	RES PUBLICA	ABCIIJMOST	JACOBITISM
ABCEELOPRW	PACE BOWLER	ABCEIMOORT	COIMBATORE	ABCIILLNRY	BRILLIANCY
ABCEELORRT	CELEBRATOR	ABCEIMORRT	BAROMETRIC	ABCIILLSST	BALLISTICS
ABCEEMMRST	CAMEMBERTS	ABCEINRRST	TRANSCRIBE	ABCIILMOPS	BIOPLASMIC
ABCEEMOOTY	AMOEBOCYTE	ABCEIORSUU	RUBIACEOUS	ABCIILRTUY	CURABILITY
ABCEENORSV	OBSERVANCE	ABCEJKLMRU	LUMBERJACK	ABCIINNOTU	INCUBATION
ABCEENRRTY	BARYCENTRE	ABCEKKORST	BACKSTROKE	ABCIINOSSS	ABSCISSION
ABCEEOPPRS	SPACE PROBE	ABCEKLLNOU	UNLOCKABLE	ABCIIOSSTT	BIOSTATICS
ABCEEPRRSU	CUPBEARERS	ABCEKLNORU	COALBUNKER	ABCIKLLSST	BLACKLISTS
ABCEFHLSSU	FLASHCUBES	ABCEKLOPRW	BLACK POWER	ABCILMOPTY	COMPATIBLY
ABCEFHOSTW	FOB WATCHES	ABCEKLRTTU	TURTLEBACK	ABCILMOSUX	MUSICAL BOX
ABCEFLNOSU	CONFUSABLE	ABCELLLORU	BLUE-COLLAR	ABCILMRUUV	VIBRACULUM
ABCEGIKLNN	BLACKENING	ABCELLMOOP	CAMPOBELLO	ABCILMSSTY	CYMBALISTS
ABCEGIKNRT	BRACKETING	ABCELLNOOR	COLLARBONE	ABCILNORSU	BINOCULARS
ABCEGILMNR	CLAMBERING	ABCELLNOOS	CONSOLABLE	ABCILNRSTU	LUBRICANTS
ABCEGILNOZ	COGNIZABLE	ABCELLOORU	COLOURABLE	ABCILORRTU	LUBRICATOR
ABCEGINNNY	BENIGNANCY	ABCELLOOST	BLASTOCOEL	ABCILPSTUY	SUBTYPICAL
ABCEGJLNOU	CONJUGABLE	ABCELLRSSW	SCREWBALLS	ABCIMMOPRU	PROCAMBIUM
ABCEGLNOOT	CONGLOBATE	ABCELMMNOO	COMMONABLE	ABCINORSTU	INCUBATORS
ABCEHHJOTT	HATCHET JOB	ABCELMMOTU	COMMUTABLE	ABCIORRRTU	RUBRICATOR
ABCEHIIRST	HEBRAISTIC	ABCELMNRSU	UNSCRAMBLE	ABCKKNOOTU	KNOCKABOUT
ABCEHILPRT	BIRTHPLACE	ABCELMOPTU	COMPUTABLE	ABCKLOPSST	BLACK SPOTS
ABCEHILRST	CHRISTABEL	ABCELNORRY	BARLEYCORN	ABCKNPRTUY	BANKRUPTCY
ABCEHILSTW	SWITCHABLE	ABCELNOSST	CONSTABLES	ABCKOOPRSS	SCRAPBOOKS
ABCEHINRRY	CHINABERRY	ABCELRRTUU	TUBERCULAR	ABCLOORRSU	COLOUR BARS
ABCEHIOOPR	AEROPHOBIC	ABCEMNOPRU	PERNAMBUCO	ABCLORRTUU	LUCUBRATOR
ABCEHKLLOS	BLACK HOLES	ABCEMOOPRT	AMBOCEPTOR	ABCLORRTUY	ROTARY CLUB
ABCEHKMNRS	BENCH MARKS	ABCENNSTUY	SUBTENANCY	ABCLOSSTTY	BLASTOCYST
ABCEHKORSY	CHEBOKSARY	ABCENRRTUY	CANTERBURY	ABCNORSTTY	BY CONTRAST
ABCEHLLOTT	TABLECLOTH	ABCENSSSTU	SUBSTANCES	ABDDEEEFLN	DEFENDABLE
ABCEHMMNRU	MACH	ABCEOORRST	SERBO-CROAT	ABDDEEEHNO	BONEHEADED
NUMBER		ABCERRSTTU	SUBTRACTER	ABDDEEELNP	DEPENDABLE
ABCEHMOPRT	CHAMBER POT	ABCFGIIKNR	BACKFIRING	ABDDEEGGLR	BEDRAGGLED
ABCEHMOSTX	MATCHBOXES	ABCFILMORU	BACULIFORM	ABDDEEGHIR	BRIDGEHEAD
ABCEHORTTX	CHATTERBOX	ABCGGIKPSY	PIGGYBACKS	ABDDEEHLLU	BULLHEADED
ABCEIILLMT	BIMETALLIC	ABCGHIINOT	COHABITING	ABDDEEKORY	KEYBOARDED
ABCEIILLNN	INCLINABLE	ABCGHIIOPR	BIOGRAPHIC	ABDDEELNPY	DEPENDABLY
ABCEIILLNR	BRILLIANCE	ABCGHIKMNU	BUCKINGHAM	ABDDEELOTU	DOUBLE DATE

ABDDEEPRSS	BEDSPREADS	ABDEEHLMPS	BLASPHEMED	ABDEHIILLS	DISHABILLE
ABDDEERSTY	TEDDY BEARS	ABDEEHLOTT	TABLE D'HOTE	ABDEHINRRS	BRANDISHER
ABDDEGINRU	UNABRIDGED	ABDEEHORST	BROADSHEET	ABDEHINRTT	HARD-BITTEN
ABDDEGIRRW	DRAWBRIDGE	ABDEEIILLT	DEBILITATE	ABDEHIORTW	WHITEBOARD
ABDDEHHINN	BEHINDHAND	ABDEEIINRT	INEBRIATED	ABDEHLOSTW	DEATHBLOWS
ABDDEHILNR	HILDEBRAND	ABDEEIKNNY	KIDNEY BEAN	ABDEHMNNSU	HUSBANDMEN
ABDDEHILOR	HARD-BOILED	ABDEEILMRY	REMEDIABLY	ABDEHNORTU	EARTHBOUND
ABDDEHINRS	BRANDISHED	ABDEEILMTT	TIMETABLED	ABDEHNRSTU	SUBTRAHEND
ABDDEHMOTU		ABDEEILNNU	UNDENIABLE	ABDEHNRTUY	THUNDER BAY
	BAD-MOUTHED	ABDEEILNRS	BREADLINES	ABDEHORRST	SHORTBREAD
ABDDEIIMRS	BRIDESMAID	ABDEEILPRU	REPUDIABLE	ABDEIIKLLS	DISLIKABLE
ABDDEILLLS	SADDLEBILL	ABDEEILPRV	DEPRIVABLE	ABDEIILMSS	ADMISSIBLE
ABDDEILNST	BLIND DATES	ABDEEILRSV	VERBALISED	ABDEIILSST	STABILISED
ABDDEIORSS	BROADSIDES,	ABDEEILRVZ	VERBALIZED	ABDEIILSTZ	STABILIZED
	SIDEBOARDS	ABDEEINNRR	BERNARDINE	ABDEIINOST	ANTIBODIES
ABDDELNORR	BORDERLAND	ABDEEIRRVW	WEAVERBIRD	ABDEIKNRSW	WINDBREAKS
ABDDELNRTU	BLADDERNUT	ABDEEISTTU	BEATITUDES	ABDEILLLNY	BLIND ALLEY
ABDDGIINNS	DISBANDING	ABDEEKLOTU	DOUBLE TAKE	ABDEILMSTU	SUBLIMATED
ABDDGORSUY	BODYGUARDS	ABDEEKORRY	KEYBOARDER	ABDEILNNUW	UNWINDABLE
ABDDIMNOOY	DAIMYO BOND	ABDEELLOPR	DEPLORABLE	ABDEILNNUY	UNDENIABLY
ABDDLMOORU	MOULDBOARD	ABDEELLORS	SOLDERABLE	ABDEILOPSS	DISPOSABLE
ABDDOORRSW	BROADSWORD	ABDEELLSTY	SELL-BY DATE	ABDEILPSTU	DISPUTABLE
ABDEEEELMR	REDEEMABLE	ABDEELMNOZ	EMBLAZONED	ABDEILRRSY	EARLY BIRDS
ABDEEEFHRT	FEATHER BED	ABDEELMRRU	DEMURRABLE	ABDEILRSTU	BRUTALISED
ABDEEEFILS	DEFEASIBLE	ABDEELNOPR	PONDERABLE	ABDEILRTTW	WATTLEBIRD
ABDEEEFLRR	DEFERRABLE	ABDEELNORS	BANDOLEERS,	ABDEILRTUZ	BRUTALIZED
ABDEEEGGLR	BARELEGGED		ENDORSABLE	ABDEIMNRST	DISBARMENT
ABDEEEGGRW	BEGGARWEED	ABDEELNSST	STEEL BANDS	ABDEIMMNSU	SUBMEDIANT
ABDEEEHQTU	BEQUEATHED	ABDEELOPRT	DEPORTABLE	ABDEIMRRTY	TIMBERYARD
ABDEEEILMR	REMEDIABLE	ABDEELORTT	BATTLEDORE	ABDEIMRTUW	DUMBWAITER
ABDEEEILRT	DELIBERATE	ABDEELSTTY	DETESTABLY	ABDEINORSU	BOUNDARIES
ABDEEELLPT	DEPLETABLE	ABDEEMRRSU	EMBRASURED	ABDEIRRSTW	WATER BIRDS
ABDEEELMRY	REDEEMABLY	ABDEENOPSU	SUBPOENAED	ABDEIRTTTU	ATTRIBUTED
ABDEEELNPX	EXPENDABLE	ABDEENPRRY	PREBENDARY	ABDEJORSTT	OBJETS D'ART
ABDEEELNRR	RENDERABLE	ABDEENRRST	BARTENDERS	ABDEKLLNOR	BANKROLLED
ABDEEELNRT	TENDERABLE	ABDEENSTTU	DEBUTANTES	ABDEKLLOTU	DOUBLE-TALK
ABDEEELSTT	DETESTABLE	ABDEEOPSST	SPEEDBOATS	ABDEKLOPRU	DOUBLE-PARK
ABDEEEMNST	DEBASEMENT	ABDEERRSST	REDBREASTS	ABDEKNORSW	BREAKDOWNS
ABDEEENRTT	BERNADETTE	ABDEFFGLSU	DUFFEL BAGS	ABDEKNPRTU	BANKRUPTED
ABDEEERSTW	SWEETBREAD	ABDEFFORSS	BRASSED OFF	ABDELLNOSW	SNOWBALLED
ABDEEFFHLU	BUFFLEHEAD	ABDEFIILMO	MODIFIABLE	ABDELLOPRY	DEPLORABLY
ABDEEFHLRS	HALF-BREEDS	ABDEFILMOR	FORMIDABLE	ABDELLORUY	LABOUREDLY
ABDEEFHNOR	BEFOREHAND	ABDEFINRRS	FIREBRANDS	ABDELMORST	BLASTODERM
ABDEEFIITU	BEAUTIFIED	ABDEFIRRTU	BREADFRUIT	ABDELMRRUY	LUMBERYARD
ABDEEFLMOR	DEFORMABLE	ABDEFLORST	STABLEFORD	ABDELNORTU	ROUND-TABLE
ABDEEFLNRU	REFUNDABLE	ABDEGGIRRU	BUDGERIGAR	ABDELOOORT	BOOTLOADER
ABDEEFORRS	FREEBOARDS	ABDEGGNOOT	TOBOGGANED	ABDELORSUV	BOULEVARDS
ABDEEGILNS	DESIGNABLE	ABDEGHINSU	SUBHEADING	ABDELORTUY	OBDURATELY
ABDEEGLORT	GOLD-BEATER	ABDEGIMNRT	ABRIDGMENT	ABDENRRSST	ST BERNARDS
ABDEEHIKNR	BIRKENHEAD	ABDEGINNOR	BROADENING	ABDENRSSTY	BYSTANDERS
ABDEEHILLS	DESHABILLE	ABDEGIRRTW	BRIDGWATER	ABDENSSTUY	SUNDAY BEST
ABDEEHILRR	HALBERDIER	ABDEGJSTUU	SUBJUGATED	ABDERRTTYY	DRY BATTERY
ABDEEHIMRT	TIMBERHEAD	ABDEGLNNRU	BURGENLAND	ABDFILMORY	FORMIDABLY
ABDEEHIMSV	MISBEHAVED	ABDEGNNRUU	GRAUBUNDEN	ABDFILNORU	FLORIBUNDA
ABDEEHINRT	HIBERNATED				

ABDFINSSTU	IFS AND BUTS	
ABDFLOOORR	FLOORBOARD	
ABDFORRSSU	SURFBOARDS	
ABDGHIINNSU	HUSBANDING	
ABDGIINPRU	UPBRAIDING	
ABDGIINRRS	DISBARRING	
ABDGIINSSU	DISABUSING	
ABDGINNRUU	BURGUNDIAN	
ABDGINORTU	GROUND BAIT	
ABDHILMOOR	RHOMBOIDAL	
ABDHIOPRSS	SHIPBOARDS	
ABDIIILSTY	DISABILITY	
ABDIIILTUY	AUDIBILITY	
ABDIIKNNRY	BRADYKININ	
ABDIILMNOU	ALBUMINOID	
ABDIILORRT	TAILORBIRD	
ABDIILPTUY	DUPABILITY	
ABDIILRTUY	DURABILITY	
ABDIINOTTU	DUBITATION	
ABDIIRSSUY	SUBSIDIARY	
ABDILMNNOR	ROMAN BLIND	
ABDILNOOST	BLOODSTAIN	
ABDILNORSU	SUBORDINAL	
ABDILOORTY	BOTRYOIDAL	
ABDILPSTUY	DISPUTABLY	
ABDIMPQSSU	DAMP SQUIBS	
ABDINOSWWY	BAY WINDOWS	
ABDINRSSTW	WRISTBANDS	
ABDLMOORYY	BLOODY MARY	
ABDMOORRRS	BOARDROOMS	
ABDNOORTUU	ROUNDABOUT	
ABDOORRTUU	TROUBADOUR	
ABEEEEFRST	BEEFEATERS	
ABEEEERSSZ	SEA BREEZES	
ABEEEEFLPRR	PREFERABLE	
ABEEEEGGLRS	SEGREGABLE	
ABEEEEGLSTV	VEGETABLES	
ABEEEGNNRS	GREEN BEANS	
ABEEEEHITTV	HEBETATIVE	
ABEEEEHLSSW	WHEELBASES	
ABEEEHQRTU	BEQUEATHER	
ABEEEEHRSTT	HARTEBEEST	
ABEEEIKRRT	TIEBREAKER	
ABEEEILLRV	RELIEVABLE	
ABEEEILRVW	REVIEWABLE	
ABEEELLLPX	EXPELLABLE	
ABEEEELLNVY	ABNEY LEVEL	
ABEEEELLSTT	SETTLEABLE	
ABEEEELMPRT	TEMPERABLE	
ABEEEELMRSS	REASSEMBLE	
ABEEEELNPRT	PENETRABLE	
ABEEELQSUZ	SQUEEZABLE	
ABEEEELRRSV	RESERVABLE	

ABEEENNOZZ	AZOBENZENE	
ABEEENNRTT	BANNERETTE	
ABEEEORSTT	STEREOBATE	
ABEEERRSST	BASSE-TERRE	
ABEEERRTTV	VERTEBRATE	
ABEEFFLMNT	BAFFLEMENT	
ABEEFFLRSU	SUFFERABLE	
ABEEFGINRS	FREE-BASING	
ABEEFGKNPR	KAPFENBERG	
ABEEFIILRV	VERIFIABLE	
ABEEFIKRRS	FIREBREAKS	
ABEEFILLLR	REFILLABLE	
ABEEFILLRT	FILTERABLE	
ABEEFILNTT	FLEA-BITTEN	
ABEEFILRSS	BAS-RELIEFS	
ABEEFIRRSU	FEBRUARIES	
ABEEFLOPRR	PERFORABLE	
ABEEFLPRRY	PREFERABLY	
ABEEFLSTTY	SAFETY BELT	
ABEEFMOOTT	BEEF TOMATO	
ABEEGHNORU	HAUBERGEON	
ABEEGHNTTU	BEAT THE GUN	
ABEEGIKNPS	BESPEAKING	
ABEEGILLNY	EYEBALLING	
ABEEGILMNR	GERMINABLE	
ABEEGILNOT	NEGOTIABLE	
ABEEGILNRT	INTEGRABLE	
ABEEGIMNRS	BESMEARING	
ABEEGINRSU	AUBERGINES	
ABEEGLNORV	GOVERNABLE	
ABEEGLNSTW	WEST BENGAL	
ABEEGLOPRS	BARGE POLES	
ABEEGNRSTT	ABSTERGENT	
ABEEHHRRTY	HEATHBERRY	
ABEEHILLRS	RELISHABLE	
ABEEHILPRS	PERISHABLE	
ABEEHIMRSV	MISBEHAVER	
ABEEHINOTT	HEBETATION	
ABEEHKNORS	BONESHAKER	
ABEEHKORSS	BRAKE SHOES	
ABEEHLMPRS	BLASPHEMER	
ABEEHMORTT	BATHOMETER	
ABEEHNORSU	OBERHAUSEN	
ABEEHOORRS	SEBORRHOEA	
ABEEHORSTU	HEREABOUTS	
ABEEHPRRSY	BARYSPHERE	
ABEEIILLMN	ELIMINABLE	
ABEEIILLRS	LIBERALISE	
ABEEIILLRZ	LIBERALIZE	
ABEEIILNPX	INEXPIABLE	
ABEEIILNTV	INEVITABLE	
ABEEIILSST	BESTIALISE	
ABEEIILSTZ	BESTIALIZE	
ABEEIINRST	INEBRIATES	

ABEEIIRSST	BESTIARIES	
ABEEILLMNR	BELLARMINE	
ABEEILLMOR	MELIORABLE	
ABEEILLNNT	TABLE LINEN	
ABEEILLNRU	UNRELIABLE	
ABEEILLNST	LISTENABLE	
ABEEILLNTV	VENTILABLE	
ABEEILLRTT	LITTLE BEAR	
ABEEILMNRT	TERMINABLE	
ABEEILMNSU	ALBUMENISE	
ABEEILMNUZ	ALBUMENIZE	
ABEEILMOST	METABOLISE	
ABEEILMOTT	METABOLITE	
ABEEILMOTZ	METABOLIZE	
ABEEILMRTT	REMITTABLE	
ABEEILMSSS	ASSEMBLIES	
ABEEILMSTT	TIMETABLES	
ABEEILNNUV	UNENVIABLE	
ABEEILNOPR	INOPERABLE	
ABEEILNORX	INEXORABLE	
ABEEILNPSX	EXPANSIBLE	
ABEEILNRSS	BLEARINESS	
ABEEILNRST	EAST BERLIN, INSERTABLE
ABEEILNRTU	REUNITABLE	
ABEEILNRWY	BARLEY WINE	
ABEEILNSTV	INVESTABLE	
ABEEILORTT	OBLITERATE	
ABEEILPPTZ	PEPTIZABLE	
ABEEILPRRS	RESPIRABLE	
ABEEILQRRU	REQUIRABLE	
ABEEILQRTU	REQUITABLE	
ABEEILRRSV	VERBALISER	
ABEEILRRVZ	VERBALIZER	
ABEEILRSST	ASSERTIBLE	
ABEEILRSSU	REISSUABLE	
ABEEILSSTT	BEASTLIEST	
ABEEIRRSSS	BRASSERIES, BRASSIERES
ABEEJLLMSU	JUMBLE SALE	
ABEEJLLNSY	JELLY BEANS	
ABEEJMMNNT	ENJAMBMENT	
ABEEKLNRSV	BLANK VERSE	
ABEEKLNTTW	WET BLANKET	
ABEEKMMMNT	EMBANKMENT	
ABEEKMMNRT	EMBARKMENT	
ABEEKNOPST	KEEP TABS ON	
ABEELLMNTU	ANTEBELLUM	
ABEELLMOPY	EMPLOYABLE	
ABEELLNRUV	VULNERABLE	
ABEELLORSV	RESOLVABLE	
ABEELLORVV	REVOLVABLE	
ABEELLPRUV	PULVERABLE	
ABEELMMMNT	EMBALMMENT	
ABEELMNRST	RESEMBLANT	

ABEELMNRSU	LEBENSRAUM, MENSURABLE	ABEGHMRRSU	HAMBURGERS
ABEELMNTTT	BATTLEMENT	ABEGHNRRSU	BUSHRANGER
ABEELMORST	BLASTOMERE	ABEGHQSUUU	USQUEBAUGH
ABEELMPRSU	PRESUMABLE	ABEGIILNNT	INTANGIBLE
ABEELNOPRS	PERSONABLE	ABEGIILNOR	OIL-BEARING
ABEELNRRTU	RETURNABLE	ABEGIILNRT	LIBERATING
ABEELNSSST	STABLENESS	ABEGIILOTV	OBLIGATIVE
ABEELOPRRT	REPORTABLE	ABEGIINNRT	BRIGANTINE
ABEELOPRRV	REPROVABLE	ABEGIINORS	ABORIGINES
ABEELOPRTX	EXPORTABLE	ABEGIINOST	ABIOGENIST
ABEELORRST	RESTORABLE	ABEGIKLNNT	BLANKETING
ABEELPSTTU	UPSETTABLE	ABEGILLNTY	BLEATINGLY
ABEELRSUVY	SURVEYABLE	ABEGILMNSS	ASSEMBLING
ABEEMORRST	BAROMETERS	ABEGILNSSU	SUBLEASING
ABEEMRRSSU	EMBRASURES	ABEGILRRSU	BURGLARIES
ABEENNNRRU	RUNNER BEAN	ABEGINNOTY	BAYONETING
ABEENNRRSS	BARRENNESS	ABEGINNQTU	BANQUETING
ABEENNRRSU	URBANENESS	ABEGINNRST	STRING BEAN
ABEENNRSSZ	BRAZENNESS	ABEGINRSTU	GAS TURBINE
ABEENORRTW	WATERBORNE	ABEGKRSSTU	GRUBSTAKES
ABEENORSSS	BARONESSES	ABEGLLNOOY	BALNEOLOGY
ABEEOPRRRT	REPROBATER	ABEGLNORRY	LOGANBERRY
ABEEOPRRST	REPROBATES	ABEGLNORSU	LOUNGE BARS
ABEEOPRSSW	POWER BASES	ABEGLOOSTZ	GO TO BLAZES
ABEFFGILRU	FEBRIFUGAL	ABEGLORRRV	VORARLBERG
ABEFFHINRS	BANFFSHIRE	ABEGMNOORS	BOOMERANGS
ABEFFILLOR	BILL OF FARE	ABEGMNOOTY	MONTEGO BAY
ABEFGIINTY	BEATIFYING	ABEGMORSUU	UMBRAGEOUS
ABEFGILORV	FORGIVABLE	ABEGNNSTTU	SUBTANGENT
ABEFGILRLS	FIBREGLASS, GLASS FIBRE	ABEGNOORTU	BATON ROUGE
ABEFGINORR	FORBEARING	ABEHHILLST	SHEATHBILL
ABEFHIRRTT	AFTERBIRTH	ABEHHIOOPT	THEOPHOBIA
ABEFHLLOTT	HALF-BOTTLE	ABEHHMMRSU	BUSHHAMMER
ABEFIILLLN	INFALLIBLE	ABEHHORRTT	HEARTTHROB
ABEFIILNOT	NOTIFIABLE	ABEHIILMNT	HABILIMENT
ABEFILLLOS	BILL OF SALE	ABEHIKLNRS	SHRINKABLE
ABEFILMORR	MORAL FIBRE	ABEHILNPSU	PUNISHABLE
ABEFILOPRT	PROFITABLE	ABEHILOPST	HOSPITABLE
ABEFKNORRT	BREAKFRONT	ABEHILPSTT	BATTLESHIP
ABEFLLLOOW	FOLLOWABLE	ABEHILPSTU	BISULPHATE
ABEFLLLORW	BALLFLOWER	ABEHILRSST	HERBALISTS
ABEFLLOORT	FOOTBALLER	ABEHILTWYY	WHITLEY BAY
ABEFLLOSTU	FAT-SOLUBLE	ABEHIMNNST	BANISHMENT
ABEFNNORUZ	BENZOFURAN	ABEHINNORT	ON THE BRAIN
ABEFNORSTY	FRAY BENTOS	ABEHINOOPX	XENOPHOBIA
ABEGGIMNOR	EMBARGOING	ABEHINOPRV	VIBRAPHONE
ABEGGNOORT	TOBOGGANER	ABEHINORRT	HIBERNATOR
ABEGGNOPSS	SPONGE BAGS	ABEHINRSSS	BRASHINESS
ABEGHILNRT	BLATHERING	ABEHIRRSTT	BIRTH-RATES
ABEGHINRRS	HARBINGERS	ABEHKOOPRS	PHRASEBOOK
ABEGHIOPRR	BIOGRAPHER	ABEHLMOOST	SMOOTHABLE
ABEGHLLLUY	BELLY LAUGH	ABEHLNOORU	HONOURABLE
ABEGHLNOOP	ANGLOPHOBE	ABEHLOPRSY	HYPERBOLAS
ABEHLORRTY	LAY BROTHER		
ABEHLORSTT	BETROTHALS		
ABEHLORTTU	BLUETHROAT		
ABEHMORTTY	BATHOMETRY		
ABEHMRSSTU	BUSHMASTER		
ABEHMRTTYY	BATHYMETRY		
ABEHNRSSTU	SUNBATHERS		
ABEHOOSSTU	BOATHOUSES, HOUSEBOATS		
ABEIIILMNT	INIMITABLE		
ABEIIILNSS	SENSIBILIA		
ABEIILLMRS	LIBERALISM		
ABEIILLNNY	BIENNIALLY		
ABEIILLNOV	INVIOLABLE		
ABEIILLRST	LIBERALIST		
ABEIILLRTY	LIBERALITY		
ABEIILLTUZ	UTILIZABLE		
ABEIILMNSS	LESBIANISM		
ABEIILMPRT	IMPARTIBLE		
ABEIILMRST	BIMESTRIAL		
ABEIILNORT	LIBERATION		
ABEIILNPRS	INSPIRABLE		
ABEIILNTTU	INTUITABLE		
ABEIILNTTY	TENABILITY		
ABEIILNTVY	INEVITABLY		
ABEIILQTUY	EQUABILITY		
ABEIILRSST	STABILISER		
ABEIILRSTZ	STABILIZER		
ABEIILSTTY	BESTIALITY		
ABEIINNRRT	INTERBRAIN		
ABEIINNRSS	BRAININESS		
ABEIINNRTW	NEW BRITAIN		
ABEIINRRSV	RIVER BASIN		
ABEIIOORSS	AEROBIOSIS		
ABEIIORSTU	OBITUARIES		
ABEIKNSTUZ	UZBEKISTAN		
ABEILLMSTU	STIMULABLE		
ABEILLNNOZ	BELLINZONA		
ABEILLNOSV	INSOLVABLE		
ABEILLPPSU	SUPPLIABLE		
ABEILLPSTU	STIPULABLE		
ABEILLSUXY	BISEXUALLY		
ABEILMMOST	METABOLISM		
ABEILMNNRU	MELBURNIAN		
ABEILMNQRU	LAMBREQUIN		
ABEILMOOTU	AUTOMOBILE		
ABEILMOPRV	IMPROVABLE		
ABEILMRSSU	SURMISABLE		
ABEILMSSTU	SUBLIMATES		
ABEILNNOOW	ON A BOWLINE		
ABEILNORXY	INEXORABLY		
ABEILNSTUU	UNSUITABLE		
ABEILOPRRV	PROVERBIAL		
ABEILOPSTU	BIPETALOUS		

ABEILOPSTY	POLYBASITE
ABEILORRST	LIBERATORS
ABEILORSSU	BELORUSSIA
ABEILORTVY	ABORTIVELY
ABEILRRTTU	TRITURABLE
ABEILRSTUV	VESTIBULAR
ABEILRSUVV	SURVIVABLE
ABEIMMOQUZ	MOZAMBIQUE
ABEIMNNOTT	OBTAINMENT
ABEIMNORTU	TAMBOURINE
ABEIMNRRSU	SUBMARINER
ABEIMNRSSU	SUBMARINES
ABEIMOSSTU	ABSTEMIOUS
ABEINNORTU	EBURNATION
ABEINNOSTT	ABSTENTION
ABEINNRSSW	BRAWNINESS
ABEINORTTX	EXORBITANT
ABEINRSSSS	BRASSINESS
ABEIOPPRSY	PRESBYOPIA
ABEIOPPRSTU	ABSORPTIVE
ABEIOSSSST	ASBESTOSIS
ABEIPRSTTY	BAPTISTERY
ABEIRRRSST	BARRISTERS
ABEIRRTTTU	ATTRIBUTER
ABEIRSTTTU	ATTRIBUTES
ABEKKMOORS	BOOKMAKERS
ABEKKORSTW	BASKETWORK,
WORKBASKET	
ABEKLLORWY	YELLOWBARK
ABEKLNNOUW	UNKNOWABLE
ABEKLNORUW	UNWORKABLE
ABEKLOOPST	BOOKPLATES
ABEKLOPRRR	PORK BARREL
ABEKMNNOTU	MOUNTEBANK
ABEKNOPRRW	PAWNBROKER
ABEKORRSTW	BREASTWORK
ABELLLLOVY	VOLLEYBALL
ABELLMNOYY	BALLYMONEY
ABELLMOOOP	POOL MALEBO
ABELLNRUVY	VULNERABLY
ABELLORVVY	REVOLVABLY
ABELLOSTUY	ABSOLUTELY
ABELLSSSUY	SYLLABUSES
ABELMMNOSU	SUMMONABLE
ABELMNORYZ	EMBLAZONRY
ABELMOOPRT	PROMOTABLE
ABELMPRSUY	PRESUMABLY
ABELNNORUV	VERBAL NOUN
ABELNOOPST	TABLESPOON
ABELNOPRSY	PERSONABLY
ABELNORSTU	NEUROBLAST
ABELNRRTUU	NURTURABLE
ABELNRSSTU	SUBALTERNS

ABELNRSTTU	TURNTABLES
ABELOOPPRS	PROPOSABLE
ABELOOPRST	BLASTOPORE
ABELOOSSTT	OSTEOBLAST
ABELOPPSSU	SUPPOSABLE
ABELPRRTUU	RUPTURABLE
ABEMMNRSSU	MEMBRANOUS
ABEMNNOSTU	SUBMONTANE
ABEMNOORRW	BONE
MARROW, MARROWBONE	
ABENNSSTTU	SUBTENANTS
ABENOPRRSS	PRESS BARON
ABENOPRSTU	BEANSPROUT
ABENORRRTW	BARRENWORT
ABENPRSSTU	ABRUPTNESS
ABEOOPRSTW	POWERBOATS
ABEOPSTTUY	BEAUTY SPOT
ABEOQSSUU	SUBAQUEOUS
ABERRRSTWY	STRAWBERRY
ABERSTTTUW	WATER BUTTS
ABFGILNOTY	FLYING BOAT
ABFGILORVY	FORGIVABLY
ABFGNOORRU	GO FOR A
BURN	
ABFIIILRTY	FRIABILITY
ABFIILLLNY	INFALLIBLY
ABFIILNORV	RIBOFLAVIN
ABFILOPRTY	PROFITABLY
ABFLLOSTUY	BOASTFULLY
ABFLLOSUUY	FABULOUSLY
ABGGGILNRY	BRAGGINGLY
ABGGIILNOT	OBLIGATING
ABGGIKNPSY	PIGGYBANKS
ABGHIIINNT	INHABITING
ABGHIILNOS	ABOLISHING
ABGHIIMMNR	BIRMINGHAM
ABGHIJNORS	JOBSHARING
ABGHINNSTU	SUNBATHING
ABGHINORRU	HARBOURING
ABGHIORTTU	RIGHTABOUT
ABGHIRRRSU	HARRISBURG
ABGHOORRUY	YARBOROUGH
ABGIIILNNT	NAIL-BITING
ABGIILLNSU	BILINGUALS
ABGIILNNTY	INTANGIBLY
ABGIILNOOT	OBLIGATION
ABGIILNOPR	PARBOILING
ABGIINNOTZ	BOTANIZING
ABGILLNNOO	BALLOONING
ABGILLNSUU	SUBLINGUAL
ABGILLOSST	GLOBALISTS
ABGILLOSTY	BILLY GOATS
ABGILMOSUY	BIGAMOUSLY
ABGILNOSTY	BOASTINGLY
ABGILOORTY	OBLIGATORY

ABGINNORRT	BARRINGTON
ABGINOORTW	ROWING BOAT
ABGINORTUV	OUTBRAVING
ABGJOORRTU	OBJURGATOR
ABGJORSTUU	SUBJUGATOR
ABGLLORUUU	LULUABOURG
ABGORRSSTU	STRASBOURG
ABHHNORSSW	HASH BROWNS
ABHIIMOPSU	AMPHIBIOUS
ABHIKMRRST	BIRTHMARKS
ABHILMNSTU	THUMBNAILS
ABHILNRSTY	LABYRINTHS
ABHILOPSTY	HOSPITABLY
ABHILORTUW	WHIRLABOUT
ABHIMNOOOP	MONOPHOBIA
ABHINPRSTU	PAINTBRUSH
ABHLLMSTTU	THUMBSTALL
ABHLNOORUY	HONOURABLY
ABHMNORRTU	RHUMBATRON
ABIIILLPTY	PLIABILITY
ABIIILLTVY	LIVABILITY
ABIIILMNTY	INIMITABLY
ABIIILMTXY	MIXABILITY
ABIIILNOST	SIBILATION
ABIIINOSST	ANTIBIOSIS
ABIIJLNOTU	JUBILATION
ABIILLMNSU	SUBLIMINAL
ABIILLOTVY	LOVABILITY
ABIILMOTVY	MOVABILITY
ABIILMTTUY	MUTABILITY
ABIILNOTY	NOTABILITY
ABIILOPTTY	POTABILITY
ABIIMORSSV	BRAVISSIMO
ABIINNOTTU	INTUBATION
ABIINORSTV	VIBRATIONS
ABIINOTTTU	TITUBATION
ABIIORSTTU	OBITUARIST
ABIJLLNTUY	JUBILANTLY
ABIKKNSTUY	AKTYUBINSK
ABIKLNNOPT	POINT-BLANK
ABILLNOOST	BALLOONIST
ABILLNOOTU	LOBULATION
ABILLNOPST	BALLPOINTS
ABILMNOSUU	ALBUMINOUS
ABILMNOTUX	TOXALBUMIN
ABILMOSSTU	ABSOLUTISM
ABILNNOORU	LABOR UNION
ABILNOOSTU	ABSOLUTION
ABILNOTTUU	TUBULATION
ABILORSSUU	SALUBRIOUS
ABILOSSTUY	SABULOSITY
ABILRSTTUU	SUBTITULAR
ABILRTTUUY	TUBULARITY
ABIMNORRST	BRAINSTORM

ABIMRSSSTU	STRABISMUS	ACCDEIILNY	INDELICACY	ACCEEIORSU	ERICACEOUS
ABINNOSTVV	BON VIVANTS	ACCDEIILST	DIALECTICS	ACCEEIRTUX	EXCRUCIATE
ABINOOPRST	ABSORPTION	ACCDEIKLNW	CANDLEWICK	ACCEELLNRT	CALL CENTRE
ABINOOSSST	BASSOONIST	ACCDEILLOP	PECCADILLO	ACCEELNOST	COALESCENT
ABINOSSTTU	BUS STATION,	ACCDEILNOT	OCCIDENTAL	ACCEELNOSV	CONVALESCE
SUBSTATION		ACCDEILNTU	INCULCATED	ACCEELNPRU	CRAPULENCE
ABKLLOOSST	BOOKSTALLS	ACCDEILRTU	CIRCULATED	ACCEELNRTU	RELUCTANCE
ABLOOPRTTT	PORT TALBOT	ACCDEIMNNY	MENDICANCY	ACCEELNSTT	LACTESCENT
ABLOORSTUY	ABSOLUTORY	ACCDEIMORT	DEMOCRATIC	ACCEELNSTU	CAULESCENT
ABMOOORSTT	MOTORBOATS	ACCDEINNTU	INDUCTANCE	ACCEELPSST	SPECTACLES
ABMRSSTTUU	SUBSTRATUM	ACCDEINOOS	OCCASIONED	ACCEEMNRST	MARCESCENT,
ABNORSTTUU	ABOUT-TURNS,	ACCDEINSST	DESICCANTS	SCARCEMENT	
TURNABOUTS		ACCDEIORST	DESICCATOR	ACCEEMOSTY	ASCOMYCETE
ABOOPRSSTT	BOOTSTRAPS	ACCDELLOOT	COLLOCATED	ACCEENNNOV	CONVENANCE
ABOORSTTUU	ROUSTABOUT	ACCDEMOSTU	ACCUSTOMED	ACCEENNOVY	CONVEYANCE
ACCCDEHIIL	CHALCIDICE	ACCDENORTT	CONTRACTED	ACCEENOPRR	COPARCENER
ACCCDIIIPR	PICRIC ACID	ACCDENPSSU	DUNCE'S CAPS	ACCEENORST	CONSECRATE
ACCCDIIIRT	CITRIC ACID	ACCDEOPRST	CADET CORPS	ACCEENPTXY	EXPECTANCY
ACCCEENRST	ACCRESCENT	ACCDEORRSS	SCORECARDS	ACCEENRSSS	SCARCENESS
ACCCEFHKOR	COCKCHAFER	ACCDEORSSW	SACRED COWS	ACCEEOPPRS	PEACE CORPS
ACCCEHILOT	CHALCOCITE	ACCDEORSTU	CORUSCATED	ACCEEORRSU	RACECOURSE
ACCCEHORTW	COWCATCHER	ACCDFIILTY	FLACCIDITY	ACCEEORSTU	CRETACEOUS
ACCCEIILRT	CICATRICLE	ACCDFIIMOR	FORMIC ACID	ACCEFFIINY	INEFFICACY
ACCCEIIRST	CICATRICES	ACCDGIIILT	TIGLIC ACID	ACCEFHLOST	FACECLOTHS
ACCCEILLNY	ENCYCLICAL	ACCDHHRRUY	CHURCHYARD	ACCEFHLRTY	FLYCATCHER
ACCCEILMOP	ACCOMPLICE	ACCDHIINOR	DIACHRONIC	ACCEFIIRRS	SACRIFICER
ACCCGLNOOO	GONOCOCCAL	ACCDHILORV	CLAVICHORD	ACCEFIIRSS	SACRIFICES
ACCCHINOOP	CACOPHONIC	ACCDHORSTW	CATCHWORDS	ACCEFILLOR	CALCIFEROL
ACCCHKOPST	SPATCHCOCK	ACCDIIINRT	NITRIC ACID	ACCEFILMOR	CALCEIFORM
ACCCHLOORY	OCHLOCRACY	ACCDIIIRST	DIACRITICS	ACCEFINOST	CONFISCATE
ACCCHOOTUU	CAOUTCHOUC	ACCDIILLPY	PICCADILLY	ACCEFLLOTU	FLOCCULATE
ACCCHOPRST	CATCH CROPS	ACCDIILOTU	TOLUIC ACID	ACCEGILLNN	CANCELLING
ACCCILLLYY	CYCLICALLY	ACCDIILSST	CLADISTICS	ACCEGILLNO	COLLAGENIC
ACCCILMORY	CYCLORAMIC	ACCDINOORS	ACCORDIONS	ACCEGILLOO	ECOLOGICAL
ACCCIMORTY	MACROCYTIC	ACCDINORTT	CONTRADICT	ACCEGILNNO	CONCEALING
ACCCINOPPU	CAPPUCCINO	ACCDKNORSW	CRACKDOWNS	ACCEGILNOS	COALESCING
ACCDDEEIRT	ACCREDITED	ACCDLOORSV	VOCAL CORDS	ACCEGILNOT	LACTOGENIC
ACCDDEEIST	DESICCATED	ACCDNNOORT	CONCORDANT	ACCEGINNOR	CARCINOGEN
ACCDDEIRRT	CREDIT CARD	ACCDNOORST	CONCORDATS	ACCEGINNOZ	COGNIZANCE
ACCDEEHIST	CATECHISED	ACCDORRSTU	COURT CARDS	ACCEHHIPRT	HEPTARCHIC
ACCDEEHITZ	CATECHIZED	ACCEEEEHKS	CHEESECAKE	ACCEHHMRSU	SCHUMACHER
ACCDEEHKMT	CHECKMATED	ACCEEEHRTY	EYE-CATCHER	ACCEHIILMR	CHIMERICAL
ACCDEEHNOR	ENCROACHED	ACCEEELPRT	RECEPTACLE	ACCEHIINNT	TECHNICIAN
ACCDEEHQRU	CHEQUE CARD	ACCEEHILLR	CHELICERAL	ACCEHIKNRS	RAIN CHECKS
ACCDEEIILS	DELICACIES	ACCEEHILNP	ENCEPHALIC	ACCEHILLMY	CHEMICALLY
ACCDEEINNS	INCANDESCE	ACCEEHINRS	CHANCERIES	ACCEHILLTY	HECTICALLY
ACCDEEIQSU	ACQUIESCED	ACCEEHISST	CATECHESIS	ACCEHILNOS	COCHINEALS
ACCDEELPTY	ACCEPTEDLY	ACCEEHKMST	CHECKMATES	ACCEHIMNSS	MISCHANCES
ACCDEENNTU	UNACCENTED	ACCEEHNORR	ENCROACHER	ACCEHIMSST	CATECHISMS
ACCDEFIIRS	SACRIFICED	ACCEEILLRT	ELECTRICAL	ACCEHINNRY	IN CHANCERY
ACCDEGHORT	DOGCATCHER	ACCEEILMNU	ECUMENICAL	ACCEHINNSS	CHANCINESS
ACCDEHIKRS	DECKCHAIRS	ACCEEILNTY	ACETYLENIC	ACCEHINOPT	CENOTAPHIC
ACCDEHKOST	COCKED HATS	ACCEEILORV	VARICOCELE	ACCEHINSST	CATCHINESS
ACCDEHLNOY	CHALCEDONY	ACCEEIMSST	ACCESS TIME	ACCEHIORRY	HIEROCRACY

ACCEHIORST	ESCHAROTIC
ACCEHIORTT	RHEOTACTIC,
THEOCRATIC	
ACCEHIRRST	SCRATCHIER
ACCEHIRRTT	TETRARCHIC
ACCEHIRSTT	ARCHITECTS
ACCEHISSTT	CATECHISTS
ACCEHLLNOR	CHANCELLOR
ACCEHLMOOR	HOMOCERCAL
ACCEHLOOST	CHOCOLATES
ACCEHLOSUY	CHYLACEOUS
ACCEHNNPTY	CATCHPENNY
ACCEHNNRTY	TRENCHANCY
ACCEHNOOTY	CHOANOCYTE
ACCEHNORTT	TECHNOCRAT,
TRENCH COAT	
ACCEHOPSTT	SCOTCH TAPE
ACCEIILNOT	CONCILIATE
ACCEIILRTT	TECTRICIAL
ACCEIIMSST	ASCETICISM
ACCEIINPRT	IN PRACTICE
ACCEIINRST	CISTERCIAN
ACCEIIRRST	CICATRISER
ACCEIIRRTZ	CICATRIZER
ACCEIIRSST	SCARCITIES
ACCEIKRSSW	WISECRACKS
ACCEILLLPS	SCALPELLIC
ACCEILLLRY	CLERICALLY
ACCEILLNSY	SCENICALLY
ACCEILMMOR	COMMERCIAL
ACCEILMNOO	ECONOMICAL
ACCEILMNOP	COMPLIANCE
ACCEILMOPT	COMPLICATE
ACCEILMOST	CACOMISTLE
ACCEILNRST	CALCSINTER
ACCEILOPPT	APOPLECTIC
ACCEILOPRR	RECIPROCAL
ACCEILOPRV	PREVOCALIC
ACCEIMNORS	SCIOMANCER
ACCEIMOOPR	COMIC OPERA
ACCEIMORST	MESOCRATIC
ACCEINNNOV	CONNIVANCE
ACCEINNORT	CONCERTINA
ACCEINNSSY	INCESSANCY
ACCEINOOST	CONSOCIATE
ACCEINORST	ACCRETIONS
ACCEINOSSS	ACCESSIONS
ACCEIOORSU	CORIACEOUS
ACCEIOPPSY	EPISCOPACY
ACCEIORSTX	EXSICCATOR
ACCEIOSSTU	CISTACEOUS
ACCEJNOSUU	JUNCACEOUS
ACCEKKLMOR	CLOCKMAKER
ACCEKNORRS	CORNCRAKES
ACCEKNRRTU	NUTCRACKER

ACCELLLOSS	CLOSE CALLS
ACCELLSSUU	CALCULUSES
ACCELMNOPT	COMPLACENT
ACCELNOOPY	CAPE COLONY
ACCELNOPTU	CONCEPTUAL
ACCELOOPST	LACTOSCOPE
ACCEMNNORY	NECROMANCY
ACCENNNOOS	CONSONANCE
ACCENOORSU	CORNACEOUS
ACCENORTTU	COUNTERACT
ACCEORRSSW	SCARECROWS
ACCEORSSUV	CURVACEOUS
ACCFFFFHHI	CHIFFCHAFF
ACCFGIILNY	CALCIFYING
ACCFHIRTTW	WITCHCRAFT
ACCFIIIMPR	PACIFIC RIM
ACCFIINNOT	FANTOCCINI
ACCFILSSUU	FASCICULUS
ACCFKOORST	FROCK COATS
ACCFLLNOTU	FLOCCULANT
ACCGHIILOR	OLIGARCHIC
ACCGHINRST	SCRATCHING
ACCGHIOPTY	PHAGOCYTIC
ACCGHORSSU	COUCH GRASS
ACCGIILORT	GO CRITICAL
ACCGIIMORT	TRAGICOMIC
ACCGILNSUY	ACCUSINGLY
ACCGIMNOPT	COMPACTING
ACCGINNOTT	CONTACTING
ACCGINNOTU	ACCOUNTING
ACCHHIILLN	CHINCHILLA
ACCHHORSST	CROSSHATCH
ACCHIIILST	CHILIASTIC
ACCHIIMSST	SCHISMATIC
ACCHIKMSTT	MATCHSTICK
ACCHILLOOS	ALCOHOLICS
ACCHILMOPS	ACCOMPLISH
ACCHILNNPS	SPLANCHNIC
ACCHILNOOT	CATHOLICON
ACCHILOSST	SCHOLASTIC
ACCHILRSTY	SCRATCHILY
ACCHILTTYY	TACHYLYTIC
ACCHIMNORY	CHIROMANCY
ACCHIMORST	CHROMATICS
ACCHIOPRSZ	SCHIZOCARP
ACCHIOSSTT	STOCHASTIC
ACCHNOPSST	SCOTCH SNAP
ACCHNORRST	CORNSTARCH
ACCHOPRSST	CROSSPATCH
ACCIIILLLP	PICCALILLI
ACCIIINNNT	CINCINNATI
ACCIILLLNY	CLINICALLY
ACCIILLOST	LOCALISTIC
ACCIILLRTY	CRITICALLY

ACCIILMSSS	CLASSICISM
ACCIILNNOT	CALCITONIN
ACCIILNRTU	UNCRITICAL
ACCIILORTY	CALORICITY
ACCIILSSST	CLASSICIST
ACCIIMNNNO	CINNAMONIC
ACCIIMNOOT	ICONOMANIC
ACCIIMNOST	SCIOMANTIC
ACCIINNNPY	PICCANINNY
ACCIINNOTY	CANONICITY
ACCIIOPRSU	CAPRICIOUS
ACCIIOTTVY	COACTIVITY
ACCIKKKKNN	KNICK-KNACK
ACCILLMOSY	COSMICALLY
ACCILMNNOU	COUNCILMAN
ACCILMNOOS	ICONOCLASM
ACCILNOOST	ICONOCLAST
ACCILNORTU	INCULCATOR
ACCILNOSTV	CONCLAVIST
ACCILNSSTY	SYNCLASTIC
ACCILOPPRY	POLYCARPIC
ACCILORRTU	CIRCULATOR
ACCILRRRUU	CURRICULAR
ACCIMNOOPR	MONOCARPIC
ACCIMNOORT	MONOCRATIC
ACCIMORSSY	COSMIC RAYS
ACCINNOOOS	ON OCCASION
ACCINOOPRU	CORNUCOPIA
ACCINOOPTU	OCCUPATION
ACCINOPRRS	CAPRICORNS
ACCINOPRSY	CONSPIRACY
ACCINORSTY	CARSON CITY
ACCINSSSTY	SYNTACTICS
ACCIOPRSTT	CATOPTRICS
ACCKKNOOOS	COCK A
SNOOK	
ACCKLMOORU	COCKALORUM
ACCLOPRTUY	PLUTOCRACY
ACCMMOORSS	
MACROCOSMS	
ACCNNOOSTU	
NO-ACCOUNTS	
ACCNOOORTV	CONVOCATOR
ACCNOOPRRY	PORNOCRACY
ACCNOORRTT	CONTRACTOR
ACDDEEENOS	DODECANESE
ACDDEEENRT	DEAD CENTRE
ACDDEEEPRT	DEPRECATED
ACDDEEERST	DESECRATED
ACDDEEERTU	RE-EDUCATED
ACDDEEHLOO	COOL-HEADED
ACDDEEHNOR	DECAHEDRON
ACDDEEHPST	DESPATCHED
ACDDEEIIPT	DIAPEDETIC
ACDDEEILTU	ELUCIDATED

Ten Letter Words

ACDDEEIPRT	PREDICATED
ACDDEELLSY	CLYDESDALE
ACDDEELNRY	DRY-CLEANED
ACDDEELNTY	DECADENTLY
ACDDEENNST	DESCENDANT
ACDDEENRTU	UNDERACTED
ACDDEENTUU	UNEDUCATED
ACDDEFFHNU	HANDCUFFED
ACDDEFFIRT	DIFFRACTED
ACDDEGHIRS	DISCHARGED
ACDDEGIINT	DEDICATING
ACDDEHIKNP	HANDPICKED
ACDDEHINSW	SANDWICHED
ACDDEHIPST	DISPATCHED
ACDDEHIRRS	HARD CIDERS
ACDDEHIRSV	CRASH-DIVED
ACDDEHNNOS	SECOND-HAND
ACDDEIILMS	DISCLAIMED
ACDDEIINOT	DEDICATION
ACDDEIINTV	VINDICATED
ACDDEILMOU	DUODECIMAL
ACDDEILOST	DISLOCATED
ACDDEILPTU	DUPLICATED
ACDDEILTTW	WILDCATTED
ACDDEINSTY	SYNDICATED
ACDDEIORTY	DEDICATORY
ACDDEIRSTT	DISTRACTED
ACDDEKLLNO	LANDLOCKED
ACDDEKLORS	DREADLOCKS
ACDDELNNOO	COLONNADED
ACDDELNOOW	CANDLEWOOD
ACDDENNRUY	REDUNDANCY
ACDDENORSW	SWORD DANCE
ACDDFHIORU	CHAUDFROID
ACDDGHILNR	GRANDCHILD
ACDDGIINRS	DISCARDING
ACDDHHNSSU	DACHSHUNDS
ACDDIINOST	ADDICTIONS
ACDDINORST	DISCORDANT
ACDEEEEHHS	HEADCHEESE
ACDEEEELRT	DECELERATE
ACDEEEEPRS	PREDECEASE
ACDEEEFLNR	FER-DE-LANCE, FREELANCED
ACDEEEFMNT	DEFACEMENT
ACDEEEGNRY	DEGENERACY
ACDEEEHIPS	HEADPIECES
ACDEEEHRRS	RESEARCHED
ACDEEEIPRT	DEPRECIATE
ACDEEEKNPP	KNEECAPPED
ACDEEENNTT	ANTECEDENT
ACDEEENRTV	ADVERTENCE
ACDEEEOORT	REDECORATE
ACDEEFFHRT	FARFETCHED
ACDEEFFLTY	AFFECTEDLY
ACDEEFFNTU	UNAFFECTED
ACDEEFGINT	DEFECATING
ACDEEFIIRR	FREDERICIA
ACDEEFINOT	DEFECATION
ACDEEFINRT	INTERFACED
ACDEEFKOPR	POKER-FACED
ACDEEFOPRW	FACE POWDER
ACDEEFORST	FORECASTED
ACDEEFRRSU	RESURFACED
ACDEEGHLLN	CHALLENGED
ACDEEGHNNO	HENDECAGON
ACDEEGINRR	ADRENERGIC
ACDEEGINRS	DECREASING
ACDEEGINRT	CENTIGRADE
ACDEEGNORU	ENCOURAGED
ACDEEHILNR	CHANDELIER
ACDEEHIMNS	MECHANISED
ACDEEHIMNZ	MECHANIZED
ACDEEHIMRS	ARCHIMEDES
ACDEEHLLNN	CHANNELLED
ACDEEHLNRT	ANDERLECHT
ACDEEHMNTT	DETACHMENT
ACDEEHNOPR	CHAPERONED
ACDEEHOPPR	COPPERHEAD
ACDEEHOPRR	REPROACHED
ACDEEHORRV	OVERARCHED
ACDEEHPRST	DESPATCHER
ACDEEHPSST	DESPATCHES
ACDEEHPSSY	SPEECH DAYS
ACDEEIILMP	EPIDEMICAL
ACDEEIILMS	DECIMALISE
ACDEEIILMZ	DECIMALIZE
ACDEEIILNT	INDELICATE
ACDEEIIMRT	ACIDIMETER
ACDEEIIMTV	MEDICATIVE
ACDEEIJSTV	ADJECTIVES
ACDEEIILNR	CINDERELLA
ACDEEIILOS	DELOCALISE
ACDEEIILOZ	DELOCALIZE
ACDEEIILRS	ESCADRILLE
ACDEEIILTY	DELICATELY
ACDEEILMPR	PREMEDICAL
ACDEEILNPP	APPENDICLE
ACDEEILNRT	INTERLACED
ACDEEILOSV	DEVOCALISE
ACDEEILOVZ	DEVOCALIZE
ACDEEILPRT	REPLICATED
ACDEEILPTU	PEDICULATE
ACDEEILPTX	EXPLICATED
ACDEEIMMNT	MEDICAMENT
ACDEEIMNPS	IMPEDANCES
ACDEEIMORT	ACIDOMETER
ACDEEIMPRT	MERCAPTIDE
ACDEEINNNT	INTENDANCE
ACDEEINNTU	DENUNCIATE, ENUNCIATED
ACDEEINPPS	APPENDICES
ACDEEINRTT	INTERACTED
ACDEEINSST	DESISTANCE
ACDEEIORTV	DECORATIVE
ACDEEIORTX	EXCORIATED
ACDEEIOTTX	DETOXICATE
ACDEEIPRRT	TRADE PRICE
ACDEEIPRST	PEDERASTIC, PREDICATES
ACDEEIRSTU	CAUTERISED
ACDEEIRTTV	DETRACTIVE
ACDEEIRTTX	EXTRICATED
ACDEEIRTUZ	CAUTERIZED
ACDEEITTUX	EXACTITUDE
ACDEELMORT	ECTODERMAL
ACDEELMORU	LEUCODERMA
ACDEELNOST	ADOLESCENT
ACDEELNRRY	DRY CLEANER
ACDEELOPRT	PERCOLATED
ACDEELORRT	CORRELATED
ACDEELORTU	EDULCORATE
ACDEELPSTU	SPECULATED
ACDEELPTUX	EXCULPATED
ACDEEMMNOR	COMMANDEER
ACDEEMMNPT	DECAMPMENT
ACDEEMNOTY	ADENECTOMY
ACDEENNOST	CONDENSATE
ACDEENNOTV	COVENANTED
ACDEENORST	SECOND-RATE
ACDEENRSSS	SACREDNESS
ACDEENRTTU	DETRUNCATE
ACDEEOOPRT	COOPERATED
ACDEEOPRRT	DEPRECATOR, PROCREATED
ACDEEOPRSS	PESCADORES
ACDEEOORST	DESECRATOR
ACDEEPRRTU	RECAPTURED
ACDEFFIIOT	OFFICIATED
ACDEFFIKRT	TRAFFICKED
ACDEFFLORS	SCAFFOLDER
ACDEFFLOTU	DUFFEL COAT
ACDEFFMORS	COFFERDAMS
ACDEFFOSTU	SUFFOCATED
ACDEFHILNS	CANDLEFISH
ACDEFHINRS	FRANCHISED
ACDEFHOSUV	VOUCHSAFED
ACDEFIILSS	CLASSIFIED
ACDEFIINST	SANCTIFIED
ACDEFIIRRT	FRATRICIDE
ACDEFIJKKN	JACK-KNIFED
ACDEFILLOS	COALFIELDS
ACDEFILSSY	DECLASSIFY

ACDEFINORT	FORNICATED
ACDEFIORST	FACTORISED
ACDEFIORTZ	FACTORIZED
ACDEFKLNOR	FOLK DANCER
ACDEFKLNOS	FOLK DANCES
ACDEFLMORS	COLD FRAMES
ACDEFLNOOT	FOOT-CANDLE
ACDEFLTTUU	FLUCTUATED
ACDEFNORRU	UNCARED-FOR
ACDEFNORTU	FECUNDATOR
ACDEFNRSSY	FANCY DRESS
ACDEGHIRRS	DISCHARGER
ACDEGHIRSS	DISCHARGES
ACDEGHRRSU	SURCHARGED
ACDEGIILMN	DECLAIMING
ACDEGIILMR	GERMICIDAL
ACDEGIILNS	ANGLICISED
ACDEGIILNZ	ANGLICIZED
ACDEGIIMNT	DECIMATING
ACDEGIINOR	RADIOGENIC
ACDEGIINOU	AUDIOGENIC
ACDEGIINST	DIE-CASTING
ACDEGILNRW	ARC WELDING
ACDEGILOOP	LOGOPAEDIC
ACDEGILRTT	CATTLE GRID
ACDEGIMMRS	SCRIMMAGED
ACDEGIMNOY	GEODYNAMIC
ACDEGIMNOR	ANDROGENIC
ACDEGINORR	CORRIGENDA
ACDEGINORT	DECORATING
ACDEGINRTT	DETRACTING
ACDEGINRTY	GARDEN CITY
ACDEGIORSU	DISCOURAGE
ACDEGIRRST	CARTRIDGES
ACDEGJNOTU	CONJUGATED
ACDEGKNORR	ROCK GARDEN
ACDEGMMRSU	SCRUMMAGED
ACDEGORRTU	CORRUGATED
ACDEHIIMRT	DIATHERMIC
ACDEHILMOT	METHODICAL
ACDEHIMMST	MISMATCHED
ACDEHIMNOP	CHAMPIONED
ACDEHIMORT	DICHROMATE
ACDEHINNRS	HINDRANCES
ACDEHINNST	DISENCHANT
ACDEHINOPS	DEACONSHIP
ACDEHINOPT	DICTAPHONE
ACDEHINORT	ACHONDRITE
ACDEHINSSW	SANDWICHES
ACDEHIPSST	DISPATCHES
ACDEHIRSSV	CRASH-DIVES
ACDEHKPSST	SKETCHPADS
ACDEHLNOST	DECATHLONS
ACDEHLOOPP	CEPHALOPOD

ACDEHMPRSY	PACHYDERMS
ACDEHNOORT	OCTAHEDRON
ACDEHNORST	ON THE CARDS
ACDEHNORSZ	SCHERZANDO
ACDEHORRTT	TETRACHORD
ACDEHRTTTU	DUTCH TREAT
ACDEIIILST	IDEALISTIC,
ITALICISED	
ACDEIIILTZ	ITALICIZED
ACDEIIINST	DIETICIANS
ACDEIIINTV	INDICATIVE
ACDEIIJTUV	JUDICATIVE
ACDEIIKNNR	KINCARDINE
ACDEIIKNNS	DICKENSIAN
ACDEIILLOT	IDIOLECTAL
ACDEIILMMT	DILEMMATIC
ACDEIILMPT	IMPLICATED
ACDEIILMRS	DISCLAIMER
ACDEIILMRV	VERMICIDAL
ACDEIILNNT	INCIDENTAL
ACDEIILNOS	DECISIONAL
ACDEIILOPR	PERIODICAL
ACDEIILOSS	SOCIALISED
ACDEIILOSZ	SOCIALIZED
ACDEIILPST	PESTICIDAL,
SEPTICIDAL	
ACDEIIMNOT	DECIMATION,
MEDICATION	
ACDEIIMPRU	EPICARDIUM
ACDEIIMRRS	MISCARRIED
ACDEIIMRST	MATRICIDES
ACDEIINNRY	INCENDIARY
ACDEIINOSY	ISOCYANIDE
ACDEIIORSU	IRIDACEOUS
ACDEIIOSST	DISSOCIATE
ACDEIIPRRS	PARRICIDES
ACDEIIPRST	PATRICIDES,
PEDIATRICS	
ACDEIIPRTY	PERACIDITY
ACDEIJNTUV	ADJUNCTIVE
ACDEIJRTUU	JUDICATURE
ACDEIKRSST	SIDETRACKS
ACDEILLORR	CORDILLERA
ACDEILLOST	OSCILLATED
ACDEILLTUV	VICTUALLED
ACDEILMNNO	NONMEDICAL
ACDEILMNOP	COMPLAINED
ACDEILMOPR	PROCLAIMED
ACDEILNNOR	ENDOCRINAL
ACDEILNNPS	CANDLEPINS
ACDEILNOTU	INOCULATED
ACDEILNPTU	INCULPATED
ACDEILNSUV	VULCANISED
ACDEILNUVZ	VULCANIZED
ACDEILORTU	ELUCIDATOR

ACDEILOTTU	COLATITUDE
ACDEILPSTU	DUPLICATES
ACDEILTTUV	CULTIVATED
ACDEIMMORT	DERMATOMIC
ACDEIMMORY	IMMODERACY
ACDEIMNNOT	DEMICANTON
ACDEIMNNST	MENDICANTS
ACDEIMNORU	ANDROECIUM
ACDEIMNOSU	MENDACIOUS
ACDEIMNNTY	INTENDANCY
ACDEINNORS	ORDINANCES
ACDEINNOSS	DISSONANCE
ACDEINNOST	SANCTIONED
ACDEINNRSS	RANCIDNESS
ACDEINOORT	CAROTENOID,
COORDINATE, DECORATION	
ACDEINOPRS	SCORPAENID
ACDEINORTT	DETRACTION
ACDEINOSTT	ANECDOTIST
ACDEINOTTX	DETOXICANT
ACDEINPRST	DISCREPANT
ACDEINSSTY	SYNDICATES
ACDEINSTTU	SANCTITUDE
ACDEIOOPRS	RADIOSCOPE
ACDEIOPRSU	PREDACIOUS
ACDEIOPRTT	TETRAPODIC
ACDEIOPSSU	SPADICEOUS
ACDEIORSST	OSTRACISED
ACDEIORSTZ	OSTRACIZED
ACDEIPQRSU	QUADRICEPS
ACDEIPRSTU	CUSTARD PIE
ACDEIQRSTU	QUADRISECT
ACDEIRRSTT	DISTRACTER
ACDEIRSSTT	DICTATRESS
ACDEIRSTTU	RUSTICATED
ACDEJKSTTU	DUST JACKET
ACDEKKMOPR	POCKMARKED
ACDELLOORT	DECOLLATOR
ACDELMORST	COLDSTREAM
ACDELNNOOS	COLONNADES
ACDELNOORT	DECOLORANT
ACDELNOOTY	ACOTYLEDON
ACDELOPPTU	CLAPPED-OUT
ACDELOPRRU	PROCEDURAL
ACDELOSSTU	OUTCLASSED
ACDEMMNORS	COMMANDERS
ACDEMMOSTU	
CUSTOM-MADE	
ACDEMNORST	DOC MARTENS
ACDEMOORST	MOTORCADES
ACDEMOOTVY	DEMY
OCTAVO	
ACDEMOPRSU	DAMP COURSE
ACDENNNOOR	ORDONNANCE
ACDENNNOOS	NANOSECOND

ACDENOPPSW	SNOW-CAPPED	
ACDENOPSTY	SYNCOPATED	
ACDENORSTT	CONTRASTED	
ACDENORSTU	UNDERCOATS	
ACDENPTTUU	PUNCTUATED	
ACDENRRRTU	REDCURRANT	
ACDENRRSTU	TRANSDUCER	
ACDEOORRST	DECORATORS	
ACDEOORRVW	WOODCARVER	
ACDEOORSTT	DOCTORATES	
ACDEOPPRSU	PSEUDOCARP	
ACDEOPRRTT	PROTRACTED	
ACDEOPRSUU	DRUPACEOUS	
ACDEOPSTTU	COUPS D'ETAT	
ACDEORRSTT	DETRACTORS	
ACDFGIIINY	ACIDIFYING	
ACDFGIILNU	FUNGICIDAL	
ACDFINNOST	CONFIDANTS	
ACDFLNOSSY	CANDYFLOSS	
ACDFORRSTW	SWORDCRAFT	
ACDGGIINRS	DISGRACING	
ACDGHIOPRT	DICTOGRAPH	
ACDGHNOOTU	TOUCH-AND-GO	
ACDGIIIMNR	GRAMICIDIN	
ACDGIIINNT	INDICATING	
ACDGIILNPS	DISPLACING	
ACDGIIMOOS	MOGADISCIO	
ACDGIINNRS	DINING CARS	
ACDGIINNST	DISTANCING	
ACDGIINOST	DIAGNOSTIC	
ACDGIKLNOP	PADLOCKING	
ACDGIKNOST	STOCKADING	
ACDGILLOSU	GLUCOSIDAL	
ACDGILNNOO	CANOODLING	
ACDGILNOOT	ODONTALGIC	
ACDGILOORY	CARDIOLOGY	
ACDGIMMNNO	COMMANDING	
ACDGLLOORS	DOG COLLARS	
ACDGLOTYYZ	ZYGODACTYL	
ACDGMNOPRU	CAMPGROUND	
ACDHIIIOPT	IDIOPATHIC	
ACDHILLPSY	CHILD'S PLAY	
ACDHILMNOY	MY OLD CHINA	
ACDHILRSUY	HYDRAULICS	
ACDHIORRSW	DISC HARROW	
ACDHIORTTY	TRACHYTOID	
ACDHIRSSSW	SWISS CHARD	
ACDHLOORRU	UROCHORDAL	
ACDHLOORSY	HYDROCORAL	
ACDHLOOSSY	DAY SCHOOLS	
ACDHMNORYY	HYDROMANCY	
ACDHNOOPRR	DROP ANCHOR	

ACDHORSTWW	WATCHWORDS	
ACDIIIMMRU	MIRACIDIUM	
ACDIIIMNST	DIACTINISM	
ACDIIINNOT	INDICATION	
ACDIIJLLUY	JUDICIALLY	
ACDIILLSUY	SUICIDALLY	
ACDIILMOPT	DIPLOMATIC	
ACDIILORTY	CORDIALITY	
ACDIILORUX	UXORICIDAL	
ACDIIMNNOS	DOMINICANS	
ACDIIMNORT	ANTIDROMIC	
ACDIIMNOST	MONADISTIC	
ACDIIMNOSY	ISODYNAMIC	
ACDIIMNSTY	DYNAMISTIC	
ACDIINNNOR	INDIAN CORN	
ACDIINNORY	INORDINACY	
ACDIINOORV	ORDOVICIAN	
ACDIINORST	INDICATORS	
ACDIINORTV	VINDICATOR	
ACDIINORTY	DICTIONARY, INDICATORY	
ACDIINOSTT	DICTATIONS	
ACDIIOORTX	RADIOTOXIC	
ACDIJORTUY	JUDICATORY	
ACDIKNOSSU	QUICKSANDS	
ACDIKRRSTT	DIRT TRACKS	
ACDIKRSSTY	YARDSTICKS	
ACDILNOPRS	SPINAL CORD	
ACDILNOSTU	SAINT-CLOUD	
ACDILOPRTU	DUPLICATOR	
ACDILPSSTY	DYSPLASTIC	
ACDIMMORUY	MYOCARDIUM	
ACDIMOORSU	MORDACIOUS	
ACDINOSSTU	CUSTODIANS	
ACDINSSSTU	DISCUSSANT	
ACDIOOPRSY	RADIOSCOPY	
ACDJOORSTU	COADJUTORS	
ACDKLMOSSY	LADY'S-SMOCK	
ACDKLORSTU	TRUCKLOADS	
ACDKNORSTU	SOUNDTRACK	
ACDKORSSTY	STOCKYARDS	
ACDLLOOPSW	CODSWALLOP	
ACDLLOPTYY	POLYDACTYL	
ACDLLORSTU	WORLD-CLASS	
ACDLLORSTU	COLLAR STUD	
ACDLMNOPSW	CLAMPDOWNS	
ACDMPRRSTU	TRUMP CARDS	
ACDOORRSSS	CROSSROADS	
ACDORRSTUY	COURTYARDS	
ACEEEFFKTT	TAKE EFFECT	
ACEEEFFMNT	EFFACEMENT	
ACEEEFFTTU	EFFECTUATE	
ACEEEFIPRS	FIRE ESCAPE	

ACEEEFIPRT	AFTERPIECE	
ACEEEFIRSS	CEASE-FIRES	
ACEEEFLNRR	FREELANCER	
ACEEEFLNRS	FREELANCES	
ACEEEFMNNT	ENFACEMENT	
ACEEEGILNN	INELEGANCE	
ACEEEGINRT	GREAT-NIECE	
ACEEEGNNSV	VENGEANCES	
ACEEEGNPRT	PERCENTAGE	
ACEEEGNRRY	REGENERACY	
ACEEEHIMRX	HEXAEMERIC	
ACEEEHRRRS	RESEARCHER	
ACEEEHRRSS	RESEARCHES	
ACEEEIMRRS	CREAMERIES	
ACEEEIPPPS	PEACE PIPES	
ACEEEIPPRV	APPERCEIVE	
ACEEEIRRST	SECRETAIRE	
ACEEEIRSTV	EVISCERATE, TEA SERVICE	
ACEEEIRTVX	EXECRATIVE	
ACEEEKRRST	RACKETEERS	
ACEEELLNRT	CRENELLATE	
ACEEELMNNT	ENLACEMENT	
ACEEELNPRV	PREVALENCE	
ACEEELNPSW	CLEAN SWEEP	
ACEEELORTT	ELECTORATE	
ACEEELRSTT	TELECASTER	
ACEEEMNNPR	PERMANENCE	
ACEEEMNNST	ENCASEMENT	
ACEEEMNPRT	TEMPERANCE	
ACEEEMNPST	ESCAPEMENT	
ACEEEMNRTT	METACENTRE	
ACEEEMORTT	ACETOMETER	
ACEEENNOTV	COVENANTEE	
ACEEENNPRT	PENETRANCE, REPENTANCE	
ACEEENNRRT	RE-ENTRANCE	
ACEEENNSTV	EVANESCENT	
ACEEENRSSV	SEVERANCES	
ACEEEPPPRR	CREPE PAPER	
ACEEEPPRRTU	RECUPERATE	
ACEEFFIMNY	EFFEMINACY	
ACEEFFLOTY	FEET OF CLAY	
ACEEFFLSST	AFFECTLESS	
ACEEFFNRSU	SUFFERANCE	
ACEEFHHTTW	CHEW THE FAT	
ACEEFIILTT	FELICITATE	
ACEEFIJKLT	LIFE JACKET	
ACEEFIILMNT	MALEFICENT	
ACEEFILNRS	CRANE FLIES	
ACEEFILNSS	FACILENESS	
ACEEFILPRS	FIREPLACES	
ACEEFINRST	INTERFACES	
ACEEFIOPSS	PIECE OF ASS	
ACEEFIORTV	VOCIFERATE	

ACEEFIRRTV	REFRACTIVE	ACEEHHLLRT	HATCHELLER
ACEEFIRSSS	FRICASSEES	ACEEHHLMNT	CHELTENHAM
ACEEFLLNTU	FLATULENCE	ACEEHHMNTT	HATCHET MEN
ACEEFLLORV	CLOVERLEAF	ACEEHHPTTU	HEPTATEUCH
ACEEFLLPUY	PEACEFULLY	ACEEHIIPRS	HAIRPIECES
ACEEFLNSTV	FLAVESCENT	ACEEHILMNN	MANCHINEEL
ACEEFLORST	FORECASTLE	ACEEHILPTT	TELEPATHIC
ACEEFLOSTV	VOLTE-FACES	ACEEHILRSV	CHEVALIERS
ACEEFORRST	FORECASTER	ACEEHILSTT	ESTHETICAL
ACEEGGNORT	CONGREGATE	ACEEHIMNPZ	CHIMPANZEE
ACEEGGRSTU	CURATE'S EGG	ACEEHIMNRS	MECHANISER
ACEEGHHRTW	CHEW THE	ACEEHIMNRZ	MECHANIZER
RAG		ACEEHIMRTX	HEXAMETRIC
ACEEGHINNP	CHEAPENING	ACEEHIMSST	SCHEMATISE
ACEEGHLLNR	CHALLENGER	ACEEHIMSTZ	SCHEMATIZE
ACEEGHLLNS	CHALLENGES	ACEEHIMTTT	METATHETIC
ACEEGHLNSS	CHANGELESS	ACEEHINNPT	PHENACETIN
ACEEGHNNOP	COPENHAGEN	ACEEHINPSS	PEACHINESS
ACEEGHNORV	CHANGEOVER	ACEEHINSTT	ANESTHETIC
ACEEGHNSSU	GAUCHENESS	ACEEHIORRT	CHARIOTEER
ACEEGHORRV	OVERCHARGE	ACEEHISSTT	AESTHETICS
ACEEGIKTTW	WICKET GATE	ACEEHISTUW	WHITE SAUCE
ACEEGILLNR	ALLERGENIC	ACEEHKLNRT	HALTERNECK
ACEEGILLOT	COLLEGIATE	ACEEHLLLOR	LA ROCHELLE
ACEEGILNTU	GENICULATE	ACEEHLLNNR	CHANNELLER
ACEEGILRSS	SACRILEGES	ACEEHLLNOP	CELLOPHANE
ACEEGILSTU	SLUICEGATE	ACEEHLMNOS	CHAMELEONS
ACEEGINNOS	CASEINOGEN	ACEEHLNNOP	ENCEPHALON
ACEEGINNPT	PANGENETIC	ACEEHLNPRU	LEPRECHAUN
ACEEGINNRT	RECREATING	ACEEHLNPTT	PLANCHETTE
ACEEGINRSV	GRIEVANCES	ACEEHLOPTY	POLYCHAETE
ACEEGINRTX	EXECRATING	ACEEHLOSSV	CLOSE SHAVE
ACEEGIOPTT	COTTAGE PIE	ACEEHLRSTW	CARTWHEELS
ACEEGIORST	CATEGORIES,	ACEEHMMRSU	MEERSCHAUM
CATEGORISE		ACEEHMNNST	ENCASHMENT
ACEEGIORTZ	CATEGORIZE	ACEEHMNOOR	ANEMOCHORE
ACEEGIOTTX	EXCOGITATE	ACEEHMNPRT	PREACHMENT
ACEEGIRSTT	CIGARETTES	ACEEHMNRST	MANCHESTER
ACEEGKNOPS	SPONGE CAKE	ACEEHMORTT	TACHOMETER
ACEEGKORTT	GET A ROCKET	ACEEHMRTTY	TACHYMETER
ACEEGLLOSU	COLLEAGUES	ACEEHMSSTT	STEAM-CHEST
ACEEGLMNOR	CAMERLENGO	ACEEHNNRST	ENCHANTERS
		ACEEHNPTTU	PENTATEUCH
ACEEGLNRST	RECTANGLES	ACEEHOPRRR	REPROACHER
ACEEGLNRTU	GREAT-UNCLE	ACEEHOPRRS	ARCHESPORE,
ACEEGMMOSU	GEMMACEOUS	REPROACHES	
ACEEGMOTTY	GAMETOCYTE	ACEEHORRSS	RACEHORSES
ACEEGNNORV	GOVERNANCE	ACEEHPRRSU	REPURCHASE
ACEEGNNPRU	REPUGNANCE	ACEEHPRSTY	ARCHETYPES
ACEEGNNSWY	NEWS AGENCY	ACEEHPTTTX	EXCEPT THAT
ACEEGNORRU	ENCOURAGER	ACEEHRRSTT	CHATTERERS
ACEEGNRSSV	SCAVENGERS	ACEEHRRSTU	CHARTREUSE
ACEEHHILRW	WHEELCHAIR	ACEEIILMST	ELEATICISM
ACEEHHIRRS	HERESIARCH	ACEEIILNTT	LICENTIATE
ACEEHHIRST	HATCHERIES		

ACEEIILPSS	SPECIALISE
ACEEIILPST	TAILPIECES
ACEEIILPSZ	SPECIALIZE
ACEEIILSST	ELASTICISE
ACEEIILSTZ	ELASTICIZE
ACEEIIMNPT	IMPATIENCE
ACEEIINNRT	CREATININE,
INCINERATE	
ACEEIIRTTV	RECITATIVE
ACEEIITTVX	EXCITATIVE
ACEEIJLNQU	JACQUELINE
ACEEIJLRTT	TRAJECTILE
ACEEIKLNRT	TRANCELIKE
ACEEIKNOTT	TAKE NOTICE
ACEEIKNRSS	CREAKINESS
ACEEIKPRTT	TICKERTAPE
ACEEIKRSST	ICE-SKATERS
ACEEILLMTY	EMETICALLY
ACEEILLPRX	PRELEXICAL
ACEEILLPSY	ESPECIALLY
ACEEILMNNT	CLEMENTINA
ACEEILMNOR	CEREMONIAL
ACEEILMNOT	COLEMANITE
ACEEILMNOU	LEUCOMAINE
ACEEILMNRT	MERCANTILE
ACEEILMNST	CENTESIMAL,
LEMNISCATE	
ACEEILMOSU	MELIACEOUS
ACEEILNNNT	CENTENNIAL
ACEEILNOPU	LEUCOPENIA
ACEEILNOTV	EVECTIONAL
ACEEILNPRS	PRASELENIC
ACEEILNPRT	EPICENTRAL
ACEEILNRST	CENTRALISE,
LINECASTER	
ACEEILNRTV	CANTILEVER
ACEEILNRTZ	CENTRALIZE
ACEEILRRTT	RETRACTILE
ACEEILRSSU	SECULARISE
ACEEILRSUZ	SECULARIZE
ACEEILRTTU	RETICULATE
ACEEILRTUV	ULCERATIVE
ACEEILRTVY	CREATIVELY,
REACTIVELY	
ACEEILSTUV	VESICULATE
ACEEIMNORT	ACTINOMERE
ACEEIMNRSS	CREAMINESS
ACEEIMNRSV	SERVICEMAN
ACEEIMNRTT	REMITTANCE
ACEEIMORRT	AEROMETRIC
ACEEIMORTT	EROTEMATIC
ACEEIMPRST	SPERMACETI
ACEEIMRSST	MASSETERIC
ACEEINNRST	TRANSIENCE
ACEEINORRT	RECREATION

ACEEINORSU	ERINACEOUS
ACEEINORTU	AUCTIONEER
ACEEINORTX	EXECRATION
ACEEINPPRT	APPRENTICE
ACEEINPRST	INTERSPACE
ACEEINPRSU	EPICUREANS
ACEEINRSST	ANCESTRIES,
RESISTANCE	
ACEEINRTUV	UNREACTIVE
ACEEINRTVY	INVETERACY
ACEEINSSTV	ACTIVENESS
ACEEIOOPRS	AECIOSPORE
ACEEIOPPST	EPISCOPATE
ACEEIOPSST	CAESPITOSE
ACEEIOQTUV	EQUIVOCATE
ACEEIORTVV	OVERACTIVE,
REVOCATIVE	
ACEEIPPRTY	PARTY PIECE
ACEEIPQRSU	PICARESQUE
ACEEIQRSTU	REQUIESCAT
ACEEIRRSST	CAREERISTS
ACEEIRRTTV	RETRACTIVE
ACEEIRTTUV	ERUCTATIVE
ACEEIRTTVX	EXTRACTIVE
ACEEKLLRSS	SALESCLERK
ACEEKNRRRT	RACK-RENTER
ACEEKNRTTV	TRACK EVENT
ACEEKORRSW	CASEWORKER
ACEELLNRSW	ALLEN SCREW
ACEELLRSSY	CARELESSLY
ACEELLSTTU	SCUTELLATE
ACEELMNOTY	MELANOCYTE
ACEELMNPST	PLACEMENTS
ACEELMORST	LATECOMERS
ACEELMORTT	LACTOMETER
ACEELNOPRV	PROVENCALE
ACEELNOPST	OPALESCENT
ACEELNOPSY	CLAP EYES ON
ACEELNORTU	ENUCLEATOR
ACEELNPRSY	SCREENPLAY
ACEELORRST	CORRELATES
ACEELORSSS	CASSEROLES
ACEELPPRTU	PERCEPTUAL
ACEELQRRUU	CRAQUELURE
ACEEMMNNPT	ENCAMPMENT
ACEEMMNOTT	COMMENTATE
ACEEMMORSU	COMMEASURE
ACEEMNNPRY	PERMANENCY
ACEEMMNSTT	ENACTMENTS
ACEEMNOOPS	ANEMOSCOPE
ACEEMNOPST	COMPENSATE
ACEEMNPRST	ESCARPMENT
ACEEMOSTUZ	ECZEMATOUS
ACEENNOPRS	CAN OPENERS
ACEENNOPRV	PROVENANCE

ACEENNORSS	RESONANCES
ACEENNORTV	CONTRAVENE,
COVENANTER	
ACEENNRSSV	CRAVENNESS
ACEENNSSTU	SUSTENANCE
ACEENORSSS	COARSENESS
ACEENPRRST	CARPENTERS
ACEENPRSST	CENTRE PASS
ACEENPRUVY	PURVEYANCE
ACEENRSSST	ANCESTRESS
ACEENRSSTW	NEWSCASTER
ACEENRSTTU	UTTERANCES
ACEENSTTUX	EXECUTANTS
ACEEOSSTTU	TESTACEOUS
ACEEPRSTTY	TYPECASTER
ACEERRSSTT	STREETCARS
ACEERRSSTW	WATERCRESS
ACEFFFILOT	FACT OF LIFE
ACEFFHLNOR	FRENCH LOAF
ACEFFHRSUU	CHAUFFEURS
ACEFFIILTV	AFFLICTIVE
ACEFFIKRRT	TRAFFICKER
ACEFFINOST	AFFECTIONS
ACEFFOSTUU	TUFFACEOUS
ACEFGILNST	SELF-ACTING
ACEFGINRRT	REFRACTING
ACEFGLLRUY	GRACEFULLY
ACEFHHIRRS	ARCHERFISH
ACEFHIINST	CHIEFTAINS
ACEFHILRTU	ULTRAFICHE
ACEFHINRSS	FRANCHISES
ACEFHIRSSY	CRAYFISHES
ACEFHIRTTY	CITY FATHER
ACEFHKMMOU	MAKE MUCH
OF	
ACEFHKORST	AFTERSHOCK
ACEFHORRTV	HOVERCRAFT
ACEFHORSTU	HOUSECRAFT
ACEFIIILST	FACILITIES
ACEFIILMSS	FACSIMILES
ACEFIILRSS	CLASSIFIER
ACEFIINNRS	FINANCIERS
ACEFIINRST	SANCTIFIER
ACEFIIOPRS	FAIR COPIES
ACEFIIRRST	ARTIFICERS
ACEFIIRSTV	FRICATIVES
ACEFIKLNPS	CLASP KNIFE
ACEFIKRSTU	FRUITCAKES
ACEFILLNOT	FLECTIONAL
ACEFILNOST	SELF-ACTION
ACEFILNTUU	FUNICULATE
ACEFILOSOU	FOLIACEOUS
ACEFINORRT	FOR CERTAIN,
REFRACTION	
ACEFINORTV	VOCIFERANT

ACEFINRSST	CRAFTINESS
ACEFIRRTTU	TRIFURCATE
ACEFKLNORS	CORNFLAKES
ACEFKORSST	TASK FORCES
ACEFLOOPTU	OUT OF PLACE
ACEFMNNOWY	FANCY
WOMEN	
ACEFNOPRTT	PONTEFRACT
ACEFORRRTY	REFRACTORY
ACEFRRSSTU	SURFCASTER
ACEGGHILNN	CHANGELING
ACEGGHINNX	EXCHANGING
ACEGGHINRR	RECHARGING
ACEGGILLOO	GEOLOGICAL
ACEGGILNNO	CONGEALING
ACEGGINNOO	OCEANGOING
ACEGGINNSV	SCAVENGING
ACEGGIRSST	SCRAGGIEST
ACEGHHIJKR	HIGHJACKER
ACEGHHINOT	HIGH-OCTANE
ACEGHHOPRT	HECTOGRAPH
ACEGHIILMT	MEGALITHIC
ACEGHIIMNP	IMPEACHING
ACEGHIIMTW	WHITE MAGIC
ACEGHIINNN	ENCHAINING
ACEGHIINRS	CASHIERING
ACEGHIIPPR	EPIGRAPHIC
ACEGHILMPT	PHLEGMATIC
ACEGHILNPR	NEPHRALGIC
ACEGHIMNNU	MACHINE GUN
ACEGHIMNOP	MEGAPHONIC
ACEGHINNNT	ENCHANTING
ACEGHINNST	CHASTENING
ACEGHINOPT	PATHOGENIC
ACEGHINRRT	CHARTERING
ACEGHINRTT	CHATTERING
ACEGHIOOPS	HAGIOSCOPE
ACEGHIRSTW	SWITCHGEAR
ACEGHOPRRY	CEROGRAPHY
ACEGHOPSTY	PHAGOCYTES
ACEGHRRRSU	SURCHARGER
ACEGHRRSSU	SURCHARGES
ACEGIIKNRY	A GIN RICKEY
ACEGIIKNST	ICE-SKATING
ACEGIILLRS	GALLICISER
ACEGIILLRZ	GALLICIZER
ACEGIILLST	LEGALISTIC
ACEGIILMNR	RECLAIMING
ACEGIILMNX	EXCLAIMING
ACEGIILMTY	LEGITIMACY
ACEGIILNNO	LIGNOCAINE
ACEGIIMNTT	MAGNETITIC
ACEGIIMOST	ISOGAMETIC
ACEGIIMPTT	PEGMATITIC

ACEGIINNRS	INCREASING	ACEHHOOSTT	TOOTHACHES	ACEHINRRSU	HURRICANES
ACEGIINORT	IATROGENIC	ACEHIILLPT	PHILATELIC	ACEHINRSSU	SEA URCHINS
ACEGIIOTTV	COGITATIVE	ACEHIILMOS	ISOCHEIMAL	ACEHINRRSTV	RAUNCHIEST
ACEGIIPRST	EPIGASTRIC	ACEHIIMRTT	ARITHMETIC	ACEHINRSTV	REVANCHIST
ACEGIIRRST	GERIATRICS	ACEHIINNOP	PHOENICIAN	ACEHIORSTT	RHEOSTATIC
ACEGIKLNNS	SLACKENING	ACEHIINOTV	INCHOATIVE	ACEHIPPSSS	SPACESHIPS
ACEGIKNPPR	PREPACKING	ACEHIIPRRT	PERITRICHA	ACEHIRSSTT	STARCHIEST
ACEGILLNOO	NEOLOGICAL	ACEHIIRSTT	TRACHEITIS	ACEHIRSTTT	TETRASTICH
ACEGILLNPR	PARCELLING	ACEHIKLNSS	CHALKINESS	ACEHLLMNOY	MELANCHOLY
ACEGILLOOS	OLIGOCLASE	ACEHIKMNOS	CHAIN-SMOKE	ACEHLLPRSU	SEPULCHRAL
ACEGILMNNY	MENACINGLY	ACEHIKMNSY	HACKNEYISM	ACEHLMOOST	SCHOOLMATE
ACEGILNNOT	CONGENITAL	ACEHIKORST	ARTICHOKES	ACEHLMORSY	LACHRYMOSE
ACEGILNOPY	CLAY PIGEON	ACEHILLNTY	ETHNICALLY	ACEHLNORST	CHARLESTON
ACEGILNORT	RELOCATING	ACEHILLOOS	ALCOHOLISE	ACEHLOORST	ORTHOCLASE
ACEGILNOTU	GLAUCONITE	ACEHILLOOZ	ALCOHOLIZE	ACEHLOOSSU	COALHOUSES
ACEGILNPTU	PECULATING	ACEHILLORY	HEROICALLY	ACEHLOPXYY	OXYCEPHALY
ACEGILNQRU	LACQUERING	ACEHILLPRY	CAERPHILLY	ACEHLORRST	ORCHESTRAL
ACEGILNRTT	CLATTERING	ACEHILLTTY	THETICALLY	ACEHLPRTYY	PHYLACTERY
ACEGILNRTU	ULCERATING	ACEHILMMOS	CHAMOMILES	ACEHMMNOOR	
ACEGILNTXY	EXACTINGLY	ACEHILMMST	MISCH METAL	CHROMONEMA	
ACEGILOOPT	APOLOGETIC	ACEHILMNOR	CHLORAMINE	ACEHMNPRST	PARCHMENTS
ACEGIMMRRS	SCRIMMAGER	ACEHILMOOP	PHOCOMELIA	ACEHMOORUX	AUXOCHROME
ACEGIMMRSS	SCRIMMAGES	ACEHILMOTY	HAEMOLYTIC	ACEHMORRTU	ROUTE MARCH
ACEGIMNPRS	SCAMPERING	ACEHILMSST	ALCHEMISTS	ACEHMORTTY	TACHOMETRY
ACEGIMNRST	CENTIGRAMS	ACEHILNNOT	NONETHICAL	ACEHMOSSTU	MOUSTACHES
ACEGIMOPRS	MEGASPORIC	ACEHILNORT	CHLORINATE	ACEHMRTTYY	TACHYMETRY
ACEGIMORST	GASOMETRIC	ACEHILOORZ	COLEORHIZA	ACEHNORRTT	TROCHANTER
ACEGINNNRT	ENTRANCING	ACEHILOPST	TELOPHASIC	ACEHNSSTTU	STAUNCHEST
ACEGINNORS	COARSENING	ACEHILORRT	RHETORICAL	ACEHOOPPRR	CARPOPHORE
ACEGINOPRS	SAPROGENIC	ACEHILPSST	SALES PITCH	ACEHOOSSTU	HOUSECOATS
ACEGINORTV	OVERACTING	ACEHILRSTU	HERACLITUS	ACEHOPPRTU	TOUCHPAPER
ACEGINPRRS	SCARPERING	ACEHILRSTY	HYSTERICAL	ACEHORRSST	CARTHORSES,
ACEGINPRSY	PANEGYRICS	ACEHIMMNSS	MECHANISMS	ORCHESTRAS	
ACEGINPSTT	SPECTATING	ACEHIMMSST	MISMATCHES,	ACEHORTTWW	WATCHTOWER
ACEGINRRTT	RETRACTING	SCHEMATISM		ACEHPRRSSU	PURCHASERS
ACEGINRSTT	SCATTERING	ACEHIMNNOR	ENHARMONIC	ACEIIIMNST	INTIMACIES
ACEGINRTTX	EXTRACTING	ACEHIMNORS	MONARCHIES	ACEIIISTTV	ACTIVITIES
ACEGIOSSTT	GEOSTATICS	ACEHIMNORW	CHAIRWOMEN	ACEIIJLSTU	JESUITICAL
ACEGIRRSST	STRATEGICS	ACEHIMNRSV	REVANCHISM	ACEIIKMNST	KINEMATICS
ACEGLMOSUU	GLUMACEOUS	ACEHIMNSTY	MYASTHENIC	ACEIIKRSTT	RICKETTSIA
ACEGLNOOOY	OCEANOLOGY	ACEHIMOPRS	SEMAPHORIC	ACEIILLLPT	ELLIPTICAL
ACEGLOOPSY	ESCAPOLOGY	ACEHIMOPRT	AMPHOTERIC,	ACEIILLNPR	PERICLINAL
ACEGLOOTUY	AUTECOLOGY	METAPHORIC		ACEIILLNRY	IRENICALLY
ACEGMMRRSU	SCRUMMAGER	ACEHIMOPTU	APOTHECIUM	ACEIILLOST	LOCALITIES
ACEGMMRSSU	SCRUMMAGES	ACEHIMOSTX	CHEMOTAXIS	ACEIILLOSU	LILIACEOUS
ACEGNNOSTT	COTANGENTS	ACEHIMPSTY	METAPHYSIC	ACEIILLRTY	ILLITERACY
ACEGNRSTTU	SCATTER-GUN	ACEHIMRSTU	RHEUMATICS	ACEIILLTXY	LEXICALITY
ACEGOORSUU	COURAGEOUS	ACEHINOPST	ASTHENOPIC	ACEIILMMST	MELISMATIC
ACEGOPRRSU	SUPERCARGO	ACEHINORRT	CHITARRONE	ACEIILMNST	MELANISTIC
ACEHHIKSTT	HIT THE SACK	ACEHINORST	ANCHORITES,	ACEIILMOPT	ATOMIC PILE
ACEHHILTWZ	WITCH-HAZEL	CHAIN STORE		ACEIILMPSS	SPECIALISM
ACEHHIPSTT	HEPTASTICH	ACEHINORTV	CHEVROTAIN	ACEIILMRST	SALIMETRIC
ACEHHLNNOP	CHANNEL-HOP	ACEHINPSST	PATCHINESS	ACEIILNOTT	ACTINOLITE
ACEHHNORSU	RANCH HOUSE	ACEHINPSTT	PENTASTICH	ACEIILNPST	PLASTICINE
		ACEHINPSTU	EPICANTHUS	ACEIILNRST	IN ARTICLES

ACEIILNTVY	INACTIVELY	ACEILLPSTY	SEPTICALLY	ACEIMNORST	CREMATIONS
ACEIILORSS	SOCIALISER	ACEILLRSTY	STERICALLY	ACEIMNORUY	AUREOMYCIN
ACEIILORSZ	SOCIALIZER	ACEILLRTUV	VICTUALLER	ACEIMNPSTU	PNEUMATICS
ACEIILOSST	SOCIALITES	ACEILLRTVY	VERTICALLY	ACEIMNRRTY	TERRAMYCIN
ACEIILOSTU	TILIACEOUS	ACEILMMNSS	CLAMMINESS	ACEIMNRSST	MISCREANTS
ACEIILPPRT	PARTICIPLE	ACEILMNOPR	COMPLAINER	ACEIMORSVW	MICROWAVES
ACEIILPRTT	TRIPLICATE	ACEILMNORS	SERMONICAL	ACEIMORTTT	TETRATOMIC
ACEIILPSST	PLASTICISE,	ACEILMNRST	CENTRALISM	ACEIMORTTU	TAUTOMERIC
SPECIALIST		ACEILMNRUW	LAWRENCIUM	ACEIMSSTTY	SYSTEMATIC
ACEIILPSTY	SPECIALITY	ACEILMRRUV	VERMICULAR	ACEINNNSTU	UNCANNIEST
ACEIILPSTZ	PLASTICIZE	ACEILMRSSU	SECULARISM	ACEINNORST	CONTAINERS,
ACEIILSTTY	ELASTICITY	ACEILMTUUV	CUMULATIVE	SANCTIONER	
ACEIIMNORS	MICRONESIA	ACEILNNOOP	NAPOLEONIC	ACEINNORTU	ENUNCIATOR
ACEIIMNRRU	CINERARIUM	ACEILNNORS	CORNELIANS	ACEINNRSSU	INSURANCES
ACEIIMRRST	ERRATICISM	ACEILNNOTU	NUCLEATION	ACEINNRSTY	TRANSIENCY
ACEIIMRSST	ARMISTICES	ACEILNNUVY	UNIVALENCY	ACEINNRTUU	NUNCIATURE
ACEIIMRSTT	TASIMETRIC	ACEILNOORT	ICONOLATER,	ACEINNSSST	SCANTINESS
ACEIINNRTY	ITINERANCY	RELOCATION		ACEINOORTV	REVOCATION
ACEIINOPST	SPECIATION	ACEILNOPPS	SCALOPPINE	ACEINOOSTV	EVOCATIONS
ACEIINORTT	RECITATION	ACEILNOPRT	PRATINCOLE	ACEINOPRTU	PRECAUTION
ACEIINOSTV	VESICATION	ACEILNOPST	NEOPLASTIC,	ACEINOPSTT	CONSTIPATE
ACEIINOTTX	EXCITATION,	PLEONASTIC		ACEINORRST	CONTRARIES
INTOXICATE		ACEILNOPTU	PECULATION	ACEINORRSV	CARNIVORES
ACEIINPSTT	ANTISEPTIC,	ACEILNORTU	ULCERATION	ACEINORRTT	RETRACTION
PSITTACINE		ACEILNORTY	LECTIONARY	ACEINORSSY	CESSIONARY
ACEIINRTVY	INVERACITY	ACEILNOSSS	SOCIALNESS	ACEINORTTU	ERUCTATION
ACEIINSTTU	AUSTENITIC	ACEILNOSST	COASTLINES	ACEINORTTW	TONIC WATER
ACEIIORRRT	CERTIORARI	ACEILNOSTU	INOSCULATE	ACEINORTTX	EXTRACTION
ACEIIORSTT	ATROCITIES	ACEILNOTUV	NOVACULITE	ACEINOSSST	CESSATIONS
ACEIIPPSST	EPISPASTIC	ACEILNPPSU	SUPPLIANCE	ACEINOSTTU	UNICOSTATE
ACEIIRSSST	SACRISTIES	ACEILNRSTU	LACUSTRINE	ACEINPSSSU	PUISSANCES
ACEIIRTTVY	CREATIVITY,	ACEILNRSUV	VULCANISER	ACEINQSTTU	QUITTANCES
REACTIVITY		ACEILNRTTY	CENTRALITY	ACEINRSSTW	SCRAWNIEST
ACEIJKKNSV	JACK KNIVES	ACEILNRTVY	TRIVALENCY	ACEINSSTTT	SCATTINESS
ACEIJNORTT	TRAJECTION	ACEILNRUUX	LUXURIANCE	ACEIOOPRTZ	AZEOTROPIC
ACEIKKNNTU	KENTUCKIAN	ACEILNRUVZ	VULCANIZER	ACEIOOPTTV	COOPTATIVE
ACEIKLRSTV	TRAVELSICK	ACEILOOSUV	OLIVACEOUS,	ACEIOOSTUU	AUTOECIOUS
ACEIKMPRST	STRIKE CAMP	VIOLACEOUS		ACEIOPRRSU	PRECARIOUS
ACEIKNORSS	CROAKINESS	ACEILOPPRS	SAPROPELIC	ACEIOPSTTT	PETTICOATS
ACEIKNPRST	SEPTIC TANK	ACEILOPRTX	EXPLICATOR	ACEIOQSSUU	SEQUACIOUS
ACEIKOPRST	AIRPOCKETS	ACEILOPTUV	COPULATIVE	ACEIORRSST	OSTRACISER
ACEILLLPRU	PELLICULAR	ACEILOQTUY	COEQUALITY	ACEIORRSTZ	OSTRACIZER
ACEILLMNSY	MISCELLANY	ACEILPPPRS	PAPER CLIPS	ACEIORRSTT	TRICOSTATE
ACEILLMORT	ALLOMETRIC	ACEILPPSTU	SUPPLICATE	ACEIPPRSST	SCRAPPIEST
ACEILLMRTY	METRICALLY	ACEILPRTUU	APICULTURE	ACEIPSSSTU	SPACESUITS
ACEILLNNNO	CANNELLONI	ACEILRSSTU	SECULARIST	ACEISSTTTY	CITY-STATES
ACEILLNOOT	OCELLATION	ACEILRSTTU	TESTICULAR	ACEJKKRSSY	SKYJACKERS
ACEILLNORT	CITRONELLA	ACEILRSTUY	SECULARITY	ACEJKLPPSU	SUPPLEJACK
ACEILLNRTU	LENTICULAR	ACEILRTUUV	AVICULTURE	ACEJKNOSST	JACKSTONES
ACEILLOPSW	PILLOWCASE	ACEIMMNORT	MANOMETRIC	ACEJORRTTY	TRAJECTORY
ACEILLOPTY	POETICALLY	ACEIMMRSTY	ASYMMETRIC	ACEKKMOSST	SMOKESTACK
ACEILLORTV	VORTICELLA	ACEIMNNOST	CISMONTANE	ACEKKMRRSU	MUCKRAKERS
ACEILLORTY	EROTICALLY	ACEIMNNRUY	INNUMERACY	ACEKLLRSTU	LACKLUSTRE
ACEILLOTXY	EXOTICALLY	ACEIMNOPRT	IMPORTANCE	ACEKLNOPST	ALPENSTOCK
ACEILLPRUY	PECULIARLY	ACEIMNOPSU	MENOPAUSIC		

ACEKLOPRSW	WORKPLACES
ACEKMNORRW	
CANKERWORM	
ACEKPRRSSY	SKYSCRAPER
ACELLLMORU	COLUMELLAR
ACELLLNOSSW	CALLOWNESS
ACELLOPSTU	LEUCOPLAST
ACELLOPTUY	EUCALYPTOL
ACELLORSSW	LOWER CLASS
ACELLPRUUV	VULPECULAR
ACELLSSTTY	TACTLESSLY
ACELMMNOOW	
COMMONWEAL	
ACELMMNNOTT	MALCONTENT
ACELMNOORT	MONTE CARLO
ACELNNOSSU	CONSENSUAL
ACELNNOSTU	LAUNCESTON
ACELNNOTUV	CONVENTUAL
ACELNOPRRU	PRONUCLEAR
ACELNOPRSY	NARCOLEPSY
ACELNORTRY	NECROLATRY
ACELNOSSTU	CONSULATES
ACELNOTTUX	CONTEXTUAL
ACELOOPRRT	PERCOLATOR
ACELOOSSTT	OSTEOCLAST
ACELOPPRST	PARCEL POST
ACELOPRSTU	SPECULATOR
ACELOSSSTU	LOST CAUSES
ACELPPRSSU	UPPER CLASS
ACELPRSSSU	SUPERCLASS
ACELPSTUUY	EUCALYPTUS
ACELRSSTTY	CRYSTAL SET
ACEMMNORTY	COMMENTARY
ACEMMNOSTU	CONSUMMATE
ACEMMOSTTY	MASTECTOMY
ACEMNNNOTT	CANTONMENT
ACEMNNORST	MONSTRANCE
ACEMNOOPSS	MOONSCAPES
ACEMNOOTYZ	MYCETOZOAN
ACEMNOPRRY	PYROMANCER
ACEMNOSTTY	NEMATOCYST
ACEMOOPRRS	MACROSPORE
ACEMOORSTU	OCTAMEROUS
ACEMORSTUY	MYRTACEOUS
ACENNNORSU	ANNOUNCERS
ACENNOORTV	COVENANTOR
ACENNORSTV	CONVERSANT
ACENNOSTTT	CONTESTANT
ACENNRSTTU	ENCRUSTANT
ACENOPSSTW	TOWNSCAPES
ACENORRSTU	RACONTEURS
ACENORSSTU	COURTESANS
ACENPRSSUU	PURSUANCES
ACEOOOPRRT	COOPERATOR

ACEOOPPRRS	CARPOSPORE
ACEOOPRRRT	PROCREATOR
ACEOOPSSTT	STATOSCOPE
ACEOPRSSTT	SPECTATORS
ACEORRRSVY	CARRY-OVERS
ACEORRSTTX	EXTRACTORS
ACEORSTUXY	EXCUSATORY
ACERRSTUUV	CURVATURES
ACFFGIILNT	AFFLICTING
ACFFIILLOY	OFFICIALLY
ACFFIILNOT	AFFLICTION
ACFFIILNOU	UNOFFICIAL
ACFFIIOORT	OFFICIATOR
ACFFILLNUY	FANCIFULLY
ACFGHINRSS	GRASSFINCH
ACFGIILNRY	CLARIFYING
ACFGIINRSY	SCARIFYING
ACFGILNNOT	CONFLATING
ACFGILOPRY	PROFLIGACY
ACFGINRRTU	FRACTURING
ACFHIILRST	CHAIR LIFTS
ACFHIOPRST	FACTORSHIP
ACFHLLTUWY	WATCHFULLY
ACFHLNORSW	HALF CROWNS
ACFHLORSTW	FLOWCHARTS
ACFIILNOPT	PONTIFICAL
ACFIILNORT	FRICTIONAL
ACFIIMNORT	ACTINIFORM
ACFIINNORS	INFRASONIC
ACFIINNORT	INFARCTION,
INFRACTION	
ACFIIOSTTU	FACTITIOUS
ACFILLLORU	FOLLICULAR
ACFILNNOOT	CONFLATION
ACFILNNOTU	FUNCTIONAL
ACFILNOOPT	FOCAL POINT
ACFILNOOST	TONIC SOL-FA
ACFILNRSUU	FUNICULARS
ACFILRSSST	FIRST-CLASS
ACFINOORRT	FORNICATOR
ACFKMRRSTU	TRUCK FARMS
ACFLLOOPRT	PORT OF CALL
ACFLNOORTW	CONTRAFLOW
ACFLNRRUUU	FURUNCULAR
ACFLOORSTU	COLOURFAST
ACGGHIILOO	HAGIOLOGIC
ACGGHIINNR	CHAGRINING
ACGGHINOTT	CHITTAGONG
ACGGIILLOT	GLAGOLITIC
ACGGIILNNO	GANGLIONIC
ACGGIINOTT	COGITATING
ACGGILLNNY	GLANCINGLY
ACGGILLOOY	GLACIOLOGY
ACGGIMOSTY	MYSTAGOGIC

ACGHHHIIRS	HIGH CHAIRS
ACGHHINTTW	WATCH NIGHT
ACGHIIJKNS	HIJACKINGS
ACGHIIMOPR	AMPHIGORIC
ACGHIINSST	CHASTISING
ACGHIIPRRT	TRIGRAPHIC
ACGHILLOOP	HAPLOLOGIC
ACGHILLOTY	GOTHICALLY
ACGHILMNRY	CHARMINGLY
ACGHILNSTY	SCATHINGLY
ACGHIMNNOP	CHAMPIGNON
ACGHIMNNOR	HOMORGANIC
ACGHIMNOST	STOMACHING
ACGHIMOPRR	MICROGRAPH
ACGHIMOPRY	MYOGRAPHIC
ACGHINNSTU	STAUNCHING
ACGHINOPRZ	ZINCOGRAPH
ACGHINPRSU	PURCHASING
ACGHIOOPRR	OROGRAPHIC
ACGHIOOPRZ	ZOOGRAPHIC
ACGHIOPPRT	PICTOGRAPH
ACGHMNOORR	
CHRONOGRAM	
ACGHOOPPRY	COPROPHAGY
ACGIIILLRT	ARGILLITIC
ACGIIKMNNN	NICKNAMING
ACGIILLMNS	MISCALLING
ACGIILLNOZ	LOCALIZING
ACGIILLOST	LOGISTICAL
ACGIILLOTY	LOGICALITY
ACGIILLRTU	LITURGICAL
ACGIILMNPS	MISPLACING
ACGIILMNSS	ANGLICISMS
ACGIILMORS	ALGORISMIC
ACGIILNRTU	CURTAILING,
GRANULITIC	
ACGIILNRTY	LARYNGITIC
ACGIILNTUV	VICTUALING
ACGIIMNNRU	MANICURING
ACGIIMNORR	MARCONI RIG
ACGIIMNORS	ORGANICISM
ACGIIMNRST	SCINTIGRAM
ACGIIMNSST	MISCASTING
ACGIINNNOT	CONTAINING
ACGIINNNOZ	CANONIZING
ACGIINNNST	INSTANCING
ACGIINNOTU	AUCTIONING,
CAUTIONING	
ACGIINNRTU	CURTAINING
ACGIINOOTT	COGITATION
ACGIINORST	ORGANICIST
ACGIINPRST	PRACTISING
ACGIINQTTU	ACQUITTING
ACGIJKKNSY	SKYJACKING
ACGIKKMNRU	MUCKRAKING

ACGILLNOPS	COLLAPSING, SCALLOPING
ACGILLNORR	CORRALLING
ACGILLOOOR	OROLOGICAL
ACGILLOOOT	OTOLOGICAL
ACGILLOOOZ	ZOOLOGICAL
ACGILLOPRY	PYROGALLIC
ACGILLRSUY	SURGICALLY
ACGILMNORU	CLAMOURING
ACGILNNPRY	PRANCINGLY
ACGILNOORY	CRANIOLOGY
ACGILNOPTU	COPULATING
ACGILORSUY	GLYCOSURIA, GRACIOUSLY
ACGIMNOORS	AGRONOMICS
ACGIMNOOSU	ASCOGONIUM
ACGIMNSSTY	GYMNASTICS
ACGINNNNOU	ANNOUNCING
ACGINNOOST	CONTAGIONS
ACGINNORRY	CARRYING-ON
ACGINNRTTU	TRUNCATING
ACGINOOSTU	CONTAGIOUS
ACGINOPRTY	AGRYPNOTIC
ACGINOPSUU	PUGNACIOUS
ACGINORRST	CO-STARRING
ACGIOOPRTV	VAGOTROPIC
ACGIORSTTY	GYROSTATIC
ACGJNOORTU	CONJUGATOR
ACGLMNOOOS	COSMOGONAL
ACGLNOORSU	CLANGOROUS
ACHHIILPST	PHTHISICAL
ACHHILMOPT	OPHTHALMIC
ACHHILMRTY	RHYTHMICAL
ACHHILOPTY	HALOPHYTIC
ACHHINSTUY	HYACINTHUS
ACHHIOPPST	PHOSPHATIC
ACHHIPPRSU	HIPPARCHUS
ACHHIPRSSU	PUSHCHAIRS
ACHHLOSSTU	SLOUCH HATS
ACHHLOSSTW	WASHCLOTHS
ACHHNOOTTU	AUTOCHTHON
ACHHOPPSTY	PSYCHOPATH
ACHIIIMNOY	ICHINOMIYA
ACHIIIMNST	HISTAMINIC
ACHIIIMRTY	HIMYARITIC
ACHIIIRSST	TRICHIASIS
ACHIILLMPS	PHALLICISM
ACHIILLPST	PHALLICIST
ACHIILORST	HISTORICAL
ACHIILORTU	THIOURACIL
ACHIIMNNOR	INHARMONIC
ACHIIMNSST	MACHINISTS
ACHIIMNSTU	·HUMANISTIC
ACHIIMNSUV	CHAUVINISM
ACHIINNOOT	INCHOATION

ACHIINNORT	CORINTHIAN
ACHIINNPQU	CHINQUAPIN
ACHIINORTT	ANORTHITIC
ACHIINPSSY	PHYSICIANS
ACHIINRSST	CHRISTIANS
ACHIINRSTT	ANTICHRIST
ACHIINSTUV	CHAUVINIST
ACHIIOPRST	APHORISTIC
ACHIIOPSST	PISTACHIOS
ACHIIPRSTY	PHYSIATRIC
ACHIIRRSTT	ARTHRITICS
ACHIIRSSTV	ARCHIVISTS
ACHIKLOORW	WORKAHOLIC
ACHIKMNOST	MACKINTOSH
ACHILLMOOS	ALCOHOLISM
ACHILLMSSU	MUSIC HALLS
ACHILLNNSY	CLANNISHLY
ACHILLNOOP	ALLOPHONIC
ACHILLNOPY	PHONICALLY
ACHILLOPRT	PROTHALLIC
ACHILLPSYY	PHYSICALLY
ACHILMOPTY	POLYMATHIC
ACHILMPSTY	ITCHY PALMS
ACHILNOORS	ISOCHRONAL
ACHILNORUY	HYALURONIC
ACHILORSUV	CHIVALROUS
ACHIMMNORS	MONARCHISM
ACHIMNOPTT	MATCH POINT
ACHIMNOPTY	AMPHICTYON
ACHIMNORST	MONARCHIST
ACHIMORRTT	TRICHROMAT
ACHIMORRYZ	MYCORRHIZA
ACHIMORSTT	CHROMATIST
ACHIMOSSST	MASOCHISTS
ACHIMOSSTU	MUSTACHIOS
ACHINNOSST	STANCHIONS
ACHINNOSTW	CHINATOWNS
ACHINOOPSX	SAXOPHONIC
ACHINPRSST	CHINSTRAPS
ACHIOOPPTT	POTATO CHIP
ACHIOOPSTY	SOCIOPATHY
ACHIOPRSTY	PHYSIOCRAT
ACHIOPTTUY	AUTOPHYTIC
ACHIPRSTYY	PSYCHIATRY
ACHIRSTTWW	WRISTWATCH
ACHKNOOTTU	NOUAKCHOTT
ACHKOPRSTW	PATCHWORKS
ACHLLLOOOW	LOW-ALCOHOL
ACHLLOOPSY	PLAYSCHOOL
ACHLMMOSRS	SCHOOLMARM
ACHLMNORUU	HOMUNCULAR
ACHLOOSSTU	HOLOCAUSTS
ACHNOOPSYZ	SCYPHOZOAN

ACHNOPSSTY	SYCOPHANTS
ACHORSTTTU	CUTTHROATS
ACIIILNOPT	POLITICIAN
ACIIILNPST	SINCIPITAL
ACIIILORTV	VARIOLITIC
ACIIILSTTV	VITALISTIC
ACIIINNOTT	INCITATION
ACIIINRSTT	INARTISTIC
ACIIINSTTV	NATIVISTIC
ACIIINTTVY	INACTIVITY
ACIIJRSTUY	JUSTICIARY
ACIIKNRSST	SANSKRITIC
ACIILLMNRY	CRIMINALLY
ACIILLNNOS	SCILLONIAN
ACIILLNORY	IRONICALLY
ACIILLMORST	MORALISTIC
ACIILLNOST	COALITIONS
ACIILNOPRV	PROVINCIAL
ACIILNORTT	TINCTORIAL
ACIILNPPRS	PRINCIPALS
ACIILNSSTV	CALVINISTS
ACIILOPRST	SAPROLITIC
ACIILOPTTY	TOPICALITY
ACIILORSTY	ROYALISTIC
ACIILOSSST	SOCIALISTS
ACIILOSSUV	LASCIVIOUS
ACIILPSTTY	PLASTICITY
ACIILRSTTU	ALTRUISTIC, ULTRAISTIC
ACIILRTTTY	TRACTILITY
ACIIMMNOPT	PANTOMIMIC
ACIIMMNSTU	NUMISMATIC
ACIIMNNOSS	INSOMNIACS
ACIIMNORST	MORTICIANS
ACIIMNPTTY	TYMPANITIC
ACIIMNRSSS	NARCISSISM
ACIIMNRSTU	MANICURIST
ACIIMOSTTT	STOMATITIC
ACIINNOOTV	INVOCATION
ACIINNOSTU	INSOUCIANT
ACIINNOTTX	INTOXICANT
ACIINOPRST	ASCRIPTION, CRISPATION
ACIINOPRTT	TRITANOPIC
ACIINORSTV	VICTORIANS
ACIINORSTX	SAINT CROIX
ACIINORTTU	URTICATION
ACIINOSTUU	INCAUTIOUS
ACIINRSSTU	NARCISSIST
ACIIOPSSUU	AUSPICIOUS
ACIIORSTVY	VARICOSITY
ACIISSSTTT	STATISTICS
ACIJLNNOTU	JUNCTIONAL
ACIJLORTUY	JOCULARITY
ACIKKLMNOR	KILMARNOCK

ACIKLNNOPT	PLANKTONIC	
ACIKLOORSW	SOCIAL WORK	
ACIKLORTYY	KARYOLYTIC	
ACIKOPRTYY	KARYOTYPIC	
ACIKRSSTTU	TRACKSUITS	
ACILLLOOQU	COLLOQUIAL	
ACILLMNNOO	MONOCLINAL	
ACILLMOORT	COLLIMATOR	
ACILLMOPYY	MYOPICALLY	
ACILLMSTYY	MYSTICALLY	
ACILLNOOPT	CALL OPTION	
ACILLNOOST	COLLATIONS	
ACILLNOOTU	ALLOCUTION,	
	LOCULATION	
ACILLNORSW	CORNWALLIS	
ACILLNORUU	UNILOCULAR	
ACILLNORUV	INVOLUCRAL	
ACILLOOPRT	ALLOTROPIC	
ACILLOORST	OSCILLATOR	
ACILLOPRTY	TROPICALLY	
ACILLORRTU	TRILOCULAR	
ACILMMOORS	MICROSOMAL	
ACILMMOSTT	COMMITTALS	
ACILMMRSUU	SIMULACRUM	
ACILMNOORT	MICROTONAL	
ACILMNOPST	COMPLAINTS	
ACILMNOSUU	CALUMNIOUS	
ACILMNOTUU	CUMULATION	
ACILMNRSUU	MINUSCULAR	
ACILMOOPTY	POLYATOMIC	
ACILMOPRRY	MICROPYLAR	
ACILMORSUU	MIRACULOUS	
ACILNNOPTY	NONTYPICAL	
ACILNOOORT	COLORATION	
ACILNOOPTU	COPULATION	
ACILNOORST	CONSORTIAL	
ACILNOORTU	INOCULATOR	
ACILNOORTY	ICONOLATRY	
ACILNOOSTU	OSCULATION	
ACILNOOTTT	COTTONTAIL	
ACILNORRTU	TRINOCULAR	
ACILNORRTY	CONTRARILY	
ACILNORSTU	ULTRASONIC	
ACILNOSTUY	LACUNOSITY	
ACILNPPSTU	SUPPLICANT	
ACILNRTTUY	TACITURNLY	
ACILOOPRRT	PROCTORIAL	
ACILOOPSTZ	ZOOPLASTIC	
ACILOOQSUU	LOQUACIOUS	
ACILOOSSUX	SAXICOLOUS	
ACILOPSSUY	SPACIOUSLY	
ACILOPSTUY	CAPTIOUSLY	
ACILORTTUV	CULTIVATOR	
ACILOSTUUY	CAUTIOUSLY	

ACILPRRSTU	SCRIPTURAL	
ACIMMORSSS	COMMISSARS	
ACIMMORSSY	COMMISSARY	
ACIMNNOOPS	COMPANIONS	
ACIMNNOSTY	SANCTIMONY	
ACIMNOOPRS	COMPARISON	
ACIMNOOPSS	COMPASSION	
ACIMNOORTY	CRANIOTOMY	
ACIMNOOSST	ONOMASTICS	
ACIMNOOSTY	ACTOMYOSIN	
ACIMNOPPRS	PRISON CAMP	
ACIMNOPRTY	PATRONYMIC,	
	PYROMANTIC	
ACIMNOSTTY	MYCOSTATIN	
ACIMNOTTUY	TAUTONYMIC	
ACIMNPRSTU	MANUSCRIPT	
ACIMOOPRTT	COMPATRIOT	
ACIMOORTVY	VARICOTOMY	
ACIMOPSTYY	ASYMPTOTIC	
ACINNNOSTT	INCONSTANT	
ACINNNOTTU	CONTINUANT	
ACINNOOORT	CORONATION	
ACINNOPTTU	PUNCTATION	
ACINNORSTT	CONSTRAINT	
ACINNORTTU	TRUNCATION	
ACINNSTTYY	NYCTINASTY	
ACINOOOPTT	COOPTATION	
ACINOOPPRT	PROTANOPIC	
ACINOORSTT	CARTOONIST	
ACINOORTVY	INVOCATORY	
ACINORSSST	CROISSANTS	
ACINPRRSTT	TRANSCRIPT	
ACIOPRSTTY	PYROSTATIC	
ACIORRSTTU	RUSTICATOR	
ACJKOPRSS	JOCKSTRAPS	
ACKLLNRSTU	TRUNK CALLS	
ACKLMNOORS	ROCK SALMON	
ACKLMOOORS	CLOAKROOMS	
ACKLNOPRST	ROCK PLANTS	
ACKLORSSSW	CROSSWALKS	
ACLLLOOSSY	COLOSSALLY	
ACLLLRTUUY	CULTURALLY	
ACLLMRSUUY	MUSCULARLY	
ACLLNPTUUY	PUNCTUALLY	
ACLLPRSTUU	SCULPTURAL	
ACLMMNOOTY	COMMONALTY	
ACLMOORSSS	CLASSROOMS	
ACLNNOSTTU	CONSULTANT	
ACLNNOSTTY	CONSTANTLY	
ACLNNPTUUU	UNPUNCTUAL	
ACLNNRSUUU	RANUNCULUS	
ACLNOORSTT	CONTRALTOS	
ACLNOPSTUY	POSTULANCY	
ACLOORSTUY	OSCULATORY	

ACLOPRSTTU	PLUTOCRATS	
ACLRRSTTUU	STRUCTURAL	
ACMMOORTTU	COMMUTATOR	
ACMMPPUUUV	VACUUM	
	PUMP	
ACMNNORTUY	COUNTRYMAN	
ACMNOORRST	CORMORANTS	
ACMNOOSSTU	COSMONAUTS	
ACNNNOOSST	CONSONANTS	
ACNOOPRSTY	SYNCOPATOR	
ACNOPRSSUY	SYNCARPOUS	
ACNOPRTTUU	PUNCTUATOR	
ACOOOPRRRT	CORPORATOR	
ACOOOPSTTV	POST OCTAVO	
ACOOPRRRTT	PROTRACTOR	
ACOOPRRRTU	PROCURATOR	
ACOPRRSSST	SPORTS CARS	
ADDDDEEKLS	SKEDADDLED	
ADDDEEFHIL	FIDDLEHEAD	
ADDDEEGILM	MIDDLE-AGED	
ADDDEEHNRU	DUNDERHEAD	
ADDDEEHRRU	RUDDERHEAD	
ADDDEEHRTY	DEHYDRATED	
ADDDEEILSS	SIDESADDLE	
ADDDEGNORW	DOWNGRADED	
ADDDELNOOW	DOWNLOADED	
ADDEEEEPST	DEEP-SEATED	
ADDEEEFHNR	FREE-HANDED	
ADDEEEFLOR	FREELOADED	
ADDEEEFNTU	UNDEFEATED	
ADDEEEGNNR	ENDANGERED	
ADDEEEHLRT	ETHELDREDA	
ADDEEEHNNV	EVEN-HANDED	
ADDEEEILNT	DELINEATED	
ADDEEEIRST	DESIDERATE	
ADDEEELNTT	DEAD-NETTLE	
ADDEEELRST	SADDLETREE	
ADDEEELRTT	DEAD LETTER	
ADDEEERSSS	ADDRESSEES	
ADDEEFHLNT	LEFT-HANDED	
ADDEEFHOST	SOFT-HEADED	
ADDEEFILOT	DEFOLIATED	
ADDEEFNNST	DEFENDANTS	
ADDEEGGINS	DISENGAGED	
ADDEEGHILR	HILDEGARDE	
ADDEEGHLNO	LONG-HEADED	
ADDEEGILMS	MIDDLE AGES	
ADDEEGINRR	DEAD RINGER	
ADDEEGINRT	DENIGRATED	
ADDEEGINST	DESIGNATED	
ADDEEGLLNR	GELDERLAND	
ADDEEHHNTU	HEADHUNTED	
ADDEEHLNRU	UNHERALDED	

403

ADDEEHHNNOP	OPEN-HANDED	ADDEHNORSU	ROUNDHEADS
ADDEEIIPSS	DIAPEDESIS	ADDEHORRTY	DEHYDRATOR
ADDEEIKMNW	WEAK-MINDED	ADDEIIILLSV	ILL-ADVISED
ADDEEILMMN	MIDDLE NAME	ADDEIIILMPY	EPIDIDYMAL
ADDEEILMST	MIDDLE EAST	ADDEIIILQTU	LIQUIDATED
ADDEEILNSS	DEADLINESS	ADDEIIINNRS	RED INDIANS
ADDEEILOTV	DOVETAILED	ADDEIIINOTU	AUDITIONED
ADDEEILPSS	DISPLEASED	ADDEIINNRST	DISTRAINED
ADDEEILRSS	SADDLERIES	ADDEIIPSST	DISSIPATED
ADDEEILRSV	DAREDEVILS	ADDEILLNSS	LANDSLIDES
ADDEEILRWY	WIDELY READ	ADDEILLOSW	DISALLOWED
ADDEEIMNRR	MIND READER	ADDEILMNST	DISMANTLED
ADDEEIOPTV	VIDEOTAPED	ADDEILMTTY	ADMITTEDLY
ADDEEIPRSW	WIDESPREAD	ADDEILNNOS	DANDELIONS
ADDEEIPRTU	REPUDIATED	ADDEILNSSY	DEADLY SINS
ADDEEIRSTV	ADVERTISED	ADDEINNOOT	ENDODONTIA
ADDEEIRTTX	EXTRADITED	ADDEINNOPT	ODD-PINNATE
ADDEEJRSTU	READJUSTED	ADDEINNOTU	DENUDATION
ADDEELLMTU	MEDULLATED	ADDEINNRRU	UNDERDRAIN
ADDEELMNOR	ENDODERMAL	ADDEINOORS	RADIOSONDE
ADDEELMOTU	DEMODULATE	ADDEINRSTW	TRADE WINDS
ADDEELOORV	OVERLOADED	ADDELMORRW	DREAM
ADDEELOPRR	ROPE LADDER		WORLD
ADDEELORSS	SADDLE-SORE	ADDELNNORW	WONDERLAND
ADDEELPRST	STEPLADDER	ADDELNNRSU	SUNDERLAND
ADDEEMNNRU	UNDERNAMED	ADDELNOORW	WOODLANDER
ADDEEMNOPR	PROMENADED	ADDELNOPWY	DOWNPLAYED
ADDEENNPST	DEPENDANTS	ADDELPQRUU	QUADRUPLED
ADDEENNTTU	UNATTENDED	ADDENNPRUU	
ADDEENQRSU	SQUANDERED		UP-AND-UNDER
ADDEENRRTU	UNDERRATED	ADDENNRSTU	UNDERSTAND
ADDEENSSWY	WEDNESDAYS	ADDENOORST	DEODORANTS
ADDEEOPRSS	DESPERADOS	ADDEPQRSUU	QUADRUPEDS
ADDEEORSTT	ROAD-TESTED	ADDFGIOORY	GOOD FRIDAY
ADDEFGINRU	DEFRAUDING	ADDFIILNSU	DISDAINFUL
ADDEFHILPS	PADDLEFISH	ADDGIIINNS	DISDAINING
ADDEFHNORU	FOUR-HANDED	ADDGIINSSU	DISSUADING
ADDEFIIMNR	FAIR-MINDED	ADDGILLNWY	WADDLINGLY
ADDEFLLRUY	DREADFULLY	ADDGILNNSU	UNSADDLING
ADDEGGILNN	GLADDENING	ADDGILNRST	STRADDLING
ADDEGHHHIN	HIGH-HANDED	ADDHIILMOS	OLD MAIDISH
ADDEGHLORT	GOLDTHREAD	ADDHILORSU	SHROUD-LAID
ADDEGILLNW	WINDGALLED	ADDIIILNUV	INDIVIDUAL
ADDEGINRSS	ADDRESSING	ADDIIINNOT	IN ADDITION
ADDEGIORRS	DORSIGRADE	ADDILLLLYY	DILLYDALLY
ADDEGLLMOS	GOLD MEDALS	ADDIMNOSUY	DIDYNAMOUS
ADDEGLLOPT	GOLD-PLATED	ADDIMOORSU	DIADROMOUS
ADDEHIIMRS	DIE-HARDISM	ADDNNOOTUW	
ADDEHIJMNU	MUJAHEDDIN		DOWN-AND-OUT
ADDEHILMNS	MISHANDLED	ADEEEEGNRT	DEGENERATE
ADDEHIMNOO	MAIDENHOOD	ADEEEFILRS	FEDERALISE
ADDEHIMNOS	ADMONISHED	ADEEEFILRZ	FEDERALIZE
ADDEHMNNOW		ADEEEFIRTV	FEDERATIVE
	HAND-ME-DOWN	ADEEEFLORR	FREELOADER
		ADEEEFRRRT	FREE-TRADER
ADEEEGGRST	SEGREGATED
ADEEEGLRSV	EVERGLADES
ADEEEGLRTU	DEREGULATE
ADEEEHHPSS	SHEEPSHEAD
ADEEEHLPSY	SLEEPYHEAD
ADEEEHLRTT	LETTERHEAD
ADEEEHNRTT	THREATENED
ADEEEHNSST	HEATEDNESS
ADEEEIPRRT	PIED-A-TERRE
ADEEEIRRTT	REITERATED
ADEEEIRSTT	EASTERTIDE
ADEEELLMNP	EMPANELLED
ADEEELLNRW	WELL-EARNED
ADEEELLRVY	REVEALEDLY
ADEEELNNUV	UNLEAVENED
ADEEELNRUW	LEEUWARDEN
ADEEELNSST	ELATEDNESS
ADEEELPRTY	REPEATEDLY
ADEEEMNNRT	ENDEARMENT
ADEEEMNRTU	ENUMERATED
ADEEEMNRUV	MANEUVERED
ADEEENORTX	EXONERATED
ADEEENPRTT	PENETRATED
ADEEENRRSW	NEWSREADER
ADEEENRSST	EAST ENDERS
ADEEENSSST	SEDATENESS
ADEEENTTUX	EXTENUATED
ADEEFFIMRR	REAFFIRMED
ADEEFFLNRU	FRAUENFELD
ADEEFFORST	AFFORESTED
ADEEFGHIRU	FIGUREHEAD
ADEEFGINRT	FEDERATING
ADEEFGLNNW	NEWFANGLED
ADEEFGLRRS	SELF-REGARD
ADEEFGMNRT	FRAGMENTED
ADEEFHLNRT	LEFT-HANDER
ADEEFHNRTU	UNFATHERED
ADEEFILLNS	SELF-DENIAL
ADEEFILMRS	FEDERALISM
ADEEFILORR	RELIEF ROAD
ADEEFILRST	FEDERALIST
ADEEFIMNST	MANIFESTED
ADEEFINORT	FEDERATION
ADEEFIRSTU	DISFEATURE
ADEEFISSTT	DEFEATISTS
ADEEFLLLNN	FLANNELLED
ADEEFLLORW	FALLOW DEER
ADEEFLRSTU	DEFAULTERS
ADEEFMNORW	FREEDWOMAN
ADEEFNOPRR	FREE PARDON
ADEEFNORRW	FOREWARNED
ADEEFOPRRT	PERFORATED
ADEEGGHLOR	LOGGERHEAD
ADEEGGILNT	DELEGATING

ADEEGGLNOS	GOLDEN AGES
ADEEGGMOSU	DEMAGOGUES
ADEEGGNRSS	RAGGEDNESS
ADEEGGOPSU	PEDAGOGUES
ADEEGGORUW	OWE A GRUDGE
ADEEGIINSS	DIAGENESIS
ADEEGIJLNR	DARJEELING
ADEEGILLST	LEGISLATED
ADEEGILMNR	MALINGERED
ADEEGILNOT	DELEGATION
ADEEGILNRR	RINGLEADER
ADEEGIMNNR	MEANDERING
ADEEGIMNRT	GERMINATED
ADEEGIMNST	MAGNETISED
ADEEGIMNTZ	MAGNETIZED
ADEEGIMNOT	DENEGATION
ADEEGINNRS	GRENADINES, SERENADING
ADEEGINOTT	NEGOTIATED
ADEEGINRRS	GRENADIERS
ADEEGINRRT	INTERGRADE, RETREADING
ADEEGINRTT	INTEGRATED
ADEEGIORTV	DEROGATIVE
ADEEGLLNOS	GOLDENSEAL
ADEEGLLRUW	WELL-ARGUED
ADEEGLMNNO	GOLDEN MEAN
ADEEGLNNNW	NEW ENGLAND
ADEEGLNRUZ	UNDERGLAZE
ADEEGLOPUU	GUADELOUPE
ADEEGLPPRY	DAPPLE-GREY
ADEEGLRRSS	REGARDLESS
ADEEGMNORT	DERMATOGEN
ADEEGNOTXY	OXYGENATED
ADEEGOORSV	OVERDOSAGE
ADEEGOORSW	GREASEWOOD
ADEEGORRRT	RETROGRADE
ADEEGPRTUX	EXPURGATED
ADEEHIIRRW	HEMIHEDRAL
ADEEHHILST	HEAT SHIELD
ADEEHHLOSV	SHOVELHEAD
ADEEHHMNOT	HEATHENDOM
ADEEHHNOPS	HEADPHONES
ADEEHHNORX	HEXAHEDRON
ADEEHHNPTY	HYPHENATED
ADEEHHNRTU	HEADHUNTER
ADEEHIIRRW	WIRE-HAIRED
ADEEHILNOT	ETHANEDIOL
ADEEHILNTU	HEULANDITE
ADEEHILPPR	HARELIPPED
ADEEHILPRS	DEALERSHIP, LEADERSHIP
ADEEHILSWY	DAISY WHEEL
ADEEHIMNSU	DEHUMANISE

ADEEHIMNUZ	DEHUMANIZE
ADEEHIMPSS	EMPHASISED
ADEEHIMPSZ	EMPHASIZED
ADEEHINRST	DISHEARTEN
ADEEHINRTT	THENARDITE
ADEEHIPRRS	READERSHIP
ADEEHIRRSS	SHERARDISE
ADEEHIRRSZ	SHERARDIZE
ADEEHIRRTY	HEREDITARY
ADEEHKORRW	HEADWORKER
ADEEHLLNRT	ENTHRALLED
ADEEHLLNSS	HANDLELESS
ADEEHLNOTW	DOWN-AT-HEEL
ADEEHLORUV	OVERHAULED
ADEEHMNPRU	UNHAMPERED
ADEEHMOSST	HOMESTEADS
ADEEHNNRTU	UNDERNEATH
ADEEHNOSST	HEADSTONES
ADEEHOSSWY	EYE SHADOWS
ADEEHRSSTW	WATERSHEDS
ADEEIIJNRR	JARDINIERE
ADEEIIILMNT	ELIMINATED
ADEEIILNNS	INSIDE LANE
ADEEIILNTV	EVIDENTIAL
ADEEIILRSS	SERIALISED
ADEEIILRSZ	SERIALIZED
ADEEIILSTV	DEVITALISE
ADEEIILTVZ	DEVITALIZE
ADEEIIMTTV	MEDITATIVE
ADEEIINRST	DISTRAINEE
ADEEIINSST	DESSIATINE, EAST INDIES
ADEEIIRTVV	DERIVATIVE
ADEEIJMNRS	RED JASMINE
ADEEIJOPRS	JEOPARDISE
ADEEIJOPRZ	JEOPARDIZE
ADEEIKLLWW	WEAK-WILLED
ADEEIKRSST	ASTERISKED
ADEEILLMNP	IMPANELLED
ADEEILLMRY	REMEDIALLY
ADEEILLPRS	ESPADRILLE
ADEEILLRRU	DERAILLEUR
ADEEILLRTT	ILL-TREATED
ADEEILLUVV	VAUDEVILLE
ADEEILMNPT	PEDIMENTAL
ADEEILMNRT	DERAILMENT
ADEEILMORS	DEMORALISE
ADEEILMORZ	DEMORALIZE
ADEEILMPRR	PERIDERMAL
ADEEILNNRW	NEW IRELAND
ADEEILNORT	DELINEATOR
ADEEILNPRT	INTERPLEAD
ADEEILNRTU	ADULTERINE
ADEEILNTTT	DILETTANTE

ADEEILNTTV	VENTILATED
ADEEILOPRS	DEPOLARISE
ADEEILOPRZ	DEPOLARIZE
ADEEILPRRV	PEARL DIVER
ADEEIMMORT	IMMODERATE
ADEEIMMUVW	MEDIUM WAVE
ADEEIMNNOT	DENOMINATE, EMENDATION
ADEEIMNNTT	DETAINMENT
ADEEIMNNRS	REMAINDERS
ADEEIMNRSS	DREAMINESS
ADEEIMNRTT	TERMINATED
ADEEIMORRT	RADIOMETER
ADEEIMORTU	AUDIOMETER
ADEEIMOTTV	DEMOTIVATE
ADEEIMPPRS	PIPE DREAMS
ADEEINORTT	ORIENTATED
ADEEINOTTV	DENOTATIVE, DETONATIVE
ADEEINPPSX	APPENDIXES
ADEEINPRST	PEDANTRIES, PEDESTRIAN
ADEEINRRSS	DREARINESS
ADEEINRRST	RESTRAINED
ADEEINRSSV	VARIEDNESS
ADEEINRSTT	REINSTATED, STRAITENED
ADEEINRTTT	TRIDENTATE
ADEEINSSST	STEADINESS
ADEEINSSTT	EISENSTADT
ADEEIOPRSX	PEROXIDASE
ADEEIOSXYY	OXEYE DAISY
ADEEIPRSTT	TAPESTRIED
ADEEIPRTTX	EXTIRPATED
ADEEIPRTUV	DEPURATIVE
ADEEIRRSTV	ADVERTISER
ADEEJRRSTU	READJUSTER
ADEEKMNRSS	MARKEDNESS
ADEEKMRRSS	DRESSMAKER
ADEEKNNRTU	UNDERTAKEN
ADEEKNRRTU	UNDERTAKER
ADEELLNQUU	UNEQUALLED
ADEELLNRUV	UNRAVELLED
ADEELLOPRY	ROLE-PLAYED
ADEELLOPST	SELLOTAPED
ADEELLORSS	LOSS LEADER
ADEELLOSTY	DESOLATELY
ADEELLQRRU	QUARRELLED
ADEELMMORS	MESODERMAL
ADEELMNORT	ENTODERMAL
ADEELMNPUX	UNEXAMPLED
ADEELMORTY	MODERATELY
ADEELMRSUY	MEASUREDLY
ADEELNNQSU	QUEENSLAND

ADEELNOSSY	SEASONEDLY	
ADEELNRRSS	SLANDERERS	
ADEELNRUUV	UNDERVALUE	
ADEELOPPRV	OVERLAPPED	
ADEELOPPTU	DEPOPULATE	
ADEELOPRSS	LEOPARDESS	
ADEELOPRVY	OVERPLAYED	
ADEELPPRRY	PREPAREDLY	
ADEELPRSTT	SPLATTERED	
ADEELRRSTU	ADULTERERS	
ADEELRSSTU	ADULTERESS	
ADEEMMNNRT	REMANDMENT	
ADEEMMNNST	AMENDMENTS	
ADEEMNNNRU	UNMANNERED	
ADEEMNNORT	ORNAMENTED	
ADEEMNNORV	OVERMANNED	
ADEEMNOPRR	PROMENADER	
ADEEMNOPRS	PROMENADES	
ADEEMNORSU	DEMEANOURS	
ADEEMNORTY	EMENDATORY	
ADEEMNORUV	MANOEUVRED	
ADEEMNORYY	READY MONEY	
ADEEMNPRTT	DEPARTMENT	
ADEEMNRSUU	UNMEASURED	
ADEEMOORRS	AERODROMES	
ADEEMOOSTU	OEDEMATOUS	
ADEENNOSSU	UNSEASONED	
ADEENNPTTU	UNPATENTED	
ADEENOPRTV	PONTEVEDRA	
ADEENORSUV	ENDEAVOURS	
ADEENPPRRU	UNPREPARED	
ADEENPRRTU	ENRAPTURED	
ADEENPRSST	DEPRESSANT	
ADEENPRSTY	PRESENT-DAY	
ADEENQRRSU	SQUANDERER	
ADEENRRTUV	ADVENTURER	
ADEENRRTUW	UNDERWATER	
ADEENRSTTU	UNDERSTATE	
ADEENRSTUV	ADVENTURES	
ADEEOPPRRR	ORDER PAPER	
ADEEOPRRSV	OVERSPREAD	
ADEEORRTTU	TRADE ROUTE	
ADEEORSTTV	OVERSTATED	
ADEEORSTVY	OVERSTAYED	
ADEEPPRSST	SPEED TRAPS	
ADEEPRRSTU	DEPARTURES	
ADEEPRSSST	TRESPASSED	
ADEERRSTYY	STARRY-EYED	
ADEERSSSTW	STEWARDESS	
ADEERSSTYY	YESTERDAYS	
ADEFFGGGIR	GAFF-RIGGED	
ADEFFLOOTT	FLAT-FOOTED	
ADEFGGINOR	GOD-FEARING	
ADEFGHIRST	FARSIGHTED	

ADEFGHORST	GODFATHERS	
ADEFGIILNN	ENFILADING	
ADEFGIINOR	FOREIGN AID	
ADEFGILNTU	DEFAULTING	
ADEFGILRSU	LIFEGUARDS	
ADEFGILRTZ	FITZGERALD	
ADEFGIRRSU	FIREGUARDS	
ADEFGLOOST	FLOODGATES	
ADEFGNOORR	ROOF GARDEN	
ADEFHHLOOT	HEALTH FOOD	
ADEFHHOORT	FATHERHOOD	
ADEFHILMSS	DAMSELFISH	
ADEFHILTTW	HALF-WITTED	
ADEFHINPRT	PATHFINDER	
ADEFHIRTWW	WHITE DWARF	
ADEFHLOOSS	FALSEHOODS	
ADEFHOORSW	FORESHADOW	
ADEFIILPSS	FISSIPEDAL	
ADEFIINQTU	QUANTIFIED	
ADEFIINRTU	INFURIATED	
ADEFIIRSTT	STRATIFIED	
ADEFIJORUZ	JUIZ DE FORA	
ADEFILLLSU	FULL-SAILED	
ADEFILLNTY	INFLATEDLY	
ADEFILLSSU	FUSILLADES	
ADEFILMNOR	MANIFOLDER	
ADEFILMNTU	FULMINATED	
ADEFILMORS	FORMALISED	
ADEFILMORZ	FORMALIZED	
ADEFILNOST	DEFOLIANTS	
ADEFILOORT	DEFOLIATOR	
ADEFILORTU	FLUORIDATE	
ADEFIMRRRT	DIRT FARMER	
ADEFINOORR	FOREORDAIN	
ADEFINORSS	SANFORISED	
ADEFINORSZ	SANFORIZED	
ADEFINRSTX	TRANSFIXED	
ADEFIRSSTX	FIXED STARS	
ADEFKLNOTU	OUTFLANKED	
ADEFLMORTU	FORMULATED	
ADEFLNRTUU	FRAUDULENT	
ADEFNOORRW	FOR A WONDER	
ADEFOOPSST	SOFT-SOAPED	
ADEFORRSTV	OVERDRAFTS	
ADEFRRSTTU	FRUSTRATED	
ADEGGHOSTU	SHAGGED OUT	
ADEGGIMOPS	PEDAGOGISM	
ADEGGINORT	DEROGATING	
ADEGGINSUW	WIND GAUGES	
ADEGGNOPTU	GET-UP-AND-GO	
ADEGHHIKNT	KNIGHTHEAD	
ADEGHHILNR	HIGHLANDER	
ADEGHHILST	HEADLIGHTS	

ADEGHHINST	NIGHTSHADE	
ADEGHIILNN	HEADLINING	
ADEGHILLNO	HELIGOLAND	
ADEGHILNOO	HALOGENOID	
ADEGHILNOR	LONGHAIRED	
ADEGHILNSU	LANGUISHED	
ADEGHINPRS	HEADSPRING, SPRINGHEAD
ADEGHIOPRY	IDEOGRAPHY	
ADEGHLORSS	GASHOLDERS	
ADEGHLRTUY	DAUGHTERLY	
ADEGHMOPRY	DEMOGRAPHY	
ADEGHMORSU	HOME GUARDS
ADEGHNORST	HEADSTRONG	
ADEGHORSUU	GUARDHOUSE	
ADEGIIILNZ	IDEALIZING	
ADEGIIILST	DIGITALISE	
ADEGIIILTZ	DIGITALIZE	
ADEGIILMNS	MISLEADING	
ADEGIILNOT	GADOLINITE, GELATINOID
ADEGIILNPR	LIP-READING	
ADEGIILNRT	RING-TAILED	
ADEGIILNSS	SIGNALISED	
ADEGIILNSZ	SIGNALIZED	
ADEGIIMMRT	IMMIGRATED	
ADEGIIMNRS	MISREADING	
ADEGIIMNTT	MEDITATING	
ADEGIINNRT	DETRAINING	
ADEGIINORT	ORIGINATED	
ADEGIINPRS	DESPAIRING	
ADEGIINSTT	INSTIGATED	
ADEGIIOPRR	PRAIRIE DOG	
ADEGILMNRY	DREAMINGLY	
ADEGILMORS	GLAMORISED	
ADEGILMORZ	GLAMORIZED	
ADEGILNNNO	NONALIGNED	
ADEGILNNNT	LANDING NET	
ADEGILNNRS	SANDERLING, SLANDERING
ADEGILNNRU	LAUNDERING	
ADEGILNOST	DESOLATING	
ADEGILNOTT	GLOTTIDEAN	
ADEGILNRUV	GERUNDIVAL	
ADEGILOOPS	APOLOGISED	
ADEGILOOPZ	APOLOGIZED	
ADEGILRSUV	VULGARISED	
ADEGILRUVZ	VULGARIZED	
ADEGIMNNRU	MAUNDERING	
ADEGIMNOPU	IMPOUNDAGE	
ADEGIMNORS	GORMANDISE	
ADEGIMNORT	MODERATING	
ADEGIMNORZ	GORMANDIZE	
ADEGIMNPST	STAMPEDING	

ADEGIMNSTU	MAGNITUDES
ADEGIMORST	DOGMATISER
ADEGIMORTZ	DOGMATIZER
ADEGINNOTT	DETONATING
ADEGINNRSW	WANDERINGS
ADEGINOORT	DEROGATION
ADEGINORRS	GARRISONED
ADEGINORRT	DENIGRATOR
ADEGINORST	DESIGNATOR
ADEGINPRSU	PERSUADING
ADEGIPRRST	PARTRIDGES
ADEGJLMNTU	JUDGMENTAL
ADEGKNRRRU	KRUGERRAND
ADEGLNORSU	GLANDEROUS
ADEGMMOPRR	PROGRAMMED
ADEGMNOOSU	ENDOGAMOUS
ADEGNOOORW	ORANGEWOOD
ADEGNOPRST	GODPARENTS
ADEGNORSSU	SANDGROUSE
ADEGOORRTY	DEROGATORY
ADEGOORSST	STAGE DOORS
ADEHHIIPRT	DIPHTHERIA
ADEHHIRSSW	DISHWASHER
ADEHHLLOOR	HOLOHEDRAL
ADEHIILMTU	HUMILIATED
ADEHIILNPR	NEPHRIDIAL
ADEHIILRSS	HAIR SLIDES
ADEHIINOPR	HEPARINOID
ADEHIILNOPS	SPHENOIDAL
ADEHIILNRRS	HARD-LINERS
ADEHIILNRST	DISENTHRAL
ADEHIILOPRS	SPHEROIDAL
ADEHIILPSTU	DISULPHATE
ADEHIMNORS	ADMONISHER, HARMONISED
ADEHIMNORZ	HARMONIZED
ADEHIMORTU	RHEUMATOID
ADEHIMOSSU	HOUSEMAIDS
ADEHINOSST	ASTONISHED
ADEHINQSUV	VANQUISHED
ADEHINRSTY	HYDRASTINE
ADEHIOPRSS	RHAPSODIES, RHAPSODISE
ADEHIOPRSZ	RHAPSODIZE
ADEHIORSTU	AUTHORISED
ADEHIORTUZ	AUTHORIZED
ADEHIOSSTW	SHADOWIEST
ADEHIRRTTY	TRIHYDRATE
ADEHIRRTWW	WITHDRAWER
ADEHJMPRSU	JAMSHEDPUR

ADEHKNORRW	WORK-HARDEN
ADEHKNORST	HANDSTROKE
ADEHKNOSSW	SHAKEDOWNS
ADEHKORRSS	DARK HORSES
ADEHLLNOUW	UNHALLOWED
ADEHLLOPRY	POLYHEDRAL
ADEHLLOSTT	DEATH TOLLS
ADEHLMNOSY	HANDSOMELY
ADEHLMOPTY	METHYLDOPA
ADEHLNRSTU	SUTHERLAND
ADEHLRTTWY	THWARTEDLY
ADEHMNNOSU	UNHANDSOME
ADEHMOORST	MASTERHOOD
ADEHMORRTW	THREADWORM
ADEHMORSTY	MOTHER'S DAY
ADEHNOOPRT	PARENTHOOD, THEROPODAN
ADEHOORSSU	ROADHOUSES
ADEHOORSVW	OVERSHADOW
ADEHORRSSW	SHOREWARDS
ADEIIIKNSS	DIAKINESIS
ADEIIIILLNT	INITIALLED
ADEIIIMNTT	INTIMIDATE
ADEIILLMPX	MAXILLIPED
ADEIILLSTT	DISTILLATE
ADEIILLTTT	TITILLATED
ADEIILMMTU	MULTIMEDIA
ADEIILMNOR	MERIDIONAL
ADEIILMPPS	MISAPPLIED
ADEIILNOPT	DEPILATION
ADEIILNRTT	INTERTIDAL
ADEIILNTTT	DILETTANTI
ADEIILORST	EDITORIALS, IDOLATRISE
ADEIILORTZ	IDOLATRIZE
ADEIILSSUV	VISUALISED
ADEIILSUVZ	VISUALIZED
ADEIIMNOTT	MEDITATION
ADEIIMNOTV	DOMINATIVE
ADEIIMNRST	ADMINISTER
ADEIIMPRSU	PRAESIDIUM
ADEIIMRSTT	DERMATITIS
ADEIINNNOS	INDONESIAN
ADEIINNORT	INORDINATE
ADEIINNOTW	NATIONWIDE
ADEIINNOTX	INDEXATION
ADEIINNPPT	PINNATIPED
ADEIINNSST	DAINTINESS, SAINT-DENIS
ADEIINNSTU	INSINUATED
ADEIINNSTW	WEST INDIAN
ADEIINORTV	DERIVATION
ADEIINOSTV	DEVIATIONS

ADEIINPPRS	DRAINPIPES
ADEIINPTTU	INAPTITUDE
ADEIIPRRSS	DISPRAISER
ADEIIPRSST	DISSIPATER
ADEIIPRSTV	PRIVATISED
ADEIIPRTVZ	PRIVATIZED
ADEIISSSUV	DISSUASIVE
ADEIJMMNRW	WINDJAMMER
ADEIKLLLRY	LADY-KILLER
ADEIKLLMMT	MALTED MILK
ADEIKNPPRS	KIDNAPPERS
ADEILLMNOS	MEDALLIONS
ADEILLMRST	TREADMILLS
ADEILLMSST	MEDALLISTS
ADEILLMSTW	WILLEMSTAD
ADEILLNOOS	SOLENOIDAL
ADEILLNOPT	POLLINATED
ADEILLNOSU	DELUSIONAL
ADEILLNPSS	PALLIDNESS
ADEILLNRRT	TENDRILLAR
ADEILLNRTU	ILL-NATURED
ADEILLNRUV	UNRIVALLED
ADEILLQRSU	QUADRILLES
ADEILLRRST	ILL-STARRED
ADEILMNOPR	PALINDROME
ADEILMNORS	NORMALISED
ADEILMNORZ	NORMALIZED
ADEILMNRST	DISMANTLER
ADEILMNSSS	DISMALNESS
ADEILMOTUV	MODULATIVE
ADEILMSTTU	STIMULATED
ADEILNNORT	INTERNODAL
ADEILNOOST	DESOLATION
ADEILNOOTV	DEVOTIONAL
ADEILNPRTU	PRUDENTIAL
ADEILNSSSW	WINDLASSES
ADEILNSTTU	TESTUDINAL
ADEILNSTUY	UNSTEADILY
ADEILOORST	OESTRADIOL
ADEILOPRTT	TETRAPLOID
ADEILOPRTY	DEPILATORY
ADEILOPSSU	DISEPALOUS
ADEILOPSTU	DIPETALOUS
ADEILOQSSU	ODALISQUES
ADEILORTUV	OUTRIVALED
ADEILOSSTT	SOLID-STATE
ADEILPSTTU	PLATITUDES, STIPULATED
ADEILRSTTU	STRIDULATE
ADEILRTTXY	DEXTRALITY
ADEILRTUUX	LUXURIATED
ADEIMMNRST	MASTERMIND
ADEIMMRSSU	SUMMARISED
ADEIMMRSUZ	SUMMARIZED

ADEIMNNOORT	MODERATION	ADELOOPRST	DOORPLATES	ADGHIILNOY	HOLIDAYING
ADEIMNPRRS	REPRIMANDS	ADELOPSTTU	POSTULATED	ADGHILLLSU	GUILDHALLS
ADEIMNRRTT	MITTERRAND	ADELORRWWY		ADGHIMNOPP	HOPPING MAD
ADEIMNRSSU	NURSEMAIDS	WORLD-WEARY		ADGHINNPRS	HANDSPRING
ADEIMORRTY	RADIOMETRY	ADELORSTUU	ADULTEROUS	ADGHIRRSTW	RIGHTWARDS
ADEIMORSST	DERMATOSIS	ADELPQRTUU	QUADRUPLET	ADGHIRSTTU	DISTRAUGHT
ADEIMORTUY	AUDIOMETRY	ADELPQRUUX	QUADRUPLEX	ADGHLPRSUU	SULPHA DRUG
ADEIMRSTUX	ADMIXTURES	ADEMMMNORU		ADGIIILMST	DIGITALISM
ADEINNOOTT	DENOTATION,	MEMORANDUM		ADGIIILNNV	INVALIDING
DETONATION		ADEMMOOSTU	STOMODAEUM	ADGIIIMNOR	MIGRAINOID
ADEINNOPWW	WINDOWPANE	ADEMNNORSS	RANDOMNESS	ADGIIINOTT	DIGITATION
ADEINNORSW	RAWINSONDE	ADEMNNORST	ADORNMENTS	ADGIIKNNPP	KIDNAPPING
ADEINNORTU	TRADE UNION	ADEMNORSTW	DOWNSTREAM	ADGIILMNOU	GADOLINIUM
ADEINNRSSU	UNSTRAINED	ADEMNRRSSU	SNARE DRUMS	ADGIILMNRY	ADMIRINGLY
ADEINNRSTY	TYRANNISED	ADEMNRSTTU	TRANSMUTED	ADGIILNPSY	DISPLAYING
ADEINNRTYZ	TYRANNIZED	ADEMOORRST	MODERATORS	ADGIIMNNOT	DOMINATING
ADEINOPRST	PATRONISED	ADEMOQRTUY	DEMY	ADGIIMNNTY	DYNAMITING
ADEINOPRTU	DEPURATION	QUARTO		ADGIIMNPRS	RISING DAMP
ADEINOPRTZ	PATRONIZED	ADEMORSTTU	OUTSMARTED	ADGIIMNSST	DISMASTING
ADEINOPTTU	DEPUTATION	ADENNORRRU	ROADRUNNER	ADGIINNNTU	INUNDATING
ADEINORSST	ADROITNESS	ADENNPRSTU	UNDERPANTS	ADGIINNPRW	DRAWING PIN
ADEINORSUV	ADENOVIRUS	ADENNRRSSU	RUN ERRANDS	ADGIINOSVW	DISAVOWING
ADEINOSTVY	VIDEO NASTY	ADENNSSSTW	NEWSSTANDS	ADGIJNNORU	ADJOURNING
ADEINPPRRS	SANDPIPERS	ADENOORSTT	DETONATORS	ADGIKNORWY	WORKING DAY
ADEINPPSST	STANDPIPES	ADENOPRSST	TRANSPOSED	ADGIKOORRV	KIROVOGRAD
ADEINPRRST	TRANSPIRED	ADENOPRSTV	VAN DER POST	ADGILLNOPR	POLLARDING
ADEINPRSSY	DISPENSARY	ADENPRSSUW	UPWARDNESS	ADGILLLOPRY	PRODIGALLY
ADEINRSSTW	TAWDRINESS	ADENRRSSTW	STERNWARDS	ADGILMNOTU	MODULATING
ADEINRSTTU	UNSTRIATED	ADENRRSUYY	DAY NURSERY	ADGILNNORT	DARLINGTON
ADEINSSSTU	UNASSISTED	ADEOPRRSTT	PROSTRATED	ADGILNNTUU	UNDULATING
ADEIOPPRSV	DISAPPROVE	ADEORRSSWW	SWEARWORDS	ADGILNOOPW	WADING POOL
ADEIOPRRTU	REPUDIATOR	ADEPPRSTUU	SUPPURATED	ADGILNOSTT	INGOLSTADT
ADEIOPRSTY	DEPOSITARY	ADFFGILNOO	OFF-LOADING	ADGIMOSSTT	DOGMATISTS
ADEIOPRSTZ	TRAPEZOIDS	ADFGIILRRY	GIRL FRIDAY	ADGINNOSTU	ASTOUNDING
ADEIPPRRTY	DAY-TRIPPER	ADFGINORRU	FAIRGROUND	ADGINNPSTU	UPSTANDING
ADEJMNSTTU	ADJUSTMENT	ADFGINORRW	FORWARDING	ADGINOPSTT	POSTDATING
ADEJOPSTUX	JUXTAPOSED	ADFHILLORS	DOLLARFISH	ADGINPRRSX	GRANDS PRIX
ADEKMNORTW		ADFHINNORU	FOUR-IN-HAND	ADGINRRSTW	DRAWSTRING
DOWN-MARKET		ADFHNOORST	AND SO FORTH	ADGIORSSWW	GRASS WIDOW
ADEKMOPRST	POSTMARKED	ADFIIINNPT	PINNATIFID	ADGLMNOOOY	
ADEKNOPRST	POND-SKATER	ADFIIKMNRU	FAIR DINKUM	MONADOLOGY	
ADEKNRRSSS	DRESS RANKS	ADFIILMRSU	DISULFIRAM	ADGLNNOPRU	GROUND PLAN
ADELLLPTUU	PULLULATED	ADFIILQSUY	DISQUALIFY	ADGLNOPRUY	PLAYGROUND
ADELLNORRU	ALL-ROUNDER	ADFIIOSSTU	FASTIDIOUS	ADGMNNORSU	GROUNDSMAN
ADELLNORSW	LOWLANDERS	ADFIISSSTY	DISSATISFY	ADGMNORSSU	GROUNDMASS
ADELLOORRR	ROAD ROLLER	ADFINNOOTU	FOUNDATION	ADGMOORRSU	GUARDROOMS
ADELLOORRU	EURODOLLAR	ADFLMNTUUU	MUTUAL FUND	ADGNNORSUY	GYNANDROUS
ADELMOPSTU	DEUTOPLASM	ADFMOOPSST	FOOD STAMPS	ADGNOOORRT	DRAGONROOT
ADELMORSST	OLD MASTERS	ADFNOORTUY	FOUDROYANT	ADHHNOSTTU	THOUSANDTH
ADELNOOSST	LOADSTONES	ADFNOPRSTU	STAND UP FOR	ADHIIKKNNT	KITH AND KIN
ADELNORRSV	LAND ROVERS	ADFNORRSTW	FRONTWARDS	ADHIILMNOT	MIDLOTHIAN
ADELNORSSU	SLANDEROUS	ADGGIINNOS	DIAGNOSING	ADHIIMMNPS	MIDSHIPMAN
ADELNPPSTU	SUPPLANTED	ADGGINNOOR	DRAGOONING	ADHIIMNSST	HIT-AND-MISS
ADELNRSTUW	WANDERLUST	ADGGINNORU	GAIN GROUND	ADHIIMSTTU	HUMIDISTAT
		ADGHHOPRRY	HYDROGRAPH		

ADHIINNSTU	HINDUSTANI
ADHIIPRTTY	HIT PAY DIRT
ADHILLLOPY	PHYLLODIAL
ADHILLNOSY	HOLY ISLAND
ADHILNOSTU	OUTLANDISH
ADHILOOPRS	DROSOPHILA
ADHILOQRRU	HARD LIQUOR
ADHIMNORSY	DISHARMONY
ADHINNOOOT	NATIONHOOD
ADHINOOPRT	ANTHROPOID
ADHINOOPRY	RADIOPHONY
ADHINOOPRZ	RHIZOPODAN
ADHINOSSWW	SASH
	WINDOW
ADHIOPRSST	RHAPSODIST
ADHIPRRTTY	THIRD PARTY
ADHLNOPSSW	SPLASHDOWN
ADHNORRSTW	NORTHWARDS
ADHNORSTWW	
	WANDSWORTH
ADHOORRTWY	ROADWORTHY
ADHORSSTUW	SOUTHWARDS
ADIIILMNSV	INVALIDISM
ADIIILMRSS	DISSIMILAR
ADIIILNOSV	DIVISIONAL
ADIIILNTVY	INVALIDITY
ADIIINNOTV	DIVINATION
ADIIINOOST	IODISATION
ADIIINOOTZ	IODIZATION
ADIILMMNSU	MAUDLINISM
ADIILMNOXY	MIXOLYDIAN
ADIILMOPRR	PRIMORDIAL
ADIILMOPRS	PRISMOIDAL
ADIILMSSSS	DISMISSALS
ADIILNORRY	ORDINARILY
ADIILNOSSU	SINUSOIDAL
ADIILNRSTU	INDUSTRIAL
ADIILOPPSY	POLYDIPSIA
ADIILOQRTU	LIQUIDATOR
ADIILORSSY	RADIOLYSIS
ADIILORSTY	SOLIDARITY
ADIILQSTUY	SQUALIDITY
ADIIMMMOTU	OMMATIDIUM
ADIIMNNNOO	ANNO DOMINI
ADIIMNNOOT	ADMONITION,
	DOMINATION
ADIIMNNORV	MORDVINIAN
ADIIMNOSSS	ADMISSIONS
ADIIMOPRST	DIATROPISM,
	PRISMATOID
ADIIMORTUU	AUDITORIUM
ADIINNNOTU	INUNDATION
ADIINNOORT	ORDINATION
ADIINOPPST	DISAPPOINT
ADIINOPSSS	DISPASSION

ADIINORRST	DISTRAINOR
ADIINORSTT	TRADITIONS
ADIINORTVY	DIVINATORY
ADIINOSSSU	DISSUASION
ADIIOPRSTT	PODIATRIST
ADILLLOSYY	DISLOYALLY
ADILLNSSTT	STANDSTILL
ADILLOSTYY	DISLOYALTY
ADILMMOPSU	PLASMODIUM
ADILMNOOOP	MONOPODIAL
ADILMNOOTU	MODULATION
ADILMOPSST	PSALMODIST
ADILNNOTUU	UNDULATION
ADILOORSTU	IDOLATROUS
ADIMNOORTY	ADMONITORY
ADIMNRRTUV	TRIVANDRUM
ADINNOPSTT	STANDPOINT
ADINNOSSTU	INS AND OUTS
ADINOOPRST	ADSORPTION
ADINOOSSTW	SATINWOODS
ADINORSSTW	DOWNSTAIRS
ADIORSSSTU	DISASTROUS
ADJLOPRTUU	PLAT DU JOUR
ADJMMOOORS	
	MAJOR-DOMOS
ADJMMORRSU	DRUM MAJORS
ADKNORRSTU	TRUNK ROADS
ADLMOOORSU	MALODOROUS
ADLNORSTUU	ULTRASOUND
ADLNORTUUY	UNDULATORY
ADLNORTUWY	UNTOWARDLY
ADLOOOSSTT	TOADSTOOLS
ADMNNOORSU	MONANDROUS
ADMNORSSST	SANDSTORMS
ADMOOOPSTT	STOMATOPOD
ADNNORRTUU	TURNAROUND
AEEEEGKMPR	GAMEKEEPER
AEEEEGKPRT	GATEKEEPER
AEEEEGLNRSS	SENEGALESE
AEEEEGNRRT	REGENERATE
AEEEEGRTTV	REVEGETATE
AEEEELNOPT	ELAEOPTENE
AEEEENRTTX	EXENTERATE
AEEEESTTTT	TETE-A-TETES
AEEEFFIMNT	EFFEMINATE
AEEEFGLNRU	ENFLEURAGE
AEEEFGNRST	FREE AGENTS
AEEEFHLSTT	FALSE TEETH
AEEEFHRRTT	THEREAFTER
AEEEFINRTZ	ANTIFREEZE
AEEEFIRRST	FIRE-EATERS
AEEEFLLNST	FENESTELLA
AEEEFLMNSS	FEMALENESS
AEEEFNRRST	TRANSFEREE

AEEEFPRSSS	FREE PASSES
AEEEGGGNRS	GREENGAGES
AEEEGGMNNT	ENGAGEMENT
AEEEGGRSST	EASTER EGGS
AEEEGHLPRT	TELPHERAGE
AEEEGHNRRT	GREENHEART
AEEEGILNNV	EVANGELINE
AEEEGILNRS	GENERALISE
AEEEGILNRZ	GENERALIZE
AEEEGILNSV	EVANGELISE
AEEEGILNVZ	EVANGELIZE
AEEEGIMNRS	MENAGERIES
AEEEGINNOR	AERO-ENGINE
AEEEGINRTV	GENERATIVE
AEEEGITTVV	VEGETATIVE
AEEEGKLOPR	GOALKEEPER
AEEEGLMNRT	REGALEMENT
AEEEGLNNOR	GREEN ANOLE
AEEEGLNOST	EAGLESTONE
AEEEGLRRSV	GEAR LEVERS
AEEEGLSSSY	EYEGLASSES
AEEEGMNNRT	ENRAGEMENT
AEEEGMNRSS	MEAGRENESS
AEEEGMNRST	AGREEMENTS
AEEEGNPPRR	GREEN PAPER
AEEEGPRSSX	EXPRESSAGE
AEEEGQOSTU	SQUETEAGUE
AEEEGRSTTZ	GAZETTEERS
AEEEHHINST	HEATHENISE
AEEEHHINTZ	HEATHENIZE
AEEEHHPRST	THREE-PHASE
AEEEHLLRTY	ETHEREALLY
AEEEHLRTWW	WATERWHEEL
AEEEHMNORX	HEXAEMERON
AEEEHMNRTW	WEATHERMEN
AEEEHNORTY	HONEY-EATER
AEEEHNRRTT	THREATENER
AEEEHOPRRS	AEROSPHERE
AEEEHRSTTW	SWEETHEART
AEEEIIPPRT	PERIPETEIA
AEEEILNRST	ETERNALISE
AEEEILNRTV	INTERLEAVE
AEEEILNRTZ	ETERNALIZE
AEEEIMNRRX	RE-EXAMINER
AEEEIMNSTV	VIETNAMESE
AEEEIMPRTV	PERMEATIVE
AEEEINRSTT	ENTREATIES
AEEEINRTTV	INVETERATE
AEEEINRTVV	ENERVATIVE
AEEEINRTVW	INTERWEAVE

AEEEJKRRRT	TEARJERKER	
AEEEJNRTUV	REJUVENATE	
AEEEKKPPRR	PARK KEEPER	
AEEEKMRRST	MARKETEERS	
AEEEKNSSSW	WEAKNESSES	
AEEEKPSSTW	SWEEPSTAKE	
AEEELLRTVW	WATER LEVEL	
AEEELLSSTT	TESSELLATE	
AEEELMMNPT	EMPALEMENT	
AEEELMMNRT	EMMENTALER	
AEEELMNNTT	LENTAMENTE,	
TENEMENTAL		
AEEELMNRTT	MANTELTREE	
AEEELMNRTV	REVEALMENT	
AEEELMNRTY	ELEMENTARY	
AEEELNNUVZ	VENEZUELAN	
AEEELNPRST	PLANE TREES	
AEEEMMNORT	ANEMOMETER	
AEEEMNOPSS	OPEN SESAME	
AEEEMNPRTT	PENTAMETER	
AEEEMNRRTU	REMUNERATE	
AEEEMSSTTW	SWEETMEATS	
AEEENNNSST	TENNESSEAN	
AEEENRRSST	EASTERNERS	
AEEEPPRRTT	PERPETRATE	
AEEEPPRTTU	PERPETUATE	
AEEERRSTYY	YESTERYEAR	
AEEERSSTTY	EASY STREET	
AEEFFHORRT	FOREFATHER	
AEEFFLLORR	FREE-FOR-ALL	
AEEFFORRST	REAFFOREST	
AEEFFSSTUY	SAFETY FUSE	
AEEFGGHIRT	FREIGHTAGE	
AEEFGHINRT	FEATHERING	
AEEFGHORRT	FOREGATHER	
AEEFGIINRT	FIRE-EATING	
AEEFGILLNT	LEAFLETING	
AEEFGILNRR	RIFLE RANGE	
AEEFGILPRS	PERSIFLAGE	
AEEFGLPRSU	PRESAGEFUL	
AEEFGORRRU	FOURRAGERE	
AEEFHHINRT	FAHRENHEIT	
AEEFHIKLRT	FATHER-LIKE	
AEEFHIKNST	SNEAK THIEF	
AEEFHINPRT	PINFEATHER	
AEEFHLOPPR	LEAF-HOPPER	
AEEFHLRSST	FATHERLESS	
AEEFHMMRST	HAMMERFEST	
AEEFHMORTT	FATHOMETER	
AEEFHOSSSU	SAFE HOUSES	
AEEFHPRSTT	STEPFATHER	
AEEFHRRSTW	FRESHWATER	
AEEFIIRRRS	FIRE-RAISER	
AEEFIKNPPR	PAPER KNIFE	

AEEFIKNRSS	FREAKINESS	
AEEFILMPRS	RELIEF MAPS	
AEEFILMRTY	FAMILY TREE	
AEEFILOPRT	PERFOLIATE	
AEEFILRSTV	AFTERLIVES	
AEEFIMNRRT	FREEMARTIN	
AEEFINRRST	FRATERNISE	
AEEFINRRTZ	FRATERNIZE	
AEEFLLNNOT	FONTANELLE	
AEEFLLNRUY	FUNEREALLY	
AEEFLLRSSY	FEARLESSLY	
AEEFLMOPRX	FOR EXAMPLE	
AEEFLRRSTT	FLATTERERS	
AEEFMNORSS	FREEMASONS	
AEEFNORRRW	FOREWARNER	
AEEFNSSSST	FASTNESSES	
AEEFNSSTTY	SAFETY NETS	
AEEFORRRSW	FORSWEARER	
AEEGGHILRT	LIGHTERAGE	
AEEGGHOPRR	GEOGRAPHER	
AEEGGILNRS	GINGER ALES	
AEEGGILNRT	RELEGATING	
AEEGGINNRT	GENERATING	
AEEGGINRRS	GRANGERISE	
AEEGGINRRZ	GRANGERIZE	
AEEGGINTTV	VEGETATING	
AEEGGIRSSV	AGGRESSIVE	
AEEGGMORST	MORTGAGEES	
AEEGGNNRTU	TERENGGANU	
AEEGGNRSSU	GREASE GUNS	
AEEGGORRST	SEGREGATOR	
AEEGGRRSSW	SWAGGERERS	
AEEGHHMORR	HEMORRHAGE	
AEEGHIILMP	HEMIPLEGIA	
AEEGHIKMTW	MAKEWEIGHT	
AEEGHIKNNR	HEARKENING	
AEEGHILNSS	SINGHALESE	
AEEGHILPST	LEGATESHIP	
AEEGHIMRST	HERMITAGES	
AEEGHINNRT	HEARTENING	
AEEGHINPRT	PREHEATING	
AEEGHINRRS	REHEARSING	
AEEGHINRTW	WEATHERING	
AEEGHIPPRR	EPIGRAPHER	
AEEGHKNNRS	GREENSHANK	
AEEGHLMORT	GEOTHERMAL	
AEEGHLNTVW	WAVELENGTH	
AEEGHLORTT	ALTOGETHER	
AEEGHLPRST	TELEGRAPHS	
AEEGHLPRTY	TELEGRAPHY	
AEEGHMNOOT	HOMOGENATE	
AEEGHMNOPS	MEGAPHONES	
AEEGHMORTY	HETEROGAMY	
AEEGHOSSTU	GATEHOUSES	

AEEGIILLLS	ILLEGALISE	
AEEGIILLLZ	ILLEGALIZE	
AEEGIILMTT	LEGITIMATE	
AEEGIILNST	GELATINISE	
AEEGIILNTZ	GELATINIZE	
AEEGIIMRTV	EMIGRATIVE	
AEEGIINRRT	GARNIERITE	
AEEGILLMNN	ENAMELLING	
AEEGILLORS	ALLEGORIES,	
ALLEGORISE		
AEEGILLORZ	ALLEGORIZE	
AEEGILMNNP	EMPANELING	
AEEGILMNRR	MALINGERER	
AEEGILMNRT	REGIMENTAL	
AEEGILMNSV	EVANGELISM	
AEEGILNNSV	LEAVENINGS	
AEEGILNORT	REGELATION,	
RELEGATION		
AEEGILNOTV	ELONGATIVE	
AEEGILNRST	GENERALIST	
AEEGILNRTU	ARGENTEUIL	
AEEGILNRTY	GENERALITY	
AEEGILNSTV	EVANGELIST	
AEEGILNTVY	NEGATIVELY	
AEEGILOSTY	LAY SIEGE TO	
AEEGILPSTT	TITLE PAGES	
AEEGILRRSU	REGULARISE	
AEEGILRRUZ	REGULARIZE	
AEEGILRTUV	REGULATIVE	
AEEGIMNNSV	GIVEN NAMES	
AEEGIMNPRT	IMPREGNATE,	
PERMEATING		
AEEGIMNRRS	GERMANISER	
AEEGIMNRRZ	GERMANIZER	
AEEGIMNRST	MAGNETISER	
AEEGIMNRTZ	MAGNETIZER	
AEEGIMPRRR	GRIM REAPER	
AEEGIMRRTU	MARGUERITE	
AEEGIMRRTV	GRAVIMETER	
AEEGINNNSU	ENSANGUINE	
AEEGINNORT	GENERATION	
AEEGINNPSS	PANGENESIS	
AEEGINNRRT	INTERREGNA	
AEEGINNRST	TANGERINES	
AEEGINNRTT	ENTREATING	
AEEGINNRTV	ENERVATING,	
VENERATING		
AEEGINNSUX	EXSANGUINE	
AEEGINORRS	REORGANISE	
AEEGINORRZ	REORGANIZE	
AEEGINORVY	A ROVING EYE	
AEEGINOTTV	VEGETATION	
AEEGINPRSV	GRAPEVINES	
AEEGINPRSY	PANEGYRISE	
AEEGINPRYZ	PANEGYRIZE	

AEEGINRRTT	RETREATING	AEEHIMMRSX	HEXAMERISM
AEEGINRRTX	GENERATRIX	AEEHIMNOPP	EPIPHONEMA
AEEGINRSSS	GREASINESS	AEEHIMNPRT	HEMIPTERAN
AEEGINRSSV	VERNISSAGE	AEEHIMSSTT	METATHESIS
AEEGIPPRRT	PAPER TIGER	AEEHINORST	ANTIHEROES
AEEGIRSSTT	STRATEGIES	AEEHINPRST	HEN PARTIES,
AEEGKMRRTY	GREY MARKET		INTERPHASE
AEEGLLNOSS	LOS ANGELES	AEEHINRSST	EARTHINESS,
AEEGLLORTT	ALLEGRETTO		HEARTINESS
AEEGLMNNTT	TANGLEMENT	AEEHIPPRTW	WHITE PAPER
AEEGLMRRSW	LEG-WARMERS	AEEHIRTTWW	WHITEWATER
AEEGLNORTU	OUTGENERAL	AEEHISTUVX	EXHAUSTIVE
AEEGLORTUV	TRAVELOGUE	AEEHKLNPRS	PLANK-SHEER
AEEGMNNOST	MANGOSTEEN	AEEHKMMPRS	HOMEMAKERS
AEEGMNOQSU	MONEGASQUE	AEEHKMPRST	THEME PARKS
AEEGMNRSTY	SEGMENTARY	AEEHKOPSSV	SPOKESHAVE
AEEGMORRST	STEREOGRAM	AEEHKORSTT	HEATSTROKE
AEEGMORSST	GASOMETERS	AEEHKOSSTU	STEAKHOUSE
AEEGMPRTUU	UP A GUMTREE	AEEHLLMRTY	HEMELYTRAL
AEEGMPSTTU	GET UP STEAM	AEEHLLNRRT	ENTHRALLER
AEEGMRRTTY	GREY MATTER	AEEHLLORSW	WHOLESALER
AEEGMRSSTU	GAUSSMETER	AEEHLMMRRS	HAMMERLESS
AEEGNNORSS	SENSE ORGAN	AEEHLMNNOP	PHENOMENAL
AEEGNNSSTW	NEWSAGENTS	AEEHLMPRSW	SPERM WHALE
AEEGNOPRSS	PERSONAGES	AEEHLNOSTT	ON THE SLATE
AEEGNORRST	GENERATORS	AEEHLNRSTT	NETTLE RASH
AEEGNORSTU	ENTOURAGES	AEEHLORSTW	WATERHOLES
AEEGNORSTV	GRAVESTONE	AEEHLRSTTX	TAX SHELTER
AEEGNPRSSS	PASSENGERS	AEEHLRSTTY	HATTERSLEY
AEEGNPRSST	PRESS AGENT	AEEHMNNSSU	HUMANENESS
AEEHHHINST	HEATHENISH	AEEHMOPRRU	AMPERE-HOUR
AEEHHILMOP	HAEMOPHILE	AEEHMOPRSS	SEMAPHORES
AEEHHILSTT	HEALTHIEST	AEEHMOPRST	ATMOSPHERE
AEEHHIMNST	HEATHENISM	AEEHMORRRT	ARTHROMERE
AEEHHINRST	EARTHSHINE	AEEHMORSUX	HEXAMEROUS
AEEHHKNPSS	SHEEPSHANK	AEEHMORTTY	METATHEORY
AEEHHLMSTU	METHUSELAH	AEEHNNOORT	ONE ANOTHER
AEEHHPSSTU	HEPHAESTUS	AEEHNORSSS	HOARSENESS
AEEHIILLPT	EPITHELIAL	AEEHNPPTVY	HAPPY EVENT
AEEHIISTTV	HESITATIVE	AEEHNPRRSS	SHARPENERS
AEEHIKLLRT	HALTER-LIKE	AEEHOOPRRS	HORSE OPERA
AEEHIKLMMR	HAMMER-LIKE	AEEHOOPRST	PEASHOOTER
AEEHILLORT	HELIOLATER	AEEHOOPSST	APOTHEOSES
AEEHILMRST	THERMALISE	AEEHORSSUW	WAREHOUSES
AEEHILMRTZ	THERMALIZE	AEEHORSTVW	WHATSOEVER
AEEHILMTTW	WHITE METAL	AEEHRRSSTV	HARVESTERS
AEEHILORTU	HAUTE-LOIRE	AEEIIKNRST	KERATINISE
AEEHILPPRR	PERIPHERAL	AEEIIKNRTZ	KERATINIZE
AEEHILPPSY	EPIPHYSEAL	AEEIILLRTT	ILLITERATE
AEEHILPRST	SPHALERITE	AEEIILMNRS	MINERALISE
AEEHILPSST	SHAPELIEST	AEEIILMNRZ	MINERALIZE
AEEHILRSTT	EARTHLIEST,	AEEIILNPRU	EPINEURIAL
	STEALTHIER	AEEIILRRTV	IRRELATIVE
AEEHILSTTW	WEALTHIEST	AEEIILRSST	ISRAELITES
		AEEIILRSTV	REVITALISE

AEEIILRTVZ	REVITALIZE
AEEIIMNNST	INSEMINATE
AEEIIMNNTT	TIEMANNITE
AEEIIMNRSS	SEMINARIES
AEEIIMNRSS	ANTI-SEMITE
AEEIIMPRTV	IMPERATIVE
AEEIIMRSSS	EMISSARIES
AEEIIMSTTV	ESTIMATIVE
AEEIINPPRZ	PIPERAZINE
AEEIIPRSST	ASPERITIES,
	PATISSERIE
AEEIJLOSSU	JEALOUSIES
AEEIJOPRTV	PEJORATIVE
AEEIKLNNRT	INTERLAKEN
AEEIKLNSSW	WEAKLINESS
AEEIKNNSSS	SNEAKINESS
AEEIKQSSTU	SQUEAKIEST
AEEIKRRSTW	WATER SKIER
AEEIKRSSTT	STREAKIEST
AEEILLLLNV	VILLANELLE
AEEILLMNST	ENAMELLIST
AEEILLNSVV	EVANSVILLE
AEEILLPSTT	STIPELLATE
AEEILLRSSV	VERSAILLES
AEEILLRTTY	LITERATELY
AEEILLRTVY	RELATIVELY
AEEILLSSTT	SATELLITES
AEEILLSTUV	TELEVISUAL
AEEILMMNPT	IMPALEMENT
AEEILMMNST	LINEAMENTS
AEEILMNNTT	ENTAILMENT
AEEILMNPRT	PLANIMETER
AEEILMNRST	STREAMLINE
AEEILMNSSS	MEASLINESS
AEEILMRSTT	ALTIMETERS
AEEILNNPRS	PERENNIALS
AEEILNNPST	SEPTENNIAL
AEEILNNSTT	SENTENTIAL
AEEILNNSTV	VALENTINES
AEEILNNTTU	LIEUTENANT
AEEILNOPRT	PERITONEAL
AEEILNORTV	REVELATION
AEEILNOSTV	ELEVATIONS
AEEILNPPPS	PINEAPPLES
AEEILNPRSS	PEARLINESS
AEEILNPRST	ALPESTRINE
AEEILNQSTU	SEQUENTIAL
AEEILNQTUV	EQUIVALENT
AEEILNRRTV	IRRELEVANT
AEEILNRSTU	NEUTRALISE
AEEILNRSTW	IN A SWELTER
AEEILNRTTY	ETERNALITY
AEEILNRTUZ	NEUTRALIZE
AEEILNSSST	ESSENTIALS

AEEILNSSSZ	SLEAZINESS	
AEEILNSTVX	SEXIVALENT	
AEEILORTTV	TOLERATIVE	
AEEILPPRRT	PERIPTERAL	
AEEILPRSST	PSALTERIES	
AEEILPRSSY	ERYSIPELAS	
AEEILPSTTU	ESTIPULATE	
AEEILQRSSU	EQUALISERS	
AEEILQRSUZ	EQUALIZERS	
AEEILRRSTT	AIR-LETTERS	
AEEILRRSVW	SILVERWARE	
AEEILRRTTU	LITERATURE	
AEEIMMMRST	METAMERISM	
AEEIMMOPRT	EMMETROPIA	
AEEIMNNPRT	PINE MARTEN	
AEEIMNNRTT	RETAINMENT	
AEEIMNNRTU	INNUMERATE	
AEEIMNNSZZ	MEZZANINES	
AEEIMNOPRT	PERMEATION	
AEEIMNORTT	MARIONETTE	
AEEIMNOSTT	MAISONETTE	
AEEIMNRSSS	NEAR MISSES,	
SMEARINESS		
AEEIMNRSTT	MARTENSITE	
AEEIMNRTUV	NUMERATIVE	
AEEIMNSSST	STEAMINESS	
AEEIMORRTV	VARIOMETER	
AEEIMPRRST	PRIME RATES	
AEEIMQRSUV	SEMIQUAVER	
AEEIMRSTTX	TAXIMETERS	
AEEINNNPWY	PENNINE WAY	
AEEINNNTVY	IN ANY EVENT	
AEEINNORTV	ENERVATION,	
VENERATION		
AEEINNOTTT	ANTOINETTE	
AEEINNPQTU	PENTAQUINE	
AEEINNRTUV	AVENTURINE	
AEEINNSSSU	UNEASINESS	
AEEINOPPST	APPOINTEES	
AEEINOPRST	PROTEINASE	
AEEINOPTTT	POTENTIATE	
AEEINORTVV	RENOVATIVE	
AEEINPPRSS	PAPERINESS	
AEEINPRSTU	RESUPINATE	
AEEINPRTVY	EVEN PARITY	
AEEINPSTTU	UNISEPTATE	
AEEINQRSTU	EQUESTRIAN	
AEEINQSSSU	QUEASINESS	
AEEINQSTTU	TITANESQUE	
AEEINRRRST	RESTRAINER	
AEEINRRTTV	TRAVERTINE	
AEEINRRTVY	VETERINARY	
AEEINRSSTW	WATERINESS	
AEEINRSTTT	INTERSTATE	
AEEINSSSTW	SWEATINESS	

AEEINSSSTY	YEASTINESS	
AEEIOPRSTV	OPERATIVES	
AEEIPPRRST	APPETISERS	
AEEIPPRRST	WATER PIPES	
AEEIPPRSTZ	APPETIZERS	
AEEIPPRVWY	PAY-PER-VIEW	
AEEIPRRSTV	PRIVATEERS	
AEEIPRSSTT	STRIPTEASE,	
TAPESTRIES		
AEEIPRSSTU	PASTEURISE	
AEEIPRSSUV	PERSUASIVE	
AEEIPRSTTX	SEXPARTITE	
AEEIPRSTUZ	PASTEURIZE	
AEEIPRTTUV	VITUPERATE	
AEEIRRSSTU	TREASURIES	
AEEIRSSTTV	TRAVESTIES	
AEEIRSTUVY	EASY VIRTUE	
AEEJLNORSU	JOURNALESE	
AEEJMORSTT	MAJORETTES	
AEEKLMNORW	ENAMELWORK	
AEEKMMNORY	MONEYMAKER	
AEEKMMRRRY	MERRYMAKER	
AEEKMNOPRT	OPEN MARKET	
AEEKMORRTU	EUROMARKET	
AEEKMPRRTV	VERKRAMPTE	
AEEKMRSSTY	MASTER KEYS	
AEELLMNOTV	MALEVOLENT	
AEELLMNRTU	ALLUREMENT	
AEELLNOPRT	PETRONELLA	
AEELLNRRUV	UNRAVELLER	
AEELLNRTVY	RELEVANTLY	
AEELLNRTXY	EXTERNALLY	
AEELLNTUVY	EVENTUALLY	
AEELLORSTT	ROSTELLATE	
AEELLORTTY	TEA TROLLEY	
AEELLQRRRU	QUARRELLER	
AEELLRRSTV	TRAVELLERS	
AEELLRSTTW	WALL STREET	
AEELMMNORU	NEUROLEMMA	
AEELMMNRTV	MARVELMENT	
AEELMMNOTT	MENTAL NOTE	
AEELMNOPRT	PLANOMETER	
AEELMNORTW	WATERMELON	
AEELMNOSSW	SALESWOMEN	
AEELMNSTTV	VESTMENTAL	
AEELMOPRTV	VOLT-AMPERE	
AEELMOPSTT	PALMETTOES	
AEELNNORSW	NEW ORLEANS	
AEELNNPTTU	ANTEPENULT	
AEELNPRTTW	WENTLETRAP	
AEELORSTTU	LOTUS-EATER	
AEELORSTVW	WATER VOLES	
AEELPRRSST	PLASTERERS	
AEELQRSSTU	SEQUESTRAL	

AEELRRSTUW	LUSTREWARE	
AEEMMNORST	MANOMETERS	
AEEMMNORTT	ANTE-MORTEM	
AEEMMNORTY	ANEMOMETRY	
AEEMMNSSTU	AMUSEMENTS	
AEEMMRRSST	STAMMERERS	
AEEMNNPRST	PERMANENTS	
AEEMNNPRTT	ENTRAPMENT	
AEEMNOPPRY	PAPER MONEY	
AEEMNOQRSU	ROMANESQUE	
AEEMNORRTU	ENUMERATOR	
AEEMNORRUV	MANOEUVRER	
AEEMNORSST	SARMENTOSE	
AEEMNORSUV	MANOEUVRES	
AEEMNPPRTY	PREPAYMENT	
AEEMNPRRTU	AMPERE-TURN	
AEEMNPRRTY	REPAYMENTS	
AEEMNRSSST	MARE'S NESTS	
AEEMNRSTTT	TREATMENTS	
AEEMNRSTTU	MENSTRUATE	
AEEMNSSSST	ASSESSMENT	
AEEMNSSSTT	MEANS TESTS	
AEEMNSSTTT	STATEMENTS,	
TESTAMENTS		
AEEMORRSTV	OVERMASTER	
AEEMORRTTV	OVERMATTER	
AEEMORSSSY	MAYORESSES	
AEEMPRRTTU	EAR TRUMPET	
AEEMRSSSST	SEAMSTRESS	
AEEMRSSSTT	MATTRESSES,	
SMEAR TESTS		
AEENNOOPSS	OPEN SEASON	
AEENNORSST	ORNATENESS	
AEENNPPRRT	TREPPANNER	
AEENOORRTX	EXONERATOR	
AEENOPQSSU	OPAQUENESS	
AEENOPRRTT	PENETRATOR	
AEENOPSTTT	POTENTATES	
AEENORSTUX	EXTRANEOUS	
AEENORTTUX	EXTENUATOR	
AEENPPRSSW	NEWSPAPERS	
AEENPPRSTT	STEPPARENT	
AEENPRSSSS	SPARSENESS	
AEENORSSSU	SQUARENESS	
AEENRRSSTV	TRANSVERSE	
AEENSSSSTV	VASTNESSES	
AEENSSSTTU	ASTUTENESS	
AEEOPPRSSU	PEA SOUPERS	
AEEOPRRSST	TETRASPORE	
AEEOPRRTWW	WATERPOWER	
AEEOPRSSSV	OVERPASSES	
AEEOPRSSTT	POETASTERS	
AEEPPRRTUW	TUPPERWARE	
AEEPRRSSST	TRESPASSER	
AEEPRRSSTY	SPARE TYRES	

AEEPRSSSST	TRESPASSES	
AEEPRSSWXY	EXPRESSWAY	
AEEQRSSSTU	SETSQUARES	
AEEQSSTTUU	STATUESQUE	
AEERRRSSTU	TREASURERS	
AEERRSTTVX	EXTRAVERTS	
AEESSTTTTU	STATUETTES	
AEFFHILSST	FLATFISHES	
AEFFHLLOTW	OFF-THE-WALL	
AEFFIIINST	AFFINITIES	
AEFFIIINTV	AFFINITIVE	
AEFFIKLLOW	WALK OF LIFE	
AEFFIKPSST	PIKESTAFFS	
AEFFILNSTU	INSUFFLATE	
AEFFLMOOPR	FLAMEPROOF	
AEFFLMOORW	FOAMFLOWER	
AEFFNRSSTU	STAFF NURSE	
AEFFOOSTTU	AFFETTUOSO	
AEFGHHLLNT	HALF-LENGTH	
AEFGHILSTW	WHITE FLAGS	
AEFGHINRRW	WHARFINGER	
AEFGHKNOUU	HUA	
KUO-FENG		
AEFGHNORTU	FEARNOUGHT	
AEFGIILNNR	FINGERNAIL	
AEFGIILNSV	LIFE-SAVING	
AEFGIIMNRS	MAGNIFIERS	
AEFGIINNRR	REFRAINING	
AEFGIINSTU	IGNES FATUI	
AEFGIIRTUV	FIGURATIVE	
AEFGILLNNN	FLANNELING	
AEFGILMNNU	MEANINGFUL	
AEFGILMNOS	FLAMINGOES	
AEFGILNLNTT	FLATTENING	
AEFGILNOUW	GUINEA FOWL	
AEFGILNRTT	FLATTERING	
AEFGILOPRT	PROFLIGATE	
AEFGILRSUY	LAY FIGURES	
AEFGIMNORR	FOREARMING	
AEFGINNSST	FASTENINGS	
AEFGIPRRTU	GRAPEFRUIT	
AEFGIRSSTT	GAS FITTERS	
AEFGKLNRTU	KLAGENFURT	
AEFGLLLOWY	YELLOW FLAG	
AEFGLLRTUY	GRATEFULLY	
AEFGLMRSTU	GULF STREAM	
AEFGLNOSST	FLAGSTONES	
AEFGLNRTUU	UNGRATEFUL	
AEFGLORSTW	AFTERGLOWS	
AEFHIKLRSY	FREAKISHLY	
AEFHIKMSST	MAKESHIFTS	
AEFHILNSSS	FLASHINESS	
AEFHILRSST	HALF-SISTER	
AEFHIMMNST	FAMISHMENT	
AEFHINOPTY	IN THE PAY OF	
AEFHINOSSS	OAFISHNESS	
AEFHIRSSST	STARFISHES	
AEFHLLLOVY	HALF VOLLEY	
AEFHLLMSUY	SHAMEFULLY	
AEFHLLSTUY	HASTEFULLY	
AEFHLMOSST	FATHOMLESS	
AEFHLNORTT	HALF-ROTTEN	
AEFHMORSSU	FARMHOUSES	
AEFHOOPSTU	OUT OF PHASE,	
OUT OF SHAPE		
AEFIILLNSS	FILIALNESS	
AEFIILMNSS	SEMIFINALS	
AEFIILMPRS	AMPLIFIERS	
AEFIILNOTU	UNIFOLIATE	
AEFIILNRTT	INFILTRATE	
AEFIILORTT	TRIFOLIATE	
AEFIILQRSU	QUALIFIERS	
AEFIINOPRS	SAPONIFIER	
AEFIINQRTU	QUANTIFIER	
AEFIKNOPRS	FAIR-SPOKEN	
AEFILLNNRY	INFERNALLY	
AEFILLNNUZ	INFLUENZAL	
AEFILLRTVY	RIFT VALLEY	
AEFILMNSTY	MANIFESTLY	
AEFILMORRS	FORMALISER	
AEFILMORRZ	FORMALIZER	
AEFILMORTW	WOLFRAMITE	
AEFILNORSU	LANIFEROUS	
AEFILNORTU	FLUORINATE	
AEFILNSSTU	FAULTINESS	
AEFILOQRTU	QUATREFOIL	
AEFILORSSU	SALIFEROUS	
AEFIMNOSST	MANIFESTOS	
AEFIMNRSST	FIRST NAMES	
AEFINNRSSU	UNFAIRNESS	
AEFINOOPRT	FORTE-PIANO,	
PIANOFORTE		
AEFINORRST	RAIN FOREST	
AEFINORTTU	REFUTATION	
AEFINPSSTY	SAFETY PINS	
AEFINRRTTY	FRATERNITY	
AEFIOPRSTU	FETIPAROUS	
AEFIORRSSU	AURIFEROUS	
AEFIORSTUV	FAVOURITES	
AEFKLNOSSW	SNOWFLAKES	
AEFKMORRSW	FRAMEWORKS	
AEFLLLOPWY	PLAYFELLOW	
AEFLLLORWW	WALLFLOWER	
AEFLLLPTTU	AT FULL PELT	
AEFLLLSSWY	FLAWLESSLY	
AEFLLNOSSW	FALLOWNESS	
AEFLLNSSUW	LAWFULNESS	
AEFLLSTTUY	TASTEFULLY	
AEFLLSTUWY	WASTEFULLY	
AEFLMNNSSU	MANFULNESS	
AEFLMORRSV	SALVERFORM	
AEFLNOPRRT	PREFRONTAL	
AEFLNRSSTU	ARTFULNESS	
AEFLOOPSTT	FOOTPLATES	
AEFLORRSTW	STARFLOWER	
AEFLORSTWW	WATERFOWLS	
AEFLRSTTWY	FLYSWATTER	
AEFMNORSTW	MEN OF	
STRAW		
AEFMNOSSSU	FAMOUSNESS	
AEFMOPRRST	PERMAFROST	
AEFNNOORST	AFTERNOONS	
AEFNOPPRRU	RUN-OF-PAPER	
AEFNORRRST	TRANSFEROR	
AEFNORRTTW	WATERFRONT	
AEFOOPRRRT	PERFORATOR	
AEFOOPPRRT	WATERPROOF	
AEFOORRSTT	TORT-FEASOR	
AEFOQRRSUU	FOURSQUARE	
AEFRRRSTTU	FRUSTRATER	
AEGGGILNRSY	ENGAGINGLY	
AEGGGINRST	STAGGERING	
AEGGGINRSW	SWAGGERING	
AEGGHILNRT	RIGHT ANGLE	
AEGGHINRST	GATHERINGS	
AEGGHINSSS	SHAGGINESS	
AEGGHIOPST	GEOPHAGIST	
AEGGHOOPSU	GEOPHAGOUS	
AEGGIILLNZ	LEGALIZING	
AEGGIILMPR	PILGRIMAGE	
AEGGIILNNR	REALIGNING	
AEGGIILNVW	LIVING WAGE	
AEGGIIMNRT	EMIGRATING	
AEGGIINNSV	ENVISAGING	
AEGGIINNTV	NEGATIVING	
AEGGIINPSU	GUINEA PIGS	
AEGGIJMRST	JIGGERMAST	
AEGGILLMNY	GLEAMINGLY	
AEGGILLNRV	GRAVELLING	
AEGGILNNNT	ENTANGLING	
AEGGILNNOT	ELONGATING	
AEGGILNRTU	REGULATING	
AEGGILRRST	STRAGGLIER	
AEGGIMNNTU	AUGMENTING	
AEGGIMNRRS	GRANGERISM	
AEGGINNRST	ESTRANGING	
AEGGINNRSV	ENGRAVINGS	
AEGGINORSS	AGGRESSION	
AEGGIORRSU	GREGARIOUS	
AEGGJNRTUU	JUGGERNAUT	
AEGGLLNOOY	ANGELOLOGY	
AEGGLOORTY	GERATOLOGY	
AEGGLRRSST	STRAGGLERS	

AEGGMOSTUY	MYSTAGOGUE	AEGHLMOOOT	HOMOLOGATE
AEGGNNORSU	GANGRENOUS	AEGHLNNOOP	ANGLOPHONE
AEGGNOSSUY	SYNAGOGUES	AEGHLNOORS	ALONGSHORE
AEGGNPRSSS	PRESSGANGS	AEGHLNOOSU	HALOGENOUS
AEGGORRSSS	AGGRESSORS	AEGHLNSTWY	LENGTHWAYS
AEGHHILLLS	SHILLELAGH	AEGHLOOORR	LOGORRHOEA
AEGHHILOPR	HELIOGRAPH	AEGHLOOPRY	OLEOGRAPHY
AEGHHILRTT	EARTHLIGHT	AEGHLOSSSU	GLASSHOUSE
AEGHHIMNWY	HIGHWAYMEN	AEGHMMORRT	THERMOGRAM
AEGHHIMSSS	HIGH MASSES	AEGHMNOOPR	GRAMOPHONE
AEGHHINOSS	HIGH SEASON	AEGHNOOORR	GONORRHOEA
AEGHHINSST	SHEATHINGS	AEGHNOPRRY	GRANOPHYRE
AEGHHISTTU	HAUGHTIEST	AEGHNOPRST	STENOGRAPH
AEGHHLORSU	HORSELAUGH	AEGHNORRST	SHORT-RANGE
AEGHHMOPPT	APOPHTHEGM	AEGHOOPRRR	OROGRAPHER
AEGHHNOPPR	NEPHOGRAPH	AEGHOOPRRZ	ZOOGRAPHER
AEGHHRRSTU	HEARTHRUGS	AEGHOOPSSU	OESOPHAGUS
AEGHIILMRT	ALMIGHTIER	AEGHOPPRRU	ROUGH PAPER
AEGHIIMNRS	MISHEARING	AEGHOPRRXY	XEROGRAPHY
AEGHIINSTT	HESITATING	AEGIIILNTV	INVIGILATE
AEGHIINSTU	INGUSHETIA	AEGIIIMTTV	MITIGATIVE
AEGHIIPRST	GRAPHITISE	AEGIIIRRTV	IRRIGATIVE
AEGHIIPRTZ	GRAPHITIZE	AEGIIJMNNZ	JIANG ZEMIN
AEGHIKMMNO	HOMEMAKING	AEGIIKNOPP	PIG IN A POKE
AEGHIKMNOS	SHOEMAKING	AEGIILLLTY	ILLEGALITY
AEGHIKNNRS	HANKERINGS	AEGIILMNRT	TRIGEMINAL
AEGHIKNNRT	TENGRI KHAN	AEGIILMNST	TIME SIGNAL
AEGHILLNOP	ANGLOPHILE	AEGIILMNSX	MAXISINGLE
AEGHILMNNS	ENGLISHMAN	AEGIILNNPX	EXPLAINING
AEGHILMORT	LITHOMARGE	AEGIILNNPZ	PENALIZING
AEGHILNNSU	UNLEASHING	AEGIILNNSS	GAINLINESS
AEGHILNOOT	THEOLOGIAN	AEGIILNOTV	LEVIGATION
AEGHILNRST	EARTHLINGS	AEGIILNPRV	PREVAILING
AEGHILNRSU	LANGUISHER	AEGIILNQUZ	EQUALIZING
AEGHILRSTY	LIGHT YEARS	AEGIILNRSS	GLAIRINESS
AEGHILSSTT	GHASTLIEST	AEGIILNSTV	VIGILANTES
AEGHIMMOPR	MIMEOGRAPH	AEGIILNTTV	LEVITATING
AEGHIMNRST	NIGHTMARES	AEGIILRTTT	GLITTERATI
AEGHIMSTTT	STEAMTIGHT	AEGIIMNNOT	GEMINATION
AEGHINNPPS	HAPPENINGS	AEGIIMNORT	EMIGRATION
AEGHINNPRS	SHARPENING	AEGIIMNSTT	ESTIMATING
AEGHINNRSS	HARNESSING	AEGIIMNSTV	NEGATIVISM,
AEGHINNRST	NEAR THINGS		TIMESAVING
AEGHINNRTU	UNEARTHING	AEGIIMSSTT	STIGMATISE
AEGHINPRRS	REPHRASING	AEGIIMSTTZ	STIGMATIZE
AEGHINRSSS	GARISHNESS	AEGIINNNRT	ENTRAINING
AEGHINRRST	SHATTERING,	AEGIINNOST	ISOANTIGEN
	STRAIGHTEN	AEGIINNPRT	PERTAINING
AEGHINRSTV	HARVESTING	AEGIINNRSS	GRAININESS
AEGHINSTTU	NAUGHTIEST	AEGIINORTV	INVIGORATE
AEGHINSTUX	EXHAUSTING	AEGIINPPTZ	APPETIZING
AEGHIPRRSY	SERIGRAPHY	AEGIINSTTV	NEGATIVIST
AEGHIRRSTT	STRAIGHTER	AEGIIRSTTU	GRATUITIES
AEGHIRTTTW	WATERTIGHT	AEGIKKMNRS	KINGMAKERS

AEGIKLLOOR	KALGOORLIE
AEGIKLMNOV	LOVEMAKING
AEGIKLNNSY	SNEAKINGLY
AEGIKNNSST	TAKINGNESS
AEGILLMNRV	MARVELLING
AEGILLNORY	REGIONALLY
AEGILLNPSY	PLEASINGLY
AEGILLNRTV	TRAVELLING
AEGILLOPTT	EPIGLOTTAL
AEGILLORST	ALLEGORIST,
	LEGISLATOR
AEGILLPSSX	PLEXIGLASS
AEGILLRRSU	GUERRILLAS
AEGILLRSSS	SALESGIRLS
AEGILMNNST	ALIGNMENTS
AEGILMNOOP	MONOPLEGIA
AEGILMNORS	ROSEMALING
AEGILMNORY	MINERALOGY
AEGILMORRS	GLAMORISER,
	RIGMAROLES
AEGILMORRZ	GLAMORIZER
AEGILMSTTU	MULTISTAGE
AEGILNNNRU	UNLEARNING
AEGILNNOOT	ELONGATION
AEGILNNPSS	GLANS PENIS
AEGILNNRUV	UNRAVELING
AEGILNNSSS	SLANGINESS
AEGILNNSUY	SANGUINELY
AEGILNOOSU	OLEAGINOUS
AEGILNORTT	TOLERATING
AEGILNORTU	REGULATION,
	UROGENITAL
AEGILNORVY	OVERLAYING
AEGILNOSTU	GELATINOUS
AEGILNPRST	PLASTERING
AEGILNPRTY	TAPERINGLY
AEGILNQRRU	QUARRELING
AEGILNRSTV	STARVELING
AEGILNRSWY	SWEARINGLY
AEGILNRVWY	WAVERINGLY
AEGILNRWYY	WEARINGLY
AEGILNSSSS	GLASSINESS
AEGILOOPRS	APOLOGISER
AEGILOOPRZ	APOLOGIZER
AEGILOORST	AEROLOGIST
AEGILOPRTT	GRAPTOLITE
AEGILORRSS	GRESSORIAL
AEGILORSSS	GLOSSARIES
AEGILRRRSU	IRREGULARS
AEGILRRSUV	VULGARISER
AEGILRRTUY	REGULARITY
AEGILRRUVZ	VULGARIZER
AEGILRSTTZ	SALZGITTER
AEGIMMNNRST	STAMMERING
AEGIMNNNRST	SMARTENING

AEGIMNNSST	ASSIGNMENT	AEGLNRSSUV	VULGARNESS
AEGIMNOPRS	ANGIOSPERM	AEGLNSSSSU	SUNGLASSES
AEGIMNORRT	GERMINATOR	AEGLOORRST	ASTROLOGER
AEGIMNORSU	GRAMINEOUS	AEGLOORTTY	TERATOLOGY
AEGIMNPRTY	PIGMENTARY	AEGLORRSTU	REGULATORS
AEGIMNPTTT	ATTEMPTING	AEGLORRTUY	REGULATORY
AEGIMNRRRY	REMARRYING	AEGLORSSUV	GROSS VALUE
AEGIMNRRST	RINGMASTER	AEGLPRSSUU	SURPLUSAGE
AEGIMNRSTT	SMATTERING	AEGLPSSSSY	SPYGLASSES
AEGIMRRTVY	GRAVIMETRY	AEGMMNOPRU	
AEGINNNPRT	TREPANNING		PNEUMOGRAM
AEGINNNORST	RESONATING	AEGMMNRTUU	ARGUMENTUM
AEGINNORTV	RENOVATING		
AEGINNOSSS	SEASONINGS	AEGMMOPRRR	PROGRAMMER
AEGINNPPRT	ENTRAPPING	AEGMMOPRRS	PROGRAMMES
AEGINNPRRT	PARTNERING	AEGMNOORST	GASTRONOME
AEGINNPRTT	PATTERNING	AEGMNOOSUX	XENOGAMOUS
AEGINNRSTT	ASTRINGENT	AEGMNORRSW	WARMONGERS
AEGINNRSTU	SAUNTERING	AEGMOPRRRS	PROGRAMERS
AEGINOORTT	NEGOTIATOR	AEGNNRTUUY	UNGUENTARY
AEGINORRSS	ORGANISERS	AEGNOOSTUU	AUTOGENOUS
AEGINORRSZ	ORGANIZERS	AEGNRRSSST	TRANSGRESS
AEGINORRTT	INTEGRATOR	AEGOORSTSU	OUTRAGEOUS
AEGINORRTV	OVERRATING	AEGOPRRSSU	SOUR GRAPES
AEGINORTVX	OVERTAXING	AEGOPRRTUX	EXPURGATOR
AEGINOSSTT	GESTATIONS	AEGORRSSTU	SURROGATES
AEGINPRSTT	SPATTERING	AEGORRSTTU	GREAT STOUR
AEGINPRSTU	SUPERGIANT	AEGPRRRSUY	PRAYER RUGS
AEGINPRSTY	PANEGYRIST	AEGPRRSSSU	SUPERGRASS
AEGINQRRTU	QUARTERING	AEHHIILMOP	HEMOPHILIA
AEGINRRSSU	REASSURING	AEHHILNSTU	HELIANTHUS
AEGINRRSTT	REGISTRANT	AEHHILPSSW	WHIPLASHES
AEGINRRSTU	TREASURING	AEHHINOPRT	HIEROPHANT
AEGINRRSTV	TRAVERSING	AEHHINPSST	THE SPANISH
AEGINRSSSS	GRASSINESS	AEHHIOPSST	HEPHAISTOS
AEGINRSSSU	SUGARINESS	AEHHIRSTTW	WHITE TRASH
AEGINRSSTU	SIGNATURES	AEHHMOOOPT	HOMOEOPATH
AEGINRSTWW	WATERWINGS	AEHHMOOPST	HOMEOPATHS
AEGIPRSTUV	PURGATIVES	AEHHMOOPTY	HOMEOPATHY
AEGIRRRSST	REGISTRARS	AEHHNOOPRT	ANTHOPHORE
AEGIRSSTTT	STRATEGIST	AEHHOPPSST	PHOSPHATES
AEGKMNOSXY	OXYGEN	AEHHPSSTTU	HATSHEPSUT
	MASK	AEHIIILNNS	SINHAILIEN
AEGLLLLNNO	LLANGOLLEN	AEHIIKLRTW	WRAITHLIKE
AEGLLMORRU	GLOMERULAR	AEHIILLMNW	WILHELMINA
AEGLLMRTUY	METALLURGY	AEHIILOSTX	HELIOTAXIS
AEGLLNNPTY	PLANGENTLY	AEHIIMNSTU	HUMANITIES
AEGLLNOSST	GALLSTONES	AEHIINNRRS	NAIRNSHIRE
AEGLLOPRSU	PELLAGROUS	AEHIINORTT	THORIANITE
AEGLMNORSS	LEMON GRASS	AEHIINOSTT	HESITATION
AEGLMOOSTY	SEMATOLOGY	AEHIINPPRS	SAPPHIRINE
AEGLMOPRTU	PROMULGATE	AEHIINPSST	ANTITHESIS
AEGLNNPRTY	PREGNANTLY	AEHIIPPSTT	EPITAPHIST
AEGLNRRSST	STRANGLERS	AEHIKKLMSS	MILK SHAKES
		AEHIKNRSSS	RAKISHNESS
AEHILLOPSV	SLAVOPHILE		
AEHILLORTY	HELIOLATRY		
AEHILLSTTY	STEALTHILY		
AEHILMNNUY	INHUMANELY		
AEHILMNOPY	ANEMOPHILY		
AEHILMNOSY	HAEMOLYSIN		
AEHILMORST	ISOTHERMAL,		
	THIMEROSAL		
AEHILMOSSY	HAEMOLYSIS		
AEHILNNOPS	ALPHONSINE		
AEHILNOSSS	SHOALINESS		
AEHILNOSST	HAILSTONES		
AEHILNOTTY	ETHYLATION		
AEHILNQRSU	HARLEQUINS		
AEHILNSSSV	LAVISHNESS		
AEHILNSTTY	HESITANTLY		
AEHILOPSTT	HOSPITALET		
AEHILOPTVY	TOP-HEAVILY		
AEHILPSSST	SPLASHIEST		
AEHILRSSTY	HAIRSTYLES		
AEHILRSTVY	SHRIEVALTY		
AEHIMMPRST	TRIPHAMMER		
AEHIMMRSTU	RHEUMATISM		
AEHIMNNPPS	PENMANSHIP		
AEHIMNNSTV	VANISHMENT		
AEHIMNORRS	HARMONISER		
AEHIMNORRZ	HARMONIZER		
AEHIMNOTUX	EXHUMATION		
AEHIMNRSSS	MARSHINESS		
AEHIMNRSTV	RAVISHMENT		
AEHIMNSSTU	ENTHUSIASM		
AEHIMOOPTY	MYTHOPOEIA		
AEHIMORRSY	MORAYSHIRE		
AEHIMPRSST	MASTERSHIP,		
	SHIPMASTER		
AEHIMPSSST	STEAMSHIPS		
AEHIMPSSTY	SYMPATHIES,		
	SYMPATHISE		
AEHIMPSTYZ	SYMPATHIZE		
AEHINOPRTU	EUPHORIANT		
AEHINOPSTT	ON THE TAPIS,		
	TIP ONE'S HAT		
AEHINORRTV	HOVERTRAIN		
AEHINORSTU	HOUSE-TRAIN		
AEHINOSTUX	EXHAUSTION		
AEHINPSSTT	PANTHEISTS		
AEHINQRSUV	VANQUISHER		
AEHINRSSST	TRASHINESS		
AEHINSSTTU	ENTHUSIAST		
AEHIOOPSST	APOTHEOSIS		
AEHIORRSTU	AUTHORISER		
AEHIORRTUZ	AUTHORIZER		
AEHIORSSST	AIR-HOSTESS		
AEHIORSTTT	THROATIEST		
AEHIPRSSTT	THERAPISTS		

AEHIQSSSTU	SQUASHIEST	AEIIINSTTV	NATIVITIES	AEIIMNNOTV	NOMINATIVE
AEHIRSSTTW	SWARTHIEST,	AEIIIRRTTV	IRRITATIVE	AEIIMNOSTT	ESTIMATION
SWEATSHIRT		AEIIJMORST	MAJORITIES	AEIIMNPQRU	PRIMAQUINE
AEHKLOPRSW	SHOPWALKER	AEIIKKSTTW	KITTIWAKES	AEIIMNQRTU	MARTINIQUE
AEHKMNOSTU	SNAKEMOUTH	AEIIKLLNPR	PAINKILLER	AEIIMNQTUY	EQUANIMITY
AEHKOORSTU	SOUTH KOREA	AEIILLLMMS	MILLESIMAL	AEIIMNRSTU	MINIATURES
AEHKORRSTW	EARTHWORKS	AEIILLLMNN	MILLENNIAL	AEIIMNRTUV	RUMINATIVE
AEHLLMRSSY	HARMLESSLY	AEIILLMNOR	MINERAL OIL	AEIIMOPRRS	IMPRESARIO
AEHLLMSTUU	HAUSTELLUM	AEIILLMNTU	ILLUMINATE	AEIIMOTTVV	MOTIVATIVE
AEHLLOOPRT	HARTLEPOOL	AEIILLMPRY	IMPERIALLY	AEIIMPTTUV	IMPUTATIVE
AEHLLOPRXY	PHYLLOXERA	AEIILLMRST	LITERALISM	AEIINNOTVV	INNOVATIVE
AEHLLOSSTW	SHALLOWEST	AEIILLOSTV	VOLATILISE	AEIINNPRTT	TRIPINNATE
AEHLMOOSUX	HOMOSEXUAL	AEIILLOTVZ	VOLATILIZE	AEIINNPRTY	ANTIPYRINE
AEHLMORTTY	METHYLATOR	AEIILLPRTT	TRIPLETAIL	AEIINNPSTT	IN-PATIENTS
AEHLMOSSSU	ALMS-HOUSES	AEIILLPSTT	PISTILLATE	AEIINOPPST	INAPPOSITE
AEHLNNOPTT	PENTATHLON	AEIILLRRTT	TRILITERAL	AEIINOPRTX	EXPIRATION
AEHLNOPSTU	HOUSEPLANT,	AEIILLRRTY	LITERARILY	AEIINOPSTT	POINSETTIA
SULPHONATE		AEIILLRSTT	LITERALIST	AEIINOQTTU	EQUITATION
AEHLOOPRRY	PYORRHOEAL	AEIILMMMOR	IMMEMORIAL	AEIINOSTTV	NOVITIATES
AEHLOPSSUY	PLAYHOUSES	AEIILMNORT	ELIMINATOR	AEIINOTUVX	EXUVIATION
AEHLPRSTUU	SULPHURATE	AEIILMNRSU	LUMINARIES	AEIINPSSST	ANTISEPSIS
AEHLRTTUUV	TRUTH-VALUE	AEIILMNSTY	SEMINALITY	AEIINQSTTU	QUANTITIES
AEHMNOORSU	MANOR	AEIILMNTTY	INTIMATELY	AEIINRSTTV	TRANSITIVE
HOUSE		AEIILMORST	MORALITIES	AEIINRTTTW	IN A TWITTER
AEHMNOORSW		AEIILMOSSS	ISOSEISMAL	AEIIOPPRTT	PROPITIATE
HORSEWOMAN		AEIILMRSTV	RELATIVISM	AEIIOPPSTV	APPOSITIVE
AEHMNORRTT	MATTERHORN	AEIILMRSVV	REVIVALISM	AEIIPPSSSW	PIPSISSEWA
AEHMNORRTW	HARROWMENT	AEIILMSTUV	SIMULATIVE	AEIIPRRTTT	TRIPARTITE
AEHMNPRSUU	SUPERHUMAN	AEIILMTTUV	MUTILATIVE	AEIIPRSTTV	PARTITIVES
AEHMOORSTX	MESOTHORAX	AEIILNNORS	ROSANILINE	AEIJLNORSU	JOURNALISE
AEHMORRSTW	EARTHWORMS	AEIILNNSTT	INTESTINAL	AEIJLNORUZ	JOURNALIZE
AEHMORSTTT	THERMOSTAT	AEIILNOOTT	ETIOLATION	AEIJMNOSSS	JAM SESSION
AEHNNNOOTY	HOOTENANNY	AEIILNORST	INTER ALIOS	AEIJNNSSTU	JAUNTINESS
AEHNOOPSSU	SOUSAPHONE	AEIILNORSV	REVISIONAL	AEIJNOOPRT	PEJORATION
AEHNOOPSSX	SAXOPHONES	AEIILNORTT	LITERATION	AEIKKLLOOS	LOOK-ALIKES
AEHNOPRSWY	PHONEY WARS	AEIILNOSTT	TONALITIES	AEIKLMNSTY	MISTAKENLY
AEHNOPRTUY	NEUROPATHY	AEIILNOTTV	LEVITATION	AEIKLNORST	OIL TANKERS
AEHOOPPRST	APOSTROPHE	AEIILNOTUV	ELUVIATION	AEIKLNSSST	STALKINESS
AEHOOPRYZZ	ZAPOROZHYE	AEIILNPRST	REPTILIANS	AEIKLNSSTU	ESKILSTUNA
AEHOOPSSTT	OSTEOPATHS	AEIILNQTUY	INEQUALITY	AEIKMNPRRT	PRINTMAKER
AEHOOPSTTT	TOOTHPASTE	AEIILNSSTW	WAISTLINES	AEIKNNPRSS	SPINNAKERS
AEHOOPSTTY	OSTEOPATHY	AEIILOPRST	POLARITIES	AEIKNNSSSW	SWANKINESS
AEHOORSSTY	SOOTHSAYER	AEIILORSST	SOLITAIRES,	AEIKPPQOSSU	PIPSQUEAKS
AEHOOSSSTU	OAST HOUSES	SOLITARIES		AEILLLMSTT	LITTLE SLAM
AEHOPPRSTY	SAPROPHYTE	AEIILRSSUV	VISUALISER	AEILLLOTWY	YELLOWTAIL
AEHOPRSTUY	HOUSE PARTY	AEIILRSTTV	RELATIVIST	AEILLLSUVY	ALLUSIVELY
AEHOPSSSTW	SWEATSHOPS	AEIILRSTTZ	STRELITZIA	AEILLMMORS	ALLOMERISM
AEHORRRSTW	RESTHARROW	AEIILRSTVV	REVIVALIST	AEILLMMRST	MILLSTREAM,
AEIIIILNST	INITIALISE	AEIILRSUVZ	VISUALIZER	SMALL-TIMER	
AEIIIILNTZ	INITIALIZE	AEIILRTTVY	RELATIVITY	AEILLMNPTU	MULTIPLANE
AEIIIINTTV	INITIATIVE	AEIIMMMNOR	IN MEMORIAM	AEILLMNRTY	TERMINALLY
AEIIILMRST	MILITARISE	AEIIMMNPRT	IMPAIRMENT	AEILLMRSTW	WATERMILLS
AEIIILMRTZ	MILITARIZE	AEIIMMNRST	ANTIMERISM	AEILLMTTUY	ULTIMATELY
AEIIILRSTV	TRIVIALISE	AEIIMNNNOT	INNOMINATE	AEILLNNRTY	INTERNALLY
AEIIILRTVZ	TRIVIALIZE				

AEILLNOPRT	PETRONILLA	AEILNRTTUY	NEUTRALITY	AEINNOPSSX	EXPANSIONS
AEILLNOPTT	POTENTILLA	AEILNSSSTU	SENSUALIST	AEINNOQRTU	QUATERNION
AEILLNPSST	PANELLISTS	AEILNSSTUY	SENSUALITY	AEINNORSTT	STENTORIAN
AEILLNPSSY	PAINLESSLY	AEILOOPRST	PORTLAOISE	AEINNOSSST	SENSATIONS
AEILLPRRSU	PLURALISER	AEILOOPTTZ	TOPAZOLITE	AEINNOSTTT	ATTENTIONS
AEILLPRRUZ	PLURALIZER	AEILOPPRSU	POPULARISE	AEINNOSTTV	NONSTATIVE
AEILLPSSSS	SALES SLIPS	AEILOPPRUZ	POPULARIZE	AEINNPPSSS	SNAPPINESS
AEILLPSSTT	PASTELLIST	AEILOPRSSU	PLESIOSAUR	AEINNQSSTU	QUAINTNESS
AEILLQSSTU	SQUALLIEST	AEILOPRSTY	EPISTOLARY	AEINNRRSTY	TYRANNISER
AEILLRSSTW	STAIRWELLS	AEILORRTTU	ELUTRIATOR	AEINNRRTYZ	TYRANNIZER
AEILLRSTTU	ILLUSTRATE	AEILORSTTU	STAUROLITE	AEINNSSSZZ	SNAZZINESS
AEILMMRTUY	IMMATURELY	AEILPRRSTY	PERISTYLAR	AEINOOPPRT	PROPIONATE
AEILMNNOPR	PRENOMINAL	AEILRRSSTU	SURREALIST	AEINOOPRRT	PERORATION
AEILMNNOPR	PRENOMINAL	AEILRSSSTY	LAY SISTERS	AEINOOPRST	OPERATIONS
AEILMNNOPRS	IMPERSONAL	AEILRSTTUV	LUSTRATIVE	AEINOPRRST	PATRONISER
AEILMNOPRT	TRAMPOLINE	AEILRSTTUZ	AUSTERLITZ	AEINOPRRTZ	PATRONIZER
AEILMNORTU	TOURMALINE	AEILSTTTUX	TEXTUALIST	AEINOPRSSS	ASPERSIONS
AEILMNOSTY	MELANOSITY	AEIMMNNRSS	MANNERISMS	AEINOPRSSU	PERSUASION
AEILMNPRTY	PLANIMETRY	AEIMMNOPST	PANTOMIMES	AEINOPRTTU	REPUTATION
AEILMNRSTU	NEUTRALISM	AEIMMNORST	MONETARISM	AEINOPTTTU	OUTPATIENT
AEILMNSSSU	SENSUALISM	AEIMMNSTZZ	MIZZENMAST	AEINORRSTT	REINSTATOR
AEILMNSTTU	LAST MINUTE	AEIMMPRSTU	SPERMATIUM	AEINORSSST	ASSERTIONS
AEILMOORRT	MELIORATOR	AEIMMRRSSU	SUMMARISER	AEINORSSTT	STATIONERS
AEILMOPPSS	AMPELOPSIS	AEIMMRRSUZ	SUMMARIZER	AEINORSSTY	TYROSINASE
AEILMOPRST	PERISTOMAL	AEIMNNNOST	MINNESOTAN	AEINORSTTY	STATIONERY
AEILMOPSTT	PTOLEMAIST	AEIMNNNOTT	ANOINTMENT	AEINPRRTTU	PARTURIENT
AEILMORRSS	MORALISERS	AEIMNNNQSU	MANNEQUINS	AEINPRTTTW	PATENT WRIT
AEILMORRSZ	MORALIZERS	AEIMNNORTU	NUMERATION	AEINRRSSST	STARRINESS
AEILMPPSST	PALIMPSEST	AEIMNOPRTT	ARMIPOTENT	AEINRRSSST	RESTRAINTS
AEILMPRSST	SLIPSTREAM	AEIMNOPTTT	TEMPTATION	AEINRSSSTT	STRAITNESS
AEILMPRSTU	PSALTERIUM	AEIMNOQSUU	EQUANIMOUS	AEINRSTUYZ	SUZERAINTY
AEILMPRTUU	PARI-MUTUEL	AEIMNORRTT	TERMINATOR	AEIOPRRRST	RESPIRATOR
AEILMRRSSU	SURREALISM	AEIMNORSST	STEAM IRONS	AEIOPRRTTX	EXTIRPATOR
AEILMRRSTT	TRIMESTRAL	AEIMNORSSW	WOMANISERS	AEIOPRRTXY	EXPIRATORY
AEILMSTTUX	TEXTUALISM	AEIMNORSTT	MONETARIST	AEIPRSTUUV	USURPATIVE
AEILNNNSTW	LAWN TENNIS	AEIMNORSWZ	WOMANIZERS	AEJMNNORUY	JOURNEYMAN
AEILNNOPRS	NONPAREILS	AEIMNPSTTY	TYMPANITES	AEJMPRSTUW	WATER JUMPS
AEILNNOPSY	POLYNESIAN	AEIMNRRRTY	INTERMARRY	AEKKLRTTUY	TALK TURKEY
AEILNNOPTY	ANTILEPTON	AEIMOOSTTU	AUTOTOMISE	AEKMNORTTW	MARKET
AEILNNORTT	INTOLERANT	AEIMOOTTUV	AUTOMOTIVE	TOWN	
AEILNNPRSU	PENINSULAR	AEIMOOTTUZ	AUTOTOMIZE	AEKMORRSTW	MASTERWORK
AEILNNPSUS	PENINSULAS	AEIMOPRRTT	IMPETRATOR	AEKMRRSSST	STRESS MARK
AEILNNRRTU	INTERLUNAR	AEIMOPRTUU	EUPATORIUM	AEKNOPRRSY	NOSY PARKER
AEILNOOPRT	TROPAEOLIN	AEIMORRSTU	MORTUARIES	AEKNOQRSTU	SQUARE KNOT
AEILNOOPSS	POLONAISES	AEIMORSSTT	ESTIMATORS	AEKNPRRSST	PRANKSTERS
AEILNOORTT	TOLERATION	AEIMORSSTV	MOVIE STARS	AEKOOPRRTY	PROKARYOTE
AEILNOPRST	INTERPOSAL	AEIMPRSSTU	PASTEURISM	AEKORRSTWW	WATERWORKS
AEILNOPRTU	ERUPTIONAL	AEIMPRSTUZ	TRAPEZIUMS	AELLMNOSTT	ALLOTMENTS
AEILNORRTT	TORRENTIAL	AEIMPSSTUV	ASSUMPTIVE	AELLMOORSU	ALLOMEROUS
AEILNORTTV	VENTILATOR	AEIMORSTUZ	QUIZMASTER	AELLMOPSSY	PLASMOLYSE
AEILNOTTUX	EXULTATION	AEINNNOQSU	SINE QUA NON	AELLMORSUV	MARVELLOUS
AEILNPRSST	PALTRINESS	AEINNOORST	RESONATION	AELLNOPPRT	PROPELLANT
AEILNPRSTY	PARTY LINES	AEINNOORTV	RENOVATION	AELLNOPRSY	PERSONALLY
AEILNRSTTU	NEUTRALIST	AEINNOPRSY	PENSIONARY	AELLNOPTVY	POLYVALENT

AELLNORTTY	TOLERANTLY	
AELLNOSSSW	SALLOWNESS	
AELLNPTTUY	PETULANTLY	
AELLNRSTTY	SLATTERNLY	
AELLNTTUXY	EXULTANTLY	
AELLOPPRSU	ALL-PURPOSE	
AELLOPSTUV	POLE VAULTS	
AELLRSSTVY	SYLVESTRAL	
AELLRTTUXY	TEXTURALLY	
AELMMNNOTU	MONUMENTAL	
AELMMOOPSS	PLASMOSOME	
AELMMORSST	MAELSTROMS	
AELMMOSSUU	MAUSOLEUMS	
AELMNNNRUY	UNMANNERLY	
AELMNNNTUS	ANNULMENTS	
AELMNNOOPS	MONOPLANES	
AELMNNOOTV	MONOVALENT	
AELMNOOPRT	PROTONEMAL	
AELMNOOPRY	LAMPOONERY	
AELMNOPRTY	PLANOMETRY	
AELMNORSWW	LAWNMOWERS	
AELMOOPRTU	TROPAEOLUM	
AELMOPPRUY	PROPYLAEUM	
AELMOPRTTU	PETROLATUM	
AELMOPSSST	EPSOM SALTS	
AELMOQSSUU	SQUAMULOSE	
AELMORSSTU	SOMERSAULT	
AELMORSTTT	LATTERMOST	
AELNNOPRYY	PENNYROYAL	
AELNNORSTY	RESONANTLY	
AELNNOSTWW	NEWTON'S LAW	
AELNOPPRTW	POWER PLANT	
AELNOPRSSY	LAYPERSONS	
AELNOPRSTY	PERSONALTY	
AELNORSUVY	RAVENOUSLY	
AELNOSSUUY	NAUSEOUSLY	
AELNPPRSTU	SUPPLANTER	
AELNPRRSUU	SUPERLUNAR	
AELOOPSSTV	SEVASTOPOL	
AELOPPRRRU	POURPARLER	
AELOPPRTUV	UPPER VOLTA	
AELOPSSTTU	POSTULATES	
AELORRSSTT	LAST RESORT	
AELPPSSTUY	PLATYPUSES	
AEMMNORRTT	MONTMARTRE	
AEMMNNOPTY	NONPAYMENT	
AEMNNOORSS	ROMAN NOSES	
AEMNNOOSST	STONEMASON	
AEMNNORTTT	ATTORNMENT	
AEMNNORTTU	TOURNAMENT	
AEMNNRRSUY	NURSERYMAN	
AEMNOOPRTT	PORTAMENTO	
AEMNOORRST	ASTRONOMER	
AEMNORRSTT	MONTSERRAT	
AEMNORRSTU	NUMERATORS	
AEMNORSSTT	ASSORTMENT	
AEMNRRSTTU	TRANSMUTER	
AEMOOPSTTY	SOMATOTYPE	
AEMOORSSTT	STATEROOMS	
AEMOPRSSTT	POSTMASTER	
AEMOPRSSTU	MOUSETRAPS	
AEMORRSTTY	ASTROMETRY	
AENNNOSSTW	WANTONNESS	
AENNORRSSW	NARROWNESS	
AENNORRSTT	NONSTARTER	
AENOOPRRST	PERSONATOR	
AENOORRSST	RESONATORS	
AENOPRRSST	TRANSPOSER	
AENOPRSSUV	SUPERNOVAS	
AENOPRSTTT	PROTESTANT	
AENPRRSTTU	TRANSPUTER	
AEOOPPRSTU	TROPOPAUSE	
AEOOQRRSTU	SQUARE ROOT	
AEOPPRRRTU	RAPPORTEUR	
AEOPPRSSTW	SPORTSWEAR	
AEOPRSTTUW	WATERSPOUT	
AEORSSSSTU	TROUSSEAUS	
AEORSSTUUX	TROUSSEAUX	
AEPRRSSSTU	SUPERSTARS	
AFFGIILNSY	FALSIFYING	
AFFGIMRSSU	SUFFRAGISM	
AFFGINNORT	AFFRONTING	
AFFGIRSSTU	SUFFRAGIST	
AFFHILLTUY	FAITHFULLY	
AFFHILNTUU	UNFAITHFUL	
AFFIILNPST	PLAINTIFFS	
AFFIIMNRSU	RUFFIANISM	
AFFLLORUUV	FLAVOURFUL	
AFFLOOSTTU	FOOT FAULTS	
AFFMNNRSUY	FUNNY FARMS	
AFGGGILNNU	UNFLAGGING	
AFGGIIMNNY	MAGNIFYING	
AFGGIIMNTU	FUMIGATING	
AFGGIINRTY	GRATIFYING	
AFGHHILLST	FLASHLIGHT	
AFGHHILPTT	FLIGHT PATH	
AFGHIILRTY	FAIRY LIGHT	
AFGHIINNOS	FASHIONING	
AFGHIIRSTU	GUITARFISH	
AFGHIORTWY	RIGHT OF WAY	
AFGIIILNNZ	FINALIZING	
AFGIIILNRT	AIR-LIFTING	
AFGIILMNPY	AMPLIFYING	
AFGIILNNTY	FAINTINGLY	
AFGIILNQUY	QUALIFYING	
AFGIILOSTU	FLAGITIOUS	
AFGIIMNOTU	FUMIGATION	
AFGIINORTU	FIGURATION	
AFGIINSSTY	SATISFYING	
AFGIKMNORS	KING-OF-ARMS	
AFGIKNRSST	SKIN GRAFTS	
AFGILNORUV	FLAVOURING	
AFGIMNORSU	AUSFORMING	
AFGIMNORTT	FORMATTING	
AFGINNPRSY	FRYING PANS	
AFHHLRSTTU	HALF-TRUTHS	
AFHILNOPST	FLASH POINT	
AFHIOPRRST	PARROTFISH	
AFHKLLNTUY	THANKFULLY	
AFHKLNNTUU	UNTHANKFUL	
AFHLLORSST	SHORTFALLS	
AFHLLORSUY	ROYAL FLUSH	
AFHLLRTUWY	WRATHFULLY	
AFIILLRRTY	FRITILLARY	
AFIILLNORSU	INFUSORIAL	
AFIILNORTT	FILTRATION, FLIRTATION	
AFIKLLMOST	MILK FLOATS	
AFILLMNORY	INFORMALLY	
AFILLNOPRU	PLAIN FLOUR	
AFILLNPPTY	FLIPPANTLY	
AFILLOOPRS	APRIL FOOLS	
AFILMNORTU	FULMINATOR	
AFILMORSST	FORMALISTS	
AFILNOOSTT	FLOTATIONS	
AFILNORTTY	FRONTALITY	
AFIMMORTUU	FUMATORIUM	
AFIMNNORST	INFORMANTS	
AFIMNOORST	FORMATIONS	
AFIMORRSTT	STRATIFORM	
AFLLLNUUWY	UNLAWFULLY	
AFLLNOORSU	ON ALL FOURS	
AFLMOORRTU	FORMULATOR	
AFNORSTTUU	FORTUNATUS	
AGGGGIINZZ	ZIGZAGGING	
AGGGILLNWY	WAGGLINGLY	
AGGGILNRST	STRAGGLING	
AGGGIMNORT	MORTGAGING	
AGGHIILLMN	GILLINGHAM	
AGGHIINNRS	GARNISHING	
AGGHILLNUY	LAUGHINGLY	
AGGHILMNPU	GALUMPHING	
AGGHILNNSY	GNASHINGLY	
AGGHLOOPRY	GRAPHOLOGY, LOGOGRAPHY	
AGGIIILNTT	LITIGATING	
AGGIIIMNTT	MITIGATING	
AGGIIINRRT	IRRIGATING	
AGGIILLNNS	SIGNALLING	
AGGIILNNST	TINGALINGS	
AGGIILNNTU	AGGLUTININ	

AGGIINNORZ	ORGANIZING	
AGGILLNOTY	GLOATINGLY	
AGGILNNNTU	UNTANGLING	
AGGILNNORY	GROANINGLY	
AGGILNNRST	STRANGLING	
AGGIMNOPRR	PROGRAMING	
AGGINOORRT	RARING TO GO	
AGGINORRTT	GARROTTING	
AGGLNOOORY	ORGANOLOGY	
AGGLNOOORZ	GORGONZOLA	
AGGMOORRST	MORTGAGORS	
AGHHILOPRT	LITHOGRAPH	
AGHHLOOPRY	HOLOGRAPHY	
AGHHMOOPRS	HOMOGRAPHS	
AGHHNOOPPR	PHONOGRAPH	
AGHHOOPPRT	PHOTOGRAPH	
AGHHOPPTYY	PHYTOPHAGY	
AGHHORTUWY	THROUGHWAY	
AGHIIINNSU	NINGSIA HUI	
AGHIILLMTY	ALMIGHTILY	
AGHIILLSTT	TAILLIGHTS	
AGHIIMNNUZ	HUMANIZING	
AGHIINNRST	TARNISHING	
AGHIINNRSV	VARNISHING	
AGHIINNRTU	THURINGIAN	
AGHIINPRRS	HAIRSPRING	
AGHIINRTWW	WAINWRIGHT	
AGHILLNOSW	SHALLOWING	
AGHILLNSSY	SLASHINGLY	
AGHILMORST	ALGORITHMS,
	LOGARITHMS	
AGHILNNTUY	HAUNTINGLY	
AGHILNPSTY	PLAYTHINGS	
AGHILNRSTT	STRINGHALT	
AGHILNSSWY	SWASHINGLY	
AGHILOPPSY	GYPSOPHILA	
AGHILORSTT	GASTROLITH	
AGHILPRTWY	PLAYWRIGHT	
AGHIMNNOTT	NOTTINGHAM	
AGHIMNNOOPS	SHAMPOOING	
AGHIMNRSST	HAMSTRINGS	
AGHIMORSST	HISTOGRAMS	
AGHINNOOPR	HARPOONING	
AGHINNOSTW	WASHINGTON	
AGHINOPRTY	ATROPHYING	
AGHIOPPRRS	SPIROGRAPH	
AGHLMOOSTU	GOALMOUTHS	
AGHLNOOORT	ORTHOGONAL	
AGHLNOSSTU	ONSLAUGHTS	
AGHLOPPRSY	POLYGRAPHS	
AGHLOPRSTY	STYLOGRAPH	
AGHLOPRXYY	XYLOGRAPHY	
AGHMMOOOSU	HOMOGAMOUS
AGHMNOOPRS	MONOGRAPHS	

AGHMNNOOPRY	NOMOGRAPHY	
AGHMNOORTU	MOUTH
	ORGAN	
AGHMOOPRTY	TOMOGRAPHY	
AGHNOOPRSY	NOSOGRAPHY	
AGHOOOPSUZ	ZOOPHAGOUS	
AGHOOPPRTY	TOPOGRAPHY	
AGHOPPRRYY	PYROGRAPHY	
AGHOPPRTYY	TYPOGRAPHY	
AGIIIILNNT	INITIALING	
AGIIIINNTT	INITIATING	
AGIIILMNNN	MAINLINING	
AGIIILMNTT	MILITATING	
AGIIILNOTT	LITIGATION	
AGIIIMMNXZ	MAXIMIZING	
AGIIIMMNNT	INTIMATING	
AGIIIMNNOTT	MITIGATION	
AGIIINNSTZ	SANITIZING	
AGIIINNORRT	IRRIGATION	
AGIIINNRRTT	IRRITATING	
AGIIINNRSTZ	SATIRIZING	
AGIIINTTTV	TITIVATING	
AGIIKNNNPR	NAPKIN RING	
AGIILLMMRS	MILLIGRAMS	
AGIILLNNST	INSTALLING	
AGIILLNORY	ORIGINALLY	
AGIILLNPRS	SPIRALING	
AGIILLNRTU	TRILINGUAL	
AGIILLNRTY	TRAILINGLY	
AGIILLNTVY	VIGILANTLY	
AGIILMMNOT	IMMOLATING	
AGIILMNNPT	IMPLANTING	
AGIILMNORZ	MORALIZING	
AGIILMNOST	ANTILOGISM	
AGIILMNSTU	SIMULATING	
AGIILMNTTU	MUTILATING	
AGIILNNORU	UNORIGINAL	
AGIILNNSTU	INSULATING	
AGIILNOPRZ	POLARIZING	
AGIILNPRST	SPRINGTAIL	
AGIILNRSTY	LARYNGITIS	
AGIILNSSTV	VITAL SIGNS	
AGIILOOPST	APIOLOGIST	
AGIILOOSTX	AXIOLOGIST	
AGIIMMNNRST	IMMIGRANTS	
AGIIMMORRT	IMMIGRATOR	
AGIIMMOSST	MISOGAMIST	
AGIIMMSSTT	STIGMATISM	
AGIIMNNNOT	NOMINATING	
AGIIMNNOWZ	WOMANIZING	
AGIIMNNPRS	MAINSPRING	
AGIIMNNRTU	RUMINATING	
AGIIMNORST	MIGRATIONS	
AGIIMNORTZ	AMORTIZING	

AGIIMNOTTV	MOTIVATING	
AGIIMNSSTT	MISSTATING	
AGIIMNSSUV	VAGINISMUS	
AGIIMSSTTT	STIGMATIST	
AGIINNNOTV	INNOVATING	
AGIINNOPPT	APPOINTING	
AGIINNORSS	SIGNORINAS	
AGIINNORTZ	NOTARIZING	
AGIINNOSTT	STATIONING	
AGIINNSSTU	SUSTAINING	
AGIINOORRT	ORIGINATOR	
AGIINOPRRR	RIP-ROARING	
AGIINOPRVZ	VAPORIZING	
AGIINORSTT	INSTIGATOR	
AGIINORSUV	VIRAGINOUS	
AGIIRSSTTU	GUITARISTS	
AGIKKLNRSY	SKYLARKING	
AGIKLMNOOT	TOOL-MAKING	
AGIKLNOPRT	PARKING LOT	
AGIKLNOSTT	TALKING-TOS	
AGIKLNOTTU	OUTTALKING	
AGIKMNNORW	WORKINGMAN	
AGIKMNNOTU	KUOMINTANG	
AGIKNNORTU	OUTRANKING	
AGILLNNRSY	SNARLINGLY	
AGILLNNSTY	SLANTINGLY	
AGILLNOPRT	PATROLLING	
AGILLNOSWW	SWALLOWING	
AGILLNRSUY	SINGULARLY	
AGILLNTTTY	TATTLINGLY	
AGILLOOSSS	ISOGLOSSAL	
AGILMNNOOP	LAMPOONING	
AGILMNRSTY	SMARTINGLY	
AGILMOOSTU	GLIOMATOUS	
AGILMOPSTY	POLYGAMIST	
AGILNNOPTY	POIGNANTLY	
AGILNNPPSY	SNAPPINGLY	
AGILNNTTUY	TAUNTINGLY	
AGILNNTUVY	VAUNTINGLY	
AGILNOPPRS	PROLAPSING	
AGILNOPPTU	POPULATING	
AGILNOPTUY	OUTPLAYING	
AGILNOSSTW	WAGONS-LITS	
AGILNOSTTU	OUTLASTING	
AGILOOPSST	APOLOGISTS	
AGILORSSST	GLOSSARIST	
AGIMMNOOST	MONOGAMIST	
AGIMMNSSUY	GYMNASIUMS	
AGIMNNOSVV	MOVING VANS	
AGIMNNSSUU	UNASSUMING	
AGIMNOORST	AGRONOMIST	
AGIMNOPRSU	SPORANGIUM	
AGINNNRRTU	RAT-RUNNING	
AGINNOPTTU	AT GUNPOINT	

AGINNORRRTW	WARRINGTON	AHIMNOOSTZ	MATOZINHOS
AGINNPPSUW	SWAN-UPPING	AHIMNPRTTU	TRIUMPHANT
AGINOPRRTY	PORTRAYING	AHIMORSTUU	HAUSTORIUM
AGINORSTTU	OUTSTARING	AHIMPPPRSU	PARISH-PUMP
AGINOSTTUY	OUTSTAYING	AHINOPRSUX	XIPHOSURAN
AGINPRSSSU	SURPASSING	AHIOOPSTTX	PHOTOTAXIS
AGIORSTTUU	GRATUITOUS	AHKLMOPRYY	KARYOLYMPH
AGKLORSSWS	GLASSWORKS	AHLLMORSSU	SMALL HOURS
AGKLPPRSSU	SPARK PLUGS	AHLLOPRSTU	PROTHALLUS
AGKNNNORTY	GRANNY KNOT	AHLMNNORTU	LUNAR MONTH
AGLLLLOPPU	GALLUP POLL	AHLMNOORST	SOLAR MONTH
AGLLLOOPRY	PYROGALLOL	AHLMOOPRTU	PHOTOMURAL
AGLLNOOPYY	PALYNOLOGY	AHLMOOPSTY	HOMOPLASTY
AGLMOOOSTY	SOMATOLOGY	AHLMPRSUWY	MURPHY'S
AGLMOOPSUY	POLYGAMOUS		LAW
AGLNOORSUU	LANGUOROUS	AHLNOPSTUY	POLYANTHUS
AGLOPPRSUY	PLAYGROUPS	AHLORRSSTU	ULTRASHORT
AGMMNOOOSU		AHMNNOOSTU	MONANTHOUS
	MONOGAMOUS	AHMNOOPRTU	PROTOHUMAN
AGMMNOPSUU	MAGNUM	AHNNOSTTWY	SHANTYTOWN
	OPUS	AHNOOPSTTY	PHOTONASTY
AGMNOORSTY	GASTRONOMY	AHNOPPRTTY	TRYPTOPHAN
AGMOOORSST	MATO	AHOOPPRRST	SAPROTROPH
	GROSSO	AHOOPPRTTY	PROTOPATHY
AGMOORSTTY	GASTROTOMY	AHOOPSSTTT	PHOTOSTATS
AGOORRSSST	GRASS ROOTS	AIIIIKMRTT	KIRITIMATI
AHHIIIILNTW	WITHIN HAIL	AIIIINNOTT	INITIATION
AHHIIRRSST	HAIR SHIRTS	AIIILLMNTU	ILLUMINATI
AHHIOPRSTU	AUTHORSHIP	AIIILLMRTY	MILITARILY
AHHISSWWYY	WISHY-WASHY	AIIILLMNNST	MINIMALIST
AHHMORRSTW	HARMSWORTH	AIIILLMRST	MILITARISM
AHHOPPRSUY	HAPPY HOURS	AIIILMNOTT	LIMITATION,
AHIIIMMPSX	AMPHIMIXIS		MILITATION
AHIIKMNRSS	KRISHNAISM	AIIILMRSTT	MILITARIST
AHIILMORTU	HUMILIATOR	AIIILMRSTY	SIMILARITY
AHIILRSSTT	SHIRTTAILS	AIIILORSTV	VISITORIAL
AHIIMNNOTU	INHUMATION	AIIILRTTVY	TRIVIALITY
AHIIMNNTUY	INHUMANITY	AIIIMNNOTT	INTIMATION
AHIIMNORSW	IRISHWOMAN	AIIIMNOPSS	PIANISSIMO
AHIINORSST	HISTORIANS	AIIIMNOSTT	IMITATIONS
AHIJNNOSST	SAINT JOHN'S	AIIINNOOST	IONISATION
AHIKKNNSTT	THINK TANKS	AIIINNOOTZ	IONIZATION
AHIKKSTUUY	KITAKYUSHU	AIIINNOTTV	INVITATION
AHIKNPRRSW	SHRINK-WRAP	AIIINORRTT	IRRITATION
AHILMORSST	HAILSTORMS	AIIINORTTY	INITIATORY
AHILMPSSYY	SYMPHYSIAL	AIIINOSTTV	VISITATION
AHILNOORTZ	HORIZONTAL	AIIINOTTTV	TITIVATION
AHILNOPPTY	HIPPOLYTAN	AIIIPRSSTY	PITYRIASIS
AHILNOPSTU	SULPHATION	AIIIPRTVVY	VIVIPARITY
AHILNPPSSY	SNAPPISHLY	AIIKNSSTTT	SAINT KITTS
AHILORSSTW	SHOW TRIALS	AIILLMNNTU	ILLUMINANT
AHIMMNORSU	HARMONIUMS	AIILLMNTTY	MILITANTLY
AHIMNOOOSU	HOMOOUSIAN	AIILLNOOTV	VOLITIONAL
AHIMNOORRU	HONORARIUM	AIILLNOSUV	VILLAINOUS
AHIMNOORSU	HARMONIOUS	AIILLORSTY	SOLITARILY
AIILLOSSTT	SOLSTITIAL		
AIILLOTTVY	VOLATILITY		
AIILLSTUVV	VALVULITIS		
AIILMMNNOS	NOMINALISM		
AIILMMNOOT	IMMOLATION		
AIILMMORST	IMMORALIST		
AIILMMORTY	IMMORALITY		
AIILMNNOST	NOMINALIST		
AIILMNOORT	MONITORIAL		
AIILMNORTY	MINATORILY		
AIILMNOSTU	SIMULATION		
AIILMNOTTU	MUTILATION		
AIILMNRSSU	INSULARISM		
AIILNNOOST	INSOLATION		
AIILNNOOST	INSULATION		
AIILNOOPPT	OPPILATION		
AIILNOOPST	POSITIONAL,		
	SPOLIATION		
AIILNOOSTV	VIOLATIONS		
AIILNOSSTU	SAINT-LOUIS		
AIILNRSSUY	URINALYSIS		
AIILNRSTUY	INSULARITY		
AIILORSSTU	SAILOR SUIT		
AIILPRSSTU	SPIRITUALS		
AIILRTTUVY	VIRTUALITY		
AIIMMNNOTU	AMMUNITION		
AIIMMPRRTU	IMPRIMATUR		
AIIMMRTTUY	IMMATURITY		
AIIMNNOOT	NOMINATION		
AIIMNNORTU	RUMINATION		
AIIMNNRSTT	MINISTRANT		
AIIMNOOTTV	MOTIVATION		
AIIMNOPRTV	PROVITAMIN		
AIIMNOPSTU	UTOPIANISM		
AIIMNOPTTU	IMPUTATION		
AIIMNORSSU	MISSOURIAN		
AIIMNORSSY	MISSIONARY		
AIIMNPRSTU	PURITANISM		
AIIMNPSSTT	TIMPANISTS		
AIIMNPSSTU	IMPUISSANT		
AIIMNPSTTY	TYMPANITIS		
AIIMOPRSTT	PATRIOTISM		
AIIMOSSTTT	STOMATITIS		
AIINNNOOTT	INTONATION		
AIINNNOOTV	INNOVATION		
AIINNORSTT	TRANSITION		
AIINNORSTU	INSINUATOR		
AIINOOPPST	APPOSITION		
AIINOOPRST	PARTITIONS		
AIINOPRSTV	PRIVATIONS		
AIINOORSST	STRIATIONS		
AIINORTTVY	INVITATORY		
AIINOSSTTU	SITUATIONS		
AIIOPRSUVV	VIVIPAROUS		

AIIPRSTTVY	VARITYPIST
AIJLMNORSU	JOURNALISM
AIJLNORSTU	JOURNALIST
AIJMORSSTU	MAJOR SUITS
AIKLLLOPTW	PILLOW TALK
AIKLOPSTUV	VOLAPUKIST
AIKLORSSYY	KARYOLYSIS
AILLMNOOPY	POLYNOMIAL
AILLMNPRST	SMALL PRINT
AILLMOSSYY	AMYLOLYSIS
AILLNOOPRT	POLLINATOR
AILLNOOPTY	OPTIONALLY
AILLNQRTUY	TRANQUILLY
AILLPRSSTU	PLURALISTS
AILMMSTTUU	ULTIMATUMS
AILMNNOOPR	PRONOMINAL
AILMNORSST	MORTAL SINS
AILMNORTUY	UNMORALITY
AILMNSSTTU	STIMULANTS
AILMOOPSTU	LIPOMATOUS
AILMORSSTU	SIMULATORS
AILMORSTTU	STIMULATOR
AILNOOPPTU	POPULATION
AILNOOPRSS	SPONSORIAL
AILNOOSTUV	OVULATIONS
AILNOPSSTU	PULSATIONS
AILNORSSTU	INSULATORS
AILNORSTTU	LUSTRATION
AILNOSTTUU	USTULATION
AILNPPSSTU	SUPPLIANTS
AILOPPRTUY	POPULARITY
AILOPRSTTU	STIPULATOR
AILRRSTUUV	ULTRAVIRUS
AIMMNORSTU	STRAMONIUM
AIMMNOSSTU	SUMMATIONS
AIMMOORRTU	MORATORIUM
AIMNNOOSTU	ANTIMONOUS
AIMNOOSTTU	AUTONOMIST
AIMNOOSTTX	TAXONOMIST
AIMNOPSSTU	ASSUMPTION
AIMNORRSST	RAINSTORMS
AIMNRSTTUU	NASTURTIUM
AIMOOORTVY	OVARIOTOMY
AINNOOPRTT	ANTIPROTON
AINNOORSTV	INNOVATORS
AINOOPRSTY	ANISOTROPY
AINOOQSTTU	QUOTATIONS
AINOOSTTTU	OUTSTATION
AINOPRSTUU	USURPATION
AINORRSSTT	TRANSISTOR
AINORRSSTY	TRANSITORY
AINPRSTUUV	PURSUIVANT
AIOOPRRSUU	UPROARIOUS
AIOORRSTTU	TRAITOROUS

AIOOSSTTTT	TATTOOISTS
AIOPPPRSSU	PUPIPAROUS
AIORRRTTTU	TRITURATOR
AKKKLLNUUX	KU KLUX KLAN
AKKMMNORSU	KOMMUNARSK
AKLOPRRRSY	LORRY PARKS
ALLNOPSTTU	POLLUTANTS
ALLOPRSSTW	STRAW POLLS
ALMNOPRTUY	POULTRYMAN
ALMOOPPRST	PROTOPLASM
ALMOPPSSUY	PLAY POSSUM
ALNOPSSTTU	POSTULANTS
ALOOORSTUZ	ZOOLATROUS
ALOOPPRSTT	PROTOPLAST
ALOOPPRTTY	PROTOTYPAL
ALOOPRSTTU	POSTULATOR
ALOPRTUUVY	VOLUPTUARY
AMMOOSTUXY	MYXOMATOUS
AMNNOOSTWW	TOWNSWOMAN
AMNOOOSTUU	AUTONOMOUS
AMNOOPRSUY	PARONYMOUS
AMOPPRSTTU	POSTPARTUM
ANOOOPRSTZ	PROTOZOANS
ANOPRRSSTT	TRANSPORTS
AOOORRSTTV	ROTOVATORS
AOOPQRSTTU	POST QUARTO
AORRRSTWWY	WORRYWARTS
BBBCKOOSSY	BOBBY SOCKS,
BBBEEELMSU	BUMBLEBEES
BBBEEIINRW	WINEBIBBER
BBBEGILNRU	BLUBBERING
BBBGHINNOO	HOBNOBBING
BBBHIINRSU	RUBBISH BIN
BBBLLOOWWY	BLOW-BY-BLOW
BBCDEIRSSU	SUBSCRIBED
BBCEEKNRRU	RUBBERNECK
BBCEELNOOU	BUBONOCELE
BBCEGILNOR	CLOBBERING
BBCEHINSSU	CHUBBINESS
BBCEHLOSUY	CUBBYHOLES
BBCEILRSS	SCRIBBLERS
BBCEIRRSSU	SUBSCRIBER
BBCEIRSSTU	SCRUBBIEST
BBCGIILNRS	SCRIBBLING
BBCIIILOST	BIBLIOTICS
BBDDEEIMOV	DIVE-BOMBED
BBDDEELOSU	DOUBLE BEDS
BBDDEILNOU	DOUBLE BIND
BBDEEIMORV	DIVE-BOMBER
BBDEIKNOOR	BOOKBINDER

BBDEIOSSUY	BUSYBODIES
BBDHIIOPRS	BISHOPBIRD
BBEEEIRRRTU	RUBBER TREE
BBEEIILRRS	BILBERRIES
BBEEIRRRSU	BURBERRIES
BBEELLOTTU	BLUEBOTTLE
BBEELMORTT	LETTER BOMB
BBEGHILOSS	BOBSLEIGHS
BBEGHIORRT	BIG BROTHER
BBEGILNORS	SLOBBERING
BBEGINRSSU	GRUBBINESS
BBEHHILOST	SHIBBOLETH
BBEHHOORSY	HOBBYHORSE
BBEHLLMOSS	BOMBSHELLS
BBEIILLOOP	BIBLIOPOLE
BBEIKLMOOO	BOOKMOBILE
BBEIKLNOST	KNOBBLIEST
BBEILNOSSW	WOBBLINESS
BBEINSSSTU	STUBBINESS
BBEIOOPRSY	BOOBY PRISE
BBEIOOPRYZ	BOOBY PRIZE
BBEKLORRUW	RUBBLEWORK
BBEKNORSTU	BONKBUSTER
BBEMNORSUX	BOX NUMBERS
BBENORRSTU	STUBBORNER
BBFHIINORS	RIBBONFISH
BBGHIINRSU	RUBBISHING
BBGHILLSTU	LIGHT BULBS
BBGHILNOOS	HOBGOBLINS
BBGILNNSUY	SNUBBINGLY
BBHILNOSSY	SNOBBISHLY
BBIIIIMNOT	IMBIBITION
BBIIILOSTT	BIBLIOTIST
BBIKMNOSST	STINK-BOMBS
BBJMMMOOUU	MUMBO
	JUMBO
BBLMOORSUY	BLOOMSBURY
BBLNORSTUY	STUBBORNLY
BCCCKMOOSS	COCKSCOMBS
BCCDEEEMNU	DECUMBENCE
BCCDEILNOU	CONDUCIBLE
BCCEEEMNRU	RECUMBENCE
BCCEEENPSU	PUBESCENCE
BCCEEENRSU	RUBESCENCE
BCCEEINRTY	CYBERNETIC
BCCEILORTU	BERTOLUCCI
BCCEIMNNUY	INCUMBENCY
BCCEINNOOS	CONCUBINES
BCCEKOSSTU	STOCK CUBES
BCCGIMNSUU	SUCCUMBING
BCCHHIINNY	INCH BY INCH
BCCHIINORT	BRONCHITIC
BCCIILSSTY	BICYCLISTS
BCDDEEILTU	DEDUCTIBLE

BCDDIIKRSY DICKYBIRDS	BCEEGIINOT BIOGENETIC	BCEHKLOOSU BLOCKHOUSE
BCDEEEFNOR CORNED BEEF	BCEEGINRSU SUBGENERIC	BCEHKOPSTU BUCKET SHOP
BCDEEEIINT BENEDICITE	BCEEHKLNOU HUCKLEBONE	BCEHLOSSUU CLUBHOUSES
BCDEEEMNRU ENCUMBERED	BCEEHKOOQU CHEQUEBOOK	BCEHMNNOOSY HONEYCOMBS
BCDEEHIMRS BESMIRCHED	BCEEHKORRY CHOKEBERRY	BCEHMRSTUW THUMBSCREW
BCDEEHLOST BEDCLOTHES	BCEEHMORUU EMBOUCHURE	BCEIIILMMS IMMISCIBLE
BCDEEIILNR INCREDIBLE	BCEEHNOOPR NECROPHOBE	BCEIIILMTY IMBECILITY
BCDEEINSSU SUBSIDENCE	BCEEHNORRX BRONX CHEER	BCEIIILNNV INVINCIBLE
BCDEEIPRRS PRESCRIBED	BCEEHNPRSS BENCH PRESS	BCEIIKLLLS SICKLEBILL
BCDEEKLLNU BULLNECKED	BCEEIILPST PLEBISCITE	BCEIILMMOS EMBOLISMIC
BCDEENOSST SECOND BEST	BCEEIILTYZ BELIZE CITY	BCEIJNOOST OBJECTIONS
BCDEEORRSS CROSSBREED	BCEEIJOSTV OBJECTIVE	BCEIJNOSTU SUBJECTION
BCDEEOSTWY BETWS-Y-COED	BCEEIJSTUV SUBJECTIVE	BCEILMNOSU COLUMBINES
BCDEFLOOTU CLUBFOOTED	BCEEIILLNPU BLUE-PENCIL	BCEILMOORT BOLOMETRIC
BCDEGHINOU DEBOUCHING	BCEEIILLOOS CELLOBIOSE	BCEILMRSTU CRUMBLIEST
BCDEGIINRS DESCRIBING	BCEEIILMOST COMESTIBLE	BCEILNRTUU TUBERCULIN
BCDEHIILOR BICHLORIDE	BCEEIILNOTY BY-ELECTION	BCEIMNNSTU INCUMBENTS
BCDEHILNOU DOUBLE CHIN	BCEEIOOSVX VOICE BOXES	BCEINNOSSU BOUNCINESS
BCDEEIILNRY INCREDIBLY	BCEEIPRRRS PRESCRIBER	BCEINORTTU CONTRIBUTE
BCDEIILPSU PUBLICISED	BCEEIPRRSY SPICEBERRY	BCEINOSSTU SUBSECTION
BCDEIILPUZ PUBLICIZED	BCEEIPSSSU SUBSPECIES	BCEIOPPRSY PRESBYOPIC
BCDEILOORR CORRODIBLE	BCEEJNORST JOB CENTRES	BCEIORSSTT OBSTETRICS
BCDEILOPRU PRODUCIBLE	BCEEJOSSTX SEX OBJECTS	BCEKKOOOPT POCKETBOOK
BCDEILORTT BITTER COLD	BCEEKLNOTT BOTTLENECK	BCEKLNRTUU TURNBUCKLE
BCDEIOPRRS PROSCRIBED	BCEELNOTTU CUTTLEBONE	BCEKLOORTW TOWER BLOCK
BCDEKLOOOS CLOSED BOOK	BCEELNRTUU TURBULENCE	BCEKLOOSTV BLOCK VOTES
BCDELNOORU CORDON BLEU	BCEELOPPRT COPPER BELT	BCELRSTUUU SUBCULTURE
BCDELORRUY CLOUDBERRY	BCEEMMORSU CUMBERSOME	BCEMNOPRTU PROCUMBENT
BCDEMMNRUU CUMMERBUND	BCEEMMORTY EMBRECTOMY	BCENOORSSS CROSSBONES
BCDEORSTTU OBSTRUCTED	BCEEOOORRR CORROBOREE	BCEORRSTTU OBSTRUCTER
BCDGIIOSTU DOG BISCUIT	BCEFFIOOSX BOX OFFICES	BCEPRSTTUU BUTTERCUPS
BCDHHIILRT CHILDBIRTH	BCEFFIOOSY OFFICE BOYS	BCFIIMORRR CRIBRIFORM
BCDHLNOOTU CLOTHBOUND	BCEFHNNORT FRONTBENCH	BCGHILNSTU NIGHTCLUBS
BCDIILMORU LUMBRICOID	BCEFIIKRRS FIREBRICKS	BCGIIINNRS INSCRIBING
BCDIIOPRRT TROPICBIRD	BCEFIJSTUY SUBJECTIFY	BCGIKLNNUU UNBUCKLING
BCDINOSTUU SUBDUCTION	BCEGHIINTW BEWITCHING	BCGINOOTTY BOYCOTTING
BCDKLOOOST BLOODSTOCK	BCEGHIKNNS KING'S BENCH	BCHIINORST BRONCHITIS
BCDKLOOOSW WOODBLOCKS	BCEGHINRTU BUTCHERING	BCHIIOPRSS BISHOPRICS
BCDKMRSTUU DUMBSTRUCK	BCEGIILORR CORRIGIBLE	BCHIIOPSSY BIOPHYSICS
BCDLNOOOTU BLOOD COUNT	BCEGIJNSTU SUBJECTING	BCHIMNOOOP MONOPHOBIC
BCDLORSTUU CLOUDBURST	BCEGILMNOY BECOMINGLY	BCHIMOORTT THROMBOTIC
BCDOPRSTUY BY-PRODUCTS	BCEGILOOOY BIOECOLOGY	BCHIOPRTYY BRYOPHYTIC
BCEEEEHLSU BLUE CHEESE	BCEGIMNNOU UNBECOMING	BCHLNOPSUW PUNCH BOWLS
BCEEEFFILT EFFECTIBLE	BCEHHNNOUY HONEYBUNCH	BCHMOOOSTT TOOTHCOMBS
BCEEEFINNT BENEFICENT	BCEHIINSST BITCHINESS	BCIIILNNVY INVINCIBLY
BCEEEFLLRT TREBLE CLEF	BCEHIISSSU HIBISCUSES	BCIILNOPSY PSILOCYBIN
BCEEEGHINS BESEECHING	BCEHILNOOR BRONCHIOLE	BCIILORSSU LUBRICIOUS
BCEEEHKNOS CHEEKBONES	BCEHILOPRY HYPERBOLIC	BCIILPSSTU PUBLICISTS
BCEEEILLNU EBULLIENCE	BCEHILOSTT BLOTCHIEST	BCIIMNOSTY SYMBIONTIC
BCEEEILLMRU CEREBELLUM	BCEHILRRUV BUR CHERVIL	BCIKMOORST BROOMSTICK
BCEEEILQRSU BECQUERELS	BCEHINNSSU BUNCHINESS	BCILPRSSTU STRIP CLUBS
BCEEENRSTU ERUBESCENT	BCEHINOOPX XENOPHOBIC	BCIMNOOOSS SONIC BOOMS
BCEEFORRTU BRUTE FORCE	BCEHINOSST BOTCHINESS	BCIMNOOSTU COMBUSTION
	BCEHKKOOST SKETCHBOOK	BCIOPRSSTU SUBTROPICS

BCKLLOOPSU	BOLLOCKS-UP	BDEEFLORSW	FLOWERBEDS	BDEGHLNOUU	DOUBLE-HUNG
BCKMOOORTT	ROCK BOTTOM	BDEEFOORSS	BED OF ROSES	BDEGIIILRS	DIRIGIBLES
BDDDEEEINTW	TWIN-BEDDED	BDEEGGLOOT	BOOTLEGGED	BDEGIILLNV	DIVING BELL
BDDDEELOOR	RED-BLOODED	BDEEGHILRT	LETHBRIDGE	BDEGIILNRU	REBUILDING
BDDDEIISUV	SUBDIVIDED	BDEEGIILNV	BEDEVILING	BDEGIINNRR	RING BINDER
BDDDEEEFINR	BEFRIENDED	BDEEGIILST	DIGESTIBLE	BDEGIINOSY	DISOBEYING
BDDEEEEILLV	BEDEVILLED	BDEEGIINNR	INBREEDING	BDEGIINRST	BESTRIDING
BDDEEEILRW	BEWILDERED	BDEEGIMOSU	DISEMBOGUE	BDEGIINSTU	SUBEDITING
BDDEEELMNO	EMBOLDENED	BDEEGLNORU	BLUDGEONER	BDEGIIPPRS	BIG DIPPERS
BDDEEELORU	DOUBLE-REED	BDEEHIMOOS	HOMEBODIES	BDEGIKORRW	BRIDGEWORK
BDDEEFNORW	NEW BEDFORD	BDEEHIMRSU	HUMBERSIDE	BDEGILNNRU	BLUNDERING
BDDEEGLNOU	BLUDGEONED	BDEEHIRRSY	DERBYSHIRE	BDEGILNORU	REDOUBLING
BDDEEILMSS	DISSEMBLED	BDEEHLNNOR	HORNBLENDE	BDEGIMOORR	BRIDEGROOM
BDDEEINRST	BESTRIDDEN	BDEEIILMOS	DEMOBILISE	BDEGINNORU	REBOUNDING
BDDEEENNRUU	UNBURDENED	BDEEIILMOZ	DEMOBILIZE	BDEGINNSTU	SUBTENDING
BDDEFILLOU	FULL-BODIED	BDEEIILRTV	DIVERTIBLE	BDEGINORTW	BRIDGETOWN
BDDEFLOOSU	BLOOD FEUDS	BDEEIILSTV	DIVESTIBLE	BDEGIOPRRT	BRIDGEPORT
BDDEGIILOS	DISOBLIGED	BDEEILLNNR	DINNER BELL	BDEGIORRTW	TROWBRIDGE
BDDEGILMRU	MIDDELBURG	BDEEILLOPT	POTBELLIED	BDEHIILPSU	BISULPHIDE
BDDEGIOOSS	DOGSBODIES	BDEEILMOSW	DISEMBOWEL	BDEHIIOPRT	PROHIBITED
BDDEHLNOOR	BONDHOLDER	BDEEILMOTU	DOUBLE TIME	BDEHIIRRSY	HYBRIDISER
BDDEHLOOOT	HOT-BLOODED	BDEEILMRSS	DISSEMBLER	BDEHIIRRYZ	HYBRIDIZER
BDDEIIRSUV	SUBDIVIDER	BDEEILNORR	BORDERLINE	BDEHNOOSUU	HOUSEBOUND
BDDEIISSSU	SUBSIDISED	BDEEILNOTY	OBEDIENTLY	BDEHNNRRSU	UNDERBRUSH
BDDEIISSUZ	SUBSIDIZED	BDEEILORSW	BOWDLERISE	BDEIIILNRV	BILIVERDIN
BDDEILMORW	MIDDLEBROW	BDEEILORWZ	BOWDLERIZE	BDEIIJNOSS	INSIDE JOBS
BDDFGIINOR	FORBIDDING	BDEEIMMNOT	EMBODIMENT	BDEIIKLOOS	OBELISKOID
BDDFILLNOS	BLINDFOLDS	BDEEIMORRY	EMBROIDERY	BDEIILMORS	DISEMBROIL
BDDGIINOTU	OUTBIDDING	BDEEIMRRSU	REIMBURSED	BDEIIRSSSU	SUBSIDISER
BDDHLNOOOU	BLOODHOUND	BDEEINNORZ	BENZODRINE	BDEIIRSSUZ	SUBSIDIZER
BDDIKLNNRU	BLIND DRUNK	BDEEIPRSSW	SPIDERWEBS	BDEIIRSTTU	DISTRIBUTE
BDDILLORSY	DOLLY BIRDS	BDEEIRSSTT	BED-SITTERS	BDEIJLRRUY	JERRY-BUILD
BDEEEEMMRR	REMEMBERED	BDEEKOOORV	OVERBOOKED	BDEIKNNORW	WIND-BROKEN
BDEEEEFILNS	DEFENSIBLE	BDEELLNRUY	UNDERBELLY	BDEILLORWY	YELLOWBIRD
BDEEEFLOTT	BOTTLE-FEED	BDEELMRRUU	BLUE MURDER	BDEILLOSSU	DISSOLUBLE
BDEEEGHILR	HEIDELBERG	BDEELNNOSS	BLONDENESS	BDEILLOTUX	BILLET-DOUX
BDEEEHLLNR	HELLBENDER	BDEELNRRSU	BLUNDERERS	BDEILMORSW	BOWDLERISM
BDEEEHLSST	THE BLESSED	BDEELQRSUU	BURLESQUED	BDEILMOSSY	SYMBOLISED
BDEEEHMORW	HOME-BREWED	BDEEMNNRUU	UNNUMBERED	BDEILMOSYZ	SYMBOLIZED
BDEEEEIILSV	DISBELIEVE	BDEEMNORSU	BURDENSOME	BDEILNNOST	STONE-BLIND
BDEEEIILNTX	EXTENDIBLE	BDEENOORTV	DENVER BOOT	BDEILNOOSS	BLOODINESS
BDEEEIILSTW	WILDEBEEST	BDEENORRUV	OVERBURDEN	BDEIMNORSS	MORBIDNESS
BDEEEIMRTT	EMBITTERED	BDEEOORSSY	OYSTER BEDS	BDEINOORSS	BROODINESS
BDEEEINRRT	INTERBREED	BDEERSSTTU	BUTTRESSED	BDEINOSSSU	DO BUSINESS
BDEEEIRTTW	BITTERWEED	BDEFFIILSU	DIFFUSIBLE	BDEIOORTTW	BITTERWOOD
BDEEELMTUW	TUMBLEWEED	BDEFFNOORW	BROWNED-OFF	BDEIORSSTU	SUBEDITORS
BDEEELNOSS	NOSEBLEEDS	BDEFGINOOR	FOREBODING	BDEKNNOORW	BROKEN-DOWN
BDEEELORTU	DOUBLETREE	BDEFGIOORT	FOOTBRIDGE	BDELLNOPSU	SPELLBOUND
BDEEELRRRY	ELDERBERRY	BDEFILOOST	SOFT-BOILED	BDELLORSUZ	BULLDOZERS
BDEEENRSTU	DEBENTURES	BDEFINORSY	BOYFRIENDS	BDELLORTUY	TROUBLEDLY
BDEEFGIINR	DEBRIEFING	BDEFIOPRRY	BIRD OF PREY	BDELMMNOUY	MOLYBDENUM
BDEEFILNSY	DEFENSIBLY	BDEGGGINRU	BEGRUDGING	BDELMNOOOY	BLOOD MONEY
BDEEFLLOSW	BEDFELLOWS	BDEGHHIINR	HIGHBINDER	BDELMNOTUW	TUMBLEDOWN
		BDEGHINNRU	HINDENBURG		

BDELNOOOST	BLOODSTONE
BDELOOPSTU	DOUBLE-STOP
BDELOOPSTY	BLOOD TYPES
BDENOPTTUU	BUTTONED UP
BDFLLOTUUY	DOUBTFULLY
BDFNOORSTU	FROSTBOUND
BDGHNNOOSU	SHOGUN
	BOND
BDGIINRSSU	DISBURSING
BDGIINRSTU	DISTURBING
BDGIKMNOSU	SUBKINGDOM
BDGILLNOUZ	BULLDOZING
BDGILNORWY	BLOW-DRYING
BDGLOOOPRU	BLOOD GROUP
BDHIILRRWY	WHIRLYBIRD
BDHIMNOORY	MONOHYBRID
BDHMNOSTUW	THUMBS
	DOWN
BDHNNOORTU	NORTHBOUND
BDHNOOSTUU	SOUTHBOUND
BDIIILNOSU	LIBIDINOUS
BDILNOPSST	BLIND SPOTS
BDINNOORRU	ROUND ROBIN
BDINOOSWWW	BOW
	WINDOWS
BDKNNOOORY	DONNYBROOK
BDLLOOSSTU	BLOOD LUSTS
BDLOOOPRST	BLOOD SPORT
BDMNOORSTU	STORMBOUND
BDNNOOTTUW	
	BUTTON-DOWN
BDNOOOTTUW	BUTTONWOOD
BEEEEFLNSS	FEEBLENESS
BEEEEGLSTU	BETELGEUSE
BEEEEMMRRR	REMEMBERER
BEEEFGILNN	ENFEEBLING
BEEEFOORRT	FREEBOOTER
BEEEGGINRR	GINGER BEER
BEEEGHINRS	HEISENBERG
BEEEGINRRR	GREENBRIER
BEEEGLNRST	GREEN BELTS
BEEEGNOSTW	GO-BETWEENS
BEEEHIILNW	WHEELIE BIN
BEEEHLLRTW	BELLWETHER
BEEEILMPTX	EXEMPTIBLE
BEEEILNRUV	UNBELIEVER
BEEEILNSTX	EXTENSIBLE
BEEEILRRSV	REVERSIBLE
BEEEILRRTV	REVERTIBLE
BEEEIMRRTT	EMBITTERER
BEEEIMRSSV	SEMIBREVES
BEEEINRSSZ	BREEZINESS
BEEEIRRSTW	SWEETBRIER
BEEEKKKOOPR	BOOKKEEPER
BEEELLRSST	BEST-SELLER

BEEELMMNST	EMBLEMENTS
BEEELMRSZZ	EMBEZZLERS
BEEELNNOTV	BENEVOLENT
BEEEMMNRTT	BETTERMENT
BEEEOOQSUXZ	SQUEEZEBOX
BEEFFNORUZ	BUFFER ZONE
BEEFGIINNT	BENEFITING
BEEFGRSTUU	SUBTERFUGE
BEEFIILLNX	INFLEXIBLE
BEEFIORSSU	SEBIFEROUS
BEEFLMNOTU	BEFOULMENT
BEEGGIILLN	NEGLIGIBLE
BEEGGLOORT	BOOTLEGGER
BEEGGNRRSU	REGENSBURG
BEEGHILNRT	BLETHERING
BEEGHINRRT	BRIGHTENER
BEEGHMNRTU	GREEN THUMB
BEEGIIILLN	INELIGIBLE
BEEGIILNRT	GILBERTINE
BEEGIILNST	INGESTIBLE
BEEGIINOSS	BIOGENESIS
BEEGIKNNOT	BETOKENING
BEEGILLNRR	BELL-RINGER
BEEGILMNRS	RESEMBLING
BEEGILMNZZ	EMBEZZLING
BEEGINRSTW	BESTREWING
BEEGINRTTW	WITTENBERG
BEEGMNORYY	EMBRYOGENY
BEEGNOORRS	GREENSBORO
BEEGOOORSY	GOOSEBERRY
BEEGPRRSTU	PETERSBURG
BEEHIIITVX	EXHIBITIVE
BEEHILLMOR	LIMBER HOLE
BEEHILMMOO	MOBILE HOME
BEEHILMOST	BLITHESOME
BEEHILNSST	BLITHENESS
BEEHIMMPRS	MEMBERSHIP
BEEHIORRSV	HERBIVORES
BEEHKMNOOR	BROKEN HOME
BEEHKOORRS	SHERBROOKE
BEEHLMNSSU	HUMBLENESS
BEEHLOPRSY	HYPERBOLES
BEEHMOORST	BOTHERSOME
BEEHMOORTT	
	MOTHER-TO-BE
BEEHNOOPSX	PHONE BOXES
BEEHOORSSX	HORSEBOXES
BEEIIJORTU	BIJOUTERIE
BEEIIKLMRT	KIMBERLITE
BEEIILLLRV	LIBREVILLE
BEEIILMMRS	IMMERSIBLE
BEEIILMNRT	TIMBERLINE
BEEIILMRSS	REMISSIBLE
BEEIILNNSS	INSENSIBLE

BEEIILNNTV	INVENTIBLE
BEEIILNRST	LIBERTINES
BEEIILNRTV	INVERTIBLE
BEEIILSSTX	BISSEXTILE
BEEIKKNORR	KNOBKERRIE
BEEILLLNTU	LUTINE BELL
BEEILLLOVW	BOLL WEEVIL
BEEILLLOWY	YELLOW BILE
BEEILLLTTT	LITTLE BELT
BEEILLNORS	REBELLIONS
BEEILLOPST	POTBELLIES
BEEILLORSU	REBELLIOUS
BEEILLRSTT	BELLETRIST
BEEILMNNSS	NIMBLENESS
BEEILMRRSU	MULBERRIES
BEEILNOPRS	NOBEL PRISE
BEEILNOPRZ	NOBEL PRIZE
BEEILNOSST	OSTENSIBLE
BEEILOSTTU	OUBLIETTES
BEEILSSTTU	SUBTLETIES
BEEILSSTUV	VESTIBULES
BEEIMRRRSU	REIMBURSER
BEEINNRSTU	INNER TUBES
BEEINORRTT	TORBERNITE
BEEINRSSTT	BITTERNESS
BEEINSSSSU	BUSINESSES
BEEIOSSSSV	OBSESSIVES
BEEIQRSTTU	BRIQUETTES
BEEIRSSUVV	SUBVERSIVE
BEEKLLOORS	BOOKSELLER
BEEKNNORSS	BROKENNESS
BEEKRSTUWY	TEWKESBURY
BEELMNRSSU	NUMBERLESS
BEELMRRSSU	SLUMBERERS
BEELNPRTUU	PUBERULENT
BEELNSSSTU	SUBTLENESS
BEELQRRSUU	BURLESQUER
BEELQRSSUU	BURLESQUES
BEELRRSSTU	BLUSTERERS
BEEMMNNOTT	ENTOMBMENT
BEEMMNOSST	EMBOSSMENT
BEEMNOOSXY	MONEYBOXES
BEEMNORSSS	SOMBRENESS
BEENOSSSTU	OBTUSENESS
BEENPRSSSU	SUPERBNESS
BEENQSSTUU	SUBSEQUENT
BEEOPRSSSX	PRESS BOXES
BEEPRRSTYY	PRESBYTERY
BEERSSSTTU	BUTTRESSES
BEFFHILOOT	OFF THE BOIL
BEFFNOORUY	BUFFOONERY
BEFGIINNOR	FIBRINOGEN
BEFGILNORW	FINGER BOWL
BEFGKOOORR	GO FOR BROKE

BEFHILLMTU	THIMBLEFUL	BEHILLORWW	WILLOWHERB	BEILOOPRST	POTBOILERS
BEFHIRSTTU	BUTTERFISH	BEHILMOSSV	BOLSHEVISM	BEILOOTUVV	OBVOLUTIVE
BEFIILLNXY	INFLEXIBLY	BEHILPRSSU	PUBLISHERS	BEIMMRSTYY	BISYMMETRY
BEFIILRSTU	FILIBUSTER	BEHIMSSSTU	MISS THE BUS	BEIMNNOOPT	EMBONPOINT
BEFLLLOPSY	BELLY FLOPS	BEHINORSTT	BIRTHSTONE	BEIMNORSSU	SUBMERSION
BEFNNNOSUY	FUNNY BONES	BEHINOSSYY	BOYISHNESS	BEINNOSTUV	SUBVENTION
BEGGHMRUUY	HUMBUGGERY	BEHKNOOOPS	PHONE BOOKS	BEINOOSSSS	OBSESSIONS
BEGGIILLNY	NEGLIGIBLY	BEHKNOSSUU	BUNKHOUSES	BEINOPRSTU	SUBREPTION
BEGGIINNNS	BEGINNINGS	BEHLMOOPTY	PHLEBOTOMY	BEINORSSUV	SUBVERSION
BEGGILNNOS	BELONGINGS	BEHLNOOTTU	BUTTONHOLE	BEINORSTUU	SUBROUTINE
BEGGIMNRSU	SUBMERGING	BEHLOOPSTT	BOTTLE SHOP	BEINOSSTWX	WITNESS BOX
BEGGINNORU	BURGEONING	BEHMOOORST	SMOOTHBORE	BEINSSSTTU	SUBSISTENT
BEGHIIINTX	EXHIBITING	BEHMOORSST	THROMBOSES	BEIOOQSSUU	OBSEQUIOUS
BEGHIIKNNT	BETHINKING	BEHMOORSTY	MOTHER'S BOY	BEIOORSSST	SOB STORIES
BEGHIILMNS	BLEMISHING	BEHMPRTTUU	TUB-THUMPER	BEIOORSSTU	BOISTEROUS
BEGHIILNRT	BLITHERING	BEHNOOORTU	ON THE BUROO	BEIOPSTTTU	PITOT TUBES
BEGHILMNOO	HEMOGLOBIN	BEHOOPRSSU	RUSSOPHOBE	BEIOQRSSTU	SOBRIQUETS
BEGHINNRTU	BURTHENING	BEHRRSSUWY	SHREWSBURY	BEIOQRSTUU	SOUBRIQUET
BEGHINORSU	NEIGHBOURS	BEIIILMMOS	IMMOBILISE	BEIORSTTUY	TUBEROSITY
BEGHINORTT	BETROTHING	BEIIILMMOZ	IMMOBILIZE	BEISSSTTTU	SUBSTITUTE
BEGHINRSST	BRIGHTNESS	BEIIILNOST	NOBILITIES	BEKKNOOOST	BOOK TOKENS
BEGHMNOORT	THROMBOGEN	BEIIIMNSTU	BITUMINISE	BEKNOORSTY	STONY BROKE
BEGHOORRTU	BORGERHOUT	BEIIIMNTUZ	BITUMINIZE	BELLMOPSTU	POST-BELLUM
BEGIIILLTY	LEGIBILITY	BEIIIOOPSS	BIOPOIESIS	BELLNOSUUY	NEBULOUSLY
BEGIILLNTT	BELITTLING	BEIIILLNOTU	EBULLITION	BELLOOOPRT	PORTOBELLO
BEGIILMNOR	EMBROILING	BEIIILLOSSU	SOLUBILISE	BELLORSTUY	TROLLEYBUS
BEGIILNRST	BLISTERING	BEIIILLOSUZ	SOLUBILIZE	BELMMOORRU	LUMBER-ROOM
BEGIILNRTT	BITTERLING	BEIIILMOPSS	IMPOSSIBLE	BELMOOSSTT	BOTTOMLESS
BEGIINRRST	BESTIRRING	BEIIILMRTUY	MULIEBRITY	BELMORSSUU	SLUMBEROUS
BEGIJRSTTU	JITTERBUGS	BEIIILNNSSY	INSENSIBLY	BELOOPRSTT	LOBSTERPOT
BEGIKLNRUY	REBUKINGLY	BEIIILNRSTT	LITTERBINS	BEMNOOSSTT	TOMBSTONES
BEGILMNRSU	SLUMBERING	BEIIILORSTT	TRILOBITES	BENNOORSTW	BROWNSTONE
BEGILNORST	BOLSTERING	BEIIILORSTU	BOILER SUIT	BENORSSSTU	ROBUSTNESS
BEGILNORSY	SOBERINGLY	BEIIILRSSTU	SUBTILISER	BEORRTTTUW	BUTTERWORT
BEGILNRSTU	BLUSTERING	BEIIILRSSTY	RESISTIBLY	BFFFFILOTU	BIT OF FLUFF
BEGILNSTTU	SUBLETTING	BEIIILRSTTT	LIBRETTIST	BFFFIOSTTU	BIT OF STUFF
BEGILOOOXY	EXOBIOLOGY	BEIIILRSTTW	BIRTWISTLE	BFGHIINRSU	FURBISHING
BEGINNNNOT	BENNINGTON	BEIIILRSTUZ	SUBTILIZER	BFGHILLSTU	BULLFIGHTS
BEGINPRRTU	PERTURBING	BEIIMSSSUV	SUBMISSIVE	BFGHILNTYY	FLY-BY-NIGHT
BEGINRSTUV	SUBVERTING	BEIINORSTY	INSOBRIETY	BFGILLMNUY	FUMBLINGLY
BEGLMOORYY	EMBRYOLOGY	BEIJLRRTUY	JERRY-BUILT	BFIIILSTUY	FUSIBILITY
BEGLMORUUX	LUXEMBOURG	BEIKLMRTTU	BUTTERMILK	BFIIIORSST	FIBROSITIS
BEGLNNNOOT	LONGBENTON	BEIKMOORST	MOTORBIKES	BFIIKORSTT	BIT OF SKIRT
BEGMOORRSV	BROMSGROVE	BEIKMORRTW	TIMBERWORK	BFIILMMORU	UMBILIFORM
BEGNORRUYY	YOUNGBERRY	BEIKNOORUY	ON YOUR BIKE	BFILLLNOUW	IN FULL BLOW
BEHHIIRSTT	THE BRITISH	BEILLMNPSU	PLUMB LINES	BFILLLSSUY	BLISSFULLY
BEHIIIINTV	INHIBITIVE	BEILMNOOSW	SNOWMOBILE	BFLMOOPTUU	OUT OF PLUMB
BEHIIINOTX	EXHIBITION	BEILMNOOTT	BOTTOM LINE	BGGIILLNOY	OBLIGINGLY
BEHIILPSTU	BISULPHITE	BEILMOOOST	LOBOTOMIES	BGGIINNPRU	UPBRINGING
BEHIIOPRRT	PROHIBITER	BEILNOSSTY	OSTENSIBLY	BGHHIIRRTT	BIRTHRIGHT
BEHIIORSTX	EXHIBITORS	BEILNOSSWZ	BLOWZINESS	BGHIIIINNT	INHIBITING
BEHIIORTXY	EXHIBITORY	BEILNOSTUY	NEBULOSITY	BGHIILNPSU	PUBLISHING
BEHIIRRSST	BRITISHERS	BEILNPRSTU	BLUEPRINTS	BGHIINNRSU	BURNISHING
BEHIKLOSSV	BOLSHEVIKS				

BGHIKNOORU	KINBOROUGH	BILMOORSWW	LOWBROWISM	CCDEENORSS	CRESCENDOS
BGHIKORRTW	BRIGHTWORK	BILNOOOTUV	OBVOLUTION	CCDEFILNOT	CONFLICTED
BGHILLMNUY	HUMBLINGLY	BILOOPRSTU	POLITBUROS	CCDEHILLOS	COLD CHISEL
BGHILLNSUY	BLUSHINGLY	BIMNOORSTT	TROMBONIST	CCDEHILNOR	CHRONICLED
BGHILLOUWY	WILLOUGHBY	BIMOOPPRRU	OPPROBRIUM	CCDEHLNTUU	DUTCH UNCLE
BGHILMOORU	MILBOROUGH	BKLLMNSSUU	NUMBSKULLS	CCDEIIIRST	CRITICISED
BGHILNNSSU	UNBLUSHING	BKMOOOPPRT	PROMPTBOOK	CCDEIIIRTZ	CRITICIZED
BGHIPRSTTU	PITTSBURGH	BMMOOOSTTT	BOTTOMMOST	CCDEIILOPY	EPICYCLOID
BGHLOOPSUY	PLOUGHBOYS	BOOPPRRSTU	TURBOPROPS	CCDEIINNOR	ENDOCRINIC
BGIIILMNOZ	MOBILIZING	CCCEEINNOS	CONSCIENCE	CCDEIINNOT	COINCIDENT
BGIIILNOTY	IGNOBILITY	CCCEEINORT	ECOCENTRIC	CCDEIJKOSY	DISC JOCKEY
BGIIJNNOSU	SUBJOINING	CCCEEINRST	CRESCENTIC,	CCDEIILOORS	CROCODILES
BGIIKLNNNU	UNBLINKING	CCCEEINRST	ECCENTRICS	CCDEIMOOOT	OCTODECIMO
BGIIILMOORS	IMBROGLIOS	CCCEELNSUU	SUCCULENCE	CCDEINNOST	DISCONNECT
BGIILOOSST	BIOLOGISTS	CCCEENORRU	OCCURRENCE	CCDEINOOPS	ENDOSCOPIC
BGIIMNSTTU	SUBMITTING	CCCEHIILMY	HEMICYCLIC	CCDEINOOST	DECOCTIONS
BGIINORSUU	RUBIGINOUS	CCCEHIILNO	COLCHICINE	CCDEINOPUU	UNOCCUPIED
BGIINSSSTU	SUBSISTING	CCCEHKORSS	CROSSCHECK	CCDEINORST	DISCONCERT
BGIJLLMNUY	JUMBLINGLY	CCCEIILPRY	PERICYCLIC	CCDEINOTUV	CONDUCTIVE
BGIKNOPRSS	SPRINGBOKS	CCCEIIMRSU	CIRCUMCISE	CCDENOOPRU	RED PUCCOON
BGILLMMNUY	MUMBLINGLY	CCCEILOTUY	LEUCOCYTIC	CCDGIIINNO	COINCIDING
BGILLMNRUY	RUMBLINGLY	CCCEINNOOP	CONCEPCION	CCDGIILOSY	GLYCOSIDIC
BGILMNOOSS	BLOSSOMING	CCCEINNORT	CONCENTRIC	CCDGIKLNOU	CUCKOLDING
BGILNNORTU	BURLINGTON	CCCEINOOTV	CONCOCTIVE	CCDGILNNOU	CONCLUDING
BGILOORSTY	BRYOLOGIST	CCCEINOOTY	COENOCYTIC	CCDGINNOTU	CONDUCTING
BGILORSUUU	LUGUBRIOUS	CCCEKLNOOR	CORNCOCKLE	CCDHIINORT	CHONDRITIC
BGIMNNOSOU	UNBOSOMING	CCCGINNOOT	CONCOCTING	CCDIMNOSTU	MISCONDUCT
BGINNOOORU	BUON GIORNO	CCCGNOOOSU	GONOCOCCUS	CCDINNOOTU	CONDUCTION
BGINNORUUY	RUGBY UNION	CCCHILMOOY	HOMOCYCLIC	CCDNOORSTU	CONDUCTORS
BGINOORRSW	BORROWINGS	CCCIIMORTY	MICROCYTIC	CCEEEEHIKP	CHEEKPIECE
BHHIMORSTY	BIORHYTHMS	CCCILLOPYY	POLYCYCLIC	CCEEEELLNX	EXCELLENCE
BHHOORSTTU	TOOTHBRUSH	CCCILMNOOY	MONOCYCLIC	CCEEEENNSS	SENESCENCE
BHIIIINNOT	INHIBITION	CCCILNSTUY	SUCCINCTLY	CCEEEFNNOR	CONFERENCE
BHIILLNOST	BILLIONTHS	CCCILOPSTY	POST-CYCLIC	CCEEEFNRSU	RUFESCENCE
BHIILLRSTT	STILLBIRTH	CCCINNOOOT	CONCOCTION	CCEEEGINOS	GEOSCIENCE
BHIILMRTTU	MULTIBIRTH	CCCIOOPRSY	CRYOSCOPIC	CCEEEIINPR	RECIPIENCE
BHIMOORSST	THROMBOSIS	CCDDEELNOY	CONCEDEDLY	CCEEEINPRS	PRESCIENCE
BHIMOSSTUU	BISMUTHOUS	CCDDEEENNOS	CONDESCEND	CCEEEINQSU	QUIESCENCE
BHKNOOOTTU	BUTTONHOOK	CCDEEEENPR	PRECEDENCE	CCEEEINRSV	VIRESCENCE
BHLLOOOSTT	TOLLBOOTHS	CCDEEEHINS	DEHISCENCE	CCEEEIOPSS	ECOSPECIES
BHLLOOSSUU	HOLUS-BOLUS	CCDEEENRST	DECRESCENT	CCEEELLNXY	EXCELLENCY
BHLLRRUUYY	HURLY-BURLY	CCDEEERRSU	RECRUDESCE	CCEEEMMNOR	RECOMMENCE
BHNOPSTTUU	PUSH-BUTTON	CCDEEFIINY	DEFICIENCY	CCEEEMMNOPT	COMPETENCE
BHOOOOPSUZ	ZOOPHOBOUS	CCDEEFINNO	CONFIDENCE	CCEEEMNSTU	TUMESCENCE
BIIIILRSTY	RISIBILITY	CCDEEGINSU	SUCCEEDING	CCEEENRRRU	RECURRENCE
BIIIILSTVY	VISIBILITY	CCDEEHHTUW	CHEW THE CUD	CCEEENRSTX	EXCRESCENT
BIIILMMOTY	IMMOBILITY	CCDEEHIORT	RICOCHETED	CCEEFFIINY	EFFICIENCY
BIILLOSTUY	SOLUBILITY	CCDEEHNOSY	SYNECDOCHE	CCEEFFILNO	OFF-LICENCE
BIILLOTUVY	VOLUBILITY	CCDEEIIIPT	EPIDEICTIC	CCEEFHHRRU	FREE CHURCH
BIILMOPSSY	IMPOSSIBLY	CCDEEIILRT	DIELECTRIC	CCEEFILLSY	LIFE CYCLES
BIIMNOSSSU	SUBMISSION	CCDEEIIPPR	PRECIPICED	CCEEFLNNOU	CONFLUENCE
BIIMNOSTUU	BITUMINOUS	CCDEEIKLRV	CLEVER DICK	CCEEGHINRS	SCREECHING
BIIOQSTUUU	UBIQUITOUS	CCDEEILNOR	RECONCILED	CCEEGINNOR	CONGENERIC
BIKLLORSST	STORKSBILL	CCDEELNNOO	CONDOLENCE	CCEEGINORS	CONCIERGES

CCEEGINORT	EGOCENTRIC, GEOCENTRIC
CCEEGNNORU	CONGRUENCE
CCEEHHIRST	CHICHESTER
CCEEHINOSS	CHOICENESS
CCEEHLORST	COLCHESTER
CCEEHNOSTU	ESCUTCHEON
CCEEHOSTTU	COUCHETTES
CCEEIIINNN	INCIPIENCE
CCEEIILMRS	SEMICIRCLE
CCEEIIPPRS	PRECIPICES
CCEEIKRRST	CRICKETERS
CCEEILLOTV	COLLECTIVE
CCEEILMNNY	INCLEMENCY
CCEEILNOPU	LEUCOPENIC
CCEEILNORR	RECONCILER
CCEEILNORT	ELECTRONIC
CCEEILOPST	TELESCOPIC
CCEEILORVY	COERCIVELY
CCEEINNNOT	CONTINENCE
CCEEINNOTV	CONNECTIVE
CCEEINNRRU	INCURRENCE
CCEEINNRST	INCRESCENT
CCEEINOPRW	CROWNPIECE
CCEEINOPTV	CONCEPTIVE
CCEEINORST	CONCRETISE
CCEEINORTV	CONCRETIVE
CCEEINORTX	EXOCENTRIC
CCEEINORTZ	CONCRETIZE
CCEEINOSSV	CONCESSIVE
CCEEINOTVV	CONVECTIVE
CCEEINRRSU	CURRENCIES
CCEEIOPRSS	CROSSPIECE
CCEEIORRTV	CORRECTIVE
CCEEISSSUV	SUCCESSIVE
CCEEJNORTU	CONJECTURE
CCEELMORTY	CYCLOMETER
CCEELNOPRU	CORPULENCE
CCEELNORTY	CONCRETELY
CCEELNRTUU	TRUCULENCE
CCEELOSTTU	COS LETTUCE
CCEELOSTUY	LEUCOCYTES
CCEEMNOPTY	COMPETENCY
CCEENOPRRT	PRECONCERT
CCEFHIIMOR	MICROFICHE
CCEFIIINST	SCIENTIFIC
CCEFIINPSU	UNSPECIFIC
CCEFIIRSUX	CRUCIFIXES
CCEFIKLSTT	CLEFT STICK
CCEFILMRUX	CIRCUMFLEX
CCEFIMRSUU	CIRCUMFUSE
CCEFINNOOT	CONFECTION
CCEFLLNOTU	FLOCCULENT
CCEFLSSSUU	SUCCESSFUL

CCEGGHOSST	SCOTCH EGGS
CCEGGILNOY	GLYCOGENIC
CCEGHHORRU	CHURCHGOER
CCEGHIIIOP	PICHICIEGO
CCEGHINORT	CROCHETING
CCEGIILNNR	ENCIRCLING
CCEGIINNOV	CONCEIVING
CCEGILLNOT	COLLECTING
CCEGIMMNNO	COMMENCING
CCEGINNNOR	CONCERNING
CCEGINNNOS	ENSCONCING
CCEGINNNOT	CONNECTING
CCEGINNORT	CONCRETING
CCEGINORRT	CORRECTING
CCEGINORSY	CRYOGENICS
CCEHHILOTV	CLOVE HITCH
CCEHIINNNO	CINCHONINE
CCEHIINNOS	CINCHONISE
CCEHIINNOZ	CINCHONIZE
CCEHIKLSST	CHECKLISTS
CCEHIKMOOR	MOCK-HEROIC
CCEHIKNOPT	CHECKPOINT
CCEHIKNOPX	CHICKEN POX
CCEHILNOPR	CHRONICLER
CCEHILNORS	CHRONICLES
CCEHIMOSSY	ECCHYMOSIS
CCEHINRSTU	CRUNCHIEST
CCEHKMOORS	CHECKROOMS
CCEHKOORSS	COCKHORSES
CCEHKOPSST	SPOT CHECKS
CCEHKORTUU	CHUCKER-OUT
CCEHMOORTY	CYTOCHROME
CCEIIINNPY	INCIPIENCY
CCEIIIRRST	CRITICISER
CCEIIIRRTZ	CRITICIZER
CCEIIIRSTV	CERVICITIS
CCEIIKNPRS	PICNICKERS
CCEIILMNOR	MICROCLINE
CCEIILOSST	SOLECISTIC
CCEIIMOORS	SERIOCOMIC
CCEIIMOTXY	MEXICO CITY
CCEIIMPSST	SCEPTICISM
CCEIINOTVV	CONVICTIVE
CCEIINRTTY	CENTRICITY
CCEIIOPPRS	PERISCOPIC
CCEIIORTVY	COERCIVITY
CCEIKKOPPT	PICKPOCKET
CCEIKMNOSY	COCKNEYISM
CCEILLLOSU	CELLULOSIC
CCEILLNOOT	COLLECTION
CCEILMNNOU	COUNCILMEN
CCEILNNOSU	NUCLEONICS
CCEILNOSUV	CONCLUSIVE
CCEILOOQTU	COQUELICOT

CCEIMNNOOU	UNECONOMIC
CCEIMNRTUV	CIRCUMVENT
CCEIMOOPRS	MICROSCOPE
CCEINNNOOT	CONNECTION
CCEINNOOPT	CONCEPTION
CCEINNOORT	CONCERTINO, CONCRETION
CCEINNOOSS	CONCESSION
CCEINNOOTV	CONVECTION
CCEINOOOPS	ICONOSCOPE
CCEINOORRT	CORRECTION
CCEINOSSSU	SUCCESSION
CCEINOSSUV	CONCUSSIVE
CCEIOOPRSU	PRECOCIOUS
CCEIOPRSST	COST PRICES
CCEISSSSUV	SUCCUSSIVE
CCEKLOORTW	CLOCK TOWER
CCEKORRSSW	CORKSCREWS
CCELLOORST	COLLECTORS
CCELLOSTYY	CYCLOSTYLE
CCELMOORTY	MOTORCYCLE
CCELMOOSTY	CYCLOSTOME
CCELMORTYY	CYCLOMETRY
CCELNSSTUU	SUCCULENTS
CCELOPRSSU	CORPUSCLES
CCEMOSTTYY	CYSTECTOMY
CCENNORRTU	CONCURRENT
CCENOORRSU	CONCOURSES
CCENOORSTV	CONVECTORS
CCENOPSSTU	CONSPECTUS
CCEOOPSSTY	CYSTOSCOPE
CCEORSSSSU	SUCCESSORS
CCFGHIKOST	COCKFIGHTS
CCFGIINRUY	CRUCIFYING
CCFILMORUU	CUCULIFORM
CCGHHHHIRU	HIGH CHURCH
CCGHINNRSU	SCRUNCHING
CCGHLNOOOY	CONCHOLOGY
CCGIIIKNNP	PICNICKING
CCGIINNNOV	CONVINCING
CCGIINNOTV	CONVICTING
CCGILORSUY	GLYCOSURIC
CCGIMNOOOS	COSMOGONIC
CCGINNORRU	CONCURRING
CCGINNOSSU	CONCUSSING
CCGINORSUU	SUCCOURING
CCGIOOPRSY	GYROSCOPIC
CCHHOOPTT	HOTCHPOTCH
CCHHIIOTTY	ICHTHYOTIC
CCHIIIRSTT	TRISTICHIC
CCHIILMOOX	XOCHIMILCO
CCHIILNNOO	CONCHIOLIN
CCHIILOPRY	CRYOPHILIC
CCHIIMNNOS	CINCHONISM

CCHIIMOPRS	MICROCHIPS
CCHIINORTY	CHRONICITY
CCHIKLOSTT	LOCKSTITCH
CCHIKOPSST	CHOPSTICKS
CCHIMOSSTT	SCOTCH MIST
CCHINNORSY	SYNCHRONIC
CCHIOOOPRS	HOROSCOPIC
CCHIOPSSTY	PSYCHOTICS
CCHIORSTTY	TRICHOCYST
CCHKLNOSUU	NO SUCH LUCK
CCHNOOSTUY	COCONUT SHY
CCHOOPSSUU	HOCUS-POCUS
CCIIIMRSST	CRITICISMS
CCIILLNOPY	POLYCLINIC
CCIILMNNOO	MONOCLINIC
CCIILMOPTY	COMPLICITY
CCIILNSTUY	UNICYCLIST
CCIILOOPRT	COPROLITIC
CCIIMMOORT	MICROTOMIC
CCIIMOPRST	COMIC STRIP
CCIIMOSSTT	SCOTTICISM
CCIINNNOTY	CONCINNITY
CCIINNOOTV	CONVICTION
CCIINOOPRS	SCORPIONIC
CCIIOOPRTX	PICROTOXIC
CCIIORSTUU	CIRCUITOUS
CCIKNOOPTU	CUCKOOPINT
CCILLNOORU	COUNCILLOR
CCILLOOPTY	COLLOTYPIC
CCILMRRUUU	CURRICULUM
CCILNNOOSU	CONCLUSION
CCIMMOORSS	MICROCOSMS
CCIMOOPRSY	MICROSCOPY
CCINNNOOSU	CONCINNOUS
CCINNOOSSU	CONCUSSION
CCINOPRSST	CONSCRIPTS
CCINOSSSUU	SUCCUSSION
CCINOSTUVY	VISCOUNTCY
CCIOOPRTYZ	CRYPTOZOIC
CCIOPPRRTY	PROCRYPTIC
CCIORRSSSS	CRISSCROSS
CCNOORRTUW	CROWN COURT
CCNORSSTTU	CONSTRUCTS
CCOOPSSTYY	CYSTOSCOPY
CDDEEEEENNP	DEPENDENCE
CDDEEEHIPR	DECIPHERED
CDDEEEEINRT	INTERCEDED
CDDEEEINUV	UNDECEIVED
CDDEEEIRRT	REDIRECTED
CDDEEEJLTY	DEJECTEDLY
CDDEEENNPY	DEPENDENCY
CDDEEENNST	DESCENDENT
CDDEEFFIIN	DIFFIDENCE
CDDEEGINNS	DESCENDING
CDDEEIINSS	DISSIDENCE
CDDEEIJPRU	PREJUDICED
CDDEEIMNOR	ENDODERMIC
CDDEEINORS	CONSIDERED
CDDEEINRTU	UNDIRECTED
CDDEEIORSV	DISCOVERED
CDDEELMOSU	CUDDLESOME
CDDEEMNOTU	DOCUMENTED
CDDEEMOOPS	DECOMPOSED
CDDEEOOPRRU	REPRODUCED
CDDEFNNOOU	CONFOUNDED
CDDEHIILOR	DICHLORIDE
CDDEIIOSSV	VIDEODISCS
CDDEIMMNOO	INCOMMODED
CDDEIMMOOS	DISCOMMODE
CDDEINNOOT	ENDODONTIC
CDDEINNOSW	SECOND WIND
CDDEINORTU	INTRODUCED
CDDEINOSTU	DEDUCTIONS, DISCOUNTED
CDDEIORSSU	DISCOURSED
CDDEMNOOPU	COMPOUNDED, DECOMPOUND OUT
CDDENOPRTU	END PRODUCT
CDDEOORTUW	CROWDED OUT
CDDHILLOSY	CLODDISHLY
CDDIIILNRY	CYLINDROID
CDDILOOPSU	DIPLODOCUS
CDDINNOOTY	DICYNODONT
CDEEEEINPX	EXPEDIENCE
CDEEEENRRT	DETERRENCE
CDEEEENRRV	REVERENCED
CDEEEFFHOS	CHEESED OFF
CDEEEFFINR	DIFFERENCE
CDEEEFFIST	SIDE EFFECT
CDEEEFHIKR	KERCHIEFED
CDEEEFILTV	DEFLECTIVE
CDEEEFMNNS	MEND FENCES
CDEEEGINRV	DIVERGENCE
CDEEEGNRTY	DETERGENCY
CDEEEHIPRR	DECIPHERER
CDEEEHLRSU	RESCHEDULE
CDEEEHNNRT	ENTRENCHED
CDEEEHNRRT	RETRENCHED
CDEEEIINNV	IN EVIDENCE
CDEEEIINRS	DECREE NISI
CDEEEIKNPR	PENDERECKI
CDEEEILOPV	VELOCIPEDE
CDEEEILQSU	DELIQUESCE
CDEEEIMNNN	COMEDIENNE
CDEEEIMNNP	IMPENDENCE
CDEEEINNST	TENDENCIES
CDEEEINPST	CENTIPEDES
CDEEEINPXY	EXPEDIENCY
CDEEEINRRT	INTERCEDER
CDEEEINRSS	RESIDENCES
CDEEEINRSW	WIDE-SCREEN
CDEEEINRUV	UNDECEIVER
CDEEEISTTV	DETECTIVES
CDEEELOPST	TELESCOPED
CDEEELORST	ELECTRODES
CDEEEMNNOT	ENCODEMENT
CDEEENNRSU	UNSCREENED
CDEEENPRST	PRECEDENTS
CDEEENPTUX	UNEXPECTED
CDEEEPRSTU	PERSECUTED
CDEEFGILNT	DEFLECTING
CDEEFIINRT	DENTIFRICE
CDEEFILNNU	INFLUENCED
CDEEFILNOT	DEFLECTION
CDEEFINORR	REINFORCED
CDEEFINOST	DEFECTIONS
CDEEFINTUV	DEFUNCTIVE
CDEEFKLPSY	FLYSPECKED
CDEEFLNORT	CENTRE-FOLD
CDEEFLNORY	ENFORCEDLY
CDEEFLOORS	FORECLOSED
CDEEFNORSS	FORCEDNESS
CDEEGHHITT	GET HITCHED
CDEEGIIMRS	GERMICIDES
CDEEGIINOR	CEREDIGION
CDEEGIKNNR	RING-NECKED
CDEEGILNNU	INDULGENCE
CDEEGILNUV	DIVULGENCE
CDEEGINOPR	PROCEEDING
CDEEGINORS	RECOGNISED
CDEEGINORZ	RECOGNIZED
CDEEGINRVY	DIVERGENCY
CDEEHIILOP	OPHICLEIDE
CDEEHIMNOR	ECHINODERM
CDEEHINNRT	INTRENCHED
CDEEHINRST	CHRISTENED
CDEEHKNPUY	KEYPUNCHED
CDEEHLRTWY	WRETCHEDLY
CDEEHMNOPR	COMPREHEND
CDEEHORRST	DORCHESTER
CDEEIIINSV	INDECISIVE
CDEEIILSVY	DECISIVELY
CDEEIIMNRS	REMINISCED
CDEEIIMPRS	SPERMICIDE
CDEEIIMRST	METRICISED
CDEEIIMRTZ	METRICIZED
CDEEIINRST	INDISCREET, INDISCRETE, IRIDESCENT
CDEEIIORRT	CORDIERITE, DIRECTOIRE
CDEEIIPRTV	PREDICTIVE
CDEEIIPSST	PESTICIDES

CDEEIIRSSV	DISSERVICE	CDEENSSSSU	CUSSEDNESS	CDEHNOSTUV	DUTCH OVENS
CDEEIIRSTV	DIRECTIVES	CDEEOPPRST	PROSPECTED	CDEHOPTTUY	TOUCH-TYPED
CDEEIJPRSU	PREJUDICES	CDEEOPRRRU	REPRODUCER	CDEIIILNNS	DISINCLINE
CDEEIKNSSW	WICKEDNESS	CDEEOPRRSU	PROCEDURES	CDEIIILNPS	DISCIPLINE
CDEEILLNST	STENCILLED	CDEEOPRSTU	PROSECUTED	CDEIIIMRSV	RECIDIVISM
CDEEILNNOS	DECLENSION	CDEERSSSTU	SEDUCTRESS	CDEIIIMSTV	VICTIMISED
CDEEILNNSU	UNLICENSED	CDEFFIIRTU	FRUCTIFIED	CDEIIIMTVZ	VICTIMIZED
CDEEILNNTY	INDECENTLY	CDEFGHIKLT	FLIGHT DECK	CDEIIINNOS	INDECISION
CDEEILNOOS	DECOLONISE	CDEFGIINSU	FUNGICIDES	CDEIIINTVV	VINDICTIVE
CDEEILNOOZ	DECOLONIZE	CDEFGIKNOR	DEFROCKING	CDEIIIRSTV	RECIDIVIST
CDEEILNOSU	NUCLEOSIDE	CDEFHILOSS	COLD FISHES	CDEIILNPPR	PRINCIPLED
CDEEILNOTU	NUCLEOTIDE	CDEFHLMORS	CHELMSFORD	CDEIILNRTY	INDIRECTLY
CDEEILNRVY	INVERCLYDE	CDEFILNOUU	FLUID OUNCE	CDEIILOSTU	SOLICITUDE
CDEEILOORS	DECOLORISE	CDEFINNNOU	UNCONFINED	CDEIIMNNTT	INDICTMENT
CDEEILOORZ	DECOLORIZE	CDEFINNOTU	FUNCTIONED	CDEIIMNOST	MIDSECTION
CDEEILORST	CLOISTERED	CDEFINOORV	CONFERVOID	CDEIIMOORT	IODOMETRIC
CDEEILRSTY	DISCREETLY,	CDEFLNOSUY	CONFUSEDLY	CDEIIMORRS	MISERICORD
	DISCRETELY	CDEFNNOORT	CONFRONTED	CDEIIMORST	DOSIMETRIC
CDEEIMMOXY	MYXOEDEMIC	CDEFNNOORU	CONFOUNDER	CDEIIMORTY	IRIDECTOMY,
CDEEIMNNTU	INDUCEMENT	CDEFNORRTU	UNDERCROFT		MEDIOCRITY
CDEEIMNOOS	ECONOMISED	CDEGGILLNU	CUDGELLING	CDEIIMPPSU	PIPED MUSIC
CDEEIMNOOZ	ECONOMIZED	CDEGHILNSU	SCHEDULING	CDEIINOPRT	PREDICTION
CDEEIMNOSU	EUDEMONICS	CDEGIINNRS	DISCERNING,	CDEIINOPST	DEPICTIONS
CDEEIMNPRU	IMPRUDENCE		RESCINDING	CDEIINORST	DIRECTIONS,
CDEEINNRSW	WINDSCREEN	CDEGIINPRT	PREDICTING		DISCRETION
CDEEINNSSU	SECUNDINES	CDEGIINSST	DISSECTING	CDEIINORTY	TYROCIDINE
CDEEINOPRV	PROVIDENCE	CDEGILNOPU	DECOUPLING	CDEIINOSST	DISSECTION
CDEEINOPST	DECEPTIONS	CDEGILNPRU	PRECLUDING	CDEIINRSTT	INTERDICTS
CDEEINORRS	CONSIDERER,	CDEGILNSUY	SEDUCINGLY	CDEIIOORRS	SORORICIDE
	RECONSIDER	CDEGIMMNNO	COMMENDING	CDEIIPRSTU	PEDICURIST
CDEEINORTT	CREDIT NOTE	CDEGIMNNNO	CONDEMNING	CDEIIRSSUV	DISCURSIVE
CDEEINPRRU	UNDERPRICE	CDEGINNNOS	CONDENSING	CDEIKLOPST	STOCKPILED
CDEEINPRSY	PRESIDENCY	CDEGINNNOT	CONTENDING	CDEIKNRRTU	UNDERTRICK
CDEEINRSST	DIRECTNESS	CDEGINNNOU	DENOUNCING	CDEIKNRSUW	WINDSUCKER
CDEEINRSTY	DYSENTERIC	CDEGINORRS	RECORDINGS	CDEIKNSSTY	STICKY ENDS
CDEEIORRSV	DISCOVERER	CDEGMNORUU	CURMUDGEON	CDEILLLPUY	PELLUCIDLY
CDEEIPRSST	DISRESPECT	CDEGNORRUW	GROUND	CDEILNOSSU	CLOUDINESS
CDEEIRRSST	DIRECTRESS		CREW	CDEILOPSUU	PEDICULOUS
CDEEIRRSTT	RESTRICTED	CDEHHHIIKT	HITCHHIKED	CDEILORSSS	CROSS-SLIDE
CDEEKKKNNO	KNOCK-KNEED	CDEHHIIRRT	THIRD REICH	CDEILORSSU	DISCLOSURE
CDEEKOOPRW	WOODPECKER	CDEHIIISTT	DITHEISTIC	CDEIMMNOPU	COMPENDIUM
CDEELLNOSU	COUNSELLED	CDEHIILNNR	INNER CHILD	CDEIMNNOST	CONDIMENTS
CDEELLNRSU	CULLENDERS	CDEHIILOPS	DISCOPHILE	CDEIMNOOST	ENDOSMOTIC
CDEELNOSSY	CLOYEDNESS	CDEHIILORU	HIERODULIC	CDEIMNOPRS	PRINCEDOMS
CDEEMNNOST	SECONDMENT	CDEHIILPTY	DIPHYLETIC	CDEIMNOSTU	MISCOUNTED
CDEEMOOPRS	DECOMPOSER	CDEHIINOST	HEDONISTIC	CDEIMOOPSS	DISCOMPOSE
CDEEMOOPRSS	COMPRESSED,	CDEHILOPTW	LOW-PITCHED	CDEIMOSSTU	CUSTOMISED
	DECOMPRESS	CDEHIMOPRY	HYPODERMIC	CDEIMOSTUZ	CUSTOMIZED
CDEENNORSS	CONDENSERS	CDEHINOPST	DOCENTSHIP	CDEINNOSTT	DISCONTENT
CDEENNORST	CONTENDERS	CDEHINOPTY	ENDOPHYTIC	CDEINOORSU	INDECOROUS
CDEENOORRS	ROOD SCREEN	CDEHINOSTW	SWITCHED-ON	CDEINORRTU	INTRODUCER
CDEENOOSTT	COTTONSEED	CDEHLNOOSU	UNSCHOOLED	CDEINORSSX	CROSS-INDEX
CDEENORRSU	UNDERSCORE	CDEHLOOPPR	CLODHOPPER	CDEINORSTU	DISCOUNTER,
CDEENORRUV	UNDERCOVER	CDEHLOOPRY	COPYHOLDER		REDISCOUNT, REDUCTIONS
CDEENOSTUU	CONSUETUDE	CDEHLOOPSS	CLOSED SHOP	CDEINPRSTU	UNSCRIPTED

CDEINRSTTU	INSTRUCTED	CDIKLLORST	DRILLSTOCK	CEEEHINRSS	CHEERINESS
CDEIOPRTUV	PRODUCTIVE	CDIKMRSSTU	DRUMSTICKS	CEEEHINSSS	CHEESINESS
CDEIORRSSU	DISCOURSER	CDIKORSSTW	SWORDSTICK	CEEEHKPRTU	UP THE CREEK
CDEIORSSSU	DISCOURSES	CDILLMOOSU	MOLLUSCOID	CEEEHLLSSY	SEYCHELLES
CDEKLORTUY	COLD TURKEY	CDILMOOORX	LOXODROMIC	CEEEHLPSSS	SPEECHLESS
CDEKNORSTU	UNDERSTOCK	CDILMOOPUY	LYCOPODIUM	CEEEHMMNSY	MESENCHYME
CDELLNOORT	CONTROLLED	CDIMMOOOSU	COMMODIOUS	CEEEHNNRRT	ENTRENCHER
CDELNOORUY	EUROCLYDON	CDIMNOORTY	MONOCYTOID	CEEEHOQRUU	EUROCHEQUE
CDELNOOSSW	CLOSEDOWNS	CDINOOPRTU	PRODUCTION	CEEEIILNRS	RESILIENCE
CDELNOOTUV	CONVOLUTED	CDINORSSSW	CROSSWINDS	CEEEIIMPST	TIMEPIECES
CDELNORSSU	SCOUNDRELS	CDLMOORSTU	STORM CLOUD	CEEEIINRSV	VICEREINES
CDELOORSUY	DECOROUSLY	CDMNNORSUU	CONUNDRUMS	CEEEIILLMNO	EMOLLIENCE
CDELPRSTUU	SCULPTURED	CDNNOOSTUW	COUNTDOWNS	CEEEIILLNST	CLIENTELES
CDEMMOOORS		CDNOOOOTTW		CEEEIILMNNT	CLEMENTINE
COMMODORES, COSMODROME		COTTONWOOD		CEEEIILMORT	CEILOMETER
CDEMNOOPRU	COMPOUNDER	CDOORRSSSW	CROSSWORDS	CEEEIILMRTT	TELEMETRIC
CDENNOOPRU	PRONOUNCED	CEEEEFFRSV	EFFERVESCE	CEEEIILNORT	RE-ELECTION
CDENOOPRRS	CORRESPOND	CEEEEFNPRR	PREFERENCE	CEEEIILNPRT	PERCENTILE
CDEOORTTUW	WOODCUTTER	CEEEEFNRRR	REFERENCER	CEEEIILNPST	PESTILENCE
CDEORRSTTU	DESTRUCTOR	CEEEEFNRRS	REFERENCES	CEEEIIMNNTT	ENTICEMENT
CDERRSTTUU	STRUCTURED	CEEEEGIPTX	EPEXEGETIC	CEEEIIMNORS	CEREMONIES
CDFFIILTUY	DIFFICULTY	CEEEEHIPRT	THREE-PIECE	CEEEIIMNRST	MESENTERIC
CDFIMOORST	DISCOMFORT	CEEEEHNPRT	THREEPENCE	CEEEIIMNRSV	SERVICEMEN
CDFLNOORST	COLD FRONTS	CEEEEIMRST	CEMETERIES	CEEEIIMNRTT	CENTIMETRE,
CDGHIILMOU	GLOCHIDIUM	CEEEEINPRX	EXPERIENCE	REMITTENCE	
CDGHILOORY	HYDROLOGIC	CEEEELLNPR	REPELLENCE	CEEEIIMNTTX	EXCITEMENT
CDGIILLNRU	RIDICULING	CEEEENRRRV	REVERENCER	CEEEIINNPRT	PERTINENCE
CDGIIKNNOO	IN GOOD NICK	CEEEENRRSV	REVERENCES	CEEEIINPRSS	CREEPINESS
CDGIILNOSS	DISCLOSING	CEEEFFGLNU	EFFULGENCE	CEEEIINPRST	EPICENTRES
CDGIINSSSU	DISCUSSING	CEEEFFLORS	EFFLORESCE	CEEEIINSSTX	EXISTENCES
CDGIKLLOOS	GOLDILOCKS	CEEEFGLNRU	REFULGENCE	CEEEIINTTWY	WINCEYETTE
CDGILLNOSY	SCOLDINGLY	CEEEFILNSS	FLEECINESS	CEEEIORRST	CORSETIERE
CDHHIILLSY	CHILDISHLY	CEEEFILRTV	REFLECTIVE	CEEEIORRSV	RECOVERIES
CDHHILOSST	DISHCLOTHS	CEEEFINNRS	INFERENCES	CEEEIPPRTV	PERCEPTIVE,
CDHIIINOOP	IDIOPHONIC	CEEEFINRRT	CENTRE-FIRE	PRECEPTIVE	
CDHIINPSSY	SYNDICSHIP	CEEEFINRSS	FIERCENESS	CEEEIPRSTV	RESPECTIVE
CDHIIOSSTU	DISTICHOUS	CEEEFIPRTV	PERFECTIVE	CEEEISTUVX	EXECUTIVES
CDHILORTYY	HYDROLYTIC	CEEEFNORRR	RE-ENFORCER	CEEEJLORTT	ELECTROJET
CDHINOOPRY	HYDROPONIC	CEEEFPRRTU	PREFECTURE	CEEEKKLOPR	LOCK KEEPER
CDHIOPRSTY	DYSTROPHIC	CEEEGGILNN	NEGLIGENCE	CEEEKRRSSU	SEERSUCKER
CDHKNNPRUU	PUNCH-DRUNK	CEEEGIINPT	EPIGENETIC	CEEELNOORU	NEUROCOELE
CDHLLOOOSS	OLD SCHOOLS	CEEEGIINSX	EXIGENCIES	CEEELNRSSV	CLEVERNESS
CDHNOOSTUW	TOUCHDOWNS	CEEEGIILNRT	RE-ELECTING	CEEELNSSST	SELECTNESS
CDIIILNOTY	INDOCILITY	CEEEGINORS	RECOGNISEE	CEEELOPSST	TELESCOPES
CDIIINNSTT	INDISTINCT	CEEEGINORZ	RECOGNIZEE	CEEEMNOPRS	RECOMPENSE
CDIIKRRTTY	DIRTY TRICK	CEEEGINRST	ENERGETICS	CEEEMNORRT	CENTROMERE
CDIILNOOSU	NIDICOLOUS	CEEEGINRTV	VICEGERENT	CEEEMNOTYZ	ECTOENZYME
CDIILNSTTY	DISTINCTLY	CEEEGLNORS	CONGER EELS	CEEEMNRSTU	SECUREMENT
CDIILOPPSY	POLYDIPSIC	CEEEGNRRSU	RESURGENCE	CEEENNRSST	RECENTNESS
CDIILORUSU	RIDICULOUS	CEEEHHLORS	HORSELEECH	CEEENOPRST	OPEN SECRET
CDIIMNORST	DOCTRINISM	CEEEHIKNSS	CHEEKINESS	CEEENRSSSU	SECURENESS
CDIINNOOST	CONDITIONS	CEEEHIMSTT	CHEMISETTE	CEEENRSSTT	SCREEN TEST
CDIINNOSTU	INDUCTIONS	CEEEHINPRR	ENCIPHERER	CEEEPRRSST	RESPECTERS
CDIINOSSSU	DISCUSSION	CEEEHINPTT	EPENTHETIC	CEEFFHIMOO	HOME OFFICE
				CEEFFHOOPS	COFFEE SHOP

CEEFFOOPST	COFFEEPOTS	CEEGMOTYYZ	ZYGOMYCETE
CEEFGHINNR	GREENFINCH	CEEGNNORTV	CONVERGENT
CEEFGILNRT	REFLECTING	CEEGNOOSTU	ECTOGENOUS
CEEFGINPRT	PERFECTING	CEEGNORSSS	CONGRESSES
CEEFGINRTU	CENTRIFUGE	CEEGNRSTTU	TURGESCENT
CEEFGLLNTU	NEGLECTFUL	CEEGORSTTU	COURGETTES
CEEFHHNORT	HENCEFORTH	CEEHHHIMOR	HOCHHEIMER
CEEFHLLRUY	CHEERFULLY	CEEHHIMORT	COME HITHER
CEEFHORTTU	FOURCHETTE	CEEHHOPSST	HOPE CHESTS
CEEFIIILST	FELICITIES	CEEHIIMRST	ERETHISMIC
CEEFIILNTV	INFLECTIVE	CEEHIKNRST	THICKENERS
CEEFIIORST	FEROCITIES	CEEHIKPPRS	SCHIPPERKE
CEEFIIRRST	RECTIFIERS	CEEHIKSSTT	SKETCHIEST
CEEFIKLNSS	FICKLENESS	CEEHILLRSS	CHISELLERS
CEEFIILNRU	INFLUENCER	CEEHILNORU	EUCHLORINE
CEEFILNNSU	INFLUENCES	CEEHILOPRT	HELICOPTER
CEEFILNORT	REFLECTION	CEEHILORRT	LOIR-ET-CHER
CEEFINOPRT	PERFECTION	CEEHILOSVY	COHESIVELY
CEEFKLLSSY	FECKLESSLY	CEEHILQRSU	SQUELCHIER
CEEFLNOORW	CONEFLOWER	CEEHIMNNRT	ENRICHMENT
CEEFLORRST	REFLECTORS	CEEHIMNTTU	TECHNETIUM
CEEFLPPRTU	PLUPERFECT	CEEHIMOPTU	MOUTHPIECE
CEEFLPRSTU	RESPECTFUL	CEEHIMORRT	RHEOMETRIC
CEEFMNNORT	CONFERMENT	CEEHIMORTX	EXOTHERMIC
CEEFNRSTTU	FRUTESCENT	CEEHIMSSTU	SHEET MUSIC
CEEFOORRSU	FORECOURSE	CEEHINNORT	INCOHERENT
CEEFORRRSS	CROSS-REFER	CEEHINOPPR	HIPPOCRENE
CEEGGILNNT	NEGLECTING	CEEHINQSTU	TECHNIQUES
CEEGHIILMP	HEMIPLEGIC	CEEHINRRST	CHRISTENER,
CEEGHIMOST	GEOCHEMIST	RECHRISTEN	
CEEGHINNOT	ETHNOGENIC	CEEHINRSTW	WINCHESTER
CEEGHKMNRU	KREMENCHUG	CEEHINSSST	CHESTINESS
CEEGHLOPST	CLOTHES PEG	CEEHINSSTT	TETCHINESS
CEEGIINOPR	EPIROGENIC	CEEHIOPPRS	PROPHECIES
CEEGIINOTV	GIVE NOTICE	CEEHIOPSSW	SHOWPIECES
CEEGIINPRV	PERCEIVING	CEEHIORSTT	THEORETICS
CEEGIINRSX	EXERCISING	CEEHIRRSTT	STRETCHIER
CEEGIINSTT	GENETICIST	CEEHKKOOYY	HOKEY COKEY
CEEGIINSTU	EUGENICIST	CEEHKNPRUY	KEYPUNCHER
CEEGINNNST	SENTENCING	CEEHKNPSUY	KEYPUNCHES
CEEGINNORU	NEUROGENIC	CEEHLLNOSW	WELL-CHOSEN
CEEGINNOSS	CONSIGNEES	CEEHLNORTY	COHERENTLY
CEEGINNQSU	SEQUENCING	CEEHLPRSSU	SEPULCHRES
CEEGINNRSS	SCREENINGS	CEEHMMOORR	CHROMOMERE
CEEGINNRST	NIGRESCENT	CEEHNNOSSU	NONESUCHES
CEEGINNRSU	INSURGENCE	CEEHNOOPPS	NEPHOSCOPE
CEEGINOORT	EROTOGENIC	CEEHNOOPRT	CTENOPHORE
CEEGINORRS	RECOGNISER	CEEHRRSSTT	STRETCHERS
CEEGINORRV	RE-COVERING	CEEIIKLNPR	PINCERLIKE
CEEGINORRZ	RECOGNIZER	CEEIILLLOS	ICE LOLLIES
CEEGINOSTV	CONGESTIVE	CEEIILLMRV	VERMICELLI
CEEGINPRST	RESPECTING	CEEIILLORS	COLLIERIES
CEEGINRSTY	SYNERGETIC	CEEIILNOSU	ISOLEUCINE
CEEGLORSTU	GLOUCESTER	CEEIILNRSY	RESILIENCY
CEEIILNRTT	CENTILITRE		
CEEIILOSTV	VELOCITIES		
CEEIILPPST	EPILEPTICS		
CEEIILPRSV	LIP SERVICE		
CEEIILRTTY	ERECTILITY		
CEEIILTTVY	ELECTIVITY		
CEEIIMNNTT	INCITEMENT		
CEEIIMORTT	METEORITIC		
CEEIIMPRRT	PERIMETRIC		
CEEIINNSST	INSISTENCE		
CEEIINNSTV	INCENTIVES		
CEEIINOPST	CENTIPOISE		
CEEIINPPRT	PERCIPIENT		
CEEIINPRST	RECIPIENTS		
CEEIINPSTV	INSPECTIVE		
CEEIINRSTT	INTERSTICE		
CEEIINTTVX	EXTINCTIVE		
CEEIIORRST	ESCRITOIRE		
CEEIIRSSTU	SECURITIES		
CEEIJLOPRT	PROJECTILE		
CEEIJNORST	REJECTIONS		
CEEIJOPRTV	PROJECTIVE		
CEEIJRSTUV	SURJECTIVE		
CEEIJRSTYY	JERSEY CITY		
CEEIKLNRSS	SILK SCREEN		
CEEIKNPRTY	PERNICKETY		
CEEIKNSSSS	SICKNESSES		
CEEILLNRST	STENCILLER		
CEEILLNSTT	INTELLECTS		
CEEILLOOPT	COLEOPTILE		
CEEILLORSS	RECOILLESS		
CEEILLRSSU	SCULLERIES		
CEEILMNOPT	INCOMPLETE		
CEEILMNORT	CLINOMETER		
CEEILMNOSS	COMELINESS		
CEEILMOPTV	COMPLETIVE		
CEEILNOSST	SELECTIONS		
CEEILNQSTU	LIQUESCENT		
CEEILNRSTV	VENTRICLES		
CEEILNRSUY	INSECURELY		
CEEILNRTTY	RETICENTLY		
CEEILPRSTT	TELESCRIPT		
CEEILPRSUV	PRECLUSIVE		
CEEILSSUVX	EXCLUSIVES		
CEEIMMOPRT	EMMETROPIC		
CEEIMMORRT	MICROMETER		
CEEIMMOSTT	COMMITTEES		
CEEIMNNOPR	PROMINENCE		
CEEIMNNRST	INCREMENTS		
CEEIMNOORS	ECONOMISER		
CEEIMNOORZ	ECONOMIZER		
CEEIMORSTV	VISCOMETER		
CEEIMOSSTV	VICOMTESSE		
CEEINNNOTV	CONVENIENT		

CEEINNPSST	SPINESCENT	CEENOSSSTU	COUNTESSES	CEGGHIMNUW	CHEWING GUM
CEEINOPPRT	PERCEPTION	CEENPRSSSU	SPRUCENESS	CEGGILNOSS	CLOGGINESS
CEEINOPRSS	PRECESSION	CEENPRSTTU	PUTRESCENT	CEGGINNORV	CONVERGING
CEEINOPRST	RECEPTIONS	CEEOPRRSTT	RETROSPECT	CEGGINOOST	GEOGNOSTIC
CEEINOPSTX	EXCEPTIONS	CEEOPRRSTU	PERSECUTOR	CEGHHIINRS	CHERISHING
CEEINORRST	CORRIENTES	CEEOQRSTTU	CROQUETTES	CEGHIIKNNT	THICKENING
CEEINORSSS	RECESSIONS	CEEORRSSST	CROSSTREES	CEGHIIKNRW	WHICKERING
CEEINORSST	SECRETIONS	CEFFFFHOTU	OFF THE CUFF	CEGHIILLNS	CHISELLING
CEEINORSTV	VENTRICOSE	CEFFHIINOR	CHIFFONIER	CEGHIILOOR	HIEROLOGIC
CEEINORSTX	EXCRETIONS	CEFFIIKKLN	FLICK KNIFE	CEGHIINNUY	UNHYGIENIC
CEEINOSSTX	EXOTICNESS	CEFFIINSTU	SUFFICIENT	CEGHIINORZ	RHIZOGENIC
CEEINOSTTX	COEXISTENT	CEFFIIRRTU	FRUCTIFIER	CEGHILMNSY	SCHEMINGLY
CEEINOSTUX	EXECUTIONS	CEFFIOOPST	POST OFFICE	CEGHILNOOT	ETHNOLOGIC
CEEINPRSSS	PRINCESSES	CEFFIRSSTU	SCRUFFIEST	CEGHILNOPY	PHYLOGENIC
CEEINPRSTU	PUTRESCINE	CEFFLLORUY	FORCEFULLY	CEGHILNOST	CLOSE THING
CEEINRRSTU	SCRUTINEER	CEFGHILNST	FLETCHINGS	CEGHILNPPS	SCHLEPPING
CEEINRSSTY	SYNCRETISE	CEFGHILNTY	FETCHINGLY	CEGHILNQSU	SQUELCHING
CEEINRSTTV	VITRESCENT	CEFGIIKLNR	FLICKERING	CEGHIMMNOO	HOMECOMING
CEEINRSTYZ	SYNCRETIZE	CEFGIIILNT	INFLECTING	CEGHIMOOPR	GEOMORPHIC
CEEIOORSVV	VOICE-OVERS	CEFGIINPSY	SPECIFYING	CEGHINOOPT	PHOTOGENIC
CEEIOPPRSS	PERISCOPES	CEFGIINRTY	CERTIFYING, RECTIFYING,	CEGHINOORT	ORTHOGENIC
CEEIOPRTTV	PROTECTIVE			CEGHINOPTY	PHYTOGENIC, TYPHOGENIC
CEEIOQRSTU	COQUETRIES	CEFGINNORR	CONFERRING	CEGHINORTU	RETOUCHING
CEEIORSSTU	COURTESIES	CEFGINNOSS	CONFESSING	CEGHINORTY	TRICHOGYNE
CEEIPRSSUV	PERCUSSIVE	CEFGLOORSU	GOLF COURSE	CEGHINOTUU	HUGUENOTIC
CEEIPSSTUV	SUSCEPTIVE	CEFHHNNORR	FRENCH HORN	CEGHINRSTT	STRETCHING
CEEKLLRSSY	RECKLESSLY	CEFHIILLSS	FISH SLICES	CEGHIOPSSY	GEOPHYSICS
CEEKLNRTTU	TURTLENECK	CEFHIIRRST	FIRST REICH	CEGHIORSTU	GROUCHIEST
CEEKLORRWW	CREWELWORK	CEFHIKNRSS	FRENCH KISS	CEGHKNORSU	ROUGHNECKS
CEELLMOPTY	COMPLETELY	CEFHIKRSSU	SUCKERFISH	CEGHLNOOTY	TECHNOLOGY
CEELMMNOPT	COMPLEMENT	CEFHILSTTU	CUTTLEFISH	CEGIIIMNNT	MENINGITIC
CEELMNNOOS	SOMNOLENCE	CEFIIILNTV	INFLICTIVE	CEGIIKLLNN	NICKELLING
CEELMOORTU	COULOMETER	CEFIIILNTY	INFELICITY	CEGIIKNNQU	QUICKENING
CEELNORSSU	ENCLOSURES	CEFIILNNOT	INFLECTION	CEGIIKNNRS	SNICKERING
CEELNORSVY	CONVERSELY	CEFIILNOQU	CINQUEFOIL	CEGIIKPRST	PIGSTICKER
CEELORRSTY	CLERESTORY	CEFIILOSTU	FELICITOUS	CEGIILLNNP	PENCILLING
CEEMMOTXYY	MYXOMYCETE	CEFIIMNNTU	MUNIFICENT	CEGIILNNPR	PRINCELING
CEEMNNSTTY	ENCYSTMENT	CEFIINNOST	INFECTIONS	CEGIILNNSS	CLINGINESS
CEEMNOORST	CENTROSOME	CEFIINOPRT	PROFICIENT	CEGIILNNST	STENCILING
CEEMNOPRTU	RECOUPMENT	CEFIINOSTU	INFECTIOUS	CEGIILNNTY	ENTICINGLY
CEEMNOPRTY	PYCNOMETER	CEFILLMRUY	MERCIFULLY	CEGIILNOSU	GENIUS LOCI
CEEMNORTUY	NEURECTOMY	CEFILMNRUU	UNMERCIFUL	CEGIILNPRY	PIERCINGLY
CEEMNPSSTU	SPUMESCENT	CEFILMOORS	FROLICSOME	CEGIILNTXY	EXCITINGLY
CEEMOPRSSS	COMPRESSES	CEFIMORSUY	CYMIFEROUS	CEGIILORTU	OLIGURETIC
CEEMOSSSTY	ECOSYSTEMS	CEFINNOOSS	CONFESSION	CEGIILOSTU	EULOGISTIC
CEENNOQSTU	CONSEQUENT	CEFINOORSU	CONIFEROUS	CEGIINNOST	SECTIONING
CEENNORSTU	ENCOUNTERS	CEFIOORSUV	VOCIFEROUS	CEGIINNPST	INSPECTING
CEENNPRSSY	PENNYCRESS	CEFKLOPSTU	POCKETFULS	CEGIINORXZ	EXORCIZING
CEENOORSTV	COVER NOTES	CEFLNOORRW	CORNFLOWER	CEGIINOSTX	COEXISTING
CEENOPPPRR	PEPPERCORN	CEFMNOORRS	CONFORMERS	CEGIINRRTU	RECRUITING
CEENOPPRTY	PREPOTENCY	CEFMOORRST	COMFORTERS	CEGIINRSTT	TRISECTING
CEENOPRRST	PRECENTORS	CEFNNOORRT	CONFRONTER	CEGIJNOPRT	PROJECTING
CEENORRSTV	CONVERTERS	CEFNOORSSS	CONFESSORS	CEGIKNNORS	RECKONINGS
CEENORTTUX	CONTEXTURE	CEFOORRSTU	FORECOURTS		

432

CEGIKNOOPR	PRECOOKING	CEHIIMNORT	THERMIONIC	CEHIORRSST	CHORISTERS
CEGIKNORST	RESTOCKING	CEHIIMNORY	HIERONYMIC	CEHKOOOSSU	COOKHOUSES
CEGILLMNOP	COMPELLING	CEHIIMOPPR	EPIMORPHIC	CEHLMOOPRY	POLYCHROME
CEGILLOOXY	LEXICOLOGY	CEHIIMOPRT	HEMITROPIC	CEHLMOPTYY	LYMPHOCYTE
CEGILMNOOP	MONOPLEGIC	CEHIIMRSTY	MYTHICISER	CEHLOOOPRT	TOCOPHEROL
CEGILMNOPT	COMPLETING	CEHIIMRTYZ	MYTHICIZER	CEHLOOPPRS	PREP SCHOOL
CEGILNNOST	CLINGSTONE	CEHIIMSTTW	TIME SWITCH	CEHLOOPRSS	PRESCHOOLS
CEGILNRSTU	CLUSTERING	CEHIINPRSS	CHIRPINESS	CEHLORRTTY	TERRYCLOTH
CEGILNRTTU	CLUTTERING	CEHIINPSST	PITCHINESS	CEHMMNOOOR	
CEGILOOSST	ECOLOGISTS	CEHIINSSTT	IN STITCHES	MONOCHROME	
CEGILOOSTT	CETOLOGIST	CEHIINSTTZ	CHINTZIEST	CEHMMOOORS	
CEGIMMNNOT	COMMENTING	CEHIIOSTTY	HISTIOCYTE	CHROMOSOME	
CEGIMNOORS	ERGONOMICS	CEHIIPPSST	PSESPHITIC	CEHMOOPRTY	CORMOPHYTE,
CEGIMNOORV	OVERCOMING	CEHIIPRSTY	SPHERICITY	ECTOMORPHY	
CEGINNNORU	RENOUNCING	CEHIIPSTUU	EUPHUISTIC	CEHNNORSTU	TRUNCHEONS
CEGINNNOST	CONSENTING	CEHIIRRTTU	URETHRITIC	CEHNOOOPPS	PHONOSCOPE
CEGINNNOTT	CONTENTING,	CEHIIRSSTU	HEURISTICS	CEHNOOSTTU	TOUCHSTONE
CONTINGENT		CEHIKNNSSU	CHUNKINESS	CEHNOPRSTU	SCUNTHORPE
CEGINNOOST	CONGESTION	CEHIKOPPST	HIP POCKETS	CEHNOPRSTY	PHENOCRYST
CEGINNOQRU	CONQUERING	CEHIKPRSSW	SHIPWRECKS	CEHNORSTVY	CHERNOVTSY
CEGINNORSV	CONSERVING,	CEHILNNPSU	PUNCH LINES	CEHOOOPRSS	HOROSCOPES
CONVERSING		CEHILNOSTU	TOUCHLINES	CEHOORSTUU	COURTHOUSE
CEGINNORTU	COUNTERING,	CEHILNSSTZ	SCHNITZELS	CEHORSTTTU	OUTSTRETCH
RECOUNTING		CEHILOPRST	LECTORSHIP	CEIIIILSTV	CIVILITIES
CEGINNORTV	CONVERTING	CEHILORSTY	CHRYSOLITE,	CEIIIINSTV	VICINITIES
CEGINNORUV	UNCOVERING	CHRYSOTILE		CEIIILLMNO	LIMICOLINE
CEGINNOSTT	CONTESTING	CEHIMMNSSU	CHUMMINESS	CEIIILLNNP	PENICILLIN
CEGINNRSTY	STRINGENCY	CEHIMNOOPR	MICROPHONE	CEIIILNPTX	INEXPLICIT
CEGINNRSUW	UNSCREWING	CEHIMNOOTT	NOMOTHETIC	CEIIILNSVY	INCISIVELY
CEGINNRSUY	INSURGENCY	CEHIMNOPTY	CHIMNEYPOT	CEIIILOPST	POLITICISE
CEGINOORRZ	RECOGNIZOR	CEHIMOOORT	HOMOEROTIC	CEIIILOPTZ	POLITICIZE
CEGINOORST	CREOSOTING	CEHIMOOPTY	HOMEOTYPIC,	CEIIIMMPRS	EMPIRICISM
CEGINOPRSS	PROCESSING	MYTHOPOEIC		CEIIIMPRST	EMPIRICIST
CEGINOPRTT	PROTECTING	CEHIMOPRTY	MICROPHYTE	CEIIIMRSTV	VICTIMISER
CEGINOSSTT	COSSETTING	CEHIMOPSTY	MESOPHYTIC	CEIIIMRTVZ	VICTIMIZER
CEGINPPRSU	SCUPPERING	CEHIMRSTUY	EURYTHMICS	CEIIINPPRT	PRECIPITIN
CEGINPSSTU	SUSPECTING	CEHINNNPPY	PINCHPENNY	CEIIIOPSST	ISOPIESTIC
CEGLNOOSYY	SYNECOLOGY	CEHINNPSSU	PUNCHINESS	CEIIJNNOST	INJECTIONS
CEGNORRSSU	SCROUNGERS	CEHINNRSTY	STRYCHNINE	CEIIJNNTUV	INJUNCTIVE
CEGOOPRSSY	GYROSCOPES	CEHINOORRS	RHINOCEROS	CEIIJNSSTU	INJUSTICES
CEHHHIIKRT	HITCHHIKER	CEHINOPPRR	PRONEPHRIC	CEIIKKLNPT	TICKLE PINK
CEHHIILMNT	HELMINTHIC	CEHINOPPSS	CHOPPINESS	CEIIKLMORT	KILOMETRIC
CEHHILNRTU	IN THE LURCH	CEHINOPPTY	PHENOTYPIC	CEIIKLNRST	CRINKLIEST
CEHHIMRTUY	EURHYTHMIC	CEHINOPRSS	CENSORSHIP	CEIIKLNSSS	SICKLINESS
CEHHIOOPST	THEOSOPHIC	CEHINOPSST	PITCHSTONE	CEIIKLPRST	PRICKLIEST
CEHHKLLOSS	SHELLSHOCK	CEHINOPTTY	ENPHYTOTIC,	CEIIKNPRST	NITPICKERS
CEHHLORTTW	LETCHWORTH	ENTOPHYTIC		CEIIKNRSST	TRICKINESS
CEHHOOPSSU	CHOPHOUSES	CEHINOSSTU	TOUCHINESS	CEIIKNSSST	STICKINESS
CEHIIINRST	TRICHINISE	CEHINPRSST	SPHINCTERS	CEIILLLSTU	CELLULITIS
CEHIIINRTZ	TRICHINIZE	CEHIOOPRRT	RHEOTROPIC	CEIILLNNOT	CENTILLION
CEHIILLNSS	CHILLINESS	CEHIOOORRT	RETROCHOIR	CEIILLNRTU	CITRULLINE
CEHIILMOST	HOMILETICS,	CEHIOPRSTT	PROSTHETIC	CEIILLOSSU	SILICULOSE
MESOLITHIC		CEHIOPRSTY	HYPOCRITES	CEIILLPTXY	EXPLICITLY
CEHIILNOTX	XENOLITHIC	CEHIOPRTXY	XEROPHYTIC	CEIILMOPST	POLEMICIST
CEHIILOPTY	HELIOTYPIC	CEHIOQSTTU	COQUETTISH	CEIILNNORS	CRINOLINES

CEIILNOSTU	LICENTIOUS	CEILNNNOTY	INNOCENTLY	CEINOPRSTT	INTROSPECT
CEIILNOSTV	NOVELISTIC	CEILNNOSVY	INSOLVENCY	CEINOPRSTU	SUPERTONIC
CEIILNPPRS	PRINCIPLES	CEILNOOPRS	NECROPOLIS	CEINOPSTTY	STENOTYPIC
CEIILOQRSU	LIQUORICES	CEILNOORRS	RESORCINOL	CEINOQTUYZ	QUEZON CITY
CEIILPRSST	LIST PRICES	CEILNOORSS	COLONISERS	CEINORRSTW	TOWN CRIERS
CEIIMMORSS	MICROSEISM	CEILNOORSZ	COLONIZERS	CEINORSSUX	EXCURSIONS
CEIIMNNOST	OMNISCIENT	CEILNOPRSU	PRECLUSION	CEINOSSTUU	INCESTUOUS
CEIIMNRSSU	SINECURISM	CEILNORSSU	INCLOSURES	CEINOSTTTU	CONSTITUTE
CEIIMORSST	ISOMETRICS	CEILNORTTY	CONTRITELY	CEINRSSTTT	STRICTNESS
CEIIMOSTTT	TOTEMISTIC	CEILNOSSST	COSTLINESS	CEINRSSSTU	CRUSTINESS
CEIIINNOPST	INCEPTIONS,	CEILNOSUVV	CONVULSIVE	CEINRSSSUV	SCURVINESS
INSPECTION		CEILOPRSTY	PROSELYTIC	CEINRSSTTY	SYNCRETIST
CEIINNOTTX	EXTINCTION	CEILOPRSUY	PRECIOUSLY	CEIOOPRRTU	PUERTO RICO
CEIINOPRSS	PRECISIONS	CEILOPSSUY	SPECIOUSLY	CEIOOPRRTY	CORPOREITY
CEIINOPRST	ISENTROPIC	CEILORSTTU	COURTLIEST	CEIOPRRTUV	CORRUPTIVE
CEIINOPRSU	PERNICIOUS	CEIMMMNOTT	COMMITMENT	CEIOPRRTUY	EURYTROPIC
CEIINOPRTV	VOICEPRINT	CEIMMNOORT	METRONOMIC	CEIOPRRTWY	COPYWRITER
CEIINOPSTT	NEPOTISTIC	CEIMMNOQUU	COMMUNIQUE	CEIORRSSSY	RESCISSORY
CEIINORRST	CRITERIONS	CEIMMNORTY	METRONYMIC	CEIORRSTUU	COUTURIERS
CEIINORSSS	RESCISSION	CEIMMOOPRS	COMPROMISE	CEIPPRRSST	PRESCRIPTS
CEIINPRSSS	CRISPINESS	CEIMMOORST	OSMOMETRIC	CEIPPRSTTY	TYPESCRIPT
CEIINRSSTU	SCRUTINIES,	CEIMMORRTY	MICROMETRY	CEIRRSSTTU	STRICTURES
SCRUTINISE, SINECURIST		CEIMMORSSU	COMMISSURE	CEJOOPRRST	PROJECTORS
CEIINRSTUY	INSECURITY	CEIMNOOOSU	MONOECIOUS	CEKKORSSTY	SKYROCKETS
CEIINRSTUZ	SCRUTINIZE	CEIMNOOPSS	MECONOPSIS	CEKLMOOORR	LOCKER ROOM
CEIINSSSTT	SCIENTISTS	CEIMNOORTT	TONOMETRIC	CEKLNORSTW	TOWN CLERKS
CEIIOORSTU	TRIOECIOUS	CEIMNOOSTT	ECONOMISTS	CELLNOORRT	CONTROLLER
CEIIOPRSTY	PRECIOSITY	CEIMNOPRSU	PROSCENIUM	CELLNOORSU	COUNSELLOR
CEIIOPSSTY	SPECIOSITY	CEIMNORSTT	METRIC TONS	CELLOORSSU	COLOURLESS
CEIIORSTVV	VIVISECTOR	CEIMNORSUU	CERUMINOUS	CELMOORSSU	LOOSE SCRUM
CEIJNOOPRT	PROJECTION	CEIMNRSSTY	SYNCRETISM	CELMOORSTY	SCLEROTOMY
CEIJNORSTU	SURJECTION	CEIMOOPRRS	MICROSPORE	CELNOPRSUU	PRONUCLEUS
CEIKKORRWW	WICKERWORK	CEIMOOPRTT	COMPETITOR,	CELOOSSSSU	COLOSSUSES
CEIKLNNOST	CLINKSTONE	OPTOMETRIC		CELOOSTUVY	COVETOUSLY
CEIKLNPSSU	PLUCKINESS	CEIMOOPSST	COMPOSITES	CELPRSSSTU	SCULPTRESS
CEIKLOPRST	STOCKPILER	CEIMOORSTY	SOCIOMETRY	CELPRSSTUU	SCULPTURES
CEIKLOPSST	STOCKPILES	CEIMOPRRTY	PYROMETRIC	CEMMNNOOSS	COMMONNESS
CEIKNOSSST	STOCKINESS	CEIMORSSTU	COSTUMIERS	CEMMNNOOTW	COMMON
CEIKPQSSTU	QUICKSTEPS	CEIMORSTVY	VISCOMETRY	NEWT	
CEIKRRSSTT	TRICKSTERS	CEIMOSSTUV	MUSCOVITES	CEMNNOOPST	COMPONENTS
CEILLNOORS	COLOR LINES	CEINNNOOTT	CONTENTION	CEMNNORTUY	COUNTRYMEN
CEILLOOQSU	COLLOQUIES	CEINNNOOTV	CONVENTION	CEMOOPRRSS	COMPRESSOR
CEILMMNOPT	COMPLIMENT	CEINNNOSTT	CONTINENTS	CENNOOPRRU	PRONOUNCER
CEILMNOOPT	COMPLETION	CEINNOORSV	CONVERSION	CENOOQRRSU	CONQUERORS
CEILMNOOPX	COMPLEXION	CEINNOPTUX	EXPUNCTION	CENOORRTTV	CONTROVERT
CEILMNOOSS	SEMICOLONS	CEINNORSTU	CENTURIONS	CENOPRSTUY	COUNTERSPY
CEILMNORTY	CLINOMETRY	CEINNOSSTT	CONSISTENT	CENORSSSTW	CROW'S NESTS
CEILMNSSSU	CLUMSINESS	CEINOOPRSS	PROCESSION	CEOOPPRRST	PROSPECTOR
CEILMOOOTV	LOCOMOTIVE	CEINOOPRTT	PROTECTION	CEOOPRRSSS	PROCESSORS
CEILMOOPST	LEPTOSOMIC	CEINOORSSU	CENSORIOUS	CEOOPRRSTT	PROTECTORS
CEILMOPSUV	COMPULSIVE	CEINOOSSUY	SYNOECIOUS	CEOOPRRSTU	PROSECUTOR
CEILMOPTXY	COMPLEXITY	CEINOPPRSU	PORCUPINES	CEOOPRRTTY	PROTECTORY
CEILMORSTU	SCLEROTIUM	CEINOPRSST	INSPECTORS	CEOOPPRSSTU	PROSPECTUS
CEILMORTUV	VOLUMETRIC	CEINOPRSSU	PERCUSSION,	CEOPRRRSSU	PRECURSORS
CEILMOSTUU	METICULOUS	SUPERSONIC			

CEOPRRRSUY	PRECURSORY	CGHILLOORS	SCHOOLGIRL	CGINNOOSTT	COTTON GINS
CEPPRRSTUU	UPPER CRUST	CGHILNOTUY	TOUCHINGLY	CGINNORSTU	CONSTRUING
CERRSSTTUU	STRUCTURES	CGHILOORTY	TRICHOLOGY	CGINNPRTUU	PUNCTURING
CFFFIISSTU	FISTICUFFS	CGHINOOOPR	GONOPHORIC	CGINOOPRST	PROGNOSTIC
CFFGIIKNOT	TICKING OFF	CGHINOOPRY	GYNOPHORIC	CGINOOSTUU	CONTIGUOUS
CFFGILNOSY	SCOFFINGLY	CGHINOOSYZ	SCHIZOGONY	CGINOPRRTU	CORRUPTING
CFGIIILNNT	INFLICTING	CGHIOPRSTY	COPYRIGHTS	CGIOOPRSYZ	ZYGOSPORIC
CFGIIKLNOR	FROLICKING	CGHLNOOORY	CHRONOLOGY	CGLOOOPRTY	PROCTOLOGY
CFGIIMNNOR	CONFIRMING	CGHLOOPSYY	PSYCHOLOGY	CHHIIOSSTY	ICHTHYOSIS
CFGIINNORU	FINNO-UGRIC	CGHOPRTUUU	CUT UP ROUGH	CHHIIPSTTW	WHIPSTITCH
CFGIKNNORU	UNFROCKING	CGIIIILNVZ	CIVILIZING	CHHILLRSUY	CHURLISHLY
CFGILOUYZZ	FUZZY LOGIC	CGIIIJNOST	JINGOISTIC	CHHILOOPTY	HOLOPHYTIC
CFGIMNNOOR	CONFORMING	CGIIIKNNPT	NITPICKING	CHHIMNOOOP	HOMOPHONIC
CFGIMNOORT	COMFORTING	CGIIILNNTY	INCITINGLY	CHHINSTTUW	WITCH-HUNTS
CFGOOPRSUU	FOCUS GROUP	CGIIILNOST	SOLICITING	CHHIOOPPRS	PHOSPHORIC
CFHIIKSSST	FISH STICKS	CGIIILNSTU	LINGUISTIC	CHHKLLOOSY	HOLLYHOCKS
CFHIIKSSTT	SHIFT STICK, STICK SHIFT	CGIIILPSTU	PUGILISTIC	CHIIIILNST	NIHILISTIC
CFHIINOORS	HONORIFICS	CGIIIORRST	RIGORISTIC	CHIIILLOPP	LIPOPHILIC
CFHIKOPRST	PITCHFORKS	CGIIJNNNOO	CONJOINING	CHIIILPPPS	PHILIPPICS
CFHIMOPRSY	SCYPHIFORM	CGIIKLLNOR	ROLLICKING	CHIIILPSTY	SYPHILITIC
CFHKOOOPRS	SHOCKPROOF	CGIIKLNRTY	TRICKINGLY	CHIIINORST	HISTRIONIC
CFHLLOOORT	FLOOR CLOTH	CGIILNNOOZ	COLONIZING	CHIIKLLSTY	TICKLISHLY
CFHLMOOORR	CHLOROFORM	CGIILOOSTT	ISOGLOTTIC	CHIILMNOOT	MONOLITHIC
CFIIILNNOT	INFLICTION	CGIIMMNOTT	COMMITTING	CHIILMOOTT	LITHOTOMIC
CFIIINOSTT	FICTIONIST	CGIIMNNORS	CRIMSONING	CHIILNOOPT	PHONOLITIC
CFIIIIOSTTU	FICTITIOUS	CGIIMNOPRS	COMPRISING	CHIILOSTTY	HISTOLYTIC
CFIIKKLNSS	SKIN FLICKS	CGIINNNOTU	CONTINUING	CHIIMOOPRS	ISOMORPHIC
CFIILLLNOU	FOLLICULIN	CGIINNOPRS	CONSPIRING	CHIIMOPRRT	TRIMORPHIC
CFIILMMORS	MICROFILMS	CGIINNORTV	CONTRIVING	CHIIMORRST	TRICHROISM
CFIILORSST	FLORISTICS	CGIINNOSST	CONSISTING	CHIIMORSTU	HUMORISTIC
CFIINNNOOT	NONFICTION	CGIINOTTUY	CONTIGUITY	CHIINNOPSU	PINCUSHION
CFIIRSTTUU	FUTURISTIC	CGIKOOPSST	POGO STICKS	CHIINORSTU	TRICHINOUS
CFIKLLNOST	FLINTLOCKS	CGILLNOOPS	SCOLLOPING	CHIIOOOPRT	OOPHORITIC
CFILMMORUU	CUMULIFORM	CGILLNOSWY	SCOWLINGLY	CHIIPSSSTY	PHYSICISTS
CFIMNOORST	CONFORMIST	CGILLOSSYY	GLYCOLYSIS	CHIKLMOSST	LOCKSMITHS
CFIMNOORTY	CONFORMITY	CGILMOOSTY	MYCOLOGIST	CHIKOOPSTT	TOOTHPICKS
CFLLNORSUY	SCORNFULLY	CGILMOOSUY	MUSICOLOGY	CHILLNOOST	LOINCLOTHS
CFLOOORRUU	FOUR-COLOUR	CGILNNOPUU	UNCOUPLING	CHILLNOSWY	CLOWNISHLY
CFLOORSSUU	SCROFULOUS	CGILNNORSY	SCORNINGLY	CHILNOOPPY	POLYPHONIC
CGGIIKNPSU	SUCKING PIG	CGILNNOSTU	CONSULTING	CHILNOOPXY	XYLOPHONIC
CGGIINNNOS	CONSIGNING	CGILNNOSUV	CONVULSING	CHILNOPSSU	CONSULSHIP
CGGINNORSU	SCROUNGING	CGILNOOOST	NOSTOLOGIC, ONCOLOGIST	CHILOOPTTY	PHOTOLYTIC
CGHHHILOOS	HIGH SCHOOL	CGILNOORSU	COLOURINGS	CHIMNNOOOP	MONOPHONIC
CGHHILORTT	TORCHLIGHT	CGILNOPSUV	LOVING CUPS	CHIMOOOPRZ	ZOOMORPHIC
CGHHIORSTU	HIGH COURTS	CGILOOOPRT	TROPICOLOGY	CHIMOORTTY	TRICHOTOMY
CGHIIKNSTT	NIGHTSTICK	CGILOOOTXY	TOXICOLOGY	CHIMPSSTYY	SYMPHYSTIC
CGHIIKSTTT	STICKTIGHT	CGILOOSTTY	CYTOLOGIST	CHINOOOPTT	PHOTOTONIC
CGHIILLOOT	LITHOLOGIC	CGIMNOOPRT	COMPORTING	CHINOOPPTY	PHONOTYPIC
CGHIILOPST	PHLOGISTIC	CGIMNOOPST	COMPOSTING	CHINOOPRSY	RHINOSCOPY
CGHIILPRTY	TRIGLYPHIC	CGINNOORSS	CONSIGNORS	CHIOOORSSU	ISOCHROOUS
CGHIINNOSU	CUSHIONING	CGINNOORST	CONSORTING	CHIOOPRRRY	PYROPHORIC
CGHIKLNOSY	SHOCKINGLY	CGINNOORTT	CONTORTING	CHIOOPPTTY	PHOTOTYPIC
CGHILLNRUY	LURCHINGLY	CGINNOORTU	CONTOURING	CHIOPRSSTU	COURTSHIPS
				CHIORSTTTW	STITCHWORT

CHKLOOOORSW	SCHOOLWORK
CHLMNOSUUU	HOMUNCULUS
CHLMOOPRYY	POLYCHROMY
CIIIILNTVY	INCIVILITY
CIIILLMPTY	IMPLICITLY
CIIILMPSST	SIMPLISTIC
CIIILMPSTY	SIMPLICITY
CIIILNTUVY	UNCIVILITY
CIIILPRTTY	TRIPLICITY
CIIIMNNOST	NICOTINISM
CIIIMNPPRU	PRINCIPIUM
CIIIMOPSTT	OPTIMISTIC
CIIIMSSTTW	WITTICISMS
CIIINNNOTT	INTINCTION
CIIINNOSTU	UNIONISTIC
CIIJLNOPST	CLIP JOINTS
CIIJNNNOTU	INJUNCTION
CIIKOSTTTU	STICK IT OUT
CIILLMOOSU	LIMICOLOUS
CIILLNOOSS	COLLISIONS
CIILLNOOST	COTILLIONS
CIILLNOOTU	ILLOCUTION
CIILLOSTTY	STYLOLITIC
CIILMMNTUU	NUMMULITIC
CIILNNOSSU	INCLUSIONS
CIILNOPSTU	PUNCTILIOS
CIILOORSST	SOLICITORS
CIILOOSSTU	SOLICITOUS
CIILOPRTVY	PROCLIVITY
CIILRRSTUY	SCURRILITY
CIILSSSTTY	STYLISTICS
CIIMMNOOSS	COMMISSION
CIIMNNOOTZ	MONZONITIC
CIIMNOPRRT	MICROPRINT
CIIMORRSST	TRICROTISM
CIINNOORTT	CONTRITION
CIINNORSSU	INCURSIONS
CIINNOTTUY	CONTINUITY
CIINOOPRTX	PICROTOXIN
CIINOPSSSU	SUSPICIONS
CIIOORSTUV	VICTORIOUS
CIIOPSSSUU	SUSPICIOUS
CIIPSTTTYY	STYPTICITY
CIJKOSSSST	JOSS STICKS
CIJLNNOOTY	CONJOINTLY
CIJNNOSTTU	T-JUNCTIONS
CIKLLOSSTT	STOCK-STILL
CIKLNOOSTT	SILK COTTON
CILLMOOQUU	COLLOQUIUM
CILLOPRSTU	PORTCULLIS
CILLOSSUUY	LUSCIOUSLY
CILMNOOOOT	LOCOMOTION
CILMNOOPSU	COMPULSION
CILMNOSSTU	COLUMNISTS

CILNNOOSUV	CONVULSION
CILOORRSTU	TRICOLOURS
CILORRSSUU	SCURRILOUS
CIMMNNOOSU	COMMUNIONS
CIMMNOOOST	COMMOTIONS
CIMMNOSSTU	COMMUNISTS
CIMNNOOOPP	NINCOMPOOP
CIMNNOSTUU	CONTINUOUS
CIMNOORSTU	CONSORTIUM
CIMOOOPRST	COMPOSITOR
CIMOPSTTUU	PUT TO MUSIC
CINNOOORTT	CONTORTION
CINNOOSSTU	CONTUSIONS
CINNOOSTUU	CONTINUOUS
CINOOPRRTU	CORRUPTION
CINOORSSTY	CONSISTORY
CINORRSTTU	INSTRUCTOR
CINOSTTUUY	UNCTUOSITY
CIOOPRSSTU	UROSCOPIST
CIOOPRSTTT	PROTOCTIST
CIOPPRSSTT	POSTSCRIPT
CIPPRRSTUU	STIRRUP CUP
CKLLOORRSW	SCROLLWORK
CKMNOORSTU	MOONSTRUCK
CKMOOORSST	STOCKROOMS
CKOPRSSTTU	TRUCK STOPS
CLMMNNOOUY	UNCOMMONLY
CLMOOOORTU	OCULOMOTOR
CLMOOPRSUY	COMPULSORY
CLNOOOOTTW	COTTON WOOL
CLNOOPRSSU	PROCONSULS
CLNOSTUUUY	UNCTUOUSLY
CLOOOPRRTU	PROLOCUTOR
CLOPRSSUUU	SCRUPULOUS
CMMMNOOOOR	COMMON ROOM
CMMNNNOOOU	COMMON NOUN
CNNNOOSTUU	COUNT NOUNS
CNNOOTTUWY	COUNTY TOWN
DDDDDFUUYY	FUDDY-DUDDY
DDDEEEFNNU	UNDEFENDED
DDDEEFIOST	EISTEDDFOD
DDDEEIOORS	DEODORISED
DDDEEIOORZ	DEODORIZED
DDDEEIORRS	DISORDERED
DDDEFILOOW	FIDDLEWOOD
DDEEEEGGNR	ENGENDERED
DDEEEFLORW	DEFLOWERED
DDEEEFORST	DEFORESTED
DDEEEHHPRS	SHEPHERDED
DDEEEHNOWY	HONEYDEWED

DDEEEEILSTT	TITLE DEEDS
DDEEEIMNOR	DOMINEERED
DDEEEIMNRT	DETERMINED
DDEEEINORZ	ZENER DIODE
DDEEEINRST	TENDERISED
DDEEEINRTZ	TENDERIZED
DDEEELLMOR	REMODELLED
DDEEELMMOS	MEDDLESOME
DDEEELMNTY	DEMENTEDLY
DDEEELOPRY	REDEPLOYED
DDEEELRSVY	DESERVEDLY
DDEEENRRTU	UNDETERRED
DDEEENRSUX	UNDERSEXED
DDEEEOOPRT	DEEP-ROOTED
DDEEEPRSSU	SUPERSEDED
DDEEFIIINT	IDENTIFIED
DDEEFIINTU	DEFINITUDE
DDEEFLNORU	FLOUNDERED
DDEEFMOOOR	FOREDOOMED
DDEEGGHOOP	HODGEPODGE
DDEEGGNOSS	DOGGEDNESS
DDEEGILNSY	DESIGNEDLY
DDEEGJLLUW	WELL-JUDGED
DDEEHIISSS	SIDE DISHES
DDEEHILMOS	DEMOLISHED
DDEEHINNSS	HIDDENNESS
DDEEHLORSU	SHOULDERED
DDEEHNORSU	ENSHROUDED
DDEEHOORTU	OUT-HERODED
DDEEIIKLMN	LIKE-MINDED
DDEEIILMNV	EVIL-MINDED
DDEEIINRSW	SIDEWINDER
DDEEIIORSX	DEOXIDISER
DDEEIIORXZ	DEOXIDIZER
DDEEIIPSSW	SIDESWIPED
DDEEIIQSTU	DISQUIETED
DDEEILMSTW	MIDDLE WEST
DDEEILNNRU	UNDERLINED
DDEEILNOSY	ONE-SIDEDLY
DDEEILNOTT	DOTTED LINE
DDEEILRTVY	DIVERTEDLY
DDEEIMNNOP	OPEN-MINDED
DDEEIMNNRU	UNDERMINED
DDEEIMNORS	ENDODERMIS, MODERNISED
DDEEIMNORZ	MODERNIZED
DDEEINNNTU	UNINTENDED
DDEEINNRTU	INDENTURED
DDEEINNSSW	WINDEDNESS
DDEEINORRV	OVERRIDDEN
DDEEINORSW	DISENDOWER, EIDERDOWNS
DDEEINRSSU	UNDERSISED
DDEEINRSUZ	UNDERSIZED
DDEEIOORRS	DEODORISER

DDEEIOORRZ	DEODORIZER	
DDEEIORRSS	SIDE ORDERS	
DDEEIRSSST	DISTRESSED	
DDEELLOORW	OLDE WORLDE	
DDEELLORWW	WELL-WORDED	
DDEELMORSU	SMOULDERED	
DDEELRRSSU	RUDDERLESS	
DDEENNOPST	DESPONDENT	
DDEENNOSSS	SODDENNESS	
DDEENNPRSU	UNDERSPEND	
DDEENNSSSU	SUDDENNESS	
DDEFGIIRSU	DISFIGURED	
DDEFGILLOS	GOLDFIELDS	
DDEFHIIIMU	HUMIDIFIED	
DDEFHIIMUY	DEHUMIDIFY	
DDEFIIILOS	SOLIDIFIED	
DDEFILOOST	FLOOD TIDES	
DDEFIMNORR	DENDRIFORM	
DDEFLORSSU	DUSSELDORF	
DDEGGGILOR	GOLD DIGGER	
DDEGHHIIMN	HIGH-MINDED	
DDEGHINRSU	SHUDDERING	
DDEGIINNST	DISTENDING	
DDEGILLMNY	MEDDLINGLY	
DDEGILNNOW	LONGWINDED	
DDEGINNORU	REDOUNDING	
DDEGIOOPRR	DO PORRIDGE	
DDEGLLLOOR	ROLLED GOLD	
DDEGLNOORY	DENDROLOGY	
DDEHHNRSTU	HUNDREDTHS	
DDEHIIIMNS	DIMINISHED	
DDEHIILNSW	WINDSHIELD	
DDEHIILPSU	DISULPHIDE	
DDEHIKNOOW	HOODWINKED	
DDEHINOSSS	SHODDINESS	
DDEHLNOSTU	HUDDLESTON	
DDEIIILQSU	LIQUIDISED	
DDEIIILQUZ	LIQUIDIZED	
DDEIIIMPSY	EPIDIDYMIS	
DDEIIIPRST	DISPIRITED	
DDEIIIJNOST	DISJOINTED	
DDEIIKRSSV	DISK DRIVES	
DDEIIMNNOU	DIMINUENDO	
DDEIINOPSS	INDISPOSED	
DDEIINOSTU	DUODENITIS	
DDEIINSSST	DISSIDENTS	
DDEIIOPRSS	DISPERSOID	
DDEIKNNRUW	WUNDERKIND	
DDEILLNPSY	SPLENDIDLY	
DDEILORRSY	DISORDERLY	
DDEIMNOSTU	DISMOUNTED	
DDEINOPRUV	UNPROVIDED	
DDEINOPSUW	UPSIDE DOWN	
DDEINORSSS	SORDIDNESS	

DDEINPSTUU	UNDISPUTED	
DDEIRSSTTU	DISTRUSTED	
DDELNORRUW	UNDERWORLD	
DDENOOPPRU	PROPOUNDED	
DDENOORSTU	UNDERSTOOD	
DDENORRSUU	SURROUNDED	
DDENRSTUUY	UNDERSTUDY	
DDEOPRRSTU	RUDDERPOST	
DDGGIILNOS	DISLODGING	
DDGGOOOOYY	GOODY-GOODY	
DDGHRRUUYY	HURDY-GURDY	
DDGIINPRRY	DRIP-DRYING	
DDGILLMNUY	MUDDLINGLY	
DDGILLNOPY	PLODDINGLY	
DDHILORRTW	THIRD WORLD	
DDHINOOPTY	DIPHYODONT	
DDHOOOOUWY	HOW DO YOU DO	
DDINOPPRTY	PONTYPRIDD	
DEEEEFPRRZ	DEEP FREEZE	
DEEEEFFLRS	SELF-FEEDER	
DEEEEFNRTT	TENDERFEET	
DEEEEGINNR	ENGINEERED	
DEEEEGNNRR	ENGENDERER	
DEEEEHLLLW	WELL-HEELED	
DEEEEKNRSW	WEEKENDERS	
DEEEEPRRSV	PERSEVERED	
DEEEFGIKNS	KNIFE-EDGES	
DEEEFHILNS	NEEDLEFISH	
DEEEFHLORR	FREEHOLDER	
DEEEFILMNT	DEFILEMENT	
DEEEFILNTV	FIELD EVENT	
DEEEFINRRT	INTERFERED	
DEEEFINRTW	WINTERFEED	
DEEEFINSSV	DEFENSIVES	
DEEEFLORRW	DEFLOWERER	
DEEEFMNRRU	REFERENDUM	
DEEEFMNRST	DEFERMENTS	
DEEEFNQRTU	FREQUENTED	
DEEEFNRTTU	UNFETTERED	
DEEEFORRST	DEFORESTER, REFORESTED	
DEEEGGGLOY	GOGGLE-EYED	
DEEEGHHINT	HEIGHTENED	
DEEEGHLNNT	LENGTHENED	
DEEEGHOOWZ	GOOD WHEEZE	
DEEEGIIMRV	DEMIVIERGE	
DEEEGIKNNW	WEEKENDING	
DEEEGILMTY	GIMLET-EYED	
DEEEGIMNRT	REGIMENTED	
DEEEGINRSS	GREEDINESS	
DEEEGIRRST	REGISTERED	
DEEEGNRSTT	DETERGENTS	
DEEEHIPRSS	HESPERIDES	

DEEEHLLSSY	HEEDLESSLY	
DEEEHLNOPT	TELEPHONED	
DEEEHNORTY	HETERODYNE	
DEEEHNRRTU	THEREUNDER	
DEEEIILRSV	DELIVERIES	
DEEEIKLLRW	WEEDKILLER	
DEEEILLMOS	DEMOISELLE	
DEEEILLMPS	MILLEPEDES	
DEEEILMRSS	REMEDILESS	
DEEEILNRSS	SLENDERISE	
DEEEILNRSZ	SLENDERIZE	
DEEEILNRUV	UNRELIEVED	
DEEEILRRVY	REDELIVERY	
DEEEILRSVW	SILVERWEED	
DEEEIMMRSS	MESMERISED	
DEEEIMMRSZ	MESMERIZED	
DEEEIMNOST	DEMONETISE	
DEEEIMNOTZ	DEMONETIZE	
DEEEIMNRRT	DETERMINER	
DEEEIMNRST	DENSIMETER	
DEEEIMORTU	EUDIOMETER	
DEEEIMRSSY	MERSEYSIDE	
DEEEINNPTV	PENDENTIVE	
DEEEINNRTV	INTERVENED	
DEEEINPRST	PREDESTINE	
DEEEINPSSS	SPEEDINESS	
DEEEINPSTX	EXPEDIENTS	
DEEEINRRST	TENDERISER	
DEEEINRRTZ	TENDERIZER	
DEEEINRSTT	INTERESTED	
DEEEIPRSSV	DEPRESSIVE	
DEEEIPRSTX	PREEXISTED	
DEEEIRSSTT	SIDE STREET	
DEEEKLNORW	NEEDLEWORK	
DEEEKOOPRR	DOORKEEPER	
DEEELLMORR	REMODELLER	
DEEELLNORW	NE'ER-DO-WELL	
DEEELLNSSY	NEEDLESSLY	
DEEELLOWWY	YELLOWWEED	
DEEELNRTTU	UNLETTERED	
DEEELOPRSV	DEVELOPERS	
DEEELRRSVY	RESERVEDLY	
DEEEMNNOTT	DENOTEMENT	
DEEEMNNOTU	DENOUEMENT	
DEEEMNNOYZ	ENDOENZYME	
DEEEMNOTTV	DEVOTEMENT	
DEEEMNRSSU	DEMURENESS	
DEEEMNSSTV	VESTMENTED	
DEEENNRSST	TENDERNESS	
DEEENPRRST	PRETENDERS	
DEEENPRSUV	SUPERVENED	
DEEENRRSTT	DETERRENTS	
DEEENRRSUV	UNRESERVED	

DEEEOPPRRY	EYEDROPPER	DEEGIINNRT	INGREDIENT	DEEIILNSTT	DISENTITLE
DEEEORSSTV	STEVEDORES	DEEGIINPTX	EXPEDITING	DEEIILOPPT	EPILEPTOID
DEEEPPPRRS	RED PEPPERS	DEEGIIRSSV	DIGRESSIVE	DEEIILORST	SIDEROLITE
DEEEPRRSSU	SUPERSEDER	DEEGIISSTV	DIGESTIVES	DEEIILPRRV	PILE DRIVER
DEEERSSUVX	DEUX-SEVRES	DEEGILMNOR	REMODELING	DEEIILRSST	STERILISED
DEEFFHLRSU	RESHUFFLED	DEEGILNNOW	GWENDOLINE	DEEIILRSTZ	STERILIZED
DEEFGHINRT	FRIGHTENED	DEEGILNOPV	DEVELOPING	DEEIILRSVY	DERISIVELY
DEEFGINPRY	DEEP FRYING	DEEGILNRSY	RESIGNEDLY	DEEIIMMNPT	IMPEDIMENT
DEEFGINRTY	GENTRIFYED	DEEGILOOSU	IDEOLOGUES	DEEIIMNRST	MINISTERED
DEEFGINSST	GIFTEDNESS	DEEGILOPRS	RIDGEPOLES	DEEIIMOPST	EPITOMISED
DEEFGIPRRU	PREFIGURED	DEEGINNPRT	PRETENDING	DEEIIMOPTZ	EPITOMIZED
DEEFIIINNT	INDEFINITE	DEEGINNRRS	RENDERINGS	DEEIINNRTT	TRIDENTINE
DEEFIIINRT	IDENTIFIER	DEEGINOOPT	PIGEON-TOED	DEEIINNSTW	DISENTWINE
DEEFIIINTV	DEFINITIVE	DEEGINORSS	DEGRESSION	DEEIINOPTT	PETITIONED
DEEFIIIRVV	REVIVIFIED	DEEGINOTTU	TONGUE-TIED	DEEIINOPTX	EXPEDITION
DEEFIILMNS	MINEFIELDS	DEEGINPRSS	DEPRESSING	DEEIINPTTU	INEPTITUDE
DEEFIILMSU	EMULSIFIED	DEEGINPRSS	REDRESSING	DEEIINQTUU	INQUIETUDE
DEEFIILNRR	FRIENDLIER	DEEGKNOTTT	GET KNOTTED!	DEEIINSSST	SENSITISED
DEEFIILNRS	FRIENDLIES,	DEEGKOPRSW	POWDER KEGS	DEEIINSSTW	WEST INDIES
INFIELDERS		DEEGLLNORU	GOLDEN RULE	DEEIINSSTZ	SENSITIZED
DEEFIILNTY	DEFINITELY	DEEGNNOOSU	ENDOGENOUS	DEEIIOPRTT	PERIDOTITE
DEEFIILRST	FERTILISED	DEEGNNOPRU	GREEN POUND	DEEIIPRSSV	DISPERSIVE
DEEFIILRTZ	FERTILIZED	DEEGOPRRSS	PROGRESSED	DEEIIPRSSW	SIDESWIPER
DEEFIINRVW	VIEWFINDER	DEEHHIILMS	HILDESHEIM	DEEIIPRSSW	SIDESWIPES
DEEFIIPRTT	PRETTIFIED	DEEHHISSTW	THE SWEDISH	DEEIISSSSU	SIDE ISSUES
DEEFILLLSW	SELF-WILLED	DEEHIINPRS	HESPERIDIN	DEEIJNORRS	REJOINDERS
DEEFILLRSU	FLEUR-DE-LIS	DEEHIIRSTT	HEREDITIST	DEEIJNOSTT	JETTISONED
DEEFILMOSU	FIELDMOUSE	DEEHILLRSV	SHRIVELLED	DEEIKNNRSU	ISKENDERUN
DEEFILNOST	FIELDSTONE	DEEHILMORS	DEMOLISHER	DEEIKNNSSS	KINDNESSES
DEEFILNRSS	FRIENDLESS	DEEHILOOTT	THEODOLITE	DEEIKORSST	SIDESTROKE
DEEFILNRYZ	FRENZIEDLY	DEEHIMORST	METHODISER	DEEILLMPSS	MISSPELLED
DEEFILORTU	OUTFIELDER	DEEHIMORTZ	METHODIZER	DEEILLORRS	DROLLERIES
DEEFILSSTT	FIELD-TESTS	DEEHINOOPV	VIDEOPHONE	DEEILLRRSV	DRIVELLERS
DEEFINNPRS	PEN FRIENDS	DEEHINORST	THRENODIES	DEEILLRSSU	SLIDE RULES
DEEFIORRRT	FERRITE-ROD	DEEHINRSSW	SWINEHERDS	DEEILLSUVY	DELUSIVELY
DEEFKNORSS	FORKEDNESS	DEEHIOPPRS	PROPHESIED	DEEILMNOSS	SOLEMNISED
DEEFLLRSUY	FLEUR-DE-LYS	DEEHIORSTV	SHROVETIDE	DEEILMNOSU	EMULSIONED
DEEFLLSSTY	SELF-STYLED	DEEHIOSSTU	TIED HOUSES	DEEILMNOSZ	SOLEMNIZED
DEEFLMNNOT	ENFOLDMENT	DEEHKNOOSS	HOOKEDNESS	DEEILNNORT	TENDERLOIN
DEEFLOORVW	OVERFLOWED	DEEHLLMOPR	PHELLODERM	DEEILNNQTU	DELINQUENT
DEEFNOORTT	TENDERFOOT	DEEHNNORSS	HORNEDNESS	DEEILNPRST	SPLINTERED
DEEFOORSTU	SUREFOOTED	DEEHNOORTT	HETERODONT	DEEILNRSSW	WILDERNESS
DEEFORRSST	DEFROSTERS	DEEHNNRRSTU	THUNDERERS	DEEILNRSTU	INTERLUDES
DEEGGNRSSU	RUGGEDNESS	DEEHNRSSSW	SHREWDNESS	DEEILPRSUV	PULVERISED
DEEGGRSTUY	GREEDY-GUTS	DEEHOORTXY	HETERODOXY	DEEILPRUVZ	PULVERIZED
DEEGHIJNNZ	JINGDEZHEN	DEEHSSSTTU	DUSTSHEETS	DEEIMMNOSU	EUDEMONISM
DEEGHINOPS	DIPHOSGENE	DEEIIINPPR	PIPERIDINE	DEEIMNNNTT	INTENDMENT
DEEGHINRRR	RED HERRING	DEEIIINSTT	IDENTITIES	DEEIMNNRRU	UNDERMINER
DEEGHINSTU	GESUNDHEIT	DEEIILLMPR	IMPERILLED	DEEIMNOOTV	MONTEVIDEO
DEEGHIOTUW	OUTWEIGHED	DEEIILLMPS	MILLIPEDES	DEEIMNOPRT	REDEMPTION
DEEGIILNRV	DELIVERING	DEEIILLNOS	LINSEED OIL	DEEIMNOPTT	IDEMPOTENT
DEEGIILNSU	GUIDELINES	DEEIILLOPT	LEPIDOLITE	DEEIMNORRS	MODERNISER
DEEGIILOOS	IDEOLOGIES	DEEIILMPST	SPEED LIMIT	DEEIMNORRZ	MODERNIZER
DEEGIILPRV	PRIVILEGED	DEEIILNNVY	VINYLIDENE	DEEIMNORSS	SERMONISED

DEEIMNORSZ	SERMONIZED	DEELORTTUV	TURTLEDOVE	DEFIIIILNTY	INFIDELITY
DEEIMNRRTU	ERMINTRUDE	DEELPRSTTU	SPLUTTERED	DEFIIIILORS	SOLIDIFIER
DEEIMNRSTT	DETRIMENTS	DEEMMNNORSS	MODERNNESS	DEFIIINNOT	DEFINITION
DEEIMNRSTW	MIDWESTERN,	DEEMMNNORTW	WONDERMENT	DEFIIINNTU	INFINITUDE
STEM-WINDER		DEEMMNNOSTW	ENDOWMENTS	DEFIILLNRY	FRIENDLILY
DEEIMNRSTY	DENSIMETRY	DEEMNOORRY	MONEY ORDER	DEFIILLRRS	FIRE DRILLS
DEEIMNSTTV	DIVESTMENT	DEEMNOPRTT	DEPORTMENT	DEFIILOSSS	FOSSILISED
DEEIMOPRST	TEMPORISED	DEEMNORSTU	TREMENDOUS	DEFIILOSSZ	FOSSILIZED
DEEIMOPRTZ	TEMPORIZED	DEEMNRRTUY	ERMYNTRUDE	DEFIILPRST	FIELD TRIPS
DEEIMORTUY	EUDIOMETRY	DEENNOOSSW	WOODENNESS	DEFIILSTTU	STULTIFIED
DEEINNNOSU	INNUENDOES	DEENNOPRST	RESPONDENT	DEFIINOPTX	FIXED-POINT
DEEINNRSST	TRENDINESS	DEENNORSTU	UNDERTONES	DEFIIOPRSU	PERFIDIOUS
DEEINNRSSU	INUREDNESS	DEENNORSVW	NEWSVENDOR	DEFILLORWW	WILDFOWLER
DEEINNRSTU	INDENTURES	DEENOQRTUU	UNDERQUOTE	DEFILMNORY	INFORMEDLY
DEEINNSSTU	UNITEDNESS	DEENORRTUV	OVERTURNED	DEFILNNRUY	UNFRIENDLY
DEEINOPRSS	DEPRESSION	DEENORRTUW	UNDERWROTE	DEFILNORWW	WINDFLOWER
DEEINOPRST	INTERPOSED	DEENORSSSU	ROUSEDNESS	DEFILNOSSW	SNOWFIELDS
DEEINOQSTU	QUESTIONED	DEENORSUVZ	RENDEZVOUS	DEFILPRSUU	SUPERFLUID
DEEINORSST	DESERTIONS	DEENOSSTUV	DEVOUTNESS	DEFIMNNORU	UNINFORMED
DEEINPRRST	RINDERPEST	DEENPRSSSU	SUSPENDERS	DEFINNRRSUW	WIND-SURFER
DEEINPRSSS	DISPENSERS	DEENRRRSSU	SURRENDERS	DEFLNOORRU	UNDERFLOOR
DEEINPRSST	PRESIDENTS	DEENRSSSTU	UNSTRESSED	DEFNOOPRRU	UNDERPROOF
DEEINQRTUU	UNREQUITED	DEEOOPPRTV	OVERTOPPED	DEGGHIILNT	DELIGHTING
DEEINRRTUW	UNDERWRITE	DEEOOPRRSU	UREDOSPORE	DEGGHIIPRS	SHIP-RIGGED
DEEINRSSSS	DRESSINESS	DEEOOPRRSU	SUPERORDER	DEGGIILRSU	GIRL GUIDES
DEEINRSSST	DISSENTERS	DEEORRSSTY	DESTROYERS	DEGGIINRSS	DIGRESSING
DEEINSTTTV	VENDETTIST	DEEPPRRSUU	SUPERDUPER	DEGGIJNPRU	PREJUDGING
DEEIOPPRRT	PROPERTIED	DEEPPRSSUU	SUPPRESSED	DEGGIJRRUY	JURY-RIGGED
DEEIOPPRSS	PREDISPOSE	DEFFGINOOR	FINGER FOOD	DEGGINNORU	UNDERGOING
DEEIOPRSUX	SUPEROXIDE	DEFFINNOST	SOFT-FINNED	DEGGINORUV	GIVE GROUND
DEEIOPRSVW	POWER DIVES	DEFFOPPRUW	POWDER PUFF	DEGHIILSST	SIDELIGHTS
DEEIOPRTTU	PIROUETTED	DEFGGILLNS	FLEDGLINGS	DEGHIMNRSU	HUMDINGERS
DEEIORRRST	TERRORISED	DEFGGILLRU	FULL-RIGGED	DEGHINNORT	DETHRONING
DEEIORRRTZ	TERRORIZED	DEFGHILLTU	DELIGHTFUL	DEGHINNRTU	THUNDERING
DEEIPRRTUY	EURYPTERID	DEFGHOOOSU	HOUSE OF	DEGHINRSST	NIGHTDRESS
DEEIPRSSUV	SUPERVISED	GOD		DEGHIORRRU	ROUGHRIDER
DEEKLLNORS	SNORKELLED	DEFGIIILNRR	GIRLFRIEND	DEGHIOSTTU	DOUGHTIEST
DEEKLMRTTU	KETTLEDRUM	DEFGIIILNYY	EDIFYINGLY	DEGHLNOORU	GOLDEN HOUR
DEEKLOOORV	OVERLOOKED	DEFGIIINNUY	UNEDIFYING	DEGHLORSSU	GOLD RUSHES
DEEKLRSSUU	LESSER KUDU	DEFGIIRRSU	DISFIGURER	DEGHMOORST	GODMOTHERS
DEEKOORRVW	OVERWORKED	DEFGINNORU	FOUNDERING	DEGHNORSUY	GREYHOUNDS
DEELLMOORS	ROLE MODELS	DEFGINORST	DEFROSTING	DEGIIILMNT	DELIMITING
DEELLNRTUW	WELL-TURNED	DEFGNOORRU	FOREGROUND	DEGIIILNNS	SIDELINING
DEELMMNOPU	NOM DE	DEFHIIIMRU	HUMIDIFIER	DEGIIIRSST	DIGITISERS
PLUME		DEFHIIILNSY	FIENDISHLY	DEGIIIRSTZ	DIGITIZERS
DEELMNOPTY	DEPLOYMENT	DEFHIINNSU	UNFINISHED	DEGIIKLNNR	REKINDLING
DEELMNOPUY	UNEMPLOYED	DEFHIINPRS	FRIENDSHIP	DEGIILLMRX	MIXED GRILL
DEELMPRSUY	PRESUMEDLY	DEFHILOPST	SHOPLIFTED	DEGIILLNPS	DISPELLING
DEELNNOOSU	UNLOOSENED	DEFHILORSU	FLOURISHED	DEGIILLNRV	DRIVELLING
DEELNNORWY	RENOWNEDLY	DEFHLNOSUW	FLESH WOUND	DEGIILLNTY	DILIGENTLY
DEELNOOSSTU	LODESTONES	DEFHLOOOSW	WHOLEFOODS	DEGIILLNYY	YIELDINGLY
DEELNORSUV	UNRESOLVED	DEFHNOOPRU	UNHOPED-FOR	DEGIILMNPY	IMPEDINGLY
DEELNOSTUU	EDENTULOUS	DEFHORRRTU	RUTHERFORD	DEGIILNNUY	UNYIELDING
DEELNPRRSU	PLUNDERERS	DEFIIIILMPS	SIMPLIFIED	DEGIILNOPS	DESPOILING
DEELOPRRTY	REPORTEDLY				

DEGIIILNORS	SOLDIERING	
DEGIILOOST	IDEOLOGIST	
DEGIINNOSU	INDIGENOUS	
DEGIINNOSV	NOSEDIVING	
DEGIINNPSS	DISPENSING	
DEGIINNSST	DISSENTING	
DEGIINOPST	DEPOSITING	
DEGIINORRV	OVERRIDING	
DEGIINORSS	DIGRESSION	
DEGIINOSST	DIGESTIONS	
DEGIINPRSS	DISPERSING	
DEGIINPRST	SPRING TIDE	
DEGIINPTUZ	DEPUTIZING	
DEGIIQSSTU	SQUIDGIEST	
DEGILLOOTY	DELTIOLOGY	
DEGILMNORS	SMOLDERING	
DEGILMNORU	MOULDERING,	
REMOULDING		
DEGILMNRSU	MUDSLINGER	
DEGILNNPRU	PLUNDERING	
DEGILNNRSU	UNDERLINGS	
DEGILNNRUY	ENDURINGLY,	
UNDERLYING		
DEGILNOORS	GONDOLIERS	
DEGILNOOSS	GOODLINESS	
DEGILNOSTU	LONGITUDES	
DEGILNRSTU	DISGRUNTLE	
DEGILOOPST	PEDOLOGIST	
DEGIMNSSSU	SMUDGINESS	
DEGINNOPRS	RESPONDING	
DEGINNOPRT	PORTENDING	
DEGINNOPUX	EXPOUNDING	
DEGINNORST	GRINDSTONE,	
STRINGENDO		
DEGINNORSU	RESOUNDING	
DEGINNPSSU	SUSPENDING	
DEGINNRSSU	UNDRESSING	
DEGINOOPRT	TORPEDOING	
DEGINOORSV	OVERDOSING	
DEGINOPPST	SIGNPOSTED	
DEGINORSTY	DESTROYING	
DEGINOSSST	STODGINESS	
DEGKLOOOOR	GOOD LOOKER	
DEGLMNOOOY	DEMONOLOGY	
DEGLMOOORT	MOTOR LODGE	
DEGLNNRSUU	UNDERSLUNG	
DEGLNOOOTY	DEONTOLOGY	
DEGLNOORSU	LOSE GROUND	
DEGLNORRUU	GROUND RULE	
DEGLNORSSU	GROUNDLESS	
DEGLOORTTY	TROGLODYTE	
DEGMNNORSU	GROUNDSMEN	
DEGNNORRTU	GROUND RENT	
DEGNNORRUW	UNDERGROWN	
DEGNOORRSW	WRONGDOERS	

DEGORRSSTU	DRUGSTORES	
DEHHIKMOSS	SHEIKHDOMS	
DEHHILOPRS	HOLDERSHIP	
DEHHILORTW	WITHHOLDER	
DEHHIMOORR	HEMORRHOID	
DEHHLOOSSU	HOUSEHOLDS	
DEHHLORSST	THRESHOLDS	
DEHHMOOORT	MOTHERHOOD	
DEHHOOOOPP	POOH-POOHED	
DEHIIINOTT	DITHIONITE	
DEHIIINRST	DISINHERIT	
DEHIIKLLOO	LIKELIHOOD	
DEHIIKMRSS	SKIRMISHED	
DEHIILLOOV	LIVELIHOOD	
DEHIILLSVY	DEVILISHLY	
DEHIILMNPU	DELPHINIUM	
DEHIILNPSY	SYLPHIDINE	
DEHIIMMNPS	MIDSHIPMEN	
DEHIIMNOPR	PREHOMINID	
DEHIIMNPRU	NEPHRIDIUM	
DEHIIOPRST	EDITORSHIP	
DEHIIRSTVW	WHIST DRIVE	
DEHIKNOORW	HOODWINKER	
DEHIKNRSZZ	DZERZHINSK	
DEHILNNOOP	INDOPHENOL	
DEHILOOPSS	SHOPSOILED	
DEHILORSTV	SHORT-LIVED	
DEHILOSSTW	DISH TOWELS	
DEHIMMNORR	HORN-RIMMED	
DEHIMNORST	HINDERMOST	
DEHIMNOSSS	MODISHNESS	
DEHIMOOPPR	HIPPODROME	
DEHIMOSSTT	METHODISTS	
DEHINNPSUU	UNPUNISHED	
DEHINOPSTY	HYPNOTISED	
DEHINOPTYZ	HYPNOTIZED	
DEHINORRSS	HORRIDNESS	
DEHINOSSTY	DISHONESTY	
DEHINRRSTU	UNDERSHIRT	
DEHIOOPRST	PRIESTHOOD	
DEHIOORSST	SISTERHOOD	
DEHIOPPRSW	WORSHIPPED	
DEHKLOOSST	STOKEHOLDS	
DEHLLOOSSU	DOLL'S HOUSE	
DEHLNOOPRY	POLYHEDRON	
DEHLORRSYY	HYDROLYSER	
DEHMMOORSU		
MUSHROOMED		
DEHMNOOPRY	ENDOMORPHY	
DEHNNOSSUW	NEWSHOUNDS	
DEHNOORRSU	HORRENDOUS	
DEHNOORSTU	UNDERSHOOT	
DEHNOORSUU	ROUNDHOUSE	
DEHNORSTUU	THUNDEROUS	

DEHOOPRSUU	HOUSE-PROUD	
DEHOOSSSSU	DOSSHOUSES	
DEIIIINSTV	DIVINITIES	
DEIIIKNSTT	IDENTIKITS	
DEIIILMSTU	SIMILITUDE	
DEIIILORSU	LIQUIDISER	
DEIIILORUZ	LIQUIDIZER	
DEIIILSVVY	DIVISIVELY	
DEIIIMNPRY	PYRIMIDINE	
DEIIIMNTUV	DIMINUTIVE	
DEIIIMSSSV	DISMISSIVE	
DEIIJMNORS	MISJOINDER	
DEIIKLNNSS	KINDLINESS	
DEIIKNRSSV	SKIN DIVERS	
DEIILLMPTU	MULTIPLIED	
DEIILLNOTU	TOLLUIDINE	
DEIILLNUWY	UNWIELDILY	
DEIILLRSST	DISTILLERS	
DEIILLRSTY	DISTILLERY	
DEIILMNOOT	DEMOLITION	
DEIILNPRTY	INTREPIDLY	
DEIILNPSST	SPINDLIEST	
DEIILORRSY	DERISORILY	
DEIILPRSTY	SPIRITEDLY	
DEIIMNNOSS	DIMENSIONS	
DEIIMNOPRS	IMPRISONED	
DEIIMNPRST	MISPRINTED	
DEIIMOPRSV	IMPROVISED	
DEIIMORTXY	OXIDIMETRY	
DEIIMPRSSU	PRESIDIUMS	
DEIINNOPPT	PINPOINTED	
DEIINNORST	RENDITIONS	
DEIINNOSSS	DISSENSION	
DEIINNOSST	DISTENSION	
DEIINNPRSU	UNINSPIRED	
DEIINNSSTU	UNTIDINESS	
DEIINOOPST	DEPOSITION,	
POSITIONED		
DEIINOPRSS	DISPERSION	
DEIINOPRXY	PYRIDOXINE	
DEIINORSSV	DIVERSIONS	
DEIINPPRST	PINSTRIPED	
DEIINRSSTU	INDUSTRIES	
DEIINSTTTU	INSTITUTED	
DEIIORSTTV	DISTORTIVE	
DEIIPRSTUV	DISRUPTIVE	
DEIJNNNOOR	NONJOINDER	
DEIKMPPRSU	MUDSKIPPER	
DEIKNNNORR	NONDRINKER	
DEIKNNNSSU	UNKINDNESS	
DEIKNRRSTU	UNDERSKIRT	
DEILLMNSSY	MINDLESSLY	
DEILLNNOTY	INDOLENTLY	
DEILLNORSS	LORDLINESS	

DEILLORSTW	WORLDLIEST	DEMNOPSSUY	PSEUDONYMS
DEILMMOSTY	IMMODESTLY	DEMNORSTUU	SURMOUNTED
DEILMNOSSU	MOULDINESS	DEMNPRRTUU	UNDERTRUMP
DEILMNPTUY	IMPUDENTLY	DEMOOOPRRW	POWDER
DEILMRSSUY	SURMISEDLY		ROOM
DEILMSTTUU	MULTITUDES	DENNORSSUW	SUNDOWNERS
DEILNNNTUW	WIND TUNNEL	DENOOPPRRU	PROPOUNDER
DEILNOOTUV	DEVOLUTION	DENOPRRTTU	PROTRUDENT
DEILNRSTTY	STRIDENTLY	DENOPSSTUU	STUPENDOUS
DEILOORRTV	LORD IT OVER	DEOORRSSUU	UREDOSORUS
DEILOSTTWW	SLOW-WITTED	DEPRSSSSTU	PRESS-STUDS
DEIMMNORSS	MODERNISMS	DFFFOOSSTU	FOODSTUFFS
DEIMNNOSTW	DISOWNMENT	DFGGIIINNY	DIGNIFYING
DEIMNOOSSS	ENDOSMOSIS	DFGHILLOOT	FLOODLIGHT
DEIMNOPRTU	IMPORTUNED	DFGIIIMORT	DIGITIFORM
DEIMNOPRUV	UNIMPROVED	DFGIINOSUU	NIDIFUGOUS
DEIMNORSST	MODERNISTS	DFGILLNNOY	FONDLINGLY
DEIMOPRSSU	DISPERMOUS	DFGILNNOSU	FOUNDLINGS
DEIMRSSTTU	MISTRUSTED	DFHILOORSY	HYDROFOILS
DEINOOPRSS	DROOPINESS	DFHLNOOSUW	WOLFHOUNDS
DEINOOPTTU	OUTPOINTED	DFHLNSSSSU	SLUSH FUNDS
DEINOORSWW	ROSE WINDOW	DFHLOOOOPT	PHOTOFLOOD
DEINOOSSST	ENDOSTOSIS	DFHLOOORTU	HOLD OUT FOR
DEINOOSSSU	ODIOUSNESS	DFIKLOPPSY	FLOPPY DISK
DEINOOSTTX	EXODONTIST	DFINOPRTUY	PROFUNDITY
DEINOPSSSU	SUSPENSOID	DFINORSSTW	SNOWDRIFTS
DEINORSSSS	DROSSINESS	DFLNOOPRUY	PROFOUNDLY
DEINORSSSW	DROWSINESS	DFNOOOPRSU	SOUNDPROOF
DEINPSSSTU	STUPIDNESS	DFNOOORRST	FRONT DOORS
DEINRSSSTU	STURDINESS	DFNRSSTTUU	TRUST FUNDS
DEIOOPRSST	DEPOSITORS	DFOOOORSTU	OUT OF
DEIOOPRSTY	DEPOSITORY		DOORS
DEIOPRRSTW	SPIDERWORT	DGGGIINORS	DISGORGING
DEIOPSSSSS	DISPOSSESS	DGGGILNRUY	GRUDGINGLY
DEIRRSSTTU	DISTRUSTER	DGGGINNRUU	UNGRUDGING
DEKKNOORWY	DONKEYWORK	DGGIIIINTZ	DIGITIZING
DEKLORSSVV	SVERDLOVSK	DGGIIINSSU	DISGUISING
DEKNOOPRUV	UNPROVOKED	DGGIIJMNSU	MISJUDGING
DEKNOORRWW		DGGIILMNNO	GOLD-MINING
	WONDERWORK	DGGIINSSTU	DISGUSTING
DEKOOORRWW		DGGILNNORU	GROUNDLING
	WOODWORKER	DGGINNOORW	WRONGDOING
DELLOOOWWY	YELLOWWOOD	DGHHIKNOOT	KNIGHTHOOD
DELLORSSWY	WORDLESSLY	DGHHINOPST	DIPHTHONGS
DELLOSSUUY	SEDULOUSLY	DGHIILLNNO	HILLINGDON
DELNNOPSSU	NONPLUSSED	DGHILMOSST	GOLDSMITHS
DELNOOPRTU	PLEURODONT	DGHINNNOTU	HUNTINGDON
DELNOPRSUU	PLUNDEROUS	DGHLNOORST	STRONGHOLD
DELOOPRRWW	WORLD	DGIIIKNNSV	SKIN DIVING
	POWER	DGIIILLNST	DISTILLING
DELOPPSSUY	SUPPOSEDLY	DGIIIMNSSS	DISMISSING
DELORRTTUY	TORTUREDLY	DGIIINNSTU	DISUNITING
DEMMOORSUW		DGIIINPTUY	PINGUIDITY
	SUMMERWOOD	DGIIILNOOST	INDOLOGIST
DEMNOPPRTU	UNPROMPTED	DGIIILNOSSV	DISSOLVING
DGIIMNNOOR	DINING ROOM
DGIIMNNOPU	IMPOUNDING
DGIINNPRSY	SPIN-DRYING
DGIINOPRST	DISPORTING
DGIINOPRSV	DISPROVING
DGIINORSTT	DISTORTING
DGIINPRSTU	DISRUPTING
DGIIOOPRSU	PRODIGIOUS
DGILNNOUWY	WOUNDINGLY
DGINOOPRSW	SPRINGWOOD
DGINOPRRTU	PROTRUDING
DGKNOORRUW	
	GROUNDWORK
DGLNOOOOTY	ODONTOLOGY
DGNNORSTUU	GROUNDNUTS
DHIILNRSWW	WHIRLWINDS
DHIIMMOPRS	DIMORPHISM
DHILLOPSUY	DIPHYLLOUS
DHILMMOOSU	HOODLUMISM
DHILORSSYY	HYDROLYSIS
DHIMOOPRSU	DIMORPHOUS
DHINOOOPRT	ORNITHOPOD
DHINOOPSWW	
	WINDOW-SHOP
DHINOPRSSU	WHIP-ROUNDS
DHIOOPPRRY	PORPHYROID
DHLMOOSTUU	LOUDMOUTHS
DHNNOSTUUW	
	SHUNT-WOUND
DHNOOORTUX	UNORTHODOX
DHNOOSSTUW	SOUTH
	DOWNS
DIIIINPSTY	INSIPIDITY
DIIILSTTUY	DISUTILITY
DIIIMMORSU	OSMIRIDIUM
DIIIMNNOTU	DIMINUTION
DIILLNOSWW	WINDOWSILL
DIIMMOPRRU	PRIMORDIUM
DIINOORSTT	DISTORTION
DIINOPRSTU	DISRUPTION
DILLLOSSTY	LLOYD'S LIST
DILLOOPPYY	POLYPLOIDY
DILORSSTUU	STRIDULOUS
DILOSSTUUY	STUDIOUSLY
DIMMNOOOPU	MONOPODIUM
DIMNORSSTW	WINDSTORMS
DIMOPRSSUY	DYSPROSIUM
DINOPRRSTU	ROUND TRIPS
DIOOPQQRUU	QUID PRO QUO
DLLOOORSUY	DOLOROUSLY
DLOOOPPSUY	POLYPODOUS
DMORSSSTTU	DUST STORMS
DNNORRSTUU	TURNROUNDS
DNOOPSSTUW	DOWNSPOUTS
DNOOSSTTUY	NOT SO DUSTY

EEEEEHMTTY	MEET THE EYE	EEEGINOPRY	EPEIROGENY
EEEEEFFNSST	EFFETENESS	EEEGINORSV	OVERSEEING
EEEEFGINRR	REFEREEING	EEEGINORTY	EROGENEITY
EEEEFKLRSS	SELF-SEEKER	EEEGIRRRST	REGISTERER
EEEEFLMSST	SELF-ESTEEM	EEEGIRRSSV	REGRESSIVE
EEEEGHHLLTT	GET THE HEEL	EEEGLNNSST	GENTLENESS
EEEEGIPSSX	EPEXEGESIS	EEEGMNRSSS	MESSENGERS
EEEEGNRRSV	EVERGREENS	EEEGNNORST	GREENSTONE
EEEEHIMRSU	EUHEMERISE	EEEHHIMPRS	HEMISPHERE
EEEEHIMRUZ	EUHEMERIZE	EEEHHLOSUW	WHEELHOUSE
EEEEHPSSSY	SHEEP'S EYES	EEEHHOTTTT	TO THE TEETH
EEEEHRRVWY	EVERYWHERE	EEEHIKLLMT	HELMET-LIKE
EEEEIKMPRT	TIMEKEEPER	EEEHILLNRS	HELLENISER
EEEEKMRRSY	KERSEYMERE	EEEHILLNRZ	HELLENIZER
EEEELLSSSV	SLEEVELESS	EEEHILMORT	HELIOMETER
EEEENNRRVV	NEVER-NEVER	EEEHILNPRS	PREHENSILE
EEEENNRSSS	SERENENESS	EEEHILPSSS	LESSEESHIP
EEEENNTWYY	TEENY WEENY	EEEHIMMRSU	EUHEMERISM
EEEENOPRSY	EYE-OPENERS	EEEHIMPRSU	EUPHEMISER
EEEENRSSSV	SEVERENESS	EEEHIMPRUZ	EUPHEMIZER
EEEENRSSTW	SWEETENERS	EEEHIMRSTU	EUHEMERIST
EEEERRRTTV	TERRE-VERTE	EEEHIMSSTT	TIME SHEETS
EEEFGIINRR	FIRE ENGINE	EEEHINNNTT	NINETEENTH
EEEFGILNRS	GREENFLIES	EEEHINNTTV	IN THE EVENT
EEEFGIMRSU	REFUGEEISM	EEEHINPSST	EPENTHESIS
EEEFGINORS	FORESEEING	EEEHINSSWZ	WHEEZINESS
EEEFGLNRUV	REVENGEFUL	EEEHINSTTV	SEVENTIETH
EEEFHOORRT	HERETOFORE	EEEHJNOSST	THE JONESES
EEEFHORRSW	WHEREFORES	EEEHKLOPTT	KEEL THE POT
EEEFHORRSU	FREE HOUSES	EEEHKOPPRS	SHOPKEEPER
EEEFIINRRS	REFINERIES	EEEHLMNTVY	VEHEMENTLY
EEEFILRRSV	FILE SERVER	EEEHLMSSTV	THEMSELVES
EEEFILRSVX	REFLEXIVES	EEEHLNOPRT	TELEPHONER
EEEFIMNNRT	REFINEMENT	EEEHLNOPST	TELEPHONES
EEEFINRRRT	INTERFERER	EEEHMOPRSS	MESOSPHERE
EEEFKNOPRS	FREE-SPOKEN	EEEHMORSST	THREESOMES
EEEFLLORRT	FORETELLER	EEEHNORSSS	HORSE SENSE
EEEFMNPRRT	PREFERMENT	EEEHNORSVW	WHENSOEVER
EEEFNNORSU	UNFORESEEN	EEEHNPRSTT	THE PRESENT
EEEFNQRRTU	FREQUENTER	EEEHNSSSTW	NEWSSHEETS
EEEGHHINRT	HEIGHTENER	EEEHOPPRRT	TREEHOPPER
EEEGHHINTT	EIGHTEENTH	EEEHORRTVY	EVERY OTHER
EEEGHIMNOT	EIGHTEENMO	EEEHRSSTTU	USHERETTES
EEEGHKLNNT	KNEE-LENGTH	EEEIIINRST	ETERNITIES
EEEGHLNNRT	LENGTHENER	EEEIIPRTTV	REPETITIVE
EEEGHNNOST	STONEHENGE	EEEIIRSSTV	SEVERITIES
EEEGHNORSU	GREENHOUSE	EEEIJLMRSS	IJSSELMEER
EEEGHNORTW	GET NOWHERE	EEEIKLMSWY	SEMIWEEKLY
EEEGIINPSS	EPIGENESIS	EEEIKLNSSS	LIKENESSES
EEEGIJNNST	JET ENGINES	EEEIKNNPRS	INNKEEPERS
EEEGIMNORT	GEOMETRISE	EEEILMMORT	MILEOMETER
EEEGIMORTZ	GEOMETRIZE	EEEILMNRST	RESILEMENT
EEEGINNPST	STEEPENING	EEEILMNRTV	REVILEMENT
EEEGINNSTW	SWEETENING	EEEILMNSSS	SEEMLINESS

EEEILMNSTY	MESITYLENE
EEEILNPRRT	TERREPLEIN
EEEILNPSSS	SLEEPINESS
EEEILNSSST	STEELINESS
EEEILORRTU	EURE-ET-LOIR
EEEILPSTVX	EXPLETIVES
EEEILRRTTW	TELEWRITER
EEEILRSSSW	WIRELESSES
EEEILRSSTW	WESTERLIES
EEEIMMRRSS	MESMERISER
EEEIMMRRSZ	MESMERIZER
EEEIMNNPRT	PRE-EMINENT
EEEIMNORST	REMONETISE
EEEIMNORTZ	REMONETIZE
EEEIMNPRTX	EXPERIMENT
EEEIMNRRTT	RETIREMENT
EEEIMNRSTT	TENSIMETER
EEEIMORSTT	METEORITES
EEEIMPPRTV	PRE-EMPTIVE
EEEIMPPRTS	PERIMETERS
EEEIMRRSTV	TIMESERVER
EEEINNPRSS	PERSIENNES
EEEINNPRST	SERPENTINE
EEEINNPRTV	PREVENIENT
EEEINNRRTV	INTERVENER
EEEINNRSST	ENTIRENESS
EEEINPRRST	ENTERPRISE
EEEINPRSTV	VESPERTINE
EEEINPRTVV	PREVENTIVE
EEEINQTTTU	NETIQUETTE
EEEINRRRTV	IRREVERENT
EEEINRSSTW	WESTERNISE
EEEINRSTWZ	WESTERNIZE
EEEINSSTWY	EYEWITNESS
EEEIOPRRRT	REPERTOIRE
EEEIPRRSSV	REPRESSIVE
EEEIPRSSVX	EXPRESSIVE
EEEIRRRSTV	RETRIEVERS
EEEIRSSTTV	SERVIETTES
EEEIRSSTTW	STREETWISE
EEEJRSSTTT	JET-SETTERS
EEEKLNRSUV	LEVERKUSEN
EEEKMRSSTU	MUSKETEERS
EEELLNPRST	REPELLENTS
EEELLNPSUV	ELEVEN-PLUS
EEELLNRSST	RELENTLESS
EEELLNRTVY	ENTRY-LEVEL
EEELMMOSTT	METTLESOME
EEELMNOPST	ELOPEMENTS
EEELMNOSTT	NETTLESOME
EEELMNOTVV	EVOLVEMENT
EEELMNSTTT	SETTLEMENT
EEELNOPRTT	OPEN LETTER
EEELNOSTTV	NOVELETTES

EEELNOTTVW	TWELVE-TONE	EEFHIINRRS	REFINISHER	EEGGINRRSS	REGRESSING
EEELNRRTVY	REVERENTLY	EEFHILLSSV	SHELF LIVES	EEGGINRRTT	REGRETTING
EEELNRSTTW	NEWSLETTER	EEFHILNSSS	FLESHINESS	EEGGISSTUV	SUGGESTIVE
EEELORSVWW	WEREWOLVES	EEFHILORSS	HORSEFLIES	EEGGNOORTW	GEORGETOWN
EEELPRRSVY	PERVERSELY	EEFHILOSSU	HOUSEFLIES	EEGHHIISTT	EIGHTIETHS
EEEMNNORST	MESENTERON	EEFHILRSVY	FEVERISHLY	EEGHHILNST	THE ENGLISH
EEEMNNRSTT	RESENTMENT	EEFHLNOORS	HOLOFERNES	EEGHHINOTT	EIGHTH NOTE
EEEMNORSST	REMOTENESS	EEFHNNORTU	FOURTEENTH	EEGHHINSSS	HIGHNESSES
EEEMNRSTTV	REVETMENTS	EEFIILLMPS	SIMPLE LIFE	EEGHHIRSTT	HIGH STREET
EEENNNSSUV	UNEVENNESS	EEFIILMRSU	EMULSIFIER	EEGHHORSTU	SEE-THROUGH
EEENORSTWZ	SNEEZEWORT	EEFIILNSSW	WIFELINESS	EEGHIKLRSU	KIESELGUHR
EEENPRRSST	PRESENTERS	EEFIILRRST	FERTILISER	EEGHIKNSTW	WEEKNIGHTS
EEENPRSSTX	EXPERTNESS	EEFIILRRTZ	FERTILIZER	EEGHILMNNS	ENGLISHMEN
EEENRRSSTW	WESTERNERS	EEFIIMNNNU	UNFEMININE	EEGHILNRST	SHELTERING
EEEOOPRSVX	OVEREXPOSE	EEFIINNNRS	SINN FEINER	EEGHILNSTT	LENGTHIEST
EEEOPRRRTX	RE-EXPORTER	EEFIINNRRST	FINISTERRE	EEGHILNSTY	SEETHINGLY
EEEOPRSTTY	STEREOTYPE	EEFIKLLORW	FLOWER-LIKE	EEGHILNWYZ	WHEEZINGLY
EEEORRRSTV	RETROVERSE	EEFIKLORST	FOREST-LIKE	EEGHILOOST	THEOLOGIES,
EEEPPPRSTU	PUPPETEERS	EEFILLLSSY	LIFELESSLY		THEOLOGISE
EEEPRRRSSV	PRESERVERS	EEFILLNOTU	FEUILLETON	EEGHILOOTZ	THEOLOGIZE
EEEPRSTTTY	TYPESETTER	EEFILLSSTY	LIFESTYLES	EEGHILSSTW	WEIGHTLESS
EEFFFKLRSU	KERFUFFLES	EEFILMNOQU	MEFLOQUINE	EEGHIMNOOS	HOMOGENISE
EEFFGIINRV	FIVE-FINGER	EEFILMRSTT	FILMSETTER	EEGHIMNOOZ	HOMOGENIZE
EEFFGINORR	FOREFINGER	EEFILNNORT	FLORENTINE	EEGHINOPST	PHOSGENITE
EEFFHINSTT	FIFTEENTHS	EEFILNPPTT	FELT-TIP PEN	EEGHINPRST	REGENTSHIP
EEFFHLRRSU	REFRESHFUL	EEFILNRTUV	INTERFLUVE	EEGHINRTVY	EVERYTHING
EEFFHLRSSU	RESHUFFLES	EEFILOSTWX	FELIXSTOWE	EEGHIORTVW	OVERWEIGHT
EEFFILSUVY	EFFUSIVELY	EEFINNORRT	INTERFERON	EEGHIRSSST	SIGHTSEERS
EEFFINOSSV	OFFENSIVES	EEFINNQRTU	INFREQUENT	EEGHLNORST	GLENROTHES
EEFFINRSST	STIFFENERS	EEFIOPRRST	PROFITEERS	EEGHLOORTY	HETEROLOGY
EEFFIORRST	FORFEITERS	EEFIORRRTX	FOX TERRIER	EEGHMNOSST	THEME SONGS
EEFFIORRTU	FORFEITURE	EEFIORRSTT	FORSTERITE	EEGHNNORRS	GREENHORNS
EEFFLORSST	EFFORTLESS	EEFIRRRSTU	FRUITERERS	EEGHNNRSTT	STRENGTHEN
EEFFNORRTY	EFFRONTERY	EEFKLNOOST	FOLKESTONE	EEGHNOORTY	HETEROGONY
EEFGHHIILR	HIGH RELIEF	EEFLLLSSSY	SELFLESSLY	EEGHOSSTUU	GUESTHOUSE
EEFGHINNRS	FRESHENING	EEFLLNTUVY	EVENTFULLY	EEGIIILMST	LEGITIMISE
EEFGHINNRS	REFRESHING	EEFLLORSSW	FLOWERLESS	EEGIIILMTZ	LEGITIMIZE
EEFGHINRRT	FRIGHTENER	EEFLMORRSU	REMORSEFUL	EEGIIKLPRS	KRIEGSPIEL
EEFGHIRRST	FREIGHTERS	EEFLNNTUUV	UNEVENTFUL	EEGIILNNNV	ENLIVENING
EEFGHLOOSS	GOOSEFLESH	EEFLNOSSUW	WOEFULNESS	EEGIILNSTV	TELEVISING
EEFGIILLNS	SINGLE FILE	EEFLNQRTUY	FREQUENTLY	EEGIILPRSV	PRIVILEGES
EEFGIILNRV	FREE-LIVING	EEFLNRSSUU	RUEFULNESS	EEGIINNOPR	PIONEERING
EEFGILLNRU	REFUELLING	EEFLNSSSUU	USEFULNESS	EEGIINNQTU	QUIETENING
EEFGILLNTY	FLEETINGLY	EEFMOPRRRS	PERFORMERS	EEGIINPRRV	REPRIEVING
EEFGILNRTW	LEFT-WINGER	EEFNNORRRU	FORERUNNER	EEGIINPRVW	PREVIEWING
EEFGIMNNRT	FERMENTING	EEFNNORSSZ	FROZENNESS	EEGIINRRTV	RETRIEVING
EEFGINNRRT	REFRINGENT	EEFNOOPRRS	FOR OPENERS	EEGIINRSSV	INGRESSIVE
EEFGINORRS	FOREIGNERS	EEFNOORSTY	FESTOONERY	EEGIIRRSST	REGISTRIES
EEFGINPRRR	PREFERRING	EEFORRSSST	FORTRESSES	EEGIKLLNNN	KENNELLING
EEFGKLLNOT	GENTLEFOLK	EEGGHILNRT	GREEN LIGHT	EEGILMNORS	MONGRELISE
EEFGLLMNOR	FELLMONGER	EEGGHOORTT	GO TOGETHER	EEGILMNORZ	MONGRELIZE
EEFGLLNUVY	VENGEFULLY	EEGGIINNRZ	ENERGIZING	EEGILNNOPV	ENVELOPING
EEFGLMNNTU	ENGULFMENT	EEGGIMNNST	SEGMENTING	EEGILNNRSY	SNEERINGLY
EEFHHLORSS	HORSEFLESH	EEGGINOTUV	GIVE TONGUE		

EEGILNNRTU	REUTLINGEN	
EEGILNNSSS	SINGLENESS	
EEGILNNSUY	UNSEEINGLY	
EEGILNOSST	TELEGNOSIS	
EEGILNPPRX	PERPLEXING	
EEGILNPSWY	SWEEPINGLY	
EEGILNRSTT	RESETTLING	
EEGILNRSTW	SWELTERING	
EEGIMNNOTT	MIGNONETTE	
EEGIMNNTTU	INTEGUMENT	
EEGIMNOORT	GONIOMETER	
EEGIMNOPPT	PEEPING TOM	
EEGIMNOPRW	EMPOWERING	
EEGIMNPPRT	PRE-EMPTING	
EEGINNOOTT	OTTO ENGINE	
EEGINNOPPS	PEPSINOGEN	
EEGINNPRST	PRESENTING	
EEGINNPRTV	PREVENTING	
EEGINOPSSY	PYOGENESIS	
EEGINORRSS	REGRESSION	
EEGINORRSV	SOVEREIGNS	
EEGINORSTY	GENEROSITY	
EEGINORSXY	OXYGENISER	
EEGINORXYZ	OXYGENIZER	
EEGINPRRSS	REPRESSING	
EEGINPRRSV	PRESERVING	
EEGINPRRTV	PERVERTING	
EEGINPRSSX	EXPRESSING	
EEGINPRSTT	PRESETTING	
EEGINQRSTU	REQUESTING	
EEGLLLOSWY	YELLOWLEGS	
EEGLLNOOSY	SELENOLOGY	
EEGLLOOPSY	SPELEOLOGY	
EEGLLORRSV	GROVELLERS	
EEGLMORSUY	GRUESOMELY	
EEGLNORSTT	LORGNETTES	
EEGLNORSUY	GENEROUSLY	
EEGLOORRST	ERGOSTEROL	
EEGMNNOORT	MONTENEGRO	
EEGMNNORTV	GOVERNMENT	
EEGNNORSUU	UNGENEROUS	
EEGNNOTTXY	OXYGEN TENT	
EEGOOPSSST	GOOSESTEPS	
EEGOPRRSSS	PROGRESSES	
EEGOPRSTUU	PORTUGUESE	
EEGOQRSSTU	GROTESQUES	
EEGORRRSST	RETROGRESS	
EEGPPPRTUY	UPPER EGYPT	
EEHHILMPTT	PITH HELMET	
EEHHILPSSY	SHEEPISHLY	
EEHHIMNOST	HENOTHEISM	
EEHHINOSSS	SHOESHINES	
EEHHINOSTT	HENOTHEIST	
EEHHINRTTT	THIRTEENTH	
EEHHIOPSTW	WHITE HOPES	
EEHHIORRSS	SHIRE HORSE	
EEHHIORSTW	WHITEHORSE	
EEHHIOSTUW	WHITE HOUSE	
EEHHIPRRST	PERTHSHIRE	
EEHHOORSSS	HORSESHOES	
EEHHOORSUW	WHOREHOUSE	
EEHHOPSSTY	HYPOTHESES	
EEHIILMPTU	EPITHELIUM	
EEHIILNOPR	PERIHELION	
EEHIIMNNOT	METHIONINE	
EEHIINNSTT	NINETIETHS	
EEHIJRSTTT	THE JITTERS	
EEHIKNPSSS	SHEEPSKINS	
EEHIKOSSTT	TO THE SKIES	
EEHIKPPTUW	KEEP UP WITH	
EEHILLLMSW	MILLWHEELS	
EEHILLRSWW	WELL-WISHER	
EEHILMNOSS	HOMELINESS	
EEHILMOPRT	THERMOPILE	
EEHILMORTY	HELIOMETRY	
EEHILNNOOS	HOLES IN ONE	
EEHILNNRTY	INHERENTLY	
EEHILNOSSS	HOLINESSES	
EEHILOOPRT	HELIOTROPE	
EEHILOPRST	PRIEST-HOLE	
EEHILORSST	HOSTELRIES	
EEHILOSTTU	SILHOUETTE	
EEHILPRSTU	SPHERULITE	
EEHIMMOOSV	HOME MOVIES	
EEHIMMPSSS	EUPHEMISMS	
EEHIMNNOTY	IN THE MONEY	
EEHIMNOPPS	HIPPOMENES	
EEHIMNOPRT	HEMIPTERON	
EEHIMNPRST	RESHIPMENT	
EEHINNOPRS	PREHENSION	
EEHINNOPRT	INTERPHONE	
EEHINNORST	RHINESTONE	
EEHINOOPRS	IONOSPHERE	
EEHINSSSTX	SIXTH SENSE	
EEHINSSSTY	SYNTHESISE	
EEHINSSTTX	SIXTEENTHS	
EEHINSSTYZ	SYNTHESIZE	
EEHINSTTTW	TWENTIETHS	
EEHIOPPRRS	PROPHESIER	
EEHIOPPRSS	PROPHESIES	
EEHIOSSUVW	HOUSEWIVES	
EEHIPRRSSW	WHISPERERS	
EEHKKOOPYY	HOKEY-POKEY	
EEHKLOOOWY	WOOKEY HOLE	
EEHKMOOSSU	SMOKEHOUSE	
EEHKNOORTT	TENTERHOOK	
EEHLLLPSSY	HELPLESSLY	
EEHLLMNOOP	MELLOPHONE	
EEHLLMORTW	MOTHERWELL	
EEHLLNOOPS	HENLE'S LOOP	
EEHLLNOPST	HELLESPONT	
EEHLLOPSSY	HOPELESSLY	
EEHLLORSST	HOSTELLERS	
EEHLMNOOYZ	HOLOENZYME	
EEHLMNORTY	HEMELYTRON	
EEHLMORSST	MOTHERLESS	
EEHLNOOSSV	SHOVELNOSE	
EEHLNOOSTW	WHOLE NOTES	
EEHLOORSUW	LOWER HOUSE	
EEHMNNNOOP	PHENOMENON	
EEHMNOOPRT	PHONOMETER	
EEHMNOORSW	HORSEWOMEN	
EEHMNOORTY	HETERONOMY	
EEHMNORSTT	NETHERMOST	
EEHMNPSTTU	UMPTEENTHS	
EEHMOOPRTT	PHOTOMETER	
EEHMOPRSSU	MORPHEUSES	
EEHMOPPRST	STEPMOTHER	
EEHMOQRSUU	HUMORESQUE	
EEHMRRSSTY	RHYMESTERS	
EEHNNOPSSY	PHONEYNESS	
EEHNNORRRT	NORTHERNER	
EEHNNOSSST	HONESTNESS	
EEHNOORTTU	ON THE OUTER	
EEHNOPSSTU	PENTHOUSES	
EEHNOPSTUY	HYPOTENUSE	
EEHNORRSTU	SOUTHERNER	
EEHNOSSTTW	WHETSTONES	
EEHNPPRSSU	PEN PUSHERS	
EEHNRSSSTU	HUNTRESSES	
EEHOOPRRSW	HORSEPOWER	
EEHOOPRSUW	POWERHOUSE	
EEHOOPRTTY	HETEROTOPY	
EEHOOPSTTY	OSTEOPHYTE	
EEHOORSSTU	STOREHOUSE	
EEHOOSTTTW	SWEET TOOTH	
EEHOPPRSSU	UPPER HOUSE	
EEHOPRRSTV	SHREVEPORT	
EEIIINOSTU	INEQUITIES	
EEIIKLNPRW	PERIWINKLE	
EEIILLMMRT	MILLIMETRE	
EEIILLNSSV	LIVELINESS	
EEIILMNSST	TIMELINESS	
EEIILNNRRT	INTERLINER	
EEIILNOSTV	TELEVISION	
EEIILORSTT	TOILETRIES	
EEIILPRRST	PRIESTLIER	
EEIILRRSST	STERILISER	
EEIILRRSTZ	STERILIZER	
EEIIMMNRTU	MEITNERIUM	
EEIIMNNPTT	IMPENITENT	
EEIIMNORST	ENORMITIES	

444

EEIIMNPRUU	EPINEURIUM	EEILMOSSVW	SEMIVOWELS
EEIIMNRSTX	IN EXTREMIS	EEILMPRSTU	PULSIMETER
EEIIMNRTTW	WINTERTIME	EEILNNOQTU	INELOQUENT
EEIIMNRTZZ	INTERMEZZI	EEILNNPTTY	PENITENTLY
EEIIMOPRST	EPITOMISER	EEILNNSSST	SILENTNESS
EEIIMOPRTZ	EPITOMIZER	EEILNOPRRT	INTERLOPER
EEIIMPRSSV	IMPRESSIVE,	EEILNOPSTU	POLITENESS
PERMISSIVE		EEILNPRTXY	INEXPERTLY
EEIINNNNTY	NINETY-NINE	EEILOOPRST	TELIOSPORE
EEIINNNSTT	INSENTIENT	EEILOPRSTX	EXPLOITERS
EEIINNRTTW	INTERTWINE	EEILOPSSVX	EXPLOSIVES
EEIINNSSSW	SINEWINESS	EEILORRSTU	IRRESOLUTE
EEIINNSSTT	INTESTINES	EEILORRTTW	ROTTWEILER
EEIINNSTTX	INEXISTENT	EEILPPRTXY	PERPLEXITY
EEIINOPRTT	PETITIONER,	EEILPPSTUV	SUPPLETIVE
REPETITION		EEILPRRSTY	SPERRYLITE
EEIINRSSST	SENSITISER	EEILPRRSUV	PULVERISER
EEIINRSSTZ	SENSITIZER	EEILPRRUVZ	PULVERIZER
EEIINRSTVW	INTERVIEWS	EEILPRSSTY	PERISTYLES
EEIIORRSST	ROTISSERIE	EEILRSSSST	RESISTLESS
EEIIPQRSTU	PERQUISITE	EEIMMMRSTU	SUMMERTIME
EEIIQRSSTU	REQUISITES	EEIMMOPRRV	PRIME MOVER
EEIJLORSSV	OVERIJSSEL	EEIMMRSSST	MESMERISTS
EEIJMNNNOT	ENJOINMENT	EEIMMRSSTY	SYMMETRISE
EEIKKORSST	KOEKSISTER	EEIMMRSTYZ	SYMMETRIZE
EEIKLMORST	KILOMETRES	EEIMNNNRTT	INTERNMENT
EEIKMORRTW	TIMEWORKER	EEIMNNOPTT	PENTIMENTO
EEIKMRSSTU	MUSKETRIES	EEIMNNORST	MINESTRONE
EEIKNRRSTT	RENT STRIKE	EEIMNNRSTT	INTERMENTS
EEIKORRRWW	WIREWORKER	EEIMNNSSTT	SENTIMENTS
EEILLLPSTV	SPLIT-LEVEL	EEIMNNSSTU	MINUTENESS
EEILLMMORT	IMMORTELLE	EEIMNNSTTV	INVESTMENT
EEILLMNOST	EMOLLIENTS	EEIMNOPPRT	PRE-EMPTION
EEILLMNSSS	SMELLINESS	EEIMNOPRTU	PERITONEUM
EEILLMPPPR	PEPPER MILL	EEIMNOPSTX	EXEMPTIONS
EEILLMSSTY	TIMELESSLY	EEIMNORRSS	SERMONISER
EEILLNNOSS	LONELINESS	EEIMNORRSZ	SERMONIZER
EEILLNOSSV	LOVELINESS	EEIMNORRTT	NITROMETER
EEILLNRSSV	SNIVELLERS	EEIMNORTZZ	INTERMEZZO
EEILLORSTT	TITLE ROLES	EEIMNPPPRT	PEPPERMINT
EEILLRSSTY	TIRELESSLY	EEIMNPRSTU	EPISTERNUM
EEILMMNPST	IMPLEMENTS	EEIMNRSSSS	REMISSNESS
EEILMMORST	MILOMETERS	EEIMNRSSTU	TERMINUSES
EEILMNNSTT	ENLISTMENT	EEIMNRSSTW	WESTERNISM
EEILMNOPRT	MONTPELIER	EEIMOPRRST	SPIROMETER,
EEILMNORSS	SOLEMNISER	TEMPORISER	
EEILMNORSZ	SOLEMNIZER	EEIMOPRRTZ	TEMPORIZER
EEILMNOSST	MILESTONES	EEIMOPRSTU	PERIOSTEUM
EEILMNOSSU	MOUSSELINE	EEIMPPRRUU	PUERPERIUM
EEILMNPPRS	PIMPERNELS	EEIMPRSTUV	RESUMPTIVE
EEILMNPSSS	SIMPLENESS	EEIMRRSSTT	TRIMESTERS
EEILMOPRSY	POLYMERISE	EEIMRSSSST	MISTRESSES
EEILMOPRYZ	POLYMERIZE	EEIMRSSSTY	SYSTEMISER
EEILMORSTY	TIRESOMELY	EEIMRSSTYZ	SYSTEMIZER
EEILMOSSTV	MOTIVELESS		
EEINNNSSTT	INTENTNESS
EEINNOPRSS	PENSIONERS
EEINNOPRST	PRETENSION,
TIN OPENERS	
EEINNOPRTV	PREVENTION
EEINNORTVW	INTERWOVEN
EEINNOSSTX	EXTENSIONS
EEINNPRTTU	TURPENTINE
EEINNPSSSU	SUPINENESS
EEINNQSSUU	UNIQUENESS
EEINOPPRST	PEPTONISER
EEINOPPRTZ	PEPTONIZER
EEINOPQTTU	EQUIPOTENT
EEINOPRRSS	REPRESSION
EEINOPRRST	INTERPOSER
EEINOPRRSV	PERVERSION
EEINOPRSSV	RESPONSIVE
EEINOPRSSX	EXPRESSION
EEINOPRSXY	EPOXY RESIN
EEINOPRTXY	PYROXENITE
EEINOQRSTU	QUESTIONER
EEINOSSTVV	VOTIVENESS
EEINPRSSTT	PERSISTENT,
PRETTINESS	
EEINPSSSUV	SUSPENSIVE
EEIOPPRRST	PROPERTIES
EEIOPPRSSV	OPPRESSIVE
EEIOPRRSTV	RESORPTIVE
EEIOPRSSST	STEREOPSIS
EEIOPRSTTT	OPERETTIST
EEIOPRSTTU	PIROUETTES
EEIOPSSSSV	POSSESSIVE
EEIORRRRST	TERRORISER
EEIORRRRTZ	TERRORIZER
EEIORRRSST	ROISTERERS
EEIORRRSSV	RESERVOIRS
EEIPPRTTUY	PERPETUITY
EEIPRRSSSU	PRESSURISE
EEIPRRSSUZ	PRESSURIZE
EEIPRRSTVY	PERVERSITY
EEIPRRTTWY	TYPEWRITER
EEIPRSSSTT	STEPSISTER
EEIRRRSSTV	RESERVISTS
EEJMNNORUY	JOURNEYMEN
EEJMNNOSTY	ENJOYMENTS
EEKLLNOPSW	WELL-SPOKEN
EEKLOOPPRW	WORKPEOPLE
EEKLORSSTW	STEELWORKS
EELLMNOOSS	LEMON SOLES
EELLMNOSSW	MELLOWNESS
EELLNNSSSU	SULLENNESS
EELLNOPPRT	PROPELLENT
EELLNOQTUY	ELOQUENTLY
EELLNOSSTY	TONELESSLY
EELLNSSTUY	TUNELESSLY

EELLOPPRRS	PROPELLERS	EFFGIINORT	FORFEITING	EFGINNORUV	UNFORGIVEN
EELLORSTUY	RESOLUTELY	EFFGIINOST	FFESTINIOG	EFGINOPRSS	PROFESSING
EELLRSSSSTY	RESTLESSLY	EFFGILLNOT	TELLING-OFF	EFGINPRTUY	PUTREFYING
EELMMNOPTY	EMPLOYMENT	EFFGINOPRR	PROFFERING	EFGINPSTUY	STUPEFYING
EELMMNOSTU	EMOLUMENTS	EFFGINOSTT	OFFSETTING	EFGLOOSTUV	TUGS-OF-LOVE
EELMNNORST	ENROLMENTS	EFFGINRSSU	SUFFERINGS	EFHHIOORTT	HIT THE ROOF
EELMNNOSSS	SOLEMNNESS	EFFIIKLOSS	KISS OF LIFE	EFHHLOSSTU	HOT FLUSHES
EELMNOOSSZ	ZOOM LENSES	EFFIILRSTU	FRUIT FLIES	EFHIIKNSSV	FISH KNIVES
EELMNPPSTU	SUPPLEMENT	EFFIIORRST	FORTIFIERS	EFHIILNRST	FLINTSHIRE
EELMNPTUZZ	PUZZLEMENT	EFFIIQSSTU	SQUIFFIEST	EFHIILNSST	FILTHINESS
EELMOOPSTT	TOTEM POLES	EFFILLMNTU	FULFILMENT	EFHIILRSSV	SILVERFISH
EELNOPRSTW	SPLEENWORT	EFFINNSSSU	SNUFFINESS	EFHIINSSST	SHIFTINESS
EELNORSTUV	VOLUNTEERS	EFFINSSSTU	STUFFINESS	EFHIIRSTTT	THRIFTIEST
EELNPPRSSU	PURPLENESS	EFFNNOOSTU	OFF ONE'S NUT	EFHIISSSTT	FETISHISTS
EELNPPSSSU	SUPPLENESS	EFGGHIINRT	FREIGHTING	EFHILLOPSW	FELLOWSHIP
EELOOPRSTT	PROTOSTELE	EFGGIILNNR	FINGERLING	EFHILOPRST	SHOPLIFTER
EELOOPRSTU	POULTERERS	EFGGIILNNY	FEIGNINGLY	EFHILORRSU	FLOURISHER
EELOPRSSTY	PROSELYTES	EFGGIINNRR	RING FINGER	EFHILORSSU	FLOURISHES
EELORSSUVY	YOURSELVES	EFGGINOORS	FOREGOINGS	EFHILRSSTT	THRIFTLESS
EELPRRSTTU	SPLUTTERER	EFGGINORTT	FORGETTING	EFHIMNNOPR	PHENFORMIN
EELPSSTTUX	SEXTUPLETS	EFGHHIILRS	HIGH-FLIERS	EFHINORSST	FROTHINESS
EEMMNOORST	METRONOMES	EFGHIIKNRS	KINGFISHER	EFHLLOOPRS	SHELLPROOF
EEMNNOPSTT	PENTSTEMON	EFGHIILSTT	FLIGHTIEST	EFHLLOSSUU	FULL HOUSES
EEMNNRRSUY	NURSERYMEN	EFGHIIPRST	PRISEFIGHT	EFHLOOPSSU	FLOPHOUSES
EEMNOORSSS	MOROSENESS	EFGHIIPRTZ	PRIZEFIGHT	EFHNORSTUX	FOXHUNTERS
EEMNOORTTY	ENTEROTOMY	EFGHILLSST	FLIGHTLESS	EFIIIINNTV	INFINITIVE
EEMOOPPRRT	PRO TEMPORE	EFGHILORTV	OVERFLIGHT	EFIIIILMPRS	SIMPLIFIER
EEMOORSTTY	STEREOTOMY	EFGHILSTWY	FLYWEIGHTS	EFIIILNNTY	INFINITELY
EEMOPPRRTY	PEREMPTORY,	EFGHIMNORS	FISHMONGER	EFIIIMNNTY	FEMININITY
	PRE-EMPTORY	EFGHINNRRTU	FURTHERING	EFIIKNRSSS	FRISKINESS
EEMORSSTTU	METOESTRUS	EFGHIORSST	GIFT HORSES	EFIILLLSST	STILL LIFES
EEMPRRSTTU	TRUMPETERS	EFGHLLLNTU	FULL-LENGTH	EFIILLNRSS	FRILLINESS
EEMQRSSTUU	SEQUESTRUM	EFGHLLNORU	FLUGELHORN	EFIILMNSSS	FLIMSINESS
EENNNNOOSS	NO-NONSENSE	EFGHOOPPRR	FROGHOPPER	EFIILNNSST	FLINTINESS
EENNOOOSST	ON ONE'S	EFGIIILLNNR	FIRING LINE	EFIILOPRSU	PILIFEROUS
	TOES	EFGIIILNQUY	LIQUEFYING	EFIILPRSTT	FILTER TIPS
EENNOPSSTT	POTENTNESS	EFGIIMNORS	FOREIGNISM	EFIILRSTTU	STULTIFIER
EENNORSSTT	ROTTENNESS	EFGIINNNTU	FINE-TUNING	EFIIMORRSU	FOURIERISM
EENNOSSSUV	VENOUSNESS	EFGIINNPRST	FINGERTIPS	EFIINORSUV	VINIFEROUS
EENOOPPSSS	POPE'S NOSES	EFGIINNPRSY	PRESIGNIFY	EFIINRSSTU	FRUITINESS
EENOPPRRSS	PROPERNESS	EFGIINNPRTY	PETRIFYING	EFIINRSSZZ	FRIZZINESS
EEOOSSTTTV	VOETSTOETS	EFGIINNRRTT	FRITTERING	EFIIORRSTU	FOURIERIST
EEOPPPPRST	PEPPER POTS	EFGIINNRRY	TERRIFYING	EFIKLNOSSS	FOLKSINESS
EEOPPPRRTW	PEPPERWORT	EFGIINNRSTU	SURFEITING	EFILLMORST	STELLIFORM
EEOPPPRSSU	PRESUPPOSE	EFGIINNSTTY	TESTIFYING	EFILLNSSUW	WILFULNESS
EEOPPRRSUW	SUPERPOWER	EFGILLLUUY	GUILEFULLY	EFILLOOPRW	LOW PROFILE
EEOPPRRSSS	PREPOSSESS	EFGILLNNNU	FUNNELLING	EFILLPSTUY	SPITEFULLY
EEOPPRRSST	PROTESTERS	EFGILLORRW	FLOWER GIRL	EFILMNPTTU	UPLIFTMENT
EEOPRSTTYY	STEREOTYPY	EFGILNORST	FOSTERLING	EFILMOOPRS	SIMFEROPOL
EEORRSTTVX	EXTROVERTS	EFGILNORVY	OVERFLYING	EFILNNSSSU	SINFULNESS
EEORSSSTUW	SOU'WESTERS	EFGILNRSTU	FLUSTERING	EFILNOPPSS	FLOPPINESS
EERRSSTTTU	STUTTERERS	EFGILNRTTU	FLUTTERING	EFILNORTWW	TWINFLOWER
EFFFILNSSU	FLUFFINESS	EFGIMNOPRR	PERFORMING	EFILOPRSST	PROFITLESS
EFFGHIIINRS	FISH FINGER	EFGINNOOST	FESTOONING	EFIMNORSTU	MISFORTUNE
EFFGIINNST	STIFFENING				

EFIMOOPRSU	POMIFEROUS	EGGINOSSTU	SUGGESTION
EFIMORRSST	FIRESTORMS	EGGIOPRSTT	GET TO GRIPS
EFINNORRTY	FORTY-NINER	EGGIORRSTU	OUTRIGGERS
EFINOORPSS	PROFESSION	EGGLLOOOPX	GOOGOLPLEX
EFINOORSSU	SONIFEROUS	EGGLOOPTYY	EGYPTOLOGY
EFINORSSST	FROSTINESS	EGGLOORSUY	GORGEOUSLY
EFINORSSWZ	FROWZINESS	EGHHHIORSS	HIGH HORSES
EFINORSTTU	STONE FRUIT	EGHHIINRTT	IN THE RIGHT
EFIOOPRRSU	PORIFEROUS	EGHHIIPRST	HIGH PRIEST
EFIOORSSSU	OSSIFEROUS	EGHHIJMPRU	HIGH JUMPER
EFIOORSSTX	SIX-FOOTERS	EGHHILOPRY	HIEROGLYPH
EFIOPRSTTU	PETIT FOURS	EGHHILOSTU	LIGHTHOUSE
EFIORSTTTU	OUTFITTERS	EGHHINORTU	IN THE ROUGH
EFJLNOSSUY	JOYFULNESS	EGHHOORSUU	ROUGHHOUSE
EFKNOOPSST	SOFT-SPOKEN	EGHIIINNRT	INHERITING
EFKOORRSTU	FOUR-STROKE	EGHIIKNNRT	RETHINKING
EFLLMORSSY	FORMLESSLY	EGHIILNRST	SLITHERING
EFLLOPRUWY	POWERFULLY	EGHIILNRSV	SHRIVELING
EFLMNOOORW	MOONFLOWER	EGHIILNTVY	THIEVINGLY
EFLMOOORTY	TOMFOOLERY	EGHIIMMNRS	SHIMMERING
EFLNORSSUW	SUNFLOWERS	EGHIIMNPRW	WHIMPERING
EFLOOPRSTW	FLOWERPOTS	EGHIIMNSST	MIGHTINESS
EFLOPPRSUU	PURPOSEFUL	EGHIINNNRS	ENSHRINING
EFMOOPRRTU	OUTPERFORM	EGHIINNPRT	TREPHINING
EFMORRSTTU	FORT SUMTER	EGHIINNPSS	ENSIGNSHIP
EFNNOORRSU	NONFERROUS	EGHIINORTZ	THEORIZING
EFOOPRRSSS	PROFESSORS	EGHIINPRSW	WHISPERING
EFOOPRRSTU	FOUR-POSTER	EGHIINSSTY	HYGIENISTS
EGGGIINNRS	SNIGGERING	EGHIINSTUX	EXTINGUISH
EGGGIINRRT	TRIGGERING	EGHILLNOST	HOSTELLING
EGGGINORSS	GROGGINESS	EGHILLNOSV	SHOVELLING
EGGGINSSTU	SUGGESTING	EGHILMOOOS	HOMOLOGISE
EGGHHIPRSU	HIPHUGGERS	EGHILMOOOZ	HOMOLOGIZE
EGGHIIINNV	INVEIGHING	EGHILNNOST	NEON LIGHTS
EGGHIILNNT	LIGHTENING	EGHILNORVY	HOVERINGLY
EGGHIINNTT	TIGHTENING	EGHILNSSST	SLIGHTNESS
EGGHINNORU	ROUGHENING	EGHILOOPPT	PHLOGOPITE
EGGHINNOTU	TOUGHENING	EGHILOORST	RHEOLOGIST
EGGIIILNNV	INVEIGLING	EGHILOOSTT	ETHOLOGIST
EGGIILMMNR	GLIMMERING	EGHILOSSTT	GHOSTLIEST
EGGIILNNST	GLISTENING	EGHILRSTVY	VERY LIGHTS
EGGIILNOUZ	EULOGIZING	EGHIMNORST	SMOTHERING
EGGIILNRTT	GLITTERING	EGHINNNORT	ENTHRONING
EGGIILNRVY	GRIEVINGLY	EGHINNORST	SHORTENING
EGGIINNTTV	VIGNETTING	EGHINNRSSU	HUNGRINESS
EGGILLNORV	GROVELLING	EGHINORSST	SHOESTRING
EGGILMOOST	GEMOLOGIST	EGHINRSTTU	SHUTTERING
EGGILNSSUY	GUESSINGLY	EGHIOPRSTT	TIGHTROPES
EGGILOOSST	GEOLOGISTS	EGHIORSSTV	OVERSIGHTS
EGGINNORSS	ENGROSSING	EGHIORSTTW	GHOSTWRITE
EGGINNPSTU	TUNING PEGS	EGHIORTTWY	TROY WEIGHT
EGGINNRSTU	GINGER NUTS	EGHJMNPTUU	JUMP THE GUN
EGGINOORSV	GOINGS-OVER	EGHLLOORSY	GLORY HOLES
EGGINOPRRU	REGROUPING	EGHLNOOPRY	PHRENOLOGY
EGHLOOPPSY	PSEPHOLOGY
EGHLOPPRTY	PETROGLYPH
EGHMNOOOSU	HOMOGENOUS
EGHMOOOTYZ	HOMOZYGOTE
EGIIILMMST	LEGITIMISM
EGIIILMSTT	LEGITIMIST
EGIIILNORR	IRRELIGION
EGIIIMNNOS	IGNOMINIES
EGIIIMNNST	MENINGITIS
EGIIKLNNSS	KINGLINESS
EGIIKNPPRS	SKIPPERING
EGIIKNRSTT	SKITTERING
EGIILLNNSV	SNIVELLING
EGIILLNOTU	GUILLOTINE
EGIILLNRVY	REVILINGLY
EGIILLNSVW	SWIVELLING
EGIILNOPTX	EXPLOITING
EGIILNRSSS	GRISLINESS
EGIILNRVVY	REVIVINGLY
EGIILNSSTU	GUILTINESS
EGIILOPSTT	EPIGLOTTIS
EGIILRSSTT	GRISTLIEST
EGIIMMNORZ	MEMORIZING
EGIIMMNNOT	MENTIONING
EGIIMMNOST	MOISTENING
EGIIMNPRSS	IMPRESSING
EGIIMNPRST	SPRINGTIME
EGIIMNPRTT	PERMITTING
EGIINNNOPS	PENSIONING
EGIINNORSS	INGRESSION
EGIINNPRRT	REPRINTING
EGIINNRRSU	REINSURING
EGIINNSSST	STINGINESS
EGIINNSSTW	WITNESSING
EGIINPPRRS	PERSPIRING
EGIINPRSST	PERSISTING, SPRINGIEST
EGIINRSSTT	GRITTINESS, STRINGIEST
EGIINRTTTW	TWITTERING
EGIINSTTTV	VIGNETTIST
EGIJKNNSTU	JUNKETINGS
EGIJNNORUY	JOURNEYING
EGIKLNNOOS	INGLENOOKS
EGIKLNNPSU	SPELUNKING
EGIKLNORVY	REVOKINGLY
EGIKNNOORS	SNOOKERING
EGIKNNORTW	NETWORKING
EGILLMMNPU	PUMMELLING
EGILLMOSTU	GUILLEMOTS
EGILLNNTUU	TUNNELLING
EGILLNNOTW	WELLINGTON
EGILLNOPPR	PROPELLING
EGILLNORWY	LOWERINGLY

447

EGILLNOSTU	OUTSELLING	EGINPRSTTU	SPUTTERING	EHIIRSSSTW	IRISH STEWS
EGILLNPRSW	WELLSPRING	EGINRSTTTU	STUTTERING	EHIIRSSTTT	THIRTSIEST
EGILLNTUXY	EXULTINGLY	EGJLLOORRY	JOLLY ROGER	EHIKLNORTW	KENILWORTH
EGILLORSSY	SYLLOGISER	EGJLMNOPRU	LONG-JUMPER	EHIKNORSTW	IN THE WORKS
EGILLORSYZ	SYLLOGIZER	EGLLMORSSY	GORMLESSLY	EHILLMOORS	HERMOSILLO
EGILMMNORS	MONGRELISM	EGLLMORSUU	GLOMERULUS	EHILLMNOOS	HOMOLOSINE
EGILMMNPTU	PLUMMETING	EGLMNOOOSU	MONOLOGUES	EHILMNSSSU	MULISHNESS
EGILMNOOSS	GLOOMINESS,	EGLMNOOOTY	ENTOMOLOGY	EHILMOPSTY	POLYTHEISM
	NEOLOGISMS	EGLMNOORUY	NUMEROLOGY	EHILNNOSSU	UNHOLINESS
EGILMNOPTT	MELTING POT	EGLMNOOYYZ	ENZYMOLOGY	EHILNOPNTR	NEUTROPHIL
EGILMNOSUU	LEGUMINOUS	EGLNNOSSUU	SUN LOUNGES	EHILNSSSSU	SLUSHINESS
EGILMNPTTY	TEMPTINGLY	EGLOOORRWW		EHILOPRSSU	RUSSOPHILE
EGILMOOSSY	SEISMOLOGY		WOOLGROWER	EHILOPSTTY	POLYTHEIST
EGILNNOSST	SINGLETONS	EGMMNOORTY		EHILORRTTY	ERYTHRITOL
EGILNNRRUY	UNERRINGLY		MONTGOMERY	EHILPRSSUU	SULPHURISE
EGILNNRSSU	NURSELINGS	EGMMNOPRSY	GYMNOSPERM	EHILPRSUUZ	SULPHURIZE
EGILNNSTTU	UNSETTLING	EGMNNOOOSU		EHIMMNOOST	MONOTHEISM
EGILNOOOST	OENOLOGIST		MONOGENOUS	EHIMMOPRTU	PROMETHIUM
EGILNOOPST	PENOLOGIST	EGMOORSSTU	GUESTROOMS	EHIMNNPSTU	PUNISHMENT
EGILNOPRTT	PORT-GENTIL	EGNNNRRSUU	GUNRUNNERS	EHIMNOOSTT	MONOTHEIST
EGILNORRUV	OVERRULING	EGNNORSSST	STRONGNESS	EHIMNOPSSY	SYMPHONIES
EGILNOSSSS	GLOSSINESS	EGNORRSTU	OVERSTRUNG	EHIMNOPSUU	EUPHONIUMS
EGILNOSTUU	LOUNGE SUIT	EGNORSSSST	SONGSTRESS	EHIMNORSUY	HIERONYMUS
EGILNPRSSY	PRESSINGLY	EGNORSSTUY	YOUNGSTERS	EHIMNSSTTY	SYNTHETISM
EGILNQSTUY	QUESTINGLY	EHHIILLSTVY	THIEVISHLY	EHIMORRSTT	THERMISTOR
EGILNRSVWY	SWERVINGLY	EHHIIMSTTW	WHITESMITH	EHINNORSST	THORNINESS
EGILOORSST	SEROLOGIST	EHHIIRSTTT	THIRTIETHS	EHINNSSSTU	NISSEN HUTS
EGILOOSSTX	SEXOLOGIST	EHHILOPRSU	HEROPHILUS	EHINOOPSUU	EUPHONIOUS
EGILORSUVY	GRIEVOUSLY	EHHILOPSTU	THEOPHILUS	EHINOOSSTT	TOOTHINESS
EGILOSUUXY	EXIGUOUSLY	EHHILOPTTY	LITHOPHYTE	EHINOPPRTY	PERIPHYTON
EGIMNNOORR	IRONMONGER	EHHILORTWW	WORTHWHILE	EHINOPPSSS	POPISHNESS
EGIMNNORTT	TORMENTING	EHHILRSSWY	SHREWISHLY	EHINORSSTW	WORTHINESS
EGIMNNORTU	REMOUNTING	EHHIMORSTT	HITHERMOST	EHINORSTUU	RUTHENIOUS
EGIMNOORTY	GONIOMETRY	EHHIOPRRSS	SHROPSHIRE	EHINPPSSSU	UPPISHNESS
EGIMNPRSSU	GRUMPINESS	EHHIOPSSTY	HYPOTHESIS	EHINRRTTUW	WINTERTHUR
EGIMNPRTTU	TRUMPETING	EHHLOOOPPR	LOPHOPHORE	EHINSSSTTY	SYNTHESIST
EGIMOOPRST	GEOTROPISM	EHHMNOOOPS	HOMOPHONES	EHINSSTTTY	SYNTHETIST
EGINNOPSSS	SPONGINESS	EHHOOOPPRT	PHOTOPHORE	EHIOOPRSTW	POOR WHITES
EGINNRSSTU	INSURGENTS	EHIIILNPPP	PHILIPPINE	EHIOORSSTX	SIX-SHOOTER
EGINNRSSTY	TRYINGNESS	EHIIILNPST	PHILISTINE	EHIOPPRRSW	WORSHIPPER
EGINNRSTTU	ENTRUSTING	EHIIKMRRSS	SKIRMISHER	EHIOPRRSTY	PREHISTORY
EGINNRSTUW	WET-NURSING	EHIIKMRSSS	SKIRMISHES	EHIOPRRTTY	PYRRHOTITE
EGINNRSUVW	UNSWERVING	EHIILLOOPS	HELIOPOLIS	EHIOPRSSST	PROSTHESIS
EGINOOPRRT	PROGENITOR	EHIILLOPSY	LYOPHILISE	EHJMOPRSUW	SHOW JUMPER
EGINOPPRRS	PROSPERING	EHIILLOPYZ	LYOPHILIZE	EHKOORRSSW	WORKHORSES
EGINOPPRSS	OPPRESSING	EHIILNOOPS	EOSINOPHIL	EHLLNOOSSW	HOLLOWNESS
EGINOPPRST	STOPPERING	EHIILNQRSU	RELINQUISH	EHLLRSSTUY	RUTHLESSLY
EGINOPRRTU	INTERGROUP	EHIILPRTTY	TRIPHYLITE	EHLMNOPPTY	NYMPHOLEPT
EGINOPRSUY	PERIGYNOUS	EHIIMNPSSS	IMPISHNESS	EHLMORSSUU	HUMOURLESS
EGINOPSSSS	POSSESSING	EHIIMOPRSV	IMPOVERISH	EHLNOOPRST	NORTH POLES
EGINORRSTW	SONGWRITER	EHIIMPPRSU	UMPIRESHIP	EHLNOOPSXY	XYLOPHONES
EGINORSSTT	GROTTINESS	EHIINNPRST	INTERNSHIP	EHLNOORSSU	HONOURLESS
EGINORSTUW	OUTSWINGER	EHIIQSSSTU	SQUISHIEST		
EGINPRRSSU	PRESSURING	EHIIRRSTTU	URETHRITIS		

EHLOORRRTY	HOLY TERROR	EIILLNOPST	SEPTILLION
EHLOPRSTUY	UPHOLSTERY	EIILLNOSTX	SEXTILLION
EHMMOOPRSY	MESOMORPHY	EIILLPSSTY	PITILESSLY
EHMMOORSUU		EIILMMNNTY	IMMINENTLY
HUMOURSOME		EIILMNNSTT	INSTILMENT
EHMNNOOOSY	HONEYMOONS	EIILMNOSST	LENTISSIMO
EHMNOOPRTY	NEPHROTOMY	EIILMNOSSU	LIMOUSINES
EHMNOOSSST	SMOOTHNESS	EIILMNPPSS	PIMPLINESS
EHMNOPSTTU	ON THE STUMP	EIILMOSTTV	LEITMOTIVS
EHMOOOPRSS	SOPHOMORES	EIILNPPSSS	SLIPPINESS
EHMOOPRTTY	PHOTOMETRY	EIILNPTUVY	PUNITIVELY
EHMOORRTTW	MOTHERWORT	EIILOPSTVY	POSITIVELY
EHNNOPRTWY	PENNYWORTH	EIILPRSSST	SPIRITLESS
EHNOORRTVW	OVERTHROWN	EIIMMPRSUY	PERIMYSIUM
EHNOORTTWY	NOTEWORTHY	EIIMNNORSU	REUNIONISM
EHNOOSSTUW	TOWN HOUSES	EIIMNOPRRS	IMPRISONER
EHNOPRSTTU	POTHUNTERS	EIIMNOPRSS	IMPRESSION,
EHNOQSTTUU	QUONSET HUT	PERMISSION	
EHNORSTWWY	NEWSWORTHY	EIIMNORSSS	REMISSIONS
EHOOOPPRRS	SPOROPHORE	EIIMOOPSTY	EPISIOTOMY
EHOOOPRSSU	POORHOUSES	EIIMOPRRSV	IMPROVISER
EHOOPPRSTY	SPOROPHYTE	EIIMOPRSUV	IMPERVIOUS
EHOOPPRTTY	TROPOPHYTE	EIIMORSSTU	MOISTURISE
EHOORRSTVW	OVERTHROWS	EIIMORSTUZ	MOISTURIZE
EHOPPSTTUU	UP THE SPOUT	EIIMPSSSST	PESSIMISTS
EHORRSTTUV	OVERTHRUST	EIINNNOSTT	INTENTIONS
EIIIINQSTU	INIQUITIES	EIINNNOSTV	INVENTIONS
EIIILLLMRT	MILLILITRE	EIINNORSST	INSERTIONS
EIIILMMSTT	TIME LIMITS	EIINNORSSV	INVERSIONS
EIIILORSTV	VITRIOLISE	EIINNORSTU	REUNIONIST
EIIILORTVZ	VITRIOLIZE	EIINNPPSSS	SNIPPINESS
EIIIMNORST	MINORITIES	EIINNRSSTW	WINTRINESS
EIIIMNPSTU	IMPUNITIES	EIINOOPRST	REPOSITION
EIIIMNRSST	MINISTRIES	EIINOOPSTX	EXPOSITION
EIIIMPRSTU	IMPURITIES	EIINOPPTTT	PETIT POINT
EIIIMPRSTV	PRIMITIVES	EIINOPPRSV	PREVISIONS
EIIIMSSTVY	EMISSIVITY	EIINOPSTVW	VIEWPOINTS
EIIINPRRST	INSPIRITER	EIINORTTWZ	ZWITTERION
EIIIOPRRST	PRIORITIES,	EIINPPRSST	PINSTRIPES
PRIORITISE		EIINPRSSSS	PRISSINESS
EIIIOPRRTZ	PRIORITIZE	EIINRSTUVY	UNIVERSITY
EIIJLNTUVY	JUVENILITY	EIINSSTTTU	INSTITUTES
EIIJMNRTUY	INJURY TIME	EIIOORRSST	SORORITIES
EIIJMNSTTU	JUST-IN-TIME	EIIOPPSSTT	PETITS POIS
EIIKLLORST	KILOLITRES	EIIPRTTUVY	ERUPTIVITY
EIIKLNNSSS	SLINKINESS	EIJLMNPSTU	MINT JULEPS
EIIKLNORST	TRISKELION	EIJLMPPRTU	TRIPLE JUMP
EIIKMNPSSS	SKIMPINESS	EIKLNPRRSS	SPRINKLERS
EIIKNNNSSS	SKINNINESS	EIKNNORRST	NON-STRIKER
EIIKNQRSSU	QUIRKINESS	EIKNNOSSTT	STINKSTONE
EIILLLOSUV	LOUISVILLE	EIKNNPSSSU	SPUNKINESS
EIILLMMNNU	MILLENNIUM	EIKNOOPSSS	SPOOKINESS
EIILLMOPTY	IMPOLITELY	EIKORSTTTY	TROTSKYITE
EIILLMPRTU	MULTIPLIER	EILLLOORTT	TOILET ROLL
EILLLSSSTY	LISTLESSLY		
EILLMNOSST	MILLSTONES		
EILLMORSTU	LUMISTEROL		
EILLNNOSTY	INSOLENTLY		
EILLNOORRT	RITORNELLO		
EILLNOOSSW	WOOLLINESS		
EILLNOSTVW	TOWNSVILLE		
EILLNRTUVY	VIRULENTLY		
EILLOOPRSY	ROLY-POLIES		
EILLOPRSSV	OVERSPILLS		
EILLOPRSUY	PERILOUSLY		
EILLORTTTU	LITTERLOUT		
EILMMOPRSY	POLYMERISM		
EILMNOOOPS	MONOPOLIES,		
MONOPOLISE			
EILMNOOOPZ	MONOPOLIZE		
EILMNOOSST	MOTIONLESS		
EILMNOPSST	SIMPLETONS		
EILMNOPTTY	IMPOTENTLY		
EILMNOSSSS	LISSOMNESS		
EILMNRSSTY	MINSTRELSY		
EILMOOPRST	METROPOLIS		
EILMOPPRRY	IMPROPERLY		
EILNNNOOTV	NONVIOLENT		
EILNNOOSTW	LOW-TENSION		
EILNNOSSTV	INSOLVENTS		
EILNNRSSUU	UNRULINESS		
EILNOOPSSX	EXPLOSIONS		
EILNOORSTU	RESOLUTION		
EILNOORTUV	REVOLUTION		
EILNOPPRTW	NIPPLEWORT		
EILNOPPSSS	SLOPPINESS		
EILNOPPSTU	SUPPLETION		
EILNOPRSST	PORTLINESS		
EILNOPRSSU	REPULSIONS		
EILNOPSSUX	EXPULSIONS		
EILNORSSTY	STORY LINES		
EILNOSTUUV	VELUTINOUS		
EILNPQTTUU	QUINTUPLET		
EILNPRRTUY	PRURIENTLY		
EILNRSSSTU	SULTRINESS		
EILNRSSTTU	TURNSTILES		
EILOOPPRST	PETROPOLIS		
EILOORSSTT	SITOSTEROL		
EILOPPRSUV	PROPULSIVE		
EILOPRRSTU	PROTRUSILE		
EILOPRSTUY	PYROLUSITE		
EILOPRSTVY	SPORTIVELY,		
VERY PISTOL			
EILOPRSUVY	PREVIOUSLY		
EILOPSSTTT	TEST PILOTS		
EIMMNOPRSS	PERSIMMONS		
EIMNOOPTT	OMNIPOTENT		
EIMNNOSSYY	SYNONYMISE		
EIMNNOSYYZ	SYNONYMIZE		

EIMNNRSTTU	INSTRUMENT	EJNOOSSSUY	JOYOUSNESS	FFGIILNNSY	SNIFFINGLY
EIMNOOPRSS	SPOONERISM	EKLOOPRRSW	SLOPWORKER	FFGIINORTY	FORTIFYING
EIMNOOSTTT	TENOTOMIST	EKLOORRTUW	WORK-TO-RULE	FFGILNNSUY	SNUFFINGLY
EIMNOPRRTU	IMPORTUNER			FFGINOPTTU	OFF-PUTTING
EIMNOPRSTU	RESUMPTION	EKMNNOORSS	NONSMOKERS	FFILLRTUUY	FRUITFULLY
EIMNORSSST	STORMINESS	EKMNNOSTUY	MONKEY NUTS	FFILNRTUUU	UNFRUITFUL
EIMNOSTTZZ	MEZZOTINTS	EKNORRTTUU	TRUNK ROUTE	FFILOORRST	FIRST FLOOR
EIMNPSSSTU	STUMPINESS	EKOORRSTUW	OUTWORKERS	FFIORSSTTU	SOFT FRUITS
EIMNSSSTTU	SMUTTINESS	ELLLOSSSUY	SOULLESSLY	FGGHHIILNY	HIGH-FLYING
EIMOOQSSTU	MOSQUITOES	ELLOPSSSTY	SPOTLESSLY	FGGHIIINNT	INFIGHTING
EIMOPPSSSU	MISSUPPOSE	ELMNOOORSU	ENORMOUSLY	FGGIIINNNR	INFRINGING
EIMOPRRSTY	SPIROMETRY	ELMNOOSUVY	VENOMOUSLY	FGGIIINNSY	SIGNIFYING
EIMOPRSSTU	IMPOSTURES	ELMNORSUYY	NUMEROUSLY	FGGIIILNORY	GLORIFYING
EIMORSSTUY	MYSTERIOUS	ELMOOPRSUY	POLYMEROUS	FGHHIINSTT	NIGHT SHIFT
EIMRRSSTTU	MISTRUSTER	ELMOOPRTUY	PLEUROTOMY	FGHHIORRTT	FORTHRIGHT
EINNOOSSST	SNOOTINESS	ELMOOPRTXY	PROTOXYLEM	FGHHLOTTUU	THOUGHTFUL
EINNOPSSSU	SUSPENSION	ELMOOPSSUY	POLYSEMOUS	FGHIILNSTU	INSIGHTFUL
EINNOSSSTT	SNOTTINESS	ELNOSSSUUY	SENSUOUSLY	FGHIILNSTY	SHIFTINGLY
EINNOSSTTU	SUSTENTION	ELOPPRSTUY	SUPPLETORY	FGHIINNRSU	FURNISHING
EINOOOPPRS	OPPRESSION	EMMNOOORSU	MONOMEROUS	FGHIINORRY	HORRIFYING
EINOOOPPRS	OPPRESSION	EMMOOPRSTT	POSTMORTEM	FGHIINRSTT	FIRST NIGHT
EINOOPPRTW	POWER POINT	EMNNOOORTU	MOTONEURON	FGHIINSSTW	SWING SHIFT
EINOOPRRST	RESORPTION	EMNNOOOSST	MOONSTONES	FGHIIOTTTU	FIGHT IT OUT
EINOOPSSSS	POSSESSION	EMNOOOPRST	MONOPTEROS	FGHILLRTUY	RIGHTFULLY
EINOOPTTTT	TOTIPOTENT	EMNOORRSTT	TORMENTORS	FGHILOOSST	FOOTLIGHTS
EINOORSTTX	EXTORTIONS	EMNOPPRSST	PROMPTNESS	FGHINNOTUX	FOXHUNTING
EINOPPRSTY	PROPENSITY	EMNORRSTUU	SURMOUNTER	FGHINOOOTT	HOTFOOTING
EINOPRSSST	SPORTINESS	EMNORSSTUU	MENSTRUOUS	FGHINORSTT	FORTNIGHTS
EINOPSSSTT	SPOTTINESS	EMOOORRSST	STOREROOMS	FGIIINRTVY	VITRIFYING
EINOQRRTTU	TOURNIQUET	EMOOORRSTV	SERVOMOTOR	FGIIJNSTUY	JUSTIFYING
EINORRSSTV	INTROVERTS	ENNOOPPRRU	PROPER NOUN	FGIILLMNOY	MOLLIFYING
EINORSSTUX	EXTRUSIONS	ENNOOPPRSY	PROPONENTS	FGIILLNNUY	NULLIFYING
EINRSSSTTU	TRUSTINESS	ENOOPRRSSY	RESPONSORY	FGIILLNRTY	FLIRTINGLY,
EIOOOPRSTZ	SPOROZOITE	ENOOPRSSSU	POROUSNESS		TRIFLINGLY
EIOOPPRRRT	PROPRIETOR	ENOOPRSTTU	PORTENTOUS	FGIILLNSTY	STIFLINGLY
EIOOPRRSST	POSTERIORS	ENOPRSSSUY	SUSPENSORY	FGIILMNORU	LINGUIFORM
EIOOPRRSTY	REPOSITORY	EOOOPRRSSU	POROUSNESS	FGIILNOSUU	FULIGINOUS
EIOOPRSTXY	EXPOSITORY	EOOOPRSSUX	EXOSPOROUS	FGIIMMMNUY	MUMMIFYING
EIOORRSSTU	ROISTEROUS	EOOPPRRSSU	OPPRESSORS	FGIIMNORTY	MORTIFYING
EIOORRTVWY	IVORY TOWER	EOOPPRRSSU	PROSPEROUS	FGIIMNSTYY	MYSTIFYING
EIOPPRRSTY	PROSPERITY	EOOPPRSTTY	PROTOTYPES	FGIIMORRST	STRIGIFORM
EIOPPRSSTT	STROPPIEST	EOOPRRSSTU	PRO-OESTRUS	FGIINOTTTU	OUTFITTING
EIOPPRSTUV	SUPPORTIVE	EOOPRSSSSS	POSSESSORS	FGIINRRSTY	STIR-FRYING
EIOPRRSSUV	SUPERVISOR	EOOPRSSSSY	POSSESSORY	FGIKNNORTU	TUNING FORK
EIOPRRSTTU	TRIPTEROUS	EOORRSSTTU	STERTOROUS	FGILLNOOSW	FOLLOWINGS
EIOPRRSTUV	PROTRUSIVE	EOPPRRSSTU	SUPPRESSOR	FGILLNOTUY	FLOUTINGLY
EIOPRSTTTU	PROSTITUTE	EOPPRRSSTU	SUPPORTERS	FGILMMNOUX	FLUMMOXING
EIOQRSSTUU	TURQUOISES	EOPRSSSSUU	SOURPUSSES	FGILNNORWY	FROWNINGLY
EIORRRSSTT	TERRORISTS	FFFFIITTYY	FIFTY-FIFTY	FGLLNORUWY	WRONGFULLY
EIORRRSTUV	RETROVIRUS	FFGHHIOSTY	FIGHT SHY OF	FGLOORTUUY	FUTUROLOGY
EIPPRRSUVY	PRIVY PURSE	FFGHIILNSY	FLYING FISH,	FGNNOOSSSU	SONS-OF-GUNS
EJLLLLORSY	JELLY ROLLS		FLY-FISHING	FHILLMRTUY	MIRTHFULLY
EJMOSSSTTU	MOTS JUSTES	FFGHIIOPPR	HIPPOGRIFF	FHILMOORRR	HORROR FILM
EJNNSSSTUU	UNJUSTNESS	FFGHORSTUU	ROUGH STUFF		
EJ.OORRSSU	SOJOURNERS	FFGIILLLNU	FULFILLING		

FHILOPRSUW	WORSHIPFUL	
FHIMORSSTX	SIXTH FORMS	
FHINORRSTT	SHIRTFRONT	
FHLLLOSTUY	SLOTHFULLY	
FHLLOTUUYY	YOUTHFULLY	
FHLLRTTUUY	TRUTHFULLY	
FHLNRTTUUU	UNTRUTHFUL	
FHLOOORSSW	FLOOR SHOWS	
FIIKLNNSST	SKINFLINTS	
FIILMMNOOR	MONILIFORM	
FIILMPRSST	FILMSTRIPS	
FIIMNORTUY	UNIFORMITY	
FIIMOORSST	FORTISSIMO	
FIIMORSTTU	FORTUITISM	
FIIORSTTTU	FORTUITIST	
FIKLLOORST	FOLKLORIST	
FIKNORSTWY	FORTY WINKS	
FILLLMORSU	FLOURMILLS	
FILLOOSTUW	FOLLOW SUIT	
FILOOOPRSS	PORTFOLIOS	
FINOOOPSTT	SOFT OPTION	
FINOOPRSTT	FOOTPRINTS	
FIOORSTTUU	FORTUITOUS	
FLLMNORUUY	MOURNFULLY	
FLLRSTTUUY	TRUSTFULLY	
FLOOOOSSTT	FOOTSTOOLS	
FMNOOORRST	FRONT ROOMS	
FMOOOPRRST	STORMPROOF	
FOOORSSTTU	OUT OF SORTS	
GGGILLNRUY	GURGLINGLY	
GGGILNRSTU	STRUGGLING	
GGHHHIILST	HIGHLIGHTS	
GGHHIILNTT	NIGHTLIGHT	
GGHHINRSTU	HIGH-STRUNG	
GGHIIILRSW	WHIRLIGIGS	
GGIILLNNST	LIGHTNINGS	
GGHIILPRSY	PRIGGISHLY	
GGHILLSSUY	SLUGGISHLY	
GGIIIINSTV	GINGIVITIS	
GGIIIMNSSV	MISGIVINGS	
GGIIINNRTU	INTRIGUING	
GGIILLNNTY	TINGLINGLY	
GGIILNNSTY	STINGINGLY	
GGIILNNSWY	SWINGINGLY	
GGIILNPPRY	GRIPPINGLY	
GGILLLNOOR	LOGROLLING	
GGILLNTTUY	GLUTTINGLY	
GGILNNOOPR	PROLONGING	
GGILNNRTUY	GRUNTINGLY	
GGINNNNRUU	GUNRUNNING	
GGINOOPRRU	PROROGUING	
GGINOORTUW	OUTGROWING	
GGLLNNOOOW	WOLLONGONG	

GHHIILPSST	LIGHTSHIPS	
GHHIINOPST	HIGH POINTS	
GHHIINRSTT	NIGHTSHIRT	
GHHIIPRSTW	SHIPWRIGHT	
GHHILRSSTU	RUSHLIGHTS	
GHHINOPRTT	TRIPHTHONG	
GHHLOORTUY	THOROUGHLY	
GHHNORRTUU	RUN-THROUGH	
GHHOORTTUU	THROUGHOUT	
GHHOOTTTUU	THOUGHT-OUT	
GHHOPRTTUU	THROUGHPUT	
GHIIKNNNTU	UNTHINKING	
GHIILLMRTW	MILLWRIGHT	
GHIILLNOTW	LINLITHGOW	
GHIILLNRWY	WHIRLINGLY	
GHIILLOPTT	PILOT LIGHT	
GHIILNRTWY	WRITHINGLY	
GHIILNSSWY	SWISHINGLY	
GHIILNSTTW	WHITTLINGS	
GHIIMNPRTU	TRIUMPHING	
GHIINNORSU	NOURISHING	
GHIINNOSTU	OUTSHINING	
GHIINOPRSW	WORSHIPING	
GHILMNPTUY	THUMPINGLY	
GHILMOOORU	HOROLOGIUM	
GHILNOOPST	PHLOGISTON	
GHILNOOSTY	SOOTHINGLY	
GHILNORTTT	THROTTLING	
GHILNOSSST	SLINGSHOTS	
GHILNRRUYY	HURRYINGLY	
GHILOOORST	HOROLOGIST	
GHILOOPSYY	PHYSIOLOGY	
GHILOPSSTT	SPOTLIGHTS	
GHLLOOPTYY	TYPHLOLOGY	
GHLMOOOOSU	HOMOLOGOUS	
GHLMOOOPRY	MORPHOLOGY	
GHLNOOPSUW	SNOWPLOUGH	
GHMNOOOOSU	HOMOGONOUS	
GHMOOOSUYZ	HOMOZYGOUS	
GHNOOSSTTW	GHOST TOWNS	
GHOORSTTUW	OUTGROWTHS	
GIIIIMMNNZ	MINIMIZING	
GIIIILLNNST	INSTILLING	
GIIILNNTVY	INVITINGLY	
GIIIMMNNNZ	IMMUNIZING	
GIIIMMNNPRT	IMPRINTING	
GIIIMNOPTZ	OPTIMIZING	
GIIINNNOUZ	UNIONIZING	
GIIKLLNNSY	SLINKINGLY	
GIIKLMNRSY	SMIRKINGLY	
GIIKLNNPRS	SPRINKLING	
GIIKLNNSTW	TWINKLINGS	
GIIKLNNSTY	STINKINGLY	

GIIKLNRSTY	STRIKINGLY	
GIIKNRSTWY	SKYWRITING	
GIILLNNOPR	ROLLING PIN	
GIILLNOPRY	PILLORYING	
GIILLNPPRY	RIPPLINGLY	
GIILLNPPSY	SLIPPINGLY	
GIILLNRSWY	SWIRLINGLY	
GIILMMNSWY	SWIMMINGLY	
GIILMNNOTW	WILMINGTON	
GIILMNOORV	LIVING ROOM	
GIILMNOPSY	IMPOSINGLY	
GIILMOOSST	MISOLOGIST	
GIILNNOPRU	PURLOINING	
GIILNNOSTV	LIVINGSTON	
GIILNNRTUY	UNTIRINGLY	
GIILNOORSU	INGLORIOUS	
GIILNOOSST	SINOLOGIST	
GIILNPPRTY	TRIPPINGLY	
GIILNPRSST	SPLIT RINGS, STRIPLINGS	
GIILNRRSTY	STIRRINGLY	
GIILNSTTWY	TWISTINGLY	
GIILOORSTV	VIROLOGIST	
GIIMNNNORU	IN MOURNING	
GIIMNNOORT	MONITORING	
GIIMNNOPSU	UNIMPOSING	
GIIMNOORTZ	MOTORIZING	
GIIMNOQSTU	MISQUOTING	
GIIMNOSSTY	MISOGYNIST	
GIINNNSTTU	UNSTINTING	
GIINNOOPRT	PORTIONING	
GIINNOPRST	PISTON RING	
GIINNRSTTU	INTRUSTING	
GIINOTTTUW	OUTWITTING	
GIINPRRSSU	SURPRISING	
GIJNNOORSU	SOJOURNING	
GIKMNNNOOS	NONSMOKING	
GIKNNOOPRR	NORRKOPING	
GILLMOSSSY	SYLLOGISMS	
GILLNOPRRS	SPRING ROLL	
GILLNPUYYZ	PUZZLINGLY	
GILLNRSTUY	RUSTLINGLY	
GILLOORSUY	GLORIOUSLY	
GILMMNOOUY	IMMUNOLOGY	
GILMNOOOST	MONOLOGIST, NOMOLOGIST
GILMOOOPST	POMOLOGIST	
GILMOOSTYZ	ZYMOLOGIST	
GILNNNSTUY	STUNNINGLY	
GILNNOOSWY	SWOONINGLY	
GILNNORSTY	SNORTINGLY	
GILNOOOPSY	OLIGOPSONY	
GILNOOOSST	NOSOLOGIST	
GILNOOPPSY	OPPOSINGLY	
GILNOOPPTY	TYPING POOL	

GILNOOPSTY	STOOPINGLY	HILOOPSSTY	PHOTOLYSIS	IKLOOPPRSU	PRUSIK LOOP
GILNOPRSTY	SPORTINGLY	HILOPPSTUY	HIPPOLYTUS	IKMORSSTTY	TROTSKYISM
GILNOPSTYY	POLYGYNIST	HILORSSSTT	SHORT LISTS	IKORSSTTTY	TROTSKYIST
GILNORRWYY	WORRYINGLY	HIMMNOOTYY	HOMONYMITY	ILLMNOSUUY	LUMINOUSLY
GILNPRSUUY	USURPINGLY	HIMNOPSSTY	SYMPHONIST	ILLNOORSSU	ROUSSILLON
GILOOOPSTT	TOPOLOGIST	HINOOPTTXY	PHYTOTOXIN	ILLOOSSSVY	SOLVOLYSIS
GILOOOSSTZ	ZOOLOGISTS	HINOPSSTTY	HYPNOTISTS	ILMMNOOOPS	MONOPOLISM
GILOOPPRST	PROGLOTTIS	HIOOOSTTTU	SHOOT IT OUT	ILMNOOOPST	MONOPOLIST
GILOOPSTTY	TYPOLOGIST	HIOOPPRSST	TROOPSHIPS	ILMNOOOSTW	SLOW MOTION
GILOORRSUY	RIGOROUSLY	HIOOPRTTXY	THIXOTROPY	ILMNOOSUUV	VOLUMINOUS
GILOORSUVY	VIGOROUSLY	HIORSSTTUU	STRUTHIOUS	ILMNOSTUUY	MUTINOUSLY
GIMMNNOSSU	SUMMONSING	HLLOOPPRSY	SPOROPHYLL	ILMOORSTUY	TIMOROUSLY
GIMMNPSSUU	SUMMINGS-UP	HLMOORSUUY	HUMOROUSLY	ILMOOSTTXY	XYLOTOMIST
GIMMPPTUYY	GIPPY TUMMY	HLOPRSSUUU	SULPHUROUS	ILMOSTTUUY	TUMULOSITY
GIMMNNOORSS	MONSIGNORS	HMOOPRSTTU	PORTSMOUTH	ILNOOOSSYZ	OZONOLYSIS
GIMNNOOSTY	MONOGYNIST	HMOOPSSTUU	POSTHUMOUS	ILNOOPPRSU	PROPULSION
GIMNOOSSUY	MISOGYNOUS	HNOOOPSTTU	PHOTOTONUS	ILOOPPRSST	SPOILSPORT
GINNNORTUU	OUTRUNNING	HOORRSSTTY	SHORT STORY	ILOPPRSSUY	SPURIOUSLY
GINNOOPPST	POSTPONING	IIILLMMNSU	ILLUMINISM	ILORSTUUVY	VIRTUOUSLY
GINNOOPRSS	SPONSORING	IIILLMNSTU	ILLUMINIST	IMMOOPRSTU	PROSTOMIUM
GINNOPPSTU	UNSTOPPING	IIILMMOTTY	IMMOTILITY	IMMOPSSSUY	SYMPOSIUMS
GINOOPRTUU	OUTPOURING	IIILNOSSTV	VIOLINISTS	IMNNOSTYYY	SYNONYMITY
GINOPPRRTU	PURPORTING	IIIMNOOPST	IMPOSITION	IMNOOOPRST	PROMOTIONS
GINOPPRSTU	SUPPORTING	IIIMNOPRSS	MISPRISION	IMNOOOPSTT	MOOT POINTS
GINTTTTTUU	TUT-TUTTING	IIIMOPSSTV	POSITIVISM	IMNOOORSUV	OMNIVOROUS
GLNOOPSUYY	POLYGYNOUS	IIINNOSTTU	INTUITIONS	IMOOPRRSSY	PROMISSORY
GLNOOSTTUU	GLUTTONOUS	IIINOQORSU	INQUISITOR	IMOOPRSSTU	IMPOSTROUS
GMNNOOOSUY	MONOGYNOUS	IIINOQSTUU	INIQUITOUS	INOOOPPRRT	PROPORTION
GMNOOOORRST	STRONG ROOM	IIIOPSSTTV	POSITIVIST	INOOPPRSTU	PROTRUSION
GNNOOSTUWY	YOUNGSTOWN	IILLLLNWYY	WILLY-NILLY	INRSSTTTUU	UNIT TRUSTS
HHILOOPPSY	PHILOSOPHY	IILLLORSUY	ILLUSORILY	IOOOPRSSTU	ISOTROPOUS
HHILOOPPTY	PHOTOPHILY	IILLNOOPSS	POLLINOSIS	IOOPPRRSTU	POTPOURRIS
HHIMOOPRRZ	RHIZOMORPH	IILMNOOPSS	IMPLOSIONS	IOOPPRSSTU	PROPOSITUS
HHLMOPRTYY	POLYRHYTHM	IILMNOPSSU	IMPULSIONS	IOORSTTTUY	TORTUOSITY
HHOOPPRSSU	PHOSPHORUS	IILMNOPSTY	POSTLIMINY	KKLMMOOOSS	KOMSOMOLSK
HIIKLSSTTY	SKITTISHLY	IILMNOSTUY	LUMINOSITY	LLORSSTUUY	LUSTROUSLY
HIILLMNOST	MILLIONTHS	IILNNOOSTU	IN SOLUTION	LMOOOSTUXY	XYLOTOMOUS
HIILLNORTT	TRILLIONTH	IILNNOOTUV	INVOLUTION	LMOSTTUUUU	TUMULTUOUS
HIILMOOPSZ	ZOOPHILISM	IILNOOPSST	POSTILIONS	LNOOORSSUY	SONOROUSLY
HIILOPRSTY	HOLY SPIRIT	IIMNNOOOUX	OXONIUM ION	LOOPSTUUVV	VOLUPTUOUS
HIILORTTTY	LITHOTRITY	IIMNNOOSSU	INSOMNIOUS	LOORSTTUUY	TORTUOUSLY
HIILOSSSTY	HISTOLYSIS	IIMNORSSTU	MINOR SUITS	MMOOPRRSUU	RUMPUS ROOM
HIIMMNOPRS	MORPHINISM	IINNORSSTU	INTRUSIONS	MNNOOOOSTU	MONOTONOUS
HIINOORSST	ORNITHOSIS	IINOOOPPST	OPPOSITION	MNNOOSSUYY	SYNONYMOUS
HIIOOOPRST	OOPHORITIS	IINOOPRSSV	PROVISIONS	MNOOOPRRTY	PROMONTORY
HIIOOTTTYY	HOITY-TOITY	IINOPPRRST	IRRUPTIONS	MNOORSSSTW	SNOWSTORMS
HIKLMOOSTT	MILK TOOTHS	IINORSSSTU	SINISTROUS	NOOOPSSSSU	SOUP SPOONS
HILLOOPRSW	WHIRLPOOLS	IINORSTTTU	INSTITUTOR	OPRSTTUVVY	TOPSY-TURVY
HILMNORTTY	TRIMONTHLY	IINORSTTUU	NUTRITIOUS		
HILNORTUWY	UNWORTHILY	IIOOOPRSTV	OVIPOSITOR		
HILOOOPSUZ	ZOOPHILOUS	IIOOPPRSTU	PROPITIOUS		
		IIOPRSSTUU	SPIRITUOUS		
		IIORSTTUVY	VIRTUOSITY		

AAAAABBCDRR	ABRACADABRA	AAACCDEILMS	ACADEMICALS
AAAAADGJLRU	GUADALAJARA	AAACCDHIRTY	TACHYCARDIA
AAAABBCEINR	ARABICA BEAN	AAACCEEHSTT	ATTACHE CASE
AAAABBCHILN	BAHIA BLANCA	AAACCEHINPU	IPECACUANHA
AAAABBCORSS	CABORA BASSA	AAACCEILLOR	CALCEOLARIA
AAAABBINRST	SABBATARIAN	AAACCEILPRT	PALAEARCTIC
AAAABCCHILN	BACCHANALIA	AAACCHILLRY	ARCHAICALLY
AAAABDGHMNR	GRAND BAHAMA	AAACCIKNPTT	PANIC ATTACK
AAAABDIIRSU	SAUDI ARABIA	AAACCILLNRU	CANALICULAR
AAAABEKMSTT	MAKE A STAB AT	AAACCILLPRT	PARALLACTIC
AAAACDGLLNU	GUADALCANAL	AAACCILMNOT	ACCLAMATION
AAAACHHKKLM	MAKHACHKALA	AAACCILOSVV	CAVACO SILVA
AAAADEGLMMT	AMALGAMATED	AAACCILPSTT	CATAPLASTIC
AAAADELMRSS	DAR ES SALAAM	AAACCLMORTY	ACCLAMATORY
AAAAFGNOSTT	ANTOFAGASTA	AAACDEEGKLP	PACKAGE DEAL
AAAAFINRRST	RASTAFARIAN	AAACDEEIKMR	MADEIRA CAKE
AAAAGHIPPRR	PARAGRAPHIA	AAACDEEIMRR	CAMARADERIE
AAAAGJNNNRY	NARAYANGANJ	AAACDEEMRRY	CAMERA-READY
AAAAGORRSTZ	STARA ZAGORA	AAACDEERSWY	CARAWAY SEED
AAAAHHMRRST	MAHARASHTRA	AAACDEILMPR	PARAMEDICAL
AAAAILNRSTU	AUSTRALIANA	AAACDEILNRT	CARDINALATE
AAAAILRSSTU	AUSTRALASIA	AAACDEILPSS	PAS-DE-CALAIS
AAABBCEELLN	BALANCEABLE	AAACDEIMMRS	MACADAMISER
AAABBCILSST	SABBATICALS	AAACDEIMMRZ	MACADAMIZER
AAABCDDIRRY	BRADYCARDIA	AAACDGNNRRY	GRAND CANARY
AAABCDEIORS	SCARABAEOID	AAACDIINNSV	SCANDINAVIA
AAABCEEIMRT	BACTERAEMIA	AAACDILNOPS	PINA COLADAS
AAABCEGGGRS	BAGGAGE CARS	AAACDILOPRX	PARADOXICAL
AAABCEGGNRS	GARBAGE CANS	AAACEEFLMNS	MALFEASANCE
AAABCEGILLR	ALGEBRAICAL	AAACEENPPRS	APPEARANCES
AAABCEGKPSS	BACK PASSAGE	AAACEFLQSTU	CATAFALQUES
AAABCEHINRT	ABRANCHIATE	AAACEGILLNN	GALLINACEAN
AAABCELRTTT	ATTRACTABLE	AAACEGILMNO	EGOMANIACAL
AAABCIKLMRS	BLACK MARIAS	AAACEGIRRWY	CARRIAGEWAY
AAABDDENORW	DRAW A BEAD ON	AAACEHKRTTT	HEART ATTACK
AAABDEGGNOV	VAGABONDAGE	AAACEHLMNNP	PANCHEN LAMA
AAABDMORSSS	AMBASSADORS	AAACEHLMRST	STEAL A MARCH
AAABEEGLLSV	SALVAGEABLE	AAACEILLMNR	ALL-AMERICAN
AAABEHIMNPS	AMPHISBAENA	AAACEIMNNPR	PAN-AMERICAN
AAABEHINRSU	BEAUHARNAIS	AAACEINPSST	SEA CAPTAINS
AAABEIILNRS	RABELAISIAN	AAACELMNPTU	CAMPANULATE
AAABEIKLLLZ	ALKALIZABLE	AAACELMNRST	SACRAMENTAL
AAABEILLNUV	UNAVAILABLE	AAACELMOPRT	PARACETAMOL
AAABELLNPTU	UNPALATABLE	AAACENOPRRT	NOT CARE A RAP
AAABELNRRTW	WARRANTABLE	AAACERRSTTU	TARTAR SAUCE
AAABGHIOOPR	AGORAPHOBIA	AAACFIIORST	AFRO-ASIATIC
AAABHIOPRST	ASTRAPHOBIA	AAACFILLNTY	FANATICALLY
AAABHMPRRTU	BRAHMAPUTRA	AAACFIMNRRT	AIRCRAFTMAN
AAABIKNNNSS	BANANA SKINS	AAACGHIMNOP	PHAGOMANIAC
AAABILNNSST	SAINT ALBANS	AAACGHIMNSU	AS MUCH AGAIN
AAACCCEINPT	CAPACITANCE	AAACGHIPPRR	PARAGRAPHIC
AAACCCILSTT	CATACLASTIC	AAACGHNOOTT	CHATTANOOGA
AAACCCISTTU	CATACAUSTIC	AAACGIINNRU	AURIGNACIAN
AAACCDEIIMN	ACADEMICIAN	AAACGILMMRT	GRAMMATICAL

AAACGINNNRV	CARAVANNING	AAAEEGRTTVX	EXTRAVAGATE
AAACHIKPPRT	APPARATCHIK	AAAEEHINSST	ANAESTHESIA
AAACHILMRRT	MATRIARCHAL	AAAEEHLLSST	TALLAHASSEE
AAACHILNOTU	ANACOLUTHIA	AAAEELNPRTY	PENALTY AREA
AAACHILPRRT	PATRIARCHAL	AAAEERSTTVX	EXTRAVASATE
AAACIKLMNPS	PACK ANIMALS	AAAEFHHKMOS	MAKE A HASH OF
AAACILLMNRU	ANIMALCULAR	AAAEFLLMRSS	FALSE ALARMS
AAACILLMORT	CLAMATORIAL	AAAEGGILMNT	GAMETANGIAL
AAACILLNOTT	LACTATIONAL	AAAEGIILNRT	EGALITARIAN
AAACILLNRST	SCARLATINAL	AAAEGIKNSTT	TAKE AGAINST
AAACILLNSTY	SATANICALLY	AAAEGILMMNO	MEGALOMANIA
AAACILLQTUY	AQUATICALLY	AAAEGILNNST	EAST ANGLIAN
AAACILNNRST	LANCASTRIAN	AAAEGKLPTTU	TAKE A PLUG AT
AAACILPPRST	PARAPLASTIC	AAAEGNRTTVX	EXTRAVAGANT
AAADDDIMNNU	DAMAN AND DIU	AAAEGORSSSS	SARGASSO SEA
AAADDFHNRST	HARD-AND-FAST	AAAEHILNOPR	AEOLIAN HARP
AAADEEJNRWY	JAYAWARDENE	AAAEHIMNNRT	AMARANTHINE
AAADEELQRSU	A SQUARE DEAL	AAAEHIMOSST	HAEMOSTASIA
AAADEENRRTW	WEAR AND TEAR	AAAEHKLMPSS	MAKE A SPLASH
AAADEGILMNN	MAGDALENIAN	AAAEHPPRRSS	PARAPHRASES
AAADEGMNORR	ROAD MANAGER	AAAEIKLLNNT	ANTALKALINE
AAADEGMNPRR	RAMP AND RAGE	AAAEILMNNOT	EMANATIONAL
AAADEGNOTTV	TO ADVANTAGE	AAAEILNPSTT	PALATINATES
AAADEHLPRST	HARD PALATES	AAAEILPPRRS	REAPPRAISAL
AAADEHPPRRS	PARAPHRASED	AAAEIMNQRSU	AQUAMARINES
AAADEILMRRR	REAR ADMIRAL	AAAEIMOPRRT	AMOR PATRIAE
AAADEILNNRX	ALEXANDRINA	AAAEINSSSST	ASSASSINATE
AAADEILNRSS	ALESSANDRIA	AAAEKNPTTTU	TAKE A PUNT AT
AAADEILRRSV	ADVERSARIAL	AAAELLNRSTT	TARANTELLAS
AAADELLMPRT	MAR DEL PLATA	AAAELNRRSTV	TRANSVAALER
AAADELLOSTV	VALLE D'AOSTA	AAAENNPRSTU	PUNTA ARENAS
AAADELMNRSS	SALAMANDERS	AAAEPPRSSTU	APPARATUSES
AAADELMPPSS	ADAM'S APPLES	AAAFGHINNST	AFGHANISTAN
AAADENNPRST	TRANSPADANE	AAAFIKPRRSS	SAFARI PARKS
AAADGGINRRT	AGGRADATION	AAAGGGINRTV	AGGRAVATING
AAADGIILMNR	MADRIGALIAN	AAAGGHHIOPR	HAGIOGRAPHA
AAADGILNORT	GRADATIONAL	AAAGGINORTV	AGGRAVATION
AAADGINNPST	GIANT PANDAS	AAAGIIMNRRS	AGRARIANISM
AAADHHLPRYZ	HAPHAZARDLY	AAAGIINRSTT	SAGITTARIAN
AAADHILNRSS	HARD AS NAILS	AAAGILNNPQU	AQUAPLANING
AAADHMMMNSU	MUHAMMADANS	AAAGIMMNNRS	GRAMMARIANS
AAADIILNORR	RADIOLARIAN	AAAGLLORSSV	VARGAS LLOSA
AAADIILNORT	RADIATIONAL	AAAGMMRRRSS	MARRAM GRASS
AAADIKKLVVZ	VLADIKAVKAZ	AAAGMPPRSSS	PAMPAS GRASS
AAADILLLNOT	ALLANTOIDAL	AAAHILNPSXY	ANAPHYLAXIS
AAADILMORRS	RADIO ALARMS	AAAIILNORTV	VARIATIONAL
AAADILNNRSS	ARAN ISLANDS	AAAIIMNNRTU	MAURITANIAN
AAADILNORSV	SALVADORIAN	AAAIINNQRTU	ANTIQUARIAN
AAADINOPSTT	ADAPTATIONS	AAAILLNOSTV	SALVATIONAL
AAADLLNRSTW	WARTS AND ALL	AAAILLNOTUV	VALUATIONAL
AAADLNORSSV	SAN SALVADOR	AAAILLORSTT	SALTATORIAL
AAAEEGGLRSS	GARAGE SALES	AAAILMNOPPR	MALAPROPIAN
AAAEEGGMNST	STAGE-MANAGE	AAAILMRRSTT	MARTIAL ARTS
AAAEEGMSSTU	SAUSAGE MEAT	AAAILNNOSTY	ANALYSATION

AAAILNRSSTU	AUSTRALIANS, SATURNALIAS
AAAINNNNOST	SAN ANTONIAN
AAAINNOOPST	PIANO SONATA
AABBBEHRSTY	BABY'S-BREATH
AABBCDEINRT	BRACE AND BIT
AABBCDEKLLL	BLACKBALLED
AABBCDKLORS	BLACKBOARDS
AABBCEEELMR	EMBRACEABLE
AABBCEINORT	BICARBONATE
AABBCIJKRST	JACKRABBITS
AABBDDDDENOR	BED AND BOARD
AABBDDEORRS	BREADBOARDS
AABBDEEIRTV	ABBREVIATED
AABBDEEKRST	BREADBASKET
AABBDEEORRV	BEAVERBOARD
AABBEEIRRTV	REBARBATIVE
AABBEEKLLRR	BALLBREAKER
AABBEEKLNRU	UNBREAKABLE
AABBEFGLRST	FLABBERGAST
AABBEGILLNR	BALL BEARING
AABBEHIILNT	INHABITABLE
AABBEHNRSUW	BHUBANESWAR
AABBEIILLNV	ABBEVILLIAN
AABBEIIRRST	BARBARITIES
AABBEIORRTV	ABBREVIATOR
AABBEIRRTTU	BARBITURATE
AABBGIINRRZ	BARBARIZING
AABBIIILMNO	BIBLIOMANIA
AABBKKMOOOO	AMABOKOBOKO
AABBLORRSUY	BARBAROUSLY
AABCCDDIRRY	BRADYCARDIC
AABCCDEIIIT	ABIETIC ACID
AABCCDEKKRT	BACKTRACKED
AABCCEEHHIRS	BEACHCHAIRS
AABCCEILPRT	PRACTICABLE
AABCCEKKPRS	BACKPACKERS
AABCCELLMUU	ACCUMULABLE
AABCCELNOTU	ACCOUNTABLE
AABCCERRUUY	BUREAUCRACY
AABCCGIKKNP	BACKPACKING
AABCCILPRTY	PRACTICABLY
AABCCKNNOTU	BANK ACCOUNT
AABCCLNRRUU	CARBUNCULAR
AABCDDEEKLP	BACKPEDALED
AABCDDIKMNO	DIAMONDBACK
AABCDEEEERTX	EXACERBATED
AABCDEEFLRY	BAREFACEDLY
AABCDEFIIIL	ACIDIFIABLE
AABCDEHIMMR	CHAMBERMAID
AABCDEHKNRS	BACKHANDERS
AABCDEIILNT	INDICATABLE
AABCDEIKLLM	BLACKMAILED
AABCDEILNST	ELASTIC BAND
AABCDEINOOR	RADIO BEACON
AABCDEKNRRS	BANKER'S CARD
AABCDELMNRU	CANDELABRUM
AABCDELNOTU	OUTBALANCED
AABCDEORRST	BROADCASTER
AABCDGGIOOR	BRAGGADOCIO
AABCDGIINRR	BARRICADING
AABCDGKLRSU	BLACKGUARDS
AABCDHKLORS	CHALKBOARDS
AABCDHMNORY	RHABDOMANCY
AABCDIINOST	ABDICATIONS
AABCDIIORTU	BIQUADRATIC
AABCDINOORR	RADIOCARBON
AABCEEEELLPR	REPLACEABLE
AABCEEELRRT	RETRACEABLE
AABCEEFLRRT	REFRACTABLE
AABCEEFNORR	FORBEARANCE
AABCEEHILMP	IMPEACHABLE
AABCEEHKLRT	LEATHERBACK
AABCEEHLMPS	PEACH MELBAS
AABCEEHMNRT	ANTECHAMBER
AABCEEILLMR	RECLAIMABLE
AABCEEILMNV	AMBIVALENCE
AABCEEILNPS	INESCAPABLE
AABCEEILNRS	INCREASABLE
AABCEEILPPR	APPRECIABLE
AABCEELNORV	OVERBALANCE
AABCEELNRST	TABERNACLES
AABCEELORTT	BRACTEOLATE
AABCEELRRTT	RETRACTABLE
AABCEELRSTT	SCATTERABLE
AABCEELRTTX	EXTRACTABLE
AABCEFIIRTV	FABRICATIVE
AABCEFLMNOY	FLAMBOYANCE
AABCEFLNOTU	CONFABULATE
AABCEFLRRTU	FRACTURABLE
AABCEGIRRRS	CARRIER BAGS
AABCEGLMNNS	BLANCMANGES
AABCEHILLRY	HEBRAICALLY
AABCEHILMNR	CHAMBERLAIN
AABCEHILSST	CHASTISABLE
AABCEHLNPUX	BLUE PANCHAX
AABCEHLNSTU	STAUNCHABLE
AABCEHLPRSU	PURCHASABLE
AABCEHMRRST	STAR CHAMBER
AABCEHNOOTV	A NOTCH ABOVE
AABCEIILNNS	CANNIBALISE
AABCEIILNNZ	CANNIBALIZE
AABCEIINPUV	BUPIVACAINE
AABCEIINSTU	BEAUTICIANS
AABCEIKLLMR	BLACKMAILER
AABCEILLLOZ	LOCALIZABLE
AABCEILMNRY	CARBYLAMINE
AABCEILNPSY	INESCAPABLY
AABCEILNRTT	INTRACTABLE

455

AABCEILPPRY	APPRECIABLY
AABCEIMNPRR	PRECAMBRIAN
AABCEIOQRSU	AQUAEROBICS
AABCEIRSTTV	ABSTRACTIVE
AABCEKKLMRT	BLACK MARKET
AABCEKLMSSS	BLACK MASSES
AABCEKLPPRS	BACKSLAPPER
AABCEKNRRSU	SAARBRUCKEN
AABCELLOORT	COLLABORATE
AABCELLQRTU	RACQUETBALL
AABCELMOPSS	COMPASSABLE
AABCELOORST	CAR-BOOT SALE
AABCELORSXY	CARBOXYLASE
AABCELORTXY	CARBOXYLATE
AABCENOPPRR	CARBON PAPER
AABCENOPRST	ABSORPTANCE
AABCEOORTTZ	AZOTOBACTER
AABCERRSTUU	BUREAUCRATS
AABCFGIINRT	FABRICATING
AABCFIINORT	FABRICATION
AABCGHIOOPR	AGORAPHOBIC
AABCGHIOPRR	BAROGRAPHIC
AABCGIILNRT	CALIBRATING
AABCGILNNNU	UNBALANCING
AABCGINRSTT	ABSTRACTING
AABCGLRRSTU	CAT BURGLARS
AABCHIINNTY	INHABITANCY
AABCHIINORT	BRACHIATION
AABCHILNSTU	BALUCHISTAN
AABCHIOPRST	ASTRAPHOBIC
AABCIIILMTY	AMICABILITY
AABCIIILPTY	PLACABILITY
AABCIILMNNS	CANNIBALISM
AABCIILNORT	CALIBRATION
AABCIILSTUY	CAUSABILITY
AABCILLMNTU	LACTALBUMIN
AABCILLNOTY	BOTANICALLY
AABCILNNRUU	INCUNABULAR
AABCILNRTTY	INTRACTABLY
AABCILOSTTY	BIOCATALYST
AABCINNOORT	CARBONATION
AABCINORSTT	ABSTRACTION
AABCKLMOORS	BLACKAMOORS
AABCLLLRSTY	CRYSTAL BALL
AABCLLNNNOS	CANNONBALLS
AABCLPRSSUU	SUBSCAPULAR
AABDDDEFMNU	DEAF-AND-DUMB
AABDDEGGORR	DAGGERBOARD
AABDDEGLLLR	GALL BLADDER
AABDDEHHNRT	HANDBREADTH
AABDDEHMORY	HEBDOMADARY
AABDDEILSSU	DISSUADABLE
AABDDEINOST	BASTINADOED
AABDDEIRSST	BASTARDISED
AABDDEIRSTZ	BASTARDIZED
AABDDELNNOY	ABANDONEDLY
AABDDELNSST	SANDBLASTED
AABDDNRSSTU	SUBSTANDARD
AABDEEFKRST	BREAKFASTED
AABDEEHHRRS	HABERDASHER
AABDEEHINRR	HAREBRAINED
AABDEEILLMP	IMPLEADABLE
AABDEELNSST	DATABLENESS
AABDEELPRSU	PERSUADABLE
AABDEEMRRSS	EMBARRASSED
AABDEGGORSU	BROAD GAUGES
AABDEGHILNS	BANGLADESHI
AABDEGILNOS	DIAGNOSABLE
AABDEHHIRRT	HAIRBREADTH
AABDEHINRSW	BRAINWASHED
AABDEHLRSTT	HALBERSTADT
AABDEHRSTWY	BREADTHWAYS
AABDEIILLNT	DENTILABIAL
AABDEIILNSV	INADVISABLE
AABDEIILRTY	READABILITY
AABDEIKNORT	DEBARKATION
AABDEILLNOT	LABIODENTAL
AABDEILLRVY	ADVERBIALLY
AABDEILNOUV	UNAVOIDABLE
AABDEILORRT	LABRADORITE
AABDEIMRTUV	ADUMBRATIVE
AABDEINOSST	BASTINADOES
AABDEKORSST	SKATEBOARDS
AABDELLNSTU	UNBALLASTED
AABDELNORST	BAROTSELAND
AABDELNRSST	SANDBLASTER
AABDELNRSTU	SALAD BURNET
AABDELRSSTU	BALUSTRADES
AABDEMNNNOS	ONE-MAN BANDS
AABDEMNNNOT	ABANDONMENT
AABDEMNRSST	BANDMASTERS
AABDEMRSTTU	MASTURBATED
AABDEOPRSST	PASTEBOARDS
AABDFIIINPS	SPINA BIFIDA
AABDGGGINNS	SANDBAGGING
AABDGIILRTY	GRADABILITY
AABDGIMNOSV	VAGABONDISM
AABDGIMNRTU	ADUMBRATING
AABDHIILNTU	HABITUDINAL
AABDHIKLNOY	BANK HOLIDAY
AABDHINNOPS	ABANDON SHIP
AABDHIOSTTV	BODHISATTVA
AABDHLOPRSS	SPLASHBOARD
AABDHMMOORY	RHABDOMYOMA
AABDIILLTUY	LAUDABILITY
AABDIILMNTY	DAMNABILITY
AABDIILMQRU	LIQUIDAMBAR
AABDIINNRRS	BRAIN DRAINS

AABDIJOORSU	OUIJA BOARDS
AABDIMNORSU	SAMURAI BOND
AABDIMNORTU	ADUMBRATION
AABDLLMOOPS	BLOOD PLASMA
AABDMOORRRT	MORTARBOARD
AABDNOOPRSX	PANDORA'S BOX
AABEEEEGRRV	EAGER BEAVER
AABEEEFKRRS	SAFEBREAKER
AABEEEGLLNR	ENLARGEABLE
AABEEELRRST	TALEBEARERS
AABEEFHORST	FEATHER BOAS
AABEEFLLRTT	FLATTERABLE
AABEEGINNRT	ANNABERGITE
AABEEGLMNTU	AUGMENTABLE
AABEEGLMSSS	ASSEMBLAGES
AABEEHILNTZ	ELIZABETHAN
AABEEHILPST	ALPHABETISE
AABEEHILPTZ	ALPHABETIZE
AABEEHKLNSU	UNSHAKEABLE
AABEEHLRSTY	BREATHALYSE
AABEEIILLNN	INALIENABLE
AABEEILLNPX	EXPLAINABLE
AABEEILLNRT	INALTERABLE
AABEEILNPRS	INSEPARABLE
AABEEILORTV	ELABORATIVE
AABEEILPRRR	IRREPARABLE
AABEEINRRRT	TRAINBEARER
AABEEINRRST	BRAINTEASER
AABEEINSSTT	BASTNAESITE
AABEEJKRRSW	JAWBREAKERS
AABEEKLNPSU	UNSPEAKABLE
AABEEKLRRSW	LAW-BREAKERS
AABEELLMNOT	BALLETOMANE
AABEELLNRTU	UNALTERABLE
AABEELLORTY	ELABORATELY
AABEELLPRRS	PALLBEARERS
AABEELLPRSU	PLEASURABLE
AABEELMNSST	TAMABLENESS
AABEELMPRTU	PERAMBULATE
AABEELMPTTT	ATTEMPTABLE
AABEELNORST	TREASONABLE
AABEELNRTTU	ENTABLATURE
AABEELNSSSV	SAVABLENESS
AABEELPRSTT	BREASTPLATE
AABEELRRSTU	TREASURABLE
AABEELRRSTV	TRAVERSABLE
AABEELRRTWY	BARLEY WATER
AABEELRSTTW	WATER TABLES
AABEEMMOPRT	MEPROBAMATE
AABEFFIILLS	FALSIFIABLE
AABEFGIILMN	MAGNIFIABLE
AABEFHILNOS	FASHIONABLE
AABEFIILLMP	AMPLIFIABLE
AABEFIILLQU	QUALIFIABLE
AABEFIILSST	SATISFIABLE
AABEFILLMMN	INFLAMMABLE
AABEFILLRTT	FILTRATABLE
AABEFLLNPPU	UNFLAPPABLE
AABEGGGMOOR	BAGGAGE ROOM
AABEGIILNNV	INVAGINABLE
AABEGIKLNRW	LAWBREAKING
AABEGILNORT	ELABORATING
AABEGIRRRTU	ARBITRAGEUR
AABEGLLMOST	MEGALOBLAST
AABEGLNORRR	BARREL ORGAN
AABEGLRRSUY	BARLEY SUGAR
AABEHIILLNN	ANNIHILABLE
AABEHILNRST	TARNISHABLE
AABEHILORUV	BEHAVIOURAL
AABEHINRRSW	BRAINWASHER
AABEHLPRRSV	PHRASAL VERB
AABEIILLMSS	ASSIMILABLE
AABEIILLSTY	SALEABILITY
AABEIILMMOR	MEMORABILIA
AABEIILMNTY	AMENABILITY
AABEIILNRRT	LIBERTARIAN
AABEIILNSSX	AIX-LES-BAINS
AABEIILRTWY	WEARABILITY
AABEIKMNORT	EMBARKATION
AABEILLLRTY	BILATERALLY
AABEILLOPRZ	POLARIZABLE
AABEILLRRST	LIBERAL ARTS
AABEILLRRTZ	TRAILBLAZER
AABEILLRVZZ	BRAZZAVILLE
AABEILMMRSU	BARIUM MEALS
AABEILMORTZ	AMORTIZABLE
AABEILNOORT	ELABORATION
AABEILNPRSY	INSEPARABLY
AABEILNRSSU	BELARUSSIAN
AABEILNRSTT	TRANSITABLE
AABEILNSSTU	SUSTAINABLE
AABEILOPRVZ	VAPORIZABLE
AABEILPRRRY	IRREPARABLY
AABEILPRTUU	BUILT-UP AREA
AABEIMNRRTT	ARBITRAMENT
AABEIMPRSTV	VAMPIRE BATS
AABEINOPSTT	BE AT PAINS TO
AABEINORRST	ABERRATIONS
AABEIOPPRTV	APPROBATIVE
AABEKLNPSUY	UNSPEAKABLY
AABELLLOSWW	SWALLOWABLE
AABELLORSUV	SLAVE LABOUR
AABELLORTTY	BATTLE ROYAL
AABELLPRSUY	PLEASURABLY
AABELMMNSSY	ASSEMBLYMAN
AABELNORSSY	TREASONABLY
AABELOPRRTY	PORTRAYABLE
AABELORSSST	ALBATROSSES

457

AABELPRSSSU	SURPASSABLE	AACCCEJKKRR	CRACKERJACK
AABFIKNORSU	BURKINA-FASO	AACCCGHIOPR	CACOGRAPHIC
AABFLLMOOSY	BOYOMA FALLS	AACCCIIILRT	CICATRICIAL
AABFLLNPPUY	UNFLAPPABLY	AACCCILMSTY	CATACLYSMIC
AABGGGGINNN	GANG-BANGING	AACCCNNOTUY	ACCOUNTANCY
AABGHHIOOPP	PHAGOPHOBIA	AACCDDEIINS	CANDIDACIES
AABGHIINTTU	HABITUATING	AACCDEEELRT	ACCELERATED
AABGHILNOOP	ANGLOPHOBIA	AACCDEELNOR	ACCELERANDO
AABGIILNORS	ABORIGINALS	AACCDEENTTU	ACCENTUATED
AABGIILNOST	SAILING BOAT	AACCDEGHRRS	CHARGE CARDS
AABGIIMNNOT	ABOMINATING	AACCDEHNORS	ARCHDEACONS
AABGIINRRTT	ARBITRATING	AACCDEIILLT	DIALECTICAL
AABGIKNNSSV	SAVINGS BANK	AACCDEIIMMS	ACADEMICISM
AABGILMNRSU	SUBMARGINAL	AACCDEIMNOP	ACCOMPANIED
AABGINOORST	ABROGATIONS	AACCDEIRRTU	CARICATURED
AABGIRSSSTU	BASS GUITARS	AACCDELMTUU	ACCUMULATED
AABGKLOOTUW	GO WALKABOUT	AACCDEMMOOT	ACCOMMODATE
AABGLLMORSY	SYLLABOGRAM	AACCDEORSUU	CARDUACEOUS
AABHIILORTT	HABILITATOR	AACCDERSSTY	SCAREDY CATS
AABHIILSTWY	WASHABILITY	AACCDGIIILN	ALGINIC ACID
AABHIINNSTT	INHABITANTS	AACCDHILNOR	CHANCROIDAL
AABHIINOSTT	HABITATIONS	AACCDHPRSST	SCRATCHPADS
AABHIINOTTU	HABITUATION	AACCDIIILRT	DIACRITICAL
AABHIMNPSST	BATSMANSHIP	AACCDIILMNO	MALONIC ACID
AABHIMRSTVZ	BAR MITZVAHS	AACCDIOSSTU	CAUSTIC SODA
AABHLLLOOSU	HULLABALOOS	AACCEEFILNT	CALEFACIENT
AABIIILRTVY	VARIABILITY	AACCEEINRRT	INCARCERATE
AABIIILSTTY	SATIABILITY	AACCEELLNOT	COLLECTANEA
AABIIKLLTTY	TALKABILITY	AACCEELNSTU	ACAULESCENT
AABIILLNORT	LIBRATIONAL	AACCEELORRT	ACCELERATOR
AABIILLPPTY	PALPABILITY	AACCEENNOTT	CONCATENATE
AABIILLSTVY	SALVABILITY	AACCEFHSTTY	SAFETY CATCH
AABIILMNRUU	ALBUMINURIA	AACCEFILNOT	CALEFACTION
AABIILNORTV	VIBRATIONAL	AACCEFLORTY	CALEFACTORY
AABIILORSTU	ATRABILIOUS	AACCEGHILNR	ARCHANGELIC
AABIILRRRTY	ARBITRARILY	AACCEGHNRTT	GNATCATCHER
AABIIMNNOOT	ABOMINATION	AACCEGIKNPS	PACKING CASE
AABIINORRTT	ARBITRATION	AACCEGILMOR	ACROMEGALIC
AABILLRSUXY	SUBAXILLARY	AACCEGILORT	CATEGORICAL
AABILMNORTY	ABNORMALITY	AACCEGORRTY	ERGATOCRACY
AABILNOOPRT	PROBATIONAL	AACCEHHMOST	STOMACHACHE
AABILNORTUY	ABLUTIONARY	AACCEHHPRST	CATCHPHRASE
AABILNOSTTU	TABULATIONS	AACCEHIIMNN	MECHANICIAN
AABILNSSTTU	SUBSTANTIAL	AACCEHILLNT	CHALCANLITE
AABINOOPPRT	APPROBATION	AACCEHILMOT	MACHICOLATE
AABIORRRSTT	ARBITRATORS	AACCEHILMST	CATECHISMAL
AABKKOORRSU	KOOKABURRAS	AACCEHIOORZ	ARCHAEOZOIC
AABLOPRRTUY	LABOUR PARTY	AACCEHIRSST	CATACHRESIS
AABNOORRSTW	NARROW BOATS	AACCEHLNNHO	NONCHALANCE
AABNOORSTTY	ASTROBOTANY	AACCEIILMST	ACCLIMATISE
AACCCDENORS	ACCORDANCES	AACCEIILMTZ	ACCLIMATIZE
AACCCDEOSUY	CYCADACEOUS	AACCEILLSTY	ASCETICALLY
AACCCDHRRST	SCRATCHCARD	AACCEILMPRT	MALPRACTICE
AACCCEENPST	ACCEPTANCES	AACCEILNORU	COUNCIL AREA

AACCEILNOSS	ACCESSIONAL
AACCEILORSS	ACCESSORIAL
AACCEILOSSU	SALICACEOUS
AACCEIMNOPR	ACCOMPANIER
AACCEINOPTT	ACCEPTATION
AACCEINOTTU	ACQUITTANCE
AACCEIORSTU	AUTOCRACIES
AACCEIRRSTU	CARICATURES
AACCEISSTUV	ACCUSATIVES
AACCEKLLNOY	CYCLOALKANE
AACCEKMNOTT	MAKE CONTACT
AACCELNRTUU	CARUNCULATE
AACCELPRSTU	SPECTACULAR
AACCELRTTUU	ACCULTURATE
AACCENNORSS	CARCASSONNE
AACCENOPRRY	COPARCENARY
AACCENRSSTU	CRUSTACEANS
AACCFIIILRS	SACRIFICIAL
AACCFIILLPY	PACIFICALLY
AACCFIILRTY	FARCICALITY
AACCFIIMNOR	ACINACIFORM
AACCFINNRSS	FRANCISCANS
AACCGHIMOPR	MACROPHAGIC
AACCGIINNTV	VACCINATING
AACCGILLNTU	CALCULATING
AACCHIIMRST	CHARISMATIC
AACCHIINRST	ANARCHISTIC
AACCHIINRTT	ANTHRACITIC
AACCHILLOTY	CHAOTICALLY
AACCHILMNOR	MONARCHICAL
AACCHILMOST	STOMACHICAL
AACCHILNOTU	ANACOLUTHIC
AACCHLNOOTY	CHOANOCYTAL
AACCIILLNTY	ACTINICALLY
AACCIILMPRT	IMPRACTICAL
AACCIILNNOT	CALCINATION
AACCIILNSTT	ANTICLASTIC
AACCIILORSS	SACROILIACS
AACCIILSTTT	STALACTITIC
AACCIINNOTV	VACCINATION
AACCIINOSTU	ACOUSTICIAN
AACCIINRTTZ	CICATRIZANT
AACCIINTTVY	VATICAN CITY
AACCILLLNOY	LACONICALLY
AACCILLNOTU	CALCULATION
AACCILLNRTU	CURTAIN CALL
AACCILLNSUU	CANALICULUS
AACCILLPRTY	PRACTICALLY
AACCILLSTUY	CAUSTICALLY
AACCILNOSST	CLASS ACTION
AACCILNOSTU	SACCULATION
AACCILNPRTU	UNPRACTICAL
AACCILOPPTY	APOCALYPTIC
AACCILOPSUY	CAPACIOUSLY

AACCILRRSUW	CIRCULAR SAW
AACCIMNOPST	ACCOMPANIST
AACCINOORTT	COARCTATION
AACCINOSSTU	ACCUSATIONS
AACCIORRSTY	ARISTOCRACY
AACCKLLMORS	ALARM CLOCKS
AACCLLORSTU	CALCULATORS
AACCLMORTUU	ACCUMULATOR
AACCLNORTTU	CONTRACTUAL
AACCNNOSTTU	ACCOUNTANTS
AACCOOPRRSU	ACROCARPOUS
AACCORRSTTY	STRATOCRACY
AACDDDEIJTU	ADJUDICATED
AACDDEEEHLR	CLEAR-HEADED
AACDDEEELST	DE-ESCALATED
AACDDEEHMRS	DEAD MARCHES
AACDDEEIMPS	AIDES-DE-CAMP
AACDDEEIPTT	DECAPITATED
AACDDEGLNOO	DODECAGONAL
AACDDEHINPP	HANDICAPPED
AACDDEHLNRS	CRASH-LANDED
AACDDEILNOR	ENDOCARDIAL
AACDDEILNSS	SCANDALISED
AACDDEILNSZ	SCANDALIZED
AACDDIJORTU	ADJUDICATOR
AACDEEEGHRST	GATECRASHED
AACDEEHILMX	HEXADECIMAL
AACDEEHNRTU	HARDECANUTE
AACDEEIILNT	ACETANILIDE
AACDEEIIRTV	ERADICATIVE
AACDEEILRTV	DECLARATIVE
AACDEEIMNPT	EMANCIPATED
AACDEEINRST	ASCERTAINED
AACDEEIPPRT	APPRECIATED
AACDEEIRTTV	REACTIVATED
AACDEELLSTT	CASTELLATED
AACDEELMSTU	EMASCULATED
AACDEELRTUW	CATERWAULED
AACDEEMNNTV	ADVANCEMENT
AACDEENNSTT	ATTENDANCES
AACDEENQRSU	SQUARE DANCE
AACDEFGLMOU	CAMOUFLAGED
AACDEFIILTT	FACILITATED
AACDEFILNOT	DEFALCATION
AACDEGHHNNS	CHANGE HANDS
AACDEGHHNRS	CHARGE HANDS
AACDEGIIMNT	DIAMAGNETIC
AACDEGIINRT	ERADICATING
AACDEGIMNRT	DEMARCATING
AACDEGMNOPR	CAMPO GRANDE
AACDEHILLPY	EDAPHICALLY
AACDEHILORS	ICOSAHEDRAL
AACDEHINOTT	ANTICATHODE
AACDEHINPPR	HANDICAPPER

AACDEHINRSS	SEDAN CHAIRS	AACDIINNOTY	CYANIDATION
AACDEHINRST	CANTHARIDES	AACDIIOPRTY	RADIOPACITY
AACDEHINRTU	HARDICANUTE	AACDIIORRTV	DIVARICATOR
AACDEHMOORR	CHOREODRAMA	AACDILLMNOY	NOMADICALLY
AACDEIILPST	CAPITALISED	AACDILLMNYY	DYNAMICALLY
AACDEIILPTZ	CAPITALIZED	AACDILLRSTY	DRASTICALLY
AACDEIINNRT	INCARDINATE	AACDILNOSTY	ANISODACTYL
AACDEIINORT	ERADICATION	AACDILNPSST	LANDSCAPIST
AACDEIINPTT	ANTICIPATED	AACDILORTTY	ARTIODACTYL
AACDEIIORTV	RADIOACTIVE	AACDILOSUUY	AUDACIOUSLY
AACDEIIPRST	PAEDIATRICS	AACDIMOORST	SARCOMATOID
AACDEILMNOT	DECLAMATION	AACDINNOOTU	COADUNATION
AACDEILMNTU	CALUMNIATED	AACDLLORTYY	LOYALTY CARD
AACDEILNORT	DECLARATION, REDACTIONAL	AACDMMNNOST	COMMANDANTS
AACDEILNOTU	EDUCATIONAL	AACDMOORSTU	CATADROMOUS
AACDEILNRSS	RADICALNESS, SCANDALISER	AACEEEEHLMOT	HAEMATOCELE
AACDEILNRSZ	SCANDALIZER	AACEEEHPRST	SPACE HEATER
AACDEILPTTU	CAPITULATED	AACEEENPRST	EASTERN CAPE
AACDEILRSTT	STRAITLACED	AACEEFFMNRT	RAMAN EFFECT
AACDEILRTTU	ARTICULATED	AACEEFIMNSS	MISFEASANCE
AACDEILRTTY	DAIRY CATTLE	AACEEFLLPTT	CLEFT PALATE
AACDEIMNNOP	PANDEMONIAC	AACEEFNNNOS	NONFEASANCE
AACDEIMNORT	DEMARCATION	AACEEGHLMPY	MEGACEPHALY
AACDEIMNORY	AERODYNAMIC	AACEEGHLRST	CASTLEREAGH
AACDEINOTUV	COADUNATIVE	AACEEGHNOPR	CHAPERONAGE
AACDEIOPRTT	DECAPITATOR	AACEEGHRRST	GATECRASHER
AACDEIORRST	ERADICATORS	AACEEGILLLY	ELEGIACALLY
AACDEIORTTV	DEACTIVATOR	AACEEGILLNS	ALLEGIANCES
AACDELMNNOR	ROMAN CANDLE	AACEEGILLNV	EVANGELICAL
AACDELMORTY	DECLAMATORY	AACEEGINPRT	PARAGENETIC
AACDELNPTTY	PENTADACTYL	AACEEGMMORT	MACROGAMETE
AACDELNSSST	SANDCASTLES	AACEEHHLTUX	HEXATEUCHAL
AACDELORRTY	DECLARATORY	AACEEHHMMOR	HAEMACHROME
AACDEMORRRU	ARMOURED CAR	AACEEHILNST	CHATELAINES
AACDEMRRSST	MASTER CARDS	AACEEHIMNPT	TAPE MACHINE
AACDFHINRST	HANDICRAFTS	AACEEHIMPPR	PAPIER-MACHE
AACDFIILRRT	FRATRICIDAL	AACEEHINSTT	ANAESTHETIC
AACDFIINOOS	AFICIONADOS	AACEEHKPSST	CHEAPSKATES
AACDGGHIIST	HAGGADISTIC	AACEEHLMNOP	ENCEPHALOMA
AACDGHIOPRR	CARDIOGRAPH	AACEEHLNNSV	CLEAN-SHAVEN
AACDGILNNPS	LANDSCAPING	AACEEHMPRST	SPERMATHECA
AACDGILNNVY	ADVANCINGLY	AACEEHPPRSS	PAPER CHASES
AACDGILNPRY	PLAYING CARD	AACEEHRRTTT	TETRARCHATE
AACDGIMRRTU	DRAMATURGIC	AACEEIIMNRS	AMERICANISE
AACDGINNSST	SAND-CASTING	AACEEIIMNRZ	AMERICANIZE
AACDGORSSTU	COASTGUARDS	AACEEIIMPST	SEPTICAEMIA
AACDHIIOPRS	APHRODISIAC	AACEEIJLTUV	EJACULATIVE
AACDHLNOSYY	HALCYON DAYS	AACEEIKLMNR	AMERICAN ELK
AACDHMOPRSY	PSYCHODRAMA	AACEEILLMNS	MESALLIANCE, MISCELLANEA
AACDIILNOTT	DICTATIONAL	AACEEILLRTV	VARICELLATE
AACDIILNOTU	ACIDULATION	AACEEILNRTT	INTERCALATE
AACDIILNSTV	VANDALISTIC	AACEEILPRST	ALTARPIECES
AACDIILORTT	DICTATORIAL	AACEEILRRST	SECRETARIAL
AACDIIMNOPS	DIPSOMANIAC	AACEEILSSTT	ATELECTASIS

AACEEIMNNNT	MAINTENANCE
AACEEIMSSST	SIAMESE CATS
AACEEINNNRT	CENTENARIAN
AACEEINNRRT	REINCARNATE
AACEEINNRSS	RENAISSANCE
AACEEIPRRTV	PREVARICATE
AACEEIRRSTT	SECRETARIAT
AACEEKLMPRT	MARKETPLACE
AACEELNPSTU	ENCAPSULATE
AACEENRRSSU	REASSURANCE
AACEFFHINRS	AFFRANCHISE
AACEFFIIRTV	AFFRICATIVE
AACEFFILNOT	AFFECTIONAL
AACEFFINOTT	AFFECTATION
AACEFGHINRR	FAR-REACHING
AACEFGLMOSU	CAMOUFLAGES
AACEFGLOOTT	COTTAGE LOAF
AACEFHMSTTY	SAFETY MATCH
AACEFIILNRV	ACRIFLAVINE
AACEFIIINSTV	FASCINATIVE
AACEFIILMNOT	MALEFACTION
AACEFILTTUV	FACULTATIVE
AACEFIMNRRT	AIRCRAFTMEN
AACEFINORRT	RAREFACTION
AACEFINORSU	FARINACEOUS
AACEFINORTT	FRACTIONATE
AACEFLMORST	MALEFACTORS
AACEFLNSSTU	FACTUALNESS
AACEFMNRTUU	MANUFACTURE
AACEGGGGKLRU	LUGGAGE RACK
AACEGGILPTU	TEGUCIGALPA
AACEGGINRRU	GUN CARRIAGE
AACEGGINRSV	SAVING GRACE
AACEGHHNOTT	CHAETOGNATH
AACEGHILOPR	ARCHIPELAGO
AACEGHLLMNS	SMALL CHANGE
AACEGHLLSSV	CHEVAL GLASS
AACEGHLOORY	ARCHAEOLOGY
AACEGHNORST	COAT HANGERS
AACEGHNORTU	AUTOCHANGER
AACEGHPRTTU	GUTTA-PERCHA
AACEGIIMRRS	MISCARRIAGE
AACEGIJLNTU	EJACULATING
AACEGILLLNY	ANGELICALLY
AACEGILLLOR	ALLEGORICAL
AACEGILLOPS	PLAGIOCLASE
AACEGILMNPS	PLASMAGENIC
AACEGILNPRY	PANEGYRICAL
AACEGILOTUV	COAGULATIVE
AACEGILPPRS	PARAPLEGICS
AACEGIMNPRS	CAMPAIGNERS
AACEGINNRTW	WATERING CAN
AACEGINPPRT	RATE-CAPPING
AACEGKOPRTU	PACKAGE TOUR

AACEGLNRRTU	RECTANGULAR
AACEGMNOORR	GRAECO-ROMAN
AACEGNOORSU	ONAGRACEOUS
AACEGRRSSTU	CASTER SUGAR
AACEHHIKNNV	NAKHICHEVAN
AACEHIILMPT	EPITHALAMIC
AACEHIILSTT	ATHEISTICAL
AACEHIIMMNS	MANICHAEISM
AACEHILLMNO	MELANCHOLIA
AACEHILLNTU	HALLUCINATE
AACEHILLPTY	APHETICALLY
AACEHILRSTT	THEATRICALS
AACEHIMMSTT	MATHEMATICS
AACEHIMNNOY	HAEMOCYANIN
AACEHIMORST	ACHROMATISE
AACEHIMORTT	HAEMATOCRIT
AACEHIMORTZ	ACHROMATIZE
AACEHIMOSTT	HAEMOSTATIC
AACEHINOTTY	THIOCYANATE
AACEHJKMMRS	JACKHAMMERS
AACEHKMMRST	MATCHMAKERS
AACEHKMRSTW	WATCHMAKERS
AACEHMMNNRT	MERCHANTMAN
AACEHMNORSU	RHAMNACEOUS
AACEHMNSTTT	ATTACHMENTS
AACEHMSSSTU	MASSACHUSET
AACEHNNORST	ANTHRACNOSE
AACEHOPRSTT	CATASTROPHE
AACEHOPSSTU	SPATHACEOUS
AACEHPRRSTY	SEARCH PARTY
AACEHPRSTUX	PURCHASE TAX
AACEIILLMNS	MISALLIANCE
AACEIILLNRS	ANCILLARIES
AACEIILLNRT	LACERTILIAN
AACEIILLPRS	CAPILLARIES
AACEIILMRSV	CAVALIERISM
AACEIILNPRR	PERICRANIAL
AACEIILNRRT	INTERRACIAL
AACEIILPPRR	PERICARPIAL
AACEIILPPTV	APPLICATIVE
AACEIILSTTU	ACTUALITIES
AACEIIMMNRS	AMERICANISM
AACEIIMNRTV	CARMINATIVE
AACEIIMQSTU	SEMIAQUATIC
AACEIINORTT	RATIOCINATE
AACEIIOSSTV	ASSOCIATIVE
AACEIIPPRTT	PARTICIPATE
AACEIJLNOTU	EJACULATION
AACEILLLSTY	ELASTICALLY
AACEILLMPRY	MIRACLE PLAY
AACEILLMPUX	AMPLEXICAUL
AACEILLNTTY	TETANICALLY
AACEILLPRRT	CATERPILLAR
AACEILLPTVY	CAPITAL LEVY

AACEILLRRTY	ERRATICALLY	AACEOPPRSUY	PAPYRACEOUS
AACEILMMPST	METAPLASMIC	AACFFIJMRST	TRAFFIC JAMS
AACEILMNORT	RECLAMATION	AACFFIORRTT	TRAFFICATOR
AACEILMNOTX	EXCLAMATION	AACFFMORRTY	FACTORY FARM
AACEILMNSSU	MAIN CLAUSES	AACFGIINNST	FASCINATING
AACEILMRTTU	MATRICULATE	AACFHIORSTU	SOUTH AFRICA
AACEILNNOSS	ASCENSIONAL	AACFHKNRSST	CRANKSHAFTS
AACEILNNRTU	ANTINUCLEAR	AACFHMORSSU	FORASMUCH AS
AACEILNORST	LACERATIONS	AACFIILLNNY	FINANCIALLY
AACEILNORTT	ALTERCATION	AACFIILORTT	FACILITATOR
AACEILNOTTY	ACETYLATION	AACFIINNOST	FASCINATION
AACEILNPSTU	INCAPSULATE	AACFILLNRTY	FRANTICALLY
AACEILNRRTU	RETINACULAR	AACFILMORRS	SCALARIFORM
AACEILNRRTY	INTERCALARY	AACFILNORST	INFRACOSTAL
AACEILPRSTU	SPIRACULATE	AACFINORRTY	FRACTIONARY
AACEILPRTTU	PARTICULATE	AACFKLMSUUV	VACUUM FLASK
AACEILSSTTT	STALACTITES	AACFMNORTUY	MANUFACTORY
AACEILSTUVY	CAUSATIVELY	AACFMOORSST	COATS OF ARMS
AACEIMMNOST	SCAMMONIATE	AACFNORSTUU	ANFRACTUOUS
AACEIMNNOTT	CONTAMINATE	AACGGIIMNNP	CAMPAIGNING
AACEIMNOORT	EROTOMANIAC	AACGGIINSTT	CASTIGATING
AACEIMNOPRT	EMANCIPATOR	AACGGILLOOR	AGROLOGICAL
AACEIMOPRTV	COMPARATIVE	AACGGILNOSY	SYNAGOGICAL
AACEINNORTT	RECANTATION	AACGGILNOTU	CATALOGUING, COAGULATING
AACEINORRTY	REACTIONARY	AACGHHOPRST	TACHOGRAPHS
AACEINORSTU	AERONAUTICS	AACGHIKMMNT	MATCHMAKING
AACEINORSTV	VACATIONERS	AACGHIKMNTW	WATCHMAKING
AACEINOSTUV	EVACUATIONS	AACGHILLOPR	ALLOGRAPHIC
AACEINOSTVX	EXCAVATIONS	AACGHILLPRY	CALLIGRAPHY, GRAPHICALLY
AACEINPRSST	PERSIAN CATS	AACGHINOPPR	APPROACHING
AACEINRSSTU	SANCTUARIES	AACGHINPRTU	PARACHUTING
AACEIORSSTT	AEROSTATICS	AACGHIOPRTU	AUTOGRAPHIC
AACEJLORTUY	EJACULATORY	AACGHKNNOWW	KWANGCHOWAN
AACEKLLNOPR	PANCAKE ROLL	AACGHLMOORU	CHAULMOOGRA
AACEKLMRSST	SMART ALECKS	AACGHNOOPRR	CORONAGRAPH
AACEKLMRSTY	SMART ALECKY	AACGHOPRRTY	CARTOGRAPHY
AACEKLRRSTY	TRACKLAYERS	AACGHOPRSSU	SARCOPHAGUS
AACELLLRSST	SALTCELLARS	AACGIILLNPY	CALLIPYGIAN
AACELLNOOST	CELLO SONATA	AACGIILLNTV	VACILLATING
AACELLOPRSU	ACARPELLOUS	AACGIILLOOX	AXIOLOGICAL
AACELMMRSUU	MARE CLAUSUM	AACGIILMNNS	ANGLICANISM
AACELMORSTU	EMASCULATOR	AACGIILMSTT	STALAGMITIC, STIGMATICAL
AACELMORTXY	EXCLAMATORY	AACGIILNNOR	CAROLINGIAN
AACELMRSSST	MASTERCLASS	AACGIIMNSTT	MASTICATING
AACELNOOSSU	SOLANACEOUS	AACGIINNNRT	INCARNATING
AACELNORSTT	TRANSLOCATE	AACGIINNOTV	VACATIONING
AACELNRRSUV	VERNACULARS	AACGIINNQTU	ACQUAINTING
AACELOPPSSY	APOCALYPSES	AACGIINOSST	ASSOCIATING
AACELPRSSTT	PLASTER CAST	AACGIINOSTT	CASTIGATION
AACELQRTUUU	AQUACULTURE	AACGIINPTTV	CAPTIVATING
AACENNNORTW	WATER CANNON	AACGILLNORY	ORGANICALLY
AACENOOPSSU	SAPONACEOUS	AACGILLOPST	POSTGLACIAL
AACENORRTVY	CONTRAYERVA	AACGILNOOPR	CARPOGONIAL
AACEOOPSSTU	SAPOTACEOUS	AACGILNOOTU	COAGULATION

AACGILNORSS	CORS ANGLAIS
AACGILNPTTU	CATAPULTING
AACGILOSSUY	SAGACIOUSLY
AACGINNRSTT	TRANSACTING
AACGINPRVYZ	CRAZY PAVING
AACGLMNOOPY	CAMPANOLOGY
AACGORRSSTU	CASTOR SUGAR
AACHHIIMPRT	AMPHITRICHA
AACHHILMOPT	OPHTHALMIAC
AACHIIINRST	CHRISTIANIA
AACHIIMNNOT	MACHINATION
AACHIIMNSST	SHAMANISTIC
AACHIINRSSU	SAURISCHIAN
AACHIKMNORV	MARKOV CHAIN
AACHIKMNPRU	KANCHIPURAM
AACHILLOPRY	PAROCHIALLY
AACHILMNOOS	MONOCHASIAL
AACHILMOPPP	HIPPOCAMPAL
AACHIMMNNOTY	MYTHOMANIAC
AACHIMMORST	ACHROMATISM
AACHIMNNORS	ANACHRONISM
AACHIMNORSS	MARASCHINOS
AACHIMOPPRR	PARAMORPHIC
AACHIMPRSST	PHARMACISTS
AACHINNNOTY	ANTHOCYANIN
AACHIPRSTTU	PARACHUTIST
AACHLLOOSTU	HOLOCAUSTAL
AACHLNNOOTU	ANACOLUTHON
AACHMMRRSUU	HARUM-SCARUM
AACHMNOSTWY	YACHTSWOMAN
AACHMOORSTU	ACHROMATOUS
AACHPRSSTTW	WATCHSTRAPS
AACIIIILNNOT	LACINIATION
AACIIILNOST	LAICISATION
AACIIILNOTZ	LAICIZATION
AACIIILPPRT	PARTICIPIAL
AACIIJNOTTT	JACTITATION
AACIILLMRTU	MULTIRACIAL
AACIILLNOOT	COALITIONAL
AACIILLNOTV	VACILLATION
AACIILLNTTY	TITANICALLY
AACIILLPRTY	CAPILLARITY, PIRATICALLY
AACIILLRSTY	SATIRICALLY
AACIILMNORT	LACRIMATION
AACIILMNOST	ANOMALISTIC
AACIILNNNOT	LANCINATION
AACIILNOPPT	APPLICATION
AACIILNPRTU	PURITANICAL
AACIILOPRST	PISCATORIAL
AACIILPSSTT	CAPITALISTS
AACIILSSTTT	STATISTICAL
AACIIMNNOTU	ACUMINATION
AACIIMNORTT	INTRA-ATOMIC
AACIIMNOSTT	MASTICATION

AACIIMORTTY	AROMATICITY
AACIINNNORT	INCARNATION
AACIINNNOTT	INCANTATION
AACIINOOSST	ASSOCIATION
AACIINOPRTT	ANTICIPATOR
AACIINOPSTT	CAPITATIONS
AACIINOPTTV	CAPTIVATION
AACIINPPRTT	PARTICIPANT
AACILLLMOPS	ALLOPLASMIC
AACILLLPSTY	PLASTICALLY
AACILLMNOSY	MASONICALLY
AACILLMOSTY	SOMATICALLY
AACILLNOOST	ALLOCATIONS
AACILLNOPRS	RAPSCALLION
AACILLOPRSY	PROSAICALLY
AACILLOSSUY	SALACIOUSLY
AACILLPRTUU	APICULTURAL
AACILLPSSTY	SPASTICALLY
AACILLSTVWY	CAVITY WALLS
AACILMNNOPT	COMPLAINANT
AACILMNOPST	COMPLAISANT
AACILMNRTTU	MATRICULANT
AACILMORRTY	LACRIMATORY
AACILMPPRSY	PARALYMPICS
AACILNOOTUV	VACUOLATION
AACILNOPRTY	COPLANARITY
AACILNOPSTU	CAPSULATION
AACILNORSTT	INTRACOSTAL
AACILNORTVY	CLAIRVOYANT
AACILOPPRTY	APPLICATORY
AACILOPRSUY	RAPACIOUSLY
AACILOPRTTU	CAPITULATOR
AACILOPSTTU	AUTOPLASTIC
AACILORRTTU	ARTICULATOR
AACILPRRSTU	PARTICULARS
AACILPRSSTT	PLASTIC ARTS
AACILRSTUVY	VASCULARITY
AACIMMNNOOS	MONOMANIACS
AACIMNNNOTT	CONTAMINANT
AACIMNOORST	ARONOMASTIC
AACIMNOOSTT	ANASTOMOTIC
AACIMNOPRSY	PYROMANIACS
AACIMORSTTY	MASTICATORY
AACINNNORTU	ANNUNCIATOR
AACINNORSTT	TRANSACTION
AACINNRRSTU	TRANSURANIC
AACINOOOPPT	APOCOPATION
AACINORSTTT	ATTRACTIONS
AACINORSTTU	ASTRONAUTIC
AACIORRSSTT	ARISTOCRATS
AACLLNRUUVY	AVUNCULARLY
AACLNNNOOST	CONSONANTAL
AACLOOORTVY	ROYAL OCTAVO
AACLOOPPRSY	LAPAROSCOPY

AACLOORRSTU	COLORATURAS	AADEEHINRRV	RAVEN-HAIRED
AACLORSTTUU	AUSCULTATOR	AADEEHLNNRT	NEANDERTHAL
AACMNOPRTUY	PARAMOUNTCY	AADEEHLRRTT	TETRAHEDRAL
AADDDEGINRS	GRANDADDIES	AADEEHLRTTT	DEATH RATTLE
AADDDEIILPT	DILAPIDATED	AADEEHMRRTW	WARM-HEARTED
AADDDEILRRT	TARRADIDDLE	AADEEHMRSST	HEADMASTERS
AADDEEEHPRS	SPEARHEADED	AADEEHNRSVW	HEAVENWARDS
AADDEEFGRSU	SAFEGUARDED	AADEEIILNNN	DAIL EIREANN
AADDEEHHNVY	HEAVY-HANDED	AADEEILMORT	AMELIORATED
AADDEEHHRRT	HARD-HEARTED	AADEEIMMNNS	MAIDEN NAMES
AADDEEHHSST	DEATH'S-HEADS	AADEEIMRRRS	SIERRA MADRE
AADDEEHIMNS	MAIDENHEADS	AADEEINPPRT	APPERTAINED
AADDEEHLPRY	PARALDEHYDE	AADEEIPPRRS	REAPPRAISED
AADDEEILNST	DESALINATED	AADEEIPRRTT	REPATRIATED
AADDEEIPPRS	DISAPPEARED	AADEEIPRTTX	EXPATRIATED
AADDEELLNRS	DARDANELLES	AADEEIRRSSV	ADVERSARIES
AADDEELLPTW	WELL-ADAPTED	AADEEIRRTTV	RETARDATIVE
AADDEELRTTU	ADULTERATED	AADEEIRSTVV	ADVERSATIVE
AADDEEMQRSU	MASQUERADED	AADEEISTTVV	DEVASTATIVE
AADDEEMRRSY	DAYDREAMERS	AADEEKOPRTW	TAKE A POWDER
AADDEENPPRS	SANDPAPERED	AADEELLLLPR	PARALLELLED
AADDEGILLNY	LEADING LADY	AADEELLNPTT	DENTAL PLATE
AADDEGIMNRY	DAYDREAMING	AADEELLPPRW	WALLPAPERED
AADDEGINORT	DEGRADATION	AADEEMORTWW	WATER MEADOW
AADDEGINRRS	DISARRANGED	AADEEMQRRSU	MASQUERADER
AADDEHIMNNS	HANDMAIDENS	AADEEMQRSSU	MASQUERADES
AADDEHNORTY	READY TO HAND	AADEEMRRSTU	ESTREMADURA
AADDEHQSSTU	DEATH SQUADS	AADEENNRTWY	TYNE AND WEAR
AADDEIILNTV	INVALIDATED	AADEENRSTVY	VETERANS DAY
AADDEILMRRS	RED ADMIRALS	AADEENRSWYY	NEW YEAR'S DAY
AADDEINRSST	STANDARDISE	AADEEORRTWY	READY-TO-WEAR
AADDEINRSTZ	STANDARDIZE	AADEFGHNRRT	GRANDFATHER
AADDEJLMSTU	MALADJUSTED	AADEFGMNNSU	FUN AND GAMES
AADDELPQRUU	QUADRUPEDAL	AADEFHLNRST	FATHERLANDS
AADDGINPRRS	GRAND RAPIDS	AADEFIKLNNR	RANK AND FILE
AADDGNNRSST	GRANDSTANDS	AADEFIMRRRY	DAIRY FARMER
AADDIIINNRT	TRINIDADIAN	AADEFLMNNTU	FUNDAMENTAL
AADDIILOPRT	DILAPIDATOR	AADEFLSSTTY	STEADFASTLY
AADDNNNORST	NONSTANDARD	AADEFNNNORS	SAN FERNANDO
AADEEEGGRTX	EXAGGERATED	AADEGGGHLNU	HAND LUGGAGE
AADEEEGLPRS	SPREAD-EAGLE	AADEGGHNRSS	HAGGARDNESS
AADEEEHHLRT	LEATHERHEAD	AADEGGILNNR	LANDING GEAR
AADEEEHLNNR	ENNEAHEDRAL	AADEGGINRRS	AGGRANDISER
AADEEEPRSTX	EXASPERATED	AADEGGINRRZ	AGGRANDIZER
AADEEERSSTV	ASSEVERATED	AADEGGOSSSU	SAUSAGE DOGS
AADEEFGLLLT	FLAGELLATED	AADEGHIINRS	HEARING AIDS
AADEEFHHLRT	HALF-HEARTED	AADEGHINRRW	HARDWEARING
AADEEGIKNTV	GIVE-AND-TAKE	AADEGHOPRTU	AUTOGRAPHED
AADEEGILOPR	A RIPE OLD AGE	AADEGIILNTT	INTAGLIATED
AADEEGNORVW	AVERAGE DOWN	AADEGIILPRS	PLAGIARISED
AADEEGNPRRR	PREARRANGED	AADEGIILPRZ	PLAGIARIZED
AADEEHHLPRT	HEPTAHEDRAL	AADEGIINRTT	INGRATIATED
AADEEHHRTXY	HEXAHYDRATE	AADEGILLNNP	PINEAL GLAND
AADEEHILRTX	EXHILARATED	AADEGILLNTV	GALLIVANTED

AADEGILNNRS	GARDEN SNAIL	AADENNRRTUW	UNWARRANTED
AADEGILNNRV	VLAARDINGEN	AADENRSSWWY	WAYWARDNESS
AADEGILNPRT	PLANTIGRADE	AADENRSTTUU	UNSATURATED
AADEGINNOST	ANTAGONISED	AADEQRRSTUY	QUARTER DAYS
AADEGINNOTZ	ANTAGONIZED	AADFFORRSTW	FAST-FORWARD
AADEGINRTUU	INAUGURATED	AADFGHINNST	HANDFASTING
AADEGINSTTV	DEVASTATING	AADFHHILLOY	HALF-HOLIDAY
AADEGLNQRSU	QUADRANGLES	AADFILLNTWX	WINDFALL TAX
AADEGLNRSSU	GRADUALNESS	AADFILRSSTU	FRUIT SALADS
AADEGLNSSTW	SWEAT GLANDS	AADFLLLOOSY	ALL FOOLS' DAY
AADEGMNMRST	GRAND MASTER	AADGGIINPRS	DISPARAGING
AADEGMNNPRT	GRANDPARENT	AADGGOOOUUU	OUAGADOUGOU
AADEGNOPRRS	GRAND OPERAS	AADGHHOPRSW	SHADOWGRAPH
AADEGNPRRTY	GARDEN PARTY	AADGHILMNNN	MANHANDLING
AADEHIILNNT	ANNIHILATED	AADGHILNNNP	PANHANDLING
AADEHIILNRT	ANTHERIDIAL	AADGHINOSSW	WASHING SODA
AADEHILLNOS	HOLLANDAISE	AADGHINRSWW	WASH DRAWING
AADEHILMNNT	THE MAINLAND	AADGHINSSWY	WASHING DAYS
AADEHIPSTXY	ASPHYXIATED	AADGHIOPRRY	RADIOGRAPHY
AADEHLNNPRS	PANHANDLERS	AADGHLPRSSU	SPLASH GUARD
AADEHMMMNOS	MOHAMMEDANS	AADGHMNRSTU	DRAUGHTSMAN
AADEIIIRRTV	IRRADIATIVE	AADGIIINRRT	IRRADIATING
AADEIILMNST	MEDIASTINAL	AADGIIKLNNR	KALININGRAD
AADEIILMSST	ASSIMILATED	AADGIILMRST	MADRIGALIST
AADEIILNRRT	INTERRADIAL	AADGIILNNNO	ANGLO-INDIAN
AADEIILPRTY	PRAEDIALITY	AADGIILNNVZ	VANDALIZING
AADEIIMNNOT	DEAMINATION	AADGIILNORR	RAILROADING
AADEIINORRT	RERADIATION	AADGIIMNRTZ	DRAMATIZING
AADEILLLMOT	METALLOIDAL	AADGINNOPRS	GRAND PIANOS
AADEILLNOPT	PLANETOIDAL	AADGINORSTU	GRADUATIONS
AADEILMNPTU	MANIPULATED	AADGLLNPPUY	PLUG-AND-PLAY
AADEILMNRRT	INTRADERMAL	AADGNNOPRSS	SNAPDRAGONS
AADEILNNQRU	QUADRENNIAL	AADGNOOPRST	GASTROPODAN
AADEILNORTY	ARYTENOIDAL	AADHHINSTTT	THIS AND THAT
AADEILNOTUV	DEVALUATION	AADHIIMOPRS	ADIAPHORISM
AADEILNRSTU	NATURALISED	AADHIIOPRST	ADIAPHORIST
AADEILNRTUZ	NATURALIZED	AADHILRSTWW	WITHDRAWALS
AADEILPRSTY	DISPARATELY	AADHIOOPRSU	ADIAPHOROUS
AADEIMMNNRST	DISARMAMENT	AADHIOPPRTY	PARATYPHOID
AADEIMNRSTV	MAIDSERVANT	AADHIOPRRTY	PARATHYROID
AADEIMRSTTU	TRAUMATISED	AADHKNOORTT	NORTH DAKOTA
AADEIMRTTUZ	TRAUMATIZED	AADHKOOSTTU	SOUTH DAKOTA
AADEINNQRTU	QUARANTINED	AADHLORSUYZ	HAZARDOUSLY
AADEINOPRTV	DEPRAVATION	AADHORRSSUU	HADROSAURUS
AADEINORRTT	RETARDATION	AADIIIINNNOR	INDO-IRANIAN
AADEINORSST	DIATESSARON	AADIIIINORRT	IRRADIATION
AADEINOSTTV	DEVASTATION	AADIIJNOSTU	JUDAISATION
AADEINPQRSU	PASQUINADER	AADIIJNOTUZ	JUDAIZATION
AADEKNRSSWW	AWKWARDNESS	AADIILLNTTU	ALTITUDINAL, LATITUDINAL
AADELLNNORT	RALLENTANDO	AADIILNOOTX	OXIDATIONAL
AADELMMOPSS	PLASMODESMA	AADIILNOPSS	ANADIPLOSIS
AADELMNORST	ALDERMASTON	AADIILNORTT	TRADITIONAL
AADELORRTTU	ADULTERATOR	AADIILNORTV	INVALIDATOR
AADEMNORSTW	TRADESWOMAN	AADIILNOSTV	VALIDATIONS

AADIILNOSTY	DIALYSATION	AAEEGINRRTW	GRANITEWARE
AADIILNTTTU	ATTITUDINAL	AAEEGINRSTV	VEGETARIANS
AADIILOSUUV	AUDIO-VISUAL	AAEEGLMMRSU	RUMMAGE SALE
AADIIMNORST	ADMIRATIONS	AAEEGLMNOPT	PLANOGAMETE
AADIINNORSU	DINOSAURIAN	AAEEGLNNPTT	PLANTAGENET
AADIINNOTTX	ANTIOXIDANT	AAEEGLNRTTV	TRAVEL AGENT
AADIIPRSSST	ASPIDISTRAS	AAEEGLORTVY	LAEVOGYRATE
AADILLMNOOT	AMONTILLADO	AAEEGLPRSTY	PEARLY GATES
AADILLMORTY	MALADROITLY	AAEEGMMNNST	MANAGEMENTS
AADILMNORTY	MANDATORILY	AAEEGMMORRS	AEROGRAMMES
AADILOORSTV	VASODILATOR	AAEEGMNNRRT	ARRANGEMENT
AADILOPPRSV	DISAPPROVAL	AAEEGMNOPRT	POMEGRANATE
AADIMNNOPRS	PRIMA DONNAS	AAEEGMNRSTY	EAST GERMANY
AADJMNNPRSU	PANJANDRUMS	AAEEGMNSSTU	ASSUAGEMENT
AADJNNORRST	TRANS-JORDAN	AAEEGNPRRRR	PREARRANGER
AADLMNNOSS	NO-MAN'S-LANDS	AAEEHHLNNPT	NAPHTHALENE
AAEEEFFLMMT	FEMME FATALE	AAEEHILMOPR	HEMERALOPIA
AAEEEGNSTTT	ESTATE AGENT	AAEEHILNNST	SAINT HELENA
AAEEEGRSTWY	STEERAGEWAY	AAEEHIMMNPT	AMPHETAMINE
AAEEEHNRRTW	EARTHENWARE	AAEEHIMNRTT	METATHERIAN
AAEEEHNRTVW	WEATHER VANE	AAEEHIOSTUV	HAUTE-SAVOIE
AAEEEIKPSSS	SPEAKEASIES	AAEEHIPRSST	PARESTHESIA
AAEEEMNNOSS	SEA ANEMONES	AAEEHKMOPTY	TAKE-HOME PAY
AAEEEMNNPPST	APPEASEMENT	AAEEHKQRSTU	EARTHQUAKES
AAEEEMPRSTU	TAPE MEASURE	AAEEHLLOSTW	AT WHOLESALE
AAEEENNRRST	NEAR EASTERN	AAEEHLLSTTU	HAUSTELLATE
AAEEEPRRSTX	EXASPERATER	AAEEHLNPTTV	HEPTAVALENT
AAEEFGHLMRT	MAGHERAFELT	AAEEHLPSSTU	HAUTES-ALPES
AAEEFGMRRRW	GERM WARFARE	AAEEHMNOORR	AMENORRHOEA
AAEEFHHILRT	FAITH HEALER	AAEEIILLTVV	ALLEVIATIVE
AAEEFHIRRTW	FAIR-WEATHER	AAEEIILMRST	MATERIALISE
AAEEFHLMTWY	MEET HALFWAY	AAEEIILMRTZ	MATERIALIZE
AAEEFHRSSTV	AFTERSHAVES	AAEEIILRRST	ARTERIALISE
AAEEFKLMRST	FLEA MARKETS	AAEEIILRRTZ	ARTERIALIZE
AAEEFLSTVVY	SAFETY VALVE	AAEEIILRTTV	RETALIATIVE
AAEEFNRRSST	TRANSFERASE	AAEEIINRSSV	SANSEVIERIA
AAEEFRSSTTT	AFTERTASTES	AAEEIKLLMRT	ALKALIMETER
AAEEEGGLMORT	AGGLOMERATE	AAEEILLMNNT	LINEAMENTAL
AAEEGGORRTX	EXAGGERATOR	AAEEILLNPRT	PANTELLERIA
AAEEGHHMORR	HAEMORRHAGE	AAEEILLPPTV	APPELLATIVE
AAEEGHLOOPS	OESOPHAGEAL	AAEEILLQRTU	EQUILATERAL
AAEEGHNPPRR	PAPERHANGER	AAEEILMMPST	SEMIPALMATE
AAEEGHRRRTZ	EARTH-GRAZER	AAEEILNNPRT	PENETRALIAN
AAEEGIKLNTV	LEAVE TAKING	AAEEILNRTTV	ALTERNATIVE
AAEEGILLLNS	SELAGINELLA	AAEEIMNNRSS	SAN MARINESE
AAEEGILLLTT	TAGLIATELLE	AAEEIMSSSTT	METASTASISE
AAEEGILLNNT	GENTIANELLA	AAEEIMSSTTZ	METASTASIZE
AAEEGILMSSX	SEXAGESIMAL	AAEEIOPRTVV	EVAPORATIVE
AAEEGILNPPT	EATING APPLE	AAEEIPPRRTV	PREPARATIVE
AAEEGILPRTT	TETRAPLEGIA	AAEEIPRSTTX	EXPATRIATES
AAEEGINNNRT	ARGENTINEAN	AAEEKLNRSTT	RATTLESNAKE
AAEEGINPPRR	REAPPEARING	AAEELLNRTTY	ALTERNATELY
AAEEGINPRSS	PARAGENESIS	AAEELLNSTTV	AT ALL EVENTS
AAEEGINPRST	GREASEPAINT	AAEELLOOSST	A SLATE LOOSE

AAEELLPRSTY	PLATELAYERS
AAEELMNSTTT	TESTAMENTAL
AAEELMQRSSU	SQUARE MEALS
AAEELNNPTTV	PENTAVALENT
AAEELNPSSTT	PLEASANTEST
AAEELNPSTTV	SEPTAVALENT
AAEELNRTTTV	TETRAVALENT
AAEELOPRTTX	EXTRAPOLATE
AAEEMNORTUX	AUXANOMETER
AAEEMQRSSTU	MARQUESSATE
AAEENNRSSUW	UNAWARENESS
AAEFFIIMRTV	AFFIRMATIVE
AAEFFILORSV	LOVE AFFAIRS
AAEFGHILNRT	FARTHINGALE
AAEFGILPRST	SEPTIFRAGAL
AAEFGLLLNST	FLAGELLANTS
AAEFGLSSSTY	SAFETY GLASS
AAEFGMNRRTY	FRAGMENTARY
AAEFHILNRTW	FATHER-IN-LAW
AAEFIIIILMRS	FAMILIARISE
AAEFIIIILMRZ	FAMILIARIZE
AAEFIIORRSV	SAVOIR-FAIRE
AAEFILMMNRT	FIRMAMENTAL
AAEFILMMNSY	FAMILY NAMES
AAEFILMNRTY	FILAMENTARY
AAEFLLNRRTY	FRATERNALLY
AAEFLMPSSTY	SAFETY LAMPS
AAEFLOPSSTT	SOFT PALATES
AAEFLRSSSTT	FALSE STARTS
AAEFORRSTYZ	SAFETY RAZOR
AAEGGGGINRT	AGGREGATING
AAEGGGINORT	AGGREGATION
AAEGGGLNSUV	LUGGAGE VANS
AAEGGIIMNTW	WAITING GAME
AAEGGILNTTU	AGGLUTINATE
AAEGGIMMNTU	GAMETANGIUM
AAEGGINNRRR	REARRANGING
AAEGGLRRUUY	A REGULAR GUY
AAEGGNORRUW	NARROW GAUGE
AAEGHHIIKST	HIGH AS A KITE
AAEGHIINRVW	HAIRWEAVING
AAEGHIMNORR	MENORRHAGIA
AAEGHINNNSS	SHENANIGANS
AAEGHLLNOXY	HEXAGONALLY
AAEGHLMOOTY	HAEMATOLOGY
AAEGHLNPRTU	HEPTANGULAR
AAEGHLOPPRY	PALEOGRAPHY
AAEGHMNOPRY	ANEMOGRAPHY
AAEGHMOPRRS	PHRASEOGRAM
AAEGHNOPRTY	PYTHAGOREAN
AAEGHNPRRST	STRAPHANGER
AAEGHNSTTTU	SET AT NAUGHT
AAEGIIIMNTV	IMAGINATIVE
AAEGIILLNTV	ALLEVIATING
AAEGIILMRST	MAGISTERIAL
AAEGIILNRTT	RETALIATING
AAEGIILPRRS	PLAGIARISER
AAEGIILPRRZ	PLAGIARIZER
AAEGIIMNNRT	REANIMATING
AAEGIIMNRSS	MINAS GERAIS
AAEGIINNOTV	EVAGINATION
AAEGIINORTV	VARIEGATION
AAEGIINPTTX	EXPATIATING
AAEGIIRTTVV	GRAVITATIVE
AAEGIKMNPST	MASKING TAPE
AAEGILLLNPR	PARALLELING
AAEGILLNNST	SAINT GALLEN
AAEGILLNOST	ALLEGATIONS
AAEGILLNPPR	APPARELLING
AAEGILLNPPY	APPEALINGLY
AAEGILLNRST	GALLANTRIES
AAEGILMMNOS	MAGLEMOSIAN
AAEGILMNRTT	MALTREATING
AAEGILMNSTT	STALEMATING
AAEGILMSSTT	STALAGMITES
AAEGILNNRTT	ALTERNATING
AAEGILNORTY	LEGATIONARY
AAEGILNOSTT	GESTATIONAL
AAEGILNQRUU	EQUIANGULAR
AAEGILNRTTU	TRIANGULATE
AAEGILNRTUV	GRANULATIVE
AAEGIMNNRRT	ARRAIGNMENT
AAEGIMRSSTT	MAGISTRATES
AAEGINNOPRS	SINGAPOREAN
AAEGINNTTTU	ATTENUATING
AAEGINOPRTV	EVAPORATING
AAEGIOPPRTV	PROPAGATIVE
AAEGIOPSTTY	STEATOPYGIA
AAEGIPRSSTT	STAG PARTIES
AAEGKMNRTUU	KUMARATUNGE
AAEGLLNNSST	GALLANTNESS
AAEGLLOPRTY	PYROGALLATE
AAEGLLORSSU	SAUSAGE ROLL
AAEGLMOPRRU	PARLOUR GAME
AAEGLNNPRTU	PENTANGULAR
AAEGLNRSTTU	STRANGULATE
AAEGNNRSSTV	VAGRANTNESS
AAEHHIILMOP	HAEMOPHILIA
AAEHHOPPSST	PHOSPHATASE
AAEHHOTUVWY	WHAT HAVE YOU
AAEHIIMNOPS	HEMIANOPSIA
AAEHIIMNSST	HISTAMINASE
AAEHIINPSTT	ANTIPATHIES
AAEHIKLNRRS	LANARKSHIRE
AAEHILLMTTY	I'LL EAT MY HAT
AAEHILNOSTT	EAST LOTHIAN
AAEHILNPSTW	WESTPHALIAN
AAEHILORRTX	EXHILARATOR

AAEHIMOSSST	HAEMOSTASIS	AAEILMOPTTT	TOTIPALMATE
AAEHKLORSTT	HOLKAR STATE	AAEILNNOPTX	EXPLANATION
AAEHKLRSSST	SALT SHAKERS	AAEILNNORTT	ALTERNATION
AAEHLNOPPRY	ALPHA PYRONE	AAEILNNOSST	SENSATIONAL
AAEHLNPRSTY	PHALANSTERY	AAEILNNPRST	TRANSALPINE
AAEHMNOOOTZ	HAEMATOZOON	AAEILNOOPRT	OPERATIONAL
AAEHMNORSTU	ATHERMANOUS	AAEILNOPPRY	PLAYER PIANO
AAEHMNNORSWW	WASHERWOMAN	AAEILNOPRRT	PROLETARIAN
AAEHMOPRTTU	THAUMATROPE	AAEILNORSTT	ALTERATIONS
AAEHMOSSTTY	STAY-AT-HOMES	AAEILNORSTX	RELAXATIONS
AAEIIIKNNOS	ANISEIKONIA	AAEILNORTUV	REVALUATION
AAEIIILRSUX	AUXILIARIES	AAEILNOSTUV	EVALUATIONS
AAEIIJNRSSS	JANISSARIES	AAEILNPRSSS	PARTIALNESS
AAEIILLMNNR	MILLENARIAN	AAEILNPRSTT	PATERNALIST
AAEIILLMNRT	MATRILINEAL	AAEILNPRSTW	LAWN PARTIES
AAEIILLNOTV	ALLEVIATION	AAEILNRRSTU	SERTULARIAN
AAEIILLNPRT	PATRILINEAL	AAEILNRSTTV	AT INTERVALS
AAEIILLPSTV	PALLIATIVES	AAEILOPRRTT	PROLETARIAT
AAEIILMMRST	MATERIALISM	AAEILORRTTY	RETALIATORY
AAEIILMNRRT	AIR TERMINAL	AAEILORSSSS	ASSESSORIAL
AAEIILMRSTT	MATERIALIST	AAEIMMOOPST	MESOPOTAMIA
AAEIILMRTTY	MATERIALITY	AAEIMNNOSSY	MAYONNAISES
AAEIILNNOST	NATIONALISE	AAEIMNNSSTT	ATTAINMENTS
AAEIILNNOTZ	NATIONALIZE	AAEIMOPPRTX	APPROXIMATE
AAEIILNNPST	PALESTINIAN	AAEINNNOSTX	ANNEXATIONS
AAEIILNORST	RATIONALISE, REALISATION	AAEINNOSSTT	ASSENTATION
AAEIILNORTT	RETALIATION	AAEINNOSSTT	NATION STATE
AAEIILNORTZ	RATIONALIZE, REALIZATION	AAEINNOTTTU	ATTENUATION
AAEIILPPRSS	PARALEIPSIS	AAEINNRRSVY	ANNIVERSARY
AAEIILQTTUV	QUALITATIVE	AAEINOOPRTV	EVAPORATION
AAEIIMNNORT	REANIMATION	AAEINOORSTT	AEROSTATION
AAEIIMNNOTX	EXAMINATION, EXANIMATION	AAEINOPPRRT	PREPARATION
AAEIIMNRSST	ERASTIANISM	AAEINOPRRST	REPARATIONS
AAEIINNPPRT	PARIPINNATE	AAEINOPRSST	SEPARATIONS
AAEIINOPTTX	EXPATIATION	AAEINORSSTU	AUSTRONESIA
AAEIINOSTTV	AESTIVATION	AAEINOSTTTT	ATTESTATION
AAEIKLLMRTY	ALKALIMETRY	AAEIOPPPRRT	APPROPRIATE
AAEIKLMNOPT	KLEPTOMANIA	AAEIORSSTTV	ASSORTATIVE
AAEIKLMRSTT	STERLITAMAK	AAEIPRSSSTT	SEPARATISTS
AAEILLLMNOT	LAMELLATION	AAEKMRSSSTT	TASKMASTERS
AAEILLLMPRS	PARALLELISM	AAELLNOPRSS	SOLAR PANELS
AAEILLLOSTV	SAL VOLATILE	AAELLOPSSTT	ELASTOPLAST
AAEILLLPRST	PARALLELIST	AAELLORRSTT	STELLARATOR
AAEILLNNPTY	TIN PAN ALLEY	AAELMNORSVV	REMOVAL VANS
AAEILLNOOTV	ALVEOLATION	AAELMNPQTUU	QUANTUM LEAP
AAEILLNOPPT	APPELLATION	AAELMOPRRTU	ARMOUR PLATE
AAEILLQRSTU	AQUARELLIST	AAELNNRSSTU	NATURALNESS
AAEILMMNRST	MATERNALISM	AAELNOPRTXY	EXPLANATORY
AAEILMNNOTT	LAMENTATION	AAELNORRSTT	ALTERNATORS
AAEILMNNORST	MONASTERIAL	AAELNRRSSTV	TRANSVERSAL
AAEILMNPRST	PARLIAMENTS, PATERNALISM	AAELNRRSTUV	TRANSVALUER
AAEILMNPRTU	PLANETARIUM	AAELNRSSTUX	TRANSSEXUAL
AAEILMNRRTU	ULTRAMARINE	AAELPRRSTTT	RATTLETRAPS
AAEILMOORRT	AMELIORATOR	AAEMNNRSSTV	MANSERVANTS

AAEMNOPRTTU	PORTMANTEAU	AAGHIRSTTWY	STRAIGHTWAY
AAEMNOSSTTW	STATESWOMAN	AAGHLNOPPRY	PLANOGRAPHY
AAEMOOPRSTZ	SPERMATOZOA	AAGHLOOPPRR	POLAROGRAPH
AAEMORSSTTT	TOASTMASTER	AAGHMMMOPRY	MAMMOGRAPHY
AAEMPRSSSTT	PAST MASTERS	AAGHNOPPRST	PANTOGRAPHS
AAENNPPRTTU	APPURTENANT	AAGHNOPPRTY	PANTOGRAPHY
AAENNPRRSTT	TRANSPARENT	AAGHNOPPRRUY	URANOGRAPHY
AAENNPRSTTU	SUPERNATANT	AAGIIILMNRY	IMAGINARILY
AAENRRSSTTU	RESTAURANTS	AAGIIIMNNNT	MAINTAINING
AAEOOPPRRRT	PARATROOPER	AAGIIIMNNOT	IMAGINATION
AAEOPPRRRTY	PREPARATORY	AAGIIKNNPST	PAINSTAKING
AAEOPRRTUVW	WATER VAPOUR	AAGIILMNORT	MIGRATIONAL
AAEOPRSSTTU	STRATOPAUSE	AAGIILMNRTY	MARGINALITY
AAEPPRSSTTY	A PRETTY PASS	AAGIILMPRSS	PLAGIARISMS
AAFFGIIILNT	AFFILIATING	AAGIILNNTTZ	TANTALIZING
AAFFGILOPST	GAFF-TOPSAIL	AAGIILNPPTT	PALPITATING
AAFFGIMNRSU	RAGAMUFFINS	AAGIILOPRRT	GLORIA PATRI
AAFFIIILNOT	AFFILIATION	AAGIILPRSST	PLAGIARISTS
AAFFIIMNORT	AFFIRMATION	AAGIIMMNNTY	MAGNANIMITY
AAFGHILNNOU	FIONNGHUALA	AAGIIMMSSTT	ASTIGMATISM
AAFGHIMNOSV	SHAVING FOAM	AAGIIMNNORT	MARGINATION
AAFGIINNSTZ	FANTASIZING	AAGIIMSSSSU	MISSISSAUGA
AAFGILLNRST	FALLING STAR	AAGIINNOSST	ASSIGNATION
AAFGINORRSU	FARRAGINOUS	AAGIINORTTV	GRAVITATION
AAFIIILMRTY	FAMILIARITY	AAGIIRSSTTU	SAGITTARIUS
AAFIINNOTTU	INFATUATION	AAGIJKNOPRT	JOKING APART
AAFILLMNORW	LAMINAR FLOW	AAGILLLNPPY	APPALLINGLY
AAFILMNOORT	FORMATIONAL	AAGILLLOOSS	GLOSSOLALIA
AAFILNOOSTT	FLOATATIONS	AAGILLMNNTY	MALIGNANTLY
AAFIMNNNRTY	INFANTRYMAN	AAGILLMRSTY	MAGISTRALLY
AAFINNOOPRT	PROFANATION	AAGILLNRTUV	VULGAR LATIN
AAFLNNOORST	NASOFRONTAL	AAGILMMMOST	MAMMALOGIST
AAFNOOPRRTY	PROFANATORY	AAGILNNORTU	GRANULATION
AAGGGHILNSU	LAUGHING GAS	AAGILNNPPUU	PULAU PINANG
AAGGHHIINNS	SHANGHAIING	AAGILNNRSTT	TRANSLATING
AAGGHHIOPRY	HAGIOGRAPHY	AAGILNOSUVY	YUGOSLAVIAN
AAGGHIIJMNT	THINGAMAJIG	AAGILNRRTUY	GRANULARITY
AAGGIILNNVZ	GALVANIZING	AAGILOPRRTU	PURGATORIAL
AAGGIIMMNNS	MISMANAGING	AAGIMMNNOSU	MAGNANIMOUS
AAGGIINRTTV	GRAVITATING	AAGIMNNOSST	ANTAGONISMS
AAGGIKLMNSS	GLASS-MAKING	AAGIMNOOSSU	ANISOGAMOUS
AAGGILLNOST	ALGOLAGNIST	AAGIMNOOSTU	ANGIOMATOUS
AAGGILNNNUY	LIANYUNGANG	AAGIMPRSSTT	PRAGMATISTS
AAGGILNNTTU	AGGLUTINANT	AAGINNOSSTT	ANTAGONISTS
AAGGINOPPRT	PROPAGATING	AAGINOOPPRT	PROPAGATION
AAGGNNORSTU	ORANGUTANGS	AAGINORRTUU	INAUGURATOR
AAGHHLOPPRY	HAPLOGRAPHY	AAGINOSSSTT	GAS STATIONS
AAGHIIINRRS	HAIR-RAISING	AAGLLMNRTUU	MULTANGULAR
AAGHIILLNOP	ANGLOPHILIA	AAGLNNOOSSX	ANGLO-SAXONS
AAGHIJKNOUZ	ZHANGJIAKOU	AAGLNOOPRTW	PATROL WAGON
AAGHIKLLMNR	HALLMARKING	AAGOOPPRRST	PROPAGATORS
AAGHILLMNPY	LYMPHANGIAL	AAHIIILMNNOT	HAMILTONIAN
AAGHILLMNRS	MARSHALLING	AAHIIILNNORT	ANNIHILATOR
AAGHILNRSSY	HARASSINGLY		

AAHIILNNOST	INHALATIONS	AAILMNRSTTT	TRANSMITTAL
AAHIILNNRSV	NAIL VARNISH	AAILNNOPSTT	PLANTATIONS
AAHIINPRSST	ANTIPHRASIS	AAILNNORSTT	TRANSLATION
AAHILMPRSTY	AMPHISTYLAR	AAILNOPPSSY	PASSION PLAY
AAHIMMNNOPY	NYMPHOMANIA	AAILNOSSTTU	SALUTATIONS
AAHIMMNOPRS	ANAMORPHISM	AAILNRSSTTU	NATURALISTS
AAHIMNOPRSS	OARSMANSHIP	AAILOORTTTZ	TOTALIZATOR
AAHIMNOSSTT	SAINT THOMAS	AAILOPRRTUV	VAPOUR TRAIL
AAHINNOPRTY	ANTIPHONARY	AAIMMNOPSTT	MAIN-TOPMAST
AAHIOPRSTXY	ASPHYXIATOR	AAIMMNOSSUY	IMMUNOASSAY
AAHKOPRRSWW	SPARROWHAWK	AAIMNOOSSST	ANASTOMOSIS
AAHLLMMORSW	MARSHMALLOW	AAIMNOPSTTU	AMPUTATIONS
AAHMNNRSTTU	TRANSHUMANT	AAIMNORSSTU	SANATORIUMS
AAHNNOPRSXY	NASOPHARYNX	AAINNNOOSTT	ANNOTATIONS
AAHNNRRSTUY	THYRSANURAN	AAINNNOPRST	NONPARTISAN
AAHNOPRSTTU	NATUROPATHS	AAINNOOQRTU	QUINTANA ROO
AAHNOPRTTUY	NATUROPATHY	AAINNOPRSTT	PATRON SAINT
AAIIILMNOTT	IMITATIONAL	AAINOPSSTTY	PAY STATIONS
AAIIILNRTTU	UTILITARIAN	AAKKNORRSSY	KRASNOYARSK
AAIIJKLMNOR	KILIMANJARO	AAKLLMPRUUU	KUALA LUMPUR
AAIIKNNOSTY	KYANISATION	AAKLORRVVYY	KARLOVY VARY
AAIIKNNOTYZ	KYANIZATION	AALLMNOOSUY	ANOMALOUSLY
AAIILLLPSUZ	LAPIS LAZULI	AALLNNRTUUY	UNNATURALLY
AAIILLMPRTY	IMPARTIALLY	AALMMOOPSST	SOMATOPLASM
AAIILMMNORT	MATRIMONIAL	AALNNPRSSTT	TRANSPLANTS
AAIILMNNOST	NATIONALISM	AALNORRSSTT	TRANSLATORS
AAIILMNOPRT	PATRIMONIAL	AALOOQRRTUY	ROYAL QUARTO
AAIILMNOPST	MAINTOPSAIL	AALORSSTTTU	ALTOSTRATUS
AAIILMNORST	RATIONALISM	AAMNPRSSTTY	SMARTY-PANTS
AAIILNNOSTT	NATIONALIST	ABBBDELOORW	WOBBLE BOARD
AAIILNNOTTY	NATIONALITY	ABBBDENRRSU	RUBBER BANDS
AAIILNOORTV	VARIOLATION	ABBBELOPSSU	SOAP BUBBLES
AAIILNOPPTT	PALPITATION	ABBCCEEHKNR	BACKBENCHER
AAIILNORSTT	RATIONALIST	ABBCCEEHKNS	BACKBENCHES
AAIILNORTTT	ATTRITIONAL	ABBCCEEHMOR	BEACHCOMBER
AAIILNORTTY	RATIONALITY	ABBCCGIKMNO	BACKCOMBING
AAIILNOSTTU	SITUATIONAL	ABBCDEEFIKO	BIOFEEDBACK
AAIIMMNNOOT	AMMONIATION	ABBCDEEILRS	DESCRIBABLE
AAIIMMNORSV	MORAVIANISM	ABBCDEENRSS	CRABBEDNESS
AAIIMNNORST	MASTROIANNI	ABBCDEMRRSU	BREADCRUMBS
AAIIMNNRSTT	SAINT MARTIN	ABBCEEEHRRS	BEAR'S-BREECH
AAIIMNOOSTT	ATOMISATION	ABBCEEEKNRU	BECKENBAUER
AAIIMNOOTTZ	ATOMIZATION	ABBCEEJLSTU	SUBJECTABLE
AAIIMNOPRTT	IMPARTATION	ABBCEEKLORT	BETA-BLOCKER
AAIIMNOPSTT	IMPASTATION	ABBCEHIILOT	BIBLIOTHECA
AAIIMNOORST	ROTARIANISM	ABBCEHIOPRY	CYBERPHOBIA
AAIIMNRSSTU	SANITARIUMS	ABBCEIILNRS	INSCRIBABLE
AAIINOPPRST	APPARITIONS	ABBCEKMNRSU	BACK NUMBERS
AAIINOPRSST	ASPIRATIONS	ABBCHHIRTTU	RABBIT HUTCH
AAILLLOSTWW	SWALLOWTAIL	ABBCHINPRTU	RABBIT PUNCH
AAILLORRSTY	SARTORIALLY	ABBCIILMNOY	BIBLIOMANCY
AAILMMNOSTU	SUMMATIONAL	ABBCKMOOORY	BACKROOM BOY
AAILMMOPPRS	MALAPROPISM	ABBCKNNNORU	BANNOCKBURN
AAILMNOPRTU	MANIPULATOR	ABBDDEGIORR	BRIDGEBOARD

ABBDDEIINRR	BIRD-BRAINED	ABCCEGINNOU	CONCUBINAGE
ABBDEELORTU	REDOUBTABLE	ABCCEIILPTY	PECCABILITY
ABBDEGNNRRU	BRANDENBURG	ABCCEIKKLST	STICKLEBACK
ABBDEIILNTU	INDUBITABLE	ABCCEILNOTV	CONVICTABLE
ABBDEIINRRU	INDIA RUBBER	ABCCEILNOVY	CONCEIVABLY
ABBDEILRSSU	DISBURSABLE	ABCCEILOSTT	ECTOBLASTIC
ABBDEIMNRSY	BABY-MINDERS	ABCCEINORRT	CENTROBARIC
ABBDEIMORRS	BOMBARDIERS	ABCCELMOOST	CLOSE COMBAT
ABBDELLNRSU	LANDLUBBERS	ABCCELORSUU	SUCCOURABLE
ABBDELORTUY	REDOUBTABLY	ABCCHIKSSTW	SWITCHBACKS
ABBDEMMNORT	BOMBARDMENT	ABCCIIMOORT	MACROBIOTIC
ABBDGIIINNS	BIAS BINDING	ABCCIINOTVY	BICONCAVITY
ABBDHIINORZ	BIROBIDZHAN	ABCCILLLOUY	BUCOLICALLY
ABBDIILNTUY	INDUBITABLY	ABCCILORSTU	SUBCORTICAL
ABBEELPRRTU	PERTURBABLE	ABCCINOOSTT	TOBACCONIST
ABBEEMNSSTU	SUBBASEMENT	ABCCIOORSUV	BACCIVOROUS
ABBEENRSTTU	BUTTER BEANS	ABCCKNORTUY	BACK COUNTRY
ABBEGIKLMOO	GO LIKE A BOMB	ABCCMOPSSTU	SUBCOMPACTS
ABBEGILNORU	BELABOURING	ABCCNORSTTU	SUBCONTRACT
ABBEGINORTW	BROWBEATING	ABCDDEEEELNS	DESCENDABLE
ABBEHHIKSSS	SHISH KEBABS	ABCDDEEFIIN	BID DEFIANCE
ABBEHIIILNT	INHIBITABLE	ABCDDEEFLOU	DOUBLE-FACED
ABBEHILLPSU	PUBLISHABLE	ABCDDEEILRS	SLICED BREAD
ABBEHILNRSU	BURNISHABLE	ABCDDEFINOR	FORBIDDANCE
ABBEIILLMOZ	MOBILIZABLE	ABCDDEKLORS	BADDERLOCKS
ABBEILMSTTU	SUBMITTABLE	ABCDEEEERRT	DECEREBRATE
ABBEINRSTUU	SUBURBANITE	ABCDEEEILPR	DEPRECIABLE
ABBEIRSSTTY	BABY-SITTERS	ABCDEEFHNRR	FRENCH BREAD
ABBEKLNOSTT	BOTTLE BANKS	ABCDEEGGKLL	BLACKLEGGED
ABBELMSSSUY	SUBASSEMBLY	ABCDEEIILMM	IMMEDICABLE
ABBELNPRRTU	RUBBER PLANT	ABCDEEIILLMN	CLEAN-LIMBED
ABBELPRRTUY	PERTURBABLY	ABCDEEIILNRS	RESCINDABLE
ABBEMPRRSTU	RUBBER STAMP	ABCDEEIILORV	DIVORCEABLE
ABBGIINSTTY	BABY-SITTING	ABCDEEIILPRT	PREDICTABLE
ABBGILMNOOZ	BAMBOOZLING	ABCDEEINORS	DECARBONISE
ABBGILNORSY	ABSORBINGLY	ABCDEEINORZ	DECARBONIZE
ABBIILLORTY	BIBLIOLATRY	ABCDEELLNRY	BELLY DANCER
ABBIILMOPRS	PROBABILISM	ABCDEELLNSY	BELLY DANCES
ABBIILLOPRST	PROBABILIST	ABCDEELLPRU	PRECLUDABLE
ABBIILOPRTY	PROBABILITY	ABCDEELMMNO	COMMENDABLE
ABCCCHKKLOO	CHOCK-A-BLOCK	ABCDEELMNNO	CONDEMNABLE
ABCCDEEELSU	SUCCEEDABLE	ABCDEELMORU	DOUBLE CREAM
ABCCDEEIIRT	BACTERICIDE, TEREBIC ACID	ABCDEELNNOS	CONDENSABLE
ABCCDEHHKNU	HUNCHBACKED	ABCDEELNRRY	CANDLEBERRY
ABCCDEKLMOY	BLACK COMEDY	ABCDEELOPSU	DOUBLE-SPACE
ABCCDENNORT	CONCERT BAND	ABCDEENORRT	CENTREBOARD
ABCCDHHORRU	BROAD CHURCH	ABCDEHILSTW	SWITCHBLADE
ABCCEEILNOV	CONCEIVABLE	ABCDEHIRRTW	BIRD-WATCHER
ABCCEEKLOPU	PEACOCK BLUE	ABCDEHORSSS	CHESSBOARDS
ABCCEILLLOT	COLLECTABLE	ABCDEIILOSS	DISSOCIABLE
ABCCEELORRT	CORRECTABLE	ABCDEIILTUY	EDUCABILITY
ABCCEEMNNRU	ENCUMBRANCE	ABCDEIIORTT	OBITER DICTA
ABCCEFILNOS	CONFISCABLE	ABCDEIKLLST	BLACKLISTED
ABCCEFIORSU	BACCIFEROUS	ABCDEIKLRSS	BACKSLIDERS

ABCDEILNOST	ENDOBLASTIC
ABCDEILPRTY	PREDICTABLY
ABCDEINOORT	NOTICE BOARD
ABCDEINRRST	TRANSCRIBED
ABCDEINRSTU	DISTURBANCE
ABCDELMMNOY	COMMENDABLY
ABCDELMNRSU	UNSCRAMBLED
ABCDEOORRSS	SCOREBOARDS
ABCDGIIKLNS	BACKSLIDING
ABCDGKNORSU	BACKGROUNDS
ABCDHIIMRTY	DITHYRAMBIC
ABCDHIIRSTU	HUDIBRASTIC
ABCDHINOOPR	BRANCHIOPOD
ABCDHIOPSTX	DISPATCH BOX
ABCDHIORSTW	SWITCHBOARD
ABCDHNOORRY	HYDROCARBON
ABCDIIILOST	IDIOBLASTIC
ABCDIILLSSY	DISSYLLABIC
ABCDIILORUV	VIBRACULOID
ABCDIIMNOSY	BIODYNAMICS
ABCDIKLOSWW	BLACK WIDOWS
ABCDMNORRUU	CARBORUNDUM
ABCEEEFFKOR	COFFEE BREAK
ABCEEEFFLOT	COFFEE TABLE
ABCEEEFLNOR	ENFORCEABLE
ABCEEEHIKRT	BREAK THE ICE
ABCEEEIKRRS	ICEBREAKERS
ABCEEEILPRV	PERCEIVABLE
ABCEEEILRSV	RECEIVABLES, SERVICEABLE
ABCEEEILRSX	EXERCISABLE
ABCEEEILRTV	CELEBRATIVE
ABCEEELMNRS	RESEMBLANCE
ABCEEELORRV	RECOVERABLE
ABCEEELPRST	RESPECTABLE
ABCEEEMMNRR	REMEMBRANCE
ABCEEEMMNRT	EMBRACEMENT
ABCEEFHNNRS	FRENCH BEANS
ABCEEFIILPS	SPECIFIABLE
ABCEEFIILRT	CERTIFIABLE, RECTIFIABLE
ABCEEFIINRY	BENEFICIARY
ABCEEFILLMR	LEAF-CLIMBER
ABCEEFINNOT	BENEFACTION
ABCEEFINRTU	RUBEFACIENT
ABCEEFNORST	BENEFACTORS
ABCEEGIINOT	ABIOGENETIC
ABCEEGILNRT	CELEBRATING
ABCEEHHILRS	CHERISHABLE
ABCEEHKLNQU	BLANK CHEQUE
ABCEEHLORTU	RETOUCHABLE
ABCEEHLRSTT	STRETCHABLE
ABCEEHORRRT	TORCHBEARER
ABCEEIJKKRT	BIKER JACKET
ABCEEILLNTU	INELUCTABLE
ABCEEILNORT	CELEBRATION

ABCEEILNPST	INSPECTABLE
ABCEEILNSUX	INEXCUSABLE
ABCEEILORRV	IRREVOCABLE
ABCEEILRRSU	IRRECUSABLE
ABCEEILRRTU	RECRUITABLE
ABCEEILRSTT	BATTLE CRIES
ABCEEILRSVY	SERVICEABLY
ABCEEINNRTY	BICENTENARY
ABCEEINORRT	CEREBRATION
ABCEEINORST	BARONETCIES
ABCEEINORTX	EXORBITANCE
ABCEEINRRRS	CRANBERRIES
ABCEEKLPPPR	BLACK PEPPER
ABCEEKLRRRW	KERB CRAWLER
ABCEEKRSSTT	BACK STREETS
ABCEEKSSTTU	BUCKET SEATS
ABCEELNORSV	CONSERVABLE, CONVERSABLE
ABCEELOPRSW	PACE BOWLERS
ABCEELOSTUU	BETULACEOUS
ABCEELPRSTY	RESPECTABLY
ABCEELRTTUU	TUBERCULATE
ABCEENNORTU	BEAN COUNTER
ABCEENORRST	ARBORESCENT
ABCEENORSSV	OBSERVANCES
ABCEEOPPRSS	SPACE PROBES
ABCEFHNOOPR	FRANCOPHOBE
ABCEFIMNORY	BY MAIN FORCE
ABCEFINORTU	RUBEFACTION
ABCEFKLORST	BLACK FOREST
ABCEFLMNOOR	CONFORMABLE
ABCEFLMOORT	COMFORTABLE
ABCEGHILLNY	BELLYACHING
ABCEGHORRTU	TURBOCHARGE
ABCEGILLMTU	MAGIC BULLET
ABCEGILNNOS	CONSIGNABLE
ABCEGILNOST	BLASTOGENIC
ABCEHHIOOPT	THEOPHOBIAC
ABCEHHJOSTT	HATCHET JOBS
ABCEHHKRSUW	BUSHWHACKER
ABCEHIILPRT	BLEPHARITIC
ABCEHIKLNSY	CHELYABINSK
ABCEHILNORV	OLIVE BRANCH
ABCEHILOPSU	BICEPHALOUS
ABCEHILPRST	BIRTHPLACES
ABCEHIMORTT	BATHOMETRIC
ABCEHIMRTTY	BATHYMETRIC
ABCEHINOOPR	NECROPHOBIA
ABCEHKNOORS	ON HORSEBACK
ABCEHKPSSTU	PASS THE BUCK
ABCEHLLOSTT	TABLECLOTHS
ABCEHLNOTUU	UNTOUCHABLE
ABCEHLNRSUU	UNCRUSHABLE
ABCEHMOPRST	CHAMBER POTS
ABCEIIIJLSTU	JUSTICIABLE

ABCEIILNOTX	INTOXICABLE		ABCHHIOPRSS	ARCHBISHOPS
ABCEIILRTUV	LUBRICATIVE		ABCHHLNOOPR	LOPHOBRANCH
ABCEIIMNOTV	COMBINATIVE		ABCHIIIMOPT	AMPHIBIOTIC
ABCEIINRSTU	SAINT-BRIEUC		ABCHIILOPSY	BIOPHYSICAL
ABCEIKNORTW	CABINETWORK		ABCHIKLMSST	BLACKSMITHS
ABCEILLLOPS	COLLAPSIBLE		ABCHIKLRSST	BLACKSHIRTS
ABCEILLMORU	BIMOLECULAR		ABCHILLOOST	HOLOBLASTIC
ABCEILLNOOZ	COLONIZABLE		ABCHILNOORR	BRONCHIOLAR
ABCEILLNTUY	INELUCTABLY		ABCHINOOPTY	NYCTOPHOBIA
ABCEILLRTUV	CARVEL-BUILT		ABCHINORRSY	CHRYSAROBIN
ABCEILMOPRS	COMPRISABLE		ABCHKLMORUU	BLACK HUMOUR
ABCEILMOPRT	PROBLEMATIC		ABCHKOOSSUY	YAH BOO SUCKS
ABCEILMORST	BLASTOMERIC, MEROBLASTIC		ABCIIILOSTY	SOCIABILITY
ABCEILMOTVY	COMBATIVELY		ABCIIIMNORT	IMBRICATION
ABCEILNOSTT	ENTOBLASTIC		ABCIIINOSTT	ANTIBIOTICS
ABCEILNPRSU	REPUBLICANS		ABCIILLMRSU	LUMBRICALIS
ABCEILNRSTU	INSCRUTABLE		ABCIILLPTUY	CULPABILITY
ABCEILNSUXY	INEXCUSABLY		ABCIILNOPTU	PUBLICATION
ABCEILORRVY	IRREVOCABLY		ABCIILNORTU	LUBRICATION
ABCEIMNNORT	RECOMBINANT		ABCIIMNNOOT	COMBINATION
ABCEIMNOORT	EMBROCATION		ABCIINORRTU	RUBRICATION
ABCEINNORTY	CYBERNATION		ABCIINORSTT	ABSTRICTION
ABCEINRRRST	TRANSCRIBER		ABCIKLLMMSU	BLACK MUSLIM
ABCEIOORRRV	BARCOO RIVER		ABCILMMORUU	COLUMBARIUM
ABCEIRSTTUV	SUBTRACTIVE		ABCILNORTUU	LUCUBRATION
ABCEJKLMRSU	LUMBERJACKS		ABCILNRSTUY	INSCRUTABLY
ABCEKKORSST	BACKSTROKES		ABCILOOPRST	BLASTOPORIC
ABCEKLNORSU	COALBUNKERS		ABCILOPRSTU	SUBTROPICAL
ABCELLLMNOO	COLLEMBOLAN		ABCILORRSTU	LUBRICATORS
ABCELLNOORS	COLLARBONES		ABCINNOORTU	CONURBATION
ABCELMNNRSU	UNSCRAMBLER		ABCINOORSTU	OBSCURATION
ABCELNNOTUU	UNCOUNTABLE		ABCINORSTTU	SUBTRACTION
ABCELNPRTUU	PUNCTURABLE		ABCLLRSTUUU	SUBCULTURAL
ABCEOOORRRT	CORROBORATE		ABCNORRSTUY	SUBCONTRARY
ABCEORRRTTU	CARBURETTOR		ABDDDEELOTU	DOUBLE DATED
ABCEORSTUUY	BUTYRACEOUS		ABDDDEIMNOR	BROADMINDED
ABCFGIINRTU	BIFURCATING		ABDDEEEILRT	DELIBERATED
ABCFGINOSTU	OBFUSCATING		ABDDEEEENSS	DEBASEDNESS
ABCFHINOOST	SON-OF-A-BITCH		ABDDEEIILTT	DEBILITATED
ABCFIILLMOR	BACILLIFORM		ABDDEEIKMRS	DISEMBARKED
ABCFIINORTU	BIFURCATION		ABDDEELOSTU	DOUBLE DATES
ABCFINOOSTU	OBFUSCATION		ABDDEFFILNN	EFF AND BLIND
ABCFLMNOORY	CONFORMABLY		ABDDEGIRRSW	DRAWBRIDGES
ABCFLMOORTY	COMFORTABLY		ABDDEHKLNNU	BUNDELKHAND
ABCGHHIOOPP	PHAGOPHOBIC		ABDDEHLLNOO	LO AND BEHOLD
ABCGHOORRSU	SCARBOROUGH		ABDDEHOOSWX	SHADOW-BOXED
ABCGIIKNOUV	BIVOUACKING		ABDDEIMNNST	DISBANDMENT
ABCGIILNRTU	LUBRICATING		ABDDELMOORW	WARM-BLOODED
ABCGIINNORZ	CARBONIZING		ABDDELNORRS	BORDERLANDS
ABCGILLOORY	BRYOLOGICAL		ABDDELORRTW	BLADDERWORT
ABCGILNPRUW	PUB-CRAWLING		ABDDGIINORV	DIVINGBOARD
ABCGINRSTTU	SUBTRACTING		ABDDOORRSSW	BROADSWORDS
ABCHHIILOTT	BATHOLITHIC		ABDEEEEGLRU	BELEAGUERED
ABCHHILOOOP	OCHLOPHOBIA		ABDEEEFHRST	FEATHER BEDS

ABDEEEFRRST	FAST-BREEDER	ABDEGGIRRSU	BUDGERIGARS
ABDEEEHILRT	HEREDITABLE	ABDEGHINSSU	SUBHEADINGS
ABDEEEHLLVW	WELLBEHAVED	ABDEGIILNNT	DINING TABLE
ABDEEEILLRV	DELIVERABLE	ABDEGIILSSU	DISGUISABLE
ABDEEELLOPV	DEVELOPABLE	ABDEGIKNORY	KEYBOARDING
ABDEEELMNRU	DENUMERABLE	ABDEGIMNRST	ABRIDGMENTS
ABDEEELNSST	BELATEDNESS	ABDEGLNNOOU	GO A BUNDLE ON
ABDEEELRRSS	REDRESSABLE	ABDEGOOORRV	GO OVERBOARD
ABDEEEMNSST	DEBASEMENTS	ABDEHIINNPR	HAIRPIN BEND
ABDEEEPRSTT	BESPATTERED	ABDEHIINNTU	UNINHABITED
ABDEEERSSTW	SWEETBREADS	ABDEHIORSTW	WHITEBOARDS
ABDEEFGIIRR	FIRE BRIGADE	ABDEHLNSSSU	HUSBANDLESS
ABDEEFIILNN	INDEFINABLE	ABDEIIJLNOS	DISJOINABLE
ABDEEFILLTT	BATTLEFIELD	ABDEIILLLST	DISTILLABLE
ABDEEGGINRR	GINGERBREAD	ABDEIILLTWY	WELDABILITY
ABDEEGLLOUZ	DOUBLE-GLAZE	ABDEIILMNOT	INDOMITABLE
ABDEEGLNOTU	DOUBLE AGENT	ABDEIIRSSTU	ABSURDITIES
ABDEEGMNOOR	BOOMERANGED	ABDEIKLNNRU	UNDRINKABLE
ABDEEHILRTY	HEREDITARY	ABDEILLLNSY	BLIND ALLEYS
ABDEEHILSST	ESTABLISHED	ABDEILLLSSY	DISSYLLABLE
ABDEEHNPRRS	SHARPBENDER	ABDEILLOSSV	DISSOLVABLE
ABDEEHORSST	BROADSHEETS	ABDEILMOTTU	TOLBUTAMIDE
ABDEEIILLRS	LIBERALISED	ABDEILMSSSY	DISASSEMBLY
ABDEEIILLRZ	LIBERALIZED	ABDEILNRSUY	UNDESIRABLY
ABDEEIILRST	DETRIBALISE	ABDEILOPRSV	DISPROVABLE
ABDEEIILRTZ	DETRIBALIZE	ABDEIMRSTUW	DUMBWAITERS
ABDEEIILSST	DESTABILISE	ABDEINORSTU	SUBORDINATE
ABDEEIILSTZ	DESTABILIZE	ABDELMOORST	BLOODSTREAM
ABDEEIKNNSY	KIDNEY BEANS	ABDELMRRSUY	LUMBERYARDS
ABDEEILMNNO	DENOMINABLE	ABDELOPRRTU	PROTRUDABLE
ABDEEILMNST	DISABLEMENT	ABDEMNORRST	BARNSTORMED
ABDEEILMSSS	DISASSEMBLE	ABDENOPRSUU	SUPERABOUND
ABDEEILNNRT	DINNER TABLE	ABDFILMOORR	DOLABRIFORM
ABDEEILNPSS	DISPENSABLE	ABDFLOOORRS	FLOORBOARDS
ABDEEILNRSU	UNDESIRABLE	ABDGHIINNRS	BRANDISHING
ABDEEILORRT	DELIBERATOR	ABDGHIMNOTU	BAD-MOUTHING
ABDEEILORTT	OBLITERATED	ABDGINOPRRS	SPRINGBOARD
ABDEEINNRRW	BREADWINNER	ABDGINORRST	STRINGBOARD
ABDEEKLOSTU	DOUBLE TAKES	ABDGMOORRSS	SMORGASBORD
ABDEEKNORSZ	BAKER'S DOZEN	ABDHHIOOPRY	HYDROPHOBIA
ABDEEKORRSY	KEYBOARDERS	ABDHINOOPRS	ON SHIPBOARD
ABDEELLLORR	ROLLERBLADE	ABDIIILTTUY	DUTIABILITY
ABDEELLNPRU	PLUNDERABLE	ABDIILMNOTY	INDOMITABLY
ABDEELLSSTY	SELL-BY DATES	ABDIINOSTUU	SUBAUDITION
ABDEELMNORZ	BRONZE MEDAL	ABDILNOOSST	BLOODSTAINS
ABDEELMNOTU	DEMOUNTABLE	ABDIMNNOSTU	SUBDOMINANT
ABDEELORRTW	WORLD-BEATER	ABDINORRSUY	SUBORDINARY
ABDEELORSTY	DESTROYABLE	ABDLNOOOSTT	ODONTOBLAST
ABDEFGINORR	FINGERBOARD	ABDNOORSTUU	ROUNDABOUTS
ABDEFGIRSSU	FIGURED BASS	ABDOORRSTUU	TROUBADOURS
ABDEFIILNNY	INDEFINABLY	ABEEEEFLORS	FORESEEABLE
ABDEFIRRSTU	BREADFRUITS	ABEEEEGLNRR	REGENERABLE
ABDEFLLOTUU	DOUBLE FAULT	ABEEEEIKLMV	MAKE-BELIEVE
ABDEGGILNOT	GOLD-BEATING	ABEEEEMNRTV	BEREAVEMENT

ABEEEERRRTV	REVERBERATE
ABEEEFLMNRT	FERMENTABLE
ABEEEGLORSW	ELBOW GREASE
ABEEEGLRRTT	REGRETTABLE
ABEEEHHINPR	HEBEPHRENIA
ABEEEHMNRRV	BREMERHAVEN
ABEEEHRSSTT	HARTEBEESTS
ABEEEIKRRST	TIEBREAKERS
ABEEEIILLPRV	REPLEVIABLE
ABEEEIILMMPR	IMPERMEABLE
ABEEEIILMMST	EMBLEMATISE
ABEEEIILMMTZ	EMBLEMATIZE
ABEEEIILPRRV	REPRIEVABLE
ABEEEIILRRTV	RETRIEVABLE
ABEEEIMNSST	ABSENTEEISM
ABEEELMNNTT	ENTABLEMENT
ABEEELMNNRRU	REMUNERABLE
ABEEELNPRST	PRESENTABLE
ABEEELNPRTV	PREVENTABLE
ABEEELPRRSV	PRESERVABLE
ABEEELPSTUY	BEAUTY SLEEP
ABEEENQTUUY	BEAUTY QUEEN
ABEEENRRRTV	REVERBERANT
ABEEERRSTTV	VERTEBRATES
ABEEFFILORT	FORFEITABLE
ABEEFFRSTTU	BUFFER STATE
ABEEFGILNRR	REFRANGIBLE
ABEEFGLORTT	FORGETTABLE
ABEEFIILLQU	LIQUEFIABLE
ABEEFIILNRT	ANTIFEBRILE
ABEEFILPRTU	PUTREFIABLE
ABEEFILRRTU	IRREFUTABLE
ABEEFLLNSSU	BALEFULNESS
ABEEFLMOPRR	PERFORMABLE
ABEEFLSSTTY	SAFETY BELTS
ABEEFNRRRTU	AFTERBURNER
ABEEGGILNPS	SLEEPING BAG
ABEEGGLRUUY	RUGBY LEAGUE
ABEEGHINQTU	BEQUEATHING
ABEEGIINOSS	ABIOGENESIS
ABEEGILMNPR	IMPREGNABLE
ABEEGILNRRY	GENE LIBRARY
ABEEGILRRST	REGISTRABLE
ABEEGINORRV	OVERBEARING
ABEEGINRRTU	TRUE BEARING
ABEEGLLLNSU	ANGELUS BELL
ABEEGLRRTTY	REGRETTABLY
ABEEHHPRSTY	BATHYSPHERE
ABEEHIILNRT	INHERITABLE
ABEEHILMPES	BLASPHEMIES
ABEEHILPRSS	PERISHABLES
ABEEHILRSST	ESTABLISHER
ABEEHILSTUX	EXHAUSTIBLE
ABEEHINRSSS	BEARISHNESS
ABEEHINRSST	BREATHINESS
ABEEHKNORRT	HEARTBROKEN
ABEEHKNORSS	BONESHAKERS
ABEEHLMPRSS	BLASPHEMERS
ABEEHLOORRS	SEBORRHOEAL
ABEEHLORRWW	WHEELBARROW
ABEEHORSTTU	THEREABOUTS
ABEEHORSTUW	WHEREABOUTS
ABEEIILLRRS	LIBERALISER
ABEEIILLRRZ	LIBERALIZER
ABEEIILMNPS	PLEBEIANISM
ABEEIILMNST	INESTIMABLE
ABEEIILNQTU	INEQUITABLE
ABEEIILQRTU	EQUILIBRATE
ABEEIKLLNSS	LIKABLENESS
ABEEIKLLRSV	BASKERVILLE
ABEEIKLMORR	BOILERMAKER
ABEEIKLNNST	LINEN BASKET
ABEEIILLNORT	INTOLERABLE
ABEEIILLNRSS	LIBERALNESS
ABEEIILLNSSV	LIVABLENESS
ABEEIILLOPRT	BOILERPLATE
ABEEIILLOPTX	EXPLOITABLE
ABEEIILLRUVZ	ULVERIZABLE
ABEEIILMMORZ	MEMORIZABLE
ABEEIILMMRRU	MARE LIBERUM
ABEEIILMNNOT	MENTIONABLE
ABEEIILMNNRU	INNUMERABLE
ABEEIILMORRV	IRREMOVABLE
ABEEIILMORST	STEAM-BOILER
ABEEIILNNOPS	PENSIONABLE
ABEEIILNNSTT	TABLE TENNIS
ABEEIILNPRSU	INSUPERABLE
ABEEIILNRRTV	INVERTEBRAL
ABEEIILNRSST	TRIABLENESS
ABEEIILNSSST	BEASTLINESS
ABEEIILNSSSZ	SIZABLENESS
ABEEIILNSSTW	WITNESSABLE
ABEEIILORSTT	BITTER ALOES
ABEEIILRRSST	LIBERATRESS
ABEEIILRRTVY	RETRIEVABLY
ABEEIINNQRTU	BARQUENTINE
ABEEIINORSSU	BUENOS AIRES
ABEEIINRSSTW	BEAR WITNESS
ABEEIINRSTUX	EXURBANITES
ABEEIINSSSUV	ABUSIVENESS
ABEEIIOPRRTV	REPROBATIVE
ABEEIIPRRRSS	RASPBERRIES
ABEEJLLMSSU	JUMBLE SALES
ABEEKLNSTTW	WET BLANKETS
ABEEKMMNNST	EMBANKMENTS
ABEELLLMSSY	BLAMELESSLY
ABEELLLMTUU	UMBELLULATE
ABEELMMNSSY	ASSEMBLYMEN

ABEELMNPRTU	NUMBERPLATE
ABEELMNSTTT	BATTLEMENTS
ABEELNNOOPR	NONOPERABLE
ABEELNNOSST	NOTABLENESS
ABEELNPRSTY	PRESENTABLY
ABEELNPRTVY	PREVENTABLY
ABEELNRTTUU	UNUTTERABLE
ABEELNRTUXY	EXUBERANTLY
ABEELOSTUUY	BEAUTEOUSLY
ABEELPRRSTY	PRESBYTERAL
ABEELQQRUUU	ALBUQUERQUE
ABEEMNRSSTU	SURBASEMENT
ABEENNNRRSU	RUNNER BEANS
ABEFFIILORT	FORTIFIABLE
ABEFFILLORS	BILLS OF FARE
ABEFFLNORRU	BARREL OF FUN
ABEFGIIILNS	SIGNIFIABLE
ABEFGIILLOR	GLORIFIABLE
ABEFGIILNNR	INFRANGIBLE
ABEFGIINTUY	BEAUTIFYING
ABEFHHLORRT	HALF-BROTHER
ABEFHIRRSTT	AFTERBIRTHS
ABEFHLNSSSU	BASHFULNESS
ABEFIIILNRT	NITRIFIABLE
ABEFIIILRTV	VITRIFIABLE
ABEFIIILSTY	FEASIBILITY
ABEFIIJLSTU	JUSTIFIABLE
ABEFIILLLMO	MOLLIFIABLE
ABEFIILLOOT	BIFOLIOLATE
ABEFIILNOSS	FISSIONABLE
ABEFILLLOSS	BILLS OF SALE
ABEFILLTUUY	BEAUTIFULLY
ABEFILRRTUY	IRREFUTABLY
ABEFLLOORST	FOOTBALLERS
ABEFLMOORTT	FOOT-LAMBERT
ABEFLMOOSTT	FALSE BOTTOM
ABEGGHRSSTU	STAGGERBUSH
ABEGGIILNOR	GLOBIGERINA
ABEGHIIMNSV	MISBEHAVING
ABEGHIINNRT	HIBERNATING
ABEGHIIOPRS	BIOGRAPHIES
ABEGHILMNOO	HAEMOGLOBIN
ABEGHILMNPS	BLASPHEMING
ABEGHIOPRRS	BIOGRAPHERS
ABEGHLLLSUY	BELLY LAUGHS
ABEGHLNOOPS	ANGLOPHOBES
ABEGIIINNRT	INEBRIATING
ABEGIILMNTT	TIMETABLING
ABEGIILNRVZ	VERBALIZING
ABEGIILRTUV	GIVE IT A BURL
ABEGIIRRSTU	SUBIRRIGATE
ABEGIKNOSST	BASINGSTOKE
ABEGILMNNOZ	EMBLAZONING
ABEGILMNOTY	AMBLYGONITE
ABEGILMNPRY	IMPREGNABLY
ABEGILNNRTY	BANTERINGLY
ABEGILNORSU	SUBREGIONAL
ABEGILNOSSX	SIGNAL BOXES
ABEGILRRYZZ	GRIZZLY BEAR
ABEGINNOPSU	SUBPOENAING
ABEGINNORRT	INTERROBANG
ABEGINNRSST	STRING BEANS
ABEGINRSSTU	GAS TURBINES
ABEGLLORSSW	GLASSBLOWER
ABEGMORRSTU	BURGOMASTER
ABEHHIRRSSU	HAIRBRUSHES
ABEHHJOORRU	JOHORE BAHRU
ABEHHORRSTT	HEARTTHROBS
ABEHIILMOPT	AMPHIBOLITE
ABEHIILPSTT	BLEPHATITIS
ABEHIINNORT	HIBERNATION
ABEHIKLNNTU	UNTHINKABLE
ABEHILMNOST	ABOLISHMENT
ABEHILNRSSU	NAILBRUSHES
ABEHILOOPRU	AILUROPHOBE
ABEHILOPRSW	WORSHIPABLE
ABEHILPSSTT	BATTLESHIPS
ABEHINOORTT	BOTHERATION
ABEHINOPRSV	VIBRAPHONES
ABEHKOOPRSS	PHRASEBOOKS
ABEHLMOORTW	BARTHOLOMEW
ABEHLMOPSSU	BLASPHEMOUS
ABEHLMORTWY	BLAMEWORTHY
ABEHLMOSTYZ	SZOMBATHELY
ABEHLORRSSU	HARBOURLESS
ABEHLORRSTY	LAY BROTHERS
ABEHNNOOTTY	ETHNOBOTANY
ABEHRSTTWYY	ABERYSTWYTH
ABEIIIILLST	LIABILITIES
ABEIIILLLMT	ILLIMITABLE
ABEIIILLNOR	BILLIONAIRE
ABEIIILLRTY	RELIABILITY
ABEIIINNORT	INEBRIATION
ABEIILLLLRY	ILLIBERALLY
ABEIILLMMST	BIMETALLISM
ABEIILLMPSU	IMPLAUSIBLE
ABEIILLMTTY	MELTABILITY
ABEIILLRSTT	BRISTLETAIL
ABEIILMNSTY	INESTIMABLY
ABEIILMSSUX	BISEXUALISM
ABEIILNQRTU	EQUILIBRANT
ABEIILNQTUY	INEQUITABLY
ABEIILNRRTT	INTERTRIBAL
ABEIILNRTTY	RENTABILITY
ABEIILOPPRT	PROPITIABLE
ABEIILOPRTY	OPERABILITY
ABEIILORTXY	EXORABILITY
ABEIILRSSST	STABILISERS

ABEIILRSSTZ	STABILIZERS
ABEIILRSTTU	BRUTALITIES
ABEIILRSTUY	REUSABILITY
ABEIILSTTTY	TESTABILITY
ABEIILSTUXY	BISEXUALITY
ABEIILTTTWY	WETTABILITY
ABEIINNOSTT	SINO-TIBETAN
ABEIINRRSSV	RIVER BASINS
ABEIIRRSTTU	TRIBUTARIES
ABEIIRTTTUV	ATTRIBUTIVE
ABEILLMORTU	RAMBOUILLET
ABEILLNORTY	INTOLERABLY
ABEILLNRSSY	BRAINLESSLY
ABEILLOPRSX	PILLAR BOXES
ABEILMMOSST	METABOLISMS
ABEILMOOSTU	AUTOMOBILES
ABEILNNPRTU	UNPRINTABLE
ABEILNOOSSS	OBSESSIONAL
ABEILNOSTTY	OBSTINATELY
ABEILNPRSUY	INSUPERABLY
ABEILOORRTT	OBLITERATOR
ABEILORSSTW	BELOW STAIRS
ABEILORSSUY	BYELORUSSIA
ABEILQRRTUY	BIQUARTERLY
ABEILRRSTTT	BRITTLE-STAR
ABEIMNNSSSU	BUSINESSMAN
ABEIMNORSTU	TAMBOURINES
ABEIMNRRSSU	SUBMARINERS
ABEINNNRSTU	BURNT SIENNA
ABEINNORSTV	INOBSERVANT
ABEINNOSSTT	ABSTENTIONS
ABEINOOPRRT	PROBATIONER, REPROBATION
ABEINOORSTV	OBSERVATION
ABEINORSTUV	SUBORNATIVE
ABEINOSSTTU	ABSTENTIOUS
ABEINSSTTUV	SUBSTANTIVE
ABEIRSSTTUV	SUBSTRATIVE
ABEKKORSSTW	WORKBASKETS
ABEKLOPRRRS	PORK BARRELS
ABEKMNNOSTU	MOUNTEBANKS
ABEKNOPRRSW	PAWNBROKERS
ABEKOOSTTTU	STATUTE BOOK
ABELLNNORVY	NONVERBALLY
ABELMNORRSY	SALMONBERRY
ABELNNORSUV	VERBAL NOUNS
ABELNOOPPST	POSTPONABLE
ABELNOOPSST	TABLESPOONS
ABELNOPPSTU	UNSTOPPABLE
ABELNRTTUUY	UNUTTERABLY
ABELOPPRSTU	SUPPORTABLE
ABELRRSTTUU	SURREBUTTAL
ABEMNNOTTTU	MOUNTBATTEN
ABEMNOORRSW	BONE MARROWS, MARROWBONES

ABEMNORRRST	BARNSTORMER
ABENOPRRSSS	PRESS BARONS
ABENOPRRTTU	PROTUBERANT
ABENOPRSSTU	BEANSPROUTS
ABEOORRSTVY	OBSERVATORY
ABEOPSSTTUY	BEAUTY SPOTS
ABFGHNOORRU	FARNBOROUGH
ABFGILNOSTY	FLYING BOATS
ABFIIILLLTY	FALLIBILITY
ABFIIIMNORT	FIMBRIATION
ABFIIJLSTUY	JUSTIFIABLY
ABFILMNSTUU	FUNAMBULIST
ABFIMOORSTU	FIBROMATOUS
ABGGGINNOOT	TOBOGGANING
ABGGIIMTUUY	AMBIGUGUITY
ABGGIJNSTUU	SUBJUGATING
ABGGILOOORY	AGROBIOLOGY
ABGHIINRSTT	BRATTISHING
ABGHIINSTTU	BATHING SUIT
ABGHIKPRRST	BRIGHT SPARK
ABGHILMOOPY	AMPHIBOLOGY
ABGHINNTTUY	ANYTHING BUT
ABGHLMOORRU	MARLBOROUGH
ABGIIILNSTZ	STABILIZING
ABGIIILNTTY	TANGIBILITY
ABGIILMNSTU	SUBLIMATING
ABGIILNOOST	OBLIGATIONS
ABGIILNRTUZ	BRUTALIZING
ABGIILNRTVY	VIBRATINGLY
ABGIINRTTTU	ATTRIBUTING
ABGIJNOORTU	OBJURGATION
ABGIJNOSTUU	SUBJUGATION
ABGIKKLNOOT	TALKING BOOK
ABGIKLLNNOR	BANKROLLING
ABGIKNNOPRW	PAWNBROKING
ABGIKNNPRTU	BANKRUPTING
ABGILLNNOSW	SNOWBALLING
ABGILLNORUY	LABOURINGLY
ABGILMOSUUY	AMBIGUOUSLY
ABGIMNOSUUU	UNAMBIGUOUS
ABGINOORSTU	SUBROGATION
ABGINOORSTW	ROWING BOATS
ABGJOORRTUY	OBJURGATORY
ABGLNORSTUY	GLASTONBURY
ABHHIKRSTTU	TURKISH BATH
ABHHIOOOPPT	PHOTOPHOBIA
ABHILMMNOPT	PHANTOM LIMB
ABHIMNORRTU	NORTHUMBRIA
ABHIOOPRSSU	RUSSOPHOBIA
ABHLLMOPSTY	LYMPHOBLAST
ABHLOOPRSTT	TROPHOBLAST
ABIIIILMTTY	IMITABILITY
ABIIIILNTVY	INVIABILITY
ABIIILLOSTY	ISOLABILITY

ABIIILLOTVY	VIOLABILITY	ACCCEHORSTW	COWCATCHERS
ABIIILNRSTY	RINSABILITY	ACCCEIILMRT	CLIMACTERIC
ABIIILNSTTY	INSTABILITY	ACCCEIILNSY	ENCYCLICALS
ABIIILPSSTY	PASSIBILITY	ACCCEILMOPS	ACCOMPLICES
ABIIILRTTVY	VIBRATILITY	ACCCEILORTU	LEUCOCRATIC
ABIIILSTTUY	SUITABILITY	ACCCELMNOPY	COMPLACENCY
ABIIINOPRTT	BIPARTITION	ACCCHIILLOT	LACCOLITHIC
ABIIKLORTWY	WORKABILITY	ACCCHILOORT	OCHLOCRATIC
ABIILLMPSUY	IMPLAUSIBLY	ACCCHOOPRTY	PTOCHOCRACY
ABIILLOSTVY	SOLVABILITY	ACCCIIOOPRS	CAPRICCIOSO
ABIILMNOSTU	SUBLIMATION	ACCCILLOOSU	CALCICOLOUS
ABIILMOSTUY	AMBITIOUSLY	ACCCIMMOORS	MACROCOSMIC
ABIILNORTTU	TRIBULATION	ACCCIMOOPRS	MACROSCOPIC
ABIILNRSTUY	INSALUBRITY	ACCCIOPRSTY	CYSTOCARPIC
ABIILOPRTTY	PORTABILITY	ACCDDEEIINO	DECANEDIOIC
ABIILOPRTVY	PROVABILITY	ACCDDEHNPRU	PUNCHED CARD
ABIILOQTTUY	QUOTABILITY	ACCDDEIIRST	DISACCREDIT
ABIILRRTTUY	TRIBUTARILY	ACCDDEINORS	DISCORDANCE
ABIIMNNOORT	BROMINATION	ACCDDEIRRST	CREDIT CARDS
ABIIMNOSTUU	UNAMBITIOUS	ACCDDELLMOU	MALOCCLUDED
ABIINNORTTU	TURBINATION	ACCDDELOPPU	CLOUD-CAPPED
ABIINOOPSTT	OBSTIPATION	ACCDDIIIMST	DIDACTICISM
ABIINOORSTT	ABORTIONIST	ACCDEEEENNT	ANTECEDENCE
ABIINORTTTU	ATTRIBUTION	ACCDEEEFNRT	FACE-CENTRED
ABILLNOOSST	BALLOONISTS	ACCDEEELNOS	ADOLESCENCE
ABILLOORSUY	LABORIOUSLY	ACCDEEELNST	DECALESCENT
ABILLORSTTU	SUBLITTORAL	ACCDEEFIILR	DECALCIFIER
ABILNNOORSU	LABOR UNIONS	ACCDEEFNORY	CONFEDERACY
ABIMNORRSST	BRAINSTORMS	ACCDEEGOPRU	COUP DE GRACE
ABINNOOOPRT	ON PROBATION	ACCDEEHIMNO	MACHINE CODE
ABINNOORSTU	SUBORNATION	ACCDEEHIORS	ARCHDIOCESE
ABINOORRSTU	BRONTOSAURI	ACCDEEHORSU	CHEQUE CARDS
ABINOOSSSST	BASSOONISTS	ACCDEEIISTV	DESICCATIVE
ABINOSSSTTU	BUS STATIONS, SUBSTATIONS	ACCDEEIKRSW	WISECRACKED
ABINRRSSTTU	BRAINS TRUST	ACCDEEIMORS	DEMOCRACIES
ABOORSSTTUU	ROUSTABOUTS	ACCDEEIORTT	DECORTICATE
ACCCDEHILNO	CHALCEDONIC	ACCDEELNOSV	CONVALESCED
ACCCDEIILNU	NUCLEIC ACID	ACCDEEMNSUU	SUCCEDANEUM
ACCCDENNOOR	CONCORDANCE	ACCDEENORST	CONSECRATED
ACCCDENNOTU	CONDUCTANCE	ACCDEFINOST	CONFISCATED
ACCCDILLOOP	DIPLOCOCCAL	ACCDEFNOSTU	SAFE-CONDUCT
ACCCDIMOPST	COMPACT DISC	ACCDEGHORST	DOGCATCHERS
ACCCEEELNOS	COALESCENCE	ACCDEGIINST	DESICCATING
ACCCEEELNST	LACTESCENCE	ACCDEHHITTT	CHITCHATTED
ACCCEEEMNRS	MARCESCENCE	ACCDEHHRSSU	ARCHDUCHESS
ACCCEEHILRS	ECCLESIARCH	ACCDEHILPRY	DIPHYCERCAL
ACCCEELMNOP	COMPLACENCE	ACCDEHNPRSU	CARDPUNCHES
ACCCEELNOPT	CONCEPTACLE	ACCDEHNRSTU	UNSCRATCHED
ACCCEFHKORS	COCKCHAFERS	ACCDEHOPSTT	SCOTCH TAPED
ACCCEHIISTT	CATECHISTIC	ACCDEIIIMRT	ACIDIMETRIC
ACCCEHIMOTT	CHEMOTACTIC	ACCDEIILLTY	DEICTICALLY
ACCCEHIOPRT	ECHOPRACTIC	ACCDEIILNOT	CONCILIATED
ACCCEHKOORS	COCKROACHES	ACCDEIINOST	DESICCATION
ACCCEHNORTY	TECHNOCRACY	ACCDEIKLNST	CANDLESTICK

ACCDEIKLNSW	CANDLEWICKS	ACCEEHLLNRY	CHANCELLERY
ACCDEILLOPS	PECCADILLOS	ACCEEHLNOXY	CYCLOHEXANE
ACCDEILMOPT	COMPLICATED	ACCEEIILNRT	ELECTRICIAN
ACCDEILNOST	OCCIDENTALS	ACCEEIIMPST	SEPTICAEMIC
ACCDEINOOTU	COEDUCATION	ACCEEIISTVX	EXSICCATIVE
ACCDEINPRSY	DISCREPANCY	ACCEEIKNPRS	SCIENCE PARK
ACCDEIPRRTU	PICTURE CARD	ACCEEIKRRSW	WISECRACKER
ACCDEKORRRT	TRACK RECORD	ACCEEILNNST	INCALESCENT
ACCDELMOPTY	COMPACTEDLY	ACCEEIMNOPS	CINEMASCOPE
ACCDELNOSSS	SECOND CLASS	ACCEEIMNRTT	METACENTRIC
ACCDENNOTUU	UNACCOUNTED	ACCEEINQSTU	ACQUIESCENT
ACCDFIIINOP	INDO-PACIFIC	ACCEEINNOSV	CONVERSANCE
ACCDGILNORY	ACCORDINGLY	ACCEENNORTT	CONCENTRATE, CONCERTANTE
ACCDHHNSSUU	SUCH AND SUCH	ACCEENNORVY	CONVEYANCER
ACCDHHRRSUY	CHURCHYARDS	ACCEENNOSVY	CONVEYANCES
ACCDHIIILOP	ACIDOPHILIC	ACCEENPSSTU	SUSCEPTANCE
ACCDHIIMORT	DICHROMATIC	ACCEEOPRSUY	CYPERACEOUS
ACCDHIINORT	ACHONDRITIC	ACCEEORRSSU	RACECOURSES
ACCDHILORSV	CLAVICHORDS	ACCEFFHHINS	CHAFFINCHES
ACCDHINOPRY	HYDNOCARPIC	ACCEFFIIOSU	EFFICACIOUS
ACCDHINORYY	HYDROCYANIC	ACCEFHLRSTY	FLYCATCHERS
ACCDIILLNRY	CYLINDRICAL	ACCEFIINRRY	FERRICYANIC
ACCDIILLORY	CODICILLARY	ACCEFILORSU	CALCIFEROUS
ACCDIILNOOR	CROCODILIAN	ACCEFINORRY	FERROCYANIC
ACCDIILOPST	OPTICAL DISC	ACCEFMNNOOR	CONFORMANCE
ACCDIIOOPRS	RADIOSCOPIC	ACCEGGIKNRT	GET CRACKING
ACCDIIPRSSU	PRUSSIC ACID	ACCEGHHITTW	CATCHWEIGHT
ACCDIMOSSTU	DISACCUSTOM	ACCEGHIINTZ	CATECHIZING
ACCDNNOOTTY	COTTON CANDY	ACCEGHIKMNT	CHECKMATING
ACCEEEEHKSS	CHEESECAKES	ACCEGHIKNQU	QUICK-CHANGE
ACCEEEEHMRS	CREAM CHEESE	ACCEGHINNOR	ENCROACHING
ACCEEEENNSV	EVANESCENCE	ACCEGHIOPRR	CEROGRAPHIC
ACCEEEFIKOP	PIECE OF CAKE	ACCEGIINQSU	ACQUIESCING
ACCEEEFILMN	MALEFICENCE	ACCEGILLOOT	CETOLOGICAL
ACCEEEFLNRT	REFLECTANCE	ACCEGILLOPY	CYCLOPLEGIA
ACCEEEHILRT	CHELICERATE	ACCEGINNORS	CARCINOGENS
ACCEEEIKKLO	COCK-A-LEEKIE	ACCEGINNOSZ	COGNIZANCES
ACCEEELNOPS	OPALESCENCE	ACCEHHHHIIR	CHICHIHAERH
ACCEEELNRST	RECALESCENT	ACCEHHIISTX	HEXASTICHIC
ACCEEELPRST	RECEPTACLES	ACCEHHISSTY	HESYCHASTIC
ACCEEFIIRTT	CERTIFICATE	ACCEHIILOST	CATHOLICISE
ACCEEFIKRRR	FIRECRACKER	ACCEHIILOTT	HELIOTACTIC
ACCEEFINORV	VOCIFERANCE	ACCEHIILOTZ	CATHOLICIZE
ACCEEGHILMO	GEOCHEMICAL	ACCEHIIMNST	MECHANISTIC
ACCEEGHINTY	EYE-CATCHING	ACCEHIINNST	TECHNICIANS
ACCEEGHORRV	COVER CHARGE	ACCEHIIORRT	HIEROCRATIC
ACCEEGILRRT	GREAT CIRCLE	ACCEHIIRSTU	EUCHARISTIC
ACCEEHHIRST	CHESHIRE CAT		
ACCEEHIINRS	CHICANERIES		
ACCEEHILMNO	CHAMELEONIC		
ACCEEHILNRT	CHANTICLEER		
ACCEEHINRRT	ARCHENTERIC		
ACCEEHIRRTU	CHARCUTERIE		
ACCEEHKORTW	WEATHERCOCK		

ACCEHILLMNO	MELANCHOLIC
ACCEHILLNTY	TECHNICALLY
ACCEHILMOOZ	ZOOCHEMICAL
ACCEHILOPPR	PROCEPHALIC
ACCEHILOPXY	OXYCEPHALIC
ACCEHIMNNOR	CHROMINANCE
ACCEHIMORTT	TACHOMETRIC
ACCEHIMORTU	EUCHROMATIC
ACCEHIMRTTY	TACHYMETRIC
ACCEHIRSSTT	SCRATCHIEST
ACCEHKOPPTT	PATCH POCKET
ACCEHLLMNOY	COLLENCHYMA
ACCEHLLNORS	CHANCELLORS
ACCEHLOOSSW	SLOWCOACHES
ACCEHNORSTT	TECHNOCRATS, TRENCH COATS
ACCEHOOSTWZ	CZESTOCHOWA
ACCEIIILLNN	ACLINIC LINE
ACCEIIIILSTV	ACCLIVITIES
ACCEIIINPRT	ACCIPITRINE
ACCEIIINRST	INTRICACIES
ACCEIILLNPR	PRECLINICAL
ACCEIILMOSV	SEMIVOCALIC
ACCEIILPRRT	PRECRITICAL
ACCEIILPRST	PERICLASTIC
ACCEIILRRSU	CIRCULARISE
ACCEIILRRUZ	CIRCULARIZE
ACCEIILRTUV	CIRCULATIVE
ACCEIIMNOST	COSMETICIAN, ENCOMIASTIC
ACCEIINNOSU	INSOUCIANCE
ACCEIINOSTV	CONCAVITIES
ACCEIINOSTX	EXSICCATION
ACCEIKKOTTT	TICK-TACK-TOE
ACCEIKNRSSS	CARSICKNESS
ACCEILLPSTY	SCEPTICALLY
ACCEILMMORS	COMMERCIALS
ACCEILMOPST	ECTOPLASMIC
ACCEILNNOTY	ANTICYCLONE
ACCEILNOPRT	NARCOLEPTIC
ACCEILNORTT	CONTRACTILE
ACCEILNORTU	CORNICULATE
ACCEILOPRST	CEROPLASTIC
ACCEILORSSY	ACCESSORILY
ACCEIMMNOTU	COMMUNICATE
ACCEIMNNORT	NECROMANTIC
ACCEIMOOPRS	COMIC OPERAS
ACCEIMORRTY	MERITOCRACY
ACCEINNNOTU	CONTINUANCE
ACCEINNORST	CONCERTINAS
ACCEINNORSU	COINSURANCE
ACCEINNORTV	CONTRIVANCE
ACCEINOORRY	COERCIONARY
ACCEINOOTVV	CONVOCATIVE
ACCEINORTTV	CONTRACTIVE
ACCEINSSSTU	CAUSTICNESS
ACCEIOORSSU	SCORIACEOUS
ACCEIORSTUU	URTICACEOUS
ACCEJLNORTU	CONJECTURAL
ACCEKNRRSTU	NUTCRACKERS
ACCELLOSTTU	COALSCUTTLE
ACCELMMNOOP	COMMONPLACE
ACCELNNOSTT	CONTACT LENS
ACCELORSSSU	SUCCESSORAL
ACCELPRRSUU	CREPUSCULAR
ACCEMNOPSST	COMPACTNESS
ACCENNNOOSS	CONSONANCES
ACCENNORSVY	CONSERVANCY
ACCENOOPRTU	POCOCURANTE
ACCENOORRST	CONSECRATOR
ACCENOPRRTT	PRECONTRACT
ACCENORRTTU	CONTRACTURE
ACCENPRTUUU	ACUPUNCTURE
ACCEOORSSTU	ECTOSARCOUS
ACCEORSSTUU	CRUSTACEOUS
ACCFGIIINRS	SACRIFICING
ACCFGILOSUU	CALCIFUGOUS
ACCFIIMOORR	CORACIIFORM
ACCFINOORST	CONFISCATOR
ACCGHIIOOPS	HAGIOSCOPIC
ACCGIILNNTU	INCULCATING
ACCGIILNOTU	GLAUCONITIC
ACCGIILNRTU	CIRCULATING
ACCGIINNOOS	OCCASIONING
ACCGILLMOOY	MYCOLOGICAL
ACCGILLNOOO	ONCOLOGICAL
ACCGILLNOOT	COLLOCATING
ACCGILLOOTY	CYTOLOGICAL
ACCGIMNOSTU	ACCUSTOMING
ACCGIMOPRTY	CRYPTOGAMIC
ACCGINNORTT	CONTRACTING
ACCGINORSTU	CORUSCATING
ACCHHIILLNS	CHINCHILLAS
ACCHHIIMOPR	AMPHICHROIC
ACCHHIINSTT	CHAIN STITCH
ACCHHMNORUW	CHURCHWOMAN
ACCHIILLSTY	STICHICALLY
ACCHIILMOST	CATHOLICISM
ACCHIILOSST	SCHOLIASTIC
ACCHIILOTTY	CATHOLICITY
ACCHIIMNORT	CHROMATINIC
ACCHIIMOSST	MASOCHISTIC
ACCHIIMSSST	SCHISMATICS
ACCHIIOOPST	SOCIOPATHIC
ACCHIIOPPRT	HIPPOCRATIC
ACCHIIORSTT	RHOTACISTIC
ACCHIIPRSTY	PSYCHIATRIC
ACCHIKMSSTT	MATCHSTICKS
ACCHILLNORY	CHRONICALLY
ACCHILLPSYY	PSYCHICALLY

ACCHILMOTYY	CYCLOTHYMIA
ACCHILOPTTY	PHYLOTACTIC
ACCHINOPSTY	SYCOPHANTIC
ACCHIOOPTTT	PHOTOTACTIC
ACCHIOORRSU	CHIAROSCURO
ACCHNOOOPSU	CACOPHONOUS
ACCIIIKKNPW	PICKWICKIAN
ACCIIILNSTV	CALVINISTIC
ACCIIILOSST	SOCIALISTIC
ACCIILNNOTU	INCULCATION
ACCIILNNQUU	QUINCUNCIAL
ACCIILNOORT	CONCILIATOR
ACCIILNORTU	CIRCULATION
ACCIILNOTVY	VOLCANICITY
ACCIILOSTUV	ACCLIVITOUS
ACCIILRRTUY	CIRCULARITY
ACCIILSSSST	CLASSICISTS
ACCIIMNNOTY	ACTINOMYCIN
ACCIIMNOTTY	ANTIMYCOTIC
ACCIINNSTTY	NYCTINASTIC
ACCIINOORTT	CORTICATION
ACCIJNNOTUV	CONJUNCTIVA
ACCIKKKKNNS	KNICK-KNACKS
ACCILLNOOOT	COLLOCATION
ACCILLPRTYY	CRYPTICALLY
ACCILMNRRUU	CIRCUMLUNAR
ACCILMOPRRU	CIRCUMPOLAR
ACCILMOPSTY	CYTOPLASMIC
ACCILNOOSST	ICONOCLASTS
ACCILNOOTTU	OCCULTATION
ACCILOPRSTY	PYROCLASTIC
ACCILOPRTTU	PLUTOCRATIC
ACCILORRTUY	CIRCULATORY
ACCIMMNNOTU	COMMUNICANT
ACCIMNNOOTT	CONCOMITANT
ACCINNNOSTY	INCONSTANCY
ACCINNOOOTV	CONVOCATION
ACCINNOORTT	CONTRACTION
ACCINOOPRSU	CORNUCOPIAS
ACCINOOPSTU	OCCUPATIONS
ACCINOORRRW	CARRION CROW
ACCINOORSTU	CORUSCATION
ACCINOPRRSU	CAPRICORNUS
ACCIORSSSTY	SYSSARCOTIC
ACCLLLOOORU	LOCAL COLOUR
ACCLNNOSTUY	CONSULTANCY
ACCLOPRRSUU	CORPUSCULAR
ACCNOORRSTT	CONTRACTORS
ACDDDEEILTY	DEDICATEDLY
ACDDDEEINRTU	CUT-AND-DRIED
ACDDEEEELRT	DECELERATED
ACDDEEEEPRS	PREDECEASED
ACDDEEEIPRT	DEPRECIATED
ACDDEEEOORRT	REDECORATED

ACDDEEFFIST	DISAFFECTED
ACDDEEGIKLR	GRIDDLECAKE
ACDDEEHHIKT	THICKHEADED
ACDDEEHHKOS	SHOCKHEADED
ACDDEEHLORT	COLD-HEARTED
ACDDEEHNORW	CROWNED HEAD
ACDDEEHNRSU	DUDE RANCHES
ACDDEEIILMS	DECIMALISED
ACDDEEIILMZ	DECIMALIZED
ACDDEEIIPRS	RICE PADDIES
ACDDEEIKRST	SIDETRACKED
ACDDEEINRSX	CARD INDEXES
ACDDEENNRST	TRANSCENDED
ACDDEENNSST	DESCENDANTS
ACDDEGIORSU	DISCOURAGED
ACDDEHLLOST	SADDLECLOTH
ACDDEHNNOSS	SECOND HANDS
ACDDEHNOOPY	DODECAPHONY
ACDDEIINOST	DEDICATIONS
ACDDEIIOSST	DISSOCIATED
ACDDEILLMSS	MIDDLE CLASS
ACDDEIMNORU	ENDOCARDIUM
ACDDEINOORT	COORDINATED
ACDDENORRSW	SWORD DANCER
ACDDENORSSW	SWORD DANCES
ACDEEEEHLRR	CHEERLEADER
ACDEEEFFTTU	EFFECTUATED
ACDEEEFILNR	ILE-DE-FRANCE
ACDEEEFNORT	CONFEDERATE
ACDEEEGLLOT	DECOLLETAGE
ACDEEEHLRTW	CARTWHEELED
ACDEEEHORRV	OVERREACHED
ACDEEEILNRV	DELIVERANCE
ACDEEEIPRTT	DECREPITATE
ACDEEEIPRTV	DEPRECATIVE
ACDEEEIRSTV	EVISCERATED
ACDEEELLNRT	CRENELLATED
ACDEEELORRT	DECELERATOR
ACDEEENNSTT	ANTECEDENTS
ACDEEEOORRTV	OVERREACTED
ACDEEEPRRTU	RECUPERATED
ACDEEFFHRUU	CHAUFFEURED
ACDEEFHLSTT	FLAT-CHESTED
ACDEEFIILTT	FELICITATED
ACDEEFIORTV	VOCIFERATED
ACDEEFLNRUU	FRAUDULENCE
ACDEEFMORRS	ARMED FORCES
ACDEEGGNORT	CONGREGATED
ACDEEGHNRRU	UNDERCHARGE
ACDEEGHORRV	OVERCHARGED
ACDEEGINPRT	DEPRECATING
ACDEEGINRST	DESECRATING
ACDEEGINRTU	RE-EDUCATING
ACDEEGIORST	CATEGORISED

ACDEEGIORTZ	CATEGORIZED	ACDEEIPRRST	TRADE PRICES
ACDEEGIOTTT	TIED COTTAGE	ACDEEIRSTTX	DIRECT TAXES
ACDEEGKLNOW	ACKNOWLEDGE	ACDEEISSSTU	CASE STUDIES
ACDEEHIINOT	ETHANEDIOIC	ACDEEKNORSW	DAWSON CREEK
ACDEEHILNOT	ENDOTHECIAL	ACDEEKQRRTU	QUARTERDECK
ACDEEHILNPP	CHIPPENDALE	ACDEELLMORU	LEUCODERMAL
ACDEEHILNRS	CHANDELIERS	ACDEELMORRS	SCLERODERMA
ACDEEHILPSY	PSYCHEDELIA	ACDEELNOPRW	CANDLEPOWER
ACDEEHIMNRS	MERCHANDISE	ACDEELNOSST	ADOLESCENTS
ACDEEHIMSST	SCHEMATISED	ACDEELNPTUU	PEDUNCULATE
ACDEEHIMSTZ	SCHEMATIZED	ACDEELNRRSY	DRY CLEANERS
ACDEEHINRTW	WINDCHEATER	ACDEEMMNNOT	COMMENTATED
ACDEEHIORTT	OCTAHEDRITE	ACDEEMNOPSS	ENCOMPASSED
ACDEEHLLOSU	CLOSE-HAULED	ACDEEMNOPST	COMPENSATED
ACDEEHMNORW	REACH-ME-DOWN	ACDEEMNRTTU	TRADUCEMENT
ACDEEHMNSTT	DETACHMENTS	ACDEENNORTV	CONTRAVENED
ACDEEHNRRTU	UNCHARTERED	ACDEENORRST	SECOND-RATER
ACDEEIILLTY	EIDETICALLY	ACDEEOPRRTY	DEPRECATORY
ACDEEIILMTV	MALEDICTIVE	ACDEFFIIRTV	DIFFRACTIVE
ACDEEIILPSS	SPECIALISED	ACDEFFLOSTU	DUFFEL COATS
ACDEEIILPSZ	SPECIALIZED	ACDEFGHMORR	FROGMARCHED
ACDEEIILTUV	ELUCIDATIVE	ACDEFGILRSU	DISGRACEFUL
ACDEEIIMMNN	MEDICINE MAN	ACDEFHILPST	FELDSPATHIC
ACDEEIINNRT	INCINERATED	ACDEFHLORTW	FLOWCHARTED
ACDEEIIOPPS	EPIDIASCOPE	ACDEFHMOOST	SMOOTH-FACED
ACDEEIIPRTV	PREDICATIVE	ACDEFIIINNT	INFANTICIDE
ACDEEIKMRTT	DREAM TICKET	ACDEFIIINOT	DEIFICATION, EDIFICATION
ACDEEILLMNY	ENDEMICALLY	ACDEFIILSTU	FEUDALISTIC
ACDEEILLNRS	CINDERELLAS	ACDEFIIORTY	EDIFICATORY
ACDEEILLNNST	CLANDESTINE	ACDEFIIRRST	FRATRICIDES
ACDEEILNOTT	DELECTATION	ACDEFINNOTU	FECUNDATION
ACDEEILNRST	CENTRALISED, CREDENTIALS	ACDEFKLNORS	FOLK DANCERS
ACDEEILNRSY	INCREASEDLY	ACDEFLLNORU	UNCALLED-FOR
ACDEEILNRTZ	CENTRALIZED	ACDEFLMMNOS	SELF-COMMAND
ACDEEILNTTU	DENTICULATE	ACDEFNORTUY	FECUNDATORY
ACDEEILPRTU	REDUPLICATE	ACDEGHHIOWY	HIGHWAY CODE
ACDEEILRSSU	SECULARISED	ACDEGHIILOT	GLOCHIDIATE
ACDEEILRSTT	DECRETALIST	ACDEGHIIMNR	MICHIGANDER
ACDEEILRSUZ	SECULARIZED	ACDEGHILLNT	CANDLELIGHT
ACDEEILRTTU	RETICULATED	ACDEGHILLRR	CHAR-GRILLED
ACDEEIMMNST	MEDICAMENTS	ACDEGHIMOPR	DEMOGRAPHIC
ACDEEIMNPRT	PREDICAMENT	ACDEGHINPST	DESPATCHING
ACDEEIMORRR	MICROREADER	ACDEGHLOORS	GRADE SCHOOL
ACDEEIMORST	DEMOCRATISE	ACDEGIILLOO	IDEOLOGICAL
ACDEEIMORTZ	DEMOCRATIZE	ACDEGIILNNN	LINE DANCING
ACDEEIMOSTT	DOMESTICATE	ACDEGIILNTU	ELUCIDATING
ACDEEINOPRT	DEPRECATION	ACDEGIIMNSU	MISGUIDANCE
ACDEEINORST	CONSIDERATE, DESECRATION	ACDEGIINPRT	PREDICATING
ACDEEINORTU	RE-EDUCATION	ACDEGIINSST	DIE-CASTINGS
ACDEEINPPRT	APPRENTICED	ACDEGILLOOP	PEDOLOGICAL
ACDEEIOPRRT	DEPRECIATOR	ACDEGILNNRY	DRY-CLEANING
ACDEEIOQTUV	EQUIVOCATED	ACDEGILOOPS	LOGOPAEDICS
ACDEEIORRSV	SERVICE ROAD	ACDEGILRSTT	CATTLE GRIDS
ACDEEIORRTT	DIRECTORATE	ACDEGIMNOSY	GEODYNAMICS

ACDEGIMORTY	TRAGICOMEDY	ACDEIINOTTX	INTOXICATED
ACDEGINNOOU	QUINDECAGON	ACDEIIRSTTV	DISTRACTIVE
ACDEGINNRTU	UNDERACTING	ACDEIJRSTUU	JUDICATURES
ACDEGIORRSU	DISCOURAGER	ACDEIKRSTTU	TRACKSUITED
ACDEGKNORRS	ROCK GARDENS	ACDEILLLMOY	MELODICALLY
ACDEGLOORST	COLD STORAGE	ACDEILLMNOY	DEMONICALLY
ACDEHIILMPS	DICEPHALISM	ACDEILLNOOT	DECOLLATION
ACDEHIIOPRT	DIAPHORETIC	ACDEILLORRS	CORDILLERAS
ACDEHIKLNST	STICKHANDLE	ACDEILMNOPS	ENDOPLASMIC
ACDEHIKMNOS	CHAIN-SMOKED	ACDEILMOPRR	DIMERCAPROL
ACDEHILNORT	CHLORINATED	ACDEILNOOST	CONSOLIDATE
ACDEHILOPSU	DICEPHALOUS	ACDEILNORSY	SECONDARILY
ACDEHIMOPRS	COMRADESHIP	ACDEILNORTU	RADIOLUCENT, REDUCTIONAL
ACDEH'IMOSTU	MUSTACHIOED	ACDEILNORTY	DECLINATORY
ACDEHINOORS	ICOSAHEDRON	ACDEILORTUY	ELUCIDATORY
ACDEHINOPST	DICTAPHONES	ACDEILORTVY	VALEDICTORY
ACDEHIOOPRT	ORTHOPAEDIC	ACDEILPPSTU	SUPPLICATED
ACDEHKMRSTU	DEUTSCHMARK	ACDEIMNNORU	ENDOCRANIUM
ACDEHLLLOPY	PHYLLOCLADE	ACDEIMNORRS	MORRIS DANCE
ACDEHLMOSUY	CHLAMYDEOUS	ACDEINNORST	CONSTRAINED
ACDEHLNPRTU	THUNDERCLAP	ACDEINNORTU	DENUNCIATOR
ACDEHLRSTTY	STRATHCLYDE	ACDEINNOSSS	DISSONANCES
ACDEHMNNOOR	ENCHONDROMA	ACDEINOOPRS	SCORPAENOID
ACDEHMNORRY	HYDROMANCER	ACDEINOORST	COORDINATES, DECORATIONS
ACDEHOORRTU	UROCHORDATE	ACDEINOPSTT	CONSTIPATED
ACDEHORRTWW	DRAW THE CROW	ACDEINOSSTU	DECUSSATION
ACDEHORRTYY	CRYOHYDRATE	ACDEINOSTTU	OUTDISTANCE
ACDEHRSTTTU	DUTCH TREATS	ACDEINOSTTW	WAINSCOTTED
ACDEIIILMOT	DOMICILIATE	ACDEINPRSTU	UNPRACTISED
ACDEIIINSTV	INDICATIVES	ACDEIOOPRSU	ADIPOCEROUS
ACDEIIJLPRU	PREJUDICIAL	ACDEIOPRRTY	PREDICATORY
ACDEIIKNRST	INSIDE TRACK	ACDEIPRSSTU	CUSTARD PIES
ACDEIILLMNY	MEDICINALLY	ACDEJKSSTTU	DUST JACKETS
ACDEIILLNTY	IDENTICALLY	ACDELLNOOTY	COTYLEDONAL
ACDEIILLORV	VARICELLOID	ACDELOPRTTY	PTERODACTYL
ACDEIILMNOT	MALEDICTION	ACDEMMMNNOT	COMMANDMENT
ACDEIILMRSS	DISCLAIMERS	ACDEMMNOSTU	CONSUMMATED
ACDEIILNNOT	DECLINATION	ACDEMNNORTU	COUNTERMAND
ACDEIILNNST	INCIDENTALS	ACDEMNORTUY	DOCUMENTARY
ACDEIILNORT	DIRECTIONAL	ACDEMOORRST	OSTRACODERM
ACDEIILNOST	SLIDE-ACTION	ACDEMOPRSSU	DAMP COURSES, MASS-PRODUCE
ACDEIILNOTU	ELUCIDATION	ACDENNNNOUU	UNANNOUNCED
ACDEIILNOTV	VALEDICTION	ACDENRRRSTU	REDCURRANTS
ACDEIILNPTU	INDUPLICATE	ACDEORRSSST	STAR-CROSSED
ACDEIILOPRS	PERIODICALS	ACDFFGHINNU	HANDCUFFING
ACDEIILORRT	DIRECTORIAL	ACDFFGIINNT	FACT-FINDING
ACDEIILPTUV	DUPLICATIVE	ACDFFGIINRT	DIFFRACTING
ACDEIIMNOST	MEDICATIONS	ACDFFGILNOS	SCAFFOLDING
ACDEIIMORRT	RADIOMETRIC	ACDFFIILMOO	OFFICIALDOM
ACDEIIMORTU	AUDIOMETRIC	ACDFFIINORT	DIFFRACTION
ACDEIIMPRRU	PERICARDIUM	ACDFGHHIINS	CHAFING DISH
ACDEIINNRTY	TYRANNICIDE	ACDFGIIMNOR	ACID-FORMING
ACDEIINOPRT	PREDICATION	ACDGGHIINRS	DISCHARGING
ACDEIINORRT	DOCTRINAIRE	ACDGHIIIOPR	IDIOGRAPHIC

ACDGHIINNSW	SANDWICHING
ACDGHIINPST	DISPATCHING
ACDGHIINRSV	CRASH-DIVING
ACDGHIMOOSU	DICHOGAMOUS
ACDGHIOPRSY	DISCOGRAPHY
ACDGHIRRRYY	HYDRARGYRIC
ACDGIIILMNS	DISCLAIMING
ACDGIIILOST	DIALOGISTIC
ACDGIIINNTV	VINDICATING
ACDGIILNOST	DISLOCATING
ACDGIILNPTU	DUPLICATING
ACDGIINNSTY	SYNDICATING
ACDGIINOPRR	ROAD PRICING
ACDGIINOSST	DIAGNOSTICS
ACDGIINRSTT	DISTRACTING
ACDGILLOOOX	DOXOLOGICAL
ACDGILNRTUY	TRADUCINGLY
ACDGIMNNOPU	UP AND COMING
ACDGINOORVW	WOODCARVING
ACDGLLOOTYY	DACTYLOLOGY
ACDGMNOPRSU	CAMPGROUNDS
ACDHHIMOTUW	WITH MUCH ADO
ACDHHIOPRRS	HARPSICHORD
ACDHIIIMRTT	MITHRIDATIC
ACDHIILLMOY	HOMICIDALLY
ACDHIILOPSU	ACIDOPHILUS
ACDHIINOOPR	RADIOPHONIC
ACDHIIOPRST	DIASTROPHIC
ACDHIMNOORT	TRICHOMONAD
ACDHIMNORTY	HYDROMANTIC
ACDHINNORYY	CYANOHYDRIN
ACDHIORRSSW	DISC HARROWS
ACDHIRSSSSW	SWISS CHARDS
ACDHLLOOOOW	WOOD ALCOHOL
ACDHLNOOORT	NOTOCHORDAL
ACDIIIILNPS	DISCIPLINAL
ACDIIIILLOTY	IDIOTICALLY
ACDIIILMORY	DOMICILIARY
ACDIIIMNOST	DIATONICISM
ACDIIIMOTTY	DIATOMICITY
ACDIIINNOST	INDICATIONS
ACDIIINNOTV	VINDICATION
ACDIILLLLYY	IDYLLICALLY
ACDIILLORST	CLOSTRIDIAL
ACDIILMNNRU	CLINANDRIUM
ACDIILMNOPR	PALINDROMIC
ACDIILMNSSY	SYNDICALISM
ACDIILNNOOT	CONDITIONAL
ACDIILNNOTU	INDUCTIONAL
ACDIILNOOST	DISLOCATION
ACDIILNOPTU	DUPLICATION
ACDIILNSSTY	SYNDICALIST
ACDIILOORRS	SORORICIDAL
ACDIILPRSTU	TRICUSPIDAL

ACDIIMNORSS	SARDONICISM
ACDIIMORSTY	MYOCARDITIS
ACDIINNOSTY	SYNDICATION
ACDIINOPSTU	CUSPIDATION
ACDIINORSTT	DISTRACTION
ACDIINORTVY	VINDICATORY
ACDIKKPSTUU	KICK UP A DUST
ACDIKLNOOSS	COOK ISLANDS
ACDIKNOPRTW	DOWNPATRICK
ACDILLORSTY	CRYSTALLOID
ACDILNOPRSS	SPINAL CORDS
ACDILOPRSTU	DUPLICATORS
ACDINNNOOOT	CONDONATION
ACDINOOORRT	COORDINATOR
ACDKLLNOORR	ROCK-AND-ROLL
ACDKNORSSTU	SOUNDTRACKS
ACDLLORSSTU	COLLAR STUDS
ACDLNOOORTY	CONDOLATORY
ACDNNOOPRSS	PROS AND CONS
ACDOOORSSTU	OSTRACODOUS
ACEEEFFFRTT	AFTEREFFECT
ACEEEFFKNOT	TAKE OFFENCE
ACEEEFHILNS	CHINESE LEAF
ACEEEFHLNRV	FRENCH LEAVE
ACEEEFIOPPP	PIPE OF PEACE
ACEEEFIPRSS	FIRE ESCAPES
ACEEEFLNRRU	NUCLEAR-FREE
ACEEEGHHRST	CHARGE SHEET
ACEEEGIMNRT	RACE MEETING
ACEEEGIMNTT	METAGENETIC
ACEEEGNPRST	PERCENTAGES
ACEEEGNRSTT	SECRET AGENT
ACEEEHIMNRS	ARCHENEMIES
ACEEEHIMNTV	ACHIEVEMENT
ACEEEHINNTT	CANINE TEETH
ACEEEHIORVV	OVERACHIEVE
ACEEEHIRRST	TREACHERIES
ACEEEHIRSTT	CATHETERISE
ACEEEHIRTTZ	CATHETERIZE
ACEEEHLLNRT	CHANTERELLE
ACEEEHLLRSV	SACHEVERELL
ACEEEHMNNNT	ENHANCEMENT
ACEEEHMORTT	TACHEOMETER
ACEEEHRRRSS	RESEARCHERS
ACEEEIKLNNW	WANNE-EICKEL
ACEEEILMNPT	MANTELPIECE
ACEEEILNPPR	PIPE CLEANER
ACEEEILNQUV	EQUIVALENCE
ACEEEILNRRV	IRRELEVANCE
ACEEEIMNRRS	MERCENARIES
ACEEEIMPRST	MASTERPIECE
ACEEEINNRST	CENTENARIES
ACEEEINRSSS	NECESSARIES
ACEEEINSSTT	NECESSITATE

ACEEEIPTTVX	EXPECTATIVE	ACEEGIKSTTW	WICKET GATES
ACEEEIRRSST	SECRETARIES	ACEEGILLNRY	GENERICALLY
ACEEEIRSSTV	TEA SERVICES	ACEEGILLNTY	GENETICALLY
ACEEEJKLPST	STEEPLEJACK	ACEEGILLNUY	EUGENICALLY
ACEEEJORSTT	EJECTOR SEAT	ACEEGILNPRS	SLEEPING CAR
ACEEELLMNOT	METALLOCENE	ACEEGILNPSS	SINGLE-SPACE
ACEEELLMNOV	MALEVOLENCE	ACEEGILSTTU	GESTICULATE
ACEEELLSSSY	CEASELESSLY	ACEEGIMMORT	MICROGAMETE
ACEEELMMNPT	EMPLACEMENT	ACEEGINNPRS	PREGNANCIES
ACEEELMNPRT	REPLACEMENT	ACEEGINORTT	TERATOGENIC
ACEEELMNRRT	RECREMENTAL	ACEEGINOTTU	AUTOGENETIC
ACEEELMNRTX	EXCREMENTAL	ACEEGIRRRTY	CERARGYRITE
ACEEELNPSSW	CLEAN SWEEPS	ACEEGKNOPSS	SPONGE CAKES
ACEEELORSTT	ELECTORATES	ACEEGLLRSSY	GRACELESSLY
ACEEEMNPSST	ESCAPEMENTS	ACEEGLMNNOT	CONGEALMENT
ACEEEMNRRT.T	RETRACEMENT	ACEEGMNORRS	SCAREMONGER
ACEEENRRSSV	SCREENSAVER	ACEEGNPRSSY	PRESS AGENCY
ACEEEOPRTTX	EXPECTORATE	ACEEHHIIRRS	HIERARCHIES
ACEEFFIILOS	OFFICIALESE	ACEEHHIKLTT	HATCHET-LIKE
ACEEFFILNTU	INEFFECTUAL	ACEEHHILRSW	WHEELCHAIRS
ACEEFFLLTUY	EFFECTUALLY	ACEEHHLMRST	CRASH HELMET
ACEEFGILNNR	FREELANCING	ACEEHHMMOOR	HAEMOCHROME
ACEEFHINNRS	ENFRANCHISE	ACEEHHMMSTU	MUCH THE SAME
ACEEFHLLOOR	ALCOHOL-FREE	ACEEHHNORST	SHEET ANCHOR
ACEEFHNRRTU	FURTHERANCE	ACEEHIILNST	LECITHINASE
ACEEFIILOPT	PIECE OF TAIL	ACEEHIINNRT	INHERITANCE
ACEEFIJKLST	LIFE JACKETS	ACEEHIIRSTT	HETAERISTIC
ACEEFILRSTV	SERVICE FLAT	ACEEHIKNRTW	KITCHENWARE
ACEEFIMNORS	FREEMASONIC	ACEEHILLNNP	PANHELLENIC
ACEEFIMNTTU	TUMEFACIENT	ACEEHILLRTY	HERETICALLY
ACEEFINOPTT	TEPEFACTION	ACEEHILMOPR	HEMERALOPIC
ACEEFLLNRST	CRESTFALLEN	ACEEHILMPRT	HALTEMPRICE
ACEEFLNRSSU	CAREFULNESS	ACEEHILNRTT	CHAIN LETTER
ACEEFLORSUU	FERULACEOUS	ACEEHILNSST	ETHICALNESS
ACEEFLPRRTU	PREFECTURAL	ACEEHILORTT	THEORETICAL
ACEEFMNOPRR	PERFORMANCE	ACEEHIMMNPT	IMPEACHMENT
ACEEFORRSST	FORECASTERS	ACEEHIMNNNT	ENCHAINMENT
ACEEFPPRSTT	PAST PERFECT	ACEEHIMNPSZ	CHIMPANZEES
ACEEGGIMMNO	EMMENAGOGIC	ACEEHIMORTT	THEOREMATIC
ACEEGGIMNOT	GAMETOGENIC, GAMOGENETIC,	ACEEHIMRTTY	ERYTHEMATIC
GEOMAGNETIC		ACEEHINNSTZ	NIETZSCHEAN
ACEEGHILOOT	OLIGOCHAETE	ACEEHINPRNT	PARENTHETIC
ACEEGHILPRT	TELEGRAPHIC	ACEEHINSSTT	ANESTHETICS
ACEEGHINNRT	INTERCHANGE	ACEEHIOPRST	SPIROCHAETE
ACEEGHINORV	HERCEGOVINA	ACEEHIORRST	CHARIOTEERS
ACEEGHINRRS	RESEARCHING	ACEEHIPRSTT	PARESTHETIC
ACEEGHLLNRS	CHALLENGERS	ACEEHIPRTTU	THERAPEUTIC
ACEEGHLNOOS	LOOSE CHANGE	ACEEHIPRTVY	HYPERACTIVE
ACEEGHNORSV	CHANGEOVERS	ACEEHKLNRST	HALTERNECKS
ACEEGHNRRSU	CHARGE NURSE	ACEEHLLNTTU	CALL THE TUNE
ACEEGHORRSV	OVERCHARGES	ACEEHLMMNSY	MESENCHYMAL
ACEEGHPRRSU	SUPERCHARGE	ACEEHLMNRUU	HERCULANEUM
ACEEGIILNNT	GEANTICLINE	ACEEHLMOPSY	MESOCEPHALY
ACEEGIKNNPP	KNEECAPPING	ACEEHLNOPSU	ENCEPHALOUS

ACEEHLNPRSU	LEPRECHAUNS	ACEEILNQUVY	EQUIVALENCY
ACEEHLOORRU	LEUCORRHOEA	ACEEILNRSST	TREACLINESS
ACEEHLOPRRT	PERCHLORATE	ACEEILNRSSY	NECESSARILY
ACEEHLOSSSV	CLOSE SHAVES	ACEEILNRSTV	CANTILEVERS
ACEEHMMNNRT	MERCHANTMEN	ACEEILNSTTT	CLIENT STATE
ACEEHMMRSSU	MEERSCHAUMS	ACEEILOORVV	CAVO-RELIEVO
ACEEHMNNNTT	ENCHANTMENT	ACEEILOPRTV	PERCOLATIVE
ACEEHMNNRRT	TRENCHERMAN	ACEEILOPSST	POLICE STATE
ACEEHMNOSTU	MENTHACEOUS	ACEEILORRTV	CORRELATIVE
ACEEHMORSTT	TACHOMETERS	ACEEILORTUX	EXECUTORIAL
ACEEHMSSTTT	TEST MATCHES	ACEEILPRRTY	PRELITERACY
ACEEHNNORRT	ARCHENTERON	ACEEILPSTUV	SPECULATIVE
ACEEHNNRSST	ENCHANTRESS	ACEEILRRSSU	SECULARISER
ACEEHNOPRTT	ON THE CARPET	ACEEILRRSUZ	SECULARIZER
ACEEHORRSTT	ORCHESTRATE	ACEEILSTTTU	TESTICULATE
ACEEHORRSTU	TREACHEROUS	ACEEIMMNORT	ANEMOMETRIC
ACEEIILLNPT	PENICILLATE	ACEEIMMORST	COMMISERATE
ACEEIILNRRT	RECTILINEAR	ACEEIMNNOTT	CEMENTATION
ACEEIILNSTT	LICENTIATES	ACEEIMNOPRT	ARMIPOTENCE
ACEEIILPRTV	REPLICATIVE	ACEEIMNORRT	CRANIOMETER
ACEEIILPTVX	EXPLICATIVE	ACEEIMNORTT	ACTINOMETER
ACEEIIMNRRT	RECRIMINATE	ACEEIMNOSTX	INCOME TAXES
ACEEIINNTUV	ENUNCIATIVE	ACEEIMNQRTU	ACQUIREMENT
ACEEIINRSST	RESISTENCIA	ACEEIMNRSTT	REMITTANCES
ACEEIINRSTT	CERTAINTIES	ACEEIMOSSTV	VASECTOMIES
ACEEIINRTTV	INTERACTIVE	ACEEINNNSST	ANCIENTNESS
ACEEIIPPRTT	PERIPATETIC, PRECIPITATE	ACEEINNORTV	NONCREATIVE
ACEEIIRSSTT	CASSITERITE	ACEEINNRRSU	REINSURANCE
ACEEIIRSTTV	RECITATIVES	ACEEINNSSTX	INEXACTNESS
ACEEIKMPRRT	MARKET PRICE	ACEEINOPTTX	EXPECTATION
ACEEIKNSSSS	SEASICKNESS	ACEEINORRST	RECREATIONS
ACEEILLNNSS	CLEANLINESS	ACEEINORSTU	AUCTIONEERS
ACEEILLNPST	SPLENETICAL	ACEEINORSTX	EXECRATIONS
ACEEILMNNRT	INCREMENTAL	ACEEINPPRST	APPRENTICES
ACEEILMNORS	CEREMONIALS	ACEEINPRRST	TRANSPIERCE
ACEEILMNORT	TRINCOMALEE	ACEEINRRSTV	TRANSCEIVER
ACEEILMNRRY	MERCENARILY	ACEEINRSSST	RESISTANCES
ACEEILMORRT	CALORIMETER	ACEEIOOPRTV	COOPERATIVE
ACEEILMORST	ELASTOMERIC	ACEEIOPPRSU	PIPERACEOUS
ACEEILMPSST	ESEMPLASTIC	ACEEIORRSTV	EVISCERATOR
ACEEILMPSTU	TIME CAPSULE	ACEEIORRTTV	RETROACTIVE
ACEEILMRTUV	VERMICULATE	ACEEIPPRSTY	PARTY PIECES
ACEEILNNNST	CENTENNIALS	ACEEIRSSTTU	RESUSCITATE
ACEEILNNORT	INTOLERANCE	ACEEJNPRSTU	SUPERJACENT
ACEEILNNOTU	ENUCLEATION	ACEEKLLRSSS	SALESCLERKS
ACEEILNNTUY	LIEUTENANCY	ACEEKNRSTTV	TRACK EVENTS
ACEEILNOPTX	EXCEPTIONAL	ACEEKORRSSW	CASEWORKERS
ACEEILNORSS	RECESSIONAL	ACEELLMNRSS	SMALL SCREEN
ACEEILNORST	RESECTIONAL	ACEELLNOSTT	CONSTELLATE
ACEEILNOSSS	SECESSIONAL	ACEELMNNOOV	MONOVALENCE
ACEEILNOSST	COESSENTIAL	ACEELMNOPTT	CONTEMPLATE
ACEEILNPRTT	CENTRIPETAL	ACEELMOPRRU	COME A PURLER
ACEEILNPSSS	SPECIALNESS	ACEELNNNSSU	UNCLEANNESS
ACEEILNPSST	PLICATENESS	ACEELNOOPRT	COLEOPTERAN

ACEELNOOSSS	CLOSE SEASON	ACEFINNORST	FOR INSTANCE
ACEELNOPSTT	PENTECOSTAL	ACEFINOTTUV	CONFUTATIVE
ACEELNORRTX	RENAL CORTEX	ACEFIOORRTV	VOCIFERATOR
ACEELNPRSSY	SCREENPLAYS	ACEFIPRRSTT	PRIESTCRAFT
ACEELNPTTXY	EXPECTANTLY	ACEFLNSSTTU	TACTFULNESS
ACEELOPPPRT	COPPERPLATE	ACEFOOPSTTX	EX POST FACTO
ACEELORSTTW	WATER CLOSET	ACEGGHILLNN	CHALLENGING
ACEEMMMOORT	COMMEMORATE	ACEGGHILNNS	CHANGELINGS
ACEEMMNNPST	ENCAMPMENTS	ACEGGILLMOO	GEMOLOGICAL
ACEEMNOOSWY	COME ONE'S WAY	ACEGGILOORT	GERATOLOGIC
ACEEMNPRSST	ESCARPMENTS	ACEGGINNORU	ENCOURAGING
ACEENNOPRTU	COUNTERPANE	ACEGGINRSSS	SCRAGGINESS
ACEENNORRTV	CONTRAVENER	ACEGGLNOOYY	GYNAECOLOGY
ACEENNORSTT	CONSTERNATE	ACEGGNOORRT	CONGREGATOR
ACEENNRSSUY	UNNECESSARY	ACEGHHILOPR	HELICOGRAPH
ACEENOORSTT	COTONEASTER	ACEGHHILRST	SEARCHLIGHT
ACEENOPRSTV	VAPORESCENT	ACEGHHILNORW	WEIGH ANCHOR
ACEENOPRTTX	EXPECTORANT	ACEGHHMNRRU	HUNGER MARCH
ACEENRSSSTW	NEWSCASTERS	ACEGHHNORST	SHORT-CHANGE
ACEEOPRRRTU	RECUPERATOR	ACEGHHOOPRR	CHOREOGRAPH
ACEEORRSTUW	WATERCOURSE	ACEGHHOPRTY	HECTOGRAPHY
ACEEPPRRTTU	PAPER-CUTTER	ACEGHIIIMNT	MICHIGANITE
ACEFFFILOST	FACTS OF LIFE	ACEGHIILORS	OLIGARCHIES
ACEFFGHILNR	CLIFFHANGER	ACEGHIIMNNZ	MECHANIZING
ACEFFGILNTY	AFFECTINGLY	ACEGHIKLLNS	SHELLACKING
ACEFFIITTVY	AFFECTIVITY	ACEGHIKMNOP	EPOCH-MAKING
ACEFFIKRRST	TRAFFICKERS	ACEGHILLNNN	CHANNELLING
ACEFFIOSTUV	SUFFOCATIVE	ACEGHILLOOR	RHEOLOGICAL
ACEFGHLLNOT	FOCAL LENGTH	ACEGHILLOOT	THEOLOGICAL
ACEFGIIMNNT	MAGNIFICENT	ACEGHILNRSY	SEARCHINGLY
ACEFGIINNRT	INTERFACING	ACEGHILOOPR	OLEOGRAPHIC
ACEFGILNRTU	CENTRIFUGAL	ACEGHILOPSY	GEOPHYSICAL
ACEFGINORST	FORECASTING	ACEGHIMNNSU	MACHINEGUNS
ACEFGINRRSU	RESURFACING	ACEGHIMNORR	MENORRHAGIC
ACEFHILNOPR	FRANCOPHILE	ACEGHIMNORU	ARCHEGONIUM
ACEFHIRSTTY	CITY FATHERS	ACEGHIMNRSY	CRYING SHAME
ACEFHLNRTUY	HALF-CENTURY	ACEGHINNOPR	CHAPERONING
ACEFHLOPRRU	REPROACHFUL	ACEGHINOPRR	REPROACHING
ACEFHMNNORW	FRENCHWOMAN	ACEGHINORRV	OVERARCHING
ACEFHNNOOPR	FRANCOPHONE	ACEGHIOPRRX	XEROGRAPHIC
ACEFHNORSTT	FRENCH TOAST	ACEGHLNOPTT	PLECTOGNATH
ACEFHORRSTV	HOVERCRAFTS	ACEGHLOOSTY	ESCHATOLOGY
ACEFIIINORT	REIFICATION	ACEGHNOPRSY	SCENOGRAPHY
ACEFIILORTT	FELICITATOR	ACEGHOOPRSU	CREOPHAGOUS
ACEFIILPRSU	SUPERFICIAL	ACEGHORRSTU	ROUGHCASTER
ACEFIINOPTT	PONTIFICATE	ACEGIIKNPRS	ASKING PRICE
ACEFIINORST	FRACTIONISE	ACEGIILLOOT	ETIOLOGICAL
ACEFIINORTZ	FRACTIONIZE	ACEGIILLOTV	COLLIGATIVE
ACEFILLLOTU	FOLLICULATE	ACEGIILNNRT	INTERLACING
ACEFILLORUW	CAULIFLOWER	ACEGIILNPRT	REPLICATING
ACEFILMMOTU	COMME IL FAUT	ACEGIILNPTX	EXPLICATING
ACEFILORSTU	LACTIFEROUS	ACEGIILOSTT	EGOTISTICAL
ACEFILOSTUY	FACETIOUSLY	ACEGIILRSST	SACRILEGIST
ACEFIMNOTTU	TUMEFACTION	ACEGIIMNOST	ISOMAGNETIC

ACEGIIMRRTV	GRAVIMETRIC
ACEGIINNNTU	ENUNCIATING
ACEGIINNRTT	INTERACTING
ACEGIINORTX	EXCORIATING
ACEGIINRTTX	EXTRICATING
ACEGIINRTUZ	CAUTERIZING
ACEGIJNOTUV	CONJUGATIVE
ACEGIKLNRST	SINGLE-TRACK
ACEGILLMRTU	METALLURGIC
ACEGILLNNOY	CONGENIALLY
ACEGILLNOOO	OENOLOGICAL
ACEGILLNOOP	PENOLOGICAL
ACEGILMNRSY	SCREAMINGLY
ACEGILMOSTY	CLEISTOGAMY
ACEGILNNOOT	CONGELATION
ACEGILNNPRS	SPRING-CLEAN
ACEGILNOPRT	PERCOLATING
ACEGILNOPSY	CLAY PIGEONS
ACEGILNORRT	CORRELATING
ACEGILNPSTU	SPECULATING
ACEGILNPTUX	EXCULPATING
ACEGILNRSSY	CARESSINGLY
ACEGILNTUUU	UNGUICULATE
ACEGILOOPST	APOLOGETICS
ACEGILOORTT	TERATOLOGIC
ACEGILRRTUU	AGRICULTURE
ACEGIMNOTVY	VAGINECTOMY
ACEGIMORSST	MESOGASTRIC
ACEGINNNOTV	COVENANTING
ACEGINNRSTY	ASTRINGENCY
ACEGINOOPRT	COOPERATING
ACEGINOPRRT	PROCREATING
ACEGINOSTTV	CASTING VOTE
ACEGINPRRTU	RECAPTURING
ACEGINPSTYC	TYPECASTING
ACEGIOORTTX	EXCOGITATOR
ACEGIOPSTTY	STEATOPYGIC
ACEGKRSSTTU	STAGESTRUCK
ACEGLNOPRTY	CALYPTROGEN
ACEGLNORTUY	GRANULOCYTE
ACEGLRSSTTU	GLASSCUTTER
ACEGMNNORSS	CONGRESSMAN
ACEGMOPRRST	SPECTROGRAM
ACEGMORSTTY	GASTRECTOMY
ACEGNORRSST	CROSS-GARNET
ACEGOOPRSST	GASTROSCOPE
ACEHHIILMOP	HAEMOPHILIC, HEMOPHILIAC
ACEHHIIMRRS	HIERARCHISM
ACEHHIINNTY	HYACINTHINE
ACEHHIMOOPT	HOMEOPATHIC
ACEHHINOSTX	HEXASTICHON
ACEHHNORSSU	RANCH HOUSES
ACEHIIINPSS	HISPANICISE
ACEHIIINPSZ	HISPANICIZE

ACEHIILLOPT	PALEOLITHIC
ACEHIILLOST	ISOLECITHAL
ACEHIILMSTT	ATHLETICISM
ACEHIILNOPR	NECROPHILIA
ACEHIILOSTT	CHIASTOLITE, HELIOSTATIC
ACEHIILSTWW	WELWITSCHIA
ACEHIINNOPT	PHONETICIAN
ACEHIINORRT	RHETORICIAN
ACEHIINPSTT	PANTHEISTIC
ACEHIKKLMMO	HAMMOCK-LIKE
ACEHIKLPRRS	PARISH CLERK
ACEHIKLPRTY	PRICKLY HEAT
ACEHIKMNORS	CHAIN-SMOKER
ACEHIKMRTUY	RHEUMATICKY
ACEHILLMORY	HOMERICALLY
ACEHILLORTW	WHITE-COLLAR
ACEHILMNOOT	MACHINE TOOL
ACEHILMNOST	SLOT MACHINE
ACEHILNPRST	SPHINCTERAL
ACEHILNSTTY	SYNTHETICAL
ACEHILRSSSY	CHRYSALISES
ACEHIMMOPRT	METAMORPHIC
ACEHIMNORSS	MARCHIONESS
ACEHIMNORTU	EUCHROMATIN
ACEHIMOOSTT	HOMEOSTATIC
ACEHIMOPRST	ATMOSPHERIC
ACEHIMORRRT	ARTHROMERIC
ACEHIMORRST	CHOIRMASTER
ACEHIMORTTX	THERMOTAXIC
ACEHIMPSSTY	METAPHYSICS
ACEHIMPSTTY	SYMPATHETIC
ACEHIMRSSST	CHRISTMASES
ACEHINNOOTT	CANINE TOOTH
ACEHINNPSSU	PAUNCHINESS
ACEHINNRSSU	RAUNCHINESS
ACEHINOOPRZ	PHANEROZOIC
ACEHINOPRRS	CHAIRPERSON
ACEHINOPRRT	CHIROPTERAN
ACEHINOPRTU	NEUROPATHIC
ACEHINORSST	CHAIN STORES
ACEHINRSSST	STARCHINESS
ACEHIOOPSTT	OSTEOPATHIC
ACEHIOOPTTV	PHOTOACTIVE
ACEHIOPPRST	HIPPOCRATES
ACEHIORSSTY	CASE HISTORY
ACEHIPRRSST	STRIP-SEARCH
ACEHIQRRSUY	SQUIREARCHY
ACEHKMRRSTT	STRETCHMARK
ACEHLLMSSTY	MATCHLESSLY
ACEHLMMNOOR	CHROMONEMAL
ACEHLMOOSST	SCHOOLMATES
ACEHLMRSSUV	SCRUMHALVES
ACEHLNNRTTY	TRENCHANTLY
ACEHLORSTUY	LYTHRACEOUS

ACEHMNOPRSY	PROSENCHYMA
ACEHMOORTTY	TRACHEOTOMY
ACEHMOPRSTU	CHAMPERTOUS
ACEHNNOOPRT	CTENOPHORAN
ACEHNNSSSTU	STAUNCHNESS
ACEHOPPRSTU	TOUCHPAPERS
ACEHOPRRSSY	CHRYSOPRASE
ACEHOPRRTYY	CRYOTHERAPY
ACEHOPSSTTW	STOPWATCHES
ACEHORSTTTWW	WATCHTOWERS
ACEIIIKNNOS	ANISEIKONIC
ACEIIILMPTV	IMPLICATIVE
ACEIIILNOTT	ELICITATION
ACEIIIMNNRT	INCRIMINATE
ACEIIIMNOST	SEMIOTICIAN
ACEIIIMNSTT	ANTI-SEMITIC
ACEIIIQSTUV	ACQUISITIVE
ACEIIKLLNTY	KINETICALLY
ACEIIKLRSTT	RICKETTSIAL
ACEIIKNOTTU	AUTOKINETIC
ACEIIKNRSSS	AIRSICKNESS
ACEIILLMMTY	MIMETICALLY
ACEIILLMNNU	ILLUMINANCE
ACEIILLMOTY	MEIOTICALLY
ACEIILLMPRY	EMPIRICALLY
ACEIILLMSSY	SEISMICALLY
ACEIILLNSTT	SCINTILLATE
ACEIILMNPRT	PLANIMETRIC
ACEIILMNSTT	MENTALISTIC
ACEIILMOPST	ATOMIC PILES
ACEIILMORST	ISOMETRICAL
ACEIILMOTTU	ITACOLUMITE
ACEIILMPSSS	SPECIALISMS
ACEIILNNORT	RECLINATION
ACEIILNOPPR	PILOCARPINE
ACEIILNOPRT	REPLICATION
ACEIILNOPTX	EXPLICATION
ACEIILNOQTU	EQUINOCTIAL
ACEIILNOTUV	INOCULATIVE
ACEIILNPRUY	PECUNIARILY
ACEIILNRRUV	CURVILINEAR
ACEIILNRSTT	CLARINETIST
ACEIILNRSTU	UNREALISTIC
ACEIILNRTTY	INTRICATELY
ACEIILOPRST	TROPICALISE
ACEIILOPRTZ	TROPICALIZE
ACEIILPPRST	PARTICIPLES
ACEIILPRSST	PLASTICISER
ACEIILPRSTT	PERISTALTIC, TRIPLICATES
ACEIILPRSTZ	PLASTICIZER
ACEIILPRTUY	PECULIARITY
ACEIILPSSST	SPECIALISTS
ACEIILRTTVY	VERTICALITY
ACEIIMNNRST	MANNERISTIC

ACEIIMNOPRT	IMPRECATION
ACEIIMNORST	ANISOMETRIC, MISCREATION, REACTIONISM, ROMANTICISE
ACEIIMNORTT	INTERATOMIC, METRICATION
ACEIIMNORTZ	ROMANTICIZE
ACEIIMNPRRU	PERICRANIUM
ACEIIMNPSSU	IMPUISSANCE
ACEIIMNRSTT	MARTENSITIC
ACEIIMNRSTU	INSECTARIUM
ACEIIMNSSTT	SEMANTICIST
ACEIINNNOTU	ENUNCIATION
ACEIINNOPTT	PECTINATION
ACEIINNORRT	INCINERATOR
ACEIINNORTT	INTERACTION
ACEIINNPSTT	PINNATISECT
ACEIINOORTX	EXCORIATION
ACEIINOPRTT	CREPITATION
ACEIINOPSTT	PECTISATION
ACEIINOPTTZ	PECTIZATION
ACEIINORSTT	RECITATIONS
ACEIINORTTX	EXTRICATION
ACEIINPPRTT	PRECIPITANT
ACEIINPRTTY	ANTIPYRETIC, PERTINACITY
ACEIINPSSTT	ANTISEPTICS
ACEIIOOPPST	APOSIOPETIC
ACEIKKLNPTY	PENALTY KICK
ACEIKLLPSTY	SKEPTICALLY
ACEIKLNPSSV	CLASP KNIVES
ACEIKLPPRRY	PRICKLY PEAR
ACEIKNPSSTT	SEPTIC TANKS
ACEILLLMNOR	LAMELLICORN
ACEILLLMOPY	POLEMICALLY
ACEILLLNORT	CITRONELLAL
ACEILLLNRUU	UNICELLULAR
ACEILLMNNOT	NONMETALLIC
ACEILLMNRUY	NUMERICALLY
ACEILLMOTTY	TOTEMICALLY
ACEILLMRRUY	MERCURIALLY
ACEILLNNOOO	NEOCOLONIAL
ACEILLNOPTU	CUPELLATION
ACEILLNRSTY	CRYSTALLINE
ACEILLOORRS	COROLLARIES
ACEILLOPSSW	PILLOWCASES
ACEILLOQUVY	EQUIVOCALLY
ACEILLRSSTY	CRYSTALLISE
ACEILLRSTTY	CRYSTALLITE
ACEILLRSTYZ	CRYSTALLIZE
ACEILLRTUVY	LUCRATIVELY
ACEILMMNOSU	COMMUNALISE
ACEILMMNOTY	METONYMICAL
ACEILMMNOUZ	COMMUNALIZE
ACEILMMRSTY	SYMMETRICAL
ACEILMNOOPS	SCOPOLAMINE
ACEILMNOOPW	POLICEWOMAN

489

ACEILMNOPRS	COMPLAINERS
ACEILMNOPRT	PLANOMETRIC
ACEILMNOPTY	AMYLOPECTIN
ACEILMNRTTU	CURTAILMENT
ACEILMNRTUU	RETINACULUM
ACEILMNSSSU	MUSICALNESS
ACEILMORRTY	CALORIMETRY
ACEILMRRTUU	MARICULTURE
ACEILNNNOSS	NONSENSICAL
ACEILNNNOTT	CONTINENTAL
ACEILNNNOTU	ANTINUCLEON
ACEILNNORTU	CRENULATION
ACEILNNRTUY	UNCERTAINLY
ACEILNNSSTY	INCESSANTLY
ACEILNOOPRR	INCORPOREAL
ACEILNOOPRT	PERCOLATION
ACEILNOORRT	CORRELATION
ACEILNOORSU	ARENICOLOUS
ACEILNOPRST	INSPECTORAL
ACEILNOPSTU	PECULATIONS, SPECULATION
ACEILNOPTUX	EXCULPATION
ACEILNOQUUV	UNEQUIVOCAL
ACEILNORSTT	INTERCOSTAL
ACEILNORTUV	COUNTERVAIL, INVOLUCRATE
ACEILNOSSST	STOICALNESS
ACEILNOSTUY	TENACIOUSLY
ACEILNPSSTY	TYPICALNESS
ACEILNRRTUV	VENTRICULAR
ACEILOOPPRS	POLARISCOPE
ACEILOOSSST	OSTEOCLASIS
ACEILOPRRTT	PROTRACTILE
ACEILORSUVY	VERACIOUSLY
ACEILORTVYY	VICEROYALTY
ACEILPRSTTY	SPECTRALITY
ACEILQRTUUU	AQUICULTURE
ACEILRRTTUU	TURRICULATE
ACEIMMOOSSU	MIMOSACEOUS
ACEIMMORRTU	CREMATORIUM
ACEIMMOTTUV	COMMUTATIVE
ACEIMNNNOTT	CONTAINMENT
ACEIMNOPRRS	MARINE CORPS
ACEIMNORRTU	MERCURATION
ACEIMNORRTY	CRANIOMETRY
ACEIMNORTTY	ACTINOMETRY
ACEIMOPRRTY	IMPRECATORY
ACEIMORRSTT	ASTROMETRIC
ACEIMPRSSTU	SUPREMACIST
ACEIMSSSTTY	SYSTEMATICS
ACEINNNOSTT	CONSTANTINE
ACEINNOOTTV	CONNOTATIVE
ACEINNORRST	CONSTRAINER
ACEINNORSTT	TRANSECTION
ACEINNPTUUV	NUNCUPATIVE
ACEINNRSSSW	SCRAWNINESS
ACEINNRTTUY	UNCERTAINTY
ACEINOOOPRT	COOPERATION
ACEINOOPRRT	INCORPORATE, PROCREATION
ACEINOOPRTU	APONEUROTIC
ACEINOORRTT	RETROACTION
ACEINOORSTV	REVOCATIONS
ACEINOPRRTU	PUERTO RICAN
ACEINOPRSSS	PROSAICNESS
ACEINOPRSTU	PRECAUTIONS
ACEINORRSTT	RETRACTIONS
ACEINORRTTY	CONTRARIETY
ACEINORSTTU	ERUCTATIONS
ACEINORSTTV	CONTRASTIVE
ACEINORSTTX	EXTRACTIONS
ACEINPPRSSS	SCRAPPINESS
ACEINPRRTUY	PARTURIENCY
ACEINRRTUUV	INCURVATURE
ACEINRSSSSU	NARCISSUSES
ACEIOOPRRTV	CORPORATIVE
ACEIOOPRTVV	PROVOCATIVE
ACEIOPRRSTT	TETRASPORIC, TRICERATOPS
ACEIOPRRTTV	PROTRACTIVE
ACEIOPRSTUU	PRECAUTIOUS
ACEKKLOPTTU	TAKE POTLUCK
ACEKKMORSTT	STOCK MARKET
ACEKKMOSSST	SMOKESTACKS
ACEKNNORSTU	COUNTERSANK
ACEKNOPPRRS	COPPER'S NARK
ACEKPRRSSSY	SKYSCRAPERS
ACELLMNOPSU	NUCLEOPLASM
ACELLNOPRUY	POLYNUCLEAR
ACELLNOPVYY	POLYVALENCY
ACELLNOSSSU	CALLOUSNESS
ACELLNRTTUY	RELUCTANTLY
ACELLOOPRRY	CORPOREALLY
ACELMNNOORT	NOMENCLATOR
ACELMNNOORU	MONONUCLEAR
ACELMNNOSTT	MALCONTENTS
ACELMRSTUUU	MUSCULATURE
ACELNNOOPVX	PLANO-CONVEX
ACELNNRSTTU	TRANSLUCENT
ACELNORSUVY	CAVERNOUSLY
ACELNORTTUX	CONTEXTURAL
ACELNOSTTTU	TALENT SCOUT
ACELOOPRRST	PERCOLATORS
ACELOOPRRTT	PROTECTORAL
ACELOOPRRTY	CORPORATELY
ACELOORRTUW	WATERCOLOUR
ACELOPRSSTU	SPECULATORS
ACELOPRTUXY	EXCULPATORY
ACELRSSSTTY	CRYSTAL SETS
ACEMMNOORRT	COMMENTATOR
ACEMMNOPRTT	COMPARTMENT
ACEMNNORSST	MONSTRANCES

ACEMNOOPRST	COMPENSATOR
ACEMORSSTTU	SCOUTMASTER
ACENNOSSTTT	CONTESTANTS
ACENOORRSTV	CONSERVATOR
ACENOPRRSTU	PROCRUSTEAN
ACENOPRRTTU	COUNTERPART
ACENORSSSSU	RAUCOUSNESS
ACENORSTTUY	COUNTRY SEAT
ACENOSSSUUV	VACUOUSNESS
ACEOOOPRRST	COOPERATORS
ACEOOOPRSSTU	STAUROSCOPE
ACFFGIIINOT	OFFICIATING
ACFFGIIKNRT	TRAFFICKING
ACFFGINOSTU	SUFFOCATING
ACFFIIIINOOT	OFFICIATION
ACFFIILNOST	AFFLICTIONS
ACFFILMNOOR	FALCONIFORM
ACFFINOOSTU	SUFFOCATION
ACFGHIINNRS	FRANCHISING
ACFGHINOSUV	VOUCHSAFING
ACFGIIINNST	SIGNIFICANT
ACFGIIJKKNN	JACK-KNIFING
ACFGIILNSSY	CLASSIFYING
ACFGIINNORT	FORNICATING
ACFGIINNSTY	SANCTIFYING
ACFGIINORTZ	FACTORIZING
ACFGIINSTTU	FUNGISTATIC
ACFGIKNORRV	CARVING FORK
ACFGILNTTUU	FLUCTUATING
ACFGINRSSTU	SURFCASTING
ACFIIINNOTU	UNIFICATION
ACFIIINNORTV	VINIFICATOR
ACFIILLNOTY	FICTIONALLY
ACFIILMNORU	CALIFORNIUM
ACFIILMORST	FORMALISTIC
ACFIILNOPST	PONTIFICALS
ACFIIMNOORT	FORMICATION
ACFIINNOORT	FORNICATION
ACFIINNORST	INFRACTIONS
ACFIIOPRRTU	PURIFICATOR
ACFILLMORUY	FORMULAICLY
ACFILMNNOTU	MALFUNCTION
ACFILNNOOST	CONFLATIONS
ACFILNOTTUU	FLUCTUATION
ACFILORSTUY	FRACTIOUSLY
ACFINNOOTTU	CONFUTATION
ACFINNORTUY	FUNCTIONARY
ACFLLOOPRST	PORT OF CALLS
ACFLNOORSTW	CONTRAFLOWS
ACFORRRUUVY	CURRY FAVOUR
ACGGHILOOPR	GRAPHOLOGIC
ACGGHINRRSU	SURCHARGING
ACGGIIILNNZ	ANGLICIZING
ACGGIILMNRY	GRIMACINGLY
ACGGIIMMNRS	SCRIMMAGING
ACGGIJNNOTU	CONJUGATING
ACGGIMMNRSU	SCRUMMAGING
ACGHHILOOPR	HOLOGRAPHIC
ACGHHIMOOPR	HOMOGRAPHIC
ACGHHINOPRY	ICHNOGRAPHY
ACGHHIOPRRY	CHIROGRAPHY
ACGHHNOOPRR	CHRONOGRAPH
ACGHHOOPRRY	CHOROGRAPHY
ACGHHOPPRSY	PSYCHOGRAPH
ACGHIIILMNPT	ITCHING PALM
ACGHIIILMORT	ALGORITHMIC, LOGARITHMIC
ACGHIIILNORT	GRANOLITHIC
ACGHIIMMNST	MISMATCHING
ACGHIIMNNOP	CHAMPIONING
ACGHIIPRSST	SPHRAGISTIC
ACGHIKMOPRY	KYMOGRAPHIC
ACGHILLMOOO	HOMOLOGICAL
ACGHILMOOPR	LAGOMORPHIC
ACGHILMOORT	COLOGARITHM
ACGHILMOOST	LOGOMACHIST
ACGHILOPPRY	POLYGRAPHIC
ACGHILOPRXY	XYLOGRAPHIC
ACGHIMNOOPR	MONOGRAPHIC, NOMOGRAPHIC, PHONOGRAMIC
ACGHIMOPRRY	MICROGRAPHY
ACGHINOOPRS	NOSOGRAPHIC
ACGHINOOPRY	ICONOGRAPHY
ACGHINOPRRY	GRANOPHYRIC
ACGHINOPRYZ	ZINCOGRAPHY
ACGHIOOPPRT	TOPOGRAPHIC
ACGHIOPPRRY	PYROGRAPHIC
ACGHIOPPRTY	TYPOGRAPHIC
ACGHIORRSTT	GASTROTRICH
ACGHOPPRRTY	CRYPTOGRAPH
ACGIIIIILNTZ	ITALICIZING
ACGIIILMNPT	IMPLICATING
ACGIIILNOST	LOGISTICIAN
ACGIIILNOSZ	SOCIALIZING
ACGIIILNPST	SALPINGITIC
ACGIILLLLOY	ILLOGICALLY
ACGIILLNOOS	SINOLOGICAL
ACGIILLNOOT	COLLIGATION
ACGIILLNOST	OSCILLATING
ACGIILLNTUV	VICTUALLING
ACGIILLOORV	VIROLOGICAL
ACGIILMNNOP	COMPLAINING
ACGIILMNOPR	PROCLAIMING
ACGIILNNOTU	INOCULATING
ACGIILNNPTU	INCULPATING
ACGIILNNUVZ	VULCANIZING
ACGIILNTTUV	CULTIVATING
ACGIIMNOSST	AGNOSTICISM
ACGIIMNRRSY	MISCARRYING

491

ACGIINNNOST	SANCTIONING	ACHILLOPRTY	TROPHICALLY
ACGIINNNOTZ	INCOGNIZANT	ACHILMOOPST	HOMOPLASTIC
ACGIINNOSTW	WAINSCOTING	ACHILMOPSUY	POLYCHASIUM
ACGIINOOSTT	COGITATIONS	ACHILMORRYZ	MYCORRHIZAL
ACGIINORSTZ	OSTRACIZING	ACHILNOORRT	CHLORINATOR
ACGIINRSTTU	RUSTICATING	ACHIMMNOOSU	MONOCHASIUM
ACGIJKKNSSY	SKYJACKINGS	ACHIMNNNOOR	NONHARMONIC
ACGIJLNOTUY	CONJUGALITY	ACHIMNOPSTT	MATCH POINTS
ACGIJNNOOTU	CONJUGATION	ACHIMNOPTYY	AMPHICTYONY
ACGIKKNOSTT	STOCKTAKING	ACHIMNORSST	MONARCHISTS
ACGILLMNOOO	NOMOLOGICAL	ACHIMOPPPSU	HIPPOCAMPUS
ACGILLMOOOP	POMOLOGICAL	ACHIMOPSSTY	SCYPHISTOMA
ACGILLMOORS	OSCILLOGRAM	ACHIMORRSTY	CHRISMATORY
ACGILLMOOTY	CLIMATOLOGY	ACHINNOOPTY	APOCYNTHION
ACGILLNOOOS	NOSOLOGICAL	ACHINOOPSTT	PHOTONASTIC
ACGILLNOOOT	ONTOLOGICAL	ACHIOOPPRTT	PROTOPATHIC
ACGILLOOPTY	TYPOLOGICAL	ACHIOOPPSTT	POTATO CHIPS
ACGILLOTYYZ	ZYGOTICALLY	ACHIOOPRTTU	AUTOTROPHIC
ACGILMOOOST	SOMATOLOGIC	ACHIOOPSTTT	PHOTOSTATIC
ACGILNOSSTU	OUTCLASSING	ACHIOPPRSTY	SAPROPHYTIC
ACGILOOPRST	CARPOLOGIST	ACHIOPRRSTU	CURATORSHIP
ACGILOOSSTT	SCATOLOGIST	ACHKMNOOPRT	ROCKHAMPTON
ACGIMNNOORT	MORNING COAT	ACHLLOOPRST	CHLOROPLAST
ACGIMNOOPRU	CARPOGONIUM	ACHLLOOPSSY	PLAYSCHOOLS
ACGIMNOORST	GASTRONOMIC	ACHLMMOOORS	CHROMOSOMAL
ACGINNOPSTY	SYNCOPATING	ACHLMMOOPRS	CHROMOPLASM
ACGINNORSTT	CONTRASTING	ACHLMOOORSS	SCHOOLMARMS
ACGINNPTTUU	PUNCTUATING	ACHLMOOPRST	CHROMOPLAST
ACGINOORRTU	CORRUGATION	ACHMMNOOORT	MONOCHROMAT
ACGINOORSTY	COSIGNATORY	ACHMMOPPSTU	STOMACH PUMP
ACGINOPRRTT	PROTRACTING	ACHMOOORTTY	THORACOTOMY
ACGIORSSTTY	GYROSTATICS	ACIIILMNOPT	IMPLICATION
ACGLLNOOOVY	VOLCANOLOGY	ACIIILMNRTY	CRIMINALITY
ACGLMNNOOUY	AGONY COLUMN	ACIIILNNNOT	INCLINATION
ACGMOOPRSSY	GYROCOMPASS	ACIIILNOPST	POLITICIANS
ACGOOPRSSTY	GASTROSCOPY	ACIIILRSTTU	RITUALISTIC
ACHHIILLPTY	ITHYPHALLIC	ACIIINNOTTT	NICTITATION
ACHHILLMOOT	HOMOTHALLIC	ACIIINOQSTU	ACQUISITION
ACHHILOPRSS	SCHOLARSHIP	ACIIILLLOPTY	POLITICALLY
ACHHOPPSSTY	PSYCHOPATHS	ACIILLMNOOS	COLONIALISM
ACHHOPPSTYY	PSYCHOPATHY	ACIILLMNOOT	COLLIMATION
ACHIIIMNPSS	HISPANICISM	ACIILLMNPUY	MUNICIPALLY
ACHIIINPSST	HISPANICIST	ACIILLMOSUY	MALICIOUSLY
ACHIIILLMSWY	WHIMSICALLY	ACIILLMOTTY	MITOTICALLY
ACHIIILMPSSY	PHYSICALISM	ACIILLNOOST	COLONIALIST, OSCILLATION
ACHIIILOOPPR	COPROPHILIA	ACIILLNOPTU	UNPOLITICAL
ACHIIILOSTTT	STATOLITHIC	ACIILLNOVVY	CONVIVIALLY
ACHIIILPSSTY	PHYSICALIST	ACIILLNPPRY	PRINCIPALLY
ACHIIMNORST	HARMONISTIC	ACIILLOPRTY	PICTORIALLY
ACHIINNRSTU	UNCHRISTIAN	ACIILLPRSTU	PLURALISTIC
ACHIINSSTUV	CHAUVINISTS	ACIILLQUYZZ	QUIZZICALLY
ACHIIPRSSTY	PHYSIATRICS	ACIILMNNOPT	INCOMPLIANT
ACHIKLOORSW	WORKAHOLICS	ACIILMNNOTU	CULMINATION
ACHILLMOOPR	ALLOMORPHIC	ACIILMNOOPT	COMPILATION

492

ACIILMNORTU	TOURMALINIC	ACILNOOSTTT	COTTONTAILS
ACIILMNSTUY	MASCULINITY	ACILNORSSTU	ULTRASONICS
ACIILNNOOTU	INOCULATION	ACILNPPSSTU	SUPPLICANTS
ACIILNNOPTU	INCULPATION	ACILNPTTUUY	PUNCTUALITY
ACIILNOPRSV	PROVINCIALS	ACILOOPRRTY	CORPORALITY
ACIILNOPSSU	SUSPICIONAL	ACILOORSTUY	ATROCIOUSLY
ACIILNOTTUV	CULTIVATION	ACILOORSUVY	VORACIOUSLY
ACIILOPRTTY	TROPICALITY	ACILORSTTUV	CULTIVATORS
ACIILORSTTU	STAUROLITIC	ACIMMNOORTY	COMMINATORY
ACIILORSUVY	VICARIOUSLY	ACIMMNOOTTU	COMMUTATION
ACIILOSUVVY	VIVACIOUSLY	ACIMMOPSTTY	SYMPTOMATIC
ACIIMMMNOST	MAMMONISTIC	ACIMNNOORTU	MUCRONATION
ACIIMMNNOOT	COMMINATION	ACIMNOOPRSS	COMPARISONS
ACIIMMNORST	ROMANTICISM	ACIMNOOPTTU	COMPUTATION
ACIIMMNOSST	MONASTICISM	ACIMNOPPRSS	PRISON CAMPS
ACIIMMNSSTU	NUMISMATICS	ACIMNOPRSTY	PATRONYMICS
ACIIMNOORSU	ACRIMONIOUS	ACIMNPRSSTU	MANUSCRIPTS
ACIIMNORSTT	ROMANTICIST	ACIMOOPRSTT	COMPATRIOTS
ACIIMNRSSTU	MANICURISTS	ACINNNOOSNT	INCONSONANT
ACIIMOPRSTT	TROPISMATIC	ACINNNOOOTT	CONNOTATION
ACIINNOOSTV	INVOCATIONS	ACINNOOORST	CORONATIONS
ACIINNORRTU	IRON CURTAIN	ACINNOOPRTT	CONTRAPTION
ACIINNORTUV	INCURVATION	ACINNOOPSTY	SYNCOPATION
ACIINNOSTTX	INTOXICANTS	ACINNOORTTU	CONTINUATOR
ACIINOOPRST	ANISOTROPIC	ACINNOPTTUU	PUNCTUATION
ACIINOORTTX	INTOXICATOR	ACINNORSSTT	CONSTRAINTS
ACIINOPRTTU	UNPATRIOTIC	ACINOOOPRRT	CORPORATION
ACIINORSTTU	RUSTICATION	ACINOOPRRTV	PROVOCATION
ACIINRSSSST	NARCISSISTS	ACINOOPRRST	CONSPIRATOR
ACIINRTTTUY	TACITURNITY	ACINOOPRRTT	PROTRACTION
ACIIOPSSSTT	PSITTACOSIS	ACINOOPRRTU	PROCURATION
ACIJNNOORTU	CONJURATION	ACINOORRSUV	CARNIVOROUS
ACIKNNORSYY	SYNKARYONIC	ACINOORSSTT	CARTOONISTS
ACILLMNOORY	MORONICALLY	ACINPRRSSTT	TRANSCRIPTS
ACILLMNOPTY	COMPLIANTLY	ACIOOPPRSTT	POTATO CRISP
ACILLMOOSTY	OSMOTICALLY	ACIORSSSSSY	SYSSARCOSIS
ACILLMOPSTY	PLASMOLYTIC	ACLLMOSTUUU	ALTOCUMULUS
ACILLMOTYYZ	ZYMOTICALLY	ACLLNNORTUY	NOCTURNALLY
ACILLNNOTUY	CONTINUALLY	ACLNNOOSTTU	CONSULTANTS
ACILLNOOOPT	LOCAL OPTION	ACLNOOORSTY	CONSOLATORY
ACILLOORRTT	TORTICOLLAR	ACLNOOPRRSU	PROCONSULAR
ACILLOORSST	OSCILLATORS	ACLNOORRSUY	RANCOROUSLY
ACILLOORSTY	OSCILLATORY	ACLOOPRSUXY	XYLOCARPOUS
ACILMMMNOSU	COMMUNALISM	ACMMNOORSTU	CONSUMMATOR
ACILMMNNOOU	COMMUNIONAL	ACMMOORSTTU	COMMUTATORS
ACILMMNOOOT	COMMOTIONAL	ACMMPPSUUUV	VACUUM PUMPS
ACILMMNOSTU	COMMUNALIST	ACMNNOOPTWY	COMPANY TOWN
ACILMMNOTUY	COMMUNALITY	ACMOOOSSTTU	SCOTOMATOUS
ACILMMORSSU	COMMISSURAL	ACOOPRRRSTT	PROTRACTORS
ACILMMRSSUU	SIMULACRUMS	ADDDDENNOSS	ODDS AND ENDS
ACILMOOPSTX	TOXOPLASMIC	ADDDEEERRSS	READDRESSED
ACILMORSTUY	CUSTOMARILY	ADDDEEGIRRS	DISREGARDED
ACILMRSTUUY	MUSCULARITY	ADDDEEHNRSU	DUNDERHEADS
ACILNNOOOST	CONSOLATION	ADDDEEILORS	DEAD SOLDIER

ADDDEEILSSS	SIDESADDLES	ADDEEELOPPTU	DEPOPULATED
ADDDEGIKLNS	SKEDADDLING	ADDEEELOPRRS	ROPE LADDERS
ADDDERSSTTU	STAR-STUDDED	ADDEEELPRSST	STEPLADDERS
ADDEEEEGNRT	DEGENERATED	ADDEEEMNNNRU	UNDERMANNED
ADDEEEEHLLV	LEVEL-HEADED	ADDEEEMNOPPR	NAMEDROPPED
ADDEEEEGLRTU	DEREGULATED	ADDEEENORTWW	WATERED-DOWN
ADDEEEHIKNS	HIDE-AND-SEEK	ADDEEENRSTTU	UNDERSTATED
ADDEEEHMPTY	EMPTY-HEADED	ADDEFFFHLNOY	OFFHANDEDLY
ADDEEEHNPPR	APPREHENDED	ADDEFIKRRST	FREDRIKSTAD
ADDEEEHRSSS	HEADDRESSES	ADDEFILORTU	FLUORIDATED
ADDEEEIMNRR	REMAINDERED	ADDEGGHORTU	GODDAUGHTER
ADDEEELRSTT	DEAD LETTERS	ADDEGGIIIRT	DIGITIGRADE
ADDEEENORUV	ENDEAVOURED	ADDEGHHINRT	RIGHT-HANDED
ADDEEEOPRSS	DESPERADOES	ADDEGHINRTY	DEHYDRATING
ADDEEFHLRUY	FURALDEHYDE	ADDEGHNORTU	DREADNOUGHT
ADDEEFLOPST	SOFT-PEDALED	ADDEGIIMNNR	MIND READING
ADDEEFMNORU	UNDREAMED-OF	ADDEGIKNRRS	KIND REGARDS
ADDEEFMNRTU	DEFRAUDMENT	ADDEGILLNRW	GRINDELWALD
ADDEEGGHILT	LIGHT-HEADED	ADDEGILMNNY	MADDENINGLY
ADDEEGHILPY	PIGHEADEDLY	ADDEGILNNSY	SADDENINGLY
ADDEEGHNORW	WRONGHEADED	ADDEGIMNNNU	UNDEMANDING
ADDEEGILMNR	LARGE-MINDED	ADDEGIMNORS	GORMANDISED
ADDEEGINNRS	DEAD RINGERS	ADDEGIMNORZ	GORMANDIZED
ADDEEGIRRRS	DISREGARDER	ADDEGJMNTUY	JUDGMENT DAY
ADDEEGNRSSU	GUARDEDNESS	ADDEGNOORTU	GOOD-NATURED
ADDEEHHLOTY	HOTHEADEDLY	ADDEHHNORST	SHORT-HANDED
ADDEEHIKNRT	KIND-HEARTED	ADDEHIILMOT	THALIDOMIDE
ADDEEHIMNSU	DEHUMANISED	ADDEHILNORS	RHODE ISLAND
ADDEEHIMNUZ	DEHUMANIZED	ADDEHILOPSU	DIADELPHOUS
ADDEEHISTTU	DEATH DUTIES	ADDEHINORTY	DEHYDRATION
ADDEEHMNPTY	EMPTY-HANDED	ADDEHINOSWW	WINDOW SHADE
ADDEEHNORTW	DOWNHEARTED	ADDEHIOPRRS	RHAPSODISED
ADDEEHPRRSS	HARD-PRESSED	ADDEHIOPRSZ	RHAPSODIZED
ADDEEIILSTV	DEVITALISED	ADDEHMNNOSW	HAND-ME-DOWNS
ADDEEIILTVZ	DEVITALIZED	ADDEHMORSUY	HYDROMEDUSA
ADDEEIINNNW	WINE AND DINE	ADDEIIIMNTT	INTIMIDATED
ADDEEIJOPRS	JEOPARDISED	ADDEIIINOOR	RADIOIODINE
ADDEEIJOPRZ	JEOPARDIZED	ADDEIIINTUV	INDIVIDUATE
ADDEEILLSVW	WELL-ADVISED	ADDEIILLMMNS	SMALL-MINDED
ADDEEILMMNS	MIDDLE NAMES	ADDEILNSUVY	UNADVISEDLY
ADDEEILNRRT	INTERLARDED	ADDEILOSVWY	DISAVOWEDLY
ADDEEILRRVY	DAREDEVILRY	ADDEILRSTTU	STRIDULATED
ADDEEIMNNOT	DENOMINATED	ADDEIOPPRSV	DISAPPROVED
ADDEEIMNPRR	REPRIMANDED	ADDELMOORTU	DEMODULATOR
ADDEEIMNRRS	MIND READERS	ADDELMORRSW	DREAM WORLDS
ADDEEIMORRS	DROMEDARIES	ADDELNNORSW	WONDERLANDS
ADDEEIMOTTV	DEMOTIVATED	ADDELNNRTUY	REDUNDANTLY
ADDEEIMRSTU	DESIDERATUM	ADDEMNOOORT	RODOMONTADE
ADDEEINOPRR	PREORDAINED	ADDGGINNORW	DOWNGRADING
ADDEEINOPRT	DEPREDATION	ADDGHILNOOR	ROADHOLDING
ADDEEIRTTWY	READY-WITTED	ADDGILNNOOW	DOWNLOADING
ADDEELNNSTU	SUDETENLAND	ADDIIIIMNOT	DIMIDIATION
ADDEELNPRUY	UNDERPLAYED	ADDIIILNSUV	INDIVIDUALS
ADDEELNRUUV	UNDERVALUED	ADDILLNNOUV	NULL AND VOID

ADDILMNORTY	DIRTY OLD MAN	ADEEELNNRSS	LEARNEDNESS
ADDNNOOSTUW	DOWN-AND-OUTS	ADEEELNRSST	RELATEDNESS
ADDNNOPSSUW	UPS AND DOWNS	ADEEELNRTTU	LAUNDERETTE
ADEEEEFGHRT	FEATHEREDGE	ADEEELNSSTX	EXALTEDNESS
ADEEEEFHRRT	FREE-HEARTED	ADEEELPRSTY	DESPERATELY
ADEEEEGGRST	DESEGREGATE	ADEEEMNNRST	ENDEARMENTS
ADEEEEGNRRT	REGENERATED	ADEEEMNRRTU	REMUNERATED
ADEEEEGNRST	DEGENERATES	ADEEEMOSTWW	MEADOWSWEET
ADEEEEHKNTY	THE NAKED EYE	ADEEENOPRTU	DEUTERANOPE
ADEEEFILNRT	DEFERENTIAL	ADEEENORRUV	ENDEAVOURER
ADEEEFLORRS	FREELOADERS	ADEEENRRSSW	NEWSREADERS
ADEEEFNRSTT	FENESTRATED	ADEEEPPRRTT	PERPETRATED
ADEEEGGLLNO	GOLDEN EAGLE	ADEEEPPRTTU	PERPETUATED
ADEEEGHLPRT	TELEGRAPHED	ADEEEPRSSSU	SUPERSEDEAS
ADEEEGILMNR	LEGERDEMAIN	ADEEFFIINRT	DIFFERENTIA
ADEEEGILNRS	GENERALISED	ADEEFFORSTV	OVERSTAFFED
ADEEEGILNRZ	GENERALIZED	ADEEFGGLOPR	LEAPFROGGED
ADEEEGILNSV	EVANGELISED	ADEEFGHIRSU	FIGUREHEADS
ADEEEGILNVZ	EVANGELIZED	ADEEFGHORRT	FORGATHERED
ADEEEGIMNNR	GENDARMERIE	ADEEFGIINNR	FINE-GRAINED
ADEEEGIMNST	DEMAGNETISE	ADEEFGILNOR	FREELOADING
ADEEEGIMNTZ	DEMAGNETIZE	ADEEFGINNRR	RANGE FINDER
ADEEEGINNRT	TRAGEDIENNE	ADEEFHLNRST	LEFT-HANDERS
ADEEEGLLNRT	LEGAL TENDER	ADEEFHORSTT	SOFTHEARTED
ADEEEGLNNRR	GREENLANDER	ADEEFILORRS	RELIEF ROADS
ADEEEGMNNRT	DERANGEMENT	ADEEFILRSST	FEDERALISTS
ADEEEGNOTXY	DEOXYGENATE	ADEEFINORST	FEDERATIONS
ADEEEGNRRRT	GRANDE-TERRE	ADEEFINRRST	FRATERNISED
ADEEEHLLORS	LEASEHOLDER	ADEEFINRRTZ	FRATERNIZED
ADEEEHLPSSY	SLEEPYHEADS	ADEEFIOPSST	SAFE-DEPOSIT
ADEEEHLRSTT	LETTERHEADS	ADEEFLLORST	FORESTALLED
ADEEEHMORST	HOMESTEADER	ADEEFLRSSSU	SELF-ASSURED
ADEEEHNNNOR	ENNEAHEDRON	ADEEFNOPRRS	FREE PARDONS
ADEEEHNOPRT	OPENHEARTED	ADEEFNRRRST	TRANSFERRED
ADEEEHNNRRSU	UNREHEARSED	ADEEFOOPRRR	PROOFREADER
ADEEEHPRSST	SPREADSHEET	ADEEGGHLORS	LOGGERHEADS
ADEEEHRRTTU	TRUEHEARTED	ADEEGGIINRS	DISAGREEING
ADEEEIILNTV	DELINEATIVE	ADEEGGILRVY	AGGRIEVEDLY
ADEEEIIMMOR	AIDE-MEMOIRE	ADEEGGINNNR	ENDANGERING
ADEEEILOPRS	OIL-SEED RAPE	ADEEGGLORTW	WATERLOGGED
ADEEEILSSUX	DESEXUALISE	ADEEGGMORUY	DEMAGOGUERY
ADEEEILSUXZ	DESEXUALIZE	ADEEGGNPRSS	PRESSGANGED
ADEEEIMNRTT	DETERMINATE	ADEEGHINRST	NEARSIGHTED
ADEEEIMPRTT	PREMEDITATE	ADEEGHIRRST	SIGHT-READER
ADEEEINNRTT	ENTERTAINED	ADEEGHLRSTU	SLAUGHTERED
ADEEEIORRTT	DETERIORATE	ADEEGHMOPRR	DEMOGRAPHER
ADEEEIPRRST	PIEDS-A-TERRE	ADEEGHNORTY	HYDROGENATE
ADEEEJNRTUV	REJUVENATED	ADEEGIILNNT	DELINEATING
ADEEEKLLPSW	SLEEPWALKED	ADEEGIINSTV	DESIGNATIVE
ADEEEKLRRST	DEERSTALKER	ADEEGIIRSST	GREAT DIESIS
ADEEEKLSTTW	SWEET-TALKED	ADEEGILNNRY	ENDEARINGLY
ADEEELLNSWY	WENSLEYDALE	ADEEGILNNST	DISENTANGLE
ADEEELLSSTT	TESSELLATED	ADEEGILNOST	DELEGATIONS
ADEEELMNNOW	NEEDLEWOMAN	ADEEGILNRRS	RINGLEADERS

ADEEGILNTTU	DEGLUTINATE
ADEEGILRRSU	REGULARISED
ADEEGILRRUZ	REGULARIZED
ADEEGIMNNRS	MEANDERINGS
ADEEGIMNPRT	IMPREGNATED
ADEEGINORRS	REORGANISED
ADEEGINORRZ	REORGANIZED
ADEEGKRRTUU	GREATER KUDU
ADEEGLPPRSY	DAPPLE-GREYS
ADEEGMNNORY	DANGER MONEY
ADEEGMNRRRY	GERRYMANDER
ADEEGMORTUY	DEUTEROGAMY
ADEEHHILSST	HEAT SHIELDS
ADEEHHIMRTY	HEMIHYDRATE
ADEEHHISTWW	WHITEWASHED
ADEEHHLORRS	SHAREHOLDER
ADEEHHNOPRT	HEPTAHEDRON
ADEEHHNRSTU	HEADHUNTERS
ADEEHIINPRS	HESPERIDIAN
ADEEHIIOPRS	ISODIAPHERE
ADEEHILLNOT	ENDOTHELIAL
ADEEHILNOPT	ELEPHANTOID
ADEEHILNORT	LION-HEARTED
ADEEHILNPRR	PHILANDERER
ADEEHILNSST	DEATHLINESS
ADEEHILPRSS	DEALERSHIPS
ADEEHILSSWY	DAISY WHEELS
ADEEHINRSST	THREADINESS
ADEEHIPRRSS	READERSHIPS
ADEEHIRRRSS	HAIRDRESSER
ADEEHIRRSTW	HARRIS TWEED
ADEEHKLORST	STAKEHOLDER
ADEEHLLNOSW	SWOLLEN HEAD
ADEEHLLSSTY	DEATHLESSLY
ADEEHLMNOTT	MENTHOLATED
ADEEHLNNRST	NETHERLANDS
ADEEHLOORTW	LEATHERWOOD
ADEEHNNOPRT	PENTAHEDRON
ADEEHNORRTT	TETRAHEDRON
ADEEIILMMSV	MEDIEVALISM
ADEEIILMMTY	IMMEDIATELY
ADEEIILMNOT	MATINEE IDOL
ADEEIILMSTV	MEDIEVALIST
ADEEIILNNOT	DELINEATION
ADEEIILNRST	RESIDENTIAL
ADEEIILRSTV	REVITALISED
ADEEIILRTVZ	REVITALIZED
ADEEIIMMNPT	IMPEDIMENTA
ADEEIIMNNST	INSEMINATED
ADEEIIMNSST	DISSEMINATE
ADEEIINRRTV	VERATRIDINE
ADEEIIPRSTV	DEPRAVITIES
ADEEIIPRTUV	REPUDIATIVE
ADEEIIRSSTV	ADVERSITIES
ADEEIIRSTVV	DERIVATIVES
ADEEILLMNNR	ILL-MANNERED
ADEEILLMRSV	SILVER MEDAL
ADEEILMNNST	ENLISTED MAN
ADEEILMNORT	ENDOMETRIAL
ADEEILMNRST	DERAILMENTS, STREAMLINED
ADEEILMNRTT	DETRIMENTAL
ADEEILMNRVY	DELIVERYMAN
ADEEILMORRS	DEMORALISER
ADEEILMORRZ	DEMORALIZER
ADEEILMORTT	DILATOMETER
ADEEILMTUUZ	DEMUTUALIZE
ADEEILNNPTT	PENTLANDITE
ADEEILNNPUX	UNEXPLAINED
ADEEILNNRTT	INTERDENTAL
ADEEILNRSTU	NEUTRALISED
ADEEILNRSTY	SEDENTARILY
ADEEILNRTUZ	NEUTRALIZED
ADEEILNSTTT	DILETTANTES
ADEEILOPRRS	DEPOLARISER
ADEEILOPRRZ	DEPOLARIZER
ADEEILPRRSV	PEARL DIVERS
ADEEILPRSSU	DISPLEASURE
ADEEILRRSVV	SLAVE DRIVER
ADEEIMNNOST	EMENDATIONS
ADEEIMNNPTU	ANTEPENDIUM
ADEEIMNNRTT	DETERMINANT, DETRAINMENT
ADEEIMNOPRT	PREDOMINATE
ADEEIMNPRRR	REPRIMANDER
ADEEIMNRSTY	SEDIMENTARY
ADEEIMORSTT	STADIOMETER
ADEEIMRTTTY	TETRADYMITE
ADEEINNRTTV	INADVERTENT
ADEEINOPRST	DESPERATION
ADEEINORRST	RAISON D'ETRE
ADEEINOSTTT	DETESTATION
ADEEINPRSST	PEDESTRIANS
ADEEIPRSSTU	PASTEURISED
ADEEIPRSTUZ	PASTEURIZED
ADEEIRRSSTV	ADVERTISERS
ADEEKLOPRSU	LOUDSPEAKER
ADEEKMRRSSS	DRESSMAKERS
ADEEKNRRSTU	UNDERTAKERS
ADEELLMNNSSW	MENDEL'S LAWS
ADEELLMRSSY	DREAMLESSLY
ADEELLNOSTW	STONEWALLED
ADEELLNRTUV	UNTRAVELLED
ADEELLOPTUV	POLE VAULTED
ADEELLORSSS	LOSS LEADERS
ADEELMNOORT	DEMONOLATER
ADEELMNRTUW	UNTERWALDEN
ADEELNOORST	ALDOSTERONE
ADEELNOORUV	NUEVO LAREDO
ADEELNRRUUV	UNDERVALUER

ADEELNRTTVY	ADVERTENTLY	ADEGGILNRUU	UNGULIGRADE
ADEELRRSSUY	REASSUREDLY	ADEGHHILNNP	HELPING HAND
ADEEMMNORTY	DYNAMOMETER	ADEGHHILNRS	HIGHLANDERS
ADEEMNNNSSU	MUNDANENESS	ADEGHHINNTU	HEADHUNTING
ADEEMNNOOOW	WOOD ANEMONE	ADEGHHINNRRT	RIGHT-HANDER
ADEEMNOPPRR	NAMEDROPPER	ADEGHHINSST	NIGHTSHADES
ADEEMNORSTT	DEMONSTRATE	ADEGHHORRTU	READ-THROUGH
ADEEMNPRSTT	DEPARTMENTS	ADEGHINOORT	IN GOOD HEART
ADEEMNRSTTU	MENSTRUATED	ADEGHMNORRT	GRANDMOTHER
ADEENNNPPSY	SPEND A PENNY	ADEGHMNRSTU	DRAUGHTSMEN
ADEENPRSSSU	UNDERPASSES	ADEGHORRTUV	OVERDRAUGHT
ADEENQRRSSU	SQUANDERERS	ADEGHORSSUU	GUARDHOUSES
ADEENRRSTUV	ADVENTURERS	ADEGIIILNTV	INVIGILATED
ADEENRSSSSU	ASSUREDNESS	ADEGIIINRST	DIGNITARIES
ADEENRSSTUV	ADVENTURESS	ADEGIILNNRW	LINE DRAWING
ADEEOPPRRRS	ORDER PAPERS	ADEGIILNNRY	INGRAINEDLY
ADEEORRSTTU	TRADE ROUTES	ADEGIILNOST	DIGESTIONAL
ADEFFILNRTU	FAULT-FINDER	ADEGIILNOTV	DOVETAILING
ADEFFIMMNOR	FRAME OF MIND	ADEGIILNPSS	DISPLEASING
ADEFFINRSST	FAST FRIENDS	ADEGIIMNTTU	UNMITIGATED
ADEFFIORSST	DISAFFOREST	ADEGIIMSSTT	STIGMATISED
ADEFFLOOTTU	FOOT FAULTED	ADEGIIMSTTZ	STIGMATIZED
ADEFGHLOORT	HEART OF GOLD	ADEGIINNORT	DENIGRATION
ADEFGIILNOT	DEFOLIATING	ADEGIINNOST	DESIGNATION
ADEFGILLNOS	SELF-LOADING	ADEGIINOPRR	PERIGORDIAN
ADEFGILNORS	DRAGONFLIES	ADEGIINOPTV	VIDEOTAPING
ADEFGIPPRTW	GIFT-WRAPPED	ADEGIINORSS	DISORGANISE
ADEFGKNOORS	GODFORSAKEN	ADEGIINORSZ	DISORGANIZE
ADEFGNOORRS	ROOF GARDENS	ADEGIINORTV	INVIGORATED
ADEFHHLOOST	HEALTH FOODS	ADEGIINPRTU	REPUDIATING
ADEFHIKOSST	KISS OF DEATH	ADEGIINRSTV	ADVERTISING
ADEFHINPRST	PATHFINDERS	ADEGIINRTTU	INGRATITUDE
ADEFHINRRTY	FIRE HYDRANT	ADEGIINRTTX	EXTRADITING
ADEFHIRSTWW	WHITE DWARFS	ADEGIIOPRRS	PRAIRIE DOGS
ADEFIILNNRS	LINDISFARNE	ADEGIJNRRSU	GRAND JURIES
ADEFIILNOOT	DEFOLIATION	ADEGIJNRSTU	READJUSTING
ADEFIILNQUU	UNQUALIFIED	ADEGIKMNRSS	DRESSMAKING
ADEFIILNRTT	INFILTRATED	ADEGIKNNRTU	UNDERTAKING
ADEFIIMNRSU	FREUDIANISM	ADEGILLOSSU	GLADIOLUSES
ADEFIINSSTU	UNSATISFIED	ADEGILLPTUY	PLEAD GUILTY
ADEFILLORUV	ILL-FAVOURED	ADEGILNNNST	LANDING NETS
ADEFILNOORT	DEFLORATION	ADEGILNNRWY	WANDERINGLY
ADEFILSSTTU	DISTASTEFUL	ADEGILNOORV	OVERLOADING
ADEFIMNOORT	DEFORMATION	ADEGILNORST	TSELINOGRAD
ADEFIMRRRST	DIRT FARMERS	ADEGILNRRTY	RETARDINGLY
ADEFLLNOSST	DENTAL FLOSS	ADEGILOOPST	PAEDOLOGIST
ADEFLNOORRS	FOOL'S ERRAND	ADEGIMNNOPR	PROMENADING
ADEFLOOPSTY	SPLAYFOOTED	ADEGIMNNOPR	GORMANDISER
ADEFMNORRST	TRANSFORMED	ADEGIMNORRZ	GORMANDIZER
ADEFNORRSSW	FORWARDNESS	ADEGIMNORSU	GOURMANDISE
ADEGGGIINNS	DISENGAGING	ADEGINNNORS	UNORGANISED
ADEGGHILNRT	RIGHT-ANGLED	ADEGINNORUZ	UNORGANIZED
ADEGGIINNRT	DENIGRATING	ADEGINNPRUY	UNDERPAYING
ADEGGIINNST	DESIGNATING	ADEGINNQRSU	SQUANDERING

ADEGINNRRTU	UNDERRATING
ADEGINORRVW	OVERDRAWING
ADEGINORSTT	ROAD TESTING
ADEGKNRRRSU	KRUGERRANDS
ADEGLMOORTY	DERMATOLOGY
ADEGLMOPRTU	PROMULGATED
ADEGLNORSUY	DANGEROUSLY
ADEGMMMNNOOR	MONOGRAMMED
ADEGNNOORSU	ANDROGENOUS
ADEHHIORRSS	HORSERADISH
ADEHHIRSSSW	DISHWASHERS
ADEHIIMNRTU	ANTHERIDIUM
ADEHIIOPRSS	DIAPHORESIS
ADEHIIORSTT	HISTORIATED
ADEHIKOORST	THEODORAKIS
ADEHILLNRST	DISENTHRALL
ADEHILLORSU	LOUDHAILERS
ADEHIMMPPUY	HAPPY MEDIUM
ADEHIMORRTY	RADIOTHERMY
ADEHIMPSSTY	SYMPATHISED
ADEHIMPSTYZ	SYMPATHIZED
ADEHINNRSUV	UNVARNISHED
ADEHINNRTTW	HANDWRITTEN
ADEHINOORTZ	ANTHEROZOID
ADEHINOSSSW	SHADOWINESS
ADEHINQRRTU	HINDQUARTER
ADEHINRSTTW	WITHSTANDER
ADEHIPRSSTW	STEWARDSHIP
ADEHIPRSTTW	SHARP-WITTED
ADEHLLLMORS	SMALLHOLDER
ADEHLLLORST	STALLHOLDER
ADEHLORSTYY	HYDROLYSATE
ADEHMNOORTY	MONOHYDRATE
ADEHNNOPSTU	OPEN-AND-SHUT
ADEHNOORTTW	DOWN-TO-EARTH
ADEHOPRSSTW	SHOP STEWARD
ADEIIILMRST	MILITARISED
ADEIIILMRTZ	MILITARIZED
ADEIIILMSST.	DISSIMILATE
ADEIIILRSTV	TRIVIALISED
ADEIIILRTVZ	TRIVIALIZED
ADEIIIMOSTT	OTITIS MEDIA
ADEIIIMRSTY	SEMIARIDITY
ADEIIINNTTU	UNINITIATED
ADEIIIPRSST	DISPARITIES
ADEIIIPSSTV	DISSIPATIVE
ADEIILLLOPS	ELLIPSOIDAL
ADEIIILLMNTU	ILLUMINATED
ADEIIILLORTY	EDITORIALLY
ADEIIILMNNOS	DIMENSIONAL
ADEIILMNRSU	SEMIDIURNAL
ADEIILMSSTU	DISSIMULATE
ADEIILNORSV	DIVERSIONAL
ADEIILORRST	IDOLATRISER

ADEIILORRTZ	IDOLATRIZER
ADEIIMMNSTU	MEDIASTINUM
ADEIIMNOPSS	IMPASSIONED
ADEIIMNOSTT	MEDITATIONS
ADEIIMPRSSU	PRAESIDIUMS
ADEIIMRSTTX	TAXIDERMIST
ADEIINNNOTT	INDENTATION
ADEIINNOOPT	OPINIONATED
ADEIINNORTT	DENITRATION
ADEIINNOSTT	DESTINATION
ADEIINOPRTT	PARTITIONED, TREPIDATION
ADEIINOPRTU	REPUDIATION
ADEIINOPRTV	DEPRIVATION
ADEIINOPSST	PASSIONTIDE
ADEIINORSTV	DERIVATIONS
ADEIINORSTY	SEDITIONARY
ADEIINORTTX	EXTRADITION
ADEIINPRSTY	STIPENDIARY
ADEIINQSTTU	EQUIDISTANT
ADEIINRSTVY	VINEYARDIST
ADEIIOPPRTT	PROPITIATED
ADEIJMMNRSW	WINDJAMMERS
ADEIKLLLRSY	LADY-KILLERS
ADEIKLLMMST	MALTED MILKS
ADEILLMRRST	DRILLMASTER
ADEILLORSST	ILL-ASSORTED
ADEILLORTUV	OUTRIVALLED
ADEILLOSVWW	SWALLOW DIVE
ADEILLRSTTU	ILLUSTRATED
ADEILMMOOTY	MYELOMATOID
ADEILMNNSSU	MAUDLINNESS
ADEILMNOPRS	PALINDROMES
ADEILMNOPTU	DEPLUMATION
ADEILMORTTY	DILATOMETRY
ADEILNOOPRT	PERIODONTAL
ADEILNRSTWZ	SWITZERLAND
ADEILNSSTUY	SUSTAINEDLY
ADEILOPPRSS	PREDISPOSAL
ADEILOPPRSU	POPULARISED
ADEILOPPRUZ	POPULARIZED
ADEILOPRRTY	PREDATORILY
ADEIMMNNOPU	PANDEMONIUM
ADEIMMNRSST	MASTERMINDS
ADEIMMNSSTT	DISMASTMENT
ADEIMNNOORT	DENOMINATOR
ADEIMNNOPRT	PREDOMINANT
ADEIMNNQRUU	QUADRENNIUM
ADEIMNOPSTU	DESPUMATION
ADEIMNRRTUY	RUDIMENTARY
ADEIMNRSTTT	TRANSMITTED
ADEIMNRSTUV	ADVENTURISM
ADEINNOOSTT	DENOTATIONS, DETONATIONS
ADEINNOPSWW	WINDOWPANES
ADEINNORSTU	TRADE UNIONS

ADEINOOPPRT	APPORTIONED	ADGHIINRTWW	WITHDRAWING
ADEINOOPRTT	DEPORTATION	ADGHIOPRTTY	DITTOGRAPHY
ADEINOPSTTU	DEPUTATIONS	ADGHLPRSSUU	SULPHA DRUGS
ADEINRSTTUV	ADVENTURIST	ADGHMRRRUYY	HYDRARGYRUM
ADEIOPPRRSV	DISAPPROVER	ADGHNOOOPRT	ODONTOGRAPH
ADEIOPRRTUY	REPUDIATORY	ADGIIILNQTU	LIQUIDATING
ADEJMNNORTU	ADJOURNMENT	ADGIIINNNOT	INDIGNATION
ADEJMNSSTTU	ADJUSTMENTS	ADGIIINNOTU	AUDITIONING
ADELLMNORSW	SMALL WONDER	ADGIIINNRST	DISTRAINING
ADELLNNNOOP	LONDON PLANE	ADGIIINPSST	DISSIPATING
ADELLNORRSU	ALL-ROUNDERS	ADGIILLNOSW	DISALLOWING
ADELLNSSTUY	DAUNTLESSLY	ADGIILMNNST	DISMANTLING
ADELLOOPRRT	PETRODOLLAR	ADGIILNNNTY	INDIGNANTLY
ADELLOORRRS	ROAD ROLLERS	ADGIILOORST	RADIOLOGIST
ADELLOORRSU	EURODOLLARS	ADGIILOOSTU	AUDIOLOGIST
ADELMNOORTY	DEMONOLATRY	ADGIILOPRTY	PRODIGALITY
ADELMNORRTU	ULTRAMODERN	ADGIINNPRSW	DRAWING PINS
ADELOOPRRST	POSTAL ORDER	ADGIINOPTUY	AUDIOTYPING
ADELOPPRSUU	DUAL-PURPOSE	ADGIINORSTY	GRANDIOSITY
ADELOPRRRSY	LORD'S PRAYER	ADGIKNNOORT	GORDIAN KNOT
ADELPQRSTUU	QUADRUPLETS	ADGIKNORSWY	WORKING DAYS
ADEMMMNORSU	MEMORANDUMS	ADGILNNOPWY	DOWNPLAYING
ADEMMNNOUUY	MAUNDY MONEY	ADGILNOOPSW	WADING POOLS
ADEMMNORTYY	DYNAMOMETRY	ADGILNPQRUU	QUADRUPLING
ADEMNNOPTWY	DOWN PAYMENT	ADGIMMNORSU	GOURMANDISM
ADENNOPRRST	TRANSPONDER	ADGIMNOORRW	DRAWING ROOM
ADENOPRRSTT	TRANSPORTED	ADGINNOSTTU	OUTSTANDING
ADENORSSSUU	ARDUOUSNESS	ADGINOPRSTT	TRADING POST
ADENORSTUUV	ADVENTUROUS	ADGINRRSSTW	DRAWSTRINGS
ADENPRSSSUU	UNSURPASSED	ADGIORSSSWW	GRASS WIDOWS
ADFFFFHNPUU	HUFF AND PUFF	ADGLNNOPRSU	GROUND PLANS
ADFFGNORSTU	GROUND STAFF	ADGLNOPRSUY	PLAYGROUNDS
ADFFHINOSST	STANDOFFISH	ADGNNOORSUY	ANDROGYNOUS
ADFGHIINNPT	PATHFINDING	ADHHNOSSTTU	THOUSANDTHS
ADFGHIINOOT	IN GOOD FAITH	ADHIIOPPSSY	DIAPOPHYSIS
ADFGIILRRSY	GIRL FRIDAYS	ADHIIORRSST	DIARTHROSIS
ADFGIINQRSU	FIRING SQUAD	ADHILMNOOSW	OLD-WOMANISH
ADFGILNNOST	SOFT LANDING	ADHILNNORST	NORTH ISLAND
ADFGILNQSUY	FLYING SQUAD	ADHILNOSSTU	SOUTH ISLAND
ADFGINORRSU	FAIRGROUNDS	ADHINNOPRSX	ANDROSPHINX
ADFHHNOOSSW	SHOW OF HANDS	ADHINOSSSWW	SASH WINDOWS
ADFIIIILLNNU	NULLIFIDIAN	ADHLNOPSSSW	SPLASHDOWNS
ADFIIIMNNTU	AD INFINITUM	ADIIILNOOST	IDOLISATION
ADFINNOOSTU	FOUNDATIONS	ADIIILNOOTZ	IDOLIZATION
ADFLMNSTUUU	MUTUAL FUNDS	ADIIILNOQTU	LIQUIDATION
ADFLNOOOPTU	FOOT-POUNDAL	ADIIIMNORTT	INTIMIDATOR
ADGGGHIILNN	HANG GLIDING	ADIIIMOSSTT	MASTOIDITIS
ADGGLNORSSU	GROUND GLASS	ADIIINNOSTV	DIVINATIONS
ADGHHIINRTT	HARD-HITTING	ADIIINOOSTX	OXIDISATION
ADGHHILNOPT	DIPHTHONGAL	ADIIINOOTXZ	OXIDIZATION
ADGHHOPRRYY	HYDROGRAPHY	ADIIINOPSST	DISSIPATION
ADGHIILMNNS	MISHANDLING	ADIILLMNOOT	TOIL AND MOIL
ADGHIIMNNOS	ADMONISHING	ADIILLNOQRU	QUADRILLION
ADGHIINNRTW	HANDWRITING	ADIILMNNOST	MANDOLINIST

ADIILMOPSTT	DIPLOMATIST	AEEEGHORRTT	THEATREGOER
ADIILOQRSTU	LIQUIDATORS	AEEEGILNRRS	GENERALISER
ADIIMNNOOST	ADMONITIONS	AEEEGILNRRZ	GENERALIZER
ADIIMNOOPST	ADOPTIONISM	AEEEGILNRSV	EVANGELISER
ADIIMORSTUU	AUDITORIUMS	AEEEGILNRVZ	EVANGELIZER
ADIINNNOSTU	INUNDATIONS	AEEEGIMNNST	STEAM-ENGINE
ADIINNOORST	ORDINATIONS	AEEEGIMNSST	METAGENESIS
ADIINOOPSTT	ADOPTIONIST	AEEEGINORTT	RENEGOTIATE
ADIINOPSTTU	DISPUTATION	AEEEGINPRRT	PEREGRINATE
ADIIOOPRSUV	AVOIRDUPOIS	AEEEGKLOPRS	GOALKEEPERS
ADIIOPRSSTT	PODIATRISTS	AEEEGKLPRRU	KEEP REGULAR
ADIIOPSTTUY	AUDIOTYPIST	AEEEGLMNNRT	ENLARGEMENT
ADIKLNRSSTU	TRUK ISLANDS	AEEEGLNNRSS	GENERALNESS
ADIKLOOSTVV	VLADIVOSTOK	AEEEGLNSSSS	AGELESSNESS
ADILLLOOPPY	POLYPLOIDAL	AEEEGMNNRSS	GERMANENESS
ADILMNOOSTU	MODULATIONS	AEEEGNPPRRS	GREEN PAPERS
ADILNNOSTUU	UNDULATIONS	AEEEHHNNSST	HEATHENNESS
ADILOOSSTWW	SOW WILD OATS	AEEEHILNNPT	ELEPHANTINE
ADILORRSTTU	STRIDULATOR	AEEEHILRTTY	ETHEREALITY
ADILOSSSUUY	ASSIDUOUSLY	AEEEHIMSSTT	METATHESISE
ADIMOOPRSUY	MYRIAPODOUS	AEEEHIMSTTZ	METATHESIZE
ADINNOPSSTT	STANDPOINTS	AEEEHINNTUV	HAUTE-VIENNE
ADJLOPRSTUU	PLATS DU JOUR	AEEEHINSSTT	ANESTHETISE
ADLNOOPRSUY	POLYANDROUS	AEEEHINSTTZ	ANESTHETIZE
ADLNOOPRSWY	PLAY ON WORDS	AEEEHIRSTWW	WEATHER-WISE
ADNNORRSTUU	TURNAROUNDS	AEEEHKMOOPW	MAKE WHOOPEE
ADNOOPRRSTU	PROTANDROUS	AEEEHLLMPRY	EPHEMERALLY
ADOOOPRSSUU	SAUROPODOUS	AEEEHLMPPRT	PAMPHLETEER
AEEEEGKMPRS	GAMEKEEPERS	AEEEHLPRRWY	PRAYER WHEEL
AEEEEGKPRST	GATEKEEPERS	AEEEHLRSTWW	WATERWHEELS
AEEEEHILRST	ETHEREALISE	AEEEHNNORRW	NOWHERE NEAR
AEEEEHILRTZ	ETHEREALIZE	AEEEHNPRSST	PARENTHESES
AEEEEHLRTTT	LEATHERETTE	AEEEHRSSTTW	SWEETHEARTS
AEEEENRSVWY	NEW YEAR'S EVE	AEEEIILNRRT	INERTIA REEL
AEEEFFLOPPT	TOFFEE APPLE	AEEEIINPPRT	PERIPETEIAN
AEEEFFLORRT	FREE-FLOATER	AEEEIIRRTTV	REITERATIVE
AEEEFGIKNPS	SAFEKEEPING	AEEEILNORRS	SIERRA LEONE
AEEEFGIRRRT	REFRIGERATE	AEEEILNRRTT	INTERRELATE
AEEEFHINRRT	HEREINAFTER	AEEEILNRRTV	REVERENTIAL
AEEEFILNRRT	REFERENTIAL	AEEEILNRSTX	EXTERNALISE
AEEEFLLNNTT	FLANNELETTE	AEEEILNRTXZ	EXTERNALIZE
AEEEFLNSSSU	EASEFULNESS	AEEEILPRRTT	PRELITERATE
AEEEFLRSSTU	FEATURELESS	AEEEIMNPRTT	INTEMPERATE
AEEEFPRSTTU	SUPERFETATE	AEEEIMNRTTX	EXTERMINATE
AEEEGGHIMTV	GIVE THE GAME	AEEEIMNRTUV	ENUMERATIVE
AEEEGGIKMNP	GAMEKEEPING	AEEEINNRRTT	ENTERTAINER
AEEEGGILNOS	GENEALOGIES	AEEEINOPRSU	EUROPEANISE
AEEEGGIRSTV	SEGREGATIVE	AEEEINOPRUZ	EUROPEANIZE
AEEEGGMMNOU	EMMENAGOGUE	AEEEINORTVX	EXONERATIVE
AEEEGGMNNST	ENGAGEMENTS	AEEEINPRTTV	PENETRATIVE
AEEEGGNNRRT	GRETNA GREEN	AEEEINRRTVW	INTERWEAVER
AEEEGHLPRRT	TELEGRAPHER	AEEEINSSSVV	EVASIVENESS
AEEEGHNPRTW	GREAT-NEPHEW	AEEEJKRRRST	TEARJERKERS
AEEEGHNRTWY	GET ANYWHERE	AEEEJLMSSTY	LESE-MAJESTY

AEEEKKPPRRS	PARK KEEPERS
AEEEKLLOSTX	EXOSKELETAL
AEEEKLLPRSW	SLEEPWALKER
AEEEKPSSSTW	SWEEPSTAKES
AEEELLOPPSS	SALESPEOPLE
AEEELLORTTT	TEETOTALLER
AEEELLRSTVW	WATER LEVELS
AEEELMMNNPT	EMPANELMENT
AEEELMNNSTV	ENSLAVEMENT
AEEELMRSSSU	MEASURELESS
AEEELNOPPVY	PAY ENVELOPE
AEEELRSTTUV	STREET VALUE
AEEEMMNORST	ANEMOMETERS
AEEEMMNPRTT	TEMPERAMENT
AEEEMMNRSTU	MEASUREMENT
AEEEMNNNRST	ENSNAREMENT
AEEEMNNRTTT	ENTREATMENT
AEEEMNOPSSS	OPEN SESAMES
AEEEMNOSSSW	AWESOMENESS
AEEEMNPRSTT	PENTAMETERS
AEEEMNRSTTT	RESTATEMENT
AEEEMPRRTTU	TEMPERATURE
AEEENNRSSST	EARNESTNESS
AEEENOPRSTT	STEAROPTENE
AEEENPRRSTV	PERSEVERANT
AEEENRSSSTU	AUSTERENESS
AEEEQRSSTTU	SEQUESTRATE
AEEFFGRSTTU	SUFFRAGETTE
AEEFFHORRST	FOREFATHERS
AEEFFILMRTU	FEATURE FILM
AEEFFLLORRS	FREE-FOR-ALLS
AEEFFLNRSSU	FEARFULNESS
AEEFFLNSSTU	FATEFULNESS
AEEFGHORRTT	HETEROGRAFT
AEEFGILLNSS	SELF-SEALING
AEEFGILNPRT	FINGERPLATE
AEEFGILNRRS	RIFLE RANGES
AEEFGINRRRT	REFRIGERANT
AEEFHHIKNST	SHEATH KNIFE
AEEFHHORSTU	HOUSEFATHER
AEEFHILNNPS	HALFPENNIES
AEEFHLLMNST	MANTELSHELF
AEEFHLNSSTU	HATEFULNESS
AEEFIILNNRT	INFERENTIAL
AEEFIILOTVX	EXFOLIATIVE
AEEFIIRRRSS	FIRE-RAISERS
AEEFILLNRST	SELF-RELIANT
AEEFILMRSTY	FAMILY TREES
AEEFILOPRRT	PROLIFERATE
AEEFIMNNRRT	REFRAINMENT
AEEFIMNOSST	MANIFESTOES
AEEFIMOPRRT	IMPERFORATE
AEEFIMORRTV	REFORMATIVE
AEEFINRRRST	FRATERNISER
AEEFINRRRTZ	FRATERNIZER
AEEFIOPRRTV	PERFORATIVE
AEEFKLNSSUW	WAKEFULNESS
AEEFLLORRST	FORESTALLER
AEEFLLPRSUU	PLEASUREFUL
AEEFLNRSSTU	TEARFULNESS
AEEFLRRSSTT	SELF-STARTER
AEEFMNNORRSY	FREEMASONRY
AEEFNNOPRSS	PROFANENESS
AEEFNORRSVW	WAR OF NERVES
AEEFOQRRRTU	FOREQUARTER
AEEGGGINRST	SEGREGATING
AEEGGHIOPRS	GEOGRAPHIES
AEEGGHOPRRS	GEOGRAPHERS
AEEGGIINORS	SEIGNIORAGE
AEEGGIKLNOP	GOALKEEPING
AEEGGILNOST	GENEALOGIST
AEEGGIMNOSS	GAMOGENESIS
AEEGGINORST	SEGREGATION
AEEGGINQSTU	GIGANTESQUE
AEEGGINRRRS	GRANGERISER
AEEGGINRRRZ	GRANGERIZER
AEEGGIRRTTU	REGURGITATE
AEEGGORSTTY	GEOSTRATEGY
AEEGHHITVWY	HEAVYWEIGHT
AEEGHHMORRS	HEMORRHAGES
AEEGHIIILMNS	HEGELIANISM
AEEGHILNPRS	GENERALSHIP
AEEGHILNPSS	SINGLE-PHASE
AEEGHINNRTT	THREATENING
AEEGHINORRV	OVERHEARING
AEEGHINORVZ	HERZEGOVINA
AEEGHIPPRTW	PAPERWEIGHT
AEEGHLNOPRS	SELENOGRAPH
AEEGHLNSTVW	WAVELENGTHS
AEEGHLORSTT	ALTOGETHERS
AEEGHLRRSTU	SLAUGHTERER
AEEGHMOOPRT	GAMETOPHORE
AEEGHMOPTTY	GAMETOPHYTE
AEEGHOPRRRX	XEROGRAPHER
AEEGHOPRRST	STEREOGRAPH
AEEGHOPSSSU	ESOPHAGUSES
AEEGIILLSTV	LEGISLATIVE
AEEGIILNNOR	LEGIONNAIRE
AEEGIILNORS	LEGIONARIES
AEEGIILNRST	GELATINISER
AEEGIILNRTZ	GELATINIZER
AEEGIINRRTT	REITERATING
AEEGIINRTTV	INTEGRATIVE, VINAIGRETTE
AEEGIINSTTV	INVESTIGATE
AEEGILLMNNP	EMPANELLING
AEEGILLMNNW	WELL-MEANING
AEEGILLNNTY	INELEGANTLY
AEEGILLNRVY	REVEALINGLY

AEEGILLRSTU	LEGISLATURE
AEEGILMNNRT	ENGRAILMENT, REALIGNMENT
AEEGILMNNSS	MEANINGLESS
AEEGILMNRRS	MALINGERERS
AEEGILMNRST	REGIMENTALS
AEEGILNNRRT	INTERREGNAL
AEEGILNRSTV	EVERLASTING
AEEGILNSSTV	EVANGELISTS
AEEGIMNNRTU	ENUMERATING
AEEGIMNNRUV	MANEUVERING
AEEGIMNSSTU	MUTAGENESIS
AEEGIMSSTTU	GUESSTIMATE
AEEGINNORST	GENERATIONS
AEEGINNORTX	EXONERATING
AEEGINNPRTT	PENETRATING
AEEGINNRSTV	EVENING STAR
AEEGINNTTUX	EXTENUATING
AEEGINORRRS	REORGANISER
AEEGINORRRZ	REORGANIZER
AEEGINORRTT	INTERROGATE
AEEGINOSSTU	AUTOGENESIS
AEEGIOPRRTV	PREROGATIVE
AEEGIPPRRST	PAPER TIGERS
AEEGLLMNNTY	GENTLEMANLY
AEEGLLMORTU	GLOMERULATE
AEEGLLOPSWY	YELLOW PAGES
AEEGLMNNOTW	GENTLEWOMAN
AEEGLMNOOPR	PROLEGOMENA
AEEGLOOPRRT	PORTO ALEGRE
AEEGLORSTUV	TRAVELOGUES
AEEGMNNNORT	MONTENEGRAN
AEEGMNORRTV	OVERGARMENT
AEEGMNRSTWY	WEST GERMANY
AEEGNNORRTY	ROENTGEN RAY
AEEGNNORSSS	SENSE ORGANS
AEEGNNRSSST	STRANGENESS
AEEGNORSSTV	GRAVESTONES
AEEGNOSSSSU	GASEOUSNESS
AEEGNPRSSTT	PRESS AGENTS
AEEHHHOSTTV	HAVE THE HOTS
AEEHHILNSST	HEALTHINESS
AEEHHILRTWW	WHEREWITHAL
AEEHHIPRSTW	WEATHER SHIP
AEEHHIRSTWW	WHITEWASHER
AEEHHISSTWW	WHITEWASHES
AEEHHMORSTV	HARVEST HOME
AEEHHNORSTT	HEARTHSTONE
AEEHIILMOPT	EPITHELIOMA
AEEHIILNRST	SAINT HELIER
AEEHIKLLLRW	KILLER WHALE
AEEHIKLNRSS	HARNESS-LIKE
AEEHIKNSTTV	HAVE KITTENS
AEEHIKPPRSS	SPEAKERSHIP
AEEHIKPSSTT	TAKE THE PISS

AEEHILLMOST	MESOTHELIAL
AEEHILLMRTY	HEMIELYTRAL
AEEHILMMNTY	METHYLAMINE
AEEHILMSTTW	WHITE METALS
AEEHILNNOST	STENOHALINE
AEEHILNNSST	SAINT HELENS
AEEHILNPPRS	PLANISPHERE
AEEHILNPSSS	SHAPELINESS
AEEHILNRSST	EARTHLINESS
AEEHILNSSTW	WEALTHINESS
AEEHILPPRRS	PERIPHERALS
AEEHILPSTTT	TELEPATHIST
AEEHILRSTVW	WHITE-SLAVER
AEEHILSSTTT	STEALTHIEST
AEEHIMMNRST	HAMMERSTEIN
AEEHIMNSTTY	AMETHYSTINE
AEEHINPRSST	PARENTHESIS
AEEHINSSTTT	ANESTHETIST
AEEHIOOPRTT	HETEROTOPIA
AEEHIOOPSST	APOTHEOSISE
AEEHIOOPSTZ	APOTHEOSIZE
AEEHIORSTTX	HETEROTAXIS
AEEHIORTTVX	EXHORTATIVE
AEEHIPPRRSS	PERIPHRASES
AEEHIPPRSTW	WHITE PAPERS
AEEHKMPRRTY	HYPERMARKET
AEEHLLMSSSY	SHAMELESSLY
AEEHLLORSSW	WHOLESALERS
AEEHLLPSSSY	SHAPELESSLY
AEEHLLRSSTY	HEARTLESSLY
AEEHLMNNRTT	ENTHRALMENT
AEEHLMORSTY	HEARTSOMELY
AEEHLMOSSTV	STEAM SHOVEL
AEEHLMOSTTY	STATELY HOME
AEEHLMPRSSW	SPERM WHALES
AEEHLMRRTUY	EURYTHERMAL
AEEHLNORTVW	LEAVENWORTH
AEEHLNPSSSS	HAPLESSNESS
AEEHLNRSSSS	HARNESSLESS
AEEHLOOPRRT	HETEROPOLAR
AEEHLPPRRTU	PURPLE HEART
AEEHLRSSSTV	HARVESTLESS
AEEHLRSSTTX	TAX SHELTERS
AEEHMNOPRST	METANEPHROS
AEEHMNORSWW	WASHERWOMEN
AEEHMOPRSST	ATMOSPHERES
AEEHMOPRSTU	HEPTAMEROUS
AEEHMORSSTU	HOUSEMASTER
AEEHNOPRSTU	HOUSEPARENT
AEEHNORRSTT	NORTHEASTER
AEEHNPPSTVY	HAPPY EVENTS
AEEHOOPRRSS	HORSE OPERAS
AEEHOOPRSST	PEASHOOTERS
AEEHOPRRSST	ASTROSPHERE

AEEHORRSSTU	HOUSE ARREST	AEEILMNSSSS	AIMLESSNESS
AEEHORSSTTU	SOUTHEASTER	AEEILMNSSWY	WESLEYANISM
AEEHRSSSTUU	THESAURUSES	AEEILMOPRRT	POLARIMETER
AEEIIILMNTV	ELIMINATIVE	AEEILMORRST	SOLARIMETER
AEEIIIINNNST	EINSTEINIAN	AEEILMOSTTT	TEETOTALISM
AEEIIINRRST	ITINERARIES	AEEILMPPRRS	PERISPERMAL
AEEIIKLNNST	IN-LINE SKATE	AEEILNNOPTX	EXPONENTIAL
AEEIILLRRST	ARTILLERIES	AEEILNNOSTX	EXTENSIONAL
AEEIILLRSTW	WATER LILIES	AEEILNNSSST	SALIENTNESS
AEEIILMMORS	MEMORIALISE	AEEILNNSSTU	UNESSENTIAL
AEEIILMMORZ	MEMORIALIZE	AEEILNNSTTU	LIEUTENANTS
AEEIILMNRRS	MINERALISE	AEEILNOPRSS	PERSONALISE
AEEIILMNRRZ	MINERALIZER	AEEILNOPRSZ	PERSONALIZE
AEEIILMNSTT	MENTALITIES	AEEILNOPRTT	INTERPOLATE
AEEIILMORTV	MELIORATIVE	AEEILNORSTV	REVELATIONS
AEEIILMRRST	SEMITRAILER	AEEILNPSTTV	SEPTIVALENT
AEEIILNNPTT	PENITENTIAL	AEEILNPSVXY	EXPANSIVELY
AEEIILNNRRT	INTERLINEAR	AEEILNQSTUV	EQUIVALENTS
AEEIILNNRST	INTERNALISE	AEEILNRRSTU	NEUTRALISER
AEEIILNNRTZ	INTERNALIZE	AEEILNRRTUZ	NEUTRALIZER
AEEIILNNSST	INESSENTIAL	AEEILNRSSSS	AIRLESSNESS
AEEIILNORST	ORIENTALISE	AEEILNRSTTX	EXTERNALIST
AEEIILNORTZ	ORIENTALIZE	AEEILNRSTUX	INTERSEXUAL
AEEIILNSTTX	EXISTENTIAL	AEEILNRTTXY	EXTERNALITY
AEEIILNTTVV	VENTILATIVE	AEEILNSSSTT	STATELINESS
AEEIILQRRSU	RELIQUARIES	AEEILNTTTVY	ATTENTIVELY, TENTATIVELY
AEEIIMNRTTV	TERMINATIVE	AEEILNTTUVY	EVENTUALITY
AEEIIMNSSTT	ANTI-SEMITES	AEEILOPPRTT	TOILET PAPER
AEEIIMNSSTW	SIAMESE TWIN	AEEILOPRRRT	REPERTORIAL
AEEIIMPRSTV	IMPERATIVES	AEEILORTTTW	TOILET WATER
AEEIIMPRTTV	IMPETRATIVE	AEEILPPRRSV	SILVER PAPER
AEEIINNTTTV	INATTENTIVE	AEEILPRSTUV	SUPERLATIVE
AEEIINOPRTV	INOPERATIVE	AEEILPRSVVY	PERVASIVELY
AEEIINORRTT	REITERATION	AEEILPSTTUX	EXSTIPULATE
AEEIIPRSSST	PATISSERIES	AEEILQRRSTU	QUARTERLIES
AEEIIPRTTVX	EXTIRPATIVE	AEEILRRRSTT	TERRESTRIAL
AEEIIRSSTTU	AUSTERITIES	AEEILRRSTTU	LITERATURES
AEEIKMNSTTU	MINUTE STEAK	AEEILRRTTTU	LITTERATEUR
AEEIKNPPRSV	PAPER KNIVES	AEEILRSSTVY	ASSERTIVELY
AEEIKNRSSST	STREAKINESS	AEEIMMNNPRT	IMPERMANENT
AEEIKRRSSTW	WATER SKIERS	AEEIMMRRSTT	TETRAMERISM
AEEILLMMNPT	IMPLEMENTAL	AEEIMNNNOQU	MENAQUINONE
AEEILLMNOPS	PSILOMELANE	AEEIMNNNRRT	ENTRAINMENT
AEEILLMPRXY	EXEMPLARILY	AEEIMNNORTU	ENUMERATION, MOUNTAINEER
AEEILLNNPRY	PERENNIALLY	AEEIMNNPRST	PINE MARTENS
AEEILLNOPPT	EN PAPILLOTE	AEEIMNNSSTT	INSTATEMENT
AEEILLNRSST	LITERALNESS	AEEIMNOPRST	IMPERSONATE
AEEILLNSSTY	ESSENTIALLY	AEEIMNOPRSU	EUROPEANISM
AEEILLPRSTV	SILVER PLATE	AEEIMNORSST	MONASTERIES
AEEILMMNSTT	SENTIMENTAL	AEEIMNORSTT	MARIONETTES
AEEILMNORST	SALINOMETER	AEEIMNOSSTT	MAISONETTES
AEEILMNPRST	SEMPITERNAL	AEEIMNRSTUV	MENSURATIVE
AEEILMNPTTU	PENULTIMATE	AEEIMNSSSSV	MASSIVENESS
AEEILMNRSTX	EXTERNALISM	AEEIMOPRRTV	VAPORIMETER

AEEIMORRSTU	TEMERARIOUS
AEEIMQRSSUV	SEMIQUAVERS
AEEIMQRSTTU	MARQUISETTE
AEEIMSSSTTY	SYSTEMATISE
AEEIMSSTTYZ	SYSTEMATIZE
AEEINNOORTX	EXONERATION
AEEINNOPRTT	PENETRATION
AEEINNORSTV	ANTEVERSION
AEEINNOTTUV	EVENTUATION
AEEINNOTTUX	EXTENUATION
AEEINOPRSTV	PERSONATIVE
AEEINORRSTV	RESERVATION
AEEINPSSSSV	PASSIVENESS
AEEIOPPRRTX	EXPROPRIATE
AEEIORRSTTV	RESTORATIVE
AEEIORSSTTX	STEREOTAXIS
AEEIPRRSSTU	PASTEURISER
AEEIPRSSTUZ	PASTEURIZER
AEEIPRSSSTT	SPESSARTITE, STRIPTEASES
AEEJNORRTUV	REJUVENATOR
AEEKLLORRST	ROLLER SKATE
AEEKLMORRTW	METALWORKER
AEEKMMNORSY	MONEYMAKERS
AEEKMMRRRSY	MERRYMAKERS
AEEKMPRRSTU	SUPERMARKET
AEEKNPRRSTU	SUPERTANKER
AEELLMNRSTU	ALLUREMENTS
AEELLMORRST	STEAMROLLER
AEELLNORRTT	RETROLENTAL
AEELLNORSTW	STONEWALLER
AEELLNPRTVY	PREVALENTLY
AEELLNSSSSW	LAWLESSNESS
AEELLOPRTUV	POLE VAULTER
AEELLORSTTY	TEA TROLLEYS
AEELLPPRTUY	PERPETUALLY
AEELLSSSTTY	TASTELESSLY
AEELMMORTTV	VOLTAMMETER
AEELMNNOSTT	MENTAL NOTES
AEELMNNPRTY	PERMANENTLY
AEELMNNRTUV	UNRAVELMENT
AEELMNORSTW	WATERMELONS
AEELMOPRSTT	PLASTOMETER
AEELMOQRRSU	QUARRELSOME
AEELMPRRTUY	PREMATURELY
AEELNNPRTTY	REPENTANTLY
AEELNNQSSUU	UNEQUALNESS
AEELNNSSSSU	SENSUALNESS
AEELNOPRSSS	SALESPERSON
AEELNOPRSST	PROLATENESS
AEELNOSSSUZ	ZEALOUSNESS
AEELNRSSSST	ARTLESSNESS
AEELOPSTTUX	EXPOSTULATE
AEELORSSTTU	LOTUS-EATERS
AEEMNOPRRTY	PYRANOMETER

AEEMNOPRSTU	PENTAMEROUS
AEEMNORRRTU	REMUNERATOR
AEEMNORRSTT	REMONSTRATE
AEEMNORSSTT	EASTERNMOST
AEEMNSSSSST	ASSESSMENTS
AEEMORRSTTU	TETRAMEROUS
AEEMPPRRSTTU	EAR TRUMPETS
AEENNOOPSSS	OPEN SEASONS
AEENNOPRRTU	NEUROPTERAN
AEENOPRRSTT	PATERNOSTER
AEENOQRRTTU	QUARTER NOTE
AEENORTTUXY	EXTENUATORY
AEENNPPRSSTT	STEPPARENTS
AEENQRSSTTU	SEQUESTRANT
AEEOOPSTTTW	SWEET POTATO
AEEOPPRRRTT	PERPETRATOR
AEEPRSSSWXY	EXPRESSWAYS
AEFFGIIMNRR	REAFFIRMING
AEFFGIMSTUU	SUFFUMIGATE
AEFFGINORST	AFFORESTING
AEFFHHILTTU	THE FAITHFUL
AEFFHIKMOTW	MAKE OFF WITH
AEFFHINRSSS	RAFFISHNESS
AEFFHLLPSUY	SHUFFLE PLAY
AEFFIIMNORR	FORAMINIFER
AEFFIKLLOSW	WALKS OF LIFE
AEFFIRSSTTY	SAFETY-FIRST
AEFFKNRRRTU	FRANKFURTER
AEFFNRSSSTU	STAFF NURSES
AEFGGHIRSTT	STAGE FRIGHT
AEFGGIMNNRT	FRAGMENTING
AEFGHORSTTU	SOUGHT-AFTER
AEFGIIINRRS	FIRE-RAISING
AEFGIILNNRS	FINGERNAILS
AEFGIIMNNST	MANIFESTING
AEFGILLLNNN	FLANNELLING
AEFGILLNRST	FINGERSTALL
AEFGILLNRTY	FALTERINGLY
AEFGILNNRTU	UNFALTERING
AEFGILNNSSU	GAINFULNESS
AEFGILOPRST	PROFLIGATES
AEFGINNNSSW	FAWNINGNESS
AEFGINNORRW	FOREWARNING
AEFGINOPRRT	PERFORATING
AEFGINORRSW	FORSWEARING
AEFGINRRSTU	TRANSFIGURE
AEFGIPRRSTU	GRAPEFRUITS
AEFHHLLLTUY	HEALTHFULLY
AEFHILLSSTY	FAITHLESSLY
AEFHILRSSST	HALF-SISTERS
AEFHIMNOPRS	FOREMANSHIP
AEFHKOORTTU	OUT OF THE ARK
AEFHLLLOSVY	HALF VOLLEYS
AEFHLMNRSSU	HARMFULNESS

AEFHMORRSTT	FARTHERMOST
AEFHOOTTUWY	OUT-OF-THE-WAY
AEFIIIMNRRS	INFIRMARIES
AEFIIKLNNRT	FRANKLINITE
AEFIILLNNTU	INFLUENTIAL
AEFIILMORST	FORMALITIES
AEFIILNNRTY	INFERNALITY
AEFIILNOOTX	EXFOLIATION
AEFIILOPRRW	PRAIRIE WOLF
AEFIIMNORTV	INFORMATIVE
AEFIINNOSTT	FESTINATION, INFESTATION, SINFONIETTA
AEFIINNRSTT	TRANSFINITE
AEFIINOPRST	PROFANITIES
AEFIINORSTT	FIRE STATION
AEFIINQRSTU	QUANTIFIERS
AEFILLLMMOR	LAMELLIFORM
AEFILLMOPRT	PATELLIFORM
AEFILLRRTTU	ULTRAFILTER
AEFILLRSTVY	RIFT VALLEYS
AEFILMORRSU	FORMULARISE
AEFILMORRUZ	FORMULARIZE
AEFILMORTVY	FORMATIVELY
AEFILMPRSUY	SUPERFAMILY
AEFILNNPSSU	PAINFULNESS
AEFILNORSUY	NEFARIOUSLY
AEFILOOPRST	FORE-TOPSAIL
AEFILOOPSTY	PLAY FOOTSIE
AEFILOPRRTY	PREFATORILY
AEFIMMMORSU	MAMMIFEROUS
AEFIMNNNRTY	INFANTRYMEN
AEFIMNNOOTT	FOMENTATION
AEFIMNOORRT	REFORMATION
AEFINNNOPTU	FOUNTAIN PEN
AEFINNRRRST	TRANSFERRIN
AEFINOOPRRT	PERFORATION
AEFINOORSTT	FORESTATION
AEFINORRSST	RAIN FORESTS
AEFINORSTTU	REFUTATIONS
AEFINRSSTUV	TRANSFUSIVE
AEFKLLOORRW	FLOORWALKER
AEFLLLOPRUW	ALL-POWERFUL
AEFLLLOPSWY	PLAYFELLOWS
AEFLLLORSWW	WALLFLOWERS
AEFLLLSSTUY	FAULTLESSLY
AEFLLMRSTUY	MASTERFULLY
AEFLLNPSSUY	PLAYFULNESS
AEFLLORSSUV	FLAVOURLESS
AEFLMOORSUV	FLAVOURSOME
AEFLNORTTUY	FORTUNATELY
AEFLORRSTWW	STRAWFLOWER
AEFLRSSTTWY	FLYSWATTERS
AEFMNORRRST	TRANSFORMER
AEFMOOPRSTT	FORE-TOPMAST

AEFMOORRRTY	REFORMATORY
AEFNNORTTUU	UNFORTUNATE
AEFNORRSTTW	WATERFRONTS
AEFNOSSSTUU	FATUOUSNESS
AEFOOPRRSTW	WATERPROOFS
AEGGGNORSTU	GO GREAT GUNS
AEGGHHINSSS	HAGGISHNESS
AEGGHIILLNT	NIGHTINGALE
AEGGHIIRRRT	HAIR TRIGGER
AEGGHILNRST	RIGHT ANGLES
AEGGHINSSSW	WAGGISHNESS
AEGGHLOOPRR	LOGOGRAPHER
AEGGHMNORTU	GRANGEMOUTH
AEGGIILLNST	LEGISLATING
AEGGIILMNNR	MALINGERING
AEGGIILMPRS	PILGRIMAGES
AEGGIIMNNRT	GERMINATING
AEGGIIMNNTZ	MAGNETIZING
AEGGIINNOTT	NEGOTIATING
AEGGIINNRTT	INTEGRATING
AEGGIINRTTU	INGURGITATE
AEGGILNNORW	LONGWEARING
AEGGILNNRSS	GLARINGNESS
AEGGILRSSTT	STRAGGLIEST
AEGGIMNOSST	MAGGOTINESS
AEGGINNOTXY	OXYGENATING
AEGGINPRTUX	EXPURGATING
AEGGINRRTTU	REGURGITANT
AEGGJNRSTUU	JUGGERNAUTS
AEGHHILOPRS	HELIOGRAPHS
AEGHHILOPRY	HELIOGRAPHY
AEGHHINNPTY	HYPHENATING
AEGHHINORST	HIGH TREASON
AEGHHINSSTU	HAUGHTINESS
AEGHHLOPRSU	PLOUGHSHARE
AEGHHLORSSU	HORSELAUGHS
AEGHHMOPRRT	THERMOGRAPH
AEGHHNOPRTY	ETHNOGRAPHY
AEGHHNOSTTU	THAT'S ENOUGH!
AEGHIIKMNNT	IN THE MAKING
AEGHIILMSTT	ALMIGHTIEST
AEGHIIMNPSZ	EMPHASIZING
AEGHIIMNRST	TIME-SHARING
AEGHIIPPRST	EPIGRAPHIST
AEGHILLNNRT	ENTHRALLING
AEGHILLNOPS	ANGLOPHILES
AEGHILLRRSY	ARGYLLSHIRE
AEGHILNNSST	HALTINGNESS
AEGHILNOOST	ANTHOLOGIES, ANTHOLOGISE, THEOLOGIANS
AEGHILNOOTZ	ANTHOLOGIZE
AEGHILNORUV	OVERHAULING
AEGHILNOTTU	GLUTATHIONE
AEGHILNSSST	GHASTLINESS

AEGHIMMOPRS	MIMEOGRAPHS
AEGHIMNNRST	GARNISHMENT
AEGHIMOPRSS	SEISMOGRAPH
AEGHINNSSTU	NAUGHTINESS
AEGHIRSSTTT	STRAIGHTEST
AEGHIRSTTWW	STRAWWEIGHT
AEGHLNOOOORR	GONORRHOEAL
AEGHLOOPRSY	PHRASEOLOGY
AEGHLOPPRYY	PYELOGRAPHY
AEGHLOPRRXY	XYLOGRAPHER
AEGHLORSSSU	HOURGLASSES
AEGHLOSSSSU	GLASSHOUSES
AEGHMNOOOPRR	MONOGRAPHER, NOMOGRAPHER
AEGHMNOOPRS	GRAMOPHONES
AEGHMNOPPRU	PNEUMOGRAPH
AEGHNOOPRRS	NOSOGRAPHER
AEGHNOPRSTY	STENOGRAPHY
AEGHNOPSSTU	STENOPHAGUS
AEGHOOPPRRT	TOPOGRAPHER
AEGHOPPRRRY	PYROGRAPHER, REPROGRAPHY
AEGHOPPRRSS	GRASSHOPPER
AEGHOPPRRTY	PETROGRAPHY, TYPOGRAPHER
AEGIIILLMNNT	ELIMINATING
AEGIIILNRSZ	SERIALIZING
AEGIIINSTTV	INSTIGATIVE
AEGIIKLLNRT	GIANT KILLER
AEGIIKNRSST	ASTERISKING
AEGIIKNRSTW	WATER SKIING
AEGIILLMNNP	IMPANELLING
AEGIILLNOST	LEGISLATION
AEGIILLNRTT	ILL-TREATING
AEGIILLSTVY	VESTIGIALLY
AEGIILMNORS	REGIONALISM
AEGIILMNSST	TIME SIGNALS
AEGIILNNRTU	INTERLINGUA
AEGIILNNTTV	VENTILATING
AEGIILNORST	REGIONALIST
AEGIILNRSSU	SINGULARISE
AEGIILNRSUZ	SINGULARIZE
AEGIILOOSTT	AETIOLOGIST
AEGIILRSTUV	VULGARITIES
AEGIIMMMNNUW	MINIMUM WAGE
AEGIIMMORRR	MIRROR IMAGE
AEGIIMNNORT	GERMINATION
AEGIIMNNRTT	TERMINATING
AEGIIMNORST	EMIGRATIONS
AEGIIMPRSTU	EPIGASTRIUM
AEGIIMRSSTT	STIGMATISER
AEGIIMRSTTZ	STIGMATIZER
AEGIINNOOTT	NEGOTIATION
AEGIINNORST	RESIGNATION
AEGIINNORTT	INTEGRATION, ORIENTATING
AEGIINNRRST	RESTRAINING
AEGIINNRSTT	REINSTATING
AEGIINORSST	SIGNATORIES
AEGIINPPRTW	WIRE-TAPPING
AEGIINPRTTX	EXTIRPATING
AEGIJLNRUUV	JUGULAR VEIN
AEGIKMMNNOY	MONEYMAKING
AEGIKMMNRRY	MERRYMAKING
AEGILLMNNTY	LAMENTINGLY
AEGILLMOOPS	MEGALOPOLIS
AEGILLNNRUV	UNRAVELLING
AEGILLNOPRY	ROLE PLAYING
AEGILLNOPST	SELLOTAPING
AEGILLNQRRU	QUARRELLING
AEGILLORSST	LEGISLATORS
AEGILLPRSSU	ASPERGILLUS
AEGILLRRRUY	IRREGULARLY
AEGILMMNOTU	GEMMULATION
AEGILMNOORT	GLOMERATION
AEGILMNOPRU	PELARGONIUM
AEGILMNORST	GILA MONSTER
AEGILMNOSTU	LIGAMENTOUS
AEGILMOOSSY	SEMASIOLOGY
AEGILNNOOST	ELONGATIONS
AEGILNOOSSX	XENOGLOSSIA
AEGILNOPPRV	OVERLAPPING
AEGILNOPRVY	OVERPLAYING
AEGILNORSTU	REGULATIONS
AEGILNPRSTT	SPLATTERING
AEGILNQRUVY	QUAVERINGLY
AEGILNRRSTY	ARRESTINGLY
AEGILNRSSTV	STARVELINGS
AEGILOOSTTU	TAUTOLOGIES, TAUTOLOGISE
AEGILOOTTUZ	TAUTOLOGIZE
AEGILRSTTUU	GUTTURALISE
AEGILRTTUUZ	GUTTURALIZE
AEGIMMOPRSU	GEMMIPAROUS
AEGIMNNNORT	ORNAMENTING
AEGIMNNNORV	OVERMANNING
AEGIMNNNRTU	RUNNING MATE
AEGIMNNORUV	MANOEUVRING
AEGIMNNSSST	ASSIGNMENTS
AEGIMNOPRRT	IMPREGNATOR
AEGIMNORSSU	IGNORAMUSES
AEGIMNRRSST	RINGMASTERS
AEGIMNRSSTT	SMATTERINGS
AEGINNNORSU	UNREASONING
AEGINNOORRV	VINEGARROON
AEGINNOOTXY	OXYGENATION
AEGINNOPSTV	PAVING STONE
AEGINNOSSUU	SANGUINEOUS
AEGINNPRRTU	ENRAPTURING
AEGINNPRSSS	SPARINGNESS
AEGINNRSSTT	ASTRINGENTS
AEGINOORSTT	NEGOTIATORS
AEGINOPRTUX	EXPURGATION

AEGINOQSTTU	QUESTION TAG
AEGINORSTTV	OVERSTATING
AEGINORSTVY	OVERSTAYING
AEGINPRSSST	TRESPASSING
AEGIPRRRTYY	PYRARGYRITE
AEGIRSSSTTT	STRATEGISTS
AEGKLORRSSW	GLASS-WORKER
AEGKMNOSSXY	OXYGEN MASKS
AEGLOORRSST	ASTROLOGERS
AEGMMOPRRRS	PROGRAMMERS
AEGMNOORSST	GASTRONOMES
AEGNOOPRSSY	GREASY SPOON
AEGOORRRTUV	ROTOGRAVURE
AEGOPRRTUXY	EXPURGATORY
AEHHIIILNNS	HSIN-HAI-LIEN
AEHHIKNSSSW	HAWKISHNESS
AEHHILLNTUY	UNHEALTHILY
AEHHIMMMRST	HAMMERSMITH
AEHHIMOPRTY	HYPOTHERMIA
AEHHINNOPTY	HYPHENATION
AEHHIOPPSST	PHOSPHATISE
AEHHIOPPSTZ	PHOSPHATIZE
AEHHIORTTTW	WHITETHROAT
AEHHLLOPTTY	THALLOPHYTE
AEHHLMMOORT	HOMOTHERMAL
AEHHMOOOPST	HOMOEOPATHS
AEHHMOOOPTY	HOMOEOPATHY
AEHHMOSSTUW	MOUTHWASHES
AEHHNOPRRTY	TENORRHAPHY
AEHHOOPPRST	PHOSPHORATE
AEHIIILMTUV	HUMILIATIVE
AEHIILLOPRU	AILUROPHILE
AEHIILLPSTT	PHILATELIST
AEHIILOPSST	HOSPITALISE
AEHIILOPSTZ	HOSPITALIZE
AEHIIMNRSTT	MARTINETISH
AEHIINOPRRS	PARISHIONER
AEHIINOSSTT	HESITATIONS
AEHIIORSTTU	AUTHORITIES
AEHIIPPRRSS	PERIPHRASIS
AEHIIRSSTUW	WHITE RUSSIA
AEHIKLNOOPR	HARPOON-LIKE
AEHIKLNRSSS	LARKISHNESS
AEHIKMNSSSW	MAWKISHNESS
AEHILLOPPTY	APOPHYLLITE
AEHILLOPRST	HOSPITALLER
AEHILMNNOOP	AMINOPHENOL
AEHILMNORTW	MOTHER-IN-LAW
AEHILMNOTTY	METHYLATION
AEHILMNRSTU	LUTHERANISM
AEHILMQSSUY	SQUEAMISHLY
AEHILMRRSTY	ERYTHRISMAL
AEHILNOSTTW	WEST LOTHIAN
AEHILNPRRTY	PLATYRRHINE

AEHILNPSSSS	SPLASHINESS
AEHILNSSSSV	SLAVISHNESS
AEHIMNNNSSS	MANNISHNESS
AEHIMNOOPPR	APOMORPHINE
AEHIMNOOPSS	HOMO SAPIENS
AEHIMNOPRST	MISANTHROPE
AEHIMNOSTUX	EXHUMATIONS
AEHIMNSSSTU	ENTHUSIASMS
AEHIMOOSSST	HOMEOSTASIS
AEHIMOPSSTY	HAEMOPTYSIS
AEHIMORSTTX	THERMOTAXIS
AEHIMPPRSTU	HIPPEASTRUM
AEHIMPRSSTY	SYMPATHISER
AEHIMPRSTYZ	SYMPATHIZER
AEHINNPPSSU	UNHAPPINESS
AEHINOORSTT	ANORTHOSITE
AEHINOORTTX	EXHORTATION
AEHINOPSSTT	STEPHANOTIS
AEHINORRSST	ENARTHROSIS
AEHINORSSTT	THROATINESS
AEHINPRRSST	PARTNERSHIP
AEHINPSSSSW	WASPISHNESS
AEHINQSSSSU	SQUASHINESS
AEHINRSSSTW	SWARTHINESS
AEHINSSSTTU	ENTHUSIASTS
AEHIRSSSTTW	SWEATSHIRTS
AEHJNOORRST	TROJAN HORSE
AEHKLLNSSTY	THANKLESSLY
AEHKLOPRSSW	SHOPWALKERS
AEHLLMOOSTY	LOATHSOMELY
AEHLLNOSSSW	SHALLOWNESS
AEHLMNOQSSU	LEMON SQUASH
AEHLMOOSSUX	HOMOSEXUALS
AEHLMOPPRRY	LAMPROPHYRE
AEHLNNOPSTT	PENTATHLONS
AEHLNOPSSTU	HOUSEPLANTS
AEHLOPPRSXY	PROPHYLAXES
AEHMMOOOPRT	OMMATOPHORE
AEHMMNOORSSU	MANOR HOUSES
AEHMNOORSTV	HARVEST MOON
AEHMORSSTTT	THERMOSTATS
AEHNOOPRRTT	ORTHOPTERAN
AEHNOOPSSSU	SOUSAPHONES
AEHOOOPSTTT	HOT POTATOES
AEHOOPPRSST	APOSTROPHES
AEHOOPRRRST	ARTHROSPORE
AEHOOPRRSTT	TRAPSHOOTER
AEHOORSSSTY	SOOTHSAYERS
AEHOQRRRTUU	QUARTER-HOUR
AEIIIINSTTV	INITIATIVES
AEIIILLMNOR	MILLIONAIRE
AEIIILLMNST	SILLIMANITE
AEIIILLTTTV	TITILLATIVE
AEIIILMMPRS	IMPERIALISM

AEIIILMNNOT	ELIMINATION
AEIIILMNRST	MINISTERIAL
AEIIILMNSST	ANTIMISSILE
AEIIILMPRST	IMPERIALIST
AEIIILMRRSV	VERISIMILAR
AEIIILMTTVY	IMITATIVELY
AEIIIMNOSST	ANIMOSITIES
AEIIIMNOSTT	ITEMISATION
AEIIIMNOTTZ	ITEMIZATION
AEIIIMNRSTU	MINIATURISE
AEIIIMNRTUZ	MINIATURIZE
AEIIINNORTT	ITINERATION
AEIIINNSTUV	INSINUATIVE
AEIIINORSSV	VISIONARIES
AEIIINPRSTV	INSPIRATIVE
AEIIINQSTTU	ANTIQUITIES
AEIIINRSSTT	INITIATRESS
AEIIIPRSTTU	PITUITARIES
AEIIKLLNPRS	PAINKILLERS
AEIIKLLOPRT	REALPOLITIK
AEIIKNNRSST	KRISTIANSEN
AEIILLMNORS	MINERAL OILS
AEIILLMSTTU	SATELLITIUM
AEIILLNPTVY	PLAINTIVELY
AEIILLNTUUX	LUXULIANITE
AEIILLPRSTU	PLURALITIES
AEIILMMORST	IMMORTALISE, MEMORIALIST
AEIILMMORTZ	IMMORTALIZE
AEIILMNNOPS	MINNEAPOLIS
AEIILMNOORT	MELIORATION
AEIILMNORST	ORIENTALISM
AEIILMNOSTT	TESTIMONIAL
AEIILMNPRRY	PRELIMINARY
AEIILMNPTTY	IMPATIENTLY
AEIILMNRTTY	AMYL NITRITE
AEIILMORSTT	MORTALITIES
AEIILMPSSVY	IMPASSIVELY
AEIILMSTTUV	STIMULATIVE
AEIILNNNOST	INTENSIONAL
AEIILNNNOTT	INTENTIONAL
AEIILNNNOTV	INVENTIONAL
AEIILNNORST	INSERTIONAL
AEIILNNORTV	INVENTORIAL
AEIILNNOTTV	VENTILATION
AEIILNNRRST	LINERTRAINS
AEIILNNRTTY	INTERNALITY
AEIILNNSSST	SAINTLINESS
AEIILNORSSS	INSESSORIAL
AEIILNORSTT	ORIENTALIST
AEIILNORTTU	ELUTRIATION
AEIILNRSSTW	SISTER-IN-LAW
AEIILORRRTT	TERRITORIAL
AEIILPRSSST	PERISTALSIS
AEIILPRTTVY	PARTITIVELY

AEIILRSSTVV	REVIVALISTS
AEIILRSTTVY	VERSATILITY
AEIIMMNRSTT	MARTINETISM
AEIIMMNNOPRY	AMINOPYRINE
AEIIMMNNORST	INSEMINATOR, NITROSAMINE
AEIIMMNNORTT	TERMINATION
AEIIMMNNORTV	VERMINATION
AEIIMMNNOSTV	NOMINATIVES
AEIIMMNOPRTT	IMPETRATION
AEIIMOOPRST	ISOMETROPIA
AEIIMOPPRRT	IMPROPRIATE
AEIIMOPRRSS	IMPRESARIOS
AEIIMRRTTUV	TRIUMVIRATE
AEIINNNORTV	INNERVATION
AEIINNNOSVV	NONINVASIVE
AEIINNNOTTT	INATTENTION
AEIINNOORTT	ORIENTATION
AEIINOPPSTT	PEPTISATION
AEIINOPPTTZ	PEPTIZATION
AEIINOPRRST	RESPIRATION
AEIINOPRRTT	PARTITIONER, REPARTITION
AEIINOPRTTX	EXTIRPATION
AEIINOPRTTY	PETITIONARY
AEIINOPSSTT	POINSETTIAS
AEIINPRSSTY	ANTIPYRESIS
AEIINRSSTTV	TRANSITIVES
AEIINSSTTUV	ANTITUSSIVE
AEIIOOPPSSS	APOSIOPESIS
AEIIOOPRRST	A POSTERIORI
AEIJLNORRSU	JOURNALISER
AEIJLNORRUZ	JOURNALIZER
AEIJMNOSSSS	JAM SESSIONS
AEIKKLMNORW	WORKMANLIKE
AEIKLNNOPPS	PLAINSPOKEN
AEIKLNOPSTT	KINETOPLAST
AEILLLLMOSTY	LAMELLOSITY
AEILLMMRSST	SMALL-TIMERS
AEILLMNOOTY	EMOTIONALLY
AEILLMNOSTY	SEMITONALLY
AEILLMNOTTW	LITTLE WOMAN
AEILLMNTTUV	MULTIVALENT
AEILLNOPTTY	POTENTIALLY
AEILLNOSSSY	SILLY SEASON
AEILLNRSTUV	SURVEILLANT
AEILLNRSUVY	UNIVERSALLY
AEILLORSSTT	TALL STORIES
AEILLORTTUV	ULTRAVIOLET
AEILMMNORTY	MOMENTARILY
AEILMNNNSSU	UNMANLINESS
AEILMNNOPRT	MINOR PLANET
AEILMNNOSSW	WOMANLINESS
AEILMNNSSTT	INSTALMENTS
AEILMNOOSTT	MOLESTATION
AEILMNOPRRT	TRAMPOLINER

AEILMNOPRSS	PERSONALISM
AEILMNOPRST	TRAMPOLINES
AEILMNORSTY	SALINOMETRY
AEILMOPRRSU	LEPROSARIUM
AEILMOPRRTY	POLARIMETRY, TEMPORARILY
AEILMOPRTTY	TEMPORALITY
AEILMOPRTXY	PROXIMATELY
AEILMPPSSST	PALIMPSESTS
AEILMPRSSST	SLIPSTREAMS
AEILMPRSTUU	PARI-MUTUELS
AEILNNOPRSU	UNIPERSONAL
AEILNOOPRTX	EXPLORATION
AEILNOPPTTY	PLATINOTYPE
AEILNOPRSST	PERSONALIST
AEILNOPRSTY	PERSONALITY
AEILNOPSSSS	PASSIONLESS
AEILNORRSTU	SERRULATION
AEILNORSTTV	VENTILATORS
AEILNORSTUV	VOLUNTARIES
AEILNORTTVY	VENTILATORY
AEILNSSSSTU	SENSUALISTS
AEILOPPRRSU	POPULARISER
AEILOPPRRUZ	POPULARIZER
AEILOSSSTTY	STEATOLYSIS
AEILOSTUVXY	VEXATIOUSLY
AEILRRSSSTU	SURREALISTS
AEIMMNRSSSU	SUMMARINESS
AEIMMORSTTU	TAUTOMERISM
AEIMMPRSSTU	SUPREMATISM
AEIMMSSSTTY	SYSTEMATISM
AEIMNNNOSTT	ANOINTMENTS
AEIMNNOPPTT	APPOINTMENT
AEIMNNORSTU	MENSURATION, NUMERATIONS
AEIMNNSSTTU	SUSTAINMENT
AEIMNOORSSU	ANISOMEROUS
AEIMNOPRTTU	IMPORTUNATE, PERMUTATION
AEIMNOPSTTT	TEMPTATIONS
AEIMNORRTTY	TERMINATORY
AEIMNORSSTT	MONETARISTS
AEIMNRRSTTT	TRANSMITTER
AEIMPRSSTTU	SUPREMATIST
AEIMQRSSTUZ	QUIZMASTERS
AEIMSSSTTTY	SYSTEMATIST
AEINNNOQSSU	SINE QUA NONS
AEINNNORTTU	ANTINEUTRON
AEINNOOPRST	PERSONATION
AEINNOORSTV	RENOVATIONS
AEINNOOSTTT	OSTENTATION
AEINNOPSTTY	SPONTANEITY
AEINNORSTUV	INTRAVENOUS
AEINNOSSSUX	ANXIOUSNESS
AEINOOPPRRT	APPORTIONER, REAPPORTION
AEINOOPRRST	PERORATIONS
AEINOOPRSSU	APONEUROSIS

AEINOOPRTTX	EXPORTATION
AEINOORRSTT	RESTORATION
AEINOORSUVX	OVERANXIOUS
AEINOPRSTT	POSTER PAINT
AEINOPRSSSU	PERSUASIONS
AEINOPRSSSV	VASOPRESSIN
AEINOPRSTTU	REPUTATIONS
AEINOPSTTTU	OUTPATIENTS
AEINOQRSTUY	QUESTIONARY
AEINORSSSUV	VARIOUSNESS
AEIOPPRRRTY	PROPRIETARY
AEIOPRRRSST	RESPIRATORS
AEIOPRRRSTY	RESPIRATORY
AEIOPRRRTTU	PORTRAITURE
AEIOPRRTTUV	VITUPERATOR
AEIPPRSTUUV	SUPPURATIVE
AEKMNOOPSSW	SPOKESWOMAN
AEKMNORSTTW	MARKET TOWNS
AEKMORRSSTW	MASTERWORKS
AEKMRRSSSST	STRESS MARKS
AEKNOPRRSSY	NOSY PARKERS
AEKNOQRSSTU	SQUARE KNOTS
AELLNOOPSTY	STANLEY POOL
AELLNOPPRST	PROPELLANTS
AELLNPRSTUU	NE PLUS ULTRA
AELLOPRSSUX	SOLAR PLEXUS
AELMNOPRRSU	SUPERNORMAL
AELMOPRSTTY	PLASTOMETRY
AELMOPSSTUY	SYMPETALOUS
AELMORSSSTU	SOMERSAULTS
AELMORSSSTY	SOLAR SYSTEM
AELMPRSTYYY	MYSTERY PLAY
AELNNNOPRTW	TOWN PLANNER
AELNOORSWXY	LOWER SAXONY
AELNOPPRSTW	POWER PLANTS
AELNOPPSTTY	PENALTY SPOT
AELNPRRSUUY	SUPERLUNARY
AELOOPRRTXY	EXPLORATORY
AELOOPSSTTY	OSTEOPLASTY
AELPPRSTUWY	WATER SUPPLY
AEMNNOOSSST	STONEMASONS
AEMNNORRSTT	REMONSTRANT
AEMNNORSTTU	TOURNAMENTS
AEMNOOPRSTY	TRYPANOSOME
AEMNOORRSST	ASTRONOMERS
AEMNOORSSSU	AMOROUSNESS
AEMNOORSTUU	NEUROMATOUS
AEMNORSSSTT	ASSORTMENTS
AEMNOSTTTUX	MANTOUX TEST
AEMOOPPRRRU	AMOUR-PROPRE
AEMOPRSSSTT	POSTMASTERS
AENNOOPRSSS	PARSON'S NOSE
AENNOOPSSTU	SPONTANEOUS
AENNOPPRSST	PRESTONPANS

AENNORRSSTT	NONSTARTERS		AFIIMORSTUV	FAVOURITISM
AENOPRRRSTT	TRANSPORTER		AFIINNORSTT	FIRST NATION
AENOPRSSTTT	PROTESTANTS		AFIINNORSTX	TRANSFIXION
AENORRSTTTU	STERNUTATOR		AFIIOPRSSSU	FISSIPAROUS
AENPPRSSSTU	SUPPRESSANT		AFILMNOORTU	FORMULATION
AENPRRSSTTU	TRANSPUTERS		AFILMNORTUY	FULMINATORY
AEOOOPPPRRTY	PARTY POOPER		AFINNORSSTU	TRANSFUSION
AEOOORRSSTU	SQUARE ROOTS		AFINOOPPRST	PORT OF SPAIN
AEOPPRRTTVY	POVERTY TRAP		AFINORRSTTU	FRUSTRATION
AEOPRSSTTUW	WATERSPOUTS		AGGHHIIKNNR	HIGH-RANKING
AFFGHIIMNRS	FISH FARMING		AGGHHLOPPRY	GLYPHOGRAPH
AFFGHLOPSTU	PLOUGHSTAFF		AGGHIILNNSU	LANGUISHING
AFFILNORSTU	INSUFFLATOR		AGGHIILOOST	HAGIOLOGIST
AFFOOORTUUV	OUT OF FAVOUR		AGGHINORRTW	RIGHT A WRONG
AFGGILNRTUU	FULGURATING		AGGHMMOPRSY	SPHYGMOGRAM
AFGHHIILNTU	HIGHFALUTIN		AGGIIILNNSZ	SIGNALIZING
AFGHHILLSST	FLASHLIGHTS		AGGIIIMMNRT	IMMIGRATING
AFGHHILPSTT	FLIGHT PATHS		AGGIIINNORT	ORIGINATING
AFGHIILRSTY	FAIRY LIGHTS		AGGIIINNSTT	INSTIGATING
AFGHILMOPRY	FILMOGRAPHY		AGGIILMNORZ	GLAMORIZING
AFGHIORSTWY	RIGHTS OF WAY		AGGIILNNOYZ	AGONIZINGLY
AFGHIPPTTUU	PUT UP A FIGHT		AGGIILNOOPZ	APOLOGIZING
AFGIIINNRTU	INFURIATING		AGGIILNRUVZ	VULGARIZING
AFGIILLMNNY	INFLAMINGLY		AGGIINNORRS	GARRISONING
AFGIILLNNUY	UNFAILINGLY		AGGIINORTTU	GURGITATION
AFGIILMNNTU	FULMINATING		AGGIMMNOPRR	PROGRAMMING
AFGIILMNORZ	FORMALIZING		AGGINOPSSTT	STAGING POST
AFGIILNNOTU	ANTIFOULING		AGGLLNOORYY	LARYNGOLOGY
AFGIINNQTUY	QUANTIFYING		AGGLOOORSTY	AGROSTOLOGY
AFGIINNRSTX	TRANSFIXING		AGHHIIMNRST	NIGHTMARISH
AFGIINRSTTY	STRATIFYING		AGHHILOPRST	LITHOGRAPHS
AFGIINSSTUU	IGNIS FATUUS		AGHHILOPRTY	LITHOGRAPHY
AFGIKLNNOTU	OUTFLANKING		AGHHIMNRSTU	HUMAN RIGHTS
AFGILLNNTUY	FLAUNTINGLY		AGHHNOOPPRS	PHONOGRAPHS
AFGILMNORTU	FORMULATING		AGHHNOOPPRY	PHONOGRAPHY
AFGILNORSUV	FLAVOURINGS		AGHHOOPPRST	PHOTOGRAPHS
AFGILNORTUU	FULGURATION		AGHHOOPPRTY	PHOTOGRAPHY
AFGILNORUVY	FAVOURINGLY		AGHHOOPRRTY	ORTHOGRAPHY
AFGILNRSTTY	FLYING START		AGHHOPPRTYY	PHYTOGRAPHY
AFGINOOPSST	SOFT-SOAPING		AGHHORSTUWY	THROUGHWAYS
AFGINRRSTTU	FRUSTRATING		AGHIIILMNTU	HUMILIATING
AFHILNOPSST	FLASH POINTS		AGHIIILNNTZ	NIZHNI TAGIL
AFIIIILNNTV	INFINITIVAL		AGHIILMNOOS	HOOLIGANISM
AFIIILMNNST	INFANTILISM		AGHIILNNSVY	VANISHINGLY
AFIIILNNTTY	INFANTILITY		AGHIILNRSVY	RAVISHINGLY
AFIIINNORTU	INFURIATION		AGHIIMNNORZ	HARMONIZING
AFIILLMORTW	FORT WILLIAM		AGHIIMOSTTX	THIGMOTAXIS
AFIILMNNOTU	FULMINATION		AGHIINNOSST	ASTONISHING
AFIILMNORTY	INFORMALITY		AGHIINNQSUV	VANQUISHING
AFIILNORRTT	INFILTRATOR		AGHIINORTUZ	AUTHORIZING
AFIILNORSTT	FLIRTATIONS		AGHIINPRRSS	HAIRSPRINGS
AFIILORSTTU	FLIRTATIOUS		AGHIINPRSTY	PHARYNGITIS
AFIIMNNOORT	INFORMATION		AGHILNOOSTT	ANTHOLOGIST
AFIIMNOORSU	OMNIFARIOUS		AGHILNORRWY	HARROWINGLY

AGHILOOPSTT	PATHOLOGIST	AGILMNPPRSS	PALM SPRINGS
AGHILPRSTWY	PLAYWRIGHTS	AGILMOOPRTY	PRIMATOLOGY
AGHIMNOPRST	PROGNATHISM	AGILMOPSSTY	POLYGAMISTS
AGHINOPRSTT	PARTING SHOT	AGILNNPPSTU	SUPPLANTING
AGHIORSTTTU	STRAIGHT-OUT	AGILNNPRSUY	UNSPARINGLY
AGHLOOPSUXY	XYLOPHAGOUS	AGILNOOOPRS	SPOROGONIAL
AGHLOPRSTYY	STYLOGRAPHY	AGILNOPPRVY	APPROVINGLY
AGHMNOOOPSU	MONOPHAGOUS	AGILNOPSTTU	POSTULATING
AGHMNOORSTU	MOUTHORGANS	AGILNORSUVY	SAVOURINGLY
AGHMOOOPRRT	GRAPHOMOTOR	AGILOORSSYY	ASSYRIOLOGY
AGHNOOPPRRY	PORNOGRAPHY	AGIMNNORRST	MORNING STAR
AGHNOOPRSTU	PROGNATHOUS	AGIMNNRSTTU	TRANSMUTING
AGIIIILLNNT	INITIALLING	AGIMNOOPRST	PROTAGONISM
AGIIIILLMNST	MAILING LIST	AGIMNORSTTU	OUTSMARTING
AGIIIILLNTTT	TITILLATING	AGINNOPRSST	TRANSPOSING
AGIIIILNNOPT	OIL PAINTING	AGINOOOPRRT	PROROGATION
AGIIIILNNORS	ORIGINAL SIN	AGINOOPRSTT	PROTAGONIST
AGIIIILNORTV	INVIGILATOR	AGINOOORRSTU	SURROGATION
AGIIIILNORTY	ORIGINALITY	AGINOORRSUV	GRANIVOROUS
AGIIIILNPSST	SALPINGITIS	AGINOPRRSTT	PROSTRATING
AGIIIILNSTTW	WAITING LIST	AGINPPRSTUU	SUPPURATING
AGIIIILNSUVZ	VISUALIZING	AGKNNNORSTY	GRANNY KNOTS
AGIIIMMNORT	IMMIGRATION	AGLLLLOPPSU	GALLUP POLLS
AGIIINNNSTU	INSINUATING	AGLLMOORSUY	GLAMOROUSLY
AGIIINNOORT	ORIGINATION	AGLLOOPSTTT	GLOTTAL STOP
AGIIINNOSTT	INSTIGATION	AGLLORRSUUY	GARRULOUSLY
AGIIINPRTVZ	PRIVATIZING	AGLMNOORTYY	LARYNGOTOMY
AGIIKNNNPRS	NAPKIN RINGS	AGLMOOOSTTY	STOMATOLOGY
AGIILLLNNOPT	POLLINATING	AGLMOOPRRTU	PROMULGATOR
AGIILMNNORZ	NORMALIZING	AGLMOORRTYY	MARTYROLOGY
AGIILMNPPSY	MISAPPLYING	AGMOORSSTTY	GASTROSTOMY
AGIILMNSTTU	STIMULATING	AHHIIIPRSST	PHTHIRIASIS
AGIILNNRSTY	STRAININGLY	AHHILMOPSTY	HALOPHYTISM
AGIILNORTUV	OUTRIVALING	AHHILNOORTU	HOLOTHURIAN
AGIILNPSTTU	STIPULATING	AHHIMNOPSSW	SHOWMANSHIP
AGIILNRSTUY	SINGULARITY	AHHLLNOPTXY	XANTHOPHYLL
AGIILNRTUUX	LUXURIATING	AHIIILMNOTU	HUMILIATION
AGIIMMNRSUZ	SUMMARIZING	AHIIIMNNOSY	NISHINOMIYA
AGIIMNNOPTU	IMPUGNATION	AHIIILLORSUY	HILARIOUSLY
AGIIMNNPRSS	MAINSPRINGS	AHIIILMORTUY	HUMILIATORY
AGIIMNOORTW	WAITING ROOM	AHIIILOPSTTY	HOSPITALITY
AGIINNNRTYYZ	TYRANNIZING	AHIIILRSSTTY	HAIRSTYLIST
AGIINNOPRTZ	PATRONIZING	AHIIMNNRRTU	ANTIRRHINUM
AGIINNPRRST	TRANSPIRING	AHIIMNOOOSU	HOMOIOUSIAN
AGIINOORRST	ORIGINATORS	AHIIMOOPPPT	HIPPOPOTAMI
AGIINOORRTV	INVIGORATOR	AHIKKOORRSW	KWASHIORKOR
AGIINORSSTT	INSTIGATORS	AHIKLMOORSW	WORKAHOLISM
AGIJNOPSTUX	JUXTAPOSING	AHIKLOTTUWW	WALK OUT WITH
AGIKLNOPRST	PARKING LOTS	AHIKMNOPRSW	WORKMANSHIP
AGIKMNOPRST	POSTMARKING	AHILLOPSTXY	PHYLLOTAXIS
AGILLLNPTUU	PULLULATING	AHILLOTUWWY	WHAT YOU WILL
AGILLMNNOOU	MONOLINGUAL	AHILNOORSTZ	HORIZONTALS
AGILLNPRTTY	PRATTLINGLY	AHILNOPRSTY	RHINOPLASTY
AGILLNRSTTY	STARTLINGLY	AHILOORRTTY	HORTATORILY

AHILOPPRSXY	PROPHYLAXIS
AHILOPRRUXY	PYRRHULOXIA
AHIMNOORRSU	HONORARIUMS
AHIMNOPRSTY	MISANTHROPY
AHIMOORSTUZ	RHIZOMATOUS
AHINOOPSSTX	SAXOPHONIST
AHINORSTTTT	THAT'S TORN IT
AHKNNOPSSSY	SHANKS'S PONY
AHLMNNORSTU	LUNAR MONTHS
AHLMNOTUXYZ	ZANTHOXYLUM
AHLMOOPRSUY	AMORPHOUSLY
AHMNNOOOPRTT	NORTHAMPTON
AHMNOOPSTTU	SOUTHAMPTON
AHNNOSSTTWY	SHANTYTOWNS
AIIIINNOSTT	INITIATIONS
AIIILLLLNPTU	LILLIPUTIAN
AIIILLLNOTTT	TITILLATION
AIIILLLNOTUV	ILLUVIATION
AIIILMNOSST	IN ALTISSIMO
AIIILMNOSTT	LIMITATIONS
AIIILMNPRTT	TRIPALMITIN
AIIILMRSSTT	MILITARISTS
AIIILNNOOST	LIONISATION
AIIILNNOOTZ	LIONIZATION
AIIILNNOTTU	INTUITIONAL
AIIILNOSTTU	UTILISATION
AIIILNOTTUZ	UTILIZATION
AIIIMNNOSTT	INTIMATIONS
AIIIMNRSTTU	MINIATURIST
AIIIMPPRRTY	PRIMIPARITY
AIIIMPSSTVY	IMPASSIVITY
AIIINNNOSTU	INSINUATION
AIIINNOPRST	INSPIRATION
AIIINNOSTTV	INVITATIONS
AIIINORRSTT	IRRITATIONS
AIIINOSSTTV	VISITATIONS
AIIKLRSTUVV	SURVIVAL KIT
AIIKNRSSSTT	SANSKRITIST
AIILLMMNOTU	MULTINOMIAL
AIILLMNORTU	ILLUMINATOR
AIILLNNOOPT	POLLINATION
AIILLNORSUY	ILLUSIONARY
AIILLPRSTUY	SPIRITUALLY
AIILLPSTTUY	PULSATILITY
AIILMMORTTY	IMMORTALITY
AIILMNOOPRT	IMPLORATION
AIILMNOOPST	MALPOSITION
AIILMNOOSST	SOLMISATION
AIILMNOOSTZ	SOLMIZATION
AIILMNOSSSU	SIMULATIONS
AIILMNOSTTU	MUTILATIONS, STIMULATION
AIILMNOSTUY	ALUMINOSITY
AIILMPRTTUY	MULTIPARITY
AIILNNORSTU	INTRUSIONAL
AIILNNORTTU	NUTRITIONAL
AIILNOOPRSV	PROVISIONAL
AIILNOPRTUY	UNIPOLARITY
AIILNOPSTTU	STIPULATION
AIILNORTUUX	LUXURIATION
AIILNOSSTTY	STYLISATION
AIILNOSTTYZ	STYLIZATION
AIILNQRTTUY	TRANQUILITY
AIILORSSSTU	SAILOR SUITS
AIIMMNOPSTT	PANTOMIMIST
AIIMMNSSTTU	NUMISMATIST
AIIMMPRRSTU	IMPRIMATURS
AIIMNNNOOST	NOMINATIONS
AIIMNNORSTU	RUMINATIONS
AIIMNNRSSTT	MINISTRANTS
AIIMNOOPRTT	IMPORTATION
AIIMNOOPRTX	PROXIMATION
AIIMNOPSTTU	IMPUTATIONS
AIIMNORSTTZ	SAINT MORITZ
AIIMOPPRRSU	PRIMIPAROUS
AIINNNOOSTT	INTONATIONS
AIINNNOOSTV	INNOVATIONS
AIINNNORRTT	NONIRRITANT
AIINNOOOSTZ	OZONISATION
AIINNOOOTZZ	OZONIZATION
AIINNOORRST	IRON RATIONS
AIINNORSSTT	TRANSITIONS
AIINOPRRSTY	INSPIRATORY
AIINOPRRTTU	PARTURITION
AIINORRTTTU	TRITURATION
AIIOOPPRRTT	PROPITIATOR
AIIOPRRSTTT	PORTRAITIST
AIIOPRSSTTT	PROSTATITIS
AIJLNORSSTU	JOURNALISTS
AIKNOORSTTW	WORKSTATION
AILLLLMNOOPP	LOLLIPOP MAN
AILLLNOOPRU	ALLOPURINOL
AILLLNOPTUU	PULLULATION
AILLMOPSSSY	PLASMOLYSIS
AILLNOPRSUU	NULLIPAROUS
AILLNORTUVY	VOLUNTARILY
AILLNRTUUXY	LUXURIANTLY
AILLORRSTTU	ILLUSTRATOR
AILMNNOSUUY	UNANIMOUSLY
AILMNOOOPRT	PROMOTIONAL
AILMNOOPPSSS	SIMPLON PASS
AILMNOPRTTY	IMPORTANTLY
AILMNORSTUV	VOLUNTARISM
AILMOOPRRTY	IMPLORATORY
AILMOOPRUYZ	POLYZOARIUM
AILMOPRSTUU	MULTIPAROUS
AILNNORTUVY	INVOLUNTARY
AILNOOPPSTU	POPULATIONS
AILNOOPRSTU	SPORULATION

512

AILNOOPSTTU	POSTULATION	BBEEERRRSTU	RUBBER TREES
AILNOPPSTTU	POSTNUPTIAL	BBEEGIILLNR	GIBBERELLIN
AILNOPSTTUU	PUSTULATION	BBEEHIRRSSU	SHRUBBERIES
AILNORSTTUV	VOLUNTARIST	BBEEILMRSSU	SUBMERSIBLE
AILNORSUUVY	UNSAVOURILY	BBEELLOSTTU	BLUEBOTTLES
AILNRSSTUUU	LAURUSTINUS	BBEELMORSTT	LETTER BOMBS
AILOPRSTTUY	STIPULATORY	BBEENORRSYY	BOYSENBERRY
AILORSTTTUY	STATUTORILY	BBEFILORSSU	BULBIFEROUS
AIMMOOSSTXY	MYXOMATOSIS	BBEGIINSSSU	BIG BUSINESS
AIMNNOOPTTU	MOUNTAINTOP	BBEGINOSSSU	GIBBOUSNESS
AIMNNOOSTUU	MOUNTAINOUS	BBEHHILOSST	SHIBBOLETHS
AIMNOPSSSTU	ASSUMPTIONS	BBEHHOORSSY	HOBBYHORSES
AIMNRSSTTUU	NASTURTIUMS	BBEHIIILLOP	BIBLIOPHILE
AINNNOOORTT	TORONTONIAN	BBEHINRSSSU	SHRUBBINESS
AINOOPRRSTT	PROSTRATION	BBEHLORSTTU	BOTTLEBRUSH
AINOPPRSTUU	SUPPURATION	BBEIKLMOOOS	BOOKMOBILES
AINORRSSSTT	TRANSISTORS	BBEIOOPRSSY	BOOBY PRISES
AINORRSSTUU	SUSURRATION	BBEIOOPRSYZ	BOOBY PRIZES
AKLNNOOOPTZ	ZOOPLANKTON	BBELLMOOSTT	BELL-BOTTOMS
ALLNOOOPPRR	PROPRANOLOL	BBELLNOTTUY	BELLY BUTTON
ALLOORSTWWW	SWALLOWWORT	BBEMNNOORTU	NEUTRON BOMB
ALMNNOOSUYY	ANONYMOUSLY	BBENORSSTTU	STUBBORNEST
ALMNOOORSTU	MONOLATROUS	BBGHILNORTY	THROBBINGLY
ALMNOORSTTU	SALMON TROUT	BBGIILLNQUY	QUIBBLINGLY
ALOPRRSTUUY	RAPTUROUSLY	BBHIIILMOPS	BIBLIOPHISM
AMNOOPRSSTW	SPORTSWOMAN	BCCDEEHKLOU	DOUBLE-CHECK
BBBEGIIINNW	WINEBIBBING	BCCDEILNOTU	CONDUCTIBLE
BBBHIINRSSU	RUBBISH BINS	BCCEEEEFINN	BENEFICENCE
BBCCEEHKLOR	BREECHBLOCK	BCCEEEENRSU	ERUBESCENCE
BBCDEHIRRTU	BUTCHERBIRD	BCCEEIILNOR	INCOERCIBLE
BBCEELNOOST	COBBLESTONE	BCCEEILNNOT	CONNECTIBLE
BBCEILMOSTU	COMBUSTIBLE	BCCEEILNOSS	CONCESSIBLE
BBCEINRSSSU	SCRUBBINESS	BCCEEINRSTY	CYBERNETICS
BBCEIRRSSSU	SUBSCRIBERS	BCCEFFIKLOO	OFFICE BLOCK
BBCEJKOORST	STOCKJOBBER	BCCEFIIPSSU	SUBSPECIFIC
BBCEKLORSTU	BLOCKBUSTER	BCCEHINOOPR	NECROPHOBIC
BBCELMORSTU	CLUSTER BOMB	BCCEIILNNOV	CONVINCIBLE
BBCGIINRSSU	SUBSCRIBING	BCCEIINOORT	NECROBIOTIC
BBDDEEELLOOU	BLUE-BLOODED	BCCHHOORSST	SCOTCH BROTH
BBDDEILLNOU	DOUBLE-BLIND	BCCHINOOPTY	NYCTOPHOBIC
BBDDEILNOSU	DOUBLE BINDS	BCCLNORTUUY	COUNTRY CLUB
BBDEEELOUYY	BLUE-EYED BOY	BCDDDELLOOO	COLD-BLOODED
BBDEEGHILOS	BOBSLEIGHED	BCDDEEEILNS	DESCENDIBLE
BBDEEHHLOOY	HOBBLEDEHOY	BCDDEEIIRTT	DIRECT DEBIT
BBDEEILLLOW	I'LL BE BLOWED	BCDDEENORTY	BODY-CENTRED
BBDEEIMORSV	DIVE-BOMBERS	BCDDEHLOTUU	DOUBLE-DUTCH
BBDEELLORWY	LLOYD WEBBER	BCDEEEIINNT	BENEDICTINE
BBDEFFLLOUU	DOUBLE BLUFF	BCDEEEIORRS	CEREBROSIDE
BBDEGIIMNOV	DIVE-BOMBING	BCDEEHILNPT	PITCHBLENDE
BBDEIKNOORS	BOOKBINDERS	BCDEEHMNOOY	HONEYCOMBED
BBDEIKNOORY	BOOKBINDERY	BCDEEHMNOTU	DEBOUCHMENT
BBDELNRSSUU	BLUNDERBUSS	BCDEEIIILRT	LIBERTICIDE
BBDGIIKNNOO	BOOKBINDING	BCDEEIIILNRS	DISCERNIBLE
BBEEEILRRSU	BLUEBERRIES	BCDEEIILRRU	IRREDUCIBLE

BCDEEIILSST	DISSECTIBLE
BCDEEIINNOT	BENEDICTION
BCDEEIMNRSU	DISENCUMBER
BCDEEINORTY	BENEDICTORY
BCDEEINSSSU	SUBSIDENCES
BCDEEORRSSS	CROSSBREEDS
BCDEGHNRRSU	BERGSCHRUND
BCDEHILNNOR	HORNBLENDIC
BCDEHILNOSU	DOUBLE CHINS
BCDEHILORSU	SUBCHLORIDE
BCDEIIILRTY	CREDIBILITY
BCDEIILNRSY	DISCERNIBLY
BCDEIILRRUY	IRREDUCIBLY
BCDEIILSSSU	DISCUSSIBLE
BCDEIKLOQUU	DOUBLE-QUICK
BCDEINORTTU	CONTRIBUTED
BCDEIOOPRSS	PROBOSCIDES
BCDEKLOORSU	BLOODSUCKER
BCDELMNOSUU	MUSCLE-BOUND
BCDELOORSSU	DOUBLE-CROSS
BCDEMMNRSUU	CUMMERBUNDS
BCDGIIKMNOR	MOCKINGBIRD
BCDGIIOSSTU	DOG BISCUITS
BCDGILLLOPU	BULLDOG CLIP
BCDIILOOPTY	BODY POLITIC
BCDIINRTUUY	RUBICUNDITY
BCDILLNOORU	COLOUR-BLIND
BCDLNOOOSTU	BLOOD COUNTS
BCDLORSSTUU	CLOUDBURSTS
BCEEEEHLSSU	BLUE CHEESES
BCEEEELNNOV	BENEVOLENCE
BCEEEFILPRT	PERFECTIBLE
BCEEEFLLRST	TREBLE CLEFS
BCEEEHHINPR	HEBEPHRENIC
BCEEEHNNQSU	QUEEN'S BENCH
BCEEEIILRST	CELEBRITIES
BCEEEILPPRT	PERCEPTIBLE
BCEEEILPRTX	EXCERPTIBLE
BCEEENQSSUU	SUBSEQUENCE
BCEEFKLNRRU	BUCKLER-FERN
BCEEGILNOST	CONGESTIBLE
BCEEGIMNNRU	ENCUMBERING
BCEEGIMNORY	EMBRYOGENIC
BCEEGKLMNRU	MECKLENBURG
BCEEHINORRS	BRECONSHIRE
BCEEHJKLOWY	CHEEK BY JOWL
BCEEHKLRRUY	HUCKLEBERRY
BCEEHKNORSW	WORKBENCHES
BCEEHNORRSX	BRONX CHEERS
BCEEIILPSST	PLEBISCITES
BCEEIILRSSS	RESCISSIBLE
BCEEIINOSST	OBSCENITIES
BCEEIJLOTVY	OBJECTIVELY
BCEEILMNNOT	CONTEMNIBLE
BCEEILMOSST	COMESTIBLES
BCEEILNORTV	CONVERTIBLE
BCEEILNOSTY	BY-ELECTIONS
BCEEILPPRTY	PERCEPTIBLY
BCEEILPSSTU	SUSCEPTIBLE
BCEEINSSSTU	SUBSISTENCE
BCEEIPRRSSU	SUPERSCRIBE
BCEEKKLNNOU	KNUCKLEBONE
BCEEKLNOSTT	BOTTLENECKS
BCEELMMOOTY	EMBOLECTOMY
BCEELNOOSST	OBSOLESCENT
BCEEMMORTYY	EMBRYECTOMY
BCEFFKORSTU	BUFFER STOCK
BCEFHILLNSU	BULLFINCHES
BCEFIIOPRST	FIBRE OPTICS
BCEGHHIMOWY	HIGH WYCOMBE
BCEGHIIMNRS	BESMIRCHING
BCEGHILLNNY	BLENCHINGLY
BCEGIIINPRRS	PRESCRIBING
BCEGILNOOOY	BIOCENOLOGY
BCEHIIIMNRS	HIBERNICISM
BCEHIILRRSV	SILVER BIRCH
BCEHILMOOPT	PHLEBOTOMIC
BCEHILNOSST	BLOTCHINESS
BCEHILOPSUU	PUBLIC HOUSE
BCEHKLOOSSU	BLOCKHOUSES
BCEHKOPSSTU	BUCKET SHOPS
BCEHLORRSSY	CHRYSOBERYL
BCEHMOORTTY	THROMBOCYTE
BCEHMRSSTUW	THUMBSCREWS
BCEIIJMOSTV	OBJECTIVISM
BCEIIJOSTTV	OBJECTIVIST
BCEIIJOTTVY	OBJECTIVITY
BCEIIILLOSTY	BELLICOSITY
BCEIIMMRSTY	BISYMMETRIC
BCEIINOORSS	NECROBIOSIS
BCEIIORSSTU	OBSCURITIES
BCEIJNSTUUV	SUBJUNCTIVE
BCEIKOOPRTU	PICTURE BOOK
BCEILLORSSU	BRUCELLOSIS
BCEILOPRRTU	CORRUPTIBLE
BCEINOSSSTU	SUBSECTIONS
BCEIOOPRSSS	PROBOSCISES
BCEIORSTTUV	OBSTRUCTIVE
BCEKKOOOORY	COOKERY BOOK
BCEKKOOOPST	POCKETBOOKS
BCEKKOORRST	STOCKBROKER
BCEKLOORSTW	TOWER BLOCKS
BCELORSTUUU	TUBERCULOUS
BCELRSSTUUU	SUBCULTURES
BCEOOOPRSST	STROBOSCOPE
BCGIIILNPUZ	PUBLICIZING
BCGIINOPRRS	PROSCRIBING
BCGILOOORYY	CRYOBIOLOGY

BCGINORSTTU	OBSTRUCTING
BCHHIOOOPPT	PHOTOPHOBIC
BCHIIIPSSTU	SHIP BISCUIT
BCHIOOPRSSU	RUSSOPHOBIC
BCHMOOOTTTU	TOUCH BOTTOM
BCHNOORSSTU	HOT-CROSS BUN
BCIIIILMSTY	MISCIBILITY
BCIILMOSSTY	SYMBOLISTIC
BCIJNNOSTUU	SUBJUNCTION
BCIKLOPRSUW	PUBLIC WORKS
BCIKMOORSST	BROOMSTICKS
BCILMOSTTUU	CUSTOM-BUILT
BCINOORRTTU	CONTRIBUTOR
BCINOORSTTU	OBSTRUCTION
BCKLLOOPSSU	BOLLOCKS-UPS
BDDDEEEGLOU	DOUBLE-EDGED
BDDDEEEINRT	INTERBEDDED
BDDDEEIIMOS	DISEMBODIED
BDDDEEINRRU	UNDERBIDDER
BDDDEFILLNO	BLINDFOLDED
BDDDEFMNOUU	DUMBFOUNDED
BDDEEEIILSV	DISBELIEVED
BDDEEEIMMRS	DISMEMBERED
BDDEEEIMNRT	DEBRIDEMENT
BDDEEEIMORR	EMBROIDERED
BDDEEIINOST	DISOBEDIENT
BDDEEIILMRTU	TUMBLE-DRIED
BDDEEIILORSW	BOWDLERISED
BDDEEIILORWZ	BOWDLERIZED
BDDEELOOPRU	PUREBLOODED
BDDEENSSSUU	SUBDUEDNESS
BDDEFLLLOOU	FULL-BLOODED
BDDEFMNORUU	DUMBFOUNDER
BDDEGIIMNNN	MIND-BENDING
BDDEGIIINORV	OVERBIDDING
BDDEHINRRTU	THUNDERBIRD
BDDEHLNOORS	BONDHOLDERS
BDDEIIRSTTU	DISTRIBUTED
BDDEILMORSW	MIDDLEBROWS
BDDELNOTUUY	UNDOUBTEDLY
BDDGIIINSUV	SUBDIVIDING
BDDHIIIMRSY	DIHYBRIDISM
BDDHLNOOOSU	BLOODHOUNDS
BDEEEEIIMRR	BIEDERMEIER
BDEEEHILLMS	EMBELLISHED
BDEEEHILMTW	THIMBLEWEED
BDEEEIILRSV	DISBELIEVER
BDEEEILMNTV	BEDEVILMENT
BDEEEILPRSS	DEPRESSIBLE
BDEEEILSSTW	WILDEBEESTS
BDEEEIMMRRS	DISMEMBERER
BDEEEIMORRR	EMBROIDERER
BDEEELNSSSS	BLESSEDNESS
BDEEFGIINNR	BEFRIENDING

BDEEFHIRRSU	REFURBISHED
BDEEGGHIIRW	WEIGHBRIDGE
BDEEGGINSUU	DUNE BUGGIES
BDEEGHILNTY	BENIGHTEDLY
BDEEGIILLNV	BEDEVILLING
BDEEGIILNRW	BEWILDERING
BDEEGILMNNO	EMBOLDENING
BDEEHILMNSU	UNBLEMISHED
BDEEIILNSST	DISTENSIBLE
BDEEIILLNRS	DINNER BELLS
BDEEIILLNPRS	SPELLBINDER
BDEEIILMNOTY	MOLYBDENITE
BDEEIILMRSSS	DISSEMBLERS
BDEEIILNORSS	BORDERLINES
BDEEIILNPSSU	SUSPENDIBLE
BDEEIIMNORST	DISROBEMENT
BDEEINNSSSU	BUSINESS END
BDEEINORSTX	TINDERBOXES
BDEEIOORSXY	DEOXYRIBOSE
BDEELLOOSSV	BLOOD VESSEL
BDEELMRRSUU	BLUE MURDERS
BDEELMRRTUY	TUMBLE DRYER
BDEELNRRSSU	BLURREDNESS
BDEEMNORTUU	OUTNUMBERED
BDEENPRRTUU	UNPERTURBED
BDEFGINOORS	FOREBODINGS
BDEFGIOORST	FOOTBRIDGES
BDEFIOPRRSY	BIRDS OF PREY
BDEGGILNNOU	BLUDGEONING
BDEGIILLNNS	SINGLE-BLIND
BDEGIILLNSV	DIVING BELLS
BDEGIILMNSS	DISSEMBLING
BDEGIINNRRS	RING BINDERS
BDEGIMORRSY	DOGBERRYISM
BDEGINNNRUU	UNBURDENING
BDEGIORRSTU	STOURBRIDGE
BDEHHOOORRT	BROTHERHOOD
BDEHIIILNTY	INHIBITEDLY
BDEHIIINNTU	UNINHIBITED
BDEHIILPRSU	SHIPBUILDER
BDEHIINNPTU	NIP IN THE BUD
BDEHIKLNOTU	DOUBLETHINK
BDEHILLSTTU	BULLSHITTED
BDEHILNPSUU	UNPUBLISHED
BDEHLNOOTTU	BUTTONHOLED
BDEHLNORTTU	THUNDERBOLT
BDEIIIILNSV	INDIVISIBLE
BDEIIIILNTY	INEDIBILITY
BDEIIILMMOS	IMMOBILISED
BDEIIILMMOZ	IMMOBILIZED
BDEIIILMSSS	DISMISSIBLE
BDEIIILNTVY	VENDIBILITY
BDEIILMRSUU	SUBDELIRIUM
BDEIINNRTUW	WIND TURBINE

BDEIIRSSSSU	SUBSIDISERS
BDEIIRSSSUZ	SUBSIDIZERS
BDEIKNORSTU	STRIKEBOUND
BDEILLLNORR	ROLLER BLIND
BDEILLOSTUX	BILLETS-DOUX
BDEILNNOOOS	IN ONE'S BLOOD
BDEILNORSTY	BLINDSTOREY
BDEIMMNOPRU	PREMIUM BOND
BDEINOOSWWX	WINDOW BOXES
BDEINOSSSSU	DUBIOUSNESS
BDEISSTTTUU	SUBSTITUTED
BDELLLOOSSY	BLOODLESSLY
BDELLNOSSUY	BOUNDLESSLY
BDELMNOOSUY	MOLYBDENOUS
BDGGIIIILNOS	DISOBLIGING
BDGGILRSUUW	LUDWIGSBURG
BDGHIIMMNRU	HUMMINGBIRD
BDGIIINSSUZ	SUBSIDIZING
BDGIILMNNOW	MIND-BLOWING
BDGIILNOTUU	OUTBUILDING
BDGLOOOPRSU	BLOOD GROUPS
BDHIILRRSWY	WHIRLYBIRDS
BDIIIIILNSVY	INDIVISIBLY
BDIIINOSSUV	SUBDIVISION
BDIIMNORTUY	MORIBUNDITY
BDIIORRSTTU	DISTRIBUTOR
BDINNOORRSU	ROUND ROBINS
BDLMNOOTTUU	BUTTONMOULD
BDLOOOPRSST	BLOOD SPORTS
BEEEFHINRSS	FINES HERBES
BEEEFOORRST	FREEBOOTERS
BEEEGGINRRS	GINGER BEERS
BEEEGIINNOR	BIOENGINEER
BEEEGILLNRT	BELLIGERENT
BEEEGILMNTU	BEGUILEMENT
BEEEGIMMNRR	REMEMBERING
BEEEGLNORTT	BOTTLE GREEN, GREENBOTTLE
BEEEHILLMRS	EMBELLISHER
BEEEHILLNOR	HELLEBORINE
BEEEILNRSUV	UNBELIEVERS
BEEEILPRRSS	REPRESSIBLE
BEEEILPRRTV	PERVERTIBLE
BEEEILPRSSX	EXPRESSIBLE
BEEEIMMMRRS	MISREMEMBER
BEEEINORSST	BETES-NOIRES
BEEEIRSTTTW	BITTERSWEET
BEEEKKOOPRS	BOOKKEEPERS
BEEELLRSSST	BEST-SELLERS
BEEELMNNNOT	ENNOBLEMENT
BEEELORSTTX	LETTERBOXES
BEEENOPPRTY	TEENYBOPPER
BEEFFNORSUZ	BUFFER ZONES
BEEFGLLOORW	GLOBEFLOWER
BEEFGRSSTUU	SUBTERFUGES

BEEFILRSTTU	BUTTERFLIES
BEEGGILSSTU	SUGGESTIBLE
BEEGGLOORST	BOOTLEGGERS
BEEGHINNORR	HERRINGBONE
BEEGIIMNRTT	EMBITTERING
BEEGIIOORSU	BOURGEOISIE
BEEGIKKNOOP	BOOKKEEPING
BEEGILLNSST	BEST-SELLING
BEEGIMNOSTT	MISBEGOTTEN
BEEGKLNTTUU	TELUKBETUNG
BEEHILMMOOS	MOBILE HOMES
BEEHILMNOOP	MOBILE PHONE
BEEHILPRRSU	REPUBLISHER
BEEHIMMPRSS	MEMBERSHIPS
BEEHIMNOORT	THEOBROMINE
BEEHKNOORSU	HOUSEBROKEN
BEEHLMNORUW	WHOLE NUMBER
BEEHMNOOSST	MESOBENTHOS
BEEHMOORSTT	MOTHERS-TO-BE
BEEHOPRRSTT	STEPBROTHER
BEEIIILMPRSS	IMPRESSIBLE, PERMISSIBLE
BEEIILNSSSV	VISIBLENESS
BEEIIRRTTUV	RETRIBUTIVE
BEEILLLNTUY	EBULLIENTLY
BEEILLLOSVW	BOLL WEEVILS
BEEILLORRSU	IRRESOLUBLE
BEEILLRRRTU	BULL TERRIER
BEEILMMNORT	EMBROILMENT
BEEILNNOSTW	TENNIS ELBOW
BEEILNOPRSS	NOBEL PRISES, RESPONSIBLE
BEEILNOPRSZ	NOBEL PRIZES
BEEILNRSSTT	BRITTLENESS
BEEIMMNPRRU	PRIME NUMBER
BEEIMNNSSSU	BUSINESSMEN
BEEINORSTTY	TENEBROSITY
BEEINRSSTUV	SUBSERVIENT
BEEIRSSSUVV	SUBVERSIVES
BEEJOORTTUV	OBJET TROUVE
BEEKLLOORSS	BOOKSELLERS
BEEKOOPRRRW	POWER BROKER
BEELLNOSSSU	SOLUBLENESS
BEELMOORSTU	TROUBLESOME
BEEMMNNOSTT	ENTOMBMENTS
BEENORSSTXY	SENTRY BOXES
BEENQRSSSUU	BRUSQUENESS
BEERRRSTTUU	SURREBUTTER
BEFGHILLRTU	BULLFIGHTER
BEFGIILNTTY	BEFITTINGLY
BEFGILNORSW	FINGER BOWLS
BEFHIILLLLT	FILL THE BILL
BEFHILLMSTU	THIMBLEFULS
BEFHILLOOTT	FOOT THE BILL
BEFHLMORTUU	RULE OF THUMB
BEFIIIILLTXY	FLEXIBILITY

BEFIILNORRU	NEUROFIBRIL
BEFIILRSSTU	FILIBUSTERS
BEFINORSSSU	FIBROUSNESS
BEFINORSTTT	FROSTBITTEN
BEFLLOOPRTU	BULLETPROOF
BEGGGILNOOT	BOOTLEGGING
BEGGHILNORS	HELSINGBORG
BEGGIILLNNR	BELL-RINGING
BEGGIILLNUY	BEGUILINGLY
BEGGINOORRS	BOGNOR REGIS
BEGHILNORUY	NEIGHBOURLY
BEGHILORSTT	STROBE LIGHT
BEGIIIILLTY	ELIGIBILITY
BEGIIMNRRSU	REIMBURSING
BEGIKNOOORV	OVERBOOKING
BEGILLMNRTY	TREMBLINGLY
BEGILLMNRUY	LUMBERINGLY
BEGILLNNNOY	ENNOBLINGLY
BEGILNQRSUU	BURLESQUING
BEGINRSSTTU	BUTTRESSING
BEGNOORSSTX	STRONGBOXES
BEHIIILLLLS	HILLBILLIES
BEHIIINOSTX	EXHIBITIONS
BEHIIIOPRTV	PROHIBITIVE
BEHIKNOOSSS	BOOKISHNESS
BEHILLNSSSU	BULLISHNESS
BEHINOORSSS	BOORISHNESS
BEHINRSSSTU	BRUTISHNESS
BEHIOORRSUV	HERBIVOROUS
BEHLNOOSTTU	BUTTONHOLES
BEHLOORRSTU	SOUL BROTHER
BEHMNOORTUU	BOURNEMOUTH
BEHMOORSSTY	MOTHER'S BOYS
BEHMPRSTTUU	TUB-THUMPERS
BEIIILMMORS	IMMOBILISER
BEIIILMMORZ	IMMOBILIZER
BEIIILMNRST	LIBERTINISM
BEIIILMQRUU	EQUILIBRIUM
BEIIILNSSTY	SENSIBILITY
BEIIILNSTTY	TENSIBILITY
BEIIILQRSTU	EQUILIBRIST
BEIILLNOSSW	BILLOWINESS
BEIILLORTUV	BLUE VITRIOL
BEIILMPRSSY	PERMISSIBLY
BEIILNOSSSU	BILIOUSNESS
BEIILORSSTU	BOILER SUITS
BEIILRSSTTT	LIBRETTISTS
BEIINORRTTU	RETRIBUTION
BEILLLLOSUY	LIBELLOUSLY
BEILLMPSTUU	SUBMULTIPLE
BEILLNOSTTU	BLUE STILTON
BEILMNOOSSW	SNOWMOBILES
BEILNOPRSSY	RESPONSIBLY
BEILORSTUVY	OBTRUSIVELY

BEIMPSSTUUV	SUBSUMPTIVE
BEINNOSSTUV	SUBVENTIONS
BEINOOSSSUV	OBVIOUSNESS
BEINORSSTUU	SUBROUTINES
BEINORSTUUV	UNOBTRUSIVE
BEINSSTTTUU	SUBSTITUENT
BEIOQRSSTUU	SOUBRIQUETS
BEISSSTTTUU	SUBSTITUTES
BELLNRTTUUY	TURBULENTLY
BELMMOORRSU	LUMBER-ROOMS
BELNOOSTUUY	BOUNTEOUSLY
BELOOPRSSTT	LOBSTERPOTS
BELOOPRSTTU	TROUBLE SPOT
BEMOOPRRSTY	PORT MORESBY
BENNOORSSTW	BROWNSTONES
BFFFFILOSTU	BIT OF FLUFFS
BFGIIILNTUY	FUNGIBILITY
BFILLLMNOOU	IN FULL BLOOM
BGGILLMNRUY	GRUMBLINGLY
BGHHIIRRSTT	BIRTHRIGHTS
BGHIIINOPRT	PROHIBITING
BGHIIINRRTV	VIRGIN BIRTH
BGHIINOPPWY	WHIPPING BOY
BGHIMNPTTUU	TUB-THUMPING
BGIIILLLTUY	GULLIBILITY
BGIILLNSTTU	SITTING BULL
BGIILMNOSYZ	SYMBOLIZING
BGILLMNSTUY	STUMBLINGLY
BGILLNORTUY	TROUBLINGLY
BGILMNNOOOT	BLOOMINGTON
BGILMOOSSTY	SYMBOLOGIST
BHIIIINNOST	INHIBITIONS
BHIIINOOPRT	PROHIBITION
BHIIILLRSTT	STILLBIRTHS
BHIIOOPRRTY	PROHIBITORY
BHILMOOSTYY	TOMBOYISHLY
BHIMNOOPRRT	PROTHROMBIN
BIIIILOPSSTY	POSSIBILITY
BIIIILORSTTY	TORSIBILITY
BIIKNOORSSV	NOVOSIBIRSK
BIILLOOSUVY	OBLIVIOUSLY
BIILOOQSTUU	OBLIQUITOUS
BIIMNOSSSSU	SUBMISSIONS
BILMOPSTUUY	BUMPTIOUSLY
BILNOOOSUXY	OBNOXIOUSLY
BIMNOORSSTT	TROMBONISTS
BIMNOPSSTUU	SUBSUMPTION
BIMORSSTUUU	RUMBUSTIOUS
BIOOOPPRRSU	OPPROBRIOUS
CCCCIMOORSU	MICROCOCCUS
CCCCKKLOOOU	CUCKOO CLOCK
CCCDEEEENRS	DECRESCENCE
CCCDEEIINNO	COINCIDENCE
CCCDEHINOSY	SYNECDOCHIC

CCCDEIIMRSU	CIRCUMCISED	CCDEIJKOSSY	DISC JOCKEYS
CCCDGINOOOO	GONOCOCCOID	CCDEIMNOORS	MICROSECOND
CCCDIIIOOSS	COCCIDIOSIS	CCDEINNNOUV	UNCONVINCED
CCCDILOOPSU	DIPLOCOCCUS	CCDEINOPRST	CONSCRIPTED
CCCEEEEENRSX	EXCRESCENCE	CCDEINORSTT	CONSTRICTED
CCCEEEENRSXY	EXCRESCENCY	CCDELLOSTYY	CYCLOSTYLED
CCCEEFIIOPS	ECOSPECIFIC	CCDENORSSTU	CONDUCTRESS
CCCEEFLLNOU	FLOCCULENCE	CCDENORSTTU	CONSTRUCTED
CCCEEFOORSS	FRESCO SECCO	CCDFLMOOORT	COLD COMFORT
CCCEEIILMST	ECLECTICISM	CCDHHILLOOS	SCHOOLCHILD
CCCEEINNOSS	CONSCIENCES	CCDHIOORTTW	WITCHDOCTOR
CCCEENNORRU	CONCURRENCE	CCDHIOOSTUU	STUDIO COUCH
CCCEENORRSU	OCCURRENCES	CCDKMOSUUVY	MUSCOVY DUCK
CCCEFIINOPS	CONSPECIFIC	CCEEEEILRTY	ELECTRIC EYE
CCCEFIOORSU	COCCIFEROUS	CCEEEEINPRT	CENTREPIECE
CCCEIMPRSTU	CIRCUMSPECT	CCEEEFHIKNR	NECKERCHIEF
CCCEINNOTTU	CONNECTICUT	CCEEEFHIRTV	HECTIC FEVER
CCCEIRSSTUY	CYSTICERCUS	CCEEEFLNORS	FLORESCENCE
CCCHILMOTYY	CYCLOTHYMIC	CCEEEFNNORS	CONFERENCES
CCCIIMMOORS	MICROCOSMIC	CCEEEFNRSTU	FRUTESCENCE
CCCIIMOOPRS	MICROSCOPIC	CCEEEGINNRS	NIGRESCENCE
CCCINNOOOST	CONCOCTIONS	CCEEEGINRVY	VICEGERENCY
CCCIOOOPPST	POCTOSCOPIC	CCEEEGNNORV	CONVERGENCE
CCCIOOPSSTY	CYSTOSCOPIC	CCEEEGNRSTU	TURGESCENCE
CCDDELNNOUU	UNCONCLUDED	CCEEEHHLOST	CHEESECLOTH
CCDEEEEINNR	NICENE CREED	CCEEEHINNOR	INCOHERENCE
CCDEEEEFHIKN	CHICKENFEED	CCEEEIINPPR	PERCIPIENCE
CCDEEEGINOT	GENETIC CODE	CCEEEILNORT	COELENTERIC
CCDEEEIINRS	IRIDESCENCE	CCEEEILNQSU	LIQUESCENCE
CCDEEELLORT	RECOLLECTED	CCEEEINNNOV	CONVENIENCE
CCDEEENRRST	RED CRESCENT	CCEEEINNPSS	SPINESCENCE
CCDEEFINNOS	CONFIDENCES	CCEEEINOPRV	PRECONCEIVE
CCDEEHHMOSY	ECHCHYMOSED	CCEEEINOPSS	CENOSPECIES
CCDEEHILPSY	PSYCHEDELIC	CCEEEINOSTX	COEXISTENCE
CCDEEHINORS	SECOND REICH	CCEEEINRRST	CIRENCESTER
CCDEEHIORTT	RICOCHETTED	CCEEEINRSTV	VITRESCENCE
CCDEEHKOPST	SPOT CHECKED	CCEEEKOOPRR	COOPER CREEK
CCDEEIIINST	INSECTICIDE	CCEEELORTTU	ELECTROCUTE
CCDEEIKLRSV	CLEVER DICKS	CCEEEMNPSSU	SPUMESCENCE
CCDEEILNOTY	CONCEITEDLY	CCEEENNOQSU	CONSEQUENCE
CCDEEILRRSS	DRESS CIRCLE	CCEEENPRSTU	PUTRESCENCE
CCDEEIINNORT	ENDOCENTRIC	CCEEENRRRSU	RECURRENCES
CCDEEIOPPRU	PREOCCUPIED	CCEEFFIINOT	COEFFICIENT
CCDEEJNORTU	CONJECTURED	CCEEFFILNOS	OFF-LICENCES
CCDEELLLOTY	COLLECTEDLY	CCEEFIIMNNU	MUNIFICENCE
CCDEELNNOOS	CONDOLENCES	CCEEFLNNOSU	CONFLUENCES
CCDEELNNORY	CONCERNEDLY	CCEEFLNOPST	SELF-CONCEPT
CCDEELNORTY	CONCERTEDLY	CCEEGINNNOT	CONTINGENCE
CCDEENNNORU	UNCONCERNED	CCEEGINOOTT	GEOTECTONIC
CCDEENNNOTU	UNCONNECTED	CCEEGNNORVY	CONVERGENCY
CCDEHILLOSS	COLD CHISELS	CCEEGNOORRT	CONCERTGOER
CCDEHIOOPRS	DICHROSCOPE	CCEEHHKORRY	CHOKECHERRY
CCDEHLNSTUU	DUTCH UNCLES	CCEEHINORTT	THEOCENTRIC
CCDEIILOORT	CROCIDOLITE	CCEEHKLLLOS	COCKLESHELL

CCEEHMOPTYY	PHYCOMYCETE		CCEHINOOSTZ	ZOOTECHNICS
CCEEHNOSSTU	ESCUTCHEONS		CCEHINOPRTY	PYROTECHNIC
CCEEIILMRSS	SEMICIRCLES		CCEHKLOSTTU	SHUTTLECOCK
CCEEIILORST	ISOELECTRIC		CCEHNOOOPRS	CHRONOSCOPE
CCEEIILRTTY	ELECTRICITY		CCEIIINSSTT	SCIENTISTIC
CCEEIIMNNOS	OMNISCIENCE		CCEIIKLRSTY	CITY SLICKER
CCEEIIMNOSV	MISCONCEIVE		CCEIIKNSSTT	STICK INSECT
CCEEIINOPTV	NOCICEPTIVE		CCEIILMNORT	CLINOMETRIC
CCEEIILLOSTV	COLLECTIVES		CCEIIMMORRT	MICROMETRIC
CCEEILNNOTV	CONVENTICLE		CCEIIMOORST	SOCIOMETRIC
CCEEILNORST	ELECTRONICS		CCEIIMORSTV	VISCOMETRIC
CCEEILPPRTU	PEPTIC ULCER		CCEIINOORST	COERCIONIST
CCEEIMNNOOT	ECONOMETRIC		CCEIIOPRRTY	RECIPROCITY
CCEEIMNNORRT	CENTROMERIC		CCEIJNNOTUV	CONJUNCTIVE
CCEEIMNRSTU	MUSIC CENTRE		CCEIKKOPPST	PICKPOCKETS
CCEEINOSTUV	CONSECUTIVE		CCEIKLNOPRU	CUPRONICKEL
CCEEIOPRSSS	CROSSPIECES		CCEILLNOOST	COLLECTIONS
CCEEIOPRSTU	EURO-SCEPTIC		CCEILNNOTTU	NOCTILUCENT
CCEEIORRSTV	CORRECTIVES		CCEILNORRTY	INCORRECTLY
CCEEJNORRTU	CONJECTURER		CCEIMNOORST	CENTROSOMIC
CCEEJNORSTU	CONJECTURES		CCEIMNOPRTY	PYCNOMETRIC
CCEELOSSTTU	COS LETTUCES		CCEIMOOPRSS	MICROSCOPES
CCEENORRSST	CORRECTNESS		CCEINNNOOST	CONNECTIONS
CCEFFIINSUY	SUFFICIENCY		CCEINNOOPST	CONCEPTIONS
CCEFHHILSTU	HECTIC FLUSH		CCEINNOOSSS	CONCESSIONS
CCEFHIIMORS	MICROFICHES		CCEINNOOSTU	CONSECUTION
CCEFIIIPSTY	SPECIFICITY		CCEINNOPRRW	CROWN PRINCE
CCEFIILNOTV	CONFLICTIVE		CCEINNOSSTY	CONSISTENCY
CCEFIINOPRY	PROFICIENCY		CCEINOORRST	CORRECTIONS
CCEFIKLSSTT	CLEFT STICKS		CCEINOSSSSU	SUCCESSIONS
CCEFINNOOST	CONFECTIONS		CCEJNNORTUU	CONJUNCTURE
CCEFIORRSUU	CRUCIFEROUS		CCEKLOORSTW	CLOCK TOWERS
CCEGHHORRSU	CHURCHGOERS		CCEKMNOSTUU	COME UNSTUCK
CCEGHIILNOR	CHOLINERGIC		CCELMOORSTY	MOTORCYCLES
CCEGHIINORT	RICOCHETING		CCENORRSTTU	RECONSTRUCT
CCEGHIMNOOR	CHROMOGENIC		CCEOOOPPRST	PROCTOSCOPE
CCEGHINOPSY	PSYCHOGENIC		CCFGIILNNOT	CONFLICTING
CCEGIILNNOR	RECONCILING		CCFIIINORUX	CRUCIFIXION
CCEGIINOOTX	TOXICOGENIC		CCFIILNNOOT	CONFLICTION
CCEGILNOORY	ECCRINOLOGY		CCGGHHINORU	CHURCHGOING
CCEGILNOOSY	SYNECOLOGIC		CCGHIILNNOR	CHRONICLING
CCEGINNNOTY	CONTINGENCY		CCGIIIINRTZ	CRITICIZING
CCEGINNOOST	COGNOSCENTI		CCGIOOPRSSY	GYROSCOPICS
CCEGINOPRTY	CRYPTOGENIC		CCHHILOOORS	CHOIR SCHOOL
CCEHHKOOORT	CROCHET HOOK		CCHIIILNOPS	SILICON CHIP
CCEHIILNOPR	NECROPHILIC		CCHIIIOSTTY	HISTIOCYTIC
CCEHIKNOPST	CHECKPOINTS		CCHIILORSTY	CHRYSOLITIC
CCEHILNOORT	TECHNICOLOR		CCHIIMNOOPR	MICROPHONIC
CCEHILNOPTY	POLYTECHNIC		CCHIIMNOOST	MONOSTICHIC
CCEHILNORRS	CHRONICLERS		CCHIIMOORTT	TRICHOTOMIC
CCEHIMMOOST	CHEMOSMOTIC		CCHIIMOPRTY	MICROPHYTIC
CCEHIMNOORT	HOMOCENTRIC		CCHIINOOPRS	RHINOSCOPIC
CCEHIMOOPRT	CHEMOTROPIC, ECTOMORPHIC		CCHILMOPTYY	LYMPHOCYTIC
CCEHINNRSSU	CRUNCHINESS		CCHIMMNOOOR	MONOCHROMIC

CCHIMOOPRTY	CORMOPHYTIC	CDDEIINOSUU	INDECIDUOUS
CCHIMOSSSTT	SCOTCH MISTS	CDDEIKOPSTT	SPOTTED DICK
CCHIOOOPRST	ORTHOSCOPIC	CDDEILNOOTY	DICOTYLEDON
CCHIORSSSST	CROSS-STITCH	CDDEILNOSSU	UNDISCLOSED
CCIILOORSTU	COLOURISTIC	CDDEILOORSU	DISCOLOURED
CCIIMMNOSTU	COMMUNISTIC	CDDEIMOOPSS	DISCOMPOSED
CCIIMOOPRRS	MICROSPORIC	CDDEINNOOST	ENDODONTICS
CCIIMOPRSST	COMIC STRIPS	CDDELLLMOOY	MOLLYCODDLE
CCIINNOOSTV	CONVICTIONS	CDDENOORSTU	COTES-DU-NORD
CCIINOPRTTY	NYCTITROPIC	CDDENOPRSTU	END PRODUCTS
CCIJNNNOOTU	CONJUNCTION	CDEEEEEFFLNS	SELF-DEFENCE
CCIKLMNOOTU	COCONUT MILK	CDEEEEEFFRSV	EFFERVESCED
CCILLNOORSU	COUNCILLORS	CDEEEEEFLNSS	DEFENCELESS
CCILMRRSUUU	CURRICULUMS	CDEEEEINPRX	EXPERIENCED
CCILNNOOSSU	CONCLUSIONS	CDEEEEFFFILT	FIELD-EFFECT
CCILNOOSSUY	CONSCIOUSLY	CDEEEEFFINRS	DIFFERENCES
CCIMNNOOPTU	COMPUNCTION	CDEEEEFFISST	SIDE EFFECTS
CCINNOOSSUU	UNCONSCIOUS	CDEEEEFGLNTU	GENUFLECTED
CCINOOPSSUU	CONSPICUOUS	CDEEEEFHIIPS	SPEECHIFIED
CCINOORRSTT	CONSTRICTOR	CDEEEEFHORUV	CHEF D'OEUVRE
CCLNNOOORWY	CROWN COLONY	CDEEEEFIILNS	FIN DE SIECLE
CCNOORRSTTU	CONSTRUCTOR	CDEEEEFIILRT	ELECTRIFIED
CCNOORRSTUW	CROWN COURTS	CDEEEEFILTVY	DEFECTIVELY
CCNOORTTUUY	COUNTY COURT	CDEEEEFLNRST	SELF-CENTRED
CCOOOOPPRSTY	PROCTOSCOPY	CDEEEEFLNRTU	UNREFLECTED
CDDDEEEEGKL	DECKLE-EDGED	CDEEEEFMNORT	DEFORCEMENT
CDDDEEIIRST	DISCREDITED	CDEEEEGILNXY	EXCEEDINGLY
CDDDEEILNUY	UNDECIDEDLY	CDEEEEGINRSV	DIVERGENCES
CDDDEIMMOOS	DISCOMMODED	CDEEEIIMMNN	MEDICINE MEN
CDDEEEEHLRSU	RESCHEDULED	CDEEEIINNRS	IN-RESIDENCE
CDDEEEIIPRTU	DECREPITUDE	CDEEEIIOPPR	PERIOD PIECE
CDDEEEMMNOR	RECOMMENDED	CDEEEIJNRTT	INTERJECTED
CDDEEEOOPRRR	PRERECORDED	CDEEEILNSTT	DELITESCENT
CDDEEFIINST	DISINFECTED	CDEEEILOPSV	VELOCIPEDES
CDDEEFILNSU	SELF-INDUCED	CDEEEILORTT	LIE DETECTOR
CDDEEHLNSUU	UNSCHEDULED	CDEEEILPTVY	DECEPTIVELY
CDDEEHNNRSU	SUNDRENCHED	CDEEEINPRTT	INTERCEPTED
CDDEEIIMRST	MISDIRECTED	CDEEEINRSTT	INTERSECTED
CDDEEIINORT	RODENTICIDE	CDEEEINSSTX	EXCITEDNESS
CDDEEILNOOS	DECOLONISED	CDEEEMMNORR	RECOMMENDER
CDDEEILNOOZ	DECOLONIZED	CDEEEMNOPRS	RECOMPENSED
CDDEEILTUVY	DEDUCTIVELY	CDEEENNOPRS	RESPONDENCE
CDDEELOORUV	OVERCLOUDED	CDEEENNORTU	ENCOUNTERED
CDDEENNOPSY	DESPONDENCY	CDEEEOPRRSS	PREDECESSOR, REPROCESSED
CDDEENORRSU	UNDERSCORED	CDEEERRRSTU	RESURRECTED
CDDEENORSSW	CROWDEDNESS	CDEEFFIKNST	STIFF-NECKED
CDDEEOORRVW	OVERCROWDED	CDEEFHIKLOY	FIELD HOCKEY
CDDEFIIMOST	DISCOMFITED	CDEEFIILNTY	DEFICIENTLY
CDDEGHILNOR	GODCHILDREN	CDEEFIINPSU	UNSPECIFIED
CDDEHIILMNR	CHILDMINDER	CDEEFILLTUY	DECEITFULLY
CDDEIIILNNS	DISINCLINED	CDEEFILNORY	ECOFRIENDLY
CDDEIIILNPS	DISCIPLINED	CDEEFILNOST	DEFLECTIONS
CDDEIILPPSS	SLIPPED DISC	CDEEFILOSST	CLOSEFISTED
CDDEIINNOOT	CONDITIONED	CDEEFINORRT	FREDERICTON

CDEEFLNORST	CENTRE-FOLDS	CDEEIRSTTUV	DESTRUCTIVE
CDEEFLNOSSY	CONFESSEDLY	CDEEKKORSTY	SKYROCKETED
CDEEFNNORST	FRONDESCENT	CDEEKNOORSS	CROOKEDNESS
CDEEFOORRTU	TOUR DE FORCE	CDEEKOOPRSW	WOODPECKERS
CDEEFOPRRTW	WORD-PERFECT	CDEEKOORSTV	OVERSTOCKED
CDEEGGINTTU	CUTTING EDGE	CDEELNNOTTY	CONTENTEDLY
CDEEGGLORSS	CROSS-LEGGED	CDEEMNNOSST	SECONDMENTS
CDEEGHIINPR	DECIPHERING	CDEENNORTUV	UNCONVERTED
CDEEGIINNRT	INTERCEDING	CDEENNOSTTU	UNCONTESTED
CDEEGIINNUV	UNDECEIVING	CDEENOORRRT	TROCORNERED
CDEEGIINRRT	REDIRECTING	CDEENOORRSS	ROOD SCREENS
CDEEGILNNSU	INDULGENCES	CDEENPSSTUU	UNSUSPECTED
CDEEGINOPRS	PROCEEDINGS	CDEEOOPPRRV	OVERCROPPED
CDEEGNOSSSU	SECOND-GUESS	CDEEOOPPRUV	OVERPRODUCE
CDEEHIINNOS	INDOCHINESE	CDEEOOPRRSU	REPRODUCERS
CDEEHIINNST	INDEHISCENT	CDEFFGIOOOS	GOOD OFFICES
CDEEHIKPRSW	SHIPWRECKED	CDEFGHIKLST	FLIGHT DECKS
CDEEHILOPRR	PERCHLORIDE	CDEFGHILNOS	GOLDFINCHES
CDEEHIMNORT	ENDOTHERMIC	CDEFHIKOPRT	PITCHFORKED
CDEEHIMNOTU	ENDOTHECIUM	CDEFHNOORRS	FRENCH DOORS
CDEEHIOQSTU	DISCOTHEQUE	CDEFIIILMSU	SEMIFLUIDIC
CDEEHPRSTTU	UPSTRETCHED	CDEFIILMMOR	MICROFILMED
CDEEIIILSTV	DECLIVITIES	CDEFIIMORST	DISCOMFITER
CDEEIIKLNSS	SLICKENSIDE	CDEFIINORST	DISINFECTOR
CDEEIIILNORT	DERELICTION	CDEFIINORTU	COUNTRIFIED
CDEEIIMNRST	DENSIMETRIC	CDEFILNNOTY	CONFIDENTLY
CDEEIIMORTU	EUDIOMETRIC	CDEFILNOSUU	FLUID OUNCES
CDEEIIMPRSS	SPERMICIDES	CDEGHHHIIPT	HIGH-PITCHED
CDEEIINORRT	REDIRECTION	CDEGHINOSST	SECOND SIGHT
CDEEIINRSTV	VIRIDESCENT	CDEGIIJNPRU	PREJUDICING
CDEEIINRTTU	INCERTITUDE	CDEGIINNORS	CONSIDERING
CDEEIIORRST	DIRECTORIES	CDEGIINORSV	DISCOVERING
CDEEIIORSSV	DISCOVERIES	CDEGIMNNOTU	DOCUMENTING
CDEEIIPRSTV	DESCRIPTIVE	CDEGIMNOOPS	DECOMPOSING
CDEEIKLNNOO	NICKELODEON	CDEGIMNORRU	CORRIGENDUM
CDEEIKLNORT	INTERLOCKED	CDEGINOPRRU	REPRODUCING
CDEEILMOOSW	LOW COMEDIES	CDEGMNORSUU	CURMUDGEONS
CDEEILNNOSS	DECLENSIONS	CDEGNORRSUW	GROUND CREWS
CDEEILNNQUY	DELINQUENCY	CDEHHNOOOPR	CHORDOPHONE
CDEEILSTUVY	SEDUCTIVELY	CDEHIIKTTTW	THICK-WITTED
CDEEIMNNRST	DISCERNMENT, RESCINDMENT	CDEHIILLNOT	DECILLIONTH
CDEEIMNNSTU	INDUCEMENTS	CDEHIILOOTT	THEODOLITIC
CDEEIMNOPRS	ENDOSPERMIC	CDEHIILORRT	TRICHLORIDE
CDEEIMNORTV	DIVORCEMENT	CDEHIIMOOST	DICHOTOMIES, DICHOTOMISE
CDEEIMOOSTX	SEXTODECIMO	CDEHIIMOOTZ	DICHOTOMIZE
CDEEINNRSSW	WINDSCREENS	CDEHIINOOPV	VIDEOPHONIC
CDEEINOPRSV	PROVIDENCES	CDEHIIPSSTW	DIPSWITCHES
CDEEINOPRTV	OPEN VERDICT	CDEHILPRTUU	PULCHRITUDE
CDEEINORRTU	REINTRODUCE	CDEHIMNOOPR	ENDOMORPHIC
CDEEINORSTT	CREDIT NOTES	CDEHIMNORST	CHRISTENDOM
CDEEINPRSUU	SUPERINDUCE	CDEHIMOPRSY	HYPODERMICS
CDEEIORRSSV	DISCOVERERS	CDEHINOPRRY	PONDICHERRY
CDEEIORRTXY	EX-DIRECTORY	CDEHIOOOPPT	PHOTOCOPIED
CDEEIRRRSVW	SCREWDRIVER	CDEHKLOORST	STOCKHOLDER

CDEHLOOPPRS	CLODHOPPERS	CDEINNOOSTU	CONTUSIONED
CDEHLOOPSSS	CLOSED SHOPS	CDEINNOPRST	NONDESCRIPT
CDEIIILNPRS	DISCIPLINER	CDEINNORSTU	DSCONTINUER
CDEIIILNPSS	DISCIPLINES	CDEINOOPSST	ENDOSCOPIST
CDEIIILNSUV	UNCIVILISED	CDEINORSTTU	DESTRUCTION
CDEIIILNUVZ	UNCIVILIZED	CDEINORSTUY	COUNTRYSIDE
CDEIIILOPST	POLITICISED	CDEINOSTTTU	CONSTITUTED
CDEIIILOPTZ	POLITICIZED	CDEIORSSTUY	DISCOURTESY
CDEIIIMORTX	OXIDIMETRIC	CDEKKNOOORR	DOORKNOCKER
CDEIIINNORT	INDIRECTION	CDELLORSUUY	CREDULOUSLY
CDEIIINSTTV	DISTINCTIVE	CDENOORRTUW	COUNTERWORD
CDEIIIOPRTT	PERIDOTITIC	CDEOORSTTUW	WOODCUTTERS
CDEIIIOPRTY	PERIODICITY	CDEOPRRRUWY	CURRY POWDER
CDEIIIRSSTV	RECIDIVISTS	CDFGIIILNNOY	CONFIDINGLY
CDEIIISSTUV	VICISSITUDE	CDFGINNNOOU	CONFOUNDING
CDEIIJNSTUV	DISJUNCTIVE	CDFIMOORSST	DISCOMFORTS
CDEIIKQTTUW	QUICK-WITTED	CDFINNOSTUY	DYSFUNCTION
CDEIILLMNOS	MILLISECOND	CDGIIKNNSUW	WIND-SUCKING
CDEIILLOORV	COD-LIVER OIL	CDGIIKNSTTU	SITTING DUCK
CDEIILLOSUY	DELICIOUSLY	CDGIIMMNNOO	INCOMMODING
CDEIILLPTUY	PELLUCIDITY	CDGIINNORTU	INTRODUCING
CDEIILNRTUY	INCREDULITY	CDGIINNOSTU	DISCOUNTING
CDEIILNTUVY	INDUCTIVELY	CDGIINORSSU	DISCOURSING
CDEIILOORST	SCLEROTIOID	CDGILOORTTY	TROGLODYTIC
CDEIILOPSSU	PEDICULOSIS	CDGIMNNOOPU	COMPOUNDING
CDEIILOSTUV	DECLIVITOUS	CDGINOOTTUW	WOODCUTTING
CDEIIMMOOST	COMMODITIES	CDGINOPRSTU	CROP-DUSTING
CDEIIMMNSTT	INDICTMENTS	CDHIIIMOOPR	IDIOMORPHIC
CDEIIMNORST	MODERNISTIC	CDHIILPRSUU	DISULPHURIC
CDEIIMOSTTY	DOMESTICITY	CDHIIMOOSTT	DICHOTOMIST
CDEIIMPPRUY	CYPRIPEDIUM	CDHIIOOPRST	CHIROPODIST
CDEIINNOORT	CONDITIONER, RECONDITION	CDHIMOOOSTU	DICHOTOMOUS
CDEIINNOSTU	DISCONTINUE	CDHINOOORTT	ORTHODONTIC
CDEIINOOPRT	PERIODONTIC	CDHINOOPRSY	HYDROPONICS
CDEIINOOPRST	DESCRIPTION, PREDICTIONS	CDIIIJNOSUU	INJUDICIOUS
CDEIINORRTT	INTERDICTOR	CDIIILNTTUY	INDUCTILITY
CDEIINOSSST	DISSECTIONS	CDIIINNNOOT	IN CONDITION
CDEIINRSSTU	SCRUTINISED	CDIIINNOSTT	DISTINCTION
CDEIINRSTUZ	SCRUTINIZED	CDIIJLOSUUY	JUDICIOUSLY
CDEIIPRSSTU	PEDICURISTS	CDIIJNNOSTU	DISJUNCTION
CDEIJLNNOOY	CONJOINEDLY	CDIIKRRSTTY	DIRTY TRICKS
CDEIJNRSTUU	DISJUNCTURE	CDIILMORSTU	CLOSTRIDIUM
CDEIJOOSTTU	DO JUSTICE TO	CDIIMMNNOOU	CONDOMINIUM
CDEIKLNORTW	TRICKLE-DOWN	CDIINOSSSSU	DISCUSSIONS
CDEILNNNOOU	ON CLOUD NINE	CDIIOOOOSTV	VOODOOISTIC
CDEILNOPSST	SPLIT SECOND	CDILLORSUUY	LUDICROUSLY
CDEILNORSUU	INCREDULOUS	CDILMOOORSX	LOXODROMICS
CDEILORSSSU	DISCLOSURES	CDILOOORUUU	DOUROUCOULI
CDEIMMNOPSU	COMPENDIUMS	CDINNOOPRTY	CYPRINODONT
CDEIMMNNOTTU	UNCOMMITTED	CDINOOPRSTU	PRODUCTIONS
CDEIMMOOPRS	COMPROMISED	CDLMOORSSTU	STORM CLOUDS
CDEIMNOOPSU	COMPENDIOUS	CDOORRSSSSW	CROSS SWORDS
CDEIMNOSSTY	SYNDESMOTIC	CEEEEFNPRRS	PREFERENCES
CDEINNOORSU	ENDOCRINOUS	CEEEEGIMNRS	EMERGENCIES

CEEEEHHRRST	THREE CHEERS
CEEEEHNPRST	THREEPENCES
CEEEEILNORT	ELECTIONEER
CEEEEIMNNPR	PRE-EMINENCE
CEEEEIMNNSS	MISE-EN-SCENE
CEEEEINPRSX	EXPERIENCES
CEEEEINRRRV	IRREVERENCE
CEEEENNRRTV	NERVE CENTRE
CEEEFFGINOV	GIVE OFFENCE
CEEEFFHOOSU	COFFEE HOUSE
CEEEFFIINTV	INEFFECTIVE
CEEEFFILTVY	EFFECTIVELY
CEEEFHIIPRS	SPEECHIFIER
CEEEFIILRRT	ELECTRIFIER
CEEEFIKQRUZ	QUICK-FREEZE
CEEEFILRSSV	SELF-SERVICE
CEEEFINQRSU	FREQUENCIES
CEEEFIORRST	REFECTORIES
CEEEFLPRSST	SELF-RESPECT
CEEEFMNNORT	ENFORCEMENT
CEEEFPRRSTU	PREFECTURES
CEEEGGHINNS	GEGENSCHEIN
CEEEGGNORRR	GREENGROCER
CEEEGIKNORT	GREENOCKITE
CEEEGINNOTX	XENOGENETIC
CEEEGINNRRV	REVERENCING
CEEEGINOSST	ECTOGENESIS
CEEEHHKLNOP	HECKELPHONE
CEEEHHMOPRS	CHEMOSPHERE
CEEEHHNRSTT	THE TRENCHES
CEEEHIKNTTT	KITCHENETTE
CEEEHILORTT	HETEROCLITE
CEEEHIMNRTU	HERMENEUTIC
CEEEHIMORST	HETEROECISM
CEEEHISSSSW	SWISS CHEESE
CEEEHLLRSSY	CHEERLESSLY
CEEEHLOPRST	CLEETHORPES
CEEEHMNNRRT	TRENCHERMEN
CEEEHOQRSUU	EUROCHEQUES
CEEEHRRSTWY	SWEET CHERRY
CEEEIIKLNTT	TELEKINETIC
CEEEIIMNNPT	IMPENITENCE
CEEEIINNNRT	INTERNECINE
CEEEIINNNST	INSENTIENCE
CEEEIINNSTX	INEXISTENCE
CEEEIINSSST	NECESSITIES
CEEEILLSTVY	SELECTIVELY
CEEEILNNOQU	INELOQUENCE
CEEEILNOPST	PLEISTOCENE
CEEEILNORST	RE-ELECTIONS
CEEEILNPSST	PESTILENCES
CEEEILPRTVY	RECEPTIVELY
CEEEILRSTVY	SECRETIVELY
CEEEILSSVXY	EXCESSIVELY

CEEEIMMNRTX	CEMENT MIXER
CEEEIMMPSUU	MUSEUM PIECE
CEEEIMNNSTT	ENTICEMENTS
CEEEIMNRSTT	CENTIMETRES
CEEEIMNSTTX	EXCITEMENTS
CEEEINNOSTV	VENESECTION
CEEEINORTUX	EXECUTIONER
CEEEINOSTVX	COEXTENSIVE
CEEEINPRSSS	PRECISENESS
CEEEINPRSST	PERSISTENCE
CEEEIPPRSTV	PERSPECTIVE
CEEEIPRSTUV	PERSECUTIVE
CEEEJNNSTUV	JUVENESCENT
CEEEKKLOPRS	LOCK KEEPERS
CEEEKMNORSS	SMOKESCREEN
CEEELLLNTXY	EXCELLENTLY
CEEELLORSTY	ELECTROLYSE
CEEELLORTTY	ELECTROLYTE
CEEELMNOSSW	WELCOMENESS
CEEELMORRST	ELECTROMERS, SCLEROMETER
CEEELNNOORT	COELENTERON
CEEELOPRTTY	ELECTROTYPE
CEEELORSTVW	SWEET CLOVER
CEEEMNOPRRS	RECOMPENSER
CEEENNORRTU	ENCOUNTERER
CEEENOPRSST	OPEN SECRETS
CEEENRSSSTT	SCREEN TESTS
CEEEOOPRSST	STEREOSCOPE
CEEFFHIIORS	IRISH COFFEE
CEEFFHINRRS	FRENCH FRIES
CEEFFHOOPSS	COFFEE SHOPS
CEEFFIIINNT	INEFFICIENT
CEEFFIILLOS	SLICE OF LIFE
CEEFFIILNTY	EFFICIENTLY
CEEFGIMOORT	COME TO GRIEF
CEEFGINNRRY	REFRINGENCY
CEEFGINRSTU	CENTRIFUGES
CEEFGLNORTU	GENUFLECTOR
CEEFHHNORTT	THENCEFORTH
CEEFHILMRST	FLETCHERISM
CEEFHILORSU	CHELIFEROUS
CEEFHLOTUYY	TOUCHY-FEELY
CEEFIKKNOPT	POCKETKNIFE
CEEFIKOOPRW	PIECE OF WORK
CEEFILMPRTY	IMPERFECTLY
CEEFILNORST	REFLECTIONS
CEEFILNORSU	FLUORESCEIN
CEEFIMNNNOT	CONFINEMENT
CEEFIMOPRSS	FORM SPECIES
CEEFINNQRUY	INFREQUENCY
CEEFINOPRST	IN RESPECT OF
CEEFINORTTU	COUNTERFEIT
CEEFINOSSTY	OF NECESSITY
CEEFLMOORRT	ELECTROFORM

CEEFLNORSTU	FLUORESCENT
CEEFLOORRSU	FORECLOSURE
CEEFLORRSUU	RESOURCEFUL
CEEFMNNORST	CONFERMENTS
CEEGHILLNOP	PHELLOGENIC
CEEGHILNRSS	SCHLESINGER
CEEGHINNNRT	ENTRENCHING
CEEGHINNNRT	RETRENCHING
CEEGHINRSST	SIGHTSCREEN
CEEGHLOPSST	CLOTHES PEGS
CEEGIINPRST	STRINGPIECE
CEEGIINSSTT	GENETICISTS
CEEGIIOOTVV	GIVE VOICE TO
CEEGILNNOSY	GEOSYNCLINE
CEEGILNOPST	TELESCOPING
CEEGILNOPTY	POLYGENETIC
CEEGILNOSTT	TELEGNOSTIC
CEEGIMNNOOT	MONOGENETIC
CEEGIMNORST	EGOCENTRISM
CEEGINOORST	OESTROGENIC
CEEGINOSSTY	CYTOGENESIS
CEEGINPRSTU	PERSECUTING
CEEGMNNORSS	CONGRESSMEN
CEEHHIIMPRS	HEMISPHERIC
CEEHHILMOOR	HELIOCHROME
CEEHHILNOPT	TECHNOPHILE
CEEHHIMRSTT	HEMSTITCHER
CEEHHKMOORV	CHEREMKHOVO
CEEHHMORSTT	HOME STRETCH
CEEHHIIINORS	CHINOISERIE
CEEHHIILLNST	HELLENISTIC
CEEHIILMORT	HELIOMETRIC
CEEHIIMPRTU	PERITHECIUM
CEEHIIMPSTU	EUPHEMISTIC
CEEHIKNSSST	SKETCHINESS, THICKNESSES
CEEHILLNOPU	NUCLEOPHILE
CEEHILLNOST	CLOTHESLINE
CEEHILMNORT	THERMOCLINE
CEEHILOPRST	ELECTORSHIP, HELICOPTERS
CEEHILORTTY	HETEROLYTIC
CEEHILPRSTU	LECTURESHIP
CEEHILQSSTU	SQUELCHIEST
CEEHIMNOPRS	MESONEPHRIC
CEEHIMOPRSS	MESOSPHERIC
CEEHIMOPRTT	PITCHOMETER
CEEHIMOPSTU	MOUTHPIECES
CEEHIOOPRTT	HETEROTOPIC
CEEHIOPRTTY	HETEROTYPIC
CEEHIRSSTTT	STRETCHIEST
CEEHKLNOSUY	HONEYSUCKLE
CEEHKNORSUY	HONEYSUCKER
CEEHKNPRSUY	KEYPUNCHERS
CEEHLLOORST	CHOLESTEROL
CEEHLLORSUY	LECHEROUSLY

CEEHLNOOPRR	CHLOROPRENE
CEEHMNOORRT	CHRONOMETER
CEEHMNOPRTY	NEPHRECTOMY
CEEHMOOPRST	THERMOSCOPE
CEEHNOORRTT	ORTHOCENTRE
CEEHOOPSSTT	STETHOSCOPE
CEEHORRTTYY	ERYTHROCYTE
CEEIIIKNSWZ	SIENKIEWICZ
CEEIIINNRST	INNER CITIES
CEEIIKNRSST	RICKETINESS
CEEIIILMRTUV	VERMICULITE
CEEIIILNNRSY	INSINCERELY
CEEIIILSTTVY	SELECTIVITY
CEEIIMMPRST	METEMPIRICS
CEEIIMNNRST	REMINISCENT
CEEIIMOPRTZ	PIEZOMETRIC
CEEIIMOPTTV	COMPETITIVE
CEEIIMORSST	ESOTERICISM
CEEIIMORSTX	EXOTERICISM
CEEIINORSTV	INSECTIVORE
CEEIINOSTVX	CONVEXITIES
CEEIINRSSTT	INTERSTICES
CEEIIPRTTVY	RECEPTIVITY
CEEIIRRSTTV	RESTRICTIVE
CEEIJLOPRST	PROJECTILES
CEEIJNORRTT	INTERJECTOR
CEEIKLNORRT	INTERLOCKER
CEEIKMMOSUY	MICKEY MOUSE
CEEIKNPRSTY	PERSNICKETY
CEEILLMRSSY	MERCILESSLY
CEEILLSUVVXY	EXCLUSIVELY
CEEILMNNNSTU	LUMINESCENT
CEEILMNOOPW	POLICEWOMEN
CEEILMNOSTU	CONTUMELIES
CEEILMNRSTU	MULTISCREEN
CEEILMOORRT	COLORIMETER
CEEILMOOSTU	LEUCOTOMIES
CEEILNNNOOV	NONVIOLENCE
CEEILNQSTUY	QUIESCENTLY
CEEILRRSTUU	SERICULTURE
CEEIMMORRST	MICROMETERS
CEEIMNNOOPT	OMNIPOTENCE
CEEIMNNOPRS	PROMINENCES
CEEIMNNOPTT	INCOMPETENT
CEEIMNNORTU	COUNTERMINE
CEEIMNNSTTU	INTUMESCENT
CEEIMNOORSU	CEREMONIOUS
CEEIMNRRTTU	RECRUITMENT
CEEIMOOPSSS	SEISMOSCOPE
CEEIMOORRSV	ROOM SERVICE
CEEIMOPRSSV	COMPRESSIVE
CEEIMOPRSTU	COMPUTERISE
CEEIMOPRTUZ	COMPUTERIZE
CEEINNNOSTT	CONSENTIENT

CEEINNOORRT	RECONNOITRE	CEFHINRSTUW	SCHWEINFURT
CEEINNOOSTX	COEXTENSION	CEFHOOSSTTU	SOFT TOUCHES
CEEINOOPRST	RETINOSCOPE	CEFIIKKLNSV	FLICK KNIVES
CEEINOPPRSS	SNIPERSCOPE	CEFIILNOST	INFLECTIONS
CEEINOPRRTT	INTERCEPTOR	CEFIINORSUZ	ZINCIFEROUS
CEEINOPRSSS	PRECESSIONS	CEFILMORSUU	CULMIFEROUS
CEEINOPRSTU	PERSECUTION	CEFILNOORTU	COUNTERFOIL
CEEINOPRTTX	EXCERPTTION	CEFILOORSUY	FEROCIOUSLY
CEEINORRSST	INTERCESSOR	CEFINNOOSSS	CONFESSIONS
CEEINORRSTU	INTERCOURSE	CEFIOPRRSUU	CUPRIFEROUS
CEEINOSSSTU	NECESSITOUS	CEFLLNOORST	SELF-CONTROL
CEEINRRSSTU	SCRUTINEERS	CEFLMOORSST	COMFORTLESS
CEEIOPPRSTV	PROSPECTIVE	CEFLNOORRSW	CORNFLOWERS
CEEIOPRSTTY	STEREOTYPIC	CEFLOOOPRSU	FLUOROSCOPE
CEEIPQRSTUU	PICTURESQUE	CEFNOPRRTUY	PERFUNCTORY
CEEIRSTTVVY	CIVVY STREET	CEGGIINNORZ	RECOGNIZING
CEEJLNORSWW	CROWN JEWELS	CEGHIILNRST	CHRISTINGLE
CEEKLNRSTTU	TURTLENECKS	CEGHIINNNRT	INTRENCHING
CEEKMNNOOPTY	POCKET MONEY	CEGHIINNRST	CHRISTENING
CEEKOORRRTT	RETRO-ROCKET	CEGHIMMNOOS	HOMECOMINGS
CEELMMNOPST	COMPLEMENTS	CEGHINORSSU	GROUCHINESS
CEELMNNOSTU	LOCUM TENENS	CEGHIOOPRST	GEOSTROPHIC
CEELMNOPSTY	SPLENECTOMY	CEGIIIMNNRS	REMINISCING
CEELMNOPTTY	COMPETENTLY	CEGIIIMNRTZ	METRICIZING
CEELNRRRTUY	RECURRENTLY	CEGIIKLNNSY	SICKENINGLY
CEEMMMNNOOSS	COMMON SENSE	CEGIILLNNST	STENCILLING
CEEMMNOPTUY	PNEUMECTOMY	CEGIILLNORY	RECOILINGLY
CEEMMNOPTTY	COMPTOMETER	CEGIILMNOST	CLOSING TIME
CEEMMOORSTT	COME TO TERMS	CEGIILMOOSS	SEISMOLOGIC
CEEMMOORSTU	COUNTERMOVE	CEGIILNNOST	NEOLOGISTIC
CEEMNNOTTTT	CONTENTMENT	CEGIILNORST	CLOISTERING
CEEMNOORTUV	COUNTERMOVE	CEGIILNOTVY	COGNITIVELY
CEEMNOPRRTU	PROCUREMENT	CEGIILOOPST	GEOPOLITICS
CEEMNOPRSTT	CONTRETEMPS	CEGIIMMNNOU	IMMUNOGENOU
CEENNOOORRST	CORNERSTONE	CEGIIMNNOOZ	ECONOMIZING
CEENNOSSSSU	CONSENSUSES	CEGIIMNOORT	GONIOMETRIC
CEENOPPPRRS	PEPPERCORNS	CEGIINNOORT	RECOGNITION
CEENOPRTTUY	COUNTERTYPE	CEGIINORSTU	CONGRUITIES
CEENORSTTTU	STONECUTTER	CEGIINRRSTT	RESTRICTING
CEEOOPRRTTV	OVERPROTECT	CEGILLNNOSU	COUNSELLING
CEEOOPRSSTY	STEREOSCOPY	CEGILNNOSSY	CLOYINGNESS
CEEOPRRSSTT	PROTECTRESS	CEGILNOORST	NECROLOGIST
CEEOPRRSSTU	PERSECUTORS	CEGILNOOSTY	SCIENTOLOGY
CEEERRRSTTUU	RESTRUCTURE	CEGILNORSSS	SINGLE-CROSS
CEFFHIIINORS	CHIFFONIERS	CEGILNRRRUY	RECURRINGLY
CEFFHIRSSTT	FESTSCHRIFT	CEGIMNNNOST	CONSIGNMENT
CEFFIOOPSST	POST OFFICES	CEGIMNOOOSS	COSMOGONIES
CEFGIILNNNU	INFLUENCING	CEGIMNOPRSS	COMPRESSING
CEFGIINNORR	REINFORCING	CEGIMOOORRV	MICROGROOVE
CEFGIKLLNOS	SELF-LOCKING	CEGIMOOPRST	COME TO GRIPS
CEFGILNOORS	FORECLOSING	CEGINNOSTT	CONTINGENTS
CEFGLOORSSU	GOLF COURSES	CEGINNORSTU	COUNTERSIGN
CEFHHNNORRS	FRENCH HORNS	CEGINOPPRST	PROSPECTING
CEFHIIISSTT	FETISHISTIC	CEGINOPRSTU	PROSECUTING
CEFHILLRTUY	FILTHY LUCRE		

CEGLMMOORYY	MYRMECOLOGY
CEGLMOOSSTY	GLOSSECTOMY
CEGLNNORTUY	CONGRUENTLY
CEGORRRSUYY	CRYOSURGERY
CEHHHIIKRST	HITCHHIKERS
CEHHIIILLOT	HELIOLITHIC
CEHHIIMMOPR	HEMIMORPHIC
CEHHILMRSUY	HELICHRYSUM
CEHHIMRSTUY	EURHYTHMICS
CEHHINRTTUW	WITCH-HUNTER
CEHHIOPRRST	CHRISTOPHER
CEHHIOPSTYZ	SCHIZOPHYTE
CEHHLOOOSSU	SCHOOLHOUSE
CEHHMNORSSY	SYNCHROMESH
CEHHMOOOPRR	CHROMOPHORE
CEHHOOOPRRT	TROCHOPHORE
CEHIIINPSST	CITISENSHIP
CEHIIINPSTZ	CITIZENSHIP
CEHIIJPSSTU	JUSTICESHIP
CEHIIJSTTUW	WITH JUSTICE
CEHIIKLNOPS	PICK HOLES IN
CEHIIKNSSTT	IN THE STICKS
CEHIILOOPRT	HELIOTROPIC
CEHIILPRSTU	SPHERULITIC
CEHIIMNORST	THERMIONICS
CEHIIMOPPRR	PERIMORPHIC
CEHIIMOSSUV	MISCHIEVOUS
CEHIINOOPRS	IONOSPHERIC
CEHIINOORSS	ISOCHRONISE
CEHIINOORSZ	ISOCHRONIZE
CEHIIOPPTTY	EPIPHYTOTIC
CEHIIOPRRST	PREHISTORIC
CEHIIOPRSVY	VICEROYSHIP
CEHIIOSSSVY	VICHYSSOISE
CEHIKMRSSTU	HUCKSTERISM
CEHIKNOPSTU	SOUP KITCHEN
CEHIKNPSSSU	PUCKISHNESS
CEHILLMOPSY	MESOPHYLLIC
CEHILMOOPPR	PLEOMORPHIC
CEHILMOOPRS	PLEOCHROISM
CEHILMORTTY	THERMOLYTIC
CEHILNOOQRU	CHLOROQUINE
CEHILNOSSST	COLTISHNESS
CEHILNOSSSU	SLOUCHINESS
CEHIMMOOPRS	MESOMORPHIC
CEHIMMOOSSS	CHEMOSMOSIS
CEHIMNOOPRS	MICROPHONES
CEHIMNOOPRT	PHONOMETRIC
CEHIMNOOPRX	XENOMORPHIC
CEHIMNOPSTY	CHIMNEYPOTS
CEHIMOOPRRX	XEROMORPHIC
CEHIMOOPRTT	PHOTOMETRIC
CEHIMOOSSST	SCHISTOSOME
CEHIMOPPRST	COPPERSMITH
CEHIMORSTTY	STICHOMETRY
CEHINNORSSY	SYNCHRONISE
CEHINNORSYZ	SYNCHRONIZE
CEHINOOPRRS	CORONERSHIP
CEHIOOOPPRT	PHOTOCOPIER
CEHIOOOPPST	PHOTOCOPIES
CEHIOOPSTTY	OSTEOPHYTIC
CEHIOPRSSTT	PROSTHETICS
CEHKNOOSSTT	ON THE STOCKS
CEHLOOPPRSS	PREP SCHOOLS
CEHMMNOORSW	COMMON SHREW
CEHMMOOORSS	CHROMOSOMES
CEHMMOOORSX	X CHROMOSOME
CEHMMOOORSY	Y CHROMOSOME
CEHMNOORRTY	CHRONOMETRY
CEHMOPRSTYY	PSYCHOMETRY
CEHNNOSSTUU	UNCOUTHNESS
CEHNOORRRST	SHORT CORNER
CEHNOOSSTTU	TOUCHSTONES
CEHOOPSSTTY	STETHOSCOPY
CEHOORSSTUU	COURTHOUSES
CEIIILLMNPU	PENICILLIUM
CEIIILLPTTY	ELLIPTICITY
CEIIILNNPTY	INCIPIENTLY
CEIIIMNOPRS	IMPRECISION
CEIIIMNOSST	MISONEISTIC
CEIIIMPSSST	PESSIMISTIC
CEIIINNRSTY	INSINCERITY
CEIIINNSTTV	INSTINCTIVE
CEIIINOPRTT	PERITONITIC
CEIIINOSTVV	VIVISECTION
CEIIINPRSTV	INSCRIPTIVE
CEIIIOPRSTT	PERIOSTITIC
CEIIIORSSTU	CURIOSITIES
CEIIIOSSTTV	SOVIETISTIC
CEIIKLLPSTT	LICKSPITTLE
CEIIKLNNRSS	CRINKLINESS
CEIIKLNPRSS	PRICKLINESS
CEIIKLQRSUV	QUICKSILVER
CEIIKNOSSTY	CYTOKINESIS
CEIIKNRSSST	TRICKSINESS
CEIIKPRSSTT	SPITSTICKER
CEIILLNSUVY	INCLUSIVELY
CEIILNRTUUV	VINICULTURE
CEIILRTTUUV	VITICULTURE
CEIILRTTUVY	RELUCTIVITY
CEIIMMNOSTU	COMMUNITIES
CEIIMNOOPTT	COMPETITION
CEIIMNOPSUU	IMPECUNIOUS
CEIIMNORRTT	NITROMETRIC
CEIIMNORSTU	NEUROTICISM
CEIIMNPRSSS	SCRIMPINESS
CEIIMOPRRST	SPIROMETRIC
CEIIMOPRSST	SEMITROPICS

CEIINNNNOTT	INCONTINENT
CEIINNNORTU	INTERNUNCIO
CEIINNOPSST	INSPECTIONS
CEIINORRSTT	RESTRICTION
CEIINOSSSUV	VICIOUSNESS
CEIINRRSSTU	SCRUTINISER
CEIINRRSTUZ	SCRUTINIZER
CEIINRSTTUV	INSTRUCTIVE
CEIIOPPRSTU	PRECIPITOUS
CEIIORRRSTT	TERRORISTIC
CEIIORSTUVY	VOYEURISTIC
CEIIPPRSTUY	PERSPICUITY
CEIJNOOPRST	PROJECTIONS
CEIKLLMOORS	ROLLICKSOME
CEIKLMOORST	MORTISE LOCK
CEIKLNNSSUU	UNLUCKINESS
CEIKLNOORRT	CRINKLEROOT
CEIKNNORSTU	COUNTERSINK
CEILLLNOOOV	VIOLONCELLO
CEILLNOPRSU	CURL ONE'S LIP
CEILMMNOPST	COMPLIMENTS
CEILMMOPRUY	PROMYCELIUM
CEILMNOOPSX	COMPLEXIONS
CEILMNOTYYZ	ENZYMOLYTIC
CEILMOOOPST	COSMOPOLITE
CEILMOOOSTV	LOCOMOTIVES
CEILMOPRTUU	POMICULTURE
CEILNOOPRTU	PERLOCUTION
CEILNORSSTU	COURTLINESS
CEILNRSTUUV	VENTRICULUS
CEILOOPRSTT	PROTOSTELIC
CEILOOPRTTY	PROTEOLYTIC
CEILOORRSTU	TERRICOLOUS
CEILOORRSUV	VERSICOLOUR
CEILOORRSVY	CORROSIVELY
CEIMMMNOSTT	COMMITMENTS
CEIMMNOQSUU	COMMUNIQUES
CEIMMNORSSU	CONSUMERISM
CEIMMOOPRRS	COMPROMISER
CEIMMOOPRSS	COMPROMISES
CEIMNOOPRSS	COMPRESSION
CEIMNOOPRTU	MUCOPROTEIN
CEIMNOORSTU	COTERMINOUS
CEIMNOPRSSU	PROSCENIUMS
CEIMNOPSTUV	CONSUMPTIVE
CEIMNORSSTU	MISCONSTRUE
CEIMOOPRSTT	COMPETITORS
CEINNNOOSTT	CONTENTIONS
CEINNNOOSTV	CONVENTIONS
CEINNOORSSU	CONNOISSEUR
CEINNOORSSV	CONVERSIONS
CEINNOOSTTU	CONTENTIOUS
CEINNOSTTTU	CONSTITUENT
CEINOOPRSSS	PROCESSIONS
CEINOOPRSTT	PROTECTIONS, STENOTROPIC
CEINOOPRSTU	PROSECUTION
CEINOOPRSTY	RETINOSCOPY
CEINOOPTTTY	TOTIPOTENCY
CEINOPRSSSU	SUPERSONICS
CEINORSSSUU	CURIOUSNESS
CEINORSTTTU	CONSTITUTER
CEINOSSSSUV	VISCOUSNESS
CEINOSSSTUV	VISCOUNTESS
CEIOOOPRRTZ	PROTEROZOIC
CEIOOPRTTYZ	CRYPTOZOITE
CEIOPPRSSUU	PERSPICUOUS
CEIOPRRSTWY	COPYWRITERS
CEIORRSTUVY	VERRUCOSITY
CEIPPRRSSTU	SUPERSCRIPT
CEIPPRSSTTY	TYPESCRIPTS
CEKLMOOORRS	LOCKER ROOMS
CEKNNORSTUU	COUNTERSUNK
CEKNOORRTUW	COUNTERWORK
CELLMOOPRRT	COMPTROLLER
CELLNNOOPTU	POLLEN COUNT
CELLNOORRST	CONTROLLERS
CELLNOORSSU	COUNSELLORS
CELLNRTTUUY	TRUCULENTLY
CELMNOORTUU	MONOCULTURE
CELMOOPRTYY	PYLORECTOMY
CELNOOPRTTU	COUNTERPLOT
CELOORSTUUY	COURTEOUSLY
CEMMNOOPRTT	COMPORTMENT
CEMOOPRRSSS	COMPRESSORS
CENOOPRRSTY	CONTROVERSY
CENOPRRSSTU	CORRUPTNESS
CENORSTTUWY	WEST COUNTRY
CEOOPPRRSST	PROSPECTORS
CEOOPRRSSTU	PROSECUTORS
CEPRRSSTTUU	SUPERSTRUCT
CFFGIIKNOST	TICKINGS OFF
CFFGIINRTUY	FRUCTIFYING
CFFHILMNOTU	FIFTH COLUMN
CFFIIINOOSU	INOFFICIOUS
CFFIILOOSUY	OFFICIOUSLY
CFGHIILLNNY	FLINCHINGLY
CFGHIILNNNU	UNFLINCHING
CFGHIMNOORT	FORTHCOMING
CFGIINNNOTU	FUNCTIONING
CFGILNNOSUY	CONFUSINGLY
CFGINNNOORT	CONFRONTING
CFGINOSTUUY	YOUNG FUSTIC
CFHHIKMNOTU	THINK MUCH OF
CFHHIIKSSSTT	SHIFT STICKS, STICK SHIFTS
CFHLLOOORST	FLOOR CLOTHS
CFIIILNOST	INFLICTIONS
CFIIILMORSTU	FORMULISTIC
CFIIINORSSTU	FIRST COUSIN

CFIMNOORSST	CONFORMISTS
CFINNOORSTU	INNS OF COURT
CFLOOOPRSUY	FLUOROSCOPY
CGGHIILOOPR	LOGOGRIPHIC
CGGIIIKNPST	PIGSTICKING
CGGIIKNPSSU	SUCKING PIGS
CGGILNORSUY	SCOURGINGLY
CGHHHIIIKNT	HITCHHIKING
CGHHHILOOSS	HIGH SCHOOLS
CGHHILNOOST	NIGHT SCHOOL
CGHHILOOTYY	ICHTHYOLOGY
CGHIIILRSTV	CIVIL RIGHTS
CGHIIKNSSTT	NIGHTSTICKS
CGHIILNTTWY	TWITCHINGLY
CGHILLNOSUY	SLOUCHINGLY
CGHILMOOOPR	MORPHOLOGIC
CGHILOOPSTY	PHYCOLOGIST
CGHILOOORSTY	CHRISTOLOGY
CGHIMNOORST	SHORTCOMING
CGHIMOOOTYZ	HOMOZYGOTIC
CGHIMOOPRYZ	ZYGOMORPHIC
CGHINOPTTUY	TOUCH-TYPING
CGIIIIMNTVZ	VICTIMIZING
CGIIIKLNOPT	POLITICKING
CGIIILNSSTU	LINGUISTICS
CGIIILRSTTU	LITURGISTIC
CGIIKLNORS	ROLLICKINGS
CGIIKLLNRTY	TRICKLINGLY
CGIIKLNOPST	STOCKPILING
CGIILLOSSTY	SYLLOGISTIC
CGIILMMNOOU	IMMUNOLOGIC
CGIILMNOORY	CRIMINOLOGY
CGIILNNNSUU	CUNNILINGUS
CGIILNOOOST	ICONOLOGIST
CGIILOOOSST	SOCIOLOGIST
CGIIMNNOSTU	MISCOUNTING
CGIIMNOSTUZ	CUSTOMIZING
CGIINNORTUY	INCONGRUITY
CGIINNRSTTU	INSTRUCTING
CGILLNNOORT	CONTROLLING
CGILMOOOSST	COSMOLOGIST
CGILNPRSTUU	SCULPTURING
CGILOOSSTTY	CYTOLOGISTS
CGIMNOOOSST	COSMOGONIST
CGINNNOOPRU	PRONOUNCING
CGINNOORSUU	INCONGRUOUS
CGINRRSTTUU	STRUCTURING
CHHIILOPTTY	LITHOPHYTIC
CHHIIMORSTY	ISORHYTHMIC
CHHIIMRTTYY	RHYTHMICITY
CHHILLMOOPY	HOMOPHYLLIC
CHHILMOOOPR	HOLOMORPHIC
CHHIMMOOOPR	HOMOMORPHIC
CHHIOORSTTY	ORTHOSTICHY

CHHLLLOOPRY	CHLOROPHYLL
CHIIILPSSTY	SYPHILITICS
CHIIIMORSST	HISTORICISM
CHIIINORSST	HISTRIONICS, TRICHINOSIS
CHIIIORSSTT	HISTORICIST
CHIIIORSTTY	HISTORICITY
CHIILLNOOTT	OCTILLIONTH
CHIILOOPRTT	PROTOLITHIC
CHIINNOPSSU	PINCUSHIONS
CHIINORRTTY	TYROTHRICIN
CHIIOOPRTTX	THIXOTROPIC
CHIIOPPRRTY	PORPHYRITIC
CHIIORRSSTY	SCIRRHOSITY
CHIIORSSTTU	TRISTICHOUS
CHIIOSSSTTY	SCHISTOSITY
CHILNOPSSSU	CONSULSHIPS
CHILOOPPRTY	POLYTROPHIC
CHILOORSTUU	ULOTRICHOUS
CHIMMNOOOPR	MONOMORPHIC
CHIMNNORSSY	SYNCHRONISM
CHIMNOOPRRS	PROCHRONISM
CHIOOOPPRTT	PHOTOTROPIC
CHIOOOPRRTT	ORTHOTROPIC
CHIOOPPRSTY	SPOROPHYTIC
CHIOOPPRTTY	TROPOPHYTIC
CHIOPSTTTUY	TOUCH-TYPIST
CHKOOOPRSST	SHOCK TROOPS
CHMNOOPSTTU	MUTTONCHOPS
CHMNOOPTTUU	NOT UP TO MUCH
CHMOOOPRSTY	PSYCHOMOTOR
CHNNOORRSTY	SYNCHROTRON
CHNNOORSSUY	SYNCHRONOUS
CIIILLMMNOR	MILLIMICRON
CIIILOPSSST	SOLIPSISTIC
CIIILRSTTUU	UTRICULITIS
CIIINNOPRST	INSCRIPTION
CIIINOOSTTY	ISOTONICITY
CIIINORSTUY	INCURIOSITY
CIIJNNNOSTU	INJUNCTIONS
CIILLOORSTT	TORTICOLLIS
CIILMMNNOOS	MONOCLINISM
CIILNOPSTUU	PUNCTILIOUS
CIIMMNNOOTU	COMMINUTION
CIIMMNOOSSS	COMMISSIONS
CIIMMOORSTT	MICROTOMIST
CIIMNOOOPST	COMPOSITION
CIIMOPRRSTU	SCRIPTORIUM
CIIMOPRSTUY	PROMISCUITY
CIINNORSTTU	INSTRUCTION
CIIOOPRSSUV	PISCIVOROUS
CILMNNOOOSU	MONOCLINOUS
CILMNOOPSSU	COMPULSIONS
CILNNOOOTUV	CONVOLUTION
CILNNOOSSUV	CONVULSIONS

CILNNOOSUUY	INNOCUOUSLY	DDEEGINNRSU	UNDERSIGNED
CIMNNOOOPPS	NINCOMPOOPS	DDEEGNOPRSU	GROUNDSPEED
CIMNNOOPSTU	CONSUMPTION	DDEEHIILRSS	DISRELISHED
CIMNOORSSTU	CONSORTIUMS	DDEEHHNNORSW	SEND HER DOWN
CIMNOPPSTUU	SUCTION PUMP	DDEEIILPPSS	SIDESLIPPED
CIMOOOPRSST	COMPOSITORS	DDEEIINRRST	DISINTERRED
CIMOOPRSSUU	PROMISCUOUS	DDEEIIQSTUU	DISQUIETUDE
CIMOPRSSTUU	SCRUMPTIOUS	DDEEIKNNRSS	KINDREDNESS
CINNOOORSTT	CONTORTIONS	DDEEILNOSTT	DOTTED LINES
CINOOPRRSTU	CORRUPTIONS	DDEEINNNPRU	UNDERPINNED
CINORRSSTTU	INSTRUCTORS	DDEEINORRRV	ORDER-DRIVEN
CIOPPRSSSTT	POSTSCRIPTS	DDEEINSSSTU	STUDIEDNESS
CIPPRRSSTUU	STIRRUP CUPS	DDEEIOPPRSS	PREDISPOSED
CIRRSSTTTUU	STRUCTURIST	DDEELLNORUW	WELL-ROUNDED
CLLNOOSUUVV	CONVOLVULUS	DDEENNNORSSU	ROUNDEDNESS
CMMMNOOOORS	COMMON ROOMS	DDEFFIILNTY	DIFFIDENTLY
CMMNNNOOOSU	COMMON NOUNS	DDEGGGILORS	GOLD DIGGERS
CNNOOSTTUWY	COUNTY TOWNS	DDEGGIINNRW	WEDDING RING
DDDEEFIOSST	EISTEDDFODS	DDEGHIIMNRT	RIGHT-MINDED
DDDEEIILMSS	MIDDLE-SISED	DDEGIILMSUY	MISGUIDEDLY
DDDEEIILMSZ	MIDDLE-SIZED	DDEGIINOORZ	DEODORIZING
DDDEELMNSSU	MUDDLEDNESS	DDEGIINORRS	DISORDERING
DDDEGILNORY	DODDERINGLY	DDEGILMNOST	DISLODGMENT
DDDENNOORTW	DOWNTRODDEN	DDEGILNRSTU	DISGRUNTLED
DDEEEEFIRRZ	FREEZE-DRIED	DDEGILSSTUY	DISGUSTEDLY
DDEEEEHNPRR	REPREHENDED	DDEGNNORRUU	UNDERGROUND
DDEEEELOPRV	REDEVELOPED	DDEHHIIOPRT	DIPHTHEROID
DDEEEFILLNW	WELL-DEFINED	DDEHIILNSSW	WINDSHIELDS
DDEEEFILSTT	FIELD-TESTED	DDEHINOORSU	DISHONOURED
DDEEEGHIRRT	THIRD-DEGREE	DDEHINORSTW	SHORT-WINDED
DDEEEGIPRST	PREDIGESTED	DDEHLMOOTUU	LOUDMOUTHED
DDEEEHILLSV	DISHEVELLED	DDEIIMNNOSU	DIMINUENDOS
DDEEEILNRSS	SLENDERISED	DDEILMNORTY	DIRTY OLD MEN
DDEEEILNRSZ	SLENDERIZED	DDEINNOOSTT	ENDODONTIST
DDEEEIMNOST	DEMONETISED	DDELNNOORRY	LONDONDERRY
DDEEEIMNOTZ	DEMONETIZED	DDGGGGIILNO	GOLD-DIGGING
DDEEEIMPRST	DISTEMPERED	DDGIILNOORS	SLIDING DOOR
DDEEEINNNPT	INDEPENDENT	DDGILMNPPUU	PLUM PUDDING
DDEEEINPRST	PREDESTINED	DDHOOOOSUWY	HOW DO YOU DOS
DDEEEIPPSST	SIDESTEPPED	DDIIKLNSTWY	TIDDLYWINKS
DDEEELLNOWW	WELL-ENDOWED	DDINOOOPRTT	DIPROTODONT
DDEEELNOPUV	UNDEVELOPED	DEEEEEFHLRW	FREEWHEELED
DDEEELNPRTY	PRETENDEDLY	DEEEEEFPRSZ	DEEP FREEZES
DDEEENOSSTV	DEVOTEDNESS	DEEEEHILRSW	SIDE-WHEELER
DDEEENNRRSU	SURRENDERED	DEEEEHNPRRR	REPREHENDER
DDEEEORRSSV	OVERDRESSED	DEEEELMNNOW	NEEDLEWOMEN
DDEEFFGLLLU	FULL-FLEDGED	DEEEELOPRRV	REDEVELOPER
DDEEFHILNOT	ON THE FIDDLE	DEEEEMOPRST	SPEEDOMETER
DDEEFIIIMNN	INDEMNIFIED	DEEEENPRRST	REPRESENTED
DDEEFIIIRSV	DIVERSIFIED	DEEEEQRSSTU	SEQUESTERED
DDEEFIIMNNU	DEFINIENDUM	DEEEFFGHIRT	FIFTH-DEGREE
DDEEFIIMSTY	DEMYSTIFIED	DEEEFFNOOST	TOFFEE-NOSED
DDEEFIORSST	DISFORESTED	DEEEFGIRRST	FIRST-DEGREE
DDEEFLLNOUW	WELL-FOUNDED	DEEEFHLNSSU	HEEDFULNESS

DEEEFHLORRS	FREEHOLDERS	DEEEMNNORST	ENDORSEMENT
DEEEFIILMPX	EXEMPLIFIED	DEEEMNNOSTU	DENOUEMENTS
DEEEFILNSTV	FIELD EVENTS, SELF-EVIDENT	DEEEMPRTTUW	TRUMPETWEED
DEEEFILNSVY	DEFENSIVELY	DEEEMRRSSSU	MURDERESSES
DEEEFIOPRRT	PROFITEERED	DEEENOPRSUX	UNDEREXPOSE
DEEEFLNNSSU	NEEDFULNESS	DEEENOPSSSX	EXPOSEDNESS
DEEEFMNRRSU	REFERENDUMS	DEEENPRSSUX	UNEXPRESSED
DEEEGGINNNR	ENGENDERING	DEEENRRRRSU	SURRENDERER
DEEEGHHOPPR	HEDGEHOPPER	DEEENRRSTTT	TRENDSETTER
DEEEGHILNNT	ENLIGHTENED	DEEEOOPRRVW	OVERPOWERED
DEEEGLORRSU	GUELDER-ROSE	DEEEOOPRSVX	OVEREXPOSED
DEEEHHPRSSS	SHEPHERDESS	DEEEOPPRSTV	OVERSTEPPED
DEEEHIINNPT	PHENETIDINE	DEEEOPRSSSS	REPOSSESSED
DEEEHILNPRS	REPLENISHED	DEEEOPRSTTY	STEREOTYPED
DEEEHIMRRSU	RUDESHEIMER	DEEEORRRTTV	RETROVERTED
DEEEHLMORVW	OVERWHELMED	DEEEORRTTVX	EXTROVERTED
DEEEHMOPRTT	HOT-TEMPERED	DEEEPRRSSST	PRESTRESSED
DEEEIIJORVV	JOIE DE VIVRE	DEEEPRRSSUU	SUPERSEDURE
DEEEIIMPRSS	EPIDERMISES	DEEFFIINNRT	INDIFFERENT
DEEEIINNPTX	INEXPEDIENT	DEEFFILNRTY	DIFFERENTLY
DEEEIINRTVW	INTERVIEWED	DEEFFINSSSU	DIFFUSENESS
DEEEIINSSST	DESENSITISE	DEEFFIOOPRR	FIREPROOFED
DEEEIINSSTZ	DESENSITIZE	DEEFFORSTUV	OVERSTUFFED
DEEEILLMPRT	ILL-TEMPERED	DEEFGHIORST	FORESIGHTED
DEEEILMMNPT	IMPLEMENTED	DEEFGIINNRX	INDEX FINGER
DEEEILMMNUV	MENDELEVIUM	DEEFGILNNSY	SELF-DENYING
DEEEILMNNST	ENLISTED MEN	DEEFGILNORW	DEFLOWERING
DEEEILMNRVY	DELIVERYMEN	DEEFGILNORST	DEFORESTING
DEEEILNNOPT	NEEDLEPOINT	DEEFHILLLOR	FIELD-HOLLER
DEEEILNPTXY	EXPEDIENTLY	DEEFIIIMNNR	INDEMNIFIER
DEEEILORSTU	DELETERIOUS	DEEFIIINNST	INTENSIFIED
DEEEIMNRRST	DETERMINERS	DEEFIIIRRSV	DIVERSIFIER
DEEEINPRRTT	INTERPRETED	DEEFIILMRSU	DEMULSIFIER
DEEEINPRTUX	EXPENDITURE	DEEFIILNRST	FRIENDLIEST
DEEEINRRSSV	VINEDRESSER	DEEFIIMORST	DEFORMITIES
DEEEINRSSTW	DESSERT WINE, WESTERNISED	DEEFIINOPRS	PERSONIFIED
DEEEINRSTWZ	WESTERNIZED	DEEFIINRSVW	VIEWFINDERS
DEEEIPPRSST	SIDESTEPPER	DEEFIKLORRW	FIELDWORKER
DEEEIRSSSTT	SIDE STREETS	DEEFILLRSSU	FLEURS-DE-LIS
DEEEJMPQUUU	QUEUE-JUMPED	DEEFILMNNRU	DUNFERMLINE
DEEEKOOPRRS	DOORKEEPERS	DEEFILMOPSS	SELF-IMPOSED
DEEELLNORSW	NE'ER-DO-WELLS	DEEFILORSTU	OUTFIELDERS
DEEELLNRRSU	UNDERSELLER	DEEFLLNOSSU	DOLEFULNESS
DEEELLPPRXY	PERPLEXEDLY	DEEFLOPRSSY	PROFESSEDLY
DEEELMNNORY	MONEYLENDER	DEEFNOORSTT	TENDERFOOTS
DEEELMNOPTV	DEVELOPMENT	DEEFNOPRSSU	UNPROFESSED
DEEELMNOTVV	DEVOLVEMENT	DEEGGINNOOV	GOOD EVENING
DEEELNNPRST	RESPLENDENT	DEEGHHINPRS	SHEPHERDING
DEEELNNRSSS	SLENDERNESS	DEEGHHINRST	RING THE SHED
DEEELNNSSSS	ENDLESSNESS	DEEGHHIOPRW	HIGH-POWERED
DEEELNORTUV	VOLUNTEERED	DEEGHILLNWY	WHEEDLINGLY
DEEELNRRTTU	UNDERLETTER	DEEGHILNOOP	PIGEONHOLED
DEEELOOPRVV	OVERDEVELOP	DEEGHIMNOOS	HOMOGENISED
DEEELPRRTVY	PERVERTEDLY	DEEGHIMNOOZ	HOMOGENIZED

DEEGHINORSY	HYDROGENISE
DEEGHINORYZ	HYDROGENIZE
DEEGHINRRRS	RED HERRINGS
DEEGHINRTUW	UNDERWEIGHT
DEEGHNORSTU	GROUNDSHEET
DEEGIIILMST	LEGITIMISED
DEEGIIILMTZ	LEGITIMIZED
DEEGIIINSTV	INDIGESTIVE
DEEGIIMNNOR	DOMINEERING
DEEGIIMNNRT	DETERMINING
DEEGIINNRST	INGREDIENTS
DEEGIINNRTZ	TENDERIZING
DEEGILLMNOR	REMODELLING
DEEGILNOPRY	REDEPLOYING
DEEGILNORUV	OVERINDULGE
DEEGILNRSVY	DESERVINGLY
DEEGILNRTVY	DIVERGENTLY
DEEGINPRSSU	SUPERSEDING
DEEGJMNPRTU	PREJUDGMENT
DEEGLLMOORW	WELL-GROOMED
DEEGLNORSSY	ENGROSSEDLY
DEEGLNOSSSS	GODLESSNESS
DEEHHLOORSU	HOUSEHOLDER
DEEHIIMPRSU	HESPERIDIUM
DEEHILLORTT	TITLEHOLDER
DEEHILMNOTU	ENDOTHELIUM
DEEHILOORST	THEODOLITES
DEEHILOSTTU	SILHOUETTED
DEEHIMOSTTW	WISDOM TEETH
DEEHINOSSSU	HIDEOUSNESS
DEEHINRRSSU	HURRIEDNESS
DEEHINSSSTY	SYNTHESISED
DEEHINSSTYZ	SYNTHESIZED
DEEHLOPRSTU	UPHOLSTERED
DEEHLOPSUUX	DUPLEX HOUSE
DEEHMNNOOOY	HONEYMOONED
DEEHMNOOPTU	OPEN-MOUTHED
DEEHMOORRTY	HYDROMETEOR
DEEHOORRSUV	HORS D'OEUVRE
DEEIIIMMNST	INDEMNITIES
DEEIIKLLMSS	SEMISKILLED
DEEIIKLNNRT	INTERLINKED
DEEIILLLRVY	LILY-LIVERED
DEEIILMNSSU	DISSEMINULE
DEEIILMPSST	SPEED LIMITS
DEEIILNOPRS	LEPIDOSIREN
DEEIILOPRSY	ERYSIPELOID
DEEIILPRRSV	PILE DRIVERS
DEEIIMMNPST	IMPEDIMENTS
DEEIIMMNRST	DETERMINISM
DEEIIMNOPTT	PIEDMONTITE
DEEIIMNPSST	DISSEPIMENT
DEEIIMNRRST	IRREDENTISM
DEEIIMNRSTT	DETERMINIST
DEEIINNRTTW	INTERTWINED
DEEIINNSSTT	DISSENTIENT
DEEIINOPSTX	EXPEDITIONS
DEEIINPRSTY	SERENDIPITY
DEEIINRRSTT	IRREDENTIST
DEEIINRSSTT	DISINTEREST
DEEIIOPSTUX	EXPEDITIOUS
DEEIIOQSSUX	SESQUIOXIDE
DEEIIRSTTUV	DIVESTITURE
DEEIKMNPPSU	PUMPKINSEED
DEEILMNOPST	DESPOILMENT
DEEILNNQSTU	DELINQUENTS
DEEILNORRSS	ORDERLINESS
DEEILNSSSTT	STILTEDNESS
DEEILOPPPTY	POLYPEPTIDE
DEEILORRSSW	WORLD SERIES
DEEILQRRRSU	RED SQUIRREL
DEEIMMNORTU	ENDOMETRIUM
DEEIMNNORUU	ENDONEURIUM
DEEIMNOSSTU	SEDIMENTOUS
DEEIMOOPRTT	DIOPTOMETER
DEEIMOPRRST	MISREPORTED
DEEIINNORST	NONRESIDENT
DEEINNOPSST	POINTEDNESS
DEEINNOSTTU	TENDENTIOUS
DEEINNPRSTU	SUPERINTEND
DEEINNSSTUW	UNWITNESSED
DEEINOPRSSS	DEPRESSIONS
DEEINOQRTUV	QUOTE-DRIVEN
DEEINORRRVW	OWNER-DRIVER
DEEINORRTTV	INTROVERTED
DEEINORSSUW	SERIES-WOUND
DEEINOSSSTU	TEDIOUSNESS
DEEINOSSSUV	DEVIOUSNESS
DEEINPRRTTU	INTERRUPTED
DEEINRRRTUW	UNDERWRITER
DEEIPRRSSSU	PRESSURISED
DEEIPRRSSUZ	PRESSURIZED
DEEKLMRSTTU	KETTLEDRUMS
DEEKNNNRSSU	DRUNKENNESS
DEELMMNOPSU	NOMS DE PLUME
DEELMNOOTTU	TOUT LE MONDE
DEELMNORTTY	TORMENTEDLY
DEELORSTTUV	TURTLEDOVES
DEELORSTUXY	DEXTEROUSLY
DEEMNOORRSY	MONEY ORDERS
DEENNOPRSST	RESPONDENTS
DEENNORSSVW	NEWSVENDORS
DEENNPRSSTU	PRUDENTNESS
DEENNSSSTTU	STUNTEDNESS
DEEOPPPRSSU	PRESUPPOSED
DEFFIINORSU	REDIFFUSION
DEFFILLLNUU	UNFULFILLED
DEFFOPPRSUW	POWDER PUFFS

DEFGGIILNTY	FIDGETINGLY
DEFGGLOOOST	FOOTSLOGGED
DEFGHIISTTT	TIGHTFISTED
DEFGHILOOTT	LIGHT-FOOTED
DEFGIIINNTY	IDENTIFYING
DEFGIILNNSW	SELF-WINDING
DEFGIILNPRS	SPRINGFIELD
DEFGIILNRRS	GIRLFRIENDS
DEFGILNNORU	FLOUNDERING
DEFGJMNORTU	FORJUDGMENT
DEFGNOORRSU	FOREGROUNDS
DEFHHLOORTT	HOLD THE FORT
DEFHIIIMRSU	HUMIDIFIERS
DEFHIINPRSS	FRIENDSHIPS
DEFHINPRSTT	SPENDTHRIFT
DEFHIOORRSX	OXFORDSHIRE
DEFHIORSSSW	SWORDFISHES
DEFHLLMOTUU	FULL-MOUTHED
DEFHLMOORTU	FOUL-MOUTHED
DEFHLNOSSUW	FLESH WOUNDS
DEFHMOOOPRT	MOTHPROOFED
DEFIIINNOST	DEFINITIONS
DEFIIJNSTUU	UNJUSTIFIED
DEFIILMSTYY	MYSTIFIEDLY
DEFIIMMNORS	MISINFORMED
DEFIIMORRSV	DIVERSIFORM
DEFIINNNPSY	SPINY-FINNED
DEFIINORRRU	FOURDRINIER
DEFILMNNSSU	MINDFULNESS
DEFILNSSTUU	DUTIFULNESS
DEFILRSSSTU	DISTRESSFUL
DEFINRRSSUW	WIND-SURFERS
DEFIOOORRSU	ODORIFEROUS
DEFKLNOOORU	UNLOOKED-FOR
DEFLLNORUWY	WONDERFULLY
DEFOOPRRSTU	RUSTPROOFED
DEFOOPSSTUY	PUSSYFOOTED
DEGGHHHIILT	HIGHLIGHTED
DEGGHILNOST	LONGSIGHTED
DEGGIINNNSU	UNDESIGNING
DEGGILOOPRS	SLOOP-RIGGED
DEGGKLRSUUY	SKULDUGGERY
DEGHIIINRTV	DIVINE RIGHT
DEGHIILMNOS	DEMOLISHING
DEGHIILNNRY	HINDERINGLY
DEGHIILPPTT	TIGHT-LIPPED
DEGHILNORSU	SHOULDERING
DEGHINNORSU	ENSHROUDING
DEGHINOORTU	OUT-HERODING
DEGHINOPSTT	POTTING SHED
DEGHLMOOOTY	METHODOLOGY
DEGHNOORSUY	HYDROGENOUS
DEGHNOORXYY	OXYHYDROGEN
DEGHNORRTUW	UNDERGROWTH
DEGIIIINNST	INDIGNITIES
DEGIIINNOST	INDIGESTION
DEGIIINPSSW	SIDESWIPING
DEGIIINQSTU	DISQUIETING
DEGIIKNRSTW	WRITING DESK
DEGIILLMRSX	MIXED GRILLS
DEGIILLNOTU	GUILLOTINED
DEGIIILNNNRU	UNDERLINING
DEGIILNOTTU	DEGLUTITION
DEGIILNRTVY	DIVERTINGLY
DEGIIMNNNRU	UNDERMINING
DEGIIMNNORZ	MODERNIZING
DEGIIMNNPSS	MISSPENDING
DEGIINNNRTU	INDENTURING
DEGIINORSSS	DIGRESSIONS
DEGIINPRSST	SPRING TIDES
DEGIINRSSST	DISTRESSING
DEGIJMMNSTU	MISJUDGMENT
DEGILLNNTUY	INDULGENTLY
DEGILLNOPRY	DEPLORINGLY
DEGILMNORSU	SMOULDERING
DEGILNNORWY	WONDERINGLY
DEGILNNOSSU	UNGODLINESS
DEGILNORUVY	DEVOURINGLY
DEGILOOPRTY	PTERIDOLOGY
DEGINNORSST	GRINDSTONES
DEGINOPRSST	TOPDRESSING
DEGKLOOOORS	GOOD LOOKERS
DEGKOPRRRSU	KRUGERSDORP
DEGLLNORSUW	GROUNDSWELL
DEGLMOOORST	MOTOR LODGES
DEGLNOOOPTT	GOLDEN POTTO
DEGLNOPRSUY	GOLDEN SYRUP
DEGLNORRSUU	GROUND RULES
DEGLOORSTTY	TROGLODYTES
DEGNNOORSTU	STONE-GROUND
DEGNNORRSTU	GROUND RENTS
DEHHIILMNOT	HELMINTHOID
DEHHILMOORS	HOLOHEDRISM
DEHHILNOOSW	HINSHELWOOD
DEHHIMOORRS	HEMORRHOIDS
DEHHLNOSTUU	SLEUTHHOUND
DEHIIINOTTT	INDO-HITTITE
DEHIIKNNNST	THIN-SKINNED
DEHIILLOOSV	LIVELIHOODS
DEHIILMNPSU	DELPHINIUMS
DEHIILPRSTU	TRISULPHIDE
DEHIINSTTUW	WHITSUNTIDE
DEHIIRSSTVW	WHIST DRIVES
DEHILNOSSTY	DISHONESTLY
DEHILNOSTTW	THISTLEDOWN
DEHILOPSUXY	OXYSULPHIDE
DEHILORSSTT	SHORT-LISTED
DEHINOORRSU	DISHONOURER

DEHINOPPRST	THIRD PERSON
DEHINPRSSSU	PRUDISHNESS
DEHINPSSTTU	STUDENTSHIP
DEHINRRSSTU	UNDERSHIRTS
DEHIOOOPPRT	PHOTOPERIOD
DEHIOORSSST	SISTERHOODS
DEHLLOOSSSU	DOLL'S HOUSES
DEHLNNOOOSW	HOLD ONE'S OWN
DEHMMNNRSSU	HUMDRUMNESS
DEHMMORSTUW	MUM'S THE WORD
DEHMOOPPRSU	PSEUDOMORPH
DEHNOOOOPRT	ODONTOPHORE
DEHNRRSTTUU	UNDERTHRUST
DEHOOOPRTTW	TOOTH POWDER
DEIIILLSSUV	DISILLUSIVE
DEIIILQRSSU	LIQUIDISERS
DEIIILQRSUZ	LIQUIDIZERS
DEIIIMNORSS	MINOR DIESIS
DEIIIMNSTUV	DIMINUTIVES
DEIIINPRTTY	INTREPIDITY
DEIIIOPRRST	PRIORITISED
DEIIIOPRRTZ	PRIORITIZED
DEIIIPSSTTU	STUPIDITIES
DEIIKKLMMMS	SKIMMED MILK
DEIILLORSUY	DELIRIOUSLY
DEIILMNOOST	DEMOLITIONS
DEIILMPRSTW	LIMP-WRISTED
DEIILNOORWW	ORIEL WINDOW
DEIILNOPRRY	PYRROLIDINE
DEIILOPRSTW	LOW-SPIRITED
DEIILOSSTUV	DISSOLUTIVE
DEIILOSSTUY	SEDITIOUSLY
DEIIMNOPRTV	IMPROVIDENT
DEIIMOORRST	DORMITORIES
DEIIMORSSTU	MOISTURISED
DEIIMORSTUZ	MOISTURIZED
DEIIMQRTTUU	TERTIUM QUID
DEIIINNNOOTW	DOWN IT IN ONE
DEIINNOSSSS	DISSENSIONS
DEIINOOPRSV	PROVISIONED
DEIINOOPSST	DEPOSITIONS
DEIINORSTTU	ROTUNDITIES
DEIINOSSSTU	DISSENTIOUS
DEIINOSTTTU	DESTITUTION
DEIILLMOOSUY	MELODIOUSLY
DEIILLNORSSW	WORLDLINESS
DEIILLORSTUY	DESULTORILY
DEIILLORSWWY	WORLDLY-WISE
DEIILLOSSTUY	DISSOLUTELY
DEIILMNOOOPS	MONOPOLISED
DEIILMNOOOPZ	MONOPOLIZED
DEIILMNPRTUY	IMPRUDENTLY
DEIILMOORRTY	DOLORIMETRY
DEIILNNNSTUW	WIND TUNNELS
DEIILNOPRTVY	PROVIDENTLY
DEIILPRRSSUY	SURPRISEDLY
DEIIMMRSSTYY	DISSYMMETRY
DEIIMNOSSSSY	SYNDESMOSIS
DEIIMOOPRTTY	DIOPTOMETRY
DEIIMOPPRTTU	PROMPTITUDE
DEIINNPSSUUY	SUNNY-SIDE UP
DEIINOORSSWW	ROSE WINDOWS
DEIIOPPRSTTU	OUTSTRIPPED
DEIIOPRSTTTU	PROSTITUTED
DEIKLLOOPRST	ROLLTOP DESK
DEIKNOORRSWW	WORK WONDERS
DEILLNOPSUUY	PENDULOUSLY
DEILLNOSSSUY	SOUNDLESSLY
DEILMORRSUUY	MURDEROUSLY
DEILNOOPRSSU	SPLENDOROUS
DEILNOOPRSUY	PONDEROUSLY
DEILOOPRRSWW	WORLD POWERS
DEMOOOPRRSW	POWDER ROOMS
DENNOOOOPSW	WOODEN SPOON
DENOOOPRSSU	ENDOSPOROUS
DENOOORSSSU	ODOROUSNESS
DEOOOPPRRST	DOORSTOPPER
DFFIIISTUVY	DIFFUSIVITY
DFGGIIINRSU	DISFIGURING
DFGHIIIMNUY	HUMIDIFYING
DFGHILLOOST	FLOODLIGHTS
DFGIIILNOSY	SOLIDIFYING
DFGIIKNNNSU	SINKING FUND
DFGIILLNOWW	WILDFOWLING
DFGIIINNRSUW	WIND-SURFING
DFGLNOOOORRU	GROUND FLOOR
DFIKLOPPSSY	FLOPPY DISKS
DFILRSSTTUU	DISTRUSTFUL
DGGIIILLNRR	DRILLING RIG
DGGIIILLNNUY	INDULGINGLY
DGGIIILMNNSU	MUDSLINGING
DGGIIKLNOOOO	GOOD-LOOKING
DGGIILNNORSU	GROUNDLINGS
DGGIIMNNOOOR	GOOD MORNING
DGGIINNOORSW	WRONGDOINGS
DGHHHIIOOPTU	UP TO HIGH DOH
DGHHIILLNOTW	WITHHOLDING
DGHHIKNOOST	KNIGHTHOODS
DGHIIIIMNNS	DIMINISHING
DGHIIINNSSTU	DISTINGUISH
DGHIIKNNOOW	HOODWINKING
DGHIIMNNSTU	MIDNIGHT SUN
DGHILOORSTY	HYDROLOGIST
DGHLNOORSST	STRONGHOLDS
DGHLNOORUUY	UNGODLY HOUR
DGIIIILNOQUZ	LIQUIDIZING
DGIIIINPRST	DISPIRITING
DGIILLNNSWY	SWINDLINGLY

DGIILNNRTUY	INTRUDINGLY	EEEFHILRRSW	FERRIS WHEEL
DGIIMNNOORS	DINING ROOMS	EEEFHMNNRST	REFRESHMENT
DGIIMNNOSTU	DISMOUNTING	EEEFHOORRTT	THERETOFORE
DGIINRSSTTU	DISTRUSTING	EEEFIILMPRX	EXEMPLIFIER
DGIKNOOORWW	WOODWORKING	EEEFILSSSTT	TSETSE FLIES
DGINNOOPPRU	PROPOUNDING	EEEFILSTTZZ	TZETZE FLIES
DGINNORRSUU	SURROUNDING	EEEFIMMRRSW	FREE-SWIMMER
DHHMNOOOSTU	SMOOTH HOUND	EEEFIMNNRST	REFINEMENTS
DHIIIORSTTY	THYROIDITIS	EEEFLLORVWY	YELLOW FEVER
DHILLNOOPPY	PODOPHYLLIN	EEEFMOORRRV	FOR EVERMORE
DHIMOOOSTTW	WISDOM TOOTH	EEEFNNRSSTV	FERVENTNESS
DHIOOOPRSUZ	RHIZOPODOUS	EEEGGHORTTT	GET-TOGETHER
DHLOOPRXYYY	POLYHYDROXY	EEEGGIINNNR	ENGINEERING
DHMNOOORXYY	MONOHYDROXY	EEEGGIINNRV	VEREENIGING
DIIIIMNOSSV	DIVISIONISM	EEEGGMNNORT	ENGORGEMENT
DIIIINOSSTV	DIVISIONIST	EEEGHHINSTT	EIGHTEENTHS
DIIILLNOSSU	DISILLUSION	EEEGHILNNRT	ENLIGHTENER
DIIILNOSSUY	INSIDIOUSLY	EEEGHNORSSU	GREENHOUSES
DIIILNOSUVY	INVIDIOUSLY	EEEGIINPSST	EPIGENESIST
DIIIMNNOSTU	DIMINUTIONS	EEEGILLLNST	TELESELLING
DIIINOOPSST	DISPOSITION	EEEGINNNSSU	GENUINENESS
DIILLNOSSWW	WINDOWSILLS	EEEGINNORVW	OVERWEENING
DIILNOOSSTU	DISSOLUTION	EEEGINNOSSX	XENOGENESIS
DIILNOPSSTY	SPONDYLITIS	EEEGINNRRTW	WINTERGREEN
DIINOORSSTT	DISTORTIONS	EEEGINPRRSV	PERSEVERING
DIINOPRSSTU	DISRUPTIONS	EEEGLMNNOTW	GENTLEWOMEN
DIINORSSTUU	INDUSTRIOUS	EEEGLNOORVY	VENEREOLOGY
DILMOOPSTUY	STYLOPODIUM	EEEGLNOPRRV	GREEN PLOVER
DIOOPQQRSUU	QUID PRO QUOS	EEEGNORSSSV	GOVERNESSES
DLOOOPRRSTV	LORD PROVOST	EEEHHILLLNP	PHILHELLENE
EEEEFKLRSSS	SELF-SEEKERS	EEEHHILPPTW	HEPPLEWHITE
EEEEFLRSTTT	FLEET STREET	EEEHHIMPRSS	HEMISPHERES
EEEEGLNNSST	GENTEELNESS	EEEHHLOSSUW	WHEELHOUSES
EEEEGNPPPRR	GREEN PEPPER	EEEHHOPRTTY	HETEROPHYTE
EEEEHIMNPRT	HEMITERPENE	EEEHIILNNPT	NEPHELINITE
EEEEHKOPRSU	HOUSEKEEPER	EEEHIIPPRRS	PERIPHERIES
EEEEHNNSTTV	SEVENTEENTH	EEEHILNPRRS	REPLENISHER
EEEEHORRSVW	WHERESOEVER	EEEHILRSSTV	SHIRTSLEEVE
EEEEIINRTVW	INTERVIEWEE	EEEHIMNRSST	SMITHEREENS
EEEEIKMPRST	TIMEKEEPERS	EEEHINNNSTT	NINETEENTHS
EEEEIMNPRSW	MINESWEEPER	EEEHINPSSSV	PEEVISHNESS
EEEEKOPRRST	STOREKEEPER	EEEHINSSTTV	SEVENTIETHS
EEEELNPRSST	REPLETENESS	EEEHIPPPRTW	WHITE PEPPER
EEEELRRSTTT	TRESTLETREE	EEEHKOPPRSS	SHOPKEEPERS
EEEEMNRSSTX	EXTREMENESS	EEEHLNNOSST	NONETHELESS
EEEENNRRSVV	NEVER-NEVERS	EEEHMMORRTT	THERMOMETER
EEEEPPPRSTW	SWEET PEPPER	EEEHMNOQRTU	QUEEN MOTHER
EEEFFHILRTW	WHIFFLETREE	EEEHMOPRRST	SPHEROMETER
EEEFFILORTW	EIFFEL TOWER	EEEIIKLNSST	TELEKINESIS
EEEFGIINNRS	FIRE ENGINES	EEEIIMRSTTX	EXTREMITIES
EEEFGIKLNSS	SELF-SEEKING	EEEIINNPSVX	INEXPENSIVE
EEEFGLLNSSU	GLEEFULNESS	EEEIINRRTTV	IRRETENTIVE
EEEFHIKNRRT	FREETHINKER	EEEIINRRTVW	INTERVIEWER
EEEFHILNSSY	FISHEYE LENS	EEEIIORRSTX	EXTERIORISE

EEEIIORRTXZ	EXTERIORIZE
EEEIIPRRTTV	PRETERITIVE
EEEIKLNOSST	SKELETONISE
EEEIKLNOSTZ	SKELETONIZE
EEEILMMNPRT	IMPLEMENTER
EEEILMNNNTV	ENLIVENMENT
EEEILMNNTTT	ENTITLEMENT
EEEILNNQSSU	QUEENLINESS
EEEILNPRRTT	TELEPRINTER
EEEILNPSVXY	EXPENSIVELY
EEEILNRTTVY	RETENTIVELY
EEEILNSSSUV	ELUSIVENESS
EEEILNSTVXY	EXTENSIVELY
EEEIMNNNTTW	ENTWINEMENT
EEEIMNORSTT	TENSIOMETER
EEEIMNOSSTV	EMOTIVENESS
EEEIMNPRSTX	EXPERIMENTS
EEEIMNQRRTU	REQUIREMENT
EEEIMNQRTTU	REQUITEMENT
EEEIMNRRSTT	RETIREMENTS
EEEIMOPRSTX	EXTEMPORISE
EEEIMOPRTXZ	EXTEMPORIZE
EEEIMRRSSTV	TIMESERVERS
EEEINNPRSTT	PRESENTIENT
EEEINNPSSSV	PENSIVENESS
EEEINORRRSV	REVERSIONER
EEEINORSSSV	EROSIVENESS
EEEINPRRRST	ENTERPRISER
EEEINPRRRTT	INTERPRETER
EEEINPRRSST	ENTERPRISES, INTERSPERSE
EEEINPRSTTX	PRE-EXISTENT
EEEINPRSTVV	PREVENTIVES
EEEINRSSSTV	RESTIVENESS
EEEIOPRRRST	REPERTOIRES, REPERTORIES
EEEJMPQRUUU	QUEUE-JUMPER
EEEKKLNOSTY	SKELETON KEY
EEEKLNOOSTX	EXOSKELETON
EEEKLORRSTW	STEELWORKER
EEELLLPSSSY	SLEEPLESSLY
EEELLNRSSVY	NERVELESSLY
EEELLNSSSSY	SENSELESSLY
EEELMNNOPTV	ENVELOPMENT
EEELMNSSTTT	SETTLEMENTS
EEELMOOPPRV	PEOPLE MOVER
EEELMORRSSS	REMORSELESS
EEELNNOOPPS	PELOPONNESE
EEELNOPRSTT	OPEN LETTERS
EEELNRSSTTW	NEWSLETTERS
EEELNSSSSSU	USELESSNESS
EEELNSSSSSX	SEXLESSNESS
EEELPRRSSTT	LETTERPRESS
EEEMMNOPRTW	EMPOWERMENT
EEEMMNNOOPRT	MONOTERPENE
EEEMNNPRSTT	PRESENTMENT
EEEMNORSTUV	VENTURESOME
EEEMNPRSSSU	SUPREMENESS
EEEMORRSTTY	STEREOMETRY
EEEMPRSSSTT	TEMPTRESSES
EEEOPRRSTTY	STEREOTYPER
EEEOPRSSTTY	STEREOTYPES
EEEPRSSTTTY	TYPESETTERS
EEFFGHIIRRT	FIRE FIGHTER
EEFFGILNRSU	GLUE-SNIFFER
EEFFGINORRS	FOREFINGERS
EEFFHLNSSTU	THE SNUFFLES
EEFFIILLORY	LIFE OF RILEY
EEFFIILMOPR	PRIME OF LIFE
EEFFIINNOSV	INOFFENSIVE
EEFFILNOSVY	OFFENSIVELY
EEFFIOORRST	OFFERTORIES
EEFFIORRRSU	FERRIFEROUS
EEFFLNRSSTU	FRETFULLNESS
EEFGGIOPRTT	PETTIFOGGER
EEFGHIILRRT	FIRELIGHTER
EEFGIINNRRT	INTERFERING
EEFGILLNORT	FORETELLING
EEFGILNRSTW	LEFT-WINGERS
EEFGINNQRTU	FREQUENTING
EEFGINORRST	REFORESTING
EEFGINORSSV	FORGIVENESS
EEFGLLRRTUY	REGRETFULLY
EEFGMNOORTT	FORGET-ME-NOT
EEFHIJLLSSY	JELLYFISHES
EEFHILLNSSS	FLESHLINESS
EEFHILNSSSS	SELFISHNESS
EEFHILOSUWY	HOUSEWIFELY
EEFHIORSUWY	HOUSEWIFERY
EEFHLLNPSSU	HELPFULLNESS
EEFHLNOPSSU	HOPEFULLNESS
EEFHMORRRTU	FURTHERMORE
EEFHNOORRST	FORESHORTEN
EEFHNORSTTU	FOURTEENTHS
EEFHOORRSTW	FOR THE WORSE
EEFIIINNRST	INTENSIFIER
EEFIILORSST	LIFE STORIES
EEFIILRRSST	FERTILISERS
EEFIILRRSTZ	FERTILIZERS
EEFIKLLNOWY	YELLOWKNIFE
EEFILLLMRSU	MILLEFLEURS
EEFILLMORSU	MELLIFEROUS
EEFILNORSSW	FLOWERINESS
EEFILNPPSTT	FELT-TIP PENS
EEFILOOPRRT	PROFITEROLE
EEFILOOORSST	LOOSESTRIFE
EEFINRSSTUV	FURTIVENESS
EEFIOPRSSTU	PESTIFEROUS
EEFIORRRSTX	FOX TERRIERS
EEFLLNRSTUY	RESENTFULLY

EEFLMNOSSSU	FULSOMENESS	EEGILLMOOST	TELEOLOGISM
EEFLMOORRTU	FLUOROMETER	EEGILLNORSV	OVERSELLING
EEFLNNSSTUU	TUNEFULNESS	EEGILLOOSTT	TELEOLOGIST
EEFLNPSSSUU	SUSPENSEFUL	EEGILMOOSTY	ETYMOLOGIES
EEFLNRSSSTU	RESTFULNESS	EEGILNNNRTU	UNRELENTING
EEFLNSSSTUZ	ZESTFULNESS	EEGILNOPSSY	POLYGENESIS
EEFMOOPRTTU	OUT OF TEMPER	EEGILNPRSTY	PESTERINGLY
EEFNNORRRSU	FORERUNNERS	EEGILOPRSTT	POLTERGEIST
EEFNOPRSSSU	PROFUSENESS	EEGIMNNOOSS	MONOGENESIS
EEGGHHIINNT	HEIGHTENING	EEGIMNNORSU	MONSEIGNEUR
EEGGHIINSST	SIGHTSEEING	EEGIMNNRRTU	INTERREGNUM
EEGGHILNNNT	LENGTHENING	EEGIMNNSTTU	INTEGUMENTS
EEGGIIMNNRT	REGIMENTING	EEGIMNOPPST	PEEPING TOMS
EEGGIINNPRW	WINNIPEGGER	EEGIMNOSSYZ	ZYMOGENESIS
EEGGIINRRST	REGISTERING	EEGINNPRSUV	SUPERVENING
EEGGILLNNTY	NEGLIGENTLY	EEGINORRSTU	TERRIGENOUS
EEGGILNNRVY	REVENGINGLY	EEGINORSTVY	SOVEREIGNTY
EEGGILORSUY	EGREGIOUSLY	EEGINPRSTTU	GUTTERSNIPE
EEGHHHLOOTW	THE WHOLE HOG	EEGIOPRRSSV	PROGRESSIVE
EEGHHILRTWW	WHEELWRIGHT	EEGKLLMNSUU	MUSKELLUNGE
EEGHIINSSTW	WEIGHTINESS	EEGKORRSTUW	GUEST WORKER
EEGHILNNOPT	TELEPHONING	EEGLMOOORTY	METEOROLOGY
EEGHILNNSST	LENGTHINESS	EEGLNSSSSTU	GUTLESSNESS
EEGHILNOOPS	PIGEONHOLES	EEGLOPPPTUU	GLOVE PUPPET
EEGHILOORST	THEOLOGISER	EEGLOQRSTUY	GROTESQUELY
EEGHILOORTZ	THEOLOGIZER	EEGMNNORSST	ENGROSSMENT
EEGHILRSTTT	STREETLIGHT	EEGMNNORSTV	GOVERNMENTS
EEGHIMNOORS	HOMOGENISER	EEGNNOSTTXY	OXYGEN TENTS
EEGHIMNOORZ	HOMOGENIZER	EEGOQRRSTUY	GROTESQUERY
EEGHIMNOOTY	HOMOGENEITY	EEGPRRSSTTU	GUTTER PRESS
EEGHIMOORST	ISOGEOTHERM	EEHHIKLOTTW	THE WHOLE KIT
EEGHINNOSTT	ETHNOGENIST	EEHHILLNSSS	HELLISHNESS
EEGHINNPTWY	PENNYWEIGHT	EEHHILMPSTT	PITH HELMETS
EEGHINOORTV	IN THE GROOVE	EEHHILOPRST	LITHOSPHERE
EEGHLOOPRTY	HERPETOLOGY	EEHHINRSTTT	THIRTEENTHS
EEGHMNOOOSU	HOMOGENEOUS	EEHHIOPRRSZ	RHIZOSPHERE
EEGHOSSSTUU	GUESTHOUSES	EEHHIORRSSS	SHIRE HORSES
EEGIILLNNTT	INTELLIGENT	EEHHIORSSTW	WHITE HORSES
EEGIILMNNRT	INTERMINGLE	EEHHMOORSTU	HOUSEMOTHER
EEGIIMMNNPT	IMPINGEMENT	EEHHMOPRTUV	OVER THE HUMP
EEGIIMMNRSZ	MESMERIZING	EEHHNOOPRTY	HETEROPHONY
EEGIIMNNOPT	OPENING TIME	EEHHNOORRTW	WHETHER OR NO
EEGIIMNRSTV	TIMESERVING	EEHHOOPPRST	PHOTOSPHERE
EEGIINNNRTV	INTERVENING	EEHHOORSSUW	WHOREHOUSES
EEGIINNORST	NITROGENISE	EEHIIKNPSTY	PIE IN THE SKY
EEGIINNORTZ	NITROGENIZE	EEHIILNOPRS	PERIHELIONS
EEGIINNRSTT	INTERESTING	EEHIIMNRSTT	THEREMINIST
EEGIINNRTTW	WIRE NETTING	EEHIIMPPRRS	PREMIERSHIP
EEGIINOPRTV	PROGENITIVE	EEHILLRSSWW	WELL-WISHERS
EEGIINPRSTX	PRE-EXISTING	EEHILMMOSTU	MESOTHELIUM
EEGIKKNORWW	WORKING WEEK	EEHILMNORTY	HEMIELYTRON
EEGIKLNORTW	TELEWORKING	EEHILMOORTT	LITHOMETEOR
EEGILLLNPRY	REPELLINGLY	EEHILMOPPRS	SPERMOPHILE
EEGILLLSSUY	GUILELESSLY	EEHILNOPRRT	LEPTORRHINE

EEHILNOPSTT	TELEPHONIST	EEIILNSSTVY	SENSITIVELY
EEHILOOPRST	HELIOTROPES	EEIILPRSSTT	PRIESTLIEST
EEHILORSSSY	HETEROLYSIS	EEIILQSTUXY	EXQUISITELY
EEHILOSSTTU	SILHOUETTES	EEIILRRSSST	STERILISERS
EEHIMOPPRRS	EMPERORSHIP	EEIILRRSSTZ	STERILIZERS
EEHIMOPRSTU	HEMIPTEROUS	EEIIMNNPRTT	IMPERTINENT
EEHINNORSST	RHINESTONES	EEIIMNOSSTT	TESTIMONIES
EEHINNOSSSU	HEINOUSNESS	EEIIMNPRRUU	PERINEURIUM
EEHINPSSSST	PETTISHNESS	EEIINNNNSTY	NINETY-NINES
EEHINRSSSTU	HIRSUTENESS	EEIINNNOSTT	NONENTITIES
EEHINRSSSTY	SYNTHESISER	EEIINNOOPRT	POINTE-NOIRE
EEHINRSSTYZ	SYNTHESIZER	EEIINNORSTV	INVENTORIES
EEHIPRSSTTU	TRUSTEESHIP	EEIINOPRRTT	PRETERITION
		EEIINOPRSTT	PETITIONERS, REPETITIONS
EEHKNOORSTT	TENTERHOOKS	EEIINRSTTUV	INVESTITURE
EEHKNOSTUVY	YEVTUSHENKO	EEIINRTTTVY	RETENTIVITY
EEHKOORRSUW	HOUSEWORKER	EEIIOPPRRST	PROPRIETIES
EEHLMNOOSUW	UNWHOLESOME	EEIIOPPRSTV	PREPOSITIVE
EEHLMNOTTVW	TWELVEMONTH	EEIIOPRSSTT	POSTERITIES
EEHLOPORRSTU	REUPHOLSTER, UPHOLSTERER	EEIIOPRSTTU	REPETITIOUS
EEHLORSTTYY	HETEROSTYLY	EEIIORRRSTT	TERRITORIES
EEHMMORRTTY	THERMOMETRY	EEIIORRSSST	ROTISSERIES
EEHMMORSSUU	SUMMERHOUSE	EEIIPORSSTU	PERQUISITES
EEHMNNOOORY	HONEYMOONER	EEIIRSTTTUV	RESTITUTIVE
EEHMNOOORTV	OVER THE MOON	EEIKNRRSSTT	RENT STRIKES
EEHMNOOPRSS	MESONEPHROS	EEILLMNOPRT	MONTPELLIER
EEHNNORRRST	NORTHERNERS	EEILLMOOPRT	TROMPE L'OEIL
EEHNNORSSTT	HORNET'S NEST	EEILLMPPPRS	PEPPER MILLS
EEHNOOOPRSZ	OZONOSPHERE	EEILLMPRTUX	MULTIPLEXER
EEHNORRSSTU	SOUTHERNERS	EEILLNOPQTU	EQUIPOLLENT
EEHNORRSTTW	NORTHWESTER	EEILLNOSSSY	NOISELESSLY
EEHOOPPRRST	TROPOSPHERE	EEILLNPSSSY	SPINELESSLY
EEHOOPRRSTU	PORTERHOUSE	EEILLOPSVXY	EXPLOSIVELY
EEHOOPRRSTY	HETEROSPORY	EEILLPRSUVY	REPULSIVELY
EEHOOPRSSUW	POWERHOUSES	EEILMNNOTVV	INVOLVEMENT
EEHOOPRSTTT	PHOTOSETTER	EEILMNNSSTT	ENLISTMENTS
EEHOORSSSTU	STOREHOUSES	EEILMNOOSST	EMOTIONLESS
EEHORSSTTUW	SOUTHWESTER	EEILMOPRTUV	PLUVIOMETER
EEIIIMNNSTU	EINSTEINIUM	EEILNNPRTTY	PERTINENTLY
EEIIINNSSTV	INSENSITIVE	EEILNSSSSSS	SINLESSNESS
EEIIINSTTVV	INVESTITIVE	EEILNOPRRST	INTERLOPERS
EEIIKLLNNNS	ENNISKILLEN	EEILNSSSSTW	WITLESSNESS
EEIIKLNPRSW	PERIWINKLES	EEILOPRSSTY	PROSELYTISE
EEIILLMMRST	MILLIMETRES	EEILOPRSTYZ	PROSELYTIZE
EEIILLNRSTY	RESILIENTLY	EEIMMNOPRTV	IMPROVEMENT
EEIILLNRTUV	TIRUNELVELI	EEIMMNPRSST	IMPRESSMENT
EEIILLPPRST	PIPISTRELLE	EEIMMNRSSSU	SUMMERINESS
EEIILLPRSTV	SPIRIT LEVEL	EEIMMOPRRSS	PRIME MOVERS
EEIILMNOSST	SOLEMNITIES	EEIMNNNORTV	ENVIRONMENT
EEIILMNRSSS	MISERLINESS	EEIMNNNRSTT	INTERNMENTS
EEIILNNPRRT	LINE PRINTER	EEIMNNOOSSS	NOISOMENESS
EEIILNNSTVY	INTENSIVELY	EEIMNNOPRST	OMNIPRESENT
EEIILNNTVVY	INVENTIVELY	EEIMNNORSSV	MONS VENERIS
EEIILNOSSTV	TELEVISIONS	EEIMNNOSSSW	WINSOMENESS
EEIILNRSSSV	SILVERINESS		

EEIMNNSSTTV	INVESTMENTS
EEIMNOPRSTU	PERITONEUMS
EEIMNORSTZZ	INTERMEZZOS
EEIMNPPPRST	PEPPERMINTS
EEIMNPPRTUU	IN PERPETUUM
EEIMNRSSTTW	WESTMINSTER
EEIMOPPRSSU	SUPERIMPOSE
EEIMPPRSTUV	PRESUMPTIVE
EEINNNORRTU	INTERNEURON
EEINNNOSTTX	NONEXISTENT
EEINNOPRSST	PRETENSIONS
EEINNOSSSUV	ENVIOUSNESS
EEINNOSSTTU	SENTENTIOUS
EEINOPRRSSS	REPRESSIONS
EEINOPRRSSV	PERVERSIONS
EEINOPRRSSX	EXPRESSIONS
EEINOPRSTTU	PRETENTIOUS
EEINOPSSSTU	PITEOUSNESS
EEINOQRSSTU	QUESTIONERS
EEINORRSTUV	ENTEROVIRUS
EEINORSSSSU	SERIOUSNESS
EEINPRRRTTU	INTERRUPTER
EEINPRTTTWY	TYPEWRITTEN
EEIOPSSSSSV	POSSESSIVES
EEIPPRSSSUV	SUPPRESSIVE
EEIPRRRSSSU	PRESSURISER
EEIPRRRSSUZ	PRESSURIZER
EEIPRRSTTWY	TYPEWRITERS
EEIPRSSSSTT	STEPSISTERS
EEJLNOSSSSY	JOYLESSNESS
EEKKOORRRTV	VOORTREKKER
EEKLORRSTTW	TRESTLEWORK
EEKMNNPSSTU	UNKEMPTNESS
EEKNOORRSTW	STONEWORKER
EELLLLOPSTU	LULL TO SLEEP
EELLLOORRTW	ROLLER TOWEL
EELLNNOSSSW	SWOLLENNESS
EELLNOOSTWY	YELLOWSTONE
EELLNOPSTUY	PLENTEOUSLY
EELLNPRTUUV	PULVERULENT
EELLOPRSSWY	POWERLESSLY
EELLORRSTTY	STORYTELLER
EELMMNOPSTY	EMPLOYMENTS
EELMNOSSSUU	EMULOUSNESS
EELMNPPSSTU	SUPPLEMENTS
EELNNSSSSSU	SUNLESSNESS
EELNOOPPSTW	TOWNSPEOPLE
EELNOORRSUY	ERRONEOUSLY
EELNOPRSTYY	POLYSTYRENE
EELOPPRSSSU	PURPOSELESS
EELOPRRSSUW	LOW-PRESSURE
EEMNNRSTTTU	ENTRUSTMENT
EEMNOORSTTY	ENTEROSTOMY
EEMNORSSTTW	WESTERNMOST

EEMOORRSTTU	TORTURESOME
EEMOPSSTTUU	TEMPESTUOUS
EENNOORSSSU	ONEROUSNESS
EENNOORSTTT	ROTTENSTONE
EENNOPRSTWW	NEWPORT NEWS
EENNORSSSSUV	NERVOUSNESS
EENNOSSSTUU	TENUOUSNESS
EENNPPRTTYY	PRETTY PENNY
EEOOPRRSSSS	REPOSSESSOR
EEOOPQRSSTTU	REQUEST STOP
EFFGHHHIIRS	HIGH SHERIFF
EFFGHIINNOT	IN THE OFFING
EFFGHIINOTT	IN THE GIFT OF
EFFGHIINRSS	FISH FINGERS
EFFGHILNRSU	RESHUFFLING
EFFGILLNOST	TELLING-OFFS
EFFGILNOSXY	FLYING FOXES
EFFGILNRSUY	SUFFERINGLY
EFFGLLORTUY	FORGETFULLY
EFFHOOOPSTT	PHOTO-OFFSET
EFFIOORRSTT	FIRST-FOOTER
EFGGHIINNRT	FRIGHTENING
EFGGHIIRRST	TRIGGERFISH
EFGGIINNRRS	RING FINGERS
EFGGIINNRTY	GENTRIFYING
EFGGIINPRRU	PREFIGURING
EFGHHIILOPR	HIGH PROFILE
EFGHHOORTTU	FORETHOUGHT
EFGHIIKNRSS	KINGFISHERS
EFGHIILNOST	LINE OF SIGHT
EFGHIILNSST	FLIGHTINESS
EFGHIIPRSST	PRISEFIGHTS
EFGHIIPRSTZ	PRIZEFIGHTS
EFGHILOOSST	LOSE SIGHT OF
EFGHIMNORSS	FISHMONGERS
EFGHINORSSU	SURGEONFISH
EFGIIILLNNR	FRINGILLINE
EFGIIILNRTZ	FERTILIZING
EFGIIINRVVY	REVIVIFYING
EFGIILLMORU	FLORILEGIUM
EFGIILMNSTT	FILMSETTING
EFGIILMNSUY	EMULSIFYING
EFGIILNPSTY	SELF-PITYING
EFGIINNPRRT	FINGERPRINT
EFGIINPRTTY	PRETTIFYING
EFGILLLORWY	GILLYFLOWER
EFGILLORRSW	FLOWER GIRLS
EFGILNOORVW	OVERFLOWING
EFGILNORSTY	FOSTERINGLY
EFGINORRSUU	FERRUGINOUS
EFGIOPRSSUY	GYPSIFEROUS
EFGLNNOSSSU	SONGFULNESS
EFHIINRSSTT	THRIFTINESS
EFHILLOPSSW	FELLOWSHIPS

EFHILLOSTWW	WOLF WHISTLE	EGGHHIILTTW	LIGHTWEIGHT
EFHILLSSSTY	SHIFTLESSLY	EGGHHINOSSS	HOGGISHNESS
EFHILNOOSSS	FOOLISHNESS	EGGHIINOTUW	OUTWEIGHING
EFHILNOSSSW	WOLFISHNESS	EGGHIINPSSS	PIGGISHNESS
EFHILNSSSUW	WISHFULNESS	EGGHIINRRTW	RIGHT-WINGER
EFHILOPRSST	SHOPLIFTERS	EGGHLNOORSW	HORNSWOGGLE
EFHIMORRSTX	SIXTH-FORMER	EGGIILLNNRY	LINGERINGLY
EFHINOPPSSS	FOPPISHNESS	EGGIILQSSTU	SQUIGGLIEST
EFHLNOOOPRR	FORLORN HOPE	EGGIINNRTWW	WRINGING WET
EFHLNRSSTUU	HURTFULNESS	EGGILLLNRUY	GRUELLINGLY
EFHMORRSTTU	FURTHERMOST	EGGILLNORWY	GLOWERINGLY
EFHOOOPRRSW	SHOWERPROOF	EGGINOPRRSS	PROGRESSING
EFIIIIMNRST	INFIRMITIES	EGGINOSSSTU	SUGGESTIONS
EFIIIINNSTV	INFINITIVES	EGGLNOOORTY	GERONTOLOGY
EFIIILNRTTY	INFERTILITY	EGHHIIKNTTW	WHITE KNIGHT
EFIIILORSTV	FRIVOLITIES	EGHHIINNOST	HIGH-TENSION
EFIIIMNNNSS	SINN FEINISM	EGHHIIPRSST	HIGH PRIESTS
EFIIINORRTY	INFERIORITY	EGHHIJMPRSU	HIGH JUMPERS
EFIIKRRSSTT	FIRST STRIKE	EGHHILLNNORS	ENGLISH HORN
EFIILNPSSTU	PITIFULNESS	EGHHILOPRSY	HIEROGLYPHS
EFIINNORSTU	INTERFUSION	EGHHILOSSTU	HOUSE LIGHTS, LIGHTHOUSES
EFIINOOPTVW	POINT OF VIEW	EGHHLLORSTU	SELL-THROUGH
EFIINOPRSSU	SPINIFEROUS	EGHHLOSSTTU	THOUGHTLESS
EFIINORRSSU	URINIFEROUS	EGHIILLNRSV	SHRIVELLING
EFIIOPRRSSU	SPIRIFEROUS	EGHIILLNRSY	RELISHINGLY
EFIKLLNSSSU	SKILFULNESS	EGHIILLNSWW	WELL-WISHING
EFIKLOORTTU	OUT OF KILTER	EGHIILNPRSY	PERISHINGLY
EFILLLMOSUU	MELLIFLUOUS	EGHIILNRSSS	GIRLISHNESS
EFILLLNPTUY	PLENTIFULLY	EGHIILNRSVY	SHIVERINGLY
EFILLOOPRSW	LOW PROFILES	EGHIILNSSST	SIGHTLINESS
EFILLRSSTUY	FRUITLESSLY	EGHIILOORST	HIEROLOGIST
EFILNSSSTUW	WISTFULNESS	EGHIINNOPSS	SPHINGOSINE
EFILOOPRRSU	PROLIFEROUS	EGHIIOPPRSU	HIPPO REGIUS
EFILPRSTUUY	SUPERFLUITY	EGHIIRSSSTU	RIGHTS ISSUE
EFIMNNORSSU	UNIFORMNESS	EGHILMNOORT	MOONLIGHTER
EFIMNORSSTU	MISFORTUNES	EGHILMOOORS	HOMOLOGISER
EFINNORRRTU	IN RETURN FOR	EGHILMOOORZ	HOMOLOGIZER
EFINOOORSUZ	OZONIFEROUS	EGHILMOOSTY	MYTHOLOGIES, MYTHOLOGISE
EFINOOPRSSS	PROFESSIONS	EGHILMOOTYZ	MYTHOLOGIZE
EFINOPRRSST	FIRST PERSON	EGHILNOOPST	NEPHOLOGIST, PHENOLOGIST
EFINORSSSUU	FURIOUSNESS	EGHILNOOSTT	ETHNOLOGIST
EFINORSSTTU	STONE FRUITS	EGHILNOSSST	GHOSTLINESS
EFIORRSTTUY	YTTRIFEROUS	EGHILORSTUY	RIGHTEOUSLY
EFLLNOSSSSU	SOULFULNESS	EGHIMNNORSU	NURSING HOME
EFLLNSSSTUU	LUSTFULNESS	EGHIMNOSTUU	HUGUENOTISM
EFLMOOORRTUY	FLUOROMETRY	EGHIMOOTTUV	GIVE MOUTH TO
EFLNNOORRSS	FORLORNNESS	EGHINNNOSST	NOTHINGNESS
EFLNNORTUUX	NEUTRON FLUX	EGHINNPSSSU	PUSHINGNESS
EFLOPRSSUUU	SUPERFLUOUS	EGHINOPPRSY	PROPHESYING
EFNNNOORRTU	FRONT-RUNNER	EGHINORSSST	SHOESTRINGS
EFNOOPRRTTY	PORT OF ENTRY	EGHINORSSSU	ROGUISHNESS
EFOOPRRSSTU	FOUR-POSTERS	EGHINORSTUU	UNRIGHTEOUS
EGGGINOPRRU	GINGER GROUP	EGHINPRSSTU	UPRIGHTNESS
EGGHHHIILRT	HIGHLIGHTER	EGHIORRSTTW	GHOSTWRITER

EGHKNOOPRSU	ROUGH-SPOKEN
EGHLLLPPTUU	PULL THE PLUG
EGHOOORRTUVW	OVERWROUGHT
EGIIILLMNPR	IMPERILLING
EGIIILMNORS	RELIGIONISM
EGIIILNNNRT	INTERLINING
EGIIILNRSTZ	STERILIZING
EGIIILORRSU	IRRELIGIOUS
EGIIILORSTY	RELIGIOSITY
EGIIIMNNRST	MINISTERING
EGIIIMNOPTZ	EPITOMIZING
EGIIINNOPRT	PRE-IGNITION
EGIIINNOPTT	PETITIONING
EGIIINNSSTZ	SENSITIZING
EGIIJNNOSTT	JETTISONING
EGIIKNPRSTT	SPIRKETTING
EGIILLMNPSS	MISSPELLING
EGIILLNNSSW	WILLINGNESS
EGIILLNORTU	GUILLOTINER
EGIILLNORTY	LOITERINGLY
EGIILLNOSTU	GUILLOTINES
EGIILLORSUY	RELIGIOUSLY
EGIILMMNRSY	SIMMERINGLY
EGIILMNNOSU	EMULSIONING
EGIILMNNOSZ	SOLEMNIZING
EGIILMNNSSS	SMILINGNESS
EGIILMNPRSY	SIMPERINGLY
EGIILLNNOSTU	LENTIGINOUS
EGIILNNOSUY	INGENIOUSLY
EGIILNNPRST	SPLINTERING
EGIILNPRUVZ	PULVERIZING
EGIILNQRUVY	QUIVERINGLY
EGIILNRSSST	GRISTLINESS
EGIILNRSSTY	RESISTINGLY
EGIILNRTTTY	TITTERINGLY
EGIIMNNORSZ	SERMONIZING
EGIIMNNRTTU	UNREMITTING
EGIIMNOPRTZ	TEMPORIZING
EGIINNNNNSW	WINNINGNESS
EGIINNOPRST	INTERPOSING
EGIINNOQSTU	QUESTIONING
EGIINNPRSSS	SPRINGINESS
EGIINNRSSST	STRINGINESS
EGIINOPRSSU	SERPIGINOUS
EGIINOPRTTU	PIROUETTING
EGIINORRRTZ	TERRORIZING
EGIINORSTUV	VERTIGINOUS
EGIINPRSSUV	SUPERVISING
EGIINPRTTWY	TYPEWRITING
EGIIOPRSSTU	PRESTIGIOUS
EGIKLLNNORS	SNORKELLING
EGIKLNOOORV	OVERLOOKING
EGIKNOORRVW	OVERWORKING
EGILLLNOTXY	EXTOLLINGLY
EGILLLOOVXY	VEXILLOLOGY
EGILLLSSTUY	GUILTLESSLY
EGILLNNOSTW	WELLINGTONS
EGILLNORTVY	REVOLTINGLY
EGILLNORVVY	REVOLVINGLY
EGILLNPRSSW	WELLSPRINGS
EGILMNOORTY	TERMINOLOGY
EGILMNOPSTT	MELTING POTS
EGILMNPRSUY	PRESUMINGLY
EGILMNRTTUY	MUTTERINGLY
EGILMOORSTT	METROLOGIST
EGILMOOSTTY	ETYMOLOGIST
EGILNNNOOSU	UNLOOSENING
EGILNNOPSSS	SLOPINGNESS
EGILNNOSUUY	INGENUOUSLY
EGILNNRSTTY	STRINGENTLY
EGILNOOOPST	STOOLPIGEON
EGILNOORSTU	NEUROLOGIST
EGILNOPRRVY	REPROVINGLY
EGILNOSSTUU	LOUNGE SUITS
EGILNPRSTTU	SPLUTTERING
EGILOOOSSTT	OSTEOLOGIST
EGILOOPRSTT	PETROLOGIST
EGILOOSSSTX	SEXOLOGISTS
EGIMNNOORRS	IRONMONGERS
EGIMNNOORRY	IRONMONGERY
EGIMNOORRSV	MISGOVERNOR
EGIMNOORRTT	TRIMETROGON
EGINNNORRUV	OVERRUNNING
EGINNOORSTU	NITROGENOUS
EGINNOPRSTY	TRYPSINOGEN
EGINNORRTUV	OVERTURNING
EGINOOPPRTV	OVERTOPPING
EGINOOPRRSS	PROGRESSION
EGINOOPRRST	PROGENITORS
EGINPPRSSSU	SUPPRESSING
EGJLMNOPRSU	LONG JUMPERS
EGLMNNOOPRT	PROLONGMENT
EGNOOOPRSSU	SPOROGENOUS
EHHILOOPPRS	PHILOSOPHER
EHHIMOOPRRT	THERIOMORPH
EHHIMOOPSST	THEOSOPHISM
EHHINNNSSSU	HUNNISHNESS
EHHIOOPPRST	PHOSPHORITE
EHHIOOPRRSW	HERO WORSHIP
EHHIOOPSSTT	THEOSOPHIST
EHHLOOSTTUY	YOUTH HOSTEL
EHIIILNPPPS	PHILIPPINES
EHIIILNPSST	PHILISTINES
EHIIILOSSTT	HOSTILITIES
EHIIIPRSTTW	WHITE SPIRIT
EHIIKLNSTTY	KITTENISHLY
EHIIKMNOOSS	SHIMONOSEKI
EHIIKMRRSSS	SKIRMISHERS

EHIILMRSSTV	SILVERSMITH
EHIILNOOPRT	HELIOTROPIN
EHIILOOPTTX	TOXOPHILITE
EHIIMMOPRST	HEMITROPISM
EHIIMNOSSTT	SMITHSONITE
EHIINNPRSST	INTERNSHIPS
EHIINNSSSSW	SWINISHNESS
EHIINPRSSST	SPINSTERISH
EHIINRSSSTT	THIRSTINESS
EHIIOPRSSST	SOPHISTRIES
EHILLMRSSTY	MIRTHLESSLY
EHILMMNOSTY	SEMIMONTHLY
EHILMNOOPTY	ENTOMOPHILY
EHILMOOPRSU	HERMOUPOLIS
EHILMORSSTY	THERMOLYSIS
EHILNOORSSZ	HORIZONLESS
EHILNOSSSTU	LOUTISHNESS
EHILNSSSSTY	STYLISHNESS
EHILOOPRSUX	XEROPHILOUS
EHILOPSSTTY	POLYTHEISTS
EHIMMOOORST	HOMOEROTISM
EHIMMOOPSTY	MYTHOPOEISM
EHIMMOORSTU	MESOTHORIUM
EHIMNNORSTU	NOURISHMENT
EHIMNNPSSTU	PUNISHMENTS
EHIMNOORTTU	NOTOTHERIUM
EHIMNOOSSTT	MONOTHEISTS
EHIMNORRSTU	MOTHER'S RUIN
EHIMOOPRRST	RHEOTROPISM
EHIMOOPSTTY	MYTHOPOEIST
EHIMOPRSTXY	XEROPHYTISM
EHINNRSSSTU	RUNTISHNESS
EHINOOPRRTT	ORNITHOPTER
EHINOSSSSTT	SOTTISHNESS
EHINRSSSTTU	RUTTISHNESS
EHIOOOPRTTZ	TROPHOZOITE
EHIOORSSSTX	SIX-SHOOTERS
EHIOPPRRSSW	WORSHIPPERS
EHJMOPRSSUW	SHOW JUMPERS
EHKNOOPRSST	SHORT-SPOKEN
EHLLORSSTWY	WORTHLESSLY
EHLMNOPPSYY	NYMPHOLEPSY
EHLMNOPTUWY	NEW PLYMOUTH
EHLOPRSSUUU	SULPHUREOUS
EHMNOOOPRST	MONOSTROPHE
EHMOOOPRSTU	HOMOPTEROUS
EHNNOPRSTWY	PENNYWORTHS
EHNOORSSTTW	STONE'S THROW
EHNOQSSTTUU	QUONSET HUTS
EHOOPPRSSTW	SHOWSTOPPER
EIIIINOSTUV	INQUISITIVE
EIIILLLMRST	MILLILITRES
EIIILMPRTVY	PRIMITIVELY
EIIILNTTUVY	INTUITIVELY
EIIIMMNRSTU	MINISTERIUM
EIIIMNORSSV	REVISIONISM
EIIINOPRSTT	PERITONITIS
EIIINOQRSTU	REQUISITION
EIIINORSSTV	REVISIONIST
EIIINOSSSTU	SINUOSITIES
EIIINSSTTVY	SENSITIVITY
EIIINSTTTUV	INSTITUTIVE
EIIIOPRSSTT	PERIOSTITIS
EIIIRSSTTVY	RESISTIVITY
EIILLLLMSSTY	LIMITLESSLY
EIILLMPSUVY	IMPULSIVELY
EIILLOOQSSU	SOLILOQUIES, SOLILOQUISE
EIILLOOQSUZ	SOLILOQUIZE
EIILMOPRSUY	IMPERIOUSLY
EIILNNSSTTY	INSISTENTLY
EIILNOOPPRT	LIPOPROTEIN
EIILNOPRSTV	SILVERPOINT
EIIMNNOOPRT	PREMONITION
EIIMNNOPRTU	PREMUNITION
EIIMNOPRSSS	IMPRESSIONS
EIIMNOPSSSU	IMPIOUSNESS
EIIMNORRTTT	INTERMITTOR
EIIMOORRSTU	MERITORIOUS
EIIMOPPRRTY	IMPROPRIETY
EIIMOPRSSST	PRESTISSIMO
EIIMOPSTTUY	IMPETUOSITY
EIIMORRSSTU	MOISTURISER
EIIMORRSTUZ	MOISTURIZER
EIINOOPPRST	PREPOSITION
EIINOOPRRSV	PROVISIONER
EIINOOPSSTX	EXPOSITIONS
EIINOPRSSUV	SUPERVISION
EIINORRSSST	SINISTRORSE
EIINORSTTTU	RESTITUTION
EIIOPPSSTUV	SUPPOSITIVE
EIIOPRRSTUY	SUPERIORITY
EIKLLORRSTW	TRELLISWORK
EILLLMNOOPP	LOLLIPOP MEN
EILLLOORSTT	TOILET ROLLS
EILLNOPSSTY	POINTLESSLY
EILLORSTTTU	LITTERLOUTS
EILMNNOPRTY	PROMINENTLY
EILMNOOOPRS	MONOPOLISER
EILMNOOOPRZ	MONOPOLIZER
EILMNOSSSYYZ	ENZYMOLYSIS
EILMOPRSSTY	PROSELYTISM
EILMOPRTUVY	PLUVIOMETRY
EILMOPSTUUY	IMPETUOUSLY
EILMORSTTUY	MULTISTOREY
EILNOORSSTU	RESOLUTIONS
EILNOORSTUV	REVOLUTIONS
EILNOPRSUUY	PENURIOUSLY
EILNPQSTTUU	QUINTUPLETS

EILOOPRSSTY	PROTEOLYSIS
EIMNNOOSSSU	OMINOUSNESS
EIMNNRSSTTU	INSTRUMENTS
EIMNOOPRRTY	PREMONITORY
EIMNOOPRSSS	SPOONERISMS
EIMNOOQSTTU	MOSQUITO NET
EIMNOORSTTU	NEUROTOMIST
EIMNOPPRSSU	PRESUMPTION
EIMOOPRSTTT	OPTOMETRIST
EIMOORRSUVV	VERMIVOROUS
EINNOOPPRTU	INOPPORTUNE
EINNOOPRSSS	RESPONSIONS
EINNOOSSSUX	NOXIOUSNESS
EINNOPSSSSU	SUSPENSIONS
EINNOQRSTUU	NON SEQUITUR
EINNOSSSSUU	SINUOUSNESS
EINOOPPRSTW	POWER POINTS
EINOOPSSSSS	POSSESSIONS
EINOORSSTUU	RIOTOUSNESS
EINOPPRSSSU	SUPPRESSION
EINOPSSTTTY	STENOTYPIST
EINOQRSTTUU	TOURNIQUETS
EINORSSTTUY	STRENUOSITY
EIOOPPRRRST	PROPRIETORS
EIOORRSTVWY	IVORY TOWERS
EIOPRRSSSUV	SUPERVISORS
EIOPRRSSUVY	SUPERVISORY
EIOPRSSTTTU	PROSTITUTES
EIOORRSTTUU	TRIQUETROUS
EKKOOPPRSVY	PROKOPYEVSK
EKLNOOPSTUY	OUTSPOKENLY
EKNNNNOSSUW	UNKNOWNNESS
EKNORRSTTUU	TRUNK ROUTES
ELLMNNOOSTY	SOMNOLENTLY
ELLMORSTUUY	TREMULOUSLY
ELLOQRSUUUY	QUERULOUSLY
ELMNOPPSUYY	MONEY SUPPLY
ELNOOORTTUY	ONLY TOO TRUE
ELNOOPPRTUY	OPPORTUNELY
ELNORSSTUUY	STRENUOUSLY
EMMOOPRSSTT	POSTMORTEMS
EMNOOPPSSSU	POMPOUSNESS
EMOOORRSSTV	SERVOMOTORS
EMORRSTTUYY	MYSTERY TOUR
ENNOOPPRRSU	PROPER NOUNS
EOPPRRSSSSU	SUPPRESSORS
FFGHILLRTUY	FRIGHTFULLY
FGGHIINOTTU	OUTFIGHTING
FGGIILNORVY	FORGIVINGLY
FGHHIINSSTT	NIGHT SHIFTS
FGHIILNOPST	SHOPLIFTING
FGHIILNORSU	FLOURISHING
FGHIINNRSSU	FURNISHINGS
FGHIINRSSTT	FIRST NIGHTS
FGHILNORTTY	FORTNIGHTLY
FGHILOPTTTU	PUT TO FLIGHT
FGIIILMNPSY	SIMPLIFYING
FGIIILNOSSZ	FOSSILIZING
FGIILLNOORT	ROOT FILLING
FGIILMNNORY	INFORMINGLY
FGIILNSTTUY	STULTIFYING
FGIINRRSSTT	FIRST-STRING
FGIKNNORSTU	TUNING FORKS
FGIOORRSUUV	FRUGIVOROUS
FHHIINOOPST	PHOTO FINISH
FHHIORRSSTT	SHORT SHRIFT
FHILMOORRRS	HORROR FILMS
FHINORRSSTT	SHIRTFRONTS
FHMOOORTUUU	OUT OF HUMOUR
FIIIMNNOSSU	INFUSIONISM
FIIINNOSSTU	INFUSIONIST
FIIOOPPRRST	PROOF SPIRIT
FIIRTTTTTUU	TUTTI FRUTTI
FILLOORSUVY	FRIVOLOUSLY
FILMRSSTTUU	MISTRUSTFUL
FILNOORSSTY	FRONTOLYSIS
FINOOOPSSTT	SOFT OPTIONS
FLLOORRSUWY	SORROWFULLY
GGGIILLNRWY	WRIGGLINGLY
GGHHIILNSTT	NIGHTLIGHTS
GGHIILLNSTY	SLIGHTINGLY
GGHIIMNNSTU	GUNSMITHING
GGIILNOPSSY	GOSSIPINGLY
GGIINNOPSST	SIGNPOSTING
GGILNOOORWW	WOOLGROWING
GHHHIORTTUW	THROUGH WITH
GHHIINRSSTT	NIGHTSHIRTS
GHHIIPRSSTW	SHIPWRIGHTS
GHHINOOOOPP	POOH-POOHING
GHHINOOPRTU	THOROUGHPIN
GHHMNNOOOPT	MONOPHTHONG
GHHNORRSTUU	RUN-THROUGHS
GHHOPRSTTUU	THROUGHPUTS
GHIIIKMNRSS	SKIRMISHING
GHIIKLNNRSY	SHRINKINGLY
GHIILLLNRTY	THRILLINGLY
GHIILLOOPST	PHILOLOGIST
GHIILLOOSTT	LITHOLOGIST
GHIILLOPSTT	PILOT LIGHTS
GHIILNNPSUY	PUNISHINGLY
GHIILNOORST	RHINOLOGIST
GHIILOOORST	OPHIOLOGIST
GHIILOOSSTT	HISTOLOGIST
GHIINNOPTYZ	HYPNOTIZING
GHIINOPPRSW	WORSHIPPING
GHIINOPTTUW	WHITING POUT
GHIJMNOPSUW	SHOW JUMPING
GHILLOOOPST	HOPLOLOGIST

GHILLOOPSYY	SYPHILOLOGY	GILNNNOPSSU	NONPLUSSING
GHILMOOSTTY	MYTHOLOGIST	GILNOOPPSTY	TYPING POOLS
GHILNOOOPST	PHONOLOGIST	GILNORRTTUY	TORTURINGLY
GHILNOOORTY	ORNITHOLOGY	GILNRSTTTUY	STRUTTINGLY
GHILOOOPRTY	OLIGOTROPHY	GIMNNORSTUU	SURMOUNTING
GHIMMNNOORSU	MUSHROOMING	GIMNOOOPRSU	SPOROGONIUM
GHIMNOOPSYY	PHYSIOGNOMY	GINNOOPRSTT	STRONG POINT
GHIMOOOSSYZ	HOMOZYGOSIS	GINOOPRSTUU	OUTPOURINGS
GHINOORRTUW	WROUGHT IRON	GMNOOOORRSST	STRONG ROOMS
GHLNOOPSSUW	SNOWPLOUGHS	GNOOOPRSTUY	PROTOGYNOUS
GIIIKLMNNSS	MISSING LINK	HHIMOOOPRSS	PHOSPHORISM
GIIIKNNNPRT	PRINTING INK	HHMNOOOOPSU	HOMOPHONOUS
GIIILLNNORT	ROLLING IN IT	HHOOOOPPRSSU	PHOSPHOROUS
GIIILNNPRSY	INSPIRINGLY	HIILLNNNOOT	NONILLIONTH
GIIILNNQRUY	INQUIRINGLY	HIILLNORSTT	TRILLIONTHS
GIIIMNNOOSU	IGNOMINIOUS	HIILMOOSTTT	LITHOTOMIST
GIIIMNNOPRS	IMPRISONING	HIILNORTTYY	HOLY TRINITY
GIIIMNNPRST	MISPRINTING, STRIP MINING	HIIMMOOPRSS	ISOMORPHISM
GIIIMNOPRSV	IMPROVISING	HIIMMOPRRST	TRIMORPHISM
GIIINNNOPPT	PINPOINTING	HIIMNOOPRST	MONITORSHIP
GIIINNNPRSU	UNINSPIRING	HILNOOPSTXY	XYLOPHONIST
GIIINNOOPST	POSITIONING	HILNOORSSTU	HONOURS LIST
GIIINNSTTTU	INSTITUTING	HIMMOOOPRSZ	ZOOMORPHISM
GIIKLNNPRSS	SPRINKLINGS	HIMNOOPSSUY	SYMPHONIOUS
GIILLLLMNOR	ROLLING MILL	HINOOPPRSSS	SPONSORSHIP
GIILLLNNUWY	UNWILLINGLY	HINOOPPSTTY	PHONOTYPIST
GIILLMNOOST	LIMNOLOGIST	HINOOPRRTTY	THYROTROPIN
GIILLMNOPRY	IMPLORINGLY	HLNOOOPPSUY	POLYPHONOUS
GIILLMNPTUY	MULTIPLYING	HMOOOOPRSSU	HOMOSPOROUS
GIILLNNOPRS	ROLLING PINS	HORRSTTTUWY	TRUSTWORTHY
GIILMNOORSV	LIVING ROOMS	IIIILMNNQSU	INQUILINISM
GIILMNOPRSY	PROMISINGLY	IIIIMMPRSTV	PRIMITIVISM
GIILMNOPRVY	IMPROVINGLY	IIIIMNSTTUV	INTUITIVISM
GIILMNQRSUY	SQUIRMINGLY	IIIIMPPSSSS	MISSISSIPPI
GIILNNTTUWY	UNWITTINGLY	IIIIMPRSTTV	PRIMITIVIST
GIILNOOSSST	SINOLOGISTS	IIIINNOQSTU	INQUISITION
GIIMNNOPRSU	UNPROMISING	IIIINSTTTUV	INTUITIVIST
GIIMNNOPRTU	IMPORTUNING	IIILLMNOPST	POINTILLISM
GIIMNOORSTT	SITTING ROOM	IIILLMNOSSU	ILLUSIONISM
GIIMNOSSSTY	MISOGYNISTS	IIILLNNOQTU	QUINTILLION
GIIMNRSSTTU	MISTRUSTING	IIILLNOPSTT	POINTILLIST
GIIMOORRRST	RIGOR MORTIS	IIILLNOSSTT	TONSILLITIS
GIIINNNOOPRS	SPRING ONION	IIILLNOSSTU	ILLUSIONIST
GIIINNNOPSTW	WINNING POST	IIILLNOQSUU	INQUILINOUS
GIIINNNOOPTTU	OUTPOINTING	IIIMNOOPSST	IMPOSITIONS
GIIINNOPRSS	PISTON RINGS	IIINNNORTTU	INNUTRITION
GIIINOORSTUV	VORTIGINOUS	IIINNOSTTTU	INSTITUTION
GIINRTTTTYY	NITTY-GRITTY	IIINOOOPSTV	OVIPOSITION
GIJMNNNPRUU	RUNNING JUMP	IIINOQRSSTU	INQUISITORS
GIKLNNNOUWY	UNKNOWINGLY	IIIOPSSSTTV	POSITIVISTS
GIKLNOOPRVY	PROVOKINGLY	IIJLNORSUUY	INJURIOUSLY
GILLMOOPSTY	POLYGLOTISM	IILLNNOOOPP	OPINION POLL
GILLNOPRRSS	SPRING ROLLS	IILLOOQSSTU	SOLILOQUIST
GILMMNRRUUY	MURMURINGLY	IILLORSSTUU	ILLUSTRIOUS

IILMOORTTUY	UTILITY ROOM	ILOOPPRSSST	SPOILSPORTS
IILOOPRRSVY	PROVISORILY	IMNOOPPRSTU	OPPORTUNISM
IILOSSSTTXY	STYLOSTIXIS	IMNOORSSTTY	MONSTROSITY
IIMNOOPRSTU	POSITRONIUM	IMPPPRRSTUU	STIRRUP PUMP
IIMNOPRTTUY	IMPORTUNITY	INOOOPPRRST	PROPORTIONS
IINOOOPPRST	PROPOSITION	INOOPPRSTTU	OPPORTUNIST
IINOOOPPSST	OPPOSITIONS	INOOPPRTTUY	OPPORTUNITY
IINOOPPSSTU	SUPPOSITION	INOOPRRSSTU	PROTRUSIONS
IINOPPQRTUY	PROPINQUITY	IOOPPRSSTUY	SUPPOSITORY
IKORSSSTTTY	TROTSKYISTS	IOOPRRSTTTU	PROSTITUTOR
ILLOPSSUWWY	PUSSY WILLOW	LMNOOOSSTUY	MONOSTYLOUS
ILLORSUUUXY	LUXURIOUSLY	LMNOORSSTUY	MONSTROUSLY
ILMNOOOPSST	MONOPOLISTS	LMOPSSTUUUY	SUMPTUOUSLY
ILNOOOPSSUY	POISONOUSLY	LOORRSTTUUY	TORTUROUSLY
ILNOOORSTUY	NOTORIOUSLY	MMOOPRRSSUU	RUMPUS ROOMS

AAAAAALMRSTT	TARAMASALATA	AAAABEHLMOSTT	HAEMATOBLAST
AAAAABBCDRRS	ABRACADABRAS	AAAABEIILMNNT	MAINTAINABLE
AAAAABBINRSST	SABBATARIANS	AAAABEILLNSSU	UNASSAILABLE
AAAABCCHILNN	BACCHANALIAN	AAAABEILNNTTU	UNATTAINABLE
AAAABDEIKNNR	BANDARANAIKE	AAAABEINNSSST	SAN SEBASTIAN
AAAACCCCIRTU	ACCIACCATURA	AAAABELLLPRRS	PARALLEL BARS
AAAACDIILPRS	PARADISIACAL	AAAABELLNRSTT	TRANSLATABLE
AAAACDIMMNTU	MACADAMIA NUT	AAAABELNOOPTY	PALAEOBOTANY
AAAACEHHKTVW	HAVE A WHACK AT	AAAABGIILNRRT	GIBRALTARIAN
AAAACEHKMSTV	HAVE A SMACK AT	AAAABGLLMRRRU	BURGLAR ALARM
AAAACEINRRSV	CARAVANSERAI	AAAABHIILNOTT	HABITATIONAL
AAAACGIMMNRT	ANAGRAMMATIC	AAAABIIILLTVY	AVAILABILITY
AAAACHILNPPS	APPALACHIANS	AAAABIILLPTTY	PALATABILITY
AAAACIMNRSST	ANTIMACASSAR	AAAABIKKLNOTU	KOTA KINABALU
AAAADEHMRSTT	MAD AS A HATTER	AAAABILLNQRRU	BARRANQUILLA
AAAADHNPRRUU	ANURADHAPURA	AAACCCDHIRTY	TACHYCARDIAC
AAAAEGGLLNPRU	PARALANGUAGE	AAAACCCEHKPTT	CATCH A PACKET
AAAAEGNRTVXZ	EXTRAVAGANZA	AAACCDEIIMNS	ACADEMICIANS
AAAAFGILLNRS	NIAGARA FALLS	AAACCDEIILMY	ACADEMICALLY
AAAAFINRRSST	RASTAFARIANS	AAACCDEILMNO	DECALCOMANIA
AAAAGGILLMNT	AMALGAMATING	AAACCDHNRRSY	CASH AND CARRY
AAAAGILLMMNOT	AMALGAMATION	AAACCDIINRRT	INTRACARDIAC
AAAAILLMNPRTY	MALAYAN TAPIR	AAACCDIIRRTT	TARTARIC ACID
AAAAILLPRRSS	SARSAPARILLA	AAACCEEHSSTT	ATTACHE CASES
AAAAILMNPRTY	MALAYAN TAPIR	AAACCEGILMTT	METAGALACTIC
AAAAILNNRSTV	TRANSVAALIAN	AAACCEGIORSU	AGARICACEOUS
AAAAILNRSSTU	AUSTRALASIAN	AAACCEHNOSTU	ACANTHACEOUS
AAAAINNNORTV	ANTANANARIVO	AAACCEIINPTT	INCAPACITATE
AAABBCEEINRS	CARIBBEAN SEA	AAACCEINNQTU	ACQUAINTANCE
AAABBCEGIRRY	BABY CARRIAGE	AAACCHILLNRY	ANARCHICALLY
AAABBCILLRRY	BARBARICALLY	AAACCHILNPTY	ANAPHYLACTIC
AAABBIIMNRRS	BARBARIANISM	AAACCIILMRST	MARCASITICAL
AAABBCCDERRSS	SACRED SCARAB	AAACCIINOPTT	CAPACITATION
AAABCDEHLNNU	BECHUANALAND	AAACCILMNOST	ACCLAMATIONS
AAABCCEGKPSSS	BACK PASSAGES	AAACCILORSTU	ACCUSATORIAL
AAABCEHILLPT	ALPHABETICAL	AAACDEEGKLPS	PACKAGE DEALS
AAABCEHILNPT	ANALPHABETIC	AAACDEELNRRY	CALENDAR YEAR
AAABCEHLOPPR	APPROACHABLE	AAACDEGILMOR	MEGALOCARDIA
AAABCEILLRWY	CABLE RAILWAY	AAACDEGIMPRS	PARADIGM CASE
AAABCELNRRTU	TABERNACULAR	AAACDEINRSTT	TRADESCANTIA
AAABCGIINNRT	CANTABRIGIAN	AAACDENNOPSU	PANDANACEOUS
AAABDDJNNORY	DARBY AND JOAN	AAACDGIIMMRT	DIAGRAMMATIC
AAABDEELLMNT	MATABELELAND	AAACDGIIMPRT	PARADIGMATIC
AAABDEILMRTZ	DRAMATIZABLE	AAACDIINNNSV	SCANDINAVIAN
AAABDEMRSSSS	AMBASSADRESS	AAACDILLMRTY	DRAMATICALLY
AAABDGHMNRSS	SMASH-AND-GRAB	AAACEEENPPRR	REAPPEARANCE
AAABDIILPTTY	ADAPTABILITY	AAACEEFLMNSS	MALFEASANCES
AAABDIJMNNRS	BANDJARMASIN	AAACEEGNRTVX	EXTRAVAGANCE
AAABDILLOOPR	PARABOLOIDAL	AAACEESSSTVW	SWEET CASSAVA
AAABDILNNSST	BATAN ISLANDS	AAACEFIMNORR	AFRO-AMERICAN
AAABEEGILMRR	MARRIAGEABLE	AAACEGGGLOTU	GALACTAGOGUE
AAABEEGLMNNU	UNMANAGEABLE	AAACEGILMMNO	MEGALOMANIAC
AAABEELLNPPU	UNAPPEALABLE	AAACEGIMNPRT	PARAMAGNETIC
AAABEHIKPPPT	PHI BETA KAPPA	AAACEGIRRSWY	CARRIAGEWAYS

545

AAACEHHNRTTU	HARTHACANUTE
AAACEHILMMTT	MATHEMATICAL
AAACEHIPRRTT	PATRIARCHATE
AAACEHKNSSTW	SASKATCHEWAN
AAACEHKRSTTT	HEART ATTACKS
AAACEHLMORTY	HAEMATOCRYAL
AAACEILMOOST	OSTEOMALACIA
AAACEILNORTU	AERONAUTICAL
AAACELNOSSTU	SANTALACEOUS
AAACFGILNNRU	LINGUA FRANCA
AAACFIINRRTT	ANTI-AIR-CRAFT
AAACFLMNRTUU	MANUFACTURAL
AAACGGILLNOY	ANAGOGICALLY
AAACGGILLOPY	APAGOGICALLY
AAACGIILNPST	CAPITAL GAINS
AAACGIIMNSTT	ANASTIGMATIC
AAACGILLNVY	GALVANICALLY
AAACGILLMMMO	MAMMALOGICAL
AAACHIKPPRST	APPARATCHIKS
AAACHILLLMTY	THALAMICALLY
AAACHILMNRST	CHARLATANISM
AAACHIMNORTU	TAUROMACHIAN
AAACHIPPRRST	PARAPHRASTIC
AAACIILNNOST	CANALISATION
AAACIILNNOTZ	CANALIZATION
AAACIILNNRRT	INTRACRANIAL
AAACILLLNTYY	ANALYTICALLY
AAACILLMNOTY	ANATOMICALLY
AAACILLMORTY	AROMATICALLY
AAACILMMNNOO	MONOMANIACAL
AAACILMNOPRY	PYROMANIACAL
AAACILNSTTTY	ANTICATALYST
AAADDEGINSTV	DISADVANTAGE
AAADDEGLNOPT	PONTA DELGADA
AAADDFHLLOOO	ALL OF A DOODAH
AAADDGILLMOY	AMYGDALOIDAL
AAADDLMNPRST	STANDARD LAMP
AAADEEGGMNST	STAGE-MANAGED
AAADEEGINNRV	EVER AND AGAIN
AAADEEINRRSV	SIERRA NEVADA
AAADEGIMQRSU	QUADRAGESIMA
AAADEGMNORRS	ROAD MANAGERS
AAADEGNOSTUV	ADVANTAGEOUS
AAADEHNRRTTW	DEATH WARRANT
AAADEILMNNRS	SALAMANDRINE
AAADEILMRRRS	REAR ADMIRALS
AAADEINSSSST	ASSASSINATED
AAADEMNNSSWY	WAYS AND MEANS
AAADFIINORST	FARADISATION
AAADFIINORTZ	FARADIZATION
AAADGIILLORT	GLADIATORIAL
AAADGLNQRRUU	QUADRANGULAR
AAADGLOORSVW	AVOGADRO'S LAW
AAADGMNNNOOR	MOAN AND GROAN
AAADHIINOPRS	ANAPHRODISIA
AAADIILLNOTT	DILATATIONAL
AAADILMNOSSS	SAMOA ISLANDS
AAAEEGGLMNTU	METALANGUAGE
AAAEEGGMNRST	STAGE MANAGER
AAAEEGILMNRT	MARIE GALANTE
AAAEEGINNRSX	SEXAGENARIAN
AAAEEGMNNPRT	PERMANGANATE
AAAEEHIMNSTT	ANATHEMATISE
AAAEEHIMNTTZ	ANATHEMATIZE
AAAEEHIPRSST	PARAESTHESIA
AAAEEKRRSTTT	STEAK TARTARE
AAAEELNPRSTY	PENALTY AREAS
AAAEGGNNRSTU	NUSA TENGGARA
AAAEGHLOPPRY	PALAEOGRAPHY
AAAEGILLMNRY	MANAGERIALLY
AAAEGIMNPRST	SERINGAPATAM
AAAEGINNNNOR	NONAGENARIAN
AAAEGNOPRRST	PERSONA GRATA
AAAEHMOPRRTY	AROMATHERAPY
AAAEIILNQRTU	EQUALITARIAN
AAAEIINNRSTZ	SAINT-NAZAIRE
AAAEILLLNPRT	ANTIPARALLEL
AAAEILLNPSST	PALATIALNESS
AAAEILMRRTTX	EXTRAMARITAL
AAAEILNNNOTX	ANNEXATIONAL
AAAEILPPRRSS	REAPPRAISALS
AAAELQQRSUUV	QUAQUAVERSAL
AAAEMMRRSSTT	MASTER-AT-ARMS
AAAGGINORSTV	AGGRAVATIONS
AAAGGIOPPRTU	APPOGGIATURA
AAAGHINPPRRS	PARAPHRASING
AAAGHIRSTTWY	STRAIGHTAWAY
AAAGIILNNOTV	NAVIGATIONAL
AAAGIINNOPST	PAGANISATION
AAAGIINNOPTZ	PAGANIZATION
AAAGIINNOSTV	GAVANISATION
AAAGIINNOTVZ	GAVANIZATION
AAAGILLLORRT	GRALLATORIAL
AAAHHHJNPRSU	SHAHJAHANPUR
AAAHIILNNOTT	ANTIHALATION
AAAHIIMNNRTU	HUMANITARIAN
AAAHIKLTWWWY	WALK AWAY WITH
AAAHILLNSTTT	HALLSTATTIAN
AAAHLLLMNPRS	MARSHALL PLAN
AAAHLNNOSTXY	SAXONY-ANHALT
AAAIILMNPRSU	MARSUPIALIAN
AAAIILMPRRTY	PARAMILITARY
AAAIILNNOSST	NASALISATION
AAAIILNNOSTZ	NASALIZATION
AAAIILNORTTT	TOTALITARIAN
AAAIIMMNRSST	SAMARITANISM
AAAIINNQRSTU	ANTIQUARIANS
AAAIKLNNOPRT	NATIONAL PARK

AAAILMNORTTU	MATURATIONAL
AAAILNNRSTVY	TRANSYLVANIA
AAAILNOPRSTY	PARALYSATION
AAAINOOPPSST	APPASSIONATO
AABBCCEMOOSU	BOMBACACEOUS
AABBCDEKLLNU	BLACK AND BLUE
AABBCCEGIKKNR	BACKBREAKING
AABBCGIKLLLN	BLACKBALLING
AABBCIIILMNO	BIBLIOMANIAC
AABBDEEFLOTU	FEEL BAD ABOUT
AABBEGIINRTV	ABBREVIATING
AABBEGILLNRS	BALL BEARINGS
AABBEIIKLLOS	BIELSKO-BIALA
AABBEIINORTV	ABBREVIATION
AABBEILRTTTU	ATTRIBUTABLE
AABBEIMMNPSY	NAMBY-PAMBIES
AABBEINRRRTW	RABBIT WARREN
AABBEIRRSTTU	BARBITURATES
AABBHIIILTTY	HABITABILITY
AABBHNNORRTT	NORTH BRABANT
AABCCDEIILRT	BACTERICIDAL
AABCCDEIKNRR	CRACKBRAINED
AABCCDEILLSY	DECASYLLABIC
AABCCEEHLNRT	CARTE BLANCHE
AABCCEELNPTU	UNACCEPTABLE
AABCCEILLLNU	INCALCULABLE
AABCCEILMNOR	MICROBALANCE
AABCCEIRRTUU	BUREAUCRATIC
AABCCENOORSU	CARBONACEOUS
AABCCGIKKNRT	BACKTRACKING
AABCCHHIIMPR	AMPHIBRACHIC
AABCCIILOTTY	BIOCATALYTIC
AABCCILLLNUY	INCALCULABLY
AABCCINRSTTU	SUBANTARCTIC
AABCCKLNRRTU	BLACKCURRANT
AABCCKNNOSTU	BANK ACCOUNTS
AABCDDEEILNT	BALANCED DIET
AABCDDEEKLLP	BACKPEDALLED
AABCDDEHKLNY	BACKHANDEDLY
AABCDDEKLRRW	BLADDERWRACK
AABCDDGINORR	BOARDING CARD
AABCDEEHKLRT	BLACK-HEARTED
AABCDEEIIILNR	INERADICABLE
AABCDEEILLPS	DISPLACEABLE
AABCDEELLLNW	WELL-BALANCED
AABCDEELLLSY	DECASYLLABLE
AABCDEELNORV	OVERBALANCED
AABCDEENOSTU	SUBDEACONATE
AABCDEFLNOTU	CONFABULATED
AABCDEGIKLNP	BACKPEDALING
AABCDEHIINRT	DIBRANCHIATE
AABCDEHIMMRS	CHAMBERMAIDS
AABCDEHORRTY	CARBOHYDRATE
AABCDEIILNNS	CANNIBALISED

AABCDEIILNNZ	CANNIBALIZED
AABCDEIILNRY	INERADICABLY
AABCDEILNSST	ELASTIC BANDS
AABCDEINOORS	RADIO BEACONS
AABCDEINOSTU	SUBDIACONATE
AABCDEKNRRSS	BANKER'S CARDS
AABCDEKNRSSW	BACKWARDNESS
AABCDELLOORT	COLLABORATED
AABCDELMNRSU	CANDELABRUMS
AABCDELOPPRR	CLAPPERBOARD
AABCDELRSTTY	ABSTRACTEDLY
AABCDENOPRSW	BOW AND SCRAPE
AABCDEORRSST	BROADCASTERS
AABCDGINNORT	CARBON DATING
AABCDGINORST	BROADCASTING
AABCDGKLLRUY	BLACKGUARDLY
AABCDIILLLOY	DIABOLICALLY
AABCDKMNOOSW	BACKWOODSMAN
AABCEEEFFILN	INEFFACEABLE
AABCEEEGHLNX	EXCHANGEABLE
AABCEEEHLNST	BALANCE SHEET
AABCEEEHLRRS	RESEARCHABLE
AABCEEFIPRRT	PREFABRICATE
AABCEEGGPRRT	CARPETBAGGER
AABCEEGINRTX	EXACERBATING
AABCEEHLMNRT	MERCHANTABLE
AABCEEHLNRSU	UNSEARCHABLE
AABCEEHLOPRR	REPROACHABLE
AABCEEHMNRST	ANTECHAMBERS
AABCEEIKMNRT	CABINET-MAKER
AABCEEINORTX	EXACERBATION
AABCEELLNOOT	OBLANCEOLATE
AABCEELLNSSS	SCALABLENESS
AABCEFHKMOOT	MAKE A BOTCH OF
AABCEFIILLSS	CLASSIFIABLE
AABCEFIILLTY	BEATIFICALLY
AABCEFIILNST	SANCTIFIABLE
AABCEFLNRSTU	BLAST FURNACE
AABCEGGKRRTU	GARBAGE TRUCK
AABCEHIIMNPS	AMPHISBAENIC
AABCEHILMNRS	CHAMBERLAINS
AABCEHILNRTU	UNCHARITABLE
AABCEHIRRRRS	CRASH BARRIER
AABCEHKLLOPR	ALPHA-BLOCKER
AABCEHKLNPRT	BLACK PANTHER
AABCEHKMNNRT	MERCHANT BANK
AABCEHLLORTT	CALL TO THE BAR
AABCEHLMNORS	ELASMOBRANCH
AABCEHLOPRRY	REPROACHABLY
AABCEHMRRSST	STAR CHAMBERS
AABCEHOPRSSU	HABEAS CORPUS
AABCEIIILPST	CAPABILITIES
AABCEIILLNPP	INAPPLICABLE
AABCEIILLOSZ	SOCIALIZABLE

AABCEIILLRTY	LACERABILITY	AABDEELNOPRS	LEOPARD'S-BANE
AABCEIILRTTY	TRACEABILITY	AABDEGGLNOUY	BODY LANGUAGE
AABCEIILRTUU	BIAURICULATE	AABDEGIIMSTU	DISAMBIGUATE
AABCEIKLLMRS	BLACKMAILERS	AABDEHHIRRST	HAIR'S BREADTH
AABCEILLLORT	BICOLLATERAL	AABDEHILRTWW	WITHDRAWABLE
AABCEILLNUVZ	VULCANIZABLE	AABDEIILNRST	DISTRAINABLE
AABCEILMNOPR	INCOMPARABLE	AABDEIKNORST	DEBARKATIONS
AABCEILNNOST	SANCTIONABLE	AABDEILLLOSW	DISALLOWABLE
AABCEILORSTZ	OSTRACIZABLE	AABDEILNNOTT	NATIONAL DEBT
AABCEILORSUV	VOCABULARIES	AABDEIMRRSSS	DISEMBARRASS
AABCEILSSTTT	BALTIC STATES	AABDELOPRRST	PLASTERBOARD
AABCEINRRSTT	SCATTERBRAIN	AABDGIINNOST	BASTINADOING
AABCEKLPPRSS	BACKSLAPPERS	AABDGIINRSTZ	BASTARDIZING
AABCENOPPRRS	CARBON PAPERS	AABDGILNNSST	SANDBLASTING
AABCENORSSST	CONTRABASSES	AABDHIKLNOSY	BANK HOLIDAYS
AABCFIINORST	FABRICATIONS	AABDIIILLTTY	DILATABILITY
AABCFLNOORTU	CONFABULATOR	AABDIIILSTVY	ADVISABILITY
AABCGHIILOPR	BIOGRAPHICAL	AABDIIILMNRTY	MILITARY BAND
AABCGHIOOPRS	AGORAPHOBICS	AABDIMNORSTU	ADUMBRATIONS
AABCGHKLLNOY	BY A LONG CHALK	AABDINOOTTUY	AUTOANTIBODY
AABCGIIKLLMN	BLACKMAILING	AABDMOORRRST	MORTARBOARDS
AABCGIKLNPPS	BACKSLAPPING	AABEEEEGRRSV	EAGER BEAVERS
AABCGILNNOTU	OUTBALANCING	AABEEEEFKRRSS	SAFEBREAKERS
AABCHIIMORTT	MICROHABITAT	AABEEEEHKRRRT	HEARTBREAKER
AABCHIINOOTT	COHABITATION	AABEEEEILMNRX	RE-EXAMINABLE
AABCHILNRTUY	UNCHARITABLY	AABEEEELMNRUV	MANEUVERABLE
AABCIIILNPTY	INCAPABILITY	AABEEFGILLLT	BIFLAGELLATE
AABCIILLNPPY	INAPPLICABLY	AABEEFGILRRR	IRREFRAGABLE
AABCIILLPRSY	PARISYLLABIC	AABEEFHINRRT	FEATHERBRAIN
AABCIILNNOTU	INCUBATIONAL	AABEEFILMNST	MANIFESTABLE
AABCIILNORST	CALIBRATIONS	AABEEFLMOSTV	MOVABLE FEAST
AABCIILRTTTY	TRACTABILITY	AABEEFLNRRST	TRANSFERABLE
AABCILLLLSYY	SYLLABICALLY	AABEEGGLMORT	MORTGAGEABLE
AABCILMNOPRY	INCOMPARABLY	AABEEGILMNTZ	MAGNETIZABLE
AABCILRRSUUU	SUBAURICULAR	AABEEGLNNTUW	BLAENAU GWENT
AABCINORSSTT	ABSTRACTIONS	AABEEGMMORRU	OBERAMMERGAU
AABCLLLRSSTY	CRYSTAL BALLS	AABEEHIILRTT	REHABILITATE
AABCLLOOORRT	COLLABORATOR	AABEEHILNSTZ	ELIZABETHANS
AABCLNORSTUY	CONSTABULARY	AABEEHILPRST	ALPHABETISER
AABCMNNNOOTT	NONCOMBATANT	AABEEHILPRTZ	ALPHABETIZER
AABCNNORSTTU	ABSTRACT NOUN	AABEEHLMQRSU	ALHAMBRESQUE
AABDDEEELMNR	REDEMANDABLE	AABEEHLRRSTY	BREATHALYSER
AABDDEGLLLRS	GALL BLADDERS	AABEEHLRRTYZ	BREATHALYZER
AABDDEHLLMOY	HEBDOMADALLY	AABEEILMMRSU	IMMEASURABLE
AABDDGHORRTU	DRAUGHTBOARD	AABEEILNRRST	RESTRAINABLE
AABDDGINORRW	DRAWING BOARD	AABEEINRRRST	TRAINBEARERS
AABDEEEGILRS	DISAGREEABLE	AABEEINRRSST	BRAINTEASERS
AABDEEGILRSY	DISAGREEABLY	AABEELLNSSUV	VALUABLENESS
AABDEEHHRRSS	HABERDASHERS	AABEELMNNRST	TABLE MANNERS
AABDEEHHRRSY	HABERDASHERY	AABEELMNORUV	MANOEUVRABLE
AABDEEHORRTW	WEATHERBOARD	AABEELMNRSUU	UNMEASURABLE
AABDEEILRTTX	EXTRADITABLE	AABEELNNORSU	UNREASONABLE
AABDEEJLRSTU	READJUSTABLE	AABEELNNOSSU	UNSEASONABLE
AABDEELMPRTU	PERAMBULATED	AABEELNNRSUW	UNANSWERABLE

AABEELNRSTTU	SUBALTERNATE	AABEKLMORRTU	LABOUR MARKET
AABEELORUVYY	A BY-YOUR-LEAVE	AABELLORSTTY	BATTLE ROYALS
AABEENNRRSTU	SUBTERRANEAN	AABELMMNOSTU	SOMNAMBULATE
AABEENNRTUUV	BUENAVENTURA	AABELMNRSTTU	TRANSMUTABLE
AABEFFLORTUW	WATER BUFFALO	AABELMOPRRTU	PERAMBULATOR
AABEFGIKNRST	BREAKFASTING	AABELNNORSUY	UNREASONABLY
AABEFHLMNOTU	UNFATHOMABLE	AABELNNOSSUY	UNSEASONABLY
AABEFIILNOPS	SAPONIFIABLE	AABELNOPRSST	TRANSPOSABLE
AABEFIILNQTU	QUANTIFIABLE	AABFGIIILTTY	FATIGABILITY
AABEFLLMMNNO	NONFLAMMABLE	AABFHLMNOTUY	UNFATHOMABLY
AABEFLNORUUV	UNFAVOURABLE	AABFIILLMMTY	FLAMMABILITY
AABEGGGMOORS	BAGGAGE ROOMS	AABFIILLOTTY	FLOATABILITY
AABEGGILLNTU	AGGLUTINABLE	AABFLLMNOTYY	FLAMBOYANTLY
AABEGHIKNRTT	BREATHTAKING	AABFLNORUUVY	UNFAVOURABLY
AABEGHILLOSU	HELIOGABALUS	AABGHIINNRSW	BRAINWASHING
AABEGHIMNTTW	BANTAMWEIGHT	AABGIIILNTVY	NAVIGABILITY
AABEGIILMNNU	UNIMAGINABLE	AABGIIILLNOOT	OBLIGATIONAL
AABEGIINRRTT	GREAT BRITAIN	AABGIIILLNRTZ	TRAILBLAZING
AABEGIINSSUU	GUINEA-BISSAU	AABGIILNOSST	SAILING BOATS
AABEGILNOPRU	ABELIAN GROUP	AABGIKNNSSSV	SAVINGS BANKS
AABEGIMNRRSS	EMBARRASSING	AABGILNORSUV	LABOURSAVING
AABEGIMNRRTT	BATTERING RAM	AABGIMNRSTTU	MASTURBATING
AABEGIRRRSTU	ARBITRAGEURS	AABHIIILNOTT	HABILITATION
AABEGLLRSSTU	GLAUBER'S SALT	AABHIIILRSSZ	BILHARZIASIS
AABEGLMMOPRR	PROGRAMMABLE	AABHIIINNOTT	INHABITATION
AABEGLNORRRS	BARREL ORGANS	AABHIILOOPRU	AILUROPHOBIA
AABEGLRRSSUY	BARLEY SUGARS	AABIIILNOSST	ASSIBILATION
AABEHIINORST	HEBRAISATION	AABIIILNSTTY	STAINABILITY
AABEHIINORTZ	HEBRAIZATION	AABIILNOORTY	ABOLITIONARY
AABEHILMNNOT	HAMBLETONIAN	AABIILRSTTUY	SATURABILITY
AABEHILMNORZ	HARMONIZABLE	AABIIMNNOOST	ABOMINATIONS
AABEHILNQSUV	VANQUISHABLE	AABIINNORSTU	URBANISATION
AABEHILNSSTU	HABITUALNESS	AABIINNORTUZ	URBANIZATION
AABEHLPRRSSV	PHRASAL VERBS	AABIINOORRST	ARBORISATION
AABEIIILLNTY	ALIENABILITY	AABIINOORRTZ	ARBORIZATION
AABEIIILLMTY	MALLEABILITY	AABIKLMNSTUY	UNMISTAKABLY
AABEIILLRTTY	ALTERABILITY	AABILLMRSUXY	SUBMAXILLARY
AABEIILNRRST	LIBERTARIANS	AABILNSSTTUV	SUBSTANTIVAL
AABEIIILPRTY	REPARABILITY	AABILOPRRSTU	SUPRAORBITAL
AABEIIILPRSTY	SEPARABILITY	AABIMNORSTTU	MASTURBATION
AABEIIILQTTUY	EQUATABILITY	AABINOOPRRTY	PROBATIONARY
AABEIKLMNSTU	UNMISTAKABLE	AABLMMNNOSTU	SOMNAMBULANT
AABEIKMNORST	EMBARKATIONS	AABMNNOOTTUW	MAN-ABOUT-TOWN
AABEIKNORSTT	STATION BREAK	AACCCEEHILTT	CATECHETICAL
AABEILLMNTVY	AMBIVALENTLY	AACCCEGNORYY	GYNAECOCRACY
AABEILLNRRTU	TURBELLARIAN	AACCCEHIRSTT	CATACHRESTIC
AABEILLPRRTY	LIBERAL PARTY	AACCCEIINRSU	INACCURACIES
AABEILMMRSUY	IMMEASURABLY	AACCDDEHIIRS	DISACCHARIDE
AABEILMMRSUZ	SUMMARIZABLE	AACCDDEMMOOT	ACCOMMODATED
AABEILNOORST	ELABORATIONS	AACCDDIILLTY	DIDACTICALLY
AABEILNPRRST	TRANSPIRABLE	AACCDDIILOPR	DIPLOCARDIAC
AABEILOORRST	LABORATORIES	AACCDEEFHHTT	HATCHET-FACED
AABEILOPPPRR	APPROPRIABLE	AACCDEEHHIKS	SICK HEADACHE
AABEINSSTTTU	SUBSTANTIATE	AACCDEEIMORS	ICE-CREAM SODA

AACCDEEINRRT	INCARCERATED	AACCEILMOSSU	SMILACACEOUS
AACCDEENNOTT	CONCATENATED	AACCEILMPRST	MALPRACTICES
AACCDEHINORS	ARCHDIOCESAN	AACCEILMTUUV	ACCUMULATIVE
AACCDEHNORRY	ARCHDEACONRY	AACCEILNORVY	CLAIRVOYANCE
AACCDEIIILNT	DIALECTICIAN	AACCEILNRRTT	RECALCITRANT
AACCDEIILMST	ACCLIMATISED	AACCEILNRTUY	INACCURATELY
AACCDEIILMTZ	ACCLIMATIZED	AACCEINNORST	TRANSOCEANIC
AACCDEILLNTY	ACCIDENTALLY	AACCEINNOTTU	ACCENTUATION
AACCDEKMPUUV	VACUUM-PACKED	AACCEINOORTV	COACERVATION
AACCDGINRRRY	CARD-CARRYING	AACCEINORRRT	INCARCERATOR
AACCDIIILRST	RADICALISTIC	AACCEIOPRTVY	OVERCAPACITY
AACCDIILNOTU	CLAUDICATION	AACCELLRRSTY	CRYSTAL CLEAR
AACCDIIOPRTT	CATADIOPTRIC	AACCELNNOOPV	PLANO-CONCAVE
AACCDILLLTYY	DACTYLICALLY	AACCELPRSSTU	SPECTACULARS
AACCDILLNORY	DRACONICALLY	AACCENOOPSUY	APOCYNACEOUS
AACCEEEILRTV	ACCELERATIVE	AACCEORSSTUY	STYRACACEOUS
AACCEEGHILMP	MEGACEPHALIC	AACCFIIINOPT	PACIFICATION
AACCEEGHOSST	STAGECOACHES	AACCFIILMOPT	FAIT ACCOMPLI
AACCEEGILNRT	ACCELERATING	AACCFIILSTTU	FACTUALISTIC
AACCEEHIMNOR	AEROMECHANIC	AACCFIIORRST	SCARIFICATOR
AACCEEHIRRST	CHARACTERISE	AACCFINNORSS	SAN FRANCISCO
AACCEEHIRRTZ	CHARACTERIZE	AACCGHHIKNOW	CHANGCHIAKOW
AACCEEIILLPR	CAPERCAILLIE	AACCGHHLOPRY	CHALCOGRAPHY
AACCEEILNORT	ACCELERATION	AACCGHIILLPR	CALLIGRAPHIC
AACCEELORRST	ACCELERATORS	AACCGHIMOPRR	MACROGRAPHIC
AACCEELPPSSU	SPACE CAPSULE	AACCGHIOPRRT	CARTOGRAPHIC
AACCEERSSTTU	EASTER CACTUS	AACCGIINRRTU	CARICATURING
AACCEFHLRRTU	CHARACTERFUL	AACCGILLOOPR	CARPOLOGICAL
AACCEGHIILPR	ARCHIPELAGIC	AACCGILLOOST	SCATOLOGICAL
AACCEGIKNPSS	PACKING CASES	AACCGILMNTUU	ACCUMULATING
AACCEGINNTTU	ACCENTUATING	AACCGIMNNOPY	ACCOMPANYING
AACCEHHIILRR	HIERARCHICAL	AACCHIIINRTT	ANTIRACHITIC
AACCEHHMOSST	STOMACHACHES	AACCHIINNNOT	CACHINNATION
AACCEHHPRSST	CATCHPHRASES	AACCHIINRSTY	SACCHARINITY
AACCEHIILNPS	CHAPLAINCIES	AACCHILLORTY	TROCHAICALLY
AACCEHIIMNRV	VICE-CHAIRMAN	AACCHILLOSST	SCHOLASTICAL
AACCEHILLMNO	MELANCHOLIAC	AACCHILMOPRS	ARCHOPLASMIC
AACCEHILLMNY	MECHANICALLY	AACCHIMNOPRT	PANCHROMATIC
AACCEHILNPRT	PENTARCHICAL	AACCHIMOOPRT	APOCHROMATIC
AACCEHILPRTY	ARCHETYPICAL	AACCHINOOSTT	COACH STATION
AACCEHIMORTT	METATHORACIC	AACCHIOPRSTT	CATASTROPHIC
AACCEHINOOSX	HEXACOSANOIC	AACCIILLLMTY	CLIMATICALLY
AACCEHPPRRST	SCRATCH PAPER	AACCIILLSSTY	CLASSICALITY
AACCEIILLNRT	ANTICLERICAL	AACCIILNTTTY	ATLANTIC CITY
AACCEIILMRST	ACCLIMATISER	AACCIILPRTTY	PRACTICALITY
AACCEIILMRTZ	ACCLIMATIZER	AACCIINNOSTV	VACCINATIONS
AACCEILLMSTU	MISCALCULATE	AACCIINRSTTU	TRACUCIANIST
AACCEILLNNOT	CANCELLATION	AACCIIORRSTT	ARISTOCRATIC
AACCEILLNOSS	NEOCLASSICAL	AACCIIRRSTTU	CARICATURIST
AACCEILLOPSU	CAPILLACEOUS	AACCILLLNOVY	VOLCANICALLY
AACCEILLPRSS	PRECLASSICAL	AACCILLNOOSY	OCCASIONALLY
AACCEILLSTTY	ECSTATICALLY	AACCILLNORTY	NARCOTICALLY
AACCEILMMORT	MACROCLIMATE	AACCILLNOSTU	CALCULATIONS
AACCEILMNOPS	COMPLAISANCE	AACCILLNRSTU	CURTAIN CALLS

AACCILLORSTY	ACROSTICALLY
AACCILLOSTUY	ACOUSTICALLY
AACCILMNOTUU	ACCUMULATION
AACCILNOOPTU	OCCUPATIONAL
AACCILNOSSST	CLASS ACTIONS
AACCILRRSSUW	CIRCULAR SAWS
AACCIMNOPSST	ACCOMPANISTS
AACCINOPRSTY	PANTISOCRACY
AACCIORRSTTT	STRATOCRATIC
AACCLMORSTUU	ACCUMULATORS
AACDDDEEEHLOR	DODECAHEDRAL
AACDDEEEHLTY	ACETALDEHYDE
AACDDEFIILSS	CLASSIFIED AD
AACDDEGNNNOS	SONG AND DANCE
AACDDGIIJNTU	ADJUDICATING
AACDDIIJNOTU	ADJUDICATION
AACDDIJORSTU	ADJUDICATORS
AACDDIKMNNRU	MANDARIN DUCK
AACDDLNORSTY	SCOTLAND YARD
AACDEEFHLMSY	SHAMEFACEDLY
AACDEEGHIMNT	MAGNETIC HEAD
AACDEEGHLNNO	HENDECAGONAL
AACDEEGILNST	DE-ESCALATING
AACDEEIIMNRS	AMERICANISED
AACDEEIIMNRZ	AMERICANIZED
AACDEEIINQSU	INADEQUACIES
AACDEEILMMNT	MEDICAMENTAL
AACDEEILMRVY	DEVIL-MAY-CARE
AACDEEILNNOW	NEW CALEDONIA
AACDEEILNOST	DE-ESCALATION
AACDEEINNRRT	REINCARNATED
AACDEEIPRRTV	PREVARICATED
AACDEENQRSSU	SQUARE DANCES
AACDEFILNSTY	FASCINATEDLY
AACDEFMNRTUU	MANUFACTURED
AACDEGIIINPTT	DECAPITATING
AACDEGILLOOP	PAEDOLOGICAL
AACDEGILMORY	CARDIOMEGALY
AACDEGLNOPRR	DROP A CLANGER
AACDEHILLLRY	HERALDICALLY
AACDEHILLNTU	HALLUCINATED
AACDEHIMNRTY	DIATHERMANCY
AACDEHINORRT	RIDE AT ANCHOR
AACDEHLMOSUY	ACHLAMYDEOUS
AACDEHLNOOPP	CEPHALOPODAN
AACDEHLOPRRT	PROCATHEDRAL
AACDEHLORRTT	TETRACHORDAL
AACDEHNOPRTY	HYDNOCARPATE
AACDEIIIINPRT	PEDIATRICIAN
AACDEIIIPRST	PARASITICIDE
AACDEIINNORT	DERACINATION
AACDEIINOPTT	DECAPITATION
AACDEIINOTTV	DEACTIVATION
AACDEIIOSSST	DISASSOCIATE

AACDEIIPPRTT	PARTICIPATED
AACDEIJLLTVY	ADJECTIVALLY
AACDEILLMNOY	DAEMONICALLY, DEMONIACALLY
AACDEILLNOSW	DISALLOWANCE
AACDEILLNPTY	PEDANTICALLY
AACDEILMMORT	MELODRAMATIC
AACDEILMNOST	DECLAMATIONS
AACDEILMRTTU	MATRICULATED
AACDEILNORST	DECLARATIONS
AACDEILNPPRU	APPENDICULAR
AACDEIMNNOTT	CONTAMINATED
AACDEIMNORSY	AERODYNAMICS
AACDEIMOOSTU	DIATOMACEOUS
AACDEINNOPRS	CAPARISONNED
AACDEINNOSSY	ASCENSION DAY
AACDEINNQTUU	UNACQUAINTED
AACDEINOPSSU	SAPINDACEOUS
AACDEKKNRRSY	KNACKER'S YARD
AACDELMNNORS	ROMAN CANDLES
AACDELMOPRSU	CAMELOPARDUS
AACDEMORRRSU	ARMOURED CARS
AACDFFIINRTY	AFFINITY CARD
AACDFGILNNRT	LANDING CRAFT
AACDFHIKNSTT	THICK AND FAST
AACDFIIILNNT	INFANTICIDAL
AACDGHIINNPP	HANDICAPPING
AACDGHIIOPRR	RADIOGRAPHIC
AACDGHILNNRS	CRASH LANDING
AACDGHIOPRRY	CARDIOGRAPHY
AACDGIILLOOR	RADIOLOGICAL
AACDGIILLOOU	AUDIOLOGICAL
AACDGIILNNSZ	SCANDALIZING
AACDGIILRSTU	GRADUALISTIC
AACDGILLMOTY	DOGMATICALLY
AACDGILNPRSY	PLAYING CARDS
AACDHHILORRY	ACHLORHYDRIA
AACDHIILLLNS	ACHILL ISLAND
AACDHIIOPRSS	APHRODISIACS
AACDHINOPQRU	QUADRAPHONIC
AACDIIINORTV	DIVARICATION
AACDIIJLORTU	JUDICATORIAL
AACDIILLLTYY	DIALYTICALLY
AACDIILLNOTY	DIATONICALLY
AACDIILLSSTY	SADISTICALLY
AACDIILMNOST	DISCLAMATION
AACDIILNNRTY	TYRANNICIDAL
AACDIIMNNORS	DRACONIANISM
AACDIIMNOPSS	DIPSOMANIACS
AACDIIMNRSTU	TRADUCIANISM
AACDIINNORRT	DOCTRINARIAN
AACDIKNNPPSS	SPICK-AND-SPAN
AACDILLNORSY	SARDONICALLY
AACDILLOPRSY	SPORADICALLY

AACDIMMNOORT	MONODRAMATIC
AACDLLNOSSUY	SCANDALOUSLY
AACEEEGHNRTX	EXCHANGE RATE
AACEEEGNSTTY	ESTATE AGENCY
AACEEEEHPRSST	SPACE HEATERS
AACEEENPRSVY	SEVERANCE PAY
AACEEFFIMNRR	REAFFIRMANCE
AACEEFFINOTT	AFFECTIONATE
AACEEFLLPSTT	CLEFT PALATES
AACEEFLMRSST	MALEFACTRESS
AACEEGGILLNO	GENEALOGICAL
AACEEGGMNNOT	AGAMOGENETIC
AACEEGHIMNOT	HAEMATOGENIC
AACEEGHNPRTX	PART EXCHANGE
AACEEGHRRSST	GATECRASHERS
AACEEGIMNPTT	MAGNETIC TAPE
AACEEGIMNRST	EAST GERMANIC
AACEEGINORSU	GERANIACEOUS
AACEEGLMORTT	GALACTOMETER
AACEEGLNRTVY	TRAVEL AGENCY
AACEEHHIKRTT	TAKE THE CHAIR
AACEEHIINSTT	AESTHETICIAN
AACEEHINSSTT	ANAESTHETICS
AACEEHINTTTU	AUTHENTICATE
AACEEHIOPRST	APOTHECARIES
AACEEHIPRSTT	PARAESTHETIC
AACEEHKMNRRS	SNAKE CHARMER
AACEEHLMPRST	SPERMATHECAL
AACEEHLMRTTY	METHACRYLATE
AACEEHNNPPST	HAPPENSTANCE
AACEEIILPRST	RECAPITALISE
AACEEIILPRTZ	RECAPITALIZE
AACEEIIMNPTV	EMANCIPATIVE
AACEEIIMNRRS	AMERICANISER
AACEEIIMNRRZ	AMERICANIZER
AACEEIIPPRTV	APPRECIATIVE
AACEEIKLNNRS	RANKINE SCALE
AACEEILMMMNY	MECAMYLAMINE
AACEEILMPPRS	PRE-ECLAMPSIA
AACEEILMSTUV	EMASCULATIVE
AACEEILNORRT	RECREATIONAL
AACEEILPRTTU	RECAPITULATE
AACEEINNNRST	CENTENARIANS
AACEEINNRSSS	RENAISSANCES
AACEEIOPRSTT	ECTOPARASITE
AACEEIRRSSTT	SECRETARIATS
AACEEKLMPRST	MARKETPLACES
AACEEKLNQSUY	SQUEAKY-CLEAN
AACEELMRRSUU	REAUMUR SCALE
AACEELNRRTUX	EXTRANUCLEAR
AACEELNRTTVY	TETRAVALENCY
AACEEMNORSTU	RAMENTACEOUS
AACEEMOPRTTV	CAVEAT EMPTOR
AACEENNPPRTU	APPURTENANCE

AACEENRRSSSU	REASSURANCES
AACEFFHHNSSU	SCHAFFHAUSEN
AACEFFINOSTT	AFFECTATIONS
AACEFFMORTTT	MATTER-OF-FACT
AACEFIIILTTV	FACILITATIVE
AACEFIIINORT	AERIFICATION
AACEFILNORRT	REFRACTIONAL
AACEFIORRSTU	SURFACE-TO-AIR
AACEFLLNORTU	CALL OF NATURE
AACEFLNNORRT	CONFRATERNAL
AACEFMNRRTUU	MANUFACTURER
AACEGGGKLRSU	LUGGAGE RACKS
AACEGGHILOPR	GEOGRAPHICAL
AACEGGHINRST	GATECRASHING
AACEGGINRRSU	GUN CARRIAGES
AACEGGINRSSV	SAVING GRACES
AACEGHHIMORR	HAEMORRHAGIC
AACEGHILLPRR	CALLIGRAPHER
AACEGHILMOOT	HAEMATOLOGIC
AACEGHILOPRS	ARCHIPELAGOS
AACEGHIMNOPR	ANEMOGRAPHIC,
PHANEROGAMIC	
AACEGHIMNRSV	SHAVING CREAM
AACEGHNOOPRY	OCEANOGRAPHY
AACEGHOPRRRT	CARTOGRAPHER
AACEGIIINRRT	GERIATRICIAN
AACEGIILLNNT	GEANTICLINAL
AACEGIILLNRT	INTERGLACIAL
AACEGIILLOOT	AETIOLOGICAL
AACEGIILMNNS	MALIGNANCIES
AACEGIIMMPRT	EPIGRAMMATIC
AACEGIIMNNPT	EMANCIPATING
AACEGIIMNNTT	ANTIMAGNETIC
AACEGIIMRRSS	MISCARRIAGES
AACEGIIMRSST	MAGISTRACIES
AACEGIINNRST	ASCERTAINING
AACEGIINPPRT	APPRECIATING
AACEGIINRTTV	REACTIVATING
AACEGILLMNTY	MAGNETICALLY
AACEGILLNOSU	GALLINACEOUS
AACEGILLORSU	ARGILLACEOUS
AACEGILLPRSU	SUPERGLACIAL
AACEGILMNNRT	MAGIC LANTERN
AACEGILMNSTU	EMASCULATING
AACEGILNOOSU	LOGANIACEOUS
AACEGILNRTUW	CATERWAULING
AACEGINNOORT	OCTOGENARIAN
AACEGINNRSTW	WATERING CANS
AACEGINPPRRT	TRACING PAPER
AACEGKOPRSTU	PACKAGE TOURS
AACEGLMORTTY	GALACTOMETRY
AACEGLNOOPSV	GALVANOSCOPE
AACEGLNORTTU	CONGRATULATE
AACEGLRRSTYZ	CRYSTAL GAZER

AACEHHIILMOP	HAEMOPHILIAC
AACEHIILLOPT	PALAEOLITHIC
AACEHIILLRTY	HIERATICALLY
AACEHIILNTTT	ANTITHETICAL
AACEHIIMRRST	MATRIARCHIES
AACEHIINPTTT	ANTIPATHETIC
AACEHIINRRST	CHRISTIAN ERA
AACEHIIPRRST	PATRIARCHIES
AACEHILLLTTY	ATHLETICALLY
AACEHILLMPTY	EMPATHICALLY, EMPHATICALLY
AACEHILLMTTY	THEMATICALLY
AACEHILLPTTY	PATHETICALLY
AACEHILLRTTY	THEATRICALLY
AACEHILMNPRU	ALPHANUMERIC
AACEHILMOPRT	METAPHORICAL
AACEHILMOTXY	HAEMATOXYLIC
AACEHILMPSTY	METAPHYSICAL
AACEHILOPRRS	ARCHESPORIAL
AACEHIMNORRT	NORTH AMERICA
AACEHIMORSTU	SOUTH AMERICA
AACEHIMPRSTT	METAPHRASTIC
AACEHMNNRSTU	TRANSHUMANCE
AACEHMNNRTVY	MERCHANT NAVY
AACEHOPRSSTT	CATASTROPHES
AACEIIINPTTV	ANTICIPATIVE
AACEIIKLLMRT	ALKALIMETRIC
AACEIILLMNSS	MISALLIANCES
AACEIILLMNTU	NAUTICAL MILE
AACEIILLMRTT	ALTIMETRICAL
AACEIILMNSTX	ANTICLIMAXES
AACEIILNOPPS	EPISCOPALIAN
AACEIILNOSTT	ELASTICATION
AACEIILNPRTT	ANTIPARTICLE
AACEIILNRTTU	INARTICULATE
AACEIIMMNRSS	AMERICANISMS
AACEIIMNNOPT	EMANCIPATION
AACEIIMNORST	RACEMISATION
AACEIIMNORTZ	RACEMIZATION
AACEIIMNRSST	SECTARIANISM
AACEIINNNTUV	ANNUNCIATIVE
AACEIINOPPRT	APPRECIATION
AACEIINORTTV	REACTIVATION
AACEIIPRSSTT	SEPARATISTIC
AACEIJKRSTTT	STRAITJACKET
AACEIJLLMSTY	MAJESTICALLY
AACEIJLNOSTU	EJACULATIONS
AACEIKLLSTTY	SALT LAKE CITY
AACEIKLMNOPT	KLEPTOMANIAC
AACEILLLLMTY	METALLICALLY
AACEILLMMTUY	IMMACULATELY
AACEILLMNSTY	SEMANTICALLY
AACEILLMPRSY	MIRACLE PLAYS
AACEILLNOORT	REALLOCATION
AACEILLNOSTT	CASTELLATION
AACEILLOPRTY	OPERATICALLY
AACEILLPRRST	CATERPILLARS
AACEILLRTTUY	ARTICULATELY
AACEILLSTTUY	EUSTATICALLY
AACEILMMNORT	COMMENTARIAL
AACEILMNOSTU	EMASCULATION
AACEILMNOSTX	EXCLAMATIONS
AACEILNNOPTT	PLACENTATION
AACEILNNRRTU	INTRANUCLEAR
AACEILNORSTT	ALTERCATIONS
AACEILRSTTTU	STRATICULATE
AACEILRTTTVY	ATTRACTIVELY
AACEIMNNOOPT	COMPANIONATE
AACEIMNOPRTY	EMANCIPATORY
AACEIMNNNORST	NONSECTARIAN
AACEINNORSTT	RECANTATIONS
AACEINOPSSTT	SPACE STATION
AACEINRTTTUV	UNATTRACTIVE
AACEIOPRRRTV	PREVARICATOR
AACEJKLNNORT	JACK-O'-LANTERN
AACEKLLNOPRS	PANCAKE ROLLS
AACEKLNOORRT	CENTRAL KAROO
AACEKNNNORSTU	CANTANKEROUS
AACELLMOPSUU	AMPULLACEOUS
AACELMNORSTW	SCARLET WOMAN
AACELPRSSSTT	PLASTER CASTS
AACENNNNORSTW	WATER CANNONS
AACENNPRRSTY	TRANSPARENCY
AACFFIORRSTT	TRAFFICATORS
AACFFMORRSTY	FACTORY FARMS
AACFGGILMNOU	CAMOUFLAGING
AACFGIIILNTT	FACILITATING
AACFGIIINOST	GASIFICATION
AACFIIILLRTY	ARTIFICIALLY
AACFIIILNOST	SALIFICATION
AACFIIILNOTT	FACILITATION
AACFIIIMNORT	RAMIFICATION
AACFIIINORTT	RATIFICATION
AACFIILMNOST	FACTIONALISM
AACFIILNOOST	FOCALISATION
AACFIILNOOTZ	FOCALIZATION
AACFIILNOSTT	FACTIONALIST
AACFIINOSSTT	SATISFACTION
AACFILLLOSUY	FALLACIOUSLY
AACFILLNORTY	FRACTIONALLY
AACFILMORSTT	STALACTIFORM
AACFINOORRTT	FRACTIONATOR
AACFIORSSTTY	SATISFACTORY
AACFKLMSSUUV	VACUUM FLASKS
AACGGHHIIOPR	HAGIOGRAPHIC
AACGGIILLNTY	GIGANTICALLY
AACGHIILLNOP	ANGLOPHILIAC
AACGHILLNOOT	ANTHOLOGICAL
AACGHILLOOPT	PATHOLOGICAL

AACGHILNOPPR	PLANOGRAPHIC
AACGHINOPPRT	PANTOGRAPHIC
AACGHINOPRRU	URANOGRAPHIC
AACGHMOOPRY	PHARMACOLOGY
AACGHMMOORRT	CHROMATOGRAM
AACGHOOPPRSU	CARPOPHAGOUS
AACGIIILNPTZ	CAPITALIZING
AACGIIILPRST	PLAGIARISTIC
AACGIIINNPTT	ANTICIPATING
AACGIILLMOPX	PLAGIOCLIMAX
AACGIILMNNTU	CALUMNIATING
AACGIILNPTTU	CAPITULATING
AACGIILNRTTU	ARTICULATING
AACGIILOPRST	PARALOGISTIC
AACGIIMPRSTT	PRAGMATISTIC
AACGIINNOSTT	ANTAGONISTIC
AACGILLMOOST	MALACOLOGIST
AACGILLOORST	ASTROLOGICAL
AACGILLOOTTU	TAUTOLOGICAL
AACGILLRRTUU	AGRICULTURAL
AACGILNNOOTV	LONG VACATION
AACGIMMNNOOU	COMMON IGUANA
AACGIMMOPRRT	PROGRAMMATIC
AACGINOPPRTU	GROUP CAPTAIN
AACGLMOOSTUU	GLAUCOMATOUS
AACGLNOOPSVY	GALVANOSCOPY
AACHHIIMNPRS	CHAIRMANSHIP
AACHIIINNSTY	HINAYANISTIC
AACHIILMOPRS	PAROCHIALISM
AACHIIMNNOST	MACHINATIONS
AACHIKLMOOTY	OKLAHOMA CITY
AACHILLMNORY	HARMONICALLY
AACHILLMOPSY	HYALOPLASMIC
AACHILLNORTU	HALLUCINATOR
AACHILMNNOSU	NO SUCH ANIMAL
AACHIMMNNOPY	NYMPHOMANIAC
AACHIMNNORSS	ANACHRONISMS
AACHIMNOPRRS	PARACHRONISM
AACHINOPRTTU	NATUROPATHIC
AACHIPRSSTTU	PARACHUTISTS
AACHLLNNNOTY	NONCHALANTLY
AACHMOORSTTU	TRACHOMATOUS
AACIIINNOPTT	ANTICIPATION
AACIIINNOTTV	INACTIVATION
AACIIINNRSSU	UNCINARIASIS
AACIIINSSTTT	STATISTICIAN
AACIILLMOTTY	AMITOTICALLY
AACIILLNOOST	LOCALISATION
AACIILLNOOTZ	LOCALIZATION
AACIILLNOSTV	VACILLATIONS
AACIILLORSTY	AORISTICALLY
AACIILLRSTTY	ARTISTICALLY
AACIILLSTTUY	AUTISTICALLY
AACIILMMORSS	COMMISSARIAL

AACIILMNNOTU	CALUMNIATION
AACIILNNOOTV	INVOCATIONAL
AACIILNOOSTV	VOCALISATION
AACIILNOOTVZ	VOCALIZATION
AACIILNOPPST	APPLICATIONS
AACIILNOPTTU	CAPITULATION
AACIILNORTTU	ARTICULATION
AACIILNRSTTU	NATURALISTIC
AACIILORSUVY	AVARICIOUSLY
AACIIMMORSST	COMMISSARIAT
AACIINNNNOTU	ANNUNCIATION
AACIINNNOOST	CANONISATION
AACIINNNOOTZ	CANONIZATION
AACIINNNORST	INCARNATIONS
AACIINNNOSTT	INCANTATIONS
AACIINNORSST	INCRASSATION
AACIINOORRTT	RATIOCINATOR
AACIINOOSSST	ASSOCIATIONS
AACIINOPRTTY	ANTICIPATORY
AACIINORRSTU	CURARISATION
AACIINORRTUZ	CURARIZATION
AACIINPPRSTT	PARTICIPANTS
AACIIOPPRRTT	PARTICIPATOR
AACIKLMOPRSY	KARYOPLASMIC
AACILLLNOPTY	PLATONICALLY
AACILLLNOSVY	SLAVONICALLY
AACILLMNORTY	ROMANTICALLY
AACILLMNOSTY	MONASTICALLY
AACILLMOSTUY	CALAMITOUSLY
AACILLNNRTYY	TYRANNICALLY
AACILLNOPPTY	PANOPTICALLY
AACILLNOPRSS	RAPSCALLIONS
AACILLNPSTYY	SYNAPTICALLY
AACILLOOORTY	ORATORICALLY
AACILLPRRTUY	PARTICULARLY
AACILLQRTUUU	AQUICULTURAL
AACILMNNOPST	COMPLAINANTS
AACILMNOOPRT	PROCLAMATION
AACILMNOORST	ASTRONOMICAL
AACILMNORSTY	MICROANALYST
AACILMORRTTU	COURT-MARTIAL, MATRICULATOR
AACILNORSTVY	CLAIRVOYANTS
AACILNOSTTUU	AUSCULTATION
AACILORRTTUY	ARTICULATORY
AACIMMOPSTTY	ASYMPTOMATIC
AACIMNNNOSTT	CONTAMINANTS
AACIMNNOOPWY	COMPANIONWAY
AACIMNNOORTT	CONTAMINATOR
AACIMNNOOSTT	ANTONOMASTIC
AACIMOORSSST	SARCOMATOSIS
AACINNORRSST	TRANSACTIONS
AACINORSSTTU	ASTRONAUTICS
AACLNNOPRTTU	CONTRAPUNTAL

AACLNPRSTTYY	CRYPTANALYST	AADEEJLNNRTW	LANTERN-JAWED
AACMOOPRSSST	ASTROCOMPASS	AADEELLLLNPRU	UNPARALLELED
AADDDEGIRSSU	SUGAR DADDIES	AADEELLNPSTT	DENTAL PLATES
AADDDEINRSST	STANDARDISED	AADEELLRZZZZ	RAZZLE-DAZZLE
AADDDEINRSTZ	STANDARDIZED	AADEELMNPRTT	DEPARTMENTAL
AADDDGLNORST	GOLD STANDARD	AADEELOPRTTX	EXTRAPOLATED
AADDEEEGLPRS	SPREAD-EAGLED	AADEEMNNRTUX	EXTRAMUNDANE
AADDEEEHHMMR	HAMMERHEADED	AADEEMORSTWW	WATER MEADOWS
AADDEEHHRTXY	HEXAHYDRATED	AADEEMQRRSSU	MASQUERADERS
AADDEEHNSSWY	ASH WEDNESDAY	AADEFFHLNOTT	FAT OF THE LAND
AADDEEILOPRT	PORT ADELAIDE	AADEFFIIILST	DISAFFILIATE
AADDEEIMNRTV	ANIMADVERTED	AADEFGGINRSU	SAFEGUARDING
AADDEFFIILST	FIT AS A FIDDLE	AADEFGHNRRST	GRANDFATHERS
AADDEFINORTU	DEFRAUDATION	AADEFGILNORT	DEFLAGRATION
AADDEFLLNOSU	ALL OF A SUDDEN	AADEFHILLMRS	FIELD MARSHAL
AADDEGINORST	DEGRADATIONS	AADEFHINNOTU	FOUNTAINHEAD
AADDEGNOPRRU	PARADE GROUND	AADEFIIILMRS	FAMILIARISED
AADDEIMNRSTT	STANDARD TIME	AADEFIIILMRZ	FAMILIARIZED
AADDEINRRSST	STANDARDISER	AADEFIKMNNOR	AFRIKANERDOM
AADDEINRRSTZ	STANDARDIZER	AADEFILMORTY	DEFAMATORILY
AADDELNOORTV	VOLTA REDONDA	AADEFILNORTY	DEFLATIONARY
AADDHIILORRT	DIARTHRODIAL	AADEFILNSSTY	SAFETY ISLAND
AADDIIILNOPT	DILAPIDATION	AADEFILNTTUY	INFATUATEDLY
AADDIILLNOTY	ADDITIONALLY	AADEFIMRRRSY	DAIRY FARMERS
AADDLLNNRSUY	ALL AND SUNDRY	AADEFLMNNSTU	FUNDAMENTALS
AADEEEGMMNNT	ENDAMAGEMENT	AADEFLOOSSST	A DOSE OF SALTS
AADEEEHHRTVY	HEAVYHEARTED	AADEGGILNNST	LANDING STAGE
AADEEEHIRSST	HEART DISEASE	AADEGHIMMORX	HEXAGRAMMOID
AADEEELNNRWZ	NEW ZEALANDER	AADEGHIOPRRR	RADIOGRAPHER
AADEEFFNORRT	FORE-AND-AFTER	AADEGHNOPRRY	PARAHYDROGEN
AADEEFHINRTT	FAINT-HEARTED	AADEGIILNNST	DESALINATING
AADEEFILLMRT	FLEET ADMIRAL	AADEGIILPQRU	QUADRIPLEGIA
AADEEFLNRSST	EAST FLANDERS	AADEGIIMMNST	DIAMAGNETISM
AADEEGGLMORT	AGGLOMERATED	AADEGIINPPRS	DISAPPEARING
AADEEGHINPRS	SPEARHEADING	AADEGILLNNPS	PINEAL GLANDS
AADEEGKMNRRT	MARKET GARDEN	AADEGILNRTTU	ADULTERATING
AADEEGKNOPTW	TAKE DOWN A PEG	AADEGILNSSST	STAINED GLASS
AADEEHILNQRU	HARLEQUINADE	AADEGIMNQRSU	MASQUERADING
AADEEHIMNOTZ	DIAZOMETHANE	AADEGINNPPRS	SANDPAPERING
AADEEHLNNRST	NEANDERTHALS	AADEGINOPPRS	PROPAGANDISE
AADEEHLRSTTT	DEATH RATTLES	AADEGINOPPRZ	PROPAGANDIZE
AADEEHQRRSTU	HEADQUARTERS	AADEGLLNNSUY	AULD LANG SYNE
AADEEIIKMTVW	TAKE A DIM VIEW	AADEGLNPRSST	STAR-SPANGLED
AADEEIILMRST	MATERIALISED	AADEGLNRSTTU	STRANGULATED
AADEEIILMRTZ	MATERIALIZED	AADEGMNRRSST	GRAND MASTERS
AADEEIIMNNRT	ANTEMERIDIAN	AADEGNNPRRST	GRANDPARENTS
AADEEIILNQTUY	INADEQUATELY	AADEGOPRSTTU	POSTGRADUATE
AADEEIILNRSST	EASTER ISLAND	AADEHHIILLPP	PHILADELPHIA
AADEEIILNRSTU	DENATURALISE	AADEHIKLMORY	HOLIDAYMAKER
AADEEIILNRTUZ	DENATURALIZE	AADEHILNORRT	ENARTHRODIAL
AADEEIMMNNRR	REMAINDERMAN	AADEHINOPRST	HEROD ANTIPAS
AADEEIMMNNST	MISDEMEANANT	AADEHIOPRRTY	RADIOTHERAPY
AADEEINOPRST	ENDOPARASITE	AADEHMNNRSTT	HERMANNSTADT
AADEEINOPRTU	DEUTERANOPIA	AADEHPRRSTTU	UTTAR PRADESH

AADEIIILNOST	IDEALISATION
AADEIIILNOTZ	IDEALIZATION
AADEIILLNUVV	VAUDEVILLIAN
AADEIILMNNOT	DELAMINATION
AADEIILMNNOS	DESALINATION, NATIONALISED
AADEIILNNOTZ	NATIONALIZED
AADEIILNNTUV	ANTEDILUVIAN
AADEIILNORST	RATIONALISED
AADEIILNORTV	DERIVATIONAL
AADEIILNORTZ	RATIONALIZED
AADEIILNRSTT	INTERSTADIAL
AADEIIMNRSTT	ADMINISTRATE
AADEIINNORST	TARDENOISIAN
AADEILNNORST	SAINT LEONARD
AADEILNNSSTT	STATEN ISLAND
AADEILNORTTU	ADULTERATION
AADEILNOSTUV	DEVALUATIONS
AADEILNQRTUV	QUADRIVALENT
AADEIMNOQSTU	DESQUAMATION
AADEIMNRSSTV	MAIDSERVANTS
AADEIMOPPRTX	APPROXIMATED
AADEIMPRRSTY	TRYPARSAMIDE
AADEINNORTTU	DENATURATION
AADEINNRSSTW	SAINT ANDREWS
AADEIOPPPRRT	APPROPRIATED
AADELLNNORST	RALLENTANDOS
AADELMNNRTUU	ULTRAMUNDANE
AADELMOPRRTU	ARMOUR-PLATED
AADELNMPRSTT	TRANSPLANTED
AADELNOPRSSU	SAN PEDRO SULA
AADEMNNNRSTU	TRANSMUNDANE
AADEMNOPPRTU	PUT A DAMPER ON
AADFFFHHLNOST	STANDOFF HALF
AADFHHILLOSY	HALF-HOLIDAYS
AADFILNNOOTU	FOUNDATIONAL
AADFINNOOSTU	SODA FOUNTAIN
AADGGIINNRRS	DISARRANGING
AADGGILMMNOR	MID GLAMORGAN
AADGHHILRSTZ	HAZARD LIGHTS
AADGHHIMNNRT	RIGHT-HAND MAN
AADGHIINPRSU	GUARDIANSHIP
AADGHILNORSZ	LOSING HAZARD
AADGHINRSSWW	WASH DRAWINGS
AADGHLPRSSSU	SPLASH GUARDS
AADGIIILNNTV	INVALIDATING
AADGIILMRTUV	MULTIGRAVIDA
AADGIILNNNOS	ANGLO-INDIANS
AADGIILQRUUV	GUADALQUIVIR
AADGILLNPPUY	APPLAUDINGLY
AADGIMNOPPRS	PROPAGANDISM
AADGIMNPRSTT	TRADING STAMP
AADGINOPPRST	PROPAGANDIST
AADHIIKNSTTZ	TADZHIKISTAN
AADHIILOPPSY	DIAPOPHYSIAL
AADHILNOOPRT	ANTHROPOIDAL
AADHINPRSSTY	DANISH PASTRY
AADHIOPRRSTY	PARATHYROIDS
AADHJKLMMORS	HAMMARSKJOLD
AADIIILNNOPS	INDIANAPOLIS
AADIIIILNNOTV	INVALIDATION
AADIIINORRST	IRRADIATIONS
AADIIKNNRSST	KRISTIANSAND
AADIIKNRSSTT	KRISTIANSTAD
AADIILMNOQRU	QUADRINOMIAL
AADIILMOPRST	PRISMATOIDAL
AADIILNOOSTV	VASODILATION
AADIINOOTTUX	AUTOXIDATION
AADIIRRSSTUV	STRADIVARIUS
AADILNOPPRST	POSTPRANDIAL
AADLMNNORUWY	LAUNDRYWOMAN
AADMNOQRSUUU	QUADRUMANOUS
AADNORRSTTUY	TRANSUDATORY
AAEEEFLRSTTW	WELFARE STATE
AAEEEGGHRTUW	WEATHER GAUGE
AAEEEGGIRTVX	EXAGGERATIVE
AAEEEGMNRSSS	MANAGERESSES
AAEEEGNSSTTT	ESTATE AGENTS
AAEEEHILRTTY	AETHEREALITY
AAEEEHILSSTT	TELAESTHESIA
AAEEEHIMMSST	HAEMATEMESIS
AAEEEHINSSTT	ANAESTHETISE
AAEEEHINSTTZ	ANAESTHETIZE
AAEEEHLNPRST	ELEPHANT'S-EAR
AAEEEHLPQRSU	RAPHAELESQUE
AAEEEHNRSTVV	WEATHER VANES
AAEEELMNPSTX	SET AN EXAMPLE
AAEEELOPRTTU	POET LAUREATE
AAEEEMNPPSST	APPEASEMENTS
AAEEEMPRRSTT	TAPE STREAMER
AAEEEMPRSSTU	TAPE MEASURES
AAEEENPRSSST	SEPARATENESS
AAEEFFGLNRST	GENERAL STAFF
AAEEFHHILRST	FAITH HEALERS
AAEEFHILRRTU	HEART FAILURE
AAEEFHLMRSSU	HALF MEASURES
AAEEFIILRSSZ	LAISSEZ-FAIRE
AAEEFLSSTVVY	SAFETY VALVES
AAEEFMNNRRTT	TENANT FARMER
AAEEFNNPRSST	SNAP FASTENER
AAEEGGGINRTX	EXAGGERATING
AAEEGGIMNOSS	AGAMOGENESIS
AAEEGGIMNRTV	GRAM-NEGATIVE
AAEEGGINNRTU	GUARANTEEING
AAEEGGINORTX	EXAGGERATION
AAEEGGLNNOTU	TONE LANGUAGE
AAEEGHLOPPRR	PALEOGRAPHER
AAEEGHLRSSTW	WEATHERGLASS
AAEEGHNNORTU	HAUTE-GARONNE

AAEEGHNPPRRS	PAPERHANGERS
AAEEGIKLNSTV	LEAVE TAKINGS
AAEEGILNOTTV	VEGETATIONAL
AAEEGILNPPST	EATING APPLES
AAEEGILRSSUV	LIVER SAUSAGE
AAEEGIMNORST	MENAGE A TROIS
AAEEGIMNTTUV	AUGMENTATIVE
AAEEGIMPSSTU	SEPTUAGESIMA
AAEEGINPRSTX	EXASPERATING
AAEEGINRSSTV	ASSEVERATING
AAEEGJLMNORR	MAJOR GENERAL
AAEEGLMMRSSU	RUMMAGE SALES
AAEEGLMNORTV	GALVANOMETER
AAEEGLNRSTTV	TRAVEL AGENTS
AAEEGLOPRSSS	OPERA GLASSES
AAEEGMNNRRST	ARRANGEMENTS
AAEEGMNOPRST	POMEGRANATES
AAEEHHIMPRTT	AMPHITHEATRE
AAEEHHORRTTT	HEART-TO-HEART
AAEEHIIKNSST	KINAESTHESIA
AAEEHIILRTVX	EXHILARATIVE
AAEEHIIMPRST	HEMIPARASITE
AAEEHIKNOSTT	TAKE A SHINE TO
AAEEHILPRSTU	LAUREATESHIP
AAEEHIMMNPST	AMPHETAMINES
AAEEHINNRSTU	NEURASTHENIA
AAEEHINPPRRT	HEIR APPARENT
AAEEHINSSSTY	SYNAESTHESIA
AAEEHINSSTTT	ANAESTHETIST
AAEEHIRRSSTY	EAST AYRSHIRE
AAEEHLNOPPRS	APLANOSPHERE
AAEEHMNORSUW	WAREHOUSEMAN
AAEEHOORRSTT	STEATORRHOEA
AAEEIIKKLLTW	WALKIE-TALKIE
AAEEIILLMRSS	MARSEILLAISE
AAEEIILLRTTV	ALLITERATIVE
AAEEIILMNTTV	ALIMENTATIVE
AAEEIILMORTV	AMELIORATIVE
AAEEIILMRRST	MATERIALISER
AAEEIILMRRTZ	MATERIALIZER
AAEEIILNQSTU	ITALIANESQUE
AAEEIILLMNPST	PLANETESIMAL
AAEEIILNORTV	REVELATIONAL
AAEEIILNRSTW	ARTESIAN WELL
AAEEIILLPRSTT	SEPTILATERAL
AAEEIILMNRRTW	MINERAL WATER
AAEEIILNNORTV	VENERATIONAL
AAEEIILNPRSST	PLEASANTRIES
AAEEIILNRSTTV	ALTERNATIVES
AAEEIILQRSSTU	SESQUIALTERA
AAEEIINOPRSTX	EXASPERATION
AAEEIINORSTV	ASSEVERATION
AAEEKLNRSSTT	RATTLESNAKES
AAEELLNOSTVY	SEATON VALLEY

AAEELMMNRTTT	MALTREATMENT
AAEELNNOSSSS	SEASONALNESS
AAEELNNPSSST	PLEASANTNESS
AAEELPQRRTTU	QUARTER PLATE
AAEEMNNPPRSW	NEWSPAPERMAN
AAEEMNNPRTWY	PERMANENT WAY
AAEEMNORSSTW	WESTERN SAMOA
AAEEMNRSTTTY	TESTAMENTARY
AAEENNPPRSST	APPARENTNESS
AAEENNPRSTUU	SUPERANNUATE
AAEERRRSTTUU	RESTAURATEUR
AAEFFIIMRSTV	AFFIRMATIVES
AAEFFQRRSTTU	QUARTERSTAFF
AAEFGGILLLNT	FLAGELLATING
AAEFGHHIILNT	FAITH HEALING
AAEFGILLLNOT	FLAGELLATION
AAEFGINNORTT	ENGRAFTATION
AAEFHHLOSUWY	HALFWAY HOUSE
AAEFHIKLNSUV	HAVE A SKINFUL
AAEFHILNRSTW	FATHERS-IN-LAW
AAEFIIILMRRS	FAMILIARISER
AAEFIIILMRRZ	FAMILIARIZER
AAEFIIILMNRSS	FAMILIARNESS
AAEFIIILMPSTT	FISSIPALMATE
AAEFILLNSSSY	SELF-ANALYSIS
AAEFILMNRRST	FRATERNALISM
AAEFILNORRTY	REFLATIONARY
AAEFILNQRRTU	QUARTERFINAL
AAEFILORSSTY	FORESTAYSAIL
AAEFLLNOPSTU	PULL A FAST ONE
AAEFMORRSSTT	MASTER OF ARTS
AAEFORRSSTYZ	SAFETY RAZORS
AAEGGGILNNSU	SIGN LANGUAGE
AAEGGGINORST	AGGREGATIONS
AAEGGHHIOPRR	HAGIOGRAPHER
AAEGGHINNPPR	PAPERHANGING
AAEGGHMNOPRT	MAGNETOGRAPH
AAEGGINNPRRR	PREARRANGING
AAEGGINRSTTT	STARTING GATE
AAEGGNORRSUW	NARROW GAUGES
AAEGHHIKNRST	EARTHSHAKING
AAEGHHOPPRRS	PHRASEOGRAPH
AAEGHIILNRTX	EXHILARATING
AAEGHILNNOOT	HALOGENATION
AAEGHIMMNPSS	GAMESMANSHIP
AAEGHIMMNSTT	METAGNATHISM
AAEGHIMNRRTW	HEARTWARMING
AAEGHIMORRRT	METRORRHAGIA
AAEGHLLNNOTT	TEN-GALLON HAT
AAEGHLMNNRSU	MANSLAUGHTER
AAEGHLOPRTTU	TELAUTOGRAPH
AAEGHMNOSTTU	METAGNATHOUS
AAEGHNOPPRRT	PANTOGRAPHER
AAEGHNOPRRRU	URANOGRAPHER

AAEGHNPRRSST	STRAPHANGERS
AAEGIIKKLLMN	MAKE A KILLING
AAEGIILLNOST	LEGALISATION
AAEGIILLNOTZ	LEGALIZATION
AAEGIILMNORT	AMELIORATING, EMIGRATIONAL
AAEGIILNRSTU	ANGULARITIES
AAEGIIMNNORT	EMARGINATION
AAEGIINNPPRT	APPERTAINING
AAEGIINOQSTU	GIANT SEQUOIA
AAEGIINPPRRS	REAPPRAISING
AAEGIINPRRTT	REPATRIATING
AAEGIINPRTTX	EXPATRIATING
AAEGILLLLNPR	PARALLELLING
AAEGILLNNTTY	TANGENTIALLY
AAEGILLNPPRW	WALLPAPERING
AAEGILLNNSTUY	NAUSEATINGLY
AAEGIMNNOTTU	AUGMENTATION
AAEGIMNNRRST	ARRAIGNMENTS
AAEGIMNRRSTT	TRANSMIGRATE
AAEGIMRRSTTU	MAGISTRATURE
AAEGINNOPTTV	VANTAGEPOINT
AAEGLLORSSSU	SAUSAGE ROLLS
AAEGLMNORTVY	GALVANOMETRY
AAEGLMOOPSSU	GAMOSEPALOUS
AAEGLMOOPSTU	GAMOPETALOUS
AAEGLMOPRRSU	PARLOUR GAMES
AAEGLMOPRSST	ERGASTOPLASM
AAEGMOPPSSTT	POSTAGE STAMP
AAEHHNOPRTTW	ON THE WARPATH
AAEHIIILNNTV	ANNIHILATIVE
AAEHIILMMPTU	EPITHALAMIUM
AAEHIILNORTX	EXHILARATION
AAEHIINOPRTZ	AZATHIOPRINE
AAEHILLMORSV	VILLAHERMOSA
AAEHILMNOTXY	HAEMATOXYLIN
AAEHILMNPSSS	SALESMANSHIP
AAEHILMOSSTY	HAEMATOLYSIS
AAEHILMRSTUY	AMATEURISHLY
AAEHILNNOPTY	PAY ON THE NAIL
AAEHIMMRSSTU	SHAMATEURISM
AAEHIMNPRSTW	WATERMANSHIP
AAEHKKLLNPTW	WALK THE PLANK
AAEHLMNOOTXY	HAEMATOXYLON
AAEHLRSSTTTW	THE LAST STRAW
AAEHMOORSTTU	ATHEROMATOUS
AAEHMOPRSSTY	MASSOTHERAPY
AAEIIILMSSTV	ASSIMILATIVE
AAEIIIILPRSTT	PARTIALITIES
AAEIILLLNOSV	LEVALLOISIAN
AAEIILLMNNRS	MILLENARIANS
AAEIILLNORTT	ALLITERATION
AAEIILMMPRST	MARITIME ALPS
AAEIILMNNOTT	ALIMENTATION
AAEIILMNNRRT	INTERLAMINAR

AAEIILMNOORT	AMELIORATION
AAEIILMNPTUV	MANIPULATIVE
AAEIILMNRRST	AIR TERMINALS
AAEIILMNRSST	INERTIAL MASS
AAEIILMRSSTT	MATERIALISTS
AAEIILNNOPST	PENALISATION
AAEIILNNOPTZ	PENALIZATION
AAEIILNOQSTU	EQUALISATION
AAEIILNOQTUZ	EQUALIZATION
AAEIILNORRST	RATIONALISER
AAEIILNORRTZ	RATIONALIZER
AAEIILNORSST	REALISATIONS
AAEIILNORSTV	VELARISATION
AAEIILNORSTZ	REALIZATIONS
AAEIILNORTVZ	VELARIZATION
AAEIILNPRSTT	INTERSPATIAL
AAEIIMNNOSTX	EXAMINATIONS
AAEIINNOSTTT	TETANISATION
AAEIINNOTTTZ	TETANIZATION
AAEIINNRSSST	SANITARINESS
AAEIINOPRRTT	REPATRIATION
AAEIINOPRTTX	EXPATRIATION
AAEIINQTTTUV	QUANTITATIVE
AAEIKMNPPSTY	MAKE IT SNAPPY
AAEILLLMPRSS	PARALLELISMS
AAEILLLMRTTU	MULTILATERAL
AAEILLLNRTUY	UNILATERALLY
AAEILLMNRRTY	ARTILLERYMAN
AAEILLMPRRTY	PREMARITALLY
AAEILLMPRRXY	PREMAXILLARY
AAEILLNOPPST	APPELLATIONS
AAEILLNSSTTU	SAINT AUSTELL
AAEILMNNOSTT	LAMENTATIONS
AAEILMNPRSTU	PLANETARIUMS
AAEILNNNPSVY	PENNSYLVANIA
AAEILNNOPSTX	EXPLANATIONS
AAEILNNOPTTX	EXPLANTATION
AAEILNNORSTT	ALTERNATIONS
AAEILNNRSTTU	SAINT LAURENT
AAEILNOPPRSY	PLAYER PIANOS
AAEILNOPRRST	PROLETARIANS
AAEILNOPSSTY	PASSIONATELY
AAEILNORSTUV	REVALUATIONS
AAEILNPRSSTT	PATERNALISTS
AAEILNRSSSTU	SALUTARINESS
AAEILORRSTUW	LOWER AUSTRIA
AAEIMMMOSSTT	METASOMATISM
AAEIMMNOOPST	MESOPOTAMIAN
AAEIMNOOOOPT	ONOMATOPOEIA
AAEINNOPRSXY	EXPANSIONARY
AAEINNORSSTU	AUSTRONESIAN
AAEINNOSSTTT	NATION STATES
AAEINOPPRRST	PREPARATIONS
AAEINOSSTTTT	ATTESTATIONS

AAEIPPRRSTTV	PRIVATE PARTS
AAEIPPRRSTUU	UPPER AUSTRIA
AAEKLMORRTWW	LOW-WATER MARK
AAEKLOPRSTTY	KERATOPLASTY
AAEKNOQRRSUW	NARROW SQUEAK
AAELLMNNORTY	ORNAMENTALLY
AAELLNNPSTUY	UNPLEASANTLY
AAELMMNNORRU	ROMAN NUMERAL
AAELMNNORTTU	ULTRAMONTANE
AAELMNPQSTUU	QUANTUM LEAPS
AAELMOOPRSTZ	SPERMATOZOAL
AAELNNPRRSTT	TRANSPLANTER
AAELNPRRSTUU	SUPERNATURAL
AAELNRSSSTTW	STALWARTNESS
AAELOOPRRTTX	EXTRAPOLATOR
AAEMNNOPRSST	MONTPARNASSE
AAEMNOPRSTTU	PORTMANTEAUS
AAEMNOPRTTUX	PORTMANTEAUX
AAEMORSSSTTT	TOASTMASTERS
AAEOOPPRRRST	PARATROOPERS
AAEOPPRSSTTU	PASSE-PARTOUT
AAFFIIIILNOST	AFFILIATIONS
AAFFIIMNORST	AFFIRMATIONS
AAFGILLNRSST	FALLING STARS
AAFHLMOSTUUY	SAY A MOUTHFUL
AAFIIIILNNOST	FINALISATION
AAFIIILNNOTZ	FINALIZATION
AAFIIILNRTTU	FUTILITARIAN
AAFIILMMNNOT	INFLAMMATION
AAFIILNNORTY	INFLATIONARY
AAFIINNOSSTU	INFATUATIONS
AAFILMMNOORT	MALFORMATION
AAFILMMNORTY	INFLAMMATORY
AAFINNOOPRST	PROFANATIONS
AAGGHIIJMNST	THINGAMAJIGS
AAGGHINNPRST	STRAPHANGING
AAGGHINOPRTU	AUTOGRAPHING
AAGGHNOOPRRY	ORGANOGRAPHY
AAGGIIILNPRZ	PLAGIARIZING
AAGGIIINNRTT	INGRATIATING
AAGGIILLNNTV	GALLIVANTING
AAGGIINNNOTZ	ANTAGONIZING
AAGGIINNRTUU	INAUGURATING
AAGGLMMOORTY	GRAMMATOLOGY
AAGHHIIJNSUZ	SHIJIAZHUANG
AAGHIIILNNNT	ANNIHILATING
AAGHIILMNRST	ANIMAL RIGHTS
AAGHIINPSTXY	ASPHYXIATING
AAGHILOORSTU	HAGIOLATROUS
AAGHIPRRSTTY	STRATIGRAPHY
AAGHLMOOTTUY	THAUMATOLOGY
AAGHLOOPPRRY	POLAROGRAPHY
AAGHOOPPRSSU	SAPROPHAGOUS
AAGIIIILLNNPS	PLAIN SAILING

AAGIIIILMNSST	ASSIMILATING
AAGIIILNORRT	IRRIGATIONAL
AAGIIIMNNOST	IMAGINATIONS
AAGIIINNNOTV	INVAGINATION
AAGIIINNORTT	INGRATIATION
AAGIIILLNNPTW	WALL PAINTING
AAGIIILMNNPTU	MANIPULATING
AAGIILNNRSUY	SANGUINARILY
AAGIIILNNRTUZ	NATURALIZING
AAGIIILNPPRSY	APPRAISINGLY
AAGIIMNRRTTUZ	TRAUMATIZING
AAGIINNNQRTU	QUARANTINING
AAGIINNOORST	ORGANISATION
AAGIINNOORTZ	ORGANIZATION
AAGIINNORTUU	INAUGURATION
AAGIINNOSSST	ASSIGNATIONS
AAGILLMNTUWY	MULLIGATAWNY
AAGILLNOUVVV	VULVOVAGINAL, APPALLING
AAGILMNNNNOT	NONMALIGNANT
AAGILNORSTTU	GASTRULATION
AAGILOOPRSTY	PARASITOLOGY
AAGIMNNRRSTT	TRANSMIGRANT
AAGINNOOSTTW	STATION WAGON
AAGLLOPRSTTU	SUPRAGLOTTAL
AAGLNOOPRSTW	PATROL WAGONS
AAHHIOPPRSTU	PHOSPHATURIA
AAHHIPRSSTTW	ATHWARTSHIPS
AAHIIILLOPRU	AILUROPHILIA
AAHIIILNNNOT	ANNIHILATION
AAHIIMNNOSTU	HUMANISATION
AAHIIMNNOTUZ	HUMANIZATION
AAHIINOPSTXY	ASPHYXIATION
AAHIINPPRSST	PARTISANSHIP
AAHIKMMNPRSS	MARKSMANSHIP
AAHILLMOOTXY	HOMOTAXIALLY
AAHILLMOPRSX	MORPHALLAXIS
AAHILLOPRSTX	TROPHALLAXIS
AAHILMNOOPRT	PROTHALAMION
AAHILNNNOTTU	NATIONAL HUNT
AAHIMMOPPRRS	PARAMORPHISM
AAHIMNOOPRSS	ANAMORPHOSIS
AAHLLMMORSSW	MARSHMALLOWS
AAIIILMNOSST	ASSIMILATION
AAIIILMPRTTY	IMPARTIALITY
AAIIILNNOSTT	LATINISATION
AAIIILNNOSTV	INSALIVATION
AAIIILNNOTTZ	LATINIZATION
AAIIILNOPRTT	TRIPOLITANIA
AAIIILNOSTTV	VISITATIONAL, VITALISATION
AAIIILNOTTVZ	VITALIZATION
AAIIILORSTTV	VISITATORIAL
AAIIIMMNOSTX	MAXIMISATION
AAIIIMMNOTXZ	MAXIMIZATION
AAIIIMNNRSTU	UNITARIANISM

AAIIIMNOSSTV	AVITAMINOSIS
AAIIIINORSSTT	SATIRISATION
AAIIIINORSTTZ	SATIRIZATION
AAIILLLPSSUZ	LAPIS LAZULIS
AAIILLMMNRTU	MULTILAMINAR
AAIILLMNPRSU	SUPRALIMINAL
AAIILLLNNOSTT	INSTALLATION
AAIILLNORRTY	IRRATIONALLY
AAIILMNNOPTT	IMPLANTATION
AAIILMNNOPTU	MANIPULATION
AAIILMNOORST	MORALISATION
AAIILMNOORTZ	MORALIZATION
AAIILMNOOTTV	MOTIVATIONAL
AAIILMNOSSTV	SALVATIONISM
AAIILNNNOOTT	INTONATIONAL
AAIILNNNOOTV	INNOVATIONAL
AAIILNNOOSTV	VIOLIN SONATA
AAIILNNORSTT	TRANSITIONAL
AAIILLNNOSSTT	NATIONALISTS
AAIILNOOPRST	POLARISATION
AAIILNOOPRTZ	POLARIZATION
AAIILNOORSST	SOLARISATION
AAIILNOORSTV	VALORISATION
AAIILNOORSTZ	SOLARIZATION
AAIILNOORTVZ	VALORIZATION
AAIILNOPPSTT	PALPITATIONS
AAIILNORRSTU	RURALISATION
AAIILNORRTUZ	RURALIZATION
AAIILNORSSTT	RATIONALISTS
AAIILNORSTTY	STATIONARILY
AAIILNOSSTTV	SALVATIONIST
AAIILNPTTVYY	NATIVITY PLAY
AAIIMNOORSTT	AMORTISATION
AAIIMNOORTTZ	AMORTIZATION
AAIINNOQSTTU	QUANTISATION
AAIINNOQTTUZ	QUANTIZATION
AAIINOOPRSTV	VAPORISATION
AAIINOOPRTVZ	VAPORIZATION
AAIILMNOPRTT	ALL-IMPORTANT
AAIILMOPRTYY	MORALITY PLAY
AAIILLORSTTUY	SALUTATORILY
AAILMMOPPRSS	MALAPROPISMS
AAILMNOPRTUY	MANIPULATORY
AAILNNORSSTT	TRANSLATIONS
AAILNOPPSSSY	PASSION PLAYS
AAILOORSTTTZ	TOTALIZATORS
AAILOPRRSTUV	VAPOUR TRAILS
AAINNOPRSSTT	PATRON SAINTS
AAINNORSTTUU	UNSATURATION
AAINOOORTTTU	AUTOROTATION
AAKLNNNNOOPT	NANOPLANKTON
AALMNOOPRSTY	TRYPANOSOMAL
ABBBCEHLOPSY	PSYCHOBABBLE
ABBBCGINNOUY	BOUNCING BABY

ABBBDEEIILSS	SIDI-BEL-ABBES
ABBBEESTTTUY	TEST-TUBE BABY
ABBBEHLMORTU	BLABBERMOUTH
ABBCCEEHKNRS	BACKBENCHERS
ABBCCEEHMORS	BEACHCOMBERS
ABBCDEFKNOOY	BACK OF BEYOND
ABBCEEGGHISU	BEACH BUGGIES
ABBCEEIKLRRS	BLACKBERRIES
ABBCFIILORST	FIBROBLASTIC
ABBCKMOOORSY	BACKROOM BOYS
ABBDDEEFLORSS	SELF-ABSORBED
ABBDEELOSSSU	DOUBLE BASSES
ABBDEHIILRYZ	HYBRIDIZABLE
ABBDEIILSSUZ	SUBSIDIZABLE
ABBDEILNNORS	ROBBEN ISLAND
ABBDEILOPSYY	PLAY BOBSY-DIE
ABBDELLLNRUY	LANDLUBBERLY
ABBDEMMNNORST	BOMBARDMENTS
ABBDEOOPPRTY	BOOBY-TRAPPED
ABBEEEHNORST	THE BARE BONES
ABBEEEILLNUV	UNBELIEVABLE
ABBEEEILLNUVY	UNBELIEVABLY
ABBEEILMRRSU	REIMBURSABLE
ABBEELORRRSU	RABBLE-ROUSER
ABBEENNOTWWY	NEWTOWNABBEY
ABBEHIJMNNSU	BENJAMIN BUSH
ABBEINRSSTTU	SUBURBANITES
ABBELNPRRSTU	RUBBER PLANTS
ABBEMPRRSSTU	RUBBER STAMPS
ABBGHIILOPRY	BIBLIOGRAPHY
ABBHLOORTWWY	THROW A WOBBLY
ABBHMOOOOSST	BAMBOO SHOOTS
ABCCCIILMSTU	SUBCLIMACTIC
ABCCDEEEELPST	BESPECTACLED
ABCCDEHILORU	COACHBUILDER
ABCCDHILNSUW	CLUB SANDWICH
ABCCDIILORXY	DICARBOXYLIC
ABCCEEEELRSU	CAUSE CELEBRE
ABCCEEEEHLNRT	TREBLE CHANCE
ABCCEEEELNORT	CONCELEBRATE
ABCCEEENORRS	ARBORESCENCE
ABCCEEIILNSS	INACCESSIBLE
ABCCEEILLNOR	RECONCILABLE
ABCCEEILOSST	ACCESSIBLE TO
ABCCEEMNNRRU	ENCUMBRANCER
ABCCEEMNNRSU	ENCUMBRANCES
ABCCEHIIMNOS	BIOMECHANICS
ABCCEHILLRUY	CHERUBICALLY
ABCCEHIMMRSU	CHAMBER MUSIC
ABCCEHOPRSST	BATCH PROCESS
ABCCEIILNSS	INACCESSIBLE
ABCCEIINRRSU	CABIN CRUISER
ABCCEIKKLSST	STICKLEBACKS
ABCCEILLNORY	RECONCILABLY

ABCCEILMMNOU	COMMUNICABLE
ABCCEILNNOOS	CONSCIONABLE
ABCCEILNORTT	CONTRACTIBLE
ABCCEILORSTU	SCROBICULATE
ABCCEINOOPRS	CARBON COPIES
ABCCEKLMNOOY	BLACK ECONOMY
ABCCHILLMORU	CHLORAMBUCIL
ABCCILLOOSTY	OCTOSYLLABIC
ABCCILMMNOUY	COMMUNICABLY
ABCCINOOSSTT	TOBACCONISTS
ABCCKLNORTUY	BLACK COUNTRY
ABCDDGIKLNPU	BLACK PUDDING
ABCDEEEILHPR	DECIPHERABLE
ABCDEEEHIRSU	DEBAUCHERIES
ABCDEEEHLORR	BREECHLOADER
ABCDEEEILNUV	UNDECEIVABLE
ABCDEEFILNOS	BEACONSFIELD
ABCDEEHOQRRU	CHEQUERBOARD
ABCDEEIILLNN	INDECLINABLE
ABCDEEIILLORS	LOCAL DERBIES
ABCDEEILMNSS	DISSEMBLANCE
ABCDEEILMOST	DOMESTICABLE
ABCDEEILNORS	CONSIDERABLE
ABCDEEILORSV	DISCOVERABLE
ABCDEEIMNNTY	AMBITENDENCY
ABCDEEINORRS	DECARBONISER
ABCDEEINORRZ	DECARBONIZER
ABCDEELLNRSY	BELLY DANCERS
ABCDEELMOOPS	DECOMPOSABLE
ABCDEGHIILNR	CHILDBEARING
ABCDEGHORRTU	TURBOCHARGED
ABCDEGILNOTU	DOUBLE-ACTING
ABCDEHILSSTW	SWITCHBLADES
ABCDEHIRRSTW	BIRD-WATCHERS
ABCDEHMOORST	HORS DE COMBAT
ABCDEHNORSTY	BODY SNATCHER
ABCDEIIILLRT	LIBERTICIDAL
ABCDEIILRSTT	DISTRACTIBLE
ABCDEIINNSST	CITISENS' BAND
ABCDEIINNSTZ	CITIZENS' BAND
ABCDEILMORST	BLASTODERMIC
ABCDEILNORSY	CONSIDERABLY
ABCDEILNOSTU	DISCOUNTABLE
ABCDEINOOPRS	PROBOSCIDEAN
ABCDEINOORST	NOTICE BOARDS
ABCDEINRSSTU	DISTURBANCES
ABCDEKMNOOSW	BACKWOODSMEN
ABCDEKNORRTU	ROUND BRACKET
ABCDELOOPRUV	CUPBOARD LOVE
ABCDEOOORRTT	CORROBORATED
ABCDHIORSSTW	SWITCHBOARDS
ABCDHNOORRSY	HYDROCARBONS
ABCDIILLOPST	DIPLOBLASTIC
ABCEEEEFFKORS	COFFEE BREAKS

ABCEEEEFFLOST	COFFEE TABLES
ABCEEEEFNRSST	BENEFACTRESS
ABCEEEEHLNRRT	RETRENCHABLE
ABCEEEELMNRSS	RESEMBLANCES
ABCEEEMMNRRR	REMEMBRANCER
ABCEEEMMNRRS	REMEMBRANCES
ABCEEENORSUV	VERBENACEOUS
ABCEEFFIINRT	FEBRIFACIENT
ABCEEFIILLNY	BENEFICIALLY
ABCEEFINNOST	BENEFACTIONS
ABCEEFLLOORS	FORECLOSABLE
ABCEEGILNORZ	RECOGNIZABLE
ABCEEHKLNQSU	BLANK CHEQUES
ABCEEHLORSUY	HERBACEOUSLY
ABCEEHMMNNRT	EMBRANCHMENT
ABCEEHORSTTX	CHATTERBOXES
ABCEEIILLNPX	INEXPLICABLE
ABCEEIILNRTX	INEXTRICABLE
ABCEEILLSSTU	SUBCELESTIAL
ABCEEILNORST	CELEBRATIONS
ABCEEILNORSU	RIBONUCLEASE
ABCEEILRSSTU	RESUSCITABLE
ABCEEINNORSV	INOBSERVANCE
ABCEEINRRTVY	INVERTEBRACY
ABCEEJKLMRTU	LUMBERJACKET
ABCEEKLNNORU	UNRECKONABLE
ABCEEKLRRRSW	KERB CRAWLERS
ABCEELOPRSTU	PROSECUTABLE
ABCEENOPRRTU	PROTUBERANCE
ABCEEORRSSUU	BURSERACEOUS
ABCEGGGIKLLN	BLACKLEGGING
ABCEGGILNNOO	BELGIAN CONGO
ABCEGHIKLLNS	BLACK ENGLISH
ABCEGHORRRTU	TURBOCHARGER
ABCEGIKLNRRW	KERB CRAWLING
ABCEGILMNOST	SINGLE COMBAT
ABCEGILNORYZ	RECOGNIZABLY
ABCEGILOORTY	BACTERIOLOGY
ABCEHIJKNOTX	JACK-IN-THE-BOX
ABCEHIKNRSSS	BRACKISHNESS
ABCEHILMNRUU	HIBERNACULUM
ABCEHILSTTTY	CHASTITY BELT
ABCEHIRRRRSU	CRUSH BARRIER
ABCEHKLRSSUW	SWASHBUCKLER
ABCEHLNOSTUU	UNTOUCHABLES
ABCEIIILLRST	LIBERALISTIC
ABCEIIILTTXY	EXCITABILITY
ABCEIILLNPXY	INEXPLICABLY
ABCEIILMNOPT	INCOMPATIBLE
ABCEIILNRTXY	INEXTRICABLY
ABCEIILOORST	BOROSILICATE
ABCEIILORTVY	REVOCABILITY
ABCEIINORSTT	OBSTETRICIAN
ABCEIIRSTTUW	WATER BISCUIT

ABCEIKNPRSTU	BANKRUPTCIES
ABCEILLNNOOS	INCONSOLABLE
ABCEILMMNOTU	INCOMMUTABLE
ABCEILMNNOSU	INCONSUMABLE
ABCEILMNOPTU	INCOMPUTABLE
ABCEILMOSSUX	MUSICAL BOXES
ABCEILNOOPPRR	INCORPORABLE
ABCEILOOSSTT	OSTEOBLASTIC
ABCEILPRTUUV	TUVA REPUBLIC
ABCEIMNOORST	EMBROCATIONS
ABCELLLNOORT	CONTROLLABLE
ABCELLLOOSTY	OCTOSYLLABLE
ABCELMNOSTTU	MESCAL BUTTON
ABCELNORSTTU	COUNTERBLAST
ABCENOSSTUUU	SUBCUTANEOUS
ABCEORRRSTTU	CARBURETTORS
ABCFIILLMORY	MORBIFICALLY
ABCFIINORSTU	BIFURCATIONS
ABCFLNOOORRU	FLUOROCARBON
ABCGHLOORSUY	BRACHYLOGOUS
ABCGIIKLLNST	BLACKLISTING
ABCGIILLLOOY	BIOLOGICALLY
ABCGIINNRRST	TRANSCRIBING
ABCGILLMOOSY	SYMBOLOGICAL
ABCGILMNNRSU	UNSCRAMBLING
ABCGILNNOOOT	CONGLOBATION
ABCHIIKLOSTY	SHOCKABILITY
ABCHIMORSSTX	CHRISTMAS BOX
ABCIIIILRSTY	IRASCIBILITY
ABCIIILMNOTU	UMBILICATION
ABCIIILNRTUY	INCURABILITY
ABCIILLMNOOY	BIONOMICALLY
ABCIILMNOPTY	INCOMPATIBLY
ABCIILNNOTUY	CONNUBIALITY
ABCIILNOPPRY	PRINCIPAL BOY
ABCIILNOPSTU	PUBLICATIONS
ABCIILNPPRSU	SUBPRINCIPAL
ABCIILORRTUY	ORBICULARITY
ABCIIMNNOOST	COMBINATIONS
ABCIJKNNOORS	JACK ROBINSON
ABCIKLLMMSSU	BLACK MUSLIMS
ABCILLLMOSYY	SYMBOLICALLY
ABCILLLOPSYY	POLYSYLLABIC
ABCILLMNOOSY	MONOSYLLABIC
ABCILLNNOOSY	INCONSOLABLY
ABCILMMNNOTU	NOCTAMBULISM
ABCILMNNOOSU	NO-CLAIM BONUS
ABCILMNOSTTU	NOCTAMBULIST
ABCIMNORSSTU	OBSCURANTISM
ABCIMNORSTUU	RAMBUNCTIOUS
ABCINNOORSTU	CONURBATIONS
ABCINORSSTTU	OBSCURANTIST, SUBTRACTIONS
ABCOOOORRRRT	CORROBORATOR
ABDDEEEHLLTU	BULLET-HEADED

ABDDEEEEHLNYZ	BENZALDEHYDE
ABDDEEEEHLORU	DOUBLE-HEADER
ABDDEEEELLORU	DOUBLE-DEALER
ABDDEEGGLORU	DOUBLE DAGGER
ABDDEEGLLOUZ	DOUBLE-GLAZED
ABDDEEEHLLLUY	BULLHEADEDLY
ABDDEEIILSST	DESTABILISED
ABDDEEIILSTZ	DESTABILIZED
ABDDEEIMNNST	ABSENT-MINDED
ABDDEEEKLLOTU	DOUBLE-TALKED
ABDDEEKLOPRU	DOUBLE-PARKED
ABDDEGILNOTU	DOUBLE-DATING
ABDDEILNOOST	BLOODSTAINED
ABDDEINORSTU	SUBORDINATED
ABDDEKMOOOSY	DOMESDAY BOOK
ABDDGIINORSV	DIVINGBOARDS
ABDDGIMNNPRU	BUMP AND GRIND
ABDEEEEILMRR	IRREDEEMABLE
ABDEEEEERRRTV	REVERBERATED
ABDEEEFIILNS	INDEFEASIBLE
ABDEEEIILMRR	IRREMEDIABLE
ABDEEEIILRTV	DELIBERATIVE
ABDEEEIILRTY	DELIBERATELY
ABDEEEILMNRT	DETERMINABLE
ABDEEEILMRRY	IRREDEEMABLY
ABDEEEINPRRS	PREBENDARIES
ABDEEELMNTZZ	BEDAZZLEMENT
ABDEEELPRSSU	SUPERSEDABLE
ABDEEFGIIRRS	FIRE BRIGADES
ABDEEFHILMRT	HALF-TIMBERED
ABDEEFIIILNT	IDENTIFIABLE
ABDEEFILLSTT	BATTLEFIELDS
ABDEEFINSTUU	SUBINFEUDATE
ABDEEGIILNRT	DELIBERATING
ABDEEGLNOSTU	DOUBLE AGENTS
ABDEEHNORTUW	WEATHER-BOUND
ABDEEIIILTTV	DEBILITATIVE
ABDEEIIKLRST	EAST KILBRIDE
ABDEEIILMRRY	IRREMEDIABLY
ABDEEIILNORT	DELIBERATION
ABDEEIILLNORR	BANDERILLERO
ABDEEILMNOPR	IMPONDERABLE
ABDEEILMNNSST	DISABLEMENTS
ABDEEILNOSSV	VOIDABLENESS
ABDEEILNRSSU	UNDESIRABLES
ABDEEILPRSTY	DISREPUTABLE
ABDEEINNRRSW	BREADWINNERS
ABDEEINNRSTU	NUBIAN DESERT
ABDEEINNSSSU	UNBIASEDNESS
ABDEEIRRSTTY	DRY BATTERIES
ABDEEKNORRRS	BANKER'S ORDER
ABDEELMNORST	DEMONSTRABLE
ABDEELMNORSZ	BRONZE MEDALS
ABDEELORRSTW	WORLD-BEATERS

ABDEEOORRSTT	BORED TO TEARS
ABDEFFHLORSU	SHUFFLEBOARD
ABDEFGINORRS	FINGERBOARDS
ABDEFIIILLLOS	SOLIDIFIABLE
ABDEFLLOSTUU	DOUBLE FAULTS
ABDEGIIILNTT	DEBILITATING
ABDEGIIKMNRS	DISEMBARKING
ABDEGIILNNST	DINING TABLES
ABDEGIKNOPRW	BAKING POWDER
ABDEGILLLNNY	BELLY-LANDING
ABDEGILNORTW	WORLD-BEATING
ABDEGINNPSTU	BE UPSTANDING
ABDEHHLMOORR	RHOMBOHEDRAL
ABDEHHNOSSUU	HOUSE HUSBAND
ABDEHIIILMNS	DIMINISHABLE
ABDEHIILSSST	DISESTABLISH
ABDEHIINNPRS	HAIRPIN BENDS
ABDEHLLORSYY	HYDROLYSABLE
ABDEHNNORSSU	RUB ONE'S HANDS
ABDEIIIILSST	DISABILITIES
ABDEIIILMNSS	INADMISSIBLE
ABDEIIILMTXY	MIXED-ABILITY
ABDEIIILNOTT	DEBILITATION
ABDEIIILRSTY	DESIRABILITY
ABDEIIIRSSSU	SUBSIDIARIES
ABDEIIILNPSTU	INDISPUTABLE
ABDEIILNRTUY	ENDURABILITY
ABDEIIOOPRSS	BASIDIOSPORE
ABDEILMNOSTU	DISMOUNTABLE
ABDEILPRSTUY	DISREPUTABLY
ABDEIMORSTUX	AMBIDEXTROUS
ABDEINORRRSU	SOUND BARRIER
ABDEINORSSTU	SUBORDINATES
ABDELMNORSTY	DEMONSTRABLY
ABDELMOORSST	BLOODSTREAMS
ABDEMOORRTTW	BOTTOM DRAWER
ABDENOQRRTUU	QUARTER-BOUND
ABDFGIIILLLNO	BILL OF LADING
ABDFIILNNRUU	INFUNDIBULAR
ABDFIILNOOOV	BIOFLAVONOID
ABDGHINOOSWX	SHADOW-BOXING
ABDGIILOOORY	RADIOBIOLOGY
ABDGIINNOORR	IRONING BOARD
ABDGINOPRRSS	SPRINGBOARDS
ABDGMOORRSSS	SMORGASBORDS
ABDIIIILNTUY	INAUDIBILITY
ABDIIILMNSSY	INADMISSIBLY
ABDIIILRSSUY	SUBSIDIARILY
ABDIIIMORSST	TROMBIDIASIS
ABDIILLMOTUY	MODULABILITY, MOULDABILITY
ABDIILNPSTUY	INDISPUTABLY
ABDIIRRSTTUY	DISTRIBUTARY
ABDLNNOSSTTU	NUTS AND BOLTS
ABEEEEMNRSTV	BEREAVEMENTS
ABEEEFLNQRTU	FREQUENTABLE
ABEEEGGILNRU	BELEAGUERING
ABEEEGILNORT	RENEGOTIABLE
ABEEEHILMPTU	EAT HUMBLE PIE
ABEEEHKORRSU	HOUSEBREAKER
ABEEEHLOPRST	OBLATE SPHERE
ABEEEIIILLRRV	IRRELIEVABLE
ABEEEIILMNPRT	IMPENETRABLE
ABEEEIILMNRTX	EXTERMINABLE
ABEEEIILNNSSV	ENVIABLENESS
ABEEEIILNRRST	EAST BERLINER
ABEEEIIMNQSTU	MESQUITE BEAN
ABEEEIINRRTTV	INVERTEBRATE
ABEEEILOOPTTT	POTATO BEETLE
ABEEELQRSSTU	SEQUESTRABLE
ABEEEMPRSTTU	SUBTEMPERATE
ABEEENQSTUUY	BEAUTY QUEENS
ABEEEORRRRTV	REVERBERATOR
ABEEEPRRSTTY	PRESBYTERATE
ABEEFFILNRSU	INSUFFERABLE
ABEEFFRSSTTU	BUFFER STATES
ABEEFGHILNRT	FRIGHTENABLE
ABEEFIIILLMSU	EMULSIFIABLE
ABEEFIIILLRTZ	FERTILIZABLE
ABEEFKLNOORW	FOREKNOWABLE
ABEEFLLMNSSU	BLAMEFULNESS
ABEEFLLMSSSY	SELF-ASSEMBLY
ABEEGGILNPSS	SLEEPING BAGS
ABEEGGILNRSS	BEGGARLINESS
ABEEGHMNOOPR	GERMANOPHOBE
ABEEGIIILNSTV	INVESTIGABLE
ABEEGIKNPSTU	SPEAKING TUBE
ABEEGILNORRS	LOGANBERRIES
ABEEGILNOXYZ	OXYGENIZABLE
ABEEGLNNORUV	UNGOVERNABLE
ABEEHHPRSSTY	BATHYSPHERES
ABEEHIILMPRS	IMPERISHABLE
ABEEHILLMORT	THERMOLABILE
ABEEHILOPPRS	PROPHESIABLE
ABEEHILRRSTW	WELSH RAREBIT
ABEEHIQRRSUU	HARQUEBUSIER
ABEEHKLNNOTT	ON THE BLANKET
ABEEHLMORSTT	THERMOSTABLE
ABEEHLOPRSST	BLASTOSPHERE
ABEEHLORRSWW	WHEELBARROWS
ABEEIIILLRST	LIBERALITIES
ABEEIIILLRSTZ	STERILIZABLE
ABEEIIILMMMOR	IMMEMORIABLE
ABEEIIILMNNRT	INTERMINABLE
ABEEIIILMNRTX	INTERMIXABLE
ABEEIIILMPRTY	PERMEABILITY
ABEEIIILNPRTX	INEXTIRPABLE
ABEEIIILNPSST	PITIABLENESS
ABEEIIILNRTVY	VENERABILITY

ABEEIIILNRTWY	RENEWABILITY
ABEEIILORTTV	OBLITERATIVE
ABEEIILPRRRS	IRRESPIRABLE
ABEEIKLNNSST	LINEN BASKETS
ABEEILLMNSSY	ASSEMBLY LINE
ABEEILLNNRUV	INVULNERABLE, VILLEURBANNE
ABEEILLORRSV	IRRESOLVABLE
ABEEIILRSTVY	LIVERY STABLE
ABEEILMMOORS	AEROEMBOLISM
ABEEILMNRRSU	SERIAL NUMBER
ABEEILNOPRST	INTERPOSABLE
ABEEILNOQSTU	QUESTIONABLE
ABEEILNSSSTU	SUITABLENESS
ABEEILOPPRRX	EXPROPRIABLE
ABEEILPRRSTY	PRESBYTERIAL
ABEEINORRTTV	VERTEBRATION
ABEEINPRRSTY	PRESBYTERIAN
ABEEIRRRSSTW	STRAWBERRIES
ABEEKLMORRTU	TROUBLEMAKER
ABEEKMRRSTUY	BUYER'S MARKET
ABEEKORRSSTT	BREASTSTROKE
ABEELLMNOPUY	UNEMPLOYABLE
ABEELLMNOTTT	BALLOTTEMENT
ABEELMMNNOTZ	EMBLAZONMENT
ABEELMNPRSTU	NUMBERPLATES
ABEELNNNOSTT	NANSEN BOTTLE
ABEELNOSSSTU	ABSOLUTENESS
ABEELNOSSTUV	SOLVENT ABUSE
ABEELOORSTUZ	ABSOLUTE ZERO
ABEELOPPRSSU	SUPERPOSABLE
ABEENPRTTTUU	PEANUT BUTTER
ABEENRSSSSTU	ABSTRUSENESS
ABEFFIIILNTY	INEFFABILITY
ABEFFILNRSUY	INSUFFERABLY
ABEFGILNORRY	FORBEARINGLY
ABEFGILNORUV	UNFORGIVABLE
ABEFGINNNRTU	AFTERBURNING
ABEFHHILLLOT	BILL OF HEALTH
ABEFHHLORRST	HALF-BROTHERS
ABEFIILLOSSZ	FOSSILIZABLE
ABEFIILRTTUY	REFUTABILITY
ABEFILNOPRTU	UNPROFITABLE
ABEFILNRSSTU	TRANSFUSIBLE
ABEFLLOOORUV	LABOUR OF LOVE
ABEFLMOOSSTT	FALSE BOTTOMS
ABEFLNOSSSTU	BOASTFULNESS
ABEFLNOSSSUU	FABULOUSNESS
ABEGGHIOOPRY	BIOGEOGRAPHY
ABEGGIMNNOOR	BOOMERANGING
ABEGHIILNSST	ESTABLISHING
ABEGHJNNORSU	JOHANNESBURG
ABEGHNOORTTU	ATTENBOROUGH
ABEGIIILLNRZ	LIBERALIZING
ABEGIILLNOUV	BOUGAINVILLE
ABEGIILNORTT	OBLITERATING
ABEGIILNPRTY	PREGNABILITY
ABEGIKLNNOOR	BOOK-LEARNING
ABEGILLLNOWY	BOWLING ALLEY
ABEGILLNOOST	BALNEOLOGIST
ABEGILNNRTTU	TABLE-TURNING
ABEGILRRSSST	BRISTLE-GRASS
ABEGILRRSYZZ	GRIZZLY BEARS
ABEGLLORSSSW	GLASSBLOWERS
ABEGLNORSSSU	GLABROUSNESS
ABEHIIILNNSU	HUSEIN IBN-ALI
ABEHIIILRTTY	HERITABILITY
ABEHIIIMNNRS	HIBERNIANISM
ABEHIILNNRTY	LABYRINTHINE
ABEHIILNOPST	INHOSPITABLE
ABEHIIMORSUV	BEHAVIOURISM, MISBEHAVIOUR
ABEHIIORSTUV	BEHAVIOURIST
ABEHILNORRTW	BROTHER-IN-LAW
ABEHINPRSSTU	PAINTBRUSHES
ABEHLORRSTTY	ERYTHROBLAST
ABEIIILLLRTY	ILLIBERALITY
ABEIIILLNNRT	BRILLIANTINE
ABEIIILLNSTY	ENSILABILITY
ABEIIILRSTVY	REVISABILITY
ABEIIILRTVVY	REVIVABILITY
ABEIIKLORTVY	REVOKABILITY
ABEIIILLLMPTU	MULTIPLIABLE
ABEIIILMMORTY	MEMORABILITY
ABEIIILMNNRTY	INTERMINABLY
ABEIIILMORTVY	REMOVABILITY
ABEIIILNNOSTU	NEBULISATION
ABEIIILNNOTUZ	NEBULIZATION
ABEIIILNNTTUY	UNTENABILITY
ABEIIILNOORTT	OBLITERATION
ABEIIILOQRRTU	EQUILIBRATOR
ABEIIILPRSTUY	SUPERABILITY
ABEIIILPRTTUY	REPUTABILITY
ABEIIMOQRSTU	BARQUISIMETO
ABEIIINORSSTU	SUBERISATION
ABEIIINORSTUZ	SUBERIZATION
ABEILLNNRUVY	INVULNERABLY
ABEILLNOPPRT	BIPROPELLANT
ABEIILLOPRRVY	PROVERBIALLY
ABEILMOSSTUY	ABSTEMIOUSLY
ABEILNOQSTUY	QUESTIONABLY
ABEILNORSSUY	BYELORUSSIAN
ABEILNORTTXY	EXORBITANTLY
ABEILNPRSSUU	PRUSSIAN BLUE
ABEINOOPRRST	PROBATIONERS
ABEINOORSSTV	OBSERVATIONS
ABEINOPRRTTU	PERTURBATION
ABEINSSSTTUV	SUBSTANTIVES
ABELLLLOPSYY	POLYSYLLABLE
ABELLLMNOOSY	MONOSYLLABLE

ABELMNORSTUU	SURMOUNTABLE
ABEMNNOOTTUW	MEN-ABOUT-TOWN
ABEMNORRRSST	BARNSTORMERS
ABFGIIILNRTY	FRANGIBILITY
ABFIIIILLNORT	FIBRILLATION
ABGGILLNOSSW	GLASS-BLOWING
ABGHIIMMNSTW	SWIMMING BATH
ABGHIINSSTTU	BATHING SUITS
ABGIIIILNTTY	IGNITABILITY
ABGIIILLMNSU	BILINGUALISM
ABGIILLMRSUW	WILLIAMSBURG
ABGIILLOORTY	OBLIGATORILY
ABGILNOOPSST	SPONGIOBLAST
ABGILOOORSTY	ASTROBIOLOGY
ABGIMNNORRST	BARNSTORMING
ABHHIKRSSTTU	TURKISH BATHS
ABHIIKMNNPRS	BRINKMANSHIP
ABHIILNOPSTY	INHOSPITABLY
ABHIINOPRSTV	VIBRAPHONIST
ABHIMNNORRTU	NORTHUMBRIAN
ABIIIILRRTTY	IRRITABILITY
ABIIILLPSTUY	PLAUSIBILITY
ABIIILMMOTVY	IMMOVABILITY
ABIIILMMTTUY	IMMUTABILITY
ABIIILMNOOST	ABOLITIONISM, MOBILISATION
ABIIILMNOOTZ	MOBILIZATION
ABIIILMPTTUY	IMPUTABILITY
ABIIILNOOSTT	ABOLITIONIST
ABIIILNPRTTY	PRINTABILITY
ABIIILNRSTUY	INSURABILITY
ABIIILSTTTWY	TWISTABILITY
ABIILMOOSTTU	AUTOMOBILIST
ABIILNOORSTT	STROBILATION
ABIILNORSSUU	INSALUBRIOUS
ABIILNRSSTTU	TRIBULATIONS
ABIILOOPPSTY	OPPOSABILITY
ABIILRSTTTUY	TRUSTABILITY
ABIIMNORSTTU	TAMBOURINIST
ABIINOORSSTT	ABORTIONISTS
ABIIOPRSTTVY	ABSORPTIVITY
ABILMMMNOSSU	SOMNAMBULISM
ABILMMNOSSTU	SOMNAMBULIST
ABILMNORSTUY	SUBNORMALITY
ABIMNORSSTTU	NIMBOSTRATUS
ABINRRSSSTTU	BRAINS TRUSTS
ABNOORRSSTUU	BRONTOSAURUS
ACCCCEIILRRT	ARCTIC CIRCLE
ACCCDEEEELNS	DECALESCENCE
ACCCDENNOORS	CONCORDANCES
ACCCDIMOPSST	COMPACT DISCS
ACCCEEEEELNRS	RECALESCENCE
ACCCEEEEILNNS	INCALESCENCE
ACCCEEEINQSU	ACQUIESCENCE
ACCCEEIILSST	ECCLESIASTIC
ACCCEEILLLTY	ECLECTICALLY
ACCCEGIINNOR	CARCINOGENIC
ACCCEHILMOTY	CYTOCHEMICAL
ACCCEIILMRST	CLIMACTERICS
ACCCEIMNNOOT	CONCOMITANCE
ACCCEIMNRSTU	CIRCUMSTANCE
ACCCHIIOPRRT	CHIROPRACTIC
ACCCIIILLOSS	LOCI CLASSICI
ACCCIIILSSST	CLASSICISTIC
ACCCIILNNOTY	ANTICYCLONIC
ACCCIILNOOST	ICONOCLASTIC
ACCDDEEHINOOP	DODECAPHONIC
ACCDDEHNPRSU	PUNCHED CARDS
ACCDDEIINORT	ENDOCARDITIC
ACCDDEINORTT	CONTRADICTED
ACCDEEFIIRTT	CERTIFICATED
ACCDEEFILLLMS	MACCLESFIELD
ACCDEEFLLOTU	DEFLOCCULATE
ACCDEEGOPRSU	COUPS DE GRACE
ACCDEEHIILNP	DIENCEPHALIC
ACCDEEHIMNOS	MACHINE CODES
ACCDEEHIORSS	ARCHDIOCESES
ACCDEEIILNOT	INDOLEACETIC
ACCDEEILLOPS	PECCADILLOES
ACCDEEILNOPY	ENCYCLOPEDIA
ACCDEEINNNST	INCANDESCENT
ACCDEEINNORT	CONCERTINAED
ACCDEEIOPRRT	RECIPROCATED
ACCDEELMORTT	CLOTTED CREAM
ACCDEELOOPRU	CAPE COLOURED
ACCDEENNNOTU	COUNTENANCED
ACCDEENNORTT	CONCENTRATED
ACCDEENORTTU	COUNTERACTED
ACCDEENOSSUU	SUCCEDANEOUS
ACCDEEOOPRRS	CERRO DE PASCO
ACCDEGHORTUU	DUTCH COURAGE
ACCDEGIILRSY	LYSERGIC ACID
ACCDEGNNORRT	CONCERT GRAND
ACCDEHHNNRRUW	CHURCHWARDEN
ACCDEHILMOPS	ACCOMPLISHED
ACCDEHILOOPP	CEPHALOPODIC
ACCDEHIOORSU	ORCHIDACEOUS
ACCDEHNRRRUY	HARD CURRENCY
ACCDEIIILNST	INSECTICIDAL
ACCDEIIIPRRT	PERICARDITIC
ACCDEIILLOPY	EPICYCLOIDAL
ACCDEIILNNOT	COINCIDENTAL
ACCDEIILRRSU	CIRCULARISED
ACCDEIILRRUZ	CIRCULARIZED
ACCDEIKLNSST	CANDLESTICKS
ACCDEILNOPTU	CONDUPLICATE
ACCDEIMMNOTU	COMMUNICATED
ACCDEIMNORTU	UNDEMOCRATIC
ACCDEINORRTT	CONTRADICTER

ACCDEIOORRTT	DECORTICATOR	ACCEEMNOPPSU	COME-UPPANCES
ACCDEIPRRSTU	PICTURE CARDS	ACCEEMNORTTU	ACCOUTREMENT
ACCDEKORRRST	TRACK RECORDS	ACCEEMOOPPRR	COME A CROPPER
ACCDEMNOSTUU	UNACCUSTOMED	ACCEENNNOSTU	COUNTENANCES
ACCDENNORTUY	COUNTRY DANCE	ACCEENNORSTT	CONCENTRATES
ACCDFIIINOOT	CODIFICATION	ACCEFGIIINNS	SIGNIFICANCE
ACCDHIINORTW	IN ACCORD WITH	ACCEFIILLMRY	FAMILY CIRCLE
ACCDHINOTTUU	DUTCH AUCTION	ACCEFIILLPSY	SPECIFICALLY
ACCDIINOORST	ACCORDIONIST	ACCEGHHIOPRT	HECTOGRAPHIC
ACCDIINOSTTY	SYNDIOTACTIC	ACCEGHINOPRS	SCENOGRAPHIC
ACCDILNOOSSS	COCOS ISLANDS	ACCEGIIKNRSW	WISECRACKING
ACCEEEGINNOT	CAENOGENETIC	ACCEGIINNNOZ	INCOGNIZANCE
ACCEEEHILNPP	EPENCEPHALIC	ACCEGIINRTUX	EXCRUCIATING
ACCEEEHLORRT	HETEROCERCAL	ACCEGILLLOOY	ECOLOGICALLY
ACCEEENOPRSV	VAPORESCENCE	ACCEGILLNOOR	NECROLOGICAL
ACCEEFFHKLOT	COFFEE KLATCH	ACCEGILNNOSV	CONVALESCING
ACCEEFGIIMNN	MAGNIFICENCE	ACCEGILNOSUW	WAGES COUNCIL
ACCEEFHIMSTU	FACE THE MUSIC	ACCEGINNNOVY	CONVEYANCING
ACCEEFHMNORT	FRANCHE-COMTE	ACCEGINNORST	CONSECRATING
ACCEEFIIRSTT	CERTIFICATES	ACCEGNOORRTY	GERONTOCRACY
ACCEEFIKRRRS	FIRECRACKERS	ACCEHHLMNORY	CHLORENCHYMA
ACCEEGHIMNOS	GEOMECHANICS	ACCEHIILLNST	CALLISTHENIC
ACCEEGHNNORX	CORN EXCHANGE	ACCEHIILNOPR	NECROPHILIAC
ACCEEGHORRSV	COVER CHARGES	ACCEHIILNSST	CALISTHENICS
ACCEEGILRRST	GREAT CIRCLES	ACCEHIILNTTY	TECHNICALITY
ACCEEGINNORZ	RECOGNIZANCE	ACCEHIIRSTTT	TETRASTICHIC
ACCEEHHIRSST	CHESHIRE CATS	ACCEHIKMNSTY	CHIMNEYSTACK
ACCEEHIILNPT	ENCEPHALITIC	ACCEHILLLORY	CHOLERICALLY
ACCEEHILMOPS	MESOCEPHALIC	ACCEHILMOPRS	ACCOMPLISHER
ACCEEHILRRST	RICHTER SCALE	ACCEHILMOPRY	MICROCEPHALY,
ACCEEHIMORTT	TACHEOMETRIC	PYROCHEMICAL	
ACCEEHIORTTT	HETEROTACTIC	ACCEHILNNNOT	NONTECHNICAL
ACCEEHIRRTTU	ARCHITECTURE	ACCEHILNOOOT	ECHOLOCATION
ACCEEHKORSTW	WEATHERCOCKS	ACCEHILOPRTY	CHALCOPYRITE
ACCEEHLMNRSY	SCLERENCHYMA	ACCEHIMOORST	MESOTHORACIC
ACCEEHLMORTY	THE REAL MCCOY	ACCEHINNNOPT	PANTECHNICON
ACCEEHMNNORT	ENCROACHMENT	ACCEHINRSSST	SCRATCHINESS
ACCEEIILNRST	ELECTRICIANS	ACCEHIOPSTVY	PSYCHOACTIVE
ACCEEIINPPRT	PRECIPITANCE	ACCEHKLOOSVZ	CZECHOSLOVAK
ACCEEIKNPRSS	SCIENCE PARKS	ACCEHKOPPSTT	PATCH POCKETS
ACCEEILLLRTY	ELECTRICALLY	ACCEHLOOPRTY	PYROCATECHOL
ACCEEILLMNUY	ECUMENICALLY	ACCEHLOORSSU	SCHORLACEOUS
ACCEEILNPTTU	CENTUPLICATE	ACCEHMNOOORT	COME TO ANCHOR
ACCEEILNRTTY	TETRACYCLINE	ACCEHOPRSSST	CROSSPATCHES
ACCEEIMNOTTY	ACTINOMYCETE	ACCEIIILPSST	SPECIALISTIC
ACCEEINOPPRV	CAPE PROVINCE	ACCEIIINNNPS	PICCANINNIES
ACCEEIORSTTT	STEREOTACTIC	ACCEIIKKMNRS	CAMI-KNICKERS
ACCEELLOORTT	COLLECTORATE	ACCEIILLLNTY	ENCLITICALLY
ACCEELMNOPTU	ACCOUPLEMENT	ACCEIILLLPTY	ECLIPTICALLY
ACCEELNNOPTY	CYCLOPENTANE	ACCEIILMMORT	MICROCLIMATE
ACCEELNNOSTV	CONVALESCENT	ACCEIILMNNOP	INCOMPLIANCE
ACCEELNNRSTU	TRANSLUCENCE	ACCEIILMORRT	CALORIMETRIC
ACCEELPRRWYY	CREEPY-CRAWLY	ACCEIILMRRSU	SEMICIRCULAR
ACCEEMNNORRS	NECROMANCERS	ACCEIILNORTV	INTERVOCALIC

ACCEIILORRTV	OVERCRITICAL	ACCGHHIINTTT	CHITCHATTING
ACCEIILRRRSU	CIRCULARISER	ACCGHHIIOPRR	CHIROGRAPHIC
ACCEIILRRRUZ	CIRCULARIZER	ACCGHHIOOPRR	CHOROGRAPHIC
ACCEIILRSSTU	SECULARISTIC	ACCGHIIKNORR	ROCKING CHAIR
ACCEIIMNORRT	CRANIOMETRIC	ACCGHIILLNOO	ICHNOLOGICAL
ACCEIIMNORTT	ACTINOMETRIC	ACCGHIILNNOP	CHILPANCINGO
ACCEIIMNOSST	COSMETICIANS	ACCGHIIMOPRR	MICROGRAPHIC
ACCEIINOPRSS	CONSPIRACIES	ACCGHIIMOTTT	THIGMOTACTIC
ACCEIINORTUX	EXCRUCIATION	ACCGHIINOOPR	ICONOGRAPHIC
ACCEIIPPRSTY	PERSPICACITY	ACCGHIINOPRZ	ZINCOGRAPHIC
ACCEILLMMORY	COMMERCIALLY	ACCGHILLOOPY	PHYCOLOGICAL
ACCEILLMNOOY	ECONOMICALLY	ACCGHINOPSTT	SCOTCH TAPING
ACCEILLMOSTY	COSMETICALLY	ACCGIIILNNOT	CONCILIATING
ACCEILLNNORT	CENTROCLINAL	ACCGIIINORST	ORGANICISTIC
ACCEILLNOTTY	TECTONICALLY	ACCGIILLMOOT	CLIMATOLOGIC
ACCEILLOPRRY	RECIPROCALLY	ACCGIILLNOOO	ICONOLOGICAL
ACCEILLOPTYY	ECOTYPICALLY	ACCGIILLOOOS	SOCIOLOGICAL
ACCEILMMNORU	UNCOMMERCIAL	ACCGIILMNOPT	COMPLICATING
ACCEILMNNOOU	UNECONOMICAL	ACCGILLMOOOS	COSMOLOGICAL
ACCEILMNORTU	COUNTERCLAIM	ACCGILNORTUY	GRANULOCYTIC
ACCEILNNNOOT	CONNECTIONAL	ACCGIOOPRSST	GASTROSCOPIC
ACCEILNNOOPT	CONCEPTIONAL	ACCHHIOPPSTY	PSYCHOPATHIC
ACCEILNNOOTV	CONVECTIONAL	ACCHIIINSTUV	CHAUVINISTIC
ACCEILNNOSTY	ANTICYCLONES	ACCHIILLOOTY	ALCOHOLICITY
ACCEILNOSSSU	SUCCESSIONAL	ACCHIILOPRTY	HYPOCRITICAL
ACCEILOOSSTT	OSTEOCLASTIC	ACCHIIMMORST	CHROMATICISM
ACCEILOPRSTU	PLUTOCRACIES	ACCHIIMNOPTY	AMPHICTYONIC
ACCEIMNOSTTY	NEMATOCYSTIC	ACCHIIMNORST	MONARCHISTIC
ACCEIMNRTTUU	CIRCUMNUTATE	ACCHIIMOORST	ISOCHROMATIC
ACCEINNNNOOS	INCONSONANCE	ACCHIIMORRTT	TRICHROMATIC
ACCEINNOORST	CONSECRATION	ACCHIIMORTTY	CHROMATICITY
ACCEINNORSTV	CONTRIVANCES	ACCHIINOOPTT	PHOTOACTINIC
ACCEIOOPRRRT	RECIPROCATOR	ACCHIIOPRSTY	PHYSIOCRATIC
ACCELLMNOPTY	COMPLACENTLY	ACCHILLNNOOO	NONALCOHOLIC
ACCELLNOPTUY	CONCEPTUALLY	ACCHILOOPSSY	PSYCHOSOCIAL
ACCELLOOORSU	COROLLACEOUS	ACCHILOPPRTY	PROPHYLACTIC
ACCELLOSSTTU	COALSCUTTLES	ACCHIMOPRSSY	MACROPHYSICS
ACCELMMNOOPS	COMMONPLACES	ACCHINOOPSTT	PHONOTACTICS
ACCELMNORSUU	MACRONUCLEUS	ACCHIOOPRRRT	CHIROPRACTOR
ACCELMOOSTTY	CYCLOSTOMATE	ACCHIOORRSSU	CHIAROSCUROS
ACCELNNRSTUY	TRANSLUCENCY	ACCIIILNNOOT	CONCILIATION
ACCELORSUUVY	CURVACEOUSLY	ACCIIINRSSST	NARCISSISTIC
ACCEMOOSSTUY	ASCOMYCETOUS	ACCIILLNRTUY	UNCRITICALLY
ACCENNOORRTT	CONCENTRATOR	ACCIILLRSTTY	CRYSTALLITIC
ACCENOORRSTY	CONSECRATORY	ACCIILMNOOPT	COMPLICATION
ACCFGHHIOSTT	CATCH SIGHT OF	ACCIILNOORST	CONCILIATORS
ACCFGIINNOST	CONFISCATING	ACCIILNOORTY	CONCILIATORY
ACCFIIMNNOSU	CONFUCIANISM	ACCIILOPRSUY	CAPRICIOUSLY
ACCFIINNOOST	CONFISCATION	ACCIIMOOPRTT	COMPATRIOTIC
ACCFIINNOSTU	CONFUCIANIST	ACCIINNOOOST	CONSOCIATION
ACCFILLNOOTU	FLOCCULATION	ACCIJLNNOTUV	CONJUNCTIVAL
ACCFINOORSTY	CONFISCATORY	ACCILLMNOOSU	MALOCCLUSION
ACCGGHHIKNOU	HACKING COUGH	ACCILLNOOOST	COLLOCATIONS
ACCGHHIINOPR	ICHNOGRAPHIC	ACCIMMNNOSTU	COMMUNICANTS

ACCIMMNOORTU	COMMUNICATOR	ACDEEEILNRTZ	DECENTRALIZE
ACCIMNNOOSTT	CONCOMITANTS	ACDEEEILNSST	DELICATESSEN
ACCIMNOOSTUU	CONTUMACIOUS	ACDEEEINNRTV	INADVERTENCE
ACCIMOORSSTY	MACROCYTOSIS	ACDEEEINRSSV	DISSEVERANCE
ACCINNOOOSTV	CONVOCATIONS	ACDEEEINSSTT	NECESSITATED
ACCINNOORSTT	CONTRACTIONS	ACDEEEOPRRRT	TAPE RECORDER
ACCJLNNORTUU	CONJUNCTURAL	ACDEEEOPRTTX	EXPECTORATED
ACDDDEEHNOOR	DODECAHEDRON	ACDEEFFLNTUY	UNAFFECTEDLY
ACDDDEGINOOR	GOOD RIDDANCE	ACDEEFFNORRT	FORT-DE-FRANCE
ACDDEEEFLSTU	SELF-EDUCATED	ACDEEFHHIKNR	HANDKERCHIEF
ACDDEEEFNORT	CONFEDERATED	ACDEEFHINNRS	ENFRANCHISED
ACDDEEEHIMST	SEMIDETACHED	ACDEEFIILRST	FEDERALISTIC
ACDDEEEELLTUW	WELL-EDUCATED	ACDEEFIINRRY	FERRICYANIDE
ACDDEEEMMNOR	COMMANDEERED	ACDEEFILMTTU	MULTIFACETED
ACDDEEFIILSS	DECLASSIFIED	ACDEEFILOPPR	PRIDE OF PLACE
ACDDEEGHNRRU	UNDERCHARGED	ACDEEFINORRY	FERROCYANIDE
ACDDEEHIMNRS	MERCHANDISED	ACDEEFNOSSTW	TWO-FACEDNESS
ACDDEEHINNST	DISENCHANTED	ACDEEFNRRSUU	UNDERSURFACE
ACDDEEHNORSW	CROWNED HEADS	ACDEEGHILRST	CLEAR-SIGHTED
ACDDEEILPRTU	REDUPLICATED	ACDEEGHINNRT	INTERCHANGED
ACDDEEIMORST	DEMOCRATISED	ACDEEGHLLNNU	UNCHALLENGED
ACDDEEIMORTZ	DEMOCRATIZED	ACDEEGHPRRSU	SUPERCHARGED
ACDDEEIMOSTT	DOMESTICATED	ACDEEGIINPRT	DEPRECIATING
ACDDEEINNRSU	REDUNDANCIES	ACDEEGIINRST	GARDEN CITIES
ACDDEFIRSTUV	FIVE-CARD STUD	ACDEEGILNORS	CLOSE-GRAINED
ACDDEFNNNOOR	CANNON FODDER	ACDEEGILSTTU	GESTICULATED
ACDDEGHINRSU	UNDISCHARGED	ACDEEGINORRT	REDECORATING
ACDDEGIILLNO	DIALLING CODE	ACDEEGIOSTTT	TIED COTTAGES
ACDDEIILNORU	RADIONUCLIDE	ACDEEGKLNORW	ACKNOWLEDGER
ACDDEIINNOTV	NONADDICTIVE	ACDEEGNNORTV	COVENT GARDEN
ACDDEEIINORST	ENDOCARDITIS	ACDEEGNNOSTT	DECONGESTANT
ACDDEEIINRTTY	IDENTITY CARD	ACDEEGNOORVW	COVERED WAGON
ACDDEILNOOST	CONSOLIDATED	ACDEEHHIMORT	HEMICHORDATE
ACDDEILRSTTY	DISTRACTEDLY	ACDEEHILMNOR	ECHINODERMAL
ACDDEINOSTTU	OUTDISTANCED	ACDEEHILNNOP	DIENCEPHALON
ACDDEINPRSTY	CANDY-STRIPED	ACDEEHIMNRRS	MERCHANDISER
ACDDEMOPRSSU	MASS-PRODUCED	ACDEEHINNRST	DISENCHANTER
ACDDENORRSSW	SWORD DANCERS	ACDEEHINRSTW	WINDCHEATERS
ACDDHIMNORYY	HYDRODYNAMIC	ACDEEHINSTTW	WATTENSCHEID
ACDDILNORSTY	DISCORDANTLY	ACDEEHKMRSTU	DEUTSCHE MARK
ACDDOOOORRRUY	CORDUROY ROAD	ACDEEHLORTTY	HETERODACTYL
ACDEEEEHLRRS	CHEERLEADERS	ACDEEHMNORSW	REACH-ME-DOWNS
ACDEEEFFNSST	AFFECTEDNESS	ACDEEHORRSTT	ORCHESTRATED
ACDEEEFNORST	CONFEDERATES	ACDEEIILLNTY	INDELICATELY
ACDEEEGILNRT	DECELERATING	ACDEEIILLTTY	DIETETICALLY
ACDEEEGINOPT	PAEDOGENETIC	ACDEEIIMNRRT	RECRIMINATED
ACDEEEGINPRS	PREDECEASING	ACDEEIIMNRTY	INTERMEDIACY
ACDEEEGLLOST	DECOLLETAGES	ACDEEIINOPRT	DEPRECIATION
ACDEEEGLNOOU	EAU DE COLOGNE	ACDEEIINQSTU	EQUIDISTANCE
ACDEEEHINRUV	UNDERACHIEVE	ACDEEIINTTUX	INEXACTITUDE
ACDEEEILNORT	DECELERATION	ACDEEIIPPRTT	PRECIPITATED
ACDEEEILNPRT	PRECEDENTIAL	ACDEEIJKNNRT	DINNER JACKET
ACDEEEILNRST	DECENTRALISE	ACDEEIKLOOPS	KALEIDOSCOPE
		ACDEEILLNNOS	DECLENSIONAL

ACDEEILLNRTY	INTERLACEDLY	ACDEHIIMNNOT	INDOMETHACIN
ACDEEILMNPST	DISPLACEMENT	ACDEHIIMORST	RADIOCHEMIST
ACDEEILNPQTU	QUINDECAPLET	ACDEHILLMOTY	METHODICALLY
ACDEEILNRSTT	DECENTRALIST	ACDEHINNOPSW	OPEN SANDWICH
ACDEEILORTVY	DECORATIVELY	ACDEHINOPTTU	PUT THE ACID ON
ACDEEIMMORST	COMMISERATED	ACDEHIOOPRST	ORTHOPAEDICS
ACDEEIMNNOPR	PREDOMINANCE	ACDEHKMRSSTU	DEUTSCHMARKS
ACDEEIMNPRST	PREDICAMENTS	ACDEHLNPRSTU	THUNDERCLAPS
ACDEEIMORRTX	XERODERMATIC	ACDEIIILNTVY	INDICATIVELY
ACDEEINOORST	AERODONETICS	ACDEIIILRTVY	VERIDICALITY
ACDEEINOPRTU	DEUTERANOPIC	ACDEIIIMNNOT	NICOTINAMIDE
ACDEEINOSSSU	EDACIOUSNESS	ACDEIIIMNNRS	INCENDIARISM
ACDEEIOPRSTU	PROPAEDEUTIC	ACDEIIIMNNRT	INCRIMINATED
ACDEEIOPRRTY	DEPRECIATORY	ACDEIIIMNRST	DISCRIMINATE
ACDEEIORRSSV	SERVICE ROADS	ACDEIIIMORST	ISODIAMETRIC
ACDEEIORRSTT	DIRECTORATES	ACDEIIINOPRT	ANTIPERIODIC
ACDEEIRSSTTU	RESUSCITATED	ACDEIIINOPRS	DICTIONARIES
ACDEEJKKNOTY	DONKEY JACKET	ACDEIIINPPST	APPENDICITIS
ACDEELMNOPTT	CONTEMPLATED	ACDEIIIOPRTY	APERIODICITY
ACDEELNOOSSS	CLOSED SEASON	ACDEIIIOSSTV	DISSOCIATIVE
ACDEELOPRRRY	RECORD PLAYER	ACDEIIIPRRST	PERICARDITIS
ACDEEMMMOORT	COMMEMORATED	ACDEIIKPRSTT	PEAK DISTRICT
ACDEEMNOPPTY	APPENDECTOMY	ACDEIILLLNNTY	INCIDENTALLY
ACDEENNNOTUV	UNCOVENANTED	ACDEIILLNSTT	SCINTILLATED
ACDEENNNRSTT	TRANSCENDENT	ACDEIILLOPRY	PERIODICALLY
ACDEENNORSTU	SECOND NATURE	ACDEIILLOPSY	EPISODICALLY
ACDEFFIINOST	DISAFFECTION	ACDEIILLRTUY	DIURETICALLY
ACDEFHIINRSS	DISFRANCHISE	ACDEIILMNOST	MALEDICTIONS
ACDEFHOORSSU	HOUSE OF CARDS	ACDEIILMORTT	DILATOMETRIC
ACDEFIIINNST	INFANTICIDES	ACDEIILNNNOT	NONIDENTICAL
ACDEFIILNNOT	CONFIDENTIAL	ACDEIILNNOST	DECLINATIONS
ACDEFIILNSSU	UNCLASSIFIED	ACDEIILNOSTV	VALEDICTIONS
ACDEFIINNSTT	DISINFECTANT	ACDEIILRRTUV	DIVERTICULAR
ACDEFIINOPTT	PONTIFICATED	ACDEIIMNORST	ROMANTICISED
ACDEFILRTTUX	FLUIDEXTRACT	ACDEIIMNORTZ	ROMANTICIZED
ACDEGHHNORST	SHORT-CHANGED	ACDEIINNNOTU	DENUNCIATION
ACDEGHIILRSY	RAYLEIGH DISC	ACDEIINNOORT	INCOORDINATE
ACDEGHIOPRRS	DISCOGRAPHER	ACDEIINNORTT	INDOCTRINATE
ACDEGHLOORSS	GRADE SCHOOLS	ACDEIINOOTTX	DETOXICATION
ACDEGIIILMNZ	DECIMALIZING	ACDEIIORSSTT	SIDEROSTATIC
ACDEGIIKNRST	SIDETRACKING	ACDEIKMNNORT	ONE-TRACK MIND
ACDEGIILLNSS	SLIDING SCALE	ACDEIKNORSTT	STOCK-IN-TRADE
ACDEGIILLOOO	IDEOLOOOGICAL	ACDEILLMOSTY	DOMESTICALLY
ACDEGIILPQRU	QUADRIPLEGIC	ACDEILLNSTYY	SYNDETICALLY
ACDEGIIOOPRT	DIAGEOTROPIC	ACDEILLOPSTY	DESPOTICALLY
ACDEGILLOOTY	DIALECTOLOGY	ACDEILLRSSTY	CRYSTALLISED
ACDEGILNNOST	LONG-DISTANCE	ACDEILLRSTYZ	CRYSTALLIZED
ACDEGINNNRST	TRANSCENDING	ACDEILMNOSUY	MENDACIOUSLY
ACDEGINORRSS	CROSS-GRAINED	ACDEILMOPSTU	DEUTOPLASMIC
ACDEHHHNOTTW	DOWN THE HATCH	ACDEILNOOORT	DECOLORATION
ACDEHHLOPRYY	HYDROCEPHALY	ACDEILNOORTU	EDULCORATION
ACDEHHOOOPTT	PHOTOCATHODE	ACDEILNOORTY	COORDINATELY
ACDEHIILLLOY	HELICOIDALLY	ACDEILNOOSST	DISCONSOLATE
ACDEHIILMMOT	IMMETHODICAL	ACDEILNORSSW	COWARDLINESS

ACDEILOORRUV	VARICOLOURED	ACDIILNSSSTY	SYNDICALISTS
ACDEIMMNNOOT	COMMENDATION	ACDIINNOOORT	COORDINATION
ACDEIMMNNORTY	DYNAMOMETRIC	ACDIINORSSTT	DISTRACTIONS
ACDEIMMOOORR	AIR COMMODORE	ACDIINORSSYY	IDIOSYNCRASY
ACDEIMNNNOOT	CONDEMNATION	ACDILMNSSTYY	SYNDACTYLISM
ACDEIMNORRRS	MORRIS DANCER	ACDILNOOORST	CONSOLIDATOR
ACDEIMNORRSS	MORRIS DANCES	ACDILNOOPRTU	PRODUCTIONAL
ACDEIMOORSTT	DOMESTICATOR	ACDINNORSTTU	TRANSDUCTION
ACDEINNNOOST	CONDENSATION	ACDINOOQRSTU	CONQUISTADOR
ACDEINNNOSTU	UNSANCTIONED	ACDLOOOPRSTT	POSTDOCTORAL
ACDEINNORTTU	DETRUNCATION	ACEEEEFJKRRT	REEFER JACKET
ACDEINNORTUY	DENUNCIATORY	ACEEEEHLPSST	STEEPLECHASE
ACDEINOOPRRT	INCORPORATED	ACEEEELMNRTT	TRACE ELEMENT
ACDELMOPRTUW	TALCUM POWDER	ACEEEELNORTT	COELENTERATE
ACDELNOORTYY	COTYLEDONARY	ACEEEENPRRSV	PERSEVERANCE
ACDELOPRRTTY	PROTRACTEDLY	ACEEEFFFRSTT	AFTEREFFECTS
ACDELOPRSTTY	PTERODACTYLS	ACEEEFILLNRS	SELF-RELIANCE
ACDEMMMNNOST	COMMANDMENTS	ACEEEFIOPPPS	PIPES OF PEACE
ACDEMMNOORTY	COMMENDATORY	ACEEEFLNPSSU	PEACEFULNESS
ACDEMNNOORTY	CONDEMNATORY	ACEEEFLNSSSS	FACELESSNESS
ACDEMOPRRSSU	MASS-PRODUCER	ACEEEFLORRST	STEER CLEAR OF
ACDEOPRSTTUW	WASTE PRODUCT	ACEEEFLRRSTV	SCARLET FEVER
ACDFIIIINNOT	NIDIFICATION	ACEEEFNNRRST	TRANSFERENCE
ACDFIIIIMNOT	MODIFICATION	ACEEEGHHRSST	CHARGE SHEETS
ACDFIIMOORTY	MODIFICATORY	ACEEEGHINNRS	SEARCH ENGINE
ACDFILMOORTY	FAMILY DOCTOR	ACEEEGHINPRS	CHEESEPARING
ACDGGIINORSU	DISCOURAGING	ACEEEGIIMNNR	ANCIEN REGIME
ACDGHHIOPRRY	HYDROGRAPHIC	ACEEEGILLTXY	EXEGETICALLY
ACDGHIIOPRTT	DITTOGRAPHIC	ACEEEGIMNRST	RACE MEETINGS
ACDGIIINNOSS	DISSOCIATING	ACEEEGINNOSS	CAENOGENESIS
ACDGIIINRSTV	VISITING CARD	ACEEEGINNSSW	NEWS AGENCIES
ACDGIILOORST	CARDIOLOGIST	ACEEEGNNRRUY	UNREGENERACY
ACDGIINNOORT	COORDINATING	ACEEEGNRSSTT	SECRET AGENTS
ACDHHINOOPRY	HYPOCHONDRIA	ACEEEHHILLLS	ACHILLES' HEEL
ACDHHIOPRRSS	HARPSICHORDS	ACEEEHHILNOT	ACE IN THE HOLE
ACDHIIMMORST	DICHROMATISM	ACEEEHILSTTT	TELAESTHETIC
ACDHIIOPRSST	RHAPSODISTIC	ACEEEHIMNQTU	CINEMATHEQUE
ACDHIIOPRSTT	DICTATORSHIP	ACEEEHIMNSTV	ACHIEVEMENTS
ACDHILLOORTY	TROCHOIDALLY	ACEEEHINOSST	COENESTHESIA
ACDHIMNOOPTY	PHOTODYNAMIC	ACEEEHLMOPRT	CEPHALOMETER
ACDHLNOOSSUY	SUNDAY SCHOOL	ACEEEHLNNOPP	EPENCEPHALON
ACDHNRSTTTUU	CUT AND THRUST	ACEEEHMNNNST	ENHANCEMENTS
ACDIIILNPRSY	DISCIPLINARY	ACEEEILLLNTT	LENTICELLATE
ACDIIIMNNOOT	NONIDIOMATIC	ACEEEILLNPST	LICENSE PLATE
ACDIIIMNNRST	DISCRIMINANT	ACEEEILMNPST	MANTELPIECES
ACDIIINNOORT	AIR-CONDITION	ACEEEILNNNSV	VALENCIENNES
ACDIIINOOSST	DISSOCIATION	ACEEEILNPPRS	PIPE CLEANERS
ACDIIIOSSTTU	ADSCITITIOUS	ACEEEILNRRSV	IRRELEVANCES
ACDIILLLOOTY	COLLOIDALITY	ACEEEIMMNNPR	IMPERMANENCE
ACDIILLMNPTU	MULTIPLICAND	ACEEEIMNNPRT	INTEMPERANCE
ACDIILLOPRTY	DIOPTRICALLY	ACEEEIMNRSVX	EX-SERVICEMAN
ACDIILNOOSST	DISLOCATIONS	ACEEEIMPRSST	MASTERPIECES
ACDIILNORTTY	DOCTRINALITY	ACEEEINRSSTV	REACTIVENESS
ACDIILNOSSSU	DISCUSSIONAL	ACEEEIPPPRTV	APPERCEPTIVE

ACEEEIPRRTUV	RECUPERATIVE
ACEEEJKLPSST	STEEPLEJACKS
ACEEEJORSSTT	EJECTOR SEATS
ACEEELLOPRTT	ELECTROPLATE
ACEEELLORSVV	CLOVERLEAVES
ACEEELMMNPST	EMPLACEMENTS
ACEEELMNPRST	REPLACEMENTS
ACEEELNOTXYY	OXYACETYLENE
ACEEELNRSSSS	CARELESSNESS
ACEEEMNNNRTT	ENTRANCEMENT
ACEEENNRRTTY	TERCENTENARY
ACEEENNRSTXY	SEXCENTENARY
ACEEEOPPRRTT	PRECEPTORATE
ACEEFFFGILNS	SELF-EFFACING
ACEEFFGHILNO	CHANGE OF LIFE
ACEEFFGINTTU	EFFECTUATING
ACEEFFHOTTTT	TO THAT EFFECT
ACEEFFILTTUY	EFFECTUALITY
ACEEFFINOTTU	EFFECTUATION
ACEEFFNNORSU	ON SUFFERANCE
ACEEFGILNRST	SELF-CATERING
ACEEFGLNRSSU	GRACEFULNESS
ACEEFGNNOOST	AGE OF CONSENT
ACEEFHINNNRS	ENFRANCHISER
ACEEFHLNORSV	FRENCH LOAVES
ACEEFHLOPRRS	SELF-REPROACH
ACEEFHMORTTY	AT THE MERCY OF
ACEEFHNOPRTU	PUT HER FACE ON
ACEEFHNORSTU	ON THE SURFACE
ACEEFHOPPRST	PART OF SPEECH
ACEEFIIIRTVV	VERIFICATIVE
ACEEFIILNQTU	LIQUEFACIENT
ACEEFIILQTUV	LIQUEFACTIVE
ACEEFIKNNNRS	FRANKINCENSE
ACEEFILLNORT	REFLECTIONAL
ACEEFILLNRTY	FRENETICALLY
ACEEFILNNORT	CONFERENTIAL
ACEEFILNNOST	LINE OF ASCENT
ACEEFILOPRRT	PREFECTORIAL
ACEEFILRSSTV	SERVICE FLATS
ACEEFINPSTTU	STUPEFACIENT
ACEEFIPRTTUV	PUTREFACTIVE
ACEEFKMORRST	MARKET FORCES
ACEEFMNOPRRS	PERFORMANCES
ACEEFPPRSSTT	PAST PERFECTS
ACEEGGINORTV	CONGREGATIVE
ACEEGHILNOSU	CHAISE LONGUE
ACEEGHILNRTW	CARTWHEELING
ACEEGHILOORS	ARCHEOLOGIES
ACEEGHINNNRST	INTERCHANGES
ACEEGHINOPTT	PATHOGENETIC
ACEEGHINORRV	OVERREACHING
ACEEGHIRRSST	CASH REGISTER
ACEEGHLLNSSY	CHANGELESSLY

ACEEGHLOPRRT	ELECTROGRAPH
ACEEGHMNNORY	MONEYCHANGER
ACEEGHNOPRRS	SCENOGRAPHER
ACEEGHNRRSSU	CHARGE NURSES
ACEEGHPRRRSU	SUPERCHARGER
ACEEGIILNNPT	PALINGENETIC
ACEEGIILNSTV	EVANGELISTIC
ACEEGIINRSTV	EVISCERATING
ACEEGIIOTTVX	EXCOGITATIVE
ACEEGIKMSSST	MESSAGE STICK
ACEEGIKNNRRV	NERVE-RACKING
ACEEGILLLNTY	TELGENICALLY
ACEEGILLLOOT	TELEOLOGICAL
ACEEGILMNOPT	MAGNETIC POLE
ACEEGILNPRSS	SLEEPING CARS
ACEEGILNPSTT	PLACE SETTING
ACEEGIMNORTY	ATOMIC ENERGY
ACEEGINNSSTX	EXACTINGNESS
ACEEGINORRTV	OVERREACTING
ACEEGINPRRTU	RECUPERATING
ACEEGLMNOORT	CONGLOMERATE
ACEEGMNORRSS	SCAREMONGERS
ACEEHHIPRRSU	HIRE PURCHASE
ACEEHHKNPPRU	KERENHAPPUCH
ACEEHHLMRSST	CRASH HELMETS
ACEEHHLNORSU	CHARNEL HOUSE
ACEEHHMOPRTY	CHEMOTHERAPY
ACEEHHNORSST	SHEET ANCHORS
ACEEHHOPRSTU	CHAPTERHOUSE
ACEEHHOPRTTY	TRACHEOPHYTE
ACEEHIIKNSTT	KINAESTHETIC
ACEEHIILNPST	ENCEPHALITIS
ACEEHIIMOOPT	HAEMOPOIETIC
ACEEHIIMSSTT	AESTHETICISM
ACEEHIINNRST	INHERITANCES
ACEEHIINORTT	THEORETICIAN
ACEEHIINSTUU	HAUTE CUISINE
ACEEHILLLLNY	HELLENICALLY
ACEEHILLMRTY	HERMETICALLY
ACEEHILLSTTY	ESTHETICALLY
ACEEHILNORSS	HEROICALNESS
ACEEHILNRSTT	CHAIN LETTERS
ACEEHILPSSST	SALES PITCHES
ACEEHIMMNTTY	ENTHYMEMATIC
ACEEHIMNSSTT	CHASTISEMENT
ACEEHIMOPRTV	OVEREMPHATIC
ACEEHIMRSSTV	CHRISTMAS EVE
ACEEHINNRSTU	NEURASTHENIC
ACEEHINORUUV	NOUVEAU RICHE
ACEEHINSSTTY	SYNAESTHETIC
ACEEHIOSTTUW	WITHOUT CEASE
ACEEHIPRSTTU	THERAPEUTICS
ACEEHLLOORRU	LEUCORRHOEAL
ACEEHLLOORSV	SCHOOL-LEAVER

ACEEHLMOPRTY	CEPHALOMETRY
ACEEHLPSSTTU	SPACE SHUTTLE
ACEEHMNNNSTT	ENCHANTMENTS
ACEEHMORRSTU	ROUTE MARCHES
ACEEHNNSSSTU	UNCHASTENESS
ACEEHOPPRRRS	SHARECROPPER
ACEEHORTTUUU	HAUTE COUTURE
ACEEIIILPSST	SPECIALITIES
ACEEIILLMNSS	MISCELLANIES
ACEEIILLRTTV	VERTICILLATE
ACEEIILMMPRT	METEMPIRICAL
ACEEIILMRRSU	MERCURIALISE
ACEEIILMRRUZ	MERCURIALIZE
ACEEIILNOSST	SECTIONALISE
ACEEIILNOSTZ	SECTIONALIZE
ACEEIIMMRSTT	MERISTEMATIC
ACEEIIMNPRSU	EPICUREANISM
ACEEIINNORST	CONTAINERISE
ACEEIINNORTZ	CONTAINERIZE
ACEEIINNRTUV	RENUNCIATIVE
ACEEIINORSTV	EVISCERATION
ACEEIIPPRSTT	PRECIPITATES
ACEEIJORRSTT	TRAJECTORIES
ACEEIKKNOPST	TAKE ONE'S PICK
ACEEIKMPRRST	MARKET PRICES
ACEEIKNOSSTT	SEASON TICKET
ACEEILLLNTTU	INTELLECTUAL
ACEEILLMMRSY	MESMERICALLY
ACEEILLMMNORY	CEREMONIALLY
ACEEILLMORTY	METEORICALLY
ACEEILLNNORT	CRENELLATION
ACEEILLNORTY	NEOTERICALLY
ACEEILLNOTUV	INVOLUCELATE
ACEEILLNRSUV	SURVEILLANCE
ACEEILLORSTY	ESOTERICALLY
ACEEILLORTXY	EXOTERICALLY
ACEEILMMNPST	MISPLACEMENT
ACEEILMPSSTU	TIME CAPSULES
ACEEILNOPRTT	PERCEPTIONAL
ACEEILNOPRRT	PRECENTORIAL
ACEEILNOPRSS	PRECESSIONAL
ACEEILNORSSS	RECESSIONALS
ACEEILNPRTTY	PETIT LARCENY
ACEEILNSSTTT	CLIENT STATES
ACEEILOPPRRT	PRECEPTORIAL
ACEEILOPSSTT	POLICE STATES
ACEEILORRSTV	CORRELATIVES
ACEEILPPSTTU	SEPTUPLICATE
ACEEILPSTTUX	SEXTUPLICATE
ACEEIMMMNOTT	COMMITTEEMAN
ACEEIMMNNORST	COMMENTARIES
ACEEIMMOSSTT	MASTECTOMIES
ACEEIMNOPSTV	COMPENSATIVE
ACEEIMNORSSX	CROSS-EXAMINE
ACEEINOOORRTV	OVERREACTION
ACEEINOPPPRT	APPERCEPTION
ACEEINOPRRTU	RECUPERATION
ACEEINOPRSTT	INSPECTORATE
ACEEINOPSTTX	EXPECTATIONS
ACEEINORRSTY	SECRETIONARY
ACEEINORSTVV	CONSERVATIVE
ACEEIOOPRSTV	COOPERATIVES
ACEELLORSSSW	LOWER CLASSES
ACEELMNNORTU	NOMENCLATURE
ACEELMNOOSTU	LOMENTACEOUS
ACEELMNORSTW	SCARLET WOMEN
ACEELMORSSST	MALTESE CROSS
ACEELNOOSSSS	CLOSE SEASONS
ACEELNPRTTYY	PETTY LARCENY
ACEELNSSSSTT	TACTLESSNESS
ACEELOOPPPTT	POPOCATEPETL
ACEELORSSTTW	WATER CLOSETS
ACEELPSSTUUY	EUCALYPTUSES
ACEEMMNNORSU	COMMENSURATE
ACEEMNNNNOTU	ANNOUNCEMENT
ACEEMNNORRST	REMONSTRANCE
ACEEMOPRSTTY	SPERMATOCYTE
ACEENNOPRSTU	COUNTERPANES
ACEENOPRSTUU	PERCUTANEOUS
ACEEOOPRRTTT	PROTECTORATE
ACEEOOPRRTTX	EXPECTORATOR
ACEEORRSSTUW	WATERCOURSES
ACEFFFFHIOST	CHIEF OF STAFF
ACEFFFFIORST	STAFF OFFICER
ACEFFGHILNRS	CLIFFHANGERS
ACEFFGHINRUU	CHAUFFEURING
ACEFFILNNSSU	FANCIFULNESS
ACEFFILOSSUU	USUAL OFFICES
ACEFFORRSUUU	FURFURACEOUS
ACEFGIIILNTT	FELICITATING
ACEFGIIKNNRV	CARVING KNIFE
ACEFGIINORTV	VOCIFERATING
ACEFGILNRSUY	FLYING SAUCER
ACEFHIIMNRTU	FRUIT MACHINE
ACEFHLNSSTUW	WATCHFULNESS
ACEFHNORSTTU	COUNTERSHAFT
ACEFHORRSSTU	RHESUS FACTOR
ACEFIIIILNOST	FICTIONALISE
ACEFIIILNOTT	FELICITATION
ACEFIIILNOTZ	FICTIONALIZE
ACEFIIINORTV	VERIFICATION
ACEFIILLNNOT	INFLECTIONAL
ACEFIILLRRTY	TERRIFICALLY
ACEFIILNOQTU	LIQUEFACTION
ACEFIILORSTU	LATICIFEROUS
ACEFIINOORTV	VOCIFERATION
ACEFIINOPRTT	PETRIFACTION
ACEFIINOPSTT	PONTIFICATES

ACEFIIPRRSUY	SUPERFICIARY
ACEFILLNORSY	FORENSICALLY
ACEFILLORSUW	CAULIFLOWERS
ACEFILNNOOSS	CONFESSIONAL
ACEFILORRRTY	REFRACTORILY
ACEFINOORRTT	TORREFACTION
ACEFINOPRTTU	PUTREFACTION
ACEFINOPSTTU	STUPEFACTION
ACEFINOSSSTU	FACTIOUSNESS
ACEFLLMOOPRW	CAMP FOLLOWER
ACEGGGINNORT	CONGREGATING
ACEGGHINORRV	OVERCHARGING
ACEGGIILLNNST	SINGLE-ACTING
ACEGGIINNSST	GIGANTICNESS
ACEGGIINORTZ	CATEGORIZING
ACEGGILLLOOY	GEOLOGICALLY
ACEGGIMNORTY	GYROMAGNETIC
ACEGGINNOORT	CONGREGATION
ACEGHHIILOPR	HELIOGRAPHIC
ACEGHHILRSST	SEARCHLIGHTS
ACEGHHINOPRT	ETHNOGRAPHIC
ACEGHHIOPRRR	CHIROGRAPHER
ACEGHHNOPRTY	TECHNOGRAPHY
ACEGHHNORRST	SHORT-CHANGER
ACEGHHOOPRRR	CHOROGRAPHER
ACEGHHOOPRRS	CHOREOGRAPHS
ACEGHHOOPRRY	CHOREOGRAPHY
ACEGHIILLNYY	HYGIENICALLY
ACEGHIIMNSTZ	SCHEMATIZING
ACEGHIKLLNSS	SHELLACKINGS
ACEGHILLNNOU	HALLUCINOGEN
ACEGHILLNOOP	NEPHOLOGICAL, PHENOLOGICAL
ACEGHILLNOOT	ETHNOLOGICAL
ACEGHILLRTUY	THEURGICALLY
ACEGHILOPPRY	PYELOGRAPHIC
ACEGHILOPRXY	LEXICOGRAPHY
ACEGHIMOOPRT	GAMETOPHORIC
ACEGHIMOPRRR	MICROGRAPHER
ACEGHIMOPTTY	GAMETOPHYTIC
ACEGHINOOPRR	ICONOGRAPHER
ACEGHINOPRRZ	ZINCOGRAPHER
ACEGHINOPRST	STENOGRAPHIC
ACEGHINORRSU	HARE COURSING
ACEGHIOPPRRR	REPROGRAPHIC
ACEGHIOPPRRT	PETROGRAPHIC
ACEGHIOPRRST	CEROGRAPHIST
ACEGHLMNOOUY	HUMAN ECOLOGY
ACEGHOPPRRST	SPECTROGRAPH
ACEGIIIILLMTY	ILLEGITIMACY
ACEGIIILNPSZ	SPECIALIZING
ACEGIIINNNRT	INCINERATING
ACEGIIINSTTV	NEGATIVISTIC
ACEGIIKNPRSS	ASKING PRICES
ACEGIILLNRRV	INVERCARGILL

ACEGIILLOOPT	GEOPOLITICAL
ACEGIILLOSTY	EGOISTICALLY
ACEGIILNNOST	SINGLE-ACTION
ACEGIILNNOTU	GENICULATION
ACEGIILNNOTY	CONGENIALITY
ACEGIILNNRSY	INCREASINGLY
ACEGIILNNRTZ	CENTRALIZING
ACEGIILNPRSS	ALICE SPRINGS
ACEGIILNRSUZ	SECULARIZING
ACEGIILORSSU	SACRILEGIOUS
ACEGIINNPPRT	APPRENTICING
ACEGIINOOTTX	EXCOGITATION
ACEGIINOQTUV	EQUIVOCATING
ACEGIKLNOOPP	COOKING APPLE
ACEGILLLNOOY	NEOLOGICALLY
ACEGILLMOORT	METROLOGICAL
ACEGILLMOOTY	ETYMOLOGICAL
ACEGILLNNOSY	GEOSYNCLINAL
ACEGILLNNOTY	CONGENITALLY
ACEGILLNOORU	NEUROLOGICAL
ACEGILLNOORY	OROGENICALLY
ACEGILLOOOST	OSTEOLOGICAL
ACEGILLOOPRT	PETROLOGICAL
ACEGILMMOPSY	OLYMPIC GAMES
ACEGILNNNRTY	ENTRANCINGLY
ACEGILNNOTTU	CONGLUTINATE
ACEGILNOOPRT	ORGANOLEPTIC
ACEGILOOPSST	ESCAPOLOGIST
ACEGILORSTTU	GESTICULATOR
ACEGIMMNNOTT	COMMENTATING
ACEGIMNNOPSS	ENCOMPASSING
ACEGIMNNOPST	COMPENSATING
ACEGINNNORTV	CONTRAVENING
ACEGINNNORST	NONSTRATEGIC
ACEGINORSSSU	GRACIOUSNESS
ACEGINOSSTTV	CASTING VOTES
ACEGIOOOPPRT	APOGEOTROPIC
ACEGLNOOPRSY	LARYNGOSCOPE
ACEGLOORSUUY	COURAGEOUSLY
ACEGLRSSSTTU	GLASSCUTTERS
ACEHHIILMOPS	HEMOPHILIACS
ACEHHIIMMPTU	AMPHITHECIUM
ACEHHIINOPRT	HIEROPHANTIC
ACEHHILMOPTX	EXOPHTHALMIC
ACEHHILOPTTY	HYPOTHETICAL
ACEHHINOPRTT	THEANTHROPIC
ACEHHLLLOOTY	ETHYL ALCOHOL
ACEHHLOOPRTY	ORTHOCEPHALY
ACEHIIINRSST	CHRISTIANISE
ACEHIIINRSTZ	CHRISTIANIZE
ACEHIIKRRSWW	WARWICKSHIRE
ACEHIILLMPTY	MEPHITICALLY
ACEHIILLMRTY	HERMITICALLY
ACEHIILLSTTY	THEISTICALLY

ACEHIILNPPRS	PLANISPHERIC
ACEHIINNOPPR	HIPPOCRENIAN
ACEHIINNOPST	PHONETICIANS
ACEHIINORRST	RHETORICIANS
ACEHIINSSTTU	ENTHUSIASTIC
ACEHIINTTTUY	AUTHENTICITY
ACEHIIOPSSTT	SOPHISTICATE
ACEHIIPPRRST	PERIPHRASTIC
ACEHIKLPRRSS	PARISH CLERKS
ACEHIKMNORSS	CHAIN-SMOKERS
ACEHIKMNOSST	MACKINTOSHES
ACEHILLLMNOY	MELANCHOLILY
ACEHILLLPTYY	PHYLETICALLY
ACEHILLMNNTU	MULTICHANNEL
ACEHILLMNOPY	PHONEMICALLY
ACEHILLNOPST	PLAIN-CLOTHES
ACEHILLNOPTY	PHONETICALLY
ACEHILLNOPUY	EUPHONICALLY
ACEHILLOPRUY	EUPHORICALLY
ACEHILLORRTY	RHETORICALLY
ACEHILLRSTYY	HYSTERICALLY
ACEHILMNOOST	MACHINE TOOLS
ACEHILMNOSST	SLOT MACHINES
ACEHILMOOPSU	AMPHICOELOUS
ACEHILMOPTYY	POLYCYTHEMIA
ACEHILNNNSSS	CLANNISHNESS
ACEHILNPSSSY	PHYSICALNESS
ACEHIMOPRSST	ATMOSPHERICS
ACEHIMORRSST	CHOIRMASTERS
ACEHIMORSTTT	THERMOSTATIC
ACEHINNOOPRT	NEOANTHROPIC
ACEHINOPRRSS	CHAIRPERSONS
ACEHINOPRRTT	TRICHOPTERAN
ACEHIOPRRSTT	ORCHESTRA PIT
ACEHIRSSTTWW	WRISTWATCHES
ACEHKMRRSSTT	STRETCHMARKS
ACEHLMMNOOTW	COMMONWEALTH
ACEHLMOORSST	SCHOOLMASTER
ACEHLNOOPRTU	PHOTONUCLEAR
ACEHLOOPSTUY	POLYCHAETOUS
ACEHLOPSSUXY	PSYCHOSEXUAL
ACEHMOORSTTY	TRACHEOSTOMY
ACEHNNOOPRRS	ANCHORPERSON
ACEIIILLRSTT	LITERALISTIC
ACEIIILMNNSS	INIMICALNESS
ACEIIILMNPSU	MUNICIPALISE
ACEIIILMNPUZ	MUNICIPALIZE
ACEIIILNNOTT	LICENTIATION
ACEIIILNSTTY	INELASTICITY
ACEIIILRSTTV	RELATIVISTIC
ACEIIILRSTVV	REVIVALISTIC
ACEIIIMNOSST	SEMIOTICIANS
ACEIIIMNPRSS	PRECISIANISM
ACEIIINNNORT	INCINERATION

ACEIIINOTTVX	INTOXICATIVE
ACEIIKKNORTY	KARYOKINETIC
ACEIILLLLPTY	ELLIPTICALLY
ACEIILLLNSUV	ALL-INCLUSIVE
ACEIILLMNSST	MISCELLANIST
ACEIILLMPTTU	MULTIPLICATE
ACEIILMMNRST	MERCANTILISM
ACEIILMNORST	SALINOMETRIC
ACEIILMNOSST	SECTIONALISM
ACEIILMNRSTT	MERCANTILIST
ACEIILMOPPSS	EPISCOPALISM
ACEIILMOPRRT	POLARIMETRIC
ACEIILMOPRST	SEMITROPICAL
ACEIILNNNRTU	INTERNUNCIAL
ACEIILNNOPST	INSPECTIONAL
ACEIILNOPRST	REPLICATIONS
ACEIILNORTTU	RETICULATION
ACEIILNOSSTT	SECTIONALIST
ACEIILNOSTUV	VESICULATION
ACEIILNRSTTT	CLARINETTIST
ACEIILNRSTVV	CIVIL SERVANT
ACEIILOQSSUU	SILIQUACEOUS
ACEIILOQTUVY	EQUIVOCALITY
ACEIILPRRSUY	SUPERCILIARY
ACEIILRRSSTU	SURREALISTIC
ACEIILRRTTTY	RETRACTILITY
ACEIIMMNNORST	CREMATIONISM
ACEIIMMORSSS	COMMISSARIES
ACEIIMNOPRST	IMPRECATIONS
ACEIIMNORRRT	RECRIMINATOR
ACEIIMNORSTT	CREMATIONIST
ACEIINNNORTU	RENUNCIATION
ACEIINNNSTTV	SAINT VINCENT
ACEIINNORRST	INCINERATORS
ACEIINNORRTY	INCRETIONARY
ACEIINNORRST	INTERACTIONS
ACEIINNOTTUV	CONTINUATIVE
ACEIINOOQTUV	EQUIVOCATION
ACEIINOORSTX	EXCORIATIONS
ACEIINOPRRTT	PRACTITIONER
ACEIINOPRSTU	PERTINACIOUS
ACEIINORRSTW	CONTRARIWISE
ACEIIOPPRRTT	PRECIPITATOR
ACEIJKLLNOSV	JACKSONVILLE
ACEIJLNOOPRT	PROJECTIONAL
ACEIKKNORRST	NOT A SKERRICK
ACEIKLOORRSW	SOCIAL WORKER
ACEIKLPPRRSY	PRICKLY PEARS
ACEIKNNORSST	IN ONE'S TRACKS
ACEIKORRRTTT	TRICK OR TREAT
ACEILLMMNNOY	MNEMONICALLY
ACEILLMMNOOT	MONOMETALLIC
ACEILLMNRTUU	MULTINUCLEAR
ACEILLMNTUVY	MULTIVALENCY

ACEILLMORRTU	TRIMOLECULAR
ACEILLMSSTYY	SYSTEMICALLY
ACEILLMTUUVY	CUMULATIVELY
ACEILLNNORRU	CARILLONNEUR
ACEILLNOOTYZ	ENZOOTICALLY
ACEILLNORTUY	NEUROTICALLY
ACEILLNOSTTU	SCUTELLATION
ACEILLNOTTUY	TEUTONICALLY
ACEILLRRSTUU	SERICULTURAL
ACEILMMMNOSS	COMMENSALISM
ACEILMMNNOORT	MONOMETRICAL
ACEILMNNOOPT	COMPONENTIAL
ACEILMNOORTU	NEUROTICAL
ACEILMNRSTTU	CURTAILMENTS
ACEILMOPRSTT	PLASTOMETRIC
ACEILMOPRSUU	PRIMULACEOUS
ACEILNNNOOTT	CONTENTIONAL
ACEILNNNOOTV	CONVENTIONAL
ACEILNNNOSTU	CONTINENTALS
ACEILNNOORSV	CONVERSIONAL
ACEILNOOPRSS	PROCESSIONAL
ACEILNOOPRST	PERCOLATIONS
ACEILNOOPRTT	LACTOPROTEIN
ACEILNOORRST	CORRELATIONS
ACEILNOORTUY	ELOCUTIONARY
ACEILNOPSSTU	SPECULATIONS
ACEILNORSUXY	EXCLUSIONARY
ACEILNOSTTUV	CONSULTATIVE
ACEILOOPRRTY	CORPOREALITY
ACEILOOPSSTT	OSTEOPLASTIC
ACEILOPRRSUY	PRECARIOUSLY
ACEIMMNOSTUV	CONSUMMATIVE
ACEIMMOORRST	COMMISERATOR
ACEIMMORRSTU	CREMATORIUMS
ACEIMNNOOPST	COMPENSATION
ACEIMNOOOOPT	ONOMATOPOEIC
ACEIMNORSSTV	CONSERVATISM
ACEIMOPRSTZ	ZOOSPERMATIC
ACEIMPRRRSTw	WRITER'S CRAMP
ACEIMPRSSSTU	SUPREMACISTS
ACEINNOORSTV	CONSERVATION,
CONVERSATION	
ACEINNOOSTTT	CONTESTATION
ACEINNORRSST	CONTRARINESS
ACEINNORSTTU	ENCRUSTATION
ACEINOPPRRTU	PORT-AU-PRINCE
ACEINOPSSSSU	SPACIOUSNESS
ACEINOPSSSTU	CAPTIOUSNESS
ACEINOSSSTUU	CAUTIOUSNESS
ACEIOOPRRRRT	TROOP CARRIER
ACEIOOQRTUVY	EQUIVOCATORY
ACEIOORSTUUV	OVERCAUTIOUS
ACEIORRSSTTU	RESUSCITATOR
ACEKKMORSSTT	STOCK MARKETS

ACEKMMMMNOORT	COMMON MARKET
ACELLNOTTUXY	CONTEXTUALLY
ACELMMNOSTUY	CONSUMMATELY
ACELMNOOPRTT	CONTEMPLATOR
ACELNOOPRSTU	PROCONSULATE
ACELNOSSTTTU	TALENT SCOUTS
ACELOORRSTUW	WATERCOLOURS
ACEMMMOOORRT	COMMEMORATOR
ACEMMNNOORSTT	COMMENTATORS
ACEMMNOPRSTT	COMPARTMENTS
ACEMMPRSSSTU	MASS SPECTRUM
ACEMNOOPRRTY	CONTEMPORARY
ACEMNOOPRSTY	COMPENSATORY
ACEMOOPRRSTU	MACROPTEROUS
ACEMORSSSTTU	SCOUTMASTERS
ACENNRRRSTTU	TRANSCURRENT
ACENOORRSTVY	CONSERVATORY
ACENOPRRSTTU	COUNTERPARTS
ACENOPRRTTUY	COUNTERPARTY
ACENORSSTTUY	COUNTRY SEATS
ACFFGGHIILNN	CLIFFHANGING
ACFFGHIILRTT	TRAFFIC LIGHT
ACFFIILLNOUY	UNOFFICIALLY
ACFGGHIMNORR	FROGMARCHING
ACFGHILNORTW	FLOWCHARTING
ACFGIIILNOTU	UGLIFICATION
ACFGIKNORRSV	CARVING FORKS
ACFHHLNORSSY	SYNCHROFLASH
ACFHIILLORRY	HORRIFICALLY
ACFHILNNOOST	INFANT SCHOOL
ACFHKMOOOSTU	ASK TOO MUCH OF
ACFIIIILNOTV	VILIFICATION
ACFIIIIMNNOT	MINIFICATION
ACFIIIINOTVV	VIVIFICATION
ACFIIINNOOTT	NOTIFICATION
ACFIIINOOSST	OSSIFICATION
ACFIIINOPRTU	PURIFICATION
ACFIIINOPTTY	TYPIFICATION
ACFIIILLLOPRY	PROLIFICALLY
ACFIIILNNNOOT	NONFICTIONAL
ACFIIMNNOORT	CONFIRMATION
ACFIINORRTTU	TRIFURCATION
ACFIIOPRRTUY	PURIFICATORY
ACFILLNNOTUY	FUNCTIONALLY
ACFILMNNOSTU	MALFUNCTIONS
ACFILNOSTTUU	FLUCTUATIONS
ACFIMNOOORT	CONFORMATION
ACFIMNOORRTY	CONFIRMATORY
ACFINNOOSTTU	CONFUTATIONS
ACFRRSTUUUY	USUFRUCTUARY
ACGGHIMNNOOR	CHANGING ROOM
ACGGIILLOOST	GLACIOLOGIST
ACGHHHIOPTYY	ICHTHYOPHAGY
ACGHHIILOPRT	LITHOGRAPHIC

ACGHHIOOPPRT	PHOTOGRAPHIC
ACGHHIOOPRRT	ORTHOGRAPHIC
ACGHHNOOPRRS	CHRONOGRAPHS
ACGHHOPPRSYY	PSYCHOGRAPHY
ACGHIIKMNNOS	CHAIN-SMOKING
ACGHIILLLOOP	PHILOLOGICAL
ACGHIILLNOOR	RHINOLOGICAL
ACGHIILLOOOP	OPHIOLOGICAL
ACGHIILLOOST	HISTOLOGICAL
ACGHIILMNPTY	LYMPHANGITIC
ACGHIILNNORT	CHLORINATING
ACGHIILNORTY	TRICHOGYNIAL
ACGHIIOPPRRS	SPIROGRAPHIC
ACGHIIPRSSST	SPHRAGISTICS
ACGHIKNOOSTW	WHAT'S COOKING?
ACGHILLMOOTY	MYTHOLOGICAL
ACGHILLNOOOP	PHONOLOGICAL
ACGHILLOOPRS	OSCILLOGRAPH
ACGHILOPRSTY	STYLOGRAPHIC
ACGHINOOPPRR	PORNOGRAPHIC
ACGHIOOPSSTY	PHAGOCYTOSIS
ACGHKLOPPUYY	HAPPY-GO-LUCKY
ACGHOOOPPRSU	COPROPHAGOUS
ACGHOPPRRTYY	CRYPTOGRAPHY
ACGIIILLLOTY	ILLOGICALITY
ACGIIINNOTTX	INTOXICATING
ACGIIKKLNSTW	WALKING STICK
ACGIILLLMNOO	LIMNOLOGICAL
ACGIILLLOSTY	LOGISTICALLY
ACGIILLLRTUY	LITURGICALLY
ACGIILMNOSUU	MUCILAGINOUS
ACGIILNOORST	CRANIOLOGIST
ACGIILNPPSTU	SUPPLICATING
ACGIIMMNOOST	MONOGAMISTIC
ACGIINNOOST	CONSIGNATION
ACGIINNNORST	CONSTRAINING
ACGIJNNOOSTU	CONJUGATIONS
ACGIKLNORSSW	WORKING CLASS
ACGILLLOOORY	OROLOGICALLY
ACGILLMNNOOY	GNOMONICALLY
ACGILNNNOTTU	CONGLUTINANT
ACGILNOOSTUY	CONTAGIOUSLY
ACGILNOPSUUY	PUGNACIOUSLY
ACGIMMNNOSTU	CONSUMMATING
ACGIMNNOORST	MORNING COATS
ACGINOORRSTU	CORRUGATIONS
ACGINOPPRRSY	CROP-SPRAYING
ACGLLNOORSUY	CLANGOROUSLY
ACGLMNNOOSUY	AGONY COLUMNS
ACGLNOOPRSYY	LARYNGOSCOPY
ACHHIILMNOPR	PHILHARMONIC
ACHHIIMNOPPS	CHAMPIONSHIP
ACHHIIMOSTYZ	SCHIZOTHYMIA
ACHHILLMRTYY	RHYTHMICALLY

ACHHILLOPTTY	THALLOPHYTIC
ACHHILOOPRST	HOLOPHRASTIC
ACHHILOPRSSS	SCHOLARSHIPS
ACHHIOPPRSTU	PHOSPHATURIC
ACHHNNOOOPRY	ONYCHOPHORAN
ACHIIIINRSST	TRICHINIASIS
ACHIIILMSTWY	WHIMSICALITY
ACHIIIMNPSSU	MUSICIANSHIP
ACHIIINRSTTY	CHRISTIANITY
ACHIILLLOSTY	HOLISTICALLY
ACHIILLNOSSU	HALLUCINOSIS
ACHIILLORSTY	HISTORICALLY
ACHIILNNOORT	CHLORINATION
ACHIILNOPRST	RHINOPLASTIC
ACHIIMNOPRST	MISANTHROPIC
ACHIIPRSSTTY	PSYCHIATRIST
ACHILLNOPTYY	HYPNOTICALLY
ACHILLORSUVY	CHIVALROUSLY
ACHILMORSTYY	LACHRYMOSITY
ACHILOOPPRRS	CORPORALSHIP
ACHIMNNORSSY	ASYNCHRONISM
ACHINOOPTTUY	AUTOHYPNOTIC
ACHINOPRSSTY	CORNISH PASTY
ACHIOOPRRRST	ARTHROSPORIC
ACHIOOPRRSUZ	RHIZOCARPOUS
ACHIOPRRSSTU	CURATORSHIPS
ACHIOPRSSSTY	ASTROPHYSICS
ACHMMOPPSSTU	STOMACH PUMPS
ACHNNOORSSUY	ASYNCHRONOUS
ACHOOPRRRTTU	PORT HARCOURT
ACIIIILMRSTT	MILITARISTIC
ACIIIILNOSTV	CIVILISATION
ACIIIILNOTVZ	CIVILIZATION
ACIIILMNNOST	NOMINALISTIC
ACIIILMNOPST	IMPLICATIONS
ACIIILMNPTUY	MUNICIPALITY
ACIIILNNNOST	INCLINATIONS
ACIIILNOOSTT	COALITIONIST, SOLICITATION
ACIIILNOPRTT	TRIPLICATION
ACIIILNOTVVY	CONVIVIALITY
ACIIILNPPRTY	PRINCIPALITY
ACIIILQTUYZZ	QUIZZICALITY
ACIIIMNNORRT	INCRIMINATOR
ACIIIMNORSTV	VICTORIANISM
ACIIINNOOTTX	INTOXICATION
ACIIINOPSSUU	INAUSPICIOUS
ACIIINOQSSTU	ACQUISITIONS
ACIIJLNORSTU	JOURNALISTIC
ACIIKKPRSSTU	KICK UPSTAIRS
ACIILLMNOSTY	MONISTICALLY
ACIILLNNOOPT	NONPOLITICAL
ACIILLNOOSST	COLONIALISTS, OSCILLATIONS
ACIILLNOPRVY	PROVINCIALLY
ACIILLNORSTT	SCINTILLATOR

ACIILLNRTUUV	VINICULTURAL
ACIILLOOPSTY	ISOTOPICALLY
ACIILLOQTUXY	QUIXOTICALLY
ACIILLOSSUVY	LASCIVIOUSLY
ACIILLPRSTUY	PURISTICALLY
ACIILLRTTUUV	VITICULTURAL
ACIILMMNOOSS	COMMISSIONAL
ACIILMNNOOTU	COLUMNIATION
ACIILMNOOPST	COMPILATIONS
ACIILMNORSTU	MATRICLINOUS
ACIILMOPRTUV	VICTORIA PLUM
ACIILNNOOOST	COLONISATION
ACIILNNOOOTZ	COLONIZATION
ACIILNNOOSTU	INOCULATIONS, INOSCULATION
ACIILNNOTTUY	CONTINUALITY
ACIILNOORSST	CONSISTORIAL
ACIILNOPPSTU	SUPPLICATION
ACIILNOPRSTU	PATRICLINOUS
ACIILNORSSSS	NAIL SCISSORS
ACIILNOSTUUY	INCAUTIOUSLY
ACIILOPSSUUY	AUSPICIOUSLY
ACIILPRSTTUU	APICULTURIST
ACIILRSTTUUV	AVICULTURIST
ACIIMNOPRTTU	PROTACTINIUM
ACIIMNORSSTT	ROMANTICISTS
ACIINNNOOTTU	CONTINUATION
ACIINNOOPSTT	CONSTIPATION
ACIINNORSTTU	INCRUSTATION
ACILLLLOOQUY	COLLOQUIALLY
ACILLMOOOTYZ	ZOOTOMICALLY
ACILLNNOSTYY	SYNTONICALLY
ACILLNOOOPST	LOCAL OPTIONS
ACILLNOPSTYY	SYNOPTICALLY
ACILLOOQSUUY	LOQUACIOUSLY
ACILMMNNOOTT	NONCOMMITTAL
ACILMNOOOPST	COSMOPOLITAN
ACILMOOPPRST	PROTOPLASMIC
ACILNNOOORTT	CONTORTIONAL
ACILNNOOOSST	CONSOLATIONS
ACILNNOOSTTU	CONSULTATION
ACILNNORTTUY	NOCTURNALITY
ACILNOOORSTU	ICONOLATROUS
ACILOOPPRSTT	PROTOPLASTIC
ACILOPPRSTUY	SUPPLICATORY
ACILORSSSTTU	TOURIST CLASS
ACIMMNNOOSTU	CONSUMMATION
ACIMMNOOSTTU	COMMUTATIONS
ACIMNOOPPSST	COMPASS POINT
ACIMNOOPSTTU	COMPUTATIONS
ACINNNOOOTST	CONNOTATIONS
ACINNOOPRSTT	CONTRAPTIONS
ACINNOORSTTT	IN CONTRAST TO
ACINOOOPRRRT	INCORPORATOR
ACINOOOPRRST	CORPORATIONS
ACINOOOPRSTV	PROVOCATIONS
ACINOOOPRRSST	CONSPIRATORS
ACINOOPRRSTT	STRIP CARTOON
ACIOOPPRSSTT	POTATO CRISPS
ACIORRRSSTTU	CIRROSTRATUS
ACKLNNOOPRTY	CRYOPLANKTON
ACLLRRSTTUUY	STRUCTURALLY
ACMNOOOTTXYY	CYTOTAXONOMY
ADDDDEEEHLMU	MUDDLE-HEADED
ADDDDEEFFILL	FIDDLE-FADDLE
ADDDEEEHNOOW	WOODENHEADED
ADDDEIILLLLY	DILLYDALLIED
ADDEEEEGGRST	DESEGREGATED
ADDEEEGIMNST	DEMAGNETISED
ADDEEEGIMNTZ	DEMAGNETIZED
ADDEEEIIRSTV	DESIDERATIVE
ADDEEEIMPRTT	PREMEDITATED
ADDEEEIORRTT	DETERIORATED
ADDEEELLNTTW	WELL-ATTENDED
ADDEEELRRTTY	RED-LETTER DAY
ADDEEENPRSSV	DEPRAVEDNESS
ADDEEEOPPRSV	EAVESDROPPED
ADDEEFFNRSTU	UNDERSTAFFED
ADDEEFHLMORY	FORMALDEHYDE
ADDEEFHOORSW	FORESHADOWED
ADDEEFINOORR	FOREORDAINED
ADDEEFLLOPST	SOFT-PEDALLED
ADDEEFLNRSSU	DREADFULNESS
ADDEEGHILNNS	SINGLE-HANDED
ADDEEGILNNST	DISENTANGLED
ADDEEGINPPSU	PEASE PUDDING
ADDEEGINRRSS	READDRESSING
ADDEEHHIMRTY	HEMIHYDRATED
ADDEEHLLOOWY	WOOLLY-HEADED
ADDEEHLNNOPY	OPEN-HANDEDLY
ADDEEHOORSVW	OVERSHADOWED
ADDEEIIMMNNO	DEMIMONDAINE
ADDEEIIMNRST	ADMINISTERED
ADDEEIIMNSST	DISSEMINATED
ADDEEIINORST	DESIDERATION
ADDEEIIMMNRST	MASTERMINDED
ADDEEIIMNOPRT	PREDOMINATED
ADDEEINOPRST	DEPREDATIONS
ADDEEJLLSTUW	WELL-ADJUSTED
ADDEELNOSSTT	STADDLESTONE
ADDEEMNORSTT	DEMONSTRATED
ADDEFGIILLNN	LANDING FIELD
ADDEFGILRRSU	DISREGARDFUL
ADDEFHILNOOS	OLD-FASHIONED
ADDEFIIILQSU	DISQUALIFIED
ADDEFIIISSST	DISSATISFIED
ADDEFLNNNOUW	NEWFOUNDLAND
ADDEGGIINRRS	DISREGARDING
ADDEGHHHILNY	HIGH-HANDEDLY

ADDEGHNORSTU	DREADNOUGHTS
ADDEGIIILOTV	DIGITAL VIDEO
ADDEGIINORSS	DISORGANISED
ADDEGIINORSZ	DISORGANIZED
ADDEHHLORRSU	HARD SHOULDER
ADDEHINOSSWW	WINDOW SHADES
ADDEHMNORSUY	HYDROMEDUSAN
ADDEIILMSSTU	DISSIMULATED
ADDEIINOPPST	DISAPPOINTED
ADDEILMNOOTU	DEMODULATION
ADDEILMNOPRS	PROMISED LAND
ADDEILMNSSTW	WEST MIDLANDS
ADDEIMMMRSUY	MIDSUMMER DAY
ADDEIMNNORRW	NARROW-MINDED
ADDFIILLNSUY	DISDAINFULLY
ADDGHIMNOORU	ROUGH DIAMOND
ADDGIILNSSTU	STUDDINGSAIL
ADDGILLNOOPP	PADDLING POOL
ADDHIIILMOPP	AMPHIDIPLOID
ADDIIIILLNUVY	INDIVIDUALLY
ADDIIINORTUV	INDIVIDUATOR
ADEEEEGINRTV	DEGENERATIVE
ADEEEEGLRSST	EASTER-LEDGES
ADEEEEHHNRRT	HERE AND THERE
ADEEEEFFORRST	REAFFORESTED
ADEEEEFGIRRRT	REFRIGERATED
ADEEEFIMTUUX	FAUTE DE MIEUX
ADEEEFMNSSTU	DEAF-MUTENESS
ADEEEGGILNRT	LATEENRIGGED
ADEEEGGINNRT	DEGENERATING
ADEEEGGLLNOS	GOLDEN EAGLES
ADEEEGGNRSTU	UNSEGREGATED
ADEEEGHLMMRS	SLEDGEHAMMER
ADEEEGIMNRST	DEMAGNETISER, DISAGREEMENT
ADEEEGIMNRTZ	DEMAGNETIZER
ADEEEGINNORT	DEGENERATION
ADEEEGINNRST	TRAGEDIENNES
ADEEEGINOPSS	PAEDOGENESIS
ADEEEGINRRTT	REDINTEGRATE
ADEEEGLNORTU	OUTGENERALED
ADEEEGMNNNRT	ENDANGERMENT
ADEEEGMNNRST	DERANGEMENTS
ADEEEHHLORTW	WHOLE-HEARTED
ADEEEHIMNRTT	HEREDITAMENT
ADEEEHINSSSV	ADHESIVENESS
ADEEEHINSSTT	ANESTHETISED
ADEEEHINSSTU	HAUTS-DE-SEINE
ADEEEHINSTTZ	ANESTHETIZED
ADEEEHIRRTTT	TETRAHEDRITE
ADEEEHLLORSS	LEASEHOLDERS
ADEEEHLNNRRT	NETHERLANDER
ADEEEHMNPRSS	HAMPEREDNESS
ADEEEHMORSTV	MOHAVE DESERT
ADEEEHPRSSST	SPREADSHEETS
ADEEEIILNPTX	EXPEDIENTIAL
ADEEEIIMMNRT	ANTE MERIDIEM
ADEEEIIMMRST	SEMIDIAMETER
ADEEEIIMNRTT	INTERMEDIATE
ADEEEILLMMOS	MADEMOISELLE
ADEEEILMNORT	RADIOELEMENT
ADEEEILNPRRT	INTERPLEADER
ADEEEILNRSTX	EXTERNALISED
ADEEEILNRTXZ	EXTERNALIZED
ADEEEIMNRTTX	EXTERMINATED
ADEEEINPRSTT	PREDESTINATE
ADEEEIOPPSTX	EXOPEPTIDASE
ADEEEKLLMRSS	SKELMERSDALE
ADEEEKLLNOST	ENDOSKELETAL
ADEEEKLRRSST	DEERSTALKERS
ADEEELLMNNRW	WELL-MANNERED
ADEEELLNSSWY	WENSLEYDALES
ADEEELNRSTTU	LAUNDERETTES
ADEEELOPPRST	TRADESPEOPLE
ADEEEMNORSST	MODERATENESS
ADEEEMORRSTV	OVERMASTERED
ADEEENOPPRRT	PREPONDERATE
ADEEENPPRRSS	PREPAREDNESS
ADEEENPRRTUV	PERADVENTURE
ADEEEOPPRRSV	EAVESDROPPER
ADEEEQRSSTTU	SEQUESTRATED
ADEEFFIILNRT	DIFFERENTIAL
ADEEFGHILNRS	HARD FEELINGS
ADEEFGILLSSS	FIELD GLASSES
ADEEFGINNRRS	RANGE FINDERS
ADEEFGINNRST	FREESTANDING
ADEEFHLOPSST	FELDSPATHOSE
ADEEFHOORRSW	FORESHADOWER
ADEEFHRSTTUU	DEATH FUTURES
ADEEFILOPRRT	PROLIFERATED
ADEEFLLORUVW	WELL-FAVOURED
ADEEFLNRSSTW	WEST FLANDERS
ADEEFNOPRRTU	UNPERFORATED
ADEEFOOPRRRS	PROOFREADERS
ADEEFOOPRRTW	WATERPROOFED
ADEEGGHIRSTT	STRAIGHTEDGE
ADEEGGILNRTU	DEREGULATING
ADEEGGIORRSU	SQUARE-RIGGED
ADEEGGIRRTTU	REGURGITATED
ADEEGHHILRTT	LIGHT-HEARTED
ADEEGHIMMOPR	MIMEOGRAPHED
ADEEGHINNPPR	APPREHENDING
ADEEGHINNRRT	HEARTRENDING
ADEEGHINRSTT	STRAIGHTENED
ADEEGHIRRSST	SIGHT-READERS
ADEEGHMOPRRS	DEMOGRAPHERS
ADEEGHOPRRSW	HEDGE SPARROW
ADEEGHPRSTTU	STEPDAUGHTER
ADEEGIIMNNRR	REMAINDERING

ADEEGIINRSTT	DISINTEGRATE	ADEEIINRRSTY	RESIDENTIARY
ADEEGIINSTTV	INVESTIGATED	ADEEIKLMSTTT	ATTESTED MILK
ADEEGIKNNRRT	KINDERGARTEN	ADEEILLMRSSV	SILVER MEDALS
ADEEGIKNRRST	RING-STREAKED	ADEEILLNNRST	LANTERNSLIDE
ADEEGILMNNRY	MEANDERINGLY	ADEEILLOSTVW	OLD WIVES' TALE
ADEEGILNORTU	DEREGULATION	ADEEILLSTTUW	WELL-SITUATED
ADEEGINNORUV	ENDEAVOURING	ADEEILMMORTY	IMMODERATELY
ADEEGINNORRT	INTERROGATED	ADEEILMNOPRT	REDEMPTIONAL
ADEEGMNNRRTU	UNDERGARMENT	ADEEILMPRSST	SLIPSTREAMED
ADEEGNPRTUUX	UNEXPURGATED	ADEEILNOPPRT	LEPIDOPTERAN
ADEEGNRRSSST	TRANSGRESSED	ADEEILNOPRSS	PERSONALISED
ADEEGOPRRSTT	GREAT RED SPOT	ADEEILNOPRSZ	PERSONALIZED
ADEEGORRTTXY	DEXTROGYRATE	ADEEILNOPRTT	INTERPOLATED
ADEEHHIKNRRS	HEADSHRINKER	ADEEILNRRSTY	RESTRAINEDLY
ADEEHHLLORRSS	SHAREHOLDERS	ADEEILRRSSVV	SLAVE DRIVERS
ADEEHHNNPTUY	UNHYPHENATED	ADEEIMMNORSU	MISDEMEANOUR
ADEEHIILRRTY	HEREDITARILY	ADEEIMNNRSTT	DETERMINANTS
ADEEHILMNOOT	ENDOTHELIOMA	ADEEIMNOPRST	IMPERSONATED
ADEEHILMORTT	MAITRE D'HOTEL	ADEEIMNRSTUV	MISADVENTURE
ADEEHILNPRRS	PHILANDERERS	ADEEIMOPRRTT	PREMEDITATOR
ADEEHIMNPPRS	MISAPPREHEND	ADEEIMSSSTTY	SYSTEMATISED
ADEEHINORSTU	HOUSE-TRAINED	ADEEIMSSTTYZ	SYSTEMATIZED
ADEEHIRRRSSS	HAIRDRESSERS	ADEEINNOOPRU	INDO-EUROPEAN
ADEEHKLORSST	STAKEHOLDERS	ADEEINNRRSTU	UNRESTRAINED
ADEEHLLLMOPR	PHELLODERMAL	ADEEINNRSSST	STRAINEDNESS
ADEEHLLNOSSW	HALLOWEDNESS	ADEEINNSSSTU	UNSTEADINESS
ADEEHLMMOTUY	MEALY-MOUTHED	ADEEINORRSST	RAISON D'ETRES
ADEEHMNNOSSS	HANDSOMENESS	ADEEINRRSSUY	DAY NURSERIES
ADEEHMOPRTTY	DERMATOPHYTE	ADEEIOPPRRTX	EXPROPRIATED
ADEEHNOPSTTY	SPOTTED HYENA	ADEEJMNRSTTU	READJUSTMENT
ADEEHNORSTTY	STONY-HEARTED	ADEEKLLORRST	ROLLER SKATED
ADEEHOPRRTTW	THE TOP DRAWER	ADEEKLOPRSSU	LOUDSPEAKERS
ADEEHORSTTTU	STOUTHEARTED	ADEEKNORSSYY	DONKEY'S YEARS
ADEEIIILMRST	DEMILITARISE	ADEELLMMNRTU	UNTRAMMELLED
ADEEIIILMRTZ	DEMILITARIZE	ADEELLORSSTW	WELL-ASSORTED
ADEEIIILMTTV	DELIMITATIVE	ADEELMNOSTTT	OLD TESTAMENT
ADEEIIILORST	EDITORIALISE	ADEELMORSSTU	SOMERSAULTED
ADEEIIILORTZ	EDITORIALIZE	ADEELOPSTTUX	EXPOSTULATED
ADEEIIJNOORR	RIO DE JANEIRO	ADEEMNNPRTUY	UNDERPAYMENT
ADEEIIILMMNPT	IMPEDIMENTAL	ADEEMNOPPRRS	NAMEDROPPERS
ADEEIIILMNNSS	MAIDENLINESS	ADEEMNORRSTT	REMONSTRATED
ADEEIIILMNOST	MATINEE IDOLS	ADEENNOORRST	ANDROSTERONE
ADEEIIILMTTVY	MEDITATIVELY	ADEENNOPPRRT	PREPONDERANT
ADEEIIILNNRST	INTERNALISED	ADEENOPSSTTU	UP-TO-DATENESS
ADEEIIILNNRTZ	INTERNALIZED	ADEENORSSTUW	SWEET-AND-SOUR
ADEEIIILNPRST	PRESIDENTIAL	ADEFFIMMNORS	FRAMES OF MIND
ADEEIIILOPRST	DEPILATORIES	ADEFGHHIOORT	HAIR OF THE DOG
ADEEIIILRTVVY	DERIVATIVELY	ADEFGHILNSUW	LUDWIGSHAFEN
ADEEIIMNNOTV	DENOMINATIVE	ADEFGHILRSTY	FARSIGHTEDLY
ADEEIIMNRRST	INTERMARRIED	ADEFGIILLNPY	PLAYING FIELD
ADEEIIMNRRTY	INTERMEDIARY	ADEFGIIMMNRX	MIXED FARMING
ADEEIINORSTT	DISORIENTATE	ADEFGILNOPST	SOFT-PEDALING
ADEEIINOSSTV	VIDEO NASTIES	ADEFGILNRSSY	LADY'S FINGERS
ADEEIINPRSSS	DISPENSARIES	ADEFGINOOPRR	PROOFREADING

ADEFGINRRSTU	TRANSFIGURED
ADEFHILLTTWY	HALF-WITTEDLY
ADEFHILMNORV	MILFORD HAVEN
ADEFHINRRSTY	FIRE HYDRANTS
ADEFHINRSSSW	DWARFISHNESS
ADEFIIIILNNOT	DEFINITIONAL
ADEFIIILQRSU	DISQUALIFIER
ADEFIILNOSTT	DEFLATIONIST
ADEFIILNPRSU	FREUDIAN SLIP
ADEFIINRSTTU	UNSTRATIFIED
ADEFILORRSST	FIRST SEA LORD
ADEFILOSSSTV	FAST DISSOLVE
ADEFIMNOORST	DEFORMATIONS
ADEFLLNRTUUY	FRAUDULENTLY
ADEGGHIILLNT	LEADING LIGHT
ADEGGHIINRST	SIGHT-READING
ADEGGIINNOPX	DENG XIAOPING
ADEGGINNORRR	ORGAN GRINDER
ADEGGLNRSSSU	SLUGGARDNESS
ADEGHHILNNPS	HELPING HANDS
ADEGHHILOPRT	LITHOGRAPHED
ADEGHHIMNNRT	RIGHT-HAND MEN
ADEGHHINNRRST	RIGHT-HANDERS
ADEGHHIPRSST	SHARP-SIGHTED
ADEGHHOOPPRT	PHOTOGRAPHED
ADEGHHOPRRRY	HYDROGRAPHER
ADEGHIILNNPR	PHILANDERING
ADEGHIIMNNUZ	DEHUMANIZING
ADEGHIINRSS	HAIRDRESSING
ADEGHINORRST	HORSE-TRADING
ADEGHIORRTTW	WITH REGARD TO
ADEGHLLNORST	STRANGLEHOLD
ADEGHLNORSTY	HEADSTRONGLY
ADEGHMNNORRS	GRANDMOTHERS
ADEGHNOORRTY	HYDROGENATOR
ADEGHNOPRSTU	SHARP-TONGUED
ADEGIIIILNTVZ	DEVITALIZING
ADEGIIJNOPRZ	JEOPARDIZING
ADEGIILLMNSY	MISLEADINGLY
ADEGIILLNNOT	DIALLING TONE
ADEGIILLNNTU	DENTILINGUAL
ADEGIILMNTTY	MEDITATINGLY
ADEGIILNNRRT	INTERLARDING
ADEGIILNNRSW	LINE DRAWINGS
ADEGIILNORSS	DIGRESSIONAL
ADEGIILNPRSY	DESPAIRINGLY
ADEGIIMNNNOT	DENOMINATING
ADEGIIMNNPRR	REPRIMANDING
ADEGIIMNOTTV	DEMOTIVATING
ADEGIINNOPRR	PREORDAINING
ADEGIINNOSST	DESIGNATIONS
ADEGIINOORRT	GRANODIORITE
ADEGIINORRSS	DISORGANISER
ADEGIINORRSZ	DISORGANIZER

ADEGIKNNNRSTU	UNDERTAKINGS
ADEGILNNPRUY	UNDERPLAYING
ADEGILNNRUUV	UNDERVALUING
ADEGILNOPPTU	DEPOPULATING
ADEGILOORRTY	DEROGATORILY
ADEGIMNNOPPR	NAMEDROPPING
ADEGINNNRSTU	UNDERSTATING
ADEGJLMNSTTU	LAST JUDGMENT
ADEHHILLPPSU	PHILADELPHUS
ADEHHIMOORRS	HAEMORRHOIDS
ADEHHOPRRTYY	HYDROTHERAPY
ADEHIILNSTTT	DILETTANTISH
ADEHIILOPSST	HOSPITALISED
ADEHIILOPSTZ	HOSPITALIZED
ADEHIINNNRSTY	HYDRASTININE
ADEHIIPRRSTT	THIRD PARTIES
ADEHILMNOPSU	SULPHONAMIDE
ADEHILMNORSU	MALNOURISHED
ADEHIMMPPSUY	HAPPY MEDIUMS
ADEHINQRRSTU	HINDQUARTERS
ADEHIOOPRSTT	ORTHOPAEDIST
ADEHIORSSTTW	SHORT-WAISTED
ADEHLLLMORSS	SMALLHOLDERS
ADEHLLLORSST	STALLHOLDERS
ADEHLMNOOPSU	MONADELPHOUS
ADEHLNNOPSTY	SHETLAND PONY
ADEHOOPSTTTT	PHOTOSTATTED
ADEHOPRSSSTW	SHOP STEWARDS
ADEIIIILMNOTT	DELIMITATION
ADEIIIILORSTT	EDITORIALIST
ADEIIIMNOSTV	DEVIATIONISM
ADEIIINNORRV	VIN ORDINAIRE
ADEIIINOSTTV	DEVIATIONIST
ADEIIINSTTTU	ATTITUDINISE
ADEIIINTTTUZ	ATTITUDINIZE
ADEIILLMNOST	MEDALLIONIST
ADEIILLLNPRUV	LIVERPUDLIAN
ADEIILLLOSSTY	DISLOYALTIES
ADEIILLSTUVV	VAUDEVILLIST
ADEIILMMNPRT	MALIMPRINTED
ADEIILMMORST	IMMORTALISED
ADEIILMMORTZ	IMMORTALIZED
ADEIILMNSTTT	DILETTANTISM
ADEIILNNORTY	INORDINATELY
ADEIILNOOPST	DESPOLIATION
ADEIILNOPRTV	PROVIDENTIAL
ADEIILNORSST	DILATORINESS
ADEIIMMNNRSU	INDIAN SUMMER
ADEIIMMNOORT	IMMODERATION
ADEIIMNNNOOT	DENOMINATION
ADEIIMNNOSTU	MOUNTAINSIDE
ADEIIMNNRSTT	DISTRAINMENT
ADEIIMNOOTTV	DEMOTIVATION
ADEIIMNOPRST	POSTMERIDIAN

ADEIIMNOPRXY	PYRIDOXAMINE	ADFIILOSSTUY	FASTIDIOUSLY
ADEIIMNORSST	DISSEMINATOR	ADGGIIMNNORZ	GORMANDIZING
ADEIIMORSTTU	AUDIOMETRIST	ADGGILNNNOST	LONG-STANDING
ADEIIMRSSTTX	TAXIDERMISTS	ADGHIINNSTTW	WITHSTANDING
ADEIINNOSTT	INDENTATIONS	ADGHIINOPRSZ	RHAPSODIZING
ADEIINNOPSST	DISPENSATION	ADGHIKLNORSW	WORLDSHAKING
ADEIINNORRSS	ORDINARINESS	ADGHILLLMNOS	SMALLHOLDING
ADEIINNOSSTT	DESTINATIONS	ADGHNOOOPRTY	ODONTOGRAPHY
ADEIINOOPRST	DISOPERATION	ADGIIIIMNNTT	INTIMIDATING
ADEIINOPPRST	DISAPPOINTER	ADGIIIINOSTT	DIGITISATION
ADEIINOPRSTV	DEPRIVATIONS	ADGIIIINOTTZ	DIGITIZATION
ADEIINORRSVY	DIVERSIONARY	ADGIILLNNOTU	LONGITUDINAL
ADEIINORSSTT	DISSERTATION	ADGIILNNPRST	LANDING STRIP
ADEIINORSTTX	EXTRADITIONS	ADGIILNRSTTU	STRIDULATING
ADEIINOSTTUV	ADVENTITIOUS	ADGIILOORSST	RADIOLOGISTS
ADEIIOOOPRST	RADIOISOTOPE	ADGIINOPPRSV	DISAPPROVING
ADEILLNOPPRT	DIPROPELLANT	ADGIKNNORRRU	ROARING DRUNK
ADEILLNPRTUY	PRUDENTIALLY	ADGILNNOSTUY	ASTOUNDINGLY
ADEILLOSSVWW	SWALLOW DIVES	ADGIMNNOOOST	SANTO DOMINGO
ADEILLPPRSSY	LADY'S-SLIPPER	ADGIMNNOORST	STANDING ROOM
ADEILMNNNSTU	DISANNULMENT	ADGIMNOORRSW	DRAWING ROOMS
ADEILNOOPPTU	DEPOPULATION	ADGINNOOOPRT	GONADOTROPIN
ADEILNORRSTV	DORSIVENTRAL	ADGINOPRSSTT	TRADING POSTS
ADEIMMNNOPSU	PANDEMONIUMS	ADGLNNOORTUU	LONG-DRAWN-OUT
ADEIMMOPRSUY	PRASEODYMIUM	ADGOOOPRSSTU	GASTROPODOUS
ADEIMNNOORST	DENOMINATORS	ADHHLLNNOORT	NORTH HOLLAND
ADEIMNOOPRRT	PREDOMINATOR	ADHHLLNOOSTU	SOUTH HOLLAND
ADEIMOOPRSTZ	SPERMATOZOID	ADHIIMMRSTT	MITHRIDATISM
ADEINOOPRSTT	DEPORTATIONS	ADHIIMOPRSST	DIASTROPHISM
ADEINOPRSSTY	DISPENSATORY	ADHILLNOSTUY	OUTLANDISHLY
ADEINOPRTTTY	POTTY-TRAINED	ADHILMMOOPTY	LYMPHOMATOID
ADEJLORSSSTU	LOSS ADJUSTER	ADHLNOOOOPRT	ODONTOPHORAL
ADEJMNNORSTU	ADJOURNMENTS	ADHOOOPRRSTU	ARTHROPODOUS
ADEKOOPRSTVZ	PETROZAVODSK	ADIIIIMNNOTT	INTIMIDATION
ADELLNORSSUY	SLANDEROUSLY	ADIIIINNOSTV	DIVINISATION
ADELLOOPRRST	PETRODOLLARS	ADIIIINNOTVZ	DIVINIZATION
ADELNOORRSTV	DORSOVENTRAL	ADIIILLMRSSY	DISSIMILARLY
ADELOOPRRSST	POSTAL ORDERS	ADIIILLNOSTT	DISTILLATION
ADEMNNOPSTWY	DOWN PAYMENTS	ADIIINORSTTT	TRADITIONIST
ADEMNOORRSST	DEMONSTRATOR	ADIILLMOPRRY	PRIMORDIALLY
ADENNOPRRSST	TRANSPONDERS	ADIILLNOQRSU	QUADRILLIONS
ADENNORSSTUW	UNTOWARDNESS	ADIILLNRSTUY	INDUSTRIALLY
ADFFGIILNNTU	FAULT-FINDING	ADIILLOPSTUV	POSTDILUVIAL
ADFFGNORSSTU	GROUND STAFFS	ADIILLORSTTY	DISTILLATORY
ADFGIILNORTU	FLUORIDATING	ADIILMOPSSTT	DIPLOMATISTS
ADFGIINORSSU	FIRING SQUADS	ADIILMORSSTU	DISSIMULATOR
ADFGILNNOSST	SOFT LANDINGS	ADIILNOORSTT	DISTORTIONAL
ADFGILNQSSUY	FLYING SQUADS	ADIILNOPSTUV	POSTDILUVIAN
ADFHIMNOOORU	MAID OF HONOUR	ADIILNORSTTU	STRIDULATION
ADFHMNOOOTTU	FOOT-AND-MOUTH	ADIINOPSSTTU	DISPUTATIONS
ADFIIILNNOST	DISINFLATION	ADIIOPSSTTUU	DISPUTATIOUS
ADFIIILNOSTU	FLUIDISATION	ADILLOORSTUY	IDOLATROUSLY
ADFIIILNOTUZ	FLUIDIZATION	ADILORRSTTUY	STRIDULATORY
ADFIILNOORTU	FLUORIDATION	ADILORSSSTUY	DISASTROUSLY

ADLNOOPRSSWY	PLAYS ON WORDS	AEEEIKNPRSVW	SNEAK PREVIEW
AEEEEGHLPRST	TELEGRAPHESE	AEEEILLNPRTT	INTERPELLATE
AEEEEGHMORTT	HETEROGAMETE	AEEEILMNPRTX	EXPERIMENTAL
AEEEEGINRRTV	REGENERATIVE	AEEEILNOORST	SAONE-ET-LOIRE
AEEEEGNNRRTU	UNREGENERATE	AEEEILNRSSTT	LITERATENESS
AEEEEHHPRRSS	SHEEPSHEARER	AEEEIMNRRTUV	REMUNERATIVE
AEEEEIMNNRST	SEINE-ET-MARNE	AEEEIMOPRRTV	EVAPORIMETER
AEEEEKLNNNOV	ON AN EVEN KEEL	AEEEIMORSTTV	OVERESTIMATE
AEEEELPRRSSS	PRESS RELEASE	AEEEINNORTTX	EXENTERATION
AEEEFFILMNTY	EFFEMINATELY	AEEEINNRRSTT	ENTERTAINERS
AEEEFFLOPPST	TOFFEE APPLES	AEEEINPRSTTV	PRESENTATIVE
AEEEFHINRRTT	THEREINAFTER	AEEEINRRTTUX	EXTRAUTERINE
AEEEFIKLNPTT	PALETTE KNIFE	AEEEIPRRSTVV	PRESERVATIVE
AEEEFILNPRRT	PREFERENTIAL	AEEEKLLPRSSW	SLEEPWALKERS
AEEEFIMNRTTV	FERMENTATIVE	AEEEKLRRSTTW	STREETWALKER
AEEEFLNRSSSS	FEARLESSNESS	AEEELLORSTTT	TEETOTALLERS
AEEEFMNORSSS	FEARSOMENESS	AEEELMNORSYY	ELEEMOSYNARY
AEEEGGINNRRT	REGENERATING	AEEELNOPPSVY	PAY ENVELOPES
AEEEGHLPRRST	TELEGRAPHERS	AEEELRSSTTUV	STREET VALUES
AEEEGHORRSTT	THEATREGOERS	AEEEMMNPRSTT	TEMPERAMENTS
AEEEGIILNRST	GENERALITIES	AEEEMMNRSSTU	MEASUREMENTS
AEEEGIKLNNNW	WANKEL ENGINE	AEEEMNNSTTTW	NEW TESTAMENT
AEEEGILNNRRV	LINE-ENGRAVER	AEEEMNRSSTTT	RESTATEMENTS
AEEEGILNOPTV	NEGATIVE POLE	AEEEMPRRSTTU	TEMPERATURES
AEEEGIMNNSTV	ENVISAGEMENT	AEEEMRSSSSST	SEAMSTRESSES
AEEEGINNORRT	REGENERATION	AEEFFGHIRRTU	FATHER FIGURE
AEEEGINNSSTV	NEGATIVENESS	AEEFFGILNORT	FREE-FLOATING
AEEEGINORTTV	REVEGETATION	AEEFFGRSSTTU	SUFFRAGETTES
AEEEGIRRSTTV	TERGIVERSATE	AEEFFHKOORST	FOR THE SAKE OF
AEEEGLMNNNTT	ENTANGLEMENT	AEEFFILMRSTU	FEATURE FILMS
AEEEGLMNNRST	ENLARGEMENTS	AEEFGIKRRSTU	FIGURE SKATER
AEEEGMMNORTT	MAGNETOMETER	AEEFGILNORRT	FORETRIANGLE
AEEEGMNNRSTT	ESTRANGEMENT	AEEFGILNPRST	FINGERPLATES
AEEEHHHNNNPRT	PHENANTHRENE	AEEFGINRRRST	REFRIGERANTS
AEEEHHNOTTXY	ETHOXYETHANE	AEEFGIORRRRT	REFRIGERATOR
AEEEHIKNSSTV	SNEAK THIEVES	AEEFGLNRSSTU	GRATEFULNESS
AEEEHILMPRTY	EPHEMERALITY	AEEFHHORSSTU	HOUSEFATHERS
AEEEHILNNSSV	HEAVENLINESS	AEEFHIKNRSSS	FREAKISHNESS
AEEEHILNRSST	LEATHERINESS	AEEFHILNRSST	FATHERLINESS
AEEEHINPPRSV	APPREHENSIVE	AEEFHIOORRST	RAISE THE ROOF
AEEEHINPRSST	PARENTHESISE	AEEFHLLOOSTW	FOLLOW THE SEA
AEEEHINPRSTZ	PARENTHESIZE	AEEFHLLRRSTU	FULLER'S EARTH
AEEEHLMPPRST	PAMPHLETEERS	AEEFHLMNSSSU	SHAMEFULNESS
AEEEHLNRSSTT	NETTLE RASHES	AEEFHLMORRTW	FLAME-THROWER
AEEEHLORSTUX	HETEROSEXUAL	AEEFHLOOSTTT	ATHLETE'S FOOT
AEEEHLPRRSWY	PRAYER WHEELS	AEEFHMNORRWY	ANYWHERE FROM
AEEEHLRRSTTY	HARLEY STREET	AEEFHOOPRRTW	WEATHERPROOF
AEEEHMORTTTX	METHOTREXATE	AEEFHORSTTTU	FOURTH ESTATE
AEEEHQRRRTTU	THREE-QUARTER	AEEFIILMPPRR	PREAMPLIFIER
AEEEIILMNORT	MAINE-ET-LOIRE	AEEFIINRRSTT	FRATERNITIES
AEEEIILNPRTX	EXPERIENTIAL	AEEFIKLLMOTT	MAKE LITTLE OF
AEEEIILNRRST	INERTIA REELS	AEEFIKLNNSTY	STANLEY KNIFE
AEEEIINNNSTT	SAINT-ETIENNE	AEEFILOPRSTU	PETALIFEROUS
AEEEIKNNORST	ENTEROKINASE	AEEFIMNNORTT	FERMENTATION

AEEFIMOPRRTV	PERFORMATIVE
AEEFINNORSTT	FENESTRATION
AEEFLMNORSTT	FORESTALMENT, MAN OF LETTERS
AEEFLNSSSSTTU	TASTEFULNESS
AEEFLNSSSTUW	WASTEFULNESS
AEEFLOPQRSUW	PASQUEFLOWER
AEEFLRRSSSTT	SELF-STARTERS
AEEFNORRSSVW	WARS OF NERVES
AEEGGGINNNSS	ENGAGINGNESS
AEEGGHILNPRT	TELEGRAPHING
AEEGGIILNNRZ	GENERALIZING
AEEGGIILNNVZ	EVANGELIZING
AEEGGILNOSST	GENEALOGISTS
AEEGGILRSSVY	AGGRESSIVELY
AEEGGIMMNOST	GEOMAGNETISM
AEEGGINNTTTW	WETTING AGENT
AEEGGIQRRRSU	SQUARE-RIGGER
AEEGHHILOPRR	HELIOGRAPHER
AEEGHHISTVWY	HEAVYWEIGHTS
AEEGHHNOPRRT	ETHNOGRAPHER
AEEGHHOPRRTY	HETEROGRAPHY
AEEGHILLMMRT	HELLGRAMMITE
AEEGHILMNOPR	GERMANOPHILE
AEEGHILNNRTY	HEARTENINGLY
AEEGHILNORTW	WATERING HOLE
AEEGHILORRUV	HELIOGRAVURE
AEEGHINOPSST	PATHOGENESIS
AEEGHINPTTVY	HEAVY PETTING
AEEGHINRRSTT	STRAIGHTENER
AEEGHIPPRSTW	PAPERWEIGHTS
AEEGHIPRSSTW	STAGE WHISPER
AEEGHLNOPRSY	SELENOGRAPHY
AEEGHLOORRTW	WOOLGATHERER
AEEGHMOOPRRT	METEOROGRAPH
AEEGHMOORSTU	HETEROGAMOUS
AEEGHNOOPRTV	PHOTOENGRAVE
AEEGHNOPRRST	STENOGRAPHER
AEEGHOOPSSSU	OESOPHAGUSES
AEEGHOPPRRRT	PETROGRAPHER
AEEGHOPRRSTY	STEREOGRAPHY
AEEGIIILLLST	ILLEGALITIES
AEEGIIILLMTT	ILLEGITIMATE
AEEGIIILMSTT	LEGITIMATISE
AEEGIIILMTTZ	LEGITIMATIZE
AEEGIIILLMTY	LEGITIMATELY
AEEGIILNNORS	LEGIONNAIRES
AEEGIILNNPSS	PALINGENESIS
AEEGIINNNRTT	ENTERTAINING
AEEGIINNRTVW	INTERWEAVING
AEEGIJNNRTUV	REJUVENATING
AEEGIKLLNPSW	SLEEPWALKING
AEEGIKLNSTTW	SWEET-TALKING
AEEGIKMNPRRT	PARKING METER
AEEGIKNNNSSS	SNEAKINGNESS
AEEGIKNRSTUY	KEY SIGNATURE
AEEGILLRSSST	LEGISLATRESS
AEEGILLRSSTU	LEGISLATURES
AEEGILMNNRST	REALIGNMENTS
AEEGILNNPSSS	PLEASINGNESS
AEEGILNNRTTY	ENTREATINGLY
AEEGIMNNOSTT	SEGMENTATION
AEEGIMNNRRTU	REMUNERATING
AEEGIMSSSTTU	GUESSTIMATES
AEEGINNNSSSU	SANGUINENESS
AEEGINOPRRRT	PEREGRINATOR
AEEGINPPRRRT	PERPETRATING
AEEGINPPRRTU	PERPETUATING
AEEGIOPRRSTV	PREROGATIVES
AEEGKNOORSTU	KERATOGENOUS
AEEGLLMNOOPR	PROLEGOMENAL
AEEGLLMNOPSY	SPLENOMEGALY
AEEGLLMNRUWZ	MANGEL-WURZEL
AEEGLLPRRSSY	PRESS GALLERY
AEEGLMNNORTV	GOVERNMENTAL
AEEGLNNOORTT	LOT-ET-GARONNE
AEEGMMNORTTY	MAGNETOMETRY
AEEGPRRSSSSU	SUPERGRASSES
AEEHHHILNSTY	HEATHENISHLY
AEEHHIKNSSTV	SHEATH KNIVES
AEEHHILMNSTY	MYELIN SHEATH
AEEHHILOPRTY	HELIOTHERAPY
AEEHHILRSTWW	WHEREWITHALS
AEEHHIMNPRSW	NEW HAMPSHIRE
AEEHHIPRSSTW	WEATHER SHIPS
AEEHHLOSSTTW	STEAL THE SHOW
AEEHHMORSSTV	HARVEST HOMES
AEEHHNOPPRTY	PHANEROPHYTE
AEEHIIMOOPSS	HAEMOPOIESIS
AEEHIINORSTT	ETHERISATION
AEEHIINORTTZ	ETHERIZATION
AEEHIKLLLRSW	KILLER WHALES
AEEHIKLNNPPT	PINK ELEPHANT
AEEHILLMNNPS	PANHELLENISM
AEEHILLNNPST	PANHELLENIST
AEEHILLPPRRY	PERIPHERALLY
AEEHILNSSSTT	STEALTHINESS
AEEHILORRSTU	TRAILER HOUSE
AEEHILRSTVWY	WHITE SLAVERY
AEEHILSTUVXY	EXHAUSTIVELY
AEEHIMNNORTT	NITROMETHANE
AEEHINNOPPRS	APPREHENSION
AEEHINOORSTU	HETEROOUSIAN
AEEHINOPSSTV	TOP-HEAVINESS
AEEHINSSSTTT	ANESTHETISTS
AEEHIOPPSTTV	STOVEPIPE HAT
AEEHIOPRSSTU	HOUSE PARTIES
AEEHIORRRRST	HAIR-RESTORER

AEEHIORSSSST	AIRHOSTESSES
AEEHKMPRRSTY	HYPERMARKETS
AEEHLLMMORWY	YELLOWHAMMER
AEEHLLMNNOPY	PHENOMENALLY
AEEHLLNORSTY	LONELY HEARTS
AEEHLMNORSTT	STENOTHERMAL
AEEHLMNRSSSS	HARMLESSNESS
AEEHLMORSTTW	TOWER HAMLETS
AEEHLMOSSSTV	STEAM SHOVELS
AEEHLMOSSTTY	STATELY HOMES
AEEHLNOPRTUY	POLYURETHANE
AEEHLOPRSTTY	HETEROPLASTY
AEEHLPPRRSTU	PURPLE HEARTS
AEEHMMOOPRST	METAMORPHOSE
AEEHMNORRTTU	MOTHER NATURE
AEEHMORSSSTU	HOUSEMASTERS
AEEHNNORRSTT	NORTHEASTERN
AEEHNOPRSSTU	HOUSEPARENTS
AEEHNORRSSTT	NORTHEASTERS
AEEHNORSSTTU	SOUTHEASTERN
AEEHOPRRSSTT	STRATOSPHERE
AEEHORRSSSTU	HOUSE ARRESTS
AEEIIILNQSTU	INEQUALITIES
AEEIIJNOQSSU	JE NE SAIS QUOI
AEEIIKLMNPRS	MARLINESPIKE
AEEIIKMNNSSY	KEYNESIANISM
AEEIIILLLRTTY	ILLITERATELY
AEEIIILLNOSTV	TELEVISIONAL
AEEIIILLNPSTT	PESTILENTIAL
AEEIILMMORRS	MEMORIALISER
AEEIILMMORRZ	MEMORIALIZER
AEEIILMNOOST	EMOTIONALISE
AEEIILMNOOTZ	EMOTIONALIZE
AEEIILMNSSST	ESSENTIALISM
AEEIILMPRTVY	IMPERATIVELY
AEEIILNNSSST	INESSENTIALS
AEEIILNRRSST	LITERARINESS
AEEIILNRSSUV	UNIVERSALISE
AEEIILNRSUVZ	UNIVERSALIZE
AEEIILNSSSTT	ESSENTIALIST
AEEIILNSSTTY	ESSENTIALITY
AEEIILOPTTVX	EXPLOITATIVE
AEEIIMNSSSTW	SIAMESE TWINS
AEEIINNORSTT	ETERNISATION
AEEIINNORTTZ	ETERNIZATION
AEEIINNPRTTY	PENITENTIARY
AEEIINNRRTTU	INTRAUTERINE
AEEIINORRSTT	REITERATIONS
AEEIIPRTTUVV	VITUPERATIVE
AEEIJLOPRTVY	PEJORATIVELY
AEEIJNNORTUV	REJUVENATION
AEEIKMNSSTTU	MINUTE STEAKS
AEEILLMNRTTT	ILL-TREATMENT
AEEILLNNPRTT	INTERPELLANT

AEEIILLNOSSTT	TESSELLATION
AEEIILLNQSTUY	SEQUENTIALLY
AEEIILLNQTUVY	EQUIVALENTLY
AEEIILLNRRST	INTERSTELLAR
AEEIILLNRRTVY	IRRELEVANTLY
AEEIILLNSSSUV	ALLUSIVENESS
AEEIILLTTTTT	TITTLE-TATTLE
AEEIILMNNNRSS	MANNERLINESS
AEEIILMNNPTTU	PENNULTIMATE
AEEIILMNRSSST	MASTERLINESS
AEEIILNNNOSST	NONESSENTIAL
AEEIILNNOPRTV	OPEN INTERVAL
AEEIILNOPRRTT	INTERPOLATER
AEEIILNOPRSSX	EXPRESSIONAL
AEEIILNPRRRST	LASER PRINTER
AEEIILPRSSTUV	SUPERLATIVES
AEEIILPRSSUVY	PERSUASIVELY
AEEIILRRSTTTU	LITTERATEURS
AEEIIMMNORSTT	AMORTISEMENT
AEEIIMMNORTTZ	AMORTIZEMENT
AEEIIMMNRSTTT	MISTREATMENT
AEEIIMMNSSTTT	MISSTATEMENT
AEEIIMNNORRTU	REMUNERATION
AEEIIMNNORSTT	SENARMONTITE
AEEIIMNNORSTU	ENUMERATIONS,
MOUNTAINEERS	
AEEIIMNORRTTX	EXTERMINATOR
AEEIIMRSSSTTY	SYSTEMATISER
AEEIIMRSSTTYZ	SYSTEMATIZER
AEEIINNOOPRTV	NONOPERATIVE
AEEIINNOPRSTT	PRESENTATION
AEEIINOORRSSU	AERONEUROSIS
AEEIINOORTTTX	EXTORTIONATE
AEEIINOPPRRTT	PERPETRATION
AEEIINOPPRTTU	PERPETUATION
AEEIINOPRRSTV	PRESERVATION
AEEIINOPRRSTY	ARSENOPYRITE
AEEIINORRRSVY	REVERSIONARY
AEEIINORRSSTV	RESERVATIONS
AEEIINRSSTTTV	TRANSVESTITE
AEEIINRSTTTUV	STERNUTATIVE
AEEIIORRSSTTV	RESTORATIVES
AEEIIPPRRTTTT	PITTER-PATTER
AEEKLLORRRST	ROLLER-SKATER
AEEKLLORRSST	ROLLER SKATES
AEEKLMORRSTW	METALWORKERS
AEEKMORRSSTT	MASTERSTROKE
AEEKMPRRSSTU	SUPERMARKETS
AEEKNPRRSSTU	SUPERTANKERS
AEELLLMNOTVY	MALEVOLENTLY
AEELLLORTTWY	YELLOW RATTLE
AEELLMNPPSTU	SUPPLEMENTAL
AEELLMORRSST	STEAMROLLERS
AEELLNORSSTW	STONEWALLERS

AEELLOPRSTUV	POLE VAULTERS
AEELMNPRRSTU	PREMENSTRUAL
AEELMOOPRSTU	SOMATOPLEURE
AEELNORSTUXY	EXTRANEOUSLY
AEELNRRSSTVY	TRANSVERSELY
AEELOOPPRTUV	OVERPOPULATE
AEELOPPRRRTY	REAL PROPERTY
AEEMNOORTUUV	OUTMANOEUVRE
AEENNORSSSSU	RAVENOUSNESS
AEENNOSSSSUU	NAUSEOUSNESS
AEENOPRRSSTT	PATERNOSTERS
AEENOQRRSTTU	QUARTER NOTES
AEENORRSSTXY	EXTRASENSORY
AEEOOPRSTUUX	AUTOEXPOSURE
AEEOOPSSTTTW	SWEET POTATOS
AEEOPPRRRSTT	PERPETRATORS
AEEOPRRSTTTU	TETRAPTEROUS
AEEOQRRSSTTU	SEQUESTRATOR
AEEFFGILLLMOR	FLAGELLIFORM
AEFFHILNSSTU	FAITHFULNESS
AEFFILRRSSTU	FIRST REFUSAL
AEFFKNRRRSTU	FRANKFURTERS
AEFGGGILNOPR	LEAPFROGGING
AEFGGHINORRT	FORGATHERING
AEFGHHOORRTU	THOROUGHFARE
AEFGHHOORTTU	AFORETHOUGHT
AEFGHHORTTTU	AFTERTHOUGHT
AEFGIILRTUVY	FIGURATIVELY
AEFGIINNRRTZ	FRATERNIZING
AEFGIINPPSWW	WIFE SWAPPING
AEFGILLMNNUY	MEANINGFULLY
AEFGILLNORST	FORESTALLING
AEFGILLNRSST	FINGERSTALLS
AEFGILLNRTTY	FLATTERINGLY
AEFGILLNSSUW	WINEGLASSFUL
AEFGILNNRTTU	UNFLATTERING
AEFGINNRRRST	TRANSFERRING
AEFGLLNRTUUY	UNGRATEFULLY
AEFHKLMORSST	THERMOS FLASK
AEFHKLNNSSTU	THANKFULNESS
AEFHKNOOSTTV	VOTE OF THANKS
AEFHLLORSSUY	ROYAL FLUSHES
AEFHLNRSSTUW	WRATHFULNESS
AEFHOOPRRSTT	SHATTERPROOF
AEFIIIILMNSST	SEMIFINALIST
AEFIIIILNRTTV	INFILTRATIVE
AEFIIIMNNOST	FEMINISATION
AEFIIIMNNOTZ	FEMINIZATION
AEFIIILLMOTTU	MULTIFOLIATE
AEFIIILLNOOTU	UNIFOLIOLATE
AEFIIILNRTUV	INTERFLUVIAL
AEFIIILMNORUV	FLUVIOMARINE
AEFIIILNOOPRT	PERFOLIATION
AEFIINNOSSTT	INFESTATIONS
AEFIINORSSTT	FIRE STATIONS
AEFIINORSTTU	TITANIFEROUS
AEFILMMNNOOT	MONOFILAMENT
AEFILMORRRSU	FORMULARISER
AEFILMORRRUZ	FORMULARIZER
AEFILNOOPRSS	PROFESSIONAL
AEFILNOOPRTV	FLAVOPROTEIN
AEFILOOPRRSS	PROFESSIONAL
AEFILOPPRSUU	PAPULIFEROUS
AEFILOPRRSTT	SELF-PORTRAIT
AEFIMNNORRST	FRONTIERSMAN
AEFIMNOOPRRT	PREFORMATION
AEFIMNOORRST	REFORMATIONS
AEFINNNOPSTU	FOUNTAIN PENS
AEFINNORSSTU	STANNIFEROUS
AEFINOOPRRST	PERFORATIONS
AEFKLLOORRSW	FLOORWALKERS
AEFLLMNORSTU	SMALL FORTUNE
AEFLLNNSSUUW	UNLAWFULNESS
AEFLLOOPRSSY	FOOL'S-PARSLEY
AEFMNORRRSST	TRANSFORMERS
AEFNNORSTTUU	UNFORTUNATES
AEGGGILNNOTU	AGGLUTINOGEN
AEGGGILNRSTY	STAGGERINGLY
AEGGGILNRSWY	SWAGGERINGLY
AEGGGINNPRSS	PRESSGANGING
AEGGHIIJLNNO	HEILONGJIANG
AEGGHIIKLNNU	HEILUNGKIANG
AEGGHIILNNST	NIGHTINGALES
AEGGHIIRRRST	HAIR TRIGGERS
AEGGHILNRSTU	SLAUGHTERING
AEGGHINSSSTT	GASTIGHTNESS
AEGGHIPPRRTY	TRIGGER-HAPPY
AEGGHLNOOSTT	SNAGGLETOOTH
AEGGHNOORRUY	ORANGE ROUGHY
AEGGHOOOPRYZ	ZOOGEOGRAPHY
AEGGIILNRRUZ	REGULARIZING
AEGGIIMNNPRT	IMPREGNATING
AEGGIINNORRZ	REORGANIZING
AEGGILORRSUY	GREGARIOUSLY
AEGGIMNNORRW	WARMONGERING
AEGGLOOORSTY	ASTROGEOLOGY
AEGHHIINSTWW	WHITEWASHING
AEGHHILOPRRT	LITHOGRAPHER
AEGHHLOPRSSU	PLOUGHSHARES
AEGHHMOPRRTY	THERMOGRAPHY
AEGHHNOOPPRR	PHONOGRAPHER
AEGHHOOPPRRT	PHOTOGRAPHER
AEGHHOOPRRRT	ORTHOGRAPHER
AEGHIIKLNNTY	LIKE ANYTHING
AEGHIILMNSST	ALMIGHTINESS
AEGHIILNSTTY	HESITATINGLY
AEGHIINNSTTU	UNHESITATING
AEGHIKNNRRTT	KNIGHT-ERRANT

AEGHILLPRSTU	SUGAR THE PILL	AEGIINNSTUXY	EXSANGUINITY
AEGHILMNNOSW	ENGLISHWOMAN	AEGIINORRSTT	REGISTRATION
AEGHILMNNSTU	LANGUISHMENT	AEGIINORSTTV	INVESTIGATOR
AEGHILNRSTTY	SHATTERINGLY	AEGIINPPRRTW	WRITING PAPER
AEGHILQRRTTU	QUARTERLIGHT	AEGIINPRSTUZ	PASTEURIZING
AEGHIMMNOSST	MESOGNATHISM	AEGIJLNRSUUV	JUGULAR VEINS
AEGHIMNORSNW	HOUSEWARMING	AEGIJLPSUWZZ	JIGSAW PUZZLE
AEGHIMOOPRST	MASTIGOPHORE	AEGIKLMNORTW	METALWORKING
AEGHIMOPRSSS	SEISMOGRAPHS	AEGIKMMNOPRT	TEMPO MARKING
AEGHIMOPRSSY	SEISMOGRAPHY	AEGILLMRSTTU	METALLURGIST
AEGHINNOOOPPT	PHONE-TAPPING	AEGILLNNOSTW	STONEWALLING
AEGHINOOOTTV	NOT GIVE A HOOT	AEGILLNOPTUV	POLE VAULTING
AEGHINOPRRSW	POWER-SHARING	AEGILMMNRSTY	STAMMERINGLY
AEGHINRRRTUY	TEARING HURRY	AEGILMNNNNOT	NONALIGNMENT
AEGHINRRSSTT	HEARTSTRINGS	AEGILMNNOOTU	MAGNILOQUENT
AEGHINRSSSTT	STRAIGHTNESS	AEGILMORSSTT	STIGMASTEROL
AEGHLMNNOORS	LONGSHOREMAN	AEGILNNNOSTU	SANGUINOLENT
AEGHLORSSTUU	SLAUGHTEROUS	AEGILNNRSSSU	SINGULARNESS
AEGHMNOOOPTT	PHOTOMONTAGE	AEGILNNRSTTY	ASTRINGENTLY
AEGHMNOOSSTU	MESOGNATHOUS	AEGILNRRSSUY	REASSURINGLY
AEGHMNOPSSUW	HUMP ONE'S SWAG	AEGILOORSTTT	TERATOLOGIST
AEGHNOOPPRRR	PORNOGRAPHER	AEGILORRSSTU	GROSSULARITE
AEGHOOPPRRST	TOPOGRAPHERS	AEGIMMORRSTU	MESOGASTRIUM
AEGHOOPRRTUV	PHOTOGRAVURE	AEGIMNNNRSTU	RUNNING MATES
AEGHOPPRRSSS	GRASSHOPPERS	AEGIMNNRSTTU	MENSTRUATING
AEGHOPPRRSTY	TYPOGRAPHERS	AEGINNOPSSTV	PAVING STONES
AEGHOPPRRTUY	GROUP THERAPY	AEGINOORRRTT	INTERROGATOR
AEGIIILMNOTT	LEGITIMATION	AEGINOPRSTUX	EXPURGATIONS
AEGIIILNRTVZ	REVITALIZING	AEGINOPRSTWY	STAYING POWER
AEGIIIMMNNNPRSW	INSEMINATING	AEGINOQSSTTU	QUESTION TAGS
AEGIIINMNNPRSW	AWE-INSPIRING	AEGLLNOOOPTY	PALEONTOLOGY
AEGIIINORTVV	INVIGORATIVE	AEGLNRSSTTUU	GUTTURALNESS
AEGIIINRSTVW	WEST VIRGINIA	AEGLOORSTUUY	OUTRAGEOUSLY
AEGIIKLLNRST	GIANT KILLERS	AEGMMNOPSSUU	MAGNUM OPUSES
AEGIILLMRRSU	GUERRILLAISM	AEGNOOPRSSSY	GREASY SPOONS
AEGIILLNPRVY	PREVAILINGLY	AEGNORRRSSST	TRANSGRESSOR
AEGIILMMNNST	MISALIGNMENT	AEGOOPSSTTUY	STEATOPYGOUS
AEGIILMNNRST	STREAMLINING	AEHHILOPSTTU	THIOSULPHATE
AEGIILMNORST	MINERALOGIST	AEHHIMNOPRSS	HORSEMANSHIP
AEGIILNNNSSU	UNGAINLINESS	AEHHIMOOPSTT	HOMEOPATHIST
AEGIILNNORTU	URINOGENITAL	AEHHLMOOPSTX	EXOPHTHALMOS
AEGIILNNRTUZ	NEUTRALIZING	AEHHLOOOPPRT	LOPHOPHORATE
AEGIILNPPTYZ	APPETIZINGLY	AEHHLOOPRSTU	ALTHORP HOUSE
AEGIILNPRSTT	EARSPLITTING	AEHHNOPPRTYY	HYPNOTHERAPY
AEGIILNRSTVV	VESTAL VIRGIN	AEHHOOPPRTTY	PHOTOTHERAPY
AEGIILRRRTUY	IRREGULARITY	AEHHOOPRRSST	SHARPSHOOTER
AEGIIMMMNNSUW	MINIMUM WAGES	AEHIIIMNNOST	THIOSINAMINE
AEGIIMMORRRS	MIRROR IMAGES	AEHIIIMNNSTU	INHUMANITIES
AEGIIMNNOPRT	IMPREGNATION	AEHIIILLPSSTT	PHILATELISTS
AEGIIMNNOPTT	PIGMENTATION	AEHIILLNOPRST	RELATIONSHIP
AEGIIMOPRSTV	GRAM-POSITIVE	AEHIILPRRSTT	HAIRSPLITTER
AEGIINNNRSTT	INTRANSIGENT	AEHIINNOPRTT	TREPHINATION
AEGIINNOOSTT	NEGOTIATIONS	AEHIINOORSTT	THEORISATION
AEGIINNORSST	RESIGNATIONS	AEHIINOORTTZ	THEORIZATION

AEHIINOPRRSS	PARISHIONERS
AEHIIRRSSTTW	SHIRTWAISTER
AEHILLOORSTU	HELIOLATROUS
AEHILMNOOPSU	ANEMOPHILOUS
AEHILMNORSTW	MOTHERS-IN-LAW
AEHIMMMOPRST	METAMORPHISM
AEHIMNNOOPRT	ENANTIOMORPH
AEHIMNNOOSSU	MANSION HOUSE
AEHIMNNOOPPSU	ONE-UPMANSHIP
AEHIMNNOSSSW	WOMANISHNESS
AEHIMNNOSSTT	ASTONISHMENT
AEHIMNNQSTUV	VANQUISHMENT
AEHIMNOPRSST	MISANTHROPES
AEHIMNOPRSTW	WITH OPEN ARMS
AEHIMNPRSSST	TRAMPISHNESS
AEHIMPRSSSTY	SYMPATHISERS
AEHIMPRSSTYZ	SYMPATHIZERS
AEHINNNOSTTT	ON THE INSTANT
AEHINNPPSSSS	SNAPPISHNESS
AEHINOOPRRTT	PROTOTHERIAN
AEHINOORSTTX	EXHORTATIONS
AEHINOOSSTTU	STATION HOUSE
AEHINPPRRSST	PARTNERSHIPS
AEHIOOPPRSST	APOSTROPHISE
AEHIOOPPRSTZ	APOSTROPHIZE
AEHIOOSSSTTU	SOUTH OSSETIA
AEHIOPRRSTWY	PRAISEWORTHY
AEHJNOORRSST	TROJAN HORSES
AEHLMPRSTTTU	THE LAST TRUMP
AEHLNOPSSTUY	POLYANTHUSES
AEHLOPPRSTUY	PYROSULPHATE
AEHMNOOPRTUX	PNEUMOTHORAX
AEHMNOORSSTV	HARVEST MOONS
AEHOOPRRSSUW	HOUSE SPARROW
AEIIIILMRSST	SIMILARITIES
AEIIIILRSTTV	TRIVIALITIES
AEIIILLMNORS	MILLIONAIRES
AEIIILLMNTUV	ILLUMINATIVE
AEIIILMMORST	IMMORALITIES
AEIIILMPRSST	IMPERIALISTS
AEIIILNRSTTT	INTERSTITIAL
AEIIILPRSSTU	SPIRITUALISE
AEIIILPRSTUZ	SPIRITUALIZE
AEIIIMMNSSTT	ANTI-SEMITISM
AEIIIMNNNOST	INSEMINATION
AEIIIMNORSSS	MISSIONARIES
AEIIIMNRSTTV	MINISTRATIVE
AEIIINNRSTTV	INTRANSITIVE
AEIIIOPPRTTV	PROPITIATIVE
AEIIKKNORSSY	KARYOKINESIS
AEIILLNQRSTU	TRANQUILLISE
AEIILLNQRTUZ	TRANQUILLIZE
AEIILLRSTTUV	ILLUSTRATIVE
AEIILMMNOOST	EMOTIONALISM

AEIILMMORRST	IMMORTALISER
AEIILMMORRTZ	IMMORTALIZER
AEIILMNOOSTT	EMOTIONALIST
AEIILMNOOTTY	EMOTIONALITY
AEIILMNOPRSS	IMPRESSIONAL
AEIILMNOSSTT	TESTIMONIALS
AEIILMNRSSUV	UNIVERSALISM
AEIILMNRTUVY	RUMINATIVELY
AEIILMNSTTUY	SIMULTANEITY
AEIILMPRTTTU	MULTIPARTITE
AEIILNNNQQUU	QUINQUENNIAL
AEIILNOOPSTX	EXPOSITIONAL
AEIILNOOPTTX	EXPLOITATION
AEIILNOOSTVW	VOWELISATION
AEIILNOOTVWZ	VOWELIZATION
AEIILNOPTTTY	POTENTIALITY
AEIILNORSSST	SOLITARINESS
AEIILNORSSTT	ORIENTALISTS
AEIILNRSSSTW	SISTERS-IN-LAW
AEIILNRSSTUV	UNIVERSALIST
AEIILNRSTUVY	UNIVERSALITY
AEIILNSTUUXY	UNISEXUALITY
AEIILORRRSTT	TERRITORIALS
AEIIMMNOORST	MEMORISATION
AEIIMMNOORTZ	MEMORIZATION
AEIIMNNOOSTT	MONETISATION
AEIIMNNOOTTZ	MONETIZATION
AEIIMNNOPSSX	EXPANSIONISM
AEIIMNNORSTT	TERMINATIONS
AEIIMNRSSSTV	TRANSMISSIVE
AEIIMRRSSTTU	TRIUMVIRATES
AEIINNNORTTU	ANTINEUTRINO
AEIINNNQSTTU	SAINT-QUENTIN
AEIINNOORSTT	ORIENTATIONS
AEIINNOPRSTU	RESUPINATION
AEIINNOPSSTX	EXPANSIONIST
AEIINNORSTTT	STRONTIANITE
AEIINOPPRRST	PERSPIRATION
AEIINOPRTTUV	VITUPERATION
AEIKMNNRSTTU	TURKMENISTAN
AEIKMNOQRSTU	QUESTION MARK
AEILLMMMSSTY	SYMMETALLISM
AEILLMNOPRSY	IMPERSONALLY
AEILLNNORTTY	INTOLERANTLY
AEILLNOOSTTW	WOLLASTONITE
AEILLORRRTTY	ROTARY TILLER
AEILMNNOPRST	MINOR PLANETS
AEILMNNORSST	MATRONLINESS
AEILMNNOSSTW	WINSTON-SALEM
AEILMNNRSTTU	INSTRUMENTAL
AEILMNOOPRTT	METROPOLITAN
AEILMNOSSTUU	SIMULTANEOUS
AEILMOORSTTT	STROMATOLITE
AEILNNRRTTUWW	UNWRITTEN LAW

AEILNOOOPRRT	POOR RELATION	AFFIILNNOSTU	INSUFFLATION
AEILNOOPRSTX	EXPLORATIONS	AFGGGILLNNUY	UNFLAGGINGLY
AEILNOORTUVY	EVOLUTIONARY	AFGGIILNRTYY	GRATIFYINGLY
AEILNORRSUVY	REVULSIONARY	AFGGIINPPRTW	GIFT-WRAPPING
AEILOPRSTUUV	VOLUPTUARIES	AFGIIILNNRTT	INFILTRATING
AEIMNNOPPSTT	APPOINTMENTS	AFGIILLMNORU	ANGUILLIFORM
AEIMNNORSTTU	MENSTRUATION	AFGIILLNQUYY	QUALIFYINGLY
AEIMNOPRRRST	IMPERSONATOR	AFGIILNSSTYY	SATISFYINGLY
AEIMNOPRSTTU	PERMUTATIONS	AFGIIMNOPRRT	PROFIT MARGIN
AEIMNRRSSTTT	TRANSMITTERS	AFGIKNOORSTT	TOASTING FORK
AEIMNRSSSTTV	TRANSVESTISM	AFGIMNNORRST	TRANSFORMING
AEINNNORSSTT	NONRESISTANT	AFGIMNNORRSTY	TRANSMOGRIFY
AEINNOPRSTU	PUT ONE'S OAR IN	AFIIILMNNOST	INFLATIONISM
AEINNORSTTTU	STERNUTATION	AFIIILNNORTT	INFILTRATION
AEINOOPRSTTT	PROTESTATION	AFIIILNNOSTT	INFLATIONIST
AEINOOPRSTTW	POWER STATION	AFIILMNNOSTU	FULMINATIONS
AEINOORRSSTT	RESTORATIONS	AFIILMORSTUU	MULTIFARIOUS
AEINOORRTTXY	EXTORTIONARY	AFIILNNOORTU	FLUORINATION
AEINOOSSTTTU	OSTENTATIOUS	AFIILNORRSTT	INFILTRATORS
AEINOPPRSSTT	POSTER PAINTS	AFIILORRSSST	FISSIROSTRAL
AEINOPRRSTTT	TRAIN SPOTTER	AFIIMMNNORST	MISINFORMANT
AEINOPRRSTTV	TRANSPORTIVE	AFILMNOORSTU	FORMULATIONS
AEINORRSTVWY	WINTER SAVORY	AFIMMNNORRST	TRANSFORMISM
AEIOOOOPPPRS	PROSOPOPOEIA	AFIMNORRSSTT	TRANSFORMIST
AEIOOPPRRRTX	EXPROPRIATOR	AFINNORRSSTU	TRANSFUSIONS
AEIOPPRRRSTY	PERSPIRATORY	AFINORRSSTTU	FRUSTRATIONS
AEKLLPPSSTUU	PULL UP STAKES	AGGGILLNRSTY	STRAGGLINGLY
AEKLMNNOOPRT	MEROPLANKTON	AGGHHLOPPRYY	GLYPHOGRAPHY
AELLLMORSUVY	MARVELLOUSLY	AGGHHMOPPRSY	SPHYGMOGRAPH
AELLMMNNOTUY	MONUMENTALLY	AGGHIIKLNPRT	PARKING LIGHT
AELLOOPPSSUY	POLYSEPALOUS	AGGHIIKNNSTV	THANKSGIVING
AELLOOPPSTUY	POLYPETALOUS	AGGHIIMNNRST	HAMSTRINGING
AELMNOOOPSSU	MONOSEPALOUS	AGGHILMNNRSY	RHYMING SLANG
AELMNOOOPSTU	MONOPETALOUS	AGGHILOOPRST	GRAPHOLOGIST
AELMORSSSTUY	SOLAR SYSTEMS	AGGHLNOOPRYY	PHARYNGOLOGY
AELMPRSSTYYY	MYSTERY PLAYS	AGGHLOOPRSSY	GLOSSOGRAPHY
AELNNNOPRSTW	TOWN PLANNERS	AGGHLOPPRTYY	GLYPTOGRAPHY
AELOOPRSTTUX	EXPOSTULATOR	AGGIIIILLNNTV	INVIGILATING
AEMMORRSSUVY	SUMMER SAVORY	AGGIIIMNSTTZ	STIGMATIZING
AEMNNOORSSTY	STONEMASONRY	AGGIIINNORTV	INVIGORATING
AEMNOOOPRSTZ	SPERMATOZOON	AGGIINNOPRSW	GROWING PAINS
AEMNOOOPRSZZ	MEZZO-SOPRANO	AGGIKLLNOOSS	LOOKING GLASS
AEMNOORRRSTT	REMONSTRATOR	AGGIKMNOORST	MAGNITOGORSK
AEMNOQSSSSUU	SQUAMOUSNESS	AGGILMNOPRTU	PROMULGATING
AEMPRRSSTTUU	SUPERSTRATUM	AGGILNOOORST	ORGANOLOGIST
AENNOOPRSSSS	PARSON'S NOSES	AGGINOPSSSTT	STAGING POSTS
AENOOPRSSSUV	VAPOROUSNESS	AGHHILNOPRTT	TRIPHTHONGAL
AENOPRRRSSTT	TRANSPORTERS	AGHHIOOPPRSY	PHYSIOGRAPHY
AENORRSTTTUY	STERNUTATORY	AGHHOOPPSTUY	PHYTOPHAGOUS
AEOOPPPRRSTY	PARTY POOPERS	AGHIILMNPSTY	LYMPHANGITIS
AEOPPRRSSTTU	SUPRAPROTEST	AGHIIMNPSTYZ	SYMPATHIZING
AEOPPRRSSTTVY	POVERTY TRAPS	AGHIINOPPRTU	UPRIGHT PIANO
AFFGILNOOTTU	FOOT FAULTING	AGHILMNOOOOT	HOMOLOGATION
AFFHILLNTUUY	UNFAITHFULLY	AGHILNOOSSTT	ANTHOLOGISTS

AGHILOOPSSTT	PATHOLOGISTS	AGLMOOPRRSTU	PROMULGATORS
AGHINOOPRSTT	TRAPSHOOTING	AHHIILMOPSTT	OPHTHALMITIS
AGHINOORSSTT	SHOOTING STAR	AHHILLLLSSYY	SHILLY-SHALLY
AGHINOPRSSTT	PARTING SHOTS	AHHILLMMOOST	HOMOTHALLISM
AGHIOPPSSYYZ	ZYGAPOPHYSIS	AHHILNOPPRTY	PHILANTHROPY
AGHLLMOOPSUY	GAMOPHYLLOUS	AHHINNOPRSTT	STROPHANTHIN
AGHLNOOOPRTY	ANTHROPOLOGY	AHHNOPRSSTTU	STROPHANTHUS
AGHMNOOPRTYY	PHARYNGOTOMY	AHIIILMNOSTU	HUMILIATIONS
AGIIIILMNRTZ	MILITARIZING	AHIIMNNOORSU	INHARMONIOUS
AGIIIILNNOTV	INVIGILATION	AHIKLOORTTUW	KILOWATT-HOUR
AGIIIILNRTVZ	TRIVIALIZING	AHILLMMOOPRS	ALLOMORPHISM
AGIIILLMNNTU	ILLUMINATING	AHILLNOORTYZ	HORIZONTALLY
AGIIILLMNSST	MAILING LISTS	AHILMNOORSUY	HARMONIOUSLY
AGIIILNNOPST	OIL PAINTINGS	AHILMNPRTTUY	TRIUMPHANTLY
AGIIILNORSTV	INVIGILATORS	AHILMOOOPRTY	HOMOPOLARITY
AGIIILNSSTTW	WAITING LISTS	AHILNOPRSTUU	SULPHURATION
AGIIINNOORTV	INVIGORATION	AHIMOOOPPPSTU	HIPPOPOTAMUS
AGIIINNOPRTT	PARTITIONING	AHIMOOOPPRSTT	HAPTOTROPISM
AGIIINOPPRTT	PROPITIATING	AHIMOOPPRSTU	AMPHITROPOUS
AGIIKLNNOPTT	TALKING POINT	AHINNOPRSSTU	SINANTHROPUS
AGIILLLMNTUU	MULTILINGUAL	AHINOOPSSSTU	SOUSAPHONIST
AGIILLLNRTUY	TRILINGUALLY	AHINOOPSSSTX	SAXOPHONISTS
AGIILLMNORYZ	MORALIZINGLY	AHINOOPSSTUY	AUTOHYPNOSIS
AGIILLNORTUV	OUTRIVALLING	AHINORRSSSTY	SYNARTHROSIS
AGIILLNRSTTU	ILLUSTRATING	AHKLLNNOOOPT	HOLOPLANKTON
AGIILLOPSSSS	SALPIGLOSSIS	AHNOOOPRRTTY	PROTHONOTARY
AGIILMNNRTUY	RUMINATINGLY	AIIIIMMNNOST	MINIMISATION
AGIILNNSSTUY	SUSTAININGLY	AIIIIMMNNOTZ	MINIMIZATION
AGIILNOORSUV	VAINGLORIOUS	AIIILLMNNOTU	ILLUMINATION
AGIILNOPPRUZ	POPULARIZING	AIIILLNNOSTT	INSTILLATION
AGIIMNNRSTTT	TRANSMITTING	AIIILMNOOSST	ISOLATIONISM
AGIIMNOORSTW	WAITING ROOMS	AIIILMPRSSTU	SPIRITUALISM
AGIINNOOPPRT	APPORTIONING	AIIILNOOSSTT	ISOLATIONIST
AGIKMNNOORWW	WORKINGWOMAN	AIIILPRSSTTU	SPIRITUALIST
AGIKNOPRRTWY	WORKING PARTY	AIIILPRSTTUY	SPIRITUALITY
AGILLNOOPSTY	PALYNOLOGIST	AIIIMMNNOSTU	IMMUNISATION
AGILMNNSSUUY	UNASSUMINGLY	AIIIMMNNOTUZ	IMMUNIZATION
AGILMNOOOOSY	ONOMASIOLOGY	AIIIMNNORSTT	MINISTRATION
AGILMNOOPRTU	PROMULGATION	AIIIMNOOPSTT	OPTIMISATION
AGILMOOOSSTT	SOMATOLOGIST	AIIIMNOOPTTZ	OPTIMIZATION
AGILNNNNOPTW	TOWN PLANNING	AIIIMNRSSTTU	MINIATURISTS
AGILNNOOOPRT	PROLONGATION	AIIINNNOOSTU	UNIONISATION
AGILNPRSSSUY	SURPASSINGLY	AIIINNNOOTUZ	UNIONIZATION
AGILORSTTUUY	GRATUITOUSLY	AIIINNNOSSTU	INSINUATIONS
AGIMNOORSSTT	GASTRONOMIST	AIIINNOPRSST	INSPIRATIONS
AGINNOPRRSST	APRON STRINGS	AIIINOOPPRTT	PROPITIATION
AGINNOPRRSTT	TRANSPORTING	AIIINOPRRTTT	TRIPARTITION
AGINNRRSSSTU	SATURN'S RINGS	AIIKLRSSTUVV	SURVIVAL KITS
AGINOOOPRRST	PROROGATIONS	AIILLNNOOTUV	INVOLUTIONAL
AGINOOPRSSTT	PROTAGONISTS	AIILLNORSTTU	ILLUSTRATION
AGINOPRSSTTT	STARTING POST	AIILLNQRTTUY	TRANQUILLITY
AGLLNOORSUUY	LANGUOROUSLY	AIILMNNNOOTU	MOUNTAIN LION
AGLLOOPSSTTT	GLOTTAL STOPS	AIILMNNORTTU	MALNUTRITION
AGLMMNOOOSUY	MONOGAMOUSLY	AIILNNOTTUUV	INVULTUATION

AIILNOOOPPST	OPPOSITIONAL
AIILNOPSSTTU	STIPULATIONS
AIILNORRSSST	SINISTRORSAL
AIILNORRSTTY	TRANSITORILY
AIIMMNSSSTTU	NUMISMATISTS
AIIMNORRSSST	TRANSMISSION
AIIMNOOORSTT	MOTORISATION
AIIMNOOORTTZ	MOTORIZATION
AIIMNOOPRSSU	PARSIMONIOUS
AIIMNOOPRSTT	IMPORTATIONS
AIIMNOOQSTTU	MISQUOTATION
AIIMOOPPRRRT	IMPROPRIATOR
AIINNOOOPSST	OPSONISATION
AIINNOOOPSTZ	OPSONIZATION
AIIOOPPRRTTY	PROPITIATORY
AIKNOORSSTTW	WORKSTATIONS
AILLMNNOOPRY	PRONOMINALLY
AILLNOOPSTTY	POLYTONALIST
AILLNOOPTTYY	POLYTONALITY
AILLORRSSTTU	ILLUSTRATORS
AILMNORSTUVY	VOLUNTARYISM
AILNOOOPPRRT	PROPORTIONAL
AILNOPPRTUUY	UNPOPULARITY
AILNORSTTUVY	VOLUNTARYIST
AILOOPRRSUUY	UPROARIOUSLY
AILOORRSTTUY	TRAITOROUSLY
AIMNNOOPRSSU	PONS ASINORUM
AIMNNOOPSTTU	MOUNTAINTOPS
AIMOORRRTWWY	TWO-WAY MIRROR
AINOOPRRSSTT	PROSTRATIONS
ALMNOOUSSTUY	AUTONOMOUSLY
ALMNOORSSTTU	SALMON TROUTS
BBBBBEEHLLUU	HUBBLE-BUBBLE
BBCDEEEKNRRU	RUBBERNECKED
BBCEELNOOSST	COBBLESTONES
BBCEILMOSSTU	COMBUSTIBLES
BBCEJKOORSST	STOCKJOBBERS
BBCEJKOORSTY	STOCKJOBBERY
BBCEKLORSSTU	BLOCKBUSTERS
BBCELLLOOSWY	COLLYWOBBLES
BBCELMORSSTU	CLUSTER BOMBS
BBCENOORRSTU	BRONCOBUSTER
BBDDDDEEELOU	DOUBLE-BEDDED
BBDEEEELOSUYY	BLUE-EYED BOYS
BBDEEGGKLOOO	GOBBLEDEGOOK
BBDEEHHLOOSY	HOBBLEDEHOYS
BBDEFFLLOSUU	DOUBLE BLUFFS
BBDEGGKLOOOY	GOBBLEDYGOOK
BBDEGHINRRUY	RUBBER DINGHY
BBDEGHMNOORY	HYDROGEN BOMB
BBDEHLOOORRT	BLOOD BROTHER
BBEEEHLLOTTW	BELOW THE BELT
BBEEGMNORRUY	MONEY-GRUBBER
BBEEILMRSSSU	SUBMERSIBLES

BBEENNNRRSUU	BUNSEN BURNER
BBEGGHIILNOS	BOBSLEIGHING
BBEHIIILLOPS	BIBLIOPHILES
BBEHIILLLOTY	BOIL THE BILLY
BBEHINNOSSSS	SNOBBISHNESS
BBELLNOSTTUY	BELLY BUTTONS
BBEMNNOORSTU	NEUTRON BOMBS
BBENNORSSSTU	STUBBORNNESS
BBHJNNOOOOSS	HOBSON-JOBSON
BCCCEIIMRRSU	CIRCUMSCRIBE
BCCDEEIJORTT	DIRECT OBJECT
BCCEEEEHKRRY	CHECKERBERRY
BCCEEELNOOSS	OBSOLESCENCE
BCCEEHKLMOOR	CHECKERBLOOM
BCCEEHNORRSS	CROSSBENCHER
BCCEEHNORSSS	CROSSBENCHES
BCCEEIIMNNSU	INCUMBENCIES
BCCEFFIKLOOS	OFFICE BLOCKS
BCCEHNOOOPRS	BRONCHOSCOPE
BCCEHORSTTTU	BUTTERSCOTCH
BCCEILOPRSTU	PUBLIC SECTOR
BCCHILLOOPSU	PUBLIC SCHOOL
BCCHIMOORTTY	THROMBOCYTIC
BCCHNOOOPRSY	BRONCHOSCOPY
BCCINOOSSSUU	SUBCONSCIOUS
BCCIOOOPRSST	STROBOSCOPIC
BCCLNORSTUUY	COUNTRY CLUBS
BCDDEEEIINOS	DISOBEDIENCE
BCDDEEEKLORU	DOUBLE-DECKER
BCDDEEIIRSTT	DIRECT DEBITS
BCDDEELLLOOR	RED BLOOD CELL
BCDDEIIILTUY	DEDUCIBILITY
BCDEEEIINNST	BENEDICTINES
BCDEEEKORRST	STOCKBREEDER
BCDEEFHIILNT	CHILD BENEFIT
BCDEEIINNOST	BENEDICTIONS
BCDEEILOPRRU	REPRODUCIBLE
BCDEEILRSTTU	DESTRUCTIBLE
BCDEIIILRTUY	REDUCIBILITY
BCDEIILNORTU	INTRODUCIBLE
BCDEIIMORTTU	OBITER DICTUM
BCDEKLOORSSU	BLOODSUCKERS
BCDGHHIIILTW	BIG WITH CHILD
BCDGIIKMNORS	MOCKINGBIRDS
BCDGIKNOOSTY	BODY STOCKING
BCDGILLLOPSU	BULLDOG CLIPS
BCEEEEEHKNRS	KNEE BREECHES
BCEEEEGHRRSU	CHEESEBURGER
BCEEEEGILLNR	BELLIGERENCE
BCEEEFILNNTY	BENEFICENTLY
BCEEEGILLNRY	BELLIGERENCY
BCEEEINRSSUV	SUBSERVIENCE
BCEEEIRRRSVY	SERVICEBERRY
BCEEELNORTVY	CONVEYER BELT

BCEEFHHNNORRT	FRONTBENCHER	BCHILNOORRTT	BIRTH CONTROL
BCEEFHHNNORST	FRONTBENCHES	BCHNOORSSSTU	HOT-CROSS BUNS
BCEEFILNORSS	FORCIBLENESS	BCIIIILPPRSTU	PUBLIC SPIRIT
BCEEHIIKRRSW	BERWICKSHIRE	BCIINNOORTTU	CONTRIBUTION
BCEEIIIIILMST	IMBECILITIES	BCIINOPRSSTU	SUBSCRIPTION
BCEEIIILLRSTT	BELLETRISTIC	BCILMMNOSUUU	CUMULONIMBUS
BCEEIJLSTUVY	SUBJECTIVELY	BCINOORRSSTU	CONTRIBUTORS
BCEEILMNOPTT	CONTEMPTIBLE	BCINOORRTTUY	CONTRIBUTORY
BCEEILMOPRSS	COMPRESSIBLE	BCINOORSSTTU	OBSTRUCTIONS
BCEEILNORSTV	CONVERTIBLES	BDDDEEFIILNR	BLIND FREDDIE
BCEEIMMOSTTU	SUBCOMMITTEE	BDDDEELOOTTU	DOUBLE-DOTTED
BCEEJLNOOSST	OBJECT LESSON	BDDDEILMNOOY	BLOODY-MINDED
BCEEKLLORSTT	BLOCK LETTERS	BDDEEEEFILMN	FEEBLEMINDED
BCEFFKORSSTU	BUFFER STOCKS	BDDEEEEGNNRR	GENDER-BENDER
BCEFGIIINNOR	FIBRINOGENIC	BDDEEEILMOSW	DISEMBOWELED
BCEFIMNNOORU	UNCIFORM BONE	BDDEEEINNSST	INDEBTEDNESS
BCEFIMOPRTTU	BIT OF CRUMPET	BDDEEENORRUV	OVERBURDENED
BCEFOOORSTUYY	BY COURTESY OF	BDDEEFHIORRS	BEDFORDSHIRE
BCEGHIILNTWY	BEWITCHINGLY	BDDEEILMOSUX	MIXED DOUBLES
BCEGIIILNORR	INCORRIGIBLE	BDDFGIILLNNO	BLINDFOLDING
BCEGIILOOOST	BIOECOLOGIST	BDDFGIILNORY	FORBIDDINGLY
BCEGIKLNOSTU	BLUESTOCKING	BDDFGIMNNOUU	DUMBFOUNDING
BCEHIIMORSTY	BIOCHEMISTRY	BDEEEFIILNNS	INDEFENSIBLE
BCEHIINOSTTY	BIOSYNTHETIC	BDEEEIILRSSV	DISBELIEVERS
BCEHILOPSSUU	PUBLIC HOUSES	BDEEEIIMNOST	BIDE ONE'S TIME
BCEHIMORSTWW	WEST BROMWICH	BDEEEIIMORRS	EMBROIDERIES
BCEIIIILLRTVY	CIVIL LIBERTY	BDEEEIIRSVWY	BIRD'S-EYE VIEW
BCEIIJMSSTUV	SUBJECTIVISM	BDEEEILLNRSU	UNDERBELLIES
BCEIIJSSTTUV	SUBJECTIVIST	BDEEEILMNRTW	BEWILDERMENT
BCEIIJSTTUVY	SUBJECTIVITY	BDEEFIILLNNSY	INDEFENSIBLY
BCEIIKLLNRTU	CLINKER-BUILT	BDEEFIILRSTU	FILIBUSTERED
BCEIIKLMOPRU	KOMI REPUBLIC	BDEEGGHIIRSW	WEIGHBRIDGES
BCEIILNRSTTU	INSTRUCTIBLE	BDEEGHHIINRS	DENBIGHSHIRE
BCEIINORTTUV	CONTRIBUTIVE	BDEEGIIILNST	INDIGESTIBLE
BCEIIPRSSTUV	SUBSCRIPTIVE	BDEEGIIILNSV	DISBELIEVING
BCEIJNSSTUUV	SUBJUNCTIVES	BDEEGIIMMNRS	DISMEMBERING
BCEIKNNRSUWW	NEW BRUNSWICK	BDEEGIIMNORR	EMBROIDERING
BCEIKOOPRSTU	PICTURE BOOKS	BDEEGLNOOTUU	DOUBLE-TONGUE
BCEILLOOPSUY	EBULLIOSCOPY	BDEEHINOSTUU	HEBETUDINOUS
BCEILMNOPTTY	CONTEMPTIBLY	BDEEIIMRRTTU	TURBIDIMETER
BCEILORSSTUU	TUBERCULOSIS	BDEEIIRRSTTU	REDISTRIBUTE
BCEINNNOSTTU	SUBCONTINENT	BDEEILLNPRSS	SPELLBINDERS
BCEKKOOOORSY	COOKERY BOOKS	BDEEIMNRSSTU	DISBURSEMENT
BCEKKOORRSST	STOCKBROKERS	BDEEINNORSTV	INVERTED SNOB
BCEOOOPRSSST	STROBOSCOPES	BDEELLOOSSSV	BLOOD VESSELS
BCERRSSTTUUU	SUBSTRUCTURE	BDEELMRRSTUY	TUMBLE-DRYERS
BCFIIILNORTY	FIBRINOLYTIC	BDEFHNOOORTU	DEBT OF HONOUR
BCGIIILMNNOR	CLIMBING IRON	BDEGGGILNRUY	BEGRUDGINGLY
BCGIIILNORRY	INCORRIGIBLY	BDEGHHOORRTU	THOROUGHBRED
BCGIILMOOORY	MICROBIOLOGY	BDEGIIILLNSTY	INDIGESTIBLY
BCGIINNORTTU	CONTRIBUTING	BDEGIILLNNPS	SPELLBINDING
BCGIINOOOSTT	GNOTOBIOTICS	BDEGIILNORWZ	BOWDLERIZING
BCHHIMOOORRT	ORTHORHOMBIC	BDEGILLNNRUY	BLUNDERINGLY
BCHIIIOPSSTY	BIOPHYSICIST	BDEGILLNOOTT	BLOODLETTING

BDEGILMNRTUY	TUMBLE-DRYING
BDEHHMNOOORR	RHOMBOHEDRON
BDEHHOOORRST	BROTHERHOODS
BDEHIILPRSSU	SHIPBUILDERS
BDEHLNORSTTU	THUNDERBOLTS
BDEHMOOORRTU	MOUTHBROODER
BDEIIIILLNTY	INDELIBILITY
BDEIIIRSTTUV	DISTRIBUTIVE
BDEIILLNOSSU	INDISSOLUBLE
BDEIINNRSTUW	WIND TURBINES
BDEILLLNORRS	ROLLER BLINDS
BDEIMMNOPRSU	PREMIUM BONDS
BDFGHILLOOSW	GOLDFISH BOWL
BDFIILMNNUUU	INFUNDIBULUM
BDGGGIILMNNO	MIND-BOGGLING
BDGHIIILNPSU	SHIPBUILDING
BDGHIIMMNRSU	HUMMINGBIRDS
BDGIIIIILRTY	DIRIGIBILITY
BDGIIINRSTTU	DISTRIBUTING
BDGIILNOSTUU	OUTBUILDINGS
BDHILOORSTTY	BLOODTHIRSTY
BDIIIIILSTVY	DIVISIBILITY
BDIIILLNOSUY	LIBIDINOUSLY
BDIIINORSTTU	DISTRIBUTION
BDIIINOSSSUV	SUBDIVISIONS
BDIILLNOSSUY	INDISSOLUBLY
BDIIORRSSTTU	DISTRIBUTORS
BDKNNNOOOSUW	KNOW NO BOUNDS
BEEEEEFLMNNT	ENFEEBLEMENT
BEEEEEFHINORR	HEREINBEFORE
BEEEEHILPRSS	PEEBLESSHIRE
BEEEELMMNTZZ	EMBEZZLEMENT
BEEEEOQSSUXZ	SQUEEZEBOXES
BEEEGILLNRST	BELLIGERENTS
BEEEGIMNPRSU	SUPREME BEING
BEEEGIOORRSS	GOOSEBERRIES
BEEEHHRRSTTU	THERE'S THE RUB
BEEEHIINNRTT	TEREBINTHINE
BEEEEHLNOOPTX	TELEPHONE BOX
BEEEHNNNOOPZ	BENZOPHENONE
BEEEIILNNSTX	INEXTENSIBLE
BEEEIILRRRSV	IRREVERSIBLE
BEEEILLMNTTT	BELITTLEMENT
BEEEILNNSSSS	SENSIBLENESS
BEEEILNRRSST	TERRIBLENESS
BEEEIMMNRTTT	EMBITTERMENT
BEEEINNNORTZ	NITROBENZENE
BEEEIPRRSSTY	PRESBYTERIES
BEEELLNNOTVY	BENEVOLENTLY
BEEELMNOSTTU	TOUT ENSEMBLE
BEEELNOOSSST	OBSOLETENESS
BEEENOPPRSTY	TEENYBOPPERS
BEEFGIINNRRT	BIREFRINGENT
BEEFIILRRSTU	FILIBUSTERER

BEEFILMNNOOT	BLOEMFONTEIN
BEEGGILNNORW	BOWLING GREEN
BEEGGHHILLRST	SHE'LL BE RIGHT
BEEGHIILLMNS	EMBELLISHING
BEEGHINNORRS	HERRINGBONES
BEEGHOOPRRTU	PETERBOROUGH
BEEGIIILLLNT	INTELLIGIBLE
BEEGIINNSSTT	BESETTING SIN
BEEGLOORRTTT	GLOBETROTTER
BEEHIIINORTX	EXHIBITIONER
BEEHILLLRSVY	BEVERLY HILLS
BEEHILNORRSS	HORRIBLENESS
BEEHLMNORSUW	WHOLE NUMBERS
BEEHLORRRTWY	WHORTLEBERRY
BEEHOPRRSSTT	STEPBROTHERS
BEEIIILMRRSS	IRREMISSIBLE
BEEIIIILRRSST	IRRESISTIBLE
BEEIIKLNSSSU	BUSINESSLIKE
BEEIILRRRSVY	IRREVERSIBLY
BEEILLLORSUY	REBELLIOUSLY
BEEILLRRRSTU	BULL TERRIERS
BEEILPPRSSSU	SUPPRESSIBLE
BEEILRSSUVVY	SUBVERSIVELY
BEEIMMNPRRSU	PRIME NUMBERS
BEEINNNOOQUZ	BENZOQUINONE
BEEINNORRTUW	WINTERBOURNE
BEEINOSSSTWX	WITNESS BOXES
BEEKOOPRRRSW	POWER BROKERS
BEELLORSSTUY	TROLLEYBUSES
BEELNNOSSSUU	NEBULOUSNESS
BEELNQSSTUUY	SUBSEQUENTLY
BEEOOPRRSSTU	OBSTREPEROUS
BEFGHIINRRSU	REFURBISHING
BEFGHILLRSTU	BULLFIGHTERS
BEFHINNOOORS	ONE FOR HIS NOB
BEFHLMORSTUU	RULES OF THUMB
BEFILLNSSSSU	BLISSFULNESS
BEFILMOPRSUU	PLUMBIFEROUS
BEGGHIINNORU	NEIGHBOURING
BEGHILORSSTT	STROBE LIGHTS
BEGIIIILLLTY	ILLEGIBILITY
BEGIIILLLNTY	INTELLIGIBLY
BEGIILLLNTTY	BELITTLINGLY
BEGIILLNRSTY	BLISTERINGLY
BEGIILOOOSTX	EXOBIOLOGIST
BEGIINORRSVW	VIRGIN'S-BOWER
BEGILLMNRSUY	SLUMBERINGLY
BEGILLNORSTY	BOLSTERINGLY
BEGILLNRSTUY	BLUSTERINGLY
BEGILMOORSTY	EMBRYOLOGIST
BEGILNPRRTUY	PERTURBINGLY
BEGIMNNORTUU	OUTNUMBERING
BEGIMNNORRSTT	BRING TO TERMS
BEHHOORSSTTU	TOOTHBRUSHES

BEHIIIMNSTTU	BISMUTHINITE	CCCEEILMNOTY	METONIC CYCLE
BEHIINOSSSTY	BIOSYNTHESIS	CCCEEILNNOTU	NOCTILUCENCE
BEHILMOOPSTT	PHLEBOTOMIST	CCCEENNORRSU	CONCURRENCES
BEHINOSSSSUW	SHOW BUSINESS	CCCEHINOPRTT	CONCERT PITCH
BEHLOORRSSTU	SOUL BROTHERS	CCCEILOOTTUY	LEUCOCYTOTIC
BEIIIILRRSSTY	IRRESISTIBLY	CCCEINNOPSTU	CONCUPISCENT
BEIILLORSTUY	RESOLUBILITY	CCCEINNSSSTU	SUCCINCTNESS
BEIILMMMOPRU	PRIMUM MOBILE	CCCEIOOPRSTT	STREPTOCOCCI
BEIILMSSSUVY	SUBMISSIVELY	CCCEMNOOPSUU	PNEUMOCOCCUS
BEIINNOOPRTW	BROWNIE POINT	CCCGIIIMNRSU	CIRCUMCISING
BEIINSSSSTTU	BUSINESS SUIT	CCCHHHIRRSTU	CHRISTCHURCH
BEIISSTTTUUV	SUBSTITUTIVE	CCCHIIORSTTY	TRICHOCYSTIC
BEILLOORSSTT	STILBOESTROL	CCCHINOOOPRS	CHRONOSCOPIC
BEILOOQSSUUY	OBSEQUIOUSLY	CCCIIIMNORSU	CIRCUMCISION
BEILOORSSTUY	BOISTEROUSLY	CCCIIIMORRTU	MICROCIRCUIT
BEILOPPRSTUU	PURPOSE-BUILT	CCDDDEEEENNOS	CONDESCENDED
BELMNOOPRYYY	POLYEMBRYONY	CCDDEEINNOST	DISCONNECTED
BELOOPRSSTTU	TROUBLE SPOTS	CCDDEEINORST	DISCONCERTED
BFFIIIILLMORR	FIBRILLIFORM	CCDDEIMNNOSTU	MISCONDUCTED
BFGGHIILLNTU	BULLFIGHTING	CCDEEEEILNST	DELITESCENCE
BFGHIILLORST	BILL OF RIGHTS	CCDEEEEMNSTU	DETUMESCENCE
BFIIIILNSTUY	INFUSIBILITY	CCDEEEFIIINS	DEFICIENCIES
BFIIILNNORSY	FIBRINOLYSIN	CCDEEEFIILNV	CIVIL DEFENCE
BFIIILNORSSY	FIBRINOLYSIS	CCDEEEFNNORS	FRONDESCENCE
BGGHHLOOORUU	LOUGHBOROUGH	CCDEEEHIINNS	INDEHISCENCE
BGHIILLNSTTU	BULLSHITTING	CCDEEEHIPRST	DIRECT SPEECH
BGHIINOPPSWY	WHIPPING BOYS	CCDEEEHNOSTU	ESCUTCHEONED
BGHILLNOOOPT	POLLING BOOTH	CCDEEEIINRSV	VIRIDESCENCE
BGHILNNOOTTU	BUTTONHOLING	CCDEEEINOPRV	PRECONCEIVED
BGIIIILMMNOZ	IMMOBILIZING	CCDEEELORTTU	ELECTROCUTED
BGIIILNNOOPT	BOILING POINT	CCDEEFIINNNO	IN CONFIDENCE
BGIILMNSTTUY	SUBMITTINGLY	CCDEEGILNSUY	SUCCEEDINGLY
BGIILNSSSTUY	SUBSISTINGLY	CCDEEIIINSST	INSECTICIDES
BGIINSSTTTUU	SUBSTITUTING	CCDEEIIMNOSV	MISCONCEIVED
BGILLORSUUUY	LUGUBRIOUSLY	CCDEEILRRSSS	DRESS CIRCLES
BHIIINOOPRST	PROHIBITIONS	CCDEEIMNRTUV	CIRCUMVENTED
BIIIIILNSTVY	INVISIBILITY	CCDEEINNORST	DISCONNECTER
BIIILLNOSTUY	INSOLUBILITY	CCDEEIORRTTU	CORRECTITUDE
BIIKOOORSSTV	VISITORS' BOOK	CCDEELOOPPRS	CLOSE-CROPPED
BIILOQSTUUUY	UBIQUITOUSLY	CCDEGIMNNOOS	SECOND COMING
BIINOSSTTTUU	SUBSTITUTION	CCDEHIIINNNO	CINCHONIDINE
CCCCEEENNORS	CONCRESCENCE	CCDEIIIIRSTV	RECIDIVISTIC
CCCCEHINOOSU	ECHINOCOCCUS	CCDEIMNOORSS	MICROSECONDS
CCCCHHIOPRTU	COPTIC CHURCH	CCDEINNOOSSU	SECOND COUSIN
CCCCKKLOOOSU	CUCKOO CLOCKS	CCDEIORRSSSS	CRISSCROSSED
CCCDEEHKORSS	CROSSCHECKED	CCDHHILOORRY	HYDROCHLORIC
CCCDEEIINNOS	COINCIDENCES	CCDHIOORSTTW	WITCHDOCTORS
CCCDEEILNOPY	ENCYCLOPEDIC	CCDIINOTTUVY	CONDUCTIVITY
CCCDEIIORSTY	CYSTICERCOID	CCDNNNOOOORTU	NONCONDUCTOR
CCCDHIIOOPRS	DICHROSCOPIC	CCEEEEILLNSY	EXCELLENCIES
CCCEEEEENRSSX	EXCRESCENCES	CCEEEEILLRSTY	ELECTRIC EYES
CCCEEHILORTY	HETEROCYCLIC	CCEEEEINPRST	CENTREPIECES
CCCEEHKNORTU	COUNTERCHECK	CCEEEEJNNSUV	JUVENESCENCE
CCCEEIINRTTY	ECCENTRICITY	CCEEEFHHRRSU	FREE CHURCHES

CCEEEFHIKNRS	NECKERCHIEFS
CCEEEFLNORSU	FLUORESCENCE
CCEEEGIIMNST	MISCEGENETIC
CCEEEGNNORSV	CONVERGENCES
CCEEEHIIMNPY	CHIMNEYPIECE
CCEEEHINOSTT	COENESTHETIC
CCEEEHKLLPRS	SPELLCHECKER
CCEEEHOOPRRT	PORTE-COCHERE
CCEEEIIMNNRS	REMINISCENCE
CCEEEILLORTV	RECOLLECTIVE
CCEEEILMNNRT	ENCIRCLEMENT
CCEEEILMNNSU	LUMINESCENCE
CCEEEILOPRST	SECRET POLICE
CCEEEIMNNOPT	INCOMPETENCE
CCEEEIMNNSU	INTUMESCENCE
CCEEEINNNOST	CONSENTIENCE
CCEEEINNNOSV	CONVENIENCES
CCEEEINORSSV	COERCIVENESS
CCEEELOOPRST	ELECTROSCOPE
CCEEEMMMNNOT	COMMENCEMENT
CCEEENNOQSSU	CONSEQUENCES
CCEEFFIIINNY	INEFFICIENCY
CCEEFFIINOST	COEFFICIENTS
CCEEFHIIJSTU	CHIEF JUSTICE
CCEEFINNOORT	CONFECTIONER
CCEEGGILNOTU	GLUCOGENETIC
CCEEGGILNOTY	GLYCOGENETIC
CCEEGILLNORT	RECOLLECTING
CCEEGILLOOSY	ECCLESIOLOGY
CCEEGINOSTTY	CYTOGENETICS
CCEEGNOORRST	CONCERTGOERS
CCEEHHILOSTV	CLOVE HITCHES
CCEEHHIMOPRS	CHEMOSPHERIC
CCEEHIIILNORT	HELIOCENTRIC
CCEEHIMOSTYZ	SCHIZOMYCETE
CCEEHINNORTT	ETHNOCENTRIC
CCEEHINNOSTU	INESCUTCHEON
CCEEHKLLLOSS	COCKLESHELLS
CCEEHKLOORST	ELECTROSHOCK
CCEEHLMOORSU	COLOUR SCHEME
CCEEHOPRRRTY	HYPERCORRECT
CCEEIIIILRSVV	CIVIL SERVICE
CCEEIILLOSTV	COLLECTIVISE
CCEEIILLOTVZ	COLLECTIVIZE
CCEEIILOOPTU	LEUCOPOIETIC
CCEEIIMNORSV	MISCONCEIVER
CCEEIINNNNOT	INCONTINENCE
CCEEIILLLOTVY	COLLECTIVELY
CCEEIILLNOORT	RECOLLECTION
CCEEIILLORTTY	ELECTROLYTIC
CCEEIILMORRST	SCLEROMETRIC
CCEEIILNNOSTV	CONVENTICLES
CCEEIILNOORTT	ELECTROTONIC
CCEEIILOPRRTY	PYROELECTRIC
CCEEIILORRTVY	CORRECTIVELY
CCEEIILPPRSTU	PEPTIC ULCERS
CCEEIILSSSUVY	SUCCESSIVELY
CCEEIMNOORST	ECONOMETRICS
CCEEIMNRRTUV	CIRCUMVENTER
CCEEIMNRSSTU	MUSIC CENTRES
CCEEINNNORTT	INTERCONNECT
CCEEIOOPRSST	STEREOSCOPIC
CCEENOPSSSTU	CONSPECTUSES
CCEEOOPPRSST	SPECTROSCOPE
CCEFHINOORSU	CONCHIFEROUS
CCEFIIINNSTU	UNSCIENTIFIC
CCEFLLSSSUUY	SUCCESSFULLY
CCEFLNSSSUUU	UNSUCCESSFUL
CCEGGINNNOOR	GOING CONCERN
CCEGHIINORTT	RICOCHETTING
CCEGHIKNOPST	SPOT-CHECKING
CCEGIILNOPRS	CLOSING PRICE
CCEGIJNNORTU	CONJECTURING
CCEGINOPPRUY	PREOCCUPYING
CCEHHIILMOOR	HELIOCHROMIC
CCEHIILLNOPU	NUCLEOPHILIC
CCEHIIMORSTT	STICHOMETRIC
CCEHIINOORRT	RHINOCEROTIC
CCEHIKLOSSTT	LOCKSTITCHES
CCEHILNOPSTY	POLYTECHNICS
CCEHIMNOORRT	CHRONOMETRIC
CCEHIMOOPRST	THERMOSCOPIC
CCEHIMOPRSTY	PSYCHOMETRIC
CCEHINOOSSTU	COCONUT SHIES
CCEHINOPRSTY	PYROTECHNICS
CCEHIOOPSSTT	STETHOSCOPIC
CCEHIORRTTYY	ERYTHROCYTIC
CCEHKLOSSTTU	SHUTTLECOCKS
CCEHLOOSTTUY	HECTOCOTYLUS
CCEHNOOPRSSY	SYNCHROSCOPE
CCEIIIMMORSS	MICROSEISMIC
CCEIIIINOORRT	ONEIROCRITIC
CCEIIKKSTTWY	STICKY WICKET
CCEIIKNSSSTT	STICK INSECTS
CCEIILLMOSTV	COLLECTIVISM
CCEIILLOSTTV	COLLECTIVIST
CCEIILLOTTVY	COLLECTIVITY
CCEIILMOORRT	COLORIMETRIC
CCEIILNNOSUV	INCONCLUSIVE
CCEIILPRSTUU	PISCICULTURE
CCEIILRRTTUU	CITRICULTURE
CCEIIMOOPSSS	SEISMOSCOPIC
CCEIINNOSSSU	IN SUCCESSION
CCEIINOOPRST	RETINOSCOPIC
CCEIINORSTTV	CONSTRICTIVE
CCEIINOSSTTU	VISCOUNTCIES
CCEIJNNOSTUV	CONJUNCTIVES
CCEIILLNOSUVY	CONCLUSIVELY

CCEILLOOOPSS	OSCILLOSCOPE
CCEILMNORSUU	MICRONUCLEUS
CCEILOOPRSUY	PRECOCIOUSLY
CCEILOOSSTUY	LEUCOCYTOSIS
CCEINNOPRRSW	CROWN PRINCES
CCEINNOSTTUY	CONSTITUENCY
CCEINOOPRSSU	PRECONSCIOUS
CCEINORSSSST	CROSS-SECTION
CCEINORSTTUV	CONSTRUCTIVE
CCEIORRSSSSS	CRISSCROSSES
CCEJNNORSTUU	CONJUNCTURES
CCELNNORRTUY	CONCURRENTLY
CCENORRRSSTU	CROSSCURRENT
CCEOOOPRRSSTY	SPECTROSCOPY
CCFGGHIIKNOT	COCKFIGHTING
CCFIIMNORSUU	CIRCUMFUSION
CCFILMORSUUU	CIRCUMFLUOUS
CCFILOOOPRSU	FLUOROSCOPIC
CCGHHIILOOTY	ICHTHYOLOGIC
CCGHILNOOOST	CONCHOLOGIST
CCGIILNNNOVY	CONVINCINGLY
CCGIINNNNOUV	UNCONVINCING
CCGIINNOPRST	CONSCRIPTING
CCGIINNORSTT	CONSTRICTING
CCGILLNOSTYY	CYCLOSTYLING
CCGINNORSTTU	CONSTRUCTING
CCHHIIMOSTYZ	SCHIZOTHYMIC
CCHHIIOPSTYZ	SCHIZOPHYTIC
CCHHIKOSSTWY	SCOTCH WHISKY
CCHHILOOORSS	CHOIR SCHOOLS
CCHHIMOOOPRR	CHROMOPHORIC
CCHIIILNOPSS	SILICON CHIPS
CCHIILNOOPRR	CHLOROPICRIN
CCHIIMOPRSSY	MICROPHYSICS
CCHIIORRSTTU	SHORT CIRCUIT
CCHIORSSSTUU	HORTUS SICCUS
CCIILNNNOOSU	IN CONCLUSION
CCIILNOPRUVY	PRIVY COUNCIL
CCIILORSTUUY	CIRCUITOUSLY
CCIIMOOPRSST	MICROSCOPIST
CCIINNOOPRST	CONSCRIPTION
CCIINNOORSTT	CONSTRICTION
CCIJNNNOOSTU	CONJUNCTIONS
CCILMOORSTTY	MOTORCYCLIST
CCILMORRSUUU	CIRROCUMULUS
CCIMNOOPSTUU	COMPUNCTIOUS
CCINNOOPRSTU	CONSTRUCTION
CCINOORRSSTT	CONSTRICTORS
CCINOORRSSTTU	CONSTRUCTORS
CCNOORRRSSTTU	CROSS-COUNTRY
CCNOORSTTUUY	COUNTY COURTS
CDDDEEFIIOST	EISTEDDFODIC
CDDDELLLMOOY	MOLLYCODDLED
CDDEEEEGNORS	SECOND-DEGREE

CDDEEEEINNNP	INDEPENDENCE
CDDEEEEINNPS	DEPENDENCIES
CDDEEEEJNSST	DEJECTEDNESS
CDDEEEHMNOPR	COMPREHENDED
CDDEEEINNNPY	INDEPENDENCY
CDDEEEINORRS	RECONSIDERED
CDDEEEIRRSTT	DERESTRICTED
CDDEEELNSSSU	SECLUDEDNESS
CDDEEEMOPRSS	DECOMPRESSED
CDDEEHLNNOSU	NONSCHEDULED
CDDEEIJNPRUU	UNPREJUDICED
CDDEEILMORSU	MIDDLE COURSE
CDDEEINNORSU	UNCONSIDERED
CDDEEINNOSTT	DISCONTENTED
CDDEELLNOORT	DECONTROLLED
CDDEENOOPRRS	CORRESPONDED
CDDEFIIKLSST	FIDDLESTICKS
CDDEFLNNOOUY	CONFOUNDEDLY
CDDEGIIINRST	DISCREDITING
CDDEHIILMNRS	CHILDMINDERS
CDDEHILLMOOS	MIDDLE SCHOOL
CDDEHILNOSSS	CLODDISHNESS
CDDEHLLOORSU	COLD SHOULDER
CDDEHLNORTUU	THUNDERCLOUD
CDDEIINNOSTU	DISCONTINUED
CDDEIKOPSSTT	SPOTTED DICKS
CDDEILNOOPRS	SCOLOPENDRID
CDDGHIIILMNN	CHILDMINDING
CDDGHIILOPRY	CHILD PRODIGY
CDDGIIMMNOOS	DISCOMMODING
CDDIIMMOOSTY	DISCOMMODITY
CDEEEEIILMNT	TELEMEDICINE
CDEEEEIINNPX	INEXPEDIENCE
CDEEEEIKLPRW	PICKERELWEED
CDEEEEILLRVW	WELL-RECEIVED
CDEEEELNNPRS	RESPLENDENCE
CDEEEFFGINOR	FORCE-FEEDING
CDEEEFFIINNR	INDIFFERENCE
CDEEEFHILRST	CHESTERFIELD
CDEEEFHORSUV	CHEFS D'OEUVRE
CDEEEGIKLNRS	SINGLE-DECKER
CDEEEHIMNPRT	DECIPHERMENT
CDEEEHNRSSTW	WRETCHEDNESS
CDEEEIINNSST	DISSENTIENCE
CDEEEIINORST	DECISION TREE
CDEEEIINPRSS	PRESIDENCIES
CDEEEIINSSSV	DECISIVENESS
CDEEEIIOPPRS	PERIOD PIECES
CDEEEILMNORT	DECLINOMETER
CDEEEILNQSTU	DELIQUESCENT
CDEEEILORRST	CLERESTORIED
CDEEEILORSTT	LIE DETECTORS
CDEEEIMNORTT	MINE DETECTOR
CDEEEINNNORS	NONRESIDENCE

CDEEEINRSSST	DISCREETNESS, DISCRETENESS
CDEEELMMNOPT	COMPLEMENTED
CDEEEMNNNOTU	DENOUNCEMENT
CDEEEOPRRSSS	PREDECESSORS
CDEEFFHILOOR	OFFICEHOLDER
CDEEFFHOORRT	OFF-THE-RECORD
CDEEFFIMNOOT	DOMINO EFFECT
CDEEFFNOSSTU	SOUND EFFECTS
CDEEFILNNNUU	UNINFLUENCED
CDEEFLLOORSU	SELF-COLOURED
CDEEFLRSSTTU	SELF-DESTRUCT
CDEEGHILNRSU	RESCHEDULING
CDEEGIILRRTY	TRIGLYCERIDE
CDEEGIKNOPRR	PECKING ORDER
CDEEGIMMNNOR	RECOMMENDING
CDEEGINNORSU	UNRECOGNISED
CDEEGINNORUZ	UNRECOGNIZED
CDEEGINOPRRR	PRERECORDING
CDEEHHKLLOSS	SHELLSHOCKED
CDEEHILLNORV	LOVECHILDREN
CDEEHILNPRST	STEPCHILDREN
CDEEHIOQSSTU	DISCOTHEQUES
CDEEHKLNOSUY	HONEYSUCKLED
CDEEHLNORSTU	UNDERCLOTHES
CDEEHORSTTTU	OUTSTRETCHED
CDEEIIIILNSVY	INDECISIVELY
CDEEIIILOPST	DEPOLITICISE
CDEEIIILOPTZ	DEPOLITICIZE
CDEEIIIMORST	MEDIOCRITIES
CDEEIIINNOST	DENICOTINISE
CDEEIIINNOTZ	DENICOTINIZE
CDEEIIINNSTV	DISINCENTIVE
CDEEIIINRTTV	INTERDICTIVE
CDEEIIILNOPRT	PREDILECTION
CDEEIIILNORST	DERELICTIONS
CDEEIIILNRSTY	INDISCREETLY
CDEEIIILPRTVY	PREDICTIVELY
CDEEIIMNOPRV	IMPROVIDENCE
CDEEIINNNRST	INDIRECTNESS
CDEEILMMNOPT	COMPLIMENTED
CDEEILNOOOTV	DO VIOLENCE TO
CDEEILRRSTTY	RESTRICTEDLY
CDEEIMMNOOXY	MIXED ECONOMY
CDEEIMOPRSTU	COMPUTERISED
CDEEIMOPRTUZ	COMPUTERIZED
CDEEINNOORRT	RECONNOITRED
CDEEINNOPRSTV	OPEN VERDICTS
CDEEINRRSTTU	UNRESTRICTED
CDEEIOPRRTUV	REPRODUCTIVE
CDEEIORRSTUV	DISCOVERTURE
CDEEIRRRSSVW	SCREWDRIVERS
CDEELOOORRSU	ROSE-COLOURED
CDEENNOOPRSS	SECOND PERSON
CDEENNOOPRST	CORESPONDENT

CDEENNRRRTUU	UNDERCURRENT
CDEEOORRRSSS	CROSS-DRESSER
CDEERRRSTTUU	RESTRUCTURED
CDEFFIIILLSTU	DIFFICULTIES
CDEFGIIINNST	DISINFECTING
CDEFHLMOOORR	CHLOROFORMED
CDEFIIINNOST	DISINFECTION
CDEFIIMORSTU	DISCOMFITURE
CDEFKLOOOTUW	OUT OF WEDLOCK
CDEGIIMNRST	MISDIRECTING
CDEGIILNNOOZ	DECOLONIZING
CDEGILNOORU	OVERCLOUDING
CDEGINNORRSU	UNDERSCORING
CDEGINNORSST	SECOND-STRING
CDEGINNRTTUU	UNDERCUTTING
CDEGINOORRVW	OVERCROWDING
CDEGLMNORUUY	CURMUDGEONLY
CDEHHIIIPRTT	DIPHTHERITIC
CDEHHIILNSSS	CHILDISHNESS
CDEHIIILPPSS	DISCIPLESHIP
CDEHIIKKNNST	THICK-SKINNED
CDEHIIKNORTY	HYDROKINETIC
CDEHIINOOOPR	CONIDIOPHORE
CDEHIIOPRRST	DIRECTORSHIP
CDEHILLOOOST	OLD SCHOOL TIE
CDEHILLOOPRY	POLICYHOLDER
CDEHILMNOOOR	MONOCHLORIDE
CDEHIMNOOORS	CHONDRIOSOME
CDEHINNORSSY	SYNCHRONISED
CDEHINNORSYZ	SYNCHRONIZED
CDEHKLOORSST	STOCKHOLDERS
CDEIIIILNNPS	INDISCIPLINE
CDEIIIJRSTUV	JURISDICTIVE
CDEIIILNTVVY	VINDICTIVELY
CDEIIIMNORST	MISDIRECTION
CDEIIINNORST	INDISCRETION
CDEIIINNORTT	INTERDICTION
CDEIIISSSTUV	VICISSITUDES
CDEIILMRTUUU	DIVERTICULUM
CDEIILNNPPRU	UNPRINCIPLED
CDEIILRSSUVY	DISCURSIVELY
CDEIIMMNOOSS	DECOMMISSION,
COMMISSIONED	
CDEIIMMRSSTY	DISSYMMETRIC
CDEIINNOOPRT	PRECONDITION
CDEIINNOORST	CONDITIONERS
CDEIINNSSSTT	DISTINCTNESS
CDEIINOOPRST	PERIODONTICS
CDEIINOPRSST	DESCRIPTIONS
CDEILNOORSUY	INDECOROUSLY
CDEILNOPSSST	SPLIT SECONDS
CDEILOPRTUVY	PRODUCTIVELY
CDEIMNORSSTU	MISCONSTRUED
CDEIMOOPRSSU	DISCOMPOSURE

CDEINOOPRRTU	REPRODUCTION
CDEINOPRTUUV	UNPRODUCTIVE
CDEIOORSSTUU	DISCOURTEOUS
CDEKKNOOORRS	DOORKNOCKERS
CDEKLNNOOOORT	LONDON ROCKET
CDELLNOOTUVY	CONVOLUTEDLY
CDELNNOOPRUY	PRONOUNCEDLY
CDELNOOOSTUY	COTYLEDONOUS
CDENRRSTTUUU	UNSTRUCTURED
CDFGIIIMNOST	DISCOMFITING
CDFGILNOORTY	FLYING DOCTOR
CDFHILOORRUY	HYDROFLUORIC
CDGGIKLLNUUY	UGLY DUCKLING
CDGIIIILNNPS	DISCIPLINING
CDGIIINNNOOT	CONDITIONING
CDGIIKNSSTTU	SITTING DUCKS
CDGIILNOORSU	DISCOLOURING
CDGIIMNOOPSS	DISCOMPOSING
CDGIKLNOOSTU	DUCKING STOOL
CDGINNNOOORR	NONCORRODING
CDHHILNOORRY	CHLOROHYDRIN
CDHIIOOPRSST	CHIROPODISTS
CDHIMNNOOSTY	SYNODIC MONTH
CDHINOOORSTT	ORTHODONTICS
CDIIIJNORSTU	JURISDICTION
CDIIILNNSTTY	INDISTINCTLY
CDIIINNOSSTT	DISTINCTIONS
CDIILLORSUUY	RIDICULOUSLY
CDIIMMNNOOSU	CONDOMINIUMS
CDIIMMNOOOSU	INCOMMODIOUS
CDIINNOORTTU	INTRODUCTION
CDIIOPRTTUVY	PRODUCTIVITY
CDILMMOOOSUY	COMMODIOUSLY
CDINOORRTTUY	INTRODUCTORY
CEEEEFFNRSTV	EFFERVESCENT
CEEEEFFHNORTV	OVER THE FENCE
CEEEEFINNRRT	INTERFERENCE
CEEEEHNORSVW	WHENCESOEVER
CEEEEIINNPRX	INEXPERIENCE
CEEEEIKKPRTW	WICKET KEEPER
CEEEEIMNNSSS	MISE-EN-SCENES
CEEEEIMNRSVX	EX-SERVICEMEN
CEEEEINPRSTX	PRE-EXISTENCE
CEEEELMORRTT	ELECTROMETER
CEEEENNRRSTV	NERVE CENTRES
CEEEFFGINRSV	EFFERVESCING
CEEEFFHOOSSU	COFFEE HOUSES
CEEEFFLNORST	EFFLORESCENT
CEEEFGHIIOPT	PIECE OF EIGHT
CEEEFHINRSTT	SCENESHIFTER
CEEEFHLNRSSU	CHEERFULNESS
CEEEFIIMPRTV	IMPERFECTIVE
CEEEFILNRTUV	UNREFLECTIVE
CEEEFKLNSSSS	FECKLESSNESS

CEEEGGNORRRS	GREENGROCERS
CEEEGGNORRRY	GREENGROCERY
CEEEGIILLNNT	INTELLIGENCE
CEEEGIINNPRX	EXPERIENCING
CEEEGIINRSTT	ENERGETICIST
CEEEHHIINSTW	CHINESE WHITE
CEEEHIIMRSTU	EUHEMERISTIC
CEEEHIIPRRSV	RECEIVERSHIP
CEEEHIKNSTTT	KITCHENETTES
CEEEHIMNNPRT	ENCIPHERMENT
CEEEHIMNPSWY	CHIMNEYSWEEP
CEEEHIMNNRTU	HERMENEUTICS
CEEEHINOSSST	COENESTHESIS
CEEEHINOSSSV	COHESIVENESS
CEEEHIOORSTU	HETEROECIOUS
CEEEHLLPSSSY	SPEECHLESSLY
CEEEHLNNOTTU	LUNCHEONETTE
CEEEHLNOOPRT	ELECTROPHONE
CEEEHLOQQSUU	QUELQUE CHOSE
CEEEHMNNNRRT	ENTRENCHMENT
CEEEHMNNNRTT	RETRENCHMENT
CEEEHMOORRST	STEREOCHROME
CEEEHNOPRRST	CENTROSPHERE
CEEEIILLNTTV	INTELLECTIVE
CEEEIIMNNPRT	IMPERTINENCE
CEEEIIMPPRTV	IMPERCEPTIVE
CEEEIINPRTTV	INTERCEPTIVE
CEEEIIPRRSTV	IRRESPECTIVE
CEEEILLNOPQU	EQUIPOLLENCE
CEEEILORRSST	CLERESTORIES
CEEEILPPRTVY	PERCEPTIVELY
CEEEILPRSTVY	RESPECTIVELY
CEEEIMMMNOTT	COMMITTEEMEN
CEEEIMMNRSTX	CEMENT MIXERS
CEEEIMMPSSUU	MUSEUM PIECES
CEEEIMNNOPRS	OMNIPRESENCE
CEEEIMNNORST	MESENTERONIC
CEEEIMORRSTT	STEREOMETRIC
CEEEINNNOSTX	NONEXISTENCE
CEEEINNQSSTU	QUINTESSENCE
CEEEINORSTUX	EXECUTIONERS
CEEEIORRSSTV	RETROCESSIVE
CEEEIPPRRSTV	PERSPECTIVES
CEEEIPRRSSUV	REPERCUSSIVE
CEEEKLNRSSSS	RECKLESSNESS
CEEEKMNORSSS	SMOKESCREENS
CEEELLNPRUUV	PULVERULENCE
CEEELLORRSTY	ELECTROLYSER
CEEELLORSTTY	ELECTROLYTES
CEEELMNOPSST	COMPLETENESS
CEEELMORRTTY	ELECTROMETRY
CEEELOPRRTTY	ELECTROTYPER
CEEELORRSSSU	RESOURCELESS
CEEEMNNNORTU	RENOUNCEMENT

CEEEMOPRRSTT	SPECTROMETER
CEEEOOPRRTTX	EXTEROCEPTOR
CEEFFHIIORSS	IRISH COFFEES
CEEFFIOPRTTY	PETTY OFFICER
CEEFFLNORSSU	FORCEFULNESS
CEEFGGILNNTU	GENUFLECTING
CEEFGHIINPSY	SPEECHIFYING
CEEFGIILNRTY	ELECTRIFYING
CEEFGILLNRTY	REFLECTINGLY
CEEFGILNNOTU	GENUFLECTION
CEEFGLLLNTUY	NEGLECTFULLY
CEEFHIKNRSSS	FRENCH KISSES
CEEFHILSSTTU	CUTTLEFISHES
CEEFIIMNOPRT	IMPERFECTION
CEEFIINOPRST	FRONTISPIECE
CEEFIKOOPRSW	PIECES OF WORK
CEEFILMNRSSU	MERCIFULNESS
CEEFILNNORST	INFLORESCENT
CEEFIMNNNOST	CONFINEMENTS
CEEFLLPRSTUY	RESPECTFULLY
CEEFLOORRSSU	FORECLOSURES
CEEGGILNOSSU	GLUCOGENESIS
CEEGGILNOSSY	GLYCOGENESIS
CEEGHIINOSTT	HISTOGENETIC
CEEGHILNOOST	TECHNOLOGIES
CEEGHILOOPRT	HERPETOLOGIC
CEEGHIMORSTY	GEOCHEMISTRY
CEEGHINOORTT	ORTHOGENETIC
CEEGHINOPTTY	PHYTOGENETIC
CEEGIIJNNRTT	INTERJECTING
CEEGIINNNSST	ENTICINGNESS
CEEGIINNPRTT	INTERCEPTING
CEEGIINNRSSU	INSURGENCIES
CEEGIINNRSTT	INTERSECTING
CEEGIINOPRTV	PRECOGNITIVE
CEEGIKLLNOPS	GLOCKENSPIEL
CEEGIKNNOSTV	EVENING STOCK
CEEGIMNNOPRS	RECOMPENSING
CEEGINNNORTU	ENCOUNTERING
CEEGINNOPTTX	NOT EXCEPTING
CEEGINOPRRSS	REPROCESSING
CEEGINRRRSTU	RESURRECTING
CEEGMNOORRST	COSTERMONGER
CEEHHIINOSTT	HENOTHEISTIC
CEEHHLOORSST	CLOTHESHORSE
CEEHHMOOPRRS	CHROMOSPHERE
CEEHHOOPPRSS	PHOSPHORESCE
CEEHIILNNSTT	LICHTENSTEIN
CEEHIIMNSSTZ	NIETZSCHEISM
CEEHIIMSSTTW	TIME SWITCHES
CEEHIINNNPPS	PINCH PENNIES
CEEHIKMNOSSS	HOMESICKNESS
CEEHILLNOSST	CLOTHESLINES
CEEHILMMOPRY	MYRMECOPHILE
CEEHILNNORTY	INCOHERENTLY
CEEHILPRSSTU	LECTURESHIPS
CEEHIMMORRTT	THERMOMETRIC
CEEHIMNOOSTU	HOME COUNTIES
CEEHIMNORSTT	THEOCENTRISM
CEEHINNNPPRY	PENNY PINCHER
CEEHINOOPRST	STEREOPHONIC
CEEHINOORRSS	RHINOCEROSES
CEEHINRSSSTT	STRETCHINESS
CEEHIOPRSTUX	EXECUTORSHIP
CEEHKLNOSSUY	HONEYSUCKLES
CEEHKMNNORWY	MONKEY WRENCH
CEEHLLMOORWY	CHROME YELLOW
CEEHLMOOPRTU	THERMOCOUPLE
CEEHLOPRSSST	CLOTHES-PRESS
CEEHMNOORRST	CHRONOMETERS
CEEHMNORSTUX	HERSTMONCEUX
CEEHMOORRSTY	STEREOCHROMY
CEEHMOPRRSTY	PSYCHROMETER
CEEHMORSTTYY	HYSTERECTOMY
CEEHOOPRRSTU	URETHROSCOPE
CEEHOOPSSSTT	STETHOSCOPES
CEEIIINNSSSV	INCISIVENESS
CEEIIINPRRTU	PERINEURITIC
CEEIIJNNORTT	INTERJECTION
CEEIIJNORTTV	INTROJECTIVE
CEEIILLLNNOTT	INTELLECTION
CEEIILMNNORT	INCLINOMETER
CEEIILMOPSTX	COMPLEXITIES
CEEIILNNPRSS	PRINCELINESS
CEEIILNPSSTX	EXPLICITNESS
CEEIILOOPSSU	LEUCOPOIESIS
CEEIIMNOPPRT	IMPERCEPTION
CEEIIMNOSSSS	SECESSIONISM
CEEIIMOPRSSU	SEMIPRECIOUS
CEEIIMORRSTU	MERETRICIOUS
CEEIINNNNOTV	INCONVENIENT
CEEIINNOPRTT	INTERCEPTION
CEEIINNORSST	INTERCESSION
CEEIINNORSTT	INTERSECTION
CEEIINOPRSTT	RECEPTIONIST
CEEIINORSSTV	INSECTIVORES
CEEIINOSSSST	SECESSIONIST
CEEIIPPRRSTV	PRESCRIPTIVE
CEEIIPPRTTVY	PERCEPTIVITY
CEEIIJNORRTTY	INTERJECTORY
CEEIKLMNPPRU	PUMPERNICKEL
CEEIKNNOOPST	IN ONE'S POCKET
CEEIILLMNOPTY	INCOMPLETELY
CEEIILLORSSTY	ELECTROLYSIS
CEEIILMOOPRSY	COPOLYMERISE
CEEIILMOOPRYZ	COPOLYMERIZE
CEEIILNNNOTVY	CONVENIENTLY
CEEIILNOOPRSS	NECROPOLISES

CEEILOPRTTVY	PROTECTIVELY
CEEIMMMNORTT	RECOMMITMENT
CEEIMNNOPSTT	INCOMPETENTS
CEEIMNOOPRST	CONTEMPORISE
CEEIMNOOPRTZ	CONTEMPORIZE
CEEINNNOQSTU	INCONSEQUENT
CEEINNOOORRRT	RECONNOITRER
CEEINNOORRSV	RECONVERSION
CEEINNPRTUUV	VENIPUNCTURE
CEEINNRRRTTU	INTERCURRENT
CEEINOOPRRTT	INTEROCEPTOR
CEEINOOPRST	STEREOPTICON
CEEINOOPRSTU	COUNTERPOISE
CEEINOORRSST	RETROCESSION
CEEINOPRRSSU	REPERCUSSION
CEEINOPRRST	INTERCEPTORS
CEEINOPRSSSU	PRECIOUSNESS
CEEINOPRSSTU	PERSECUTIONS
CEEINOPSSSSU	SPECIOUSNESS
CEEINORRRSTU	RESURRECTION
CEEINORRSSTY	INTERCESSORY
CEEINORSTTTU	RECONSTITUTE
CEEINPPRRRTU	PRINCE RUPERT
CEEIOOPRRSTT	STEREOTROPIC
CEEIOORRRSTT	ECOTERRORIST
CEEKOORRRSTT	RETRO-ROCKETS
CEELLNOORTTV	ELECTRONVOLT
CEELNNOQSTUY	CONSEQUENTLY
CEELNOORSTTU	ELECTROTONUS
CEELOOOPRSTU	COLEOPTEROUS
CEEMOPRRSSTY	SPECTROMETRY
CEEMOPRRSSTUU	SUPREME COURT
CEENNOOQRSTU	QUEEN CONSORT
CEENNOORRSST	CORNERSTONES
CEENNOORRTTU	COUNTERTENOR
CEENOOOPPRSS	SNOOPERSCOPE
CEENOORRRTTV	CONTROVERTER
CEENOOSSSTUV	COVETOUSNESS
CEEOPPRRSSSTU	PROSPECTUSES
CEFFHMNOOPSU	OFF ONE'S CHUMP
CEFFIIINNSTU	INSUFFICIENT
CEFFIIILOOPRT	PILOT OFFICER
CEFFIORRSTU	FRUCTIFEROUS
CEFFIORSSTUU	SUFFRUTICOSE
CEFGIIKLLNRY	FLICKERINGLY
CEFGIIKLNPTY	FLYING PICKET
CEFHHILNOPRS	FRENCH POLISH
CEFHILMNNOUY	ICHNEUMON FLY
CEFHLLLOOOSW	SCHOOLFELLOW
CEFIIILNOSTU	INFELICITOUS
CEFIIILORSTU	SILICIFEROUS
CEFIIIORRSTU	FOURIERISTIC
CEFIIILOSTUY	FELICITOUSLY
CEFIIILMNNTUY	MUNIFICENTLY
CEFIIILNOORRS	FERROSILICON
CEFIIILNOPRSS	PROLIFICNESS
CEFIIILNOPRTY	PROFICIENTLY
CEFIIILNOSTUY	INFECTIOUSLY
CEFILLORRTUU	FLORICULTURE
CEFILMOORRTU	FLUOROMETRIC
CEFILNOORSTU	COUNTERFOILS
CEFILOORSUVY	VOCIFEROUSLY
CEFKKLOORRSW	CLERK OF WORKS
CEFLNNORSSSU	SCORNFULNESS
CEFNOOOPRRTU	COUNTERPROOF
CEGHHIILOPRY	HIEROGLYPHIC
CEGHIIKNPRSW	SHIPWRECKING
CEGHIILNRSTT	CHITTERLINGS
CEGHIINNRSST	CHRISTENINGS
CEGHIIOPSSTY	GEOPHYSICIST
CEGHIKNNOSSS	SHOCKINGNESS
CEGHIKNOORRS	ROCKING HORSE
CEGHILLNQSUY	SQUELCHINGLY
CEGHILNOOORS	CHRONOLOGIES
CEGHILNOOSTT	TECHNOLOGIST
CEGHILOOPSSY	PSYCHOLOGIES, PSYCHOLOGISE
CEGHILOOPSYZ	PSYCHOLOGIZE
CEGIIIILMSTT	LEGITIMISTIC
CEGIIKLLMNRY	MERCY KILLING
CEGIIKLNNORT	INTERLOCKING
CEGIIKLNNRSY	SNICKERINGLY
CEGIILLOOSTX	LEXICOLOGIST
CEGIILMNOSST	CLOSING TIMES
CEGIILNNPSTY	INSPECTINGLY
CEGIINNOOPRT	PRECOGNITION
CEGIINNOORST	RECOGNITIONS
CEGIINOPTTYY	GENOTYPICITY
CEGIKKNORSTY	SKYROCKETING
CEGIKLNNOSSU	KING'S COUNSEL
CEGIKNOORSTV	OVERSTOCKING
CEGILLLMNOPY	COMPELLINGLY
CEGILNNNOTTY	CONTINGENTLY
CEGILNNORSTU	CURLING STONE
CEGILNOOPRTY	GLYCOPROTEIN
CEGIMNNNOSST	CONSIGNMENTS
CEGINNNNOSTU	UNCONSENTING
CEGINNNOORTW	CONNING TOWER
CEGINNORSTU	COUNTERSIGNS
CEGINNOSTTTU	STONECUTTING
CEGINNPSSTUU	UNSUSPECTING
CEGINOOPPRRV	OVERCROPPING
CEGINPRSSTTU	PRESS CUTTING
CEHHILNRSSSU	CHURLISHNESS
CEHHIMMOOOPR	HOMEOMORPHIC
CEHHIMOOPRTT	PHOTOTHERMIC
CEHHIMOOPSTT	PHOTOCHEMIST
CEHHIOOPPRST	PHOTOSPHERIC
CEHHLOOOSSSU	SCHOOLHOUSES

CEHIIIILNOOPS	EOSINOPHILIC	CEIIMMNOPRTU	MINICOMPUTER
CEHIIKLNSSST	TICKLISHNESS	CEIIMNOOPSTT	COMPETITIONS
CEHIIKNOOPTT	PHOTOKINETIC	CEIIMOOPRSTT	PROTOSEMITIC
CEHIILLNNORS	LINCOLNSHIRE	CEIIMOORSSTT	SOCIOMETRIST
CEHIILMNOPRS	NECROPHILISM	CEIINNNOSSTT	INCONSISTENT
CEHIILNQSSSU	CLIQUISHNESS	CEIINNORRSTU	INSURRECTION
CEHIILOPSTTY	POLYTHEISTIC	CEIINOOPRRTY	INCORPOREITY
CEHIIMNOOSTT	MONOTHEISTIC	CEIINOPPRRST	PRESCRIPTION
CEHIIMNOPRUY	PERIONYCHIUM	CEIINORRSSST	RESTRICTIONS
CEHIINNOPRTY	PERICYNTHION	CEIINORRSSTUX	EXCURSIONIST
CEHIIOPPRSTU	PERITRICHOUS	CEIINORSTTVY	VENTRICOSITY
CEHIKLMORSTY	LOCKSMITHERY	CEIINOSTTTUV	CONSTITUTIVE
CEHIKNOPSSTU	SOUP KITCHENS	CEIIOPPRRSTV	PROSCRIPTIVE
CEHILLOPPTYY	POLYPHYLETIC	CEIIPRRRSTTW	SCRIPTWRITER
CEHILMNOOPTY	MONOPHYLETIC	CEIIPSSTTUVY	SUSCEPTIVITY
CEHILMNOPPTY	NYMPHOLEPTIC	CEIKLMOORSST	MORTISE LOCKS
CEHILNNOSSSW	CLOWNISHNESS	CEILLLNOOOSV	VIOLONCELLOS
CEHILOQSTTUY	COQUETTISHLY	CEILLMOPSUVY	COMPULSIVELY
CEHILORRTTUU	HORTICULTURE	CEILLMOSTUUY	METICULOUSLY
CEHIMMOOPRST	CHEMOTROPISM	CEILLNOSUVVY	CONVULSIVELY
CEHIMNORRTYY	ERYTHROMYCIN	CEILLOPRSSTU	PORTCULLISSES
CEHIMOOPRRTT	THERMOTROPIC	CEILMNOOSTUU	CONTUMELIOUS
CEHIMOORSTYZ	ZOOCHEMISTRY	CEILMNOPRSTY	POLYCENTRISM
CEHINNORRSSY	SYNCHRONISER	CEILNNOSSTTY	CONSISTENTLY
CEHINNORRSYZ	SYNCHRONIZER	CEILNOORRTTU	INTERLOCUTOR
CEHIOOOPPRST	PHOTOCOPIERS	CEILNOORSSUY	CENSORIOUSLY
CEHLMMOORSSU	SUMMER SCHOOL	CEILNOSSSSUU	LUSCIOUSNESS
CEHMMOOORSSX	X CHROMOSOMES	CEILNOSSTUUY	INCESTUOUSLY
CEHMMOOORSSY	Y CHROMOSOMES	CEIMMNOOPSST	COMPOS MENTIS
CEHMNORSTUUX	HURSTMONCEUX	CEIMNNOOPRSU	MISPRONOUNCE
CEHMOOOPRSSU	PHOTOCOMPOSE	CEIMNNOORSTU	CONTERMINOUS
CEHMOOOOPRTY	OOPHORECTOMY	CEIMNOPRSTTY	STREPTOMYCIN
CEHNOOPRRTTU	PHOTOCURRENT	CEIMNOPSSTUV	CONSUMPTIVES
CEHOOPRRSTUY	URETHROSCOPY	CEIMOOORRSTV	VISCEROMOTOR
CEIIIILLNSTV	INCIVILITIES	CEINNOOPRTTU	COUNTERPOINT
CEIIILMNPSST	IMPLICITNESS	CEINNOOPRTVW	PROVINCETOWN
CEIIILOPRSTV	PROCLIVITIES	CEINNOORSSSU	CONNOISSEURS
CEIIIMNOPRSS	PRECISIONISM	CEINNOSSTTTU	CONSTITUENTS
CEIIINNORSTU	REUNIONISTIC	CEINOOPRSSTU	PROSECUTIONS
CEIIINNOSSTW	WISCONSINITE	CEINPSSSTTUU	INTUSSUSCEPT
CEIIINOPRSST	PRECISIONIST	CEJNOORRRSUY	CORONER'S JURY
CEIIINORTTWZ	ZWITTERIONIC	CELLLOORSSUY	COLOURLESSLY
CEIIINOSSTVV	VIVISECTIONS	CELLMOOPRRST	COMPTROLLERS
CEIIJNNOORTT	INTROJECTION	CELLNNOOPSTU	POLLEN COUNTS
CEIIKLSSTWZZ	SWIZZLE STICK	CELMNOPRTUUU	MUCOPURULENT
CEIIKRRSSTUY	SECURITY RISK	CELOOOPRRSTU	POSTER COLOUR
CEIILLNOSTUY	LICENTIOUSLY	CEMMNNNOOSSU	UNCOMMONNESS
CEIILLRSTUUV	SILVICULTURE	CEMMOOSTUXYY	MYXOMYCETOUS
CEIILMOPRTUV	PLUVIOMETRIC	CEMNOOPSTTUU	CONTEMPTUOUS
CEIILNOOSTTU	ELOCUTIONIST	CEMOOOORRSTT	MOTOR SCOOTER
CEIILNOPRSUY	PERNICIOUSLY	CENNOSSSTUUU	UNCTUOUSNESS
CEIILOPRSSUU	SUPERCILIOUS	CFFHILMNOSTU	FIFTH COLUMNS
CEIILRRTTUUV	VITICULTURER	CFGHIIKNOPRT	PITCHFORKING
CEIIMMNOORSS	COMMISSIONER	CFGIIILLMMNOR	MICROFILMING

CFGIILNOOSTV	COST OF LIVING
CFGILMNOORTY	COMFORTINGLY
CFIIILOSTTUY	FICTITIOUSLY
CFIIKLLOORST	FOLKLORISTIC
CFIILLNOOSTU	SOLIFLUCTION
CFIIMNNOORTY	INCONFORMITY
CFIINORSSSTU	FIRST COUSINS
CFILNORSSUUU	FURUNCULOSIS
CFIMNNOORTUY	UNCONFORMITY
CGHHIINNTTUW	WITCH-HUNTING
CGHHIINORTUW	WITCHING HOUR
CGHIIKKNNOPS	SHOCKING PINK
CGHIILOOOPRT	OLIGOTROPHIC
CGHIILOOOSTY	STOICHIOLOGY
CGHIILOORSTT	TRICHOLOGIST
CGHIIMNOOPSY	PHYSIOGNOMIC
CGHIIMOOPRTT	THIGMOTROPIC
CGHILMOOPSSY	PSYCHOLOGISM
CGHILNOOORST	CHRONOLOGIST
CGHILOOPSSTY	PSYCHOLOGIST
CGHIMNOORSST	SHORTCOMINGS
CGHINOOOPPTY	PHOTOCOPYING
CGHINOOPSSSY	PSYCHOGNOSIS
CGIIIILLNOPTZ	POLITICIZING
CGIIINNNRSTUZ	SCRUTINIZING
CGIIKLLLNORY	ROLLICKINGLY
CGIILMOOSSTU	MUSICOLOGIST
CGIILNNNOTUY	CONTINUINGLY
CGIILOOOSSST	SOCIOLOGISTS
CGIILOOOSTTX	TOXICOLOGIST
CGIIMMNOOPRS	COMPROMISING
CGIINNOSTTTU	CONSTITUTING
CGIKLLNOORST	ROLLING STOCK
CGILNOOSTUUY	CONTIGUOUSLY
CGILOOOPRSTT	PROCTOLOGIST
CGILOOPRSTTY	CRYPTOLOGIST
CGINOOPRSSTY	PYROGNOSTICS
CHHIIOOPPRST	PHOSPHORITIC
CHHILMOPRTYY	POLYRHYTHMIC
CHHIMOOOPRRT	ORTHOMORPHIC
CHHINORRSSTT	CHRIST'S-THORN
CHHMMOOOORSU	HOMOCHROMOUS
CHIIILOOPTTX	TOXOPHILITIC
CHIIMNNRSSTY	STRYCHNINISM
CHIJLNOOORSU	JUNIOR SCHOOL
CHILOOOPPRSU	COPROPHILOUS
CHIMMNOOORST	MONOCHROMIST
CHIMNOOOORST	MONOSTROPHIC
CHIMNOOORSTU	MONOTRICHOUS
CHIMNOPRSTYY	CHYMOTRYPSIN
CHIMOOOPPRRT	PROTOMORPHIC
CHIOOOPPRRTT	PROTOTROPHIC
CHIOOOPRRSTV	ROSTROPOVICH
CHMMNOOORSST	SHORT COMMONS

CIIIIOPSSTTV	POSITIVISTIC
CIIILLMPTTUY	MULTIPLICITY
CIIINNOPRSST	INSCRIPTIONS
CIILLOOSSTUY	SOLICITOUSLY
CIILMNNORSUY	SYNCLINORIUM
CIILMNOOOPST	MONOPOLISTIC
CIILOOORSTUVY	VICTORIOUSLY
CIILOPSSSUUY	SUSPICIOUSLY
CIIMMNNOOSTU	COMMUNIONIST
CIIMNOOOPSST	COMPOSITIONS
CIIMNOPRSTTY	NYCTITROPISM
CIINNOOSTTTU	CONSTITUTION
CIINNORSSTTU	INSTRUCTIONS
CIINOOPPRRST	PROSCRIPTION
CIJLNORSSTUU	JURISCONSULT
CILLMOOPRSUY	COMPULSORILY
CILLORRSSUUY	SCURRILOUSLY
CILNNOOOSTUV	CONVOLUTIONS
CILNNOOSTUUY	CONTINUOUSLY
CIMMOOORSSTU	MICROSTOMOUS
CIMNNOOPSSTU	CONSUMPTIONS
CIMNOPPSSTUU	SUCTION PUMPS
CLLOPRSSUUUY	SCRUPULOUSLY
CLNOPRSSUUUU	UNSCRUPULOUS
DDDDDEFISUUY	FUDDY-DUDDIES
DDDEEEGINNOP	PODDED ENGINE
DDDEEEENRRSSU	UNDERDRESSED
DDDEEFHILRSU	HUDDERSFIELD
DDDEEINRSTUU	UNDERSTUDIED
DDDEHNNOOOORR	RHODODENDRON
DDEEEELLRSVW	WELL-DESERVED
DDEEEEMNNSST	DEMENTEDNESS
DDEEEENNSSTX	EXTENDEDNESS
DDEEEENRSSSV	DESERVEDNESS
DDEEEFHLNOTU	DO THE NEEDFUL
DDEEEFMNORSS	DEFORMEDNESS
DDEEEIINSSST	DESENSITISED
DDEEEIINSSTZ	DESENSITIZED
DDEEEIMNNRTU	UNDETERMINED
DDEEEINNNPST	INDEPENDENTS
DDEEEINNOSSS	ONE-SIDEDNESS
DDEEELNOPRUV	UNDERDEVELOP
DDEEENOPRSUX	UNDEREXPOSED
DDEEFFGLLLUY	FULLY-FLEDGED
DDEEFGIILMNR	MIDDLE FINGER
DDEEFHIIIMRU	DEHUMIDIFIER
DDEEFIIINNTU	UNIDENTIFIED
DDEEGHIILMTW	MIDDLEWEIGHT
DDEEGHIINTWW	WHITE WEDDING
DDEEGIILMNNS	SINGLE-MINDED
DDEEGILMNOST	DISLODGEMENT
DDEEGILNORUV	OVERINDULGED
DDEEGLLNORUW	WELL-GROUNDED
DDEEHIIINRST	DISINHERITED

DDEEHIILNOOT	ENDOTHELIOID	DEEEGHNNRSTT	STRENGTHENED
DDEEIILMMNPS	SIMPLE-MINDED	DEEEGIINNRRV	ENGINE DRIVER
DDEEIILQSTUY	DISQUIETEDLY	DEEEGILNOPRV	REDEVELOPING
DDEEIINPRRST	PRIEST-RIDDEN	DEEEGINNRSSS	RESIGNEDNESS
DDEEILLOPRVW	WELL-PROVIDED	DEEEGINNRSSV	EVENING DRESS
DDEEILLOPSSW	WELL-DISPOSED	DEEEGJMNPRTU	PREJUDGEMENT
DDEEILMNNOPY	OPEN-MINDEDLY	DEEEGOOPPSST	GOOSESTEPPED
DDEEILNNORUW	LIE DOWN UNDER	DEEEGORRRSST	RETROGRESSED
DDEEILNNPSSS	SPLENDIDNESS	DEEEHHIPPRSS	SHEPHERD'S PIE
DDEEIMNNOSTW	DISENDOWMENT	DEEEHIILRTVW	WHITE-LIVERED
DDEEINRSSTUU	UNDERSTUDIES	DEEEHILMNSTV	DISHEVELMENT
DDEEIOPSSSSS	DISPOSSESSED	DEEEHINPRRSV	REVERENDSHIP
DDEELNNOPSTY	DESPONDENTLY	DEEEHINRSSTW	WITHEREDNESS
DDEFNOOOPRSU	SOUNDPROOFED	DEEEHMNNORTT	DETHRONEMENT
DDEGGIINNRSW	WEDDING RINGS	DEEEIILNORRT	INDRE-ET-LOIRE
DDEGGIOOOSY	GOODY-GOODIES	DEEEIINRSSSV	DESENSITISER
DDEGHHIILMNY	HIGH-MINDEDLY	DEEEIINRSSSV	DERISIVENESS
DDEGHILNRSUY	SHUDDERINGLY	DEEEIINRSSTZ	DESENSITIZER
DDEGHIRRSUUY	HURDY-GURDIES	DEEEILLPPQUW	WELL-EQUIPPED
DDEGHMOOORUU	GOOD-HUMOURED	DEEEILNRSSSW	WILDERNESSES
DDEGILLNNOWY	LONGWINDEDLY	DEEEILNRSTTY	INTERESTEDLY
DDEGILNNOPSS	PLODDINGNESS	DEEEIMNORSTT	DENSITOMETER
DDEGILNOORST	DENDROLOGIST	DEEEIMNRRSTW	MIDWESTERNER
DDEGIMNNORST	STRONG-MINDED	DEEEIMOPRSTX	EXTEMPORISED
DDEGINNORSSW	DRESSING-DOWN	DEEEIMOPRTXZ	EXTEMPORIZED
DDEGNNORRSUU	UNDERGROUNDS	DEEEINNRSTTU	UNINTERESTED
DDEHILNNOOPR	PHILODENDRON	DEEEINPRRSST	INTERSPERSED
DDEHINOORSTU	RIDE TO HOUNDS	DEEEINRSSSTW	DESSERT WINES
DDEEIIILPRSTY	DISPIRITEDLY	DEEEJLLOPPRT	JET-PROPELLED
DDEEIIJLNOSTY	DISJOINTEDLY	DEEEKLNNOOST	ENDOSKELETON
DDEEIILNNOORR	LIRIODENDRON	DEEEELMNNORSY	MONEYLENDERS
DDEEIIMNOSUVV	MODUS VIVENDI	DEEELMNOPRTY	REDEPLOYMENT
DDEEIMOOPPSSU	PSEUDOPODIUM	DEEELMNOPSTV	DEVELOPMENTS
DDEELNORRSUUY	SURROUNDEDLY	DEEELMNPPSTU	SUPPLEMENTED
DDEGIILNOORSS	SLIDING DOORS	DEEELNORSSSV	RESOLVEDNESS
DDEGILMNPPSUU	PLUM PUDDINGS	DEEELNRRSUVY	UNRESERVEDLY
DEEEEEMNPRTV	EVEN-TEMPERED	DEEEMNNORSST	ENDORSEMENTS
DEEEEGIILNNS	DIESEL ENGINE	DEEENRRSSTTT	TRENDSETTERS
DEEEEGMNNNRT	ENGENDERMENT	DEEEOOPPRSSS	PREPOSSESSED
DEEEEHILRSSW	SIDE-WHEELERS	DEEFFHINRRSU	UNDERSHERIFF
DEEEEHLNSSSS	HEEDLESSNESS	DEEFGIILNSTT	FIELD-TESTING
DEEEEILNNPTT	PENDENTE LITE	DEEFGIINNRSX	INDEX FINGERS
DEEEEIMNPRRT	PREDETERMINE	DEEFGINNOOPS	SPOON-FEEDING
DEEEEIMNPRTX	EXPERIMENTED	DEEFGKNOORTU	FORKED TONGUE
DEEEELLMPRTW	WELL-TEMPERED	DEEFHIINNSSS	FIENDISHNESS
DEEEELNNSSSS	NEEDLESSNESS	DEEFHOPRSTUY	DUTY-FREE SHOP
DEEEEMOPRSST	SPEEDOMETERS	DEEFIIIILNST	INFIDELITIES
DEEEENRRSSSV	RESERVEDNESS	DEEFIIILNNTY	INDEFINITELY
DEEEFGHORRTU	FOURTH-DEGREE	DEEFIIILNTVY	DEFINITIVELY
DEEEFGINRRYZ	FREEZE-DRYING	DEEFIIILNNRSS	FRIENDLINESS
DEEEFIINNSST	DEFINITENESS	DEEFIILPPRTT	FILTER-TIPPED
DEEEFLLMOPSY	SELF-EMPLOYED	DEEFIKLORRSW	FIELDWORKERS
DEEEFNNQRTUU	UNFREQUENTED	DEEFILLMNORW	WELL-INFORMED
DEEEGHINNPRR	REPREHENDING	DEEFILNRRSUY	USER-FRIENDLY

DEEFINRSTUUX	INDEX FUTURES
DEEFLOORSTUY	SUREFOOTEDLY
DEEGGHHIINOPP	HEDGEHOPPING
DEEGGIINPRST	PREDIGESTING
DEEGGIMNORST	DISGORGEMENT
DEEGHIINNSTW	WINDING SHEET
DEEGHIINSTUX	EXTINGUISHED
DEEGHINRSSST	NIGHTDRESSES
DEEGHNORSSTU	GROUNDSHEETS
DEEGIILMNNRT	INTERMINGLED
DEEGIILMOOPY	EPIDEMIOLOGY
DEEGIILNNRSZ	SLENDERIZING
DEEGIILNNSSY	YIELDINGNESS
DEEGIILOPSTT	EPIGLOTTIDES
DEEGIIMNNOTZ	DEMONETIZING
DEEGIIMNPRST	DISTEMPERING
DEEGIINNPRST	PREDESTINING
DEEGIINOPRST	PREDIGESTION
DEEGIINPPSST	SIDESTEPPING
DEEGIINPRSTW	SPEEDWRITING
DEEGIJMMNSTU	MISJUDGEMENT
DEEGILLNNRSU	UNDERSELLING
DEEGILLNOOOR	GOLDEN ORIOLE
DEEGILMNNNOY	MONEYLENDING
DEEGILNPRSSY	DEPRESSINGLY
DEEGIINNRRRSU	SURRENDERING
DEEGINNRSTTT	TRENDSETTING
DEEGINORRSSV	OVERDRESSING
DEEGJMNPRSTU	PREJUDGMENTS
DEEGLLOOSTYY	DYSTELEOLOGY
DEEGLNOOOSTU	LOOSE-TONGUED
DEEHHIIMOPRS	HEMISPHEROID
DEEHHIOPPRSW	HORSEWHIPPED
DEEHHLOORSSU	HOUSEHOLDERS
DEEHIIKRSSSW	SIDE WHISKERS
DEEHIILNQRSU	RELINQUISHED
DEEHIILNSSSV	DEVILISHNESS
DEEHIIMOPRSV	IMPOVERISHED
DEEHIINPRSST	RESIDENTSHIP
DEEHILLORSTT	TITLEHOLDERS
DEEHILMMNOST	DEMOLISHMENT
DEEHIMMNORST	ENDOTHERMISM
DEEHIMNOORTU	TIME-HONOURED
DEEHINNSSTUY	THE SUNNY SIDE
DEEHIOPPRTTY	PTERIDOPHYTE
DEEHNNORSTTU	THUNDERSTONE
DEEHOORRSSUV	HORS D'OEUVRES
DEEIIILLRSST	DISTILLERIES
DEEIIINSSSVV	DIVISIVENESS
DEEIILLNNSSUW	UNWIELDINESS
DEEIIMMOPRST	POST MERIDIEM
DEEIIMNNRSTT	DISINTERMENT
DEEIIMNORTTV	DIVERTIMENTO
DEEIIMORRTTU	DUMORTIERITE

DEEIINPRSSST	SPIRITEDNESS
DEEIIOOPRSST	DEPOSITORIES
DEEIJLNOOOST	LOOSE-JOINTED
DEEIJNORRRSU	SURREJOINDER
DEEILLNORRSS	SLENDER LORIS
DEEILMNNSSSS	MINDLESSNESS
DEEILNOOPPRT	LEPIDOPTERON
DEEILOPRSSTY	PROSELYTISED
DEEILOPRSTYZ	PROSELYTIZED
DEEIMMNNOOSS	SOMEONE'S MIND
DEEIMMNRSTTY	DENSITOMETRY
DEEIMOPPRRST	PTERIDOSPERM
DEEIMOPPRSSU	SUPERIMPOSED
DEEINNNORSST	NONRESIDENTS
DEEINNOQSTUU	UNQUESTIONED
DEEINNRRTTUW	UNDERWRITTEN
DEEINORRRSVW	OWNER-DRIVERS
DEEINRRRSTUW	UNDERWRITERS
DEEKNOORRRWW	WONDER-WORKER
DEELMNORSTUY	TREMENDOUSLY
DEELNORSSSSW	WORDLESSNESS
DEELNOSSSSUU	SEDULOUSNESS
DEENOOPRSSST	DESSERTSPOON
DEENOPRRSSTU	UNDER PROTEST
DEFFHIRSSTTU	STUFFED SHIRT
DEFFHLNOOPSU	POUND OF FLESH
DEFGGINORRUU	FIGURE-GROUND
DEFGHHIIILTY	HIGH FIDELITY
DEFGHILLLTUY	DELIGHTFULLY
DEFGIIIMNNNY	INDEMNIFYING
DEFGIIINRSVY	DIVERSIFYING
DEFGIIMNSTYY	DEMYSTIFYING
DEFGIINORSST	DISFORESTING
DEFHINPRSSTT	SPENDTHRIFTS
DEFHLOOORSSU	HOUSE OF LORDS
DEFIIILMSTUY	SEMIFLUIDITY
DEFIILOPRSUY	PERFIDIOUSLY
DEFIINOPRSTU	PROFUNDITIES
DEFILOORSTUY	DO-IT-YOURSELF
DEFINOOOPRRT	POINT OF ORDER
DEFIOORRSSUU	SUDORIFEROUS
DEFNNOOPRSSU	PROFOUNDNESS
DEGGHILNOOSU	LODGING HOUSE
DEGGINNORSSW	DRESSING GOWN
DEGHHIIIPRST	HIGH-SPIRITED
DEGHHIINOPST	DIPHTHONGISE
DEGHHIINOPTZ	DIPHTHONGIZE
DEGHHIORSSTT	SHORTSIGHTED
DEGHIIIILNRSS	DISRELISHING
DEGHILNRTUY	THUNDERINGLY
DEGHINOORSTV	OVERDO THINGS
DEGHINOPSSTT	POTTING SHEDS
DEGIIILNPPSS	SIDESLIPPING
DEGIIINNNRRST	DISINTERRING

DEGIIKNRSSTW	WRITING DESKS
DEGIILLOOSTT	DELTIOLOGIST
DEGIILNNOSUY	INDIGENOUSLY
DEGIINNNNPRU	UNDERPINNING
DEGIINNOSSUU	DISINGENUOUS
DEGIINNRRTUW	UNDERWRITING
DEGIINOPPRSS	PREDISPOSING
DEGIJMMNSSTU	MISJUDGMENTS
DEGIKNOORRRW	WORKING ORDER
DEGILLNORSTW	STRONG-WILLED
DEGILMNOOOST	DEMONOLOGIST
DEGILNNORSUY	RESOUNDINGLY
DEGILNOOOSTT	DEONTOLOGIST
DEGIMNNORRSS	MORNING DRESS
DEGIMNOORRSS	DRESSING ROOM
DEGINOOPPRST	DOORSTEPPING
DEGINOPRSSST	TOPDRESSINGS
DEGKNOORRSTU	GROUND STROKE
DEGLLNORSSUW	GROUNDSWELLS
DEGLLNORSSUY	GROUNDLESSLY
DEGMNOORRRUY	MERRY-GO-ROUND
DEHHHMMORTTY	RHYTHM METHOD
DEHHILOSSSTU	SOUTH SHIELDS
DEHIIIMMNNST	DIMINISHMENT
DEHIIKLLNOOU	UNLIKELIHOOD
DEHILLOPPSUY	POLYSULPHIDE
DEHIMMNOOPRS	ENDOMORPHISM
DEHINNORRSUU	UNDERNOURISH
DEHINOOPRSST	SPINSTERHOOD
DEHLLOORRTWY	OTHERWORLDLY
DEHLNOORRSUY	HORRENDOUSLY
DEHLNORSTUUY	THUNDEROUSLY
DEHLOOOSTTTW	TWO-TOED SLOTH
DEHMNORRSTTU	THUNDERSTORM
DEHNOOORSTUW	SOUTHERNWOOD
DEIIKLNNNSSU	UNKINDLINESS
DEIILLOOQSSU	SOLILOQUISED
DEIILLOOQSUZ	SOLILOQUIZED
DEIILNOORSWW	ORIEL WINDOWS
DEIILPRSTUVY	DISRUPTIVELY
DEIIOOPPRRST	POOR-SPIRITED
DEIJNPRRSTUU	JURISPRUDENT
DEILLOOSSSVW	SLOW DISSOLVE
DEIMNOPSTUYY	PSEUDONYMITY
DEINOOOOPPRRT	PROPORTIONED
DEINOSSSSTUU	STUDIOUSNESS
DEIOOPRSSSSS	DISPOSSESSOR
DEKLLOOPRSST	ROLLTOP DESKS
DELNNOOPSTYY	POLYSYNDETON
DELNOPSSTUUY	STUPENDOUSLY
DEMNNOPSSUUY	PSEUDONYMOUS
DENNOORSSSUW	WONDROUSNESS
DEOOOPPRRSST	DOORSTOPPERS
DFGHIINNOSTW	DOWNSHIFTING
DFGHIINOPSSY	SPINY DOGFISH
DFGIIKNNNSSU	SINKING FUNDS
DFGLNOOOORSU	GROUND FLOORS
DFHILNOOOPSU	POUND-FOOLISH
DGGHHIINNOSU	HIGH-SOUNDING
DGGHIINNNOOT	NOTHING DOING
DGGIILNSSTUY	DISGUSTINGLY
DGHIINNORSUU	DISHONOURING
DGIIILNNOOSV	LONG DIVISION
DGIILOOPRSUY	PRODIGIOUSLY
DGILNOOOOSTT	ODONTOLOGIST
DGINNORRSSUU	SURROUNDINGS
DHHIILOOPPPS	PHOSPHOLIPID
DHIIIMMOOPRS	IDIOMORPHISM
DHLNOOOPPTYY	POLYPHYODONT
DHMMPPTTUUYY	HUMPTY DUMPTY
DIIIINOOQSSTU	DISQUISITION
DIIINOOPSSST	DISPOSITIONS
DIILNOOSSSTU	DISSOLUTIONS
DIILNOOSSTUU	SOLITUDINOUS
EEEEEHHLRRTW	THREE-WHEELER
EEEEFGHILNRW	FREEWHEELING
EEEEGHMORSTW	GET SOMEWHERE
EEEEGIILNPSS	SPIEGELEISEN
EEEEGNPPPRRS	GREEN PEPPERS
EEEEHINPRRSV	REPREHENSIVE
EEEEHKOPRSSU	HOUSEKEEPERS
EEEEHLMNOPRT	NEPHELOMETER
EEEEHLNRSSTV	NEVERTHELESS
EEEEHNNSSTTV	SEVENTEENTHS
EEEEIINRSTVW	INTERVIEWEES
EEEEIMNPRRTX	EXPERIMENTER
EEEEIMNPRSSW	MINESWEEPERS
EEEEINNQRSTU	EQUESTRIENNE
EEEEINSSSTWY	EYEWITNESSES
EEEEKOPRRSST	STOREKEEPERS
EEEELMNRSTTT	RESETTLEMENT
EEEELNOPRRTT	LETTER OPENER
EEEELNRSSSST	TREELESSNESS
EEEEMNORSTTX	EXTENSOMETER
EEEENNPRRRTU	ENTREPRENEUR
EEEENNRRSSTV	REVERENTNESS
EEEENPRRSSSV	PERVERSENESS
EEEEORRTTTTT	TEETER-TOTTER
EEEEPPPRSSTW	SWEET PEPPERS
EEEFFIILLNNTT	IN FINE FETTLE
EEEFFIMORSTU	EFFUSIOMETER
EEEFFINSSSUV	EFFUSIVENESS
EEEFFLLLNNORW	FENNELFLOWER
EEEFGGINNNRS	GREEN FINGERS
EEEFGLNNSSUV	VENGEFULNESS
EEEFGNNOORSS	FOREGONENESS
EEEFHHHINOTTT	IN THE TEETH OF
EEEFHIKNRRST	FREETHINKERS

604

EEEFHILRRSSW	FERRIS WHEELS
EEEFHINNOTTV	IN THE EVENT OF
EEEFHINRRRSW	RENFREWSHIRE
EEEFHINRSSSV	FEVERISHNESS
EEEFHMNRRSST	REFRESHMENTS
EEEFIILLLLMU	MILLEFEUILLE
EEEFIILMMPRR	FILM PREMIERE
EEEFIILNRRTT	INTERFERTILE
EEEFILLNSSSS	LIFELESSNESS
EEEFILNRSSTT	SELF-INTEREST
EEEFJLNNOOSY	ENJOY ONESELF
EEEFLLNSSSSS	SELFLESSNESS
EEEFLMNORSTT	MEN OF LETTERS
EEEFLNNSSTUV	EVENTFULNESS
EEEGGHORSTTT	GET-TOGETHERS
EEEGHIKNOPSU	HOUSEKEEPING
EEEGHILRTTWW	WELTERWEIGHT
EEEGHIMNOSTU	MEETINGHOUSE
EEEGHINSTTVY	SEVENTY-EIGHT
EEEGHNNRRSTT	STRENGTHENER
EEEGHNOORSTU	HETEROGENOUS
EEEGHNORSSTT	TOGETHERNESS
EEEGHOORTTYZ	HETEROZYGOTE
EEEGIIMNNPSW	MINESWEEPING
EEEGIINNORRT	ORIENTEERING
EEEGIINORSST	GENEROSITIES
EEEGIKMNNNOY	MONKEY ENGINE
EEEGIKNOPRST	STOREKEEPING
EEEGILNOPRSV	OVERSLEEPING
EEEGINNPRRST	REPRESENTING
EEEGINNPSSSW	SWEEPINGNESS
EEEGMNORSSSU	GRUESOMENESS
EEEGNNORSSSU	GENEROUSNESS
EEEGNOOPRRST	PROGESTERONE
EEEGNOORRSUV	OVERGENEROUS
EEEHHINPSSSS	SHEEPISHNESS
EEEHHLNORTUV	ELEVENTH HOUR
EEEHHMOPRRST	THERMOSPHERE
EEEHILLOSTTT	STILETTO HEEL
EEEHIILMNORST	HERMOTENSILE
EEEHILRSSSTV	SHIRTSLEEVES
EEEHIMNNNRST	ENSHRINEMENT
EEEHIMNRSTTU	HERMENEUTIST
EEEHINNOPRRS	REPREHENSION
EEEHINNORSTW	NONE THE WISER
EEEHJMPQTUUU	JUMP THE QUEUE
EEEHLLNOPTYY	POLYETHYLENE
EEEHLLNPSSSS	HELPLESSNESS
EEEHLMNOSSSS	HOMELESSNESS
EEEHLNOPSSSS	HOPELESSNESS
EEEHLOPRSTTW	POTTER'S WHEEL
EEEHMMORRSTT	THERMOMETERS
EEEHMNNNORTT	ENTHRONEMENT
EEEHMNOQRSTU	QUEEN MOTHERS

EEEHMOORRSTU	HETEROMEROUS
EEEHNOPRRRSY	REPREHENSORY
EEEHNORSSTTT	ON THE STREETS
EEEHNOSSSTUY	SHUT ONE'S EYES
EEEHOPRRSSTZ	HERPES ZOSTER
EEEIILPRSTX	PERPLEXITIES
EEEIIMNRSSTT	MESENTERITIS
EEEIINPRRTTV	INTERPRETIVE
EEEIINPRSSVX	INEXPRESSIVE
EEEIINRRSTVW	INTERVIEWERS
EEEIIPPRSTTU	PERPETUITIES
EEEIIPQRRSTU	PREREQUISITE
EEEIIPRRSSTV	PERVERSITIES
EEEILLLOPPTT	LITTLE PEOPLE
EEEILMNNPRTY	PRE-EMINENTLY
EEEILMNNSSSU	UNSEEMLINESS
EEEILMNORSTU	SON ET LUMIERE
EEEILMNSSSST	TIMELESSNESS
EEEILMOORVZZ	MEZZO-RELIEVO
EEEILMPPRTVY	PRE-EMPTIVELY
EEEILNPRRST	TELEPRINTERS
EEEILNPRTVVY	PREVENTIVELY
EEEILNRRRTVY	IRREVERENTLY
EEEILNRSSSST	TIRELESSNESS
EEEILNRSSSTW	WESTERLINESS, WESTERN ISLES
EEEILPRRSSVY	REPRESSIVELY
EEEILPRSSVXY	EXPRESSIVELY
EEEIMNNPRSTT	PRESENTIMENT
EEEIMNNPRSTU	SUPEREMINENT
EEEIMNNRSTTV	REINVESTMENT
EEEIMNORSSST	TIRESOMENESS
EEEIMNORSSTT	SENSITOMETER
EEEIMNPRRSST	MISREPRESENT
EEEIMNQRRSTU	REQUIREMENTS
EEEIMOORRSST	STEREOISOMER
EEEIMOPRRSTX	EXTEMPORISER
EEEIMOPRRTXZ	EXTEMPORIZER
EEEIMOPRSTUX	TIME EXPOSURE
EEEINNPRSSTX	INEXPERTNESS
EEEINNPRSTUV	SUPERVENIENT
EEEINPRRRSTT	INTERPRETERS
EEEINPRSSUVX	UNEXPRESSIVE
EEEINRRTTTUX	INTERTEXTURE
EEEIORRSTVVX	EXTROVERSIVE
EEEJMPQRSUUU	QUEUE-JUMPERS
EEEKKLNOSSTY	SKELETON KEYS
EEEKLOOPPPSS	SPOKESPEOPLE
EEELLLNRSSTY	RELENTLESSLY
EEELLMORRTTU	TELLUROMETER
EEELLOPPPRWY	YELLOW PEPPER
EEELMMNOPRTY	RE-EMPLOYMENT
EEELMNNOOSSS	LONESOMENESS
EEELMNNOOSTT	ON ONE'S METTLE
EEELMNNSTTTU	UNSETTLEMENT

EEELMNPPRSTU	SUPPLEMENTER	EEGHIILNNPRS	REPLENISHING
EEELMOPPRRTT	TELEPROMPTER	EEGHIINOSSST	HISTOGENESIS
EEELNNOQSSTU	ELOQUENTNESS	EEGHIINPRRTZ	THE PRIZE RING
EEELNNOSSSST	TONELESSNESS	EEGHIINRSTUX	EXTINGUISHER
EEELNNSSSSTU	TUNELESSNESS	EEGHIKNRRSTU	HUNGER STRIKE
EEELNORSSSTU	RESOLUTENESS	EEGHILLSSTWY	WEIGHTLESSLY
EEELNRSSSSST	RESTLESSNESS	EEGHILMNORVW	OVERWHELMING
EEELOOPRSTTU	TELEUTOSPORE	EEGHINOORSST	ORTHOGENESIS
EEEMPRSSTTXY	EXPERT SYSTEM	EEGHINOPSSTY	PHYTOGENESIS
EEENOORSSTTT	TESTOSTERONE	EEGHLLOOPRST	HOT-GOSPELLER
EEEOPRRTTTVY	REVERT TO TYPE	EEGHLMNNOORS	LONGSHOREMEN
EEFFGHIIRRST	FIRE FIGHTERS	EEGHLOOORSTU	HETEROLOGOUS
EEFFGILNRSSU	GLUE-SNIFFERS	EEGHMNOORSTU	THERMOGENOUS
EEFFIIILLLORX	ELIXIR OF LIFE	EEGHMNOORTTU	MOTHER TONGUE
EEFFLLORSSTY	EFFORTLESSLY	EEGHNOOORSTU	HETEROGONOUS
EEFGHIIKNNRT	FREETHINKING	EEGHNOORSTUY	HETEROGYNOUS
EEFGHIIILNRRT	FREIGHTLINER	EEGHOORSTUYZ	HETEROZYGOUS
EEFGHIIILNRTT	FERLINGHETTI	EEGIIIINNRTVW	INTERVIEWING
EEFGHIIILRRST	FIRELIGHTERS	EEGIILLLNPPS	SLEEPING PILL
EEFGHIILRTTW	WEIGHT LIFTER	EEGIILLNNNVY	ENLIVENINGLY
EEFGHIIPRRST	PRISEFIGHTER	EEGIILMMNNPT	IMPLEMENTING
EEFGHIIPRRTZ	PRIZEFIGHTER	EEGIILNORRTV	GREEN VITRIOL
EEFGHILNRRSY	REFRESHINGLY	EEGIILOPSSTT	EPIGLOTTISES
EEFGIIILLNRTT	LITTLE FINGER	EEGIIMNNOPST	OPENING TIMES
EEFGIILMNPXY	EXEMPLIFYING	EEGIINNPRRST	ENTERPRISING
EEFGIIMMNRSW	FREE-SWIMMING	EEGIINNPRRTT	INTERPRETING
EEFGIIMNNNRT	INFRINGEMENT	EEGIINNRSTWZ	WESTERNIZING
EEFGIINOPRRT	PROFITEERING	EEGIJMNPQUUU	QUEUE-JUMPING
EEFGMNOORSTT	FORGET-ME-NOTS	EEGIKKNORSWW	WORKING WEEKS
EEFHHHMMMOOOR	HOME FROM HOME	EEGILLNOOSST	SELENOLOGIST
EEFHIILRSSSV	SILVERFISHES	EEGILLNRSTWY	SWELTERINGLY
EEFIIINNRSST	INTENSIFIERS	EEGILLOOPSST	SPELEOLOGIST
EEFIIMNORSSU	SEMINIFEROUS	EEGILLOOSSTT	TELEOLOGISTS
EEFIIINORRSSU	RESINIFEROUS	EEGILMNOOOST	ENTOMOLOGISE
EEFILLORSSTU	STELLIFEROUS	EEGILMNOOOTZ	ENTOMOLOGIZE
EEFILMOOORST	TOMFOOLERIES	EEGILMOOPPSS	GOOSE PIMPLES
EEFILMORSTTU	FLITTERMOUSE	EEGILMOOPSTY	EPISTEMOLOGY
EEFILNNQRTUY	INFREQUENTLY	EEGILNNORTUV	VOLUNTEERING
EEFILNOORRTX	RETROFLEXION	EEGILNNSSSSW	WINGLESSNESS
EEFILNPSSSTU	SPITEFULNESS	EEGILNOPRTTU	TRIPLE-TONGUE
EEFIMNNORRST	FRONTIERSMEN	EEGILOPRSSTT	POLTERGEISTS
EEFLLMORRSUY	REMORSEFULLY	EEGILQRRRSUY	GREY SQUIRREL
EEFLLNNTUUVY	UNEVENTFULLY	EEGIMNNNRRSU	INTERREGNUMS
EEFLLNOOOPSW	ONE FELL SWOOP	EEGINNPRSSSS	PRESSINGNESS
EEFLMNORSSSS	FORMLESSNESS	EEGINOOPRRVW	OVERPOWERING
EEFLNOPRSSUW	POWERFULNESS	EEGINOOPRSSS	SPOROGENESIS
EEGGGGHMRRUU	HUGGER-MUGGER	EEGINOOPRSVX	OVEREXPOSING
EEGGHIILNNNT	ENLIGHTENING	EEGINOPPRSTV	OVERSTEPPING
EEGGHIINTTUV	GIVE IT THE GUN	EEGINOPRSSSS	REPOSSESSING
EEGGIILNNRSS	GINGERLINESS	EEGINOPRSTTY	STEREOTYPING
EEGGILSSTUVY	SUGGESTIVELY	EEGINORSSSUV	GRIEVOUSNESS
EEGGNOORSSSU	GORGEOUSNESS	EEGINOSSSUUX	EXIGUOUSNESS
EEGGHHILRSTWW	WHEELWRIGHTS	EEGINPRSSTTU	GUTTERSNIPES
EEGHHIPRRSSU	HIGH-PRESSURE	EEGIOPRRSSSV	PROGRESSIVES

EEGKORRSSTUW	GUEST WORKERS
EEGKPPRSTYYZ	KYRGYZ STEPPE
EEGLMNNOOOPR	PROLEGOMENON
EEGLOPPPSTUV	GLOVE PUPPETS
EEGNNOORRSUU	NEUROSURGEON
EEGNORRRSUUY	NEUROSURGERY
EEHHIIMMOPRT	HEMIMORPHITE
EEHHIINSSSTV	THIEVISHNESS
EEHHILLNOPTY	THEOPHYLLINE
EEHHINRSSSSW	SHREWISHNESS
EEHHIOPPRRSW	HORSEWHIPPER
EEHHLLNNOORZ	HOHENZOLLERN
EEHHLLOPRTYY	HETEROPHYLLY
EEHHMOORSSTU	HOUSEMOTHERS
EEHHOOOSSSTUU	HOUSE-TO-HOUSE
EEHHOOSSUUYY	HOUSEY-HOUSEY
EEHIIIMNNRTT	IN THE INTERIM
EEHIIKKLLRRSS	SELKIRKSHIRE
EEHIILNQRRSU	RELINQUISHER
EEHIIMNPPRRU	PERINEPHRIUM
EEHIIMOPRRSV	IMPOVERISHER
EEHIIMPPRRSS	PREMIERSHIPS
EEHIINNSSSVX	VIXENISHNESS
EEHILMNORSST	MOTHERLINESS
EEHILNNPSTWY	PENNY WHISTLE
EEHILNOOPSST	SIPHONOSTELE
EEHILNOPSSTT	TELEPHONISTS
EEHIMOPRSTTY	MORE'S THE PITY
EEHINRSSSSTY	SYNTHESISERS
EEHINRSSSTYZ	SYNTHESIZERS
EEHIPRSSSTTU	TRUSTEESHIPS
EEHLNRSSSSTU	RUTHLESSNESS
EEHLOORRSTTU	RULE THE ROOST
EEHLOPRRSSTU	UPHOLSTERERS
EEHMMORSSSUU	SUMMERHOUSES
EEHMNNOOORSY	HONEYMOONERS
EEHMNOOORSTU	HETERONOMOUS
EEHMNOORSTUY	HETERONYMOUS
EEHMNRRRSUUY	NURSERY RHYME
EEHNNORRSTTW	NORTHWESTERN
EEHNNORSSSTT	HORNET'S NESTS
EEHNORSSTTUW	SOUTHWESTERN
EEHOOPRRSSTU	PORTERHOUSES
EEIIIMNRSSTV	INTERMISSIVE
EEIIIINPRRSTU	PERINEURITIS
EEIIIINRSSTUV	UNIVERSITIES
EEIIKLLNNSSU	UNLIKELINESS
EEIIILLPRSSTV	SPIRIT LEVELS
EEIIILMNNPTTY	IMPENITENTLY
EEIIILMNNSSTU	UNTIMELINESS
EEIIILMNOPSST	IMPOLITENESS
EEIIILMPRSSVY	IMPRESSIVELY, PERMISSIVELY
EEIIILNNPRRST	LINE PRINTERS
EEIIILNPPRSSS	SLIPPERINESS
EEIIILNPRSSST	PRIESTLINESS
EEIIILNPSSSST	PITILESSNESS
EEIIILNRSSSST	SISTERLINESS
EEIIILOOPPSTV	POSITIVE POLE
EEIIIMNNRTTTT	INTERMITTENT
EEIIMNOPRRSS	REIMPRESSION
EEIIMNOQSTTU	QUESTION TIME
EEIIMNPRRSTT	MISINTERPRET
EEIIMNPRSSUV	UNIMPRESSIVE
EEIIMNPRSTTY	SEMIPETERNITY
EEIIMNRRTTUX	INTERMIXTURE
EEIIMORSSTUV	SEMIVITREOUS
EEIIINNNORTTV	INTERVENTION
EEIIINNPSSTUV	PUNITIVENESS
EEIIINNRSSSST	SINISTERNESS
EEIIINOORSSTV	STEREOVISION
EEIIINOPPRSST	PROPENSITIES
EEIIINOPRRSSV	IRRESPONSIVE
EEIIINOPSSSTV	POSITIVENESS
EEIINORRSTVV	INTROVERSIVE
EEIINPRRTTUV	INTERRUPTIVE
EEIINRSSTTUV	INVESTITURES
EEIIOOPRRSST	REPOSITORIES
EEIIPRSSTVXY	EXPRESSIVITY
EEIKLMNNOSTY	MILTON KEYNES
EEIKOPRRRSTW	WORKER-PRIEST
EEILLNNOSSSV	SLOVENLINESS
EEILLNSSSSST	LISTLESSNESS
EEILLORRSTUY	IRRESOLUTELY
EEILMMNNOPTY	IN EMPLOYMENT
EEILMOOPRSST	METROPOLISES
EEILMOPPRRTY	PEREMPTORILY
EEILNNOOPSVX	NONEXPLOSIVE
EEILNOOORSSU	OLEORESINOUS
EEILNOOPPRSY	POLYISOPRENE
EEILNOORRSTU	RESOLUTIONER
EEILNOPRSSSU	PERILOUSNESS
EEILNOPRSSVY	RESPONSIVELY
EEILNPRSSTTY	PERSISTENTLY
EEILOPPRSSVY	OPPRESSIVELY
EEILOPRRSSTY	PROSELYTISER
EEILOPRRSTYZ	PROSELYTIZER
EEILOPSSSSVY	POSSESSIVELY
EEIMMMNSSTUY	IMMUNE SYSTEM
EEIMMNOPRSTV	IMPROVEMENTS
EEIMMNNNOPRSY	MONEY-SPINNER
EEIMNNNORSTV	ENVIRONMENTS
EEIMNNORSSTTY	SENSITOMETRY
EEINNOOPQSTU	OPEN QUESTION
EEINNOPRSSUV	UNRESPONSIVE
EEINNORSSSSU	RESINOUSNESS
EEINOOPPSSST	OPPOSITENESS
EEINOOPRSSSS	REPOSSESSION
EEINOORRRSTV	RETROVERSION

EEINOORRSTVX	EXTROVERSION
EEINOPRSSSSU	SUPERSESSION
EEINOPRSSSTV	SPORTIVENESS
EEINOPRSSSUV	PERVIOUSNESS, PREVIOUSNESS
EEINORSSSTUV	VITREOUSNESS
EEKLMNOPUYZZ	MONKEY-PUZZLE
EEKNNOORSTTT	STOKE-ON-TRENT
EEKNOOPPRSSS	SPOKESPERSON
EELLLOORRSTW	ROLLER TOWELS
EELLNNNOOSSV	NOLENS VOLENS
EELLNOSSSSSU	SOULLESSNESS
EELLORRSSTTY	STORYTELLERS
EELMMNNOPTUY	UNEMPLOYMENT
EELMOPRRSTTY	STORMY PETREL
EELNOORSSSST	ROOTLESSNESS
EELNOPSSSSST	SPOTLESSNESS
EEMNNOOPPSTT	POSTPONEMENT
EEMNNOORSSSU	ENORMOUSNESS
EEMNNORSSSUU	NUMEROUSNESS
EENNOOPPRSSU	ON ONE'S UPPERS
EENNOSSSSSUU	SENSUOUSNESS
EENOOPRRSTUU	NEUROPTEROUS
EEOOPPRRSSTU	PREPOSTEROUS
EEOPQRSSSTTU	REQUEST STOPS
EEOPRRRSSSTU	TROUSER PRESS
EEPPRRTTTTYY	PRETTY-PRETTY
EFFGGHIIINRT	FIRE FIGHTING
EFFGGIILLNNSU	GLUE-SNIFFING
EFFGHHHIIRSS	HIGH SHERIFFS
EFFGIINQOPRR	FIREPROOFING
EFFILNRSSTUU	FRUITFULNESS
EFGGGIINOPTT	PETTIFOGGING
EFGHHIILOPRS	HIGH PROFILES
EFGHIILNOSST	LINES OF SIGHT
EFGHIINNSSTT	SHIFTINGNESS
EFGHIINRRSTT	FIRST-NIGHTER
EFGHILNRSSTU	RIGHTFULNESS
EFGHLNOOPUUY	YOUNG HOPEFUL
EFGIIINNNSTY	INTENSIFYING
EFGIILNRRTYY	TERRIFYINGLY
EFGIINNOPRSY	PERSONIFYING
EFGIINNPRRST	FINGERPRINTS
EFGILLNRTTUY	FLUTTERINGLY
EFGILNPSTUYY	STUPEFYINGLY
EFGLNNORSSUW	WRONGFULNESS
EFHHILLOOOSY	HOLY OF HOLIES
EFHIILQRRSSU	SQUIRRELFISH
EFHILLMNORTU	RUN-OF-THE-MILL
EFHILLOSSTWW	WOLF WHISTLES
EFHILMNRSSTU	MIRTHFULNESS
EFHIMNPRSSSU	FRUMPISHNESS
EFHLLNOSSSTU	SLOTHFULNESS
EFHLNNOOPRTY	HORN OF PLENTY
EFHLNOSSTUUY	YOUTHFULNESS

EFHLNRSSTTUU	TRUTHFULNESS
EFIILMOPRSVY	OVERSIMPLIFY
EFIINOOPSTVW	POINTS OF VIEW
EFILLOPRSSTY	PROFITLESSLY
EFIOOOPRRSSU	SOPORIFEROUS
EFLLOPPRSUUY	PURPOSEFULLY
EFLMNNORSSUU	MOURNFULNESS
EFLNOPRSSSTU	SPORTFULNESS
EFLNRSSSTTUU	TRUSTFULNESS
EFNNNORRRSTU	FRONT-RUNNERS
EFNOOPRRSTTY	PORTS OF ENTRY
EGGGIILLNNRSY	SNIGGERINGLY
EGGGILNSSTUY	SUGGESTINGLY
EGGGINOPRRSU	GINGER GROUPS
EGGHHIILSTTW	LIGHTWEIGHTS
EGGHHIINSSSW	WHIGGISHNESS
EGGHIIKLNNSS	KING'S ENGLISH
EGGHIILNNOOP	PIGEONHOLING
EGGHIIMNNOOZ	HOMOGENIZING
EGGHIIINPRSS	PRIGGISHNESS
EGGHIIINRRSTW	RIGHT-WINGERS
EGGHILNSSSSU	SLUGGISHNESS
EGGHLOOOOPTY	PHOTOGEOLOGY
EGGIIIILMNTZ	LEGITIMIZING
EGGIILLMMNRY	GLIMMERINGLY
EGGIILLNNSTY	GLISTENINGLY
EGGIILLNRTTY	GLITTERINGLY
EGGILLLNORVY	GROVELLINGLY
EGGILNNORSSY	ENGROSSINGLY
EGGILOOPSTTY	EGYPTOLOGIST
EGGIMNNOOPRSS	GOSSIPMONGER
EGHHIIKNSTTW	WHITE KNIGHTS
EGHHILNNORSS	ENGLISH HORNS
EGHHILNOSSSU	GHOULISHNESS
EGHHNOORSSTU	THOROUGHNESS
EGHIIILMMNRSY	SHIMMERINGLY
EGHIILMNPRWY	WHIMPERINGLY
EGHIILNOSTTU	SILHOUETTING
EGHIILNOTTWZ	TWILIGHT ZONE
EGHIILOOPSSY	PHYSIOLOGIES
EGHIINNSSTYZ	SYNTHESIZING
EGHIINORSTWW	WIGTOWNSHIRE
EGHIIRSSSTU	RIGHTS ISSUES
EGHILMNOORST	MOONLIGHTERS
EGHILMOOOPRS	MORPHOLOGIES
EGHILMOORSTY	MYTHOLOGISER
EGHILMOORTYZ	MYTHOLOGIZER
EGHILNOOPRST	PHRENOLOGIST
EGHILNOOSSTT	ETHNOLOGISTS
EGHILNOPRSTU	UPHOLSTERING
EGHILOOPPSST	PSEPHOLOGIST
EGHIMNNNOOOY	HONEYMOONING
EGHIMNNORSSU	NURSING HOMES
EGHIMNOOORSU	ROOMING HOUSE

EGHINNOOSSST	SOOTHINGNESS
EGHINOOORSTV	OVERSHOOTING
EGHINOOPRRSV	GOVERNORSHIP
EGHINOORRTVW	OVERTHROWING
EGIIIKLNNNRT	INTERLINKING
EGIIILLNNRSV	SILVER LINING
EGIIILNNNPRT	LINE PRINTING
EGIIIMNOPSTU	IMPETIGINOUS
EGIIINNNRRTTW	INTERTWINING
EGIIKLNPPRRS	KLIPSPRINGER
EGIIKNNNSSST	STINKINGNESS
EGIIKNNRSSST	STRIKINGNESS
EGIIKNOPPPRS	SKIPPING-ROPE
EGIILLMNPSSS	MISSPELLINGS
EGIILLNNOPST	SELLING POINT
EGIILMMNORVY	LIVING MEMORY
EGIILMNNOPTT	MELTING POINT
EGIILMOOSSST	SEISMOLOGIST
EGIILNNPPSSS	SLIPPINGNESS
EGIILNPPRRSY	PERSPIRINGLY
EGIIMNOOPRRT	PRIMOGENITOR
EGIIMNOPRRST	MISREPORTING
EGIINNPRRTTU	INTERRUPTING
EGIINPRRSSUZ	PRESSURIZING
EGIKKNNOPRTY	PONY-TREKKING
EGILLNNOORST	ROLLING STONE
EGILLNORSTTY	STORYTELLING
EGILMNNORTTY	TORMENTINGLY
EGILMNOOOSTT	ENTOMOLOGIST
EGILMNOOSTYZ	ENZYMOLOGIST
EGILMOOSSTTY	ETYMOLOGISTS
EGILNOOOPSST	STOOLPIGEONS
EGILNOOPRSUY	PYROLIGNEOUS
EGILNOORSSSU	GLORIOUSNESS
EGILNOORSSTU	NEUROLOGISTS
EGILNOPPRSSY	OPPRESSINGLY
EGILNOPRSTTY	PROTESTINGLY
EGILNRSTTTUY	STUTTERINGLY
EGILOOPRSSTT	PETROLOGISTS
EGIMMNOOPRSU	SPERMOGONIUM
EGIMNOORRTTY	TRIGONOMETRY
EGINOOPRRSSS	PROGRESSIONS
EGINOORRSSSU	RIGOROUSNESS
EGINOORSSSUV	VIGOROUSNESS
EGINOPPPRSSU	PRESUPPOSING
EGINPRRSSSTU	PURSE STRINGS
EGMMNOORRRUU	RUMOURMONGER
EHHIILOOPPSS	PHILOSOPHIES, PHILOSOPHISE
EHHIILOOPPSZ	PHILOSOPHIZE
EHHIIMMMOPRS	HEMIMORPHISM
EHHILOOPPRSS	PHILOSOPHERS
EHHIMNOOPRST	THERMOSIPHON
EHHINOOOPPRS	SIPHONOPHORE
EHHLOOSSTTUY	YOUTH HOSTELS
EHHMNOOOPRTY	PHYTOHORMONE
EHIIILNNOPTW	WHIP INTO LINE
EHIIILORTTVW	WHITE VITRIOL
EHIIKNOOPSST	PHOTOKINESIS
EHIIKNORRSSS	KINROSS-SHIRE
EHIIKNSSSSTT	SKITTISHNESS
EHIILLNOPSTT	SEPTILLIONTH
EHIILLNOSTTX	SEXTILLIONTH
EHIILLOPSTWW	WILL-O'-THE-WISP
EHIILMOOPRST	HELIOTROPISM
EHIILMRSSSTV	SILVERSMITHS
EHIILNOSTTTW	WHITE STILTON
EHIIMMOPPRRS	PERIMORPHISM
EHIIMNPRSTUX	XIPHISTERNUM
EHIIMOOPPRSS	EPIMORPHOSIS
EHILLOPPRTYY	PYROPHYLLITE
EHILMMOOPPRS	PLEOMORPHISM
EHILNOORTTWY	NOTEWORTHILY
EHILNSSSSTTU	SLUTTISHNESS
EHIMMMOOPRSS	MESOMORPHISM
EHIMOOPPRRTY	PYROMORPHITE
EHIMOOPRSTTT	PHOTOMETRIST
EHINNORSSTUW	UNWORTHINESS
EHIOORRSSSTT	SHORT STORIES
EHIOPRRSSUVY	SURVEYORSHIP
EHKMNOOOPSST	SMOOTH-SPOKEN
EHLMOOOPPRTY	PHOTOPOLYMER
EHMMOOOPRSSU	MESOMORPHOUS
EHMNNOORRSTT	NORTHERNMOST
EHMNOORSSSUU	HUMOROUSNESS
EHMNOORSSTTU	SOUTHERNMOST
EHNNOOPRTTU	PHOTONEUTRON
EHOOOPRRSTTU	ORTHOPTEROUS
EHOOPPRSSSTW	SHOWSTOPPERS
EIIIMMMNORSS	IMMERSIONISM
EIIIMMNORSST	IMMERSIONIST
EIIIMNNORSST	INTERMISSION
EIIIMNNPRSTT	INSPIRITMENT
EIIIMNOOPRST	REIMPOSITION
EIIIMPRTTTVY	PERMITTIVITY
EIIINOQRSSTU	REQUISITIONS
EIIINORSSSTV	REVISIONISTS
EIIILLLLMNOPS	PLIMSOLL LINE
EIIILLNORSSSU	ILLUSORINESS
EIIILMNOOSTUV	EVOLUTIONISM
EIIILMOOPPRST	PLEIOTROPISM
EIIILNNNOSTUV	TUNNEL VISION
EIIILNOOOPPST	POLE POSITION
EIIILNOOORRSTU	IRRESOLUTION
EIIILNOOSTTUV	EVOLUTIONIST
EIIILOOPRSTXY	EXPOSITORILY
EIIMMNNOOPRST	IMPRISONMENT
EIIMNNNQQUUU	QUINQUENNIUM
EIIMNNOOPRST	PREMONITIONS

EIINNOORRSTV	INTROVERSION
EIINNOPRRTTU	INTERRUPTION
EIINOOPPRSSST	PREPOSITIONS
EIINOORSTTTX	EXTORTIONIST
EIINOPRSSTTU	SUPERSTITION
EIIOOPPSSTTV	POSTPOSITIVE
EILLMNOOSSTY	MOTIONLESSLY
EILLNNNOOTVY	NONVIOLENTLY
EILLOPPRSTUY	SUPPLETORILY
EILMOPPRSTUU	MULTIPURPOSE
EILMORSSTUYY	MYSTERIOUSLY
EIMNNNOOOTTT	NOT TO MENTION
EIMNNNOSSSUU	NUMINOUSNESS
EIMNOOOPRRST	PROMONTORIES
EIMNOOORRSST	SENSORIMOTOR
EIMNOOQSSTTU	MOSQUITO NETS
EIMNOORSSSTU	TIMOROUSNESS
EIMNOPPRSSTU	PRESUMPTIONS
EINNORSSSUW	WIN ONE'S SPURS
EINNOQRSSTUU	NON SEQUITURS
EINOORSSSUUX	UXORIOUSNESS
EINOPRRSSTTW	WINTER SPORTS
EINOPRSSSSUU	SPURIOUSNESS
EINORSSSSUUU	USURIOUSNESS
EINORSSSTUUV	VIRTUOUSNESS
EKKNNOOSTUVZ	NOVOKUZNETSK
ELNOOPPSSSUU	POPULOUSNESS
ELNOOPRSTTUY	PORTENTOUSLY
ELOOPPRRSSUY	PROSPEROUSLY
ELOOPPRRSTTY	LOST PROPERTY
ELOORRSSTTUY	STERTOROUSLY
EMMNOOOPRSSU	MONOSPERMOUS
EMOOOPRRRSTT	STORM TROOPER
EMOPPRSSTUUU	PRESUMPTUOUS
EMORRSSTTUYY	MYSTERY TOURS
ENNOOORSSSSU	SONOROUSNESS
ENOORSSSTTUU	TORTUOUSNESS
FFGIINOORSTT	FIRST-FOOTING
FFHJLOORTUUY	FOURTH OF JULY
FGGGILNOOOST	FOOTSLOGGING
FGHHLLOTTUUY	THOUGHTFULLY
FGHIILNORRYY	HORRIFYINGLY
FGHIMNOOOPRT	MOTHPROOFING
FGIIILLNOSSV	LIVING FOSSIL
FGIIIMMNNORS	MISINFORMING
FGIIJLNSTUYY	JUSTIFYINGLY
FGIILLLMNOYY	MOLLIFYINGLY
FGIILMNORTYY	MORTIFYINGLY
FGIILMNSTYYY	MYSTIFYINGLY
FGILOORSTTUU	FUTUROLOGIST
FGINOOPRRSTU	RUSTPROOFING
FGINOOPSSTUY	PUSSYFOOTING
FHLLNOOOORRU	ROLL OF HONOUR
FIILMMORTTUY	MULTIFORMITY
FILLMNOSUUUX	LUMINOUS FLUX
FILOORSTTUUY	FORTUITOUSLY
FMNNOORSSTUU	FROM SUN TO SUN
GGGHHHIIILNT	HIGHLIGHTING
GGGILLNRSTUY	STRUGGLINGLY
GGHHILNRSTUY	HIGHLY STRUNG
GGHIILMNNOOT	MOONLIGHTING
GGHIILNOPSTT	SPOTLIGHTING
GGIIILLNNOTU	GUILLOTINING
GGIIILLNNRTUY	INTRIGUINGLY
GGIILMMNOSWY	GO SWIMMINGLY
GGILMNNOORRY	MORNING GLORY
GHHMNNOOOPST	MONOPHTHONGS
GHIIKLNNNTUY	UNTHINKINGLY
GHIILLOOPSST	PHILOLOGISTS
GHIILNNORSUY	NOURISHINGLY
GHIILNORSSTT	SHORT-LISTING
GHIILOOPSSTY	PHYSIOLOGIST
GHILMOOOPRST	MORPHOLOGIST
GHILMOOSSTTY	MYTHOLOGISTS
GHILNOOOPSST	PHONOLOGISTS
GHIMMOOPRSYZ	ZYGOMORPHISM
GHINOOPPSSTW	SHOWSTOPPING
GHLMNOOOOSUY	HOMOGONOUSLY
GHLMOOOSUYYZ	HOMOZYGOUSLY
GIIIINOPRRTZ	PRIORITIZING
GIIIKLMNNNSS	MISSING LINKS
GIIIMNNPRSST	STRIP MININGS
GIIIMNORSTUZ	MOISTURIZING
GIIINNOOPRSV	PROVISIONING
GIILLLLMNORS	ROLLING MILLS
GIILLNOORSUY	INGLORIOUSLY
GIILMMNOOPSW	SWIMMING POOL
GIILMMNOOSTU	IMMUNOLOGIST
GIILMMNOOOPZ	MONOPOLIZING
GIILNPRRSSUY	SURPRISINGLY
GIIMNOORSSTT	SITTING ROOMS
GIINNNOOPRSS	SPRING ONIONS
GIINNNOOPRTTU	TURNING POINT
GIINOPPRSTTU	OUTSTRIPPING
GIINOPRSTTTU	PROSTITUTING
GIJMNNNPRSUU	RUNNING JUMPS
GINNOOPRSSTT	STRONG POINTS
GLLNOOSTTUUY	GLUTTONOUSLY
GLOOOOOPRTYZ	PROTOZOOLOGY
HHILOOOPPSTU	PHOTOPHILOUS
HHIMMMOOOPRS	HOMOMORPHISM
HHIOOTTTUUWW	TU-WHIT TU-WHOO
HHMMOOOTTTUU	MOUTH-TO-MOUTH
HIIIILMNPSTT	PHILISTINISM
HIILLOOPPRWW	WHIPPOORWILL
HIKLMMOORSTW	SILKWORM MOTH
HILMMOOPPRSY	POLYMORPHISM
HILOOOPPRSTU	TROPHILOUS

HIMMMNOOOPRS	MONOMORPHISM	IILLNNOOOPPS	OPINION POLLS
HIMOOOPPRSTT	PHOTOTROPISM	IILMNOOSTUVY	VOLUMINOSITY
HIMOOOPRRSTT	ORTHOTROPISM	IILMOORSTTUY	UTILITY ROOMS
HINOOPPPRRSY	PORPHYROPSIN	IILNORSTTUUY	NUTRITIOUSLY
HIOOOPRRSTTY	PROTOHISTORY	IILOOPPRSTUY	PROPITIOUSLY
HJKNNNOOOSTX	KNOX-JOHNSTON	IINNOOOPPTTT	POINT-TO-POINT
HLLMNOOOPSUY	MONOPHYLLOUS	IINOOOPPRSST	PROPOSITIONS
HLMOOOPPRSUY	POLYMORPHOUS	IINOOOPPSSTT	POSTPOSITION
HLMOOPSSTUUY	POSTHUMOUSLY	IINOOPPSSSTU	SUPPOSITIONS
HMOOOPSSSTUY	PHYSOSTOMOUS	IINOOPRSTTTU	PROSTITUTION
HOOOOPRRSTTU	ORTHOTROPOUS	IIOOPPSSSTUU	SUPPOSITIOUS
IIIIMNNOSTTU	INTUITIONISM	ILLMNOOOSTTY	TONSILLOTOMY
IIIINNOQSSTU	INQUISITIONS	ILLMNOOSUUVY	VOLUMINOUSLY
IIIINNOSTTTU	INTUITIONIST	ILLOPSSSUWWY	PUSSY WILLOWS
IIILLNOPSSTT	POINTILLISTS	IMPPPRRSSTUU	STIRRUP PUMPS
IIILLNOSSSTU	ILLUSIONISTS	INNNOOOOPSSU	NONPOISONOUS
IIILNOQSTUUY	INIQUITOUSLY	INOOPPRSSTTU	OPPORTUNISTS
IIIMNOORTTUV	VOMITURITION	LLMOSTTUUUUY	TUMULTUOUSLY
IIINNORSTTTU	NUTRITIONIST	LLOOPSTUUUVY	VOLUPTUOUSLY
IIINNORSTTUU	INNUTRITIOUS	LMNNOOOOSTUY	MONOTONOUSLY
IIINNOSSTTTU	INSTITUTIONS	LMNNOOSSUYYY	SYNONYMOUSLY
IIIOPRSSTTUY	SPIRITUOSITY	MNPPRRSTTUUU	TURN UP TRUMPS

AAAAACINNRSTT	SANTA CATARINA
AAAAADGGIINNN	AGAIN AND AGAIN
AAAABCCEELRTU	BACCALAUREATE
AAAABCCHILMRR	HAMILCAR BARCA
AAAABCEEKKSTT	TAKE A BACK SEAT
AAAABDILMORSS	AMBASSADORIAL
AAAACCDIIKLLS	LACKADAISICAL
AAAACCINRSSTU	TRANSCAUCASIA
AAAACCLMNORST	MALACOSTRACAN
AAAACDDGINUUY	CIUDAD GUAYANA
AAAACDEEMRSTT	ATACAMA DESERT
AAAACEIMMNORS	AMERICAN SAMOA
AAAACEINRRSSV	CARAVANSERAIS
AAAACILLLNPTY	APLANATICALLY
AAAACILLNOPRY	PARANOIACALLY
AAAACIMNRSSST	ANTIMACASSARS
AAAADEGHLMNOP	ALPHA AND OMEGA
AAAAEGIMMNRST	ANAGRAMMATISE
AAAAEGIMMNRTZ	ANAGRAMMATIZE
AAAAEGNRSTVXZ	EXTRAVAGANZAS
AAAAEHILNPPRR	PARAPHERNALIA
AAAAGILMMNOST	AMALGAMATIONS
AAAAGIMMMNRST	ANAGRAMMATISM
AAAAGIMMNRSTT	ANAGRAMMATIST
AAAAILNRSSSTU	AUSTRALASIANS
AAABBCEGIRRSY	BABY CARRIAGES
AAABCCEINORTY	CYANOBACTERIA
AAABCCILLORTY	ACROBATICALLY
AAABCCILMNOTY	BY ACCLAMATION
AAABCDEHINRTU	CHATEAUBRIAND
AAABCDIKNORTW	BACKWARDATION
AAABCEEILNRST	ASCERTAINABLE
AAABCEGILLLRY	ALGEBRAICALLY
AAABCEILLNORY	ANAEROBICALLY
AAABCEILLRSWY	CABLE RAILWAYS
AAABCEILMNRRU	ARABIC NUMERAL
AAABCEIRSSTTV	BITTER CASSAVA
AAABCILLLOPRY	PARABOLICALLY
AAABDDELNTTUW	WATTLE AND DAUB
AAABDEEINRRST	ARABIAN DESERT
AAABDEGIILMTY	DAMAGEABILITY
AAABDEGMNNNOR	RAG-AND-BONE MAN
AAABEEELLRTUV	RATEABLE VALUE
AAABEGIILMNTY	MANAGEABILITY
AAABEGILLMNPT	PAINTBALL GAME
AAABEGILNNOTZ	ANTAGONIZABLE
AAABEHIKPPPST	PHI BETA KAPPAS
AAABEILLMNPTU	MANIPULATABLE
AAABELNNRRTUW	UNWARRANTABLE
AAABGLLMRRRSU	BURGLAR ALARMS
AAABHILLMPSTU	AMPHIBLASTULA
AAABHOOQQSTWW	BASOTHO-QWAQWA
AAABIIILLNOST	LABIALISATION
AAABIIILLNOTZ	LABIALIZATION

AAABIIILNTTTY	ATTAINABILITY
AAABIIKLNNOST	BALKANISATION
AAABIIKLNNOTZ	BALKANIZATION
AAACCCEGIKNPR	A CRACKING PACE
AAACCDEIIINPT	INCAPACITATED
AAACCDHIILNOR	ARCHIDIACONAL
AAACCEEEELLNRS	CLEARANCE SALE
AAACCEEHMNRTT	CATCHMENT AREA
AAACCEGILRTTX	EXTRAGALACTIC
AAACCEINNQSTU	ACQUAINTANCES
AAACCFINNNRSS	SAN FRANCISCAN
AAACCGILLLMOO	MALACOLOGICAL
AAACCHILLRTTY	CATHARTICALLY
AAACCHLORSSTY	THALASSOCRACY
AAACCILLMNORY	MACARONICALLY
AAACCILLRSSTY	SARCASTICALLY
AAACDDIILLSTY	DADAISTICALLY
AAACDEEINPPRS	DISAPPEARANCE
AAACDEELNRRSY	CALENDAR YEARS
AAACDEGIILMRT	DIGITAL CAMERA
AAACDEGINRRSS	AIRS AND GRACES
AAACDEHHKNRRS	CHANDRASEKHAR
AAACDEIIINPRT	PAEDIATRICIAN
AAACDEIIORTTV	RADIOACTIVATE
AAACDELLNOORW	ROAD ALLOWANCE
AAACDELNPPRRT	PART AND PARCEL
AAACDFNRRSSTT	ARTS AND CRAFTS
AAACDGHIIMPRT	DIAPHRAGMATIC
AAACDHIINOPRS	ANAPHRODISIAC
AAACDIIILPRST	PARASITICIDAL
AAACDIILMNOSS	DIPSOMANIACAL
AAACDILLOPRXY	PARADOXICALLY
AAACDILMNNSSY	CAYMAN ISLANDS
AAACDILNNRSSY	CANARY ISLANDS
AAACEEGNRSTVX	EXTRAVAGANCES
AAACEEELNRSTTY	SCALY ANTEATER
AAACEENNNOPPR	NONAPPEARANCE
AAACEENOPRRSW	A NARROW ESCAPE
AAACEEOPPRSUV	PAPAVERACEOUS
AAACEFIILNNRY	FINANCIAL YEAR
AAACEFILNORRT	RAREFACTIONAL
AAACEFMORRRTT	CREAM OF TARTAR
AAACEGHILOPPR	PALAEOGRAPHIC
AAACEGIINNRSS	CASSEGRAINIAN
AAACEGILMMNOS	MEGALOMANIACS
AAACEGILMNNOR	ANGLO-AMERICAN
AAACEGILMTTUY	GUATEMALA CITY
AAACEHIILLMNV	MACHIAVELLIAN
AAACEHIIMMNTT	MATHEMATICIAN
AAACEHILLPTTY	APATHETICALLY
AAACEHIMOOPPR	PHARMACOPOEIA
AAACEHNRRRSTW	SEARCH WARRANT
AAACEIILMNNRT	LATIN AMERICAN
AAACEIKLMOSTT	STAKE A CLAIM TO

AAACEILLMNOTX	EXCLAMATIONAL	AAADHIMMMMNSU	MUHAMMADANISM
AAACEILLMOOST	OSTEOMALACIAL	AAADIIMNORSTT	DRAMATISATION
AAACEILNNSSST	SATANICALNESS	AAADIIMNORTTZ	DRAMATIZATION
AAACELRRSTUVX	EXTRAVASCULAR	AAADKLMRRSTTX	KARL-MARX-STADT
AAACENRRRSTTU	RESTAURANT CAR	AAAEEEHKNPRSS	SHAKESPEAREAN
AAACENRSTTTTX	SEX ATTRACTANT	AAAEEGGLMNSTU	METALANGUAGES
AAACFGILNNRSU	LINGUA FRANCAS	AAAEEGGMNRSST	STAGE MANAGERS
AAACFILLNSTTY	FANTASTICALLY	AAAEEGINNRSSX	SEXAGENARIANS
AAACFIMNORRTW	AIRCRAFTWOMAN	AAAEEGINNRTTT	GIANT ANTEATER
AAACGGILLOPRY	PARAGOGICALLY	AAAEEHNRRSSTW	WESTERN SAHARA
AAACGIIMNPRTT	ANTIPRAGMATIC	AAAEEJLNRSTTW	SERJEANT AT LAW
AAACGILLMMRTY	GRAMMATICALLY	AAAEEJMNRSTVY	VESTMANAEYJAR
AAACGILLMPRTY	PRAGMATICALLY	AAAEFFHINORST	AFTER A FASHION
AAACHILLMSTTY	ASTHMATICALLY	AAAEFGMOPRSSS	PASSAGE OF ARMS
AAACHILLNOPRY	ANAPHORICALLY	AAAEFGNPRRSSU	ASPARAGUS FERN
AAACHILNRSSSU	HALICARNASSUS	AAAEFIILMMRST	MATERFAMILIAS
AAACIILLMNOTX	AXIOMATICALLY	AAAEFIILMPRST	PATERFAMILIAS
AAACIILLPRSTY	PARASITICALLY	AAAEGGGIKNPRR	PARKING GARAGE
AAACIILLSTTVY	ATAVISTICALLY	AAAEGGGIMNNST	STAGE-MANAGING
AAACIILNNNOTT	INCANTATIONAL	AAAEGIILMMNOR	EMILIA-ROMAGNA
AAACIILNOSTTU	ACTUALISATION	AAAEGILNNPRTT	GREAT PLANTAIN
AAACIILNOTTUZ	ACTUALIZATION	AAAEGIMMNPRST	PARAMAGNETISM
AAACIIORSSTTU	AUSTRO-ASIATIC	AAAEGINNNNORS	NONAGENARIANS
AAACIKOPRRSST	SICK AS A PARROT	AAAEGINORTTVX	EXTRAVAGATION
AAACILLLPRTYY	PARALYTICALLY	AAAEGLLLMOPRR	PARALLELOGRAM
AAACILLMNOPRY	PANORAMICALLY	AAAEGLNRTTVXY	EXTRAVAGANTLY
AAACILLMOTTUY	AUTOMATICALLY	AAAEHIMNRSSTT	THE SAMARITANS
AAACILLMRTTUY	TRAUMATICALLY	AAAEHIOSSSTTU	SOUTHEAST ASIA
AAACILNNORSSY	NARCOANALYSIS	AAAEIILMNNOTX	EXAMINATIONAL
AAACILNNORSTT	TRANSACTIONAL	AAAEILMNPRRTY	PARLIAMENTARY
AAACILNNRSTTT	TRANSATLANTIC	AAAEINORSTTVX	EXTRAVASATION
AAACILOSSTTUY	AUTOCATALYSIS	AAAEMMRRSSSTT	MASTERS-AT-ARMS
AAADDDEELTUVX	VALUE-ADDED TAX	AAAFILMNNOSTW	TASMANIAN WOLF
AAADDDEGINSTV	DISADVANTAGED	AAAGGGILNRTVY	AGGRAVATINGLY
AAADDEGINSSTV	DISADVANTAGES	AAAGIILNORTTV	GRAVITATIONAL
AAADDEHHMPRSY	MADHYA PRADESH	AAAGIINNSSSST	ASSASSINATING
AAADDEHHNPRRS	ANDHRA PRADESH	AAAGILNOOPPRT	PROPAGATIONAL
AAADDILNPPSSY	PAY-AND-DISPLAY	AAAHIIMNNRSTU	HUMANITARIANS
AAADDLMNPRSST	STANDARD LAMPS	AAAHIINORRTTU	AUTHORITARIAN
AAADEEEINNNRS	SEANAD EIREANN	AAAHIKNRSSTUY	RATUSHINSKAYA
AAADEEFHNRRTT	TAR AND FEATHER	AAAIIILMNNOST	ANIMALISATION
AAADEEGMRRRSU	DEMERARA SUGAR	AAAIIILMNNOTZ	ANIMALIZATION
AAADEEHHLNRTY	HALE AND HEARTY	AAAIILLNNOSTT	TANTALISATION
AAADEEHIMNSTT	ANATHEMATISED	AAAIILLNNOTTZ	TANTALIZATION
AAADEEHIMNTTZ	ANATHEMATIZED	AAAIIMNNOOSTT	ANATOMISATION
AAADEGGILNNRU	GUARDIAN ANGEL	AAAIIMNNOOTTZ	ANATOMIZATION
AAADEGINORRRT	A ROARING TRADE	AAAIIMNOORSTT	AROMATISATION
AAADEHHNPRSSZ	HAPHAZARDNESS	AAAIIMNOORTTZ	AROMATIZATION
AAADEHIINPRTT	ANTI-APARTHEID	AAAIINNORSTTV	INTRAVASATION
AAADEHNRRSTTW	DEATH WARRANTS	AAAIINNOSSSST	ASSASSINATION
AAADEILLQRRTU	QUADRILATERAL	AAAIINORRSTTT	TARTARISATION
AAADEINOPPRTT	PREADAPTATION	AAAIINORRTTTZ	TARTARIZATION
AAADGIMNOORST	GOOD SAMARITAN	AAAIKLNNOPRST	NATIONAL PARKS
AAADHHILNRRSU	HARUN AL-RASHID	AAAILLNNORSTT	TRANSLATIONAL

AAAILLNNORTTU	ULTRANATIONAL
AAAILLNORRSTT	TRANSLATORIAL
AAAILMNORSTVY	SALVATION ARMY
AAAILNNNRSTVY	TRANSYLVANIAN
AAAILNNOPRSTU	SUPRANATIONAL
AABBBIILORSTY	ABSORBABILITY
AABBCEEHILNOS	BELISHA BEACON
AABBCEGINPRTU	TURNIP CABBAGE
AABBCEHIKNSTT	STAB IN THE BACK
AABBCEILNRRST	TRANSCRIBABLE
AABBCEJKORRTU	BARBOUR JACKET
AABBCILLMOSTY	BOMBASTICALLY
AABBDDEEGILOR	BIODEGRADABLE
AABBDEEFGLRST	FLABBERGASTED
AABBDIILORSTY	ADSORBABILITY
AABBEEILLMOTZ	METABOLIZABLE
AABBEHIILNNTU	UNINHABITABLE
AABBEIILLOSSU	BOUILLABAISSE
AABBEIINORSTV	ABBREVIATIONS
AABBEINRRRSTW	RABBIT WARRENS
AABBENORRSSSU	BARBAROUSNESS
AABBIIILNOTTY	OBTAINABILITY
AABCCDDEENOTU	DEAD-CAT BOUNCE
AABCCEEFIILRS	SACRIFICEABLE
AABCCEEIRRSUU	BUREAUCRACIES
AABCCEHHLPRYY	BRACHYCEPHALY
AABCCEHILNPRS	SPECIAL BRANCH
AABCCEIILMPRT	IMPRACTICABLE
AABCCEIILPTTY	ACCEPTABILITY
AABCCEIORSSSU	BRASSICACEOUS
AABCCELNNOTUU	UNACCOUNTABLE
AABCCIIILNNST	CANNIBALISTIC
AABCCIILLLTUY	CALCULABILITY
AABCCIILMPRTY	IMPRACTICABLY
AABCCIILLOSTU	LACTOBACILLUS
AABCCKLNRRSTU	BLACKCURRANTS
AABCCLNNOTUUY	UNACCOUNTABLY
AABCDDEEILNST	BALANCED DIETS
AABCDDGINORRS	BOARDING CARDS
AABCDDHINORSW	SANDWICH BOARD
AABCDEEEFNRSS	BAREFACEDNESS
AABCDEEFIPRRT	PREFABRICATED
AABCDEEGHILRS	DISCHARGEABLE
AABCDEELRRSTT	BATTLE-SCARRED
AABCDEENNORUV	OVERABUNDANCE
AABCDEGIKLLNP	BACKPEDALLING
AABCDEHIILTTY	DETACHABILITY
AABCDEHIKLNTW	BLACK AND WHITE
AABCDEHORRSTY	CARBOHYDRATES
AABCDELLMNOOR	BALLROOM DANCE
AABCDELOPPRRS	CLAPPERBOARDS
AABCDGIKLMRSU	BLACKGUARDISM
AABCDINNORSTT	CONTRABANDIST
AABCEEEELNPSS	PEACEABLENESS

AABCEEEGHLLLN	CHALLENGEABLE
AABCEEEHLNSST	BALANCE SHEETS
AABCEEEILLPRR	IRREPLACEABLE
AABCEEGGPRRST	CARPETBAGGERS
AABCEEGHIOPRT	BACTERIOPHAGE
AABCEEHILMNPU	UNIMPEACHABLE
AABCEEIILLMRR	IRRECLAIMABLE
AABCEEIKMNRST	CABINET-MAKERS
AABCEEILMNRSV	VRAISEMBLANCE
AABCEEKQRRSTU	SQUARE BRACKET
AABCEELLPRRSY	CEREBRAL PALSY
AABCEFFGHNRSU	ASCHAFFENBURG
AABCEFGIMOTTU	COMBAT FATIGUE
AABCEFIIINOTT	BEATIFICATION
AABCEFIINORTT	ABORTIFACIENT
AABCEFIOPRRRT	PREFABRICATOR
AABCEFLNRSSTU	BLAST FURNACES
AABCEGGKRRSTU	GARBAGE TRUCKS
AABCEGHIIINRV	VIRGINIA BEACH
AABCEGHIILNTY	CHANGEABILITY
AABCEGHIILRTY	CHARGEABILITY
AABCEGHINORRS	A CRASHING BORE
AABCEGILLLNOO	BALNEOLOGICAL
AABCEGILLMOST	MEGALOBLASTIC
AABCEGILNNORV	OVERBALANCING
AABCEGINOORSU	BORAGINACEOUS
AABCEHIKLPRSU	SAKHA REPUBLIC
AABCEHILLLMNR	LAMELLIBRANCH
AABCEHILMNPUY	UNIMPEACHABLY
AABCEHIRRRRSS	CRASH BARRIERS
AABCEHKMNNRST	MERCHANT BANKS
AABCEIILLPRTU	ALTAI REPUBLIC
AABCEIINORRTT	NITROBACTERIA
AABCEIIRSTTTY	TETRABASICITY
AABCEILLLMOTY	METABOLICALLY
AABCEILLOORTV	COLLABORATIVE
AABCEILLRSTTY	TETRASYLLABIC
AABCEILMNNOOP	COMPANIONABLE
AABCEILPRRTTU	TATAR REPUBLIC
AABCEIMRRSTUU	BUREAUCRATISM
AABCEINOORRST	SERBO-CROATIAN
AABCEINRRSSTT	SCATTERBRAINS
AABCELMMNNOSU	SOMNAMBULANCE
AABCFGILNNOTU	CONFABULATING
AABCFIILORTTY	FACTORABILITY
AABCFIKMNNOORT	BACK FORMATION
AABCFILNNOOTU	CONFABULATION
AABCFILORRSUV	FIBROVASCULAR
AABCFLNOORTUY	CONFABULATORY
AABCGGIIILNNNZ	CANNIBALIZING
AABCGILLNOORT	COLLABORATING
AABCHIIILMNTY	MACHINABILITY
AABCIIILLMPTY	IMPLACABILITY
AABCIIILLPPTY	APPLICABILITY

AABCIILLLLSTY	BALLISTICALLY
AABCIILLNORTU	LUBRICATIONAL
AABCIILLOSTTY	BIOSTATICALLY
AABCIILLRSTYY	SYBARITICALLY
AABCIILMOPRTY	COMPARABILITY
AABCIINNOORST	CARBONISATION
AABCIINNOORTZ	CARBONIZATION
AABCIINORRSTU	CARBURISATION
AABCIINORRTUZ	CARBURIZATION
AABCIKLMNNOTU	BLACK MOUNTAIN
AABCILLNOOORT	COLLABORATION
AABCILMNNOOPY	COMPANIONABLY
AABCINORSSSTT	CONTRABASSIST
AABCLLOOORRST	COLLABORATORS
AABCMNNNOOSTT	NONCOMBATANTS
AABCNNOOORSST	CONTRABASSOON
AABDDEGINNPRS	BANDSPREADING
AABDDEHIILNNR	HILDEBRANDIAN
AABDDGHILORTY	BROAD DAYLIGHT
AABDDGIINNORR	DRAINING BOARD
AABDDGINORRSW	DRAWING BOARDS
AABDEEFGIILNT	INDEFATIGABLE
AABDEEHIILRTT	REHABILITATED
AABDEEHORRSTW	WEATHERBOARDS
AABDEFGIILNTY	INDEFATIGABLY
AABDEFGIOPRSS	BIRD OF PASSAGE
AABDEFGKORSST	DOG'S BREAKFAST
AABDEGIINNRRT	GRIN AND BEAR IT
AABDEGLLNRTUY	ARGYLL AND BUTE
AABDEHKNNRRTU	HANDBRAKE TURN
AABDEIILNRTUY	UNREADABILITY
AABDEILNNOSTT	NATIONAL DEBTS
AABDEINNNORRS	SAN BERNARDINO
AABDEINSSTTTU	SUBSTANTIATED
AABDEKLNRSTUY	LAUNDRY BASKET
AABDENNPRSTUU	SUPERABUNDANT
AABDENOOPRSSX	PANDORA'S BOXES
AABDGLNOORUWY	ALBURY-WODONGA
AABDHIMNORSTT	RHABDOMANTIST
AABDIIILLSTYY	DIALYSABILITY
AABDIILNSSTUU	TUBUAI ISLANDS
AABEEEEGLNRSS	AGREEABLENESS
AABEEEEHHNRTTW	WEATHER-BEATEN
AABEEEFLMNSST	SELF-ABASEMENT
AABEEEELNORSST	ELABORATENESS
AABEEEELOORRTV	OVERELABORATE
AABEEFILNNOTU	FONTAINEBLEAU
AABEEFLMOSSTV	MOVABLE FEASTS
AABEEGHIKNRRT	HEARTBREAKING
AABEEIIILLRTVY	REVEALABILITY
AABEEIILPRTTY	REPEATABILITY
AABEELLLRSTTY	TETRASYLLABLE
AABEEMMNNRRSST	EMBARRASSMENT
AABEFFLORSTUW	WATER BUFFALOS

AABEFHILNNOSU	UNFASHIONABLE
AABEFIILLNQUU	UNQUALIFIABLE
AABEFILLNOPTU	FALLOPIAN TUBE
AABEFILMORSSU	BALSAMIFEROUS
AABEFLMNORRST	TRANSFORMABLE
AABEGHIMNOOPR	GERMANOPHOBIA
AABEGHIMNSTTW	BANTAMWEIGHTS
AABEGHINQRSSU	SQUARE-BASHING
AABEGIILLNOUV	BOUGAINVILLEA
AABEGILMNPRTU	PERAMBULATING
AABEGILNORRTU	GUBERNATORIAL
AABEGILNRRSTT	SABRE-RATTLING
AABEGIMNRRSST	BATTERING RAMS
AABEHILLORUVY	BEHAVIOURALLY
AABEIIILNRTTY	RETAINABILITY
AABEIIKLMRTTY	MARKETABILITY
AABEIILLLOTVZ	VOLATILIZABLE
AABEIILMNORST	ABNORMALITIES
AABEIILMRSTUY	MEASURABILITY
AABEIILMSTTTY	METASTABILITY
AABEIILNORSTV	VERBALISATION
AABEIILNORTVZ	VERBALIZATION
AABEIILNRSTWY	ANSWERABILITY
AABEIILOPRTVY	EVAPORABILITY
AABEIILRRUVXY	AUXILIARY VERB
AABEIIMNNRSTU	ANTISUBMARINE
AABEIINRRRSST	ARBITRARINESS
AABEIKNORSSTT	STATION BREAKS
AABEILMNOPRTU	PERAMBULATION
AABEILNOOPPRT	APPORTIONABLE
AABEILNOORSTV	OBSERVATIONAL
AABEILOQRSTUU	SUBEQUATORIAL
AABELMNNRRTUU	NATURAL NUMBER
AABELMOPRRSTU	PERAMBULATORS
AABELMOPRRTUY	PERAMBULATORY
AABELNOPRRSTT	TRANSPORTABLE
AABELOPRRTUUY	BEAUTY PARLOUR
AABGGILLMMNOU	GAMMA GLOBULIN
AABGHIOOPRTUY	AUTOBIOGRAPHY
AABGHLLOPRSYY	SYLLABOGRAPHY
AABGIIILNSSTY	ASSIGNABILITY
AABGIILOPPRTY	PROPAGABILITY
AABHIIILNPRRS	LIBRARIANSHIP
AABIIIILNRTVY	INVARIABILITY
AABIIIILNSTTY	INSATIABILITY
AABIIILLMPPTY	IMPALPABILITY
AABIIILMPSSTY	IMPASSABILITY
AABIIILNOSSTT	STABILISATION
AABIIILNOSTTZ	STABILIZATION
AABIIILNNNRTTU	TINTINNABULAR
AABIIILNNSSTTU	INSUBSTANTIAL
AABIIILNORSTTU	BRUTALISATION
AABIIILNORTTUZ	BRUTALIZATION
AABIIILOPRTUVY	VAPOURABILITY

AABIILOSTTTUY	AUTOSTABILITY	AACCEGIILNRTT	INTERGALACTIC
AABIINNNOORTW	RAINBOW NATION	AACCEGIINNRRT	INCARCERATING
AABILLNSSTTUY	SUBSTANTIALLY	AACCEGILLOOTU	AUTECOLOGICAL
AABILNNSSTTUU	UNSUBSTANTIAL	AACCEGILLORTY	CATEGORICALLY
AABINORSSTTTU	SUBSTANTIATOR	AACCEGILLOTTY	GEOTACTICALLY
AABLMMNOORSTU	SOMNAMBULATOR	AACCEGINNNOTT	CONCATENATING
AACCCEEILNRRT	RECALCITRANCE	AACCEHHLNPRTY	CHANTRY CHAPEL
AACCCEGHNORTU	CHARGE ACCOUNT	AACCEHIINNORT	CHAIN REACTION
AACCCEGINORTY	GYNAECOCRATIC	AACCEHIINOSTT	CATECHISATION
AACCCEIILLMRT	CLIMACTERICAL	AACCEHIINOTTZ	CATECHIZATION
AACCCFIIILNOT	CALCIFICATION	AACCEHIKMRSST	CHRISTMAS CAKE
AACCCGHHILOPR	CHALCOGRAPHIC	AACCEHILLMSTY	SCHEMATICALLY
AACCCIIILMNTT	ANTICLIMACTIC	AACCEHILOSSTT	SCHOLASTICATE
AACCCIILMMORT	MACROCLIMATIC	AACCEHILRRTTU	ARCHITECTURAL
AACCDEEHHIKSS	SICK HEADACHES	AACCEHIMMORTT	METACHROMATIC
AACCDEEHINOPT	HEPTADECANOIC	AACCEHIMPRSTU	PHARMACEUTICS
AACCDEEHIRRST	CHARACTERISED	AACCEHIPPRRST	SHARP PRACTICE
AACCDEEHIRRTZ	CHARACTERIZED	AACCEIILLMNTY	CINEMATICALLY
AACCDEEIILNRU	CLAIRAUDIENCE	AACCEIINNORRT	INCARCERATION
AACCDEEIMORSS	ICE-CREAM SODAS	AACCEIIOPRSTT	ECTOPARASITIC
AACCDEGHHNNOP	CHOP AND CHANGE	AACCEIIORRSST	ARISTOCRACIES
AACCDEHIILMOR	RADIOCHEMICAL	AACCEIJKLOPRT	PRACTICAL JOKE
AACCDEHIIRRST	TRISACCHARIDE	AACCEILLMRTUV	CIRCUMVALLATE
AACCDEIIILNST	DIALECTICIANS	AACCEILLNNOST	CANCELLATIONS
AACCDEIILNOST	DIATONIC SCALE	AACCEILLNSTUY	ENCAUSTICALLY
AACCDEIINNOPT	PENTANOIC ACID	AACCEIMMNNOPT	ACCOMPANIMENT
AACCDEIINORTT	ACCREDITATION	AACCEINNNOOTT	CONCATENATION
AACCDEILLMSTU	MISCALCULATED	AACCEINNOSTTU	ACCENTUATIONS
AACCDEILNOOTU	COEDUCATIONAL	AACCEINOPSSSU	CAPACIOUSNESS
AACCDEIMMOOTV	ACCOMMODATIVE	AACCEKNORTTTU	COUNTERATTACK
AACCDEIMNNOPU	UNACCOMPANIED	AACCELLNOOPRR	LANCE CORPORAL
AACCDFIIIINOT	ACIDIFICATION	AACCELLPRSTUY	SPECTACULARLY
AACCDGHIIOPRR	CARDIOGRAPHIC	AACCELORSSSUU	CRASSULACEOUS
AACCDGIILLOOR	CARDIOLOGICAL	AACCFIIILLRSY	SACRIFICIALLY
AACCDGIMMNOOT	ACCOMMODATING	AACCFIIILNORT	CLARIFICATION
AACCDHIMRRSST	CHRISTMAS CARD	AACCFIIINNORT	CARNIFICATION
AACCDIILLOPTY	APODICTICALLY	AACCFIIINOPRT	CAPRIFICATION
AACCDIILNOSSS	CAICOS ISLANDS	AACCFIIINORST	SCARIFICATION
AACCDIILMNOORT	CARCINOMATOID	AACCFIIILLORY	CALORIFICALLY
AACCDIMMNOOOT	ACCOMMODATION	AACCFIILLSSTY	FASCISTICALLY
AACCEEFHSSTTY	SAFETY CATCHES	AACCFIILNOSTU	FASCICULATION
AACCEEFIRSTUV	SURFACE-ACTIVE	AACCGGIILLLOO	GLACIOLOGICAL
AACCEEHHIMNNT	THE MAIN CHANCE	AACCGHILLNOOT	ANGLO-CATHOLIC
AACCEEHILMNOT	CATECHOLAMINE	AACCGIIILMNTZ	ACCLIMATIZING
AACCEEHIMNORS	AEROMECHANICS	AACCGIIILLNOOR	CRANIOLOGICAL
AACCEEHIMRRST	SACCHARIMETER	AACCGILNOOPSV	GALVANOSCOPIC
AACCEEHILMNPRY	MACRENCEPHALY	AACCHIILMNOOT	MACHICOLATION
AACCEEHILRRSST	CHARACTERLESS	AACCHIILMRSSU	MUSICAL CHAIRS
AACCEEHMORRST	SACCHAROMETER	AACCHIIMNNORT	ANTIMONARCHIC
AACCEELMNRUUV	VACUUM CLEANER	AACCHIINNORST	ANACHRONISTIC
AACCEFIIINOTT	ACETIFICATION	AACCHILLLLOOY	ALCOHOLICALLY
AACCEFILORRSU	CALCARIFEROUS	AACCHILLMORTY	CHROMATICALLY
AACCEGHHLLOPRR	CHALCOGRAPHER	AACCHILLOPRTT	TROPHALLACTIC
AACCEGHINOOPR	OCEANOGRAPHIC	AACCHILMNOORT	ROMAN CATHOLIC

AACCHINOOSSTT	COACH STATIONS	AACDEIINNRSTT	TRANSACTINIDE
AACCIIINNOOST	COCAINISATION	AACDEIINOPRST	ENDOPARASITIC
AACCIIINNOOTZ	COCAINIZATION	AACDEIINOPSTT	DECAPITATIONS
AACCIIINORSTT	CICATRISATION	AACDEIKLLNPST	SLAP AND TICKLE
AACCIIINORTTZ	CICATRIZATION	AACDEILLLORRU	CELLULAR RADIO
AACCIILLMPRTY	IMPRACTICALLY	AACDEILLMORTY	DECLAMATORILY
AACCIILLSSTUY	CASUISTICALLY	AACDEILLNSTYY	ASYNDETICALLY
AACCIILMNOOSS	OCCASIONALISM	AACDEILLORRTY	DECLARATORILY
AACCIILMNORTY	MICROANALYTIC	AACDEILNQRUVY	QUADRIVALENCY
AACCIIRRSSTTU	CARICATURISTS	AACDEILPQRTUU	QUADRUPLICATE
AACCIILLNSTTYY	SYNTACTICALLY	AACDEIMNNNOTT	DECONTAMINANT
AACCIILLOPSSST	POSTCLASSICAL	AACDEINNNORSSU	ARUNDINACEOUS
AACCIILMNOSTUU	ACCUMULATIONS	AACDEINOSSSUU	AUDACIOUSNESS
AACCIILNNOOOTV	CONVOCATIONAL	AACDELNOPRSSY	PLAY ONE'S CARDS
AACCIILNNOORTT	CONTRACTIONAL	AACDFFIILNRST	TRAFFIC ISLAND
AACCIILNORTTUU	ACCULTURATION	AACDFIIIMNNOT	DAMNIFICATION
AACCIILNPRTTYY	CRYPTANALYTIC	AACDFMNOORSTW	WOODCRAFTSMAN
AACCIINORSSTTY	SACROSANCTITY	AACDGHILNNRSS	CRASH LANDINGS
AACCILLNORTTUY	CONTRACTUALLY	AACDGIIINNOST	DIAGNOSTICIAN
AACDDEEEHLLRY	CLEAR-HEADEDLY	AACDHIIIOPRST	ADIAPHORISTIC
AACDDEEEELLNVV	ADVANCED LEVEL	AACDHILLLRUYY	HYDRAULICALLY
AACDDEEIQSUUX	DUQUE DE CAXIAS	AACDHILLOPRSY	RHAPSODICALLY
AACDDEFIILSSS	CLASSIFIED ADS	AACDHILMNOORT	TRICHOMONADAL
AACDDEIIOSSST	DISASSOCIATED	AACDHIMMOOSSS	SADOMASOCHISM
AACDDFIIINNOT	DANDIFICATION	AACDHIMOOSSST	SADOMASOCHIST
AACDDIKMNNRSU	MANDARIN DUCKS	AACDIIILLMOTY	IDIOMATICALLY
AACDEEEGHIMNST	MAGNETIC HEADS	AACDIIILPQRTU	QUADRICIPITAL
AACDEEGHNNORR	CHANDERNAGORE	AACDIIINNNORT	INCARDINATION
AACDEEGINRRRU	UNDERCARRIAGE	AACDIIIORTTVY	RADIOACTIVITY
AACDEEHINTTTU	AUTHENTICATED	AACDIIKNNNOPR	RACK-AND-PINION
AACDEEILPRTTU	RECAPITULATED	AACDIILLLSTUY	DUALISTICALLY
AACDEEIMNNOTT	DECONTAMINATE	AACDIILLORTTY	DICTATORIALLY
AACDEEINPRSSV	SPACE INVADERS	AACDIILNNOPRT	CARDINAL POINT
AACDEEIQRSTTU	ACQUIRED TASTE	AACDIIMNOPSST	ANTISPASMODIC
AACDEENNNNOTT	NONATTENDANCE	AACDIIMNORRTY	DRAMATIC IRONY
AACDEFFIIMNRS	DISAFFIRMANCE	AACDILLMOPSSY	SPASMODICALLY
AACDEFFINRRTW	TRAFFIC WARDEN	AACDIMNORSSTY	ASTRODYNAMICS
AACDEFGHIRSTT	STRAIGHT-FACED	AACEEEGHNRSTX	EXCHANGE RATES
AACDEFLLNNOOR	ONCE AND FOR ALL	AACEEEHJKLRTT	LEATHERJACKET
AACDEGGILLMOY	DEMAGOGICALLY	AACEEFHMSSTTY	SAFETY MATCHES
AACDEGGILLOPY	PEDAGOGICALLY	AACEEFLNRSSSU	SELF-ASSURANCE
AACDEGHIINRRS	CARDIGANSHIRE	AACEEGHILOPRS	ARCHIPELAGOES
AACDEGHIOPRRR	CARDIOGRAPHER	AACEEGHLLSSSV	CHEVAL GLASSES
AACDEGJLNOSUU	JUGLANDACEOUS	AACEEGHLMNOPR	ENCEPHALOGRAM
AACDEGLMNNORS	SCANDALMONGER	AACEEGHLMOPSU	MEGACEPHALOUS
AACDEGLNORTTU	CONGRATULATED	AACEEGHNOOPRR	OCEANOGRAPHER
AACDEHIIMNRRT	ARCHIMANDRITE	AACEEGHNPRSTX	PART EXCHANGES
AACDEHLMNNORT	CALENDAR MONTH	AACEEGIILLNPR	ALPINE GLACIER
AACDEIIINPRST	PEDIATRICIANS	AACEEGILNPRTW	WATERING PLACE
AACDEIIIJLRTUX	EXTRAJUDICIAL	AACEEGIMNPSTT	MAGNETIC TAPES
AACDEIIILLMRTY	DIAMETRICALLY	AACEEGINNOSTU	GENTIANACEOUS
AACDEIILLOPRY	APERIODICALLY	AACEEGLOOSTTV	COTTAGE LOAVES
AACDEIILOPPRR	PERICARPOIDAL	AACEEHIILNPST	ELEPHANTIASIC
AACDEIILRSTTU	DISARTICULATE	AACEEHILLSTTY	AESTHETICALLY

AACEEHILMPRTT	HEPTAMETRICAL	AACEHIIIMNRTT	ARITHMETICIAN
AACEEHILNPRTT	PARENTHETICAL	AACEHIILLSTTY	ATHEISTICALLY
AACEEHIPRRSST	SEARCH PARTIES	AACEHIILNOPST	CEPHALISATION
AACEEHKMNRRSS	SNAKE CHARMERS	AACEHIILNOPTZ	CEPHALIZATION
AACEEHMNOPSUY	NYMPHAEACEOUS	AACEHIILRTTTY	THEATRICALITY
AACEEIILLPSTV	CAPITAL LEVIES	AACEHIIMNNOST	MECHANISATION
AACEEIILNRTTV	INTERCALATIVE	AACEHIIMNNOTZ	MECHANIZATION
AACEEIINNRSST	NECESSITARIAN	AACEHIIMNNRST	CHRISTIAN NAME
AACEEIINORRST	REACTIONARIES	AACEHIIMNPSTY	METAPHYSICIAN
AACEEILLMMRTY	METAMERICALLY	AACEHILLNTTUY	AUTHENTICALLY
AACEEILMMNRUY	ANEMOMETRICAL	AACEHILMNPRRU	HURRICANE LAMP
AACEEILNNRSTW	SAINT LAWRENCE	AACEHINOPRTTY	ACTINOTHERAPY
AACEEILNNSUUV	NUISANCE VALUE	AACEHINORTTTU	AUTHENTICATOR
AACEEIMNNRSTT	ASCERTAINMENT	AACEHLNOPSSSY	PSYCHOANALYSE
AACEELLLRRTUX	EXTRACELLULAR	AACEHLNOPSYYZ	PSYCHOANALYZE
AACEENNPPRSTU	APPURTENANCES	AACEHMSSSSTTU	MASSACHUSETTS
AACEFGILNORTV	CONFLAGRATIVE	AACEHNOPPRRTY	PARTHENOCARPY
AACEFIILLNRTY	INTERFACIALLY	AACEIIILMRSTT	MATERIALISTIC
AACEFILLMNRUY	NUCLEAR FAMILY	AACEIIIMPRSST	SEMIPARASITIC
AACEFILMNRSST	MASSIF CENTRAL	AACEIIKLLMNTY	KINEMATICALLY
AACEFINRSTTUY	SAFETY CURTAIN	AACEIILLLRSTY	REALISTICALLY
AACEFMNRRSTUU	MANUFACTURERS	AACEIILLMNSSY	MESSIANICALLY
AACEFNOPRRSTT	TRANSPORT CAFE	AACEIILMNSTU	NAUTICAL MILES
AACEGGHJKNNNU	KANGCHENJUNGA	AACEIILLNRRTY	INTERCALARILY,
AACEGHILLLRTY	LETHARGICALLY	INTERRACIALLY	
AACEGHILLMPRY	GRAPHEMICALLY	AACEIILMMNRSU	UNICAMERALISM
AACEGHILNPRSS	GRAPHICALNESS	AACEIILMNRSTT	MATERNALISTIC
AACEGHILOORST	ARCHAEOLOGIST	AACEIILMNRSTU	UNICAMERALIST
AACEGHIMNOPRT	CINEMATOGRAPH	AACEIILNNORTT	INTERACTIONAL,
AACEGHOPRRRST	CARTOGRAPHERS	INTERCALATION	
AACEGHOPRSSSU	SARCOPHAGUSES	AACEIILNNOSTT	CAT-O'-NINE-TAILS
AACEGIIIMNNRZ	AMERICANIZING	AACEIILNOPPSS	EPISCOPALIANS
AACEGIIINRRST	GERIATRICIANS	AACEIILNPRSTT	PATERNALISTIC
AACEGIILLMNOR	MINERALOGICAL	AACEIILNRSSST	SATIRICALNESS
AACEGIILLMNTY	ENIGMATICALLY	AACEIILPRRSTU	PARTICULARISE
AACEGIILLNNTY	ANTIGENICALLY	AACEIILPRRTUZ	PARTICULARIZE
AACEGIINNNRRT	REINCARNATING	AACEIIMMOSTTU	SEMIAUTOMATIC
AACEGIINPRRTV	PREVARICATING	AACEIIMOPRRST	MICROPARASITE
AACEGILLLLORY	ALLEGORICALLY	AACEIINNNORRT	REINCARNATION
AACEGILLLMRTU	METALLURGICAL	AACEIINOPPRST	APPRECIATIONS
AACEGILLMTUYZ	ZEUGMATICALLY	AACEIINOPRRTV	PREVARICATION
AACEGILLRSTTY	STRATEGICALLY	AACEIINORSTTU	CAUTERISATION
AACEGILMNNRST	MAGIC LANTERNS	AACEIINORTTUZ	CAUTERIZATION
AACEGILMNOOSU	MAGNOLIACEOUS	AACEIINRRRSTU	CURTAIN RAISER
AACEGILMNORTV	GALVANOMETRIC	AACEIJKRSSTTT	STRAITJACKETS
AACEGIMNOPSTU	COME UP AGAINST	AACEIKLMNOPST	KLEPTOMANIACS
AACEGINNOORST	OCTOGENARIANS	AACEIKLOPRSTT	KERATOPLASTIC
AACEGINOSSSUU	SAGACIOUSNESS	AACEILLLNRRTU	INTRACELLULAR
AACEGLLMMORRU	GRAM-MOLECULAR	AACEILLMNPTUY	PNEUMATICALLY
AACEGLLOOPSUY	POLYGALACEOUS	AACEILLMORTXY	EXCLAMATORILY
AACEGLMNORRSS	MARRONS GLACES	AACEILLMPRSTY	SPERMATICALLY
AACEGLRRSSTYZ	CRYSTAL GAZERS	AACEILMNRRSUV	VERNACULARISM
AACEHHILNOPRZ	RHIZOCEPHALAN	AACEILMOPRTVY	COMPARATIVELY
AACEHHLOOPRTX	CEPHALOTHORAX	AACEILNNOPSTU	ENCAPSULATION
		AACEILNOSSSSU	SALACIOUSNESS

AACEILNRRSTUU	CRANIAL SUTURE	AACGIIILNNNOTZ	ANGLICIZATION
AACEILOOPPRSS	LAPAROSCOPIES	AACGIIIMSSTTT	ASTIGMATISTIC
AACEILRSSTTTU	TRUCIAL STATES	AACGIIINPPRTT	PARTICIPATING
AACEIMNNRSTTT	TRANSMITTANCE	AACGIILLLNTVY	VACILLATINGLY
AACEIMNOOPSST	COMPASSIONATE	AACGIILLNNORY	INORGANICALLY
AACEINNOOTTTV	CONNOTATATIVE	AACGIILMNRTTU	MATRICULATING
AACEINOPRRSTT	PROCRASTINATE	AACGIILNORSTU	CARTILAGINOUS
AACEINOPRRTUY	PRECAUTIONARY	AACGIIMNNNOTT	CONTAMINATING
AACEINOPSSSTT	SPACE STATIONS	AACGIINNNOPRS	CAPARISONNING
AACEIOPRRRSTV	PREVARICATORS	AACGIJLNNOOTU	CONJUGATIONAL
AACEJKLNNORST	JACK-O'-LANTERNS	AACGILLLNOOPY	PALYNOLOGICAL
AACELMMNOPRTT	COMPARTMENTAL	AACGILLLNOSTY	NOSTALGICALLY
AACELNORRSUUV	NEUROVASCULAR	AACGILMNOOPST	CAMPANOLOGIST
AACELNRSSTTUU	SUSTENTACULAR	AACGILNNOOSTV	LONG VACATIONS
AACELORSSSTUU	ASSAULT COURSE	AACGILNOOPRTV	GALVANOTROPIC
AACEMNNOORSTT	ENTOMOSTRACAN	AACGIMMMNOORT	MONOGRAMMATIC
AACEMNNOPPRTY	PARENT COMPANY	AACGINOPPRSTU	GROUP CAPTAINS
AACFFIIIILNOST	FALSIFICATION	AACGKNOOORRTU	KANGAROO COURT
AACFGHIILRRTT	LIGHT AIRCRAFT	AACGLNOORRTTU	CONGRATULATOR
AACFGIIIMNNOT	MAGNIFICATION	AACHHIIMNPRSS	CHAIRMANSHIPS
AACFGIIINORTT	GRATIFICATION	AACHHILPSTXYY	TACHYPHYLAXIS
AACFGIILNNSTY	FASCINATINGLY	AACHHIMNPSSTY	YACHTSMANSHIP
AACFGILNNOORT	CONFLAGRATION	AACHIILLNNNOTU	HALLUCINATION
AACFGIMNNRTUU	MANUFACTURING	AACHILLLMPTYY	LYMPHATICALLY
AACFHIMNPRSST	CRAFTSMANSHIP	AACHILLNOPPSY	PANSOPHICALLY
AACFIIIIILRTTY	ARTIFICIALITY	AACHILLNORTUY	HALLUCINATORY
AACFIIILMNOPT	AMPLIFICATION	AACHILNNOORRT	NORTH CAROLINA
AACFIIILNOQTU	QUALIFICATION	AACHILNOORSTU	SOUTH CAROLINA
AACFIIIMNORST	RAMIFICATIONS	AACHILOPRSSTY	ASTROPHYSICAL
AACFIILOQRTUY	QUALIFICATORY	AACHIMMNNOPSY	NYMPHOMANIACS
AACFIINNOORTT	FRACTIONATION	AACHIMMNOPRST	PANCHROMATISM
AACFIINOORSTT	FACTORISATION	AACHIMMOOPRST	APOCHROMATISM
AACFIINOORTTZ	FACTORIZATION	AACHIMOPRSSTT	CATASTROPHISM
AACFIINOSSSTT	SATISFACTIONS	AACHIOPRSSTTT	CATASTROPHIST
AACFINORSTTUY	ANFRACTUOSITY	AACHLNOPSSTYY	PSYCHOANALYST
AACFORRSSTTTU	FRACTOSTRATUS	AACHLOOPRSTTY	THORACOPLASTY
AACGGHIKNNSUW	KWANGSI-CHUANG	AACIIIILNOSTT	ITALICISATION
AACGGHINOOPRR	ORGANOGRAPHIC	AACIIIILNOTTZ	ITALICIZATION
AACGGILLNOOOR	ORGANOLOGICAL	AACIIILLNNNOT	INCLINATIONAL
AACGGILMMOORT	LOGOGRAMMATIC	AACIIILLPPRTY	PARTICIPIALLY
AACGGILNRSTYZ	CRYSTAL GAZING	AACIIILNNOSTT	NATIONALISTIC
AACGHHIMNNTTW	NIGHT WATCHMAN	AACIIILNOOSST	SOCIALISATION
AACGHIIILLNNTU	HALLUCINATING	AACIIILNOOSTZ	SOCIALIZATION
AACGHIILLPRST	CALLIGRAPHIST	AACIIILNORSTT	RATIONALISTIC
AACGHIIPRRSTT	STRATIGRAPHIC	AACIIINNOORTT	RATIOCINATION
AACGHILMNOOPR	NOMOGRAPHICAL	AACIIINOPPRTT	PARTICIPATION
AACGHILOOPPRT	TOPOGRAPHICAL	AACIINSSSTTTT	STATISTICIANS
AACGHILOPPRTY	TYPOGRAPHICAL	AACIILLMMNNOTY	ANTINOMICALLY
AACGHLMMOORRS	GRAMMAR SCHOOL	AACIILLMORTTY	MATRILOCALITY,
AACGHMNOOPRSY	PHARMACOGNOSY	TRIATOMICALLY	
AACGIIIILLMSTY	IMAGISTICALLY	AACIILLMOSTTY	ATOMISTICALLY
AACGIIILLNOST	GALLICISATION	AACIILLNPRTUY	PURITANICALLY
AACGIIILLNOTZ	GALLICIZATION	AACIILLOPRTTY	PATRIOTICALLY
AACGIIILNNOST	ANGLICISATION	AACIILLPRSTTY	PATRISTICALLY

AACIILLSSTTTY	STATISTICALLY	AADDEGINOPPRS	PROPAGANDISED
AACIILMNORSSY	MICROANALYSIS	AADDEGINOPPRZ	PROPAGANDIZED
AACIILMNORTTU	MATRICULATION	AADDEGNOPRRSU	PARADE GROUNDS
AACIILMPRRSTTU	PARTICULARISM	AADDEILNRSSST	DASTARDLINESS
AACIILNNOOSTV	VOLCANISATION	AADDGIINNRSTZ	STANDARDIZING
AACIILNNOOTVZ	VOLCANIZATION	AADDIIILNOPST	DILAPIDATIONS
AACIILNNOPSTU	INCAPSULATION	AADDIIILMNSSWY	MIDWAY ISLANDS
AACIILNNOSTUV	VULCANISATION	AADEEEGGLRTXY	EXAGGERATEDLY
AACIILNNOTUVZ	VULCANIZATION	AADEEEHINSSTT	ANAESTHETISED
AACIILNOPSTTU	CAPITULATIONS	AADEEEHINSTTZ	ANAESTHETIZED
AACIILNORSTTU	ARTICULATIONS	AADEEEHIRSSST	HEART DISEASES
AACIILPRRSTTU	PARTICULARIST	AADEEEIKNSSWW	WIDE-AWAKENESS
AACIILPRRTTUY	PARTICULARITY	AADEEEIMNNRRT	MEDITERRANEAN
AACIIMMNNORTU	COMMUNITARIAN	AADEEEELPRSTXY	EXASPERATEDLY
AACIIMMORSSST	COMMISSARIATS	AADEEEMMNRSTU	ADMEASUREMENT
AACIIMMNNOOTT	CONTAMINATION	AADEEEMMORSTU	MADE-TO-MEASURE
AACIIMNNORTUU	ACTINOURANIUM	AADEEFHHLLRTY	HALF-HEARTEDLY
AACIINNNOOSST	CANONISATIONS	AADEEFILLLMRST	FLEET ADMIRALS
AACIINNNOOSTZ	CANONIZATIONS	AADEEFNSSSSTT	STEADFASTNESS
AACIINNOORSTT	NARCOTISATION	AADEEGGGILNPRS	SPREAD-EAGLING
AACIINNOORTTZ	NARCOTIZATION	AADEEGILMORRT	RADIOTELEGRAM
AACIINNOPSSTT	PANIC STATIONS	AADEEGILMQRSU	MADRIGALESQUE
AACIILLMNOOTUY	AUTONOMICALLY	AADEEGIMNPRST	DISPARAGEMENT
AACIILMNOOTXY	TAXONOMICALLY	AADEEGINPRRST	GARDEN PARTIES
AACIILMNOPSTY	COMPLAISANTLY	AADEEGINRSTTT	TRADING ESTATE
AACIILMPRSTYY	SYMPATRICALLY	AADEEGKMNRRST	MARKET GARDENS
AACIILMNOOPRST	PROCLAMATIONS	AADEEGLLMNRRW	WALL GERMANDER
AACIILMNOOPTTU	COMPUTATIONAL	AADEEHLMRRTWY	WARM-HEARTEDLY
AACIILMNRRSTUU	INTRAMUSCULAR	AADEEHLOPRRTZ	TRAPEZOHEDRAL
AACIILMOOPSSTT	SOMATOPLASTIC	AADEEHLORRTTT	TETARTOHEDRAL
AACIILMORRSTTU	COURT MARTIALS,	AADEEHMNNSSSU	UNASHAMEDNESS
COURTS-MARTIAL		AADEEIILLNNOST	DENATIONALISE
AACIILNNOORSTT	TRANSLOCATION	AADEEIILLNNOTZ	DENATIONALIZE
AACIILNPRSSTYY	CRYPTANALYSIS	AADEEIILNNNORR	NORADRENALINE
AACIMNNOOPSWY	COMPANIONWAYS	AADEELNPPPRST	PEPPER-AND-SALT
AACIMNNOORSTT	CONTAMINATORS	AADEENNPRSTUU	SUPERANNUATED
AACIMNNRSTTTY	TRANSMITTANCY	AADEFFMNOORSW	MEADOW SAFFRON
AACLNNOORSSTT	SOLAR CONSTANT	AADEFGHHINORR	HARD OF HEARING
AADDDELNOORSW	RED SANDALWOOD	AADEFHILLMRSS	FIELD MARSHALS
AADDEEEEFHNSST	FATHEADEDNESS	AADEFIILNOSTU	FEUDALISATION
AADDEEEEHIRRTW	READ-WRITE HEAD	AADEFIILNOTUZ	FEUDALIZATION
AADDEEEELMPRST	PADDLE STEAMER	AADEFILNSSSTY	SAFETY ISLANDS
AADDEEGIILLNS	LEADING LADIES	AADEFILOOPRSS	FOOL'S PARADISE
AADDEEGILMPSS	MIDDLE PASSAGE	AADEFLLMNNTUY	FUNDAMENTALLY
AADDEEGINNNRRU	UNDERDRAINAGE	AADEGGILNNSST	LANDING STAGES
AADDEEGNRRTUU	UNDERGRADUATE	AADEGHILNRTUW	DAUGHTER-IN-LAW
AADDEEHHINNST	HEAD IN THE SAND	AADEGHIOPRRRS	RADIOGRAPHERS
AADDEEHHLRRTY	HARD-HEARTEDLY	AADEGIIMNNRTV	ANIMADVERTING
AADDEEELNRTTUU	UNADULTERATED	AADEGILNSTTVY	DEVASTATINGLY
AADDEFFIIILLST	DISAFFILIATED	AADEGOPRSSTTU	POSTGRADUATES
AADDEGGHNRRTU	GRANDDAUGHTER	AADEHHILMOORR	HAEMORRHOIDAL
AADDEGHNORRUY	ROUGH-AND-READY	AADEHIILMOSSY	HAEMODIALYSIS
AADDEGHOPRRSS	ADDRESSOGRAPH	AADEHIILNPSUZ	SULPHADIAZINE
AADDEGILNRSSS	SALAD DRESSING	AADEHIKLMORSY	HOLIDAYMAKERS

AADEHILNORSUY	HYALURONIDASE	AAEEEHIILLSSS	HAILE SELASSIE
AADEHIMMMMNNOS	MOHAMMEDANISM	AAEEEHILPPRRT	PRE-RAPHAELITE
AADEHIMNORSTU	DIATHERMANOUS	AAEEEHLNPRTTT	PATENT LEATHER
AADEHNORRSTTW	NORTHEASTWARD	AAEEEILNNORRS	SIERRA LEONEAN
AADEHNORSSSUZ	HAZARDOUSNESS	AAEEEILNNRTTV	ANAL RETENTIVE
AADEHORSSTTUW	SOUTHEASTWARD	AAEEELMMNPRTT	TEMPERAMENTAL
AADEIIILNOSST	IDEALISATIONS	AAEEELOPRSTTU	POETS LAUREATE
AADEIIILNOSTZ	IDEALIZATIONS	AAEEEMNNPRTVW	PERMANENT WAVE
AADEIIIMNOSTT	MEDIATISATION	AAEEFFGNRSSTT	STAFF SERGEANT
AADEIIIMNOTTZ	MEDIATIZATION	AAEEFGILLNNNS	SELF-ANNEALING
AADEIILLMORTY	MEDIATORIALLY	AAEEFHORSTTTT	STATE-OF-THE-ART
AADEIILLMPRXY	MAXILLIPEDARY	AAEEFKKMMNOOY	MAKE A MONKEY OF
AADEIILMMNRST	MALADMINISTER	AAEEFMNNRRSTT	TENANT FARMERS
AADEIIMNNORSV	ANIMADVERSION	AAEEFNNPRSSST	SNAP FASTENERS
AADEIINOPSSST	DISPASSIONATE	AAEEGGILMNRST	MARAGING STEEL
AADEIIPQRRTTU	QUADRIPARTITE	AAEEGGILMORTV	AGGLOMERATIVE
AADEILMMORSTT	MELODRAMATIST	AAEEGGILNORST	SEGREGATIONAL
AADEILMNORSST	MALADROITNESS	AAEEGGINNOPRT	GENERATION GAP
AADEIMNNRSSSU	RUSSIAN DESMAN	AAEEGGINORSTX	EXAGGERATIONS
AADEINORRRTXY	EXTRAORDINARY	AAEEGGLNNOSTU	TONE LANGUAGES
AADEINRRSTTWW	WITWATERSRAND	AAEEGHHIRRTTX	HIGHER-RATE TAX
AADEJLMMNSTTU	MALADJUSTMENT	AAEEGHLOPPRRS	PALEOGRAPHERS
AADELMOPRSTTY	DERMATOPLASTY	AAEEGHMNOOSTU	HAEMATOGENOUS
AADEMNORSTTUY	TETRADYNAMOUS	AAEEGIILMNRRS	MARRIAGE LINES
AADFFIKNRSSTT	STIFF AND STARK	AAEEGIILMPRTX	EXEMPLI GRATIA
AADFILLOOPRSY	APRIL FOOLS' DAY	AAEEGIIMMPRST	EPIGRAMMATISE
AADFINNOORTUY	FOUNDATIONARY	AAEEGIIMMPRTZ	EPIGRAMMATIZE
AADFINNOOSSTU	SODA FOUNTAINS	AAEEGIIMNRRRT	INTERMARRIAGE
AADGGIILNPRSY	DISPARAGINGLY	AAEEGIIMNRSTV	VEGETARIANISM
AADGHIIKLMNOY	HOLIDAYMAKING	AAEEGIMMMNNST	MISMANAGEMENT
AADGHIINNNRWZ	WINNING HAZARD	AAEEGIMNRTTUV	ARGUMENTATIVE
AADGIIILNNTWY	LADY-IN-WAITING	AAEEGINOPRSTU	EUSPORANGIATE
AADGIIMNOOSTT	DOGMATISATION	AAEEGJLMNORRS	MAJOR GENERALS
AADGIIMNOOTTZ	DOGMATIZATION	AAEEGJMNORRST	SERGEANT MAJOR
AADGILNNOOPRST	PROSTAGLANDIN	AAEEGLPPPRSSU	PURPLE PASSAGE
AADGIMNPRSSTT	TRADING STAMPS	AAEEGNNNOORRTT	TARN-ET-GARONNE
AADGINOPPRSST	PROPAGANDISTS	AAEEHHIMPRSTT	AMPHITHEATRES
AADHILNORRSTY	SYNARTHRODIAL	AAEEHHMOPPSST	METAPHOSPHATE
AADHMNNOORTTW	NOT WORTH A DAMN	AAEEHHORRSTTT	HEART-TO-HEARTS
AADIIIILLNPRSS	LIPARI ISLANDS	AAEEHIILNPSST	ELEPHANTIASIS
AADIIIILNNNOSS	IONIAN ISLANDS	AAEEHILLNNNPY	PHENYLALANINE
AADIIINOOSTTZ	DIAZOTISATION	AAEEHINPPRRST	HEIRS APPARENT
AADIIINOOTTZZ	DIAZOTIZATION	AAEEHINSSSTTT	ANAESTHETISTS
AADIIILLNORTTY	TRADITIONALLY	AAEEHLLLLOSVW	ALLHALLOWS EVE
AADIIMNNOORST	RANDOMISATION	AAEEHMNOSTTUX	EXANTHEMATOUS
AADIIMNNOORTZ	RANDOMIZATION	AAEEHNORSSTTT	EAST-NORTHEAST
AADIIMNORRSTT	ADMINISTRATOR	AAEEHOSSSTTTU	EAST-SOUTHEAST
AADILMNSSTUUU	ALDUS MANUTIUS	AAEEIIIILMMRST	IMMATERIALISE
AAEEEFFLMMSST	FEMMES FATALES	AAEEIIIILMMRTZ	IMMATERIALIZE
AAEEEFGHMMNOT	NAME OF THE GAME	AAEEIIIKKLLSTW	WALKIE-TALKIES
AAEEEFLRSSTTW	WELFARE STATES	AAEEIILMNNRTT	INTERLAMINATE
AAEEEGHLMPRST	GREASE THE PALM	AAEEIIMNNORTX	RE-EXAMINATION
AAEEEGLMMNRSS	GERMAN MEASLES	AAEEIINNRRSSV	ANNIVERSARIES
AAEEEGMNNRRRT	REARRANGEMENT	AAEEIKLMNSSTT	STATESMANLIKE

AAEEIKLNSSTTV	TALKATIVENESS	AAEGIILLLORST	LEGISLATORIAL
AAEEIILLNRSSTW	ARTESIAN WELLS	AAEGIILLMRSTY	MAGISTERIALLY
AAEEIILLNRTTVY	ALTERNATIVELY	AAEGIIILNNTTTY	TANGENTIALITY
AAEEILMNRRSTW	MINERAL WATERS	AAEGIIMMMPRST	EPIGRAMMATISM
AAEEILNNNOPPT	PENEPLANATION	AAEGIIMMPRSTT	EPIGRAMMATIST
AAEEILNOPRSTX	EXPLANATORIES	AAEGIIMNNORST	GERMANISATION
AAEEILNRRSTTT	TRANSLITERATE	AAEGIIMNNORTZ	GERMANIZATION
AAEEILOPRTTVX	EXTRAPOLATIVE	AAEGIIMNNOSTT	MAGNETISATION
AAEEINNPRSTTY	SPINY ANTEATER	AAEGIIMNNOTTZ	MAGNETIZATION
AAEEINORRSTTU	EURASIAN OTTER	AAEGIIMNQQSUU	QUINQUAGESIMA
AAEEINORSSSTV	ASSEVERATIONS	AAEGIKLNPPRSW	WALKING PAPERS
AAEEKMMNPRSTU	AMUSEMENT PARK	AAEGILLMNOOPT	MEGALOPOLITAN
AAEELNPRRRTTU	PRETERNATURAL	AAEGILLMNNOPST	LEAMINGTON SPA
AAEEMNNPRSTWY	PERMANENT WAYS	AAEGILNOPRTTX	EXTRAPOLATING
AAEEMPPRRSSTU	SEMPER PARATUS	AAEGIMNNNORTTU	ARGUMENTATION
AAEEMQRRRSTTU	QUARTERMASTER	AAEGIMNNOSTTU	AUGMENTATIONS
AAEEQRRSSTTUV	QUARTERSTAVES	AAEGINNOPSTTV	VANTAGE POINTS
AAEERRRSSTTUU	RESTAURATEURS	AAEGINOORSTTY	GEOSTATIONARY
AAEFFIILMNORR	FORAMINIFERAL	AAEGLLNOOOPTY	PALAEONTOLOGY
AAEFFIILMRTVY	AFFIRMATIVELY	AAEGLLOOOOPYZ	PALAEOZOOLOGY
AAEFFIIMNORRT	REAFFIRMATION	AAEGMOPPSSSST	POSTAGE STAMPS
AAEFFINOORSTT	AFFORESTATION	AAEHHILLNORTY	A ROLL IN THE HAY
AAEFFQRRSSTTU	QUARTERSTAFFS	AAEHHILMOPRTX	XEROPHTHALMIA
AAEFGILLLMNST	FLAGELLANTISM	AAEHIIILMNSSS	LEISHMANIASIS
AAEFGIMNNORTT	FRAGMENTATION	AAEHIIIMNNSTT	ANTIHISTAMINE
AAEFHHLOSSUWY	HALFWAY HOUSES	AAEHIIORTTTUV	AUTHORITATIVE
AAEFHLMORSTTW	WALTHAM FOREST	AAEHIMNPSSSTT	STATESMANSHIP
AAEFIIIILMRST	FAMILIARITIES	AAEHINNNOQRTU	ANTHRAQUINONE
AAEFIIMNNOSTT	MANIFESTATION	AAEHINPRSSSTY	PARASYNTHESIS
AAEFILMNOORRT	REFORMATIONAL	AAEHNNOPRSTTY	PARASYNTHETON
AAEFILNQRRSTU	QUARTERFINALS	AAEIIIILMMMRST	IMMATERIALISM
AAEFMORRSSSTT	MASTERS OF ARTS	AAEIIILMMRSTT	IMMATERIALIST
AAEGGGGILMNORT	AGGLOMERATING	AAEIIILMMRTTY	IMMATERIALITY
AAEGGHHIIOPRS	HAGIOGRAPHIES	AAEIIIILNNOSTT	NATIONALITIES
AAEGGHHILNNUY	LAUGHING HYENA	AAEIIILNORSST	SERIALISATION
AAEGGIILNTTUV	AGGLUTINATIVE	AAEIIILNORSTZ	SERIALIZATION
AAEGGILMNOORT	AGGLOMERATION	AAEIIMNNNPPRT	IMPARIPINNATE
AAEGGIMNNOORT	AGGIORNAMENTO	AAEIIKLMNPSST	SEMIPALATINSK
AAEGGINRSSTTT	STARTING GATES	AAEIILLMNOSTT	METALLISATION
AAEGGLMNORSTW	WEST GLAMORGAN	AAEIILLMNOTTZ	METALLIZATION
AAEGGLNOOPRTU	PROTOLANGUAGE	AAEIILLMNRSTU	UNILATERALISM
AAEGHHIKMRRTW	HIGH-WATER MARK	AAEIILLQTTUVY	QUALITATIVELY
AAEGHHOPPRRSY	PHRASEOGRAPHY	AAEIILMNNORTT	TERMINATIONAL
AAEGHIILMNOPR	GERMANOPHILIA	AAEIILNNNORTT	INTERNATIONAL
AAEGHILMOOSTT	HAEMATOLOGIST	AAEIILNNOORTT	ORIENTATIONAL
AAEGHIPRRRSTT	STRATIGRAPHER	AAEIILNNORSTV	VERNALISATION
AAEGHLLMOPRTY	METALLOGRAPHY	AAEIILNNORTVZ	VERNALIZATION
AAEGHLLNNOSTT	TEN-GALLON HATS	AAEIILNOPRRST	RESPIRATIONAL
AAEGHLOPPSYYZ	ZYGAPOPHYSEAL	AAEIILNORRTTT	TRILATERATION
AAEGHLOPRTTUY	TELAUTOGRAPHY	AAEIIMNNNOSTX	ANNEXATIONISM
AAEGHMORRTTUY	GREAT YARMOUTH	AAEIIMNOOPRST	ANISOMETROPIA
AAEGHNOOPRRTY	ORGANOTHERAPY	AAEIINNNOSTTX	ANNEXATIONIST
AAEGIIIILMNRTZ	MATERIALIZING	AAEIINOPPPRRT	INAPPROPRIATE
AAEGIIILMNTVY	IMAGINATIVELY	AAEILLNNOSSTY	SENSATIONALLY

AAEILLNOOPRTY	OPERATIONALLY	AAGIIMNNPRSTY	PRAYING MANTIS
AAEILLNOPRTXY	EXPLANATORILY	AAGIIMNOPPRTX	APPROXIMATING
AAEILMNNORSTU	MENSURATIONAL	AAGIINNOORSST	ORGANISATIONS
AAEILMNOPRTTU	PERMUTATIONAL	AAGIINNOORSTZ	ORGANIZATIONS
AAEILMOPPRTXY	APPROXIMATELY	AAGIINNORSTUU	INAUGURATIONS
AAEILNNNNPSVY	PENNSYLVANIAN	AAGIINOPPPRRT	APPROPRIATING
AAEILNNOPRRST	INTRAPERSONAL	AAGIKNNSSUUUY	AUNG SAN SUU KYI
AAEILNOOORTTV	LAEVOROTATION	AAGILMMNNOSUY	MAGNANIMOUSLY
AAEILNOOPRTTX	EXTRAPOLATION	AAGILNNNPRSTT	TRANSPLANTING
AAEILNORSTTWY	SANITARY TOWEL	AAGILNNORSTTU	STRANGULATION
AAEILOPPPRRTY	APPROPRIATELY	AAGILNOOOPRSZ	ZOOSPORANGIAL
AAEILOPPRRRTY	PREPARATORILY	AAGIMNORRRSTT	TRANSMIGRATOR
AAEIMNNNOORTT	ORNAMENTATION	AAGINNOOSSTTW	STATION WAGONS
AAEIMNORSSTTT	STATIONMASTER	AAGLMNOORSTUU	GRANULOMATOUS
AAEINNNOSSTTU	INSTANTANEOUS	AAHHNOOPPRTTY	ANTHROPOPATHY
AAEINNOPRSTTU	SUPERNATATION	AAHIILMMNSSTU	MALTHUSIANISM
AAEKLMORRSTWW	LOW-WATER MARKS	AAHIIMNNOORST	HARMONISATION
AAEKNOQRRSSUW	NARROW SQUEAKS	AAHIIMNNOORTZ	HARMONIZATION
AAELLMOOPRSTU	SOMATOPLEURAL	AAHIINOORSTTU	AUTHORISATION
AAELMMNNORRSU	ROMAN NUMERALS	AAHIINOORTTUZ	AUTHORIZATION
AAELNNNRSSTUU	UNNATURALNESS	AAHINOPSSSSTT	SHOP ASSISTANT
AAELNNPRRSTTY	TRANSPARENTLY	AAIIIILNNOPRST	INSPIRATIONAL
AAELOOORRTTVY	LAEVOROTATORY	AAIIIILNNOPRTT	TRIPOLITANIAN
AAFFGHINPRSSU	SUFFRAGANSHIP	AAIIIILNNOPSTT	PLATINISATION
AAFFIINNOPRRT	NITROPARAFFIN	AAIIIILNNOPTTZ	PLATINIZATION
AAFGIIIILMNRZ	FAMILIARIZING	AAIIIILNOORSTV	VARIOLISATION
AAFHINOOPRRST	PARROT-FASHION	AAIIIILNOORTVZ	VARIOLIZATION
AAFIIILMNRTUY	UNFAMILIARITY	AAIIIILNORRTTY	IRRATIONALITY
AAFIILMMNNOST	INFLAMMATIONS	AAIIIILNOSSTUV	VISUALISATION
AAFIILMNNOORT	INFORMATIONAL	AAIIIILNOSTUVZ	VISUALIZATION
AAFIILMNOORST	FORMALISATION	AAIIINOPRSTTV	PRIVATISATION
AAFIILMNOORTZ	FORMALIZATION	AAIIINOPRTTVZ	PRIVATIZATION
AAFILMMNOORST	MALFORMATIONS	AAIIINOPSSSTV	PASSIVISATION
AAGGILLNNOTTU	AGGLUTINATION	AAIIINOPSSTVZ	PASSIVIZATION
AAGGILNNRSTTU	STRANGULATING	AAIILLMNNOTTU	MULTINATIONAL
AAGHHINOOPPRT	ANTHROPOPHAGI	AAIILLNNOSSTT	INSTALLATIONS
AAGHIILLMNORT	ANTILOGARITHM	AAIILLNOPRSTU	PLURALISATION
AAGHIINNNOSTW	WASHINGTONIAN	AAIILLNOPRTUZ	PLURALIZATION
AAGHIMNOOPRST	MASTIGOPHORAN	AAIILMNNOORST	NORMALISATION
AAGHIORRRSTTZ	STRAIGHT RAZOR	AAIILMNNOORTZ	NORMALIZATION
AAGIIILMMNORT	IMMIGRATIONAL	AAIILMNNOPSTU	MANIPULATIONS
AAGIIILNNNOTZ	NATIONALIZING	AAIILMNOOPTTT	TOTIPALMATION
AAGIIILNNORTZ	RATIONALIZING	AAIILNOSSSTTV	SALVATIONISTS
AAGIIJNNOORST	JARGONISATION	AAIILNPSTTVYY	NATIVITY PLAYS
AAGIIJNNOORTZ	JARGONIZATION	AAIIMMNORSSTU	SUMMARISATION
AAGIIKLNNPSTY	PAINSTAKINGLY	AAIIMMNORSTUZ	SUMMARIZATION
AAGIILLNNPSTW	WALL PAINTINGS	AAIIMNOOPPRTX	APPROXIMATION
AAGIILLNNTTYZ	TANTALIZINGLY	AAIIMNORRSTTY	MARTYRISATION
AAGIILMNOORST	GLAMORISATION	AAIIMNORRTTYZ	MARTYRIZATION
AAGIILMNOORTZ	GLAMORIZATION	AAIINNOPRRSTT	TRANSPIRATION
AAGIILNNORTTU	TRIANGULATION	AAIINOOPPPRRT	APPROPRIATION
AAGIILNORSTUV	VULGARISATION	AAIJLMMOORRTY	MORAL MAJORITY
AAGIILNORTUVZ	VULGARIZATION	AAIKLNNOPRSSW	PARKINSON'S LAW
AAGIILNRRTTUY	TRIANGULARITY	AAIKMNOOQRTTU	QUOTATION MARK

AAILLMOOPPSTU	PAPILLOMATOUS
AAILLMOPRSTYY	MORALITY PLAYS
AAILNNOPPSTTU	SUPPLANTATION
AAILNNORSTTTU	NATIONAL TRUST
AAIMNNORSTTTU	TRANSMUTATION
AAINOPRRRSTTY	TRANSPIRATORY
AALMOOPSSTTTY	STOMATOPLASTY
AANNORRSSTUUY	TYRANNOSAURUS
ABBBEHLMORSTU	BLABBERMOUTHS
ABBCDEEIILNRS	INDESCRIBABLE
ABBCDEIILNRSY	INDESCRIBABLY
ABBCEEIJLNOOT	OBJECTIONABLE
ABBCEGIKLNRRY	BLACKBERRYING
ABBCEGILNOPUU	BUBONIC PLAGUE
ABBCEHIHRSTTU	RABBIT HUTCHES
ABBCEHILNORTU	BRONCHIAL TUBE
ABBCEHINPRSTU	RABBIT PUNCHES
ABBCEHKOORRSS	SHOCK ABSORBER
ABBCEIJLNOOTY	OBJECTIONABLY
ABBCGHIIILOPR	BIBLIOGRAPHIC
ABBCIIILOPRST	PROBABILISTIC
ABBDEEFNORSTU	BEAST OF BURDEN
ABBDEEMPRRSTU	RUBBER-STAMPED
ABBDEIILRSTTU	DISTRIBUTABLE
ABBDEILLNORTU	BULLETIN BOARD
ABBDFFILMNNSU	BLIND MAN'S BUFF
ABBDILOOOOSSU	BOBO-DIOULASSO
ABBEEHILLPRSU	REPUBLISHABLE
ABBEEILLMNRTY	BLANTYRE-LIMBE
ABBEEILMPRRTU	IMPERTURBABLE
ABBEELMMNOOTZ	BAMBOOZLEMENT
ABBEELMNORSTW	SAM BROWNE BELT
ABBEGGHINORTY	BIG BANG THEORY
ABBEGHIILOPRR	BIBLIOGRAPHER
ABBEGILNORRSU	RABBLE-ROUSING
ABBEIIILOPRST	PROBABILITIES
ABBEIILLMORRY	MOBILE LIBRARY
ABBEILMPRRTUY	IMPERTURBABLY
ABBEILSSTTTUU	SUBSTITUTABLE
ABBGINOOPPRTY	BOOBY TRAPPING
ABBIIILMOPRTY	IMPROBABILITY
ABCCDEEIKLMOS	BLACK COMEDIES
ABCCDEHILORSU	COACHBUILDERS
ABCCDENORSTTU	SUBCONTRACTED
ABCCDIILLMORU	UMBILICAL CORD
ABCCEEIILNNOV	INCONCEIVABLE
ABCCEGIILLOOO	BIOECOLOGICAL
ABCCEEIIILMPTY	IMPECCABILITY
ABCCEIIILSSTY	ACCESSIBILITY
ABCCEIILLMORS	SOCIAL CLIMBER
ABCCEIILNNOVY	INCONCEIVABLY
ABCCEEIILORTTY	BACTERIOLYTIC
ABCCEIIMMNRTU	CIRCUMAMBIENT
ABCCEIINRRSSU	CABIN CRUISERS
ABCCEIMMORTUY	MYCOBACTERIUM
ABCCHHIIOPRRS	ARCHBISHOPRIC
ABCCILMNOPPUY	PUBLIC COMPANY
ABCCNOORRSTTU	SUBCONTRACTOR
ABCDDEEIILRST	DISCREDITABLE
ABCDDEEILTTUX	TAX-DEDUCTIBLE
ABCDDEEIILRSTY	DISCREDITABLY
ABCDDEIINOORX	CARBON DIOXIDE
ABCDDGIKLNPSU	BLACK PUDDINGS
ABCDEEEGHNRST	BERCHTESGADEN
ABCDEEEINORRT	DECEREBRATION
ABCDEEELMMNOR	RECOMMENDABLE
ABCDEEHILPTTT	PITCHED BATTLE
ABCDEEIILOPRT	PERIODIC TABLE
ABCDEEIIMOSTY	BASIDIOMYCETE
ABCDEEILNNNOS	INCONDENSABLE
ABCDEEILNPRTU	UNPREDICTABLE
ABCDEELLOPRST	CORPS DE BALLET
ABCDEEMNOOPRY	BEYOND COMPARE
ABCDEHIOPSSTX	DISPATCH BOXES
ABCDEHNORSSTY	BODY SNATCHERS
ABCDEIIILLNPS	DISCIPLINABLE
ABCDEIIILMRTU	MIRABILE DICTU
ABCDEIIILNTUY	INEDUCABILITY
ABCDEIIILPRTY	PREDICABILITY
ABCDEIIILPSTY	DESPICABILITY
ABCDEIIILLOQTU	QUODLIBETICAL
ABCDEIIILLTUXY	EXCLUDABILITY
ABCDEILORRRRY	RECORD LIBRARY
ABCDEKNORRSTU	ROUND BRACKETS
ABCDIIIILNTVY	VINDICABILITY
ABCDIIILLPTUY	DUPLICABILITY
ABCDILNOOOSTT	ODONTOBLASTIC
ABCEEEELNRSSX	EXECRABLENESS
ABCEEEFIIINRS	BENEFICIARIES
ABCEEEFIILLRT	ELECTRIFIABLE
ABCEEEFILLNNU	INFLUENCEABLE
ABCEEEHMMRRRT	CHARTER MEMBER
ABCEEEIINNRST	BICENTENARIES
ABCEEEILNOPTX	EXCEPTIONABLE
ABCEEEILNRSUV	UNSERVICEABLE
ABCEEEILORRRV	IRRECOVERABLE
ABCEEELMNOPRS	RECOMPENSABLE
ABCEEELNSSSUX	EXCUSABLENESS
ABCEEHILLPTUW	THE PUBLIC WEAL
ABCEEHILNORSV	OLIVE BRANCHES
ABCEEHIMNRSTY	CHIMNEYBREAST
ABCEEHNPRRSTU	BUSH CARPENTER
ABCEEIILNPRSU	REPUBLICANISE
ABCEEIILNPRUZ	REPUBLICANIZE
ABCEEILMOORSU	BROMELIACEOUS
ABCEEILNNOSTT	INCONTESTABLE
ABCEEILNOPRRS	CEREBROSPINAL
ABCEEILORRRVY	IRRECOVERABLY

ABCEEILRRSTTU	BATTLE CRUISER
ABCEEJMRSTTTU	SUBJECT MATTER
ABCEELMMNORSU	COMMENSURABLE
ABCEELNNOOPRU	PRONOUNCEABLE
ABCEENOORRSSS	BEAR ONE'S CROSS
ABCEENOPRRSTU	PROTUBERANCES
ABCEFGIIILLNNT	FILING CABINET
ABCEFGIILMMNR	CLIMBING FRAME
ABCEFHIILLMRU	LIEBFRAUMILCH
ABCEFIIINORTV	VERIFICATION
ABCEFINOORRSU	CARBONIFEROUS
ABCEFLMNNOORU	UNCONFORMABLE
ABCEFLMNOORTU	UNCOMFORTABLE
ABCEGHIMNNSU	SUBMACHINE GUN
ABCEGHORRRSTU	TURBOCHARGERS
ABCEGIINNOOSU	BIGNONIACEOUS
ABCEGILLMOORY	EMBRYOLOGICAL
ABCEGINORRSSZ	ZEBRA CROSSING
ABCEHILSSTTTY	CHASTITY BELTS
ABCEHIRRRRSSU	CRUSH BARRIERS
ABCEHLOOPRSTU	CLAUSTROPHOBE
ABCEHOPRRSTUY	BRACHYPTEROUS
ABCEIIILLNNTU	ENUNCIABILITY
ABCEIIIILNOTTY	NOTICEABILITY
ABCEIIILLMORTY	BIOMETRICALLY
ABCEIIILMNPRSU	REPUBLICANISM
ABCEIIILNOPRTU	REPUBLICATION
ABCEIILORSSTY	BACTERIOLYSIS
ABCEIIMNNOORT	RECOMBINATION
ABCEIINORSSTT	OBSTETRICIANS
ABCEIIRRSSTTUW	WATER BISCUITS
ABCEILLLPSTTU	PLASTIC BULLET
ABCEILLMNORYY	EMBRYONICALLY
ABCEILLORSTTY	OBSTETRICALLY
ABCEILNNOSTTY	INCONTESTABLY
ABCEILNORTTUU	TUBERCULATION
ABCEILNSSSSSU	BUSINESS CLASS
ABCEILOORSSTU	STROBILACEOUS
ABCEILORRRTUU	ARBORICULTURE
ABCEIOOORRRTV	CORROBORATIVE
ABCEKKKLNRSSSU	BRASS KNUCKLES
ABCELNORSSTTU	COUNTERBLASTS
ABCFLMNOORTUY	UNCOMFORTABLY
ABCGGHINORRTU	TURBOCHARGING
ABCGHIKLNSSUW	SWASHBUCKLING
ABCGIKLNORSTT	STARTING BLOCK
ABCGINOOORRRT	CORROBORATING
ABCHHINOOPRST	OPISTHOBRANCH
ABCHILLMOPSTY	LYMPHOBLASTIC
ABCHILOOPRSTT	TROPHOBLASTIC
ABCIIILLNOTUY	INOCULABILITY
ABCIIILLNPTUY	INCULPABILITY
ABCIIILMOPTTY	COMPATIBILITY
ABCIIILNOSTUY	UNSOCIABILITY
ABCIIILLOPRSTT	TRIPLOBLASTIC
ABCIILMOPTTUY	COMPUTABILITY
ABCIILNOPPRSY	PRINCIPAL BOYS
ABCILMNNOOSSU	NO-CLAIMS BONUS
ABCILNOORSTTU	OBSTRUCTIONAL
ABCIMNNNOOOOP	BOON COMPANION
ABCINOOOORRRT	CORROBORATION
ABCLRRSSTTUUU	SUBSTRUCTURAL
ABCOOOORRRRST	CORROBORATORS
ABDDDEEEEFHRT	FEATHERBEDDED
ABDDDEILMNORY	BROADMINDEDLY
ABDDEEEGHINSS	BIGHEADEDNESS
ABDDEEELLORSU	DOUBLE-DEALERS
ABDDEEFILNNOY	BADLY IN NEED OF
ABDDEEGILLNOU	DOUBLE-DEALING
ABDDEEHIILNNR	HILDEBRANDINE
ABDDEEHLLORSU	SHOULDER BLADE
ABDDEEHLRTUYY	BUTYRALDEHYDE
ABDDEEIILNPTY	DEPENDABILITY
ABDDEFHLLNOOS	FLESH AND BLOOD
ABDDEILNNNSSS	SAND-BLINDNESS
ABDDGINNOORSU	SOUNDING BOARD
ABDEEEEHINRRS	ABERDEENSHIRE
ABDEEEEHLNPRR	REPREHENDABLE
ABDEEEFLORTUU	DOUBLE FEATURE
ABDEEEGKLLNOW	KNOWLEDGEABLE
ABDEEEHKNORRT	BROKEN-HEARTED
ABDEEEHLNOPTY	BEYOND THE PALE
ABDEEEIILMRTY	REDEEMABILITY
ABDEEEILMNNST	DISENABLEMENT
ABDEEFGIRSSSU	FIGURED BASSES
ABDEEFGLMOORR	GAMBREL-ROOFED
ABDEEFIIILRSV	DIVERSIFIABLE
ABDEEGIILNRST	DISINTEGRABLE
ABDEEGILNRSST	DRESSING TABLE
ABDEEGINPRSTT	SPREAD BETTING
ABDEEGKLLNOWY	KNOWLEDGEABLY
ABDEEIILNNNTV	VENETIAN BLIND
ABDEEIILNNPSS	INDISPENSABLE
ABDEEIILNORST	DELIBERATIONS
ABDEEIILNPTXY	EXPENDABILITY
ABDEEIILSTTTY	DETESTABILITY
ABDEEIIMRTTXY	AMBIDEXTERITY
ABDEEILMNOPRS	IMPONDERABLES
ABDEEKNORRRSS	BANKER'S ORDERS
ABDEFIILLORRT	DEFIBRILLATOR
ABDEGGILLNOUZ	DOUBLE-GLAZING
ABDEGHINOORSU	BOARDINGHOUSE
ABDEGIIILNSTZ	DESTABILIZING
ABDEGIKLLNOTU	DOUBLE-TALKING
ABDEGIKLNOPRU	DOUBLE-PARKING
ABDEGILLLNNSY	BELLY-LANDINGS
ABDEHHNOSSSUU	HOUSE HUSBANDS
ABDEHILMNNSST	BLANDISHMENTS

ABDEHILNOORSU	DISHONOURABLE	ABEEFIILNOPRS	PERSONIFIABLE
ABDEIILNNPSSY	INDISPENSABLY	ABEEFIILPRRTY	PREFERABILITY
ABDEIILNOPRTY	PONDERABILITY	ABEEGHHLPRSTU	BUSH TELEGRAPH
ABDEIINNORSTU	INSUBORDINATE	ABEEGHIKNORSU	HOUSEBREAKING
ABDEIINORSTUV	SUBORDINATIVE	ABEEGHLORSTTT	GHETTO BLASTER
ABDEILLNOOORT	BLOOD RELATION	ABEEGIILMNNRS	NEGRI SEMBILAN
ABDEMOORRSTTW	BOTTOM DRAWERS	ABEEGIKNPSSTU	SPEAKING TUBES
ABDFGIILLLNOS	BILLS OF LADING	ABEEGILNORRVY	OVERBEARINGLY
ABDFIIIILMOTY	MODIFIABILITY	ABEEGILNOSSST	BLASTOGENESIS
ABDFIIIILMORTY	FORMIDABILITY	ABEEHIILNSTUX	INEXHAUSTIBLE
ABDGIIKNORRST	SKIRTING BOARD	ABEEHILMNSSTT	ESTABLISHMENT
ABDGIINNOORRS	IRONING BOARDS	ABEEHILOPRTTZ	PORT ELIZABETH
ABDGIINNORSTU	SUBORDINATING	ABEEHILRRSSTW	WELSH RAREBITS
ABDHIIINORSTY	HYBRIDISATION	ABEEHKLNORRTY	HEARTBROKENLY
ABDHIIINORTYZ	HYBRIDIZATION	ABEEIILLRRSUV	AUBERVILLIERS
ABDHILNOORSUY	DISHONOURABLY	ABEEIILMPRTTY	TEMPERABILITY
ABDIIIILMSSTY	ADMISSIBILITY	ABEEIILNNORTV	INVENTORIABLE
ABDIIIILNOSSUV	SUBDIVISIONAL	ABEEIILNPRTTY	PENETRABILITY
ABDIIIILOPSSTY	DISPOSABILITY	ABEEIILRRRTVY	IRRETRIEVABLY
ABDIIILPSTTUY	DISPUTABILITY	ABEEIIOOPRRRT	RIBEIRAO PRETO
ABDIIINOSSSTU	SUBSIDISATION	ABEEIILMNSSSY	ASSEMBLY LINES
ABDIIINOSSTUZ	SUBSIDIZATION	ABEEIILLRSSTVY	LIVERY STABLES
ABDIINNOORSTU	SUBORDINATION	ABEEILMNNNOTU	UNMENTIONABLE
ABDILLMNNOPTU	PLATINUM-BLOND	ABEEILMNRRSSU	SERIAL NUMBERS
ABDMOOOORRTTU	OUTBOARD MOTOR	ABEEILNNRRSSS	BRAINLESSNESS
ABEEEEFLNORSU	UNFORESEEABLE	ABEEILNNSTTUU	SUBLIEUTENANT
ABEEEEILMMPRS	SEMIPERMEABLE	ABEEILNOORTTX	EXTORTIONABLE
ABEEEEIRRRTVV	REVERBERATIVE	ABEEINPRRSSTY	PRESBYTERIANS
ABEEEELNPRRST	REPRESENTABLE	ABEEIOORSSTTV	OBSERVATORIES
ABEEEFIILLMPX	EXEMPLIFIABLE	ABEEKLMORRSTU	TROUBLEMAKERS
ABEEEGINRRRTV	REVERBERATING	ABEEKMNNORTUY	MOUNTEBANKERY
ABEEEHILNPPRS	APPREHENSIBLE	ABEELNNNORRTU	NONRETURNABLE
ABEEEHKORRSSU	HOUSEBREAKERS	ABEFGLNORTTUY	UNFORGETTABLY
ABEEEHLOPRSST	OBLATE SPHERES	ABEFHHILLLOST	BILLS OF HEALTH
ABEEEIILLPRRV	IRREPLEVIABLE	ABEFHOOOPRSTT	A SPOT OF BOTHER
ABEEEIILRRRTV	IRRETRIEVABLE	ABEFIIIILLRTTY	FILTERABILITY
ABEEEIKKRRRST	STRIKEBREAKER	ABEFIILNORRRU	NEUROFIBRILAR
ABEEEILMNRSSS	MISERABLENESS	ABEFLLOOORSUV	LABOURS OF LOVE
ABEEEILMNSSST	ESTIMABLENESS	ABEGGIIIMSTUU	AMBIGUGUITIES
ABEEEILNPRRTT	INTERPRETABLE	ABEGIIILNOTTY	NEGOTIABILITY
ABEEEILNQSSTU	EQUITABLENESS	ABEGIIILNRTTY	INTEGRABILITY
ABEEEILNRSSTV	VERITABLENESS	ABEGIIILNORTVY	GOVERNABILITY
ABEEEIMMPRRTV	PRIVATE MEMBER	ABEGILLLNOSWY	BOWLING ALLEYS
ABEEEINORRRTV	REVERBERATION	ABEGILNOPPRTT	BLOTTING PAPER
ABEEEINRRSTTV	INVERTEBRATES	ABEGIMNOSSSUU	AMBIGUOUSNESS
ABEEEELLMNSSS	BLAMELESSNESS	ABEHHINNOORST	HEATH ROBINSON
ABEEELLNORSST	TOLERABLENESS	ABEHIIILPRSTY	PERISHABILITY
ABEEEELNRSSTTU	UTTERABLENESS	ABEHIILNSTUXY	INEXHAUSTIBLY
ABEEELOOPSTTT	POTATO BEETLES	ABEHIIORSSTUV	BEHAVIOURISTS
ABEEEORRRRTVY	REVERBERATORY	ABEHILNORRSTW	BROTHERS-IN-LAW
ABEEFFIMMORRT	FAR BE IT FROM ME	ABEHLLMOPSSUY	BLASPHEMOUSLY
ABEEFGIILNRRR	IRREFRANGIBLE	ABEIIIILNSSTT	INSTABILITIES
ABEEFGLNORTTU	UNFORGETTABLE	ABEIIIILNTTVY	INEVITABILITY
ABEEFHOPRSTTT	THE BEST PART OF	ABEIIILLNRTUY	UNRELIABILITY

ABEIIILMNRTTY	TERMINABILITY
ABEIIILNOPRTY	INOPERABILITY
ABEIIILNOQRTU	EQUILIBRATION
ABEIIILNORTXY	INEXORABILITY
ABEIIILNPSTXY	EXPANSIBILITY
ABEIIILPRRSTY	RESPIRABILITY
ABEIIILLMOPTY	EMPLOYABILITY
ABEIIILNRTUVY	VULNERABILITY
ABEIIILLORSTVY	RESOLVABILITY
ABEIIILMNRSSST	TRANSMISSIBLE
ABEIIILNRRTTUY	RETURNABILITY
ABEIILOPRTTXY	EXPORTABILITY
ABEIILRTTTUVY	ATTRIBUTIVELY
ABEIIMNOSSSTU	AMBITIOUSNESS
ABEIIMOORSTUV	OVERAMBITIOUS
ABEIINSSSTTUV	SUBSTANTIVISE
ABEIINSSTTUVZ	SUBSTANTIVIZE
ABEILMNNOSTUU	BLUE MOUNTAINS
ABEILNOORSSSU	LABORIOUSNESS
ABEILNOPPRSTU	INSUPPORTABLE
ABEILNSSTTUVY	SUBSTANTIVELY
ABEIMNNOSSSUW	BUSINESSWOMAN
ABEINNORSTUVY	SUBVENTIONARY
ABELLLLOPSSYY	POLYSYLLABLES
ABELLLMNOOSSY	MONOSYLLABLES
ABELMMNOORTWY	MELTON MOWBRAY
ABELNOPRRTTUY	PROTUBERANTLY
ABFGHIIILLORTT	BIT OF ALL RIGHT
ABFIIIILLLLNTY	INFALLIBILITY
ABFIIIILOPRTTY	PROFITABILITY
ABFLLLOOOOPST	FOOTBALL POOLS
ABGGHIIILLLNNT	BALL LIGHTNING
ABGGIIILOOORST	AGROBIOLOGIST
ABGHIIMMNSSTW	SWIMMING BATHS
ABGIIIILNNTTY	INTANGIBILITY
ABGIIINORRSTU	SUBIRRIGATION
ABGIIMNNORRST	BRAINSTORMING
ABHIIILNPSTUY	PUNISHABILITY
ABHIIINOORSTV	VASOINHIBITOR
ABIIIIILMNTTY	INIMITABILITY
ABIIIILLNOTVY	INVIOLABILITY
ABIIIILMPRTTY	IMPARTIBILITY
ABIIIILNOSTVY	INSOLVABILITY
ABIIILMNOOSST	MOBILISATIONS
ABIIILMNOOSTZ	MOBILIZATIONS
ABIIILMOPRTVY	IMPROVABILITY
ABIIILNOOSSTT	ABOLITIONISTS
ABIIILNOSSTTU	SUBTILISATION
ABIIILNOSTTUZ	SUBTILIZATION
ABIIILNSTTUUY	UNSUITABILITY
ABIIILRSTUVVY	SURVIVABILITY
ABIILMNNNTTUU	TINTINNABULUM
ABIILMNOOSSTY	SYMBOLISATION
ABIILMNOOSTYZ	SYMBOLIZATION
ABIIILMORRTTUV	MULTIVIBRATOR
ABILLMMNOOSSY	MONOSYLLABISM
ABILMMNOSSSTU	SOMNAMBULISTS
ABILNOOPPSTUU	SUBPOPULATION
ACCCDEEEINNNS	INCANDESCENCE
ACCCDEINORTTU	CREDIT ACCOUNT
ACCCEEELNNOSV	CONVALESCENCE
ACCCEEHIILRRT	ELECTRIC CHAIR
ACCCEEIILNOSS	SOCIAL SCIENCE
ACCCEEIILSSST	ECCLESIASTICS
ACCCEEIILNRTY	ECCENTRICALLY
ACCCEFFIILRRT	TRAFFIC CIRCLE
ACCCEHIILMMOR	MICROCHEMICAL
ACCCEHIILMOPR	MICROCEPHALIC
ACCCEHIINORTT	ARCHITECTONIC
ACCCEIMMNOOOR	MACROECONOMIC
ACCCEIMNRSSTU	CIRCUMSTANCES
ACCCELOOPRSTT	STREPTOCOCCAL
ACCCENNOOOVVX	CONCAVO-CONVEX
ACCCGHILLNOOO	CONCHOLOGICAL
ACCCHILOOPSTY	STAPHYLOCOCCI
ACCCIIILMMORT	MICROCLIMATIC
ACCCIIKKLOSTT	COCKTAIL STICK
ACCCIIMNOOTTY	ACTINOMYCOTIC
ACCCILOPRSTTY	CRYPTOCLASTIC
ACCDDEEHRRSTU	STARCH-REDUCED
ACCDEEEFINORS	CONFEDERACIES
ACCDEEEENNNRST	TRANSCENDENCE
ACCDEEEENORRRT	CATER-CORNERED
ACCDEEGHNORRR	RECORD-CHANGER
ACCDEEHHORRST	SCORCHED EARTH
ACCDEEIILNOST	OCCIDENTALISE
ACCDEEIILNOTZ	OCCIDENTALIZE
ACCDEEIILNPRSS	DISCREPANCIES
ACCDEEIILNOPSY	ENCYCLOPEDIAS
ACCDEEINNOPRT	ACCIDENT-PRONE
ACCDEELOOPRSU	CAPE COLOUREDS
ACCDEENNNRSTY	TRANSCENDENCY
ACCDEGNNORRST	CONCERT GRANDS
ACCDEHHIKLLTY	LATCHKEY CHILD
ACCDEHHILOPRY	HYDROCEPHALIC
ACCDEHHNNRRSUW	CHURCHWARDENS
ACCDEHINOORTW	WITH ONE ACCORD
ACCDEIIKLOOPS	KALEIDOSCOPIC
ACCDEIILMNOST	OCCIDENTALISM
ACCDEIILNNOOT	CODECLINATION
ACCDEIILNOSTT	OCCIDENTALIST
ACCDEIINOORTT	DECORTICATION
ACCDEIINORTTV	CONTRADICTIVE
ACCDEILLMOPTY	COMPLICATEDLY
ACCDEILMNOPTU	UNCOMPLICATED
ACCDENNORSTUY	COUNTRY DANCES
ACCDFIIINOOST	CODIFICATIONS
ACCDGIINNORTT	CONTRADICTING

ACCDHHINOOPRY	HYPOCHONDRIAC	ACCEELNNOSSTT	CONTACT LENSES
ACCDHIILORSTV	CLAVICHORDIST	ACCEELNNOSSTV	CONVALESCENTS
ACCDHIILPRSUU	SULPHURIC ACID	ACCEEMNORSTTU	ACCOUTREMENTS
ACCDHIMNOPSYY	PSYCHODYNAMIC	ACCEEOORRSSTU	STERCORACEOUS
ACCDHINOSTTUU	DUTCH AUCTIONS	ACCEFFIIINOSU	INEFFICACIOUS
ACCDIIILNSSTY	SYNDICALISTIC	ACCEFFIILOSUY	EFFICACIOUSLY
ACCDIIINORSTY	IDIOSYNCRATIC	ACCEFGIKRRRSU	CARRICKFERGUS
ACCDIILLLLNRYY	CYLINDRICALLY	ACCEFIIINOPST	SPECIFICATION
ACCDIIMMNNOOU	INCOMMUNICADO	ACCEFIIINORTT	CERTIFICATION, RECTIFICATION
ACCDIINNOORTT	CONTRADICTION	ACCEFIIORRTTY	CERTIFICATORY
ACCDILNOORRTU	CONDUCTOR RAIL	ACCEFINNOORTY	CONFECTIONARY
ACCDINOORRTTY	CONTRADICTORY	ACCEFIOOPRTTU	OUT OF PRACTICE
ACCEEEEGHOSTT	COTTAGE CHEESE	ACCEGHHIOOPRR	CHOREOGRAPHIC
ACCEEEELLNPRX	PAR EXCELLENCE	ACCEGHIILOPRX	LEXICOGRAPHIC
ACCEEEELMORRT	ACCELEROMETER	ACCEGHILLNOOT	TECHNOLOGICAL
ACCEEEGHIRRSV	SERVICE CHARGE	ACCEGHILNNORY	ENCROACHINGLY
ACCEEEHILLNPT	TELENCEPHALIC	ACCEGIILLLLOOX	LEXICOLOGICAL
ACCEEEHILLNRS	CHANCELLERIES	ACCEGIINNNORT	CONCERTINAING
ACCEEEHILMNPS	MESENCEPHALIC	ACCEGIINOPRRT	RECIPROCATING
ACCEEEHILMNPT	METENCEPHALIC	ACCEGILMNOORT	CONGLOMERATIC
ACCEEEILLORST	ECCLESIOLATER	ACCEGINNNNOTU	COUNTENANCING
ACCEEFFIILRSS	SELF-SACRIFICE	ACCEGINNNORTT	CONCENTRATING
ACCEEFIIIPSTV	SPECIFICATIVE	ACCEGINNORTTU	COUNTERACTING
ACCEEGHILNTYY	EYE-CATCHINGLY	ACCEGINOORRTT	GERONTOCRATIC
ACCEEGHKNOSTX	STOCK EXCHANGE	ACCEGIOPPRRTU	GROUP PRACTICE
ACCEEGHNNORSX	CORN EXCHANGES	ACCEHHIILMOST	HISTOCHEMICAL
ACCEEGHNORRTU	COUNTERCHARGE	ACCEHHIINSSTT	CHAIN STITCHES
ACCEEHHLOORST	SCHOOLTEACHER	ACCEHHILMOOPT	PHOTOCHEMICAL
ACCEEHILLNOTY	ACETYLCHOLINE	ACCEHHILOOPRT	ORTHOCEPHALIC
ACCEEHILMOPRT	CEPHALOMETRIC,	ACCEHHORRSSTT	RORSCHACH TEST
PETROCHEMICAL		ACCEHIILLNSST	CALLISTHENICS
ACCEEHMNNORST	ENCROACHMENTS	ACCEHIILNOPRS	NECROPHILIACS
ACCEEHORRSTTY	OYSTERCATCHER	ACCEHIILPRRTY	HYPERCRITICAL
ACCEEIILLNRTV	INTERCLAVICLE	ACCEHIKLLMOOT	MILK CHOCOLATE
ACCEEIIILMMNSU	ECUMENICALISM	ACCEHIKMNSSTY	CHIMNEYSTACKS
ACCEEIILMMORS	COMMERCIALISE	ACCEHILLOOPSS	SPECIAL SCHOOL
ACCEEIILMMORZ	COMMERCIALIZE	ACCEHIMNORSST	CHROMATICNESS
ACCEEIILORSSV	SOCIAL SERVICE	ACCEHINMNOPST	PANTECHNICONS
ACCEEIIMORRST	MERITOCRACIES	ACCEHIOOPSSTT	TACHISTOSCOPE
ACCEEIIOPRRTV	RECIPROCATIVE	ACCEIIKLNOSTW	ANTICLOCKWISE
ACCEEIKLNOPRS	COCKER SPANIEL	ACCEIIKNNPRST	PANIC-STRICKEN
ACCEEIILLORSTY	ECCLESIOLATRY	ACCEIIILMMORS	COMMERCIALISM
ACCEEIILNOPSTU	CONCEPTUALISE	ACCEIIILMMORST	COMMERCIALIST
ACCEEIILNOPTUZ	CONCEPTUALIZE	ACCEIIILMMORTY	COMMERCIALITY
ACCEEIILNPSSST	SCEPTICALNESS	ACCEIIILMNOSSS	NEOCLASSICISM
ACCEEIILNQSTUY	ACQUIESCENTLY	ACCEIIILNOSSST	NEOCLASSICIST
ACCEEIILORSTTT	ELECTROSTATIC	ACCEIIILOPRRTY	RECIPROCALITY
ACCEEIIMMNOTUX	EXCOMMUNICATE	ACCEIIILPRRSTU	SUPERCRITICAL
ACCEEIINNORSSV	CONSERVANCIES	ACCEIIMMNOTUV	COMMUNICATIVE
ACCEEIINNORTTV	CONCENTRATIVE	ACCEIINNNOSST	INCONSTANCIES
ACCEEIINOPRTTV	CONTRACEPTIVE	ACCEIINOOPRRT	RECIPROCATION
ACCEEIINORSSSS	ACCESSORINESS	ACCEIIOPPRSSU	PERSPICACIOUS
ACCEEIINORTTUV	COUNTERACTIVE	ACCEILLLNNOUY	NUCLEONICALLY
ACCEELLMMOORU	MACROMOLECULE	ACCEILLMNOPSU	NUCLEOPLASMIC

ACCEILMNNNOOP	NONCOMPLIANCE	ACCIILMMNOSTU	COMMUNALISTIC
ACCEILMNOPSTU	CONCEPTUALISM	ACCIILMNOOPST	COMPLICATIONS
ACCEILMNORSTU	COUNTERCLAIMS	ACCIILNORTTTY	CONTRACTILITY
ACCEILNNOSSTU	CONSULTANCIES	ACCIIMMNNOOTU	COMMUNICATION
ACCEILNOPSTTU	CONCEPTUALIST	ACCIIMNOOSSTY	ACTINOMYCOSIS
ACCEINNNOORTT	CONCENTRATION	ACCIIOORRSSTV	VICTORIA CROSS
ACCEINNOOPRTT	CONTRACEPTION	ACCIJLNNNOOTU	CONJUNCTIONAL
ACCEINNOORRTY	CONCRETIONARY	ACCILMNNOOTTY	CONCOMITANTLY
ACCEINNOORSSY	CONCESSIONARY	ACCIMMNOORTUY	COMMUNICATORY
ACCEINNOORTTU	COUNTERACTION	ACCIMNOOOTTXY	CYTOTAXONOMIC
ACCEINOOPPRTU	PREOCCUPATION	ACDDDEEEIINPV	PEACE DIVIDEND
ACCEINOPPRSSU	PERCUSSION CAP	ACDDEEEEGSSTU	EDUCATED GUESS
ACCELOOPRRSST	PECTORAL CROSS	ACDDEEEEHHNNOR	HENDECAHEDRON
ACCFGIIILNRSY	SACRIFICINGLY	ACDDEEEEHIMSST	SEMIDETACHEDS
ACCFIIINOORST	SCORIFICATION	ACDDEEEEHINRUV	UNDERACHIEVED
ACCFIINNOOSST	CONFISCATIONS	ACDDEEEEILNRST	DECENTRALISED
ACCFLMORSTUUU	FRACTOCUMULUS	ACDDEEEEILNRTZ	DECENTRALIZED
ACCGGHHIKNOSU	HACKING COUGHS	ACDDEEEEKMNOPR	PROMENADE DECK
ACCGHHHHIMNRU	HIGH CHURCHMAN	ACDDEEEENOPRTT	TOP DEAD CENTRE
ACCGHHINOOPRR	CHRONOGRAPHIC	ACDDEEEFFILSTY	DISAFFECTEDLY
ACCGHHINORSST	CROSS-HATCHING	ACDDEEEGIKNNOR	DEAD RECKONING
ACCGHHIOPPRSY	PSYCHOGRAPHIC	ACDDEEEHHIITTW	DICE WITH DEATH
ACCGHIIKNORRS	ROCKING CHAIRS	ACDDEEEHLLORTY	COLD-HEARTEDLY
ACCGHIILMNOPS	ACCOMPLISHING	ACDDEEIMNOOTY	ADENOIDECTOMY
ACCGHILLNOOOR	CHRONOLOGICAL	ACDDEEELNOORSS	SECOND SEA LORD
ACCGHILLOOPSY	PSYCHOLOGICAL	ACDDEEEMNNORTU	COUNTERMANDED
ACCGHIOPPRRTY	CRYPTOGRAPHIC	ACDDEENRSSTUV	SEVEN-CARD STUD
ACCGIIILNRRUZ	CIRCULARIZING	ACDDEFHIINRSS	DISFRANCHISED
ACCGIILLMOOSU	MUSICOLOGICAL	ACDDEGHILNNRR	GRANDCHILDREN
ACCGIILLOOOTX	TOXICOLOGICAL	ACDDEGIILLNOS	DIALLING CODES
ACCGIIMMNNOTU	COMMUNICATING	ACDDEGILLNOOR	DENDROLOGICAL
ACCGILLOOOPRT	PROCTOLOGICAL	ACDDEGLLNSSTU	DUCTLESS GLAND
ACCGILNOOPRSY	LARYNGOSCOPIC	ACDDEHIILMOSU	DICHLAMIDEOUS
ACCHHIMNOORMT	HOMOCHROMATIC	ACDDEHIMNOOPS	DODECAPHONISM
ACCHIIILPSSTY	PHYSICALISTIC	ACDDEHINOOPST	DODECAPHONIST
ACCHIILMOPRSY	MICROPHYSICAL	ACDDEIIIMNRST	DISCRIMINATED
ACCHIILMOSSST	SCHOLASTICISM	ACDDEIIILLNRTY	DENDRITICALLY
ACCHIIMNOOPRT	ACTINOMORPHIC	ACDDEIIINNORTT	INDOCTRINATED
ACCHIIMORRSSU	CHIAROSCURISM	ACDDEIINOOPRRS	PANIC DISORDER
ACCHIINOPSTTY	ANTIPSYCHOTIC	ACDDEIINRSTTY	IDENTITY CARDS
ACCHIIORRSSTU	CHIAROSCURIST	ACDDEINNOORTU	UNCOORDINATED
ACCHILLOOPRST	CHLOROPLASTIC	ACDDELMMMNOOU	COMMAND MODULE
ACCHILLOPSTYY	PSYCHOTICALLY	ACDDHIMNORSYY	HYDRODYNAMICS
ACCHILMMOOPRS	CHROMOPLASMIC	ACDDOOOORRRSUY	CORDUROY ROADS
ACCHILMOOPRTY	POLYCHROMATIC	ACDEEEEHINNSST	INDECENT HASTE
ACCHILOPPRSTY	PROPHYLACTICS	ACDEEEEHINRRUV	UNDERACHIEVER
ACCHIMMNOOORT	MONOCHROMATIC	ACDEEEEHLNOOPS	HOLD ONE'S PEACE
ACCHIMOOPSSTY	PSYCHOSOMATIC	ACDEEEEHORRSTU	TERRACED HOUSE
ACCHIOOPPRRRST	CHIROPRACTORS	ACDEEEILNSSST	DELICATESSENS
ACCHIOOPRRSSUZ	SCHIZOCARPOUS	ACDEEELNOPRST	PREADOLESCENT
ACCIIILNNORTU	IN CIRCULATION	ACDEEELNPRRSU	SUPERCALENDER
ACCIIIMMNOOST	ICONOMATICISM	ACDEEENNOPPRR	PREPONDERANCE
ACCIIINNOPSTW	IT WAS NO PICNIC	ACDEEEOPRRRST	TAPE RECORDERS
ACCIILLPRSTUU	PISCICULTURAL	ACDEEFGIILMNT	MAGNETIC FIELD

ACDEEFGINNORT	CONFEDERATING	ACDEFIINNSSTT	DISINFECTANTS
ACDEEFHHIKNRS	HANDKERCHIEFS	ACDEFILMNNOTU	MALFUNCTIONED
ACDEEFHNORRTW	THENCEFORWARD	ACDEGGHIINPRS	GRAPHIC DESIGN
ACDEEFIIILMRT	CERTIFIED MAIL	ACDEGGHINNRRU	UNDERCHARGING
ACDEEFILNNOST	SELF-CONTAINED	ACDEGGIKLNNOW	ACKNOWLEDGING
ACDEEFINNOORT	CONFEDERATION	ACDEGGINORRSS	GRADE CROSSING
ACDEEFNORRRTW	CENTRE FORWARD	ACDEGHHOOPRTU	THOROUGHPACED
ACDEEGHHOOPRR	CHOREOGRAPHED	ACDEGHIIMNNRS	MERCHANDISING
ACDEEGHIKNNRT	KITCHEN GARDEN	ACDEGIILLLOOY	IDEOLOGICALLY
ACDEEGHIMNNNU	MACHINEGUNNED	ACDEGIILLNSSS	SLIDING SCALES
ACDEEGIIMORST	TRAGICOMEDIES	ACDEGIILNPRTU	REDUPLICATING
ACDEEGILNNPRS	SPRING-CLEANED	ACDEGIIMNORTZ	DEMOCRATIZING
ACDEEGILNPRTY	DEPRECATINGLY	ACDEGIIMNOSTT	DOMESTICATING
ACDEEGIMMNNOR	COMMANDEERING	ACDEGIIMNOSTY	GEODYNAMICIST
ACDEEGNNOSSTT	DECONGESTANTS	ACDEGILLMNOOO	DEMONOLOGICAL
ACDEEGNOORSVW	COVERED WAGONS	ACDEGILLNOOOT	DEONTOLOGICAL
ACDEEHIIKMNNY	KIDNEY MACHINE	ACDEGIMMNNORW	WING COMMANDER
ACDEEHIKLOTTT	TICKLE TO DEATH	ACDEHHILNPRSS	SHIP'S CHANDLER
ACDEEHILORRTT	TETRACHLORIDE	ACDEHHLOPRSUY	HYDROCEPHALUS
ACDEEHINPRSSS	CASH DISPENSER	ACDEHIIMRSSTT	CHRISTMASTIDE
ACDEEHLNNOORR	HOLE-AND-CORNER	ACDEHIIOPSSTT	SOPHISTICATED
ACDEEIIILMSTV	MEDIEVALISTIC	ACDEHILMNOPTY	ENDOLYMPHATIC
ACDEEILLNNNQU	QUINDECENNIAL	ACDEHIMMNOPRS	COMMANDERSHIP
ACDEEIILPRTUV	REDUPLICATIVE	ACDEHIMMNORTY	THERMODYNAMIC
ACDEEIILPRTVY	PREDICATIVELY	ACDEHIMOPRTTY	DERMATOPHYTIC
ACDEEIIMNNRTY	INDETERMINACY	ACDEHLMOOPRSY	CHLAMYDOSPORE
ACDEEIIMNOPRT	PREMEDICATION	ACDEHMRSTTTUU	CUT THE MUSTARD
ACDEEIIMOSTTV	DOMESTICATIVE	ACDEHOOOPRRTT	PROTOCHORDATE
ACDEEIINNORST	CONTAINERISED,	ACDEIIIILNNTTW	IDENTICAL TWIN
INCONSIDERATE		ACDEIIIMNORST	DOSIMETRICIAN
ACDEEIINNORTZ	CONTAINERIZED	ACDEIIKLRSTTW	WILDCAT STRIKE
ACDEEIINOPRTT	DECREPITATION	ACDEIILNNOTTU	DENTICULATION
ACDEEIJKNNRST	DINNER JACKETS	ACDEIILNOPRTU	REDUPLICATION
ACDEEIKLOOPSS	KALEIDOSCOPES	ACDEIIMNOSTT	DOMESTICATION
ACDEEILLNNSTY	CLANDESTINELY	ACDEIINNNOSTU	DENUNCIATIONS
ACDEEILMNPSST	DISPLACEMENTS	ACDEIINNOORST	CONSIDERATION
ACDEEILNORSTY	CONSIDERATELY	ACDEIINOQRSTU	QUADRISECTION
ACDEEILNPPRRU	PERPENDICULAR	ACDEIINORRSTY	DISCRETIONARY
ACDEEILOPRRTY	DEPRECATORILY	ACDEIKMNNORST	ONE-TRACK MINDS
ACDEEIMMNORTV	INVERTED COMMA	ACDEIKNNNORTT	DARK CONTINENT
ACDEEIMNORSSX	CROSS-EXAMINED	ACDEILLMMOUWY	CADMIUM YELLOW
ACDEEIMNORSTU	DOCUMENTARIES	ACDEILMNORTUY	DOCUMENTARILY
ACDEEINNORSSS	SECONDARINESS	ACDEILNNOPTUU	PEDUNCULATION
ACDEEJKKNNOSTY	DONKEY JACKETS	ACDEILNNORSTY	CONSTRAINEDLY
ACDEELNOOSSSS	CLOSED SEASONS	ACDEILOOPRRTU	PARTI-COLOURED
ACDEELOPRRRSY	RECORD PLAYERS	ACDEILOPRSSTY	PERISSODACTYL
ACDEEMNNOPSTU	UNCOMPENSATED	ACDEIMMNNOOST	COMMENDATIONS
ACDEFGHHIINSS	CHAFING DISHES	ACDEIMMOOORRS	AIR COMMODORES
ACDEFGIILNSSY	DECLASSIFYING	ACDEIMMOOSTTY	MASTOIDECTOMY
ACDEFGILLRSUY	DISGRACEFULLY	ACDEIMNNOSTT	CONDEMNATIONS
ACDEFHLLOTTUY	THE CALL OF DUTY	ACDEIMNNOOTTU	DOCUMENTATION
ACDEFHOORSSSU	HOUSES OF CARDS	ACDEIMNORRRSS	MORRIS DANCERS
ACDEFIIILNOST	FICTIONALISED	ACDEINNNORSTU	UNCONSTRAINED
ACDEFIIILNOTZ	FICTIONALIZED	ACDEKLLNOORRR	ROCK-AND-ROLLER

ACDELNOOOSTUY	ACOTYLEDONOUS
ACDELOORRSTUW	STRAW-COLOURED
ACDEMMNNOSTUU	UNCONSUMMATED
ACDEOPRSSTTUW	WASTE PRODUCTS
ACDFIIIMNOOST	MODIFICATIONS
ACDFILMOORSTY	FAMILY DOCTORS
ACDGHINOOOPRT	ODONTOGRAPHIC
ACDGIIINRSSTV	VISITING CARDS
ACDGIILNNOOST	CONSOLIDATING
ACDGIINNOSTTU	OUTDISTANCING
ACDGILLNOOOOT	ODONTOLOGICAL
ACDGILMOSTYYZ	ZYGODACTYLISM
ACDGIMNOPRSSU	MASS-PRODUCING
ACDGLOOSTUYYZ	ZYGODACTYLOUS
ACDHIIKKNPSUY	KICK UP A SHINDY
ACDHIILMNOORT	MITOCHONDRIAL
ACDHIIINOPSSTU	CUSTODIANSHIP
ACDHIIOPRSSTT	DICTATORSHIPS
ACDHILMNOOORS	CHONDRIOSOMAL
ACDHIMNOOPSTY	PHOTODYNAMICS
ACDHKLORRSTUY	HARD-LUCK STORY
ACDHLNOOSSSUY	SUNDAY SCHOOLS
ACDHMNOOORSTU	CHONDROMATOUS
ACDIIILNNOPTU	INDUPLICATION
ACDIIIMNORRST	DISCRIMINATOR,
DOCTRINAIRISM	
ACDIIIOOOPRST	RADIOISOTOPIC
ACDIILLLLNSSSY	SCILLY ISLANDS
ACDIILLNNOOTY	CONDITIONALLY
ACDIILNNNOOTU	UNCONDITIONAL
ACDIILNNOOOST	CONSOLIDATION
ACDIILNOOOORST	DISCOLORATION
ACDIILPQRTUUY	QUADRUPLICITY
ACDIINNOORRTT	INDOCTRINATOR
ACDINOOQRSSTU	CONQUISTADORS
ACDLLOOPSTUYY	POLYDACTYLOUS
ACDLMNOOOSTUY	CONDYLOMATOUS
ACEEEEEKNOOPS	KEEP ONE'S PEACE
ACEEEEFJKRRST	REEFER JACKETS
ACEEEEHLPRSST	STEEPLECHASER
ACEEEEHLPSSST	STEEPLECHASES
ACEEEELMNRSTT	TRACE ELEMENTS
ACEEEENNPPPRY	CAYENNE PEPPER
ACEEEEPPRRSTW	CARPET SWEEPER
ACEEEFFGINOPR	PEACE OFFERING
ACEEEFGGNNOOS	EGG ON ONE'S FACE
ACEEEFHHITTVY	HAVE ITCHY FEET
ACEEEFMORRRTT	REFRACTOMETER
ACEEEGILLNRTY	ENERGETICALLY
ACEEEGIINPRSS	PRESS AGENCIES
ACEEEGLMNORTT	ELECTROMAGNET
ACEEEGLNNRRUY	NUCLEAR ENERGY
ACEEEGLNRSSSS	GRACELESSNESS
ACEEEGMNNORTU	ENCOURAGEMENT

ACEEEHHILLLSS	ACHILLES' HEELS
ACEEEHHPPRSTY	SPEECH THERAPY
ACEEEHIKMNSTY	SMACK IN THE EYE
ACEEEHINRSTVY	SEVEN-YEAR ITCH
ACEEEHLLNNOPT	TELENCEPHALON
ACEEEHLMNNOPS	MESENCEPHALON
ACEEEHLMNNOPT	METENCEPHALON
ACEEEHNNRSSST	ENCHANTRESSES
ACEEEIINNRSTV	INTENSIVE CARE
ACEEEIINSSTTV	NECESSITATIVE
ACEEEIKNOPTTX	TAKE EXCEPTION
ACEEEILLNPSST	LICENSE PLATES
ACEEEILMNNRTT	INTERLACEMENT
ACEEEILNRSSVY	NECESSARY EVIL
ACEEEILOPPRRR	PEOPLE CARRIER
ACEEEIMNNRRSS	MERCENARINESS
ACEEEIMNORSVY	YEOMAN SERVICE
ACEEEINNOPRVX	AIX-EN-PROVENCE
ACEEEINOSSTVV	EVOCATIVENESS
ACEEEILLNORTTV	ELECTROVALENT
ACEEEILLOPRRTT	ELECTROPLATER
ACEEEFFHINNPRS	AFFENPINSCHER
ACEEEFFILLNTUY	INEFFECTUALLY
ACEEEFGIIMNRRT	FERRIMAGNETIC
ACEEEFGIMNORRT	FERROMAGNETIC
ACEEEFHHIRSTTT	FEATHERSTITCH
ACEEEFHIMNNRST	FRANCHISEMENT
ACEEEFHMNOSTUV	VOUCHSAFEMENT
ACEEEFHOPPRSST	PARTS OF SPEECH
ACEEEFINOSSSTU	FACETIOUSNESS
ACEEEFMNORSTUU	FRUMENTACEOUS
ACEEEFMORRRTTY	REFRACTOMETRY
ACEEEGGINNOORT	ORGANOGENETIC
ACEEEGHHIOPRRT	HETEROGRAPHIC
ACEEEGHHLNORST	CLOTHES HANGER
ACEEEGHHMNRRRU	HUNGER MARCHER
ACEEEGHHMNRRSU	HUNGER MARCHES
ACEEEGHHOOPRRR	CHOREOGRAPHER
ACEEEGHIIMNNSW	SEWING MACHINE
ACEEEGHILNOPRS	SELENOGRAPHIC
ACEEEGHILNORSU	CLEARINGHOUSE
ACEEEGHILNOSSU	CHAISE LONGUES
ACEEEGHILOPRRX	LEXICOGRAPHER
ACEEEGHIOPRRST	STEREOGRAPHIC
ACEEEGHIRRSSST	CASH REGISTERS
ACEEEGHLOPRRTY	ELECTROGRAPHY
ACEEEGHMNNORSY	MONEYCHANGERS
ACEEEGHPRRRSSU	SUPERCHARGERS
ACEEEGIILSTTUV	GESTICULATIVE
ACEEEGIIMMNOST	MISCEGENATION
ACEEEGIINNNRST	INTRANSIGENCE
ACEEEGIINNSSTT	NECESSITATING
ACEEEGIINOPRRR	CARRIER PIGEON
ACEEEGILLLOOPS	SPELEOLOGICAL

ACEEGILLMORTY	GEOMETRICALLY	ACEEIKNOSSSTT	SEASON TICKETS
ACEEGILMNNOQU	MAGNILOQUENCE	ACEEILLLNRRTU	INTERCELLULAR
ACEEGILMNOPST	MAGNETIC POLES	ACEEILLLNSTTU	INTELLECTUALS
ACEEGILNNORRT	CENTRAL REGION	ACEEILLMNNRTY	INCREMENTALLY
ACEEGILNPSSTT	PLACE SETTINGS	ACEEILLMNOSSU	MISCELLANEOUS
ACEEGIMMNORTT	MAGNETOMETRIC	ACEEILLMOQRUU	EQUIMOLECULAR
ACEEGINNNSSSU	UNCEASINGNESS	ACEEILLNNNSSU	UNCLEANLINESS
ACEEGINOPRRTX	EXPECTORATING	ACEEILLNOPTXY	EXCEPTIONALLY
ACEEGLMNOORST	CONGLOMERATES	ACEEILLPSTUVY	SPECULATIVELY
ACEEHHILLORTT	HETEROTHALLIC	ACEEILLRRSSTY	RECRYSTALLISE
ACEEHHIRVWWYY	EVERY WHICH WAY	ACEEILLRRSTYZ	RECRYSTALLIZE
ACEEHHLNORSSU	CHARNEL HOUSES	ACEEILMNOPTTV	CONTEMPLATIVE
ACEEHIILMMNPS	SIMPLE MACHINE	ACEEILMNRRSSU	MERCURIALNESS
ACEEHIIORSSST	CASE HISTORIES	ACEEILMOPRSTU	PRECIOUS METAL
ACEEHIIQRRSSU	SQUIREARCHIES	ACEEILNNOPRTV	CONVERTIPLANE
ACEEHIKNRSSST	HEARTSICKNESS	ACEEILNNOPTUX	UNEXCEPTIONAL
ACEEHILLORTTY	THEORETICALLY	ACEEILNNOQSTU	CONSEQUENTIAL
ACEEHILNPRSSS	SPHERICALNESS	ACEEILNNRRTUW	NUCLEAR WINTER
ACEEHILOPRSTT	HETEROPLASTIC	ACEEILNNRSSUY	UNNECESSARILY
ACEEHIMNORSSS	MARCHIONESSES	ACEEILNORSTTU	INTEROSCULATE
ACEEHIMNSSSTT	CHASTISEMENTS	ACEEILNOSTTUX	CONTEXTUALISE
ACEEHIMRRSSTT	CHRISTMAS TREE	ACEEILNOTTUXZ	CONTEXTUALIZE
ACEEHINOPRRST	TERPSICHOREAN	ACEEILNRTTUUV	ENCULTURATIVE
ACEEHIPRRSSTY	SECRETARYSHIP	ACEEILOOPRTVY	COOPERATIVELY
ACEEHLLMOOORT	ALCOHOLOMETER	ACEEILOPPRSSW	SPECIAL POWERS
ACEEHLLNNNNTU	CHANNEL TUNNEL	ACEEILOPRSTTY	STEREOTYPICAL
ACEEHLLOORSSV	SCHOOL-LEAVERS	ACEEILORRTTVY	RETROACTIVELY
ACEEHLLOPPSTU	LEPTOCEPHALUS	ACEEILORTTUVV	OVERCULTIVATE
ACEEHLMMNOOTW	THE COMMON WEAL	ACEEIMMMOORTV	COMMEMORATIVE
ACEEHLMNORRTU	THERMONUCLEAR	ACEEIMNORRSSX	CROSS-EXAMINER
ACEEHLMNSSSST	MATCHLESSNESS	ACEEIMNPRTTUY	PNEUMATIC TYRE
ACEEHLORRSTUY	TREACHEROUSLY	ACEEINNNRSSTU	UNCERTAINNESS
ACEEHLPPRSTUY	SUPPLY TEACHER	ACEEINNOORSVZ	CONVERSAZIONE
ACEEHLPSSSTTU	SPACE SHUTTLES	ACEEINNOSSSTU	TENACIOUSNESS
ACEEHMNOPPRRT	RAPPROCHEMENT	ACEEINOOPRSTU	PROTEINACEOUS
ACEEHNNOORSTU	SOUTHERN OCEAN	ACEEINOOPRTTX	EXPECTORATION
ACEEIIILPRSTU	PECULIARITIES	ACEEINOORRSTV	CONSERVATOIRE,
ACEEIIIMNRRTV	RECRIMINATIVE		OVERREACTIONS
ACEEIIIPPRTTV	PRECIPITATIVE	ACEEINOPRSSTT	INSPECTORATES
ACEEIILLLPPTY	EPILEPTICALLY	ACEEINORSSSUV	VERACIOUSNESS
ACEEIILMMNORS	CEREMONIALISM	ACEEINORSSTVV	CONSERVATIVES
ACEEIILMNOPRS	SEMIPORCELAIN	ACEEIOPRRSTTV	PRIVATE SECTOR
ACEEIILMNORST	CEREMONIALIST	ACEELLNOOPRSU	PORCELLANEOUS
ACEEIILMNPRSS	EMPIRICALNESS	ACEELLNSSSSSS	CLASSLESSNESS
ACEEIILNNNRTT	TRICENTENNIAL	ACEELLOORRRST	ROLLER COASTER
ACEEIILNRTTVY	INTERACTIVELY	ACEELMMNOPRTY	COMPLEMENTARY
ACEEIILPPRTTY	PRECIPITATELY	ACEELMNNOPRST	NOMENCLATURES
ACEEIIMMORSTV	COMMISERATIVE	ACEELNNOPRRTY	PENALTY CORNER
ACEEIIMNNOSTT	AMNIOCENTESIS	ACEEMMNNOPSST	ENCOMPASSMENT
ACEEIIMNORRST	MERCERISATION	ACEEMNNNNOSTU	ANNOUNCEMENTS
ACEEIIMNORRTZ	MERCERIZATION	ACEEMNNORRSST	REMONSTRANCES
ACEEIINNOSSTT	NECESSITATION	ACEEOOPRRSTTT	PROTECTORATES
ACEEIINORSSVV	VARICOSE VEINS	ACEFFFFHIOSST	CHIEFS OF STAFF
ACEEIIRSSTTUV	RESUSCITATIVE	ACEFFFFIORSST	STAFF OFFICERS

ACEFGHIINNNRS	ENFRANCHISING
ACEFGIIIINSTV	SIGNIFICATIVE
ACEFGIILMNNTY	MAGNIFICENTLY
ACEFGIILNNRTU	LUNATIC FRINGE
ACEFGIKKOOTTU	GET A KICK OUT OF
ACEFGILNRSSUY	FLYING SAUCERS
ACEFHHIIINPST	CHIEFTAINSHIP
ACEFHIIMNRSTU	FRUIT MACHINES
ACEFHLLOPRRUY	REPROACHFULLY
ACEFIIIJLLNOT	JELLIFICATION
ACEFIIILNOSTT	FELICITATIONS
ACEFIIINNORTU	REUNIFICATION
ACEFIIINNORSTV	VERSIFICATION
ACEFIIINOSTTT	TESTIFICATION
ACEFIILLPRSUY	SUPERFICIALLY
ACEFIILNORSTY	FORENSICALITY
ACEFIINNORSTU	FUNCTIONARIES
ACEFIINOORSTV	VOCIFERATIONS
ACEFILNNOOSSS	CONFESSIONALS
ACEFILNOOPRSS	FALSE SCORPION
ACEFINNOORSSY	CONFESSIONARY
ACEFINNORRTTY	CONFRATERNITY
ACEFINORSSSTU	FRACTIOUSNESS
ACEFJKKLNOORT	NORFOLK JACKET
ACEFLLMOOPRSW	CAMP FOLLOWERS
ACEFOOORRTTWW	WATER CROWFOOT
ACEGGGHIINNNR	CHANGE RINGING
ACEGGHIINNNRT	INTERCHANGING
ACEGGHINPRRSU	SUPERCHARGING
ACEGGHIOOOPRZ	ZOOGEOGRAPHIC
ACEGGIILNSTTU	GESTICULATING
ACEGGILLOOPTY	EGYPTOLOGICAL
ACEGGILNNORUY	ENCOURAGINGLY
ACEGGILNOOSTY	GYNAECOLOGIST
ACEGGINNOORST	CONGREGATIONS
ACEGGLLRSSSTU	CLASS STRUGGLE
ACEGHHIMOPRRT	THERMOGRAPHIC
ACEGHHNOOPRRR	CHRONOGRAPHER
ACEGHIIMNNRTU	TURING MACHINE
ACEGHIIMOPRSS	SEISMOGRAPHIC
ACEGHILLLOOTY	ETHOLOGICALLY, THEOLOGICALLY
ACEGHILLNOOPR	PHRENOLOGICAL
ACEGHILLOOPPS	PSEPHOLOGICAL
ACEGHILNOPRRY	REPROACHINGLY
ACEGHILNORSSU	SOUL-SEARCHING
ACEGHILOOSSTT	ESCHATOLOGIST
ACEGHIMNNORTT	MAGNETIC NORTH
ACEGHINORRSTT	ORCHESTRATING
ACEGHNOOPPRSY	PHARYNGOSCOPE
ACEGHOPPRRRTY	CRYPTOGRAPHER
ACEGHOPPRRSTY	SPECTROGRAPHY
ACEGIIILNOPT	GEOPOLITICIAN
ACEGIIIMNNRRT	RECRIMINATING

ACEGIIINORTTY	IATROGENICITY
ACEGIIINPPRTT	PRECIPITATING
ACEGIIKNNRSVV	CARVING KNIVES
ACEGIIILLLOOTY	ETIOLOGICALLY
ACEGIILLNNSSW	LICENSING LAWS
ACEGIILLOSTTY	EGOTISTICALLY
ACEGIILNNOORT	RECOGNITIONAL
ACEGIILNOSTTU	GESTICULATION
ACEGIIMMNNORST	COMMISERATING
ACEGIINOORSST	COSIGNATORIES
ACEGIINOPRSTY	SAPROGENICITY
ACEGIINPRRSTT	STARTING PRICE
ACEGIINRSSTTU	RESUSCITATING
ACEGIKLNOOPPS	COOKING APPLES
ACEGILLMNNOOOT	ENTOMOLOGICAL
ACEGILLMNOORU	NUMEROLOGICAL
ACEGILLMNOORY	ERGONOMICALLY
ACEGILLMNOOYZ	ENZYMOLOGICAL
ACEGILLNNOOTY	ONTOGENICALLY
ACEGILLOOPRTY	GEOTROPICALLY
ACEGILLSTYYYZ	SYZYGETICALLY
ACEGILMNNOPTT	CONTEMPLATING
ACEGILMNOPSTY	SALPINGECTOMY
ACEGILMOOSSTU	CLEISTOGAMOUS
ACEGILNNNOSUY	SANGUINOLENCY
ACEGILNNOORSS	CONGRESSIONAL
ACEGILNORRSUU	NEUROSURGICAL
ACEGILOOPSSST	ESCAPOLOGISTS
ACEGIMMMNOORT	COMMEMORATING
ACEGIMNOPRSTU	PNEUMOGASTRIC
ACEGINOOPRSTT	PROGNOSTICATE
ACEGLNOOOPSUY	POLYGONACEOUS
ACEGMNNOORSSW	CONGRESSWOMAN
ACEHHIIINOPRSX	HIERACOSPHINX
ACEHHIINOPRSZ	SCHIZOPHRENIA
ACEHHILMOPRTX	XEROPHTHALMIC
ACEHHLLLMOOTY	METHYL ALCOHOL
ACEHHMMNRSTUY	CHRYSANTHEMUM
ACEHHMOOOPRRT	CHROMATOPHORE
ACEHHOPPRSTYY	PSYCHOTHERAPY
ACEHIIINRRSST	CHRISTIANISER
ACEHIIINRRSTZ	CHRISTIANIZER
ACEHIIILLLMOTY	HOMILETICALLY
ACEHIILLPPTYY	EPIPHYTICALLY
ACEHIILLRSTUY	HEURISTICALLY
ACEHIILMNSSSW	WHIMSICALNESS
ACEHIILOOPPRT	APHELIOTROPIC
ACEHIIMMRSSTT	CHRISTMASTIME
ACEHIIOPSSSTT	SOPHISTICATES
ACEHIJKLPRSSY	PHYSICAL JERKS
ACEHILLMMOPRY	MORPHEMICALLY
ACEHILLNORSSS	SCHOLARLINESS
ACEHILLNSTTYY	SYNTHETICALLY
ACEHILLOOPRTY	ORTHOEPICALLY

ACEHILLOPPRTY	PROPHETICALLY	ACEIKLOORRSSW	SOCIAL WORKERS
ACEHILLOPRTTY	PROTHETICALLY	ACEILLLLMRTUU	MULTICELLULAR
ACEHILMOPRSTT	THERMOPLASTIC	ACEILLLLPSTYY	SYLLEPTICALLY
ACEHILOOPRSTV	PRIVATE SCHOOL	ACEILLLOPPRTY	PROLEPTICALLY
ACEHILPPRSSUY	SUPERPHYSICAL	ACEILLMMRSTYY	SYMMETRICALLY
ACEHIMOORSTTT	TRACHEOTOMIST	ACEILLNNNOSSY	NONSENSICALLY
ACEHIMORSSTTT	THERMOSTATICS	ACEILLNNOOSTT	CONSTELLATION
ACEHINOORRSTT	ORCHESTRATION	ACEILLNOOPRRY	INCORPOREALLY
ACEHIOPRRSSTT	ORCHESTRA PITS,	ACEILLNOQUUVY	UNEQUIVOCALLY
STRATOSPHERIC		ACEILLOPSTUUY	EUCALYPTUS OIL
ACEHIORSSTTTU	TETRASTICHOUS	ACEILMMNOPRTY	COMPLIMENTARY
ACEHLMOORSSST	SCHOOLMASTERS	ACEILMNNOOPTT	CONTEMPLATION
ACEHLNOORTTTW	CHARLOTTETOWN	ACEILMNNORRTU	INTERCOLUMNAR
ACEHMMOPSTTYY	SYMPATHECTOMY	ACEILMNNSSSUU	UNMUSICALNESS
ACEHNNOOPRRSS	ANCHORPERSONS	ACEILMNOOPRSS	COMPRESSIONAL
ACEHNNOORRTTY	ON THE CONTRARY	ACEILMNOPRVYY	LIVERY COMPANY
ACEHNOORRTTTY	TO THE CONTRARY	ACEILNNORTTUU	ENCULTURATION
ACEIIIILMPRST	IMPERIALISTIC	ACEILNOORRSTV	CONTROVERSIAL
ACEIIILLNNOPT	PENICILLATION	ACEILOOPRTVVY	PROVOCATIVELY
ACEIIILNORSTT	ORIENTALISTIC	ACEIMMMNOOORT	COMMEMORATION
ACEIIILNOSTVV	VIVISECTIONAL	ACEIMNNORRTTU	MACRONUTRIENT
ACEIIILQSTUVY	ACQUISITIVELY	ACEINNNOORSTT	CONSTERNATION
ACEIIIMNNORRT	RECRIMINATION	ACEINNNOORTTV	CONTRAVENTION
ACEIIINOPPRTT	PRECIPITATION	ACEINNOORSSTV	CONVERSATIONS
ACEIIINRTTTVY	INTERACTIVITY	ACEINOORSSSTU	ATROCIOUSNESS
ACEIIKLMOSTTU	STICK OUT A MILE	ACEINOPRRSSST	CONSPIRATRESS
ACEIILLNNORTY	ACRYLONITRILE	ACEIOORPRRRST	TROOP CARRIERS
ACEIILLNRRTTU	INTRATELLURIC	ACELLMMNOOORU	MONOMOLECULAR
ACEIILLNRSTXY	EXTRINSICALLY	ACELLNOORSTTY	CONSTELLATORY
ACEIILLOOPTYZ	EPIZOOTICALLY	ACELMNOPRRSUU	SUPERCOLUMNAR
ACEIILMNOPSST	NEOPLASTICISM	ACELMNORRSUUU	NEUROMUSCULAR
ACEIILMNORTUV	VERMICULATION	ACELNOOPRSSTU	PROCONSULATES
ACEIILMNOSSSU	MALICIOUSNESS	ACELOOPRSSSVY	SOLVAY PROCESS
ACEIILNOOPSTT	POLICE STATION	ACEMOOPRSTTTY	PROSTATECTOMY
ACEIILNOPRRTT	INTERTROPICAL	ACENNOOOOPRRT	NONCOOPERATOR
ACEIILNOPRSST	PERSONALISTIC	ACENNOORRSSSU	RANCOROUSNESS
ACEIILNORSTTU	RETICULATIONS	ACFFGHIILRSTT	TRAFFIC LIGHTS
ACEIILNPQTTUU	QUINTUPLICATE	ACFFGILNOSTUY	SUFFOCATINGLY
ACEIILNRSSTTT	CLARINETTISTS	ACFFIIINOORTT	FORTIFICATION
ACEIILNRSSTVY	CIVIL SERVANTS	ACFFIIINNOOPTT	IN POINT OF FACT
ACEIIMMNOORST	COMMISERATION	ACFGIIIILNNOT	LIGNIFICATION
ACEIIMNNOOOST	ECONOMISATION	ACFGIIIINNNST	INSIGNIFICANT
ACEIIMNNOOOTZ	ECONOMIZATION	ACFGIIIINNOST	SIGNIFICATION
ACEIIMNORRRTY	RECRIMINATORY	ACFGIIILNNSTY	SIGNIFICANTLY
ACEIINNNORSTU	RENUNCIATIONS	ACFGIIILNOORT	GLORIFICATION
ACEIINNOOPRST	PRECONISATION	ACFGIIINNOPTT	PONTIFICATING
ACEIINNOOPRTZ	PRECONIZATION	ACFGIINNOORTU	CONFIGURATION
ACEIINOOPRRTV	INCORPORATIVE	ACFHIIINOORRT	HORRIFICATION
ACEIINOOQSTUV	EQUIVOCATIONS	ACFHIILLNOORY	HONORIFICALLY
ACEIINOPRRSTT	PRACTITIONERS	ACFIIIILNOSTV	VILIFICATIONS
ACEIINORSSSUV	VICARIOUSNESS	ACFIIIINNORTT	NITRIFICATION
ACEIINORSSTTU	RESUSCITATION	ACFIIIINORTTV	VITRIFICATION
ACEIINOSSSUVV	VIVACIOUSNESS	ACFIIIJLLNOOT	JOLLIFICATION
ACEIIORRTTTVY	RETROACTIVITY	ACFIIIJNOSTTU	JUSTIFICATION

ACFIIILLMNOOT	MOLLIFICATION
ACFIIILLNNOTU	NULLIFICATION
ACFIIIMMMNOTU	MUMMIFICATION
ACFIIIMNOORTT	MORTIFICATION
ACFIIIMNOSTTY	MYSTIFICATION
ACFIIINNOOSTT	NOTIFICATIONS
ACFIIJORSTTUY	JUSTIFICATORY
ACFIIILLLORSTY	FLORISTICALLY
ACFIIILLOOPRSY	SOPORIFICALLY
ACFIILMNNOSTU	FUNCTIONALISM
ACFIILNNOSTTU	FUNCTIONALIST
ACFIIMNNOORST	CONFIRMATIONS
ACFILLLORRTUU	FLORICULTURAL
ACFILNNNNOOTU	NONFUNCTIONAL
ACFIMNNOOORST	CONFORMATIONS
ACFINNNOOORTT	CONFRONTATION
ACGGHHILOPPRY	GLYPHOGRAPHIC
ACGGHHINNORST	SHORT-CHANGING
ACGGHIKLNOSTU	LAUGHINGSTOCK
ACGGHILOPPRTY	GLYPTOGRAPHIC
ACGGHIMNNOORS	CHANGING ROOMS
ACGHHIIOPPRSY	PHYSIOGRAPHIC
ACGHHILMOOOPR	HOMOLOGRAPHIC
ACGHHIMNOOSTT	SHOOTING MATCH
ACGHIILLOOPSY	PHYSIOLOGICAL
ACGHILLLMOOOY	HOMOLOGICALLY
ACGHILLMOOOPR	MORPHOLOGICAL
ACGHILLOOPRSY	OSCILLOGRAPHY
ACGHIMNNOOOPT	PATHOGNOMONIC
ACGHNOOPPRSSY	PHARYNGOSCOPY
ACGIIIILMNNNRT	INCRIMINATING
ACGIIIILLNNSTT	SCINTILLATING
ACGIIIMNNORTZ	ROMANTICIZING
ACGIIKKLNSSTW	WALKING STICKS
ACGIIILLLOSSTY	SYLLOGISTICAL
ACGIIILLMNNOPY	COMPLAININGLY
ACGIIILLMOOSTT	CLIMATOLOGIST
ACGIIILLNRSTYZ	CRYSTALLIZING
ACGIIILMNNNOPU	UNCOMPLAINING
ACGIIILRRSTTUU	AGRICULTURIST
ACGIIMMNOORRS	MICROORGANISM
ACGIINNNOSTUY	CONSANGUINITY
ACGIINNOOPRRT	INCORPORATING
ACGILLLLMNOOOY	NOMOLOGICALLY
ACGILLLNOOOSY	NOSOLOGICALLY
ACGILLLNOOOTY	ONTOLOGICALLY
ACGILLLOOOPTY	TOPOLOGICALLY
ACGILLNOOOSTV	VOLCANOLOGIST
ACGINNNOOOSTU	NONCONTAGIOUS
ACGIOOPRSSSTT	GASTROSCOPIST
ACHHIIINNORST	ORNITHISCHIAN
ACHHIILLOOPPS	PHILOSOPHICAL
ACHHIILNOPPRT	PHILANTHROPIC
ACHHIIMNOPPSS	CHAMPIONSHIPS

ACHHIIMOPRSTU	AMPHITRICHOUS
ACHHIINOOSTTW	IN CAHOOTS WITH
ACHHILMMOORSS	SCHOOLMARMISH
ACHHIMNOORSTX	XANTHOCHROISM
ACHHIMNOOSTHN	AUTOCHTHONISM
ACHHLLNOOOSTU	ALLOCHTHONOUS
ACHHNOOOSTTUU	AUTOCHTHONOUS
ACHIIIJPRSSTU	JUSTICIARSHIP
ACHIIIMNOSTTY	MYTHICISATION
ACHIIIMNOTTYZ	MYTHICIZATION
ACHIIILLOPSSTY	SOPHISTICALLY
ACHIIMMORRSTT	TRICHROMATISM
ACHIIMNNOOPPS	COMPANIONSHIP
ACHIIOOPRSSTT	SOPHISTICATOR
ACHIIPRSSSTTY	PSYCHIATRISTS
ACHILLMNOPSYY	SYMPHONICALLY
ACHILLMPSSYYY	SYMPHYSICALLY
ACHILLORRTTUU	HORTICULTURAL
ACHILMOOPRRSY	PRIMARY SCHOOL
ACHILMOORSTYS	CHROMATOLYSIS
ACHILMOPSTTYY	SYMPATHOLYTIC
ACIIIILNOSSTV	CIVILISATIONS
ACIIIILNOSTVZ	CIVILIZATIONS
ACIIIIMNNNORT	INCRIMINATION
ACIIIIMNOSTTV	VICTIMISATION
ACIIIIMNOTTVZ	VICTIMIZATION
ACIIILLLORTVY	VITRIOLICALLY
ACIIILLNNOSTT	SCINTILLATION
ACIIILLNNRSTY	INTRINSICALLY
ACIIILMNNORTU	ANTICLINORIUM
ACIIILMNOPRSV	PROVINCIALISM
ACIIILNNOPRST	INSCRIPTIONAL
ACIIILNOOSSTT	SOLICITATIONS
ACIIILNOPRTVY	PROVINCIALITY
ACIIIMNNORRTY	INCRIMINATORY
ACIILLLMOOQSU	COLLOQUIALISM
ACIILLLRSTUUV	SILVICULTURAL
ACIILLLSSTTYY	STYLISTICALLY
ACIILLNOORTUY	ILLOCUTIONARY
ACIILNRSTTYY	CRYSTALLINITY
ACIILMNOOOPST	COMPOSITIONAL
ACIILMNOORSUY	ACRIMONIOUSLY
ACIILMNOORTTY	MICROTONALITY
ACIILMOORSTTT	STROMATOLITIC
ACIILMOPRSTUV	VICTORIA PLUMS
ACIILNNORSTTU	INSTRUCTIONAL
ACIILNOOPSSTU	SUPPLICATIONS
ACIILNORSTTUV	VOLUNTARISTIC
ACIILQRSTTUUU	AQUICULTURIST
ACIIMMNNOOSTU	COMMUNISATION
ACIIMMNNOOTUZ	COMMUNIZATION
ACIIMMNNOSTTU	ANTI-COMMUNIST
ACIIMMOOPRSTT	COMPATRIOTISM
ACIIMNNOOSSTU	SANCTIMONIOUS

ACIINNNOOPRTU	PRONUNCIATION
ACIINNNOOSTTU	CONTINUATIONS
ACIINNOOOPRRT	INCORPORATION
ACIINNOPRRSTT	TRANSCRIPTION
ACIINNORSSTTU	INCRUSTATIONS
ACILMMOOPSSSY	MYCOPLASMOSIS
ACILMNOOOPSST	COSMOPOLITANS
ACILMOOPRRRUY	PRIMARY COLOUR
ACILMRRSSTTUU	STRUCTURALISM
ACILNNOOSSTTU	CONSULTATIONS
ACILRRSSTTTUU	STRUCTURALIST
ACIMMNNOOSSTU	CONSUMMATIONS
ACIMNOOPPSSST	COMPASS POINTS
ACINNOPRSTTTU	CONTRAPUNTIST
ACINOOPRRSSTT	STRIP CARTOONS
ACKKMNNOOPSST	POSTMAN'S KNOCK
ACLMORSSTTUUU	CUMULOSTRATUS,
STRATOCUMULUS	
ADDDEEEEFLRSSS	SELF-ADDRESSED
ADDDEEEGILLMNN	MIDDLE ENGLAND
ADDDEEHLNNRUY	UNDERHANDEDLY
ADDDEGGLLNOSY	DADDY LONGLEGS
ADDEEEEHNRRTT	TENDERHEARTED
ADDEEEGHINPSS	PIGHEADEDNESS
ADDEEEGHNORSV	DEHYDROGENASE
ADDEEEGHNORTY	DEHYDROGENATE
ADDEEEGMNRRRY	GERRYMANDERED
ADDEEEHHNOSST	HOT-HEADEDNESS
ADDEEEHLLNOSW	SWOLLEN HEADED
ADDEEEILMNRST	MIDDLE EASTERN
ADDEEEIINOPPST	ENDOPEPTIDASE
ADDEEELRRSSTTY	RED-LETTER DAYS
ADDEEENOPPRRT	PREPONDERATED
ADDEEFFHHNNOSS	OFFHANDEDNESS
ADDEEFFIORSST	DISAFFORESTED
ADDEEFLNNPRUY	PENNY-DREADFUL
ADDEEGHHILLTY	LIGHT-HEADEDLY
ADDEEGHLNORWY	WRONGHEADEDLY
ADDEEGIINRSTT	DISINTEGRATED
ADDEEGNNRSSUU	UNGUARDEDNESS
ADDEEHIKLNRTY	KIND-HEARTEDLY
ADDEEHLNORTWY	DOWNHEARTEDLY
ADDEEIIILMRST	DEMILITARISED
ADDEEIIILMRTZ	DEMILITARIZED
ADDEEIIINORSTT	DISORIENTATED
ADDEEIMNNSSSY	MANY-SIDEDNESS
ADDEEINNSSSUV	UNADVISEDNESS
ADDEFGIILLNNS	LANDING FIELDS
ADDEGHILNOOTU	GO INTO A HUDDLE
ADDEGINNNRSTU	UNDERSTANDING
ADDEGINNORRST	STANDING ORDER
ADDEGLNOORTUY	GOOD-NATUREDLY
ADDEHHLORRSSU	HARD SHOULDERS
ADDEHILNORTUY	THE DAILY ROUND

ADDEIIIILNSUV	INDIVIDUALISE
ADDEIIIILNUVZ	INDIVIDUALIZE
ADDEIIINOOSTX	DEOXIDISATION
ADDEIIINOOTXZ	DEOXIDIZATION
ADDEIILNNOTTY	AN OLD IDENTITY
ADDEIINOOOORST	DEODORISATION
ADDEIINOOOORTZ	DEODORIZATION
ADDEIINOPRSTU	SUPERADDITION
ADDEIKMNOOSST	IT MAKES NO ODDS
ADDEILMNOPRSS	PROMISED LANDS
ADDEIMNNRSSTU	MISUNDERSTAND
ADDEIMNOOPRSU	MODUS OPERANDI
ADDGHIMNOORSU	ROUGH DIAMONDS
ADDGIILLLLNYY	DILLYDALLYING
ADDGILLNOOPPS	PADDLING POOLS
ADDIIIILMNSUV	INDIVIDUALISM
ADDIIIILNSTUV	INDIVIDUALIST
ADDIIIILNTUVY	INDIVIDUALITY
ADDIIIINNOTUV	INDIVIDUATION
ADEEEEEHLLRRW	WHEELER-DEALER
ADEEEEFHINRTV	FEATHER-VEINED
ADEEEEGHHNOTV	HAVE THE EDGE ON
ADEEEEGHKLPTT	TAKE THE PLEDGE
ADEEEEHHLORSV	HEAD OVER HEELS
ADEEEEHNRTTVY	THREE-DAY EVENT
ADEEEFFGILNST	SELF-DEFEATING
ADEEEFFIINRTT	DIFFERENTIATE
ADEEEFILLNRTY	DEFERENTIALLY
ADEEEGGGINRST	DESEGREGATING
ADEEEGGIMMNNST	DISENGAGEMENT
ADEEEGGINORST	DESEGREGATION
ADEEEGHLMMRRS	SLEDGEHAMMERS
ADEEEGIMNRSSS	DISAGREEMENTS
ADEEEGLLNORTU	OUTGENERALLED
ADEEEGOPRRTUY	DAGUERREOTYPE
ADEEEHIMNRSTT	HEREDITAMENTS
ADEEEHLNOPRTY	OPENHEARTEDLY
ADEEEIIMNNRTT	INDETERMINATE
ADEEEIIMNRTTV	DETERMINATIVE
ADEEEIIMPRTTV	PREMEDITATIVE
ADEEEIINPRSSS	PEDESTRIANISE
ADEEEIINPRSTZ	PEDESTRIANIZE
ADEEEIIORRTTV	DETERIORATIVE
ADEEEILNNNRUV	INLAND REVENUE
ADEEEILNOPRSS	DEPERSONALISE
ADEEEILNOPRSZ	DEPERSONALIZE
ADEEEILOPRTTY	RADIOTELETYPE
ADEEEILORSSTW	LOWER EAST SIDE
ADEEEIMNRSTTU	UNDERESTIMATE
ADEEEIMNRSTTV	ADVERTISEMENT
ADEEEIMORSTTV	OVERESTIMATED
ADEEEINNRSSST	SEDENTARINESS
ADEEEINOPQRTU	EQUIPONDERATE
ADEEELLMNOPTV	DEVELOPMENTAL

ADEEEELLMORRST	STEAMROLLERED
ADEEEENRSSSTUV	ADVENTURESSES
ADEEEOPPRRSSV	EAVESDROPPERS
ADEEFFIILNRST	DIFFERENTIALS
ADEEFFIILSSST	SELF-SATISFIED
ADEEFGLNRRSSU	REGARDFULNESS
ADEEFIILLLQUW	WELL-QUALIFIED
ADEEFILLNOORV	OIL OF LAVENDER
ADEEFILNOPPST	SELF-APPOINTED
ADEEFINOORSTT	DEFORESTATION
ADEEGGGINSSZZ	ZIGZAGGEDNESS
ADEEGGHINNNSX	HANG SENG INDEX
ADEEGGHIRSSTT	STRAIGHTEDGES
ADEEGGIIMMNNTZ	DEMAGNETIZING
ADEEGGLNNPRSU	GELANDESPRUNG
ADEEGHHNORVYY	HEAVY HYDROGEN
ADEEGHILNRSTY	NEARSIGHTEDLY
ADEEGHLMNORST	GOLDEN HAMSTER
ADEEGHOPRRSSW	HEDGE SPARROWS
ADEEGIINNNRSS	INGRAINEDNESS
ADEEGIINNNRRTT	INTERGRADIENT
ADEEGIINORRTT	DETERIORATING
ADEEGIINORSTY	TAYSIDE REGION
ADEEGIKNNRRST	KINDERGARTENS
ADEEGILNNOOPS	OLD AGE PENSION
ADEEGIMORSTTU	DEUTEROGAMIST
ADEEGINNOOTXY	DEOXYGENATION
ADEEGINOPPRSV	EAVESDROPPING
ADEEGJLMNTUUV	VALUE JUDGMENT
ADEEGLNNORSTU	DENTAL SURGEON
ADEEGMNNRRSTU	UNDERGARMENTS
ADEEGOPRRTUYY	DAGUERREOTYPY
ADEEHHIKNRRSS	HEADSHRINKERS
ADEEHHILNOOTT	TOAD-IN-THE-HOLE
ADEEHHIMOPRRT	HERMAPHRODITE
ADEEHHLMNOOSU	HOUSEHOLD NAME
ADEEHIILMNNPY	DIPHENYLAMINE
ADEEHIIMNORTT	TRIMETHADIONE
ADEEHILMNORST	SIDEREAL MONTH
ADEEHIMMOPRTX	MIXED METAPHOR
ADEEHIMNSSTUU	HUMANE STUDIES
ADEEHMMOOPRST	METAMORPHOSED
ADEEHMNOORRSY	DYSMENORRHOEA
ADEEHNNOOSSTU	SOUTHEND-ON-SEA
ADEEHNOOPRRTZ	TRAPEZOHEDRON
ADEEHORSSTUVY	SHROVE TUESDAY
ADEEIIIILORRST	EDITORIALISER
ADEEIIIILORRTZ	EDITORIALIZER
ADEEIIIMMNPRR	PRIME MERIDIAN
ADEEIIIMNSSTV	DISSEMINATIVE
ADEEIIINPRSST	STIPENDIARIES
ADEEIIILMNNSTT	DISENTAILMENT
ADEEIIILMNPSST	DISSEPIMENTAL
ADEEIIILMNRSTY	SEDIMENTARILY
ADEEIIILNORTTT	TOILET-TRAINED
ADEEIIIMNNORTT	DETERMINATION
ADEEIIIMNNOSTT	SEDIMENTATION
ADEEIIIMNOPRTT	PREMEDITATION
ADEEIIIMNORRTT	INTERMEDIATOR
ADEEIIINNORSTT	TENDERISATION
ADEEIIINNORTTZ	TENDERIZATION
ADEEIIINOORRTT	DETERIORATION
ADEEIIINOPRTXY	EXPEDITIONARY
ADEEIIILLMNRTY	DETRIMENTALLY
ADEEIIILLNNRSST	LANTERNSLIDES
ADEEIIILLNOPPTW	WELL-APPOINTED
ADEEIIILLNORRVY	ORDINARY LEVEL
ADEEIIILLOSSTVW	OLD WIVES' TALES
ADEEIIILLLTTTTT	TITTLE-TATTLED
ADEEIIILMMNNSTT	DISMANTLEMENT
ADEEIIILMNOORTZ	METRONIDAZOLE
ADEEIIILNNRTTVY	INADVERTENTLY
ADEEIIMMNORSSU	MISDEMEANOURS
ADEEIIMNORSTTV	DEMONSTRATIVE
ADEEIIMNPRRTTT	PRINTED MATTER
ADEEIIMNRSSTUV	MISADVENTURES
ADEEIINNOPORTU	EQUIPONDERANT
ADEEIINOSSSTTW	AT ONE'S WITS' END
ADEEIINOPRRSST	PREDATORINESS
ADEEIINOPRRSTU	SUPERORDINATE
ADEEJMMORRTTU	DRUM MAJORETTE
ADEEJMNRSSTTU	READJUSTMENTS
ADEELOOPPRRTUV	OVERPOPULATED
ADEEMMNOORTUUV	OUTMANOEUVRED
ADEEMNRSTTTUU	MATURE STUDENT
ADEFFHILLNOSU	FULL-FASHIONED
ADEFFHIORRSST	STAFFORDSHIRE
ADEFGHHILNOST	SLEIGHT OF HAND
ADEFGHINOORSW	FORESHADOWING
ADEFGIILLNPSY	PLAYING FIELDS
ADEFGIINNOORR	FOREORDAINING
ADEFGILLNOPST	SOFT-PEDALLING
ADEFGNNOOOORT	GOOD AFTERNOON
ADEFHILNOORSS	FOOLHARDINESS
ADEFIILNPRSSU	FREUDIAN SLIPS
ADEFILLSSSTTUY	DISTASTEFULLY
ADEFLLOOPSTYY	SPLAYFOOTEDLY
ADEGGHIILLNST	LEADING LIGHTS
ADEGGIILNNNST	DISENTANGLING
ADEGGIILNNRSS	NIGGARDLINESS
ADEGGINNORRS	ORGAN GRINDERS
ADEGHIKNNORRW	WORK-HARDENING
ADEGHINNNOSTT	ONE-NIGHT STAND
ADEGHINNOORTY	HYDROGENATION
ADEGHINOORSVW	OVERSHADOWING
ADEGHLLNORSST	STRANGLEHOLDS
ADEGIIIMNNRST	ADMINISTERING
ADEGIIIMNNSST	DISSEMINATING

ADEGIIKNNRRTW	DRINKING WATER	ADEIINNORSTTU	TRADE UNIONIST
ADEGIIILLNNOST	DIALLING TONES	ADEIINORSSSTT	DISSERTATIONS
ADEGIILNNOTTU	DEGLUTINATION	ADEILLNRSTTUU	UNILLUSTRATED
ADEGIIMMNNRST	MASTERMINDING	ADEILMNNOPRTY	PREDOMINANTLY
ADEGIIMNNOPRT	PREDOMINATING	ADEILNOORTUVY	DEVOLUTIONARY
ADEGIIMOOPRST	DIAGEOTROPISM	ADEIMNNOORSTT	DEMONSTRATION
ADEGIINNNPRTU	UNDERPAINTING	ADEINOSSSSSUU	ASSIDUOUSNESS
ADEGIINORRSTT	DISINTEGRATOR	ADEJLORSSSSTU	LOSS ADJUSTERS
ADEGIKLNNOTWY	TAKE LYING DOWN	ADELNOPRRSTTY	TRANSPORTEDLY
ADEGILMOORSTT	DERMATOLOGIST	ADELNORSTUUVY	ADVENTUROUSLY
ADEGILNNOQRTU	GRANDILOQUENT	ADEMNOORRSSTT	DEMONSTRATORS
ADEGILNNQRSUY	SQUANDERINGLY	ADENNORSTUUUV	UNADVENTUROUS
ADEGIMNNNORST	DEMONSTRATING	ADFFHILNOSSTY	STANDOFFISHLY
ADEGIMNNORRSUY	YOUNG MARRIEDS	ADFGGHHIILLNN	HIGHLAND FLING
ADEHHIIILMOOP	HAEMOPHILIOID	ADFGIIILLNQSUY	DISQUALIFYING
ADEHIIILMNPSTY	LYMPHADENITIS	ADFGIIINSSSTY	DISSATISFYING
ADEHIIMNOOSTT	METHODISATION	ADFGIINNOPRTY	INFANT PRODIGY
ADEHIIMNOOTTZ	METHODIZATION	ADFHIMNOOORSU	MAIDS OF HONOUR
ADEHILNNOPRSW	LANDOWNERSHIP	ADFIKLLNNOORS	NORFOLK ISLAND
ADEHINNRSSTWW	WITHDRAWNNESS	ADGGHHHIIMNTY	HIGH-AND-MIGHTY
ADEHINRSTUVYY	HEAVY INDUSTRY	ADGHIILMNNOSY	ADMONISHINGLY
ADEHIOOOPPRSST	APOSTROPHISED	ADGHILLLLMNOSS	SMALLHOLDINGS
ADEHIOOOPPRSTZ	APOSTROPHIZED	ADGHMNNOOPRRY	GYNANDROMORPH
ADEHLLOOPPSUY	POLYADELPHOUS	ADGIIILMNNSSTU	DISSIMULATING
ADEHLOPRRSSTU	SHOULDER STRAP	ADGIIINNOPPST	DISAPPOINTING
ADEHNORRSTTWW	NORTHWESTWARD	ADGIIILNNPRSST	LANDING STRIPS
ADEHORSSTTUWW	SOUTHWESTWARD	ADGIIMNNOSTUU	MAGNITUDINOUS
ADEIIIILMSSTV	DISSIMILATIVE	ADGILNNOSTTUY	OUTSTANDINGLY
ADEIIIILMSSTUV	DISSIMULATIVE	ADHIIILLNOQRTU	QUADRILLIONTH
ADEIIIILNPSTTU	PLATITUDINISE	ADHIIILNOPPSST	SPIT AND POLISH
ADEIIIILNPTTUZ	PLATITUDINIZE	ADHIIMNOORSSU	DISHARMONIOUS
ADEIIILNRSSTU	INDUSTRIALISE	ADHILNOORSTYY	HYDROLYSATION
ADEIIILNRSTUZ	INDUSTRIALIZE	ADHIMNOPRSSSW	SWORDSMANSHIP
ADEIIIMMNNOSST	DISSEMINATION	ADIIIIILMNOSST	DISSIMILATION
ADEIIINOSSTTV	DEVIATIONISTS	ADIIIIILMNPRTU	PLATINIRIDIUM
ADEIIINRSSTTV	DITRANSITIVES	ADIIIILMRSSTY	DISSIMILARITY
ADEIIINRSTTTU	ATTITUDINISER	ADIIIILLNOSSTT	DISTILLATIONS
ADEIIINRTTTUZ	ATTITUDINIZER	ADIIILMNOSSTU	DISSIMULATION
ADEIIKPRRSTTY	STRIKE PAY DIRT	ADIIILMNRSSTU	INDUSTRIALISM
ADEIIILLNORSTU	TRANQUILLISED	ADIIILMORSSTY	DISSIMILATORY
ADEIIILLNQRTUZ	TRANQUILLIZED	ADIIILNOOPSST	DISPOSITIONAL
ADEIIILMNOPSSY	IMPASSIONEDLY	ADIIILNRSSTTU	INDUSTRIALIST
ADEIIILNOOTTVY	DEVOTIONALITY	ADIILNNNORSTU	NONINDUSTRIAL
ADEIIMMNNOOTT	TIME-AND-MOTION	ADIILNOPSTTUU	PLATITUDINOUS
ADEIIMMNNRSSU	INDIAN SUMMERS	ADIKLNRSSUUYY	RYUKYU ISLANDS
ADEIIMMNNNOOST	DENOMINATIONS	ADIMNNOORSSWY	IN SO MANY WORDS
ADEIIMMNNOOPRT	PREDOMINATION	AEEEEEINPRRRS	ARRIERE-PENSEE
ADEIIMMNNOORST	MODERNISATION	AEEEEFHNRTTTV	AFTER THE EVENT
ADEIIMMNNOORTZ	MODERNIZATION	AEEEEHHNNSTVV	SEVENTH HEAVEN
ADEIIMMNNORSTU	TRADE UNIONISM	AEEEEILNRRSST	RENSSELAERITE
ADEIIMMNOSSTU	MOUNTAINSIDES	AEEEEIMNPRSST	PASSEMENTERIE
ADEIIINNNOSTTU	UNITED NATIONS	AEEEELPRRSSSS	PRESS RELEASES
ADEIIINNOOPRRT	PREORDINATION	AEEEEMNPRSSTT	TEMPERATENESS
ADEIIINNOPSSST	DISPENSATIONS	AEEEFGHHIRTTW	FEATHERWEIGHT

AEEEFGHLNRTTU	FEATURE-LENGTH
AEEEFGIIRRRTV	REFRIGERATIVE
AEEEFILRSSSTV	SELF-ASSERTIVE
AEEEFINQRTTUV	FREQUENTATIVE
AEEEFNORRSTTW	WATER SOFTENER
AEEEGGIMNOSST	GAMETOGENESIS
AEEEGHHINPRSS	SHEEPSHEARING
AEEEGHLLOPPRT	TELEGRAPH POLE
AEEEGHLNOPRRS	SELENOGRAPHER
AEEEGHMNOPRST	MAGNETOSPHERE
AEEEGIKLMNRTT	TELEMARKETING
AEEEGIKLNRRST	GENERAL STRIKE
AEEEGILMNNORT	NOLI-ME-TANGERE
AEEEGILNOPSTV	NEGATIVE POLES
AEEEGIMNPRRTY	PRAYER MEETING
AEEEGLMNNNSTT	ENTANGLEMENTS
AEEEGMNNRSSTT	ESTRANGEMENTS
AEEEGNOOPRRST	OPERATOR GENES
AEEEHHILNPTTW	WHITE ELEPHANT
AEEEHHNOPRSST	ASTHENOSPHERE
AEEEHHOPPRSTU	PAPER THE HOUSE
AEEEHIIMMNNTT	IN THE MEANTIME
AEEEHILMNNOPP	EPIPHENOMENAL
AEEEHIMOPRSSV	OVEREMPHASISE
AEEEHIMOPRSVZ	OVEREMPHASIZE
AEEEHLLMNSSTV	MANTELSHELVES
AEEEHLMNSSSNS	SHAMELESSNESS
AEEEHLNPSSSSS	SHAPELESSNESS
AEEEHLNRSSSST	HEARTLESSNESS
AEEEHLORSSTUX	HETEROSEXUALS
AEEEHMNORSSST	HEARTSOMENESS
AEEEIIILLLNTV	ILLE-ET-VILAINE
AEEEIIIMMNRST	SEINE-MARITIME
AEEEIILNSTTUV	EVENTUALITIES
AEEEIIMNRTTVX	EXTERMINATIVE
AEEEIKLLOPPST	SLEEP LIKE A TOP
AEEEIKLNPSTTV	PALETTE KNIVES
AEEEIKNPRSSVW	SNEAK PREVIEWS
AEEEILLNRRTVY	REVERENTIALLY
AEEEILMNPRSSX	EXEMPLARINESS
AEEEILMNPRTTY	INTEMPERATELY
AEEEILNPRTTVY	PENETRATIVELY
AEEEIMNNNRTTT	ENTERTAINMENT
AEEEIMNNRSTTT	REINSTATEMENT
AEEEIMNORSSSW	WEARISOMENESS
AEEEIMORSSSTV	OVERESTIMATES
AEEEINNPSSSVX	EXPANSIVENESS
AEEEINNSSTTTV	ATTENTIVENESS, TENTATIVENESS
AEEEINOPRRSTV	PERSEVERATION
AEEEINOPRSSTV	OPERATIVENESS
AEEEINPRSSSVV	PERVASIVENESS
AEEEINRSSSSTV	ASSERTIVENESS
AEEEIPRRSSTVV	PRESERVATIVES

AEEEKLLMRRSST	SELLER'S MARKET
AEEEKLRRSSTTW	STREETWALKERS
AEEELLNSSSSUV	VALUELESSNESS
AEEELNPRSTTTT	LETTERS PATENT
AEEELNSSSSSTT	STATELESSNESS, TASTELESSNESS
AEEEMMNOPRRTU	PNEUMATOMETER
AEEEMNORSTTTV	OVERSTATEMENT
AEEEMNPRRSSTU	PREMATURENESS
AEEENOPRSSTTT	POSTE RESTANTE
AEEEORRRSTTUV	TREASURE TROVE
AEEFFGHIRRSTU	FATHER FIGURES
AEEFFGINORRST	REAFFORESTING
AEEFFHIMOPPTW	WIPE OFF THE MAP
AEEFGGIINRRRT	REFRIGERATING
AEEFGIINORRRT	REFRIGERATION
AEEFGIIPRRTUV	PREFIGURATIVE
AEEFGIKRRSSTU	FIGURE SKATERS
AEEFGINORRSU	ARGENTIFEROUS
AEEFGIORRRRST	REFRIGERATORS
AEEFHHLLNSSTU	HEALTHFULNESS
AEEFHILNSSSST	FAITHLESSNESS
AEEFHKMMOOSTT	MAKE THE MOST OF
AEEFHLMOOPRRT	MOTHER-OF-PEARL
AEEFHLMORRSTW	FLAME-THROWERS
AEEFHLNOOPRST	ELEPHANT'S-FOOT
AEEFIIILLNNRTY	INFERENTIALLY
AEEFIILOPRRTV	PROLIFERATIVE
AEEFILLMORSTU	METALLIFEROUS
AEEFILNORSSST	SELF-ASSERTION
AEEFILNRRSSTT	SELF-RESTRAINT
AEEFIMNORSSTV	FORMATIVENESS
AEEFIMOORRRST	REFORMATORIES
AEEFINNOQRTTU	FREQUENTATION
AEEFINORSSSU	NEFARIOUSNESS
AEEFINOORRSTT	REFORESTATION
AEEFINOPRSTTU	SUPERFETATION
AEEFIOOPRRSST	PROFESSORIATE
AEEFLLNSSSSTU	FAULTLESSNESS
AEEFLMNRSSSTU	MASTERFULNESS
AEEGGHOOOPRRZ	ZOOGEOGRAPHER
AEEGGIILNNNRV	LINE-ENGRAVING
AEEGGILNNORTU	OUTGENERALING
AEEGGINNOORSS	ORGANOGENESIS
AEEGGINNSTTTW	WETTING AGENTS
AEEGGLLORRSUY	ROGUES' GALLERY
AEEGHHMOPRRRT	THERMOGRAPHER
AEEGHHMPRSTUV	HAVE THE GRUMPS
AEEGHHNOPRRST	ETHNOGRAPHERS
AEEGHIINNSTTZ	ANESTHETIZING
AEEGHILMOORST	ISOGEOTHERMAL
AEEGHILNNRTTY	THREATENINGLY
AEEGHILNORSTW	WATERING HOLES
AEEGHIMOPRRSS	SEISMOGRAPHER

AEEGHIPRSSSTW	STAGE WHISPERS	AEEIIILMNPRRS	PRELIMINARIES
AEEGHNOOPRRTV	PHOTOENGRAVER	AEEIIIMNSSTTV	IMITATIVENESS
AEEGHNOPRRSST	STENOGRAPHERS	AEEIIILLNNPTTY	PENITENTIALLY
AEEGIIINSTTVV	INVESTIGATIVE	AEEIILMNOPRSS	IMPERSONALISE
AEEGIILMNORSS	GENERALISSIMO	AEEIILMNOPRSZ	IMPERSONALIZE
AEEGIILNNRTXZ	EXTERNALIZING	AEEIILMNRSTUV	UNIVERSAL TIME
AEEGIIMNNORTT	REGIMENTATION	AEEIILNNORRTT	INTERRELATION
AEEGIIMNNRTTX	EXTERMINATING	AEEIILNNPSSTV	PLAINTIVENESS
AEEGIIMNRSTTU	TIME SIGNATURE	AEEIILNNTTTVY	INATTENTIVELY
AEEGIINNOORTT	RENEGOTIATION	AEEIILNOPQTTU	EQUIPOTENTIAL
AEEGIINNOPRRT	PEREGRINATION	AEEIILNOPRSST	PERSONALITIES
AEEGIINORRTTV	INTERROGATIVE	AEEIILNOPRTTV	INTERPOLATIVE
AEEGIKMNPRRST	PARKING METERS	AEEIILNORSTTV	REVELATIONIST
AEEGIKNRSSTUY	KEY SIGNATURES	AEEIILNORSTVY	TELEVISIONARY
AEEGILLLNPRST	SELLING-PLATER	AEEIILNQSTTUY	SEQUENTIALITY
AEEGILLMNNSSY	MEANINGLESSLY	AEEIILORRRTTX	EXTERRITORIAL
AEEGILLNRSTVY	EVERLASTINGLY	AEEIIMMNORSST	MESMERISATION
AEEGILNNPRTTY	PENETRATINGLY	AEEIIMMNORSTZ	MESMERIZATION
AEEGILNNTTUXY	EXTENUATINGLY	AEEIIMNNORTTX	EXTERMINATION
AEEGIMMNOOTTV	MAGNETOMOTIVE	AEEIIMNPSSSSV	IMPASSIVENESS
AEEGIMNNRTTUY	INTEGUMENTARY	AEEIIMNQRSSTU	EQUESTRIANISM
AEEGIMNORRSTV	OVERMASTERING	AEEIINNOQRSTU	QUESTIONNAIRE
AEEGINNRSTTUU	SIGNATURE TUNE	AEEIKNOPRSSTT	STREPTOKINASE
AEEGINQRSSTTU	SEQUESTRATING	AEEILLLMNNSST	MENTAL ILLNESS
AEEGINRRSSSTV	TRANSGRESSIVE	AEEILLMNNSTTY	SENTIMENTALLY
AEEGIORRRSTTV	TERGIVERSATOR	AEEILLNNOPTXY	EXPONENTIALLY
AEEGLLMNRSUWZ	MANGEL-WURZELS	AEEILLNNORSSU	LONS-LE-SAUNIER
AEEHHIINNOPTZ	PHENOTHIAZINE	AEEILLNOPRRTT	INTERPELLATOR
AEEHHILLMNSVW	WILHELMSHAVEN	AEEILLPRSTUVY	SUPERLATIVELY
AEEHHILMMNNTT	NEMATHELMINTH	AEEILLRRRSTTY	TERRESTRIALLY
AEEHHILNNSSTU	UNHEALTHINESS	AEEILLRTTTTTT	TITTLE-TATTLER
AEEHHMOPRRTTY	THERMOTHERAPY	AEEILMNNNORTV	ENVIRONMENTAL
AEEHIILLNNOST	HELLENISATION	AEEILMOPRRTXY	EXTEMPORARILY
AEEHIILLNNOTZ	HELLENIZATION	AEEILNNNOOPPS	PELOPONNESIAN
AEEHIKLNNPPST	PINK ELEPHANTS	AEEILNNNOPRST	ANTIPERSONNEL
AEEHILMMNNOPS	PHENOMENALISM	AEEILNNOPRRST	INTERPERSONAL
AEEHILMNNOPST	PHENOMENALIST	AEEILNNPRRSTT	SILENT PARTNER
AEEHILNNRSSTU	UNEARTHLINESS	AEEIILNNQQTUUV	QUINQUEVALENT
AEEHILORRSSTU	TRAILER HOUSES	AEEILNNRSSSUV	UNIVERSALNESS
AEEHIMNNQSSSU	SQUEAMISHNESS	AEEILNOORSTVV	LATEROVERSION
AEEHINNOPPRSS	APPREHENSIONS	AEEILNPRRRSST	LASER PRINTERS
AEEHINORSSSTW	SEAWORTHINESS	AEEILOPRSSTUY	ERYSIPELATOUS
AEEHIOPPSSTTV	STOVEPIPE HATS	AEEILPPRSSTUW	WATER SUPPLIES
AEEHIORRRRSST	HAIR-RESTORERS	AEEIMMNSSSTTT	MISSTATEMENTS
AEEHIPRRRSSTU	TREASURERSHIP	AEEIMNNOPPRTT	REAPPOINTMENT
AEEHKLNNSSSST	THANKLESSNESS	AEEIMNOPRRRST	TEMPORARINESS
AEEHLMNOOSSST	LOATHSOMENESS	AEEIMNOPRSSTX	PROXIMATENESS
AEEHLNORRSTTY	NORTHEASTERLY	AEEIMNORRSTTV	REMONSTRATIVE
AEEHLORSSTTUY	SOUTHEASTERLY	AEEIMNORRSTTX	EXTERMINATORS
AEEHMMOOPRSSS	METAMORPHOSES	AEEINNNRSSSTU	SATURNINENESS
AEEHMMOPSSTUU	EMPHYSEMATOUS	AEEINNOPRSSTT	PRESENTATIONS
AEEHMNOOPPRTU	PNEUMATOPHORE	AEEINOOPRRTTX	RE-EXPORTATION
AEEHMOOPPRRST	SPERMATOPHORE	AEEINOORRSTUV	ARTERIOVENOUS
AEEHMOPPRSTTY	SPERMATOPHYTE	AEEINOQRSSTTU	SEQUESTRATION

AEEINOSSSTUVX	VEXATIOUSNESS
AEEINRSSSTTTV	TRANSVESTITES
AEEIOOPPRSTTV	POSTOPERATIVE
AEEIPPRRSSSTT	ASSET-STRIPPER
AEEKLLORRRSST	ROLLER-SKATERS
AEEKMORRSSSTT	MASTERSTROKES
AEELMNPPRSTUY	SUPPLEMENTARY
AEELNOOPSSTTU	STENOPETALOUS
AEEMMNOPRTTUY	PNEUMATOMETRY
AEEMNOOPRSTTU	TREPONEMATOUS
AEEMNPRRRSUUY	SUPERNUMERARY
AEFFGIMRSSTTI	SUFFRAGETTISM
AEFGGIIKNRSTU	FIGURE-SKATING
AEFGHHOORRSTU	THOROUGHFARES
AEFGHHORSTTTU	AFTERTHOUGHTS
AEFGHIKMNNOOT	MAKE NOTHING OF
AEFGHINNNPRTY	PENNY-FARTHING
AEFGIILLORRSU	ARGILLIFEROUS
AEFGIILNOPRRT	PROLIFERATING
AEFGIINOPRRTU	PREFIGURATION
AEFGILLNNRTUY	UNFALTERINGLY
AEFGILNNORRWY	FOREWARNINGLY
AEFGILNOORTTV	FLOATING VOTER
AEFGINOOPRRTW	WATERPROOFING
AEFHKLMORSSST	THERMOS FLASKS
AEFHKNOOSSTTV	VOTES OF THANKS
AEFHLOOSTTUUU	OUT OF THE USUAL
AEFIIIILMNNST	INFINITESIMAL
AEFIIIILMNSST	SEMIFINALISTS
AEFIIILNORSTT	FERTILISATION
AEFIIILNORTTZ	FERTILIZATION
AEFIILLLNNTUY	INFLUENTIALLY
AEFIILMNORSUU	ALUMINIFEROUS
AEFIILMNORTVY	INFORMATIVELY
AEFIILNOOPRRT	PROLIFERATION
AEFIILNOPRSTU	PLATINIFEROUS
AEFIIMNOOPRRT	IMPERFORATION
AEFIIMNORSSTU	STAMINIFEROUS
AEFIINRRSTTTY	INTERSTRATIFY
AEFILLOPRSSTW	LOW-PASS FILTER
AEFILMNOPRSTT	SELF-IMPORTANT
AEFILNOOPRSSS	PROFESSIONALS
AEFILNOOPRSSW	PASSIONFLOWER
AEFILNOOQSTUW	QUESTION OF LAW
AEFINOOPRRRSW	PRISONER OF WAR
AEFIOOQRRSTUU	QUARTZIFEROUS
AEFLLMNORSSTU	SMALL FORTUNES
AEFLNNORTTUUY	UNFORTUNATELY
AEGGGIINRRTTU	REGURGITATING
AEGGHHLOPPRRY	GLYPHOGRAPHER
AEGGHIILNRRTT	RIGHT TRIANGLE
AEGGHIIMMNOPR	MIMEOGRAPHING
AEGGHIINNRSTT	STRAIGHTENING
AEGGHILNOORTW	WOOLGATHERING
AEGGHLOOPRRSS	GLOSSOGRAPHER
AEGGHLOPPRRTY	GLYPTOGRAPHER
AEGGIIIMNPSTT	SPITTING IMAGE
AEGGIIINNSTTV	INVESTIGATING
AEGGIINNORRTT	INTERROGATING
AEGGIINORRTTU	REGURGITATION
AEGGIINRSTTTT	SITTING TARGET
AEGGINNNOORSS	NONAGGRESSION
AEGGINNRRSSST	TRANSGRESSING
AEGHHILNORSSY	ROYAL HIGHNESS
AEGHHIOPPRRSY	PHYSIOGRAPHER
AEGHHOOPPRRST	PHOTOGRAPHERS
AEGHIIKNNPRSS	PINKING SHEARS
AEGHIILNNOORT	LOTHIAN REGION
AEGHIINNSTTUX	EXTINGUISHANT
AEGHIIPRRRSST	REGISTRARSHIP
AEGHIKLNORSST	STALKING-HORSE
AEGHIKNNRRSTT	KNIGHTS-ERRANT
AEGHILLLNNRTY	ENTHRALLINGLY
AEGHILNORSTUV	VAULTING HORSE
AEGHILOOPRSST	PHRASEOLOGIST
AEGHIMNORSSUW	HOUSEWARMINGS
AEGHIMNORTTUW	MOUTH-WATERING
AEGHINNOORSST	ON A SHOESTRING
AEGHIOPRRSSTU	SURROGATESHIP
AEGHLMMOORTTY	THREMMATOLOGY
AEGHMNOOOPSTU	ENTOMOPHAGOUS
AEGHNNOOPTTUY	PUT ON THE AGONY
AEGHNOOPPRRRS	PORNOGRAPHERS
AEGIIIILNNNRTZ	INTERNALIZING
AEGIIIILNRSSTU	SINGULARITIES
AEGIIINNOSTTV	INVESTIGATION
AEGIILLOPRSSS	ASPERGILLOSIS
AEGIILMNNNOOR	INNER MONGOLIA
AEGIILMNORSST	MINERALOGISTS
AEGIILMNORSYY	SYRINGOMYELIA
AEGIILMNPRSST	SLIPSTREAMING
AEGIILMOOSSST	SEMASIOLOGIST
AEGIILNNOPRSZ	PERSONALIZING
AEGIILNOPRTT	INTERPOLATING
AEGIILNNNRRTY	RESTRAININGLY
AEGIILNRSSTVV	VESTAL VIRGINS
AEGIIMNNOPRST	IMPERSONATING
AEGIIMNNRRRTY	INTERMARRYING
AEGIIMNSSTTYZ	SYSTEMATIZING
AEGIINNOORRTT	INTERROGATION
AEGIINOPPRRTX	EXPROPRIATING
AEGIINORRSSTT	REGISTRATIONS
AEGIINORSSTTV	INVESTIGATORS
AEGIJLPSSUWZZ	JIGSAW PUZZLES
AEGIKLLNORRST	ROLLER SKATING
AEGILLLMNSSST	SMELLING SALTS
AEGILLMNOORSS	LEMON GRASS OIL
AEGILLMRSSTTU	METALLURGISTS

AEGILMNORSSTU	SOMERSAULTING	AEIIILNORSTTZ	STERILIZATION
AEGILNOOPRRSS	PROGRESSIONAL	AEIIILNORTTUZ	REUTILIZATION
AEGILNOPSTTUX	EXPOSTULATING	AEIIILPRRSSTU	SPIRITUALISER
AEGIMNNOPRRRY	MORNING PRAYER	AEIIILPRRSTUZ	SPIRITUALIZER
AEGIMNNORRSTT	REMONSTRATING	AEIIIMNOOPSTT	EPITOMISATION
AEGIMNOOPRSSU	ANGIOSPERMOUS	AEIIIMNOOPTTZ	EPITOMIZATION
AEGIMOOOPPRST	APOGEOTROPISM	AEIIIMNOORSST	ISOMERISATION
AEGINNORRSSST	TRANSGRESSION	AEIIIMNOORSTZ	ISOMERIZATION
AEGINOORRRSTT	INTERROGATORS	AEIIINNORSSSV	VISIONARINESS
AEGINOORRRTTY	INTERROGATORY	AEIIINNOSSSTT	SENSITISATION
AEGLMNOORSSSU	GLAMOROUSNESS	AEIIINNOSSTTZ	SENSITIZATION
AEGLMOOSSTTYY	SYSTEMATOLOGY	AEIIINOOSSTTV	SOVIETISATION
AEGLNORRSSSUU	GARRULOUSNESS	AEIIINOOSTTVZ	SOVIETIZATION
AEGNORRRSSSST	TRANSGRESSORS	AEIIILLNNNOTTY	INTENTIONALLY
AEHHHINOPRRRY	HERNIORRHAPHY	AEIIILLNOQRTUV	VENTRILOQUIAL
AEHHIIILMNSST	HELMINTHIASIS	AEIIILLNQRRSTU	TRANQUILLISER
AEHHIILORSTTV	HEALTH VISITOR	AEIIILLNQRRTUZ	TRANQUILLIZER
AEHHIINORSTTW	WITHIN EARSHOT	AEIIILMNNOOPRS	PRONOMINALISE
AEHHILLLMNPTTY	PLATYHELMINTH	AEIIILMNNOOPRZ	PRONOMINALIZE
AEHHIMNOPRSTT	THEANTHROPISM	AEIIILMNNOOSST	SOLEMNISATION
AEHHINOPRSTTT	THEANTHROPIST	AEIIILMNNOOSTZ	SOLEMNIZATION
AEHHINORRRSTY	NORTH AYRSHIRE	AEIIILMNNOPSTU	EMULSION PAINT
AEHHIOPPRSTYY	PHYSIOTHERAPY	AEIIILMNOORSTT	TOLERATIONISM
AEHHLLMORSSTU	THE SMALL HOURS	AEIIILMNOPRSTY	IMPERSONALITY
AEHHLNORRTUUY	UNEARTHLY HOUR	AEIIILNNNNOTTU	UNINTENTIONAL
AEHHLOOPPRSSY	PHOSPHORYLASE	AEIIILNNNORTTU	INTERLUNATION
AEHHOOPPPRSSY	PYROPHOSPHATE	AEIIILNNOOPRTT	INTERPOLATION
AEHHOOPRRSSST	SHARPSHOOTERS	AEIIILNOOPPRST	PREPOSITIONAL
AEHIILNOPRSST	RELATIONSHIPS	AEIIILNOOPSTTX	SEXPLOITATION
AEHIILNORSSSU	HILARIOUSNESS	AEIIILNOORSTTT	TOLERATIONIST
AEHIINNORSSTW	AIRWORTHINESS	AEIIILNOPRSTUV	PULVERISATION
AEHIIRRSSSTTW	SHIRTWAISTERS	AEIIILNOPRTUVZ	PULVERIZATION
AEHILMMNORTUY	ALUMINOTHERMY	AEIIILOOPRRRT	PROPRIETORIAL
AEHILMOOSTUXY	HOMOSEXUALITY	AEIIILOPPRRRTY	PROPRIETARILY
AEHILMOPPRSTY	AMPHIPROSTYLE	AEIIIMMNOOPRST	IMPERSONATION
AEHIMMNOPRTUY	IMMUNOTHERAPY	AEIIMNOOPRRTT	REIMPORTATION
AEHIMMOOPRSST	METAMORPHOSIS	AEIIMNOOPRSTT	TEMPORISATION
AEHIMNNPRSSTT	TRANSSHIPMENT	AEIIMNOOPRTTZ	TEMPORIZATION
AEHIMNPRSTUUY	SUPERHUMANITY	AEIIMNOSSSSTY	SYSTEMISATION
AEHINNORSSTT	NORTH OSSETIAN	AEIIMNOSSTTYZ	SYSTEMIZATION
AEHINOOSSSTTU	STATION HOUSES	AEIINNOOPPSTT	PEPTONISATION
AEHINOPRSSSUV	VAPOURISHNESS	AEIINNOOPPTTZ	PEPTONIZATION
AEHLLNNOORRTT	NORTHALLERTON	AEIINNOPSSSTX	EXPANSIONISTS
AEHLMNOOPRTVW	WOLVERHAMPTON	AEIINOOPPRRTX	EXPROPRIATION
AEHMNOOPRRTTY	ANTHROPOMETRY	AEIINOOPRSSTT	ESPIRITO SANTO
AEHMNOOPRSSSU	AMORPHOUSNESS	AEIINOOPRSTTX	EXTRAPOSITION
AEHMNOQRTTUUY	QUANTUM THEORY	AEIINOORRRSTT	TERRORISATION
AEHOOPRRSSSUW	HOUSE SPARROWS	AEIINOORRRTTZ	TERRORIZATION
AEIIILLLLMNNST	MILLENNIALIST	AEIINORRSSSTT	TRANSISTORISE
AEIIILLMNORSS	MILLIONAIRESS	AEIINORRSSTTZ	TRANSISTORIZE
AEIIILLMNPRRY	PRELIMINARILY	AEIKLMNOPRSST	SPORTSMANLIKE
AEIIILLMNRSTY	MINISTERIALLY	AEIKMNOQRSSTU	QUESTION MARKS
AEIIILNORSSTT	STERILISATION	AEILLLLMNOOSSS	SALMONELLOSIS
AEIIILNORSTTU	REUTILISATION	AEILLMMMNOOST	MONOMETALLISM

AEILLMMNOOSTT	MONOMETALLIST
AEILLNOPRTTWW	WILLOW PATTERN
AEILLNOPSSSSY	PASSIONLESSLY
AEILLORRRSTTY	ROTARY TILLERS
AEILMMNNOTTUY	MONUMENTALITY
AEILMNOOPRSTT	METROPOLITANS
AEILMNOPRTTUY	IMPORTUNATELY
AEILMNOPSYLSY	PNEUMATOLYSIS
AEILNNORSSTUV	VOLUNTARINESS
AEILNNORSTUVY	INTRAVENOUSLY
AEILNNRSTTUWW	UNWRITTEN LAWS
AEILNOOOPRRST	POOR RELATIONS
AEILNOOPRSTTT	PETROL STATION
AEILNOOPSTTUX	EXPOSTULATION
AEILNOORRTUVY	REVOLUTIONARY
AEILOOOOPPPRS	PROSOPOPOEIAL
AEIMNNOOPPRTT	APPORTIONMENT
AEIMNNOORRSTT	REMONSTRATION
AEIMNNORSSTTU	MENSTRUATIONS
AEIMNOOPRRSST	IMPERSONATORS
AEIMNOPRSSTTT	PROTESTANTISM
AEIMPRRRSSSTY	PRIMARY STRESS
AEINNORSSSUUV	UNSAVOURINESS
AEINOOOPPRRTT	PROPORTIONATE
AEINOOPRSSTTT	PROTESTATIONS
AEINOOPRSSTTW	POWER STATIONS
AEIOOPPRRRSTX	EXPROPRIATORS
AEKLOOPPRSTVV	PETROPAVLOVSK
AELNNOOPSSTUY	SPONTANEOUSLY
AELOOPRSTTUXY	EXPOSTULATORY
AEMMNOOORSTTU	MONOTREMATOUS
AEMNOOOPRSSZZ	MEZZO-SOPRANOS
AENNNORSSSTUY	TYRANNOUSNESS
AENOOOPPRRTXY	PROPAROXYTONE
AENOPRRSSSTUU	RAPTUROUSNESS
AFFGIIMNOSTUU	SUFFUMIGATION
AFGGHHIIRSTTT	STRAIGHT FIGHT
AFGGIINNRRSTU	TRANSFIGURING
AFGHIINOPRRST	PROFIT SHARING
AFGHIKNOORTUW	FOR AUGHT I KNOW
AFGIIILNNRTUY	INFURIATINGLY
AFGIILNNOOPTT	FLOATING-POINT
AFGIIMNNOPRST	PROFIT MARGINS
AFGIKNOORSSTT	TOASTING FORKS
AFIIILNNORSTT	INFILTRATIONS
AFIIILNOOSSST	FOSSILISATION
AFIIILNOOSSTZ	FOSSILIZATION
AFIILLNOOOPRS	FLORIANOPOLIS
AFIILLORSTTUY	FLIRTATIOUSLY
AFILMOPPRSTUY	FAMILY SUPPORT
AFILNOPPRRUUV	FLAVOPURPURIN
AGGHHIILNOPRT	LITHOGRAPHING
AGGHHINOOPPRT	PHOTOGRAPHING
AGGHHMOPPRSYY	SPHYGMOGRAPHY

AGGHIIKLNPRST	PARKING LIGHTS
AGGHIIKNNSSTV	THANKSGIVINGS
AGGHILOOPRSST	GRAPHOLOGISTS
AGGIIILNNOSTU	ISOAGGLUTININ
AGGIIIILNNSTTY	INSTIGATINGLY
AGGIIINNORTTU	INGURGITATION
AGGIIJNNRUUXY	XINJIANG UYGUR
AGGIILNNOPPRR	GRAPPLING IRON
AGGILLNOORSTY	LARYNGOLOGIST
AGHHIILMNRSTY	NIGHTMARISHLY
AGHHILMNOPPSU	PLOUGHMANSHIP
AGHHIMNOORSTT	ORTHOGNATHISM
AGHHLLMOOOPTY	OPHTHALMOLOGY
AGHHLMNNOOOPT	MONOPHTHONGAL
AGHHNOOORSTTU	ORTHOGNATHOUS
AGHIIILLMNTUY	HUMILIATINGLY
AGHIIILNOPSTZ	HOSPITALIZING
AGHIIILNPRSTT	HAIR-SPLITTING
AGHIILNNOSSTY	ASTONISHINGLY
AGHIINOPPRSTU	UPRIGHT PIANOS
AGHINOOPSTTTT	PHOTOSTATTING
AGHINOORSSSTT	SHOOTING STARS
AGHLLMOORSUUW	GALLOWS HUMOUR
AGIIILLLNTTTY	TITILLATINGLY
AGIIILLMNRSTU	TRILINGUALISM
AGIIILMMNNPRT	MALIMPRINTING
AGIIILMMNORTZ	IMMORTALIZING
AGIIILNNNOOPT	NO OIL PAINTING
AGIIKLNNOPSTT	TALKING POINTS
AGIILLMNSTTUY	STIMULATINGLY
AGIIILLNOOSSTY	SYLLOGISATION
AGIILLNOOSTYZ	SYLLOGIZATION
AGIIILMOOPPRST	PLAGIOTROPISM
AGIIILNNNRTYYZ	TYRANNIZINGLY
AGIIILNNOPRTYZ	PATRONIZINGLY
AGIIILOORSSSTY	ASSYRIOLOGIST
AGIIMNOORRSUV	GRAMINIVOROUS
AGIINNOPRTTTY	POTTY-TRAINING
AGILMMNOOSTUY	NUMISMATOLOGY
AGILMOORRSTTY	MARTYROLOGIST
AGILNNOOOPRST	PROLONGATIONS
AGIMNOOOPRSUZ	ZOOSPORANGIUM
AHHNOOOPPRSTY	ANTHROPOSOPHY
AHIIIILNOOPRRT	HORRIPILATION
AHIIILNOPSTTY	INHOSPITALITY
AHIIMMNOOOSSU	HOMOOUSIANISM
AHIJNNOPRSTUZ	ZINJANTHROPUS
AHIMNOPPRSSST	SPORTSMANSHIP
AHKLNNOOPPTTY	PHYTOPLANKTON
AHLLMMMOOOTWY	WOOLLY MAMMOTH
AHMMOOOOPRSTU	OMMATOPHOROUS
AIIIILLNNOQSTU	INQUISITIONAL
AIIIILNOQRSTU	INQUISITORIAL
AIIIIMNPPSSSS	MISSISSIPPIAN

AIIILLMNNOSTU	ILLUMINATIONS
AIIILLMNPSTUY	PUSILLANIMITY
AIIILNNOSTTTU	INSTITUTIONAL
AIIILNOOSSSTT	ISOLATIONISTS
AIIILPRSSSTTU	SPIRITUALISTS
AIIIMMNNOSSTU	IMMUNISATIONS
AIIIMMNNOSTUZ	IMMUNIZATIONS
AIIIMNOOPPRRT	IMPROPRIATION
AIIIMNOOPRSTV	IMPROVISATION
AIIINNNOOSTTV	INNOVATIONIST
AIIIOOPPRSTTU	PROPITIATIOUS
AIIJNOOPSTTUX	JUXTAPOSITION
AIILLMNOPSSUU	PUSILLANIMOUS
AIILLNNORTUVY	INVOLUNTARILY
AIILLNOOPRSVY	PROVISIONALLY
AIILLNORSSTTU	ILLUSTRATIONS
AIILMNNNOOSTU	MOUNTAIN LIONS
AIILNOOOPPRST	PROPOSITIONAL
AIILNOOPPSSTU	SUPPOSITIONAL
AIILNOOPSSTTU	SAN LUIS POTOSI
AIIMNNORSSSST	TRANSMISSIONS
AIIMNOOQSSTTU	MISQUOTATIONS
AIINNOOPRSSTT	TRANSPOSITION
AIIOOOPRSUVVV	OVOVIVIPAROUS
AILMOOOPSSSTX	TOXOPLASMOSIS
AIMOORRRSTWWY	TWO-WAY MIRRORS
BBCDEELMORSTU	CLUSTER-BOMBED
BBCDGIIKLLNOU	BUILDING BLOCK
BBCEEGIKNNNRU	RUBBERNECKING
BBCEEIORRSSUV	OVERSUBSCRIBE
BBCEHMOORRSTU	BUTCHER'S-BROOM
BBCEIILMNOSTU	INCOMBUSTIBLE
BBCGGHIILNNTU	NIGHTCLUBBING
BBDEELNRSSSUU	BLUNDERBUSSES
BBDEGHMNOORSY	HYDROGEN BOMBS
BBDEHLOOORRST	BLOOD BROTHERS
BBDIIILNOOSVY	DIVISION LOBBY
BBEEEEEEHIIJS	HEEBIE-JEEBIES
BBEEFGHIMORRT	FIGHTER-BOMBER
BBEEGMNORRSUY	MONEY-GRUBBERS
BBEENNNNRRSSUU	BUNSEN BURNERS
BBEGGIMNNORUY	MONEY-GRUBBING
BBINNOOORRSTT	TORN TO RIBBONS
BCCCDEIIMRRSU	CIRCUMSCRIBED
BCCCEEHILPRUZ	CZECH REPUBLIC
BCCCHINOOOPRS	BRONCHOSCOPIC
BCCDDEEEHKLOU	DOUBLE-CHECKED
BCCDEEIJORSTT	DIRECT OBJECTS
BCCEEHIKKKTTU	KICK THE BUCKET
BCCEEHNORRSSS	CROSSBENCHERS
BCCEEIILORRTT	TRIBOELECTRIC
BCCEEIINRSTTY	CYBERNETICIST
BCCEEILORRTTU	TURBO-ELECTRIC
BCCEHHINOOOSS	HOBSON'S CHOICE

BCCEIIIJOSTTV	OBJECTIVISTIC
BCCEIIILNNNOV	INCONVINCIBLE
BCCEILNORSTTU	CONSTRUCTIBLE
BCCHILLOOPSSU	PUBLIC SCHOOLS
BCDDDELLLOOOY	COLD-BLOODEDLY
BCDDEEEKLORSU	DOUBLE-DECKERS
BCDDEEFGIITTU	BUDGET DEFICIT
BCDDEELLOORS	RED BLOOD CELLS
BCDDEELOORSSU	DOUBLE-CROSSED
BCDDEFIINORTY	FORBIDDEN CITY
BCDDEIIILTTUY	DEDUCTIBILITY
BCDDGILLNOORU	BLOODCURDLING
BCDEEEILLLNPU	BLUE-PENCILLED
BCDEEEKORRSST	STOCKBREEDERS
BCDEEGIKNORST	STOCKBREEDING
BCDEEGINORRSS	CROSSBREEDING
BCDEEIIILNRS	INDISCERNIBLE
BCDEELOORRSSU	DOUBLE-CROSSER
BCDEELOORSSSU	DOUBLE-CROSSES
BCDEIIIILNRTY	INCREDIBILITY
BCDEIILNORTUY	INDOLEBUTYRIC
BCDGHIIKKRRTU	KIRKCUDBRIGHT
BCDGIKNOOSSTY	BODY STOCKINGS
BCDIIILOORRTY	CORRODIBILITY
BCDIIILOPRTUY	PRODUCIBILITY
BCEEEEFFILRSV	EFFERVESCIBLE
BCEEEEFKNOORR	REFERENCE BOOK
BCEEEFGIINNRR	BIREFRINGENCE
BCEEEGIINORST	BIOENERGETICS
BCEEEGILLNORT	COBELLIGERENT
BCEEEHIKLRRSU	HUCKLEBERRIES
BCEEEHLNNOORZ	CHLOROBENZENE
BCEEEIILMPPRT	IMPERCEPTIBLE
BCEEEIJNOSSTV	OBJECTIVENESS
BCEEEILNOPRWY	EYEBROW PENCIL
BCEEEELNORSTVY	CONVEYER BELTS
BCEEFHNNORRST	FRONTBENCHERS
BCEEGILMNNRUY	ENCUMBERINGLY
BCEEHIILRRSU	SILVER BIRCHES
BCEEIILMPPRTY	IMPERCEPTIBLY
BCEEIILNNORTV	INCONVERTIBLE
BCEEIILNPSSTU	INSUSCEPTIBLE
BCEEIILPPRRST	PRESCRIPTIBLE
BCEEIMMOSSTTU	SUBCOMMITTEES
BCEEJLNOOSSST	OBJECT LESSONS
BCEFFIOOOPSTX	POST OFFICE BOX
BCEFHIMNOOOTT	FINE-TOOTH COMB
BCEFHINOOSSST	SONS-OF-BITCHES
BCEFJMOOORRST	JOB'S COMFORTER
BCEGHILNOOOTY	BIOTECHNOLOGY
BCEGIKLNOSSTU	BLUESTOCKINGS
BCEIIIILQRSTU	EQUILIBRISTIC
BCEIILNOPRRTU	INCORRUPTIBLE
BCEILMNOOPRYY	POLYEMBRYONIC

BCEILORSTTUVY	OBSTRUCTIVELY
BCEINNNOSSTTU	SUBCONTINENTS
BCERRSSSTTUUU	SUBSTRUCTURES
BCFGIIMMNNOOR	COMBINING FORM
BCGHILNOOOORY	CHRONOBIOLOGY
BCGHILOOOPSYY	PSYCHOBIOLOGY
BCGHNOOORTUUY	COUNTY BOROUGH
BCGIIIILORRTY	CORRIGIBILITY
BCGIIILMNNORS	CLIMBING IRONS
BCGIILOOORSTY	CRYOBIOLOGIST
BCIIIIILMMSTY	IMMISCIBILITY
BCIIIIILNNTVY	INVINCIBILITY
BCIILNOPRRTUY	INCORRUPTIBLY
BCIINNOORSTTU	CONTRIBUTIONS
BCIINOPRSSSTU	SUBSCRIPTIONS
BDDEEEEGNNRRS	GENDER-BENDERS
BDDEEEGINNNRU	UNDERBREEDING
BDDEEEEILLMOSW	DISEMBOWELLED
BDDEEIILNOSTY	DISOBEDIENTLY
BDDEEIIMMNOST	DISEMBODIMENT
BDDEEIIRRSTTU	REDISTRIBUTED
BDDEEIJLNOOTU	DOUBLE-JOINTED
BDDEEIMNNRSTU	DISBURDENMENT
BDDEGHILMORSU	MIDDLESBROUGH
BDDEIILMMORSW	MIDDLEBROWISM
BDDEIINRSTTUU	UNDISTRIBUTED
BDDEILNNORSSW	WORD BLINDNESS
BDDEMNRSSTUUY	BURY ST EDMUNDS
BDEEEEFILNOSS	BESIDE ONESELF
BDEEEFGIKRRRS	FREDERIKSBERG
BDEEEFGILNOTT	BOTTLE-FEEDING, FEEDING BOTTLE
BDEEEGIINNRRT	INTERBREEDING
BDEEEGIJLLNOU	GOLDEN JUBILEE
BDEEEIIRSSVWY	BIRD'S-EYE VIEWS
BDEEEIMMMNRST	DISMEMBERMENT
BDEEELNNSSSSU	UNBLESSEDNESS
BDEEFGILORSUU	DOUBLE FIGURES
BDEEFIIIKNNNT	BENEFIT IN KIND
BDEEFIIILNSTY	DEFENSIBILITY
BDEEGIILLNRWY	BEWILDERINGLY
BDEEGIILMNOSW	DISEMBOWELING
BDEEGIILMNSSX	MIXED BLESSING
BDEEGIINORSUW	BROWNIE GUIDES
BDEEGINNNNSSU	UNBENDINGNESS
BDEEGINNORRUV	OVERBURDENING
BDEEGINOORRRS	BORDERS REGION
BDEEIIILNTTXY	EXTENDIBILITY
BDEEIMNRSSSTU	DISBURSEMENTS
BDEEINNORSSTV	INVERTED SNOBS
BDEELLNOOSSSS	BLOODLESSNESS
BDEELNNOSSSSU	BOUNDLESSNESS
BDEELOOPRRSSU	BLOOD PRESSURE
BDEFFNOOOPRRU	BURDEN OF PROOF

BDEFHNOOOORSTU	DEBTS OF HONOUR
BDEGHHINOOORU	NEIGHBOURHOOD
BDEGHHOORRSTU	THOROUGHBREDS
BDEGIIIILSTTY	DIGESTIBILITY
BDEHIIIILNNTUY	UNINHIBITEDLY
BDEHNOOOPRSTU	BOUSTROPHEDON
BDEILNNNOSSSW	SNOW BLINDNESS
BDEKLNOOORTWY	OLD-BOY NETWORK
BDFFIIIILSTUY	DIFFUSIBILITY
BDFGHILLOOSSW	GOLDFISH BOWLS
BDGGIIILLNOSY	DISOBLIGINGLY
BDIIILLOSSTUY	DISSOLUBILITY
BDIIINORSSTTU	DISTRIBUTIONS
BEEEEHILNPRRS	REPREHENSIBLE
BEEEELLLRSSTT	BELLES-LETTRES
BEEEFFGIINNRT	FRINGE BENEFIT
BEEEHIKMOPRRS	PEMBROKESHIRE
BEEEHIKRRSSTW	WEST BERKSHIRE
BEEEHILLMMNST	EMBELLISHMENT
BEEEHILNPRRSY	REPREHENSIBLY
BEEEIIJLLRSUV	SILVER JUBILEE
BEEEIIILNPRSSX	INEXPRESSIBLE
BEEEIILPRRRSS	IRREPRESSIBLE
BEEEILNPRSSSU	SUPERSENSIBLE
BEEEIMMNRRSTU	REIMBURSEMENT
BEEEINOSSSSSV	OBSESSIVENESS
BEEFGINRRSTTU	BUTTERFINGERS
BEEFHIMNRRSTU	REFURBISHMENT
BEEFILLMORSUU	UMBELLIFEROUS
BEEGGILNNORSW	BOWLING GREENS
BEEGHNRRSTTTU	BRUTE STRENGTH
BEEGIILLNNUVY	UNBELIEVINGLY
BEEGLOORRSTTT	GLOBETROTTERS
BEEHILMRRTUWY	WHITE MULBERRY
BEEHILNOOORTZ	BELO HORIZONTE
BEEHILNORRSST	BROTHERLINESS
BEEIIILMMPRSS	IMPERMISSIBLE
BEEIIILNSTTXY	EXTENSIBILITY
BEEIIILRRSTVY	REVERSIBILITY
BEEIIILNOPRSS	IRRESPONSIBLE
BEEIIILNPRRTTU	INTERRUPTIBLE
BEEIIILNPRSSXY	INEXPRESSIBLY
BEEIIILPRRRSSY	IRREPRESSIBLY
BEEILNRSSTUVY	SUBSERVIENTLY
BEEINORSSSTUV	OBTRUSIVENESS
BEENNOOSSSTUU	BOUNTEOUSNESS
BEFFGINNORRTU	BURNT OFFERING
BEFGIIILNRSTU	FILIBUSTERING
BEFGIILNOOPRS	BE SPOILING FOR
BEFGIILLOORSU	GLOBULIFEROUS
BEFIIIILLNTXY	INFLEXIBILITY
BEFILNNOSSTUU	BOUNTIFULNESS
BEFINNNSSSUUY	FUNNY BUSINESS
BEGGIIIILLNTY	NEGLIGIBILITY

BEGGILNOORTTT	GLOBETROTTING
BEGHHIORRRSUX	ROXBURGHSHIRE
BEGHNOOORRTTU	ROTTEN BOROUGH
BEGIIIIILLNTY	INELIGIBILITY
BEGIILLMMNNUU	MILLENNIUM BUG
BEGIILNNNOPTW	TENPIN BOWLING
BEHIIIIMNOSTX	EXHIBITIONISM
BEHIIINOSTTX	EXHIBITIONIST
BEHIIILOPRTVY	PROHIBITIVELY
BEHILOORRSUVY	HERBIVOROUSLY
BEIIIILMRSSTY	REMISSIBILITY
BEIIIILNNSSTY	INSENSIBILITY
BEIIIILNRTTVY	INVERTIBILITY
BEIIIILOPSSST	POSSIBILITIES
BEIIIILRSSTTY	RESISTIBILITY
BEIIILNOSSTTY	OSTENSIBILITY
BEIILNOOSSSUV	OBLIVIOUSNESS
BEIILNOPRRSSY	IRRESPONSIBLY
BEIINNOOPRSTW	BROWNIE POINTS
BEIINSSSSSTUU	BUSINESS SUITS
BEIIOPRSSTTUU	SUBREPTITIOUS
BEILNORSTUUVY	UNOBTRUSIVELY
BEIMNOPSSSTUU	BUMPTIOUSNESS
BEINNOOOSSSUX	OBNOXIOUSNESS
BFGHIILLORSST	BILLS OF RIGHTS
BFILLLMNOOSSU	IN FULL BLOSSOM
BFILLOORSTUUU	TUBULIFLOROUS
BGHILLNOOOPST	POLLING BOOTHS
BGIIILNNOOPST	BOILING POINTS
BIIIIILMOPSSY	IMPOSSIBILITY
BIIKOOORSSSTV	VISITORS' BOOKS
BIINOSSSTTTUU	SUBSTITUTIONS
BILOOOPPRRSUY	OPPROBRIOUSLY
CCCCEEINNOPSU	CONCUPISCENCE
CCCDEEEENRRSU	RECRUDESCENCE
CCCDEIILORSTU	CLOSED-CIRCUIT
CCCDEIIMNRSUU	UNCIRCUMCISED
CCCEEEFIMNRRU	CIRCUMFERENCE
CCCEEEIILNOPT	POETIC LICENCE
CCCEEILOOPRST	ELECTROSCOPIC
CCCEGHIKNORSS	CROSSCHECKING
CCCEHIIMOSTYZ	SCHIZOMYCETIC
CCCEIIILORSUV	VICIOUS CIRCLE
CCCEIIMNOOOOS	SOCIOECONOMIC
CCCEIINNORTTY	CONCENTRICITY
CCCEILMPRSTUY	CIRCUMSPECTLY
CCCEIOOPPRSST	SPECTROSCOPIC
CCCEOOPRSSTTU	STREPTOCOCCUS
CCCIIIMNORSSU	CIRCUMCISIONS
CCCILNNOOTUUY	COUNTY COUNCIL
CCDDEEEELLMNNO	CONDEMNED CELL
CCDDEEGINNNOS	CONDESCENDING
CCDDENOORTTUU	CONDUCTED TOUR
CCDEEEEILNQSU	DELIQUESCENCE

CCDEEEELLNNOTW	WELL-CONNECTED
CCDEEHILORRTY	HYDROELECTRIC
CCDEEIINNOSTV	DISCONNECTIVE
CCDEEILMNOPSY	ENCYCLOPEDISM
CCDEEILNOPSTY	ENCYCLOPEDIST
CCDEEIMOORRTT	MICRODETECTOR
CCDEEINNNOOSS	CONDESCENSION
CCDEEINNOSSUV	CONDUCIVENESS
CCDEEINOOPRUW	OWNER-OCCUPIED
CCDEEINRRRTTU	DIRECT CURRENT
CCDEELNNNORUY	UNCONCERNEDLY
CCDEENNOOPRSY	CO-RESPONDENCY
CCDEENORRSTTU	RECONSTRUCTED
CCDEGIINNNOST	DISCONNECTING
CCDEGIINNNORT	DISCONCERTING
CCDEGINNNOORT	CONNECTING ROD
CCDEHIOOSSTUU	STUDIO COUCHES
CCDEHKLNOORTU	ROUND THE CLOCK
CCDEIINNOOST	DISCONNECTION
CCDEIINNOORT	DISCONCERTION
CCDEIMNOORSTU	SEMICONDUCTOR
CCDEINNOOSSSU	SECOND COUSINS
CCDGIIMNNOSTU	MISCONDUCTING
CCDNNNOOORSTU	NONCONDUCTORS
CCEEEEEFFNRSV	EFFERVESCENCE
CCEEEEFFLNORS	EFFLORESCENCE
CCEEEEHIKNRSV	NECKERCHIEVES
CCEEEEIRRSSTV	SECRET SERVICE
CCEEEFFIOSTTV	COST-EFFECTIVE
CCEEEFILNNORS	INFLORESCENCE
CCEEEFILORRRT	FERROELECTRIC
CCEEEFNOORRRT	FERROCONCRETE
CCEEEHIIMNPSY	CHIMNEYPIECES
CCEEEHMOOPRRT	CHEMORECEPTOR
CCEEEIILOPRTZ	PIEZOELECTRIC
CCEEEIIMNNRSS	REMINISCENCES
CCEEEIINNNNOV	INCONVENIENCE
CCEEEILMNNORT	RECONCILEMENT
CCEEEILMORRTT	ELECTROMETRIC
CCEEEIMNORRTX	CONCRETE MIXER
CCEEEINNNOQSU	INCONSEQUENCE
CCEEEINNRRRTU	INTERCURRENCE
CCEEEMMMNNOST	COMMENCEMENTS
CCEEFFIIINSSU	SUFFICIENCIES
CCEEFFIIILOOPR	POLICE OFFICER
CCEEFHIIJSSTU	CHIEF JUSTICES
CCEEFINNOORST	CONFECTIONERS
CCEEFINNOORTY	CONFECTIONERY
CCEEGHIINOSTZ	SCHIZOGENETIC
CCEEGHINOPSTY	PSYCHOGENETIC
CCEEGIINNNOST	CONTINGENCIES
CCEEGIINORTTY	EGOCENTRICITY
CCEEGILNORTTU	ELECTROCUTING
CCEEHIIILLOPRT	ELECTROPHILIC

CCEEHILNOOPRT	ELECTROPHONIC
CCEEHILOOPRTT	PHOTOELECTRIC
CCEEHILOOPRTU	HEROIC COUPLET
CCEEHIMMNOOOS	HOME ECONOMICS
CCEEHIMNNORRY	CHIMNEY CORNER
CCEEHLMOORSSU	COLOUR SCHEMES
CCEEHMMOORRRU	MERCUROCHROME
CCEEIIIORRSTV	OVERCRITICISE
CCEEIIIORRTVZ	OVERCRITICIZE
CCEEIIJOPSTTU	POETIC JUSTICE
CCEEIILNOORST	ISOELECTRONIC
CCEEIINNOSSST	CONSISTENCIES
CCEEILLNOORST	RECOLLECTIONS
CCEEILNOORTTU	ELECTROCUTION
CCEEILNOSSSUV	OCCLUSIVENESS
CCEEILNOSTUVY	CONSECUTIVELY
CCEEIMOPRRSTT	SPECTROMETRIC
CCEEINNOOPPRT	PRECONCEPTION
CCEEINNOORRST	INCORRECTNESS
CCEEINOOPRRUW	OWNER-OCCUPIER
CCEENNOOOVVXX	CONVEXO-CONVEX
CCEEOOPPRSSST	SPECTROSCOPES
CCEFFIIINNSUY	INSUFFICIENCY
CCEFIILMNORUX	CIRCUMFLEXION
CCEFILNOOSSSU	SELF-CONSCIOUS
CCEGHIIKNNPRS	SPRING CHICKEN
CCEGIIIMNNOSV	MISCONCEIVING
CCEGIILLNNORY	RECONCILINGLY
CCEGIILNNRRTU	TURNING CIRCLE
CCEGIILNOPRSS	CLOSING PRICES
CCEGIIMNNRTUV	CIRCUMVENTING
CCEHHIINOPRSZ	SCHIZOPHRENIC
CCEHHIMOOPRRS	CHROMOSPHERIC
CCEHIIKNOPSTY	PSYCHOKINETIC
CCEHILMNOORTY	CHLOROMYCETIN
CCEHIMOPRSSTY	PSYCHOMETRICS
CCEHIMORSTTYY	CYTOCHEMISTRY
CCEHIOOPRRSTU	URETHROSCOPIC
CCEHIORSSSSTT	CROSS-STITCHES
CCEHMOOPSTUYY	PHYCOMYCETOUS
CCEIIIILLOSTTV	COLLETIVISTIC
CCEIIMNNOOPST	MISCONCEPTION
CCEIIMNNORTUV	CIRCUMVENTION
CCEIIMNOOSSSU	SEMICONSCIOUS
CCEIINNNOSSTY	INCONSISTENCY
CCEIINNOOSSTT	CONSCIENTIOUS
CCEIKKKLLOORW	LIKE CLOCKWORK
CCEILNNOOORSW	CROWN COLONIES
CCEIMMOOPRRTU	MICROCOMPUTER
CCEINNOOPRRST	PRINCE CONSORT
CCEINNOOSSSSU	CONSCIOUSNESS
CCEINNOPRRSSW	CROWN PRINCESS
CCEINOORSSSST	CROSS-SECTIONS
CCENNNNOORRTU	NONCONCURRENT
CCENOORRRSTTU	RECONSTRUCTOR
CCENORRRSSSTU	CROSSCURRENTS
CCGHILNOOOSST	CONCHOLOGISTS
CCGHINOOPSSTY	PSYCHOGNOSTIC
CCGIIKNNOOPTT	COTTON-PICKING
CCGIINORRSSSS	CRISSCROSSING
CCHHHIIIMNOTY	HO CHI MINH CITY
CCHHIILOPPRSY	PSYCHROPHILIC
CCHHIOPPSSSYY	PSYCHOPHYSICS
CCHIINNORSSTY	SYNCHRONISTIC
CCHIIOPRRSSTU	CORPUS CHRISTI
CCHIIORRSSTTU	SHORT CIRCUITS
CCHILMOOPTTYY	LYMPHOCYTOTIC
CCIINNOOPSSUU	INCONSPICUOUS
CCIINNOORSSTT	CONSTRICTIONS
CCILMOORSSTTY	MOTORCYCLISTS
CCILNNOOSSUUY	UNCONSCIOUSLY
CCILNOOPSSUUY	CONSPICUOUSLY
CCINNOORSSTTU	CONSTRUCTIONS
CCINNOORSTUUY	COUNTRY COUSIN
CDDDEEEINNSSU	UNDECIDEDNESS
CDDEEEENNPRTU	UNPRECEDENTED
CDDEEEGNOSSSU	SECOND-GUESSED
CDDEEEHIORRTT	OTHER-DIRECTED
CDDEEIILLNORS	ILL-CONSIDERED
CDDEEIINNOORT	RECONDITIONED
CDDEEIKLMNNOS	CONDENSED MILK
CDDEHHILOORRY	HYDROCHLORIDE
CDDEHILLMOOSS	MIDDLE SCHOOLS
CDDEHLNORSTUU	THUNDERCLOUDS
CDDEIIILNNPSU	UNDISCIPLINED
CDDEIINNNOOTU	UNCONDITIONED
CDDEILMOOPSSY	DISCOMPOSEDLY
CDDGILLLMNOOY	MOLLYCODDLING
CDDIIMMOOOSSU	DISCOMMODIOUS
CDEEEEEHMMNRT	CREME DE MENTHE
CDEEEEFILPSTV	SELF-DECEPTIVE
CDEEEEFINSSTV	DEFECTIVENESS
CDEEEEHNORRRT	THREE-CORNERED
CDEEEEIINNPRX	INEXPERIENCED
CDEEEEINNPRUX	UNEXPERIENCED
CDEEEEINPSSTV	DECEPTIVENESS
CDEEEEIQRSTUZ	CREDIT SQUEEZE
CDEEEFFLNOSSS	SELF-CONFESSED
CDEEEFHILRSST	CHESTERFIELDS
CDEEEFILLNNST	INFLECTEDNESS
CDEEEFILNOPST	SELF-DECEPTION
CDEEEFILNSSTU	DECEITFULNESS
CDEEEFINORTTU	COUNTERFEITED
CDEEEFORRRSS	CROSS-REFERRED
CDEEEGHINOPST	PIGEON-CHESTED
CDEEEGIIKNNSV	KING'S EVIDENCE
CDEEEGIKLNRSS	SINGLE-DECKERS
CDEEEGLOORRRT	TORRE DEL GRECO

CDEEEIILNNQSU	DELINQUENCIES	CDEGIIMOOOPSS	SIGMOIDOSCOPE
CDEEEIINNRRSV	DINNER SERVICE	CDEGIINNNOSTT	DISCONTENTING
CDEEEIINPRSTV	VICE PRESIDENT	CDEGIKNNNORUW	UNCROWNED KING
CDEEEIKMPQRTU	QUICK-TEMPERED	CDEGILLNNOORT	DECONTROLLING
CDEEEIMNORSTT	MINE DETECTORS	CDEGILNNOOORY	ENDOCRINOLOGY
CDEEEIMOPRSSV	DECOMPRESSIVE	CDEGINNOOPRRS	CORRESPONDING
CDEEEINNOPRVW	NEW PROVIDENCE	CDEGINORRSSSS	CROSS-DRESSING
CDEEEINNORSST	RECONDITENESS	CDEHHIOOORRST	RHODOCHROSITE
CDEEEINSSSTUV	SEDUCTIVENESS	CDEHIIIOPRSTY	SPHEROIDICITY
CDEEFFHILOORS	OFFICEHOLDERS	CDEHIIKMNSTTU	STICK-IN-THE-MUD
CDEEFFIILLNST	SELF-INFLICTED	CDEHIIKNORSTY	HYDROKINETICS
CDEEFFILNNOST	SELF-CONFIDENT	CDEHIIMNOPRRU	PERICHONDRIUM
CDEEFHKMOOORT	DOME OF THE ROCK	CDEHIIOOOPPRT	PHOTOPERIODIC
CDEEFIIIKLMRT	CERTIFIED MILK	CDEHIIOPPRTTY	PTERIDOPHYTIC
CDEEFIIILMRSS	MID-LIFE CRISES	CDEHIIOPRRSST	DIRECTORSHIPS
CDEEFIIILNSTUV	SELF-INDUCTIVE	CDEHILLOOOSST	OLD SCHOOL TIES
CDEEFILPRSSTU	DISRESPECTFUL	CDEHIMOOPPRSU	PSEUDOMORPHIC
CDEEFINNOORTV	OVERCONFIDENT	CDEHIMOORTTYY	THYROIDECTOMY
CDEEGGHIINPTW	PITCHING WEDGE	CDEHKNRRSTTUU	THUNDERSTRUCK
CDEEGHIMNNOPR	COMPREHENDING	CDEIIIINNSTTV	INDISTINCTIVE
CDEEGIINNORRS	RECONSIDERING	CDEIIILNSTTVY	DISTINCTIVELY
CDEEGIKNOPRRS	PECKING ORDERS	CDEIIIMPRSSTV	DESCRIPTIVISM
CDEEGIMNOPRSS	DECOMPRESSING	CDEIIINNORSST	INDISCRETIONS
CDEEGINNORSTU	COUNTERSIGNED	CDEIIJNOSSSUU	JUDICIOUSNESS
CDEEGLOORSTUX	DEXTROGLUCOSE	CDEIIMNOOOPST	DECOMPOSITION
CDEEHIINOPRTY	DRYOPITHECINE	CDEIINNOOPRST	PRECONDITIONS
CDEEHILLNSSSS	CHILDLESSNESS	CDEIINOPRTUWW	PICTURE WINDOW
CDEEIIIMNRSTT	DETERMINISTIC	CDEILLMOORTUU	MULTICOLOURED
CDEEIIIMOSSTT	DOMESTICITIES	CDEILLNORSUUY	INCREDULOUSLY
CDEEIIINNSSTV	DISINCENTIVES	CDEILMNOOPSUY	COMPENDIOUSLY
CDEEIIILNOPRST	PREDILECTIONS	CDEILNORSSSUU	LUDICROUSNESS
CDEEIIILNOSSSU	DELICIOUSNESS	CDEINNOOPRTUV	NONPRODUCTIVE
CDEEIIILPRSTVY	DESCRIPTIVELY	CDEINOOPRRSTU	REPRODUCTIONS
CDEEIIMNORSTT	DENSITOMETRIC	CDEINOORSSTTU	DISCOUNT STORE
CDEEIINNOORRT	RECONDITIONER	CDELLNOOOPTYY	POLYCOTYLEDON
CDEEIIORSSSTU	DISCOURTESIES	CDELMNOOOOTY	MONOCOTYLEDON
CDEEIJNPRRSUU	JURISPRUDENCE	CDEOOOPRRRSSW	WORD PROCESSOR
CDEEIKNORRTTY	KITTY-CORNERED	CDFGILNOORSTY	FLYING DOCTORS
CDEEILNNOOPRS	SCOLOPENDRINE	CDFIIMNOORSTY	DISCONFORMITY
CDEEILRSTTUVY	DESTRUCTIVELY	CDGGIKLLNSUUY	UGLY DUCKLINGS
CDEEIMNOOPRSS	DECOMPRESSION	CDGIIINNNOSTU	DISCONTINUING
CDEEINOOPRSTU	COUNTERPOISED	CDGIIMOOOPSSY	SIGMOIDOSCOPY
CDEEINORSTTTU	RECONSTITUTED	CDGIKLNOOSSTU	DUCKING STOOLS
CDEEIOPPRRSST	ESPRIT DE CORPS	CDHIIMNNOOORT	MITOCHONDRION
CDEEKKLNRSTUU	KNUCKLE-DUSTER	CDIIIJLNOSUUY	INJUDICIOUSLY
CDEENNOOPRRST	CORRESPONDENT	CDIIINNOSTTUY	DISCONTINUITY
CDEENNOOPRSST	CO-RESPONDENTS	CDIINNOORSTTU	INTRODUCTIONS
CDEENNRRRSTUU	UNDERCURRENTS	CDIINNOOSSTUU	DISCONTINUOUS
CDEEORRRSSSSS	CROSS-DRESSERS	CEEEEEILNORRT	ELECTIONEERER
CDEFHINNORSWW	FRENCH WINDOWS	CEEEEEFFILPRTT	PELTIER EFFECT
CDEFIIIILMRSS	MID-LIFE CRISIS	CEEEEEFFINSSTV	EFFECTIVENESS
CDEFIILNNOSTU	SELF-INDUCTION	CEEEEEFLPRRTTT	LETTER-PERFECT
CDEFOOOOPRRSS	FOOD PROCESSOR	CEEEEEFMNNORRT	RE-ENFORCEMENT
CDEGHHNOOSTTU	SECOND THOUGHT	CEEEEEGHINORTT	HETEROGENETIC

CEEEEGIIMNNRS	EMINENCE GRISE	CEEFIINOPRSTT	PERFECTIONIST
CEEEEEHLNRSSSS	CHEERLESSNESS	CEEFINOORSSSU	FEROCIOUSNESS
CEEEEEIKKPRSTW	WICKET KEEPERS	CEEFLLORRSUUY	RESOURCEFULLY
CEEEEILNSSSTV	SELECTIVENESS	CEEGHIINOSSSZ	SCHIZOGENESIS
CEEEEIMNNPRSU	SUPEREMINENCE	CEEGHIIRRSTUW	CRUISERWEIGHT
CEEEEINNPRSUV	SUPERVENIENCE	CEEGHIMNOOPRT	MORPHOGENETIC
CEEEEINRSSSSV	RECESSIVENESS	CEEGHINOPSSSY	PSYCHOGENESIS
CEEEEIRSSSTV	SECRETIVENESS	CEEGHINORTTUW	COUNTERWEIGHT
CEEEEINSSSSVX	EXCESSIVENESS	CEEGHLNNOOTWY	NEW TECHNOLOGY
CEEEEIOPRTTVX	EXTEROCEPTIVE	CEEGIIMMNNOTU	IMMUNOGENETIC
CEEEEJNNRSTUV	REJUVENESCENT	CEEGIKLLNOPSS	GLOCKENSPIELS
CEEEFFIILNTVY	INEFFECTIVELY	CEEGILLNORSSV	LEVEL CROSSING
CEEEFFPRRTTUU	FUTURE PERFECT	CEEGILMMNNOPT	COMPLEMENTING
CEEEFGHIIOPST	PIECES OF EIGHT	CEEGILMMNOTTU	TELECOMMUTING
CEEEFHINRSSST	SCENESHIFTERS	CEEGMNOORRSST	COSTERMONGERS
CEEEFIINNSSTV	INFECTIVENESS	CEEHHIMMORSTT	THERMOCHEMIST
CEEEFIMNNORRT	REINFORCEMENT	CEEHHIMOOPRRT	HETEROMORPHIC
CEEEFINORRTTU	COUNTERFEITER	CEEHHIOOPRRTT	HETEROTROPHIC
CEEEFNOORSTUV	VOTE OF CENSURE	CEEHHLOORSSST	CLOTHESHORSES
CEEEGGINORRTU	GEIGER COUNTER	CEEHHNORSSTTU	HORSE CHESTNUT
CEEEGHIKLNNRS	GELSENKIRCHEN	CEEHIMNNOOPRS	COMPREHENSION
CEEEGHILLNOPT	PHELLOGENETIC	CEEHIMNNORSTT	ETHNOCENTRISM
CEEEGIIILNNRV	CIVIL ENGINEER	CEEHINNNPPRSY	PENNY-PINCHERS
CEEEGIIKNNRTY	KINETIC ENERGY	CEEHIOPPPRRST	PRECEPTORSHIP
CEEEHIILNNSTT	LIECHTENSTEIN	CEEHIOPRSTTTW	WITH RESPECT TO
CEEEHILLLMOSU	HEMICELLULOSE	CEEHLNOOOPRTT	PHOTOELECTRON
CEEEHILLOPRST	ELECTROPHILES	CEEHLOOPRRSTU	ELECTROPHORUS
CEEEHIMNOPRSV	COMPREHENSIVE	CEEHNOORSSTTW	STONE THE CROWS
CEEEHIMNPSSWY	CHIMNEYSWEEPS	CEEHOOOPPRRTT	PHOTORECEPTOR
CEEEHLNNOSTTU	LUNCHEONETTES	CEEIIIILMRSSU	CRUISE MISSILE
CEEEHLNORRSSU	LECHEROUSNESS	CEEIIIMMPRSTT	METEMPIRICIST
CEEEHNSSTTTUW	SWEET CHESTNUT	CEEIIINNORSST	SENIOR CITISEN
CEEEIIMNNRTTT	INTERMITTENCE	CEEIIINNORSTZ	SENIOR CITIZEN
CEEEIINOPRTTV	INTEROCEPTIVE	CEEIIJNNORSTT	INTERJECTIONS
CEEEILMMORRST	ELECTROMERISM	CEEIILMOPTTVY	COMPETITIVELY
CEEEILMNRSSST	MERCILESSNESS	CEEIILRRSTTVY	RESTRICTIVELY
CEEEILMOORTTV	ELECTROMOTIVE	CEEIIMNOPTTUV	UNCOMPETITIVE
CEEEILNOSSSSV	VOICELESSNESS	CEEIIMPPRSSTV	PERSPECTIVISM
CEEEILNPRSSSS	PRICELESSNESS	CEEIINNOPRSTT	INTERCEPTIONS
CEEEILNSSSSUV	SECLUSIVENESS	CEEIINNORSSST	INTERCESSIONS
CEEEILNSSSSUVX	EXCLUSIVENESS	CEEIINNORSSTT	INTERSECTIONS
CEEEINRSSSUVX	EXCURSIVENESS	CEEIINOPRSSST	RECEPTIONISTS
CEEEIOPRRSTTV	RETROSPECTIVE	CEEIINOPRSTTV	INTROSPECTIVE
CEEELNNOQSSUU	QUEEN'S COUNSEL	CEEIINOSSSSST	SECESSIONISTS
CEEEOPRRRSSSV	PROCESS-SERVER	CEEIKLNNOSTUU	KINETONUCLEUS
CEEFFFGIINOOR	FOREIGN OFFICE	CEEILMNNOPTTY	INCOMPETENTLY
CEEFFIIILNNTY	INEFFICIENTLY	CEEILMNOORSUY	CEREMONIOUSLY
CEEFFIJNORSTY	JEFFERSON CITY	CEEILNNOOPRTU	NUCLEOPROTEIN
CEEFFIOPRSTTY	PETTY OFFICERS	CEEILNOOPRRST	SCLEROPROTEIN
CEEFGILNNOSTU	GENUFLECTIONS	CEEILNOSSSTUY	NECESSITOUSLY
CEEFIIKLNORSU	NICKELIFEROUS	CEEILOOPRSTTU	TELEUTOSPORIC
CEEFIIMNOPRST	IMPERFECTIONS,	CEEILPQRSTUUY	PICTURESQUELY
PERFECTIONISM		CEEIMNNOORSUU	UNCEREMONIOUS
CEEFIINOPRSST	FRONTISPIECES	CEEIMNOOOPRRT	RECEPTION ROOM

CEEINNORSTTTU	RECONSTITUENT
CEEINOOPRRSTT	RETROSPECTION
CEEINOOPRSSTU	COUNTERPOISES, PRECIOUS STONE
CEEINOORRSSSV	CORROSIVENESS
CEEINOORRSSTV	CONTROVERSIES
CEEINOPRRSSSU	REPERCUSSIONS
CEEINORRRSSTU	RESURRECTIONS
CEEINOSSSSTUV	VISCOUNTESSES
CEEIOOPRSSSTT	STEREOSCOPIST
CEELMNOOORRTT	REMOTE CONTROL
CEELPQRSSTUUU	SCULPTURESQUE
CEEMMNNOOPTUY	PNEUMONECTOMY
CEEMNNNOOPRTU	PRONOUNCEMENT
CEENNOOQRSSTU	QUEENS CONSORT
CEENNOORRSTTU	COUNTERTENORS
CEENOORSSSTUU	COURTEOUSNESS
CEFFFGIILNORY	FLYING OFFICER
CEFFIILOOPRST	PILOT OFFICERS
CEFFIINOOSSTU	OFFICIOUSNESS
CEFGIIKLNPSTY	FLYING PICKETS
CEFHIMMOORRRU	FERROCHROMIUM
CEFHLLLOOOSSW	SCHOOLFELLOWS
CEFIINNNOOSTU	NONINFECTIOUS
CEFILNOPRRTUY	PERFUNCTORILY
CEFKKLOORRSSW	CLERKS OF WORKS
CEGGHHLNOOOORY	GEOCHRONOLOGY
CEGHHIILOPRSY	HIEROGLYPHICS
CEGHIIILLNNPS	SPINE-CHILLING
CEGHIINNNNPPY	PENNY-PINCHING
CEGHIKNOORRSS	ROCKING HORSES
CEGHILNOOSSTT	TECHNOLOGISTS
CEGHINNOOSTUU	COUNTINGHOUSE
CEGHOPRRSSUYY	PSYCHOSURGERY
CEGIIILNOORST	CORELIGIONIST
CEGIIINNORSTU	INCONGRUITIES
CEGIIKLLMNRSY	MERCY KILLINGS
CEGIILMMNNOPT	COMPLIMENTING
CEGIILMNORSYY	SYRINGOMYELIC
CEGIILNNORRTY	NITROGLYCERIN
CEGIILNOOSSTT	SCIENTOLOGIST
CEGIIMMNNOSTU	TIME-CONSUMING
CEGIIMNOORRTT	TRIGONOMETRIC
CEGIIMNNOPRTU	MOVING PICTURE
CEGIIMNOPRTUZ	COMPUTERIZING
CEGIINNNOORRT	RECONNOITRING
CEGIKLNNOSSSU	KING'S COUNSELS
CEGILMMOORSTY	MYRMECOLOGIST
CEGIMNNNNOOST	ON CONSIGNMENT
CEGINNNOORSTW	CONNING TOWERS
CEGINPRSSSTTU	PRESS CUTTINGS
CEGINRRRSTTUU	RESTRUCTURING
CEHHIIMMOOORT	HOMOIOTHERMIC
CEHHIIMOOPRRT	THERIOMORPHIC
CEHHOOPRTTTTU	PUT TO THE TORCH
CEHHOOPTTTTUU	PUT TO THE TOUCH
CEHIIKNOPSSSY	PSYCHOKINESIS
CEHIILMOOPPTY	LYMPHOPOIETIC
CEHIILMOSSUVY	MISCHIEVOUSLY
CEHIILNOOPSST	SIPHONOSTELIC
CEHIIMMOOORST	HOMOEROTICISM
CEHIIMNOOPRST	CHEMISORPTION
CEHIIMOORSTTY	STOICHIOMETRY
CEHIINOPPRSST	INSPECTORSHIP
CEHIMMMNOOTUY	COMMUNITY HOME
CEHIMNOOOPRRT	CHROMOPROTEIN
CEHLMMOORSSSU	SUMMER SCHOOLS
CEHLNOORRSSUY	NURSERY SCHOOL
CEHMNOORRTTUY	MOTHER COUNTRY
CEHMOOOOOPPRST	PHOTOCOMPOSER
CEIIIILNNSTTVY	INSTINCTIVELY
CEIIJNOOPRSTT	PROJECTIONIST
CEIIKLSSSTWZZ	SWIZZLE STICKS
CEIIKRRSSSTUY	SECURITY RISKS
CEIILLLNOOSTV	VIOLONCELLIST
CEIILMNOPSUUY	IMPECUNIOUSLY
CEIILNNOORTTU	INTERLOCUTION
CEIILNRSTTUVY	INSTRUCTIVELY
CEIILOOPPRSTW	POWER POLITICS
CEIILOPPRSTUY	PRECIPITOUSLY
CEIILRRSSTTUU	SERICULTURIST
CEIIMMNOORSSS	COMMISSIONERS
CEIIMMNOPRSTU	MINICOMPUTERS
CEIIMNNORRTTU	MICRONUTRIENT
CEIIMNOOOPRST	RECOMPOSITION
CEIIMNOOPRSTT	PROTECTIONISM
CEIIMNOOPRTTU	MOTION PICTURE
CEIINNOOPRSTT	INTROSPECTION
CEIINNORRSSTU	INSURRECTIONS
CEIINOOPRSSTT	RETINOSCOPIST
CEIINOOPRSTTT	PROTECTIONIST
CEIINOORSSTUV	INSECTIVOROUS
CEIINOPPRRSST	PRESCRIPTIONS
CEIINOPRSSSTU	PERCUSSIONIST
CEIIPRRRSSTTW	SCRIPTWRITERS
CEILLMNOOSTTY	TONSILLECTOMY
CEILMNNOOOSSU	MONONUCLEOSIS
CEILMNOORSTUY	COTERMINOUSLY
CEILNNOOSTTUY	CONTENTIOUSLY
CEILNOORRSTTU	INTERLOCUTORS
CEILNOORRTTUY	INTERLOCUTORY
CEIMMMNOORSUU	EUROCOMMUNISM
CEIMNOOPPRSTU	INCOME SUPPORT
CEINNNOOSSSUU	INNOCUOUSNESS
CEINNOOPRSTTU	COUNTERPOINTS
CEINOOQRSSSTU	CROSS-QUESTION
CEIOOOPPPRRRT	PROPRIOCEPTOR
CELLNOOSSUUVV	CONVOLVULUSES

CELOOOPRRSSTU	POSTER COLOURS
CEMOOOORRSSTT	MOTOR SCOOTERS
CEOOPPRRSSSSU	CROSS-PURPOSES
CFFIKKLORRTTU	FORKLIFT TRUCK
CFGHIILLNNNUY	UNFLINCHINGLY
CFGHILMNOOOORR	CHLOROFORMING
CFGILLNOORSUY	FLYING COLOURS
CFHINNORTTTUU	TRUTH-FUNCTION
CFIMMNNNOOORS	NONCONFORMISM
CFIMNNNOOORST	NONCONFORMIST
CFIMNNNOOORTY	NONCONFORMITY
CGGHHINOOOPUW	WHOOPING COUGH
CGGILNNOORRWY	CROWNING GLORY
CGHHIILOOSTTY	ICHTHYOLOGIST
CGHIIKNNOOSTT	SHOOTING STICK
CGHIILOORSSTT	CHRISTOLOGIST,
TRICHOLOGISTS	
CGHIINNNORSYZ	SYNCHRONIZING
CGHILOOPSSSTY	PSYCHOLOGISTS
CGIIIKNNOPSTT	STICKING POINT
CGIIILLOOOPST	OLIGOPOLISTIC
CGIIILMNOORST	CRIMINOLOGIST
CGIIILNOOSSTU	SOCIOLINGUIST
CGIIIMMNNOOSS	COMMISSIONING
CGIIINPRRSTTW	SCRIPTWRITING
CGIILOOOSSTTX	TOXICOLOGISTS
CGIIMNNORSSTU	MISCONSTRUING
CGILNNOORSUUY	INCONGRUOUSLY
CHHIOOORSSTTU	ORTHOSTICHOUS
CHHIOOPRSSTYY	PSYCHOHISTORY
CHIIILOOPRSST	SOLICITORSHIP
CHIIOOOPRRSTT	PROTOHISTORIC
CHIJLNOOORSSU	JUNIOR SCHOOLS
CHILMMNNOOOUY	HOLY COMMUNION
CHILMOOPSSTYY	LYMPHOCYTOSIS
CHILOOPSSSTUY	PHYSOCLISTOUS
CIIIIIMPRSTTV	PRIMITIVISTIC
CIIIILLNOSSTU	ILLUSIONISTIC
CIIILNRSTTUUV	VINICULTURIST
CIIILNOPSTUUY	PUNCTILIOUSLY
CIILMMOOOPSST	COSMOPOLITISM
CIIMNNOOOPSST	MONOPSONISTIC
CIINNOOORSTTT	CONTORTIONIST
CIINNOOSSTTTU	CONSTITUTIONS
CIINOOPPRRSST	PROSCRIPTIONS
CIINOOPPRSTTU	OPPORTUNISTIC
CIINOOPRRSTTU	CORRUPTIONIST
CILMOOPRSSUUY	PROMISCUOUSLY
DDDEEGGILNNOW	GOLDEN WEDDING
DDDEHNNOOORRS	RHODODENDRONS
DDEEEEIMNPRRT	PREDETERMINED
DDEEEELLLOPVW	WELL-DEVELOPED
DDEEEELOOPRVV	OVERDEVELOPED
DDEEEGHINORSY	DEHYDROGENISE

DDEEEGHINORYZ	DEHYDROGENIZE
DDEEEIIMPRRST	RED SPIDER MITE
DDEEEIINRSSTT	DISINTERESTED
DDEEEILMNRSTW	MIDDLE WESTERN
DDEEEILNNNPTY	INDEPENDENTLY
DDEEEINNPRSTU	SUPERINTENDED
DDEEELMNOPRUY	UNDEREMPLOYED
DDEEEFGIILMNRS	MIDDLE FINGERS
DDEEFNNOSSSUU	UNFOUNDEDNESS
DDEEGHHINRTUW	HUNDREDWEIGHT
DDEEGHIILMSTW	MIDDLEWEIGHTS
DDEEGHIINSTWW	WHITE WEDDINGS
DDEEGIIILMSSU	GUIDED MISSILE
DDEEGIILNRSVW	SILVER WEDDING
DDEEHILNOOTWY	DYED-IN-THE-WOOL
DDEEIIKMNNRST	KIDDERMINSTER
DDEEIIMNSSTTW	DIM-WITTEDNESS
DDEEINORRSSWW	WINDOW-DRESSER
DDEFINOOPRRUV	UNPROVIDED FOR
DDEGHHIOORRSU	RIDE ROUGHSHOD
DDEGHIIINSSTU	DISTINGUISHED
DDEGIIKMNNOTU	UNITED KINGDOM
DDEGINNRSTUUY	UNDERSTUDYING
DDEGLNNOOOOTY	ENDODONTOLOGY
DDEHIIKNOORZZ	ORDZHONIKIDZE
DDEHINOOPPSWW	WINDOW-SHOPPED
DDEIIIILMSSTU	DISSIMILITUDE
DDEIIIILLNOSSU	DISILLUSIONED
DDEIMNOORSSTU	MISUNDERSTOOD
DDEMNNOORSSWY	DOWN'S SYNDROME
DEEEEFFGIRRRZ	FRIDGE-FREEZER
DEEEEFGGINNRR	GREEN-FINGERED
DEEEEFINNSSSV	DEFENSIVENESS
DEEEEGIILLNSS	DIESEL ENGINES
DEEEEHHPRSSSS	SHEPHERDESSES
DEEEEIMNPRRRT	PREDETERMINER
DEEEELLPRRSVW	WELL-PRESERVED
DEEEELMNOPRTV	REDEVELOPMENT
DEEEENNPRRSTU	UNREPRESENTED
DEEEENPRRSSTV	PERVERTEDNESS
DEEEFGJMNORTU	FOREJUDGEMENT
DEEEFGKLLNOSW	SELF-KNOWLEDGE
DEEEFGKLNOORW	FOREKNOWLEDGE
DEEEFHHIORRRS	HEREFORDSHIRE
DEEEFHNOOORST	FORESHORTENED
DEEEFIILMPRSS	SEMPER FIDELIS
DEEEFILLNSTVY	SELF-EVIDENTLY
DEEEFLLLOPPRS	SELF-PROPELLED
DEEEFLNORSSUW	SUNFLOWER SEED
DEEEFLOPSSSSS	SELF-POSSESSED
DEEEGGHILNPST	SIGN THE PLEDGE
DEEEGHILNNNTU	UNENLIGHTENED
DEEEGIINNRRSV	ENGINE DRIVERS
DEEEGJMNPRSTU	PREJUDGEMENTS

DEEEHLMNNOOWY	HONEYDEW MELON
DEEEHMOPRRSTT	SHORT-TEMPERED
DEEEILLORSTUY	DELETERIOUSLY
DEEEINOQSTUVX	VEXED QUESTION
DEEEKLMMRRTTU	KETTLEDRUMMER
DEEELLNNORRSU	ENROLLED NURSE
DEEELLNNPRSTY	RESPLENDENTLY
DEEENOPRRSUUX	UNDEREXPOSURE
DEEENORSSSTUX	DEXTEROUSNESS
DEEFFFINORRST	FIRST OFFENDER
DEEFFIILNNRTY	INDIFFERENTLY
DEEFFLNNRSSUU	UNRUFFLEDNESS
DEEFFOORSTUWW	SWEET WOODRUFF
DEEFGGHIILNRT	LIGHT-FINGERED
DEEFGIIMNRSTU	DISFIGUREMENT
DEEFGIINNPRRT	FINGERPRINTED
DEEFGILLNNSTU	SELF-INDULGENT
DEEFHHIORRRST	HERTFORDSHIRE
DEEFHIIMRRSSU	DUMFRIESSHIRE
DEEFHIMNORSTT	THETFORD MINES
DEEFILNOPRSSU	SPLENDIFEROUS
DEEFLNNORSSUW	WONDERFULNESS
DEEGHHIPRRSSU	HIGH-PRESSURED
DEEGHIINNSSTW	WINDING SHEETS
DEEGHILLNOSUW	DWELLING HOUSE
DEEGHILMOOOST	METHODOLOGIES
DEEGIIINNSSTZ	DESENSITIZING
DEEGIJMMNSSTU	MISJUDGEMENTS
DEEGILMNOOSTY	SEDIMENTOLOGY
DEEGILNORSTUV	SILVER-TONGUED
DEEGIMNNNOPSY	SPENDING MONEY
DEEGINNOPRSUX	UNDEREXPOSING
DEEGINNORSTTW	DOWNING STREET
DEEHHIINNOSSS	HOIDENISHNESS
DEEHHINNOSSSY	HOYDENISHNESS
DEEHHNORRSTUW	THUNDERSHOWER
DEEHIINNPRSTU	INDENTURESHIP
DEEHINNORSTTY	NORTH TYNESIDE
DEEHINOSSTTUY	SOUTH TYNESIDE
DEEIIIMMNNRST	INDETERMINISM
DEEIIIMNNRSTT	INDETERMINIST
DEEIIINOQRSTU	REQUISITIONED
DEEIIILLNORSS	SOLDIERLINESS
DEEIIILMNNOSS	DIMENSIONLESS
DEEIIILNORSSU	DELIRIOUSNESS
DEEIIILOPPRST	LEPIDOPTERIST
DEEIIILOPSTUXY	EXPEDITIOUSLY
DEEIIMNNRSTTU	DISINTERMENTS
DEEIIMNNSSTTV	DISINVESTMENT
DEEIIMNOORSST	ENDOMETRIOSIS
DEEIIMNOORSTU	DEMERITORIOUS
DEEIINOSSSSTU	SEDITIOUSNESS
DEEILMNOOSSSU	MELODIOUSNESS
DEEILNNOSTTUY	TENDENTIOUSLY
DEEILNORSSSTU	DESULTORINESS
DEEILNOSSSSTU	DISSOLUTENESS
DEEILOOPPRSTU	LEPIDOPTEROUS
DEEIMNOSSSTUW	WOMEN'S STUDIES
DEEINNPRRTTUU	UNINTERRUPTED
DEELLOPPRSTUW	WELL-SUPPORTED
DEELNNOSSSSSU	SOUNDLESSNESS
DEEMNORRSSSUU	MURDEROUSNESS
DEEMOOOPRRSST	DEPRESSOMOTOR
DEENNOOPRSSSU	PONDEROUSNESS
DEENOOPRSSSST	DESSERTSPOONS
DEFFHIRSSSTTU	STUFFED SHIRTS
DEFFIIILNOOSV	FIELD OF VISION
DEFHILMRRTTYY	MERTHYR TYDFIL
DEFHIMORRRTUU	RUTHERFORDIUM
DEFIILPRSTUUY	SUPERFLUIDITY
DEFIMNNOOOSTU	OUT OF ONE'S MIND
DEFINOOOPRRST	POINTS OF ORDER
DEGGHILNOOSSU	LODGING HOUSES
DEGGIILNNORUV	OVERINDULGING
DEGGINNORSSSW	DRESSING GOWNS
DEGHHNOOORRTY	ORTHOHYDROGEN
DEGHIIIINNRST	DISINHERITING
DEGHIIINRSSTU	DISTINGUISHER
DEGHILMOOOSTT	METHODOLOGIST
DEGHIMNOOOSTT	DO SOMETHING TO
DEGHMNOOOSTTU	SMOOTH-TONGUED
DEGIIILNPSSTT	SIDESPLITTING
DEGIIILMNNNRUY	UNDERMININGLY
DEGIILNNOORRS	SOLDERING IRON
DEGIILNRSSSTY	DISTRESSINGLY
DEGIILOOPRSTT	PTERIDOLOGIST
DEGIINNNNPRSU	UNDERPINNINGS
DEGIINOPSSSSS	DISPOSSESSING
DEGIKNNOORRWW	WONDER-WORKING
DEGIMNOORRSSS	DRESSING ROOMS
DEGKNOORRSSTU	GROUND STROKES
DEGMNOORRRSUY	MERRY-GO-ROUNDS
DEHHIILOOPPSS	PHILOSOPHISED
DEHHIILOOPPSZ	PHILOSOPHIZED
DEHINOOPPRSWW	WINDOW-SHOPPER
DEHMNORRSSTTU	THUNDERSTORMS
DEIIILMNOOSTT	DEMOLITIONIST
DEIIINNNOOSSS	INSIDIOUSNESS
DEIIINNOSSSUV	INVIDIOUSNESS
DEIIIOPSSSSTU	UTI POSSIDETIS
DEIIILMNOPRTVY	IMPROVIDENTLY
DEIINOOOPPRST	PROPOSITIONED
DEIINOOPSSSSS	DISPOSSESSION
DEINNNOSSTTUU	STUDENTS' UNION
DEIOOPRSSSSSY	DISPOSSESSORY
DFGGHIIILLNOOT	FLOODLIGHTING
DFGHHIMOOOSST	SMOOTH DOGFISH
DFGIINNOOOOPS	FOOD POISONING

DFGINNOOOPRSU	SOUNDPROOFING
DFIINOORSTTUU	FORTITUDINOUS
DFILLRSSTTUUY	DISTRUSTFULLY
DGGHINNNORTTU	HUNTING GROUND
DGGINNOOPRRUV	PROVING GROUND
DGLMNOOOOSSTU	ODONTOGLOSSUM
DHIIIMMOOPRSS	ISODIMORPHISM
DHIIMOOOPRSSU	ISODIMORPHOUS
DIIIINNOOPSST	INDISPOSITION
DIIIINOQSSSTU	DISQUISITIONS
DIILMNNOSTTUU	MULTITUDINOUS
DIILLNORSSTUUY	INDUSTRIOUSLY
DIINOOOOPPRRST	DISPROPORTION
DILNOOOPSSSUY	ISOSPONDYLOUS
DLNOOOOPPRTTY	POLYPROTODONT
EEEEFHILNSSSY	FISH-EYE LENSES
EEEEFILNRSSVX	REFLEXIVENESS
EEEEFILPRRRSV	LIFE PRESERVER
EEEEFKLNOOPST	KEEP TO ONESELF
EEEEFLNOOPSSX	EXPOSE ONESELF
EEEEGHILNRSTW	STEERING WHEEL
EEEEGHINORSST	HETEROGENESIS
EEEEGHINORTTY	HETEROGENEITY
EEEEGHINOORSTU	HETEROGENEOUS
EEEEGNOPRRRSS	REPRESSOR GENE
EEEEHKLLRRSTT	HELTER-SKELTER
EEEEINNPSSSVX	EXPENSIVENESS
EEEEINNRSSTTV	RETENTIVENESS
EEEEINNSSSTVX	EXTENSIVENESS
EEEELLMOPPRST	ELLESMERE PORT
EEEELLNPSSSSS	SLEEPLESSNESS
EEEELNNRSSSSV	NERVELESSNESS
EEEELNNSSSSSS	SENSELESSNESS
EEEELNOPRRSTT	LETTER OPENERS
EEEELPRRSSSTT	LETTERPRESSES
EEEENNPRRRSTU	ENTREPRENEURS
EEEEORRSTTTTT	TEETER-TOTTERS
EEEFFGILLLNOW	FELLOW FEELING
EEEFFINNOSSSV	OFFENSIVENESS
EEEFGILNNNSSU	UNFEELINGNESS
EEEFGIMNPRRTU	PREFIGUREMENT
EEEFGLNRRSSTU	REGRETFULNESS
EEEFIILMMPRRS	FILM PREMIERES
EEEFLLNORRTTU	FORTUNE-TELLER
EEEFLNNRSSSTU	RESENTFULNESS
EEEFLNOPRSSSU	REPOSEFULNESS
EEEGGINORSSSU	EGREGIOUSNESS
EEEGHILMNNNTT	ENLIGHTENMENT
EEEGHILNNQSSU	QUEEN'S ENGLISH
EEEGHILRSTTWW	WELTERWEIGHTS
EEEGHIMNORSST	THERMOGENESIS
EEEGHIMNOSSTU	MEETINGHOUSES
EEEGIIMNNPRTX	EXPERIMENTING
EEEGILLNNPRSS	REPELLINGNESS

EEEGILLNSSSSU	GUILELESSNESS
EEEGILNNORVWY	OVERWEENINGLY
EEEGILNOORSTV	VENEREOLOGIST
EEEGINOPRRSTW	POWER STEERING
EEEGIORRRSSTV	RETROGRESSIVE
EEEGNOQRSSSTU	GROTESQUENESS
EEEHHIILNPRTW	THREE-LINE WHIP
EEEHHNOOSSTTW	SHOW ONE'S TEETH
EEEHIIILNNPPT	IN THE PIPELINE
EEEHILLOSSTTT	STILETTO HEELS
EEEHILMNNPRST	REPLENISHMENT
EEEHILMOPRRTY	PYRHELIOMETER
EEEHILMPPRSSX	HERPES SIMPLEX
EEEHIMNNNOOPP	EPIPHENOMENON
EEEHINNOSTTTX	SIXTEENTH NOTE
EEEHLLNOOPSTT	TELEPHOTO LENS
EEEHLMNOOSSSW	WHOLESOMENESS
EEEHLOPRSSTTW	POTTER'S WHEELS
EEEHMMNNNORST	ENTHRONEMENTS
EEEHOOPRRSTTU	HETEROPTEROUS
EEEIIILLNRSSU	LEISURELINESS
EEEIIILNNPSVY	INEXPENSIVELY
EEEIIINNSSTVV	INVENTIVENESS
EEEIIINNSSSTV	SENSITIVENESS
EEEIIINQSSSTUX	EXQUISITENESS
EEEIIINRSSSTV	RESISTIVENESS
EEEIIPQRRSSTU	PREREQUISITES
EEEILLNNNPSSS	PENNILESSNESS
EEEILNNOSSSSS	NOISELESSNESS
EEEILNNPSSSSS	SPINELESSNESS
EEEILNOPSSSVX	EXPLOSIVENESS
EEEILNPRSSSUV	REPULSIVENESS
EEEIMNNORSSSV	MONS VENERISES
EEEIMNNPRSSTT	PRESENTIMENTS
EEEIMNOOPRTTT	POTENTIOMETER
EEEIMOPRSSTUX	TIME EXPOSURES
EEELLMORRSSSY	REMORSELESSLY
EEELMOPPRRSTT	TELEPROMPTERS
EEELNNOPSSSTU	PLENTEOUSNESS
EEELNOPRSSSSW	POWERLESSNESS
EEEMPRSSSTTXY	EXPERT SYSTEMS
EEENNOORRSSSU	ERRONEOUSNESS
EEFFFGGHIIORTU	FIGURE OF EIGHT
EEFFGLNORSSTU	FORGETFULNESS
EEFFIILLNNOSVY	INOFFENSIVELY
EEFGHIIILNRRST	FREIGHTLINERS
EEFGHIILRSTTW	WEIGHT LIFTERS
EEFGHIIPRRSST	PRISEFIGHTERS
EEFGHIIPRRSTZ	PRIZEFIGHTERS
EEFGHILORSSTU	SELF-RIGHTEOUS
EEFGIILLNRSTT	LITTLE FINGERS
EEFGIIILNRRTY	INTERFERINGLY
EEFGIIMNNNRST	INFRINGEMENTS
EEFGIIINNOPRTZ	FREEZING POINT

EEFGINNOORSST	FRONTOGENESIS	EEGINOPRRSTTU	INTEREST GROUP
EEFGINOORRRRT	REIGN OF TERROR	EEGINORSTTTUW	TONGUE TWISTER
EEFHHINOORSTT	IN THE THROES OF	EEGOPPRRRSSUU	PRESSURE GROUP
EEFHILNSSSSSU	UNSELFISHNESS	EEHHIILLLMNPS	PHILHELLENISM
EEFHILNSSSSST	SHIFTLESSNESS	EEHHIMNNNOOPP	PHI-PHENOMENON
EEFHNNORRTTUU	FORTUNE HUNTER	EEHHMMNOOOPPR	MORPHOPHONEME
EEFIIILLMNOSTU	FEUILLETONISM	EEHIIMOOPSSTV	PHOTOEMISSIVE
EEFIILLNOSTTU	FEUILLETONIST	EEHIKORRSSTWY	WEST YORKSHIRE
EEFILLNNPSSTU	PLENTIFULNESS	EEHILLOORSSTT	TORTOISESHELL
EEFILNNOOSSSU	FELONIOUSNESS	EEHILMNRSSSST	MIRTHLESSNESS
EEFILNRSSSSTU	FRUITLESSNESS	EEHILNNPSSTWY	PENNY WHISTLES
EEGGHHHLOOOTW	GO THE WHOLE HOG	EEHILNORSSSTU	SOUTHERLINESS
EEGGHINNNRSTT	STRENGTHENING	EEHIMNOPTTTUU	UP-TO-THE-MINUTE
EEGGIJKOPRRYY	JIGGERY-POKERY	EEHIMORSSSSTU	HOUSEMISTRESS
EEGGINOOPPSST	GOOSESTEPPING	EEHKNNOOORSTT	ON TENTERHOOKS
EEGGINORRRSST	RETROGRESSING	EEHLNORRSSTTWY	NORTHWESTERLY
EEGHHIILOPSVX	HIGH EXPLOSIVE	EEHLNRSSSSSTW	WORTHLESSNESS
EEGHIILNNNPSW	SPINNING WHEEL	EEHLOORSSTTUY	HETEROSTYLOUS
EEGHIINNRSSTW	WITHERINGNESS	EEHLORSSTTUWY	SOUTHWESTERLY
EEGHIINRSSTUX	EXTINGUISHERS	EEHMNOOOSSSTT	TOOTHSOMENESS
EEGHIKNOOSSTT	SKEET SHOOTING	EEHMNOORRSSTT	NORTH SOMERSET
EEGHIKNRRRSTU	HUNGER STRIKER	EEHMNRRRSSUYY	NURSERY RHYMES
EEGHIKNRRSSTU	HUNGER STRIKES	EEHNORSSTTTWW	WEST-NORTHWEST
EEGHILNSSSSST	SIGHTLESSNESS	EEHOOOPRRSSTU	HETEROSPOROUS
EEGHILOOPRSTT	HERPETOLOGIST	EEHOSSSTTTUWW	WEST-SOUTHWEST
EEGHIMNOOPRSS	MORPHOGENESIS	EEIIIILNNSSTVY	INSENSITIVELY
EEGHIMNORSTTT	THERMOSETTING	EEIIIIMMNPRRST	PRIME MINISTER
EEGHINNOSSTTW	SWEET NOTHINGS	EEIIIIMNPRSSTV	PRIMITIVENESS
EEGHINORSSSTU	RIGHTEOUSNESS	EEIIIMOPPRRST	IMPROPRIETIES
EEGHIOORSSTYZ	HETEROZYGOSIS	EEIIINNSSTTUV	INTUITIVENESS
EEGHLLOOPRSST	HOT-GOSPELLERS	EEIIINOQRRSTU	REQUISITIONER
EEGHLMNNOOOPY	PHENOMENOLOGY	EEIIILLMNSSSST	LIMITLESSNESS
EEGHLMNOOOSUY	HOMOGENEOUSLY	EEIIILMNNPRTTY	IMPERTINENTLY
EEGHMNOORSTTU	MOTHER TONGUES	EEIIILMNPSSSUV	IMPULSIVENESS
EEGIIILLLNNTTY	INTELLIGENTLY	EEIIILMOOSSTTY	OSTEOMYELITIS
EEGIIILLLNPPSS	SLEEPING PILLS	EEIIILNOORSTUV	REVOLUTIONISE
EEGIIILLNNNTTU	UNINTELLIGENT	EEIIILNOORTUVZ	REVOLUTIONIZE
EEGIIILMNOORST	TERMINOLOGIES	EEIIILNOQRRSTU	VENTRILOQUISE
EEGIIILNNRSTTY	INTERESTINGLY	EEIIILNOQRTUVZ	VENTRILOQUIZE
EEGIIILNORSSSU	RELIGIOUSNESS	EEIIILOOPPSSTV	POSITIVE POLES
EEGIIMNOPRRTU	PRIMOGENITURE	EEIIMNOPRSSSU	IMPERIOUSNESS
EEGIIMNOPRTXZ	EXTEMPORIZING	EEIIMNOPRSSSX	EXPRESSIONISM
EEGIINNPRRSST	INTERSPERSING	EEIINNNORSTTV	INTERVENTIONS
EEGILLNNNRTUY	UNRELENTINGLY	EEIINNOPRRSST	INTERSPERSION
EEGILLNSSSSTU	GUILTLESSNESS	EEIINOPRSSSTX	EXPRESSIONIST
EEGILLOOPSSST	SPELEOLOGISTS	EEILLMNOOSSTY	EMOTIONLESSLY
EEGILMNNPPSTU	SUPPLEMENTING	EEILLMOPRSTTU	MULTIPLE STORE
EEGILMOOORSTT	METEOROLOGIST	EEILLNOOPQRSU	NOLLE PROSEQUI
EEGILOPRRSSVY	PROGRESSIVELY	EEILMPPRSTUVY	PRESUMPTIVELY
EEGIMMNNORSVT	MISGOVERNMENT	EEILNNOPSSSST	POINTLESSNESS
EEGINNNOSSSUU	INGENUOUSNESS	EEILNNOSSTTUY	SENTENTIOUSLY
EEGINNOPPSSTT	STEPPING-STONE	EEILNOPRSTTUY	PRETENTIOUSLY
EEGINOORRRSST	RETROGRESSION	EEILOPRRSSSTY	PROSELYTISERS
EEGINOPPRSSSS	PREPOSSESSING	EEILOPRRSSTYZ	PROSELYTIZERS

EEIMNNNOPRSST	PROMINENTNESS
EEIMNNNOPRSSY	MONEY-SPINNERS
EEIMNNORSSSSUV	VERMINOUSNESS
EEIMNOOPRSSTV	PROMOTIVENESS
EEIMNOPSSSTUU	IMPETUOUSNESS
EEIMOOPRRSSTT	STEREOTROPISM
EEINNOPRSTTUU	UNPRETENTIOUS
EEINOOPPRSSSS	PREPOSSESSION
EEINOPPRRSSTU	PRESSURE POINT
EEINOPPRSSSUV	PURPOSIVENESS
EEKLMNOPSUYZZ	MONKEY-PUZZLES
EEKNNOOPSSSSTU	OUTSPOKENNESS
EELLNOOOPPPRYY	POLYPROPYLENE
EELLOPPRSSSUY	PURPOSELESSLY
EELMNORSSSTUU	TREMULOUSNESS
EELMOPRRSSTTY	STORMY PETRELS
EELMOPSSTTUUY	TEMPESTUOUSLY
EELNOQRSSSUUU	QUERULOUSNESS
EEMNNOOPPSSTT	POSTPONEMENTS
EEMNORSSSTUVY	NERVOUS SYSTEM
EENNOOPPRSSTU	OPPORTUNENESS
EENNORSSSSTUU	STRENUOUSNESS
EFFGGILNNORSU	LONGSUFFERING
EFFGHILNRSSTU	FRIGHTFULNESS
EFFIILOORSSSU	FOSSILIFEROUS
EFFIILPPPRSTU	STIFF UPPER LIP
EFGGHIIILNTTW	WEIGHT LIFTING
EFGGHIIINPRST	PRISEFIGHTING
EFGGHIIINPRTZ	PRIZEFIGHTING
EFGGHIILNNRTY	FRIGHTENINGLY
EFGGIINNORSSV	FORGIVINGNESS
EFGHHLLOOTTUW	WELL-THOUGHT-OF
EFGIIILLNPSTYY	SELF-PITYINGLY
EFGIKLNNOORWY	FOREKNOWINGLY
EFHHIINOOPSST	PHOTO FINISHES
EFHIOOPPRRSSS	PROFESSORSHIP
EFHLNNOOPRSTY	HORNS OF PLENTY
EFHMMNOORTTTU	MOMENT OF TRUTH
EFHOOOPPRTTTU	PUT TO THE PROOF
EFIIIMNRRSSTT	FIRST MINISTER
EFIILLNOOPRSU	POLLINIFEROUS
EFILNOOORSSTU	STOLONIFEROUS
EFILNOORSSSSU	FRIVOLOUSNESS
EFLLOPRSSUUUY	SUPERFLUOUSLY
EFLNOORRSSSUW	SORROWFULNESS
EGGHIIINNSTUX	EXTINGUISHING
EGGHILLNOOPST	HOT-GOSPELLING
EGGHLMOOOOPRY	GEOMORPHOLOGY
EGGIIILMNNNRT	INTERMINGLING
EGGILNOOORSTT	GERONTOLOGIST
EGHHIILOPRSTY	HIEROGLYPHIST
EGHHIINOPPRSW	HORSEWHIPPING
EGHHILLMNOOTY	HELMINTHOLOGY
EGHHLLOSSTTUY	THOUGHTLESSLY
EGHIIILLNNQRSU	RELINQUISHING
EGHIIILNRRSST	STIRLINGSHIRE
EGHIIIMNOPRSV	IMPOVERISHING
EGHIILMNNOPSY	SPHINGOMYELIN
EGHIILNNSSSTU	UNSIGHTLINESS
EGHIILNPRSSST	SPRIGHTLINESS
EGHIIMNOOPSSY	PHYSIOGNOMIES
EGHIIMNOPSSTY	PHYSOSTIGMINE
EGHILOOPPSSST	PSEPHOLOGISTS
EGHIMNOOORSSU	ROOMING HOUSES
EGIIIILNNORRST	IRRELIGIONIST
EGIIIILNOSSSTU	LITIGIOUSNESS
EGIIJNNNNNPSY	SPINNING JENNY
EGIILLLOOSTVX	VEXILLOLOGIST
EGIILLNNNSSUW	UNWILLINGNESS
EGIILLNNOPSST	SELLING POINTS
EGIILMNNOPSTT	MELTING POINTS
EGIILMNNNRTTUY	UNREMITTINGLY
EGIILMNNOORSTT	TERMINOLOGIST
EGIILMNOPRTYZ	TEMPORIZINGLY
EGIILMOOSSSST	SEISMOLOGISTS
EGIILNNOPRSSY	INTERPOSINGLY
EGIILNNOQSTUY	QUESTIONINGLY
EGIILNOPRSTYZ	PROSELYTIZING
EGIIMMNNOPRSS	PROMISINGNESS
EGIIMMNOPPRSSU	SUPERIMPOSING
EGIIMOPRRSSSV	PROGRESSIVISM
EGIINNNOQSTUU	UNQUESTIONING
EGIINNOORRSST	INTROGRESSION
EGIINNPPRRSST	PRINTING PRESS
EGIINPRSTTTTY	SITTING PRETTY
EGIIOPRRSSSTV	PROGRESSIVIST
EGILLNNOORSST	ROLLING STONES
EGILMNOOOSSTT	ENTOMOLOGISTS
EGILNNOSSSTUU	GLUTINOUSNESS
EGILNOPPRRSTU	SPLINTER GROUP
EGIMMMNOPRSSY	GYMNOSPERMISM
EGMMNOOPRRSSU	GYMNOSPERMOUS
EGMMNOOPRRSSUU	RUMOURMONGERS
EHHIILOOPPRSS	PHILOSOPHISER
EHHIILOOPPRSZ	PHILOSOPHIZER
EHHIMMMOOOPRS	HOMEOMORPHISM
EHHIMMNOORSTU	MONMOUTHSHIRE
EHIILLOPSSTWW	WILL-O'-THE-WISPS
EHIILMOOPSSSY	LYMPHOPOIESIS
EHIIMNOOOPSST	PHOTOEMISSION
EHILLNNOOPQUY	PHYLLOQUINONE
EHILMNOOOPSTU	ENTOMOPHILOUS
EHILNOPSSSTYY	POLYSYNTHESIS
EHIMMOOPRRSTT	THERMOTROPISM
EHLLLOOPPSTUY	LEPTOPHYLLOUS
EHLLNOOPSSTUY	STENOPHYLLOUS
EIIIILLNQSTUVY	INQUISITIVELY
EIIIINNSSTTVY	INSENSITIVITY

EIIIILLMOOPSTY	POLIOMYELITIS	FGHIIILLNORSUY	FLOURISHINGLY
EIIIIMMNOPRSSS	IMPRESSIONISM	FGIIIILLNOSSSV	LIVING FOSSILS
EIIIMNNORSSST	INTERMISSIONS	FHLLNOOOOORRSU	ROLL OF HONOURS
EIIIMNOPRSSST	IMPRESSIONIST	FILLMRSSTTUUY	MISTRUSTFULLY
EIIINNOOPRSTT	INTERPOSITION	GGGHHINOOORTU	THOROUGHGOING
EIIILLLLMNOPSS	PLIMSOLL LINES	GGHIIILNPRSTT	STRIP LIGHTING
EIILMNOQRSTUV	VENTRILOQUISM	GHIILLOOPSSTY	SYPHILOLOGIST
EIILMOORRSTUY	MERITORIOUSLY	GHIILNOOORSTT	ORNITHOLOGIST
EIILNOOOOPPSST	POLE POSITIONS	GHIILNOPPRSWY	WORSHIPPINGLY
EIILNOORSTTUV	REVOLUTIONIST	GHIILOOPSSSTY	PHYSIOLOGISTS
EIILNOQRSTTUV	VENTRILOQUIST	GHIIMMOOPRSTT	THIGMOTROPISM
EIIMNOORSSSST	MONSTROSITIES	GHIIMNOOPSSTY	PHYSIOGNOMIST
EIINNOPRRSTTU	INTERRUPTIONS	GIIIIILNNPRSTY	INSPIRITINGLY
EIINOOPPRRSSTU	SUPERPOSITION	GIIIILLNOOQSUZ	SOLILOQUIZING
EIINOOPPRSTTU	OPPORTUNITIES	GIIIILMNNOOSUY	IGNOMINIOUSLY
EIINOORSSTTTX	EXTORTIONISTS	GIILMMNOOPSSW	SWIMMING POOLS
EIINOPRSSSTTU	SUPERSTITIONS	GIILMNRSSTTUY	MISTRUSTINGLY
EIIOOPPRSSSTU	SUPPOSITORIES	GIINNNOPRSTTU	TURNING POINTS
EIIOPRRSSTTUU	SURREPTITIOUS	GIINNOOOOPPRRT	PROPORTIONING
EIIOPRSSSTTUU	SUPERSTITIOUS	GILLLMOOPSSYY	POLYSYLLOGISM
EIJLNOOPPRSTU	JET PROPULSION	HHIMOOOPRRSUZ	RHIZOMORPHOUS
EILNNOOPPRTUY	INOPPORTUNELY	HIIIILLNNOQTTU	QUINTILLIONTH
EINNOOOPRSSSU	POISONOUSNESS	HIILLOOPPRSWW	WHIPPOORWILLS
EINNOOORSSSTU	NOTORIOUSNESS	HILORRSTTTUWY	TRUSTWORTHILY
EMNOPSSSSTUUU	SUMPTUOUSNESS	IIINOOPPSSTNT	OPPOSITIONIST
EMOOOPRRRSSTT	STORM TROOPERS	IIIINOOPRRSSTV	PRISON VISITOR
FFIIINNOOSSSU	FISSION-FUSION	IILLLORSSTUUY	ILLUSTRIOUSLY
FFLLLLNOOOORR	ROLL-ON ROLL-OFF	IIMNOOOPPRRST	MISPROPORTION
FGHHLLOOORTUW	FOLLOW-THROUGH	IINNOOOPPSTTT	POINT-TO-POINTS
FGHIIILLMNOOTT	MOONLIGHT FLIT		

AAAABCCEELRSTU	BACCALAUREATES
AAAABEHKLLLMRU	MAHALLA EL KUBRA
AAAACCDEINORSU	ANACARDIACEOUS
AAAACCILLPRTTY	PARATACTICALLY
AAAACCINNRSSTU	TRANSCAUCASIAN
AAAACDIIMMNOST	MACADAMISATION
AAAACDIIMMNOTZ	MACADAMIZATION
AAAACEGILLMMNO	MEGALOMANIACAL
AAAACEHMNORSTU	AMARANTHACEOUS
AAAACEIMNNRRST	SACRAMENTARIAN
AAAACHIILNNRSS	HALICARNASSIAN
AAAADEGINNQRRU	QUADRAGENARIAN
AAAADELLLNORRV	ANDORRA LA VELLA
AAAAEGLNRSTTUW	NATURAL WASTAGE
AAAAEHILNPPRRS	PARAPHERNALIAS
AAAAFIILNNPRRS	INFRALAPSARIAN
AAAAFIIMNRRSST	RASTAFARIANISM
AAAAGHIMNOPRST	PHANTASMAGORIA
AAAAHHIKMNPSTV	VISHAKHAPATNAM
AAAAIILLNOPSTT	PALATALISATION
AAAAIILLNOPTTZ	PALATALIZATION
AAAABBCEILNNPRU	BANANA REPUBLIC
AAABCCDHILRTYY	BRACHYDACTYLIA
AAABCCEIILLMTZ	ACCLIMATIZABLE
AAABCCILMNNOOY	CYANOCOBALAMIN
AAABCDEEFLSNRT	BALANCE OF TRADE
AAABCDEGINOSTU	SANTIAGO DE CUBA
AAABCEFLMNRTUU	MANUFACTURABLE
AAABCEHILLLPTY	ALPHABETICALLY
AAABCEHILMOSTT	HAEMATOBLASTIC
AAABCEHILNOPPR	INAPPROACHABLE
AAABCEHLNOPPRU	UNAPPROACHABLE
AAABCEILMNOSSU	BALSAMINACEOUS
AAABCEILMNRRSU	ARABIC NUMERALS
AAABDDEEEHORST	BEAT A DEAD HORSE
AAABDDEELLLLNN	BE-ALL AND END-ALL
AAABDDEENRRRST	STANDARD-BEARER
AAABDEEELMPSTX	SET A BAD EXAMPLE
AAABDEEMRSSSSS	AMBASSADRESSES
AAABDHIMOPRSSS	AMBASSADORSHIP
AAABDIINORSSTT	BASTARDISATION
AAABDIINORSTTZ	BASTARDIZATION
AAABEEELLRSTUV	RATEABLE VALUES
AAABEGGIILNNPR	PLEA BARGAINING
AAABEIILLMNNPRR	PRIMA BALLERINA
AAABEILNOOPSTT	PALAEOBOTANIST
AAABELLNNPRSTT	TRANSPLANTABLE
AAABIILNOOPRST	PARABOLISATION
AAABIILNOOPRTZ	PARABOLIZATION
AAABIILNRRTTWY	WARRANTABILITY
AAACCDEHIINORT	ARCHIDIACONATE
AAACCDEHINRRSS	CASH AND CARRIES
AAACCDEIMNNOOR	ADENOCARCINOMA
AAACCDEIOPPRSU	CAPPARIDACEOUS
AAACCDILORRSUV	CARDIOVASCULAR
AAACCEEELLNRSS	CLEARANCE SALES
AAACCEEFFHHKLTT	AT THE CHALKFACE
AAACCEEHILMNOR	AEROMECHANICAL
AAACCEEHMNRSTS	CATCHMENT AREAS
AAACCEGHILLOOR	ARCHAEOLOGICAL
AAACCEHILMPRTU	PHARMACEUTICAL
AAACCEILNNORTX	EXTRACANONICAL
AAACCELMNOPSUU	CAMPANULACEOUS
AAACCGHILOPRRT	CARTOGRAPHICAL
AAACCGIIINNPTT	INCAPACITATING
AAACCHIILNRSTT	CHARLATANISTIC
AAACCHILLMORTY	ACHROMATICALLY
AAACCIIINNOPTT	INCAPACITATION
AAACCILLORTTUY	AUTOCRATICALLY
AAACCLMOORSSTU	MALACOSTRACOUS
AAACDDEGGKLNOR	CLOAK-AND-DAGGER
AAACDEEGHILNRR	HEGIRA CALENDAR
AAACDEEINPPRSS	DISAPPEARANCES
AAACDEFGNORRUV	GRACE-AND-FAVOUR
AAACDEGIKLNNNP	PANCAKE LANDING
AAACDEIIIMNNNR	AMERICAN INDIAN
AAACDEIIINNPRST	PAEDIATRICIANS
AAACDFHIMNNRST	HANDICRAFTSMAN
AAACDHILNOOPRS	ACHONDROPLASIA
AAACDHINNRSTTU	TRISTAN DA CUNHA
AAACDIILNNOSST	SCANDALISATION
AAACDIILNNOSTZ	SCANDALIZATION
AAACEEGILNSSTU	AGUASCALIENTES
AAACEEILLNORRS	ALSACE-LORRAINE
AAACEEILNORSUV	VALERIANACEOUS
AAACEFGIORSSUX	SAXIFRAGACEOUS
AAACEFIILNNRSY	FINANCIAL YEARS
AAACEFILLLNSTY	SELF-ANALYTICAL
AAACEGILMNNORS	ANGLO-AMERICANS
AAACEHIILMRRSV	AIR VICE-MARSHAL
AAACEHIIMMNSTT	MATHEMATICIANS
AAACEHILLMMTTY	MATHEMATICALLY
AAACEHILMOOPPR	PHARMACOPOEIAL
AAACEHILNOPPRT	PALAEANTHROPIC
AAACEHIMOOPPRS	PHARMACOPOEIAS
AAACEHNRRRSSTW	SEARCH WARRANTS
AAACEIIMMNNPRS	PAN-AMERICANISM
AAACEILLMNNSTY	ANAMNESTICALLY
AAACEILLMSTTTY	METASTATICALLY
AAACEILMMNRSST	SACRAMENTALISM
AAACEILMNRSSTT	SACRAMENTALIST
AAACEILMNRSTTY	SACRAMENTALITY
AAACENRRRSSTTU	RESTAURANT CARS
AAACFIILLLSTTY	FATALISTICALLY
AAACFIILNOSSTT	SATISFACTIONAL
AAACGHIKLNSSTT	SLASHING ATTACK
AAACGHIMNOPRST	PHANTASMAGORIC
AAACGIILLMSTTY	ASTIGMATICALLY

AAACGIILLNPSTY	PAGANISTICALLY
AAACGIILMRRTTY	GRAMMATICALITY
AAACGILLMNORTY	MORGANATICALLY
AAACGLORRSSTUV	GASTROVASCULAR
AAACHILLLLOPTY	ALLOPATHICALLY
AAACHILMMNNOPY	NYMPHOMANIACAL
AAACHILMOPRTTU	THAUMATROPICAL
AAACIIIILNOPSTT	CAPITALISATION
AAACIIIILNOPTTZ	CAPITALIZATION
AAACILLLLOPRTY	ALLOPATRICALLY
AAADEEGHHMSTTW	WHAT'S THE DAMAGE?
AAADEEHLLORTTT	LEAD TO THE ALTAR
AAADEEHLMNNNRT	NEANDERTHAL MAN
AAADEGGILNNRSU	GUARDIAN ANGELS
AAADEGLNOSTUVY	ADVANTAGEOUSLY
AAADEHMNPSTTYY	TEA AND SYMPATHY
AAADEIILNNRTUV	VALETUDINARIAN
AAADEILLQRRSTU	QUADRILATERALS
AAADEIMNNORRSY	ORDINARY SEAMAN
AAADFIILLMORRY	FAIRY ARMADILLO
AAADGHIOOPRRTU	AUTORADIOGRAPH
AAADGIILLMNORT	GIANT ARMADILLO
AAADGIMNOORSST	GOOD SAMARITANS
AAADIIIILNNRTTU	LATITUDINARIAN
AAADIIMNORSSTT	DRAMATISATIONS
AAADIIMNORSTTZ	DRAMATIZATIONS
AAADIJNNNORRST	TRANS-JORDANIAN
AAAEEFGIKMOPRS	MAKE A PIG'S EAR OF
AAAEEGINNNPRSTU	SEPTUAGENARIAN
AAAEEGMNRRSSTT	SERGEANT-AT-ARMS
AAAEEHHLMMORTT	HAEMATOTHERMAL
AAAEEHIIMNRRTT	HENRIETTA MARIA
AAAEEHMNRRSTWX	MANX SHEARWATER
AAAEEIILLPRTXY	EPITAXIAL LAYER
AAAEEJMNRRSSTT	SERJEANT-AT-ARMS
AAAEGGGIKNPRRS	PARKING GARAGES
AAAEGHIIMNNTTZ	ANATHEMATIZING
AAAEGHLNNOPRSY	NASOPHARYNGEAL
AAAEGIIILMNRST	EGALITARIANISM
AAAEGLLLMOPRRS	PARALLELOGRAMS
AAAEGLMOPRRSSU	MASSAGE PARLOUR
AAAEHILMNNNOTT	NATIONAL ANTHEM
AAAGIIILNNOORST	ORGANISATIONAL
AAAGIIILNNOORTZ	ORGANIZATIONAL
AAAGIIMMNPRSTT	ANTIPRAGMATISM
AAAGIINNNOOSTT	ANTAGONISATION
AAAGIINNNOOTTZ	ANTAGONIZATION
AAAGINOORRSSTTV	ASTRONAVIGATOR
AAAHIINORRSTTU	AUTHORITARIANS
AAAIILLNNOORSTU	NATURALISATION
AAAIILLNNORTTUZ	NATURALIZATION
AAAIILNORSTTWY	RAILWAY STATION
AAAIIMNORSTTTU	TRAUMATISATION
AAAIIMNORTTTUZ	TRAUMATIZATION

AAAIINNOSSSSST	ASSASSINATIONS
AAAILNNORSTTUV	TRANSVALUATION
AABBCEEFINORST	ABSORBEFACIENT
AABBCEEHILNOSS	BELISHA BEACONS
AABBDDEEGILORS	BIODEGRADABLES
AABBDDEENRRTTU	BREAD-AND-BUTTER
AABBDEEHIMNORT	BROAD IN THE BEAM
AABBEEELNNRSSU	UNBEARABLENESS
AABBEFGGILNRST	FLABBERGASTING
AABBEIILLOSSSU	BOUILLABAISSES
AABBELOPRRRSWY	BLOW A RASPBERRY
AABBHIIIILNTTY	INHABITABILITY
AABCCCDHILRTYY	BRACHYDACTYLIC
AABCCCEEHHILPRY	BRACHYCEPHALIC
AABCCDEKKLLNOT	BLOCK AND TACKLE
AABCCEELNNORTU	COUNTERBALANCE
AABCCEGHIIOPRT	BACTERIOPHAGIC
AABCCEHILLMOPS	ACCOMPLISHABLE
AABCCEHNOOORSU	OROBANCHACEOUS
AABCCEIIORSTTT	BACTERIOSTATIC
AABCCEILMMRTUU	CIRCUMAMBULATE
AABCCIIIILPRTY	PRACTICABILITY
AABCCIILNOTTUY	ACCOUNTABILITY
AABCDDEEHKNNSS	BACKHANDEDNESS
AABCDDHINORSSW	SANDWICH BOARDS
AABCDEEEGHNRUU	BUREAU DE CHANGE
AABCDEEEMMNNRY	REMEMBRANCE DAY
AABCDEEFIILLSS	DECLASSIFIABLE
AABCDEEHLOTTTU	CHATEAU BOTTLED
AABCDEEHNNRUZZ	NEBUCHADNEZZAR
AABCDEEHORTTUY	CATHODE RAY TUBE
AABCDEEIKRRSTV	BACK-SEAT DRIVER
AABCDEEINRRSTT	SCATTERBRAINED
AABCDEEKMNOPPY	KEEP BAD COMPANY
AABCDEENNPRSUU	SUPERABUNDANCE
AABCDEENRSSSTT	ABSTRACTEDNESS
AABCDEGIILLNNV	ADVANCE BILLING
AABCDEGIKLNRRT	BLANK CARTRIDGE
AABCDEHOORRSST	ACROSS-THE-BOARD
AABCDEIILLNOSS	DIABOLICALNESS
AABCEEEEFLNOSV	LEAVE OF ABSENCE
AABCEEEGHLNNSS	CHANGEABLENESS
AABCEEEHKNRTTT	THE BEATEN TRACK
AABCEEEKKLMRRT	BLACK MARKETEER
AABCEEFLNOOPRW	BALANCE OF POWER
AABCEEGHLNORUX	LABOUR EXCHANGE
AABCEEGILNRTXY	EXACERBATINGLY
AABCEEHIKLMNNS	BLACKEN HIS NAME
AABCEEHILNRSST	CHARITABLENESS
AABCEEHILOPRRR	IRREPROACHABLE
AABCEEHINSTTUU	EUSTACHIAN TUBE
AABCEEIILLPRTY	REPLACEABILITY
AABCEEILLLMMTY	EMBLEMATICALLY
AABCEEKQRRSSTU	SQUARE BRACKETS

AABCEFGIINPRRT	PREFABRICATING
AABCEFIIINOSTT	BEATIFICATIONS
AABCEFIIINOTTU	BEAUTIFICATION
AABCEFIIINOPRRT	PREFABRICATION
AABCEGHHIIMNNT	BATHING MACHINE
AABCEHIIILMPTY	IMPEACHABILITY
AABCEHIIILLRSTY	HEBRAISTICALLY
AABCEHILOPRRRY	IRREPROACHABLY
AABCEIIILLORSST	AEROBALLISTICS
AABCEIILNNPRTU	ANTIREPUBLICAN
AABCEIILRRTTTY	RETRACTABILITY
AABCEIILRTTTXY	EXTRACTABILITY
AABCEIIORSSSTT	BACTERIOSTASIS
AABCEILLMORRTY	BAROMETRICALLY
AABCEILNORSSTU	CONSTABULARIES
AABCEIMOORSSUU	SIMAROUBACEOUS
AABCFIKMNOORST	BACK FORMATIONS
AABCFILNNOOSTU	CONFABULATIONS
AABCGGIILLOOOR	AGROBIOLOGICAL
AABCGHIILLMOOP	AMPHIBIOLOGICAL
AABCGHIILLOPRY	BIOGRAPHICALLY
AABCGHIIOOPRTU	AUTOBIOGRAPHIC
AABCGHIMOOPRRR	MICROBAROGRAPH
AABCHIILPRSTY	PURCHASABILITY
AABCHILOOPRSTU	CLAUSTROPHOBIA
AABCIIILLMPRSY	IMPARISYLLABIC
AABCIIILNRTTTY	INTRACTABILITY
AABCIIMNORSSTT	ABSTRACTIONISM
AABDDEEIMNNORT	ONE-ARMED BANDIT
AABDDEELNNRSTU	UNDERSTANDABLE
AABDDEFIIOPRRS	BIRD OF PARADISE
AABDDELNNRSTUY	UNDERSTANDABLY
AABDDGIINNORRS	DRAINING BOARDS
AABDEEEFHINRRT	FEATHERBRAINED
AABDEEEHHIRRSS	HABERDASHERIES
AABDEEEHILNNNR	BANNER HEADLINE
AABDEFGIOPRSSS	BIRDS OF PASSAGE
AABDEFIIIILLQSU	DISQUALIFIABLE
AABDEIIKMNORST	DISEMBARKATION
AABDEIILPRSTUY	PERSUADABILITY
AABDEKLNRSSTUY	LAUNDRY BASKETS
AABDHHNPRSSUUW	WASH AND BRUSH-UP
AABDHILMNOSSUY	BUSMAN'S HOLIDAY
AABDIIIILNSTYY	INADVISABILITY
AABDIIIILNOTUVY	UNAVOIDABILITY
AABDIINOOPPRST	DISAPPROBATION
AABEEEFMNNOOST	BEMOAN ONE'S FATE
AABEEEINORRSWY	RAISE AN EYEBROW
AABEEEKLMNRRSS	REMARKABLENESS
AABEEELNNORSSS	REASONABLENESS
AABEEELNNOSSSS	SEASONABLENESS
AABEEFGILNNOST	SELF-ABNEGATION
AABEEFLNORSSUV	FAVOURABLENESS
AABEEGIKMNORRR	BROKEN MARRIAGE

AABEEHIIILRTTV	REHABILITATIVE
AABEEHIILLPRSS	HERPES LABIALIS
AABEEHIILRTTWY	WEATHERABILITY
AABEEHJKMNORST	JAM ON THE BRAKES
AABEEIMNNORTUV	MOUNTAIN BEAVER
AABEEMMNRRSSST	EMBARRASSMENTS
AABEFGHLLORRSU	BARREL OF LAUGHS
AABEFILLMMNNNO	NONINFLAMMABLE
AABEFILLNOPSTU	FALLOPIAN TUBES
AABEGHIIILNRTT	REHABILITATING
AABEGHIOOPRRTU	AUTOBIOGRAPHER
AABEGIILLNOSUV	BOUGAINVILLEAS
AABEGILMNNRSSY	EMBARRASSINGLY
AABEHIIILNORTT	REHABILITATION
AABEIIIILLNNTY	INALIENABILITY
AABEIIILLNORST	LIBERALISATION
AABEIIILLNORTZ	LIBERALIZATION
AABEIIILLNRTTY	INALTERABILITY
AABEIIILMNRRST	LIBERTARIANISM
AABEIIILNPRSTY	INSEPARABILITY
AABEIIIILPRRRTY	IRREPARABILITY
AABEIILRRSUVXY	AUXILIARY VERBS
AABEIINSSTTTUV	SUBSTANTIATIVE
AABEILMNOPRSTU	PERAMBULATIONS
AABEILNNORSTTU	SUBALTERNATION
AABEKMRRRSTWY	STRAWBERRY MARK
AABELOPRRSTUUY	BEAUTY PARLOURS
AABENORRRSTWY	STRAWBERRY ROAN
AABFIIILLMMNTY	INFLAMMABILITY
AABFIILLNPPTUY	UNFLAPPABILITY
AABGIINNSSTTTU	SUBSTANTIATING
AABHIIINPPRSST	BIPARTISANSHIP
AABIIILLMNPTUY	MANIPULABILITY
AABIILMNSSSTTU	SUBSTANTIALISM
AABIILNSSSTTTU	SUBSTANTIALIST
AABIILNSSTTTUY	SUBSTANTIALITY
AABIINNOSSTTTU	SUBSTANTIATION
AABILMMNNOOSTU	SOMNAMBULATION
AACCCCENNOOOVV	CONCAVO-CONCAVE
AACCCDHIIINOTY	THIOCYANIC ACID
AACCCEEHILLTTY	CATECHETICALLY
AACCCEEIILLSST	ECCLESIASTICAL
AACCCEEGHNORSTU	CHARGE ACCOUNTS
AACCCEHIIRRSTT	CHARACTERISTIC
AACCCHLLOOPSTY	STAPHYLOCOCCAL
AACCDDDEEHHNNRT	CATCH RED-HANDED
AACCDDEMMNOOTU	UNACCOMMODATED
AACCDEHILOPRSY	POLYSACCHARIDE
AACCDEHIMNOORS	MONOSACCHARIDE
AACCDEIINNORTT	CONTRAINDICATE
AACCDEILLMORTY	DEMOCRATICALLY
AACCDHIMOPRSTY	PSYCHODRAMATIC
AACCDHIMRRSSST	CHRISTMAS CARDS
AACCDIIINRSTTU	TRADUCIANISTIC

AACCDIINNNORTT	CONTRAINDICANT	AACCHILMNOORST	ROMAN CATHOLICS
AACCDIMMNOOOST	ACCOMMODATIONS	AACCHILNOPSTYY	PSYCHOANALYTIC
AACCEEGHILLMOP	MEGALOCEPHALIC	AACCIIILMPRTTY	IMPRACTICALITY
AACCEEGIILNTTT	TELANGIECTATIC	AACCIIIMOPRRST	MICROPARASITIC
AACCEEILNNRSTU	NATURAL SCIENCE	AACCIILLMNOSTU	MISCALCULATION
AACCEEINNNORSS	RECONNAISSANCE	AACCIILLNNOORR	CONRAIL, CONRAIL
AACCEELMNRSUUV	VACUUM CLEANERS	AACCIILMNRSTTU	CIRCUMSTANTIAL
AACCEELNORRRTU	NUCLEAR REACTOR	AACCIILNPRTTUY	UNPRACTICALITY
AACCEGGHINRRRY	CARRYING CHARGE	AACCIIMNOORSST	CARCINOMATOSIS
AACCEGGILLNOOY	GYNAECOLOGICAL	AACCIILLNOOPTUY	OCCUPATIONALLY
AACCEGHIINRRTZ	CHARACTERIZING	AACCKLNNNOPSTT	PLANCK CONSTANT
AACCEGHILLOOST	ESCHATOLOGICAL	AACDDDEKKNRSSU	DUCKS AND DRAKES
AACCEGIILOOPTT	GALACTOPOIETIC	AACDDEEEELLNSVV	ADVANCED LEVELS
AACCEGIIMNRTUV	CIRCUMNAVIGATE	AACDDEEILOSTVV	DEVIL'S ADVOCATE
AACCEGINNOSTUY	NYCTAGINACEOUS	AACDDEEIMNNOTT	DECONTAMINATED
AACCEHHIILLRRY	HIERARCHICALLY	AACDDEILNOTTUU	ADULT EDUCATION
AACCEHHLNPRSTY	CHANTRY CHAPELS	AACDEEEFFHMNSSS	SHAMEFACEDNESS
AACCEHIILOPPRS	ARCHIEPISCOPAL	AACDEEGHHNORST	CHASE THE DRAGON
AACCEHIINNORST	CHAIN REACTIONS	AACDEEGIILLNRT	LEADING ARTICLE
AACCEHIKLOOSSV	CSECHOSLOVAKIA	AACDEEGINRRRSU	UNDERCARRIAGES
AACCEHIKMRSSST	CHRISTMAS CAKES	AACDEEGIPPRRRT	CARTRIDGE PAPER
AACCEHILLNOOPT	PLAIN CHOCOLATE	AACDEEILLNQTUW	WELL-ACQUAINTED
AACCEHILLORTTY	THEOCRATICALLY	AACDEEILOPPRTU	PROPAEDEUTICAL
AACCEHILLPRTYY	ARCHETYPICALLY	AACDEEIQRSSTTU	ACQUIRED TASTES
AACCEHINOPPRRT	PARTHENOCARPIC	AACDEELNNNRSTT	TRANSCENDENTAL
AACCEIIILPRSTT	PRACTICALITIES	AACDEENORSSSUV	CADAVEROUSNESS
AACCEIILRRTUUV	CURRICULA VITAE	AACDEFFINRRSTW	TRAFFIC WARDENS
AACCEIJKLOPRST	PRACTICAL JOKES	AACDEGILLMOORT	DERMATOLOGICAL
AACCEILLLOPPTY	APOPLECTICALLY	AACDEGINOPRSST	DATA PROCESSING
AACCEILLMTUUVY	ACCUMULATIVELY	AACDEGLMNNORSS	SCANDALMONGERS
AACCEIMMNNOPST	ACCOMPANIMENTS	AACDEHIIMNNRST	ARCHIMANDRITES
AACCEEINNNOOSTT	CONCATENATIONS	AACDEHILORRSST	TRISOCTAHEDRAL
AACCEKNORSTTTU	COUNTERATTACKS	AACDEHLMNNORST	CALENDAR MONTHS
AACCELLMMOORRU	MACROMOLECULAR	AACDEHLNOPSSYY	PSYCHOANALYSED
AACCELLNOOPRRS	LANCE CORPORALS	AACDEHMOPRSTUY	PACHYDERMATOUS
AACCELNNORSUUU	RANUNCULACEOUS	AACDEIIILLLSTY	IDEALISTICALLY
AACCELOOPRSTUU	PORTULACACEOUS	AACDEIIIILMNOST	DECIMALISATION
AACCFHOORRRRTY	CARRY A TORCH FOR	AACDEIIIILMNOTZ	DECIMALIZATION
AACCFIIILNORST	CLARIFICATIONS	AACDEIILLNOOST	DELOCALISATION
AACCFIIILNOSST	CLASSIFICATION	AACDEIILLNOOTZ	DELOCALIZATION
AACCFIIINNOSTT	SANCTIFICATION	AACDEIILMMNOST	DOMESTIC ANIMAL
AACCFIILMOPSST	FAITS ACCOMPLIS	AACDEIILNNOPTY	PLATINOCYANIDE
AACCFIILORSSTY	CLASSIFICATORY	AACDEIILNOSTTU	EDUCATIONALIST
AACCFLOOOOPSTV	FOOLSCAP OCTAVO	AACDEIILPRRSTU	PARTICULARISED
AACCFNNORTTTUU	TURF ACCOUNTANT	AACDEIILPRRTUZ	PARTICULARIZED
AACCGHHHHIINSU	SHIHCHIACHUANG	AACDEIINORTTTX	DIRECT TAXATION
AACCGHIILLORY	OLIGARCHICALLY	AACDEILMOPRSTT	DERMATOPLASTIC
AACCGHILLNOOST	ANGLO-CATHOLICS	AACDEILMORRTTU	COURT-MARTIALED
AACCGIIILLMNSTU	MISCALCULATING	AACDEILNOPRSSS	SPORADICALNESS
AACCGIIILLMORTY	TRAGICOMICALLY	AACDEIMNNNOTTU	UNCONTAMINATED
AACCGILLLNOOOV	VOLCANOLOGICAL	AACDEIMNNOORTT	DECONTAMINATOR
AACCGINNOSSTUV	SAVINGS ACCOUNT	AACDEINOPRRSST	PROCRASTINATED
AACCHIIILLMSSTY	SCHISMATICALLY	AACDELNNOSSSSU	SCANDALOUSNESS
AACCHILLOSSTTY	STOCHASTICALLY	AACDFFIIILNRSST	TRAFFIC ISLANDS

AACDGHIMOOPRRY	MYOCARDIOGRAPH	AACEFILLNOSSSU	FALLACIOUSNESS
AACDGIIINOSSST	DISASSOCIATING	AACEFINRSSTTUY	SAFETY CURTAINS
AACDGIILLNOSTY	DIAGNOSTICALLY	AACEFNOPRRSSTT	TRANSPORT CAFES
AACDHIMOOSSSST	SADOMASOCHISTS	AACEGGHILLOPRY	GEOGRAPHICALLY
AACDIIIIILNNPRS	DISCIPLINARIAN	AACEGGHINNORRT	GREGORIAN CHANT
AACDIIINOOSSST	DISASSOCIATION	AACEGGILNNOORT	CONGREGATIONAL
AACDIILLLMOPTY	DIPLOMATICALLY	AACEGGHHIIMNNSW	WASHING MACHINE
AACDIILNNOOPRST	CARDINAL POINTS	AACEGHHIOPPRRS	PHRASEOGRAPHIC
AACDIILORRSTTU	DISARTICULATOR	AACEGHIILLPPRY	EPIGRAPHICALLY
AACDIKNNPQRSSU	QUIPS AND CRANKS	AACEGHIILMOPSU	MALPIGHIACEOUS
AACDILNOOSSTUY	ANISODACTYLOUS	AACEGHIINNTTTU	AUTHENTICATING
AACDILOORSTTUY	ARTIODACTYLOUS	AACEGHIJKRSTTT	STRAIGHTJACKET
AACEEEEGINSSTT	ESTATE AGENCIES	AACEGHILLLMPTY	PHLEGMATICALLY
AACEEEEFGHNORTX	RATE OF EXCHANGE	AACEGHILLMNOPY	MEGAPHONICALLY
AACEEEFHINRSTT	STARE IN THE FACE	AACEGHILLMOPRT	METALLOGRAPHIC
AACEEEEGILNRSTV	TRAVEL AGENCIES	AACEGHILLOOPRS	PHRASEOLOGICAL
AACEEEEGIPPRRTT	CIGARETTE PAPER	AACEGHILOORSST	ARCHAEOLOGISTS
AACEEEHIMNNOST	IN THE SAME CANOE	AACEGHILOPRTTU	TELAUTOGRAPHIC
AACEEEHKMRRRST	MARKET RESEARCH	AACEGHIMNOPRTY	CINEMATOGRAPHY
AACEEEHLMOSTUY	THYMELAEACEOUS	AACEGIILLLLSTY	LEGALISTICALLY
AACEEEHMMORTTY	HAEMACYTOMETER	AACEGIILLMOOSS	SEMASIOLOGICAL
AACEEEILLRSTUV	RELATIVE CLAUSE	AACEGIILNPRTTU	RECAPITULATING
AACEEFFILNOTTY	AFFECTIONATELY	AACEGIILOOPSST	GALACTOPOIESIS
AACEEGGILLLNOY	GENEALOGICALLY	AACEGIINNOPRST	ANGINA PECTORIS
AACEEGHHLNOPPR	ENCEPHALOGRAPH	AACEGIINOORSTT	CATEGORISATION
AACEEGHILNNRTT	CENTRAL HEATING	AACEGIINOORTTZ	CATEGORIZATION
AACEEGHNOOPRRS	OCEANOGRAPHERS	AACEGILLLLOOPTY	APOLOGETICALLY
AACEEGIIILLMNSV	EVANGELICALISM	AACEGILLMNOORT	ORGANOMETALLIC
AACEEGIIILNSSTT	TELANGIECTASIS	AACEGILNRRTTUY	RECTANGULARITY
AACEEGIIPRSVWY	GIVEAWAY PRICES	AACEHHILNNOPY	PHTHALOCYANINE
AACEEGILLNNPTY	PANGENETICALLY	AACEHIIIMNRSTT	ARITHMETICIANS
AACEEGILNPRSTW	WATERING PLACES	AACEHIILLLLPTY	PHILATELICALLY
AACEEHHMNOPRTY	MECHANOTHERAPY	AACEHIILLMRTTY	ARITHMETICALLY
AACEEHHNNOPPRST	ON THE SCRAPHEAP	AACEHIILLNTTTY	ANTITHETICALLY
AACEEHIIMOOPTT	HAEMATOPOIETIC	AACEHIILMNSTUV	MALE CHAUVINIST
AACEEHILLLLPTTY	TELEPATHICALLY	AACEHIIMNNRSST	CHRISTIAN NAMES
AACEEHILMNPSST	EMPHATICALNESS	AACEHIIMNOSSTT	SCHEMATISATION
AACEEHILRRTUVX	EXTRAVEHICULAR	AACEHIIMNOSTTZ	SCHEMATIZATION
AACEEHIMNNRSTV	MERCHANT NAVIES	AACEHIINNOTTTU	AUTHENTICATION
AACEEHIPRSSTTY	CRYPTAESTHESIA	AACEHILLLNNOUY	UNHOLY ALLIANCE
AACEEIIIINNPPRTV	INAPPRECIATIVE	AACEHILLMNNORY	ENHARMONICALLY
AACEEIILOPRSTV	OVERCAPITALISE	AACEHILLMOPRSY	SEMAPHORICALLY
AACEEIILOPRSTVZ	OVERCAPITALIZE	AACEHILLMOPRTY	METAPHORICALLY
AACEEIIILPPRTVY	APPRECIATIVELY	AACEHILLMPSTYY	METAPHYSICALLY
AACEEIIILPRTTUV	RECAPITULATIVE	AACEHILMNPRRSU	HURRICANE LAMPS
AACEEIINNPPRTU	UNAPPRECIATIVE	AACEHIMMMORSTT	METACHROMATISM
AACEEILNPPPRRT	RICE-PAPER PLANT	AACEHIMOOPPRST	PHARMACOPOEIST
AACEEILNPRTTUV	VENTURE CAPITAL	AACEHLNOPRSYYZ	PSYCHOANALYZER
AACEEILNRSSTTU	ARTICULATENESS	AACEHMNOOOPPRS	ANAMORPHOSCOPE
AACEEINNPRRSST	TRANSPARENCIES	AACEHMNNOPRSTU	PARENCHYMATOUS
AACEEINRSSTTTV	ATTRACTIVENESS	AACEIIILNOPSST	SPECIALISATION
AACEFFINORRRTW	WARRANT OFFICER	AACEIIILNOPSTZ	SPECIALIZATION
AACEFFLMORTTTY	MATTER-OF-FACTLY	AACEIILLMNNOOT	CALAMINE LOTION
AACEFIINPRRTTU	PARTURIFACIENT	AACEIILLNPSTTY	ANTISEPTICALLY

AACEIILLNRTTUY	INARTICULATELY	AACGHILLLOOPTY	PATHOLOGICALLY
AACEIIILMOOPRTV	IMPERIAL OCTAVO	AACGHILLMOPRYY	MYOGRAPHICALLY
AACEIILNNORSTT	CENTRALISATION	AACGHILLOOPRRY	OROGRAPHICALLY
AACEIILNNORTTZ	CENTRALIZATION	AACGHILMOOPRST	PHARMACOLOGIST
AACEIILNOPRTTU	RECAPITULATION	AACGHLMMOORRSS	GRAMMAR SCHOOLS
AACEIILNORSSTU	SECULARISATION	AACGHLOOPPRSYY	PARAPSYCHOLOGY
AACEIILNORSTUZ	SECULARIZATION	AACGILLLOORSTY	ASTROLOGICALLY
AACEIILPPPRSTT	PAST PARTICIPLE	AACGILLLOOTTUY	TAUTOLOGICALLY
AACEIILPRRRSTU	PARTICULARISER	AACGILLMOORRTY	MARTYROLOGICAL
AACEIILPRRRTUZ	PARTICULARIZER	AACGILMNOOPSST	CAMPANOLOGISTS
AACEIINNNORRST	REINCARNATIONS	AACGILNNOORTTU	CONGRATULATION
AACEIINOPRRSTV	PREVARICATIONS	AACGKNOOORRSTU	KANGAROO COURTS
AACEIINRRRSSTU	CURTAIN RAISERS	AACGLNOORRTTUY	CONGRATULATORY
AACEIILLNOPSTY	PLEONASTICALLY	AACHHINOOPPRTT	ANTHROPOPATHIC
AACEILLMMNORTY	MANOMETRICALLY	AACHIILLNNOSTU	HALLUCINATIONS
AACEILLMMRSTYY	ASYMMETRICALLY	AACHIILLNOOOST	ALCOHOLISATION
AACEILLMNORRTU	INTRAMOLECULAR	AACHIILLNOOOTZ	ALCOHOLIZATION
AACEILLMSSTTYY	SYSTEMATICALLY	AACHIIMNNORSTT	ANTIMONARCHIST
AACEILNNNRSSTY	TYRANNICALNESS	AACHILLOORTTUY	LOCAL AUTHORITY
AACEILNNOORSTV	CONSERVATIONAL,	AACHILLOPTTUYY	AUTOPHYTICALLY
CONVERSATIONAL		AACHILNOPSSSYY	PSYCHOANALYSIS
AACEILNNOPSSTU	ENCAPSULATIONS	AACHLLLLMOOPYU	MALACOPHYLLOUS
AACEILNORSTTUX	EXCLAUSTRATION	AACHLNOPSSSTYY	PSYCHOANALYSTS
AACEIMNOPRSTTU	STORM IN A TEACUP	AACIIIILLNRSTTY	INARTISTICALLY
AACEINNORSTTUU	INTRACUTANEOUS	AACIIILMNOPPST	MISAPPLICATION
AACEINOPRSSSST	CAST ASPERSIONS	AACIIILNOPRTTY	ANTICIPATORILY
AACEKLNNORSTUY	CANTANKEROUSLY	AACIIILNOPSSTT	PLASTICISATION
AACELLLOPPRRYY	POLYCARPELLARY	AACIIILNOPSTTZ	PLASTICIZATION
AACELLMNOOPRRY	MONOCARPELLARY	AACIIIMNOOSSST	ASSOCIATIONISM
AACELLMOPRRSUU	SUPRAMOLECULAR	AACIIILLMORSTY	MORALISTICALLY
AACELORSSSSTUU	ASSAULT COURSES	AACIIILLLRSTTUY	ALTRUISTICALLY
AACFFGIMNORRTY	FACTORY FARMING	AACIIILMOOPTTTU	AUTOMATIC PILOT
AACFFIIILNOSST	FALSIFICATIONS	AACIILNOOPRRST	CONSPIRATORIAL
AACFGHIIILRRSTT	LIGHT AIRCRAFTS	AACIILNORSTTU	STRATICULATION
AACFGIIIMNNOST	MAGNIFICATIONS	AACIILNPPPRRST	PRINCIPAL PARTS
AACFGIIINORSTT	GRATIFICATIONS	AACIILOPRSSTTY	SOCIALIST PARTY
AACFGILNNOORST	CONFLAGRATIONS	AACIINNOOSSSTT	ACTION STATIONS
AACFGILNORRTUV	VULGAR FRACTION	AACILLLLOOPRTY	ALLOTROPICALLY
AACFIIILNOQSTU	QUALIFICATIONS	AACILLLNORSTUY	ULTRASONICALLY
AACFIIIMMNNOOT	AMMONIFICATION	AACILLMNOORSTY	ASTRONOMICALLY
AACFIIINNOOPST	SAPONIFICATION	AACILLMOPSTTYY	ASYMPTOTICALLY
AACFIIINNOQTTU	QUANTIFICATION	AACINOOOPRRTTX	CORPORATION TAX
AACFIIINORSTTT	STRATIFICATION	AACINOOPRRRSTT	PROCRASTINATOR
AACFIIILLMORTTU	MULTIFACTORIAL	AACLLNNOPRTTUY	CONTRAPUNTALLY
AACFIIILORSSTTY	SATISFACTORILY	AADDDEEEEHHNRSS	HARD-HEADEDNESS
AACFINORSSTTUY	UNSATISFACTORY	AADDEEEELMPRSST	PADDLE STEAMERS
AACFLOOOPQRSTU	FOOLSCAP QUARTO	AADDEEFGHLOORS	FLOG A DEAD HORSE
AACGGILLLNOORY	LARYNGOLOGICAL	AADDEEGNRRSTUU	UNDERGRADUATES
AACGGILLMOSTYY	MYSTAGOGICALLY	AADDEEIILLNNOST	DENATIONALISED
AACGGILNNORTTU	CONGRATULATING	AADDEEIILLNNOTZ	DENATIONALIZED
AACGHHIILOOPRRT	ORTHOGRAPHICAL	AADDEELNOQRRSU	SQUADRON LEADER
AACGHHIMNNSTTW	NIGHT WATCHMANS	AADDEGGHHNRRSTU	GRANDDAUGHTERS
AACGHHMOOPRRTY	CHROMATOGRAPHY	AADDEGILNRSSSS	SALAD DRESSINGS
AACGHIIILLPRSST	CALLIGRAPHISTS	AADDEGINNRSTVW	GRANDSTAND VIEW

AADDHMNRSTUUYY	MAUNDY THURSDAY	AADEIILNNOPSST	DISPENSATIONAL
AADEEEFGIOPRST	PATE DE FOIE GRAS	AADEIILNOOPRST	DEPOLARISATION
AADEEEGKMNNRRT	MARKET GARDENER	AADEIILNOOPRTZ	DEPOLARIZATION
AADEEEHLLRTTTY	TETRAETHYL LEAD	AADEIILNORSSTT	DISSERTATIONAL
AADEEEHLRRRSSS	DRESS REHEARSAL	AADEEIIMNNORSSV	ANIMADVERSIONS
AADEEEILLLPPPR	PARALLELEPIPED	AADEILNNORTUUV	UNDERVALUATION
AADEEELMNRSSST	ELDER STATESMAN	AADEILNOOPSSST	AT ONE'S DISPOSAL
AADEEEMNNNNPRSY	PYRENEAN DESMAN	AADEINOPPPRRTU	UNAPPROPRIATED
AADEEFGHILMNRY	FLYING HEAD MARE	AADELLOPSSTTTU	SLOTTED SPATULA
AADEEFGILLLNOT	DINOFLAGELLATE	AADELMPRRSSTTU	MUSTARD PLASTER
AADEEFGLLNRRUV	GLANDULAR FEVER	AADFFGIIIILNST	DISAFFILIATING
AADEEFHILNRTTY	FAINT-HEARTEDLY	AADFFIIIILNOST	DISAFFILIATION
AADEEFIILNORST	FEDERALISATION	AADGGIINNOPPRZ	PROPAGANDIZING
AADEEFIILNORTZ	FEDERALIZATION	AADGIIIILNOSTT	DIGITALISATION
AADEEGGIMNNRST	AGGRANDISEMENT	AADGIIIILNOTTZ	DIGITALIZATION
AADEEGGIMNNRTZ	AGGRANDIZEMENT	AADIIILMNORSTT	TRADITIONALISM
AADEEGHILOPRRT	RADIOTELEGRAPH	AADIIILNORSTTT	TRADITIONALIST
AADEEGIMNNNRRST	DISARRANGEMENT	AADIIIMNNORSTT	ADMINISTRATION
AADEEGIMNPRSST	DISPARAGEMENTS	AADIIIMNRRSTTX	ADMINISTRATRIX
AADEEGINRSSTTT	TRADING ESTATES	AADIIMNORRSSTT	ADMINISTRATORS
AADEEHHIMPRSST	HEADMASTERSHIP	AAEEEFGMNNORRS	FERROMANGANESE
AADEEIILNPQSSU	SESQUIPEDALIAN	AAEEEGGGHINRTT	IN THE AGGREGATE
AADEEIINNPRRST	PREDESTINARIAN	AAEEEGHIMNOSST	HAEMATOGENESIS
AADEEIKLMOPRTV	EVAPORATED MILK	AAEEEGMNNPRRRT	PREARRANGEMENT
AADEEILNRRSTTT	TRANSLITERATED	AAEEEGMNNRRRST	REARRANGEMENTS
AADEEINNPRSSTT	ANTIDEPRESSANT	AAEEEHHIMRSSTT	THERMAESTHESIA
AADEEINNQSSTTU	ANTIQUATEDNESS	AAEEEHILPPRRST	PRE-RAPHAELITES
AADEEPRRSSTTUU	SUPERSATURATED	AAEEEINPRSSSTV	SEPARATIVENESS
AADEFFHLNOSSTV	STANDOFF HALVES	AAEEELNOPRSSTT	PERSONAL ESTATE
AADEFFIIILNSTU	DIVINE AFFLATUS	AAEEEMNNPRSTVW	PERMANENT WAVES
AADEFILMNNSTU	FUNDAMENTALISM	AAEEFFGNRSSSTT	STAFF SERGEANTS
AADEFILMNNSTTU	FUNDAMENTALIST	AAEEFFHIIMRTTV	THE AFFIRMATIVE
AADEFILMNNTTUY	FUNDAMENTALITY	AAEEFFILLNOOSV	AVAIL ONESELF OF
AADEGHILNRSTUW	DAUGHTERS-IN-LAW	AAEEFGIMNNORRS	FERROMAGNESIAN
AADEGIINNORRTT	INTERGRADATION	AAEEFHHLORSTTT	SALT OF THE EARTH
AADEGINOORRRTT	RETROGRADATION	AAEEFILNNRRSTT	TRANSFERENTIAL
AADEGOORRRRTTY	RETROGRADATORY	AAEEGGGILNRTXY	EXAGGERATINGLY
AADEHHKLLNNOOV	HOEK VAN HOLLAND	AAEEGHIINNSTTZ	ANAESTHETIZING
AADEHIILLMNPSU	SULPHANILAMIDE	AAEEGHLLMOPRRT	METALLOGRAPHER
AADEHIIMNNOSTU	DEHUMANISATION	AAEEGHLLNOOPTY	PALAEETHNOLOGY
AADEHIIMNNOTUZ	DEHUMANIZATION	AAEEGHLMNNOOPX	HAPAX LEGOMENON
AADEHIINNORSST	SHERARDISATION	AAEEGIILNNORST	GENERALISATION
AADEHIINNORSTZ	SHERARDIZATION	AAEEGIILNNORTZ	GENERALIZATION
AADEHIINPRSSST	DANISH PASTRIES	AAEEGIILNNOSTV	EVANGELISATION
AADEHIIOPRRSTT	RADIOTHERAPIST	AAEEGIILNNOTVZ	EVANGELIZATION
AADEHINNOPSSSU	DIAPHANOUSNESS	AAEEGILNPRSTXY	EXASPERATINGLY
AADEHORSSSTTUW	SOUTHEASTWARDS	AAEEGJMNORRSST	SERGEANT MAJORS
AADEEIIILNOSTTV	DEVITALISATION	AAEEGLMNPRSSTU	SUPRASEGMENTAL
AADEEIIILNOTTVZ	DEVITALIZATION	AAEEGLPPPRSSSU	PURPLE PASSAGES
AADEIIIMNRSTTV	ADMINISTRATIVE	AAEEGMNOPRSSSU	RAMPAGEOUSNESS
AADEIIKLRSSTTW	SIDEWALK ARTIST	AAEEGOPRRRSTTW	GREAT SPEARWORT
AADEIILMNNNOOT	DENOMINATIONAL	AAEEHIIMOOPSST	HAEMATOPOIESIS
AADEIILMNOORST	DEMORALISATION	AAEEHIMNRSSSTU	AMATEURISHNESS
AADEIILMNOORTZ	DEMORALIZATION	AAEEHINORSTTTW	WEATHER STATION

AAEEHMNOPRSTTU	APARTMENT HOUSE	AAEHILLMNOPSTT	MENTAL HOSPITAL
AAEEHMOOPRRRST	SPERMATORRHOEA	AAEHIMOPRSSSTT	MASSOTHERAPIST
AAEEIILLLRTTVY	ALLITERATIVELY	AAEHLMOOPPRRST	SPERMATOPHORAL
AAEEIIILMMPRSST	ALPES MARITIMES	AAEIIIKNNORSTT	KERATINISATION
AAEEIIILNNNORTT	INTERNATIONALE	AAEIIIKNNORTTZ	KERATINIZATION
AAEEIIILNNORSTT	ETERNALISATION	AAEIIIILLMMNNNRS	MILLENARIANISM
AAEEIIILNNORTTZ	ETERNALIZATION	AAEIIIILMNNORST	MINERALISATION
AAEEIKLNRRSSTU	KAISERSLAUTERN	AAEIIILMNNORTZ	MINERALIZATION
AAEEILNNOPRSTT	PRESENTATIONAL	AAEIIILNORSSST	SERIALISATIONS
AAEEILNNPRRTTY	INTERPLANETARY	AAEIIILNORSSTZ	SERIALIZATIONS
AAEEIMNPRSTTTV	PAVEMENT ARTIST	AAEIIILNORSTTV	REVITALISATION
AAEEINNOPSSSSS	PASSIONATENESS	AAEIIILNORTTVZ	REVITALIZATION
AAEEINRRSSTTTW	WATER-RESISTANT	AAEIIIMMPRSSST	SEMIPARASITISM
AAEEKMMNPRSSTU	AMUSEMENT PARKS	AAEIIINNNRSSST	INSANITARINESS
AAEELNNNPSSSTU	UNPLEASANTNESS	AAEIIINNPPRTTT	PINNATIPARTITE
AAEEMQRRRSSTTU	QUARTERMASTERS	AAEIIILLNNORSTT	REINSTALLATION
AAEFFFFGIINORRS	FOREIGN AFFAIRS	AAEIIILMNNOSSST	SENSATIONALISM
AAEFFIIMNORRST	REAFFIRMATIONS	AAEIIILMNOOPRST	OPERATIONALISM
AAEFGLLNOOPRTT	FORE-TOPGALLANT	AAEIIILMNOPRRST	PROLETARIANISM
AAEFHHMMOOTTTU	FOAM AT THE MOUTH	AAEIIILMNSSTYZZ	MIZZEN STAYSAIL
AAEFHINNORRRST	FINSTERAARHORN	AAEIIILMOPQRRTU	IMPERIAL QUARTO
AAEFIIIMNNOSSTT	MANIFESTATIONS	AAEIIILNNNORST	INTERNATIONALS
AAEFIIINNORRST	FRATERNISATION	AAEIIILNNORSTTU	NEUTRALISATION
AAEFIIINNORRTTZ	FRATERNIZATION	AAEIIILNNORTTUZ	NEUTRALIZATION
AAEFILOPPRRSST	PLASTER OF PARIS	AAEIIILNNOSSSTT	SENSATIONALIST
AAEFIMNORRSTTV	TRANSFORMATIVE	AAEIIILNQTTTUVY	QUANTITATIVELY
AAEFLLNOPRRRUU	FUNERAL PARLOUR	AAEIIMOPPPRRST	MISAPPROPRIATE
AAEGGGGLNNORSTU	STRONG LANGUAGE	AAEIINNORSSSTT	STATIONARINESS
AAEGGGHIILMNNTU	HAEMAGGLUTININ	AAEIINNPPRRSTT	ANTIPERSPIRANT
AAEGGIINNORRST	GRANGERISATION	AAEIINOPRSSTTU	PASTEURISATION
AAEGGIINNORRTZ	GRANGERIZATION	AAEIINOPRSTTUZ	PASTEURIZATION
AAEGGILMNOORST	AGGLOMERATIONS	AAEIKKKLMNRSSU	KAMENSK-URALSKI
AAEGGILMNOSSYZ	GLOSSY MAGAZINE	AAEILLLLMORRST	LAMELLIROSTRAL
AAEGHHIKMRRSTW	HIGH WATER MARKS	AAEILLLLMRTTUY	MULTILATERALLY
AAEGHIILLNRTXY	EXHILARATINGLY	AAEILMOOPPRSTT	SPATIOTEMPORAL
AAEGHILMNRRTWY	HEARTWARMINGLY	AAEILNORRRSTTT	TRANSLITERATOR
AAEGIIIILLLNOST	ILLEGALISATION	AAEILNORSSTTWY	SANITARY TOWELS
AAEGIIIILLLNOTZ	ILLEGALIZATION	AAEIMNORSSTTT	STATIONMASTERS
AAEGIIIILNNOSTT	GELATINISATION	AAEINNNOPRSTUU	SUPERANNUATION
AAEGIIIILNNOTTZ	GELATINIZATION	AAELLNPRRSTUUY	SUPERNATURALLY
AAEGIIILLNOORST	ALLEGORISATION	AAELMNSSSSTTYY	SYSTEMS ANALYST
AAEGIIILLNOORTZ	ALLEGORIZATION	AAENNNOPPRSSST	NANSEN PASSPORT
AAEGIIILNORRSTT	REGISTRATIONAL	AAFGIILLMNNNPY	FAMILY PLANNING
AAEGIIILNORRSTU	REGULARISATION	AAFIIIMNNORRTU	UNIFORMITARIAN
AAEGIIILNORRTUZ	REGULARIZATION	AAFIILLMMNORTY	INFLAMMATORILY
AAEGIIMNRRSTTV	TRANSMIGRATIVE	AAFIMNNOORRSTT	TRANSFORMATION
AAEGIIINNNRSSSU	SANGUINARINESS	AAGGHINOOPRRST	ORGANOGRAPHIST
AAEGIIINNOORRST	REORGANISATION	AAGGIIIILNNRTTY	INGRATIATINGLY
AAEGIIINNOORRTZ	REORGANIZATION	AAGGILMMOORSTT	GRAMMATOLOGIST
AAEGIILMNOOPRST	SPERMATOGONIAL	AAGHIIIINOPRSTT	GRAPHITISATION
AAEGIILNOOPRSTT	PROGESTATIONAL	AAGHIIIINOPRTTZ	GRAPHITIZATION
AAEGIMNNRRTTTY	MATERNITY GRANT	AAGHIILMNORSTT	ANTILOGARITHMS
AAEHHIILLOPSTUZ	SULPHATHIAZOLE	AAGIIIMNOSSTTT	STIGMATISATION
AAEHIIIMNNSSTT	ANTIHISTAMINES	AAGIIIMNOSTTTZ	STIGMATIZATION

AAGIIILNORSSTUV	VULGARISATIONS
AAGIIILNORSTUVZ	VULGARIZATIONS
AAGIILOOPRSSTT	PARASITOLOGIST
AAGIIMNNORRSTT	TRANSMIGRATION
AAGILMNOOPRSTV	GALVANOTROPISM
AAGIMNORRRSTTY	TRANSMIGRATORY
AAHHIIMOPRRSST	AMPHIARTHROSIS
AAHIINNORSSTTU	AUTHORISATIONS
AAHIINOORSTTUZ	AUTHORIZATIONS
AAHILMOPPRRSTY	AMPHIPROSTYLAR
AAHILNOOOPRRTT	PROTHONOTARIAL
AAHILNORRSTTUY	NATURAL HISTORY
AAHINOPSSSSSTT	SHOP ASSISTANTS
AAHLLOPPSSTTYY	STAPHYLOPLASTY
AAIIIIILNNOSTT	INITIALISATION
AAIIIIILNNOTTZ	INITIALIZATION
AAIIIILMNORSTT	MILITARISATION
AAIIIILMNORTTZ	MILITARIZATION
AAIIIILMNRSTTU	UTILITARIANISM
AAIIIILNORSSTV	TRIVIALISATION
AAIIIILNORTTVZ	TRIVIALIZATION
AAIIIILLNOOSTTV	VOLATILISATION
AAIIIILLNOOTTVZ	VOLATILIZATION
AAIIINNOOSSTTU	AUTOIONISATION
AAIIINNOOOTTUZ	AUTOIONIZATION
AAIIJLNNOORSTU	JOURNALISATION
AAIIJLNNOORTUZ	JOURNALIZATION
AAIILLLNORSTTU	ILLUSTRATIONAL
AAIILLMNNOSTTU	MULTINATIONALS
AAIILLMOOPPSST	PAPILLOMATOSIS
AAIILLNNORSTTY	TRANSITIONALLY
AAIILNOOPPRSTU	POPULARISATION
AAIILNOOPPRTUZ	POPULARIZATION
AAIIMNOOPPRSTX	APPROXIMATIONS
AAIINOOPPPRRST	APPROPRIATIONS
AAIKMNOOQRSTTU	QUOTATION MARKS
AAILMMNNORSTTU	ULTRAMONTANISM
AAILMNNORSTTTU	ULTRAMONTANIST
AAIMNNORSTTTUU	TRANSMUTATIONS
AAINNOOPRRSTTT	TRANSPORTATION
ABBBEEEISSSTTTU	TEST-TUBE BABIES
ABBCDEEEEIORRSU	BERBERIDACEOUS
ABBCEHILNORSTU	BRONCHIAL TUBES
ABBCEHKOORRSSS	SHOCK ABSORBERS
ABBCEIIJLSTTUY	SUBJECTABILITY
ABBCEIKLLLRRYY	BLACKBERRY LILY
ABBCGHILLNOORU	RUBBING ALCOHOL
ABBDDEEEELORSTU	DOUBLE-BREASTED
ABBDEEFNORSSTU	BEASTS OF BURDEN
ABBDEILLNORSTU	BULLETIN BOARDS
ABBDIIIILNTTUY	INDUBITABILITY
ABBEEEEFHLLLLOT	BELLE OF THE BALL
ABBEEEELNORSSSV	OBSERVABLENESS
ABBEEFHNORRTTU	BEAR THE BRUNT OF
ABBEEHINNOOPRT	PHENOBARBITONE
ABBEGHIIILOPRS	BIBLIOGRAPHIES
ABBEGHIIILOPRRS	BIBLIOGRAPHERS
ABBEGIMNPRRSTU	RUBBER-STAMPING
ABCCCEEIIMMNRU	CIRCUMAMBIENCE
ABCCCEIORSTUUU	CUCURBITACEOUS
ABCCDEEHOPRSST	BATCH PROCESSED
ABCCDEHILNSSUW	CLUB SANDWICHES
ABCCDIILLMORSU	UMBILICAL CORDS
ABCCEEEEELRSSU	CAUSES CELEBRES
ABCCEEEELORRRTX	CEREBRAL CORTEX
ABCCEEFHILNOST	CHIEF CONSTABLE
ABCCEEIIKRRRTU	CIRCUIT BREAKER
ABCCEEIILLNORR	IRRECONCILABLE
ABCCEEIILLNRTYY	CYBERNETICALLY
ABCCEEILMMNOUX	EXCOMMUNICABLE
ABCCEEILNNOORT	CONCELEBRATION
ABCCEHIINORSST	BRONCHIECTASIS
ABCCEHIKLNPSST	PITCH-BLACKNESS
ABCCEIILLMORSS	SOCIAL CLIMBERS
ABCCEIILLNORRY	IRRECONCILABLY
ABCCEIILMMNNOU	INCOMMUNICABLE
ABCCEIILNNPSUU	PUBLIC NUISANCE
ABCCEILNNNOOSU	UNCONSCIONABLE
ABCCGINNORSTTU	SUBCONTRACTING
ABCCHHIIOPRRSS	ARCHBISHOPRICS
ABCCHILOOPRSTU	CLAUSTROPHOBIC
ABCCILNNNOOSUY	UNCONSCIONABLY
ABCCNOORRSSTTU	SUBCONTRACTORS
ABCDEEEEEFHMMMR	FEMME DE CHAMBRE
ABCDEEEEILNSSV	DECEIVABLENESS
ABCDEEEEELLNSST	DELECTABLENESS
ABCDEEEHIILNPR	INDECIPHERABLE
ABCDEEEIIILRSSV	DISSERVICEABLE
ABCDEEEEILNRSST	CREDITABLENESS
ABCDEEEILPRSST	DISRESPECTABLE
ABCDEEELLOOORT	COLORADO BEETLE
ABCDEEGIKNORRR	RECORD-BREAKING
ABCDEEHIILNPRY	INDECIPHERABLY
ABCDEEHILPSTTT	PITCHED BATTLES
ABCDEEIILNNORS	INCONSIDERABLE
ABCDEGIIIILPRTY	CREDIBILITY GAP
ABCDEIIIILPRTTY	PREDICTABILITY
ABCDEIILNNOSTY	CONDENSABILITY
ABCDEIMNNOOOORX	CARBON MONOXIDE
ABCDENOOOORRRTU	UNCORROBORATED
ABCDGHILNOOORS	BOARDING SCHOOL
ABCDIIIILOSSTY	DISSOCIABILITY
ABCEEEHMMRRRST	CHARTER MEMBERS
ABCEEFIILNORTY	ENFORCEABILITY
ABCEEGHIKLOORT	GLOBE ARTICHOKE
ABCEEGIIILLNOTY	BIOGENETICALLY
ABCEEGIINORSUZ	ZINGIBERACEOUS
ABCEEGILNNORUZ	UNRECOGNIZABLE

ABCEEGKKOORRST	STOCKBROKERAGE	ABDDEEEEHLLNSSU	BULLHEADEDNESS
ABCEEGKNNOOSTW	GET ONE'S OWN BACK	ABDDEEHIILSSST	DISESTABLISHED
ABCEEHHHRTTTUY	BURY THE HATCHET	ABDDEEEHLLORSSU	SHOULDER BLADES
ABCEEHIIKSTTTU	TAKE THE BISCUIT	ABDDEEEHLNOOSTU	DOUBLET AND HOSE
ABCEEHIJKNOSTX	JACK-IN-THE-BOXES	ABDDEEIIJLMNOU	DIAMOND JUBILEE
ABCEEHIMNRSSTY	CHIMNEYBREASTS	ABDDEEEILMNNSTY	ABSENT-MINDEDLY
ABCEEHIOOPRSUU	EUPHORBIACEOUS	ABDDEEMMNNOOSTU	METES AND BOUNDS
ABCEEIIIILPRTVY	PERCEIVABILITY	ABDDGINNOORSSU	SOUNDING BOARDS
ABCEEIIIILRSTVY	SERVICEABILITY	ABDEEEEILNRSST	DELIBERATENESS
ABCEEIILORRTVY	RECOVERABILITY	ABDEEEFFIILNRT	DIFFERENTIABLE
ABCEEIILPRSTTY	RESPECTABILITY	ABDEEEFLORSTUU	DOUBLE FEATURES
ABCEEILNNSTUUY	SUBLIEUTENANCY	ABDEEEGHIIRTVW	GIVE A WIDE BERTH
ABCEEILRRSSTTU	BATTLE CRUISERS	ABDEEEGILNRSST	SINGLE-BREASTED
ABCEEMMMNORSUU	MUCOUS MEMBRANE	ABDEEEIILMNNRT	INDETERMINABLE
ABCEFGIIILLNNST	FILING CABINETS	ABDEEEIMNNOOTV	ABOVE-MENTIONED
ABCEFGIIILMMNRS	CLIMBING FRAMES	ABDEEEELLNOPRSS	DEPLORABLENESS
ABCEGHIMNNSSUU	SUBMACHINE GUNS	ABDEEFIIIILNNTU	UNIDENTIFIABLE
ABCEGIIJNRSSTU	SUBJECT-RAISING	ABDEEFIOOPSSTX	SAFE-DEPOSIT BOX
ABCEGIILOORSTT	BACTERIOLOGIST	ABDEEGHIOSTWYY	GO BY THE WAYSIDE
ABCEGILNNORSWW	BROWN LACEWINGS	ABDEEGILNRSSST	DRESSING TABLES
ABCEGINORRSSSZ	ZEBRA CROSSINGS	ABDEEHIIILRTTY	HEREDITABILITY
ABCEHIILRSTTTY	STRETCHABILITY	ABDEEIILLRSSTU	LIBERAL STUDIES
ABCEHILLLOPRYY	HYPERBOLICALLY	ABDEEIILMNNRTY	INDETERMINABLY
ABCEHILORRSTTY	ERYTHROBLASTIC	ABDEEIILNNNSTV	VENETIAN BLINDS
ABCEHIMORSSSTX	CHRISTMAS BOXES	ABDEFIINNOSTUU	SUBINFEUDATION
ABCEIIILLNTTUY	INELUCTABILITY	ABDEFINORSTUUY	SUBINFEUDATORY
ABCEIIILNSTUXY	INEXCUSABILITY	ABDEFMOOORRSTW	FROM BAD TO WORSE
ABCEIIILORRTVY	IRREVOCABILITY	ABDEGHINOORSSU	BOARDINGHOUSES
ABCEIINOOPSSUV	ABOVE SUSPICION	ABDEGHLMNORTUU	ROUGH-AND-TUMBLE
ABCEIILLLMOORTY	BOLOMETRICALLY	ABDEGIIILLNNRRY	LENDING LIBRARY
ABCEIILLLPSSTTU	PLASTIC BULLETS	ABDEHHLMNRSSTU	RHYTHM AND BLUES
ABCEIILLMNOPSUU	PNEUMOBACILLUS	ABDEHLMNNORRTU	NORTHUMBERLAND
ABCEIILLMNOSSSY	SYMBOLICALNESS	ABDEIIIILMNOOST	DEMOBILISATION
ABCEIILMNNOOSSU	NO-CLAIM BONUSES	ABDEIIIILMNOOTZ	DEMOBILIZATION
ABCEIILNNNOSTTU	SUBCONTINENTAL	ABDEIIILNPSSTY	DISPENSABILITY
ABCELLLNNOORTU	UNCONTROLLABLE	ABDEIIILNRSTUY	UNDESIRABILITY
ABCELNOSSTUUUY	SUBCUTANEOUSLY	ABDEIIIINRSSSU	SUBSIDIARINESS
ABCEMMMNOORSUU	MUCOMEMBRANOUS	ABDEIILNOORSTW	BOWDLERISATION
ABCFFFLMOOORTY	COMFORTABLY OFF	ABDEIILNOORTWZ	BOWDLERIZATION
ABCFIIILMNOORTY	CONFORMABILITY	ABDEILLMNNOPTU	PLATINUM BLONDE
ABCGIIILLMOOOTY	BIOCLIMATOLOGY	ABDEILLMOPRUWY	UPWARDLY-MOBILE
ABCGIILNOOPSST	SPONGIOBLASTIC	ABDEILLNOOORST	BLOOD RELATIONS
ABCGIKLNORSSTT	STARTING BLOCKS	ABDEILMORSTUXY	AMBIDEXTROUSLY
ABCHIIILNOTTUUY	UNTOUCHABILITY	ABDEILRRRSTWWY	WILD STRAWBERRY
ABCHILMOOPRSTT	THROMBOPLASTIC	ABDGHIMNOOSTTU	DOUBTING THOMAS
ABCIIIIJLSTTUY	JUSTICIABILITY	ABDGIIILOOORST	RADIOBIOLOGIST
ABCIIIILLLOPSTY	COLLAPSIBILITY	ABDGIIKNORSST	SKIRTING BOARDS
ABCIIIILNRSTTUY	INSCRUTABILITY	ABDIIIILMNOTTY	INDOMITABILITY
ABCIILLMNOSTYY	SYMBIONTICALLY	ABDIIIILLOSSTVY	DISSOLVABILITY
ABCIILMNNOSSTU	SOMNAMBULISTIC	ABDIIILNORSTTU	DISTRIBUTIONAL
ABCIILNOORRTTU	CONTRIBUTORIAL	ABDIIOOOPRSSSU	BASIDIOSPOROUS
ABCILMNORSTUUY	RAMBUNCTIOUSLY	ABDMOOOORRSTTU	OUTBOARD MOTORS
ABCIMNNNOOOOPS	BOON COMPANIONS	ABEEEEFGIKLNTV	VEGETABLE KNIFE
ABDDEEEFGHINRT	FEATHERBEDDING	ABEEEFFILNNOOS	BANE OF ONE'S LIFE

ABEEEEFILNNRRTT	ENFANT TERRIBLE
ABEEEGHHIMNSTV	MIGHT-HAVE-BEENS
ABEEEEHLNRSSSST	BREATHLESSNESS
ABEEEIKKRRRSST	STRIKEBREAKERS
ABEEEEIMMPRRSTV	PRIVATE MEMBERS
ABEEEINORRRSTV	REVERBERATIONS
ABEEEELNNOPRSSS	PERSONABLENESS
ABEEFIILMNRTTY	FERMENTABILITY
ABEEGHIILNSTUX	EXTINGUISHABLE
ABEEGHILMMNOOT	METHAEMOGLOBIN
ABEEGHLORSSRTTT	GHETTO BLASTERS
ABEEGIIKKNRRST	STRIKEBREAKING
ABEEGILNRRSSST	TRANSGRESSIBLE
ABEEGNOORRRTTU	TURBOGENERATOR
ABEEHILMNSSSTT	ESTABLISHMENTS
ABEEHILNOPSSST	HOSPITABLENESS
ABEEHLNNOORSSU	HONOURABLENESS
ABEEHLOORTTTTW	HOT-WATER BOTTLE
ABEEIIILMMPRTY	IMPERMEABILITY
ABEEIIILRRTTVY	RETRIEVABILITY
ABEEIILMNNOSSU	EMISSION NEBULA
ABEEIILMNOPRSS	IMPRESSIONABLE
ABEEIILMNRRTUY	REMUNERABILITY
ABEEIILPRRSTVY	PRESERVABILITY
ABEEILMNNNOSTU	UNMENTIONABLES
ABEEILNNOQSTUU	UNQUESTIONABLE
ABEEILNNSSTTUU	SUBLIEUTENANTS
ABEEILRRRSSTTU	SUBTERRESTRIAL
ABEEIMNOSSSSTU	ABSTEMIOUSNESS
ABEEKLNNNOSSUW	UNKNOWABLENESS
ABEFGIIILNNRTY	REFRANGIBILITY
ABEFIIIILRRTTUY	IRREFUTABILITY
ABEFILNOOPRSST	SELF-ABSORPTION
ABEGGHHINORRTU	ROUGH BREATHING
ABEGHILMNOOOXY	OXYHAEMOGLOBIN
ABEGHLMNNRSSTU	BREMSSTRAHLUNG
ABEGIIIILMNPRTY	IMPREGNABILITY
ABEGIILORRSSTY	GYROSTABILISER
ABEGIILORRSTYZ	GYROSTABILIZER
ABEHIIIILNRTTY	INHERITABILITY
ABEHIIILSTTUXY	EXHAUSTIBILITY
ABEIIIILMNSTTY	INESTIMABILITY
ABEIIILLNORTTY	INTOLERABILITY
ABEIIILMNNRTUY	INNUMERABILITY
ABEIIILMORRTVY	IRREMOVABILITY
ABEIIILNPRSTUY	INSUPERABILITY
ABEIILMNOPRSSY	IMPRESSIONABLY
ABEIIMNOPRRTTU	IMPERTURBATION
ABEIINNORRTTTUV	NONATTRIBUTIVE
ABEILMNORRSSTU	INSURMOUNTABLE
ABEILNNOQSTUUY	UNQUESTIONABLY
ABEILNORSSSSUU	SALUBRIOUSNESS
ABFGIIIILLNNRTY	INFRANGIBILITY
ABFIIIIILRRTTVY	VITRIFIABILITY

ABFIIIIJLSTTUY	JUSTIFIABILITY
ABFIIIILNOSSTY	FISSIONABILITY
ABHIIIKLNNTTUY	UNTHINKABILITY
ABHIIINOOPRRTY	PROHIBITIONARY
ABHIIINOORSTVY	VASOINHIBITORY
ABHILLMNOPSTTU	PUT IN MOTHBALLS
ABHILMNOOPRSTT	THROMBOPLASTIN
ABIIIIILLLMRTTY	ILLIMITABILITY
ABIIIILLMPSTUY	IMPLAUSIBILITY
ABIIIILMMNOOST	IMMOBILISATION
ABIIIILMMNOOTZ	IMMOBILIZATION
ABIIIIMNNOSTTU	BITUMINISATION
ABIIIIMNNOTTUZ	BITUMINIZATION
ABIILOPPRSTTUY	SUPPORTABILITY
ACCCDEIIIILNOR	RICINOLEIC ACID
ACCCDEINORSTTU	CREDIT ACCOUNTS
ACCCEEEIILLNPS	SPECIAL LICENCE
ACCCEEHILLNORV	VICE-CHANCELLOR
ACCCEEIILNOSSS	SOCIAL SCIENCES
ACCCEENNOOOVVX	CONVEXO-CONCAVE
ACCCEFFIILRRST	TRAFFIC CIRCLES
ACCCEFINOOPRRT	TROPIC OF CANCER
ACCCEHHILMOPSY	PSYCHOCHEMICAL
ACCCEHIINORSTT	ARCHITECTONICS
ACCCEIMMNOOORS	MACROECONOMICS
ACCCENNORRTTUU	CURRENT ACCOUNT
ACCCHIIOOPSSTT	TACHISTOSCOPIC
ACCCHLOOPSSTUY	STAPHYLOCOCCUS
ACCCIIKKLOSSTT	COCKTAIL STICKS
ACCCILLOSSSSUU	LOCUS CLASSICUS
ACCCILNOOSSSSU	CLASS-CONSCIOUS
ACCDDDEKLOOOOO	COCK-A-DOODLE-DOO
ACCDEEEELNOPRS	PREADOLESCENCE
ACCDEEEHHIKNRT	CHICKENHEARTED
ACCDEEFILNNSTU	SELF-INDUCTANCE
ACCDEEHINRRRSU	HARD CURRENCIES
ACCDEEIILLLRTY	DIELECTRICALLY
ACCDEEIILMMORS	COMMERCIALISED
ACCDEEIILMMORZ	COMMERCIALIZED
ACCDEEILMNORTY	DYNAMOELECTRIC,
ELECTRODYNAMIC	
ACCDEEILNNNSTY	INCANDESCENTLY
ACCDEEILNOPSTU	CONCEPTUALISED
ACCDEEILNOPTUZ	CONCEPTUALIZED
ACCDEEILOORRST	CROCODILE TEARS
ACCDEEIMMNNOTUX	EXCOMMUNICATED
ACCDEEIMNOPPTY	APPENDICECTOMY
ACCDEEINNNOSTU	DISCOUNTENANCE
ACCDEELLMOSTUW	WELL-ACCUSTOMED
ACCDEFILLNOOTU	DEFLOCCULATION
ACCDEFNNOORTUU	UNACCOUNTED-FOR
ACCDEHHIMNORSY	HYDROMECHANICS
ACCDEHILMNOPSU	UNACCOMPLISHED
ACCDEHINORSSUW	SANDWICH COURSE

ACCDEHKLNOORTU	AROUND THE CLOCK
ACCDEIILLNNOTY	COINCIDENTALLY
ACCDEIINNNOSTU	DISCONTINUANCE
ACCDEINOOPSTTU	DEPOSIT ACCOUNT
ACCDHHINOOPRSY	HYPOCHONDRIACS
ACCDHIIIMMORST	DICHROMATICISM
ACCDHIMNOPSSYY	PSYCHODYNAMICS
ACCDIILNNOOPTU	CONDUPLICATION
ACCDIINNOORSTT	CONTRADICTIONS
ACCDILNOORRSTU	CONDUCTOR RAILS
ACCEEEEFFHKLOST	COFFEE KLATCHES
ACCEEEEFILNPTXY	LIFE EXPECTANCY
ACCEEEGHIRRSSV	SERVICE CHARGES
ACCEEEHILLMNPY	MYELENCEPHALIC
ACCEEEILOPSTVY	ESCAPE VELOCITY
ACCEEEILPRRSWY	CREEPY-CRAWLIES
ACCEEELLMOPRTX	ELECTRA COMPLEX
ACCEEELLNORTVY	ELECTROVALENCY
ACCEEENNOPSTUX	EXPENSE ACCOUNT
ACCEEEORRSSTUW	WORCESTER SAUCE
ACCEEFFHHNNOOT	ON THE OFF CHANCE
ACCEEFILLMORTV	COLLECTIVE FARM
ACCEEFIMORRRTT	REFRACTOMETRIC
ACCEEGHILOPRRT	ELECTROGRAPHIC
ACCEEGHKNOSSTX	STOCK EXCHANGES
ACCEEGILLNORTY	EGOCENTRICALLY,
GEOCENTRICALLY	
ACCEEHHIILNNPR	RHINENCEPHALIC
ACCEEHHIILMMORT	THERMOCHEMICAL
ACCEEHHLOORSST	SCHOOLTEACHERS
ACCEEHIIILNLST	TECHNICALITIES
ACCEEHILMOPRST	PETROCHEMICALS
ACCEEHKLNORRTU	ROCKET-LAUNCHER
ACCEEHORRSSTTY	OYSTERCATCHERS
ACCEEIILORSSSV	SOCIAL SERVICES
ACCEEIIMNNOORT	ECONOMETRICIAN
ACCEEIINNOORSS	CONCESSIONAIRE
ACCEEIKLNOPRSS	COCKER SPANIELS
ACCEEILLLNORTY	ELECTRONICALLY
ACCEEILLLOPSTY	TELESCOPICALLY
ACCEEILORSSTTT	ELECTROSTATICS
ACCEEILORSSTUU	STERCULIACEOUS
ACCEEINOPRSTTV	CONTRACEPTIVES
ACCEFGGHHIINNT	FIGHTING CHANCE
ACCEFGIIIINNNS	INSIGNIFICANCE
ACCEFIIIILLNSTY	SCIENTIFICALLY
ACCEFIIINOPSST	SPECIFICATIONS
ACCEFIIINORSTT	RECTIFICATIONS
ACCEGHIIILLNNOU	HALLUCINOGENIC
ACCEGHIIIMNNPRR	PRINCE CHARMING
ACCEGHIOPPRRST	SPECTROGRAPHIC
ACCEGIILNRTUXY	EXCRUCIATINGLY
ACCEGIKLLNOOTU	COCKTAIL LOUNGE
ACCEGILLMMOORY	MYRMECOLOGICAL

ACCEGIOPPRRSTU	GROUP PRACTICES
ACCEHHORRSSSTT	RORSCHACH TESTS
ACCEHIKLLMOORY	MOCK-HEROICALLY
ACCEHILLOOPSSS	SPECIAL SCHOOLS
ACCEHILMMNOPST	ACCOMPLISHMENT
ACCEHILMOOPRSU	MICROCEPHALOUS
ACCEHILOORSSTU	HORATIUS COCLES
ACCEIIILNNOORT	RECONCILIATION
ACCEIIILNOORRT	ONEIROCRITICAL
ACCEIIILLMOORSY	SERIOCOMICALLY
ACCEIIILLOPPRSY	PERISCOPICALLY
ACCEIIILNOORRTY	RECONCILIATORY
ACCEIILORSSTUY	SOCIAL SECURITY
ACCEIINNOORSTT	CONCRETISATION
ACCEIINNOORTTZ	CONCRETIZATION
ACCEIINOPRSSSU	CAPRICIOUSNESS
ACCEILLMNNOOUY	UNECONOMICALLY
ACCEILNOORSSST	CROSS-SECTIONAL
ACCEIMMNOORTUX	EXCOMMUNICATOR
ACCEINNNOORSTT	CONCENTRATIONS
ACCEINOORSTTTU	COUNTERACTIONS
ACCEINOOPPRSTU	PREOCCUPATIONS
ACCEINOPPRSSSU	PERCUSSION CAPS
ACCFFIIINORTTU	FRUCTIFICATION
ACCFIIIIILNOST	SILICIFICATION
ACCFIMMNNOOORT	COMMON FRACTION
ACCGHIILLOOPRS	OSCILLOGRAPHIC
ACCGHIILLOORST	CHRISTOLOGICAL
ACCGHILOPRSSUY	PSYCHOSURGICAL
ACCGHINOOPPRSY	PHARYNGOSCOPIC
ACCGIIILLMNNOOR	CRIMINOLOGICAL
ACCGILLLLOOOSY	SOCIOLOGICALLY
ACCHHILOPPSSYY	PSYCHOPHYSICAL
ACCHHIMOOOPRRT	CHROMATOPHORIC
ACCHHIMOOORRTT	ORTHOCHROMATIC
ACCHIIILNORSTT	ANTICHLORISTIC
ACCHIIINNNOOST	CINCHONISATION
ACCHIIINNNOOTZ	CINCHONIZATION
ACCHIILOPRTYY	HYPOCRITICALLY
ACCHILLNNORSYY	SYNCHRONICALLY
ACCHIMOOPSSSTY	PSYCHOSOMATICS
ACCIIIILLOOOPST	SOCIOPOLITICAL
ACCIILNNOOPRST	CONSCRIPTIONAL
ACCIIMMNNOOSTU	COMMUNICATIONS
ACCIIMNNORTTUU	CIRCUMNUTATION
ACCILLOPPRRTYY	PROCRYPTICALLY
ACCILMNOOSTUUY	CONTUMACIOUSLY
ACCILNNOOSTTUU	CONSTRUCTIONAL
ACDDDEEIILMNST	MIDDLE-DISTANCE
ACDDEEEKMNOPRS	PROMENADE DECKS
ACDDEEGILNNNOR	ENDOCRINE GLAND
ACDDEGLLNSSSTU	DUCTLESS GLANDS
ACDDEIIINNNOORT	AIR-CONDITIONED
ACDDELMMMNOOSU	COMMAND MODULES

ACDEEEEEINSSTTV	STATE'S EVIDENCE	ACDEGHIMNORRS	MARCHING ORDERS
ACDEEEHINRRSUV	UNDERACHIEVERS	ACDEGHIMNORSTY	HYDROMAGNETICS
ACDEEEHNORSSSY	DO THE NECESSARY	ACDEGHINNORSTU	COUNTERSHADING
ACDEEEHORRSSTU	TERRACED HOUSES	ACDEGIILLLOOOY	IDEOLOOGICALLY
ACDEEEIIMNNPTT	PATENT MEDICINE	ACDEGIILLOOPRT	PTERIDOLOGICAL
ACDEEEILOOPRST	RADIO TELESCOPE	ACDEGIILLOOSTT	DIALECTOLOGIST
ACDEEEIMNOPPST	APPENDECTOMIES	ACDEGILNNNRSTY	TRANSCENDINGLY
ACDEEEINNOPQRU	EQUIPONDERANCE	ACDEGIMMNNNORSW	WING COMMANDERS
ACDEEEENRRRSTUY	UNDERSECRETARY	ACDEGIMNNNORTU	COUNTERMANDING
ACDEEFFIMORRTT	DIFFRACTOMETER	ACDEGINOOPRSTT	PROGNOSTICATED
ACDEEFGIILMNST	MAGNETIC FIELDS	ACDEGMMNNOOORR	COMMON-OR-GARDEN
ACDEEFHIINNRSS	DISENFRANCHISE	ACDEHHIILOORTZ	CHLOROTHIAZIDE
ACDEEFHORRSSTW	CHEST OF DRAWERS	ACDEHHIIMOPRRT	HERMAPHRODITIC
ACDEEFINNOORST	CONFEDERATIONS	ACDEHHILNPRSSS	SHIP'S CHANDLERS
ACDEEFINOQRRUY	RADIO FREQUENCY	ACDEHIILLMMOTY	IMMETHODICALLY
ACDEEFNORRRSTW	CENTRE FORWARDS	ACDEHIILLOPRSY	SPHEROIDICALLY
ACDEEGHIIIMNNVV	VENDING MACHINE	ACDEHIIMORRSTY	RADIOCHEMISTRY
ACDEEGHIINNRUV	UNDERACHIEVING	ACDEHILLMOPRYY	HYPODERMICALLY
ACDEEGHIKNNRST	KITCHEN GARDENS	ACDEHILLNOPTYY	ENDOPHYTICALLY
ACDEEGHILLRSTY	CLEAR-SIGHTEDLY	ACDEHILMOOPPRR	CHLORPROPAMIDE
ACDEEGHILOOSSW	WILD-GOOSE CHASE	ACDEHIMMNORSTY	THERMODYNAMICS
ACDEEGIILNNRTZ	DECENTRALIZING	ACDEHINOORRSTT	TRISOCTAHEDRON
ACDEEGIIMNORRS	ORGANISED CRIME	ACDEHLOOOPPRSV	APPROVED SCHOOL
ACDEEGIIMNORRZ	ORGANIZED CRIME	ACDEIIIIMNNRST	INDISCRIMINATE
ACDEEGIINORSTT	STAGE DIRECTION	ACDEIIILNNORTU	UNIDIRECTIONAL
ACDEEGILNNOQRU	GRANDILOQUENCE	ACDEIIILNNSTTW	IDENTICAL TWINS
ACDEEGIMNNORSU	DISCOURAGEMENT	ACDEIIILNORTTY	DIRECTIONALITY
ACDEEGKLMNNOTW	ACKNOWLEDGMENT	ACDEIIINORSSSY	IDIOSYNCRASIES
ACDEEHIIINNRST	DISINHERITANCE	ACDEIIKLRSSTTW	WILDCAT STRIKES
ACDEEHIIKMNNSY	KIDNEY MACHINES	ACDEIILLMNPRTU	PNEUMATIC DRILL
ACDEEHILMNOSST	METHODICALNESS	ACDEIILLMOORTY	IODOMETRICALLY
ACDEEHIMNNSTT	DISENCHANTMENT	ACDEIILNNOOOST	DECOLONISATION
ACDEEHINNOPSSW	OPEN SANDWICHES	ACDEIILNNOOOTZ	DECOLONIZATION
ACDEEHINPRSSSS	CASH DISPENSERS	ACDEIILNOOORST	DECOLORISATION
ACDEEIILNRSSTU	DIURETICALNESS	ACDEIILNOOORTZ	DECOLORIZATION
ACDEEIKORRRTTT	TRICK OR TREATED	ACDEIINNOORSST	CONSIDERATIONS
ACDEEILLLNNOSY	DECLENSIONALLY	ACDEILLMNOOSTY	ENDOSMOTICALLY
ACDEEILLNORSTV	CLOSED INTERVAL	ACDEILLNOOSSTY	DISCONSOLATELY
ACDEEILNPPRRSU	PERPENDICULARS	ACDEIMMNNOPSUY	PNEUMODYNAMICS
ACDEEIMMNNOORT	RECOMMENDATION	ACDEINNOOPRRTU	UNINCORPORATED
ACDEEIMMNORSTV	INVERTED COMMAS	ACDEINNORSTUUY	CONSUETUDINARY
ACDEEIMNNOSSSU	MENDACIOUSNESS	ACDEINOOQRSSTU	CONQUISTADORES
ACDEEIMNNOSTWW	CASEMENT WINDOW	ACDFGHIIINNRSS	DISFRANCHISING
ACDEEINOPRSSSU	PREDACIOUSNESS	ACDFHIIIIMNOTU	HUMIDIFICATION
ACDEELNNNRSTTY	TRANSCENDENTLY	ACDFIIIIILNOOST	SOLIDIFICATION
ACDEEMMNNOORRTY	RECOMMENDATORY	ACDGGIILNORSUY	DISCOURAGINGLY
ACDEENNORRSUVY	ORDNANCE SURVEY	ACDGHILLLOORYY	HYDROLOGICALLY
ACDEENOPRRSSTT	PROTRACTEDNESS	ACDGHILMNNOOPY	HOLDING COMPANY
ACDEFGHILMNORR	FRENCH MARIGOLD	ACDGIIIIMNNRST	DISCRIMINATING
ACDEFGIKNNOORY	DAY OF RECKONING	ACDGIIINNNORTT	INDOCTRINATING
ACDEFIIIIINNOTT	IDENTIFICATION	ACDHHIIOPRRSST	HARPSICHORDIST
ACDEFIIILLNNOTY	CONFIDENTIALLY	ACDHIIOOOPPRTT	DIAPHOTOTROPIC
ACDEGGINNORSSS	GRADE CROSSINGS	ACDIIIIILNNNOST	DISINCLINATION
ACDEGHILLMOOOT	METHODOLOGICAL	ACDIIIIMNNORST	DISCRIMINATION

ACDIIIJLNORSTU	JURISDICTIONAL	ACEEGHIIMNNSSW	SEWING MACHINES
ACDIIILNNOOTTY	CONDITIONALITY	ACEEGHIKLNNRSU	RECKLINGHAUSEN
ACDIIIMNORRSTY	DISCRIMINATORY	ACEEGHILNORSSU	CLEARINGHOUSES
ACDIIINNNOOORT	INCOORDINATION	ACEEGHILNOSSSU	CHAISES LONGUES
ACDIIINNNOORTT	INDOCTRINATION	ACEEGHILOPRRSX	LEXICOGRAPHERS
ACDIIILNNOOOSST	CONSOLIDATIONS,	ACEEGHIMMNORTT	THERMOMAGNETIC
DISCONSOLATION		ACEEGHIMOOPRRT	METEOROGRAPHIC
ACDIIILNOOORSST	DISCOLORATIONS	ACEEGIIINNNORTT	TRACTION ENGINE
ACDILLLMOOORXY	LOXODROMICALLY	ACEEGIINOPRRRS	CARRIER PIGEONS
ACDIMNOOPRSSTU	MASS PRODUCTION	ACEEGILLLLOOTY	TELEOLOGICALLY
ACEEEEFFFLMNST	SELF-EFFACEMENT	ACEEGILLMOOORT	METEOROLOGICAL
ACEEEEFHHLNPRT	THREE-HALFPENCE	ACEEGILLNRSTYY	SYNERGETICALLY
ACEEEEFLNPRSST	FALSE PRETENCES	ACEEGLNRRSTTUU	STRUCTURAL GENE
ACEEEEGILLPTXY	EPEXEGETICALLY	ACEEGNOORSSSUU	COURAGEOUSNESS
ACEEEEHHILNRTW	CATHERINE WHEEL	ACEEHHIIKSSTTV	THICK AS THIEVES
ACEEEEILMNNPPRS	MALICE PREPENSE	ACEEHHILNNNOPR	RHINENCEPHALON
ACEEEEINNNRRSTT	TERCENTENARIES	ACEEHHIMOPRSTT	CHEMOTHERAPIST
ACEEEEPPRRSSTW	CARPET SWEEPERS	ACEEHIIILNPSTT	LICENTIATESHIP
ACEEEFFGINOPRS	PEACE OFFERINGS	ACEEHIIINSTTTU	AUTHENTICITIES
ACEEEFHIMRRTUV	RHEUMATIC FEVER	ACEEHIILLNNPST	PANHELLENISTIC
ACEEEFINRRSSTV	REFRACTIVENESS	ACEEHIILMMNPSS	SIMPLE MACHINES
ACEEEGGILNNRSW	GREEN LACEWINGS	ACEEHIINPPPRST	APPRENTICESHIP
ACEEEGHINNNOSTU	CHANGE ONE'S TUNE	ACEEHILLMNNOSS	MELANCHOLINESS
ACEEEGIILLNPTY	EPIGENETICALLY	ACEEHILLMORTXY	EXOTHERMICALLY
ACEEEGIMMOSTTT	COMMITTEE STAGE	ACEEHILNNOPSSU	EUPHONICALNESS
ACEEEGMNNORSTU	ENCOURAGEMENTS	ACEEHIMMNORSSV	SERVOMECHANISM
ACEEEHHILLORTT	HETEROLECITHAL	ACEEHIMRRSSSTT	CHRISTMAS TREES
ACEEEHILNNNRST	CHINESE LANTERN	ACEEHINORSUUVX	NOUVEAUX RICHES
ACEEEHILNORSST	CHOLINESTERASE	ACEEHKMNORSTTT	SHOCK TREATMENT
ACEEEHLLMNNOPY	MYELENCEPHALON	ACEEHLNNOOPPRS	PROSENCEPHALON
ACEEEHLMLORRTT	ELECTROTHERMAL	ACEEHLPPRSSTUY	SUPPLY TEACHERS
ACEEEHMMOORTTY	HAEMOCYTOMETER	ACEEHMNOPPRRST	RAPPROCHEMENTS
ACEEEHNORTTTTU	TO THE UTTERANCE	ACEEHPRRRSTTTY	STRETCHER PARTY
ACEEEHOORRSTUV	HAVE RECOURSE TO	ACEEIIIILLLMPST	SEMIELLIPTICAL
ACEEEIILMNNNST	SEMICENTENNIAL	ACEEIIIJLNNORTT	INTERJECTIONAL
ACEEEEILLLMRTTY	TELEMETRICALLY	ACEEIIILLLNPSST	ELLIPTICALNESS
ACEEEILMNORTTU	ROMAINE LETTUCE	ACEEIIILLMPRRTY	PERIMETRICALLY
ACEEEILMORRSTT	STEREOMETRICAL	ACEEIIILLRRSTTV	VERTICILLASTER
ACEEEEILNNNOQUV	NONEQUIVALENCE	ACEEIIILNNNOPTT	EPICONTINENTAL
ACEEEILNPRSTTY	PETTY LARCENIES	ACEEIIILNNORSST	INTERCESSIONAL
ACEEELMORSSSST	MALTESE CROSSES	ACEEIIILNNORSTT	INTERSECTIONAL
ACEEEMNOOPRSTV	OVERCOMPENSATE	ACEEIIILNOPTTXY	EXCEPTIONALITY
ACEEEMNORRSTUU	COUNTERMEASURE	ACEEIIILNOSSTTY	COESSENTIALITY
ACEEFFGLNNORSU	LONG-SUFFERANCE	ACEEIIILNPRSTTT	PETIT LARCENIST
ACEEFFIILLNTTUY	INEFFECTUALITY	ACEEIIINORSSTTV	SERVICE STATION
ACEEFHIIINORTT	ETHERIFICATION	ACEEIKLNRSSSTV	TRAVELSICKNESS
ACEEFHILORSSTW	AS THE CROW FLIES	ACEEILLLLNTTUY	INTELLECTUALLY
ACEEFIIIINORSTT	ESTERIFICATION	ACEEILLMNORRTU	INTERMOLECULAR
ACEEFILMNOPRST	SELF-IMPORTANCE	ACEEILMNOOOPSU	POLEMONIACEOUS
ACEEFILMPRRSTU	SIMPLE FRACTURE	ACEEILMOPRSSTU	PRECIOUS METALS
ACEEFINORRRSTY	REFRACTORINESS	ACEEILNNQQUUVY	QUINQUEVALENCY
ACEEGHHLNORSST	CLOTHES HANGERS	ACEEILNNRRSTUW	NUCLEAR WINTERS
ACEEGHHMNRRRSU	HUNGER MARCHERS	ACEEILNORRRSTU	RESURRECTIONAL
ACEEGHHOOPRRRS	CHOREOGRAPHERS	ACEEILNORSTVVY	CONSERVATIVELY

ACEEIMMNNORSTU	INCOMMENSURATE
ACEEIMNOOOORRT	RECREATION ROOM
ACEEIMNOOPRRST	CONTEMPORARIES
ACEEIMNOPPRRTU	MERCAPTOPURINE
ACEEIMNORRSSSX	CROSS-EXAMINERS
ACEEINNOOOPRTV	NONCOOPERATIVE
ACEEINOORRSSTV	CONSERVATOIRES,
CONSERVATORIES	
ACEEINOPRRSSSU	PRECARIOUSNESS
ACEELLOORRRSST	ROLLER COASTERS
ACEFFIIOSSTTUY	SUFFICE IT TO SAY
ACEFFINOOQSTTU	QUESTION OF FACT
ACEFGIIINNORTT	GENTRIFICATION
ACEFGIIINNORTTU	CENTRIFUGATION
ACEFHHIIINPSST	CHIEFTAINSHIPS
ACEFHIIIOTTVVY	HIVE OF ACTIVITY
ACEFIIIILMPSTV	SIMPLIFICATIVE
ACEFIIIINORTVV	REVIVIFICATION
ACEFIIILMNOSTU	EMULSIFICATION
ACEFIIILPRSTUY	SUPERFICIALITY
ACEFIIINOSSSTTU	FACTITIOUSNESS
ACEFINOOPPRRRT	PROPER FRACTION
ACEFINRRRSTTUU	INFRASTRUCTURE
ACEFJKKLNOORST	NORFOLK JACKETS
ACEFLNOORSSSTU	COLOURFASTNESS
ACEGGHHINOOPRR	CHOREOGRAPHING
ACEGGHIIMNNNNU	MACHINEGUNNING
ACEGGIILNNNPRS	SPRING-CLEANING
ACEGGILLNOOORT	GERONTOLOGICAL
ACEGGILNOOSSTY	GYNAECOLOGISTS
ACEGHILLLNOOTY	ETHNOLOGICALLY
ACEGHILLNOOPTY	PHOTOGENICALLY
ACEGHILLNOORTY	ORTHOGENICALLY
ACEGHLMOOPSTYY	METAPSYCHOLOGY
ACEGHMMOOPRSUY	MYRMECOPHAGOUS
ACEGHOPPRRRSTY	CRYPTOGRAPHERS
ACEGIIINNNORTZ	CONTAINERIZING
ACEGIILLLOSTUY	EULOGISTICALLY
ACEGIILLMNOORT	TERMINOLOGICAL
ACEGIILLORSSUY	SACRILEGIOUSLY
ACEGIILNNORTUV	COUNTERVAILING
ACEGIILNNOTTUV	CONGLUTINATIVE
ACEGIILNOQTUVY	EQUIVOCATINGLY
ACEGIILNOSSTTU	GESTICULATIONS
ACEGIIMNNORSSX	CROSS-EXAMINING
ACEGIINPRRSSTT	STARTING PRICES
ACEGILLLMOOTYY	ETYMOLOGICALLY
ACEGILLLOOOSTY	OSTEOLOGICALLY
ACEGILMNNOOORT	CONGLOMERATION
ACEGILNOPRSSTU	PLASTIC SURGEON
ACEGILPRRSSTUY	PLASTIC SURGERY
ACEGIMMMOPRRSU	PROGRAMME MUSIC
ACEGINNNOOSSUU	CONSANGUINEOUS
ACEGINNOOSSSTU	CONTAGIOUSNESS
ACEGINNOPSSSUU	PUGNACIOUSNESS
ACEHHIINOPRRTT	THERIANTHROPIC
ACEHHILLOOPSTY	THEOSOPHICALLY
ACEHHILLOPTTYY	HYPOTHETICALLY
ACEHHILOOPRSUZ	RHIZOCEPHALOUS
ACEHHLMOOOPPST	OPHTHALMOSCOPE
ACEHHMMNRSSTUY	CHRYSANTHEMUMS
ACEHIIIILMSSTW	WHIMSICALITIES
ACEHIILLPSTUUY	EUPHUISTICALLY
ACEHIILNORSSST	HISTORICALNESS
ACEHIIMNNOOPRT	ENANTIOMORPHIC
ACEHIINNSSTTUU	UNENTHUSIASTIC
ACEHIINOOPRTTU	EUTROPHICATION
ACEHIINOPPRSST	SPINTHARISCOPE
ACEHIINOPRSSST	CORNISH PASTIES
ACEHIIOOPRSSST	SPIROCHAETOSIS
ACEHIIOORRSTTT	OSTEOARTHRITIC
ACEHILLNOPPTYY	PHENOTYPICALLY
ACEHILLOPRSTYY	PROSTHETICALLY
ACEHILLOPRTXYY	XEROPHYTICALLY
ACEHILMNOOPRRZ	CHLORPROMAZINE
ACEHILMOPRSSTT	THERMOPLASTICS
ACEHILOOPRSSTV	PRIVATE SCHOOLS
ACEHIMNOOPRRTT	ANTHROPOMETRIC
ACEHIMOPPRSTTY	SPERMATOPHYTIC
ACEHINNNORSSSTY	NARCOSYNTHESIS
ACEHINOORRSSTT	ORCHESTRATIONS
ACEIIIILMNPSTU	MUNICIPALITIES
ACEIIIILNPPRST	PRINCIPALITIES
ACEIIILLMOPRTY	MILITARY POLICE
ACEIIILLMPTTUV	MULTIPLICATIVE
ACEIIILLNORTTV	VERTICILLATION
ACEIIILLOPSSTY	ISOPIESTICALLY
ACEIIILMNOOSTT	EMOTIONALISTIC
ACEIIILNRRTUVY	CURVILINEARITY
ACEIIILNRSSTUV	UNIVERSALISTIC
ACEIIIMMNOORSS	COMMISSIONAIRE
ACEIIIMNNORRST	RECRIMINATIONS
ACEIIINNOPSSTX	EXPANSIONISTIC
ACEIIINOPPRSTT	PRECIPITATIONS
ACEIILLLNRTUUY	UNICELLULARITY
ACEIILLMNNOOOS	NEOCOLONIALISM
ACEIILLNNOOOST	NEOCOLONIALIST
ACEIILMNNNOOST	CONTINENTALISM
ACEIILNNNNOSTT	CONTINENTALIST
ACEIILNNNOTTTY	CONTINENTALITY
ACEIILNNOOPRST	IN LOCO PARENTIS
ACEIILNNORRSTU	INSURRECTIONAL
ACEIILNOOPSSTT	POLICE STATIONS
ACEIILNOPRSTUY	PERTINACIOUSLY
ACEIILNOSSSSUV	LASCIVIOUSNESS
ACEIIMMNNOORTU	IMMUNOREACTION
ACEIIMMNOORSST	COMMISERATIONS
ACEIINNOOORSVZ	CONVERSAZIOONI

ACEIINNORSSTTY	SYNCRETISATION
ACEIINNORSTTYZ	SYNCRETIZATION
ACEIINNOSSSTUU	INCAUTIOUSNESS
ACEIINOPSSSSUU	AUSPICIOUSNESS
ACEILLLLMORTUVY	VOLUMETRICALLY
ACEILLMMOORSTY	OSMOMETRICALLY
ACEILLMNOOORRSS	CRIMSON ROSELLA
ACEILLMOPRRTYY	PYROMETRICALLY
ACEILLNNNOOTVY	CONVENTIONALLY
ACEILLNNOOSSTT	CONSTELLATIONS
ACEILLNOOPRSST	CROSS-POLLINATE
ACEILLNOPRSSUY	SUPERSONICALLY
ACEILMNOOORTUV	MACROEVOLUTION
ACEILMNOOPRRTY	CONTEMPORARILY
ACEILNNNNOOTUV	UNCONVENTIONAL
ACEILNNOOOPSTT	CONSTANTINOPLE
ACEILNNOOOPRST	SPIRONOLACTONE
ACEILNOOPRRTUY	PERLOCUTIONARY
ACEILNOPRRRTUV	PROVENTRICULAR
ACEILOORRSTTUW	WATERCOLOURIST
ACEIMMNNOORSTU	COMMENSURATION
ACEINNNOOOOPRT	NONCOOPERATION
ACEINNNOORSSTTV	CONTRAVENTIONS
ACELLMNNOOPRSU	PERSONAL COLUMN
ACELNOPRSSSSWY	LAWSON'S CYPRESS
ACELRRRSTTTUUU	ULTRASTRUCTURE
ACEMNOOORSSTTU	ENTOMOSTRACOUS
ACFFIIINOORSTT	FORTIFICATIONS
ACFGIIIILNNOTZ	FICTIONALIZING
ACFGIIIINNOSST	SIGNIFICATIONS
ACFGIIILNOORST	GLORIFICATIONS
ACFGIILMNNNOTU	MALFUNCTIONING
ACFGIINNOORSTU	CONFIGURATIONS
ACFIIIILMNOPST	SIMPLIFICATION
ACFIIIJLLNOOST	JOLLIFICATIONS
ACFIIILNOSTTTU	STULTIFICATION
ACFIIILLRSTTUUY	FUTURISTICALLY
ACFIILNNOSSTTU	FUNCTIONALISTS
ACFIMNOOOORSTTT	COMFORT STATION
ACFINNNOOORSTT	CONFRONTATIONS
ACGGHHIMOPPRSY	SPHYGMOGRAPHIC
ACGGHIKLNOSSTU	LAUGHINGSTOCKS
ACGHHHIOOPSTUY	ICHTHYOPHAGOUS
ACGHIIILNOPSTT	ANTIPHLOGISTIC
ACGHIIKNNOSTTT	STICK AT NOTHING
ACGHIILLLLOOPY	PHILOLOGICALLY
ACGHIILLLLOOTY	LITHOLOGICALLY
ACGHIILLLOOSTY	HISTOLOGICALLY
ACGHIILLNOOORT	ORNITHOLOGICAL
ACGHILLLNOOOPY	PHONOLOGICALLY
ACGIIILLLNSTUY	LINGUISTICALLY
ACGIIILLLPSTUY	PUGILISTICALLY
ACGIIILLNNOTTXY	INTOXICATINGLY
ACGIIILPRRSSTU	SURGICAL SPIRIT

ACGIILRRSSTTUU	AGRICULTURISTS
ACGIIMMNOOORRSS	MICROORGANISMS
ACGILNOOOPRSSTY	LARYNGOSCOPIST
ACGINOOOPRRSTT	PROGNOSTICATOR
ACHHILLMNOOOPY	HOMOPHONICALLY
ACHHIMMMOOORST	HOMOCHROMATISM
ACHHINOOOPPRST	ANTHROPOSOPHIC
ACHHLMOOOPPSTY	OPHTHALMOSCOPY
ACHIIIINNORSTT	TRICHINISATION
ACHIIIINNORTTZ	TRICHINIZATION
ACHIIILLLPSTYY	SYPHILITICALLY
ACHIIILLNORSTY	HISTRIONICALLY
ACHIIIMNOORSST	TRICHOMONIASIS
ACHIIINOOPSSTT	SOPHISTICATION
ACHIILLLMNOOTY	MONOLITHICALLY
ACHIILLLOSTTYY	HISTOLYTICALLY
ACHIIOPRSSSTTY	ASTROPHYSICIST
ACHILLLNOOOPYY	POLYPHONICALLY
ACHILLOOOPPTYY	PHOTOTYPICALLY
ACHILMMOOOPRST	POLYCHROMATISM
ACHILMOOOPRRSSY	PRIMARY SCHOOLS
ACHIMMMNOOOORST	MONOCHROMATISM
ACIIIILNOOPSTT	POLITICISATION
ACIIIILNOOPTTZ	POLITICIZATION
ACIIIILPRSSTTU	SPIRITUALISTIC
ACIIIILLMPSSTY	SIMPLISTICALLY
ACIIILLMNOPTTU	MULTIPLICATION
ACIIILLMOPSTTY	OPTIMISTICALLY
ACIIILMNOPRSSV	PROVINCIALISMS
ACIIILNOPSSUUY	INAUSPICIOUSLY
ACIILLLLMOOQSSU	COLLOQUIALISMS
ACIILNNOOSTTTU	CONSTITUTIONAL
ACIINNNOOPRSTU	PRONUNCIATIONS
ACIINNOOPRSSTT	CONTRAPOSITION
ACIINNOPRRSSTT	TRANSCRIPTIONS
ACIKMNNOORSTUY	ROCKY MOUNTAINS
ACILLMMNNOOTTY	NONCOMMITTALLY
ACILMOOPRRRSUY	PRIMARY COLOURS
ACIMMOOORSSTTU	MICROSTOMATOUS
ACIMNOOOSTTTXY	CYTOTAXONOMIST
ADDDDEGIIMNNOW	DIAMOND WEDDING
ADDDEIIIILNSUV	INDIVIDUALISED
ADDDEIIIILNUVZ	INDIVIDUALIZED
ADDEEEEHHNNNSSV	EVEN-HANDEDNESS
ADDEEEFFIINRTT	DIFFERENTIATED
ADDEEEFHLNNSST	LEFT-HANDEDNESS
ADDEEEFILMNTXY	EXTENDED FAMILY
ADDEEEHIMNPPRS	MISAPPREHENDED
ADDEEEHNNNOPSS	OPEN-HANDEDNESS
ADDEEEIKMNNSSW	WEAK-MINDEDNESS
ADDEEEILMPRTTY	PREMEDITATEDLY
ADDEEEILNNNPSS	PINS AND NEEDLES
ADDEEEIMNPRTTU	UNPREMEDITATED
ADDEEEIMNRSTTU	UNDERESTIMATED

ADDEEFFHLRRUUY	FURFURALDEHYDE
ADDEEFIIMMNNRSS	FAIR-MINDEDNESS
ADDEEFLNNNORUW	NEWFOUNDLANDER
ADDEEFLNNPRSUY	PENNY DREADFULS
ADDEEGHHHINNSS	HIGH-HANDEDNESS
ADDEEHIIMMNNRTY	DIMENHYDRINATE
ADDEEILMNNPRSU	NIL DESPERANDUM
ADDEEINNNORSWY	NINE DAYS' WONDER
ADDEGILNOORRSU	RIO GRANDE DO SUL
ADDEGINNNRSSTU	UNDERSTANDINGS
ADDEGINNORRSST	STANDING ORDERS
ADDEIIIILNRSUV	INDIVIDUALISER
ADDEIIIILNRUVZ	INDIVIDUALIZER
ADDEIIILNRSSTU	INDUSTRIALISED
ADDEIIILNRSTUZ	INDUSTRIALIZED
ADDEIILLNNOPTW	WIND-POLLINATED
ADDEIILNOPPSTY	DISAPPOINTEDLY
ADDIIIILNSSTUV	INDIVIDUALISTS
ADEEEEEGNNRSST	DEGENERATENESS
ADEEEEEHLLRRSW	WHEELER-DEALERS
ADEEEEFHINRSUW	AUF WIEDERSEHEN
ADEEEEGHILLNRW	WHEELER-DEALING
ADEEEEHHLMMPST	HEMEL HEMPSTEAD
ADEEEEHNRSTTVY	THREE-DAY EVENTS
ADEEEEIMNPRRTT	PREDETERMINATE
ADEEEELMNRSSTT	ELDER STATESMEN
ADEEEELNNNRRVV	NEVER-NEVER LAND
ADEEEFGILORRTU	TIERRA DEL FUEGO
ADEEEFHOOPRRTW	WEATHERPROOFED
ADEEEFIMNNOORT	AFOREMENTIONED
ADEEEFIMNRSTTU	DISFEATUREMENT
ADEEEFINNORSTT	DEFENESTRATION
ADEEEGHHMMNPRS	GERMAN SHEPHERD
ADEEEGHNOORRRY	HONORARY DEGREE
ADEEEGIILLMNRST	LEGERDEMAINIST
ADEEEGIINRRTTV	REDINTEGRATIVE
ADEEEGIKNNRRRT	KINDERGARTENER
ADEEEGLNRRSSSS	REGARDLESSNESS
ADEEEGOPRRRTUY	DAGUERREOTYPER
ADEEEGOPRRSTUY	DAGUERREOTYPES
ADEEEHHLLORTWY	WHOLE-HEARTEDLY
ADEEEHIINRRSST	HEREDITARINESS
ADEEEHIKMNOSSU	HOUSEMAID'S KNEE
ADEEEHILNOOPRT	RADIOTELEPHONE
ADEEEHIMNNRSTT	DISHEARTENMENT
ADEEEHIRRSSTTV	THE DRIVER'S SEAT
ADEEEIIIMNRRST	INTERMEDIARIES
ADEEEIIMMQRSUV	DEMISEMIQUAVER
ADEEEIIMNSSTTV	MEDITATIVENESS
ADEEEILMORRTTY	RADIOTELEMETRY
ADEEEIMNRSSTTU	UNDERESTIMATES
ADEEEMNNRSTTTU	UNDERSTATEMENT
ADEEENNPPRRSSU	UNPREPAREDNESS
ADEEFFIIINORRTT	DIFFERENTIATOR
ADEEFGHINRSST	FARSIGHTEDNESS
ADEEFGINNOSTTU	DETONATING FUSE
ADEEFGLLOOPRSU	GOLD-OF-PLEASURE
ADEEFHILLNOSTU	THE LIFE AND SOUL
ADEEFHILNSSTTW	HALFWITTEDNESS
ADEEFIMNNOORRT	FOREORDAINMENT
ADEEFLLLMOORWY	FOLLOW-MY-LEADER
ADEEGGIMNNRRRY	GERRYMANDERING
ADEEGGHHNOOOSTV	HAVE THE GOODS ON
ADEEGHILNNRTY	HEARTRENDINGLY
ADEEGHILNRSSTU	DAUGHTERLINESS
ADEEGHNNORSSST	HEADSTRONGNESS
ADEEGIIINRSTTV	DISINTEGRATIVE
ADEEGIINORRTT	REDINTEGRATION
ADEEGINNOPPRRT	PREPONDERATING
ADEEGINOORRSTV	DEROGATORINESS
ADEEGJLMNSTUUV	VALUE JUDGMENTS
ADEEGLNNORSSTU	DENTAL SURGEONS
ADEEHHIILMOPRS	HEMISPHEROIDAL
ADEEHHIMOPRRST	HERMAPHRODITES
ADEEHHLMNNOOSSU	HOUSEHOLD NAMES
ADEEHILMNNRSTT	DISENTHRALMENT
ADEEHILNNOPSTY	SHETLAND PONIES
ADEEHILNOOPRTY	RADIOTELEPHONY
ADEEHIMMOPRSTX	MIXED METAPHORS
ADEEHLMNOORRSY	DYSMENORRHOEAL
ADEEHMNNNOSSSU	UNHANDSOMENESS
ADEEIIINORSSTV	RADIOSENSITIVE
ADEEIILNNNORST	NONRESIDENTIAL
ADEEIILOPRRSTV	PRIVATE SOLDIER
ADEEIIMNNOOSTT	DEMONETISATION
ADEEIIMNNOOTTZ	DEMONETIZATION
ADEEIINNOPRSTT	PREDESTINATION
ADEEIINSSSSSUV	DISSUASIVENESS
ADEEILLNORRSVY	ORDINARY LEVELS
ADEEILNNRRSTUY	UNRESTRAINEDLY
ADEEILNORRSSWW	WORLD-WEARINESS
ADEEIMNNORRSST	ARRONDISSEMENT
ADEEINNOOPPRRT	PREPONDERATION
ADEEJMMORRSTTU	DRUM MAJORETTES
ADEELNNOPPRRTY	PREPONDERANTLY
ADEELLNNORSSSSU	SLANDEROUSNESS
ADEEMNRSSTTTUU	MATURE STUDENTS
ADEFFGHINNORTU	FOUNDING FATHER
ADEFFGIIINORSST	DISAFFORESTING
ADEFFHILLNOSUY	FULLY-FASHIONED
ADEFGHIMOORRTY	FAIRY GODMOTHER
ADEFGIIMNOORRST	TRANSMOGRIFIED
ADEFIIIINNOSSTT	DISINFESTATION
ADEFIIINOORSSTT	DISFORESTATION
ADEFIIINOSSSTTU	FASTIDIOUSNESS
ADEGGIIINNRSTT	DISINTEGRATING
ADEGGILLNRSSSU	SLUGGARDLINESS
ADEGHIKNNOORTT	THE GORDIAN KNOT

ADEGHINNNOSSTT	ONE-NIGHT STANDS
ADEGIIIILMNRTZ	DEMILITARIZING
ADEGIIINNORSTT	DISINTEGRATION,
DISORIENTATING	
ADEGIIILLMNPRSY	PYRAMID SELLING
ADEGIILMNNPRRY	REPRIMANDINGLY
ADEGILMOORSSTT	DERMATOLOGISTS
ADEGINNNPSSSTU	UPSTANDINGNESS
ADEHHIILLLLSSY	SHILLY-SHALLIED
ADEHHIMOPRRSTU	HERMAPHRODITUS
ADEHILNNOSSSTU	OUTLANDISHNESS
ADEHIMOOOOPPRSS	PAEDOMORPHOSIS
ADEHIMOOORTTUW	WITHOUT MORE ADO
ADEHINOORRSSTW	ROADWORTHINESS
ADEHLOPRRSSSTU	SHOULDER STRAPS
ADEHORSSSTTUWW	SOUTHWESTWARDS
ADEIIIILMNNORST	TRIDIMENSIONAL
ADEIIIILMNNOSTY	DIMENSIONALITY
ADEIIILNPRSTTU	PLATITUDINISER
ADEIIILNPRTTUZ	PLATITUDINIZER
ADEIIINNOORSTT	DISORIENTATION
ADEIIILLMNRRTUY	RUDIMENTARILLY
ADEIIILLNOPRTVY	PROVIDENTIALLY
ADEIILMNNNOOSX	MASON-DIXON LINE
ADEIILMNNOOSTW	TWO-DIMENSIONAL
ADEIIMNNOORSST	MODERNISATIONS
ADEIIMNNOORSTZ	MODERNIZATIONS
ADEIIMNNOOPPSST	DISAPPOINTMENT
ADEIINNOOPRRST	PREORDINATIONS
ADEIINNORSSTTU	TRADE UNIONISTS
ADEIINORRSSSTT	TRANSISTORISED
ADEIINORRSSTTZ	TRANSISTORIZED
ADEILMMNORRSTU	ULTRAMODERNISM
ADEILMNORRSTTU	ULTRAMODERNIST
ADEIMMNNOORSST	DEMONSTRATIONS
ADEINOOORRTTTX	DEXTROROTATION
ADEOOOORRRTTTXY	DEXTROROTATORY
ADFGGHHIILLNNS	HIGHLAND FLINGS
ADFGGIINNOORT	TO-ING AND FRO-ING
ADFGIKLNOOORRW	FORWARD-LOOKING
ADFHNNOOOOORRST	AND SO ON *OR* FORTH
ADGGGHOORSSTYY	SHAGGY-DOG STORY
ADGGIMNNOPRSTU	STAMPING GROUND
ADGHILOOORRSVV	VOROSHILOVGRAD
ADGIILLLNNOTUY	LONGITUDINALLY
ADGIIILNOPPRSVY	DISAPPROVINGLY
ADIIILMNOSSSTU	DISSIMULATIONS
ADIIILNRSSSTTU	INDUSTRIALISTS
ADIILOPSSTTUUY	DISPUTATIOUSLY
AEEEEFHLNOOPSTTX	AT THE EXPENSE OF
AEEEEFLNOOPPSY	APPLE OF ONE'S EYE
AEEEEGINSSSTTVV	VEGETATIVENESS
AEEEEILMNNRSST	ELEMENTARINESS
AEEEEINNPRRTTT	INTERPENETRATE

AEEEEINPRRSSTTV	REPRESENTATIVE
AEEEELLNPRRTTW	WATER-REPELLENT
AEEEFGHHIRSSTTW	FEATHERWEIGHTS
AEEEFHOQRSTTTU	AT THE REQUEST OF
AEEEFIILNNRRTT	INTERFERENTIAL
AEEEFILLNPRRTY	PREFERENTIALLY
AEEEFNORRSSTTW	WATER SOFTENERS
AEEEGGGIMNNNRT	ENGAGEMENT RING
AEEEGGINRSSSSV	AGGRESSIVENESS
AEEEGHLLOPPRST	TELEGRAPH POLES
AEEEGHLNPRSTTT	GRASP THE NETTLE
AEEEGIILLNNRSST	LARGE INTESTINE
AEEEGIKLNRRSST	GENERAL STRIKES
AEEEGILLPRRSSS	PRESS GALLERIES
AEEEGIMNPRRSTY	PRAYER MEETINGS
AEEEGNNOOPQRTU	ROENTGENOPAQUE
AEEEGNNOORRSTT	ENTEROGASTRONE
AEEEHHHHILRTTWW	THE WHEREWITHAL
AEEEHHHINNSSST	HEATHENISHNESS
AEEEHHILNPSTTW	WHITE ELEPHANTS
AEEEHIINNPPRSV	INAPPREHENSIVE
AEEEHILNPPRSVY	APPREHENSIVELY
AEEEHIMNNRSTTT	MAN IN THE STREET
AEEEHINSSSTUVX	EXHAUSTIVENESS
AEEEHLLORSTUXY	HETEROSEXUALLY
AEEEIIINNPRSTT	PENITENTIARIES
AEEEIILMNNSSTT	SENTIMENTALISE
AEEEIILMNNSTTZ	SENTIMENTALIZE
AEEEIINPRRTTTV	INTERPRETATIVE
AEEEILLMNPRTXY	EXPERIMENTALLY
AEEEILMMRSSTTY	REAL-TIME SYSTEM
AEEEILMNRRTUVY	REMUNERATIVELY
AEEEILNOPRSTUV	SUPERELEVATION
AEEEIMNNNRSTTT	ENTERTAINMENTS
AEEEIMNNRSSTTT	REINSTATEMENTS
AEEEIINNPRRTTT	INTERPENETRANT
AEEEIINNOPRRSTT	REPRESENTATION
AEEEINPRSSSSUV	PERSUASIVENESS
AEEEIOOPRRRTTV	RETRO-OPERATIVE
AEEELLNOOPRRRU	EUROPEAN ROLLER
AEEELMNNNRSSSS	MANNERLESSNESS
AEEELNOOPRRSST	PERSONAL STEREO
AEEEMNOOPRSTUX	EXTEMPORANEOUS
AEEEMNORSSTTTV	OVERSTATEMENTS
AEEENNORSSSTUX	EXTRANEOUSNESS
AEEENNRRSSSSTV	TRANSVERSENESS
AEEENQSSSSTTUU	STATUESQUENESS
AEEEOORRRSSTTUV	TREASURE TROVES
AEEFGGHILNRSTT	FLIGHT SERGEANT
AEEFGHJLLNOTUW	LAW OF THE JUNGLE
AEEFGIIMMNRRST	FERRIMAGNETISM
AEEFGIINRSTUV	FIGURATIVENESS
AEEFGILMNNNSSU	MEANINGFULNESS
AEEFGIMMNNORRST	FERROMAGNETISM

AEEFGLNNRSSTUU	UNGRATEFULNESS	AEEIILNNQSSTTU	QUINTESSENTIAL
AEEFHINNOSTTTT	NOT THE FAINTEST	AEEIILNRSTTUXY	INTERSEXUALITY
AEEFHLNNNNPPYY	PENNY-HALFPENNY	AEEIILPRTTUVVY	VITUPERATIVELY
AEEFIILNOQQTUU	QUINQUEFOLIATE	AEEIIMNNOORSTT	REMONETISATION
AEEFNOOPRRSSTW	WATERPROOFNESS	AEEIIMNNOORTTZ	REMONETIZATION
AEEGGHHLNORSTTT	TO GREAT LENGTHS	AEEIIMNOORSSTV	OVERESTIMATION
AEEGGIINORSSTT	SEGREGATIONIST	AEEIINNOPRRTTT	INTERPRETATION
AEEGGILLNNORTU	OUTGENERALLING	AEEIINNOQRSSTU	QUESTIONNAIRES
AEEGGINORRSSSU	GREGARIOUSNESS	AEEIINNORSSTTW	WESTERNISATION
AEEGGIOSSTTUUV	AUTOSUGGESTIVE	AEEIINNORSTTWZ	WESTERNIZATION
AEEGHHLORSSTUU	SLAUGHTERHOUSE	AEEIINNRSSSTTV	TRANSITIVENESS
AEEGHILNNOOPTY	PILE ON THE AGONY	AEEIINPQQRTTUU	QUINQUEPARTITE
AEEGHIMNSSSTTT	STEAMTIGHTNESS	AEEIILLNNRSSSTT	SLATTERNLINESS
AEEGHINRSSTTTW	WATERTIGHTNESS	AEEIILNNPRRSSTT	SILENT PARTNERS
AEEGIIILLLMTTY	ILLEGITIMATELY	AEEILNOORTTTXY	EXTORTIONALITY
AEEGIIIILLNNRST	INERTIA SELLING	AEEIMNOQRSSTTU	QUESTION MASTER
AEEGIIILLNNSTT	INTELLIGENTSIA	AEEINOQRSSSTTU	SEQUESTRATIONS
AEEGIIILRRRSTU	IRREGULARITIES	AEEFFHILNSSSTUU	UNFAITHFULNESS
AEEGIILMNORSSS	GENERALISSIMOS	AEEFFHLNOOORRUW	FLOWER-OF-AN-HOUR
AEEGIILNNNRTTY	ENTERTAININGLY	AEFGGHIKNSTUWY	GUY FAWKES NIGHT
AEEGIIMNNNORTU	MOUNTAINEERING	AEFGHIILMPRRST	PILGRIM FATHERS
AEEGIIMNORSTTV	OVERESTIMATING	AEFGHINNNNPRSTY	PENNY-FARTHINGS
AEEGIIMNRSSTTU	TIME SIGNATURES	AEFGIINOORRRST	ROARING FORTIES
AEEGIINNOPRRST	PEREGRINATIONS	AEFGIINPORRSTU	PREFIGURATIONS
AEEGIINORRSTTV	INTERROGATIVES,	AEFGILNOORSTTV	FLOATING VOTERS
TERGIVERSATION		AEFFHHLNNOOPRTWY	HALFPENNYWORTH
AEEGILLMNORRST	STEAMROLLERING	AEFHKLNNNSSTUU	UNTHANKFULNESS
AEEGINNRSSTTUU	SIGNATURE TUNES	AEFIILNOOPRRST	PROLIFERATIONS
AEEGIORRRSTTVY	TERGIVERSATORY	AEFILLNOOPRSSY	PROFESSIONALLY
AEEGNOORSSSTUU	OUTRAGEOUSNESS	AEFILLOOPRRSSY	PROFESSORIALLY
AEEHHLMNNOPSTU	SULPHONMETHANE	AEFILNNOOPRSSU	UNPROFESSIONAL
AEEHHOPPPRRSSTU	SUPERPHOSPHATE	AEFILNOOPRSSSW	PASSIONFLOWERS
AEEHIKNOOPRRUY	KEEP YOUR HAIR ON!	AEFINOOPRRRSSW	PRISONERS OF WAR
AEEHILLMNOTTTW	THE LITTLE WOMAN	AEGGHHOOPRTYY	PHYTOGEOGRAPHY
AEEHILLNOPRVXY	VINE PHYLLOXERA	AEGGHIILNRRSTT	RIGHT TRIANGLES
AEEHILOOPRRTTY	HETEROPOLARITY	AEGGHINNOOPRTV	PHOTOENGRAVING
AEEHIMNORSSTUV	OVERENTHUSIASM	AEGGIIIMNPSSTT	SPITTING IMAGES
AEEHINPPPPRRSW	WHIPPERSNAPPER	AEGGIILLNNOSST	ILL-GOTTEN GAINS
AEEIIILMMMMORT	TIME IMMEMORIAL	AEGGIINRSSTTTT	SITTING TARGETS
AEEIIILMNSSTTX	EXISTENTIALISM	AEGGIKLLNOOSSS	LOOKING GLASSES
AEEIIILNNSSTTY	INESSENTIALITY	AEGGINOOSSTTUU	AUTOSUGGESTION
AEEIIILNOPSTTT	POTENTIALITIES	AEGHHLMOPPRSTY	PLETHYSMOGRAPH
AEEIIILNSSTTTX	EXISTENTIALIST	AEGHIIILNOOOSTT	THEOLOGISATION
AEEIIILORRRSTT	TERRITORIALISE	AEGHIIILNOOOTTZ	THEOLOGIZATION
AEEIIILORRRTTZ	TERRITORIALIZE	AEGHIIMNNOOOST	HOMOGENISATION
AEEIILLMMNNSST	SMALL INTESTINE	AEGHIIMNNOOOTZ	HOMOGENIZATION
AEEIILLNNOPRTT	INTERPELLATION	AEGHIKNNRRRTTY	KNIGHT-ERRANTRY
AEEIILMMNNOPTT	IMPLEMENTATION	AEGHILNORSSTUV	VAULTING HORSES
AEEIILMMNNSSST	SENTIMENTALISM	AEGHIMMNOOPRST	METAMORPHOSING
AEEIILMNNSSTTT	SENTIMENTALIST	AEGHLLMOOPPRSY	MEGASPOROPHYLL
AEEIILMNNSTTTY	SENTIMENTALITY	AEGHLNOOPRTUY	NEUROPATHOLOGY
AEEIILNNNORTTV	INTERVENTIONAL	AEGHMMOOPRRTTY	PHOTOGRAMMETRY
AEEIILNNORRSTT	INTERRELATIONS	AEGHNNNOORTTUY	TURN ON THE AGONY
AEEIIILNNOSTTXY	EXTENSIONALITY	AEGIIIILLMNOSTT	LEGITIMISATION

AEGIIIILMNOTTZ	LEGITIMIZATION
AEGIIILNNORTTT	TOILET TRAINING
AEGIIILNNPRSWY	AWE-INSPIRINGLY
AEGIIIMNNORRTT	INTERMIGRATION
AEGIIIINNORSTTT	INTEGRATIONIST
AEGIIIINNOSSTTV	INVESTIGATIONS
AEGIIKMNOPSSSV	PASSIVE SMOKING
AEGIIKNOPRRSTW	WORKING PARTIES
AEGIILLLNNRSTW	ALL-IN WRESTLING
AEGIILLNTTTTTT	TITTLE-TATTLING
AEGIILMNNOORST	MONGRELISATION
AEGIILMNNOORTZ	MONGRELIZATION
AEGIILNNNRSTTY	INTRANSIGENTLY
AEGIINNOORRSTT	INTERROGATIONS
AEGIINPPRSSSTT	ASSET-STRIPPING
AEGILLNOOOPSTT	PALEONTOLOGIST
AEGIMMNOOPRSTU	SPERMATOGONIUM
AEGIMNNOORTUUV	OUTMANOEUVRING
AEGINNORRSSSST	TRANSGRESSIONS
AEGINNPRSSSSSU	SURPASSINGNESS
AEGINORSSSTTUU	GRATUITOUSNESS
AEGKKMNOORSSTU	UST-KAMENOGORSK
AEGLLMOPRRTUYY	PYROMETALLURGY
AEHHHILNOORTTU	HOLIER-THAN-THOU
AEHHHOOOPPRSTT	ORTHOPHOSPHATE
AEHHIILLLLRSSY	SHILLYSHALLIER
AEHHNNOORRSTTT	NORTH-NORTHEAST
AEHHOOSSSTTTUU	SOUTH-SOUTHEAST
AEHIIKLLMOOPRT	POIKILOTHERMAL
AEHIILOPRRSTWY	PRAISEWORTHILY
AEHIINNOSSSTTY	SYNTHESISATION
AEHIINNOSSTTTY	SYNTHETISATION
AEHIINNOSSTTYZ	SYNTHESIZATION
AEHIINNOSTTTYZ	SYNTHETIZATION
AEHIIOORRSSTTT	OSTEOARTHRITIS
AEHIJKMOOOOSTV	KOSOVO-METOHIJA
AEHILLOOPSSUXZ	SULPHISOXAZOLE
AEHILNNOORSSTZ	HORIZONTALNESS
AEHIMNNOORSSSU	HARMONIOUSNESS
AEHIMOOPPPSSTU	HIPPOPOTAMUSES
AEIIILMORRRSTT	TERRITORIALISM
AEIIILNNNOTTTY	INTENTIONALITY
AEIIILNNRSTTVY	INTRANSITIVELY
AEIIILORRRSTTT	TERRITORIALIST
AEIIILORRRTTTY	TERRITORIALITY
AEIIINOQRRSTUY	REQUISITIONARY
AEIIJLNNORSTUV	UNIVERSAL JOINT
AEIILLLMNNOPST	POSTMILLENNIAL
AEIILLLRSTTUVY	ILLUSTRATIVELY
AEIILLMNOPRSSY	IMPRESSIONALLY
AEIILLNNOSSSUV	VILLAINOUSNESS
AEIILLNQRRSSTU	TRANQUILLISERS
AEIILLNQRRSTUZ	TRANQUILLIZERS
AEIILMNNOPSSTU	EMULSION PAINTS

AEIILMNOOPRSTY	POLYMERISATION
AEIILMNOOPRTYZ	POLYMERIZATION
AEIILNNOOPRSTT	INTERPOLATIONS
AEIILNNOPRSTUY	UNIPERSONALITY
AEIIMMNORSSTTY	SYMMETRISATION
AEIIMMNORSTTYZ	SYMMETRIZATION
AEIIMNNOOPRSST	IMPERSONATIONS
AEIINNORRSSTTY	TRANSITORINESS
AEIINOOPPRRSTX	EXPROPRIATIONS
AEIINOPRRSSSTU	PRESSURISATION
AEIINOPRRSSTUZ	PRESSURIZATION
AEILLMNOSSTUUY	SIMULTANEOUSLY
AEILLOOPPRRRTY	PROPRIETORALLY
AEILMNOPRRSTUY	SUPERNORMALITY
AEILNOOOPPRTUV	OVERPOPULATION
AEILNOOPRSSTTT	PETROL STATIONS
AEILNOOPSSTTUX	EXPOSTULATIONS
AEILNOOSSTTTUY	OSTENTATIOUSLY
AEIMNNOOPPRSTT	APPORTIONMENTS
AEINOORRSSSTTU	TRAITOROUSNESS
AELLMNOOOPPRT	MONOPROPELLANT
AFFGHNNOOSSTUW	SAWN-OFF SHOTGUN
AFGGHHIIRSSTTT	STRAIGHT FIGHTS
AFGIIIILLNNOSTT	FILLING STATION
AFIIIMMNNOORST	MISINFORMATION
AFIILLMORSTUUY	MULTIFARIOUSLY
AGGHIIIKNNRSUU	SINKIANG-UIGHUR
AGGHILNOOPRSTY	PHARYNGOLOGIST
AGGIIILNNORTVY	INVIGORATINGLY
AGGIILNNOPPRRS	GRAPPLING IRONS
AGGLLNOOOORTYY	OTOLARYNGOLOGY
AGHHIIOOPRRSTY	HISTORIOGRAPHY
AGHHILOOOPSTTY	HISTOPATHOLOGY
AGHHLOOOPPTTYY	PHYTOPATHOLOGY
AGHIILLMNPSTYY	SYMPATHIZINGLY
AGHIINOOPRSTZ	APOSTROPHIZING
AGHILNOOOPRSTT	ANTHROPOLOGIST
AGIIIILLNNNQRTUZ	TRANQUILLIZING
AGIIILNOSTUVVV	VULVOVAGINITIS
AGIILLNOOPSTT	POLLING STATION
AGIILMNNNOSTTU	NONSTIMULATING
AGINOPPPRRSTTU	SUPPORTING PART
AGLMMOOOPSTTYY	SYMPTOMATOLOGY
AHHIILNOPPRSTT	PHILANTHROPIST
AHHLLNOOPSTUXY	XANTHOPHYLLOUS
AHIIIMMNOOOSSU	HOMOIOUSIANISM
AHIILMNNOORSUY	INHARMONIOUSLY
AHIILMOOPSSSST	HISTOPLASMOSIS
AHIILNOPRSSTUU	SULPHURISATION
AHIILNOPRSTUUZ	SULPHURIZATION
AIIIILNOORSTTV	VITRIOLISATION
AIIIILNOORTTVZ	VITRIOLIZATION
AIIIMNOOPRSSTV	IMPROVISATIONS
AIIIMNRSSSTTVY	TRANSMISSIVITY

AIIINNNOOSTTUW	NO-WIN SITUATION	BCEIIIILNORTTVY	CONVERTIBILITY
AIIINNORSTTTUY	INSTITUTIONARY	BCEIIILPSSTTUY	SUSCEPTIBILITY
AIILMNNOOOOPST	MONOPOLISATION	BCFGIIMMNNOORS	COMBINING FORMS
AIILMNNOOOOPTZ	MONOPOLIZATION	BCGIIILMOOORST	MICROBIOLOGIST
AIILMNOOPRSSUY	PARSIMONIOUSLY	BCIIILOPRRTTUY	CORRUPTIBILITY
AIILNOOOPPSSTT	POSTPOSITIONAL	BCIIMNOORSSTTU	OBSTRUCTIONISM
AIINNOOPRSSSTT	TRANSPOSITIONS	BCIINOORSSTTTU	OBSTRUCTIONIST
AILLNOOOPPRRTY	PROPORTIONALLY	BCIKMNNOOPRTUUY	COUNTRY BUMPKIN
BBBCGHINRRSSUU	SCRUBBING BRUSH	BDDEEEELNNORTU	DOUBLE ENTENDRE
BBCDEEIORRSSUV	OVERSUBSCRIBED	BDDEEEILNOOPRX	PEROXIDE BLONDE
BBCDGIIKLLNOSU	BUILDING BLOCKS	BDDEFFIINORRTU	FORBIDDEN FRUIT
BBCEGILMNORSTU	CLUSTER BOMBING	BDDEFGIINNORSS	FORBIDDINGNESS
BBCGIKLLMNOSTU	STUMBLING BLOCK	BDEEEFGILNOSTT	FEEDING BOTTLES
BBCIIILMOSTTUY	COMBUSTIBILITY	BDEEEGIJLLNOSU	GOLDEN JUBILEES
BBCILNOOOOPPRU	PRO BONO PUBLICO	BDEEEGIMMNOSTU	DISEMBOGUEMENT
BBDEEGHIINRRSU	RUBBER DINGHIES	BDEEEHHIIMNSTT	BEHIND THE TIMES
BBDEEGILNOOOSU	BOIS DE BOULOGNE	BDEEEEHINORTTTT	TO THE BITTER END
BBEEEGILLNOOSS	NOBLESSE OBLIGE	BDEEEIINNNORTZ	DINITROBENZENE
BBEIIILMRSSTUY	SUBMERSIBILITY	BDEEEILMMNOSTW	DISEMBOWELMENT
BCCCGIIIMNRRSU	CIRCUMSCRIBING	BDEEFILMNPRRSU	PLUMBER'S FRIEND
BCCCIIMOOPRSSU	SUBMICROSCOPIC	BDEEGGHILMNOST	THE MIND BOGGLES
BCCDEEEGHIKLNOU	DOUBLE-CHECKING	BDEEGIIILLNSVY	DISBELIEVINGLY
BCCDEEIIJNORTT	INDIRECT OBJECT	BDEEGIILLMNOSW	DISEMBOWELLING
BCCEEEEGILRTTU	ICEBERG LETTUCE	BDEEGILLNRSTUW	TUNBRIDGE WELLS
BCCEEIKKKNORRS	KNICKERBOCKERS	BDEEIMNOOORRTW	ON BORROWED TIME
BCCEEIIIJSSTTUV	SUBJECTIVISTIC	BDEELOOPRRSSSU	BLOOD PRESSURES
BCCHINOOORPSST	BRONCHOSCOPIST	BDEGHHINOOORSU	NEIGHBOURHOODS
BCCILNOOSSSUUY	SUBCONSCIOUSLY	BDEGHIILNNNSST	NIGHT BLINDNESS
BCDEEEEILRRSTT	STREET-CREDIBLE	BDEGIIINRRSTTU	REDISTRIBUTING
BCDEEHHNOORSUU	BOUCHES-DU-RHONE	BDEIIIILMQRSUU	DISEQUILIBRIUM
BCDEEHILLLOOTW	WHITE BLOOD CELL	BDEIIIILNSSTTY	DISTENSIBILITY
BCDEEIILNRSTTU	INDESTRUCTIBLE	BDEIIILLNNOSSU	LIBIDINOUSNESS
BCDEELOORRSSSU	DOUBLE-CROSSERS	BDEIIILNPSSTUY	SUSPENDIBILITY
BCDEEMOOOPPRTT	COPPER-BOTTOMED	BDEIIILRSTTUVY	DISTRIBUTIVELY
BCDEGILNOORSSU	DOUBLE-CROSSING	BDEIIINORRSTTU	REDISTRIBUTION
BCDEIIIILRRTUY	IRREDUCIBILITY	BDGIILNNOOOOPS	BLOOD POISONING
BCDEIIILPPRSTU	PUBLIC-SPIRITED	BDHIILLOORSTTY	BLOODTHIRSTILY
BCDEIILNRSTTUY	INDESTRUCTIBLY	BDIIIIIILNSTVY	INDIVISIBILITY
BCEEEEEFKNOORRS	REFERENCE BOOKS	BEEEEHLNOOPSTX	TELEPHONE BOXES
BCEEEHILMNOPRS	COMPREHENSIBLE	BEEEELMNORSTUV	BOULEVERSEMENT
BCEEEILNOPRSWY	EYEBROW PENCILS	BEEEFFGIINNRST	FRINGE BENEFITS
BCEEFIIILPRTTY	PERFECTIBILITY	BEEEFFGIKNOOST	GET OFF ONE'S BIKE
BCEEGIILLLLNNPU	BLUE-PENCILLING	BEEEGGIIINNNOR	BIOENGINEERING
BCEEGIMNNNOSSU	UNBECOMINGNESS	BEEEHHLNOOOPTT	TELEPHONE BOOTH
BCEEHIILNOPRSY	HYPERBOLIC SINE	BEEEHILLMMNSST	EMBELLISHMENTS
BCEEHILMNOPRSY	COMPREHENSIBLY	BEEEHILORRRSTW	WHORTLEBERRIES
BCEEIIILPPRTTY	PERCEPTIBILITY	BEEEIIJLLRSSUV	SILVER JUBILEES
BCEEIILMNNOSTU	BIOLUMINESCENT	BEEEILLNORSSSU	REBELLIOUSNESS
BCEEIILMNOPRSS	INCOMPRESSIBLE	BEEEIMMNNRRSTU	REIMBURSEMENTS
BCEEILNOORRTTV	CONTROVERTIBLE	BEEEINRSSSSUVV	SUBVERSIVENESS
BCEEIMNNPRSTUU	SUPERINCUMBENT	BEEELLNOOOSSTT	LOSE ONE'S BOTTLE
BCEFHIKLOOOSTT	LICK THE BOOTS OF	BEEGIIIILLLNNTU	UNINTELLIGIBLE
BCEFHIMNOOOSTT	FINE-TOOTH COMBS	BEEGIIOOPRSTTU	PETIT BOURGEOIS
BCEFJMOOOORRSST	JOB'S COMFORTERS	BEEGIOOPRSTTUY	PETTY BOURGEOIS

BEEHHHILMNTTTU	HUNT THE THIMBLE	CCDEGIILNNOOOR	ENDOCRINOLOGIC
BEEHLOOORRSTTU	TROUBLESHOOTER	CCDEGINNNOORST	CONNECTING RODS
BEEIIILNOSSTVWY	LIVE BY ONE'S WITS	CCDEHHILLNOORS	SCHOOLCHILDREN
BEEIILNPPRSSSU	INSUPPRESSIBLE	CCDEHIIORRSTTU	SHORT-CIRCUITED
BEEIILOPRSSTVX	VISIBLE EXPORTS	CCDEIIINPRRTTU	PRINTED CIRCUIT
BEEIIMNSSSSSUV	SUBMISSIVENESS	CCDEIIMNNOOSTU	SEMICONDUCTION
BEEIKMNNOSSSUY	MONKEY BUSINESS	CCDEIINNNOOSST	DISCONNECTIONS
BEEIMNOOPPRSTU	OPPOSITE NUMBER	CCDEIIOOORRSTT	CORTICOSTEROID
BEEINOOQSSSSUU	OBSEQUIOUSNESS	CCDEIMNOORSSTU	SEMICONDUCTORS
BEEINOORSSSSTU	BOISTEROUSNESS	CCDENOOPPRRSTUU	SUPERCONDUCTOR
BEELMNORSSSSUU	SLUMBEROUSNESS	CCDGIIIMOOOPSS	SIGMOIDOSCOPIC
BEELOOPRRSSTUY	OBSTREPEROUSLY	CCDHHHOOOORRTUX	ORTHODOX CHURCH
BEFFGINNORRSTU	BURNT OFFERINGS	CCDHNOOOOPRTTU	PHOTOCONDUCTOR
BEFGILNRSSTTUY	FLYING BUTTRESS	CCEEEEEEJNNRSUV	REJUVENESCENCE
BEGGIIILSSTTUY	SUGGESTIBILITY	CCEEEEFHIITUUVX	CHIEF EXECUTIVE
BEGGILNOORSTTT	GLOBETROTTINGS	CCEEEEFNNNORSW	NEWS CONFERENCE
BEGHNOOORRSTTU	ROTTEN BOROUGHS	CCEEEEFNORRRSS	CROSS-REFERENCE
BEGILNORSSSUUU	LUGUBRIOUSNESS	CCEEEEMMMNNORT	RECOMMENCEMENT
BEHHIKNOOPSTTU	PUT THE KIBOSH ON	CCEEEFIIOPRSST	STEREOSPECIFIC
BEHIIIINOSSTTX	EXHIBITIONISTS	CCEEEGJLNNORTU	CONCRETE JUNGLE
BEIIIILMPRSSTY	PERMISSIBILITY	CCEEEHILMORRTT	THERMOELECTRIC
BEIIIILLORRSTUY	IRRESOLUBILITY	CCEEEHILMORSTT	ELECTROCHEMIST
BEIIIILMOPRSSTV	VISIBLE IMPORTS	CCEEEIIKLNORTT	ELECTROKINETIC
BEIIILNOPRSSTY	RESPONSIBILITY	CCEEEIINNNOSV	INCONVENIENCES
BEIINOQSSSTUUU	UBIQUITOUSNESS	CCEEEIMNORRSTX	CONCRETE MIXERS
BELOPRRSSSSTUU	BRUSSELS SPROUT	CCEEEINSSSSSUV	SUCCESSIVENESS
BGIILLMMNNOOUU	IMMUNOGLOBULIN	CCEEFFIILOOPRS	POLICE OFFICERS
BHIIIIMNOOPRST	PROHIBITIONISM	CCEEFFIILOORST	CORIOLIS EFFECT
BHIIIINOOPRSTT	PROHIBITIONIST	CCEEFHIINOPRST	CHIEF INSPECTOR
CCCDEEEENRRSSU	RECRUDESCENCES	CCEEFLNSSSSSUU	SUCCESSFULNESS
CCCDEEHIIOOPRT	CERCOPITHECOID	CCEEGHHHINNOSU	CHECHENO-INGUSH
CCCDGILOOORRTU	GLUCOCORTICORD	CCEEGIILLOOSST	ECCLESIOLOGIST
CCCEEEFIMNRRSU	CIRCUMFERENCES	CCEEHHIMNOSTTY	CHEMOSYNTHETIC
CCCEEEHHHIINNR	CHINCHERINCHEE	CCEEHIINORTTTY	THEOCENTRICITY
CCCEEEIIINRSTT	ECCENTRICITIES	CCEEHILOOPRSTU	HEROIC COUPLETS
CCCEEFIIINNOST	SCIENCE FICTION	CCEEHIMNNORRSY	CHIMNEY CORNERS
CCCEHHINOPSSTY	PSYCHOTECHNICS	CCEEHINOPRSSTY	PYROTECHNICSES
CCCEIIILMNRSSU	CIRCUMSCISSILE	CCEEIINNOSSTTU	CONSTITUENCIES
CCCEIIILORSSUV	VICIOUS CIRCLES	CCEEILLMOORSTT	COLLECTOR'S ITEM
CCCEIIMMNOOORS	MICROECONOMICS	CCEEILLNNOOTUV	COLLECTIVE NOUN
CCCEIIMNOPRSTU	CIRCUMSPECTION	CCEEILNOORSTTU	ELECTROCUTIONS
CCCIIIMORRRTUY	MICROCIRCUITRY	CCEEINNOOPPRST	PRECONCEPTIONS
CCCIILMNOORTUU	CIRCUMLOCUTION	CCEEINOOORRSTT	CORTICOSTERONE
CCCILMOORRTUUY	CIRCUMLOCUTORY	CCEEINOOPRRSUW	OWNER-OCCUPIERS
CCCILNNOOSTUUY	COUNTY COUNCILS	CCEEINOOPRSSSU	PRECOCIOUSNESS
CCDDEEEILLMNNOS	CONDEMNED CELLS	CCEEINORRSTTUV	RECONSTRUCTIVE
CCDDEEILNNOSTY	DISCONNECTEDLY	CCEGHIIKNNPRSS	SPRING CHICKENS
CCDEEEEIILLLRST	DIESEL-ELECTRIC	CCEGIILNNRRSTU	TURNING CIRCLES
CCDEEEFFILNNOS	SELF-CONFIDENCE	CCEGINNORRSTTU	RECONSTRUCTING
CCDEEEHIINPRST	INDIRECT SPEECH	CCEHHIIKOSSSTW	SCOTCH WHISKIES
CCDEEEIINNNNOV	INCONVENIENCED	CCEHHIINOPRSSZ	SCHIZOPHRENICS
CCDEEEIINPRSVY	VICE-PRESIDENCY	CCEHHIOOPSSUYZ	SCHIZOPHYCEOUS
CCDEEEENNOOPRRS	CORRESPONDENCE	CCEHIIIMOORSTT	STOICHIOMETRIC
CCDEEGIIILNNRV	DRIVING LICENCE	CCEHIIMMORRSTY	MICROCHEMISTRY

CCEHIMMNOSTTUY	COMMUNITY CHEST
CCEHIMOOSSTUYZ	SCHIZOMYCETOUS
CCEHINOOPRSTUY	PSYCHONEUROTIC
CCEIILLNNOSUVY	INCONCLUSIVELY
CCEIIMNNOOPSST	MISCONCEPTIONS
CCEILNORSTTUVY	CONSTRUCTIVELY
CCEILOOORRSSTU	STERCORICOLOUS
CCEIMMOOPRRSTU	MICROCOMPUTERS
CCEIMOOOPRRRSS	MICROPROCESSOR
CCEIMORRRSTTUU	MICROSTRUCTURE
CCEINNOOPRRSST	PRINCES CONSORT
CCEINNOORRSTTU	RECONSTRUCTION
CCEINOORRSSSTU	CROSS-COUNTRIES
CCEIOOPPRSSSTT	SPECTROSCOPIST
CCGHIILOOPSSTY	PSYCHOLOGISTIC
CCGIILNNNNOUVY	UNCONVINCINGLY
CCHIINOOOPRRTT	CORTICOTROPHIN
CCHIIOPRRRTVYY	PYRRHIC VICTORY
CCIIIJNNOSTTUV	CONJUNCTIVITIS
CCIIILPRSSTTUU	PISCICULTURIST
CCIILMNOORTUUV	CIRCUMVOLUTION
CCIIMNORSTTUVW	CONSTRUCTIVISM
CCIINORSSTTTUV	CONSTRUCTIVIST
CCILMOORRTUUVY	CIRCUMVOLUTORY
CCINNOORSSTUUY	COUNTRY COUSINS
CDDDEEHLLOORSU	COLD SHOULDERED
CDDDEEEEFLRSSTTU	SELF-DESTRUCTED
CDDEEEELLMNOTUW	WELL-DOCUMENTED
CDDEEILNNOSTTY	DISCONTENTEDLY
CDDEGHIIILOPRS	CHILD PRODIGIES
CDDEHIIILMOORSU	SODIUM CHLORIDE
CDDEILNOOOSTUY	DICOTYLEDONOUS
CDEEEEEIINNQSUV	QUEEN'S EVIDENCE
CDEEEEHNOPPRRST	REPORTED SPEECH
CDEEEEEILNPRSTT	PRESIDENT-ELECT
CDEEEEEIORSTTTV	STORE DETECTIVE
CDEEEEEIQRSSTUZ	CREDIT SQUEEZES
CDEEEEENNPSSTUX	UNEXPECTEDNESS
CDEEEEFGILLNNSU	SELF-INDULGENCE
CDEEEEFILORRTTT	LETTER OF CREDIT
CDEEEEFIMNNOPRS	PRESENCE OF MIND
CDEEEGILNNORUV	OVERINDULGENCE
CDEEEIIMMNOOSX	MIXED ECONOMIES
CDEEEIINNRSSV	DINNER SERVICES
CDEEEILOOPRSTT	ELECTRODEPOSIT
CDEEEINRRSSSTT	RESTRICTEDNESS
CDEEELNNNOOORT	NOLO CONTENDERE
CDEEENNNOQRUUW	UNCROWNED QUEEN
CDEEFGHINNNRRSS	FRENCH DRESSING
CDEEFHHILNOPRS	FRENCH POLISHED
CDEEFIIIILLNPSS	SELF-DISCIPLINE
CDEEFLLLNOORST	SELF-CONTROLLED
CDEEGGINNOSSSU	SECOND-GUESSING
CDEEHILNNORSSW	CHINLESS WONDER

CDEEHLLLOORSUY	HYDROCELLULOSE
CDEEIIINNSSTVV	VINDICTIVENESS
CDEEIIINOPPRST	EDITIO PRINCEPS
CDEEIINRSSSTUV	DISCURSIVENESS
CDEEILLNNOOPTUY	POLYNUCLEOTIDE
CDEEILMOOOPPSUX	OEDIPUS COMPLEX
CDEEIMNNNOOPTT	DISCONTENTMENT
CDEEINNOOORSSSU	INDECOROUSNESS
CDEEINOPRSSTUV	PRODUCTIVENESS
CDEEKKLNRSSTUU	KNUCKLE-DUSTERS
CDEENNOOPRRSST	CORRESPONDENTS
CDEFIIIMMMOSSU	FIDEICOMMISSUM
CDEFOOOOPRRSSS	FOOD PROCESSORS
CDEGHHIIILNPPR	HIGH-PRINCIPLED
CDEGHHILLOORUY	HIGHLY COLOURED
CDEGHHNOOSSTTU	SECOND THOUGHTS
CDEGIIINNNOORT	RECONDITIONING
CDEGINOOPRRSSW	WORD PROCESSING
CDEHILMNNOOPTT	HOLD IN CONTEMPT
CDEHINOOORRSTY	HYDROCORTISONE
CDEIIIILRSTTUV	DIVERTICULITIS
CDEIIILORSSTUV	DIVERTICULOSIS
CDEIIIINNSSTT	INDISTINCTNESS
CDEIIILNNOOPRTU	PRODUCTION LINE
CDEIILNORSSSUU	RIDICULOUSNESS
CDEIINNNOORRTTU	REINTRODUCTION
CDEIINNOOPRSSU	UNDER SUSPICION
CDEIINNOPRSSUU	SUPERINDUCTION
CDEIINOPRSTUWW	PICTURE WINDOWS
CDEIINORSSTTTU	DESTRUCTIONIST
CDEILOORSSTUUY	DISCOURTEOUSLY
CDEINOOOPRRTUV	OVERPRODUCTION
CDEINOORSSSTTU	DISCOUNT STORES
CDEOOOPRRRSSSW	WORD PROCESSORS
CDFIINNOOOOTTU	OUT OF CONDITION
CDGIILMNOOPSSY	DISCOMPOSINGLY
CDHHILLLOOOPRY	CHLOROPHYLLOID
CDHINOOOPRSSTT	PROSTHODONTICS
CDIIJNNNNOOSTU	NONDISJUNCTION
CDIILMMNOOOSUY	INCOMMODIOUSLY
CDIILNOORRTTUY	INTRODUCTORILY
CEEEEFFLNRSTVY	EFFERVESCENTLY
CEEEEFILNRSSTV	REFLECTIVENESS
CEEEEFNPPRRSTT	PRESENT PERFECT
CEEEEGIILNNORT	ELECTIONEERING
CEEEEHLNPSSSSS	SPEECHLESSNESS
CEEEFFGHIOPRSU	FIGURE OF SPEECH
CEEEFFGIIORRST	REGISTER OFFICE
CEEEFFGILNRSVY	EFFERVESCINGLY
CEEEFFLLPRSSTU	SELF-RESPECTFUL
CEEEFGILNPRSST	SELF-RESPECTING
CEEEFGLLNNSSTU	NEGLECTFULNESS
CEEEFIIOPRRSTV	IRRESPECTIVE OF
CEEEFIMNNORRST	REINFORCEMENTS

CEEEFINORRSTTU	COUNTERFEITERS
CEEEFLNPRSSSTU	RESPECTFULNESS
CEEEFNOORSSTUV	VOTES OF CENSURE
CEEEGGINORRSTU	GEIGER COUNTERS
CEEEGIIILNNRSV	CIVIL ENGINEERS
CEEEGIILLNNNTU	UNINTELLIGENCE
CEEEGIIMNNOPRT	SPERMIOGENETIC
CEEEGILNORRTTV	COVERING LETTER
CEEEGLORRRSTUY	ELECTROSURGERY
CEEEHIKNNOPPSU	KEEP ONE'S CHIN UP
CEEEHIMNOPRSSV	COMPREHENSIVES
CEEEHIMORSSTTY	HYSTERECTOMIES
CEEEHKMNNORSWY	MONKEY WRENCHES
CEEEHLMNOORRTT	THERMOELECTRON
CEEEHNOORRTTUV	OVER THE COUNTER
CEEEIIKNNPRSST	PERNICKETINESS
CEEEIIMMOORRTT	MICROMETEORITE
CEEEIILMMNOPRST	COMPLEMENTISER
CEEEIILMMNOPRTZ	COMPLEMENTIZER
CEEEIILMNNOPSST	INCOMPLETENESS
CEEEIMMNNOPRTV	PINCER MOVEMENT
CEEEINOPRSSTTV	PROTECTIVENESS
CEEEIOPRRSSTTV	RETROSPECTIVES
CEEEKOOPRRRSSU	PRESSURE COOKER
CEEELNNOQSSSUU	QUEEN'S COUNSELS
CEEEMMNNORRSTU	COUNTERMENSURE
CEEENNOPPPRRRT	PEPPERCORN RENT
CEEFFFIILNSSTU	SELF-SUFFICIENT
CEEFFGIIORRSTY	REGISTRY OFFICE
CEEFGIINNORTTU	COUNTERFEITING
CEEFGINORRRSS	CROSS-REFERRING
CEEFHIILMNNOSU	ICHNEUMON FLIES
CEEFIILNOSSSTU	FELICITOUSNESS
CEEFIILORRSSTT	CROSS-FERTILISE
CEEFIILORRSSTZ	CROSS-FERTILIZE
CEEFIINNOSSSTU	INFECTIOUSNESS
CEEFIINOPRSSTT	PERFECTIONISTS
CEEFILNOOPRSTT	SELF-PROTECTION
CEEFINOOOOPSTV	TOP OF ONE'S VOICE
CEEFINOORSSSUV	VOCIFEROUSNESS
CEEGHINNOPPRST	SHOPPING CENTRE
CEEGIILNNORRTY	NITROGLYCERINE
CEEGIIMMNNOSTU	IMMUNOGENETICS
CEEGIINNNPRRST	SCREEN PRINTING
CEEGILLLLNOOSU	LIGNOCELLULOSE
CEEGILLNORSSSV	LEVEL CROSSINGS
CEEHHIMNOSSSTY	CHEMOSYNTHESIS
CEEHHMOOOORRSTU	HETEROCHROMOUS
CEEHHNOOPPRSST	PHOSPHORESCENT
CEEHHNORSSTTTU	HORSE CHESTNUTS
CEEHIILMOPRRTY	PYRHELIOMETRIC
CEEHIIMOPRSTYZ	PIEZOCHEMISTRY
CEEHIIOOPRRTTY	ERYTHROPOIETIC
CEEHIMMOPSSSTY	METEMPSYCHOSIS

CEEHIMNNOOPRSS	COMPREHENSIONS
CEEHIMNNORSSTT	ETHNOCENTRISMS
CEEHIMOPRRSTTY	PETROCHEMISTRY
CEEHNOPRSSTTUW	PUT THE SCREWS ON
CEEIIILMRSSSSU	CRUISE MISSILES
CEEIIIMPPRTTVY	IMPERCEPTIVITY
CEEIIINNORSSST	SENIOR CITISENS
CEEIIINNORSSTZ	SENIOR CITIZENS
CEEIIILLMNORSTT	SCINTILLOMETER
CEEIIILMORRSTUY	MERETRICIOUSLY
CEEIIILNNNNOTVY	INCONVENIENTLY
CEEIIILNNOSSSTU	LICENTIOUSNESS
CEEIIILNORSSTTW	WINTER SOLSTICE
CEEIIILPPRRSTVY	PRESCRIPTIVELY
CEEIIINNOPRSSSY	PERNICIOUSNESS
CEEIIINNORSSTTV	NONRESTRICTIVE
CEEIIOOPPPRRTV	PROPRIOCEPTIVE
CEEIKLNOORSTTT	SILK-COTTON TREE
CEEIKNORRRRSTT	TERROR-STRICKEN
CEEILLLNOORSTU	NITROCELLULOSE
CEEILMMORSSSTU	SUMMER SOLSTICE
CEEILMNOPSSSUV	COMPULSIVENESS
CEEILMNOSSSTUU	METICULOUSNESS
CEEILNORRSTTUU	INTERLOCUTRESS
CEEILNORRSSUYY	YOURS SINCERELY
CEEIIMMOOPRRRTY	MICROPYROMETER
CEEIMNOOOPRRST	RECEPTION ROOMS
CEEINNORSSSSUU	CENSORIOUSNESS
CEEIINNOSSSSTUU	INCESTUOUSNESS
CEEINOOOPRRTTV	OVERPROTECTION
CEEINOOPRSSTTU	PRECIOUS STONES
CEELLNOORSSSSU	COLOURLESSNESS
CEEMNNNOOPRSTU	PRONOUNCEMENTS
CEEPRRRSSTTUUU	SUPERSTRUCTURE
CEFFFGIIILNORSY	FLYING OFFICERS
CEFFIIIILLNNOST	SELF-INFLICTION
CEFFIIIILLNNSTUY	INSUFFICIENTLY
CEFGHIMNOORSUZ	GNOMES OF ZURICH
CEFGIIKLLNORST	STOCKING-FILLER
CEFHMMNOOOOSSU	HOUSE OF COMMONS
CEFIIINOSSSTTU	FICTITIOUSNESS
CEGGHHHIILNOOTY	HIGH TECHNOLOGY
CEGGIINNNORSTU	COUNTERSIGNING
CEGHIJNOOPRSTU	HOUSING PROJECT
CEGHIMMNPRSSTU	SPRECHSTIMMUNG
CEGHINNOOSSTUU	COUNTINGHOUSES
CEGIIILNOORSST	CORELIGIONISTS
CEGIIKNNNORSTU	COUNTERSINKING
CEGIIMNOPRSTUV	MOVING PICTURES
CEGIINNOOPRSTI	COUNTERPOISING
CEGIINNORSTTTU	RECONSTITUTING
CEHHIIMORSSTTY	HISTOCHEMISTRY
CEHHIMMNOOOOPPR	MORPHOPHONEMIC
CEHHIMOOPRSTTY	PHOTOCHEMISTRY

CEHHINOOPSTTTY	PHOTOSYNTHETIC	CHIIOOORSSTTXY	THYROTOXICOSIS
CEHHOOOOPPPRSS	PHOSPHOROSCOPE	CHILMOOORSTTUY	TRICHOTOMOUSLY
CEHIINOPRRSTTT	STREPTOTHRICIN	CIIILLRSSTTUUV	SILVICULTURIST
CEHIJMNNOORTTU	THERMOJUNCTION	CIINNOOORSSTTT	CONTORTIONISTS
CEHIKNOORRRRST	HORROR-STRICKEN	CLLNOPRSSUUUUY	UNSCRUPULOUSLY
CEHILMMOOPRSUY	MYRMECOPHILOUS	DDDEEGGILNNOSW	GOLDEN WEDDINGS
CEHILMOORSSSST	SCHOOLMISTRESS	DDEEEEEGNRRSWY	DYER'S-GREENWEED
CEHIMMMNOOSTUY	COMMUNITY HOMES	DDEEEEIMNNRSST	DETERMINEDNESS
CEHINOOPRSSNOS	PSYCHONEUROSIS	DDEEEEINNNPRTT	INTERDEPENDENT
CEHLNOORRSSSUY	NURSERY SCHOOLS	DDEEEELMMNOSSS	MEDDLESOMENESS
CEIIIINOSSTTVY	VIVISECTIONIST	DDEEEIIKLMNNSS	LIKE-MINDEDNESS
CEIIIILNOOSTTUV	EVOLUTIONISTIC	DDEEEIILMNNSSV	EVIL-MINDEDNESS
CEIIIMPPRRSSTV	PRESCRIPTIVISM	DDEEEIINQSSSTU	DISQUIETEDNESS
CEIIINORRSSTTT	RESTRICTIONIST	DDEEEIMNNNOPSS	OPEN-MINDEDNESS
CEIIIPPRRSSTTV	PRESCRIPTIVIST	DDEEEIMNNNORTU	UNDERMENTIONED
CEIIJNOOPRSSTT	PROJECTIONISTS	DDEEGHHIIMNSSU	HIGH-MINDEDNESS
CEIILLOPRSSUUY	SUPERCILIOUSLY	DDEEGIIILMSSSU	GUIDED MISSILES
CEIILNNNOSSTTY	INCONSISTENTLY	DDEEGIIILLMNNSY	SINGLE-MINDEDLY
CEIILNOORRRSTT	TRINITROCRESOL	DDEEGIILNRSSVW	SILVER WEDDINGS
CEIILNOOSSSSTU	SOLICITOUSNESS	DDEEGILNNNOSSW	LONGWINDEDNESS
CEIIMMNNNOORTU	INTERCOMMUNION	DDEEHINNORRSUU	UNDERNOURISHED
CEIIMNNOOOPSSU	PNEUMOCONIOSIS	DDEEIIJNNOSSST	DISJOINTEDNESS
CEIIMNOOPRSTTU	MOTION PICTURES	DDEEIILNORRSSS	DISORDERLINESS
CEIINNOORSTTTU	RECONSTITUTION	DDEEINNOPSSSUW	UPSIDE-DOWNNESS
CEIINOOPRSSTTT	PROTECTIONISTS	DDEGGHINNOSTUW	SHOTGUN WEDDING
CEIINOORSSSTUV	VICTORIOUSNESS	DDEGHLMOOORUUY	GOOD-HUMOUREDLY
CEIINOPPRRSSTU	SUPERSCRIPTION	DDEGIINNORSSWW	WINDOW DRESSING
CEIINOPRRSSSTU	PERCUSSIONISTS	DDEGILMNNORSTY	STRONG-MINDEDLY
CEIINOPSSSSSUU	SUSPICIOUSNESS	DDEHIILNOPSSSS	SLIPSHODDINESS
CEILLMNOOSTUUY	CONTUMELIOUSLY	DDEHIMNNOPSTUW	DOWN IN THE DUMPS
CEILNOPRRSTUUV	PROVENTRICULUS	DEEEEFFGIRRRSZ	FRIDGE-FREEZERS
CEILNORRSSSSUU	SCURRILOUSNESS	DEEEEFILNRSSTT	SELF-INTERESTED
CEIMMMMOOORTTY	COMMIT TO MEMORY	DEEEEGHHNORTTT	TO THE NTH DEGREE
CEKLMOOPRSTTUU	MOCK TURTLE SOUP	DEEEEGINNRSSSV	EVENING DRESSES
CELMNOOPSTTUUY	CONTEMPTUOUSLY	DEEEEHMNORRRTV	REVEREND MOTHER
CELNOPRSSSSUUU	SCRUPULOUSNESS	DEEEEILLMMOSSS	MESDEMOISELLES
CFFHIILMNOSTTU	FIFTH COLUMNIST	DEEEEIMNPRRRST	PREDETERMINERS
CFFIKKLORRSTTU	FORKLIFT TRUCKS	DEEEEIMNPRRSST	MISREPRESENTED
CFIILLORRSTTUU	FLORICULTURIST	DEEEEINRSSTTTV	VESTED INTEREST
CFIINOOQRRTUUY	COURT OF INQUIRY	DEEEELMNOPRSTV	REDEVELOPMENTS
CFIMNNNOOORSST	NONCONFORMISTS	DEEEENNRRSSSUV	UNRESERVEDNESS
CGHHIIIMMNOOSS	HIGH COMMISSION	DEEEFFGOORRSST	DEGREES OF FROST
CGHIIKNOOSSTTT	SHOOTING STICKS	DEEEFIIINNNSST	INDEFINITENESS
CGHIILNOPSSTUY	PSYCHOLINGUIST	DEEEFILNNRSSSS	FRIENDLESSNESS
CGHILOOOOPSTYY	PHYTOSOCIOLOGY	DEEEFNOORSSSTU	SUREFOOTEDNESS
CGIIIKNNOPSSTT	STICKING POINTS	DEEEGIIKLNNNTT	KNITTING NEEDLE
CGIIILMNOORSST	CRIMINOLOGISTS	DEEEGIIMNNPRRT	PREDETERMINING
CGIIILNNRSTUYZ	SCRUTINIZINGLY	DEEEGILNOOPRVV	OVERDEVELOPING
CGIIILNOOOPSST	OLIGOPSONISTIC	DEEEGIOPRRSSTT	REGISTERED POST
CGIIMMNNOOPRSU	UNCOMPROMISING	DEEEHHLLOORSTT	THREE-TOED SLOTH
CHHKNOORSSTTUW	NOT WORTH SHUCKS	DEEEHHPPRRSSUU	SHEPHERD'S-PURSE
CHHLLLOOOPRSUY	CHLOROPHYLLOUS	DEEEHLLMOOOPPS	OLD PEOPLE'S HOME
CHIILORRSTTTUU	HORTICULTURIST	DEEEHLMNNOOSWY	HONEYDEW MELONS
CHIINOPRRSSTTU	INSTRUCTORSHIP	DEEEIIMNPRRSTT	MISINTERPRETED

DEEEIIMNRSSTTV	DIVERTISSEMENT
DEEEIINORRSSVV	REVISED VERSION
DEEEILNPRRSSTY	INTERSPERSEDLY
DEEEINNNPRSTTU	SUPERINTENDENT
DEEEINOQSSTUVX	VEXED QUESTIONS
DEEELLNNORRSSU	ENROLLED NURSES
DEEEMNNORSSSTU	TREMENDOUSNESS
DEEFFFINORRSST	FIRST OFFENDERS
DEEFFIIIMNNRST	INDIFFERENTISM
DEEFFIIINNRSTT	INDIFFERENTIST
DEEFGHILLNSSTU	DELIGHTFULNESS
DEEFGHINOORSTW	THE WRONG SIDE OF
DEEFGIIMNRSSTU	DISFIGUREMENTS
DEEFIIILMOPRSV	OVERSIMPLIFIED
DEEFIIILNNRSSU	UNFRIENDLINESS
DEEFIIINOPRSSU	PERFIDIOUSNESS
DEEFILOORRSTUY	DO-IT-YOURSELFER
DEEFLOORRRTTUW	FOUR-LETTER WORD
DEEGHILLNOSSUW	DWELLING HOUSES
DEEGIIIILMOOPST	EPIDEMIOLOGIST
DEEGIINNNOSSSU	INDIGENOUSNESS
DEEGIINNNPRSTU	SUPERINTENDING
DEEGILMNNRSTTU	DISGRUNTLEMENT
DEEGLNNORSSSSU	GROUNDLESSNESS
DEEHHIOOOPPRRSW	HERO WORSHIPPED
DEEHNNOORRSSSU	HORRENDOUSNESS
DEEIIIILMRSTUV	VERISIMILITUDE
DEEIIILNOPRSTV	VESPERTILIONID
DEEIIILNOORSTUV	REVOLUTIONISED
DEEIIILNOORTUVZ	REVOLUTIONIZED
DEEKNOOPPRRSTV	DNEPROPETROVSK
DEENNOOOOPRSST	ON ONE'S DOORSTEP
DEENNOPSSSSTUU	STUPENDOUSNESS
DEFFIIIILNOOSSV	FIELDS OF VISION
DEFHILLNOQTTUU	NOT THE FULL QUID
DEGHHIIIILMNOTT	THE MIDNIGHT OIL
DEGHHIIKLRSTTU	TURKISH DELIGHT
DEGHHILORSSTTY	SHORTSIGHTEDLY
DEGHILNOORSSYY	HYDROGENOLYSIS
DEGIIKLNNNOSSV	LOVING KINDNESS
DEGIIILNNOORRSS	SOLDERING IRONS
DEGIILNNOSSUUY	DISINGENUOUSLY
DEGIINOOPRSSSU	PRODIGIOUSNESS
DEGILNOORSSTUY	SOUL-DESTROYING
DEHIIMOOOPPRST	PHOTOPERIODISM
DEHIMMOOPPRSSU	PSEUDOMORPHISM
DEHINOOPPRSSWW	WINDOW-SHOPPERS
DEIIINOOPPRSST	PREDISPOSITION
DEIILOOPPRRSTY	POOR-SPIRITEDLY
DEIIMNNNRSTTUW	WIND INSTRUMENT
DEILMNOOPSSTU	DIPLOSTEMONOUS
DEILNNNOPSSUU	SUN IN SPLENDOUR
DEILNORSSSSTUU	STRIDULOUSNESS
DEINNNOSSSTTUU	STUDENTS' UNIONS
DFGGHINNOOOORT	GOOD-FOR-NOTHING
DGGHIIIINNSSTU	DISTINGUISHING
DGGHINNNORSTUU	HUNTING GROUNDS
DGGINNOOPRRSUV	PROVING GROUNDS
DGHIINNOOPPSWW	WINDOW-SHOPPING
DGIIIIILLNNOSSU	DISILLUSIONING
DHINOOOPRSSTTT	PROSTHODONTIST
DIIIINNOOPSSST	INDISPOSITIONS
EEEEEFINPRRRST	FREE ENTERPRISE
EEEEEKMNOPPRST	KEEP ONE'S TEMPER
EEEEELPRSTTTTY	TELETYPESETTER
EEEEFHINNOORTY	ONE IN THE EYE FOR
EEEEFILPRRRSSV	LIFE PRESERVERS
EEEEFIMNORRRTT	INTERFEROMETER
EEEEGHILNRSSTW	STEERING WHEELS
EEEEGINRRSSSSV	REGRESSIVENESS
EEEEGJLLORRSUW	JEWELLER'S ROUGE
EEEEHKLLRRSSTT	HELTER-SKELTERS
EEEEIINPRSSTTV	REPETITIVENESS
EEEEIMNPRRRSST	MISREPRESENTER
EEEEINNPRSSTVV	PREVENTIVENESS
EEEEINPRRSSSSV	REPRESSIVENESS
EEEEINPRSSSSVX	EXPRESSIVENESS
EEEELLNNRSSSST	RELENTLESSNESS
EEEELMNOOPRSST	LOSE ONE'S TEMPER
EEEEFFLNORSSSST	EFFORTLESSNESS
EEEFGLMNNORSTV	SELF-GOVERNMENT
EEEFIMNORRRTTY	INTERFEROMETRY
EEEFLLMMNOPSTY	SELF-EMPLOYMENT
EEEFLLNORRSTTU	FORTUNE-TELLERS
EEEFLMNORRSSSU	REMORSEFULNESS
EEEFLNNNSSTUUV	UNEVENTFULNESS
EEEGGINSSSSTUV	SUGGESTIVENESS
EEEGHILNSSSSTW	WEIGHTLESSNESS
EEEGIIMNOPRSST	SPERMIOGENESIS
EEEHHIILNPRSTW	THREE-LINE WHIPS
EEEHHILMOPPSST	MEPHISTOPHELES
EEEHIINPRSSTVY	HYPERSENSITIVE
EEEHINNOSSTTTX	SIXTEENTH NOTES
EEEIILMNOPSSST	IMPOLITENESSES
EEEIILMNPRSSTT	SIMPLE INTEREST
EEEIIMNPRRRSTT	MISINTERPRETER
EEEIIMNPRSSSSV	IMPRESSIVENESS, PERMISSIVENESS
EEEILMNOSSSSTV	MOTIVELESSNESS
EEEIILNOPRSSSSX	EXPRESSIONLESS
EEEIMNOPPRRTSY	PEREMPTORINESS
EEEINNOPRSSSSV	RESPONSIVENESS
EEEINNPSSSSSUV	SUSPENSIVENESS
EEEINOPPRSSSSV	OPPRESSIVENESS
EEEINOPSSSSSSV	POSSESSIVENESS
EEEJLLLMOPRTUY	PETROLEUM JELLY
EEEMMMNNOOSTVW	WOMEN'S MOVEMENT
EEEOPRRRSSSSTU	TROUSER PRESSES

EEFFGGHIIORSTU	FIGURES OF EIGHT
EEFGGHINOOSTTT	NOT THE FOGGIEST
EEFGGIIIKLNNNS	SINKING FEELING
EEFGHINNOORRSU	FORESHORTENING
EEFGIINNOPRSTZ	FREEZING POINTS
EEFGINOORRRRST	REIGNS OF TERROR
EEFHIIINNORRST	IRONS IN THE FIRE
EEFHILNRSSSSTT	THRIFTLESSNESS
EEFHNNORRSTTUU	FORTUNE HUNTERS
EEFIIIILNRRTTY	INTERFERTILITY
EEFILNOOPSSSSS	SELF-POSSESSION
EEFLNOPPRSSSUU	PURPOSEFULNESS
EEGGHHIILLNNSTT	SHEET LIGHTNING
EEGGHIILLNNNTY	ENLIGHTENINGLY
EEGGIILNNNSTTT	STINGING NETTLE
EEGHHIIILLMNTT	IN THE LIMELIGHT
EEGHHIILOPSSVX	HIGH EXPLOSIVES
EEGHIIILNNNPSSW	SPINNING WHEELS
EEGHIIMNNSTTUX	EXTINGUISHMENT
EEGHIKNRRRSSTU	HUNGER STRIKERS
EEGHILLMNORVWY	OVERWHELMINGLY
EEGHINOOPPRRTY	PORPHYROGENITE
EEGHLNOOORSTUY	HETEROGONOUSLY
EEGIIILMNORTTU	ULTIMOGENITURE
EEGIILMOOPSSTT	EPISTEMOLOGIST
EEGIILNNPRRSTY	ENTERPRISINGLY
EEGILMOOORSSTT	METEOROLOGISTS
EEGILNOOPRRVWY	OVERPOWERINGLY
EEGINNOOPRRSSV	NONPROGRESSIVE
EEGINNOPPSSSTT	STEPPING-STONES
EEGINOPRRSSTTU	INTEREST GROUPS
EEGINORSSTTTUW	TONGUE TWISTERS
EEGINPRRSSSSTU	PURSE STRINGSES
EEGOPPRRRSSSUU	PRESSURE GROUPS
EEHHILNOORSSTWW	WORTH ONE'S WHILE
EEHHILNOORSSTWW	WORTHWHILENESS
EEHHIMMOOPRRST	HETEROMORPHISM
EEHHLLOOPRSTUY	HETEROPHYLLOUS
EEHHLLOORSSTUY	YOUTH HOSTELLER
EEHIILMNNQRSTU	RELINQUISHMENT
EEHIILNOPPRSTY	PYELONEPHRITIS
EEHIINOOPSSSTT	PHOTOSENSITISE
EEHIINOPSSTTV	PHOTOSENSITIVE
EEHIINOOPSSTTZ	PHOTOSENSITIZE
EEHIIOOPRRSSTY	ERYTHROPOIESIS
EEHILLOORSSTTT	TORTOISESHELLS
EEHIMOOPRRRSTU	MOTHER SUPERIOR
EEHINNOORSSTTW	NOTEWORTHINESS
EEHINNOPRRTTTU	THREE-POINT TURN
EEHINNORSSSTWW	NEWSWORTHINESS
EEHINOOPPQSTTU	POP THE QUESTION
EEHINOPQSTTTUU	PUT THE QUESTION
EEHLMNOOORSTUY	HETERONOMOUSLY
EEHLMNOORSTUYY	HETERONYMOUSLY
EEHLMNORSSSSUU	HUMOURLESSNESS
EEHMOOOPPRRTTY	PYROPHOTOMETER
EEIIIMMNPRRSST	PRIME MINISTERS
EEIILMNNRTTTTY	INTERMITTENTLY
EEIIILNOORRSTUV	REVOLUTIONISER
EEIIILNOORRTUVZ	REVOLUTIONIZER
EEIIILNPRSSSST	SPIRITLESSNESS
EEIINNOPRSTUVY	OPEN UNIVERSITY
EEIINOPRSSSSTX	EXPRESSIONISTS.
EEILLMOPRSSTTU	MULTIPLE STORES
EEILMNNOOSSSST	MOTIONLESSNESS
EEIMNORSSSSTUY	MYSTERIOUSNESS
EEINOOPRSSSSST	PREPOSSESSIONS
EEINOPPRRSSSTU	PRESSURE POINTS
EEINOPRRSSSTUV	PROTRUSIVENESS
EELOOPPRRSSTUY	PREPOSTEROUSLY
EEMNORSSSSTUVY	NERVOUS SYSTEMS
EENNOOOPPRRSST	PERSON-TO-PERSON
EENNOOPRSSSTTU	PORTENTOUSNESS
EENOOPPRSSSSUU	PROSPEROUSNESS
EENOORRSSSSTTU	STERTOROUSNESS
EFFGHHLLOORTTUU	FORETHOUGHTFUL
EFFGIIJLNSSTUY	SELF-JUSTIFYING
EFFILNNRSSTUUU	UNFRUITFULNESS
EFGGIIIINNNPRRT	FINGERPRINTING
EFGHHINORRSSTT	FORTHRIGHTNESS
EFGHHLNOSSTTUU	THOUGHTFULNESS
EFGHLNOOORSTWY	GLORY-OF-THE-SNOW
EFGILNOPPRSSTU	SELF-SUPPORTING
EFHILNOPRSSSUW	WORSHIPFULNESS
EFHIOOPPRRSSSS	PROFESSORSHIPS
EFHMMNOORSTTTU	MOMENTS OF TRUTH
EFINOORSSSTTUU	FORTUITOUSNESS
EGGHHIIINPRRSU	HIGH-PRESSURING
EGGIILMNNOORRS	MORNING GLORIES
EGHHILNNOOOTTT	LONG IN THE TOOTH
EGHHILNNORRSTT	NORTHERN LIGHTS
EGHHILNORSSTTU	SOUTHERN LIGHTS
EGIIIINNOQRSTU	REQUISITIONING
EGIIILMNNRTTTY	INTERMITTINGLY
EGIIILNNNRTTWY	INTERTWININGLY
EGIINNPRRSSSSU	SURPRISINGNESS
EGILNOPPRRSSTU	SPLINTER GROUPS
EHHINOOOPPPRST	PHOSPHOPROTEIN
EHHINOOPSSSTTY	PHOTOSYNTHESIS
EHHNNOORRSTTTW	NORTH-NORTHWEST
EHHOOSSSTTTUUW	SOUTH-SOUTHWEST
EHIIILNNOOPRTT	TRINITROPHENOL
EHILMNOPSSSTYY	POLYSYNTHESISM
EHINNOOPRSSTTU	PUT ONE'S SHIRT ON
EHLNOPRSSSSUUU	SULPHUROUSNESS
EHMOOOPPRRTTYY	PYROPHOTOMETRY
EIIIMNOPRSSSST	IMPRESSIONISTS
EIIINNOOPRSSTT	INTERPOSITIONS

EIILNOQRSSTTUV	VENTRILOQUISTS
EIINNORSSSTTUU	NUTRITIOUSNESS
EIINOOPPPRSSTU	PRESUPPOSITION
EIINOOPPRSSSTU	PROPITIOUSNESS
EIKNNNNOOOOSSW	KNOW ONE'S ONIONS
EILMNNOOSSSUUV	VOLUMINOUSNESS
EIMNNOOOPPRRTT	PROPORTIONMENT
EIMNOPRSSSSTTU	STIR ONE'S STUMPS
EINNOOPQRRSTUU	NON PROSEQUITUR
ELMNOSSSTTUUUU	TUMULTUOUSNESS
ELMOPPRSSTUUUY	PRESUMPTUOUSLY
ELNOOPSSSTUUUV	VOLUPTUOUSNESS

EMNNNOOSSSSUYY	SYNONYMOUSNESS
FGHHLLOOORSTUW	FOLLOW-THROUGHS
FGHIILLMNOOSTT	MOONLIGHT FLITS
GHHIIILNOOPPSZ	PHILOSOPHIZING
GHIILNOOORSSTT	ORNITHOLOGISTS
GIIINNOOOPPRST	PROPOSITIONING
GIIKMMNNRSSTUW	SWIMMING TRUNKS
GILOOOOOPRSTTZ	PROTOZOOLOGIST
HHINOOOOPPRSSU	SIPHONOPHOROUS
IIIIINNOQSSTTU	INQUISITIONIST
IIINOOPRRSSSTV	PRISON VISITORS

AAAAACDEHHMMRRS	MAD AS A MARCH HARE
AAAAADDEGINSTTV	AT A DISADVANTAGE
AAAABBDIKKLNORR	KABARDINO-BALKAR
AAAABCEILLNOOPT	PALAEOBOTANICAL
AAAABGHKKNNOORR	NAGORNO-KARABAKH
AAAACCDIIKLLLSY	LACKADAISICALLY
AAAACCEHHLNNOPT	ACANTHOCEPHALAN
AAAACCILLLLPRTY	PARALLACTICALLY
AAAACDEGILRRUWY	DUAL CARRIAGEWAY
AAAACEFFMORSTTT	AS A MATTER OF FACT
AAAACEGHILLOPPR	PALAEOGRAPHICAL
AAAACEILLMNNRTY	ALIMENTARY CANAL
AAAACFGHHILMNSU	HALF AS MUCH AGAIN
AAAACGHILLPRRYY	PARAGRAPHICALLY
AAAAEIILMNNPRRT	PARLIAMENTARIAN
AAAAFIIMNRRSSST	RASTAFARIANISMS
AAABBCEILNNPRSU	BANANA REPUBLICS
AAABBDDIIILNNQZ	INQILAB ZINDABAD
AAABCEEHINRRTTT	TETRABRANCHIATE
AAABCHIILOPPRTY	APPROACHABILITY
AAABCIIILNNNOTZ	CANNIBALIZATION
AAABDGHKKNNOORS	GORNO-BADAKHSHAN
AAABDHIMOPRSSSS	AMBASSADORSHIPS
AAABEGHHINOTTUV	HAVE A THING ABOUT
AAABEGIIILMRRTY	MARRIAGEABILITY
AAABEHIILNOPSTT	ALPHABETISATION
AAABEHIILNOPTTZ	ALPHABETIZATION
AAABEIILLMNNPRRS	PRIMA BALLERINAS
AAABIILLNRSTTTY	TRANSLATABILITY
AAABILNNRSSTTTU	TRANSUBSTANTIAL
AAACCDEEILOPSSU	ASCLEPIADACEOUS
AAACCDHIMMNOPRY	PHARMACODYNAMIC
AAACCEEFHILMRRW	CHEMICAL WARFARE
AAACCEGHIKNRRY	HACKNEY CARRIAGE
AAACCEEINORRSSU	SARRACENIACEOUS
AAACCEFHILLPTTY	PATHETIC FALLACY
AAACCEFIIRRRRT	AIRCRAFT CARRIER
AAACCEMOPPRRSTU	CARPOMETACARPUS
AAACCGHILLMOOPR	PHARMACOLOGICAL
AAACCHIILLNRSTY	ANARCHISTICALLY
AAACCIIILMNOSTT	ACCLIMATISATION
AAACCIIILMNOTTZ	ACCLIMATIZATION
AAACCILLLOPPTYY	APOCALYPTICALLY
AAACDEEEMMNRSTU	AMUSEMENT ARCADE
AAACDEEFFGHIRRS	CHARGE D'AFFAIRES
AAACDEFGIORRRRW	CARRIAGE FORWARD
AAACDEFJKLLORST	JACK-OF-ALL-TRADES
AAACDEGIILLMNTY	DIAMAGNETICALLY
AAACDEILLMNORYY	AERODYNAMICALLY
AAACDEILLMORSUY	AMARYLLIDACEOUS
AAACDEIMNNOORTT	ANIMATED CARTOON
AAACDFGIILMNORR	AFRICAN MARIGOLD
AAACDIIINOORTTV	RADIOACTIVATION
AAACDIILLNOOORT	RADIOLOCATIONAL

AAACEEGILLNPRTY	PARAGENETICALLY
AAACEEHIMMMSTTT	METAMATHEMATICS
AAACEFFHHIILMRRS	AIR CHIEF MARSHAL
AAACEFILLLMNOWY	FAMILY ALLOWANCE
AAACEGILMNOPRTY	MALACOPTERYGIAN
AAACEHIILMRRSSV	AIR VICE-MARSHALS
AAACEHIIMNNPRSS	SPANISH-AMERICAN
AAACEHIMPPRSSTY	PARASYMPATHETIC
AAACEIIIMNNORST	AMERICANISATION
AAACEIIIMNNORTZ	AMERICANIZATION
AAACEIKLMMNORTX	EXCLAMATION MARK
AAACGGHIJKLNSSU	LAUGHING JACKASS
AAACHIIMNOORTTZ	ACHROMATIZATION
AAACIILLLMNOSTY	ANOMALISTICALLY
AAACIILNORSSTUV	VASCULARISATION
AAACIILNORSTUVZ	VASCULARIZATION
AAACILLNORSTTUY	ASTRONAUTICALLY ·
AAADDDEEELSTUVX	VALUE-ADDED TAXES
AAADDEGINOSSTTV	DISADVANTAGEOUS
AAADDIINNORSSTT	STANDARDISATION
AAADDIINNORSTTZ	STANDARDIZATION
AAADEEEEHIIKLSV	A HEAD LIKE A SIEVE
AAADEEEILLRTVWY	ELEVATED RAILWAY
AAADEEGNNOOSTTV	TO ONE'S ADVANTAGE
AAADEFHHOOPRTTT	AT THE DROP OF A HAT
AAADEIILNNRSTUV	VALETUDINARIANS
AAADGHILLMNNRSY	MARSHALLING YARD
AAADGHIOOPRRTUY	AUTORADIOGRAPHY
AAAEEFHMMNNNORV	MANNA FROM HEAVEN
AAAEEGGHILMNTTU	HAEMAGGLUTINATE
AAAEEGINNPRSSTU	SEPTUAGENARIANS
AAAEEGLMMNNRSTT	GENTLEMAN-AT-ARMS
AAAEEGMNRRSSSTT	SERGEANTS-AT-ARMS
AAAEFIILMNNOSTT	MANIFESTATIONAL
AAAEGGHIINNRSTT	AGAINST THE GRAIN
AAAEGHLNOOPPRTY	PALAEONTOGRAPHY
AAAEGIINNNQQRUU	QUINQUAGENARIAN
AAAEGINORSSTTVW	STARVATION WAGES
AAAEGLMOPRRSSSU	MASSAGE PARLOURS
AAAEGNNNOOPRRST	PERSONA NON GRATA
AAAEHILMNNNOSTT	NATIONAL ANTHEMS
AAAEIIILMNQRSTM	EQUALITARIANISM
AAAEIIILNORRSTT	ARTERIALISATION
AAAEIIILNORRTTZ	ARTERIALIZATION
AAAEILMNNPRRTUY	UNPARLIAMENTARY
AAAEMORRSSSTTTU	TARSOMETATARSUS
AAAFFIKMMNNNRRTU	FRANKFURT AM MAIN
AAAFIIIILMNORST	FAMILIARISATION
AAAFIIIILMNORTZ	FAMILIARIZATION
AAAGIINNOORSTTV	ASTRONAVIGATION
AAAHIIIMMNNRSTU	HUMANITARIANISM
AAAHIIIMNNRSTTU	HUMANITARIANIST
AAAIIILLMMNOSST	MALASSIMILATION
AAAIIILMNORSTTT	TOTALITARIANISM

AAAIIILNNNOOSTT	NATIONALISATION
AAAIIILNNNOOTTZ	NATIONALIZATION
AABBCGHIIIILLOPR	BIBLIOGRAPHICAL
AABCCCELMOORSUU	COOL AS A CUCUMBER
AABCCDEEHILLNSY	HENDECASYLLABIC
AABCCDEELNNORTU	COUNTERBALANCED
AABCCDEGHHLMNNO	MONCHEN-GLADBACH
AABCCDEKKLLNOST	BLOCK AND TACKLES
AABCCEELNNORSTU	COUNTERBALANCES
AABCCEELORRRSUV	CEREBROVASCULAR
AABCCEEMNOORSST	CRAB SOMEONE'S ACT
AABCCEGIILLOORT	BACTERIOLOGICAL
AABCCEGIILMNRUV	CIRCUMNAVIGABLE
AABCDEEEHLLLNSY	HENDECASYLLABLE
AABCDEEHORSTTUY	CATHODE RAY TUBES
AABCDEEIKRRSSTV	BACK-SEAT DRIVERS
AABCDEGIKLNRRST	BLANK CARTRIDGES
AABCDEEIILNOORST	ANABOLIC STEROID
AABCDEIINNOORST	DECARBONISATION
AABCDEIINNOORTZ	DECARBONIZATION
AABCDEILNOORTXY	DECARBOXYLATION
AABCDGIIIILLOOOR	RADIOBIOLOGICAL
AABCDGILLMNNOOR	BALLROOM DANCING
AABCDHIILLMRTYY	DITHYRAMBICALLY
AABCEEEFKLRRTVW	BLACKWATER FEVER
AABCEEEKKLMRRST	BLACK MARKETEERS
AABCEEFFIIILLNTY	INEFFACEABILITY
AABCEEGGIIMNNRT	MAGNETIC BEARING
AABCEEGHIILNTXY	EXCHANGEABILITY
AABCEEGHILNNRTY	INTERCHANGEABLY
AABCEEGHLNORSUX	LABOUR EXCHANGES
AABCEEHINSSTTUU	EUSTACHIAN TUBES
AABCEEINOQRSSTU	SESQUICARBONATE
AABCEFHKLOORRTY	THE BACK OF A LORRY
AABCEGGHIILOOPR	BIOGEOGRAPHICAL
AABCEGHHIIMNNST	BATHING MACHINES
AABCEGHIOOPRSTU	BACTERIOPHAGOUS
AABCEGILMNOPSUU	PLUMBAGINACEOUS
AABCEILLLMOPRTY	PROBLEMATICALLY
AABCEILLLMORSTY	MEROBLASTICALLY
AABCFIIIILLNOSTY	SYLLABIFICATION
AABCGHKLLNNOOTY	NOT BY A LONG CHALK
AABCHIILLNRTYY	LABYRINTHICALLY
AABCHILLLLOOSTY	HOLOBLASTICALLY
AABCIIIILLNPPTY	INAPPLICABILITY
AABCIIILMNOPRTY	INCOMPARABILITY
AABCIINOORSSTTU	BIOASTRONAUTICS
AABDDDGGILNNOOR	BOARD AND LODGING
AABDDEEIMNNORST	ONE-ARMED BANDITS
AABDDEFIIOPRRSS	BIRDS OF PARADISE
AABDEEEHILNNNRS	BANNER HEADLINES
AABDEEFFHIORRST	BIRDS OF A FEATHER
AABDEEGHINORRTW	WEATHERBOARDING
AABDEIIILNORSTT	DETRIBALISATION

AABDEIIILNORTTZ	DETRIBALIZATION
AABDEIIILNOSSTT	DESTABILISATION
AABDEIIILNOSTTZ	DESTABILIZATION
AABDHILMNOSSSUY	BUSMAN'S HOLIDAYS
AABEEEEFIKLMNOR	MAKE A BEELINE FOR
AABEEELNNORSSST	TREASONABLENESS
AABEEFHILNNOSSS	FASHIONABLENESS
AABEEGHIILRTTTY	A TIGER BY THE TAIL
AABEEGHIKLNRRTY	HEARTBREAKINGLY
AABEFGIIILRRRTY	IRREFRAGABILITY
AABEFIILNRRSTTY	TRANSFERABILITY
AABEFLNORRTTUZZ	BURNT TO A FRAZZLE
AABEGHHMOOPRRRT	THERMOBAROGRAPH
AABEGHIILMNOORU	HAEMOGLOBINURIA
AABEGHIIOOPRSTU	AUTOBIOGRAPHIES
AABEIIIILMMRSTUY	IMMEASURABILITY
AABEIILMNORTUVY	MANOEUVRABILITY
AABEKMRRRRSSTWY	STRAWBERRY MARKS
AABGGIIILLNTTUY	AGGLUTINABILITY
AABIILNOPRSSTTY	TRANSPOSABILITY
AACCCCEIILNRRTT	ANTARCTIC CIRCLE
AACCDEEHHLOOPRT	CEPHALOCHORDATE
AACCDEEKNORTTTU	COUNTERATTACKED
AACCDEGHIILOORS	OLIGOSACCHARIDE
AACCDEGIILLLOOT	DIALECTOLOGICAL
AACCDEGIIMNRTUV	CIRCUMNAVIGATED
AACCDEHHILMNORY	HYDROMECHANICAL
AACCDEIIILLMRTY	ACIDIMETRICALLY
AACCDEILMOORSST	SOCIAL DEMOCRATS
AACCDEIMNPPRRSS	SCRIMP AND SCRAPE
AACCDGILMMNOOTY	ACCOMMODATINGLY
AACCDHIIMOOSSTC	SADOMASOCHISTIC
AACCDHILNOOPRST	ACHONDROPLASTIC
AACCDIILLOOPRSY	RADIOSCOPICALLY
AACCEEEGILNPRRT	GENERAL PRACTICE
AACCEEGHILMMNOT	MAGNETOCHEMICAL
AACCEEHIIOPPRST	ARCHIEPISCOPATE
AACCEEHILMNORSV	SERVOMECHANICAL
AACCEEHILORSSTT	THE COAST IS CLEAR
AACCEEILLNNOPRT	PRECANCELLATION
AACCEEILLNORTTY	ELECTROANALYTIC
AACCEEILLNNOPST	PENTATONIC SCALE
AACCEEILNNRRSSTU	NATURAL SCIENCES
AACCEEINNNORSSS	RECONNAISSANCES
AACCEEKNORRTTTU	COUNTERATTACKER
AACCEELNORRSTTU	NUCLEAR REACTORS
AACCEFIILOOPRSU	CAPRIFOLIACEOUS
AACCEGGHINRRRSY	CARRYING CHARGES
AACCEGHIIMNOPRT	CINEMATOGRAPHIC
AACCEHHILMNOOPT	PHOTOMECHANICAL
AACCEHIILLMNSTY	MECHANISTICALLY
AACCEHIILLRSTUY	EUCHARISTICALLY
AACCEHILLLLMNOY	MELANCHOLICALLY
AACCEHILLMORTTY	TACHOMETRICALLY

AACCEHILLMRTTYY	TACHYMETRICALLY	AACDHIILLNOOPRY	RADIOPHONICALLY
AACCEHILLRRTTUY	ARCHITECTURALLY	AACDIIIILNNPRSS	DISCIPLINARIANS
AACCEIIILLMNRST	ANTICLERICALISM	AACDIIILNORSTTU	DISARTICULATION
AACCEIIILLMNOSTY	ENCOMIASTICALLY	AACDIILNOPQRTUU	QUADRUPLICATION
AACCEIIILLNRRTUV	INTERCLAVICULAR	AACEEEFGHNORSTX	RATE OF EXCHANGES
AACCEILRRRRTUUX	EXTRACURRICULAR	AACEEEFHORRSTTW	WEATHER FORECAST
AACCFFFGHKLOOOT	GO OFF AT HALF-COCK	AACEEEGIPPRRSTT	CIGARETTE PAPERS
AACCFIIILNOSSST	CLASSIFICATIONS	AACEEEILLRSSTUV	RELATIVE CLAUSES
AACCFNNORSTTTUU	TURF ACCOUNTANTS	AACEEEILNRSSSST	SALES RESISTANCE
AACCGHHIMOOPRRT	CHROMATOGRAPHIC	AACEEENNQRRTTUY	QUATERCENTENARY
AACCGHIMMNOORRT	CHRONOGRAMMATIC	AACEEFFHIMNNRST	AFFRANCHISEMENT
AACCGHIMNOOPRST	PHARMACOGNOSTIC	AACEEFGHLMNORRT	FARM THE LONG ACRE
AACCGIIMNORRTUV	CIRCUMNAVIGATOR	AACEEFHINNOSTTT	AT THE INSTANCE OF
AACCGINNOSSSTUV	SAVINGS ACCOUNTS	AACEEFIILLMNRSU	NUCLEAR FAMILIES
AACCHHIINNRRTUU	UNITARIAN CHURCH	AACEEFIINOORSST	FREE ASSOCIATION
AACCHHIIOOPPRTT	HIPPOCRATIC OATH	AACEEGHHLNOPPRY	ENCEPHALOGRAPHY
AACCHIIILNOOSTT	CATHOLICISATION	AACEEGHILLLPRTY	TELEGRAPHICALLY
AACCHILLNOPSTYY	SYCOPHANTICALLY	AACEEGHIMNOPRRT	CINEMATOGRAPHER
AACCIIILLLOSSTY	SOCIALISTICALLY	AACEEGHLLLNORWY	YELLOW ARCHANGEL
AACCIIILNORRSTU	CIRCULARISATION	AACEEHIINORTTTZ	CATHETERIZATION
AACCIIILNORRTUZ	CIRCULARIZATION	AACEEHILLMORTTY	THEOREMATICALLY
AACCIIILPRRSTTU	PARTICULARISTIC	AACEEHILLNPRTTY	PARENTHETICALLY
AACCIILLMNORTUV	CIRCUMVALLATION	AACEEHILLPRTTUY	THERAPEUTICALLY
AACCIILLMNOSSTU	MISCALCULATIONS	AACEEHMNOPRRTWW	COME THE RAW PRAWN
AACCILLLLOPRTTUY	PLUTOCRATICALLY	AACEEIILLPPRTTY	PERIPATETICALLY
AACDDEEEEHLNRSS	CLEAR-HEADEDNESS	AACEEIILNNORSTV	NATIONAL SERVICE
AACDDEEEGNSSTUU	AN EDUCATED GUESS	AACEEIILLNPRSTU	INTERNAL CAPSULE
AACDDEEILOSSTVV	DEVIL'S ADVOCATES	AACEFFINORRRSTW	WARRANT OFFICERS
AACDDHIKMNORRTY	TOM, DICK, AND HARRY	AACEFHHIMRRSSTT	FATHER CHRISTMAS
AACDEEEEGIORSST	ASSOCIATE DEGREE	AACEFILOOPRSSSU	PASSIFLORACEOUS
AACDEEEEHNPRRSTV	CHAPTER AND VERSE	AACEGGHINNNORRST	GREGORIAN CHANTS
AACDEEGIIILLNPPS	SPECIAL PLEADING	AACEGHHIIMNNSSW	WASHING MACHINES
AACDEEGIIILLNRST	LEADING ARTICLES	AACEGHHMOOPRRRT	CHROMATOGRAPHER
AACDEEHIKLMMNRS	HAMMER AND SICKLE	AACEGHIJKRSSTTT	STRAIGHTJACKETS
AACDEEHIMNNOTUU	HUMANE EDUCATION	AACEGHILLOPRRXY	XEROGRAPHICALLY
AACDEEHKKNRRSTY	THE KNACKER'S YARD	AACEGHILOOPSTTT	COTTAGE HOSPITAL
AACDEEIIILNPRSTU	UNDERCAPITALISE	AACEGIIMNORSSTV	MOVING STAIRCASE
AACDEEIIILNPRTUZ	UNDERCAPITALIZE	AACEHILLNOPRTUY	NEUROPATHICALLY
AACDEEIILOPRSTV	OVERCAPITALISED	AACEHILLOOPSTTY	OSTEOPATHICALLY
AACDEEIILOPRTVZ	OVERCAPITALIZED	AACEHLMORSSTUUW	WALRUS MOUSTACHE
AACDEEIIMNNOTTV	DECONTAMINATIVE	AACEIIILMNOPPSS	EPISCOPALIANISM
AACDEEILNNSSTTU	INDECENT ASSAULT	AACEIIILNOPSSST	SPECIALISATIONS
AACDEGIIIKKLNNV	ALIVE AND KICKING	AACEIIILNOPSSTZ	SPECIALIZATIONS
AACDEGIIMNNNOTT	DECONTAMINATING	AACEIIILPRRSTTU	PARTICULARITIES
AACDEHOORRSSSTT	AT THE CROSSROADS	AACEIIIMNNOPSTT	EMANCIPATIONIST
AACDEIILLMORTUY	AUDIOMETRICALLY	AACEIILLLLMNSTY	MENTALISTICALLY
AACDEIILMMNOSST	DOMESTIC ANIMALS	AACEIILLLPRSTTY	PERISTALTICALLY
AACDEIILNOSSTTU	EDUCATIONALISTS	AACEIILLMNNRSTY	MANNERISTICALLY
AACDEIIMNOORSTT	DEMOCRATISATION	AACEIILMNOPRRTT	MALPRACTITIONER
AACDEIIMNOORTTZ	DEMOCRATIZATION	AACEIILNNPRSSTU	PURITANICALNESS
AACDEILLMORRTTU	COURT-MARTIALLED	AACEIILNOPRSTTU	RECAPITULATIONS
AACDEILNNOOSSTT	SEA ISLAND COTTON	AACEIILPPPRSSTT	PAST PARTICIPLES
AACDFIIINOSSSTT	DISSATISFACTION	AACFGILNORRSTUV	VULGAR FRACTIONS
AACDFIIORSSSTTY	DISSATISFACTORY	AACFIIINNOORSTT	FRACTIONISATION

AACFIIINNOORTTZ	FRACTIONIZATION
AACFIIINORSSTTT	STRATIFICATIONS
AACGGHILLNOOPRY	PHARYNGOLOGICAL
AACGHHILLLOOPRY	HOLOGRAPHICALLY
AACGHIIILMNORTT	ANTILOGARITHMIC
AACGHIILLLMORTY	ALGORITHMICALLY,
	LOGARITHMICALLY
AACGHILLLLOPPRYY	POLYGRAPHICALLY
AACGHILLMNOOPRY	MONOGRAPHICALLY,
	NOMOGRAPHICALLY
AACGHILLLNOOOPRT	ANTHROPOLOGICAL
AACGHILLOOOPPRTY	TOPOGRAPHICALLY
AACGHILLOPPRTYY	TYPOGRAPHICALLY
AACGHILMOOOPRSST	PHARMACOLOGISTS
AACGIIILNPRRTUZ	PARTICULARIZING
AACGIILMNORRTTU	COURT-MARTIALING
AACGIINNOPRRSTT	PROCRASTINATING
AACGILLMNOORSTY	GASTRONOMICALLY
AACGILNNOORSTTU	CONGRATULATIONS
AACGILNOORSSTUY	AGRANULOCYTOSIS
AACGIMMNOOPRRSU	MACROSPORANGIUM
AACHIINOPSICISATION	HISPANICISATION
AACHIIIINNOPSTZ	HISPANICIZATION
AACHIILLMNORSTY	HARMONISTICALLY
AACHILLLMOOPSTY	HOMOPLASTICALLY
AACHILLOPPRSTYY	SAPROPHYTICALLY
AACHILLOPPSSTTY	STAPHYLOPLASTIC
AACIIILLLLRSTTUY	RITUALISTICALLY
AACIIIMNNOORSTT	ROMANTICISATION
AACIIIMNNOORTTZ	ROMANTICIZATION
AACIILLLMOPSTUY	POLITICAL ASYLUM
AACIILLNORSSTTY	CRYSTALLISATION
AACIILLNORSTTYZ	CRYSTALLIZATION
AACIILMMNNOOSTU	COMMUNALISATION
AACIILMMNNOOTUZ	COMMUNALIZATION
AACIILMNOOSSSSY	ANCYLOSTOMIASIS
AACIILMOOPSTTTU	AUTOMATIC PILOTS
AACIILNNOPRRSTT	TRANSCRIPTIONAL
AACIINNOOPRRSTT	PROCRASTINATION
AACIKMNNOPRTTUU	PUNCTUATION MARK
AACILLLMOPSTYYY	PLASMOLYTICALLY
AACILLMMOPSTTYY	SYMPTOMATICALLY
AACLLRRRSTTTUUU	ULTRASTRUCTURAL
AADDDEINNNORSST	NONSTANDARDISED
AADDDEINNNORSTZ	NONSTANDARDIZED
AADDDELMNNPPSUY	SUPPLY AND DEMAND
AADDEHILNOOSTWW	WHITE SANDALWOOD
AADDEIILNOPRSTU	SUPERADDITIONAL
AADEEEEEIILNRSSV	VENEREAL DISEASE
AADEEEEELMNOPRTV	DEVELOPMENT AREA
AADEEEFFHHLNRSST	HALF-HEARTEDNESS
AADEEEFHIMNOOST	AHEAD OF ONE'S TIME
AADEEEGKMNNRRST	MARKET GARDENERS
AADEEEGLMOOPSTX	SET A GOOD EXAMPLE
AADEEEHLRRRSSSS	DRESS REHEARSALS

AADEEEHMNRRSSTW	WARM-HEARTEDNESS
AADEEEILMNPRSTT	DEPARTMENTALISE
AADEEEILMNPRTTZ	DEPARTMENTALIZE
AADEEEMNPRSTTTT	STATE DEPARTMENT
AADEEGGIKMNNRRT	MARKET GARDENING
AADEEGHILOPRRTY	RADIOTELEGRAPHY
AADEEGIIMMNNOSTT	DEMAGNETISATION
AADEEGIIMMNNOTTZ	DEMAGNETIZATION
AADEEHIIIMNNRRST	HEREDITARIANISM
AADEEIILNOSSTUX	DESEXUALISATION
AADEHIIOPRRSSTT	RADIOTHERAPISTS
AADEIIKLRSSSTTW	SIDEWALK ARTISTS
AADEIILNOPSSSTY	DISPASSIONATELY
AADEIILNORRRTXY	EXTRAORDINARILY
AADEIIMOPPPRRST	MISAPPROPRIATED
AADEILMNNOORSTT	DEMONSTRATIONAL
AADEINPRRSSSSTT	STARS AND STRIPES
AADELLOPSSSTTTU	SLOTTED SPATULAS
AADELMPRRSSSTTU	MUSTARD PLASTERS
AADELNOPRSTTUUY	POLYUNSATURATED
AADEMNOOPRRTTUW	PORTMANTEAU WORD
AADFGHIORRRSTTW	STRAIGHTFORWARD
AADFHMNNOOSSTUY	A MONTH OF SUNDAYS
AADFIIILNNORSTY	DISINFLATIONARY
AADGHHIMNPRSSTU	DRAUGHTSMANSHIP
AADGIIINNOORSST	DISORGANISATION
AADGIIINNOORSTZ	DISORGANIZATION
AADIIILNORSSTTT	TRADITIONALISTS
AADIIIMNNORSSTT	ADMINISTRATIONS
AADIIMMNNSSTTTUU	MUTATIS MUTANDIS
AAEEEEEHNOPRTWY	A WEATHER EYE OPEN
AAEEEFGLMMNNRRT	GENTLEMAN FARMER
AAEEEGILLNNRRTT	ETERNAL TRIANGLE
AAEEEGLMMNNRSTT	GENTLEMEN-AT-ARMS
AAEEEILMNNPTTTU	ANTEPENULTIMATE
AAEEELLMMNPRTTY	TEMPERAMENTALLY
AAEEFFINOORRSTT	REAFFORESTATION
AAEEFGIMNNRRSST	FRAGMENTARINESS
AAEEFHILRSSTTVV	HARVEST FESTIVAL
AAEEFIIILMRSSSZ	LAISSEZ-FAIREISM
AAEEFIIILMNNOSTX	SELF-EXAMINATION
AAEEFLLNOPRSTXY	SELF-EXPLANATORY
AAEEGGIIINNRSTV	NEGATIVE-RAISING
AAEEGHHINRRSTTT	EARTHSHATTERING
AAEEGIILNNORSST	GENERALISATIONS
AAEEGIILNNORSTZ	GENERALIZATIONS
AAEEGILMNRRTTUVY	ARGUMENTATIVELY
AAEEHINOPRRSTVY	AVERSION THERAPY
AAEEHINORSSTTTW	WEATHER STATIONS
AAEEHMNOPRSSTTU	APARTMENT HOUSES
AAEEIILLNNORSTTX	EXTERNALISATION
AAEEIILLNNORTTXZ	EXTERNALIZATION
AAEEIINNOOPRSTU	EUROPEANISATION
AAEEIINNOOPRTUZ	EUROPEANIZATION

AAEEILNNOPRRSST	PROLETARIANNESS	AAHHHLOPPRRSTYY	STAPHYLORRHAPHY
AAEEIMNPRSSTTTV	PAVEMENT ARTISTS	AAHHIINOOPPSSTT	PHOSPHATISATION
AAEEINOPPPRRSST	APPROPRIATENESS	AAHHIINOOPPSTTZ	PHOSPHATIZATION
AAEELLNPRRRTTUY	PRETERNATURALLY	AAHIIILNOOPSTTZ	HOSPITALISATION
AAEENNNPRRSSSTT	TRANSPARENTNESS	AAHIIILNOOPSTTZ	HOSPITALIZATION
AAEFLLNOPRRRSUU	FUNERAL PARLOURS	AAIIIIMNNORSTTU	MINIATURISATION
AAEGHIILLNOTTTU	LET IT ALL HANG OUT	AAIIIIMNNORTTUZ	MINIATURIZATION
AAEGIIILNNOSTTV	INVESTIGATIONAL	AAIIILMMNOORSTT	IMMORTALISATION
AAEGIIKNNNPSSST	PAINSTAKINGNESS	AAIIILMMNOORTTZ	IMMORTALIZATION
AAEGIILNNOORTT	INTERROGATIONAL	AAIIILMNOOPRSTV	IMPROVISATIONAL
AAEGIILNNRRTTT	TRANSLITERATING	AAIIJLNOOPSTTUX	JUXTAPOSITIONAL
AAEGIIMNNPRSSTY	PRAYING MANTISES	AAIILLNNORTTUVY	INVOLUNTARILY
AAEGILLNOOOPSTT	PALAEONTOLOGIST	AAIILNNOOPRSSST	TRANSPOSITIONAL
AAEGILLOOOOPSTZ	PALAEOZOOLOGIST	AAIIMNOOPRSSSTY	TRYPANOSOMIASIS
AAEGIMMNNNOSSSU	MAGNANIMOUSNESS	AAIINNOOPRSTTTU	SATURATION POINT
AAEHIILORTTTUVY	AUTHORITATIVELY	ABBCCEFIIMNNORU	FIBONACCI NUMBER
AAEHILLMNOPSSTT	MENTAL HOSPITALS	ABBCEEEEFFKLOOOT	COFFEE-TABLE BOOK
AAEIIIILLMMNPRST	ANTI-IMPERIALISM	ABBDDEEEELLLORRU	DOUBLE-BARRELLED
AAEIIIILLMNPRSTT	ANTI-IMPERIALIST	ABBDEEELNORSSTU	REDOUBTABLENESS
AAEIIILLMMNOORST	MEMORIALISATION	ABBDEGHILORRTYY	DAYLIGHT ROBBERY
AAEIIILMMNOORTZ	MEMORIALIZATION	ABBEEIIILLMORRS	MOBILE LIBRARIES
AAEIIILMNNNORTT	INTERLAMINATION	ABBEEIIILLNTUVY	UNBELIEVABILITY
AAEIIILNNNORSTT	INTERNALISATION	ABBEIIIILMOPRST	IMPROBABILITIES
AAEIIIILNNOORTTZ	ORIENTALIZATION	ABCCCDEIIILNORU	RIBONUCLEIC ACID
AAEIIILNPRSSSTT	ANTIPERISTALSIS	ABCCEEFHILNOSST	CHIEF CONSTABLES
AAEIILLMNNRSTTU	TRANSILLUMINATE	ABCCEEIIKRRRSTU	CIRCUIT BREAKERS
AAEIILLNNNORTTY	INTERNATIONALLY	ABCCEEILLNOOPST	POLICE CONSTABLE
AAEIILMORRRRTTY	TERRITORIAL ARMY	ABCCEFIIIJNOOTT	OBJECTIFICATION
AAEIILNNOOPRSST	PERSONALISATION	ABCCEFIIILLPSSUY	SUBSPECIFICALLY
AAEIILNNOOPRSTZ	PERSONALIZATION	ABCCEGHINOPRSST	BATCH PROCESSING
AAEIILNNORRSTTT	TRANSLITERATION	ABCCEIIIILNSSTY	INACCESSIBILITY
AAEIILNNOSSSSTT	SENSATIONALISTS	ABCCEIIILLNORTY	RECONCILABILITY
AAEIILNOPPPRRTY	INAPPROPRIATELY	ABCCEIIILMNOPPSU	PUBLIC COMPANIES
AAEIIMNOSSSTTTY	SYSTEMATISATION	ABCCEIIILNNPSSUU	PUBLIC NUISANCES
AAEIIMNOSSTTTYZ	SYSTEMATIZATION	ABCCIIIILNORTTY	CONTRACTIBILITY
AAEIINNPPRRSSTT	ANTIPERSPIRANTS	ABCCIIKLMNNOOOT	COMBINATION LOCK
AAEILLLMNNNPSTT	INSTALLMENT PLAN	ABCDEEEEEGHLORRS	BACHELOR'S DEGREE
AAEILLMNPRRSSTUU	SUPERNATURALISM	ABCDEEELLOOORST	COLORADO BEETLES
AAEILNNNOSSTTUY	INSTANTANEOUSLY	ABCDEEHIIILPRTY	DECIPHERABILITY
AAEILNPRRSSTTUU	SUPERNATURALIST	ABCDEEIILORRRRS	RECORD LIBRARIES
AAEINNNNOPSSSTT	ANTS IN ONE'S PANTS	ABCDEELMNORRSUU	CONSUMER DURABLE
AAELMNSSSSSTTYY	SYSTEMS ANALYSTS	ABCDEGHIKNNORTU	IN THE BACKGROUND
AAENNORRSSSTUUY	TYRANNOSAURUSES	ABCDEGIIIILPRSTY	CREDIBILITY GAPS
AAFGGGIILMNNSSY	MAGNIFYING GLASS	ABCDEIILLLOQTUY	QUODLIBETICALLY
AAFGIINNORRSTTU	TRANSFIGURATION	ABCDEIIILMOOPSTY	DECOMPOSABILITY
AAFIIIILMNRSTTU	FUTILITARIANISM	ABCDEIIMOOSSTUY	BASIDIOMYCETOUS
AAFIILLNORRTTTU	ULTRAFILTRATION	ABCEEEIIILLNOSTV	CABLE TELEVISION
AAFIILMNOOORSTU	FORMULARISATION	ABCEEEILNNOPTUX	UNEXCEPTIONABLE
AAFIILMNOOORTUZ	FORMULARIZATION	ABCEEGHIKLOORST	GLOBE ARTICHOKES
AAFIMNNOORSSTTT	TRANSFORMATIONS	ABCEEGHINORSSTT	TOSSING THE CABER
AAGIIIILNNORSSTU	SINGULARISATION	ABCEEHHLMNNOOPR	RHOMBENCEPHALON
AAGIIIILNNORSTUZ	SINGULARIZATION	ABCEEILMMNNORSU	INCOMMENSURABLE
AAGIILNORSTTTUU	GUTTURALISATION	ABCEEILMNNNOOOU	ONCE IN A BLUE MOON
AAGIILNORTTTUUZ	GUTTURALIZATION	ABCEEILNNOPTUXY	UNEXCEPTIONABLY

689

ABCEELNNNOOPRUU	UNPRONOUNCEABLE
ABCEGIIILNORTYZ	RECOGNIZABILITY
ABCEGIILOORSSTT	BACTERIOLOGISTS
ABCEIIIILLNPTXY	INEXPLICABILITY
ABCEIIIILNRTTXY	INEXTRICABILITY
ABCEIIILLMMRSTYY	BISYMMETRICALLY
ABCEIIILLNOPRSTU	PUBLIC RELATIONS
ABCGIILLNOOOTTY	GNOTOBIOTICALLY
ABCIIIIILMNOPTTY	INCOMPATIBILITY
ABCIIIILLNNOOSTY	INCONSOLABILITY
ABCIIILMMNOTTUY	INCOMMUTABILITY
ABCIIILMMNOPTTUY	INCOMPUTABILITY
ABCIIILNNOORSUV	BINOCULAR VISION
ABCIILLLMOSSTYY	SYMBOLISTICALLY
ABDDDEEIMNNORSS	BROADMINDEDNESS
ABDDDEHLNNOORTU	BLOOD-AND-THUNDER
ABDDEEEHNOORSUW	BONDED WAREHOUSE
ABDDEEIIJLMNOSU	DIAMOND JUBILEES
ABDDEELMMOORSSW	WARM-BLOODEDNESS
ABDEEEHILLLSSTW	WELL-ESTABLISHED
ABDEEEHKLNORRTY	BROKEN-HEARTEDLY
ABDEEEIIIILMRRTY	IRREDEEMABILITY
ABDEEEILNORRTVY	BEYOND RETRIEVAL
ABDEIIIILMNOPRTY	IMPONDERABILITY
ABDEIIIILPRSTTUY	DISREPUTABILITY
ABDEIIILMNORSTTY	DEMONSTRABILITY
ABDEIIILNNORSTUY	INSUBORDINATELY
ABDEILLMNNOPSTU	PLATINUM BLONDES
ABDIIIIILMNSSTY	INADMISSIBILITY
ABDIIIIILNPSTTUY	INDISPUTABILITY
ABDIIINNNOORSTU	INSUBORDINATION
ABEEEEGIKLNSTVV	VEGETABLE KNIVES
ABEEEEILNNPRRTT	INTERPENETRABLE
ABEEEELNNPRSSST	PRESENTABLENESS
ABEEEFHHLMORSTT	STAR-OF-BETHLEHEM
ABEEEFHOPRRTTTT	THE BETTER PART OF
ABEEEGHHHLNOSTW	THE WHOLE SHEBANG
ABEEEHKNNORRSST	HEARTBROKENNESS
ABEEHILMNORSSTW	BLAMEWORTHINESS
ABEEIIILNNORSTUV	LABOUR-INTENSIVE
ABEEIIMNPRRSSTY	PRESBYTERIANISM
ABEEINNSSSSTTUV	SUBSTANTIVENESS
ABEGHHIMNOORSTT	SMOOTH BREATHING
ABEHIIIILMPRSTY	IMPERISHABILITY
ABEHIILMORSTTTY	THERMOSTABILITY
ABEHILMNOOORRTT	TRIBROMOETHANOL
ABEIIIILLNNRTUVY	INVULNERABILITY
ABEIIILLORRSTVY	IRRESOLVABILITY
ABEIILLMNOPTUYY	UNEMPLOYABILITY
ABEINOOOPRSSTTV	OBSERVATION POST
ABFIIILNOPRTTUY	UNPROFITABILITY
ABFILMMNOOORSTY	SYMBOL-FORMATION
ABHNNOOORTTTTUW	NOT WORTH A BUTTON
ACCCCEGHIKNNOTU	CHECKING ACCOUNT

ACCCDDKLLNOOOUU	CLOUD-CUCKOO-LAND
ACCCEEGIILLLOOS	ECCLESIOLOGICAL
ACCCEEHILLNORSV	VICE-CHANCELLORS
ACCCEEIIILMSSST	ECCLESIASTICISM
ACCCEEILOORSTTU	ELECTROACOUSTIC
ACCCEFIIKNNOOTY	COCKNEYFICATION
ACCCEHHIILMOPSY	PHYSICOCHEMICAL
ACCCEHHILNOOTT	PSYCHOTECHNICAL
ACCCEIIIILMMORST	COMMERCIALISTIC
ACCCEIILNOPSTTU	CONCEPTUALISTIC
ACCCEILOOPRSTUU	ACOUSTIC COUPLER
ACCCENNORRSTTUU	CURRENT ACCOUNTS
ACCCHIOOPSSSTUY	PSYCHOACOUSTICS
ACCCIILLMOOPRSY	MICROSCOPICALLY
ACCDDDEKLOOOOOS	COCK-A-DOODLE-DOOS
ACCDDEEINNNOSTU	DISCOUNTENANCED
ACCDDEIMMNNNOOS	SECOND-IN-COMMAND
ACCDEEEEEHQRRRU	CHEQUERED CAREER
ACCDEEHILLLPSYY	PSYCHEDELICALLY
ACCDEEHINOOPSU	CHENOPODIACEOUS
ACCDEEILMNOPSST	COMPLICATEDNESS
ACCDEEILMNORSTY	ELECTRODYNAMICS
ACCDEFFFGHKLOOO	GO OFF HALF-COCKED
ACCDEFGHHLNNORU	CHURCH OF ENGLAND
ACCDEHINORSSSUW	SANDWICH COURSES
ACCDEIIILMNNSTU	INCIDENTAL MUSIC
ACCDEINOOPSSTTU	DEPOSIT ACCOUNTS
ACCDEIOPPRRSTTU	PICTURE POSTCARD
ACCDFHIIINNOORT	CHONDRIFICATION
ACCEEEFIMNORSST	MASTER OF SCIENCE
ACCEEEGILMNORTT	ELECTROMAGNETIC,
MAGNETOELECTRIC	
ACCEEEIINORSTVV	ON ACTIVE SERVICE
ACCEEENNOPSSTUX	EXPENSE ACCOUNTS
ACCEEFHIIINOPST	SPEECHIFICATION
ACCEEFIIIILNORTT	ELECTRIFICATION
ACCEEFIILMNRRTU	CIRCUMFERENTIAL
ACCEEFILLMORSTV	COLLECTIVE FARMS
ACCEEFINNOOOSSS	SENSE OF OCCASION
ACCEEGILLORRSTU	ELECTROSURGICAL
ACCEEHHIMOORRTT	HETEROCHROMATIC
ACCEEHILOORRSTT	ATHEROSCLEROTIC
ACCEEIIMMNNOTUVX	EXCOMMUNICATIVE
ACCEEIIINNOOSSR	CONCESSIONAIRES
ACCEEILNORTTXYY	OXYTETRACYCLINE
ACCEFFGIIIILNRSS	SELF-SACRIFICING
ACCEFGIIIPRSTYY	SPECIFIC GRAVITY
ACCEFHHMMNOSSUU	MUCH OF A MUCHNESS
ACCEGHIIILNNORT	ANTICHOLINERGIC
ACCEGHIIMNNPRRS	PRINCE CHARMINGS
ACCEGHILLLNOOTY	TECHNOLOGICALLY
ACCEGHILLNOPSYY	PSYCHOGENICALLY
ACCEGIIILMMNORZ	COMMERCIALIZING
ACCEGIILLNNOPRSS	PELICAN CROSSING

ACCEGIILNNOPTUZ	CONCEPTUALIZING	ACDEEGIIILLMOOP	EPIDEMIOLOGICAL
ACCEGIIMMNNOTUX	EXCOMMUNICATING	ACDEEGIINORSSTT	STAGE DIRECTIONS
ACCEGIKLLNOOSTU	COCKTAIL LOUNGES	ACDEEGIMNORSSTU	DISCOURAGEMENTS
ACCEGILLLNOOSYY	SYNECOLOGICALLY	ACDEEGKLMNNOOSTW	ACKNOWLEDGMENTS
ACCEHHILLMNOOPR	CHLORAMPHENICOL	ACDEEHIIILNOOPRT	RADIOTELEPHONIC
ACCEHIIILLPRRTYY	HYPERCRITICALLY	ACDEEHILLLMNORTY	ENDOTHERMICALLY
ACCEHIIILNORSSTT	INTERSCHOLASTIC	ACDEEIIILNNORSTY	INCONSIDERATELY
ACCEHIIMMNOPRSTY	PSYCHOMETRICIAN	ACDEEIIMMOORRMRT	RADIOMICROMETER
ACCEHIILLMNOORTY	HOMOCENTRICALLY	ACDEEIIINNOORRST	RECONSIDERATION
ACCEHILLMOOPRTY	CHEMOTROPICALLY	ACDEEILLNPPRRUY	PERPENDICULARLY
ACCEHILMMNOPSST	ACCOMPLISHMENTS	ACDEEIMMNNOORST	RECOMMENDATIONS
ACCEHINNOOPRRTT	ANTHROPOCENTRIC	ACDEEIMNNOSSTWW	CASEMENT WINDOWS
ACCEIIKNNORSSTW	STICK IN ONE'S CRAW	ACDEELMOORRSSTU	SCLERODERMATOUS
ACCEIILMRRTUUUV	CURRICULUM VITAE	ACDEEMNNNOORSTY	STAND ON CEREMONY
ACCEIILNNOPRSUY	INSURANCE POLICY	ACDEENORRSSSSTY	SECONDARY STRESS
ACCEIILOPPRSSUY	PERSPICACIOUSLY	ACDEFGIKNNOORSY	DAYS OF RECKONING
ACCEIIMMNNOOTUX	EXCOMMUNICATION	ACDEFIIIIMNNNOT	INDEMNIFICATION
ACCEIIMMNNOTUUV	UNCOMMUNICATIVE	ACDEFIIIINNORTT	DENITRIFICATION
ACCEIIOORRSSSTV	VICTORIA CROSSES	ACDEFIIIINORSTV	DIVERSIFICATION
ACCEILMOOPRRSTU	ULTRAMICROSCOPE	ACDEFIIIINORTTV	DEVITRIFICATION
ACCELLNOOOSUUVV	CONVOLVULACEOUS	ACDEFIIILMNOSTU	DEMULSIFICATION
ACCFIMMNNOOOORST	COMMON FRACTIONS	ACDEFIIILNNOTTY	CONFIDENTIALITY
ACCGHIIIILLOOOST	STOICHIOLOGICAL	ACDEGIKNOOPSSTT	SPIGOT AND SOCKET
ACCGHILLLNOOORTY	CHRONOLOGICALLY	ACDEGILNNNOSTTU	CONSENTING ADULT
ACCGHILLLOOPSYY	PSYCHOLOGICALLY	ACDEGINORSTTTUY	COTTAGE INDUSTRY
ACCHHILMOOOPPST	OPHTHALMOSCOPIC	ACDEHIIILNPSSTU	DUAL CITISENSHIP
ACCHIILNNOORTTY	THYROCALCITONIN	ACDEHIIILNPSTUZ	DUAL CITIZENSHIP
ACCIKLLMOOOOTTV	MOLOTOV COCKTAIL	ACDEHIILLMOSTTY	METHODISTICALLY
ACDDEEEELNNPSTU	DEPENDENT CLAUSE	ACDEHIINOPSSTTU	UNSOPHISTICATED
ACDDEEEEHHIKNSST	THICKHEADEDNESS	ACDEHIKLORRSSTU	HARD LUCK STORIES
ACDDEEEHILMSSTU	DUTCH ELM DISEASE	ACDEHLOOOPPRSSV	APPROVED SCHOOLS
ACDDEEEHLNORSST	COLD-HEARTEDNESS	ACDEHMNNOOORSTU	ENCHONDROMATOUS
ACDDEEGILNNNORS	ENDOCRINE GLANDS	ACDEIIIILMNNOORT	OMNIDIRECTIONAL
ACDDEEHIIILLRSUY	DIESEL-HYDRAULIC	ACDEIIIILNORRSTY	DISCRETIONARILY
ACDDEMMNNOORRSY	SECONDARY MODERN	ACDEIIINNNOORST	INCONSIDERATION
ACDDEFLMOOORSSW	SWORD OF DAMOCLES	ACDEIIINNORRSTY	INDISCRETIONARY
ACDDIIIIILNSTUV	INDIVIDUALISTIC	ACDEIILLMNORSTY	MODERNISTICALLY
ACDEEEEEGGHLRRT	THREE-LEGGED RACE	ACDEIILLMNPRSTU	PNEUMATIC DRILLS
ACDEEEEFILMNTTV	MENTAL DEFECTIVE	ACDGHIMNNOOPRRY	GYNANDROMORPHIC
ACDEEEEILNNORTT	ENTENTE CORDIALE	ACDGIIIINNNOORT	AIR-CONDITIONING
ACDEEEEFHILLNORS	HALL OF RESIDENCE	ACDHIIILLMOOPRY	IDIOMORPHICALLY
ACDEEEFIIIILNRTT	DEFINITE ARTICLE	ACDHIIIMNOOOSTT	DICHOTOMISATION
ACDEEEGHILORRTT	CIGARETTE HOLDER	ACDHIIIMNOOOTTZ	DICHOTOMIZATION
ACDEEEIIMNNPSTT	PATENT MEDICINES	ACDIIIILNNNOSST	DISINCLINATIONS
ACDEEEINNORSSST	CONSIDERATENESS	ACDIIIINRSSTUVY	VICISSITUDINARY
ACDEEEMNOOPRSTV	OVERCOMPENSATED	ACDIIINNNOOSTTU	DISCONTINUATION
ACDEEFHORRSSSTW	CHESTS OF DRAWERS	ACDILLLNNOOOTUY	UNCONDITIONALLY
ACDEEFILNORRRTU	FUNERAL DIRECTOR	ACEEEEELNOPSSUV	ACE UP ONE'S SLEEVE
ACDEEFLMNNORRRT	CLERMONT-FERRAND	ACEEEEGILLNNORT	GENERAL ELECTION
ACDEEFMMNNOORSY	COMEDY OF MANNERS	ACEEEEGILNORTTV	ELECTRONEGATIVE
ACDEEGGHIINPRRS	GRAPHIC DESIGNER	ACEEEEHHILNRSTW	CATHERINE WHEELS
ACDEEGHHIINORTU	HIGHER EDUCATION	ACEEEFGGHINNORX	FOREIGN EXCHANGE
ACDEEGHIIMNNNSV	VENDING MACHINES	ACEEEFGILNNOPRR	PEREGRINE FALCON
ACDEEGHILOOSSSW	WILD-GOOSE CHASES	ACEEEFHIMNNNRST	ENFRANCHISEMENT

ACEEEGIILLNORTT	INTERCOLLEGIATE
ACEEEGIMMOSSTTT	COMMITTEE STAGES
ACEEEGIMNOPRSTT	SPERMATOGENETIC
ACEEEHHHLNOOPRX	HEXACHLOROPHENE
ACEEEHHIPPRSSTT	SPEECH THERAPIST
ACEEEHILLMNRTUY	HERMENEUTICALLY
ACEEEHILNNNRSST	CHINESE LANTERNS
ACEEEHNORRSSSTU	TREACHEROUSNESS
ACEEEIILLLLNSTTU	INTELLECTUALISE
ACEEEIILLLNTTUZ	INTELLECTUALIZE
ACEEEILNNOPSSTX	EXCEPTIONALNESS
ACEEEILNORRSSTV	CORRELATIVENESS
ACEEEILNPSSSTUV	SPECULATIVENESS
ACEEEIMMNOPRSSU	MENISPERMACEOUS
ACEEEMNNORRSSTU	COUNTERMEASURES
ACEEEENOPPRSSSTY	PAY ONE'S RESPECTS
ACEEFHHMNOOOORRT	REACH FOR THE MOON
ACEEFHLNOPRRSSU	REPROACHFULNESS
ACEEFIIIILMNOPTX	EXEMPLIFICATION
ACEEFIINNORRSTT	CONFRATERNITIES
ACEEFILMPRRSSTU	SIMPLE FRACTURES
ACEEGGIILLNNORT	TRAINING COLLEGE
ACEEGHINNOOPRTT	ANTHROPOGENETIC
ACEEGIILLMOOPST	EPISTEMOLOGICAL
ACEEGIINNNORSTT	TRACTION ENGINES
ACEEGIINORRSTTT	GASTROENTERITIC
ACEEGILLLNOOPTYY	POLYGENETICALLY
ACEEGILLNOOSTYY	OESTROGENICALLY
ACEEHHIIKNNOTTT	TAKE IT ON THE CHIN
ACEEHHIMNOORRTT	HETEROCHROMATIN
ACEEEHHINOOPPRST	PHOSPHOCREATINE
ACEEHHIILLLLNSTY	HELLENISTICALLY
ACEEHHIINPPPRSST	APPRENTICESHIPS
ACEEHILOORRSSST	ATHEROSCLEROSIS
ACEEHHIMMNORSSSV	SERVOMECHANISMS
ACEEIIIINQSSSTUV	ACQUISITIVENESS
ACEEIIILLLMNSTTU	INTELLECTUALISM
ACEEIIILLLNSTTTU	INTELLECTUALIST
ACEEIIILLLNTTTUY	INTELLECTUALITY
ACEEIIILLMOPRTYZ	PIEZOMETRICALLY
ACEEIILMNOPRSVY	LIVERY COMPANIES
ACEEIILNNNOOSTV	CONVENTIONALISE
ACEEIILNNNOOTVZ	CONVENTIONALIZE
ACEEIILNNNOQSTU	INCONSEQUENTIAL
ACEEIINORSSSTTV	SERVICE STATIONS
ACEEILLLMNOOSSUY	MISCELLANEOUSLY
ACEEILLLNOOSSTUY	ELECTROLYSATION
ACEEILMMNORSSSTY	SYMMETRICALNESS
ACEEINOOPRSSTVV	PROVOCATIVENESS
ACEEILMNRRROSTUY	RESURRECTIONARY
ACEELMNROOQRRSUU	LOURENCO MARQUES
ACEEMNNOOOPRSTU	CONTEMPORANEOUS
ACEFFGIJLMNOPPU	JUMPING-OFF PLACE
ACEFIIIIINNNOSTT	INTENSIFICATION

ACEFIIIILMNNOOST	SOLEMNIFICATION
ACEFIIIINNOOPRST	PERSONIFICATION
ACEFIILORRSTTUV	ARTICLES OF VIRTU
ACEFINOOPPRRRST	PROPER FRACTIONS
ACEFINRRRSSTTUU	INFRASTRUCTURES
ACEGHHIMNOOSSTT	SHOOTING MATCHES
ACEGHIIIKMNNNTT	KNITTING MACHINE
ACEGHILLLOOPPSY	PSEPHOLOGICALLY
ACEGHIMMOOPRRTT	PHOTOGRAMMETRIC
ACEGHLLOOPSUYYZ	ZYGOPHYLLACEOUS
ACEGIIILLMMNNOUY	IMMUNOGENICALLY
ACEGIILLMNOOORT	TERMINOLOGICAL
ACEGIINOOPRSTTV	PROGNOSTICATIVE
ACEGILLNORRSUUY	NEUROSURGICALLY
ACEGILMNNOOORST	CONGLOMERATIONS
ACEGILNOPRSSSTU	PLASTIC SURGEONS
ACEHHIILLMNPTTY	PLATYHELMINTHIC
ACEHHIKNORTTUVW	HAVE NO TRUCK WITH
ACEHHINNPSSSTTU	SPANISH CHESTNUT
ACEHHINOPPRSTTU	PITHECANTHROPUS
ACEHHIOPPRSSTTY	PSYCHOTHERAPIST
ACEHIILLLOOPRTY	HELIOTROPICALLY
ACEHIILLLOPRRSTY	PREHISTORICALLY
ACEHIILOOPSTTTY	PHOTOELASTICITY
ACEHIIMMMOPSTTY	SYMPATHOMIMETIC
ACEHILLMNOOPRXY	XENOMORPHICALLY
ACEHILLMOOPRTTY	PHOTOMETRICALLY
ACEHILOPSSTUXYY	PSYCHOSEXUALITY
ACEHINOPRRSTUYY	NEUROPSYCHIATRY
ACEHMNOOPRSSTUY	PROSENCHYMATOUS
ACEIIIILLMPSSSTY	PESSIMISTICALLY
ACEIIIIMMNOORSSS	COMMISSIONAIRES
ACEIIILLORSTUVYY	VOYEURISTICALLY
ACEIILMNNNOOSTV	CONVENTIONALISM
ACEIILNNNOOSSTV	CONVENTIONALIST
ACEIILNNNOOTTVY	CONVENTIONALITY
ACEIILNNOOPRSTT	INTROSPECTIONAL
ACEIILNNOORSTTU	INTEROSCULATION
ACEIIMNNOORSSTV	CONSERVATIONISM
ACEIIMNOOPRSSTTU	COMPUTERISATION
ACEIIMNOOPRTTUZ	COMPUTERIZATION
ACEIINNOORSSTTV	CONSERVATIONIST
ACELNOOOPPRRSTU	COUNTERPROPOSAL
ACELPRRRSSTTUUU	SUPERSTRUCTURAL
ACEOOPPRRSSSSTU	AT CROSS-PURPOSES
ACFGIIIILNNNSTY	INSIGNIFICANTLY
ACFIIIILMNOPSST	SIMPLIFICATIONS
ACFIIMNNOOOSTTY	COMITY OF NATIONS
ACFIMNOOORSSTTT	COMFORT STATIONS
ACGGIINNOOPRSTT	PROGNOSTICATING
ACGHHIIIOOPRRST	HISTORIOGRAPHIC
ACGHHIMOOOPPRRT	MICROPHOTOGRAPH, PHOTOMICROGRAPH
ACGHHINOOOPPRTZ	PHOTOZINCOGRAPH

ACGHHLLMNNOPSUU	PLOUGHMAN'S LUNCH	ADEEHILNNOORSTW	LET ONE'S HAIR DOWN
ACGHHLOOOOPPSTYY	PSYCHOPATHOLOGY	ADEEHINPRSSSTTW	SHARP-WITTEDNESS
ACGHILLLLMOOOPRY	MORPHOLOGICALLY	ADEEIIINNOSSSTT	DESENSITISATION
ACGIIILLLNNSTTY	SCINTILLATINGLY	ADEEIIINNOSSTTZ	DESENSITIZATION
ACGIIINNNNOOTTX	NONINTOXICATING	ADEEIILOPRRSSTV	PRIVATE SOLDIERS
ACHHMOOOOPRRSTU	CHROMATOPHOROUS	ADEEIIMNNOPRTTU	UNPREMEDITATION
ACHIIIMOOSSSSST	SCHISTOSOMIASIS	ADEEIIMNNORSTTU	UNDERESTIMATION
ACHIINNNOORSSTY	SYNCHRONISATION	ADEEIINNOOPSSST	OPINIONATEDNESS
ACHIINNNOORSTYZ	SYNCHRONIZATION	ADEEILMNOPRRSTU	MENSTRUAL PERIOD
ACHIIOPRSSSSTTY	ASTROPHYSICISTS	ADEEILMNORSTTVY	DEMONSTRATIVELY
ACHIKLNNOOPPTTY	PHYTOPLANKTONIC	ADEEIMNNORSTTUV	UNDEMONSTRATIVE
ACHILLLORRTTUUY	HORTICULTURALLY	ADEFFGHINNORSTU	FOUNDING FATHERS
ACIIILNNOPQTTUU	QUINTUPLICATION	ADEFFHINNOSSSST	STANDOFFISHNESS
ACIILMMNOOOPSST	COSMOPOLITANISM	ADEFGHIMOORRSTY	FAIRY GODMOTHERS
ACIILMNNOOSSTUY	SANCTIMONIOUSLY	ADEFGIIILLNQSTU	SELF-LIQUIDATING
ACIILNNOOSSTTTU	CONSTITUTIONALS	ADEGHLLMORRTUYY	HYDROMETALLURGY
ADDDDEGIIMNNOSW	DIAMOND WEDDINGS	ADEGIIIOPRRSSTT	PRESTIDIGITATOR
ADDDEEEHNNNRSSU	UNDERHANDEDNESS	ADEHHIIMMOPRRST	HERMAPHRODITISM
ADDDEEFHILMOORT	MIDDLE-OF-THE-ROAD	ADEHILMNOOPSTTU	PENTOTHAL SODIUM
ADDEEEEEHLLNSSV	LEVEL-HEADEDNESS	ADEHIMOOPRSSTTY	DERMATOPHYTOSIS
ADDEEEEHLNRRTTY	TENDERHEARTEDLY	ADEIIIIILMRSSST	DISSIMILARITIES
ADDEEEGHHILNSST	LIGHT-HEADEDNESS	ADEIIINORSSSTTT	DISSERTATIONIST
ADDEEEGHHNNORSSW	WRONGHEADEDNESS	ADEIIJLNPRRSTUU	JURISPRUDENTIAL
ADDEEEHIKNNRSST	KIND-HEARTEDNESS	ADEIILNORRSSTTX	SINISTRODEXTRAL
ADDEEGHHINNRSST	RIGHT-HANDEDNESS	ADEIILNORRSTTVY	DORSIVENTRALITY
ADDEEGHINNOORTY	DEHYDROGENATION	ADEIIMNNOPPSSTT	DISAPPOINTMENTS
ADDEEGNNOORSSTU	GOOD-NATUREDNESS	ADEILMOPSTTUUUY	PSEUDOMUTUALITY
ADDEEHHNNORSSST	SHORT-HANDEDNESS	ADGGIMNNORSSTU	STAMPING GROUNDS
ADDEEILLMMNNSSS	SMALL-MINDEDNESS	ADGHIINNNOSTTTW	NOTWITHSTANDING
ADDEEINNNORSSWY	NINE DAYS' WONDERS	ADGIIIILNNRSTUZ	INDUSTRIALIZING
ADDEGHIIKNRRSTW	WITH KIND REGARDS	ADGIIILNNOPPSTY	DISAPPOINTINGLY
ADDEIMNNNOPQSSS	MIND ONE'S P'S AND Q'S	AEEEFHIIKNNNOSV	HAVE ONE'S KNIFE IN
ADDGIIIIILNNUVZ	INDIVIDUALIZING	AEEEFHOORRRSTWW	THE WORSE FOR WEAR
ADEEEEEGHHORTVV	HAVE THE EDGE OVER	AEEEFIILNPRRTTY	PREFERENTIALITY
ADEEEEGILLNRRVY	GENERAL DELIVERY	AEEEFLLLLORRTVW	FELLOW TRAVELLER
ADEEEEHHNRRTTUW	UNDER THE WEATHER	AEEEGGGIMNNNRST	ENGAGEMENT RINGS
ADEEEEHHNNOPRSST	OPENHEARTEDNESS	AEEEGGILLORRSSU	ROGUES' GALLERIES
ADEEEFGHINORSTU	UNDER THE AEGIS OF	AEEEGGLNNOORRRV	GOVERNOR-GENERAL
ADEEEFHNORSSSTT	SOFTHEARTEDNESS	AEEEGHHILNORTT	IN THE ALTOGETHER
ADEEEGHHMNPRRSS	GERMAN SHEPHERDS	AEEEGHINNOORSST	PARTHENOGENESIS
ADEEEGHINNRSSST	NEARSIGHTEDNESS	AEEEGIILLNNRSST	LARGE INTESTINES
ADEEEGILMNNNSTT	DISENTANGLEMENT	AEEEGILLMNNNSSS	GENTLEMANLINESS
ADEEEGILNNOOPRS	OLD AGE PENSIONER	AEEEGILMNNNSSSS	MEANINGLESSNESS
ADEEEHIMNNRSSTT	DISHEARTENMENTS	AEEEGILNNPPRRST	SLEEPING PARTNER
ADEEEIIINNNSSST	SEINE-SAINT-DENIS	AEEEGILNNRSSSTV	EVERLASTINGNESS
ADEEEIILMNNSSTT	SENTIMENTALISED	AEEEGIMNOPRSSST	SPERMATOGENESIS
ADEEEIILMNNSTTZ	SENTIMENTALIZED	AEEEHHILMNOPPST	MEPHISTOPHELEAN
ADEEEMNNRSSTTTU	UNDERSTATEMENTS	AEEEHIIMMNNORST	IMMERSION HEATER
ADEEEMNOPRRSTTT	DEPARTMENT STORE	AEEEHIIMNPPRSSV	MISAPPREHENSIVE
ADEEFFFHHLLNOTY	FLY OFF THE HANDLE	AEEEHILORSTTUXY	HETEROSEXUALITY
ADEEFFGIIINNRTT	DIFFERENTIATING	AEEEHORRRSSTTUW	WEAR THE TROUSERS
ADEEFFIIIINNORTT	DIFFERENTIATION	AEEEIILLMMNPRSTX	EXPERIMENTALISM
ADEEFILNSSSSTTU	DISTASTEFULNESS	AEEEIILMNPRSTTX	EXPERIMENTALIST
ADEEGIIMNNRSTTU	UNDERESTIMATING	AEEEIIMNNOPRTTX	EXPERIMENTATION

AEEEIINNNSSTTTV	INATTENTIVENESS
AEEEILNPRSSSTUV	SUPERLATIVENESS
AEEEIMNOPRRSSTX	EXTEMPORARINESS
AEEEIMNPRRRSSUU	SUPERNUMERARIES
AEEEINNOPRRSSTT	REPRESENTATIONS
AEEELMNOQRRSSSU	QUARRELSOMENESS
AEEELNOOPRSSTTT	PERSONAL STEREOS
AEEELOPRRRSSSTW	LESSER SPEARWORT
AEEFGGHILNRSSTT	FLIGHT SERGEANTS
AEEFGHIMNNORRTT	THE MORNING AFTER
AEEFGHINOOPRRTW	WEATHERPROOFING
AEEFGIMNNRRSTTU	TRANSFIGUREMENT
AEEFHILLLLOTVYY	LILY OF THE VALLEY
AEEFIILNNRSTTTU	FIRST LIEUTENANT
AEEFNNNORSSSTTU	UNFORTUNATENESS
AEEFNOOOPRRTTWY	POWER OF ATTORNEY
AEEGGHHOOPPRRTY	PHYTOGEOGRAPHER
AEEGGHLORRSSTTW	LET THE GRASS GROW
AEEGHHILNORSSSY	ROYAL HIGHNESSES
AEEGHHLOOPPRTTY	PHOTOTELEGRAPHY,
TELEPHOTOGRAPHY	
AEEGHHLORSSSTUU	SLAUGHTERHOUSES
AEEGHIKLOPRRTTW	TIGHTROPE WALKER
AEEGHINNOOPRSST	ANTHROPOGENESIS
AEEGHLLMNOOSSTZ	THOMSON'S GAZELLE
AEEGIILNORRTTVY	INTERROGATIVELY
AEEGIINOORRRSTT	INTERROGATORIES
AEEGIINORRSSTTT	GASTROENTERITIS
AEEGIMNOPRSSTTY	OPERATING SYSTEM
AEEHHHILLNNOPPT	PHENOLPHTHALEIN
AEEHHIJNOSSSTVW	JEHOVAH'S WITNESS
AEEHIILMOOPSTTU	EPITHELIOMATOUS
AEEHIIMNNOPPRSS	MISAPPREHENSION
AEEHIKLNOPRTUY	PHENYLKETONURIA
AEEHILMMNOOPRRY	HOLY ROMAN EMPIRE
AEEHINPPPPRRSSW	WHIPPERSNAPPERS
AEEIIILMMMMORST	TIMES IMMEMORIAL
AEEIIINOORRSTTX	EXTERIORISATION
AEEIIINOORRTTXZ	EXTERIORIZATION
AEEIIILLMNNSSSTT	SMALL INTESTINES
AEEIIILMNNSSSTTT	SENTIMENTALISTS
AEEIILNNOPPRTTY	PLENIPOTENTIARY
AEEIILNOORRSTUV	REVOLUTIONARIES
AEEIIMNNOPRSSTT	PRESENTATIONISM
AEEIIMNOOPRSSTTX	EXTEMPORISATION
AEEIIMNOOPRTTXZ	EXTEMPORIZATION
AEEIINNOPRRSTTT	INTERPRETATIONS
AEEIINNOPRSSTTT	PRESENTATIONIST
AEEIILLMMNOOOPSS	OIL SOMEONE'S PALM
AEEIILLMNNORTVY	ENVIRONMENTALLY
AEEIILLMNNPRSTUY	SUPPLEMENTARILY
AEEIILMNNOOPPRUU	PLEUROPNEUMONIA
AEEIILMNNOPPSTTU	SUPPLEMENTATION
AEEIILNNOOPRRTUV	RELATIVE PRONOUN

AEEIILNNOPSSSSSS	PASSIONLESSNESS
AEEIILNORRSSTTUU	RUSSIAN ROULETTE
AEEIIMNOQRSSSTTU	QUESTION MASTERS
AEEIMPRRRSSSSTY	PRIMARY STRESSES
AEEIINOQRRSSSSTU	QUARTER SESSIONS
AEENNNOOPSSSSTU	SPONTANEOUSNESS
AEFGGHJLOORRTUU	GO FOR THE JUGULAR
AEFIIIIILLMNNSTY	INFINITESIMALLY
AEFIILLLLNNOOPST	SELF-POLLINATION
AEFIILMNOOPRSSS	PROFESSIONALISM
AEFIILNOOPRSSST	PROFESSIONALIST
AEFIILNORSSSTTU	FLIRTATIOUSNESS
AEFILLMNOPRSTTY	SELF-IMPORTANTLY
AEGGHILLNOORSTY	SHOOTING GALLERY
AEGGIILNNORRTTY	INTERROGATORILY
AEGGILNNRRSSTY	TRANSGRESSINGLY
AEGHHIIMNNRSSST	NIGHTMARISHNESS
AEGHHIIOOPRRRST	HISTORIOGRAPHER
AEGHIINNOPRSSTW	WITHIN ONE'S GRASP
AEGIIINNNOORSTT	NITROGENISATION
AEGIIINNNOORTTZ	NITROGENIZATION
AEGIIINNNRSSTTT	INTRANSIGENTIST
AEGIILNOORRRTTY	INTERROGATORILY
AEGILLNOOOPSSTT	PALEONTOLOGISTS
AEGILLNOPSTTUXY	EXPOSTULATINGLY
AEHHIIMNOPRRSTT	THERIANTHROPISM
AEHHIIOPPRSSTTY	PHYSIOTHERAPIST
AEHIIJJMNOORTTY	JOIN THE MAJORITY
AEHIIMMNNOOPRST	ENANTIOMORPHISM
AEHIMNOOPPRSTTT	ANTHROPOMETRIST
AEIIIILMMMNNRSSX	MARXISM-LENINISM
AEIIIILMNNRSSTTX	MARXIST-LENINIST
AEIIIJLNNORSSTUV	UNIVERSAL JOINTS
AEIILLNOOPRSSTIU	PREPOSITIONALLY
AEIILLLNOORRTUVY	REVOLUTIONARILY
AEIILMMNNRSSTTU	INSTRUMENTALISM
AEIILMMNOOPRSTT	METROPOLITANISM
AEIILMNNRSSTTTU	INSTRUMENTALIST
AEIILMNNRSTTTUY	INSTRUMENTALITY
AEIILNNNORSSTUV	INVOLUNTARINESS
AEIIILNOOPRSSTTY	PROSELYTISATION
AEIIILNOOPRSTTYZ	PROSELYTIZATION
AEIIMNNNORSTTTU	INSTRUMENTATION
AEILNOOOPPRRTTY	PROPORTIONATELY
AELNNNOOOPPRRSU	PERSONAL PRONOUN
AFFGHNNOOSSSTUW	SAWN-OFF SHOTGUNS
AFFHILLORSTTUUYY	YOURS FAITHFULLY
AFGGIIMNNORRSTY	TRANSMOGRIFYING
AFGHLMOOOOPRRTU	PHOTOFLUOROGRAM
AFGIIIILLNNOSST	FILLING STATIONS
AFGIIKMNNNOOPRT	NON-PROFIT-MAKING
AGHHHILOOOPPRTT	PHOTOLITHOGRAPH
AGHHIILLLLNSSYY	SHILLY-SHALLYING
AGHHIIMNOOPSSTT	OPISTHOGNATHISM

AGHHILLMOOOPSTT	OPHTHALMOLOGIST	BCGHIILOOOPSSTY	PSYCHOBIOLOGIST
AGHHINOOOPSSTTU	OPISTHOGNATHOUS	BCGIIIIILNORRTY	INCORRIGIBILITY
AGHHOOOOPPPRTTY	PHOTOTOPOGRAPHY	BCGIIIILMOOORSST	MICROBIOLOGISTS
AGHHOOOPPPRTTYY	PHOTOTYPOGRAPHY	BCGIINNNNOORRTTU	NONCONTRIBUTING
AGHIILMNOOOSTTY	MYTHOLOGISATION	BCIINOORSSSTTTU	OBSTRUCTIONISTS
AGHIILMNOOOTTYZ	MYTHOLOGIZATION	BCINNNOOORRTTUY	NONCONTRIBUTORY
AGHILNOOOPRSSTT	ANTHROPOLOGISTS	BDDEEEELNNORSTU	DOUBLE ENTENDRES
AGIIINNORRSSTTZ	TRANSISTORIZING	BDDEEEILNOOPRSX	PEROXIDE BLONDES
AGIILLNNOOPSSTT	POLLING STATIONS	BDDEEFLLLNOOSSU	FULL-BLOODEDNESS
AGINOPPPRRSSTTU	SUPPORTING PARTS	BDEEFIIIILNNSTY	INDEFENSIBILITY
AHHIILNOPPRSSTT	PHILANTHROPISTS	BDEEFILMNPRRSSU	PLUMBER'S FRIENDS
AHIJLMNOOOOPRSTU	PHOTOJOURNALISM	BDEGIIIIILNSTTY	INDIGESTIBILITY
AHIJLNOOOPRSTTU	PHOTOJOURNALIST	BDFFIIILMNNORUU	INFUNDIBULIFORM
AHINOOOPRRSSTTT	PHOTOTRANSISTOR	BDIIIILLNOSSTUY	INDISSOLUBILITY
AIIIILLNQORSTUY	INQUISITORIALLY	BEEEEFILNNNOOSS	FEEL IN ONE'S BONES
AIIINNNOOSSTTUW	NO-WIN SITUATIONS	BEEEGGILNSSSSTU	SUGGESTIBLENESS
AIILLLLMNOPSSUUY	PUSILLANIMOUSLY	BEEEIINNNORRTTZ	TRINITROBENZENE
AIILNOOOPPRRTTY	PROPORTIONALITY	BEEEILNNOPRSSSS	RESPONSIBLENESS
AIKNNNNOQTTUUWY	UNKNOWN QUANTITY	BEEELMNOORSSSTU	TROUBLESOMENESS
BBBBEEFGIIILRTT	FLIBBERTIGIBBET	BEEGHHIILLNOOTW	THE WHOLE BOILING
BBBDEEHLLLMNOOS	BLONDE BOMBSHELL	BEEGHIILNNORSSU	NEIGHBOURLINESS
BBCEEKKLLOORRSTT	STOCKBROKER BELT	BEEHIIINOPRSSTV	PROHIBITIVENESS
BBCGIKLLMNOSSTU	STUMBLING BLOCKS	BEEHILNOOPSTTUW	UP TO THE ELBOWS IN
BBCHIIIIIILLOPST	BIBLIOPHILISTIC	BEEHINOORRSSTUV	HERBIVOROUSNESS
BBDEIIIIILNOOSSV	DIVISION LOBBIES	BEEHLOOORRSSTTU	TROUBLESHOOTERS
BBDIMOORRRSTUUY	DORMITORY SUBURB	BEEIIIIILNNSSST	INSENSIBILITIES
BBEHILMMMOOORST	THROMBOEMBOLISM	BEEIIIILNNSTTXY	INEXTENSIBILITY
BCCDEEIIJNORSTT	INDIRECT OBJECTS	BEEIIIILRRRSTVY	IRREVERSIBILITY
BCCEEEEGILRSTTU	ICEBERG LETTUCES	BEEIMNOOPPRSSSS	OPPOSITE NUMBERS
BCCEEEIILMNNOSU	BIOLUMINESCENCE	BEEINNORSSSSTUUV	UNOBTRUSIVENESS
BCCEEEIMNNPRSUU	SUPERINCUMBENCE	BEFHHLMOOOOTTUY	THE BLOOM OF YOUTH
BCCEEILNORRSTTU	RECONSTRUCTIBLE	BEGIIIIILLLNTTY	INTELLIGIBILITY
BCCEEINOPRSSSTU	SUBSISTENCE CROP	BEIIIIILMRRSSTY	IRREMISSIBILITY
BCCEGHIMNNNRRUU	NUMBER-CRUNCHING	BEIIIIILRRSSTTY	IRRESISTIBILITY
BCDDDEELLNOOOSS	COLD-BLOODEDNESS	BEIMNORSSSSTUUU	RUMBUSTIOUSNESS
BCDEEEIMMNNRSTU	DISENCUMBERMENT	BELLLORSSTUUWYY	SLOWLY BUT SURELY
BCDEEHILLLOOSTW	WHITE BLOOD CELLS	BELOPRRSSSSSTUU	BRUSSELS SPROUTS
BCDEGIIILNOSTUY	BUILDING SOCIETY	BFILLNOPPSSUUUY	BOUNTIFUL SUPPLY
BCDEIIILOPRRTUY	REPRODUCIBILITY	BHIIIINOOPRSSTT	PROHIBITIONISTS
BCDEIIILRSTTTUY	DESTRUCTIBILITY	CCCDEEEIIMNOSST	DOMESTIC SCIENCE
BCDEILLNNOORSSU	COLOUR BLINDNESS	CCCDEEFIIKNNORT	CONFIDENCE TRICK
BCEEEFFGILNORTY	BENEFIT OF CLERGY	CCCEEEIMNNNOOSY	CONSCIENCE MONEY
BCEEEFGHIIOPRTT	TIP OF THE ICEBERG	CCCEEHLMOOSTTYY	CHOLECYSTECTOMY
BCEEEFIIKNNSSST	SICKNESS BENEFIT	CCCEEIILMNOORRT	MICROELECTRONIC
BCEEEILNPSSSSTU	SUSCEPTIBLENESS	CCCEIILNORSTUUY	SECURITY COUNCIL
BCEEFFIOOOPSSTX	POST OFFICE BOXES	CCCIIIMNOPRRSTU	CIRCUMSCRIPTION
BCEEHILLOOPRSSS	PHLEBOSCLEROSIS	CCCIILMNOORSTUU	CIRCUMLOCUTIONS
BCEEIIILMPPRRST	IMPRESCRIPTIBLE	CCDDDEEHHILNOOOS	SECOND CHILDHOOD
BCEEINORSSSSTTUV	OBSTRUCTIVENESS	CCDEEEFFNOORRTT	CONCERTED EFFORT
BCEGHIILNOOSTTU	BIOTECHNOLOGIST	CCDEEEFINNNOOOV	CONVENIENCE FOOD
BCEHIIIIINOSTTX	EXHIBITIONISTIC	CCDEEEIIMORSSTV	DOMESTIC SERVICE
BCEHIILNOPPRSUW	PUBLIC OWNERSHIP	CCDEEEENNNNORSSU	UNCONCERNEDNESS
BCEIIILMNOPTTTY	CONTEMPTIBILITY	CCDEEEENNNNOSSTU	UNCONNECTEDNESS
BCEIIILMOPRSSTY	COMPRESSIBILITY	CCDEEGIIIILNNRSV	DRIVING LICENCES

CCDEEEINOPRSTUUV	SUPERCONDUCTIVE
CCDEELLNORSTTUW	WELL-CONSTRUCTED
CCDEGIILNNORSTY	DISCONCERTINGLY
CCDEIIINPRRSTTU	PRINTED CIRCUITS
CCDEINNOOPRSTUU	SUPERCONDUCTION
CCDENOOPRRSSTUU	SUPERCONDUCTORS
CCDHIIKLLOSUWWW	CHUCK-WILL'S-WIDOW
CCDHINNOOOOPTTU	PHOTOCONDUCTION
CCEEEEFNNNORSSW	NEWS CONFERENCES
CCEEEEFNNOPRRSS	PRESS CONFERENCE
CCEEEEFNORRRSSS	CROSS-REFERENCES
CCEEEEHHINQRSSU	CHINESE CHEQUERS
CCEEEEILMMOSTTT	SELECT COMMITTEE
CCEEEFFILOSTTVY	COST-EFFECTIVELY
CCEEEFIINNOORST	CONFECTIONERIES
CCEEEGJLNNORSTU	CONCRETE JUNGLES
CCEEEHHNOOPPRSS	PHOSPHORESCENCE
CCEEEHILOOPRRTT	ELECTROPHORETIC
CCEEEIIKLNORSTT	ELECTROKINETICS
CCEEEFFFIILNSSUY	SELF-SUFFICIENCY
CCEEEFHIINOPRSST	CHIEF INSPECTORS
CCEEEGIIINNNNNOV	INCONVENIENCING
CCEEEHIIILNORTTY	HELIOCENTRICITY
CCEEEHIINNORTTTY	ETHNOCENTRICITY
CCEEEHNORRSTTTUU	TECHNOSTRUCTURE
CCEEEIIINNNOSSST	INCONSISTENCIES
CCEEEIILOPRRTTYY	PYROELECTRICITY
CCEEEIINNNNOORTT	INTERCONNECTION
CCEEEILLMOORSSTT	COLLECTOR'S ITEMS
CCEEEILLNNOOSTUV	COLLECTIVE NOUNS
CCEEEIMMNNORTTUU	COMMUNITY CENTRE
CCEEEINNOPRRSSSW	CROWN PRINCESSES
CCEEFILLNOOSSSUY	SELF-CONSCIOUSLY
CCEEHIIMMOOPSTTY	PSYCHOTOMIMETIC
CCEEHIMMNOSSTTUU	COMMUNITY CHESTS
CCEEIILLNOOORSSU	COLLISION COURSE
CCEEIILNNOOSSTUY	CONSCIENTIOUSLY
CCEEIMOOOOPRRRSSS	MICROPROCESSORS
CCEEINNNOOSSSSUU	UNCONSCIOUSNESS
CCEEINNOOPSSSSUU	CONSPICUOUSNESS
CCEEINNOORRSSTTU	RECONSTRUCTIONS
CCGHIIINORRSTTU	SHORT-CIRCUITING
CCGIIIILNOOSSTU	SOCIOLINGUISTIC
CCIIINNOOORSTTT	CONTORTIONISTIC
CCIIINNOOPRSSTT	CONSCRIPTIONIST
CCIILLNOOPRRUVY	PRIVY COUNCILLOR
CCIILNOOPSSSUUY	INCONSPICUOUSLY
CCIIMNNOORSSTTU	MISCONSTRUCTION
CDDEEEEEINNNPRT	INTERDEPENDENCE
CDDEEEELNNPRTUY	UNPRECEDENTEDLY
CDDEEFIIIILLNPSS	SELF-DISCIPLINED
CDDEEFIIINNORRT	DIRECTION FINDER
CDDEFNNOOOOPSTU	FOOT-POUND-SECOND
CDDEGHILLNOORSU	COLD-SHOULDERING

CDDEINNOOPRRTUU	UNDERPRODUCTION
CDEEEEEINNQSSUV	QUEEN'S EVIDENCES
CDEEEEFLNNRSSST	SELF-CENTREDNESS
CDEEEEINNNPRSTU	SUPERINTENDENCE
CDEEEEIORSSTTTV	STORE DETECTIVES
CDEEEFILORRSTTT	LETTERS OF CREDIT
CDEEEHHILPRSTUW	WHITED SEPULCHRE
CDEEEHNNORRTTUU	UNDER-THE-COUNTER
CDEEEIINNPRRSWW	WINDSCREEN WIPER
CDEEEIINPRSSSTV	DESCRIPTIVENESS
CDEEEIMNNPRSTUU	SUPERINDUCEMENT
CDEEEINNNPRSTUY	SUPERINTENDENCY
CDEEEINRSSSTTUV	DESTRUCTIVENESS
CDEEELLMMNOOPSW	COMMON SPEEDWELL
CDEEFFILLNNOSTY	SELF-CONFIDENTLY
CDEEFGILNRSSTTU	SELF-DESTRUCTING
CDEEFIILNORSTYY	FRIENDLY SOCIETY
CDEEFIILORRSSST	CROSS-FERTILISED
CDEEFIILORRSSTZ	CROSS-FERTILIZED
CDEEFILLPRSSTUY	DISRESPECTFULLY
CDEEFILNORSSTTU	SELF-DESTRUCTION
CDEEHIIKNSSTTTW	THICK-WITTEDNESS
CDEEHILNNORSSSW	CHINLESS WONDERS
CDEEIIIIMNNRSTTC	INDETERMINISTIC
CDEEIIINNSSSTTV	DISTINCTIVENESS
CDEEIIKNQSSTTUW	QUICK-WITTEDNESS
CDEEILMNNOOPTWY	ENDOWMENT POLICY
CDEEILNNORSSSUU	INCREDULOUSNESS
CDEEINOOQRSSSTU	CROSS-QUESTIONED
CDEGIILNNOOORST	ENDOCRINOLOGIST
CDEGILNNOOPRRSY	CORRESPONDINGLY
CDEIIIINNOSSTTU	DISCONTINUITIES
CDEIIIJNNOSSSUU	INJUDICIOUSNESS
CDEIILNOOPPRSTU	PRODUCTION LINES
CDHIILNOPRSTUUU	PULCHRITUDINOUS
CDIILNNOOSSTUUY	DISCONTINUOUSLY
CDIINNOOPRTTUVY	NONPRODUCTIVITY
CEEEEEELOOPRSTT	TELESTEREOSCOPE
CEEEEFFIINNSSTV	INEFFECTIVENESS
CEEEEFHORRRRSSU	REFRESHER COURSE
CEEEEGIIMNNRSSS	EMINENCES GRISES
CEEEEKLNNOORSTU	KEEP ONE'S COUNSEL
CEEEFFGHIOPRSSU	FIGURES OF SPEECH
CEEEFFGIIORRSST	REGISTER OFFICES
CEEEFIIMNORRRTT	INTERFEROMETRIC
CEEEFLNORRSSSUU	RESOURCEFULNESS
CEEEGGILNNOOSSU	GLUCONEOGENESIS
CEEEGHILORRSSTU	GLOUCESTERSHIRE
CEEEGILNORRSSTV	COVERING LETTERS
CEEEHIIMNNOPRSV	INCOMPREHENSIVE
CEEEHILMNOPRSVY	COMPREHENSIVELY
CEEEHILOOPRRSST	ELECTROPHORESIS
CEEEHIMORRSSTTY	STEREOCHEMISTRY
CEEEIILLNNOSUUV	NOUVELLE CUISINE

CEEEIILOOPRSTTV	ELECTROPOSITIVE
CEEEIIMNOPSSTTV	COMPETITIVENESS
CEEEIIMOORRSSTT	STEREOISOMETRIC
CEEEIINRRSSSTTV	RESTRICTIVENESS
CEEEILOPRRSTTVY	RETROSPECTIVELY
CEEEIMMNNOPRSTV	PINCER MOVEMENTS
CEEEIMNNOORSSSU	CEREMONIOUSNESS
CEEEINPQRSSSTUU	PICTURESQUENESS
CEEEKOOPRRRSSSU	PRESSURE COOKERS
CEEENNOPPPRRRST	PEPPERCORN RENTS
CEEFFGIIORRSSTY	REGISTRY OFFICES
CEEFHIIIKMNNOTT	IN THE NICK OF TIME
CEEFIIIILLNOSTTU	FEUILLETONISTIC
CEEFINNOPRRSSTU	PERFUNCTORINESS
CEEGHIIILNNORSST	CROSSING THE LINE
CEEGHINNOPPRSST	SHOPPING CENTRES
CEEGIIIKMOSSTTV	GIVE IT SOME STICK
CEEGLLLNOOPPRYY	PROPYLENE GLYCOL
CEEHHIMMORRSTTY	THERMOCHEMISTRY
CEEHIIMNNOOPRS	INCOMPREHENSION
CEEHIIMNOSSSSSUV	MISCHIEVOUSNESS
CEEHIINOPRRSSTT	HISTORIC PRESENT
CEEHILLNOORRSXY	HEXYLRESORCINOL
CEEHIMNOORRSTTU	MOTHER COUNTRIES
CEEIIINOPRSSSTX	EXPRESSIONISTIC
CEEIIILNOPRSTTVY	INTROSPECTIVELY
CEEIIMNNOPSSSUU	IMPECUNIOUSNESS
CEEIIMNORRRSSTN	RESURRECTIONISM
CEEIINOPPRSSSTU	PRECIPITOUSNESS
CEEIINORRRSSTTU	RESURRECTIONIST
CEEIINPSSSTTUUV	INTUSSUSCEPTIVE
CEEIKNOPRRSTTVY	POVERTY-STRICKEN
CEEILMNNOORSUUY	UNCEREMONIOUSLY
CEEIMNNNOOOOSTW	COME INTO ONE'S OWN
CEEINNNOOSSSTTU	CONTENTIOUSNESS
CEEINNOOQRRSSTU	CORONER'S INQUEST
CEEINOOQQRRSSTU	CROSS-QUESTIONER
CEEINOPPRSSSSUU	PERSPICUOUSNESS
CEEPRRRSSSTTUUU	SUPERSTRUCTURES
CEFGHHIILLNNOPRS	FRENCH POLISHING
CEFGHIIILNNNNSSU	UNFLINCHINGNESS
CEFGIIKLLNORSST	STOCKING-FILLERS
CEGHIJNOOPRSSTU	HOUSING PROJECTS
CEGIIKMNNNORSSS	MORNING SICKNESS
CEGIIMMMNOSSTUW	SWIMMING COSTUME
CEGILNOOPPSSSTY	SYNOPTIC GOSPELS
CEGINNNOORSSSUU	INCONGRUOUSNESS
CEGINOOOPRRSSTY	CROSSOPTERYGION
CEHHIMMNOOOPPRS	MORPHOPHONEMICS
CEHIIMMMNORSTUY	IMMUNOCHEMISTRY
CEHLNOOOORSSSUW	SHOW ONE'S COLOURS
CEHNNNOORSSSSUY	SYNCHRONOUSNESS
CEIIIIMNOPRSSST	IMPRESSIONISTIC
CEIIIINOSSSTTVV	VIVISECTIONISTS
CEIILNNOPSSSSTUU	PUNCTILIOUSNESS
CEIINNOPSSSTTUU	INTUSSUSCEPTION
CEIMMNNNOOOOPSST	NON COMPOS MENTIS
CEIMNOOPRSSSSUU	PROMISCUOUSNESS
CEIMNOPRSSSSTUU	SCRUMPTIOUSNESS
CEKLLNOOPPSSSUU	PULL ONE'S SOCKS UP
CFFHIILMNOSSTTU	FIFTH COLUMNISTS
CFGHHHLOOOOSTTU	SCHOOL OF THOUGHT
CFGHHIIILNNOOSS	FINISHING SCHOOL
CFHILMNOOOORRRT	NITROCHLOROFORM
CFIINOOQRRSTUUY	COURTS OF INQUIRY
CGHHIIIMMNOOSSS	HIGH COMMISSIONS
CHHHINNOORSRTUY	ORNITHORHYNCHUS
CHILLMOOOPPRRSY	MICROSPOROPHYLL
DDDEEEHLNOORRSUU	ROUND-SHOULDERED
DDEEEFHILMNOORW	MIDDLE OF NOWHERE
DDEFGHLNOOOPSSU	SLOUGH OF DESPOND
DDEGGHINNOSSTUW	SHOTGUN WEDDINGS
DDEGHIIINNSSTU	UNDISTINGUISHED
DEEEEGINRRRSSTU	REGISTERED NURSE
DEEEEHMNORRRSTV	REVEREND MOTHERS
DEEEEINRSSSTTTV	VESTED INTERESTS
DEEEELMNOOPRTVV	OVERDEVELOPMENT
DEEEFGHINORSSTT	FORESIGHTEDNESS
DEEEFLLOPSSSSSY	SELF-POSSESSEDLY
DEEEHLLMOOOOPPSS	OLD PEOPLE'S HOMES
DEEEIILLNNNOTTW	WELL-INTENTIONED
DEEEIILMMNRRSTS	DELIRIUM TREMENS
DEEEIINOPSSSTUX	EXPEDITIOUSNESS
DEEEINNNOSSSTTU	TENDENTIOUSNESS
DEEEINNNPRSSTTU	SUPERINTENDENTS
DEEELMMNNOPRTUY	UNDEREMPLOYMENT
DEEHIINOOPSSSTT	PHOTOSENSITISED
DEEHIINOOPSSTTZ	PHOTOSENSITIZED
DEEHIMOORRSTTTU	RIDE OUT THE STORM
DEEILNNPRRTTUUY	UNINTERRUPTEDLY
DEFFIIILLNNORSTY	FLY INTO FLINDERS
DEFGGHIIKLNNORT	FORKED LIGHTNING
DEFHHLLNOOOSTUW	FOLLOW THE HOUNDS
DEFHIIMNNOORSTU	FOURTH DIMENSION
DEFILNRSSSSTTUU	DISTRUSTFULNESS
DEGHHIIILNRRSVW	WHIRLING DERVISH
DEGHHIINNNORSTU	HUNTINGDONSHIRE
DEIIIILLMNNOSSTU	DISILLUSIONMENT
DEIIINOOPPRSSST	PREDISPOSITIONS
DEIIMNNNRSSTTUW	WIND INSTRUMENTS
DEIINNORSSSSTUU	INDUSTRIOUSNESS
DEIINNRRSSSTUUY	SUNRISE INDUSTRY
EEEEGILNPSTTTTY	TELETYPESETTING
EEEEGNNNOORSSTV	GET ON ONE'S NERVES
EEEEHLLNOOPSSTT	TELEPHOTO LENSES
EEEEHNOPQSTTUUZ	PUT THE SQUEEZE ON
EEEEIINNNPSSSVX	INEXPENSIVENESS
EEEEELMNORRSSSSS	REMORSELESSNESS

EEEEMNNORSSSTUV	VENTURESOMENESS
EEEEFFIINNNOSSSV	INOFFENSIVENESS
EEEEFHIILNOSSSUW	HOUSEWIFELINESS
EEEEFHNNOOOORRSTW	NONE THE WORSE FOR
EEEFILMMNOPRSTV	SELF-IMPROVEMENT
EEEEGHMNNOOOSSSU	HOMOGENEOUSNESS
EEEGIILLMOSTVWY	GIVE IT SOME WELLY
EEEGIIMNNPRRSST	MISREPRESENTING
EEEGIINNOPRSSTV	PROGENITIVENESS
EEEGILORRRSSTVY	RETROGRESSIVELY
EEEIIIILNNOPRSTV	VESPERTILIONINE
EEEIIMMOORRSSST	STEREOISOMERISM
EEEIIINOPRSSSTTU	REPETITIOUSNESS
EEEILLLLMNOPPRWY	YELLOW PIMPERNEL
EEEILNNOOPPRSTT	POISON-PEN LETTER
EEEIMNPPRSSSTUV	PRESUMPTIVENESS
EEEINNNOSSSSTTU	SENTENTIOUSNESS
EEEINNOPRSSSTTU	PRETENTIOUSNESS
EEELNOPPRSSSSSU	PURPOSELESSNESS
EEEMNNOPSSSSTTUU	TEMPESTUOUSNESS
EEEFFFHILNOORSST	SHIFT FOR ONESELF
EEFGHILLORSSTUY	SELF-RIGHTEOUSLY
EEFGHNOORRSTTTW	TOWER OF STRENGTH
EEFGIOOOPRRRSSSU	REGIUS PROFESSOR
EEFHMMNOOOPRSTTU	SPUR-OF-THE-MOMENT
EEFILLLLMNOSSSUU	MELLIFLUOUSNESS
EEFLNOPRSSSSSUU	SUPERFLUOUSNESS
EEFMMNNOORRSSTTT	FROM STEM TO STERN
EEGGIILNNNSSTTT	STINGING NETTLES
EEGHHLNOSSSSTTU	THOUGHTLESSNESS
EEGHIMNOORSSSSTY	MOOG SYNTHESISER
EEGHIMNOORSSTYZ	MOOG SYNTHESIZER
EEGIIIJNNNNNPSS	SPINNING JENNIES
EEGIIIMNNPRRSTT	MISINTERPRETING
EEGIINNORSSSTUV	VERTIGINOUSNESS
EEGIINNPPRRSSST	PRINTING PRESSES
EEGIINOPRSSSSTU	PRESTIGIOUSNESS
EEHHILNOORTTTWW	THROW IN THE TOWEL
EEHHLLOORSSTTUY	YOUTH HOSTELLERS
EEHIKNOOPRRSTUY	KEEP YOUR SHIRT ON
EEHILNNOOORSSST	LOSE ONE'S SHIRT ON
EEHIMOOPRRRSSTU	MOTHER SUPERIORS
EEHINNOPRRSTTTU	THREE-POINT TURNS
EEHLNOPRSSSSUUU	SULPHUREOUSNESS
EEIIIIINNQSSSTUV	INQUISITIVENESS
EEIIIIMNNNORSTTV	INTERVENTIONISM
EEIIIINNNORSTTTV	INTERVENTIONIST
EEIILLNNOORRTTTU	TRINITROTOLUENE
EEIINNNNNOORTTV	NONINTERVENTION
EEILNNOPRSTTUUY	UNPRETENTIOUSLY
EEINNNOOPPRSSTU	INOPPORTUNENESS
EFGIIIILMNOPRSVY	OVERSIMPLIFYING
EFIIIIIILNNPSTTV	SPLIT INFINITIVE
EFILMNRSSSSTTUU	MISTRUSTFULNESS
EGGHIIIKLNNRSTT	LIGHTNING STRIKE
EGHHIIILLMNOOSTT	HELMINTHOLOGIST
EGHHIINOOPPRSSW	HERO-WORSHIPPING
EGHHILLNOOSTTUY	YOUTH HOSTELLING
EGHHILNOOPRSTTT	PLIGHT ONE'S TROTH
EGHIIIKLNNNORSTV	SHRINKING VIOLET
EGHILNOOOPRSUYY	NEUROPHYSIOLOGY
EGIIIILNNOORTUVZ	REVOLUTIONIZING
EHHINOOPPRSSUYY	NEUROHYPOPHYSIS
EHIIIKLMMOOPRST	POIKILOTHERMISM
EHIILLMOOPPRRTTU	PHOTOMULTIPLIER
EHILOOPRSSTTTUW	WHISTLE-STOP TOUR
EHINORRSSSTTTUW	TRUSTWORTHINESS
EIIIMNOOPPRSSTU	SUPERIMPOSITION
EIILOPRRSSTTUUY	SURREPTITIOUSLY
EIILOPRSSTTUUY	SUPERSTITIOUSLY
EIINOOPPPRSSSTU	PRESUPPOSITIONS
FFGHIINNORSSSTU	SOFT FURNISHINGS
FGHHIIIKLNNSTUW	WISHFUL THINKING
FGHIINNNNOOOSWW	NO SHOW OF WINNING

AAAAACDDEELLPPSS	CALL A SPADE A SPADE
AAAAACEEEKMNNPPR	MAKE AN APPEARANCE
AAAAACGILLMMMNRTY	ANAGRAMMATICALLY
AAAABBDGGILNORTT	RAGTAG AND BOBTAIL
AAAABCEHILLLNPTY	ANALPHABETICALLY
AAAACCHILLLNPTYY	ANAPHYLACTICALLY
AAAACDEGILRRSUWY	DUAL CARRIAGEWAYS
AAAACDEHHLNPRRSU	ARUNACHAL PRADESH
AAAACDGIILLMMRTY	DIAGRAMMATICALLY
AAAACDGIILLMPRTY	PARADIGMATICALLY
AAAACEEHILMMMTTT	METAMATHEMATICAL
AAAACEELLNOPPRST	TO ALL APPEARANCES
AAAACEILLMNNRSTY	ALIMENTARY CANALS
AAAADEGHIIRSSSTT	AS STRAIGHT AS A DIE
AAAAEHIIMNNOSTTT	ANATHEMATISATION
AAAAEHIIMNNOTTTZ	ANATHEMATIZATION
AAAAEIILMNNPRRST	PARLIAMENTARIANS
AAAABBDDEEFKNRSST	BED AND BREAKFASTS
AAABCCEILLRRSTUUY	BUREAUCRATICALLY
AAABCDDHHMMNNOOTT COMBAT	HAND-TO-HAND
AAABCDEGGIIILORR	REGGIO DI CALABRIA
AAABCEEGHHILNNNT	HANG IN THE BALANCE
AAABCEEKKLLNRSTT	BLACK RATTLESNAKE
AAABCEFILLMNOORT	AMERICAN FOOTBALL
AAABCGHIILOOPRTU	AUTOBIOGRAPHICAL
AAABEEEKPPRSSTTW	WASTEPAPER BASKET
AAABEEGGLLMNSSUY	ASSEMBLY LANGUAGE
AAABEINNRSSTTTTU	TRANSUBSTANTIATE
AAACCCFHIIINORST	SACCHARIFICATION
AAACCDHIMMNOPRSY	PHARMACODYNAMICS
AAACCDIIILLLRSTY	RADICALISTICALLY
AAACCEEGHIKNRRSY	HACKNEY CARRIAGES
AAACCEEHHIKKRRSS	KARACHAI-CHERKESS
AAACCEEHHILLMNPT	THALAMENCEPHALIC
AAACCEEIILNOPSSU	CAESALPINIACEOUS
AAACCEFIIRRRRRST	AIRCRAFT CARRIERS
AAACCEGHILLLOORY	ARCHAEOLOGICALLY
AAACCEHIINNPQSTU	ACQUAINTANCESHIP
AAACCEHIINORRSTT	CHARACTERISATION
AAACCEHIINORRTTZ	CHARACTERIZATION
AAACCEHILLMPRTUY	PHARMACEUTICALLY
AAACCFIIILLNOSST	CLASSIFICATION
AAACCGHIILLLLPRY	CALLIGRAPHICALLY
AAACCHILLOPRSTTY	CATASTROPHICALLY
AAACCIIILLORRSTY	ARISTOCRATICALLY
AAACDEEEMMNRSSTU	AMUSEMENT ARCADES
AAACDEEFFGHIRRSS	CHARGES D'AFFAIRES
AAACDEGINORRRSTU	REARGUARD ACTIONS
AAACDEILLLMMORTY	MELODRAMATICALLY
AAACDEIMNNOORSTT	ANIMATED CARTOONS
AAACEEEILMNNOPRT	AMERICAN ANTELOPE
AAACEEGGILLMNOTY	AGAMOGENETICALLY
AAACEEGHIMMNORST	ARCHAEOMAGNETISM

AAACEEHHLLMNNOPT	THALAMENCEPHALON
AAACEEKLLNOORRTW	LOCAL AREA NETWORK
AAACEFHHIILMRRSS	AIR CHIEF MARSHALS
AAACEGHILLMNOPRY	ANEMOGRAPHICALLY
AAACEGHILNOOPPRT	PALAEONTOGRAPHIC
AAACEGHINNOPRTTY	ACANTHOPTERYGIAN
AAACEGIILLMMPRTY	EPIGRAMMATICALLY
AAACEGILLLNOOOPT	PALAEONTOLOGICAL
AAACEGILLLOOOOPZ	PALAEOZOOLOGICAL
AAACEHIILLNPTTTY	ANTIPATHETICALLY
AAACEHILLLMNPRUY	ALPHANUMERICALLY
AAACEHILLMPRSTTY	METAPHRASTICALLY
AAACEIIILNOPRSTT	RECAPITALISATION
AAACEIIILNOPRTTZ	RECAPITALIZATION
AAACEIKLMMNORSS	EXCLAMATION MARKS
AAACEINNORTTTTTT	ATTRACT ATTENTION
AAACFHIIILLNSSST	ATLANTIC SAILFISH
AAACGHILLLNOPPRY	PLANOGRAPHICALLY
AAACGHILLNOPPRTY	PANTOGRAPHICALLY
AAACGIILLNNOSTTY	ANTAGONISTICALLY
AAACIILLLNRSTTUY	NATURALISTICALLY
AAACILLMMOPSTTYY	ASYMPTOMATICALLY
AAACILLMNNOOSTTY	ANTONOMASTICALLY
AAACILLMNNOOPRSTY	PARONOMASTICALLY
AAADDDEEKLNNRSSS	SNAKES AND LADDERS
AAADDEEFHLMOPRRY	PARAFORMALDEHYDE
AAADEEEILLRSTVWY	ELEVATED RAILWAYS
AAADEEGNNOSSSTUV	ADVANTAGEOUSNESS
AAADEEIMNOPRRSST	DRAMATIS PERSONAE
AAADEFJLMMNOSSTT	FLOTSAM AND JETSAM
AAADEGHIMPPRRSSY	DIAPHRAGM PESSARY
AAADEGIILNNORRTT	INTERGRADATIONAL
AAADEIILLNNORSTTU	DENATURALISATION
AAADEIILNNORTTUZ	DENATURALIZATION
AAADGHILLMNNRRSY	MARSHALLING YARDS
AAADIILLMMNORRSST	MALADMINISTRATOR
AAAEEEEGLNRSSTTT	REAL ESTATE AGENTS
AAAEEEEHHKMRTVWY	MAKE HEAVY WEATHER
AAAEEEGLMNPRSTY	PAYMASTER GENERAL
AAAEEEJLNNNPRSST	JAPANESE LANTERNS
AAAEEFLLMMMNNNORS	ALL MANNER OF MEANS
AAAEEGIILLNOQRTUU	EQUATORIAL GUINEA
AAAEEHIINNOSSTTT	ANAESTHETISATION
AAAEEHIINNOSTTTZ	ANAESTHETIZATION
AAAEEIIMNNOPPRTX	EXAMINATION PAPER
AAAEILLMNNOOPSYY	MALAYO-POLYNESIAN
AAAFILMNNOORRSTT	TRANSFORMATIONAL
AAAGIILLNNOORSTY	ORGANISATIONALLY
AAAGIILLNNOORTYZ	ORGANIZATIONALLY
AAAGIILMNNORSTTT	TRANSMIGRATIONAL
AAAHIIIMNNORRSTTU	AUTHORITARIANISM
AAAIIILNNOORSSTT	RATIONALISATIONS
AAAIIILNNOORSTTZ	RATIONALIZATIONS
AAAIILLMNNORSTTU	ULTRANATIONALISM

AAAIILLNNORSTTTU	ULTRANATIONALIST	AACCDIIINNNOORTT	CONTRAINDICATION
AAAIILMNNOPRSSTU	SUPRANATIONALISM	AACCEEFGIKNNOOTZ	TAKE COGNIZANCE OF
AABBDDELNNOPSSUY	BY LEAPS AND BOUNDS	AACCEEHILLMORTTY	TACHEOMETRICALLY
AABBEIIILLMOTTYZ	METABOLIZABILITY	AACCEEILLORSTTTY	STEREOTACTICALLY
AABCCDEIIIMNNOOZ	AMINOBENZOIC ACID	AACCEEKNORRSTTTU	COUNTERATTACKERS
AABCCEEGGLLOORRT	GARBAGE COLLECTOR	AACCEELLNOOSSTTW	COALS TO NEWCASTLE
AABCCEEHHMORRRST	CHAMBER ORCHESTRA	AACCEEMNOPRRSTYY	COMPANY SECRETARY
AABCCEGILNNORTU	COUNTERBALANCING	AACCEGHHILLOPRTY	HECTOGRAPHICALLY
AABCCIIIILMPRTTY	IMPRACTICABILITY	AACCEGHIIMMPSTTY	SYMPATHETIC MAGIC
AABCCIILMMNORTUU	CIRCUMAMBULATION	AACCEGHILLNOPRSY	SCENOGRAPHICALLY
AABCCILMMORRTUUY	CIRCUMAMBULATORY	AACCEGIKNNORTTTU	COUNTERATTACKING
AABCDEEIIMNNOORW	AMERICAN WOODBINE	AACCEGILLLNRSTUU	INTEGRAL CALCULUS
AABCDEIILNOORSST	ANABOLIC STEROIDS	AACCEEHHHILNNOPRY	RHYNCHOCEPHALIAN
AABCDGILMNOOPTUY	GUNBOAT DIPLOMACY	AACCEEHHIIIMNPRSV	VICE-CHAIRMANSHIP
AABCEEEEILLMMNSST	EMBLEMATICALNESS	AACCEEHIILMNSSSST	SCHISMATICALNESS
AABCEEHILNNRSSTU	UNCHARITABLENESS	AACCEEHILLOOPRSUY	CARYOPHYLLACEOUS
AABCEFGILLMNORRU	AMERICAN BULLFROG	AACCEEIILLLLNORTVY	INTERVOCALICALLY
AABCEEHIIILMNPTUY	UNIMPEACHABILITY	AACCFILOOPRRRSTU	PROCURATOR FISCAL
AABCEIIIIILLMRRTY	IRRECLAIMABILITY	AACCGGIIIMNNRTUV	CIRCUMNAVIGATING
AABCGIILNORSSTUU	SUBCARTILAGINOUS	AACCGHIILLMNOOST	ANGLO-CATHOLICISM
AABCIILLMNOOORST	COLLABORATIONISM	AACCGHIILLMOPRRY	MICROGRAPHICALLY
AABCIILLNOOORSTT	COLLABORATIONIST	AACCGHILLOPRRSTY	CRYSTALLOGRAPHIC
AABCILLLLLOPSYYY	POLYSYLLABICALLY	AACCGIIIMNNORTUV	CIRCUMNAVIGATION
AABCILLLLMNOOSYY	MONOSYLLABICALLY	AACCHHILLOPPSTYY	PSYCHOPATHICALLY
AABCINNOOORSSSTT	CONTRABASSOONIST	AACCHIIILLNSTUVY	CHAUVINISTICALLY
AABDDEEFGIKNRSTW	WEDDING BREAKFAST	AACCHIIINNNORSST	ANACHRONISNISTIC
AABDEEEEFFNNRTWW	FEW AND FAR BETWEEN	AACCHIILMMNOORST	ROMAN CATHOLICISM
AABDEEEEGILNRSSS	DISAGREEABLENESS	AACCHILLLOPPRTYY	PROPHYLACTICALLY
AABDEEEIMNOORRRT	ANEROID BAROMETER	AACCIILLMNRSTTUY	CIRCUMSTANTIALLY
AABDEEFHILLSTWYY	FALL BY THE WAYSIDE	AACCILLOOPRSSTUY	STAUROSCOPICALLY
AABDEEIMMNRRSSST	DISEMBARRASSMENT	AACDDEEIILNPRSTU	UNDERCAPITALISED
AABDEFGIIIILNTTY	INDEFATIGABILITY	AACDDEEIILNPRTUZ	UNDERCAPITALIZED
AABEEEGHLLLMNOWW	WHOLE NEW BALL GAME	AACDDEGHLNOOSSTT	GOODS AND CHATTELS
AABEEEGLMORRSTVW	VEGETABLE MARROWS	AACDDEHLLNNOOOTT	NOT HOLD A CANDLE TO
AABEEELNNNORSSSU	UNREASONABLENESS	AACDDHILLMNORYYY	HYDRODYNAMICALLY
AABEEELNNNOSSSSU	UNSEASONABLENESS	AACDEEEEGIORSSST	ASSOCIATE DEGREES
AABEEFGHIKLNRSST	ENGLISH BREAKFAST	AACDEEEELORRSSUY	DAY RELEASE COURSE
AABEEFLNNORSSUUV	UNFAVOURABLENESS	AACDEEEIMNNNORRT	MAINTENANCE ORDER
AABIIILNNNSTTTUU	TINTINNABULATION	AACDEEFGILLNORTT	FLAGRANTE DELICTO
AABIIILNNSSTTTUY	INSUBSTANTIALITY	AACDEEGHIILOPRRT	RADIOTELEGRAPHIC
AABIILLNNSSTTTUY	UNSUBSTANTIALITY	AACDEEGIILMRRRST	MEDICAL REGISTRAR
AABIIILNOPRRSTTTY	TRANSPORTABILITY	AACDEEHIIOPRRTTU	RADIOTHERAPEUTIC
AACCCDEFIILNOORR	AFRICAN CROCODILE	AACDEEIILNNRTUN	QUADRICENTENNIAL
AACCCDEHIINNORTW	IN ACCORDANCE WITH	AACDEEIILLNNORST	DECENTRALISATION
AACCCDIIINORRSTY	IDIOSYNCRACRATIC	AACDEEIILNNORTTZ	DECENTRALIZATION
AACCCEEIILLLSSTY	ECCLESIASTICALLY	AACDEEILNNSSSSTU	INDECENT ASSAULTS
AACCCEHIKMRRRSST	CHRISTMAS CRACKER	AACDEELLNNNRSTUY	TRANSCENDENTALLY
AACCCIILLLNOOSTY	ICONOCLASTICALLY	AACDEFIILMNNSTTU	FUNDAMENTALISTIC
AACCDEEHHIILPRTT	TEREPHTHALIC ACID	AACDEHHIILNPRSST	CHRISTADELPHIANS
AACCDEEILNNOORTV	DEUTEROCANONICAL	AACDEHIIKKMMNNRST	KITCHEN-SINK DRAMA
AACCDEFGHKLNORRT	GRANDFATHER CLOCK	AACDEIIILKLMMNORTY	DILATOMETRICALLY
AACCDEFIIIILNOSST	DECLASSIFICATION	AACDEINOPRSSSSST	SCISSORS-AND-PASTE
AACCDEFIILLOPTTY	FILLED TO CAPACITY	AACDFIIIIILNOQSTU	DISQUALIFICATION
AACCDEGILLLNNOST	LONGDISTANCE CALL	AACDGHHILLOPRRYY	HYDROGRAPHICALLY

AACDIIIILMNNORST	DISCRIMINATIONAL
AACDIIIILNORSTTT	TRADITIONALISTIC
AACDIIILNNORSTTU	INDUSTRIAL ACTION
AACEEEEGLNRRRSTY	SECRETARY-GENERAL
AACEEEEFHORRSSTTW	WEATHER FORECASTS
AACEEEHHHLNOORTX	HEXACHLOROETHANE
AACEEEIINPPRSSTV	APPRECIATIVENESS
AACEEFFMNORSSTTT	MATTER-OF-FACTNESS
AACEEFHKNNOORTTV	ARK OF THE COVENANT
AACEEGHILLMNPSST	PHLEGMATICALNESS
AACEEGIILLLNNPTY	PALINGENETICALLY
AACEEGIILLLNSTVY	EVANGELISTICALLY
AACEEGILLNPRSSTT	LAST RESTING PLACE
AACEEGLMNOOPRTUU	ANALOGUE COMPUTER
AACEEGNOOPRRTTUV	AGENT PROVOCATEUR
AACEEHILLNNRSTUY	NEURASTHENICALLY
AACEEHILMNOPRSST	METAPHORICALNESS
AACEEHIMOPRSSTTU	MASSOTHERAPEUTIC
AACEEIIILLNNPSTV	CAPITAL-INTENSIVE
AACEEIIIMNNRSSST	NECESSITARIANISM
AACEEIILLRRSTTTV	VERTICILLASTRATE
AACEEIIILMNRRSSSU	MACLAURIN'S SERIES
AACEEIILNNRSSTTU	INARTICULATENESS
AACEEIKMNNOORSTV	MAKE CONVERSATION
AACEEILLNNORSTTU	NATURAL SELECTION
AACEEILLNOOPRTUV	PALACE REVOLUTION
AACEEILMMNOPRSTT	COMPARTMENTALISE
AACEEILMMNOPRTTZ	COMPARTMENTALIZE
AACEEILMNSSSSTTY	SYSTEMATICALNESS
AACEEKNNNORSSSTU	CANTANKEROUSNESS
AACEFFIILNOSSSTT	SELF-SATISFACTION
AACEFGILLNRRTTUU	ULTRACENTRIFUGAL
AACEFIINORSSSSTT	SATISFACTORINESS
AACEGHHIILNOPSTT	TEACHING HOSPITAL
AACEGHHILLNOPRTY	ETHNOGRAPHICALLY
AACEGHILLOPPRRTY	PETROGRAPHICALLY
AACEGHILOOPSSTTT	COTTAGE HOSPITALS
AACEGHLLOPRRRSTY	CRYSTALLOGRAPHER
AACEGIIILNOPRTVZ	OVERCAPITALIZING
AACEGIIMNORSSSTV	MOVING STAIRCASES
AACEHHIIILLNOPRTY	HIEROPHANTICALLY
AACEHIILLNSSTTUY	ENTHUSIASTICALLY
AACEHIILLOORSTTU	LOCAL AUTHORITIES
AACEHIILLPPRRSTY	PERIPHRASTICALLY
AACEHIILMNNORRTV	HARMONIC INTERVAL
AACEHILLMORSTTTY	THERMOSTATICALLY
AACEHLMORSSSTUUW	WALRUS MOUSTACHES
AACEIIILLLLRSTTY	LITERALISTICALLY
AACEIIILLLRSTTVY	RELATIVISTICALLY
AACEIIILMNORRSTU	MERCURIALISATION
AACEIIILMNORRTUZ	MERCURIALIZATION
AACEIIILNNOOSSTT	SECTIONALISATION
AACEIIILNNOOSTTZ	SECTIONALIZATION
AACEIIILNNOSSSTT	SENSATIONALISTIC
AACEIIILNOOPRSTT	OPERATIONALISTIC
AACEIIINNNOORSTT	CONTAINERISATION
AACEIIINNNOORTTZ	CONTAINERIZATION
AACEIIINNNNORSTT	REINCARNATIONIST
AACEIILLLRRSSTUY	SURREALISTICALLY
AACEIILNORRRTTUV	ATRIOVENTRICULAR
AACEIIMNNOORSSTX	CROSS-EXAMINATION
AACEILLLMNNOPRTY	PLANNOMETRICALLY
AACEILLMNOOOOPTY	ONOMATOPOEICALLY
AACEILLNNOORSTVY	CONVERSATIONALLY
AACEILNNNNORSTTT	TRANSCONTINENTAL
AACELOOOPRRSTUVY	SUPER ROYAL OCTAVO
AACFIIIILNNOOSTT	FICTIONALISATION
AACFIIIILNNOOTTZ	FICTIONALIZATION
AACGHHIILLLOPRTY	LITHOGRAPHICALLY
AACGHHILLLMOOOPT	OPHTHALMOLOGICAL
AACGHHILLOOPPRTY	PHOTOGRAPHICALLY
AACGHHILLOOPRRTY	ORTHOGRAPHICALLY
AACGHIIILLNNPRTY	PHYSICAL TRAINING
AACGHILLLOPRSTYY	STYLOGRAPHICALLY
AACGHILLNOOPPRRY	PORNOGRAPHICALLY
AACGIIINNNOPPRTT	NONPARTICIPATING
AACGIILLMNORRTTU	COURT-MARTIALLING
AACHHHILLOPPRRSTY	STAPHYLORRHAPHIC
AACHIIIINNORSSTT	CHRISTIANISATION
AACHIIIINNORSTTZ	CHRISTIANIZATION
AACHIILLMNOPRSTY	MISANTHROPICALLY
AACHILLNOOPTTUYY	AUTOHYPNOTICALLY
AACIIIILLLMRSTTY	MILITARISTICALLY
AACIIIILMNNOPSTU	MUNICIPALISATION
AACIIIILMNNOPTUZ	MUNICIPALIZATION
AACIIILLLMNOPTTU	MULTIPLICATIONAL
AACIIILLNOOPRRSTY	CONSPIRATORIALLY
AACIKMNNOPRSTTUU	PUNCTUATION MARKS
AACILNNORRSTTTUU	TRANSCULTURATION
AADDDDEEEGILMPRS	MIDDLE AGED SPREAD
AADDEEEGILMMMNNT	MIDDLE MANAGEMENT
AADDEEGHHKLNNOSS	GOLDEN HANDSHAKES
AADDEEIIKMPRRSST	MAKE RAPID STRIDES
AADDFGIILNNORSTV	STANDARD OF LIVING
AADEEEEEIILNRSSSV	VENEREAL DISEASES
AADEEEELMNOPRSTV	DEVELOPMENT AREAS
AADEEEFFGIILNRRT	DIFFERENTIAL GEAR
AADEEEFHINNRSSTT	FAINT-HEARTEDNESS
AADEEEGHHNRSTTUW	THE GREAT UNWASHED
AADEEHILMORRRSTT	TETARROHEDRALISM
AADEEHLNNOOPRSVY	OVERPLAY ONE'S HAND
AADEEIIKNRSTTTTU	STRIKE AN ATTITUDE
AADEEIILNRSSTTTU	INDUSTRIAL ESTATE
AADEFFIIILNOORRT	AFFILIATION ORDER
AADEFFIILNOORSTT	DISAFFORESTATION
AADEIIILLMNORSTT	DEMILITARISATION
AADEIIILLMNORTTZ	DEMILITARIZATION
AADEIIIILNOORSTT	EDITORIALISATION

AADEIIIILNOORTTZ	EDITORIALIZATION
AADEIIIILMNRSTTVY	ADMINISTRATIVELY
AADEMNOOPRRSTTUW	PORTMANTEAU WORDS
AAEEEFGOOPPPRRRS	GREASEPROOF PAPER
AAEEEGLNNORRSTTY	ATTORNEY GENERALS
AAEEEILNNOPRRSTT	REPRESENTATIONAL
AAEEEILRRRRSTTTX	EXTRATERRESTRIAL
AAEEFFHIIIMNRTTV	IN THE AFFIRMATIVE
AAEEFHILRSSSTTVV	HARVEST FESTIVALS
AAEEFHLMNOOPRTUY	POLYURETHANE FOAM
AAEEGHHIILMNSTVY	TIME HANGS HEAVILY
AAEEGHIJNNOPRRTU	EUROPEAN NIGHTJAR
AAEEGHILLNOOPSTT	PALAEETHNOLOGIST
AAEEGILOOPRRRTVY	ROYAL PREROGATIVE
AAEEGPPRRRRSSTUY	SPARE-PART SURGERY
AAEEIIILNNOSTTST	INTERNATIONALISE
AAEEIIIILNNNORTTZ	INTERNATIONALIZE
AAEEIIILNNOPRRTTT	INTERPRETATIONAL
AAEEIIILNNORSSSTTX	EXTERNALISATIONS
AAEEIIILNNORSTTXZ	EXTERNALIZATIONS
AAEEIILORRRRTTTX	EXTRATERRITORIAL
AAEEILMNPRRRSTTU	PRETERNATURALISM
AAEEILMNPRRTTUWY	MANUAL TYPEWRITER
AAEELNNPRRSSSTUU	SUPERNATURALNESS
AAEFFHIOOOPRSSTV	HAVE A SOFT SPOT FOR
AAEFHIIIILLNNNOST	SELF-ANNIHILATION
AAEGGIIILNOSSTTVV	ISOAGGLUTINATIVE
AAEGIIIIILMNOSTTT	LEGITIMATISATION
AAEGIIIIILMNOTTTZ	LEGITIMATIZATION
AAEGIIILNNORSSTTT	GASTROINTESTINAL
AAEIIILMNNNORSTT	INTERNATIONALISM
AAEIIILMNNOOOTTZ	EMOTIONALISATION
AAEIIILMNNOOOTTZ	EMOTIONALIZATION
AAEIIILNNNORSTTT	INTERNATIONALIST
AAEIIILNNNORTTTY	INTERNATIONALITY
AAEIIILNNORSSTTUV	UNIVERSALISATION
AAEIIILNNORSTTUVZ	UNIVERSALIZATION
AAEIIIKNNOORRSTTW	SANITATION WORKER
AAEIIILNNORRSSTTT	TRANSLITERATIONS
AAEIILNOPRRSSSSYY	SENSORY PARALYSIS
AAELOOPQRRRSTUUY	SUPER ROYAL QUARTO
AAFGIINNORRSSTTU	TRANSFIGURATIONS
AAGGIIILNNOOSTTN	ISOAGGLUTINATION
AAGHHOOOPPRRSTTY	ASTROPHOTOGRAPHY
AAGIIIMNOPPPRRST	MISAPPROPRIATING
AAIIIIILNOPRSSTTU	SPIRITUALISATION
AAIIIILNOPRSTTUZ	SPIRITUALIZATION
AAIIIILLNNOQRSTTU	TRANQUILLISATION
AAIIIILLNNOQRTTUZ	TRANQUILLIZATION
AAIIIMNOOPPPRRST	MISAPPROPRIATION
AAIIILLMNNORSTTTU	TRANSILLUMINATOR
AAIIMNNORSSTTTTU	TRANSMUTATIONIST
ABBBCDEEIKNRSTTU	BEST BIB AND TUCKER
ABBCDDEEGHIKMPRU	HUMPBACKED BRIDGE
ABBCDEIIIILNRSTY	INDESCRIBABILITY
ABBCEEEFFKLOOOST	COFFEE-TABLE BOOKS
ABBCEHLNOORSSTTU	BACHELOR'S-BUTTONS
ABBCEIIIJLNOOTTY	OBJECTIONABILITY
ABBDEEEGMNRRTTUW	BADEN-WURTTEMBERG
ABBDEELNORRRSTWY	STRAWBERRY BLONDE
ABBEEEEINNNNOOST	A BEE IN ONE'S BONNET
ABBEIIILMPRRTTUY	IMPERTURBABILITY
ABBIIIILSSTTTTUUY	SUBSTITUTABILITY
ABCCDKLLNOORSTUY	COCK-AND-BULL STORY
ABCCEEEIKLLNRSTT	ELECTRIC BLANKETS
ABCCEEHILNOPRSTY	HYPERBOLIC SECANT
ABCCEEILLNOOPSST	POLICE CONSTABLES
ABCCEFIIIJNOSTTU	SUBJECTIFICATION
ABCCEGHIIILLNOOT	BIOTECHNOLOGICAL
ABCCEIIIILNNOTVY	INCONCEIVABILITY
ABCCGHIIILLOOOPSY	PSYCHOBIOLOGICAL
ABCCIIKLMNNOOOST	COMBINATION LOCKS
ABCCILLOOOPRSSTY	STROBOSCOPICALLY
ABCDDEEEEMNOORTT	BOTTOM DEAD CENTRE
ABCDEEEEGHLORRSS	BACHELOR'S DEGREES
ABCDEEEHHLLOOOTW	THE WHOLE CABOODLE
ABCDEEGILNNORSSU	CUDGEL ONE'S BRAINS
ABCDEEHIMNNOPRRS	DOBERMAN PINSCHER
ABCDEELMNORRSSUU	CONSUMER DURABLES
ABCDEGIILLNOSSTT	DISCLOSING TABLET
ABCDEGKNNOOOORSW	GO BACK ON ONE'S WORD
ABCDEIIIILNNNOSTY	INCONDENSABILITY
ABCDEIIIILNPRTTUY	UNPREDICTABILITY
ABCEEEEFILNRRRRY	REFERENCE LIBRARY
ABCEEEEHRRRRSSTT	STRETCHER-BEARERS
ABCEFFIINOOOPRRT	PROBATION OFFICER
ABCEFGIIILLNNORY	FIBRINOGENICALLY
ABCEHIILLNOSTTYY	BIOSYNTHETICALLY
ABCEHIMNNNOOOPRU	BRONCHOPNEUMONIA
ABCEIIIIILLLMSSST	BALLISTIC MISSILE
ABCEIIIILNNOSTTTY	INCONTESTABILITY
ABCEIMNNORSSSTUU	RAMBUNCTIOUSNESS
ABCFIILMNNOORTUY	UNCONFORMABILITY
ABDDEEEEHNOORSSUW	BONDED WAREHOUSES
ABDDEEEIMNNRSSST	ABSENT-MINDEDNESS
ABDDEHLNNNOOOOSS	BLOOD ON ONE'S HANDS
ABDEEEEFIIILLNSST	IDENTIFIABLENESS
ABDEEEFIOOPSSSTX	SAFE-DEPOSIT BOXES
ABDEEEILNPRSSSTU	DISREPUTABLENESS
ABDEEFIIMNNORRST	FIRE-AND-BRIMSTONE
ABDEEFIOOPSSTTXY	SAFETY-DEPOSIT BOX
ABDEEGGILMNPRRSU	GINGERBREAD PLUMS
ABDEEGIIILLNNRSS	LENDING LIBRARIES
ABDEEHIILMNSSSTT	DISESTABLISHMENT
ABDEEKNNOORRSUVW	NERVOUS BREAKDOWN
ABDEFIIIIIILRSTVY	DIVERSIFIABILITY
ABDEGHIMNOOSSTTU	DOUBTING THOMASES

ABDEIIIIILLLMTTY	LIMITED LIABILITY	ACCEEIILOORRRSTT	ARTERIOSCLEROTIC
ABDEIIIIILNNPSSTY	INDISPENSABILITY	ACCEEIIMMNNORRTTU	INTERCOMMUNICATE
ABDFIIILNOOORSUV	DIVISION OF LABOUR	ACCEEIKNOOPRRTTT	PROTECTION RACKET
ABDFILNNOOORSSTU	BLOOD TRANSFUSION	ACCEEILLOOPRSSTY	STEREOSCOPICALLY
ABEEEFILNNRRSSTT	ENFANTS TERRIBLES	ACCEEIMNNOOPRSSTY	COPERNICAN SYSTEM
ABEEEGLNNNORSSUV	UNGOVERNABLENESS	ACCEFIIIILLNNSTUY	UNSCIENTIFICALLY
ABEEEIIILMMPRSTY	SEMIPERMEABILITY	ACCEGIILNNOPRSSS	PELICAN CROSSINGS
ABEEEIILMNNNRRSST	INTERMINABLENESS	ACCEHIINOPRRSTUY	NEUROPSYCHIATRIC
ABEEEIILNPRRSTTY	REPRESENTABILITY	ACCEHILLMOPRSTYY	THERMOSCOPICALLY
ABEEEILNNOQSSSTU	QUESTIONABLENESS	ACCEHILLMOPRSTYY	PSYCHOMETRICALLY
ABEEGHIIILNNSTUX	INEXTINGUISHABLE	ACCEIIILLNOOSSTTV	COLLECTIVISATION
ABEEGIIMPRRRTTUZ	PIETERMARITZBURG	ACCEIIILLNOOTTVZ	COLLECTIVIZATION
ABEEIIIILRRRTTVY	IRRETRIEVABILITY	ACCEIIILOSSSTTTX	LEXICOSTATISTICS
ABEEIIIILNPRRTTTY	INTERPRETABILITY	ACCEIILLMNORRSTY	MICROCRYSTALLINE
ABEELMNNORSSSTUU	SURMOUNTABLENESS	ACCEIIILLNOOPRSTY	RETINOSCOPICALLY
ABEFGIIIILNRRRTY	IRREFRANGIBILITY	ACCEIIMMNNNOOSTUX	EXCOMMUNICATIONS
ABEHIIIILNSTTUXY	INEXHAUSTIBILITY	ACCEIINOORSSTTVV	VASOCONSTRICTIVE
ABEHILOORRSSSTTY	ERYTHROBLASTOSIS	ACCFILLLOOOPRSUY	FLUOROSCOPICALLY
ABEINOOOPRSSSTTV	OBSERVATION POSTS	ACCGHHIIILLLOOTYY	ICHTHYOLOGICALLY
ABIIIILMNRSSSTTY	TRANSMISSIBILITY	ACCGIILLMMOOORTY	MICROCLIMATOLOGY
ACCCCEEEILNNOSSU	CONSCIENCE CLAUSE	ACCHHIIOOPRRSTTY	ORTHOPSYCHIATRIC
ACCCCEGHIKNNOSTU	CHECKING ACCOUNTS	ACCIINNOOORSSTTV	VASOCONSTRICTION
ACCCDDHHIILOORRY	HYDROCHLORIC ACID	ACCIKLLMOOOOSTTV	MOLOTOV COCKTAILS
ACCCDEEILLLLNOPYY	ENCYCLOPEDICALLY	ACDDDEFILNNOOSTU	CONSOLIDATED FUND
ACCCDFHHLNOORSTU	CHURCH OF SCOTLAND	ACDDEEEELNNPSSTU	DEPENDENT CLAUSES
ACCCEEEEGHILLLNOT	TECHNICAL COLLEGE	ACDDEEMNNOORRSSY	SECONDARY MODERNS
ACCCEEEILNOSSSUV	CONCESSIVE CLAUSE	ACDDEFHIIIIMNOTU	DEHUMIDIFICATION
ACCCEEGHHILLORTU	COLLEGIATE CHURCH	ACDDEGHILLNOSSTW	SWADDLING CLOTHES
ACCCEEHIIINNRSST	CHRISTIAN SCIENCE	ACDDGHIIMNPRSSTU	CHRISTMAS PUDDING
ACCCEEIIILLNOPST	POLITICAL SCIENCE	ACDDHHJNNOPSUUWY	PUNCH-AND-JUDY SHOW
ACCCEEILOORSSTTU	ELECTROACOUSTICS	ACDEEEEEGGHLRRST	THREE-LEGGED RACES
ACCCEHHIINNOPSTY	PSYCHOTECHNICIAN	ACDEEEEFILMNSTTV	MENTAL DEFECTIVES
ACCCEILOOPRSSTUU	ACOUSTIC COUPLERS	ACDEEEEHIMMNNRTUV	UNDERACHEIVEMENT
ACCCIILMOOPRRSTU	ULTRAMICROSCOPIC	ACDEEEEIKMMNNOST	TAKE ONE'S MEDICINE
ACCDDEIMMNNNOOSS	SECONDS-IN-COMMAND	ACDEEEEIIPRTTTVV	PRIVATE DETECTIVE
ACCDEEEMMNNOOPRRT	PROMENADE CONCERT	ACDEEEEINRRRSSTU	UNDERSECRETARIES
ACCDEEFHIIMMNNOR	COMMANDER IN CHIEF	ACDEEEFHILLNORSS	HALLS OF RESIDENCE
ACCDEEHHIKLLNRTY	LATCHKEY CHILDREN	ACDEEEFIIILNRSTT	DEFINITE ARTICLES
ACCDEFHIKLOOOSVW	FIVE O'CLOCK SHADOW	ACDEEEFIINOQRRSU	RADIO FREQUENCIES
ACCDEFMNOOPRRTUU	COMPOUND FRACTURE	ACDEEEFLLOORRUVV	FOUR-LEAVED CLOVER
ACCDEGIINNNNOSTU	DISCOUNTENANCING	ACDEEEGHILNRSSST	CLEAR-SIGHTEDNESS
ACCDEHHIILLMOOPS	DOLICHOCEPHALISM	ACDEEEGHILORRSTT	CIGARETTE HOLDERS
ACCDEHIIMOOSSTTY	HOMOSCEDASTICITY	ACDEEEGHKLPSTTUU	TAKE UP THE CUDGELS
ACCDEIOPPRRSSTTU	PICTURE POSTCARDS	ACDEEEIIILNPRSTV	VICE-PRESIDENTIAL
ACCEEEEFIILNPSTX	LIFE EXPECTANCIES	ACDEEEIILLLNSTTU	INTELLECTUALISED
ACCEEEEGLLLLOORT	ELECTORAL COLLEGE	ACDEEEIIMMNPRSSSV	MANIC-DEPRESSIVES
ACCEEEELLMOPRSTX	ELECTRA COMPLEXES	ACDEEEEILNNNOSTTU	SECOND LIEUTENANT
ACCEEEFFIIILORRV	OFFICIAL RECEIVER	ACDEEENNNNRSSSTT	TRANSCENDENTNESS
ACCEEEFHIINOOPTT	PIECE OF THE ACTION	ACDEEFHIIMMNNRSST	DISFRANCHISEMENT
ACCEEEFIMNNORSSST	MASTERS OF SCIENCE	ACDEEFHINORRTTUU	FURTHER EDUCATION
ACCEEFMOORRRSSTTU	CREATURE COMFORTS	ACDEEFIIMNNOORST	CONFEDERATIONISM
ACCEEHIILLLNORTY	HELIOCENTRICALLY	ACDEEFIINNOORSTT	CONFEDERATIONIST
ACCEEHILLNNORTTY	ETHNOCENTRICALLY	ACDEEFILNORRRSTU	FUNERAL DIRECTORS
ACCEEHLMNORSSTUY	SCLERENCHYMATOUS	ACDEEFINNOPRSTUU	SUPERFECUNDATION

ACDEEGGHIINPRRSS	GRAPHIC DESIGNERS
ACDEEGINNOORRRTU	RECREATION GROUND
ACDEEGMMOOPRRRSU	PROGRAMMED COURSE
ACDEEHIILMNOPRTY	DIACETYLMORPHINE
ACDEEIIILLMNOSTUY	EUDEMONISTICALLY
ACDEEIIILMNNORSTU	RADIOLUMINESCENT
ACDEEIILMOPRRTUY	PERPENDICULARITY
ACDEEJKLNOORSSVY	DAVY JONES'S LOCKER
ACDEFIIIIMNNNOST	INDEMNIFICATIONS
ACDEFIILNNNORTTT	CONTINENTAL DRIFT
ACDEFINNOOORSTUU	FOUNDATION COURSE
ACDEGHIILMNNOOPS	HOLDING COMPANIES
ACDEGHILLLMOOOTY	METHODOLOGICALLY
ACDEGIIIKNNRSSTT	STRIKING DISTANCE
ACDEGIILMOPRSTTU	DIGITAL COMPUTERS
ACDEGILNNNOSSTTU	CONSENTING ADULTS
ACDEGMNOOPRRSSTU	SOUND SPECTROGRAM
ACDEHILLMOPSTTUY	SHUTTLE DIPLOMACY
ACDEIIIILMNNRSTY	INDISCRIMINATELY
ACDEIIIILLMNORTTU	MULTIDIRECTIONAL
ACDEIILMNORRSTTU	ULTRAMODERNISTIC
ACDEIINORRSTTTTY	DISTRICT ATTORNEY
ACDEILOOPRSSSTUY	PERISSODACTYLOUS
ACDIIIIIMNNNORST	INDISCRIMINATION
ACDIIIILMNORRSTY	DISCRIMINATORILY
ACEEEEEEFFFMNORRR	FRAME OF REFERENCE
ACEEEEGILLNNORST	GENERAL ELECTIONS
ACEEEEHLLQRRSTUV	TRAVELLER'S CHEQUE
ACEEEFGILNNOPRRS	PEREGRINE FALCONS
ACEEEGGHIILRRTTT	CIGARETTE LIGHTER
ACEEEGHKLNOPSSTU	GET ONE'S HACKLES UP
ACEEEGIIINPRRRSV	VIRGINIA CREEPERS
ACEEEGILMMNORSTT	ELECTROMAGNETISM
ACEEEGINNOOPRSTU	COUNTERESPIONAGE
ACEEEHHILNNPRSTY	CHRYSELEPHANTINE
ACEEEHHIPPRSSSST	SPEECH THERAPISTS
ACEEEHIILLMRSTUY	EUHEMERISTICALLY
ACEEEHIPRRRSSTTT	STRETCHER PARTIES
ACEEEHLLMNOORSTY	ELEMENTARY SCHOOL
ACEEEIILLLLNRSTTU	INTELLECTUALISER
ACEEEIILLLLNRTTUZ	INTELLECTUALIZER
ACEEEIILNNNQSSTU	SESQUICENTENNIAL
ACEEEILLMNPPRRST	SCARLET PIMPERNEL
ACEEFGINORRSTTVY	CENTRES OF GRAVITY
ACEEFHILLNNNOSTT	CONTINENTAL SHELF
ACEEFIIILMNOPSTX	EXEMPLIFICATIONS
ACEEFIKNOOPRSTWY	NASTY PIECE OF WORK
ACEEGGIILLNNORST	TRAINING COLLEGES
ACEEGHHILOOPPRTT	PHOTOTELEGRAPHIC,
TELEPHOTOGRAPHIC	
ACEEGHIIILLNOSTTY	HISTOGENETICALLY
ACEEGHILLLLOOPRTY	HERPETOLOGICALLY
ACEEGHILLMNNOOOP	PHENOMENOLOGICAL
ACEEGHILLNOORTTY	ORTHOGENETICALLY

ACEEGHILLNOPTTYY	PHYTOGENETICALLY
ACEEGHIMMNORSTTY	MAGNETOCHEMISTRY
ACEEGIILLNOORRST	SOLICITOR GENERAL
ACEEGIILNORSSSSU	SACRILEGIOUSNESS
ACEEGIIMNORSTTTV	MAGNETOSTRICTIVE
ACEEGIMNNOOPRSTV	OVERCOMPENSATING
ACEEGLMMNOOPRTTV	GLOVE COMPARTMENT
ACEEHHIINNOPPRTT	PITHECANTHROPINE
ACEEHHIMMOORRSTT	HETEROCHROMATISM
ACEEHHIOOPPRTTTU	PHOTOTHERAPEUTIC
ACEEHIILMNORSTVV	THERMIONIC VALVES
ACEEHIINORSSTTUV	OVERENTHUSIASTIC
ACEEHILLMMORRTTY	THERMOMETRICALLY
ACEEHILLNOOPRSTY	STEREOPHONICALLY
ACEEIILLOPPSSTVX	PLASTIC EXPLOSIVE
ACEEIILNNNNORTTT	INTERCONTINENTAL
ACEEIILNNOQSTTUY	CONSEQUENTIALITY
ACEEIILOORRRSSST	ARTERIOSCLEROSIS
ACEEIMNNOOOPRSTV	OVERCOMPENSATION
ACEEINNOOOPRSTTY	PRESENTATION COPY
ACEELMNOOPPRRSTU	PERSONAL COMPUTER
ACEEMNOOOPRRSTVY	OVERCOMPENSATORY
ACEFFGIJLMNOPPSU	JUMPING-OFF PLACES
ACEFIIINNOOPRSST	PERSONIFICATIONS
ACEFIIMNOOPPRRRT	IMPROPER FRACTION
ACEFLLMNNOORTUWY	FELLOW COUNTRYMAN
ACEGGHILLMOOOOPR	GEOMORPHOLOGICAL
ACEGHHIILLLMNOOT	HELMINTHOLOGICAL
ACEGHHIILLLLOPRYY	HIEROGLYPHICALLY
ACEGIIKLNPRSSSTT	STICKING PLASTERS
ACEGIILNNOORSSST	CONGRESSIONALISM
ACEGIIMNNOORSTTT	MAGNETOSTRICTION
ACEGILNNNOOSSUUY	CONSANGUINEOUSLY
ACEHHILLMOOPRTTY	PHOTOTHERMICALLY
ACEHHILMOOPPRSXY	CHEMOPROPHYLAXIS
ACEHHILMOOPRSSST	SCHOOLMASTERSHIP
ACEHHIOOPPRSSSTTY	PSYCHOTHERAPISTS
ACEHIIKLLNOOPTTY	PHOTOKINETICALLY
ACEHIIILLLOPSTTYY	POLYTHEISTICALLY
ACEHIILLMNOOSTTY	MONOTHEISTICALLY
ACEHIILMOPRSTTTY	THERMOPLASTICITY
ACEHILLLLLOPPTYYY	POLYPHYLETICALLY
ACEHIMNNOOPPRSTT	ANTHROPOCENTRISM
ACEIIIKKNNRSSTTW	KNICKERS IN A TWIST
ACEIIINNOPSSSSUU	INAUSPICIOUSNESS
ACEIILLLLMOPRTUVY	PLUVIOMETRICALLY
ACEIILLNNNOQTTTU	CONTINENTAL QUILT
ACEIILMNOOOPRSTY	COPOLYMERISATION
ACEIILMNOOOPRTYZ	COPOLYMERIZATION
ACEIILMNOORRSSTV	CONTROVERSIALISM
ACEIILNNOOOPRSST	CONSOLATION PRISE
ACEIILNNOOOPRSTZ	CONSOLATION PRIZE
ACEIILNOORRSSTTV	CONTROVERSIALIST
ACEIINNOORSSSTTV	CONSERVATIONISTS

ACEIKNNOOPRSSSTT	STOP IN ONE'S TRACKS
ACEILLNOPRSSTTUY	PERSONALITY CULTS
ACFGIIIMNNOORSTU	CONFIGURATIONISM
ACFGIIINNOORSTTU	CONFIGURATIONIST
ACFIIIILLNNOSTTU	NULLIFICATIONIST
ACGHHHILMOOOPRRT	CHROMOLITHOGRAPH
ACGHHIMOOOPPRRTY	MICROPHOTOGRAPHY,
	PHOTOMICROGRAPHY
ACGHHINOOOPPRTYZ	PHOTOZINCOGRAPHY
ACGHIILLLNOOORTY	ORNITHOLOGICALLY
ACGHIILLMNOOPSYY	PHYSIOGNOMICALLY
ACGIINNOOOPRSSTT	PROGNOSTICATIONS
ACHHIOOOOPPRTTTU	PHOTOAUTOTROPHIC
ACHIILLORRSTTTUU	HORTICULTURALIST
ACIIIILLOPSSTTVY	POSITIVISTICALLY
ACIIIMNNNOOPRSTU	MISPRONUNCIATION
ACIILLLLMNOOOPSTY	MONOPOLISTICALLY
ACIILLNNOOOPRSST	CROSS-POLLINATION
ACIILLNNOOSTTTUY	CONSTITUTIONALLY
ACIILNNNOOSTTTUU	UNCONSTITUTIONAL
ADDDDEEEEEHLMNSSU	MUDDLE-HEADEDNESS
ADDEEEEFIIILMNSTX	EXTENDED FAMILIES
ADDEEEEIMNNNNPST	INDEPENDENT MEANS
ADDEEGINNNOOORRRT	RIO GRANDE DO NORTE
ADDEEIIIKKLLNSSS	LIKES AND DISLIKES
ADDEEIMMMMNNRSSSU	MIDSUMMER MADNESS
ADDEEIMNNNORRSSW	NARROW-MINDEDNESS
ADDEGIIMNNNRSSTU	MISUNDERSTANDING
ADEEEEFHHLOORSTU	LEADER OF THE HOUSE
ADEEEEHHLNNORSTW	WHOLEHEARTEDNESS
ADEEEEIIMNPRRTTV	PREDETERMINATIVE
ADEEEFGHMNOORTUY	YEOMEN OF THE GUARD
ADEEEFGIIILNNRTT	DEFINITE INTEGRAL
ADEEEGGIINORSSTT	DESEGREGATIONIST
ADEEEGHILNOOPRRT	GARDEN HELIOTROPE
ADEEEGILNNOOPRSS	OLD AGE PENSIONERS
ADEEEHIILMNNORST	THREE-DIMENSIONAL
ADEEEHHNNORSSSTTY	STONY-HEARTEDNESS
ADEEEHNORSSSTTTU	STOUTHEARTEDNESS
ADEEEIIMNNOPRRTT	PREDETERMINATION
ADEEEINNNRRSSSTU	UNRESTRAINEDNESS
ADEEEMNOPRRSSTTT	DEPARTMENT STORES
ADEEFFIIINNORSTT	DIFFERENTIATIONS
ADEEGGGHIILNNRST	GREASED LIGHTNING
ADEEGHHINPRSSSST	SHARP-SIGHTEDNESS
ADEEGIILNNOQSSTU	LEADING QUESTIONS
ADEEGILNNOOPRRTY	PREPONDERATINGLY
ADEEHHHHIINRRTTT	HITHER AND THITHER
ADEEHHILMMNRRRUU	MULHEIM AN DER RUHR
ADEEHIINNNOORSSTU	A THORN IN ONE'S SIDE
ADEEILMNOPRRSSTU	MENSTRUAL PERIODS
ADEFHINOOOORRTTUY	OUT OF THE ORDINARY
ADEFINNNOOOSSTTU	FOUNDATION STONES
ADEGGGHIOOORSSSTY	SHAGGY-DOG STORIES
ADEGIIIINOPRSTTT	PRESTIDIGITATION
ADEHHHINOOOPPSSYY	ADENOHYPHOPHYSIS
ADEIIIINORSSTTVY	RADIOSENSITIVITY
ADEIIMNOPRRRTTTX	DOT-MATRIX PRINTER
ADEIINOOOPPRRSTT	DISPROPORTIONATE
ADELLNOOORSSSWWW	SWALLOW ONE'S
	WORDS
ADFGIIIKNNNNORTU	DRINKING FOUNTAIN
ADGHHIIIINNOOPSTT	DIPHTHONGISATION
ADGHHIIIINNOOPTTZ	DIPHTHONGIZATION
ADGHIMMMNNOOPRRSY	GYNANDROMORPHISM
ADHHINOPRSSSTTTY	SHORTHAND TYPISTS
AEEEEFGLMMNNNRRST	GENTLEMEN FARMERS
AEEEEFIMNNRSSTTV	FERMENTATIVENESS
AEEEEHHIKLNOPSTW	A SPOKE IN THE WHEEL
AEEEEHINNPPRSSSV	APPREHENSIVENESS
AEEEEIINNPRRTTTV	INTERPENETRATIVE
AEEEEINNPRSSSTTV	PRESENTATIVENESS
AEEEFFFHLMOORSTT	FLAME-OF-THE-FOREST
AEEEFHILNNNNPPSY	PENNY-HALFPENNIES
AEEEFILNOPRRSSTV	SELF-PRESERVATION
AEEEFLLLLORRSTVW	FELLOW TRAVELLERS
AEEEGGIIILLLMNOR	REGGIO NELL'EMILIA
AEEEGGINNORSSSST	SEASON'S GREETINGS
AEEEGGLNNOORRRSV	GOVERNORS-GENERAL,
	GOVERNOR-GENERALS
AEEEGHIINNNRRTWY	RING IN THE NEW YEAR
AEEEGHIMNOOOSSVW	GIVE SOMEONE A SHOW
AEEEGHNOPRRRSTUY	OPEN-HEART SURGERY
AEEEGILNNPPRSSTU	SLEEPING PARTNERS
AEEEHHILMNNPRTTY	TRIPHENYLMETHANE
AEEEHIILMMNNOPPS	EPIPHENOMENALISM
AEEEHIILMNNOPPST	EPIPHENOMENALIST
AEEEHIIMMNNORRST	IMMERSION HEATERS
AEEEIINNNOPRRTTT	INTERPENETRATION
AEEELMNOOPRSTUXY	EXTEMPORANEOUSLY
AEEFGHIILLNNTTTU	FLIGHT LIEUTENANT
AEEFIIILMNOOPRSS	SEMIPROFESSIONAL
AEEFIIILNNRSSTTU	FIRST LIEUTENANTS
AEEFNOOOPRRSTTWY	POWERS OF ATTORNEY
AEEGGHHHIILTTVWY	LIGHT HEAVYWEIGHT
AEEGGIIILMNNNRST	MINISTERING ANGEL
AEEGGLNOOORRSTTY	GASTROENTEROLOGY
AEEGHIKLOPRRSTTW	TIGHTROPE WALKERS
AEEGHMMMNOOPRSTY	SPHYGMOMANOMETER
AEEGIIILMNNNSTTZ	SENTIMENTALIZING
AEEGIIJKMNNORSSV	KING JAMES VERSION
AEEGIMNOPRSSSTTY	OPERATING SYSTEMS
AEEHIIMNNOOPPRSSS	MISAPPREHENSIONS
AEEHIINOPRRSSSTW	PRAISEWORTHINESS
AEEHHMNOORSSSTTTU	SOUTHEASTERNMOST
AEEIIIILNLNSSSTTX	EXISTENTIALISIST
AEEIIIILNOPQTTTUY	EQUIPOTENTIALITY
AEEIIIILORRRTTTXY	EXTERRITORIALITY
AEEIIILLNNQSSTTUY	QUINTESSENTIALLY

AEEIILMMNNNORSTV	ENVIRONMENTALISM	BBEHHIILMOOPRSTT	THROMBOPHLEBITIS
AEEIILMNNNORSTTV	ENVIRONMENTALIST	BCCDEEIILNOORUXY	DEOXYRIBONUCLEIC
AEEIIMNNRSSSSSTV	TRANSMISSIVENESS	BCCEEHIILNOOPRSY	HYPERBOLIC COSINE
AEEIIMNOOPRSSTTX	EXTEMPORISATIONS	BCCEEIIILORRTTTY	TRIBOELECTRICITY
AEEIIMNOOPRSTTXZ	EXTEMPORIZATIONS	BCCEEINOPRSSSSTU	SUBSISTENCE CROPS
AEEILMNNOSSSSTUU	SIMULTANEOUSNESS	BCCEILOOPPRRSTUU	PUBLIC PROSECUTOR
AEEILNNOPRSSSTUV	RELATIVE PRONOUNS	BCCEINNOOSSSSSUU	SUBCONSCIOUSNESS
AEELNOOPPPRRRSTY	PERSONAL PROPERTY	BCCIIIIILNNNOTVY	INCONVINCIBILITY
AEFFGIILLNORRSSU	SELF-RAISING FLOUR	BCDDEEGKNOOORTTW	GET DOWN TO BEDROCK
AEFGIIILLMNNOPRRT	MORNING-AFTER PILL	BCDDEGHIILNNPTUU	IN THE PUDDING CLUB
AEFHIOPPRSSSTTTT	FIRST PAST THE POST	BCEEEHIILMNNNOPRS	INCOMPREHENSIBLE
AEFIIKMNOOOPRRSV	MAKE PROVISION FOR	BCEEELMOOOPRRSST	SPECTROBOLOMETER
AEFIILLNOOPPRSTY	PELLITORY OF SPAIN	BCEEFINNNNOOOOTT	BONE OF CONTENTION
AEFIILMNORSSSTUU	MULTIFARIOUSNESS	BCEEHIILMNNOPRSY	INCOMPREHENSIBLY
AEFIILNNNOOOPRRT	NONPROLIFERATION	BCEEIIIILMPPRTTY	IMPERCEPTIBILITY
AEFILLNNOOPRSSUY	UNPROFESSIONALLY	BCEEIILMNNORSTTU	TRIBOLUMINESCENT
AEGHIIILLNNORTTWW	WRITING ON THE WALL	BCEEIILNNOORSTTV	INCONTROVERTIBLE
AEGHILNOOOPRSTTU	NEUROPATHOLOGIST	BCEIIIILNNORTTVY	INCONVERTIBILITY
AEGHIMMOOPRRSTTT	PHOTOGRAMMETRIST	BCEIIILNPSSTTUUY	INSUSCEPTIBILITY
AEHHIIOPPRSSSTTY	PHYSIOTHERAPISTS	BCEIIILLPPRRSTTY	PRESCRIPTIBILITY
AEHHIMNOOOPPRRST	ANTHROPOMORPHISE	BCEIILNNOORTTVY	INCONTROVERTIBLY
AEHHIMNOOOPPRRTZ	ANTHROPOMORPHIZE	BCIIIILNOPRRTTUY	INCORRUPTIBILITY
AEHIIMNNOORSSSSU	INHARMONIOUSNESS	BDDDEEILMNNOOSSY	BLOODY-MINDEDNESS
AEIIIIILLLMMNORTU	MULTIMILLIONAIRE	BDDEEEEEFILMNNSS	FEEBLEMINDEDNESS
AEIIIIILNOSSTTTU	INSTITUTIONALISE	BDEEGIINNOPRSSSU	SUSPENSION BRIDGE
AEIIIIILNNOSTTTUZ	INSTITUTIONALIZE	BDEHIILNOORSSSTT	BLOODTHIRSTINESS
AEIIILMNRSSSTTTX	MARXIST-LENINISTS	BEEEELNQRRRSSUUY	QUEENSBERRY RULES
AEIIILLNOPPRSSTY	SPLIT PERSONALITY	BEEEGHILNORSTTTU	TEETHING TROUBLES
AEIILMNNRSSSTTTU	INSTRUMENTALISTS	BEEEGIIOOPRSSTTU	PETIT BOURGEOISES
AEIIMNNOOPRSSSSU	PARSIMONIOUSNESS	BEEEGIOOPRSSTTUY	PETTY BOURGEOISES
AEINOQRRSTTUUVYY	QUANTITY SURVEYOR	BEEEHIIILNPRRSTY	REPREHENSIBILITY
AELNNNOOOPPRRSSU	PERSONAL PRONOUNS	BEEENOOPRRSSSSTU	OBSTREPEROUSNESS
AFILLMOOOPPRRSTT	FROM PILLAR TO POST	BEEFGILNRSSSTTUY	FLYING BUTTRESSES
AGGIILMMMNOPRRTU	MULTIPROGRAMMING	BEEIIIILNOPRSSST	RESPONSIBILITIES
AGGILLNOOOPRRTTY	OTOLARYNGOLOGIST	BEEIIIMLNPRSSTXY	INEXPRESSIBILITY
AGHHHILOOOPRRTTY	PHOTOLITHOGRAPHY	BEEIIIILPRRRSSTY	IRREPRESSIBILITY
AGHHILLMOOOPSSTT	OPHTHALMOLOGISTS	BEEIIILNOPRSSTVX	INVISIBLE EXPORTS
AGHHILOOOPPSTTTY	PHYTOPATHOLOGIST	BEIIIIILMMPPRSSTY	IMPERMISSIBILITY
AHHIIILNOOOPPSST	PHILOSOPHISATION	BEIIIILMNOPRSSTY	INVISIBLE IMPORTS
AHHIIILNOOOPPSTZ	PHILOSOPHIZATION	BEIIIILNOPRRSSTY	IRRESPONSIBILITY
AHHIMMNOOOPPRRST	ANTHROPOMORPHISM	CCCDEEFIIKNNORST	CONFIDENCE TRICKS
AHHIMMNOOOPPRRTS	ANTHROPOMORPHIST	CCCEEEINNNNOOOSS	ON ONE'S CONSCIENCE
AHHMNOOOOPPRRSTU	ANTHROPOMORPHOUS	CCCEEIILMNOORRST	MICROELECTRONICS
AIIIILMNNOSSTTTU	INSTITUTIONALISM	CCCEEIKLNOORSTUW	COUNTERCLOCKWISE
AIIIILNNOSSTTTTU	INSTITUTIONALIST	CCCHLNNOOOORRSTYY	SYNCHROCYCLOTRON
AKKLMMMNOOORSSU		CCDEEEFFINNOOOTV	VOTE OF CONFIDENCE
KOMSOMOLSK-ON-AMUR		CCDEEEFINNNOOOSV	CONVENIENCE FOODS
BBBBEEFGIIILRSTT	FLIBBERTIGIBBETS	CCDEEHIILORRTTYY	HYDROELECTRICITY
BBBCEGHINRRSSSUU	SCRUBBING BRUSHES	CCDIINOOPRRTTUVYY	PYROCONDUCTIVITY
BBCEEKKLOORRSSTT	STOCKBROKER BELTS	CCEEEEFNNOPRRSSS	PRESS CONFERENCES
BBCEKLNOOOOOPSTY	BLOT ONE'S COPYBOOK	CCEEEEIILMMOSSTTT	SELECT COMMITTEES
BBCIIIILMNOSTTUY	INCOMBUSTIBILITY	CCEEEELOOPPRSSTT	TELESPECTROSCOPE
BBDEEEIINNORRSTVY	INVERTED SNOBBERY	CCEEEFIILORRRTTY	FERROELECTRICITY
BBEEHHNNOOOORSSY	ON ONE'S HOBBYHORSE	CCEEEHIILMMNNSTU	CHEMILUMINESCENT

CCEEEEHILMORRSTTY	ELECTROCHEMISTRY
CCEEEIIIILOPRTTYZ	PIEZOELECTRICITY
CCEEHIILOOPRTTTY	PHOTOELECTRICITY
CCEEIILNNOSSSSUV	INCONCLUSIVENESS
CCEEIILNOORRSTTT	ELECTROSTRICTION
CCEEIMMNNORSTTUY	COMMUNITY CENTRES
CCEEINNOOPRSSSSU	PRECONSCIOUSNESS
CCEEINNORSSTTUV	CONSTRUCTIVENESS
CCEHIIIOPRRRSTVY	PYRRHIC VICTORIES
CCEIILLNOOORSSSU	COLLISION COURSES
CCGHIIILNOPSSTUY	PSYCHOLINGUISTIC
CCGIIIILNOOSSSTU	SOCIOLINGUISTICS
CCIILLNOOPRRSUVY	PRIVY COUNCILLORS
CCIIMNNOORSSSTTU	MISCONSTRUCTIONS
CDDDEEEEILORRRVY	RECORDED DELIVERY
CDDEEEEHILMNOPRY	HYPODERMIC NEEDLE
CDDEEEINNNOSSSTT	DISCONTENTEDNESS
CDDEEFIIINNORRST	DIRECTION FINDERS
CDDEGHIIILRRSTTT	RED-LIGHT DISTRICT
CDDEGHLNOOOORRY	DENDROCHRONOLOGY
CDEEEEINNOPRSTUX	INDECENT EXPOSURE
CDEEEFHIMNOORSTW	DEMISE OF THE CROWN
CDEEEHHILPRSSTUW	WHITED SEPULCHRES
CDEEEIINNPRRSSWW	WINDSCREEN WIPERS
CDEEEILMOOPPSSUX	OEDIPUS COMPLEXES
CDEEEINOPRRSSTUV	REPRODUCTIVENESS
CDEEELLMNOOOORTT	REMOTE-CONTROLLED
CDEEHIIJOPRTTUUW	WITHOUT PREJUDICE
CDEEIMNNOOPRSTTU	COMPOUND INTEREST
CDEEINOORSSSSTUU	DISCOURTEOUSNESS
CDEFFGIILNOOOOPR	COOLING-OFF PERIOD
CDEGIIKLMMNNOOTU	UNTIL KINGDOM COME
CDELLNOOOOPSTUYY	POLYCOTYLEDONOUS
CDELMNNOOOOOSTUY	MONOCOTYLEDONOUS
CEEEEEFFGHNORSTU	GREENHOUSE EFFECT
CEEEEEFFMNORRRST	TERMS OF REFERENCE
CEEEEEKKNOPPPRSU	KEEP ONE'S PECKER UP
CEEEEFHORRRRSSSU	REFRESHER COURSES
CEEEEHHLNOPPRSTU	THE UPPER ECHELONS
CEEEEJLLMORSTUWY	COSTUME JEWELLERY
CEEEFFINNOORSTUV	COUNTEROFFENSIVE
CEEEGGIIIILNNNRV	CIVIL ENGINEERING
CEEEGIIKLNNPSSSS	SLEEPING SICKNESS
CEEEHHMMOOOORRST	HETEROCHROMOSOME
CEEEHLOOOPPRTTTY	PHOTOELECTROTYPE
CEEEHMOORRRTTTYY	ERYTHROCYTOMETER
CEEEIIMNNORRSSSV	MERETRICIOUSNESS
CEEEIINOPRRSSSTV	PRESS INTO SERVICE
CEEEFFGIINNORRTU	RETURNING OFFICER
CEEEFLOOORSTTTUU	SETTLE OUT OF COURT
CEEEGIILLLNNOPPPR	PROPELLING PENCIL
CEEEGILMMOOOORRTY	MICROMETEOROLOGY
CEEEHHLNOOPPRSSTY	PHOSPHORESCENTLY
CEEEHILMNNOOPSTTU	PHOTOLUMINESCENT
CEEEHMOORRRTTTYYY	ERYTHROCYTOMETRY
CEEEIILNOPRSSSSUU	SUPERCILIOUSNESS
CEEEIINOPPRRSSSTV	PROSCRIPTIVENESS
CEEEINOOQRRSSSTTU	CROSS-QUESTIONERS
CEEELLMNOOPPRSTUU	COLOUR SUPPLEMENT
CEFGIIILNORRSSTZ	CROSS-FERTILIZING
CEGHHIIIMMNOORSS	HIGH COMMISSIONER
CEGHIMNNOOPRSSSV	CHYMOTRYPSINOGEN
CEGIIILNNORRRTTY	TRINITROGLYCERIN
CEGIIMMMNOSSSTUW	SWIMMING COSTUMES
CEGIINNOOQRSSSTU	CROSS-QUESTIONING
CEIIINNOPRSSTTT	INTROSPECTIONIST
CEIIINNORRSSSTTU	INSURRECTIONISTS
CELNNOPRSSSSUUUU	UNSCRUPULOUSNESS
CFGHHHLOOOOSSTTU	SCHOOLS OF THOUGHT
CFGHHIIILNNOOSSS	FINISHING SCHOOLS
CGGHLLNOOOOORTTY	GLOTTOCHRONOLOGY
CGHHILOOOPPSSYYY	PSYCHOPHYSIOLOGY
CGHIIILOOOPPSSTTY	PHYTOSOCIOLOGIST
CGIIIMMNNOOORSSV	ROVING COMMISSION
CGIILMMNNOOPRSUY	UNCOMPROMISINGLY
CHIIMNOOOOOPPSTT	PHOTOCOMPOSITION
DDEEEEILNNNPRTTY	INTERDEPENDENTLY
DDEEEELMNNOPRTUV	UNDERDEVELOPMENT
DDEEEGHINOOPRRXY	HYDROGEN PEROXIDE
DDEEEGIILMNNNSSS	SINGLE-MINDEDNESS
DDEEEIILMMNNPSSS	SIMPLE-MINDEDNESS
DDEEGGGGHIILLPYY	HIGGLEDY-PIGGLEDY
DDEEGIMNNNORSSST	STRONG-MINDEDNESS
DDEEHIKNNOPRRSZZ	DNEPRODZERZHINSK
DDEEHILOORRSSSUY	DISORDERLY HOUSES
DDEGHIIKNOPRRSUU	YORKSHIRE PUDDING
DEEEEEGMNNORRSTY	GREEN-EYED MONSTER
DEEEEGINRRRSSSTU	REGISTERED NURSES
DEEEEINNNRSSSTTU	UNINTERESTEDNESS
DEEEHILLNORRSTVW	SELL DOWN THE RIVER
DEEEHIMMNOSSSTVW	SWEDISH MOVEMENTS
DEEFFFILNOOORRSTU	SOLDIER OF FORTUNE
DEEGGIKKLNNOORWW	WORKING KNOWLEDGE
DEEGHHIIINPRSSST	HIGH-SPIRITEDNESS
DEEGHHIILNOPRSTUY	HYDROGEN SULPHITE
DEEGHHINORSSSSTT	SHORTSIGHTEDNESS
DEEGHLMOOOORRTTY	HYDROMETEOROLOGY
DEEGHNNOOOOSSSTT	HONEST-TO-GOODNESS
DEEGIINNNOSSSSUU	DISINGENUOUSNESS
DEEHILLNOORRSSTW	OTHERWORLDLINESS
DEEHIMMNOOORSSTT	MONTESSORI METHOD
DEEHIMNNNORRSTUU	UNDERNOURISHMENT
DEEILLNOOOPPRRTW	WELL-PROPORTIONED
DEFFIIIIMNSTUUVX	DIMINUTIVE SUFFIX
DEHIIINNOOORRTTY	TRIIODOTHYRONINE
EEEEEEGHINOSTTVY	GIVE ONE'S EYETEETH
EEEEEHHILNNRTTVW	REINVENT THE WHEEL
EEEEEHLLMMORSTTU	MEURTHE-ET-MOSELLE

EEEEGHINNOOSTTTT	GET ONE'S TEETH INTO	EEGHHHHIOPRSTTTU	PERISH THE THOUGHT!
EEEEHINNPPRRRSTU	ENTREPRENEURSHIP	EEGHINOOPPSTTTTY	PHOTOTYPESETTING
EEEEINNPRSSSSUVX	UNEXPRESSIVENESS	EEGHLLMNOOOOPRSY	SELENOMORPHOLOGY
EEEFGHIIINRRSTUX	FIRE EXTINGUISHER	EEHMNNOORRSSTTTW	NORTHWESTERNMOST
EEEFGIILNNOORRTW	OIL OF WINTERGREEN	EEHMNOORSSSTTTUW	SOUTHWESTERNMOST
EEEGHHIIMMPSTTUV	IT GIVES ME THE HUMP	EEMNOPPRSSSSTUUU	PRESUMPTUOUSNESS
EEEGHHMMOOOORRSTY	MOTHER GOOSE RHYME	EFFGIILLNORRSSSU	SELF-RISING FLOURS
EEEHIIMPPRRSSTUV	HEIRS PRESUMPTIVE	EFIIIIILNNPSSTTV	SPLIT INFINITIVES
EEEILLNOPRSSSSXY	EXPRESSIONLESSLY	EGGHHILNNOOPRSTU	HOUGHTON-LE-SPRING
EEEILNNOOPPRSSTT	POISON-PEN LETTERS	EGGHIIIKLNNRSSTT	LIGHTNING STRIKES
EEENOOPPRRSSSSTU	PREPOSTEROUSNESS	EGHIIIKLNNORSSTV	SHRINKING VIOLETS
EEFGHNOORRSSTTTW	TOWERS OF STRENGTH	EGHIIINNOOPSSTTZ	PHOTOSENSITIZING
EEFHHIILOOPRTTWW	WIPE THE FLOOR WITH	EHIIINOOPSSTTTVY	PHOTOSENSITIVITY
EEFHIILMNNNOTTTY	FLY IN THE OINTMENT	EHILOOPRSSSTTTUW	WHISTLE-STOP TOURS
EEFIIIILMMNNOPRST	LIFE IMPRISONMENT	EIINOOPPSSSSSTUU	SUPPOSITIOUSNESS

PALINDROMES

3			5	6
AHA	HUH	TNT	CIVIC	DENNED
BIB	MAM	TOT	KAYAK	HALLAH
BOB	MOM	TUT	LEVEL	HANNAH
DAD	MUM	WOW	MADAM	REDDER
DID	NUN		MINIM	TERRET
DUD	OHO	**4**	RADAR	TUT-TUT
ERE	PAP	BOOB	REFER	
EVE	PEP	DEED	ROTOR	
EWE	PIP	KOOK	SAGAS	**9**
EYE	POP	MA'AM	SEXES	
GAG	PUP	NOON	SHAHS	MALAYALAM
GIG	SIS	PEEP	SOLOS	ROTAVATOR
HAH	SOS	POOP	TENET	
HEH	TAT	SEES		
	TIT	TOOT		

BACKWORDS

2

AH – HA	GEL – LEG	SUB – BUS
AM – MA	GOB – BOG	SUP – PUS
AT – TA	GOD – DOG	TAB – BAT
EH – HE	GOT – TOG	TAP – PAT
HA – AH	GUM – MUG	TAR – RAT
HE – EH	GUT – TUG	TEN – NET
HO – OH	HOD – DOH	TIN – NIT
IT – TI	JAR – RAJ	TIP – PIT
MA – AM	LAG – GAL	TOD – DOT
MP – PM	LAP – PAL	TOG – GOT
NO – ON	LEE – EEL	TON – NOT
OH – HO	LEG – GEL	TOP – POT
ON – NO	MAD – DAM	TOR – ROT
PM – MP	MAR – RAM	TUB – BUT
TA – AT	MAY – YAM	TUG – GUT
TI – IT	MID – DIM	WAR – RAW
	MUG – GUM	WAY – YAW
3	NAB – BAN	WED – DEW
AND – DNA	NAP – PAN	WON – NOW
BAD – DAB	NET – TEN	YAM – MAY
BAG – GAB	NIB – BIN	YAP – PAY
BAN – NAB	NIP – PIN	YAW – WAY
BAT – TAB	NIT – TIN	YOB – BOY
BIN – NIB	NOD – DON	
BOG – GOB	NOT – TON	**4**
BOY – YOB	NOW – WON	ABLE – ELBA
BUD – DUB	NUB – BUN	ABUT – TUBA
BUN – NUB	PAL – LAP	BARD – DRAB
BUS – SUB	PAN – NAP	BATS – STAB
BUT – TUB	PAR – RAP	BRAG – GARB
DAB – BAD	PAT – TAP	BUNS – SNUB
DAM – MAD	PAY – YAP	BUTS – STUB
DEW – WED	PER – REP	DEER – REED
DIM – MID	PIN – NIP	DIAL – LAID
DNA – AND	PIT – TIP	DOOM – MOOD
DOG – GOD	POT – TOP	DOOR – ROOD
DOH – HOD	PUS – SUP	DRAB – BARD
DON – NOD	RAJ – JAR	DRAW – WARD
DOT – TOD	RAM – MAR	DRAY – YARD
DUB – BUD	RAP – PAR	DUAL – LAUD
EEL – LEE	RAT – TAR	EDAM – MADE
GAB – BAG	RAW – WAR	EDIT – TIDE
GAL – LAG	REP – PER	ELBA – ABLE
GAS – SAG	ROT – TOR	EMIR – RIME
	SAG – GAS	EMIT – TIME

BACKWORDS (Continued)

ERGO	-	OGRE	POOL	-	LOOP
ET AL	-	LATE	POTS	-	STOP
EVIL	-	LIVE	RAIL	-	LIAR
FLOG	-	GOLF	RAPS	-	SPAR
FLOW	-	WOLF	RATS	-	STAR
GALS	-	SLAG	REED	-	DEER
GARB	-	BRAG	REEL	-	LEER
GNAT	-	TANG	RIAL	-	LAIR
GOLF	-	FLOG	RIME	-	EMIR
GULP	-	PLUG	ROOD	-	DOOR
GUMS	-	SMUG	ROOM	-	MOOR
GUNS	-	SNUG	SCAM	-	MACS
HOOP	-	POOH	SLAG	-	GALS
KEEL	-	LEEK	SLAP	-	PALS
KEEP	-	PEEK	SMUG	-	GUMS
LAID	-	DIAL	SNAP	-	PANS
LAIR	-	RIAL	SNIP	-	PINS
LATE	-	ET AL	SNOT	-	TONS
LAUD	-	DUAL	SNUB	-	BUNS
LEEK	-	KEEL	SNUG	-	GUNS
LEER	-	REEL	SPAM	-	MAPS
LIAR	-	RAIL	SPAN	-	NAPS
LIVE	-	EVIL	SPAR	-	RAPS
LOOP	-	POOL	SPAT	-	TAPS
LOOT	-	TOOL	SPAY	-	YAPS
MACS	-	SCAM	SPIN	-	NIPS
MADE	-	EDAM	SPIT	-	TIPS
MAPS	-	SPAM	SPOT	-	TOPS
MAWS	-	SWAM	STAB	-	BATS
MEET	-	TEEM	STAR	-	RATS
MOOD	-	DOOM	STEP	-	PETS
MOOR	-	ROOM	STEW	-	WETS
NAPS	-	SPAN	STOP	-	POTS
NIPS	-	SPIN	STUB	-	BUTS
NUTS	-	STUN	STUN	-	NUTS
OGRE	-	ERGO	SWAM	-	MAWS
PALS	-	SLAP	SWAP	-	PAWS
PANS	-	SNAP	SWAY	-	YAWS
PART	-	TRAP	SWOT	-	TOWS
PAWS	-	SWAP	TANG	-	GNAT
PEEK	-	KEEP	TAPS	-	SPAT
PETS	-	STEP	TEEM	-	MEET
PINS	-	SNIP	TIDE	-	EDIT
PLUG	-	GULP	TIME	-	EMIT
POOH	-	HOOP	TIPS	-	SPIT

TONS	-	SNOT
TOOL	-	LOOT
TOPS	-	SPOT
TORT	-	TROT
TOWS	-	SWOT
TRAP	-	PART
TROT	-	TORT
TUBA	-	ABUT
WARD	-	DRAW
WETS	-	STEW
WOLF	-	FLOW
YAPS	-	SPAY
YARD	-	DRAY
YAWS	-	SWAY

5

ANNAM	-	MANNA
ATLAS	-	SALTA
CARES	-	SERAC
DARAF	-	FARAD
DECAL	-	LACED
DENIM	-	MINED
DEVIL	-	LIVED
FARAD	-	DARAF
FIRES	-	SERIF
KEELS	-	SLEEK
LACED	-	DECAL
LAGER	-	REGAL
LEPER	-	REPEL
LEVER	-	REVEL
LIVED	-	DEVIL
LOOPS	-	SPOOL
MANNA	-	ANNAM
MINED	-	DENIM
PACER	-	RECAP
PARTS	-	STRAP
POOLS	-	SLOOP
PORTS	-	STROP
REBUT	-	TUBER
RECAP	-	PACER
REGAL	-	LAGER
REMIT	-	TIMER
REPEL	-	LEPER
REVEL	-	LEVER
SALTA	-	ATLAS

BACKWORDS (continued)

SERAC - CARES
SERIF - FIRES
SLEEK - KEELS
SLOOP - POOLS
SMART - TRAMS
SNIPS - SPINS
SPINS - SNIPS
SPOOL - LOOPS
SPOTS - STOPS
STOPS - SPOTS
STRAP - PARTS
STRAW - WARTS
STROP - PORTS
TIMER - REMIT
TRAMS - SMART
TUBER - REBUT
WARTS - STRAW

6

ANIMAL - LAMINA
DELIAN - NAILED
DENIER - REINED
DIAPER - REPAID
DRAWER - REWARD
HARRIS - SIRRAH
LAMINA - ANIMAL
LOOTER - RETOOL
NAILED - DELIAN
PUPILS -
   SLIP-UP
RECAPS - SPACER
REINED - DENIER
RENNET - TENNER
REPAID - DIAPER
RETOOL - LOOTER

REWARD - DRAWER
SERVES - SEVRES
SEVRES - SERVES
SIRRAH - HARRIS
SLIP-UP - PUPILS
SNOOPS - SPOONS
SPACER - RECAPS
SPOONS - SNOOPS
TENNER - RENNET

8

DESSERTS -
   STRESSED
STRESSED -
   DESSERTS